BOOK PRICES:
USED AND RARE
1995

BOOK PRICES:
USED AND RARE
1995

Edited by

Edward N. Zempel

and

Linda A. Verkler

THE SPOON RIVER PRESS

Published by:
The Spoon River Press
2319-C West Rohmann Avenue
Peoria, IL 61604
(309) 672-2665
Fax: (309) 672-7853

ISBN 0-930358-12-0.

Manufactured in the United States of America

This book is printed on acid-free paper meeting the requirements of the American National Standard for Permanence of Paper for Printed Library Materials.

Introduction

Book Prices: Used and Rare, 1995 is the third volume in a series of book price guides. Published annually, *Book Prices: Used and Rare* is a reference for the secondhand and antiquarian book dealer, general and rare book librarian, and the private collector seeking to place a value on a book. The over 30,000 titles in the present volume have been selected from the 1994 catalogs of over 165 book dealers in the United States and Great Britain, both generalists and specialists. The dealers who provided catalogs—and kindly gave their permission to reproduce their entries—represent a broad spectrum of the American and British book trade, not only geographically, but in the subject matter range and the price range of the books offered.

With a large variety of possible subject categories, we have attempted to balance the entries in this guide. Our general goal has been to provide pricing information on books in those subject categories and that price range most likely to be found in the day-to-day trade of the average generalist bookseller. This volume, then, contains entries on books in a wide variety of subject areas. Among them are modern first editions, travel and voyages, Americana and the West, natural history, science, medicine, art, architecture, children's literature, and books on books. Only books published in English have been listed. No foreign language publications have been included.Though this guide includes several entries for books priced over $5,000 and some entries for books priced under $20, 90 percent of the titles listed in this guide are priced between $20 and $300.

All prices are given in both U.S. dollars and pounds sterling.

Entry Alphabetizing

Entries have been alphabetized word-for-word by the author's surname. Every effort has been made to present the correct spelling of surnames. However, variant spellings were sometimes found, especially in names beginning with de and De, le and Le, Mac and Mc, etc. (Such inconsistencies extend also to the entry of such names in reference works and library catalog files.)

Names preceded by de or de la should correctly be alphabetized under the family surname. For example, Simone de Beauvoir should be alphabetized under B—i.e., Beauvoir, Simone de. However, in the interests of clarity, ease of reference, and in anticipation of where many readers would first look, we have alphabetized such names under D. The same practice was used for surnames beginning with di, le, la, von, etc. Please take this into consideration when searching for an entry for a particular author. If not in one place, the name may be in another.

In the case of U.S. government publications such as House and Senate documents, the user is advised to check for the title of the work, as well as for the work's author. Some works have been entered with the government agency as the author. For example, publications of the Bureau of American Ethnology (BAE) have generally been alphabetized under BAE.

An entry for which the author is unknown has been entered alphabetically in the general list by its title. Pseudonymous entries give, if known, the author's real name in parentheses after the pseudonym. Generally, in the interest of more efficient alphabetizing, military ranks and other titles have been deleted from the author's name.

Some edited works (letters, diaries, and journals, especially) were listed in catalogs under the name of the author; others were listed under the name of the editor. In searching such titles in this guide, check first under the name of the author, and then under the name of the editor. Though there are exceptions, translated works have generally been entered under the name of the author, not the translator.

Entry Information

Each entry in *Book Prices: Used and Rare* includes the following information (when offered in the catalog): author's name (in CAPITAL letters), title of book, publisher and/or place and date of publication, condition, the price at which the book was cataloged, and the name (perhaps shortened) of the dealer who cataloged the book. The key to these dealer abbreviations is found in the listing of contributing book dealers, which begins on page 8.

If the condition of the book is not noted, it may be assumed that the book is in good or better collectible condition. Specific faults are usually listed in parentheses following the general condition of the book or its dust jacket. In the case of modern first editions, careful attention was given to noting those defects, both of the dust jacket and the book itself, affecting the book's value. The following are general definitions applying to a book's condition.

As New: In "as published" condition. The dust jacket (dj), if issued with the book, must be flawless.

Very Fine (VF): Nearly as new.

Fine: Without defect, but not "as new."

Near Fine (NF): Approaching Fine condition.

Very Good (VG): Minimal wear with no defects.

Good: In average condition.

Poor: Text complete, but book worn and binding defective.

Ex-library copies and book club editions are noted.

First editions are so noted. All titles are hardcover, unless the entry mentions otherwise. Every book is presumed to be in its original binding unless the entry mentions otherwise.

A dust jacket (dj) is mentioned when present. The dust jacket is assumed to be in the same general condition as the book unless the entry mentions otherwise. Slipcases also are noted.

In the case of certain older books, where collation is a factor in determining the book's edition, the collation (if given in the dealer's catalog) has been provided. Generally, if mentioned in the dealer's catalog description, folding maps, folding plates, and folding illustrations have been mentioned in the entry, regardless of the value of the book. In the case of entries for limited editions, the number of copies in the edition has been noted, if included in the catalog entry.

When a "point" (a typographical or binding feature bearing on the edition of the book and thus on its value) was mentioned in the book dealer's catalog entry, we have included that "point" in our entry. For some Americana entries we have also included the Howes reference number included in the dealer's catalog entry (e.g., Howes E 231). These numbers are keyed to entries in the second edition of *U.S.iana* by Wright Howes. Similarly, some entries carry numbers referencing the *Bibliography of American Literature* (BAL), e.g., BAL 14356.

For some titles we have provided multiple entries, suggesting a price agreement or a price range, usually across a range of conditions or editions. As mentioned, most of the entries provide information on books in the $20-$300 price range. Generally, then—though there are exceptions—this guide does not contain entries for unique copies, association copies, or books published in very small limited editions. While most of the books listed are hardcovers, prices on some vintage paperback first editions also have been included.

The prices listed are retail prices at which the books were cataloged in 1994.

Identifying First Editions

First Editions: A Guide to Identification is the standard reference for identifying first editions. A new edition of this book will be published in mid-1995. To receive information on this forthcoming edition, send your name and address to the publisher: The Spoon River Press, 2319-C West Rohmann Avenue, Peoria, IL 61604. The Spoon River Press also publishes and distributes a wide range of books about books. Write for our free catalog.

Abbreviations

To allow the inclusion of as much useful information as possible, certain standard abbreviations were used. A list of those abbreviations is on page 14.

A Caution

The prices listed in this guide are not the prices that book dealers will pay for the books listed. The prices listed are the prices at which dealers offered books for sale in 1994. The prices listed are, then, retail prices. Like any other retail business, the selling of rare, scarce, and used books depends on a markup for its profitability. The price a dealer is willing to pay for a book depends on its condition and scarcity, as well as the demand for the book.

While the prices listed in this guide are the prices at which the books were advertised for retail sale, the books may not have sold at these prices.

Standing Orders

Book Prices: Used and Rare is published annually in early March. Annual volumes may be placed on standing order *at preferential discounts well below the post-publication price.*

Annual volumes on standing order will be shipped in March each year. To place *Book Prices: Used and Rare* on standing order, contact the publisher: The Spoon River Press, 2319-C West Rohmann Avenue, Peoria, IL 61604. Send no payment. An invoice will be enclosed with the book when it is shipped.

We are intent on making *Book Prices: Used and Rare* the most comprehensive, affordable, and useful book price guide obtainable. If you have suggestions on how future annual editions might be improved regarding focus or coverage, please let us know.

Contributing Book Dealers

We are grateful to the book dealers listed below, who generously provided copies of their 1994 catalogs for our use in compiling this price guide. The name in parentheses below the name of the dealer is the name by which the dealer's catalog entries are identified in this guide.

Charles Agvent
(AGVENT)
RD 2, Box 377A
Mertztown, PA 19539
(610) 682-4750

a/k/a Fine Used Books
(AKA)
4142 Brooklyn NE
Seattle, WA 98105
(206) 632-5870

Antic Hay Rare Books
(ANTIC HAY)
P.O. Box 2185
Asbury Park, NJ 07712
(908) 774-4590

Appelfeld Gallery
(APPELFELD)
1372 York Avenue
New York, NY 10021
(212) 988-7835

Archaeologia
(ARCHAEOLOGIA)
707 Carlston Avenue
Oakland, CA 94610
(510) 832-1405

Argosy Book Store
(ARGOSY)
116 E. 59th Street
New York, NY 10022
(212) 753-4455

Ars Artis
(ARS ARTIS)
31 Abberbury Road
Oxford OX4 4ET
United Kingdom

Artis Books
(ARTIS BOOKS)
P.O. Box 822
201 N. Second Avenue
Alpena, MI 49707
(517) 354-3401

Ash Rare Books
(ASH)
25 Royal Exchange
London EC3V 3LP
United Kingdom

Authors of the West
(AUTHORS OF THE WEST)
191 Dogwood Drive
Dundee, OR 97115
(503) 538-8132

Gene W. Baade
(BAADE)
824 Lynnwood Avenue N.E.
Renton, WA 98056

Beasley Books
(BEASLEY)
1533 W. Oakdale
Chicago, IL 60657
(312) 472-4528

Benchmark Books
(BENCHMARK)
331 Rio Grande Street
Suite 300
Salt Lake City, UT 84109
(801) 532-3100

Steven C. Bernard
(BERNARD)
15011 Plainfield Lane
Darnestown, MD 20874
(301) 948-8423

Between the Covers
(BETWEEN THE COVERS)
132 Kings Highway East
Haddonfield, NJ 08033
(609) 354-7665

David Bickersteth
(BICKERSTETH)
4 South End, Bassingbourn
Royston, Herts. SG8 5NG
United Kingdom

The Bishop of Books
(BISHOP)
328 Market Street
Salt Lake City, UT 84109
(801) 532-3100

The Blue Dragon Book Shop
(BLUE DRAGON)
Box 216
Ashland, OR 97520
(503) 482-2142

Blue Mountain Books
(BLUE MOUNTAIN)
P.O. Box 363
Catskill, NY 12414
(518) 943-4771

Bohling Book Company
(BOHLING)
P.O. Box 204
Decatur, MI 49045
(616) 423-8786

Nelson Bond
(BOND)
4724 Easthill Drive
Roanoke, VA 24018
(703) 774-2674

The Book Block
(BOOK BLOCK)
8 Loughlin Avenue
Cos Cob, CT 06807
(203) 629-2990

The Book Broker
(BOOK BROKER)
P.O. Box 1283
Charlottesville, VA 22902
(804) 296-2194

Book Finders International
(BOOK FINDERS)
701 Gervais Street
Columbia, SC 29201
(803) 252-1589

The Book Market
(BOOK MARKET)
Box 74
Altadena, CA 91003
(818) 797-9527

The Bookpress Ltd.
(BOOKPRESS)
P.O. Box KP
Williamsburg, VA 23187
(804) 229-1260

Meyer Boswell Books, Inc.
(BOSWELL)
2141 Mission Street
San Francisco, CA 94110
(415) 255-6400

Judith Bowman Books
(BOWMAN)
Pound Ridge Road
Bedford, NY 10506
(914) 234-7543

Brooks Books
(BROOKS)
P.O. Box 21473
Concord, CA 94521
(510) 672-4566

Carroll Burcham, Bookseller
(BURCHAM)
5546 17th Place
Lubbock, TX 79416
(806) 799-0416

Richard Cady Rare Books
(CADY)
1927 N. Hudson Avenue
Chicago, IL 60614
(312) 944-0856

Andrew Cahan, Bookseller
(CAHAN)
3000 Blueberry Lane
Chapel Hill, NC 27516
(919) 968-0538

Cattermole
(CATTERMOLE)
9880 Fairmount Road
Newbury, OH 44065
(216) 338-3253

Chapel Hill Rare Books
(CHAPEL HILL)
P.O. Box 456
Carrboro, NC 27510
(919) 929-8351

Children's Book Adoption
 Agency
(BOOK ADOPTION)
P.O. Box 643
Kensington, MD 20895
(301) 565-2834

Stan Clark Military Books
(CLARK)
915 Fairview Avenue
Gettysburg, PA 17325
(717) 337-1728

Connolly
(CONNOLLY)
2810 Kansas Avenue
Joplin, MO 64804-2931
(417) 624-5602

Claude Cox
(COX)
3 & 5 Silent Street
Ipswich IP1 1TF
United Kingdom

Thomas Cullen
(CULLEN)
Box 134
Cattaraugus, NY 14719
(716) 257-5121

James Cummins Bookseller
(CUMMINS)
699 Madison Avenue
New York, NY 10021
(212) 688-6441

D & D Galleries
(D & D)
Box 8413
Somerville, NJ 08876
(908) 874-3162

Dalian Books
(DALIAN)
81 Albion Drive
London Fields
London E8 4LT
United Kingdom

Ursula C. Davidson, Books
(DAVIDSON)
134 Linden Lane
San Rafael, CA 94901
(415) 454-3939

Dawson's Book Shop
(DAWSON)
535 N. Larchmont Blvd.
Los Angeles, CA 90004
(213) 469-2186

Joseph A. Dermont
(DERMONT)
13 Arthur Street
P.O. Box 654
Onset, MA 02558
(508) 295-4760

Dramatis Personae
(DRAMATIS PERSONAE)
71 Lexington Avenue
New York, NY 10010
(212) 679-3705

Drusilla's Books
(DRUSILLA'S)
P.O. Box 16
Lutherville, MD 21094
(410) 321-6687

I. D. Edrich
(EDRICH)
17 Selsdon Road
London E11 2QF
United Kingdom

Francis Edwards
(EDWARDS)
The Old Cinema
Castle Street
Hay-on-Wye
via Hereford HR3 5DF
United Kingdom

Francis Edwards of London
(EDWARDS)
13 Great Newport Street
Charing Cross Road
London WC2H 7JA
United Kingdom

Else Fine Books
(ELSE FINE)
P.O. Box 43
Dearborn, MI 48121
(313) 834-3255

Europa Books
(EUROPA)
15 Luttrell Avenue
London SW15 6PD
United Kingdom

Joseph J. Felcone Inc.
(FELCONE)
P.O. Box 366
Princeton, NJ 08542
(609) 924-0539

Fine Books
(FINE BOOKS)
781 E. Snell Road
Rochester, MI 48306
(810) 651-8799

Five Quail Books
(FIVE QUAIL)
Route 1, Box 157A
Spring Grove, MN 55974
(507) 498-3346

Fuller and Saunders, Books
(FULLER & SAUNDERS)
1531 33rd Street N.W.
Washington, DC 20007
(202) 337-3235

W. Bruce Fye
(FYE)
1607 N. Wood Avenue
Marshfield, WI 54449
(715) 384-8128

John Gach Books
(GACH)
5620 Waterloo Road
Columbia, MD 21045
(410) 465-9023

Michael Ginsberg Books
(GINSBERG)
Box 402
Sharon, MA 02067
(617) 784-8181

Edwin V. Glaser Rare Books
(GLASER)
P.O. Box 1765
Sausalito, CA 94966
(415) 332-1194

Glenn Books
(GLENN)
323 E. 55th Street
Kansas City, MO 64113
(816) 444-4447

James Tait Goodrich
(GOODRICH)
214 Everett Place
Englewood, NJ 07631
(201) 567-0199

William A. Graf
(GRAF)
717 Clark Street
Iowa City, IA 52240-5640
(319) 337-7748

David A.H. Grayling
Lyvennet
Crosby Ravensworth
Penrith
Cumbria CA10 3JP
United Kingdom

Great Epic Books
(GREAT EPIC)
15918-20th Place West
Lynnwood, WA 98037
(206) 745-3113

John R. Gretton
(GRETTON)
5 Quebec Road, Dereham
Norfolk NR19 2DP
United Kingdom

Emmett Harrington
(HARRINGTON)
P.O. Box 27326
San Francisco, CA 94127
(415) 587-4604

Hartfield Fine & Rare Books
(HARTFIELD)
117 Dixboro Road
Ann Arbor, MI 48105
(313) 662-6035

Robert G. Hayman
(HAYMAN)
Box 188
Carey, OH 43316
(419) 396-6933

Heinoldt Books
(HEINOLDT)
1325 W. Central Avenue
South Egg Harbor, NJ 08215
(609) 965-2284

Joshua Heller Rare Books
(HELLER)
P.O. Box 39114
Washington, DC 20016-9114
(202) 966-9411

Hemlock Books
(HEMLOCK)
170 Beach 145th Street
Neponsit, NY 11694
(718) 318-0737

John Henly Bookseller
(HENLY)
Brooklands
Walderton, Chichester
West Sussex PO18 9EE
United Kingdom

Heritage Book Shop, Inc.
(HERITAGE)
8540 Melrose Avenue
Los Angeles, CA 90069
(310) 659-3674

The Hermitage Bookshop
(HERMITAGE)
290 Fillmore Street
Denver, CO 80206
(303) 388-6811

High Latitude
(HIGH LATITUDE)
P.O. Box 11254
Bainbridge Island, WA 98110
(206) 842-0202

Peter Murray Hill (Rare Books)
(HILL)
10 Beverley Gardens
Stamford
Lincolnshire PE9 2UD
United Kingdom

Hobbyhorse Books
(HOBBYHORSE)
P.O. Box 591
Ho Ho Kus, NJ 07423
(201) 327-4717

R.F.G. Hollett and Son
(HOLLETT)
6 Finkle Street, Sedbergh
Cumbria LA10 5BZ
United Kingdom

George J. Houle
(HOULE)
7260 Beverly Boulevard
Los Angeles, CA 90036
(213) 937-5858

J & J House Booksellers
(HOUSE)
P.O. Box 919
Unionville, PA 19375
(215) 444-0490

James S. Jaffe Rare Books
(JAFFE)
18 Haverford Station Road
2nd Floor
Haverford, PA 19041
(215) 649-4221

Janus Books, Ltd.
(JANUS)
P.O. Box 40787
Tucson, AZ 85717
(602) 881-8192

Priscilla Juvelis
(JUVELIS)
1166 Massachusetts Avenue
Cambridge, MA 02138
(617) 497-7570

Kenneth Karmiole
(KARMIOLE)
P.O. Box 464
Santa Monica, CA 90406
(310) 451-4342

John K. King Books
(KING)
901 W. Lafayette Boulevard
Detroit, MI 48226
(313) 961-0622

Knollwood Books
(KNOLLWOOD)
P.O. Box 197
Oregon, WI 53575-0197
(608) 835-8861

Maggie Lambeth Rare Books
(LAMBETH)
Star Route 4, Box 361
Blanco, TX 78606
(210) 833-5252

Lame Duck Books
(LAME DUCK)
90 Moraine Street
Jamaica Plain, MA 02130-4330
(617) 522-6657

James and Mary Laurie
(LAURIE)
251 S. Snelling Avenue
St. Paul, MN 55105
(612) 699-1114

Edward J. Lefkowicz, Inc.
(LEFKOWICZ)
P.O. Box 630
Fairhaven, MA 02719
(508) 997-6839

Barry R. Levin
(LEVIN)
2265 Westwood Blvd., #669
Los Angeles, CA 90064
(310) 458-6111

John Lewis
(LEWIS)
35 Stoneham Street
Coggeshall
Essex CO6 1UH
United Kingdom

L.J. Lewton
(LEWTON)
Old Station House
Freshford
Bath BA3 6EQ
United Kingdom

Lien's Book Shop
(LIEN'S)
57 South 9th Street
Minneapolis, MN 55402
(612) 332-7081

Limestone Hills Book Shop
(LIMESTONE)
P.O. Box 1125
Glen Rose, TX 76043
(817) 897-4991

MacDonnell Rare Books
(MACDONNELL)
9307 Glenlake Drive
Austin, TX 78730
(512) 345-4139

Robert A. Madle
(MADLE)
4406 Bestor Drive
Rockville, MD 20853
(301) 460-4712

Marlborough Rare Books Ltd.
(MARLBOROUGH)
144-146 New Bond Street
London W1Y 9FD
United Kingdom

C.J. Martin
(MARTIN)
45 New Mill Lane
Mansfield
Woodhouse NG19 9BU
United Kingdom

David A. McClintock
(MCCLINTOCK)
1454 Sheridan Avenue N.E.
Warren, OH 44483
(216) 372-4425

McGowan Book Company
(MCGOWAN)
P.O. Box 16325
Chapel Hill, NC 27516
(919) 968-1121

Frank Mikesh
(MIKESH)
1356 Walden Road
Walnut Creek, CA 94596
(510) 934-9243

Ming Books
(MING)
110 Gloucester Avenue
Primrose Hill
London NW1 8JA
United Kingdom

Hartley Moorhouse
(MOORHOUSE)
17 Hampstead Lane
Highgate
London N6 4RT
United Kingdom

Mordida Books
(MORDIDA)
P.O. Box 79322
Houston, TX 77279
(713) 467-4280

Nicholas Morrell
(MORRELL)
77 Falkland Road
Kentish Town
London NW5 2XB
United Kingdom

V.J. Moss
(MOSS)
83 Chaigley Road
Longridge
Preston PR3 3TQ
United Kingdom

Murder by the Book
(MURDER)
1281 North Main Street
Providence, RI 02904
(401) 331-9140

Oak Knoll Books
(OAK KNOLL)
414 Delaware Street
New Castle, DE 19720
(302) 328-7232

October Farm
(OCTOBER FARM)
2609 Branch Road
Raleigh, NC 27610
(919) 772-0482

Oregon Territorial Books
(OREGON)
P.O. Box 22
Sublimity, OR 97385
(503) 769-7356

Other Worlds Bookstore
(OTHER WORLDS)
1281 North Main Street
Providence, RI 02904-1827
(401) 331-9140

Parker Books of the West
(PARKER)
P.O. Box 8390
Sante Fe, NM 87504
(505) 988-1076

Parmer Books
(PARMER)
7644 Forrestal Road
San Diego, CA 92120-2203
(619) 287-0693

Ian Patterson
(PATTERSON)
21 Bateman Street
Cambridge CB1 2NB
United Kingdom

Peninsula Books
(PENINSULA)
451 N. Madison
Traverse City, MI 49684
(616) 941-2032

Dick Perier
(PERIER)
P.O. Box 1
Vancouver, WA 98666
(206) 696-2033

The Petersfield Bookshop
(PETERSFIELD)
16 A Chapel Street
Petersfield
Hampshire GU32 3DS
United Kingdom

R. & A. Petrilla
(PETRILLA)
Box 306
Roosevelt, NJ 08555-0306
(609) 426-4999

Pettler & Lieberman
(PETTLER)
8033 Sunset Boulevard #977
Los Angeles, CA 90046
(310) 474-2479

Pharos Books
(PHAROS)
P.O. Box 17
Fair Haven Station
New Haven, CT 06513
(203) 562-0085

Philip J. Pirages
(PIRAGES)
P.O. Box 504
2205 Nut Tree Lane
McMinnville, OR 97128
(503) 472-0476

R. Plapinger
(PLAPINGER)
P.O. Box 1062
Ashland, OR 97520
(503) 488-1220

The Poetry Bookshop
(POETRY)
West House
Broad Street
Hay-on-Wye
via Hereford HR3 5DB
United Kingdom

Polyanthos
(POLYANTHOS)
Park Avenue Books
P.O. Box 343
Huntington, NY 11743
(516) 271-5558

Wallace D. Pratt, Bookseller
(PRATT)
1801 Gough Street, #304
San Francisco, CA 94109
(415) 673-0178

Quest Rare Books
(QUEST)
774 Santa Ynez
Stanford, CA 94305
(415) 324-3119

David Rees
(REES)
18a Prentis Road
London SW16 1QD
United Kingdom

William Reese Co.
(REESE)
409 Temple Street
New Haven, CT 06511
(203) 789-8081

Jo Ann Reisler, Ltd.
(REISLER)
360 Glyndon Street, N.E.
Vienna, VA 22180
(703) 938-2967

Revere Books
(REVERE)
P.O. Box 420
Revere, PA 18953
(610) 847-2709

Alice Robbins, Bookseller
(ROBBINS)
3002 Round Hill Road
Greensboro, NC 27408
(910) 282-1964

Leona Rostenberg and
  Madeleine Stern Rare Books
(ROSTENBERG
 & STERN)
40 E. 88th Street
New York, NY 10128
(212) 831-6628

Sadlon's Old and Rare Books
(SADLON)
1207 Fox River Dr.
De Pere, WI 54115
(414) 336-6665

Savona Books
(SAVONA)
9 Wilton Road
Hornsea
N. Humberside HV18 1QV
United Kingdom

Schoyer's Antiquarian Books
(SCHOYER)
1404 S. Negley Avenue
Pittsburgh, PA 15217
(412) 521-8464

Andrew Sclanders
(SCLANDERS)
11 Albany Road
Stroud Green
London N4 4RR
United Kingdom

Second Life Boooks, Inc.
(SECOND LIFE)
P.O. Box 242
Lanesborough, MA 01237
(413) 447-8010

Florian J. Shasky
(SHASKY)
970 Terra Bella Avenue
Suite 1
Mountain View, CA 94043
(415) 967-5330

Gregory Shifrin
(SHIFRIN)
15 Schoonmaker Lane
Woodstock, NY 12498
(914) 679-8472

The Silver Door
(SILVER DOOR)
P.O. Box 3208
Redondo Beach, CA 90277
(310) 379-6005

Smithfield Rare Books
(SMITHFIELD)
20 Deer Run Trail
Smithfield, RI 02917
(401) 231-8225

A. Sokol Books
(SOKOL)
Berghersh Place
Witnesham, Ipswich
Suffolk IP6 9EZ
United Kingdom

Monroe Stahr Books
(STAHR)
4420 Ventura Canyon Ave., #2
Sherman Oaks, CA 91423
(818) 784-0870

Sumner & Stillman
(SUMNER & STILLMAN)
P.O. Box 973
Yarmouth, ME 04096
(207) 846-6070

Raymond M. Sutton, Jr.
(SUTTON)
430 Main Street
Williamsburg, KY 40769
(606) 549-3464

Peter Taylor & Son
(PETER TAYLOR)
1 Ganders Ash
Leavesden
Watford
Hertfordshire WD2 7HE
United Kingdom

Michael Taylor Rare Books
(MICHAEL TAYLOR)
The Gables
8 Mendham Lane
Harleston, Norfolk 1P20 9DE
United Kingdom

Robert Temple
(TEMPLE)
65 Mildmay Road
London N1 4PU
United Kingdom

Trophy Room Books
TROPHY ROOM
Box 3041
Agoura, CA 91301
(818) 889-2469

H.E. Turlington Books
(TURLINGTON)
P.O. Box 190
Carrboro, NC 27510-0190
(919) 968-3656

Ulysses
(ULYSSES)
31 & 40 Museum Street
London WC1A 1LH
United Kingdom

Len Unger
(UNGER)
631 N. Wilcox Avenue, 3B
Los Angeles, CA 90004
(213) 962-7929

T.S. Vandoros Rare Books
(VANDOROS)
5827 Highland Terrace
Middleton, WI 53562
(608) 836-8254

The Veatchs
(VEATCHS)
20 Veronica Court
Smithtown, NY 11787-1323
(516) 265-3357

Virgo Books
(VIRGO)
Little Court, South Wraxall
Bradford on Avon
Wiltshire BA 15 2SE
United Kingdom

Waiting for Godot Books
(GODOT)
P.O. Box 331
Hadley, MA 01035
(413) 585-5126

Patrick Walcot
(WALCOT)
60 Sunnybank Road
Sutton Coldfield
West Midlands B73 5RJ
United Kingdom

Andrew D. Washton
(WASHTON)
411 E. 83rd Street
New York, NY 10028
(212) 481-0479

Waterfield's
(WATERFIELD)
36 Park End Street
Oxford OX1 1HJ
United Kingdom

Jeff Weber
(WEBER)
P.O. Box 3368
Glendale, CA 91201
(818) 848-9704

Wheldon & Wesley Ltd.
(WHELDON & WESLEY)
Lytton Lodge, Codicote
Hitchin Herts. SG4 8TE
United Kingdom

David White
(WHITE)
17 High Street
Bassingbourn
Royston, Herts. SG8 5NE
United Kingdom

F.E. Whitehart
(WHITEHART)
40 Priestfield Road
Forest Hill
London SE23 2RS
United Kingdom

Edna Whiteson, A.B.A.
(WHITESON)
66 Belmont Avenue
Cockfosters
Herts. EN4 9LA
United Kingdom

Nigel Williams
(WILLIAMS)
7 Waldeck Grove
West Norwood,
London SE27 0BE
United Kingdom

Willow House Books
(WILLOW HOUSE)
58A Chapel Street
Chorley, Lancs. PR7 1BS
United Kingdom

Words Etcetera
(WORDS ETC)
Hinton Lodge
Crown Road, Marnhull
Dorset DT10 1DE
United Kingdom

Worldwide Antiquarian
(WORLDWIDE)
P.O. Box 391
Cambridge, MA 02141
(617) 876-6220

ABBREVIATIONS

To allow us to provide the maximum amount of information in a limited space, we have used the following abbreviations in editing the entries for this guide. Most of these abbreviations are standard.

4to	a book with a height of approximately 12"	ex-libris	bookplate present	OUP	Oxford University Press
8vo	a book with a height of approximately 9"	extrem(s)	extremities	pb	paperback
		facs	facsimile	Phila	Philadelphia
12mo	a book with a height of approximately 7-8"	fep	free end paper, front end paper, front free end paper, flyleaf	pict	pictorial
add'l	additional			prelims	preliminary pages
aeg	all edges gilt	fig(s)	figure(s)	plt(s)	plate(s)
adv	advance	fldg	folding, fold-out, folded	pg/pp	page(s)
als	autograph letter, signed	fr	front	port(s)	portrait(s)
assoc	association	frontis	frontispiece	promo	promotional
BAE	Bureau of American Ethnology	FSG	Farrar, Straus, and Giroux	pseud	pseudonym
BAL	Bibliography of American Literature	G&D	Grosset & Dunlap	ptd	printed
		GC	Garden City	ptg	printing
Balt	Baltimore	GPO	Government Printing Office	ptr	printer
bd(s)	board(s)	grn	green	pub's	publisher's
bkpl(s)	bookplate(s)	hb	hardback, hardcover	rev	revised, reviser
brn	brown	hist	historical	rev copy	review copy
b/w	black and white	HMSO	Her (His) Majesty's Stationery Office	rep	rear end paper, rear free end paper
C&W	Chatto & Windus	illus	illustration(s), illustrated, illustrator	rt	right
ca	circa			rmdr mk	remainder mark
cat(s)	catalog(s)	imp	impression	rpt	reprint
CCC	Collins Crime Club	incl	included, including	rptd	reprinted
cent	century	inscrip	non-authorial inscription	S&S	Simon & Schuster
cl	cloth	L.A.	Los Angeles	SF	San Francisco
comp	compiler/complimentary	LEC	Limited Editions Club	sig(s)	non-authorial signature(s); signature(s) (gathering of book pages)
contemp	contemporary	lib	library		
CUP	Cambridge University Press	litho	lithograph, lithographic		
cvr(s)	cover(s)	lg	large	sl	slight, slightly, minor,
cvrd	covered	ltd	limited	sm	small
dbl	double	lt	light, lightly, moderately	soc	society
DCC	Doubleday Crime Club	mk(s)	mark(s), marking(s)	SPCK	Society for the Promotion of Christian Knowledge
dec	decorative, decorated	mkd	marked		
diag(s)	diagram(s)	MMA	Metropolitan Museum of Art	subs	subscription
dj	dust jacket, dust wrapper	mod	modern	supp	supplement
dk	dark	MOMA	Museum of Modern Art	teg	top edge gilt
dknd	darkened	ms	manuscript	tls	typed letter, signed
dkng	darkening	mtd	mounted	tp	title page
dup	duplicate	n.d.	no date	trans	translated, translator, t tion
dwgs	drawings	n.p.	no place, no publisher		
ed(s)	editor(s), edited by, edition(s)	NAL	New American Library	univ	university
emb	embossed	NF	near fine	unptd	unprinted
engr(s)	engraving(s), engraved	#	number	VF	very fine
enlgd	enlarged	NY	New York	VG	very good
ep(s)	endpaper(s)	NYGS	New York Graphic Society	vol(s)	volume(s)
esp	especially	o/w	otherwise	w/	with
et al	and others	OJ	Orange Judd	w/o	without
ex-lib	ex-library	orig	original		

A

A'BECKETT, GILBERT ABBOTT (rev). The Comic Blackstone. London: Bradbury, Agnew, 1887. Rev, extended ed. Blue pict cl (worn; hinges cracked). Good. *Boswell.* $125/£81

A. (Pseud of Matthew Arnold.) The Strayed Reveller, and Other Poems. London: B. Fellows, 1849. 1st ed, 1st bk. 128pp. Orig grn cl. VG (hinges cracked internally; spine wear). *Chapel Hill.* $450/£290

AARONSON, BERNARD and HUMPHREY OSMOND (eds). Psychedelics: The Uses and Implications of Hallucinogenic Drugs. London: Hogarth Press, 1971. 1st UK ed. NF in dj (lt worn). *Sclanders.* $47/£30

ABBE, JAMES E. I Photograph Russia. NY: Robert M. McBride, (1934). 1st ed. Ink numeral top tp, else NF in VG pict dj (tape repair spine verso, abrasions). *Chapel Hill.* $50/£32

ABBEY, EDWARD. Cactus Country. NY: Time-Life, 1973. 1st ed. Fine. *Connolly.* $30/£19

ABBEY, EDWARD. Jonathan Troy. NY: Dodd Mead, (1954). 1st ed, 1st bk. Inscribed at later date. Fine in NF dj (2 triangular chips internally repaired, few tears). *Between The Covers.* $3,000/£1,935

ABBEY, KLERAN. (Pseud of Helen Reilly). Beyond the Dark. Scribner's, 1944. 1st ed. VG (sm tear, name, lt soiled) in dj (lt worn, chipped). *Murder.* $50/£32

ABBOT, ANTHONY. The Shudders. NY: Farrar & Rinehart, 1943. 1st ed. Fine in dj (lt wear). *Else Fine.* $45/£29

ABBOT, ANTHONY. The Shudders. NY: Farrar & Rinehart, 1943. 1st ed. VG in dj (sl dknd spine, ends chipped). *Mordida.* $135/£87

ABBOT, CHARLES GREELEY. Smithsonian Scientific Series. NY: Smithsonian Inst, 1931. 12 vols complete. Fine. *Bishop.* $100/£65

ABBOT, W.W. The Royal Governors of Georgia 1754-1775. Chapel Hill: UNC Press, (1959). 1st ed. Grn cl. Red pencil notes, else NF in VG dj. *Chapel Hill.* $45/£29

ABBOTT, A.O. Prison Life in the South.... NY: Harper, 1866. 2nd ptg. Frontis, 374pp + (10)pp ads. Orig grn cl. Bkpl; bkseller's inkstamp; hinges tender, else VG-. *Chapel Hill.* $85/£55

ABBOTT, BERENICE. Berenice Abbott Photographs. NY: Horizon Press, 1970. 1st ed. NF in NF dj. *Bishop.* $60/£39

ABBOTT, BERENICE. The World of Atget. NY: Horizon, (1964). 180 photo plts. NF in dj (chipped). *Artis.* $125/£81

ABBOTT, H.P. The Nazi SS Made Believers. OH, 1946. VG. *Clark.* $45/£29

ABBOTT, JOHN S.C. Captain Kidd and Others of the Buccaneers. NY: Dodd, Mead, 1898. 373pp. Good. *Hayman.* $20/£13

ABBOTT, LEE K. Love Is a Crooked Thing. Chapel Hill: Algonquin, 1986. 1st ed. Signed, dated. Fine in Fine dj. *Revere.* $45/£29

ABBOTT, LEE K. Strangers in Paradise. NY: Putnam's, 1987. 1st ed. Signed, dated. Fine in Fine dj. *Revere.* $40/£26

ABBOTT, LYMAN. Reminiscences. NY, 1915. 1st ed. *Hayman.* $20/£13

ABBOTT, MAUDE. Atlas of Congenital Cardiac Disease. NY, 1936. 1st ed. Good. *Fye.* $250/£161

ABBOTT, MAUDE. Atlas of Congenital Cardiac Disease. NY, 1954. 1st ed, rpt. Good. *Fye.* $125/£81

ABDILL, GEORGE B. Civil War Railroads. NY: Bonanza Books, (1961). Later ptg. NF in VG dj (spine split). *Mcgowan.* $35/£23

ABE, K. The Box Man. Knopf, 1974. 1st ed. Fine in dj. *Fine Books.* $37/£24

ABEEL, DAVID. Journal of a Residence in China, and the Neighboring Countries. NY: J. Abeel Williamson, 1836. 2nd ed. Orig cl (faded); paper spine label. *Karmiole.* $100/£65

ABERCROMBIE, JOHN. Inquiries Concerning the Intellectual Powers and the Investigation of Truth. Edinburgh/London, 1833. 4th ed. xv,441pp. 1/2 calf, marbled bds (lt spotting; upper hinge, joint sl tender; sl worn; spine faded). *Edwards.* $124/£80

ABERCROMBIE, JOHN. Pathological and Practical Researches on Diseases of the Brain and Spinal Cord. Phila, 1843. 324pp. Leather. (Backstrip worn; fr hinge broken.) *Fye.* $150/£97

ABERCROMBIE, JOHN. Pathological and Practical Researches on Diseases of the Stomach.... Phila, 1838. 3rd Amer ed. 320pp + 8pp ads. (Worn; upper cvr detached; heavily browned.) *Argosy.* $50/£32

ABERCROMBIE, LASCELLES. The Sale of Saint Thomas in Six Acts. Secker, 1930. #118/480 signed. Name, date; spine faded, o/w Fine. *Poetry.* $31/£20

ABERNATHY, JOHN. Catch 'Em Alive Jack. NY: Association, 1936. 1st ed. *Lambeth.* $60/£39

ABERNETHY, JAMES. The Hunterian Oration, for the Year 1819...Royal College of Surgeons.... London, 1819. (1); 66pp ad leaf. Uncut; new marbled bds. Good. *Goodrich.* $75/£48

ABERNETHY, JOHN. Lectures on Anatomy, Surgery, and Pathology. London, 1828. 1st ed. 580pp (lib stamps prelims; index bound upside down). New 1/4 calf. *Whitehart.* $140/£90

ABERNETHY, JOHN. The Surgical and Physiological Works of.... London: Longman, et al, 1830. 4 vols. Vols 1&2 in early 1/4 sheep; vols 3&4 in orig sheep w/new cl backs. Ex-lib w/mks; foxing, o/w internally Good set. *Goodrich.* $250/£161

ABERNETHY, JOHN. Surgical Observations on Diseases Resembling Syphilis. London, 1810. 234pp (sl foxing; lib stamp tp). New 1/2 red morocco. *Whitehart.* $171/£110

ABERNETHY, JOHN. Surgical Observations on Diseases Resembling Syphilis. London, 1814. 3rd ed. 234pp (lib stamps, sigs). New 1/2 calf. *Whitehart.* $124/£80

ABERNETHY, JOHN. Surgical Observations on the Constitutional Origin and Treatment of Local Diseases.... Phila, 1811. 1st Amer ed. 325pp. Full leather. Good. *Fye.* $300/£194

ABERNETHY, JOHN. Surgical Observations on the Constitutional Origin and Treatment of Local Diseases.... London: Longman etc, 1826. 8th ed. xii,346pp. Contemp 1/2 calf, gilt; marbled bds (rubbed). Internally Very Clean. *White.* $116/£75

ABERNETHY, JOHN. Surgical Observations on the Constitutional Origin and Treatment of Local Diseases.... London, 1829. 11th ed. xii,346pp (sl foxing). New paper spine, binding & eps fitted. (Bd edges damaged.) *Whitehart.* $93/£60

ABERNETHY, JOHN. Surgical Observations. Part the Second. London, 1806. 1st ed. viii,246pp (lib stamps prelims). *Whitehart.* $217/£140

ABERNETHY, JOHN. The Surgical Works of John Abernethy. London: Longman etc, 1827. New ed. 2 vols. Engr plt vol 2; tp each vol. Good. *White.* $287/£185

ABERNETHY, THOMAS PERKINS. From Frontier to Plantation in Tennessee. Chapel Hill: Univ of NC Press, 1932. 1st ed. Tan cl. Bkpl, else Fine in VG dj (verso tape repaired). *Chapel Hill.* $95/£61

ABERNETHY, THOMAS PERKINS. Western Lands and the American Revolution. NY: D. Appleton-Century, 1937. 1st ed. 4 fldg maps. VG + in dj (chipped, soiled). *Bohling.* $85/£55

ABERT, JAMES W. Through the Country of the Comanche Indians in the Fall of the Year 1845. John Galvin (ed). SF: John Howell, 1970. Color frontis, 25 color plts, 2 fldg maps. VF in VF dj. *Oregon.* $95/£61

ABERT, JAMES W. Through the Country of the Comanche Indians in the Fall of the Year 1845.... John Galvin (ed). SF: John Howell, 1970. White cl, gilt. Dj (lt soiled). *Glenn.* $55/£35

ABERT, JAMES W. Through the Country of the Comanche Indians in...1845. (SF): John Howell Bks, 1970. New ptg. 22 color plts, 3 maps (2 fldg). VG. Howes A 10. *Schoyer.* $45/£29

ABNEY, W. Colour Vision. London, 1895. 1st ed. 231pp. Good. *Fye.* $100/£65

ABORDEN, MRS. JOHN. The Cruise of the Northern Light. NY: Macmillan, 1928. VG. *High Latitude.* $45/£29

Above and Beyond: A History of the Medal of Honor from the Civil War to Vietnam. Boston, 1985. VG in VG dj. *Clark.* $37/£24

ABRAHAM, DOROTHY. Lone Cone. n.d. (ca 1946). 3rd ed. VG in wraps. *Oregon.* $30/£19

ABRAHAM, GEORGE D. British Mountain Climbs. London: Mills & Boon, 1932. 3rd ed. VG in dj (worn). *Hollett.* $54/£35

ABRAHAM, GEORGE D. The Complete Mountaineer. London: Methuen, 1907. 1st ed. 75 plts. Orig cl gilt (rebacked in matching levant morocco gilt). *Hollett.* $132/£85

ABRAHAM, GEORGE D. Mountain Adventures at Home and Abroad. London: Methuen, 1910. 1st ed. 26 plts. (Spine sl faded; flyleaves sl browned.) *Hollett.* $93/£60

ABRAHAM, GEORGE D. On Alpine Heights and British Crags. London: Methuen, 1919. 1st ed. 24 plts. (Spine sl faded). *Hollett.* $101/£65

ABRAHAM, JAMES JOHNSTON. Lettsom. His Life.... London, 1933. Frontis port. Cl (sl faded). *Edwards.* $54/£35

ABRAHAM, KARL. Selected Papers of.... London: Hogarth/Inst of Psycho-Analysis, 1949. 1st ed. Grn cl. VG in dj. *Gach.* $35/£23

ABRAMS, LE ROY. Flora of Los Angeles and Vicinity. Stanford: Stanford Univ, 1904. Fine. *Quest.* $45/£29

ABSE, DANNIE. Ash on a Young Man's Sleeve. London, 1954. 1st ed. Inscribed. VG in dj. *Words Etc.* $43/£28

ABSE, DANNIE. Lunchtime. London: Poem-of-the-Month Club Ltd, 1974. 1st Eng ed. Signed. VG. *Ulysses.* $28/£18

ABSE, DANNIE. Some Corner of an English Field. London, 1956. 1st ed. VG in dj (sl rubbed). *Words Etc.* $23/£15

ABU-LUGHOD, JANET L. Cairo. Princeton, NJ: Princeton Univ Press, 1971. 1st ed. VG (upper part of leaves wrinkled by dampness) in dj. *Worldwide.* $45/£29

Account of a New Process in Painting.... (By Miss Cleaver.) London: Rivington, 1821. xi,174pp. Bds (respined). *Marlborough.* $349/£225

ACHESON, SAM. 35,000 Days in Texas. NY: Macmillan, 1938. Signed, inscribed. VG. *Burcham.* $45/£29

ACIER, M. (ed). From Spanish Trenches. NY, 1937. 1st ed. Dull, else Good in wrappers. *Whiteson.* $28/£18

ACKERKNECHT, E.H. A Short History of Medicine. NY, 1955. Nice. *Goodrich.* $35/£23

ACKERLEY, J.R. E.M. Forster, A Portrait. London, 1970. 1st ed. VG in ptd wrappers. *Argosy.* $25/£16

ACKERLEY, J.R. My Father and Myself. NY: Coward-McCann, 1969. 1st Amer ed. Black cl. Fine in dj w/wraparound band. *Cady.* $20/£13

ACKROYD, PETER. Country Life. London: Ferry Press, 1978. One of 324 (of 350) trade copies. NF in wrappers. *Rees.* $39/£25

ACKROYD, PETER. Country Life. Ferry Press, 1978. One of 324 (of 350) trade copies. Signed. NF in wrappers. *Rees.* $54/£35

ACKROYD, PETER. Dickens. London: Sinclair-Stevenson, 1990. One of 150 specially bound, numbered, signed. Fine in glassine dj. *Rees.* $70/£45

ACKROYD, PETER. The Diversions of Purley. London: Hamilton, 1987. 1st UK ed. Signed. Fine in dj. *Lewton.* $34/£22

ACKROYD, PETER. Dressing Up. London: Thames & Hudson, 1979. 1st ed. Fine in dj (sl nicked). *Rees.* $93/£60

ACKROYD, PETER. Dressing Up. London: Thames & Hudson, 1979. 1st UK ed. Fine in VG + dj (sl scratch rear). *Williams.* $186/£120

ACKROYD, PETER. Ezra Pound and His World. Thames & Hudson, 1980. 1st ed. Fine in dj. *Poetry.* $19/£12

ACKROYD, PETER. First Light. London: Hamish Hamilton, 1989. 1st ed. Signed. Fine in dj. *Limestone.* $30/£19

ACKROYD, PETER. Hawksmoor. London: Hamilton, 1985. 1st UK ed. Bkpl, o/w Fine in dj. *Lewton.* $42/£27

ACKROYD, PETER. The Last Testament of Oscar Wilde. Hamish Hamilton, 1983. 1st ed. Dj. *Edwards.* $23/£15

Across the Atlantic. (By John Delaware Lewis.) London: George Earle, 1851. 1st ed. x,274pp + ads. Grn blind-stamped cl. Sm gouge on spine, o/w Very Nice. *Karmiole.* $75/£48

ACTON, HAROLD. Five Saints and an Appendix. London: Robert Holden, 1927. 1st ed. Cl-backed batik bds, paper spine label; unopened. Stamp rear pastedown; fep torn, else Fine. *Pharos.* $45/£29

ACTON, HAROLD. Nancy Mitford. A Memoir. London: Hamish Hamilton, 1976. 1st ed. NF in dj. *Limestone.* $55/£35

ACTON, LORD. The Cambridge Modern History. NY: Macmillan, 1903. 5 vols. VG + . *Bishop.* $22/£14

ACTON, WILLIAM. A Complete Practical Treatise on Venereal Diseases, and Their Immediate and Remote Consequences. NY, 1846. 1st Amer ed. 334pp. Contents Fine (spine chipped; fr bd detached). *Fye.* $150/£97

Acts of the General Assembly of the State of Virginia, Passed in 1861-2, in the Eighty-Sixth Year of the Commonwealth. Richmond: William F. Ritchie, 1862. Sheep-backed marbled bds, embrowned but sound. *Boswell.* $150/£97

Acts Passed at the First Session of the Eighteenth General Assembly for the Commonwealth of Kentucky...1809. Frankfort: William Gerard, 1810. 1st ed. 172pp. Later cl. Lacks last leaf of index; few pp w/portions missing, else VG. *Mcgowan.* $125/£81

ADACHI, KINNOSUKE. Tales of Three Cities in Manchuria. (Tokyo): South Manchuria Railway Co, 1933. Color ptd wrappers, remnants of lettering on fr cvr. Color ptd wrappers. *Schoyer.* $40/£26

ADAIR, GILBERT. Vietnam on Film: From the 'The Green Berets' to 'Apocalypse Now.' NY: Proteus, (1981). 1st US ed. VG+ in dj (lt worn; lamination piece peeled). *Aka.* $50/£32

ADAIR, JAMES. The History of the American Indians. Johnson City, TN: Watauga Press, 1930. 2nd ed. One of 750. Fldg map. Teg; unopened. Blue cl (spine sl soiled). Fine. Howes A 38. *Chapel Hill.* $175/£113

ADAM, EVELYN. Behind the Shoji. London, 1910. 1st ed. (Lt discolored.) *Edwards.* $43/£28

ADAMIC, LOUIS. The House in Antigua: A Restoration. NY/London: Harper, 1937. 1st ed. Orig cl, photo cvr label (spine sl discolored). *Sadlon.* $10/£6

ADAMS, ALICE. Return Trips. NY: Knopf, 1985. 1st ed. Fine in dj (lt used, lt edgewear). *Aka.* $20/£13

ADAMS, ANDREW LEITH. Field and Forest Rambles. London: Henry S. King, (1873). Aeg. Full tan calf, gilt school badge. *Petersfield.* $87/£56

ADAMS, ANDREW LEITH. Notes of a Naturalist in the Nile Valley and Malta. Edinburgh: Edmonston & Douglas, 1870. xvi,(296)pp, color map. Sturdy buckram (ex-lib rebound). *Schoyer.* $45/£29

ADAMS, ANDY. The Corporal Segundo. Wilson M. Hudson (ed). Austin: Encino Press, 1968. 1st ed. #22/750. Signed by Hudson. Pict bds. Fine. *Harrington.* $40/£26

ADAMS, ANDY. The Outlet. Boston, 1905. 1st Amer ed. Pict cvrs, gilt. Fine (spine sl sunned, extrems sl rubbed). *Polyanthos.* $75/£48

ADAMS, ANDY. The Outlet. Boston: Houghton Mifflin, 1905. 1st ed. Cvr worn, else VG. *Parker.* $50/£32

ADAMS, ANDY. Reed Anthony, Cowman. Boston: Houghton Mifflin, 1907. 1st ed. VG- (sm hole in spine, 1st 4pp). *Parker.* $35/£23

ADAMS, ANDY. A Texas Matchmaker. Boston, 1904. 1st ed. *Lambeth.* $30/£19

ADAMS, ANDY. Why the Chisholm Trail Forks and Other Tales of the Cattle Country. Wilson Hudson (ed). Austin: Univ of TX, 1956. 1st thus. NF in dj (lt wear; chip). *Parker.* $35/£23

ADAMS, ANDY. Why the Chisholm Trail Forks and Other Tales of the Cattle Country. Wilson M. Hudson (ed). Austin: Univ of TX, 1956. 1st ed. Dj. *Lambeth.* $35/£23

ADAMS, ANSEL. Ansel Adams. Images 1923-1974. Boston, 1974. 1st ptg. Signed. 115 photos. Fine in dj, orig monographed slipcase (tape reinforced; stains, sl peeling). *Baade.* $425/£274

ADAMS, ANSEL. Death Valley. SF: 5 Associates, 1959. 2nd ed. Pict wrappers (sl stain lower margin). *Shasky.* $35/£23

ADAMS, ANSEL. Examples: The Making of 40 Photographs. NYGS, (1983). 1st ed. VF in VF dj. *Oregon.* $45/£29

ADAMS, ANSEL. An Introduction to Hawaii. SF: 5 Associates, (1964). 1st ed. VG in pict color wrappers. *Shasky.* $40/£26

ADAMS, ANSEL. Making a Photograph. London/NY: Studio Ltd/Studio Pub, 1935. 1st ed. 32 tipped-in plts, all Fine. Glossy pict paper-cvrd bds (dull, extrems worn, bumped). VG (eps lt foxed, ink name, date) in dj (dampstain, short tears, else VG). *Godot.* $250/£161

ADAMS, ANSEL. Photographs of the Southwest. Boston, 1976. 1st ptg. Gilt cl. Fine in dj (sl creased). *Baade.* $90/£58

ADAMS, ANSEL. Yosemite and the Range of Light. Boston: NYGS, 1979. 1st ed. Signed. VG+ in VG dj. *Parker.* $125/£81

ADAMS, ANSEL. Yosemite Valley. Nancy Newhall (ed). SF: 5 Associates, 1959. 1st ed. Pict wrappers (corner crease). *Dawson.* $60/£39

ADAMS, ARTHUR. Travels of a Naturalist in Japan and Manchuria. London: Hurst and Blackett, 1870. 1st ed. 8vo. Engr frontis, x,334pp. Contemp tan half calf, marbled bds. VG (few mks; sl rubbed, short splits lower joint). *Morrell.* $256/£165

ADAMS, BERNARD. London Illustrated, 1604-1851. (Phoenix): Oryx Press, 1983. 1st ed. One of 500. Frontis. Fine. *Bookpress.* $110/£71

ADAMS, C. Great Campaigns. London: Blackwood, 1877. 5 fldg maps. 1/2 maroon calf, marbled sides (lg piece torn away), gilt backstrip (faded), leather label. *Petersfield.* $81/£52

ADAMS, DOUGLAS. The Hitch Hiker's Guide to the Galaxy. NY: Harmony Books, (1980). 1st Amer ed. 1st bk. NF in dj. *Godot.* $45/£29

ADAMS, DOUGLAS. The Hitch Hiker's Guide to the Galaxy. London: Arthur Baker, (1980). 1st hb ed. NF in NF dj. *Levin.* $200/£129

ADAMS, DOUGLAS. The Hitch Hiker's Guide to the Galaxy. London: Barker, 1979. 1st UK ed. Fine in dj. *Lewton.* $62/£40

ADAMS, DOUGLAS. The Restaurant at the End of the Universe. London: Barker, 1980. 1st UK ed. Fine in dj. *Lewton.* $54/£35

ADAMS, E. Francis Danby: Varieties of Poetic Experience. Yale Univ Press, 1973. 6 color, 160 b/w plts. Sound in dj. *Ars Artis.* $116/£75

ADAMS, EDWARD F. The Modern Farmer in His Business Relations.... SF: Stone, 1899. 1st ed. 662pp. VG. *Second Life.* $65/£42

ADAMS, ELIZABETH. Women Professional Workers. Chautauqua, NY, 1921. 1st ed. 2-inch piece clipped fep, o/w Fine. *Fye.* $80/£52

ADAMS, GEORGE WORTHINGTON. Doctors in Blue, The Medical History of the Union Army in the Civil War. NY, (1952). 1st ed. VG+ in VG+ dj. *Pratt.* $47/£30

ADAMS, H.G. Favorite Song Birds. London: Groombridge & Sons, n.d. (ca 1857). 3rd ed. 192pp, 12pp cat; 5 full-pg hand-colored plts. Mod brn cl; paper shelf label. Good+. *Smithfield.* $65/£42

ADAMS, H.G. The Language and Poetry of Flowers. NY: Derby, Jackson, 1860. Frontis, 272,60pp; 4 hand-colored plts, guards. Gilt dec cl (rubbed, spine ends worn). Text, plts Fine. *Quest.* $110/£71

ADAMS, HAROLD. The Missing Moon. NY: Charter, 1983. 1st ed. VF in wrappers. *Mordida*. $25/£16

ADAMS, HAROLD. Paint the Town Red. NY: Charter, 1982. 1st ed. VF in wrappers. *Mordida*. $25/£16

ADAMS, HENRY. The Education of Henry Adams. Boston: Riverside, 1918. 1st trade ed. VG + (lacks dj). *Lame Duck*. $45/£29

ADAMS, HERBERT. Oddways. Phila: Lippincott, 1929. 1st ed. VG in dj (dknd spine, chipped, closed tears). *Mordida*. $45/£29

ADAMS, HERBERT. The Queen's Gate Mystery. Lippincott, 1927. 1st ed. Top pg edges soiled; cvrs lt stained, else VG. *Murder*. $30/£19

ADAMS, J. WINSTEAD. Psychoanalysis of Drug Dependence. NY: Grune & Stratton, (1978). 1st ed. Ptd black cl. (Ex-lib.) *Gach*. $30/£19

ADAMS, JAMES TRUSLOW. America's Tragedy. NY: Scribner's, 1934. 1st ed. VG. *Mcgowan*. $45/£29

ADAMS, JOHN GLOVER. Discourse Commemorative of Alex Hodgson Stevens Life and Character. NY, (1871). 1st ed. 42pp. Mtd photo. VG. *Argosy*. $85/£55

ADAMS, JOHN QUINCY. The Birth of Mormonism. Boston, 1916. Ex-lib, o/w VG. *Benchmark*. $40/£26

ADAMS, JOHN QUINCY. Writings, 1779-1823. Worthington C. Ford (ed). NY, 1913-1917. 1st ed. 7 vols. (Few spines sl faded.) *Ginsberg*. $275/£177

ADAMS, JOHN. The Earliest Diary of John Adams. June 1753-April 1754. September 1758-January 1759. Cambridge: Harvard, 1966. 1st ed. 8 plts. Fine in VG dj. *Connolly*. $27/£17

ADAMS, JOHN. Legal Papers of John Adams. L. Kinvin Wroth & Hiller B. Zobel (eds). Cambridge: Harvard Univ Press, 1965. 3 vols. In djs (vol 3 chipped). *Argosy*. $125/£81

ADAMS, JULIA DAVIS. Stonewall. Dutton, (c1931). (1st ed). VG. *Book Broker*. $45/£29

ADAMS, LEONIE. High Falcon and Other Poems. NY, 1920. 1st ed. Fine. *Bond*. $85/£55

ADAMS, LEONIE. Those Not Elect. NY: McBride, 1925. 1st ed. White bds. VG in dj (reinforced verso). *Argosy*. $175/£113

ADAMS, N. A Voyage Around the World. Boston: Henry Hoyt, (1871). 1st separate ed. Frontis, (x),9-152pp, 2 plts. (Spine faded.) *Lefkowicz*. $135/£87

ADAMS, R.H. Illustrated Catalogue of Indian Portraits...Painted by Henry Cross. N.p.: R.H. Adams, 1927. Gray wrapper, cl spine. VG. *Laurie*. $75/£48

ADAMS, RAMON F. The Best of the American Cowboy. Norman: Univ of OK, 1957. 1st ed. *Lambeth*. $30/£19

ADAMS, RAMON F. Come and Get It. The Story of the Old Cowboy Cook. Norman: Univ of OK, 1952. 1st ed. VG + *Parker*. $35/£23

ADAMS, RAMON F. The Cowboy and His Humor. Austin: Encino, 1968. #504/850 signed. Gold paper over bds. *Lambeth*. $40/£26

ADAMS, RAMON F. Cowman Says It Salty. Tucson: Univ of AZ, 1971. 1st ed. Dj. *Lambeth*. $25/£16

ADAMS, RAMON F. More Burs under the Saddle. Norman: Univ of OK, 1979. 1st ed. Dj. *Lambeth*. $35/£23

ADAMS, RAMON F. The Old-Time Cowhand. NY: Macmillan, 1961. 1st trade ed. Tan cl. Fine in VG + dj (sl rubbed, chipped). *Harrington*. $30/£19

ADAMS, RAMON F. The Rampaging Herd. Norman: Univ of OK, (1959). (1st ed.) VG + in dj. *Bohling*. $150/£97

ADAMS, RAMON F. The Rampaging Herd. Norman, 1959. 1st ed. Fine in dj (sl worn, closed tear). *Baade*. $195/£126

ADAMS, RAMON F. Rampaging Hero, A Bibliography of Books and Pamphlets on Men and Events in the Cattle Industry. Norman, Univ of OK, (1959). (1st ed). Tp facs. VG + in dj. *Bohling*. $150/£97

ADAMS, RAMON F. Six-Guns and Saddle Leather. Norman: Univ of OK, 1954. 1st ed. NF (sl stain spine) in VG- dj. *Parker*. $150/£97

ADAMS, RAMON F. and HOMER BRITZMAN. Charles M. Russell: The Cowboy Artist. Pasadena, CA: Trail's End Pub Co, (1948). 1st ed. Pict eps. Burgundy cl. Fine in Fine dj. *Glenn*. $100/£65

ADAMS, RAMON F. and HOMER BRITZMAN. Charles Russell, the Cowboy Artist. Pasadena: Trails End, 1948. 1st ed. Ltd to 600. Signed presentation by Britzman. 2 vols. 1/4 leather, gold lettering. VF set. *Perier*. $395/£255

ADAMS, RANDOLPH C. Three Americanists. Phila: Univ of PA Press, 1939. 1st ed. Frontis; 3 plts. Fine. *Bookpress*. $65/£42

ADAMS, RICHARD. The Girl in a Swing. London: Allen Lane, 1980. 1st UK ed. 1st issue (w/pub's name on tp; heroine's name ptd as Kathe throughout). VG + in dj. *Williams*. $39/£25

ADAMS, RICHARD. The Plague Dogs. London: Allen Lane, 1977. 1st ed. A. Wainwright (illus). Dj (price-clipped). *Hollett*. $31/£20

ADAMS, RICHARD. Watership Down. London, 1972. 1st UK ed. VG (name) in dj (sl grubby, sm chips to spine corners, few long closed tears to hinges). *Williams*. $240/£155

ADAMS, RICHARD. Watership Down. London: Collins, 1972. 1st UK ed. VG (spine rubbed; fep sl mkd) in NF dj. *Williams*. $349/£225

ADAMS, RICHARD. Watership Down. Macmillan, 1974. 1st Amer ed, 1st bk. Fine in dj. *Fine Books*. $60/£39

ADAMS, ROBERT. Land Behind Baghdad: A History of Settlement on the Diyala Plains. Chicago: Univ of Chicago Press, (1965). 22 plts, 9 maps. Good. *Archaeologia*. $65/£42

ADAMS, ROBERT. The Narrative of Robert Adams Wrecked on the Western Coast of Africa in 1810.... London, 1816. 1st ed. xxxix,231pp (tp edges worn); lg fldg map. 1/2 calf (rebound). *Lewis*. $271/£175

ADAMS, ROBERT. Summer Nights. NY: Aperture, 1985. 1st ed. Fine in illus dj. *Cahan*. $40/£26

ADAMS, SAMUEL HOPKINS. The Pony Express. NY: Random House, 1950. 1st trade ed. Lee J. Ames (illus). Good in dj. *Cattermole*. $30/£19

ADAMS, W.H. The French Garden 1500-1800. London: Scolar, 1979. VF in dj. *Europa*. $31/£20

ADAMS, W.I. LINCOLN. Amateur Photography. NY: Baker & Taylor, 1893. 1st ed. 90pp + 10pp ads. Illus stiff wrappers. Spine lt chipped, else VG. *Cahan*. $65/£42

ADAMS, W.I. LINCOLN. Photographing in Old England, with Some Snap Shots in Scotland and Wales. NY, 1910. 1st ed. Pict cl (soiled). *Argosy*. $75/£48

ADAMS, WILLIAM. BAE Bulletin 188. Shonto. Washington, 1963. 10 plts, 3 maps (1 fldg), 12 charts. (Ex-lib, ink stamps, #s.) *Edwards.* $25/£16

ADCOCK, FLEUR. In Focus. London: Poem-of-the-Month Club Ltd, 1977. 1st Eng ed. Signed. VG (sm paper flaw; corner sl creased). *Ulysses.* $28/£18

ADDAMS, JANE. The Second Twenty Years at Hull-House. NY: Macmillan, 1930. 1st ed. Top edge dusted, else VG in VG- dj (tape repairs). *Lame Duck.* $45/£29

ADDAMS, JANE. The Spirit of Youth and the City Streets. NY: Macmillan, 1912. Good. *Hayman.* $20/£13

ADDAMS, JANE. Twenty Years at Hull-House. NY: Macmillan, 1910. 1st ed. Norah Hamilton (illus). Brn cl, gilt; paper illus. VG (fr hinge starting; spine sl skewed; soiled). *Hermitage.* $60/£39

ADDISON, CHARLES G. Damascus and Palmyra: a Journey to the East. London: Richard Bentley, 1838. 1st ed. 2 vols. 8vo. xxvii,(i)errata,440 (inner margins of frontis stained); x,(ii),484pp, half titles. (Foxing, browning.) 10 hand-colored litho plts. Green cl (rebacked; new eps, part of orig backstrips preserved; corners bumped; upper corners strengthened). *Morrell.* $527/£340

ADDISON, CHARLES G. The History of the Knights Templars, The Temple Church and the Temple. London: Longman et al, 1842. 1st ed. Frontis. Orig gilt/blindstamped brn cl (expertly rebacked). VG. *Houle.* $275/£177

ADDISON, JOSEPH et al. The Sir Roger de Coverly Papers. (NY): LEC, 1945. Ltd to 1500 signed by Gordon Ross (illus). Frontis, tp vignette, 10 color plts. Good in slipcase. *Karmiole.* $50/£32

ADDISON, JOSEPH. Miscellaneous Works. London: Ptd for J. & R. Tonson, 1753. 3 vols. 62 plts. (Feps lt browned, 1 lacks sm piece.) Contemp mottled calf, dec gilt, raised bands, leather spine labels (spines sl cracked). *Edwards.* $233/£150

ADDISON, JOSEPH. Remarks on Several Parts of Italy.... London: Tonson, 1736. 5th ed. Contemp polished calf, gilt. VG (joints split; lacks leather label). *Agvent.* $125/£81

ADDISON, JOSEPH. The Vision of Mirzah. SF: Book Club of CA, 1917. #277/300. Frontis port. Uncut. Orig bds, linen spine. VG. *Hartfield.* $75/£48

ADDISON, JOSEPH. Works. London: Bell, 1883. Reprint. 6 vols. 1/2 maroon morocco; marbled bds; gilt. (Rubbed; spines sl dknd.) *Agvent.* $200/£129

ADE, GEORGE. Breaking Into Society. NY: Harper, 1904. 1st ed. Very Nice. *Hermitage.* $30/£19

ADE, GEORGE. Doc' Horne. NY: Grosset & Dunlap, 1899. 292pp, 4pp ads. Fine. *Connolly.* $27/£17

ADE, GEORGE. In Babel. Stories of Chicago. NY: McClure, Phillips, 1903. 1st ed. Good (white lettering flaked). *Connolly.* $10/£6

ADE, GEORGE. More Fables. Chicago: Stone, 1900. 1st Amer ed. Dec cl. VG (discoloration rear cvr; sig). *Agvent.* $45/£29

ADE, GEORGE. People You Know. NY: Harper, 1903. 1st ed. VG. *Hermitage.* $35/£23

Adelaide, or the Rainy Evening. Boston: Christian Register Office, 1827. 34pp. Woodcut vignette tp, cvr; 3 Fine 1/2 pg cuts. Pict buff paper wrappers. VG (spine top chipped). *Hobbyhorse.* $75/£48

ADELMAN, BOB. Down Home: Camden, Alabama. NY: McGraw-Hill, (1972). (Lt edgewear.) Dj (chipped; shelfwear). *Aka.* $30/£19

ADHEMAR, JEAN and FRANCOISE CACHIN. Degas. The Complete Etchings, Lithographs and Monotypes. London: Thames & Hudson, 1973. Fine in dj. *Heller.* $200/£129

ADHEMAR, JEAN and FRANCOISE CACHIN. Degas. The Complete Etchings.... London, 1974. 18 color plts. (Ex-lib w/ink stamp, bkpl.) Dj (spine sl faded). *Edwards.* $62/£40

ADHEMAR, JEAN. Toulouse-Lautrec, His Complete Lithographs and Drypoints. NY, n.d. (1965). Sm spot fep, else VG in dj (sl worn). *King.* $175/£113

ADHEMAR, JEAN. Toulouse-Lautrec. London, 1965. 370 plts. Orange cl (soiled). *Edwards.* $85/£55

ADHEMAR, JEAN. Toulouse-Lautrec. His Complete Lithographs and Drypoints. London: Thames & Hudson, 1965. Orig ed. 368 plts (54 color). Sound in dj. *Ars Artis.* $163/£105

ADLER, KATHLEEN. Manet. Oxford: Phaidon, 1986. 1st ed. Dj. *Edwards.* $47/£30

ADLUM, JOHN. Memoirs of the Life of John Adlum in the Revolutionary War. Chicago: Caxton Club, 1968. One of 1100. Blue cl. VG + in glassine wrapper (chipped). *Bohling.* $45/£29

ADNEY, EDWIN T. and HOWARD I. CHAPELLE. The Bark Canoes and Skin Boats of North America. Washington: Smithsonian, 1964. 1st ed. VG. *High Latitude.* $45/£29

ADRIAN, E.D. The Basis of Sensation. NY, 1928. 1st Amer ed. Good. *Fye.* $60/£39

ADRIAN, E.D. The Mechanism of Nervous Action, Electrical Studies of the Neurone. Phila, 1932. 1st Amer ed. (Ex-lib.) *Fye.* $50/£32

ADRIAN, E.D. The Mechanism of Nervous Action, Electrical Studies of the Neurone. London, 1932. 1st ed. Good. *Fye.* $100/£65

ADRIAN, E.D. The Physical Background of Perception. Oxford, 1947. 1st ed. (Ex-lib.) *Fye.* $35/£23

ADRIANI, GOTZ. Degas. London, 1985. 1st UK ed. Dj. *Edwards.* $54/£35

ADRIANI, GOTZ. Toulouse-Lautrec, the Complete Graphic Works. (NY): Thames and Hudson, (1988). 1st Amer ed. Frontis. Minor rubbing dj; else Fine. *Bookpress.* $200/£129

ADRIANI, GOTZ. Toulouse-Lautrec. The Complete Graphic Works, a Catalogue Raisonne. London: Thames & Hudson, 1988. Sound in dj. *Ars Artis.* $59/£38

Adventures of a Pincushion. (By Mary Ann Kilner.) London: John Marshall, n.d. (ca 1780). 2 vols in 1. Sm 12mo. Full-pg frontis (verso reinforced at spine), ix,124pp; 35 half-pg VF wood engrs. Dutch floral bds (rubbed, corners rounded; ink scribbles inside). Internally VG (lacks eps, pp95-6). *Hobbyhorse.* $250/£161

Adventures of Congo.... London: John Harris, n.d. (ca 1825). 2nd ed. 12mo. x,191,2pp list, 24 Fine engrs in 12 plts, dated 10 Nov 1823. Pict buff paper on bds, red roan spine, gilt title. VG (sl internal foxing; lt soiling, rubbing). *Hobbyhorse.* $250/£161

Adventures of Ferdinand Count Fathom. (By Tobias Smollett.) London: W. Johnston, 1753. 1st ed. 2 vols. 8vo. 262; 315pp. Early 20th cent full speckled calf in period style w/morocco spine labels; gilt. Paper repairs to title, other leaves Vol 1; lacks half-titles, final blank leaf Vol 1; label; else Lovely. *Chapel Hill.* $700/£452

Adventures of Mother Hubbard and Her Dog. London: J.L. Marks, n.d. (ca 1840). 12mo. 15pp + 1pg ad on back wrapper; 8 Fine wood engrs. Ptd dec stiff wrapper; pp 2, 15 pasted down. Internally Fine (cvrs sl soiled). *Hobbyhorse.* $255/£165

Adventures of Peregrine Pickle in which are included Memoirs of a Lady of Quality. (By Tobias Smollett.) London: Strahan et al, 1784. 7th ed. 4 vols. Engr frontis each vol, (xii),268; 298; 282; 304pp. Full contemp calf, gilt. Nice set. *Hartfield.* $425/£274

Adventures of Roderick Random. (By Tobias Smollett.) London: J. Osborn, 1748. 1st ed, 1st bk. One of 2000. 2 vols. 8vo. 324; 366pp. Contemp full calf, gilt-ruled borders, raised bands. Fr cvr Vol 1 reattached, other joints cracked, sig; else VG in brn cl chemises, 1/4 morocco dbl slipcase. *Chapel Hill.* $800/£516

Adventures of the Old Woman, Her Dog and the Pedlar. London: J.L. Marks, n.d. (ca 1830). 12mo. 6 leaves + 1pg list on lower wrapper. Five 1/2pg, six 1/3pg hand-colored wood engrs. Good (sm chip to wrapper, 1st pg; split at spine; sm spots). *Hobbyhorse.* $155/£100

Adventures of Tuffy. London: Robert Edwards, 1948. 25x21 cm. 4 dbl-pg pop-ups. Heavy cards. Spine sl worn, o/w VG-. *Book Finders.* $60/£39

AESOP. Aesop's Fables. London: T. Hepstinstall, 1797. 12mo. Full-pg copper engr tp, xii,(8),267pp. Full leather on bds, gilt, red label. Lt rubbed; sm scuff upper cvr, else Fine. *Hobbyhorse.* $400/£258

AESOP. Aesop's Fables. NY: Cassell, 1884. Enlgd ed. 4to. 390 numbered pp. Ernest Griset (illus). Illus bds (sl edgewear). *Reisler.* $350/£226

AESOP. Aesop's Fables. V.S. Vernon Jones (trans). London: Heinemann, 1912. 13 color plts by Arthur Rackham (sl foxing throughout). *Petersfield.* $101/£65

AESOP. Aesop's Fables. V. Jones (trans). London: Heinemann, 1912. #814/1450. Signed by Arthur Rackham (illus). 13 color plts, 58 b/w illus mtd on brn paper. NF in slipcase. *Davidson.* $1,450/£935

AESOP. Aesop's Fables. Samuel Croxall (trans). Oxford: LEC, 1933. Teg, rest untrimmed. Vellum spine, marbled sides, gilt title. Lovely in pub's slipcase. *Book Block.* $175/£113

AESOP. Fables of Aesop and Other Eminent Mythologists. (By Roger L'Estrange.) London: D. Brown et al, 1724. 7th ed corrected. 2 vols in 1. Thick 8vo. Full-pg copper engr port, plt, x,550pp + 1pg list; 266pp + 2pp list. Full tooled leather on bds (corners rubbed, rounded; spine lt frayed; worm hole internal part lower bd; line crack along fr hinges). Internally Fine (bkpl; ink sig fep). *Hobbyhorse.* $300/£194

AESOP. Fables of Aesop and Others. Samuel Croxall (trans). London: J. Brambles et al, 1804. New ed. 12mo. Engr frontis (faded spot lower corners) w/impt dated Aug 1, 1803; xxiv,329pp + 7pp index. VF cuts. 3/4 red grain morocco (rebound); marbled paper on bds; new eps. (Dated ink sig fr flyleaf; sm wormholes fr edges last few pp.) *Hobbyhorse.* $150/£97

AESOP. Fables of Aesop with a Life of the Author. NY: Hurd and Houghton, 1867. Herrick (engrs). xiii + 311pp. Red tooled cl on bds, gilt. VG (hinges lt shaken, cvr rubbed, spine chipped). *Hobbyhorse.* $125/£81

AESOP. The Fables of Aesop. London: Hodder & Stoughton, (1909). 1st ed. Lg 4to. 23 mtd color plts by Edward J. Detmold. Brn cl, gold lettering, design. VG. *Reisler.* $685/£442

AESOP. The Fables of Aesop. Samuel Croxall (trans). London: Frederick Warne, n.d. (1874). Revised Ed. Lg 12mo. Full-pg wood engr, by two, frontis; viii,152 + 1pg list lower cvr. 'Warne's Edition of Aesop's Fables' upper cvr. Pict yellow paper on bds, grn cl spine. Internally VG (dry seal of dealer; dated ink sig tp; soiled, corners worn; damp spot lower edge rear cvr). *Hobbyhorse.* $150/£97

AESOP. The Fables of Aesop. London: Milner & Co, n.d. (ca 1860). Title on upper cvr reads: The Illustrated Aesop's Fables—School Edition. Sm 8vo. Full-pg wood engr frontis, vii,134 + 4pp list. Dk grn sand grain cl on bds; tooled title. VG (ink sig fep; eps browning; 1 bk list, 1 ad pg pasted down on cvrs; corners lt rubbed). *Hobbyhorse.* $125/£81

AESOP. Fabulae Aesopi Selectae. London: W. Strahan, E. Johnston et al, 1774. 8th ed. viii + 155pp. Brown linen on bds. Text ptd in Latin, English. VG (dated ink sig, Latin dedication eps; upper cvr split). *Hobbyhorse.* $200/£129

AESOP. The Medici Aesop, Spencer MS 50. Bernard McTigue (trans). NY: Abrams, 1989. 151 color plts. Gilt-dec cl. VG in dj. *Argosy.* $75/£48

AESOP. Selected Fables of Esop and Other Fabulists. London: Ptd for R. & J. Dodsley, 1761. 8vo. Full-pg copper engr frontis (ink sig verso), lxiii,204 + 28pp; 15 full-pg engrs (sl foxing, lt browning). Full grained leather, blind tooled, gilt fillets; gilt label title spine; brn eps. Good (cvr edge rubbed; lacks backstrip; fr cvr partly loose). *Hobbyhorse.* $400/£258

AESOP. Some of Aesop's Fables. Alfred Caldecott (trans). NY: Macmillan, 1883. 1st Amer ed. Randolph Caldecott (designs). 4to. vi,79pp. Pict pink cl on bds (lt soiled; corners bumped). Internally Fine. *Hobbyhorse.* $175/£113

AESOP. Three Hundred Aesop Fables. London/NY: George Routledge, n.d. (ca 1865). G.F. Townsend (trans); J. Greenaway (engrs). 12mo, xxxii + 224pp. Pict brn cl on bds, gilt dec spine, upper cvr stamped w/black dec frame. VG (ink sig; sigs lt pulled; 2 sm tears edge of pp62-63, repaired; cvrs lt soiled; spine chipped). *Hobbyhorse.* $225/£145

AESOP. Three Hundred Aesop's Fables. Geo. Fyler Townsend (trans). NY: McLoughlin Bros, n.d. (ca 1875). 8vo. x,230pp. Dec tooled red cl on bds (edges lt rubbed; spine lt faded); gilt title, vignette upper cvr, spine; yellow eps. VG (pencil sig fep). *Hobbyhorse.* $125/£81

AFLALO, F.G. Fishermen's Weather. London: A&C Black, 1906. 1st ed. 8 color plts by Charles Whymper. VG. *Hollett.* $47/£30

AFLALO, F.G. Sunset Playgrounds. NY: Scribner's, 1909. 1st ed. Lt blue cl, gilt titles. VG +. *Bowman.* $50/£32

AGAPIDA, FRAY ANTONIO. (Pseud of Washington Irving.) A Chronicle of the Conquest of Granada. Phila: Carey, Lea & Carey, 1829. 1st ed, sm paper issue (3000 thus). 2 vols. Untrimmed. Orig muslin-backed bds. Sound set (lt foxing; edgeworn, rubbed; spines soiled; labels eroded). BAL 10125. *Reese.* $75/£48

AGASSIZ, ELIZABETH C. (ed). Louis Agassiz. His Life and Correspondence. Boston: HM, 1885. 1st ed. 2 vols in 1. 794pp + ads, 12 engrs. Teg. VG. *Mikesh.* $45/£29

AGASSIZ, ELIZABETH C. (ed). Louis Agassiz. His Life and Correspondence. Boston, 1888. 8th ed. 2 vols. (Sl bumped.) *Goodrich.* $30/£19

AGASSIZ, ELIZABETH C. and ALEXANDER. Seaside Studies in Natural History. Boston, 1865. 1st ed. vi,155pp. Emb cl (bumped, rubbed). VG. *Shifrin.* $125/£81

AGASSIZ, LOUIS and MRS. A Journey in Brazil. Boston: Ticknor & Fields, 1868. xix,540pp. (Hinges cracked; discolored.) *Parmer.* $115/£74

AGASSIZ, LOUIS. Methods of Study in Natural History. Boston, 1863. 1st ed. 319pp + ads. VG. Sig of I.M. Sathrop. *Argosy.* $125/£81

AGASSIZ, LOUIS. The Structure of Animal Life. Six Lectures.... NY, 1866. 1st ed. 128pp. (Sunned; backstrip chipped.) *Argosy.* $150/£97

AGEE, JAMES and WALKER EVANS. Let Us Now Praise Famous Men. Boston: Houghton-Mifflin, (1960). Rev ed. Fine in dj. *Pharos.* $95/£61

AGEE, JAMES and WALKER EVANS. Let Us Now Praise Famous Men. London, 1965. 1st UK ed. Dj (chipped, sl loss). *Edwards.* $54/£35

AGEE, JAMES. The Collected Short Prose of James Agee. Robert Fitzgerald (ed). Boston: Houghton-Mifflin, 1968. 1st ed. Fine in dj. *Pharos.* $60/£39

AGEE, JAMES. The Collected Short Prose. Houghton Mifflin, 1968. 1st ed. NF in dj (spine dknd, lt soiled). *Stahr.* $75/£48

AGEE, JAMES. A Death in the Family. NY: McDowell, Obolensky, (1957). 1st ed, adv rev copy. Bound in wrappers made from dj. VG (extrems sl rubbed). *Hermitage.* $300/£194

AGEE, JAMES. A Death in the Family. NY: McDowell, Obolensky, (1957). 1st ed. Ink name fep; extrems faded; sl shelfwear, else VG in dj (worn, chipped). *Hermitage.* $100/£65

AGEE, JAMES. A Death in the Family. NY: McDowell Oblensky, 1957. 1st ed, 1st issue. VG+ in VG+ dj. *Pettler.* $80/£52

AGEE, JAMES. Four Early Stories. West Branch: Cummington Press, 1964. One of 285 numbered. 4to. Blue leather spine; patterned bds. Fine in handmade paper dj, as issued. *Dermont.* $350/£226

AGEE, JAMES. Letters of James Agee to Father Flye. NY: George Braziller, 1962. 1st ed. Fine in NF dj. *Hermitage.* $40/£26

AGEE, JAMES. Letters of James Agee to Father Flye. NY: Braziller, 1962. 1st ed. Fine in dj. *Pharos.* $60/£39

AGNEW, FRANKLIN H. The Lay of a Summer's Day or 'Love Is Mightier Than All.' L.A.: Faun Press, 1933. One of 100 1st ed copies, designed, ptd by Ward Ritchie. Gilt dec bds, paper title label. Fine in NF dj. *Connolly.* $125/£81

AHLBERG, HAKON. Swedish Architecture of the Twentieth Century. NY: Scribner's, 1925. 1st ed. 152 leaves of photo plts. Blue cl (faded, sl soiled; spine extrems sl frayed). *Karmiole.* $100/£65

AHLBERG, HAKON. Swedish Architecture of the Twentieth Century. NY: Scribner's, 1925. 1st ed. 152 plts. Cvrs lt rubbed, # on spine. *Bookpress.* $375/£242

AIKEN, CONRAD. Among the Lost People. NY: Scribner's, 1934. 1st ed. Fine (except for tape reinforcement top of spine). *Cahan.* $40/£26

AIKEN, CONRAD. And in the Human Heart. NY: Duell, Sloan & Pearce, (1940). 1st ed. VG (sl fade, browning) in white dj (browning). *Antic Hay.* $75/£48

AIKEN, CONRAD. Blue Voyage. NY, 1927. 1st ed. VF. *Bond.* $60/£39

AIKEN, CONRAD. Brownstone Eclogues and Other Poems. NY: Duell, Sloan & Pearce, (1942). 1st ed. Fine in dj (lt chipped). *Hermitage.* $45/£29

AIKEN, CONRAD. The Charnel Rose; Senlin: A Biography. Boston: Four Seas, 1918. 1st ed. Lt blue cl. VG. *Argosy.* $75/£48

AIKEN, CONRAD. The Jig of Forslin. Boston: Four Seas, 1916. 1st ed. VG in pict dj (edges chipped). *Argosy.* $85/£55

AIKEN, CONRAD. The Kid. Lehmann, 1947. 1st ed. VF in dj (sl soiled). *Poetry.* $23/£15

AIKEN, CONRAD. The Pilgrimage of Festus. NY, 1923. 1st ed. Patterned bds; paper label. VG. *Argosy.* $30/£19

AIKEN, CONRAD. Punch: The Immortal Liar. NY, 1921. 1st ed. Patterned bds; paper label. VG. *Argosy.* $30/£19

AIKEN, CONRAD. Selected Poems. NY, 1929. 1st Amer ed. VG (names). *Polyanthos.* $30/£19

AIKEN, CONRAD. Ushant, An Essay. NY, (1952). 1st ed. VG in dj (sl edgeworn). *King.* $35/£23

AIKEN, G.D. Pioneering with Wildflowers. Putney, (1933). 48 plts. (Some pp browned.) *Sutton.* $25/£16

AIKIN, JOHN. A View of John Howard's Life, Travels and Philanthropic Labors. Phila: Omrod & Woodward, 1794. 1st Amer ed. Frontis port;196pp + ads,11pp subs list, 3 leaves pub's ads. Contemp tree calf (back mended). VG. *Argosy.* $150/£97

AIKIN, JOHN. A View of the Life, Travels, and Philanthropic Labours of the Late John Howard. NY: David Huntington et al, 1814. Contemp mottled sheep. Nice (sl rubbed, chafed). *Boswell.* $225/£145

AIKIN, LUCY. Memoirs of the Court of King James the First. London: Longman et al., 1822. 2nd ed. 2 vols. 444,413pp. Paper-backed bds w/paper label; uncut. VG (worn). *Second Life.* $125/£81

AIKMAN, DUNCAN (ed). The Taming of the Frontier. NY: Minton, Balch, 1925. VG in dj (torn). *Schoyer.* $45/£29

AIMARD, GUSTAVE. The Pirates of the Prairies. London: Ward & Lock, 1861. viii,370pp. Contemp 1/2 calf, marbled bds (faded; sl rubbed). (Edges sl browned; upper joint cracked.) *Hollett.* $31/£20

AINSLIE, DOUGLAS. Chosen Poems. Hogarth Press, 1926. 1st ed. (Spine split.) *Words Etc.* $54/£35

AINSLIE, KATHLEEN. Catharine Susan and Me Goes Abroad. London: Castell Bros, ca 1909. 1st ed. Wraps, tied w/silk ribbon. 1909 inscrip, o/w VG. *Davidson.* $125/£81

AINSLIE, KATHLEEN. Catharine Susan and Me's Coming Out. London: Castell Brothers, (1910). 12mo. Pict paper cvrs w/silk ribbon. Good. *Reisler.* $150/£97

AINSLIE, KATHLEEN. Catharine Susan's Little Holiday. London: Castell Brothers, (1905). 12mo. Pict paper cvrs w/silk ribbon (minor spine wear). *Reisler.* $120/£77

AINSLIE, KATHLEEN. Oh! Poor Amelia Jane! London: Castell Bros, ca 1900. Illus pict wraps, bound w/silk ribbon. VG (sm soiling, inscrip). *Davidson.* $125/£81

AINSWORTH, ED. Beckoning Desert. NJ: Prentice-Hall, (1962). 1st ed. Fine in Fine dj. *Book Market.* $20/£13

AINSWORTH, ED. California Jubilee. Culver City, CA: Murray & Gee, 1948. 1st ed. Signed presentation. Beige cl (lt soiled) in illus dj. *Karmiole.* $30/£19

AINSWORTH, ED. California. L.A.: House-Warven, 1951. 1st ed. Fine in Fine dj. *Book Market.* $15/£10

AINSWORTH, ED. The Cowboy in Art. NY: World, (1968). 1st ed. Fine in Fine dj. *Book Market.* $60/£39

AINSWORTH, ED. Eagles Fly West. Macmillan, 1946. 1st ed. VG in VG dj. *Oregon.* $27/£17

AINSWORTH, ED. Golden Checkerboard. Palm Desert: Desert-Southwest, (1965). 1st ed. Fine in Fine dj. *Book Market.* $125/£81

AINSWORTH, WILLIAM HARRISON. Cardinal Pole. London: Chapman & Hall, 1863. 1st ed. 3 vols. 1/2 titles each vol. Grn cl blocked in blind, gilt spines. Good (lib label each vol; short slits in cl at joints). *Bickersteth.* $171/£110

AINSWORTH, WILLIAM HARRISON. Old Saint Paul's: A Tale of the Plague and the Fire. London, 1841. 1st ed. 3 vols. John Franklin (illus). Half calf, marbled bds, edges. *Argosy.* $400/£258

AINSWORTH, WILLIAM HARRISON. The Star-Chamber in Historical Romance. London: George Routledge, n.d. 3/4 blue morocco, marbled bds. Very Attractive. *Boswell.* $175/£113

Air Land and See in Pop-up Action Pictures. London: Birn Bros, n.d. (196?). 23x17 cm. 4 dbl-pg pop-ups. Glazed pict bds. VG. *Book Finders.* $40/£26

AIRY, OSMUND. Charles II. London: Goupil & Co., 1901. Ltd ed, #963/1250. Hand-tinted frontis port. 1/2 red morocco, gilt. Teg, others uncut. *D & D.* $290/£187

AITKEN, CORA KENNEDY. Legends and Memories of Scotland. London, 1874. 1st ed. Pict cvrs gilt. Fine. *Polyanthos.* $95/£61

AKELEY, CARL E. In Brightest Africa. London, 1924. 1st ed. (Feps lt browned; upper hinge cracked; sl staining, bubbling upper bd.) *Edwards.* $85/£55

AKELEY, CARL E. Work of...in Field Museum of Natural History. (Chicago, 1927). 42 photograv plts. Loose as issued in bd slipcase. VG. *Argosy.* $75/£48

AKEN, DAVID. Pioneers of the Black Hills, or Gordon's Stockade Party of 1874. (Milwaukee, 1911). Port. VG in ptd wrapper. Howes A 93. *Bohling.* $75/£48

AKEN, DAVID. Pioneers of the Black Hills.... (Milwaukee, 1920?). Professionally repaired, else VG in wraps. Howes A 93. *Perier.* $75/£48

AKERMAN, JOE A., JR. Florida Cowman. Kissimmee, 1976. 1st ed. Fine. *Baade.* $40/£26

AKURGAL, EKREM. The Art of the Hittites. NY: Abrams, (1962). 174 plts (26 color). Good in dj. *Archaeologia.* $150/£97

AKURGAL, EKREM. The Art of the Hittites. Constance McNab (trans). NY: Abrams, n.d. (ca 1962). 1st US ed. 174 plts (24 color). Sl rubbed; sl tear spine, o/w VG. *Worldwide.* $95/£61

ALARCON, PEDRO. A Friend of Death. Cassell, 1891. 1st ed. VG. *Madle.* $50/£32

ALBANESE, ANTHONY GERALD. The Plantation School. Vantage, (c. 1976). VG in VG dj. *Book Broker.* $25/£16

ALBAUGH, WILLIAM A. Tyler, Texas. Harrisburg: Stackpole, 1958. 1st ed. 8 plts, map. VG in dj (worn). *Connolly.* $47/£30

ALBAUGH, WILLIAM A., III. Confederate Faces. (Solano Beach, CA: Verde Publishers, 1970). 1st ed, ltd to 400. Orig cl (sl soiled). VG. *Mcgowan.* $650/£419

ALBAUGH, WILLIAM A., III. More Confederate Faces. (Washington, DC: ABS Printers, 1972). 1st ed, ltd to 400. Orig cl. Pristine in NF dj. *Mcgowan.* $450/£290

ALBEE, EDWARD. Box and Quotations from Chairman Mao Tse-Tung. NY: Atheneum, 1969. 1st ed. Signed. Fine in NF dj. *Antic Hay.* $100/£65

ALBEE, EDWARD. Everything in the Garden. NY: Atheneum, 1968. 1st ed. Fine in dj. *Antic Hay.* $35/£23

ALBEE, EDWARD. The Lady from Dubuque. NY, 1980. 1st ed. Fine in dj. *Whiteson.* $23/£15

ALBEE, EDWARD. Malcolm. NY: Atheneum, 1966. 1st ed. NF in dj (sl wear). *Antic Hay.* $35/£23

ALBEE, EDWARD. Malcolm: Adapted by Edward Albee from the Novel by James Purdy. NY: Atheneum, 1966. 1st ed. NF in dj (sl wear, lt rubbing). *Cahan.* $45/£29

ALBEE, EDWARD. The Play: The Ballad of the Sad Cafe. Boston: Houghton Mifflin, 1963. 1st ed. Fine in dj (lt worn). *Hermitage.* $65/£42

ALBEE, EDWARD. Seascape. NY, 1975. 1st Amer ed. Signed. Fine in dj. *Polyanthos.* $40/£26

ALBEE, EDWARD. Tiny Alice. NY: Atheneum, 1965. 1st ed. Black cl. Fine in dj (sl wear). *Antic Hay.* $40/£26

ALBEE, EDWARD. Who's Afraid of Virginia Woolf? London: Cape, 1964. 1st UK ed. VG in dj. *Lewton.* $57/£37

ALBEE, EDWARD. The Zoo Story and Other Plays. London: Cape, (1962). 1st ed. NF in dj. *Hermitage.* $100/£65

ALBERS, ANNI. On Weaving. Middletown: Wesleyan Univ Press, 1965. 1st ed. 112 plts. Fine in dj (sl chipped). *Cahan.* $75/£48

ALBERTS, ROBERT C. The Most Extraordinary Adventures of Major Robert Stobo. Houghton Mifflin, 1965. 1st ed. VG in Good dj. *Book Broker.* $35/£23

Album of American Battle Art 1755-1918. Washington: GPO, 1947. VG. *Hermitage.* $50/£32

Album of American Battle Art, 1755-1918. Washington: GPO, 1947. 1st ed. (Bkpl, fr hinge internally cracked, text lt browned.) *Bookpress.* $85/£55

ALCALA-GALIANO, ALVARO. The Fall of a Throne. Mrs. Steuart Erskine (trans). London: Thornton Butterworth, 1933. 1st ed. VG (sunned). *Patterson.* $54/£35

ALCOCK, C.W. Famous Cricketers and Cricket Grounds. London: Hudson & Kearns, 1895. Full black leather (neatly rebacked), gilt dec. *Petersfield.* $186/£120

ALCOTT, LOUISA M. The Candy Country. Boston: Little Brown, (1900). 8vo. 52pp; 2 b/w plts. Taupe cl, gilt. Good+. *Drusilla's.* $22/£14

ALCOTT, LOUISA M. Little Men. Boston: Roberts Bros, 1871. 1st Amer ed, 1st issue, w/ads listing Pink and White Tyranny as 'nearly ready.' 376pp. Grn cl. VG. BAL 167. *Chapel Hill.* $300/£194

ALCOTT, LOUISA M. Little Men. Life at Plumfield with Jo's Boys. Boston: Roberts Bros, 1871. 1st Amer ed, 1st issue w/'Pink and White Tyranny nearly ready'. 4 plts (sl dampstain to lower forecorner). Dk grn cl (rebound) orig backstrip, cvr panel laid on. BAL 167. Sadlon. $150/£97

ALCOTT, LOUISA M. Little Men. Life at Plumfield's with Jo's Boys. Boston: Roberts Bros, 1871. 1st Amer ed. Ads at fr list Pink & White Tyranny as 'nearly ready'. 12mo. Purple cl (backstrip faded). BAL 167. Argosy. $200/£129

ALCOTT, LOUISA M. May Flowers. Boston: Little Brown, (1899). 8vo. 56pp; 4 b/w plts. Taupe cl, gilt. NF. Drusilla's. $25/£16

ALCOTT, LOUISA M. An Old-Fashioned Girl. London: Sampson Low, Martson, 1907. 1st Eng ed. Thick, 4to. 12 full-pg illus by Jessie Wilcox Smith. Teg. Illus brn cl; gold dec stamped on spine (foxing; eps faded). Reisler. $150/£97

ALCOTT, WILLIAM A. The House I Live In. Part First. The Frame. Boston: Lilly et al, 1834. 12mo. 2 square wood engr frontispieces, xii,144pp. Black roan, gilt title, grn paper on bds (lt rubbed). VG (ink, pencil sigs chipped fep). Hobbyhorse. $125/£81

ALDEN, JOHN RICHARD. General Gage in America.... Baton Rouge: LSU Press, 1948. 1st ed. Frontis port. Brn cl. Bkpl, else NF in dj (price-clipped). Chapel Hill. $50/£32

ALDEN, PAULETTE BATES. Feeding the Eagles. Saint Paul: Graywolf, 1988. 1st ed, 1st bk. Fine in NF dj. Robbins. $20/£13

ALDIN, CECIL and JOHN HASSALL. The Happy Annual. NY: E.P. Dutton, (1907). 1st Amer ed. Lg, 4to. Cl-backed illus bds (minor edgewear; sm spot rear cvr; fr hinge cracked). Reisler. $385/£248

ALDINGTON, RICHARD. The Berkshire Kennet. (Hurst, Reading, Berks: Peacock Press, 1955.) One of 310. Fine. Pharos. $75/£48

ALDINGTON, RICHARD. The Colonel's Daughter. London: C&W, 1931. 1st ed. #50/210. Signed. Teg. Full buckram, beveled bds. Spine faded, o/w VG. Virgo. $85/£55

ALDINGTON, RICHARD. The Complete Poems. London, (1948). 1st ed. VG in dj. Argosy. $40/£26

ALDINGTON, RICHARD. The Crystal World. London, (1937). 1st ed. Cl (sl faded). Bickersteth. $31/£20

ALDINGTON, RICHARD. D.H. Lawrence: Portrait of a Genius But.... NY, (1950). 1st Amer ed. VG in dj. Argosy. $45/£29

ALDINGTON, RICHARD. A Dream in the Luxembourg. London: C&W, 1930. 1st Eng ed. Blue cl gilt. Name, else Very Nice in dj (sl wear, repaired). Cady. $25/£16

ALDINGTON, RICHARD. Exile and Other Poems. London: Allen & Unwin, 1923. 1st ed, ltd to 750. Blue cl gilt. Very Nice in dj (sl worn). Cady. $25/£16

ALDINGTON, RICHARD. Frauds. London: Heinemann, (1957). 1st Eng ed. Violet cl. Very Nice in dj. Cady. $20/£13

ALDINGTON, RICHARD. Lawrence of Arabia. London, 1955. 1st ed w/errata slip. Sl bumped, else Good in dj (defective). King. $25/£16

ALDINGTON, RICHARD. Life Quest. London: C&W, 1935. 1st ed. Fine in Fine dj. Beasley. $65/£42

ALDINGTON, RICHARD. Literary Studies and Reviews. London: Allen & Unwin, (1924). 1st ed. (Sl foxed; backstrip faded, torn). Petersfield. $16/£10

ALDINGTON, RICHARD. Love and the Luxembourg. NY: Covici, Friede, 1930. Ltd to 475 signed by Aldington and Frederick Warde (designer). Teg. Maroon cl gilt. Very Nice in pub's slipcase. Cady. $50/£32

ALDINGTON, RICHARD. The Love of Myrrhine and Konallis and Other Prose Poems. Chicago: Pascal Covici, 1926. Ltd to 1010 numbered. NF in dj (chipped, edgeworn). Sadlon. $15/£10

ALDINGTON, RICHARD. The Romance of Casanova. NY: Duell et al, (1946). 1st ed. Fine in dj (sl edgeworn). Sadlon. $20/£13

ALDINGTON, RICHARD. Soft Answers. London: C&W, 1932. 1st Eng ed. Red cl gilt. Very Nice in dj (sl wear). Cady. $30/£19

ALDINGTON, RICHARD. Soft Answers. Chatto, 1932. Signed ltd ed, #20/110. VG+ (ep hinges sl starting; spine lt faded). Williams. $101/£65

ALDINGTON, RICHARD. Stepping Heavenward. Florence: G. Orioli, 1931. 1st ed. #98/808 on hand-made paper, signed. Unopened. Cl-backed yellow bds. NF in dj (lt soiled, frayed). Cox. $85/£55

ALDINGTON, RICHARD. W. Somerset Maugham, an Appreciation. NY: Doubleday, Doran, (1939). 1st ed. Paper wrappers (soiled). Oak Knoll. $15/£10

ALDINGTON, RICHARD. War and Love (1915-1918). Boston: Four Seas Co, 1919. 1st Amer ed. Patterned bds (extrems sl rubbed). Fine. Polyanthos. $100/£65

ALDINGTON, WILLIAM (trans). The XI Bookes of the Golden Asse. London: Golden Cockerel, 1923. #144/450. Cl-backed bds (sl soiled). Edwards. $74/£48

ALDISS, BRIAN. The Brightfount Diaries. Faber, 1955. 1st ed, 1st bk. Edges sl faded, else Good in dj (sl dull). Whiteson. $43/£28

ALDISS, BRIAN. The Brightfount Diaries. Faber, 1955. 1st ed, 1st bk. Presentation copy. VG in VG dj. Whiteson. $116/£75

ALDISS, BRIAN. The Brightfount Diaries. London: Faber & Faber, 1955. 1st ed. VG in dj (sl chipped spine extrems). Limestone. $95/£61

ALDISS, BRIAN. Helliconia Summer. NY: Atheneum, 1983. 1st ed. Signed. Promo material laid-in. Fine in dj. Antic Hay. $45/£29

ALDISS, BRIAN. The Male Response. London: Dobson, 1961. 1st ed. Top edge dusty, o/w VG in dj. Rees. $31/£20

ALDISS, BRIAN. Report on Probability A. Doubleday, 1969. 1st US ed. VG in dj. Madle. $30/£19

ALDISS, BRIAN. Space, Time and Nathaniel. London: Faber, 1957. 1st ed. Signed. Sl foxed; cvrs sl faded, shelfwear, o/w Good in dj (worn, price-clipped). Virgo. $101/£65

ALDISS, BRIAN. Starship. Criterion Books, 1959. 1st Amer ed. Grn bds. Fading, else NF in NF dj (sl wear spine extrems). Aronovitz. $80/£52

ALDISS, BRIAN. The Trillion Year Spree. Atheneum, 1986. 1st US ed. NF in dj. Madle. $30/£19

ALDRICH, F.L.S. My Child and I in Sickness and Health, From Pre-Natal Life Until Sixteen. Phila, 1903. 1st ed. Good. Fye. $75/£48

ALDRICH, MILDRED. On the Edge of the War Zone. Boston: Small, Maynard, (1917). 1st ed. Port; 12 plts. Dec grn cl. VG. Petrilla. $35/£23

ALDRICH, THOMAS BAILEY. The Ballad of Babie Bell and Other Poems. NY, 1859. 1st issue. Fine (spine top rubbed; bkpl). Polyanthos. $100/£65

ALDRICH, THOMAS BAILEY. Daisey's Necklace and What Came of It. NY: Derby & Jackson, 1857. 1st ed. Stamped in blind (spine, edges lightened; spot rear cvr; extrems sl rubbed; lt foxing). BAL 249. *Sadlon.* $25/£16

ALDRICH, THOMAS BAILEY. Judith of Bethulia: A Tragedy. Boston/NY: Houghton Mifflin, 1904. 1st lg paper ed w/'Published Nov. 1904' on copyright pg. Orig cl, paper spine label (spine lightened; lt dampstain lower right corner, sig starting). BAL 394. *Sadlon.* $25/£16

ALDRICH, THOMAS BAILEY. Mercedes, and Later Lyrics. Boston: Houghton, Mifflin, 1884. 1st ed. Pub's gray cl, paper spine label (sl chipped; sl worn). BAL 325. *Book Block.* $30/£19

ALDRICH, THOMAS BAILEY. Ponkapog Papers. Boston: Houghton, 1903. 1st ed, sm paper issue. Teg. Gilt cl. VG. BAL 393. *Reese.* $20/£13

ALDRICH, THOMAS BAILEY. The Story of a Bad Boy. Boston: Fields, Osgood, 1870. 1st ed, 1st issue. 261pp + 23pp pub's cat. Full red morocco, aeg. Fine. BAL 269. *Schoyer.* $150/£97

ALDRIDGE, REGINALD. Life on a Ranch: Ranch Notes in Kansas, Colorado...and Northern Texas. NY: D. Appleton, 1884. 12mo. vii,227,4pp ads; 4 plts. Nice (lt rubbed, soiled; spine chipped) in ptd wrappers. Howes A 110. *Bohling.* $950/£613

ALEICHEM, SHOLOM. Inside Kasrilevke. NY: Schocken Books, (1965). 1st ed in English. Signed. Fine in dj. *Godot.* $325/£210

ALEXANDER, EDWARD PORTER. Military Memoirs of a Confederate. NY: Scribner's, 1907. 1st ed. VG (sl speckling; sl dampstaining). Howes A 114. *Mcgowan.* $250/£161

ALEXANDER, EDWARD PORTER. Military Memoirs of a Confederate. NY: Scribner's, 1907. 1st ed. Frontis port, fldg map at rear. Grn cl (spine top chipped). VG. Howes A 114. *Chapel Hill.* $275/£177

ALEXANDER, FRANZ and HUGO STAUB. The Criminal, the Judge and the Public. Gregory Zilboorg (trans). Glencoe, IL: Free Press, (1956). (Rev ed), 1st ptg. Black cl. VG in dj. *Gach.* $28/£18

ALEXANDER, FRANZ and HUGO STAUB. The Criminal, the Judge, and the Public. Glencoe, IL, 1956. Signed by Alexander. Good. *Fye.* $95/£61

ALEXANDER, FRANZ and SHELDON SELESNICK. The History of Psychiatry. NY, 1966. 1st ed. Good. *Fye.* $35/£23

ALEXANDER, FRANZ and THOMAS FRENCH. Studies in Psychosomatic Medicine. NY: Ronald Press Co, (1948). 1st ed. Red cl. VG in dj (worn). *Gach.* $40/£26

ALEXANDER, FRANZ and WILLIAM HEALY. The Roots of Crime. NY: Knopf, 1935. 1st ptg. Blue cl. (Cvrs dull.) *Gach.* $35/£23

ALEXANDER, FRANZ et al. Psychoanalytic Pioneers. NY: Basic Books, (1966). 1st ed. Beige cl. Good (lib bkpl, stamps; hinges cracked). *Gach.* $35/£23

ALEXANDER, FRANZ. Our Age of Unreason. Phila: Lippincott, (1942). 1st ed. Blue cl. VG in dj (worn). *Gach.* $25/£16

ALEXANDER, J.J.G. and A.C. DE LA MARE. The Italian Manuscripts in the Library of Major J.R. Abbey. London: Faber & Faber, 1969. 6 color, 80 b/w plts. Dj. *Edwards.* $85/£55

ALEXANDER, SAMUEL. Space, Time and Deity. London: Macmillan, 1920. 1st ed. 2 vols. VG + . *Lame Duck.* $200/£129

ALEXANDER, T.H. Loot. Dallas, TX: Southwest Press, 1932. 1st ed. Signed. VG. *Burcham.* $40/£26

ALEXANDER, WILLIAM L. List of Ex-Soldiers, Sailors and Marines, Living in Iowa. Des Moines: Roberts, 1886. 1st ed. (8),772pp. Contemp 1/2 calf (fr bd loose). *Ginsberg.* $175/£113

ALEXANDRIAN, SARANE. Man Ray. Eleanor Levieux (trans). Chicago: Philip O'Hara, (1974). 1st ed. VG in dj. *Argosy.* $60/£39

ALFORD, M. Needlework as Art. London, 1886. Royal 8vo. Frontis; xxiii,422pp; 85 plts; aeg. (Upper hinge cracked; sl shaken; soiled.) *Edwards.* $147/£95

ALFRED, WILLIAM. Agamemnon: A Verse Play in Four Acts. NY: Knopf, 1954. 1st Amer ed, ltd to 1250; 1st bk. Fine in dj (sl used). *Pharos.* $45/£29

ALGER, HORATIO, JR. The Young Miner. (SF): Book Club of CA, 1965. Ltd to 450. Cl-backed pict bds. VG. *Shasky.* $65/£42

ALGER, HORATIO, JR. The Young Miner; or Tom Nelson in California. Boston: Loring, Publishers, (1879). 1st ed. Grn dec cl. Fine. *Appelfeld.* $125/£81

ALGREN, NELSON. Chicago. GC: Doubleday, 1951. 1st ed. Bkpl, else NF in dj (sl rubbed). *Hermitage.* $50/£32

ALGREN, NELSON. The Last Carousel. NY: Putnam, 1973. 1st ed. Signed. VG + in dj. *Limestone.* $95/£61

ALGREN, NELSON. Nelson Algren's Own Book of Lonesome Monsters. NY: Lancer, 1962. Correct 1st ed. NF in wraps. *Beasley.* $40/£26

ALGREN, NELSON. A Walk on the Wild Side. NY: Farrar, (1956). 1st ed. Fine in crisp dj (sl soiled). *Reese.* $45/£29

ALGREN, NELSON. Who Lost an American? NY: Macmillan, 1963. 1st ed. Fine (sl bowed) in Fine dj. *Beasley.* $40/£26

Ali Baba; or the Forty Thieves. London: Ryle & Paul, n.d. (ca 1840). Chapbook. 12mo. 12pp + 1pg list on lower wrapper. Internally Fine (edges chipped, reinforced spine cracking). *Hobbyhorse.* $100/£65

ALI, SALIM. The Birds of Sikkim. (London): OUP, 1962. 1st ed. 17 color plts, 9 b/w photos. Lt blue cl. Fine in ptd dj. *House.* $150/£97

ALI, SALIM. The Birds of Travancore and Cochin. (London): OUP, (1953). 1st ed. 22 color plts. Brn cl. NF in ptd dj w/color plt mtd on cvr. *House.* $200/£129

Alibaba and the Forty Thieves. London: Bancroft, 1960. 20x29 cm. 2 dbl-pg pop-ups. Pict bds. VG. *Book Finders.* $100/£65

Alice's Adventures in Wonderland. NY: Delacorte, 1980. 21x30 cm. 6 pop-ups, pull-tabs. Jenny Thorne (illus). Glazed pict bds. VG. *Book Finders.* $35/£23

All Around the Christmas Tree. Kenosha, WI: John Martin's House, 1949. 16x21 cm. 2 VG pop-ups. Glazed pict bds (rubbed; white showing through blue on spine). *Book Finders.* $80/£52

All's Not Gold That Glitters. (By Emily Neal Haven.) NY: Appleton, 1853. 1st ed. 214,(2)pp, chromolitho extra-title. Orig cl, stamped in gilt, blind. Spine faded, sl frayed, foxing, else Good. *Reese.* $55/£35

ALLAN, J. Australian Shells. Melbourne, 1959. 2nd rev ed. Color frontis; 11 color, 32 plain plts. *Wheldon & Wesley.* $54/£35

ALLAN, LUKE. The Black Opal. London: Arrowsmith, 1935. 1st ed. VG in VG dj (internal tape mks). *Ming.* $31/£20

ALLAN, LUKE. Scotland Yard Takes a Holiday. London: Arrowsmith, 1934. 1st ed. Foxing pg edges, o/w Fine in dj (price-clipped; label removed). *Mordida.* $75/£48

ALLAN, MEA. The Tradescants. London: Michael Joseph, (1964). Fldg chart. Fine in dj. *Quest.* $90/£58

ALLAN, P.B.M. A Moth-Hunter's Gossip. London, 1937. 4 plts. (Sl used.) *Wheldon & Wesley.* $39/£25

ALLBEURY, TED. The Other Side of Silence. London: Granada, 1981. 1st ed. NF in dj. *Limestone.* $30/£19

ALLBEURY, TED. The Seeds of Treason. London: NEL, 1986. 1st ed. Fine in dj. *Silver Door.* $30/£19

ALLBUTT, T. CLIFFORD. The Historical Relations of Medicine and Surgery to the End of the Sixteenth Century.... London: Macmillan, 1905. (Ex-lib.) *Goodrich.* $65/£42

ALLDREDGE, EUGENE PERRY. Cowboys and Coyotes. Nashville: Vanity, 1945. 1st ed. VG in dj (taped). *Parker.* $50/£32

ALLEGRETTO, MICHAEL. Death on the Rocks. NY: Scribner's, 1987. 1st ed. VF in dj. *Mordida.* $35/£23

ALLEMAN, MRS. TILLIE. At Gettysburg, or, What a Girl Saw and Heard of the Battle. NY: W. Lake Borland, 1889. 1st ed. 118pp; 4 maps (1 fldg). Sm ad tipped at back. VG. *Petrilla.* $85/£55

ALLEN, A.J. Ten Years in Oregon. Ithaca, 1850. 2nd ed. 430pp. Orig cl, spine gilt (extrems worn; short tears top of joints). VG (lt foxing). Howes A 131. *Reese.* $300/£194

ALLEN, ALICE MAYHEW. Early Roads and Trails in California. SF: Nat'l Soc of Colonial Dames of America, 1942. 4 maps; ptd wrappers. *Dawson.* $30/£19

ALLEN, CHARLES DEXTER. American Book-Plates. NY, 1894. 1st ed. 437pp, 10 engrs. (Upper hinge cracked.) *Argosy.* $50/£32

ALLEN, CLIFFORD. The Sexual Perversions and Abnormalities...the Psychology of Paraphilia. London, 1949. 2nd ed. Good. *Fye.* $40/£26

ALLEN, DOUGLAS and DOUGLAS ALLEN, JR. N.C. Wyeth. The Collected Paintings, Illustrations, and Murals. NY: Bonanza, 1972. Sound in dj. *Ars Artis.* $70/£45

ALLEN, DOUGLAS and DOUGLAS ALLEN, JR. N.C. Wyeth: The Collected Paintings, Illustrations and Murals. NY: Bonanza Books, 1972. Fabricoid. VG in dj. *Argosy.* $100/£65

ALLEN, DURWARD L. Wolves of Minong. Boston: HM, 1979. 1st ed. Dec cl. NF in VG dj. *Mikesh.* $35/£23

ALLEN, DURWARD L. (ed). Pheasants of North America. Harrisburg: Stackpole, 1956. 1st ed. Fine in Fine+ dj. *Bowman.* $35/£23

ALLEN, DURWARD L. (ed). Pheasants of North America. Harrisburg/Washington: Stackpole/W.L.M.I., 1956. 1st ed. 82 plts. NF in VG dj. *Mikesh.* $45/£29

ALLEN, EDWARD WEBER. The Vanishing Frenchman: The Mysterious Disappearance of Laperouse. Rutland, VT: Tuttle, (1959). 1st ed. Fine in dj. *Lefkowicz.* $45/£29

ALLEN, EVERETT S. Arctic Odyssey. NY: Dodd, Mead, 1962. 1st ed. VG in VG- dj. *Blue Dragon.* $35/£23

ALLEN, FRED. Much Ado About Me. Boston: Atlantic, Little Brown, (1956). 1st ed. NF in VG+ dj (lt worn; sm tears;   nicks). *Between The Covers.* $50/£32

ALLEN, GRANT. Strange Stories. London: C&W, 1885. 2nd ed. Frontis. Dec brn cl. Bright (sl hinge crack). *Agvent.* $25/£16

ALLEN, H. A Monograph of the Bats of North America. Washington: Nat. Mus. Bull., 1893. iv,198pp; 38 plts. Cl (sl rubbed). *Wheldon & Wesley.* $62/£40

ALLEN, HERVEY and THOMAS OLLIVE MABBOTT. Poe's Brother, the Poems of William Henry Leonard Poe.... NY, (1926). 1st ed, ltd to 1000 numbered. Teg. Fresh in dj (spine stained), box (frayed, stained). *King.* $75/£48

ALLEN, HERVEY. Action at Aquila. NY: Farrar & Rinehart, (1938). 1st ed. Orig blue cl. NF (spine lt rubbed) in pict dj. *Chapel Hill.* $45/£29

ALLEN, HERVEY. Action at Aquila. NY, 1938. 1st ed. VG in VG dj (sl chipping). *Pratt.* $42/£27

ALLEN, HERVEY. Anthony Adverse. NY: Farrar & Rinehart, 1933. 1st ed. Stamped in gilt over flexible bds (sl bubbles). Dj (spine rubbed, edgeworn). *Sadlon.* $20/£13

ALLEN, HERVEY. Anthony Adverse. NY, 1934. 1st ed w/these illus. 2 vols. 2 color frontispieces by N.C. Wyeth. VG. *Argosy.* $125/£81

ALLEN, HERVEY. Bedford Village. NY: Farrar & Rinehart, (1944). 1st ed. (Lt soiled, bumped.) Dj (frayed). *Hermitage.* $40/£26

ALLEN, HERVEY. Christmas Epithalamium. NY: William Edwin Rudge, 1925. 1st ed thus. One of 325 ptd. 8 leaves. Paper-cvrd bds, paper label. Fine in tissue wrapper. *Hermitage.* $75/£48

ALLEN, HERVEY. Israfel, the Life and Times of Edgar Allan Poe. NY: George H. Doran, 1926. 1st ed, 1st state. 2 vols. Maroon cl, gilt. In 1st state, a wine glass is seen on table in port of Longfellow p529. Fine set (lt offsetting ep vol 1 from clipping once laid in) in Excellent box (rear panel faded). *Macdonnell.* $250/£161

ALLEN, HERVEY. Toward the Morning. NY: Rinehart, (1948). 1st ed. NF in dj (sl worn, frayed). *Hermitage.* $40/£26

ALLEN, J. ROMILLEY. Celtic Art in Pagan and Christian Times. London: Methuen, 1904. 1st ed. Red gilt cl (sl rubbed). *Hollett.* $101/£65

ALLEN, J.A. History of North American Pinnipeds.... Washington, 1880. xvi,785pp. (Ex-lib.) *Wheldon & Wesley.* $93/£60

ALLEN, JAMES LANE. The Kentucky Warbler. GC: Doubleday, 1918. 1st Amer ed. VG. *Agvent.* $35/£23

ALLEN, JAMES TURNEY. The Greek Theater of the Fifth Century Before Christ. Berkeley: Univ of CA Press, (1919). Dj spine faded, o/w Fine. *Archaeologia.* $45/£29

ALLEN, JOHN. Passage through the Garden. Univ of IL, (1975). 1st ed. 47 maps. VF in VF dj. *Oregon.* $50/£32

ALLEN, JULIAN. Autocracy in Poland and Russia. NY: Wiley, 1854. 200pp. Brn blind-stamped cl (ex-lib, pocket removed). *Schoyer.* $75/£48

ALLEN, L.F. The American Herd Book—1846. Buffalo, 1846. xxiv,(9-)240pp (lt foxing), 4 plts (browned). 1/2 leather (worn, spotted). *Sutton.* $145/£94

ALLEN, LEE. The Hot Stove League. Barnes, 1955. 1st ed. VG (browning). *Plapinger.* $110/£71

ALLEN, R.S. Lucky Forward. NY, 1947. VG. *Clark.* $35/£23

ALLEN, R.W. The Opsonic Method of Treatment. Phila, 1907. 1st Amer ed. Good. *Fye.* $40/£26

ALLEN, RICHARD. Covered Bridges of the Middle Atlantic States. NY: Bonanza Books, (1959). Frontis. Fine in dj. *Bookpress.* $25/£16

ALLEN, RICHARD. Covered Bridges of the Middle West. Brattleboro, VT: Stephen Greene Press, 1970. 1st ed. Dj rubbed, o/w Fine. *Bookpress.* $50/£32

ALLEN, RICHARD. Covered Bridges of the Northeast. Brattleboro, VT: Stephen Greene Press, 1957. 1st ed. Ink name, else VG in dj (chipped). *Bookpress.* $35/£23

ALLEN, RICHARD. Covered Bridges of the South. NY: Bonanza Books, (1970). Fine in dj. *Bookpress.* $25/£16

ALLEN, ROBERT PORTER. Birds of the Caribbean. NY: Viking, 1961. 1st ed. VG. Kip Farrington's copy, w/his bkpl. *Bowman.* $40/£26

ALLEN, TIMOTHY. Ophthalmic Therapeutics. NY, 1876. 1st ed. Good. *Fye.* $100/£65

ALLEN, V.C. Rhea and Meigs Counties (Tennessee) in the Confederate War. (N.p., 1909.) 1st ed. Gray cl. Sm bkseller label, else NF. *Chapel Hill.* $150/£97

ALLEN, VELTA MYRLE. Within Adobe Walls. Sunland, CA: Cecil L. Anderson, 1948. Signed. VG. *Burcham.* $100/£65

ALLEN, W.W. and R.B. AVERY. California Gold Book. SF/Chicago: Donohue & Henneberry, 1893. 1st ed. (Cl sl worn; sticker removed fep.) *Glenn.* $125/£81

ALLEN, WALTER C. Hendersonia. Highland Park, NJ: W.C. Allen, 1973. 1st ed. NF (lt sunned spine). *Beasley.* $100/£65

ALLEN, WILLIAM H. Al Smith's Tammany Hall. NY: Institute for Public Service, 1928. 1st ed. 4 photo plts. VG. *Connolly.* $25/£16

ALLEN, WOODY. Getting Even. R-H, 1971. 1st ed. Signed. Fine in dj. *Fine Books.* $225/£145

ALLEN, WOODY. Side Effects. NY, 1980. 1st Amer ed. Signed. Fine (bkpl) in dj. *Polyanthos.* $75/£48

ALLEN, WOODY. Without Feathers. NY: Random House, (1975). 1st ed. NF in dj. *Antic Hay.* $35/£23

ALLENDE, ISABEL. Eva Luna. NY: Knopf, 1988. 1st Amer ed. NF in NF dj. *Revere.* $35/£23

ALLENDE, ISABEL. Eva Luna. Margaret Sayers Peden (trans). PA: Franklin Lib, 1988. 1st Amer ed. Ltd to unspecified # signed. Full brown dec leather. Issued w/o dj. *Godot.* $65/£42

ALLENDE, ISABEL. Eva Luna. Hamilton, 1989. 1st UK ed. Signed. Fine in dj. *Lewton.* $36/£23

ALLENDE, ISABEL. The House of the Spirits. London: Cape, 1985. 1st UK ed. Fine in dj. *Lewton.* $26/£17

ALLENDE, ISABEL. The Infinite Plan. Harper, 1993. 1st UK ed. Signed, w/signed promo pict. *Lewton.* $28/£18

ALLEY, B.F. History of Clarke County, Washington Territory. Portland: Washington Pub Co, 1885. 399pp. 1/4 leather. VG. *Perier.* $600/£387

ALLEY, R. Francis Bacon. London: Thames & Hudson, 1964. 27 mtd color illus. 1pg laser print facs, else Good in dj (sl frayed). *Ars Artis.* $1,938/£1,250

ALLINGHAM, MARGERY. The China Governess. GC: Doubleday, 1962. 1st ed. Fine in dj. *Mordida.* $45/£29

ALLINGHAM, MARGERY. The Gyrth Chalice Mystery. GC: DCC, 1931. 1st Amer ed. Label, o/w VG in dj (chipping; closed tears). *Mordida.* $65/£42

ALLINGHAM, MARGERY. The Mind Readers. NY: William Morrow, 1965. 1st ed. Fine in dj (internal spotting; sl wear). *Mordida.* $45/£29

ALLINGHAM, MARGERY. The Return of Mr. Campion: Uncollected Stories. J.E. Morpurgo (ed). London: Hodder & Stoughton, 1989. 1st ed. Fine in dj (sl crinkling top edge). *Janus.* $35/£23

ALLINGHAM, MARGERY. The Tiger in the Smoke. London: C&W, 1952. 1st ed. Spotting pg edges, o/w VG in dj (nicks, wear). *Mordida.* $65/£42

ALLISON, DOROTHY. Trash. Ithaca: Firebrand, (1988). 1st ed. Fine. *Robbins.* $45/£29

ALLISON, DRUMMOND. The Yellow Night. Fortune Press, 1944. 1st Eng ed, 1st issue. Black cl, gilt. VG in dj. *Edrich.* $70/£45

ALLISON, JOHN. Dropped Stitches in Tennessee History. Nashville: Marshall & Bruce, 1897. 150pp; 7 plts. Dec cl. VG. *Schoyer.* $45/£29

ALLSHOUSE, ROBERT H. Photographs for the Tsar. NY, 1980. VG in dj. *Argosy.* $75/£48

ALLSOPP, BRUCE. Decoration and Furniture. London: Pitman, (1952). 1st ed. 2 vols. Frontis, 7 plts; frontis, 11 plts. VG in djs (lt chipped). *Bookpress.* $135/£87

ALLSOPP, FRED W. Albert Pike. Little Rock: Parke-Harper, 1928. 1st ed. 12 plts. NF. *Blue Dragon.* $75/£48

ALLSOPP, FRED W. Folklore of Romantic Arkansas. N.p.: Grolier Soc., 1931. 2 vols. Blue cl, gilt spine titles. VG (faded). *Bohling.* $75/£48

ALLSOPP, FRED W. Folklore of Romantic Arkansas. N.p.: Grolier Soc, 1931. 2 vols. Uncut, partly unopened. Ink note fep, o/w Fine set. *Hayman.* $100/£65

ALLWOOD, M.C. Carnations and All Dianthus. London, 1937. 2nd ed. Color frontis, 82 plain plts. Mint. *Henly.* $39/£25

ALOTTA, ROBERT I. Stop the Evil. A Civil War History of Desertion and Murder. San Rafael, CA, (1978). 1st ed. Fine in Fine dj. *Mcgowan.* $35/£23

ALPATOV, M.W. Art Treasures of Russia. NY: Abrams, (1967). 104 hand-tipped color plts. VG in dj. *Argosy.* $75/£48

ALPERS, SVETLANA. Rembrandt's Enterprise; the Studio and the Market. London: Thames & Hudson, 1988. 12 color plts. Fine in Mint dj. *Europa.* $25/£16

Alphabet Annotated for Youth and Adults. London: Ackermann, n.d. (ca 1850). 1st ed. Folio. x,54pp. G.W. Terry (illus). Dec stiff paper wrappers. Enclosed in folder w/red cl on bds, gilt spine title. Fine (sl soiling wrapper edges, trace of glue). *Hobbyhorse.* $350/£226

Alphabet of Country Scenes. NY: McLoughlin Bros, (1873). Folio. 12 leaves + 1pg list lower wrapper, 24 chromolithos; all text, illus ptd one side of leaf only; upper wrapper w/designed title, lg vignette of girl and boy picking berries (bkpl; label; sm crease corner of upper wrapper). Fine. *Hobbyhorse.* $225/£145

Alphabet of Country Scenes. NY: McLoughlin Bros, 1899. 4to. 6pp chromos. Spine rubbed, o/w VG in gilt chromo wraps. *Drusilla's.* $75/£48

ALSTON, CHARLES HENRY. Wild Life in the West Highlands. Glasgow, 1912. 1st ed. Color frontis. (Edges, feps foxed; discoloring, lt stain upper bd.) *Edwards.* $39/£25

ALSTON, J.W. Hints to Young Practitioners in the Study of Landscape Painting. London: Longman, n.d. 3rd ed. Aquatint frontis (edge frayed), engr tp, 2ff,67pp, 4 plts (1 etched line, 3 aquatints). Orig bds w/label (worn, rebacked). *Ars Artis.* $194/£125

ALTER, J. CECIL. Early Utah Journalism. Salt Lake City, 1938. 1st ed. *Ginsberg.* $50/£32

ALTER, J. CECIL. Early Utah Journalism. Salt Lake City: UT State Hist Soc, 1938. 1st ed. VG in stiff wrappers. *Cahan.* $60/£39

ALTER, J. CECIL. Jim Bridger. Norman, 1962. 1st ptg of new ed. Rev card laid in. Fine in dj (sl worn). Howes A 191. *Baade.* $47/£30

ALTER, J. CECIL. Through the Heart of the Scenic West. Salt Lake City, UT: Shepherd Book, 1927. Ltd to 1000. Signed. VG. *Lien.* $45/£29

ALTER, J. CECIL. Utah: the Storied Domain.... Chicago, 1932. 1st ed. Vols 1-3. Dec emb cvrs; marbled eps, pg edges. VG + . *Benchmark.* $150/£97

ALTGELD, JOHN P. Live Questions: Including Our Penal Machinery and Its Victims. Chicago: Donohue & Henneberry, 1890. Ex-lib, but sound. *Boswell.* $50/£32

ALTHER, LISA. Kin-Flicks. NY: Knopf, 1976. 1st ed, 1st bk. New in dj. *Bernard.* $25/£16

ALTIERI, JAMES. The Spearheaders. Indianapolis: Bobbs-Merrill, (1960). 1st ed. Signed, inscribed. Fine in Fine dj. *Glenn.* $35/£23

ALTROCCHI, JULIA COOLEY. The Old California Trail. Caldwell: Caxton Printers, 1945. VG in dj. *Schoyer.* $40/£26

ALTSHELER, JOSEPH. The Sun of Quebec. NY, 1919. 1st ed. VG. *Clark.* $28/£18

ALVAREZ, A. Lost. Turret, 1968. One of 250. Fine. *Poetry.* $19/£12

ALVAREZ, A. The Savage God. NY, (1971). 1st Amer ed. Cl-backed bds. VG in dj. *King.* $25/£16

ALVAREZ, AL. The Legacy. London: Poem-of-the-Month Club Ltd, 1972. 1st Eng ed. Signed. VG (sm mk verso). *Ulysses.* $31/£20

ALVAREZ, JULIA. How the Garcia Girls Lost Their Accents. Chapel Hill: Algonquin, 1991. 1st ed. NF in Fine dj. *Robbins.* $35/£23

ALVAREZ, OCTAVIO. The Celestial Brides. Stockbridge, MA, 1978. 152 plts. VG in dj. *Argosy.* $100/£65

ALVAREZ, WALTER. Nervous Indigestion. NY, 1930. 1st ed. Good. *Fye.* $50/£32

ALVORD, CLARENCE W. Cahokia Records 1778-1790. Springfield: IL State Hist Lib v2, VA Series v1, 1907. 1st ed. 5 plts, fldg map. *Oregon.* $45/£29

ALVORD, CLARENCE W. The County of Illinois. IL State Hist Lib, 1907. Wraps (scuffed). *Schoyer.* $15/£10

ALVORD, CLARENCE W. Kaskaskia Records 1778-1790. Springfield: IL State Hist Lib v5, VA Series v2, 1909. 1st ed. 7 plts. *Oregon.* $45/£29

ALVORD, CLARENCE W. The Mississippi Valley in British Politics. Cleveland: Clark, 1917. 2 vols. 4 color maps. Gilt spine titles, tops; unopened. Prelim leaf roughly opened vol 1, else Fine. Howes A 195. *Bohling.* $350/£226

ALVORD, CLARENCE W. The Mississippi Valley in British Politics. Cleveland: Clark, 1917. 1st ed. 2 vols. Howes A 195. *Ginsberg.* $300/£194

ALVORD, CLARENCE W. and CLARENCE E. CARTER (eds). The New Regime, 1765-1767. Springfield: IL State Hist Lib, 1921. Blue cl. VG. *Schoyer.* $45/£29

ALVORD, CLARENCE W. and CLARENCE E. CARTER (eds). Trade and Politics, 1767-1769. Springfield: IL State Hist Lib, 1921. Blue cl. VG. *Schoyer.* $50/£32

AMADO, JORGE. The Miracle of the Birds. Barbara Shelby Merello (trans). NY: Targ Editions, 1983. 1st ed. One of 250 signed. Fine in glassine dj. *Juvelis.* $90/£58

AMADO, JORGE. The Two Deaths of Quincas Wateryell. NY: Knopf, 1965. 1st Amer ed. Fine in dj. *Hermitage.* $45/£29

AMADO, JORGE. The Violent Land. Samuel Putnam (trans). NY: Knopf, 1945. 1st Amer ed. Pg edges lt foxed; fr pastedown dknd at hinge, else NF in VG dj (sl nicking, tears). *Between The Covers.* $50/£32

AMANN, WILLIAM FRAYNE (ed). Personnel of the Civil War. NY, (1961). 2 vols. Vol 1 spine lt spotted, else VG in slipcase (soiled). *King.* $45/£29

AMARAL, ANTHONY. Movie Horses, Their Treatment and Training. Indianapolis: Bobbs-Merrill, 1967. 1st ed. VG in VG dj. *October Farm.* $45/£29

AMBLER, CHARLES HENRY. History of Transportation in the Ohio Valley.... Glendale: Clark, 1932. 1st ed. *Ginsberg.* $150/£97

AMBLER, ERIC. Passage of Arms. NY: Knopf, 1960. 1st Amer ed. Peach cl, gilt-titled. VG in dj (sl worn). *Cady.* $20/£13

AMBLER, ERIC. State of Siege. NY: Knopf, 1956. 1st Amer ed. Fine in dj. *Hermitage.* $35/£23

AMBROSINI, M. and M. WILLIS. The Secret Archives of the Vatican. Eyre & Spottiswoode, 1970. 25 plts. Black cl. VG. *Moss.* $28/£18

AMEDEO, LUIGI. On the Polar Star in the Arctic Sea...with the Statements of Commander U. Cagni.... London: Hutchinson, 1903. 1st Eng ed. 2 vols. 16 plts; 2 fldg panoramas; 2 maps in pocket. Orig dec cl. VG. *High Latitude.* $275/£177

American and English Genealogies in the Library of Congress. Washington: GPO, 1919. 2nd ed. Maroon cl (sl rubbed). *Karmiole.* $75/£48

American Angler's Guide: Containing the Opinions and Practice of the Best English and American Anglers.... (By John J. Brown.) NY: H. Long & Bros., 1849. 4th ed. 2 full-pg engr plts. Ltr black leatherette. VG. *Houle.* $135/£87

American Art Today. (NY): Natl Art Soc, (1939). 1st ed. Good (bkpl) in yellow ptd wrappers (lt faded). *Karmiole.* $60/£39

American Primer. Phila: Matthew Carey, 1813. 4th improved ed. 36pp. 32 woodcuts. Pict paper cvrs, black paper spine (rebacked); oval woodcuts upper wrapper, tp. Internally Fine. (Chipped orig wrappers laid down on new papers and rebacked w/black paper as orig issued.) *Hobbyhorse.* $175/£113

AMERINGER, OSCAR. If You Don't Weaken. NY: Henry Holt, (1940). Rev copy, slip laid in. NF. *Sadlon.* $15/£10

AMERINGER, OSCAR. If You Don't Weaken. NY: Holt, 1940. 1st ed. Frontis port, 9 photo-plts. 1940 article laid in. VG in dj (heavily chipped). *Connolly.* $35/£23

AMERY, L.S. The Times History of the War in South Africa, 1899-1902. London, 1900-1909. Vol 1: 2nd ed; rest 1st eds. 7 vols. Lt foxing, o/w VG set in red cl, gilt medallions to spines (faded; damp mks few vols; sunned, rubbed). *Edwards.* $271/£175

AMES, AZEL. The May-Flower and Her Log; July 15, 1620—May 6, 1621. Boston, 1901. 1st ed. Howes A 218. *Ginsberg.* $150/£97

AMES, DELANO. Death of a Fellow Traveller. NY: Rinehart, 1950. 1st ed. Fine in NF dj. *Beasley.* $35/£23

AMES, ERNEST. The Tremendous Twins. London, 1900. 2nd ed. (Sl worn; bumped.) *Edrich.* $39/£25

AMES, O. Orchids in Retrospect. Cambridge, 1948. Frontis. Orig wrappers (sl faded, chipped). *Sutton.* $65/£42

AMES, V.B. Matrimonial Primer.... SF: Paul Elder, n.d. (ca 1905). 1st ed. Sm 8vo. 39 leaves, 10 full-pg lithos in red/black, incl frontis; dec eps. Pict label on blue/white cl. Ink dedication, soiling, else Fine. *Hobbyhorse.* $55/£35

AMES-LEWIS, FRANCIS. Drawing in Early Renaissance Italy. Yale Univ Press, 1982. 8 color plts; in dj. *Edwards.* $31/£20

AMHERST, A. A History of Gardening in England. London, 1895. 1st ed. xvi,399pp. *Wheldon & Wesley.* $78/£50

AMIS, KINGSLEY. The Folks That Live on the Hill. London: Hutchinson, 1990. 1st ed. Fine in dj. *Virgo.* $16/£10

AMIS, KINGSLEY. The Green Man. NY: Harcourt, Brace & World, (1970). 1st Amer ed. Fine in NF dj. *Hermitage.* $40/£26

AMIS, KINGSLEY. I Like It Here. H-B, 1958. 1st Amer ed. Some lt dust soil tp, else Fine in VG+ dj (sl sunned spine). *Fine Books.* $65/£42

AMIS, KINGSLEY. Jake's Thing. London: Hutchinson, 1978. 1st UK ed. Fine in dj. *Lewton.* $23/£15

AMIS, KINGSLEY. The James Bond Dossier. London: Cape, 1965. 1st ed. NF in dj (price-clipped, lt edgewear). *Janus.* $55/£35

AMIS, KINGSLEY. Lucky Jim's Politics. London: Conservative Political Centre, 1968. 1st ed. Fine in wrappers. *Limestone.* $75/£48

AMIS, KINGSLEY. Lucky Jim. London: Gollancz, 1953. 1st UK ed. VG in yellow dj (spine browning, sl chipping). *Williams.* $1,008/£650

AMIS, KINGSLEY. New Maps of Hell. Gollancz, 1961. 1st UK ed. Sm bkseller's label, o/w Excellent in dj (sl frayed; missing sm pieces at corners). *Sclanders.* $54/£35

AMIS, KINGSLEY. The Old Devils. London: Hutchinson, 1986. 1st ed. Signed. Fine in dj. *Rees.* $39/£25

AMIS, KINGSLEY. The Old Devils. Hutchinson, 1986. 1st UK ed. Fine in dj. *Lewton.* $23/£15

AMIS, KINGSLEY. One Fat Englishman. London: Gollancz, 1963. 1st ed. Fine in dj. *Rees.* $39/£25

AMIS, KINGSLEY. The Riverside Villas Murder. NY: Harcourt Brace, 1973. 1st US ed. Fine in NF dj. *Janus.* $20/£13

AMIS, KINGSLEY. Take a Girl Like You. London: Gollancz, 1960. 1st UK ed. VG (occasional lt foxing) in dj. *Lewton.* $39/£25

AMIS, KINGSLEY. That Uncertain Feeling. Gollancz, 1955. 1st UK ed. NF in dj (spine sl dknd). *Sclanders.* $62/£40

AMIS, KINGSLEY. Wasted and Kipling at Bateman's. London: Poem-of-the-Month Club Ltd, 1973. 1st Eng ed. Signed. VG. *Ulysses.* $93/£60

AMIS, MARTIN. Dead Babies. London: Cape, 1975. 1st UK ed. Fine in dj (price-clipped). *Moorhouse.* $271/£175

AMIS, MARTIN. Einstein's Monsters. London: Cape, 1987. 1st ed. Inscribed. Fine in dj. *Rees.* $47/£30

AMIS, MARTIN. Einstein's Monsters. Cape, 1987. 1st UK ed. Fine in dj. *Lewton.* $28/£18

AMIS, MARTIN. Einstein's Monsters. NY: Harmony, 1987. 1st US ed. Signed. Fine in Fine dj. *Beasley.* $75/£48

AMIS, MARTIN. Invasion of the Space Invaders. London: Hutchinson, 1982. 1st ed. NF in pict wrappers. *Rees.* $54/£35

AMIS, MARTIN. Invasion of the Space Invaders. London: Hutchinson, 1982. 1st UK ed. Generally VG (sl creasing of cvrs). *Lewton.* $45/£29

AMIS, MARTIN. London Fields. NY: Harmony, (1989). 1st ed. Fine in NF dj. *Robbins.* $20/£13

AMIS, MARTIN. London Fields. NY: Harmony, 1989. 1st U.S. ed. Inscribed. Fine in Fine dj. *Beasley.* $50/£32

AMIS, MARTIN. London Fields. Cape, 1989. 1st UK ed. Fine in dj. *Lewton.* $28/£18

AMIS, MARTIN. London Fields. London: Cape, 1989. One of 150 specially bound numbered, signed. Fine in glassine dj. *Rees.* $116/£75

AMIS, MARTIN. Money. Cape, 1984. 1st UK ed. Fine in dj. *Lewton.* $62/£40

AMIS, MARTIN. The Moronic Inferno. London: Cape, 1986. 1st UK ed. Signed. Fine in dj. *Lewton.* $39/£25

AMIS, MARTIN. Other People. London: Cape, 1981. 1st UK ed. Fine in dj. *Lewton.* $73/£47

AMIS, MARTIN. Other People: A Mystery Story. Cape, 1981. 1st ed. Signed, dated (1984). Fine in dj. *Rees.* $116/£75

AMIS, MARTIN. The Rachel Papers. London: Cape, 1973. 1st UK ed, 1st bk. Fine in NF dj. *Williams.* $465/£300

AMIS, MARTIN. The Rachel Papers. NY: Knopf, 1974. 1st Amer ed, 1st bk. 'BTP' sticker fr pastedown, else Fine in NF dj (extrems lt worn). *Between The Covers.* $125/£81

AMIS, MARTIN. The Rachel Papers. NY: Knopf, 1974. 1st US ed. NF in dj (sm tear top edge; sl crease fr flap). *Bernard.* $100/£65

AMIS, MARTIN. Success. NY: Harmony Books, (1987). 1st Amer ed. Fine in dj. *Antic Hay.* $25/£16

AMIS, MARTIN. Success. London: Cape, 1978. 1st UK ed. Fine in dj. *Lewton.* $109/£70

AMIS, MARTIN. Time's Arrow. London: Cape, 1991. Fine in dj. *Limestone.* $30/£19

AMIS, MARTIN. Time's Arrow. NY: Harmony, 1991. 1st ed. Inscribed. Fine in Fine dj. *Beasley.* $45/£29

AMIS, MARTIN. Time's Arrow. London: Cape, 1991. 1st ed. Signed. Fine in dj. *Rees.* $39/£25

AMIS, MARTIN. Time's Arrow. London: London Limited Editions, 1991. One of 200 numbered, signed preceding trade ed. Fine in opaque wraps. *Williams.* $85/£55

AMIS, MARTIN. Time's Arrow. London: Cape, 1991. One of 200 specially bound by London Ltd Eds, numbered, signed. Fine in glassine dj. *Rees.* $101/£65

AMMEN, DANIEL. The Atlantic Coast. NY: Scribner's, (1885). Subscription ed. Frontis, x,273pp. Spine ends sl rubbed, else VG. *Mcgowan.* $45/£29

AMMONS, A.R. Diversifications. NY: Norton, (1975). 1st ed. Signed. VF in VF dj. *Pharos.* $40/£26

AMMONS, A.R. Sphere: A Form of Motion. NY: Norton, (1974). Signed. 1st ed. VF in dj. *Pharos.* $75/£48

Among the Arabs: Adventures in the Desert, and Sketches of Life.... NY: Nelson, n.d. (ca 1877). 248pp. Blue cl stamped in black/gilt (sl worn). *Schoyer.* $40/£26

Among the Pimas. (By Charles Cook.) Albany: Ladies Union Mission School, 1893. 1st ed. 136pp. *Ginsberg.* $100/£65

AMORY, R. and R.L. EMERSON. Wharton and Stille's Medical Jurisprudence. Vol. II—Poisons. Rochester, NY, 1905. 5th ed. Vol II only. Contemp calf (rebacked; 2 labels on spine, 1 orig). *Whitehart.* $147/£95

AMORY, ROBERT. A Treatise on Electrolysis and Its Applications.... NY: Wood, 1886. 'Wood Library ed'. vii; 307pp. VG. *Goodrich.* $65/£42

AMOS, SHELDON. The Science of Law. NY: D. Appleton, 1874. Crimson cl; gilt. Sound (worn; faded). *Boswell.* $65/£42

AMSDEN, CHARLES AVERY. Navaho Weaving. Albuquerque: Univ of NM, 1949. 2nd ed. Color repro laid in. VG (edgewear). *Parker.* $150/£97

AMSDEN, CHARLES AVERY. Navaho Weaving. Glorieta: Rio Grande, 1964. Rpt. VG + . *Parker.* $50/£32

AMUNDSEN, ROALD and LINCOLN ELLSWORTH. First Crossing of the Polar Sea. NY: George H. Doran, 1927. 1st ed in English. Fldg map. Excellent in dj (lt chipped). *High Latitude.* $95/£61

AMUNDSEN, ROALD and LINCOLN ELLSWORTH. Our Polar Flight. NY: Dodd, Mead, 1925. 1st ed. Excellent in orig ptd, illus dj (few minor chips top/bottom edges; split over lower spine). *High Latitude.* $110/£71

AMUNDSEN, ROALD. My Polar Flight. London: Hutchinson, n.d. (1925). 1st Eng ed. VG + . *Walcot.* $62/£40

AMUNDSEN, ROALD. The Northwest Passage...Record of a Voyage of...the Ship 'Gjoa' 1903-1907.... NY: E.P. Dutton, 1908. 1st US ed. 2 vols. 2 fldg maps laid in. Orig dec cl; teg. Minor fold split in one map else VG. *High Latitude.* $400/£258

AMUNDSEN, ROALD. The South Pole, an Account of the Norwegian Antarctic Expedition in the 'Fram' 1910-1912. London: John Murray, 1912. 1st Eng ed. 2 vols. Good + (sl rubbed, minor mks). *Walcot.* $426/£275

AMUNDSEN, ROALD. The South Pole. A.G. Chater (trans). NY/London: Keedick/Murray, 1913. 1st Amer ed. 2 vols. 8vo. Blue cl, gilt titles (internal foxing; spine titles faded, sl wear; hinges reinforced vol 1). *Parmer.* $900/£581

Amusing History of Tom Thumb. Bath, NY: R.L. Underhill, n.d. (ca 1830). 24mo. 8pp, eight 1/2pg woodcuts, incl title pg. Orig marbled paper wrappers (pencil sig; lt foxed). VG w/VF cuts. *Hobbyhorse.* $200/£129

ANAND, MULK RAJ. Kama Kala. Geneva, 1958. 69 plts. VG in dj. *Argosy.* $45/£29

ANDERSEN, HANS CHRISTIAN. Fairy Tales by Hans Andersen. Phila: David McKay. 1st Amer ed. 12 full-pg color illus, 59 b/w illus by Arthur Rackham. Rose-red cl, pict gold stamping. NF in dj (multiple pieces missing). *Davidson.* $285/£184

ANDERSEN, HANS CHRISTIAN. Fairy Tales of Hans Christian Andersen. NY: Brentano's, (1916). 1st Amer ed (Eng sheets). Lg 4to. Teg. Harry Clarke (illus). Grey cl, b/w decs (spine lt faded; cl lt spotted, darkened; lt foxing few pp). *Reisler.* $600/£387

ANDERSEN, HANS CHRISTIAN. Fairy Tales. London/Bombay/Sydney: Harrap, (1930). 4to, 319 + (i)pp (tape-repaired tear 1pg); 16 color, 24 b/w plts by Harry Clarke. Mod 3/4 morocco, gilt; orig grn pict cl (stained, rubbed) mtd on fr, back cvrs; new eps. NF. *Blue Mountain.* $250/£161

ANDERSEN, HANS CHRISTIAN. Fairy Tales. NY: George H. Doran, 1924. 1st Amer ed. 280pp, 12 tipped-in color plts, illus eps by Kay Nielson. Black cl, silver pict onlay. VG (back bd lt soiled, spine lt faded). *Davidson.* $650/£419

ANDERSEN, HANS CHRISTIAN. Fairytales. London: Hodder & Stoughton, 1924. 1st Eng ed. 197pp, 12 tipped-in color plts, lettered guards, illus eps. Kay Nielson (illus). Black cl, gilt. VG (spine head, tail worn; fep stained; sm hole spine). *Davidson.* $650/£419

ANDERSEN, HANS CHRISTIAN. Hans Andersen's Fairy Tales. England: Boots the Chemists, (1913). 8vo, 320pp, 16 tipped-in color plts by W. Heath Robinson. Red cl, gilt. VG (spine lt faded). *Davidson.* $250/£161

ANDERSEN, HANS CHRISTIAN. Hans Andersen's Fairy Tales. NY: Henry Holt, 1913. 1st Amer ed. 4to. 16 full color mtd plts by W. Heath Robinson. (Foxing.) Wine-red cl, gilt, add'l white coloring (spine sl darkened). *Reisler.* $350/£226

ANDERSEN, HANS CHRISTIAN. Hans Andersen's Fairy Tales. London: Blackie & Son, n.d. (1906 inscrip). Folio. 3 dbl-pg color plts, 24 color plts, 31 illus by Helen Stratton. Gray spine cl (water mks); color pict bds. Edges rubbed, o/w VG. *Drusilla's.* $100/£65

ANDERSEN, HANS CHRISTIAN. Hans Christian Andersen. The Maker of Fairy Tales. (Fairy Tales, vol II). Jean Hersholt (ed, trans). NY: LEC, 1942. 2 vols. Ltd to 1500 numbered, signed by Hersholt and Fritz Kredel (dwgs). This copy further inscribed by Hersholt. Frontis port. Brn cl over dec brn bds. Good in slipcase. *Karmiole.* $150/£97

ANDERSEN, HANS CHRISTIAN. The Little Mermaid. NY: Macmillan, 1939. 1st ed thus. 6 full-color plts by Dorothy Lathrop. Black cl, gilt. VG in dj (lt torn). *Davidson.* $295/£190

ANDERSEN, HANS CHRISTIAN. The Sand-Hills of Jutland. Ticknor & Fields, 1860. 1st Amer ed. Spine sl worn, else VG. *Fine Books.* $175/£113

ANDERSEN, HANS CHRISTIAN. The Snow Queen. NY: Dial, 1982. 1st ed. 4to, 40pp. Susan Jeffers (illus). Grey cl bds. Fine in VG dj. *Davidson.* $45/£29

ANDERSEN, HANS CHRISTIAN. Thumbelina. Vernon Ives (ed). (NY): Holiday House, 1939. One of 1200 hand-colored. Sq 16mo. 28 leaves. Good (one loose leaf reglued). *Hobbyhorse.* $25/£16

ANDERSEN, HANS CHRISTIAN. The Wild Swan. NY: Dial, 1981. 1st ed. 4to, 40pp. Susan Jeffers (illus). Blue cl bds. Fine in VG dj. *Davidson.* $45/£29

ANDERSON, ANTONY. Elmer Wachtel. (L.A.: Carl A. Bundy Quill & Press), 1930. Gold-stamped cl in dj (torn). Inscrip from Marion Wachtel. *Dawson.* $125/£81

ANDERSON, ARCHER. The Campaign and Battle of Chickamauga. Richmond: William Ellis Jones, 1881. 1st ed. 38pp. Orig ptd wraps. Good + (lt chipped, worn, sm hole last 3 leaves affecting few words). *Chapel Hill.* $150/£97

ANDERSON, B. Fragrance among Old Volumes. Kegan Paul, 1910. 14 plts. Teg. Fine. *Moss.* $34/£22

ANDERSON, C.W. Big Red. NY: Macmillan, 1942. 1st ed. VG in Fair dj. *October Farm.* $45/£29

ANDERSON, C.W. Blaze and Thunderbolt. NY: Macmillan, 1955. 1st ed. 7.5x10. 32pp. Fine. *Cattermole.* $40/£26

ANDERSON, C.W. Thoroughbreds. NY: Macmillan, 1942. 1st ed. VG in Good dj. *October Farm.* $45/£29

ANDERSON, C.W. A Touch of Greatness. NY: Macmillan, 1945. 1st ed. 2mo, 96pp. Grn cl, black title. VG in dj (lt torn). *Davidson*. $47/£30

ANDERSON, CHARLES C. Fighting by Southern Federals. NY: Neale Publ Co, 1912. 1st ed. Cl (worn; ex-lib, mks; lacks fep). *King*. $85/£55

ANDERSON, CHARLES C. Fighting by Southern Federals. NY: Neale, 1912. 1st ed. Orig blue cl. Sm hole fr gutter, else VG + . *Chapel Hill*. $175/£113

ANDERSON, CHESTER. James Joyce and His World. NY: Viking/Studio, (1968). 1st ed, Amer issue (British sheets). NF in dj. *Reese*. $35/£23

ANDERSON, D.G. and C.F. KEEFER. The Therapeutic Value of Penicillin, a Study of 10,000 Cases. Ann Arbor, 1948. 1st ed. Good. *Fye*. $75/£48

ANDERSON, E.L. Six Weeks in Norway. Cincinnati: Robert Clarke, 1877. 1st ed. Frontis map, 80pp. Grn cl, gilt. Good. *Karmiole*. $40/£26

ANDERSON, EVA GREENSLIT. Dog-Team Doctor. Caldwell, ID: Caxton, 1940. 1st ed. Inscribed. Dec cl. Joints rubbed, else VG in dj (tattered). *High Latitude*. $35/£23

ANDERSON, ISABEL. From Corsair to Riffian. Boston/NY: Houghton Mifflin, 1927. 1st ed. 24 plts. VG in dj (torn). *Worldwide*. $16/£10

ANDERSON, ISABEL. The Great Sea Horse. Boston: Little Brown, 1909. 1st ed. 4to. 251pp; 24 color plts. Teg. Red cl, gilt. NF. *Drusilla's*. $155/£100

ANDERSON, ISABEL. A Yacht Voyage in Mediterranean Seas. Boston: Marshall Jones, 1930. 1st ed. Color frontis. *Lefkowicz*. $30/£19

ANDERSON, J. RINGLAND. Detachment of the Retina: A Contribution to the Study.... Cambridge, 1931. 1st ed. Good. *Fye*. $150/£97

ANDERSON, J. RINGLAND. Hydrophthalmia or Congenital Glaucoma. Cambridge, 1939. 1st ed. Good in dj. *Fye*. $100/£65

ANDERSON, J.K. Ancient Greek Horsemanship. Berkeley/LA: Univ of CA, 1961. 39 b/w plts. VG in dj (price-clipped). *Schoyer*. $50/£32

ANDERSON, JACK and BILL PRONZINI. The Cambodia File. GC: Doubleday, 1981. 1st ed. NF in VG dj (closed tear; ink mk fep). *Aka*. $35/£23

ANDERSON, JAMES H. (ed). Life and Letters of Judge Thomas J. Anderson and Wife.... (Columbus): Press of F.J. Heer, 1904. Grn cl, gilt. *Boswell*. $75/£48

ANDERSON, JOHN HENRY. American Civil War: The Operations in the Eastern Theatre.... London: Hugh Rees, 1910. 1st ed. 13 (of 14) fldg maps in pocket. Spine sl darkened, else NF. *Mcgowan*. $350/£226

ANDERSON, JOHN Q. Tales of Frontier Texas 1830-1860. Dallas: SMU, 1966. 1st ed. Dj. *Lambeth*. $25/£16

ANDERSON, JOHN R.L. Death in the Thames. London: Gollancz, 1974. 1st ed. Pg edges lt discolored, spine sl slanted, else NF in Fine dj. *Murder*. $50/£32

ANDERSON, JOHN. Mandalay to Momien...Two Expeditions to Western China of 1868 and 1875. London: Macmillan, 1876. Frontis, xvi,(480)pp, 3 fldg maps, 15 plts. Grn dec cl stamped in gilt/black (ex-lib, internal mks; recased, rebacked, new eps). *Schoyer*. $250/£161

ANDERSON, M.D. The Medieval Carver. CUP, 1935. 1st ed. Frontis, 20 plts. Gilt device upper bd. *Edwards*. $39/£25

ANDERSON, MARGARET. My 30 Years War. Knopf, 1930. 1st ed. Sl dull, else Good. *Whiteson*. $31/£20

ANDERSON, MAXWELL. Off Broadway, Essays About the Theatre. NY, (1947). 1st ed. VG in dj (sl used). *King*. $35/£23

ANDERSON, NANCY MAE. Swede Homestead. Caldwell: Caxton, 1942. 1st ed. Name, else VG in dj (torn). *Perier*. $40/£26

ANDERSON, POUL and GORDON DICKSON. Earthman's Burden. Gnome, 1957. 1st ed. Fine in Mint dj. *Madle*. $100/£65

ANDERSON, POUL. The Avatar. NY: Berkley Pub Corp, (1978). 1st ed. Fine in dj. *Sadlon*. $20/£13

ANDERSON, POUL. Beyond the Beyond. Gollancz, 1970. 1st Eng, 1st trade hb ed. Signed. Fine in VG + dj. *Aronovitz*. $60/£39

ANDERSON, POUL. Brain Wave. Heinemann, 1955. 1st Eng, 1st hb ed. Signed. VG + in dj. *Aronovitz*. $375/£242

ANDERSON, POUL. Brain Wave. Walker, 1969. 1st US hb ed. VG in dj. *Madle*. $75/£48

ANDERSON, POUL. Flight to Forever. Malian Press, 1954. 1st ed. VG + in wraps. *Aronovitz*. $45/£29

ANDERSON, POUL. Murder Bound. NY: Macmillan, 1962. 1st ed. Fine (browning to pg borders) in NF dj. *Janus*. $75/£48

ANDERSON, POUL. Perish by the Sword. NY: Macmillan, 1959. 1st ed. Fine (bump, pp browned) in NF dj (short closed tears). *Janus*. $125/£81

ANDERSON, POUL. Three Hearts and Three Lions. Doubleday, 1961. 1st ed. VF in dj. *Madle*. $400/£258

ANDERSON, POUL. Vault of the Ages. Winston, 1952. 1st ed. Fine in dj (sl frayed). *Madle*. $125/£81

ANDERSON, POUL. Virgin Planet. Avalon, 1959. 1st ed. Fine in dj. *Madle*. $100/£65

ANDERSON, R.C. Naval Wars in the Baltic During the Sailing-Ship Epoch 1522-1850. London: G. Gilbert-Wood, 1910. Teg. *Petersfield*. $62/£40

ANDERSON, R.C. The Rigging of Ships in the Days of the Spritsail Topmast 1600-1720. Salem, MA: Marine Research Soc, 1927. Frontis; 24 full-pg plts. (Eps discolored due to laid-in clippings). VG in dj (sl worn; few tears reinforced on verso). *Hayman*. $50/£32

ANDERSON, ROBERT J. The Metallurgy of Aluminum and Aluminum Alloys. NY: Henry Carey Baird, 1925. 1st ed. Grn cl, gilt. Corner bumped, o/w Fine. *Karmiole*. $35/£23

ANDERSON, SHERWOOD. A New Testament. NY, 1927. 1st Amer ed. Fine in Fine dj. *Polyanthos*. $150/£97

ANDERSON, SHERWOOD. A New Testament. NY: B&L, 1927. 1st ed. Fine. *Else Fine*. $45/£29

ANDERSON, SHERWOOD. A Story Teller's Story. NY: B.W. Huebsch, 1924. 1st ed, 1st issue, w/top edge stained yellow. Brn pebbled cl. Bkpl of Estelle Doheny. Fr inner hinge cracked; name stamp, o/w Fine in NF dj. *Chapel Hill*. $125/£81

ANDERSON, SHERWOOD. The Triumph of the Egg. NY: B.W. Huebsch, 1921. 1st ed, 1st issue, w/top edge stained yellow. Dk grn cl. Bkpl of Estelle Doheny. VG (bkseller label; gift inscrip). *Chapel Hill*. $75/£48

ANDERSON, SHERWOOD. Windy McPherson's Son. NY: John Lane, 1916. 1st ed, 1st bk. Dec lt brn cl. Bkpl of Estelle Doheny. VG (inner hinges tender). *Chapel Hill*. $140/£90

ANDERSON, SHERWOOD. Windy McPherson's Son. NY: John Lane, 1916. 1st ed, 1st bk. Gilt-dec tan cl. Good (pencil name erased title; spine gilt sl dull; corners sl worn). *Reese.* $150/£97

ANDERSON, TROYER S. The Command of the Howe Brothers During the American Revolution. NY/London: OUP, 1936. 1st ed. Dbl-port frontis. Dk blue cl. Good (contemp newspaper review tipped to fr pastedown, tp soiled). *Chapel Hill.* $50/£32

ANDERSON, WILLIAM. The Architecture of the Renaissance in Italy. London: Batsford, 1896. 1st ed. Frontis; xvii,(i),155,(3)pp; 54 illus on plts. Red gilt cl. Teg. Corners bruised; spine sl sunned; bkpl, else VG. *Bookpress.* $50/£32

ANDERSON, WILLIAM. Descriptive and Historical Catalogue of a Collection of Japanese and Chinese Paintings in the British Museum. London, 1886. xvi,554pp,(i)ad, 31 plts. Parts uncut, unopened. (Browning to margins, fep; cl rubbed; bumped, chipped.) *Edwards.* $116/£75

ANDERSON, WILLIAM. The Pictorial Arts of Japan. London: Sampson et al, 1886. xix,276pp, 80 plts (incl 16 chromolithos). (Ex-lib w/ink stamps text, margins of plts, sl affecting illus; sporadic soiling margins). Marbled eps, aeg. (Rebacked, orig morocco spine laid down; lib bkpl.) *Edwards.* $388/£250

Andes and the Amazon.... (By James Orton.) NY: Harper, 1870. Frontis; fldg map. (Ink name; lt worn, frayed.) *Hermitage.* $85/£55

ANDRAL, G. Medical Clinic: Diseases of the Encephalon.... Phila, 1843. 1st Eng trans. 303pp. 1/2 leather. Good. *Fye.* $150/£97

ANDRE, EUGENE. A Naturalist in the Guianas. London: Smith, Elder, 1904. 1st ed. 34 plts, lg fldg color map. Orig red cl, gilt (rubbed, soiled). *Karmiole.* $65/£42

ANDRE, MAJOR. Journal (1777-1778). H.C. Lodge (ed). Boston: Bibliophile Soc, 1903. 1st ed. One of 467. 2 vols. 3 engr titles; 2 ports; 7 facs; 38 maps. Full vellum, gold-stamped. Howes A 239. *Ginsberg.* $500/£323

ANDREANO, RALPH. No Joy in Mudville. Schenckman, 1965. 1st ed. Fine in VG dj. *Plapinger.* $25/£16

Andree's Story, the Complete Record of His Polar Flight, 1897. (By S.A. Andree.) NY: Viking, (1930). Fine in NF dj. *Hermitage.* $100/£65

ANDREE, S.A. The Andree Diaries. London: John Lane, 1931. 1st ed. VG. *Walcot.* $47/£30

ANDREE, S.A. The Andree Diaries.... London: John Lane, Bodley Head, 1931. Red cl (soiled, worn; bkpl). *Parmer.* $100/£65

ANDREEV, LEONID. The Dark. Hogarth Press, 1922. 1st ed. Pp sl brittle, o/w VG in wrappers (sl dusty). *Words Etc.* $78/£50

ANDREW, A.M. and R.E. JOHNSON. Pilot Jack Knight. Wheeler, 1950. 1st ed. VG. *Madle.* $20/£13

ANDREW, LAUREL B. The Early Temples of the Mormons. Albany, 1978. VG+ in dj. *Benchmark.* $35/£23

ANDREW, LAUREL B. The Early Temples of the Mormons. Albany: St. Univ of NY, 1978. 1st ed. VF in VF dj. *Oregon.* $35/£23

ANDREWS, ALLEN. The Pig Plantagenet. NY: Viking, 1981. 1st ed. Full-pg frontis, 11 full-pg b/w illus, tailpieces by Michael Foreman. Gray paper on bds, brn cl spine w/gilt title. Pict eps. Mint in dj. *Hobbyhorse.* $95/£61

ANDREWS, C.L. The Eskimo and His Reindeer in Alaska. Caldwell, ID: Caxton, 1939. Frontis map. VG in dj. *High Latitude.* $60/£39

ANDREWS, C.L. The Story of Sitka. Seattle, (1922). 1st ed. 15 plts (incl fldg map). VG in Good+ dj (spine ends chipped). *Oregon.* $75/£48

ANDREWS, C.L. The Story of Sitka. Seattle: Lowman & Hanford, c 1922. 1st ed. Frontis, fldg map. Grn cl, gilt. Sig, lt spots, else VG; text Fine. *Parmer.* $85/£55

ANDREWS, CAROL. Ancient Egyptian Jewelry. NY: Abrams, (1991). Good in dj. *Archaeologia.* $85/£55

ANDREWS, JOHN. History of the War with America, France, Spain and Holland.... London, 1785-1786. 1st ed. 4 vols. (2),448; (2),445; (2),445; (2),416,(6)pp + subs list; 31 plts and maps. Vol 3 marbled; paper spines (lt cracked, worn; few bds loose; portions of orig ms spine labels); entirely uncut. Howes A 259. *Ginsberg.* $750/£484

ANDREWS, MARIETTA MINNIGERODE. Memoirs of a Poor Relation.... Dutton, (c. 1927). (2nd ptg). Good. *Book Broker.* $25/£16

ANDREWS, MARIETTA MINNIGERODE. Scraps of Paper. NY: E.P. Dutton, (1929). 1st ed. VG. *Mcgowan.* $65/£42

ANDREWS, MARY RAYMOND SHIPMAN. His Soul Goes Marching On. NY: Scribner's, 1922. Untrimmed. VG. *Burcham.* $35/£23

ANDREWS, MATTHEW PAGE. The Soul of a Nation. Scribner, 1943. 1st ed. VG. *Book Broker.* $35/£23

ANDREWS, MATTHEW PAGE. Virginia the Old Dominion. Doubleday, Doran, 1937. Boxed ed. 2 vols. Blue leather (rubbed). Box (broken). *Book Broker.* $60/£39

ANDREWS, ROBERT HARDY. A Corner of Chicago. Boston: Little, Brown, 1963. 1st ed. VG in dj (chipped). *Burcham.* $25/£16

ANDREWS, ROBERT W. The Life and Adventures of Capt. Robert W. Andrews, of South Carolina. Boston: E.P. Whitcomb, 1887. 1st ed. Frontis port, 87,(1)pp. Orig ptd wraps. Lacks rear wrap, spine worn, o/w VG. *Chapel Hill.* $95/£61

ANDREWS, ROY CHAPMAN. Whale Hunting with Gun and Camera. NY: Appleton, 1916. 1st ed. Cl (sl rubbed). Good+ (spine lettering dull). *Walcot.* $56/£36

ANDREWS, ROY CHAPMAN. Whale Hunting with Gun and Camera. NY: D. Appleton, 1916. 1st ptg. Orig cl; teg. VG. *High Latitude.* $75/£48

ANDREWS, ROY CHAPMAN. Whale Hunting with Gun and Camera. NY: Appleton-Century, 1935. 2nd ed. VG (name) in Poor dj. *Perier.* $35/£23

ANDREWS, V.C. Flowers in the Attic. NY: S&S, 1979. 1st hb ed. 1st bk. VF in dj. *Else Fine.* $50/£32

ANDREWS, W. On the Extra-Illustration of Books. London: Zaehnsdorf, 1910. Good in ptd cvrs. *Moss.* $25/£16

ANDREWS, WAYNE. Architecture in New England. Brattleboro, VT: Stephen Greene Press, (1973). 1st ed. VG in dj (creased, chipped). *Bookpress.* $45/£29

ANDREWS, WILLIAM. Antiquities and Curiosities of the Church. London: William Andrews, 1897. 1st ed. 285,(x)pp (1/2 title removed; title, final leaf lt browned; few spots). Gilt cl (sl bubbled). *Hollett.* $39/£25

ANDREWS, WILLIAM. Curious Church Customs. London: Hull, 1895. Frontis, 274pp + (x)pp list (feps sl browned); teg. Gilt-ruled 2-tone cl (sl worn). *Edwards.* $56/£36

ANDREWS, WILLIAM. Ecclesiastical Curiosities. London: William Andrews, 1899. 1st ed. (iv),250,(v)pp (flyleaves lt browned). Teg. Upper hinge frayed. *Hollett.* $54/£35

ANDREWS, WILLIAM. England in the Days of Old. London: William Andrews, 1897. 1st ed. (iv),279,(x)pp (1/2 title browned). Teg. Cl over beveled bds (lt rubbed), gilt. *Hollett.* $54/£35

ANDREWS, WILLIAM. Famous Frosts and Frost Fairs in Great Britain. London: George Redway, 1887. 1st ed. #375/400 ptd. Frontis, viii,91pp; 2 engr plts. *Cox.* $70/£45

ANDREWS, WILLIAM. Old Church Lore. Hull: William Andrews, 1891. 1st ed. (iv),255,(vi)pp. Levant morocco (rebacked), gilt. VG. *Hollett.* $62/£40

ANDREWS, WILLIAM. Old-Time Punishments. Hull/London, 1890. x,251pp (margins lt browned). Teg. (Hinges tender, sl shaken; sl rubbed; spine sl chipped.) *Edwards.* $54/£35

ANDREYEV, L. Abyss. John Cournos (trans). London: Golden Cockerel Press, 1929. #300/500. Frontis, 3 wood-engrs; uncut, teg. Buckram-backed bds. Good. *Cox.* $59/£38

ANDREYEV, L. The Seven Who Were Hanged. Oglive, 1909. 1st ed. VG +. *Fine Books.* $55/£35

ANDRIC, IVO. Bosnian Story. Kenneth Johnstone (trans). London: Lincolns-Prager, (1958). 1st Eng ed. Red cl (extrems sl worn). Nice. *Shasky.* $35/£23

Anecdotes of Animals. London: Harvey & Darton, 1832. Sq 12mo. viii,147pp + 4pp list, 5 VF full-pg copper engrs. Red roan back, marbled paper, gilt title. VG (3 sm holes leaf 79 affecting few letters; ink sig; rubbed, bumped; spine cracked). *Hobbyhorse.* $115/£74

Anecdotes of Mr. Hogarth. London: Thomas Cook & G.&J. Robinson, 1803. viii,386pp. Contemp 1/2 calf (sl rubbed), gilt. *Hollett.* $78/£50

ANGEL, MARIE. Beasts in Heraldry. VT: Stephen Greene, 1974. 1st ed. 12mo, unpaginated. Marie Angel (illus). VG + (lt soiled, corner split, ink name on fly) in orig box. *Davidson.* $85/£55

ANGEL, MYRON (ed). History of Nevada with Illustrations and Biographical Sketches.... Oakland: Thompson & West, 1881. 1st ed. 680pp; 116 plts. Recased in orig leather spine, dec cl. VG. Howes A 273. *Perier.* $695/£448

ANGEL, MYRON. History of Nevada with Illustrations and Biographical Sketches.... Oakland: Thompson & West, 1881. 1st ed. 680pp, 80 litho plts (4 dbl-pg), 36 steel-engr port plts, dbl-pg chart; 4pp facs of Territorial Enterprise vl #26 + 34pp bio text not incl in pagination. Prelims incl t.p. creased, repaired, o/w contents Fine. VG. Howes A 273. *Oregon.* $850/£548

ANGELL, NORMAN. After All. The Autobiography of Sir Norman Angell. London: Hamish Hamilton, (1951). 1st ed. Fine in dj (sl used). *Pharos.* $25/£16

ANGELL, ROGER. Five Seasons: A Baseball Companion. NY: S&S, (1977). 1st ed. Fine in NF dj. *Aka.* $25/£16

ANGELL, ROGER. The Stone Arbor and Other Stories. Boston: Little Brown, 1960. 1st ed, 1st bk. VG + in VG dj. *Pettler.* $40/£26

ANGELOU, MAYA. The Heart of a Woman. NY: Random House, (1981). 1st ed. VG in dj (nicks, short tears, else VG). *Godot.* $40/£26

ANGELOU, MAYA. The Heart of a Woman. NY: Random House, (1981). 1st ed. Inscribed. Black cl-backed bds. NF in NF dj. *Chapel Hill.* $100/£65

ANGLE, PAUL M. The Great Chicago Fire, the Human Account. Chicago: Chicago Hist Soc, 1946. 1st ed. VG in dj (edge-torn). *Perier.* $25/£16

ANGLE, PAUL M. A Pictorial History of the Civil War Years. GC, NY, (1967). 1st ed. NF in VG dj. *Mcgowan.* $25/£16

ANGLE, PAUL M. (ed). The Lincoln Reader. New Brunswick: Rutgers Univ, 1947. 1st ed. NF in chipped but VG dj. *Mcgowan.* $25/£16

Angler's Note-Book and Naturalist's Record. London: William Satchell, 1880. 6 woodcuts. *Petersfield.* $43/£28

ANGLESEY, MARQUESS OF. One-Leg. The Life and Letters of Henry William Paget...:1768-1854. London, 1961. 2nd imp. Frontis port; 22 plts; 2 fldg charts. VG in dj (sl scuffed). *Edwards.* $25/£16

ANGLUND, JOAN WALSH. Book of Good Tidings. NY: Harcourt Brace, 1965. 1st ed. 4.25x3. Pict cl (faded spots). Fine in Fine dj. *Book Adoption.* $30/£19

ANGUS, JOHN W. A Dictionary of Crimes and Offences According to the Law of Scotland.... Edinburgh: William Green, 1895. Gilt. Cl worn, but sound. *Boswell.* $125/£81

Animal and Train ABC. London: Dean & Sons, (ca 1908). Untearable lt grn cl, gilt title, horse. NF (1908 inscrip). *Davidson.* $250/£161

Animal Tales. NY: Philomel, 1980. 5th ptg. 23x29 cm. 5 pull-down pp. Glazed pict bds. VG. *Book Finders.* $25/£16

ANISIMOV, A.I. et al. Masterpieces of Russian Painting. London: Zwemmer, 1930. 20 color plts, 43 monochrome repros. Fine. *Europa.* $62/£40

ANLEY, GWENDOLYN. Irises. London, 1946. 1st ed. Good. *Brooks.* $20/£13

ANNESLEY, JAMES. Sketches of the Most Prevalent Diseases of India.... London, 1829. 2nd ed. 501pp. 1/2 leather (ex-lib; backstrip rubbed). *Fye.* $325/£210

Annie Nelles: or, The Life of a Book Agent. Cincinnati: For author, 1868. 8vo. Port, x,385pp. Grn pebbled cl. Bubbled, worn at tips, spine; inner hinges splitting, o/w Good. *Veatchs.* $160/£103

Annual Report of Alaska Agriculture Experiment Stations For 1906. Washington: GPO, 1907. 10th annual report. 10 plts. VG in wraps. *Perier.* $20/£13

Annual Report of the Architect of the United States. Washington: GPO, 1899. 1st ed. 44pp; 53 plts (9 fldg). Internally VG in wrappers (chipped). *Bookpress.* $150/£97

Annual Report of the Gettysburg National Military Park Commission to the Secretary of the War, 1893-1904. Washington, 1905. VG +. *Pratt.* $45/£29

ANSON, ADRIAN C. A Ball Player's Career. Era Pub Co, 1900. 1st ed. Good +; no dj as issued. *Plapinger.* $500/£323

ANSTED, D.T. Scenery, Science and Art. London, 1854. 1st ed. viii,323pp + 4pp ads, 4 tinted litho plts. (Lower joint starting.) *Henly.* $132/£85

ANSTEY, F. The Black Poodle. London, 1884. 1st ed. VG. *Madle.* $125/£81

ANSTIE, FRANCIS. Neuralgia and the Diseases that Resemble It. NY, 1882. 1st Amer ed. 233pp. Good. *Fye.* $50/£32

ANTAL, FREDERICK. Florentine Painting and Its Social Background. London, 1965. 2nd ed. 160 plts. Good. *Washton.* $85/£55

ANTHONY, EDGAR WATERMAN. A History of Mosaics. Boston: Porter Sargent, (1935). 1st ed. 80 plts. Black cl; gilt. Prospectus laid in. Good (bkpl) in illus dj (sl soiled). *Karmiole.* $125/£81

ANTHONY, EDWARD and JOSEPH (verses). The Fairies Up-to-Date. Boston: Little, Brown, 1923. 1st Amer ed. Jean de Bosschere (illus). Lg 8vo, 200pp. Red cl, pict insert fr cvr. Fine. *Godot.* $125/£81

ANTHONY, GORDON. Ballet Camera Studies. London: Geoffrey Bless, (1937). 1st ed. 96 mtd plts. 2-tone red/beige linen (spine sl soiled). Nice. *Appelfeld.* $200/£129

ANTHONY, HELEN B. Lisbon: West of the Trinity (Texas). Dallas, TX: SMU, 1971. Signed. VG in dj. *Burcham.* $25/£16

ANTIN, MARY. The Promised Land. Boston: Houghton Mifflin, 1912. 1st Amer ed. Partly unopened. Dec cl. NF. *Agvent.* $175/£113

ANTIN, MARY. The Promised Land. Boston/NY, 1912. 1st ed. *Hayman.* $25/£16

ANTON, FERDINAND and FREDERICK J. DOCKSTADER (eds). Primitive Art: Pre-Columbian; North American Indian; Africa; Oceanic. NY: Abrams, (1979). 7 maps, 2 charts. Good in dj. *Archaeologia.* $85/£55

ANTON, FERDINAND. Art of the Maya. NY: Putnam's, 1970. 1st Amer ed. Dec eps. Grey cl, gilt spine titles. NF in VG dj. *Parmer.* $75/£48

ANTONINUS, BROTHER. (Pseud of William Everson.) The Last Crusade. (Berkeley): Oyez, (1969). 1st ed. One of 165 numbered, signed. 1/2 white calf, cl over bds. NF. *Reese.* $200/£129

ANTONINUS, BROTHER. (Pseud of William Everson.) Who Is She That Looketh Forth as Morning. Santa Barbara: Capricorn Press, 1972. 1st ed. One of 250 numbered, signed. Gilt cl. Fine. *Reese.* $100/£65

ANTONINUS, BROTHER. (Pseud of William Everson.) Who Is She That Looketh Forth as the Morning. Santa Barbara: Capricorn Press, 1972. 1st ed. #227/250 numbered, signed. 9-pg note laid in. Grn leatherette. Fine. *Houle.* $165/£106

APENSZLAK, JACOB (ed). The Black Book of Polish Jewry. (NY?), (1943). Inner rear hinge cracked, else Good in dj (torn, worn). *King.* $35/£23

APOLLINAIRE, GUILLAUME. Apollinaire on Art. Essays and Review, 1902-1918. (NY): Viking, 1972. 1st ed. Promo photo laid in. Fine (sl cocked) in NF dj (lt faded spine). *Beasley.* $65/£42

APOLLONIUS OF TYRE. Historia Apollonii Regis Tyri. Paul Turner (trans). London: Golden Cockerel Press, 1956. #210/300. 6 collotype plts by Mark Severin; teg. Tan morocco-backed maroon cl, blocked in gilt. Fine. *Cox.* $101/£65

APPELFELD, AHARON. Badenheim 1939. Boston: Godine, (1980). 1st Amer ed. Fine in NF dj (sl rubbed). *Between The Covers.* $35/£23

APPERLEY, CHARLES JAMES. Memoirs of the Life of the Late John Mytton.... London: Ackermann, 1837. 2nd ed. 8vo. x,206pp, 1f, 8pp ads, engr title, 18 hand-colored aquatints by Alken. Crimson morocco gilt by Riviere, aeg (spine darkened, joints cracking). *Marlborough.* $1,008/£650

APPERSON, G.L. Bygone London Life. NY: James Pott, 1904. 1st Amer ed. Pict cl; gilt-lettered. Fore-edges untrimmed. VG. *Dramatis Personae.* $70/£45

APPERT, FRANCOIS. The Art of Preserving All Kinds of Animal and Vegetable Substances for Several Years. London: Black, Parry & Kingsbury, 1812. 2nd Eng ed. 164pp + ad; fldg plt. Mod cl-back bds; uncut. Fine. *Second Life.* $500/£323

APPLE, MAX. The Oranging of America and Other Stories. NY: Grossman, 1976. 1st ed. Fine in dj. *Reese.* $35/£23

APPLEGATE, JESSE. A Day with the Cow Column in 1843. Portland: Champoeg Press, 1952. #214/225. VG. *Perier.* $85/£55

APPLEGATE, JESSE. A Day with the Cow Column in 1843. Portland: Champoeg Press, 1952. Ltd to 225. 1st thus. Gilt-stamped spine. Fine. *Oregon.* $115/£74

Appleton's Illustrated Hand-Book of American Travel. NY: Appleton, 1860. 216pp + 12pp ads, fldg color map. Pink cl (sunned). *Schoyer.* $150/£97

APPLETON, LE ROY H. Indian Art of the Americas. NY, (1950). 1st ed (w/errata). 79 full color plts. Ex-lib blind-stamp rep; lt discolored, else VG in dj (torn, chipped). *King.* $50/£32

APTHEKER, HERBERT. The Negro in the Civil War. NY: International, (1938). 1st ed. VG in ptd stiff wraps. *Petrilla.* $45/£29

APTHEKER, HERBERT. Negro Slave Revolts in the United States, 1526-1860. NY: International, (1939). 1st ed. VG in ptd stiff wraps. *Petrilla.* $50/£32

APULIEUS, LUCIUS. The Golden Ass. NY: LEC, 1932. #229/1500 signed by Percival Goodman (illus). VG (bkpl) in slipcase. *Williams.* $116/£75

ARAMILEV, IVAN. Beyond the Ural Mountains. Michael Heron (trans). London: Allen & Unwin, (1961). VG in dj. *Schoyer.* $25/£16

ARBER, AGNES. Herbals, Their Origin and Evolution...1470-1670. Cambridge, 1938. 2nd ed, rewritten, enlgd. 27 plts. Lacks fr flyleaf, o/w Nice. *Wheldon & Wesley.* $116/£75

ARBER, AGNES. Herbals, Their Origin and Evolution...1470-1670. Cambridge: University Press, 1938. 2nd ed. 26 plts. (Cvrs faded; spine spotted, hole in cl.) *Oak Knoll.* $45/£29

ARBUTHNOT, JOHN. An Essay Concerning the Effects of Air on Human Bodies. London: Ptd for J&R Tonson, 1751. (xv),224pp (lower margin sl wormed throughout, upper margin last few leaves; lt ink stamp; bkpl.) Full gilt-edged calf (sl rubbed; new eps; upper bd, 1/2 title detached; lower joint tender), leather label (sl chipped). *Edwards.* $194/£125

ARCHER, JEFFREY. Shall We Tell the President. Cape, 1977. 1st UK ed. NF in NF dj (extrems sl worn). *Martin.* $25/£16

ARCHER, LIEUTENANT. Circumstantial Account of the Wreck of His Majesty's Ship Phoenix.... London: Thomas Tegg, n.d. (1810). Fldg aquatint frontis, trimmed close, (5)-28pp. *Lefkowicz.* $175/£113

ARCHER, THOMAS. The Frog's Parish Clerk. London: Sampson, Low, Son & Marston, 1866. 1st ed. 18 engrs. Forest grn cl, gilt. Fine. *Glenn.* $150/£97

ARCHER, THOMAS. William Ewart Gladstone and His Contemporaries.... London: Blackie & Son, 1883. 2 vols. 1/4 tan morocco, gilt dec spines. *D & D.* $100/£65

Architectural Details (Ornamental and Structural) of the Renaissance Period in England. NY: Wm. Helburn, n.d. (ca 1910). 52 plts. 1/2 leather (worn). *Argosy.* $85/£55

Arctic World. (By W.H. Adams.) London: Nelson, 1876. 1st ed. 276pp, map (torn, repaired). Orig dec gilt cl. Good+ (extrems rubbed). *Walcot.* $59/£38

Arctic World: Its Plants, Animals and Natural Phenomena. (By W.H.D. Adams.) London, 1876. viii,9-276pp 15 full-pg engrs. Good. *Henly.* $74/£48

ARD, WILLIAM. Hell Is a City. NY: Rinehart, 1955. 1st ed. Pp dknd, o/w VG in dj (sm chips; crease-tears; closed tears). *Mordida.* $45/£29

ARD, WILLIAM. The Perfect Frame. NY: William Morrow, 1951. 1st ed. Fine in VG dj (chipping; short closed tears). *Mordida.* $50/£32

ARENDT, HANNAH. Eichmann in Jerusalem. Viking Press, 1963. 1st ed. NF in NF dj. *Bishop.* $22/£14

ARENDT, HANNAH. Eichmann in Jerusalem. NY: Viking, 1963. 1st ed. NF in dj. *Lame Duck.* $50/£32

ARENSBERG, ANN. Sister Wolf. NY: Knopf, 1980. 1st ed, 1st bk. Fine in dj. *Reese.* $25/£16

ARGALL, PHYLLIS. The Truth about Jesse James. Sullivan, MO: Lester Dill & Trudy Turilli, 1955. Pict wrappers (lt bent, soiled). *Glenn.* $20/£13

ARGENTI, PHILIP P. The Costumes of Chios. London: Batsford, (1953). One of 500. 111 plts (88 color). Fine in dj (torn). *Bookpress.* $475/£306

ARGUS, ARABELLA. The Adventures of a Donkey. London: William Darton, June 1815. 1st ed. Signed, dated October 29th, 1814 by 'Jemmy.' 12mo. (iii),231pp + (16pp) ads, VF full-pg engr frontis. Marbled paper on bds (rubbed), red roan spine (lt worn), gilt title, fillets. VG (sig loose). *Hobbyhorse.* $300/£194

ARGUS, ARABELLA. Further Adventures of Jemmy Donkey.... London: William Darton, 1821. 1st ed. 12mo. iv,154pp + 3pp list, full-pg copper engr frontis, 2 other VF full-pg engrs w/imprint dated 1821. (Inked names on dedication pg.) Marbled paper on bds (soiled, rubbed, sl scratching), red roan spine, gilt title, fillets. Internally Fine. *Hobbyhorse.* $300/£194

ARGUS, ARABELLA. The Juvenile Spectator. London: W. Darton, June 1813/1812. 2 vols in 1. 12mo. xi,225pp + 1pg ad; iv,220pp, 8 full-pg VF copper engrs. Mod 3/4 red leather, marbled paper, gilt title. Fine (lt rubbing spine). *Hobbyhorse.* $250/£161

ARIS, ERNEST. Bunkum Brown Bandit. London: Gale & Polden, (ca 1930). 4to. 10 full-color plts (lt foxing prelims). Stiff paper wrappers w/stapled binding. *Reisler.* $110/£71

ARIS, ERNEST. Sir Francis Duck Adventurer. London: Gale & Polden, (ca 1930). 4to. 10 full-color plts (lt foxing prelims). Stiff paper wrappers w/stapled binding. *Reisler.* $110/£71

ARISTOPHANES. The Eleven Comedies. NY: Horace Liveright, 1928. 1st ed thus. #1879/2000 ptd for suscribers only. 2 vols. Jean de Bosschere (illus). Black cl. Fine in djs. *Chapel Hill.* $85/£55

ARISTOPHANES. Lysistrata. Gilbert Seldes (trans). NY: LEC, 1934. #904/1500 numbered, signed by Pablo Picasso (illus). Dec paper-cvrd bds. Fine in tissue dj (sl chipped, torn), card liner (sl fading), slipcase (lt worn). *Hermitage.* $3,750/£2,419

ARISTOTLE. Aristotle's Master-Piece, Completed in Two Parts. London, 1830. 142pp. Good. *Fye.* $75/£48

ARISTOTLE. The Works of Aristotle. London, 1798. 407pp. Leather. Good. *Fye.* $100/£65

ARKIN, ARTHUR M. et al (eds). The Mind in Sleep. Hillsdale, NJ: Erlbaum/Wiley, (1978). 1st ed. Grn cl. VG in dj (lt worn). *Gach.* $65/£42

ARLEN, MICHAEL. The Green Hat. London: Collins, (1924). 1st ed. VG in dj (sl worn). *Limestone.* $225/£145

ARMATAGE, GEORGE. Every Man His Own Horse Doctor. NY: OJ, 1888. 830pp. Good. *October Farm.* $58/£37

ARMBRUSTER, EUGENE L. Brooklyn's Eastern District. Brooklyn, NY, 1942. 1st ed. Leather label (cvr wear). *Heinoldt.* $35/£23

ARMES, GEORGE A. Ups and Downs of an Army Officer. Washington, 1900. 1st ed. Pict cl (sl discolorations corners; spine faded). Howes A 316. *Ginsberg.* $225/£145

ARMES, GEORGE A. Ups and Downs of an Army Officer. Washington, DC: N.p., 1900. 1st ed. Frontis. Brn cl, silver-stamped design. Very Nice. Howes A 316. *Karmiole.* $250/£161

ARMITAGE, A.B. Cadet to Commodore. London: Cassell, 1925. Frontis port. Orig cl. VG. *High Latitude.* $50/£32

ARMITAGE, A.B. Two Years in the Antarctic. London: Edward Arnold, 1905. 1st ed. Fldg map. Mod 1/2 calf. VG. *Walcot.* $388/£250

ARMITAGE, A.B. Two Years in the Antarctic. Edward Arnold, 1905. 1st ed. Fldg map. Cl sl discolored fr edge bds, o/w VG. *Walcot.* $496/£320

ARMITAGE, E. LIDDALL. Stained Glass History, Technology and Practice. London, 1959. Color frontis, 117 plts. (Eps sl spotted.) Dj (chipped). *Edwards.* $39/£25

ARMITAGE, MERLE (ed). Martha Graham. L.A.: Merle Armitage, 1937. Ltd to 1000. 24pp photo plts. Gray cl. Good. *Karmiole.* $75/£48

ARMITAGE, MERLE et al. Klee. NY: Duell, Sloan & Pearce, (1950). 1st ed. One of 1050 signed. Fine in pub's slipcase (soiled). *Hermitage.* $75/£48

ARMITAGE, MERLE. Accent on Life. Ames: IA State, 1965. 1st ed. NF in NF dj. *Parker.* $45/£29

ARMITAGE, MERLE. The Lithographs of Richard Day. NY, 1932. One of 500 numbered. Signed frontis; 12 other plts; port. VG. *Argosy.* $200/£129

ARMITAGE, MERLE. Rendezvous with the Book. NY: George McKibben, 1949. 1st ed. VG+. *Parker.* $50/£32

ARMOR, WILLIAM C. Lives of the Governors of Pennsylvania...Incidental History...1609-1872. Phila, 1872. 528pp; 29 ports (lacks plt/map in front?). VG-. *Artis.* $25/£16

ARMOUR, MARGARET (trans). The Nibelungenlied. NY: LEC, 1960. One of 1500 numbered, signed by Edy Legrand (illus). Fine in pub's slipcase. *Hermitage.* $95/£61

ARMS, CEPHAS. Long Road to California: The Journal of Cephas Arms Supplemented with Letters. Mount Pleasant, MI: John Cumming, (1985). Good. *Hayman.* $20/£13

ARMS, DOROTHY NOYES. Kerr Eby. NY, 1930. 12 mtd repros. Orig bds (rebacked in cl; worn; upper hinge cracked). *Argosy.* $50/£32

ARMSTRONG, ALEXANDER. A Personal Narrative of the Discovery of the North West Passage.... London: Hurst & Blackett, 1857. 1st ed. xxii,2,616pp (pg #s in sig K have been duplicated but text is complete, in correct sequence), tinted litho frontis, fldg map. Good+ (rubbed but sound, inner hinges strengthened). *Walcot.* $581/£375

ARMSTRONG, ALEXANDER. A Personal Narrative of the Discovery of the Northwest Passage...Under Sir John Franklin. London: Hurst & Blackett, 1857. xxii(2)616pp. Tinted litho frontis; fldg map. Orig pebbled cl. (Sm faint lib stamp on title, back of plt, map.) VG. *High Latitude.* $850/£548

ARMSTRONG, ELIZABETH. Robert Estienne, Royal Printer. Cambridge: University Press, 1954. 1st ed. 8 plts. Fine in dj. *Bookpress.* $135/£87

ARMSTRONG, JAMES LESLIE. Scenes in Craven. York: Ptd at Herald-Office, 1835. 1st ed. 136,(ii),ii,(iii). Patterned cl (neatly rebacked in matching calf gilt). (Bkpl, sig; spots.) *Hollett.* $132/£85

ARMSTRONG, JOHN. Practical Illustrations of Typhus Fever, of the Common Continued Fever, and of Inflammatory Diseases. NY, 1824. 3rd Amer ed. 432pp. Full leather. Good. *Fye.* $60/£39

ARMSTRONG, LOUIS. Swing That Music. London: Longmans, Green, 1936. 1st ed. 11 fldg plts. Nice in dj (heavily chipped). *Bookpress.* $185/£119

ARMSTRONG, MARGARET. The Man with No Face. NY: Random House, 1940. 1st ed. NF in VG+ dj (lt edgewear, sl crease). *Janus.* $85/£55

ARMSTRONG, MARTIN. The Puppet Show. London: Golden Cockerel Press, 1922. Black cl backstrip (sl rubbed), lt blue sides (faded). *Petersfield.* $19/£12

ARMSTRONG, MOSES. Early Empire Builders of Great West. St. Paul, 1901. 1st ed. 22 plts. Corner, spine end wear, o/w VG. *Oregon.* $50/£32

ARMSTRONG, N. After Big Game in the Upper Yukon. London, 1937. 3 maps. VG. *Trophy Room.* $225/£145

ARMSTRONG, N. Yukon Yesterdays. London, 1936. VG (tear rep). *Trophy Room.* $600/£387

ARMSTRONG, RICHARD and RICHARD MARSHALL. Five Painters in New York. (NY: Whitney Museum of Art, 1984.) VG in stiff ptd wrappers. *Argosy.* $35/£23

ARMSTRONG, WALTER. Gainsborough and His Place in English Art. London: Heinemann, 1898. xi,214pp; 62 photogravures, 10 litho facs. Internally Excellent (loose, spine tear). *Ars Artis.* $163/£105

ARMSTRONG, WALTER. Gainsborough and His Place in English Art. London/NY, 1898. 62 photogravure plts, 10 litho facs. Red cl. Fine. *Argosy.* $175/£113

Army Regulations Adopted for the Use of the Army of the Confederate States.... New Orleans: Bloomfield, 1861. 198,(2)pp. Contemp 1/2 morocco (joints worn; lacks eps; spine crown chipped). *Ginsberg.* $600/£387

Army Regulations, Adopted for the Use of the Army of the Confederate States.... Richmond: West & Johnston, 1861. 1st ed. 198,(2)pp. Red sheep-backed bds. Good (bkpl; rubbed, soiled; last sig nearly detached; long closed tear 1 leaf). *Chapel Hill.* $400/£258

Army Regulations...of the Army of the Confederate States.... Raleigh, NC: Inst for Deaf & Dumb & Blind, 1861. 3rd ed. 198,(2),32pp. Orig flexible cl. VG (soiled, foxed, dampstain nearly throughout). *Chapel Hill.* $400/£258

ARNETT, ETHEL STEPHENS. Confederate Guns Were Stacked, Greensboro, North Carolina. Greensboro, NC: Piedmont Press, 1965. 1st ed. Frontis. Gilt-titled cl. Mks, else Fine in dj. *Cahan.* $150/£97

ARNETT, MARALEA. The Annals and Scandals of Henderson County Kentucky 1775-1975. Corydon, KY: Freman, 1976. Signed. VG in dj (chipped). *Burcham.* $28/£18

ARNO, PETER. Hell of a Way to Run a Railroad. NY, 1956. 1st ed. VF in Good dj (nibbled). *Bond.* $25/£16

ARNOLD, EDWIN LESTER. Phra the Phoenician. London, 1893. VG. *Madle.* $50/£32

ARNOLD, EDWIN. Seas and Lands. London: Longmans, Green, 1891. 1st ed. x,535,24pp, 42 full-pg illus. Pict cl (rubbed, dulled; sl fingered). *Hollett.* $70/£45

ARNOLD, HUGH. Stained Glass of the Middle Ages in England and France. A&C Black, 1913. 50 guarded plts. Pict cl. VG. *Peter Taylor.* $59/£38

ARNOLD, HUGH. Stained Glass of the Middle Ages in England and France. London: A&C Black, 1913. 1st ed. Color frontis, 49 color plts. (Eps browned; hinges cracked; spine sl faded, split.) *Edwards.* $62/£40

ARNOLD, ISAAC N. The Life of Benedict Arnold, His Patriotism and His Treason. Chicago: Jansen, McClurg, 1880. 1st ed. Frontis port, 444pp. 1/2 black morocco, marbled bds, morocco spine labels (lt chipped). Hinges tender, else VG. *Chapel Hill.* $200/£129

ARNOLD, L.B. American Dairying. Rochester, 1876. 354pp (6pp marginal dampstaining). (Worn; fr hinge cracked.) *Sutton.* $55/£35

ARNOLD, LLOYD. High on the Wild with Hemingway. Caldwell: Caxton, 1969. 1st ed. Signed presentation, signed by Arnold, Jack Hemingway, and Tillie Arnold. VF in VG dj. *Oregon.* $100/£65

ARNOLD, MATTHEW. Culture and Anarchy. London: Smith, Elder, 1869. 1st ed. VG (sm area discolored lower spine where label removed). *Lame Duck.* $300/£194

ARNOLD, MATTHEW. Discourses in America. London: Macmillan, 1885. 1st ed. Presentation slip tipped in. Gilt cl (sl edgeworn; blemish fr cvr). Good (eps lt foxed; inscrip). *Reese.* $40/£26

ARNOLD, MATTHEW. Essays in Criticism. Boston: Ticknor & Fields, 1865. 1st Amer ed. Fine (pencil sig). *Pharos.* $85/£55

ARNOLD, MATTHEW. Merope. A Tragedy. London: Longman et al, 1858. 1st ed, 1st issue binding. lii,138pp + ads. Grn cl. Hinges cracked, spine sl worn, else VG. *Godot.* $100/£65

ARNOLD, MATTHEW. New Poems. London: Macmillan, 1867. 1st ed. Grn cl. NF. *Sumner & Stillman.* $150/£97

ARNOLD, MATTHEW. Poems. Second Series. London: Longman et al, 1855. 1st ed. v,(3),210,vi,(ad)pp + 24pp pub's cat; uncut. Brn eps, ptd ads pastedowns. Blocked in blind, lettered in gold. VG (sig; sl wear backstrip). *Cox.* $70/£45

ARNOLD, MATTHEW. Poems...A New Edition. London: Longman, 1853. 1st ed. Ptd pastedown ads (variant ads from those described by Tinker). Grn cl stamped in blind, gilt (spine lt sunned; sm rubbed spot 1 joint). VG (inscrip). *Reese.* $250/£161

ARNOLD, MATTHEW. Reports on Elementary Schools 1852-1881... London: Macmillan, 1889. 1st ed. Gilt cl (sl flecked). Good (bkpl; eps lt foxed). *Reese.* $55/£35

ARNOLD, MATTHEW. The Scholar Gipsy and Thyrsis. London: Philip Lee Warner, 1910. #35/100, signed by W. Russell Flint (illus). 10 tipped-in color plts. Pict vellum (cvrs bowed); teg. *Schoyer.* $150/£97

ARNOLD, MATTHEW. Thyrsis, a Monody, and The Scholar Gypsy. Portland: Thomas B. Mosher, 1910. Ltd ed, one of 100. VG in ptd wrappers. *Argosy.* $50/£32

ARNOLD, OREN and JOHN P. HALE. Hot Irons: Heraldry of the Range. NY: Macmillan, 1945. 1940 ed, rpt. VG in dj (chipped). *Burcham.* $45/£29

ARNOLD, OREN. Wild Life in the Southwest. Dallas, (1936). 2nd ptg. Pict leatherette. Fine. *Artis.* $25/£16

ARNOLD, THOMAS W. The Library of A. Chester Beatty, a Catalogue of the Indian Miniatures. Bloomsbury: Emery Walker, 1936. 1st ed. 3 vols, complete. Lg folio. Partly uncut. Ex-lib w/bkpl removed, tips bruised; else Fine. *Bookpress.* $1,200/£774

ARNOT, HUGO. The History of Edinburgh.... Edinburgh: Creech, 1788. xii,677, map, 19 engr plts. (Foxing.) Calf (rebacked). *Marlborough.* $519/£335

ARNOUX, CHARLES A. D'BERTALL. The Communists of Paris: 1871. London: Buckingham, (1873). Pict title, 40 color plts. 1/2 morocco. VG. *Argosy.* $250/£161

ARNOW, HARRIETTE. The Weedkiller's Daughter. NY, 1970. 1st ed. VG in dj (sl used). *King.* $35/£23

ARONSON, JOSEPH. The Encyclopedia of Furniture. NY, (1941). (4th ptg). VG in dj. *Hayman.* $20/£13

ARP, JEAN. Arp on Arp. NY: Viking, 1972. 1st ed. Promo photo laid in. Fine (cocked) in Fine dj (few short tears). *Beasley.* $65/£42

ARP, JEAN. Sculpture: His Last Ten Years. NY: Abrams, 1968. VG in dj. *Argosy.* $85/£55

ARREDONDO, ANTONIO DE. Arredondo's Historical Proof of Spain's Title to Georgia. Herbert E. Bolton (ed). Berkeley: Univ of CA Press, 1925. 1st ed. Unopened. Blue cl. NF. Howes A 336. *Chapel Hill.* $150/£97

ARRHENIUS, SVANTE. Immunochemistry: The Application of the Principles of Physical Chemistry.... NY, 1907. 1st Eng trans. Good. *Fye.* $400/£258

ARRHENIUS, SVANTE. Quantitative Laws in Biological Chemistry. London, 1915. 1st ed. *Fye.* $125/£81

ARRINGTON, LEONARD J. Great Basin Kingdom: An Economic History of the Latter-Day Saints 1830-1900. Cambridge, 1958. 1st ed. VG +. *Benchmark.* $55/£35

Art of Alexander and John Robert Cozens. New Haven: Yale Ctr for British Art, 1980. 61 plts. Good in wrappers. *Washton.* $20/£13

Art of Claude Lorrain. London, 1969. 41 illus on plts. Good in wrappers (sl soiled). *Washton.* $35/£23

Art of Preserving the Feet. London: Colburn, 1818. 3rd ed. xvi,239pp. Uncut, partially unopened. Orig bds, paper spine label. Excellent (hinges starting). *Hemlock.* $275/£177

ART STUDENTS LEAGUE OF NEW YORK. Hundredth Anniversary Exhibition of Paintings and Sculptures by 100 Artists.... NY, 1975. VG in ptd wrappers. *Argosy.* $30/£19

ARTHUR, GEORGE. Life of Lord Kitchener. London: Macmillan, 1920. 1st ed. 3 vols. 11 plts/maps. (Sl mkd.) Sound. *Cox.* $23/£15

ARTHUR, TIMOTHY SHAY. Advice to Young Ladies on Their Duties and Conduct in Life. Boston: Phillips, Sampson, 1851. Stereotype ed. 204pp, engr 1/2 title. Aeg. Red cl (spine frayed; inner hinge cracked; bkpl). *Weber.* $20/£13

Artist's Assistant. (By Carrington Bowles.) London: Ostell, 1807. Engr frontis, xvi,296pp, 10 plts (6 fldg). (Sl staining.) Later roan-backed bds. *Marlborough.* $581/£375

ARTMAN, W. and L.V. HALL. Beauties and Achievements of the Blind. Auburn, 1859. 387pp. Good. *Fye.* $40/£26

ARTRIP, LOUISE and FULLEN. Memoirs of Daniel Fore (Jim) Chisholm and the Chisholm Trail. (Booneville, AR: Artrip Pub, 1949.) Presentation signed by both. Wraps. *Cullen.* $65/£42

ASBURY, HERBERT. A Methodist Saint. NY: Knopf, 1927. 1st ed. Fine in dj (sl chipped, spine dknd). *Reese.* $30/£19

ASBURY, HERBERT. Up From Methodism. NY, 1926. 1st Amer ed, 1st bk. Fine (spine extrems, corners sl rubbed). *Polyanthos.* $30/£19

ASCH, SHOLEM. The Nazarene. Maurice Samuel (trans). NY: Putnam's, (1939). 1st Amer ed. Signed. Fine in dj. *Godot.* $65/£42

ASH, GEORGE. His Adventures and Life Story as Cowboy, Ranger and Soldier. London: Drane's, (1923). Dj. Howes 348. *Lambeth.* $75/£48

ASHBERY, JOHN and JAMES SCHUYLER. A Nest of Ninnies. NY: Dutton, 1969. 1st ed. As New in dj. *Jaffe.* $75/£48

ASHBERY, JOHN. Self-Portrait in a Convex Mirror. NY: Viking, (1975). 1st ed. Fine in dj. *Antic Hay.* $25/£16

ASHE, SAMUEL A'COURT. History of North Carolina. Vol 1: Greensboro, NC, 1925; Vol 2: Raleigh, 1925. Rubbed, stamp vol 1; hinge starting vol 2, o/w VG. *Cahan.* $125/£81

ASHE, THOMAS. Poems. London: Geo. Bell & Sons, 1886. 1st collected ed. vi,334pp. Grn cl, gilt. Uncut. Nice. *Cox.* $43/£28

ASHENDEN. (Pseud of Sidney E.P. Nowill.) The Mountains of My Life. London: William Blackwood & Sons, 1954. 1st ed. 28 plts. (Spine sl damp-spotted.) Dj (sl worn; lacks piece). *Hollett.* $47/£30

ASHFORD, DAISY. The Young Visitors. NY: George H. Doran, (1919). 1st ed. Pict bds. NF. *Macdonnell.* $50/£32

ASHLEIGH, CHARLES. Rambling Kid. Faber & Faber, 1930. Grn cl. Nice. *Patterson.* $39/£25

ASHLEY, CLIFFORD W. The Ashley Book of Knots. NY, 1944. 1st ed. Dj (sl rubbed, chipped). *Edwards.* $54/£35

ASHLEY, CLIFFORD W. The Yankee Whaler. NY, (1942). (3rd ed). 15 color, 111 b/w plts. Fine in dj. *Lefkowicz.* $100/£65

ASHLEY, CLIFFORD W. The Yankee Whaler. Boston/NY: Houghton, Mifflin, 1926. 1st ed. 16 Fine color plts. VG. Howes A 356. *Hayman.* $200/£129

ASHLEY, CLIFFORD W. The Yankee Whaler. Boston/NY, 1926. 1st ed. One of 1625. Inscribed on 1/2 title. 16 color plts. (Cvrs sl soiled; edges sl worn.) VG. Howes A 356. *Lefkowicz.* $450/£290

ASHLEY, CLIFFORD W. The Yankee Whaler. Boston, 1938. Popular Edition. Good. *King.* $65/£42

ASHLEY, GEORGE T. Reminiscenses of a Circuit Rider. Hollywood: by author, 1941. 1st ed. VG. *Perier.* $20/£13

ASHLEY, WILLIAM H. The West of William H. Ashley. Dale L. Morgan (ed). Denver: Old West Pub Co, 1964. One of 250 numbered, signed. Fldg map. 3/4 brn leather. Nice (sl scuffing, bkpl) in slipcase. *Bohling.* $500/£323

ASHLEY, WILLIAM H. The West of William H. Ashley. Dale L. Morgan (ed). Denver: Fred A. Rosenstock, Old West Pub Co, 1964. One of 250 numbered. Signed. Lg fldg map. Half calf; cl bds; red morocco spine label lettered in gilt. Fine in VG slipcase. *Laurie.* $450/£290

ASHMOLE, BERNARD. Architect and Sculptor in Classical Greece. NY: NY Univ Press, 1972. In dj. *Edwards.* $47/£30

ASHTON, DORE. Yes But...: A Critical Study of Philip Guston. NY: Viking, 1976. 1st ed. NF in VG pict dj. *Cahan.* $45/£29

ASHTON, F. Alas, That Great City. A. Dakers, 1948. 1st ed. NF in VG dj (dust-soil). *Aronovitz.* $25/£16

ASHTON, JOHN (comp). Humour, Wit, and Satire of the Seventeenth Century. London: C&W, 1883. 1st ed. 454pp + 32pp ads. Pict grn cl, gilt. NF. *Hartfield.* $145/£94

ASHTON, JOHN. A Century of Ballads. London: Elliot Stock, 1887. 1st ed. xx + 354pp (top corner prelims sl creased). 3/4 leather, marbled bds (spine lacking portions; joints split). NF internally. *Blue Mountain.* $65/£42

ASHTON, JOHN. The Legendary History of the Cross. London: T. Fisher Unwin, 1887. Tp,clxxvipp; 64 woodcuts. Fore, lower edges uncut. (Feps lt browned; lower pastedown sl worn; upper joint cracked; worn; spine surface cut away 2 places; spine head bumped w/sl loss.) *Edwards.* $101/£65

ASHTON, JOHN. Old Times: A Picture of Social Life at the End of the Eighteenth Century. London: John C. Nimmo, 1885. 88 plts. 3/4 red morocco, raised bands, gilt top. Nice. *Appelfeld.* $85/£55

ASHTON, JOHN. Varia. London: Ward & Downey, 1894. 1st ed. 219pp. Brn cl, gilt. (Bumped, gilt faded; tp foxed.) Text Excellent. *Hartfield.* $65/£42

ASHTON, WENDELL J. Voice in the West. NY: Duell, Sloan & Pearce, 1950. 1st ed. VG in dj (worn). *Parker.* $30/£19

ASHTON, WILLIAM. The Evolution of a Coast-Line. London/Southport, 1920. (Spine sl rubbed.) *Edwards.* $31/£20

ASIMOV, ISAAC and STEPHEN H. DOLE. Planets for Man. London: Methuen, 1965. 1st Eng ed. Purple cl. Fine in dj (price-clipped). *Dalian.* $31/£20

ASIMOV, ISAAC. Earth Is Room Enough. Doubleday, 1957. 1st ed. Fine in NF dj. *Aronovitz.* $160/£103

ASIMOV, ISAAC. Foundation's Edge. Whispers Press, 1982. 1st ed. One of 1000 numbered, signed. Fine w/o dj, as issued. *Madle.* $100/£65

ASIMOV, ISAAC. Future Days. London, 1986. 1st ed. Fine in dj. *Madle.* $35/£23

ASIMOV, ISAAC. I Robot. NY: Gnome, (1950). 1st ed. Rear bd top, 2 corners bumped, else NF in VG + dj (spine ends worn, frayed; closed tear rear panel). *Other Worlds.* $450/£290

ASIMOV, ISAAC. It's Such a Beautiful Day. Creative Education, 1985. 1st ed. VF. *Aronovitz.* $45/£29

ASIMOV, ISAAC. The Martian Way and Other Stories. Dobson, 1964. 1st Eng ed. NF in VG + dj (spine lt worn). *Aronovitz.* $65/£42

ASIMOV, ISAAC. Murder at the ABA. GC: Doubleday, 1976. 1st ed. Black cl-backed mauve bds. NF in dj. *Cady.* $25/£16

ASIMOV, ISAAC. The Naked Sun. London, 1958. 1st Eng ed. VG in dj (sl soiled). *Words Etc.* $116/£75

ASIMOV, ISAAC. Nightfall 20 SF Stories. Gollancz, 1970. 1st Eng ed. NF in VG + dj. *Aronovitz.* $65/£42

ASIMOV, ISAAC. Nine Tomorrows. London: Dennis Dobson, 1963. 1st Eng ed. Black cl. Fine in dj. *Dalian.* $39/£25

ASIMOV, ISAAC. Pebble in the Sky. Doubleday, 1950. 1st ed, 1st bk. Inscribed. VG in VG dj (wear, tear). *Fine Books.* $225/£145

ASKIN, JOHN. The John Askin Papers 1747-1820. M.M. Quaife (ed). Detroit: Detroit Lib Commission, 1928-1931. 1st ed. 2 vols. 13 maps/plts. Teg. 1/2 morocco, gilt. NF set. Howes A 359. *Cahan.* $275/£177

ASKIN, JOHN. The John Askin Papers, 1747-1820. Milo M. Quaife (ed). Detroit, 1928-1931. 1st ed. 2 vols. 13 maps and plts. 1/2 morocco. (Sm emb lib stamps; bkpl removed.) Howes A 359. *Ginsberg.* $250/£161

ASKIN, JOHN. The John Askin Papers. 1747-1820. M.M. Quaife (ed). N.p.: Detroit Public Lib, 1928 & 1931. 1st ed. One of 1000. 2 vols. Frontis; 11 illus. Blue cl, gilt. VG. *Laurie.* $150/£97

ASKINS, CHARLES. The African Hunt. Harrisburg: Stackpole, 1958. 1st ed. VG + in dj. *Bowman.* $50/£32

ASPIN, J. Ancient Customs, Sports, and Pastimes, of the English, Explained from Authentic Sources.... London: John Harris, 1835. 2nd ed. Engr frontis. 1/4 leather (hinges, ends rubbed). *Dramatis Personae.* $125/£81

ASPLUND, KARL. Anders Zorn, His Life and Work. London: The Studio, 1921. 64 plts. Teg, rest uncut. Orig vellum-backed ptd bds, gilt. Sl mks, o/w VF. *Europa.* $132/£85

ASPRIN, ROBERT. The Bug Wars. St. Martin's, 1979. 1st ed. Fine in dj. *Madle.* $35/£23

ASQUITH, CYNTHIA (ed). The Third Ghost Book. London, 1955. 1st ed. VG in NF dj. *Madle.* $45/£29

ASQUITH, CYNTHIA. This Mortal Coil. Arkham House, 1947. 1st ed. Fine in dj. *Madle.* $110/£71

ASQUITH, CYNTHIA. The Queen. London: Hutchinson, (1937). 1st ed. #42/250, signed. 1/2 blue morocco, cl (cvrs sl soiled, inscrip). *Chapel Hill.* $125/£81

ASQUITH, CYNTHIA. What Dreams May Come. London, 1951. 1st ed. VG. *Mcclintock.* $35/£23

ASTAIRE, FRED. Steps in Time. NY: Harper, (1959). 1st ed ('E-I'). Signed. VG in dj (long tear upper cvr). *Houle.* $225/£145

ASTLE, THOMAS. The Origin and Progress of Writing. London, 1803. 2nd ed. Engr frontis;(viiii),xxiv,240pp; 31 plts. 1/2 calf (leather split along joints; edges worn), marbled bds, spine gilt, morocco label, all edges sprinkled. (Lt foxing to prelim, endleaves.) *Veatchs.* $400/£258

ASTOR, JOHN JACOB. A Journey to Other Worlds. Appleton, 1894. 1st ed. New eps, else VG. *Madle.* $100/£65

ASTRUP, EIVIND. With Peary Near the Pole. London: C. Arthur Pearson, 1896. 362pp. Frontis port, fldg map. Orig dec cl; teg. VG. *High Latitude.* $195/£126

ASWELL, JAMES. We Know Better. Gordon Lewis, 1927. #211/500. Signed by Don Miller (illus). Paper cvr. Boxed. *Book Broker.* $45/£29

ATCHLEY, S.C. Wild Flowers of Attica. W.B. Turrill (ed). London, 1938. 22 color plts. Good. *Henly.* $59/£38

ATHEARN, ROBERT G. Forts of the Upper Missouri. Englewood Cliffs: Prentice-Hall, 1967. 1st ed. VG+ in VG- dj (repaired). *Parker.* $50/£32

ATHEARN, ROBERT G. Rebel of the Rockies: The Denver and Rio Grande Western Railroad. New Haven: Yale Univ Press, 1962. 1st ed. Signed. Beige pict cl. NF in VG+ dj (lt chipped, rubbed). *Harrington.* $40/£26

ATHEARN, ROBERT G. William Tecumseh Sherman and the Settlement of the West. Norman, (1956). 1st ed. Fine in Fine dj. *Pratt.* $45/£29

ATHERTON, GERTRUDE. Adventures of a Novelist. NY: Liveright, 1932. 1st ed. VG in dj (sl chipped, loose fitting). *Hermitage.* $40/£26

ATHERTON, GERTRUDE. The Immortal Marriage. NY: Boni & Liveright, 1927. 1st ed. VG. *Second Life.* $35/£23

ATHERTON, GERTRUDE. The Jealous Gods. NY: Liveright, 1928. 1st ed. Fine in dj. *Second Life.* $75/£48

ATHERTON, GERTRUDE. The Splendid Idle Forties. NY: Stokes, 1902. 1st ed. Good+ (mkd; eps waterstained) in VG+ dj (not orig). *Parker.* $60/£39

ATHERTON, HERBERT M. Political Prints in the Age of Hogarth. OUP, 1974. Fldg frontis map. Dj (sl chipped). *Edwards.* $39/£25

ATHERTON, JOHN. The Fly and the Fish. NY: Macmillan, 1951. 1st trade ed. VF in dj. *Bowman.* $175/£113

ATIL, ESIN. Suleymanname. The Illustrated History of Suleyman the Magnificent. Washington/NY: Nat'l Gallery of Art/Abrams, 1986. 1st ed. VG in dj. *Worldwide.* $65/£42

ATKINS, EDWIN F. Sixty Years in Cuba. Cambridge, MA: Privately ptd, 1926. 1st ed. *Ginsberg.* $150/£97

ATKINS, WILLIAM. The Art and Practice of Printing.... London: New Era Pub, (1931). 6 vols. Gilt-lettered blue cl. Fine set. *House.* $200/£129

ATKINSON, E. MILES. Abscess of the Brain: Its Pathology, Diagnosis and Treatment. London, 1934. 1st ed. Good. *Fye.* $75/£48

ATKINSON, F.W. 100 Years in the Pajaro Valley from 1769 to 1868. (Watsonville, Jan 1935.) Rev ed. Frontis; port; plt. Stiff ptd wraps (lt soiled; label added). *Bohling.* $30/£19

ATKINSON, GEORGE F. Mushrooms: Edible, Poisonous, Etc. Studies of American Fungi. Ithaca: Andrus & Church, 1900. 1st ed. 6 color, 200 b/w plts. Silver/black pict gray cl. VG. *House.* $130/£84

ATKINSON, GEORGE W. (ed). Bench and Bar of West Virginia. Charleston: Virginian Law Book, 1919. Pebbled buckram (sl dusty, stained). *Boswell.* $75/£48

ATKINSON, HERBERT. Cock-Fighting and Game Fowl. Bath: George Bayntun, 1938. 1st ed. 22 plts (10 color). Uncut, partly unopened. VG in dj. *Hollett.* $341/£220

ATKINSON, J.C. The Last of the Giant Killers—or The Exploits of Sir Jack of Danby Dale. MacMillan, 1891. 1st ed. VG+. *Fine Books.* $90/£58

ATKINSON, JAMES. Epitome of the Art of Navigation. W. Montaine (rev). London, W&J Mount et al, 1759. 447,(1)pp; 10 plts (the 10th complete w/moving part). Contemp calf (rebacked, new eps; dampstains). *Lefkowicz.* $350/£226

ATKINSON, JAMES. The Expedition Into Affghanistan: Notes and Sketches Descriptive of the Country...1839 and 1840.... London: W.H. Allen, 1842. 1st ed. Frontis, map. Orig maroon cl (extrems worn). *Appelfeld.* $200/£129

ATKINSON, R.H.M. BUDDLE and G.A. JACKSON (eds). Brougham and His Early Friends, Letters to James Loch 1798-1809. London: privately ptd, 1908. Vellum-backed bds. Attractive. *Boswell.* $225/£145

ATKINSON, SAMUEL C. A Catechism of American Law. Phila: S.C. Atkinson, 1838. Cl-backed bds. Worn, but sound. *Boswell.* $175/£113

ATKINSON, THOMAS DINHAM. English and Welsh Cathedrals. London, 1912. 1st ed. Color frontis, 19 color plts, 20 b/w plts, 48 plans. Newspaper clipping loosely inserted. (Spine lt faded.) *Edwards.* $39/£25

ATKINSON, THOMAS WITLAM. Travels in the Regions of the Upper and Lower Amoor and the Russian Acquisitions.... NY, 1860. 1st Amer ed. 448pp+ads; 83 wood engrs; fldg map. Gilt dec cl (upper cvr stained, joint cracked). *Argosy.* $150/£97

ATKINSON, W.N. and J.B. Explosions in Coal Mines. London, 1886. 144pp. 12 plans. Orig cl. VG. *Argosy.* $125/£81

ATLAY, J.B. (ed). Trial of the Stauntons. London: William Hodge, 1952. Rev copy. Good in dj (worn). *Boswell.* $50/£32

ATLEE, WASHINGTON. General and Differential Diagnosis of Ovarian Tumors. Phila, 1873. 1st ed. 482pp. Good. *Fye.* $350/£226

ATMORE, CHARLES. Serious Advice, from a Father to His Children.... Phila: J.H. Cunningham, 1819. 12mo. 36pp+1pg list lower wrapper, full-pg VF wood engr frontis. Ptd blue paper wrappers. Leaves lt browned, sl chipped, fore-edge rubbed, else Fine. *Hobbyhorse.* $80/£52

ATTAWAY, WILLIAM. Calypso Song Book. NY: McGraw Hill, 1957. 1st ed. Fine in dj (minor edgewear, tears). *Else Fine.* $85/£55

ATTAWAY, WILLIAM. Calypso Song Book. Lyle Kenyon Engel (ed). NY: McGraw-Hill, (1957). 1st ed. VG in dj (short creased tears, else VG). *Godot.* $50/£32

ATTLEE, C.R. As It Happened. London: Heinemann, 1954. 1st ed. Nice in dj (nicked). *Patterson.* $54/£35

ATWATER, CALEB. Remarks Made on a Tour to Prairie du Chien.... Columbus: Isaac N. Whiting, 1831. 1st ed, 1st issue. 8vo. Contemp full calf (rubbed; foxing). VG in gilt stamped red morocco-backed fldg box. Howes A 379. *Houle.* $1,250/£806

ATWATER, RICHARD and FLORENCE. Mr. Popper's Penguins. Boston: Little, Brown, 1938. 1st ed. Robert Lawson (illus). 8vo. Illus lt grey cl. Good in pict dj (worn). *Reisler.* $100/£65

ATWOOD, EVANGELINE. We Shall Be Remembered. Anchorage, AK: Methodist Univ, 1966. VG+ (underlining, notes rep) in dj (edgeworn). *Bohling.* $35/£23

ATWOOD, MARGARET. Bluebeard's Egg. McClelland & Stewart, 1983. 1st ed. Fine in dj. *Stahr.* $45/£29

ATWOOD, MARGARET. Bluebeard's Egg. London: Cape, 1987. 1st UK ed. Signed. Fine in dj. *Lewton.* $29/£19

ATWOOD, MARGARET. Dancing Girls. Cape, 1982. 1st UK ed. Signed. Fine in dj. *Lewton*. $39/£25

ATWOOD, MARGARET. The Handmaid's Tale. London: Cape, 1986. 1st UK ed. Fine in dj. *Williams*. $28/£18

ATWOOD, MARGARET. Lady Oracle. McClelland & Stewart, 1976. 1st Canadian ed. Fine in dj (sl rubbed, chipped). *Virgo*. $39/£25

ATWOOD, MARGARET. Life Before Man. London: Cape, 1980. 1st UK ed. Signed. Fine in dj. *Lewton*. $37/£24

ATWOOD, MARGARET. Procedures for Underground. Toronto: OUP, 1970. 1st ed. Signed. Spine lt creased, name, else VG in stiff pict wrappers. *Godot*. $85/£55

ATWOOD, MARGARET. The Robber Bride. London: Bloomsbury, (1993). One of 150 numbered, signed. Cl, marbled bds. Fine in tissue dj. *Dermont*. $100/£65

ATWOOD, MARGARET. Up in the Tree Colouring Book. (Toronto): McClelland & Stewart, n.d. (1978). 1st ed. 4to. 8pp. Stapled wrappers. *Between The Covers*. $250/£161

ATWOOD, MARGARET. You Are Happy. NY: Harper, 1974. 1st US ed. Fine in Fine dj. *Beasley*. $60/£39

AUBREY, JOHN. Brief Lives.... Cresset, 1949. 1st thus. Gilt-dec buckram. Eps sl mkd, else VG. *Whiteson*. $23/£15

AUBREY, JOHN. Monumenta Britannica or a Miscellany of British Antiquities. John Fowles (ed). Boston, 1980. #67/250 signed. Fine in Fine box. *Polyanthos*. $200/£129

AUCHINCLOSS, LOUIS. Diary of a Yuppie. Franklin Center, PA: Franklin Lib, 1986. Signed ltd ed. Frontis. Gilt-worked black full-morocco leather; aeg; marbled eps. Fine. *Antic Hay*. $75/£48

AUCHINCLOSS, LOUIS. Edith Wharton. A Woman in Her Time. NY: Viking, (1971). 1st ed. Ivory gilt-stamped cl. Gold pict dj. *Juvelis*. $50/£32

AUCHINCLOSS, LOUIS. Exit Lady Masham. Boston: Houghton, Mifflin, 1983. 1st ed. Signed. Fine in dj. *Antic Hay*. $45/£29

AUCHINCLOSS, LOUIS. Exit Lady Masham. Franklin Center, PA: Franklin Lib, 1983. Signed ltd ed. Gilt-worked; red full-morocco leather; aeg; ribbon marker. Mint. *Antic Hay*. $75/£48

AUCHINCLOSS, LOUIS. The House of the Prophet. Boston: Houghton Mifflin, 1980. 1st ed. Signed. Fine in Fine dj (sl wear). *Revere*. $35/£23

AUCHINCLOSS, LOUIS. The Injustice Collectors. Boston: Houghton Mifflin, 1950. 1st ed. Fine in dj (lt used). *Juvelis*. $100/£65

AUCHINCLOSS, LOUIS. Motiveless Malignity. Boston: Houghton, Mifflin, 1969. 1st ed. Fine in dj (sl wear). *Antic Hay*. $25/£16

AUCHINCLOSS, LOUIS. Pioneers and Caretakers. Minneapolis, (1965). 1st ed. Rev copy. VG in dj. *Argosy*. $45/£29

AUCHINCLOSS, LOUIS. The Winthrop Covenant. Boston: Houghton, Mifflin, 1976. 1st ed. Signed. NF in dj. *Antic Hay*. $50/£32

AUCHINCLOSS, LOUIS. A World of Profit. Boston: Houghton Mifflin, 1968. 1st ed. Fine in dj (sl worn). *Hermitage*. $30/£19

AUCHTER, E.C. and H.B. KNAPP. Orchard and Small Fruit Culture. NY, 1949. 3rd ed. (Soiled; ink inscrip.) *Sutton*. $40/£26

AUDEN, W.H. About the House. London: Faber & Faber, (1966). 1st British ed. NF in dj. *Reese*. $30/£19

AUDEN, W.H. The Age of Anxiety. NY, (1947). 1st ed. Fine in VG + dj (2 sm nicks, abrasion, sm hole). *Fuller & Saunders*. $75/£48

AUDEN, W.H. The Age of Anxiety. NY: Random House, (1947). 1st ed. Ltd to 3500. Fine in dj. *Reese*. $85/£55

AUDEN, W.H. The Age of Anxiety. NY, 1947. 1st Amer ed. Fine (sl rubbed) in dj (sl rubbed, soiled, 3 sm holes). *Polyanthos*. $60/£39

AUDEN, W.H. A Certain World. London: Faber & Faber, 1971. 1st Eng ed. NF in dj (sm chip). *Limestone*. $55/£35

AUDEN, W.H. City Without Walls and Other Poems. London: Faber & Faber, (1969). 1st ed. Fine in dj. *Reese*. $45/£29

AUDEN, W.H. Collected Longer Poems. NY: Random House, (1969). 1st Amer ed. Rmdr mk ep, else Fine in dj. *Reese*. $20/£13

AUDEN, W.H. Collected Shorter Poems 1927-1957. NY, 1966. 1st Amer ed. Fine (sl rubbed) in dj (sm edge tear, nicks, sl rubbed, price-clipped). *Polyanthos*. $30/£19

AUDEN, W.H. The Dance of Death. London: Faber & Faber, (1933). 1st ed. Grn bds (sl rubbed, sl discolored, sl foxing). Good in dj (rubbed, sl chipped). *Ash*. $116/£75

AUDEN, W.H. Elegy for Young Lovers. Mainz: B. Schott's Sohne, 1961. 1st ed. VG + in wraps. *Sclanders*. $31/£20

AUDEN, W.H. The Enchafed Flood. NY, (1950). 1st ed. Fine in VG dj (price-clipped, sl dknd, sm chips). *Fuller & Saunders*. $45/£29

AUDEN, W.H. The Enchafed Flood. NY: Random House, (1950). 1st ed. Ltd to 2500. Very Nice (lt offset endsheet from clipping; sig, sl pencil notes) in dj (lt frayed). *Reese*. $55/£35

AUDEN, W.H. The Enchafed Flood. London: Faber, 1951. 1st UK ed. Fine in VG dj (dulled, spine browned; closed tears). *Williams*. $39/£25

AUDEN, W.H. The Enchafed Flood. London: Faber, 1951. 1st UK ed. Sl offsetting to eps, o/w VG in dj (spotted, sl soiled, 2 closed tears, spine faded). *Virgo*. $54/£35

AUDEN, W.H. Epistle to a Godson and Other Poems. Faber & Faber, (1972). 1st ed. Dj. *Bickersteth*. $31/£20

AUDEN, W.H. Homage to Clio. NY: Random House, (1960). 1st ed. Rev copy, slip laid in. (Sl foxing fore-edge, eps. Sl soiling to cl, dj.) *Shasky*. $60/£39

AUDEN, W.H. Litany and Anthem for S. Matthew's Day. Northampton: For Church of S. Matthew, 21 Sept 1946. 1st ed. Single sheet folded twice. Sm splashes fr cvr, o/w VG. *Rees*. $70/£45

AUDEN, W.H. Making Knowing and Judging. OUP, 1956. 1st ed. Wrappers. (Sl faded; spotted). Contents Good. *Whiteson*. $16/£10

AUDEN, W.H. Nones. NY, 1951. 1st Amer ed. Fine in dj (spine sl sunned, sm chips, edgetear, sl soiled). *Polyanthos*. $40/£26

AUDEN, W.H. On This Island. NY: Random House, (1937). 1st Amer ed. Fine in dj (sl dknd, lt chipped). *Reese*. $65/£42

AUDEN, W.H. Poems. Faber & Faber, (Nov 1932). (2nd ed.) (Lt soiled; ink inscrip fr fly.) *Bickersteth*. $39/£25

AUDEN, W.H. Poems. London: Faber, 1930. 1st ed. Paper wrapper over card cvrs (sl soiled, rubbed, chipped; spine chipped, split). Good (feps browned). *Virgo.* $310/£200

AUDEN, W.H. Secondary Worlds, Essays. NY: Random House, (1968). 1st Amer ed. Fine in dj (price-clipped; sl dusty). *Hermitage.* $30/£19

AUDEN, W.H. Spain. (London): Faber & Faber, (1937). 1st ed, probably preceding Hours Press ed. Ptd wrapper over plain wrapper. Sl smudge fr wrapper, else Fine. *Reese.* $100/£65

AUDEN, W.H. Spain. London: Faber, 1937. 1st ed. VF. *Patterson.* $147/£95

AUDEN, W.H. Thank You, Fog. NY: Random House, (1974). 1st ed. VG in dj. *Hermitage.* $25/£16

AUDEN, W.H. (ed). 19th Century British Minor Poets. NY: Delacorte, (1966). 1st ed. VG (sm sticker mk pastedown) in dj (price-clipped, lt edgeworn). *Reese.* $30/£19

AUDEN, W.H. (ed). Van Gogh, A Self-Portrait. Greenwich: NYGS, 1961. 1st ed. Fine in dj. *Beasley.* $65/£42

AUDEN, W.H. and CHESTER KALLMAN. The Rake's Progress. (NY): Boosey & Hawkes, 1953. 1st Amer ed. Sm nick, else NF in ptd wrappers. *Godot.* $75/£48

AUDEN, W.H. and CHRISTOPHER ISHERWOOD. The Ascent of F6. London: Faber, (1936). 1st ed. VG in dj (sm chip back cvr; tape repairs; sm nicks, tears). *Houle.* $225/£145

AUDEN, W.H. and CHRISTOPHER ISHERWOOD. The Ascent of F6. Faber, 1936. 1st ed. Name; cl soiled, o/w VG. *Poetry.* $19/£12

AUDEN, W.H. and CHRISTOPHER ISHERWOOD. The Dog Beneath the Skin or Where Is Francis? London: Faber & Faber, (1935). 1st ed. NF in dj (chipped). *Hermitage.* $100/£65

AUDEN, W.H. and CHRISTOPHER ISHERWOOD. Journey to a War. London, 1939. 1st Eng ed. VG. *Edrich.* $70/£45

AUDEN, W.H. and CHRISTOPHER ISHERWOOD. On the Frontier. A Melodrama in Three Acts. London: Faber, 1938. 1st UK ed. VG in dj. *Lewton.* $116/£75

AUDEN, W.H. and CHRISTOPHER ISHERWOOD. On the Frontier: A Melodrama in Three Acts. London: Faber & Faber, (1938). 1st ed. NF. *Sadlon.* $30/£19

AUDEN, W.H. and CHRISTOPHER ISHERWOOD. On the Frontier: A Melodrama in Three Acts. London: Faber & Faber, (1938). 1st ed. Nice in VG dj. *Reese.* $50/£32

AUDEN, W.H. and LOUIS MacNEICE. Letters from Iceland. NY, (1937). 1st Amer ed. Fine in dj (spine sl sunned, 2 sm tears, chips). *Polyanthos.* $95/£61

AUDEN, W.H. and LOUIS MacNEICE. Letters from Iceland. London: Faber, 1937. 1st ed. Fldg map. (Extrems sl rubbed.) *Hollett.* $47/£30

AUDEN, W.H. and LOUIS MacNEICE. Letters from Iceland. London: Faber & Faber, 1937. 1st ed. VG in dj (lacks 1/2-inch piece spine head). *Limestone.* $145/£94

AUDIOSIO, GABRIEL. Harun Al-Rashid, Caliph of Bagdad. NY: McBride, 1931. 1st ed. 8 plts. Sl rubbed; bkpl, o/w VG. *Worldwide.* $35/£23

AUDSLEY, GEORGE ASHDOWN. The Ornamental Arts of Japan. London: Sampson et al, 1882-4. 2 vols. Frontispieces, 100 plts, incl 70 chromolithos (minor surface loss to several, due to adhesion to guards). (Tps, prelims browned; vol 1 half-title, frontis stained; tissue guard torn; vol 2 rear pgs lt spotted w/sm stain affecting margin 2 plts; ink owner stamps half-titles.) Full black calf, red/grn inlaid, gilt (minor wear to joints; minor surface scratching; corners straightened), aeg. VG set. *Edwards.* $2,480/£1,600

AUDSLEY, W. and G. Cottage, Lodge and Villa Architecture. London: W. Mackenzie, n.d. (c. 1860). 58pp text; 140 engr plts; fldg table (loose). Orig 1/2 leather, gilt; cl-cvrd bds (worn, mks); spine raised in bands. Generally VG. *Willow House.* $233/£150

AUDSLEY, W. and G. Guide to the Art of Illuminating and Missal Painting. G. Rowney, 1862. Blind-stamped cl, gilt title. Inner hinge cracked, sl wear, o/w clean. *Moss.* $93/£60

AUDSLEY, W. and G. Guide to the Art of Illuminating and Missal Painting. London: George Rowney, 1862. 4th ed. Color frontis, 8 litho plts. 1/2 calf over marbled bds (rebound). Joints starting, extrems scuffed, lt stain pp corner, else VG. *Glenn.* $125/£81

AUDSLEY, W. and G. Guide to the Art of Illuminating and Missal Painting. London, 1864. 6th ed. Frontis (partially detached), 72pp + 40pp ads, 7 litho plts (4 color). (Spine dknd, chipped.) *Edwards.* $31/£20

AUDUBON, JOHN JAMES. Journal of.... Howard Corning (ed). Cambridge, MA, 1939. New ed. Howes A 387. *Ginsberg.* $150/£97

AUDUBON, JOHN JAMES. Letters of John James Audubon, 1826-1840. Boston, 1930. 1st ed. One of 225. 2 vols. Lt blue bds, muslin spines. Howes A 388. *Ginsberg.* $450/£290

AUDUBON, JOHN JAMES. The Original Water-Color Paintings...for the Birds of America. NY: American Heritage, 1966. Orig ed. 2 vols. 431 color repros. Fine in slipcase (lt worn). *Glenn.* $150/£97

AUDUBON, JOHN JAMES. Ornithological Biography. Edinburgh: Adam Black, 1831-39. 1st eds. 5 vols (vol 5 states 1849 rather than actual 1839). Three 1/2 titles. 19th cent 1/2 morocco over marbled bds (vol 1 in black morocco, 2-5 in maroon), paper spine label. Good set (bindings faded, scuffed; bkpl; sl text foxing). Howes A 389. *Cullen.* $1,850/£1,194

AUDUBON, M.R. Audubon and His Journals.... NY, 1897. 2 vols. xiv,532; viii,554,(1)pp (corner creased 2pp). (Lt scuffed; hinges cracked or starting; # sticker on spines; ex-lib.) *Sutton.* $135/£87

AUEL, JEAN. The Clan of the Cave Bear. NY: Crown Books, 1980. 1st ed, 1st bk. NF in NF dj. *Pettler.* $80/£52

AUEL, JEAN. The Mammoth Hunters. NY, (1985). 1st ed. Cl-backed bds. Sl stained, bumped, else Good in dj. *King.* $25/£16

AUGHEY, JOHN H. The Fighting Preacher. Chicago, 1899. 1st ed. 361pp. Pict cl. VG+. *Pratt.* $185/£119

AUGHEY, JOHN H. Tupelo. Lincoln, 1888. 595pp. Pict cl. Sl cvr wear, soiling, o/w VG+. *Pratt.* $47/£30

AULT, NORMAN and LENA. The Podgy Book of Tales. London: E. Grant Richards, (1907). 1st ed. Thick, 16mo. 16 full-color plts. Full pict cl cvrs (rubbing of images). *Reisler.* $300/£194

Aunt Louisa's Old Nursery Friends. (By Laura Belinda Valentine.) London: Frederick Warne, n.d. (ca 1880). 4to. 3 stories, each w/6 Fine full-pg chromolithos. Gilt pict bd w/label (lt rubbed; spine extrems chipped). *Hobbyhorse*. $100/£65

AUSCHER, E.S. A History and Description of French Porcelain. London, 1905. One of 1250. 24 color plts (edges sl foxed; feps lt browned). 2-tone cl; teg. *Edwards*. $56/£36

AUSLANDER, JOSEPH. Hell in Harness. NY: Doubleday, Doran, 1929. 1st ed. (Spine ends, corners sl rubbed; sm spots.) *Sadlon*. $15/£10

AUSTEN LEIGH, WILLIAM and MONTAGU GEORGE KNIGHT. Chawton Manor and Its Owners. London: Smith, Elder, 1911. 1st ed. 14 ports, 8 plts. Teg. Vellum-backed cl, gilt. Flyleaves sl spotted. *Hollett*. $248/£160

AUSTEN, JANE. Emma. NY: LEC, 1964. One of 1500 ptd, signed by Fritz Kredel (illus). Fine in pub's slipcase. *Hermitage*. $90/£58

AUSTEN, JANE. Lady Susan. Oxford: Clarendon Press, 1925. 1st separate ed. Uncut. Bds, cl spine, ptd paper label. *Bickersteth*. $39/£25

AUSTEN, JANE. The Novels and Letters. NY: Frank S. Holby, 1914. Hampshire Ed, ltd to 1250. 12 vols. 1/2 blue morocco, ribbed gilt dec spines, teg. *D & D*. $3,500/£2,258

AUSTEN, JANE. The Works of Jane Austen. London: Richard Bentley & Son, 1882. 6 vols. 8vo; teg. 1/2 grn calf, gilt dec spines (rubbed; spines uniformly faded to brn). *D & D*. $695/£448

AUSTEN, JANE. The Works of Jane Austen. Boston: Dana Estes, 1906. Illus Cabinet Ed. 12 vols, incl 2 vols of letters illus in color by Hugh Thompson. 1/2 blue morocco, ribbed gilt dec spine. Teg, others uncut. *D & D*. $1,750/£1,129

AUSTER, PAUL. Ghosts. LA: Sun and Moon Press, 1986. 1st Amer ed. Signed. Fine in dj. *Polyanthos*. $45/£29

AUSTER, PAUL. Ground Work. Faber, 1990. 1st ed. Fine in dj (sl rubbed). *Rees*. $16/£10

AUSTER, PAUL. In the Country of Last Things. NY: Viking, 1987. 1st ed. Fine in NF dj. *Pettler*. $25/£16

AUSTER, PAUL. In the Country of Last Things. Faber, 1988. 1st UK ed. Signed. Rev slip laid in. Fine in dj. *Sclanders*. $34/£22

AUSTER, PAUL. The Invention of Solitude. NY: Sun, 1982. 1st ed. Fine in wraps. *Beasley*. $85/£55

AUSTER, PAUL. Leviathan. NY: Viking, 1992. 1st ed. Inscribed. Fine in Fine dj. *Beasley*. $45/£29

AUSTER, PAUL. Moon Palace. NY: Viking, 1989. 1st ed. Inscribed. Fine in Fine dj. *Beasley*. $75/£48

AUSTER, PAUL. The New York Trilogy. Faber, 1966. 1st UK ed. Signed. Fine in dj. *Lewton*. $47/£30

AUSTIN, ALFRED. Haunts of Ancient Peace. A&C Black, 1908. 1st ed. 20 color plts. Teg. (Lt browning; hinges sl tender; sl worn.) *Edwards*. $39/£25

AUSTIN, EDMUND O. The Black Challenge. NY: Vantage, (1959). 1st ed. VG in VG dj (sl chipped). *Godot*. $65/£42

AUSTIN, LEONARD. Around the World in San Francisco. Stanford: James Ladd Delkin, 1940. Ltd to 500. 27 plts. Edgewear, o/w VG. *Oregon*. $90/£58

AUSTIN, MARY and ANSEL ADAMS. Taos Pueblo. Boston: NYGS, 1977. Facs of 19030 ed. Ltd to 950 numbered, signed by Adams. 12 full-pg photos. Tan calf over orange linen. Fine in matching linen slipcase. *Karmiole*. $750/£484

AUSTIN, MARY and SUTTON PALMER. California, the Land of the Sun. London: A&C Black, (1914). 1st ed. 32 tipped-in color plts, fldg map at rear. Grn pict cl (lt worn, rubbed, sl bumped). VG + . *Harrington*. $250/£161

AUSTIN, MARY. The American Rhythm. NY: Harcourt, (1923). 1st ed. Brn cl; uncut. Nice in dj (sl chipped, soiled). *Second Life*. $150/£97

AUSTIN, MARY. Earth Horizon. Boston: Houghton Mifflin, 1932. 1st ed. Fine in dj (lt chipped, faded; price-clipped; 1/2 inch missing spine head). *Hermitage*. $75/£48

AUSTIN, MARY. The Land of Little Rain. Boston: Houghton Mifflin, 1903. 1st ed, 1st bk. Frontis. Teg. Olive cl. Fine. *Reese*. $350/£226

AUSTIN, MARY. The Land of Little Rain. H-M, 1950. 1st ed thus. 48 b/w photo plts by Ansel Adams. NF in dj (wear, tear, chipping). *Fine Books*. $110/£71

AUSTIN, MARY. The Land of Little Rain. Boston, 1950. 1st ed thus. Ansel Adams (photos). VG in dj (frayed). *King*. $150/£97

AUSTIN, MARY. The Lands of the Sun. Boston: Houghton Mifflin, 1927. 1st ed. Color frontis. Ink inscrip; spine faded, o/w Fine. *Hermitage*. $65/£42

AUSTIN, MARY. Starry Adventure. Boston/NY: Houghton Mifflin, 1931. 1st ed. Lt spotted, else NF in silver foil ptd dj (chips, tears, spine faded, else VG). *Godot*. $65/£42

AUSTIN, MOSES and STEPHEN F. The Austin Papers. Eugene C. Barker (ed). Washington: GPO, 1924. 3 vols. VG. *Laurie*. $250/£161

AUSTIN, SARAH. The Story without an End. London: Sampson et al, 1872. New ed. Tinted frontis, vi,40pp, 15 chromolithos w/new tissues. Gilt dec cl (edge repairs). *Hollett*. $302/£195

AUSTIN, STEPHEN F. The Austin Papers. E.C. Barker (comp/ed). Washington, 1924-8. 1st ed. 3 vols. *Ginsberg*. $200/£129

AVALLONE, MIKE. The Crazy Mixed-Up Corpse. Greenwich: Fawcett, 1957. 1st ed: pb orig. NF. *Janus*. $18/£12

AVARY, MYRTA LOCKETT. Dixie After the War. Doubleday, Page, 1906. (1st ed). VG. *Book Broker*. $45/£29

AVEDON, RICHARD. Avedon Photographs 1947-1977. (NY, 1978). 1st ed. 162 photos. Pict bds. Inscrip, else VG in glassine dj (sl chipped). *King*. $125/£81

AVEDON, RICHARD. In the American West: 1979-1984. NY: Abrams, 1985. 1st ed. Signed, dated. 109 full-pg b/w photos. Mtd photo fr, rear cvrs. Owner blindstamp, else Fine in acetate dj. *Cahan*. $200/£129

AVEDON, RICHARD. Portraits. NY, 1977. 1st ed. Inscribed. VF in dj. *Pharos*. $150/£97

AVERSON, WILLIAM. Tendril in the Mesh. (N.p.): Cayucos Books, 1973. 1st ed. One of 250 numbered, signed. 1/2 calf, bds. Fine. *Reese*. $75/£48

AVERY, CHARLES. Giambologna; the Complete Sculpture. Oxford: Phaidon/Christie's, 1987. 16 color plts. Fine in Mint dj. *Europa*. $147/£95

AVERY, OSWALD. Studies on the Chemical Nature of the Substance Inducing Transformation of the Pneumococcal Types.... 1944. Ex-lib. *Fye.* $150/£97

AVEY, ELIJAH. The Capture and Execution of John Brown. Chicago, (1906). 1st ed. Navy blue cl. NF. *Glenn.* $15/£10

AVI-YONAH, MICHAEL. Israel: Ancient Mosaics. NYGS, (1960). 32 color plts. (Inscrip.) Dj (tattered). *Archaeologia.* $85/£55

Awful Disclosures...of the Hotel Dieu Nunnery of Montreal.... (By Maria Monk.) NY, 1855. 261pp. (Extrems worn; 1 side of spine reglued.) *Hayman.* $35/£23

AXFORD, H. WILLIAM. Giplin County Gold. Peter McFarlane 1848-1929 Mining Entrepreneur.... Chicago: Swallow Press, 1976. VG in dj. *Burcham.* $20/£13

AYDEN, ERJE. The Crazy Green of Second Avenue. (NY: New Wave, 1965.) 1st ed. NF. *Pharos.* $25/£16

AYER, EMMA BURBANK. A Motor Flight through Algeria and Tunisia. Chicago: A.C. McClurg, 1911. 1st ed. Frontis. Pict tan cl (inner hinges strained). *Petrilla.* $35/£23

AYER, ETHAN. The Beneficiary and Other Poems. IA City: Prairie Press, (1967). Fine in dj. *Graf.* $25/£16

AYER, I. WINSLOW. The Great Treason Plot in the North during the War. Chicago: U.S. Pub Co, (1895). Enlgd ed. 253pp + 3pp ads. Pict cl (sl mks). Howes A 426. *Schoyer.* $85/£55

AYLMER, FELIX. Dickens Incognito. London: Rupert Hart-Davis, 1959. 1st Eng ed. Very Nice in dj. *Cady.* $25/£16

AYLMER, G.E. and REGINALD CANT. A History of York Minster. Oxford: Clarendon Press, 1977. Color frontis, 6 plans. Brn cl, gilt. Fine in dj. *Peter Taylor.* $60/£39

AYLMER, G.E. and REGINALD CANT. A History of York Minster. Oxford: Clarendon Press, 1977. 1st ed. Frontis; 6 plans. Gilt cl. VG in dj. *Hollett.* $70/£45

AYRE, WILLIAM. Memoirs of the Life and Writings of Alexander Pope. London: For the Author, 1795. 2 vols. Early full calf, gilt rules (spines worn, leather labels replaced). Contents VG (bkpls). *Hartfield.* $225/£145

AYRES, ATLEE B. Mexican Architecture. NY: William Helburn, (1926). 1st ed. Frontis, 150 plts. Grn gilt cl. Nice. *Karmiole.* $150/£97

AYRES, ATLEE B. Mexican Architecture. NY, 1926. (Sl worn; chipped w/sl loss.) *Edwards.* $109/£70

AYRES, JAMES. English Naive Painting 1750-1900. London, 1980. 48 color plts. Dj. *Edwards.* $31/£20

AYRES, JAMES. English Naive Painting 1750-1900. London: Thames & Hudson, 1980. 1st ed. 151 plts (48 color). Fine in Fine dj. *Willow House.* $23/£15

AYRTON, ELISABETH. The Cretan. London: Hodder & Stoughton, 1963. 1st ed. VG in dj. *Hollett.* $47/£30

AYRTON, MICHAEL and HENRY MOORE. Giovanni Pisano, Sculptor. NY, 1969. Good in dj. *Washton.* $85/£55

AYRTON, MICHAEL. British Drawings. London: Collins, 1946. 1st ed. 8 color plts. VG in dj. *Hollett.* $47/£30

AYRTON, MICHAEL. Drawings and Sculpture. (London, 1962.) VG in dj. *Argosy.* $50/£32

AYRTON, MICHAEL. Fabrications. London: Secker & Warburg, 1972. 1st ed. Fine in dj. *Hollett.* $101/£65

AYRTON, MICHAEL. Giovanni Pisano, Sculptor. London; Thames & Hudson, 1969. Color frontis, 370 plts. Sound in dj. *Ars Artis.* $194/£125

AYRTON, MICHAEL. Halloween Who's Who. London: Hulton Press, 1953. 4pp of plts. Orig pict wrappers (staples sl rusted). *Hollett.* $47/£30

AYRTON, MICHAEL. The Maze Maker. London: Longmans, 1967. 1st ed. VG in dj. *Hollett.* $70/£45

AYRTON, MICHAEL. The Midas Consequence. London: Secker & Warburg, 1974. 1st ed. VG in dj. *Hollett.* $47/£30

AYRTON, MICHAEL. The Minotaur. London: Genevieve Restaurants, 1970. 1st ed. 13 plts by Ayrton. Pict bds (hinges sl rubbed). *Hollett.* $132/£85

AYRTON, MICHAEL. The Rudiments of Paradise. London: Secker & Warburg, 1971. 1st ed. 73 plts. Press cuttings loosely inserted. VG in dj. *Hollett.* $101/£65

AYRTON, MICHAEL. The Testament of Daedalus. London: Methuen, 1962. 1st ed. 16 litho plts. Cl-backed marbled bds, gilt. VG in dj (price-clipped). *Hollett.* $116/£75

AYRTON, MICHAEL. Tittivulus or the Verbiage Collector. London: Max Reinhardt, 1953. 1st ed. VG in dj (price-clipped, sl worn, chipped). *Hollett.* $85/£55

B

BABBITT, CHARLES. Early Days at Council Bluffs. Washington: Byron Adams, 1916. 1st ed. 2 maps. VG. Howes B 4. *Oregon.* $95/£61

BABCOCK, HAVILAH. I Don't Want to Shoot an Elephant. NY, 1958. 1st ed. VF in VG dj (chipped). *Bond.* $85/£55

BABCOCK, HAVILAH. Jaybirds Go to Hell on Friday. NY, 1965. 1st ed. VF (dated inscrip) in dj. *Bond.* $65/£42

BABCOCK, HAVILAH. My Health Is Better in November. Columbia: Univ of SC, 1947. 1st ed. Few sm spots on fore-edge, else Fine in illus dj (sm tears spine top). *Cahan.* $125/£81

BABCOCK, HAVILAH. My Health Is Better in November. Columbia, SC, 1948. 2nd ptg. Mint in VG dj. *Bond.* $50/£32

BABELON, ERNEST. Manual of Oriental Antiques.... B.T.A. Evetts (trans). London: Grevel, 1889. New ed. xx,352,xiipp. Sl rubbed, o/w VG ex-lib. *Worldwide.* $60/£39

BABER, D.F. Injun Summer. Caldwell: Caxton, 1952. 1st ed. Dj. *Heinoldt.* $25/£16

Babes in the Wood. (May Bell Series.) NY: McLoughlin Bros, n.d. (ca 1890). 4 leaves, 4 full-pg wood engrs; upper wrapper w/2 children walking in woods, signed Beuton; lower wrapper w/2 horsemen, each carrying 1 of the children; 1st, last pg of text ptd on wrappers. Good (split lower portion of 1st leaf fold and spine; sm dampstain center folds). *Hobbyhorse.* $40/£26

BABINGTON, S.H. Navajo Gods and Tom-Toms. NY: Greenberg Pub, (1950). Ink name, else VG in dj (torn). *Perier.* $37/£24

BABSON, MARIAN. Murder on Show. London: Collins, 1972. VG in VG dj (rubbed, price-clipped). *Ming.* $70/£45

BABSON, MARIAN. Untimely Guest. London: CCC, 1976. 1st ed. VF in dj. *Mordida.* $40/£26

Baby's Red Letter Days. Syracuse: Just's Foods, (1901). 1st ptg. 8vo. Tinted illus by Jessie Wilcox Smith. Growth chart, order form laid in. Stiff paper wrappers w/emb decs; silk ties. Clean, bright (few pgs filled in). *Reisler.* $120/£77

Baby's Red Letter Days. Syracuse: Just's Foods, (1906). 2nd ptg. 8vo. Growth chart bound in. Ptd color cvr. Clean, bright (sm tape mk cvr). *Reisler.* $85/£55

BACHER, OTTO H. With Whistler in Venice. NY: Century, 1908. 1st ed. 44 plts. Orig brn cl over bds, gilt. (Sl soiled.) *Karmiole.* $75/£48

BACHMAN, LAWRENCE. The Lorelei. London: Collins, 1957. 1st ed. Inscribed. Fine in dj (lt soiled back panel; short creases fr panel). *Mordida.* $45/£29

BACHMAN, RICHARD. (Pseud of Stephen King.) Thinner. NAL, 1984. 1st ed. Fine in dj w/wraparound band. *Madle.* $125/£81

BACK, GEORGE. Narrative of an Expedition in H.M.S. Terror...1836-7. London: John Murray, 1838. vii,456pp. 12 plts, fldg map. Recent 1/4 calf, well done. Nice, plts very clean. *High Latitude.* $590/£381

BACK, GEORGE. Narrative of the Arctic Land Expedition to the Mouth of the Great Fish River.... London: John Murray, 1836. 1st ed. x,663pp, fldg map, 16 plts. 19th cent 1/2 calf, marbled bds. VG. *Walcot.* $388/£250

BACK, GEORGE. Narrative of the Arctic Land Expedition to the Mouth of the Great Fish River...1833, 1834, and 1835. London: John Murray, 1836. 1st ed. 16 full-pg engr plts; fold-out map. Rebound in 1/4 leather, marbled bds. Foxing, o/w VG. *Laurie.* $600/£387

BACKES, MAGNUS and REGINE DOLLING. Art of the Dark Ages. NY: Abrams, 1969. Dec eps. Fine in Mint dj. *Europa.* $25/£16

BACKHOUSE, E. and J.O.P. BLAND. Annals and Memoirs of the Court of Peking. London: Heinemann, 1914. 25 plts. Edges spotted, o/w Very Nice. *Hollett.* $147/£95

BACKUS, JOSEPH. The Complete Constable. Hartford: For the Author, 1812. 134,(8)pp (sl worming holes blank edges last pp). Full contemp leather, leather spine label. *Schoyer.* $100/£65

Backwoods of Canada: Being Letters From the Wife of an Emigrant Officer.... London: Charles Knight, 1836. 1st ed. 51pp; 20 wood engrs. Pub's cl (lt worn; sl discolored; spine rebacked, orig cl laid down). Ink ownership, else VG. *Hermitage.* $250/£161

BACON, ALICE MABEL. Japanese Interior. Boston/NY: Houghton, Mifflin, 1893. (xx),267pp. Grey cl stamped in silver. VG. *Schoyer.* $40/£26

BACON, FRANCIS and FRANCIS GODWYN. The History of the Reigns of Henry the Seventh, Henry the Eight, Edward the Sixth, and Queen Mary.... London: R. Scot et al, 1676. Frontis port; (12),138,(12),202pp. Orig calf (spine rubbed, chipped). *Karmiole.* $350/£226

BACON, FRANCIS. The Elements of the Common Lawes of England, Branched into a Double Tract.... London, 1639. Contemp sheep (rebacked, rubbed). Sound. *Boswell.* $850/£548

BACON, FRANCIS. The Essayes or Counsels Civill and Morall. NY: LEC, 1944. One of 1100 numbered, ptd by William Rudge under direction of Bruce Rogers, and signed by him. Uncut; unopened. Cl box. *Argosy.* $175/£113

BACON, FRANCIS. The Essays or Counsels Civill and Morall. NY: LEC, 1944. #46/1100. VG (corners sl worn). *Graf.* $125/£81

BACON, FRANCIS. Works. London: Rivington, 1778. 5 vols. 4 frontispieces. Contemp calf (worn, rebacked; 1st vol considerably dampstained). *Argosy.* $250/£161

BACON, J. Theory of Colouring. London: Geo. Rowney, 1872. 4th ed. ix,58pp + 22pp ads, 6 color plts; aeg. Emb cl. NF (foxing). *Cahan.* $125/£81

BACON, LEE. Our Houseboat on the Nile. Boston/NY: Houghton, Mifflin, 1902. Frontis, 12 plts. (Tears at spine, label removed.) *Archaeologia.* $35/£23

BACON, LIONEL. Alpines. Newton Abbot, Eng., 1973. 20 b/w photo plts. Ex-lib. Dj. *Brooks.* $25/£16

BACON, MARTHA. Sophia Scrooby Preserved. Boston: Little, Brown, (1968). 1st ed. VG in dj. *Petrilla.* $25/£16

Bad Boy's Diary. NY: J.S. Ogilvie, (1880). 276pp + ads. Cl (faded, lt worn). *Hayman.* $25/£16

BADEN-POWELL, GEORGE S. New Homes for the Old Country. London, 1872. 1st ed. 512pp. Gilt dec cl. VG. *Argosy.* $125/£81

BADEN-POWELL, R.S.S. Sketches in Mafeking and East Africa. London, 1907. 1st ed. Color frontis, 8 other color plts, map. Rebacked, new eps, o/w VG in pict khaki cl (sl soiled). *Edwards.* $147/£95

BADEN-POWELL, ROBERT. Pig-Sticking or Hog Hunting. London, 1924. 1st ed, rev. Color frontis. (Sl foxing.) *Edwards.* $54/£35

BADEN-POWELL, ROBERT. Pig-Sticking or Hog-Hunting.... London: Herbert Jenkins, 1924. 4 color plts. VG in dj (sl defective). *Cox.* $39/£25

BADGER, JOSEPH. A Memoir of.... Henry Noble Day (ed). Hudson, OH: Sawyer, Ingersoll, 1851. 1st ed. Frontis, 185pp + (2)pp ads. Orig cl (rubbed; text foxed). Good. Howes B 25. *Cahan.* $200/£129

BADLAM, ALEXANDER. The Wonders of Alaska. SF: Bancroft, 1890. 2nd ed. vii,(2),148,(1)pp. Dec red cl. Overall VG. *Parmer.* $75/£48

BADT, F.B. Bell-Hangers' Hand-Book. Chicago: Electrician Pub Co, 1895. 3rd ed. Maroon cl (lt wear). *Glenn.* $25/£16

BAE. 4th Annual Report. Washington: Smithsonian, 1886. 1st ed. 532pp, 83 plts. Gilt dec cl. VG. *Mikesh.* $75/£48

BAE. 6th Annual Report. Washington: GPO, 1888. lviii,675pp. Leather (rebound). *Schoyer.* $65/£42

BAE. 8th Annual Report. Washington: GPO, 1891. xxxvi,298pp. Orig grn pict cl (sm lib mks). *Schoyer.* $125/£81

BAE. 8th Annual Report. Washington: GPO, 1891. 1st ed. (36),298pp + plts. Plan in rear pocket. Dk olive grn cl, gilt. VG (soiled; tender joints; bkpl, sig). *Chapel Hill.* $175/£113

BAE. 9th Annual Report. Washington: GPO, 1892. xlvi,617pp, 2 maps, 6 chromolitho plts. Orig grn cl (sl shaken; lib bkpl). *Schoyer.* $85/£55

BAE. 17th Annual Report, Part 2. Washington, DC: GPO, 1898. Gilt-pict cl (sm tears top, bottom spine; bkpl). *Archaeologia.* $150/£97

BAE. 19th Annual Report, Part II. Washington, 1900. *Hayman.* $60/£39

BAE. 25th Annual Report. Washington: Smithsonian, 1907. Gold-stamped pict cl (bumped). *Dawson.* $60/£39

BAE. 30th Annual Report. Washington D.C.: GPO, 1915. Grn cl. VG. *Perier.* $75/£48

BAE. 31st Annual Report. Washington: GPO, 1916. NF in grn cl. *Perier.* $75/£48

BAE. 33rd Annual Report. Washington: GPO, 1919. Orig grn cl. VG. *Schoyer.* $65/£42

BAE. 42nd Annual Report. Washington, 1928. Fldg color map. (Ex-lib.) *Edwards.* $31/£20

BAE. Bulletin 147. Washington, 1952. Ptd wrappers. *Ginsberg.* $50/£32

BAEDEKER, KARL. Austria, Together with Budapest, Prague, Karlsbad.... Leipzig: Baedeker, 1929. 12th rev ed. 80 maps, plans; 2 panoramas. *Petersfield.* $16/£10

BAEDEKER, KARL. Austria-Hungary with Excursions to Cetinje, Belgrade and Bucharest. Leipzig/London/NY: Karl Baedeker/T. Fisher Unwin/Scribner's, 1911. 11th ed. 71 maps, 77 plans, 2 panoramas. Name, else Fine. *Cahan.* $125/£81

BAEDEKER, KARL. Belgium and Holland. Leipzig, 1905. 14th ed. Nice in dj. *Gretton.* $16/£10

BAEDEKER, KARL. Berlin and Its Environs. Leipsic, 1903. 1st ed. 4 maps, 19 plans. All edges marbled. (Pencil notes; upper hinge cracked; spine sl sunned, frayed.) *Edwards.* $54/£35

BAEDEKER, KARL. Berlin and Its Environs. Leipsic, 1905. 2nd ed. 6 maps, 18 plans. All edges marbled. (Lacks fep; spine sl sunned, chipped w/loss; sm hole.) *Edwards.* $39/£25

BAEDEKER, KARL. Berlin and Its Environs. Leipsic: Karl Baedeker, 1905. 2nd ed. 6 maps, 18 plans. Red cl stamped in blind, gilt. NF. *Schoyer.* $40/£26

BAEDEKER, KARL. The Dominion of Canada with Newfoundland and an Excursion to Alaska. Leipzig/London/NY: Karl Baedeker/T. Fisher Unwin/Scribner's, 1922. 4th ed. 14 maps, 12 plans. Fine. *Cahan.* $200/£129

BAEDEKER, KARL. The Eastern Alps. Leipsic: Baedeker, 1899. 9th ed. 47 maps, 10 plans, 7 panoramas. (Backstrip torn; sl foxed.) *Petersfield.* $16/£10

BAEDEKER, KARL. Egypt and the Sudan. Leipzig, 1908. 6th remodelled ed. 23 (of 24) maps; 76 plans. Rubbed; spine frayed, o/w Good. *Worldwide.* $65/£42

BAEDEKER, KARL. Egypt and the Sudan. Leipzig: Baedeker, 1908. 6th remodelled ed. 24 maps, 76 plans, 57 vignettes. (Fr cvr stained.) *Petersfield.* $70/£45

BAEDEKER, KARL. Egypt and the Sudan. Leipzig, 1914. 7th ed. 22 maps; 85 plans. Sl rubbed; sl tears spine; fr inner hinges strengthened, o/w VG. *Worldwide.* $85/£55

BAEDEKER, KARL. Egypt. Leipsic, 1892. xxxviii,365pp, 11 maps, 26 plans. (Upper hinge split, crudely taped; notes; worn.) *Edwards.* $70/£45

BAEDEKER, KARL. Egypt. Leipzig: Baedeker, 1902. 5th remodelled ed. 23 maps, 66 plans, 59 vignettes. (Backstrip sl chipped.) *Petersfield.* $87/£56

BAEDEKER, KARL. Egypt. Leipsic, 1902. 5th remodelled ed. 23 maps; 66 plans. VG (hinges sl rubbed). *Hollett.* $186/£120

BAEDEKER, KARL. Egypt. Leipsic: Karl Baedeker, 1902. 5th remodelled ed. 23 maps, 66 plans, 59 vignettes. Pencil marginalia, else NF. *Cahan.* $200/£129

BAEDEKER, KARL. Egypt. Leipzig, 1914. 7th ed. Good+. *Gretton.* $47/£30

BAEDEKER, KARL. Egypt; Part First: Lower Egypt and the Peninsula of Sinai. Leipsic/London: Karl Baedeker/Dulau, 1895. 3rd ed, rev. ccxvi,293pp, 14 maps, 33 plans, 7 views. Fine. *Cahan.* $225/£145

BAEDEKER, KARL. Greece. Handbook for Travelers. Leipzig: Karl Baedeker, 1894. 2nd rev ed. cxii,376pp, 8 maps (incl lg fldg in pocket), 15 plans. Red cl (faded, rubbed). *Karmiole.* $65/£42

BAEDEKER, KARL. London and Its Environs. Leipzig, 1911. Internally VG. (Head of spine sl torn; sl rubbed.) *Patterson.* $31/£20

BAEDEKER, KARL. London and Its Environs. Leipzig, 1930. 19th rev ed. 48 maps/plans. *Edwards.* $43/£28

BAEDEKER, KARL. Munich and Its Environs. Hamburg et al: Karl Baedeker, 1956. 15 maps, plans. Red cl stamped in blind, gilt (paper browning). Dj. *Schoyer.* $20/£13

BAEDEKER, KARL. Northern Germany. Leipsic: Baedeker, 1893. 11th ed. 32 maps, 56 plans. (Backstrip faded; sl foxed.) *Petersfield.* $16/£10

BAEDEKER, KARL. Northern Italy Including Florence. Leipzig, 1930. 15th ed. VG. *Gretton.* $23/£15

BAEDEKER, KARL. Norway, Sweden, and Denmark.... Leipzig: Baedeker, 1909. 9th ed, rev. 43 maps, 26 plans. (Backstrip sl faded.) *Petersfield.* $34/£22

BAEDEKER, KARL. Palestine and Syria. Leipzig, 1906. 4th ed. 20 maps, 52 plans, panorama, tipped-in warning against confiscation by Turkish authorities (spine sl rubbed, faded). *Schoyer.* $100/£65

BAEDEKER, KARL. Paris and Environs. Leipzig, 1907. 16th rev ed. 14 maps, 38 plans. All edges marbled. (Sl wear.) *Edwards.* $28/£18

BAEDEKER, KARL. The Rhine from Rotterdam to Constance. Coblenz/Leipsic: Karl Baedeker, 1873. 5th ed. 15 maps; 16 town plans. Mod 1/2 morocco gilt. VG. *Hollett.* $186/£120

BAEDEKER, KARL. The Rhine from Rotterdam to Constance. Leipsic: Karl Baedeker, 1889. 11th rev ed. xxiv,386pp; 36 maps; 22 plans. Red cl (rubbed; short splits in hinges; sl shaken). *Cox.* $28/£18

BAEDEKER, KARL. The Rhine, including the Black Forest and the Vosges. Leipzig: Baedeker, 1911. 17th ed. 69 maps, 59 plans. *Petersfield.* $16/£10

BAEDEKER, KARL. Russia with Tehran, Port Arthur and Peking. Leipzig/London/NY: Karl Baedeker/T. Fisher Unwin/Scribner's, 1914. 1st ed. 40 maps, 78 plans. As New. Laid in clamshell box. *Cahan.* $850/£548

BAEDEKER, KARL. Southern Germany and Austria, including Hungary, Dalmatia and Bosnia. Leipsic et al: Karl Baedeker, 1891. 7th ed. xvi,495pp, 16 maps (1 split, others brittle), 31 plans. Red cl stamped in blind, gilt (spine worn). *Schoyer.* $50/£32

BAEDEKER, KARL. Southern Germany, Including Wurtemberg and Bavaria. Leipsic: Karl Baedeker, 1895. 8th rev ed. xxviii,266pp, 16 maps, 15 plans. Lg map torn w/o loss; few corners turned down, pencil marginalia, sm puncture along spine, else VG. *Cahan.* $50/£32

BAEDEKER, KARL. Switzerland. Leipzig, 1928. 27th ed. VG. *Gretton.* $12/£8

BAEDEKER, KARL. Tyrol and the Dolomites.... Leipzig: Baedeker, 1927. 13th rev ed. 65 maps, 19 plans, 11 panoramas. (Backstrip faded.) *Petersfield.* $28/£18

BAEDEKER, KARL. The United States with Excursions to Mexico, Cuba, Porto Rico, and Alaska. Leipzig/NY/London: Karl Baedeker/Scribner's/T. Fisher Unwin, 1909. 4th rev ed. 33 maps, 41 town plans, 7 ground plans.Pencil mkd, tp lt worn, else VG. *Cahan.* $125/£81

BAERLEIR, A. Daze, the Magician. Barker, 1936. 1st ed. VG. *Aronovitz.* $38/£25

BAGGETT, W.T. (ed). Pacific Coast Law Journal. SF: W.T. Baggett, 1878. 10 vols. Contemp sheep. Worn, few joints cracking, but Sound set. *Boswell.* $250/£161

BAGGULEY, WILLIAM H. (ed). Andrew Marvell 1621-1678. Tercentenary Tributes.... London: OUP, 1922. 1st ed. Rmdr binding. VF in ptd dj. *Pharos.* $150/£97

BAGLEE, CHRISTOPHER and ANDREW MORLEY. Street Jewellery. London: New Cavendish Books, 1979. Good in pict cl, mtd cvr enamel sign. *Cox.* $39/£25

BAGLEY, CLARENCE B. The Acquisition and Pioneering of Old Oregon. Seattle: Argus, 1924. 1st ed. Ptd wrappers. *Ginsberg.* $125/£81

BAGNOLD, ENID. Letters to Frank Harris and Other Friends. R.P. Lister (ed). (Gloucestershire): Whittington Press, W. Heinemann, (1980). Ltd ed of 400 numbered. Signed. Tipped-in color frontis; 4 tipped-in plts. Good in slipcase. *Karmiole.* $75/£48

BAGNOLD, ENID. Letters to Frank Harris and Other Friends. R.P. Lister (ed). London: Whittington Press & William Heinemann, 1980. 1st ed. #292/400, signed. 5 tipped-in plts. Orig floral cl, paper label; slip-case. Fine. *Cox.* $70/£45

BAGOT, RICHARD. The Italian Lakes. London: A&C Black, (1908). 68 color plts; teg. Pict blue cl. VG +. *House.* $50/£32

BAGSTER-COLLINS, JEREMY F. George Colman, The Younger. 1762-1836. Morningside Heights: King's Crown, 1946. 1st ed. Frontis. VG. *Dramatis Personae.* $30/£19

BAHR, A.W. Old Chinese Porcelain and Works of Art in China. London, 1911. 121 plts (12 color). (Corners worn.) *Argosy.* $175/£113

BAIKIE, JAMES. Egyptian Antiquities in the Nile Valley: A Descriptive Handbook. London: Methuen, (1932). 31 plts. (Corner bumped.) *Archaeologia.* $75/£48

BAIKIE, JAMES. Egyptian Papyri and Papyrus-Hunting. London: Religious Tract Soc, 1925. (Sig.) *Archaeologia.* $65/£42

BAIKIE, JAMES. A History of Egypt. London, 1929. 2 vols. 48 plts, 2 fldg maps. (Ex-libris; spines faded.) *Edwards.* $47/£30

BAIKIE, JAMES. The Life of the Ancient East, Being Some Chapters of the Romance of Modern Excavation. NY: Macmillan, 1923. 1st ed. 32 plts; fldg map. Sl rubbed, soiled, o/w VG. *Worldwide.* $30/£19

BAILEY, B.H. The Raptorial Birds of Iowa. Des Moines: Geo Surv, 1918. 1st ed. Blind-stamped dec cl. NF. *Mikesh.* $35/£23

BAILEY, F.M. China-Tibet-Assam. A Journey, 1911. London: Jonathan Cape, (1945). Fldg map. Red cl (rubbed, shaken). *Schoyer.* $40/£26

BAILEY, H.C. The Great Game. CCD, 1939. 1st ed. NF in dj (lt used; sm piece missing spine foot; closed tears). *Murder.* $75/£48

BAILEY, H.C. Mr. Fortune Here. NY: DCC, 1940. 1st Amer ed. VG in dj (tape mend; chipped; wear). *Mordida.* $45/£29

BAILEY, HAMILTON (ed). Surgery of Modern Warfare. Edinburgh, 1941. VG. *Argosy.* $100/£65

BAILEY, HAMILTON. Emergency Surgery. NY: Wood, 1930. 2 vols. NF. *Goodrich.* $50/£32

BAILEY, HARRIET. Nursing Mental Diseases. NY, 1921. Good. *Fye.* $30/£19

BAILEY, JOHN WEDELL. The Mammals of Virginia.... Williams Prnt Co, 1946. (1st ed). VG in Good dj. *Book Broker.* $35/£23

BAILEY, KENNETH P. The Ohio Company of Virginia: And the Westward Movement, 1748-1792. Glendale, CA: Clark, 1939. 1st ed. Teg; unopened. Fine in plain dj. *Cahan.* $145/£94

BAILEY, L.H. The Cultivated Evergreens. NY: Macmillan, 1923. 1st ed. 58 full-pg plts. Teg. 2-color gilt-stamped buckram. NF. *Quest.* $60/£39

BAILEY, L.H. Cyclopaedia of American Horticulture. NY: Macmillan, 1900-1902. 1st ed. 4 vols. 50 duotone plts. Gilt-stamped binding (scuffed, shaken). *Quest.* $195/£126

BAILEY, L.H. Farm and Garden Rule-Book. NY, (1915). New ed. (Pp tanned; name.) *Sutton.* $45/£29

BAILEY, L.H. The Forcing-Book. NY, 1897. 1st ed. xiii,266pp. (Lt worn, soiled.) *Sutton.* $40/£26

BAILEY, L.H. The Holy Earth. Ithaca, (1915). (Fading, spotting; sl text browning.) *Sutton.* $27/£17

BAILEY, L.H. Manual of Gardening. NY, 1910. 1st ed. 25 b/w plts. NF. *Shifrin.* $55/£35

BAILEY, L.H. and E.Z. Hortus Third. A Concise Dictionary of Plants Cultivated in the United States and Canada. NY/London, 1976. NF in NF dj. *Shifrin.* $125/£81

BAILEY, PAUL. At the Jerusalem. London: Cape, 1967. 1st UK ed, 1st bk. Fine in dj. *Moorhouse.* $47/£30

BAILEY, PAUL. A Distant Likeness. Cape, 1973. 1st ed. Inscribed. Fine in dj (sl rubbed, sl trimmed). *Rees.* $16/£10

BAILEY, PAUL. An English Madam: The Life and Work of Cynthia Payne. Cape, 1982. 1st ed. Fine in dj. *Rees.* $16/£10

BAILEY, PAUL. Holy Smoke. L.A.: Westernlore, 1978. 1st ed. VF in VF dj. *Oregon.* $25/£16

BAILEY, PAUL. Peter Smart's Confessions. Cape, 1977. 1st UK ed. Fine in dj (price-clipped). *Williams.* $19/£12

BAILEY, PAUL. Walkara; Hawk of the Mountains. L.A.: Westernlore, 1954. 1st ed. VG in VG- dj (sm spine chips). *Parker.* $45/£29

BAILEY, PEARCE. Accidents and Injury, Their Relations to Diseases of the Nervous System. NY, 1899. 1st ed. 430pp. Good. *Fye.* $200/£129

BAILEY, PEARL. The Raw Pearl. NY, (1968). 1st Amer ed. Signed, adding the word 'love'. Fine in dj (sl edge rubbed). *Polyanthos.* $25/£16

BAILEY, PERCIVAL et al. Intracranial Tumors of Infancy and Childhood. Chicago, 1939. 23 plts. Internally Good (ex-lib). *Goodrich.* $85/£55

BAILEY, PERCIVAL et al. Intracranial Tumours of Infancy and Childhood. Chicago, 1939. 1st ed. 23 photo plts. Good. *Fye.* $200/£129

BAILEY, PHILIP. Golden Mirages. Macmillan, 1940. 1st ed. Frontis; 24pp photos; 8pp maps. VG in Good + dj. *Oregon.* $50/£32

BAILEY, ROBERT G. Hell's Canyon: A Story of the Deepest Canyon on the North American Continent. Lewiston, ID: R.G. Bailey Ptg, 1943. 1st ed. Ltd to 1500, signed. Illus eps. Good (spine sl faded). *Lien.* $140/£90

BAILEY, ROBERT G. River of No Return. Lewiston, ID: Bailey-Blake Ptg, 1935. 1st ed. Ltd to 1400, signed. Good (lt wear corners, spine). *Lien.* $145/£94

BAILLIE, MATTHEW. The Morbid Anatomy of Some of the Most Important Parts of the Human Body. To which are prefixed, Preliminary Observations on Diseased Structures, by James Wardrop. London, 1833. Later ed. xvi,343pp (foxing first/last few pp). Uncut. Orig cl, paper label. (Hinges partially split; rubbed.) Uncut. Fine. *Hemlock.* $425/£274

BAILLIE-GROHMAN, W.A. Camps in the Rockies. London: Sampson Low et al, 1882. Stated 2nd ed (i.e. ptg). viii,438pp + 4pp ads, 4 plts, fldg map. VG. *Schoyer.* $175/£113

BAILLIE-GROHMAN, W.A. Fifteen Years' Sport and Life in the Hunting Grounds of Western America and British Columbia. London: Horace Cox, 1900. 1st ed. Teg. 77 plts, 3 maps in pocket. Cl over beveled bds, gilt. Eps browned, joints cracked, but VG. *Hollett.* $287/£185

BAILLIE-GROHMAN, W.A. Sport in the Alps. NY, 1896. 1st ed. xv,356pp + (ii)pub's ads; 18 plts. Teg. Dec cl (head, tail spine replaced; lower bd lt dampspotted; sl shaken). *Edwards.* $101/£65

BAILLIE-GROHMAN, W.A. Tyrol. A&C Black, 1908. 1st ed. 24 color plts by E. Harrison Compton (illus), map. Teg. Dec cl. *Edwards.* $31/£20

BAIN, ALEXANDER. The Senses and the Intellect NY: Appleton, 1879 3rd ed, 1st bk. (ii) + xxviii + 714pp. Pebbled brn cl. VG. *Gach.* $65/£42

BAIN, IAIN. The Watercolours and Drawings of Thomas Bewick and His Workshop Apprentices. Cambridge: MIT, 1981. 2 vols. Uniform orig cl, gilt. VF set in slipcase. *Europa.* $124/£80

BAIN, IAIN. The Watercolours and Drawings of Thomas Bewick and His Workshop Apprentices. London: Gordon Fraser, 1981. 2 vols. Slipcase. *Ars Artis.* $209/£135

BAIN, JOHN. Tobacco in Song and Story. NY/Boston, 1896. Frontis port. Few leaves unopened; dec eps. Tan suede, gilt. VG (few pp w/tears). *Shifrin.* $60/£39

BAIN, JOHN. Tobacco in Song and Story. NY, 1896. 1st ed. Frontis port, 144pp. Teg, rest uncut. Pict title (sl rubbed). *Edwards.* $23/£15

BAINBRIDGE, BERYL. Sweet William. London: Duckworth, 1975. 1st ed. Signed. Fine in dj (price-clipped). *Rees.* $31/£20

BAINBRIDGE, BERYL. Young Adolf. Duckworth, 1978. 1st UK ed. NF in dj. *Williams.* $23/£15

BAINBRIDGE, HENRY C. Peter Carl Faberge. London, (1949). 1st ed. 127 plts. VG in dj. *Argosy.* $75/£48

BAINBRIDGE, HENRY C. Peter Carl Faberge. London: Batsford, 1949. 1st ed. 126 plts (16 color). (Sm split upper joint, spine faded; ex libris). *Edwards.* $70/£45

BAINE, RODNEY. Robert Munford. Athens: Univ of GA, (1967). 1st ed. VG in dj. *Dramatis Personae.* $30/£19

BAINES, ANTHONY. European and American Musical Instruments. NY: Viking/Studio Book, 1966. 1st US ed. VG in dj. *Cahan.* $85/£55

BAINES, THOMAS. The Gold Regions of South Eastern Africa. London: Edward Stanford et al, 1877. 1st ed. xxiv,240pp, mtd photo frontis port, 3 other mtd photos, 2-pg fldg facs of letter, lg fldg map in pocket. Grn gilt-stamped pict cl (recent reback using orig backstrip; wear). *Schoyer.* $400/£258

BAINES, THOMAS. The Gold Regions of South Eastern Africa.... London: Edward Stanford, 1877. 1st ed. 8vo. Photo frontis port, xxiv,240pp. 3 mounted photo plts; fldg facs letter, vignettes; lg fldg map in pocket. Brn cl, dec in black/gilt. VG (joints, hinges well repaired; sl rubbed, scratched). *Morrell.* $295/£190

BAIR, EVERETT. This Will Be an Empire. NY: Pageant Press, (1959). 1st ed. Yellow cl. Fine in dj (worn; price-clipped). *Laurie.* $40/£26

BAIR, PATRICK. Faster! Faster! Viking, 1950. 1st ed, 1st bk. Lt soiled, else Fine in dj (lt worn). *Murder.* $35/£23

BAIRD, CHARLES W. History of the Huguenot Emigration to America. NY: Dodd, Mead, (1885). 354; 448pp; fldg map, 2 fldg plts, lg fldg facs. (Fade mk base of spines; stamp top, bottom edges.) Howes B 43. *Schoyer.* $100/£65

BAIRD, G.W. A Report to the Citizens.... Ashland: Lewis Osborne, 1972. Ltd to 600 numbered. VG. *Oregon.* $50/£32

BAIRD, S.F. Pacific Railroad Survey. Vol 8. Mammals. Washington, 1857. Quarto ed. xlviii,757pp (browned; 2 stamps), 44 plts (some browned). Contemp 1/2 morocco (worn, scuffed; fr hinge tender, splitting). *Sutton.* $135/£87

BAIRD, S.F. Pacific Railroad Survey. Vol 9. Birds. Washington, 1858. Quarto ed. lvi,1005pp (browned). Cl over contemp bds (rebacked, orig backstrip laid down; scuffed, worn). *Sutton.* $115/£74

BAIRD, S.F. et al. The Water Birds of North America. Boston, 1884. 2 vols. xi,537; (4),552pp (sl browned). Gilt dec cl (worn; spine ends frayed; paper to inner hinges cracked). *Sutton.* $375/£242

BAIRNSFATHER, P. Sport and Nature in the Himalayas. London, 1914. VG + in gilt pict cl (spine faded). *Trophy Room.* $350/£226

BAKARICH, SARAH. Gunsmoke, the True Story of Tombstone. Tombstone Press, 1954. 1st ed. VG (name on cvr) in pict wraps. *Oregon.* $17/£11

BAKARICH, SARAH. Gunsmoke. Privately ptd, 1947. VG in wraps. *Cullen.* $75/£48

BAKELESS, JOHN. Daniel Boone. NY: Morrow, 1939. 3rd ptg. Tan cl. Spine dknd, else VG. *Chapel Hill.* $40/£26

BAKER, B. GRANVILLE. The Passing of the Turkish Empire in Europe. London, 1913. Map (detached; soiled, spine chipped w/puncture mk; hinges cracked; foxing.) *Edwards.* $43/£28

BAKER, CARLOS. Ernest Hemingway: A Life Story. NY: Scribner's, (1969). 1st ed. Sl bump top edge, o/w Fine in dj (lt edgeworn). *Sadlon.* $15/£10

BAKER, CHARLES H., JR. The Gentleman's Companion. Vol I: An Exotic Cookery Book... Vol II: An Exotic Drinking Book. NY: Derrydale, 1939. One of 1250. 2 vols. Uncut. VG in slipcase (broken). *Argosy.* $150/£97

BAKER, DENYS VAL. The Face in the Mirror. Arkham House, 1971. 1st ed. Fine in dj. *Madle.* $35/£23

BAKER, E.C. STUART. Mishi the Man-Eater. London: Witherby, 1928. Red cl. VG + . *Bowman.* $45/£29

BAKER, GEORGE PIERCE. Charles Dickens and Maria Beadnell; Private Correspondence. Boston: Bibliophile Soc, 1908. 1st ed. One of 493. Uncut. Parchment-backed bds, gilt. Nice (eps foxed; sl aging). *Macdonnell.* $100/£65

BAKER, HENRY. The Microscope Made Easy. London, 1743. 2nd ed. 14 fldg plts. Contemp calf (cvrs detached). Contents VG. *Petersfield.* $140/£90

BAKER, L.C. The United States Secret Service in the Late War. Chicago, 1894. 398pp. 1902 Reprint. Pict cl. VG +. *Pratt.* $40/£26

BAKER, MARCUS. Geographic Dictionary of Alaska. Washington: GPO, 1906. 2nd ed. Antique black cl (newly rebound). VG (ex-lib). *Perier.* $85/£55

BAKER, NATHAN ADDISON. Nathan Addison Baker (1843-1934).... Nolie Mumey (ed). Denver, CO: Old West Pub Co, 1965. Ltd ed to 500 numbered, signed by Mumey. Frontis port; 4 fldg facs rear pocket. Tan linen; gilt leather spine, cvr labels. Good. *Karmiole.* $85/£55

BAKER, NICHOLSON. The Mezzanine. NY: Weidenfield & Nicholson, 1988. 1st ed, 1st bk. Fine in Fine dj. *Revere.* $75/£48

BAKER, NICHOLSON. Room Temperature. NY: Grove Weidenfeld, (1990). 1st ed. Fine in dj. *Between The Covers.* $45/£29

BAKER, NICHOLSON. Room Temperature. NY: Grove Weidenfeld, 1990. 1st ed. Signed. Fine in Fine dj. *Beasley.* $100/£65

BAKER, NICHOLSON. Room Temperature. Granta Books, 1990. 1st Eng ed. Rev slip inserted. Fine in dj. *Ulysses.* $70/£45

BAKER, NICHOLSON. Room Temperature. Granta, 1990. 1st UK ed. Fine in dj. *Lewton.* $23/£15

BAKER, NICHOLSON. Room Temperature. NY: Grove Weidenfeld, 1990. 1st US ed. VF in VF dj. *Pettler.* $30/£19

BAKER, NICHOLSON. Room Temperature. Grove Weidenfeld, 1990. 1st US ed. Fine in dj. *Williams.* $31/£20

BAKER, NICHOLSON. U and I. London: Granta, 1991. 1st UK ed. Fine in dj. *Moorhouse.* $12/£8

BAKER, NICHOLSON. Vox. NY: Random House, (1992). 1st ed, 1st ptg. Fine in Fine dj (sm rubbed spot fr panel). *Between The Covers.* $85/£55

BAKER, NICHOLSON. Vox. NY: Random House, 1992. 1st ed. Inscribed. Fine in NF dj. *Beasley.* $75/£48

BAKER, OLIVER. Black Jacks and Leather Bottells. London, n.d. c.(1921). #236 of signed, ltd ed. 190,(viii)pp (prelims lt browned). 24 plts, incl 3 color (plt 17 sm marginal tear). Gilt lettering, shield to upper bd. (Ex-libris.) *Edwards.* $194/£125

BAKER, P.J. Disarmament and the Coolidge Conference. Hogarth Press, 1927. 1st ed. VG in wrappers. *Words Etc.* $62/£40

BAKER, P.J. Disarmament. Hogarth Press, 1926. 1st Eng ed. Lt doodling fep, o/w VG. *Edrich.* $54/£35

BAKER, PEARL. The Wild Bunch at Robbers Roost. NY, (1965). 1st ed. Fine in dj (wear). *Pratt.* $30/£19

BAKER, R.T. Building and Ornamental Stones of Australia. (New South Wales: Dept of Public Instruction), 1915. 1st ed. Frontis, 1 plt. VG. *Bookpress.* $125/£81

BAKER, RUSSELL. So This Is Depravity. NY: Congdon & Lattes, (1980). 1st ed. One of 500 numbered, signed. Fine in slipcase. *Hermitage.* $75/£48

BAKER, S. JOSEPHINE. The Division of Child Hygiene of the Department of Health of the City of New York. NY, 1912. 1st ed. (Ex-lib.) Wrappers. *Fye.* $100/£65

BAKER, SAMUEL W. The Albert N'Yanza Great Basin of the Nile.... London: Macmillan, 1867. 2 vols. xxx,371; xii,372pp, lg fldg map, 35 maps; uncut. Good in orig grn cl (vol 1 sides badly faded by damp). *Cox.* $116/£75

BAKER, SAMUEL W. The Albert N'Yanza, Great Basin of the Nile, and Explorations of the Nile Sources. London: Macmillan, 1867. 1st ed. 2 vols. 8vo. xxx,371; x,(ii),372pp. 2 maps (1 fldg); port frontis, 13 engr plts. Grn cl, gilt. (Mks, ink stamps, bkpls; sl rubbed; lower cvr vol 1 damp spotted.) *Morrell.* $202/£130

BAKER, SAMUEL W. Ismailia. NY, 1875. 1st Amer ed. 542pp. Dec cvr (mottled; top, bottom spine worn; lt foxing). *Heinoldt.* $60/£39

BAKER, SAMUEL W. The Nile Tributaries of Abyssinia.... Phila, 1868. 4th ed. 413pp. (Ink, stamped names; inner hinges broken; cvrs worn.) *King.* $75/£48

BAKER, SAMUEL W. The Rifle and Hound in Ceylon. Phila: Lippincott, 1875. Frontis, 305pp + ads. Grn pict cl, gilt dec spine. VG (stamps to eps). *Bowman.* $45/£29

BAKER, SAMUEL W. The Rifle and the Hound in Ceylon. London: Longmans, Green, 1884. New ed. xx,353pp; 6 plts. Contemp full calf gilt (nicely rebacked to match). Raised band, spine label. VG. *Hollett.* $186/£120

BAKER, SAMUEL W. Wild Beasts and Their Ways. London, 1898. xiv,455pp + (iv)pub's ads. Gilt-illus cl (spotted; spine faded; rubbed; feps lt browned; hinges tender). *Edwards.* $70/£45

BAKER, W.S. Bibliotheca Washingtoniana: A Descriptive List of the Biographies and Biographical Sketches of George Washington. Phila: R.M. Lindsay, 1889. One of 400. 179pp. Unopened. Rebacked. VG. *Moss.* $93/£60

BAKER, WILLIAM AVERY. Colonial Vessels. Barre Pub, 1962. 1st ed. 3 sheets of plans laid in. *Lefkowicz.* $45/£29

BAKER, Z. The Cottage Builder's Manual. Worcester: Z. Baker, 1856. 1st ed. Frontis, (iv),9-176pp (complete), 2pp. Pub's blindstamped cl (spine, tips repaired; text foxed; cvrs sl rubbed). *Bookpress.* $350/£226

BALABAN, JOHN. After Our War. Pittsburgh: Univ of Pittsburgh, (1974). 1st ed. Award material laid in. Fine in dj. *Reese.* $30/£19

BALABAN, JOHN. Vietnam Poems. (Oxford): Carcanet Press, (1970). 1st ed, 1st bk. One of 600. Fine in ptd wrappers. *Heller.* $65/£42

BALANCHINE, GEORGE. Choreography...A Catalogue of Works. Harvey Simmonds (ed). NY: Eakins Press Foundation, 1983. 1st ed, 1/2000 ptd by Stamperia Valdonega. Prospectus. VG in mylar wrapper, bd slipcase. *Argosy.* $100/£65

BALCH, E.S. Antarctica. Phila: Press of Allen Lane & Scott, 1902. 1st ed. 3 fldg maps. Good + (ex-lib, sl rubbed). *Walcot.* $155/£100

BALDASS, L. Jan van Eyck. Phaidon, 1952. 170 plts (8 color). Internally Good in dj (sl frayed). *Ars Artis.* $116/£75

BALDICK, ROBERT. The Duel: A History of Duelling. NY: Clarkson N. Potter, 1965. 1st ed. Illus cl. VG in dj (chipped; offset). *Cahan.* $25/£16

BALDWIN, ALICE BLACKWOOD. An Army Wife on the Frontier. Salt Lake City, (1975). 1st ed, ltd to 1200. Fine in Fine dj. *Pratt*. $45/£29

BALDWIN, DOROTHY ARNO. The May Party Mystery and Other Stories. Nashville, TN: Cokesbury Press, (1926). Folio, 40 leaves. 4 color plts by Imogene Watson Foster; pict eps. Orange cl, pict paper label. NF in Good pict dj (sm edgetears; sm piece out of spine). *Blue Mountain*. $95/£61

BALDWIN, HANSON W. Sea Fights and Shipwrecks: True Tales of the Seven Seas. NY: Hanover House, 1955. 1st ed. Fine in dj (sl edgeworn). *Sadlon*. $15/£10

BALDWIN, J.H. The Large and Small Game of Bengal and the North-Western Provinces of India. London, 1877. 2nd ed. xxiv,380pp. (Ex-lib.) *Wheldon & Wesley*. $85/£55

BALDWIN, JAMES and MARGARET MEAD. A Rap on Race. Phila: Lippincott, (1971). 1st ed. VG in dj. *Petrilla*. $25/£16

BALDWIN, JAMES. Another Country. NY, 1962. 1st Amer ed. Fine (sl rubbed) in dj (spine sl sunned, sm tear, sl rubbed, price-clipped). *Polyanthos*. $125/£81

BALDWIN, JAMES. The Evidence of Things Not Seen. NY: Holt et al, (1985). 1st ed. Signed. Fine in dj. *Godot*. $135/£87

BALDWIN, JAMES. The Fire Next Time. NY: Dial, 1963. 1st ed. Sm edgetear fep, else Fine in dj. *Godot*. $45/£29

BALDWIN, JAMES. Giovanni's Room. London: Michael Joseph, (1957). 1st Eng ed. VG in dj (soiled, short tears, else VG). *Godot*. $65/£42

BALDWIN, JAMES. Giovanni's Room. NY, 1956. 1st Amer ed. Fine (sm name label; sl crease). *Polyanthos*. $40/£26

BALDWIN, JAMES. Go Tell It on the Mountain. London: Joseph, 1954. 1st ed. NF in dj. *Rees*. $116/£75

BALDWIN, JAMES. Going to Meet the Man. NY: Dial Press, 1965. 1st ed. Fine in NF dj. *Revere*. $45/£29

BALDWIN, JAMES. Going to Meet the Man. NY: Dial, 1965. 1st ed. NF in dj (spine lt worn, short creased tear, else NF). *Godot*. $50/£32

BALDWIN, JAMES. If Beale Street Could Talk. London: Michael Joseph, (1974). 1st UK ed. Fine in NF dj. *Robbins*. $35/£23

BALDWIN, JAMES. If Beale Street Could Talk. London: Joseph, 1974. 1st Eng ed. Fine in dj. *Limestone*. $45/£29

BALDWIN, JAMES. Little Man, Little Man, a Story of Childhood. (London): Michael Joseph, (1976). 1st ed (Eng ed precedes). Fine in dj. *Heller*. $75/£48

BALDWIN, JAMES. Little Man, Little Man. NY: Dial Press, 1976. 1st ed. NF. *Pettler*. $40/£26

BALDWIN, JAMES. Nobody Knows My Name. NY, 1961. 1st Amer ed. Fine (sl rubbed) in dj (sl rubbed). *Polyanthos*. $75/£48

BALDWIN, JAMES. One Day, When I Was Lost. London: Michael Joseph, (1972). 1st ed. Fine in Fine dj (price-clipped). *Godot*. $85/£55

BALDWIN, THOMAS. Kick Off. Goldsmith, 1932. 1st ed. Fine in dj (sl frayed). *Madle*. $20/£13

BALDWIN, THOMAS. Narrative of the Massacre, by the Savages.... NY, 1835. 24pp; fldg woodcut. 1/2 morocco, bds. Good. Howes B 63. *Ginsberg*. $425/£274

BALFOUR, GRAHAM. The Life of Robert Louis Stevenson. London: Methuen, 1901. 1st ed. 2 vols. 3/4 morocco, marbled bds; gilt. (Lt foxing vol II; sl foxing vol I fore-edge.) *Sadlon*. $60/£39

BALINT, ALICE. The Early Years of Life. NY: Basic Books, (1954). 1st Amer ed, 1st ptg. Gray cl. VG in dj (chipped). *Gach*. $28/£18

BALL, EVE. Ma'am Jones of the Pecos. Tucson, 1969. 1st ed. Fine (ink info on feps) in dj. *Baade*. $65/£42

BALL, J. William Caslon, Master of Letters. Roundwood Press, 1973. Color frontis, 64 plts. Fine in dj. *Moss*. $47/£30

BALL, JOHN. The Eyes of Buddha. Boston: Little, 1976. 1st ed. Signed, inscribed. *Silver Door*. $37/£24

BALL, JOHN. In the Heat of the Night. NY: Harper & Row, (1965). 1st Amer ed. Inscribed. Fine (lt erasure) in dj. *Between The Covers*. $500/£323

BALL, KATHERINE M. Decorative Motives of Oriental Art. London/NY: John Lane/Dodd, Mead, (1927). 1st ed. Teg. Black cl. VG +. *House*. $200/£129

Ballads of Robin Hood. CUP, 1977. #494/1600 signed by David Gentleman (illus). Fine in slipcase (sl worn). *Hermitage*. $75/£48

BALLANCE, C. The History of Peoria, Illinois. Peoria: Ptd by N.C. Nason, 1870. viii,271pp. Nice (spine lt faded; ends frayed). Howes B 72. *Bohling*. $300/£194

BALLANCE, CHARLES. Some Points in the Surgery of the Brain and Its Membranes. London, 1907. 1st ed. Good. *Fye*. $500/£323

BALLANTYNE, R.M. The Young Trawler. London: Nisbet, 1884. 1st UK ed. 5 plts. Dec cl. VG (hinges partly cracked; sl edge wear). *Agvent*. $50/£32

BALLARD, ADOLPHUS. The Domesday Inquest. London: Methuen, 1923. 2nd ed. 27 plts. VG. *Hollett*. $85/£55

BALLARD, GEORGE. Memoirs of British Ladies. London: T. Evans, 1775. 3rd ed, 1st bk. 320pp + index. Contemp calf. VG. *Second Life*. $350/£226

BALLARD, H.C. Poems. Chicago: Church, 1870. 1st ed. 164pp. *Ginsberg*. $150/£97

BALLARD, J.G. The Atrocity Exhibition. London: Cape, 1970. 1st UK ed. Faded red lettering on spine, o/w Fine in dj. *Lewton*. $85/£55

BALLARD, J.G. Chronopolis and Other Stories. Putnam, 1971. 1st ed. Fine in dj. *Fine Books*. $95/£61

BALLARD, J.G. Concrete Island. NY: FSG, 1974. 1st ed. VF in dj. *Else Fine*. $50/£32

BALLARD, J.G. Concrete Island. London: Cape, 1974. 1st UK ed. Signed. Fine in dj. *Lewton*. $76/£49

BALLARD, J.G. Crash. Cape, 1973. 1st UK ed. Signed. Edge bds sl faded, o/w NF in Fine dj (price-clipped). *Sclanders*. $124/£80

BALLARD, J.G. The Crystal World. NY: FSG, (1966). 1st Amer ed. VG (sm sticker shadow fep; edges bds sl faded) in VG dj (tears; rubbed). *Between The Covers*. $100/£65

BALLARD, J.G. The Drowned World and the Wind from Nowhere. Doubleday, 1965. 1st ed. Fine in dj (spine sl frayed). *Madle*. $135/£87

BALLARD, J.G. Empire of the Sun. London: Gollancz, 1984. 1st issue, w/only 2 blurbs (by Angela Carter and Graham Greene) on rear of dj. Fine in dj. *Williams*. $54/£35

BALLARD, J.G. Empire of the Sun. Gollancz, 1984. 1st UK ed. Signed. Mint in Mint dj (1st state w/2 quotes on back panel). *Martin*. $37/£24

BALLARD, J.G. Hello America. London: Cape, 1981. 1st ed. Fine in dj. *Virgo*. $39/£25

BALLARD, J.G. Hello America. Cape, 1981. 1st UK ed. Signed. Fine in dj. *Lewton*. $36/£23

BALLARD, J.G. High Rise. NY: HRW, 1977. 1st ed. VF in dj (minor rubs at corners). *Else Fine*. $35/£23

BALLARD, J.G. High-Rise. NY: Holt, 1977. 1st ed. Inscribed. Fine in dj (lt used) *Beasley*. $50/£32

BALLARD, J.G. Myths of the Near Future. London: Cape, 1982. 1st UK ed. Fine in dj. *Lewton*. $22/£14

BALLARD, J.G. Running Wild. London et al: Hutchinson, 1988. 1st Eng ed. VF in dj. *Limestone*. $45/£29

BALLARD, J.G. The Unlimited Dream Company. London: Cape, 1979. 1st UK ed. Fine in dj. *Lewton*. $26/£17

BALLARD, J.G. The Unlimited Dream Company. Cape, 1979. 1st UK ed. Signed. Fine in dj. *Lewton*. $39/£25

BALLENTINE, GEORGE. Autobiography of an English Soldier in the United States Army. William H. Goetzmann (ed). Chicago: Lakeside Classic, 1986. Pict cl. Fine. *Pratt*. $35/£23

BALLIET, WHITNEY. New York Notes. Boston: Houghton Mifflin, 1976. 1st ed. NF in NF dj (sm tear, wrinkling). *Aka*. $35/£23

BALLIET, WHITNEY. Such Sweet Thunder. Indianapolis: Bobbs-Merrill, (1966). 1st ed. VG + in dj (sl edgeworn, scuffed). *Aka*. $40/£26

BALLOU, MATURIN M. Due West. Boston/NY: Houghton Mifflin (Riverside), 1888. 6th ed. xii,387,8pp. Sl rubbed, o/w VG. *Worldwide*. $24/£15

BALLOU, MATURIN M. The New Eldorado. Boston, 1889. 1st ed. *Heinoldt*. $25/£16

BALLOU, MATURIN M. The New Eldorado. Boston: Houghton Mifflin, 1889. 1st ed. xi,352pp + 8pp ads. Brn pict cl, gilt lettering. VG. *Oregon*. $85/£55

BALLOU, ROBERT. Early Klickitat Valley Days. Goldendale, WA: (Irving Bath, 1938). 1st ed. Incl separately ptd index (1972). Fine. *Perier*. $100/£65

BALNEAVES, E. Elephant Valley. Chicago: R.M., 1963. 1st ed. Dbl-pg map. NF in Fine dj. *Mikesh*. $37/£24

BALSTON, THOMAS. James Whatman: Father and Son. London: Methuen, 1957. 1st ed. Fine in dj (sl chipped). *Oak Knoll*. $95/£61

BALSTON, THOMAS. The Life of Jonathan Martin.... London: Macmillan, 1945. 1st ed. 16 plts. Gilt cl. VG in dj (lt spotted). *Hollett*. $39/£25

BALSTON, THOMAS. Sitwelliana 1915-1927. London: Duckworth, 1928. 1st ed. Inscribed. 3 ports. Good (lt spotting) in dec bds, paper label. Bkpl of Lord Kenyon. *Cox*. $54/£35

BALSTON, THOMAS. William Balston, Paper Maker, 1759-1849. London: Methuen, 1954. 1st ed. (Sl cocked.) *Oak Knoll*. $125/£81

BALTHUS (BALTHASAR KLOSSOWSKI DE ROLA). Mitsou. NY: Abrams/MMA, 1984. 60pp. Fine in dj. *Cattermole*. $50/£32

BANCROFT, CAROLINE. Gulch of Gold. Boulder, (1969). 3rd ptg. Fldg view. Fine in Good dj. *Artis*. $25/£16

BANCROFT, FREDERIC and COBB PILCHER (eds). Surgical Treatment of the Nervous System. Phila, 1946. 1st ed. Good. *Fye*. $150/£97

BANCROFT, FREDERIC and HENRY MARBLE (eds). Surgical Treatment of the Motor-Skeletal System. Part I. Phila, 1951. 2nd ed. Good. *Fye*. $50/£32

BANCROFT, GEORGE. The History of the Colonization of the United States. Boston: Little, Brown, 1870. 23rd ed. 9 vols. 1/2 brn morocco, ribbed gilt dec spines. *D & D*. $590/£381

BANCROFT, HUBERT HOWE. Annals of the California Gold Era. NY: Bancroft Co, n.d. Cl w/paper spine label (fr inner hinge weak; few gatherings sl loose). *Dawson*. $100/£65

BANCROFT, HUBERT HOWE. Essays and Miscellany. From the Works of H.H. Bancroft. SF: History Co, 1890. vi,764 pp; all edges marbled. Orig leather, black morocco labels, gilt (hinges cracked; deep chip, lesser one to spine; eps edges browned). Contents Fine. *Connolly*. $45/£29

BANCROFT, HUBERT HOWE. History of Arizona and New Mexico, 1530-1888. SF, 1889. xxxviii,829pp; fldg map. 3/4 brn leather, marbled bds (fr bd sl bowed, rear hinge split; wear). Howes B 91. *Bohling*. $90/£58

BANCROFT, HUBERT HOWE. History of Mexico— 1516-1887. SF: A.L. Bancroft, 1883-88. 1st ed. 6 vols (9-14 inclusive). Full leather, marbled edges. Overall Good + set (shelfworn, stains; hinges weak). Howes B 91. *Parmer*. $200/£129

BANCROFT, HUBERT HOWE. History of Oregon Vol 1: 1834-1838. Vol 2: 1848-1888. Vols XXIX & XXX of Works, 1886-1888. 1st ed. xxxix,789; xv,808pp, fldg map. Full calf (fr hinges cracked, glued; corners worn). Internally VG. *Oregon*. $70/£45

BANCROFT, HUBERT HOWE. History of the North Mexican States and Texas. Vols XV & XVI of Works, 1884/1889. 1st ed. xlviii,751; xvi,814pp. Full calf, black morocco spine labels. Internally VG (hinges cracked, glued; corners worn). Howes B 91. *Oregon*. $100/£65

BANCROFT, HUBERT HOWE. History of the Northwest Coast 1543-1846. From the Works of H.H. Bancroft. SF: History Co, 1884/1886. 2 vols. 1,555pp, fldg map; all edges marbled. Orig leather, black morocco labels, gilt (hinges cracked 1st vol, fr bd detached but present; spine end wear both vols; eps browned). Contents Fine. Howes B91. *Connolly*. $75/£48

BANCROFT, HUBERT HOWE. History of Utah: 1540-1886. SF, 1889. 1st ed. 808pp. Full leather (extrems worn; fr hinge severely cracked but attached; rear hinge cracked). Internally clean. *Benchmark*. $75/£48

BANCROFT, HUBERT HOWE. History of Washington, Idaho, and Montana 1845-1889. From the Works of H.H. Bancroft. SF: History Co, 1890. xxvi,836pp; all edges marbled. Orig leather, black morocco labels, gilt (hinges cracked; chipping, not affecting labels). Contents Fine. Howes B91. *Connolly*. $45/£29

BANCROFT, HUBERT HOWE. Literary Industries. From the Works of H.H. Bancroft. SF: History Co., 1890. 1st ed. Engr frontis port, tissue, viii,808pp; all edges marbled. Speckled calf, morocco labels. Hinges cracking, weak; else VG. Howes 91. *Connolly*. $65/£42

BANCROFT, LAURA. Prince Mud-Turtle. Chicago: Reilly & Britton, (1906). 1st ed. 12mo. 14 full-pg color plts + color tp by Maginel Wright Enright. Dec tan cl (rubbed; marginal tears within). *Reisler*. $335/£216

BANDELIER, A.F. An Outline of the Documentary History of the Zuni Tribe. Boston: Houghton Mifflin, 1892. 1st ed. VG (rebound). *Parker.* $195/£126

BANDELIER, ADOLF. Delight Makers. NY: Dodd Mead, 1890. 1st ed. Newspaper article pasted on ep. Good (worn; name). *Parker.* $150/£97

BANDELIER, ADOLPH. Southwestern Journals of Adolph F. Bandelier 1880-1882. Univ of NM, (1966). 1st ed. Frontis; 21pp photos; journal facs. VF in VF dj. *Oregon.* $60/£39

BANDELIER, ADOLPHE. The Gilded Man. NY: D. Appleton, 1893. 1st ed. VG. *Parker.* $175/£113

BANDI, HANS-GEORG. Eskimo Prehistory. Univ of AK, (1969). 1st US ed. VG + in VG- dj. *Blue Dragon.* $25/£16

BANDLE, EUGENE. Frontier Life in the Army, 1854-1861. Glendale: Clark, 1932. 10 plts, fldg map. Red cl. VG. *Schoyer.* $125/£81

BANDLER, SAMUEL. The Expectant Mother. Phila, 1921. Good. *Fye.* $20/£13

BANDLER, SAMUEL. Uterine and Tubal Gestation. NY, 1903. 1st ed. Good. *Fye.* $60/£39

BANGS, E. GEOFFREY. Portals West. (SF): CA Hist Soc, (1960). Ltd to 1000 numbered. 36 photo plts. Beige gilt-stamped cl. Fine in ptd dj. *Karmiole.* $65/£42

BANGS, JOHN KENDRICK and P. NEWELL. The Enchanted Typewriter. Harpers, 1899. 1st ed. Spine sunned, else VG + . *Fine Books.* $20/£13

BANGS, JOHN KENDRICK. The Bicyclers and Three Other Farces. Harpers, 1896. 1st ed. VG + . *Aronovitz.* $24/£15

BANGS, JOHN KENDRICK. The Bicyclers and Three Other Farces. NY: Harper, 1896. 1st ed. Signed presentation. Dec blue cl. VG. BAL 728. *Antic Hay.* $175/£113

BANGS, JOHN KENDRICK. Songs of Cheer. Boston: Sherman French & Co., 1910. 1st ed. Inscribed, dated. 1/2 cl. Fine in Fine dj. BAL 783. *Chapel Hill.* $150/£97

BANGS, JOHN KENDRICK. The Water Ghost and Others. NY: Harper, 1894. 1st ed. Frontis; 296pp; 40 plts. Grn cl, gilt/silver dec. Ink presentation, o/w VG. *Hermitage.* $75/£48

BANKART, GEORGE P. The Art of the Plasterer. London: B.T. Batsford, n.d. (c. 1909). 2nd ed. Gray cl. VG (eps soiled; marginal smudges). *House.* $150/£97

BANKOFF, GEORGE. Plastic Repair of Genito-Urinary Defects. NY, 1956. 1st ed. Good in dj. *Fye.* $100/£65

BANKS, CHARLES EDWARD. The History of Martha's Vineyard, Dukes County, Massachusetts. Boston, 1911; Boston, 1911; Edgartown, 1925. 1st ed. 3 vols. Howes B 98. *Argosy.* $400/£258

BANKS, EDGAR JAMES. Bismya or the Lost City of Adab. NY/London: Putnam's, 1912. Map; teg. Dk blue cl, gilt (sl spotted, rubbed). *Schoyer.* $85/£55

BANKS, ELEANOR. Wandersong. Caldwell: Caxton, 1950. 1st ed. NF in VG + dj (sl losses spine top). *Harrington.* $45/£29

BANKS, ERNIE and JIM ENRIGHT. Mr. Cub. Follet, 1971. 1st ed. Fine in VG dj. *Plapinger.* $40/£26

BANKS, IAIN M. Consider Phlebas. Macmillan, 1987. One of 176 numbered, signed. Fine in dj, slipcase. *Rees.* $194/£125

BANKS, IAIN M. The Player of Games. Macmillan, 1988. One of 201 specially bound, numbered, signed. Fine in slipcase. *Rees.* $194/£125

BANKS, IAIN M. Walking on Glass. London: Macmillan, 1985. 1st ed. Fine in dj. *Rees.* $39/£25

BANKS, IAIN M. Walking on Glass. Macmillan, 1985. 1st UK ed. Fine in dj. *Lewton.* $22/£14

BANKS, IAIN M. The Wasp Factory. London: Macmillan, 1984. 1st ed, 1st bk. Signed. Fine in dj. *Rees.* $93/£60

BANKS, IAIN M. The Wasp Factory. London: Macmillan, 1984. 1st UK ed. Fine in dj. *Lewton.* $73/£47

BANKS, JOSEPH. Joseph Banks in Newfoundland and Labrador. A.M. Lysaght (ed). London, 1971. Frontis; 8 color maps; 12 color plts. *Wheldon & Wesley.* $109/£70

BANKS, MARY ROSS. Bright Days in the Old Plantation. Boston: Lee & Shepard, 1891 (c. 1882). 1st ed. Pict cl. NF. *Pharos.* $30/£19

BANKS, MICHAEL. Commando Climber. London: Dent, 1955. 1st ed. Color frontis port. VG in dj (sl worn). *Hollett.* $31/£20

BANKS, MICHAEL. Rakaposhi. London: Secker & Warburg, 1959. 1st ed. Color frontis, 35 plts. VG in dj (price-clipped). *Hollett.* $39/£25

BANKSON, RUSSELL A. The Klondike Nugget. Caldwell, ID: Caxton, 1935. VG. *High Latitude.* $65/£42

BANNERMAN, DAVID ARMITAGE. The Birds of the British Isles. London, 1953-63. 12 vols. 386 color, 2 plain plts by G.E. Lodge. Good (lacks djs). *Henly.* $442/£285

BANNERMAN, DAVID ARMITAGE. The Birds of Tropical West Africa. Vol 5 (only). London, 1939. 11 color plts, dbl-pg map, fldg map. (Feps lt foxed, cl sl stained.) Dj (ragged). *Edwards.* $78/£50

BANNERMAN, DAVID ARMITAGE. The Birds of West and Equatorial Africa. Edinburgh, 1953. 2 vols. 30 color plts, 24 plts. Djs (ragged, tape-repaired, some loss). *Edwards.* $140/£90

BANNERMAN, HELEN. Little Black Mingo. London: Nisbet, c. 1941. Lg 24mo. Pict cl (wear). Good+ in Good+ dj (sm tears). *Book Adoption.* $60/£39

BANNERMAN, HELEN. Little Black Sambo. NY: Golden/Western, (1976). 2nd ptg. Lg 4to. Bonnie & Bill Rutherford (illus). Glazed pict paper-cvrd bds (sl worn). VG + . *Book Adoption.* $75/£48

BANNERMAN, HELEN. Little Black Sambo. NY: Samuel Gabriel, 1948. 4to. Mary LaFetra Russell (illus). VG in pict cardboard wraps (spine sl worn). *Book Adoption.* $50/£32

BANNERMAN, HELEN. Little Black Sambo. NY: Platt & Munk, 1955. Sm 8vo. Eulalie (illus). Orange pict paper-cvrd bds. NF in VG + dj (sm tears). *Book Adoption.* $75/£48

BANNERMAN, HELEN. Little Black Sambo. NY: Platt & Munk, 1972. Eulalie (illus). VF. *Bond.* $25/£16

BANNERMAN, HELEN. Little Black Sambo. NY: Platt & Munk, 1972. Sm 8vo. Eulalie (illus). White pict paper-cvrd bds. NF. *Book Adoption.* $75/£48

BANNERMAN, HELEN. Little Black Sambo/Red Hen/Peter Rabbit. Akron: Saalfield, 1942. Ethel Hays (illus). Linenette, spiral bound. VG (corners bumped). *Davidson.* $185/£119

BANNERMAN, HELEN. Little White Squibba. London: C&W, 1966. 1st ed. Lg 24mo. Pict paper-cvrd bds (sl rubbed). Fine in NF dj (sl rubbed). *Book Adoption.* $95/£61

BANNERMAN, HELEN. The Story of Little Black Mingo. London: James Nisbet, (1901). 1st ed. 16mo. 144pp. White cl, red lettering, line dwg set in emb frame (presentation binding); red/black spine lettering (cvr worn). *Reisler*. $750/£484

BANNERMAN, HELEN. The Story of Little Black Mingo. London: James Nisbet, (1902). Red cl. VG (ink name tp, fr bd corner discolored) in VG dj. *Davidson*. $225/£145

BANNERMAN, HELEN. The Story of Little Black Mingo. London: Nisbet, (ca 1935). 12mo. Rose-pink cl, black lettering, dec devices. Good in pict dj (sm spots). *Reisler*. $85/£55

BANNERMAN, HELEN. The Story of Little Black Quasha. London: James Nisbet, (1908). Yellow cl. VG (ink name tp) in VG dj. *Davidson*. $225/£145

BANNERMAN, HELEN. The Story of Little Black Sambo. Chicago: M.A. Donohue, (1919). Peter Rabbit Series. Sm 8vo. Red cl bds, pict label. Good (2 articles glued in). *Davidson*. $200/£129

BANNERMAN, HELEN. The Story of Little Black Sambo. London: C&W, 1941. 12mo, 113pp. White eps w/vignettes inside fr, rear cvrs. Helen Bannerman (illus). Blind-stamped blue bds w/pict onlay. NF in dj (lt chipped). *Davidson*. $250/£161

BANNERMAN, HELEN. The Story of Little Black Sambo. London: Grant Richards, Nov 1899. 2nd ed. 32mo. Pict cl (wear; rear hinge torn; possibly recased in orig binding). VG (pencil inscrip). *Book Adoption*. $1,400/£903

BANNERMAN, HELEN. The Story of Little Kettle-Head. NY: Frederick A. Stokes, 1904. 1st Amer ed. 16mo. 144pp. Cl-backed illus bds (edgewear; rubbed). Lt spoting, o/w Internally Fine. *Reisler*. $400/£258

BANNERMAN, HELEN. The Story of Sambo and the Twins. NY: F.A. Stokes, 1936. 1st ed. Lg 24mo. Pict cl (back cvr soiled). VG+ (pp31-32, 41-42 repaired) in partial dj. *Book Adoption*. $250/£161

BANNING, MARGARET CULKIN. Women for Defense. NY: Duell, Sloan & Pearce, (1942). 1st ed. Gray cl. VG. Dj (worn). *Petrilla*. $25/£16

BANNING, WILLIAM and GEORGE HUGH BANNING. Six Horses. NY: Century, (1930). 2nd ptg. VG in dj. *Schoyer*. $30/£19

BANNISTER, MANLY. Conquest of Earth. Avalon, 1957. 1st ed. Fine in dj. *Madle*. $30/£19

BANTA, POLLY. Goat Gruff. An Action Book. Cincinnati: Artcraft, n.d. (195?). 15x20 cm. 5 3D spring-ups. Pict bds (spine worn). Internally VG. *Book Finders*. $45/£29

BANTA, R.E. Indiana Authors and Their Books 1816-1916. Crawfordsville, IN: Wabash College, 1949. Fine. *Sadlon*. $60/£39

BANTA, R.E. The Ohio. NY, (1949). 1st ed. Spine sl soiled, else VG in dj (discolored, lt torn, worn). *King*. $25/£16

BANTA, WILLIAM and J.W. CALDWELL, JR. Twenty-Seven Years on the Texas Frontier. Council Hill, OK, (1933). Frontis port. Fine in ptd wrappers. *Bohling*. $75/£48

BANVILLE, JOHN. Doctor Copernicus. Secker & Warburg, 1976. 1st ed. NF in dj. *Rees*. $70/£45

BANVILLE, JOHN. Ghosts. London: Secker & Warburg, 1993. 1st ed. Fine in dj. *Rees*. $31/£20

BANVILLE, JOHN. Kepler. Secker, 1981. 1st UK ed. Fine in dj ('Staff Library' in ink on flyleaf). *Williams*. $93/£60

BANVILLE, JOHN. Mefisto. London: Secker & Warburg, 1986. 1st ed. Signed. Fine in dj. *Rees*. $39/£25

BANVILLE, JOHN. Nightspawn. NY: Norton, 1971. 1st US ed. Fine (last pg soiled) in VG dj. *Beasley*. $45/£29

BARAKA, AMIRI. A Black Value System. NY: Jihad, 1970. 1st ed. NF in stapled wraps. *Lame Duck*. $85/£55

BARAKA, AMIRI. Reggae or Not! NY: Contact II Publications, 1981. 1st ed. NF in ptd wraps. *Revere*. $35/£23

BARAKA, AMIRI. The Sidney Poet Heretical. NY: I. Reed Books, 1979. 1st ed. Fine in ptd glossy wraps. *Revere*. $35/£23

BARBAULD, A.L. (Pseud of Anna Laetitia Aikin). Selections from Hymns in Prose. Phila: Chapman, 1854. 12mo. iv,72pp. Full-pg wood engr frontis, 10 VF full-pg engrs. Grn tooled cl on bds, gilt title upper cvr. VG (dated ink inscrip fep, stamped # lower ep, lt discoloration eps). *Hobbyhorse*. $100/£65

BARBAULD, MRS. (Pseud of Anna Laetitia Aikin.) Hymns for Children in Prose. New Haven: S. Babcock, 1840. 1 3/4 x 2 7/8 inches. 8pp, 3 full-pg engrs, engr tp. Paper wrappers, wood engr illus (cvr resewn; spine worn; rear cvr marginal tear, mks). *Reisler*. $150/£97

BARBAULD, MRS. (Pseud of Anna Laetitia Aikin.) Lessons for Children. London: Longman, 1867. New ed. 12mo. iv,176pp. Full-pg copper engr frontis; engr vignette tp. Grn tooled cl on bds, gilt title spine, speckled edges. NF (lib ink stamp; #s; dry seal margin 3 leaves; repaired lower ep). *Hobbyhorse*. $90/£58

BARBE, MURIEL CULP. A Union Forever. Glendale, CA: Barbe Assoc, 1949. 1st ed. Fine in dj (lt soiled). *Glenn*. $55/£35

BARBEAU, MARIUS. Alaska Beckons. Caldwell: Caxton, 1947. 1st ed. VG in VG dj. *Perier*. $60/£39

BARBEAU, MARIUS. The Downfall of Temlaham. Toronto: Macmillan, 1928. 1st ed. VG (name) in Poor (torn) dj. *Perier*. $97/£63

BARBER, A.W. (comp). The Benevolent Raid of General Lew Wallace. Washington: R. Beresford, 1914. 1st ed. Staple rust, o/w VG in wraps. *Oregon*. $125/£81

BARBER, B. AQUILA. The Art of Frank O. Salisbury. Leigh-on-Sea, 1936. #13/250. Signed by Salisbury. Color frontis port, 27 color plts. (Eps sl spotted.) Teg, rest uncut. Full vellum, gilt. *Edwards*. $155/£100

BARBER, RED. The Broadcasters. Dial, 1970. 1st ed. Fine in VG dj. *Plapinger*. $30/£19

BARBOUR, RALPH HENRY and LAMAR SARRA. How to Play Better Baseball. Appleton-Century, 1935. 1st ed. VG. *Plapinger*. $35/£23

BARBOUR, RALPH HENRY. Weatherby's Inning. Appleton, 1903. 1st ed. Pict cl. VG-. *Fine Books*. $65/£42

BARBUSSE, HENRI. Chains. Steppen Haden Guest (trans). NY: International Publishers, 1925. 1st ed in English. 2 vols. VG. *Argosy*. $50/£32

BARCLAY, J. An Inquiry into the Opinions, Ancient and Modern, Concerning Life and Organization. Edinburgh, 1822. xvi,542pp (foxing). Full calf (spine sl rubbed). *Whitehart*. $186/£120

BARCLAY, J. The Muscular Motions of the Human Body. Edinburgh, 1808. xxii,591pp. New 1/2 morocco. (Lt foxing.) *Whitehart*. $372/£240

BARD, FLOYD C. Horse Wrangler, Sixty Years in the Saddle in Wyoming and Montana. Norman: Univ of OK, (1960). 1st ed. Yellow cl. VG in VG dj. *Laurie.* $60/£39

BARD, SAMUEL. A Compendium of the Theory and Practice of Midwifery. NY, 1817. 4th ed. Contemp calf (warped, worn). *Argosy.* $125/£81

BARD, SAMUEL. A Compendium of the Theory and Practice of Midwifery: Containing Practical Instructions.... NY, 1815. 3rd ed. 269pp. Full leather. Scattered foxing, but Fine. *Fye.* $400/£258

BARDIN, SHLOMO. Pioneer Youth in Palestine. NY: Bloch, 1932. 1st ed. VG in dj (sl torn). *Worldwide.* $25/£16

BARDSWELL, F.A. The Herb Garden. London, 1911. 16 color plts. *Wheldon & Wesley.* $39/£25

BARES, GEORGE S. The Naval Cadet's Guide. London: Portsea, 1860. Blue cl (rubbed, faded; margins sl soiled, spotted); canvas/string cvring. *Petersfield.* $33/£21

BARETTI, JOSEPH. A Journey from London to Genoa.... London: T. & L. Davies, 1770. 1st 8vo ed. 4 vols. Full early speckled calf, gilt fillets, raised bands, dbl leather labels. Very Nice set (18th cent bkpls). *Hartfield.* $795/£513

BARING, MAURICE. Cecil Spencer. Heinemann, 1929. #128/525 signed. Parchment bds sl soiled, o/w NF. *Poetry.* $39/£25

BARING, MAURICE. Dead Letters. London: Martin Secker, (1920). 1st ed. Paper spine label. Hinges sl weak; bkpls, else Fine. *Pharos.* $35/£23

BARING, MAURICE. The Glass Mender and Other Tales. London: James Nisbit, 1910. 1st ed. 8vo. 260pp; 12 color plts by Baring. Teg. Blue cl, gilt. Spine sl faded, fr hinge cracked, o/w VG. *Drusilla's.* $55/£35

BARING, MAURICE. Orpheus in Mayfair and Other Stories and Sketches. Mills & Boon, 1909. 1st ed. VG (spine sl faded). *Aronovitz.* $135/£87

BARING, MAURICE. The Puppet Show of Memory. Boston: Little Brown, 1922. 1st Amer ed. VG. *Burcham.* $25/£16

BARING, MAURICE. Unreliable History. London: Heinemann, 1934. 1st thus. NF (spine sl faded) in dj. *Williams.* $23/£15

BARING-GOULD, SABINE. Curious Myths of the Middle Ages. Longmans, 1892. VG. *Madle.* $60/£39

BARING-GOULD, SABINE. Siegfried: A Romance Founded on Wagner's Operas.... London: Dean & Son, 1904. 1st ed. Spine sl faded, edges lt foxed, o/w Very Nice. *Temple.* $47/£30

BARING-GOULD, SABINE. The Silver Store Collected from Mediaeval Christian and Jewish Mines. London: Longmans, Green, 1868. 1st ed. 197, (ii)pp. (Lib stamp back title; few marginal blind stamps; spine faded; recased.) *Hollett.* $101/£65

BARING-GOULD, WILLIAM and CECIL. The Annotated Mother Goose. NY: Bramhall House, (1962). (Sl abrasion rear joint.) Dj (rubbed, sl edgeworn). *Sadlon.* $35/£23

BARING-GOULD, WILLIAM and CECIL. The Annotated Mother Goose: Nursery Rhymes Old and New. (NY: Potter, 1962). 1st ed. 4to. VG in dj (nicks, creases; rubbing). *Houle.* $75/£48

BARING-GOULD, WILLIAM and CECIL. The Annotated Mother Goose: Nursery Rhymes, Old and New. NY: Clarkson N. Potter, 1962. 1st ed. 350pp. Yellow linen on bds; dec eps; pict red dj. Minor rubbing dj corners; else Fine. *Hobbyhorse.* $95/£61

BARING-GOULD, WILLIAM. The Annotated Sherlock Holmes. NY: Clarkson N. Potter, (1967). 1st ed. 2 vols. Fine in djs, pub's slipcase (sl shelfworn). *Sadlon.* $125/£81

BARING-GOULD, WILLIAM. The Annotated Sherlock Holmes. Clarkson Potter, 1967. 1st ed. 2 vols. NF in VG+ dj and VG+ slipcase. *Bishop.* $52/£34

BARING-GOULD, WILLIAM. Nero Wolfe of West 35th Street. Viking, 1969. 1st ed. Edges lt worn, else NF in dj (lt chipped, tape-repaired tears). *Murder.* $50/£32

BARING-GOULD, WILLIAM. Sherlock Holmes of Baker Street. NY: Clarkson N. Potter, 1962. 1st ed. Fine (sl corner bumps) in dj (lt edgewear). *Janus.* $65/£42

BARING-GOULD, WILLIAM. Sherlock Holmes of Baker Street. NY: Clarkson N. Potter, 1962. 1st ed. Fine in dj. *Mordida.* $75/£48

BARKER, A.J. The Neglected War. Mesopotamia, 1914-1918. London, 1967. 1st ed. 24 plts. VG in dj. *Edwards.* $54/£35

BARKER, ALAN. The Civil War in America. London, (1961). 1st ed. Fine in Fine dj. *Mcgowan.* $30/£19

BARKER, BURT BROWN. McLoughlin Empire and Its Rulers. Clark, 1959. 1st ed. Fldg map. Fine. *Oregon.* $45/£29

BARKER, CICELY MARY. Book of the Flower Fairies. London: Blackie, n.d. Lg 12mo. 72 full-color plts bound in. Grn pict cl, gilt decs. NF (lt spotting text). *Book Adoption.* $300/£194

BARKER, CICELY MARY. Fairies of the Trees. London: Blackie, n.d. 5.5x4.25. 24 color plts. Pict paper-cvrd bds; pict label. VG+ in VG+ dj (clipped). *Book Adoption.* $80/£52

BARKER, CICELY MARY. Flower Fairies of the Spring. London: Blackie, n.d. Tiny Tots Series ed. 5.5x4.25. 24 color plts. Pict paper-cvrd bds; pict label. NF (lt foxing text pp; sl wear) in VG dj (chipped). *Book Adoption.* $85/£55

BARKER, CICELY MARY. A Flower Fairy Alphabet. London: Blackie, n.d. 5.5x4.25. 24 color plts. Pict paper-cvrd bds; pict label. Lacks spine, else VG+ in VG dj (soiled). *Book Adoption.* $80/£52

BARKER, CLIVE. The Damnation Game. London: W&N, 1985. 1st UK ed. Fine in dj. *Lewton.* $54/£35

BARKER, EDWARD HARRISON. Wanderings by Southern Waters. Eastern Aquitaine. London: Bentley, 1893. (iv),(404)pp. Brn cl stamped in gilt, blind (ex-lib, pockets removed; bumped). *Schoyer.* $50/£32

BARKER, ETHEL ROSS. Rome of the Pilgrims and Martyrs. Methuen, 1913. 1st ed. (Sm stamp.) *Edwards.* $25/£16

BARKER, EUGENE C. Mexico and Texas 1821-1835. Dallas, TX: P.L. Turner, (1928). 1st ed. Dk red cl (dull). Pencil notes, else VG. *Chapel Hill.* $75/£48

BARKER, F.A. The Modern Prison System of India. London: Macmillan, 1944. *Boswell.* $50/£32

BARKER, F.D. An Angler's Paradise. London: Faber & Gwyer, 1929. 1st ed. VG. *Bowman.* $50/£32

BARKER, G. Eros in Dogma. Faber, 1944. 1st ed. Fine in dj (dull; sl chipped). *Whiteson.* $25/£16

BARKER, G. Janus. Faber, 1935. 1st ed. VG. *Whiteson.* $23/£15

BARKER, GEORGE. The Dead Seagull. NY: FSG, (1950). 1st Amer ed. NF in illus dj. *Cahan.* $35/£23

BARKER, GEORGE. Thrilling Adventures of the Whaler Alcyone. Peabody, MA: George Barker, 1916. 1st ed. Port. VG (lt foxing). *Lefkowicz.* $125/£81

BARKER, LEWELLYS. The Nervous System and Its Constituent Neurones. NY, 1899. 1132pp; fldg plt (fold torn). Full leather. (Marginal water stain affecting few leaves; fr hinge top torn; soiled.) *Fye.* $250/£161

BARKER, NICHOLAS. Stanley Morison. (London): Macmillan, (1972). 1st ed. Fine in dj (short tears). *Heller.* $45/£29

BARKER, RICHARD (ed). The Fatal Caress...and Other Accounts of English Murders from 1551 to 1888. NY: Duell et al, (1947). 1st ed. NF in dj (brittle, repairs to verso, lacks 1-inch piece spine foot). *Sadlon.* $15/£10

BARKER, T.C. Pilkington Brothers and the Glass Industry. London: Allen & Unwin, 1960. 20 plts, 12 graphs, 5 charts, 4 plans. VG (stamp, bkpl ep). *Peter Taylor.* $36/£23

BARKER, W.G.M. JONES. The Three Days of Wensleydale. London: Charles Dolman, 1854. 1st ed. Engr frontis, xxiii,296pp + 8pp ads. Blue gilt cl (sl rubbed). Very Nice (spots). *Hollett.* $93/£60

BARKSDALE, JAMES WORSHAM. A Comparative Study of Contemporary White and Negro Standards in Health, Education and Welfare. Charlottesville, VA, 1949. 1st ed. NF in orig stiff ptd wrappers. *Mcgowan.* $75/£48

BARKSDALE, LENA. The First Thanksgiving. Knopf, 1942. 1st ed. Inscribed. 57pp. Lois Leski (illus). Fair (dknd) in Fair dj (dknd). *Book Broker.* $15/£10

BARLEY, M.W. The English Farmhouse and Cottage. London, 1961. 1st ed. 24 plts; 8 tables. Dj (sl chipped). *Edwards.* $47/£30

BARLOW, JAMES. Essays on Surgery and Midwifery. London, 1822. 417pp; 5 copper plts (2 fldg). 1/2 calf (worn; joints cracked). Lib stamp; plts sl foxed, else internally Fine. *Argosy.* $300/£194

BARLOW, JANE. The Battle of the Frogs and Mice. (London): Methuen, 1894. 1st ed. Francis D. Bedford (engrs). Pict cl (soil, wear). *Glenn.* $150/£97

BARLY, JOSEPH. Judging Saddle Horses and Roadsters. Milwaukee, 1945. 1st ed. VG in Good dj. *October Farm.* $45/£29

BARMAN, CHRISTIAN. Sir John Vanbrugh. NY: Scribner's, 1924. 1st ed. Frontis, 33 plts. Sunned; text sl yellowed, else VG. *Bookpress.* $45/£29

Barn Plans and Outbuildings. (By Bryan David Halsted.) NY: OJ, 1882. 2nd ed. Frontis,235,(5)pp. Pub's cl (lt rubbed). *Bookpress.* $145/£94

BARNARD, EVAN G. A Rider of the Cherokee Strip. Boston: Houghton Mifflin, 1936. 1st ed. Good (sm snag spine). Howes B 147. *Lien.* $45/£29

BARNARD, GEORGE. Drawing from Nature: A Series of Progressive Instructions.... London: Longmans, Green et al, 1865. 1st ed. 18 color litho plts. Teg. Forest grn beveled cl, gilt (wear, esp joints, extrems). Very Nice. *Glenn.* $175/£113

BARNARD, GEORGE. The Theory and Practice of Landscape Painting in Water-Colours. London: Hamilton Adams, 1858. New, enlgd ed. 286pp (few edges frayed), 30 chromolithos. (Sl worn, spine torn.) *Ars Artis.* $116/£75

BARNARD, GEORGE. The Theory and Practice of Landscape Painting in Water-Colours. George Routledge & Sons, 1871. New ed. (viii),286pp; ad leaf; 26 color litho plts. Blue cl, blocked in blind lower cvr, gilt. VF. *Bickersteth.* $147/£95

BARNARD, J.G. The Phenomena of the Gyroscope, Analytically Examined. NY: D. Van Nostrand, 1858. 1st ed. (vi),537-560, 529-536; 299-304pp. Aeg. Contemp full morocco (edges, spine sl rubbed). *Bookpress.* $425/£274

BARNARD, ROBERT. Death on the High C's. NY: Walker, 1977. 1st ed. Fine in dj (minor rubs to corners). *Else Fine.* $50/£32

BARNARD, ROBERT. The Disposal of the Living. London: CCC, 1985. 1st ed. Inscribed. Fine in dj. *Mordida.* $75/£48

BARNARD, SEYMOUR. A Child's Garden of Relatives. NY/Toronto: Rinehart, 1950. 84pp. 34 full-pg color lithos by Edna Eicke. Green cl on bds, gilt title spine. Lt soiled cvr edges; else Fine. *Hobbyhorse.* $75/£48

BARNEBY, W. HENRY. Life and Labour in the Far, Far, West. London: Cassell, 1884. 1st ed. xvi,432pp + 8pp ads, lg fldg color map. Pict red cl (spine sl sunned). *Schoyer.* $200/£129

BARNEBY, W. HENRY. New Far West and The Old Far East. London: Stanford, 1889. (xii),316pp + 4pp ads. 3 fldg color maps, 6 plts, Grn cl stamped in gilt, black. 9Ex-lib; lettering traces, spine worn.) *Schoyer.* $125/£81

BARNES, AL. Vinegar Pie and Other Tales of the Grand Traverse Region. Detroit, 1959. 1st ed. Fine in dj. *Artis.* $25/£16

BARNES, BURT. The Scissors Mother Goose. NY: Dodd, Mead, 1910. 1st ed. 9x12. 24pp. Cl spine, pict bds. Good. *Cattermole.* $60/£39

BARNES, CLARE, JR. John F. Kennedy: Scrimshaw Collector. Boston/Toronto: Little, Brown, n.d. (1969). 1st ed. Lt fading lower edge, else Fine in NF illus dj. *Cahan.* $100/£65

BARNES, DAVID M. The Draft Riots in New York, July, 1863. NY: Baker & Godwin, 1863. 117pp. Orig wraps (worn but sound). *Boswell.* $150/£97

BARNES, DJUNA. Ah My God. (Paris): Le Nouveau Commerce, (1987). 1st ed, ltd to 500 numbered. Single lg folio sheet folded into 12pp, cord bound. Unopened. Fine. *Godot.* $50/£32

BARNES, DJUNA. Greenwich Village as It Is. NY: Phoenix Bookshop, 1978. 1st ed. One of 300. Fine. *Second Life.* $65/£42

BARNES, DJUNA. The Selected Works of Djuna Barnes. NY: Farrar, Straus & Cudahy, (1962). 1st ed. VG (extrem fading) in dj (worn; closed tear). *Hermitage.* $50/£32

BARNES, JAMES and WILLIAM ROBINSON. Asparagus Culture. NY: Routledge, n.d. (1881). 84pp. Good. *Brooks.* $31/£20

BARNES, JAMES J. Free Trade in Books. Oxford: Clarendon, 1964. 1st ed. Blue cl. Good in dj. *Karmiole.* $30/£19

BARNES, JAMES M. Picture Analysis of Golf Strokes, a Complete Book of Instruction. Phila, 1919. 1st ed. Newspaper photos attached to feps (eps soiled; inscrips; frayed, rubbed). *King.* $125/£81

BARNES, JULIAN. Before She Met Me. London: Cape, 1982. 1st ed. Fine in dj. *Rees.* $70/£45

BARNES, JULIAN. Before She Met Me. Cape, 1982. 1st UK ed. Signed. Fine in dj. *Lewton.* $54/£35

BARNES, JULIAN. Flaubert's Parrot. NY: Knopf, 1985. 1st Amer ed. Fine in dj. *Hermitage.* $45/£29

BARNES, JULIAN. A History of the World in 10 1/2 Chapters. London: Cape, 1989. 1st ed. Signed. Fine in dj. *Rees.* $54/£35

BARNES, JULIAN. History of the World in 10 1/2 Chapters. Cape, 1989. 1st UK ed. Signed. Fine in dj. *Lewton.* $47/£30

BARNES, JULIAN. Metroland. London: Cape, 1980. 1st ed, 1st bk. Fine in dj. *Rees.* $116/£75

BARNES, JULIAN. Metroland. London: Cape, 1980. 1st ed. Signed. Fine in dj (price-clipped). *Virgo.* $124/£80

BARNES, JULIAN. The Porcupine. NY: Knopf, (1992). 1st Amer ed. Signed. Fine in dj. *Godot.* $45/£29

BARNES, JULIAN. Staring at the Sun. London: Cape, 1986. 1st ed. Signed. Fine in dj. *Rees.* $39/£25

BARNES, JULIAN. Staring at the Sun. NY, 1987. 1st ed. Fine in Fine dj. *Fuller & Saunders.* $25/£16

BARNES, JULIAN. Talking It Over. London: London Ltd Editions, (1991). 1st ed. Ltd to 200 signed. Cl-backed marbled bds. As New in glassine dj. *Jaffe.* $175/£113

BARNES, JULIAN. Talking It Over. London: Cape, 1991. 1st ed. Signed. Fine in dj. *Rees.* $39/£25

BARNES, JULIAN. Talking It Over. London: Cape, 1991. One of 200 specially bound by London Ltd Eds, numbered, signed. Fine in glassine dj. *Rees.* $70/£45

BARNES, LEMUEL CALL. Two Thousand Years of Missions before Carey. Chicago: Christian Culture Press, 1900. (xviii),504pp, fldg map. Red cl stamped in gilt (spine dknd; soil). *Schoyer.* $30/£19

BARNES, LINDA. A Trouble of Fools. NY: St. Martin's, 1987. 1st ed. VF in dj. *Mordida.* $65/£42

BARNES, MARGARET AYER. Westward Passage. Boston: Houghton Mifflin, 1931. 1st ed. Signed. Bkpl, o/w Fine in art deco dj (used; internally mended). *Pharos.* $75/£48

BARNES, MELVYN. Murder in Print. London, 1986. 1st ed. Fine in Fine dj. *Polyanthos.* $35/£23

BARNES, R. MONEY. A History of the Regiments and Uniforms of the British Army. London: Seeley Service & Co, (1951). 2nd ed. 24 color plts. Red cl. VG in color pict dj (chipped). *House.* $85/£55

BARNES, W.H. The Grape in Kansas. Topeka, 1901. Frontis (tear). Grn cl (wrinkling to spine, crease fr cvr). *Sutton.* $50/£32

BARNES, WILL C. Western Grazing Grounds and Forest Ranges. Chicago: Breeder's Gazette, 1913. Gold-stamped cl (sl loose; article by author tipped to fep; lt wear; bkpl). *Dawson.* $150/£97

BARNES, WILLIAM H. The Contemporary American Organ.... Glen Rock, NJ, 1959. 6th ed. (Spine faded; cvrs sl worn.) *King.* $50/£32

BARNES, WILLIAM H. History of the Thirty-Ninth Congress of the United States. NY: Harper, 1868. Presentation copy. ix,636pp; 18 steel-engr ports. VG. *Schoyer.* $85/£55

BARNES, WILLIAM. Poems of Rural Life. London: John Russell Smith, 1844. 1st ed. Inscrip; soiling, o/w VG in contemp 1/2 morocco (fraying; upper joint sl weak). *Poetry.* $112/£72

BARNETT, DONALD L. Mau Mau from Within. London: MacGibbon & Kee, (1966). Fine in NF dj (edgewear; lacks sm piece at spine). *Aka.* $35/£23

BARNEY, MARY (ed). A Biographical Memoir of the Late Commodore Joshua Barney. Boston: Gray & Bowen, 1832. xvi,328pp (lacks port). Untrimmed. (Spine sunned; stains.) Howes B 160. *Schoyer.* $50/£32

BARNEY, MARY (ed). A Biographical Memoir of the Late Commodore Joshua Barney. Boston: Gray, 1832. 1st ed. (16),238pp, port. Cl-backed bds. Howes B 160. *Ginsberg.* $150/£97

BARNICOT, A.M. The Shadow of the Woman. London: Grayson, 1934. 1st ed. VG in Good dj. *Ming.* $39/£25

BARNITZ, ALBERT. The Mystic Delvings. Cincinnati: A Watson, 1857. 1st ed. Inscribed. Frontis port, 288pp. Brn gilt cl (sl soiled, frayed). *Karmiole.* $35/£23

BARNS, T. ALEXANDER. Across the Great Craterland to the Congo. London: Benn, 1923. 1st ed. Tan cl, gilt titles. VG+. *Bowman.* $90/£58

Barns, Plans, and Outbuildings. NY: OJ, 1881. 1st ed. VG. *Bishop.* $37/£24

BARNSTONE, HOWARD. The Galveston That Was. NY/Houston: Macmillan/Museum of Fine Arts, (1967). 2nd ptg. Lt foxing 1st, last pg, else VG in pict dj (closed tears; sl rubbing). *Cahan.* $75/£48

BARO, GENE. Claes Oldenburg. London/NY, 1969. 368 plts. (Ex-lib w/ink stamp, label; tape mk.) Dj (sl soiled). *Edwards.* $70/£45

BARON, JOHN. The Life of Edward Jenner. London, 1838. 2 vols. 624; 471pp. 1/2 leather. (Owner letters tipped in; ink notations.) *Fye.* $300/£194

BARR, ALFRED H. (ed). Fantastic Art, Dada, Surrealism. NY: MOMA, 1937. 2nd ed. Gilt design on cl. VG (eps discolored). *Cahan.* $35/£23

BARR, ALFRED H. (ed). Fantastic Art, Dada, Surrealism. NY, 1947. 3rd ed. Color frontis. Dj (lt soiled, chipped, sl loss spine). *Edwards.* $109/£70

BARR, ALFRED H. (ed). Masters of Modern Art. NY: MOMA, (1954). 356 plts (77 color). VG. *Argosy.* $65/£42

BARR, BERYL and BARBARA TURNER SACHS. The Artists' and Writers' Cookbook. Sausalito, CA: Contact Editions, (1961). 1st ed. Bkpl, else NF in pub's slipcase box (lt worn). *Godot.* $65/£42

BARR, ROBERT. Unchanging East. Boston: Page, 1900. 2 vols. (256); 256pp; teg. Grn dec cl (faded). *Schoyer.* $45/£29

BARR, WILLIAM. Journal of a March from Delhi to Peshawur.... London: James Madden, 1844. 1st ed. 8vo. xvi,410,(2)ads, half title, 6 sepia litho plts (incl frontis). Orig brick blind-stamped cl, gilt lettered spine. Good (sl foxing in margins of plts, lib stamp on title, leaf partly erased w/o loss; upper cvr, spine faded, sm tears at foot of spine). *Morrell.* $667/£430

BARRETT, C.R.B. Somersetshire: Highways, Byways, and Waterways. London, 1894. 1st ed. xv,366pp (feps lt browned), 4 etchings. (Spine discolored, chipped.) *Edwards.* $47/£30

BARRETT, JAY A. Evolution of the Ordinance of 1787. NY: Putnam's, 1891. (vi),94pp; 3 maps. (Bds stained.) *Schoyer.* $35/£23

BARRETT, JOHN G. Sherman's March Through the Carolinas. Chapel Hill, (1956). 1st ed. Signed. VG+ in VG+ dj (sm piece torn). *Pratt.* $45/£29

BARRETT, JOHN G. Sherman's March Through the Carolinas. Chapel Hill: Univ of NC, 1956. 1st ed. VG in dj (worn). *Chapel Hill.* $40/£26

BARRETT, TIMOTHY. Japanese Papermaking: Traditions, Tools, and Techniques. NY/Tokyo: Weatherhill, (1983). Frontis. Japanese eps. Brn cl bds, gilt. Fine in dj. *Heller.* $75/£48

BARRETT, WILLIAM E. The Lilies of the Field. GC: Doubleday, 1962. 1st ed. NF in dj. *Bernard.* $25/£16

BARRIE, J.M. Auld Licht Idylls. London: Hodder & Stoughton, 1888. 1st ed. Buckram, beveled edges. Fine. *Pharos.* $150/£97

BARRIE, J.M. Courage. London: Hodder & Stoughton, 1922. 1st UK ed. NF in VG dj (spine sl chipped). *Williams.* $23/£15

BARRIE, J.M. The Entrancing Life. London: Hodder & Stoughton, (1930). 1st ed. NF. *Sadlon.* $25/£16

BARRIE, J.M. George Meredith—1909. Portland: Mosher, 1919. 1st thus, one of 950 ptd. VF in wraps, slipcase. *Pharos.* $40/£26

BARRIE, J.M. George Meredith—1909. NY: William Edwin Rudge, 1924. 1st ed thus. One of 500 ptd. Paper-cvrd bds. Fine in tissue wrapper. *Hermitage.* $75/£48

BARRIE, J.M. George Meredith—1909. NY: Rudge, 1924. 1st ed. Sl wear spine head, foot, o/w Nice in orig glassine (chipped, worn). *Pharos.* $20/£13

BARRIE, J.M. The Greenwood Hat. Peter Davies, 1937. 1st trade ed. NF in dj (chipped). *Fine Books.* $20/£13

BARRIE, J.M. The Greenwood Hat. London: Peter Davies, 1937. 1st trade ed. NF in dj (chipped, torn, browned). *Williams.* $28/£18

BARRIE, J.M. Half Hours. London: Hodder & Stoughton, (1914). Later issue of 1st Eng ed w/an added color frontis, no ads. VG. *Pharos.* $20/£13

BARRIE, J.M. The Little Minister. London: Cassell, 1891. 1st ed. 3 vols. Brn cl. Good (cvrs worn). *Pharos.* $200/£129

BARRIE, J.M. The Little White Bird or Adventures in Kensington Gardens. Scribner's, 1902. 1st Amer ed. Pict cl. VG +. *Aronovitz.* $65/£42

BARRIE, J.M. The Little White Bird. London: Hodder & Stoughton, 1902. 1st ed. Frontis, teg. Dk blue cl (sl faded; lt chipped). VG. *Chapel Hill.* $125/£81

BARRIE, J.M. M'Connachie and J.M.B. London: Peter Davies, 1938. 1st ed. VG. *Cahan.* $35/£23

BARRIE, J.M. Margaret Ogilvy. London: Hodder & Stoughton, 1896. 1st Eng ed. Frontis port, 204 + (4)pp ads. Dk blue cl. Bkpl; offsetting prelims, else NF. *Chapel Hill.* $95/£61

BARRIE, J.M. Mary Rose: A Play in Three Acts. London: Hodder & Stoughton, 1924. (Spine label sl yellowed.) *Sadlon.* $35/£23

BARRIE, J.M. Peter Pan and Wendy. London: Hodder & Stoughton, (n.d., Boots ed). Thick 4to. Gwynedd M. Hudson (illus). Illus dk blue cl, black/gold lettering (spine faded). Pict dj (worn; sm pieces missing spine). *Reisler.* $285/£184

BARRIE, J.M. Peter Pan and Wendy. NY, 1921. 1st ed thus. 10x7 inches. 12 full-pg color plts, 20 b/w dwgs by Mabel Lucie Attwell. Pict cl. (Ink inscrip; eps browned; sm marginal hole 1 pg, cvrs worn, spotted.) *King.* $60/£39

BARRIE, J.M. Peter Pan in Kensington Gardens. London: Hodder & Stoughton, (1910). 7th Eng ed. 4to, 125pp text, 50 mtd color plts by Arthur Rackham. Brown-red cl, gold pict stamping. Corners, bottom of spine worn, else VG. *Davidson.* $450/£290

BARRIE, J.M. Peter Pan in Kensington Gardens. London: Hodder & Stoughton, 1906. 1st ed. Sm 4to. 50 color plts by Arthur Rackham. Pict cl (spine ends creased), gilt image. VG +; contents NF. *Book Adoption.* $750/£484

BARRIE, J.M. Peter Pan in Kensington Gardens. London: Hodder & Stoughton, 1906. 1st trade ed. 49 (of 50) mtd color plts by Arthur Rackham. Worn, dknd. *Hollett.* $186/£120

BARRIE, J.M. Peter Pan in Kensington Gardens. NY, 1907. 50 tipped-in full-pg plts by Arthur Rackham, guards (few plts unhinged). Gilt pict cl (stained, bumped, rubbed, soiled; stamped names). *King.* $150/£97

BARRIE, J.M. Peter Pan in Kensington Gardens. H&S, n.d. (ca 1925). 16 tipped-in full color illus. Gold-gilt pict cl. Spine faded, else VG. *Fine Books.* $110/£71

BARRIE, J.M. Tommy and Grizel. London: Cassell, 1900. 1st ed. Teg. Bkpl, hinges cracking, sm nick spine, else Good. *Reese.* $20/£13

BARRIE, J.M. When Wendy Grew Up. Sidney Blow (ed). (London): Nelson, 1957. 1st ed. 8vo. Frontis, 32pp. Blue cl. NF in dj (spine faded). *Chapel Hill.* $35/£23

BARRINGER, PAUL B. et al. University of Virginia. Lewis Pub, 1904. 2 vols. Aeg. Half leather (wear, rubbing; pencil, ink mks). *Book Broker.* $100/£65

BARRINGTON, DAINES. The Possibility of Approaching the North Pole Asserted.... A New Edition. London: T. & J. Allman, 1818. xxiv,258. Uncut. Fldg map (offsetting to tp). Paper-cvrd bds (sl rubbed). Good. *Walcot.* $233/£150

BARRON, ARCHIBALD F. Vines and Vine Culture. London, 1887. 2nd ed. xv,189pp + ads (pencil underlining), 30 plts. Gilt-dec cl (scuffing; dampstained, affecting few pp; fraying). *Sutton.* $40/£26

BARRON, ARCHIBALD F. Vines and Vine Culture. London: Journal of Horticulture, 1892. 3rd ed, rev. 199pp + ad; 30 engrs. VG. *Second Life.* $75/£48

BARROW, ELFRIDA DE RENNE and LAURA PALMER BELL. Anchored Yesterdays. Savannah: Press of the Review Publishing & Ptg, 1923. 1st ed. Fine. *Pharos.* $30/£19

BARROW, JOHN. A Chronological History of Voyages into the Arctic Regions. London: John Murray, 1818. 1st ed. 6,379pp, fldg map. Uncut; new eps. Orig bds (rebacked w/linen). Good +. (lacks 48pp appendix). *Walcot.* $233/£150

BARROW, JOHN. A Visit to Iceland by Way of Tronyem in the 'Flower of Yarrow' Yacht in the Summer of 1834. London, 1835. 1st ed. xxiv,320pp; 9 woodcuts (foxed). Orig bds. *Lewis.* $132/£85

BARROW, JOHN. Voyages of Discovery and Research within the Arctic Regions.... London: John Murray, 1846. 1st ed. Frontis port, xiv,530pp + ads, 2 maps. Good + (sl worn). *Walcot.* $302/£195

BARROW, W.J. Procedures and Equipment Used in the Barrow Method of Restoring Manuscripts and Documents. Richmond, 1945. 1st ed. Spine browning, else Fine in wrappers. *Bookpress.* $85/£55

BARROWS, JOHN R. A Wisconsin Youth in Montana 1880-1882. Missoula, 1932. Rpt. (Cvr soiled; lib stamp.) *Bohling.* $45/£29

BARROWS, R.M. (comp). The Kit Book for Soldiers, Sailors and Marines. Chicago: Consolidated Book Pub, 1943. 1st ed, 2nd issue. Issued w/o dj; illus bds (extrems worn). *Pettler.* $50/£32

BARROWS, R.M. (comp). The Kit Book for Soldiers, Sailors, and Marines. Chicago: Consolidated Book Pub, 1943. 1st ed, 2nd issue w/1943 rather than 1942 copyright date. VG (pp edge browned; lt rubbing). *Chapel Hill*. $100/£65

BARROWS, WALTER B. and E.A. SCHWARZ. The Common Crow of the United States. Washington, 1895. 98pp. Uncut. Ptd wrappers. VG. *Argosy*. $40/£26

BARRUS, CLARA. Our Friend John Burroughs. Boston: Houghton Mifflin, 1914. 1st ed. Photogravure frontis port. VG (sl bumped). *Shifrin*. $12/£8

BARRY, JOSEPH. The Strange Story of Harper's Ferry with Legends of the Surrounding Country. Martinsburg, WV: Thompson Bros, 1903. 1st ed. 2 plts. Good+ in wraps. *Oregon*. $25/£16

BARRY, P. Barry's Fruit Garden. NY, (1872). Rev, enlgd ed. Frontis, 491pp (name, bkpl). Gilt-dec cl (lt wear, insect mks). *Sutton*. $65/£42

BARRY, P. Barry's Fruit Garden. NY: OJ, 1872. 1st ed as such. Frontis, v-xvi,491pp. Gilt-dec cvr, spine. Fine. *Quest*. $60/£39

BARRY, P. The Fruit Garden. NY, 1851. 1st ed. xiv,398pp (foxing; blank pg missing edge; tp torn). Cl (worn, soiled, spine missing piece). *Sutton*. $95/£61

BARSNESS, LARRY. Heads, Hides and Horns. The Compleat Buffalo Book. Fort Worth: TX Christian Univ, 1985. 1st ed. NF in NF dj. *Parker*. $40/£26

BARTH, JOHN. The End of the Road. GC: Doubleday, 1958. 1st ed. Blue cl. VG (eps lt dust-soiled) in dj (flaps lt soiled). *Chapel Hill*. $250/£161

BARTH, JOHN. The Floating Opera. NY: Appleton-Century-Crofts, (1956). 1st ed, 1st bk. Signed. Brn cl. VG (spine nick; sl offsetting eps) in VG dj. *Chapel Hill*. $250/£161

BARTH, JOHN. The Floating Opera. GC, 1967. Rev ed, 1st thus. Fine in Fine dj (price-clipped). *Fuller & Saunders*. $65/£42

BARTH, JOHN. The Friday Book Essays and Other Nonfiction. NY: Putnam's, (1984). 1st ed. Fine in dj. *Reese*. $25/£16

BARTH, JOHN. Letters. A Novel. NY: Putnam's, (1979). 1st ed. One of 500 numbered, differently bound, signed. Fine in slipcase. *Reese*. $75/£48

BARTH, JOHN. Lost in the Funhouse. GC: Doubleday, 1968. 1st ed. NF in NF dj (few closed tears; sl wear). *Revere*. $45/£29

BARTH, JOHN. Sabbatical. NY: Putnam's, (1982). 1st ed. One of 750 numbered, specially bound, signed. Mint in cl slipcase. *Reese*. $50/£32

BARTH, JOHN. The Sot-Weed Factor. GC: Doubleday, 1960. 1st ed. Bottom spine edge sm nick, o/w VG+ in dj (spine bottom chipped; edges sl worn; rear panel lt soiled). *Bernard*. $300/£194

BARTHELME, DONALD. City Life. NY: FSG, (1970). 1st ed. Fine in dj. *Bernard*. $35/£23

BARTHELME, DONALD. City Life. NY: FSG, (1970). 1st ed. NF (sl worn) in dj. *Between The Covers*. $65/£42

BARTHELME, DONALD. Great Days. NY: FSG, (1979). 1st ed. New in dj. *Bernard*. $12/£8

BARTHELME, DONALD. Snow White. London: Jonathan Cape, (1968). 1st Eng ed. Fine in dj. *Heller*. $65/£42

BARTHELME, DONALD. Snow White. NY: Atheneum, 1967. 1st ed. Fine in dj. *Heller*. $75/£48

BARTHES, ROLAND. Elements of Semiology. NY: H&W, 1968. 1st US ed. NF in VG dj (spine faded). *Lame Duck*. $35/£23

BARTHOLOW, ROBERTS. Cholera: Its Causes, Symptoms, Pathology and Treatment. Phila: Lea Bros, 1893. vii,1342,16pp. Pub's file copy (spine sticker). Good. *Goodrich*. $75/£48

BARTHOLOW, ROBERTS. The Principles and Practice of Disinfection. Cincinnati, 1867. 1st ed. 111pp. *Fye*. $150/£97

BARTLETT, ELISHA. The History, Diagnosis, and Treatment of the Fevers of the United States. Phila, 1856. 4th ed. 610pp. Good. *Fye*. $125/£81

BARTLETT, ELISHA. The History, Diagnosis, and Treatment of Typhoid and Typhus Fever.... Phila, 1842. 1st ed. 393pp. 1/2 leather. Contents VF (hinges weak; piece missing backstrip top). *Fye*. $300/£194

BARTLETT, ELLEN STRONG. Historical Sketches of New Haven. New Haven: Tuttle, Morehouse & Taylor, 1897. 98pp (frontis? leaf excised). Beveled-edge cl. *Schoyer*. $35/£23

BARTLETT, MARY. Gentians. Poole, Dorset, 1975. 1st ed. 21 color plts. Fine in dj. *Brooks*. $21/£14

BARTLETT, ROBERT A. and RALPH T. HALE. Northward Ho! The Last Voyage of the Karluk. Boston: Small, Maynard, 1919. 2nd ptg. Orig dec cl. Fine in orig dj. *High Latitude*. $65/£42

BARTLEY, NUMAN V. The Rise of Massive Resistance. Baton Rouge: LA State Univ Press, (1969). 1st ed. VG in dj. *Petrilla*. $35/£23

BARTOCCI, BARBARA. Christmas in Many Lands. Kansas City: Hallmark, n.d. (1976). 17x23 cm. 8 dbl-pg pop-ups. Judy Griffith (illus). Glazed pict bds. Fine. *Book Finders*. $60/£39

BARTON, ALBERT. The Story of Primrose, 1831-1895. (Madison, WI), 1895. 1st ed. 112pp. *Ginsberg*. $75/£48

BARTON, BERNARD. Memoir, Letters, and Poems. Phila: Lindsay & Glakiston, 1850. 1st Amer ed. Frontis port, xii,405pp(2pp ads). Blind-stamped cl, gilt; silk ribbon marker. Name stamps, else VG. *Hartfield*. $225/£145

BARTON, CLARA. The Red Cross in Peace and War. Washington, 1899. 1st ed. 703pp. Good. *Fye*. $100/£65

BARTON, D. PLUNKET et al. The Story of the Inns of Court. Boston: Houghton Mifflin, 1928. (Sl worn; bds spine, top faded.) Sound. *Boswell*. $65/£42

BARTON, E.H. The Cause and Prevention of Yellow Fever at New Orleans and Other Cities in America. With Addition of a Supplement. NY, 1857. 3rd ed. 282pp; lg fldg map of New Orleans. (Spine head, tail chipped.) *Fye*. $225/£145

BARTON, JAMES L. Story of Near East Relief (1915-1930). NY: Macmillan, 1930. 1st ed. 63 plts. Sl rubbed; spine sl frayed, o/w VG. *Worldwide*. $35/£23

BARTON, JOHN RECTOR. Rural Artists of Wisconsin. Madison: Univ of WI, 1948. 1st ed. VG. *Cahan*. $45/£29

BARTON, PHYLLIS. Cecil C. Bell. (Kansas City, 1976.) VG in dj. *Argosy*. $50/£32

BARTON, WILLIAM. A Flora of North America. Phila, 1821-22-23. 3 vols. xix,138; x,107; vii,100pp; 106 plts. 1/2 red leather (extrems rubbed), marbled bds. Text, plts generally clean (spines fraying). *Brooks*. $3,995/£2,577

BARTON, WILLIAM. Memoirs of the Life of David Rittenhouse...Late President of the American Philosophic Society. Phila, 1813. Frontis port, 614pp. Uncut (foxing throughout). Orig bds (crudely rebacked in cl). *Argosy.* $125/£81

BARTTELOT, WALTER GEORGE. The Life of Edmund Musgrave Barttelot. London, 1890. 3rd ed. Mtd photo frontis port, xi,(iv),413pp, 3 plts, 2 fldg maps. (Edges dampstained; spine faded, soiled; edges sl foxed; ex-libris.) *Edwards.* $70/£45

BARZUN, JACQUES and WENDELL HERTIG TAYLOR. A Catalogue of Crime. NY: Harper, 1971. 1st ed, 1st ptg. Fine in Fine dj (lt edgewear). *Janus.* $85/£55

BASHFORD, HERBERT and HARR WAGNER. A Man Unafraid. SF: Harr Wagner, (1927). 1st ed. Grn cl. Lt offsetting to eps, else VG +. *Chapel Hill.* $40/£26

BASICEVIC, DIMITRIJE. Primitive Painting: An Anthology.... NY, 1980. VG in dj. *Argosy.* $125/£81

BASILE, GIAMBATTISTA. Stories from the Pentamerone. E.G. Strange (ed). London: Macmillan, 1911. One of 150. 32 mtd color plts by Warwick Goble. Teg, others untrimmed. VG (soiling). *Schoyer.* $400/£258

BASINSKY, EARLE. The Big Steal. NY: Dutton, 1955. 1st ed, 1st bk. NF in dj (lt rubbed). *Murder.* $50/£32

BASKIN, ESTHER. Creatures of Darkness. Boston: Little, Brown, (1962). 1st ed. Ownership fep, else VG in dj. *Hermitage.* $35/£23

BASKIN, ESTHER. Creatures of Darkness. Boston: Little, Brown, (1962). 1st ed. Signed by Leonard Baskin (illus). 4to. Orange cl (spine faded); in pict dj (edges darkened). *Reisler.* $125/£81

BASKIN, LEONARD. Ars Anatomica: A Medical Fantasia. NY: Medicina Rara, 1972. Ltd ed of 2500. 13 plts. Unbound gatherings laid in a cl fldg slipcase. Good. *Goodrich.* $175/£113

BASKIN, LEONARD. Hosie's Alphabet. NY: Viking, (1972). 1st ed. Orig pict bds. Fine in dj. *Sadlon.* $35/£23

BASKIN, LEONARD. Hosie's Zoo. NY: Viking, 1981. 1st ed. 4to, unpaginated. Fine in VG dj. *Davidson.* $40/£26

BASKIN, LEONARD. Imps, Demons, Hobgoblins, Witches, Fairies. NY: Pantheon, 1984. 1st ed. Fine in Fine dj. *Davidson.* $47/£30

BASKIN, R.N. Reminiscences of Early Utah. Salt Lake City, 1914. 1st ed. Inscribed. Good + (sl stained, warped, bumped; fr hinge cracked). *Benchmark.* $75/£48

BASON, FRED. Fred Bason's Third Diary. Michael Sadleir (ed). (London): Deutsch, (1955). 1st ed. Fine in dj. *Oak Knoll.* $40/£26

BASS, RICK. The Watch. NY: W.W. Norton, (1989). 1st ed. Fine in dj. *Godot.* $35/£23

BASS, RICK. The Watch. NY: Norton, 1989. 1st ed. Fine in Fine dj. *Pettler.* $25/£16

BASS, RICK. Wild to the Heart. Harrisburg: Stackpole, 1987. 1st ed. Fine in Fine dj. *Revere.* $40/£26

BASS, RICK. Wild to the Heart. Harrisburg: Stackpole, 1987. 1st ed. Fine in Fine dj. *Parker.* $60/£39

BAST, THEODORE and BARRY ANSON. The Temporal Bone and the Ear. Springfield, 1949. 1st ed. Good. *Fye.* $50/£32

BASYE, ARTHUR HERBERT. The Lords Commissioners of Trade and Plantations. New Haven: Yale, 1925. VG. *Schoyer.* $45/£29

BATAILLE, GEORGES. Death and Sensuality. NY: Walker, 1962. 1st ed in English. Fine in dj (lt worn). *Beasley.* $100/£65

BATCHELOR, DENZIL. British Boxing. London: Collins, 1948. 1st ed. 8 color plts. Dj. *Petersfield.* $23/£15

BATCHELOR, JOHN CALVIN. The Birth of the People's Republic of Antarctica. NY: Dial, (c 1983). 1st ed. Fine in dj (lt rubbed, sm repaired tear). *Heller.* $45/£29

BATE, PERCY. Modern Scottish Portrait Painters. Edinburgh: Otto Schulze, 1910. Ltd to 375. 34 plts (foxing), guards. Red calf over cl (spine extrems rubbed), gilt. *Karmiole.* $125/£81

BATEMAN, R. When the Whites Went. Dobson, 1963. 1st ed. Fine in dj. *Aronovitz.* $45/£29

BATEMAN, ROBERT. The Art of Robert Bateman. NY, 1981. 1st ed. Debossed cl. Fine in dj. *Baade.* $175/£113

BATEMAN, T. A Practical Synopsis of Cutaneous Diseases and A Succint Account of the Contagious Fever of This Country. London, 1814. 3rd ed. 2 works in 1. Color frontis plt,344 + 178pp (prelims foxed). *Whitehart.* $372/£240

BATEMAN, T. A Practical Synopsis of Cutaneous Diseases. London, 1813. 2nd ed. Frontis plt,xxiv,336pp. New calf (imperfectly bound at end not affecting text). *Whitehart.* $698/£450

BATES, ALBERT C. An Early Connecticut Engraver (Amos Doolittle) and His Work. Hartford, 1906. Ltd ed. VG in ptd wrappers (spine chipped). *Argosy.* $65/£42

BATES, CHARLES. Custer's Indian Battles. Bronxville, NY: Privately ptd, (1936). 1st ed. Frontis. 2 surface peels cvr, o/w Fine in wraps. *Oregon.* $60/£39

BATES, CHARLES. Custer's Indian Battles. Bronxville, NY: (By author, 1936). VG + in ptd wraps. *Bohling.* $25/£16

BATES, DAISY. Long Shadow of Little Rock. NY: David McKay, 1962. VG in dj (price-clipped). *Aka.* $35/£23

BATES, ELISHA. The Doctrines of Friends. Mountpleasant: By the Author, 1825. 2nd ed. 320pp. Leather (upper joints cracking; sm chip spine). *Hayman.* $50/£32

BATES, ELISHA. The Doctrines of Friends: or Principles of the Christian Religion. Mountpleasant, (OH): Ptd by author, 1825. 320pp (foxing). Orig full calf. *Cullen.* $125/£81

BATES, H.E. Charlotte's Row. London: Cape, (1931). 1st ed. VG in dj (spine lt browned, nicks). *Godot.* $85/£55

BATES, H.E. Charlotte's Row. Cape, 1931. 1st ed. VG in dj (dull; sl chipped). *Whiteson.* $109/£70

BATES, H.E. The Country of White Clover. London: Michael Joseph, 1952. 1st ed. Very Nice in VG dj (sl faded). *Virgo.* $39/£25

BATES, H.E. A Crown of Wild Myrtle. London: Michael Joseph, 1962. 1st UK ed. Fine in VG dj. *Williams.* $23/£15

BATES, H.E. The Cruise of the Breadwinner. London: Joseph, 1946. 1st ed. VG in dj (sl torn, chipped). *Rees.* $31/£20

BATES, H.E. The Cruise of the Breadwinner. London: Michael Joseph, 1946. 1st ed. Sl rubbed, o/w VG in dj (nicked, rubbed). *Virgo.* $39/£25

BATES, H.E. Cut and Come Again. London: Jonathan Cape, (1935). 1st ed. Sl bumped, edges sl spotted, o/w Nice in dj (sl frayed). *Ash.* $155/£100

BATES, H.E. The Daffodil Sky. London, (1955). 1st ed. Fine in dj. *Argosy*. $45/£29

BATES, H.E. The Day of the Tortoise. Joseph, 1961. 1st ed. VG in VG dj. *Whiteson*. $23/£15

BATES, H.E. Down the River. London: Gollancz, 1937. 1st ed. 83 wood engrs by Agnes Miller Parker. Inscrip, o/w VG + . *Willow House*. $70/£45

BATES, H.E. The Fabulous Mrs. V. London, 1964. 1st ed. Fine (spine heel sl creased) in NF dj. *Polyanthos*. $30/£19

BATES, H.E. The Fallow Land. London, 1932. 1st ed. Fine in dj. *Argosy*. $175/£113

BATES, H.E. The Fallow Land. London, 1932. 1st ed. VG in dj (spine sl dknd). *Words Etc*. $194/£125

BATES, H.E. The Four Beauties. London, (1968). 1st ed. Fine in dj. *Argosy*. $40/£26

BATES, H.E. A German Idyll. Golden Cockerel, 1932. 1st ed, ltd to 307 signed. Uncut. Dec cl. Sl dull, else NF. *Whiteson*. $194/£125

BATES, H.E. The Golden Oriole. London: Michael Joseph, 1962. 1st UK ed. NF in VG + dj (price-clipped). *Williams*. $39/£25

BATES, H.E. The Jacaranda Tree. London: Joseph, 1949. 1st ed. Sig, edges foxed, o/w VG in dj (worn). *Rees*. $16/£10

BATES, H.E. The Jacaranda Tree. Joseph, 1949. 1st ed. Spine edges sl faded, else Good in dj (sl torn). *Whiteson*. $22/£14

BATES, H.E. Love for Lydia. London: Michael Joseph, 1952. Eps sl browned, gilt sl dull, o/w VG in dj (soiled, nicked). *Virgo*. $20/£13

BATES, H.E. Mrs. Esmonds Life. London: By D. White & Son, 1931. #292/300. Signed. Yellow buckram, gilt titles. Sl scuffed, else VG. *Heller*. $175/£113

BATES, H.E. The Poacher. London: Cape, 1935. 1st ed. Staining, o/w Nice in VG dj (tears, spine sunned). *Beasley*. $50/£32

BATES, H.E. The Scarlet Sword. London: Michael Joseph, 1950. 1st ed. Spine rubbed, faded, fr joint sl cracked, o/w VG in dj (worn, price-clipped, chipped). *Virgo*. $39/£25

BATES, H.E. The Seasons and the Gardener. Cambridge, 1941. C.F. Tunnicliffe (engrs). Limp ptd wrappers. Dj. *Petersfield*. $28/£18

BATES, H.E. Seven Tales and Alexander. London: Scholartis Press, 1929. 1st ed, ltd to 950. Partially unopened. Fine in VG dj. *Godot*. $85/£55

BATES, H.E. Through the Woods. NY, 1936. 1st Amer ed. Fine (3 cvr nicks). *Polyanthos*. $75/£48

BATES, H.E. The Vanished World. 1969. 1st UK ed. Fine in NF dj. *Sclanders*. $19/£12

BATES, H.E. The Yellow Meads of Asphodel. London, (1976). 1st ed. VG in dj. *Argosy*. $25/£16

BATES, HENRY WALTER. The Naturalist on the River Amazons. London/Boston: John Murray/Roberts Bros, 1875. 3rd ed. Pebbled grn cl (wear). Good (bkpl removal). *Glenn*. $65/£42

BATES, JOSEPH D., JR. Atlantic Salmon Flies and Fishing. Stackpole, (1970). 1st ed. 8 color plts. Fine in dj (lacks 2-inch piece). *Artis*. $50/£32

BATES, MOSES. The Plymouth (MA) Almanac. Containing the Names of the Citizens...1860.... Plymouth, MA: Charles C. Doten, 1860. 1st ed. 116pp, 28pp ads. Brn cl (spine sl rubbed). *Karmiole*. $50/£32

BATES, MRS. D.B. Incidents on Land and Water, or Four Years on the Pacific Coast. Boston: James French, 1857. 1st ed. Frontis, 336pp. Black cl stamped in gilt, blind. Lt rubbed, o/w Very Nice (2 sm bkpls; inscrip). *Karmiole*. $150/£97

BATES, MRS. D.B. Incidents on Land and Water, or Four Years on the Pacific Coast.... Boston: Libby, 1858. 7th ed. 336pp; 4 plts, guards. Blind-stamped red cl (lt rubbed, stained), gilt vignettes. *Petrilla*. $60/£39

BATES, MRS. D.B. Incidents on Land and Water. Boston: Published for Author, 1860. 9th ed. Frontis, 336pp, 3 full-pg illus. Blind, gold-stamped cl. Bkpl of Carl I. Wheat. *Dawson*. $50/£32

BATES, RALPH. Lean Men: An Episode in a Life. London: Peter Davies, 1934. 1st ed. *Patterson*. $70/£45

BATES, RALPH. The Miraculous Horde. London: Cape, 1939. 1st ed. Fine in pict dj. *Patterson*. $78/£50

BATESTON, W. Mendel's Principles of Heredity. CUP, 1909. Frontis port, xiv,396pp, 6 color plts. Cl (hinges cracked; worn; accession label; dampstained edges). *Edwards*. $70/£45

BATSFORD, HARRY and CHARLES FRY. The Greater English Church of the Middle Ages. London: Batsford, 1940. 1st ed. (Cl lt spotted.) Dj. *Hollett*. $39/£25

BATSFORD, HERBERT. English Mural Monuments and Tombstones. London, (1916). 1st ed. Dec gilt cl (backstrip chipped). *Argosy*. $60/£39

BATSFORD, HERBERT. English Mural Monuments and Tombstones. Batsford, 1916. 84 b/w plts. (Eps spotted; ex-libris; discoloring.) *Edwards*. $116/£75

BATTEN, A. Flowers of Southern Africa. Sandton, 1986. 100 Fine color plts. Dj. *Sutton*. $225/£145

BATTEN, JOHN M. Reminiscences of Two Years in the United States Navy. Lancaster, PA: Inquirer Ptg & Publ Co, 1881. 1st ed. Signed presentation copy. 125pp. Orig blue-gray cl. VG. *Chapel Hill*. $150/£97

BATTEN, M.I. English Windmills. London: Architectural Press, 1930-32. 1st ed. 2 vols. (Cl lt faded.) Dj vol 2. *Hollett*. $101/£65

BATTERSBY, MARTIN. The Decorative Twenties. NY, 1969. VG in dj. *Argosy*. $60/£39

BATTEY, THOMAS C. The Life and Adventures of a Quaker Among the Indians. Boston: Lee & Shepard, 1876. xii,339pp. Orig cl (extrems worn; damped). (Sm lib label.) *Hollett*. $186/£120

BATTLE, KEMP. History of the University of North Carolina. Raleigh: Ptd by Edwards and Broughton, 1907-1912. 1st ed. 2 vols. 1pg supplement (foxed) tipped in vol 2. Rubbed, stained; sig vol 1 loose, else VG. *Cahan*. $135/£87

Battle-Fields of the South, from Bull Run to Fredericksburg. (By Thomas E. Caffey.) London: Smith, Elder, 1863. 1st ed. 2 vols. 8vo, 339; 399pp, 2 fldg maps; unopened. Purple cl. Nice set (spine ends rubbed, vol II chipped). Howes B 238. *Chapel Hill*. $600/£387

BATTS, J. British Manuscript Diaries of the 19th Century. Rowman & Littlefield, 1976. Fine in dj. *Moss*. $54/£35

BATTY, J.H. How to Hunt and Trap. Phila: Porter & Coates, 1878. 220,(4)pp; added illus title pg. Rust cl, stamped in gold/black (lower spine frayed). *Karmiole*. $75/£48

BATTY, J.H. Practical Taxidermy, and Home Decoration. NY: OJ, 1906. Brn cl, gilt stamped. VG + . *Bohling*. $65/£42

BAUD-BOVY, DANIEL. Peasant Art in Switzerland. Arthur Palliser (trans). The Studio, 1924. Tipped-in color frontis (2 corners sl torn), 14 tipped-in color plts. Mod cl (rebound; ex-lib, ink stamps, margins sl thumbed). *Edwards.* $54/£35

BAUDELAIRE, CHARLES. Flowers of Evil. London: LEC, 1940. #904/1500 numbered. 2 vols. Jacob Epstein (stone lithos). Eng text brick red cl. French facs ed in wrappers & tissue dj. Both NF in slipcase (cl vol rubbed). *Hermitage.* $225/£145

BAUDELAIRE, CHARLES. Paris Spleen 1869. Louise Varese (trans). (NY): New Directions, (1947). Cl-backed patterned bds. Sl discolored, else Good in slipcase (worn; splitting). *King.* $20/£13

BAUDOUIN, FRANS. Rubens. NY, 1977. Good in dj. *Washton.* $75/£48

BAUDUY, JEROME K. Diseases of the Nervous System. Phila: Lippincott, 1892. 2nd ed. 352pp. Orig cl, recently recased saving orig spine. Final 50 leaves bottom outer corner chipped. *Goodrich.* $150/£97

BAUER, CLYDE. The Story of Yellowstone Geysers. Yellowstone Park, WY: Haynes, (1937). 1st ed. Tipped-in color frontis; dbl-pg map. Tan cl (bumped, rubbed). NF. *Blue Mountain.* $25/£16

BAUER, CLYDE. Yellowstone Geysers. Yellowstone Park: Haynes, (1947). Rev ed. Tipped-in frontis. VG in Good+ dj. *Oregon.* $40/£26

BAUER, JOHANN. Kafka and Prague. NY, (1971). 1st ed. VG. *Argosy.* $60/£39

BAUER, K. JACK. The Mexican War 1846-1848. NY, (1974). 1st ed. Dj spine faded, o/w VG+. *Pratt.* $50/£32

BAUER, K. JACK. The Mexican War 1846-1848. NY, 1974. 1st ed. VG in VG dj. *Clark.* $50/£32

BAUER, K. JACK. Surfboats and Horse Marines. Annapolis, 1969. 1st ed. VG in VG dj. *Clark.* $45/£29

BAUER, MAX. Precious Stones. L.J. Spencer (trans). London: Charles Griffin, 1904. 19 plts (8 color) only (of 20; lacks plt 9). Teg. (Marbled eps, few leaves spotted.) 1/2 morocco (bkpl; upper hinge cracked; sl splitting head), gilt spines w/raised bands. *Edwards.* $233/£150

BAUM, DWIGHT JAMES (ed). Great Georgian Houses of America. NY: Architects Emergency Committee, 1933 and 1937. 1st ed. 2 vols. Sl rubbed; vol 2 foxed eps, 1st and last leaves, else VG set. *Bookpress.* $235/£152

BAUM, DWIGHT JAMES. Great Georgian Houses of America. Volume 1. NY: Architects Emergency Committee, 1933. 1st ed. Frontis. (Waterstained bottom edge; eps foxed; cvrs worn.) *Bookpress.* $95/£61

BAUM, JULIUS (ed). Romanesque Architecture in France. NY: B. Westermann, (1928). 2nd ed. Grn cl stamped in black/gold (bkpl). *Karmiole.* $75/£48

BAUM, JULIUS (ed). Romanesque Architecture in France. London: Country Life, (1928). 2nd ed. Lt foxing, else Fine. *Pharos.* $125/£81

BAUM, JULIUS (ed). Romanesque Architecture in France. London: Country Life, (1928). 2nd ed. Lt foxing, else Fine. *Pharos.* $125/£81

BAUM, L. FRANK. The Army Alphabet. Chicago: Geo. M. Hill, 1900. 1st ed. Lg 4to. Harry Kennedy (illus). Cl-backed illus bds (worn). Text, pictures Fine (pg edges folded). *Reisler.* $600/£387

BAUM, L. FRANK. The Cowardly Lion of Oz. Chicago: Reilly & Lee, Pre-1935. 266pp, 12 color plts by John R. Neill. VG in dj (lt chipped). *Davidson.* $400/£258

BAUM, L. FRANK. The Emerald City of Oz. Chicago: Reilly & Britton, (1910). 1st ed. 8vo. 296pp; 16 color plts w/metallic grn ink by John R. Neill. Lt blue cl, pict paste label; pict eps. VG. *Drusilla's.* $600/£387

BAUM, L. FRANK. Father Goose, His Book. Chicago: M.A. Donahue, ca 1910. 6th ed. 4to, unpaginated. W.W. Denslow (illus). Pict bds. VG in dj (several pieces missing). *Davidson.* $385/£248

BAUM, L. FRANK. The Land of Oz. Chicago, 1939. John R. Neil (illus). 9x6.5 inches. 287pp. Cl w/pict label. Bkpl mostly removed; tape mks eps, else Nice in dj (tape repairs). *King.* $35/£23

BAUM, L. FRANK. The Lost Princess of Oz. Reilly & Lee, 1917. 12 full-pg, color plts by J.R. Neill. NF. *Fine Books.* $135/£87

BAUM, L. FRANK. The Magic of Oz. Chicago, (1919). 1st ed, 1st state. 9x6.5 inches. 266pp; 12 full-pg color plts (1 illus loose). Cl, color label. (Ink, stamped names; ink inscrip; fr inner hinge cracked; cvrs worn, soiled; foxing.) *King.* $195/£126

BAUM, L. FRANK. The Magic of Oz. Chicago: Reilly & Lee, (1919). 1st ed, 1st state. 4to. 12 color plts by John R. Neill. Olive-grn cl, color paste label (edges chipped; marginal tear rep). *Reisler.* $485/£313

BAUM, L. FRANK. The Magic of Oz. Chicago: Reilly & Lee, (1935). John R. Neill (illus). Color plt mtd to fr cvr. Lower corner tp creased, else Fine, As New in color ptd dj (sm spot on spine). *Cahan.* $125/£81

BAUM, L. FRANK. The Magic of Oz. Chicago: Reilly & Lee, (ca 1935). Early ptg. Sm 4to. John R. Neill (illus). Dk orange cl. VG in dj w/back flap listing 26 titles through 'Ojo in Oz' (nicks). *Houle.* $125/£81

BAUM, L. FRANK. The Magical Monarch of Mo. Indianapolis: Bobbs-Merrill, (1903). 1st ed, 2nd state, w/variant eps from The Enchanted Island of Yew. 4to. 12 color plts by Frank Verbeck (sl coloring one dwg). Blue cl w/paste label, black outlines (sm ink stains; minor wear corners, base spine). *Reisler.* $275/£177

BAUM, L. FRANK. The Navy Alphabet. Chicago: George M. Hill, 1900. 1st ed. Lg, 4to. Harry Kennedy (illus). Cvrs rubbed, edgewear. *Reisler.* $550/£355

BAUM, L. FRANK. The New Wizard of Oz. Indianapolis: Bobbs-Merrill, (1939). 8vo, 208pp. 8 inserted color plts, pict eps w/scenes from MGM movie. W.W. Denslow (illus). Grn cl w/pict, black lettering, spine gilt lettered. VG in dj (tattered). *Davidson.* $275/£177

BAUM, L. FRANK. The New Wizard of Oz. Indianapolis: Bobbs-Merrill, (1944). Ltr ptg. 4to. 6 full-pg color illus by Evelyn Copelman. VG in dj (chips). *Houle.* $95/£61

BAUM, L. FRANK. Ozma of Oz. Chicago, (1907). Later ptg (1946?). John R. Neill (illus). 9x6.5 inches. 270pp. Cl, pict label. Sl tape residue eps, else Nice in dj (taped reinforcements). *King.* $35/£23

BAUM, L. FRANK. Rinkitink in Oz. Reilly & Lee, 1916. 12 full-pg, full color plts by J.R. Neill. NF in dj (lt worn; chipped). *Fine Books.* $225/£145

BAUM, L. FRANK. Rinkitink in Oz. Chicago: Reilly & Lee, pre-1935. 314pp, 12 color plts by John R. Neill, w/captions. Red cl, pict label. NF in dj (lt torn). *Davidson.* $400/£258

BAUM, L. FRANK. The Royal Book of Oz. Ruth Plumly Thompson (ed). Chicago: Reilly & Lee, (1921). 1st ed, 1st state. 4to. 12 color plts by John R. Neill. Lt grey cl, color paste label. (Sm marginal stain.) Pict dj (worn, largely complete). *Reisler.* $2,850/£1,839

BAUM, L. FRANK. The Scarecrow of Oz. Chicago: Reilly & Lee, ca 1940s (dj list thru Magic Mimic). 8vo, 288pp. John R. Neill (illus). Grn cl w/pict onlay. VG in dj (tattered). *Davidson.* $150/£97

BAUM, L. FRANK. The Sea Fairies. Chicago: Reilly & Britton, (1911). 1st ed. 4to. (240pp); 12 duo-tone plts by John R. Neill. Grn ribbed cl, dk grn lettering, red fish; pict paste label; illus eps. VG + . *Drusilla's.* $350/£226

BAUM, L. FRANK. Sky Island. Chicago: Reilly & Britton, 1912. 1st ed. 4to. 12 full-pg color plts by John R. Neill; color eps (minor mks; owner block filled in). Red cl w/color paste label (corner chipped; spine sl darkened). *Reisler.* $400/£258

BAUM, L. FRANK. Tik-Tok of Oz. Chicago: Reilly & Lee, (1935). John R. Neill (illus). Color plt mtd to fr cvr. Fine, As New in color ptd dj. *Cahan.* $125/£81

BAUM, L. FRANK. The Tin Woodman of Oz. Reilly & Britton, 1918. 1st ed, 1st state. 4to, 288pp, 12 color plts by John R. Neill. Red cl, pict paste-on w/ads listing thru present title. VG (1-inch defect illus ep). *Davidson.* $1,000/£645

BAUM, L. FRANK. The Tin Woodman of Oz. Chicago: Reilly & Lee, ca 1940s. This ed b/w. 8vo, 287pp. John R. Neil (illus). Beige cl, pict onlay. VG (ink inscrip) in dj (chipped). *Davidson.* $150/£97

BAUM, L. FRANK. The Wizard of Oz and The Land of Oz. NY: Looking Glass Library, (1960). 1st ed thus. 8vo. Rita Fava (illus). Illus grn bds (mild edgewear). Pict dj (edges, folds worn). *Reisler.* $85/£55

BAUM, L. FRANK. The Wizard of Oz. Akron: Saalfield, (1944). 6 VG movable color plts (1 tab creased) by Julian Wehr. Orange pict paper-cvrd bds, spiral bound. VG. *Davidson.* $200/£129

BAUMANN, FREDRICK. Gonorrhea: Its Diagnosis and Treatment. NY, 1908. 1st ed. 206pp. Good. *Fye.* $60/£39

BAUMGARTNER, LEONA and JOHN F. FULTON. A Bibliography of the Poem, Syphilis Sive Morbus Gallicus. (By Girolamo Fracastoro of Verona). New Haven: Yale Univ Press, 1935. 1st ed. Frontis, 9 facs. Blue cl, gilt spine. Good. *Karmiole.* $50/£32

BAUMLER, ERNST. Paul Ehrlich: Scientist for Life. NY, 1984. 1st Eng trans. Good. *Fye.* $35/£23

BAUR, JOHN E. Christmas on the American Frontier, 1800-1900. Caldwell: Caxton, 1961. 1st ed. Dec eps. Red cl. Fine in NF dj. *Harrington.* $50/£32

BAUR, JOHN I.H. The Inlander: Life and Work of Charles Burchfield, 1893-1967. Newark, 1982. VG in dj. *Argosy.* $125/£81

BAUSCH, EDWARD. Manipulation of the Microscope. Rochester, NY: Bausch & Lomb, 1897. 3rd ed, 15th thousand. 200pp (name stamps; pencil notes, mks). Good in maroon cl (worn, spotted; bds sl warped). *Knollwood.* $60/£39

BAX, CLIFFORD and LEON M. LION. Hemlock for Eight. Frederick Muller, (1946). 1st ed. Inscribed presentation. Dj (spine head, foot defective). *Bickersteth.* $47/£30

BAX, CLIFFORD. Pretty Witty Nell. London: Chapman & Hall, 1932. 13 plts. 1/2 cl, gilt. Fine. *Peter Taylor.* $25/£16

BAXANDALL, MICHAEL. Giotto and the Orators. Clarendon, 1971. (Ex-lib, bkpl, ink stamps.) Dj. *Edwards.* $31/£20

BAXT, GEORGE. A Queer Kind of Death. London: Jonathan Cape, 1967. 1st ed. VG in Good dj. *Ming.* $39/£25

BAXT, GEORGE. Swing Low, Sweet Harriet. NY: S&S, 1967. 1st ed. Fine in NF dj (short closed tear). *Janus.* $45/£29

BAXTER, CHARLES. First Light. NY: Viking, 1987. 1st ed. Inscribed. Fine in Fine dj. *Beasley.* $75/£48

BAXTER, DOREEN. Woodland Frolics. Leicester: Brockhampton Press, (1952). 1st ed. 4to. 6 full-pg color plts. Grey cl (sl shelfwear), green lettering, illus. Pict dj (worn; chipped). *Reisler.* $165/£106

BAXTER, GLEN. Atlas. NY: Knopf, 1983. 1st Amer ed. Fine in glossy bds as issued. *Between The Covers.* $45/£29

BAXTER, JAMES PHINNEY. The Pioneers of New France in New England. Albany: Joel Munsell's Sons, 1894. 450pp. NF. Howes B 249. *Schoyer.* $150/£97

BAXTER, JAMES PHINNEY. The Pioneers of New France in New England. Albany: Munsell, 1894. 1st ed. (2),450pp. Ptd yellow bds (worn). Howes B 249. *Ginsberg.* $150/£97

Bay of San Francisco. Chicago: Lewis Pub Co, 1892. 2 vols. 708; 680pp. Aeg. Full calf, gilt (vol 1 rebacked; vol 2 outer hinges cracked). *Karmiole.* $200/£129

BAY, J. CHRISTIAN. A Handful of Western Books.... Cedar Rapids, IA, 1935/1936/1936. One of 350; 400; 400. 1st, 3rd vols inscribed. 3 vols. Cl-backed bds, ptd labels. *Bohling.* $250/£161

BAYER, OLIVER WELD (ed). Cleveland Murders. NY, (1947). 1st ed. Cl-backed bds. VG in dj (sl frayed, price-clipped). *King.* $25/£16

BAYER, OLIVER WELD. Paper Chase. Crime Club, 1943. 1st ed, 1st bk. Cl edges lt faded, else NF in dj (lt worn). *Murder.* $45/£29

BAYLEY, DENIS. A Londoner in Rupert's Land. Thomas Bunn of the Hudson's Bay Company. Chichester, Eng: Moore & Tillyer, 1969. 1st ed. Fldg chart, ep maps; prospectus sheet laid in. VF in VF dj. *Oregon.* $45/£29

BAYLEY, F.W.N. Drolleries for Little Folks.... NY: C. Shepard, n.d. (ca 1850). 8vo. 32pp. Dec paper wrappers. Sigs, damp spots, sl soiled, spine tender, else VG. *Hobbyhorse.* $150/£97

BAYLEY, N. and W. MAYNE. The Mouldy. NY: Knopf, 1982. 1st Amer ed. Nicola Bayley (illus). Mint in Mint dj. *Davidson.* $50/£32

BAYLISS, JOSEPH E. and ESTELLE L. River of Destiny, the Saint Marys. Detroit, 1955. 1st ed, signed by both authors. Lt spotted, else Good in dj (used). *King.* $35/£23

BAYLISS, WILLIAM. The Vaso-Motor System. London, 1923. 1st ed. Good. *Fye.* $125/£81

BAYLOR, GEORGE. Bull Run to Bull Run. Richmond: B.F. Johnson, 1900. 1st ed. Frontis port. Orig gilt, silverstamped blue buckram. Lt rubbed, else NF. *Chapel Hill.* $300/£194

BAYLOR, GEORGE. Bull Run to Bull Run; or, Four Years in the Army of Northern Virginia. Richmond: B.F. Johnson, 1900. 1st ed. VG. *Mcgowan.* $300/£194

BAYNE, SAMUEL G. On an Irish Jaunting Car Through Donegal and Connemara. NY: Harper, 1902. 1st ed. VG + . *Bishop.* $30/£19

BAZANCOURT, CESAR LECAT. Crimean Expedition, to the Capture of Sebastopol. Robert Howe Gould (trans). London: Sampson Low, 1856. 2 vols. 2 frontis port lithos, xxxvi,413; 538pp. Maroon cl stamped in blind, gilt (faded, chipped). *Schoyer.* $150/£97

BAZIN, GERMAIN. The Loom of Art. J. Griffin (trans). NY, (1962). VG. *Argosy.* $35/£23

BAZIN, HERVE. Viper in the Fist. NY: Prentice-Hall, 1951. 1st US ed. VG (sl foxing; fading) in VG + dj. *Lame Duck.* $45/£29

BEACH, REX. Padlocked. NY, 1926. Stated 1st ed. Good. *Hayman.* $15/£10

BEACH, S.A. The Apples of New York. Albany, 1905. 2 vols. 130 color, 68 b/w plts. Gilt-stamped cl (bumped; stamp). Bright set. *Sutton.* $195/£126

BEACH, SYLVIA. Shakespeare and Company. NY: Harcourt, Brace, (1959). 1st ed. Fine in dj. *Oak Knoll.* $35/£23

BEACH, SYLVIA. Shakespeare and Company. NY: Harcourt Brace, n.d. (c. 1959). 1st ed. Inscrip, bumped, o/w VG in dj (chipped, soiled). *Virgo.* $47/£30

BEACH, SYLVIA. Ulysses in Paris. Harcourt, Brace, 1956. 1st ed, privately ptd. Illus bds; cvr photo. VG. *Whiteson.* $37/£24

BEADLE, ERASTUS F. To Nebraska in '57, a Diary of Erastus F. Beadle. NY Pub Lib, 1923. Frontis facs; 2 plts. Ptd wraps (lt soiled; spine ends chipped). *Bohling.* $45/£29

BEADLE, ERASTUS F. To Nebraska in '57. NY Pub Lib, 1923. Wraps. *Heinoldt.* $18/£12

BEADLE, J.H. Life in Utah. Phila, 1870. 1st ed. Frontis, 540pp. Lt staining, lt edgewear, name, o/w VG. *Benchmark.* $55/£35

BEADLE, J.H. Polygamy or The Mysteries and Crimes of Mormonism.... N.p., (1904). (Lt rubbed, soiled; spine ends frayed; fr hinge cracked, rep removed.) *Bohling.* $45/£29

BEADLE, J.H. Western Wilds, and the Men Who Redeem Them. Cincinnati: Jones Bros, 1878. Dbl-pg map. 3/4 leather (spine sunned; scuffed). Howes B 269. *Schoyer.* $75/£48

BEAGLE, PETER S. The Fantasy Worlds of Peter Beagle. NY: Viking, 1978. 1st ed thus. Fine in dj. *Limestone.* $40/£26

BEAGLE, PETER S. A Fine and Private Place. NY: Viking, 1960. 1st ed, 1st bk. Name, sm spots endsheets, else NF in VG dj (sm nicks, rear panel tanned). *Reese.* $75/£48

BEAGLE, PETER S. A Fine and Private Place. NY: Viking, 1960. 1st ed, 1st bk. Sm owner label, scuff fr bd, else NF in NF dj (lt rubbed). *Between The Covers.* $125/£81

BEAGLE, PETER S. A Fine and Private Place. Muller, 1960. 1st Eng ed, 1st bk. Fine in dj. *Aronovitz.* $95/£61

BEAGLE, PETER S. The Last Unicorn. NY: Viking, (1968). 1st ed. Fine in black dj (lt mkd, 2 short tears). *Heller.* $125/£81

BEAGLE, PETER S. The Last Unicorn. Viking, 1968. 1st ed. Fine in dj. *Madle.* $175/£113

BEAGLE, PETER. The Last Unicorn. Viking, 1968. 1st ed. Fine in dj. *Fine Books.* $125/£81

BEAL, M.D. A History of Southeastern Idaho. Caldwell: Caxton, 1942. 1st ed. VG. *Oregon.* $70/£45

BEAL, MERRILL D. The Story of Man in Yellowstone. Caldwell: Caxton, 1949. 1st ed. VG in VG dj. *Perier.* $45/£29

BEAL, REBECCA J. Jacob Eichholtz 1776-1842: Portrait Painter of Pennsylvania. Phila: Hist Soc of PA, 1969. 1st ed. Fine in dj. *Cahan.* $50/£32

BEALBY, J.T. How to Make an Orchard in British Columbia. London, 1912. Dec, emb cl (minor soiling). *Brooks.* $29/£19

BEALE, LIONEL S. Disease Germs; Their Nature and Origin. London, 1872. 2nd ed. 472pp. Inner hinges cracked. *Fye.* $75/£48

BEALE, LIONEL S. How to Work with the Microscope. London: Harrison, 1868. 4th ed. 383pp, photo frontis, 69 plts. VG (sig). *Savona.* $93/£60

BEALE, LIONEL S. The Microscope and Its Application to Practical Medicine. London, 1867. 3rd ed. xxiv,320pp; 58 plts. New eps; short tear half title; spine defective; cl worn, o/w VG. *Whitehart.* $54/£35

BEALE, MARIE. Decatur House and Its Inhabitants. (Washington: Nat'l Trust for Hist Preservation), 1954. 1st ed. Fine in dj (tattered). *Bookpress.* $45/£29

BEALE, RICHARD LEE TUBERVILLE. History of the Ninth Virginia Cavalry in the War Between the States. Richmond, VA: B.F. Johnson, 1899. 1st ed. 192pp. Sl extrem wear, else VG. Howes B 274. *Mcgowan.* $1,500/£968

BEAN, R.B. Sir William Osler from His Bedside Teachings and Writings. William Bennett Bean (ed). NY: Schuman, 1950. Nice in dj. *Goodrich.* $75/£48

BEAN, W.J. Trees and Shrubs Hardy in the British Isles. London, 1950-51. 7th ed. 3 vols. Fine in dj. *Henly.* $74/£48

BEAR, GREG. Blood Music. Arbor House, 1985. 1st ed. Fine in dj. *Madle.* $45/£29

BEAR, GREG. Eon. (NY): Bluejay International, (1985). 1st ed. Fine in NF dj. *Antic Hay.* $50/£32

BEAR, GREG. The Wind From a Burning Woman. Arkham House, 1983. 1st ed. VF in dj. *Madle.* $125/£81

BEAR, STANDING. Land of the Spotted Eagle. Boston/NY: Houghton Mifflin, 1933. 1st ed. Frontis. Black-stamped cl (2 spots top edge; pencil marginalia). Dj (edgewear). *Dawson.* $40/£26

BEARD, CHARLES R. A Catalogue of the Collection of Martinware Formed by Mr. Frederick John Nettlefold.... London: Waterlow & Sons, 1936. 1st ed, presentation copy. 69 plts (incl 31 mtd, colored). Gilt-edged cl (ex-lib w/perf, ink stamps, bkpl, #s; soiled; chipped); teg, rest uncut. *Edwards.* $233/£150

BEARD, GEOFFREY. Georgian Craftsmen. NY, 1967. 1st US ed. (Ex-lib, bkpl, ink stamps.) Dj (#s). *Edwards.* $39/£25

BEARD, GEORGE and A.D. ROCKWELL. A Practical Treatise on the Medical and Surgical Uses of Electricity. NY, 1875. 2nd ed. 794pp. *Fye.* $150/£97

BEARD, GEORGE. Sexual Neurasthenia (Nervous Exhaustion). NY, 1884. 1st ed. 270pp. Good. *Fye.* $150/£97

BEARD, GEORGE. Stimulants and Narcotics; Medically, Philosophically, and Morally Considered. NY, 1871. 1st ed. 155pp. Good. *Fye.* $250/£161

BEARD, PETER. Longing for Darkness. Harcourt, Brace & Jovanovich, 1975. 1st ed. Fine in Fine dj. *Bishop.* $90/£58

BEARDSLEY, AUBREY. A Book of Fifty Drawings. London: Leonard Smithers, 1897. 1st ed. One of 500 on japon paper. Teg. Pict cl (sl worn, mkd, sl splashed). Good (few pp sl creased). *Ash.* $380/£245

BEARDSLEY, AUBREY. The Later Work.... London: John Lane, 1930. 174 plts. Blue cl. Good. *Cox.* $54/£35

BEARDSLEY, AUBREY. Letters from Aubrey Beardsley to Leonard Smithers. R.A. Walker (ed). (London): First Edition Club, 1937. 2 photogravure ports. Gilt-stamped black cl. NF. *House.* $60/£39

BEARDSLEY, AUBREY. The Letters of Aubrey Beardsley. London: Cassell, 1971. 1st ed. Sl bruised, o/w Very Nice in dj (soiled, nicked, price-clipped). *Virgo.* $70/£45

BEARDSLEY, AUBREY. The Uncollected Works. London: John Lane, (1925). 1st ed. Blue dec cl. *Appelfeld.* $150/£97

BEARDSLEY, AUBREY. Under the Hill and Other Essays in Prose and Verse. London: John Lane, Bodley Head, 1904. 1st ed. Teg. Dec cl, gilt. Nice (lt worn, lib label). *Ash.* $380/£245

BEARE, W. The Roman Stage: A Short History of Latin Drama.... London: Methuen, (1964). 8 plts. Good in dj. *Archaeologia.* $45/£29

BEARSS, EDWIN C. Hardluck Ironclad, The Sinking and Salvage of the Cairo. Baton Rouge, 1966. 1st ed. Cvr soiling o/w VG +. *Pratt.* $35/£23

BEARSS, EDWIN C. and A.M. GIBSON. Fort Smith: Little Gibraltar on the Arkansas. Norman: Univ of OK, (1969). 1st ed. VG in dj (sl worn). *Lien.* $30/£19

BEASLEY, H. The Druggist's General Receipt Book.... London, 1861. 5th ed. viii,494pp. Later paper-cvrd bds, new eps. Pp sl grubby, o/w VG. *Whitehart.* $62/£40

BEATIE, R.H., JR. Road to Manassas. N.p., 1961. 1st ed. VG + in VG + dj. *Pratt.* $37/£24

BEATON, CECIL. Ashcombe. London, 1949. 1st Eng ed. VG in dj (sl frayed). *Edrich.* $47/£30

BEATON, CECIL. The Face of the World. John Day. 1st ed. NF in VG + dj. *Bishop.* $42/£27

BEATON, CECIL. The Face of the World. London, 1957. 1st ed. (Feps lt spotted.) Dj (sl chipped). *Edwards.* $62/£40

BEATON, CECIL. Far East. London: Batsford, (1945). 1st ed. Color frontis. Dj. *Petersfield.* $23/£15

BEATON, CECIL. Near East. Batsford, 1943. 1st Eng ed. (Name.) Dj. *Edrich.* $47/£30

BEATON, CECIL. Photobiography. Doubleday, 1951. 1st ed. VG +. *Bishop.* $25/£16

BEATON, CECIL. Photobiography. London, 1951. 1st ed. Frontis port (sl foxing); in dj (sl chipped, browned). *Edwards.* $31/£20

BEATON, CECIL. Photobiography. NY: Doubleday, 1951. 1st ed. 100 b/w plts. VG in illus dj. *Cahan.* $60/£39

BEATON, MAUDE. From Cairo to Khyber to Celebes. NY: Liveright, (1942). Lt blue cl stamped in gilt, black. In dj (chipped). *Schoyer.* $25/£16

BEATTIE, ANN. Alex Katz. NY: Abrams, (1987). 1st ed. 26 plts. Fine in Fine dj. *Robbins.* $35/£23

BEATTIE, ANN. Chilly Scenes of Winter. GC: Doubleday, 1976. 1st ed. Fine in VG dj (price-clipped; spine ends chipped; creases). *Chapel Hill.* $75/£48

BEATTIE, ANN. Chilly Scenes of Winter. GC: Doubleday, 1976. 1st ed. Fine in NF dj. *Pettler.* $80/£52

BEATTIE, ANN. Distortions. GC: Doubleday, (1976). 1st ed. Name, else Fine in VG dj (price-clipped). *Chapel Hill.* $75/£48

BEATTIE, ANN. Distortions. GC: Doubleday, 1976. 1st ed, 1st bk. Fine (edges sl dknd) in NF dj (lt rubbed). *Between The Covers.* $100/£65

BEATTIE, ANN. Secrets and Surprises. NY: Random House, (1978). 1st ed. Effaced pub's stamp bottom edge, o/w Fine in dj (lt worn; price-clipped). *Hermitage.* $30/£19

BEATTIE, SUSAN. The New Sculpture. New Haven/London: Yale Univ, 1983. Dj (sl torn spine head). *Edwards.* $47/£30

BEATTY, JOHN. Memoirs of a Volunteer 1861-1863. Harve S. Ford (ed). Cincinnati, 1879. 1946 reprint. 317pp; map. VG + in VG + dj (lt wear). *Pratt.* $40/£26

BEATTY, K.J. Human Leopards. London: Hugh Rees, 1915. 1st ed. 33 plts. VG in dj (sl defective at edges). *Hollett.* $101/£65

BEAUFORT, DUKE OF and MOWBRAY MORRIS. Hunting. London: Longmans, Green, 1894. 7th ed, rev. xii,385pp + ad leaf; uncut. (Lt spotting.) Pict brn cl. Good. *Cox.* $39/£25

BEAUFORT, DUKE OF. Driving. London, 1889. Frontis, tp vignette, xvi,426pp + (iv)pub's ads, 11 plts. Unopened. (Lt foxing; spine discolored, wrinkled.) *Edwards.* $54/£35

BEAUFORT, EMILY A. Egyptian Sepulchres and Syrian Shrines, Including a Visit to Palmyra. London: Macmillan, 1874. New ed. viii,(iii),546pp. Blue morocco; gilt-dec spine; leather label; dentelles. VG. *Petrilla.* $75/£48

BEAUMONT, C. The Intruder. Putnam, 1959. 1st ed. NF in VG + dj. *Aronovitz.* $85/£55

BEAUMONT, CYRIL. Ballet Design: Past and Present. (London, 1946). VG in dj. *Argosy.* $60/£39

BEAUMONT, CYRIL. Serge Diaghilev. London: C.W. Beaumont, 1933. 1st ed. 7 plts. (Fep excised; sl soiled, chipped.) *Shasky.* $25/£16

BEAUMONT, ROBERTS. Colour in Woven Design. London: Whittaker, George Bell, 1890. 1st ed. xxiv,440,(32)pp; 32 color plts. VG. *Bookpress.* $275/£177

BEAUMONT, WILLIAM. Experiments and Observations on the Gastric Juice, and the Physiology of Digestion. Plattsburgh, 1833. 1st ed. 280pp (foxed, browned), 3 engr plts. Good in orig bds (spine worn, faded). In 1/4 calf & linen clamshell box. *Goodrich.* $1,275/£823

BEAUMONT, WILLIAM. Experiments and Observations on the Gastric Juice, and the Physiology of Digestion. Boston: Lilly, Wait, 1835. 2nd Amer ed. 280pp (heavily foxed, browned). Orig bds (rebacked). Good. *Goodrich.* $575/£371

BEAUMONT, WILLIAM. Experiments and Observations on the Gastric Juice, and the Physiology of Digestion. Edinburgh: Maclachlan & Stewart, mdcccxxxviii (1838). 1st British ed, rpt from Plattsburgh ed. 1/2 title; xx,319pp + ads. Orig cl (wear to headpiece), paper label; uncut. VG. *Goodrich.* $775/£500

BEAUMONT, WILLIAM. The Physiology of Digestion with Experiments on the Gastric Juice. Burlington: Chauncey Goodrich, 1848. 2nd ed. 303,(1)pp. Good in orig bds (newly rebacked, orig label laid down; text heavily foxed, browned). *Goodrich.* $475/£306

BEAUMONT, WILLIAM. The Physiology of Digestion.... Burlington: Chauncey Goodrich, 1847. 2nd ed. 303pp. Pub's blind-stamped ribbed brn cl, gilt spine. Bkpl traces pastedown, else VG. *Hermitage.* $425/£274

BEAUREGARD, G.T. A Commentary on the Campaign and Battle of Manassas of July, 1861. NY: Putnam's, 1891. 1st ed. xiv,187pp; 2 fldg maps. VG. *Cahan.* $150/£97

BEAUREGARD, G.T. A Commentary on the Campaign and Battle of Manassas of July, 1861. NY/London: Putnam, 1891. 1st ed. 187pp, 2 fldg maps. Maroon cl. Spine ends lt rubbed, edges dknd, else VG. *Chapel Hill.* $200/£129

Beautiful Book of Nursery Rhymes, Stories and Pictures. London: Blackie, n.d. 4to. 84 color plts by Frank Adams. Red cl, blind-stamped decs, gold lettering. (Internal foxing.) *Reisler.* $535/£345

Beauty and the Beast. L.A.: Intervisual, 1976. Carousel Book. Pop-up. Karen Avery (illus). Lg 16mo. Glazed pict paper-cvrd bds. Fine. *Book Adoption.* $50/£32

Beauty and the Beast. London: C&W, 1976. Peepshow Book. Pop-up. Karen Avery (illus). Lg 16mo. Glazed pict paper-cvrd bds. Fine. *Book Adoption.* $60/£39

BEAVER, HERBERT. Reports and Letters of...1836-1838. Champoeg, 1959. 1st ed. One of 750. VF. *Oregon.* $60/£39

BEAZLEY, J.D. Attic Black-Figure Vase-Painters. NY: Hacker, 1978. Fine. *Archaeologia.* $150/£97

BEAZLEY, J.D. Attic Red-Figure Vase-Painters. Oxford: Clarendon, 1963. 2nd ed. 3 vols. Good in dj. *Archaeologia.* $650/£419

BEAZLEY, J.D. The Development of Attic Black-Figure. Berkeley: Univ of CA Press, 1951. 49 plts. (Bkpl.) *Archaeologia.* $85/£55

BEAZLEY, J.D. Etruscan Vase-Painting. Oxford: Clarendon Press, 1947. 40 plts. (Sig; lt bumped.) *Archaeologia.* $450/£290

BEAZLEY, J.D. Greek Vases in Poland. Oxford: Clarendon, 1928. 32 plts. (Spine lt chipped.) *Archaeologia.* $500/£323

BECCARIA. An Essay on Crimes and Punishments.... Phila: William Young, 1793. x,(13)-230pp. Contemp sheep. Sound (spine worn; head chipped away). *Felcone.* $275/£177

BECHER, A.B. Navigation of the Pacific Ocean.... London: J.D. Potter, 1864. (iv),264pp (early leaves clipped, no loss). 3/4 blue morocco (rubbed; pocket removed). *Schoyer.* $40/£26

BECHTEL, EDWIN DE T. Jacques Callot. NY: Braziller, 1955. 3 dbl-pg plts. Fine. *Europa.* $37/£24

BECHTEL, EDWIN DE T. Jacques Callot. NY, 1955. VG in dj. *Argosy.* $50/£32

BECK, HENRY C. More Forgotten Towns of Southern New Jersey. NY, 1937. 1st ed. Reviews pasted in. *Heinoldt.* $25/£16

BECK, JOHN. An Inaugural Dissertation on Infanticide. NY, 1817. 1st ed. 96pp. (2-inch piece cut top tp; foxed.) Wrappers. *Fye.* $300/£194

BECK, JOSEPH C. Applied Pathology in Diseases of the Nose, Throat, and Ear. St. Louis, 1923. 4 colored plts. Nice. *Goodrich.* $45/£29

BECK, L. ADAMS. Openers of the Gate. Cosmopolitan, 1930. 1st ed. VG. *Madle.* $50/£32

BECK, LEWIS C. Botany of the Northern and Middle States. Albany: Webster & Skinners, 1833. 471pp (lt foxing). 1/4 calf (rebound). *Cullen.* $225/£145

BECK, SYDNEY and ELIZABETH ROTH. Music in Prints. NY, 1965. 52 full-pg prints. As New. *Bond.* $30/£19

BECKER, ROBERT H. Designs on the Land. SF: Book Club of CA: 1969. One of 500. 64 maps. 1/2 leather. Cl faded, else Very Nice. *Bohling.* $350/£226

BECKER, ROBERT H. Designs on the Land: Disenos of California Ranchos and Their Makers. SF: Book Club of CA, 1969. 1st ed, 500 ptd. 64 facs maps. Suede-backed cl. Fine. *Cahan.* $350/£226

BECKER, STEPHEN. The Season of the Stranger. NY: Harpers, (1951). 1st ed, 1st bk. Fine in Fine dj. *Pharos.* $75/£48

BECKETT, HUGH. The Montreal Snow Shoe Club, Its History and Record.... Montreal: Becket Bros, 1882. 1st ed. 521pp. VG. *Oregon.* $75/£48

BECKETT, OLIVER. J.F. Herring and Sons. London, 1981. (Lower fore-edge cvr sl damaged.) *Argosy.* $60/£39

BECKETT, R.B. Hogarth. London, 1949. 202 plts. Good. *Washton.* $75/£48

BECKETT, SAMUEL (trans). An Anthology of Mexican Poetry. Thames & Hudson, 1958. 1st ed. VG in dj. *Whiteson.* $54/£35

BECKETT, SAMUEL. All Strange Away. London: Calder, 1979. 1st ed. Fine in dj. *Rees.* $19/£12

BECKETT, SAMUEL. All That Fall. NY: Grove, (1957). 1st trade ed. Fine in dj (lt edgeworn, sm tear). *Reese.* $100/£65

BECKETT, SAMUEL. All That Fall: A Play for Radio. London: Faber & Faber, (1957). 1st ed. Orig dec ptd wrappers (spine ends sl worn). *Sadlon.* $75/£48

BECKETT, SAMUEL. As the Story Was Told. London: Calder, 1990. 1st ed. Fine in dj. *Rees.* $19/£12

BECKETT, SAMUEL. Company. London: Calder, 1980. 1st ed. NF in dj. *Rees.* $31/£20

BECKETT, SAMUEL. From an Abandoned Work. London: Faber & Faber, (1958). 1st ed. Fine in pict wraps. *Pharos.* $60/£39

BECKETT, SAMUEL. Happy Days. Faber, 1962. 1st UK ed. Fine in NF dj (spine sl rubbed). *Sclanders.* $39/£25

BECKETT, SAMUEL. Krapp's Last Tape and Embers. Faber, 1959. 1st ed. Stiff wraps in integral dj. NF. *Poetry.* $70/£45

BECKETT, SAMUEL. Malone Dies. Grove Press, 1956. 1st US ed. Orig pb ed. VG (unevenly faded). *Williams.* $28/£18

BECKETT, SAMUEL. Mercier and Camier. London: Calder & Boyars, 1974. 1st ed. Fine in dj. *Rees.* $19/£12

BECKETT, SAMUEL. Molloy, Malone Dies, the Unnamable: A Trilogy. Paris: Olympia Press, (1959). 1st 1-vol ed, Olympia Press issue, variant issue w/'Francs: 1.800/18 N F.' on lower rt corner rear cvr. Rear cvr states: 'Francs: 1.800/ 18 N F./ not to be sold in/ the U.S.A. or U.K.' (Lt creased, short edgetears, lt wear.) *Godot.* $65/£42

BECKETT, SAMUEL. Our Exagmination Round His Factification for Incamination of Work in Progress. Paris: Shakespeare, 1929. 1st ed. Wrappers sl soiled, else NF. *Pharos.* $350/£226

BECKETT, SAMUEL. Play. London: Faber, 1964. 1st ed. VG in dj (rubbed, creased). *Rees.* $31/£20

BECKETT, SAMUEL. Poems in English. London: Calder, 1961. 1st ed. VG in dj. *Rees.* $70/£45

BECKETT, SAMUEL. Stories and Texts for Nothing. NY: Grove Press, (1967). 1st Amer ed. Sm spots fore-edge, else Fine in Fine dj (sm smudge). *Between The Covers.* $65/£42

BECKETT, SAMUEL. Texts for Nothing. Calder & Boyars, 1974. 1st ed. Fine in dj (price-clipped). *Rees.* $19/£12

BECKETT, SAMUEL. Waiting for Godot. Faber & Faber, (1956). 1st Eng ed. Tipped in Pub's note after title. (Press cutting pasted inner fr cvr; inscrip; sm piece paper pasted in.) Dj. *Bickersteth.* $59/£38

BECKETT, SAMUEL. Waiting for Godot. London: Faber & Faber, (1956). 1st Eng ed. Eps foxed, else NF in dj. *Godot.* $250/£161

BECKETT, SAMUEL. Watt. NY: Grove Press, (1959). 1st Amer ed, clothbound issue ltd to 100 numbered, specially bound. Paper-cvrd bds. Cl spine evenly faded, else Fine; issued w/o dj. *Godot.* $385/£248

BECKETT, SAMUEL. Watt. Paris: Olympia Press, 1953. 1st regular trade ed. One of 1100 numbered. VG + (sm chip backstrip head) in wraps. *Sclanders.* $155/£100

BECKETT, SAMUEL. Worstward Ho. London: Calder, 1983. 1st ed. Fine in dj. *Rees.* $19/£12

BECKFORD, PETER. Thoughts on Hunting. London, 1798. New ed. xv,340pp (tp, frontis browned; rest of text sl blued). Early 1/2 calf, marbled bds (sl loss corners), dec gilt spine, morocco label. *Edwards.* $132/£85

BECKFORD, WILLIAM. Vathek, an Arabian Tale. (NY): LEC, 1945. #904/1500 numbered, signed by Valenti Angelo (illus). Full leather. NF in tissue dj (sl chipped), liner, pub's slipcase. *Hermitage.* $75/£48

BECKFORD, WILLIAM. Vathek. NY: John Day, 1928. Dj; slipcase (worn, incomplete). *Glenn.* $65/£42

BECKFORD, WILLIAM. Vathek. Herbert B. Grimsditch (trans). Bloomsbury: Nonesuch, 1929. One of 1550 copies. Parchment-backed gilt bds; marbled eps. Fine. *Pharos.* $75/£48

BECKHAM, BARRY. Runner Mack. NY: Morrow, 1972. 1st ed. Fine in NF dj. *Lame Duck.* $85/£55

BEDDARD, FRANK E. A Book of Whales. London/NY, 1900. 1st ed. Frontis, 20 plts. (Spine sl rubbed, faded.) *Lefkowicz.* $150/£97

BEDFORD, F.G.D. The Sailor's Pocket Book. Portsmouth: Griffin, (1877). 3rd ed. 526pp, index. New reps. 1882 prize label. Very Nice. *Limestone.* $125/£81

BEDFORD, GUNNING. Clinical Lectures on the Diseases of Women and Children. NY, 1856. 4th ed. 602pp. Good. *Fye.* $50/£32

BEDFORD, GUNNING. The Principles and Practice of Obstetrics. NY, 1866. 3rd ed. 743pp. Full leather. Good. *Fye.* $75/£48

BEDFORD, SYBILLE. The Trial of Dr. Adams. NY: S&S, 1959. *Boswell.* $25/£16

BEDFORD-JONES, H. The Mesa Trail. Doubleday, 1920. 1st ed. NF in dj (spine worn). *Madle.* $50/£32

BEDFORD-JONES, H. The Mission and the Man. Pasadena: San Pasqual Press, 1939. Red ptd 2-tone cl. Dj (short tear). *Dawson.* $75/£48

BEDFORD-JONES, M. and H. D'Artagnan's Letter. NY: Covici-Friede, 1931. 1st ed. Good in dj (worn). *Hayman.* $25/£16

Bee, a Collection of Poems Chiefly Designed for the Young. Dublin: J. Jones, 1824. 12mo. viii,180pp. Full-pg wood engr frontis, vignette tp (bkpl; dated pencil sig fep; lib sticker; ep edges browned). Full leather on bds (upper cvr reattached; lower bd reinforced; spine scuffed; lt rubbed). Internally VG. *Hobbyhorse.* $55/£35

BEEBE, GILBERT. Contraception and Fertility in the Southern Appalachians. Balt, 1942. 1st ed. Good. *Fye.* $40/£26

BEEBE, LUCIUS and CHARLES CLEGG. Cable Car Carnival. Oakland: G. Hardy, 1951. 1st ed. Signed by both authors. Pict eps. NF in NF dj. *Harrington.* $35/£23

BEEBE, LUCIUS and CHARLES CLEGG. Great Railroad Photographs, U.S.A. Berkeley: Howell-North, 1964. 1st and only ed. #1894/2000, signed by authors. Pict eps. Red gilt-lettered cl. Fine in Fine slipcase. *Harrington.* $75/£48

BEEBE, LUCIUS and CHARLES CLEGG. Narrow Gauge in the Rockies. Berkeley: Howell-North, 1958. 1st ed. #582/850 deluxe 'Clear Board' ed, signed by authors. Fldg map in rear pocket; pict eps. Black gilt-lettered cl. Fine in pict slipcase (sl rubbed). *Harrington.* $175/£113

BEEBE, LUCIUS and CHARLES CLEGG. Rio Grande, Mainline of the Rockies. Berkeley: Howell-North, 1962. 1st ed. #1185/1250 deluxe 'Timberline' ed, signed by authors. Fldg map in rear pocket; pict eps. Grey gilt-lettered cl. Fine in orig pict slipcase (rubbed). *Harrington.* $110/£71

BEEBE, LUCIUS and CHARLES CLEGG. Steamcars to the Comstock. Berkeley: Howell-North, 1957. 1st ed. Pict eps. VG in Good + dj. *Oregon.* $35/£23

BEEBE, LUCIUS. The Central Pacific and the Southern Pacific Railroads. Berkeley: Howell-North, 1963. 1st ed. Signed. 121 photos. Pict eps. Fine in dj (chipped, rubbed). *Harrington.* $70/£45

BEEBE, LUCIUS. Mansions on Rails: The Folklore of the Private Railway Car. Berkeley: Howell-North, 1959. 1st ed. #1950/1950 signed. Tipped-in color frontis, fldg plan in rear pocket; pict eps. Red gilt-lettered cl. Fine in orig pict slipcase (sl rubbed). *Harrington.* $110/£71

BEEBE, LUCIUS. Mixed Train Daily, a Book of Short-Line Railroads. Berkeley: Howell-North, 1961. 4th ed. 6 color plts; pict eps. Beige cl. Fine in VG + dj (sl rubbed, chipped). *Harrington.* $35/£23

BEEBE, LUCIUS. Mr. Pullman's Elegant Palace Car. GC: Doubleday, 1961. Pict eps. Black/grn cl. Fine in dj (rubbed). *Harrington.* $75/£48

BEEBE, LUCIUS. The Overland Limited. Berkeley: Howell-North, 1963. 1st ed. 2 color repros; pict eps. Red cl. Fine in NF dj. *Harrington.* $35/£23

BEEBE, WILLIAM. The Arcturus Adventure. NY, 1926. 8 color plts. Gilt stamped cl (sm marginal tear 1pg). *Sutton.* $50/£32

BEEBE, WILLIAM. The Arcturus Adventure. London: Putnam, 1926. 7 color plts. VG. *Hollett.* $116/£75

BEEBE, WILLIAM. Beneath Tropic Seas. NY, 1928. 1st ed. Color frontis, pict eps. (Spine faded; spotted.) *Sutton.* $37/£24

BEEBE, WILLIAM. Edge of the Jungle. NY: Henry Holt, 1921. 1st ed. Unopened. NF (eps sl yellowed) in dj (edgeworn). *Sadlon.* $20/£13

BEEBE, WILLIAM. Galapagos, World's End. Putnam's, (1924). 9 color plts, 83 photos. (Few pp sl foxed.) Dj. *Petersfield.* $70/£45

BEEBE, WILLIAM. Galapagos, World's End. NY/London, 1924. 1st ed. 9 color plts. Contents Good. (Joints loose.) *Wheldon & Wesley.* $78/£50

BEEBE, WILLIAM. Half Mile Down. NY: Harcourt, Brace, (1934). 1st ed. Stamped in blind/silver (spine head sl rubbed). *Sadlon.* $35/£23

BEEBE, WILLIAM. High Jungle. NY: Duell et al, (1949). 1st ed. (Spine sl lightened; gilt sl rubbed.) *Sadlon.* $20/£13

BEEBE, WILLIAM. Pheasants. GC: Doubleday, 1926. 1st trade ed. 2 vols. Grn cl. Lt spots, o/w Fine. *Bowman.* $120/£77

BEECHER, CATHERINE and HARRIET BEECHER STOWE. The American Woman's Home. NY: J.B. Ford, 1869. 1st ed. Frontis, (vi),500,(12)pp. Pub's grn cl. Text lt browned, dec tp lt foxed, else VG. *Bookpress.* $185/£119

BEECHER, CATHERINE. Letters to the People on Health and Happiness. NY, 1855. 1st ed. 29pp. Good. *Fye.* $125/£81

BEECHER, GEORGE ALLEN. A Bishop of the Great Plains 1910-1943. Phila: Church Hist Soc, 1950. Dent, else VG. *Burcham.* $40/£26

BEECHER, H.W. New Star Papers.... NY, 1859. 1st ed. 402pp. (Bkpl; ink inscrip; chipped; spotted, worn.) *King.* $22/£14

BEECHER, H.W. Norwood. NY, 1868. 1st ed. 549pp. (Spine ends frayed; cvrs discolored, worn; sl cocked.) *King.* $22/£14

BEECHER, H.W. Plain and Pleasant Talk about Fruits, Flowers and Farming. NY, 1859. 1st ed. 420pp. (Dampstaining several pp, browning; extrems worn, cvrs scuffed.) *Sutton.* $65/£42

BEECHER, MISS. Miss Beecher's Domestic Receipt-Book. NY: Harper, 1856. 3rd ed. xvi,306pp + 24pp;40 figs. Stamped cl. Pps damp mkd; backstrip, corners worn; 2-inch section lower backstrip missing; all else Good. *Connolly.* $85/£55

BEECHER, MRS. H.W. All Around the House; or, How to Make Homes Happy. NY: Appleton, 1879. xii,461pp,(6)ads. Dec brn cl. (Lt wear spine ends; inner hinge reinforced.) *Petrilla.* $50/£32

BEECHER, MRS. H.W. Letters from Florida. NY: D. Appleton, 1879. 85pp + ads (lacks fep). *Hayman.* $40/£26

BEECHER, MRS. H.W. Letters from Florida. NY: Appleton, 1879. Inscribed. VG. *Schoyer.* $100/£65

BEECHEY, F.W. Narrative of a Voyage to the Pacific and Beering's Strait. London: H. Colburn and R. Bentley, 1831. New Ed. 2 vols. xxii,472; lv,452pp, 23 plts, 3 fldg maps. Antique style 1/2 calf, marbled bds (rebound). Good (lt foxing, dust mks). *Walcot.* $659/£425

BEECHEY, F.W. Narrative of a Voyage to the Pacific and Beering's Strait.... London: Henry Colburn & Richard Bentley, 1831. (3rd ed.) 2 vols. Lg 8vo. xviii,472; iv,452pp. 23 plts, 3 fldg charts. Orig drab bds (rebacked, sl rubbed); orig spines (soiled) and paper labels laid down. *Karmiole.* $750/£484

BEECHING, H.C. (selected by). A Book of Christmas Verse. NY: Dodd, Mead, 1895. 1st Amer ed. Walter Crane (designs). Teg, rest untrimmed. Pub's biscuit-color buckram, pict design, gilt title spine. Fine. *Book Block.* $105/£68

BEECHING, JACK. The Galleys at Lepanto. NY: Scribner's, 1983. 1st US ed. 8 plts. VG in dj. *Worldwide.* $20/£13

BEEDE, A. McG. Sitting Bull—Custer. Bismarck, ND: Bismarck Tribune Co, (1913). Tan suede. Good. *Lien.* $175/£113

BEEDHAM, R.J. Wood Engraving. Ditchling: St. Dominic's Press: Pepler & Sewell, 1935. Woodcut vignette tp. VF. *Europa.* $70/£45

BEEDHAM, R.J. Wood Engraving. Faber, 1948. VG. *Moss.* $47/£30

BEEDING, FRANCIS. Death Walks in Eastrepps. NY: Mystery League, 1931. 1st ed. NF in dj (lt edgewear, closed triangular tear). *Else Fine.* $65/£42

BEEDOME, THOMAS. Select Poems Divine and Humane. London: Nonesuch, 1928. #826/1250. Uncut. VG in full parchment, pigskin thongs. Card slipcase (lt soiled). *Cox.* $54/£35

BEELER, JOE. Cowboys and Indians. Norman: Univ of OK Press, (1967). 1st ed. Author's signed orig dwg ffep. 80 plts. Dj lt rubbed, spine sunned; else Fine. *Bookpress.* $300/£194

BEER, PATRICIA. Spanish Balcony. London: Poem-of-the-Month Club Ltd, 1973. 1st Eng ed. Signed. VG. *Ulysses.* $25/£16

BEER, THOMAS. The Mauve Decade. NY, 1926. Ltd lg paper ed, 69/150 (of 165) signed. Fine (cvrs sl rubbed) in NF box. *Polyanthos.* $100/£65

BEERBOHM, MAX. Cartoons.... London: Stephen Swift, n.d. (1901). 1st ed. 15 VG color plts. Portfolio (worn). *Bookpress.* $300/£194

BEERBOHM, MAX. Fifty Caricatures. NY: E.P. Dutton, 1913. 1st ed, Amer issue. 48 inserted plts. Pict grn cl, gilt. Fine. *Macdonnell.* $150/£97

BEERBOHM, MAX. The Happy Hypocrite. New Fairfield: Bruce Rogers/October House, 1955. One of 600. Cl-backed patterned bds. VF in orig glassine & slipcase. *Pharos.* $85/£55

BEERBOHM, MAX. Lytton Strachey. CUP, 1943. 1st Amer ed. Fine in ptd wraps (spine sl sunned). *Polyanthos.* $25/£16

BEERBOHM, MAX. Observations. London: Heinemann, 1925. 1st ed. Color frontis; 51 plts. Cvrs sl soiled, else internally Fine. *Pharos.* $95/£61

BEERBOHM, MAX. A Peep into the Past. (NY): Privately ptd, 1923. 1st ed, ltd to 300 on Japan Vellum. Labels worn, sm tear cvr label, sl corner wear, else VG. *Godot.* $175/£113

BEERBOHM, MAX. The Poet's Corner. London: Heinemann, 1904. 1st ed, earlier issue, in bds, not wraps. 20 VG color lithos. Orig bds, design (spine cracked, broken; contents loose). *Ash.* $380/£245

BEERBOHM, MAX. Rossetti and His Circle. Heinemann, (1922). 1st ed, #178/380 numbered, signed. Color frontis; 22 color plts, guards. Aeg. White buckram (sl soiled). *Bickersteth.* $233/£150

BEERBOHM, MAX. Rossetti and His Circle. London: Heinemann, 1922. 1st ed. Frontis, 22 tipped-in color plts. Orig cl (lt mks). Nice in dj (rubbed). *Ash.* $194/£125

BEERBOHM, MAX. Seven Men. London: Heinemann, 1919. 1st ed. (Back faded.) *Petersfield.* $33/£21

BEERBOHM, MAX. A Survey. NY, 1921. 1st ed, Amer issue. Brn cl-backed brn bds. Fine in dj (sl worn, torn). *Heller.* $150/£97

BEERBOHM, MAX. A Survey. Heinemann, 1921. 1st ed. Contents VG (binding dull; sl stained). *Whiteson.* $26/£17

BEERBOHM, MAX. Things New and Old. London: Heinemann, 1923. 1st ed. Color frontis, 49 plts, guards. Good in orig buckram (sl mottled); dj (lt soiled, frayed). *Cox.* $101/£65

BEERBOHM, MAX. Things New and Old. London: Heinemann, 1923. 1st ed. Yellow-brn cl. Good. *Appelfeld.* $125/£81

BEERBOHM, MAX. The Works of Max Beerbohm. London: Heinemann, 1922. One of 780 sets. Signed. Red cl. Lacks dj, else Fine. *Pharos.* $85/£55

BEERBOHM, MAX. The Works. NY: Scribner's, 1896. 1st ed. One of 1000. Teg, uncut. Dec stamped brn cl. Foxing, else Fine. *Macdonnell.* $350/£226

BEERS, FANNIE A. Memories. Phila: Lippincott, 1891. 1st ed. 20pp ads. Brn olive cl, Gilt title. (Sl edgewear.) *Hermitage.* $75/£48

BEERS, FANNIE A. Memories. Phila: Lippincott, 1891. 2nd ed. Frontis port, 336pp. Orig brn cl. Lib bkpl, blindstamp, hinges starting, else VG. *Chapel Hill.* $45/£29

BEERS, FRANK. The Green Signal or Life on the Rail. Kansas City, MO: Franklin Hudson Pub Co, (c. 1904). Port; 6 plts. VG (pulp paper dknd) in pict wraps (spine chipped). *Bohling.* $35/£23

BEETON, ISABELLA. The Book of Household Management. London: S.O. Beeton, 1861. 1st ed. Contemp 1/2 morocco, new black morocco backstrip, gilt (some pp, plts misbound). *Petersfield.* $744/£480

BEGBIE, HAROLD. The Political Struwwelpeter. London: Grant Richards, 1899. 2nd ed. 8vo, 24pp. F.C. Gould (illus). Cl-backed pict bds. VG (sm dkng, edges bumped). *Davidson.* $275/£177

BEGBIE, J. WARBURTON. Selections from the Works of...Begbie. Dyce Duckworth (ed). London: New Sydenham Soc, 1882. Port,xxiv,422pp. *Bickersteth.* $37/£24

BEGG, ALEXANDER. History of British Columbia, from Its Earliest Discovery to the Present Time. Toronto, 1894. 1st ed. 568pp, errata tipped in, lg fldg map. Gilt-stamped cl. VG. *Oregon.* $135/£87

BEGGS, WESLEY. Under the Sunny Blue Skies of the Western Plains. Denver: Eastwood-Kirchner, 1912. Name, else VG. *Perier.* $50/£32

BEGLEY, LOUIS. As Max Saw It. NY, 1994. 1st Amer ed. Signed. Mint in Mint dj. *Polyanthos.* $40/£26

BEHAN, BRENDAN. Brendan Behan's Island. (NY): Bernard Geis, (1962). 1st ed. Signed by Behan and Paul Hogarth (dwgs). Fine in NF dj. *Dermont.* $200/£129

BEHAN, BRENDAN. Brendan Behan's New York. Bernard Geis, 1964. 1st ed. VG + in VG + dj. *Bishop.* $25/£16

BEHAN, BRENDAN. Hold Your Hour and Have Another. Hutchinson, 1963. 1st Eng ed. Fine in dj (sl rubbed). *Ulysses.* $85/£55

BEHAN, BRENDAN. The Quare Fellow. London: Methuen, 1956. 1st ed, 1st bk. Sig, o/w Fine in dj (sl rubbed). *Pharos.* $150/£97

BEHM, MARC. The Queen of the Night. Boston: Houghton Mifflin, 1977. 1st ed. Fine in Fine dj. *Pettler.* $45/£29

BEHRENDT, WALTER CURT. Modern Building, Its Nature, Problems, and Forms. NY: Harcourt Brace, (1937). 1st ed. Rubber stamps, sm bkseller label feps, else VG. *Bookpress.* $85/£55

BEHRMAN, S.N. Conversation with Max. London: Hamish Hamilton, 1960. 1st Eng ed. Signed, dated presentation. Fine in dj (sl discolored) laid in gilt-emb leather overwrapper. *Cahan.* $75/£48

BEHRMAN, S.N. Wine of Choice. NY: Random House, 1938. 1st ed. VG + in dj (drknd spine, edges). *Else Fine.* $45/£29

BEILENSON, PETER. The Story of Frederic W. Goudy. Mt. Vernon: Peter Pauper, 1965. 1st ed. One of 1950 ptd. Fine in tissue wrapper. *Hermitage.* $35/£23

BEIRNE, FRANCIS F. The War of 1812. NY: Dutton, 1949. 1st ed. Blue cl. VG in dj (worn). *Chapel Hill.* $55/£35

BEKASSY, FERENC. Adriatica and Other Poems. Hogarth Press, 1925. 1st ed. Head, foot spine sl nicked, o/w VG. *Words Etc.* $155/£100

BELDEN, ALBERT. The Fur Trade of America and Some of the Men Who Made and Maintain It. NY: Peltries Pub Co, (1917). 1st ed. Gilt-titled brn cl (wear, hinges weak). *Bohling.* $125/£81

BELDEN, L. BURR. The Mississippians and the Georgians of Death Valley 1849 Party. L.A.: DV 49ers, 1975. 1st ed, ltd hb copy. Fine. *Book Market.* $20/£13

BELGRAVE, C. DALRYMPLE. Siwa. The Oasis of Jupiter Ammon. London: John Lane The Bodley Head, 1923. 1st ed. 22 plts (incl color frontis), map. Blue ribbed cl, gilt. VG. *Hollett.* $116/£75

BELKIN, JOHN N. The Mosquitoes of the South Pacific. Berkeley, 1962. 2 vols. 412 plts. VG, boxed. *Argosy.* $60/£39

BELKNAP, BOYNTON H. Yankee Josh, the Rover. NY, 1893. Beadle Pocket Lib, vol XXXVIII. 1st ed. Sl aging; marginal tears, else VG- in pict wrappers. *Pharos.* $30/£19

BELKNAP, CHARLES E. History of the Michigan Organizations at Chickamauga, Chattanooga and Missionary Ridge, 1863. Lansing, 1899. 2nd ed. 375pp. Cvr wear, o/w Fine. *Pratt.* $65/£42

BELKNAP, CHARLES E. History of the Michigan Organizations at Chickamauga, Chattanooga, and Missionary Ridge 1863. Lansing, MI: Robert Smith Ptg Co, 1899. 2nd ed on heavier paper than 1st. 374,(1)pp. Sl wear extrems, inscrip, else VG. *Mcgowan.* $250/£161

BELKNAP, JEREMY. The History of New-Hampshire. (Dover, NH): O. Crosby & J. Varney, 1812. 3 vols, complete. Fldg maps (2-inch tear; another repaired). Contemp calf (lt worn; vol 3 spine neatly rebacked; text browned, lt foxed; bkpl). *Bookpress.* $300/£194

BELKNAP, WALDRON P. American Colonial Painting. Cambridge, MA: Harvard Univ Press, 1959. 75pp plts. (Spine faded.) Pub's box. *Argosy.* $165/£106

BELL, ALEXANDER GRAHAM. The Mechanism of Speech. NY, 1908. 3rd ed. Good. *Fye.* $30/£19

BELL, B. A System of Surgery. Edinburgh, 1801. 7th ed. 7 vols. 478pp, 48 plts; 472pp; 445pp, 11 plts; 588pp; 29 plts; 581pp, 28 plts; 536pp, 20 plts; 460pp, 26 plts. Full calf (worn; lt foxing). *Whitehart.* $388/£250

BELL, C.F. (ed). Annals of Thomas Banks: Sculptor Royal Academician. Cambridge, 1938. 1st ed. 43 plts. VG. *Argosy.* $150/£97

BELL, CHARLES (ed). The Journal of Henry Kelsey (1691-1692). Winnipeg: Dawson Richard Pub, 1928. Plt; 9 maps (1 extending; 1 dbl-pg). Orig bds (spine cracking). *Hollett.* $23/£15

BELL, CHARLES. The Anatomy and Philosophy of Expression as Connected with the Fine Arts. London: Bohn, 1872. 6th ed. viii,275pp, 4 engr plts. (Spine rebacked.) Ars Artis. $54/£35

BELL, CHARLES. Essays on the Anatomy of Expression in Painting. London, 1806. 1st ed. 186pp. 1/2 leather; marbled bds; new eps. Fine. Fye. $1,500/£968

BELL, CHARLES. The Hand, Its Mechanism and Vital Endowments as Evincing Design. London: William Pickering, 1837. 4th ed. xvi,368pp. Contemp calf. Sm split spine top; ends, sides sl chipped; lib bkpl, o/w VG. White. $121/£78

BELL, CHARLES. Institutes of Surgery: Arranged in the Order of the Lectures Delivered in the University of Edinburgh. Phila: Waldie, 1840. 446pp (lt foxing). Contemp 1/4 sheep, bds (worn; weak, cracked joints). Goodrich. $145/£94

BELL, CHARLES. Letters Concerning the Diseases of the Urethra. Boston, 1811. 1st Amer ed. 6 engr plts. (Text browned.) Mod polished calf. Goodrich. $250/£161

BELL, CHARLES. Manuscript of Drawings of the Arteries. Editions Medicina Rare, 1970. Ltd ed, #1165/2500. Prospectus, bio tipped in. Fine in slipcase. Goodrich. $65/£42

BELL, CLIVE. An Account of French Painting. London: C&W, 1931. VG+ (ink name) in dj (rubbed, chipped, creased). Williams. $54/£35

BELL, CLIVE. Proust. London: Hogarth, 1928. 1st ed. Ltd to 1200. Red/black cl. Label sl tanned, else Fine. Reese. $85/£55

BELL, CURRER, ELLIS, and ACTON. (Pseud of Charlotte, Emily and Anne Bronte.) Poems. London: Smith, Elder, 1846. 1st ed, 2nd issue. 1pg undated ads, contents leaf, errata; 'Westley's & Co.' binder's ticket rep. Usual binding: blind-stamped grn cl (damp-mkd, ends worn; eps reinforced), harp design, floral border. Good. Sumner & Stillman. $475/£306

BELL, CURRER. (Pseud of Charlotte Bronte). The Professor, a Tale. NY: Harper, 1857. 1st Amer ed. Orig cl stamped in gilt/blind (spine ends, corners sl frayed; lt foxing). Henry C. Carey's copy. Sadlon. $175/£113

BELL, CURRER. (Pseud of Charlotte Bronte.) The Professor. London: Smith, Elder, 1857. 1st ed. 2 vols. viii,294,(2)pp ads; iv,258,(6)pp ads+16pp pub's cat. 1st issue dk grayish purple cl (spine expertly rebuilt, corners worn). Lg case, blue leather spine. Schoyer. $400/£258

BELL, GERTRUDE. The Letters of Gertrude Bell, Selected and Edited by Lady Bell. NY: Boni & Liveright, 1927. 1st US ed. 2 vols. 2 maps (1 fldg). Sl rubbed; sl foxing, o/w VG. Worldwide. $40/£26

BELL, GERTRUDE. The Letters of Gertrude Bell. NY: Boni & Liveright, 1927. 1st Amer ed. 2 vols. Beveled blue buckram (lt spotting). Sl rubbing, else NF set. Great Epic. $95/£61

BELL, GERTRUDE. The Letters of Gertrude Bell. London, 1928. Rpt. 2 vols. Fldg map in pocket. Stiff card cvr as issued. Djs (repaired tears). Lewis. $56/£36

BELL, GRAHAM. The Artist and His Public. Hogarth Press, 1939. Words Etc. $47/£30

BELL, HORACE. On the Old West Coast. Lanier Bartlett (ed). NY: William Morrow, 1930. 1st ed. Frontis. 2-tone cl. Dj (top edge worn). Dawson. $60/£39

BELL, HORACE. On the Old West Coast. Lanier Bartlett (ed). NY: William Morrow, 1930. 1st trade ed. Pict eps. Grey cl, paper labels. Fine in sl chipped, price-clipped dj, o/w NF. Harrington. $75/£48

BELL, HORACE. Reminiscences of a Ranger. Santa Barbara: Wallace Hebberd, 1927. 2nd ed. Frontis. Pict gilt-stamped cl. Soiling, corner wear, o/w VG. Howes B 325. Oregon. $45/£29

BELL, ISAAC. Foxiana. London: Country Life, 1929. 1st ed. (Spine bubbled.) October Farm. $40/£26

BELL, J. Bell's New Pantheon. London: J. Bell, 1790. 2 vols in 1. 29 full-pg copper plts. Full tree calf. (Worn; joints cracked.) Argosy. $350/£226

BELL, J. Discourses on the Nature and Cure of Wounds. Edinburgh, 1800. 2 vols bound in 1. x,250,235pp; 2 plts. Contemp bds (rebacked). Whitehart. $279/£180

BELL, J. MUNRO. The Furniture Designs of Chippendale, Hepplewhite and Sheraton. NY: Robert M. McBride, 1938. Worn; text margins lt sunned, else VG. Bookpress. $85/£55

BELL, J. MUNRO. The Furniture Designs of Chippendale, Hepplewhite and Sheraton. NY: Tudor Pub, 1940. Patterned cl. Fine in VG dj (lt soil, chipping). House. $40/£26

BELL, J. MUNRO. The Furniture Designs of Thomas Chippendale. London, 1910. 63 plts. Spine title (rpt incl in this vol): The Gentleman and Cabinet Maker's Director. (Backstrip worn at head, tail; corners worn.) Argosy. $150/£97

BELL, J.H.B. A Progress in Mountaineering. Scottish Hills to Alpine Peaks. London, 1950. 1st ed. 24 photo plts. Dj. Bickersteth. $23/£15

BELL, JAMES MACKINTOSH. Wilds of Maoriland. London: Macmillan, 1914. 2 fldg maps; teg. Blue cl, gilt (scuffed, rubbed). Schoyer. $75/£48

BELL, JAMES. The Homoeopathic Therapeutics of Diarrhoea, Dysentery.... NY, 1879. 168pp. Good. Fye. $75/£48

BELL, JOHN and CHARLES. The Anatomy and Physiology of the Human Body. London: Longmans et al, 1829. 7th ed. 3 vols. xxxiv,604; xvi,592; xii,471pp. Uncut. (Vol 1 lacks title label, hinge cracked; vol 2 shaken, text lt foxed, browned.) Goodrich. $225/£145

BELL, JOHN and D.F. CONDIE. All the Material Facts in the History of Epidemic Cholera. Phila, 1832. 1st ed. (Ex-lib; sl tears tp, not affecting text; bds stained.) Argosy. $200/£129

BELL, JOHN and D.F. CONDIE. All the Material Facts in the History of Epidemic Cholera: Being a Report of the College of Physicians of Philadelphia.... Phila, 1832. 2nd ed. 188pp. Contents Fine (much of backstrip missing). Fye. $150/£97

BELL, JOSEPHINE. The Alien. London: Bles, 1964. 1st ed. NF in NF dj. Ming. $39/£25

BELL, JOSEPHINE. Death at the Medical Board. London: Longman, 1944. 1st ed. VG+ in dj (chipped; sm pieces missing). Murder. $50/£32

BELL, JULIAN. Winter Movement and Other Poems. London, 1930. 1st ed. Extra paper label tipped in. Partly unopened. Excellent (edges sl spotted) in dj (spine dknd; sl chipped; sm stain; dust-mks). Waterfield. $132/£85

BELL, KATHERINE M. Swinging the Censer. Santa Barbara: (Katherine Bell Cheney), 1931. 1st ed. Frontis port. Teg. Black/burgundy gilt cl. Good (bkpl) in dj (sl chipped, faded). Karmiole. $40/£26

BELL, LILIAN. The Love Affairs of an Old Maid. NY: Harper, 1893. 1st ed, 1st bk. 188pp. VG. Second Life. $65/£42

BELL, MADISON SMARTT. Straight Cut. NY: Ticknor & Fields, 1986. 1st ed. Fine in Fine dj. *Revere.* $30/£19

BELL, MADISON SMARTT. Waiting for the End of the World. NY: Ticknor & Fields, 1985. 1st ed. NF in VG dj. *Revere.* $50/£32

BELL, MADISON SMARTT. The Washington Square Ensemble. NY: Viking, 1983. 1st ed. 1st bk. VF in dj (short closed tear). *Else Fine.* $135/£87

BELL, MALCOLM. Major Butler's Legacy. Athens: Univ of GA Press, (1987). 1st ed. Fine in Fine dj. *Mcgowan.* $45/£29

BELL, MALCOLM. Old Pewter. London: B.T. Batsford, (1913). 1st ed. Frontis; 106 plts. Blue gilt cl. Good. *Karmiole.* $45/£29

BELL, MRS. ARTHUR. Nurembourg. A&C Black, 1905. 1st ed. 20 color plts. Teg. Dec cl (spine sl faded, rubbed; feps browned, lacks sm piece fore-edge; hinges cracked). *Edwards.* $47/£30

BELL, MRS. N.S. Pathways of the Puritans. Framingham, MA, (1930). 1st ed. Fldg map. Sl corner wear, o/w VG. *Artis.* $17/£11

BELL, N. The Lord of Life. Little-Brown, 1933. 1st Amer ed. Foxing fore-edge, else VG+ in VG pict dj (inner reinforcement). *Aronovitz.* $95/£61

BELL, NEIL. Precious Porcelain. London: Gollancz, 1931. 1st ed. Map on verso 1/2 title. Very Nice. *Temple.* $26/£17

BELL, SOLOMON. Tales of Travels West of the Mississippi. Boston: Gray & Bowen, 1830. 1st ed. Frontis, 162pp; dbl-pg map. VG (rebound). Howes S 739. *Oregon.* $795/£513

BELL, T. A History of British Quadrupeds Including the Cetacae. London, 1874. 2nd ed. xviii,474,2pp; 160 wood engrs. (Spine faded.) *Henly.* $47/£30

BELL, THOMAS. The Anatomy, Physiology, and Diseases of the Teeth. London: For S. Highley, 1829. 1st ed. 8vo. xiii,(1 ad),329,(1),(4 ads)pp; 11 plts (offsetting). Untrimmed. New 1/4 cl over orig marbled bds. VG (lt foxing; lib bkpls; stamp title verso). *Glaser.* $950/£613

BELL, W. BLAIR. The Pituitary. NY, 1919. 1st Amer ed. Good. *Fye.* $150/£97

BELL, WALTER GEORGE. The Great Plague in London in 1665. London: John Lowe, 1924. 1st ed. VG (sm mks fr cvr). *White.* $62/£40

BELL, WALTER GEORGE. The Great Plague in London in 1665. London, 1924. 1st ed. Good. *Fye.* $125/£81

BELL, WILLIAM DIXON. The Moon Colony. Goldsmith, 1937. 1st ed. Fine in dj. *Madle.* $50/£32

BELL, WILLIAM DIXON. The Secret of Tibet. Goldsmith, 1938. 1st ed. Fine in dj (sl frayed). *Madle.* $75/£48

BELL, WILLIAM GARDNER. Will James. Flagstaff, 1987. 1st ed. Gilt debossed cl. Fine. *Baade.* $45/£29

BELLAMY, EDWARD. Equality. NY: Appleton, 1897. 1st ed. Bkpl, else VG+ in dj (chipped, worn). *Lame Duck.* $350/£226

BELLAMY, EDWARD. Looking Backward 2000-1887. Boston: Ticknor, 1888. 1st ed, 1st ptg. Lt grn cl, gilt. VG. BAL 956. *Macdonnell.* $225/£145

BELLAMY, EDWARD. Looking Backward. Hollywood: LEC, 1941. #904/1500 numbered, signed by Elise (illus). Fine in new slipcase. *Hermitage.* $90/£58

BELLAMY, EDWARD. Looking Backward: 2000-1887. Boston: Ticknor, 1888. 1st ed. Earliest ptg w/J.J. Arakelyan imprint on copyright pg. Dec gray cl. VG (lt wear; eps quite foxed). BAL 956. *Antic Hay.* $250/£161

BELLAMY, H.S. and P. ALLAN. The Calendar of Tiahuanaco. Faber, 1956. 3 fldg illus. Dj. *Edwards.* $43/£28

BELLARD, ALFRED. Gone for a Soldier, The Civil War Memoirs of Private Alfred Bellard. David Herbert Donald (ed). Boston, 1975. 1st ed. Map. VG+ in VG+ dj. *Pratt.* $45/£29

BELLARD, ALFRED. Gone for a Soldier. Boston: Little, Brown, 1975. 1st ed. NF in VG dj. *Mcgowan.* $35/£23

BELLOC, HILAIRE. Advice. London, 1960. 1st ed. Fine in dj (sl sunned). *Polyanthos.* $30/£19

BELLOC, HILAIRE. Avril. London: Sheed & Ward, 1945. 1st ed. Frontis. Orig cl gilt. VG in dj (sl worn). *Hollett.* $39/£25

BELLOC, HILAIRE. The Battle Ground. Cassell, 1936. 1st ed. VG in dj. *Whiteson.* $23/£15

BELLOC, HILAIRE. The Chanty of the Nona. London, 1928. Ltd 1st ed, one of 500 signed. Bds. VG. *Argosy.* $50/£32

BELLOC, HILAIRE. Characters of the Reformation. NY: Sheed & Ward, 1936. 1st Amer ed. 23 color ports. Fine in dj (sl frayed, nicked). *Hermitage.* $40/£26

BELLOC, HILAIRE. A Conversation with an Angel and Other Essays. London: Jonathan Cape, (1928). 1st ed. (Spine lightened.) *Sadlon.* $10/£6

BELLOC, HILAIRE. The Emerald of Catherine the Great. NY: Harper, 1926. 1st US ed. Top edge stained grn. Blue cl dec in emerald grn. Very Nice in dj (sl worn). *Cady.* $40/£26

BELLOC, HILAIRE. The Four Men, a Farrago. Indianapolis, (1912). Feps sl spotted, else VG in dj (chipped, torn, rubbed, dknd). *King.* $35/£23

BELLOC, HILAIRE. The Four Men. Nelson, (1911). 1st ed. VG-. *Fine Books.* $20/£13

BELLOC, HILAIRE. The Jews. Constable, 1922. 1st ed. Sl dull, else VG. *Whiteson.* $47/£30

BELLOC, HILAIRE. The Jews. London: Constable, 1937. Rev ed. Part of dj laid in. Few pencil notes, o/w Fine. *Patterson.* $78/£50

BELLOC, HILAIRE. The Old Road. London, 1911. Fldg map. (Feps, edges lt foxed.) *Edwards.* $54/£35

BELLOC, HILAIRE. Places. Essays. London: Cassell, 1942. 1st ed. Fine in Fine pict dj. *Patterson.* $93/£60

BELLOC, HILAIRE. The Postmaster-General. London, (1932). 1st Eng ed. 30 dwgs by G.K. Chesterton. Bkpl, else VG in dj (chipped, torn, dknd). *King.* $85/£55

BELLOC, HILAIRE. Selected Essays. London: Methuen, 1948. 1st ed. (Spine sl faded.) Dj. *Hollett.* $39/£25

BELLOC, HILAIRE. The Servile State. London/Edinburgh: T.N. Foulis, 1912. 1st ed. Text lt foxed, spine lt browned, else VG. *Godot.* $45/£29

BELLOC, HILAIRE. The Stane Street. London, 1913. 24 maps (20 sketch maps, 1 fldg). (Edges sl foxed.) *Edwards.* $39/£25

BELLOC, HILAIRE. The Stane Street. Constable, 1913. 1st ed. 16 plts by William Hyde; fldg map at end. Bds, cl spine (sl spotted). *Bickersteth.* $39/£25

BELLOC, HILAIRE. Sussex. London: A&C Black, 1906. 1st ed. 75 color plts by Wilfrid Ball (edges of 3 bruised), captioned guards; fldg sketch map. Dec cl (sl rubbed). Teg. Good. *Cox.* $70/£45

BELLOC, HILAIRE. The Verse of Hilaire Belloc. W.N. Roughead (ed). London: Nonesuch Press, 1954. One of 1650 numbered. Fine in dj (sm nicks). *Ulysses.* $85/£55

BELLOSTE, AUGUSTIN. The Hospital Surgeon. London: J&B Sprint et al, 1713. 3rd ed. Engr frontis, (24),456pp. Contemp full calf (recently rebacked). Text browning, else Good. *Goodrich.* $450/£290

BELLOW, SAUL. Dangling Man. London: Lehmann, 1946. 1st UK ed, 1st bk. VG w/o dj. *Williams.* $43/£28

BELLOW, SAUL. The Dean's December. NY: Harper, (1982). 1st trade ed. Rev slip, photo laid in. Fine in dj. *Reese.* $25/£16

BELLOW, SAUL. Herzog. NY: Viking, (1964). 1st ed. Fine in dj (sl rubbed). *Between The Covers.* $100/£65

BELLOW, SAUL. Herzog. NY: Viking, 1964. 1st ed. Signed. Sm white patch fr bd, else Fine in NF dj (price mkd in pen). *Lame Duck.* $275/£177

BELLOW, SAUL. Humboldt's Gift. NY: Viking, (1975). Advance reading copy. Text lt foxed, else NF in yellow ptd wrappers. *Godot.* $45/£29

BELLOW, SAUL. Humboldt's Gift. Viking, 1975. Advance Reading Copy. NF in yellow wraps (spine dknd). *Stahr.* $35/£23

BELLOW, SAUL. Mosby's Memoirs and Other Stories. NY: Viking, (1968). 1st ed. Fine in dj (sm closed tear). *Reese.* $25/£16

BELLOW, SAUL. Mr. Sammler's Planet. London: W&N, 1970. 1st UK ed. VG in dj. *Lewton.* $17/£11

BELLOW, SAUL. Nobel Lecture. (NY): Targ Editions, (1979). 1st ed thus. One of 350 numbered, signed. Fine in plain dj. *Reese.* $100/£65

BELLOW, SAUL. Nobel Lecture. (NY): Targ Editions, (1979). Ltd to 350 numbered, signed. Fine. *Karmiole.* $100/£65

BELLOW, SAUL. A Silver Dish. NY: Albondocani, 1979. One of 300 numbered (of 326), signed. Cl, marbled bds, ptd label. VF. *Reese.* $125/£81

BELLOW, SAUL. Summations. Bennington: Bennington Chapbooks in Literature, 1987. #286/1000 numbered. Fine in ptd wraps. *Revere.* $30/£19

BELLOW, SAUL. The Victim. NY: Vanguard Press, (1947). 1st ed. Black cl. NF in VG dj (price-clipped). *Chapel Hill.* $250/£161

BELLOW, SAUL. The Victim. Lehmann, 1948. 1st UK ed. VG + in dj (lacks 1-inch x 2 1/2-inch chip to bottom fr panel). *Williams.* $62/£40

BELLOWS, EMMA S. (comp). The Paintings of George Bellows. NY, 1929. Ltd 1st ed. (Rubbed, soiled.) *Argosy.* $200/£129

BELLROSE, FRANK C. et al. Ducks, Geese and Swans of North America. Harrisburg, PA, 1976. 2nd ed. VG in dj (chipped). *Burcham.* $35/£23

BELOTE, JAMES and WILLIAM. Corregidor: The Saga of a Fortress. NY, 1967. 1st ed. VG in VG dj. *Clark.* $35/£23

BELT, THOMAS. The Naturalist in Nicaragua. London: John Murray, 1874. 1st ed. (Spine dknd; wear.) *Hermitage.* $100/£65

BEMELMANS, LUDWIG. The Elephant Cutlet. Alhambra, CA: Audrey Arellanes, 1966. Ltd to 100 ptd. 4pp (French fold), heavy wrappers, sewn w/red yarn. Fine. *Cady.* $25/£16

BEMELMANS, LUDWIG. The Golden Basket. NY: Viking, 1936. 1st ed. 8vo, 96pp. Ludwig Bemelmans (illus). Orange cl. VG (some soil). *Davidson.* $85/£55

BEMELMANS, LUDWIG. Hansi. NY: Viking, 1934. 1st ed, 1st bk. Illus blue cl. NF. *Drusilla's.* $125/£81

BEMELMANS, LUDWIG. Hotel Splendide. NY: Viking, 1941. 1st ed. Fr gutter foxed, else Fine in VG dj (sl loss to crown; nicks, tears). *Between The Covers.* $45/£29

BEMELMANS, LUDWIG. Hotel Splendide. Viking, 1941. 1st ed. One of 305 specially bound, signed. NF in glassine dj (worn) & Fine slipcase. *Fine Books.* $250/£161

BEMELMANS, LUDWIG. Life Class. NY: Viking, 1938. 1st ed. Red cl, pict inset. VG in dj (sl worn). *Cady.* $30/£19

BEMELMANS, LUDWIG. Madeline and the Bad Hat. NY: Viking, (1956). 1st trade ed. VG in VG dj. *Davidson.* $275/£177

BEMELMANS, LUDWIG. Madeline and the Gypsies. NY: Viking, 1959. 1st ed. Tall 4to. 56pp. Grn cl bds. VG (ink inscrip) in dj (lt torn, crayon mks). *Davidson.* $225/£145

BEMELMANS, LUDWIG. Madeline's Rescue. NY: Viking, 1959. 1st ed. Tall 4to. 56pp. Grn cl bds. VG (black smudges base of 2 pp) in dj (lt torn). *Davidson.* $250/£161

BEMELMANS, LUDWIG. My Life in Art. Harpers, 1958. 1st ed. NF in dj (lt soiling). *Fine Books.* $40/£26

BEMELMANS, LUDWIG. Quito Express. NY: Viking, 1938. 1st ed. Obl 4to. Cl-backed illus bds. Good in pict dj (chipped). *Reisler.* $85/£55

BEMROSE, WILLIAM. Manual of Buhl-Work and Marquetry. London: Bemrose, n.d. (ca 1860). 1st ed. 26,(8)pp, 14 chromolitho plts. Pub's cl (lt soiled). VG. *Bookpress.* $485/£313

BEMROSE, WILLIAM. Manual of Wood Carving. London: Bemrose, n.d. (?1900). 18th ed. 15 plts; patterned eps; edges red. Orig grn cl, gilt/black emb cvr design. Spine top sl worn, o/w Fine. *Europa.* $50/£32

BENAVIDEZ, ROY and OSCAR GRIFFIN. The Three Wars of Roy Benavidez. San Antonio: Coronoa, (1986). VG (lt bumped) in dj. *Aka.* $40/£26

Bench and Bar of California 1937-38. Chicago: C.W. Taylor, 1937. Buckram, gilt (Worn.) *Boswell.* $50/£32

BENCH, JOHNNY with WILLIAM BRASHLER. Catch You Later. Harper & Row, 1979. 1st ed. Fine in VG + dj. *Plapinger.* $30/£19

BENCHLEY, NATHANIEL. One to Grow On. NY: McGraw-Hill, (1958). 1st ed. Rev slip, photo laid in. Fine in dj. *Hermitage.* $35/£23

BENCHLEY, PETER. Jaws. GC: Doubleday, 1974. 1st ed. NF in VG + dj. *Pettler.* $150/£97

BENCHLEY, PETER. Jaws. Deutsch, 1974. 1st Eng ed. VG in dj. *Whiteson.* $23/£15

BENCHLEY, ROBERT. After 1903- What? NY: Harper, 1938. 1st ed. Fine in VG dj (1-inch creased tear, short tears). *Godot.* $85/£55

BENCHLEY, ROBERT. After 1903—What? NY/London: Harper, 1938. 1st ed. Gluyas Williams (illus). Pict cl. (Ink name.) Dj (torn; sl defective spine top). *Bickersteth.* $47/£30

BENCHLEY, ROBERT. Benchley on Business. NY: Dictophone Products, 1929. 1st (separate) ed. Fine in stapled grn wrappers. *Godot.* $275/£177

BENCHLEY, ROBERT. From Bed to Worse. NY/London: Harper, 1934. 1st ed. (Ink name; cvrs sl faded.) Dj (spine top defective). *Bickersteth.* $47/£30

BENCHLEY, ROBERT. Of All Things. London: Bodley Head, 1922. 1st Eng ed. VG. *Limestone.* $85/£55

BENCHLEY, ROBERT. Of All Things. London: John Lane, the Bodley Head, 1922. 1st Eng ed. Gluyas Williams (illus). VG (cvr edges rubbed). *Ulysses.* $132/£85

BENDER, LAURETTA. A Visual Motor Gestalt Test and Its Clinical Use. NY, 1938. Internally Good. (Ex-lib; cl rubbed, worn.) *Goodrich.* $25/£16

BENDIEN, S.G.T. Specific Changes in the Blood Serum, A Contribution to the Serological Diagnosis of Cancer and Tuberculosis. London, 1931. 1st Eng trans. Good. *Fye.* $75/£48

BENE, F. The Feeding and Related Behavior of Hummingbirds.... Boston, (1947). 12 plts. (Gilt title dulled.) *Sutton.* $40/£26

BENEDEK, THERESE. Psychoanalytic Investigations. NY: Quadrangle Books, (1973). 1st ed. VG. *Gach.* $50/£32

BENEDICT, CARL PETERS. Tenderfoot Kid on Gyp Water. Austin/Dallas, 1943. 1st ed. One of 550 ptd. Dec cl. *Ginsberg.* $300/£194

BENEDICT, DOROTHY. Fabulous. NY: Pantheon, 1961. 1st ed. VG in VG dj. *October Farm.* $25/£16

BENEDICT, H.Y. and JOHN A. LOMAX. The Book of Texas. NY: Doubleday, 1916. 1st ed. *Lambeth.* $40/£26

BENEDICTUS, DAVID. You're a Big Boy Now. NY: Dutton, 1964. 1st Amer ed. Fine in dj (sl rubbed). *Between The Covers.* $45/£29

BENESCH, OTTO. Collected Writings. Vol I: Rembrandt. London, 1970. Good in dj. *Washton.* $50/£32

BENESCH, OTTO. The Drawings of Rembrandt. London: Phaidon, 1954-57. 6 vols. Buckram. VF set. *Europa.* $721/£465

BENESCH, OTTO. The Drawings of Rembrandt. Eva Benesch (ed). London: Phaidon, 1973. 5 vols (of 6; lacks vol I). Maroon cl, gilt. (Ex-lib w/ink stamp, label remains.) *Edwards.* $233/£150

BENET, STEPHEN VINCENT. The Beginning of Wisdom. NY: Holt, 1921. 1st ed. Black cl stamped in orange. VG. *Reese.* $35/£23

BENET, STEPHEN VINCENT. Celebrated Stories Made into Movies. Chicago: Royce, 1944. 1st ed. Pict wrappers. Sl rubbed, else VG. *Pharos.* $75/£48

BENET, STEPHEN VINCENT. Five Men and Pompey. Boston: Four Seas, 1915. 1st ed, 2nd state in brn rather than purple wrappers; 1st bk. Inscribed. Ptd wrappers over bds. Good. *Karmiole.* $150/£97

BENET, STEPHEN VINCENT. Jean Huguenot. NY: Holt, 1923. 1st ed. VG. *Reese.* $25/£16

BENET, STEPHEN VINCENT. John Brown's Body. (GC: Doubleday, Doran, 1928). 1st trade ed. Fine in NF dj. *Mcgowan.* $85/£55

BENET, STEPHEN VINCENT. John Brown's Body. NY, 1928. 1st ed. VG+. *Pratt.* $40/£26

BENET, STEPHEN VINCENT. Nancy Hanks—Song. N.p., n.d. 1st ed. Orig music taped into hand-lettered wrappers (edges sl chipped). VG. *Pharos.* $90/£58

BENET, STEPHEN VINCENT. Nightmare at Noon. NY: Farrar & Rinehart, (1940). 1st ed. Ptd bds. Very Nice (ep stained). *Second Life.* $75/£48

BENET, STEPHEN VINCENT. Tales Before Midnight. NY: Farrar, (1939). 1st ed. Inscribed, signed. VG (pastedowns dknd; nick 1 joint) in dj (lt frayed). *Reese.* $75/£48

BENET, STEPHEN VINCENT. They Burned the Books. NY: Farrar & Rinehart, (1942). 1st issue w/pub's device on copyright pg. Nice (Spine faded). *Pharos.* $75/£48

BENET, STEPHEN VINCENT. Western Star. (NY): Editions for Armed Services, n.d. Fine. *Pharos.* $35/£23

BENET, STEPHEN VINCENT. Young People's Pride. NY: Holt, 1922. 1st ed. Frontis. VG. *Reese.* $25/£16

BENET, WILLIAM ROSE. The Burglar of the Zodiac and Other Poems. New Haven: Yale Univ, 1918. 1st ed. NF (pp browned) in dj (sl browning; chips, tear). *Antic Hay.* $50/£32

Bengo to the Rescue. London: Purnell, 1956. 24x17 cm. 3 pop-ups. Glazed pict bds. VG. *Book Finders.* $50/£32

BENGTSSON, FRANS. The Long Ships. Michael Meyer (trans). Stockholm: Norstedts, (1954). 1st ed. Map eps. Fine in pict dj (spine corners lt worn). *Else Fine.* $60/£39

BENHAM, CHARLES. The Fourth Napoleon. Stone, 1897. 1st ed. VG. *Madle.* $125/£81

BENJAMIN, ASHER. The American Builder's Companion.... Boston: R.P. & C. Williams, April 1816. 3rd ed. 4to. 104pp (foxed, dampstained); 59 engr plts (3 w/marginal tears repaired; 1 lacks part of border). Contemp sheep (rubbed, soiled). Sound. *Felcone.* $650/£419

BENJAMIN, ASHER. The Builder's Guide.... Boston: Perkins & Marvin, 1839. 1st ed. 4to. 83pp; 66 plts (lacks plt 7, extra copy plt 5). Later 1/2 calf, contemp marbled sides. Lt foxing, else VG. *Bookpress.* $875/£565

BENJAMIN, PARK. The United States Naval Academy.... NY/London: Putnam's, 1900. 1st ed. *Lefkowicz.* $85/£55

BENJAMINS, MR. (Pseud of Bret Harte.) Lothaw. London: John Camden Hotten, n.d. (1871). Unpaginated. Frontis, 7 full-pg illus. Bkpl. Orig wraps; fldg slipcase (bkpl of Morris L. Parrish). BAL 7430 (2nd issue). *Schoyer.* $175/£113

BENNET, JAMES A. Forts and Forays. Brooks & Reeve (eds). Albuquerque: Univ of NM, 1948. 1st ed thus. VG+ in VG- dj. *Parker.* $55/£35

BENNET, R.A. Thyra. Holt, 1901. 1st ed. VG. *Aronovitz.* $75/£48

BENNET, ROBERT AMES. Sheepman's Gold. Washburn, 1939. 1st Amer ed. NF in dj (lt chipped; worn). *Stahr.* $35/£23

BENNETT, A. The Author's Craft. Hodder & Stoughton, 1914. 1st ed. Good in dj (sl dull, rubbed). *Whiteson.* $20/£13

BENNETT, A.G. Whaling in the Antarctic. NY: Henry Holt, 1932. 1st US ed. VG. *High Latitude.* $45/£29

BENNETT, A.W. and G. MURRAY. A Handbook of Cryptogamic Botany. London, 1889. 1st ed. viii,473,(2)pp. (Worn; spine faded; spotted, stained.) *Sutton.* $40/£26

BENNETT, ARNOLD and EDWARD KNOBLOCK. London Life: A Play in Three Acts and Nine Scenes. London: C&W, 1924. 1st ed. (Spine label sl rubbed.) *Sadlon.* $10/£6

BENNETT, ARNOLD. The Lion's Share. London: Cassell, 1916. 1st ed. Inscribed, initialed. (Backstrip faded; sl dampstained.) *Petersfield.* $233/£150

BENNETT, ARNOLD. Mr. Prohack. London: Methuen, (1922). 1st ed. Inscribed. Fine. *Hermitage*. $75/£48

BENNETT, ARNOLD. The Old Wive's Tale. Oxford: LEC, 1941. #904/1500 numbered, signed by John Austin (illus). Cl-backed paper-cvrd bds. Fine in djs & pub's slipcase (lt worn). *Hermitage*. $100/£65

BENNETT, ARNOLD. The Price of Love. NY: Harper, 1914. 1st Amer ed. Ink name, o/w NF. *Hermitage*. $25/£16

BENNETT, ARNOLD. These Twain. London: Methuen, 1916. 1st UK ed. NF in VG dj (rear strengthened). *Williams*. $233/£150

BENNETT, B.A. and D.G. WILKINS. Donatello. Phaidon, 1984. Sound in dj. *Ars Artis*. $93/£60

BENNETT, C.H. The Surprising, Unheard of and Never-to-be-Surpassed Adventures of Young Munchausen.... Routledge, Warne & Routledge, 1865. 1st ed. Sq 8vo. Frontis, (iv),107pp; 10 plts (edges waterstained). Pebble-grained blue cl (sl soiled), blocked in blind, gilt-lettered. *Bickersteth*. $116/£75

BENNETT, E.A. Journalism for Women. A Practical Guide. London, 1898. 1st ed. Uncut, unopened. Pict cvrs. Fine. *Polyanthos*. $200/£129

BENNETT, EMERSON. The Trapper's Bride. Cincinnati: U.P. James, (1860). 5th ed. 154pp + ad leaf, 2pp illus. Unopened. Pict wrappers (separating at spine; soiling, edgewear; worm holes). *Dawson*. $40/£26

BENNETT, G.J. The Pedestrian's Guide Through North Wales. London: Henry Colburn, 1838. 1st ed. viii,391pp, add'l illus tp, 19 etched plts, 7 fldg plts. Blind-emb cl (spine chipped, faded; foxed, shaken, ex-libris). *Edwards*. $70/£45

BENNETT, GEORGE FLETCHER. Early Architecture of Delaware. NY: Bonanza, n.d. Frontis. VG. *Bookpress*. $45/£29

BENNETT, H.S. Life on the English Manor. CUP, 1956. 6 plts, 4 woodcuts. VG in dj. *Hollett*. $47/£30

BENNETT, HARRIETT M. Calendar for the Year 1890. London: Raphael Tuck, 1890. Oblong, 16mo. Paper wrappers w/twisted ribbon binding. Generally Fine (sl edge chip). *Reisler*. $75/£48

BENNETT, JOHN. Madame Margot: A Legend of Old Charleston. Columbia: Univ of SC, 1951. 1st ed. Pristine in orig tissue remnants. *Pharos*. $30/£19

BENNETT, JOHN. The Pathology and Treatment of Pulmonary Tuberculosis.... Phila, 1854. 1st Amer ed. 130pp. Good. *Fye*. $100/£65

BENNETT, LERONE, JR. Pioneers in Protest. Chicago: Johnson, 1968. 1st ed. VG in dj (edgeworn). *Petrilla*. $30/£19

BENNETT, MONICA. Encyclopedia of Chrysanthemums. NY, 1958. 8 color plts. Good. *Brooks*. $27/£17

BENNETT, NORMAN. The Science and Practice of Dental Surgery. London, 1931. 2nd ed. 2 vols. (Lib ink stamp.) *Edwards*. $47/£30

BENNETT, T.P. Architectural Design in Concrete. London: 1927. 100 plts. (Margins of plts sl browned; joints tender; worming upper bd; spine chipped w/loss.) *Edwards*. $47/£30

BENNETT, WHITMAN. A Practical Guide to American Nineteenth Century Color Plate Books. NY: Bennett Book Studios, 1949. 1st ed. Red cl. VG. *Glenn*. $65/£42

BENNETT, WHITMAN. A Practical Guide to American Nineteenth Century Color Plate Books. NY: Bennett Book Studios, 1949. 1st ed. 8vo. xxii,133pp; 8pp supplement, errata slip. Cl. Fine. *Bookpress*. $110/£71

BENSON, A.E. History of the Massachusetts Horticultural Society. N.p., 1929. Frontis. Cl (lt wear; damp-stained; fr hinge starting). *Sutton*. $60/£39

BENSON, ARTHUR C. The Child of the Dawn. Smith-Elder, 1912. 1st ed. Extrems sl rubbed, else VG. *Aronovitz*. $38/£25

BENSON, ARTHUR C. The Hill of Trouble. London, 1903. 1st ed. VG. *Madle*. $75/£48

BENSON, ARTHUR C. The Isles of Sunset. London, 1908. VG. *Madle*. $35/£23

BENSON, D.R. Irene, Good-Night. NY: Targ Editions, 1982. 1st ed, one of 250 signed by Benson and Edward Gorey (illus). Frontis. Purple Japanese silk over bds. Glassine dj. *Juvelis*. $175/£113

BENSON, E.F. Daisy's Aunt. London: Thomas Nelson, (1910). 1st ed. Color frontis. Bkpl, edges foxed, o/w VG. Enamel spine title-piece VG. *Ash*. $70/£45

BENSON, E.F. Paul. London: Heinemann, 1906. 1st ed. Pale yellow pict cl. VG (bkpl; lt wear, foxing). *Ash*. $78/£50

BENSON, JOHN HOWARD and ARTHUR GRAHAM CAREY. The Elements of Lettering. Newport: John Stevens, 1940. One of 100 rag paper copies, signed. Red cl, teg. NF (spine faded; sm spot fore-edge, not affecting leaves). *Veatchs*. $120/£77

BENSON, LUTHER. Fifteen Years in Hell. Indianapolis, 1879. 208pp. Good. *Hayman*. $25/£16

BENSON, N.P. The Log of the El Dorado. SF: James H. Barry, (1915). 1st ed in bk form. 6 plts. Marginal damp-stain 2 leaves, o/w Attractive in orig pict wrappers. *Lefkowicz*. $115/£74

BENSON, ROBERT (ed). Holford Collection. London: OUP, 1927. #XL/400. 2 vols. 200 plts. Marbled eps (ex-libris); teg. *Edwards*. $194/£125

BENSON, ROBERT HUGH. Lord of the World. London: Sir Isaac Pitman & Sons, 1915. 1st ed. Spine faded; sl foxing; o/w Very Nice. *Temple*. $45/£29

BENSUSAN, S.L. Morocco. London: A&C Black, 1904. 74 color plts. Teg. Pict cl, gilt. *Petersfield*. $93/£60

BENT, ARTHUR C. Life Histories of North American Birds. Washington, 1919-68. All 1st eds. 23 vols, complete. 2 vols in buckram (browned pp); 20 vols in orig wrappers (chipped, creased; spine chipped, split or spotted 4 vols); 1 vol in plain brn wrappers (sm edge tears to frontis taped). Clean. *Sutton*. $535/£345

BENT, ARTHUR C. Life Histories of North American Gulls and Terns. Washinton: GPO, 1921. 93 full-pg plts. Paper cvrs feathered, o/w Good. *Bishop*. $50/£32

BENT, J. THEODORE. The Ruined Cities of Mashonaland. London: Longmans, 1892. 1st ed. 8vo. xi,(i)blank,376,24 pub's list, half title (lib stamp, ink mk on title), 3 fldg maps, 2 plans, 12 plts. Blue cl (sm blind stamp; sl edge-rubbed), gilt. VG. *Morrell*. $163/£105

BENT, NEWELL. American Polo. NY, 1929. 1st ed. VG (cl faded). *Argosy*. $85/£55

BENTLEY, E.C. Elephant's Work. London: Hodder & Stoughton, 1950. 1st ed. Top edge dknd, o/w VG in dj (tear, sl wear). *Mordida*. $45/£29

BENTLEY, E.C. Trent's Last Case. London: Nelson, n.d. (1913). 1st UK ed. Fine. *Lewton*. $70/£45

BENTLEY, E.C. and H. WARNER ALLEN. Trent's Own Case. NY: Knopf, 1936. 1st Amer ed. VG w/o dj. *Mordida.* $30/£19

BENTLEY, GERALD EADES. The Jacobean and Caroline Stages, Dramatic Companies and Players. Oxford: Clarendon, 1949-56. Rpt. 5 vols. VG set in djs. *Petersfield.* $264/£170

BENTLEY, JOHN. Health Made Easy for the People; or, Physical Training.... Phila, 1854. 171pp. Good. *Fye.* $60/£39

BENTLEY, NICHOLAS. The Tongue-Tied Canary. NY: Duell, Sloan & Pearce, 1949. 1st ed. Rev copy. Fine in dj. *Cahan.* $40/£26

BENTLEY, NICOLAS. Nicolas Bentley's Book of Birds. London: Andre Deutsch, 1965. 1st ed. Lg 8vo. Fine in Fine dj. *Book Adoption.* $35/£23

BENTLEY, RICHARD. Designs for Six Poems by Mr. T. Gray.... London: Dodsley, 1789. 2nd ed. Port, 6 plts, 13 engr head- or tail-pieces, russia (joints cracked, spine rubbed). *Marlborough.* $279/£180

BENTLEY, THOMAS. False Honor. NY: Edward Walker, 1879. 1st ed. 270pp. Good. *Hayman.* $35/£23

BENTON, F. The Honey Bee. Washington, 1896. 118pp (fep gutter cracked), 11 plts. (Corners worn; lower backstrip gone.) *Sutton.* $45/£29

BENTON, THOMAS HART. Thirty Years' View. NY: Appleton, 1854. 2 vols. Frontis port, ix,739; frontis view, 788pp. Spines faded, else Very Nice set. *Bohling.* $150/£97

BENTWRIGHT, JEREMIAH. The American Horse Tamer. NY, 1858. 1st ed? 86pp. Gilt, debossed cl. VG (sig, lt foxing, bumped corners). *Baade.* $150/£97

BENWELL, GWEN and ARTHUR WAUGH. Sea Enchantress: The Tale of the Mermaid and Her Kin. London: Hutchinson, (1961). 1st ed. 16 plts, map. Very Nice in dj. *Cady.* $30/£19

BERAUD, H. Lazarus. Macmillan, 1925. 1st ed. VG+ in VG dj (lt wear, tear; inner reinforcement). *Aronovitz.* $85/£55

BERCOVICI, ALFRED. That Blackguard Burton! Indianapolis/NY: Bobbs-Merrill, 1962. 1st ed. Sl rubbed, o/w VG. *Worldwide.* $20/£13

BERCOVICI, KONRAD. Crimes of Charity. NY: Knopf, 1917. VG in dj (soiled). *Schoyer.* $35/£23

BERCOVICI, KONRAD. The Incredible Balkans. NY: Putnam's, 1932. 1st ed. Sl rubbed; spine fading; lib # spine, o/w VG ex-lib. *Worldwide.* $16/£10

BERENS, CONRAD and JOHN KING. An Atlas of Ophthalmic Surgery. Phila, 1961. 1st ed. Good in dj. *Fye.* $75/£48

BERENSON, BERNARD. Caravaggio. NY, 1953. 88 plts. Cl sl rubbed. *Washton.* $30/£19

BERENSON, BERNARD. The Drawings of the Florentine Painters. Chicago: Univ of Chicago Press, 1938. 1st ed. 3 vols. Pub's blue buckram, gilt spines. Good. *Karmiole.* $300/£194

BERENSON, BERNARD. Homeless Paintings of the Renaissance. Bloomington, 1970. Good in dj. *Washton.* $75/£48

BERENSON, BERNARD. The Italian Painters of the Renaissance. GC: Phaidon, (1953). 2nd ptg. Color frontis, 16 color plts. VG. *Bookpress.* $100/£65

BERENSON, BERNARD. Italian Pictures of the Renaissance. London, 1968. 4to. 3 vols. 1988 plts. VG (ex-lib; bkpls; deaccession stamps). *Washton.* $900/£581

BERENSON, BERNARD. The Passionate Sightseer: From the Diaries, 1947-1956. London: Thames & Hudson, 1966. 2nd imp. 3 plts. Blue cl over bds. VG in dj. *Heller.* $30/£19

BERESFORD, J.D. The Hampdenshire Wonder. S&J, 1911. 1st ed. Inscribed. Good. *Aronovitz.* $375/£242

BERESFORD, M.W. and J.K.S. ST. JOSEPH. Medieval England. CUP, 1958. 1st ed. 111 figs, map (feps lt browned). *Edwards.* $70/£45

BERGAN, WILLIAM M. Old Nantasket. (Boston, 1968.) Black buckram, gilt title. VG. *Bohling.* $30/£19

BERGENGREN, RALPH. David the Dreamer. Boston: Atlantic Monthly, (1922). 1st ed. Oblong 4to. Tom (Seidmann)-Freud (illus). Grn cl, color paste label, gold stamping (edgewear). Color dj (taped; sm pieces missing). *Reisler.* $750/£484

BERGER, JOHN and JEAN MOHR. Another Way of Telling. Pantheon, 1982. 1st ed. NF in NF dj. *Bishop.* $22/£14

BERGER, JOHN. The Foot of Clive. London: Methuen, 1962. 1st ed. VG in dj. *Rees.* $16/£10

BERGER, JOHN. A Fortunate Man. London: Allen Lane, 1967. 1st ed. NF in dj (nick). *Rees.* $23/£15

BERGER, THOMAS. Crazy in Berlin. Scribners, 1958. 1st ed, 1st bk. Fine in VG+ dj. *Fine Books.* $125/£81

BERGER, THOMAS. The Feud. NY: Delacorte/Lawrence, (1983). 1st ed. NF in dj. *Antic Hay.* $25/£16

BERGER, THOMAS. Little Big Man. Dial, 1964. 1st ed. NF in dj (lt rubbed). *Fine Books.* $110/£71

BERGER, THOMAS. Reinhart in Love. NY: Scribner's, 1962. 1st ed. VF in dj. *Else Fine.* $75/£48

BERGER, THOMAS. Rinehart's Women. NY: Delacorte, 1981. 1st ed. Fine in Fine dj. *Revere.* $20/£13

BERGER, VICTOR. Berger's Broadsides. Milwaukee: Social-Democratic Pub, 1912. 1st ed. VG (hinges going). *Beasley.* $125/£81

BERGHOLD, ALEXANDER. The Indians' Revenge. SF, 1891. 1st Amer ed. 240pp. Pict cl. Howes B 373. *Ginsberg.* $150/£97

BERGLER, EDMUND. The Basic Neurosis. NY: Grune & Stratton, (1949). Later ptg. Black cl. VG in dj. *Gach.* $25/£16

BERGLER, EDMUND. Homosexuality: Disease or Way of Life? NY: Hill & Wang, 1956. 1st ed, 1st ptg. Red cl. VG. *Gach.* $27/£17

BERGLER, EDMUND. Selected Papers of.... NY/London: Grune & Stratton, (1969). 1st ed. Blue cl, painted labels. VG. *Gach.* $100/£65

BERGMAN, ANDREW. The Big Kiss-Off of 1944. NY: Holt, 1974. 1st ed. Fine (scuff fep) in NF dj. *Janus.* $35/£23

BERGMAN, RAY. Fresh-Water Bass. NY: Penn, (1942). 1st ed. 10 color plts. Ex-lib w/outside mks removed; glue mks, o/w Good. *Artis.* $35/£23

BERGMAN, RAY. With Fly, Plug and Bait. NY, 1947. 1st ed. 7 color plts. Fine in dj (chipped). *Artis.* $45/£29

BERGSTROM, INGVAR. Dutch Still-Life Painting in the Seventeenth Century. NY: Thomas Yoseloff, (1956). 1st ed. 8 color plts. Dj. *Bookpress.* $400/£258

BERGSTROM, INGVAR. Dutch Still-Life Painting in the Seventeenth Century. NY, 1956. 8 color plts. Fine. *Europa.* $256/£165

BERJANE, J. French Dishes for English Tables. London, 1931. Dj (sl chipped). *Edwards.* $23/£15

BERJEAU, J.P. The Homoeopathic Treatment of Syphilis, Gonorrhoea, Spermatorrhoea, and Urinary Diseases. Phila, 1869. Rev ed. 256pp. Good. *Fye.* $75/£48

BERKEBILE, DON H. Carriage Terminology: An Historical Dictionary. Smithsonian, 1978. 1st ed. *Lambeth.* $200/£129

BERKELEY, EDMUND C. Giant Brains, or Machines That Think. NY: Wiley, 1949. 1st ed. NF in VG dj (few lg chips). *Lame Duck.* $85/£55

BERKELEY, GRANTLEY F. Reminiscences of a Huntsman. London: Arnold, 1897. 'Sportsman's Library' ed. 344pp; teg. Orig 3/4 parchment vellum, marbled bds. VG. *Bowman.* $70/£45

BERKMAN, ALEXANDER and EMMA GOLDMAN. Anarchism on Trial. Trial and Speeches...1917. NY: Mother Earth, 1917. 1st ed. VG in wraps. *Beasley.* $150/£97

BERKMAN, ALEXANDER and EMMA GOLDMAN. Deportation. Its Meaning and Menace. Ellis Island/NY: M.E. Fitzgerald, 1919. 1st ed. NF (dknd; rusting staples) in wraps. *Beasley.* $100/£65

BERKMAN, ALEXANDER and EMMA GOLDMAN. Trials and Speeches. NY: Mother Earth Pub, 1917. 1st ed. VG + in wraps. *Beasley.* $125/£81

BERKOFF, STEVEN. Gross Intrusion and Other Stories. London/Dallas: Calder/Riverrun, 1979. 1st UK ed. Fine in dj. *Williams.* $47/£30

BERLANDIER, JEAN LOUIS. Indians of Texas in 1830. Smithsonian, 1969. 1st ed. 20 color plts. VF in Fine dj. *Oregon.* $50/£32

BERLINER, M.L. Biomicroscopy of the Eye, Slit Lamp Microscopy of the Living Eye. NY, 1949. 1st ed. 2 vols. Good. *Fye.* $200/£129

BERMAN, ELEANOR D. Thomas Jefferson among the Arts: A Essay in Early American Esthetics. NY: Philosophical Library, (c. 1947). VG in Good dj. *Book Broker.* $25/£16

BERMAN, MYRON. Richmond's Jewry: Shabbat in Shockoe, 1769-1976. Univ Press of VA, 1979. (1st ed). VG in VG dj. *Book Broker.* $35/£23

BERNACCHI, L.C. Saga of the Discovery. London/Glasgow: Blackie & Son, 1938. 1st ed. 3 maps (1 fldg). Blue cl. Edges foxed, else VG. *Parmer.* $125/£81

BERNACCHI, L.C. A Very Gallant Gentleman. London: Thornton Butterworth, 1933. 1st ed, 3rd imp. Spine faded, chipped; inscrip. *Parmer.* $60/£39

BERNANOS, GEORGES. A Diary of My Times. Pamela Morris (trans). London: Boriswood, 1938. 1st ed. VG. *Patterson.* $62/£40

BERNARD, CLAUDE. An Introduction to the Study of Experimental Medicine. NY: Macmillan, 1927. 1st Amer ed. Good. *Goodrich.* $45/£29

Bernardo Cavalinno of Naples 1616-1656. Cleveland, 1984. Good in dj. *Washton.* $65/£42

BERNAU, J.H. Missionary Labours in British Guiana.... London, 1847. 1st ed. 12mo. 242pp; 15 engrs; fldg map. 1/2 blue calf; gilt spine. *Argosy.* $250/£161

BERNERS, JULIANA. The Treatyse of Fysshinge wyth an Angle. London: William Pickering, 1827. Frontis, 41pp. Full mottled calf, gilt, red lettering piece. Joints sl tender, but sound. *Petersfield.* $310/£200

BERNERS, LORD. A Distant Prospect. London: Constable, (1945). 1st ed. Fine (lacks dj). *Petersfield.* $23/£15

BERNHARD, THOMAS. The Lime Works. Sophie Wilkins (trans). NY: Knopf, 1973. 1st Amer ed. Fine in dj. *Hermitage.* $35/£23

BERNHARDT, C. Indian Raids in Lincoln County, Kansas, 1864 and 1869. Lincoln, KS: Lincoln Sentinel, 1910. 1st ed. Fldg map. Subs list bound in. Ptd wraps (lacks backstrip). *Cullen.* $125/£81

BERNHEIM, H. Suggestive Therapeutics. NY, 1889. 1st Eng trans. 420pp. Good. *Fye.* $100/£65

BERNSTEIN, ALINE. The Martha Washington Doll Book. N.p.: Howell, Soskin, (1945). 1st ed. Obl 4to. (21) leaves, 12 color plts. Comb binding (lt rubbed). VG. *Bookpress.* $125/£81

BERNSTEIN, ALINE. Three Blue Suits. NY: Equinox Cooperative, 1933. One of 600. Frontis. Belgian linen, paper spine, cvr labels. Spine sl age-dknd, else Fine in slipcase (defective). *Pharos.* $95/£61

BERRA, YOGI and ED FITZGERALD. Yogi. Doubleday, 1961. 1st ed. Fine in VG + dj. *Plapinger.* $30/£19

BERRIGAN, DANIEL and ROBERT COLES. Geography of Faith: Conversations When Underground. Boston: Beacon Press, (1971). 1st ed. Fine in NF dj. *Aka.* $35/£23

BERRIGAN, DANIEL. The Dark Night of Resistance. NY, 1971. Signed presentation. Fine in dj (spine sl rubbed, sl soiled). *Polyanthos.* $30/£19

BERRIGAN, DANIEL. Night Flight to Hanoi: War Diary with 11 Poems. NY: Macmillan, (1968). Stated 1st. NF in VG + dj (price-clipped). *Aka.* $40/£26

BERRIGAN, TED. Many Happy Returns. NY: Corinth Books, 1969. Ltd to 1500. This copy signed. Pict cvrs (sl rubbed). Fine. *Polyanthos.* $30/£19

BERRY, BURTON Y. Out of the Past: The Istanbul Grand Bazaar. NY: Arco, (1977). Dj. *Schoyer.* $40/£26

BERRY, DON. A Majority of Scoundrels. Harper, (1961). 1st ed. 2 maps in pocket. VF. *Oregon.* $60/£39

BERRY, DON. A Majority of Scoundrels. Harper, (1961). 1st ed. 2 maps in pocket. VG in Fine dj. *Oregon.* $80/£52

BERRY, DON. A Majority of Scoundrels. NY, (1961). 1st ed. Pub photo. VG in dj (sl worn). *King.* $35/£23

BERRY, DON. A Majority of Scoundrels. NY: Harper, (1961). 1st ptg. 2 fldg maps (folds repaired). Dj. *Schoyer.* $50/£32

BERRY, DON. A Majority of Scoundrels. NY: Harper, 1961. 1st ed. VG (bkpl) in VG- dj. *Parker.* $90/£58

BERRY, DON. To Build a Ship. Viking, (1963). 1st ed. Fine in VG dj. *Oregon.* $75/£48

BERRY, G.A. Subjective Symptoms in Eye Diseases. Edinburgh/London, 1886. 118pp; 13 figs. (Cl sl dull, duststained, worn.) *Whitehart.* $39/£25

BERRY, HENRY. Boston Red Sox. Rutledge, 1975. 1st ed. Fine in VG + dj. *Plapinger.* $30/£19

BERRY, W. TURNER and A.F. JOHNSON. Catalogue of Specimens of Printing Types by English and Scottish Printers and Founders, 1665-1830. London: OUP, 1935. 24 plts. 1/4 cl, bds. Tips rubbed; eps, untrimmed paper edges foxed, else NF in ptd dj (spine chipped). *Veatchs.* $450/£290

BERRY, W. TURNER and A.F. JOHNSON. Encyclopaedia of Type Faces. Blandford Press, 1953. 1st ed. Dj. *Edwards.* $47/£30

BERRY, WENDELL. A Continuous Harmony, Essays Cultural and Agricultural. NY: Harcourt, (1972). 1st ed. Fine in dj. *Second Life.* $65/£42

BERRY, WENDELL. Findings. (IA City): Prairie Press, 1969. Fine in dj. *Graf.* $40/£26

BERRY, WENDELL. Nathan Coulter, a Novel. Boston, 1960. 1st ed. 1st bk. Nice in dj (sl worn; nicks, stains to flap). *Second Life.* $200/£129

BERRY, WENDELL. November Twenty Six Nineteen Hundred Sixty Three.... NY: Braziller, (1964). 1st ed, unsigned issue. Fine in slipcase (lt rubbed). *Reese.* $35/£23

BERRY, WENDELL. A Place on Earth. NY: Harcourt Brace, (1967). 1st ptg. Excellent in dj (sl faded; 1-inch closed tear; sm chips). *Second Life.* $250/£161

BERRY-HILL, HENRY and SIDNEY. Chinnery and China Coast Paintings. Leigh-on-Sea: F. Lewis, 1970. Ltd to 600. Tipped-in color frontis. VG in dj (sl chipped, price-clipped). *Hollett.* $116/£75

BERRYMAN, JOHN. Berryman's Sonnets. NY: FSG, (1967). 1st ed. VG in dj. *Hermitage.* $40/£26

BERRYMAN, JOHN. Collected Poems 1937-1971. London, 1990. 1st Eng ed. Fine in dj. *Words Etc.* $31/£20

BERRYMAN, JOHN. Delusions, etc. London: Faber & Faber, (1972). 1st Eng ed. Fine in dj. *Heller.* $35/£23

BERRYMAN, JOHN. Delusions, Etc. London: Faber, 1972. 1st ed. NF in dj (sl rubbed, creased). *Rees.* $19/£12

BERRYMAN, JOHN. The Dream Songs. NY: FSG, (1969). 1st complete 1-vol ed. NF in dj. *Hermitage.* $40/£26

BERRYMAN, JOHN. The Dream Songs. London, 1990. 1st Eng ed. Fine in dj. *Words Etc.* $31/£20

BERRYMAN, JOHN. Henry's Fate and Other Poems. NY: FSG, 1977. 1st ed. Fine in dj. *Aka.* $35/£23

BERRYMAN, JOHN. His Toy, His Dream, His Rest. NY: FSG, (1968). 1st ed. Fine in NF dj (tear). *Antic Hay.* $35/£23

BERRYMAN, JOHN. Homage to Mistress Bradstreet. NY: Farrar, Straus & Cudahy, (1956). 1st ed. Ben Shahn (illus). Fine in NF dj. *Antic Hay.* $175/£113

BERRYMAN, JOHN. Stephen Crane. (NY): William Sloane Assoc, (1950). 1st ed. VG in dj (spine faded, short tears; else VG). *Godot.* $125/£81

BERTON, PIERRE. Drifting Home. Toronto, 1973. 1st ed. Fine in dj (sl edgeworn). *Baade.* $27/£17

BERTON, PIERRE. The Impossible Railway. NY: Knopf, 1972. (1st Amer ed). VG+ in dj (lacks piece). *Bohling.* $35/£23

BERTON, PIERRE. Klondike. Toronto, 1972. 1st ptg of rev ed. Sl bumped, o/w NF in dj. *Baade.* $30/£19

BERTON, PIERRE. The Last Spike. Toronto, 1971. 1st ed. Fine in dj (sl shelfworn). *Baade.* $40/£26

BERTON, PIERRE. The Mysterious North. Toronto, 1956. 1st ed. Dec cl. Tape residue ep, o/w VG in dj (sl chipped). *Baade.* $42/£27

BERTON, PIERRE. The National Dream. Toronto, 1970. 1st ed. Fine in dj (sl edgeworn; closed tears). *Baade.* $40/£26

BERTRAM, ANTHONY. Paul Nash: The Portrait of an Artist. London: Faber & Faber, 1955. Red buckram, gilt spine title. Sl shelfwear, else Fine. *Heller.* $40/£26

BERTRAM, ANTHONY. Paul Nash: The Portrait of an Artist. London: Faber & Faber, 1955. 1st ed. Frontis. As New in dj (sl sunned; tape-reinforced; closed tear). *Great Epic.* $55/£35

BERTRAM, ANTHONY. The Pleasures of Poverty. London: Hollis & Carter, 1950. 1st Eng ed. Grn paper bds. Very Nice. *Cady.* $20/£13

BERVE, HELMUT and GOTTFRIED GRUBEN. Greek Temples, Theatres and Shrines. NY: Abrams, n.d. (ca 1962). 36 mtd color plts. Good in dj. *Karmiole.* $200/£129

BERVE, HELMUT and GOTTFRIED GRUBEN. Greek Temples, Theatres, and Shrines. NY: Abrams, n.d. (1962). 36 mtd color plts. VG. *Argosy.* $85/£55

BESANT, WALTER. London City. London, 1910. 1st ed. Fldg map. Teg. Dec gilt spine. (Top edge sl faded.) *Edwards.* $47/£30

BESANT, WALTER. London. A&C Black, 1903-12. 10 vols. Maroon cl (sl bumped, edges lt discolored), dec gilt spines (lt faded, bumped, chipped). *Edwards.* $504/£325

BESANT, WALTER. South London. London, 1912. New ed. Etched frontis. Teg. Gilt illus upper bd, spine. (Feps browned; sl worn.) *Edwards.* $43/£28

BESKOW, ELSA. Aunt Brown's Birthday. NY: Harper, (1930). Obl 8vo. 12 full-color lithos. Cl-backed pict bds. (Edges, corners worn; bds soiled.) Internally VG. *Davidson.* $65/£42

BESSIE, ALVAH. Men in Battle. A Story of Americans in Spain. NY, 1939. 1st Amer ed. Fine (spine edges sunned) in dj (sl sunned, chipped, lacks piece). *Polyanthos.* $45/£29

BESSIE, ALVAH. Men in Battle. A Story of Americans in Spain. NY: Scribner's, 1939. 1st ed. Nice in dj (worn, chipped, repaired, but complete). *Patterson.* $186/£120

BESSON, MAURICE. The Scourge of the Indies. London: Routledge, 1929. One of 960. 5 full-pg hand-colored repros. Brick red cl. Rubbed, else Fine. *Glenn.* $175/£113

BEST, GERALD M. Snowplow: Clearing Mountain Rails. Berkeley: Howell-North, 1966. 1st ed. Pict eps. Grn cl. Fine in NF dj. *Harrington.* $35/£23

BEST, THOMAS. A Concise Treatise of the Art of Angling. for B. Crosby, 1807. New ('Seventh') ed. Frontis, 186pp + (4)pp ads. Contemp mottled calf gilt. *Hill.* $171/£110

BESTE, RICHARD. The Wabash. London, 1855. 1st ed. 2 vols. Color litho frontis views, (12),329; (8),352pp (vol 1 lacks ep; marginal staining; vol 2 tp lacks corner affecting few words; marginal staining; sigs starting; spine mended), 2 plts. Howes B 401. *Ginsberg.* $150/£97

BESTER, ALFRED. The Demolished Man. Shasta, 1953. 1st ed. Fine in Fine dj (3 short closed tears). *Aronovitz.* $350/£226

BESTER, ALFRED. Extro. London: Eyre Methuen, 1975. 1st Eng ed. Blue cl. Pp sl tanned, o/w Fine in dj. *Dalian.* $39/£25

BESTERMAN, THEODORE (ed). The Pilgrim Fathers. London: Golden Cockerel, 1939. Rpt. One of 300 numbered. 8 engrs. Patterned bds; teg. Prospectus laid in. VG (bkpl). *Cahan.* $200/£129

BESTON, HENRY. Northern Farm. NY: Rinehart, 1948. 1st ed. Fine in dj. *Bowman.* $45/£29

BETENSON, LULA PARKER. Butch Cassidy, My Brother. Provo, (1975). 2nd ptg. Frontis. VG in Good+ dj. *Oregon.* $35/£23

BETJEMAN, JOHN. Antiquarian Prejudice. Hogarth, 1939. 1st ed. Wraps sl dull, else Good. *Whiteson.* $26/£17

BETJEMAN, JOHN. Antiquarian Prejudice. London: Hogarth Press, 1939. 1st ed. Saddle-stitched in wrapper. Sl bumped, else NF. *Between The Covers.* $150/£97

BETJEMAN, JOHN. Collins Guide to English Parish Churches. London: Collins, 1958. 1st ed. VG in dj. *Hollett.* $39/£25

BETJEMAN, JOHN. English Cities and Small Towns. London: Collins, 1943. 1st ed. Pict bds. Fine in dj. *Argosy.* $50/£32

BETJEMAN, JOHN. A Few Late Chrysanthemums. London: John Murray, 1954. 1st ed. VG in dj (roughly price-clipped). *Hollett.* $39/£25

BETJEMAN, JOHN. A Few Late Chrysanthemums. London: Murray, 1954. 1st UK ed. Fine in VG dj (sl grubby). *Williams.* $39/£25

BETJEMAN, JOHN. Ghastly Good Taste. London: Chapman & Hall, 1933. 1st ed, 2nd issue, w/errata slip, spare label. Fldg illus. 1/2 cl over ptd bds, paper spine label (spine ends sl rubbed). *Sadlon.* $20/£13

BETJEMAN, JOHN. A Nip in the Air. Murray, 1974. 1st UK ed. Fine in dj. *Lewton.* $22/£14

BETJEMAN, JOHN. An Oxford University Chest.... London, (1938). 1st ed. L. Moholy-Nagy et al (illus). Cl-backed marbled bds (corners worn). Nice. *Waterfield.* $101/£65

BETJEMAN, JOHN. A Pictorial History of English Architecture. London: John Murray, 1972. One of 100 numbered, signed. Buckram-backed marbled paper bds; teg. Fine in slipcase. *Ulysses.* $349/£225

BETJEMAN, JOHN. A Ring of Bells. London: John Murray, 1962. 1st ed. Edward Ardizzone (illus). Pict bds. VG. *Hollett.* $47/£30

BETJEMAN, JOHN. Summoned by Bells. Murray, 1960. 1st ed. Fine in VG + dj. *Fine Books.* $30/£19

BETJEMAN, JOHN. Summoned by Bells. London: John Murray, 1960. 1st UK ed. Fine (sm bruise upper bd) in dj. *Williams.* $47/£30

BETJEMAN, JOHN. Vintage London. London, 1942. 1st ed. 11 tipped-in color plts. (Eps lt spotted.) Dj (sl chipped). *Edwards.* $47/£30

BETT, WALTER R. (ed). The History and Conquest of Common Diseases. Norman: Univ of OK Press, 1954. 1st ed. VG in dj. *White.* $28/£18

BETT, WALTER R. (ed). The History and Conquest of Common Diseases. Norman, OK, 1954. 1st ed. Good. *Fye.* $75/£48

BETTELHEIM, BRUNO. Surviving and Other Essays. NY: Knopf, 1979. 1st ed. Ptd white linen. VG in dj (price-clipped, lt worn). *Gach.* $28/£18

BETTEN, H.L. Upland Game Shooting. Phila: Penn Publishing, 1940. 1st trade ed. Color frontis, 8 full-pg color plts. Bkpl, else NF. *Cahan.* $75/£48

BETTS, DORIS. The Insurrection. NY: Putnam's, (1954). 1st ed, 1st bk. Rev slip laid in. Fine in NF dj. *Hermitage.* $125/£81

BETTS, EDWIN M. and HAZLEHURST BOLTON PERKINS. Thomas Jefferson's Flower Garden at Monticello. Dietz Press, 1941. Signed by Perkins. VG. *Book Broker.* $25/£16

BETZ, D.O. Tuners Handbook and Manual. Lima, OH, 1908. (Sl shelfwear.) *Artis.* $15/£10

BEVAN, ANEURIN et al. What We Saw in Russia. Hogarth Press, 1931. 1st ed. VG in wrappers. *Words Etc.* $93/£60

Beverages and Sauces of Colonial Virginia. (By Laura S. Fitchett.) Neale Pub, 1906. 1st ed. Teg. Dec cl (rubbed; spine snagged, frayed). Contents VG. *Book Broker.* $200/£129

BEVERIDGE, ALBERT J. Abraham Lincoln 1809-1858. Boston/NY: Houghton Mifflin, (1928). 2 vols. Blue cl (sl rubbed; bumped); gilt titles. VG (several leaves roughly opened). *Blue Mountain.* $15/£10

BEVERIDGE, ALBERT J. Abraham Lincoln, 1809-1858. Boston, 1928. 'Standard Library Edition.' 4 vols. VG + . *Pratt.* $95/£61

BEVERIDGE, ALBERT J. Abraham Lincoln, 1809-1858. Houghton Mifflin, 1928. Standard Lib ed. 4 vols. 4 frontispieces; 32 plts. Sm cut cl vol 2; sm nicks vol 4, o/w Fine. Howes B 408. *Oregon.* $30/£19

BEVERIDGE, ALBERT J. The Life of John Marshall. Boston/NY: Houghton Mifflin, 1916. 4 vols in 2. Red cl (spines faded). Sound. *Boswell.* $100/£65

BEVERIDGE, ALBERT J. The Life of John Marshall. Boston: Houghton Mifflin, 1919. 4 vols. Crimson cl, leather labels. Faded, but Sound. *Boswell.* $75/£48

BEVERIDGE, ALBERT J. The Life of John Marshall. Boston: Houghton Mifflin, 1919. Autograph ed, signed on frontis. 4 vols, 8vo. 4 color frontispieces, 4 color photogrv plts. 3/4 blue morocco, ribbed gilt dec spines. Teg, others uncut. *D & D.* $400/£258

BEWICK, THOMAS. 21 Engravings. St. Charles, IL: Privately ptd, 1951. Ltd to 500 sets. 2 vols. (42;40)pp; 21 orig woodcuts each vol. Brn morocco over dec bds. Good in slipcase. *Karmiole.* $175/£113

BEWICK, THOMAS. Figures of British Land Birds. Newcastle upon Tyne: S. Hodgson for R. Beilby & T. Bewick, 1800. 1st ed, 500 ptd. Mod 1/2 tan morocco. VG (sl spotting 1st, final leaves; from lib of Pamela & Raymond Lister). *Cox.* $271/£175

BEWICK, THOMAS. A General History of Birds and Quadrupeds. Phila: Robert Desilver, 1824. 1st Amer combined ed. 2 vols in 1. 70,142pp. 64 handcolored plts. Full sheep w/morocco spine label. VG (leather cracked, abraded; spine chipped; browning). *Chapel Hill.* $150/£97

BEWICK, THOMAS. A General History of Quadrupeds. Newcastle-Upon-Tyne, 1790. 1st ed. viii,456pp (tears upper margin pp12-14, repaired, no loss). Calf, gilt (rebacked, preserving spine), new label. *Henly.* $349/£225

BEWICK, THOMAS. A General History of Quadrupeds. Newcastle Upon Tyne: S. Hodgson et al, 1792. 3rd ed. Full tan calf w/gilt bands, black gilt spine label. Prelims sl foxed, else Very Nice. *Limestone.* $275/£177

BEWICK, THOMAS. A General History of Quadrupeds. Newcastle upon Tyne: Edw. Walker for T. Bewick and Son, 1820. 7th ed. x,528pp. 1/2 levant morocco, raised bands, old spine label. VG. *Hollett.* $217/£140

BEWICK, THOMAS. A History of British Birds. Newcastle, 1832. 7th ed. 2 vols. Calf. Internally Good (refixed; joints cracked; 1884 cuttings pasted in; pencil notes; 2 leaves vol 2 stained). *Wheldon & Wesley.* $217/£140

BEWICK, THOMAS. A Memoir of Thomas Bewick. Newcastle/London, 1862. xix,314pp. (Margins lt browned; frontis, prelims lt spotted; bkpl; hinges tender; joints sl worn, frayed; spine faded, sl chipped.) *Edwards.* $93/£60

BEWICK, THOMAS. A Memoir. Written by Himself 1822-1828. London, 1924. 1st ed. Frontis port. Illus to upper bd. *Edwards.* $39/£25

BEWICK, THOMAS. Memorial Edition of Thomas Bewick's Works. London: Bernard Quaritch, 1885-1887. Ltd to 750 numbered, signed by Quaritch. 5 vols, complete. 1/2 brn morocco over lt brn cl; teg, others uncut. (Hinges rubbed; leather tips dknd.) *Oak Knoll.* $450/£290

BEWICK, THOMAS. Wood Engravings of Thomas Bewick Reproduced in Collotype. London: Hart-Davis, 1953. 1st ed. Ltd to 1000 signed by Reynolds Stone (intro). Eps, fore-edges lt foxed, o/w Fine in dj (lt foxed). *Jaffe.* $225/£145

BEYLE, MARIE-HENRI (STENDHAL). The Red and the Black. NY: LEC, 1947. #904/1500 numbered, signed by Rafaello Busoni (illus). Leather-backed cl binding. Fine in pub's slipcase (sl used). *Hermitage.* $75/£48

BEZA, MARCU. Byzantine Art in Roumania. London: Batsford, 1940. 1st ed. 29 color, 67 monochr plts (marginal browning); in dj (ragged w/loss). *Edwards.* $39/£25

BEZZERIDES, A.I. Thieves' Market. Scribners, 1949. 1st ed. NF in VG+ dj. *Fine Books.* $38/£25

BI'KIS, DINEH. The Upward Trail. Grand Rapids: Eerdman's, 1935. 1st ed. VG (sl slanted). *Parker.* $45/£29

BIANCHI, DANIEL B. Some Recollections of the Merrymount Press. (Berkeley): George L. Harding & Roger Levenson, 1976. Ltd to 125. Black cl, gilt. Good. *Karmiole.* $30/£19

BIANCO, MARGERY WILLIAMS. The Hurdy-Gurdy Man. NY: OUP, (1933). 1st ed. Signed by Robert Lawson (illus). Sq 8vo. Grn/black illus bds (chipped; few pp lack marginal pieces). *Reisler.* $150/£97

BIANCO, PAMELA. The Doll in the Window. NY: OUP, 1953. 1st ed. Square, 8vo. Blue-grey cl, decs. Good in Fine color pict dj. *Reisler.* $55/£35

BIBBY, GEOFFREY. Looking for Dilmun. NY: Knopf, 1969. 1st ed. VG in dj. *Worldwide.* $20/£13

Bibelot: A Reprint of Poetry and Prose for Book Lovers.... Portland, ME: for Thomas B. Mosher, 1895-1925. 21 vols. Fine in djs (1 worn), slipcases (shelfworn; lacking 1; 3 lacking backstrips). *Sadlon.* $150/£97

Bibliography of Carlyle. (By Richard Herne Shepherd). London: Elliot Stock, (1881). 1st ed. Blue cl; gilt spine. Good. *Karmiole.* $40/£26

BICHAT, XAVIER. Physiological Researches Upon Life and Death. Phila, 1809. 1st Eng trans. 300pp. Full leather. Good. *Fye.* $750/£484

BICK, EDGAR M. Sourcebook of Orthopaedics. Balt: Williams & Wilkins, 1937. Nice. *Goodrich.* $85/£55

BICKEL, LENNARD. Mawson's Will. NY: Stein & Day, (1977). 1st ed. VG in VG dj. *Blue Dragon.* $25/£16

BICKERSTAFF, LAURA M. Pioneer Artists of Taos. Denver: Sage Books, (1955). 1st ed. Fine in NF dj. *Harrington.* $175/£113

BICKERTON, L.M. An Illustrated Guide to Eighteenth-Century English Drinking Glasses. Cirencester, 1971. Dj (price-clipped). *Edwards.* $70/£45

BICKERTON, THOMAS H. A Medical History of Liverpool from the Earliest Days to the Year 1920. London: John Murray, 1936. 1st ed. 24 plts, 8 maps and plans (2 fldg, linen-backed), 50 ports. Fine. *Hollett.* $116/£75

BICKHAM, G. Deliciae Britannicae, or the Curiosities of Kensington, Hampton Court, and Windsor Castle.... London, (1742). 2nd ed. viii,184pp, 10 engr plts. Contemp calf. *Marlborough.* $465/£300

BICKHAM, GEORGE. The Universal Penman. NY: Paul A. Struck, 1941. Ltd ed to 1000 numbered. 205 full-pg plts. Brn cl; gilt-stamped. Good in dj. *Karmiole.* $125/£81

BICKHAM, WARREN STONE. Operative Surgery Covering the Operative Technic Involved in the Operations of General and Special Surgery. Phila: Saunders, 1930. (1st reprinting). 6 vols. (Sl worn; spines faded.) Internally Good. *Goodrich.* $150/£97

BICKHAM, WILLIAM D. From Ohio to the Rocky Mountains. Dayton, 1879. Inscribed. 178pp. Spine extrems worn; inner fr hinge cracked, else VG. *Ginsberg.* $200/£129

BICKNELL, A.J. Detail, Cottage and Constructive Architecture. NY: A.J. Bicknell, 1873. 1st ed. Frontis; (iv)pp; 75 plts. Pub's cl (rebacked w/orig spine laid on; cvrs worn). (Ink inscrip; water damage along outer margin early leaves; text handled.) *Bookpress.* $350/£226

BICKNELL, A.J. Detail, Cottage and Constructive Architecture. NY: A.J. Bicknell, 1873. 1st ed. Frontis, (iv)pp, 75 plts. Pub's cl (soiled, worn). Fr hinge internally cracked; bkpl, else VG. *Bookpress.* $450/£290

BIDDLE, ELLEN McGOWAN. Reminiscences of a Soldier's Wife. Phila: Lippincott, 1907. 1st ed. Inscribed. VG (spine sl frayed). Howes B 426. *Parker.* $250/£161

BIDDLE, GEORGE. The Art of Adolphe Borie. Washington, 1937. Color frontis, 46 plts. VG in dj. *Argosy.* $85/£55

BIDDLE, TYRREL E. The Corinthian Yachtsman, or Hints on Yachting. London, 1886. 1st ed. (6),87,(xvi),(8)pp, 2 plts. *Lefkowicz.* $85/£55

BIDDLE, TYRREL E. Hints to Beginners in Amateur Yacht Designing.... London: Norie & Wilson, 1890. 1st ed. Frontis, 19,(2 ads)pp, 2 fldg plts. (Spine chipped, fr cvr tender.) *Lefkowicz.* $100/£65

BIDDLE, TYRREL E. How to Make Knots, Bends and Splices as Used at Sea. London: Norie & Wilson, (1879). 16,4pp ads. *Lefkowicz.* $40/£26

BIDDLECOMB, GEORGE. The Art of Rigging. Salem: Marine Research Soc Pub 8, 1925. 17 plts, tables. Fine. *Lefkowicz.* $95/£61

BIDDLECOMBE, GEORGE. The Art of Rigging. Salem, MA: Marine Research Soc, 1925. 1st ed. 17 plts. Grn cl, gilt spine. Good in dj (soiled). *Karmiole.* $40/£26

BIDERMANAS, IZIS. The World of Marc Chagall. NY: Doubleday, 1968. 1st ed. Fine. *Cahan.* $65/£42

BIDLAKE, JOHN. Poetical Works. London, 1804. Rev 2nd ed. Fine engr frontis. Contemp mottled calf, neatly gilt. VG. *Argosy.* $150/£97

BIDWELL, JOHN. Echoes of the Past about California bound with In Camp and Cabin by Rev. John Steele. Chicago: Lakeside Press, 1928. Fldg map. Teg. Red cl (extrems sl worn). *Harrington.* $35/£23

BIDWELL, JOHN. The First Emigrant Train to California. Menlo Park: Penlitho Press, (1966). Ltd to 500 numbered. Port. Gilt-stamped buckram, leather spine label. VF in plain paper dj that folds to completely enclose bk. *Oregon.* $75/£48

BIDWELL, JOHN. In California Before the Gold Rush. L.A.: Ward Ritchie, 1948. Ltd to 1000. 1st thus. Uncut, unopened. Pict bds. Fine. *Oregon.* $50/£32

BIDWELL, JOHN. A Journey to California, 1841. Friends of Bancroft Lib, 1964. Facs ed. Fldg map. VF. *Oregon.* $60/£39

BIEBER, MARGARETE. The History of the Greek and Roman Theater. Princeton: Princeton Univ Press, (1971). 2nd ed. Good in dj (torn). *Archaeologia.* $150/£97

BIENFANG, RALPH. The Subtle Sense: Key to the World of Odors. Norman, OK, 1946. 1st ed. Good in dj. *Fye.* $40/£26

BIERCE, AMBROSE and GUSTAV A. DANZIGER. The Monk and the Hangman's Daughter. Chicago: F.J. Schulte, 1892. 1st ed, clothbound issue. Khaki cl stamped in black (sl foxing; corner sl worn). VG. *Reese.* $175/£113

BIERCE, AMBROSE. Black Beetles in Amber. SF/NY: Western Author's Pub Co, 1892. 1st ed. Port. Gray cl, gilt-stamped. Sl soiled, spine rubbed, else Good. BAL 1111. *Reese.* $100/£65

BIERCE, AMBROSE. Black Beetles in Amber. SF: Western Authors, 1892. 1st issue, in gray cl. Frontis port, 280pp. (Spine rubbed, binding scuffed.) BAL 1111. *Schoyer.* $200/£129

BIERCE, AMBROSE. The Collected Works of Ambrose Bierce. NY: Neale Pub Co, 1909-1912. 1st ed. 12 vols. Frontis port. Teg. Cream cl over bds, paper spine label. (Waterstains vol 12 spine, lt soiling other spines.) *Karmiole.* $250/£161

BIERCE, AMBROSE. In the Midst of Life. London: C&W, 1892. 1st British ed. This copy has blue coated eps (not white), inserted cat (dated Oct 1891), other variations from Starrett's description (Starrett 11). Gilt-dec dk blue cl. Bkpl, owner sigs, sm square adhesive paper ep, o/w NF. *Reese.* $450/£290

BIERCE, AMBROSE. In the Midst of Life. NY: Putnam's, 1898. 1st ed. Fr bd sl bowed, joints lt scuffed, o/w VG. *Hermitage.* $125/£81

BIERCE, AMBROSE. The Shadow on the Dial and Other Essays. Robertson, 1909. 1st ed. Fine in Fine dj (spine, panel margins faded). *Aronovitz.* $200/£129

BIERCE, AMBROSE. The Shadow on the Dial and Other Essays. SF: A.M. Robertson, 1909. 1st ed. Sl offsetting eps, o/w Fine in dj (sl faded). *Hermitage.* $275/£177

BIERCE, AMBROSE. A Son of the Gods and a Horseman in the Sky. SF: Paul Elder, (1907). 1st ed thus. Photogravure frontis. Vellum-backed paper-cvrd beveled bds. NF in dj & box (sl chipped). *Hermitage.* $175/£113

BIERCE, AMBROSE. Tales of Soldiers and Civilians. NY: LEC, 1943. #904/1500 numbered, signed by Paul Landacre (illus). Pict cl, leather. Sl rubbed, else Very Nice. *Hermitage.* $75/£48

BIGELOW, H.B. and W.C. SCHROEDER. Fishes of the Western North Atlantic. Part 2. New Haven, 1953. One of 2500. 2 maps. (Spine faded, splotchy; lt scuffed; eps foxed.) Dj (tattered.) *Sutton.* $100/£65

BIGELOW, HORATIO. Gunnerman. NY: Derrydale, (1939). 1st ed, #442/950. NF. *Mcgowan.* $150/£97

BIGELOW, HORATIO. An International System of Electro-Therapeutics. Phila, 1895. 1st ed. 1179pp. Good. *Fye.* $250/£161

BIGELOW, JACOB. Elements of Technology. Boston: Hilliard Gray et al, 1829. 1st ed. xii,507pp, 22 plts (8 fldg). (Hinges reinforced, cvrs worn, foxing, frontis folded.) Good. *Bookpress.* $225/£145

BIGELOW, JOHN, JR. The Campaign of Chancellorsville.... (Dayton, OH: Morningside House, 1984). Facs rpt of 1st ed. Errata, 39 color maps, 3 sketches, 5 plans. Fine. *Mcgowan.* $200/£129

BIGELOW, JOHN, JR. The Campaign of Chancellorsville: A Strategic and Tactical Study. New Haven: Yale, 1910. 1st ptg. #427/1000. 4to. 39 maps (some in rear pocket), 3 sketches, 5 plans. VG. *Schoyer.* $550/£355

BIGELOW, L.J. Bench and Bar: A Complete Digest of the Wit, Humor, Asperities and Amenities of the Law. NY: Harper, 1867. 1st ed. 364,(4)pp. *Ginsberg.* $125/£81

BIGGAR, HENRY. The Early Trading Companies of New France. Toronto, 1901. 1st ed. Ltd to 600. Fldg map. 1/4 morocco (top edge of spine chipped, cracked 7cm down fr hinge). Howes B 438. *Oregon.* $350/£226

BIGGS, DONALD C. The Pony Express. SF: Privately pub, 1961. One of 500. Fine in ptd wraps. *Parmer.* $47/£30

BIGMORE, E.C. and C.W.H. WYMAN. A Bibliography of Printing, With Notes and Illustrations. NY: Duschnes, 1945. 2 vols. *Veatchs.* $125/£81

BIHALJI-MERIN, OTO. Primitive Artists of Yugoslavia. NY: McGraw-Hill, 1964. Tan cl in dj. (Pp1-18 sl water damaged to corner.) *Karmiole.* $65/£42

BILL, ALFRED HOYT. The Beleaguered City, Richmond 1861-1865. NY, 1946. 1st ed. Fldg map. Sm piece torn from dj, o/w VG. *Pratt.* $30/£19

BILL, ALFRED HOYT. The Campaign of Princeton 1776-1777. Princeton, NJ: Princeton Univ Press, 1948. 1st ed. Signed. Brn cl. Fine. *Chapel Hill.* $40/£26

BILL, LEDYARD. A Winter in Florida. NY: Wood & Holbrook, 1869. 2nd ed. 222pp + 6pp ads, 5 plts, map. Grn cl. (Sl stain edge of rear flyleaves.) *Schoyer.* $100/£65

BILLINGS, FRANK. The Relation of Animal Diseases to the Public Health, and Their Prevention. NY, 1884. 1st ed. Inscribed. 446pp. (Ex-lib.) *Fye.* $225/£145

BILLINGS, JOHN D. Hardtack and Coffee. Chicago, (1960). Lakeside Classic. VG. *Schoyer.* $25/£16

BILLINGS, JOHN S. (ed). Physiological Aspects of the Liquor Problem.... Boston, 1903. 1st ed. 2 vols. Good. *Fye.* $150/£97

BILLINGS, JOHN S. et al. The Liquor Problem: A Summary of Investigations...1893-1903. Cambridge, 1905. 1st ed. Good. *Fye.* $75/£48

BILLINGS, ROBERT WILLIAM. Architectural Illustrations and Description of the Cathedral Church at Durham. London: T. and W. Boone, 1843. 1st ed. viii(incl 2pp subs list)+54pp+(iv)text. Tp vignette, 75 engr plts (lt marginal spotting; sm ink spots margin plt 69; prelims lt spotted). Gilt-edged morocco (lt soiled, rubbed; ex-libris), marbled eps. *Edwards.* $310/£200

BILLINGS, WARREN M. (ed). The Old Dominion in the Seventeenth Century: A Documentary History of Virginia, 1606-1689. Univ of NC, (1976). 2nd ptg. VG. *Book Broker.* $25/£16

BILLINGTON, C. Ferns of Michigan. Bloomfield Hills, 1952. Frontis, 16 plts. Cl (bkpl). Dj (spine faded). *Sutton.* $30/£19

BILLON, FREDERIC L. Annals of St. Louis. St. Louis: For Author, 1886-1888. 2 vols. Frontis ports, viii,507; iv,465pp. Internally Fine (vol 1 sunned, stained). *Schoyer.* $350/£226

BILLROTH, T. Clinical Surgery. C.T. Dent (trans). London: New Sydenham Soc. Vol XCIV, 1881. xx,518pp, 9 lithos, 29 woodcuts. Emb cl, gilt device (spine sl rubbed, lower joint sl split). *Edwards.* $47/£30

BILLROTH, T. The Medical Sciences in the German Universities. NY: Macmillan, 1924. 1st ed in English. (Ink name.) *Bickersteth.* $171/£110

BILOVSKY, FRANK and RICH WESTCOTT. The Phillies Encyclopedia. Leisure Press, 1984. 1st ed. Fine in VG+ dj. *Plapinger.* $45/£29

BINDMAN, DAVID and D. TOOMEY. The Complete Graphic Works of William Blake. London: Thames & Hudson, 1978. Dj. *Ars Artis.* $116/£75

BINDMAN, DAVID. William Blake. Thames & Hudson, 1982. 1st ed. 21 color plts. Fine in dj. *Poetry.* $31/£20

BINET, ALFRED and THEODORE SIMON. The Intelligence of the Feeble-Minded. Balt, 1916. 1st Eng trans. Good. *Fye.* $125/£81

BINET, ALFRED. On Double Consciousness.... Chicago: Open Court, 1896 (1890). 1st ed. (vi) + 89 + (5)pp. Early russet cl. VG (ex-lib, lt mkd). *Gach.* $45/£29

BING, ROBERT. Compendium of Regional Diagnosis in Affections of the Brain and Spinal Cord. NY, 1909. 1st Eng trans. Good. *Fye.* $75/£48

BINGER, CARL. Thomas Jefferson: A Well-Tempered Mind. Norton, (ca 1970). 1st ed. VG- (few pp underlined, check mks). *Book Broker.* $25/£16

BINGHAM, CLIFTON and L.L. WEEDON (verses). The Pet's Panorama: A Novel Picture Book for Children. London: Ernest Nister, (ca 1900). 4to. 3 panorama pop-ups (one tab needs regluing). Cl-backed color illus bds (minor edgewear). Fine. *Reisler.* $750/£484

BINGHAM, CLIFTON. Kittenland. London: Collins, (1903). Sm folio. 8 full-pg color plts by Louis Wain. (Marginal tears, smudges, plts unaffected.) Cl-backed illus stiff paper cvrs (worn; spine split). *Reisler.* $485/£313

BINGHAM, D.A. The Marriages of the Bonapartes. London, 1881. 1st ed. 2 vols. vi,357; 365pp. Foxing to eps both vols; sl tear tp vol I, o/w VG. Dk grn cl, emb devices, gilt titles. *Edwards.* $47/£30

BINGHAM, HIRAM. Inca Land, Explorations in the Highlands of Peru. Boston: Houghton Mifflin, 1922. 1st ed. Blue cl (lt rubbed). VG. *Hermitage.* $75/£48

BINGHAM, J. ELLIOT. Narrative of the Expedition to China.... London: Henry Colburn, 1843. 2nd ed. 2 vols. viii,426,(i); vi,446pp; 1 hand-colored litho; 3 etchings. Orig cl gilt (neatly recased). Lacks fldg map, o/w Very Nice. *Hollett.* $457/£295

BINGHAM, JOHN. Five Roundabouts to Heaven. London: Gollancz, 1953. 1st ed. Pp sl dknd, o/w Fine in dj (sm stain; sl dknd spine). *Mordida.* $50/£32

BINGHAM, JOHN. A Fragment of Fear. London: Gollancz, 1965. 1st ed. Fine in dj. *Mordida.* $45/£29

BINGHAM, JOHN. I Love, I Kill. London: Gollancz, 1968. 1st ed. Fine in dj (stain). *Mordida.* $45/£29

BINGHAM, ROBERT W. The Cradle of the Queen City. A History of Buffalo to the Incorporation of the City. Vol XXXI. Buffalo: Buffalo Hist Soc, 1931. 1st ed. 17 plts. Brn cl, gilt. Good. *Karmiole.* $35/£23

BINION, RUDOLPH. Frau Lou: Nietzsche's Wayward Disciple. Princeton, NJ: Princeton Univ Press, (1969). 1st ed, 2nd corrected ptg. Gray cl. VG in dj (lt worn). *Gach.* $50/£32

BINKLEY, WILLIAM C. Expansionist Movement in Texas, 1836-1850. Berkeley: Univ of CA, 1925. NF (lt spine wear) in ptd wraps. *Bohling.* $250/£161

BINKLEY, WILLIAM C. The Texas Revolution. Baton Rouge: LSU Press, (1952). 1st ed. Beige cl. NF in dj. *Chapel Hill.* $40/£26

BINNEY, GEORGE. With Seaplane and Sledge in the Arctic. London: Hutchinson, (1925). 1st ed. Fldg map. Good+ (spine, fr bd faded). *Walcot.* $31/£20

BINNEY, W.G. A Manual of American Land Shells. Washington: Nat. Mus. Bull., 1885. 528pp. Good (ex-lib) in wrappers. *Wheldon & Wesley.* $93/£60

BINNS, ARCHIE. Peter Skene Ogden: Fur Trader. Binfords & Mort, (1967). 1st ed. 2 dbl-pg maps. Fine in Fine dj. *Oregon.* $25/£16

BINYON, LAURENCE. The Drawings and Engravings of William Blake. Geoffrey Holme (ed). London: The Studio, 1922. 104 plts (16 color mtd, 2 text ports). VG. *Argosy.* $250/£161

BINYON, LAURENCE. The Engraved Designs of William Blake. London/NY, 1926. 82 plts (20 color). (Lt spotting; extrems sl worn.) *Edwards.* $140/£90

BINYON, LAURENCE. The Engraved Designs of William Blake. London: Ernest Benn, 1926. 1st ed. White linen-backed dec bds (spine sl yellowed, corners bumped). *Sadlon.* $200/£129

BINYON, LAURENCE. The Engraved Designs of William Blake. London/NY: Ernest Benn/Scribner's, 1926. Orig ed. 82 plts. Ornamental bds. Excellent. *Ars Artis.* $194/£125

BINYON, LAURENCE. The Engraved Designs of William Blake. Da Capo, 1967. *Ars Artis.* $93/£60

BINYON, LAURENCE. The Followers of William Blake. London: Halton & Truscott Smith, 1925. 1st ed. Teg. Orig cl, gilt-ruled (spine ends sl rubbed). *Sadlon.* $150/£97

BINYON, LAURENCE. The North Star and Other Poems. Macmillan, 1941. 1st ed. Inscribed presentation. (Cvrs sl soiled; inscrip.) *Bickersteth.* $54/£35

BINYON, LAURENCE. The Wonder Night. (London: Faber, 1927). 1st ed. Ptd wraps (sl soiled). *Second Life.* $20/£13

Biographia Scoticana: or, A Brief Historical Account of the Lives.... (By John Howie). Glasgow: Khull, Blackie, 1821. 1st ed. Engr frontis, 552,Lpp; 4 engr ports. Contemp calf (rebacked), red calf spine label. *Karmiole.* $125/£81

Biographical Anecdotes of William Hogarth. (By John Nichols and George Steevens.) London: Nichols, 1782. 2nd ed. iv,474pp. Contemp full calf (nicely rebacked, orig label laid down), gilt. VG (wear, lt foxed). *Hartfield.* $295/£190

BIRCH, JOHN. Examples of Stables.... London: William Blackwood, 1892. 64pp, 30 litho plts (2 fldg). Gilt cl (sm mk upper bd). *Hollett.* $217/£140

BIRCH, S. Ancient History from the Monuments: Egypt...to B.C. 300. London: SPCK, 1879. Frontis, 192,4pp. Ex-lib. *Worldwide.* $25/£16

BIRCH, WALTER de GRAY. Seals. NY: Putnam, 1907. 52 plts. *Boswell.* $125/£81

BIRD, ISABELLA L. The Golden Chersonese and the Way Thither. London: John Murray, 1883. 1st ed. Frontis; xvi,384 + 32pp ads; 10 plts; fldg map. Mod 1/2 morocco gilt. VG. *Hollett.* $147/£95

BIRD, ISABELLA L. A Lady's Life in the Rocky Mountains. Norman: Univ of OK Press, (1960). 1st ed. Fine in Fine dj. *Book Market.* $20/£13

BIRD, ISABELLA L. A Lady's Life in the Rocky Mountains. NY: Putnam's, 1879-80. 1st Amer ed. xii,296pp + 4pp ads, 6 plts. Bright pict cl (19th cent lib bkpl; sl spine label remnant). *Schoyer.* $150/£97

BIRD, MARIA. Andy Pandy's Jump-Up Book. London: Purnell, n.d. (1955). 27x21 cm. 5 pop-ups. Marvyn Wright (illus). Glazed pict bds (stamp). VG. *Book Finders.* $60/£39

BIRDSONG, JAMES C. Brief Sketches of the North Carolina State Troops in the War Between the States. Raleigh: Josephus Daniels, 1894. 1st ed. 213pp. Orig cream wraps, color insignia. NF. *Chapel Hill.* $350/£226

BIRGE, JULIUS C. The Awakening of the Desert. Boston: Gorham, 1912. 1st ed. Internally VG (cvr worn). Howes B 463. *Parker.* $60/£39

BIRKBECK, GEOFFREY. Old Norfolk Houses. London: Jarrold & Sons, n.d. 1st ed. 36 tipped-in color plts, guards. Lib cl, gilt. Birkbeck arms from orig dj laid on to pastedown. *Hollett.* $132/£85

BIRKBECK, MORRIS. Letters from Illinois. London: Taylor & Hessey, 1818. xv,114pp + (6)pp ads dated Sept 1818. Orig bds (spine repaired, chipped spine label laid down). Sl dampstain, lt foxing, else Fine. Howes B 467. *Cahan.* $150/£97

BIRKENHEAD, SHEILA. Against Oblivion. Cassell, 1943. 1st ed. VG in dj (worn). *Poetry.* $19/£12

BIRKET-SMITH, KAJ. The Eskimos. NY: Dutton, 1935. 1st ed. Map eps. VG in dj. *Walcot.* $37/£24

BIRKETT, NORMAN. The Game of Cricket. London: B.T. Batsford, 1955. (Spine tail sl faded.) Dj. *Edwards.* $47/£30

BIRLEY, ERIC. Research on Hadrian's Wall. Kendal: Titus Wilson, 1961. 1st ed. 18 plts. Gilt cl. (Eps sl browned.) Dj. *Hollett.* $85/£55

BIRNEY, HOFFMAN. Mountain Chief: An Indian Legend for Children. Phila: Penn Pub Co, (1938). 1st ed. Lg 8vo, 82pp. Pict paper over cl. Pict eps, bkpl carelessly removed, else NF in dj (worn, price-clipped, 2-inch chip). *Godot.* $85/£55

BIRRELL, FRANCIS. A Letter from a Black Sheep. Hogarth Press, 1932. 1st ed. VG in wrappers. *Words Etc.* $31/£20

BIRRELL, FRANCIS. A Letter from a Black Sheep. London: Hogarth, 1932. 1st ed. VG in wrappers (stain). *Cahan.* $65/£42

Birth of Christ from the Gospel According to Saint Luke. N.p.: Golden Cockerel, 1925. #21/360. 1/4 morocco over bds. Respectable (rubbed; lt wear, dkng). *Hermitage.* $75/£48

Birth of Christ from the Gospel According to Saint Luke. London: Golden Cockerel, 1925. One of 370. 1/4 leather, blue paper bds. Spine lt rubbed, else VG. *Heller.* $175/£113

BISCHOFF, ERNEST. Microscopic Analysis of the Anastomoses Between the Cranial Nerves. Hanover, 1977. 1st Eng trans. Good in dj. *Fye.* $50/£32

BISCHOFF, WILLIAM. The Jesuits in Old Oregon, 1840-1940. Caxton, 1945. 1st ed. Fine in VG dj. *Oregon.* $45/£29

BISHOP, CHARLES. The Journal and Letters of Captain Charles Bishop...1794-1799. Michael Roe (ed). Cambridge: Pub for Hakluyt Soc at University Press, 1967. 1st ed. Facs frontis; 5 maps (2 fldg). Blue gilt cl. Good in dj (sl soiled, chipped). *Karmiole.* $35/£23

BISHOP, ELIZABETH. The Ballad of the Burglar of Babylon. NY: FSG, (1968). 1st ed. Fine in dj (price-clipped, sm tears, else Fine). *Godot.* $135/£87

BISHOP, ELIZABETH. North and South. Boston: Houghton Mifflin, 1946. 1st ed, 1st bk. Fine in dj (lt wear). *Godot.* $575/£371

BISHOP, ELIZABETH. Poems. London: C&W, 1956. 1st ed. One of 500. Paper-cvrd bds. Fine in dj (spine lt browned, else NF). *Godot.* $125/£81

BISHOP, ELIZABETH. Questions of Travel. NY: Farrar Straus, (1965). 1st ed. Fine in dj. *Pharos.* $85/£55

BISHOP, ERNEST. The Narcotic Drug Problem. NY, 1921. 1st ed, 2nd ptg. (Pencil underlining.) *Fye.* $30/£19

BISHOP, ERNEST. The Timber Wolf of the Yukon. Chicago, (1925). 1st ed. Signed presentation. Color frontis; plt. Fine. *Oregon.* $35/£23

BISHOP, H.H. Pictorial Architecture in Greece and Italy. London: S.P.C.K., 1887. 1st ed. 135pp. Very Nice. *Hollett.* $85/£55

BISHOP, JIM. The Day Lincoln Was Shot. NY: Harper, (1955). Inscribed. Black cl-backed grn bds (bumped). NF in dj (sl chipped). *Blue Mountain.* $15/£10

BISHOP, JOHN PEALE. The Collected Essays. NY: Scribner's, 1948. 1st ed. NF in dj. *Hermitage.* $65/£42

BISHOP, MRS. J.F. The Yangtze Valley and Beyond. London, 1899. 1st ed. xv,557pp, fldg map. Lib cl (rebound; gilt # spine; sl spotting; bkpl, inkstamps). *Edwards.* $70/£45

BISHOP, NATHANIEL H. Voyage of the Paper Canoe. Edinburgh: David Douglas, 1878. Frontis, xv,351,(i)pp + 16pp pub's list (marginal browning); 10 maps, 6 plts. Gilt-ruled cl (recased, repairs spine). *Edwards.* $388/£250

BISHOP, RUFUS and SETH Y. WELLS (eds). Testimonies of the Life, Character, Revelations and Doctrines of Mother Ann Lee, and the Elders with Her.... Albany: 1888. 2nd ed. 302pp. Calf; raised bands, label; devices in blind, gauffered edges. VG. *Petrilla.* $225/£145

BISHOP, S.C. Notes on the Habits and Development of the Mudpuppy. Albany, 1926. 11 plts (1 fldg). Wrappers (browned). *Sutton.* $25/£16

BISHOP, ZEALIA. The Curse of Yig. Sauk City: Arkham House, 1953. 1st ed. Fine in NF dj (lt rubbed). *Other Worlds.* $150/£97

BISHOP, ZEALIA. The Curse of Yig. Arkham House, 1953. 1st ed. Fine in dj. *Madle.* $175/£113

BISSELL, MARY. Physical Development and Exercise for Women. NY, 1891. 108pp. Good. *Fye.* $80/£52

BISSOONDATH, NEIL. Digging Up the Mountains. Deutsch, 1986. 1st UK ed, 1st bk. Fine in dj. *Lewton.* $23/£15

BITTING, KATHERINE GOLDEN. Gastronomic Bibliography. SF: The Author, 1939. 1st ed. 5 plts. (Sl foxing eps; both hinges internally strengthened.) *Bookpress.* $350/£226

BITTING, SAMUEL TILDEN. Rural Land Ownership Among the Negroes of Virginia With Special Reference to Albemarle County. Charlottesville, VA, 1915. 1st ed. NF in orig stiff ptd wrappers. *Mcgowan.* $75/£48

BJORNSTROM, F. Hypnotism. Nils Posse (trans). NY: Humboldt, 1887. Trans from 2nd Swedish ed. 126pp. Orig binding. (Ex-lib; sl rubbed; stamp tp.) *Goodrich.* $135/£87

Black Book. (NY): Jewish Black Book Committee, 1946. Black cl. VG. *Cullen.* $75/£48

Black Book; or, Corruption Unmasked! (By John Wade.) London, 1820. 1st ed. 480pp. Mod buckram (hinges cracked). *Argosy.* $250/£161

BLACK, C.B. Guide to Touraine and Brittany. London, 1892. 11th ed. 10 maps, 12 plans. *Edwards.* $31/£20

BLACK, JOHN JANVIER. Forty Years in the Medical Profession: 1858-1898. Phila, 1900. (Few pp dog-eared.) *Argosy.* $35/£23

BLACK, JOHN LOGAN. Crumbling Defenses or Memoirs and Reminiscences of John Logan, Colonel C.S.A. Macon, GA: Eleanor D. McSwain, (1960). 1st ed, ltd to 500. Orig cl. NF. *Mcgowan.* $95/£61

BLACK, JOHN LOGAN. Crumbling Defenses. Eleanor D. McSwain (ed). Macon, GA: Eleanor D. McSwain, (1960). 1st ed. Full-pg port, full-pg fldg facs. Orig grey cl. Fine. *Chapel Hill.* $75/£48

BLACK, MARY and JEAN LIPMAN. American Folk Painting. NY: Potter, 1966. 1st ed. NF in dj. *Cahan.* $45/£29

BLACK, ROBERT G. The Little Miami Railroad. Cincinnati, n.d. (not before 1936). VG in dj (sl worn). *Hayman.* $75/£48

BLACK, W.G. Folk-Medicine A Chapter in the History of Culture. NY: Franklin, 1970. Facs rpt of 1883 ed. Good. *Goodrich.* $45/£29

BLACKBURN, HENRY. Artists and Arabs, or Sketching in Sunshine. Boston: Osgood & Co, 1874. (216)pp + 1pp, errata tipped in. Royal blue cl stamped in blind, gilt (bkpls, sigs, possibly ex-lib). *Schoyer.* $60/£39

BLACKBURN, HENRY. Randolph Caldecott: A Personal Memoir.... NY: Routledge, 1886. 1st Amer ed. 216pp (emb lib stamp tp). Grn cl, beveled bds (sl rubbed); pict stamped black; gilt. Good. *Hermitage.* $75/£48

BLACKBURN, I.W. Intracranial Tumors Among the Insane. Washington, 1903. 1st ed. Good. *Fye.* $100/£65

BLACKBURN, JOHN. Bury Him Darkly. NY: Putnam's, (1970). 1st ed. NF in dj (sl soil). *Antic Hay.* $45/£29

BLACKBURN, PAUL. Gin: Four Journal Pieces. Mt. Horeb, WI: Perishable Press, 1970. 1st ed. Ltd to 136. Vellum-backed cockerel bds. Fine. *Jaffe.* $275/£177

BLACKBURN, PAUL. It Might as Well Be Spring. (Madison, WI): Perishable Press, 1967. 1st 'correct and separate' ed. Ltd to 100 ptd. Fine. *Jaffe.* $350/£226

BLACKBURN, PAUL. The Selection of Heaven. Mt. Horeb, WI: Perishable Press, 1980. 1st ed. Ltd to 170. Fine in wrappers. *Jaffe.* $125/£81

BLACKER, IRWIN R. (ed). The Old West in Fiction. NY: Ivan Obolenshy, 1961. 1st ed. VG. *Burcham.* $25/£16

BLACKFAN, K.D. and L.K. DIAMOND. Atlas of the Blood in Children. NY, 1944. 70 plts. Good. *Goodrich.* $40/£26

BLACKFORD, CHARLES M. Annals of the Lynchburg Home Guard. Lynchburg, VA: John W. Rohr, 1891. 1st ed. Frontis port, 185pp. Orig black cl. VG (spine sl faded). *Chapel Hill.* $1,200/£774

BLACKFORD, CHARLES M. (ed). Letters from Lee's Army. NY/London: Scribner, 1947. 1st ed. Gilt-emb cl. VG in dj (lt chipped). *Cahan.* $40/£26

BLACKIE, AGNES. A.C. Blackie and Son, 1809-1959. London: Blackie & Son, (1959). 1st ed. Fine. *Bookpress.* $75/£48

BLACKIE, AGNES. A.C. Blackie and Son. 1809-1959. London/Glasgow: Blackie & Son, (1959). 1st ed. Comp copy, slip laid in. Fine. *Limestone.* $30/£19

BLACKMUR, R.P. The Double Agent. NY, (1935). 1st ed. VG in dj. *Argosy.* $125/£81

BLACKMUR, R.P. The Expense of Greatness. NY: Arrow Editions, (1940). 1st ed. Fine in VG dj (spine sunned). *Hermitage.* $75/£48

BLACKSTOCK, CHARITY. The Foggy, Foggy Dew. London: Hodder & Stoughton, 1958. 1st ed. Fine in VG + dj. *Janus.* $25/£16

BLACKSTONE, WILLIAM. An Analysis of the Laws of England. Oxford: Clarendon, 1759. 4th ed. *Boswell.* $350/£226

BLACKSTONE, WILLIAM. Commentaries on the Laws of England. Dublin: John Exshaw, 1773. 5th ed. 4 bks. Contemp polished calf (sl rubbed). Exceptionally Nice. *Boswell.* $1,750/£1,129

BLACKSTONE, WILLIAM. Commentaries on the Laws of England. London: T. Cadell, 1791. 11th ed. 4 vols. 8vo. Frontis port vol 1; 2 engr tables vol 2. Full contemp calf, gilt lettered red/black spine labels (2 spines rubbed). Excellent. *D & D.* $1,750/£1,129

BLACKSTONE, WILLIAM. Commentaries on the Laws of England. In Four Books. London: for T. Cadell et al, 1791. 11th ed. Contemp calf (joints cracked, spines worn). Usable only. *Boswell.* $350/£226

BLACKSTONE, WILLIAM. Commentaries on the Laws of England.... Phila: Lippincott, 1860. 2 vols. Contemp sheep. Working set only (cvrs loose). *Boswell.* $150/£97

BLACKSTONE, WILLIAM. A Discourse on the Study of the Law (etc). Oxford: Clarendon, 1758. 1st ed. Early speckled 1/2 calf. Sl chipped, but well preserved. *Boswell.* $4,500/£2,903

BLACKWELL, ALICE STONE. Lucy Stone. Little Brown, 1930. 2nd ptg. Unsigned presentation. Frontis, 7 plts. 3pp letter dated 1932 tipped to reps; chronology tipped to fep. VG. *Oregon.* $35/£23

BLACKWOOD, ALGERNON. The Dance of Death. Dial, 1928. 1st ed. VG. *Madle.* $75/£48

BLACKWOOD, ALGERNON. The Doll and One Other. Arkham House, 1946. 1st ed. VF in dj. *Madle.* $60/£39

BLACKWOOD, ALGERNON. Full Circle. London: Elkin Mathews & Marrot, 1929. 1st ed. One of 530 numbered, signed. Fine in NF dj (lt wear; sm chips to sl sunned spine). *Beasley.* $125/£81

BLACKWOOD, ALGERNON. John Silence. London, 1910. 3rd ptg. Grn cl, gold lettering; medallion port on fr cvr. Nice (rubbed, incl port). *Mcclintock.* $45/£29

BLACKWOOD, ALGERNON. Julius Le Vallon. NY, 1916. 1st Amer ed. VG. *Argosy.* $50/£32

BLACKWOOD, ALGERNON. A Prisoner in Fairyland. Macmillan, 1913. 1st ed. VG-. *Madle.* $30/£19

BLACKWOOD, ALGERNON. The Wave. London, 1916. 1st ed. Grn cl. VG. *Argosy.* $125/£81

BLACKWOOD, WILLIAM. Atlas of Neuropathology. Balt, 1949. 1st ed. Good. *Fye.* $30/£19

BLADES, WILLIAM. The Enemies of Books. London: Elliot Stock, 1896. xviii,151pp; teg, others uncut. Red cl, gilt (backstrip faded; sl worn; lib labels, stamps). *Cox.* $23/£15

BLAIKIE, W. GARDEN. The Personal Life of David Livingstone Chiefly from His Unpublished Journals.... NY, 1881. 1st Amer ed. Lacks map, else VF. *Fye.* $40/£26

BLAINE, DELABERE P. An Encyclopaedia of Rural Sports. London: Longman et al, 1840. 1st ed. xv,(i),1,240pp, 600 wood engrs (name; minor flaws). Full brown calf (rubbed, scuffed), gilt, leather label. NF. *Blue Mountain.* $185/£119

BLAIR, CLAUDE. Arms, Armour and Base-Metalwork. London, 1974. 1st ed. Dj. *Edwards.* $194/£125

BLAIR, DOROTHY. A History of Glass in Japan. Kodansha International/Corning Museum of Glass, 1973. 1st ed. 240 photos (37 color). 2-tone cl in protective dj. *Edwards.* $194/£125

BLAIS, MARIE-CLAIRE. Mad Shadows. Merloyd Lawrence (trans). Boston: Little, Brown, (1960). 1st Amer ed. VG (extrems sunned) in dj (sunned; edges worn; price-clipped). *Hermitage.* $30/£19

BLAISDELL, ANNE. (Pseud of Elizabeth Linington.) Nightmare. NY: Harper, 1961. 1st ed. Fine in VG + dj. *Janus.* $50/£32

BLAKE, J.L. First Book in Astronomy. Boston: Lincoln & Emands, 1831. 115pp; 8 plts. (Ex-lib w/mks; corners worn; spine taped; pp browned). *Knollwood.* $45/£29

BLAKE, JOHN. The Farmer's Every-Day Book.... Auburn: Miller, Orton & Mulligan, 1854. 12th thousand. 654pp. Leatherbound. (Edges worn; fr hinge split 1-inch.) *October Farm.* $45/£29

BLAKE, MARY E. On the Wing. Rambling Notes of a Trip to the Pacific. Boston: Lee & Shepard, 1883. 1st ed. 235pp + 4pp ads. *Schoyer.* $85/£55

BLAKE, PETER. Marcel Breuer: Architect and Designer. NY: Architectural Record & MOMA, (1949). 1st ed. Ink inscrip; sl rubbed, else VG. *Bookpress.* $45/£29

BLAKE, PETER. Marcel Breuer: Sun and Shadow. London: Longman, Green, (1955). 1st ed. Frontis. Fine. *Bookpress.* $85/£55

BLAKE, ROBERT. The Unknown Prime Minister. London, 1955. 1st ed. Frontis; 10 plts. VG in dj (sl worn). *Edwards.* $39/£25

BLAKE, S.F. and A.C. ATWOOD. Geographical Guide to Floras of the World. Washington, 1942-61. 2 vols. Cl (lt scuffed). *Sutton.* $65/£42

BLAKE, VIVIENNE. Follow Me Animal Book. Akron: Saalfield, 1945. 26x21 cm. 8 animations by Martha Paulsen. Pict bds, spiral binding (sl wear extrems). Internally VG. *Book Finders.* $60/£39

BLAKE, W.O. The History of Slavery and the Slave Trade, Ancient and Modern.... Columbus, OH, 1857. 1st ed. 832pp. Full leather (stained, spine chipped, fr cvr bubbled, rear hinge splitting). *King.* $150/£97

BLAKE, WILLIAM. The Book of Thel. London/NY: Gollancz/Payson, 1928. Ltd to 1700. Spine sl rubbed, o/w Fine. *Europa.* $28/£18

BLAKE, WILLIAM. Letters from William Blake to Thomas Butts 1800-1803. Oxford: Clarendon, 1926. One of 350. Marbled bds; label. Lib bkpl; stamp tp verso; nick backstrip, o/w VG. *Poetry.* $116/£75

BLAKE, WILLIAM. The Letters of William Blake. Geoffrey Keynes (ed). Clarendon, 1980. 3rd ed. Fine (inscrip) in dj (price-clipped). *Poetry.* $34/£22

BLAKE, WILLIAM. The Poems of William Blake. Pickering, 1874. Few pg corners turned, tp edges dknd, o/w VG in blue-grn cl (dull; rubbed). *Poetry.* $186/£120

BLAKE, WILLIAM. The Poetical Works of William Blake. Edwin J. Ellis (ed). C&W, 1906. 1st ed. 2 vols. Teg, rest uncut. Spare label present. Internally Fine (reversed calf backstrip split, disintegrating). *Poetry.* $23/£15

BLAKE, WILLIAM. Poetry and Prose of William Blake. Geoffrey Keynes (ed). Nonesuch Press, 1927. Cl over beveled bds. Spine lightened, o/w Fine. *Sadlon.* $75/£48

BLAKE, WILLIAM. Poetry and Prose. Geoffrey Keynes (ed). London: Nonesuch, 1941. Good in dj (frayed). *Cox.* $19/£12

BLAKE, WILLIAM. The Writings of William Blake. Geoffrey Keynes (ed). Nonesuch, 1925. #781/1500. 3 vols. Edges uncut (sl dknd). 1/4 vellum dknd, rubbed; sl bumped, o/w NF set. *Poetry.* $388/£250

BLAKE, WILLIAM. The Writings of William Blake. Geoffrey Keynes (ed). London: Nonesuch, 1925. One of 1500 numbered sets. 3 vols. Largely unopened. Photogravure frontis. 1/4 vellum, marbled bds (spines tanned, rubbed; corners sl worn). Good set (eps lt tanned). *Reese.* $275/£177

BLAKE, WILLIAM. The Writings. Geoffrey Keynes (ed). Nonesuch Press, 1925. Ltd to 1500. 3 vols. Pub's variant binding(?): full brn calf. Spine heads 2 vols sl dknd, rubbed, o/w Very Handsome set. *Words Etc.* $310/£200

BLAKELOCK, DENYS. Finding My Way. Hollis & Carter, (1958). 1st ed. 1958 inscribed presentation. Frontis; 6 photos. Dj. *Bickersteth.* $39/£25

BLAKENEY, ROBERT. A Boy in the Peninsular War. Julian Sturgis (ed). London, 1899. 1st ed. xviii,382pp; fldg map at rear. Hinges cracked; eps browned, faintly foxed, o/w VG. Red cl (bumped; fraying spine head, tail), gilt. *Edwards.* $233/£150

BLAKENEY, THOMAS S. Sherlock Holmes: Fact or Fiction. London: Murray, 1932. 1st UK ed. VG in dj (browned, chipped). *Williams.* $85/£55

BLAKEY, R. Historical Sketches of the Angling Literature of All Nations. London: J.R. Smith, 1856. 1st ed. 335pp. Blind-stamped dec cl. Lacks spine, else Good + . *Mikesh.* $37/£24

BLAKISTON, JOHN. Twenty Years in Retirement.... London: A.J. Valpy, 1836. 2 vols. Later 1/2 calf (backstrips rubbed; lib stamps tps; paper label fr cvrs). Tls from Humphrey Milford loosely inserted. *Waterfield.* $85/£55

BLAKISTON, T.W. Five Months on the Yang-Tze; With a Narrative.... London, 1862. xv,380pp; 2 maps, 24 engrs. Mod cl. *Lewis.* $147/£95

BLANC, MEL and PHILIP BASHE. That's 'Not' All Folks! (NY): Warner, (1988). Fine in dj (lt rubbed). *Aka.* $35/£23

BLANCO, ANTONIO de FIERRO. (Pseud of Walter Nordhoff). The Journey of the Flame. Boston, 1933. 1st ed. Dec cl. Fine in dj (sl worn, price-clipped). *Baade.* $100/£65

BLAND, J.O.P. Recent Events and Present Policies in China. Phila/London: Lippincott/Heinemann, 1912. 2 fldg maps (1 color). Tipped-in errata. Yellow cl (soiled; foxing; pencil notes). *Schoyer.* $50/£32

BLAND, J.O.P. Recent Events and Present Policies in China. London: Heinemann, 1912. 1st ed. 50pp plts; fldg color map. VG (lower joint tender). *Hollett.* $132/£85

BLAND, J.O.P. and E. BACKHOUSE. China Under the Empress Dowager. Peking, 1939. New rev ed. Frontis port, 2 fldg maps. (Spine sl soiled.) *Edwards.* $93/£60

BLAND-SUTTON, JOHN. Orations and Addresses. London, 1924. 1st ed. Good. *Fye.* $75/£48

BLANDFORD, G. Fielding. Insanity and Its Treatment: Lectures.... Phila, 1871. 1st ed. 471pp. Good. *Fye.* $200/£129

BLANKAART, STEPHEN. The Physical Dictionary. Sam. Crouch and John & Benj. Sprint, 1715. 6th ed. (iv),376pp; ad leaf; 2 engr plts. Orig panelled calf (rubbed; pale waterstaining few pp; lt spotting). *Bickersteth.* $178/£115

BLANKENSHIP, WILLIAM D. The Leavenworth Irregulars. Indianapolis: Bobbs-Merrill, (1974). Stated 1st ptg. VG in dj (edgewear). *Aka.* $50/£32

BLANKERT, A. Vermeer of Delft. Oxford: Phaidon, 1978. Sound in dj. *Ars Artis.* $54/£35

BLATCHLEY, W.S. In Days Agone: Notes on the Fauna and Flora of Subtropical Florida.... Indianapolis: Nature Pub Co, 1932. 1st ed. 15 full-pg b/w photo plts. Fine. *Cahan.* $75/£48

BLATTY, WILLIAM PETER. The Exorcist. London, 1971. 1st ed. VG in dj (rubbed). *Words Etc.* $19/£12

BLATTY, WILLIAM PETER. The Exorcist. H&R, 1971. 1st ed. NF in NF dj. *Aronovitz.* $55/£35

BLATTY, WILLIAM PETER. Which Way to Mecca, Jack? B. Geis, 1960. 1st ed, 1st bk. Fine in NF dj (sm tear, abrasion). *Fine Books.* $40/£26

BLAVATSKY, HELENA PETROVNA. From the Caves and Jungles of Hindostan. London: Theosophical Soc, 1892. 1st ed. 318pp + ads. Pub's cl. VG (name stamp). *Second Life.* $125/£81

BLAYLOCK, JAMES P. The Digging Leviathan. Bath: Avon, Morrigan, 1988. 1st hb ed. One of 300 numbered, signed by author, artist, Tim Powers, and K.W. Jeter. Fine in Fine dj, slipcase. *Other Worlds.* $125/£81

BLECH, GUSTAVUS. Clinical Electrosurgery. London, 1938. 1st ed. Good. *Fye.* $150/£97

BLECH, GUSTAVUS. The Practitioner's Guide to the Diagnosis and Treatment of Diseases of Women. Chicago, 1903. 1st ed. Good. *Fye.* $125/£81

BLEECK, OLIVER. (Pseud of Ross Thomas.) The Highbinders. NY: Morrow, 1973. 1st ed. Signed. VG in VG + dj. *Lame Duck.* $200/£129

BLEECK, OLIVER. (Pseud of Ross Thomas). The Procane Chronicle. NY: William Morrow, 1972. 1st ed. Fine in dj (price-clipped; short closed tear). *Mordida.* $165/£106

BLEGBOROUGH, R. Facts and Observations Respecting the Air-Pump Vapour-Bath, in Gout...and Other Diseases. London, 1803. Frontis,152pp (sl foxing). Orig bds (corners worn). *Whitehart.* $140/£90

BLEGEN, THEODORE C. Minnesota. St. Paul: Univ of MN, 1963. 1st ed. 12 photo plts. VG in Good dj. *Connolly.* $35/£23

BLEILER, EVERETT. The Checklist of Fantastic Literature. Shasta, 1948. 1st ed. Fine in Mint dj. *Madle.* $200/£129

BLEILER, EVERETT. The Checklist of Fantastic Literature. Chicago, 1948. Stated 1st ed. (Ex-lib w/mks.) *Hayman.* $35/£23

BLESH, RUDI and HARRIET JANIS. They All Played Ragtime. NY: Knopf, 1950. 1st ed. Fine in VG dj (tape mends at edges). *Beasley.* $40/£26

BLESH, RUDI and HARRIET JANIS. They All Played Ragtime. London: Sidgwick & Jackson, 1958. 1st ed. Top edge speckled, o/w VG in dj (sl soiled, chipped, sm closed tears). *Virgo.* $43/£28

BLESH, RUDI. Shining Trumpets. NY: Knopf, 1946. 1st ed. NF (name) in VG dj (chips, tears, spine sunning). *Beasley.* $75/£48

BLESH, RUDI. This Is Jazz. London: Jazz Music Books, 1943. 1st UK ed, 1st bk. VG + in wraps (lt worn). *Beasley.* $75/£48

BLEVINS, WINFRED. Give Your Heart to the Hawks. L.A.: Nash, (1973). 1st ed, (true) 1st ptg. 2.5cm thick. 6 plts, 5 maps. Tan cl. Fine in VG dj. *Oregon.* $50/£32

BLIGH, WILLIAM. A Narrative of the Mutiny on Board His Majesty's Ship Bounty.... London, 1790. 1st ed. 88pp; plan; 2 charts. Recent 3/4 tree calf; marbled bds. Ink name; plts/plans rebacked; lacks 'Track of the Bounty Launch'; sl textual staining, offset, else Attractive. *King.* $3,500/£2,258

BLIGH, WILLIAM. A Voyage to the South Seas. Adelaide: LEC, 1975. One of 2000 numbered, signed by Alan Villiers (intro) & Geoffrey C. Ingleton (illus). Full pict cl, leather label. Fine in slipcase. *Hermitage.* $150/£97

BLINN, LEROY J. A Practical Workshop Companion for Tin, Sheet Iron, and Copper Plate Workers. Phila, 1869. 184pp; fldg diagram. VG, largely unopened. *Argosy.* $75/£48

BLISH, HELEN H. A Pictographic History of the Oglala Sioux. Lincoln: Univ of NE Press, (1967). 1st trade ed. 32 color plts. Yellow/black cl. Fine in VG + slipcase (sl bumped, soiled). *Harrington.* $90/£58

BLISH, JAMES and ROBERT W. LOWNDES. The Duplicated Man. Avalon, 1959. 1st ed. Fine in dj. *Madle.* $30/£19

BLISH, JAMES. Black Easter. Doubleday, 1968. 1st ed. VG + in VG + dj. *Aronovitz.* $125/£81

BLISH, JAMES. Black Easter. Doubleday, 1968. 1st ed. Fine in dj. *Madle.* $350/£226

BLISH, JAMES. A Case of Conscience. London: Faber & Faber, (1964). 2nd imp. Bumped, else NF in dj (price-clipped). *Other Worlds.* $45/£29

BLISH, JAMES. A Case of Conscience. Faber, 1958. 1st Eng, 1st hb ed. VG + in VG + dj. *Aronovitz.* $395/£255

BLISH, JAMES. Earthman Come Home. NY: Putnam's, (1955). 1st ed. Fine in dj (sl dust soiling). *Levin.* $100/£65

BLISH, JAMES. The Frozen Year. NY: Ballantine, (1957). 1st ed. Fine in NF dj (lt soil). *Antic Hay.* $150/£97

BLISH, JAMES. Jack of Eagles. Greenberg, 1952. 1st ed. NF in dj (sl nicked). *Madle.* $60/£39

BLISH, JAMES. Mission to the Heart Stars. NY: Putnam's, (1965). 1st ed. Fine in dj (sl wear, soiled). *Antic Hay.* $125/£81

BLISH, JAMES. The Seedling Stars. NY: Gnome, (1957). 1st ed. Grn bds, brn lettering. VG + in dj (short tears; spine chipped). *Other Worlds.* $20/£13

BLISH, JAMES. The Seedling Stars. NY: Gnome Press, 1957. 1st Amer ed. (Paper browned.) Fine in dj (sm edge tears rear panel). *Polyanthos.* $30/£19

BLISH, JAMES. The Star Trek Reader. NY: Dutton, (1976). 1st ed. NF in NF dj. *Other Worlds.* $25/£16

BLISH, JAMES. Titan's Daughter. London: White Lion, 1975. 1st ed. VF in dj. *Else Fine.* $50/£32

BLISS, EUGENE. Anorexia Nervosa. NY, 1960. 1st ed. Good. *Fye.* $50/£32

BLISS, FREDERICK JONES. A Mound of Many Cities or, Tell El Hesy Excavated. NY: Macmillan, 1894. (Extrems sl shelfworn.) *Archaeologia.* $75/£48

BLISS, WALTER. Twainiana Notes. Hartford: Hobby Shop, (1930). Ltd to 1000 numbered. Fine. *Agvent.* $40/£26

BLISS, WALTER. Twainiana Notes. Hartford: Hobby Shop, 1930. 1st ed. Ltd to 1000. Fine. *Cahan.* $40/£26

BLOCH, DOROTHY. So the Witch Won't Eat Me. Fantasy and the Child's Fear of Infanticide. Boston: Houghton, Mifflin, 1978. 1st ed. Ptd black cl. VG in dj. *Gach.* $25/£16

BLOCH, IWAN. Marquis de Sade. N.p.: Julian, 1931. 1st Amer ed. (Sl cvr spotting, wear.) *King.* $35/£23

BLOCH, RAYMOND. Etruscan Art. Greenwich, CT: NYGS, 1959. 71 mtd color illus; 2 fldg illus. VG. *Argosy.* $150/£97

BLOCH, ROBERT. Blood Runs Cold. S&S, 1961. 1st ed. Fine in dj (rubbed). *Madle.* $100/£65

BLOCH, ROBERT. The Dead Beat. NY: S&S, 1960. 1st ed. (Pg edges browned; sl cocked, sm bump bottom edge). Dj (lt soiled). *Aka.* $65/£42

BLOCH, ROBERT. The Dead Beat. S&S, 1960. 1st ed. Fine in dj. *Madle.* $100/£65

BLOCH, ROBERT. Dragons and Nightmares. Mirage, 1968. 1st ed. One of 1000. VF in dj. *Madle.* $75/£48

BLOCH, ROBERT. The Eighth Stage of Fandom. Advent, 1962. 1st ed. Fine in wraps. *Madle.* $50/£32

BLOCH, ROBERT. The King of Terrors: Tales of Madness and Death. NY: Mysterious, 1977. 1st ed, #8/250 numbered, signed. Fine in dj, black cl slipcase. *Houle.* $100/£65

BLOCH, ROBERT. The Opener of the Way. Arkham House, 1945. 1st ed. Signed. VG. *Aronovitz.* $90/£58

BLOCH, ROBERT. Pleasant Dreams. Arkham House, 1960. 1st ed. Fine in dj. *Madle.* $125/£81

BLOCHMAN, LAWRENCE G. Clues for Dr. Coffee: A Second Casebook. Phila: Lippincott, 1964. 1st ed. Fine in NF dj. *Janus.* $35/£23

BLOCK, ANDREW. The Book Collector's Vade Mecum. Archer, 1932. VG. *Moss.* $39/£25

BLOCK, ANDREW. Key Books of British Authors, 1600-1932. London: Archer, 1933. 1st ed. VG in dj. *Moss.* $31/£20

BLOCK, ARTHUR. Murphy's Law. L.A.: Price/Stern/Sloan, 1984. 15x20 cm. 3 pop-ups, 9 pull-tabs. Glazed pict bds. VG. *Book Finders.* $35/£23

BLOCK, EUGENE. Great Train Robberies of the West. NY: Coward, McCann, (1959). 1st ed. VG in VG dj. *Oregon.* $25/£16

BLOCK, EUGENE. Great Train Robberies of the West. NY, (1959). 1st ed. Dj sl worn, chipped, o/w Fine. *Pratt.* $30/£19

BLOCK, LAWRENCE. The Burglar in the Closet. NY: Random House, 1978. 1st ed. Fine in Fine dj. *Janus.* $45/£29

BLOCK, LAWRENCE. The Burglar Who Painted Like Mondrian. NY: Random House, 1983. 1st ed. Fine in dj. *Mordida.* $45/£29

BLOCK, LAWRENCE. The Burglar Who Painted Like Mondrian. Arbor, 1983. 1st ed. Inscribed. Fine in dj. *Murder.* $40/£26

BLOCK, LAWRENCE. Me Tanner, You Jane. NY: Macmillan, 1970. 1st ed. Fine in dj (lt crease fr flap; pinhole rear flap). *Janus.* $45/£29

BLOCK, LAWRENCE. The Topless Tulip Caper. London: Allison, (1984). 1st Eng ed. Fine in Fine dj. *Unger.* $50/£32

BLOCK, LAWRENCE. The Topless Tulip Caper. London: Allison & Busby, 1984. 1st hb ed. VF in dj. *Mordida.* $35/£23

BLOCKSON, CHARLES L. (ed). The Underground Railroad. NY: Prentice Hall, (1987). 1st ed. VG in dj. *Petrilla.* $30/£19

BLODGETT, HENRY WILLIAMS. Autobiography of Henry W. Blodgett. Waukegan, IL, 1906. 1st ed. Howes B 540. *Ginsberg.* $300/£194

BLODGETT, JEAN. Kenojuak. Toronto, 1985. VG in dj. *Argosy.* $75/£48

BLOGG, M.W. Bibliography of the Writings of Sir William Osler...Revised and Enlarged.... Balt, 1921. (Emb stamp on title.) *Goodrich.* $75/£48

BLOK, ALEXANDER. The Twelve. Babette Deutsch & Abraham Yarmolinsky (trans). NY: B.W. Huebsch, 1920. 1st ed in English. VG in ptd wrappers. *Godot.* $65/£42

BLOK, ALEXANDER. The Twelve. Babette Deutsch (trans). NY: B.W. Huebsch, 1920. 1st ed. Ptd wrappers (tear fr panel). *Heller.* $75/£48

BLOMFIELD, REGINALD. The Formal Garden in England. London: Macmillan, 1892. xii,244. *Marlborough.* $140/£90

BLOMFIELD, REGINALD. The Formal Garden in England. London: Macmillan, 1901. 3rd ed. Gilt-dec pict cvr. Spine dknd; sl cvr soil, else VG. *Quest.* $70/£45

BLOMFIELD, REGINALD. A Short History of Renaissance Architecture in England 1500-1800. London: George Bell, 1900. 27 plts. VG. *Hollett.* $23/£15

BLOMFIELD, REGINALD. The Touchstone of Architecture. Oxford: Clarendon Press, 1925. 1st ed. Text sl yellowed; inscrip; cvrs sl worn, else Fine. *Bookpress.* $75/£48

BLOND, GEORGES. The Great Whale Game. London: Weidenfeld & Nicolson, (1954). 1st Eng ed. Frontis, 12 plts. Good + . *Blue Dragon.* $15/£10

BLOOM, A. The Farm in the Fen. London, 1944. 3 maps (2 fldg). Dj. *Sutton.* $25/£16

BLOOM, J. HARVEY. English Seals. London: Methuen, 1906. 1st ed. (Spine sl faded.) *Hollett.* $62/£40

BLOOMFIELD, ARTHUR. A Bibliography of Internal Medicine—Communicable Diseases. Chicago, 1958. 1st ed. (Ex-lib.) *Fye.* $75/£48

BLOOMFIELD, B.C. Philip Larkin: A Bibliography 1933-1976. Faber & Faber, 1979. 1st Eng ed. Blue cl. VF in Fine dj. *Dalian.* $70/£45

BLOOMFIELD, ROBERT. Rural Tales. London, 1802. 2nd ed. Frontis port; 11 wood engrs by Bewick. Contemp calf (sl rubbed). Nice (no 1/2 title). *Poetry.* $47/£30

BLORE, EDWARD. The Monumental Remains of Noble and Eminent Persons. London, 1826. 1/2 morocco (marginal spotting; ex-libris; sl rubbed), raised bands, teg. Sm cat descrip tipped in. *Edwards.* $85/£55

BLOSS, ROY S. Pony Express—The Great Gamble. Berkeley: Howell-North, 1959. 1st ed. Fldg map; pict eps. Grey cl. NF in VG- dj (loss). *Harrington.* $30/£19

Blossoms of Morality. (By Richard Johnson.) London: E. Newbery, 1789. 1st ed, pub w/o woodcuts of Bewick. Sm 8vo. Full-pg copper engr frontis, (4),212pp. Rebacked w/orig leather bds, cvrs, gilt spine title. VG (foxing spot upper corner frontis, tp; ink name, ink stamp reps; ink dated name both eps; edges lt rubbed). *Hobbyhorse.* $300/£194

Blossoms of Morality.... (By Richard Johnson.) London: J. Harris/G. & W.B. Whittaker, 1821. 7th ed. 12mo. 235pp + 4pp ads; 47 cuts by I. Bewick. Marble paper on bd, gilt leather spine (lt rubbed). VG (sig, date; lt foxed). *Hobbyhorse.* $200/£129

BLUEGUM, TOM. (Pseud of Warren G. Payne.) The Backblocks' Parson. A Story of Australian Life. London: Charles H. Kelly, 1899. 1st ed. 221pp. Dec cl *Lefkowicz.* $65/£42

BLUEMEL, CARL. Greek Sculptors at Work. London: Phaidon, (1955). Good in dj. *Archaeologia.* $50/£32

BLUM, ANDRE. On the Origin of Paper. Harry Miller Lydenberg (trans). NY: R.R. Bowker, 1934. 1st ed in English. (Ink names.) *Oak Knoll.* $55/£35

BLUM, DANIEL. A Pictorial History of the American Theatre 1900-1956. NY, (1956). VG in dj (edgeworn). *Artis.* $22/£14

BLUM, DANIEL. A Pictorial History of the American Theatre. 100 Years, 1860-1960. NY: Bonanza, (1960). Fine in Good dj. *Artis.* $22/£14

BLUM, E.C. In Satan's Realm. R-M, 1899. 1st ed. VG (dust-soiling). *Aronovitz.* $70/£45

BLUMENTHAL, JOSEPH. The Printed Book in America. Boston: David Godine, (1977). 1st ed. 70 plts. Fine in dj (price-clipped). *Bookpress.* $85/£55

BLUMENTHAL, WALTER HART. Bookman's Bedlam. New Brunswick: Rutgers Univ Press, 1955. 1st ed. 16 full-pg plts. Red cl, gilt title. Nice in dj (sl worn). *Cady.* $45/£29

BLUNDELL, MICHAEL. The Wild Flowers of Kenya. London, 1982. 48 plts, map. Fine in dj. *Brooks.* $45/£29

BLUNDEN, EDMUND. English Poems. London: Cobden-Sanderson, 1925. 1st ed. Uncut. Fine (prelims, margins foxed) in dj (spine sunned; torn, chipped). *Polyanthos.* $45/£29

BLUNDEN, EDMUND. Nature in English Literature. Hogarth Press, 1929. 1st ed. VG in dj (tears). *Words Etc.* $19/£12

BLUNDEN, EDMUND. Nature in Literature. Hogarth Press, 1929. 1st ed. VG in dj (sl frayed; internally repaired spine). *Words Etc.* $19/£12

BLUNDEN, EDMUND. Pastorals: a Book of Verses. London, (1916). 1st ed. Ltd to 1050. Fine (split spine head; 2pp carelessly opened) in brn wrappers. *Waterfield.* $194/£125

BLUNDEN, EDMUND. Undertones of War. London: Cobden-Sanderson, (1928). 1st ed. Black cl. Fine in dj (dknd). *Jaffe.* $175/£113

BLUNDEN, EDMUND. Undertones of War. London: R. Cobden Sanderson, 1928. 1st ed. Bkpl, edges foxed, sm spine tear, else VG in dj (sl nicked, browned spine). *Limestone.* $250/£161

BLUNDEN, EDMUND. Undertones of War. NY, 1929. 1st Amer ed. Fine (sl soiled; bkpl). *Polyanthos.* $35/£23

BLUNDEN, EDMUND. The Waggoner and Other Poems. London, 1920. Ltd to 500, this one of 1st issue of 250. VG in dj. *Edrich.* $124/£80

BLUNDEN, EDMUND. Winter Nights, a Reminiscence.... London: Faber & Gwyer, 1928. 1st ed, deluxe issue. One of 500 numbered, signed. Bds lt dust-soiled, else Fine. *Reese.* $65/£42

BLUNDEN, EDMUND. Winter Nights. London: Faber & Gwyer, 1928. 1st ed. One of 500 numbered, signed. Sugar blue bds, gilt. VF. *Macdonnell.* $75/£48

BLUNT, ANN. Bedouin Tribes of the Euphrates....Wilfred S. Blunt (ed). NY: Harper, 1879. 1st Amer ed. 445pp. 12 plts; 1 color fldg map. Sl rubbed, o/w VG. *Worldwide.* $225/£145

BLUNT, ANTHONY. Art and Architecture in France, 1500-1700. London: Penguin, 1953. Dj. *Petersfield.* $28/£18

BLUNT, ANTHONY. The French Drawings in the Collection...at Windsor Castle. London/Oxford: Phaidon, 1945. Red buckram. Fine in dj. *Europa.* $37/£24

BLUNT, ANTHONY. The French Drawings in the Collection...at Windsor Castle. London: Phaidon, 1945. Frontis, 127 plts; in dj (sl worn, discolored). *Edwards.* $43/£28

BLUNT, ANTHONY. Nicolas Poussin. NY: Pantheon Books, (1967). 1st ed. 2 vols. 265 plts. Fine (bkpl) in djs, slipcase (faded). *Bookpress.* $450/£290

BLUNT, ANTHONY. Nicolas Poussin. NY, 1967. 2 vols. 265 plts. Good in dj, slipcase. *Washton.* $200/£129

BLUNT, ANTHONY. Nicolas Poussin. The A.W. Mellon Lectures in the Fine Arts 1958. Washington, (1966). 2 vols. VG, lacks slipcase. *Argosy.* $250/£161

BLUNT, ANTHONY. Nicolas Poussin. The A.W. Mellon Lectures in the Fine Arts, 1958. Washington: Bollingen Foundation/Pantheon, 1967. 2 vols. Orig cl w/djs. VF set; Vol 2 in slipcase; both in 2nd slipcase. *Europa.* $512/£330

BLUNT, ANTHONY. The Paintings of Nicolas Poussin. London: Phaidon, 1966. Internally Fine (binding sl mkd). *Europa.* $178/£115

BLUNT, EDMUND M. The American Coast Pilot. NY: Edmund & George W. Blunt, 1842. 14th ed. (xxii,2 blank),686pp,(1 appendix, dated February, 1844, 1 blank, 2 ads);19 plts (2 not called for). Orig calf (lacks spine label; chipped; gatherings started). *Lefkowicz.* $225/£145

BLUNT, EDMUND M. The American Coast Pilot. NY: Edmund & George W. Blunt, 1842. 14th ed. (xxii,2 blank),686,(1 appendix, 1 blank w/tipped-in errata slip dated August 1845, 2 ads)pp. 19 plts (2 not called for in directions to binder). Orig calf (spine dried). Sound (label fr pastedown). *Lefkowicz.* $250/£161

BLUNT, JOSEPH. The Merchant and Shipmaster's Assistant.... NY: Edmund M. Blunt, 1822. 1st ed. vii,(1),464,viii,(24)pp. Contemp sheep. Dampstaining, o/w Fine. *Felcone.* $400/£258

BLUNT, JOSEPH. The Merchant and Shipmaster's Assistant.... NY: E. & G.W. Blunt, 1832. (viii),474,(viii index)pp. Orig calf (worn, head spine chipped). Sound (dampstains). *Lefkowicz.* $175/£113

BLUNT, WILFRID S. A New Pilgrimage and Other Poems. London: Kegan Paul Trench, 1889. 1st ed. Grn cl gilt, beveled edges. Sig; 2 stickers, else Very Nice. *Pharos.* $40/£26

BLUNT, WILFRID. The Art of Botanical Illustration. London: Collins, 1950. 1st ed. 47 color plts; 32 b/w plts. Nice in dj (chipped, torn). *Second Life.* $75/£48

BLUNT, WILFRID. The Art of Botanical Illustration. London, 1950. 1st ed. 47 color plts, 37 b/w plts. (Feps lt browned, cl lt discolored.) Dj (sl foxing upper portion). *Edwards.* $147/£95

BLUNT, WILFRID. The Art of Botanical Illustration. London: Collins, 1950. 1st ed. 47 color plts. VF in VF dj. *Quest.* $150/£97

BLUNT, WILFRID. Cockerell. NY: Knopf, 1965. VG in dj. *Veatchs.* $30/£19

BLUNT, WILFRID. Omar. London: Chapman & Hall, (1966). 1st Eng ed. VG in dj. *Hermitage.* $30/£19

BLUNT, WILFRID. Pietro's Pilgrimage: A Journey to India and Back at the Beginning of the Seventeenth Century. London: James Barrie, 1953. 30 plts. Good in dj (tattered). *Archaeologia.* $35/£23

BLUNT, WILFRID. Sweet Roman Hand. Five Hundred Years of Italic Cursive Script. London, 1952. 2nd ed. Dj (corners, spine sl chipped). *Edwards.* $23/£15

BLUNT, WILFRID. Tulipomania. Penguin Books, 1950. 1st ed. 16 color plts. Dj (sl chipped). *Edwards.* $23/£15

BLUNT, WILFRID. Tulipomania. London: Penguin Books, 1950. 1st ed. 16 full-pg color plts. Pict bds. NF in VG dj. *Shifrin.* $35/£23

BLY, ROBERT. Iron John. Reading: Addison-Wesley, 1990. 1st ed. Fine in Fine dj (sl wear). *Revere.* $45/£29

BLYTH, ALEXANDER and MEREDITH. Poisons: Their Effects and Detection. London, 1906. 4th ed. VG (hinges broken). *Argosy.* $125/£81

BOADEN, JAMES. Memoirs of Mrs. Siddons. Phila: Lippincott, 1893. #89/150 lg-paper copies. xv,471pp, 5 ports. 3/4 leather, gilt. Teg, others untrimmed. Unopened. VG. *Schoyer.* $125/£81

BOARDMAN, JOHN and EUGENIO LAROCCA. Eros in Greece. NY: Erotic Art Book Soc, (1978). Good in dj. *Archaeologia.* $35/£23

BOARDMAN, JOHN. Archaic Greek Gems: Schools and Artists.... Evanston: Northwestern Univ Press, 1968. Good in dj. *Archaeologia.* $45/£29

BOARDMAN, JOHN. Engraved Gems: The Ionides Collection. Evanston: Northwestern Univ Press, 1968. Good in dj. *Archaeologia.* $55/£35

BOARDMAN, JOHN. Greek Gems and Finger Rings: Early Bronze Age to Late Classical. NY: Abrams, (1972). 51 color plts. Good in dj. *Archaeologia.* $250/£161

BOARDMAN, PETER. The Shining Mountain. London: Hodder & Stoughton, 1978. 1st ed. VG in dj. *Hollett.* $70/£45

BOARDMAN, SAMUEL L. Maine Cattle. Augusta: For author, 1875. 1st ed. 48pp. VG in ptd wraps (sl worn). *Second Life.* $75/£48

BOAS, FRANZ. BAE Bulletin 59. Kutenai Tales. Washington, 1918. (Ex-lib, #, ink stamps prelims; surface scratching, tear.) *Edwards.* $23/£15

BOAS, FRANZ. Primitive Art. Oslo: H. Aschehoug, 1927. 1st ed. 15 plts. Sl offsetting eps, else NF in dj. *Cahan.* $100/£65

BOASE, T.S.R. English Art 1100-1216. Oxford, 1953. 95 plts. Good. *Washton.* $65/£42

BOASE, T.S.R. Giorgio Vasari. Princeton, 1979. Good in dj. *Washton.* $45/£29

BOASE, T.S.R. The Sculpture of David Wynne 1949-1967. London, 1968. 1st UK ed. Color frontis. *Edwards.* $39/£25

Bobby Bear. Magic Action Book. Racine, WI: Whitman, 1935. 19x19cm. 3 dbl-pg pop-ups. Pict bds. VG-. *Book Finders.* $90/£58

BOBER, PHYLLIS PRAY. Drawings after the Antique by Amico Aspertini. London, 1957. 64 plts. Good. *Washton.* $95/£61

BOCCACCIO, GIOVANNI. The Decameron. Frances Winwar (trans). NY: LEC, 1930. 1/1500 numbered, signed by T.M. Cleland (decs). 2 vols. VG. *Argosy.* $200/£129

BOCKER, DOROTHY. Birth Control Methods. NY, 1924. 1st ed. Good in wrappers. *Fye.* $50/£32

BODDY, ALEXANDER A. With Russian Pilgrims. London: Wells Gardner, (1892). (xiv),(348)pp, 2 dbl-pg maps. Grn pict cl (worn, lib pocket removed). *Schoyer.* $40/£26

BODE, WINSTON. A Portrait of Pancho. Austin: Pemberton Press, 1965. #44/150, signed. Full brn leather, gilt title. Fine in slipcase. *Bohling.* $350/£226

BODE, WINSTON. A Portrait of Pancho. Austin: Pemberton Press, 1965. 1st ed, trade issue. Signed. Gilt cl. Top edge dusty, else Fine in NF dj. *Reese.* $35/£23

BODEN, F.C. A Derbyshire Tragedy. London: Dent, 1935. 1st ed. Soil fr bd, o/w Fine in dj (lt used; chips). *Beasley.* $45/£29

BODEN, F.C. Miner. London: J.M.Dent, 1932. 1st ed. Fine in NF dj (sm chips). *Beasley.* $60/£39

BODENHEIM, MAXWELL. Lights in the Valley. NY, (1942). 1st ed. VG in dj. *Argosy.* $30/£19

BODENHEIM, MAXWELL. My Life and Loves in Greenwich Village. NY: Bridgehead, 1954. 1st ed. VG + (name) in VG dj. *Bishop.* $22/£14

BODENHEIM, MAXWELL. The Sardonic Arm. Chicago, 1923. 1st ed, ltd to 575 numbered. Extra label present. (Cvrs sl worn; sl chip spine label.) *King.* $50/£32

BODLEY, HAL. The Team That Wouldn't Die. Serendipity, 1981. 1st ed. Fine in VG + dj. *Plapinger.* $35/£23

BODLEY, TEMPLE. George Rogers Clark. Boston/NY: Houghton Mifflin, (1926). 1st ed. Frontis. Dk red cl. Tape mk reps, else VG. *Chapel Hill.* $40/£26

BOECK, WILHELM and JAIME SABARTES. Picasso. Abrams, (1955). 1st ed. 38 color plts, 2 dbl spreads in color offset, 4pp in color offset; 414 halftones. VG (sigs) in VG dj. *Oregon.* $95/£61

BOECK, WILHELM and JAIME SABARTES. Picasso. NY: Abrams, (1955). 1st ed. 38 full-pg color plts. Dec cl. Fine in dj. *Hermitage.* $125/£81

BOECK, WILHELM and JAIME SABARTES. Picasso. NY: Abrams, n.d. (1955). Fine in illus dj. *Cahan.* $100/£65

BOECK, WILLIAM and CHARLES STILES. Studies on Various Intestinal Parasites (Especially Amoebae) of Man. Washington, 1923. 1st ed. Good in wrappers. *Fye.* $40/£26

BOEHM, MRS. A.G. History of the New Richmond Cyclone of June 12th, 1899. St. Paul: Dispatch Job Ptg, 1900. 1st ed. Frontis port, 15 plts/illus. Red gilt cl. Nice. *Cady.* $30/£19

BOELTER, HOMER H. Portfolio of Hopi Kachinas. Hollywood: Homer H. Boelter, (1969). 1st ed. Ltd to 1000 signed. Separate suite of 16 color plts accompanies portfolio. VG in slipcase. *Lien.* $350/£226

BOERHAAVE, HERMAN. De Viribus Medicamentorum: or, a Treatise of the Virtue and Energy of Medicines. London: For J. Wilcox et al, 1720. 1st ed in English. (xxxii),328pp (lt waterstaining at foot throughout book). Old calf (edges defective; adequately rebacked; new eps). *Bickersteth.* $457/£295

BOGAN, LOUISE. Dark Summer. NY: Scribner's, 1929. 1st ed. Sticker, paper adhered to half title, else VG+ in VG- dj (spine extrems, folds chipped). *Lame Duck.* $165/£106

BOGAN, LOUISE. Journey Around My Room. NY: Viking, (1980). 1st ed. Top edge bumped, o/w VG in dj (chip). *Hermitage.* $20/£13

BOGARDE, DIRK. A Postillion Struck by Lightning. Chatto, 1977. 1st ed. 1st bk. VG in VG dj. *Whiteson.* $28/£18

BOGG, EDMUND. Lakeland and Ribblesdale. London: Leeds, 1898. 1st ed. xii,256pp (eps browned). Gilt cl (spine sl faded). *Hollett.* $39/£25

BOGGS, CHARLES. Marine Aviation in the Philippines. Washington, 1951. VG (covers sl chipped). *Clark.* $85/£55

BOGGS, KATE DOGGETT. Prints and Plans of Old Gardens. Richmond: Garrett & Massie, 1932. 39 plts. Dec cl. Fine in dj. *Quest.* $85/£55

BOGGS, KATE DOGGETT. Prints and Plants of Old Gardens. Richmond: Garrett & Massie, (1932). 1st ed. Cl sl used; spine sunned, o/w VG. *Pharos.* $60/£39

BOGGS, MAE H.B. My Playhouse Was a Concord Coach. (Oakland: Howell-North, 1942.) 1st ed. 8 fldg maps. Howes B 570. *Ginsberg.* $500/£323

BOGGS, MAE H.B. (comp). My Playhouse Was a Concord Coach. (Oakland, CA: Howell-North, 1942). 1st ed. Signed presentation copy. 21 maps (8 fldg). Blue cl, gilt spine. Good. *Karmiole.* $375/£242

BOGGS, WM. R. Military Reminiscences of General Wm. R. Boggs, C.S.A. Durham, NC: Seeman Printery, 1913. 1st ed. Frontis port. Grey cl (spotted). VG (offsetting tp). *Chapel Hill.* $125/£81

BOGLE, DONALD. Brown Sugar: Eighty Years of America's Black Female Superstars. NY: Harmony, (1980). 1st ed. Fine in NF dj (lt wrinkled). *Aka.* $65/£42

BOHLEN, DIANE DEGRAZIA. Prints and Related Drawings by the Carracci Family. A Catalogue Raisonne. Washington, D.C.: Nat'l Gallery of Art, 1979. Good in wrappers. *Washton.* $90/£58

BOHN, DAVID. Glacier Bay, the Land and the Silence. SF: Sierra Club, (1967). 1st ed. Fine in Fine dj. *Oregon.* $60/£39

BOHN, DAVID. Rambles through an Alaskan Wild: Katmai and the Valley of the Smokes. Santa Barbara: Capra Press, 1979. 1st ed. One of 5000. Inscribed. Tipped-in color frontis; pict eps. Gilt brn cl. Fine in Fine dj. *Harrington.* $35/£23

BOHR, NIELS. Atomic Theory and the Description of Nature. NY, 1934. 1st Amer ed. Fine (spine sl sunned, extrems rubbed, sl soiled). *Polyanthos.* $45/£29

BOHUN, WILLIAM. The Law of Tithes.... London: E. and R. Nutt, and R. Gosling et al, 1731. 2nd ed. Contemp calf, paper label (rubbed). *Boswell.* $450/£290

BOIES, HENRY M. Prisoners and Paupers. NY: Putnam's, 1893. Brn cl, gilt (worn). *Boswell.* $125/£81

BOKER, GEORGE HENRY. The Legend of the Hounds. NY: William Edwin Rudge, 1929. Ltd to 800. Cl-backed marbled paper over bds. Fine. *Glenn.* $50/£32

Bold Little Cowboy with Pop-Up Pictures. London/Somerset: Purnell, n.d. (197?). 23x17 cm. 3 dbl-pg pop-ups. Glazed pict bds (fr cvr sl concave). Pict dj. *Book Finders.* $30/£19

BOLES, ROBERT. Curling. Boston: Houghton Mifflin, 1968. 1st ed. VG in dj (nicks; sl rubbing). *Houle.* $75/£48

BOLINGBROKE, HENRY ST. JOHN. A Letter to Sir William Windham. London: A. Millar, 1753. 1st ed. (4),532pp. Engr port. Old calf (rebacked), red morocco label. Good. *Karmiole.* $150/£97

BOLIO, ANTONIO MEDIZ. The Land of the Pheasant and the Deer. Enid Eder Perkins (trans). Mexico: Editorial Cultura, 1935. One of 900. 3 full-pg illus by Diego Rivera. Pict bds (sl bowed; newspaper stain fep). *Dawson.* $60/£39

BOLITHO, HECTOR (ed). A Batsford Century. Batsford, 1943. 1st ed. Color frontis. Teg, rest uncut. (Edges, spine sl discolored; bumped; sl worn; bkpl.) *Edwards.* $23/£15

BOLITHO, HECTOR. The Queen's Tact. London, 1938. 1st ed. Signed. NF in ptd stiff wraps. *Polyanthos.* $25/£16

BOLL, HEINRICH. Adam and the Train. NY: McGraw-Hill, (1970). 1st Amer ed. VG in dj (lt stain, else VG). *Godot.* $35/£23

BOLL, HEINRICH. Bread of Our Early Years. Mervyn Savill (trans). London: ARCO, 1957. 1st ed. Sl offsetting eps, o/w VG in dj (sl soiled, chipped). *Virgo.* $39/£25

BOLL, HEINRICH. The Lost Honour of Katharina Blum. London: Secker & Warburg, 1975. 1st UK ed. Fine in dj (sl rubbed). *Virgo.* $14/£9

BOLLER, ALFRED P. Practical Treatise on the Construction of Iron Highway Bridges. NY: John Wiley, 1893. 4th ed. Frontis,x,(i),8-144pp (text lt browned; occasional pencil; ink name). Pub's cl (lt rubbed; tips sl worn). *Bookpress.* $100/£65

BOLLER, HENRY A. Among the Indians. Chicago, (1959). Lakeside Classic. VG. *Schoyer.* $20/£13

BOLLER, HENRY A. Among the Indians. Phila, 1868. 1st ed. 428pp, lg fldg map. Mod full leather. Howes B 579. *Ginsberg.* $750/£484

BOLLER, HENRY A. Among the Indians. Chicago, 1959. Fldg map. Fine. *Oregon.* $35/£23

BOLLER, WILLY. Masterpieces of the Japanese Color Woodcut. (N.p.): Boston Book & Art Shop, (1957). Maroon cl, bds. Fine in Good dj (creased, corner torn). *House.* $85/£55

BOLLINGER, EDWARD T. and FREDERICK BAUER. The Moffat Road. Denver: Sage Books, (1962). 1st ed. #129/2000 signed by authors. Pict eps. Brn gilt-lettered cl. Fine in VG+ dj. *Harrington.* $55/£35

BOLLINGER, EDWARD T. and FREDERICK BAUER. The Moffat Road. Denver: Sage Books, (1962). One of 2000, signed by both. Color plt; pict ep. Fine in dj. *Bohling.* $175/£113

BOLT, ROBERT. A Man for All Seasons. London: Samuel French, (1960). 1st acting ed. Sm edge tears tp, o/w Fine. *Polyanthos.* $35/£23

BOLT, ROBERT. A Man for All Seasons. NY: Random House, 1962. 1st ed. Fine in dj (few sl soiled spots). *Else Fine.* $85/£55

BOLTON, ARTHUR T. The Architecture of Robert and James Adam, 1758-1794. Country Life, 1922. 2 vols. Contents VG (ex-lib, labels feps, rubber stamps; sl soiled, rubbed). *Petersfield.* $310/£200

BOLTON, ARTHUR T. The Architecture of Robert and James Adam. (1758-1794). London/NY: Country Life/Scribner's, 1922. 1st ed. 2 vols. Aeg. Emb cameo fr bds. (Lt rubbed.) Nice. *Bookpress.* $425/£274

BOLTON, ARTHUR T. The Gardens of Italy. London: Country Life, 1919. Color frontis plt tipped in. Teg. Fine. *Quest.* $325/£210

BOLTON, ARTHUR T. The Portrait of Sir John Soane, R.A. (1753-1837). London, n.d. c.(1927). Frontis port, 47 plts. (Eps lt spotted.) Gilt-edged cl. *Edwards.* $70/£45

BOLTON, CHARLES KNOWLES. The Founders: Portraits of Persons Born Abroad Who Came to the Colonies.... Boston Athenaeum, 1919-26. 3 vols. Cl, teg. *Marlborough.* $302/£195

BOLTON, HERBERT E. Font's Complete Diary. Berkeley, 1933. Howes B 585. *Ginsberg.* $85/£55

BOLTON, HERBERT E. Fray Juan Crespi: Missionary Explorer on the Pacific Coast, 1769-1774. Berkeley, CA, 1927. 1st ed. 11 maps/plts. Howes B 586. *Ginsberg.* $150/£97

BOLTON, HERBERT E. The Padre on Horseback. SF: Sonora, 1932. Frontis. Unopened. Marbled bds; coarse cl spine, label. Dj. *Dawson.* $75/£48

BOLTON, HERBERT E. Texas in the Middle Eighteenth Century. Berkeley: Univ of CA Press, 1915. 1st ed. Partly unopened. Blue cl. NF. Howes B 589. *Chapel Hill.* $250/£161

BOLTON, HERBERT E. (ed). Historical Memoirs of New California by Fray Francisco Palou. Berkeley: Univ of CA, 1926. 4 vols. Inscribed by Bolton vol 1. Unopened (lt wear). *Dawson.* $350/£226

BOLTON, HERBERT E. and MARY ROSS. The Debatable Land. Berkeley: Univ of CA Press, 1925. 1st ed. Frontis. Blue cl. Sm inkstamp fep, tp lt spotted, else NF. *Chapel Hill.* $150/£97

BOLTON, J. and H. BOLTEN-REMPT. The Hidden Rembrandt. Oxford: Phaidon, 1978. Sound. *Ars Artis.* $78/£50

BOLTON, J.S. The Brain in Health and Disease. London, 1914. VG. *Whitehart.* $62/£40

Bomba's Adventure. London: Bancroft, 1967. Animal; Magic Pop-Up Series PU5/2. 14x20 cm. 6 fan-fld pop-ups. G. Seda & J. Pavlin (illus). Pict wraps. Sm tear on rear cvr, o/w Good-. *Book Finders.* $80/£52

BOMBERGER, C.M. The Battle of Bushy Run. Jeanette, 1928. 1st ed. VG. *Clark.* $40/£26

BOMPAS, GEORGE C. Life of Frank Buckland by His Brother-in-Law. London, 1886. 11th ed. Frontis port, ix,433pp (feps foxed). Marbled eps, edges. Calf, gilt (spine chipped, discolored; head of joints splitting; sl rubbed). *Edwards.* $31/£20

BONAR, HORATIUS. The Desert of Sinai: Notes of a Spring Journey from Cairo to Beersheba. NY: Carter, 1857. 1st ed. vii,408pp (feps foxed; sl foxing, o/w VG. *Worldwide.* $125/£81

BOND, C.J. The Leucocyte in Health and Disease Being an Enquiry into Certain Phases of Leucocytic Activity. London, 1924. 1st ed. 48 plts. Good. *Fye.* $75/£48

BOND, FRANCIS. The Chancel of English Churches. OUP, 1916. Fine. *Peter Taylor.* $48/£31

BOND, FRANCIS. The Chancel of English Churches. OUP, 1916. *Edwards.* $62/£40

BOND, FRANCIS. Fonts and Font Covers. London, 1908. (Eps spotted.) *Edwards.* $62/£40

BOND, FRANCIS. Fonts and Font Covers. London: OUP, 1908. 1st ed. Blue cl. VG. *Hollett.* $62/£40

BOND, FRANCIS. Wood Carvings in English Churches—Misericords. OUP, 1910. Orig blue cl (sl rubbed). VG. *Peter Taylor.* $42/£27

BOND, FRANCIS. Wood Carvings in English Churches. London: OUP, 1910. 1st ed. (Eps lt spotted; spine sl rubbed.) *Hollett.* $47/£30

BOND, FRANCIS. Wood Carvings in English Churches. 1. Misericords. OUP, 1910. 1st ed. Presentation copy, inscribed. Blue cl. (Flyleaves lt spotted.) *Hollett.* $85/£55

BOND, FRANCIS. Wood Carvings in English Churches: Stalls and Tabernacle Work. London, 1910. 1st ed. VG (inscrip; spine sl faded, rubbed). *Willow House.* $54/£35

BOND, FREDERICK W. The Negro and the Drama. Washington: Associated Pub, 1940. 1st ed. Spine faded, else Fine. *Cahan.* $75/£48

BOND, JAMES. Field Guide of Birds of the West Indies. NY: Macmillan, 1947. 1st ed. Sm spot bottom pg edges, o/w Fine in dj (short closed tear; wear). *Mordida.* $75/£48

BOND, MICHAEL. Paddington Helps Out. London: Collins, 1960. 1st ed. 8vo. Peggy Fortnum (dwgs). Orange cl, silver spine lettering. Good in pict dj (chip). *Reisler.* $125/£81

BOND, NELSON. Exiles of Time. Prime, 1949. 1st ed. Fine in dj (sl edgeworn). *Madle.* $35/£23

BOND, NELSON. Exiles of Time. Phila, 1949. 1st ed. As New in perfect dj. *Bond.* $60/£39

BOND, NELSON. Lancelot Biggs: Spaceman. Doubleday, 1950. 1st ed. Fine in dj (sl nicked). *Madle.* $60/£39

BOND, NELSON. Mr. Mergenthwirker's Lobblies and Other Fantastic Tales. NY, 1946. 1st ed. VF in VG dj (sl chipped). *Bond.* $50/£32

BOND, NELSON. Nightmares and Daydreams. Sauk City, WI, 1968. 1st and only ed, ltd to 2000. As New in Fine dj. *Bond.* $60/£39

BOND, NELSON. Nightmares and Daydreams. Arkham House, 1968. 1st ed. Fine in dj (sl frayed). *Madle.* $35/£23

BOND, NELSON. The Thirty-First of February. NY: Gnome Press, 1949. As New in VF dj. *Bond.* $70/£45

BOND, NELSON. The Thirty-First of February. Gnome, 1949. 1st ed. VF in dj. *Madle.* $27/£17

BOND, RAYMOND T. Handbook for Poisoners. NY/Toronto: Rinehart, (1951). 1st ed. Black cl. VG in dj. *Weber.* $25/£16

BOND, W.H. (ed). Eighteenth Century Studies in Honor of Donald F. Hyde. NY: Grolier Club, 1970. 1st ed. One of 1650. Linen bds, gilt titles. Fine in patterned box. *Hartfield.* $95/£61

BONE, MUIRHEAD. The Western Front. NY, 1917. 1st Amer ed. 2 vols in 10 parts. 200 plts. Cl-backed bd portfolios (worn). *Argosy.* $100/£65

BONE, STEPHEN. Albion, an Artist's Britain. London: A&C Black, 1939. 24 color plts (binding sl soiled). *Petersfield.* $23/£15

BONER, CHARLES. Chamois Hunting in the Mountains of Bavaria and the Tyrol. London: Chapman & Hall, 1860. 2nd ed. xiii,446pp, 7 color litho plts (lt spotting). Contemp blue calf (rebacked, repaired). Good. *Bickersteth.* $248/£160

BONEY, KNOWLES. Liverpool Porcelain of the Eighteenth Century and its Makers. Batsford, 1957. 1st ed. 57 b/w plts. Cl (lt soiled); gilt spine title. (Ex-libris.) *Edwards.* $271/£175

BONHAM-CARTER, VICTOR. Exploring Parish Churches. London: Routledge & Kegan Paul, 1961. 1st ed. 8 plts. VG in dj (sl worn, price-clipped). *Hollett.* $23/£15

BONIME, WALTER. The Clinical Use of Dreams. NY: Basic Books, (1962). 1st ed. Gray cl. VG in dj (worn). *Gach.* $30/£19

BONINGTON, CHRIS et al. Changabang. NY: Oxford, 1976. 1st ed. VG- (ex-libris; fep removed) in dj. *Aka.* $23/£15

BONINGTON, CHRIS. Annapurna South Face. London: Cassell, 1971. 1st ed. 48 color plts. (Spine faded.) *Hollett.* $47/£30

BONINGTON, CHRIS. Everest the Hard Way. London: Hodder & Stoughton, 1976. 1st ed. 80 color plts. Mint in dj. *Hollett.* $54/£35

BONN, FRANZ. The Children's Theatre. London: Kestrel/Penguin, 1978. 22x25 cm. 5 3D scenes. Glazed pict bds. VG. *Book Finders.* $35/£23

BONNER, M.G. with ALAN GOULD (eds). The Big Baseball Book for Boys. McLoughlin Bros, 1931. Presumed 1st ed. Good+ in Good+ dj. *Plapinger.* $125/£81

BONNER, T.D. The Life and Adventures of James P. Beckwourth.... NY: Harper, 1856. 1st ptg. 537pp, 11 (of 12) plts (lacks frontis). Orig cl (sl worn). Howes B 601. *Schoyer.* $150/£97

BONNER, THOMAS. The Life and Adventures of James P. Beckwourth. Univ of NE, (1972). 1st thus. Fine. Howes B 601. *Oregon.* $30/£19

BONNEY, CECIL. Looking Over My Shoulder. Roswell: Hall-Poorbaugh, 1971. 1st ed. NF in VG- dj. *Parker.* $60/£39

BONNEY, T.G. The Building of the Alps. London: Fisher Unwin, (1913). 2nd ptg. Grn cl stamped in gilt, blind (bump; ex-lib w/mks). *Schoyer.* $65/£42

BONNEY, T.G. The Building of the Alps. London, 1912. 1st ed. 32 plts. (Foxing.) *Henly.* $37/£24

BONNEY, THERESE. Europe's Children 1939-1943. N.p.: Rhode Pub, (1943). 1st ed. VG (worn) in dj (worn; price-clipped). *Hermitage.* $30/£19

BONNEY, WILLIAM PIERCE. History of Pierce County, Washington. Chicago: Pioneer Hist Pub., 1927. 1st ed. 3 vols. VG set. *Perier.* $200/£129

BONNYCASTLE, JOHN. An Introduction to Astronomy. London, 1811. 6th ed. Frontis, viii,384pp; 19 plts. Orig bds (new canvas back w/paper label); uncut. VG. *Cox.* $54/£35

BONNYCASTLE, R.H. Spanish America. Phila: Abraham Small, 1819. Fldg frontis map, 482pp, fldg color plt. 3/4 black polished calf, marbled bds (rubbed). *Schoyer.* $250/£161

BONSAL, STEPHEN. Edward Fitzgerald Beale: A Pioneer in the Path of Empire, 1822-1903. NY, 1912. 1st ed. Howes B 608. *Ginsberg.* $125/£81

BONTEMPS, ARNA and JACK CONROY. Slappy Hooper, the Wonderful Sign Painter. Boston: Houghton Mifflin, 1946. 1st ed. Fine in dj (chipped). *Beasley.* $275/£177

BONTEMPS, ARNA. Chariot in the Sky. Phila: John Winston, 1951. 1st ed. Fine in NF dj (lt wear). *Beasley.* $50/£32

BONTEMPS, ARNA. Lonesome Boy. Boston: HMCo, 1955. 1st Amer ed. VG (name; lt dampstaining) in VG- dj (lt stained; chipped). *Between The Covers.* $65/£42

BONTEMPS, ARNA. Lonesome Boy. Cambridge: Riverside Press, 1955. 1st ed. Blue cl in pict dj. *Petrilla.* $85/£55

BONTEMPS, ARNA. Lonesome Boy. Boston: HMCo, 1955. 2nd ed. Felix Topolski (illus). 28pp. Cl. Fine in dj (price-clipped). *Cattermole.* $40/£26

Book of Beloit. Daily News Pub, 1936. 1st ed. Pict heavy wrappers. Good (worn). *Connolly.* $35/£23

Book of Common Prayer, and Administration of the Sacraments, and Other Rites.... Oxford: Ptd by T. Wright & W. Gill, 1773. Unpaginated. Contemp black paneled calf, gilt. Good (text foxing). *Karmiole.* $200/£129

Book of Common Prayer, and Administration of the Sacraments, and Other Rites.... London: Ptd by John Jarvis, for Joseph Good, 1791. Unpaginated; 10 copper-engr plts. Contemp black straight-grained morocco, gilt; marbled eps, aeg. Good. *Karmiole.* $150/£97

Book of Fairy Poetry. London: Longmans, Green, 1920. 1st ed. 4to. 16 mtd color plts by Warwick Goble. Grey cl w/blue lettering, decs (spine sl darkened; red spot fr guard). *Reisler.* $300/£194

Book of Fun; or Laugh and Learn for Boys and Girls. London: James Gilbert, n.d. (ca 1850). iv,215pp. Tinted full-pg copper engr 1/2 title; marbled eps. 3/4 leather w/corners; marble paper on bds; raised bands; gilt title spine (sm bkseller label; spine, corners lt rubbed). Fine. *Hobbyhorse.* $225/£145

Book of Nursery and Mother Goose Rhymes. NY: Doubleday, 1954. 1st ed. 4to, 192pp, 260 illus (14 full-color) by Marguerite de Angeli. Beige cl w/Mother Goose. VG (ink name) in dj (tattered). *Davidson.* $65/£42

Book-Lover's Almanac for the Year 1893. NY: Duprat & Co, 1893. Ltd to 400. 56pp; 12 color plts. Red fabricoid, gilt spine w/orig color-illus wrappers preserved. Good. *Karmiole.* $50/£32

BOOKWALTER, JOHN W. Siberia and Central Asia. Springfield, OH: 1899. (xxxii),548pp. Red cl, gilt (spine sl cocked; pocket removed). *Schoyer.* $100/£65

BOOLE, GEORGE. A Treatise on Differential Equations. Cambridge: Macmillan, 1859. 1st ed, 2nd issue w/Appendix, pp 487-494, containing Notes to Chapter XIV, and Corrections. xv,(i),494pp; plt; ad leaf; 12pg cat. (Dk stain upper cvr; slits in cl at joints.) *Bickersteth.* $302/£195

BOONE and CROCKETT CLUB. 18th Big Game Awards 1980-1982. Alexandria, 1984. 1st ed. Fine in dj. *Artis.* $35/£23

BOONE and CROCKETT CLUB. Records of North American Big Game. Alexandria, (1984). 8th ed, 2nd ptg. VF in dj. *Artis.* $35/£23

BOONE, ROBERT. Hack. Highland Press, 1978. 1st ed. Fine in VG dj (lt worn). *Plapinger.* $50/£32

BOOTH, CHARLES et al. Life and Labour of the People in London. London, 1902-3. 7 vols. 18 color linen-backed fldg maps. Some vols partly unopened. Teg. Full japon bds, gilt dec spines (ex-lib, #s; bkpls removed feps; soiling; marginal foxing). *Edwards.* $310/£200

BOOTH, CHARLES G. Mr. Angel Comes Aboard. GC: DCC, 1944. 1st ed. Fine in dj (sl wear). *Mordida.* $45/£29

BOOTH, EVANGELINE and GRACE LIVINGSTON HILL. The War Romance of the Salvation Army. Phila: Lippincott, (1919). 1st ed. 2 ports. VG. *Petrilla.* $30/£19

BOOTH, JOHN. The Battle of Waterloo. London: For J. Booth & T. Egerton, 1815. 3rd ed. Fldg frontis map, xcviii,116pp; 2 plts. Mod 1/4 grn cl, grn marbled bds. Fine (few spots). *Weber.* $250/£161

BOOTH, JOHN. Booth's Manual of Domestic Medicine and Guide to Health and Long Life. Cincinnati, 1884. 1st ed. 1024pp. Good. *Fye.* $75/£48

BOOTH, WILLIAM. In Darkest England and the Way Out. London: Int'l Headquarters of the Salvation Army, (1890). 1st ed. Frontis, (vi),285,(29)pp. Pub's cl (spine sl shaken; cvrs rubbed; spine, tips worn). (Eps foxed.) *Bookpress.* $150/£97

BORCHGREVINK, C.E. First on the Antarctic Continent. London: George Newnes, 1901. 1st ed. Mod cl (rebound). Good+ (map trimmed at head). *Walcot.* $287/£185

BORDEN, MRS. JOHN. The Cruise of the Northern Light. NY: Macmillan, 1928. 1st ed. NF (emb lib stamp on tp). *Bowman.* $45/£29

Border Beagles; A Tale of Mississippi. (By William Gilmore Simms.) Phila: Carey & Hart, 1840. 1st ed. Binding A. 2 vols. 8vo. 300; 337pp. Purple cl, paper spine labels. Spines, edges sunned; pencil mks; sl foxing, else VG. BAL 18068. *Chapel Hill.* $650/£419

BORDMAN, SID. Expansion to Excellence. Walsworth, 1980. 1st ed. Fine in VG+ dj (lt shelfwear). *Plapinger.* $85/£55

BOREHAM, FRANK W. A Tuft of Comet's Hair. London: Epworth Press, (1926). 1st ed. Orig cl stamped in gilt/blind. 2 sl rubbed spots, o/w NF. *Sadlon.* $15/£10

BORENIUS, TANCRED. Forty London Statues and Public Monuments. London: Methuen, 1926. 1st ed. 40 tipped-in plts. Fine. *Europa.* $62/£40

BORGES, JORGE LUIS and ADOLFO BIOY-CASARES. Chronicles of Bustos Domecq. London: Allen Lane, 1967. 1st ed. NF in dj. *Rees.* $16/£10

BORGES, JORGE LUIS. The Congress. Norman Thomas di Giovanni (trans). London: Enitharmon Press, 1974. 1st ed, ltd to 250 numbered. Tipped-in frontis port. Fine in dj. *Godot.* $150/£97

BORGES, JORGE LUIS. Ficciones. Grove Press, 1962. 1st ed. Fine in dj (sl rubbed). *Fine Books.* $295/£190

BORGES, JORGE LUIS. Labyrinths. Donald A. Yates & James E. Irby (eds). (NY): New Directions Book, (1962). 1st Amer ed. Fine in dj (price-clipped, nicks, lt edgewear, else VG). *Godot.* $175/£113

BORGES, JORGE LUIS. Other Inquisitions 1937-52. London: Souvenir, 1973. 1st ed. Fine in dj. *Rees.* $31/£20

BORING, EDWIN. A History of Experimental Psychology. NY: Appleton et al, 1950. 2nd ed. Pub's buckram (sl rubbed). VG. *Peter Taylor.* $47/£30

BORING, EDWIN. History, Psychology, and Science: Selected Papers. NY, 1963. 1st ed. Good in dj. *Fye.* $50/£32

BORKENAU, FRANZ. The Spanish Cockpit. London: Faber, 1937. 1st ed. *Patterson.* $116/£75

BORLAND, HAL. High, Wide and Lonesome. Phila: Lippincott, 1956. 1st ed. VG (bkpl partly removed; sl faded) in dj (lt rubbed). *Hermitage.* $25/£16

BORLAND, HAL. The Seventh Winter. Phila: Lippincott, 1960. 1st ed. Rev slip laid in. Fine in NF dj. *Hermitage.* $25/£16

BORNEMAN, ERNEST. A Critic Looks At Jazz. London: Jazz Music Books, 1946. 1st ed. NF in wraps. *Beasley.* $60/£39

BORROW, GEORGE. The Bible in Spain. London, 1843. 4th ed. 3 vols. xxiii,370; viii,391; viii,398pp, ads each vol. Later 1/2 calf. *Lewis.* $178/£115

BORROW, GEORGE. Lavengro, The Scholar, The Gypsy, The Priest. London: LEC, 1936. #904/1100 numbered, signed by Barnett Freedman (illus). Vol 1 label rubbed, else Fine set in pub's slipcase. *Hermitage.* $85/£55

BORROW, GEORGE. Lavengro; the Scholar, the Gypsy, the Priest. London: John Murray, 1851. 3 vols. Frontis port (tear). Contemp 1/2 calf (lib labels cvrs; press mks spine; lib stamps tps; lack 1/2 titles). *Waterfield.* $78/£50

BORROW, GEORGE. The Romany Rye; a Sequel to Lavengro. London: John Murray, 1857. 2 vols. Pub's cl (worn; lib label fr cvrs; pub's ptd label remains; sewing vol 1 breaking). *Waterfield.* $101/£65

BORROW, GEORGE. The Zincali; or, an Account of the Gypsies of Spain. London, 1841. 1st ed. 2 vols. 3/4 calf. VG. *Argosy.* $350/£226

BORSOOK, EVE. The Mural Painters of Tuscany, from Cimabue to Andrea del Sarto. London: Phaidon, (1960). 1st ed. Ink name, else VG. *Bookpress.* $100/£65

BOSANQUET, W.C. Serums, Vaccines and Toxines in Treatment and Diagnosis. London, 1904. 1st ed. Good. *Fye.* $60/£39

BOSBYSHELL, OLIVER C. (ed). Pennsylvania at Antietam. Harrisburg, 1906. Fldg color map. 3/4 leather. VG. *Schoyer.* $35/£23

BOSSAOGLIA, ROSSANA et al. 1200 Years of Italian Sculpture. NY, n.d. (1968). 64 tipped-in color plts. Good in dj. *Washton.* $150/£97

BOSSERT, H. An Encyclopaedia of Colour Decoration.... London, 1928. 120 color plts. Rebound lib morocco-backed cl bds (ink stamps, #s; sl spotting; inner margin sl split half-title; marginal thumbing; soiled, rubbed). *Edwards.* $93/£60

BOSSERT, H. Peasant Art in Europe. NY: E. Weyhe, 1927. 1st ed. 100 full color, 32 b/w plts. Ex-lib w/stamps on fr blanks, title leaf, # on spine, else VG. *Bookpress.* $175/£113

BOSTOCK, J. An Elementary System of Physiology. London, 1824. 1st ed. Vol 1 only (of 3). xxiii,518pp. Contemp 3/4 roan (rebacked). List of contents partly misbound at back but complete, o/w VG. *Whitehart.* $101/£65

Boston Directory. Boston: E. Cotton, 1816. 1st ed. 252pp (lacks map). Ptd marbled wrappers (chipped, rubbed). *Karmiole.* $50/£32

BOSTON, NOEL. Old Guns and Pistols. London: Ernest Benn, (1958). 1st ed. 4 plts. Grn cl. VG in dj. *Weber.* $25/£16

BOSWELL, HAZEL. French Canada. NY: Viking, 1938. 1st ed. Obl 16mo, 83pp, 25 full-pg illus. Beige cl. NF in NF dj. *Davidson.* $75/£48

BOSWELL, JAMES. An Account of Corsica, the Journal of a Tour to That Island. London: Edw. & Chas. Dilly, 1768. 2nd ed. Fldg map frontis,xxii,384pp (tape mks blank prelims; bk ticket). Early leather cvrs (nicely rebacked; some wear), tooled spine, leather label, gilt. Internally Fine. *Hartfield.* $395/£255

BOSWELL, JAMES. Boswell in Holland (1763-1764). Frederick A. Pottle (ed). London: Heinemann, 1952. 1st ed. 3 plts; 2 facs. VG in dj (lower hinge torn). *Hollett.* $39/£25

BOSWELL, JAMES. Boswell on the Grand Tour. Frank Brady & Frederick A. Pottle (eds). London: Heinemann, 1953. 1st ed. 9 plts. VG in dj (sl worn, torn). *Hollett.* $47/£30

BOSWELL, JAMES. Boswell on the Grand Tour: Germany and Switzerland 1764. F.A. Pottle (ed). London: Heinemann, (1953). 1st British trade ed. Inscribed, signed by Pottle 1977. Teg. 1/2 vellum, gilt cl. Vellum mellowing, o/w Fine in slipcase (lt worn). *Reese.* $150/£97

BOSWELL, JAMES. Boswell on the Grand Tour: Germany and Switzerland 1764. Frederick A. Pottle (ed). London, 1953. De Luxe ed, ltd to 1000 numbered. Teg; uncut. Vellum-backed cl. VG in Poor slipcase. *King.* $150/£97

BOSWELL, JAMES. Boswell on the Grand Tour: Italy, Corsica and France 1765-1766. F. Brady & F.A. Pottle (eds). London: Heinemann, (1955). 1st British trade ed. VG in dj (edges sl tanned). *Reese.* $35/£23

BOSWELL, JAMES. Boswell's Life of Johnson. Including Journal of a Tour to the Hebrides and Diary of a Journey into North Wales. George Birkbeck (ed). NY: Harper, 1891. 6 vols. Frontispieces;604; 551; 526; 514; 524; 323pp. Dk blue cl, gilt. Teg; uncut. Excellent in acetate djs. *Hartfield.* $245/£158

BOSWELL, JAMES. Boswell's London Journal 1762-1763. F.A. Pottle (ed). M-H, 1950. 1st ed. Fine in NF dj. *Fine Books.* $35/£23

BOSWELL, JAMES. Dorando. London: Elkin Mathews & Marrot, 1930. Ltd ed, one of 600. (Ex-lib; few marginal blind stamps; stamp verso title.) Cl-backed dec bds. Dj (sl worn, soiled; sl defective spine top, base). *Hollett.* $23/£15

BOSWELL, JAMES. Dorando. London: Elkin Mathews, 1930. Rpt of 1767 ed, #79/600. Blue cl spine, dec paper bds; uncut. Nice in dj. *Hartfield.* $95/£61

BOSWELL, JAMES. The Hypochondriack. Margery Bailey (ed). Stanford, CA: Stanford Univ, 1928. 1st ed. 2 vols. Frontispieces; 6 plts. Black cl. Fine set. *Karmiole.* $65/£42

BOSWELL, JAMES. The Journal of a Tour to the Hebrides with Samuel Johnson, LL.D. London: T. Cadell & W. Davies, 1813. 6th ed. Contemp calf (rebacked; new eps), leather labels. *Glenn.* $300/£194

BOSWELL, JAMES. The Journal of a Tour to the Hebrides with Samuel Johnson. London: Baldwin for C. Dilly, 1785. 2nd ed. Ad leaf, 1/2 title present; '5' on p475 dropped. Old calf (rebacked), recent leather label. (Bkpl; 1854 sig laid down; stain edges 1/2 title; cvrs worn). *Agvent.* $500/£323

BOSWELL, JAMES. The Journal of a Tour to the Hebrides with Samuel Johnson. NY: Viking, 1936. 1st complete pub of orig mss. One of 790 numbered. 4-pg prospectus. NF (spine sl sunned; sm stain from bkpl) in slipcase (lacks paper label). *Agvent.* $150/£97

BOSWELL, JAMES. The Journal of a Tour to the Hebrides, With Samuel Johnson. London: Charles Dilly, 1785. 2nd ed. 543pp + (1)p ad. Orig full calf, morocco spine label. Joints cracked externally but holding, else VG. *Chapel Hill.* $300/£194

BOSWELL, JAMES. The Journal of the Tour to the Hebrides with Samuel Johnson LL.D. London: Henry Baldwin, 1785. 2nd ed. 8vo. (xx)(i)(534)(i)pp (1st 4pp lt stained, else internally fresh). Points: F5 canceled; pp475 w/'5' missing; final ad leaf for forthcoming 'Life of Johnson'. Orig lt blue bds (cvrs detached, rubbed; lacks most of spine), orig eps. Felt-lined full brn morocco solander case, raised bands, gilt lettered spin *D & D.* $1,100/£710

BOSWELL, JAMES. The Life of Samuel Johnson LL.D. London: for Charles Dilly, 1793. 2nd ed. 3 vols. Thick 8vo. (41)(603); (ii)(634); (iii)(711)pp. Engr frontisport; 'Round Robin' engr fldg pl vol 2; engr fldg pl vol 3. Vol 1 has 2 leaves of 'Corrections' and 'Additional Corrections' leaf, and the 'Chronological Catalog of Johnson's Prose' and 21pp supplement added after bk was ptd. Orig lt blue paper-cvrd bds. Uncut, as issued (spines expertly relined, retaining orig spines). Brn cl slipcase. *D & D.* $2,500/£1,613

BOSWELL, JAMES. The Life of Samuel Johnson, LL.D. London: Charles Dilly, 1791. 1st ed, 2nd state of 1st ptg w/'give' on p. 135 corrected, w/all cancels and other points indicated by Pottle (79). 2 vols. 4to. With the stipple-engr port, the Round-Robin, and the facs of Johnson's handwriting. Rebound in period style w/morocco spines, marbled bds, gilt extra, double leather labels. Fine. *Hartfield.* $3,950/£2,548

BOSWELL, JAMES. The Life of Samuel Johnson, LL.D. London: Baldwin for Dilly, 1791. 1st issue. 2 vols. 4to. 2 plts. Mod 1/4 red morocco. (Lacks port; 2 leaves w/sm repairs; few leaves w/stains; vol 1 lt rubbing, crown wear). *Agvent.* $2,500/£1,613

BOSWELL, JAMES. The Life of Samuel Johnson, LL.D. London: John Murray, 1835. 10 vols. 10 engr frontispieces; 1 fldg plt (lt spotting). Contemp 1/2 calf; gilt spine (sl worn; few sm chips). *Hollett.* $271/£175

BOSWELL, JAMES. The Life of Samuel Johnson. Dublin, 1792. 3 vols. Tree calf (spine split vols 1-2; waterstaining to last few leaves vol 3). *Argosy.* $250/£161

BOSWELL, JAMES. The Life of Samuel Johnson. London: For Charles Dilly, 1793. 2nd ed. 3 vols. Chestnut leather spines, marbled bds (rebound in period style), raised bands, red leather labels, gilt, blind dec spine. Fine set. *Hartfield.* $895/£577

BOSWELL, JAMES. The Life of Samuel Johnson. Oxford: William Pickering/Talboys & Wheeler, 1826. 4 vols. xxii,(v-)xii,394, (4),416; (4),395; (4),428pp; engr port; 2 fldg facs plts. Contemp diced calf, double morocco labels. Good set (inscrip). *Cox.* $171/£110

BOSWELL, JAMES. The Life of Samuel Johnson. London: LEC, 1938. 3 ports. Lacks box, else Fine. *Argosy.* $125/£81

BOSWELL, JAMES. The Life of Samuel Johnson.... London: Ptd for T. Cadell & W. Davies, 1807. 5th ed. 4 vols. Port, plt (2 examples bound in vols I and II, w/o facs leaf). Late 19th cent binder's cl. Good set (lt foxing). *Reese.* $100/£65

BOSWELL, JAMES. The Life of Samuel Johnson.... NY: Doubleday, Page, 1922. Temple Bar ed, ltd to 785 sets. 10 vols. Cream parchment paper over brn paper bds w/paper spine label; teg. Extra labels tipped in back each vol. Fine (scattered, marginal stains 1 vol) in orig djs. *Agvent.* $400/£258

BOSWELL, JAMES. The Life of Samuel Johnson.... E.G. Fletcher (ed). NY: Heritage, (ca 1963). 3 vols. Sm bkpl each vol, else Fine in slipcases. *Reese.* $60/£39

BOSWELL, JOHN and RON BARRETT. The Pop-Up White House. NY: Bantam Books, 1983. 35x23 cm. 1 dbl-pg pop-up w/envelope of pieces. Ron Barret & Gary Hallgren (illus). Glazed pict bds. Fine. *Book Finders.* $40/£26

BOSWELL, PEYTON. George Bellows. NY, (1942). VG. *Argosy.* $35/£23

BOSWELL, ROBERT. Dancing in the Movies. Univ of IA Press, 1986. 1st ed, 1st bk. Fine in dj. *Stahr.* $100/£65

BOSWELL, ROBERT. Dancing in the Movies. Iowa City, 1986. 1st ed, 1st bk. Fine in dj. *Lame Duck.* $150/£97

BOSWELL, THOMAS. How Life Imitates the World Series. Doubleday, 1982. 1st ed. Fine in VG+ dj (lt crease spine). *Plapinger.* $45/£29

BOSWELL, THOMAS. Why Time Begins on Opening Day. Doubleday, 1984. 1st ed. Fine in VG dj. *Plapinger.* $25/£16

BOTKIN, B.A. (ed). Lay My Burden Down. Chicago: Univ of Chicago, (1945). 1st Amer ed. Fine (spine sl rubbed, bkpl) in dj (lacks sm pieces, rubbed). *Polyanthos.* $45/£29

BOTKIN, B.A. (ed). New York City Folklore. NY: Random House, (1956). 1st ptg. VG in dj. *Schoyer.* $30/£19

BOTTA, PAOLO EMILIO. Observations on the Inhabitants of California, 1827-1828. L.A.: Glen Dawson, 1952. One of 140 ptd. 'James Kirker, the Only Surviving Portrait' ptd letterpress laid in. *Dawson.* $150/£97

BOTTOME, MARGARET. Sunshine Trip: Glimpses of the Orient.... NY/London: Edward Arnold, 1897. Frontis port, 215pp. Teg. Cl stamped in gilt (foxing; owner mks fep; leaf repaired w/tape). *Schoyer.* $40/£26

BOTTOMLEY, GORDON. Chambers of Imagery. London: Elkin Mathews, 1907. 1st ed. Wrappers (sl stained). *Hollett.* $31/£20

BOTTOMS, DAVID. Easter Weekend. Boston: Houghton Mifflin, 1990. 1st ed. Fine in Fine dj. *Revere.* $40/£26

BOTTOMS, DAVID. In a U-Haul North of Damascus. NY: Wm. Morrow, 1983. 1st ed. Signed. Fine in Fine dj. *Revere.* $50/£32

BOTTOMS, DAVID. Shooting Rats at the Bibb County Dump. NY: Morrow, 1980. 1st ed. Inscribed, signed. Fine in dj. *Pharos.* $85/£55

BOUCHER, ANTHONY. The Case of the Baker Street Irregulars. NY: S&S, 1940. 1st ed. Lt spotting eps; sm stain fore-edge, o/w VG in dj (chipped, frayed; short closed tears). *Mordida.* $150/£97

BOUCHER, JONATHAN. Reminiscences of an American Loyalist 1738-1789. Boston/NY: Houghton Mifflin, 1925. 1st ed. Ltd to 575. NF. Howes B640. *Mcgowan.* $95/£61

BOUCHER, JONATHAN. Reminiscences of an American Loyalist, 1738-1789. Boston, 1925. 1st ed. One of 575. (Sm emb lib stamp; bkpl removed.) Howes B 640. *Ginsberg.* $100/£65

BOUGH, R.B. The Life of Sir John Falstaff. London: Longman et al, 1857. xx,196pp, 20 full-pg engrs, 1 full-pg woodcut by George Cruikshank. Full morocco, dec spine panels, leather spine labels; aeg. VG. *Schoyer.* $600/£387

BOUGHTON, ALICE. Photographing the Famous. NY: Avondale Press, 1928. 1st ed. 28 photos. Edges soiled, else VG. *Cahan.* $225/£145

BOUILLON, JEAN-PAUL. Art Nouveau, 1870-1914. NY: Rizzoli, (1985). 1st ed. Rear dj rubbed. *Bookpress.* $100/£65

BOULDON, POWHATAN. Home Reminiscences of John Randolph of Roanoke. Danville/Richmond: Pub by Author/Clemmitt & Jones, 1878. ix,320pp; port, illus tp. (Notes; rear pocket removed.) *Schoyer.* $45/£29

BOULET, ROGER H. The Tranquility and the Turbulence: The Life and Work of Walter J. Phillips. Markham, Ontario, (1981). 1st ed, signed. Silver bds. VG in dj. *Argosy.* $100/£65

BOUQUET, HENRY. The Papers of Henry Bouquet. Harrisburg: PA Hist & Museum Comm, 1951. Frontis. (Sm spot.) *Heinoldt.* $25/£16

BOURDON, DAVID. Warhol. NY: Abrams, (1989). VG in dj. *Argosy.* $75/£48

BOURJAILY, VANCE. Confessions of a Spent Youth. NY, 1960. Signed presentation copy by author. Fine (top edges sl rubbed) in Fine dj. *Polyanthos.* $30/£19

BOURJAILY, VANCE. The End of My Life. Scribners, 1947. 1st ed, 1st bk. Fine in VG dj (chip). *Fine Books.* $50/£32

BOURKE, JOHN G. An Apache Campaign. NY: Scribner's, 1886. 1st ed. Good (soiled, worn). Howes 652. *Parker.* $175/£113

BOURKE, JOHN G. On the Border with Crook. NY, (1891). 1st ed. 491pp. Pict cvr. VG (6 of 7 plts removed; 2 pp torn out but neatly replaced w/typed pp). *Pratt.* $125/£81

BOURKE, JOHN G. On the Border with Crook. NY: Scribner's, 1891. 1st ed. 491pp. Pict cl. Good. Howes B654. *Lien.* $250/£161

BOURKE, JOHN G. On the Border with Crook. NY: Scribner's, 1891. 1st ed. VG- (spine lt worn; hinge starting). Howes B 654. *Parker.* $350/£226

BOURKE, JOHN G. The Snake Dance of the Moquis of Arizona. NY: Scribner's, 1884. 1st ed. VG (fep torn). Howes B 655. *Parker.* $300/£194

BOURKE-WHITE, MARGARET. Dear Fatherland, Rest Quietly: A Report on the Collapse of Hitler's 'Thousand Years'. NY: S&S, 1946. 1st ed. Signed presentation. Gray cl, maroon lettering. Sl worn, else Fine. *Cummins.* $300/£194

BOURKE-WHITE, MARGARET. Eyes on Russia. NY: S&S, 1931. 1st ed, 1st bk. Ink name; lt soiling, o/w Fine. *Hermitage.* $225/£145

BOURKE-WHITE, MARGARET. Halfway to Freedom. NY: S&S, 1949. 1st ed. Fine in dj (lt worn). *Hermitage.* $75/£48

BOURKE-WHITE, MARGARET. Portrait of Myself. NY: S&S, 1963. 1st ed. Signed. Marbled bds. NF in pict dj (spine rubbed; edgeworn). *Blue Mountain.* $125/£81

BOURKE-WHITE, MARGARET. They Called It Purple Heart Valley. NY: S&S, 1944. 1st ed. VG+ in VG dj. *Bishop.* $60/£39

BOURNE, GEOFFREY and NELLY GOLARZ (eds). Muscular Dystrophy in Man and Animals. NY, 1963. 1st ed. (Ex-lib.) *Fye.* $75/£48

BOURNE, GEORGE. The Bettesworth Book, Talks with a Surrey Peasant. Lamley, 1901. 1st ed. (Sl faded.) *Petersfield.* $39/£25

BOURNE, GEORGE. Change in the Village. Duckworth, 1912. 1st ed. (Ex-lib, tp stamp; backstrip sl mkd.) *Petersfield.* $39/£25

BOURNE, GILBERT C. A Text-Book of Oarsmanship. London: OUP, 1925. Frontis. (Sl worn.) *Edwards.* $54/£35

BOURNE, RANDOLPH. History of a Literary Radical and Other Essays. NY: B.W. Huebsch, 1920. 1st ed. Bkseller label fr pastedown, o/w Fine. *Heller.* $25/£16

BOURNE, RANDOLPH. Untimely Papers. NY: Huebsch, 1919. 1st ed. Sl wear extrems, else VG + . *Lame Duck.* $50/£32

BOUSQUET, JACQUES. Mannerism. NY, 1964. 32 tipped-in color plts. VG in dj. *Washton.* $125/£81

BOUSQUET, JACQUES. Mannerism: The Painting and Style of the Late Renaissance. Simon Watson Taylor (trans). NY: Braziller, 1964. 32 color mtd illus. VG in dj (torn). *Argosy.* $75/£48

BOUTCHER, WILLIAM. A Treatise on Forest-Trees. (Dublin: William Wilson & John Exshaw, 1784.) 4th ed. 2 p.l.,xxvii,(4),307pp. Contemp tree calf (sl dulled), gilt-ruled spine, red morocco label. VF (corner sl worn). *Pirages.* $200/£129

BOUTELL, CHARLES. Christian Monuments in England and Wales.... London: George Bell, 1854. viii,156pp (sl spotting); partially unopened. Blind emb cl (spine faded). *Edwards.* $62/£40

BOUTELL, CHARLES. A Manual of British Archaeology. London: Lovell Reeve, 1858. 1st ed. xvi,384pp, 20 full-pg hand colored plts. Brn cl blocked in blind/gilt. Superb. *Cady.* $125/£81

BOUTELL, CHARLES. Monumental Brasses and Slabs. London: G. Bell, 1847. xv + 235pp, 23 stone engrs. (Lt spotting, fore-edge few leaves sl water-stained.) 1/2-calf, cl bds, gilt spine bands (upper hinge tender; lt water-stained, extrems sl worn); relevant clippings tipped in. *Edwards.* $85/£55

BOUTELL, CHARLES. The Monumental Brasses of England. London, 1849. xii,53pp. (Ex-lib; spotting; re-bound, sl soiled; #s spine.) *Edwards.* $39/£25

BOUTELL, H.S. First Editions of To-Day and How to Tell Them. Phila: Lippincott, 1929. Rpt of 1928 ed. (Spine faded.) *Oak Knoll.* $15/£10

BOUTON, JIM. Ball Four. Leonard Schecter (ed). World, 1970. 1st ed. VG + in Good + dj. *Plapinger.* $25/£16

BOUVET, F. Bonnard, the Complete Graphic Work. London: Thames & Hudson, 1981. 60 color plts. Dj. *Ars Artis.* $59/£38

BOUVIER, JACQUELINE. One Special Summer. Delacorte Press, 1974. 1st ed, ltd to 500; signed by Jacqueline & Lee Bouvier. Fine in NF slipcase. *Bishop.* $400/£258

BOVA, BEN. The Star Conquerors. Winston, 1959. 1st ed. Fine in dj. *Madle.* $275/£177

BOVINI, GIUSEPPE. Ravenna Mosaics. Greenwich, CT: NYGS, (1956). 1st ed. 45 color plts, 1 mtd color plt in text. Gold cl, gilt. Good in dj, cardboard slipcase. *Karmiole.* $60/£39

BOWDITCH, HENRY I. (ed). First Annual Report of the State Board of Health, Lunacy, and Charity of Massachusetts, 1879. Boston, 1880. 1st ed. 277pp. Good. *Fye.* $150/£97

BOWDITCH, HENRY I. (ed). Ninth (and Tenth) Annual Report(s) of the State Board of Health of Massachusetts. Boston, 1878, 1879. 1st eds. 2 vols. 529; 309pp. Good. *Fye.* $150/£97

BOWDITCH, NATHANIEL INGERSOLL. Memoir of Nathaniel Bowditch. Cambridge, 1884. 3rd ed. (4),178pp; 8 plts. *Lefkowicz.* $200/£129

BOWDITCH, NATHANIEL. The New American Practical Navigator. Newburyport: Edmund M. Blunt, 1807. 2nd ed. xiv,15-312,(284 tables),613-679,(1 ad)pp; 11 plts. Includes text of 1804 Appendix. Contemp calf (cvrs dried; spine top chipped; lt foxing throughout). *Lefkowicz.* $850/£548

BOWDITCH, NATHANIEL. The New American Practical Navigator. NY: E.M. Blunt, and Samuel A. Burtus, 1817. 1st stereotype (4th) ed. (xvi),274,280,(555)-597, (13 ads)pp. 12 charts (fldg chart frayed at edges and repaired at one fold, w/minor loss), plts. Pg 214 misnumbered '412'; pg 264 correctly numbered. Orig calf (rebacked). (Worming to margins, pp browned throughout; top of tp torn w/o loss.) *Lefkowicz.* $325/£210

BOWDITCH, NATHANIEL. The New American Practical Navigator. NY: Edmund M. Blunt, 1821. 5th stereotype ed. (xvi),272,296,(555)-594pp (lacks last text leaf + 6pp ads; last leaf present w/tears, loss); 12 charts (one very worn, affecting image) and plts. Orig calf (worn; shaken). *Lefkowicz.* $200/£129

BOWDITCH, NATHANIEL. The New American Practical Navigator. NY: E. & G.W. Blunt, 1853. 23rd new stereotype ed. (2),4,(iii-xx),319,(1 blank),460,2 ads pp; 14 charts & plts (incl plt facing p452, not called for). Orig calf (worn). *Lefkowicz.* $175/£113

BOWDITCH, NATHANIEL. The New American Practical Navigator. NY: E. & G.W. Blunt, 1861. 30th new stereotype ed. (2),8,(iii-xx),1-289,(1 blank),460 tables,(2 ads)pp; 14 charts (tear to chart fold) and plts. Orig calf (wear; gatherings started; dampstains, lt foxing; label inside fr cvr). *Lefkowicz.* $225/£145

BOWDLER, JANE. Poems and Essays.... Bath: R. Cruttwell, 1797. 9th ed. Contemp calf; greek key border; red morocco lettering-piece; marbled eps (fr joint cracked). *Waterfield.* $62/£40

BOWEN, B.B. A Blind Man's Offering. Boston: Author, 1877. 432pp; port. VG. *Petrilla.* $20/£13

BOWEN, ELIZABETH. Bowen's Court. NY: Knopf, 1942. 1st Amer ed. VF in dj. *Hermitage.* $45/£29

BOWEN, ELIZABETH. Early Stories. NY, 1951. 1st ed. NF in dj (sl chipped, rubbed). *Rees.* $16/£10

BOWEN, ELIZABETH. Eva Trout, or Changing Scenes. London: Cape, 1969. 1st Eng ed. Fine in dj. *Limestone.* $30/£19

BOWEN, ELIZABETH. The Heat of the Day. NY: Knopf, 1949. 1st Amer ed. Fine in dj (sl edgeworn). *Sadlon.* $20/£13

BOWEN, ELIZABETH. The House in Paris. NY: Knopf, 1936. 1st Amer ed. NF in dj (sl edgeworn). *Sadlon.* $20/£13

BOWEN, ELIZABETH. A Time in Rome. London: Longmans, 1960. 1st ed. Inscrip; sm mk fep, o/w VG in dj (sl mkd, rubbed; price-clipped). *Virgo.* $22/£14

BOWEN, FRANK C. From Carrack to Clipper. London/NY, 1927. 67 full-pg b/w, 4 color plts. (Faded cvr edges; few pp browned.) *Hayman.* $25/£16

BOWEN, FRANK C. The Sea: Its History and Romance. London, (1926). 1st ed in bk form. 4 vols. Dec cl (sl rubbed). VG set. *Lefkowicz.* $250/£161

BOWEN, J.J. The Strategy of Robert E. Lee. NY: Thomas Y. Crowell, (1914). 1st ed. Blue cl. Cvr lt spotted, else VG. *Chapel Hill.* $60/£39

BOWEN, ROBERT SIDNEY. Dave Dawson with the Flying Tigers. Saalfield, 1943. 1st ed. NF in dj (chip). *Madle.* $20/£13

BOWERS, A.C. Under Head-Hunters' Eyes. Phila, 1929. 1st ed. Fldg map. Blind-emb cl (fading, sl soiled; hinges cracked). *Edwards.* $31/£20

BOWERS, C.G. Winter-Hardy Azaleas and Rhododendrons. Boston, 1954. Frontis, 16 plts. Cl (bkpl). Dj (lt wear). *Sutton.* $38/£25

BOWERS, CLAUDE. My Mission to Spain: Watching the Rehearsal for World War II. London: Gollancz, 1954. 1st ed. VG (bds sl cocked, eps spotted) in dj. *Patterson.* $47/£30

BOWERS, JOHN Z. and E.F. PURCELL. Advances in American Medicines: Essays on the Bicentennial. NY, 1976. 2 vols. NF in glassine wrappers. *Goodrich.* $75/£48

BOWLES, E.A. A Handbook of Crocus and Colchicum for Gardeners. London, 1952. Rev ed. 12 color, 20 plain plts. (Fore-edge sl foxed.) Dj. *Henly.* $43/£28

BOWLES, JANE. In the Summer House. NY: Random House, (1954). 1st ed. Fine in dj (sm chip fr panel). *Pharos.* $150/£97

BOWLES, JANE. Plain Pleasures. London: Peter Owen, (1966). 1st ed. Handsome (top edge soiled; stamp rep) in dj (lt wear). *Robbins.* $100/£65

BOWLES, JANE. Two Serious Ladies. NY: Knopf, 1943. 1st ed. 1st bk. Eps sl soiled, sl wear, else VG in dj (chip, lt wear, else VG). *Godot.* $450/£290

BOWLES, PAUL. Let It Come Down. R-H, 1952. 1st ed. NF in NF dj. *Fine Books.* $120/£77

BOWLES, PAUL. Let It Come Down. London: John Lehmann, 1952. 1st Eng ed. Fine in NF illus dj (few sm chips at crown). *Cahan.* $185/£119

BOWLES, PAUL. A Little Stone. London: John Lehmann, 1950. 1st UK ed. Prelims, fore-edge sl spotted, o/w VG in dj (sl rubbed, frayed, closed tears). *Moorhouse.* $132/£85

BOWLES, PAUL. The Spider's House. London: Macdonald, 1957. 1st British ed. VG + in dj (spine chipped). *Lame Duck.* $200/£129

BOWLES, PAUL. Their Heads Are Green and Their Hands Are Blue. NY: Random House, (1963). 1st ed. Name, NF in NF dj (price-clipped; sl worn; lt sunned). *Chapel Hill.* $40/£26

BOWLES, PAUL. Two Years Beside the Strait. P. Owen, 1990. 1st ed, ltd to 75 signed. Fine in dj. *Whiteson.* $47/£30

BOWLES, PAUL. Up Above the World. NY, 1966. 1st Amer ed. NF (sl rubbed; name) in dj (sl rubbed, lacks sm piece). *Polyanthos.* $50/£32

BOWLES, PAUL. Up Above the World. London: Peter Owen, 1967. 1st ed. VG in dj (sl rubbed). *Rees.* $31/£20

BOWLES, PAUL. Without Stopping. NY: Putnam, 1972. 1st ed. 24 plts. NF in dj. *Worldwide.* $18/£12

BOWLES, SAMUEL. Across the Continent: A Summer's Journey to the Rocky Mountains.... Springfield, MA, 1865. 1st ed, 1st issue. 452pp; fldg map. Howes 1089. *Ginsberg.* $125/£81

BOWLES, SAMUEL. Our New West. Springfield: Bill, Nichols, 1872. Later ptg. Presentation. Steel-engr frontis, 524pp, map, 12 plts. Orig 3/4 leather (spine #). *Schoyer.* $45/£29

BOWLES, SAMUEL. Our New West: Records of Travel between the Mississippi River and the Pacific Ocean. Hartford: Hartford Pub Co, 1869. 1st ed. 528 (i.e. 524)pp, map. Orig 3/4 morocco, pebble-grained cl (sl wear). NF. *Harrington.* $75/£48

BOWLKER, CHARLES. The Art of Angling. London: Swinney & Walker, 1792. 6th ed. Engr frontis, 118pp + 2pp ads (sl foxed). Full leather (rebound; joints cracked; later eps). *Petersfield.* $620/£400

BOWLKER, CHARLES. The Art of Angling. Ludlow: Richard Jones, 1833. Tinted frontis. Uncut. Blue ptd pict bds. *Hill.* $271/£175

BOWMAN, A.K. The Life and Teachings of Sir William Macewen. London, 1942. 1st ed. Good. *Fye.* $90/£58

BOWNESS, ALAN (ed). The Complete Sculpture of Barbara Hepworth 1960-69. London: Lund Humphries, 1971. Dec paper over bds; gilt title. Fine (sm bkseller label) in dj. *Heller.* $150/£97

BOWNESS, ALAN and LUIGI LAMBERTINI. Victor Pasmore. London, 1980. 1st UK ed. 249 plts, 51 color plts; in dj (sl rubbed). *Edwards.* $155/£100

BOWNESS, ALAN and LUIGI LAMBERTINI. Victor Pasmore. A Catalogue Raisonne.... NY: Rizzoli, 1980. 249 plts (51 color). Sound. *Ars Artis.* $93/£60

BOWNESS, ALAN. Barbara Hepworth. London, 1966. 1st ed. Frontis port; 76 plts (20 color). Dj (sl chipped). *Edwards.* $54/£35

BOWRING, JOHN. Observations on the Oriental Plague and on Quarantines.... Edinburgh, 1838. 1st ed. 45pp. (Lib stamp.) Wrappers. *Fye.* $40/£26

BOX, EDGAR. (Pseud of Gore Vidal.) Death in the Fifth Position. NY: Dutton, 1952. 1st ed. NF (sm # stamp fep) in VG dj (chipped, edgewear, rubbed, internal reinforcement). *Janus.* $85/£55

Boy's and Girl's Book of Sports. NY/Phila: Turner & Fisher, n.d. (ca 1840). 12mo. 24pp, full-pg hand-colored wood engr frontis, lg engr vignette tp, engr 1/2 title, 10 VF wood engrs, diag. Pict paper wrappers. (Lt dampstain corners of few leaves, not affecting text or engrs; sm chip upper corner spine). In all, Fine. *Hobbyhorse.* $215/£139

Boy's Picture Book. (Toy Books Series #3.) Concord, NH: R. Merrill, n.d. (ca 1845). 70 x 60mm. 2 full-pg wood engrs. Illus upper wrapper (ink cancellation; lt offsetting). VG. *Hobbyhorse.* $80/£52

BOYCE, RUBERT. Mosquito or Man? London, 1909. 1st ed. Good. *Fye.* $150/£97

BOYD, BELLE. Belle Boyd in Camp and Prison. NY: Blelock, 1865. 1st Amer ed. 464pp. Orig grn cl. Spine sl faded, sl worn, else Good + . Howes H 190. *Chapel Hill.* $100/£65

BOYD, CYRUS F. The Civil War Diary of Cyrus F. Boyd. Mildred Thorne (ed). IA City: State Hist Soc of IA, 1953. 1st ed. Blue buckram, gold lettering on spine. VG (edges faded). *Graf.* $25/£16

BOYD, JAMES. Long Hunt. NY: Scribner's, 1930. One of 260 signed. Teg. Cl, morocco spine label. (Lt rubbed.) VG. *Cahan.* $75/£48

BOYD, JAMES. Marching On. NY, 1927. Stated 1st ed. Good in dj (sl worn). *Hayman.* $25/£16

BOYD, JULIAN P. The Murder of George Wythe. Phila: Philobiblon Club, 1949. 1st ed. Fine in glassine dj (sl chipped). *Cahan.* $60/£39

BOYD, NANCY. (Pseud of Edna St. Vincent Millay.) Distressing Dialogues. NY/London: Harper, (c 1924). 1st ed. Black cl stamped in gold. Gold on backstrip flaking, o/w VG. *Heller.* $35/£23

BOYD, THOMAS M. Worship in Wood. Chicago: American Seating Co, 1927. 1st ed. 10 full-pg gravure plts. Leather-backed plum cl. Sm owner stamp tp, eps, o/w Fine. *House.* $50/£32

BOYD, WILLIAM KENNETH. The Story of Durham. Durham, NC: Duke Univ, 1925. 1st ed. Frontis port. Gilt cl. Panel of dj laid in. Corner bumped, sm sticker, else Fine. *Cahan.* $85/£55

BOYD, WILLIAM. The Blue Afternoon. London: Sinclair-Stevenson, (1990). One of 150 numbered, signed. Cl, marbled bds. Fine in tissue dj, as issued. *Dermont.* $100/£65

BOYD, WILLIAM. The Blue Afternoon. S&S, 1993. 1st UK ed. Signed. Fine in dj. *Lewton.* $31/£20

BOYD, WILLIAM. Brazzaville Beach. London: Sinclair-Stevenson, (1990). One of 150 numbered, signed. Cl, marbled bds. New in glassine. *Dermont.* $100/£65

BOYD, WILLIAM. Brazzaville Beach. London: Sinclair-Stevenson, 1990. 1st ed. Signed. Fine in dj. *Virgo.* $54/£35

BOYD, WILLIAM. A Good Man in Africa. London: Hamish Hamilton, 1981. 1st ed, 1st bk. NF in dj (price-clipped). *Lame Duck.* $750/£484

BOYD, WILLIAM. A Good Man in Africa. Hamish Hamilton, 1981. 1st UK ed, 1st bk. Signed. Fine in Fine dj. *Sclanders.* $465/£300

BOYD, WILLIAM. A Good Man in Africa. NY: Morrow, 1982. 1st ed. 1st bk. VF in dj. *Else Fine.* $75/£48

BOYD, WILLIAM. An Ice-Cream War. London: Hamish Hamilton, 1982. 1st ed. VG in dj. *Cox.* $31/£20

BOYD, WILLIAM. Physiology and Pathology of the Cerebro-Spinal Fluid. NY, 1920. 1st ed. Good. *Fye.* $50/£32

BOYD, WILLIAM. School Ties. Hamish Hamilton, 1985. 1st UK ed. Fine in dj. *Sclanders.* $147/£95

BOYD, WILLIAM. Stars and Bars. London: Hamilton, 1984. 1st UK ed. Fine in dj. *Williams.* $25/£16

BOYD, WILLIAM. Stars and Bars. Hamilton, 1984. 1st UK ed. Signed. Fine in dj. *Williams.* $39/£25

BOYD, WILLIAM. Stars and Bars. Morrow, 1985. 1st Amer ed. Uncorrected proof. Fine in wraps. *Fine Books.* $40/£26

BOYER, L. BRYCE and PETER L. GIOVACCHINI. Psychoanalytic Treatment of Schizophrenic, Borderline, and Characterologic Disorders. NY: Aronson, (1980). 2nd rev & enlgd ed, 1st ptg. Black cl. VG in dj (chipped). *Gach.* $35/£23

BOYER, L. BRYCE. The Regressed Patient. NY/London: Aronson, (1983). 1st ed. Ptd grn fabrikoid. VG (name stamps). *Gach.* $30/£19

BOYER, MARY G. Arizona in Literature. Glendale, CA: Clark, 1935. Frontis. VG+. *Bohling.* $75/£48

BOYER, NATHALIE ROBINSON. A Virginia Gentleman and His Family. Phila: For author, 1939. 1st ed. #113/300 signed. VG-. *Book Broker.* $45/£29

BOYER, RICK. Billingsgate Shoal. Houghton, 1982. 1st ed. Lt wrinkling bottom bd edges, else Fine in dj (sm nick spine head). *Murder.* $65/£42

BOYKIN, EDWARD M. The Falling Flag. Evacuation of Richmond, Retreat and Surrender at Appomatox. NY: E.J. Hale & Son, 1874. 3rd ed. 140pp. Orig cl. Lacking 1 plt; cvr speckling, else VG. Howes B676. *Mcgowan.* $350/£226

BOYKIN, EDWARD. Beefsteak Raid. NY, (1960). 1st ed. Dj worn, o/w VG+. *Pratt.* $45/£29

BOYLAN, GRACE DUFFIE. The Steps to Nowhere. NY: Baker & Taylor, 1910. 1st ed. 4to. 8 full-pg color plts (incl frontis) by Ike Morgan. Blue cl, color paste label, white lettering (spine lettering rubbed). *Reisler.* $110/£71

BOYLE, F. The Culture of Greenhouse Orchids.... London, 1902. 3 color plts. *Wheldon & Wesley.* $62/£40

BOYLE, KAY et al (eds). 365 Days. NY: Harcourt, 1936. 1st ed. Fine in dj (lt used). *Beasley.* $100/£65

BOYLE, KAY. Avalanche. NY: S&S, 1944. 1st ed. VF in dj (sl rubbed). *Hermitage.* $45/£29

BOYLE, KAY. Thirty Stories. NY: S&S, (1946). 1st ed. Lt fading upper edges, o/w NF in dj (sl rubbing). *Hermitage.* $45/£29

BOYLE, ROBERT. The Hon. Robert Boyle's 'Occasionall Reflections'. London, 1808. Engr frontis, xlviii,155,(3)pp. Good. *Goodrich.* $85/£55

BOYLE, T. CORAGHESSAN. East Is East. (NY): Viking, (1990). 1st ed. Inscribed in 1990. Fine in dj. *Godot.* $65/£42

BOYLE, T. CORAGHESSAN. Greasy Lake. NY: Viking, 1985. 1st ed. NF in NF dj. *Revere.* $50/£32

BOYLE, T. CORRAGHESSAN. World's End. (NY): Viking, (1987). 1st ed. Fine in dj. *Between The Covers.* $35/£23

BOYLES, KATE and VIRGIL D. The Hoosier Volunteer. NY: A.L. Burt, (1914). 1st ed. VG. *Mcgowan.* $25/£16

BOYNTON, CHARLES B. The History of the Navy During the Rebellion. NY: Appleton, 1867-68. 1st ed. 2 vols. 576; (580)pp + (8)pp ads, 30 plts. Pub's sheep (sl dried). *Lefkowicz.* $300/£194

BRABY, D. The Way of Wood Engraving. London, (1935). Good in dj. *Veatchs.* $35/£23

BRABY, D. The Way of Wood-Engraving. London: Studio Publications, 1953. Red cl over bd, black spine title. Fine (sl worn) in dj. *Heller.* $85/£55

BRACE, CHARLES LORING. The Dangerous Classes of New York, and Twenty Years' Work Among Them. NY: Wynkoop & Hallenbeck, 1872. 448pp; 13 plts. (Sig pulled.) *Schoyer.* $65/£42

BRACKEN, DOROTHY and MAURINE REDWAY. Early Texas Homes. Dallas: SMU, 1956. 1st ed. Dj. *Lambeth.* $35/£23

BRACKEN, DOROTHY and MAURINE REDWAY. Early Texas Homes. Dallas: Southern Methodist Univ Press, 1956. 2nd ptg. Sig; dj rubbed, lt chipped, else VG. *Bookpress.* $45/£29

BRACKENRIDGE, HENRY MARIE. Views of Louisiana...Voyage up the Missouri River, in 1811. Pittsburgh: Cramer et al, 1814. 1st ed. 304pp. 3/4 bright red morocco, marbled bds, gilt spine. Good. Howes B 688. *Schoyer.* $850/£548

BRACKENRIDGE, HENRY MARIE. Views of Louisiana; Together with a Journal of the Voyage Up the Mississippi River in 1811. Pittsburgh: Cramer, Spear & Eichbahn, 1814. 1st ed. 8vo. Full contemp calf (scuffed); upper hinge tender). Howes B 688. *Glenn.* $875/£565

BRACKETT, LEIGH. The Starmen. Gnome, 1952. 1st ed. Fine in dj. *Madle.* $125/£81

BRACKETT, LEIGH. The Sword of Rhiannon. Boardman, 1955. 1st Eng, 1st separate, 1st hb ed. Fine in NF dj (lt wear, tear). *Aronovitz.* $225/£145

BRADAM, TONY and COLIN HAWKINS. See You Alligator. NY: Dial, 1986. 29x24 cm. 5 tab-operated movables. Glazed pict bds. VG. *Book Finders.* $25/£16

BRADBURY, MALCOLM. Eating People Is Wrong. London: Secker & Warburg, 1959. 1st ed, 1st bk. Fine in dj. *Pharos.* $50/£32

BRADBURY, MALCOLM. Eating People Is Wrong. London: Secker & Warburg, 1959. 1st ed. Signed. Foxing to edges, eps, o/w NF in dj (sl rubbed, chipped). *Rees.* $78/£50

BRADBURY, MALCOLM. Eating People is Wrong. Secker, 1959. 1st UK ed, 1st bk. Signed. NF in VG dj (sl rubbed; sl extrem wear, repaired w/archival tape). *Williams.* $93/£60

BRADBURY, MALCOLM. Evelyn Waugh. London: Oliver & Boyd, 1964. 1st ed. VG (name) in wrappers. *Rees.* $31/£20

BRADBURY, MALCOLM. Phogey! London: Max Parrish, 1960. 1st ed. Signed. NF in dj (sl rubbed, mkd). *Rees.* $39/£25

BRADBURY, MALCOLM. Phogey. M. Parrish, 1960. 1st ed. Fine in VG + dj. *Fine Books.* $35/£23

BRADBURY, MALCOLM. Rates of Exchange. London: Secker, 1983. 1st UK ed. Fine in dj. *Williams.* $23/£15

BRADBURY, MALCOLM. Stepping Westward. Boston: Houghton Mifflin, 1966. Uncorrected proof of 1st Amer ed. Title label lower edge, else Fine in spiral bound wrappers. *Reese.* $60/£39

BRADBURY, RAY and A. SESSA. The Ghosts of Forever. Rizzoli, 1980. 1st ed. One of 1500. Signed. Fine in dj (closed tear). *Aronovitz.* $80/£52

BRADBURY, RAY. The Attic Where the Meadow Greens. Northridge: Lord John, 1979. 1st ed. #28/75 specially bound, signed. VF. *Hermitage.* $125/£81

BRADBURY, RAY. Beyond 1984: Remembrance of Things Future. Targ Editions, (1979). One of 300 numbered, signed. Fine in plain dj. *Dermont.* $75/£48

BRADBURY, RAY. Dandelion Wine. London: Hart-Davis, 1957. 1st ed. VG in dj (sl rubbed, chipped, spine tanned). *Rees.* $54/£35

BRADBURY, RAY. Dark Carnival. Sauk City, WI: Arkham House, 1947. One of 3112, 1st bk. Fine in dj (lt soiled rear panel). *Bernard.* $750/£484

BRADBURY, RAY. Dark Carnival. London: Hamish Hamilton, 1948. 1st ed. 1st bk. VG (sm inscrip) in dj (sl rubbed, chipped, price-clipped, tear). *Rees.* $70/£45

BRADBURY, RAY. Dark Carnival. Hamilton, 1948. 1st UK ed, 1st bk. VG in Good dj (worn, browned; price-clipped; closed tear spine bottom, strengthened to rear). *Williams.* $101/£65

BRADBURY, RAY. The Day It Rained Forever. RHD, 1959. 1st ed. Inscribed. Lt foxing top edge, fore-edge, else VG + in VG dj. *Fine Books.* $150/£97

BRADBURY, RAY. Death Is a Lonely Business. NY: Knopf, 1985. 1st ed. Inscribed. Rev slip laid in. Fine in dj. *Reese.* $60/£39

BRADBURY, RAY. Fahrenheit 451. London, 1954. 1st Eng ed. Good. *Waterfield.* $39/£25

BRADBURY, RAY. Forever and the Earth. Croissant, 1984. 1st ed. One of 300. Signed. As New in dj. *Fine Books.* $65/£42

BRADBURY, RAY. The Golden Apples of the Sun. London, 1953. 1st British ed. VG in dj (sl chipped, frayed). *Madle.* $75/£48

BRADBURY, RAY. The Golden Apples of the Sun. Doubleday, 1953. 1st ed. Rev copy, slip laid in. Signed. Fine in VG + dj (1-inch tear, wrinkle rear panel). *Fine Books.* $235/£152

BRADBURY, RAY. The Halloween Tree. NY: Knopf, (1972). 1st ed. Fine in dj. *Bernard.* $50/£32

BRADBURY, RAY. The Haunted Computer and the Android Pope. NY: Knopf, 1981. 1st ed. Fine in Fine dj (extrems sl dknd). *Between The Covers.* $45/£29

BRADBURY, RAY. Hollerbochen Comes Back. L.A.S.F.L., 1938. 1st ed. Inscribed. 2 pp stapled to make 4. Fine. *Fine Books.* $275/£177

BRADBURY, RAY. The Illustrated Man. Doubleday, 1951. 1st ed. Signed. Foxing eps, else NF in NF dj. *Fine Books.* $285/£184

BRADBURY, RAY. Long after Midnight. NY: Knopf, 1976. 1st ed. Fine in dj. *Reese.* $35/£23

BRADBURY, RAY. Long after Midnight. London: Hart-Davis, 1977. 1st Eng ed. Top edges sl dusty, else Fine in dj. *Limestone.* $85/£55

BRADBURY, RAY. The Machineries of Joy. NY, 1964. 1st ed. As New in perfect dj. *Bond.* $75/£48

BRADBURY, RAY. The Martian Chronicles. Avon: LEC, 1974. 1st thus. One of 2000 numbered, signed by author and artist. Fine (binding inverted?) in slipcase (corner starting; lacks plain tissue dj). *Other Worlds.* $125/£81

BRADBURY, RAY. The Martian Chronicles. LEC, 1974. One of 2000 signed by author & Joseph Mugniani (illus). Fine in glassine dj & slipcase. *Fine Books.* $175/£113

BRADBURY, RAY. The October Country. London: Hart-Davis, 1956. 1st Eng ed. VF in color pict dj. *Limestone.* $175/£113

BRADBURY, RAY. The October Country. Rupert Hart-Davis, 1956. 1st UK ed. NF in VG dj (sl dusty; sl edgewear; creasing). *Williams.* $85/£55

BRADBURY, RAY. The October Country. NY, 1970. 1st hb ed. Pub's rev slip. As New in dj. *Bond.* $50/£32

BRADBURY, RAY. Old Ahab's Friend and Friend to Noah, Speaks His Piece. Squires, 1971. 1st ed. One of 485. Signed. As New in wraps. *Fine Books.* $55/£35

BRADBURY, RAY. The Pedestrian. Roy A. Squires, 1964. One of 280. Fine. *Madle.* $150/£97

BRADBURY, RAY. S Is for Space. Doubleday, 1966. 1st ed. Signed. VG + in VG + dj. *Aronovitz.* $80/£52

BRADBURY, RAY. The Silver Locusts. London: Rupert Hart-Davis, 1951. 1st British ed, 1st ptg. VG in dj (soil, wear). *Glenn.* $210/£135

BRADBURY, RAY. The Silver Locusts. RHD, 1951. 1st ed. Signed. Corner lt bumped, else Fine in NF dj (lt rubbed). *Fine Books.* $175/£113

BRADBURY, RAY. Something Wicked This Way Comes. S&S, 1962. 1st ed. Fine in VG + dj (lt wear, tear). *Aronovitz.* $195/£126

BRADBURY, RAY. Something Wicked This Way Comes. London: Rupert Hart-Davis, 1963. 1st Eng ed. Signed, dated July 13, 1983. Fine in dj (price-clipped). *Hermitage.* $225/£145

BRADBURY, RAY. Something Wicked This Way Comes. London: Hart-Davis, 1965. 1st Eng ed. NF in dj. *Limestone.* $135/£87

BRADBURY, RAY. Switch on the Night. Pantheon, 1955. 1st ed. Signed. VG in dj (lt sunning, dust soiling). *Fine Books.* $225/£145

BRADBURY, RAY. This Attic Where the Meadow Greens. Northridge: Lord John, 1979. 1st ed. One of 300 numbered (of 375) signed. Cl, dec bds. Fine. *Reese.* $60/£39

BRADBURY, RAY. Twin Hieroglyphs That Swim the River Dust. Northridge: Lord John, 1978. 1st ed. One of 300 numbered (of 326) signed. Cl, marbled bds, paper label; spare label laid in. Fine. *Reese.* $60/£39

BRADDON, RUSSELL. The Siege. NY: Viking, 1970. 12 plts; map. NF in dj. *Worldwide.* $25/£16

BRADFORD, GAMALIEL, JR. Lee the American. Boston/NY: Houghton Mifflin, (1912). Early rpt ed. Frontis port. Teg. Burgundy cl, gilt. Lt rubbed, else Fine. *Glenn.* $35/£23

BRADFORD, ROARK. John Henry: A Play With Music. NY: Harpers, 1939. 1st ed. Pict cl. Fine in dj (sl age-dknd). *Pharos.* $45/£29

BRADFORD, SARAH H. Grandmama's Search or Tommy Lost and Found for Little Children. Dresden: E. Blockmann, (ca 1869). Oblong, 4to. 8 full-pg color lithos, each w/lift-up flap. Cl-backed illus bds. (Hinges cracked; piece missing blank fep; corner piece missing from pg.) *Reisler.* $385/£248

BRADLEY, A.G. The Wye. A&C Black, 1910. 1st ed. 20 color plts, fldg map. Teg. Dec cl. *Edwards.* $54/£35

BRADLEY, EDITH. The Story of the English Abbeys Told in Counties. London: Robert Hale, 1938. 1st ed. Map. Gilt cl. VG in dj (edges sl chipped, worn). *Hollett.* $47/£30

BRADLEY, ELIZA. An Authentic Narrative of the Shipwreck and Sufferings of Mrs. Eliza Bradley.... Boston: James Walden, 1820. 1st ed. Fldg frontis, 108pp. Mod calf-backed marbled bds. *Felcone.* $250/£161

BRADLEY, ELIZA. An Authentic Narrative of the Shipwreck and Sufferings of.... Boston: Jonathan Howe, 1823. 1st ed. Fldg woodcut frontis (tears, repairs; fraying); 103pp. Contemp wooden bds (worn; upper cvr nearly detached; rear broken; foxing, stains). Good. *Second Life.* $135/£87

BRADLEY, GLENN D. The Story of the Pony Express. Chicago: A.C. McClurg, 1913. 1st ed. Frontis. White-ptd cl. Dj (fr cvr neatly separated). *Dawson.* $40/£26

BRADLEY, J.W. and T.G. GOODWIN. A Manual of Illumination. London: Windsor & Newton, c. 1880. 11th ed. Full brn calf (sm tear backstrip; sm hole plt 10; ink stain frontis). *Petersfield.* $65/£42

BRADLEY, MARION Z. The Mists of Avalon. Knopf, 1982. 1st ed. Fine in dj. *Madle.* $75/£48

BRADLEY, TOM. The Old Coaching Days in Yorkshire. Leeds: Yorkshire Conservative Newspaper Co, 1889. xi,251pp + (iii)pp ads (lacks 3 leaves of ads fr; 1 leaf misbound at end). Mod 1/2 crimson levant morocco gilt, orig pict cl gilt preserved on upper bd (sl dull). Very Nice. *Hollett.* $186/£120

BRADLEY, VAN ALLEN. The Book Collector's Handbook of Values. NY: Putnam's, 1976-1977. 2nd ed. Fine in NF dj. *Glenn.* $40/£26

BRADLEY, WILL. Peter Poodle, Toy Maker to the King. NY: Dodd, Mead, 1906. 1st ed. 4to, 166pp. Lt edgewear, nicks, else Fine. *Godot.* $850/£548

BRADLEY, WILL. Will Bradley, His Chap Book. NY: Typophiles, 1955. One of 400. Patterned bds. Fine. *Veatchs.* $65/£42

BRADLEY-BIRT, F.B. Bengal Fairy Tales. London: Lane, 1920. 6 color plts; uncut except top edge (few pp sl foxed; faded, sl stained). *Petersfield.* $39/£25

BRADSHAW, B. B. Bradshaw's Dictionary of Mineral Waters, Climatic Health Resorts...and Hydropathic Establishments. London: Trubner, 1890. 1xxxiii,410pp + 14pp ads, lg fldg map in pocket (repairs to tears). Pict cl. *Schoyer.* $125/£81

BRADSHAW, W.R. The Goddess of Atvatabar. Douthitt, 1892. 1st ed. Pict cl. Rubbed; spine sl dknd, else VG-. *Aronovitz.* $185/£119

BRADY, FRANK. Boswell's Political Career. New Haven/London: Yale Univ, 1965. 1st ed. Fine in pict dj. *Hartfield.* $65/£42

BRAGDON, ROGER W. Down-Easter. Manchester, ME, (1954). Stated 1st ed. Good in dj (sl worn). *Hayman.* $15/£10

BRAGHINE, A. The Shadow of Atlantis. Dutton, 1940. 1st ed. Fine in NF dj. *Aronovitz.* $50/£32

BRAHAM, ALLAN. The Architecture of the French Enlightenment. London: Thames & Hudson, 1980. VF in dj. *Europa.* $101/£65

BRAIN, RUSSELL. Recent Advances in Neurology. Phila, 1929. Good. *Fye.* $40/£26

BRAINARD, DAVID L. Six Came Back. Indianapolis: Bobbs-Merrill, (1940). VG (bkpl). *Blue Dragon.* $30/£19

BRAINE, JOHN. From the Hand of the Hunter. Boston: Houghton Mifflin, (1960). 1st ed. NF in VG dj. *Hermitage.* $25/£16

BRAINE, JOHN. Life at the Top. London: Eyre & Spottiswoode, 1962. 1st UK ed. NF in VG dj. *Bernard.* $20/£13

BRAINE, JOHN. Room at the Top. Boston: Houghton, Mifflin, 1957. 1st Amer ed, 1st bk. NF in dj. *Cady.* $40/£26

BRAINE, JOHN. The Vodi. (London): Eyre & Spottiswoode, (1959). 1st UK ed. NF in dj. *Bernard.* $50/£32

BRAINERD, E. Violets of North America. Burlington, 1921. 25 color plts. Cl (faded, spotted; sig). *Sutton.* $57/£37

BRAINERD, ELEANOR HOYT. For Love of Mary Ellen. NY: Harper, 1912. 1st ed. Rose O'Neill (illus). 12mo, 44pp. Pict cl. Lt worn, else VG. *Godot.* $45/£29

BRAITHWAITE, R. The British Moss-Flora. London, 1887. 3 vols. 128 plts. Gilt device. (Lt browning, ex-libris; spines sl chipped; bumped.) *Edwards.* $233/£150

BRAKE, BRIAN et al. Art of the Pacific. NY: Abrams, 1980. 84 color plts. VG in dj. *Argosy.* $50/£32

BRAKE, HEZEKIAH. On Two Continents, a Long Life's Experience. Topeka: Crane, 1896. 240pp; 2 ports. Gilt-titled cl (spine ends frayed; etching). VG (bkpl). Howes B 178. *Bohling.* $75/£48

BRAKE, HEZEKIAH. On Two Continents. Topeka, 1896. 1st ed. 240pp; 2 ports. (Spine lt discolored.) Howes B 718. *Ginsberg.* $85/£55

BRAKE, HEZEKIAH. On Two Continents. A Long Life's Experience. Topeka: Crane, 1896. 1st ed. Good + (fep removed; edges worn). Howes B 718. *Parker.* $95/£61

BRAKE, HEZEKIAH. On Two Continents. A Long Life's Experience. Topeka: By Author, 1896. 1st ed. 240pp, ports. Red cl. Mottled, flecked, o/w VG. Howes B 718. *Cahan.* $125/£81

BRAMAH, ERNEST. English Farming and Why I Turned It Up. London: Leadenhall, 1894. 1st ed, 1st bk. Cl (sl sunned). Nice. *Ash.* $310/£200

BRAMAH, ERNEST. Kai Lung Unrolls His Mat. D-D, 1928. 1st ed. NF in VG + dj (lt wear). *Fine Books.* $150/£97

BRAMAH, ERNEST. Kai Lung Unrolls His Mat. London: Richards Press, 1928. 1st UK ed. VG + . *Williams.* $25/£16

BRAMAH, ERNEST. Kai Lung's Golden Hours. London: Grant Richards, 1922. 1st ed. VG. *Limestone.* $55/£35

BRAMAH, ERNEST. Kai Lung's Golden Hours. London: Grant Richards, 1922. 1st ed. Pict cl. Nice (sl dusty) in dj (lt browned). *Ash.* $194/£125

BRAMMER, WILLIAM. The Gay Place. H-M, 1961. 1st ed, 1st bk. Fine in VG + dj. *Fine Books.* $125/£81

BRAMWELL, B. Anaemia and Some of the Diseases of the Blood-Forming Organs and Ductless Glands. Edinburgh, 1899. (vii),450pp. Cl stained, dusty, worn, o/w VG. *Whitehart.* $62/£40

BRAMWELL, B. Diseases of the Spinal Cord. Edinburgh, 1895. 3rd ed. 659pp. Good. *Fye.* $100/£65

BRAMWELL, CRIGHTON and EDITH LONGSON. Heart Disease and Pregnancy. London, 1938. 1st ed. Good. *Fye.* $75/£48

BRANCH, E. DOUGLAS. Hunting of the Buffalo. NY, 1929. 1st ed. (Spots cvr.) *Heinoldt.* $35/£23

BRANCH, E. DOUGLAS. Hunting of the Buffalo. Appleton, 1929. 1st ed. 15 plts. VF in VG dj. *Oregon.* $75/£48

BRANCH, E. DOUGLAS. Westward. NY: D. Appleton, 1930. 1st ed. VG- (pencil underlining; hinge repaired). *Parker.* $25/£16

BRANCH-JOHNSON, W. The English Prison Hulks. London, (1957). 1st ed. Dj. *Lefkowicz.* $60/£39

Brand Book of the State of New Mexico. Issued by Cattle Sanitary Board of NM, (1915). 1st ed. All edges stained red as issued. *Shasky.* $300/£194

BRAND, CHRISTIANNA. Cat and Mouse. NY: Knopf, 1950. 1st Amer ed. Fine in dj. *Mordida.* $35/£23

BRAND, CHRISTIANNA. Green for Danger. NY: Dodd Mead, 1944. 1st Amer ed. Name on fep, o/w VG in dj (chipped, frayed; closed tears). *Mordida.* $45/£29

BRAND, CHRISTIANNA. Heaven Knows Who: The Trial of Jessie M'Lachlan. London: Michael Joseph, 1960. 1st ed. Pp dknd, o/w Fine in dj (sl wear; faint crease). *Mordida.* $65/£42

BRAND, CHRISTIANNA. Tour de Force. London: Michael Joseph, 1955. 1st ed. Fine in dj (price-clipped). *Mordida.* $65/£42

BRAND, JOHN. Observations on the Popular Antiquities of Great Britain. London: Henry Bohn, 1848-1849. 3 vols. Frontis, xx,539; frontis, v,(i),522; frontis, iv,499,(i)blank,32pp pub's list. (Neatly recased using orig backstrips, sides; sl loss of cl to spines.) *Peter Taylor.* $101/£65

BRAND, MAX. (Pseud of Frederick Faust.) The Blue Jay. H&S, 1926. 1st Eng ed. VG + in VG pict dj (inner reinforcement; chipping). *Fine Books.* $70/£45

BRAND, MAX. (Pseud of Frederick Faust.) Destry Rides Again. D-M, 1930. 1st ed. Good. *Fine Books.* $45/£29

BRAND, MAX. (Pseud of Frederick Faust.) Dr. Kildare Takes Charge. NY: Dodd-Mead, 1941. 1st ed. Faint tape shadows eps, else Fine in dj (minor wear, sm chip spine). *Else Fine.* $60/£39

BRAND, MAX. (Pseud of Frederick Faust.) The Happy Valley. D-M, 1931. 1st ed. VG + in VG dj (chipping; lt staining). *Fine Books.* $100/£65

BRAND, MAX. (Pseud of Frederick Faust.) Hunted Riders. D-M, 1935. 1st ed. VG + in pict dj (chipping; 2-inch closed tear). *Fine Books.* $85/£55

BRAND, MAX. (Pseud of Frederick Faust.) The Night Horseman. Putnams, 1920. 1st ed. VG. *Madle.* $40/£26

BRAND, MAX. (Pseud of Frederick Faust.) The Phantom Spy. NY: Dodd Mead, (1973). 1st ed. Fine in dj. *Mordida.* $35/£23

BRAND, MAX. (Pseud of Frederick Faust.) Pillar Mountain. NY: Dodd, Mead, (1928). 1st ed. NF in Fine illus dj. *Unger.* $250/£161

BRAND, MAX. (Pseud of Frederick Faust.) The Seventh Man. Putnams, 1921. 1st ed. VG. *Madle.* $40/£26

BRAND, MAX. (Pseud of Frederick Faust.) Trailin'! Putnam, 1920. 1st ed. Nice. *Fine Books.* $35/£23

BRAND, MAX. (Pseud of Frederick Faust.) Wine on the Desert. NY: Dodd, Mead, 1940. 1st ed. NF in VG + dj (spine lt faded; extrems lt chipped). *Lame Duck.* $300/£194

BRANDAU, R.S. (ed). History of Homes and Gardens of Tennessee. (Nashville): Garden Study Club of Nashville, 1936. 1st ed. One of 1500. Eps sl foxed, inscrip, margins lt browned; worn, spine shaken, else VG. *Bookpress.* $350/£226

BRANDAU, R.S. (ed). History of Homes and Gardens of Tennessee. Garden Study Club of Nashville, 1936. Ltd to 1500. Fine. *Quest.* $225/£145

BRANDEIS, LOUIS D. Other People's Money and How the Bankers Use It. NY: Frederick A. Stokes, 1914. 2nd ptg. Gilt. Cl worn, but sound. *Boswell.* $75/£48

BRANDEL, M. Rain Before Seven. Harpers, 1945. 1st ed, 1st bk. Fine in VG + dj (dust soil rear panel; spine chip). *Aronovitz.* $35/£23

BRANDER, J. Tristan Da Cunha 1506-1902. Allen & Unwin, 1940. 1st ed. VG + in VG dj. *Walcot.* $56/£36

BRANDON, JOHN G. The One-Minute Murder. NY: Dial, 1935. 1st ed. Fine in VG dj (chipping, tears). *Mordida.* $35/£23

BRANDT, BILL. Camera in London. London: Focal Press, (1948). 1st ed. Margins, eps lt browned, else VG in dj (worn, torn). *Bookpress.* $45/£29

BRANDT, BILL. Perspective of Nudes. NY: Amphoto, 1961. 1st ed. 90 photo plts ptd in gravure. Patterned bds. Closed tear 1 plt, else NF in illus dj (sm chip spine end). *Cahan.* $235/£152

BRANDT, BILL. Shadow of Light. NY: Da Capo Press, 1977. 1st Amer ed. 144 b/w plts. Owner stamp, else VG in dj (lt worn). *Cahan.* $100/£65

BRANHAM, LEVI. My Life and Travels. Dalton, GA: A.J. Showalter, 1929. 1st ed. Minor damping, sm tape repair lower margin; else VG in ptd wrappers. *Mcgowan.* $375/£242

BRANKSTON, A.D. Early Ming Wares of Chingtechen. Hong Kong/London, 1970. One of 1050. Color frontis; 44 b/w plts; sketch map. Dj (sl soiled; chipped, sl loss spine head). *Edwards.* $70/£45

BRANNER, ROBERT. St. Louis and the Court Style in Gothic Architecture. London, 1965. 160 illus on plts. Good. *Washton.* $200/£129

BRANNON, PETER A. The Organization of the Confederate Post Office Department at Montgomery and A Story of the Thomas Welsh Provisional Stamped Envelope.... Montgomery: The author, 1960. Signed. VG (pencil underlining) in VG- dj. *Book Broker.* $85/£55

BRAQUE, GEORGES. Georges Braque: His Graphic Work. NY: Abrams, (1961). 1st Amer ed. Fine in dj (lt soiled). *Hermitage.* $75/£48

BRASHER, MINNIE M. Mark Twain: Son of Missouri. Chapel Hill: Univ of NC Press, 1934. 1st ed. As New in illus dj. *Cahan.* $40/£26

BRASHLER, WILLIAM. Josh Gibson. Harper & Row, 1978. 1st ed. Fine in VG dj (lt worn). *Plapinger.* $100/£65

BRASSEY, LORD. The Navy Annual 1886. Portsmouth: Griffin, 1886. 100 plts. (Backstrip sl rubbed.) *Petersfield.* $124/£80

BRASSEY, MRS. A Voyage in the 'Sunbeam'—Our Home on the Ocean for Eleven Months. Chicago: Belford, Clarke, 1883. Frontis, xiv,511pp; fldg color map; 6 plts. Pict grn cl. VG. *Petrilla.* $45/£29

BRASSEY, MRS. A Voyage in the 'Sunbeam.' Chicago, 1881. Frontis, xiv,511pp, fldg map. Gilt device upper bd, spine (lt spotted). *Edwards.* $59/£38

BRASSEY, T.A. (ed). The Naval Annual. London, 1896. Contents VG (binding worn, roughly rebacked). *Petersfield.* $78/£50

BRATT, JOHN. Trails of Yesterday. Lincoln: University Publishing, 1921. 1st ed. Signed presentation by Mrs. Bratt. VG. Howes B 725. *Perier.* $295/£190

BRAUN, ALFRED and ISADORE FRIESNER. The Labyrinth: An Aid to the Study of Inflammations of the Internal Ear. NY, 1913. Good. *Fye.* $75/£48

BRAUN, HUGH. The Story of the English House. London: Batsford, 1940. 1st ed. VG in dj (sl worn). *Hollett.* $23/£15

BRAUN, LILLIAN JACKSON. The Cat Who Ate Danish Modern. Dutton, 1967. 1st ed. NF in dj (lt soiled). *Murder.* $100/£65

BRAUNTON, ERNEST. The Garden Beautiful in California. LA, 1940. 2nd ed. 18 b/w plts. VG in dj (lt chipped). *Brooks.* $27/£17

BRAUTIGAN, RICHARD. The Abortion. NY: S&S, (1971). 1st ed, hb issue. Orange cl. Fine in dj (few scuffs; tiny tears; internal tape repair; price-clipped). *Antic Hay.* $150/£97

BRAUTIGAN, RICHARD. The Abortion: An Historical Romance 1966. Cape, 1973. 1st Eng ed. Spine head sl bumped, else NF in NF dj. *Fine Books.* $65/£42

BRAUTIGAN, RICHARD. The Abortion: An Historical Romance 1966. London: Cape, 1973. 1st UK ed. Rev copy, pub's slip laid in. NF in dj (sl edgeworn, price-clipped). *Sclanders.* $34/£22

BRAUTIGAN, RICHARD. All Watched Over by Machines of Loving Grace. (SF): Communication Co, (1967). 1st ed, ltd to 1500. VG in stapled yellow ptd wrappers. *Godot.* $300/£194

BRAUTIGAN, RICHARD. A Confederate General from Big Sur. NY, (1964). 1st ed. VG in dj. *King.* $150/£97

BRAUTIGAN, RICHARD. A Confederate General from Big Sur. NY: Grove, 1964. 1st ed. Edges sl dusty; head, tail spine sl tender; o/w NF. Dj (lt rubbed, lt creasing spine ends). *Sclanders.* $101/£65

BRAUTIGAN, RICHARD. A Confederate General from Big Sur. London: Cape, 1970. 1st UK ed. Corner bumped, o/w NF. Dj (price-clipped, sl edgewear). *Sclanders.* $28/£18

BRAUTIGAN, RICHARD. Dreaming of Babylon. NY: Delacorte/Lawrence, 1977. 1st ed. Fine in Fine dj. *Janus.* $35/£23

BRAUTIGAN, RICHARD. The Hawkline Monster. S&S, 1974. 1st ed. Fine in dj (price-clipped). *Stahr.* $25/£16

BRAUTIGAN, RICHARD. In Watermelon Sugar. London: Cape, 1970. 1st UK ed. NF in dj. *Sclanders.* $39/£25

BRAUTIGAN, RICHARD. The Pill Versus the Springhill Mine Disaster. SF: Four Seasons Foundation, 1968. 1st ed, pb orig. Name stamp t.p., else VG in wrappers. *Pettler.* $45/£29

BRAUTIGAN, RICHARD. The Pill Versus the Springhill Mine Disaster. London: Cape, 1970. 1st UK ed. NF in dj. *Sclanders.* $39/£25

BRAUTIGAN, RICHARD. Please Plant This Book. SF/Santa Barbara: Graham Mackintosh, 1968. Card folded to create 2 pockets, w/seed packets laid in, each containing seeds. NF (lacks 2 packets). *Sclanders.* $310/£200

BRAUTIGAN, RICHARD. Please Plant This Book. SF: Graham Mackintosh, 1968. 1st ed. 8 seed packets each w/poem ptd on it in ptd cardboard folder. VG (sl foxing, 1 sl dampstain); seeds & packets Fine. *Between The Covers.* $750/£484

BRAUTIGAN, RICHARD. Revenge of the Lawn. NY: S&S, 1971. NF in dj (sl wear head of spine). *Sclanders.* $39/£25

BRAUTIGAN, RICHARD. Rommel Drives on Deep into Egypt. NY: Delacorte Press, (1970). 1st ed. Pict cl. Long tear fep, else NF in dj. *Godot.* $45/£29

BRAUTIGAN, RICHARD. Sombrero Fallout. NY: S&S, 1976. 1st ed. NF in dj. *Sclanders.* $31/£20

BRAUTIGAN, RICHARD. The Tokyo-Montana Express. NY: Targ Editions, (1979). 1st ed. Ltd to 350 signed. As New in glassine dj. *Jaffe.* $250/£161

BRAUTIGAN, RICHARD. The Tokyo-Montana Express. NY: Targ Editions, (1979). Signed ltd ed of 350. Fine in glassine dj. *Antic Hay.* $175/£113

BRAUTIGAN, RICHARD. The Tokyo-Montana Express. London: Cape, (1981). 1st Eng ed. Blue cl-backed white paper bds. NF in dj. *Cady.* $15/£10

BRAUTIGAN, RICHARD. The Tokyo-Montana Express. London: Cape, 1981. 1st UK ed. NF in dj. *Sclanders.* $23/£15

BRAUTIGAN, RICHARD. Trout Fishing in America. London: Cape, 1970. 1st UK ed. NF in dj (sl edgeworn). *Sclanders.* $47/£30

BRAUTIGAN, RICHARD. Willard and His Bowling Trophies, a Perverse Mystery. London: Jonathan Cape, (1976). 1st Eng ed. Fine in dj (backstrip faded). *Heller.* $45/£29

BRAUTIGAN, RICHARD. Willard and His Bowling Trophies. S&S, 1975. 1st ed. Fine (rmdr mk, price in marker) in dj. *Stahr.* $25/£16

BRAUTIGAN, RICHARD. Willard and His Bowling Trophies. NY: S&S, 1975. 1st ed. NF in dj. *Sclanders.* $31/£20

BRAVERMAN, KATE. Lithium for Medea. NY: Harper & Row, (1979). 1st ed. VG in dj (crumpled fr edge; chip). *Hermitage.* $25/£16

BRAY, MARY M. A Sea Trip in Clipper Ship Days. Boston: Badger, (1920). 1st ed. (Lacks fep.) *Ginsberg.* $100/£65

BRAY, N.N.E. Shifting Sands. London: Unicorn, 1934. 1st ed. Frontis; fldg map. Overall Good+. *Great Epic.* $75/£48

BRAYER, GARNET M. and HERBERT O. American Cattle Trails 1540-1900. Bayside, NY: Western Range Cattle Indus, 1952. 1st ed. Pp yellowed, else VG in pict wrappers (lt soiled). *Glenn.* $35/£23

BRAYLEY, EDWARD WEDLAKE. A Topographical History of Surrey. Dorking/London: Robert Best Ede/Tilt & Bogue, 1841(-1848). 1st ed. 5 vols. 129 plts; tp red/black. Orig polished calf, spines gilt, red/grn spine labels. Excellent set (sm mks cvrs). *Bickersteth.* $442/£285

BRAZIER, MARY. A History of the Electrical Activity of the Brain: The First Half-Century. London, 1961. 1st ed. (Ex-lib.) *Fye.* $100/£65

BRAZIL, ANGELA. A Terrible Tomboy. London: Gay & Bird, 1904. 1st ed. Pict cl (sl rubbed, dknd). Good. *Ash.* $225/£145

Bread-Winners, a Social Study. (By John Hay.) NY: Harper, 1884. 1st ed, this copy w/o 'The End' on p319. Dec grn cl (sl dust-spotted). Ink inscrip, o/w VG. BAL 7762. *Reese.* $25/£16

BREASTED, CHARLES. Pioneer to the Past: The Story of James Henry Breasted, Archaeologist.... NY: Scribner's, 1943. Frontis port. (Bkpl.) *Archaeologia.* $45/£29

BREASTED, JAMES HENRY. A History of Egypt from the Earliest Times to the Persian Conquest. NY: Scribner's, (1926). 2nd ed. 13 maps. (Sig, spine nicked.) *Archaeologia.* $75/£48

BREASTED, JAMES HENRY. A History of Egypt from the Earliest Times to the Persian Conquest. NY: Scribner's, 1942. 2nd ed. Sl rubbed, o/w VG. *Worldwide.* $40/£26

BREASTED, JAMES HENRY. A History of Egypt. London, 1920. 2nd ed. Color frontis, 13 maps (1 fldg). Blue cl (rebound, orig upper bd laid down). *Edwards.* $39/£25

BREBNER, JOHN B. The Explorers of North America 1492-1806. London: A&C Black, 1933. 1st ed. Blue cl. NF. *Chapel Hill.* $75/£48

BREBNER, JOHN B. The Explorers of North America: 1492-1806. V.T. Harlow & J.A. Williamson (eds). London: A&C Black, 1933. 1st ed. 3 fldg maps. VG in dj (sl rubbing; nicks, creases). *Houle.* $75/£48

BRECHT, BERTOLT. Tales from the Calendar. Yvonne Kapp & Michael Hamburger (trans). London: Methuen, (1961). 1st Eng ed. NF in dj. *Hermitage.* $35/£23

BRECHT, BERTOLT. The Trial of Lucullus. H.R. Hays (trans). (NY): New Directions, (1943). Hb ed. Fine in dj (spine sl used). *Pharos.* $30/£19

BREDON, JULIET. Peking. A Historical and Intimate Description.... Shanghai: Kelly & Walsh, 1922. 2nd ed. 6 fldg maps, 24 b/w photo plts. Black/gilt pict orange cl. VG. *House.* $70/£45

BREEN, PATRICK. Diary of Patrick Breen, One of the Donner Party. Berkeley: Univ of CA, 1910. 1st complete ed. Facs frontis. Fine in orig brn ptd wrappers. *Harrington.* $45/£29

BREEN, PATRICK. Diary of Patrick Breen, One of the Donner Party. Frederick J. Teggart (ed). Berkeley: Univ of CA, 1910. 1st ed. Photo plt frontis. Ptd wrappers. VG. *Shasky.* $35/£23

BREESKIN, ADELYN. Mary Cassatt. Washington, 1979. 2nd ed, rev. One of 200 signed. Leather-backed patterned bds. Aeg. Fine in slipcase. *Argosy.* $350/£226

BREESKIN, ADELYN. Milton Avery. Smithsonian, 1969. 125 repros. VG in ptd wrappers. *Argosy.* $40/£26

BREHM, ALFRED EDMUND. From North Pole to Equator. J. Arthur Thomson (ed). Margaret R. Thomson (trans). London: Blackie & Son, 1896. 1st Eng ed. xxxi,592pp. Orig pict cl gilt (extrems worn; spine label removed; 2 abraded lengths upper bd); teg. (Label removed from flyleaf; 1st section sl loose.) *Hollett.* $47/£30

BREIHAN, CARL W. The Complete and Authentic Life of Jesse James. NY: Frederick Fell, (1953). New, rev ed. Red paper over bds. Fine in NF dj. *Glenn.* $35/£23

BREIHAN, CARL W. The Complete and Authentic Life of Jesse James. NY, 1953. 1st ed. NF (sig, date) in dj (sl tears). *Baade.* $32/£21

BREIHAN, CARL W. The Day Jesse James Was Killed. NY: Frederick Fell, (1961). 1st ed. (Bumped.) Dj (lt worn; price-clipped). *Glenn.* $25/£16

BREIHAN, CARL W. The Killer Legions of Quantrill. Seattle, WA: Hangman, 1971. 1st ed. Pict bds. NF. *Glenn.* $30/£19

BREIHAN, CARL W. and CHARLES A. ROSAMOND. The Bandit Belle. Seattle: Hangman, 1970. 1st ed. Red pict fabricoid over bds. Fine. *Glenn.* $30/£19

BREIHAN, CARL W. and WAYNE MONTGOMERY. Forty Years on the Wild Frontier. Greenwich, (1985). 1st ed. Fine in Fine dj. *Pratt.* $30/£19

BREMER, FREDERIKA. The Homes of the New World. Mary Howitt (trans). NY: Harper, 1853. 1st US ed. 2 vols. VG (fr hinge of cl sl wormed; internal soiling). Howes B745. *Second Life.* $325/£210

BREMNER, M.D.K. The Story of Dentistry from the Dawn of Civilization to the Present. Brooklyn, NY, 1939. 20 plts. (Lib label remains inside fr cvr; 2 rubber date stamps fep; short slit top of upper joint.) *Bickersteth.* $54/£35

BREMNER, M.D.K. The Story of Dentistry. NY, 1946. 2nd ed. 39 plts. (Ink sig; spine sl worn; cl sl dust-stained.) *Whitehart.* $93/£60

BRENAN, GERALD. The Face of Spain. London: Turnstile Press, 1950. 1st ed. Fine in pict dj. *Patterson.* $54/£35

BRENAN, GERALD. The Spanish Labyrinth. Cambridge: CUP, 1943. 1st ed. Fine in pict dj. *Patterson.* $101/£65

BRENNAN, JOSEPH PAYNE. Nightmare Need. Arkham House, 1964. 1st ed. Fine in NF dj (lt wear). *Madle.* $200/£129

BRENNAN, JOSEPH PAYNE. Nightmare Need. Sauk City: Arkham House, 1964. 1st ed. One of 500. NF in dj (spine lt rubbed). *Other Worlds.* $250/£161

BRENNAN, JOSEPH PAYNE. Nine Horrors and a Dream. Arkham House, 1958. 1st ed. Fine in dj. *Madle.* $150/£97

BRENNAN, JOSEPH PAYNE. Nine Horrors: And a Dream. Sauk City: Arkham House, 1958. 1st ed. Fine in Fine dj. *Other Worlds.* $200/£129

BRENNAN, JOSEPH PAYNE. A Select Bibliography of H.P.L. By author, 1952. 1st ed. One of 150. Fine in wraps. *Madle.* $75/£48

BRENNAN, JOSEPH PAYNE. Stories of Darkness and Dread. Sauk City: Arkham House, 1973. 1st ed. Fine in Fine dj. *Other Worlds.* $35/£23

BRENNAN, JOSEPH PAYNE. The Wind of Time. (Sauk City): H&W Press, 1961. 1st ed. Fine in NF dj. *Other Worlds.* $125/£81

BRENNECKE, J. The Hunters and the Hunted. NY, 1957. VG in VG dj. *Clark.* $45/£29

BRENNER, ANITA. The Wind That Swept Mexico. NY, 1943. 1st ed. VG (tape mks on cvrs). *Bond.* $25/£16

BRENNER, ANITA. The Wind That Swept Mexico: The History of the Mexican Revolution 1910-1942. NY: Harper & Row, (1943). 4th ed. VG in dj (worn, lacks pieces). *Aka.* $40/£26

BRENT, JOSEPH LANCASTER. Memoirs of the War between the States. (New Orleans: Fontana Ptg Co, 1940.) 1st ed. Ltd to 100 ptd. 1/2 leather w/antique marbled paper. Howes B 746. *Mcgowan.* $850/£548

BRENTANO, CLEMENS. The Tale of Gockle, Hinkle and Gackeliah. Doris Orgel (trans). NY: Random House, 1961. 1st ed. Maurice Sendak (illus). 7.5x9.5. 144pp. Fine in dj (w/glassine wrap). *Cattermole.* $125/£81

BREON, JOHN. The Sorrows of Travel. NY: Putnam, (1955). 1st ed. NF in dj (torn, lacks piece). *Pharos.* $20/£13

Brer Rabbit's Holiday with Pop-Up Pictures. London: Birn Bros, n.d. (196?). 23x17 cm. 4 dbl-pg pop-ups. Glazed pict bds. VG. *Book Finders.* $40/£26

BRERA, VALERIAN. A Treatise on Verminous Diseases, Preceded by the Natural History of Intestinal Worms.... Boston, 1817. 1st Eng trans. 368pp; 5 fldg plts. (Recent leather spine label; outer hinges cracked.) *Fye.* $200/£129

BRERETON, F.S. The Great Aeroplane. Blackie, (1911). Pict cl. NF in VG dj (chip fr panel). *Aronovitz.* $125/£81

BRESHKOVSKY, CATHERINE. The Little Grandmother of the Russian Revolution: Reminiscences and Letters. Alice Stone Blackwell (ed). Boston: Little, Brown, 1917, 18. Later issue. Name, symbol fep. *Aka.* $20/£13

BRESLIN, JIMMY. Can't Anyone Here Play This Game? Viking, 1963. 1st ed. Fine in Fine dj. *Plapinger.* $40/£26

BRETON, NICHOLAS. The Twelve Months. Brian Rhys (ed). London: Golden Cockerel, 1927. #189/500 numbered. Orange buckram, gilt. Spine sl fraying; 4 glue spots, sl offsetting fep, else VG. *Hermitage.* $150/£97

BRETT, SIMON. The Dead Side of the Mike. London: Gollancz, 1980. 1st ed. Handwritten letter from Brett laid in. VF in dj. *Mordida.* $85/£55

BRETT, SIMON. Situation Tragedy. London: Gollancz, 1981. 1st ed. VF in dj. *Silver Door.* $35/£23

BREUIL, HENRI. Four Hundred Centuries of Cave Art. Montignac, Dordogne: Centre d'Etudes et De Documentation Prehistorique, (1952). Ltd to 500 numbered. 4 double-pg color plts. Beige linen stamped in brn (sl soiled), mtd cvr illus. *Karmiole.* $50/£32

BREWER, DOUGLAS J. and RENEE F. FRIEDMAN. Fish and Fishing in Ancient Egypt. Warminster: Aris & Phillips, (1989). Good in dj. *Archaeologia.* $85/£55

BREWER, GIL. 13 French Street. NY: Gold Medal, 1951. 1st ed. Fine in wraps. *Beasley.* $25/£16

BREWER, GIL. So Rich, So Dead. NY: Gold Medal, 1951. 1st ed. Fine in wraps. *Beasley.* $25/£16

BREWER, JOSIAH. A Residence at Constantinople, in the Year 1827. New Haven: Durrie & Peck, 1830. 2nd ed. Fldg engr frontis, 384pp (foxing); fldg hand-colored map at back. Contemp calf, gilt black leather spine label. *Karmiole.* $200/£129

BREWER, LEIGHTON. Virgin Waters. NY: Coward McCann, 1941. 1st ed. VG+ in dj. *Bowman.* $30/£19

BREWER, WILLIAM H. Up and Down California in 1860-1864. New Haven: Yale, 1930. 1st ed. VG (bkpl). Howes B 754. *Parker.* $150/£97

BREWER, WILLIS. Alabama: Her History, Resources, War Record, and Public Men. From 1540 to 1872. Montgomery, AL: Barrett & Brown, 1872. 1st ed. 712pp. Later cl. Working copy (ex libris, 2 perf lib stamps; chipping at edges of title, last pg). Howes B 755. *Mcgowan.* $450/£290

BREWERTON, GEORGE. Incidents of Travel in New Mexico. Ashland: Lewis Osborne, 1969. 1st thus. Ep map. Fine. *Oregon.* $35/£23

BREWERTON, GEORGE. Overland with Kit Carson. NY: Coward-McCann, 1930. 1st ed. Map. VG. *Pharos.* $45/£29

BREWINGTON, M.V. Shipcarvers of North America. Barre, 1962. 1st ed. Fine in dj. *Lefkowicz.* $75/£48

BREWINGTON, M.V. and DOROTHY. The Marine Paintings and Drawings in the Peabody Museum. Salem, MA, 1981. 2 vols. 74 color plts. Djs (vol 1 spine sl torn, repaired). *Edwards.* $271/£175

BREWSTER, GEORGE (ed). The Western Literary Magazine and Journal of Education, Science, Arts and Morals. Cleveland: By the ed, 1854. Signed in type by ed. 400pp, 16 full-pg engrs. *Hayman.* $60/£39

BREWSTER, WILLIAM. The Birds of the Cambridge Region of Massachusetts. Cambridge: Nuttall Ornithological Club, 1906. 4 plts, 3 maps. Brewster bkpls laid in. (Fr hinge rough.) *Schoyer.* $75/£48

BREYTENBACH, BREYTEN. The True Confessions of an Albino Terrorist. London: Faber & Faber, 1984. 1st ed. Inscribed. Fine in Fine dj. *Lame Duck.* $100/£65

BRICE, JAMES. Reminiscences of Ten Years Experience on the Western Plains. Kansas City: James Brice, (1907?). 6 full-pg dwgs. Ptd wrappers. *Dawson.* $250/£161

BRICE, WALLACE A. History of Fort Wayne, from the Earliest Known Accounts of This Point, to the Present Period.... Fort Wayne: D.W. Jones, 1868. 1st ed. xvi,324,33pp, 7 plts. Lt wear spine ends, foxing, else VG. Howes B 761. *Cahan.* $225/£145

BRICKELL, JOHN. The Natural History of North Carolina with an Account of the Trade, Manners, and Customs.... (Raleigh: Rptd by authority of Trustees of Pub Lib, 1911.) Fldg map; 4 plts. VG (bkpl). Howes B 762. *Cahan.* $200/£129

BRICKETT, ALBERT W. Sackett on Instructions to Juries.... Chicago: Callaghan and Co, 1908. 3rd ed. 3 vols. *Boswell.* $75/£48

Brickwork in Italy. Chicago: Amer Face Brick Assoc, 1925. 1st ed. Frontis, map. (Text lt yellowed; name; spine, edges worn.) *Bookpress.* $35/£23

BRIDGE, JAMES HOWARD. Millionaires and Grub Street. NY: Brentano's, 1931. 1st ed. Frontis port. Untrimmed. NF. *Connolly.* $50/£32

BRIDGES, R. Overheard in Arcady. Scribners, 1894. 1st ed. White cl, gold-gilt pict stamping. Fine in dj (sl chipped). *Fine Books.* $150/£97

BRIDGES, ROBERT. The Feast of Bacchus. Oxford: Privately ptd by H. Daniel, 1889. 1st ed. Ltd to 105 (this unnumbered). (8),94,(2)pp; uncut. Orig vellum-backed bds (sl rubbed, soiled, short split). Good. Cox. $186/£120

BRIDGES, ROBERT. The Testament of Beauty. NY, 1929. One of 250 numbered. VG in slipcase. Argosy. $125/£81

BRIDGES, ROBERT. The Testament of Beauty. NY, 1930. 1st Amer trade ed. As New. Bond. $20/£13

BRIDGES, T.C. Martin Crusoe: A Boy's Adventure on Wizard Island. London: George G. Harrap, 1920. 1st ed. Full color frontis; 4 b/w plts; map. Spine sl dknd, o/w Nice. Temple. $22/£14

Brief Extracts from High Authorities Exposing the Evils of Vaccination.... Providence, RI, 1891. 1st Amer ed. 188pp. Good. Fye. $100/£65

Brief Memoir Concerning Abel Thomas.... Phila: Benjamin & Thomas Kite, 1824. 51pp. Related clippings pasted to eps, o/w VG. Hayman. $35/£23

Brief Record of the Advance of the Egyptian Expeditionary Force under the Command of General Sir Edmund H.H. Allenby. London: HMSO, 1919. 2nd ed. Frontis port, 55 full-pg maps. Pub's cl backstrip, ptd paper bds (sl rubbed, sl soiled). Good. Peter Taylor. $54/£35

Brief Record of the Advance of the Egyptian Expeditionary Force.... London: HMSO, 1919. 2nd ed (1st ed pub by 'The Palestine News'). Port, 56 full-pg maps. Ptd bds, cl spine. Bickersteth. $171/£110

BRIEGER, PIETER. English Art 1216-1307. Oxford, 1968. 2nd ed. 96 plts. Good. Washton. $65/£42

Brigand Captain. Beadle's New Dime Novel. No. 328. ca 1880. Last # listed on back cvr is #382. VG (cvr chipped, 2 pieces cut out) in wraps (fragile). Book Market. $30/£19

BRIGANTI, GIULIANO. The View Painters of Europe. (London): Phaidon, (1970). 1st ed in English. Ink inscrip fep, spine sl shaken; else Fine. Bookpress. $100/£65

Briggs and Co., Patent Transfer Papers. NY: Briggs & Co, (1882). 8vo. 156pp; pp98-99, 119-124 illus by Kate Greenaway. Blue cl, gilt. VG. Davidson. $100/£65

BRIGGS, BARBARA. Trees of Britain. London, 1936. 1st ed. (Feps lt browned.) Dj (dknd, chipped). Edwards. $39/£25

BRIGGS, L. VERNON. Arizona and New Mexico, 1882. Boston: Privately ptd, 1932. 1st ed. (10),282pp. (Sl soiled.) Ginsberg. $125/£81

BRIGGS, MARTIN SHAW. Muhammadan Architecture in Egypt and Palestine. Oxford: Clarendon, 1924. 1st ed. Frontis. Partially unopened. Spine sl sunned, o/w VG. Bookpress. $325/£210

BRIGGS, R.A. Bungalows and Country Residences. London: B.T. Batsford, 1891. 1st ed. 29 litho plts. Orig blue cl, gilt. Good. Karmiole. $75/£48

BRIGGS, RAYMOND. Fungus the Bogeyman Plop-Up Book. London: Hamish Hamilton Children's Books, 1982. 19x27 cm. 7 dbl-pg 'plop-ups.' Glazed pict bds. VG. Book Finders. $50/£32

BRIGGS, RICHARD. The New Art of Cookery, According to the Present Practice. Phila: For W. Spotswood, R. Campbell & B. Johnson, 1792. 1st Amer ed. 557pp + ads. Later sheep (lacks fep; sig; sl staining, foxing; closely trimmed by binder). Argosy. $500/£323

BRIGHAM, CLARENCE. Paul Revere's Engravings. NY: Atheneum, 1969. 2nd ed, rev. 77 plts (3 color). Sound in dj. Ars Artis. $54/£35

BRIGHAM, CLARENCE. Paul Revere's Engravings. NY: Atheneum, 1969. Revised ed. 1 fldg illus. Red/blue cl. Good in dj. Karmiole. $60/£39

BRIGHAM, WILLIAM T. Guatemala. NY: Scribner's, 1887. 1st ed. 8vo. xv,(i)blank,453,(3),(14)ads, half title, 4 maps, charts (3 fldg), 24 plts incl frontis. Grn cl, dec in black/gilt. Good (blank leaf at end torn away; bkpl, spine, corners sl rubbed). Morrell. $147/£95

BRIGHT, JOHN. Speeches of John Bright, M.P. on the American Question. Boston: Little, Brown, 1865. 1st ed. Engr frontis port. xvi,278pp. Grn gilt cl (lt rubbed). Karmiole. $45/£29

BRIGHT, RICHARD. Travels from Vienna Through Lower Hungary...In the Year 1814. Edinburgh: for Archibald Constable, 1818. 1st ed, 1st bk. 4to. Frontis, 642(102)pp, 9 plts, 2 fldg maps. Teg. Untrimmed, errata slip tipped in. Later 19th cent calf (rebacked, orig spine neatly laid down). Traces of foxing, else Nice. Chapel Hill. $500/£323

BRIGHT, W. Bright's Single Stem, Dwarf and Renewal System of Grape Culture. Phila, 1860. 1st ed. 123pp + (2pp ads). Flexible cl (spine faded; lt soiled, spot; fr hinge reinforced w/tape). Sutton. $55/£35

BRILLAT-SAVARIN, JEAN. Physiologie du Gout, a Handbook of Gastronomy. NY: J.W. Bouton, 1884. Later ed. 52 orig etchings. Teg. Burgundy morocco-backed bds (rubbed); French signed binding, gilt. Glenn. $125/£81

BRINCKERHOFF, SIDNEY B. and ODIE B. FAULK. Lancers for the King. Phoenix: AZ Hist Found, 1965. Fldg map. Gold-stamped cl. Dj (part sunned). Dawson. $75/£48

BRININSTOOL, E.A. A Trooper with Custer and Other Historic Incidents of the Battle of Little Big Horn. Columbus, OH: Hunter-Trader-Trapper Co, 1925. Errata slip tipped in. Gold cl. Soil; else VG. Bohling. $60/£39

BRINK, ANDRE. Rumours of Rain. London: W.H. Allen, 1978. 1st British ed. NF in NF dj. Lame Duck. $45/£29

BRINKLEY, JOHN. Lettering Today. London: Studio Vista, 1964. 1st ed. VG in dj (sl torn, lacks sm piece). Michael Taylor. $31/£20

BRINKLEY, WILLIAM. Don't Go Near the Water. NY: Random House, 1956. 1st ed. Fine (sl wear) in NF dj. Revere. $35/£23

BRINLEY, FRANCIS. Life of William T. Porter. NY: Appleton, 1860. 1st ed. (7),273pp; port. Ginsberg. $200/£129

BRINNIN, JOHN MALCOLM. Dylan Thomas in America. Boston: Little, Brown, (1955). 1st ed. Fine in dj. Pharos. $35/£23

BRINNIN, JOHN MALCOLM. No Arch, No Triumph. NY: Knopf, 1945. 1st ed. Inscribed. Fine in dj (used). Pharos. $125/£81

BRINNIN, JOHN MALCOLM. The Third Rose. Little Brown, 1959. 1st ed. VG in VG dj. Bishop. $20/£13

BRINTON, DANIEL G. Essays of an Americanist. Phila: Porter & Coates, 1890. 489pp. VG. Schoyer. $100/£65

BRISAC, CATHERINE. A Thousand Years of Stained Glass. Geoffrey Culverwell (trans). NY: Doubleday, 1986. VG in dj. Hollett. $47/£30

BRISBIN, JAMES. The Beef Bonanza. Phila: Lippincott, 1885. 222pp + 6pp ads, 8 plts. Bright pict cl. VG. Howes B 780. Schoyer. $100/£65

BRISTOL, WALTER W. The Story of the Ojai Valley. Ojai: Ojai Pub Co, (1946). Frontis. Grn-stamped cl. (Lt marginal stain; gathering partly sprung.) *Dawson.* $40/£26

BRISTOW, JOHN S. et al. Diseases of the Intestines and Peritoneum. NY: William Wood, 1879. 1st Amer ed. 243pp. Emb dec cl. VG. *Glaser.* $45/£29

BRISTOW, JOSEPH QUAYLE. Tales of Old Fort Gibson. NY: Exposition Press, (1961). 1st ed. VG in dj. *Lien.* $25/£16

BRISTOW, JOSEPH. Tales of Old Fort Gibson Exposition Press, (1961). 1st ed. VG in Good+ dj. *Oregon.* $35/£23

BRISTOWE, W.S. The Comity of Spiders. NY, 1968. Rpt. 2 vols. 22 plts. *Wheldon & Wesley.* $116/£75

British Historical Portraits. A Selection from the National Portrait Gallery.... Cambridge, 1957. Good. *Washton.* $35/£23

British Sports and Sportsmen: The Story of Shipping. London: Sports & Sportsmen, n.d. (ca 1921). 1st ed. One of 1000. 10 photogravures, 8 color plts. Orig morocco, gilt (spine ends sl rubbed). *Lefkowicz.* $175/£113

BRITTEN, EMMA. The Electric Physician, or Self-Cure Through Electricity. Boston, 1875. 1st ed. 59pp. Contents Fine (binding faded). *Fye.* $100/£65

BRITTEN, F.J. Old Clocks and Watches and Their Makers. London, (1932). 6th ed. Orig cl, new black leather backstrip gilt. (Sl bumped.) *Petersfield.* $124/£80

BRITTON, JOHN and EDWARD WEDLAKE BRAYLEY. Beauties of England and Wales. London, 1801-18. 19 vols in 26. 8vo. 2 fldg maps. Rebound in green buckram, gilt. Occasional lt foxing, sm lib stamp tps, few pencil mks, else VG set. *Cahan.* $1,000/£645

BRITTON, JOHN and EDWARD WEDLAKE BRAYLEY. Memoirs of the Tower of London: Comprising Historical and Descriptive Accounts.... London: Hurst, Chance, & Co, 1830. 3/4 calf over marbled bds (rubbed). *Boswell.* $175/£113

BRITTON, JOHN. A Dictionary of the Architecture and Archaeology of the Middle Ages. London: Longman, 1838. Inscribed presentation. Frontis, xvi+xviii+498pp (margins lt browned);   39 engr plts; marbled eps. Mod gilt-edged calf (rebound), dec motifs, raised bands. *Edwards.* $209/£135

BRITTON, ROSWELL S. The Chinese Periodical Press, 1800-1912. Shanghai: Kelly & Walsh, 1933. 1st ed. Red cl, gilt (faded). *Karmiole.* $65/£42

BROADFOOT, W. Billiards. London, 1896. Frontis, tp, xii,455pp (wrinkling, marginal staining p200 on; lt foxing), 10 plts. *Edwards.* $43/£28

BROADHEAD, G.C. et al. Report on the Geological Survey of the State of Missouri.... Jefferson City, 1874. 734,xlix,4pp; 24 plts. (Cl sl worn.) *Wheldon & Wesley.* $62/£40

BROADHEAD, G.C. et al. Reports on the Geological Survey of the State of Missouri, 1855-1871. Jefferson City, 1873. 324,vipp. 3 color plts, 9 dbl color maps. Good+ (spine faded, loose). *Bohling.* $85/£55

BROADLEY, A.M. Napoleon in Caricature 1795-1821. London, 1911. 2 vols. 24 color illus. Spines faded. *Argosy.* $225/£145

Broadside Ballads of the Restoration Period From the Jersey Collection.... London: John Lane, Bodley Head, 1930. #540/750. White linen spine, marbled linen bds (lt bumped); uncut. Contents Excellent. *Hartfield.* $285/£184

BROCK, HENRY IRVING. Colonial Churches in Virginia. Richmond: Dale Press, (1930). 1st ed. Cl-backed patterned bds. Fine. *Pharos.* $45/£29

BROCK, HENRY IRVING. Colonial Churches in Virginia. Richmond: Dale Press, (1930). 1st ed. Fine. *Pharos.* $45/£29

BROCK, LYNN. The Stoke Silver Case. NY: Harper, 1929. 1st Amer ed. VG in dj (internal tape repairs; chipping; closed tears; stamp). *Mordida.* $50/£32

BROCKETT, I.P. Epidemic and Contagious Diseases: Their History, Symptoms.... NY, 1873. 1st ed. 507pp. Full leather (rubbed). *Fye.* $250/£161

BRODER, PATRICIA JANIS. Bronzes of the American West. NY: Abrams, (1974). Gold-stamped cl. Dj. *Dawson.* $100/£65

BRODHEAD, JOHN ROMEYN. History of the State of New York, 1609-1691. NY, 1853, 1871. 1st ed. 2 vols. Thick 8vo. Orig cl (dampstain margin vol I; bindings don't match as published). *Argosy.* $300/£194

BRODHEAD, L.W. The Delaware Water Gap.... Phila: Sherman & Co., 1870. 1st ed. 276pp; color ptd frontis. Purple cl (spine faded), gilt. *Karmiole.* $50/£32

BRODIE, B.C. Lectures on the Diseases of the Urinary Organs. Phila: Lea & Blanchard, 1843. 1st Amer ed. vii,(9)-214,32(ads)pp (lt foxed). Contemp cl (sl worn); paper spine label (rubbed). VG. *Glaser.* $85/£55

BRODIE, B.C. Pathological and Surgical Observations on the Diseases of the Joints. London, 1834. 3rd ed. viii,344pp (prelims foxed). 1/2 cl, marbled bds. *Whitehart.* $140/£90

BRODIE, FAWN M. The Devil Drives. NY: Norton, 1967. 1st ed. 16 plts. Name whited out on 1/2 tp, o/w VG. *Worldwide.* $22/£14

BRODIE, FAWN M. The Devil Drives: A Life of Sir Richard Burton. NY: Norton, (1967). 1st ed. Fine in dj. *Sadlon.* $15/£10

BRODIE, FAWN M. No Man Knows My History. NY, 1945. 1st ed. Spine sunned, fr hinge tender, o/w VG+. *Benchmark.* $40/£26

BRODRICK, A. HOUGHTON (ed). Animals in Archaeology. London: Barrie & Jenkins, (1972). 9 color plts. Good in dj. *Archaeologia.* $45/£29

BRODRICK, GEORGE C. English Land and English Landlords. London et al: Cassell et al, 1881. viii,515pp+8pp pub ads. Brn cl stamped in gilt, blind. Largely unopened. VG. *Schoyer.* $75/£48

BRODY, SAUL. The Disease of the Soul. Ithaca, NY, 1974. 1st ed. Good. *Fye.* $25/£16

BRODZKY, ANNE TRUEBLOOD et al. Stones, Bones and Skin. Toronto: Soc for Art Pubs, 1977. 3-pg color fold-out. VG. *Blue Dragon.* $60/£39

BROGGER, A.W. and HAAKON SHETELIG. The Viking Ships, Their Ancestry and Evolution. L.A.: Knud K. Morgensen, (1953). 1st ed in Engligh. Fine in dj. *Lefkowicz.* $50/£32

BROMBERG, RUTH. Canaletto's Etchings. A Catalogue...Describing the Known States.... London, 1974. Good in dj. *Washton.* $300/£194

BROMELL, HENRY. The Slightest Distance. Boston: Houghton Mifflin, 1974. 1st ed. Fine in dj. *Pharos.* $20/£13

BROMFIELD, LOUIS. Animals and Other People. NY: Harper, (1955). 1st ed. Fine in NF dj (sl rubbed, nicks). *Between The Covers.* $50/£32

BROMFIELD, LOUIS. A Few Brass Tacks. NY, (1946). 1st ed. VG in dj (sl discolored, worn, sm tear). *King.* $25/£16

BROMFIELD, LOUIS. A Good Woman. NY: Frederick A. Stokes, 1927. 1st ed. Top edge foxed, else Fine in dj (spine faded, else Fine). *Godot.* $45/£29

BROMFIELD, LOUIS. The Strange Case of Miss Annie Spragg. Stokes, 1928. 1st ed. VG- in Nice dj (worn). *Fine Books.* $20/£13

BROMLEY, GEORGE T. The Long Ago and the Later On, or Recollections of Eighty Years. SF: A.M. Robertson, 1904. 1st trade ed. Frontis port. Red cl (spine faded, extrems sl worn). VG+. *Harrington.* $40/£26

BROMLEY, GEORGE T. The Long Ago and the Later On. SF, 1904. (Fr inner hinges sl weak; short scratch back cvr.) *Hayman.* $35/£23

BROMMELLE, N. and P. SMITH (eds). Conservation and Restoration of Pictorial Art. London: Butterworth, 1976. Sound in dj. *Ars Artis.* $70/£45

BRONAUGH, W.C. The Youngers' Fight for Freedom. Columbia, MO: The Author, 1906. 1st ed. Burgundy cl (sl wear). *Glenn.* $125/£81

BRONGERS, GEORG A. Nicotiana Tabacum. The History of Tobacco and Tobacco Smoking in the Netherlands. (Groningen): Theodore Niemeyer, (1964). VG in dj (chipped). *Schoyer.* $40/£26

BRONK, WILLIAM. Life Supports. SF: North Point, (1981). 1st ed. VF in dj. *Pharos.* $30/£19

BRONK, WILLIAM. That Tantalus. Elizabeth, 1971. 1st ed. Fine in dj (worn). *Poetry.* $23/£15

BRONSON, EDGAR BEECHER. In Closed Territory. Chicago: McClurg, 1910. 1st Amer ed. Emb lib stamp, sm repair head of spine, o/w VG. *Bowman.* $120/£77

BRONSON, WILFRID. Children of the Sea. NY: Harcourt Brace, (1940). 1st ed. 4to. Frontis; 12fp illus. Blue striated cl, navy lettering; map eps. VG. *Drusilla's.* $60/£39

BRONTE, CHARLOTTE and EMILY. The Life and Works of the Sisters Bronte. NY: Harper Bros, 1900. Haworth ed, illus w/photogravure ports, views. 7 vols. Grn cl. Fine. *Pharos.* $250/£161

BRONTE, EMILY. Poems. Selwyn & Blount, 1923. #185/500. Bkpl; offset on fly; bds sl dknd, o/w VG. *Poetry.* $47/£30

BRONTE, EMILY. Wuthering Heights. London: Duckworth, 1931. Claire Leighton (engrs). Frontis. Top edge red. Red maroon buckram over bds; gilt spine title. VG (edges lt faded). *Heller.* $225/£145

BROOKE, JOCELYN. The Crisis in Bulgaria or Ibsen to the Rescue! London: C&W, 1956. 1st ed. NF in dj (rumpled). *Hermitage.* $25/£16

BROOKE, JOCELYN. Elizabeth Bowen. London: British Council, (1952). 1st ed. Port. NF in ptd wrappers. *Reese.* $20/£13

BROOKE, JOCELYN. The Goose Cathedral. London: Bodley Head, 1950. 1st Eng ed. Fine in dj (spine sl faded; tear top fr panel). *Ulysses.* $70/£45

BROOKE, JOCELYN. The Military Orchid. London: Bodley Head, (1948). 1st ed. Inscribed, signed, dated. Frontis. Fine in VG dj (sm chips). *Reese.* $125/£81

BROOKE, JOCELYN. The Military Orchid. London, 1948. 1st ed. Color frontis. Dj (sl chipped). *Edwards.* $31/£20

BROOKE, RICHARD. Liverpool as It Was During the Last Quarter of the Eighteenth Century. Liverpool: J. Mawdsley, 1853. 558pp, 6 plts (1 waterstained). Cl blocked in blind, gilt lettering (paper label, lib #s). VG. *Bickersteth.* $147/£95

BROOKE, RUPERT. 1914 and Other Poems. Sidgwick & Jackson, 1915. 1st ed. Frontis port. Dk blue cl. Spine label dknd, sl chipped, spare present; edges sl dknd, o/w NF. *Poetry.* $186/£120

BROOKE, RUPERT. 1914. Five Sonnets. London: Sidgwick & Jackson, 1915. 1st separate ed. VG in ptd wrappers (sl used). *Reese.* $30/£19

BROOKE, RUPERT. John Webster and the Elizabethan Drama. NY: John Lane, 1916. 1st ed. Black cl, labels. Fine in dj (spine dull). *Sumner & Stillman.* $275/£177

BROOKE, RUPERT. The Letters of Rupert Brooke. Geoffrey Keynes (ed). London: Faber, 1968. 1st ed. Fine in dj. *Virgo.* $62/£40

BROOKE, RUPERT. The Old Vicarage Grantchester. London: Sidgwick & Jackson, 1916. 1st thus. NF in gray wrappers. *Agvent.* $175/£113

BROOKE, RUPERT. The Old Vicarage Grantchester.... London: Sidgwick & Jackson, 1916. 1st separate ed. One of 2900 ptd. VG in ptd wrappers (lt use edges; sm spots upper wrapper). *Reese.* $125/£81

BROOKE-ROSE, CHRISTINE. A Grammar of Metaphor. London: Secker & Warburg, (1958). 1st ed. Corner sl bumped, else Fine in NF dj (spine sl tanned, price-clipped). *Between The Covers.* $150/£97

BROOKES, R. The Art of Angling. London: Lowndes, 1793. Later ed. Orig blue wrappers. Edges ruffled, else Fine. *Juvelis.* $75/£48

BROOKES, RICHARD. The General Practice of Physic.... London: J. Newbery, 1763. 2 vols. Contemp polished calf. (Worn; stamps on titles; leaf torn.) *Goodrich.* $175/£113

BROOKNER, ANITA. Hotel du Lac. London: Cape, 1984. 1st UK ed. Fine in dj. *Lewton.* $54/£35

BROOKNER, ANITA. Latecomers. NY: Pantheon, (1988). Rev copy, slip laid in. Fine in Fine dj. *Robbins.* $25/£16

BROOKNER, ANITA. A Misalliance. London: Cape, 1986. 1st ed. Fine in NF dj. *Limestone.* $25/£16

BROOKNER, ANITA. A Start in Life. London: Cape, 1981. 1st UK ed. Fine in dj. *Lewton.* $93/£60

BROOKNER, ANITA. Watteau. London: Hamlyn, 1967. Frontis, 47 color plts. Sm repair to dj, o/w VF. *Europa.* $23/£15

BROOKS, BRYANT B. Memoirs of Bryant B. Brooks. Glendale: Clark, 1939. 1st ed, ltd to 150. Stamp remains half-title; sm puncture top rear bd, o/w Clean. *Hermitage.* $200/£129

BROOKS, BRYANT B. Memoirs of Bryant B. Brooks. Glendale, CA: Clark, 1939. One of 150. Brown cl. Good. Howes B 814. *Karmiole.* $250/£161

BROOKS, CHARLES MATTOON, JR. Texas Missions, Their Romance and Architecture. Dallas: Dealey & Lowe, 1936. 1st ed. 20 plts. Fr inner hinge cracked, edgewear; text yellowed, else VG. *Bookpress.* $45/£29

BROOKS, COLLIN. The Ghost Hunters. NY: J.H. Sears, (1928). 1st Amer ed. Fine in VG dj (chipping; internal tape mends). *Mordida.* $45/£29

BROOKS, ELDRIDGE S. The Master of the Stronghearts. NY: E.P. Dutton, 1898. 1st ed. Frontis, xvi,314pp; 8 plts. Pict grn cl (bumped, rubbed; hinges cracked). Internally VG. *Blue Mountain.* $20/£13

BROOKS, GWENDOLYN. The Bean Eaters. NY: Harper, 1960. 1st ed. Name; spine sunned, o/w Fine in dj (chipped, torn). *Beasley.* $85/£55

BROOKS, JEREMY. Henry's War. London: Macmillan, 1962. 1st ed. Fine in dj. *Hermitage.* $40/£26

BROOKS, JUANITA. The Mountain Meadows Massacre. Norman: Univ of OK, (1962). (1st ptg of 2nd ed.) NF in dj. *Bohling.* $50/£32

BROOKS, JUANITA. The Mountain Meadows Massacre. Stanford, 1950. 1st ed. Map. VG + in dj (chip). *Benchmark.* $100/£65

BROOKS, NOAH. First Across the Continent-The Story of the Lewis and Clark Expedition. NY: Scribner's, 1901. 1st ed. VG. *Perier.* $50/£32

BROOKS, VAN WYCK. Fenollosa and His Circle. NY, 1962. 1st ed. VG in dj. *Argosy.* $40/£26

BROOKS, VAN WYCK. The Flowering of New England 1815 to 1865. (NY): E.P. Dutton, 1936. 1st ed. (Worn.) Dj (chipped, torn; lacks 1-inch spine top). *Juvelis.* $40/£26

BROOKS, VAN WYCK. New England: Indian Summer 1865-1915. NY: Dutton, 1940. 1st ed. NF in dj. *Pharos.* $20/£13

BROOKS, VAN WYCK. Opinions of Oliver Allston. NY: E.P. Dutton, (1941). 1st ed. Fine in dj. *Hermitage.* $35/£23

BROOKS, WALTER R. Freddie and the Ignormus. NY: Knopf, 1941. 6th ed. Kurt Wiese (illus). 5.5x8. 286pp. Cl. VG. *Cattermole.* $35/£23

BROOKS, WALTER R. The Story of Fredinald. NY: Knopf, 1936. 1st ed. 4to. Kurt Wiese (illus). (Pencil inscrip.) Beige cl. Color pict dj (minor edgewear, lt edge spotting). *Reisler.* $185/£119

BROOKSHIER, F. The Burro. Norman: Univ of OK, 1974. 1st ed. Fine in VG dj. *Mikesh.* $30/£19

BROOMELL, I.N. and P. FISCHELIS. Anatomy and Histology of the Mouth and Teeth. London: Kimpton, 1917. 5th ed, rev. VG. *Savona.* $39/£25

BROONZY, BIG BILL and YANNICK BRUYNOGHE. Big Bill Blues. London/NY: Cassell/Grove, 1955. 1st US ed (the Cassell bk, bound in black cl instead of brn, w/the Grove dj constitutes the 1st US ed). Fine in Fine dj. *Beasley.* $75/£48

BROPHY, BRIGID. Hackenfeller's Ape. NY: Random House, 1954. 1st US ed. VG in dj (lt soiled). *Cahan.* $40/£26

BROPHY, JOHN and ERIC PARTRIDGE (eds). Songs and Slang of the British Soldier. London, 1931. 3rd ed. VG in dj. *Edrich.* $47/£30

BROPHY, JOHN and ERIC PARTRIDGE (eds). Songs and Slang of the British Soldier: 1914-1918. London, 1930. 2nd ed. Inscrip; eps sl browned; prelims, fore-edge sl foxed, o/w Good + in dj (chipped). *Edwards.* $78/£50

BROSNAN, JIM. The Long Season. Harper & Row, 1960. 1st ed. VG + in VG dj. *Plapinger.* $60/£39

BROSSARD, CHANDLER. The Bold Saboteurs. NY: Farrar, Straus and Young, 1953. 1st ed. Fine in dj (sl rubbed). *Cahan.* $50/£32

BROSSARD, CHANDLER. Who Walk in Darkness. (NY): New Directions, (1952). 1st ed, 1st bk. VG (edges dusty) in dj (soiled). *Reese.* $50/£32

BROSSARD, CHANDLER. Who Walk in Darkness. New Directions, 1952. 1st ed, 1st bk. NF in NF dj (lt dust soil). *Fine Books.* $85/£55

BROTHERS, MARY HUDSON. A Pecos Pioneer. Albuquerque: Univ of NM, 1943. 1st ed. VG in VG dj. *Perier.* $95/£61

BROTHERS, MARY HUDSON. A Pecos Pioneer. Albuquerque: Univ of NM, 1943. 1st ed. NF in VG dj (water mks). *Parker.* $165/£106

BROTHERTON, T.W. Circling the Globe. L.A.: Times-Mirror, (1910). Grn cl stamped in gilt. *Schoyer.* $40/£26

BROTHWELL, DON and A.T. SANDISON. Diseases in Antiquity. Springfield, IL, 1967. VG. *Argosy.* $85/£55

BROTHWELL, DON and PATRICIA. Food in Antiquity. London: Thames & Hudson, (1969). 4 maps. Good in dj. *Archaeologia.* $65/£42

BROUGH, ROBERT B. The Life of Sir John Falstaff. London, 1858. 1st ed in vol form, w/woodcut bound in after plt list. 196pp, 20 plts by George Cruikshank. Full morocco, gilt spine. Aeg; dentelles. (Joints split, hinges reinforced.) *Argosy.* $300/£194

BROUN, H. Pieces of Hate. Doran, 1922. 1st ed. NF in Nice dj (chipping). *Fine Books.* $60/£39

BROUN, HEYWOOD. Seeing Things at Night. NY, 1921. 1st Amer ed, 1st bk. Fine (spine sl sunned; extrems, corners sl rubbed; name; dw piece pasted inside fr cvr). *Polyanthos.* $75/£48

BROWER, CHARLES D. Fifty Years Below Zero. NY: Dodd, Mead, 1942. 21 plts. VG in dj (worn, torn). *Hollett.* $54/£35

BROWER, DAVID (ed). Not Man Apart. SF: Sierra Club, 1965. 28 color lithos. Pict eps. Fine in dj (chipped). *Connolly.* $65/£42

BROWER, KENNETH (ed). Galapagos. SF: Sierra Club, 1968. 2 vols. VG in djs, slipcase. *Argosy.* $150/£97

Brown Book of the Hitler Terror.... NY: Knopf, 1933. 1st ed. VG + . *Bishop.* $20/£13

BROWN, A. The Kingdom in the Sky. Macmillan, 1932. 1st ed. NF in dj (sl worn). *Aronovitz.* $55/£35

BROWN, ALEC (trans). The Voyage of the Chelyuskin—by Members of the Expedition. NY: Macmillan, 1935. 1st ed. VG in Poor (torn) dj. *Perier.* $75/£48

BROWN, ALEXANDER (ed). Longboat to Hawaii. Cambridge: Cornell Maritime, (1974). 1st ed. VG. *Blue Dragon.* $25/£16

BROWN, ALEXANDER. English Politics in Early Virginia History. Russell & Russell, 1968. VG. *Book Broker.* $35/£23

BROWN, BASIL. Law Sports at Gray's Inn (1594). NY: Privately ptd by Author, 1921. Bds worn, chipped; else sound. *Boswell.* $75/£48

BROWN, CHARLES and MAGGIE. This Is a Strange Land. Byrd Gibbens (ed). Albuquerque, (1988). 1st ed. Fine in Fine dj. *Pratt.* $30/£19

BROWN, CHRISTOPHER. Scenes of Everyday Life. Dutch Genre Painting of the Seventeenth Century. London: Faber, 1984. Fine in Mint dj. *Europa.* $47/£30

BROWN, CHRISTY. My Left Foot. London: Secker, 1954. 1st UK ed. Fine in VG dj (short closed tears invisibly repaired w/archival tape). *Williams.* $147/£95

BROWN, CLARA SPALDING. Life in Shut-In Valley and Other Pacific Coast Tales. (Franklin, OH: Editor Pub Co, 1895). 1st ed. Plum cl stamped in black. VG. *Reese.* $35/£23

BROWN, CLAUDE. The Children of Ham. NY: Stein & Day, (1976). 1st ed. Fine in Fine dj. *Robbins.* $25/£16

BROWN, D. MACKENZIE (ed). China Trade Days in California. Selected Letters.... Berkeley, 1947. 1st ed. 1 plt. Fine in Fine dj. *Oregon.* $35/£23

BROWN, D. MACKENZIE (ed). China Trade Days in California: Selected Letters from the Thompson Papers, 1832-1863. Berkeley: Univ of CA Press, 1947. 1st ed. Frontis port, 1 plt. Red cl. Fine in NF dj (lt chipped). *Harrington.* $45/£29

BROWN, DEE. Killdeer Mountain. NY: Holt, Rinehart & Winston, 1983. 1st ed. Fine in Fine dj. *Connolly.* $25/£16

BROWN, DEE. Trail Driving Days. NY, 1952. 1st ed. Sl soiled, else VG in dj (badly torn). *King.* $45/£29

BROWN, DEE. Trail Driving Days. Scribner's, 1952. 1st ed. Erratum slip tipped to pg v. VG in Good+ dj. *Oregon.* $65/£42

BROWN, DOLORES CLINE. Yukon Trophy Trails. Sidney, BC: Gray's Pub, c. 1971. 1st ed. Fine in Fine dj. *Perier.* $40/£26

BROWN, DOUGLAS S. Catawba Indians. Columbia: Univ of SC Press, (1966). 1st ed. Brn cl. Fine in NF dj. *Chapel Hill.* $50/£32

BROWN, ELEANOR and BOB. Culinary Americana. NY: Roving Eye Press, (1961). Internally Fine. Grn cl (bumped, spotted). VG dj (edges chipped). *Blue Mountain.* $85/£55

BROWN, ELI. The Eclectic Physiology or Guide to Health. NY, 1886. 187pp. Good. *Fye.* $25/£16

BROWN, ELIJAH. The Real Billy Sunday. Otterbein, 1914. Rpt. VG in Good+ dj (scarce). *Plapinger.* $160/£103

BROWN, ELTON T. A History of the Great Minnesota Forest Fires.... St. Paul: Brown Bros, (1894). 233,(5)pp. Good (sl worn, soiled). *Hayman.* $40/£26

BROWN, FREDRIC. Freak Show Murders. Belen, NM: Dennis McMillan, 1985. 1st ed. Ltd to 350 signed, numbered by Richard Lupoff (intro). Fine in dj. *Murder.* $75/£48

BROWN, FREDRIC. His Name Was Death. NY: Dutton, 1954. 1st ed. VG in dj (sm chip spine; lt wear). *Else Fine.* $50/£32

BROWN, FREDRIC. Night of the Jabberwock. NY: Dutton, 1950. 1st ed. Bkpl, else NF in VG+ dj (spine faded; extrems sl worn). *Lame Duck.* $500/£323

BROWN, FREDRIC. The Pickled Punks. Hilo: Dennis McMillan, 1991. 1st ed, one of 450 numbered. Fine in Fine dj. *Janus.* $45/£29

BROWN, FREDRIC. Space on My Hands. Chicago: Shasta, 1951. 1st ed. Signed. Reps sl tanned, else NF in NF dj (spine sl faded). *Lame Duck.* $475/£306

BROWN, FREDRIC. The Water Walker. Missoula: Dennis McMillan, 1990. 1st ed. One of 425 numbered. As New in As New dj. *Janus.* $45/£29

BROWN, FREDRIC. What Mad Universe. Dutton, 1949. 1st ed. Fine in dj (sl nicked; edge-rubbed; closed tears). *Madle.* $175/£113

BROWN, G. BALDWIN. Anglo-Saxon Architecture. London, 1925. New ed. 31 plts, fldg map. (Ex-libris w/ink stamps, bkpl removed, sl spotting; worn.) *Edwards.* $39/£25

BROWN, G. BALDWIN. Ecclesiastical Architecture in England.... London, 1903. 1st ed. Fldg map. (Ex-libris; spine sl faded, joints sl rubbed; ink stamps, bkpl removed.) *Edwards.* $39/£25

BROWN, G. BALDWIN. The Life of Saxon England in Its Relation to the Arts. London, 1903. 1st ed. (Bkpl; ink stamps; bkpl removed; spine sl faded; joints sl rubbed.) *Edwards.* $39/£25

BROWN, GEORGE. Recollections of Itinerant Life. Cincinnati, 1866. 3rd ed. 456pp. *Hayman.* $75/£48

BROWN, GEORGE. Reminiscences of Gov. R.J. Walker. Rockford, IL: Privately ptd, 1902. 1st ed. Frontis, 4 plts. Cl mottled, o/w VG. *Oregon.* $40/£26

BROWN, GLENN. History of the United States Capital. Washington: GPO, 1900-03. 2 vols. (Staining, scuffing.) *Schoyer.* $300/£194

BROWN, HARRIET CONNOR. Grandmother Brown's Hundred Years: 1827-1927. Boston: Little, Brown, 1930. VG in dj (chipped). *Burcham.* $40/£26

BROWN, HARRISON (ed). A Bibliography on Meteorites. Univ of Chicago Press, 1953. Grn cl. Bumped, worn; ex-lib w/mks, o/w VG. *Knollwood.* $65/£42

BROWN, I. BAKER. On Scarlatina: Its Nature and Successful Treatment. London, 1869. 3rd ed. 116pp. Good. *Fye.* $75/£48

BROWN, ISAAC. On Some Diseases of Women Admitting of Surgical Treatment. Phila, 1876. 1st Amer ed. 276pp. Good. *Fye.* $75/£48

BROWN, J. The Forester or A Practical Treatise on the Planting.... London, 1871. 4th ed. xiii,835pp. (Rebacked preserving spine.) Good. *Henly.* $54/£35

BROWN, J. The North-West Passage.... London, 1858. Frontis, xii,463pp; 2 fldg color maps. New cl. (Map edges repaired; sm stain lower corner last few leaves.) *Wheldon & Wesley.* $388/£250

BROWN, J. HAMMOND. From Out of the Yukon. Portland: Bindfords & Mort, (1948). Signed. VG in VG- dj. *Blue Dragon.* $60/£39

BROWN, J. MORAY. Polo. London: Vinton, 1895. 1st ed. (Bumped.) *October Farm.* $85/£55

BROWN, J.Y. To the Moon and Back in Ninety Days. Lunar, 1922. 1st ed. VG. *Aronovitz.* $75/£48

BROWN, JAMES BERRY. Journal of a Journey Across the Plains in 1859. George Stewart (ed). SF: Book Club of CA, 1970. 1st ed. Ltd to 450. Frontis, map. Pict bds. VF. *Oregon.* $100/£65

BROWN, JENNIFER. Strangers in Blood. Vancouver: Univ of BC, (1980). 1st ed. Fine in VG dj. *Oregon.* $45/£29

BROWN, JEREMY. Jomo Kenyatta. E.P. Dutton, 1972. 1st ed. NF in VG+ dj. *Bishop.* $15/£10

BROWN, JESSE and A.M. WILLARD. The Black Hills Trails. John T. Milek (ed). Rapid City, SD: Rapid City Journal Co, 1924. 1st ed. VG. Howes B 850. *Lien.* $195/£126

BROWN, JOE DAVID. Stars in My Crown. NY, 1947. 1st ed. NF in VG dj. *Mcgowan.* $25/£16

BROWN, JOE. The Hard Years. London: Gollancz, 1967. 1st ed. (Spine faded.) *Hollett.* $23/£15

BROWN, JOHN HENRY. History of Texas 1685-1892. St. Louis: L.E. Daniel, 1892. 1st ed. Vol I only. 631pp. Orig gilt-stamped grey cl, dec black emb. Fine. *Lambeth.* $100/£65

BROWN, JOHN HENRY. The Indian Wars and Pioneers of Texas. Austin: L.E. Daniell, n.d. (1896). 1st ed. 124 plts. Grn cl gilt, blind-stamped. Fine (spine head, foot expertly repaired). Howes B 857. *Hermitage.* $850/£548

BROWN, JOHN MASON. Daniel Boone. NY: Random House, 1952. 1st trade ed. Lee J. Ames (illus). Dec eps. VG in dj. *Cattermole.* $15/£10

BROWN, JOHN. Letters of Dr. John Brown. London: A&C Black, 1907. 8 plts. (Title, port sl spotted.) *Bickersteth.* $54/£35

BROWN, JONATHAN. Velazquez, Painter and Courtier. New Haven: Yale Univ Press, 1986. VG in dj. *Argosy.* $125/£81

BROWN, LANGDON. The Sympathetic Nervous System in Disease. London, 1923. 2nd ed. Good. *Fye.* $40/£26

BROWN, LARRY. Big Bad Love. Chapel Hill: Algonquin, 1990. 1st ed. Fine in Fine dj. *Revere.* $30/£19

BROWN, LARRY. Big Bad Love. Chapel Hill: Algonquin, 1990. 1st ed. VF in dj. *Else Fine.* $35/£23

BROWN, LARRY. Dirty Work. Chapel Hill: Algonquin Books, 1989. 1st ed. Fine in Fine dj. *Dermont.* $25/£16

BROWN, LARRY. Dirty Work. Chapel Hill: Algonquin, 1989. 1st ed. Fine in Fine dj. *Revere.* $35/£23

BROWN, LARRY. Dirty Work. Chapel Hill: Algonquin Books, 1989. 1st ed. Signed. Fine in dj. *Bernard.* $60/£39

BROWN, LARRY. Facing the Music. Chapel Hill: Algonquin Books, 1988. 1st ed, 1st bk. Fine in dj. *Bernard.* $75/£48

BROWN, LARRY. Facing the Music. Chapel Hill: Algonquin Books, 1988. 1st ed, 1st bk. Signed. Black cl. Fine in Fine dj. *Chapel Hill.* $100/£65

BROWN, LARRY. Facing the Music. Chapel Hill: Algonquin, 1988. 1st ed. Fine in dj. *Turlington.* $50/£32

BROWN, LESLIE. British Birds of Prey. London, 1976. 1st ed. 16 plts. Dj. *Edwards.* $54/£35

BROWN, MARCIA. Dick Whittington and His Cat. NY: Scribner's, 1950. 1st ed. 4to, 32pp. Fine in dj. *Godot.* $65/£42

BROWN, MARK H. The Flight of the Nez Perce. NY: Putnam's, (1967). 1st ed. Black cl. Fine in VG+ dj (sl rubbed, chipped). *Harrington.* $40/£26

BROWN, MARK H. and W.R. FELTON. Before Barbed Wire: L.A. Huffman, Photographer on Horseback. NY: Bramhall House, (1956). Rpt. Black cl. NF in VG+ dj. *Harrington.* $35/£23

BROWN, MARK. The Plainsmen of the Yellowstone. NY: Putnam's, (1961). 1st ed. VG in dj (sl worn). *Lien.* $40/£26

BROWN, NORMAN O. Life Against Death. Wesleyan, 1947. 1st ed. Pg-corner creased, else NF in dj. *Lame Duck.* $250/£161

BROWN, O. PHELPS. The Complete Herbalist. Jersey City: By the Author, 1873. 1st ed. Litho frontis port, 504pp. Blind-stamped, gilt titles. VF. *Hemlock.* $125/£81

BROWN, PAUL. 3 Rings. NY: Scribner's, 1938. 1st ed. Good (shelfworn). *October Farm.* $125/£81

BROWN, PAUL. Draw Horses: Its Fun and Its Easy. NY, 1949. 1st ed. VF (lib pocket) in VF dj. *Bond.* $45/£29

BROWN, PAUL. Good Luck and Bad. NY: Scribner's, 1940. 1st ed, #36/780 signed. Sm scrape fr cvr, o/w VG. *October Farm.* $145/£94

BROWN, PERCY. Picturesque Nepal. A&C Black, 1912. 4 color plts, map. Dec cl (lt dampstained, spine sl chipped; feps lt browned). *Edwards.* $54/£35

BROWN, R. SHEPARD. Stringfellow of the Fourth. NY, (1960). 1st ed. Map. VG in VG dj. *Pratt.* $40/£26

BROWN, R.J. Windmills of England. London: Robert Hale, 1976. 1st ed. VG in dj. *Hollett.* $47/£30

BROWN, R.N. RUDMOSE et al. The Voyage of the 'Scotia.' Edinburgh: Wm. Blackwood, 1906. 1st ed. Good+ (spine title dull, sm 1cm tear head of spine, repaired). *Walcot.* $388/£250

BROWN, R.N. RUDMOSE. A Naturalist at the Poles. Seeley Service, 1923. 1st ed. Sl mkd, o/w Clean. *Walcot.* $62/£40

BROWN, R.N. RUDMOSE. A Naturalist at the Poles. Phila: Lippincott, 1924. 2 fldg maps. VG (lt wear). *High Latitude.* $80/£52

BROWN, R.N. RUDMOSE. The Polar Regions. Methuen, 1927. 1st ed. 23 maps. VG. *Walcot.* $59/£38

BROWN, R.N. RUDMOSE. The Polar Regions. A Physical and Economic Geography.... London: Methuen, 1927. 23 maps (2 fldg). VG. *High Latitude.* $40/£26

BROWN, RICHARD. The Principles of Practical Perspective. London: Leigh & Son, 1835. 2nd ed. 2 parts in 1 vol. viii,132pp (sl damage 1st tp); 50 plts (incl 2 aquatint frontispieces) (most plts w/sl tidemks). 1/2 leather, marbled bds. *Ars Artis.* $543/£350

BROWN, RITA MAE. Six of One. NY: Harper & Row, 1978. 1st ed. NF in NF dj. *Revere.* $35/£23

BROWN, ROBERT (ed). The Adventures of John Jewitt, Only Survivor of the Ship 'Boston'.... London, 1896. 256pp+ads. Grn cl. *Lewis.* $116/£75

BROWN, SAMUEL R. The Western Gazetteer: Or Emigrant's Directory. Auburn, NY: H.C. Southwick, 1817. 1st ed, 3rd issue. Full contemp brn leather (sl rubbing), gilt. VG. Howes B 867. *Houle.* $375/£242

BROWN, SARAH. Stained Glass. An Illustrated History. London: Studio Editions, 1992. 1st ed. VG in dj. *Hollett.* $47/£30

BROWN, STERLING A. The Collected Poems.... NY: Harper & Row, (1980). 1st ed. VG in dj. *Petrilla.* $45/£29

BROWN, T. The Taxidermist's Manual. NY: Judd, (n.d.). Rev from 20th UK ed. 77 engr. Blind-stamped gilt dec cl. VG+. *Mikesh.* $40/£26

BROWN, T. GRAHAM and GAVIN DE BEER. The First Ascent of Mount Blanc. London, 1957. 1st ed. VG in dj. *King.* $50/£32

BROWN, THADDEUS C.S. et al. Behind the Guns. Carbondale, (1965). #660/1000. Fine in slipcase. *Pratt.* $50/£32

BROWN, THADDEUS C.S. et al. Behind the Guns: The History of Battery I, 2nd Regiment, Illinois Light Artillery. Clyde C. Walton (ed). Carbondale/Edwardsville, IL: Southern IL Univ, 1965. 1st ed as such. One of 1000 signed. Cl-backed blue bds. Fine in orig acetate dj, pub's slipcase. *Cahan.* $60/£39

BROWN, VARINA DAVIS. A Colonel at Gettysburg and Spotsylvania. Columbia, SC: State Co., 1931. 1st ed. Frontis port, fldg map, 2 full-pg maps. Orig blue cl. Prelims lt foxed, else NF in VG dj. *Chapel Hill.* $350/£226

BROWN, W. SORLEY. The Life and Genius of T.W.H. Crosland. Cecil Palmer, 1928. 1st Eng ed. Blue cl (sl rubbed). VG. *Dalian.* $54/£35

BROWN, WILFRED GAVIN. Angler's Almanac. London: Frederick Muller, 1949. 1st ed. VG in dj (short edgetear, price-clipped). *Hollett.* $39/£25

BROWN, WILLIAM H. Portrait Gallery of Distinguished American Citizens.... (NY, 1931.) One of 600. 27 full-pg plts. Gilt pict buckram. VG. *Argosy*. $200/£129

BROWN, WILLIAM PERRY. A Sea-Island Romance. NY: John B. Alden, 1888. 1st ed. Dk blue-grn cl. VG (name). *Chapel Hill*. $95/£61

BROWN-SEQUARD, C.E. Lectures on the Diagnosis and Treatment of Principal Forms of Paralysis of the Lower Extremities. Phila, 1861. 1st ed. 118pp. Contents Fine (1/4 inch missing spine top; 1 inch missing spine bottom). *Fye*. $750/£484

BROWNE, D.J. The Field Book of Manures. NY, 1855. xii,(5-)422pp. (Lt dampstained; ink name; rep torn; re-backed w/orig backstrip.) *Sutton*. $110/£71

BROWNE, D.J. The Trees of America. NY: Harper, 1846. xii,520pp (eps stained). Orig brn cl, blind/gilt-stamped (bumped, rubbed; tear spine top). VG. *Shifrin*. $75/£48

BROWNE, G.W. and N.H. DOLE. The New America and the Far East. Boston, (1910). 9 vols. 2pp color map each vol. Gilt cl. VF. *Artis*. $110/£71

BROWNE, J. ROSS and JAMES TAYLOR. Reports Upon the Mineral Resources of the United States. GPO, 1867. 1st ed. 360pp. Fair (ex-lib; cl loosened; dampstained). *Oregon*. $40/£26

BROWNE, J. ROSS. Adventures in the Apache Country. NY: Harper, 1869. 1st ed. 535+4pp cat. Fair (ex-lib). Howes B 875. *Blue Mountain*. $35/£23

BROWNE, J. ROSS. Crusoe's Island. A Ramble in the Footsteps of Alexander Selkirk. NY: Harper, 1864. 1st ed. 436pp. *Lefkowicz*. $175/£113

BROWNE, J. ROSS. Etchings of a Whaling Cruise. John Seelye (ed). Cambridge: HUP, 1968. Fine in dj. *Lefkowicz*. $75/£48

BROWNE, J. ROSS. Report on the Mineral Resources of the States and Territories West of the Rocky Mountains. Washington: GPO, 1868. 674,72pp. Orig cl (spine spotted). *Schoyer*. $100/£65

BROWNE, J. ROSS. Resources of the Pacific Slope. NY: D. Appleton, 1869. 2 parts in 1. 678; 200pp. Purple cl (faded; fr hinge sl chipped). *Karmiole*. $150/£97

BROWNE, J. ROSS. Washoe Revisited. Oakland: Biobooks, (1957). Ltd to 500. Fine. *Oregon*. $45/£29

BROWNE, J. ROSS. Yusef; or the Journey of the Frangi. Harper, 1853. 1st ed. 421pp; 6pp ads. Pict cl. VG (corners worn). *Oregon*. $175/£113

BROWNE, J.H. BALFOUR. South Africa. London et al: Longmans, Green, 1904. vi,(240)pp+40pp pub's cat (some leaves dog-eared). Blue cl, gilt (sl warped). *Schoyer*. $40/£26

BROWNE, JAMES. A History of the Highlands, and of the Highland Clans. London: A. Fullerton, 1845. New ed. 4 vols. lxxii,447; vii,478; vi(2),504; viii,501pp + directions to binder; lg fldg hand-colored map (tear neatly repaired); 39 engr ports, views. Grn cl. Uncut. VG (ex-lib). *Cox*. $186/£120

BROWNE, JEFFERSON BEALE. Key West, the Old and the New. St. Augustine: Record Co, 1912. 1st ed. Minor damping, else VG. *Mcgowan*. $150/£97

BROWNE, JOHN. Myographia Nova: or, A Graphical Description of All the Muscles in Humane Body.... London, 1697. Ltd ed #1230/2500. 1/4 calf. Good in slipcase. *Goodrich*. $55/£35

BROWNE, LINA FERGUSSON. J. Ross Browne: His Letters.... Albuquerque: Univ of NM, 1969. 1st ed. VG in dj. *Burcham*. $45/£29

BROWNE, MALCOLM W. New Face of War. Indianapolis: Bobbs-Merrill, (1965). VG in dj (scuffed; edge chips). *Aka*. $35/£23

BROWNE, MONTAGU. Practical Taxidermy.... London: The Bazaar, 1922. 3rd ed. (Sm tear backstrip.) *Petersfield*. $25/£16

BROWNE, THOMAS. Browne's Religio Medici and Digby's Observations. OUP, 1909. Parchment bds w/yapped edges. Sl dusty, else VG. *Goodrich*. $65/£42

BROWNE, THOMAS. A Letter to a Friend.... London: Golden Cockerel Press, 1923. #28/115. Uncut, on handmade paper. Holland-backed grey bds, paper label (sl soiled, browned). Good. *Cox*. $85/£55

BROWNE, THOMAS. The Letters of Sir Thomas Browne. Geoffrey Keynes (ed). London, 1946. Good in dj. *Fye*. $50/£32

BROWNE, THOMAS. Religio Medici. London: J. Torbuck & C. Corbett, 1736. New Edition. Engr frontis, xxxvi,253,(11)pp. Early mottled calf (expertly rebacked); red leather spine label. VG (bkpl, inscrip). *Glaser*. $175/£113

BROWNE, THOMAS. Religio Medici. New Edition, Corrected and Amended.... London: Ptd for J. Torbuck, 1736. Engr frontis, 150 leaves. Contemp 1/4 vellum (worn, spine chipped), marbled bds. *Goodrich*. $250/£161

BROWNE, THOMAS. Sir Thomas Browne's Works, Including His Life and Correspondence. Simon Wilkins (ed). London: William Pickering, 1835. 4 vols. Engr port, 3 inserted pedigrees (2 fldg), engr facs autograph, 3 engr plts. 3/4 maroon morocco, marbled bds, gilt-panelled spines (joints rubbed). *Cummins*. $450/£290

BROWNE, THOMAS. The Works of Sir Thomas Browne. Simon Wilkin (ed). London: Bohn, 1852. 3 vols. Frontis port, lxxxii,463 (sl browning); iv,563; vii,542pp. Blind-stamped blue cl. VG (spines sl faded). *White*. $101/£65

BROWNE, THOMAS. The Works of Thomas Browne. C. Sayle (ed). Edinburgh, 1927. 3 vols. Frontis port,lv,351; frontis,x,400; ix,601pp. Cl spine, bds, leather labels. Sl dust stained, o/w VG set. *Whitehart*. $54/£35

BROWNE, THOMAS. The Works. Charles Sayle (ed). Edinburgh: John Grant, 1927. 3 vols. 5 plts. Buckram-backed bds, morocco labels. Uncut. Good. *Cox*. $59/£38

BROWNE, THOMAS. The Works. Simon Wilkins (ed). London: Pickering, 1836. 4 vols. Orig full tree calf (rebacked, orig backstrip laid down), raised bands; gilt; aeg. *Goodrich*. $350/£226

BROWNE, W.G. Travels in Africa, Egypt, and Syria...1792 to 1798. London: For T. Cadell et al, 1799. 1st ed. Frontis, xxxviii,496pp, 1 plt, 2 lg fldg maps, 8 tables. Full tree-calf (rebacked), 5 raised bands, leather label (edges lt rubbed; contemp sig). *Archaeologia*. $850/£548

BROWNING, ELIZABETH BARRETT. The Letters of Robert Browning and Elizabeth Barrett Browning. NY: Harper, 1899. 1st Amer ed. 2 vols. Teg, uncut. Grn cl, gilt. NF set. *Macdonnell*. $75/£48

BROWNING, ELIZABETH BARRETT. Sonnets from the Portuguese. NY: LEC, 1948. One of 1500. Signed by Valenti Angelo (illus). Fine in slipcase. *Pharos*. $150/£97

BROWNING, ELIZABETH BARRETT. Twenty-Two Un-published Letters. NY: United Feature Syndicate, 1935. One of 1188. Unopened. Fine in pub's box. *Heller*. $35/£23

BROWNING, ROBERT. Asolando; Fancies and Facts. London: Smith, Elder, (1889). 1st ed. viii,157pp + (3)pp ads and blank. Orig dk red beveled cl, lettered in gold (sl rubbed, sm bruise). *Cox*. $31/£20

BROWNING, ROBERT. A History of Golf, the Royal and Ancient Game. London: Dent, (1955). 8 color plts. *Petersfield*. $132/£85

BROWNING, ROBERT. The Pied Piper of Hamelin. London: Frederick Warne, (1910). Kate Greenaway (illus). 4to. 48pp, full-pg color frontis, tp vignette, perfect plts. Color pict paper on bd (corners bumped; edges, spine extrems rubbed). Good. *Hobbyhorse*. $100/£65

BROWNING, ROBERT. The Pied Piper of Hamelin. London: Harrap, 1939. 1st thus. Arthur Rackham (illus). Fine (ink inscrip) in wrappers as issued. *Williams*. $140/£90

BROWNING, ROBERT. The Poems of Robert Browning. Cambridge: LEC, 1969. One of 1500 numbered, signed by Peter Reddick (illus). Fine in pub's slipcase. *Hermitage*. $100/£65

BROWNING, ROBERT. The Ring and the Book. London: Smith, Elder & Co., 1868-69. 1st ed. 4 vols. Dk grn cl; spines #ed in Roman numerals. Fine set. *Chapel Hill*. $400/£258

BROWNING, ROBERT. The Ring and the Book. London: Smith Elder, 1868. 1st ed, 1st issue. Vols 1 & 2 in Arabic type, vols III & IV in Roman type. 4 vols. Grn cl, beveled bds. Attractive (hinges vol 1,4 repaired; crown, heel worn; rubbed). *Hermitage*. $275/£177

BROWNLEE, CHARLES. Reminiscences of Kaffir Life and History.... Lovedale, S.A., 1896. 1st ed. viii,403pp. Foxing, sl worn, o/w VG in olive combed cl, gilt titles. *Edwards*. $93/£60

BROWNLEE, RICHARD S. Gray Ghosts of the Confederacy. Baton Rouge, (1958). 1st ed. VG + . *Pratt*. $40/£26

BROWNSON, ORESTES. Works of Orestes Brownson. Henry F. Brownson (ed). Detroit, 1887. 1st ed. 20 vols. (Most vols mended/tightened.) *Ginsberg*. $450/£290

BROWSE, LILLIAN. Degas Dancers. London: Faber & Faber, 1949. Tipped-in color frontis, tp vignette, 11 tipped-in color plts, 256 b/w plts. Teg. Cl (sl soiled, faded), leather title label spine. Protective cvr (taped to pastedowns). *Edwards*. $116/£75

BRUCE, CURT. The Great Houses of New Orleans. NY: Knopf, 1977. 1st ed. Frontis. Edges worn, else VG in dj. *Bookpress*. $35/£23

BRUCE, IAN (ed). The Nun of Lebanon. London: Collins, 1951. 1st ed. 4 plts. Sl rubbed, soiled, o/w VG. *Worldwide*. $24/£15

BRUCE, JAMES. Travels...Africa, Syria...into Abyssinia, to Discover the Source of the Nile.... London: n.d. (ca 1835). Engr frontis, 1/2 title, 348 pp; aeg. Contemp morocco; tooled gilt, blind; dentelles. VG (inscrip). *Petrilla*. $85/£55

BRUCE, JOHN COLLINGWOOD. The Hand-Book to the Roman Wall. London: Newcastle upon Tyne, 1909. 6th ed. Fldg map. Gilt cl. VG. *Hollett*. $23/£15

BRUCE, JOHN COLLINGWOOD. The Roman Wall. London: John Russell Smith, 1851. 16 litho views, 2 fldg engr maps. Red cl backstrip (faded), marbled sides (rebound; 1st pp sl foxed). *Petersfield*. $59/£38

BRUCE, LENNY. How to Talk Dirty and Influence People. (Chicago, 1965). 1st ed. Sm stain last few pp, else Good in dj (torn, frayed). *King*. $40/£26

BRUCE, LENNY. How to Talk Dirty and Influence People. Playboy Press, 1965. 1st ed. NF in VG dj. *Fine Books*. $35/£23

BRUCE, LEO. A Bone and a Hank of Hair. London: Peter Davies, 1961. 1st ed. Fine in VG dj (price-clipped; internal tape mends; wear). *Mordida*. $65/£42

BRUCE, LEO. Death of a Bovver Boy. London: W.H. Allen, 1974. 1st ed. Fine in dj. *Mordida*. $65/£42

BRUCE, LEO. Death of a Commuter. London: W.H. Allen, 1967. 1st ed. VG in dj (price-clipped; internal tape repairs). *Mordida*. $65/£42

BRUCE, LEO. Death on Allhallowe'en. London: W.H. Allen, 1970. 1st ed. Fine in dj (sl wear). *Mordida*. $65/£42

BRUCE, PHILIP A. The Virginia Plutarch. UNC, 1929. 2 vols. Near VG. *Book Broker*. $40/£26

BRUCE, ROBERT (ed). Custer's Last Battle. NY: Nat. Highways Assoc, 1927. 1st ed. Fine in wraps. *Oregon*. $100/£65

BRUCE, ROBERT. The Fighting Norths and Pawnee Scouts. Lincoln: NE State Hist Soc, 1932. 1st ed. Pict wraps (worn, soiled). *Schoyer*. $30/£19

BRUCE, WILLIAM C. Below the James: A Plantation Sketch. NY: Neale, 1918. Lt purple cl (sl stain fr cvr; lt spotting). *Schoyer*. $30/£19

BRUCE-MITFORD, RUPERT. The Sutton Hoo Ship Burial. Vol 1. London: British Museum, 1975. 13 color plts, 16 fldg sheets, map pocket w/12 items. Orig buckram, gilt emblem. Neat repair lower inner joint, sl shaken, o/w Fine. *Europa*. $70/£45

BRUCKE, ERNST. The Human Figure: Its Beauties and Defects. London: H. Grevel, 1891. Midnight blue cl, gilt. (Sl soiled.) *Glenn*. $50/£32

BRUFF, J. GOLDSBOROUGH. Gold Rush, the Journals, Drawings, and Other Papers of J. Goldsborough Bruff. Columbia, 1949. 2nd ed. VG in Good + dj. *Oregon*. $95/£61

BRUMMELL, BEAU. Male and Female Costume. GC: Doubleday, Doran, 1932. 1st ed. One of 476. 85 plts. Unopened. Gilt-lettered brn cl. Fine. *House*. $100/£65

BRUNCKEN, HERBERT. Last Parade. Muscatine, IA: Prairie Press, 1938. 1st ed. Signed. Blue cl. VG in dj (chipped, worn). *Chapel Hill*. $30/£19

BRUNDAGE, FRANCES. What Happened to Tommy. Rochester: Stecher Lithographic, (1921). F. Brundage (illus). VG in pict wraps. *Davidson*. $95/£61

BRUNNER, ARNOLD and THOMAS TRYON. Interior Decoration. NY: Wm. T. Comstock, 1887. 1st ed. Frontis,(vi),65pp; 15 plts. Pub's gilt cl. Lt wear, else VG. *Bookpress*. $495/£319

BRUNNER, JOHN. The Brink. Gollancz, 1959. 1st ed. VG + in VG dj (spine sl dknd). *Aronovitz*. $85/£55

BRUNNER, JOHN. The Sheep Look Up. London: J.M. Dent, 1974. 1st Eng ed. Label removed fep, o/w Fine in dj. *Temple*. $37/£24

BRUNNER, JOHN. The Shockwave Rider. London: J.M. Dent, 1975. 1st Eng ed. Fine in dj (edges sl rubbed). *Temple*. $31/£20

BRUNNER, JOHN. Stand on Zanzibar. Doubleday, 1968. 1st ed. Fr hinge cracking, else Fine in dj. *Madle*. $200/£129

BRUNNER, JOHN. Stand on Zanzibar. Doubleday, 1968. 1st ed. Signed. Fine in VG dj. *Aronovitz.* $125/£81

BRUNNER, JOHN. Telepathist. Faber, 1965. 1st ed. Cvrs lt spotted, else Fine in NF dj. *Aronovitz.* $80/£52

BRUNNER, JOHN. Times Without Number. London: Elmfield Press, 1962. 1st Eng ed. Yellow cl. VF in Fine dj. *Dalian.* $39/£25

BRUNNER, JOHN. The Whole Man. NY: Walker, 1969. 1st ed. VF in dj. *Else Fine.* $60/£39

BRUNO, GUIDO. Adventures in American Bookshops, Antique Stores and Auction Rooms. Detroit: Douglas Book Shop, 1922. 1st ed. Fine (chipped spine label). *Beasley.* $30/£19

BRUSH, DANIEL H. Growing Up with Southern Illinois, 1820 to 1861. Chicago, (1944). Lakeside Classic. VG. *Schoyer.* $25/£16

BRUSSEL, I.R. A Bibliography of the Writings of James Branch Cabell. Phila: Centaur Book Shop, 1932. Ltd ed of 350 numbered. Frontis port tipped in. Grn cl; paper spine label. Good in dj (bit soiled). *Karmiole.* $30/£19

BRUTON, ERIC. Clocks and Watches. London, 1968. 1st ed. Dj. *Edwards.* $47/£30

BRY, DORIS and NICHOLAS CALLAWAY. Georgia O'Keefe: In the West. NY, 1989. 1st ed. Fine in dj. *Argosy.* $85/£55

BRYAN, C.D.B. Friendly Fire. NY: Putnam, (1976). 1st ed. NF in NF dj (edge tear). *Aka.* $35/£23

BRYAN, C.D.B. Friendly Fire. NY: Putnam's, 1976. 1st ed. NF in NF dj. *Revere.* $40/£26

BRYAN, C.D.B. P.S. Wilkinson. NY: Harper & Row, 1965. 1st ed. Signed. NF in VG dj. *Revere.* $60/£39

BRYAN, DANIEL. The Mountain Muse. Harrisonburg: For the Author, 1813. 252pp (soiled; lacks feps). Contemp calf (neatly rebacked), gilt red morocco spine label. *Karmiole.* $200/£129

BRYAN, EMMA LYON. 1860-1965, A Romance of the Valley of Virginia. (Harrisonburg: J. Taliaffero, 1892). 1st ed. 228,(1)pp. Text browned; bkpl; spine chipped; lt worn, else VG in orig wrappers. *Bookpress.* $135/£87

BRYAN, J., III. The Sword Over the Mantel. McGraw-Hill, (1960). (1st ed). Near VG. *Book Broker.* $30/£19

BRYAN, JULIEN. Siege. NY: Doubleday, Doran, 1940. Inscribed. VG in dj (chipped). *Schoyer.* $30/£19

BRYAN, WILLIAM S. and ROBERT ROSE. History of the Pioneer Families of Missouri.... St. Louis: Bryan, Brand, 1876. iv,528pp (fep, flyleaf corner removed). 2 plts w/composite ports (incl frontis). Blue cl, gilt spine title. Good (extrems frayed; spotted, soiled) in VG dj. *Bohling.* $250/£161

BRYAN, WM. S. and ROBERT ROSE. A History of the Pioneer Families of Missouri. Columbia, MO: Lucas Bros, (1935). Facs of 1876 ed. Frontis. VG. Howes B901. *Lien.* $125/£81

BRYANT, BILLY. Children of Ol' Man River. Chicago, (1988). Lakeside Classic. VG. *Schoyer.* $15/£10

BRYANT, BILLY. Children of Ol' Man River. Martin Ridge (ed). Chicago: (Lakeside Classic), 1988. Brn cl; gilt stamping, top. *Bohling.* $35/£23

BRYANT, BILLY. Children of Ol' Man River. Martin Ridge (ed). Chicago, 1988. Lakeside Classic. 1st ed. Pict cl. Fine. *Pratt.* $27/£17

BRYANT, EDWIN. What I Saw in California. Santa Ana: Fine Arts, 1936. Signed by ptr. Color frontis, map. Calf-backed bds, leather label, gold-stamped spine (lt wear). Howes B 903. *Ginsberg.* $200/£129

BRYANT, JACOB. A New System, or, An Analysis... London: Ptd for J. Walker, 1807. 1st ed. 6 vols. 41 copper-engr plts, port. Brn cl, orig 1/2 calf over marbled bds, gilt spines (outer hinges vol 1 cracked, hinges vols 2-6 starting; extrems rubbed; bkpls). *Karmiole.* $250/£161

BRYANT, WILLIAM CULLEN. Poems. NY: LEC, 1947. One of 1500. Signed by Thomas Nason (artist). Full black sheepskin. NF in NF case. *Agvent.* $125/£81

BRYANT, WILLIAM CULLEN. Thirty Poems. NY: Appleton, 1864. 1st ed, 1st state. Teg; partially unopened. Contemp 3/4 morocco, marbled bds (extrems lt rubbed; sm abrasion spine). BAL 1683. *Sadlon.* $75/£48

BRYANT, WILLIAM CULLEN. Thirty Poems. NY: Appleton, 1864. 1st ed, 2nd state. Cl stamped in gilt/blind (lt rubbed, sl lightened spots; lt foxing, esp 1st, last leaves). BAL 1683. *Sadlon.* $20/£13

BRYCE, GEORGE. The Remarkable History of the Hudson Bay Company.... NY: Scribner's, (1910). 3rd ed. Inner fr hinge cracked, else VG- in clear added mylar dj. *Blue Dragon.* $35/£23

BRYCE, JAMES. Impressions of South Africa. NY: Century, 1897. 1st Amer ed. (xviii),(500)pp, teg; 3 fldg maps. (Dampstains.) Brick cl (soiled). *Schoyer.* $50/£32

BRYCE, JAMES. Memories of Travel. London: Macmillan, 1933. 1st ed. Title stamped 'presentation copy.' (Feps sl mottled; lt stains.) *Hollett.* $39/£25

BRYDEN, H. ANDERSON. Gun and Camera in Southern Africa. London: Stanford, 1893. (Backstrip faded; mkd, sl loose.) *Petersfield.* $124/£80

BRYDONE, PATRICK. A Tour through Sicily and Malta. (London: Ptd for W. Strahan & T. Cadell, 1773.) 1st ed, 1st ptg. 2 vols. 1/2 titles, errata leaf present. Contemp smooth calf (nicks; insect damage), gilt spines, red morocco labels, paper shelf label bottom of spine. Leaves sl dknd; 2 branching wormholes prelims vol 1; wormhole vol 2 (no loss to text either vol), else Fine. Bkpl of Wm. Constable. *Pirages.* $350/£226

BRYDONE, PATRICK. Tour through Sicily and Malta. London: Cadell & Davis, 1806. xii, 387pp, fldg engr map (tape repairs). Panelled tree calf, gilt spine, by Sotheran (spine chipped, joints rubbed, label worn). *Schoyer.* $85/£55

BRYHER. (Pseud of W. Ellerman.) The Coin of Carthage. NY: Harcourt, (1963). 1st ed. Fine in NF dj. *Reese.* $35/£23

BRYHER. (Pseud of W. Ellerman.) Gate to the Sea. London: Collins, 1959. 1st (British) ed. Fine in VG dj (2 mended tears; dust soiling). *Reese.* $25/£16

BRYHER. (Pseud of W. Ellerman.) The Player's Boy. NY: Pantheon, (1953). 1st ed. Fine in NF dj. *Reese.* $30/£19

BRYHER. (Pseud of W. Ellerman.) Ruan. (NY): Pantheon, (1960). 1st ed. Frontis. VG (ink inscrip) in dj. *Reese.* $25/£16

BRYNER, B.C. Abraham Lincoln in Peoria, Illinois. (Peoria, IL: Privately ptd by Edward J. Jacob, Oct 16, 1924.) One of 100. Signed by Jacob. 4 fldg facs. Leather spine, corners; 5 raised bands; gilt top. Nice (sl rubbed; corner bumped; bkpl). *Bohling.* $150/£97

BRYSON, J. GORDON. One Hundred Dollars and a Horse. NY: William Morrow, 1965. 1st ed. Dj. *Lambeth.* $30/£19

BUBER, MARTIN. I and Thou. Edinburgh, 1937. 1st Eng trans. Wraps (dknd; spine defective). *King.* $95/£61

BUCHAN, JOHN (ed). Musa Piscatrix. London/Chicago: John Lane/McClurg, 1896. 1st ed. xxiv,107pp + 16pp pub's cat, 6 etchings by E. Philip Pimlott. Pict blue cl (sl bubbling). Teg, others untrimmed. *Schoyer.* $175/£113

BUCHAN, JOHN. The African Colony. Edinburgh/London: William Blackwood, 1903. 1st ed, 1st binding. Fldg color map. Orig dk blue cl. NF (sl rubbed). *Sumner & Stillman.* $185/£119

BUCHAN, JOHN. The Island of Sheep. London: Hodder & Stoughton, (1936). 1st ed. Fine in dj (lt used). *Juvelis.* $150/£97

BUCHAN, JOHN. The Marquis of Montrose. London: Nelson, 1913. 1st UK ed. VG (fr pastedown abrased). *Williams.* $62/£40

BUCHAN, JOHN. The Moon Endureth. NY: Sturgis & Walton, 1912. 1st Amer ed. Lt blue-grey cl dec in black/silver. NF in VG dj (sl chipped). *Sumner & Stillman.* $325/£210

BUCHAN, JOHN. Mountain Meadow. Boston: Houghton Mifflin, 1941. 1st Amer ed. Fine in dj (crease). *Mordida.* $75/£48

BUCHAN, JOHN. Prester John. Nelson, (1910). 1st ed. Spine flaking, else VG. *Aronovitz.* $75/£48

BUCHAN, JOHN. Sick Heart River. London: Hodder & Stoughton, 1941. 1st UK ed. VG in dj (price-clipped, sl worn, rubbed). *Williams.* $34/£22

BUCHAN, LAURA and JERRY ALLEN. Hearth in the Snow. NY: Wilfred Funk, (1952). 1st ed. Fine in Fine dj. *Perier.* $30/£19

BUCHAN, SUSAN. Funeral March of a Marionette. London: Hogarth Press, 1935. 1st ed. One of 1500. Fine in dj (sl worn). *Second Life.* $45/£29

BUCHAN, WILLIAM. Advice to Mothers, on the Subject of Their Own Health.... London: T. Cadell & W. Davies, 1803. 1st ed. (iv),419,(i)pp. 1/2-calf antique, marbled bds (new eps). *Bickersteth.* $217/£140

BUCHAN, WILLIAM. Advice to Mothers, on the Subject of Their Own Health.... Phila, 1804. 1st Amer ed. 344pp. Full leather. Good. *Fye.* $300/£194

BUCHAN, WILLIAM. Domestic Medicine, or, A Treatise on the Prevention and Cure of Diseases, by Regimen and Simple Medicines.... Exeter, 1843. 495; 48pp. Recent cl. (Ex-lib.) *Fye.* $100/£65

BUCHAN, WILLIAM. Domestic Medicine, or, A Treatise on the Prevention and Cure of Diseases.... Exeter: Williams, 1828. 22nd Eng ed. 496; xlviiipp (foxed; early leaves dampstained). New cl. *Goodrich.* $95/£61

BUCHAN, WILLIAM. Domestic Medicine. London, 1813. 21st ed. xl,762pp (foxing). 1/2 leather, marbled bds, leather spine label (incorrectly labeled 18th ed). *Whitehart.* $93/£60

BUCHAN, WILLIAM. Every Man His Own Doctor; or, a Treatise on the Prevention and Cure of Diseases.... New Haven: Whiting, 1816. 2 parts in 1 vol. 464; 138pp. (Foxing.) Orig full sheep (sl worn; edges bumped). *Goodrich.* $125/£81

BUCHANAN, ANGUS. Wild Life in Canada. Toronto: McClelland, Stewart, 1920. Map. Lt blue pict cl. Spine lt faded, o/w VG + . *Bowman.* $75/£48

BUCHANAN, BRIGGS. Early Near Eastern Seals in the Yale Collection. New Haven: Yale Univ Press, 1981. 1st ed. 218 plts. VG. *Worldwide.* $80/£52

BUCHANAN, CHARLES. Antisepsis and Antiseptics. Newark, 1895. 1st ed. 352pp. Good. *Fye.* $80/£52

BUCHANAN, ROBERT. The Fleshly School of Poetry. London: Strahan, 1872. 1st ed. Fine in wrappers (dusty; spine sl used). *Pharos.* $300/£194

BUCHANAN, ROBERT. The Pied Piper of Hamelin: A Fantastic Opera in Two Acts. London: Heinemann, 1893. 1st ed. 8vo. 12 full-pg b/w illus by Hugh Thomson. Sage cl w/grn lettering, design. Corners lt bumped; o/w NF. *Reisler.* $150/£97

BUCHANAN, THOMAS G. Who Killed Kennedy? London: Secker & Warburg, 1964. 1st UK ed. VG + (sm bruise; staining) in dj. *Williams.* $28/£18

BUCHANAN-BROWN, JOHN. Phiz! London: David & Charles, 1978. Dj. *Edwards.* $31/£20

BUCHANAN-BROWN, JOHN. Phiz! The Book Illustrations of Hablot Knight Browne. Newton Abbot: David & Charles, 1978. Sound in dj. *Ars Artis.* $39/£25

BUCHHOLZ, HANS-GUNTER and VASSOS KARAGEORGHIS. Prehistoric Greece and Cyprus. London: Phaidon, (1973). 4 color plts. (Sig.) *Archaeologia.* $95/£61

BUCHNER, ALEXANDER. Musical Instruments through the Ages. London: Spring Books, n.d. (ca 1950). 1st ed in English. 323 plts. VG + in dj (spine sl dknd). *Bookpress.* $85/£55

BUCK, FRANKLIN. A Yankee Trader in the Gold Rush. Houghton Mifflin, 1930. 1st ed. Frontis; 7 plts. VG in VG dj. *Oregon.* $50/£32

BUCK, HOWARD. The Tempering. New Haven: Yale Univ, 1919. 1st ed, 1st bk. VG. *Pharos.* $75/£48

BUCK, MITCHELL S. Book Repair and Restoration. Phila: Nicholas L. Brown, 1918. Ltd to 1000. Burgundy cl (soiled), paper spine label. Dj (chipped). *Karmiole.* $35/£23

BUCK, PEARL S. All Under Heaven. NY: John Day, (1973). Signed ltd ed of 1000. Fine in dj. *Antic Hay.* $85/£55

BUCK, PEARL S. China: Past and Present. NY: John Day, (1972). Signed ltd ed of 1000 numbered. Fine in dj (price-clipped). *Antic Hay.* $85/£55

BUCK, PEARL S. Death in the Castle. NY: John Day, (1965). 1st ed. NF in dj. *Antic Hay.* $45/£29

BUCK, PEARL S. Essay on Myself. NY: John Day, (1966). One of 1000. Signed. Fine in acetate dj (sl wear). *Antic Hay.* $125/£81

BUCK, PEARL S. The Good Earth. NY: John Day, (1931). 1st ed, 1st issue, w/'flees' for 'fleas' line 17, p100. Cl stamped in gilt/blind (spine sl dull; sl rubbed). Later dj (lt soiled, chipped). *Sadlon.* $35/£23

BUCK, PEARL S. Stories for Little Children. NY: John Day, 1940. 1st ed. Weda Yap (illus). NF in VG + dj (1-inch tear fr panel; surface loss extrems). *Lame Duck.* $150/£97

BUCK, SOLON J. The Granger Movement. Cambridge, 1913. 1st ed. (Sm emb lib stamp; bkpl removed.) Howes B 916. *Ginsberg.* $75/£48

BUCK, SOLON J. and ELIZABETH H. The Planting of Civilization in Western Pennsylvania. Pittsburgh, 1939. *Hayman.* $35/£23

BUCKBEE, EDNA. Pioneer Days of Angel's Camp. Angels Camp, CA: Calaveras Californian, (1932). 1st ed. 12 plts. Fine in pict wraps. *Oregon.* $60/£39

BUCKBEE, EDNA. The Saga of Old Tuolumne. Press of Pioneers, 1935. 1st ed. Frontis; 14 plts. Good + (faded). *Oregon.* $55/£35

BUCKERIDGE, J.O. Lincoln's Choice. The Repeating Rifle Which Cut Short the Civil War. Harrisburg, (1956). 1st ed. Dj torn, chipped, o/w VG+. *Pratt.* $32/£21

BUCKHAM, GEORGE. Notes from the Journal of a Tourist. NY: Gavin, 1890. 2 vols complete. Frontis, xx,1024pp (lt marginal staining); teg. Presentation card laid in. (Bds sl buckling.) *Archaeologia.* $85/£55

BUCKHOLTZ, L.V. (comp). Tactics for Officers of Infantry, Cavalry and Artillery. Richmond, VA: J.W. Randolph, 1861. 1st ed. 121,(2)pp ads. Brn cl. VG (contemp sig; sl spotted). *Chapel Hill.* $400/£258

BUCKINGHAM, GEORGE VILLIERS. The Rehearsal. Montague Summers (ed). Shakespeare Head, 1924. #134/510. Cl-backed bds (sl rubbed; label chipped, dknd; foxing; edges sl dusty). *Poetry.* $47/£30

BUCKINGHAM, NASH. Blood Lines. Tales of Shooting and Fishing. NY: Derrydale, (1938). #294/1250. Fine in glassine dj (sl chipped). *Polyanthos.* $250/£161

BUCKINGHAM, NASH. De Shootin'est Gentman. NY: Derrydale, 1934. One of 950 numbered. Fine+. *Bowman.* $500/£323

BUCKINGHAM, NASH. Mark Right! Tales of Shooting and Fishing. NY: Derrydale, (1936). 1st ed, #550/1250. VG. *Mcgowan.* $275/£177

BUCKINGHAM, NASH. De Shootin'est Gent'man and Other Hunting Tales. NY, (1961). 1st ed, ltd to 260 numbered, signed by author and Hamilton Greene (illus). VG in glassine dj, slipcase (sl used). *King.* $395/£255

BUCKINGHAM, NASH. Tattered Coat. NY: Putnam's, (1944). #840/995 signed. Sl soiling, else VG. *Mcgowan.* $150/£97

BUCKLAND-WRIGHT, JOHN. Etching and Engraving Techniques and the Modern Trend. London: Studio, 1953. 1st ed. VG in orig cl (sl mkd). *Cox.* $54/£35

BUCKLEY, FRANCIS. A History of Old English Glass. London, 1925. 1st ed. 60 plts. (Prelims, tp sl spotted; cl sl soiled; spine sl sunned, sm split.) *Edwards.* $140/£90

BUCKLEY, M.B. Diary of a Tour in America.... Dublin, 1889. 1st ed. (3),384pp. Dec cl. *Ginsberg.* $75/£48

BUCKLEY, W. Big Game Hunting in Central Africa. London: Cecil Palmer, (1930). 1st ed. Brn cl. VG (sig). *Chapel Hill.* $150/£97

BUCKLEY, WILLIAM F., JR. A Very Private Plot. NY: William Morrow, 1994. 1st ed. Signed. VF in dj. *Mordida.* $30/£19

BUCKMAN, DAVID LEAR. Old Steamboat Days on the Hudson River. NY: Grafton, (1907). 1st ed. 22 plts. VG. *Blue Dragon.* $45/£29

BUCKNILL, JOHN A. The Birds of Surrey. London: R.H. Porter, 1900. 1st ed. 6 photogravure plts. (Fore-edge sl foxed.) *Petersfield.* $78/£50

BUCKROSE, J.E. Rambles in the North Yorkshire Dales. London: Mills & Boon, 1913. 1st ed. Pict gilt cl. VG. *Hollett.* $47/£30

BUDD, F.E. A Book of Lullabies 1300-1900. London: Eric Partridge, 1930. 1st ed. One of 700 ptd. VG+. *Bishop.* $15/£10

BUDD, WILLIAM. Typhoid Fever. NY: (Amer Public Health Assoc), 1931. Ltd to 800. Frontis, 4 plts (1 color). Blue cl (sl rubbed), blue leather spine label. *Karmiole.* $30/£19

BUDD, WILLIAM. Typhoid Fever: Its Nature.... London, 1873. 1st ed. 193pp. Spine head frayed. *Fye.* $400/£258

BUDD, WILLIAM. Typhoid Fever: Its Nature.... NY, 1977 (facs of 1931 ed). Good. *Fye.* $40/£26

BUDDE, LUDWIG and RICHARD NICHOLLS. A Catalogue of the Greek and Roman Sculpture. CUP, 1964. 62 b/w plts. (Half-title sl creased; ex-lib w/ink stamp, label remains.) Dj (sl chipped). *Edwards.* $70/£45

BUDE, JOHN. When the Case Was Opened. London: Macdonald, 1952. 1st ed. NF in dj (lt wear bottom edge; lt soiled rear). *Murder.* $40/£26

BUDGE, E.A. WALLIS. An Account of the Sarcophagus of Seti I. London: Sir John Soane's Museum, 1908. (Spine chipped.) *Archaeologia.* $85/£55

BUDGE, E.A. WALLIS. Babylonian Life and History. London, 1925. 2nd ed. 11 plts. *Edwards.* $39/£25

BUDGE, E.A. WALLIS. The Book of the Dead. London: British Museum, 1929. Good in stiff wraps. *Archaeologia.* $25/£16

BUDGE, E.A. WALLIS. By Nile and Tigris. London: Murray, 1920. 1st ed. 2 vols. Rubbed, sl soiled, spine sl frayed; sl foxing, o/w VG. *Worldwide.* $350/£226

BUDGE, E.A. WALLIS. The Divine Origin of the Craft of the Herbalist. London: Soc of Herbalists, 1928. (Stained.) Dj (tattered). *Archaeologia.* $85/£55

BUDGE, E.A. WALLIS. Easy Lessons in Egyptian Hieroglyphics, With Sign List. London, 1899. 246pp. (Bkpl removed; stamped name; ink notes; loose; worn, stained back cvr.) *King.* $35/£23

BUDGE, E.A. WALLIS. An Egyptian Hieroglyphic Dictionary. NY: Ungar, (1960). 2 vols complete. (Sig.) *Archaeologia.* $200/£129

BUDGE, E.A. WALLIS. Egyptian Ideas of the Future Life. London: Kegan Paul et al, 1908. 8 plts. (Spine faded.) *Archaeologia.* $45/£29

BUDGE, E.A. WALLIS. Egyptian Sculptures in the British Museum. London: British Museum, 1914. 54 photo plts. (Spine chipped, torn.) *Archaeologia.* $250/£161

BUDGE, E.A. WALLIS. The Nile. London, 1898. 6th ed. 443pp (bkpl; ink, stamped names). Gilt-stamped cl (stained; spine spotted). *King.* $35/£23

BUDGE, E.A. WALLIS. The Nile. London, 1901. 7th ed. 2 maps, fldg map. Marbled eps, edges. Gilt-dec cl (sl worn, spine sl chipped; lt foxing). *Edwards.* $39/£25

BUDGE, E.A. WALLIS. The Nile. London: Thos. Cook, 1901. 7th ed. 2 maps. VG. *Hollett.* $62/£40

BUDGEN, FRANK. James Joyce and the Making of Ulysses. London: Grayson & Grayson, (1934). 1st ed. Lacks dj, else NF. *Pharos.* $35/£23

BUDGEN, L.M. Episodes of Insect Life by Acheta Domestica. Second Series. London: Reeve & Benham, 1851. Litho frontis. Aeg. Orig blue cl, blind/gilt dec. VG (lt spotting). *Shifrin.* $125/£81

BUDRYS, ALGIS. Michaelmas. Berkley, 1977. 1st ed. Inscribed. Fine in dj. *Madle.* $35/£23

BUECHNER, FREDERICK. A Long Day's Dying. NY: Knopf, 1950. 1st ed. NF in dj. *Hermitage.* $65/£42

BUECHNER, THOMAS. Norman Rockwell. NY, 1972. 1st ed. Mint in dj. *Bond.* $35/£23

BUEL, J.W. The Border Outlaws...The Younger Brothers, Jesse and Frank James, and Their Comrades in Crime... St. Louis/Phila: Hist Pub Co, 1884. Old calf (worn, stained; fr joint cracked). Text Fine. Howes B 933. *Glenn.* $75/£48

BUEL, J.W. The Border Outlaws...Younger Brothers, Jesse and Frank James.... St. Louis: Linahan, 1881. 1st ed. Frontis each section; 252,148pp; 12 color plts; 4pp ads. Pict cl. Good+ (lacks fep; stamp). Howes B 933. *Oregon.* $95/£61

BUEL, J.W. Heroes of the Plains. NY: Parks Bros, 1882. 548pp (shaken; sigs pulled). Brn cl (rubbed, bumped). Good. *Blue Mountain.* $25/£16

BUEL, J.W. Heroes of the Plains. NY/St. Louis: N.D. Thompson, 1882. 2nd ptg. 548pp. Pict cl (edgewear). Howes B 934. *Schoyer.* $85/£55

BUEL, J.W. Russian Nihilism and Exile Life in Siberia. St. Louis: Historical Pub, 1883. 1st ed. Gilt-stamped grn cl (rebound). Fine. *Beasley.* $85/£55

BUEL, J.W. The True Story of 'Wild Bill' Hickok. NY: Atomic Bks, (1946). VG in stiff pict wraps. *Schoyer.* $30/£19

BUEL, J.W. The True Story of Wild Bill Hickok. J. Brussel (ed). NY: Atomic Books, (1946). Lt erasure spot fr wrap, o/w VG. *Oregon.* $25/£16

BUEL, JESSE. The Farmer's Companion.... Boston: Marsh, et al, 1840. 2nd ed. 303pp + ad. Mod bds; paper label. Nice. *Second Life.* $95/£61

BUFFUM, E. GOULD. Six Months in the Gold Mines. Ward Ritchie, 1959. Gilt-stamped black cl spine, black/yellow patterned bds. Fine. *Oregon.* $60/£39

BUFFUM, E. GOULD. Six Months in the Gold Mines: From a Journal.... Phila, 1850. 172pp + ads. (Neat tear fr joint, expertly repaired head, toe of spine; corners worn.) VG. Howes B 943. *Reese.* $750/£484

BUIST, ROBERT. American Flower-Garden Directory.... Phila, 1851. 4th ed. xvi,339 + 20pp ads (prelims, final 30pp foxed, browned). Orig brn cl, blind/gilt-stamped pict cvr (bumped, rubbed; top 1/4-inch spine perished). VG. *Shifrin.* $50/£32

BUIST, ROBERT. The Family Kitchen Gardener. NY, 1847. 1st ed. 216pp (foxing, marginal dampstaining). Gilt-dec cl (wear, staining, splitting, loss). *Sutton.* $95/£61

BUIST, ROBERT. The Rose Manual.... Phila: Carey and Hart, 1844. 1st ed. 182,(2)pp. (Pencil notes.) Gray blind-stamped cl. Good+. *Bookpress.* $185/£119

BUKOWSKI, CHARLES. Barfly, the Continuing Saga of Henry Chinaski. Sutton West & Santa Barbara, (1984). 1st ed, one of 200 deluxe numbered, signed. VG in glassine dj (sl rubbed). *King.* $250/£161

BUKOWSKI, CHARLES. Beautiful and Other Long Poems. Stockton, CA, 1988. 1st ed, ltd to 700 numbered. VG in wraps. *King.* $25/£16

BUKOWSKI, CHARLES. Burning in Water, Drowning in Flame. L.A., 1974. 1st ed, one of 300 numbered, signed. VG in glassine dj (sm tears). *King.* $195/£126

BUKOWSKI, CHARLES. Cold Dogs in the Courtyard. (Chicago: Literary Times-Cyfoeth, 1965). One of 500. Old price in marker fr wrap, else Fine in stapled wrappers. *Between The Covers.* $250/£161

BUKOWSKI, CHARLES. Confessions of a Man Insane Enough to Live with Beasts. IL: Mimeo Press, 1965. 1st ed, ltd to 500. VG in stapled pict wrappers. *Godot.* $275/£177

BUKOWSKI, CHARLES. Horsemeat. Santa Barbara, 1982. 1st ed, ltd to 125 numbered, signed by Bukowski and Michael Montfort (photos). Orig prospectus present. VG in glassine dj (sl rubbed). *King.* $395/£255

BUKOWSKI, CHARLES. Hot Water Music. Santa Barbara: Black Sparrow, 1983. One of 100 numbered, signed. Add'l tipped-in abstract painting. VF in orig acetate. *Pharos.* $250/£161

BUKOWSKI, CHARLES. Hot Water Music. Santa Barbara: Black Sparrow, 1983. One of 350 numbered, signed. Pre-pub broadside prospectus laid in. Fine. *Pharos.* $150/£97

BUKOWSKI, CHARLES. In the Shadow of the Rose. Black Sparrow Press, 1991. Ltd to 750 numbered, signed. Fine in Fine dj. *Polyanthos.* $65/£42

BUKOWSKI, CHARLES. Love Is a Dog from Hell, Poems 1974-1977. Santa Barbara, 1977. 1st ed, one of 300 numbered, signed. Cl-backed pict bds. VG in glassine dj (sl rubbed). *King.* $85/£55

BUKOWSKI, CHARLES. Love Poem to Marina. (Santa Barbara): Black Sparrow Press, 1973. 1st ed. VG. *King.* $50/£32

BUKOWSKI, CHARLES. Luck. Santa Rosa: Black Sparrow, (1987). 1st ed. One of 200 numbered, signed. Cl, dec bds. Fine. *Reese.* $30/£19

BUKOWSKI, CHARLES. Play the Piano Drunk Like a Percussion Instrument.... Santa Barbara, 1979. 1st ed, one of 300 numbered, signed. VG in glassine dj (sl rubbed). *King.* $75/£48

BUKOWSKI, CHARLES. The Rooming-House Madrigals: Early Selected Poems 1946-1966. Santa Rosa: Black Sparrow, 1988. One of 400 numbered, signed. Cl-backed pict bds. VF in orig acetate. *Pharos.* $45/£29

BUKOWSKI, CHARLES. Septuagenarian Stew, Stories and Poems. Santa Rosa, 1990. 1st ed, one of 251 numbered, lettered, signed; handbound in bds, w/orig signed silkscreen print by Bukowski. VG in glassine dj (sl rubbed). *King.* $125/£81

BUKOWSKI, CHARLES. War All the Time: Poems 1981-1984. Santa Barbara: Black Sparrow, 1984. One of 400 hb copies numbered, signed. Cl, paper-cvrd bds. Acetate dj. *Between The Covers.* $150/£97

BUKOWSKI, CHARLES. Women. Santa Barbara, 1978. 1st ed, one of 300 numbered, signed w/sm self-port. VG in glassine dj (sl rubbed). *King.* $75/£48

BULEY, R. CARLYLE. The Old Northwest Pioneer Period 1815-1840. IN Univ Press, 1951. 2nd ed. 2 vols. VG+ in VG slipcase. *Bishop.* $40/£26

BULEY, R. CARLYLE. The Old Northwest; Pioneer Period 1815-1840. IN Univ Press, 1951. 2nd ptg. 2 vols. VG. *Artis.* $55/£35

BULL, A.J. Photo-Engraving. London: Edward Arnold, 1934. 1st ed. Color frontis, 14 plts. Black cl. Fine in dj. *Weber.* $65/£42

BULLARD, ASA. Fifty Years with the Sabbath Schools. Boston: Lockwood, Brooks, 1876. 1st ed. 336pp, frontis port. Dec grn cl. Good. *Karmiole.* $30/£19

BULLARD, ASA. The Good Scholar. Boston: Lee & Shepard, 1863. 16mo. Engr frontis, tp, 64pp + 1pg ad. Emb brn cl (sl rubbed). VG (spot pg 9 not affecting text). *Hobbyhorse.* $50/£32

BULLARD, MARION. The Somersaulting Rabbit. NY: E.P. Dutton, (1927). 12 plts (1-inch tear 1 plt). Red cl-backed pict white bds (sl soiled). Else NF. *Blue Mountain.* $65/£42

BULLEN, FRANK. The Cruise of the 'Cachalot' Round the World After Sperm Whales. NY, 1899. 1st NY ed. xx,379pp; fldg map. Pict cvr. *Lewis.* $59/£38

BULLEN, FRANK. The Cruise of the 'Cachalot' Round the World after Sperm Whales. London: Smith, Elder, 1903. 2nd ed, 11th imp. Blue cl (sl rubbed). *Hollett.* $101/£65

BULLER, WALTER LAWRY. Birds of New Zealand. E.G. Turbott (ed). London, 1967. 48 tipped-in color plts. Dec eps. Dj; in slipcase, as issued. *Edwards.* $93/£60

BULLETT, GERALD. Poems in Pencil. J.M. Dent & Sons, 1937. 1st ed. Teg, rest untrimmed. Ornamental bds, cl spine. *Bickersteth.* $28/£18

BULLINS, ED. The Reluctant Rapist. NY: Harper, 1973. 1st ed. Fine (sticker) in Fine dj (2 sm digs rear panel). *Beasley.* $35/£23

BULLOCH, JAMES D. Secret Service of the Confederate States in Europe. London: Bentley, 1883. 1st ed. 2 vols. (10),460; (6),438pp. 1/2 morocco, raised bands, gilt-dec spines. Very Nice set (sm emb lib stamps). Howes B 949. *Ginsberg.* $400/£258

BULLOCH, WILLIAM. The History of Bacteriology. London, 1938. 1st ed. Good. *Fye.* $125/£81

BULWER LYTTON, EDWARD. The Lost Tales of Miletus. NY: Harpers, 1866. 1st Amer ed. NF. *Pharos.* $45/£29

BULWER LYTTON, EDWARD. The Lost Tales of Miletus. London: John Murray, 1866. 1st ed. xii,(2),168pp + 32pp pub's cat; uncut. Brn cl (sl soiled; sl nick spine head). Good. *Cox.* $28/£18

BUND, J.W. WILLIS. Oke's Game Laws. London: Butterworth, 1897. 4th ed. Grn cl, gilt (worn, hinges cracked). *Boswell.* $85/£55

BUNIM, MIRIAM SCHILD. Space in Medieval Painting and the Forerunners of Perspective. NY: Columbia Univ, 1940. 1st ed. Frontis. Blue cl (spotted), gilt spine. Dj. *Karmiole.* $100/£65

BUNIN, IVAN. The Gentleman of San Francisco and Other Stories. Hogarth Press, 1934. 2nd ed. VG in dj. *Words Etc.* $116/£75

BUNIN, IVAN. Memories and Portraits. London: John Lehmann, (1951). 1st ed. Fine in dj (sl sunned). *Pharos.* $25/£16

BUNN, MATTHEW. Journal of the Adventures of.... Chicago, 1962. One of 2000. Ptd wrappers. *Ginsberg.* $25/£16

BUNNING, JIM with RALPH BERNSTEIN. Story of Jim Bunning. Lippincott, 1965. 1st ed. VG + in VG + dj. *Plapinger.* $35/£23

BUNT, CYRIL G.E. The Goldsmiths of Italy. London: Martin Hopkinson, 1926. 1st ed. Tipped-in color frontis, 20 b/w plts. Teg. Gilt-lettered blue buckram. NF (sl wear). *House.* $180/£116

BUNT, CYRIL G.E. The Life and Work of William James Muller of Bristol. Leigh-on-Sea, 1948. 1st ed. #229/500. Tipped-in color frontis, 8 tipped-in color plts, 34 b/w plts. Fore, lower edges uncut. *Edwards.* $70/£45

BUNTING, BASIL. Briggflatts. London: Fulcrum Press, (1966). 1st ed, regular issue, one of 400 thus. Sl fading, o/w Fine in dec wrappers. *Jaffe.* $375/£242

BUNTING, BASIL. Collected Poems. London: Fulcrum Press, 1968. 1st ed. NF in dj (sl creased, browned). *Rees.* $31/£20

BUNTING, BASIL. Collected Poems. London: Fulcrum Press, 1968. 1st trade ed. VG. *Hollett.* $70/£45

BUNTING, BASIL. Descant on Rawthey's Madrigal. (Lexington, KY): Gnomon Press, (1968). 1st ed. Ltd to 500. Frontis photo. Fine in wrappers. *Jaffe.* $75/£48

BUNTING, BASIL. Loquitur. London: Fulcrum, (1965). 1st ed, trade issue. Ptd bds. NF. *Reese.* $85/£55

BUNTING, BASIL. Loquitur. London: Fulcrum Press, (1965). 1st ed. One of 774 bound in bds of 1000 total. Fine. *Jaffe.* $225/£145

BUNTING, BASIL. Loquitur. London: Fulcrum, 1965. 1st ltd ed. One of 1000. Fine in clear plastic dj as issued. *Hollett.* $147/£95

BUNTING, BASIL. Version of Horace. Holborn, London: Officina Mauritania, 1972. 1st ed in type. One of 300 (250 for sale). Fldg leaflet. Fine in envelope (lt soiled). *Reese.* $35/£23

BUNUEL, LUIS. My Last Breath. London: Cape, 1984. 1st ed. Fine in dj. *Patterson.* $39/£25

BUNYAN, JOHN. The Pilgrim's Progress and The Life and Death of Mr. Badman. Kynoch Press, 1928. One of 1600. 8 full-pg illus by Karl Michel inserted. Teg. Marbled cl-cvrd bds, white parchment spine label. Fine (spine dknd; shelfwear). *Heller.* $125/£81

BUNYAN, JOHN. The Pilgrim's Progress. London: T. Heptinstall, 1796. 1st part frontis w/imprint dated May 2d, 1796. 2 parts in 1 w/continuous pagination. Sm 4to. 1st part frontisport w/imprint dated May 2d, 1796. 2nd part copper engr frontis. xlviii,433, viii,223,1pp. 8 full-pg copper engrs (lt offsetting facing pp). Contemp mottled full leather on bds, red label spine; gilt. Good (pencil sig fep; extrems rubbed; lower bd partly loose; lt foxing). *Hobbyhorse.* $185/£119

BUNYAN, JOHN. The Pilgrim's Progress. (London: T. Heptinstall, 1796.) 2 p.l., xlviii,208pp; (209)-434,(1)pp (sl yellowed; lt foxed); 2 engr tps; 8 engr plts (discolored w/offsetting). 19th cent 1/2 roan (scuffed; hinges cracked), marbled paper sides, raised bands, blind rules. *Pirages.* $125/£81

BUNYAN, JOHN. The Pilgrim's Progress. London: David Bogue, 1851. Frontis port, xcii,(viii),440pp; aeg. Full gilt filleted morocco, dec gilt-edged raised bands (spine rubbed, surface loss). *Edwards.* $47/£30

BUNYAN, JOHN. The Pilgrim's Progress. London: Routledge, Warne, and Routledge, 1861. Later ed. 8vo. Frontis, 407,(1)pp. Aeg. Maroon morocco, gilt-tooled; inner dentelles, raised bands. Extrems, spine sl rubbed, else VG. *Chapel Hill.* $100/£65

BUNYAN, JOHN. The Pilgrim's Progress. London: Nonesuch, 1928. #649/1600. 5 woodcuts by Karl Michel; teg, others uncut. Marbled cl, leather label. VG. *Cox.* $70/£45

BUNYAN, JOHN. The Pilgrim's Progress. NY: Payson & Clarke, 1928. 1st ed. VG. *Pharos.* $40/£26

BUNYAN, JOHN. The Pilgrim's Progress. NY: LEC, 1941. #904/1500 numbered. William Blake (illus). Fine in pub's slipcase. *Hermitage.* $150/£97

BUNYAN, JOHN. The Pilgrim's Progress. London: Ward, Lock, and Tyler, n.d. (ca 1860). xix,304pp, full-pg frontis, engr vignette tp, 100 VF engrs by Thomas Dalziel. Marbled eps, edges. Full leather on bds; gilt ti-tle spine; gilt. (Sm tear top edge 1st 3 leaves; damp stain upper cvr; shelfwear). In all, VG. *Hobbyhorse.* $125/£81

BUNYARD, EDWARD A. Old Garden Roses. London, 1936. Color frontis; 32 plain plts. *Wheldon & Wesley.* $70/£45

BUNYARD, EDWARD A. Old Garden Roses. London/NY: Country Life/Scribner's, 1936. 1st ed. Color frontis, 32 b/w plts. Fine in Fine dj. *Quest.* $90/£58

BURBRIDGE, BEN. Gorilla. London, 1928. (Lt foxing; upper hinge cracked; cl dampstained.) *Edwards.* $39/£25

BURCH, JOHN P. Charles W. Quantrell. (Vega, TX: Burch, 1923.) Bright pict cl. VG. *Schoyer.* $25/£16

BURCH, JOHN P. Charles W. Quantrell. (Vega, TX, 1923.) 1st ed. Burgundy cl, gilt. *Glenn.* $75/£48

BURCHARD, JOHN E. (ed). Rockets, Guns, and Targets. Boston: Little, Brown, 1948. 1st ed. VG in dj (chipped, worn). *Knollwood.* $50/£32

BURCHETT, WILFRED. Furtive War: The United States in Vietnam and Laos. NY: International, (1963). NF in dj (price-clipped; edges rubbed; internal tape reinforcement). *Aka.* $45/£29

BURDEKIN, K. The Rebel Passion. Morrow, 1929. 1st ed. VG + in dj (lt chipped). *Aronovitz.* $55/£35

BURDEN, W. DOUGLAS. Dragon Lizards of Komodo.... NY: Putnam's, 1927. (Faded.) *Petersfield.* $28/£18

BURDER, SAMUEL. Oriental Customs. London, 1802-7. 2 vols. xvi,400; 394pp. 1/2 calf, marbled bds (sl rubbed; ex-libris; upper joints tender). *Edwards.* $85/£55

BURDETT, OSBERT. A Little Book of Cheese. London: Gerald Howe, 1935. Black cl. Fair (sig). *Heller.* $25/£16

BURDICK, J.R. et al (eds). The Standard Guide on All Collected Cards and Their Values. East Stroudsburg, 1960. VG. *Argosy.* $35/£23

BURDSALL, RICHARD and ARTHUR B. EMMONS. Men against the Clouds. London: John Lane, The Bodley Head, 1935. 1st ed. 7 maps, charts. (Edges sl faded.) Dj (sl chipped, torn). *Hollett.* $132/£85

BUREAU OF AMERICAN ETHNOLOGY. *See* BAE

BURET, F. Syphilis in Ancient and Prehistoric Times. Volume I. Phila, 1891. 1st Eng trans. 226pp. Good. *Fye.* $75/£48

BURGE, DOLLY SUMNER. A Woman's Wartime Journal: An Account of the Passage Over a Georgia Plantation of Sherman's Army.... NY: Century, 1918. 1st ed. Dec cl. *Ginsberg.* $125/£81

BURGES, TRISTAM. Battle of Lake Erie. Phila: Marshall, 1839. 132pp (foxed); 2 diags. (Pencil, ink sigs.) *Schoyer.* $50/£32

BURGESS, ANTHONY. Beds in the East. London: Heinemann, 1959. 1st ed. VG in dj (sl faded, edge-chipped). *Hollett.* $116/£75

BURGESS, ANTHONY. A Clockwork Orange. London: Heinemann, 1962. 1st ed. NF in color pict dj. *Limestone.* $565/£365

BURGESS, ANTHONY. A Clockwork Orange. London: Heinemann, 1962. 1st ed. 1st binding (2nd being purple bds). Dk brn cl-textured bds. Top edges sl foxed, o/w Fine in dj (tape mks verso). *Temple.* $287/£185

BURGESS, ANTHONY. A Clockwork Orange: A Play with Music. London: Hutchinson, 1987. 1st ed. Fine in wrappers. *Rees.* $19/£12

BURGESS, ANTHONY. The Clockwork Testament. NY, 1974. 1st US ed. Dec cl. Fine in dj (sl dull; sl mkd). *Whiteson.* $28/£18

BURGESS, ANTHONY. Devil of a State. Heinemann, 1961. 1st ed. VG in dj (dull). *Whiteson.* $25/£16

BURGESS, ANTHONY. The End of the World News. Hutchinson, 1982. 1st UK ed. Fine in dj. *Lewton.* $23/£15

BURGESS, ANTHONY. Enderby Outside. London: Heinemann, 1968. 1st UK ed. Fine in dj. *Williams.* $116/£75

BURGESS, ANTHONY. Enderby. NY, (1968). 1st Amer ed. VG in dj (sl used, dknd). *King.* $35/£23

BURGESS, ANTHONY. Ernest Hemingway and His World. London, (1978). 1st ed. Fine in NF dj. *Polyanthos.* $30/£19

BURGESS, ANTHONY. The Eve of Saint Venus. London: Sidgwick and Jackson, 1964. 1st ed. Fine in dj. *Limestone.* $35/£23

BURGESS, ANTHONY. The Eve of St. Venus. London: S&J, 1964. 1st UK ed. NF in dj. *Lewton.* $31/£20

BURGESS, ANTHONY. Joysprick. London: Deutsch, 1973. 1st UK ed. Fine in NF dj (price-clipped). *Williams.* $101/£65

BURGESS, ANTHONY. The Kingdom of the Wicked. PA: Franklin Center, 1985. 1st ed, ltd to unspecified # signed. Aeg. Full maroon leather, gold-stamped. Fine; issued w/o dj. *Godot.* $50/£32

BURGESS, ANTHONY. Language Made Plain. London: English Universities Press, (1964). 1st ed. Top edge lt foxed, else Fine in VG dj. *Godot.* $150/£97

BURGESS, ANTHONY. A Long Trip to Teatime. London: Dempsey & Squires, 1976. 1st Eng ed. Inscribed. NF in dj (price-clipped). *Antic Hay.* $85/£55

BURGESS, ANTHONY. MF. Cape, 1971. 1st UK ed. NF in dj. *Sclanders.* $31/£20

BURGESS, ANTHONY. On Mozart: A Paean for Wolfgang. NY: Ticknor & Fields, 1991. 1st ed. Signed and dated. Fine in dj (price-clipped). *Antic Hay.* $50/£32

BURGESS, ANTHONY. The Right to an Answer. London: Heinemann, 1960. 1st UK ed. NF in VG dj (closed tears; spine sl faded). *Williams.* $101/£65

BURGESS, ANTHONY. Time for a Tiger. Heinemann, 1956. 1st UK ed. Sl signs of ownership, o/w VG + in VG dj (spine head chipped; corners sl rubbed; foxing rear panel; bkseller's label). *Martin.* $287/£185

BURGESS, ANTHONY. A Vision of Battlements. NY, 1965. 1st Amer ed. Fine in dj (spine sl sunned, small edge tears, chips). *Polyanthos.* $30/£19

BURGESS, ANTHONY. The Wanting Seed. Norton, 1963. 1st Amer ed. Fine in VG + dj. *Fine Books.* $65/£42

BURGESS, ANTHONY. The Worm and the Ring. Heinemann, 1961. 1st ed. Fading upper margins, else VG in VG dj (lt wear). *Fine Books.* $375/£242

BURGESS, ANTHONY. The Worm and the Ring. London: Heinemann, 1961. 1st UK ed. NF (fep replaced) in VG + dj. *Williams.* $543/£350

BURGESS, G. The Master of Mysteries. B-M, 1912. 1st ed. VG + . *Fine Books.* $150/£97

BURGESS, G.H.O. The Curious World of Frank Buckland. London, 1967. Frontis port; 15 plts. *Wheldon & Wesley.* $31/£20

BURGESS, GELETT. Bayside Bohemia. SF: Book Club of CA, 1954. 1st ed. One of 375. Fine. *Hermitage.* $125/£81

BURGESS, GELETT. The Maxims of Methuselah.... NY: Frederick A. Stokes, (1907). 1st ed. Pict bds, grn cl spine. VG (rear cvr soiled). *Sumner & Stillman.* $115/£74

BURGESS, GELETT. The Nonsense Almanack for 1901. NY: Frederick A. Stokes, (1901). 1st ed as such. Fine in heavy paper wrappers. *Cahan.* $125/£81

BURGESS, GELETT. The Purple Cow! SF: (Lark/William Doxey), 1895. 1st ed, 1st issue (ptd on both sides of leaves). Pict self-wrappers. NF (sm tear 1st pg) in oversized cl clamshell case. *Sumner & Stillman.* $350/£226

BURGESS, JOHN CART. An Easy Introduction to Perspective. London: pub, sold by author, 1840. 7th ed, 'rewritten, with Twelve New Plates.' 26pp, 1f, frontis, 11 litho plts. Cl (rebacked, damp stain). *Marlborough.* $186/£120

BURGESS, R.B. Angling and How to Angle. London: Warne, 1895. Brn pict cl, gilt lettering (sl worn). VG. *Glenn.* $95/£61

BURGESS, THORNTON W. The Adventures of Grandfather Frog. (Bedtime Story Series). Boston: Little, Brown, 1946. Inscribed. Harrison Cady (illus). 1/2 color pict bds. VG in VG dj. *Davidson.* $185/£119

BURGESS, THORNTON W. Bowser the Hound. Boston: Little, Brown, 1920. 1st ed. 8vo. 8 color plts by Harrison Cady. Grn cl, color paste label (mks within). *Reisler.* $70/£45

BURGESS, THORNTON W. Cubby Finds an Open Door. Racine: Whitman, (1929). 16mo. Nina R. Jordan (illus). Color-illus bds. Good in full color dj (few marginal tears). *Reisler.* $45/£29

BURGESS, THORNTON W. Farmer Brown's Boy Becomes Curious. Racine: Whitman, (1929). 16mo. Nina R. Jordan (illus). Illus color bds. Good in full color dj (few marginal tears). *Reisler.* $45/£29

BURGESS, THORNTON W. Lightfoot the Deer. Boston: Little Brown, 1921. 1st ed. Green Forest Series. 8vo. 8 color plts by Harrison Cady. Navy cl; pict paste label. NF in Good+ dj (chipped). *Drusilla's.* $75/£48

BURGESS, THORNTON W. Old Granny Fox. Boston: Little Brown, 1920. 1st ed. Green Meadow Series. 8vo. 8 color plts by Harrison Cady. Lt grn cl; pict paste label. NF in Good+ dj (chipped). *Drusilla's.* $75/£48

BURGESS, THORNTON W. Reddy Fox. (Bedtime Story Series). Boston: Little, Brown, 1946. Inscribed. Harrison Cady (illus). 1/2 color pict bds. VG in VG dj. *Davidson.* $185/£119

BURGESS, THORNTON W. While the Story-Log Burns. Boston: Little, Brown, 1938. 1st ed. 195pp, 8 full-pg color plts by Lemuel Palmer. VG (inscrip) in VG dj (sm dkng, sm tape repairs). *Davidson.* $150/£97

BURKE, BERNARD. Peerage and Baronetage. London: Berke's Peerage, 1928. 86th ed. 7 plts. Excellent (re-cased). *Hollett.* $147/£95

BURKE, EDGAR. American Dry Flies and How to Tie Them. NY: Derrydale, 1931. One of 500. Errata slip tipped in. Fine in orig glassine dj (chipped). *Bowman.* $500/£323

BURKE, EDMUND. On Conciliation with the Colonies and Other Papers on the American Revolution. Peter J. Stanlis (ed). Lunenburg, VT: LEC, 1975. One of 2000 signed by Lynd Ward (illus). Prospectus laid in. Patterned cl. VF in glassine & slipcase. *Pharos.* $150/£97

BURKE, EDMUND. Reflections on the Revolution in France. Ptd for J. Dodsley, 1770. 2nd ed. Contemp 1/2 calf (cvrs age-soiled; names on title; marginal notes). *Hill.* $70/£45

BURKE, EDMUND. The Works of the Right Honourable Edmund Burke. London: Ptd for J. Dodsley, 1792. 1st ed. 3 vols. 4to; (4),580,(4); 656; (4),602pp. 19th cent 1/2 grn calf over marbled bds, gilt; at top of each spine is crown w/capitals 'PM.' Wide margined. Very nice (extrems sl rubbed; titles sl foxed). *Karmiole.* $750/£484

BURKE, EDMUND. The Works. London, 1883-7. 9 vols. Engr port. Marbled eps, edges. Contemp 1/2 calf (sl rubbed, worn; sl dknd; upper joint vol 9 cracked), gilt. *Edwards.* $287/£185

BURKE, EDMUND. The Works. Oxford: OUP, 1906-1907. 5 vols. Grn cl, gilt, ribbon markers; teg. Lt pencil mks, else VG. *Hartfield.* $95/£61

BURKE, JAMES LEE. Black Cherry Blues. Boston: Little, Brown, 1989. 1st ed. VF in dj. *Mordida.* $65/£42

BURKE, JAMES LEE. Half of Paradise. Boston: Houghton-Mifflin, 1965. 1st ed. 1st bk. Fine in dj (extrems faintly rubbed). *Else Fine.* $2,000/£1,290

BURKE, JAMES LEE. Heaven's Prisoners. Holt, 1988. 1st ed. VF in dj (sl rubbed). *Murder.* $40/£26

BURKE, JAMES LEE. A Morning for Flamingos. Boston: Little Brown, 1990. 1st ed. VF in dj. *Mordida.* $45/£29

BURKE, JAMES LEE. The Neon Rain. NY: Henry Holt, 1987. 1st ed. VF in dj. *Mordida.* $90/£58

BURKE, JAMES LEE. To the Bright and Shining Sun. NY: Scribner's, 1970. 1st ed. Fine in dj (short closed crease-tear). *Mordida.* $800/£516

BURKE, JAMES LEE. To the Bright and Shining Sun. NY: Scribner's, 1970. 1st ed. Fine in dj (very minor wear top edge). *Else Fine.* $1,250/£806

BURKE, JAMES LEE. Two for Texas. NY: Pocket Books, 1982. 1st ed. Crease on spine, o/w Fine in wrappers. *Mordida.* $45/£29

BURKE, JOSEPH and COLIN CALDWELL. Hogarth: The Complete Engravings. NY: Abrams, (n.d. ca 1968). VG in dj. *Argosy.* $150/£97

BURKE, KATHLEEN. The White Road to Verdun. NY: Doran, (1916). 1st ed. Port; 15 plts. Blue cl, cvr inset, white lettering (flaked). *Petrilla.* $30/£19

BURKE, PETER. Celebrated Naval and Military Trials. London: Wm. H. Allen, 1876. Cl worn. *Boswell.* $150/£97

BURKE, THOMAS. More Limehouse Nights. Doran, 1921. 1st ed. VG+ in VG pict dj (inner reinforcement; wear). *Fine Books.* $65/£42

BURKS, ARTHUR J. Black Medicine. Sauk City: Arkham House, (1966). 1st ed. NF in NF dj. *Other Worlds.* $45/£29

BURKS, ARTHUR J. Black Medicine. Arkham House, 1966. 1st ed. VF in dj. *Madle.* $60/£39

BURLAND, H. The Gold Worshipers. Dillingham, 1906. 1st ed. Hinges, edges worn, else VG in VG dj. *Aronovitz.* $135/£87

BURLEIGH, T.D. Birds of Idaho. Caldwell: Caxton, 1972. 1st ed. Dec cl. VF in Fine dj. *Mikesh.* $37/£24

BURLEIGH, THOMAS D. Birds of Idaho. Caldwell: Caxton, 1972. Fine in VG dj. *Perier.* $50/£32

BURLEND, REBECCA. A True Picture of Emigration. London, (1848). 64pp. Ptd wrappers. Howes B 992. *Ginsberg.* $250/£161

BURLEY, W.J. Wycliffe and the Quiet Virgin. London: Gollancz, 1986. 1st ed. Fine in dj (price-clipped). *Murder.* $40/£26

BURLINGHAM, DOROTHY TIFFANY and ANNA FREUD. Psychoanalytic Studies of the Sighted and the Blind. NY: IUP, (1972). 1st ed. Gray cl. VG in dj (lt worn). *Gach.* $40/£26

BURLINGHAM, DOROTHY TIFFANY. Twins: A Study of Three Pairs. London: Imago Pub Co, (1952). 1st ed. Inscribed. 30 charts. Grn cl. VG. *Gach.* $75/£48

BURN, ROBERT SCOTT (ed). The New Guide to Carpentry, General Framing, and Joinery. London: Murdoch, n.d. (c. 1870). 364pp, 150 full-pg engr plts. 1/2 calf, gilt, raised bands. Good+ (wear, sl foxing). *Willow House.* $116/£75

BURNABY, FRED. On Horseback through Asia Minor. London, 1877. 2nd ed. 2 vols. xxxii,352; xx,399pp (margins lt browned, soiled; tp vol 2 sl rubbed w/loss), 3 fldg maps. Teg; marbled eps. 1/2 calf (sl worn; spines faded, sl chipped; joints splitting; ex-libris). *Edwards.* $186/£120

BURNE-JONES, EDWARD. Letters to Katie. London: Macmillan, 1925. 1st ed. (Flyleaves spotted.) Orig holland-backed bds; paper spine label. *Hollett.* $62/£40

BURNET, JACOB. Notes on the Early Settlement of the North-Western Territory. Cincinnati: Derby, Bradley, 1847. 1st ed. Frontis port (not in all copies), 501pp + 16pp ads. Dk brn cl. Foxing, spine ends lt chipped, else VG. Howes J 997. *Chapel Hill.* $200/£129

BURNET, JAMES. Diseases of the Newborn. London, 1927. 1st ed. Good. *Fye.* $50/£32

BURNET, JOHN. Practical Hints on Colour Painting. Ptd by James Carpenter, 1835. 4th ed. 64pp + 4pp pub's ads, 8 color plts. (Sl browning edges; lt foxed feps.) Cl-backed bds (sl soiled; chipped spine, title label; edges rubbed). *Edwards.* $54/£35

BURNET, JOHN. A Practical Treatise on Painting in Three Parts.... London: Carpenter, 1835. 31pp, 9 plts; 45pp, 8 plts; 64pp, 8 plts + 4pp ads. Contemp cl-backed bds. Pt 1 sl browned, spine head sl chipped, o/w Nice. *Europa.* $93/£60

BURNET, JOHN. A Practical Treatise on Painting. London: Ptd for Proprietor, 1830. New ed. 31,45,64pp text; 17 b/w, 8 color plts; marbled eps. Contemp 1/2 calf w/marbled bds (hinges reinforced; corners sl worn; rebacked), leather label. *Edwards.* $116/£75

BURNET, THOMAS. The Theory of the Earth. London: J. Hooke, 1726. 6th ed. 2 vols. Cvrs loose, o/w VG+. *Bishop.* $75/£48

BURNETT, ETIENNE. The Campaign Against Microbes. London, 1909. 1st Eng trans. Good. *Fye.* $40/£26

BURNETT, ETIENNE. Microbes and Toxins. NY, 1912. 1st Eng translation. Good. *Fye.* $40/£26

BURNETT, F.M. The Clonal Selection Theory of Acquired Immunity. Nashville, 1959. 1st ed. Good. *Fye.* $75/£48

BURNETT, F.M. Enzyme Antigen and Virus: A Study.... Cambridge, 1958. 1st ed. Ex-lib. *Fye.* $35/£23

BURNETT, F.M. Virus as Organism: Evolutionary and Ecological Aspects of Some Human Virus Diseases. Cambridge, MA, 1946. 1st ed. Good. *Fye.* $75/£48

BURNETT, FRANCES HODGSON. A Fair Barbarian. Boston: Osgood, 1881. 1st ptg. Dec grn cl. VG (sl cocked; sl rubbed). BAL 2055. *Agvent.* $75/£48

BURNETT, FRANCES HODGSON. Little Lord Fauntleroy. London: Frederick Warne, 1886. 1st ed ptd in England. Reginald B. Birch (illus). Lg 8vo. Gilt pict grn cl; beveled edges. VG (inner hinges sl cracking; edges sl rubbed). *Reese.* $375/£242

BURNETT, FRANCES HODGSON. Little Lord Fauntleroy. NY: Scribner's, 1887. R.B. Birch (illus). 4to. 209pp + 16pp ads. Pict cvr ptd in red/black on blue-grey cl on bd w/gilt vignette (dated presentation inscrip; sl rubbing; 2 red spots cvr). VG. *Hobbyhorse.* $75/£48

BURNETT, FRANCES HODGSON. A Little Princess. NY: Scribner's, 1905. 1st thus. 4to. Frontis, guard; 266pp; 12 color plts by Ethel Franklin Betts. Teg. Navy ribbed cl, pict paste label (chipped), gilt. VG. *Drusilla's.* $85/£55

BURNETT, FRANCES HODGSON. Queen Silver-Bell. NY: Century, 1906. 1st ed. Inscribed. 16mo. 132pp; 20 color plts by Harrison Cady. Lt blue cl, pict paste label. VG (spine lettering faded). *Drusilla's.* $125/£81

BURNETT, FRANCES HODGSON. The Secret Garden. NY: Stokes, (1911). Issue B (simultaneous issue). 4 color plts. Pict grn cl. Good (cvrs rubbed, lt edgeworn w/marginal loss to print; rear hinge cracked; inscrip fep; soiling; paper aged). *Agvent.* $150/£97

BURNETT, FRANCES HODGSON. The White People. NY: Harper, (1917). 1st ed. VG (foxing) in orig dj (sm chips; orig price on spine obliterated w/new price of $1.00 added, BAL notes this as occurring in the wrappered issue, which was binding C). BAL 2125, binding B, sheets 3. *Turlington.* $75/£48

BURNETT, GILBERT. Bishop Burnet's History of His Own Time. Oxford, 1823. 6 vols. Frontis. 1/2 calf (rubbed). *Argosy.* $300/£194

BURNETT, J.H. (ed). The Vegetation of Scotland. Edinburgh, 1964. 96 plts (3 color) (sm tear margin of 1). Cl (spine faded; 1pg w/underlining). *Sutton.* $75/£48

BURNETT, W.R. Adobe Walls. NY: Knopf, 1953. 1st ed. Fine in dj (spine sl dknd, else Fine). *Between The Covers.* $50/£32

BURNETT, W.R. Dark Hazard. Harper, 1933. 1st ed. NF in dj (worn). *Fine Books.* $30/£19

BURNETT, W.R. Little Caesar. NY, 1929. 1st ed. Good (used; lacks dj). *King.* $20/£13

BURNEY, CHARLES. A General History of Music...to the Present Period. London: For the Author, 1776-1789. 1st ed. 4 vols. Reynolds port. Early 3/4 leather, gilt extra, marbled bds (rebacked, orig spines laid down; bkpls, art lib blindstamp). Attractive set. *Hartfield.* $1,985/£1,281

BURNHAM, DONALD L. et al. Schizophrenia and the Need-Fear Dilemma. NY: IUP, (1969). 1st ed. Inscribed. Blue cl. VG in dj (worn). *Gach.* $40/£26

BURNHAM, JOHN. Jelliffe: American Psychoanalyst and Physician and His Correspondence with Sigmund Freud.... Chicago, 1983. Good. *Fye.* $35/£23

BURNHAM, LOUIS E. Behind the Lynching of Emmet Louis Till. (NY: Freedom Associates, 1955.) 1st ed. VG in pict self-wraps. *Petrilla.* $30/£19

BURNS, EMILE (trans). Nazi Conspiracy in Spain. (By Otto Katz and Willi Muenzenberg). London: Gollancz, 1937. 1st ed. 16 facs. Nice. *Patterson.* $78/£50

BURNS, EUGENE. The Sex Life of Wild Animals. NY: Rinehart, (1953). 1st ed. Pp sl browned, else VG in VG dj. *Pharos.* $30/£19

BURNS, JOHN. The Anatomy of the Gravid Uterus. Boston, 1808. 1st Amer ed. 248pp. 1/2 leather. (Fr bd detached; 1/2 inch missing from spine top.) *Fye.* $200/£129

BURNS, JOHN. Dissertations on Inflammation. NY, 1812. 2 vols in 1. xii,214pp. Leather binding (worn, torn, esp spine; ex-lib w/label, stamps), leather label. *Whitehart*. $279/£180

BURNS, JOHN. Dissertations on Inflammation.... Albany: E.F. Backus, 1812. 1st Amer ed. 2 vols in 1. 213; 214pp (lt browning). Contemp calf (corners rubbed), red leather label. Very Nice. *Hemlock*. $200/£129

BURNS, JOHN. Popular Directions for the Treatment of the Diseases of Women and Children. NY, 1811. 1st Amer ed. 324pp. Full leather. *Fye*. $200/£129

BURNS, OLIVE ANN. Cold Sassy Tree. Ticknor & Fields, 1984. 1st ed. Postcard of cvr laid in. NF in dj (lt rubbing ft of spine). *Stahr*. $150/£97

BURNS, REX. The Alvarez Journal. Harper, 1975. 1st ed. Lt worn, spotted, else VG in dj (spine worn, tear taped). *Murder*. $45/£29

BURNS, REX. The Farnsworth Score. Harper, 1977. 1st ed. Sm tear, else NF in dj (lt soiled). *Murder*. $35/£23

BURNS, TEX. (Pseud of Louis L'Amour). Hopalong Cassidy and the Rustlers of West Fork. London: Hodder & Stoughton, (1951). 1st Eng ed. Fine in dj. *Heller*. $75/£48

BURNS, WALTER NOBLE. The Saga of Billy the Kid. Doubleday, 1926. 1st ed. VG. *Oregon*. $35/£23

BURNS, WALTER NOBLE. Tombstone. NY: Doubleday, 1927. 1st ed. Good. *Parker*. $35/£23

BURNS, WALTER NOBLE. A Year with a Whaler. NY, 1913. 1st ed. Fine in dj. *Lefkowicz*. $100/£65

BURNS, ZED H. Confederate Forts. Natchez, 1977. 1st ed. Fine in Fine dj. *Pratt*. $32/£21

BURNS, ZED H. Confederate Forts. Natchez, MS, 1977. 1st ed. Orig cl. Fine in Fine dj. *Mcgowan*. $35/£23

BURPEE, LAWRENCE J. Among the Canadian Alps. NY: John Lane, 1914. 1st ed. Frontis; 3 color plts; 5 maps. Grn cl pict stamped blue/brn/white. Good (rubbed; spine sl dull; fore-edge sl foxed). *Hermitage*. $100/£65

BURPEE, LAWRENCE J. Among the Canadian Alps. London: John Lane, The Bodley Head, 1915. 4 color plts; 45 plts; 5 maps. Mod 1/2 grn levant morocco, gilt. VG (frontis lt spotted). *Hollett*. $109/£70

BURPEE, LAWRENCE J. The Search for the Western Sea. Toronto: Musson, n.d. (1908). 1st ed. Frontis. 9 fldg maps (lg map tape-repaired). VG. Howes 1006. *Oregon*. $350/£226

BURR, ANNA R. Weir Mitchell, His Life and Letters. NY, 1929. 1st ed. Good. *Fye*. $60/£39

BURR, MALCOLM. In Bolshevik Siberia. London: Witherby, 1931. 1st ed. Map. VG. *Walcot*. $31/£20

BURRAGE, HENRY S. The Beginnings of Colonial Maine, 1602-1658. (Portland): Ptd for the State, 1914. 27 plts. VG. *Schoyer*. $50/£32

BURRI, RENE. The Gaucho. NY: Crown, 1968. 1st US ed. Frontis. Gilt-titled cl. NF in dj (worn, torn, tape-repaired). *Cahan*. $20/£13

BURROUGHS, A. Art Criticism from a Laboratory. London: Allen & Unwin, n.d. (ca 1938). Sound. *Ars Artis*. $54/£35

BURROUGHS, EDGAR RICE. At the Earth's Core. NY: Grosset & Dunlap, (1922). 3rd ed (ca 1940). VG in dj (frayed). *King*. $35/£23

BURROUGHS, EDGAR RICE. Back to the Stone Age. Tarzana, (1937). 1st ed. Cl (worn, spotted; text stained, lacks illus). Nice dj. *King*. $150/£97

BURROUGHS, EDGAR RICE. The Beasts of Tarzan. Chicago: McClurg, 1916. 1st Amer ed. NF (spine sl sunned). *Polyanthos*. $350/£226

BURROUGHS, EDGAR RICE. The Beasts of Tarzan. Chicago: A.C. McClurg & Co., 1916. 1st ed. Frontis. VG (spine lettering dull; stain top edge, lt foxing). *Chapel Hill*. $400/£258

BURROUGHS, EDGAR RICE. The Beasts of Tarzan. Chicago: A.C. McClurg, 1916. 1st ed. Name fr pastedown, o/w VG. *Bernard*. $500/£323

BURROUGHS, EDGAR RICE. The Beasts of Tarzan. Burt, 1917. NF in dj (repaired). *Madle*. $75/£48

BURROUGHS, EDGAR RICE. Beyond Thirty and The Man-Eater. South Ozone Park, NY: Science-Fiction & Fantasy Publ, 1957. 1st ed, ltd to 3000. Dknd, else Good in dj (soiled). *King*. $50/£32

BURROUGHS, EDGAR RICE. Beyond Thirty. Eshbach, 1950. 1st ed. Mint in wraps. *Madle*. $150/£97

BURROUGHS, EDGAR RICE. Beyond Thirty. N.p.: (L.A. Eshbach, 1955). Unauthorized ptg (300 copies) in over-size wrappers. Lacks paper title label, else Fine. *Other Worlds*. $100/£65

BURROUGHS, EDGAR RICE. Carson of Venus. Burroughs, 1939. 1st ed. VG in VG dj (lt wear). *Fine Books*. $175/£113

BURROUGHS, EDGAR RICE. Carson of Venus. ERB, 1939. 1st ed. Fine in dj (1 nick). *Madle*. $350/£226

BURROUGHS, EDGAR RICE. The Cave Girl. Canaveral, 1962. NF in dj. *Madle*. $25/£16

BURROUGHS, EDGAR RICE. The Chessmen of Mars. Chicago: A.C. McClurg, 1922. 1st ed. Red cl (spine sl lightened; sl rubbed). Clean. *Sadlon*. $75/£48

BURROUGHS, EDGAR RICE. The Chessmen of Mars. Methuen, 1923. 1st Eng ed. Sm cl loss outer hinges, else VG + in VG dj (lt wear, tear). *Aronovitz*. $1,175/£758

BURROUGHS, EDGAR RICE. The Chessmen of Mars. London: Methuen, 1923. 1st UK ed. NF (sm hole) in VG dj (rear strengthened; label removal mk). *Williams*. $233/£150

BURROUGHS, EDGAR RICE. The Efficiency Expert. House of Greystoke, 1966. 1st ed. Fine in wraps. *Madle*. $100/£65

BURROUGHS, EDGAR RICE. Escape on Venus. Tarzana, (1946). 1st ed. Corners badly bumped, sl stained, else Good in dj (spine chipped). *King*. $150/£97

BURROUGHS, EDGAR RICE. Escape on Venus. ERB, 1946. 1st ed. Fine in dj (2 chips). *Madle*. $150/£97

BURROUGHS, EDGAR RICE. Escape on Venus. Canaveral, 1963. Fine in dj. *Madle*. $25/£16

BURROUGHS, EDGAR RICE. The Eternal Lover. NY: Grosset, (1927). 1st Grosset ed. Frontis by J. Allen St. John. Dk red cl stamped in black. VG in color pict dj (nicks, tears, creases; 2 sm stains lower cvr). *Houle*. $175/£113

BURROUGHS, EDGAR RICE. The Girl from Hollywood. NY: Macauley, (1923). 1st ed, 1st issue. Frontis. Sm hole spine; bottom corner tips sl frayed, o/w VG. *Bernard*. $75/£48

BURROUGHS, EDGAR RICE. The Gods of Mars. Tarzana: Burroughs, (ca 1948). Rpt. Frontis by Frank E. Schoonover. Tan bds stamped in brn, top edge stained brick red. VG in color pict dj (sm chips). *Houle*. $100/£65

BURROUGHS, EDGAR RICE. I Am a Barbarian. Tarzana, (1967). 1st ed. VG in dj. *King.* $75/£48

BURROUGHS, EDGAR RICE. I Am a Barbarian. ERB, 1967. 1st ed. Fine in NF dj. *Madle.* $75/£48

BURROUGHS, EDGAR RICE. Jungle Girl. NY: Grosset & Dunlap, (1932). 3rd ed. Sl spotted, else Good in dj (worn, soiled). *King.* $25/£16

BURROUGHS, EDGAR RICE. Jungle Girl. London: Odhams Press, 1933. 1st Eng ed. Maroon cl. Spine dull, fore-edge sl foxed, o/w VG in dj (sl dusty). *Dalian.* $101/£65

BURROUGHS, EDGAR RICE. Jungle Tales of Tarzan. Chicago, 1919. 3rd ptg, w/last illus tipped onto p312 instead of p316. Cl (rubbed, soiled; fr hinge cracked; spot on fore-edge). Repro dj. *King.* $40/£26

BURROUGHS, EDGAR RICE. The Lad and the Lion. Canaveral, 1964. Fine in dj. *Madle.* $95/£61

BURROUGHS, EDGAR RICE. Land of Terror. Tarzana, (1944). 1st ed. Inscrip, sl stain, extrems rubbed, else Good in dj (badly chipped, torn, tape-repaired). *King.* $150/£97

BURROUGHS, EDGAR RICE. Land of Terror. Tarzana: Edgar Rice Burroughs, (1944). 1st ed. Blue cl; spine, upper cvr stamped in red, top edge stained red; uncut. VG in color pict dj (sm spine chip; tape repairs; nicks, sm tears). *Houle.* $375/£242

BURROUGHS, EDGAR RICE. Land of Terror. Canaveral, 1963. Fine in dj. *Madle.* $60/£39

BURROUGHS, EDGAR RICE. The Land That Time Forgot. Canaveral, 1962. VG in dj. *Madle.* $25/£16

BURROUGHS, EDGAR RICE. Llana of Gathol. Tarzana: ERB Inc, (1948). 1st ed. Bkpl(?) removed fep, lt bumped, else NF in dj (edgeworn, frayed, spine foxed, tears fr flap fold). *Other Worlds.* $60/£39

BURROUGHS, EDGAR RICE. Llana of Gathol. Tarzana, 1948. 1st Amer ed. Fine (sl rubbed, spine sl sunned). *Polyanthos.* $60/£39

BURROUGHS, EDGAR RICE. Llana of Gathol. ERB, 1948. 1st ed. Fine in dj. *Madle.* $145/£94

BURROUGHS, EDGAR RICE. Lost on Venus. ERB, 1935. 1st ed. VG in dj (sl frayed, soiled). *Madle.* $375/£242

BURROUGHS, EDGAR RICE. The Master Mind of Mars.... NY: Grosset & Dunlap, (1929). 1st thus. Name, else VG in dj (worn, chipped). *Other Worlds.* $25/£16

BURROUGHS, EDGAR RICE. The Moon Men. Canaveral, 1962. Fine in dj. *Madle.* $25/£16

BURROUGHS, EDGAR RICE. The Moon Men. NY: Canaveral Press, 1975. Reissue of 1962 ed. New in dj. *Bernard.* $35/£23

BURROUGHS, EDGAR RICE. The Mucker. London: Methuen, 1921. 1st ed. Pub's 8pp cat inserted at end. Blue cl. Lower edges uncut. Nice (lt foxing). *Temple.* $54/£35

BURROUGHS, EDGAR RICE. The Outlaw of Torn. Chicago, 1927. 1st ed. Spine torn, sunned; sl spotted, else Fair in repro dj. *King.* $45/£29

BURROUGHS, EDGAR RICE. The Outlaw of Torn. McClurg, 1927. 1st ed. Fine in dj (spine top chipped). *Madle.* $2,000/£1,290

BURROUGHS, EDGAR RICE. The Outlaw of Torn. Chicago: McClurg, 1927. 1st ed. Fine in pict dj (closed triangular tear fr panel, minor edgewear). *Else Fine.* $2,250/£1,452

BURROUGHS, EDGAR RICE. The Return of Tarzan. Tauchnitz, 1921. 1st ed thus. NF in wraps. *Aronovitz.* $65/£42

BURROUGHS, EDGAR RICE. The Return of Tarzan. NY: A.L. Burt, n.d. (1916). Early rpt. VG in dj (spine faded; rear panel lt soiled). *Bernard.* $65/£42

BURROUGHS, EDGAR RICE. Savage Pellucidar. NY, 1963. 1st ed. Sl spotted, else good in dj (frayed, lacks lg piece). *King.* $50/£32

BURROUGHS, EDGAR RICE. Savage Pellucidar. Canaveral, 1963. 1st ed. Fine in dj. *Madle.* $100/£65

BURROUGHS, EDGAR RICE. The Son of Tarzan. NY: A.L. Burt, 1918. 6th ed. Cl (sl dknd, rubbed; stamped name). Dj (soiled, worn, torn, spine chipped). *King.* $25/£16

BURROUGHS, EDGAR RICE. The Son of Tarzan. London: Methuen, 1919. 1st Eng ed. Red cl. Faded, mkd; pp sl browned, o/w VG. *Dalian.* $70/£45

BURROUGHS, EDGAR RICE. Swords of Mars. Tarzana: Burroughs, (1936). 1st ed. Attempts to cover, erase fep inscrips, else VG + in dj (sunned spine, creasing, edgewear, chip). *Other Worlds.* $300/£194

BURROUGHS, EDGAR RICE. Swords of Mars. Tarzana: Edgar Rice Burroughs, (1936). 1st ed. 8vo. Frontis; 4 full-pg b/w illus. Blue cl; spine, upper cvr stamped in red, top edge stained red; uncut. VG in color pict dj (nicks; short tears). *Houle.* $750/£484

BURROUGHS, EDGAR RICE. Synthetic Men of Mars. Tarzana, CA: ERB, (1940). 1st ed. 5 b/w plts by John Coleman Burroughs. Fine in Flawless dj. *Bernard.* $500/£323

BURROUGHS, EDGAR RICE. Tales of Three Planets. NY, 1964. 1st ed. Sl discolored, else Good in later dj (sl soiled, torn). *King.* $65/£42

BURROUGHS, EDGAR RICE. Tales of Three Planets. Canaveral, 1964. 1st ed. Fine in dj. *Madle.* $100/£65

BURROUGHS, EDGAR RICE. Tanar of Pellucidar. Metropolitan, 1930. 1st ed. VG in VG dj (sl nicks; tears spine center). *Fine Books.* $95/£61

BURROUGHS, EDGAR RICE. Tarzan and 'The Foreign Legion.' Tarzana, (1947). 1st ed. Sl stained, else Good in dj (edgeworn). *King.* $75/£48

BURROUGHS, EDGAR RICE. Tarzan and the Ant Men. Chicago, 1924. 1st ed. Frontis. Cl (worn; spine repaired, recolored; inner hinge reinforced). *King.* $75/£48

BURROUGHS, EDGAR RICE. Tarzan and the Ant Men. Chicago: A.C. McClurg, 1924. 1st ed. Dk tan cl (sl rubbed). *Sadlon.* $75/£48

BURROUGHS, EDGAR RICE. Tarzan and the Ant Men. Chicago, 1924. 2nd ed, w/McClurg on title, G&D on spine. Cl (frayed, worn, soiled; lacks fep, frontis detached). Poor dj (lacks pieces). *King.* $65/£42

BURROUGHS, EDGAR RICE. Tarzan and the Ant Men. London: Methuen, 1925. 1st ed. Pub's 8pp cat inserted, dated '525.' Brn cl. Fore-edges rough-trimmed; lower edges uncut. Very Nice. *Temple.* $62/£40

BURROUGHS, EDGAR RICE. Tarzan and the Castaways. Canaveral, 1965. 1st ed. Fine in dj. *Madle.* $125/£81

BURROUGHS, EDGAR RICE. Tarzan and the City of Gold. Tarzana: Edgar Rice Burroughs, (1933). 1st ed. 8vo. Frontis; 4 full-pg b/w illus. Blue cl; spine, upper cvr stamped in red, top edge stained red (sl stains other edges). VG in color pict dj (nicks). *Houle.* $950/£613

BURROUGHS, EDGAR RICE. Tarzan and the Forbidden City. Tarzana: Edgar Rice Burroughs, (1948). Ltr ptg. Frontis by John Coleman Burroughs. Gray cl stamped in blue, top edge stained blue. VG in color pict dj (sm chip upper spine end; nicks). *Houle.* $100/£65

BURROUGHS, EDGAR RICE. Tarzan and the Forbidden City. Burroughs, 1938. 1st ed. NF in dj. *Fine Books.* $325/£210

BURROUGHS, EDGAR RICE. Tarzan and the Foreign Legion. Tarzana: Burroughs, (1947). 1st ed. Bkpl(?) removed fep, else NF in VG + dj (foxed). *Other Worlds.* $50/£32

BURROUGHS, EDGAR RICE. Tarzan and the Foreign Legion. ERB, 1948. 1st ed. VG in dj (frayed, soiled). *Madle.* $80/£52

BURROUGHS, EDGAR RICE. Tarzan and the Foreign Legion. London: W.H. Allen, n.d. (but 1947). 1st British ed. White cl sl soiled, else VG in dj (sl dusty). *Hermitage.* $45/£29

BURROUGHS, EDGAR RICE. Tarzan and the Golden Lion. NY: Grosset & Dunlap, (1923). 2nd ed (w/wrong plt #s). Name, spine lt sunned, else Nice in dj (defective). *King.* $60/£39

BURROUGHS, EDGAR RICE. Tarzan and the Golden Lion. Chicago, 1923. 1st ed. Cl (rubbed, soiled; illus loose). *King.* $65/£42

BURROUGHS, EDGAR RICE. Tarzan and the Golden Lion. Chicago: McClurg, 1923. 1st ed. VG + in white/red/gold dj (some edgewear, lt dust soil). *Else Fine.* $1,500/£968

BURROUGHS, EDGAR RICE. Tarzan and the Jewels of Opar. Chicago, 1918. Spine worn, sm spot, extrems rubbed, hinges broken, frontis detached but present, else VG. *King.* $85/£55

BURROUGHS, EDGAR RICE. Tarzan and the Leopard Men. Tarzana, (1935). 1st ed. Cl (frayed, spine recolored; bkpl). *King.* $35/£23

BURROUGHS, EDGAR RICE. Tarzan and the Leopard Men. Tarzana: E.R. Burroughs, (1935). 1st ed. 8vo. Blue cl; spine, upper cvr stamped in orange-red, top edge stained red. VG in color pict dj (nicks). *Houle.* $650/£419

BURROUGHS, EDGAR RICE. Tarzan and the Lost Empire. NY: Metropolitan, (1929). 1st ed. Name under fr flap, else Fine in NF dj (short tears). *Between The Covers.* $1,000/£645

BURROUGHS, EDGAR RICE. Tarzan and the Madmen. Canaveral, 1964. 1st ed. Fine in dj. *Madle.* $125/£81

BURROUGHS, EDGAR RICE. Tarzan and the Tarzan Twins. Canaveral, 1963. 1st ed thus. Fine in dj. *Madle.* $75/£48

BURROUGHS, EDGAR RICE. Tarzan of the Apes. Newnes, (1929). 1st Eng soft-cvr ed. Color pict cvr. Sm tears; sm piece missing, else VG + in wraps. *Aronovitz.* $75/£48

BURROUGHS, EDGAR RICE. Tarzan of the Apes. Burt, 1915. VG in dj (heavily chipped). *Madle.* $75/£48

BURROUGHS, EDGAR RICE. Tarzan of the Apes. Burt, 1917. VG + in VG dj (lt wear). *Fine Books.* $225/£145

BURROUGHS, EDGAR RICE. Tarzan the Invincible. Tarzana: Edgar Rice Burroughs, (1931). 1st ed. 8vo. Frontis. Blue cl; spine, upper cvr stamped in red. VG in color pict dj (nicks; tears). *Houle.* $950/£613

BURROUGHS, EDGAR RICE. Tarzan the Magnificent. Tarzana: Edgar Rice Burroughs, (1948). 2nd ed. Frontis by John Coleman Burroughs. Gray cl stamped in blue, top edge stianed blue. VG in color pict dj (nicks, tears). *Houle.* $125/£81

BURROUGHS, EDGAR RICE. Tarzan the Terrible. NY: Grosset & Dunlap, (1921). Rpt ed. Red cl (lt rubbed). Names, sm sticker, else VG in pict dj (chipped). *Glenn.* $45/£29

BURROUGHS, EDGAR RICE. Tarzan the Terrible. Chicago, 1921. 1st ed. Worn; lacks dj. *King.* $75/£48

BURROUGHS, EDGAR RICE. Tarzan the Untamed. Chicago, 1920. 1st ed. Outer hinge torn, sl frayed, else Nice. *King.* $100/£65

BURROUGHS, EDGAR RICE. Tarzan Triumphant. Tarzana: Burroughs, (1932). 1st ed. Spine lt faded, else NF in Fine dj. *Between The Covers.* $450/£290

BURROUGHS, EDGAR RICE. Tarzan's Quest. Tarzana, (1936). 1st ed. Cl (stained, rubbed, frayed; inner hinge reglued; name). *King.* $45/£29

BURROUGHS, EDGAR RICE. Tarzan's Revenge. Racine, WI, (1938). 1st ed. VG (spine tips rubbed). *Mcclintock.* $50/£32

BURROUGHS, EDGAR RICE. Tarzan, Lord of the Jungle. NY: Grosset & Dunlap, (1928). 5th ed. Map. Cl (sl stained, soiled). Dj (sl chipped, edgetorn). *King.* $25/£16

BURROUGHS, EDGAR RICE. Thuvia, the Maid of Mars. Chicago: McClurg, 1920. 1st ed. Olive grn cl. Nice (lacks dj). *Second Life.* $95/£61

BURROUGHS, EDGAR RICE. Thuvia, the Maid of Mars. G&D, 1921. VG in dj (sl chipped). *Madle.* $75/£48

BURROUGHS, JOHN. The Breath of Life. Boston: Houghton Mifflin, 1915. 1st ed. Frontis. Fine in dj (sl chipped). *Second Life.* $85/£55

BURROUGHS, JOHN. Camping and Tramping with Roosevelt. Boston, 1907. 1st Amer ed. Fine (bkpl; sl sunned). *Polyanthos.* $30/£19

BURROUGHS, JOHN. Camping with President Roosevelt. (Boston, 1906). 1st ed. Frontis; 5 plts. Good in wrappers. *Hayman.* $20/£13

BURROUGHS, JOHN. Guardian of the Grasslands. Cheyenne: Pioneer Ptg & Stationery Co, 1971. Ltd numbered ed (# unstated), signed. Color frontis. Tan calf, gilt. Good in illus slipcase (sl worn). *Karmiole.* $100/£65

BURROUGHS, JOHN. John Burroughs Talks. H-M, 1922. 1st ed. Spine spotted, else VG + . *Fine Books.* $30/£19

BURROUGHS, JOHN. Leaf and Tendril. Boston: Houghton Mifflin, 1908. 1st Amer ed. Frontis. Fine. BAL 2180. *Agvent.* $40/£26

BURROUGHS, JOHN. Literary Values. Boston: Houghton, Mifflin, 1902. 1st Amer ed. VG. BAL 2172. *Agvent.* $35/£23

BURROUGHS, JOHN. Locusts and Wild Honey. Boston, 1879. 253pp. Contemp 1/2 calf, marbled bds (sl rubbed). VG. *Shifrin.* $40/£26

BURROUGHS, JOHN. My Boyhood.... GC/NY/Toronto: Doubleday, Page, 1922. 1st ed. Frontis (starting); 2 color, 8 half-tone plts (sl worming fr hinge). Grn cl-backed bds (rubbed, soiled; spine spotted), ptd paper label. VG in pict dj (edges, spine chipped; sm pieces out). BAL 2202. *Blue Mountain.* $45/£29

BURROUGHS, JOHN. Signs and Seasons. Boston: Houghton, Mifflin, 1886. 1st Amer ed. VG (worn; bkpl). BAL 2147. *Agvent.* $50/£32

BURROUGHS, JOHN. The Summit of the Years. Boston: Houghton, Mifflin, 1913. 1st Amer ed. Frontis. Partly unopened. Fine (spine label sl faded). BAL 2186. *Agvent.* $30/£19

BURROUGHS, JOHN. Time and Chance. Boston: Houghton, Mifflin, 1912. 1st Amer ed. Frontis. Fine in Fine dj (closed tear). BAL 2185. *Agvent.* $150/£97

BURROUGHS, JOHN. Whitman, a Study. Boston: Houghton, 1896. 1st ed. Teg. Gilt grn cl. Eps lt foxed, else NF. BAL 2162. *Reese.* $75/£48

BURROUGHS, WILLIAM S. The Adding Machine. London: John Calder, 1985. 1st ed. Fine in dj. *Sclanders.* $28/£18

BURROUGHS, WILLIAM S. The Book of Breething. Berkeley: Blue Wind Press, 1975. 1st US ed, softcvr issue. NF-. *Sclanders.* $25/£16

BURROUGHS, WILLIAM S. Cobble Stone Gardens. Cherry Valley: Cherry Valley Editions, 1976. 1st ed. VG in pict wraps (crease). *Revere.* $40/£26

BURROUGHS, WILLIAM S. The Dead Star. SF: Nova Broadcast Press, 1969. 1st ed. Lt sticker shadow rear wrap, else Fine in stapled wrappers. *Between The Covers.* $50/£32

BURROUGHS, WILLIAM S. Doctor Benway, a Passage from the Naked Lunch. Santa Barbara, 1979. One of 324 bound in wrappers, signed. Prospective present. Cvrs lt worn. *King.* $95/£61

BURROUGHS, WILLIAM S. Junkie. NY: Ace Books, 1953. Ace-Double D-15, bound back-to-back w/'Narcotic Agent' by Maurice Helbrant. 1st bk. Wraps. (Sm dent fr cvr edge, 1st leaves; lt rubbed creasing cvrs; spine lt worn.) *Sclanders.* $271/£175

BURROUGHS, WILLIAM S. Junkie. London: David Bruce & Watson, 1973. Sl bump lower bd, o/w NF in dj (sl rubbed, extrems sl worn). *Sclanders.* $62/£40

BURROUGHS, WILLIAM S. The Last Words of Dutch Schultz. NY, (1975). 1st Amer ed. VG in dj (sl discolored). *King.* $35/£23

BURROUGHS, WILLIAM S. Letters to Allen Ginsberg. 1953-1957. (Geneva): Am Here Books, (1978). 1st ed. Ltd to 500 numbered. Port. Sm bump, soiled, else Good. *King.* $95/£61

BURROUGHS, WILLIAM S. The Naked Lunch. London: John Calder, 1964. 1st UK ed. Spine sl leaned, o/w NF in dj. *Sclanders.* $54/£35

BURROUGHS, WILLIAM S. The Naked Lunch. NY: Grove Press, 1966. 1st Evergreen Black Cat Edition (BC-115). 1st US pb ed. VG (short tear fr cvr). *Sclanders.* $12/£8

BURROUGHS, WILLIAM S. The Naked Lunch. NY, 1984. 25th Anniversary ed. #79/500 signed. Fine in Fine box. *Polyanthos.* $150/£97

BURROUGHS, WILLIAM S. Nova Express. NY: Grove, 1964. 1st ed. Fine (date fep) in NF dj. *Beasley.* $60/£39

BURROUGHS, WILLIAM S. Nova Express. London: Cape, 1966. 1st UK ed. Fine in dj. *Sclanders.* $54/£35

BURROUGHS, WILLIAM S. The Place of Dead Roads. London: John Calder, 1984. 1st UK ed. Fine in dj. *Sclanders.* $19/£12

BURROUGHS, WILLIAM S. Sinki's Sauna. (NY): Pequod Press, (1982). One of 500 numbered. Fine in stapled wrappers. *Between The Covers.* $125/£81

BURROUGHS, WILLIAM S. The Soft Machine. Paris: Olympia Press, 1961. Price cancelled back cvr. NF in dj (spine sl dknd). *Sclanders.* $178/£115

BURROUGHS, WILLIAM S. The Soft Machine. Paris: Olympia Press, 1961. 2nd issue, only diff being a new rubberstamped price on rear wrap of 1st issue. Sm, lt stain last pg, else Fine in NF dj (sl rubbed). *Between The Covers.* $275/£177

BURROUGHS, WILLIAM S. The Soft Machine. London: Calder & Boyars, 1968. 1st UK ed. NF in dj (lt rubbed, creased). *Sclanders.* $47/£30

BURROUGHS, WILLIAM S. The Ticket That Exploded. NY: Grove, 1967. 1st Amer ed. Signed. NF in Fine dj (price-clipped). *Revere.* $125/£81

BURROUGHS, WILLIAM S. The Ticket That Exploded. NY: Grove, 1967. 1st ed. Fine in dj (rubbed). *Beasley.* $40/£26

BURROUGHS, WILLIAM S. The Ticket That Exploded. NY: Grove Press, 1968. Evergreen Black Cat (BC-164). 1st US pb ed. NF. *Sclanders.* $14/£9

BURROUGHS, WILLIAM S. White Subway. London: Aloes, n.d. 2nd ptg. One of 500. Fine in pict wraps. *Polyanthos.* $25/£16

BURROUGHS, WILLIAM S. The Wild Boys. NY: Grove, 1971. 1st ed. Fine in Fine dj. *Beasley.* $125/£81

BURROUGHS, WILLIAM S. The Wild Boys. London: Calder & Boyars, 1972. 1st UK ed. Short snag dj spine, o/w NF in dj (sl rubbed). *Sclanders.* $31/£20

BURROUGHS, WILLIAM S. and BRION GYSIN. The Exterminator. SF: Auerhahn, 1960. 1st ed. NF in wraps. *Beasley.* $75/£48

BURROW, E.I. Elements of Conchology According to the Linnaean System. London, 1825. New (2nd) ed. xix,245pp; 28 engr plts (25 hand-colored). 1/2 calf (rubbed, sl foxed). *Wheldon & Wesley.* $155/£100

BURROWES, THOMAS H. (ed). Pennsylvania School Architecture. Harrisburg: A. Boyd Hamilton, 1855. 1st ed. Frontis, 276pp. (Fr bd spotted, lt wear; foxing.) *Bookpress.* $375/£242

BURROWS, HAROLD. Biological Actions of Sex Hormones. Cambridge, 1945. 1st ed. Good. *Fye.* $125/£81

BURROWS, HAROLD. Oestrogens and Neoplasia. Springfield, 1952. 1st ed. Good. *Fye.* $100/£65

BURT, STRUTHERS. Powder River. Let 'er Buck. NY: Farrar Rinehart, 1938. 1st ed. VG (bkpl) in VG- dj. *Parker.* $50/£32

BURT, WILLIAM H. The Mammals of Michigan. Univ of MI, 1954. 13 color plts. (Cl dull.) *Artis.* $25/£16

BURTIS, THOMSON. The War of the Ghosts. Doubleday, 1932. 1st ed. VG in dj (lt worn, nicked). *Madle.* $50/£32

BURTON, H. Ski Troops: US Army's 10th Mountain Division. NY, 1971. VG in VG dj. *Clark.* $37/£24

BURTON, ISABEL. AEI: Arabia Egypt India. A Narrative of Travel. London: William Mullen, 1879. 1st ed. *Cummins.* $400/£258

BURTON, ISABEL. The Inner Life of Syria, Palestine, and the Holy Land. London: C. Kegan Paul, 1879. Frontis port (sl spotted; marked on reverse); xi,516,32pp; 2 chromolithos; 12 woodburytypes. Mod 1/2 levant morocco gilt, gilt decs from orig cl laid on to upper bd. VG. *Hollett.* $186/£120

BURTON, J. Lectures on Female Education and Manners. Elizabeth-Town: S. Kollock, 1799. 5th Amer ed. 280,(4)pp. Contemp sheep. Spine foot chipped off, else Excellent. *Felcone.* $300/£194

BURTON, JOHN HILL. The Book Hunter. Blackwood, 1898. 427pp. Red cl (spine faded). *Moss.* $14/£9

BURTON, JOHN HILL. The Book-Hunter Etc. Edinburgh/London: Blackwood, 1862. 1st ed. viii,384pp, 1/2 title bound in; teg. 3/4 red straight-grain morocco, gilt spine. Corners sl worn, o/w attractive. *Reese.* $100/£65

BURTON, JOHN HILL. The Book-Hunter. London: Wm Blackwood & Sons, 1882. #882/1000. Lg 8vo. Etched frontis, x,civ,427pp, 4 engr plts, vignettes. Uncut in orig blue cl, gilt (extrems rubbed; head, tail of backstrip sl worn). *Cox.* $47/£30

BURTON, JOHN HILL. Narratives from Criminal Trials in Scotland. London: Chapman & Hall, 1852. 2 vols in 1. (Cl worn, buckled.) Usable only. *Boswell.* $150/£97

BURTON, MILES. (Pseud of John Rhode.) Death Takes the Living. London: Collins, 1949. 1st ed. VG in dj (sl chipped). *Limestone.* $85/£55

BURTON, MILES. (Pseud of John Rhode.) The Hardway Diamonds Mystery. Collins, 1930. 1st ed. Contents Good (binding dull; sl rubbing). *Whiteson.* $34/£22

BURTON, MILES. (Pseud of John Rhode.) Murder of a Chemist. London: Crime Club, 1936. 1st ed. VG + (name). Pict dj (lacks triangular 1 1/2-inch chip upper spine corner, spine top). *Else Fine.* $150/£97

BURTON, MILES. (Pseud of John Rhode.) Situation Vacant. London: Collins, 1946. 1st ed. VG + (bd edges soiled) in dj (spine lt sunned; edges dknd). *Janus.* $35/£23

BURTON, PERCY M. and GUY H.G. SCOTT. The Law Relating to the Prevention of Cruelty to Animals and Some Kindred Topics.... London: John Murray, 1906. (Cl quite worn.) Sound only. *Boswell.* $150/£97

BURTON, RICHARD F. The City of the Saints and across the Rocky Mountains to California. NY, 1862. 1st Amer ed. Frontis, 574pp, fldg plan (lacks fldg map; wear, bumped; lacks 1/4-inch crown, foot of spine). *Benchmark.* $100/£65

BURTON, RICHARD F. The City of the Saints.... NY: Harper, 1862. 1st Amer ed. Frontis, (xvi),574pp; 2 fldg maps, 2pp ads at end. Blindstamped cl (lt wear extrems). *Dawson.* $275/£177

BURTON, RICHARD F. Etruscan Bologna: A Study. London, 1876. 1st ed. (Rebacked; remnants of spine mtd; ex-lib; corners worn.) *Argosy.* $100/£65

BURTON, RICHARD F. Falconry in the Valley of the Indus. London: John van Voorst, 1852. 1st ed. 1/2 title, xvi,107,(viii,ads)pp, 4 tinted lithos. VG (spine, top edges sl faded; spine sl frayed). *Hollett.* $1,705/£1,100

BURTON, RICHARD F. The Gold-Mines of Midian and the Ruined Midianite Cities. London: C. Kegan Paul & Co, 1878. 1st ed. 8vo. Half title, xvi,395,(3) (sl foxing 1st, last leaves), fldg map mtd on linen. Orig maroon blind-stamped cl (variant binding, possibly remainder), gilt-lettered on spine (bkpl, lower edge of lower cvr, spine faded). *Morrell.* $512/£330

BURTON, RICHARD F. The Lake Regions of Central Africa. London, 1860. 2 vols. 12 color plts; fldg color map. 1/2 calf, leather labels. Fine. *Argosy.* $1,250/£806

BURTON, RICHARD F. The Nile Basin. London, 1864. 1st ed. 195pp. Contemp 3/4 calf. (Corners rubbed; lacks maps.) *Argosy.* $300/£194

BURTON, RICHARD F. Personal Narrative of a Pilgrimage to El-Medinah and Meccah. NY: Putnam, 1856. 1st Amer ed. Tinted litho frontis, tp, fldg map. Orig brn cl (rebacked, orig backstrip laid down). VG (text lt browned). *House.* $350/£226

BURTON, RICHARD F. Selected Papers on Anthropology, Travel and Exploration. N.M. Penzer (ed). London, 1924. (Ex-lib, ink stamp, labels, upper hinge sl cracked; spine chipped.) *Edwards.* $39/£25

BURTON, RICHARD F. Selected Papers on Anthropology, Travel and Exploration.... London, 1924. 1st ed, one of 100 numbered on hand-made paper. Teg. Cl (name, address; discolored, soiled). *King.* $195/£126

BURTON, RICHARD F. Sind Revisited. London, 1877. 1st ed. 2 vols. xii,343; iv,331pp (browned). Red cl (rebound; spines faded; upper bd vol 2 sl warped). *Edwards.* $589/£380

BURTON, RICHARD F. Tales From the Gulistan. P. Allan, 1928. 1st ed. J. Kettelwell (illus). VG + . *Fine Books.* $75/£48

BURTON, RICHARD F. Vikram and the Vampire. L-G, 1870. 1st ed. 1/2 leather; marbled bds. VG. *Fine Books.* $250/£161

BURTON, RICHARD F. (trans). Book of the Thousand Nights and a Night. N.p. (US): Privately ptd by Burton Club, (n.d.). 16 vols (6 vols Supplemental Nights). Frontispieces each vol. Black cl, gilt/silver. VG set. *Schoyer.* $450/£290

BURTON, RICHARD F. (trans). The Carmina of Caius Valerius Catullus. London: For Private Subs only, 1894. One of 1000. Engr frontis port, xxiii,313pp (eps spotted). Uncut. Japon-backed bds (soiled, worn; spine rubbed). *Edwards.* $39/£25

BURTON, RICHARD F. (trans). Il Pentamerone. London: Henry, 1893. 1st trade ed. 2 vols. xvi,282; vi,280pp (offset feps vol 1). Black cl, gold-stamped (both vols bumped, lt frayed). Good+ set. *Godot.* $275/£177

BURTON, RICHARD F. (trans). The Kama Sutra of Vatsyayana. Cosmopoli: For Kama Shastra Soc of London & Benares, 1883. 1st ed. 182pp + 2pp ads (eps foxed). Gold-stamped vellum (dknd, foxed; gilt dull, flaked). Prospectus laid in. Good + . *Godot.* $650/£419

BURTON, RICHARD F. (trans). The Kasidah of Haji Abdu El Yezdi. (NY): LEC, 1937. #904/1500 numbered, signed by Valenti Angelo (illus). Full purple leather. Very Nice in tissue dj, liner & slipcase. *Hermitage.* $125/£81

BURTON, RICHARD F. (trans). The Kasidah of Haji Abdu el Yezdi. New Haven: Yale Univ, 1937. LEC. Ltd to 1500. Signed by Valenti Angelo (illus). Full lavender crushed morocco, blind-stamped. Folder, slipcase. *Sadlon.* $100/£65

BURTON, RICHARD F. (trans). The Kasidah of Haji Abdu El-Yezdi. Portland, ME: Mosher, 1895. 1st ed. One of 250. Frontis. Untrimmed as issued. 1/2 vellum. Sl rubbed, soiled, o/w VG. *Worldwide.* $75/£48

BURTON, RICHARD F. (trans). The Kasidah of Haji Abdu El-Yezdi. London: Cook, 1900. 3rd ed. One of 250. Rubbed, spine frayed, o/w VG. *Worldwide.* $65/£42

BURTON, ROBERT. The Anatomy of Melancholy.... London, 1800. 9th ed, corrected. 2 vols. Later 19th cent 1/2 polished calf; marbled bds; gilt tooling; raised bands. Good. *Goodrich.* $295/£190

BURTON, ROBERT. The Anatomy of Melancholy.... London, 1849. Engr frontis, 748pp. Good. *Fye.* $100/£65

BURTON, VIRGINIA LEE. Maybelle the Cable Car. Boston: Houghton Mifflin, 1952. 1st ed. 9.25x9.5. Pict cl. NF. *Book Adoption.* $45/£29

BURTON, WILLIAM. A History and Description of English Earthenware.... London: Cassell, 1904. 1st ed, #669/1450. 24 color plts; 93 half-tone plts/illus. Red cl. Good. *Cox.* $70/£45

BURY, G. WYMAN. Arabia Infelix. London: Macmillan, 1915. 3 maps. Red cl, gilt. VG. *Schoyer.* $200/£129

BUSCH, FREDERICK. Closing Arguments. NY: Ticknor & Fields, 1991. 1st ed, rev copy. Promo material laid in. Fine in Fine dj. *Aka.* $40/£26

BUSCH, FREDERICK. The Mutual Friend. NY: Harper & Row, (1978). *Between The Covers.* $65/£42

BUSCH, MORITZ. Travels between the Hudson and the Mississippi, 1851-1852. (Lexington): Univ Press of KY, (1971). 1st ed in English. Blue cl. Fine in NF dj. *Harrington.* $40/£26

BUSEY, SAMUEL C. Personal Reminiscences and Recollections. Washington, 1895. 373pp. VG. *Schoyer.* $60/£39

BUSHELL, S.W. Oriental Ceramic Art. NY: Crown, (1980). NF in dj. *Schoyer.* $85/£55

BUSHELL, S.W. Oriental Ceramic Art. NY, 1899. xiii+942pp. Teg; partly unopened. (Rebound; new eps.) *Edwards.* $140/£90

BUSHNELL, DAVID. BAE Bulletin 48. Choctaw of Bayou Lacomb St. Tammy Parish Louisiana. Washington, 1909. 22 plts. (Ex-lib; spine sl rubbed.) *Edwards.* $23/£15

BUSHNELL, DAVID. BAE Bulletin 69. Native Villages and Village Sites East of the Mississippi. Washington, 1919. Color frontis map, 16 plts. (Ex-lib.) *Edwards.* $23/£15

BUSHNELL, DAVID. BAE Bulletin 71. Native Cemeteries and Forms of Burial East of the Mississippi. Washington, 1920. 17 plts, incl tinted frontis. (Ex-lib.) *Edwards.* $23/£15

BUSHNELL, DAVID. BAE Bulletin 77. Villages of the Algonquian, Siouan, and Caddoan Tribes West of the Mississippi. Washington, 1922. 55 plts. (Ex-lib.) *Edwards.* $28/£18

BUSHNELL, DAVID. BAE Bulletin 83. Burials of the Algonquian, Siouan and Caddoan Tribes West of the Mississippi. Washington, 1927. 37 plts. (Sl marginal browning, ex-lib.) *Edwards.* $28/£18

BUSHNELL, G.H.S. and ADRIAN DIGBY. Ancient American Pottery. London, 1955. 1st ed. 30 plts (4 color), 2 maps, table. Dj (sl rubbed). *Edwards.* $31/£20

BUSHONG, MILLARD K. General Turner Ashby and Stonewall's Valley Campaign. Verona, VA: McClure Ptg Co, 1980. 1st ed. NF in NF dj. *Bishop.* $20/£13

BUSK, DOUGLAS. The Delectable Mountains. London: Hodder & Stoughton, 1946. 1st ed. 37 plts; 4 maps. (Edges sl damp-stained.) *Hollett.* $39/£25

BUSTON, L.H. DUDLEY. Eastern Road. London: Kegan Paul, 1924. Maroon cl (sl faded). *Schoyer.* $45/£29

BUTEN, HARRY M. Wedgwood Rarities. Merion, PA: Buten Museum of Wedgwood, 1969. 1st ed. VG. *Argosy.* $125/£81

BUTLER, A.S.G. The Lutyens Memorial. The Architecture of Sir Edwin Lutyens. London: Country Life, 1950. 1st ed. Vol III only. Frontis, 107 plts. Dj (sl soiled, chipped). *Edwards.* $233/£150

BUTLER, A.S.G. The Substance of Architecture. London, 1926. 8 plts; fore-edge uncut. (Eps, fore-edge leaves sl spotted; bkpl.) *Edwards.* $62/£40

BUTLER, ALBAN. The Lives of the Fathers, Martyrs and Other Principal Saints. Bernard Kelly (ed). London: Virtue, 1949. 5 vols. VG set. *Hollett.* $70/£45

BUTLER, ARTHUR G. Birds of Great Britain and Ireland. Hull: Brumby & Clark, n.d. (ca 1908). 2 vols. 115 color litho plts. Gray over blue cl, gilt spine (extrms sl rubbed). *Karmiole.* $375/£242

BUTLER, ARTHUR G. Foreign Finches in Captivity. London, 1894. 1st ed. 4to. viii,332pp; 60 Fine hand-colored lithos, guards. F.W. Frohawk (illus). Gilt pict red cl (bumped, sl discolored, sunned; inside hinges weak). VG. *Shifrin.* $3,600/£2,323

BUTLER, B.S. Geology and Ore Deposits of the San Francisco and Adjacent Districts, Utah. Washington: GPO, 1913. 41 plts, fldg map (in pocket). Heavy tan wraps. Sunned, soiled, o/w VG+. *Five Quail.* $120/£77

BUTLER, BENJAMIN FRANKLIN. Autobiography and Personal Reminiscences of Major-General Benjamin F. Butler. Boston: A.M. Thayer, 1892. 1st ed. 1154,(4)pp. VG (rebacked, old spine laid down). *Mcgowan.* $85/£55

BUTLER, CHARLES. Reminiscences of Charles Butler...with...Considerations on the Present Proceedings for the Reform on the English Courts of Equity.... Boston: Wells & Lilly, 1827. Orig bds (rebacked in cl); untrimmed. Sound. *Boswell.* $250/£161

BUTLER, CHARLES. Reminiscences. London: John Murray, 1824. 4th ed. 2 vols. xii,404; vi,290pp (spotting); marbled edges. 1/2 calf, marbled bds (edges sl rubbed), leather labels. *Edwards.* $93/£60

BUTLER, CHARLES. Syphilis Sive Morbus Humanus, a Rationalization of Yaws So-Called. Brooklyn, 1936. 1st ed. Good. *Fye.* $35/£23

BUTLER, ELLIS PARKER. The Confessions of a Daddy. NY: Century, 1907. 1st ed. Pict red cl. VG. *Antic Hay.* $35/£23

BUTLER, ELLIS PARKER. Philo Gubb, Correspondence-School Detective. Boston, 1918. 1st ed. Pict cl (ink mark-outs at edges). *King.* $95/£61

BUTLER, FRANCES ANNE. Journal. Phila, 1835. 1st Amer ed. 2 vols. 252pp+12pp ads; 218pp+22pp ads. (Lt foxing; rebound.) Slipcase. *Heinoldt.* $45/£29

BUTLER, GWENDOLINE. Coffin and the Paper Man. London: CCC, 1990. 1st ed. Fine in dj. *Mordida.* $35/£23

BUTLER, GWENDOLINE. Coffin on Murder Street. London: CCC, 1991. 1st ed. Fine in dj. *Mordida.* $35/£23

BUTLER, J.R. Floralia, Garden Paths and By-Paths of the Eighteenth Century. Chapel Hill, 1938. Ltd to 500. Signed presentation. 10 plts (4 color). Dj (lt edgewear). *Sutton.* $85/£55

BUTLER, JOHN C. Historical Record of Macon and Central Georgia. Macon: J.W. Burke, 1879. 1st ed. Frontis, 351pp (inserted slip after p348)+(28)pp ads. Orig orange cl. VG (spine sl faded). Howes B 1056. *Chapel Hill.* $275/£177

BUTLER, JOSEPH T. Candleholders in America, 1650-1900. NY: Bonanza Books, (1967). 1st ed. Frontis. Bkpl; else Fine in used dj. *Bookpress.* $45/£29

BUTLER, JUNE RAINSFORD. Floralia—Garden Paths and By-Paths of the 18th Century. Chapel Hill, NC, 1938. 1st ed. Ltd to 500. Buckram (spine lt sunned). NF. *Shifrin.* $60/£39

BUTLER, OCTAVIA E. Patternmaster. GC: Doubleday, 1976. 1st ed, 1st bk. Fine in dj (lt dust soiling). *Levin.* $125/£81

BUTLER, OCTAVIA. Mind of My Mind. Doubleday, 1977. 1st ed. Fine in dj. *Madle.* $50/£32

BUTLER, ROBERT OLEN. Wabash. NY: Knopf, 1987. 1st ed. Rev slip laid in. Fine in dj. *Reese.* $35/£23

BUTLER, SAMUEL. Erewhon or Over the Range. NY: Cheshire House, 1931. One of 1200 numbered. Teg. 1/4 calf, dec bds. Fine in VG slipcase. *Reese.* $75/£48

BUTLER, SAMUEL. Erewhon. NY: LEC, 1934. #904/1500 numbered, signed by Rockwell Kent (illus). Fine in pub's slipcase. *Hermitage.* $150/£97

BUTLER, SAMUEL. Erewhon. NY: Pynson Printers, 1934. LEC. Signed by Rockwell Kent (designs). Full ivory silk, litho design. NF in pub's slipcase. *Sadlon.* $135/£87

BUTLER, SAMUEL. Hudibras. Edinburgh: For R. Clark et al, 1784. x,338pp (repairs 1 leaf; last few leaves damp-stained), 3 plts. Contemp full polished calf; raised bands, spine label. *Hollett.* $47/£30

BUTLER, SAMUEL. Hudibras. Troy, NY: Wright, Goodenow & Stockwell, 1806. 1st Amer ed. x,286,(14)pp, index. Calf, red leather spine label (extrems sl rubbed). *Karmiole.* $100/£65

BUTLER, SAMUEL. Hudibras. London: Ptd by W. Lewis, 1819. New Ed. 2 vols. lxxiv,444; 494pp, 120 hand-colored plts. Contemp mottled calf, dec gilt (lt wear, sl loss vol 1; ex-libris), leather labels (spines sl creased). *Edwards.* $194/£125

BUTLER, SAMUEL. The Posthumous Works.... R. Reily, 1730. 3rd ed, corrected. Contemp calf (joints cracked; lettering-piece defective). *Waterfield.* $62/£40

BUTLER, SAMUEL. The Way of All Flesh. London: Grant Richards, 1903. 1st ed. Teg. VG (spine sunned; name, tape marks eps; inner hinges starting). *Chapel Hill.* $350/£226

BUTLER, SAMUEL. The Way of All Flesh. NY: LEC, 1936. #904/1500 numbered, signed by Ward Johnson (illus). 2 vols. Full leather. Fine in pub's slipcase. *Hermitage.* $100/£65

BUTLER, WILLIAM ALLEN. Nothing to Wear. NY: Rudd & Carleton, 1857. 1st ed. Ribbed cl stamped in gilt/blind (spine ends, corners rubbed; text offset to plts; lt foxing). BAL 2228. *Sadlon.* $15/£10

BUTLER, WILLIAM FRANCIS. The Wild North Land. Toronto: Musson Book Co, 1924. Rpt ed. Map. VG. *Blue Dragon.* $35/£23

BUTLER, WILLIAM. The Land of the Veda. NY/Cincinnati: Eaton & Mains/Jennings & Graham, 1906. Pict cl (lower joint cracked). *Hollett.* $217/£140

BUTLIN, MARTIN and EVELYN JOLL. The Paintings of J.M.W. Turner. New Haven/London: Yale Univ, 1977. 1st ed. 2 vols. 556 plts vol 2. Uniform blue buckram, gilt. VF set. *Europa.* $194/£125

BUTLIN, MARTIN and EVELYN JOLL. The Paintings of J.M.W. Turner. Yale Univ, 1984. Rev ed. 2 vols. 572 plts. Paper in card slipcase. *Ars Artis.* $116/£75

BUTLIN, MARTIN. The Paintings and Drawings of William Blake. Yale Univ, 1981. 2 vols. Dj. *Ars Artis.* $349/£225

BUTLIN, MARTIN. The Paintings and Drawings of William Blake. Yale Univ Press, 1981. 1st ed. 2 vols. 1193 plts. VF in djs. *Poetry.* $209/£135

BUTLIN, MARTIN. William Blake: A Complete Catalogue of the Works in the Tate Gallery. Tate Gallery, 1957. Fine in dj. *Europa.* $19/£12

BUTOR, MICHAEL. Letters from the Antipodes. Athens: OH Univ, (1981). 1st Amer ed. Fine in dj. *Hermitage.* $25/£16

BUTOR, MICHEL. A Change of Heart. NY: S&S, 1957. 1st US ed. Corners bruised, else VG + in VG dj (chipping; tears). *Lame Duck.* $35/£23

BUTTERFIELD, CONSUL W. An Historical Account of the Expedition Against Sandusky.... Cincinnati, 1873. 403pp. Overall VG (name; spine ends lt worn, sm damp area fr cvr). Howes B 1062. *Hayman.* $125/£81

BUTTERFIELD, CONSUL W. An Historical Account of the Expedition Against Sandusky.... Cincinnati: R. Clarke, 1873. Frontis port, x,403pp. Grn cl (edgewear). Overall VG (bkpl). Howes B 1062. *Bohling.* $150/£97

BUTTERFIELD, CONSUL W. History of Brule's Discoveries and Explorations 1610-1626.... Cleveland, 1898. 1st ed. Frontis, xiii,185pp, 6 plts. Fine. Howes B 1063. *Oregon.* $125/£81

BUTTERFIELD, CONSUL W. History of George Rogers Clark's Conquest of the Illinois and the Wabash Towns 1778 and 1779. Columbus, 1904. Sm dampspot back cvr, o/w VG. *Hayman.* $50/£32

BUTTERFIELD, CONSUL W. History of George Rogers Clark's Conquest of the Illinois and the Wabash Towns 1778 and 1779. Columbus: Heer, 1904. 2 ports. Pict cl. VG. *Schoyer.* $90/£58

BUTTERFIELD, CONSUL W. History of George Rogers Clark's Conquest of the Illinois and the Wabash Towns 1778 and 1779. Columbus, OH: F.J. Heer, 1904. 1st ed. Frontis port. Grn cl. Inkstamp fep, else Fine. *Chapel Hill.* $165/£106

BUTTERFIELD, CONSUL W. History of the Girtys. Columbus, 1950. Rpt. Dj (worn, verso reinforced). Howes B 1066. *Hayman.* $50/£32

BUTTERWORTH, BENJAMIN. The Growth of Industrial Art.... Washington: GPO, 1892. 200pp. New 1/4 calf (sl soiling, browning, some pp torn at inner margins). *Marlborough.* $853/£550

BUTTERWORTH, HEZEKIAH. Zig Zag Journeys in the British Isles. Boston: Dana Estes, (1889). 1st ed. Pict cl. NF in dj (chipped, sl soiled). *Sadlon.* $30/£19

BUTTERWORTH, HEZEKIAH. Zig Zag Journeys in the Orient. Boston, 1882. 320pp. Illus cl (sl faded, rubbed; sm dent; hinges sl tender). *Edwards.* $54/£35

BUTTERWORTH, HEZEKIAH. Zig Zag Journeys in the Orient. Boston: Estes & Lauriat, 1882. 1st ed. Pict cl (spine ends, corners sl rubbed). *Sadlon.* $30/£19

BUTTS, EDWARD. The Swastika. Kansas City, MO, 1908. 1st ed headed 'Statement No. 1.' Gilt-stamped buckram. Bkpl. *Argosy.* $65/£42

BUTTS, I.R. Every Man His Own Counsellor. Boston: I.R. Butts, 1848. 44th ed. 108pp. Ptd wraps (chipped, but usable). *Boswell.* $75/£48

BUTTS, MARY. Ashe of Rings. Wishart, 1933. Rev ed. VG (edges worn, prelims spotted). *Patterson.* $62/£40

BUTTS, MARY. Imaginary Letters. Paris: Edward W. Titus, 1928. Ltd to 250 numbered, ptd. Flesh-colored cl, paper cvr title, spine labels (glue-stained). VG. *Weber.* $225/£145

BUTTS, MARY. Scenes from the Life of Cleopatra. London: Heinemann, 1935. 1st ed. Sl bumped; fore-edge spotted, o/w VG in Good dj (sl nicked, soiled; price-clipped). *Virgo.* $186/£120

BUXTON, E. Two African Trips. London, 1902. Pull-out rear pocket map. Nice in ptd buckram cl. *Trophy Room.* $375/£242

BUXTON, EDWARD NORTH. Epping Forest. London, 1884. 1st ed. xii,147pp; 9 maps and plans. (Soiled, spine yellowed.) *Edwards.* $31/£20

BUXTON, EDWARD NORTH. Short Stalks. London: Stanford, 1892. (Faded, loose, bumped, backstrip torn.) *Petersfield.* $54/£35

BUXTON, EDWARD NORTH. Short Stalks. London: Edward Stanford, 1893. 2nd ed. xiii,(405)pp; 25 full-pg illus. Uncut. Pict buckram (dknd, spine frayed), gilt. Flyleaves spotted. *Hollett.* $287/£185

BUXTON, J. The Redstart. London, 1950. 1st ed. 1 color, 16 plain plts. Good. *Henly.* $43/£28

BYATT, A.S. Degrees of Freedom—The Novels of Iris Murdoch. Chatto, 1965. 1st UK ed. VG (sl mks bds, eps; school lib label) in dj (sl fading; sm corner chip fr panel; sm rubbed patch bottom spine). *Williams.* $70/£45

BYATT, A.S. The Game. Scribner's, 1967. 1st Amer ed. NF in dj. *Stahr.* $45/£29

BYATT, A.S. The Game. NY: Scribner's, 1967. 1st ed. Fine in dj (minor wear). *Else Fine.* $85/£55

BYATT, A.S. Possession. NY: Random House, 1990. 1st ed. Fine in dj (price-clipped). *Else Fine.* $65/£42

BYATT, A.S. Still Life. C&W, 1985. 1st UK ed. NF in dj. *Lewton.* $28/£18

BYATT, A.S. The Virgin in the Garden. London: C&W, 1978. 1st ed. NF in dj (sl waterstained). *Virgo.* $54/£35

BYATT, A.S. The Virgin in the Garden. London: Chatto, 1978. 1st UK ed. VG + (ink inscrip) in dj (price-clipped). *Williams.* $39/£25

BYFORD, WILLIAM. A Treatise on the Chronic Inflammation and Displacement of the Unimpregnated Uterus. Phila, 1864. 1st ed. 215pp. Good. *Fye.* $200/£129

BYFORD, WILLIAM. A Treatise on the Chronic Inflammation and Displacements of the Unimpregnated Uterus. Phila, 1871. 2nd ed. 248pp. Good. *Fye.* $65/£42

BYINGTON, CYRUS. BAE Bulletin 46. Dictionary of the Choctaw Language. John R. Swanton & Henry S. Halbert (eds). Washington, 1915. Frontis port. (Ex-lib; hinges cracked through; shaken; sl staining upper bd.) *Edwards.* $28/£18

BYKOV, CONSTANTINE. The Cerebral Cortex and the Internal Organs. NY, 1957. 1st Eng trans. Good. *Fye.* $75/£48

BYLES, MARIE BUEZEVILLE. By Cargo and Mountain. London, 1931. 1st ed. *Edwards.* $54/£35

BYNE, ERIC and GEOFFREY SUTTON. High Peak. London: Secker & Warburg, 1966. 1st ed. 46 plts. VG. *Hollett.* $62/£40

BYNE, MILDRED STAPLEY and ARTHUR. Spanish Gardens and Patios. Phila/NY: Lippincott/Architectural Record, 1924. 1st ed. 4 color plts. Gilt-stamped pict cvr. *Quest.* $195/£126

BYNE, MILDRED STAPLEY and ARTHUR. Spanish Gardens and Patios.... Phila/NY: Lippincott/Architectural Record, 1928. 1st ed. 4 color plts. Blue cl, gilt. VF in dj. *Pharos.* $125/£81

BYNNER, WITTER. Book of Lyrics. NY: Knopf, 1955. 1st ed, ltd to 1750 numbered. NF in dj. *Antic Hay.* $25/£16

BYNNER, WITTER. A Book of Plays. NY: Knopf, 1922. 1st ed. Good (fr hinge cracked; dull; worn). *Godot.* $35/£23

BYNNER, WITTER. Tiger. NY: M. Kennerley, 1913. 1st Amer ed. Fine (sig; lacks dj). *Agvent.* $40/£26

BYNNER, WITTER. Tiger. NY: Mitchell Kennerley, 1913. 1st ed. VG. *Chapel Hill.* $60/£39

BYRD, CECIL K. A Bibliography of Illinois Imprints 1814-1858. Chicago/London: Univ of Chicago Press, (1966). 1st ed. Fine in dj. *Heller.* $40/£26

BYRD, RICHARD E. Little America. NY: Putnam's, 1930. 1st ed. VG. *Parmer.* $35/£23

BYRD, RICHARD E. Little America. NY: Putnam, 1930. 1st ed. VG + in dj (sl torn). *Walcot.* $39/£25

BYRD, RICHARD E. Skyward. Chicago, (1981). Lakeside Classic. VG. *Schoyer.* $15/£10

BYRD, RICHARD E. Skyward. Chicago: Lakeside Classic, 1981. Fldg map. Black cl, gilt titles. Inscrip, else VG. *Parmer.* $30/£19

BYRD, WILLIAM. Another Secret Diary of William Byrd of Westover, 1739-1741. Maude H. Woodfin (ed). Dietz, 1942. VG (ex-lib; spine label erased; cvr varnished; eps foxed). *Book Broker.* $35/£23

BYRD, WILLIAM. Another Secret Diary of William Byrd of Westover, 1739-1741. Maude H. Woodfin (ed). Richmond, VA: Dietz Press, 1942. 1st ed. Beige cl. Fine. *Chapel Hill.* $65/£42

BYRD, WILLIAM. The Writings of.... NY, 1901. One of 500. 4 plts. 1/4 art vellum, bds. Dj (worn). Howes B 1077. *Ginsberg.* $175/£113

BYRNE, BERNARD JAMES. A Frontier Army Surgeon. NY, 1962. 2nd rev ed. VG + in VG + dj. *Pratt.* $25/£16

BYRNE, DONN. Messer Marco Polo. NY: Century Co, 1921. 1st ed. NF in dj (sl edgeworn). BAL 2291. *Sadlon.* $60/£39

BYRNE, DONN. O'Malley of Shanganagh. NY, (1925). 1st ed. Fine in dj. *Argosy.* $60/£39

BYRON, LORD. The Bride of Abydos. London: John Murray, 1813. 4th ed. Good + in orig plain wrappers (sl defective). *Poetry.* $39/£25

BYRON, LORD. Childe Harold's Pilgrimage. London: John Murray, 1814. 8th ed. Fldg facs. Contemp 1/2 calf, mod cl (rebacked). VG (no 1/2 title; foxing). *Poetry.* $39/£25

BYRON, LORD. Childe Harold's Pilgrimage. Paris: Harrison, 1931. One of 660 (of 725). Red cl over bds. Fine in pub's slipcase (split top, bottom edges), label. *Juvelis.* $100/£65

BYRON, LORD. Don Juan, Cantos III, IV, and V. London: Ptd by Thomas Davidson, 1821. 1st ed. 1/2 title. Uncut. Foxing, sl staining, o/w VG in orig paper-cvrd bds (joints tender; label rubbed, chipped; spine ends defective). *Poetry.* $132/£85

BYRON, LORD. Hebrew Melodies. London: John Murray, 1815. 1st ed, 1st issue w/Rogers's Jacqueline listed 2nd on verso of 1st ad leaf. 2pp undated ads, 4 leaves prelim titles, 4pp ads dated June 1815. VG in orig unptd drab wrappers (sl edgeworn, soiled, spine chipped; ink notations inside cvrs); cl case. *Sumner & Stillman.* $550/£355

BYRON, LORD. Hours of Idleness. Newark: S.&J. Ridge, 1807. 1st ed w/1/2 title & 1st issue points: D3 & Y3 are cancels; dbl 'where' on p5; 'thunder' on p114; 'the' on p181; p171 numbered correctly. 8vo. 1/2 title,xiv,187pp.   Contemp calf (newly rebacked, labelled). Excellent. *Cox.* $853/£550

BYRON, LORD. Letters and Journals of Lord Byron. London: John Murray, 1830. 1st ed. 2 vols. viii,670; (2),823pp + errata leaf; engr plt (title facing browned). Contemp 1/2 calf (rubbed; newly rebacked, dbl morocco labels). Good (spotting). *Cox.* $186/£120

BYRON, LORD. Letters and Journals. London: John Murray, 1830. 1st British ed. 2 vols. Frontis. 1/2 calf. (Spine, corners rubbed.) *Agvent.* $325/£210

BYRON, LORD. The Letters. Dent, 1933. 1st ed. 16 plts. Buckram, gilt. VG. *Poetry.* $19/£12

BYRON, LORD. Marino Faliero, Doge of Venice. London: John Murray, 1821. 1st ed, 1st issue, w/5 1/2 lines of Doge's speech on p151, w/half-title, prelim blank leaf. xxi,261pp + ad leaf, 8pp pub's ads; uncut, partly unopened. Good (sl wear, joints cracked, lower cvr scratched; defect spine label). *Bickersteth.* $233/£150

BYRON, LORD. Marino Faliero. London: John Murray, 1821. 1st ed, 1st issue. Rebacked brn calf w/maroon leather labels, gilt, over contemp brn calf. Cvrs lt worn, else Very Nice. *Limestone.* $175/£113

BYRON, LORD. Mazeppa, a Poem. London: John Murray, 1819. 1st ed, 2nd issue, w/printer's impt on verso p71. 71pp + (8)pp ads. Untrimmed. VG (lt soiling, spine separating) in orig drab grn-gray wraps (author, title penned fr wrap). *Chapel Hill.* $300/£194

BYRON, LORD. Mazeppa, a Poem. London: John Murray, 1819. 1st ed, 2nd issue. 71,(i)pp. Mod 1/2 calf, gilt (lt spotting). *Hollett.* $186/£120

BYRON, LORD. Sardanapalus, A Tragedy. The Two Foscari, A Tragedy. Cain, A Mystery. London: John Murray, 1821. 1st ed uncut in bds, variant A. 8vo. (viii)(439)pp. Orig gray bds (lt foxing; hinges cracked, but cvrs attached; spine worn, chipped), orig ptd paper spine label priced '15s'. 1/2 blue morocco slipcase, ribbed gilt-lettered spine. *D & D.* $690/£445

BYRON, LORD. The Works. Phila: R.W. Pomeroy, 1825. 1st this ed. 8 vols. Uncut. Orig pub's bds. (Paper spines, labels renewed; pp dkng; early bkseller ticket.) Generally Good set. *Hartfield.* $450/£290

BYRON, ROBERT. The Station. NY: Knopf, 1928. 1st Amer ed w/cancel tp. Cl-backed batik bds, paper spine label. Spine faded; lacks dj, else VG. *Pharos.* $60/£39

BYRON, ROBERT. The Station. London: Lehmann, 1949. 1st ed. Pg carelessly opened, spine sl faded, rubbed, o/w VG. *Virgo.* $28/£18

BYRON, ROBERT. The Station. London: Lehmann, 1949. 1st thus. VG in dj. *Lewton.* $26/£17

BYRON. JOHN. Byron's Narrative of the Loss of the Wager...on the Coast of Patagonia. London: Henry Egatt (sic), 1832. Frontis, xvi,219,3pp ads. 3/4 morocco, gilt (rubbed). *Lefkowicz.* $100/£65

C

C.3.3. (Pseud of Oscar Wilde.) The Ballad of Reading Gaol. London: Leonard Smithers, 1898. 1st ed. One of 800. 8vo. 31 leaves. Mustard cl, cream cl spine. VG (cl sl soiled, bubbled; offsetting eps). *Chapel Hill.* $800/£516

CABELL, JAMES BRANCH. As I Remember It. McBride, 1955. 1st ed. Fine in dj. *Fine Books.* $25/£16

CABELL, JAMES BRANCH. Chivalry. NY, 1909. 1st ed. 12 full-pg color plts; teg. Dec cl. Spine dec mostly worn off, stained, ex-lib blindstamp, else Good. *King.* $65/£42

CABELL, JAMES BRANCH. The Eagle's Shadow. NY: Doubleday, Page, 1904. 1st ed, 1st issue, 1st bk. Illus eps. Gilt-titled cl (lt smudges). VG. *Cahan.* $85/£55

CABELL, JAMES BRANCH. The Jewel Merchants: a Comedy in One Act. NY: Robert M. McBride, 1921. 1st ed. Ltd to 1040. Gilt-stamped cl. Spine gilt sl dull, o/w Fine in dj (chip). *Sadlon.* $15/£10

CABELL, JAMES BRANCH. Joseph Hergesheimer: An Essay in Interpretation. Chicago: Bookfellows, 1921. 1st ed, one of 1000. VG+ (edgewear) in pict wrappers, string tie intact. *Other Worlds.* $40/£26

CABELL, JAMES BRANCH. The Line of Love. NY: Harpers, 1905. 1st state. Color insert; 10 color plts. VG (rubbed). *Agvent.* $90/£58

CABELL, JAMES BRANCH. The Music from Behind the Moon, an Epitome. NY: John Day, 1926. 1st ed. One of 3000 ptd. Nicked, else Fine in pub's slipcase (chipped, worn). *Hermitage.* $65/£42

CABELL, JAMES BRANCH. The Music from Behind the Moon. John Day, 1926. 1st ed. VG-. *Madle.* $75/£48

CABELL, JAMES BRANCH. The Silver Stallion. NY: McBride, 1926. #152/850 of lg paper ed, signed. VG (lettering faded; hinges sl exposed). *Williams.* $31/£20

CABELL, JAMES BRANCH. Some of Us. An Essay in Epitaphs. NY, 1930. #424/1295 signed. Uncut. Fine (lt sunned, sl rubbed). *Polyanthos.* $40/£26

CABELL, JAMES BRANCH. Something about Eve. London: John Lane, (1927). 1st British trade ed. Dec red cl. VG in white dj (chipped, lt soiled). *Reese.* $25/£16

CABELL, JAMES BRANCH. Something About Eve. NY, 1929. 1st illus ed. Decs, gold/black cvr. (Snag top edge spine.) *Mcclintock.* $30/£19

CABELL, JAMES BRANCH. Something about Eve. NY: McBride, 1929. 1st illus ed. Frontis. Gilt pict cl. Fine in VG dj (short creased tear mended on verso; 2 snags rear panel). *Reese.* $50/£32

CABELL, JAMES BRANCH. The Way of Ecben. NY: Robert M. McBride, (1929). 1st ed. Fine in tissue dj & slipcase (worn). *Hermitage.* $50/£32

CABLE, GEORGE WASHINGTON. The Amateur Garden. NY: Scribner, 1914. 1st ed. Fine. BAL 2382. *Second Life.* $45/£29

CABLE, GEORGE WASHINGTON. Bonaventure. NY: Scribners, 1888. 1st Amer ed. VG- (cl streaked, soiled). BAL 2346. *Agvent.* $75/£48

CABLE, GEORGE WASHINGTON. The Cavalier. NY: Scribner's, 1901. Fine. *Hermitage.* $25/£16

CABLE, GEORGE WASHINGTON. The Cavalier. NY: Scribners, 1901. 1st Amer ed. 8 plts. Dec cl. NF. BAL 2368: Ptg 3. *Agvent.* $35/£23

CABLE, GEORGE WASHINGTON. Kincaid's Battery. NY: Scribners, 1908. 1st ed. Dec cl. VG (owner sig in blue pencil). BAL 2376. *Agvent.* $40/£26

CABLE, GEORGE WASHINGTON. Old Creole Days. NY: Scribners, 1879. 1st ptg, 1st bk. VG (sig; cl sl soiled, stained). *Agvent.* $175/£113

CABLE, GEORGE WASHINGTON. Strange True Stories of Louisiana. NY: Scribner's, 1889. 1st ed. Frontis. Dec cream cl (dust soiled), pict onlay. Sound (fr inner hinge sl weak). BAL 2350. *Reese.* $40/£26

CABOT, RICHARD. A Layman's Handbook of Medicine with Special Reference to Social Workers. Boston, 1916. 1st ed. Good. *Fye.* $50/£32

CABOT, RICHARD. The Serum Diagnosis of Disease. NY, 1899. 1st ed. 154pp. Good. *Fye.* $100/£65

CABOT, W.B. In Northern Labrador. Boston: Richard Badger, 1912. 1st ed. Errata slip. Good +. *Walcot.* $109/£70

CADELL, CHARLES. Narrative of the Campaigns of the Twenty-Eighth Regiment. London, 1835. 1st ed. xx,281pp + 1pg list (Sl browned.) Good in morocco-backed bds (worn, damp-damaged). *Edwards.* $155/£100

CADILLAC and LIETTE. The Western Country in the 17th Century. Chicago, (1947). Lakeside Classic. VG. *Schoyer.* $25/£16

CADMAN, S. PARKES. The Parables of Jesus. Phila: David McKay, (1931). 1st ed. 4to. 8 color plts by N.C. Wyeth. Dk purple cl, color paste label (few minor scratches). Tp, frontis foxed; o/w Nice. *Reisler.* $675/£435

CADOGAN, WILLIAM. A Dissertation on the Gout, and all Chronic Diseases.... Ptd for J. Dodsley, 1771. 3rd ed. 99pp (lacks 1/2 title). Mod wrappers. *Bickersteth.* $124/£80

CADY, HARRISON. Holiday Time on Butternut Hill. Racine: Whitman, 1929. 1st ed. 24mo. Good (sm soil) in dj (detached, soiled). *Davidson.* $60/£39

CADY, HARRISON. Jack Frost Arrives on Butternut Hill. Racine: Whitman, 1929. 1st ed. 12mo. NF in Fine dj. *Davidson.* $75/£48

CADY, HARRISON. Time to Get Up. NY: Stoll and Edwards, (1928). 4to, 10 leaves. Grn cl-backed color pict bds (sm hole cl spine). NF. *Blue Mountain.* $45/£29

CADY, JOHN H. Arizona's Yesterday. (Patagonia, AZ, 1916.) Ptd pict wrappers (mended). Howes C 16. *Ginsberg.* $100/£65

CAESER, GENE. King of the Mountain Men, the Life of Jim Bridger. Dutton, 1961. 1st ed. VG in Good + dj. *Oregon.* $25/£16

CAHILL, JAMES. Treasures of Asia: Chinese Painting. Geneva: Skira, (1972). 2nd ed. 100 color tipped-in plts. Yellow cl. Fine in dj. *Weber.* $50/£32

CAHN, WALTER. Romanesque Bible Illumination. Ithaca, NY: Cornell Univ Press, 1982. 60 color plts. VG in dj, slipcase. *Argosy.* $100/£65

CAHUN, LEON. The Adventures of Captain Mago. Scribners, 1889. Good. *Madle.* $45/£29

CAIDIN, M. The Saga of Iron Annie. NY, 1979. VG in VG dj. *Clark.* $30/£19

CAIGER, G. Dolls on Display, Japan in Miniature. Tokyo: Hokuseido Press, (1933). Pict eps. Silk-cvrd bds. *Cullen.* $150/£97

CAIN, J. et al. Lithographs of Chagall 1962-1968. Vol 3. Boston, 1969. 2 color lithos. Excellent in dj (sm tear top). *Ars Artis.* $543/£350

CAIN, JAMES M. The Baby in the Icebox and Other Short Fiction. NY, (1981). 1st trade ed. Port. VG in dj. *King.* $25/£16

CAIN, JAMES M. The Butterfly. NY: Knopf, 1947. 1st ed. NF (bkpl) in bright dj. *Janus.* $50/£32

CAIN, JAMES M. Galatea. NY: Knopf, 1953. Stated 1st ed. (Pg edges sl browned, name). Dj (3 short closed tears). *Aka.* $30/£19

CAIN, JAMES M. Galatea. Hale, 1954. 1st ed. VG in dj (sl nicked, price-clipped). *Rees.* $31/£20

CAIN, JAMES M. Jealous Woman. Hale, 1955. 1st ed. VG in dj (sl nicked, mkd). *Rees.* $31/£20

CAIN, JAMES M. Love's Lovely Counterfeit. Knopf, 1942. 1st ed. VG in dj (lt wear; inner reinforcement). *Fine Books.* $110/£71

CAIN, JAMES M. The Magician's Wife. NY, 1965. 1st ed. VG in dj (rubbed). *King.* $25/£16

CAIN, JAMES M. The Moth. NY, 1948. 1st ed. Fine (eps lt foxed) in VG dj (sm rubbed spot, 2 closed tears, creasing). *Fuller & Saunders.* $45/£29

CAIN, JAMES M. The Moth. London: Knopf, 1948. 1st ed. VG in VG dj. *Ming.* $54/£35

CAIN, JAMES M. Our Government. Knopf, 1930. 1st ed, 1st bk. Spine sl faded, else VG. *Fine Books.* $85/£55

CAIN, JAMES M. Serenade. London: Jonathan Cape, 1938. 1st UK ed. VG. *Ming.* $39/£25

CAIN, JAMES M. Three of a Kind. NY: Knopf, 1943. 1st ed. Fine in NF dj (lt wear). *Janus.* $150/£97

CAIN, JAMES M. Three of a Kind. London: Robert Hale, n.d. (c. 1945). 1st ed. VG in dj (sl chipped, creased). *Rees.* $54/£35

CAIN, MARVIN R. Lincoln's Attorney General, Edward Bates of Missouri. Columbia, MO: Univ of MO Press, 1965. 1st ed. Frontis. Fine in NF dj. *Cahan.* $20/£13

CAIN, MARVIN R. Lincoln's Attorney General. Edward Bates of Missouri. Columbia, (1965). 1st ed. VG + in VG + dj. *Pratt.* $30/£19

CAIN, PAUL. Fast One. NY: Avon Books, 1948. Pb ed. Faint crease; sl wear, o/w Fine in wrappers. *Mordida.* $45/£29

CAINE, HALL. Life of Samuel Taylor Coleridge. Walter Scott, 1887. 1st ed. Teg; uncut. Blue cl, gilt spine. Inscrip; edges dusty, o/w VG. *Poetry.* $31/£20

CAIRD, JAMES. Prairie Farming in America. London: Longman et al, 1859. 1st ed. viii,128pp, fldg map. Blind-emb grn cl, gilt title (short tear repaired). Fine. Howes C 19. *Cahan.* $285/£184

CAIRD, MONA. Romantic Cities of Provence. London: T. Fisher Unwin, 1906. 1st ed. Teg. (Spine sl dknd; sm stain upper bd; eps foxed.) *Hollett.* $47/£30

CAIRNCROSS, DAVID. The Origin of the Silver Eel, with Remarks on Bait and Fly Fishing. London, 1862. Frontis, 96pp. Paper title label. (Fr fly leaf, ep water-stained.) *Argosy.* $75/£48

CAIRNS, MARY L. Grand Lake in the Olden Days.... (Denver, 1971). Good. *Hayman.* $25/£16

Cairo Guide. Federal Writers' Project (Illinois). Cairo: Sponsored by Cairo Public Lib, 1938. 1st ed. Color ptd wrappers. Rear wrapper edges dknd, else Fine. *Cahan.* $40/£26

CAIUS, JOHANNES. Of Englishe Dogges. Washington, DC: Milo Denlinger, (1947). 3rd ed in English, 1st Amer ptg. Facs rpt of 1880 ptg. NF in ptd wraps (sl creased). *Blue Mountain.* $75/£48

CALAS, NICOLAS. Confound the Wise. NY: Arrow, 1942. 1st ed. Fine in dj (tape-mended; chipped). *Beasley.* $100/£65

CALASANCTIUS, SISTER MARY JOSEPH. The Voice of Alaska. Lachine, Quebec: Sisters of St. Ann Press, 1935. Fldg map. VG in ptd wrapper. *High Latitude.* $50/£32

CALDECOTT, RANDOLPH. Come Lasses and Lads. London: Routledge, 1884. Obl 8vo. 24pp + 1pg ad on back cvr; 6 full-pg color plts. Color pict wrappers. Bumped, lt chipped, sl soiled, spine reinforced along internal edge, else Good. *Hobbyhorse.* $150/£97

CALDECOTT, RANDOLPH. The Farmer's Boy. George Routledge & Sons, 1881. 1st ed. 7 full-pg color illus by VG in stiff wraps. *Davidson.* $55/£35

CALDECOTT, RANDOLPH. The Fox Jumps Over the Parson's Gate. London: Routledge, 1883. Obl 8vo. 24pp + 1pg ad back cvr; 6 full-pg color plts. Color pict cream wrappers. Corners chipped, sm repaired tear, spine repaired, lt soiling, else Good. *Hobbyhorse.* $150/£97

CALDECOTT, RANDOLPH. Gleanings from the Graphic. London: Routledge, 1889. 1st ed. 4to. Frontis port, 84pp; 32 color illus by Caldecott. Color pict bds, gilt lettering; swimming scene (sl out of register). VG. *Drusilla's.* $100/£65

CALDECOTT, RANDOLPH. The Great Panjandrum Himself. London: Routledge, 1885. 1st ed. Obl 8vo. 24pp + 1pg ad back cvr; 6 full-pg color plts. Color pict cream wrappers. Fine. *Hobbyhorse.* $155/£100

CALDECOTT, RANDOLPH. The Hey Diddle Diddle Picture Book. London: Frederick Warne, n.d. (ca 1910). Oblong 8vo. 24 full-pg chromolithos. Ptd pict cl on bd (lt wear, spots on cvr). VG. *Hobbyhorse.* $75/£48

CALDECOTT, RANDOLPH. The Milkmaid, an Old Song.... London: Routledge, 1882. Obl 8vo. 24pp + 1pg ad back cvr; 6 full-pg color plts. Color pict cream wrappers. Lt chipped, else VG. *Hobbyhorse.* $150/£97

CALDECOTT, RANDOLPH. Ride A-Cock Horse to Bambury Cross and A Farmer Went Trotting Upon His Grey Mare. London: Routledge, 1884. Oblong 8vo, 4pp + 1pg ad on back cvr, 6 full-pg color plts. Color pict cream wrappers. Sl soiled, rubbed, minor repair, else VG. *Hobbyhorse.* $150/£97

CALDECOTT, RANDOLPH. A Sketch-Book of R. Caldecott's. London: Routledge, (1883). 1st ed. Obl 8vo. 48pp; 23 full-pg color lithos, 24 full-pg dwgs. Dec tan linen. VG (eps lt foxed; ink sig; rubbed). *Hobbyhorse.* $125/£81

CALDER, ISABEL M. Colonial Captivities, Marches, and Journeys. NY: Macmillan, 1935. 1st ed. Frontis, 1 plt. Maroon cl, gilt; teg. Good. *Karmiole.* $35/£23

CALDER, ISABEL M. Colonial Captivities, Marches, and Journeys. NY, 1935. 1st ed. *Ginsberg.* $75/£48

CALDERON, V.G. The White Llama Being La Venganza del Condor.... Richard Phibbs (trans). London: Golden Cockerel Press, 1938. 1st ed. Frontis; six 1/2pg wood engrs. Blue cl (sl rubbed). VG. *Cox.* $43/£28

CALDERWOOD, W.L. The Salmon Rivers and Lochs of Scotland. London: Arnold, 1909. 1st ed. Red cl, gilt titles; teg. Fine +. *Bowman.* $165/£106

CALDICOTT, J. The Values of Old English Silver and Sheffield Plate, from the XVth to the XIXth Centuries. J. Starkie Gardner (ed). London: Bemrose & Sons, 1906. 1st ed. 87 plts. Blue cl, gilt. Good. *Cox.* $85/£55

CALDWELL, DOROTHY J. (ed). Missouri Historic Sites Catalogue. Columbia: State Hist Soc of MO, 1963. 1st ed. Map. Fine in Good dj. *Connolly.* $32/£21

CALDWELL, ELSIE NOBLE. Alaska Trail Dogs. NY, 1945. 1st ed. Map. Shelfwear, o/w VG. *Artis.* $17/£11

CALDWELL, ERSKINE. The Deer at Our House. NY: Collier Books, (1966). 1st ed. Pict cl. Name, else Fine in dj (price-clipped, 1-inch creased tear, nick, else VG). *Godot.* $85/£55

CALDWELL, ERSKINE. Episode in Palmetto. NY: Duell, Sloan & Pearce, (1950). 1st ed. Owner blindstamp, o/w Fine in dj (lt chipped). *Hermitage.* $30/£19

CALDWELL, ERSKINE. In Search of Bisco. NY: FSG, (1965). Stated 1st ed. NF in dj (2 short closed tears). *Aka.* $20/£13

CALDWELL, ERSKINE. Journeyman. (NY, 1935). Ltd 1st ed. Fine in pub's box. *Argosy.* $75/£48

CALDWELL, ERSKINE. North of the Danube. Viking Press, 1939. 1st ed. Margaret Bourke White (photos). VG + in VG dj. *Bishop.* $60/£39

CALDWELL, ERSKINE. Place Called Estherville. NY: Duell et al, (1949). 1st ed. Fine in dj (lt rubbed). *Sadlon.* $40/£26

CALDWELL, ERSKINE. Poor Fool. NY: Rariora Press, 1930. 1st ed. Ltd to 1000. Recent gilt-stamped cl. (Dampstain approx 1-inch top margin leaves.) *Sadlon.* $20/£13

CALDWELL, ERSKINE. The Sacrilege of Alan Kent. Portland, ME: Falmouth Book House, 1936. 1st ed. 8 wood engrs. Fine in dj (worn, torn). *Graf.* $150/£97

CALDWELL, ERSKINE. Tenant Farmer. NY: Phalanx Press, (1935). 1st separate ed. One of 1500. Nice in grn wraps (sl streaked, faded). *Second Life.* $125/£81

CALDWELL, ERSKINE. This Very Earth. NY, (1948). 1st ed. Sl musty odor, else VG in dj (sl spotted). *King.* $35/£23

CALDWELL, ERSKINE. This Very Earth. NY: DS&P, (1948). 1st ed. Fine in VG dj (2 sm chips). *Between The Covers.* $85/£55

CALDWELL, ERSKINE. Tobacco Road. DSP, 1940. 1st illus ed. VG + in box (worn). *Fine Books.* $25/£16

CALDWELL, NORMAN. The French in the Mississippi Valley, 1740-1750. Univ IL, 1941. 1st ed. Map. Fine. *Oregon.* $40/£26

CALDWELL, WILLIAM H. The Guernsey. Peterborough, NH: American Guernsey Cattle Club, 1941. 1st ed. 2 color plts. Brn dec fabricoid, mtd cvr photo. Good in dj. *Karmiole.* $40/£26

Calendar of Alexander Graham Bell Correspondence in the Volta Bureau, Washington, D.C. (WPA). Washington, 1940. 1st ed. NF in orig stiff ptd wrappers. *Mcgowan.* $45/£29

CALEY, EARLE R. Analyses of Ancient Glasses 1790-1957. Corning: Corning Museum of Glass, 1962. (Corners lt bumped.) Dj. *Archaeologia.* $125/£81

CALHOUN, ARTHUR W. A Social History of the American Family: From Colonial Times to the Present. Cleveland: Clark, 1917-1919. 3 vols. (Ex-lib.) Howes C 27. *Schoyer.* $125/£81

CALHOUN, FREDERICK S. The Lawmen. Washington, (1989). 1st ed. Fine in Fine dj. *Pratt.* $25/£16

CALHOUN, W.L. History of the 42nd Regiment, Georgia Volunteers. Atlanta: (Sisson, print, 1900). 1st ed. Frontis port. Orig crate-paper wraps. Lt edge-spotting, else VG in 3/4 calf clamshell box, protective folder. Howes C 33. *Chapel Hill.* $475/£306

CALI, FRANCOIS. Architecture of Truth. NY: George Braziller, (1957). 1st Amer ed. Fine in dj (sl sunned, rubbed). *Bookpress.* $55/£35

California State Almanac and Annual Register for 1855. Sacramento: Democratic State Journal, 1855. 48,(6)pp + 16pp ads. Fine in ptd self-wrappers. *Dawson.* $600/£387

California Three Hundred and Fifty Years Ago. Manuelo's Narrative.... SF: Samuel Carson, 1888. Frontis, 333pp. Black, gold-stamped cl (lt worn). *Dawson.* $50/£32

California, a Guide to the Golden State. NY: Hastings House, 1939. 1st ed. Map in rear pocket. Ink name, else VG. *Perier.* $45/£29

CALISHER, HORTENSE. Textures of Life. Boston, 1963. 1st Amer ed. Signed. Fine in NF dj (price-clipped). *Polyanthos.* $25/£16

CALKINS, DICK and PHIL NOWLAN. The Pop-Up Buck Rogers. Strange Adventures in the Spider-Ship. Chicago: Pleasure, n.d. (1935). 20x23cm. 3 dbl-pg pop-ups. Illus bds. (Reinforced inside spine not affecting pop-ups.) *Book Finders.* $280/£181

CALL, LEWIS W. United States Military Reservations.... Washington: GPO, 1907. Ex-lib. *Argosy.* $100/£65

CALLAGHAN, MORLEY. A Broken Journey. NY: Scribner's, 1932. 1st ed. Fine in NF dj (sl sunned spine). *Beasley.* $175/£113

CALLAGHAN, MORLEY. It's Never Over. Scribners, 1930. 1st ed. VG+ in VG dj (worn; dust soil). *Fine Books.* $150/£97

CALLAGHAN, MORLEY. Strange Fugitive. Scribners, 1928. 1st ed, 1st bk. Corner wear, else VG. *Fine Books.* $45/£29

CALLAGHAN, MORLEY. They Shall Inherit the Earth. NY: Random House, 1935. 1st ed. Fine in VG dj (chipping; spine dknd). *Beasley.* $65/£42

CALLAHAN, ALSTON. Surgery of the Eye: Injuries. Springfield, 1950. 1st ed. Good. *Fye.* $60/£39

CALLAHAN, GENEVIEVE A. Sunset All-Western Cook Book. Stanford: Stanford Univ, 1933. 1st ed, 1st issue. Grn cl over pict wrappers stamped black on spine. VG. *Houle.* $75/£48

CALLAHAN, NORTH. Flight from the Republic. Indianapolis: Bobbs-Merrill, (1967). 1st ed. Blue cl. Fine in NF dj. *Chapel Hill.* $35/£23

CALLAWAY, JAMES E. The Early Settlement of Georgia. Athens: Univ of GA Press, (1948). 1st ed. Tan cl. VG in dj. *Chapel Hill.* $60/£39

CALMETTE, ALBERT. Tubercle Bacillus Infection and Tuberculosis in Man and Animals. Balt, 1923. 1st Eng trans. Good. *Fye.* $100/£65

CALMETTE, ALBERT. Venoms, Venomous Animals and Antivenomous Serumtherapeutics. London, 1908. 1st Eng trans. Good. *Fye.* $300/£194

CALTHROP, DION CLAYTON. English Costume. London, 1906. 4 vols. VG. *Argosy.* $275/£177

CALTHROP, DION CLAYTON. English Costume. II. Middle Ages. A&C Black, 1906. 1st ed. 15 color plts; teg. (Foxing; spine chip; dampstain upper bd.) *Edwards.* $31/£20

CALVERT, ALBERT F. Cook's Handbook for Spain. London, 1924. Red cl. VG-. *Gretton.* $31/£20

CALVERT, ALBERT F. Southern Spain. London: Black, 1908. 75 color plts; fldg map. Teg. Sl rubbed, o/w VG. *Worldwide.* $65/£42

CALVERT, GEORGE H. (ed). Illustrations of Phrenology. Balt: William & Joseph Neal, 1832. 1st ed, 1st bk. 192pp. 26 woodcuts. Grn muslin (lacks paper spine label). Spine splitting, chipped; sig; foxing, else VG. BAL 2393. *Chapel Hill.* $400/£258

CALVERTON, V. The Man Inside.... Scribner's, 1936. 1st ed. Fine in VG dj (dust soil). *Aronovitz.* $75/£48

CALVIN, ROSS. River of the Sun. Albuquerque, 1946. 1st ed. Red cl, gilt. NF in VG dj (chipped). *Five Quail.* $55/£35

CALVIN, ROSS. River of the Sun. Albuquerque: Univ of NM, 1946. 1st ed. VG+ in dj (worn). *Parker.* $65/£42

CALVIN, ROSS. Sky Determines. Albuquerque: Univ of NM, (1948). Rev ed. Pict cl. VG in dj (sl tape repair). *Schoyer.* $30/£19

CALVIN, ROSS. Sky Determines. NY: MacMillan, 1934. 1st ed. VG. *Parker.* $40/£26

CALVINO, ITALO. If on a Winter's Night a Traveler. Secker & Warburg, 1981. 1st UK ed. Fine in dj. *Sclanders.* $23/£15

CALVINO, ITALO. If on a Winter's Night a Traveler. NY: Harcourt, Brace, Jovanovich, 1981. 1st US ed. NF in dj. *Lame Duck.* $50/£32

CALVINO, ITALO. Invisible Cities. HBJ, 1972. 1st ed. NF in VG dj (lt wear). *Fine Books.* $40/£26

CALVINO, ITALO. Italian Fables. Louis Brigante (trans). NY: Orion, 1959. 1st US ed. Fine in NF dj (price-clipped). *Pettler.* $65/£42

CALVINO, ITALO. The Path to the Nest of Spiders. Boston: Beacon, 1957. 1st US ed. Lt foxing pg edges; sticker residue fep, else VG+ in VG+ dj. *Lame Duck.* $95/£61

CALVINO, ITALO. The Silent Mr. Palomar. William Weaver (trans). NY: Targ Editions, 1981. 1st ed. One of 250 signed. Black bds, dec linen spine. Mint in dj. *Juvelis.* $75/£48

CALVINO, ITALO. The Silent Mr. Palomar. NY: Targ Editions, 1981. Ltd to 250 numbered, signed. Woodcut frontis port. Fine in glassine. *Karmiole.* $100/£65

CALVINO, ITALO. The Silent Mr. Palomar. NY: Targ, 1981. One of 250 signed. VF in VF dj. *Between The Covers.* $185/£119

CALVINO, ITALO. The Silent Mr. Palomar. NY: Targ Editions, 1981. One of 250 specially bound, signed. Fine in glassine dj. *Rees.* $194/£125

CALVINO, ITALO. T Zero. H-B-W, 1969. 1st ed. Fine in VG+ dj. *Fine Books.* $75/£48

Camberwick Green TV Pop-Up Book. London: Dean, 1972. 23x17 cm. 3 pop-ups. Glazed pict bds. VG-. *Book Finders.* $25/£16

CAMERON, DONALD CLOUGH. Grave Without Grass. NY: Holt, 1940. 1st ed. Spine slant, lt edgewear, else NF in dj (rubbed, lacks sm pieces). *Murder.* $40/£26

CAMERON, G.R. Pathology of the Cell. Edinburgh, 1952. 64 plts. Bottom corner sl knocked, o/w VG in dj. *Whitehart.* $74/£48

CAMERON, H.K. A List of Monumental Brasses on the Continent of Europe. London, 1970. Good. *Washton.* $35/£23

CAMERON, KENNETH. English Place-Names. London: Batsford, 1961. 1st ed. VG in dj. *Hollett.* $31/£20

CAMP, DEBORAH. Belle Starr. NY: Harmony, (1987). 1st ed. Fine in Fine dj. *Glenn.* $20/£13

CAMP, WALTER (ed). Spalding's Official Foot Ball Guide 1896. NY: American Sports Pub Co, (1896). 137,(4)pp + ads. Wrappers. (Sm piece lacking corner 1 leaf, not affecting ptg; underlining; sl wear.) *Hayman*. $75/£48

CAMP, WALTER and LORIN F. DELAND. Football. Boston/NY, 1896. 1st ed. 425pp. Gilt-pict cl (blue binding). (Ex-lib; soiling; extrems worn; title sl chipped, mended; inner hinge cracked.) *King*. $175/£113

Campaign of the Forty Fifth Regiment Massachusetts Volunteer Militia. (By Charles Eustis Hubbard.) Boston: Ptd by James S. Adams, 1882. 1st ed. Frontis, 126pp, 12 full-pg photo plts; aeg. 19th cent full grn morocco, raised bands, gilt spine. Very Nice. *Chapel Hill*. $150/£97

Campaigns of the Civil War. NY: Scribner's, (1885). 1st ed. Subscription ed. 13 vols. Frontis plts not found in reg ed; lg paper copies in deluxe binding of 1/2 leather, cl. NF (sl wear spine extrems few vols). *Mcgowan*. $350/£226

Campaigns of the Civil War. NY: Scribner's, 1881-1883. All vols 1st eds except I, II, IV (2nd eds). 13 vols. Blue cl. Fine in pub's box (lt worn). *Chapel Hill*. $700/£452

CAMPANELLA, ROY. It's Good to Be Alive. Little-Brown, 1959. 1st ed. VG in Good+ dj (sl worn). *Plapinger*. $30/£19

CAMPBELL, ALBERT H. Pacific Wagon Roads. Washington, 1859. 1st ed. 125pp, 6 fldg maps. Mod cl. Howes C 86. *Ginsberg*. $450/£290

CAMPBELL, ALEXANDER. Christian Baptism; With its Antecedents and Consequences. Bethany, VA: Campbell, 1853. Orig full calf (sm piece missing; cvrs flecked). *Ginsberg*. $150/£97

CAMPBELL, ARCHIBALD. Armada Cannon. London, 1899. 1st ed. Sq 8vo. 63pp; frontis port, guard; 11 plts (some w/guards); letter loosely inserted. Upper hinge cracked; eps sl browned; pp awkwardly opened, o/w VG in red/white bds (sl soiled; spine tail frayed). *Edwards*. $54/£35

CAMPBELL, BRUCE and JAMES FERGUSON-LEES. A Field Guide to Birds' Nests. London: Constable, 1972. Fine in dj. *Petersfield*. $54/£35

CAMPBELL, ELIZABETH W. CROZER. The Desert Was Home. L.A.: Westernlore, 1961. 1st ed. Signed. Fine in Fine dj. *Book Market*. $60/£39

CAMPBELL, HARRY. Flushing and Morbid Blushing. London, 1890. 1st ed. 270pp. Good. *Fye*. $150/£97

CAMPBELL, HELEN. Darkness and Daylight. Hartford, 1892. 740pp. Full calf, leather spine labels. Lt spine wear, o/w VG. *Artis*. $25/£16

CAMPBELL, HEYWORTH (ed). The Body Beautiful. Vol 2. NY: Dodge Publishing, 1936. 2nd ed. 88 full-pg b/w nudes. Spiral bound. VG (lt rubbed, lt creasing). *Cahan*. $75/£48

CAMPBELL, HEYWORTH (ed). The Body Beautiful. Vol 3. NY: Dodge Publishing, 1937. 2nd ed. 89 full-pg b/w nudes. Spiral bound. VG (lt rubbed). *Cahan*. $75/£48

CAMPBELL, IAIN. Ian Fleming: A Catalogue of a Collection.... Liverpool: Campbell, 1978. 1st ed, pb orig. Signed. Fine in Fine wrappers, as issued. *Janus*. $65/£42

CAMPBELL, J.A. and W.W. LAMAR. The Venomous Reptiles of Latin America. Ithaca, 1989. 504 color photos, 115 maps (6 color). Dj (lt chipped, rubbed). *Sutton*. $55/£35

CAMPBELL, J.L. Geology and Mineral Resources of the James River Valley.... NY: Putnam's, 1882. 1st ed. (ii),119pp, 1 plt. Ex-lib w/mks, bkpls; both hinges internally cracked; sl rubbed else VG. *Bookpress*. $110/£71

CAMPBELL, JAMES HAVELOCK. McClellan: A Vindication of the Military Career of General George B. McClellan. NY: Neale Publishing, 1916. 1st ed. Sm nick base of spine, else NF. *Mcgowan*. $175/£113

CAMPBELL, JOHN A. Recollections of the Evacuation of Richmond. Balt: John Murphy, 1880. 1st ed. 27pp. Orig ptd blue wraps. VG (spine chipped, creases, name). *Chapel Hill*. $150/£97

CAMPBELL, JOHN LORD. Lives of the Admirals and Other Eminent British Seamen.... London: For J. & H. Pemberton & T. Waller, 1742-44. 1st ed. 4 vols. Cambridge calf (worn; several cvrs detached). *Argosy*. $100/£65

CAMPBELL, JOHN LORD. The Lives of the Chief Justices of England. London: John Murray, 1849-57. 1st eds. 3 vols. Contemp 3/4 calf (joints cracking). *Boswell*. $350/£226

CAMPBELL, JOHN LORD. The Lives of the Chief Justices of England. London, 1849. 2 vols. xix,588; xii,584,16pp pub's list (few leaves foxed). Blind emb cl (spines faded, chipped). *Edwards*. $54/£35

CAMPBELL, JOHN LORD. The Lives of the Lord Chancellors and Keepers of the Great Seal of England.... London: John Murray, 1845-47. 1st ed. 7 vols. Contemp calf (joints cracked, spines worn). Usable only. *Boswell*. $350/£226

CAMPBELL, JOHN W. The Black Star Passes. Fantasy, 1953. 1st ed, 2nd state binding. Fine in dj (lt wear, tear). *Aronovitz*. $35/£23

CAMPBELL, JOHN W. The Black Star Passes. Fantasy, 1953. 1st ed. Fine in dj. *Madle*. $90/£58

CAMPBELL, JOHN W. The Incredible Planet. Fantasy, 1949. 1st ed. One of 250 numbered, signed. Fine in dj (sl chipped). *Madle*. $225/£145

CAMPBELL, JOHN W. The Mightiest Machine. Hadley, 1947. 1st ed. Fine in dj (spine chipped). *Madle*. $100/£65

CAMPBELL, JOSEPH and M.J. ABADIE. The Mythic Image. Princeton Univ Press, 1974. VG in dj. *Argosy*. $75/£48

CAMPBELL, LANG. The Dinky Ducklings. (Sunny Book Series). Joliet: P.F. Volland, 1928. 1st ed. 12mo, 39pp. Cl-backed pict bds. VG (edges lt bumped). *Davidson*. $75/£48

CAMPBELL, MALCOLM. Pietro Cortona at the Pitti Palace. Princeton Univ, 1977. Fine in Mint dj. *Europa*. $65/£42

CAMPBELL, MARIA HULL. Revolutionary Services and Civil Life of General William Hull. NY, 1848. xx,(17)-482pp, 4 battle plans. Orig cl (spine chipped; foxed; bkpl; fep removed). *Bohling*. $150/£97

CAMPBELL, MARJORIE W. The Northwest Company. NY: St. Martin's, 1957. 1st ed. Fine in VG dj. *Perier*. $47/£30

CAMPBELL, RAMSEY (ed). New Tales of the Cthulhu Mythos. (Sauk City): Arkham House, 1980. 1st ed. Fine in Fine dj. *Other Worlds*. $100/£65

CAMPBELL, RAMSEY. Demons by Daylight. Arkham House, 1973. 1st ed. Fine in dj. *Aronovitz*. $25/£16

CAMPBELL, RAMSEY. Demons by Daylight. Arkham House, 1973. 1st ed. Fine in dj. *Madle*. $60/£39

CAMPBELL, RAMSEY. The Doll Who Ate His Mother. Bobbs-Merrill, 1976. 1st ed. Fine in dj. *Madle.* $125/£81

CAMPBELL, RAMSEY. The Face That Must Die. Santa Cruz: Scream Press, 1983. 1st US, hb ed, 1st ptg. Fine in Fine dj. *Other Worlds.* $100/£65

CAMPBELL, RAMSEY. The Influence. NY: Macmillan, 1988. 1st Amer ed, rev copy w/pub's slip laid in. VF in dj. *Silver Door.* $30/£19

CAMPBELL, RAMSEY. The Inhabitant of the Lake. Arkham House, 1964. 1st ed. Fine in dj. *Madle.* $150/£97

CAMPBELL, ROBERT and VERNON ALLISON. Barriers. An Encyclopedia of United States Barbed Fence Patents. Denver: Western Profiles, 1986. 1st ed. NF in NF dj. *Parker.* $45/£29

CAMPBELL, ROY. Adamastor, Poems. London: Faber & Faber, (1930). 1st ed. (Eps sl foxed; sl dusty.) NF 1st issue dj. *Hermitage.* $65/£42

CAMPBELL, ROY. Choosing a Mast. London: Faber, 1931. #278/300 signed. Lg paper ed. Fine (spine, corners sl rubbed). *Polyanthos.* $60/£39

CAMPBELL, ROY. The Flaming Terrapin. NY: Dial, (1924). 1st Amer ed. Eps sl foxed, else VG in dj (sl chipped). *Hermitage.* $50/£32

CAMPBELL, ROY. The Flaming Terrapin. NY: Dial, 1924. 1st Amer ed, 1st bk. Cl-backed batik bds. VG. *Pharos.* $60/£39

CAMPBELL, ROY. Flowering Reeds. (London): Boriswood, 1933. 1st ed. Backstrip detached, glued, else internally Nice. *Pharos.* $15/£10

CAMPBELL, ROY. The Georgiad. London: Boriswood, 1931. 1st ed. Fine (sl rubbed) in dj (sl sunned, chipped). *Polyanthos.* $50/£32

CAMPBELL, ROY. Nativity. Faber, 1953. 1st UK ed. Ariel Poem. Fine in wraps in envelope, as issued. *Sclanders.* $19/£12

CAMPBELL, ROY. Poems. Paris: Hours Press, 1930. 1st ed. One of 200 numbered, ptd by hand, signed. 1/4 orange calf, pict paper over bds. Edges sl rubbed, o/w VF in glassine dj (chipped). *Reese.* $350/£226

CAMPBELL, ROY. Talking Bronco. London: Faber & Faber, (1946). 1st ed. Fine in NF dj (price-clipped). *Hermitage.* $40/£26

CAMPBELL, ROY. Talking Bronco. London: Faber & Faber, 1946. 1st ed. VG in dj (sl frayed; repaired). *Cox.* $23/£15

CAMPBELL, RUTH. The Cat Whose Whiskers Slipped. Boston/Joliet/NY: P.F. Volland, (1925). 10th ed. 8vo, 50 leaves. Pict eps. Pict blue cl (edges rubbed, bumped). Internally Fine. *Blue Mountain.* $45/£29

CAMPBELL, THOMAS (ed). Frederick the Great and His Times. London, 1842-1843. 1st ed. 4 vols. Frontis port (browned). Blue emb cl (recased, new eps). VG (foxing). *Edwards.* $233/£150

CAMPBELL, THOMAS. Gertrude of Wyoming. London, 1809. 1st ed. Contemp calf (worn; pieces missing spine; joints cracked; hinges reinforced). Internally VG (bkpl). *Poetry.* $31/£20

CAMPBELL, THOMAS. Gertrude of Wyoming. London: Routledge, 1857. 1st ed w/these illus. viii,94,(2)pp, 35 lg wood-engrs by Brothers Dalziel. Red cl, beveled bds, blocked in blind/gold (sl worn). Fep renewed, o/w Good. *Cox.* $31/£20

CAMPBELL, THOMAS. The Movable School Goes to the Negro Farmer. Tuskegee Institute, (1936). 1st ed. Orig cl. Minor cvr speckling, else VG. *Mcgowan.* $165/£106

CAMPBELL, WILFRED. Canada. London: A&C Black, 1907. 1st ed. 77 color plts. (Spine sl faded; spotting; piece torn from 1st tissue.) *Hollett.* $62/£40

CAMPBELL, WILLIAM and L. KERR. The Surgical Diseases of Children. NY, 1912. 1st ed. Rear inner hinge cracked, o/w VF. *Fye.* $100/£65

CAMPS, F.E. Medical and Scientific Investigations in the Christie Case. London, 1953. Signed. 47 diags; 6 color plts. VG. *Whitehart.* $39/£25

CAMUS, ALBERT. The Plague. NY, 1948. 1st Amer ed. Ex-lib blindstamp, else VG in dj (rubbed, frayed). *King.* $50/£32

CAMUS, ALBERT. Resistance, Rebellion, and Death. Justin O'Brien (trans). NY: Knopf, 1961. 1st Amer ed. Fine in dj (sl edgewear). *Reese.* $45/£29

CAMUS, ALBERT. The Stranger. Stuart Gilbert (trans). LEC, 1971. #809/1500 signed by Daniel Maffia (illus). 10 color plts. Crimson leatherette. Fine in slipcase. *Cox.* $70/£45

CAMUS, CHARLES-ETIENNE. A Treatise on the Teeth of Wheels, Pinions, etc...for Millwork, Clock-Work, etc. London: Taylor, 1803. 8vo. xv,1f,144pp, 15 fldg engr plts, 4ff ads (lacks leaf of ads). Bds, uncut (dusty, spine, joints well worn). *Marlborough.* $853/£550

CANADA, J.W. Life at Eighty. La Porte, TX: J.W. Canada, 1952. Signed. VG. *Burcham.* $45/£29

CANBY, HENRY S. Thoreau. Boston: Houghton, Mifflin, 1939. 1st ed. Ltd to 265 numbered, signed. Cream cl, gilt. Fine in Fine box. *Macdonnell.* $150/£97

CANBY, HENRY S. Turn West, Turn East. Boston: Houghton, Mifflin, 1951. 1st Amer ed. VG in VG dj. *Agvent.* $35/£23

CANDEE, HELEN CHURCHILL. The Tapestry Book. NY, 1935. New ed. 4 color plts. Fore-edge uncut. Dj (sl chipped). *Edwards.* $39/£25

CANDLER, E. The Dinosaur's Egg. Blackwood, 1925. 1st ed. VG-. *Aronovitz.* $40/£26

CANDLER, EDMUND. Long Road to Baghdad. London: Cassell, 1919. 1st ed. 2 vols. Frontis photo ports, 2 fldg maps, 17 plans, 14 plts. Slate cl stamped in dk blue (sl rubbed, bumped). *Schoyer.* $175/£113

CANDLER, EDMUND. The Unveiling of Lhasa. London: Edward Arnold, 1905. 4th imp. Color frontis, fldg map. Pict cl (sl stained, damped; upper joint cracking, eps sl soiled). *Hollett.* $132/£85

CANETTI, ELIAS. Crowds and Power. NY: Viking, 1962. 1st US ed. NF in VG dj (spine-faded; sm chips). *Lame Duck.* $45/£29

CANFIELD, THOMAS HAWLEY. Life of Thomas Hawley Canfield.... Burlington, VT, 1889. Presentation copy. Engr frontis port, 48pp. Dk grn cl. VG+. Howes C 113. *Bohling.* $450/£290

CANNING, VICTOR. His Bones Are Coral. London, (1955). 1st ed. VG in dj (name, price-clipped, rubbed). *King.* $22/£14

CANNON, BETTIE WADDELL. All About Franklin, from Pioneers to Preservation. Franklin: Franklin Hist Soc, 1979. VG. *Peninsula.* $30/£19

CANNON, CURT. (Pseud of Ed McBain). I'm Cannon—For Hire. Gold Medal #814, Oct 1958. 1st ed. Pb orig. Lt worn, else Fine. *Murder.* $20/£13

Cantabrigia Depicta. A Concise and Accurate Description of the University and Town of Cambridge.... Cambridge: Bentham, 1763. Half-title, title, 117pp, 1f, fldg engr plan (margin defective), 7 plts. New wrappers. *Marlborough*. $388/£250

CANTON, WILLIAM. The Invisible Playmate. London: Isbister, 1894. 1st ed. Lt brn cl. NF (spine sl worn). *Sumner & Stillman*. $75/£48

CANTWELL, ROBERT. Laugh and Lie Down. NY: Farrar, 1931. 1st ed. Fine (spine sl faded) in 2nd state dj. *Beasley*. $150/£97

CANUCK, JANEY. Seeds of Pine. Toronto: H&S, (1914). 1st ed. Gilt-stamped cl. Fine. *Artis*. $35/£23

CAPA, ROBERT. Death in the Making. NY: Covici, Friede, 1938. 1st ed. 1st bk. Name; eps dknd along hinge; sl soiled; spine dknd, else VG. *Cahan*. $100/£65

CAPA, ROBERT. Images of War. NY: Paragraphic Books, (1964). Ptd stiff wrappers. Fine. *Cahan*. $45/£29

CAPA, ROBERT. Slightly Out of Focus. Henry Holt, 1947. 1st ed. VG in VG dj. *Bishop*. $37/£24

CAPEK, ABE. Chinese Stone-Pictures: A Distinctive Form of Chinese Art. London, (1962). 72 plts. VG in dj. *Argosy*. $50/£32

CAPEK, KAREL. Intimate Things. Dora Round (trans). London: George Allen & Unwin, 1935. 1st ed. Lt dusting, o/w Fine. *Temple*. $19/£12

CAPEK, THOMAS. The Cechs (Bohemians) in America.... Boston: Houghton, 1920. 1st ed. Inscribed presentation. *Ginsberg*. $75/£48

CAPONIGRO, PAUL. Megaliths. Boston: NYGS/Little Brown, 1986. 1st ed. Fine in Fine dj. *Parker*. $75/£48

CAPOTE, TRUMAN. Answered Prayers, the Unfinished Novel. NY, (1987). 1st ed. VG in dj. *King*. $25/£16

CAPOTE, TRUMAN. Breakfast at Tiffany's. Random House, 1958. 1st ed. NF in NF dj. *Fine Books*. $110/£71

CAPOTE, TRUMAN. Breakfast at Tiffany's. NY: Random House, 1958. 1st ed. NF in NF dj (price-clipped; short closed tear). *Pettler*. $150/£97

CAPOTE, TRUMAN. Breakfast at Tiffany's. London: Hamish Hamilton, 1958. 1st Eng ed. Fine in dj. *Limestone*. $80/£52

CAPOTE, TRUMAN. Breakfast at Tiffany's. Hamilton, 1958. 1st UK ed. VG in dj. *Lewton*. $59/£38

CAPOTE, TRUMAN. A Christmas Memory. NY, 1966. 1st ed. As New in slipcase. *Bond*. $45/£29

CAPOTE, TRUMAN. A Christmas Memory. Random House, 1966. 1st ed. One of 600. Signed. Fine in slipcase. *Fine Books*. $350/£226

CAPOTE, TRUMAN. The Dogs Bark: Public People and Private Places. NY: Random House, (1973). 1st ed. Fore-edge lt soiled, else Fine in dj. *Between The Covers*. $75/£48

CAPOTE, TRUMAN. The Grass Harp. NY: Random House, (1952). 1st ed. Tan cl, paper cvr label. Fine in NF dj (sm tear top fore-edge). Very Nice. *Chapel Hill*. $300/£194

CAPOTE, TRUMAN. In Cold Blood. NY: Random House, (1965). 1st trade ed. Fine in VG dj (sl edgewear). *Reese*. $40/£26

CAPOTE, TRUMAN. In Cold Blood. Random House, 1965. 1st ed. NF in VG dj (lt wear). *Fine Books*. $23/£15

CAPOTE, TRUMAN. Local Color. NY: Random House, (1950). 1st ed. Inscrip fep; bottom edge sl rubbed; o/w Fine in dj (lt soiled; spine sunned). *Jaffe*. $125/£81

CAPOTE, TRUMAN. Local Color. NY, 1950. 1st Amer ed. NF (corners sl rubbed, bkpl). *Polyanthos*. $35/£23

CAPOTE, TRUMAN. The Muses Are Heard. London: Heinemann, (1957). 1st British ed. Dj (lacks pieces; top edge creased, chipped). *Bickersteth*. $70/£45

CAPOTE, TRUMAN. Music for Chameleons. NY: Random House, (1980). 1st ed. One of 350 specially bound, signed. Brn cl. Mint in pub's slipcase, orig shrinkwrap. *Chapel Hill*. $325/£210

CAPOTE, TRUMAN. Observations. (NY: S&S, 1959). 1st ed. White paper-cvrd bds, silver-stamped. Sl bumped, else Fine in glassine dj (short tear, else Fine), pub's slipcase box (bumped, short tears, else VG). *Godot*. $250/£161

CAPOTE, TRUMAN. One Christmas. London, (1983). 1st Eng ed. VG in dj. *Argosy*. $40/£26

CAPOTE, TRUMAN. One Christmas. London: Hamish Hamilton, 1983. 1st Eng ed. Fine in dj. *Limestone*. $55/£35

CAPOTE, TRUMAN. Other Voices, Other Rooms. NY, (1948). 1st ed. VG + (lt bumped) in VG + dj (sm chips, spine sl dknd). *Fuller & Saunders*. $175/£113

CAPOTE, TRUMAN. Other Voices, Other Rooms. London, (1948). 1st Eng ed, 1st bk. Good. *Waterfield*. $47/£30

CAPP, AL. The Life and Times of the Shmoo. Pocket Books, 1949. 1st pb ed. VG in wraps. *Fine Books*. $12/£8

CAPPER, W.M. and D. JOHNSON. Arthur Rendle Short. London, 1954. Frontis; 2 dbl-sided plts. Lib binding, label, stamps, o/w Good. *Whitehart*. $16/£10

CAPUTO, PHILIP. Means of Escape. NY: Harper Collins, 1991. 1st ed. Fine in Fine dj. *Revere*. $25/£16

CAPUTO, PHILIP. A Rumor of War. NY: Holt, Rinehart & Winston, (1977). 1st ed, 1st bk. NF in dj (tear; edge wrinkle; 2 pinholes fep). *Aka*. $30/£19

CARD, F.W. Bush-Fruits. L.H. Bailey (ed). NY, (1898). xii,537pp (1pg underlined; cl scuffed.) *Sutton*. $45/£29

CARDAN, JEROME. The Book of My Life. NY, 1930. 1st ed. Good. *Fye*. $40/£26

CARDOZO, BENJAMIN N. The Paradoxes of Legal Science. NY: Columbia Univ, 1928. 1st ed. Burgundy cl. VG. *Glenn*. $125/£81

CARDUS, NEVILLE and JOHN ARLOTT. The Noblest Game. London, 1949. Frontis, 48 color, 16 b/w plts. Dj (chipped). *Edwards*. $39/£25

CARDWELL, EDWARD. Lectures on the Coinage of the Greek and Romans. Oxford: John Murray, 1832. 1st ed. xvi,328pp + (30)pp ads; uncut. Blue cl, paper spine label. Good. *Karmiole*. $75/£48

CAREW, THOMAS. The Works of Thomas Carew. T. Maitland (ed). Edinburgh: W.&C. Tait, 1824. 1st collected ed. xv,214pp,v. Old bds (corners sl worn); rebacked in buckram gilt. *Hollett*. $132/£85

CAREY, CHARLES H. History of Oregon. Chicago: Pioneer Hist, 1922. 1st ed. 3 vols. Fldg map; marbled eps, edges. VG. *Oregon*. $175/£113

CAREY, CHARLES H. History of Oregon. Chicago: Pioneer Hist Pub., 1922. Pub's ed. 3 vols. VG. *Perier*. $150/£97

CAREY, DAVID. Life in Paris; Comprising the Rambles, Sprees and Amours of Dick Wildfire.... London: Fairburn, 1822. 1st ed. 8vo. xxiv,489pp, frontis, 20 aquatint plts by Cruikshank. Blue morocco gilt by Tout, aeg (edges rubbed). *Marlborough.* $1,163/£750

CAREY, GEO. G. Astronomy, as It Is Known at the Present Day. London: I. Chidley, 1836. Frontis port, 166pp + 88pp supplement. Good in 1/2 leather; marbled edges, eps (bkpl; spine separating). *Knollwood.* $90/£58

CAREY, HENRY. Songs and Poems. London: Golden Cockerel Press, 1924. #315/350. 23 wood engrs by Robert Gibbings. Uncut except for top edge. Vellum backstrip (sl faded), blue sides (sl bumped). *Petersfield.* $155/£100

CAREY, PETER. Bliss. Australia: UQP, 1981. 1st ed. Fine in dj (sl rubbed). *Rees.* $62/£40

CAREY, PETER. Bliss. Faber, 1981. 1st UK ed. Fine in dj. *Lewton.* $39/£25

CAREY, PETER. The Fat Man in History and Other Stories. NY: Random, 1980. 1st ed. Review copy; promo letter, photo laid-in. Fine in dj (sm snag). *Else Fine.* $65/£42

CAREY, PETER. The Fat Man in History. London: Faber & Faber, 1980. 1st British ed. Fine in Fine dj. *Lame Duck.* $100/£65

CAREY, PETER. The Fat Man in History. London: Faber, 1980. 1st UK ed. Signed. NF in dj. *Williams.* $65/£42

CAREY, PETER. Oscar and Lucinda. NY: Harper & Row, 1988. 1st Amer ed. Fine in Fine dj. *Revere.* $25/£16

CAREY, PETER. Oscar and Lucinda. NY: Harper, 1988. 1st Amer ed. Signed. Fine in Fine dj. *Beasley.* $60/£39

CAREY, PETER. Oscar and Lucinda. Univ of Queensland Press, 1988. 1st ed. Brief inscrip; minor bumps, else Fine in dj. *Else Fine.* $85/£55

CAREY, PETER. The Tax Inspector. NY: Knopf, 1992. 1st ed. Inscribed. Fine in Fine dj. *Beasley.* $40/£26

CAREY, PETER. War Crimes. Australia: UQP, 1979. 1st ed. Pg edges sl browned, o/w Fine in dj (sl rubbed, spine sunned). *Rees.* $70/£45

CARLETON, JAMES HENRY. The Battle of Buena Vista.... NY: Harper, 1848. 1st ed. viii,238,(2)pp + 8pp ads, 2 fldg maps. Brn cl, blind, gilt-stamped (spine extrems chipped; bkpl, lib call #). *Karmiole.* $175/£113

CARLETON, WILL. City Ballads. NY: Harper & Bros, 1886. 1st ed. 180,(iv)pp (few spots). Dec pict cl, gilt, over beveled bds. *Hollett.* $47/£30

CARLETON, WILL. Farm Ballads. NY: Harper & Bros, 1882. 159pp (corner 1/2 title repaired.) Dec pict cl, gilt, over bevelled bds (extrems lt rubbed). *Hollett.* $39/£25

CARLETON, WILLIAM. Valentine M'Clutchy, the Irish Agent. Dublin: James Duffy, 1854. 468pp. 20 illus by Phiz (Hablot Knight Browne). 3/4 red morocco (bkpl). *Schoyer.* $100/£65

CARLING, JOHN R. The Viking's Skull. Little-Brown, 1904. 1st ed. VG-. *Madle.* $35/£23

CARLING, JOHN R. The Viking's Skull. Little Brown, 1904. 1st ed. VG + . *Aronovitz.* $65/£42

CARLISLE, BILL. Bill Carlisle, Lone Bandit. Pasadena, 1946. 1st ed. Dj chipped, worn, discolored, o/w Fine. *Pratt.* $37/£24

CARLISLE, D.T. The Belvidere Hounds. NY: Derrydale, 1935. 1st Amer ed. Pict cvrs. Fine. *Polyanthos.* $95/£61

CARLQUIST, SHERWIN. Hawaii. A Natural History. NY: Natural History Press, 1970. 1st ed. Fine in Fine dj. *Book Market.* $150/£97

CARLYLE, THOMAS. The Complete Works. Boston: Colonial Press, n.d. Beacon Ed. 22 vols. Teg. Fine set. *Polyanthos.* $250/£161

CARLYLE, THOMAS. Past and Present. London: Chapman & Hall, 1843. 1st ed. Ltd to 2000. Stamped in gilt, blind. Fr inner hinge cracking, rear inner hinge mended; lt foxing, soiling; sm nick spine, else Good. *Reese.* $65/£42

CARLYLE, THOMAS. Sartor Resartus. London: George Bell, 1898. 1st ed thus. Edmund J. Sullivan (illus). xxiv,352pp; aeg. Offsetting tp, else Fine. *Godot.* $125/£81

CARLYLE, THOMAS. Sartor Resartus. London: LEC, 1931. 1/1500 numbered, signed by Oliver Simon (ptr). Teg. VG (bkpl) in bd slipcase. *Argosy.* $85/£55

CARMICHAEL, HOAGY. The Stardust Road. NY: Rinehart, 1946. 1st ed. VG. *Bishop.* $10/£6

CARMICHAEL, RICHARD. An Essay on Venereal Diseases. London, 1825. 2nd ed. xvi,376pp, 5 color fldg plts. Uncut. (Ex-lib w/bkpl, ink stamps; hinges repaired, rebacked.) *Edwards.* $155/£100

CARNAP, RUDOLF. Meaning and Necessity. Chicago: Univ of Chicago, 1947. 1st ed. VG + in dj (tape reinforced). *Lame Duck.* $150/£97

CARNELL, JOHN (ed). No Place Like Earth. London, 1952. 1st ed. Signed. Fine in dj (chipped). *Madle.* $25/£16

CARNES, J.A. Journal of a Voyage from Boston to the West Coast of Africa. Boston, 1852. 479pp (browning, soiling). Contemp cl bds (orig title laid down). *Edwards.* $78/£50

CAROLINO, PEDRO. The New Guide of the Conversation in Portuguese and English. Boston: James R. Osgood & Co., 1883. 1st Amer ed. 182pp. Tan cl. Intro by Mark Twain. VG (stamp, cl sl soiled). BAL 3412. *Chapel Hill.* $350/£226

CARPENTER, EDWARD. The Drama of Love and Death. NY: Mitchell Kennerley, 1912. 1st ed. Fine in dj (lt chipped; sm hole). *Beasley.* $65/£42

CARPENTER, EDWARD. England's Ideal. London: Swan, Sonnenschein, Lowry, 1887. 1st ed. Top edge dusted; lt soiling; sl extrem wear, else VG. *Lame Duck.* $95/£61

CARPENTER, EDWARD. Love's Coming of Age. Manchester: Labor Press, 1896. 1st ed. Fr inner hinge starting; inscrip, else VG + . *Lame Duck.* $200/£129

CARPENTER, JOHN and RUE. Improving Songs for Anxious Children. NY/London, G. Schirmer, (1913). Obl folio, 50pp. Yellow cl-backed dec bds (rubbed, soiled; spine head, tail worn); ptd pink paper label fr cvr. NF internally. *Blue Mountain.* $95/£61

CARPENTER, RHYS. Greek Sculpture. Univ of Chicago Press, 1960. 1st ed. 47 plts. Dj. *Edwards.* $39/£25

CARPENTER, W.B. The Microscope and Its Revelations. London, 1891. 7th ed by W.H. Dallinger. xviii,1099pp; 21 plts (7 color). New cl. (S.H. Meakin's copy w/annotations; 2 sm notes preserved at end.) *Wheldon & Wesley.* $101/£65

CARPENTER, WILL TOM. Lucky 7. A Cowman's Autobiography. Austin: Univ of TX, 1957. 1st ed. *Parker.* $25/£16

CARPENTER, WILLIAM. On the Use and Abuse of Alcoholic Liquors, in Health and Disease. Boston, 1851. 264pp. Good. *Fye.* $100/£65

CARPENTER, WILLIAM. On the Use and Abuse of Alcoholic Liquors, in Health and Disease. Phila, 1866. 178pp. Good. *Fye.* $75/£48

CARPENTIER, ALEJO. The Lost Steps. London: Gollancz, 1956. 1st ed. Wraparound band. VG in dj (price-clipped). *Rees.* $19/£12

CARR, CALEB. Casing the Promised Land. NY: Harper, (1980). 1st ed, 1st bk. Fine in dj (lt rubbed; price-clipped). *Reese.* $30/£19

CARR, CAMILLUS. A Cavalryman in Indian Country. Ashland, OR: Lewis Osborne, 1974. #441/600. Port. Linen-backed bds. Prospectus, letter laid in. Fine in plain dj (lt soiled). *Bohling.* $60/£39

CARR, CAMILLUS. A Cavalryman in Indian Country. Ashland: Lewis Osborne, 1974. #58/600. Fine. *Perier.* $45/£29

CARR, CAMILLUS. A Cavalryman in Indian Country. Ashland: Lewis Osborne, 1974. Ltd to 600. Buckram, bds. Fine. *Oregon.* $50/£32

CARR, EDWARD HALLETT. Karl Marx. A Study in Fanaticism. London: Dent, 1934. 1st ed. Foxing, o/w Fine. *Beasley.* $50/£32

CARR, EMILY. Growing Pains. Toronto, 1946. 1st ed. Gilt cl. VG. *Baade.* $50/£32

CARR, EMILY. Hundreds and Thousands the Journals of Emily Carr. Toronto: Clarke, Irwin, 1966. 1st ed. NF (inscrip) in dj (sl foxed). *Hermitage.* $40/£26

CARR, HERBERT R.C. and GEORGE A. LISTER. The Mountains of Snowdonia in History, the Sciences, Literature and Sport. London: Crosby Lockwood, 1948. 2nd ed. 27 plts (incl color frontis); 6 maps. VG in dj. *Hollett.* $47/£30

CARR, J.L. The Harpole Report. Secker & Warburg, 1972. 1st ed. Inscribed. NF in dj (sl nicked). *Rees.* $116/£75

CARR, J.L. What Hetty Did. London: Quince Tree Press, 1988. One of 2850. Signed. Fine in wrappers. *Rees.* $31/£20

CARR, JOHN DICKSON. Below Suspicion. London: Hamilton, 1950. 1st UK ed. Fine in VG dj (closed tears; chip). *Williams.* $39/£25

CARR, JOHN DICKSON. The Blind Barber. NY: Harper, 1934. 1st ed. Stamp on fep, o/w Fine in Fine dj (tiny closed tears; sl rubbing). *Mordida.* $650/£419

CARR, JOHN DICKSON. The Demoniacs. NY: Harper & Row, (1962). 1st ed. Fine in dj (lt edgeworn). *Sadlon.* $40/£26

CARR, JOHN DICKSON. Fire Burn! London: Hamish Hamilton, 1957. 1st Eng ed. Pgs sl browned, else VG in dj (sl worn). *Limestone.* $75/£48

CARR, JOHN DICKSON. The Four False Weapons. NY: Harper, 1937. 1st ed. Fine in dj (spine faded; tiny nicks). *Mordida.* $350/£226

CARR, JOHN DICKSON. The Hungry Goblin. NY: Harper & Row, (1972). 1st ed. Fine in dj (lt worn). *Hermitage.* $40/£26

CARR, JOHN DICKSON. In Spite of Thunder. London: Hamish Hamilton, 1960. 1st Eng ed. Fine in dj. *Mordida.* $50/£32

CARR, JOHN DICKSON. The Life of Sir Arthur Conan Doyle. NY: Harper, (1949). 1st ed. Fine in dj (lt rubbed). *Sadlon.* $35/£23

CARR, JOHN DICKSON. Most Secret. NY: Harper & Row, (1964). 1st ed. NF in dj (lt edgeworn). *Sadlon.* $30/£19

CARR, JOHN DICKSON. The Murder of Sir Edmund Godfrey. NY: Harper, 1936. 1st ed. Fine in VG dj (faded spine; chipping; closed tears). *Mordida.* $300/£194

CARR, JOHN DICKSON. Panic in Box C. Harper, 1966. 1st ed. Fine in dj. *Murder.* $50/£32

CARR, JOHN DICKSON. Scandal at High Chimneys. London: Hamish Hamilton, 1959. 1st ed. Fine in Fine dj. *Ming.* $39/£25

CARR, JOHN DICKSON. The Third Bullet and Other Stories. NY: Harper, 1954. 1st ed. Fine (sl bump) in NF dj. *Janus.* $85/£55

CARR, JOHN. Pioneer Days in California. Eureka, CA: Times Pub Co, 1891. Frontis port, (4)11-452pp. Dk grn cl (wear; extrems frayed), gilt spine title. Howes C 167. *Bohling.* $250/£161

CARR, JOHN. A Vulcan Among the Argonauts.... SF: Geo. Fields, 1936. One of 500 ptd. Fine. *Oregon.* $65/£42

CARREL, ALEXIS and G. DEHILLY. The Treatment of Infected Wounds. NY: Hoeber, 1917. Fair (ex-lib; chipped, repaired; leaf loose). *Goodrich.* $25/£16

CARRICK, ALICE VAN LEER. Shades of Our Ancestors. Boston, 1928. 1st ed. Color frontis. Pict cl (sunned, soiled). *Argosy.* $85/£55

CARRIER, CONSTANCE. The Middle Voice. Denver: Swallow, 1955. 1st ed, 1st bk. Signed. VF in dj (chipped). *Pharos.* $75/£48

CARRIGHAR, SALLY. Moonlight at Midday. NY: Knopf, 1958. 1st ed. VG in dj (lt worn). *Parmer.* $25/£16

CARRINGTON, FITZROY (ed). Prints and Their Makers. London, 1913. (Eps sl spotted, feps browned.) Teg, rest uncut. Gilt-edged cl (spine head sl bumped). *Edwards.* $78/£50

CARRINGTON, FRANCES C. My Army Life and the Fort Phil. Kearney Massacre. Phila: Lippincott, 1910. 1st ed. Bright orig cl. VG. Howes C 172. *Schoyer.* $85/£55

CARRINGTON, MARGARET I. Absaraka, Home of the Crows. Chicago, (1950). Lakeside Classic. VG. *Schoyer.* $30/£19

CARROLL, GEORGE R. Pioneer Life in and around Cedar Rapids, Iowa, from 1839 to 1849. Cedar Rapids, IA: Times Ptg & Binding House, 1895. 1st ed. 251pp (few pp creased). Dk grn cl (bumped, rubbed); dec bands; gilt spine. VG. Howes C 180. *Blue Mountain.* $35/£23

CARROLL, JAMES A. The First Ten Years in Alaska. NY: Exposition, (1957). 1st ed. VG in VG- dj. *Blue Dragon.* $27/£17

CARROLL, JOHN M. The Black Military Experience in the American West. NY: Liveright, (1971). 1st trade ed. Pict eps. Brn cl in pict dj. *Petrilla.* $150/£97

CARROLL, JOHN M. (ed). Custer in Texas. NY: Sol Lewis & Liveright, 1975. VG in dj. *Lien.* $40/£26

CARROLL, JOHN M. and BYRON PRICE (comps). Roll Call on the Little Big Horn, 26 June 1876. Ft. Collins: Old Army Press, (1974). 1st ed. Mint. *Graf.* $40/£26

CARROLL, LEWIS. (Pseud of C.L. Dodgson.) Alice in Wonderland. London: Raphael Tuck, (1910). 1st ed thus. 4to. 148pp, 12 full-pg color plts by Mabel Lucie Attwell. Aeg. Grn cl, gold stamping (worn; rear hinge cracked). *Reisler.* $300/£194

CARROLL, LEWIS. (Pseud of C.L. Dodgson.) Alice in Wonderland. NY: Grosset and Dunlap, (1945). 3pp of movables by Julian Wehr. Spiral bound. Corners bumped, o/w VG. *Davidson.* $125/£81

CARROLL, LEWIS. (Pseud of C.L. Dodgson.) Alice Through the Looking Glass and Hunting of the Snark. SF: Pennyroyal Press, 1983. 1st ed. Barry Moser (illus). 9x14. 200pp. Cl. Fine in dj. *Cattermole.* $40/£26

CARROLL, LEWIS. (Pseud of C.L. Dodgson.) Alice's Adventures in Wonderland and Through the Looking Glass and What Alice Found there. NY: Random House, (1946). 2 vols. Cl-backed pict bds (spine sl lightened). Orig pub's slipcase (chip, label abrasions). *Sadlon.* $20/£13

CARROLL, LEWIS. (Pseud of C.L. Dodgson.) Alice's Adventures in Wonderland and Through the Looking Glass. NY: Platt & Peck, (1900). 16 full-pg color illus by Blanche McManus. Beige cl, illus cvr. Nice. *Reisler.* $175/£113

CARROLL, LEWIS. (Pseud of C.L. Dodgson.) Alice's Adventures in Wonderland and Through the Looking-Glass. Stockholm: Continental Book Co. AB, (1946). 1st ed thus. 12mo. 66 dwgs by Mervyn Peake. Illus cvr. Good in paper wraps (spine worn, chipped). *Reisler.* $550/£355

CARROLL, LEWIS. (Pseud of Charles L. Dodgson.) Alice's Adventures in Wonderland with Through the Looking Glass. London: Macmillan, 1866 & 1872. 1st authorized ed & 1st ed. 2 vols. 1st issue, w/inverted 'S' last line of contents leaf. Aeg. Full grn morocco (orig cl cvrs, spine bound in rear each vol), ribbed gilt-dec spines (uniformly faded), gilt-dec red morocco floral onlays. *D & D.* $5,000/£3,226

CARROLL, LEWIS. (Pseud of Charles L. Dodgson.) Alice's Adventures in Wonderland with Through the Looking Glass. Boston: Lee & Shepard, 1869 & 1872. 1st Amer ptd eds. 2 vols. Vol 1: pub's grn pebble-grained cl (inner hinges cracked, spine ends worn w/loss), triple gilt-ruled cvrs, gilt-stamped centerpieces. Aeg. Internally Fine (fep chipped). Vol 2: Pub's blue pebble-grained cl (spine ends worn w/loss; rear inner hinge starting), triple gilt-ruled fr cvr, triple blind-ruled back cvr, gilt-stamped centerpieces. Internally Fine. *D & D.* $1,700/£1,097

CARROLL, LEWIS. (Pseud of C.L. Dodgson.) Alice's Adventures in Wonderland. London: William Heinemann, (1907). 1st Arthur Rackham-illus ed. #998/1130. Color frontis, 12 tipped-in illus. Gilt-dec white cl, teg. Bright, NF. *Chapel Hill.* $1,500/£968

CARROLL, LEWIS. (Pseud of C.L. Dodgson.) Alice's Adventures in Wonderland. London, (1907). 1st ed. 13 mtd color plts by Arthur Rackham (illus). White cl (spine shows some handling; lt foxing). *D & D.* $2,000/£1,290

CARROLL, LEWIS. (Pseud of C.L. Dodgson.) Alice's Adventures in Wonderland. NY: D. Appleton, (1927). Facs repro of 1866 Amer ed. Aeg. John Tenniel (illus). Red cl, gold dec. Fine in glassine wrapper, red box (sl staining). *Reisler.* $175/£113

CARROLL, LEWIS. (Pseud of C.L. Dodgson.) Alice's Adventures in Wonderland. NY: McLoughlin, (ca. 1915). 1st ed thus. Colored frontis. Pict tan cl. Spine, extrems lt sunned; cat descrip removed from fep, else VG. *Chapel Hill.* $95/£61

CARROLL, LEWIS. (Pseud of Charles L. Dodgson.) Alice's Adventures in Wonderland. London: Macmillan, 1866. 1st authorized ed, 1st issue w/inverted 'S' in last line contents leaf. Aeg. Gilt-dec red pub's cl (spine neatly relined; lt worn). Respectable. *D & D.* $4,900/£3,161

CARROLL, LEWIS. (Pseud of C.L. Dodgson.) Alice's Adventures In Wonderland. NY: Appleton, 1866. 1st suppressed ed. Issue points (no priority): 'B' in 'By' on tp is above and to rt of 'T' in 'Tenniel'; hyphen between 'Rabbit-Hole' on contents pg. Orig gilt-dec red cl (spine relined; inner hinges reinforced). Aeg. *D & D.* $7,500/£4,839

CARROLL, LEWIS. (Pseud of C.L. Dodgson.) Alice's Adventures in Wonderland. Lee & Shepard, 1869. 1st Amer ptg. Corner tips, spine extrems worn; rear inner hinge starting, else Good in custom cl tray-case. *Aronovitz.* $1,000/£645

CARROLL, LEWIS. (Pseud of C.L. Dodgson.) Alice's Adventures in Wonderland. London: Ward, Lock, 1922. Margaret W. Tarrant (illus). Thick, 8vo. Tp, ads for book reference 48 colored plts but there are only 44, which is # listed in table of contents. Grn cl, color paste label, dec cvr (worn; hinges cracked). Color dj (corners, spine worn; tape reinforcement from back). *Reisler.* $175/£113

CARROLL, LEWIS. (Pseud of C.L. Dodgson.) Alice's Adventures in Wonderland. SF: Univ of CA, 1982. 1st ed. Barry Moser (illus). 9x14. 146pp. Fine in dj. *Cattermole.* $50/£32

CARROLL, LEWIS. (Pseud of C.L. Dodgson.) Alice's Adventures in Wonderland. Berkeley: Univ of CA, 1982. 1st ed. Incl portfolio w/orig illus of Mad Hatter signed by Barry Moser (illus). Red cl in pub's slipcase. Fine. *Davidson.* $225/£145

CARROLL, LEWIS. (Pseud of C.L. Dodgson.) Feeding the Mind. London: C&W, 1907. 1st ed. Red cl spine over grey pict bds. VG. *Houle.* $175/£113

CARROLL, LEWIS. (Pseud of C.L. Dodgson.) The Hunting of the Snark and Other Poems and Verses. NY: Harper, 1903. 1st ed thus. 4to. Some pp uncut. Peter Newell (illus). White bds, gold lettering, dec. Good in stiff grn dj, gold lettering; pub's box (edgewear), ptd paste label. *Reisler.* $675/£435

CARROLL, LEWIS. (Pseud of C.L. Dodgson.) The Letters of Lewis Carroll. Morton N. Cohen (ed). NY: OUP, 1979. 1st Amer ed. 2 vols. Fine in pub's slipcase (lt worn). *Hermitage.* $60/£39

CARROLL, LEWIS. (Pseud of C.L. Dodgson.) Nonsense Songs...from Alice in Wonderland. London/NY/Sydney: Chappell, 1908. 1st ed, Amer issue (w/$ price rubberstamped fr cvr). 4to, 64pp. Nameplate fr cvr, else VG in ptd wrappers. *Godot.* $150/£97

CARROLL, LEWIS. (Pseud of C.L. Dodgson.) Rhyme? and Reason? Macmillan, 1883. 1st ed. Lt cvr soil, dulling, else VG. *Aronovitz.* $250/£161

CARROLL, LEWIS. (Pseud of C.L. Dodgson.) Sylvie and Bruno Concluded. London: Macmillan, 1893. 1st Eng ed, 1st issue, w/chapter 8 in the table of contents given as at pg 110 instead of pg 113. Harry Furniss (illus). Gilt-worked red cl; aeg. NF (foxing, scattered spotting to eps). *Antic Hay.* $125/£81

CARROLL, LEWIS. (Pseud of C.L. Dodgson.) Three Sunsets and Other Poems. London, 1898. 1st ed, 2nd ptg. Aeg. Binding is not grn cl as issued but pale blue in which some copies are found. VF (sl rubbing). *D & D.* $450/£290

CARROLL, LEWIS. (Pseud of C.L. Dodgson.) Through the Looking Glass. NY: Frederick A. Stokes, (1905). 1st ed, later ptg. 12 full-pg illus by M.L. Kirk, 50 illus by John Tenniel. Illus purple-grey cl, gilt. Good. *Reisler.* $175/£113

CARROLL, LEWIS. (Pseud of C.L. Dodgson.) Through the Looking Glass. Boston: DeWolfe, Fiske, 1898. 12mo, 175pp, 4 chromolitho color plts by john Tenniel. Grey cl, pict stamping, gilt. VG (ink name, address fr fly; bds lt soiled). *Davidson.* $185/£119

CARROLL, LEWIS. (Pseud of C.L. Dodgson.) Through the Looking-Glass and What Alice Found There. London: Macmillan, 1872. 1st ed, 1st issue. Aeg. Orig gilt dec red pub's cl (spine relined; inner hinges strengthened; lt wear). Respectable. *D & D.* $750/£484

CARROLL, LEWIS. (Pseud of C.L. Dodgson.) Through the Looking-Glass and What Alice Found There. NY: LEC, 1935. #904/1500 numbered, signed by Alice Hargreaves. John Tenniel (illus). Full blue morocco. Fine in pub's slipcase. *Hermitage.* $1,000/£645

CARRUTH, HAYDEN. Adventures of Jones. Harper, 1895. 1st ed. VG-. *Madle.* $35/£23

CARS, A. DES. A Treatise on Pruning Forest and Ornamental Trees. Boston: A. Williams, 1900. 4th ed (trans from 7th Fr ed). 50 engrs. VG (sl cvr soil). *Second Life.* $50/£32

CARSE, ROBERT. Department of the South. Columbia, 1961. 1st ed. Fine in Fine dj (3 sm pieces torn). *Pratt.* $60/£39

CARSON, GERALD. One for a Man, Two for a Horse: A Pictorial History, Grave and Comic of Patent Medicine. NY, 1961. 1st ed. Good. *Fye.* $50/£32

CARSON, HARRIET. From the Loom to the Lawyer's Gown. London: S.W. Partridge, c. 1885. 5th ed. Frontis port, 96,16pp. Pict cl gilt (extrems sl worn). *Hollett.* $23/£15

CARSON, KIT. Kit Carson's Own Story of His Life as Dictated to Col. and Mrs. D.C. Peters about 1856-57.... Blanche C. Grant (ed). Taos: Santa Fe New Mexican, 1926. 1st ed, 1st ptg. Frontis, 12 plts. Orig wraps. Fine. Howes C 182. *Oregon.* $90/£58

CARSON, RACHEL. The Edge of the Sea. Boston: Houghton Mifflin, 1955. 1st ed. VG in dj (chip, short tear). *Aka.* $30/£19

CARSON, RACHEL. Silent Spring. H-M, 1962. 1st ed. Fine in VG+ dj. *Fine Books.* $85/£55

CARSON, RACHEL. Silent Spring. Boston: Houghton, Mifflin, 1962. 1st ed. NF (sl foxing fore-edge) in dj (lt edgewear; sl foxing white rear panel; couple tiny tears). *Antic Hay.* $125/£81

CARSON, RACHEL. Under the Sea-Wind. S&S, 1941. 1st ed, 1st bk. NF in VG+ dj (worn). *Fine Books.* $250/£161

CARSWELL, CATHERINE. The Savage Pilgrimage: A Narrative of D.H. Lawrence. NY: Harcourt Brace, (1932). 1st ed. VG. *Graf.* $25/£16

CARTER, ANGELA. The Bloody Chamber. Harper, 1980. 1st ed. Fine in dj. *Madle.* $75/£48

CARTER, ANGELA. Fireworks. London: Quartet Books, 1974. 1st ed. Sig, else Fine in dj. *Limestone.* $85/£55

CARTER, ANGELA. Honeybuzzard. NY: S&S, 1966. 1st US ed, 1st bk. Sm rmdr mk bottom pg edge, else NF in VG+ dj (price-clipped). *Pettler.* $50/£32

CARTER, ANGELA. The Passion of New Eve. NY: Harcourt, 1977. 1st ed. Fine (sl sunned) in Fine dj. *Beasley.* $30/£19

CARTER, ANGELA. Shadow Dance. London: Heinemann, 1966. 1st UK ed, 1st bk. Fine in VG dj (spine sl faded, corner rubbed). *Lewton.* $147/£95

CARTER, GEORGE. A Narrative of the Loss of the 'Grosvenor' East Indiaman.... London, 1791. 1st ed. Frontis, fldg plt, 174pp. Contemp 1/2 calf. Nice. *Lewis.* $248/£160

CARTER, HARVEY LEWIS. Dear Old Kit, The Historical Christopher Carson. Norman, (1968). 1st ed. VG+ in dj. *Pratt.* $55/£35

CARTER, HODDING. Doomed Road of Empire. A.B. Guthrie, Jr. (ed). NY: McGraw-Hill, 1963. 1st ed. Map. Dj. *Lambeth.* $25/£16

CARTER, HOWARD. The Tomb of Tutankhamen. NY: Dutton, 1954. 17 color plts. NF in dj. *Worldwide.* $22/£14

CARTER, JAMES C. The University of Virginia: Jefferson Its Father, and His Political Philosophy. Univ of VA, 1898. 38pp. Paper cvr. VG (soil, foxed). *Book Broker.* $45/£29

CARTER, JIMMY. A Government as Good as Its People. NY, (1977). 1st ed, signed. Good in dj (rubbed, sl tear). *King.* $100/£65

CARTER, JIMMY. Keeping Faith, Memoirs of a President. Norwalk, CT: Easton Press, (1982). Signed. Aeg. Full gilt-stamped gray leather. VG. *King.* $125/£81

CARTER, JOHN and GRAHAM POLLARD. The Firm of Charles Ottley.... London/NY: Rupert Hart-Davis/Scribner's, 1948. 1st ed. Extrems sl dknd, else NF in ptd wrappers. *Reese.* $50/£32

CARTER, JOHN and MICHAEL SADLEIR. Victorian Fiction, an Exhibition.... CUP, 1947. 1st ed. Black cl, gilt. *Macdonnell.* $65/£42

CARTER, JOHN and PERCY H. MUIR. Printing and the Mind of Man. (London/Cambridge: Cassell/Univ Ptg House, 1967). 1st ed. Fine in Fine dj. *Sadlon.* $250/£161

CARTER, JOHN and PERCY H. MUIR. Printing and the Mind of Man. London: Cassell, 1967. 1st ed. Dbl-pg engr title opening. VG in dj. *Cox.* $132/£85

CARTER, JOHN and PERCY H. MUIR. Printing and the Mind of Man. Cassell, 1967. 1st ed. Fine in dj. *Moss.* $140/£90

CARTER, JOHN et al. Printing and the Mind of Man. London: F.W. Bridges, 1963. 1st ed. Fine copy of exhibit cat (not published bk) in orig ptd wrappers. *Macdonnell.* $100/£65

CARTER, JOHN. Binding Variants in English Publishing, 1820-1900. London: Constable, 1932. 1st ed. One of 500. 16 collotype plts. Lt foxing on blue paper used for text, else Fine. *Bookpress.* $110/£71

CARTER, JOHN. A Handlist of the Writings of Stanley Morison. Cambridge: For Private Distribution, 1950. (Spine, part of cvr faded.) *Veatchs.* $50/£32

CARTER, JOHN. More Binding Variants. London: Constable, (1938). 1st ed. Dj sl worn, chipped; else Fine. *Bookpress.* $100/£65

CARTER, JOHN. Taste and Technique in Book-Collecting. NY: R.R. Bowker, 1948. 1st Amer ed. Gray cl (lt soiled) in dj (bit chipped). *Karmiole.* $45/£29

CARTER, KATHRYN TURNER. Stagecoach Inns of Texas. Waco: Texian, 1972. 1st ed. Dj. *Lambeth.* $40/£26

CARTER, LIN. Dreams from R'Lyeh. Sauk City: Arkham House, 1975. 1st ed. Fine in Fine dj. *Other Worlds.* $25/£16

CARTER, LIN. Dreams from R'lyeh. Arkham House, 1975. 1st ed. Fine in dj. *Madle.* $25/£16

CARTER, MORRIS. Isabella Stewart Gardner and Fenway Court. Boston/NY: Houghton Mifflin (Riverside), 1925. 1st ed. 25 plts. Sl rubbed, o/w VG. *Worldwide.* $45/£29

CARTER, SAMUEL III. The Riddle of Dr. Mudd, A Biography.... NY, (1974). 1st ed. Fine in Fine dj. *Pratt.* $27/£17

CARTER, SAMUEL III. The Siege of Atlanta, 1864. NY, (1973). 1st ed. Fine in Fine dj. *Pratt.* $30/£19

CARTER, THOMAS FRANCIS. The Invention of Printing in China and Its Spread Westward. NY: Columbia Univ, 1925. 1st ed. Fine. *Hermitage.* $100/£65

CARTER, THOMAS FRANCIS. The Invention of Printing in China. NY: Columbia Univ Press, (1925). 1st ed. Fldg chart. Fine. *Bookpress.* $125/£81

CARTER, VINCENT. The Bern Book. NY: John Day, (1973). 1st ed. VG in VG dj (tears). *Aka.* $25/£16

CARTER, W.A. McCurtain County and Southeast Oklahoma. Idabel, OK: n.p., 1923. 1st ed. Brn cl (lt soiled; spine faded). *Glenn.* $185/£119

CARTER, W.R. History of the First Regiment of Tennessee Volunteer Cavalry.... Knoxville, TN: Gaut-Ogden, 1902. 1st ed. Frontis port. Orig blue cl. Contemp sig, else VG. *Chapel Hill.* $375/£242

CARTIER-BRESSON, HENRI. The Decisive Moment. NY, (1952). 1st Amer ed. 126 photos. Pamplet of captions. Pict bds by Matisse. Sm bump, sl discolored, sl bowed, else Nice in dj (sl dknd, sl pull spine). *King.* $495/£319

CARTIER-BRESSON, HENRI. The Decisive Moment. NY: S&S, 1952. 1st Amer ed. 126 photos, booklet of captions laid in. Bound in color ptd bds. Fine in dj (repaired chip). *Cahan.* $750/£484

CARTIER-BRESSON, HENRI. The Europeans. NY: S&S, 1955. 1st US ed. 114 full-pg plts. Caption booklet laid in. Repaired tear spine top; lt rubbed, else VG. *Cahan.* $425/£274

CARTIER-BRESSON, HENRI. The Europeans. NY: S&S, 1955. 1st US ed. 114 full-pg plts. Book of captions laid in. Fine in glassine dj w/ptd flaps. *Cahan.* $600/£387

CARTIER-BRESSON, HENRI. Man and Machine. NY, (1971). 1st ed. Sl staining, wrinkling, else Good. *King.* $75/£48

CARTIER-BRESSON, HENRI. The People of Moscow. NY, 1955. 1st Amer ed. Fine (bkpl) in dj (chipped, sl soiled). *Polyanthos.* $200/£129

CARTIER-BRESSON, HENRI. The People of Moscow. NY: S&S, 1955. 1st ed. 163 photos. VG in dj (sl chipped). *Cahan.* $125/£81

CARTIER-BRESSON, HENRI. The World of Henri Cartier Bresson. NY, (1968). 1st ed. 210 photos. VG in dj (sl edgetorn). *King.* $125/£81

CARTLAND, FERNANDO G. Southern Heroes or the Friends in War Time. Cambridge, 1895. 1st ed. 482pp. (Ex-lib w/mks; inner hinges cracking.) *Hayman.* $30/£19

CARTTER, GEORGE R. Twilight of the Jackass Prospector. Morongo Valley: Sagebrush, (1982). 1st ed, ltd to 2000. Fine in wraps. *Book Market.* $30/£19

CARUTHERS, WILLIAM. Loafing Along Death Valley Trails. Death Valley Pub, 1951. Fine. *Book Market.* $12/£8

CARVALHO, SOLOMON N. Incidents of Travel and Adventure in the Far West. NY, 1857. Frontis, 380pp + ads. Lt foxing; wear, sl cocked, o/w VG. *Benchmark.* $250/£161

CARVER, CLIFFORD N. Bookplates of Princeton and Princetonians. Princeton, NJ, 1912. 1st ed. Ltd to 500 signed, this unsigned and unnumbered. 26 facs bkpls. Gilt-titled, blind-emb bds. Fine. *Cahan.* $75/£48

CARVER, J. Travels Through the Interior Parts of North America...1766, 1767, and 1768. London: Ptd for Author, 1778. 1st ed. 8vo. xvi,(17)-543pp; 2 fldg maps; 4 plts. Full leather (rebacked, orig spine laid down; scuffed, worn). Generally VG (sl internal foxing). *Parmer.* $850/£548

CARVER, J. Travels Through the Interior Parts of North America...1766, 1767, and 1768. London: For Author, 1778. 1st ed. 8vo. (xviii)543(i)pp, 2 fldg maps, 4 copper plts; aeg. (Tp loose; sm lt dampstain top inner corner leaves.) Later full-speckled calf (fr cvr detached; spine head chipped; rear cvr starting); gilt-lettered leather labels; raised bands. Fine. Howes C 215. *Blue Mountain.* $1,500/£968

CARVER, J. Travels through the Interior Parts of North America...1766, 1767, and 1768. London: For the author, 1778. 1st ed. Lg 8vo. (xx),543pp. 2 hand-colored engr maps, 4 copper plts. Tall, untrimmed in orig bds (rebacked in period style). VG. Howes C 215. *Schoyer.* $1,750/£1,129

CARVER, J. Travels through the Interior Parts of North America...1766, 1767, and 1768. Minneapolis: Ross & Haines, 1956. Facs ed. #691/1500. Frontis port, 4 plts, 2 fldg maps. Blue cl. NF (sl bumped) in VG+ dj (chipped, spine dknd). Howes C 215. *Harrington.* $45/£29

CARVER, NORMAN F., JR. Form and Space of Japanese Architecture. Tokyo: Shokokusha, (1955). 1st ed. VG. *Bookpress.* $135/£87

CARVER, NORMAN F., JR. Form and Space of Japanese Architecture. Tokyo: Shokokusha, (1955). 1st ed. Ink inscrip, else VG in dj. *Bookpress.* $185/£119

CARVER, RAYMOND. Cathedral. Knopf, 1983. 1st ed. VF in dj. *Fine Books.* $45/£29

CARVER, RAYMOND. Cathedral. NY: Knopf, 1983. 1st ed. Fine in Fine dj. *Beasley.* $50/£32

CARVER, RAYMOND. Elephant and Other Stories. London: Collins Harvill, 1988. 1st Eng ed. Fine in dj. *Ulysses.* $70/£45

CARVER, RAYMOND. Fires. London: Collins Harvill, 1985. 1st ed. VG in dj (nick). *Rees.* $31/£20

CARVER, RAYMOND. For Tess. Concord, NH: William B. Ewert, 1984. 1st ed. Ltd to 125 numbered, signed by Carver and Claire Van Vliet (printer). Framed broadside. Fine. *Jaffe.* $450/£290

CARVER, RAYMOND. Furious Seasons and Other Stories. Santa Barbara: Capra, 1977. 1st ed. Fine in wraps. *Beasley.* $150/£97

CARVER, RAYMOND. A New Path to the Waterfall. NY: Atlantic, 1989. 1st ed. Fine in Fine dj. *Beasley.* $40/£26

CARVER, RAYMOND. This Water. Ewert, NH, 1985. 1st Amer ed. Ltd ed, #100/136 signed. Fine. *Polyanthos.* $100/£65

CARVER, RAYMOND. What We Talk About When We Talk About Love. NY: Knopf, 1981. 1st ed. Fine in Fine dj. *Beasley.* $100/£65

CARVER, RAYMOND. Where I'm Calling From. NY: Atlantic, 1988. 1st ed. Fine in Fine dj. *Beasley.* $40/£26

CARVER, RAYMOND. Will You Please Be Quiet, Please? NY: McGraw-Hill, 1976. 1st ed. Fine (erasure fep) in dj (sl used; sm spot; short closed tear). *Beasley.* $250/£161

CARY, ELISABETH LUTHER. The Rossettis. NY: Putnam's, (1901). 1st ed. 30 plts. Teg; uncut. Fr hinge internally cracked, corners sl bruised, else VG. *Bookpress.* $75/£48

CARY, ELISABETH LUTHER. The Works of James McNeill Whistler. NY: Moffat, Yard, 1907. 31 plts. Sound. *Ars Artis.* $116/£75

CARY, JOYCE. The African Witch. Morrow, 1936. 1st Amer ed. VG in dj (lt worn). *Fine Books.* $75/£48

CARY, JOYCE. The African Witch. London: Gollancz, 1936. 1st ed. Gilt titling on spine dull, edges sl foxed, but Nice in VG dj (sl spine-browned dj). *Limestone.* $185/£119

CARY, JOYCE. The Drunken Sailor. London, 1947. 1st Eng ed. (Name.) Dj (sl frayed). *Edrich.* $25/£16

CARY, JOYCE. The Horse's Mouth. NY: Harper, (1944). 1st Amer ed. VG in dj (nicked). *Hermitage.* $40/£26

CARY, JOYCE. Marching Soldier. London, 1945. 1st Eng ed. VG in dj. *Edrich.* $31/£20

CARY, JOYCE. Memoir of the Bobotes. London, 1960. 1st ed. VG in dj (sl torn). *Edwards.* $23/£15

CARY, JOYCE. Mister Johnson. NY: Harper, n.d. (but 1950). 1st ed. VG in dj. *Hermitage.* $40/£26

CASADO, S. The Last Days of Madrid. Rupert Croft-Cooke (trans). London: Peter Davies, 1939. 1st ed. Nice (edges sl worn; prelims lt foxed). *Patterson.* $271/£175

CASANOVA, JACQUES. The Memoirs of Jacques Casanova de Seingalt 1725-1798. Arthur Machen (trans). Edinburgh: Ptd for Members of LEC, 1940. One of 1500 numbered sets. 8 vols. Cl, dec bds. Bkpls, o/w Fine set in slipcases (lt worn). *Reese.* $125/£81

CASANOVA, JACQUES. The Memoirs of Jacques Casanova de Seingalt. London: Navarre Soc, 1922. New ed. 2 vols. 2 ports; 10 photogravures. (Edges faded.) Fine in djs. *Hollett.* $70/£45

CASATI, GAETANO. Ten Years in Equatoria. London: Warne, 1898. 494pp, 4 fldg maps in pocket. Grn pict cl, gilt titles. VG +. *Bowman.* $125/£81

CASEMENT, DAN D. Random Recollections: The Life and Times...20th Century Cowman. Kansas City: Walker, 1955. 1st ed. *Ginsberg.* $150/£97

CASEMENT, ROGER. Some Poems of Roger Casement. Dublin/London: Talbot Press/T. Fisher Unwin, 1918. 1st ed. VG in ptd wrappers. *Cahan.* $200/£129

CASEY, BILL. A Shroud for a Journey. Boston: Houghton Mifflin, 1960. 1st ed. NF in dj (sl rubbed, price-clipped). *Reese.* $60/£39

CASEY, JOHN. An American Romance. NY: Atheneum, 1977. 1st ed. Fine in Fine dj. *Lame Duck.* $150/£97

CASEY, ROBERT J. The Texas Border and Some Borderliners. Indianapolis: Bobbs-Merrill, (1950). 1st trade ed in dj. 35pg 'The Guide' in rear pocket. VG. *Schoyer.* $40/£26

CASH, W.J. The Mind of the South. Knopf, 1970 (1941). VG (ex-lib) in VG dj. *Book Broker.* $25/£16

CASKEY, WILLIE MALVIN. Secession and Restoration of Louisiana. (Baton Rouge): LA State Univ, 1938. 1st ed. NF. *Mcgowan.* $85/£55

CASLER, JOHN OVERTON. Four Years in the Stonewall Brigade. Guthrie, OK: State Capital Ptg, 1893. 1st ed. 8vo, 495pp, fldg facs. Orig pict gilt-stamped blue cl. Fr hinge cracked internally, spine lt sunned, names, pencil notes, else VG. *Chapel Hill.* $850/£548

CASLER, JOHN OVERTON. Four Years in the Stonewall Brigade. Girard, KS: Appeal Pub Co, 1906. 2nd ed. Orig ptd wrappers bound in full blue morocco w/both wraps bound in. VG (few creases to wraps; sm glue stain lower margin tp; pp numbered in pencil lower corner). Howes 219. *Mcgowan.* $850/£548

CASPARY, VERA. Laura. London: Eyre & Spottiswoode, 1944. 1st ed. VG + in VG- dj (chipped; heavy soiling, surface loss spine panel partially obscuring lettering). *Lame Duck.* $150/£97

CASSADY, NEAL. The First Third. A Partial Autobiography and Other Writings. SF: City Lights, 1971. 1st ed. NF in wraps. *Sclanders.* $39/£25

CASSIDY, JOHN. A Station in the Delta. NY, (1979). 1st ed. NF in NF dj. *Aka.* $40/£26

CASSOU, JEAN et al. The Sources of Modern Art. London, 1962. 1st UK ed. Tipped-in color frontis, 51 tipped-in color plts, 333 b/w plts. (Lib ink stamps; sl rubbed corners.) *Edwards.* $62/£40

CASTANEDA, CARLOS. Journey to Ixtlan: The Lessons of Don Juan. NY: S&S, 1972. 1st ed. NF in dj. *Lame Duck.* $35/£23

CASTANEDA, CARLOS. The Teachings of Don Juan. Berkeley: U of CA, 1968. 1st ed. NF in NF dj (sl spine fade). *Lame Duck.* $250/£161

CASTELAR, EMILIO. Life of Lord Byron and Other Sketches. Mrs. Arthur Arnold (trans). London, 1875. 1st ed. Buckram, gilt-lettered spine (dull; dusty; 1/2 title clipped). *Poetry.* $23/£15

CASTELFRANCO, GIORGIO. Donatello. NY, n.d. (1965?). 40 color plts. Good in dj. *Washton.* $100/£65

CASTELLANI, ALDO and ALBERT J. CHALMERS. Manual of Tropical Medicine. London, 1919. 3rd ed. 16 color plts. (Ink name fr fly; sl rubbed, spotted; sm slit spine top.) *Bickersteth.* $62/£40

CASTELLO, JULIO M. The Theory and Practice of Fencing. NY, (1933). VG in dj. *Artis.* $20/£13

CASTERET, NORBERT. The Darkness under the Earth. London: Dent, 1954. 1st Eng ed. VG in dj (edges sl creased). *Hollett.* $23/£15

CASTERET, NORBERT. More Years under the Earth. Rosemary Dinnage (trans). London: Neville Spearman, 1962. 1st ed. VG in dj (sl worn). *Hollett.* $23/£15

CASTIGLIONI, ARTURO. A History of Medicine. E.B. Krumbhaar (ed). NY: Knopf, 1941. (Rubbed, spine lettering faded.) Internally Fine. *Goodrich.* $125/£81

CASTILLO-PUCHE, JOSE LUIS. Hemingway in Spain. Helen R. Lane (trans). London: New Eng Lib, 1975. 1st ed. Fine in dj. *Patterson.* $47/£30

CASTLE, EGERTON. English Book-Plates. London: George Bell, 1894. xiii,249,(ii)pp. Eps browned, spotted; spine dknd, sm snag. *Hollett.* $54/£35

CASTLE, W.E. Genetics and Eugenics. Cambridge, MA, 1920. VG. *Argosy.* $60/£39

CASTLEMAN, ALFRED L. The Army of the Potomac. Milwaukee: Strickland, 1863. (x),288pp + 6pp ads. (Spine sunned.) Howes C 230. *Schoyer.* $100/£65

CASTLEMAN, HARVEY N. Sam Bass, the Train Robber. Girard: Hadelmann-Julius, 1944. 1st ed. VG. *Parker.* $20/£13

CASTLEMAN, HARVEY N. The Texas Rangers. Girard: Haldeman-Julius, 1944. 1st ed. White wraps. *Lambeth.* $15/£10

Catalogue of Books in the Library of the British Museum.... London, 1884. 3 vols. (Ex-lib, labels, card-holder remains; sl spotting; spines discolored, chipped w/loss.) *Edwards.* $140/£90

Catalogue of European Paintings in the Minneapolis Institute of Arts. Minneapolis, 1970. Good in wrappers. *Washton.* $35/£23

Catalogue of the Books, Manuscripts, Maps and Drawings in the British Museum. NY, 1992. One of 400. 8 vols. *Sutton.* $250/£161

CATE, MARGARET DAVIS. Early Days of Coastal Georgia. St. Simons Island: Fort Frederica Assoc, (1955). Inscribed. VG in dj. *Schoyer.* $25/£16

Catechism of British Geography. (By William Pinnock.) London: G.&W.B. Whittaker, 1823. 2 vols. 12mo. vi + 106pp + 1pg summary, 3pp list on wrappers; 70pp + 5pp list and ad, full-pg engr frontis port each vol, + engr tp w/lg vignette. Fine set in dec stiff buff paper wrappers (lt dusted). *Hobbyhorse.* $125/£81

Catechism of British Law. (By William Pinnock.) London: G.B. Whittaker, 1824. 5th ed. 12mo. 72pp + 5pp list and ad on wrappers, frontis port, vignette on added engr tp. Fine in dec stiff buff paper wrappers. *Hobbyhorse.* $95/£61

Catechism of General Ancient Biography. By a Lady. Wellington, Salop: F. Houlston, 1826. 12mo. 56pp + 1pg list on back wrapper; full-pg hand-colored wood engr frontis; ports. Ptd pink paper wrappers (lt rubbed). Fine. *Hobbyhorse.* $90/£58

Catechism of German Grammar. (By William Pinnock.) London: G. & W.B. Whittaker, 1823. 12mo. 72pp + 3pp ads and list on wrapprs. VF full-pg wood-engr frontis. Dec stiff buff wrappers. Fine. *Hobbyhorse.* $55/£35

Catechism of Poetry. (By William Pinnock.) London: G. and W.B. Whittaker, (1822). 3rd ed. 12mo. 71pp + 3pp list on wrappers, frontis port, steel engr vignette on added engr tp, which carries publication date. Fine in dec wrappers. *Hobbyhorse.* $75/£48

Catechism of the Duty of Children to Parents. (By William Pinnock.) London: Geo. B. Whittaker, 1824. 12mo. 64pp + 12pp list + 3pp book list on wrappers. VG. *Hobbyhorse.* $55/£35

CATESBY, MARK. The Natural History of Carolina, Florida and the Bahama Islands. Savannah: Beehive Press, 1974. 1st ed, as such. One of 500 numbered. 50 color plts. Fine, As New in clamshell box. *Cahan.* $600/£387

CATESBY, MARK. The Natural History of Carolina, Florida, and the Bahama Islands. Savannah, GA: Beehive Press, 1974. One of 500 numbered. 50 full-color plts, each in its own ptd portfolio. Custom-made cl clam shell box. *Bookpress.* $425/£274

CATHCART, GEORGE. Commentaries on the War in Russia and Germany in 1812 and 1813. London, 1850. Signed (initials) presentation. 15,383pp. (Worn.) *Heinoldt.* $35/£23

CATHCART, LINDA L. Richard Diebenkorn. (NY), 1978. VG in cl pict wrappers. *Argosy.* $40/£26

CATHER, WILLA. Alexander's Bridge. Boston/NY: Houghton Mifflin, 1912. 1st ed, 1st ptg, 2nd issue, binding B. Purple cl. Bkpl, else NF. *Godot.* $275/£177

CATHER, WILLA. Death Comes for the Archbishop. NY: Knopf, 1927. 1st ed. Signed. VG in dk grn box. *Parker.* $650/£419

CATHER, WILLA. Death Comes for the Archbishop. NY: Knopf, 1927. 1st trade ed, 1st ptg, 1st binding. 1st ptg (20,000 copies) does not have 'First and second printings before publication' statement. 1st binding is stained ochre on top edge w/plain wove eps. Orig grn cl, labels. Fine. *Macdonnell.* $200/£129

CATHER, WILLA. A Lost Lady. Knopf, 1923. 1st ed. Spine sunned, else VG. *Fine Books.* $25/£16

CATHER, WILLA. A Lost Lady. NY: LEC, 1983. #588/1500 signed by William Bailey (illus). Frontis etching, 4 full-pg b/w illus. Plum eps; aeg. Burgundy leather spine, tips; burgundy/plum floral patterned cl. Fine in plum slipcase. *Heller.* $150/£97

CATHER, WILLA. Lucy Gayheart. NY: Knopf, 1935. 1st ed, trade issue. Grn cl. Spine lt faded, else NF in dj (short tears, else NF). *Godot.* $100/£65

CATHER, WILLA. Lucy Gayheart. NY: Knopf, 1935. 1st ed. #630/749 signed. Full blue buckram, beveled edges, gilt. Teg; uncut. VG in plain dj (sm chips), pub's slipcase. *Houle.* $450/£290

CATHER, WILLA. Lucy Gayheart. NY: Knopf, 1935. 1st ed. One of 749 lg paper copies, signed. Uncut. Blue cl. VF in dj (chipped, worn), pub's box. *Second Life.* $300/£194

CATHER, WILLA. My Mortal Enemy. NY, 1926. 1st ed. Cl-backed bds (stamped name; frayed, rubbed, soiled). *King.* $25/£16

CATHER, WILLA. The Novels and Stories of Willa Cather. Boston: Houghton Mifflin, 1937-1941. 1st ed, 1st issue, ltd to 970 numbered, signed. 13 vols. Cream linen spines, dk gray-blue cl, gilt-stamped leather labels; teg. Fine in orig pub's oversized, yapped djs (sm chips, short tears to deges; spines lt faded, else VG). *Godot.* $2,850/£1,839

CATHER, WILLA. Obscure Destinies. NY, 1932. 1st ed. Cl w/labels (spine yellowed, lt worn, lacks dj). *King.* $20/£13

CATHER, WILLA. The Old Beauty and Others. Knopf, 1948. 1st ed. Inscrip, else Fine in dj (chipped). *Authors Of The West.* $30/£19

CATHER, WILLA. The Professor's House. NY: Knopf, 1925. 1st ed. #149/225 numbered, signed. 8vo. Grn cl (spine faded), patterned bds. VG in pub's gray/grn bd slipcase w/pink paper spine label (w/holograph '149'). *Houle.* $625/£403

CATHER, WILLA. Sapphira and the Slave Girl. NY: Knopf, 1940. 1st ed. #66/520 specially bound lg paper copies, signed. Teg. Grn bds, grn buckram spine. Fine in oversized dj (1/2 inch chip head of tanned spine), in pub's slipcase (lt aged). *Chapel Hill.* $400/£258

CATHER, WILLA. Shadows on the Rock. NY: Knopf, 1931. 1st ed, 1st ptg, trade issue. Grn cl. Lt faded, else VG in rose-colored dj (spine lt faded, 2 sm tears). *Godot.* $100/£65

CATHER, WILLA. Shadows on the Rock. NY: Knopf, 1931. 1st ed, lg paper ed, ltd to 619, signed. Marble paper-cvrd bds, leather label (sl scuffed); uncut. Very nice. *Second Life.* $400/£258

CATHER, WILLA. Shadows on the Rock. Knopf, 1931. 1st ed. Fine in Fine dj. *Authors Of The West.* $125/£81

CATHER, WILLA. The Troll Garden. M-P, 1905. 1st ed, 2nd issue binding. Fep renewed, else VG + . *Fine Books.* $375/£242

CATHERWOOD, JOHN. A New Method of Curing the Apoplexy. London: ptd by J. Darby, for W. Taylor, 1715. viii; 77pp. Contemp 1/4 calf, marble bds (rebacked). Lt foxing, else VG. *Goodrich.* $595/£384

CATICH, EDWARD M. Eric Gill, His Social and Artistic Roots. Iowa City: Prairie Press, 1964. 1st ed. Photo of Fr. Catich laid in. Fine in pict dj. *Shasky*. $50/£32

CATICH, EDWARD M. Letters Redrawn from the Trajan Inscription in Rome. Davenport: Catfish Press, (1961). Signed. 44p; 93 loose plts. Folio-sized fldg case (lt wear). *Veatchs*. $150/£97

CATICH, EDWARD M. Letters Redrawn from the Trajan Inscription in Rome. Davenport, IA: St. Ambrose College, 1961. 2nd ed. Inscribed. Orange buckram. VG in matching slipcase. *Heller*. $150/£97

CATLIN, GEORGE. The Breath of Life, or Mal-Respiration.... NY: John Wiley, 1861. 1st ed. 78pp. Black cl (extrems rubbed). *Karmiole*. $150/£97

CATLIN, GEORGE. Illustrations of the Manners, Customs, and Condition of the North American Indians.... London, 1845. 5th ed. 2 vols. 264; 266pp (foxing); 360 engrs. 3/4 brn leather; marbled bds (sl wear; sm tear), red leather labels. *King*. $650/£419

CATLIN, GEORGE. Last Rambles Amongst the Indians of the Rocky Mountains and the Andes. Edinburgh: Gall & Inglis, (c. 1877). 24 woodcuts. Blue dec cl (extrems sl rubbed). VG. *Hollett*. $70/£45

CATLIN, GEORGE. Letters and Notes on the Manners, Customs, and Condition of the North American Indians. London, 1841. 2nd ed. 2 vols. Frontis, viii,264; viii,266pp; 312 numbered illus on 176 plts (actually 309 illus); 3 maps (1 fldg). Contemp 1/2 morocco, purple cl; gilt-stamped burgundy leather spine labels; marbled eps. Sm sunned strip top vol 2, o/w Fine. Howes C 241. *Oregon*. $850/£548

CATLIN, GEORGE. Letters and Notes on...the North American Indians. NY: Wiley & Putnam's, 1841. 1st Amer ed (from British sheets). 2 vols. viii,264; viii,266pp, 311 plts, 2 maps (1 fldg); tipped-in errata vol 1. Orig cl (newly rebacked, orig spine; new eps). Howes C 241. *Schoyer*. $800/£516

CATLIN, GEORGE. North American Indians. Edinburgh: John Grant, 1903. 2 vols. Partially unopened. Burgundy cl, black/gilt decs. (Lt shelfwear; inscrip, pencil note.) *Parmer*. $500/£323

CATLIN, HENRY G. Yellow Pine Basin. NY: George H. Richmond, 1897. 1st ed. Teg. Article tipped in. Gilt pict cl. Sound. *Reese*. $20/£13

CATLOW, AGNES. Drops of Water. London: Reeve & Benham, 1851. xviii,194pp + 4pp ads, 4 hand-colored litho plts; aeg. Grn gilt cl (sm gouge spine). *Karmiole*. $100/£65

CATTERMOLE, R. The Book of Raphael's Cartoons. London, 1845. 185pp. Several engr plts hors texte. Good (sl rubbed, soiled). *Washton*. $85/£55

Cattle Barons' Rebellion Against Law and Order. Evanston, 1955. Ltd to 1000. Signed, dated by Herbert Brayer of Branding Iron Press. Fine in orig ptd folder (sm edge cuts, sl soiled). *Baade*. $50/£32

CATTON, BRUCE. The American Heritage Picture History of the Civil War. American Heritage, (c. 1960). VG. *Book Broker*. $25/£16

CATTON, BRUCE. The Army of the Potomac. GC, (1962). 3 vols. Fine in dj (lt wear). *Pratt*. $40/£26

CATTON, BRUCE. A Stillness at Appomattox. GC: Doubleday, 1953. 1st ed. Internally NF in dj (sl chipped). *Blue Mountain*. $35/£23

CATTON, BRUCE. This Hallowed Ground. GC, (1956). Signed presentation ed. Dj chipped, o/w Fine. *Pratt*. $55/£35

CATTON, BRUCE. The War Lords of Washington. NY, (1948). 1st ed, 1st bk. VG in dj (chipped). *Artis*. $25/£16

CAUDWELL, SARAH. The Shortest Way to Hades. London: CCC, 1984. 1st ed. Fine in dj (sl wear). *Mordida*. $75/£48

CAUDWELL, SARAH. The Sirens Sang of Murder. London: Collins, 1989. 1st ed. Fine in Fine dj. *Janus*. $45/£29

CAUFIELD, S.F.A. and BLANCHE C. SAWARD. The Dictionary of Needlework. London: L. Upcott Gill, 1885. 2nd ed. 4to. (vi),518pp; 28 color plts (1 ragged edge); silken eps. Textured cl (hinges taped; sl fraying; rebacked, much of orig spine laid down; bubbling; spine faded). *Edwards*. $171/£110

CAUGHEY, JOHN WALTON (ed). Rushing for Gold. Berkeley: Univ of CA Press, 1949. Red cl. Fine in NF dj (sm closed tears). *Harrington*. $35/£23

CAUGHEY, JOHN WALTON (ed). Seeing the Elephant. Ward Ritchie Press, 1951. 1st ed. Ltd to 250. Pict bds. Fine. *Oregon*. $75/£48

CAUGHEY, JOHN WALTON. Gold Is the Cornerstone. Berkeley: Univ of CA, 1948. 1st ed. Fine in Fine dj. *Book Market*. $35/£23

CAUGHEY, JOHN WALTON. Gold Is the Cornerstone. Univ of CA, 1948. 1st ed. Fine in Fine dj. *Oregon*. $45/£29

CAUGHEY, JOHN WALTON. McGillivray of the Creeks. Norman: Univ of OK Press, (1958). Facs ed of 1938 orig ed. Fine in NF dj (sl chipped, spine faded). *Harrington*. $45/£29

CAUGHEY, LA REE. The Wilderness Is a Book. (L.A.): Ward Ritchie, 1966. 1st ed. Pict cl. Dj. *Dawson*. $35/£23

CAUSEY, A. Edward Burra, Complete Catalogue. Phaidon, 1985. 32 color plts. Dj. *Ars Artis*. $93/£60

CAUSLEY, CHARLES. Farewell, Aggie Weston. Kent: Hand & Flower Press, 1951. 1st UK ed. VG in wrappers (spine sl browned). *Moorhouse*. $12/£8

CAUZ, LOUIS. Baseball's Back in Town. Controlled Media, 1977. 1st ed. VG+ in VG+ dj. *Plapinger*. $100/£65

Cavaliers of Virginia, or the Recluse of Jamestown. NY: Harper, 1834-35. 1st ed. 2 vols. (Foxed; worn.) BAL 2791. *Cahan*. $250/£161

CAVE, C.J.P. Roof Bosses in Medieval Churches. CUP, 1948. 1st ed. Frontis. (Ex-libris w/ink stamp tp, bkpl removed.) *Edwards*. $85/£55

CAVE, HENRY W. Golden Tips. London: Sampson Low, 1900. 1st ed. Frontis port; fldg map. VG (sm dent in spine). *Hollett*. $116/£75

CAVE, HENRY W. Golden Tips. London, 1904. 3rd ed. Dec cl. *Wheldon & Wesley*. $54/£35

CAVE, RODERICK. The Private Press. London: Faber & Faber, (1971). 1st ed. Frontis, 72 plts. Bkpl; else VG. *Bookpress*. $85/£55

CAVE, RODERICK. The Private Press. London: Faber & Faber, 1971. 1st ed. 72 plts. VG in orig cl; dj. *Cox*. $70/£45

CAVELER, WILLIAM. Select Specimens of Gothic Architecture. London: by author, 1835. xv,3pp subs, 74 plts (6 dbl-pg, 1 tinted). (Foxing.) Full morocco, gilt (spine lt sunned, sl wear). *Edwards*. $271/£175

CECIL, HENRY. Daughters in Law. London: Joseph, 1961. 1st ed. Inscribed. Edges browned, o/w VG in dj (closed tear). *Murder*. $75/£48

CECIL, HENRY. Friends at Court. NY: Harper, (1956). 1st ed. Fine in dj (sl rubbed). *Pharos.* $30/£19

CECIL, HENRY. Friends at Court. London: Joseph, 1956. 1st ed. Signed presentation copy. NF in dj. *Limestone.* $55/£35

CECIL, HENRY. The Painswick Line. London, (1958). 1st ed. Fine in dj (spine sl rubbed). *Polyanthos.* $45/£29

CECIL, HENRY. Settled Out of Court. NY: Harper, (1959). 1st ed. Fine in dj. *Pharos.* $30/£19

CECIL, HENRY. Settled Out of Court. London: Michael Joseph, 1959. 1st ed. Spotting pg edges, o/w Fine in dj. *Mordida.* $35/£23

CECIL, HENRY. Unlawful Occasions. London: Michael Joseph, 1962. 1st ed. Inscribed. Foxing pg edges, o/w Fine in dj (faded spine). *Mordida.* $45/£29

CECINSKY, HERBERT. The Gentle Art of Faking Furniture. London, 1931. 1st ed. Frontis port, 292 plts. (Shaken; mks, joints splitting.) *Edwards.* $116/£75

CELEBONOVIC, ALEKSA. The Heyday of Salon Painting. London, 1974. 1st UK ed. 170 plts (41 color). Dj. *Edwards.* $39/£25

CELEBONOVIC, ALEKSA. Some Call It Kitsch: Masterpieces of Bourgeois Realism. NY: Abrams, n.d. Gilt-emb cl. Fine in illus dj. *Cahan.* $75/£48

Celebrated Trials, and Remarkable Cases of Criminal Jurisprudence...to the Year 1825. London: Knight & Lacey, 1825. Contemp diced calf (rebacked). Attractive. *Boswell.* $1,250/£806

CELINE, LOUIS-FERDINAND. Guignol's Band. Bernard Frechtman & Jack T. Nile (trans). (NY): New Directions, (1954). 1st Amer ed. NF in dj. *Godot.* $65/£42

CELIZ, FRANCISCO. Diary of the Alarcon Expedition into Texas, 1718-1719. L.A.: Quivira Soc, 1935. 1st ed. One of 600 numbered. 8 plts; 2 maps. Vellum spine (paper label remnants lower spine). Howes C 254. *Ginsberg.* $225/£145

CELLINI, BENVENUTO. Autobiography of Benevuto Cellini. NY: Doubleday, 1946. #798/1000 signed, dated by Salvador Dali (illus). Fine in slipcase. *Williams.* $388/£250

CELLINI, BENVENUTO. The Life of Benvenuto Cellini. Verona: LEC, 1937. #162/1500 signed by Fritz Kredel (illus). Fine in slipcase. *Williams.* $147/£95

CENDRARS, BLAISE. At the Heart of the World. (NY: O Press, 1978). 1st Amer ed, ltd to 500. Unptd black wrappers. Fine in dec dj. *Godot.* $45/£29

CENDRARS, BLAISE. Panama or The Adventures of My Seven Uncles. John Dos Passos (trans, illus). NY: Harper, 1931. 1st ed. Illus fr cvr. 2 offset tape mks inside fr cvr, fep; sl dust soiled, else VG. *Godot.* $35/£23

CENDRARS, BLAISE. Sutter's Gold. Henry Logan Stuart (trans). NY: Harper, 1926. 1st Amer ed. 5 inserted woodcuts. Pub's cl over gilt paper-cvrd bds (worn), paper spine label. *Book Block.* $35/£23

CEPEDA, ORLANDO with CHARLES EINSTEIN. My Ups and Downs in Baseball. Putnam's, 1968. 1st ed. Fine in Fine dj. *Plapinger.* $40/£26

CERF, BENNETT. Bennett Cerf's Pop-Up Riddles. NY: Random House, 1967. 1st ed. 18pp, 2 pop-ups, 10 mechanical pp. VG. *Godot.* $40/£26

CERRUTI, HENRY. Ramblings in California. Margaret Mollins & Virginia Thickens (eds). Friends of Bancroft, 1954. 1st ed. One of 500 ptd. Frontis. Vellum, bds. Fine. *Oregon.* $60/£39

CERVANTES. The History of the Renowned Don Quixote de la Mancha. Charles Henry Wilmot (trans). London: J. Cooke, 1774. 2 vols. 8vo. Copper engr frontis, xii,390; iv,398pp + 1pg list + 1pg; 29 VF full-pg plts. Full leather on bds, gilt (rebacked); orig bds (orig spine laid in; new eps), red spine label. (Bkpl, label both vols; ex-libris on inserted orig flyleaves; edges rubbed, soiled; sm hole vol 2 lower bd). *Hobbyhorse.* $495/£319

CESCINSKY, HERBERT and GEORGE LELAND HUNTER. English and American Furniture. GC: GC Pub Co, (1929). 1st ed. Eps foxed, else VG in dj (torn). *Bookpress.* $50/£32

CESCINSKY, HERBERT. The Old-World House, Its Furniture and Decoration. London: A&C Black, 1924. 1st ed. 2 vols. Frontispieces; teg. Rubbed, else VG. *Bookpress.* $225/£145

CHABON, MICHAEL. The Mysteries of Pittsburgh. NY: Morrow, (1988). 1st ed, 1st bk. Fine in dj. *Turlington.* $60/£39

CHABOT, FREDERICK C. The Alamo, Altar of Texas Liberty. San Antonio: Naylor, 1931. 1st ed. Orig ptd wraps protected in cl binding. *Lambeth.* $50/£32

CHABOT, FREDERICK C. The Alamo. San Antonio: Naylor Ptg Co, 1931. 1st ed. VG in orig pict wraps. *Chapel Hill.* $60/£39

CHACE, ELIZABETH BUFFUM and LUCY BUFFUM LOVELL. Two Quaker Sisters, from the Original Diaries of.... NY, (1937). 1st ed. Orig cl. VG. *Mcgowan.* $75/£48

CHADWICK, HENRY. The Game of Base Ball. NY, (1868). 180+ pp (ink # bottom of tp), port. Cl-backed bds (loose, rubbed, spine chipped). Good. *King.* $1,250/£806

CHADWICK, J. The Decipherment of Linear B. CUP, 1967. VG in dj. *Moss.* $31/£20

CHADWICK, W.S. Giants of the Forest. Indianapolis: Bobbs-Merrill, 1929. 1st ed. Fine. *Bowman.* $50/£32

CHADWICK, WHITNEY. Women Artists and the Surrealist Movement. London, 1985. 1st ed. Dj. *Edwards.* $31/£20

CHADWICK, WILLIAM. The Life and Times of Daniel Defoe. London: John Russell Smith, 1859. 1st ed. Engr frontis. Contemp full polished calf, banded, gilt (sl worn, spine sunned). Nice. *Ash.* $116/£75

CHAFE, WALLACE. BAE Bulletin 183. Seneca Thanksgiving Rituals. Washington, 1961. (Ex-lib.) *Edwards.* $23/£15

CHAGALL, BELLA. Burning Lights. NY: Shocken Books, (1946). 1st Amer ed. Marc Chagall (illus). Ink #s fep, else VG in dj (torn, chipped). *Hermitage.* $45/£29

CHALFANT, W.A. Death Valley. Stanford/London: Stanford Univ Press/OUP, 1930. 1st ed. Orange/gold dec cl (spine dknd; edgewear). Overall VG. *Parmer.* $45/£29

CHALFANT, W.A. Gold Guns and Ghost Towns. Stanford: Univ Press, (1947). 1st ed. Fine in Fine dj. *Book Market.* $28/£18

CHALFANT, W.A. Outposts of Civilization. Boston: Christopher, (1928). Fine in Fine dj. *Book Market.* $100/£65

CHALK, THOMAS. Journals of the Lives, Travels, and Gospel Labours of Thomas Wilson, and James Dickinson. London: C. Gilpin, 1847. xxx,217pp (book label). Mod 1/2 calf, buckram bds, gilt. *Hollett.* $101/£65

CHALKER, FUSSELL M. Pioneer Days among the Ocmulgee. Carrollton, GA: F.M. Chalker, 1970. 1st ed. Signed. Grn cl. NF in VG dj (price-clipped). *Chapel Hill.* $40/£26

CHALKLEY, THOMAS. The Journal of.... NY, 1808. 7,556pp. New buckram (rebound). *Heinoldt.* $35/£23

CHALMERS MITCHELL, PETER. My House in Malaga. London: Faber, 1938. 1st ed. VG in dj (worn). *Patterson.* $70/£45

CHALMERS, GEORGE. Caledonia: Or, An Account, Historical and Topographic, of North Britain, from the Most Ancient to the Present Times. London: T. Cadell/A. Constable, 1810/1824. Vols II, III 1st eds. 3 vols. xii,904pp, lg fldg map, 5 plts; viii,1007pp; iv,914pp. (Rebound; tape repair 2 places, few short closed tears, foxing, pencil mks, numerous pencil marginalia vol III.) *Cahan.* $200/£129

CHALMERS, GEORGE. The Life of Thomas Ruddiman.... Ptd for John Stockdale, 1794. Frontis port; 2pp facs (1 fldg). Later 1/2 sheep. *Waterfield.* $132/£85

CHALMERS, HARVEY. Joseph Brant: Mohawk. East Lansing: MI State Univ Press, (1955). 1st ed. Frontis port. Rust cl. NF in dj. *Chapel Hill.* $40/£26

CHALON, H. BERNARD. Chalon's Drawing Book of Animals and Birds.... London: Chalon & Nattes, 1804. Title, 16 engr or etched plts, 3ff letterpress. Later half morocco (rubbed). *Marlborough.* $1,163/£750

CHAMBERLAIN, GEORGE AGNEW. African Hunting Among the Thongas. NY: Harper, 1923. 1st ed. Photo paste-down fr cvr. VG+. *Bowman.* $50/£32

CHAMBERLAIN, PAUL M. It's About Time. London: Holland Press, 1978 (1941). Rpt. Gilt-illus blue cl. VG. *Knollwood.* $45/£29

CHAMBERLAIN, SAMUEL. Beyond New England Thresholds. NY: Hastings House, (1937). 1st ed. Fine. *Bookpress.* $25/£16

CHAMBERLAIN, SAMUEL. My Confession. NY: Harper & Bros, 1956. 16 plts. Fine in Fair dj (chipped). *Connolly.* $27/£17

CHAMBERLAINE, WILLIAM W. Memoirs of the Civil War.... Washington: Byron S. Adams, 1912. 1st ed. Sm 8vo, frontis port. Orig red cl. Handwritten corrections in few places, else Fine. *Chapel Hill.* $900/£581

CHAMBERLAYNE, JOHN HAMPDEN. Ham Chamberlayne, Virginian: Letters and Papers.... Richmond, VA: Press of Dietz Ptg, 1932. 1st ed. #662/1000. Frontis port, dbl-pg map, fldg map. 2-tone cl. Fore-edge lt spotted, else Fine in NF dj. *Chapel Hill.* $250/£161

CHAMBERLAYNE, JOHN HAMPDEN. Ham Chamberlayne—Virginian Letters and Papers of an Artillery Officer.... Richmond, VA: Dietz Ptg Co, 1932. 1st ed, ltd to 1000 numbered. Fine in NF dj. *Mcgowan.* $250/£161

CHAMBERLIN, BERNARD PEYTON. The Negro and Crime in Virginia. Charlottesville, VA, 1936. 1st ed. NF in orig stiff ptd wrappers. *Mcgowan.* $75/£48

CHAMBERS, ANDREW. Recollections. N.p.: Privately ptd, 1947. 1st ed. VF in stapled wraps. Howes C 270. *Oregon.* $150/£97

CHAMBERS, DAVID. Joan Hassall Engravings and Drawings. London: Private Libraries Assoc, 1985. 1st ed. VG. *Cox.* $31/£20

CHAMBERS, E.K. The Elizabethan Stage. Oxford: Clarendon, (1951). Rpts. 5 vols. Frontispieces. Fine in 4 djs (torn, neatly repaired). *Petersfield.* $217/£140

CHAMBERS, E.K. The Mediaeval Stage. Oxford: Clarendon, 1954. Rpt. 2 vols. Frontispieces. Fine in djs. *Petersfield.* $133/£86

CHAMBERS, GEORGE. Historical Sketch of Pottsville, Schuylkill County, PA. Pottsville, PA, 1876. 1st ed. 19pp. Orig ptd wrappers sl chipped, else VG. *Mcgowan.* $65/£42

CHAMBERS, HENRY E. Mississippi Valley Beginnings, an Outline.... NY/London: Putnam's, 1922. 13 plts & maps. Good (worn, dull; lt foxing). *Bohling.* $65/£42

CHAMBERS, R. The Book of Days. London, 1864. 2 vols. 832; 840pp. Teg; dec eps. 1/2 leather (faded; rubbed; lt soiled). *Edwards.* $78/£50

CHAMBERS, R. Police!!! Appleton, 1915. 1st ed. VG+ in Nice dj (wear, tear, soiling; inner reinforcement). *Aronovitz.* $125/£81

CHAMBERS, ROBERT W. The Mystery of Choice. Appleton, 1899. NF. *Madle.* $50/£32

CHAMBERS, ROBERT W. The Red Republic. NY: Putnam's, 1895. 1st ed. Bit worn spine heel, lower corners, else NF in illus cl cvrs. *Else Fine.* $250/£161

CHAMBERS, ROBERT W. The Rogue's Moon. NY, 1928. 1st ed. Yellow cl. VG in pict dj (torn). *Argosy.* $40/£26

CHAMBERS, ROBERT W. The Rogue's Moon. NY: Appleton, 1929. Pict cl. NF in dj (sl soiled, edgeworn). *Sadlon.* $50/£32

CHAMBERS, WILLIAM. American Slavery and Colour. London, 1861. 2nd Eng ed, enlgd. Sl wear spine ends; else VG. *Mcgowan.* $150/£97

CHAMBLESS, E. Roadtown. Roadtown Press, 1910. 1st ed. NF. *Aronovitz.* $95/£61

CHAMBLISS, WILLIAM H. Chambliss' Diary; or, Society as It Really Is. NY: Chambliss, 1895. xiv,408,(1)pp. Gilt/silver stamping. Spine rubbed, lt bumped; fep removed, else VG. *Bohling.* $200/£129

CHAMPION, F.W. With a Camera in Tiger-land. London, 1928. 74 plts. (Sm worm holes inside fr cvrs, affecting prelims.) *Wheldon & Wesley.* $39/£25

CHAMPLIN, JAMES. Travels and Adventures of Rev. James Champlin.... Columbus, OH: Charles Scott's Power Press, 1842. 1st ed. 192pp. Lacks eps, sm chip expertly repaired, o/w VG. *Cahan.* $275/£177

CHAMPLIN, JOHN DENISON, JR. The Chronicle of the Coach. NY: Scribner's, 1886. 1st ed. Good+ (bumped; tp torn). *October Farm.* $60/£39

CHAMPLIN, JOHN DENISON, JR. The Chronicle of the Coach.... London: C&W, 1886. xv,298,32pp (owner stamp, cutting laid on to fr pastedown). Pict red cl (damped, faded, sl bumped), gilt. *Hollett.* $47/£30

CHAMPNEY, ELIZABETH W. and FRERE CHAMPNEY. Romance of Old Japan. NY, 1917. 1st Amer ed. Teg, rest uncut. Gilt dec cvrs. Fine (inscrip; nick, spine sl sunned). *Polyanthos.* $45/£29

CHANCE, JOSEPH E. The Second Texas Infantry. Austin, TX, (1984). 1st ed. VG in dj. *King.* $25/£16

CHANCELLOR, E. BERESFORD. The Annals of the Strand. London, 1912. Fldg illus. Gilt device upper bd. (Lt foxing; spine faded.) *Edwards.* $54/£35

CHANCELLOR, E. BERESFORD. The Lives of the Rakes. NY: Brentano's, 1926. 6 vols. Navy blue cl. VG (bkpl). *Weber.* $45/£29

CHANDLEE, EDWARD. Six Quaker Clockmakers. Phila: Hist Soc of PA, 1943. 1st trade ed. Dec eps. Gilt-stamped cl. VG. *Argosy.* $75/£48

CHANDLER, A. BERTRAM. The Rim of Space. Avalon, 1961. 1st ed. Fine in dj (spine sl faded). *Madle.* $40/£26

CHANDLER, ASA. Hookworm Disease. NY, 1929. 1st ed. Good. *Fye.* $50/£32

CHANDLER, MELBOURNE C. Of Garryowen in Glory. Chandler, 1960. 1st ed. NF in VG dj. *Parker.* $110/£71

CHANDLER, RAYMOND and ROBERT PARKER. Poodle Springs. London: Macdonald, 1990. #16/250 signed by Parker. Fine in slipcase. *Lewton.* $42/£27

CHANDLER, RAYMOND. The Big Sleep. Knopf, 1939. 1st ed, 1st bk. Owner stamp; sm worm hole through entire book, else VG-. *Fine Books.* $125/£81

CHANDLER, RAYMOND. Farewell, My Lovely. NY: Knopf, 1940. 1st ed. NF in dj (spine re-touched; lt rubbing folds). *Hermitage.* $2,500/£1,613

CHANDLER, RAYMOND. Finger Man. NY: Avon, 1950. Paperback reprint ed. VG in wrappers. *Mordida.* $30/£19

CHANDLER, RAYMOND. Five Murderers. Avon, 1944. 1st pb ed. VG in wraps. *Fine Books.* $45/£29

CHANDLER, RAYMOND. Killer in the Rain. London: Hamish Hamilton, 1964. 1st ed. NF (lt spotting top edge) in VG + dj. *Janus.* $175/£113

CHANDLER, RAYMOND. Killer in the Rain. London: Hamish Hamilton, 1964. 1st Eng ed. NF in dj. *Limestone.* $195/£126

CHANDLER, RAYMOND. Killer in the Rain. London: Hamilton, 1964. 1st UK ed. NF in dj. *Williams.* $116/£75

CHANDLER, RAYMOND. Killer in the Rain. Boston: Houghton Mifflin, 1964. 1st US ed. Fine in bright dj (lt edgewear). *Janus.* $225/£145

CHANDLER, RAYMOND. The Lady in the Lake. Hamish Hamilton, (1944). 1st Eng ed, 1st ptg. Yellow cl (edges sl soiled). Orig dj (sl defective at spine head, foot; strengthened inner side). *Bickersteth.* $543/£350

CHANDLER, RAYMOND. The Little Sister. London: Hamish Hamilton, 1949. 1st ed. Spotting pg edges, o/w Fine in dj (sl faded spine; sl wear; tiny closed tears). *Mordida.* $800/£516

CHANDLER, RAYMOND. The Long Good-Bye. London: Hamilton, 1953. 1st UK ed. VG (bds sl dulled). *Williams.* $28/£18

CHANDLER, RAYMOND. The Long Good-Bye. London: Hamilton, 1953. 1st UK ed. VG (sl tape mks feps) in dj (sl edgewear, scuff mk). *Williams.* $147/£95

CHANDLER, RAYMOND. The Long Goodbye. London: Hamish Hamilton, 1953. 1st ed. VG in dj (sl worn). *Limestone.* $185/£119

CHANDLER, RAYMOND. The Midnight Raymond Chandler. Boston: Houghton Mifflin, 1971. 1st ed. VG in dj (nicks). *Houle.* $150/£97

CHANDLER, RAYMOND. Playback. London: Hamish Hamilton, (1958). 1st UK ed. Ep offset where bkmk was laid in, o/w Fine in NF dj (crease; internally mended tear rear panel). *Bernard.* $200/£129

CHANDLER, RAYMOND. Playback. Boston: Houghton Mifflin, 1958. 1st Amer ed. Name, o/w Fine in dj (sl wear). *Mordida.* $125/£81

CHANDLER, RAYMOND. Raymond Chandler Speaking. Dorothy Gardiner & Kathrine Sorley Walker (eds). Boston: Houghton, Mifflin, 1962. 1st ed, 1st Amer ptg. Fine in NF dj. *Hayman.* $80/£52

CHANDLER, RAYMOND. Red Wind. Cleveland, (1946). 1st ed. Lt stained, else Good in dj (price-clipped, heavily chipped). *King.* $25/£16

CHANDLER, RAYMOND. Spanish Blood. Cleveland, (1946). 1st ed. Cl (worn, bumped; text yellowed). Dj (rubbed, heavily chipped). *King.* $25/£16

CHANDLER, RAYMOND. Spanish Blood. Cleveland/NY: World Publishing, (1946). 1st ed. Pp browned, o/w NF in Attractive dj. *Bernard.* $65/£42

CHANNING, GRACE ELLERY. The Sister of a Saint and Other Stories. Chicago: Stone & Kimball, 1895. 1st ed. 261pp. Uncut. VG. *Second Life.* $45/£29

CHANNING, MARK. King Cobra. Lippincott, 1934. 1st ed. VG. *Madle.* $20/£13

CHANNING, MARK. White Python. Lippincott, 1934. 1st US ed. Fine in dj. *Madle.* $150/£97

CHANNING, WALTER. A Treatise on Etherization in Childbirth. Boston, 1848. 1st ed. 8vo. 400pp. Mod cl. Sl soiling last 2 leaves, else internally Fine. *Argosy.* $850/£548

CHAPEL, CHARLES EDWARD. Guns of the Old West. NY: Coward-McCann, (1961). 1st ed. Blue cl. NF in VG + dj (sl chipped). *Harrington.* $45/£29

CHAPELLE, HOWARD I. The Baltimore Clipper, Its Origin and Development. Salem: Marine Research Soc Pub 22, 1930, 1st ed. One of 97 lg paper copies. xii,192,(1)pp. (Spine head tear.) Howes C 288. *Lefkowicz.* $225/£145

CHAPELLE, HOWARD I. The Baltimore Clipper. Salem, MA: Marine Research Soc, 1930. 1st ed. Frontis, 35 plts; 48 plans. Textured blue cl; gilt spine. Fine. *Karmiole.* $125/£81

CHAPELLE, HOWARD I. The Baltimore Clipper. Salem, MA: Marine Research Soc, 1930. 1st ed. 36 plts. Good in dj (sl worn). Howes C 288. *Hayman.* $125/£81

CHAPELLE, HOWARD I. The History of American Sailing Ships. NY: Bonanza, 1935. Pict cl. Fine in Good dj. *Connolly.* $35/£23

CHAPELLE, HOWARD I. The Search for Speed Under Sail 1700-1855. NY, 1967. 36 halftones, 16 fldg plts. VG in dj. *Argosy.* $75/£48

CHAPIN, ANNA ALICE. The Now-A-Days Fairy Book. NY: Dodd, Mead, 1911. 1st ed. 6 tipped-in full-pg color illus by Jessie Wilcox Smith; orange backing sheets, lettered guards. Red-brn cl, color pict cvr. VG (spine faded, wavy; back bd spotted). *Davidson.* $285/£184

CHAPIN, CHARLES. The Sources and Modes of Infection. NY, 1916. 2nd ed. (Ex-lib.) *Fye.* $75/£48

CHAPIN, HOWARD MILLAR. The Tartar: The Armed Sloop of the Colony of Rhode Island in King George's War.... Providence: Soc of Colonial Wars, 1922. 1st ed. 6 plts, fldg map. (Cvrs sl soiled.) *Lefkowicz.* $70/£45

CHAPLIN, CHARLES. My Autobiography. London, 1966. Rpt. Fine in dj. *Artis.* $25/£16

CHAPLIN, RALPH. Wobbly. Chicago, (1948). 1st ed. (Cvrs stained.) *King.* $25/£16

CHAPLIN, S. My Fate Cries Out. Phoenix, 1949. 1st ed. VG in dj (torn, dull). *Whiteson.* $37/£24

CHAPMAN, ABEL. Bird-Life of the Borders on Moorland and Sea.... London, 1907. 2nd ed, re-written & enlgd. Color map. Orig buckram (repaired). *Wheldon & Wesley.* $78/£50

CHAPMAN, ABEL. Bird-Life of the Borders. London: Gurney & Jackson, 1889. 1st ed. xii,286,16pp, uncut. Gilt cl (sl rubbed). Very Nice. *Hollett.* $171/£110

CHAPMAN, ABEL. The Borders and Beyond. London, 1924. 19 color plts by W.H. Riddell, 2 fldg sketch maps. *Edwards.* $116/£75

CHAPMAN, ABEL. Memories, of Fourscore Years Less Two, 1851-1929. London, 1930. 1st ed. (Feps lt foxed.) *Edwards.* $85/£55

CHAPMAN, ABEL. Retrospect. Reminiscences and Impressions of a Hunter Naturalist in Three Continents, 1851-1928. Gurney & Jackson, 1928. Teg, rest uncut. *Petersfield.* $59/£38

CHAPMAN, ABEL. Retrospect. Reminiscences...1851-1928. London, 1928. 1st ed. Teg. (Extrems sl rubbed.) *Edwards.* $78/£50

CHAPMAN, ABEL. Savage Sudan. London: Gurney & Jackson, 1921. 1st ed. Ribbed grn cl gilt (extrems sl worn; string mks upper hinge, fore-edge). Teg, uncut. *Hollett.* $287/£185

CHAPMAN, CHARLES F. and F.W. HORENBURGER (eds). Practical Boat Building. NY: Motor Boating, (1953). 1st ed. *Lefkowicz.* $45/£29

CHAPMAN, F. SPENCER. Northern Lights. The Official Account of the British Arctic Air-Route Expedition 1930-1931. London: C&W, 1932. 1st ed. 64 plts, 4 fldg maps. Blue cl (lt soiled). VG. *House.* $75/£48

CHAPMAN, F. SPENCER. Northern Lights. The Official Account of the British Arctic Air-Route Expedition 1930-31. London: C&W, 1933. 3rd imp. Fldg map. Good. *Walcot.* $26/£17

CHAPMAN, F. SPENCER. Northern Lights. The Official Account of the British Arctic Air-Route Expedition. 1930-1931. London: C&W, 1932. Frontis, 64 plts, fldg map. Overall VG (sl foxing to edges). *Parmer.* $95/£61

CHAPMAN, GEOFFREY. The Siege of Lyme Regis. Lyme Regis: Serendip Books, 1982. 1st ed. Tipped-in erratum. Fine in orig wrappers. *Rees.* $16/£10

CHAPMAN, HENRY C. A Manual of Medical Jurisprudence and Toxicology. Phila: Saunders, 1892. 237pp + ads. Good. *Goodrich.* $35/£23

CHAPMAN, JOHN WIGHT. A Camp on the Yukon. Cornwall-on-Hudson: Idlewild Press, c.1948. Map as frontis. VG in dj (stained). *High Latitude.* $45/£29

CHAPMAN, OLIVE MURRAY. Across Lapland with Sledge and Reindeer. London, (1932). 1st ed. Map. Sl shelfwear. *Artis.* $35/£23

CHAPMAN, R.W. Cancels. London, 1930. 1st ed, one of 500. 11 collotype facs on fldg plts. Vellum-backed marbled bds (ex-lib w/ink stamps verso half title; bkpl; cardholder remains; sm dent). *Edwards.* $233/£150

CHAPMAN, WALKER. The Golden Dream, Seekers of El Dorado. Bobbs Merrill, (1967). 1st ed. 5 maps. VF in VF dj. *Oregon.* $30/£19

CHAPMAN, WENDALL and LUCIE. Wilderness Wanderers. NY: Scribner's, 1937. 1st ed. Tan cl, pict pastedown fr cvr. VG. *Bowman.* $45/£29

CHAPPELL, E. Voyage of His Majesty's Ship Rosamund to Newfoundland and the Southern Coast of Labrador. London: J.Mawman, 1818. xix,270pp. Fldg map, 3 plts. Recent half calf, marbled bds, gilt spine. VG (lt foxing). *Walcot.* $287/£185

CHAPPELL, EDWIN (ed). The Tangier Papers of Samuel Pepys. London: Navy Records Soc, 1935. 1st ed. 3 maps. Good + (ex-lib w/ink stamps, labels to spine) in blue/white buckram. *Edwards.* $39/£25

CHAPPELL, FRED. Dagon. NY: Harcourt, (1968). 1st ed. Dj spine faded, o/w VG. *Turlington.* $75/£48

CHAPPELL, FRED. The Gaudy Place. NY: Harcourt Brace Jovanovich, (1973). 1st ed. Fine in dj. *Godot.* $35/£23

CHAPPELL, FRED. The Inkling. NY: Harcourt, (1965). 1st ed. Fine in dj (tears). *Turlington.* $75/£48

CHAPPELL, FRED. It Is Time, Lord. NY: Atheneum, 1963. 1st ed, 1st bk. NF in dj (sl soiling). *Chapel Hill.* $125/£81

CHAPPELL, FRED. Wind Mountain. Baton Rouge: LSU, 1979. 1st ed. Fine in dj. *Pharos.* $30/£19

CHAPPELL, FRED. The World Between the Eyes. Baton Rouge: LA State Univ, 1971. 1st ed. Inscribed. VF in dj. *Pharos.* $85/£55

CHAPPELL, WARREN. A Short History of the Printed Word. NY: Knopf, 1970. 1st ed. Fine in dj. *Second Life.* $35/£23

CHAPPLE, JOE MITCHELL. To Bagdad and Back. Boston: Chapple, 1928. 1st ed. 34 plts (2 color). Worn, ex-lib, #, o/w VG. *Worldwide.* $30/£19

CHARAKA CLUB. Proceedings of.... NY, 1903-1985. Vols 1-12. VG set (some spines lt soiled). *Goodrich.* $1,195/£771

CHARAKA CLUB. Proceedings of...Volume 2. NY: Wood, 1906. Ltd ed, #33/315. Linen-backed bds (lt soiled). Internally Fine. *Goodrich.* $150/£97

CHARAKA CLUB. Proceedings of...Volume 3. NY, 1910. Ltd ed. Sound (ex-lib). *Goodrich.* $115/£74

CHARAKA CLUB. Proceedings of...Volume 3. NY: Wood, 1910. Ltd ed. #275/350. Linen-backed bds (soiled; bds chipped). Internally Fine. *Goodrich.* $125/£81

CHARAKA CLUB. Proceedings of...Volume 4. NY, 1916. Ltd ed. Sound (ex-lib). *Goodrich.* $115/£74

CHARAKA CLUB. Proceedings of...Volume 4. NY, 1916. Ltd ed. Sound (ex-lib). *Goodrich.* $115/£74

CHARAKA CLUB. Proceedings of...Volume 5. NY, 1919. Good. *Goodrich.* $85/£55

CHARAKA CLUB. Proceedings of...Volume 8. NY: Columbia Univ Press, 1938. 1st Eng trans. Linen-backed bds (lt soiled). Internally Fine. *Goodrich.* $115/£74

CHARAKA CLUB. Proceedings of...Volume 9. NY, 1938. (Spine dusty; fr hinge beginning to split.) *Goodrich.* $95/£61

CHARAKA CLUB. Proceedings of...Volume 9. NY, 1938. Ltd ed. Good. *Fye.* $125/£81

CHARAKA CLUB. Proceedings of...Volume 10. NY, 1941. Good. *Goodrich.* $75/£48

CHARAKA CLUB. Proceedings of...Volume 12. NY, 1985. *Goodrich.* $75/£48

CHARBONNEAUX, JEAN (preface). Treasures of the Louvre. London: Weidenfeld and Nicolson, 1966. 2 vols. 120 tipped-in color plts. Djs (spines sl yellowed; sm tear vol 2). *Edwards.* $116/£75

CHARBONNEAUX, JEAN. Greek Bronzes. London: Elek, (1962). 32 plts. Good in dj (tattered). *Archaeologia.* $35/£23

CHARCOT, J.B. The Voyage of the 'Why Not?' in the Antarctic. London: Hodder & Stoughton, 1911. 1st Eng ed. Chart. Orig pict gilt cl (sl rubbed, fr bd bubbled). Good. *Walcot.* $233/£150

CHARCOT, J.M. Clinical Lectures on Diseases of the Nervous System Delivered at the Infirmary of La Salpetriere. Vol 3. T. Savill (trans). London, 1889. xviii,438pp; 86 woodcuts. (Spine ends, corners sl worn.) *Whitehart.* $140/£90

CHARCOT, J.M. Clinical Lectures on Senile and Chronic Diseases. W.S. Tuke (trans). London: New Sydenham Soc, 1881. xvi,307pp; 6 plts. Spine marked, sl defective, o/w VG. *Whitehart.* $147/£95

CHARCOT, J.M. Clinical Lectures on Senile and Chronic Diseases. London, 1881. 1st Eng trans. 303pp. Good. *Fye.* $200/£129

CHARCOT, J.M. Clinical Lectures on the Diseases of Old Age. NY, 1881. 1st Amer ed. 280pp. Good. *Fye.* $150/£97

CHARCOT, J.M. Lectures on Localisation of Cerebral and Spinal Diseases. London, 1883. 1st Eng trans. 341pp. Good. *Fye.* $300/£194

CHARDIN, JOHN. Sir John Chardin's Travels in Persia. London: Aronout Press, 1927. 3rd ed. #569/975. 7 plts (2 fldg). Untrimmed, unopened. Sl rubbed, o/w VG. *Worldwide.* $225/£145

CHARDON, FRANCOIS. Chardon's Journal at Fort Clark 1834-1839. Annie H. Abel (ed). Pierre, SD, 1932. 1st ed. 3 plts. Uncut, unopened. VG (sig). Howes C 303. *Oregon.* $140/£90

CHARLES, C.J. Elizabethan Interiors. London/NY, (1917). Ltd, numbered ed; presentation copy. 2 vols. Vellum-backed bds, 1/2 leather (mismatched bindings; lacks spine). *Argosy.* $150/£97

CHARLES, C.J. Elizabethan Interiors. NY: F. Greenfield, n.d. #481/500. 40 plts. 1/2 japon (soiled), cl bds (lt stained; sm dent). *Edwards.* $70/£45

CHARLES, C.J. Elizabethan Interiors. London: George Newnes, n.d. 1st ed. One of 800. 1/2 leather (spine, bds rubbed; tips worn). Rubber stamps, else VG. *Bookpress.* $150/£97

CHARLES, MRS. TOM. Tales of the Tularosa. Alamogordo, 1953. 1st ed in pict wraps. Signed. (Sl wear at cvr edges.) *Baade.* $60/£39

CHARLES, RAY and DAVID RITZ. Brother Ray. Ray Charles' Own Story. NY: Dial, 1978. 1st ed. Fine in Fine dj (short tears). *Beasley.* $35/£23

CHARLES, ROLLO. Continental Porcelain of the Eighteenth Century. London: Ernest Benn, (1964). 1st ed. 62 monochrome, 12 color plts. Good in dj (chipped). *Karmiole.* $50/£32

CHARLES, ROLLO. Continental Porcelain of the Eighteenth Century. London, 1964. 1st ed. 12 color, 64 b/w plts; map. (Fep sl soiled.) Dj (sl ragged). *Edwards.* $39/£25

CHARLES-PICARD, GILBERT (ed). Larousse Encyclopedia of Archaeology. Anne Ward (trans). NY: Putnam's, 1972. 1st ed. 40 color, 600 monochrome plts; pict eps. Fine in Fine dj. *Connolly.* $45/£29

CHARMET, RAYMOND and CLAUDE ROGER MARX. Ira Moskowitz. NY, 1966. Inscribed tp; frontis signed by artist. 63 facs plts (18 color, 45 duotones). VG in dj (torn). *Argosy.* $150/£97

CHARNAS, SUZY McKEE. Vampire Tapestry. NY: S&S, 1980. 1st ed. NF in VG + dj. *Parker.* $100/£65

CHARNOCK, JOHN. Biographia Navalis; or, Impartial Memoirs of the Lives and Characters of Officers...1660.... London, 1794-1798. 1st eds. 4 vols & 2 vols continuation. Lt foxing, o/w VG. Contemp 1/2 calf on marbled bds; spine gilt in compartments; ship devices; double lettering pieces (spine head vol II chipped, worn). *Edwards.* $1,163/£750

CHARRIERE, GEORGES. Scythian Art: Crafts of the Early Eurasian Nomads. NY, 1979. VG in dj. *Argosy.* $125/£81

CHARTERIS, EVAN. The Life and Letters of Sir Edmund Gosse. London, 1931. 1st ed. VG. *Words Etc.* $28/£18

CHARTERIS, LESLIE. Prelude for War. NY: DCC, 1938. 1st Amer ed. Spine stained, o/w VG in dj (chipping; short closed tears; wear). *Mordida.* $125/£81

CHARTERIS, LESLIE. The Saint Goes West. GC: DCC, 1942. 1st ed. VG in dj. *Else Fine.* $75/£48

CHARTERIS, LESLIE. The Saint in Miami. GC: DCC, 1940. 1st ed. VG in dj. *Else Fine.* $90/£58

CHARTERIS, LESLIE. The Saint Steps In. GC: DCC, 1943. 1st ed. NF in pict dj (minor chips spine corners). *Else Fine.* $85/£55

CHARVAT, WILLIAM. Literary Publishing in America: 1790-1850. Phila: Univ of PA Press, (1959). 2nd ptg. Fine in dj. *Bookpress.* $50/£32

CHARYN, JEROME. Once upon a Droshky. NY: McGraw-Hill, (1964). 1st ed, 1st bk. Ink price fep, else Fine in NF dj. *Hermitage.* $30/£19

CHARYN, JEROME. War Cries over Avenue C. NY: Donald Fine, (1985). 1st ptg. As New in Fine dj. *Aka.* $35/£23

CHASE, A.W. Dr. Chase's Recipes. Ann Arbor, 1872. 400pp. Good. *Fye.* $40/£26

CHASE, J. SMEATON. California Coast Trails. London: Grant Richards, 1913. 1st ed. VG- (sm hole 1st few pp; hinge starting). *Parker.* $37/£24

CHASE, J. SMEATON. California Desert Trails. Boston: Houghton Mifflin, (1919). Grn gilt-dec pict cl (extrems sl worn). NF (inscrip). *Harrington.* $40/£26

CHASE, J. SMEATON. Cone-Bearing Trees of the California Mountains. Chicago: McClurg, 1911. Pict orange cl (soiled, sl worn). *Bohling.* $25/£16

CHASE, J. SMEATON. Our Araby: Palm Springs and the Garden of the Sun. Pasadena: Star News, 1920. 1st ed. Pocket map. VG. *Book Market.* $75/£48

CHASE, J. SMEATON. The Penance of Magdalena and Other Tales of the California Missions. Boston: Houghton Mifflin, (1915). Pict bds. VG + . *Bohling.* $24/£15

CHASE, J. SMEATON. Yosemite Trails: Camp and Pack-Train.... Boston/NY: Houghton Mifflin, (March 1911). 16 plts (2 dbl); dbl map. Navy cl. Good (spine rubbed, dull; leaves roughly opened; ink notes). *Bohling.* $45/£29

CHASE, SALMON P. Inside Lincoln's Cabinet: The Civil War Diaries of Salmon P. Chase. David Donald (ed). NY, 1954. 1st ed. VG + in VG + dj. *Pratt.* $30/£19

CHASE, WILL HENRY. Pioneers of Alaska: The Trail Blazers of Bygone Days. Kansas City, 1951. 1st ed. Leatherette. Fine. *Artis.* $20/£13

CHASE, WILLIAM HENRY. Pioneers of Alaska. Kansas City, MO, (1951). VG (bds sl bowed). *Bohling.* $45/£29

CHATTERTON, E. KEBLE. Old Sea Paintings. London/NY: John Lane, The Bodley Head/Dodd, Mead, (1928). 1st ed. 109 plts (14 color). *Lefkowicz.* $175/£113

CHATTERTON, E. KEBLE. Old Ship Prints. London/NY, (1927). 1st ed. 105 plts (15 color). *Lefkowicz.* $165/£106

CHATTERTON, E. KEBLE. Steamship Models. London, 1924. 1st ed. One of 1000, numbered, signed. 128 plts. (Text foxed, cvrs soiled.) *Lefkowicz.* $175/£113

CHATTERTON, E. KEBLE. The Yachtsman's Pilot to the Harbours of England.... London, 1937. 3rd rev ed. 52 harbour plans. Eps sl foxed, o/w VG in dj (spine sunned). *Edwards.* $39/£25

CHATTERTON, FREDERICK. Shop Fronts. London, 1927. 1st ed. (Ex-lib; soiled; lower joint splitting.) *Edwards.* $70/£45

CHATTERTON, THOMAS. The Works. London: Ptd by Biggs & Cottle, 1803. 3 vols. Fldg plt; marbled eps, edges (lt browning). Contemp 1/2 calf, marbled bds, dec gilt ruled raised bands, leather spine labels (lt soiled, sl rubbed). *Edwards.* $194/£125

CHATTERTON, THOMAS. The Works. Robert Southey (ed). London: Longman & Rees, 1803. 1st ed. 3 vols. 3 frontispieces; 4 plts (1 fldg; tear to fold). 1/2 calf (rebacked; hinges reinforced). Vol II lacks 1st contents pg; foxing, o/w VG set. *Poetry.* $310/£200

CHATTO, WILLIAM ANDREW. Facts and Speculations on the Origin and History of Playing Cards. London: Smith, 1848. 1st ed. 32pp ads at end; 26 wood engrs (2 color) & facs. Purple cl (spine faded, rubbed), gilt, blindstamped. VG. *Houle.* $350/£226

CHATTO, WILLIAM ANDREW. A Treatise on Wood Engraving. London, 1861. New ed. xvi + 664pp (prelims sl spotted). Morocco-backed bds (sl soiled, worn), dec gilt spine (sl rubbed). *Edwards.* $116/£75

CHATWIN, BRUCE and PAUL THEROUX. Patagonia Revisited. Salisbury: Michael Russell, 1985. 1st ed. VF in dj. *Limestone.* $35/£23

CHATWIN, BRUCE and PAUL THEROUX. Patagonia Revisited. Russell, 1985. 1st ed. One of 250 specially bound, signed by both authors. As New in tissue dj. *Fine Books.* $285/£184

CHATWIN, BRUCE and PAUL THEROUX. Patagonia Revisited. Boston: Houghton Mifflin, 1986. 1st Amer ed. Fine in Fine dj. *Revere.* $40/£26

CHATWIN, BRUCE. In Patagonia. Summit Books, 1977. 1st Amer ed, 1st bk. Fine in NF dj (closed tears; chip). *Fine Books.* $110/£71

CHATWIN, BRUCE. In Patagonia. Cape, 1977. 1st UK ed, 1st bk. NF in dj. *Sclanders.* $465/£300

CHATWIN, BRUCE. On the Black Hill. London: Cape, 1982. 1st ed. Fine in dj. *Rees.* $70/£45

CHATWIN, BRUCE. On the Black Hill. Cape, 1982. 1st UK ed. Fine in dj. *Lewton.* $43/£28

CHATWIN, BRUCE. Utz. London: Cape, 1988. 1st ed. Fine in dj. *Rees.* $31/£20

CHATWIN, BRUCE. Utz. Cape, 1988. 1st UK ed. Fine in dj. *Lewton.* $23/£15

CHATWIN, BRUCE. The Viceroy of Ouidah. Summit, 1980. 1st Amer ed. Fine in dj. *Fine Books.* $38/£25

CHATWIN, BRUCE. The Viceroy of Ouidah. London: Cape, 1980. 1st ed. Fine in dj (sl rubbed). *Rees.* $62/£40

CHATWIN, BRUCE. The Viceroy of Ouidah. London: Cape, 1980. 1st ed. VF in dj. *Limestone.* $75/£48

CHATWIN, BRUCE. What Am I Doing Here? Cape, 1989. 1st UK ed. Fine in dj. *Lewton.* $28/£18

CHATZIDAKIS, MANOLIS. Greece: Byzantine Mosaics. NY: NYGS, 1959. 32 full-pg color plts. VG in dj. *Argosy.* $60/£39

CHAUCER, GEOFFREY. The Canterbury Tales. NY, (1934). NF in dj (tears, sl sunned). *Polyanthos.* $65/£42

CHAUCER, GEOFFREY. The Canterbury Tales. Rendered into Modern English Verse by Frank Ernest Hill. London: LEC, 1934. 1/1500 numbered, signed by George W. Jones (type designer). 2 vols. Frontis port. Pict bds. VG in bd slipcase. *Argosy.* $175/£113

CHAUCER, GEOFFREY. The Canterbury Tales...Done into Modern English Verse by Frank Ernest Hill. NY: LEC, 1946. 1/1500 numbered, signed by Arthur Szyk (illus). 1 dbl-pg color plt. VG in patterned bd slipcase. *Argosy.* $250/£161

CHAUCER, GEOFFREY. The Complete Works. Walter W. Skeat (ed). Oxford: Clarendon, 1952. 2nd ed. 7 vols. Fine in djs. *Petersfield.* $326/£210

CHAUCER, GEOFFREY. The Nun's Priest's Tale Newly Rendered into Modern English by Nevill Coghill. London, Christmas 1950. Ltd to 1000, card loosely inserted. Fine in greaseproof wrapper. *Waterfield.* $39/£25

CHAUCER, GEOFFREY. The Prioress's Tale. Astolat Press, 1902. One of 500. Frontis. Teg. Prelims dknd, o/w VG in gilt-dec vellum. *Poetry.* $31/£20

CHAUCER, GEOFFREY. Troilus and Cressida. George Philip Krapp (rendered by). London: LEC, 1939. Ltd to 1500 numbered, signed by George W. Jones (ptr). White ptd linen over brn dec bds. Fine in slipcase (rubbed). *Karmiole.* $75/£48

CHAUDRON, A. DE V. Chaudron's Spelling Book. Mobile: S.H. Goetzel, 1865. 'Fourth Edition—Thirtieth Thousand,' so stated. Full-pg frontis engr, tp vignette, 48pp. Orig ptd wraps. Angular hle pp 15-16, affecting few words, o/w Fine. *Chapel Hill.* $350/£226

CHAVASSE, PYE HENRY. Advice to a Wife on the Management of Her Own Health.... NY, c. 1873. 1st Amer ed. 273pp. Good. *Fye.* $50/£32

CHAVASSE, PYE HENRY. The Physical Training of Children with a Preliminary Dissertation by F.H. Getschel, M.D. Phila, 1871. 1st ed. 368pp. Good. *Fye.* $75/£48

CHAVEZ, FRAY ANGELICO. Coronado's Friars. Washington: Academy of Am Franciscan History, 1968. 1st ed. NF. *Parker.* $75/£48

CHAYEFSKY, PADDY. The Goddess. NY: S&S, 1958. 1st ed. NF in dj (sl wear). *Antic Hay.* $45/£29

CHEESMAN, EVELYN. Islands Near the Sun. London, 1927. Dec cl cvrs. *Lewis.* $43/£28

CHEEVER, HENRY T. The Whale and His Captors. NY: Harper, 1850. 314pp + (6)pp ads. (Foxing.) Fine. *Lefkowicz.* $225/£145

CHEEVER, JOHN. The Brigadier and the Golf Widow. NY: Harper, (1964). 1st ed. Signed. Fine in NF dj. *Reese.* $185/£119

CHEEVER, JOHN. Bullet Park. NY: Knopf, 1969. 1st ed. Signed. Fine in dj. *Antic Hay.* $150/£97

CHEEVER, JOHN. The Enormous Radio and Other Stories. NY: Funk & Wagnalls, 1953. 1st ed. Nice (sl shelf rubbed) in dj (lt worn). *Reese.* $150/£97

CHEEVER, JOHN. The Enormous Radio and Other Stories. London: Gollancz, 1953. 1st Eng ed. Fine in dj (lt soiled, internally repaired tears, reinforcement). *Heller.* $125/£81

CHEEVER, JOHN. Homage to Shakespeare. Stevenson, CT: Country Squires Books, (1968). 1st ed, ltd to 150 numbered, signed. Fine in dj (lt browned, sm soil mks, else NF). *Godot.* $225/£145

CHEEVER, JOHN. Homage to Shakespeare. Stevenson, CT: Country Squires Books, (1968). 1st ed. #56/150, signed. Blue cl. Fine in lavender dj, paper label. *Chapel Hill.* $300/£194

CHEEVER, JOHN. The Housebreaker of Shady Hill and Other Stories. Harper, 1958. 1st ed. NF in NF dj. *Fine Books.* $85/£55

CHEEVER, JOHN. The Leaves, the Lion-Fish and the Bear. L.A.: Sylvester & Orphanos, 1980. 1st ed. One of 300 numbered, signed (of 330). Dec bds. Fine. *Reese.* $125/£81

CHEEVER, JOHN. The Letters of John Cheever. Benjamin Cheever (ed). London: Cape, 1989. 1st UK ed. Fine in dj. *Virgo.* $28/£18

CHEEVER, JOHN. The National Pastime. L.A.: Sylvester & Orphanos, 1982. 1st separate ed. One of 300 numbered, signed (of 330). Pict cl. Sl crease 1 leaf, else Fine. *Reese.* $75/£48

CHEEVER, JOHN. Oh, What a Paradise It Seems. NY: Knopf, 1982. 1st ed. VF in dj. *Pharos.* $30/£19

CHEEVER, JOHN. Some People, Places, and Things That Will Not Appear in My Next Novel. London: Gollancz, 1961. 1st Eng ed. Fine in dj. *Heller.* $85/£55

CHEEVER, JOHN. The Stories of John Cheever. NY: Knopf, 1978. 1st ed. Signed. Fine in NF dj. *Beasley.* $150/£97

CHEEVER, JOHN. The Stories of John Cheever. NY, 1978. Signed presentation. Fine (spine sl rubbed) in Fine dj. *Polyanthos.* $85/£55

CHEEVER, JOHN. The Wapshot Chronicle. Harper, 1957. 1st ed. Fine in NF dj. *Fine Books.* $95/£61

CHEEVER, JOHN. The Wapshot Scandal. NY: Harper & Row, 1963. 1st ed. NF in NF dj (sl wear). *Revere.* $40/£26

CHEKHOV, ANTON. The Selected Letters of Anton Chekhov. Lillian Hellman (ed). Sidonie K. Lederer (trans). NY: Farrar, Straus, (1955). 1st ed. NF in dj (sl rubbed). *Pharos.* $30/£19

CHEKHOV, ANTON. The Selected Letters of Anton Chekhov. Lillian Hellman (ed). Sidonie Lederer (trans). NY: Farrar, Straus, (1955). 1st ed. Blue cl. Name, else NF in dj (lt worn). *Chapel Hill.* $60/£39

CHENERY, WILLIAM E. (ed). Home Entertaining: Amusements for Everyone. Boston: Lothrop, Lee & Shepard, (1912). 1st ed. Color pict blue cl. VG. *Petrilla.* $20/£13

CHENERY, WILLIAM H. The Fourteenth Regiment Rhode Island Heavy Artillery.... Providence: Snow & Farnham, 1898. 1st ed. Frontis port, 343pp. Orig red cl. Spine faded, lt stains, else VG. *Chapel Hill.* $325/£210

CHENEVIERE, ANTOINE. Russian Furniture. NY: Vendome Press, (1988). 1st Amer ed. Frontis. Bkpl; else Fine. *Bookpress.* $65/£42

CHENEY, SHELDON. The Open-Air Theatre. NY: Mitchell Kennerley, 1918. 1st ed. 50 photo plts. Tp tear, dj lacks 2 inches to spine, o/w Fine. *Artis.* $15/£10

CHENEY, SHELDON. Stage Decoration. London: Chapman & Hall, 1928. 1st ed. Frontis, 127 plts. 1-inch tear fr hinge, else VG. *Bookpress.* $125/£81

CHERRY, KELLY. Sick and Full of Burning. NY: Viking, (1974). 1st ed, 1st bk. Fine in NF dj (crease). *Reese.* $35/£23

CHERRY-GARRARD, APSLEY. The Worst Journey in the World. London: Constable & Co, (1922). 2 vols. 1st ed. 10 lg fldg panoramas. Orig blue cl. VG. *High Latitude.* $990/£639

CHERRY-GARRARD, APSLEY. The Worst Journey in the World. Constable, 1922. 1st ed. 2 vols, 8vo. lxiv,300; viii,301-585, 10 lg fldg panoramas. Linen-backed spine, blue paper-cvrd bds. Dampstains Vol 2 bds, plt sl frayed fr edge; but Good+. *Walcot.* $698/£450

CHERRY-GARRARD, APSLEY. The Worst Journey in the World. London: C&W, 1952. 9 plts, 4 maps. Edges sl spotted. Dj. *Hollett.* $54/£35

CHERRY-GARRARD, APSLEY. The Worst Journey in the World. NY: George H. Doran, n.d. (1923). 2 vols. 1st US ed. Bound from sheets of 1st London ed, identical except for omitting 10 fldg panoramas and 2 sentences in preface; preface dated 1923 instead of 1922. Orig linen backed papered bds; paper spine labels. Exceptionally Fine in orig ptd djs (minor chipping to upper, lower edges; sm hole in both djs over spines). *High Latitude.* $650/£419

CHESHIRE, FRANK. The Scientific Temperance Hand-Book for Temperance Teachers and Advocates. London, ca 1890. 1st ed. 285pp. Good. *Fye.* $60/£39

CHESLEY, LARRY. Seven Years in Hanoi: A POW Tells His Story. Salt Lake City: Bookcraft, (1973). Stated 1st ed. Fine in NF dj (sm wrinkle; sl scuffing; price-clipped). *Aka.* $45/£29

CHESNEY, FRANCIS RAWDON. Narrative of the Euphrates Expedition.... London: Longmans, Green, 1868. 1st ed. 8vo. Fldg frontis, xviii,564,24pp, partly unopened (2 leaves torn across, repaired; bkpl, label), 45 litho plts, 2 maps (1 color fldg in pocket). Gilt cl (sl stained, faded; recased). *Hollett.* $853/£550

CHESNUT, MARY. The Private Mary Chesnut: The Unpublished Civil War Diaries. C. Vann Woodward and Elisabeth Muhlenfeld (eds). NY: OUP, 1984. 1st ed. NF in dj. *Cahan.* $35/£23

CHESNUTT, CHARLES W. The Colonel's Dream. NY, 1905. 1st ed, 2nd state w/correct spelling of name on spine. VG (ex-lib, spine #; bkpl removed, offset rep; # rear pastedown; sl wear; cvr spotting). *King.* $295/£190

CHESNUTT, CHARLES W. The Colonel's Dream. NY: Doubleday, Page & Co., 1905. 1st ed. Red cl. VG+. *Chapel Hill.* $325/£210

CHESNUTT, CHARLES W. The Conjure Woman. Boston/NY: Houghton, Mifflin, 1899. 1st ed, 1st bk. 12mo, 229pp. Brn pict cl. VG (bkpl, sig; spine sl dknd). *Chapel Hill.* $500/£323

CHESTER, ALFRED. The Exquisite Corpse. NY, 1967. 1st Amer ed. Fine in Fine dj. *Polyanthos.* $35/£23

CHESTER, GEORGE RANDOLPH. Get-Rich-Quick Wallingford. Phila: Altemus, 1908. 1st ed. Spine flaking; musty odor, o/w Fine. *Beasley.* $100/£65

CHESTER, SAMUEL HALL. Pioneer Days in Arkansas. Richmond, VA: Presbyterian Committee of Pub, (1927). VG in ptd wrappers. *Bohling.* $175/£113

CHESTERFIELD, LORD. Principles of Politeness and of Knowing the World. (Carlisle, PA): Ptd by Alexander & Philips, 1809. 1st ed. Calf-backed marbled bds. Poor (tp worn, stained; lacks fep, blanks, half-title). *Pharos.* $40/£26

CHESTERFIELD. Travestie; or School for Modern Manners. London: for Thomas Tegg, 1808. Title, 2ff, 70pp, 1f, engr color fldg frontis, 9 engr plts (1 fldg), by Rowlandson. Half calf (sl rubbed). *Marlborough.* $388/£250

CHESTERTON, G.K. Alarms and Discursions. NY, 1911. 1st Amer ed. (Ink inscrip; news clipping affixed inside back cvr; sl wear.) *King.* $25/£16

CHESTERTON, G.K. The Ballad of the White Horse. London: Methuen, 1911. 1st ed. Uncut. Grn cl (extrems sl worn, rubbed; sig bkpl). *Cox.* $39/£25

CHESTERTON, G.K. The Barbarism of Berlin. Cassell, 1914. 1st UK ed. VG (foxing) in wrappers as issued. *Williams.* $23/£15

CHESTERTON, G.K. Chaucer. Faber, 1932. 1st UK ed. NF in dj (browned, rubbed; closed tears). *Williams.* $70/£45

CHESTERTON, G.K. The Club of Queer Trades. NY, 1905. 1st Amer ed. (Cvr design worn away, spine dknd, extrems rubbed, author's obit affixed to feps.) *King.* $25/£16

CHESTERTON, G.K. The Coloured Lands. London: Sheed & Ward, 1938. 1st ed. Cl-backed patterned bds (sl rubbed). *Hollett.* $54/£35

CHESTERTON, G.K. The Coloured Lands.... NY: Sheed & Ward, 1938. 1st Amer ed. Grn cl. Good (owner stamp, 2 old tape mks feps) in dj (nicks; old strengthening verso). *Reese.* $50/£32

CHESTERTON, G.K. The Common Man. Sheed & Ward, 1950. 1st UK ed. NF in dj. *Williams.* $31/£20

CHESTERTON, G.K. Criticisms and Appreciations of Charles Dickens' Works. Dent, 1911. 1st UK ed. VG+ (sm bkpl). *Williams.* $70/£45

CHESTERTON, G.K. Five Types. Humphreys, 1910. 1st ed. Parchment-backed bds (sl mkd). Contents NF. *Whiteson.* $23/£15

CHESTERTON, G.K. The Glass Walking Stick. Methuen, 1955. 1st UK ed. Fine in NF dj. *Williams.* $31/£20

CHESTERTON, G.K. Greybeards at Play. London: Sheed & Ward, 1933. 1st UK ed. Fine (lacks dj). *Williams.* $19/£12

CHESTERTON, G.K. Heretics. London: Bodley Head, 1908. VG. *Hollett.* $39/£25

CHESTERTON, G.K. The Incredulity of Father Brown. London: Cassell, 1926. 1st ed. VG. *Hollett.* $101/£65

CHESTERTON, G.K. The Innocence of Father Brown. Cassell, 1911. 1st ed. Good. *Fine Books.* $195/£126

CHESTERTON, G.K. The Judgement of Dr. Johnson: A Comedy in Three Acts. London: Sheed & Ward, (1927). 1st ed. (Spine gilt sl dull.) *Sadlon.* $15/£10

CHESTERTON, G.K. The Man Who Was Thursday. D-M, 1908. 1st Amer ed. VG+. *Fine Books.* $70/£45

CHESTERTON, G.K. The Man Who Was Thursday. NY: Dodd, Mead, 1910. Later ed. Dk grn half-calf leather; cl binding; raised panels; leather title labels on spine; marbled eps. VG (wear). *Antic Hay.* $45/£29

CHESTERTON, G.K. Manalive. Nelson, 1912. 1st ed. Dec cl. Good. *Whiteson.* $23/£15

CHESTERTON, G.K. Manalive. NY: John Lane, 1912. 1st ed. Red cl. VG (sm bkpl fr pastedown). *Antic Hay.* $40/£26

CHESTERTON, G.K. The Napoleon of Notting Hill. John Lane, 1904. 1st UK ed. VG (sl spine fraying; browning bds). *Williams.* $54/£35

CHESTERTON, G.K. Orthodoxy. Bodley Head, 1909. 1st UK ed. VG (sl nicking, fading to spine). *Williams.* $31/£20

CHESTERTON, G.K. The Queen of Seven Swords. Sheed & Ward, 1926. 1st UK ed. VG+ in dj (sl dent upper cvr). *Williams.* $28/£18

CHESTERTON, G.K. The Resurrection of Rome. London: Hodder & Stoughton, (1930). 1st ed. VG in dj. *Hollett.* $39/£25

CHESTERTON, G.K. The Return of Don Quixote. London: C&W, 1927. 1st ed. (Few spots; feps lt browned; extrems rubbed). *Hollett.* $31/£20

CHESTERTON, G.K. The Return of Don Quixote. Chatto, 1927. 1st UK ed. VG (spine top bumped; bkpl). *Williams.* $39/£25

CHESTERTON, G.K. Robert Browning. London: Macmillan, 1903. 1st ed. Good (bkpl). *Cox.* $28/£18

CHESTERTON, G.K. The Scandal of Father Brown. London et al: Cassell, (1935). 1st UK ed. Name, address stamped fr pastedown, o/w NF. *Bernard.* $250/£161

CHESTERTON, G.K. Simplicity and Tolstoy. Humphreys, 1912. 1st ed. Soft suede cvrs. Dec spine sl rubbed, else Good. *Whiteson.* $23/£15

CHESTERTON, G.K. The Surprise. NY, 1953. 1st Amer ed. Fine (sl sunned); no dj as issued. *Polyanthos.* $30/£19

CHESTERTON, G.K. The Sword of Wood. London: Elkin Mathews & Marrot, 1928. #398/500 signed. Fine in dj. *Limestone.* $135/£87

CHESTERTON, G.K. The Wisdom of Father Brown. J. Lane, 1915. 1st Amer ed. Stamps on pastedowns, else VG. *Fine Books.* $45/£29

CHESTNUT, CHARLES W. The Conjure Woman. Boston/NY: HMCo, 1899. 1st Amer ed. Spine bottom, bds lt worn, else VG. *Between The Covers.* $350/£226

CHESTNUT, MARY BOYKIN. A Diary from Dixie. Ben Ames Williams (ed). Boston: Houghton Mifflin, 1950. 2nd, best ed. VG. *Mcgowan.* $45/£29

CHESTON, CHARLES. Evelyn Cheston. London: Faber & Faber, (1931). Frontis; 49 plts, guards. Red gilt cl. Good. *Karmiole.* $65/£42

CHETWOOD, CHARLES. Genito-Urinary and Venereal Diseases. Phila, 1892. 1st ed. 178pp. Good. *Fye.* $35/£23

CHETWOOD, W.R. A General History of the Stage...Down to the Present Time. London: for W. Owen, 1749. 1st ed. Later 1/2 calf; spine gilt. Fine. *Dramatis Personae.* $300/£194

CHEVALIER, MAURICE. I Remember It Well. Macmillan, 1970. 1st ed. Signed. NF in NF dj. *Bishop.* $40/£26

CHEVES, W.R. Snow Ridges and Pillboxes. n.p., 1945. 1st ed. VG. *Clark.* $150/£97

CHEYNE, GEORGE. The English Malady. London, 1734. 3rd ed. xxxii,370pp (corner torn fep; pencil mks in margins; prelims sl foxed). Old calf (weak joints). *Whitehart.* $372/£240

CHEYNE, GEORGE. An Essay of Health and Long Life. London: G. Strahan & J. Leake, 1725. 2nd ed. xx,(24),232pp. Old calf, blind-stamped tooling, red lettering piece. Bkpl, prelim margins lt stained, else VG. *Hemlock.* $150/£97

CHEYNE, GEORGE. An Essay of Health and Long Life. London, 1725. 5th ed. xx,(xxiv),232pp. New leather spine, paper-cvrd bds. Bottom margin tp defective but neatly repaired; inscrip, o/w VG. *Whitehart.* $233/£150

CHEYNE, GEORGE. An Essay of Health and Long Life. London, 1725. 6th ed. T.p.,(i)dedication, (xx)preface, (xxi)contents, 232pp (eps sl spotted; some margins sl grubby, sl loss outer margin ppC2 not affecting text). Full speckled calf (rebacked; upper bd detached, spine bumped). *Edwards.* $132/£85

CHEYNE, GEORGE. An Essay of Health and Long Life. London, 1745. 9th ed. xlvii,232pp (eps sl foxed). Full calf (sl rubbed). *Whitehart.* $109/£70

CHEYNE, GEORGE. An Essay on Health and Long Life. London, 1724. 1st ed. Contemp calf (joints cracked). *Goodrich.* $295/£190

CHEYNE, GEORGE. The Natural Method of Cureing the Diseases of the Body.... London: G. Strahan, 1742. 3rd ed. (xviii),316pp. Contemp full calf; spine w/raised bands. Clean (ends chipped; fr hinge splitting). *White.* $147/£95

CHEYNE, WILLIAM. Lister and His Achievement. London, 1925. 1st ed. Good. *Fye.* $40/£26

CHEYNEY, PETER. Ladies Won't Wait. Dodd, 1951. 1st ed. Bds lt soiled; sl top edge wear, else NF in dj (lt wear). *Murder.* $35/£23

CHIANG YEE. Chin-Pao and the Giant Pandas. London: Country Life, 1939. 1st ed. 84pp, 3 color plts. VG in dj (chips, edgetears, sl soiled). *Hollett.* $70/£45

CHIANG YEE. Chin-Pao at the Zoo. London: Methuen, 1942. 3rd ed. Color frontis, 96pp. VG in dj (price-clipped; edge chips). *Hollett.* $54/£35

CHIANG YEE. Dabbitse. London: Transatlantic Arts, 1944. 1st ed. 64pp, 4 color plts. VG in dj (sl rubbed, mkd; edgetear). *Hollett.* $70/£45

CHIANG YEE. The Men of the Burma Road. London: Methuen, 1942. 1st ed. Color frontis; 8 plts. VG (fly-leaves sl spotted) in dj (few edge tears). *Hollett.* $47/£30

CHIANG YEE. The Silent Traveller in Oxford. London: Methuen, 1944. 1st ed. 12 color, 8 monotone plts. VG in dj. *Hollett.* $39/£25

CHIANG YEE. The Silent Traveller in Paris. London: Methuen, 1956. 1st ed. 16 plts (12 color). VG in dj. *Hollett.* $47/£30

CHIANG YEE. The Silent Traveller in San Francisco. London: Methuen, 1964. 1st ed. 16 color plts. VG in dj. *Hollett.* $47/£30

CHIANG YEE. The Silent Traveller in the Yorkshire Dales. London: Methuen, 1942. 4th ed. Press cutting on feps. VG in dj (price-clipped). *Hollett.* $39/£25

CHICHESTER, FRANCIS. Gipsy Moth Circles the World. London: Hodder & Stoughton, 1967. 1st ed. 53 plts (14 color). VG in dj. *Hollett.* $39/£25

Child's Companion and Juvenile Instructor. London: RTS, 1855. Color ptd frontis (sl stain margins). *Petersfield.* $23/£15

Child's Guide. Springfield: G&C Merriam, 1842. Stereotype Ed. 12mo. Full-pg wood engr frontis, viii,180pp + 1pg ad lower bds. Pict label on bds (rubbed), 3/4 leather spine (cracked). In all, Good (foxing). *Hobbyhorse.* $75/£48

Child's Illustrated Gift Book. NY: Leavitt & Allen, 1863. 1st ed. 4to, 96pp. Red dec cl, gold-stamped. Short tear lower spine, else VG. *Godot.* $185/£119

Child's Instructor, or Picture Alphabet. Glasgow: Lumsden, n.d. (ca 1815). 16mo. 16 leaves. Oval woodcut tp; 1st, last leaves pasted on wrapper. Plain buff wrappers. VF. *Hobbyhorse.* $275/£177

Child's Picture Book. Concord, NH: Rufus Merrill, n.d. (ca 1850). 6 parts in 1. 16mo. 96pp + 1pg ad lower wrapper. VF (gilt leather ex-libris w/offset spot fep; lower spine sl splitting) in pict stiff paper wrappers. *Hobbyhorse.* $150/£97

CHILD, CHARLES, JR. Sterility and Conception. NY, 1926. 1st ed. Good. *Fye.* $50/£32

CHILD, HEATHER. Decorative Maps. London: Studio, 1956. 1st ed. VG in dj. *Michael Taylor.* $34/£22

CHILD, LYDIA MARIA. Letters from New York. NY: Francis, 1845. 1st ed, 1st state w/1st entry on pii Philothea with terminal ads. 287pp + ads. Pub's cl. Very nice. BAL 3152. *Second Life.* $85/£55

CHILD, LYDIA MARIA. Letters of.... Boston: Houghton, Mifflin, 1883. 1st ed. 280pp + 16pp cat; engr port. Grn cl, grn coated eps. VG. BAL 3220. *Second Life.* $65/£42

CHILDERS, ERSKINE (ed). The Riddle of the Sands. Barre: Imprint Society, 1971. #107/1950 numbered, signed by John O'Connor (illus). Half leather-backed dec bds. Bkpl, else Fine in pub's slipcase. *Hermitage.* $85/£55

CHILDERS, JAMES SAXON. A White Man and a Black Man in the Deep South. NY: Farrar & Rinehart, 1936. 1st ed. VF in dj (2 sm edge chips). *Else Fine.* $65/£42

Children of the Bible. NY: Amer Tract Soc, n.d. (ca 1870). 12mo. 52pp; 8 full-pg wood engrs. Blind-stamped cl on bds (corners rounded), gilt. Fine (ink sig). *Hobbyhorse.* $75/£48

Children's Picture Fable-Book. Boston: Ticknor & Fields, 1860. 1st Amer ed. Sm 8vo. Full-pg engr frontis, viii,278 + (2pp) index; 60 illus by Harrison Weir; engrs by John Greenaway. 3/4 grain morocco w/corners; marbled paper on bds; 5 raised bands, gilt; dec eps. Fine (sl rubbed edges, cvrs). *Hobbyhorse.* $225/£145

Children's Toys of Yesterday. (By Geoffrey C. Holme.) London: The Studio, 1932. 1st ed. Spine chipped, else VG in pict wrappers. *Glenn.* $75/£48

CHILDRESS, ALICE. Like One of the Family...Conversations from a Domestic's Life. NY: Independence Publ, (1956). 1st ed, 1st bk. Port. Red/gray bds. VG. *Petrilla.* $50/£32

CHILDRESS, MARK. A World Made of Fire. NY: Knopf, 1984. 1st ed. VF in dj. *Pharos.* $30/£19

CHILDRESS, MARK. A World Made of Fire. NY: Knopf, 1984. 1st ed. 1st bk. Signed. Fine in dj. *Else Fine.* $95/£61

CHILDS, HARWOOD. The Nazi Primer. Harper Brothers, 1938. NF in VG dj. *Bishop.* $20/£13

CHILDS, MARY FAIRFAX. De Namin' ob de Twins and Other Sketches from Cotton Land. NY, 1908. 1st ed. Author presentation. Orig prospectus laid in. Fine. *Mcgowan.* $125/£81

CHILTON, C. (ed). The Sub-Antarctic Islands of New Zealand. London: Wellington, 1909. 1st ed. 2 vols. Map. Good (ex-lib, blind stamps, spine #s). *Walcot.* $209/£135

CHILTON, JOHN. Billies's Blues. NY: Stein & Day, (1975). (Bkst stamp 1/2 title.) Dj (tears, edgewear). *Aka.* $40/£26

CHILTON, JOHN. Who's Who of Jazz. Phila: Chilton, 1972. 1st US ed. Fine in Fine dj (short tears). *Beasley.* $65/£42

CHILVERS, HEDLEY A. The Story of De Beers. London, 1940. 2nd ed. 1 color plt, 68 photogravure plts (lt browning). Dj (browned, sl chipped). *Edwards.* $93/£60

CHINN, GEORGE M. The Machine Gun. Washington, 1951. 1st ed. Vol I only (of 3). Navy cl; gilt. Good+. *Edwards.* $62/£40

CHIPMAN, N.P. The Tragedy of Andersonville: Trial of Captain Henry Wirz, the Prison Keeper. (Sacramento, 1911). 2nd ed. *Ginsberg.* $75/£48

CHIPP, HERSCHEL B. and BRENDA RICHARDSON. Hundertwasser. Greenwich, CT: NYGS, (1968). Pict cl. VG. *Argosy.* $60/£39

CHIPPERFIELD, JIMMY. My Wild Life. NY: Putnam, 1976. 1st US ed. VG in VG dj. *October Farm.* $25/£16

CHISHOLM, A. STUART M. Recreations of a Physician. NY, 1914. VG. *Argosy.* $35/£23

CHITTENDEN, ABRAHAM. Orderly Book of Lieut. Abraham Chittenden...1776.... Hartford, CT: Privately ptd, 1922. 1st ed. *Ginsberg.* $50/£32

CHITTENDEN, FRED J. (ed). Dictionary of Gardening. London, 1951. 1st ed. 4 vols. Good in djs. *Henly.* $132/£85

CHITTENDEN, FRED J. (ed). Dictionary of Gardening. Oxford, 1974. 2nd ed. 4 vols+ supplement. Fine in djs. *Petersfield.* $233/£150

CHITTENDEN, HIRAM M. (ed). Life, Letters and Travels of Father Pierre Jean De Smet.... NY: Harper, 1905. 4 vols. (Sm emb lib stamps each vol; bkpls removed; lt chipping.) Howes C 392. *Ginsberg.* $600/£387

CHITTENDEN, HIRAM MARTIN. The American Fur Trade of the Far West. Stanford: Academic Rpts, 1954. 2 vols. Brn cl. NF in djs (sl chipped, spines dknd). Howes C 390. *Harrington.* $75/£48

Chitty Chitty Bang Bang. Random House, 1968. 19x24 cm. Gwen Gordon and Dave Chambers (illus). Pict bds. VG-. *Book Finders.* $150/£97

CHITTY, JOSEPH. A Practical Treatise on the Law of Contracts, Not Under Seal. Springfield: G. and C. Merriam, 1848. 7th Amer ed. Contemp sheep (rubbed). *Boswell.* $125/£81

CHOLMONDELEY-PENNELL, H. Fishing. London: Longmans, 1889. 2 vols. Pict cl bds (sl rubbed; vol 1 loose; foxing). *Petersfield.* $84/£54

CHOLMONDELEY-PENNELL, H. The Modern Practical Angler.... London: Routledge, c. 1870. 50 engrs. *Petersfield.* $54/£35

CHOPIN, KATE. The Awakening. Chicago: H. Stone, 1899. 1st Amer ed. Dec grn cl. Decent (owner stamp; lt crease rear cvr; soiled; spine dull). BAL 3246. *Agvent.* $750/£484

CHOPIN, KATE. Bayou Folk. Boston: Houghton, Mifflin, 1894. 1st ed. 313pp. Good (ex-lib, bkpl, stamp tp; spine faded; extrems worn). BAL 3244. *Second Life.* $300/£194

CHORD, JACK T. The Window Display Manual. Cincinnati: Display, (1931). 1st ed. Black silver-stamped cl. Good. *Karmiole.* $65/£42

CHORLTON, WILLIAM. The American Grape Grower's Guide. NY, 1856. 171pp+6pp ads (lt foxing, eps browned). Cl (faded, worn). *Sutton.* $65/£42

CHORLTON, WILLIAM. The American Grape Grower's Guide. NY: OJ, n.d. (c. 1852). (2nd ed.) xii,11-204pp+4pp ads. (Foxing; rep removed; worn, spotted, spine ends frayed.) *Bohling.* $45/£29

CHOUKRI, MOHAMED. Tennessee Williams in Tangier. Santa Barbara: Cadmus, 1979. 1st ed. #137/200 signed by Paul Bowles (trans) and Choukri. Frontis dwg. Fine in ptd white wraps, mtd cvr illus. *Chapel Hill.* $150/£97

CHRISMAN, HARRY E. The Ladder of Rivers. Denver, 1962. 1st ed. NF in dj (sl chipped, price-clipped). *Baade.* $50/£32

Christ Church Oxford. (By Charles L. Dodgson.) London: Hodder & Stoughton, 1911. 1st ed. Tipped-in color illus p152. Teg, rest uncut. Pub's white cl-backed blue bds, gilt-lettered spine (lt soiled; corners worn). *D & D.* $180/£116

CHRIST-JANER, ALBERT. Boardman Robinson. Univ Chicago, 1946. 126 plts (9 color). Sound in dj (frayed). *Ars Artis.* $54/£35

CHRIST-JANER, ALBERT. Boardman Robinson. Chicago: Univ of Chicago, 1946. 1st ed. 126 plts. VG in dj. *Cahan.* $50/£32

CHRISTENSEN, ERWIN O. Early American Wood Carving. Cleveland: World Pub, (1952). 1st ed. VG in dj. *Schoyer.* $30/£19

CHRISTENSEN, ERWIN O. The Index of American Design. NY: Macmillan, 1950. 1st ed. VG in dj (sl worn). *Bookpress.* $65/£42

CHRISTENSEN, ERWIN O. Primitive Art. NY: Crowell, (1955). 1st ed. 32 color plts, 348 photos. Black, red cl. Good in dj (sl chipped). *Karmiole.* $85/£55

CHRISTENSON, KATHRYN and KELVIN W. MILLER. Granlund: the Sculptor and His Work. St. Peter, MN: Gustavus Adolphus College, 1978. VG in dj. *Argosy.* $85/£55

CHRISTIAN, FRANCES and SUSANNE MASSIE (eds). Homes and Gardens in Old Virginia. Richmond: Garrett & Massie, 1950. 2nd ed. (Rubbed, spotted; name, text foxed.) *Bookpress.* $35/£23

CHRISTIANSEN, KEITH. Gentile da Fabriano. NY: Cornell Univ, 1982. 110 plts. Fine in Mint dj. *Europa.* $74/£48

CHRISTIE, AGATHA. The ABC Murders. NY: Dodd, Mead, 1936. 1st US ed. VG+. *Janus.* $45/£29

CHRISTIE, AGATHA. The Adventure of the Christmas Pudding. Collins, 1960. 1st ed. Fine in NF dj. *Fine Books.* $75/£48

CHRISTIE, AGATHA. The Adventure of the Christmas Pudding. London: Collins, 1960. 1st ed. Fine in dj. *Limestone.* $125/£81

CHRISTIE, AGATHA. And Then There Were None. NY: Dodd, Mead, 1940. 1st US ed. VG (stamp). *Janus.* $35/£23

CHRISTIE, AGATHA. Appointment with Death. London: Collins, 1938. 1st ed. VG (sunned spine; bkpl). *Janus.* $35/£23

CHRISTIE, AGATHA. At Bertram's Hotel. NY: Dodd, Mead, (1965). 1st US ed. Signed. Fine in dj (sl worn, price-clipped). *Second Life.* $150/£97

CHRISTIE, AGATHA. The Body in the Library. London: Collins, 1942. 1st UK ed. VG+ (ink name) in dj (spine sl worn). *Williams.* $543/£350

CHRISTIE, AGATHA. By the Pricking of My Thumbs. London: CCC, 1968. 1st ed. VG in VG dj. *Ming.* $31/£20

CHRISTIE, AGATHA. Cards on the Table. London: CCC, 1936. 1st ed. VG w/o dj. *Mordida.* $45/£29

CHRISTIE, AGATHA. Cat Among the Pigeons. London: Crime Club, (1959). 1st ed. VG in dj (spine extrems chipped). *Argosy.* $50/£32

CHRISTIE, AGATHA. Cat Among the Pigeons. London: CCC, 1959. 1st ed. Good in Good dj. *Ming.* $31/£20

CHRISTIE, AGATHA. The Clocks. Collins, 1963. 1st ed. Fine in VG+ dj (3 short tears). *Fine Books.* $30/£19

CHRISTIE, AGATHA. Come Tell Me How You Live. London: Collins, 1946. 1st UK ed. NF in VG dj (sl dusty). *Williams.* $116/£75

CHRISTIE, AGATHA. Death Comes as the End. London: Collins, 1945. 1st ed. NF in dj. *Limestone.* $165/£106

CHRISTIE, AGATHA. Death Comes as the End. London: Collins, 1945. 1st UK ed. VG+ (sl bumped) in VG dj (lt edgewear). *Williams.* $93/£60

CHRISTIE, AGATHA. Destination Unknown. London: Collins, (1954). 1st ed. Fine in dj (soiled). *Glenn.* $65/£42

CHRISTIE, AGATHA. Destination Unknown. London: CCC, 1954. 1st ed. VG in VG dj. *Ming.* $54/£35

CHRISTIE, AGATHA. Destination Unknown. London: Collins, 1954. 1st ed. Sig, else VG in dj. *Limestone.* $55/£35

CHRISTIE, AGATHA. Elephants Can Remember. London: Crime Club, (1972). 1st ed. Fine in dj. *Argosy.* $50/£32

CHRISTIE, AGATHA. Endless Night. London: CCC, 1967. 1st ed. VG in VG dj. *Ming.* $39/£25

CHRISTIE, AGATHA. Evil Under the Sun. NY: Dodd, Mead, 1941. 1st ed. VG. *Janus.* $35/£23

CHRISTIE, AGATHA. Evil Under the Sun. London: Collins, 1941. 1st ed. Pencil sig, else VG in dj (spine extrems sl chipped). *Limestone.* $635/£410

CHRISTIE, AGATHA. Five Little Pigs. London: Collins, 1942. 1st ed. VG in VG- dj (backstrip, extrems faded; sm chip fr panel). *Limestone.* $235/£152

CHRISTIE, AGATHA. Funerals Are Fatal. NY: Dodd-Mead, 1953. 1st ed. VF in dj (lt used). *Else Fine.* $60/£39

CHRISTIE, AGATHA. Hallowe'en Party. London: CCC, 1969. 1st ed. VG (writing fep) in VG dj (sm tears). *Ming.* $39/£25

CHRISTIE, AGATHA. Hercule Poirot's Christmas. London: Collins, 1939. 1st ed. VG (sl dusty, spine sl faded). *Limestone.* $150/£97

CHRISTIE, AGATHA. Hickory Dickory Dock. London: Collins, 1955. 1st ed. VG+ in dj. *Else Fine.* $30/£19

CHRISTIE, AGATHA. The Hollow. London: Collins, 1946. 1st ed. NF in VG dj (faded spine). *Janus.* $35/£23

CHRISTIE, AGATHA. The Hollow. London: CCC, 1946. 1st ed. Good in Good dj (rubbed). *Ming.* $78/£50

CHRISTIE, AGATHA. The Hound of Death. London: Odhams, (1933). 1st ed. Good (spine gilt dulled, edges sl spotted) in dj (chipped, repaired). *Ash.* $147/£95

CHRISTIE, AGATHA. The Labours of Hercules. London: Collins, 1947. 1st ed. Fine in VG- dj (internally repaired). *Limestone.* $140/£90

CHRISTIE, AGATHA. Miss Marple's Final Cases. London: CCC, 1979. 1st ed. Fine in dj. *Mordida.* $45/£29

CHRISTIE, AGATHA. Mrs. McGinty's Dead. London: Collins, 1952. 1st ed. VG+ in dj (sl chipped spine head). *Limestone.* $60/£39

CHRISTIE, AGATHA. The Murder at Hazelmoor. NY: Dodd, Mead, 1931. 1st Amer ed. Orange cl. Spine evenly faded, else Fine. *Godot.* $65/£42

CHRISTIE, AGATHA. The Murder at the Vicarage. NY: Dodd Mead, 1930. 1st Amer ed. Faded area spine top, o/w VG in dj (half-inch piece missing; closed tears). *Mordida.* $125/£81

CHRISTIE, AGATHA. A Murder Is Announced. NY: Dodd, Mead, 1950. 1st US ed. Fine in VG+ dj (lt edgewear, lt soiling). *Janus.* $100/£65

CHRISTIE, AGATHA. A Murder Is Announced. NY: Dodd, Mead, 1950. Softbound advance copy. NF (spine slant), bound in dj (spine sunned, closed tears). *Janus.* $65/£42

CHRISTIE, AGATHA. Murder Is Easy. London: Collins, 1939. 1st UK ed. VG+ (ink name) in dj (price-clipped, long closed tear; spine sl chipped). *Williams.* $930/£600

CHRISTIE, AGATHA. The Murder of Roger Ackroyd. London: Collins, 1926. 1st ed. Ink price fr pastedown; sm mks fore-edge; faint stain, o/w Fine w/o dj. *Mordida.* $450/£290

CHRISTIE, AGATHA. The Mystery of the Blue Train. NY: Dodd Mead, 1928. 1st Amer ed. Several pp w/internal stamps, o/w VG in dj (sl faded spine, creases). *Mordida.* $300/£194

CHRISTIE, AGATHA. N or M? NY: Dodd, Mead, 1941. 1st US ed. VG+ in VG dj (chipped). *Janus.* $85/£55

CHRISTIE, AGATHA. One Two Buckle My Shoe. London: Collins, 1940. 1st UK ed. VG in dj (price-clipped; ink name, address; nicks strengthened). *Williams.* $543/£350

CHRISTIE, AGATHA. Ordeal by Innocence. London: Collins, (1958). 1st ed. Fine in dj (lt soiled). *Glenn.* $65/£42

CHRISTIE, AGATHA. Ordeal By Innocence. London: Crime Club, (1958). 1st ed. VG in dj. *Argosy.* $85/£55

CHRISTIE, AGATHA. The Pale Horse. London: Collins, 1961. 1st ed. Fine in dj. *Else Fine.* $40/£26

CHRISTIE, AGATHA. Partners in Crime. NY: Dodd-Mead, 1929. 1st ed. NF. *Else Fine.* $65/£42

CHRISTIE, AGATHA. The Patriotic Murders. NY: Dodd, Mead, 1941. 1st US ed. VG+. *Janus.* $45/£29

CHRISTIE, AGATHA. Peril at End House. NY: Dodd, Mead, 1932. 1st US ed. VG+ (label; name). *Janus.* $30/£19

CHRISTIE, AGATHA. Poems. NY: Dodd, Mead, 1973. 1st US ed. Fine in orig glassine ptd wrapper (sl creased). *Williams.* $62/£40

CHRISTIE, AGATHA. Remembered Death. D-M, 1945. 1st ed. VG+ in dj (worn). *Fine Books.* $78/£50

CHRISTIE, AGATHA. The Road of Dreams. London: Bles, 1924. 1st UK ed. VG (spine label browned, chipped; inscrip). *Williams.* $302/£195

CHRISTIE, AGATHA. Sad Cypress. London: Collins, 1940. 1st ed. VG+ in NF dj. *Limestone.* $585/£377

CHRISTIE, AGATHA. The Seven Dials Mystery. London: Collins, 1929. 1st UK ed, 1st ptg. Black cl, red lettering. VG (sl bumping). *Williams.* $147/£95

CHRISTIE, AGATHA. The Sittaford Mystery. London: Collins, 1931. 1st UK ed. VG. *Williams.* $132/£85

CHRISTIE, AGATHA. Sparkling Cyanide. London: Collins, (1945). 1st ed. VG in dj (lacks lower spine, repaired on verso). *Argosy*. $100/£65

CHRISTIE, AGATHA. Sparkling Cyanide. London: CCC, 1945. 1st ed. VG in Good dj (rubbed). *Ming*. $109/£70

CHRISTIE, AGATHA. Sparkling Cyanide. London: Collins, 1945. 1st UK ed. VG+ in VG dj (sm scratch). *Williams*. $147/£95

CHRISTIE, AGATHA. Thirteen at Dinner. NY: Dodd, Mead, 1933. 1st US ed. VG (spine sunned). *Janus*. $45/£29

CHRISTIE, AGATHA. Towards Zero. London: Collins, 1944. 1st ed. Sig, else NF in dj. *Limestone*. $250/£161

CHRISTIE, AGATHA. Towards Zero. NY: Dodd, Mead, 1944. 1st US ed. VG (spine, edges sunned). *Janus*. $20/£13

CHRISTIE, AGATHA. Triple Threat. D-M, 1943. 1st ed. NF in VG- dj (spine wear). *Fine Books*. $85/£55

CHRISTIE, AGATHA. The Underdog. London: Readers Library, 1929. 1st UK ed. VG. *Lewton*. $85/£55

CHRISTIE, AGATHA. The Underdog. (With Blackman's Wood by E. Phillips Oppenheim). Readers Library, 1929. 1st UK ed. VG, no dj. *Lewton*. $93/£60

CHRISTIE, AGATHA. The Witness for the Prosecution and Other Stories. NY: Dodd, Mead, 1948. 1st US ed. Fine in NF dj (lt edgewear). *Janus*. $200/£129

CHRISTIE, MRS. ARCHIBALD. Samplers and Stitches. London: Batsford, 1920. 1st ed. Color frontis, 33 plts (2 loose). Fore-edge uncut. Cl-backed bds (lower hinge sl tender; ex-libris; wear). *Edwards*. $70/£45

CHRISTISON, J. SANDERSON. Brain in Relation to Mind. Chicago, 1899. 1st ed. 143pp. Good. *Fye*. $40/£26

CHRISTMAN, ENOS. One Man's Gold. NY: Whittelsey House, 1930. 1st ed. Marbled cvr. VG+. *Parker*. $50/£32

Christmas Box of Pretty Stories. NY: McLoughlin Bros, n.d. 4to. Full-pg pict color litho frontis, 287pp. Emb, gilt pict red linen. VF (sig, shelfwear; 1pg expertly repaired). *Hobbyhorse*. $95/£61

CHRISTOPHER, FREDERICK. A Textbook of Surgery by American Authors. Phila: Saunders, 1942. 3rd ed. Good. *Goodrich*. $65/£42

CHRISTOPHER, JOHN. The Caves of Night. London: Eyre & Spottiswoode, 1958. 1st ed. Fine in dj (sl frayed, spine edges sl rubbed). *Temple*. $40/£26

CHRISTOPHER, JOHN. The Death of Grass. London: Michael Joseph, 1956. 1st ed. Nice in dj. *Temple*. $62/£40

CHRISTOPHER, JOHN. The Lotus Caves. London: Hamish Hamilton, 1969. 1st ed. Fine in dj (nicked). *Temple*. $40/£26

CHRISTOPHER, JOHN. The Year of the Comet. Joseph, 1955. 1st ed. Fine in NF dj. *Aronovitz*. $40/£26

CHRISTY, HOWARD CHANDLER. The Christy Girl. Indianapolis: Bobbs-Merrill, (1906). Unpaginated, 16 color plts, 4 tinted illus. Dec cl binding (sl soiled), mtd illus. *Schoyer*. $75/£48

CHRISTY, THOMAS. Thomas Christy's Road Across the Plains. Robert Becker (ed). Denver, Old West Pub Co, 1969. Frontis port; 94 strip maps. Pict cl. VG+ in dj (dknd, edgeworn). *Bohling*. $75/£48

CHUINARD, ELDON. Only One Man Died. Glendale: Clark, 1979. 1st ed. Color frontis. Corner bump, o/w Fine in VG dj. *Oregon*. $225/£145

CHUINARD, ELDON. Only One Man Died. The Medical Aspects of the Lewis and Clark Expedition. Glendale: Clark, 1979. 1st ed. One of 1020 ptd. Color frontis. VG (name, sticker) in VG dj. *Oregon*. $190/£123

CHURCH, A.H. Josiah Wedgwood: Master Potter. London: Seeley, 1903. 'New ed, rev and engld.' 4 gravure plts. Gilt-stamped pict burgundy cl; teg. VG. *Houle*. $150/£97

CHURCH, A.H. et al. Some Minor Arts as Practised in England. London, 1894. Thin folio. viii,80pp; 12 color plts. Aeg. (Corners sl rubbed.) *Edwards*. $70/£45

CHURCH, ALBERT COOK. Whale Ships and Whaling. NY, (1938). 1st ed. Pict cl. NF in dj. *Lefkowicz*. $130/£84

CHURCH, ELLA RODMAN. Artistic Embroidery. NY: Adams & Bishop, (1880). 1st ed. 132pp + (4)pp pub's ads. Dec brn cl. Good. *Karmiole*. $75/£48

CHURCH, PEGGY POND. The House at Otowi Bridge. Albuquerque: Univ of NM, 1960. 1st ed. NF in VG dj. *Parker*. $37/£24

CHURCH, THOMAS. Gardens Are for People. NY: Reinhold, 1955. 1st ed. Fine. *Quest*. $95/£61

CHURCH, THOMAS. Your Private World. A Study of Intimate Gardens. SF, 1969. Fine in dj. *Brooks*. $95/£61

CHURCHILL, FLEETWOOD (ed). Essays on the Puerperal Fever and Other Diseases Peculiar to Women. Phila, 1850. 1st Amer ed. 464pp. Good. *Fye*. $175/£113

CHURCHILL, FLEETWOOD. The Diseases of Females: Including those of Pregnancy and Childbed. Phila, 1847. 4th Amer ed. 601pp. Full leather. Good. *Fye*. $75/£48

CHURCHILL, FLEETWOOD. On the Diseases of Women, Including Diseases of Pregnancy and Childbed. Phila, 1852. 683pp. Full leather. Good. *Fye*. $75/£48

CHURCHILL, FLEETWOOD. On the Theory and Practice of Midwifery. Phila, 1846. 2nd Amer ed. 525pp. Full leather. Good. *Fye*. $100/£65

CHURCHILL, FLEETWOOD. On the Theory and Practice of Midwifery. Phila, 1860. New Amer ed. 655+32pp ads (margins browned; sigs loose). Full sheep (worn). *Argosy*. $60/£39

CHURCHILL, ROBERT. Game Shooting. London, 1963. Dj (chipped, crease to spine). *Edwards*. $31/£20

CHURCHILL, T.O. The Life of Lord Viscount Nelson, Duke of Bronte.... London, 1808. 1st ed. Frontis port, viii,100pp, 13 plts (2 fldg), facs letter. Browned, stained, o/w VG in mod calf-backed marbled bds, spine label. *Edwards*. $271/£175

CHURCHILL, T.O. The Life of Lord Viscount Nelson, Duke of Bronte.... London: T. Bensley for J. and W. MacGavin, 1808. 1st ed. 4to. viii,100pp. 15 copper-engr plts (3 fldg), incl al by Nelson in facs. Contemp 1/2 calf over marbled bds, gilt spine (spine extrems bit chipped; bkpl). *Karmiole*. $375/£242

CHURCHILL, WINSTON S. Blood, Sweat, and Tears. NY: Putnam's, (1941). 1st Amer ed of 'Into Battle.' VG in dj (chipped, lt edgewear, short tears). *Godot*. $65/£42

CHURCHILL, WINSTON S. The End of the Beginning. Boston: Little, Brown, 1943. 1st Amer ed. Red cl. VG in dj (price-clipped, short tears, lt edgewear, else VG). *Godot*. $65/£42

CHURCHILL, WINSTON S. Great Contemporaries. NY: Putnam, 1937. 1st US ed. Fine. *Graf.* $87/£56

CHURCHILL, WINSTON S. A History of the English Speaking Peoples. D-M, 1956-8. 1st Amer ed. 4 vols. Fine in djs. *Fine Books.* $150/£97

CHURCHILL, WINSTON S. A History of the English-Speaking Peoples. London, 1956-8. Vol 2, 2nd ed; rest 1st eds. 4 vols. Djs (sl foxed, chipped). *Edwards.* $93/£60

CHURCHILL, WINSTON S. Ian Hamilton's March. London: Longmans, Green, 1900. 1st ed. xii,(1),409+32pp ads; 10 plts, plans; fldg map. Orig cl gilt (neatly recased w/new eps). VG. *Hollett.* $388/£250

CHURCHILL, WINSTON S. In the Balance. H-M, 1952. 1st Amer ed. Fine in VG dj (sm chips; lt wear). *Fine Books.* $65/£42

CHURCHILL, WINSTON S. Into Battle. Cassell, 1941. 1st ed, 1st issue. VG+ in VG dj (3 sm chips). *Fine Books.* $175/£113

CHURCHILL, WINSTON S. London to Ladysmith via Pretoria. Longmans Green, 1900. 1st ed. Name, else VG in pict cl. *Fine Books.* $650/£419

CHURCHILL, WINSTON S. London to Ladysmith via Pretoria. London: Longmans, 1900. 1st ed. Pale fawn pict cl (sl dusty, sl mks, lt scoring of edges). Nice. *Ash.* $767/£495

CHURCHILL, WINSTON S. London to Ladysmith Via Pretoria. London: Longmans, 1900. Stated 2nd imp. One of 500. VG (lt foxing to few pp). *Williams.* $194/£125

CHURCHILL, WINSTON S. Lord Randolph Churchill. London, 1906. 1st ed. 2 vols. Frontis port each vol, 16 other plts (5 photogravures). Good+ (eps browned; foxed) in plum cl, gilt (sl rubbed, bumped, worn; spines sunned). *Edwards.* $233/£150

CHURCHILL, WINSTON S. Lord Randolph Churchill. London: Macmillan, 1906. 1st UK ed. 2 vols. VG set (lt spine wear, fading, lt foxing; bkpls). *Williams.* $349/£225

CHURCHILL, WINSTON S. Marlborough—His Life and Times. Harrap, 1933-1938. 1st eds. 4 vols. Vols 1-3 spines sl lightened, else NF set. *Fine Books.* $575/£371

CHURCHILL, WINSTON S. My African Journey. London, 1908. 1st ed. Red pict cl. VG. *Argosy.* $750/£484

CHURCHILL, WINSTON S. Onwards to Victory. L-B, 1944. 1st ed. NF in dj. *Fine Books.* $70/£45

CHURCHILL, WINSTON S. Painting as a Pastime. NY: Whittlesey House, (1950). 1st Amer ed. Frontis port, 18 color plts. (Lt wear.) *Shasky.* $35/£23

CHURCHILL, WINSTON S. Painting as a Pastime. McGraw-Hill, 1950. 1st ed. Fine in NF dj. *Fine Books.* $40/£26

CHURCHILL, WINSTON S. The River War; An Historical Account of the Reconquest of the Sudan. London: Longmans, Green, 1899. 1st ed. 2 vols. Orig cl; pict stamped gilt. NF (lt foxing). *Argosy.* $3,000/£1,935

CHURCHILL, WINSTON S. Savrola. London: Longmans, Green, 1900. New imp. Blue-grn cl, gilt (backstrip sl creased, lt rubbed). Foxing, spotting, but VG. *Hollett.* $186/£120

CHURCHILL, WINSTON S. The Second World War. London: Cassell, 1948-1954. 1st ed. 6 vols. VG+ set (inscrip). *Limestone.* $125/£81

CHURCHILL, WINSTON S. The Second World War. London: Cassell, 1948-1954. 1st Eng ed. 6 vols. Fine in djs (lt chipped). *Glenn.* $275/£177

CHURCHILL, WINSTON S. Thoughts and Adventures. London: Thornton Butterworth, (1932). 1st ed. Sandy-brn cl (lt worn; sm lib card fr pastedown). *Glenn.* $250/£161

CHURCHILL, WINSTON S. Winston Churchill's War Speeches. London: Cassell, (1941-1946). 1st Eng ed. 7 vols. VG set in djs (lt soiled, chipped). *Glenn.* $350/£226

CHURCHMAN, JOHN. An Account of the Gospel Labours. London, 1780. vii,351,1pp (sl spotting, tp sl thumbed). Calf-backed bds (rebound, new eps). *Edwards.* $85/£55

CHUTE, CAROLYN. The Beans. London: C&W/Hogarth, (1985). 1st British ed, 1st bk. Fine in Fine dj. *Robbins.* $45/£29

CIARDI, JOHN. The Alphabestiary. Phila: Lippincott, (1966). 1st trade ed. Signed. Milton Hebald (illus). Emb grn cl. Fine in slipcase (sl wear, spotting). *Antic Hay.* $75/£48

CIARDI, JOHN. I Marry You. New Brunswick: Rutgers Univ, 1958. 1st ed. Signed presentation. NF (lt browning eps) in dj (lt wear). *Antic Hay.* $50/£32

CIBBER, COLLEY. An Apology for the Life of Colley Cibber.... London: Ptd for R. Dodsley, 1750. 3rd ed. Engr port (sl offsetting to tp), (xxiv),555pp. Orig calf, spine gilt (rubbed), red morocco spine label. Good (18th cent bkpl). *Bickersteth.* $171/£110

CIBBER, COLLEY. An Apology for the Life of Colley Cibber.... London: Golden Cockerel, 1925. One of 450 numbered. 2 vols. Cl-backed bds, spines gilt. Sl dusty, else VG set. *Hermitage.* $150/£97

CIBBER, COLLEY. An Apology for the Life of Mr. Colley Cibber. London: John C. Nimmo, 1889 (1888). 1st ed thus, #15/20. 2 vols. 26 mezzotint port plts. R.B. Parkes (plts), Adelphe Lalauze (etchings). Full brn levant morocco; gilt; raised bands; silk eps. Teg; edges uncut. Fine (bkpl removed). *Dramatis Personae.* $400/£258

CICERO. The Familiar Epistles. Joseph Webbe (trans). London: Edward Griffin, (1620). 1st ed thus. 12mo. Fine engr architectural title, (xxiv),919,(i)pp. Sl later mottled calf, spine gilt (sl damaged at head, tail), red morocco label. Good (contemp sig; sm wormtrail blank outer margin 1st few ll; short tear 4ll w/o loss). *Sokol.* $969/£625

Cinderella and Other Fairy Stories with Realistic Pop-Up Pictures. London: Birn Bros, n.d. (197?). 27x21 cm. 5 fan-fld pop-ups (few sl slow). Glazed pict bds. *Book Finders.* $35/£23

Cinderella, A Troll Pop-Up Book. NJ: Troll, n.d. (1980). 20x27 cm. Linda Griffith (illus). Glazed pict bds. VG-. *Book Finders.* $30/£19

Cinderella. NY: Stephen Daye, 1945. 17x22 cm. 5pp Good action pictures w/tabs by Julian Wehr. Illus bds, spiral binding (fraying, 1/2 inch missing.) *Book Finders.* $100/£65

Cinderella. London: Murray, 1973. 26x9 cm. 6 fan-fld pop-ups. V. Kubasta (illus). Glazed pict bds. VG. *Book Finders.* $100/£65

Cinderella. NY: McLoughlin Bros, n.d. (1869). (Aunt Friendly's Colored Picture Books series.) 8vo. 6 leaves; 6 full-pg chromolithos. Dec stiff paper wrapper (lt soil, reinforced spine). Internally VF (inscrip). *Hobbyhorse.* $75/£48

Cinderella. Fairy Tale Pop-Up Book. London: Young World, n.d. (1973). 27x20 cm. 6 dbl-pg pop-ups. Glazed pict bds. VG- (inscrip). *Book Finders.* $35/£23

Cinderella: or, The Little Glass Slipper. Edinburgh: Oliver & Boyd, n.d. (ca 1820). 12mo. Full-pg wood engr frontis, 35pp + 1pg ad back wrapper, 14 VF 1/2pg cuts. Pict stiff paper wrappers (lt soiled, discolored, chipped, nicked). Fine. *Hobbyhorse.* $175/£113

Cinderella; or the Little Glass Slipper. York: J. Kendrew, n.d. (ca 1820). Chapbook. 16mo. 16pp; 15 woodcuts. Pict paper wrappers (sl foxing). Fine. *Hobbyhorse.* $75/£48

CIPRIANI, R. All the Paintings of Mantegna. London: Oldbourne, 1963. 2 vols. 184 plts (8 color). Sound. *Ars Artis.* $23/£15

CIST, CHARLES. Cincinnati in 1841: Its Early Annals and Future Prospects. Cincinnati: For the Author, 1841. Frontis, 300pp + ads, 4 steel engrs. Howes C 412. *Hayman.* $75/£48

CIST, CHARLES. Sketches and Statistics of Cincinnati in 1851. Cincinnati, 1851. Frontis, 363pp. Good (bkpl; contemp inscrip; lt foxing; extrems sl frayed). Howes C 412. *Ginsberg.* $125/£81

CITRON, JULIUS. Immunity, Methods of Diagnosis and Therapy and Their Practical Application. Phila, 1912. 1st Eng trans. Good. *Fye.* $100/£65

CLAESSENS, BOB and JEANNE ROUSSEAU. Bruegel. London, 1987. New ed. 104 color plts. Dj. *Edwards.* $39/£25

CLAIBORNE, JOHN F.H. Historical Account of Hancock County and the Sea Board of Mississippi. New Orleans, 1876. 1st ed. 16pp. VG in orig ptd wrappers. *Mcgowan.* $150/£97

CLAIBORNE, JOHN F.H. Life and Times of Gen. Sam Dale, the Mississippi Partisan. NY, 1860. 1st ed. 233,(6)pp incl 13 plts. (Crown chipped; joint edges wearing.) Howes C 417. *Ginsberg.* $175/£113

CLAIR, COLIN. Christopher Plantin. London: Cassell, 1960. 1st ed. 24 plts & facs. Good in dj (sl soiled). *Cox.* $39/£25

CLAIR, COLIN. A History of Printing. London: Cassell, 1965. 1st ed. VG in dj. *Cox.* $31/£20

CLANCEY, P.A. The Birds of Natal and Zululand. Edinburgh, 1964. 41 color plts, fldg map, 17 b/w plts. Dj (torn, chipped). *Edwards.* $132/£85

CLANCY, TOM. The Cardinal of the Kremlin. London, 1988. 1st UK ed. Fine in Fine dj. *Fuller & Saunders.* $35/£23

CLANCY, TOM. The Hunt for Red October. Annapolis: Naval Institute, 1984. 1st ed, 1st bk. NF in dj. *Lame Duck.* $650/£419

CLANCY, TOM. The Hunt for Red October. Annapolis: Naval Institute Press, 1984. 1st ed. Fine in dj (sm scrape; tiny closed tears). *Mordida.* $600/£387

CLANCY, TOM. The Hunt for Red October. London: Collins, 1985. 1st Eng ed. Bkseller stamp fr pastedown, else Fine in dj. *Limestone.* $250/£161

CLANCY, TOM. Patriot Games. NY: Putnam's, 1987. 1st ed. Inscribed, errata slip laid in. Fine in dj. *Mordida.* $65/£42

CLANCY, TOM. Red Storm Rising. NY: Putnam's, (1986). 1st ed. Signed presentation. Fine in NF dj. *Antic Hay.* $150/£97

CLANCY, TOM. Red Storm Rising. NY: Putnam's, (1986). 1st ed. Signed. Fine in dj. *Sadlon.* $85/£55

CLANCY, TOM. Submarine. NY: Putnam's, (1993). 1st ed. One of 300 numbered, signed. VF in VF pub's slipcase. *Unger.* $250/£161

CLANCY, TOM. The Sum of All Fears. NY: Putnam's, 1991. 1st ed. One of 600 specially bound, numbered, signed. VF in slipcase, w/o dj as issued. *Mordida.* $225/£145

CLANCY, TOM. The Sum of All Fears. London: Harper Collins, 1991. 1st Eng ed. VF in dj. *Limestone.* $50/£32

CLANCY, TOM. Without Remorse. NY: Putnam's, 1993. 1st ed. Signed. New in dj. *Else Fine.* $50/£32

CLAP, ROGER. Memoirs of Captain Roger Clap.... Boston: Clap, 1807. 39pp. Ptd wrappers. Howes C 422. *Ginsberg.* $250/£161

CLAPHAM, A.R. et al. Flora of the British Isles. Cambridge, 1962. 2nd ed. Grn cl. Ex-libris. *Brooks.* $37/£24

CLAPHAM, A.W. English Romanesque Architecture After the Conquest. OUP, 1934. 1st ed. 47 plts. (Feps lt browned, spine discolored.) *Edwards.* $47/£30

CLAPPE, LOUISE. The Shirley Letters from California Mines in 1851-52. SF: Thomas C. Russell, 1922. 1st ed thus. #241/450 numbered, signed by Russell. One of 200 on Exeter bk-paper. Hand-colored frontis; 7 full-pg plts. Beige burlap, grn bds; teg, uncut. VG. Howes C 427. *Houle.* $275/£177

CLAPPERTON, R.H. Paper and Its Relationship to Books. London: J.M. Dent, 1934. 1st Eng ed. Brn paper bds, gilt. VF in dj (sl tanned). *Dalian.* $31/£20

CLAPPERTON, R.H. and W. HENDERSON. Modern Paper-Making. London: Waverley, 1929. 1st ed. Grained cl, gilt. Lt wear, sl mks, o/w VG. *Willow House.* $47/£30

CLARE, JOHN. The Later Poems. Eric Robinson & Geoffrey Summerfield (eds). Manchester Univ Press, 1964. 1st ed. VG (inscrip). *Poetry.* $23/£15

CLARE, JOHN. Poems Chiefly from Manuscript. London: Cobden-Sanderson, 1920. Port. (Labels to feps, backstrip sl faded; sl puckered.) *Petersfield.* $33/£21

CLARE, JOHN. Poems Chiefly from Manuscript. Edmund Blunden & Alan Porter (eds). Cobden-Sanderson, 1920. 1st ed. Frontis port. Nice (sl stained; label sl rubbed). *Poetry.* $93/£60

CLARE, JOHN. Selected Letters. Mark Storey (ed). Clarendon, 1988. 1st ed. Fine in dj. *Poetry.* $31/£20

CLARE, JOHN. Sketches in the Life of John Clare Written by Himself. Cobden-Sanderson, 1931. 1st ed. Lt spotting, o/w VG in orig cl (partly faded; 3 stains). *Poetry.* $93/£60

CLARIDGE, R.T. Hydropathy. London, 1842. 1st ed. 318pp. New 1/2 calf, marbled bds, new leather labels. VG. *Whitehart.* $109/£70

CLARK, A. Barbarossa: The Russian German Conflict, 1941-1945. NY, 1950. VG in VG dj. *Clark.* $35/£23

CLARK, ARTHUR H. The Clipper Ship Era. NY/London, (1910). 1st ed. Frontis. Good. *Hayman.* $30/£19

CLARK, ARTHUR H. The Clipper Ship Era.... NY: Putnam's, 1920. *Petersfield.* $31/£20

CLARK, EDNA. Ohio Art and Artists. Richmond, VA, 1932. 143 plts. VG in dj. *Argosy.* $250/£161

CLARK, ELEANOR. Dr. Heart. A Novella and Other Stories. NY: Pantheon, (1974). 1st ed. Signed. Cl faded through dj, else Fine. *Reese.* $40/£26

CLARK, ELLA E. Indian Legends of the Pacific Northwest. Berkeley: Univ of CA, 1953. 1st ed. VG in VG dj. *Perier.* $30/£19

CLARK, ELLERY H., JR. Boston Red Sox—75th Anniversary History 1901-75. Exposition, 1975. 1st ed. Fine in VG + dj. *Plapinger.* $35/£23

CLARK, ELLERY H., JR. Red Sox Fever. Exposition, 1979. 1st ed. Fine in VG + dj. *Plapinger.* $30/£19

CLARK, FRANCIS E. Our Journey Around the World. Hartford, CT: Worthington, 1897. 641pp. Bkpl; sl rubbed, o/w VG. *Worldwide.* $45/£29

CLARK, FRANCIS E. Our Journey Around the World: An Illustrated Record of a Year's Travel.... Hartford: A.D. Worthington, 1895. 1st ed. 641,(1 ads)pp, 2 ports, fldg map. *Lefkowicz.* $100/£65

CLARK, GALEN. Indians of the Yosemite Valley and Vicinity. Yosemite Valley: Galen Clark, 1904. 1st ed. Frontis, 18 full-pg photos. Pict cl. *Dawson.* $125/£81

CLARK, GALEN. The Yosemite Valley. Yosemite Valley: Nelson L. Salter, 1911. 2nd ed. 21 full-pg photos. Grn-stamped pict cl (soiling). *Dawson.* $100/£65

CLARK, GEOFFREY (ed). Trial of James Camb. London: William Hodge, 1949. Very Nice in dj (worn). *Boswell.* $65/£42

CLARK, GEORGE ROGERS. The Conquest of the Illinois. Chicago, (1922). Lakeside Classic. VG. *Schoyer.* $40/£26

CLARK, GEORGE ROGERS. George Rogers Clark Papers 1771-1781. James Alton James (ed). IL State Hist Lib v8, VA Series v3, 1912. 1st ed. 4 plts. Howes C 433. *Oregon.* $60/£39

CLARK, J. A Treatise on Pulmonary Consumption. London, 1835. xxxiii,399pp. Old bds (rebacked). *Whitehart.* $109/£70

CLARK, JAMES C. Last Train South. Jefferson, NC, 1984. 2nd ed. Lacks rep, else Fine. *Mcgowan.* $35/£23

CLARK, JOHN G. The Grain Trade in the Old Northwest. Urbana: Univ of IL Press, 1966. VG in dj. *Schoyer.* $30/£19

CLARK, JOHN SPENCER. The Life and Letters of John Fiske. Boston, 1917. 1st ed. 2 vols. Gilt cl. Sm nick vol 2, o/w VG. *Artis.* $17/£11

CLARK, JOSEPH G. Lights and Shadows of Sailor Life.... Boston: Mussey, 1848. 324pp, 6 woodcut plts (browning). Orig cl (spine ends worn). Howes C 442. *Lefkowicz.* $175/£113

CLARK, KEITH and LOWELL TILLER. Terrible Trail: The Meek Cutoff, 1845. Caldwell: Caxton, 1966. 1st ed. Signed by both authors. Fine in Fine dj. *Perier.* $75/£48

CLARK, KENNETH and DAVID FINN. The Florence Baptistry Doors. NY: Viking, (1980). 1st ed. Fine in dj. *Pharos.* $75/£48

CLARK, KENNETH et al. Sidney Nolan. London, 1961. 199 plts (16 color). (Eps lt spotted; sl soiled; spine, edges faded.) *Edwards.* $116/£75

CLARK, KENNETH. Animals and Men. NY, 1977. Dj (sl chipped). *Edwards.* $54/£35

CLARK, KENNETH. The Drawings by Sandro Botticelli for Dante's Divine Comedy after the Originals.... NY, 1976. 1st Amer ed. Color frontis, 99 superb plts. VG in dj. *Argosy.* $100/£65

CLARK, KENNETH. The Gothic Revival. NY: Scribners, 1929. 1st Amer ed, ptd in England. Fine in dj (mended). *Pharos.* $200/£129

CLARK, KENNETH. Henry Moore Drawings. London, 1974. Dj. *Edwards.* $70/£45

CLARK, KENNETH. Henry Moore's Sheep Sketchbook. London: Thames & London, 1981. 1st ed. Tan cl bds. Fine in pict dj. *Heller.* $35/£23

CLARK, KENNETH. Piero della Francesca. London: Phaidon, 1951. 1st ed. Color frontis, 6 tipped-in plts, 148 monochrome plts. Dj torn, o/w VF (bkpl). *Europa.* $62/£40

CLARK, KENNETH. Piero della Francesca. London, 1951. 1st ed. 7 mtd color plts. VG. *Argosy.* $75/£48

CLARK, KENNETH. Piero della Francesca. Complete Edition. Phaidon, 1969. 2nd rev ed. Excellent in dj. *Ars Artis.* $132/£85

CLARK, MARY HIGGINS. The Cradle Will Fall. NY: S&S, 1980. 1st ed. Fine in Fine dj. *Janus.* $45/£29

CLARK, MARY HIGGINS. A Stranger Is Watching. NY: S&S, 1977. 1st ed. Fine in NF dj (reinforced). *Janus.* $35/£23

CLARK, ROBERT C. History of the Willamette Valley, Oregon. Chicago: S.J. Clarke, 1927. 1st ed. 3 vols. Fine set. *Perier.* $225/£145

CLARK, ROBERT STERLING and ARTHUR DE C. SOWERBY. Through Shen-Kan. C.H. Chepmell (ed). London: T. Fisher Unwin, 1912. 1st ed. Frontis map, 6 color plts, mounted on thick paper, 58 uncolored plts, lg fldg route map in pocket. Ochre cl (sl soiled, ink lib mk foot of spine), ptd in black. VG (lt ink stamps on versos of plts, map). *Morrell.* $326/£210

CLARK, ROLAND. Pot Luck. NY: A.S. Barnes, (1945). 1st ed. Butterscotch-colored cl. Fine in slipcase (worn). *Glenn.* $45/£29

CLARK, RONALD W. An Eccentric in the Alps. London: Museum Press, 1959. 1st ed. 17 plts. VG in dj (sl worn). *Hollett.* $47/£30

CLARK, RONALD W. A Picture History of Mountaineering. NY, (1956). 1st Amer ed. VG in dj (worn, sl torn). *King.* $60/£39

CLARK, RONALD W. The Victorian Mountaineers. London: Batsford, 1953. 1st ed. VG. *Hollett.* $39/£25

CLARK, RONALD W. and EDWARD C. PYATT. Mountaineering in Britain. London, 1957. 1st ed. 104 plts. Dj (sl creased, chipped). *Edwards.* $70/£45

CLARK, STERLING B.F. How Many Miles from St. Jo? SF: Privately ptd, 1929. 1st ed. 5 plts. Cl-backed pict marbled bds. Compliments slip, erratum tipped in. VG + in plain parchment wrapper as issued. *Shasky.* $55/£35

CLARK, T.M. Building Superintendence.... Boston: Ticknor & Co, 1890. (viii),336,(8)pp. (Fr hinge internally cracked; rubber stamp feps; ink inscrip; pencil inscrips p332, rep). Pub's cl (lt wear). *Bookpress.* $75/£48

CLARK, WALTER VAN TILBURG. The Track of the Cat. Random House, (1949). 1st ed. Good + (sm dampstain rear cvr, ep) in Good + dj (chipped). *Oregon.* $45/£29

CLARK, WALTER VAN TILBURG. The Track of the Cat. NY, 1949. 1st ptg. Debossed cl. VG- (bkpl; sl faded, letters sl flaking) in dj (chipped). *Baade.* $40/£26

CLARK, WALTER. Histories of the Several Regiments and Battalions from North Carolina in the Great War, 1861-'65. Raleigh/Goldsboro: E.M. Uzzel (vol 1)/Nash Bros (vols 2-5). 1st ed. 5 vols. 8vo, frontis port. Orig pict grey cl. Rear cvr vol 3 discolored, else VG + . *Chapel Hill.* $650/£419

CLARK, WILLIAM L. Hand-Book of Criminal Procedure. St. Paul: West Pub Co, 1895. Full sheep (rubbed). Usable only. *Boswell.* $50/£32

CLARK, WILLIAM. The Field Notes of Captain William Clark 1803-1805. Ernest Staples Osgood (ed). Yale, 1964. 1st ed. Fine in VG dj. *Oregon.* $300/£194

CLARK, WILLIAM. Reminiscences of the Thirty-Fourth Regiment, Mass. Vol. Infantry. Clark, 1871. 31pp. VG (lt edgewear) in ptd wraps. *Bohling.* $85/£55

CLARK, WILLIS GAYLORD. The Literary Remains...Including the Ollapodiana Papers.... Lewis Clark (ed). NY: Burgess, Stringer, 1844. Clbound issue rebound. 1/2 black morocco. Good (lib bkpls, blindstamps; foxing). BAL 3282. *Agvent.* $75/£48

CLARKE, A.B. Travels in Mexico and California: Comprising a Journal.... Boston: Wright & Hasty's Steam Press, 1852. 1st ed. Orig ptd wrappers. VF in custom-made grey cl slipcase, chemise. Howes C 451. *Parmer.* $2,400/£1,548

CLARKE, ADAM (comp). Bibliographical Dictionary. Liverpool: W. Baynes, 1802-1806. 1st eds. 8 vols. 8vo. Lt cvr wear but Very Nice in orig pub's bds. *Bookpress.* $1,350/£871

CLARKE, ALLEN. Windmill Land. London: J.M. Dent, 1916. 1st ed. 32 plts, map. Later cl, panel w/orig lettering laid onto spine. (Prelims sl mkd; leaf soiled, sl defective in margin.) *Hollett.* $70/£45

CLARKE, ARTHUR C. Across a Sea of Stars. NY: Harcourt-Brace, 1959. 1st ed. VF in dj (sm chip rear panel). *Else Fine.* $95/£61

CLARKE, ARTHUR C. Against the Fall of Night. Gnome, 1953. 1st ed. VG. *Madle.* $25/£16

CLARKE, ARTHUR C. Against the Fall of Night. Gnome, 1953. 1st ed. NF in NF dj (lt wear, tear). *Aronovitz.* $150/£97

CLARKE, ARTHUR C. Childhood's End. London: Sidgwick & Jackson, 1954. 1st ed. VG in dj (sl worn). *Rees.* $23/£15

CLARKE, ARTHUR C. Childhood's End. S&J, 1954. 1st Eng ed. NF in VG + dj. *Aronovitz.* $250/£161

CLARKE, ARTHUR C. Earthlight. NY: Ballantine Books, (1955). 1st ed. Ptd wraps. Fine (paper edges browned). *Antic Hay.* $35/£23

CLARKE, ARTHUR C. Expedition to Earth. NY: Ballantine Books, (1953). 1st ed. Ptd wraps. Fine. *Antic Hay.* $35/£23

CLARKE, ARTHUR C. A Fall of Moondust. Harcourt, 1961. 1st ed. VG in Fine dj. *Madle.* $175/£113

CLARKE, ARTHUR C. Glide Path. London: Sidgwick & Jackson, 1969. 1st ed. VG in dj. *Rees.* $31/£20

CLARKE, ARTHUR C. Going into Space. Trend Books, 1954. 1st ed. NF in wraps. *Madle.* $25/£16

CLARKE, ARTHUR C. Islands in the Sky. Phila: John C. Winston, (1952). 1st ed. Fine in dj (lt edgeworn, 2 sm rubbed spots). *Reese.* $85/£55

CLARKE, ARTHUR C. Islands in the Sky. London: Sidgwick & Jackson, n.d. (1952). 1st ed. Frontis. Fine in dj (sl frayed, torn, strengthened internally w/tissue). *Temple.* $62/£40

CLARKE, ARTHUR C. The Other Side of the Sky. NY: Harcourt-Brace, 1958. 1st ed. Fine in dj (lt edgewear, sm chip). *Else Fine.* $65/£42

CLARKE, ARTHUR C. Prelude to Space. Gnome, 1954. 1st ed. Fine in dj (spine chipped). *Madle.* $100/£65

CLARKE, ARTHUR C. Reach for Tomorrow. Gollancz, 1962. 1st Eng ed. Lt dust soiling top edge, else NF in VG + dj. *Aronovitz.* $125/£81

CLARKE, ARTHUR C. The Reefs of Taprobang. London, 1957. 1st ed. Fine in dj (worn). *Madle.* $40/£26

CLARKE, ARTHUR C. The Sands of Mars. S&J, 1951. 1st ed. VG. *Aronovitz.* $25/£16

CLARKE, ARTHUR C. The Sands of Mars. Gnome, 1952. 1st ed. Fine in dj (sl rubbed). *Madle.* $165/£106

CLARKE, ARTHUR C. Tales of Ten Worlds. NY: HBW, 1962. 1st ed. Fine in dj (minor rubs). *Else Fine.* $60/£39

CLARKE, ARTHUR C. Voices from the Sky. Gollancz, 1966. 1st Eng ed. Signed. NF in VG dj. *Aronovitz.* $50/£32

CLARKE, AUSTIN. Collected Poems. Dolmen Press, 1974. 1st Eng ed. VG in dj. *Edrich.* $39/£25

CLARKE, AUSTIN. The Third Kiss. Dublin: Dolmen Press, 1976. One of 500 unnumbered. Fine in dj. *Sclanders.* $28/£18

CLARKE, AUSTIN. Tiresias. Templeogue, Dublin: Bridge Press, 1971. One of 200. Fine in dj (spine, edges browned). *Ulysses.* $85/£55

CLARKE, B. Mental Disorder in Earlier Britain. Cardiff, 1975. Ex-lib w/stamps, label remnants, o/w Good. *Whitehart.* $28/£18

CLARKE, BASIL F.L. Church Builders of the Nineteenth Century. Devon: David & Charles, (1969). 1st ed, thus. VG in dj (chipped). *Bookpress.* $35/£23

CLARKE, BASIL. Polar Flight. London: Ian Allan, (1964). 1st ed. VG in VG dj. *Blue Dragon.* $27/£17

CLARKE, C. Mystery Flight of the Q2. R&L, 1932. 1st ed. NF in dj. *Aronovitz.* $30/£19

CLARKE, C.C. The Wonders of the World. New Haven/Charleston, SC: J. Babcock/S. Babcock, 1822. Sq 12mo. 32pp + 1pg list lower wrapper; 8 plts (4th plt bound in upside down). Buff stiff paper wrappers (corner chipped; sm repair; spine reinforced). VG (ink sig, internal foxing). *Hobbyhorse.* $225/£145

CLARKE, CAROLYN W. Evacuation 114 as Seen from Within. Boston: Hudson Ptg, 1919. 1st ed. Port; 5 plts. VG. *Petrilla.* $25/£16

CLARKE, D.L. Beaker Pottery of Great Britain and Ireland. CUP, 1970. 2 vols. Color frontis, 8 plts. Djs. *Edwards.* $93/£60

CLARKE, E. The Errors of Accommodation and Refraction of the Eye and Their Treatment. London, 1903. 1st ed. Presentation copy. Color plt. (Ink mks; reps sl affected by water; spine ends sl worn.) *Whitehart.* $28/£18

CLARKE, E.D. Travels in Various Countries of Europe, Asia and Africa. London, 1816-24. 4th ed. 11 vols. Frontis port. Mainly unopened. 1/2 roan, marbled bds, gilt spines (ex-libris; chipped; rubbed; joints cracking; upper bd, fep vol 10 nearly detached). *Edwards.* $620/£400

CLARKE, EDWARD H. The Building of a Brain. Boston: Osgood, (1874). 5th ed. 153pp. Excellent. *Second Life.* $95/£61

CLARKE, EDWARD. Visions: A Study of False Sight (Pseudopia).... Boston, 1878. 1st ed. Lacks frontis, o/w VG. *Fye.* $75/£48

CLARKE, GEORGE H. (ed). A Treasury of War Poetry. British and American Poems of the World War 1914-1917. Boston: Houghton Mifflin, 1917. 1st ed. VG in ptd khaki paper wrappers (sl dusty, sm spots, nicks). *Reese.* $85/£55

CLARKE, H.T. et al. The Chemistry of Penicillin. Princeton, 1949. 1st ed. Good. *Fye.* $75/£48

CLARKE, J. JACKSON. Congenital Dislocation of the Hip. London: Bailliere, Tindal & Cox, 1910. Good. *Goodrich.* $175/£113

CLARKE, JOHN HENRIK (ed). William Styron's Nat Turner: Ten Black Writers Respond. Boston: Beacon, 1968. 1st ed. VG in dj. *Cahan.* $40/£26

CLARKE, LE MON. The Vaginal Diaphragm: Its Fitting and Use in Contraceptive Technique. St. Louis, 1939. (Ex-lib.) *Fye.* $50/£32

CLARKE, LINDSAY. Sunday Whiteman. Cape, 1987. 1st UK ed, 1st bk. Fine in dj. *Williams.* $39/£25

CLARKE, MARY W. Chief Bowles and the Texas Cherokees. Norman: Univ of OK Press, (1971). 1st ed. Brn cl. Fine in dj (price-clipped). *Chapel Hill.* $40/£26

CLARKE, STEPHAN P. The Lord Peter Wimsey Companion. NY: Mysterious Press, 1985. 1st ed. Fine (name stamp) in Fine dj (lt rubbed). *Janus.* $65/£42

CLARKE, T. WOOD. The Bloody Mohawk. NY: Macmillan, 1940. 1st ed. Brn cl. Sig, else Fine in VG dj. *Chapel Hill.* $65/£42

CLAUDEL, PAUL. Five Great Odes. Rapp & Carroll, 1967. #69/100 signed by Edward Lucie-Smith (trans). Fine in dj (price-clipped; torn, creased). *Poetry.* $31/£20

CLAUDEL, PAUL. Three Poems of the War. New Haven: Yale, 1919. 1st Amer ed. Contents Clean (sig; rear cvr stained). *Agvent.* $25/£16

Claudine, or Humility, the Basis of All the Virtues. (By Maria Elizabeth Budden.) London: J. Harris, 1823. 2nd ed. Dedication pg signed M.E.B. 12mo. Copper engr frontis, ii,200pp; 5 Fine plts, each w/2 engrs, dated Dec 1, 1822. Pict blue cvrs, red roan spine, gilt title, vignette. VG (lt rubbed, chipped). *Hobbyhorse.* $145/£94

CLAUDY, CARL H. The Land of No Shadow. NY: Grosset & Dunlap, (1933). 1st ed. Color frontis. Blue cl stamped in black. Fine. *Weber.* $50/£32

CLAUDY, CARL. A Thousand Years a Minute. Grosset, 1933. 1st ed. NF in dj (lt chipped). *Madle.* $100/£65

CLAUS, HUGO. Karel Appel. London, 1963. 1st UK ed. Color pict bds (ex-libris; edges sl rubbed). *Edwards.* $132/£85

CLAUSEN, J. et al. Experimental Studies on the Nature of Species. Washington, Carnegie Inst, 1940-58. 4 parts in 1 vol. *Wheldon & Wesley.* $93/£60

CLAVELL, JAMES. Shogun. NY: Atheneum, 1975. 1st ed. Fine in NF dj (2 short tears). *Between The Covers.* $100/£65

CLAVELL, JAMES. Tai-Pan. M. Joseph, 1966. 1st Eng ed. Fine in VG+ dj. *Fine Books.* $38/£25

CLAVELL, JAMES. Whirlwind. NY: Wm. Morrow, (1986). 1st trade ed. Signed. Fine in dj. *Bernard.* $50/£32

CLAVIERE, ETIENNE and JACQUES P. BRISSOT DE WARVILLE. Commerce of America with Europe. NY: Swords, 1795. 1st Amer ed. (35),228pp, port (lacks sm piece). New cl. Howes C 464. *Ginsberg.* $200/£129

CLAY, ENID. Sonnets and Verses. London: Golden Cockerel, 1925. One of 450. 1/4 linen, blue paper over bds. Edges worn to paper title label, else Fine. *Heller.* $675/£435

CLAY, JEAN. Romanticism. London: Phaidon, 1981. Dj. *Edwards.* $54/£35

CLAY, JOHN. My Life on the Range. Chicago: privately ptd, (1924). Frontis. Teg. Gold-stamped cl, index written rep. (Envelope glued rear pastedown.) *Dawson.* $250/£161

CLAY, JOHN. My Life on the Range. NY: Antiquarian, 1961. Ltd to 750. NF. *Parker.* $65/£42

CLAY, JOHN. Old Days Recalled. Chicago: Privately ptd, 1915. 1st ed. *Ginsberg.* $175/£113

CLAY, REGINALD and THOMAS COURT. The History of the Microscope. London, 1975. Good. *Fye.* $75/£48

CLAY, ROTHA MARY. Julius Caesar Ibbetson 1759-1817. London: Country Life, 1948. 1st ed. Color frontis, 2 color plts, 125 photo plts. (Feps lt yellowed, worn; lacks dj.) *Edwards.* $116/£75

CLAY, ROTHA MARY. The Mediaeval Hospitals of England. London: Methuen, 1909. 1st ed. 78 plts. Red cl (spine sl faded), gilt. *Hollett.* $101/£65

CLAYTON, ALEXANDER M. Centennial Address on the History of Marshall County Delivered...1876. Washington, DC, 1880. 1st ed. 32pp. Minor soiling, chipping to orig ptd wrappers, else VG. *Mcgowan.* $150/£97

CLAYTON, MURIEL. Catalogue of Rubbings of Brasses and Incised Slabs; Victoria and Albert Museum. London: Bd of Ed, 1929. 72 plts. Fine in orig ptd wraps. *Europa.* $31/£20

CLAYTON, MURIEL. Victoria and Albert Museum. Catalogue of Rubbings of Brasses and Incised Slabs. London, 1929. Rev ed. 72 plts. Good in wrappers. *Washton.* $30/£19

CLAYTON, VICTORIA VIRGINIA. White and Black under the Old Regime. Milwaukee: Young Churchman Co, (1899). 1st ed. 195pp. Dec cl. NF. *Mcgowan.* $150/£97

CLAYTON, W.F. A Narrative of the Confederate States Navy. Weldon, NC: Harrell's Ptg House, 1910. 1st ed. Ltd to 100. 8vo, frontis port. Orig gray cl. Cvr sl soiled, else NF. *Chapel Hill.* $900/£581

CLEAGE, ALBERT B. The Black Messiah. NY: Sheed & Ward, 1968. VG in VG dj. *Peninsula.* $35/£23

CLEARY, JON. Helga's Web. NY: Morrow, 1970. 1st ed. Fine in dj. *Else Fine.* $75/£48

CLEARY, JON. The High Commissioner. NY: Morrow, 1966. 1st ed. VF in dj (sl spine darkening). *Else Fine.* $125/£81

CLEARY, JON. The Safe House. NY: Morrow, 1975. 1st Amer ed. Fine in dj (sl soiling). *Silver Door.* $22/£14

CLEATOR, P.E. Rockets Through Space. NY: S&S, 1936. 1st US ed. 23 plts. Good in blue cl, silver foil spine label (faded, name, stamps, pencil mks; spine starting to tear). *Knollwood.* $125/£81

CLEAVELAND, AGNES MORLEY. No Life for a Lady. Boston: Houghton Mifflin, (1941). VG in dj (ink on flap). *Perier.* $35/£23

CLEAVELAND, AGNES MORLEY. No Life for a Lady. Boston, (1944). *Heinoldt.* $15/£10

CLEAVES, FREEMAN. Meade of Gettysburg. Norman, 1960. 1st ed. VG in VG dj. *Clark.* $45/£29

CLEAVES, FREEMAN. Meade of Gettysburg. Norman, 1960. 1st ed. VG+ in VG+ dj. *Pratt.* $65/£42

CLELAND, ROBERT GLASS. The Cattle on a Thousand Hills: Southern California, 1850-70. San Marino: Huntington Lib, 1941. 1st ed. Inscribed. Dj (chipped). *Dawson.* $60/£39

CLELAND, ROBERT GLASS. El Molino Viejo. (L.A.): Ward Ritchie, 1950. 1st ed. 2 plts. Brn cl, pict cvr label. Fine. *Harrington.* $35/£23

CLELAND, ROBERT GLASS. The Irvine Ranch of Orange County 1810-1950. Huntington, 1952. 1st ed. Map, prospectus laid in. Fine in Fine dj. *Oregon.* $65/£42

CLELAND, ROBERT GLASS. The Place Called Sespe. Privately ptd, (1953). 2nd ptg. Fldg map frontis. Fine. *Oregon.* $45/£29

CLELAND, ROBERT GLASS. This Reckless Breed of Men. NY: Knopf, 1950. 1st ed. 4 maps. Blue cl. Fine in VG dj (sl chipped, stabilized). *Harrington.* $40/£26

CLELAND, ROBERT GLASS. This Reckless Breed of Men. NY, 1950. 1st ed. Debossed cl. Sl bumped, o/w NF in dj (sl chipped). *Baade.* $50/£32

CLELAND, T.M. The Decorative Work of T.M. Cleland. NY: Pynson Printers, 1929. Ltd to 1200. 99pp of plts (1 mtd fldg plt); litho frontis port. Black cl. Good in dj (chipped). *Karmiole.* $125/£81

CLELAND, T.M. The Decorative Work of.... NY: Pynson Printers, 1929. 1st ed. One of 1200 numbered. Port. Teg. Gilt polished buckram. Spine sl worn, else VG (portions of dj laid in). *Reese.* $90/£58

CLEMENS, FRED W. Three Hundred Years along the Rothrock Trail. (Spokane: F.M. Rothrock, 1954). 1st ed. Signed. Fine. *Perier.* $45/£29

CLEMENS, KATHARINE. Gardens and Books. Webster Groves: Int'l Mark Twain Soc, 1938. 1st ed. Inscribed, presentation tipped in. Good (hinge tender). *Second Life.* $65/£42

CLEMENS, THOMAS E. Quaint Old Landmarks in East Germantown with East Germantown: A New Name.... E. Germantown (Phila): 1939. 1st ed. 2 vols in 1; frontis; 16pp photo-views. Blue cl. VG. *Petrilla.* $45/£29

CLEMENTS, GEORGE. Clements' Customs Guide. London: Thomas Ostell, 1840. 6th annual ed. xxxi,344pp. Blind-stamped cl, gilt. VG. *Hollett.* $70/£45

CLEVELAND, DUCHESS OF. The Life and Letters of Lady Hester Stanhope, By Her Niece.... London: William Clowers, 1897. 1st ed. Frontis engr, 357pp; all edges rouged. White linen beveled bds, gilt/black titles, decs. Attractive (armorial bkpl; sl soiled). *Hartfield.* $195/£126

CLEVELAND, GROVER. Fishing and Shooting Sketches. NY: Outing Pub, 1907. 1st ed. NF. *Artis.* $30/£19

CLEVELAND, H.W.S. Hints to Riflemen. NY: Appleton, 1864. Ltd to 500. Frontis, 260pp + ads. Orig grn pebbled cl. Lt foxed, o/w VG + . *Bowman.* $85/£55

CLEVELAND, RAY L. An Ancient South Arabian Necropolis. Balt: Johns Hopkins, 1965. 1st ed. 120 plts. NF. *Worldwide.* $45/£29

CLEVELAND, RICHARD J. A Narrative of Voyages and Commercial Enterprises. London: Edward Moxon, 1843. 1st Eng ed. (iii)-xii,123(1)pp (lacks 1/2 title). Aeg. Old (orig?) cl-backed bds. Fine. *Lefkowicz.* $700/£452

CLEVENGER, S.V. Spinal Concussion: Surgically Considered as a Cause of Spinal Injury.... Phila: Davis, 1889. iv,(1),359pp. (Cl sl worn; stamp on title.) *Goodrich.* $395/£255

CLEWELL, JOHN HENRY. History of Wachovia in North Carolina...1752-1902. NY: Doubleday, Page, 1902. 1st ed. VG (few corners creased; sm stain few leaves; spine lt rubbed). *Cahan.* $85/£55

CLIFFORD, DEREK and TIMOTHY. John Crome. London: Faber, 1968. 6 color plts, 128 monochrome. Fine in Mint dj. *Europa.* $43/£28

CLIFFORD, DEREK and TIMOTHY. John Crome. London: Faber, 1968. 6 color plts. Sound. *Ars Artis.* $70/£45

CLIFFORD, DEREK. Collecting English Watercolours. Princeton, NJ, 1971. 13 color, 243 monochrome plts. VG in dj. *Argosy.* $65/£42

CLIFFORD, DEREK. Watercolours of the Norwich School. London, (1965). 1st ed. 8 hand-tipped color plts. VG in dj. *Argosy.* $50/£32

CLIFTON, LUCILLE. All Us Come Cross the Water. NY: Holt Rinehart, 1973. 1st ed. Sm 4to. Pict paper-cvrd bds. VF (inscrip) in Fine dj (sm repair). *Book Adoption.* $45/£29

CLIFTON, LUCILLE. Some of the Days of Everett Anderson. NY: Henry Holt, (1970). 1st ed. VG in dj (lt stained, lg tear, sm chip). *Godot.* $65/£42

CLIFTON, MARK and FRANK RILEY. They'd Rather Be Right. NY: Gnome, 1957. 1st ed. Pp browned, o/w NF in VG + dj (top left spine edge chipped). *Bernard.* $75/£48

CLIFTON, MARK and FRANK RILEY. They'd Rather Be Right. Gnome, 1957. 1st ed. Fine in dj. *Madle.* $125/£81

CLIFTON, VIOLET. The Book of Talbot. London: Faber, 1933. VG in dj (worn). *Bowman.* $65/£42

CLIFTON-TAYLOR, ALEC. The Pattern of English Building. London: Batsford, 1965. 2nd ed. Dj (chipped). *Edwards.* $54/£35

CLINCH, GEORGE. Bloomsbury and St. Giles's: Past and Present. London, 1890. xii,220pp. (Extrems sl rubbed; soiling.) *Edwards.* $43/£28

CLINCH, GEORGE. Bloomsbury and St. Giles's: Past and Present. London: Truslove & Shirley, 1890. xii,220pp. Pict cl, beveled bds, gilt. VG. *Hollett.* $132/£85

CLINCH, GEORGE. English Costume from Prehistoric Times to the End of the 18th Century. London: Methuen, 1909. 1st ed. Red cl (sl faded), gilt. *Hollett.* $85/£55

CLINCH, GEORGE. English Hops.... London, (1919). 12 plts. *Wheldon & Wesley.* $39/£25

CLINCH, GEORGE. Handbook of English Antiquities for the Collector and the Student. London: L. Upcott Gill, 1905. Worn, spine faded, but sound. *Boswell.* $35/£23

CLINCH, GEORGE. Mayfair and Belgravia. London: Truslove & Shirley, 1892. xii,184,(ii)pp. Dec cl, beveled bds (spine faded), gilt. *Hollett.* $132/£85

CLINE, GLORIA. Peter Skene Ogden and the Hudson's Bay Company. Univ of OK, (1974). 1st ed. 6 maps (3 dbl-pg). VF in Fine dj. *Oregon.* $50/£32

CLINTON, GEORGE. Memoirs of the Life and Writings of Lord Byron. London, 1827. (2nd ed.) Frontis port. No 1/2 title. Foxing, o/w VG in near contemp 1/2 morocco, gilt spine. *Poetry.* $85/£55

CLODD, EDWARD. Myths and Dreams. London: Chatto, 1891. 2nd ed. (Backstrip sl faded.) *Petersfield.* $25/£16

CLODD, EDWARD. Pioneers of Evolution from Thales to Huxley. London, 1897. 2nd ed. xii,250pp; 3 ports. Cl (sl used). *Wheldon & Wesley.* $31/£20

CLODE, CHARLES M. The Early History of the Guild of Merchant Taylors. London: Harrison & Sons, 1888. 1st ed. 2 vols. xvi,415; xvi,441pp; lg fldg facs. VG. *Cox.* $101/£65

CLOETE, STUART. The African Giant. London, 1956. 1st ed. Orig cl. Minor scattered foxing, else VG. *Mcgowan.* $45/£29

CLOETE, STUART. Watch for the Dawn. Boston: Houghton Mifflin, 1939. 1st ed. Bds lt soiled, o/w Fine in pict dj (lt worn). *Hermitage.* $35/£23

CLOUSTON, J.S. Vandrad the Viking. Nelson, 1898. 1st ed. VG +. *Aronovitz.* $95/£61

CLOUSTON, W.A. The Book of Noodles: Stories of Simpletons. London: Elliot Stock, 1888. 1st ed. xx,228pp. All edges uncut; unopened. Very Nice. *Cady.* $25/£16

CLOWES, WILLIAM LAIRD. The Captain of the Mary Rose. Tower, 1892. 1st ed. Pict cl stamped black, gold. VG-. *Aronovitz.* $85/£55

CLOWES, WILLIAM LAIRD. The Royal Navy: A History.... London, 1897. 1st ed. Vol 1 only (of 7). Fair (lacks frontis; ex-lib; inner hinges tender). *Lefkowicz.* $75/£48

CLOWES, WILLIAM. Profitable and Necessarie Booke of Observations. NY, 1945. (Facs of 1596 ed.) Good. *Fye.* $75/£48

CLUM, WOODWORTH. Apache Agent. The Story of John P. Clum. Boston: Houghton Mifflin, 1936. 1st ed. Frontis. Dj (top edge worn). *Dawson.* $60/£39

CLUM, WOODWORTH. Apache Agent. The Story of John P. Clum. Boston: Houghton Mifflin, 1936. 1st ed. VG + (name). *Parker.* $75/£48

CLYDE, NORMAN. Norman Clyde of the Sierra Nevada. (SF): Scrimshaw Press, 1971. One of 500 handbound by Earle Gray. Frontis, double-pg map, 16 full-pg photos. Ptd bds w/cl spine, paper spine label. *Dawson.* $175/£113

CLYNE, GERALDINE. The Jolly Jump-Up Zoo Book. Springfield, Mass: McLoughlin Bros, 1946. 27x21 cm. 6 VG- dbl-pg pop-ups. (Spine reinforced w/tape, corners worn, edges rubbed.) *Book Finders.* $90/£58

CLYNE, GERALDINE. The Jolly Jump-Ups and Their New House. Springfield: McLoughlin Bros, 1939. 27x19 cm. 6 pop-ups. Illus bds. VG-. *Book Finders.* $110/£71

CLYNE, GERALDINE. The Jolly Jump-Ups on the Farm. Springfield, MA: McLoughlin Bros, 1940. 1st ed. 8vo. 6 pop-ups (1 sl torn). Cl-backed pict bds. Lt edgewear, else Fine. *Glenn.* $125/£81

CLYNE, GERALDINE. The Jolly Jump-Ups See the Circus. Springfield, MA: McLoughlin Bros, 1944. 1st ed. 8vo. 6 pop-ups. Cl-backed pict bds. Sl rubbed, else Fine. *Glenn.* $125/£81

CLYNE, GERALDINE. The Jolly Jump-Ups See the Circus. Mass: McLoughlin Bros, 1945. 27x19 cm. 6 dbl-pg pop-ups. Pict bds. VG-. *Book Finders.* $120/£77

COALE, CHARLES B. The Life and Adventures of Wilburn Waters. Richmond: Gary, 1878. 1st ed. 265pp. Orig brn cl (lt edgewear). VG +. *Bowman.* $350/£226

COALE, WILLIAM. Hints on Health; With Familiar Instructions for the Treatment and Preservation of the Skin, Hair.... Boston, 1857. 3rd ed. 210pp. Good. *Fye.* $75/£48

COAST, JOHN. Railroad of Death. London, 1946. 1st ed. Inscrip, eps browned, o/w VG in dj (crumpled; spine torn w/loss). *Edwards.* $23/£15

COATES, JAMES. Human Magnetism or How to Hypnotise. London, 1897. 1st ed. 253pp. Good. *Fye.* $125/£81

COATES, ROBERT M. Beyond the Alps. London: Gollancz, 1962. 1st ed. VG in dj (sl rubbed, chipped, soiled). *Virgo.* $23/£15

COATES, ROBERT M. The Eater of Darkness. (Paris: Contact Editions, 1926). 1st ed. 2 chips fr wrapper; sm nick, dkng spine label; eps sl foxed, o/w Very Nice in marbled wrappers, dec slipcase. *Reese.* $500/£323

COATES, ROBERT. Yesterday's Burdens. NY: Macaulay, 1933. 1st ed. NF (spine sl sunned) in dj (lt used; spine chipped). *Beasley.* $125/£81

COATS, ALICE M. The Book of Flowers. London: Phaidon, 1973. 1st ed. 40 color plts. As New in slipcase. *Quest.* $125/£81

COATS, ALICE M. The Plant Hunters. NY: McGraw Hill, 1970. 1st Amer ed. *Quest.* $65/£42

COATS, ALICE M. The Treasury of Flowers. NY, 1975. 1st Amer ed. 118 plts (33 color). VG in dj. *Brooks.* $29/£19

COATS, PETER. Flowers in History. London: Weidenfield & Nicholson, 1970. 1st ed. 148 photos. As New. *Quest.* $55/£35

COATSWORTH, ELIZABETH. The Cat Who Went to Heaven. NY: Macmillan, (1958). 1st ed thus. 4to. Lynd Ward (illus). Brn-tan cl w/yellow cat. Good in color pict dj. *Reisler.* $50/£32

COATSWORTH, ELIZABETH. The Cat Who Went to Heaven. NY: Macmillan, 1930. 1st ed. Signed. Lynd Ward (illus). Red cl, black lettering (lt spots). *Reisler.* $110/£71

COBB, ARTHUR F. Birds of the Falkland Islands. Witherby, 1933. 1st ed. VG in remains of dj. *Walcot.* $34/£22

COBB, BERT. Hunting Dogs. NY: Crafton Collection, 1931. 1st trade ed. 12 tipped-in plts. Price list laid in. Bkpl, inscrip, else Fine. *Cahan.* $50/£32

COBB, DANIEL. The Medical Botanist, and Expositor of Diseases and Remedies. Volume I. Castile, NY, 1846. 256pp. Full leather. (Rubbed; lacks rep; foxed). *Fye.* $50/£32

COBB, FRANK. An Aviator's Luck. Saalfield, 1927. 1st ed. Fine in dj. *Madle.* $20/£13

COBB, FRANK. Dangerous Deeds. Saalfield, 1927. 1st ed. Fine in dj. *Madle.* $20/£13

COBB, HUMPHREY. Paths of Glory. NY: Viking, 1935. 1st ed. Fine in dj (lt chipped). *Hermitage.* $40/£26

COBB, HUMPHREY. Paths of Glory. NY: Viking, 1935. 1st ed. NF in NF dj. *Revere.* $75/£48

COBB, IRVIN S. Down Yonder with Judge Priest and Irvin S. Cobb. NY: Ray Long & Richard R. Smith, 1932. 1st ed, with 'quarel' for 'quarrel' on pg 251, line 11. VG in dj. *Antic Hay.* $85/£55

COBB, IRVIN S. Maine. NY: George H. Doran, (1924). 1st ed. Pict paper-cvrd bds. Fine in NF dj. *Hermitage.* $35/£23

COBB, IRVIN S. Roll Call. Indianapolis: Bobbs, Merrill, (1942). 1st ed. NF in VG dj (wear; few tears). *Antic Hay.* $17/£11

COBB, JOHN STORER. A Quartercentury of Cremation in North America. Boston: Knight & Millet, 1901. Frontis. (Rear pocket removed.) *Schoyer.* $30/£19

COBB, LYMAN. Cobb's Juvenile Reader, No. 1. Sandy Hill, (NY): Griffen, Mabbett, 1836. 12mo. 72pp + 1pg list lower cvr, full-pg frontis plus 4 full-pg wood engrs. Ptd brn paper on bds, black roan spine. Fair (internal foxing, fading; cvrs spotted, soiled w/rounded corners; name). *Hobbyhorse.* $45/£29

COBB, LYMAN. The Evil Tendencies of Corporal Punishment as a Means of Moral Discipline.... NY: Mark H. Newman, 1847. Emb cl, gilt (rubbed; lt foxed). *Boswell.* $175/£113

COBB, RUTH and RICHARD HUNTER. Dollies. London: Grant Richards, 1902. 1st ed. #15 in Dumpy series. 24mo. Olive cl w/grn pinstripes (sl spine fading, edge darkening). *Reisler.* $165/£106

COBB, TY with AL STUMP. My Life in Baseball—The True Record. Doubleday, 1961. 1st ed. VG (pencil underlining) in Good+ dj. *Plapinger.* $60/£39

COBB, TY. Busting 'Em. Clode, 1914. 1st ed. VG; no dj (not issued?). *Plapinger.* $950/£613

COBBETT, JAMES PAUL. A Grammar of the Italian Language. London: For author, 1834. 3rd ed. xiv,368pp. Old 1/2 calf gilt, raised bands, marbled bds. *Hollett.* $116/£75

COBBETT, WILLIAM. The American Gardener.... NY: Turner & Hayden, 1844. 230pp. Very Nice (sl foxed). *Second Life.* $125/£81

COBBETT, WILLIAM. Cobbett's Legacy to Labourers. London: (Author), 1834. 1st ed. 141(3)pp + ad. Orig maroon roan (backstrip reinforced w/matching cl), gilt. *Cox.* $54/£35

COBBETT, WILLIAM. Cottage Economy. London: C. Clement, 1822. 1st ed in bk form. 207,ivpp (1st, last pp sl spotted, browned). Old 1/2 calf gilt, raised bands, marbled bds. *Hollett.* $279/£180

COBBETT, WILLIAM. Cottage Economy. London, 1822. Stereotype Ed. Contemp 1/2 black calf. *Petersfield.* $70/£45

COBBETT, WILLIAM. Cottage Economy. London: C. Clement, 1822. Stereotype ed. Add'l engr frontis; iv,(i),207pp. Old 1/2 calf gilt, raised bands, marbled bds. Name cut from title top, o/w VG. *Hollett.* $233/£150

COBBETT, WILLIAM. Cottage Economy. Hartford: Andrus, 1848. Rpt. 158,68pp. Pub's cl (sl worn). NF. *Second Life.* $65/£42

COBBETT, WILLIAM. Cottage Economy. Hammersmith: Douglas Pepler, 1916. One of 250 ptd. Full-pg wood engr. Cl-backed ptd bds, paper label (sl browned, rubbed). Good. *Cox.* $85/£55

COBBETT, WILLIAM. The Emigrant's Guide; in Ten Letters, Addressed to the Tax-Payers of England.... London, 1830. Rptd 'New Edition.' 162pp. Mod 3/4 calf, leather label (soil). Good. Howes L 516. *Ginsberg.* $150/£97

COBBETT, WILLIAM. The English Gardener...Concluding with a Kalendar. London: (Author), 1833. (4),338pp; fldg plt; 12pp pub's cat inserted at end. Bds (worn; rebacked in cl), orig label. Good (browning). *Cox.* $70/£45

COBBETT, WILLIAM. The English Gardener; or, A Treatise on the Situation, Soil.... London, 1833. iv;338;fldg plt. (Text spotted; plt sl foxed; rebacked.) *Henly.* $132/£85

COBBETT, WILLIAM. A Grammar of the English Language...to Which Are Added, Six Lessons.... London: By author, 1829. (240)pp. Orig bds (neatly rebacked); uncut. One gathering foxed, o/w Good. *Cox.* $50/£32

COBBETT, WILLIAM. Life and Adventures of Peter Porcupine with Other Records of His Early Career in England and America. London: Nonesuch, 1927. Color frontis. 1/2 bds; unopened. VG. *Argosy.* $50/£32

COBBETT, WILLIAM. Life and Adventures of Peter Porcupine.... London: Nonesuch, 1927. 1st ed. #1439/1800. Hand-colored frontis. Orig cl-backed marbled bds. Sound (corners worn). *Cox.* $31/£20

COBBETT, WILLIAM. A Year's Residence in the United States of America. Part I only. London: Sherwood, Neely, & James, 1818. 1st Eng ed. 8vo. viii,168pp. Orig bds. Rubbed; uncut, paper label lacking, o/w Fine. Howes C 525. *Argosy.* $200/£129

COBBETT, WILLIAM. A Year's Residence, in the United States of America. London: E. Bensley for the author, 1828. 3rd ed. x,370pp. Contemp sponged calf w/raised bands, spine label. VG (bkpl). *Hollett.* $116/£75

COBLEIGH, ROLFE. Handy Farm Devices and How to Make Them. NY: OJ, 1910. VG (tp, frontis foxed). *Bohling.* $25/£16

COBLENTZ, STANTON A. After 12,000 Years. Fantasy Pub, 1950. 1st ed. Fine in dj. *Madle.* $20/£13

COBLENTZ, STANTON A. Under Triple Suns. Fantasy, 1955. 1st ed. One of 300 numbered, signed. Fine in dj (frayed). *Madle.* $95/£61

COBLENTZ, STANTON A. Villains and Vigilantes. NY, 1936. 1st ed. Fine (bkpl) in dj. *Baade.* $50/£32

COBLENTZ, STANTON A. Villains and Vigilantes. Wilson-Erickson, 1936. 1st ed. Fine in dj (sl frayed). *Madle.* $75/£48

COBLENTZ, STANTON A. The Wonder Stick. Cosmopolitan, 1929. 1st ed. Fine in NF dj (lt dust soil). *Aronovitz.* $35/£23

COBURN, ALVIN. The Epidemiology of Hemolytic Streptococcus During World War II in the United States Navy. Balt, 1949. 1st ed. Good. *Fye.* $40/£26

COCHRAN, DORIS M. Poisonous Reptiles of the World: A Wartime Handbook. Washington, 1943. 17 plts. Orig wraps. Good. *Goodrich.* $65/£42

COCHRAN, HAMILTON. Blockade Runners of the Confederacy. Indianapolis, (1958). Fine in dj (chipped). *Pratt.* $35/£23

COCHRAN, KEITH. Colt Peacemaker Encyclopedia. (Rapid City, SD: 1986.) Ltd to 2000 ptd in Standard Ed. VG in dj. *Lien.* $60/£39

COCHRANE, J.A. Dr. Johnson's Printer. London: Routledge & Kegan Paul, 1964. 1st ed. Blue cl, gilt. Excellent in dj. *Hartfield.* $65/£42

COCKAYNE, L. New Zealand Plants and Their Story. Wellington, 1967. 4th ed. VG (sm lib stamps; bumped). *Brooks.* $35/£23

COCKBURN, GEORGE. Extract from a Diary of.... London, 1888. 1st ed. Sm 8vo. 96pp. Eps sl browned, o/w VG. Dk grn cl, gilt title (rubbed). *Edwards.* $70/£45

COCKE, R. Veronese's Drawings. London: Sotheby, 1984. 12 color plts. Sound in dj. *Ars Artis.* $93/£60

COCKERELL, DOUGLAS. Bookbinding and the Care of Books.... London: John Hogg, 1901. 1st ed. 8 collotype plts. Orig holland-backed bds. VG (differentially faded at edges). *Cox.* $39/£25

COCKERELL, DOUGLAS. Some Notes on Bookbinding. London: OUP, 1929. 1st ed. Orig cl-backed marbled bds. Good. *Cox.* $31/£20

COCKERELL, SIDNEY C. Old Testament Miniatures. NY, (1975). 1st ed. 92 color plts. VG in dj. *Argosy.* $75/£48

COCKERELL, SIDNEY. Old Testament Miniatures. London: Phaidon, n.d. (c. 1970). 92 full-pg plts. Dj. *Edwards.* $101/£65

COCKERELL, SIDNEY. Old Testament Miniatures. NY, n.d. (ca 1975). Good in dj. *Washton.* $100/£65

COCKTON, HENRY. The Life and Adventures of Valentine Vox, the Ventriloquist. London: Routledge, 1848. Frontis, xx,620pp (marginal soiling, browning); mtd title (short tears repaired); 58 engr plts (sl marginal foxing). Contemp 1/2 calf (rebacked; rubbed), retaining old backstrip. *Cox.* $54/£35

COCKTON, HENRY. Sylvester Sound the Somnambulist. London: William Mark Clark, 1849. Frontis port, extra engr title, xvi,367pp; 43 engr plts. Contemp 1/2 blue calf (rebacked), orig backstrip. Good. *Cox.* $54/£35

COCTEAU, JEAN. Cock and Harlequin. Rollo H. Myers (trans). Egoist Press, 1921. 1st UK ed. Port, 2 monograms by Picasso. Few leaves creased top corner, o/w Excellent in wraps. *Sclanders.* $62/£40

COCTEAU, JEAN. The Infernal Machine. OUP, 1936. 1st UK ed. Lt edge bump, o/w NF- in dj (spine sl discolored). *Sclanders.* $54/£35

COCTEAU, JEAN. Opium. Ernest Boyd (trans). Allen & Unwin, 1933. 1st UK ed. VG reading copy. *Sclanders.* $19/£12

COCTEAU, JEAN. Round the World Again in 80 Days. London, 1937. 1st Eng ed. VG in dj. *Words Etc.* $54/£35

COCTEAU, JEAN. The Typewriter. Ronald Duncan (trans). Dennis Dobson, 1947. 1st UK ed. NF in dj (sl rubbed). *Sclanders.* $39/£25

COCTEAU, JEAN. The White Paper by Anonymous. Paris, 1957. 1st ed. NF in ptd wraps. *Polyanthos.* $30/£19

Code of Iowa, Passed at the Session of the General Assembly of 1850-1, and Approved 5th February, 1851. Iowa City: Palmer and Paul, State Printers, 1851. New 1/4 calf over marbled bds. Nice. *Boswell.* $250/£161

CODMAN, JOHN. Brook Farm, Historic and Personal Memoirs. Boston: Arena Pub Co, 1894. Frontis, viii,335pp + ads. VG (extrms frayed; rear hinge cracked). *Bohling.* $65/£42

CODMAN, JOHN. The Mormon Country. NY, 1874. 1st ed. Frontis map, 225pp. Spine sl dknd, worn, o/w VG. *Benchmark.* $95/£61

CODMAN, JOHN. Winter Sketches from the Saddle, by a Septuagenarian. NY: Putnam's, (1888). 1st ed. 205pp; port. VG. *Petrilla.* $20/£13

CODRESCU, ANDREI. The History of the Growth of Heaven. (SF): Grape Press, 1971. One of 350. Signed. NF in stapled pict wrappers. *Reese.* $30/£19

CODRINGTON, THOMAS. Roman Roads in Britain. London, 1918. 3rd ed. 10 maps (1 in rear pocket). (Cl faded.) *Edwards.* $31/£20

CODY, LIZA. Head Case. London: Collins, 1985. 1st ed. Fine in dj. *Murder.* $40/£26

CODY, MORRILL. Passing Stranger. NY: Macaulay, (1936). 1st ed. Lt dust soiling lower edge, o/w Fine in VG pict dj (lt nicked; dust dknd). *Reese.* $60/£39

CODY, MORRILL. This Must Be the Place. NY: Lee Furman, (1937). 1st Amer ed, bk club issue. Gilt-stamped orange cl. Fine in VG dj (nicks, old mend). *Reese.* $25/£16

COE, MICHAEL D. The Jaguar's Children: Pre-Classic Central Mexico. NY: Museum of Primitive Art, 1965. (Inscrip.) Dj (tattered). *Archaeologia.* $85/£55

COE, TUCKER. (Pseud of Donald E. Westlake.) A Jade in Aries. NY: Random House, 1970. 1st ed. Fine in dj (some lamination lifting). *Janus.* $35/£23

Coelebs in Search of a Wife. (By Hannah More.) NY: Swords, 1809. 1st US ed from 2nd London ed. 2 vols. viii,259; 254 + 2pp ads. Contemp mottled calf. VG set (ink inscrips; lt foxing). *Second Life.* $150/£97

COESTLER, A. (Arthur Koestler) et al. The Practice of Sex. London, 1936. 1st issue w/integral wallet at rear w/8 illus. VG. *Lewton.* $116/£75

COETZEE, J.M. Dusklands. Johannesburg: Ravan, 1974. 1st ed. Fine in dj. *Lame Duck.* $650/£419

COETZEE, J.M. Foe. (Toronto): Stoddart, (1986). 1st ed, Canadian issue. Sm dot bottom edge, else Fine in dj. *Godot.* $35/£23

COETZEE, J.M. Foe. NY: Viking, 1987. 1st ed. Review copy. VF in dj. *Else Fine.* $40/£26

COETZEE, J.M. From the Heart of the Country. NY: Harper, 1977. 1st ed. VF in dj (minor edgewear). *Else Fine.* $60/£39

COETZEE, J.M. Life and Times of Michael K. NY: Viking, (1983). 1st Amer ed. NF in dj. *Hermitage.* $30/£19

COETZEE, J.M. Life and Times of Michael K. Johannesburg: Ravan, 1983. 1st ed. Fine in Fine dj. *Lame Duck.* $275/£177

COFFEY, BRIAN. (Pseud of Dean Koontz.) The Face of Fear. B-M, 1977. 1st ed. NF in VG+ dj (sm tears; chip rear panel). *Fine Books.* $125/£81

COFFEY, BRIAN. (Pseud of Dean Koontz.) The Face of Fear. Bobbs-Merrill, 1977. 1st ed. Fine in dj (nick). *Madle.* $250/£161

COFFIN, DAVID R. The Villa d'Este at Tivoli. Princeton, 1960. (Extrms sl bumped.) *Washton.* $125/£81

COFFIN, DAVID R. (ed). The Italian Garden. Washington: Dumbarton Oaks, 1972. 1st ed. 8 plts. Spine sunned, else Fine in dj. *Bookpress.* $35/£23

COFFIN, GEORGE. A Pioneer Voyage to California and Round the World, 1849 to 1852. (Chicago: Gorham B. Coffin, 1908.) Frontis. (Tips sl bumped.) *Dawson.* $75/£48

COFFIN, GEORGE. A Pioneer Voyage to California and Round the World. (Chicago, 1908.) 1st ed. Inscribed presentation from author's grandson. Howes 2070. *Ginsberg.* $125/£81

COFFIN, LEWIS A., JR. and ARTHUR C. HOLDEN. Brick Architecture of the Colonial Period.... NY: Architectural Book Pub, 1919. 1st ed. 118 plts. VG (wear, hinges internally cracked, spine label rubbed). *Bookpress.* $350/£226

COFFIN, MARIE M. The History of Nantucket Island: a Bibliography.... (Nantucket: Nantucket Hist Trust, 1970.) Ltd ed. *Lefkowicz.* $35/£23

COFFIN, ROBERT. Last of the 'Logan.' Ithaca: Cornell Univ, 1941. Frontis photo port. NF in dj. *Schoyer.* $45/£29

COFFIN, TRISTRAM P. The Illustrated Book of Baseball Folklore. Seabury, 1975. 1st ed. Fine in VG dj. *Plapinger.* $35/£23

COGAN, DAVID. Neurology of the Ocular Muscles. Springfield, 1948. 1st ed. Good. *Fye.* $75/£48

COHEN, ARTHUR A. Sonia Delaunay. NY: Abrams, 1975. 1st ed. Fine in dj. *Cahan.* $125/£81

COHEN, LEONARD. Parasites of Heaven. Toronto, (1966). 1st ed. NF in pict wraps. *Polyanthos.* $45/£29

COHEN, MORTON N. Lewis Carroll, Photographer of Children: Four Nude Studies. Phila: Rosenbach Foundation/Clarkson N. Potter, 1979. Fine in dj. *Cahan.* $60/£39

COHEN, OCTAVUS ROY. Dark Days and Black Knights. NY: Dodd, Mead, 1923. 1st ed. Inscrip, else VG. *Chapel Hill.* $30/£19

COHEN, OCTAVUS ROY. Don't Ever Love Me. NY: Macmillan, 1947. 1st ed. NF (bumped) in VG+ dj (lt chipped). *Janus.* $45/£29

COHN, LOUIS HENRY. Bibliography of the Works of Ernest Hemingway. NY: Random House, 1931. Ltd to 500 numbered. Fldg facs frontis. Black cl; gilt. Good. *Karmiole.* $75/£48

COHN, WILLIAM. Chinese Painting. London, (1950). 2nd rev ed. 224 plts. (Corners bumped.) *Artis.* $25/£16

COKE, DESMOND. The Art of Silhouette. London: Martin Secker, (1913). 1st ed. Grey cl (lt wear). *Glenn.* $50/£32

COKE, EDWARD. A Systematic Arrangement of Lord Coke's First Institute of the Laws of England.... London: Ptd by S. Brooke, 1818. 3 vols. 3/4 morocco, marbled bds. Repaired but sound. *Boswell.* $450/£290

COKE, EDWARD. The Third Part of the Institutes of the Laws of England.... London: A. Crooke, 1669. 4th ed. Mod full calf (w/o port). Attractive. *Boswell.* $850/£548

COKE, HENRY J. Ride over the Rocky Mountains to Oregon and California. London: Bentley, 1852. 1st ed. (10),388,(2)pp, port. Contemp 1/2 morocco. Howes C 548. *Ginsberg.* $450/£290

COKE, LAWRENCE and LUCILLE. Mining on the Trails of Destiny. NY: Vantage, (1969). 1st ed. Fine in Fine dj. *Book Market.* $30/£19

COKE, RICHARD. The Arab's Place in the Sun. London: Thornton Butterworth, 1929. 1st ed. Map; 8 plts. (Spine faded, creased; joints tender; sl spotting; ex-libris w/label.) *Hollett.* $47/£30

COLAM, LANCE. The Death Treasure of the Khmers. London, 1939. 1st ed. (Feps lt browned.) Dj (chipped, loss). *Edwards.* $31/£20

COLAM, LANCE. The Death Treasure of the Khmers. London: Stanley Paul, 1939. 1st ed. 11 plts. Spine sl faded. *Hollett.* $39/£25

COLANGE, L. Zell's Popular Encyclopedia. Phila: T. Ellwood Zell, 1870-1873. 1st ed. 2 vols. iv,1196; (2),1152; 202pp (supplement). Grn calf over cl (sl rubbed). Very Nice. *Karmiole.* $125/£81

COLBURN, ZERAH. A Memoir of Zerah Colburn. Springfield: G.&C. Merriam, 1833. 1st ed. Engr frontis port. Orig cl (upper hinge worn), orig paper label (rubbed). *Dramatis Personae.* $200/£129

COLBY, MERLE. A Guide to Alaska. NY, 1950. 5th ptg. Fldg map in rear packet. VG. *Artis.* $20/£13

COLDEN, CADWALLADER D. The Life of Robert Fulton.... NY: Kirk & Mercein, 1817. 1st ed. vi,369,(1)pp (lt foxing; lt corner dampstain); port (old cat cutting tipped to verso); fldg table. Uncut. Period-style paper-backed bds, orig paper laid down on cvrs. Very Nice. *Felcone.* $300/£194

COLE, ALLAN B. (ed). Yankee Surveyors in the Shogun's Seas...1853-1856. Princeton: Princeton Univ, 1947. VG in dj. *High Latitude.* $30/£19

COLE, CORNELIUS. California Three Hundred and Fifty Years Ago. Manuelo's Narrative. SF: Samuel Carson, 1888. Frontis, 333pp. Gilt dec cl. VG. *Connolly.* $42/£27

COLE, ERNEST. House of Bondage. NY: Random House, (1967). VG in dj (wear). *Aka.* $35/£23

COLE, G.D.H. and MARGARET. The Brooklyn Murders. NY: Albert & Charles Boni, 1931. 1st pb ed. Fine in stiff wrappers w/cardboard slipcase. *Mordida.* $45/£29

COLE, G.D.H. and MARGARET. The Brothers Sackville. NY: Macmillan, 1937. 1st Amer ed. Pg edges, eps dknd, o/w VG in dj (sl wear). *Mordida.* $45/£29

COLE, G.D.H. and MARGARET. Knife in the Dark. London: CCC, 1942. 1st ed. Lt spotting; fading spine top, o/w VG in dj (sm piece missing; short closed tears; sm chips). *Mordida.* $50/£32

COLE, G.D.H. and MARGARET. A Lesson in Crime and Other Stories. London: Polybooks, 1946. Reprint ed. Fine in dj. *Mordida.* $65/£42

COLE, G.D.H. and MARGARET. Mrs. Warrender's Profession. NY: Macmillan, 1939. 1st Amer ed. VG in dj (sl wear; closed punch-tear; external tape mend; sm chips). *Mordida.* $45/£29

COLE, G.D.H. and MARGARET. Toper's End. London: CCC, 1942. 1st ed. Sl spotting edges, o/w Fine in dj (price-clipped; chipping; short closed tears; soiled back). *Mordida.* $75/£48

COLE, HARRY ELLSWORTH. Stagecoach and Tavern Tales of the Old Northwest. Cleveland: Clark, 1930. 1st ed. Largely unopened. Bumped, o/w VG. *October Farm.* $135/£87

COLE, J. PRESTON. The Problematic Self in Kierkegaard and Freud. New Haven: Yale Univ Press, (1971). 1st ed. Red fabrikoid. VG in dj (sl defective). *Gach.* $30/£19

COLE, REX VICAT. British Trees. London, 1907. 2 vols. Photogravure frontis. Teg. (Cl sl soiled, rubbed; spines sl bumped.) *Edwards.* $54/£35

COLE, S.W. The American Fruit Book. Boston, 1849. 288pp (mild foxing, staining; rear blank sheet missing). Contemp calf (splitting at spine). *Sutton.* $65/£42

COLEMAN, EMMA LEWIS. New England Captives Carried to Canada Between 1677 and 1760.... Portland, ME: Southworth, 1925. 2 vols. Unopened. Orig cl, dec gilt. Spines dull, else VG set. *Bohling.* $200/£129

COLEMAN, KENNETH. The American Revolution in Georgia 1763-1789. Athens: Univ of GA press, (1958). 1st ed. Blue cl. Fine in NF dj (lt edgeworn). *Chapel Hill.* $55/£35

COLEMAN, LIZZIE D. History of the Pigeon Roost Massacre. Mitchell, IN, 1904. Good (chipped remnants of fr wrap laid in, lacks rear; lower corner tp rumpled, chipped; smudges). *Bohling.* $75/£48

COLEMAN, SATIS N. Bells: Their History, Legends, Making, and Uses. Chicago, 1928. Inscribed, dated. VG. *Argosy.* $100/£65

COLEMAN, SETH. Memoirs of Doctor Seth Coleman of Amherst. New Haven: Flagg & Gray, 1817. 1st ed. (2),288pp. Contemp calf w/leather spine label (rubbed, lt foxing). *Karmiole.* $35/£23

COLEMAN, TERRY. The Railway Navvies. London: Hutchinson, 1965. Gilt cl. VG in dj. *Hollett.* $39/£25

COLEMAN, W.S. British Butterflies. London, 1867. New ed. Color frontis, 179pp + 4pp pub's ads (lacks pp1-4; sl browning); 15 plts (13 color). Mod 1/2 morocco (rebound), marbled bds. *Edwards*. $31/£20

COLEMAN, WANDA. Mad Dog Black Lady. Santa Barbara: Black Sparrow, 1979. 1st trade ed. Port. VG in stiff wraps. *Petrilla*. $30/£19

COLERIDGE, ERNEST HARTLEY. Life and Correspondence of John Duke Lord Coleridge.... London: Heinemann, 1904. 2 vols. Blue cl (worn). *Boswell*. $75/£48

COLERIDGE, MRS. S.T. Minnow among Tritons, Letters to Thomas Poole 1799-1834. Bloomsbury: Nonesuch Press, 1934. 1st ed. One of 675 numbered. 3 ports; facs. Uncut, partly unopened. Nice. *Second Life*. $65/£42

COLERIDGE, SAMUEL TAYLOR. Aids to Reflection. Henry Nelson Coleridge (ed). London: William Pickering, 1848. 2 vols. xx,338; lxvi,322pp. Contemp 1/2 calf (rebacked retaining old lettering pieces), marbled sides. Sound set. *Cox*. $70/£45

COLERIDGE, SAMUEL TAYLOR. Confessions of an Enquiring Spirit. London: Pickering, 1840. 1st ed. Ad leaf, (8),x,(2),95pp + 16pp pub's cat; uncut. Good (sl browned) in blue cl (hinges splitting, backstrip chipped, paper label defective). *Cox*. $74/£48

COLERIDGE, SAMUEL TAYLOR. The Dramatic Works. Derwent Coleridge (ed). London: Moxon, 1857. New ed. 1/2 title. Aeg. Red morocco prize binding, gilt. Fine. *Poetry*. $70/£45

COLERIDGE, SAMUEL TAYLOR. Letters, Conversations and Recollections of.... NY: Harper, 1836. 1st Amer ed. Diced cl (sl soiled), ptd spine label (sl eroded). Good (lt foxing; 2 contemp clippings on rep). *Reese*. $65/£42

COLERIDGE, SAMUEL TAYLOR. Poems. London: Longman & Rees, 1803. 3rd ed. xii,202,(2)pp pub's ads. Aeg. Full crushed morocco, dec gilt spine (sl rubbed). *Karmiole*. $175/£113

COLERIDGE, SAMUEL TAYLOR. The Poetical Works of.... London: William Pickering, 1834. 3rd ed. 3 vols. Contemp 1/2 calf, gilt spines, marbled bds (sl rubbed; hand-colored armorial bkpl). *Cummins*. $300/£194

COLERIDGE, SAMUEL TAYLOR. The Rime of the Ancient Mariner. Oxford, 1930. One of 750. VG in cl-backed Cockerell paper bds. Ptd dj (lt soiled). *Cox*. $70/£45

COLERIDGE, SAMUEL TAYLOR. The Rime of the Ancient Mariner. NY: Cheshire House, 1931. #11/1200. Uncut. Fine (spine sunned; sl rubbed) in box (sl rubbed, 2 corners split). *Polyanthos*. $75/£48

COLERIDGE, SAMUEL TAYLOR. The Rime of the Ancient Mariner. NY: LEC, 1945. One of 1500 signed by Edward A. Wilson (illus). Full leather. Envelope w/prospectus glued to fr pastedown, else Fine in slipcase. *Pharos*. $150/£97

COLERIDGE, SAMUEL TAYLOR. Specimens of the Table Talk. Vol II. Murray, 1835. 1st ed. Frontis (foxed). Teg. VG in later 1/2 morocco (sl rubbed). *Poetry*. $19/£12

COLERIDGE, SARA. Memoir and Letters of.... London: King, 1873. 1st ed. 353,466pp. Good (ex-lib; hinges loose). *Second Life*. $65/£42

COLES, ROBERT. The Darkness and the Light. NY: Aperture, 1974. 1st ed. 65 b/w plts. Fine in VG dj. *Cahan*. $85/£55

COLETTE. The Blue Lantern. London: Secker, 1963. 1st UK ed. VG in dj (price-clipped). *Williams*. $23/£15

COLETTE. The Last of Cheri. NY, (1932). 1st Amer ed. VG +. *Mcclintock*. $20/£13

COLFAX, SCHUYLER. The Laws of Kansas.... (Washington, 1856.) 1st ed. 16pp. VG in self-wraps. *Petrilla*. $35/£23

Collection of Ornamental Designs.... (By Matthias Lock.) (London: John Weale, ca1840.) Title (sl stained), 23 plts (num 1-24). Cl (spine defective, faded). *Marlborough*. $186/£120

COLLEDGE, MALCOLM A.R. The Art of Palmyra. London: Thames & Hudson, (1976). Good in dj. *Archaeologia*. $95/£61

COLLEDGE, MALCOLM A.R. The Art of Palmyra. Thames & Hudson, 1976. 1st ed. Dj. *Edwards*. $47/£30

COLLES, ABRAHAM. Practical Observations on the Venereal Disease, and on the Use of Mercury. Phila, 1837. 1st Amer ed. 211pp. Good. *Fye*. $150/£97

COLLES, CHRISTOPHER. Survey of the Roads of the United States of America 1789. Walter W. Ristow (ed). Cambridge: Harvard Univ, 1961. Fldg map. Dj (soiled, price-clipped, spotted). *Bohling*. $45/£29

COLLET, L.W. The Structure of the Alps. London, 1935. 2nd ed. Inscribed. 12 plts (4 fldg). Fine. *Henly*. $28/£18

COLLETT, RITTER. The Cincinnati Reds. Jordan-Powers, 1976. 1st ed. Fine in VG dj. *Plapinger*. $125/£81

COLLIDGE, L.A. Klondike and the Yukon Country.... Phila, 1897. Rev, enlgd ed. 251pp (tp stained). New buckram (rebound), leather label. Contents VG. *Heinoldt*. $35/£23

COLLIER, JEREMY. A Short View of the Immorality and Profaneness of the English Stage.... London: S. Keble et al, 1698. 1st ed. (xvi),288pp. Later full calf, deep border in blind on sides (rebacked, orig backstrip reinstated, title unobtrusively mtd). Nice. *Cox*. $233/£150

COLLIER, JOHN PAYNE. Punch and Judy. NY: LEC, 1937. #162/1500. George Cruikshank (illus). Fine in orig tissue guard in slipcase. *Williams*. $101/£65

COLLIER, JOHN. The Devil and All. Nonesuch, 1934. Ltd to 1000 numbered, signed. Frontis; 3 inlaid silver foils fr cvr (sl chipped, tarnished). Good. *Waterfield*. $93/£60

COLLIER, JOHN. His Monkey Wife. Davies, 1930. 1st ed, 1st bk. VG. *Aronovitz*. $65/£42

COLLIER, JOHN. The John Collier Reader. NY: Knopf, 1972. 1st ed. Fine in dj. *Mordida*. $75/£48

COLLIER, JOHN. Presenting Moonshine. NY: Viking, 1941. 1st ed. Fine in VG dj (spine torn, wrinkled). *Beasley*. $35/£23

COLLIER, WILLIAM ROSS and EDWIN VICTOR WESTRATE. Dave Cook of the Rockies. NY: Rufus Rockwell Wilson, 1936. 1st ed. VG in dj (sl chipped). *Lien*. $40/£26

COLLINGWOOD, R.G. and J.N.L. MYRES. Roman Britain and the English Settlements. Oxford: Clarendon Press, 1936. 1st ed. 10 maps. VG. *Hollett*. $39/£25

COLLINGWOOD, STUART DODGSON. The Life and Letters of Lewis Carroll. London: T. Fisher Unwin, 1898. 1st ed. 8vo. 448pp,(12)pp ads. Teg. Gilt-dec grn cl w/bevelled edges. Binding sl soiled, o/w VG. *Chapel Hill*. $85/£55

COLLINGWOOD, STUART DODGSON. The Life and Letters of Lewis Carroll. London, 1899. 2nd ed. Frontis port, xx,448pp + (xii)ads. Teg, rest uncut. (Spotting; hinges tender; spine discolored.) *Edwards*. $70/£45

COLLINGWOOD, W.G. The Limestone Alps of Savoy. London, 1884. xxiii,206pp. Unopened, uncut. (Upper fore-edge cvr dampstained.) Glassine dj (torn). *Henly.* $74/£48

COLLINGWOOD, W.G. Northumbrian Crosses of the Pre-Norman Age. London: Faber, 1927. 1st ed. Uncut. Gilt cl (spine sl dulled). Dj (fr panel taped fr pastedown). *Hollett.* $248/£160

Collins's Peerage of England; Genealogical, Biographical, and Historical. London: Ptd for F.C. and J. Rivington, 1812. 1st ed, as such. 9 vols. xv,(4),574; (iv),619; (iv),807; (iv),552; iv,732; iv,764; iv,578, ad; iv,624; iv,526pp. Full contemp polished calf, morocco spine labels; marbled edges, eps. VG set (some hinges starting, occasional foxing, armorial bkpls each vol). *Cahan.* $400/£258

COLLINS, A. FREDERICK. Jack Heaton, Oil Prospector. NY: Frederick A. Stokes, (1920). 1st ed. 237pp, 6 illus by Charles E. Cartwright. Fine in pict dj (nicks, else NF). *Godot.* $45/£29

COLLINS, CARVEL. Sam Ward in the Gold Rush. Stanford, (1949). 1st ed. Frontis; 3 plts. VG. *Oregon.* $17/£11

COLLINS, CHARLES ALSTON. A Cruise upon Wheels. London: Peter Davies, 1936. 1st ed. Partly unopened. VG in dj (spine, top edges sl dknd). *Hollett.* $39/£25

COLLINS, COLIN. The Human Mole. London, 1909. 1st ed. Good+ *Madle.* $75/£48

COLLINS, DENNIS. Indian's Last Fight. (Girard, KS, 1915.) 1st ed. Howes C 590. *Ginsberg.* $300/£194

COLLINS, HUBERT E. Warpath and Cattle Trail. NY: William Morrow, 1928. 1st ed. Good. Howes C592. *Lien.* $65/£42

COLLINS, JOHN S. Across the Plains in '64. Omaha, 1904. 1st ed. Inscribed presentation. (New fep; ink stains cvrs.) Howes C 594. *Ginsberg.* $200/£129

COLLINS, MAX ALLAN. The Million-Dollar Wound. NY: St. Martin's, 1986. 1st ed. Signed. Fine in Fine dj. *Janus.* $35/£23

COLLINS, WILKIE. No Name. London: Sampson Low, 1862. 1st ed. 3 vols. 8vo, half-titles vols 1-2. Orig orange scarlet morocco cl, gilt blocked in blind. Fine (recent name label inside each cvr; edges sl soiled). *Bickersteth.* $1,054/£680

COLLINS, WILLIAM. The Poetical Works. Nicolas (ed). London: William Pickering, 1830. 1st Aldine ed. Port. Orig cl, uncut. VG (backstrip sl faded; label lt rubbed). *Cox.* $28/£18

COLLINS, WINFIELD HAZLITT. The Truth about Lynching and the Negro in the South.... NY: Neale Pub. Co., 1918. 1st ed. NF (bkpl, sm lib blindstamp). *Mcgowan.* $250/£161

COLLINSON, HUGH. Country Monuments. London: David & Charles, 1975. 1st ed. 32 plts. VG in dj. *Hollett.* $31/£20

COLLINSON, RICHARD. Journal of H.M.S. Enterprise, on the Expedition in Search of Sir John Franklin's Ships in Behring Strait, 1850-55.... London: Sampson, Low, etc., 1889. xi,531pp. Color frontis, port, 6 fldg maps. Orig dec cl. VG (sm lib rubber stamp on title, back of frontis, maps). *High Latitude.* $900/£581

COLLIS, MAURICE. The First Holy One. Knopf, 1948. 1st ed. VG in VG- dj. *Bishop.* $18/£12

COLLIS, MAURICE. Foreign Mud.... London: Faber, 1946. 1st ed. (Sl mkd; backstrip faded.) *Petersfield.* $25/£16

COLLIS, MAURICE. The Grand Peregrination. Faber, 1949. 1st ed. Dj (chipped, crease, loss). *Edwards.* $25/£16

COLLIS, MAURICE. The Great Within. Faber, 1941. 1st ed. 3 maps (1 fldg). Dj (sl chipped). *Edwards.* $25/£16

COLLIS, MAURICE. The Land of the Great Image. Faber & Faber, 1943. 1st ed. 4 plans, fldg map. (Ex-libris.) Dj (sl rubbed, chipped). *Edwards.* $25/£16

COLLIS, MAURICE. Quest for Sita. NY, 1947. 1st Amer ed. Mervyn Peake (illus). Black cl. VF in Fine dj. *Dalian.* $194/£125

COLLIS, MAURICE. Stanley Spencer; a Biography. London: Harvill, 1962. Frontis, 24 plts; pict eps. Pub's cl. Fine. *Europa.* $19/£12

COLLODI, C. Pinocchio. NY: LEC, 1937. #162/1500 signed by Richard Floethe (illus). Fine in slipcase (sl dusty). *Williams.* $147/£95

COLLUM, CHARLES R. New York Nude: A Photographic Essay. (NY: Amphoto, 1981). 1st Amer ed. Fine in dj (price-clipped). *Between The Covers.* $65/£42

COLOMB, P. The Great War of 189-: A Forecast. London: Heinemann, 1893. 1st ed. Pict grn cl. Fine. *Cummins.* $300/£194

Colonial Churches: A Series of Sketches. Richmond: Southern Churchman, 1907. VG-. *Book Broker.* $45/£29

COLP, RALPH, JR. To Be an Invalid: The Illness of Charles Darwin. Chicago, 1977. 1st ed. Good in dj. *Fye.* $25/£16

COLQUHOUN, ARCHIBALD R. China in Transformation. London: Harper, 1898. 1st ed. viii,(iv),398pp, 17 plts. Blue gilt cl (sm snag). Few spots, but attractive, bright. *Hollett.* $186/£120

COLQUHOUN, JOHN. The Moor and the Loch. Edinburgh: Wm. Blackwood, 1840. Stamped in gilt, blind. (Upper part of spine missing; foxed throughout.) *Argosy.* $75/£48

COLQUHOUN, JOHN. The Moor and the Loch. London: Blackwood, 1884. 6th ed. 2 vols. Tipped in photo port. Gilt dec grn cl (inscrip). *Petersfield.* $96/£62

COLSON, PERCY. The Strange History of Lord George Gordon. London: Robert Hale, 1937. 1st ed. Frontis port, 15 plts. Nice. *Cady.* $25/£16

COLT, C.F. and A. MIALL. The Early Piano. London: Stainer & Bell, 1981. 1st ed. Fine in dj. *Willow House.* $31/£20

COLT, MIRIAM DAVIS. Went to Kansas.... Watertown: L. Ingalls, 1862. 1st ed. 294pp. Orig brn blindstamped cl (extrems sl worn; gilt spine lettering dull). VG+ (early sig; lt foxing, soiling). Howes C 616. *Harrington.* $425/£274

COLT, MIRIAM DAVIS. Went to Kansas.... Watertown, 1862. 1st ed. 294pp (lacks fr flyleaf). Howes C 616. *Ginsberg.* $450/£290

COLTMAN, ROBERT, JR. Beleaguered in Peking. Phila: F.A. Davis, 1901. 77 photo engrs. Lime grn cl stamped in gilt, dk grn (spine sl faded; several leaves creased). *Schoyer.* $65/£42

COLTON, HAROLD S. Black Sand. Albuquerque: Univ of NM, 1960. 1st ed. NF in VG dj (sl soil). *Parker.* $45/£29

COLTON, HAROLD S. Hopi Kachina Dolls with a Key to Their Identification. Albuquerque: Univ of NM, 1949. 1st ed. NF in VG- dj. *Parker.* $95/£61

COLTON, WALTER. The California Diary by...Late Alcalde of Monterey. Biobooks, 1948. 1st thus. Ltd to 1000 ptd. 6 plts, map, fldg facs. Marbled eps. Fine. Howes C 625. *Oregon*. $55/£35

COLTON, WALTER. The California Diary. Oakland: Biobooks, 1948. One of 1000. Map, 6 plts, fldg facs, 6 ports on 1 sheet. Red pebbled cl, gilt spine titles, dec. Gilt faded, else NF. Howes C 625. *Parmer*. $65/£42

COLTON, WALTER. Glances into California. LA: Dawson, 1955. Ltd to 250 ptd. Fine. *Oregon*. $45/£29

COLTON, WALTER. Three Years in California. Stanford Univ Press, (1949). Facs rpt. Tan cl. Fine in Fine dj. *Harrington*. $40/£26

COLTON, WALTER. Three Years in California. NY: A.S. Barnes, 1850. 1st ed. Engr frontis port, 456pp, 5 full-pg engr ports, 6 full-pg plts, map, fldg facs (sm corner tear). Black cl (extrems worn) stamped in blind/gilt. VG+ (foxing, esp eps, prelims). Howes C 625. *Harrington*. $225/£145

COLTON, WALTER. Three Years in California. NY: A.S. Barnes, 1850. 1st ed. Frontis; 456pp; 4 ports; map; fldg facs. VG. Howes C 625. *Oregon*. $275/£177

COLTON, WALTER. Visit to Constantinople and Athens. NY: Leavitt, Lord, 1836. 1st ed. 348,9,4,6pp. Orig cl. Sl rubbed, soiled; cvrs sl dampstained; spine sl frayed; lt foxing, o/w VG ex-lib. *Worldwide*. $85/£55

COLUM, PADRAIC. Creatures. NY: Macmillan, 1927. Ltd to 300. Signed by Colum and Boris Artzybashoff (illus). Cl-backed silver bds. Spine title sl rubbed, o/w Fine in pub's slipcase (worn). *Sadlon*. $100/£65

COLUM, PADRAIC. Wild Earth and Other Poems. NY: Henry Holt, 1916. 1st ed as such. VG in dj (lt chipped, rubbed). *Cahan*. $45/£29

COLVIN, F.F. and E.R. GORDON. Diary of the 9th (Q.R.) Lancers During the South African Campaign, 1899 to 1902. South Kensington: Cecil Roy, 1904. 1st ed. Fldg map in pocket. 2-tone cl, gilt; inner hinges starting, else NF. *Mcgowan*. $350/£226

COLVIN, F.F. and E.R. GORDON. Diary of the 9th Lancers During the South African Campaign, 1899 to 1902. London, 1904. 1st ed. Frontis, lg fldg map in pocket. Eps browned, sl brittle; hinges sl pulled, o/w VG in red/yellow dec cl (spine sl chipped). *Edwards*. $194/£125

COLWIN, LAURIE. Dangerous French Mistress and Other Stories. London: C&W, 1975. 1st UK ed, 1st bk. Fine in dj (price-clipped). *Robbins*. $45/£29

COLWIN, LAURIE. Passion and Affect. NY: Viking, (1974). 1st bk. NF (bd edges faded) in Fine dj. *Antic Hay*. $60/£39

COLWIN, LAURIE. Passion and Affect. Viking, 1974. 1st ed, 1st bk. Fine in NF dj (sl wear head spine). *Stahr*. $45/£29

COLWIN, LAURIE. Shine On, Bright and Dangerous Object. Viking, 1975. 1st ed. NF in dj (sm scratch). *Stahr*. $45/£29

COLWIN, LAURIE. Shine On, Bright and Dangerous Object. London: C&W, 1976. 1st UK ed. Fine in dj (spine rubbed). *Robbins*. $25/£16

COLYER, J.F. Extraction of the Teeth. London, 1912. (Lib ink stamp.) *Edwards*. $47/£30

COMBE, ANDREW. The Principles of Physiology Applied to the Preservation of Health.... NY: Fowler & Wells, 1847. 7th Edinburgh ed. 320pp; 5 woodcuts. Good+ (foxing; spine chipped; cvrs worn). *Smithfield*. $18/£12

COMBE, GEORGE. The Constitution of Man Considered in Relation to External Objects. Boston: William Ticknor, 1844. 14th ed. (ii)+xii+412+(2)pp. Pebbled brn cl. VG. *Gach*. $30/£19

COMBER, L.F. Chinese Secret Societies in Malaya. NY, 1959. 1st ed. 11 plts, 2 maps (1 fldg). Dj (sl chipped, loss). *Edwards*. $116/£75

COMELIUS, FRED. Tambalear the Tumbleweed and Other Southwestern Stories. El Paso: Carl Hertzog, 1959. 2nd ed. Signed inscription by Hertzog. Orig mailing envelope, unaddressed. Fine in pict wrapper. *Laurie*. $150/£97

COMMAGER, HENRY STEELE. The Blue and the Gray. Bobbs Merrill, 1950. 1st ed. 2 vols. VG+ in VG slipcase. *Bishop*. $40/£26

Compilation of Navy and Other Laws. Washington: Navy Dept, 1875. Full sheep (rubbed). Usable. *Boswell*. $125/£81

Complete History of the Wars in Scotland; Under the Conduct of...James Marquis of Montrose, in Two Parts. London, 1720. 1st ed. Sm 8vo. 18,200; lvipp,24pp. Inscrips; lt browning, o/w VG. Contemp full calf (worn at extrems, rebacked). *Edwards*. $194/£125

COMPTON, R.H. (ed). Our South African Flora. Cape Town, n.d. (ca 1950). 8 full-pg color plts, 100 tipped-in color cards. Paper cvrd bds (worn, lack tipped-on emblem), cl spine. *Brooks*. $24/£15

COMPTON-BURNETT, IVY. Daughters and Sons. NY, 1938. 1st Amer ed. VG. *Mcclintock*. $15/£10

COMPTON-BURNETT, IVY. A Father and His Fate. London: Gollancz, 1957. 1st ed. Nice in VG dj (soiled, nicked; price-clipped). *Virgo*. $23/£15

COMPTON-BURNETT, IVY. The Mighty and Their Fall. Gollancz, 1961. 1st UK ed. NF in dj. *Sclanders*. $16/£10

COMPTON-BURNETT, IVY. Mother and Son. London, 1955. 1st ed. VG. *Argosy*. $45/£29

COMPTON-BURNETT, IVY. Pastors and Masters. London: Heath Cranton, 1925. 1st ed. Pp sl browned; name, o/w VG in dj (soiled; sm nicks; extrems chipped). *Virgo*. $101/£65

COMPTON-BURNETT, IVY. Two Worlds and Their Ways. London, (1949). 1st ed. VG in dj. *Argosy*. $40/£26

COMROE, B.I., L.H. COLLINS and M.P. CRANE. Internal Medicine in Dental Practice. Phila, 1939. 1st rptg. 44 engr, colored plt. Good. *Goodrich*. $20/£13

COMSTOCK, ANDREW. A System of Elocution.... Phila: Butler & Williams, 1845. 364; 32pp. Mod leather (rebound). *Hayman*. $50/£32

COMSTOCK, F.G. A Practical Treatise on the Culture of Silk.... Hartford: Gleason, 1839. 2nd ed, rev. 96pp; 4 wood engrs. Linen-backed ptd bds. VG (lt foxing). *Second Life*. $125/£81

COMSTOCK, WILLIAM. Bungalows, Camps and Mountain Houses. NY, (1908). Cl-backed bds. VG (sl worn, soiled). *Bohling*. $125/£81

COMSTOCK, WILLIAM. Detail, Cottage and Constructive Architecture. NY: Comstock, 1873. 75 lg litho plts. (Lt lib stamp tp; rebacked.) *Schoyer*. $375/£242

CONARD, HOWARD L. Uncle Dick Wootton, the Pioneer Frontiersman of the Rocky Mountain Region.... Chicago: Dibble, 1890. 1st ed. 472,473-(474),ad pp. Full leather, gilt-stamped spine, presentation binding. Howes C 659. *Ginsberg*. $275/£177

CONDE, J.A. History of the Dominion of the Arabs in Spain. Mrs. Jonathan Foster (trans). London, 1854. 3 vols. Frontis. Vols 2-3 unopened. (Prelims lt browned; sl worn.) *Edwards*. $54/£35

CONDER, CLAUDE REIGNIER. Tent Work in Palestine. NY: D. Appleton, 1878. 2 vols complete. 733pp. Gilt-pict cl (extrems lt rubbed; bkpl). *Archaeologia*. $200/£129

CONDICT, JEMIMA. Jemima Condict, Her Book. Newark, NJ: Carteret Book Club, 1930. Ltd to 200. 2 plts. Beige linen over dec bds. Fine. *Karmiole*. $75/£48

CONDIE, D. FRANCIS. A Practical Treatise on the Diseases of Children. Phila, 1858. 5th ed. 762pp. Good. *Fye*. $50/£32

CONDON, EDDIE and THOMAS SUGRUE. We Called It Music. NY: Holt, 1947. 1st ed. Fine in NF dj (speckled spine). *Beasley*. $50/£32

CONDON, RICHARD. The Manchurian Candidate. M. Joseph, 1960. 1st Eng ed. Fine in VG + dj. *Fine Books*. $95/£61

CONDON, RICHARD. The Oldest Confession. NY: Appleton-Century-Crofts, 1958. 1st ed. Rev copy, pub's slip laid in. Edges shelfworn, else NF in NF dj (lt chipping). *Lame Duck*. $95/£61

CONDON, RICHARD. Prizzi's Honour. London: Joseph, 1982. 1st British ed. NF in dj. *Silver Door*. $25/£16

CONE, MARY. Two Years in California. Chicago, 1876. Dbl-pg frontis map, xii(2),238pp. Gilt-dec cl. Fr hinge broken, else VG. *Ginsberg*. $100/£65

CONE, MARY. Two Years in California. Chicago: S.C. Griggs, 1876. 1st ed. Frontis; xiii,238pp; 15 plts; fldg map; 8pp ads. Lt corner wear, o/w VG. *Oregon*. $55/£35

CONE, MARY. Two Years in California. Chicago: Griggs, 1876. 1st ed. 238pp. VG. *Second Life*. $125/£81

Confederate States Almanac...1862. Nashville, TN: Southern Methodist Publishing House, 1862. 1st ed. 32pp. Ptd wraps. VG + (lt foxing, lt fold). *Chapel Hill*. $350/£226

CONFUCIUS. The Analects of Confucius. Lionel Giles (trans). NY: LEC, 1970. #330/1500 signed by Tseng Yu-Ho (illus). Chinese brocade cl. Fine in pub's slipcase. *Hermitage*. $135/£87

CONGER, HORACE and CAROLINE CRANE. Obstetrics and Womanly Beauty. Chicago, c. 1880. 1st ed. 541pp. (Inner hinges cracked.) *Fye*. $75/£48

CONGREVE, WILLIAM. The Works of.... Birmingham: Ptd by John Baskerville, 1761. 3 vols. Frontis port, 5 engr plts. Red calf, gilt. Aeg. (Backstrips worn, joints mended, bindings not uniform; vol 1-2 waterstained; hinges reinforced.) *Argosy*. $250/£161

CONKLIN, E. Picturesque Arizona. NY: Mining Record, 1878. Frontis, 380pp. Grn cl, gilt/black stamping. Nice. *Bohling*. $300/£194

CONKLIN, EMMA BURKE. A Brief History of Logan County, Colorado.... (Denver): Elbridge Gerry Chapter, DAR, (1928). Presentation copy. Nice (sl damp damage upper edge) in dj. *Bohling*. $75/£48

CONKLING, ROSCOE P. and MARGARET B. The Butterfield Overland Mail, 1857-1869. Glendale: Clark, 1947. 1st ed. 3 vols. 77 plts; 3 fldg maps. *Argosy*. $600/£387

CONNELL, EVAN S. The Anatomy Lesson and Other Stories. Viking, 1957. 1st ed. Inscribed presentation. Fine in VG dj (fading, spine wear). *Fine Books*. $135/£87

CONNELL, EVAN S. The Connoisseur. NY, 1974. 1st ed. VG in dj (yellowed). *King*. $25/£16

CONNELL, EVAN S. Mr. Bridge. NY: Knopf, 1969. 1st ed. Fine in NF dj. *Robbins*. $45/£29

CONNELL, EVAN S. Mrs. Bridge. NY: Viking, 1959. 1st ed. NF in VG + dj (sl surface loss; sl chipped). *Lame Duck*. $150/£97

CONNELL, EVAN S. Son of the Morning Star. SF: North Point, (1984). 1st ed. Fine in Fine dj. *Unger*. $150/£97

CONNELL, EVAN S. Son of the Morning Star. SF: North Point Press, 1984. 1st ed. Fine in Fine dj. *Book Market*. $60/£39

CONNELL, EVAN S. The White Lantern. NY: Holt, (1980). 1st ed. Fine in dj (edgewear). *Robbins*. $15/£10

CONNELL, ROBERT. Arkansas. NY: Paebar Co, 1947. Six Gun 478. VG. *Perier*. $50/£32

CONNELLEY, WILLIAM ELSEY. History of Kansas Newspapers. Topeka: KS State Ptg Plant, 1916. 1st ed. Blue cl (corners worn; spine sl faded). *Glenn*. $45/£29

CONNELLEY, WILLIAM ELSEY. History of Kansas Newspapers. Topeka: KS State Ptg, 1916. 1st ed. *Oregon*. $70/£45

CONNELLEY, WILLIAM ELSEY. Ingalls of Kansas. Topeka, KS: By the Author, 1909. 1st ed. Few pp roughly opened, o/w NF in red cl. *Glenn*. $45/£29

CONNELLEY, WILLIAM ELSEY. Quantrill and the Border Wars. Cedar Rapids, 1910. 1956 Reprint. Errata. Fine in dj (sl wear). *Pratt*. $50/£32

CONNELLEY, WILLIAM ELSEY. Quantrill and the Border Wars. Cedar Rapids, IA: Torch Press, 1910. 1st ed, 1st ptg. Red cl. Howes 689. *Glenn*. $225/£145

CONNELLEY, WILLIAM ELSEY. Quantrill and the Border Wars. Cedar Rapids: Torch Press, 1910. 1st ed. 2 maps. VG in dj (chip, short tears). Howes C 689. *Cahan*. $175/£113

CONNER, DANIEL. Joseph Reddeford Walker and Arizona Adventure. Univ OK, (1956). 1st ed. 8 plts, map. VG. *Oregon*. $37/£24

CONNER, S. The Quest of the Sea Otter. R&L, 1927. 1st ed. Fine in VG + pict dj (2 chips). *Aronovitz*. $45/£29

CONNETT, EUGENE V. American Sporting Dogs. NY: D. Van Nostrand, (1948). 1st ed. Rust cl, gilt spine. Fine. *Karmiole*. $100/£65

CONNETT, EUGENE V. Feathered Game: From a Sporting Journal. NY: Derrydale Press, 1929. 1st ed. Ltd to 500. French folded unnumbered leaves, color illus tp, 10 color medallions. Bkpl, else Fine. *Cahan*. $200/£129

CONNETT, EUGENE V. Fishing a Trout Stream. NY: Derrydale, (1934). 1st ed. #567/950. 93 plts. Sl rubbing spine, else VG. *Mcgowan*. $175/£113

CONNETT, EUGENE V. Random Casts. NY: Derrydale. One of 1075 numbered. Blue/grn designed cl. Fine + in orig glassine dj. *Bowman*. $275/£177

CONNETT, EUGENE V. Wildfowling in the Mississippi Flyway. Van Nostrand, (1949). 1st ed. VG in dj remains. *Cullen*. $125/£81

CONNETT, EUGENE V. Wing Shooting and Angling. NY: Scribner's, 1922. 1st ed, 1st bk. Spine dull, o/w VG. *Bowman*. $75/£48

CONNICK, CHAS. J. Adventures in Light and Color. London: Harrap, 1937. 1st ed. 42 plts, 48 collotype plts. Black cl, gilt. (sl wear, sl foxing). *Willow House.* $194/£125

CONNOLLY, C. and J. ZERBE. Les Pavillons. London: Hamish Hamilton, 1962. Fine. *Quest.* $70/£45

CONNOLLY, CYRIL (ed). The Golden Horizon. London: Weidenfeld & Nicholson, (1953). 1st ed. Gilt cl. Smudge tp verso, o/w Nice in dj (nicked, chipped). *Reese.* $25/£16

CONNOLLY, CYRIL. The Condemned Playground. Essays 1927-1944. London: Routledge, 1945. 1st ed. Nice. *Patterson.* $78/£50

CONNOLLY, CYRIL. Previous Convictions. London: Hamish Hamilton, (1963). 1st Eng ed. Blue cl gilt. Very Nice in dj. *Cady.* $25/£16

CONNOLLY, CYRIL. The Rock Pool. NY: Scribner's, 1936. 1st Amer ed, 1st bk (w/1936 on title, Scribner's 'A' on copyright pg). Pict eps in dk blue on lt blue paper. Oatmeal cl blocked in blue. Very Nice. *Cady.* $50/£32

CONNOR and SKAGGS. Broadcloth and Britches, the Santa Fe Trade. College Station: Texas A&M, (1977). 1st ed. VF in VF dj. *Oregon.* $30/£19

CONNOR, DONALD RUSSELL. BG—Off the Record. Fairless Hills: Gaildonna Pub, 1958. 1st ed. NF (rubbing). *Beasley.* $75/£48

CONOVER, GEORGE S. (comp). Journals of the Military Expedition of Major General John Sullivan.... Auburn, 1887. 579,(2)pp, 5 fldg maps in pockets. (Fr inner hinges cracking; fr cvr spotted.) *Hayman.* $75/£48

CONRAD, BARNABY. The Death of Manolete. Boston: Houghton Mifflin, 1958. 1st ed. VG- in VG- dj. *Parker.* $50/£32

CONRAD, BARNABY. Zorro: A Fox in the City. NY: Doubleday, (1971). 1st ed. Inscribed yr of pub. 128pp. Fine in dj (short creased tears, else VG). *Godot.* $40/£26

CONRAD, HOWARD L. Uncle Dick Wootton. Chicago, (1957). Lakeside Classic. VG. *Schoyer.* $25/£16

CONRAD, JESSIE. A Handbook of Cookery for a Small House. London: Heinemann, (1923). 1st ed. Ptd cl. VG (ep sl browned). *Second Life.* $200/£129

CONRAD, JOHN. A Set of Six. Methuen, 1908. 1st ed. Ads at end. Dec cl. Contents Good (binding dull). *Whiteson.* $101/£65

CONRAD, JOSEPH. Almayer's Folly. NY, 1895. 1st Amer ed. Fine (name stamp). *Polyanthos.* $475/£306

CONRAD, JOSEPH. The Arrow of Gold. GC: Doubleday, Page, 1919. 1st ed, 1st ptg w/quotation in French on tp. Blue cl (lt rubbed). VG. *Hermitage.* $45/£29

CONRAD, JOSEPH. The Arrow of Gold. GC, 1919. 1st ed, 2nd issue. Cl (sl worn; stamped name). *King.* $40/£26

CONRAD, JOSEPH. Chance. Methuen, 1914. 1st ed, (2nd issue). Bears the cancelled 1914 tp; ads dated both July, Autumn 1913. Foxing pg edges, else VG+. *Fine Books.* $275/£177

CONRAD, JOSEPH. The Children of the Sea. NY: Dodd, Mead & Co., 1897. 1st ed. 217pp. Pict blue cl. VG (pencil sig). *Chapel Hill.* $450/£290

CONRAD, JOSEPH. Heart of Darkness. NY: LEC, 1969. #330/1500 signed by Robert Shore (illus). Vellum over illus bds. VF in pub's slipcase. *Hermitage.* $85/£55

CONRAD, JOSEPH. Heart of Darkness. NY: LEC, 1969. One of 1500 ptd. Signed by Robert Shore (illus). Dec bds. VF in glassine in slipcase. *Pharos.* $125/£81

CONRAD, JOSEPH. Laughing Anne and One Day More. London: John Castle, 1924. 1st ed. (Foxing; flyleaves browned.) *Hollett.* $47/£30

CONRAD, JOSEPH. Laughing Anne and One Day More. London: John Castle, 1924. 1st trade ed. NF. *Sadlon.* $30/£19

CONRAD, JOSEPH. Lord Jim. D-M, 1900. 1st Amer ed. Photo laid in. Orig cl laid down over new. Eps replaced; soiling, spotting rear cvr, else VG+. *Fine Books.* $100/£65

CONRAD, JOSEPH. Lord Jim. London: Blackwood, 1900. 1st UK ed. VG (bds sl damp; lt foxing). *Williams.* $225/£145

CONRAD, JOSEPH. Lord Jim. NY: LEC, 1959. One of 1500 signed by Lynd Ward (illus). Leather-backed dec bds. Fine in slipcase (spine sl sunned). *Pharos.* $200/£129

CONRAD, JOSEPH. The Medallion Edition of the Works. London: Gresham, 1925. 22 vols. Blue cl, gilt medallion. One vol sl rubbed, o/w Good set. *Petersfield.* $543/£350

CONRAD, JOSEPH. The Mirror of the Sea. Harper, 1906. 1st Amer ed. Pict cl. VG. *Fine Books.* $100/£65

CONRAD, JOSEPH. The Nigger of the Narcissus. London: Heinemann, 1898. 1st issue, w/H of Heinemann on spine same size as other letters; 16pp ads. VG+ (ink inscrip). *Williams.* $349/£225

CONRAD, JOSEPH. The Nigger of the Narcissus. London: Heinemann, 1898. 1st published Eng ed, 1st issue, w/'H' of Heinemann in larger type than other letters. 259pp,(4),(16)pp ads. Charcoal grey cl. NF (name, spine dknd). *Chapel Hill.* $400/£258

CONRAD, JOSEPH. The Nigger of the Narcissus. L.A.: LEC, 1965. One of 1500 signed by Millard Sheets (illus). 1/4 morocco cl bds. Fine in slipcase. *Pharos.* $125/£81

CONRAD, JOSEPH. Nostromo. London & NY: Harper & Bros., 1904. 1st ed. Blue cl. NF (crown of spine nicked, sl foxing). *Chapel Hill.* $400/£258

CONRAD, JOSEPH. Nostromo. SF: Taylor & Taylor for LEC, 1961. One of 1500 signed by Lima de Freitas (illus). Pict cl. VF in slipcase. *Pharos.* $125/£81

CONRAD, JOSEPH. Notes on My Books. NY/Toronto: Doubleday, Page, 1921. 1st Amer ed. Ltd to 250. Signed. Gilt-dec vellum. NF in glassine wrapper, outer blue ptd dj (repaired tears, chips). *Sadlon.* $350/£226

CONRAD, JOSEPH. Novels and Stories. NY: Doubleday, Page, 1925. 26 vols. Brn dec buckram, gilt tops. Good. *Appelfeld.* $300/£194

CONRAD, JOSEPH. An Outcast of the Islands. London: T. Fisher Unwin, 1896. 1st ed. Teg. Good (lacks fep; sl rubbed, sl discolored). *Ash.* $302/£195

CONRAD, JOSEPH. An Outcast of the Islands. London: T. Fisher Unwin, 1896. 1st ed. 391pp. Teg. Dk grn cl. VG (inscrip, hinges cracked internally; spine ends, corners worn). *Chapel Hill.* $350/£226

CONRAD, JOSEPH. An Outcast of the Islands. London: Fisher Unwin, 1896. 1st ed. Eps sl foxed, spine sl rubbed, barely affecting gilt, o/w VG. *Rees.* $388/£250

CONRAD, JOSEPH. An Outcast of the Islands. Fisher Unwin, 1896. 1st UK ed. VG. *Williams.* $543/£350

CONRAD, JOSEPH. An Outcast of the Islands. Avon: LEC, 1975. One of 1500 numbered, signed by Robert Shore (illus). Fine in pub's slipcase. *Hermitage.* $90/£58

CONRAD, JOSEPH. An Outcast of the Islands. Avon: LEC, 1975. One of 1500 signed by Robert Shore (illus). Dec cl. VF in slipcase & glassine. *Pharos.* $95/£61

CONRAD, JOSEPH. The Point of Honor. NY: McClure, 1908. 1st separate (and 1st Amer) ed; this copy in 1st binding, w/'McClure' at foot of spine. Orig grn cl pict dec in white. VG (sl shelfworn). Cagle A13c. *Sumner & Stillman.* $135/£87

CONRAD, JOSEPH. The Rescue. London, 1920. 1st ed pub'd in England. *Bickersteth.* $34/£22

CONRAD, JOSEPH. The Rescue. London/Toronto: J.M. Dent, 1920. 1st Eng ed. Cl stamped in gilt/blind. NF in dj (sm chips). *Sadlon.* $100/£65

CONRAD, JOSEPH. The Rescue. London/Toronto: Dent, 1920. 1st Eng ed. Spinal lettering sl faded, else VG in pict dj. *Limestone.* $195/£126

CONRAD, JOSEPH. The Rover. London: T. Fisher Unwin, (1923). 1st Eng ed. (Top edge spine sl lightened.) Dj (worn, chipped). *Sadlon.* $75/£48

CONRAD, JOSEPH. The Rover. GC: Doubleday, Page, 1923. 1st Amer ed. Extrems lt rubbed, o/w Fine. *Sadlon.* $20/£13

CONRAD, JOSEPH. The Rover. NY: Doubleday, Page, 1923. 1st Amer ed. One of 377 numbered, signed. Teg. Orig vegetable vellum, gilt. VG in new slipcase. *Macdonnell.* $300/£194

CONRAD, JOSEPH. The Rover. London: T. Fisher Unwin, 1923. 1st ed. (Lt spots edges; feps lt faded; sm mk spine upper bd; spine lettering faded.) Dj (edges sl chipped). *Hollett.* $116/£75

CONRAD, JOSEPH. The Secret Agent. Werner Laurie, 1923. #873/1000 numbered, signed. NF in dj w/extra title label. *Williams.* $504/£325

CONRAD, JOSEPH. The Secret Sharer. NY: LEC, (1985). 1/1500 numbered, signed by Bruce Chandler (illus). 3 etchings. Fine in cl fldg case. *Argosy.* $250/£161

CONRAD, JOSEPH. The Secret Sharer. NY: LEC, (1985). One of 1500 signed by Bruce Chandler (illus). 3 etchings. Silk; leather cvr label. VF in fldg box. *Pharos.* $225/£145

CONRAD, JOSEPH. The Shadow Line, a Confession. GC: Doubleday, Page, 1917. 1st ed. Blue cl, gilt. VG. *Hermitage.* $50/£32

CONRAD, JOSEPH. Some Reminiscences. London: Eveleigh Nash, 1912. 1st ed. One of 1000 ptd. Blue cl, gilt. Fine. *Macdonnell.* $225/£145

CONRAD, JOSEPH. Suspense. London: J.M. Dent, 1925. 1st ed. Frontis. (Spotting.) Dj (torn, creased w/sl loss). *Hollett.* $132/£85

CONRAD, JOSEPH. Suspense. GC: Doubleday, Page, 1925. 1st ed. #359/377 numbered. Teg. Parchment-cvrd bds. Pristine in orig tissue jacket, ptd blue dj, in pub's slipcase (sl wear). *Chapel Hill.* $350/£226

CONRAD, JOSEPH. Suspense. London/Toronto: J.M. Dent, 1925. 1st Eng ed. (Spine head sl rubbed.) Dj (sl edgeworn, 2 vertical creases). *Sadlon.* $100/£65

CONRAD, JOSEPH. Tales of Hearsay. London, (1925). 1st ed. Cl (sl worn, spine dull). *King.* $45/£29

CONRAD, JOSEPH. Tales of Hearsay. London: T. Fisher, Unwin, (1925). 1st ed. Tape mks eps; lacks dj, o/w Fine. *Pharos.* $95/£61

CONRAD, JOSEPH. Tales of Hearsay. GC: Doubleday, Page, 1925. 1st Amer ed. NF in dj (spine chipped; price-clipped). *Hermitage.* $75/£48

CONRAD, JOSEPH. Tales of Hearsay. London: T. Fisher Unwin, 1925. 1st ed. VG (sl mkd, spotted) in dj (sl creased; chipped, sl loss). *Hollett.* $116/£75

CONRAD, JOSEPH. Tales of Unrest. London: T. Fisher Unwin, 1898. 1st Eng ed. 14pp undated ads. Orig dk grn cl; teg. VG (spine ends sl worn). *Sumner & Stillman.* $225/£145

CONRAD, JOSEPH. Typhoon and Other Stories. London: Heinemann, 1903. 1st Eng ed, 1st issue, w/windmill device on tp, w/o 'Reserved for the Colonies only' verso 1/2-title. Charcoal grey cl. Bkpl; foxing, offsetting eps, else NF. *Chapel Hill.* $450/£290

CONRAD, JOSEPH. Under Western Eyes. London: Methuen, (1911). 1st ed. 32pp ads dated Sept 1911 (later state). Red cl, gilt. Spine sl faded, else Fine. Cagle A14a(1). *Sumner & Stillman.* $295/£190

CONRAD, JOSEPH. The Uniform Edition of the Works, plus Notes.... London: Dent, 1923-24. 21 vols. Backs unevenly faded, o/w Sound. *Petersfield.* $217/£140

CONRAD, JOSEPH. Victory, an Island Tale. London: Methuen, (1915). 1st Eng ed. (Edges lt foxed; spine lt sunned.) *Glenn.* $140/£90

CONRAD, JOSEPH. Within the Tides. Dent, 1915. 1st ed. Fine in VG+ dj (sl chipping spine head). *Fine Books.* $525/£339

CONRAD, JOSEPH. The Works of Joseph Conrad. NY: Doubleday, Page, 1920-1928. 1st ed thus, Sun Dial ed, ltd to 735 numbered, signed. 24 vols. 1/4 cl, pub's ptd spine labels (browned), paper-cvrd bds (sl frayed, bumped, few creased, lt browned, rubbed). Good set. *Godot.* $750/£484

CONRAD, JOSEPH. Youth, Typhoon, the End of the Tether. L.A.: LEC, 1972. One of 1500 signed by printer and Robert Shore (illus). 1/4 leather. VF in slipcase & glassine. *Pharos.* $95/£61

CONRAD, JOSEPH. Youth: A Narrative. Edinburgh: William Blackwood, 1902. 1st ed, earliest issue w/ads dated 10/02. Grn cl (lt rubbed; sl frayed). VG. *Hermitage.* $275/£177

CONROY, FRANK. Midair. NY: Dutton, (1985). 1st ed. VF in dj. *Pharos.* $25/£16

CONROY, FRANK. Midair. NY: Dutton, 1985. 1st ed. Inscribed. Fine in Fine dj. *Beasley.* $75/£48

CONROY, FRANK. Stop-Time. NY: Viking, (1967). 1st ed, 1st bk. Fine in Fine dj. *Dermont.* $100/£65

CONROY, JACK. A World to Win. NY: Covici Friede, 1935. 1st Amer ed. NF in dj (spine sl sunned; extrems sl chipped; sl edge worn). *Polyanthos.* $30/£19

CONROY, PAT. The Boo. Verona: McClure, 1971. 1st ed, 2nd ptg, 1st bk. Fine in dj (1/2-inch split upper rear spine fold). *Else Fine.* $300/£194

CONROY, PAT. The Great Santini. Boston: Houghton-Mifflin, 1976. 1st ed. NF (inscrip) in dj. *Else Fine.* $65/£42

CONROY, PAT. The Great Santini. Boston: HMCo, 1976. 1st ed. Signed. Fine in Fine dj (interior foxed). *Between The Covers.* $250/£161

CONROY, PAT. The Lords of Discipline. Boston: HMCo, 1980. 1st ed. Signed. 2 sm spots fore-edge, else Fine in dj. *Between The Covers.* $185/£119

CONROY, PAT. The Prince of Tides. Boston: HMC, 1986. 1st ed. Signed. Fine in dj. *Between The Covers.* $150/£97

Considerations on the French War...a Letter to William Pitt by a British Merchant. London: D.I. Eaton, 1794. 1st ed. 1/2-title; iv,66pp. Recent cl-backed bds; ptd cvr label. *Petrilla.* $60/£39

CONSIDINE, BOB. The Panama Canal. NY: Random House, 1951. 1st trade ed. Fritz Kredle (illus). Dec eps. VG in dj. *Cattermole.* $20/£13

CONSTABLE, JOHN. John Constable's Sketch-Books of 1813 and 1814. Graham Reynolds (intro). London: V&A Museum, 1985. 3 vols. 12 plts. Uniform cl. VF set in Mint slipcase. *Europa.* $42/£27

CONSTABLE, JOHN. John Constable's Sketch-Books of 1813 and 1814.... London: Victoria & Albert Museum, HMSO, 1973. 1st ed. 3 vols. 12 plts. Grn gilt cl. Good in slipcase. *Karmiole.* $75/£48

CONSTABLE, JOHN. Letters of John Constable, R.A., to C.R. Leslie, R.A. 1826-1837. Peter Leslie (ed). London, 1931. Mostly uncut. (Sl sunned.) *Washton.* $40/£26

CONSTABLE, W.G. Canaletto. OUP, 1962. 1st ed. 2 vols. Frontis port, 184 plts. (Ex-lib w/ink stamps, label remains.) Djs (sl ragged). *Edwards.* $194/£125

CONSTABLE, W.G. Canaletto. London: Clarendon, 1962. 2 vols. Frontis port, 184 b/w plts; mod marbled eps. (Sm owner ink stamp preface.) Spanish-style re-bind in fawn-crushed morocco-backed cl bds; gilt raised bands spines. *Edwards.* $233/£150

CONSTABLE, W.G. The Painter's Workshop. OUP, 1954. Frontis, 24 plts. Fine in clean pict dj. *Europa.* $37/£24

CONSTANTINE, K.C. A Fix Like This. London: Dutton, 1975. 1st ed. VG in VG dj. *Ming.* $31/£20

CONSTANTINE, K.C. Upon Some Midnights Clear. London: Hodder, 1986. 1st British ed. Pp starting to brn, o/w Fine in dj. *Silver Door.* $25/£16

Contagious Diseases of Domesticated Animals. Washington, 1881. 1st ed. 391pp. Good. *Fye.* $100/£65

CONTENAU, GEORGES. Everyday Life in Babylon and Assyria. London: Edward Arnold, (1955). 23 plts. Good in dj. *Archaeologia.* $25/£16

CONTINI, MILA. Fashion from Ancient Egypt to the Present Day. NY: Odyssey Press, (1965). 1st ed. Blue cl. Fine in color dj. *House.* $40/£26

Contrast: or Modes of Education. (By Hannah Farnham Lee.) Boston: Whipple & Damrell, 1837. 1st ed. 116pp (lacks fep; foxing). Pub's cl. VG. *Second Life.* $135/£87

Contributions to the Historical Society of Montana. Volume I. 1902. 2nd ed (ptg). Orig red cl. VG. *Schoyer.* $75/£48

Contributions to the Historical Society of Montana. Volume II. Helena, 1896. 409pp. Orig red cl. VG. *Schoyer.* $80/£52

Contributions to the Historical Society of Montana. Volume III. Helena, 1900. Orig red cl. VG. *Schoyer.* $75/£48

Contributions to the Historical Society of Montana. Volume III. 1900. 1st ed. 13 plts. Fine. *Oregon.* $100/£65

Contributions to the Historical Society of Montana. Volume IV. Helena: Independent Pub., 1903. Bkpl, else VG. *Perier.* $80/£52

Contributions to the Historical Society of Montana. Volume V. Helena, 1904. Orig red cl. VG. *Schoyer.* $60/£39

Contributions to the Historical Society of Montana. Volume V. Helena: Independent Pub., 1904. VG. *Perier.* $80/£52

Contributions to the Historical Society of Montana. Volume VI. Helena, 1907. Orig red cl. VG. *Schoyer.* $60/£39

Contributions to the Historical Society of Montana. Volume VII. Helena, 1910. Orig red cl. VG. *Schoyer.* $50/£32

Conversations on Botany. (By E. and S.M. Fitton.) London, 1828. 6th ed. xx,278pp; 21 hand-colored plts (sl offsetting most plts; bds worn). Uncut. *Wheldon & Wesley.* $47/£30

CONWAY, AGNES ETHEL. A Ride through the Balkans, on Classic Ground with a Camera. Robert Scott, 1917. Binders' cl, leather label. *Petersfield.* $28/£18

CONWAY, G.R.G. (ed). An Englishman and the Mexican Inquisition, 1556-1560. Mexico City: Privately ptd, 1927. 1st ed, one of 250 numbered. 14 plts. Black cl, paper spine label. Good. *Karmiole.* $85/£55

CONWAY, MARTIN. The Alps.... London: A&C Black, 1924. 1st ed. 70 color plts. (Prelims sl foxed; fore-edge sl spotted; sl bubbling fr cvr.) NF. *Blue Mountain.* $60/£39

CONWAY, MARTIN. The Bolivian Andes. London, 1901. Lib leather-backed cl (rebound, sl worn; accession #; ink stamps, labels). *Edwards.* $47/£30

CONWAY, MARTIN. No Man's Land. Cambridge: CUP, 1906. 1st ed. 2 fldg maps in rear pocket. Orig cl (sl rubbed). VG. *Walcot.* $233/£150

CONWAY, MONCURE DANIEL. Travels in South Kensington. NY: Harper, 1882. 1st ed. Frontis; (5)-234,(4)pp. Pub's cl. Ink name; paper yellowing, else Very Nice. *Bookpress.* $335/£216

CONWAY, WILLIAM MARTIN. Aconcagua and Tierra Del Fuego. London: Cassell, 1902. 1st ed. 27 plts; map. (Upper bd, spine damp-mkd.) *Hollett.* $217/£140

CONWAY, WILLIAM MARTIN. The Alps from End to End. London: Constable, 1895. 1st ed. xii,403pp; teg. (Plts, text water-stained; hinges cracking.) 2-tone cl gilt (sl worn; bd edges faded; upper bd damped). *Hollett.* $70/£45

CONWAY, WILLIAM MARTIN. Climbing and Exploration in the Karakoram-Himalayas. London: T. Fisher Unwin, 1894. 1st ed. xxviii,709,(i)pp; fldg map (some folds torn); uncut. Pict cl gilt (sl worn, bumped; joints cracked; lib label; stamp). *Hollett.* $388/£250

CONWAY, WILLIAM MARTIN. Literary Remains of Albrecht Durer. Cambridge, 1889. 1st ed. (Rubbed; ex-lib.) *Argosy.* $75/£48

Cook's Guide to Norway, Sweden and Denmark. London, 1893. 2nd ed. 232pp. Dec red cl. Nice. *Gretton.* $31/£20

Cook's Tourist's Handbook for Switzerland. London: Thomas Cook, 1879. 1st ed. Fldg frontis map, viii,241pp + 32pp ads. Brn bds (sl rubbed). Good. *Cox.* $54/£35

Cook's Tourist's Handbook for Switzerland. London, 1908. Red cl. VG. *Gretton.* $12/£8

Cook's Traveller's Handbook for Palestine and Syria. London: Simpkin et al, 1924. New ed. 3 fldg maps (1 in rear pocket). Sl tear 1 map, o/w VG. *Worldwide.* $45/£29

COOK, CHARLES. The Battle of Cape Esperance. NY, 1968. 1st ed. VG in VG dj. *Clark.* $35/£23

COOK, CYRIL. The Life and Work of Robert Hancock. London: Chapman & Hall, 1948. 1st ed. Frontis port, 120 plts. Blue cl, gilt title. Nice. *Cady.* $45/£29

COOK, DAVID J. Hands Up. Denver, 1897. (Enlgd 2nd ed). Frontis port, ii,442pp, port. Maroon cl, gilt title. VG (spine sl dull, frayed). Howes C 728. *Bohling*. $175/£113

COOK, DAVID J. Hands Up; or Thirty-Five Years of Detective Life in the Mountains and on the Plains. Denver, 1897. 2nd enlgd ptg. 442pp. Fine. *Book Market*. $200/£129

COOK, E.T. The Life of John Ruskin. London: George Allen, 1911. 1st ed. 2 vols. 2 frontispieces. (Lt foxing.) *Bookpress*. $65/£42

COOK, E.T. (ed). The Century Book of Gardening.... London/NY: 'Country Life'/Scribner, (1910). VG (hinges loose). *Second Life*. $75/£48

COOK, EARNSHAW. Percentage Baseball. Waverly, 1964. VG+. *Plapinger*. $100/£65

COOK, EARNSHAW. Percentage Baseball. MIT Press, 1966. 1st ptg, rev & corrected ed. Fine in Fine dj. *Plapinger*. $85/£55

COOK, G.H. The English Cathedral through the Centuries. London: Phoenix House, 1957. 1st ed. 63 plans, 115 plts. Name, o/w Fine in dj. *Petersfield*. $28/£18

COOK, G.H. The English Mediaeval Parish Church. London: Phoenix House, 1955. 2nd ed. 54 plans. Name, o/w Fine in dj. *Petersfield*. $23/£15

COOK, G.H. Mediaeval Chantries and Chantry Chapels. London: Phoenix House, 1947. 1st ed. 59 plts, 26 plans. VG in dj (lt worn, price-clipped, edges taped). *Hollett*. $39/£25

COOK, H.C.B. The Battle Honours of the British and Indian Armies 1662-1982. London, 1987. #196/750. Bkpl signed. VG in dj & slipcase. *Edwards*. $70/£45

COOK, HARVEY TOLIVER. The Life and Legacy of David Rogerson Williams. NY: Privately ptd, 1916. Engr frontis. Teg; unopened. Spine gilt rubbed, else VG. *Cahan*. $75/£48

COOK, JAMES H. Fifty Years on the Old Frontier as Cowboy, Hunter.... New Haven: Yale, 1923. 1st ed. VG (sl edgeworn; dj fragments laid in). *Parker*. $80/£52

COOK, JAMES H. Fifty Years on the Old Frontier as Cowboy.... New Haven: Yale Univ, 1923. 1st ed. (Lt soiled.) *Shasky*. $50/£32

COOK, JAMES H. Fifty Years on the Old Frontier.... Norman: Univ of OK, (1957). (1st ptg of new ed.) Fine in dj. *Bohling*. $42/£27

COOK, JAMES. The Explorations of Captain Cook in the Pacific. A. Grenfell Price (ed). NY: LEC, 1957. #893/1500, signed by Geoffrey Ingleton (illus) & Douglas Dunstan (designer). Color frontis port. Tan calf spine, bds cvrd in tapa cl (sl wear). VG slipcase. *Hartfield*. $195/£126

COOK, JAMES. A Voyage Towards the South Pole and Round the World Performed in H.M.S. Resolution.... London: W. Strahan and T. Cadell, 1779. 3rd ed. 2 vols. 4to. xl,378; 8,396pp. Orig full calf (rebacked w/old gilt dec, spine relaid). Good+ (ex-lib w/r.s.m. on rear of plts; few minor mks). *Walcot*. $2,325/£1,500

COOK, JOHN A. Pursuing the Whale. London: John Murray, 1926. 1st Eng ed. VG. *Hollett*. $54/£35

COOK, JOHN A. Pursuing the Whale; a Quarter-Century of Whaling in the Arctic. Boston/NY, 1926. 1st ed. (Prelims lt foxed; back cvr dampstained.) *Lefkowicz*. $45/£29

COOK, MRS. E.T. Highways and Byways in London. London, 1903. Teg. (Lt browning; sl worn.) *Edwards*. $31/£20

COOK, OLIVE. Movement in Two Dimensions. London: Hutchinson, 1963. 1st ed. Fine in dj. *Cahan*. $75/£48

COOK, R.M. Greek Painted Pottery. London: Methuen, (1966). 1st ed. 56 plts. Good. *Archaeologia*. $65/£42

COOK, R.M. Greek Painted Pottery. London, 1960. 1st ed. 66 plts. Dj (sl chipped). *Edwards*. $43/£28

COOK, ROY BIRD. The Family and Early Life of Stonewall Jackson. Richmond, VA: Old Dominion Press, 1925. 2nd ed. NF. *Mcgowan*. $65/£42

COOK, T.A. Old Provence. London, 1905. 2 vols. Most pp unopened, uncut. Clean, bright cvrs. *Lewis*. $56/£36

COOK, THOMAS H. The Orchids. Boston: Houghton Mifflin, 1982. 1st ed. Fine in dj (sl wear). *Mordida*. $35/£23

COOK, THOMAS L. Palmyra and Vicinity. Palmyra, 1930. 1st ed. Port. VG. *Benchmark*. $125/£81

COOKE, ALISTAIR. Christmas Eve. NY: Knopf, 1952. 1st ed. Orange/yellow paper over bds in star pattern. NF in black ptd dj. *Juvelis*. $75/£48

COOKE, ARTHUR O. A Book of Dovecotes. London, 1920. 1st ed. Tipped-in color frontis, 3 tipped-in color plts, 2 newspaper clippings taped fep. Uncut. Cl-backed bds (soiled, worn, bumped). *Edwards*. $31/£20

COOKE, ARTHUR O. The Forest of Dean. NY, 1913. 4 color plts, 56 b/w plts. Teg. (Lt browning; spine sl chipped.) *Edwards*. $47/£30

COOKE, COLIN. The Life of Stafford Cripps. London: Hodder & Stoughton, 1957. 1st ed. Nice in dj (torn). *Patterson*. $93/£60

COOKE, EDMUND VANCE. Baseballogy. Forbes, 1912. 1st ed. Pict cvr. VG; no dj as issued. *Plapinger*. $125/£81

COOKE, HARRIET N. The Trees, Fruits and Flowers of the Bible. NY: American Tract Soc, (ca 1846). 120pp (lt foxing, esp 2pp), 8pp engrs. Gilt-stamped spine. *Quest*. $40/£26

COOKE, JOHN ESTEN. A Life of Gen. Robert E. Lee. NY: D. Appleton, 1871. 1st ed. Frontis port, vi,577pp. Grn cl. Offsetting tp, else NF. BAL 3733. *Chapel Hill*. $275/£177

COOKE, JOHN ESTEN. Outlines from the Outpost. Chicago, (1961). Lakeside Classic. VG. *Schoyer*. $25/£16

COOKE, JOHN ESTEN. Stonewall Jackson and the Old Stonewall Brigade. Richard B. Harwell (ed). Univ of VA Press, (c. 1954). Port. VG. *Book Broker*. $50/£32

COOKE, JOHN ESTEN. Tamawaca Folks; A Summer Comedy. N.p.: Tamawaca Press, (1907). 1st ed. Emb cl. Good (eps foxed). *Artis*. $25/£16

COOKE, JOHN HENRY. Narrative of Events in the South of France.... London, 1835. 319pp. Contemp calf, leather label. Howes C 736. *Ginsberg*. $450/£290

COOKE, M.C. Introduction to the Study of Fungi.... London: A&C Black, 1895. 1st ed. Spine sl skewed, lt faded; hinges starting; o/w VG. *Hermitage*. $50/£32

COOKE, M.C. A Plain and Easy Account of British Fungi. London, 1876. 3rd ed, rev. 174pp. (Sl adhesion signs.) *Wheldon & Wesley*. $39/£25

COOKE, M.C. Rust, Smut, Mildew, and Mould. London: Allen, 1902. 6th ed. 16 plts. New eps. VG. *Savona*. $39/£25

COOKE, MAUD C. 20th Century Hand-Book of Etiquette.... Phila: Co-operative Pub, (1899). Color frontis, 524pp. Pict grn cl (sl mottled). *Petrilla*. $40/£26

COOKE, NICHOLAS. A Treatise on Antiseptic Medication or Declat's Method. Chicago, 1882. 1st ed. 120pp. Good. *Fye.* $75/£48

COOKE, PHILIP ST. GEORGE. Scenes and Adventures in the Army. Phila, 1859. 2nd ed. 432pp. Nice (sm nick fr joint). Howes C 740. *Ginsberg.* $500/£323

COOKE, ROBERT A. Allergy in Theory and Practice. Phila, 1947. Good. *Goodrich.* $25/£16

COOLEY, JEROME EUGENE. Recollections of Early Days in Duluth. Duluth: By the author, 1925. Signed. Frontis port. VG (lt soiled, rubbed). *Bohling.* $125/£81

COOLIDGE, DANE. Fighting Men of the West. NY: Dutton, (1932). 1st ed. Fine in Fine dj. *Book Market.* $100/£65

COOLIDGE, DANE. Gringo Gold. NY: G&D, reprint from (1939), ca 1945. Fine in Fine dj. *Book Market.* $25/£16

COOLIDGE, DANE. Horse-Ketchum. NY: Dutton, (1930). 1st ed. Fine in Fine dj. *Book Market.* $75/£48

COOLIDGE, DANE. Last of the Seris. NY: E.P. Dutton, 1939. 1st ed. Grey cl. VG (lt foxing) in dj (worn). *Parmer.* $50/£32

COOLIDGE, DANE. Silver Hat. NY: Dutton, 1934. 1st ed. VG in VG dj (torn). *Book Market.* $40/£26

COOLIDGE, DANE. The Texican. Chicago: A.C. McClurg, 1911. 1st ed. 5 color plts by Maynard Dixon. (Fr cvr sl soiled.) *Karmiole.* $40/£26

COOLIDGE, OLIVIA E. Egyptian Adventures. Boston: Houghton Mifflin, (1954). (Inscrip.) Dj. *Archaeologia.* $25/£16

COOLIDGE, W.A.B. Alpine Studies. London: Longmans, 1912. 1st ed. 16 plts. (Heavily spotted; cl faded, spine rubbed.) Untrimmed. *Hollett.* $47/£30

COOLIDGE, W.A.B. Alpine Studies. London, 1912. 1st ed. 16 plts (rubbed, spine faded). *Bickersteth.* $70/£45

COOLIDGE, W.A.B. Alps in Nature and History. London: Methuen, (1908). 8 fldg maps. Blue cl stamped in gilt (sl scuffed, bumped, pencilling, ex-lib). *Schoyer.* $65/£42

COOMBE, FLORENCE. Islands of Enchantment. London, 1911. Map. Grn cl. *Lewis.* $90/£58

COOMBS, SARAH V. South African Plants for American Gardens. NY, 1936. Sm marginal stain, foxing, but tight. *Brooks.* $36/£23

COON, NELSON. Gardening for Fragrance. NY, 1970. VG in dj. *Brooks.* $19/£12

COONEY, LORAINE M. and HATTIE C. RAINWATER. Garden History of Georgia, 1733-1933. Atlanta: Peachtree Garden Club, 1933. 1st ed. One of 1500. VG (lt foxing; cvrs handled; corners lt bruised). *Bookpress.* $250/£161

COONTS, STEPHEN. Flight of the Intruder. Annapolis: Naval Institute, (1986). 1st ed, 1st bk. Fine in Fine dj. *Aka.* $50/£32

COOPER, ARTHUR. The Sexual Disabilities of Man and Their Treatment. London, 1908. 1st ed. Good. *Fye.* $60/£39

COOPER, ASTLEY. The Anatomy and Surgical Treatment of Inguinal and Congenital Hernia. London: T. Cox, 1804. Lg atlas portfolio. vi,60pp (lt browning); 11 engr plts (1 partially colored); extra outline leaf. Contemp 1/4 calf, marbled bds (spine rebacked). *Goodrich.* $1,250/£806

COOPER, ASTLEY. The Lectures of Sir Astley Cooper on the Principles and Practice of Surgery with Additional Notes and Cases. Phila, 1835. 4th Amer ed. 648pp. Recent 1/4 leather; new eps. *Fye.* $200/£129

COOPER, ASTLEY. The Lectures of Sir Astley Cooper...on the Principles and Practice of Surgery. London, 1824, 1825, 1827. 3 vols. viii,352; vi,458, 4 plts; 538pp, 2 plts. 1/2 blue calf, gilt spines. Fine. *Whitehart.* $1,008/£650

COOPER, ASTLEY. Lectures on the Principles and Practice of Surgery. London, 1835. 8th ed. viii,612pp. 1/2 vellum (rubbed; foxing). *Whitehart.* $74/£48

COOPER, ASTLEY. Observations on the Structure and Diseases of the Testis. B.B. Cooper (ed). London, 1841. 2nd ed. xiii,328pp; 14 color plts. (Lib stamps; fr bd loose, repaired w/tape.) *Whitehart.* $434/£280

COOPER, ASTLEY. A Treatise on Dislocations and Fractures of the Joints. B.B. Cooper (ed). London, 1842. New ed. xxxi,576pp (prelims sl foxed). Orig cl (rebacked). *Whitehart.* $217/£140

COOPER, ASTLEY. A Treatise on Dislocations and on Fractures of the Joints. London, 1826. 5th ed. xxiv,518pp (tp sl foxed); 34 plts (sl foxing). Old 1/2 calf (worn; joints weak). *Whitehart.* $434/£280

COOPER, BRANSBY B. The Life of Sir Astley Cooper, Bart., Interspersed with Sketches.... London, 1848. 1st ed. 2 vols. 448; 480pp. 1/2 leather. Good. *Fye.* $200/£129

COOPER, BRANSBY B. The Life of Sir Astley Cooper. London, 1843. 2 vols. Frontis port,xxiv,448; viii,480pp. 1/2 morocco, marble bds, gilt. VG. *Whitehart.* $109/£70

COOPER, BRANSBY B. Surgical Essays: The Result of Clinical Observations made at Guy's Hospital. London, 1843. 4 color litho plts. Orig bds. Crisp. *Goodrich.* $275/£177

COOPER, C.S. and W. PERCIVAL WESTELL. Trees and Shrubs of the British Isles. London, 1909. 2 vols in 1. Frontis (foxed); 16 color, 70 b/w plts. Marbled eps. Gilt-edged 1/2 morocco (rubbed; blind lib stamp upper bd). *Edwards.* $70/£45

COOPER, DOUGLAS. Picasso Theatre. NY, (1968). Pict cl. Rear inner hinge crakced, else Good in glassine dj (incomplete). *King.* $175/£113

COOPER, ELIZABETH. My Lady of the Indian Purdah. NY: Stokes, 1927. 1st ed. Frontis; 14 photo plts. Gilt-stamped brn cl; cvr photo. VG. *Petrilla.* $15/£10

COOPER, ELLWOOD. Forest Culture and Eucalyptus Trees. SF: Cubery, 1876. 237pp, 2pp errata; 2 plts. Internally Fine (spine chipped; scuffed). *Quest.* $85/£55

COOPER, G.A. and R.E. GRANT. Permian Brachiopods of West Texas. Smithsonian, 1972-76. 4 vols in 8. 662 plts. Wrappers. *Wheldon & Wesley.* $279/£180

COOPER, JAMES FENIMORE. The History of the Navy of the United States of America. Phila: Lea & Blanchard, 1839. 1st ed. 2 vols. 394; 481,(1, errata)pp, 2 maps. Orig cl (rebacked, orig spines preserved; sl stained, bubbled; foxing within; early sigs). BAL 3888. Howes C 748. *Lefkowicz.* $250/£161

COOPER, JAMES FENIMORE. The Last of the Mohicans. London: Richard Bentley, 1836. Engr frontis; x,401pp (joints cracked; bkpl); aeg. Contemp scarlet straight-grained morocco gilt (lt rubbed). *Hollett.* $62/£40

COOPER, JAMES FENIMORE. The Last of the Mohicans. NY: Scribner's, 1919. 1st ed. N.C. Wyeth (illus). Lg 8vo. Cl, pict label. VG (sl shaken). *Book Adoption.* $75/£48

COOPER, JAMES FENIMORE. The Last of the Mohicans. NY: Scribner's, 1919. 1st ed. 4to. 14 full-pg color illus by N.C. Wyeth. Black cl, color paste label, tinted top, gold stamped spine. *Reisler.* $150/£97

COOPER, JAMES FENIMORE. The Pioneers, or the Sources of the Susquehanna; a Descriptive Tale. Richard Bentley, 1849. Revised, corrected. Frontis; xi,460pp. *Bickersteth.* $34/£22

COOPER, JAMES FENIMORE. Sketches of Switzerland. Phila: Carey, Lea & Blanchard, 1836. 1st ed, variant binding. 2 vols. 8vo. 244; 239pp. Grn cl w/paper spine labels. Sl adhesion fep to pastedown Vol 2; name, else NF. *Chapel Hill.* $750/£484

COOPER, JEREMY. Nineteenth-Century Romantic Bronzes. Newton Abbot, 1975. Dj. *Edwards.* $39/£25

COOPER, JEREMY. Nineteenth-Century Romantic Bronzes.... London: David & Charles, (1975). 1st ed. Bkpl, 2-inch tear rear cvr dj; else Fine. *Bookpress.* $35/£23

COOPER, MADISON. Sironia, Texas. Boston: Houghton Mifflin, 1952. 1st ed, 1st bk. Signed. 2 vols. Very Nice set in djs (short closed tear). *Reese.* $75/£48

COOPER, REVEREND MR. A New History of England. London: E. Newbery, 1798. 10th ed, w/additions. 12mo. xii,186pp. Full-pg engr frontis, 5 full-pg engrs in text (penciled sig, ink dated name). Grn spine, marbled paper (discolored) on bds (cvr edges rubbed, corners rounded). Internally VG. *Hobbyhorse.* $300/£194

COOPER, SAMUEL. The First Lines of the Practice of Surgery. London: Richard Phillips, 1807. 1st ed. xxiv,554pp + 3 leaves ads; 9 engr plts. Orig calf (rebacked, new eps). *Bickersteth.* $225/£145

COOPER, SUSAN ROGERS. Chasing Away the Devil. St. Martin, 1991. 1st ed. Fine in dj. *Murder.* $50/£32

COOPER, SUSAN. The Grey King. NY: Atheneum, 1975. 1st ed. NF in dj (creased). *Other Worlds.* $60/£39

COOPER, WILLIAM T. Parrots of the World. London, 1973. 1st ed. Fine in dj. *Edwards.* $543/£350

COOVER, ROBERT. A Night at the Movies Or, You Must Remember This. NY, 1987. 1st Amer ed. Signed. Fine in dj. *Polyanthos.* $35/£23

COOVER, ROBERT. The Origin of the Brunists. Putnam, 1966. 1st ed, 1st bk. NF in dj. *Fine Books.* $110/£71

COOVER, ROBERT. A Political Fable. Viking, 1980. 1st ed. NF in NF dj. *Bishop.* $20/£13

COOVER, ROBERT. The Universal Baseball Association, Inc. J. Henry Waugh, Prop. Random House, 1968. 1st ed. Fine in dj (price-clipped; lt nicked edges). *Stahr.* $75/£48

COOVER, ROBERT. The Universal Baseball Association, Inc. J. Henry Waugh, Prop. London: Rupert-Hart-Davis, 1970. 1st Eng ed. Fine in dj. *Limestone.* $45/£29

COPE, WENDY. Making Cocoa for Kingsley Amis. Faber, 1986. 1st ed. Fine in dj. *Rees.* $54/£35

COPE, WENDY. Poem from a Colour Chart of House Paints. Priapus, 1986. One of 100 signed. Fine in wrappers. *Rees.* $47/£30

COPE, ZACHARY. Almroth Wright, Founder of Modern Vaccine Therapy. London, 1966. 1st ed. Good in dw. *Fye.* $35/£23

COPE, ZACHARY. The Treatment of the Acute Abdomen Operative and Post-Operative. London, 1928. 2nd ed. Nice. *Goodrich.* $30/£19

COPELAND, R. MORRIS. Country Life. Boston: Crosby & Nichols, 1863. 2nd ed. Frontis; x,814pp; 8 plts. (1 dbl-pg). Pub's blindstamped cl. Faint waterstain lower edge; sl cvr wear, else VG. *Bookpress.* $195/£126

COPELAND, ROBERT MORRIS. Country Life: A Handbook of Agriculture.... NY: OJ, 1867. 6th ed, w/supplement. Double frontis plan, viii,(iii-v),ix-x,912pp, 9 plts. Orig grn cl, gilt spine (shelfworn, spine ends frayed, hinge weak). *Bohling.* $65/£42

COPELAND, THOMAS. Observations on the Principal Diseases of the Rectum and Anus. London: J. Callow, 1814. 2nd ed. ix,183pp + 1pg ads. Marbled bds, mod 1/2 morocco (ex-lib, rebound, new eps). *Edwards.* $287/£185

COPLAN, M.F. Pink Lemonade. NY, (1945). 1st ed. VG. *Artis.* $25/£16

COPLEY, ESTHER. Cottage Comforts.... London: Simpkin, Marshall, 1834. 11th ed. 224pp. Uncut. Paper-backed bds (chipped); paper label. VG. *Second Life.* $85/£55

COPLEY, ESTHER. The Housekeeper's Guide, or a Plain and Practical System of Domestic Cookery. London: Longman & Co. et al, 1838. 1st ed. Engr frontis, tp; 5 full-pg engr plts. Contemp brn cl over brn bds, spine w/ptd paper label; uncut. VG (rubbing; lt foxing). *Houle.* $375/£242

COPPARD, A.E. Adam and Eve and Pinch Me. London: Golden Cockerel, 1921. 1st ed. Ltd to 550, this one of 160 in white canvas binding. Unopened. VG (paper label browned). *Cox.* $171/£110

COPPARD, A.E. Clorinda Walks in Heaven. Golden Cockerel, 1922. 1st ed. One of 1200 ptd. Sl shelfworn; bumped, else VG in dj (sl chipped, rubbed). *Hermitage.* $90/£58

COPPARD, A.E. Collected Poems. NY: Knopf, 1928. 1st ed. VG. *Graf.* $30/£19

COPPARD, A.E. Count Stefan. London: Golden Cockerel, 1928. 1st ed. #596/600 ptd by Robert Gibbings (wood engrs) on hand-made paper. Frontis, 3 vignettes. Orig buckram-backed Cockerell marbled bds, uncut. VG. *Cox.* $101/£65

COPPARD, A.E. Crotty Shinkwin; The Beauty Spot. London: Golden Cockerel, 1932. #459/500. 7 wood-engrs by Robert Gibbings. Teg, rest uncut. Blue morocco-backed dec cl (backstrip sl faded). VG. *Cox.* $171/£110

COPPARD, A.E. Emergency Exit. NY: Random House, (1934). 1st ed, ltd to 350 numbered, signed. Ink name, else *Godot.* $85/£55

COPPARD, A.E. Fearful Pleasures. Sauk City: Arkham House, 1946. 1st ed. Bkpl, else VG + in dj. *Other Worlds.* $80/£52

COPPARD, A.E. Fearful Pleasures. Arkham House, 1946. 1st ed. NF in NF dj. *Madle.* $100/£65

COPPARD, A.E. The Field of Mustard. London: Cape, (1926). 1st ed. Uncut except for top edge. (Fore-edges sl foxed; sl mkd.) *Petersfield.* $47/£30

COPPARD, A.E. The Man from Kilsheelan. London: Wm. Jackson, 1930. #290/550 signed. Woodcut frontis. Very nice in glassine paper wrapper. *Virgo.* $62/£40

COPPARD, A.E. Nixey's Harlequin. London: Jonathan Cape, (1931). 1st ed. Name, eps lt foxed, else Fine in dj (short tear, sl dust soiled, else Fine). *Godot.* $85/£55

COPPARD, A.E. Nixey's Harlequin. London: Cape, 1931. 1st ed. VG in dj. *Limestone.* $75/£48

COPPARD, A.E. Pelegea and Other Poems. London: Golden Cockerel Press, 1926. 1st ed. #262/425. 6 wood engrs by Robert Gibbings. Sig of Humbert Wolfe. Canvas-backed batik dec bds. VG. *Cox.* $171/£110

COPPARD, A.E. Pink Furniture. London: Cape, (1930). #205/260 signed. Teg, uncut (few pp lt foxed). Full parchment. Dj. *Petersfield.* $81/£52

COPPARD, A.E. Silver Circus. Cape, 1928. 1st ed. VG + in VG + dj. *Fine Books.* $60/£39

COPPARD, A.E. Silver Circus. London: Cape, 1928. 1st trade ed. Edges uncut (sl browned, spotted). Sl offsetting to 1/2 title, last pg, o/w VG in dj (soiled, nicked, sm closed tears). *Virgo.* $47/£30

COPPARD, A.E. and ROBERT GIBBINGS. Rummy That Noble Game Expounded in Prose, Poetry, Diagram and Engraving.... London: Golden Cockerel, (1932). 1st ed. #29/250 on hand-made paper, signed by Coppard and Gibbings (engrs). 15 engrs, diagram. Grn morocco-backed dec cl; teg; others uncut. VG (backstrip sl faded). *Cox.* $132/£85

Copper Camp. Stories of the World's Greatest Mining Town, Butte, Montana. NY: Hastings House, (1943). 1st ed. VG in dj (edge-chipped). *Perier.* $37/£24

COPPING, ARTHUR. A Journalist in the Holy Land. London: Religious Tract Soc, 1911. 20 color plts (sl stain blank area of few plts). Illus (sl rubbed) mtd on fr cvr. *Schoyer.* $50/£32

COPPING, ARTHUR. A Journalist in the Holy Land. NY, 1912. Dec cvrs. *Lewis.* $50/£32

Coquet-Dale Fishing Songs. (By Francis Doubleday.) London: William Blackwood, 1852. viii,168pp. Blind-stamped cl (spine dulled, frayed), gilt. *Hollett.* $101/£65

Corbett and Ballenger's Ninth Annual Denver City Directory. Denver: Thomas B. Corbett & John H. Ballenger, 1881. 625(i.e. 612)pp; dbl-pg map. Ptd bds. (Lacks leather spine). *Dawson.* $225/£145

CORBETT, JIM. The Man-Eating Leopard of Rudraprayag. NY: Oxford, 1948. Fine+ in dj. *Bowman.* $60/£39

CORBETT, P.E. The Sculpture of the Parthenon. London: Penguin Books, 1959. 1st ed. 40 b/w plts. Dj. *Edwards.* $39/£25

CORBIN, BERNARD G. and WILLIAM KERKA. Steam Locomotives of the Burlington Route. (Red Oak, IA, 1960.) Gilt-stamped black buckram. VF in dj. *Bohling.* $125/£81

CORDELL, EUGENE F. The Medical Annals of Maryland 1799-1899. Balt: (Press of Williams & Wilkins), 1903. Frontis, 889pp. Grn cl. Tp detached but present, else VG, partly unopened. *Chapel Hill.* $250/£161

CORDELL, EUGENE F. The Medical Annals of Maryland, 1799-1899. Balt, 1903. 1st ed. 32 plts. Uncut, unopened. Fine. *Bookpress.* $250/£161

CORDER, E.M. The Deer Hunter. NY: Exeter, (1979). 1st hb ed. Dj. *Aka.* $40/£26

CORDER, SUSANNA (comp). Life of Elizabeth Fry. London, 1853. xvi,646pp. Full calf, gilt. *Edwards.* $93/£60

CORDIER, A.H. Some Big Game Hunts. KS City: Privately ptd, 1911. 1st ed. Lt yellow cl. Spotted, soiled, o/w VG. *Bowman.* $200/£129

CORDIER, DANIEL. The Drawings of Jean Dubuffet. Cecily Mackworth (trans). NY: George Braziller, 1960. 1st US ed. Illus paper over bds. Lt soil; sl bumped, else VG in dj. *Cahan.* $85/£55

CORDRY, MRS. T.A. The Story of the Marking of the Santa Fe Trail by the Daughters of the American Revolution.... Topeka: Crane, 1915. 1st ed. VG- (ink name; spine worn). Internally VG. *Parker.* $65/£42

CORE, E.L. Vegetation of West Virginia. Parsons, 1966. Dj (lt wear). *Sutton.* $27/£17

CORELLI, MARIE. The Love of Long Ago and Other Stories. London: Methuen, (1920). 1st ed. Inscribed. Cvrs used; inner hinges cracked, else VG-. *Pharos.* $75/£48

CORK, RICHARD. Art Beyond the Gallery. Yale Univ Press, 1985. Dj (sl chipped). *Edwards.* $47/£30

CORKRAN, DAVID H. The Creek Frontier 1540-1783. Norman: Univ of OK Press, (1967). 1st ed. Orange cl. Fine in NF dj (spine faded). *Chapel Hill.* $50/£32

CORLE, EDWIN (ed). Merle Armitage Dance Memoranda. NY: Duell, Sloan & Pearce, 1947. 1st ed. VG in dj. *Cahan.* $85/£55

CORLE, EDWIN. Billy the Kid. Duell, Sloan, Pierce, (1953). 1st ed. VG in dj (torn). *Oregon.* $30/£19

CORLE, EDWIN. Billy the Kid. NY/Boston: Duell, Sloan, Pearce/Little, Brown, (1953). 1st ed. Ink inscrip, else VG in dj. *Godot.* $35/£23

CORLE, EDWIN. Burro Alley. NY: Random House, (1938). 1st ed. Label fr pastedown, else NF in white dj (dknd). *Reese.* $35/£23

CORLE, EDWIN. Burro Alley. NY: Random, 1938. 1st ed. VF in pict dj (minor wear extrems). *Else Fine.* $75/£48

CORLE, EDWIN. Fig Tree John. NY: Liveright, (1935). 1st ed. Fine in Fine dj (chipped). *Book Market.* $100/£65

CORLE, EDWIN. The Gila River of the Southwest. NY: Rinehart, (1951). 1st ed. Fine in Fine dj. *Book Market.* $50/£32

CORLE, EDWIN. Mojave. A Book of Stories. NY: Liveright, (1934). 1st ed, 1st bk. Fine in Fine dj. *Book Market.* $325/£210

CORLE, EDWIN. The Royal Highway (El Camino Real). Indianapolis: Bobbs Merrill, 1949. 1st ltd Mission Bell ed. Signed. VG- in dj (worn). *Parker.* $40/£26

CORLE, EDWIN. The Royal Highway. Bobbs Merrill, (1949). 1st ed. 2 maps. VG in VG dj. *Oregon.* $35/£23

CORLETT, WILLIAM THOMAS. The Medicine-Man of the American Indian and His Cultural Background. Springfield, IL, 1935. 1st ed. *Argosy.* $85/£55

CORLETT, WILLIAM. A Treatise on the Acute, Infectious Exanthemata. Phila, 1901. 1st ed. (Ex-lib; inner hinges cracked; shaken.) *Fye.* $50/£32

CORLEY, DONALD. The Haunted Jester. (N.p.): Robert M. McBride, 1931. 1st ed. VG. *Hermitage.* $25/£16

CORLEY, DONALD. The Haunted Jester. NY: McBride, 1931. 1st ed. Fine in fragile gold dj (few short tears, creases top edge). *Else Fine.* $85/£55

CORMAN, CID. For Now. Origin Press, 1970. 1st ed, signed. Fine in wrappers. *Dermont.* $20/£13

CORNABY, W. ARTHUR. A String of Chinese Peach-Stones. London: Charles H. Kelly, 1895. 1st ed. Color frontis, xv,479pp. Gilt cl over beveled bds. VG. *Hollett.* $132/£85

CORNARO, LEWIS. Discourses on a Sober and Temperate Life. London: Ptd for Benjamin White, 1779. New ed, corrected. xii,188pp. Full calf, gilt. *Edwards.* $70/£45

CORNARO, LEWIS. Sure and Certain Methods of Attaining a Long and Healthful Life. London, 1737. 5th ed. 197pp (tp sl stained at margin; pp17-24 sl stained at upper corner). Orig calf (worn; joints cracked, upper joint sl wormed). *Edwards*. $101/£65

CORNELL, JULIEN. The Trial of Ezra Pound. Faber, 1967. 1st UK ed. Crease early pp, o/w Fine in dj (sl wear). *Poetry*. $19/£12

CORNELL, RALPH J. Conspicuous California Plants.... Pasadena: San Pasqual Press, 1938. 1st ed. Ltd to 1500. Pict cvr. Fine in dj. *Quest*. $65/£42

CORNELL, WALTER. Health and Medical Inspection of School Children. Phila, 1913. 1st ed. (Marginal water stain.) *Fye*. $60/£39

CORNER, E.J.H. The Natural History of Palms. Univ of CA, 1966. 1st ed. Sm dampstain rear cvr, o/w VG. *Oregon*. $45/£29

CORNER, MISS. Careless James. London: Dean & Son, n.d. (ca 1855). 16mo. Full-pg wood engr frontis, vignette tp, 7ff+1pg list lower wrapper. VG (pencil sig frontis) in pict yellow paper wrappers (lt soiled). *Hobbyhorse*. $75/£48

CORNER, WILLIAM. San Antonio De Bexar—A Guide and History. San Antonio: 1890. Six Gun 498. 166pp. 16 plts. VG. Howes C 778. *Perier*. $125/£81

CORNET, GEORGES. Tuberculosis and Acute General Miliary Tuberculosis. Phila, 1905. 1st Eng trans. 1/2 leather. *Fye*. $75/£48

CORNING, LEAVITT, JR. Baronial Forts of the Big Bend. (Austin): Trinity Univ, 1967. VG in dj. *Schoyer*. $35/£23

CORNISH, DUDLEY TAYLOR. The Sable Arm Negro Troops in the Union Army, 1861-1865. (Lawrence, KS): University Press of KS, (1987). 1st ed, thus w/new foreword by Herman Hattaway. Orig cl. Fine in Fine dj. *Mcgowan*. $45/£29

CORNWELL, BERNARD. Rebel. London: Harper Collins, 1993. 1st ed. VF in dj. *Limestone*. $30/£19

CORNWELL, BERNARD. Sharpe's Eagle. London: Collins, 1981. 1st ed. Fine in dj. *Limestone*. $65/£42

CORNWELL, BERNARD. Sharpe's Gold. London: Collins, 1981. 1st ed. Fine in dj. *Limestone*. $65/£42

CORNWELL, BERNARD. Sharpe's Regiment. London: Collins, 1986. 1st ed. Fine in dj. *Limestone*. $30/£19

CORNWELL, BERNARD. Sharpe's Rifles. London: Collins, 1988. 1st UK ed. Fine in dj. *Williams*. $39/£25

CORNWELL, BERNARD. Sharpe's Siege. London: Collins, 1987. 1st UK ed. Fine in dj. *Williams*. $39/£25

CORNWELL, BERNARD. Wildtrack. London: Michael Joseph, 1988. 1st UK ed. Fine in dj. *Williams*. $31/£20

CORNWELL, PATRICIA. Postmortem. NY: Scribner's, 1990. 1st ed, advance rev copy. Fine in Fine dj. *Janus*. $300/£194

CORNWELL, PATRICIA. A Time for Remembering. NY: Harper, (1983). 1st ed, 1st bk. Fine in NF dj (closed tear). *Robbins*. $125/£81

Corot 1796-1875. Phila: Museum of Art, 1946. Good in wrappers (sl worn). *Washton*. $15/£10

CORREDOR-MATHEOS, J. Miro's Posters. NJ: Chartwell, n.d. (1980). 119 color plts. Sound in dj. *Ars Artis*. $116/£75

CORRIGAN, A.J. A Printer and His World. London: Faber & Faber, 1944. 1st ed. VG in dj (sl spotted). *Moss*. $22/£14

CORRIGAN, DOUGLAS. That's My Story. NY: Dutton, 1938. 56 photograv illus. VG in dj (nicks). *Houle*. $85/£55

CORRY, JOHN. The Detector of Quackery. London: For B. Crosby, et al, 1802. 2nd ed, 'Amplified.' (iv),164,7,(iv)pp, deckle-edged (sm hole top title; foreedges sl creased). Contemp bds (rebacked; spine rubbed, chipped, stained). NF internally. *Blue Mountain*. $125/£81

CORSE, CARITA DOGGETT. The Key to the Golden Islands. Chapel Hill: Univ of NC, 1931. 1st ed. Map eps. Unopened. Fine in glassine dj. *Cahan*. $50/£32

CORSE, CARITA DOGGETT. The Key to the Golden Islands. Chapel Hill: Univ of NC Press, 1931. 1st ed. Ltd to 212 signed. Teg. Shelf-backed red cl, gilt dec. Dampstain, o/w VG. *Cahan*. $40/£26

CORSO, GREGORY. Bomb. SF: City Lights, 1958. 1st ed, 1st state. One of 2000. Fldg broadside. Short crease, o/w NF. *Sclanders*. $62/£40

CORSO, GREGORY. Bomb. City Light Books, 1958. 1st ed. VG+. *Fine Books*. $100/£65

CORSO, GREGORY. Earth Egg. Unmuzzled Ox Editions, (1974). #52/100 signed. Separate booklet, facs poem. Fine in pict box (corners sl rubbed). *Polyanthos*. $50/£32

CORSO, GREGORY. The Happy Birthday of Death. NY, (1960). 1st Amer ed. Signed. Cvrs edge rubbed, o/w Fine. *Polyanthos*. $35/£23

CORSO, GREGORY. The Happy Birthday of Death. (NY): New Directions, (1960). 1st ed. Fold-out broadside poem 'Bomb' inserted. VG in ptd wraps. *Antic Hay*. $45/£29

CORSO, GREGORY. Hitting the Big 5-0. NY: Catchword Papers, 1983. 'Out of series,' signed. Fine in ptd wraps. *Polyanthos*. $35/£23

CORSON, JULIET. The Cooking Manual.... NY, 1877. 1st ed. 144pp. (Cvrs rubbed, dknd.) *King*. $65/£42

CORTAZAR, JULIO. 62: A Model Kit. NY: Pantheon, 1972. 1st ed. Spine sl slanted, o/w Fine in Fine dj (tiny tears). *Beasley*. $40/£26

CORTAZAR, JULIO. Around the Day in Eighty Worlds. SF: North Point, 1986. 1st ed. NF in NF dj. *Bishop*. $17/£11

CORTAZAR, JULIO. Cronopios and Famas. NY: Pantheon, 1969. 1st Amer ed. NF in dj (spine tanned). *Lame Duck*. $125/£81

CORTAZAR, JULIO. End of the Game and Other Stories. London: Collins, 1968. 1st ed. Fine in dj (minor edgewear). *Else Fine*. $45/£29

CORTAZAR, JULIO. Hopscotch. London: Collins & Harvill, 1967. 1st British ed. NF in NF dj. *Lame Duck*. $100/£65

CORTAZAR, JULIO. A Manual for Manuel. NY: Pantheon, 1978. 1st ed. Fine in dj. *Else Fine*. $50/£32

CORTES, HERNANDO. The Despatches of Hernando Cortes, the Conqueror of Mexico. NY: Wiley & Putnam, 1843. 1st ed. xii,432pp (foxing). Brn bds (chipped), paper spine label. *Karmiole*. $100/£65

CORTISSOZ, ROYAL (intro). The Work of Charles Platt. NY: Architectural Bk Pub Corp, 1913. 183 plts. Sl dampstain traces fr bd, else Fine in dj (repaired). *Quest*. $250/£161

CORVO, BARON. (Pseud of Frederick Rolfe.) The Armed Hands and Other Stories and Pieces. Cecil Woolf (ed). London, 1974. 1st ed. VF in VF dj. *Mcclintock*. $35/£23

CORVO, BARON. (Pseud of Frederick Rolfe.) Chronicles of the House of Borgia. NY/London, (1901). 1st Amer ed. Black cl binding state. VG. *Mcclintock.* $145/£94

CORVO, BARON. (Pseud of Frederick Rolfe.) The Desire and Pursuit of The Whole. London, (1934). 1st ed, 1st issue binding. Dk grn cl; spine stamped in gilt. VG. *Argosy.* $200/£129

CORVO, BARON. (Pseud of Frederick Rolfe.) The Desire and Pursuit of the Whole. London, (1961). 3rd ed. Fine in VG dj. *Mcclintock.* $17/£11

CORVO, BARON. (Pseud of Frederick Rolfe.) The Desire and Pursuit of the Whole. London: Cassell, 1934. 1st ed, 1st issue in veridian cl. Pp sl browned, sl foxed, o/w Very Nice in VG dj (sl chipped; browned). *Virgo.* $147/£95

CORVO, BARON. (Pseud of Frederick Rolfe.) Hadrian the Seventh. NY: Knopf, 1937. 1st Alblabook issue. Bright (spine lt faded, sm ink spot fore-edge) in dj (spine sl faded, price-clipped). *Aka.* $20/£13

CORVO, BARON. (Pseud of Frederick Rolfe.) Hadrian the Seventh. (London: C&W, 1950.) New Phoenix Lib ed, 1st in the Phoenix Lib, 4th imp of A-6a. Fine in dj. *Pharos.* $35/£23

CORVO, BARON. (Pseud of Frederick Rolfe.) Letters to Harry Bainbridge. London: Enitharmon Press, 1977. 1st ed. One of 350. Fine in dj. *Polyanthos.* $40/£26

CORVO, BARON. (Pseud of Frederick Rolfe.) Letters to James Walsh. London, 1972. 1st ed, ltd to 500 numbered. Fine in dj. *Mcclintock.* $50/£32

CORVO, BARON. (Pseud of Frederick Rolfe.) Letters to James Walsh. London: Rota, 1972. 1st ed. #5A/500. Spine sl rubbed, o/w NF in dj (sl rubbed, chipped). *Virgo.* $54/£35

CORVO, BARON. (Pseud of Frederick Rolfe.) Nicholas Crabbe or The One and the Many. New Directions, 1958. 1st Amer ed. NF in NF dj (closed tear). *Fine Books.* $60/£39

CORVO, BARON. (Pseud of Frederick Rolfe.) Nicholas Crabbe or the One and the Many. London, 1958. 1st ed. Fine (sl rubbed) in dj. *Polyanthos.* $30/£19

CORVO, BARON. (Pseud of Frederick Rolfe.) Nicholas Crabbe or The One and the Many. London: C&W, 1958. 1st ed. Name; eps, edges sl foxed, o/w VG in dj (closed tear; spine faded). *Virgo.* $62/£40

CORVO, BARON. (Pseud of Frederick Rolfe.) Nicholas Crabbe. London: C&W, 1960. 1st ed, #55/215. Fine in slipcase. *Virgo.* $124/£80

CORVO, BARON. (Pseud of Frederick Rolfe.) Without Prejudice. London: Privately ptd, 1963. One of 600 w/laid in note. NF in plain dj (sl chipped, closed tear). *Virgo.* $217/£140

CORY, DONALD WEBSTER (ed). 21 Variations on a Theme. NY, (1953). 1st ed. VG. *Mcclintock.* $25/£16

CORY, H. The Bears of Jasper. London: Nelson, 1946. Fine in VG + dj. *Mikesh.* $45/£29

CORYN, M. The Chevalier D'Eon 1728-1810. London: Thornton Butterworth, (1932). 1st ed. Frontis, 3 plts. Dj fr panel, flap laid in. Nice. *Cady.* $25/£16

COSGROVE, RACHEL R. Hidden Valley of Oz. Chicago: Reilly and Lee, (1951). 1st ed. 4to. Dirk (Gringhuis) (illus). Blue cl, color pict paste label; in color dj (sl wear foot spine). *Reisler.* $325/£210

COSTON, H.E. TOWNER et al. River Management, the Making, Care and Development of Salmon and Trout Rivers. London: Seeley, c. 1936. (Backstrip sl faded.) *Petersfield.* $47/£30

COTT, H.B. Adaptive Coloration in Animals. NY: OUP, 1940. 1st ed. Blind-stamped dec cl. NF in VG dj. *Mikesh.* $45/£29

COTTAM, C. and J.B. TREFETHEN (eds). Whitewings. Princeton: Van Nost, 1968. 1st ed. 14 tables, 2 color plts. Gilt dec cl. NF in VG dj. *Mikesh.* $27/£17

COTTERAL, BONNIE. Tumbling, Pyramid Building and Stunts for Girls and Women. NY, 1931. 1st ed. Good. *Fye.* $40/£26

COTTERILL, R.S. History of Pioneer Kentucky. Cincinnati: Johnson & Hardin, 1917. 4 fldg facs maps. (Rear pocket removed.) *Schoyer.* $55/£35

COTTON, CHARLES. The Compleat Gamester. Barre: Imprint Society, 1970. #107/1950 signed by Joseph Low (illus). Full cowhide. Bkpl, else Fine in pub's slipcase. *Hermitage.* $85/£55

COTTON, CHARLES. The Compleat Gamester. Barre: Imprint Soc, 1970. 1st ed, #1750/1950. Signed by Joseph Low (illus). Hand-rubbed cowhide, gilt decs. Fine in VG marbled paper slipcase. *Connolly.* $55/£35

COTTON, HENRY. A Typographical Gazetteer.... Oxford, 1831. 2nd ed. xviii,393pp; uncut. Blue cl (sl rubbed, faded). VG. *Cox.* $186/£120

COTTON, ROBERT. Cotton Posthuma. London: Richard Lowndes, 1672. 1/2 calf over marbled bds (newly rebound). Top edge closely trimmed, leaves lt browned, else Fine. *Glenn.* $250/£161

COTTRELL, C.H. Recollections of Siberia in the Years 1840 and 1841. London, 1842. xii,410pp, errata slip, 16pp ads, fldg map. Grn cl (sm cracks). *Lewis.* $225/£145

COUES, E. Birds of the Colorado Valley. Washington, 1878. Part 1. xvi,807pp. (Back cvr loose; sl waterstaining.) *Wheldon & Wesley.* $62/£40

COUES, E. and J.A. ALLEN. Monographs of North American Rodentia. Washington, 1887. xii,x,1091pp; 7 plts. Good (ex-lib; sl loose; sl used). *Wheldon & Wesley.* $116/£75

COULSON, CONSTANCE J.D. Korea. A&C Black, 1910. 12 color plts, map. Color port laid down upper bd. (Sl spotting.) *Edwards.* $23/£15

COULSON, W. On the Diseases of the Hip-Joint. London, 1837. viii,112pp. VG. *Whitehart.* $434/£280

COULTER, E. MERTON (ed). Georgia's Disputed Ruins. Chapel Hill: Univ of NC Press, 1937. 1st ed. One of 750. Blue cl. NF in VG dj (price-clipped). *Chapel Hill.* $125/£81

COULTER, E. MERTON. The South during Reconstruction 1865-1877. Baton Rouge, 1945. Fldg map. Dj worn, chipped, o/w VG + . *Pratt.* $30/£19

COULTER, E. MERTON. Travels in the Confederate States. Norman: Univ of OK Press, (1961). 2nd ed. Red cl. NF in dj (soiled). *Chapel Hill.* $85/£55

COULTER, E. MERTON. William G. Brownlow, Fighting Parson of the Southern Highlands. Chapel Hill: UNC Press, 1937. 1st ed. Fldg map, facs. Brn cl. NF in VG dj. *Chapel Hill.* $100/£65

COULTER, E. MERTON. William G. Brownlow: Fighting Parson of the Southern Highlands. Chapel Hill: UNC Press, 1937. 1st ed. Fldg map. Tp sl foxed, else VG in dj (edge-chipped). *Cahan.* $60/£39

COULTHARD, ALFRED J. and MARTIN WATTS. Windmills of Somerset and the Men Who Worked Them. London: Research Pub., 1978. 1st ed. Signed by Martin Webb. VG in dj. *Hollett.* $62/£40

COULTON, G.G. Life in the Middle Ages. Cambridge, 1929-30. 4 vols. *Petersfield.* $37/£24

COULTON, G.G. Social Life in Britain from the Conquest to the Reformation. CUP, (1918) 1919. Rev ed. 40 plts. Uncut. Buckram gilt. VG in dj (frayed, neatly strengthened). *Peter Taylor.* $50/£32

COUPER, HEATHER and DAVID PELHAM. Universe. NY: Random House, 1985. 25x25 cm. 6 dbl-pg pop-ups, pull-tabs. Glazed pict bds. VG. *Book Finders.* $30/£19

COURLANDER, HAROLD. Negro Folk Music U.S.A. NY: Columbia Univ, 1963. 1st ed. Fine (name) in dj (lt used). *Beasley.* $50/£32

COURNAND, ANDRE. Cardiac Catheterization in Congenital Heart Disease. NY, 1950. 1st ed, 2nd ptg. (Ex-lib.) *Fye.* $150/£97

COURSEY, O.W. Pioneering in Dakota. Mitchell, SD: Educator Supply Co, (1937). Inscribed. VG. *Schoyer.* $30/£19

COURTHION, PIERRE. Georges Rouault. NY: Abrams, (1962). 1st ed. Emb cl. Fine in pict dj. *Cahan.* $100/£65

COURTHION, PIERRE. Georges Rouault. NY, n.d. (ca 1960). 49 tipped-in color illus. (Minor marginal browning). Dj (sl soiled, creased). *Edwards.* $85/£55

COURTINE, ROBERT J. Madame Maigret's Recipes. NY: Harcourt Brace, 1975. 1st ed. Fine in dj (sl crease). *Janus.* $65/£42

Courtship, Merry Marriage, and Pic-nic Dinner, of Cock Robin and Jenny Wren. London: Grant & Griffith, n.d. (ca 1850). 12mo. Frontis,16 leaves + 1pg ad back cvr. Grn ptd stiff paper wrappers (label inside; chipped). VG. *Hobbyhorse.* $150/£97

COURVILLE, CYRIL B. Cerebral Palsy. LA: San Lucas Press, 1954. Good. *Goodrich.* $75/£48

COURVILLE, CYRIL B. Commotio Cerebri: Cerebral Concussion and the Postconcussion Syndrome in Their Medical and Legal Aspects. L.A., 1953. 1st ed. Good. *Fye.* $100/£65

COURVILLE, CYRIL B. Pathology of the Central Nervous System. Mountain View, 1945. 2nd ed, rev & enlgd. Good. *Goodrich.* $35/£23

COURVILLE, CYRIL B. Untoward Effects of Nitrous Oxide Anethesia.... Mountainview, CA, 1939. 1st ed. Good. *Fye.* $65/£42

COUSINS, FRANK and PHIL M. RILEY. The Wood-Carver of Salem. Boston: Little, Brown, 1916. 1st ed. One of 930. Frontis, 127 plts. Uncut, unopened; teg. (Bkpl, rubberstamp; worn; margins browned, sl foxed.) *Bookpress.* $125/£81

COUTANT, C.G. History of Wyoming.... Argonaut, (1966). 26 plts. Fine. Howes C 810. *Oregon.* $50/£32

COVARRUBIAS, MIGUEL. The Eagle, the Jaguar, and the Serpent: Indian Art of the Americas, North America. NY, 1954. 1st ed. Dec cl. VG in dj. *Argosy.* $150/£97

COVARRUBIAS, MIGUEL. Indian Art of Mexico and Central America. NY: Knopf, 1957. 1st ed. VG- in Good dj (chipped). *Parker.* $100/£65

COVARRUBIAS, MIGUEL. Indian Art of Mexico and Central America. NY, 1957. 1st ed. 12 color plts. 2-tone dec cl. VG. *Argosy.* $125/£81

COVARRUBIAS, MIGUEL. Negro Drawings. NY: Knopf, 1927. 1st ed. 56pp. Blue bds, gilt title. VG in dj (lt chipped). *Davidson.* $1,250/£806

COVENTRY, FRANCIS. The History of Pompey the Little. London: Golden Cockerel, 1926. #351/400. Frontis. Uncut, partly unopened. VG in buckram-backed bds. Ptd dj (spotted). *Cox.* $171/£110

COVERLEY-PRICE, VICTOR. An Artist among Mountains. London: Robert Hale, 1957. 1st ed. 33 plts. VG in dj. *Hollett.* $31/£20

COWAN, J. Diseases of the Heart. London, 1914. (Few pp sl discolored.) New binder's cl. *Whitehart.* $124/£80

COWAN, ROBERT E. Booksellers of Early San Francisco. LA: Ward Ritchie, 1953. 1st ed. Ltd to 350. Fine. *Oregon.* $50/£32

COWARD, NOEL. Bitter Sweet and Other Plays. NY: Doubleday, Doran, 1929. 1st Amer ed, ltd to 1000 numbered, signed. Black cl. Crease fep, spine rubbed, sl dull, else VG. *Godot.* $275/£177

COWARD, NOEL. Point Valaine. GC: Doubleday, 1935. 1st ed. NF in dj (lt wear). *Else Fine.* $65/£42

COWARD, NOEL. Pomp and Circumstance. NY: Doubleday, 1960. 1st Amer ed. Very Nice in dj. *Cady.* $30/£19

COWARD, NOEL. Present Indicative. London: Heinemann, 1937. 1st UK ed. VG in dj (sl creased, browned). *Williams.* $70/£45

COWARD, NOEL. To Step Aside. GC: Doubleday, 1939. 1st ed. Fine in dj (minor edgewear, sm corner chips). *Else Fine.* $55/£35

COWASJEE, SAROS (ed). Stories from the Raj. London: Bodley Head, 1982. 1st ed. NF in dj. *Rees.* $31/£20

COWDERY, MAE V. We Lift Up Our Voices. Phila: Alpress, 1936. One of 350 numbered. Frontis illus. Cl-backed paper-cvrd bds (extrems dknd). VG w/o dj. *Between The Covers.* $250/£161

COWDRY, E.V. (ed). Special Cytology: The Form and Functions of.... NY, 1928. 1st ed. 2 vols. 1348pp. (Backstrip dull; spine tail, head worn.) *Fye.* $150/£97

COWLEY, ABRAHAM. The Mistress with Other Select Poems. John Sparrow (ed). London: Nonesuch, 1926. #234/1050. (Internal spotting.) Buckram (sl worn, chipped), morocco label (chipped). *Cox.* $31/£20

COWLEY, ABRAHAM. The Mistress. John Sparrow (ed). London: Nonesuch, 1926. One of 1050. Buckram. Bkpl; label sl rubbed; spine dknd; offsetting eps, else internally Fine. *Pharos.* $125/£81

COWLEY, MALCOLM. Blue Juniata: Poems. NY, 1929. 1st ed. As New. *Bond.* $150/£97

COWLEY, MALCOLM. The Dry Season. Norfolk: New Directions/Poet of the Month, (1941). 1st ed, issue in bds. Fine in dj (edge-sunned; nick). *Reese.* $75/£48

COWLEY, MALCOLM. Exile's Return. NY, 1951. Rev, expanded ed. VG in dj. *Argosy.* $40/£26

COWLEY, MALCOLM. Exile's Return. NY: LEC, 1981. One of 2000 numbered, signed by Cowley and Berenice Abbott (photos). Cl, pict bds. VF in slipcase. *Reese.* $100/£65

COWLEY, MALCOLM. Exile's Return: A Literary Odyssey of the 1920's. NY: LEC, 1981. One of 2000 numbered, signed by Cowley and Berenice Abbott (photos). Cl-backed dec bds. Fine in pub's slipcase. *Hermitage.* $125/£81

COWLEY, MALCOLM. The Literary Situation. NY: Viking, 1954. 1st ed. Gray cl. Inscrip, else NF in dj (lt used). *Chapel Hill.* $40/£26

COWLEY, MALCOLM. A Second Flowering. NY: Viking, (1973). Uncorrected pg proofs of 1st ed. VG in ptd wrappers (label residue). *Reese.* $60/£39

COWPER, WILLIAM. Memoir of the Early Life of.... Ptd for R. Edwards, 1816. 2nd ed. Port; 1 fldg, 2 other ad leaves. Uncut. Orig bds. Foot of backstrip worn, o/w Good. *Hill.* $163/£105

COWPER, WILLIAM. Poems. Ptd for J. Johnson, 1811. New ed. 2 vols. Contemp tree calf. (Old erased lib stamps eps.) *Hill.* $62/£40

COWPER, WILLIAM. Poems. London: Tilt & Bogue, 1841. 2 vols. lxxii,274pp + (ii)ads; viii,336pp; aeg. Inner gilt dentelles. Full gilt dec morocco. *Edwards.* $132/£85

COWPER, WILLIAM. Private Correspondence of William Cowper. London: Henry Colburn, 1824. 1st ed. 2 vols. Frontis ports (foxed; offsetting to tps). 1/2 title vol 1 only, as issued. Uncut. VG in mod cl; spine hand-titled. *Poetry.* $194/£125

COWPER, WILLIAM. The Task, a Poem in Six Books. Phila: Thos. Dobson, 1787. 1st Amer ed. 12mo. 218pp,(2,ads). Full contemp calf, gilt; red leather label (fading; hinges weakening). Contents Excellent. *Hartfield.* $285/£184

COWPER, WILLIAM. The Task. London: James Nisbet, 1878. 17 plts. Aeg. Dec cl. *Quest.* $225/£145

COX, DAVID. A Treatise on Landscape Painting in Water Colours. Geoffrey Holme (ed). London: The Studio, 1922. 72 plts (15 mtd color); teg. Contemp 1/2 morocco; orig wrappers bound in, gilt spine. Fine. *Europa.* $105/£68

COX, E.H.M. The Library of Edmund Gosse. London: Dulau, 1924. 1st ed. Frontis. Blue cl. Fine in dj (gouge). *Karmiole.* $85/£55

COX, E.H.M. Plant-Hunting in China. London, 1945. Color frontis; 24 photo plts. *Wheldon & Wesley.* $47/£30

COX, EARNEST SEVIER. Let My People Go. Richmond, VA: White America Soc, (1925). 1st ed. NF in orig ptd wrappers. *Mcgowan.* $75/£48

COX, J. CHARLES and ALFRED HARVEY. English Church Furniture. London: Methuen, (1907). (Binding faded.) *Petersfield.* $31/£20

COX, J. CHARLES and ALFRED HARVEY. English Church Furniture. London: Methuen, 1907. 1st ed. Gilt red cl (sl faded, rubbed; foxed). Foxed. *Hollett.* $62/£40

COX, J. CHARLES. Churchwardens' Accounts from the Fourteenth Century to the Close of the Seventeenth Century. London: Methuen, 1913. 1st ed. 36 plts. Spine sl faded. *Hollett.* $54/£35

COX, J. CHARLES. English Church Fittings, Furniture and Accessories. Batsford, 1923. (Spine faded.) *Edwards.* $47/£30

COX, J. CHARLES. English Church Fittings, Furniture, and Accessories. NY, 1923. (Spine sl sunned, frayed.) *Washton.* $50/£32

COX, J. CHARLES. The English Parish Church. Batsford, 1914. (Feps lt browned; bkpl; spines faded.) *Edwards.* $47/£30

COX, J. CHARLES. The Parish Registers of England. London: Methuen, 1910. 1st ed. 24 plts. Spotted, sl browned; spine sl faded. *Hollett.* $54/£35

COX, J. CHARLES. Pulpits, Lecterns, and Organs in English Churches. OUP, 1915. (Lt rubbed.) *Edwards.* $70/£45

COX, J. CHARLES. The Royal Forests of England. London: Methuen, 1905. 1st ed. Pp spotted; spine dknd, rubbed. *Hollett.* $70/£45

COX, J. CHARLES. The Sanctuaries and Sanctuary Seekers of Mediaeval England. London: George Allen, 1911. 1st ed. Color frontis, 20 plts. Damped, spine faded. *Hollett.* $39/£25

COX, J.R. Classics in the Literature of Mountaineering and Mountain Travel from the F.P. Farquar Collection. Univ of CA Lib, 1980. One of 500. VG. *Moss.* $70/£45

COX, JACOB DOLSON. The March to the Sea: Franklin and Nashville. NY: Scribner's, 1882. 1st ed. ix,265,(4)pp. VG. *Mcgowan.* $35/£23

COX, PETER. The Larger Species of Rhododendron. London: Batsford, 1979. 6 color plts. As New (price clip). *Quest.* $60/£39

COX, PETER. The Larger Species of Rhododendron. London: Batsford, 1979. 1st ed. 59 plts (6 color). VG in dj. *Hollett.* $54/£35

COX, ROSS. Adventures on the Columbia River...together with a Journey Across the American Continent. NY: J.&J. Harper, 1832. 1st Amer ed. 2 ad pp,(iii)-xv,(25)-335pp (eps, prelims sl foxed). Blue cl (edges, extrems sl worn; spine sl dknd; orig paper spine label rubbed off). VG +. Howes C 822. *Harrington.* $450/£290

COX, SAMUEL S. Arctic Sunbeams: or from Broadway to the Bosphorus by Way of the North Cape. NY: Putnam's, 1882. Inscribed presentation. Brn dec cl (sl rubbed, stained). *Schoyer.* $30/£19

COX, SAMUEL S. Diversions of a Diplomat in Turkey. NY: Webster, 1893. Frontis (dampstained), xix,685pp. Rubbed, soiled; spine frayed, o/w Good. *Worldwide.* $45/£29

COX, SAMUEL S. Isles of the Princes. NY/London: Putnam's, 1887. 1st ed. (x),(382)pp + 6pp ads, fldg map. Brn dec cl, stamped in black, gilt (few sigs sl pulled). *Schoyer.* $65/£42

COX, SANFORD C. Recollections of the Early Settlement of the Wabash Valley. Lafayette: Courier Steam Book & Job Ptg House, 1860. 1st ed. 160pp. Gilt-emb pub's cl (chipped). VG. Howes C 823. *Cahan.* $150/£97

COX, W.W. History of Seward County, Nebraska. Lincoln: State Journal Co, 1888. 290pp. Exterior stains, else VG. *Perier.* $97/£63

COX, WILLIAM. The Mets Will Win the Pennant. Putnam's, 1964. 1st ed. VG in Good + dj. *Plapinger.* $35/£23

COXE, GEORGE H. The Barotique Mystery. NY: Knopf, 1936. 1st ed. NF in pict dj (lt wear, edges, corners). *Else Fine.* $85/£55

COXE, GEORGE H. Dangerous Legacy. NY: Knopf, 1946. 1st ed. NF (sm stamp rep) in VG + dj (price-clipped; spine head lt chipped). *Janus.* $35/£23

COXE, GEORGE H. The Lady Is Afraid. NY: Knopf, 1940. 1st ed. NF in VG + dj (lt rubbed; price-clipped). *Janus.* $35/£23

COXE, JOHN REDMAN. The American Dispensatory. Phila: Carey & Lea, 1831. 1st ed. (8),832pp. Orig calf (scuffed), leather spine label. Overall Good (foxing; sigs loosening). *Artis.* $120/£77

COXE, LOUIS O. The Sea Faring and Other Poems. (NY): Henry Holt, (c 1947). 1st ed. Fine in NF dj (price-clipped). *Heller.* $35/£23

COXE, WILLIAM. A View of the Cultivation of Fruit Trees.... Phila, 1817. 1st ed. 253,(15)pp, 77 wood-engr plts. (Sl foxed, browned; bkpl; reps missing.) Contemp tree calf (lt orn, rubbed). *Sutton.* $550/£355

COYLE, KATHLEEN. There Is a Door. Paris: Edward W. Titus, 1931. Ltd to 525, signed. Teg. Linen over bds, paper labels. Good. *Karmiole.* $45/£29

COYLE, WILLIAM. (Pseud of Thomas Keneally). Act of Grace. London: C&W, 1988. 1st UK ed. Fine in dj. *Lewton.* $23/£15

COYLE, WILLIAM. Ohio Authors and Their Books 1796-1950. Cleveland/NY: World Pub, (1962). 1st ed. Fine in dj. *Sadlon.* $45/£29

COYNER, DAVID H. The Lost Trappers. Cincinnati: Truman, 1850. 2nd ptg. 255pp. (Sig; foxing; chipped; sigs sprung.) Howes C 836. *Schoyer.* $80/£52

COYSH, A.W. Collecting Bookmarkers. London: David & Charles, 1974. 1st ed. VG in dj (price-clipped). *Hollett.* $39/£25

COZZENS, FREDERIC S. The Sparrowgrass Papers. NY: Derby & Jackson, 1856. 1st ed, 1st issue. 8pp undated ads. Blind-stamped purple cl, gilt-dec spine. Fine. *Sumner & Stillman.* $115/£74

COZZENS, JAMES GOULD. Confusion. Boston: B.J. Brimmer, 1924. 1st ed, 1st bk. Blue rmdr binding w/o pub's device and name on spine. Spine lt dknd, o/w VG, w/o dj. *Heller.* $35/£23

COZZENS, JAMES GOULD. Confusion. Boston: B.J. Brimmer, 1924. 1st ed. Good. *Juvelis.* $75/£48

COZZENS, JAMES GOULD. Guard of Honor. NY: Harcourt, Brace, (1948). 1st ed. Fine in NF dj. *Unger.* $175/£113

COZZENS, JAMES GOULD. Michael Scarlett. NY: Albert & Charles Boni, 1925. 1st ed. VG (lacks dj). *Antic Hay.* $45/£29

COZZENS, JAMES GOULD. S.S. San Pedro. NY: Harcourt, Brace, (1931). 1st ed. NF in dj (sl edgeworn). *Sadlon.* $30/£19

CRABB, ALFRED LELAND. A Mockingbird Sang at Chickamauga, A Tale of Embattled Chattanooga. Indianapolis, (1949). 1st ed. Sl cvr fading, o/w Fine. *Pratt.* $35/£23

CRABB, RICHARD. Empire on the Platte. Cleveland: World, (1967). 1st ed. Fine in VG dj. *Oregon.* $45/£29

CRABB, RICHARD. Empire on the Platte. Cleveland/NY: World, (1967). Ltd to 250 signed. Cl-backed bds. Fine in Fine dj, box. *Glenn.* $100/£65

CRABBE, GEORGE. Poems. London: J. Hatchard, 1807. 1st ed. 1/2 title, xxvi,256pp. Contemp 1/2 calf (mod amateur reback), paper label. Gatherings spotted, o/w Good. *Cox.* $43/£28

CRABBE, GEORGE. Tales of the Hall. London: John Murray, 1819. 1st ed. 2 vols. xxiv,326; x,354+2pp ads; 1/2-titles. Mid 19th cent 1/2 black morocco over marbled bds; gilt spines (corners, edges rubbed). *Karmiole.* $150/£97

CRABBE, GEORGE. Tales. London: J. Hatchard, 1813. 3rd ed. 2 vols. Foxing, o/w VG in later buckram (2-inch split vol 1 backstrip). *Poetry.* $31/£20

CRABBE, GEORGE. The Village. London: J. Dodsley, 1783. 1st ed. Title (sl soiled; inscrip), guard,(2),38pp. Mod calf-backed bds, morocco labels; uncut. *Cox.* $248/£160

CRABBE, GEORGE. The Works. London: John Murray, 1823. 8 vols. Contemp calf (worn; joints rubbed; lacks 3 of 16 labels; top part vol IV spine missing, pieces lost crowns vols I, II). Internally VG. *Poetry.* $93/£60

CRABTREE, BETH G. Guide to the Private Manuscript Collections in the North Carolina State Archives. NC Dept of Archives & Hist, 1964. VG. *Book Broker.* $45/£29

CRACE, JIM. Continent. London: Heinemann, 1986. 1st ed. Inscribed. Fine (lt dents) in Fine dj (pub's sticker fr panel). *Beasley.* $150/£97

CRADOCK, MRS. H. Josephine, John and the Puppy. London: Blackie, (1920). 1st ed. 4to. 8 color plts by Honor C. Appleton. Cl-backed illus bds (fore-edge foxed). *Reisler.* $175/£113

CRAFTS, WILLIAM AUGUSTUS. The Southern Rebellion. Boston: Samuel Walker, 1865-67. 1st ed. 2 vols. 648;652pp. Orig parts as issued separately, each w/own wrappers bound together in cl. VG set. *Mcgowan.* $250/£161

CRAIG, ALEC. The Banned Books of England. London: George Allen & Unwin, 1937. 1st ed. Orig cl. Good. *Cox.* $31/£20

CRAIG, CHARLES. Amebiasis and Amebic Dysentery. Springfield, 1954. 1st ed. Good. *Fye.* $50/£32

CRAIG, CHARLES. The Etiology, Diagnosis, and Treatment of Amebiasis. Balt, 1944. 1st ed. Good. *Fye.* $50/£32

CRAIG, CHARLES. The Parasitic Amoebae of Man. Phila, 1911. 1st ed. (Fep torn; ex-lib.) *Fye.* $50/£32

CRAIG, CHARLES. The Wassermann Test. St. Louis, 1918. 1st ed. Good. *Fye.* $75/£48

CRAIG, EDWARD GORDON. On the Art of the Theatre. London: Heinemann, 1911. 1st trade ed. 16 plts, guards. Gilt-lettered black cl, natural bds. Lt foxing text, o/w VG. *House.* $250/£161

CRAIG, MAURICE. Irish Bookbindings, 1600-1800. London: Cassell, 1954. 1st ed. 58 plts. Tip bruised, else VG. *Bookpress.* $385/£248

CRAIG, NEWTON N. Thrills 1861 to 1887. (Oakland, CA: Craig, 1931). 2 plts, letter facs. VG. *Schoyer.* $50/£32

CRAIG, NUTE. Thrills 1861 to 1887. Oakland: Privately ptd, n.d. (1931). 1st ed. 1 plt. Leatherette. VG. *Oregon.* $75/£48

CRAIG, WILLIAM. Enemy at the Gates: The Battle for Stalingrad. NY, 1973. 1st ed. VG in dj (worn). *Clark.* $26/£17

CRAIGHEAD, F. and J. Hawks, Owls and Wildlife. Harrisburg/Washington: Stackpole/WMI, 1956. 1st ed. Fine in Good+ dj. *Mikesh.* $45/£29

CRAIGHEAD, F.C. Insect Enemies of Eastern Forests. Washington, 1950. Incl supplement. Cl (spine faded; spotted; fr hinge cracked). *Sutton.* $45/£29

CRAIGHEAD, F.C. The Trees of South Florida. Vol I. Coral Gables, 1971. Dj (lt wear). *Sutton.* $30/£19

CRAIGHILL, E.A. Confederate Surgeon, The Personal Recollections of.... Peter W. Houck (ed). Lynchburg, 1989. 1st ltd ed, 240/1000. Signed. Pict cl. Fine. *Pratt.* $17/£11

CRAIK, HENRY. A Century of Scottish History. Edinburgh/London, 1901. 2 vols. Emb cl. VG. *Argosy.* $100/£65

CRAIS, ROBERT. The Monkey's Raincoat. London: Piatkus, 1987. 1st hb ed. VF in dj (price-clipped, sticker). *Mordida.* $75/£48

CRAM, MILDRED. Old Seaport Towns of the South. NY: Dodd Mead, 1917. 1st ed. Fr inner hinge starting, else VG. *Pharos.* $20/£13

CRAM, RALPH ADAMS. The Ruined Abbeys of Great Britain. London, 1906. 1st ed. Gilt-ruled illus cl (spine sl rubbed; few pp lt foxed). *Edwards.* $39/£25

CRAMER, GERALD et al. Henry Moore. Catalogue of Graphic Work Volume II. 1973-1975. Geneva, 1976. 111 color plts; in dj. *Edwards.* $202/£130

CRAN, MARION. Gardens in America. London, 1931. 1st ed. 16 photo plts. Prelims, edges foxed, else VG. *Brooks.* $26/£17

CRANDALL, LEE S. The Management of Wild Mammals in Captivity. Chicago, 1965. Inscribed. VG. *Argosy.* $50/£32

CRANE, HART. The Bridge. NY: LEC, 1981. One of 2000 signed by Richard Benson (photos). VF in dec slipcase. *Pharos.* $150/£97

CRANE, HART. White Buildings. NY, 1926. 1st ed, 2nd issue w/corrected tp on a stub. Cl-backed batik bds. Lt pencilled underlinings; penned notes; bkpl; cvrs lt edgeworn, o/w VG. *Pharos.* $300/£194

CRANE, HART. White Buildings: Poems.... (NY): Boni & Liveright, 1926. 1st ed, 1st bk, w/2nd issue cancel title-leaf. Cl, batik bds (spine gilt dull; bumped; eps smudged, offset from clipping). Good (sig). *Reese.* $250/£161

CRANE, J.W.E. Bookbinding for Amateurs. Upcott Gill, n.d. (c 1893). Grn cl blocked in black/gilt. Good. *Moss.* $62/£40

CRANE, LEO. Desert Drums—The Pueblo Indians of New Mexico 1540-1928. Boston: Little Brown, 1928. 1st ed. VG. *Perier.* $65/£42

CRANE, LEO. Indians of the Enchanted Desert. Boston: Little, Brown, 1926. 2nd ptg. Fldg map. VG. *Perier.* $65/£42

CRANE, STEPHEN and J. SLOAN. Great Battles of the World. Lippincott, 1901. 1st ed. Spine sl lightened, else VG +. *Fine Books.* $125/£81

CRANE, STEPHEN and ROBERT BARR. The O'Ruddy. NY: Stokes, (1903). 2nd ed. Color frontis. Tan cl pict blocked in grn/black. *Cady.* $25/£16

CRANE, STEPHEN. George's Mother. NY: Edward Arnold, 1896. 1st ed. Buff cl stamped in black. NF. BAL 4073. *Macdonnell.* $125/£81

CRANE, STEPHEN. Great Battles of the World. Phila, 1901. 1st Amer ed. John Sloan (illus). Pict cvrs gilt; teg. Fine (sl edge rubbed). *Polyanthos.* $125/£81

CRANE, STEPHEN. The Little Regiment. NY: D. Appleton, 1896. 1st ed, 1st state. 6pp ads on pg 197. VG +. *Bishop.* $65/£42

CRANE, STEPHEN. The Little Regiment. Appleton, 1896. 1st ed. Lt dust soil, else VG +. *Fine Books.* $85/£55

CRANE, STEPHEN. The Monster and Other Stories. NY/London: Harper, 1899. 1st ed. Frontis, (vi),(190)pp + (2)pp ads, 11 inserted plts. Top edge stained red-orange. Gilt-lettered red cl, 3 black medallions beneath title; gilt-titled spine. BAL 4085. *Cady.* $175/£113

CRANE, STEPHEN. The Open Boat. NY: Doubleday & McClure, 1899. 1st ed. Name; sl rubbing to bds, else NF. *Between The Covers.* $350/£226

CRANE, STEPHEN. The Red Badge of Courage. Appleton, 1896. 1st ed, 2nd state w/1896 tp tipped in. NF. *Fine Books.* $75/£48

CRANE, STEPHEN. The Red Badge of Courage. NY: LEC, 1944. One of 1000 numbered, signed by John Steuart Curry (illus). Full leather. NF in slipcase (repaired). *Hermitage.* $125/£81

CRANE, STEPHEN. Stephen Crane's Love Letters to Nellie Crouse.... Edwin H. Cady & Lester G. Wells (eds). (NY): Syracuse Univ, 1954. 1st ed. Sl browned, else Fine in VG dj. BAL 4116. *Godot.* $45/£29

CRANE, STEPHEN. The Third Violet. NY: Appleton, 1897. 1st ed. VG- (sl cocked, worn, soiled; 1900 sig). *Between The Covers.* $65/£42

CRANE, STEPHEN. War Is Kind. NY: Stokes, 1899. 1st ed. 96pp. Dec grey bds, paper spine label. Spine sl dknd, else NF. BAL 4083. *Chapel Hill.* $900/£581

CRANE, WALTER. The Absurd A.B.C. George Routledge & Sons, (1870-74). 1st ed. Red leather. VG in folder, slipcase. *Davidson.* $375/£242

CRANE, WALTER. The Baby's Bouquet. NY/London: Frederick Warne, n.d. 4to, 56pp. Stiff glazed pict bds. Good (edges, corners worn; fr hinge cracked). *Davidson.* $75/£48

CRANE, WALTER. The Baby's Own Aesop, Being the Fables Condensed.... George Routledge & Sons, 1887. 1st ed. Square 8vo. 56pp; errata, addenda slip tipped in; dec eps. Glazed pict bds; cl spine. Fine (inscrip; sl soiled). *Bickersteth.* $140/£90

CRANE, WALTER. The Baby's Own Aesop. London: Routledge, 1887. 7.25-inch sq. Pict cl spine. VG + (wear). *Book Adoption.* $150/£97

CRANE, WALTER. The Baby's Own Aesop. London: Routledge, 1887. 1st ed. Sq 8vo. 56pp; all edges tinted. Cl-backed illus bds (edgewear). *Reisler.* $250/£161

CRANE, WALTER. The Bases of Design. London: George Bell & Sons, 1902. 1st ed. Teg; partly unopened. (Cvr wear; ink, pencil inscrips; lt foxing eps.) Text VG. *Bookpress.* $135/£87

CRANE, WALTER. The Bluebeard Picture Book. London: George Routledge, (1875). 1st combined ed. 4to. Blue cl (spine chipped; corner wear; hinges weak), gilt. *Reisler.* $300/£194

CRANE, WALTER. The Claims of Decorative Art. Boston: Houghton, Mifflin, 1892. 1st Amer ed. (Ex-lib w/stamps, mks.) *Bookpress.* $185/£119

CRANE, WALTER. A Flower Wedding. Cassell, 1905. 1st ed. Pict bds (edges sl rubbed), cl spine. Fine. *Bickersteth.* $147/£95

CRANE, WALTER. Legends for Lionel, in Pen and Pencil. London: Cassell, 1887. 1st ed. Sm 4to. Pict paper-cvrd bds (wear), cl spine. Contents Fine (sm tear). *Book Adoption.* $250/£161

CRANE, WALTER. Line and Form. London: Bell, 1914. Teg. Orig cl, emb white design. Spine faded, o/w Fine. *Europa.* $28/£18

CRANE, WALTER. Queen Summer. London/Paris/Melbourne: Cassell & Co, 1891. 40pp + 9pp list; leaves folded Japanese style. Dec orange eps. Dec paper on bds (lt soiled; uppper cvr spotted), cl spine. VG (ink sig fep; crack inner hinge; edges lt rubbed). *Hobbyhorse.* $125/£81

CRANE, WALTER. Walter Crane's Picture Book. London: Routledge, (1874). 1st ed. 4to. 64 color plts. Aeg. Wine red cl, black/gold dec (spotted, worn; hinges starting). *Reisler.* $600/£387

Cranford. (By Elizabeth Cleghorn Gaskell.) NY: Harper, 1853. 1st Amer ed. iv,330pp + 6pp ads. Blue (rubbed). *Karmiole.* $40/£26

CRANTZ, DAVID. The History of Greenland.... London, 1820. 2 vols in 1 (tp perforated; lacks pp355,7,9 vol 1; ex-lib). Mod 3/4 leather, marbled paper over bds. *Parmer.* $250/£161

CRANWELL, JOHN PHILIPS and WILLIAM BOWERS CRANE. Men of Marque. A History of Private Armed Vessels.... NY: WW Norton, (1940), 1st ed. Signed by both on 1/2 title. 13 charts & plts. Sailcloth cvrs (soiled). *Lefkowicz.* $175/£113

CRANWELL, JOHN PHILIPS. and SAMUEL A. SMILEY. United States Navy Waterline Models and How to Build Them. NY, (1947). Stated 1st ed. Good. *Hayman.* $15/£10

CRAPSEY, ADELAIDE. A Study in English Metrics. NY: Knopf, 1918. 1st ed. VG in dj (lt worn). BAL 4122. *Cahan.* $100/£65

CRAPSEY, ADELAIDE. Verse. Rochester: Manas Press, 1915. 1st ed, 1st bk. VG. BAL 4120. *Argosy.* $75/£48

CRARY, CATHERINE S. (ed). Dear Belle. Letters...1858-1865. Middletown, CT: Wesleyan Univ Press, (1965). 1st ed. NF in dj (lt worn). *Glenn.* $30/£19

CRASTER, E. The History of All Souls College Library. Faber, 1971. 1st ed. 7 plts. VG in dj. *Moss.* $37/£24

CRASTER, E. History of the Bodleian Library 1845-1945. Oxford: Clarendon, 1952. VG in dj (sl torn). *Moss.* $70/£45

CRAVEN, AVERY. The Coming of the Civil War. NY: Scribner's, 1942. 1st ed. (Spine sl soiled.) *Shasky.* $30/£19

CRAVEN, AVERY. The Coming of the Civil War. NY, 1942. 2nd ed Revised (1957). Signed. VG+ in VG+ dj. *Pratt.* $40/£26

CRAVEN, AVERY. Edmund Ruffin, Southerner. NY/London: D. Appleton, 1932. 1st ed. VG. *Mcgowan.* $65/£42

CRAVEN, JOHN J. Prison Life of Jefferson Davis.... Carleton, 1866. (1st ed). 377pp. Good (1-inch tear to joint; snag on spine; foxing). *Book Broker.* $45/£29

CRAVEN, THOMAS (ed). A Treasury of American Prints. NY, (1939). 1st ed. Spiral-bound bds. VG in dj. *Argosy.* $65/£42

CRAVEN, W.F. and J.L. CATE (eds). The Army Air Forces in World War II: The Pacific: Guadalcanal to Saipan, August 1942-July 1944. Chicago, 1950. Vol 4. (Ex-lib.) *Clark.* $37/£24

CRAVEN, W.F. and J.L. CATE (eds). The Army Air Forces in World War II: The Pacific: Matterhorn to Nagasaki, June 1944-August 1945. Chicago, 1953. Vol 5. (Ex-lib.) *Clark.* $37/£24

CRAVENS, R.H. Brett Weston: Photographs from Five Decades. Millerton: Aperture, 1980. 1st ed. Fine in dj. *Cahan.* $75/£48

CRAWFORD, BENJAMIN F. Her Name was Achsah. Bucyrus, OH, (1954). 1st ed. Good in wrappers. *Hayman.* $15/£10

CRAWFORD, F. MARION. Constantinople. NY: Scribner's, 1895. (x),(80)pp. Tan dec cl (dknd). *Schoyer.* $35/£23

CRAWFORD, F. MARION. Khaled, a Tale of Arabia. London, 1891. 1st ed. VG. *Madle.* $40/£26

CRAWFORD, F. MARION. Khaled, A Tale of Arabia. London: Macmillan, 1891. 1st ed. (iv),258,2pp. Sl rubbed; spine sl frayed, o/w VG. *Worldwide.* $45/£29

CRAWFORD, F. MARION. Saracinesca. London: William Blackwood, 1887. 1st ed. 3 vols. Half-title present all vols. Orig pale brn cl, gilt lettered spine. Fine set. *Bickersteth.* $225/£145

CRAWFORD, F. MARION. The Upper Berth. London, 1894. 1st ed. VG. *Madle.* $75/£48

CRAWFORD, HARRIET (ed). Subterranean Britain. London: John Baker, 1979. 1st ed. VG in dj. *Hollett.* $47/£30

CRAWFORD, J. MARSHALL. Mosby and His Men.... NY: G.W. Carleton, 1867. 1st ed. 375pp. Orig emb grn cl. VG (lt edgeworn, sl foxed). Howes C 871. *Chapel Hill.* $350/£226

CRAWFORD, J.H. Wild Life of Scotland. London, 1896. 1st ed. 280pp. (Lt browning; ex-libris; split to upper joint w/sl cl loss.) *Edwards.* $43/£28

CRAWFORD, LEWIS F. Badlands and Broncho Trails. Bismark: Capitol Book, (1922). 1st ed. VG. *Perier.* $50/£32

CRAWFORD, LEWIS F. Rekindling Camp Fires. Bismark: Capitol Book, (1926). 1st ed. Ink inscrip, else VG. Howes C 872. *Perier.* $75/£48

CRAWFORD, LEWIS F. Rekindling Camp Fires. Bismarck, ND: Capital Book, (1926). 1st ed. Map. Good (sm spot fr cover). Howes C872. *Lien.* $75/£48

CRAWFORD, MEDOREM. Journal of Medorem Crawford. Eugene, OR, 1897. 1st separate ed. 26pp, stapled. Howes C 874. *Ginsberg.* $100/£65

CRAWFORD, MICHAEL H. Roman Republican Coinage. London: CUP, 1974. 1st ed. 2 vols. 62 plts; 79 plts. Dj (sl rubbed). *Edwards.* $209/£135

CRAWFORD, OSWALD. By Path and Trail. N.p., (Salt Lake City, Intermountain), 1908. 1st ed. *Ginsberg.* $125/£81

CRAWFORD, SAMUEL W. History of the Fall of Fort Sumpter (sic). (NY: Francis P. Harper, 1896.) 2nd ed. Frontis, 486pp. Orig ptd wraps soiled, else VG. *Chapel Hill.* $85/£55

CRAWFORD, T.S. A History of the Umbrella. London: David & Charles, 1970. 1st ed. NF in dj. *Willow House.* $39/£25

CRAWFORD, THOMAS E. The West of the Texas Kid 1881-1910. Norman: Univ of OK Press, (1962). 1st ed. Fine in Fine dj. *Book Market.* $20/£13

CRAWFURD, OSWALD (ed). A Year of Sport and Natural History. London: Chapman & Hall, 1895. (Backstrip rubbed; joint split.) *Petersfield.* $59/£38

CRAWHALL, JOSEPH. The Compleatest Angling Booke. Freshet, (1970). Facs of 1881 ed. Leatherette. VF in slipcase. *Artis.* $35/£23

CRAWHALL, JOSEPH. Impresses Quaint. Newcastle upon Tyne: Mawson, Swan & Morgan, 1889. 1st ed. Ltd to 300. 100 leaves ptd recto only. Cl-backed pict bds (rubbed, sl worn). Good. *Cox.* $233/£150

CRAWHALL, JOSEPH. Old Aunt Elspa's ABC. London: Field & Tuer et al, n.d. (ca 1885). Oblong 4to. 21pp + 2pp ads (repaired tear edge 2pp). VG in pict brn paper wrappers (edges, spine lt rubbed; lower wrapper w/stamp pasted down, partially peeled). *Hobbyhorse.* $200/£129

CRAWHALL, JOSEPH. Olde Tayles Newlye Relayted. London: Leadenhall Press, 1883. 1st ed. Mod buckram. VG (ex-lib, blind emb stamp to leaves). *Cox.* $70/£45

CRAWLEY, ERNEST. Studies of Savages and Sex. Theodore Besterman (ed). London: Methuen/John Wiley, (1929). 1st ed. Grn cl. Name stamps to tp, else VG. *Gach.* $50/£32

CRAYON, GEOFFREY. (Pseud of Washington Irving.) Bracebridge Hall; or, The Humorists. John Murray, 1822. 2nd British ed. 2 vols. Contemp 1/2 red morocco (rubbed; spine scratched). BAL 10110. *Bickersteth.* $62/£40

CREAMER, ROBERT. Babe: The Legend Comes to Life. S&S, 1974. 1st ed. Fine in VG+ dj. *Plapinger.* $50/£32

CREAMER, ROBERT. Stengel: His Life and Times. S&S, 1984. 1st ed. Fine in VG+ dj. *Plapinger.* $30/£19

CREASEY, JOHN. The Case of the Innocent Victims. London: Hodder & Stoughton, 1959. 1st ed. VG in Good dj (rubbed). *Ming.* $31/£20

CREASEY, JOHN. Double for the Toff. London: Hodder & Stoughton, 1959. 1st ed. Fine in NF dj (lt edgewear). *Janus.* $50/£32

CREASEY, JOHN. Look Three Ways at Murder. London: Hodder & Stoughton, 1964. 1st ed. VG in VG dj. *Ming.* $31/£20

CREASEY, JOHN. Murder, London-New York. London: Houghton & Stoughton, 1958. 1st ed. Fine in Fine dj (sl edgewear). *Janus.* $50/£32

CREASEY, JOHN. A Prince for Inspector West. London: Hodder & Stoughton, 1956. 1st ed. NF in VG+ dj. *Janus.* $50/£32

CREASEY, JOHN. The Toff and the Sleepy Cowboy. London: Hodder & Stoughton, 1974. 1st ed. VG in VG dj. *Ming.* $39/£25

CREASEY, JOHN. The Toff and the Stolen Tresses. London: Hodder & Stoughton, 1958. 1st ed. Fine in dj (lt edgewear). *Janus.* $50/£32

CREASEY, JOHN. The Toff and the Terrified Taxman. London: Hodder & Stoughton, 1973. 1st ed. VG+ in VG+ dj. *Ming.* $31/£20

CREELEY, ROBERT. Characteristically. Cambridge: Pomegranate Press, 1972. Ltd ed of 500 numbered, signed. Fine. *Antic Hay.* $35/£23

CREELEY, ROBERT. A Day Book. NY: Scribner's, (1972). 1st ed. Fine in acetate dj (lt chipped). *Antic Hay.* $25/£16

CREELEY, ROBERT. A Day Book. NY: Scribner's, (1972). 1st ed. Fine in orig pub's glassine dj (sm tear). *Hermitage.* $30/£19

CREELEY, ROBERT. Divisions and Other Early Poems. Mt. Horeb, WI: Perishable Press, 1968. 1st ed. Ltd to 100. Fine in wrappers. *Jaffe.* $250/£161

CREELEY, ROBERT. A Form of Women. NY: Jargon/Corinth, (1959). 1st ed, 2000 ptd. VG in ptd wraps (soiled; stain inside both cvrs). *Antic Hay.* $20/£13

CREELEY, ROBERT. Hotel Schrieder, Heidelberg. (Minneapolis): Walker Art Center, 1984. 1st ed. One of 150 signed. VF. *Jaffe.* $45/£29

CREELEY, ROBERT. Numbers. NY: Poets Press, 1968. One of 150 numbered, signed. Fine in wrappers. *Ulysses.* $31/£20

CREELEY, ROBERT. St. Martins. L.A.: Black Sparrow, 1971. 1st ed. Cl-backed bds. Fine in plastic dj. *Hermitage.* $65/£42

CREELEY, ROBERT. The Whip. Worcester: Migrant Books, 1957. 1st UK ed. Lt staining upper wrapper, o/w NF. *Sclanders.* $186/£120

CREENY, W.F. Illustrations of Incised Slabs on the Continent of Europe.... N.p: n.p., 1891. 1st ed. (iv),viii,76pp, 71 facs. (Lt thumbed; orig black cl spine repaired, cvrs sl sunned, bkpl, bkseller label.) *Bookpress.* $185/£119

CREIGHTON, CHARLES. Contributions to the Physiology and Pathology of the Breast and its Lymphatics Glands. London: Macmillan, 1878. 36 text woodcuts. (Ex-lib.) *Goodrich.* $115/£74

CREIGHTON, CHARLES. A History of Epidemics in Britain from A.D. 664 to the Extinction of Plague. Cambridge, 1891. 1st ed. 706pp. (Ex-lib.) *Fye.* $100/£65

CREIGHTON, CHARLES. A History of Epidemics in Britain. Cambridge: CUP, 1891-1894. 2 vols. xii,706; xii,883pp, untrimmed. Excellent (sm slit lower joint vol 2). *Bickersteth.* $341/£220

CREIGHTON, M. A History of the Papacy During the Period of the Reformation. London: Longmans, Green, 1892. 'New Edition.' 5 vols. Pub's ads at end. Gilt-stamped dk grn cl. VG (text underlining vols 1,2,4). *Houle.* $125/£81

CRELLIN, J.K. Medical Ceramics. London, 1969. Color plt. Dj. *Whitehart.* $62/£40

CREPEAU, RICHARD C. Baseball. Univ of Central FL, 1980. 1st ed. VG+ in Good+ dj. *Plapinger.* $30/£19

CRESPELLE, JEAN-PAUL. The Fauves. Greenwich, CT: NYGS, (1962). 1st ed. 100 color plts. Orange cl. Good in dj. *Karmiole.* $65/£42

CRESSY-MARCKS, VIOLET. Journey into China. NY: Dutton, 1942. Grn cl (sl faded, scuffed). *Schoyer.* $25/£16

CREW, ALBERT. The Old Bailey, History.... London: Nicholson & Watson, 1933. Red cl (worn). Usable only. *Boswell.* $45/£29

CREWS, HARRY. All We Need of Hell. NY: Harper, 1987. 1st ed. VF in dj. *Else Fine.* $50/£32

CREWS, HARRY. Blood and Grits. NY: Harper & Row, (1979). 1st ed. Lt stain spine, inside dj, else Fine in dj (tear rear panel). *Between The Covers.* $85/£55

CREWS, HARRY. A Feast of Snakes. NY: Atheneum, 1976. 1st ed. NF in VG dj (internal dampstain). *Pettler.* $125/£81

CREWS, HARRY. A Feast of Snakes. NY: Atheneum, 1976. 1st ed. NF (lt sunned) in NF dj. *Revere.* $125/£81

CREWS, HARRY. A Feast of Snakes. NY: Atheneum, 1976. 1st ed. VF in dj. *Else Fine.* $165/£106

CREWS, HARRY. The Gospel Singer. NY: William Morrow, 1968. 1st ed, 1st bk. Blurbs by Richard E. Kim and Andrew Lytle. Blue eps mkd, unevenly faded, o/w Fine in dj (repaired short tears; expert reinforcement to spine). *Heller.* $400/£258

CREWS, HARRY. The Gypsy's Curse. NY: Knopf, 1974. 1st ed. Fine in dj. *Else Fine.* $150/£97

CREWS, HARRY. The Hawk Is Dying. Knopf, 1973. 1st ed. NF in NF dj. *Fine Books.* $110/£71

CREWS, HARRY. Karate Is a Thing of the Spirit. NY: Morrow, 1971. 1st ed. Fine in dj. *Between The Covers.* $250/£161

CREWS, HARRY. The Knockout Artist. NY: Harper & Row, (1988). 1st ed. Fine in dj (lt dust soiled). *Chapel Hill.* $40/£26

CREWS, HARRY. The Knockout Artist. NY: Harper, 1988. 1st ed. VF in dj. *Else Fine.* $35/£23

CREWS, HARRY. Madonna at Ringside. Northridge: Lord John, 1991. 1st ed, one of 275 numbered, signed. Fine w/o dj as issued. *Lame Duck.* $100/£65

CREWS, HARRY. Madonna at Ringside. Lord John Press, 1991. One of 275 numbered, signed. Fine; issued w/o dj. *Polyanthos.* $75/£48

CREWS, HARRY. Naked in the Garden Hills. NY, 1969. 1st issue. One of 5500. Fine (1/4-inch hole fr bd, tips lt rubbed) in Fine 1st issue dj (sl creasing). *Fuller & Saunders.* $225/£145

CREWS, HARRY. This Thing Don't Lead to Heaven. Morrow, 1970. 1st ed. Fine in NF dj. *Fine Books.* $140/£90

CRIBB, P.J. and G.P. LEEDAL. The Mountain Flowers of Southern Tanzania. Rotterdam, 1982. 72 b/w plts by Mair Swann. Fine in dj. *Brooks.* $46/£30

CRICHTON, ANDREW. The History of Arabia. NY: Harper, 1834. 1st Amer ed. 2 vols. Fldg map frontis, xii,418; 422,(2)pp. Grey linen (rebound, orig leather spine labels laid down), gilt. Sound set (foxing). *Hartfield.* $145/£94

CRICHTON, ANDREW. The History of Arabia. Ancient and Modern. NY: Harper, 1839. 2 vols. Frontis fldg map (stained, foxed), 2 vignette tps, 416; 422pp, 7 plts. Paper spine labels. (Ex-lib, bkpl.) *Schoyer.* $100/£65

CRICHTON, MICHAEL. The Andromeda Strain. NY: Knopf, 1969. 1st ed. VG (white spine ends browned) in dj (sl wear; lt soil; tiny tear). *Antic Hay.* $50/£32

CRICHTON, MICHAEL. Eaters of the Dead. Knopf, 1976. 1st ed. Fine in dj. *Madle.* $35/£23

CRICHTON, MICHAEL. Five Patients. NY: Knopf, 1970. 1st ed. NF in dj. *Else Fine.* $50/£32

CRICHTON, MICHAEL. Five Patients. Knopf, 1970. 1st ed. Fine in dj. *Fine Books.* $65/£42

CRICHTON, MICHAEL. The Great Train Robbery. London: Cape, 1975. 1st British ed. VG + in dj. *Silver Door.* $25/£16

CRICHTON, MICHAEL. The Great Train Robbery. NY: Knopf, 1975. 1st ed. Fine in Fine dj (spine lt faded). *Between The Covers.* $65/£42

CRICHTON, MICHAEL. Jurassic Park. NY, 1990. 1st trade ed. Extrems rubbed, sm ink smudge fep, else VG in dj (sl soiled). *King.* $50/£32

CRICHTON, MICHAEL. Jurassic Park. London: Century, 1991. 1st ed. Fine in dj. *Lewton.* $54/£35

CRICHTON, MICHAEL. Sphere. Macmillan, 1987. 1st ed. Fine in dj. *Rees.* $19/£12

CRICHTON, MICHAEL. The Terminal Man. NY, 1972. 1st ed. VG in dj (sl rubbed, mkd). *Rees.* $19/£12

CRICHTON, MICHAEL. The Terminal Man. NY: Knopf, 1972. 1st ed. VF in dj. *Else Fine.* $60/£39

CRICHTON, MICHAEL. Travels. NY: Knopf, 1988. 1st ed. Fine in Fine dj. *Revere.* $25/£16

CRICHTON-MILLER, H. Insomnia. London, 1930. 1st ed. Good. *Fye.* $60/£39

CRIDLAND, ROBERT B. Practical Landscape Gardening. NY: A.T. De La Mare, 1929. 2nd ed, rpt. Frontis. Blind-stamped, gilt-emb cl, color pict mt fr bd. Fine. *Quest.* $35/£23

CRILE, GEORGE and WILLIAM E. LOWER. Anoci-Association. Phila: Saunders, 1914. Nice (ex-lib). *Goodrich.* $75/£48

CRILE, GEORGE. George Crile. An Autobiography. Lippincott, 1947. 1st ed. 2 vols. VG + in VG + dj & VG slipcase. *Bishop.* $20/£13

CRISP, CHRISTOPHER. The Christian Experiences. Phila: Kite, 1822. 412pp. (Heavy spotting; browning; sl waterstaining; fr pastedown sl wormed; joints tender.) Full speckled calf (worn), leather label (chipped). *Edwards.* $47/£30

CRISP, FRANK. Mediaeval Gardens. London: John Lane, Bodley Head, 1924. 1st ed. Ltd to 1000. 2 vols. 225 plts; 314 plts. Teg. Gilt-dec cream buckram, gilt titles. Fine. *Quest.* $475/£306

CRISP, FREDERICK ARTHUR. Memorial Rings. London: Privately ptd, 1908. 1st ed. #94/150. 1/2 vellum (soiled). Teg; uncut. Marginal thumb-prints, o/w Good. *Cox.* $147/£95

CRISP, QUENTIN. All This and Bevin Too. London: Nicholson & Watson, 1943. 1st Eng ed. 7 full-pg dwgs by Mervyn Peake. Red/cream ptd wrappers. Cvrs foxed, sl mkd, rubbed, split along spine, o/w VG. *Dalian.* $388/£250

CRISP, QUENTIN. How to Become a Virgin. Duckworth, 1981. 1st UK ed. Signed presentation. NF in dj. *Sclanders.* $39/£25

CRISP, QUENTIN. The Naked Civil Servant: An Autobiography. NY, 1977. 1st Amer ed. Inscribed. Name, o/w NF in dj (sl rubbed). *Rees.* $23/£15

CRISPIN, E. The Moving Toyshop. Gollancz, 1946. 1st UK ed. Bds, wrapper sl mottled; spine wrapper sl faded, o/w VG in VG dj. *Martin.* $90/£58

CRISPIN, EDMUND. Fen Country. London, 1979. 1st ed. Fine in dj (price-clipped). *Polyanthos.* $25/£16

CRISWELL, ELIJAH HARRY. Lewis and Clark: Linguistic Pioneers. Columbia, MO: Univ of MO, 1940. 1st ed. Repaired tear to fr cvr, else NF in wraps as issued. *Perier.* $375/£242

CRITCHLEY, MACDONALD. The Black Hole and Other Essays. London: Pitman, 1964. 1st ed. Good in dj. *White.* $23/£15

CROCKATT, ERNEST. The Murder of Til Taylor, a Great Western Sheriff. Phila: Dorrance, (1970). 1st ed. Fldg map. Good + in dj (worn, chipped). *Oregon.* $20/£13

CROCKER, H. RADCLIFFE. Atlas of Diseases of the Skin. Edinburgh/London: Young J. Pentland, 1896. 2 vols. 48 color plts (last 2 w/sm marginal tears). Signed port laid down vol 1 tp. 1/2 calf (head, foot spines expertly repaired w/loss; inner hinges taped). *Goodrich.* $395/£255

CROCKETT, S.R. The Black Douglas. D&M, 1899. 1st ed. Top edge dknd, else VG + . *Aronovitz.* $75/£48

CROFT-COOKE, RUPERT. The Unrecorded Life of Oscar Wilde. W.H. Allen, 1972. 1st Eng ed. Black cl. Fine in dj. *Dalian.* $54/£35

CROFT-COOKE, RUPERT. The Verdict of You All. London: Secker & Warburg, 1955. 1st ed. Black cl titled in silver. Very Nice in dj. *Cady.* $25/£16

CROFTS, FREEMAN WILLS. Death of a Train. London: Hodder & Stoughton, 1946. 1st ed. VG in pict dj (sl wrinkled w/minor internal reinforcement). *Limestone.* $75/£48

CROFTS, FREEMAN WILLS. The Loss of the Jane Vosper. NY: Dodd Mead, 1936. 1st Amer ed. Lt spotting fore-edge, o/w NF in dj (faded spine; sm chips; short tears). *Mordida.* $75/£48

CROFTS, FREEMAN WILLS. Silence for the Murderer. London: Hodder & Stoughton, 1949. 1st ed. Lt spotting pg edges, o/w Fine in dj. *Mordida.* $75/£48

CROFUT, WILLIAM. Troubadour: A Different Battlefield. NY: Dutton, 1968. Stated 1st ed. VG+ in dj (rubbed; torn; price-clipped). *Aka.* $40/£26

CROGHAN, GEORGE. Army Life on the Western Frontier. Norman: Univ of OK, (1958). 1st ptg. Map. VG in dj. *Schoyer.* $30/£19

CROGHAN, GEORGE. Army Life on the Western Frontier. Francis Paul Prucha (ed). Norman, (1958). 1st ed. VG (ex-lib). *Pratt.* $25/£16

CROLY, G. Salathiel—A Tale of the Past, The Present and The Future. Colburn, 1828. 1st ed. 3 vols. Leather, marbled bds; marbled eps. Lt rubbing, else VG. *Fine Books.* $450/£290

CROLY, GEORGE. Tarry Thou Till I Come or Salathiel, the Wandering Jew. NY, 1901. 1st Amer, illus ed. NF. *Polyanthos.* $40/£26

CROMER, EARL OF. Modern Egypt. London: Macmillan, 1908. 1st ed. 2 vols. Good set (inscrips; top edges dusty, shelfwear). *Virgo.* $62/£40

CRONE, J.O. The Magnetic Healer's Guide. Kansas City, MO, 1903. 1st ed. Good. *Fye.* $40/£26

CRONIN, VINCENT. The Wise Man from the West. London: Rupert Hart-Davis, 1955. 1st ed. Color frontis; 9 plts; 2 maps. VG in dj (repaired). *Hollett.* $59/£38

CRONISE, TITUS. The Natural Wealth of California. SF: Bancroft, 1868. 1st ed. 696pp. Good (ex-lib; w/o plts). *Book Market.* $60/£39

CRONISE, TITUS. The Natural Wealth of California. SF: Bancroft, 1868. 1st ed. 696pp. Plts. Fine. *Book Market.* $200/£129

CRONISE, TITUS. The Natural Wealth of California.... SF, 1868. xvi,696pp. Spotting; stamp title, else Sound. *Ginsberg.* $200/£129

CRONQUIST, ARTHUR et al. Intermountain Flora. NY, 1972. VG+. *Brooks.* $49/£32

CRONQUIST, ARTHUR et al. Intermountain Flora. Vol 1. NY, 1972. Frontis. *Sutton.* $45/£29

CROOK, GEORGE. General George Crook: His Autobiography. Martin F. Schmidt (ed). Norman: Univ of OK Press, (1960). 2nd ed. 14 maps. Fine in dj. *Graf.* $30/£19

CROOKSHANK, EDGAR (ed). History and Pathology of Vaccination. London, 1889. 1st ed. 2 vols. 466; 610pp. 4 plts lacking, o/w VG set. *Fye.* $350/£226

CROSBY, FRANK. Life of Abraham Lincoln.... Phila: John E. Potter, 1865. 476pp; port. Full leather; aeg. Good (joints torn; cvr worn). *Book Broker.* $30/£19

CROSBY, HARRY. Transit of Venus. Paris: Black Sun Press, 1929. 2nd ed. #130/200. Orig wrappers in glassine dj. Mint in orig slipcase cvrd in silver/gold foil. *Cummins.* $350/£226

CROSBY, SUMNER. The Apostle Bas-Reliefs at Saint-Denis. New Haven, 1972. 85pp plts. Good. *Washton.* $50/£32

CROSBY, THOMAS. Up and Down the North Pacific Coast by Canoe and Mission Ship. Toronto: Missionary Soc of the Methodist Church: c.1914. Orig ptd wrapper; photo port of author mounted on front. Sm piece broken off lower corner of port; else VG. *High Latitude.* $70/£45

CROSS, AMANDA. The James Joyce Murder. NY: Macmillan, (1967). 1st ed. (Not mislabeled re-issue.) Spine cocked, else NF in dj (price-clipped). *Other Worlds.* $100/£65

CROSS, MRS. ASHTON. The Pekingese Dog. London, 1932. 1st ed. Frontis port, 45 plts. Sm gilt device upper bd. (Lt browning; eps spotted; edges, spine faded; joints sl chipped.) *Edwards.* $54/£35

CROSS, RALPH HERBERT. The Early Inns of California, 1844-1869. SF: Privately ptd, 1954. 1st ed. One of 500. Fldg map. Unopened. Cl-backed red patterned bds. Fine. *Harrington.* $65/£42

CROSS, RALPH HERBERT. The Early Inns of California, 1844-1869. SF: Privately pub, 1954. One of 500. Fldg map. Unopened. Blue cl spine, dec paper over bds. NF. *Parmer.* $35/£23

CROSSLEY, FRED H. The English Abbey. London: Batsford, 1939. 2nd ed. Color frontis, 2 fldg plans. Fore-edge lt spotted. Dj. *Hollett.* $31/£20

CROSSLEY, FRED H. English Church Craftsmanship. London: Batsford, 1941. 1st ed. VG in dj (sl rubbed, price-clipped). *Hollett.* $39/£25

CROSSLEY, FRED H. English Church Design, 1040-1540 A.D. Batsford, 1945. 1st ed. Fine in dj. *Peter Taylor.* $19/£12

CROSSLEY, FRED H. Timber Building in England. London: Batsford, (1951). 1st ed. Frontis; 202 illus on plts. Eps foxed, else Fine in dj (handled). *Bookpress.* $95/£61

Crotchet Castle. (By Thomas Love Peacock). London: T. Hookham, 1831. 1st ed. (vi),300pp, uncut, w/half-title but w/o final ad leaf; marbled eps. Later 19th cent 1/2 calf. *Bickersteth.* $853/£550

CROUSE, M. ELIZABETH. Algiers. NY, 1906. Dec blue cl. Excellent. *Lewis.* $43/£28

CROUSE, NELLIS. Lemoyne D'Iberville: Soldier of New France. Cornell Univ, (1954). 1st ed. 2 maps. VG in VG dj. *Oregon.* $45/£29

CROW, RANKIN. Rankin Crow and the Oregon Country. Ironside, OR: Privately ptd, 1970. 2nd ptg. Signed. VG in VG dj. *Oregon.* $35/£23

CROWE, GEORGE. The Commission of H.M.S. 'Terrible,' 1898-1902. London, 1903. 1st ed. Frontis. VG in pict blue cl (sl damp-mottled). *Edwards.* $132/£85

CROWE, J.A. and G.B. CAVALESELLE. The Early Flemish Painters: Notices of Their Lives and Works. London: John Murray, 1872. 2nd ed. viii,383pp (fep separating along hinge; bkpl). Teg. Full morocco, gilt tooling. NF. *Cahan.* $75/£48

CROWE, SYLVIA and SHEILA HAYWOOD. The Gardens of Mughul India. London: Thames & Hudson, 1972. 1st ed. Map, 12 color plts. Fine. *Quest.* $90/£58

CROWE, SYLVIA. Garden Design. NY: Hearthside, 1959. Fine in dj. *Quest.* $40/£26

CROWEN, MRS. T.J. The American Lady's System of Cookery.... Auburn & Buffalo: 1854. 7th thousand. 450pp. Dec cl (lt foxing). *Petrilla.* $65/£42

CROWFIELD, CHRISTOPHER. (Pseud of Harriet B. Stowe). Little Foxes. Boston: Ticknor & Fields, 1866. 1st Amer ed. Brn cl stamped in gilt/blind. Early ink name, sig starting w/fore-edge nicked, hinges sl weak, o/w Good. BAL 19441. *Reese.* $40/£26

CROWFOOT, J.W. Early Churches in Palestine. London: British Academy, 1941. 30 plts. (Bumped.) *Archaeologia.* $85/£55

CROWLEY, ALEISTER. Atlantis. (US): Dove Press, (n.d. ca 1970). 1st Amer ed. Red cl. Errata slip laid in. Ink name, scribble fep, else VG in white dj (dust soiled, nicks, short tears, else VG). *Godot.* $50/£32

CROWLEY, ALEISTER. Moonchild. London: Mandrake Press, 1929. 1st ed. VG in dj (2 one-inch chips, short creased tears mended on verso w/paper tape; lt wear). *Godot.* $185/£119

CROWLEY, ALEISTER. Moonchild. Mandrake Press, 1929. 1st UK ed. VG, lacking dj. *Sclanders.* $39/£25

CROWLEY, ALEISTER. Oracles. Inverness, 1905. 1st ed. (Rear blank detached; sl foxing.) Poor wraps. *King.* $250/£161

CROWLEY, ALEISTER. The Stratagem and Other Stories. London: Mandrake Press, (1929). 1st ed. Black cl-backed gold textured bds. Very Nice. *Cady.* $50/£32

CROWLEY, ALEISTER. The Stratagem and Other Stories. London: Mandrake Press, (n.d. 1929). 1st ed. VG in dj. *Godot.* $100/£65

CROY, HOMER. The Trial of Mrs. Abraham Lincoln. NY, (1962). 1st ed. Dj wear, o/w Fine. *Pratt.* $20/£13

CROZIER, WILLIAM ARMSTRONG (ed). Early Virginia Marriages. Southern Book Co, 1953. VG. *Book Broker.* $25/£16

CROZIER, WILLIAM ARMSTRONG (ed). Virginia Colonial Militia 1651-1776. Southern Book Co, 1954. Paper cvr. (Pencil mks; ex-lib.) *Book Broker.* $25/£16

CRUICKSHANK, BRODIE. Eighteen Years on the Gold Coast of Africa.... London: Hurst and Blackett, 1853. 1st ed. 2 vols. 8vo. viii,345,(1)16 ads; vi,335,(1)8 ads. Purple blind-stamped cl (spines faded, cvrs lt damp-spotted). Internally VG (lib stamps on titles, 2 leaves erased w/o loss). *Morrell.* $434/£280

CRUIKSHANK, GEORGE. The Bachelor's Own Book. Glasgow, ca 1880. 24 plts, extra pict t.p. 3/4 calf (worn). Orig upper wrapper bound in. *Argosy.* $85/£55

CRUIKSHANK, GEORGE. Omnibus. London, 1842. 1st ed. Aeg. 1/2 calf, raised bands (orig cvrs bound in). NF (foxing; string mk; rubbed, sl chipped). *Polyanthos.* $75/£48

Cruise of the Walnut Shell. (By Richard Andre). NY: McLoughlin Bros, n.d. (1880s). Color pict wraps (rubbed, sl chipped). *King.* $35/£23

CRUM, JOSIE MOORE. The Rio Grande Southern Railroad. Durango: San Juan History, 1961. Rev ed. Signed. Blue cl. Fine. *Harrington.* $70/£45

CRUM, MARGARET (ed). First-Line Index of English Poetry 1500-1800.... Oxford, 1969. 1st ed. 2 vols. Blue cl (sl splash-mks on fore-edges). Good set. *Cox.* $279/£180

CRUM, W.E. (ed). A Coptic Dictionary. Oxford: Clarendon Press, 1929-39. 1st ed. Wraps (spines chipped, tape remnants at spine). *Archaeologia.* $150/£97

CRUMB, ROBERT. The Yum Yum Book. SF: Scrimshaw, (1975). 1st ed. Nice in dj (sl worn). *Second Life.* $45/£29

CRUMB, ROBERT. The Yum Yum Book. SF: Scrimshaw Press, 1975. 1st ed. NF (shelfwear) in dj (lt used; rubbed). *Beasley.* $125/£81

CRUMLEY, JAMES. Dancing Bear. NY: Random House, (1983). 1st ed. NF in dj (lt used). *Aka.* $40/£26

CRUMLEY, JAMES. Dancing Bear. NY: Random House, 1983. 1st ed. Fine in dj. *Janus.* $65/£42

CRUMLEY, JAMES. The Last Good Kiss. NY: Random House, 1978. 1st ed. VF in dj. *Mordida.* $85/£55

CRUMLEY, JAMES. The Last Good Kiss. NY: Random House, 1978. 1st ed. Inscribed. NF in dj (lt used). *Beasley.* $50/£32

CRUMLEY, JAMES. The Muddy Fork. Northridge: Lord John, 1984. 1st ed. One of 250 numbered, signed. VF w/o dj as issued. *Mordida.* $150/£97

CRUMLEY, JAMES. One to Count Cadence. NY: Random House, 1969. 1st ed, 1st bk. Fine in Fine dj. *Beasley.* $275/£177

CRUMLEY, JAMES. One to Count Cadence. R-H, 1969. 1st ed. NF in VG dj (lt wear). *Fine Books.* $165/£106

CRUMLEY, JAMES. The Wrong Case. London: Hart-Davis, 1976. 1st British ed. Signed. Sl spine crease, o/w NF in dj (lt wear). *Silver Door.* $275/£177

CRUMP, SPENCER. Henry Huntington and the Pacific Electric: A Pictorial Album. L.A.: Trans-Anglo Books, (1970). 1st ed. Map. Red cl. Corners sl bumped, o/w NF in VG+ dj (sl rubbed). *Harrington.* $45/£29

CRUMP, SPENCER. Redwoods, Iron Horses, and the Pacific: The Story of the California Western Railroad. Costa Mesa: Trans-Anglo Books, 1971. 3rd ed. Pict eps. Brn cl. 2 corners lt bumped, o/w NF in VG+ dj (sl rubbed). *Harrington.* $30/£19

CRUSE, A.J. Cigarette Card Cavalcade. London, 1948. 1st ed. Color frontis, 28 plts. (Hinges cracked, lt browning; lt soiled, rubbing.) *Edwards.* $31/£20

CRUTTWELL, M. Luca and Andrea della Robbia, and Their Successors. London/NY: Dent, 1902. (Top of spine sl frayed.) *Ars Artis.* $116/£75

CRUTTWELL, M. Verrocchio. London: Duckworth, 1904. 47 plts. Sound. *Ars Artis.* $39/£25

CUDAHY, JOHN. Mananaland: Adventuring with Camera and Rifle.... NY: Duffield, 1928. Frontis. Gold-stamped cl. *Dawson.* $60/£39

CULBERTSON, THADDEUS. BAE Bulletin 147. Journal of an Expedition to the Mauvaises Terres and the Upper Missouri in 1850. Washington: GPO, 1952. 2 fldg facs maps. Fine in ptd wraps. Howes C 9410. *Schoyer.* $40/£26

CULBERTSON, THADDEUS. BAE Bulletin 147. Journal of an Expedition to the Mauvaises Terres and Upper Missouri in 1850. John F. McDermott (ed). 1952. Rpt. 2 fldg maps. VG. Howes C 941. *Oregon.* $65/£42

CULLEN, COUNTEE. Color. NY: Harper, 1925. 1st ed, 1st bk. Yellow cl, patterned bds, labels (foxing, inscrip; spine tanned). *Petrilla.* $125/£81

CULLEN, COUNTEE. Color. NY: Harper, 1925. 1st ed, 1st ptg. Nice (spine sl dknd; mks to text; ink poem rep). *Glenn.* $125/£81

CULLEN, COUNTEE. Copper Sun. NY: Harper & Row, 1927. 1st ed. Cl-backed marbled bds. Very Nice (bkpl, pencil name; short edgetears 3pp) in dj (chips; pieces missing spine extrems). *Aka.* $300/£194

CULLEN, THOMAS. Adenomyoma of the Uterus. Phila: Saunders, 1908. Internally VG (ex-lib). *Goodrich.* $95/£61

CULLEN, THOMAS. The Distribution of Adenomyomas Containing Uterine Mucosa. Chicago, 1920. 1st ed. Good. *Fye.* $25/£16

CULLEN, WILLIAM. First Lines of the Practice of Physic. NY, 1805. 2 vols in 1. 582pp. Full leather. Good. *Fye.* $250/£161

CULLEY, JOHN H. Cattle, Horses and Men of the Western Range. L.A.: Ward Ritchie, (1940). Inscribed. Frontis. (Newspaper rev tipped to rep w/offsetting; bkpl, sticker; paper, cl separated at fr hinge.) *Dawson.* $150/£97

CULLEY, JOHN H. Cattle, Horses and Men of the Western Range. L.A.: Ward Ritchie, 1940. 1st ed. VG- (ex-libris, blank bkpl; sig half loose; soil). *Parker.* $50/£32

CULLEY, JOHN H. Cattle, Horses and Men of the Western Range. Ward Ritchie, 1940. 1st ed. Howes C 942. *Lambeth.* $200/£129

CULLEY, JOHN H. Cattle, Horses and Men. L.A.: Ward Ritchie, (1940). 1st ed. Signed presentation. Fair (water stain lower part of pp; bkpl) in dj (worn, chipped). Howes C 942. *Lien.* $100/£65

CULLINGFORD, CECIL H.D. British Caving. London: Routledge & Kegan Paul, 1953. 1st ed. 48 plts. (Extrems sl rubbed.) Dj (sl worn; spine creased). *Hollett.* $54/£35

CULLINGFORD, GUY. Third Party Risk. London: Geoffrey Bles, 1962. 1st ed. Fine in dj (sl faded spine; sl wear). *Mordida.* $35/£23

CULPEPPER, NICHOLAS. Culpepper's Family Physician. James Scammon (rev). Exeter: James Scammon, 1825. 360pp (foxed; browning). Full calf. *Goodrich.* $125/£81

CULVER, FRANCIS. Blooded Horses of Colonial Days. Balt, 1922. VG. *October Farm.* $65/£42

CUMMING, C.F. GORDON. Two Happy Years in Ceylon. London, 1892. 3rd ed. 2 vols. 438pp, 19 plts, fldg map. Teg; marbled eps. 1/2 morocco, marbled bds, raised bands. *Edwards.* $233/£150

CUMMING, KATE. Gleanings from Southland. Birmingham: Roberts, 1895. 1st ed. Frontis port, 277pp. Orig red cl. Hinges sl tender, spine letters faded, else VG. *Chapel Hill.* $200/£129

CUMMING, PRIMROSE. The Great Horses. London: Dent, 1946. 1st ed. VG in Good+ dj. *October Farm.* $45/£29

CUMMING, R. GORDON. Five Years of a Hunter's Life in the Far Interior of Southern Africa. London, 1850. 2nd ed. 2 vols. Map; illus tp; 15 plts. 1/2 morocco (joints weak). *Wheldon & Wesley.* $217/£140

CUMMING, R. GORDON. Five Years' Adventures in the Far Interior of South Africa.... London: Murray, (1904). New ed. 16 full-pg engrs. Good+ (rebound; ex-lib). *Mikesh.* $25/£16

CUMMING, R. GORDON. Five Years' Hunting Adventures in South Africa. London, n.d. Complete Popular ed. Map. (Spine dknd, creased; split to lower joint hand-stitched; blind lib stamp fep, lt foxed.) *Edwards.* $70/£45

CUMMING, R. GORDON. A Hunter's Life in South Africa. London: Murray, 1850. 2 vols. 2 engr tps, map. 1/2 mod brn calf (rebound; new eps), gilt. *Petersfield.* $202/£130

CUMMINGS, E.E. 50 Poems. NY: Duell, Sloan & Pearce, (1940). 1st ed. Fine in dj (sl used). *Pharos.* $85/£55

CUMMINGS, E.E. Eimi. C-F, 1933. 1st ed. One of 1381 signed. Yellow cl sl dust soiled, else VG-. *Fine Books.* $150/£97

CUMMINGS, E.E. Eimi. NY: Covici, Friede, 1933. One of 1381 signed. Yellow cl. NF. *Pharos.* $250/£161

CUMMINGS, E.E. Fairy Tales. HBW, 1965. 1st ed. John Eaton (illus). VG+ in VG+ dj (3 sm chips; lt wear). *Fine Books.* $65/£42

CUMMINGS, E.E. I Sing of Olaf Glad and Big. (NY: Igal Roodenko, 1952). 1st separate ed, variant w/yellow ptd wrappers. Single folio sheet, folded and tipped into (as issued) wrappers; cvrs state, 'May Day 1952.' Fine. *Godot.* $50/£32

CUMMINGS, E.E. Is 5. NY: Boni & Liveright, 1926. 1st ed. Cvrs aged; lacks dj, else VG. *Pharos.* $50/£32

CUMMINGS, E.E. No Thanks. (NY, 1935). 1st ed. VG in dj (edges chipped). *Argosy.* $150/£97

CUMMINGS, E.E. Poems 1923-1954: First Complete Edition. NY: Harcourt Brace, (1954). *Aka.* $25/£16

CUMMINGS, E.E. Puella Mea. N.p.: S.A. Jacobs, Golden Eagle Press, (1949). 1st separate ptg. Pict blue bds, gilt. In matching dj (spine, top edge faded w/sm tears top). NF. *Blue Mountain.* $150/£97

CUMMINGS, E.E. Selected Letters of E.E. Cummings. NY: Harcourt, Brace & World, (1969). 1st ed. VG in dj (price-clipped; lt rubbed). *Hermitage.* $40/£26

CUMMINGS, E.E. Selected Letters of E.E. Cummings. F.W. Dupee & George Stade (eds). (London): Deutsch, (1972). 1st Eng ed. NF in dj. *Antic Hay.* $20/£13

CUMMINGS, E.E. Tulips and Chimneys. NY: Thomas Seltzer, 1924. 'Second Printing March 1924.' Paper spine label. Spine age-dknd, sl chipped, else VG. *Pharos.* $45/£29

CUMMINGS, E.E. VV. Liveright, 1931. 1st ed. Sl fraying, fading; lt scratches cvr, else VG. *Fine Books.* $45/£29

CUMMINGS, RAY. The Girl in the Golden Atom. Harper, 1923. 1st ed. VG. *Madle.* $75/£48

CUMMINGS, SAMUEL. The Western Pilot: Containing Charts of the Ohio River and of the Mississippi.... Cincinnati: Conklin, 1841. New ed. 144pp, 42 woodcut charts. Orig ptd bds (worn, faded). Howes C 948. *Ginsberg.* $500/£323

CUMMINS, D. DUANE. William Robinson Leigh, Western Artist. Univ of OK, 1980. 1st ed. 30 color plts. New sm folio. Dj. *Heinoldt.* $35/£23

CUMMINS, SARAH J. Autobiography and Reminiscences of.... (Freewater, OR: By author, 1914.) Port. VG+ in gray ptd wraps. Howes C 951. *Bohling.* $65/£42

CUNARD, NANCY. Black Man and White Ladyship: An Anniversary. (London): Privately ptd, not for sale, 1931. 1st Eng ed. Erratum slip. Ptd paper wrappers, vertical fold. Staples sl rusty, o/w Nice. *Patterson.* $140/£90

CUNARD, NANCY. GM: Memories of George Moore. London: Hart-Davis, 1956. 1st ed. Top edge sl dusty, o/w VG in Good dj (sl soiled, spotted, chipped). *Virgo.* $23/£15

CUNARD, NANCY. Grand Man. London: Secker & Warburg, 1954. 1st ed. VG in dj (sl soiled, chipped; sm closed tear). *Virgo.* $54/£35

CUNARD, NANCY. Man—Ship—Tank—Gun—Plane: a Poem. London, 1944. Ltd to 400 numbered. Single fldg sheet (creased, dusty). *Waterfield.* $47/£30

CUNARD, NANCY. Parallax. Hogarth Press, 1925. 1st ed. Spine, edges sl dknd, o/w VG. *Words Etc.* $171/£110

CUNARD, NANCY. Parallax. London: Hogarth, 1925. 1st ed. Eugene McCown (illus). Lovely (spine lt worn; cvrs uniformly sunned). Issued w/o dj. *Robbins.* $450/£290

CUNARD, NANCY. Releve into Maquis. Derby: Grasshopper Press, 1944. 1st ed, ltd to 250. Single sheet folded into 4pp. Fine. *Godot.* $45/£29

CUNARD, NANCY. Releve into Maquis. UK: Grasshopper Press, 1944. 1st ed. One of 250. Single leaf folded. Fine. *Polyanthos.* $30/£19

CUNEO, JOHN R. Robert Rogers of the Rangers. NY, 1959. 1st ed. VG + in dj (sl wear; faded spine). *Pratt.* $27/£17

CUNLIFFE, BARRY. Excavations at Portchester Castle. London, 1975. 40 plts. Dj (sl torn; chipped, loss). *Edwards.* $43/£28

CUNNINGHAM, ALBERT B. Old Black Bass. NY: Abingdon Press, 1922. 1st ed. 4 b/w plts. VG (sm cut 1st 2pp, no loss). *Bowman.* $40/£26

CUNNINGHAM, ALLAN. The Life of Sir David Wilkie. London: J. Murray, 1843. 1st ed. 3 vols. Frontis port; xi,(i),489,(3); vii(i),530,(2); vii,(i),532pp. Orig cl (backstrips faded; inner hinges cracked), paper labels. Uncut. *Cox.* $132/£85

CUNNINGHAM, EDWARD (adapted by). Gulliver in Lilliput. Kansas City: Hallmark, n.d. (1976). 17x23 cm. H. Lohnes (paper mechanics). Glazed pict bds. VG. *Book Finders.* $55/£35

CUNNINGHAM, EUGENE. Buckaroo. Boston: Houghton Mifflin, 1933. 1st ed. Signed. VG. *Parker.* $50/£32

CUNNINGHAM, EUGENE. Gun Bulldogger. Houghton Mifflin, 1939. 1st ed. NF in dj (worn, chipped). *Stahr.* $35/£23

CUNNINGHAM, EUGENE. Gypsying Through Central America. London, 1922. 1st Eng ed. Frontis port, map. (Sl browning; spine sl sunned.) *Edwards.* $23/£15

CUNNINGHAM, EUGENE. Riders of the Night. Boston: Houghton Mifflin, 1932. 1st ed. Signed. VG- (name; edgewear). *Parker.* $30/£19

CUNNINGHAM, EUGENE. Triggernometry. Caldwell: Caxton Printers, 1945. 4th ptg. VG in dj. *Schoyer.* $30/£19

CUNNINGHAM, EUGENE. Triggernometry: A Gallery of Gunfighters. Caldwell: Caxton, (1945). 3rd ptg. Good in pict cvrs. *Lien.* $45/£29

CUNNINGHAM, J.V. The Helmsman. SF: Colt Press, 1942. 1st ed. Signed. 1/4 red leather w/marbled paper sides; fr cvr blind-stamped 'JVC' and '1942.' Unopened. Fine. *Graf.* $375/£242

CUNNINGHAM, JOHN. Warhorse. Macmillan, 1956. 1st ed. VG in Good + dj (spine end chipped). *Oregon.* $27/£17

CUNNINGHAME GRAHAM, R.B. *See* GRAHAM, R.B. CUNNINGHAME

Curiosa of Flagellants [and] History of Flagellation. Privately ptd, n.d. 2 works in 1 vol. Mod cl (rebound), gilt spine title. (Lt spotting.) *Edwards.* $59/£38

Curiosities of Literature. (By Isaac D'Israeli.) London, 1793-94. 3rd ed. 2 vols. Full calf (rebacked). *Argosy.* $250/£161

CURLE, RICHARD. Into the East. Notes on Burma and Malaya.... London: Macmillan, 1923. 1st ed. Fine in dj. *Reese.* $75/£48

CURLING, T.B. A Practical Treatise on the Diseases of the Testis, and of the Spermatic Cord and Scrotum.... P.B. Goddard (ed). Phila: Carey & Hart, 1843. 1st Amer ed. xxiii,(25)-568,(8 ads)pp. Orig cl. Fine. *Glaser.* $300/£194

CURREY, J. SEYMOUR. The Story of Old Fort Dearborn. Chicago: A.C. McClurg, 1912. 1st ed. Good (cvr lt worn). *Lien.* $35/£23

CURRIE, BARTON W. and AUSTIN McHUGH. Officer 666. NY: H.K. Fly, 1912. 1st ed. Dec bds; color eps. NF. *Beasley.* $45/£29

CURRIE, GEORGE E. Warfare along the Mississippi, The Letters of.... Norman E. Clarke (ed). Mt. Pleasant, MI, (1960). 1st ed ltd to 1000. Lt stained, o/w VG +. *Pratt.* $25/£16

CURRIER, ANDREW. The Menopause. NY, 1897. 1st ed. 309pp. Good. *Fye.* $150/£97

CURRIER, THOMAS FRANKLIN. A Bibliography of John Greenleaf Whittier. Cambridge: Harvard Univ, 1937. 1st ed. Frontis port; 18 plts; orig 19th cent photo of Whittier laid in. Red cl; gilt. Good in dj (bit chipped). *Karmiole.* $40/£26

CURRIER-BRIGGS, NOEL. Virginia Settlers and English Adventurers.... Genealogical Pub, 1970. 3 vols in 1. VG. *Book Broker.* $50/£32

CURSHMANN, H. Typhoid Fever and Typhus Fever. W. Osler (ed). Phila, 1905. 1st Eng trans. Good. *Fye.* $75/£48

CURTIN, WALTER R. Yukon Vyage. Caldwell, ID: Caxton Printers, 1938. 1st ed. Frontis map. Blue cl, gilt. Good in dj (sl chipped). *Karmiole.* $50/£32

CURTIS, CHARLES H. Orchids: Their Description and Cultivation. London: Putnam's, (1950). 1st ed. 30 color, 48 b/w plts. Gilt-lettered grn cl. Fine. *House.* $110/£71

CURTIS, EDWARD S. In the Land of the Head-Hunters. Yonkers-on-Hudson: World Book Co, 1919. 1st ed. Gray cl (soiling). VG. *Between The Covers.* $350/£226

CURTIS, EDWARD S. Indian Days of the Long Ago. Yonkers-on-Hudson: World, 1915. 2nd ptg. Signed. Fine. *Oregon.* $325/£210

CURTIS, ELIZABETH GIBBON. Gateways and Doorways of Charleston, South Carolina, in the Eighteenth and the Nineteenth Centuries. NY: Architectural Book Pub Co, (1926). 1st ed. Frontis; 68 plts. Bkpl, else VG. *Bookpress.* $75/£48

CURTIS, GEORGE WILLIAM. The Howadji in Syria. NY: Harper's, 1852. 1st Amer ed. 304pp + 8pp ads. Grn cl stamped in gilt (spotted; loose sig; foxing). BAL 4261. *Schoyer.* $50/£32

CURTIS, GEORGE WILLIAM. The Howadji in Syria. NY: Harper, 1864. (Spine chipped; extrems worn.) *Archaeologia.* $65/£42

CURTIS, GEORGE. The Correspondence of John Lothrop Motley. NY, 1889. 1st ed. 2 vols complete. 395; 423pp. Fine set. *Bond.* $22/£14

CURTIS, JOHN. Harvey's Views on the Use of Circulation of the Blood. NY, 1915. Ex-lib; frontis loose. *Goodrich.* $50/£32

CURTIS, NEWTON MARTIN. From Bull Run to Chancellorsville. NY/London: Putnam's, 1906. Unopened. Navy cl, red cross, gilt lettering; gilt top. VG. *Bohling.* $90/£58

CURTIS, NEWTON MARTIN. From Bull Run to Chancellorsville. NY, 1906. 1st ed. Signed. Roster. Pict cl; gilt edge. Sl cvr spotting, wear, o/w VG +. *Pratt.* $85/£55

CURTIS, PAUL A. Sportsmen All. NY: Derrydale, 1938. One of 950 numbered. Fine. *Bowman.* $150/£97

CURTIS, W.H. The Elements of Wood Ship Construction. NY: McGraw-Hill, 1919. 1st ed. Stamp tp, o/w Fine. *Lefkowicz.* $95/£61

CURTIS, WARDON. The Strange Adventures of Mr. Middleton. Chicago: Stone, 1903. 1st ed. Pict cl (sl bubbled; extrems sl rubbed). VG (owner stamp margin 1st text pg). *Reese.* $35/£23

CURTIS, WILLIAM ELEROY. Egypt, Burma and British Malaysia. Chicago et al: Revell, 1905. Frontis map. Grey-brn dec cl (sl discolored). *Schoyer.* $45/£29

CURWEN, H. A History of Booksellers. C&W, 1873. 20 plts. Recased in orig brn dec cl, spine laid down. Good. *Moss.* $56/£36

CURWOOD, JAMES OLIVER. The Alaskan. NY: Cosmopolitan, 1923. 1st ed. Fine in dj (chipped). *Hermitage.* $40/£26

CURWOOD, JAMES OLIVER. The Country Beyond. NY, 1922. 1st ed. NF. *Artis.* $17/£11

CURWOOD, JAMES OLIVER. The Gold Hunters. IN, (1929). 1st ed. Pict cl. VG-. *Artis.* $22/£14

CURWOOD, JAMES OLIVER. The Plains of Abraham. NY, 1928. 1st ed. Good+. *Artis.* $15/£10

CURZON, EARL OF KEDLESTON. Leaves from a Viceroy's Note-Book and Other Papers. London: Macmillan, 1926. 1st ed. Frontis. Navy blue cl (rear hinge cracked). *Weber.* $75/£48

CURZON, GEORGE NATHANIEL. British Government in India. London, 1925. 2 vols. Photogravure frontis. Gilt dec cl. Mint. *Argosy.* $150/£97

CURZON, GEORGE. Problems of the Far East. Japan-Korea-China. London: Longmans, Green, 1894. 2nd ed. xx,441pp (foxed); 2 maps (1 fldg, color). Teg. Wheat buckram (lt foxed), leather spine label. Somewhat foxed. *Schoyer.* $65/£42

CURZON, ROBERT. Visits to Monasteries in the Levant. London, 1865. 5th ed. Contemp gilt-dec calf (spine faded; sm split upper joint; prelims lt spotted, sm bkpl). *Edwards.* $54/£35

CUSHING, CALEB. Reminiscences of Spain.... Boston: Carter et al, 1833. 2 vols in 1. (viii),300; 300pp. 3/4 leather (rubbed); spine lettering. *Schoyer.* $45/£29

CUSHING, FRANK HAMILTON. My Adventures in Zuni. Santa Fe: Peripatetic Press, (1941). One of 400. VG+ in dj (price-clipped; dknd, chipped). *Bohling.* $450/£290

CUSHING, FRANK HAMILTON. Zuni Folk Tales. NY: Putnam's, 1901. 1st ed. VG- (fr corners chewed; blindstamp fep). *Parker.* $175/£113

CUSHING, FULTON, J.F. Harvey Cushing. Springfield, 1946. 1st ed. Internally Good (spine sunned, faded). *Goodrich.* $65/£42

CUSHING, HARVEY and LOUISE EISENHARDT. Meningiomas. Their Classification.... Springfield: Thomas, 1938. Spine faded, o/w VG in dj. *Goodrich.* $895/£577

CUSHING, HARVEY and PERCIVAL BAILEY. A Classification of the Tumors of the Glioma Group on a Histogenetic Basis with a Correlated Study of Prognosis. Phila, 1926. 1st ed. Recent cl; new eps. (Lt lib stamp.) *Fye.* $350/£226

CUSHING, HARVEY and PERCIVAL BAILEY. A Classification of the Tumors of the Glioma Group on a Histogenetic Basis with a Correlated Study of Prognosis. NY, 1971. (Facs of 1926 ed.) Good. *Fye.* $50/£32

CUSHING, HARVEY and PERCIVAL BAILEY. Tumors Arising from the Blood-Vessels of the Brain. Springfield: Thomas, 1928. Rebound in new cl. Good. *Goodrich.* $495/£319

CUSHING, HARVEY and PERCIVAL BAILEY. Tumors Arising from the Blood-Vessels of the Brain. London, 1928. 1st ed, British imprint. Good. *Fye.* $500/£323

CUSHING, HARVEY. A Bibliography of the Writings of Harvey Cushing.... Springfield, 1939. Ltd ed of 500. Fine in dj. *Goodrich.* $175/£113

CUSHING, HARVEY. Consecratio Medici and Other Papers. Boston, 1928. 1st ed, 1st ptg. Good. *Fye.* $150/£97

CUSHING, HARVEY. From a Surgeon's Journal. London, 1936. 1st British ed. Good. *Fye.* $100/£65

CUSHING, HARVEY. From a Surgeon's Journal. Boston, 1936. 1st ed, later ptg. Good. *Fye.* $35/£23

CUSHING, HARVEY. Harvey Cushing's Seventieth Birthday Party. Springfield: Thomas, 1939. Ltd ed of 350. (Ex-lib.) *Goodrich.* $75/£48

CUSHING, HARVEY. Intracranial Tumours. Springfield, 1932. 1st ed. Good. *Fye.* $600/£387

CUSHING, HARVEY. The Life of Sir William Osler. Oxford, 1925. 1st ed, 1st imp. 2 vols. Good (lt shelf wear; lower corner vol 2 repaired). *Goodrich.* $150/£97

CUSHING, HARVEY. The Life of Sir William Osler. Oxford, 1925. 1st ed, 1st ptg. 2 vols. Full lt blue leather; gilt spines; red/black labels; gilt fore-edges. Outer hinges cracked, o/w Fine. *Fye.* $400/£258

CUSHING, HARVEY. The Life of Sir William Osler. Oxford, 1925. 1st ed, 3rd imp. 2 vols. VG set. *Goodrich.* $125/£81

CUSHING, HARVEY. The Life of Sir William Osler. Oxford, 1926. 1st ed, 2nd imp. 2 vols. Fair (ex-lib; cl rubbed; mkings). *Goodrich.* $65/£42

CUSHING, HARVEY. The Life of Sir William Osler. Oxford, 1926. 1st ed, 4th ptg. Corrigenda & Addenda published in 1936 bound into this copy. 2 vols. VF. *Fye.* $250/£161

CUSHING, HARVEY. The Life of Sir William Osler. Oxford, 1940. 1st ed, later imp. 2 vols in box. Good (lt wear). *Goodrich.* $75/£48

CUSHING, HARVEY. The Life of Sir William Osler. Oxford, 1940. 1st ed. 1 vol. Nice in dj (lt wear). *Goodrich.* $60/£39

CUSHING, HARVEY. The Medical Career and Other Papers. Boston: Little, Brown, 1940. 3rd ptg. NF in dj (sl edge fray). *Goodrich.* $45/£29

CUSHING, HARVEY. The Medical Career. Hanover, 1930. 1st ed in bk form. Good. *Fye.* $100/£65

CUSHING, HARVEY. Meningiomas, Their Classification, Regional Behaviour, Life History, and Surgical End Results. Springfield, 1938. 1st ed. Good. *Fye.* $750/£484

CUSHING, HARVEY. Papers Relating to the Pituitary Body, Hypothalamus and Parasympathetic Nervous System. Springfield, 1932. 1st ed. Cvrs spotted, o/w Fine. *Fye.* $400/£258

CUSHING, HARVEY. The Personality of a Hospital. Boston, 1930. 1st ed in bk form. Good. *Fye.* $75/£48

CUSHING, HARVEY. The Pituitary Body and Its Disorders. Phila/London: Lippincott, (1912). 1st ed, 1st issue, w/Cushing described on title as 'Associate Professor.' One of 2000. Fldg plt. Name, ink note fep, o/w Fine. *Bickersteth.* $589/£380

CUSHING, HARVEY. The Pituitary Body and Its Disorders. Phila, 1912. 1st ed, 1st imp. (Shelf wear; spine partially varnished; eps renewed; title stamp.) *Goodrich.* $495/£319

CUSHING, HARVEY. The Pituitary Body and Its Disorders. Phila, 1912. 1st ed, 1st ptg. Fine. *Fye.* $600/£387

CUSHING, HARVEY. The Pituitary Body and Its Disorders. Birmingham, 1979. Ltd ed. Nice. *Goodrich.* $90/£58

CUSHING, HARVEY. Selected Papers on Neurosurgery. Donald Matson (ed). New Haven, 1969. 1st ed. Good. *Fye.* $200/£129

CUSHING, HARVEY. Studies in Intracranial Physiology and Surgery. OUP, 1926. (Ex-lib; spine sunned.) Internally VG. *Goodrich.* $495/£319

CUSHING, HARVEY. Tumors of the Brain and Meninges and Hydrocephalus. Phila, 1910. 1st ed. Good. *Fye.* $150/£97

CUSHING, HARVEY. Tumors of the Nervus Acusticus. Phila, 1917. 1st ed. (Dept of US Army gilt stamp on backstrip.) *Fye.* $650/£419

CUSHING, HARVEY. A Visit to Le Puy-En-Velay. Cleveland: Rowfant Club, 1986. One of 500. As New. *Goodrich.* $95/£61

CUSHMAN, DAN. The Great North Trail. McGraw Hill, (1966). 1st ed. VG in VG dj. *Oregon.* $25/£16

CUSSLER, CLIVE. Deep Six. NY: S&S, (1984). 1st ed. Signed. Fine in Fine dj (crease). *Unger.* $75/£48

CUSSLER, CLIVE. Deep Six. NY: S&S, 1984. 1st ed. Fine in Fine dj. *Revere.* $20/£13

CUSSLER, CLIVE. Raise the Titanic! NY: Viking, (1976). 1st ed. Spine slant; edge tears, else VG+. *Other Worlds.* $30/£19

CUST, A.M. The Ivory Workers of the Middle Ages. London: George Bell, 1902. 1st ed. 37 photo plts. 1/2 red morocco over marbled bds, gilt spine (sl rubbed). *Karmiole.* $60/£39

CUST, LIONEL. The Cenci: A Study in Murder. London: Mandrake Press, 1929. 1st ed as such. Paper label. Bottom edge sl rubbed, else Fine in dj (dusty). *Cahan.* $25/£16

CUSTER, ELIZABETH B. Following the Guidon. NY, 1890. 1st ed. Dec cl. Sl rubbed, else Good. *King.* $45/£29

CUSTER, ELIZABETH B. Following the Guidon. NY: Harper, 1890. 1st ed. Grn cl. Very Nice (ink inscrip; abrasion leading bd edges; wear). *Hermitage.* $100/£65

CUSTER, ELIZABETH B. Following the Guidon. NY: Harper, 1890. 1st ptg. xx,341pp, 14 plts. Bright pict cl. VG. *Schoyer.* $50/£32

CUSTER, GEORGE A. My Life on the Plains. Chicago, (1952). Lakeside Classic. VG. *Schoyer.* $30/£19

CUTCHINS, JOHN A. A Famous Command: The Richmond Light Infantry Blues. Richmond: Garrett & Massie, 1934. 1st ed. Inscribed. Mtd photo on blue cl. VG in dj (fragmented). *Cahan.* $85/£55

CUTHBERT, FATHER. The Capuchins. London, 1928. 2 vols. 2 frontis ports. (Vol 1 spine head chipped; vol 2 lower joint tail damaged; ex-libris.) *Edwards.* $39/£25

CUTHBERT, MARION. April Grasses. NY: Womans Press, (1936). 1st ed. Dec paper-cvrd bds. Name, else VG. *Godot.* $185/£119

CUTLACK, F.M. Breaker Morant. Sydney, 1962. 1st ed. Tipped-in frontis port. VG in blue cl. *Edwards.* $62/£40

CUTLER, CARL C. Greyhounds of the Sea...American Clipper Ship. NY/London, 1930. 1st ed. Good. Howes C 983. *Hayman.* $50/£32

CUTLER, CHARLES D. Northern Painting from Pucell to Bruegel. Fourteenth, Fifteenth, and Sixteenth Centuries. NY, 1968. 32 color plts. Good. *Washton.* $45/£29

CUTLER, FREDERICK MORSE. The Old First Massachusetts Coast Artillery in War and Peace. Boston: Pilgrim, 1917. 1st ed. NF in pub's cl. *Cahan.* $85/£55

CUTLER, J. WESLEY. Crumbs of Comfort. Madison, WI, 1899. 1st ed. 413pp. Good. *Fye.* $40/£26

CUTRIGHT, PAUL RUSSELL. A History of the Lewis and Clark Journals. Norman: Univ of OK, (1976). 1st ed. VG in VG dj. *Perier.* $95/£61

CUTTEN, GEORGE GARTON. The Silversmiths of Virginia...from 1694 to 1850. Richmond, VA: Dietz Press, 1952. 1st ed. Silver cl. Fine. *Chapel Hill.* $35/£23

CUTTEN, GEORGE. Three Thousand Years of Mental Healing. NY, 1911. 1st ed. Good. *Fye.* $100/£65

CUTTER, CALVIN. Anatomy and Physiology: Designed for Academies and Families. Boston, 1847. 6th ed. 342pp. Full leather. Good. *Fye.* $30/£19

CUTTER, DONALD C. Malaspina in California. SF: John Howell, 1960. One of 1000. Unopened. Beige cl; gilt spine, cvr dec. Fine. *Parmer.* $125/£81

CUTTING, ELISABETH BROWN. Jefferson Davis Political Soldier. NY: Dodd, Mead, 1930. 1st ed. NF in VG pict dj. *Mcgowan.* $85/£55

CUTTING, SUYDAM. The Fire Ox and Other Years. London, 1947. 3 maps. Dj (sl grubby). *Lewis.* $37/£24

CUTTING, SUYDAM. The Fire-Ox. NY: Scribner's, 1940. 1st ed. Fine in dj (torn, repaired). *Bowman.* $65/£42

CUTTS, EDWARD L. A Manual for the Study of the Sepulchral Slabs and Crosses of the Middle Ages. London: John Henry Parker, 1849. 1st ed. Frontis; viii,93pp; 83 plts. Pub's cl (lt cvr wear spine). (Foxing.) *Bookpress.* $125/£81

CUTTS, EDWARD L. Scenes and Characters of the Middle Ages. London: Simpkin et al, 1926. 6th ed. Frontis. Grn cl, gilt spine. Fine (bkpl). *Weber.* $45/£29

CUTTS, JAMES MADISON. The Conquest of California and New Mexico...in the Years 1846 and 1847. Phila, 1847. Frontis port, engr title (sm stamp verso), 264pp, 4 plans. Outer hinges, extrems worn; ex-lib; bkpls; several sigs started, 1 detached; lt foxing, else Good. Howes C 989. *Reese.* $400/£258

CZAPLICKA, M.A. Aboriginal Siberia. Oxford, 1914. 16 plts, 2 fldg maps. Red cl (ex-lib). VG. *Schoyer.* $85/£55

CZWIKLITZER, CHRISTOPHER. Picasso's Posters. NY, (1971). 1st Amer ed. Sl staining, else VG in dj (scratched, spine chipped, cello cvr peeling). *King.* $250/£161

D

D'ABRANTES, DUCHESS. Memoirs of Napoleon, His Court and Family. London, 1836. 1st Eng ed. 2 vols. Frontis, guard, 548, 6 port plts; 520pp, 8 plts. Eps foxed both vols, o/w Good+. Navy cl, gilt. *Edwards.* $70/£45

D'ABRERA, B. Birdwing Butterflies of the World. London, 1975. Slipcase. *Wheldon & Wesley.* $155/£100

D'ABRERA, B. and A. HAYES. Sphingidae Mundi. London, 1986. 80 color plts. *Wheldon & Wesley.* $155/£100

D'ARBLAY, MADAME. Diary and Letters of Madame D'Arblay. London: Colburn, 1854. 7 vols. Engr frontis port, fldg holograph ms vol 1. Bound by Leighton in dk blue cl. Nice set. *Hartfield.* $285/£184

D'AULAIRE, INGRID and EDGAR PARIN. Abraham Lincoln. NY: Doubleday, Doran, 1939. 1st ed. Lg, 4to. Cl-backed color illus bds (sl corner wear). Pict dj (edgewear; chips spine ends). *Reisler.* $185/£119

D'AULAIRE, INGRID and EDGAR PARIN. Ola. GC: Doubleday, Doran, 1932. 1st ed. Pict paper-cvrd bds (wear); cl spine. Contents clean. *Book Adoption.* $50/£32

D'AULAIRE, INGRID and EDGAR PARIN. Trolls. GC: Doubleday, 1972. 1st ed. 4to. Pict paper-cvrd bds. As New in As New dj (sm tear). *Book Adoption.* $35/£23

D'AULNOY, MARIE. D'Aulnoy's Fairy Tales. Phila: David McKay, (1923). 4to. Gustaf Tenggren (illus). Blue cl, color paste label, tinted top, gilt-lettered spine. Pict dj (marginal tears). *Reisler.* $150/£97

D'AULNOY, MARIE. D'Aulnoy's Fairy Tales. Phila: David McKay, 1923. 1st ed. 4to. 457pp; 9 color plts by Gustaf Tenggren. Navy cl, gilt-edged pict paste label; illus eps. NF. *Drusilla's.* $150/£97

D'EASUM, DICK. Fragments of Villainy. Boise: Statesman Printing, 1959. 1st ed. Ink names, else VG in VG dj. *Perier.* $27/£17

D'ESPERANCE, E. Northern Lights and Other Psychic Stories. Office of Light, 1901. 1st ed. VG-. *Aronovitz.* $55/£35

D'HARNONCOURT, ANNE and KYNASTON McSHINE. Marcel Duchamp. London, 1974. Dj (wrinkled). *Edwards.* $70/£45

D'HERELLE, FELIX. The Bacteriophage and Its Clinical Applications. Springfield, 1930. 1st Eng trans. Cvrs spotted. *Fye.* $100/£65

D'HERELLE, FELIX. Immunity in Natural Infectious Disease. Balt, 1924. 1st Eng trans. Good. *Fye.* $125/£81

D'HULST, R.A. Jordaens Drawings. Phaidon, 1974. 4 vols. 8 plts; 272 plts; 376 plts. Good in slipcase (split, knocked). *Ars Artis.* $388/£250

D'ISRAELI, ISAAC. Romances. London: Cadell & Davies, 1799. 1st this ed. Engr frontis, xix,324,(2)pp, errata. Orig leather bds (rebacked), leather label; marbled eps. Armorial bkpl, inner hinges reinforced, else VG. *Hartfield.* $350/£226

D'OLLONE, VICOMTE. In Forbidden China. Bernard Miall (trans). London: Fisher Unwin, 1911. 1st ed in English. Frontis port, fldg map, 84 plts. Blue cl, dec in red/gilt, teg. (One gathering loose; very sl rubbed, stained). *Morrell.* $109/£70

D'ORS, EUGENIO. Paul Cezanne. NY: Weyhe, 1936. 3 color, 59 monochrome plts. 1/2 red morocco (joints cracked; hinges reinforced), orig wrappers bound in. *Argosy.* $125/£81

D., H. (Hilda Doolittle.) By Avon River. NY: Macmillan, 1949. 1st Amer ed. Fine in dj (price-clipped; sl worn). *Hermitage.* $40/£26

D., H. (Hilda Doolittle.) Helen in Egypt. NY: Grove, (1961). 1st ed. VG (spine sl frayed; sig) in dj (rubbed). *Hermitage.* $35/£23

D., H. (Hilda Doolittle). Heliodora and Other Poems. London: Jonathan Cape, (1924). 1st ed. VG (bkpl) in dj (dust soiled, lt edgewear, sm chip, else VG). *Godot.* $185/£119

D., H. (Hilda Doolittle.) Heliodora and Other Poems. London: Cape, 1924. 1st UK ed. VG (offsetting eps; edges sl spotted, browned; lt bumped, rubbed; sl fading spine ends; name) in dj (soiled; chipped; spine edges cracked). *Virgo.* $85/£55

D., H. (Hilda Doolittle). Hippolytus Temporizes. Boston, 1927. Ltd ed 500 (of 550). Uncut. Fine (name) in box. *Polyanthos.* $100/£65

D., H. (Hilda Doolittle). Hymen. London: Egoist Press, 1921. 1st ed. Dec paper (chipped) over stiff wrappers. VG. *Reese.* $175/£113

D., H. (Hilda Doolittle.) Ion of Euripides. Boston: Houghton Mifflin, 1937. 1st Amer ed. Fine in dj (sl frayed). *Hermitage.* $40/£26

D., H. (Hilda Doolittle.) Kora and Ka. Berkeley: Bios, (1978). Ltd ed to 100 hb. Fine in dj (lt soil, rubbing). *Antic Hay.* $75/£48

D., H. (Hilda Doolittle.) Palimpsest. (Boston: Houghton Mifflin, 1926). 1st Amer ed. One of 700. Cl-backed dec bds. (Extrems rubbed; sl fading; soiling.) *Hermitage.* $200/£129

D., H. (Hilda Doolittle). Palimpsest. (Boston: Houghton Mifflin, 1926). 1st ed, Amer issue. One of 700 bound up from Contact Ed sheets w/cancel title leaf. Cl, batik bds (shelfworn). Name, lt foxing, o/w Good in dj (spine dknd, nicks). *Reese.* $175/£113

D., H. (Hilda Doolittle.) Red Roses for Bronze. NY: Random House, 1929. Ltd to 475. Fine in sewn ptd wraps. *Antic Hay.* $45/£29

D., H. (Hilda Doolittle.) Red Roses for Bronze. London: C&W, 1931. 1st Eng ed. Ink name, else VG in dj (frayed). *Hermitage.* $75/£48

D., H. (Hilda Doolittle.) Red Roses for Bronze. London: C&W, 1931. 1st UK ed. Spine sl faded; lacks dj, o/w VG. *Virgo.* $47/£30

D., H. (Hilda Doolittle.) The Walls Do Not Fall. London: Oxford, 1944. 1st ed. Ptd wrapper over stiff wrapper. Nice (lt foxing, lt edgewear). *Reese.* $55/£35

D., H. (Hilda Doolittle), trans. Euripides. Boston: Houghton Mifflin, 1937. 1st Amer ed. Fine in dj (lt frayed). *Hermitage.* $40/£26

D., H. (Hilda Doolittle). Hedylus. Boston, 1928. 1st Amer ed, ltd ed #750/775. Fine (bkpl). *Polyanthos.* $150/£97

DA LAHONTAN, BARON. New Voyages to North America. McClurg, 1905. Rpt. 2 vols. 22 plts (incl 2 fldg maps). VG. Howes L 25. *Oregon.* $175/£113

DA SILVA, OWEN. Mission Music of California. (LA: Warren F. Lewis, 1941.) Ltd to 1000. Signed. Brn burlap over grn bds. Good. *Karmiole.* $125/£81

DA VINCI, LEONARDO. The Notebooks. NY, 1938. Orig ed. 2 vols. Gilt-dec red buckram. VG. *Argosy.* $85/£55

DA VINCI, LEONARDO. A Treatise on Painting. J.F. Rigaud (trans). London: For J. Taylor, 1802. Engr frontis port, xcv,236pp, 22 engr plts (spotting). Contemp 1/2 calf, marbled bds. Sl rubbed, rebacked, corners repaired, o/w Fine. *Europa.* $85/£55

DABNEY, OWEN P. True Story of the Lost Shackle. (Salem: Capital Ptg Co, c.1897). Frontis, 98pp. VG (paper dknd) in blue ptd wraps. *Bohling.* $150/£97

DABNEY, R.L. Life and Campaigns of Lieut.-Gen. Thomas J. Jackson. NY: Blelock, 1866. 1st Amer ed. (12),741pp, engr port. (Sm emb lib stamps; bkpl removed.) Howes D 2. *Ginsberg.* $125/£81

DACUS, J.A. Illustrated Lives and Adventures of Frank and Jesse James and the Younger Brothers.... St. Louis: N.D. Thompson, 1881. 2nd ed. Brn cl (nearly detached), gilt. Internally VG (sl browning). Howes D 6. *Glenn.* $125/£81

DADD, GEORGE H. The Modern Horse Doctor. NY: OJ, 1885. Frontis, 432pp. Maroon cl, gilt spine. VG (spine sl faded, frayed). *Bohling.* $45/£29

DAGGETT, R.M. Braxton's Bar. A Tale of Pioneer Years in California. NY: Carleton, 1882. 1st ed. (Shabby.) *Reese.* $20/£13

DAGUE, R.A. HENRY ASHTON. Alameda. The author, 1903. 1st ed. Fine (sm abrasion rep). *Beasley.* $125/£81

DAHL, GEORGE LEIGHTON. Portals, Doorways and Windows of France. NY: Architectural Book Pub Co, (1925). 1st ptg. Dec cl. VG. *Schoyer.* $85/£55

DAHL, KAI R. The Teddy Expedition among the Ice Floes of Greenland. NY: D. Appleton, 1925. 1st ed. Map. VG. *Walcot.* $31/£20

DAHL, ROALD. Charlie and the Great Glass Elevator. Knopf, 1972. 1st ed. VG + in dj (short closed tears). *Fine Books.* $40/£26

DAHL, ROALD. Charlie and the Great Glass Elevator. Knopf, 1972. 1st ed. VG + in dj (short closed tears). *Aronovitz.* $40/£26

DAHL, ROALD. Charlie and the Great Glass Elevator. NY: Knopf, 1972. 1st ed. 4to, 163pp. J. Schindelman (illus). Blue cl bds, beige pict cvr. Ink name, o/w VG in VG dj. *Davidson.* $65/£42

DAHL, ROALD. Going Solo. NY: Farrar Straus, 1986. 1st US ed. Lg 8vo. Paper-cvrd bds, cl spine. Fine in Fine dj. *Book Adoption.* $35/£23

DAHL, ROALD. Kiss Kiss. London: Joseph, (1960). 1st Eng ed. Dk grn cl gilt. Very Nice in dj (sl worn). *Cady.* $40/£26

DAHL, ROALD. The Magic Finger. Allen & Unwin, 1968. 1st UK ed. Pict bds sl mottled, o/w VG +. *Martin.* $59/£38

DAHL, ROALD. My Uncle Oswald. London: Michael Joseph, 1979. 1st ed. VG in dj. *Hollett.* $31/£20

DAHL, ROALD. Over to You. Hamilton, 1946. 1st UK ed. Signed. VG in dj. *Lewton.* $217/£140

DAHL, ROALD. Switch Bitch. London: Joseph, 1974. 1st ed. Fine in dj. *Limestone.* $25/£16

DAHL, ROALD. The Wonderful Story of Henry Sugar. London: Cape, 1977. 1st UK ed. NF in dj. *Lewton.* $31/£20

DAHLBERG, EDWARD. The Confessions of Edward Dahlberg. NY, 1971. 1st Amer ed. Signed. Fine in Fine box. *Polyanthos.* $60/£39

DAHLBERG, EDWARD. The Flea of Sodom. London: Nevill, 1950. 1st ed. Signed. NF in glassine dj. *Rees.* $54/£35

DAHLBERG, EDWARD. From Flushing to Calvary. NY: Harcourt, 1932. 1st ed. Fine in NF dj (spine sl dknd). *Beasley.* $175/£113

DAHLBERG, EDWARD. The Sorrows of Priapus. CT, New Directions. Fine (nick) in dj (spine sl sunned; rubbed, nicked, edgetear). *Polyanthos.* $25/£16

DAHLBERG, EDWARD. Those Who Perish. NY: John Day, 1934. 1st ed. Black binding. Offsetting 2pp, o/w Fine in Fine dj. *Beasley.* $150/£97

Daisy; or Cautionary Stories, in Verse. (By Elizabeth Turner.) London: Griffith and Farran, n.d. (ca 1860). 27th ed. 12mo. 66 + 6pp ads, 29 (of 30) 1/2pg hand-colored VF woodcuts, attributed to Samuel Williams. Green cl w/dec gilt title, blind motif. Good (lt internal foxing; ink name, label; lacks pp 23-4; binding worn; few blisters fr cvr). *Hobbyhorse.* $75/£48

DAIX, P. and J. ROSSELET. Picasso. The Cubist Years 1907-1916. London: Thames & Hudson, 1979. Sound in dj. *Ars Artis.* $147/£95

DALE, EDWARD E. and GASTON LITTON. Cherokee Cavaliers: Forty Years of Cherokee History.... Norman: Univ of OK, 1939. 1st ed. VG in dj (sl worn). *Lien.* $75/£48

DALE, EDWARD EVERETT. The Range Cattle Industry. Ranching on the Great Plains from 1865 to 1925. Norman: Univ of OK Press, (1960). 1st ptg of new ed. 17 maps. Tan cl. VG + in dj (lt rubbed). *House.* $90/£58

DALE, EDWARD EVERETT. The Range Cattle Industry: Ranching...from 1865 to 1925. Norman: Univ of OK, (1960). (1st ptg of new ed.) Fine in Fine dj. *Bohling.* $50/£32

DALGLIESH, ALICE. Long Live the King! NY: Scribner's, 1937. 4to. Frontis, 77pp, 27 full-pg b/w dwgs, 3 full-pg double spreads, pict color litho eps. Pict paper on bds (edges lt worn w/sm chips; rebacked). Internally Fine. *Hobbyhorse.* $35/£23

DALI, SALVADOR. Dali. 50 Secrets of Magic Craftmanship. NY: Dial, 1948. 1st Amer ed. (Spine extrems rubbed; heal sl chipped.) *Polyanthos.* $100/£65

DALI, SALVADOR. Hidden Faces. NY: Dial, 1944. 1st ed. Frontis. NF in dj (chipped; sl rubbed). *Hermitage.* $75/£48

DALI, SALVADOR. The Secret Life of Salvador Dali. NY: Dial, 1942. Fine in dj (sl rubbed). *Williams.* $186/£120

DALI, SALVADOR. The Secret Life of Salvador Dali. NY: Dial, 1942. 1st Amer ed. Rear hinge repaired; faint tape shadows, else NF in Fair dj (heavily taped repaired). 1/2 leather slipcase w/Dali's first name misspelled on spine. *Between The Covers.* $125/£81

DALI, SALVADOR. The Secret Life of Salvador Dali. NY: Dial Press, 1942. 1st ed. Dbl-pg color frontis, color plt. Black buckram, 2 ptd labels. VF in color pict dj. *House.* $300/£194

DALI, SALVADOR. The Secret Life of Salvador Dali. Haakon M. Chevalier (trans). London: Vision, 1948. Ltd to 1000. Dbl color frontis, 16 plts. Sl soiled, o/w Fine. *Europa.* $124/£80

DALI, SALVADOR. The Secret Life of Salvador Dali. Haakon M. Chevalier (trans). London: Vision Press, 1949. Ltd to 1000. Color dbl-pg title; 1 color, 16 monochrome plts. Mod 1/2 black levant morocco gilt, buckram bds. Excellent (lt fingering). *Hollett.* $217/£140

DALLAS, PAUL. The Lost Planet. Winston, 1956. 1st ed. Fine in dj. *Madle.* $125/£81

DALLAS, SANDRA. Cherry Creek Gothic. Victorian Architecture in Denver. Norman, 1971. 1st ed. Fine in dj. *Baade.* $30/£19

DALLAS, SANDRA. No More than Five in a Bed. Norman: Univ of OK, (1967). 1st ed. Red cl. Fine in VG dj. *Glenn.* $30/£19

DALLIMORE, W. Holly, Yew and Box with Notes on Other Evergreens. London, 1908. 1st ed. 41 plts. Pict cl, gilt; new eps. (Ex-lib w/stamps on title, plts.) *Henly.* $50/£32

DALLIMORE, W. and A.B. JACKSON. A Handbook of Conifereae including Ginkgoaceae. London, 1948. 3rd ed. 40 plts. Good. *Henly.* $43/£28

DALRYMPLE, JOHN. Memoirs of Great Britain and Ireland. London, 1771-88. 2nd ed. 2 vols. Engr tp vignette vol 2. Contemp speckled calf, raised bands, gilt ruling, leather title labels (joints cracked; vol 2 spine cracked, sl chipped; bkpls). *Edwards.* $155/£100

DALRYMPLE, WILLIAM. Travels through Spain and Portugal, in 1774. London: for J. Almon, 1777. 1st ed. Frontis engr, iv,187pp, fldg map (early leaves dampstained). Recent 3/4 red morocco, marbled paper. *Schoyer.* $275/£177

DALTON, CHARLES. Waterloo Roll Call. London: Eyre, 1904. 2nd ed. *Petersfield.* $33/£21

DALTON, JOHN and THOMAS THOMSON. A System of Chemistry. Edinburgh/London/Dublin: Bell & Bradfute, E. Balfour/John Murray/Gilbert & Hodges, 1807. 3rd ed. 5 vols. 4 engr plts. New bds, calf spines, morocco labels. *Bickersteth.* $434/£280

DALTON, JOHN. Topographical Anatomy of the Brain. Phila, 1885. Vols 1 & 3. Orig cl. Good. *Fye.* $400/£258

DALTON, MICHAEL. The Countrey Justice. London: H. Sawbridge, S. Roycroft & W. Rawlings, 1682. Folio. (xvi),535,(32)pp. Contemp calf (sm area upper fr cvr damaged). Excellent. *Cox.* $349/£225

DALTON, O.M. Catalogue of the Engraved Gems of the Post-Classical Periods.... London: British Museum, 1915. Frontis, 37 plts. (Feps sl browned; spine sl faded.) *Edwards.* $465/£300

DALY, ELIZABETH. Somewhere in the House. NY: Rinehart, 1946. 1st ed. NF (stamp) in NF dj (lt edgewear, lt soiled). *Janus.* $85/£55

DALZIEL, H. The St. Bernard. London: Gill, n.d. (ca late 19th cent). Color frontis, 132pp, 2 full-pg engrs, 12pp ads. Blind-stamped dec cl. Lacks fep, else VG +. *Mikesh.* $75/£48

Dame Partlet's Farm. London: Grant and Griffith, n.d. (ca 1840). New Ed. 12mo. Full-pg frontis, 12 VF 1/2pg engrs (hand-colored); 48pp + 1pg list. Yellow stiff paper wrappers (spine strengthened). Fine (sig; sl spotting 1 plt). *Hobbyhorse.* $150/£97

Dame Wiggins of Lee, and Her Seven Wonderful Cats. London: A.K. Newman, 1823. 12mo. Full-pg hand colored engr frontis (repaired tear), 16 leaves. Mod red morocco on bds. Lacks orig wrappers; ink name, label; lt soiling throughout; sm chip 1 leaf, else Fine. *Hobbyhorse.* $500/£323

DAMI, LUIGI. The Italian Garden. NY, (1924). 351 plts. Mod 1/2 red morocco, linen; gilt-lettered spine. Faint internal soiling, else NF. *Brooks.* $299/£193

DAMISCH, HUBERT and HENRY MARTIN. Adami. NY, 1924. 3 dbl-pg color lithos. VG in dj. *Argosy.* $60/£39

DAMON, BERTHA. Green Corners. London: Joseph, (1947). 1st Eng ed. 6 full-pg color plts by Clare Leighton. VG in 1st state dj w/corrections to fr panel blurb (nicks). *Houle.* $75/£48

DAMON, ETHEL M. The Stone Church at Kawaiahao, 1820-1944. Honolulu: Honolulu Star-Bulletin Press, 1945. 1st ed. Blue cl (sl rubbed). *Karmiole.* $40/£26

DAN, HORACE and E.C. MORGAN WILLMOTT. English Shop-Fronts Old and New. London: Batsford, 1907. Binder's cl (dampstained). *Petersfield.* $25/£16

DANA, CHARLES A. Eastern Journeys. NY: Appleton, 1898. (iv),146pp + 10pp pub's ads; teg. Brn dec cl (spine faded; pocket removed). *Schoyer.* $40/£26

DANA, FREEMAN. (Pseud of Phoebe Atwood Taylor). Murder at the New York World's Fair. NY, (1938). 1st ed. VG in dj (worn, creased, transparent tape exterior reinforcement). *Mcclintock.* $125/£81

DANA, J.D. Corals and Coral Islands. NY, 1872. 1st ed. Color frontis, 398 pp; 3 plts; 3 maps (2 fldg). Pict cl, gilt. Binding sl worn; tear tp repaired, o/w Good. *Henly.* $194/£125

DANA, J.D. Corals and Coral Islands. London, 1875. 2nd Eng ed. Color frontis, xx,348pp; 40 ads, 3 maps (2 fldg). Pict cl. (Inner hinges cracked.) *Henly.* $74/£48

DANA, JOHN COTTON and HENRY W. KENT (eds). Old Librarian's Almanack. Woodstock, VT: Elm Tree Press, 1909. 1st ed. Frontis facs. Tan cl-backed marbled bds, paper labels. Very Nice. *Cady.* $75/£48

DANA, JUAN FRANCISCO. The Blond Ranchero. LA: Dawson's, (1960). 1st ed. Ltd to 500 ptd. Frontis, 4 plts. Fine. *Oregon.* $75/£48

DANA, RICHARD HENRY. Richard Henry Dana, Jr. Speeches in Stirring Times.... Boston: Houghton Mifflin, 1910. 1st ed. 5 photograv plts, map. VG. BAL 4487. *Shasky.* $50/£32

DANA, RICHARD HENRY. The Seaman's Friend. Boston: Thomas Groom, 1851. 6th ed. 225,(1 blank)pp + (2)pp ads, 5 plts. (Label; early inscrip fep.) *Lefkowicz.* $100/£65

DANA, RICHARD HENRY. Two Years Before the Mast. Chicago: Lakeside, 1930. One of 1000. Teg. Gilt-dec cl. White spine sl tanned, o/w Fine in VG slipcase (lt staining back panel). *Reese.* $85/£55

DANA, RICHARD HENRY. Two Years Before the Mast. Chicago: Lakeside Press, 1930. One of 1000. Edw. A. Wilson (illus). Beige/blue linen, gilt. Fine in slipcase (lt worn). *Bohling.* $165/£106

DANA, RICHARD HENRY. Two Years Before the Mast. NY: LEC, 1947. #796/1500 signed by Hans Alexander Mueller (illus). Fine in slipcase (sl dusty). *Williams.* $116/£75

DANA, RICHARD HENRY. Two Years Before the Mast. LEC, 1947. Ltd to 1500 numbered, signed by Hans Alexander Mueller (engrs). Sm bkpl, no slipcase, o/w Fine. *Oregon.* $65/£42

DANA, SAMUEL L. A Muck Manual for Farmers. Lowell, MA: Bixby, 1842. 1st ed. 242pp, 1f. Bds. *Marlborough.* $186/£120

DANA, SAMUEL L. A Muck Manual for Farmers. Boston, 1851. 3rd ed. xx,(17-)345pp. (Lacks fep; pencil mks blank sheets; ex-lib; part of backstrip missing, spine split). *Sutton.* $50/£32

DANDRIDGE, RAYMOND GARFIELD. Zalka Peetruza and Other Poems. Cincinnati: McDonald Press, 1928. 1st ed. Cl spine, paper-cvrd bds. Inscrip, else VG. *Godot.* $135/£87

DANE, J. Prince Madog—Discoverer of America. Eliot Stock, n.d. (but 1909). 1st ed. Presentation copy. Spine foxed, soiled; else VG +. *Fine Books.* $95/£61

DANE, JOEL Y. The Christmas Tree Murders. GC: DCC, 1938. 1st ed. VG in dj. *Else Fine.* $45/£29

DANE, RICHARD. Sport in Asia and Africa. London: Andrew Melrose, 1921. 1st ed. 24 plts. (Worn; fore-edge, spine string-marked; label removed from pastedown; sl shaken; lower joint cracked.) *Hollett.* $54/£35

DANIEL, DAN. The Real Babe Ruth. Spink, 1949. Ltr ptg. Fine; no dj as issued. *Plapinger.* $65/£42

DANIEL, F.E. The Strange Case of Dr. Bruno. Guarantee Pub, 1906. 1st ed. New eps(?), else Good. *Aronovitz.* $65/£42

DANIEL, HOWARD. Devils, Monsters, and Nightmares: An Introduction to the Grotesque and Fantastic in Art. London, 1964. VG in dj. *Argosy.* $50/£32

DANIEL, JEAN HOUSTON and PRICE. Executive Mansions and Capitols of America. Waukesha, WI: Country Beautiful, (1969). 1st ed. Bkpl, short tear spine, else Fine. *Bookpress.* $45/£29

DANIEL, JOHN WARWICK. The Campaign and Battles of Gettysburg. Lynchburg, VA: Bell, Browne, 1875. 1st ed. 45pp. NF in orig plain wrappers. *Mcgowan.* $250/£161

DANIELS, ELAM J. An Exposure of 'Father Divine,' the Negro Worshipped by Millions as God. N.p., n.d. (ca 1949). 9th rev ed. VG in pict stiff wraps. *Petrilla.* $65/£42

DANIELS, JONATHAN. The Devil's Backbone. NY: McGraw-Hill, (1962). 1st ed. Brn cl. NF in dj (lt browned). *Chapel Hill.* $45/£29

DANIELS, JONATHAN. Stonewall Jackson. NY, 1959. 1st ed. Fine in dj (sl wear). *Pratt.* $17/£11

DANIELS, W.H. (ed). The Temperance Reform and Its Great Reformers. NY, 1878. 612pp. Good. *Fye.* $90/£58

DANIELSON, RICHARD E. Martha Doyle and Other Sporting Memories. NY: Derrydale, (1938). 1st Amer ed. Uncut. Fine (sl rubbed). *Polyanthos.* $100/£65

DANKERS, JASPAR and PETER SLUYTER. Journal of a Voyage to New York and a Tour in Several of the American Colonies in 1679-80. Henry C. Murphy (trans, ed). Brooklyn, 1867. 1st ed. Lg 8vo. 440pp; 6 color litho plts, 3 fldg; 6 fldg sepia plts. *Argosy.* $450/£290

DANNATT, TREVOR (ed). Architects' Year Book 7. London, 1956. (Ex-lib.) *Edwards.* $39/£25

DANNETT, SYLVIA G.L. She Rode with the Generals, but Her Regiment Thought She Was a Man. NY, (1960). 1st ed. VG + in VG + dj. *Pratt.* $37/£24

DANNETT, SYLVIA G.L. A Treasury of Civil War Humor. NY, (1963). 1st ed. VG + in VG + dj. *Pratt.* $35/£23

DANOT, SERGE. Magic Roundabout Fun Pop-Up Book. London: Dean, 1974. 23x17 cm. 3 pop-ups. Glazed pict bds (rough edges bottom cvrs, fr label mk). Inside VG. *Book Finders.* $28/£18

DANZIG, ALLISON and JOE REICHLER. The History of Baseball. Prentice-Hall, 1959. 1st ed. VG in Good + dj. *Plapinger.* $50/£32

DANZIGER, JAMES. Cecil Beaton. Viking, 1980. 1st ed. NF in NF dj. *Bishop.* $40/£26

DARBY, WILLIAM. A Tour from the City of New York, to Detroit.... NY: Kirk, 1819. 1st ed. 228,64,(7)pp, errata slip, 3 fldg maps (1 color). Contemp calf (rebacked). Howes D 66. *Ginsberg.* $500/£323

DARDEN, GENEVIEVE M. (comp). My Dear Husband. (Taunton, MA): Descendants of Whaling Masters, (1980). 1st ed. Errata slip. Dj. *Lefkowicz.* $35/£23

Dark Side of the Moon. London: Faber & Faber, (1946). 1st ed. Dk blue cl. Fine in VG dj. *Sumner & Stillman.* $75/£48

DARLEY, F.O.C. A Selection of War Lyrics with Illustrations on Wood. NY: James G. Gregory, 1864. 1st ed. 32pp. VG. *Mcgowan.* $45/£29

DARLEY, LIONEL S. Bookbinding Now and Then. Faber, 1959. 19 plts. VG in dj. *Moss.* $37/£24

DARLEY, LIONEL S. Bookbinding Then and Now. London: Faber & Faber, 1950. VG + in dj. *Limestone.* $45/£29

DARLEY, LIONEL S. Introduction to Bookbinding. Faber, 1965. 1st ed. VG in dj. *Moss.* $31/£20

DARLING, F. FRASER. Natural History in the Highlands and Islands. London: Collins, (1947). 1st ed. Dj (faded). *Petersfield.* $47/£30

DARLING, F. FRASER. The Seasons and the Farmer. Cambridge, 1944. C.F. Tunnicliffe (engrs). (Sl faded.) *Petersfield.* $23/£15

DARLING, WILL Y. The Bankrupt Bookseller. Edinburgh: Robert Grant, 1947. 1st ed. Fine in dj. *Graf.* $25/£16

DARLING, WILLY. The Bankrupt Bookseller. Edinburgh: R. Grant, 1947. Good in dj (worn). *Moss.* $19/£12

DARLINGTON, C.D. Chromosome Botany and the Origins of Cultivated Plants. London, 1973. 3rd rev ed. Frontis map, 24 tables. Fine in dj. *Brooks.* $30/£19

DARNELL, ERMINA JETT. Forks of Welkhorn Church. Louisville, KY, 1946. 1st ed. VG. *Mcgowan.* $65/£42

DARRELL, MARGERY (ed). Once upon a Time, The Fairy Tale World of Arthur Rackham. NY: Viking, (1972). 1st ed. Arthur Rackham (illus). Cl-backed paper-cvrd bds. VG in dj. *Hermitage.* $85/£55

DARROW, CLARENCE S. Farmington. Chicago: A.C. McClurg, 1904. 1st ed. Inscribed. Grn cl (spine sl dknd). Very Nice. *Glenn.* $300/£194

DARTON, F.J. HARVEY. Dickens. Positively the First Appearance. London: Argonaut Press, 1933. Cl-backed bds, paper spine label (chipped). Endleaves browned, else VG. *Glenn.* $90/£58

DARTON, F.J. HARVEY. Modern Book-Illustration in Great Britain and America. Studio Special Winter 1931. Sl pulled, o/w VG in plastic-covered dj. *Willow House.* $85/£55

DARTON, N.H. Guidebook of the Western United States. Part C. The Santa Fe Route. Washington: GPO, 1916. 2nd ptg, corrected. 42 plts (incl fldg map), 25 fldg color sheet maps. Black cl. VG. *Schoyer.* $50/£32

DARTON, N.H. Story of the Grand Canyon of Arizona. Kansas City, MO: Fred Harvey, 1926. 9th ed. Wraps. *Burcham.* $15/£10

DARWIN, BERNARD (ed). The Dickens Advertiser. London: Elkin Mathews & Marrot, 1930. Pict cl (sl faded). *Petersfield.* $23/£15

DARWIN, CHARLES. Charles Darwin's Notebooks 1836-1844.... P.H. Barrett, et al (eds). Ithaca, NY, 1987. *Wheldon & Wesley.* $124/£80

DARWIN, CHARLES. The Descent of Man and Selection in Relation to Sex. NY: D. Appleton, 1871. 1st Amer ed, 1st issue w/corrective note in vol 2. 2 vols. 409; v,436pp (lt stains few leaves; fore-edge sl stained). Dec gilt cl (extrems lt worn). Nice. *Shasky.* $185/£119

DARWIN, CHARLES. The Descent of Man and Selections in Relation to Sex. NY: LEC, 1971. #727/1500. Signed by Fritz Kredel (illus). Morocco leather spine, wood veneer sides, gold-stamped spine. Fine in VG slipcase. *Graf.* $90/£58

DARWIN, CHARLES. The Descent of Man, and Selection in Relation to Sex. London: 1890. 2nd ed, 27th thousand. xvi,693,32pp. Good. *Henly.* $47/£30

DARWIN, CHARLES. The Descent of Man. London: John Murray, 1883. 2nd ed. 17th thousand. xvi,693pp (flyleaves foxed). Contemp 1/2 calf (sl rubbed), gilt. *Hollett.* $70/£45

DARWIN, CHARLES. The Expression of the Emotions in Man and Animals. NY: D. Appleton, 1873. 1st Amer ed. viii,374pp (eps foxed; few pp roughly opened); 7 heliotype plts; teg. Blue-grn cl (spine, label browned w/fraying; lt dampstain lower cvr), ptd pub's label on spine (rmdr binding?). *Godot.* $100/£65

DARWIN, CHARLES. The Expression of the Emotions in Man and Animals. London, 1873. 1st ed, 10th thousand. 394pp. Good. *Fye.* $600/£387

DARWIN, CHARLES. The Expression of the Emotions in Man and Animals. NY, 1897. 372pp. 1/2 leather. VF. *Fye.* $125/£81

DARWIN, CHARLES. The Formation of Vegetable Mould through the Action of Worms.... London: John Murray, 1882. 7th thousand. Grn sand-grain cl. Good. *Waterfield.* $93/£60

DARWIN, CHARLES. The Formation of Vegetable Mould, Through the Action of Worms.... London, 1883. 8th thousand. vii,328pp; ad. (Refixed in case; sm stamp fore-edge, 1 in text.) *Henly.* $59/£38

DARWIN, CHARLES. The Formation of Vegetable Mould, Through the Action of Worms.... NY, 1898. 326pp. 1/2 leather. Good. *Fye.* $45/£29

DARWIN, CHARLES. Journal of Researches by...into the Natural History and Geology of the Countries Visited.... Heritage, (1957). VF in Fine slipcase. *Oregon.* $20/£13

DARWIN, CHARLES. Journal of Researches into the Natural History and Geology...During the Voyage of H.M.S. Beagle. NY: Heritage, (1957). Dec cl. NF in VG slipcase. *Mikesh.* $30/£19

DARWIN, CHARLES. Journal of Researches into the Natural History and Geology...During the Voyage, etc. of H.M.S. Beatle, etc. London: Murray, (1901). 26 plts. Dec cl. Good + . *Mikesh.* $37/£24

DARWIN, CHARLES. The Movements and Habits of Climbing Plants. London, 1891. 5th thousand. ix,208pp; 32 ads. Stamp in text, o/w Fine. *Henly.* $65/£42

DARWIN, CHARLES. A Naturalist's Voyage. London, 1888. 17th Thousand. x,519pp; 32ads. (Inner joints sl weak.) *Henly.* $39/£25

DARWIN, CHARLES. A Naturalist's Voyage. London: John Murray, 1888. 18th thousand. Grn sand-grain cl. Good. *Waterfield.* $70/£45

DARWIN, CHARLES. On the Origin of Species by Means of Natural Selection. London, 1860. 2nd ed. 5th thousand. Murray's cat dated Jan 1860 at end. 8vo. x,502pp; fldg diag. Orig grn cl. *Wheldon & Wesley.* $698/£450

DARWIN, CHARLES. On the Origin of Species by Means of Natural Selection. 41st Thousand. John Murray, 1891. 6th ed. xxi,432pp; ad leaf. Grn cl. *Bickersteth.* $43/£28

DARWIN, CHARLES. On the Origin of Species by Means of Natural Selection. 5th Thousand. John Murray, 1860. 2nd ed, 2nd issue. ix,(i),502pp; fldg plt; pub's 32pg cat. Grn cl blocked in blind, gilt spine. (Ink name 1/2 title; upper joint slit; inner joint cracked; sewing sl loose.) *Bickersteth.* $233/£150

DARWIN, CHARLES. The Various Contrivances by which Orchids are Fertilised by Insects. London, 1904. 2nd ed, 7th imp. Good. *Henly.* $37/£24

DARWIN, CHARLES. The Various Contrivances by Which Orchids Are Fertilized by Insects. London: John Murray, 1882. 2nd ed. xvi,300pp. Contemp 1/2 calf, gilt, contrasting spine labels. VG. *Hollett.* $93/£60

DARWIN, ERASMUS. Zoonomia; or, The Laws of Organic Life. London, 1801. 3rd ed. 4 vols. 516; 565; 512; 493pp. Full leather (rubbed; hinges cracked). Contents VG (tps, 1 leaf clipped). *Fye.* $400/£258

DARWIN, F. (ed). Charles Darwin: His Life.... London: Murray, (1908). Abridged ed. Frontis port. Dec cl. Good + . *Mikesh.* $30/£19

DARWIN, FRANCIS (ed). The Life and Letters of Charles Darwin. London: John Murray, 1887. 2nd ed. 3 vols. Gray-blue cl (worn, dusty; vol 1 rear joint split; lib label cvrs). *Waterfield.* $116/£75

DARWIN, FRANCIS (ed). The Life and Letters of Charles Darwin. London, 1887. 3rd ed. 3 vols. (Sl foxing; spine vol 2 sl worn.) *Wheldon & Wesley.* $124/£80

DARWIN, FRANCIS (ed). More Letters of Charles Darwin. London, 1903. 2 vols. 15 ports. *Wheldon & Wesley.* $124/£80

DASENT, ARTHUR IRWIN. The History of St. James's Square. London, 1895. Frontis port (lt stained), xii,300pp, fldg plan. Teg. Gilt illus upper bd. (Marginal browning; spine sl chipped.) *Edwards.* $40/£26

DASENT, GEORGE WEBBE. The Story of Burnt Njal or Life in Iceland at the End of the Tenth Century. Edinburgh, 1861. 1st ed. 2 vols. 8 maps, plans. Gilt dec cl. VG. *Argosy.* $250/£161

DASENT, GEORGE WEBBE. The Story of Burnt Njal. Edinburgh: Edmonston & Douglas, 1861. 2 vols. xxx,cciv,256; xii,507pp; 2 engr frontispieces; 5 maps, plans. Very Nice. *Hollett.* $233/£150

DASENT, GEORGE WEBBE. The Story of Burnt Njal. Edinburgh, 1861. 1st ed. 2 vols. Frontis, cciv,256; xiii,507pp. Emb cl. (Upper hinge vol 2 cracked.) *Edwards.* $116/£75

Dash's Holiday. (Uncle John's Drolleries Series.) NY: McLoughlin Bros, n.d. (ca 1865). 4to. 6 leaves + 1pg list lower wrapper, 1 center spread, 4 full-pg, 2 double-pg chromolithos; 1st, last chromos pasted on wrappers; cvr w/designed title of dog at table being served. VG (ink sig, sl chipped 2 leaves) in wrappers (lt soiled). *Hobbyhorse.* $185/£119

DASHWOOD, RICHARD LEWES. Chiploquorgan. Dublin: White, 1871. 1st ed. 293pp, 2 engr plts; teg. 3/4 red morocco, raised bands, gilt titles; silk ribbon marker. Lt edgewear, o/w Fine. *Bowman.* $325/£210

DATER, JUDY and JACK WELPOTT. Women and Other Visions. Dobbs Ferry, NY: Morgan & Morgan, 1975. 1st ed. 107 full-pg b/w photos. Silver-emb cl. Fine in pict dj. *Cahan.* $60/£39

DAUBOURG, E. Interior Architecture. London: Chapman and Hall, 1877. 8pp, 40 engr plts. Recent buckram. *Marlborough.* $388/£250

DAUGHERTY, JAMES. Abraham Lincoln. NY: Viking, 1943. 1st ed. Sm 4to. 34 full-pg illus. Pict cl, linen spine. NF in VG+ dj (chipped). *Book Adoption.* $85/£55

DAUGHERTY, JAMES. Daniel Boone. NY: Viking, 1939. 1st ed. Sm 4to. Pict cl. Fine in NF dj. *Book Adoption.* $95/£61

DAUGHERTY, JAMES. The Landing of the Pilgrims. NY: Random House, 1950. 1st trade ed. Dec eps. VG in dj. *Cattermole.* $35/£23

DAULBY, DANIEL. A Descriptive Catalogue of the Works of Rembrandt.... Liverpool, 1796. Engr frontis port. (Spotted; tp sl browned.) Marbled eps, edges; inner gilt dentelles; gilt edges. Calf (hinges repaired; rebacked w/orig dec gilt spine laid down). *Edwards.* $233/£150

DAUMAS, E. The Horses of the Sahara, and the Manners of the Desert.... James Hutton (trans). London: Wm. H. Allen, 1863. 1st Eng ed. 8vo. xi,(i)blank,355. Contemp red half calf, marbled bds (upper edge faded; upper joint, hinge cracked; edge-rubbed). Internally VG (few pencil mks). *Morrell.* $233/£150

DAUMIER, HONORE. 240 Lithographs. NY, 1946. 1st ed. 240 plts. (Sl soiled.) *Argosy.* $100/£65

DAVENPORT, CYRIL. English Embroidered Bookbindings. London: Kegan Paul, 1899. 113pp, 52 full-pg plts. 1/2 morocco over marbled bds (extrems scuffed). *Cullen.* $125/£81

DAVENPORT, CYRIL. Mezzotints. NY, 1903. 1st Amer ed. Frontis; 39 Fine plts, guards. VG. *Argosy.* $100/£65

DAVENPORT, CYRIL. Mezzotints. London, 1904. Frontis port. (Eps spotted.) Teg, rest uncut, parts unopened. Dec gilt title (edges sl faded). *Edwards.* $47/£30

DAVENPORT, CYRIL. Royal English Bookbindings. Seeley, 1896. 8 Fine color plts. Good in maroon dec cl. *Moss.* $93/£60

DAVENPORT, GUY. The Bowman of Shu. NY: Grenfell Press, 1983. 1st ed. Ltd to 115 signed. 1/4 grn morocco, pict bds. As New. *Jaffe.* $225/£145

DAVENPORT, GUY. Goldfinch Thistle Star. (NY): Red Ozier Press, (1983). 1st ed. One of 155 softbound dated, signed. As New in dec wrappers. *Jaffe.* $100/£65

DAVENPORT, GUY. The Resurrection in Cookham Churchyard. NY: Jordan Davies, 1982. 1st ed. One of 250 signed. New in dj. *Jaffe.* $100/£65

DAVENPORT, JOHN. Aphrodisiacs and Anti-Aphrodisiacs: Three Essays. London, 1869. 1st ed. 154pp; 7 plts. 1/4 leather. Contents Fine (hinges cracked; 2 pieces missing spine). *Fye.* $150/£97

DAVENPORT, RICHARD. The Amateur's Perspective. London: The Author, 1828. xii,84pp, 15 fldg plts. 1/2 leather, raised bands, marbled bds, gilt (sl worn). *Ars Artis.* $233/£150

DAVEY, NORMAN. A History of Building Materials. London, 1961. 1st ed. 73 plts. Dj (sl rubbed). *Edwards.* $59/£38

DAVID, ELIZABETH. French Country Cooking. London, 1951. 1st ed. VG in pict dj (chip). *Words Etc.* $101/£65

DAVID, RONALD L. A History of Opera in the American West. Englewood Cliffs: Prentice-Hall, 1965. 1st ed. VG+ in VG dj. *Parker.* $30/£19

DAVID, VILLIERS. The Guardsman and Cupid's Daughter, and Other Poems. (London), 1930. 1/500, signed by David & John Austen (illus). VG. *Argosy.* $75/£48

DAVIDOFF, LEO. Brain Tumors: Their Pathology, Symptomatology.... Utica, NY, 1931. 1st ed. Good. *Fye.* $125/£81

DAVIDS, KENNETH. The Softness on the Other Side of the Hole. NY: Grove, (1968). 1st ed. Rev copy, slip laid in. Fine in dj. *Reese.* $30/£19

DAVIDS, R.C. Lords of the Arctic. NY/London: Macmillan/Collier, 1982. 1st ed. Fine in VG+ dj. *Mikesh.* $37/£24

DAVIDSON, ANGUS. Edward Lear: Landscape Painter and Nonsense Poet (1812-1888). NY: Dutton, 1939. 11 plts. (Sig.) *Archaeologia.* $45/£29

DAVIDSON, BRUCE. East 100th Street. Cambridge, MA: Harvard Univ Press, 1970. 1st ed. Fine in pict stiff wrappers. *Cahan.* $175/£113

DAVIDSON, DONALD. The Tennessee. NY, (1946, 1948). 1st eds. 2 vols. Name, date; sl stain vol 1, else Good set in djs (worn, faded, sl torn, price-clipped). *King.* $65/£42

DAVIDSON, DONALD. The Tennessee. NY: Rinehart, (1946-8). 1st ed. 2 vols. Tape mks vol 1 pastedowns; nick vol 2 spine; o/w Good set in djs (spines sunned; chipped). *Reese.* $50/£32

DAVIDSON, ELLIS A. A Practical Manual of House-Painting, Graining, Marbling and Sign-Writing. London: Crosby Lockwood, 1896. 11th ed. xxi,394pp (early sig), 9 color plts. Orig emb cl (water-stained), paper spine label. *Europa.* $101/£65

DAVIDSON, H.A. David Otis Mears, D.D.: An Autobiography, 1842-1893. Boston: Pilgrim, (1920). 1st ed. *Ginsberg.* $75/£48

DAVIDSON, H.C. (ed). The Book of the Home. London, 1904. 8 vols. Color frontispieces (sl marginal foxing). *Edwards.* $155/£100

DAVIDSON, JOHN. A Full and True Account of the Wonderful Mission of Earl Lavender.... Ward & Downey Ltd, 1895. 1st ed. Frontis by Aubrey Beardsley, xii,290pp + (ii)pub's ads. (Spine sunned, chip.) *Edwards.* $50/£32

DAVIE, DONALD. The Heyday of Sir Walter Scott. London: Routledge, (1961). 1st ed. Fine in dj. *Reese.* $30/£19

DAVIE, ROBERT E. Diary of William Barret Travis: August 30, 1833-June 26, 1834. Waco: Texian, 1966. 1st ed. Dj. *Lambeth.* $50/£32

DAVIES, ARTHUR. Essays on the Man and His Art. (Cambridge): Phillips Publications, 1924. VG in dj, slipcase. *Argosy.* $100/£65

DAVIES, CHARLES. A Treatise on Shades and Shadows, and Linear Perspective. NY: Harper, 1832. 157pp, 20 fldg engr plts. (Last ff sl foxed; waterstain.) Contemp 1/2 leather, marbled bds (joints cracked; sl worn). *Ars Artis.* $147/£95

DAVIES, G. Bibliography of British History: Stuart Period 1603-1714. Oxford: Clarendon, 1928. VG. *Moss.* $56/£36

DAVIES, GEORGE R. Collection of Old Chinese Porcelains. NY, 1913. Color frontis, 24 color plts. Teg, rest uncut. (Fore-edge upper bd lt water-stained; cl sl bumped; joint heads sl splitting.) *Edwards.* $155/£100

DAVIES, GERALD S. Charterhouse in London. London, 1921. Marbled eps, edges. Prize calf binding, gilt shield, raised bands (ink stamp, sl loss to tail). *Edwards.* $54/£35

DAVIES, HUGH WILLIAM. Devices of the Early Printers, 1457-1560, Their History and Development. London: Grafton, 1935. VG (spine faded; ink notes; pastedowns lt foxed) in blue buckram case. *Heller.* $100/£65

DAVIES, J. SANGER. Dolomite Strongholds. London: George Bell & Sons, 1896. 1st ed. Color frontis; 176,(iii)pp; map; 8 plts. (Extrems sl rubbed.) *Hollett.* $85/£55

DAVIES, K.G. The Royal African Company. London: Longmans, (1957). 1st ed. VG in Good+ dj. *Oregon.* $35/£23

DAVIES, MARTIN. The National Gallery, London. Antwerp, 1953. 2 vols. 462 plts (2 color). (Sm repaired damage to lower backstrip vol 2.) *Washton.* $250/£161

DAVIES, MARTIN. Rogier van der Weyden. London, 1972. Good in dj (sl worn). *Washton.* $250/£161

DAVIES, NINA M. Picture Writing in Ancient Egypt. London: Griffith Inst, 1958. 17 plts (12 color). Good in dj (chipped). *Archaeologia.* $85/£55

DAVIES, R.H. and C.D. GIBSON. About Paris. Harpers, 1895. 1st ed. VG+. *Fine Books.* $35/£23

DAVIES, RANDALL (ed). Old Water-Colour Society's Club 1924-1925. London, 1925. 2nd annual vol. Color frontis, 38 plts. (Feps browned; bds sl rubbed.) *Edwards.* $74/£48

DAVIES, REGINALD. The Camel's Back. London, 1957. 1st ed. 6 plts. Sig; sl foxing eps, edges, o/w Good. Dk grn cl, gilt. *Edwards.* $23/£15

DAVIES, RHYS. A Bed of Feathers. London: Mandrake Press, (1929). 1st ed. Cl-backed patterned bds. Edge rubbed, else Fine in dj (rubbed, dusty). *Cahan.* $30/£19

DAVIES, RHYS. My Wales. NY: Funk & Wagnalls, 1938. 1st ed. Stamp fr pastedown; eps lt browned, o/w Fine in dj (lt worn; spine lacks piece). *Hermitage.* $45/£29

DAVIES, RHYS. Pig in a Poke. London: Joiner & Steele, 1931. One of 1000 numbered. VG in dj (soiled; spine head, heel chipped). *Agvent.* $45/£29

DAVIES, RHYS. Rings on Her Fingers. London: Harold Shaylor, 1930. 1st ed. Fine in NF dj (spine sl dknd). *Beasley.* $75/£48

DAVIES, RHYS. Rings on Her Fingers. NY: Harcourt, 1930. 1st US ed. Fine in dj (lt chipped; dknd spine). *Beasley.* $25/£16

DAVIES, RHYS. The Stars, the World, and the Women. London: William Jackson, 1930. 1st ed. #58/550 signed. Teg, others uncut. Orig buckram. Good. *Cox.* $28/£18

DAVIES, RHYS. The Withered Root. London: Holden, 1927. 1st ed. Fine in NF dj (spine dknd). *Beasley.* $75/£48

DAVIES, ROBERTSON and TYRONE GUTHRIE. Renown at Stratford, a Record of the Shakespeare Festival in Canada 1953. Toronto, (1953). 1st ed. Sl tear, else Good in dj (tattered). *King.* $65/£42

DAVIES, ROBERTSON. A Jig for the Gypsy. Toronto, 1954. 1st ed. Sl mkd, o/w NF in dj (sl rubbed). *Rees.* $194/£125

DAVIES, ROBERTSON. A Jig for the Gypsy. London: Clarke, Irwin, 1954. 1st Eng ed. Fine in dj (extrems sl rubbed). *Ulysses.* $240/£155

DAVIES, ROBERTSON. The Lyre of Orpheus. Toronto: Macmillan of Canada, (1988). 1st ed, Canadian issue. Signed. Fine in dj. *Godot.* $85/£55

DAVIES, ROBERTSON. The Lyre of Orpheus. (London): Viking, (1988). 1st Eng ed, ltd to 150 numbered, signed. Cl spine, marbled paper-cvrd bds. Fine in pub's tissue dj. *Godot.* $150/£97

DAVIES, ROBERTSON. The Manticore. Toronto, 1972. 1st ed. NF in dj (sl rubbed, nicked). *Rees.* $16/£10

DAVIES, ROBERTSON. The Manticore. Toronto: Macmillan, 1972. 1st ed. Fine in dj. *Juvelis.* $100/£65

DAVIES, ROBERTSON. A Mixture of Frailties. NY: Scribner's, (1958). 1st Amer ed. Good in dj (lt soiled, price-clipped, sm chip). *Reese.* $45/£29

DAVIES, ROBERTSON. A Mixture of Frailties. Scribners, 1958. 1st Amer ed. Spine top bumped, torn, else VG+ in NF dj. *Fine Books.* $38/£25

DAVIES, ROBERTSON. One Half of Robertson Davies. Toronto: Macmillan, 1977. 1st ed. Fine in VG dj. *Revere.* $35/£23

DAVIES, ROBERTSON. The Papers of Samuel Marchbanks. (NY): Viking, (1986). 1st Amer ed. Fine in dj. *Between The Covers.* $45/£29

DAVIES, ROBERTSON. The Rebel Angels. NY: Viking, 1982. 1st Amer ed. Fine in Fine dj. *Revere.* $45/£29

DAVIES, ROBERTSON. The Table Talk of Samuel Marchbanks. Toronto: Clark, Irwin, 1949. 1st ed. NF in VG dj (sl bleedthrough; sm hole). *Revere.* $100/£65

DAVIES, ROBERTSON. The Table Talk of Samuel Marchbanks. Toronto: Clarke, Irwin, 1949. 1st ed. Red cl, silver-stamped. Fine in VG dj (nick, lt wear, sl soiled). *Godot.* $150/£97

DAVIES, ROBERTSON. The Table Talk of Samuel Marchbanks. London: C&W, 1951. 1st ed. VG in dj (short closed tear). *Rees.* $62/£40

DAVIES, ROBERTSON. Tempest-Tost. Toronto: Clarke, Irwin, 1951. 1st ed. Grn cl. Bold ink name, date; spine faded, else VG in dj (2 sm brn stains, spine lt faded, else VG). *Godot.* $150/£97

DAVIES, ROBERTSON. Tempest-Tost. London: C&W, 1952. 1st ed. VG in dj (sl frayed, nicked, mkd). *Rees.* $116/£75

DAVIES, ROBERTSON. A Voice from the Attic. Knopf, 1960. 2nd ptg. NF in VG+ dj. *Bishop.* $17/£11

DAVIES, ROBERTSON. The Well-Tempered Critic. Toronto: McClelland & Stewart, 1981. 1st ed. Fine in Fine dj. *Revere.* $50/£32

DAVIES, ROBERTSON. What's Bred in the Bone. (NY): Viking/Elizabeth Sifton Books, (1985). 1st Amer ed. Fine in dj. *Godot.* $40/£26

DAVIES, ROBERTSON. World of Wonders. London, 1977. 1st ed. VG+ (browning) in VG+ dj. *Fuller & Saunders.* $35/£23

DAVIES, T. WITTON. Magic, Divination, and Demonology Among the Hebrews and Their Neighbours.... London: James Clark, (1898). Inscribed presentation. 8vo. xvi,130,(2)pp. Pub's cl w/gilt stamped title; uncut. VG. *Laurie.* $125/£81

DAVIES, THOMAS. Memoirs of the Life of David Garrick, Esq. London: for the Author, 1780. 1st ed. 2 vols. Engr frontis. Full contemp tree calf (worn; backstrip head chipped); morocco labels. *Dramatis Personae.* $120/£77

DAVIES, THOMAS. Memoirs of the Life of David Garrick.... For Author, 1780. New ed. 2 vols. Frontis. Continental 1/2 calf. *Hill.* $109/£70

DAVIES, W.H. The Adventures of Johnny Walker, Tramp. London: Cape, (1926). One of 125 numbered, signed. 1st collective ed. Edges sl sunned, eps foxed, o/w Very Nice in white dj (heavily tanned). *Reese.* $60/£39

DAVIES, W.H. The Adventures of Johnny Walker, Tramp. London: Cape, 1926. 1st ed. (Flyleaves lt browned.) *Hollett.* $23/£15

DAVIES, W.H. The Hour of Magic. Cape, 1922. 1st ed. Sl mkd, else contents Good. *Whiteson.* $28/£18

DAVIES, W.H. Later Days. London: Cape, 1925. 1st ed. VG. *Hollett.* $31/£20

DAVIES, W.H. Nature Poems and Others. Fifield, 1908. 1st ed. Foxing; bds discolored, sl worn, o/w VG. *Poetry.* $23/£15

DAVIES, W.H. New Poems. Elkin Mathews, 1907. 1st ed. NF (bkpl; fore-edge spotted). *Poetry.* $28/£18

DAVIOT, GORDON. Claverhouse. London, 1937. 1st ed. Frontis port; 5 ports; map. Buff cl. VG. *Edwards.* $23/£15

DAVIS, ANDREW JACKSON. The Children's Progressive Lyceum. Boston: Bela Marsh, 1866. 5th ed. Full-pg frontis w/plt guard; full-pg cut. Full leather on bds, gilt title on spine, gilt edges (sl rubbing cvrs). Fine (ink name, scribble fep). *Hobbyhorse.* $95/£61

DAVIS, ANGELA. If They Come in the Morning. NY: Third Press/Joseph Okpaku, (1971). 1st ed, 1st bk. VG in dj. *Petrilla.* $50/£32

DAVIS, ANGELA. If They Come in the Morning. NY: Third Press, (1971). Stated 1st ed. Fine in dj (sl rubbed). *Aka.* $40/£26

DAVIS, BRIAN L. German Army Uniforms and Insignia 1933-1945. London, 1973. 2nd rev ed. VG in dj (sl sunned). *Edwards.* $25/£16

DAVIS, BRITTON. The Truth about Geronimo. Chicago, (1951). Lakeside Classic. VG. *Schoyer.* $30/£19

DAVIS, BRITTON. The Truth about Geronimo. Milo Milton Quaife (ed). New Haven, 1926. 1951 reprint, Lakeside Classic #49. Fine in pict cl. *Pratt.* $35/£23

DAVIS, BURKE. Gray Fox: Robert E. Lee and the Civil War. Rinehart, (c. 1956). 1st ed. VG in Good dj. *Book Broker.* $25/£16

DAVIS, BURKE. Jeb Stuart, The Last Cavalier. NY, 1957. 1st ed. Fine in dj (sl wear). *Pratt.* $37/£24

DAVIS, BURKE. Jeb Stuart. The Last Cavalier. NY: Rinehart, (1957). 1st ed. Grey cl. Name, edgewear, else VG in Good dj (1/2-inch chip top spine). *Chapel Hill.* $75/£48

DAVIS, BURKE. The Long Surrender. NY: Random House, (1985). 1st ed. Fine in NF dj. *Mcgowan.* $35/£23

DAVIS, CARLYLE CHANNING and WILLIAM A. ALDERSON. The True Story of 'Ramona.' Dodge, (1914). 1st ed. Teg. Pict cvr. Fine. *Authors Of The West.* $50/£32

DAVIS, CHARLES G. The ABC of Yacht Design. NY: Rudder, (1930). 1st ed. Ptd wrapppers. *Lefkowicz.* $35/£23

DAVIS, CHARLES G. The Built-Up Ship Model. Salem, 1933. 1st ed. 37 plts. Dj. *Lefkowicz.* $95/£61

DAVIS, CHARLES G. The Ship Model Builder's Assistant. Salem, MA: Marine Research Soc, 1926. 1st ed. Good in dj (sl worn). *Hayman.* $60/£39

DAVIS, CHARLES G. The Ship Model Builder's Assistant. Salem: Marine Research Soc Pub 12, 1926. 1st ed. Dj (badly torn). *Lefkowicz.* $65/£42

DAVIS, CHARLES G. The Ship Model Builder's Assistant. NY, 1970. Rpt. *Lefkowicz.* $35/£23

DAVIS, CHARLES G. Shipping and Craft in Silhouette. Salem, MA: Marine Research Soc, 1929. VG in dj (neatly reinforced). *Hayman.* $50/£32

DAVIS, CHARLES G. Shipping and Craft in Silhouette. Salem: Marine Research Soc Pub 20, 1929. 1st ed. 102 plts. VF in dj. *Lefkowicz.* $65/£42

DAVIS, CHARLES G. Ships of the Past. Salem, MA: Marine Research Soc, 1929. 12 dbl-pg plts. Good. *Hayman.* $75/£48

DAVIS, CHARLES G. Ships of the Past. Salem: Marine Research Soc Pub 19, 1929. 1st ed. (Shelfwear.) *Lefkowicz.* $90/£58

DAVIS, DANIEL. A Practical Treatise Upon the Authority and Duty of Justices of the Peace in Criminal Prosecutions. Boston: Cummings, Hilliard & Co, 1824. Contemp sheep (rubbed). *Boswell.* $175/£113

DAVIS, DAVID D. Acute Hydrocephalus or Water in the Head.... London: Taylor & Walton, 1840. 1st ed. xi,309pp. 1/2 roan, marbled bds. VG (lt foxing). *Goodrich.* $795/£513

DAVIS, DAVID D. Acute Hydrocephalus, or Water in the Head, and Inflammatory Disease.... Phila, 1840. 1st Amer ed. 126pp. Good in stiff wrappers. *Fye.* $75/£48

DAVIS, ELLIS A. and EDWIN H. GROBE. The New Encyclopedia of Texas. Dallas, (ca 1926). 1st ed. 4 vols. Dec cl. *Ginsberg.* $250/£161

DAVIS, EVANGELINE and BURKE. Rebel Raider, A Biography of Admiral Semmes. Phila, (1966). 1st ed. Fine in dj (sm tear, sm piece torn off). *Pratt.* $27/£17

DAVIS, EVANGELINE. Charleston Houses and Gardens. Preservation Soc of Charleston, (c. 1975). Unpaged; color photo. VG. *Book Broker.* $25/£16

DAVIS, FANNY. The Palace of Topkapi in Istanbul. NY: Scribner's, (1970). VG in dj. *Schoyer.* $35/£23

DAVIS, FANNY. The Palace of Topkapi in Istanbul. NY: Scribner, 1970. 1st ed. Color frontis. VG in dj. *Worldwide.* $35/£23

DAVIS, GEORGE. Coming Home. NY: Random House, (1971). 1st ed. Fine in dj. *Reese.* $75/£48

DAVIS, H.L. Honey in the Horn. Harper, 1935. 1st ed, 1st bk. Erasures, foxing, else Fine in dj (chipped). *Authors Of The West.* $50/£32

DAVIS, HENRY T. Solitary Places Made Glad. Cincinnati, 1890. Frontis, 422pp, port. (Sm rubber lib stamp tp; label removed spine.) Howes D 114. *Ginsberg.* $100/£65

DAVIS, J.K. With the 'Aurora' in the Antarctic 1911-1914. London: Andrew Melrose, (1919). 1st ed. Fldg map. VG (lettering sl dull, lt foxing). *Walcot.* $465/£300

DAVIS, JEFFERSON. The Rise and Fall of the Confederate Government. NY: D. Appleton, 1881. 1st ed. 2 vols. Sl extrem wear, else NF set. Howes D 120. *Mcgowan.* $300/£194

DAVIS, JEFFERSON. The Rise and Fall of the Confederate Government. NY: Appleton, 1881. 1st ed. 2 vols. Frontis port, 707,(4)pp ads; 808,(4)pp ads. Pub's 1/2 morocco binding. VG (bkpl; rubbed). *Chapel Hill.* $375/£242

DAVIS, JOHN FRANCIS. Chinese: A General Description.... NY: Harper, 1836. 2 vols. Engr fldg frontis map, 383; 440pp + 4pp ads (foxed). 3/4 leather (rubbed). *Schoyer.* $125/£81

DAVIS, JOHN STAIGE. Plastic Surgery. Its Principles and Practice. Phila: Blakiston, (1919). 1st ed. 8vo. VG (ex-lib). *Glaser.* $600/£387

DAVIS, JOHN. Travels of John Davis in the United States of America 1798 to 1802. J.V. Cheney (ed). Boston: Bibliophile Soc, 1910. One of 487 sets. 2 vols. Vellum spines. Boxed. Howes D 123. *Ginsberg.* $175/£113

DAVIS, JOHN. Travels of John Davis in the United States of America, 1798 to 1802. John Vance Cheney (ed). Boston: Privately ptd, MDCDX. 2 vols. VG. Howes D123. *Lien.* $95/£61

DAVIS, JULIA. Never Say Die: The Glengarry McDonalds of Virginia. American History Press, (c. 1980). Signed. Stiff paper. VG. *Book Broker.* $25/£16

DAVIS, LEELA B. A Modern Argonaut. SF: Whitaker & Ray, (1896). 1st ed. Gilt white cl. (Foxed; name, note; bkpl scar.) *Reese.* $45/£29

DAVIS, LEVERETT, JR. et al. Exterior Ballistics of Rockets. Princeton, NJ: D. Van Nostrand, 1958. Blue cl (ex-lib). Extrems sl worn, lib mks, o/w Good. *Knollwood.* $60/£39

DAVIS, LINDSEY. Shadows in Bronze. London: S&J, 1990. 1st UK ed. Fine (sl bumped) in dj. *Lewton.* $62/£40

DAVIS, LINDSEY. Venus in Copper. Hutchinson, 1991. 1st ed. Fine in dj. *Rees.* $31/£20

DAVIS, LOYAL. Intracranial Tumors Roentgenologically Considered. NY, 1933. 1st ed. Good. *Fye.* $200/£129

DAVIS, LOYAL. Neurological Surgery. Chicago, 1936. 1st ed. Good. *Fye.* $125/£81

DAVIS, LOYAL. The Principles of Neurological Surgery. Phila, 1942. 2nd ed. Good. *Fye.* $50/£32

DAVIS, MARY LEE. Uncle Sam's Attic. Boston: W.A. Wilde, (1930). Fine in VG dj. *Perier.* $30/£19

DAVIS, N. Carthage and Her Remains. NY: Harper, 1861. Frontis, xv,504pp, 3 plts (2 color), 3 maps and plans. Gilt-pict cl (extrems rubbed, spine chipped). *Archaeologia.* $125/£81

DAVIS, N. Carthage and Her Remains. NY: Harper, 1861. 1st Amer ed. 504pp + 2pp ads, 2 fldg maps, 2 color plts. Lavender cl, blind/gilt-stamped (faded, rubbed). *Schoyer.* $100/£65

DAVIS, N. Ruined Cities within Numidian and Carthaginian Territories. London: John Murray, 1862. xiv,391pp + 32pp ads; fldg map. Orig blind-stamped cl gilt. Very Nice. *Hollett.* $209/£135

DAVIS, NATHAN SMITH. History of the American Medical Association....to January, 1855. S.W. Butler (ed). Phila, 1855. 1st ed. 191pp + ads; 9 engr ports. Orig cl (backstrip chipped; foxed). *Argosy.* $150/£97

DAVIS, RICHARD HARDING. The Bar Sinister. NY, 1903. 1st ed, 1st issue w/gold spine lettering. VG. *Argosy.* $50/£32

DAVIS, RICHARD HARDING. Vera: The Medium. NY: Scribner's, 1908. 1st ed. Pict purple cl. VG (spine sl faded). BAL 4548. *Antic Hay.* $35/£23

DAVIS, RICHARD HARDING. The West from a Car Window. NY: Harpers, 1892. 1st ed. 243pp. *Lambeth.* $40/£26

DAVIS, STEPHEN CHAPIN. California Gold Rush Merchant; The Journal of.... Benjamin B. Richards (ed). San Marino: Huntington Lib, 1956. Map. Cl-backed bds, ptd spine label. VG + (bkpl) in plastic dj (torn). *Bohling.* $40/£26

DAVIS, TERENCE (ed). Decorative Art. The Studio, 1960. Vol 50. (Margins lt browned; ex-lib; tape mks, #s.) Protected dj. *Edwards.* $47/£30

DAVIS, TERENCE. The Gothick Taste. London: David & Charles, (1974). 1st ed. Fine in dj. *Bookpress.* $65/£42

DAVIS, W.H. El Gringo. NY: Harper, 1857. 1st ed. 432pp, 13 plts. New cl, bds; new eps (lib name copyright; lt foxing). Howes D 139. *Schoyer.* $200/£129

DAVIS, WALTER BICKFORD and DANIEL S. DURRIE. An Illustrated History of Missouri.... St. Louis/Cincinnati: A.J. Hall/Robert Clarke, 1876. Frontis, xx,639pp; 98 plts. Gilt/blindstamped cl (spine sl faded, rubbed). *Bohling.* $150/£97

DAVIS, WILLIAM C. Battle of New Market. GC, (1975). 1st ed. Fine. *Pratt.* $25/£16

DAVIS, WILLIAM C. The Orphan Brigade. GC: Doubleday, 1980. 1st ed. Fine in Fine dj. *Mcgowan.* $30/£19

DAVIS, WILLIAM C. (ed). The Image of War 1861-1865. GC: Doubleday, 1981-4. 6 vols. NF in NF djs. *Mcgowan.* $250/£161

DAVIS, WILLIAM HEATH. Seventy-Five Years in California. SF: John Howell, 1929. One of 2000. 38 plts, fldg facs (dknd), color view on fep; partially unopened. (Worn, spine sunned, ends frayed; nscrip.) Good. Howes D 136. *Bohling.* $60/£39

DAVIS, WILLIAM HEATH. Seventy-Five Years in California.... Harold A. Small (ed). SF: John Howell, 1967. Gilt-lettered, dec brn cl. Fine. *Harrington.* $45/£29

DAVIS, WILLIAM M. Nimrod of the Sea. NY: Harper, 1874. 1st ed. 403pp (corners worn; tears); 16 plts. Peach cl-backed tan bds (bumped, rubbed, soiled; slit; spine dknd). Fair. Howes D 137. *Blue Mountain.* $45/£29

DAVIS, WILLIAM T. (ed). The New England States. Boston: D.H. Hurd, (1897). 1st ed. 4 vols. Contemp brn morocco over marbled bds, gilt calf spine labels. Good set. *Karmiole.* $200/£129

DAVISON, GRACE L. The Gates of Memory. Solvang: Santa Ynez Valley News, (1955). Signed. Black-ptd cl. Dj (wrinkle). *Dawson.* $35/£23

DAVISON, LAWRENCE H. (Pseud of D.H. Lawrence.) Movements in European History. London: Humphrey Milford, OUP, 1921. 1st ed, 1st binding. 14 maps at end (2 fldg). Brn cl, black-titled spine. Very Nice. *Cady.* $250/£161

DAVSON, HUGH. The Physiology of the Eye. London, 1949. 1st ed. Good. *Fye.* $50/£32

DAVY, HUMPHRY. Elements of Agricultural Chemistry.... London: Longman, et al, 1814. 2nd ed. 479pp; 9 fldg plts. Calf-backed bds (worn). *Second Life.* $225/£145

DAVY, HUMPHRY. On the Safety Lamp for Coal Miners; With Some Reflections on Flame. London: Ptd for R. Hunter, 1818. Fldg enr frontis, viii,148pp (lib stamp tp, eps). 3/4 leather (joints, corners rubbed). *Schoyer.* $750/£484

DAWE, GEORGE. The Life of George Morland. London, (ca 1895). Color frontis, 221pp; 55 gravure illus, guards. Uncut. (Cl stained.) *Argosy.* $125/£81

DAWS, GAVAN. Shoal of Time. A History of the Hawaiian Islands. NY: Macmillan, (1968). 1st ed. Fine in Fine dj. *Book Market.* $50/£32

DAWSON, FIELDING. The Dream / Thunder Road. L.A.: Black Sparrow, 1972. 1st ed. One of 200 numbered, signed. VF. *Reese.* $25/£16

DAWSON, FIELDING. The Greatest Story Ever Told: A Transformation. Black Sparrow, 1973. One of 200 numbered, signed. Fine in acetate dj. *Dermont.* $35/£23

DAWSON, FIELDING. Krazy Kat and 76 More. Santa Barbara: Black Sparrow, 1982. 1st ed. One of 250 numbered, signed. Fine. *Reese.* $30/£19

DAWSON, FIELDING. Open Road. Black Sparrow, 1970. One of 200 numbered, signed. Acetate dj. *Dermont.* $35/£23

DAWSON, FIELDING. The Sun Rises Into the Sky. Black Sparrow, 1974. One of 200 numbered, signed. Fine dj. *Dermont.* $35/£23

DAWSON, FIELDING. Will She Understand? Santa Rosa: Black Sparrow, 1988. One of 150 numbered, signed. Cl, pict bds. Fine. *Reese.* $30/£19

DAWSON, FIELDING. The Yin and Yang Radio Repair Man. Black Sparrow, 1970. One of 126 numbered, signed. Fine in dec wrappers. *Dermont.* $25/£16

DAWSON, GEORGE. Pleasures of Angling with Rod and Reel for Trout and Salmon. NY: Sheldon, 1876. 1st ed. xiv,(ii)264pp, 4 plts. (Fr hinge starting; bumped, rubbed.) VG. *Blue Mountain.* $285/£184

DAWSON, JOHN P. A History of Lay Judges. Cambridge: Harvard Univ Press, 1960. Nice in dj. *Boswell.* $85/£55

DAWSON, MARY. The Mary Dawson Game Book.... Phila: McKay, (1916). 1st ed. Blue cl. VG. *Petrilla.* $35/£23

DAWSON, W.F. Christmas: Its Origin and Associations.... London, 1902. Teg. Illus cl (sl soiled, spine chipped; hinges sl cracked). *Edwards.* $116/£75

DAWSON, WARREN R. Magician and Leech. London: Methuen, (1929). 3 plts. Good. *Archaeologia.* $85/£55

DAWSON, WILLIAM LEON and LYNDS JONES. The Birds of Ohio...Description of the 320 Species of Birds.... Columbus, 1903. 1st ed. 2 vols. 80 color plts. Buckram. *Argosy.* $250/£161

DAWSON, WILLIAM LEON. The Birds of California. San Diego: South Moulton, 1923. Students' ed. 3 vols. Grn cl (sl edgewear; spine faded). Overall VG. *Parker.* $325/£210

DAWSON, WILLIAM LEON. The Birds of Ohio. Columbus: Wheaton, 1903. 1st ed. Spine ends lt worn, else VG. *Mikesh.* $75/£48

Day in a Child's Life. London: Routledge, (1881). 1st ed, 1st issue, in sunflower binding. Kate Greenaway (illus). Post 4to. Glazed, beveled, linen-backed pict bds (sl wear, lt mks). Good. *Ash.* $302/£195

DAY, DONALD and HARRY HERBERT ULLOM (eds). The Autobiography of Sam Houston. Norman: Univ of OK, 1954. 1st ed. VG (fore-edge lt foxed) in dj. *Cahan.* $35/£23

DAY, HAROLD A.E. East Anglican Painters. Eastbourne: Fine Art Publishers, 1968-9. One of 1000. 3 vols, all inscribed. Vol 1 bound in cl, vols 2-3 in buckram. All with b/w illus mtd on upper bds. Vols 2,3 in protective cellophane cvr (sl taped to pastedowns). *Edwards.* $271/£175

DAY, HAROLD A.E. John Constable, R.A. 1776-1837. Eastbourne: Fine Art Publishers, 1975. 218 b/w, 5 color plts. Dj. *Edwards.* $70/£45

DAY, J. WENTWORTH. Here Are Ghosts and Witches. London: Batsford, 1954. 1st ed. 10 full-pg illus by Michael Ayrton. VG in dj (sl rubbed). *Hollett.* $85/£55

DAY, JEREMIAH. An Introduction to Algebra. New Haven: Durrie & Peck, 1839. 332pp; 2 fldg plts. Full leather. Good (fr cvr loose; foxing; lt pencilling). *Smithfield.* $25/£16

DAY, LEWIS F. Lettering in Ornament. London: Batsford, (1914). 2nd rev ed. Olive grn cl. Fine. *Glenn.* $65/£42

DAY, LEWIS F. Nature in Ornament. London: Batsford, 1929. 2nd ed rev. 81 plts. VG + in dj (sl worn). *Willow House.* $31/£20

DAY, LEWIS F. Pensmanship of the XVI, XVII, and XVIIth Centuries. London: Batsford, n.d. Unpaginated. Frontis, 112 plts. (Sl soiled, spine lt faded.) *Edwards.* $70/£45

DAY, LEWIS F. and MARY BUCKLE. Art in Needlework. London: Batsford, 1900. 1st ed. (Fr hinge internally cracked, foxing, contemp ink inscrip half-title.) *Bookpress.* $125/£81

DAY, LEWIS F. and MARY BUCKLE. Art in Needlework. London: Batsford, 1907. 3rd ed, rev, enlgd. (Soil; hinges cracked; sm nick.) *Edwards.* $39/£25

DAY, THOMAS. The History of Sandford and Merton. Phila: Lippincott, 1868. 8vo. 532pp; 6 VF full-pg engrs; brn eps. Burgundy tooled cl, gilt. VF (spine faded). *Hobbyhorse.* $100/£65

DAY, WILLIAM. Headaches. Phila, 1882. 322pp. Good. *Fye.* $50/£32

DAY-LEWIS, C. Beechen Vigil and Other Poems. Fortune, 1925. 1st ed, 1st bk. Inscrip; wrappers frayed along yapped edges, o/w Fine. *Poetry.* $93/£60

DAY-LEWIS, C. The Buried Day. London, 1960. 1st ed. Photo frontis. Fine in dj (sl soiled). *Polyanthos.* $35/£23

DAY-LEWIS, C. Country Comets. London: Martin Hopkinson, 1928. 1st ed. Possible rmdr binding. Faded/mottled, o/w Nice in dj. *Pharos.* $125/£81

DAY-LEWIS, C. Dick Willoughby. Blackwell, n.d. 1st ed. Color frontis. Contents Good (corners sl rubbed). *Whiteson.* $37/£24

DAY-LEWIS, C. The Friendly Tree. Cape, 1936. 1st ed. VG in dj (sl rubbed). *Whiteson.* $62/£40

DAY-LEWIS, C. From Feathers to Iron. London: Hogarth, 1931. 1st ed. Ptd yellow bds (sl rubbed, dust soiled). *Cox.* $39/£25

DAY-LEWIS, C. From Feathers to Iron. London: Hogarth Press, 1931. 1st ed. Yellow bds. Fine. *Pharos.* $45/£29

DAY-LEWIS, C. From Feathers to Iron. Hogarth Press, 1931. Rev copy. VG. *Words Etc.* $101/£65

DAY-LEWIS, C. The Magnetic Mountain. Hogarth Press, 1933. 1st ed. VG. *Words Etc.* $85/£55

DAY-LEWIS, C. The Magnetic Mountain. Hogarth, 1933. 1st trade ed. Ltd to 500. Red-lettered pict bds. (Pencil notes reps.) *Waterfield.* $23/£15

DAY-LEWIS, C. Noah and the Waters. London: Hogarth Press, 1936. 1st UK ed. VG + in VG dj (foxed, spine sl grubby). *Williams.* $39/£25

DAY-LEWIS, C. The Poet's Task. Oxford: Clarendon, 1951. 1st ed. VG in ptd wraps. *Antic Hay.* $20/£13

DAY-LEWIS, C. The Poet's Task: An Inaugural Lecture Delivered...on 1 June 1951. Oxford: Clarendon Press, 1951. Presumably 1st issue; untrimmed. VG in sewn wraps. *Pharos.* $30/£19

DAY-LEWIS, C. Requiem for the Living. NY: Harper & Row, (1964). 1st Amer ed. Rev copy w/inserted slip. NF (stain top edge) in dj. *Antic Hay.* $45/£29

DAY-LEWIS, C. Revolution in Writing. London, 1935. 1st Eng ed. VG (edges lt spotted; spine faded) in wrappers. *Ulysses.* $39/£25

DAY-LEWIS, C. Starting Point. NY: Harper, 1938. 1st Amer ed. Ink name, 1938 date, else VG in dj (nicks, short tears, lt edgewear). *Godot.* $75/£48

DAY-LEWIS, C. Transitional Poem. Hogarth Press, 1929. Rev copy. VG. *Words Etc.* $101/£65

DAYES, EDWARD. A Picturesque Tour in Yorkshire and Derbyshire. London: John Nichols, 1825. 2nd ed. viii,204pp, uncut, 14 steel-engr plts (some sl spotted). Blue bds (worn, rebacked). *Hollett.* $248/£160

DAYTON, FRED ERVING. Steamboat Days. NY: Stokes, 1925. 1st ed. Color frontis by John Wolcott Adams. Gilt stamped dk blue cl. VG. *Houle.* $95/£61

DE AMICIS, E. Morocco; Its People and Places. London, 1882. 392pp. Contemp 1/2 calf (sl worn; ex-lib). *Lewis.* $65/£42

DE ARMENT, ROBERT K. Bat Masterson. Norman, 1979. 1st ed. Fine in dj (sl shelfworn). *Baade.* $50/£32

DE ARMENT, ROBERT K. Knights of the Green Cloth. Univ of OK, (1982). 1st ed. VF in VF dj. *Oregon.* $30/£19

DE BALZAC, HONORE. Old Goriot. NY: LEC, 1948. #904/1500 numbered, signed by Rene Ben Sussan (illus). Half leather, marbled bds. Fine in slipcase (sl rubbed). *Hermitage.* $75/£48

DE BALZAC, HONORE. The Works of H. De Balzac. Phila: Gebbie Pub Co., 1897, 98, 99. #21/1000. 24 vols. 3/4 red morocco, ribbed gilt dec spines. Teg, others uncut. *D & D.* $975/£629

DE BARTHE, JOE. Life and Adventures of Frank Grouard. Univ of OK, (1958). Rpt of 1894 ed. 2 maps. VG in VG dj. Howes D 183. *Oregon.* $45/£29

DE BEAUVOIR, MARQUIS. Voyage Round the World. London: John Murray, 1870-2. 3 vols. Fldg frontis, xii,(308); vi,388; (xii),(292)pp, 14 plts (2 fldg); aeg. 3/4 dk blue morocco (spine mks; bkpls). *Schoyer.* $225/£145

DE BEAUVOIR, SIMONE. All Men Are Mortal. Leonard Friedman (trans). Cleveland/NY: World, (1955). 1st US ed. Nice in dj (chipped, worn). *Second Life.* $65/£42

DE BEAUVOIR, SIMONE. Force of Circumstance. NY: Putnam's, (1963). 1st Amer ed. Fine in dj (price-clipped). *Hermitage.* $40/£26

DE BEAUVOIR, SIMONE. The Long March. Cleveland/NY: World, (1958). 1st ed. Nice in dj (sl soiled). *Second Life.* $65/£42

DE BEAUVOIR, SIMONE. Memoirs of a Dutiful Daughter. Cleveland: World, (1959). 1st ed. VG + (lt stain top) in dj (shelfworn, snag, spine lt faded). *Aka.* $25/£16

DE BEAUVOIR, SIMONE. The Second Sex. NY: Knopf, 1953. 1st US ed. VG+ in VG- dj (shallow chipping; abrasion rear flap fold wearing through in places). *Lame Duck.* $50/£32

DE BEER, G.R. Alps and Men. London, 1932. 1st ed. 16 plts. *Bickersteth.* $34/£22

DE BEER, G.R. Alps and Men. London: Edward Arnold, 1932. 1st ed. 16pp of plts, sketch-map, ep maps. VG. *Hollett.* $54/£35

DE BEER, G.R. Early Travellers in the Alps. London, 1930. 1st ed. 40 plts. *Bickersteth.* $54/£35

DE BEER, G.R. Early Travellers in the Alps. London: Sidgwick & Jackson, 1930. 1st ed. 40 plts. Lt spots to flyleaves, fore-edges, o/w Fine in dj. *Hollett.* $70/£45

DE BEERSKI, P. JEANNERAT. Angkor. Boston/NY, 1924. 1st ed. Map, plan. (Spine sl rubbed; sm chip.) *Edwards.* $54/£35

DE BERNIERES, LOUIS. Captain Corelli's Mandolin. Secker & Warburg, 1994. 1st issue, in white bds. Signed, dated. Fine in dj. *Rees.* $47/£30

DE BERNIERES, LOUIS. The Troublesome Offspring of Cardinal Guzman. London: Secker & Warburg, 1992. 1st ed. Signed. Bump, o/w Fine in dj. *Rees.* $31/£20

DE BERNIERES, LOUIS. The War of Don Emmanuel's Nether Parts. Secker & Warburg, 1990. 1st ed. Signed, dated. Upper edges bumped, o/w Fine in dj. *Rees.* $54/£35

DE BETHEL, DAVID (comp). The Tyrolese Cookery Book. London: Medici Soc, 1937. Dec paper over bds, buckram spine. Sl dirty, eps browned, else VG. *Heller.* $25/£16

DE BETHEL, DAVID. Bouquet Garni: Good Dishes from la Belle France. London: Medici Soc, 1939. Dec paper bds. Sl worn, eps browned, o/w Good. *Heller.* $25/£16

DE BLES, ARTHUR. How to Distinguish the Saints in Art. NY: Art Culture Publications Inc, 1925. 1st ed. Blue cl, gilt. Good. *Karmiole.* $30/£19

DE BRUNHOFF, JEAN. Babar and Father Christmas. Merle S. Haas (trans). NY: Random House, (1940). 1st Amer ed in English ($3 on dw). Folio, unpaginated. L. de Brunhoff (illus). VG (ink inscrip, bkpl) in VG dj. *Davidson.* $375/£242

DE BRUNHOFF, LAURENT. Babar's Picnic. Merle Haas (trans). NY: Random House, (1949). 1st Amer ed. Sm folio. Cl-backed illus bds (sl edge chipping). *Reisler.* $250/£161

DE BRUNHOFF, LAURENT. Babar's Visit to Bird Island. London: Methuen, (1952). 1st Eng ed. Sm folio. Cl-backed illus bds (minor edgewear). *Reisler.* $300/£194

DE CAMP, L. SPRAGUE and CATHERINE C. Ancient Ruins and Archaeology. GC, NY: Doubleday, 1964. 1st ed. VG in dj. *Worldwide.* $24/£15

DE CAMP, L. SPRAGUE and CATHERINE. The Day of the Dinosaur. Doubleday, 1968. 1st ed. Fine in dj. *Madle.* $150/£97

DE CAMP, L. SPRAGUE and FLETCHER PRATT. The Carnelian Cube. Gnome, 1948. NF in dj (frayed; spine chipped). *Madle.* $65/£42

DE CAMP, L. SPRAGUE and FLETCHER PRATT. Wall of Serpents. Avalon, 1960. 1st ed. Author sig laid in. Fine in dj. *Madle.* $175/£113

DE CAMP, L. SPRAGUE and P. SCHUYLER MILLER. Genus Homo. Fantasy, 1950. 1st ed. VG in Good dj. *Aronovitz.* $35/£23

DE CAMP, L. SPRAGUE and P. SCHUYLER MILLER. Genus Homo. Fantasy, 1950. 1st ed. Fine in dj (sl frayed). *Madle.* $75/£48

DE CAMP, L. SPRAGUE and P. SCHUYLER MILLER. Genus Homo. Reading, PA: Fantasy, 1950. 1st ed. One of 500 numbered, signed on tipped-in sheet. Lt offset from old dj protector, else Fine in dj. *Reese.* $200/£129

DE CAMP, L. SPRAGUE and STANLEY WEINBAUM. Fantasy Twin. Fantasy Pub, 1951. 1st ed. Fine in dj (sl frayed). *Madle.* $100/£65

DE CAMP, L. SPRAGUE. The Arrows of Hercules. GC: Doubleday, 1965. 1st ed. Fine in dj (sl wear). *Antic Hay.* $65/£42

DE CAMP, L. SPRAGUE. The Arrows of Hercules. Doubleday, 1965. 1st ed. Fine in dj. *Madle.* $75/£48

DE CAMP, L. SPRAGUE. The Castle of Iron. Gnome, 1950. 1st ed. NF in dj. *Madle.* $45/£29

DE CAMP, L. SPRAGUE. Demons and Dinosaurs. Sauk City: Arkham House, 1970. 1st ed. Bkpl, else Fine in dj (lt soiled; chip, edgewear). *Other Worlds.* $200/£129

DE CAMP, L. SPRAGUE. Demons and Dinosaurs. Arkham House, 1970. 1st ed. Fine in dj (dust soiled). *Madle.* $300/£194

DE CAMP, L. SPRAGUE. Divide and Rule. Fantasy, 1948. 1st ed. Signed. Fine in dj (sm chip). *Madle.* $60/£39

DE CAMP, L. SPRAGUE. The Dragon of the Ishtar Gate. GC: Doubleday, 1961. NF in dj (sl wear; price-clipped). *Antic Hay.* $50/£32

DE CAMP, L. SPRAGUE. The Glory That Was. Avalon, 1960. 1st ed. Fine in dj (tear). *Madle.* $60/£39

DE CAMP, L. SPRAGUE. The Golden Wind. Doubleday, 1969. 1st ed. NF in dj (chipped). *Madle.* $50/£32

DE CAMP, L. SPRAGUE. The Golden Wind. GC: Doubleday, 1969. 1st ed. NF (sl soil) in dj (browning; 1-inch tear). *Antic Hay.* $50/£32

DE CAMP, L. SPRAGUE. Lovecraft: A Biography. London, 1975. 1st British ed. Fine in dj. *Madle.* $40/£26

DE CAMP, L. SPRAGUE. Rogue Queen. Doubleday, 1951. 1st ed. Fine in dj (frayed). *Madle.* $85/£55

DE CAMP, L. SPRAGUE. Scribblings. NESFA Press, 1972. 1st ed. One of 500 numbered. Signed. Fine in dj. *Madle.* $90/£58

DE CAMP, L. SPRAGUE. The Search for Zei. NY: Avalon, (1962). 1st ed. VG (sl stain rear cvr; few pp edges browned) in dj. *Antic Hay.* $45/£29

DE CAMP, L. SPRAGUE. The Search for Zei. Avalon, 1962. 1st ed. Fine in dj. *Madle.* $75/£48

DE CAMP, L. SPRAGUE. Solomon's Stone. Avalon, 1957. 1st ed. Fine in dj. *Madle.* $75/£48

DE CAMP, L. SPRAGUE. The Tower of Zanid. Avalon, 1958. 1st ed. Fine in dj (sl frayed). *Madle.* $75/£48

DE CAMP, L. SPRAGUE. Wheels of If. Shasta, 1948. 1st ed. NF in dj (sl chipped). *Madle.* $90/£58

DE CASSERES, BENJAMIN. Mencken and Shaw. NY, (1930). 1st ed. (Eps browned; cvrs discolored; sl cocked.) Poor dj. *King.* $25/£16

DE CASSERES, BENJAMIN. The Shadow-Eater. NY: Albert & Charles Boni, 1915. 1st ed, 1st issue; one of 500 trade copies of 650. 1st bk. Unopened. Lt edgewear, o/w VG. *Reese.* $50/£32

DE CHAIR, SOMERSET. The Golden Carpet. London: Faber & Faber, 1946. 3rd imp. Color fldg map. Sl rubbed, soiled, o/w VG. *Worldwide.* $30/£19

DE CHARDIN, PIERRE TEILHARD. The Future of Man. London: Collins, 1964. 1st Eng ed. Red cl. NF in dj (soiled). *Dalian.* $23/£15

DE CHARDIN, TEILHARD. Letters from a Traveller. London, 1962. 1st Eng ed. 4 plts; dbl-pg map. Fine. *Henly.* $14/£9

DE CORONADO, FRANCISCO VAZQUEZ. Journey of Francisco Vazquez de Coronado. SF: Grabhorn, 1933. 1st thus. VG-. *Parker.* $225/£145

DE COSTER, CHARLES. The Glorious Adventures of Tyl Ulenspiegl. Harlem: LEC, 1934. #1150/1500 signed by Richard Floethe (illus). Fine in slipcase (sl worn). *Williams.* $62/£40

DE COSTER, CHARLES. The Glorious Adventures of Tyl Ulenspiegl. Allan Ross MacDougal (trans). Haarlem: LEC, 1934. #904/1500 numbered, signed by Richard Floethe (illus). Fine in pub's slipcase. *Hermitage.* $85/£55

DE CRESPIGNY, CLAUDE CHAMPION. Forty Years of a Sportsman's Life. London, 1925. New & rev ed. Frontis port. (Feps lt browned; chip, sl dented.) *Edwards.* $31/£20

DE CRESPIGNY, E.C. A New London Flora. London, 1877. xxiv,179pp + 20pp ads. (Text underlining.) *Henly.* $23/£15

DE FONTERIZ, LUIS. Red Terror in Madrid. London: Longmans, Green, 1937. 1st ed. Nice. *Patterson.* $78/£50

DE GAURY, GERALD. Arabian Journey and Other Desert Travels. London: Harrap, 1950. 1st ed. Sl sun staining, else NF. *Great Epic.* $45/£29

DE GIUSTINO, DAVID. Conquest of Mind-Phrenology and Victorian Social Thought. London, 1975. 1st ed. Good in dj. *Fye.* $40/£26

DE GONCOURT, EDMOND and JULES. The Woman of the Eighteenth Century. Jacques Le Clercq & Ralph Roeder (trans). NY: Balch, 1927. 1st ed. Good (hinge tender; cvrs sl soiled). *Second Life.* $45/£29

DE GRAZIA, TED. Father Junipero Serra. Ward Ritchie, (1969). 1st ed. VG in VG dj. *Oregon.* $45/£29

DE GROOT, IRENE and ROBERT VORSTMAN. Sailing Ships. Prints by the Dutch Masters.... NY, 1980. Good in dj. *Washton.* $45/£29

DE HAAS, ARLINE. The Jazz Singer. NY: Grosset, (1927). Motion picture ed. 2pp pub's ads at end. VG in color pict dj (sm chips). *Houle.* $85/£55

DE HASS, FRANK S. Buried Cities Recovered. Phila: Bradley, 1892. Rev ed. 610pp. Edges rubbed, o/w VG. *Worldwide.* $45/£29

DE HASS, WILLS. History of the Early Settlement and Indian Wars of Western Virginia. Wheeling: H. Hoblitzell, 1851. 1st ed. Frontis; 416pp; 5 plts. Pub's blindstamped cl. (Ex-lib w/mks; bkpl; waterstains through text; binding worn.) Howes D 223. *Bookpress.* $285/£184

DE HOVEDEN, ROGER. Annals of Roger de Hoveden. London: H.G. Bohn, 1853. 2 vols. xii,564; (i)556pp. Teg. 1/2 morocco, gold spine, raised bands; marbled eps. NF (extrems lt rubbed, owner blindstamp). *Cahan.* $85/£55

DE HUFF, ELIZABETH W. Say the Bells of Old Missions. St Louis: B. Herder, 1943. 1st ed. VG- (ink name; fep corner clipped). *Parker.* $30/£19

DE JONG, MEINDERT. The House of Sixty Fathers. NY: Harper, (1956). 1st ed. 8vo. Maurice Sendak (illus). Lt tan cl, red lettering, dec. Good in illus dj (lt worn). *Reisler.* $275/£177

DE JONG, MEINDERT. The Singing Hill. London: Lutterworth, (1963). 1st Eng ed. 8vo. Maurice Sendak (illus). Illus grn bds; in matching dj (sl marginal wear). *Reisler.* $75/£48

DE KAY, J.E. Natural History of New York. Part One. Zoology. NY: Appleton, 1843. 4to. 2 parts. iv,(2),271; (3),70pp; 53 plts. (Foxed; bottom outer corner leaves chewed.) Gilt cl (rebacked, orig spine; very worn). *Goodrich.* $250/£161

DE KAY, J.E. Zoology of New York or The New York Fauna. Part III, IV. Albany, 1842. 2 vols. vi,(1),98; xiv,(1),415pp, 102 plts (fore-edges dampstained; few browned). (Rebacked w/most of orig backstrips; wear; lt foxed.) Sutton. $195/£126

DE KAY, J.E. Zoology of New York. Part 1. Mammalia. Bound w/intro to the Series. Albany, 1842. (3),188; xiii,(1),146pp (prelims foxed); 30 (of 35) plts incl 24 (of 29) hand-colored plts of mammals. (Corners worn; backstrip partially gone, reinforced w/tape; starting to split in center.) Sutton. $285/£184

DE KOCK, PAUL. Memoirs.... Leonard Smithers, 1899. 1st Eng ed. Pub's blue rib-grain blindstamped cl. Excellent (spine sl dknd). Waterfield. $54/£35

DE KUN, NICHOLAS. The Mineral Resources of Africa. Amsterdam/London/NY: Elsevier, 1965. VG. Schoyer. $75/£48

DE LA BECHE, H.T. The Geological Observer. London, 1853. 2nd ed. xxviii,740pp. Good. Henly. $81/£52

DE LA FAILLE, J.B. The Works of Vincent Van Gogh. (NY): Reynal & Co, (1970). 1st ed. 56 color plts. Gray linen. Good in illus dj (sl chipped). Karmiole. $150/£97

DE LA FAYETTE, MME. The Death of Madame. Paris: Harrison of Paris, 1931. One of 325. Signed by Monroe Wheeler (pub). Aeg. Full vellum, gilt title; sewing threads worked through spine. Pub's gilt-titled case (sl worn). Book Block. $125/£81

DE LA MARE, WALTER. Alone. London: Faber & Gwyer, (1927). 1st ed. One of 350 numbered. Flexible pict bds. VF in glassine dj. Macdonnell. $40/£26

DE LA MARE, WALTER. Alone. (London: Faber & Gwyer, n.d.) Ordinary issue. Sl dusty, else Fine in red pict wrappers. Pharos. $25/£16

DE LA MARE, WALTER. Broomsticks and Other Tales. Constable, 1925. 1st ed. (Sl faded one side.) Bickersteth. $34/£22

DE LA MARE, WALTER. The Burning Glass and Other Poems. Faber & Faber, (1945). 1st ed. Untrimmed. (Ink inscrip.) Dj (sl defective spine top; sl soiled). Bickersteth. $31/£20

DE LA MARE, WALTER. The Connoisseur and Other Stories. W. Collins Sons, (1926). 1st ed. Bds, buckram spine, pict design upper cvr. Bickersteth. $39/£25

DE LA MARE, WALTER. The Connoisseur and Other Stories. London: Collins, 1926. 1st ed. Uncut. Cl-backed bds, gilt. VG. Hollett. $39/£25

DE LA MARE, WALTER. Crossings: A Fairy Play.... London, (1923). 1st Eng trade ed. Cl-backed bds, grn morocco lettering piece. Good in dj (spine-faded; sl frayed). Waterfield. $47/£30

DE LA MARE, WALTER. Desert Islands and Robinson Crusoe. London/NY: Faber & Faber/Fountain Press, 1930. 1st ed ltd to 650, this being out of series (written in ink), signed. (iii),286pp. VF full-pg engr 1/2 title by Rex Whistler (lt offsetting facing pg). Engr head-, tailpieces w/tissue guards. Fine. Hobbyhorse. $150/£97

DE LA MARE, WALTER. Desert Islands and Robinson Crusoe. Faber & Faber, 1930. 1st ed. Add'l pict tp; pict eps. (Spine faded.) Pict inscrip by J.B. Priestley. Bickersteth. $93/£60

DE LA MARE, WALTER. Ding Dong Bell. London: Selwyn & Blount, 1924. 1st ed. Browned pastedowns, spine sl rubbed, o/w VG w/spare paper label in VG dj (sl chipped, spine browned). Virgo. $62/£40

DE LA MARE, WALTER. Down-Adown-Derry. London: Constable, (1922). Lg paper copy of 1st Eng ed. 193pp, 3 color plts by Dorothy P. Lathrop. Pict blue cl. Schoyer. $125/£81

DE LA MARE, WALTER. The Dutch Cheese and Other Stories. London: Faber & Faber, (1946). 1st ed. NF in dj (tears; sm spine chip). Antic Hay. $25/£16

DE LA MARE, WALTER. The Fleeting and Other Poems. Constable, (1933). 1st ed. (Ink name.) Bickersteth. $34/£22

DE LA MARE, WALTER. A Forward Child. Faber & Faber, (1934). Dj (sl creased; upper edge chipped). Bickersteth. $31/£20

DE LA MARE, WALTER. Henry Brocken, His Travels and Adventures.... London: John Murray, 1904. 1st ed, 1st issue, w/plain top edge; lacks closing bracket after 'Ramal' on tp. Dec cl, gilt. Nice (lt mks, signs of age). Ash. $132/£85

DE LA MARE, WALTER. Inward Companion. London: Faber, 1950. 1st ed. Untrimmed. VG. Hollett. $23/£15

DE LA MARE, WALTER. Lewis Carroll. London: Faber & Faber, (1932). 1st ed. VG (spine cocked) in dj (sm chips, tears; spine browning). Antic Hay. $45/£29

DE LA MARE, WALTER. Lewis Carroll. London: Faber & Faber, 1932. 62pp. Linen on bd, gilt spine title (water spots cvrs; eps foxed). Good. Hobbyhorse. $50/£32

DE LA MARE, WALTER. Memoirs of a Midget. London, (1921). 1st issue, w/o 'Printed in Great Britain' on verso tp. Fine in dj (rubbed; spine frayed). Waterfield. $47/£30

DE LA MARE, WALTER. Mr. Bumps and His Monkey. Phila: John C. Winston, (1942). 1st ed. Pict paper over bds (spine chipped; edgewear). VG in dj (lt worn). Glenn. $65/£42

DE LA MARE, WALTER. News. London: Faber & Faber, 1930. Signed ltd ed of 300. Blue bds. VG (wear; cvrs spotted). Antic Hay. $45/£29

DE LA MARE, WALTER. O Lovely England and Other Poems. London: Faber & Faber, (1953). 1st ed. NF in dj (chipped). Sadlon. $15/£10

DE LA MARE, WALTER. On the Edge. Faber & Faber, (1930). 1st ed. Dj (top chipped; spine top defective; ink name). Bickersteth. $34/£22

DE LA MARE, WALTER. On the Edge. London: Faber, 1930. 1st ed. (Sl faded.) Hollett. $31/£20

DE LA MARE, WALTER. On the Edge. London: Faber & Faber, 1930. Signed ltd ed of 300 numbered. Pink cl; teg. VG (sm stain spine head). Antic Hay. $75/£48

DE LA MARE, WALTER. On the Edge: Short Stories. London: Faber & Faber, 1930. Lg-paper ed ltd to 300 signed. Teg. Unopened. Rose cl, gilt. Spine sl mkd, else Very Nice. Cady. $35/£23

DE LA MARE, WALTER. Poems 1901 to 1918. London: Constable, (1920). 1st trade ed. 2 vols. Gilt-dec cl (sl lightened spots). Sadlon. $30/£19

DE LA MARE, WALTER. Poems 1919 to 1934. Constable, (1935). 1st ed. Untrimmed. Good (lt spotting eps) in dj. Bickersteth. $39/£25

DE LA MARE, WALTER. Poems. London: John Murray, 1906. 1st ed. Dec grn cl. VG (lt foxing). Antic Hay. $75/£48

DE LA MARE, WALTER. The Return. London: W. Collins Sons, (1922). Rev ed. Signed ltd ed of 250 numbered. Leather spine label. Good (binding browned). Antic Hay. $50/£32

DE LA MARE, WALTER. The Riddle and Other Stories. Selwyn & Blount, (May, 1923). 1st ed. (Sm slit spine top.) *Bickersteth.* $34/£22

DE LA MARE, WALTER. Self to Self. London: Faber & Gwyer, 1928. 1st ed. One of 500 numbered, signed. White bds, gilt. Fine. *Macdonnell.* $45/£29

DE LA MARE, WALTER. Self to Self. (London: Faber & Gwyer, 1928.) Ordinary issue. Fine in yellow wrappers. *Pharos.* $25/£16

DE LA MARE, WALTER. A Snowdrop. (London: Faber & Faber, n.d.) Ordinary issue. Fine in grn wrappers. *Pharos.* $20/£13

DE LA MARE, WALTER. Stories from the Bible. Faber & Gwyer, 1929. 1st ed. Dec eps. (Upper cvr edges, spine faded.) Dj (upper edge chipped.) *Bickersteth.* $34/£22

DE LA MARE, WALTER. Stuff and Nonsense and So On. Constable, 1927. 1st ed. Teg, rest untrimmed. (Upper cvr sl spotted.) *Bickersteth.* $39/£25

DE LA MARE, WALTER. Thus Her Tale. Edinburgh: Porpoise Press, 1923. 1st ed. Ptd wrappers. *Bickersteth.* $28/£18

DE LA MARE, WALTER. Two Tales: I. The Green Room. II. The Connoisseur. London: The Bookman's Journal, (1925). Ltd to 250. Signed. Teg. Vellum-backed dec bds. *Sadlon.* $75/£48

DE LA MARE, WALTER. The Winnowing Dream. London: Faber & Faber, (1954). 1st ed. NF in sewn ptd wraps w/orig mailing envelope. *Antic Hay.* $20/£13

DE LA NOY, MICHAEL. Denton Welch; the Making of a Writer. London, 1984. 1st ed. Fine in dj. *Words Etc.* $31/£20

DE LA PENA, JOSE ENRIQUE. With Santa Anna in Texas. Carmen Perry (trans, ed). College Station: TX A&M, 1975. 1st ed. Dj. *Lambeth.* $30/£19

DE LA REE, GERRY (ed). The Book of Virgil Finlay. Gerry De La Ree, 1975. 1st ed. Fine in dj. *Madle.* $150/£97

DE LA REE, GERRY (ed). The Fourth Book of Virgil Finlay. Gerry De La Ree, 1979. 1st ed. Fine in dj. *Madle.* $75/£48

DE LA REE, GERRY (ed). The Second Book of Virgil Finlay. Gerry De La Ree, 1978. 1st ed. Fine in dj. *Madle.* $100/£65

DE LA REE, GERRY et al. Bok.... Saddle River: De La Ree, 1974. 1st ed. One of 500 numbered. Rear cvr creased, else NF in pict wrappers. *Other Worlds.* $20/£13

DE LA TORRE, LILLIAN. Dr. Sam: Johnson, Detector. NY: Knopf, 1946. 1st Amer ed. NF in dj (price-clipped). *Cady.* $30/£19

DE LA TORRE, LILLIAN. Dr. Sam: Johnson, Detector. NY: Knopf, 1946. 1st ed. Fine in dj. *Mordida.* $45/£29

DE LA VEGA, GARCILASO. The Florida of the Inca. John Grier Varner & Jeannette Johnson Varner (trans). Austin: Univ of TX, 1951. 1st ed thus. VG in dj (chipped). *Schoyer.* $35/£23

DE LABORDE, M. LEON. Journey through Arabia Petraea. London: John Murray, 1838. 2nd ed. Frontis port, xxviii,340pp (2pp sl torn, feps sl spotted), fldg map (foxed), 28 plts (1 w/crease tear). Teg; marbled eps. Contemp gilt-ruled calf bds (corners repaired; sl surface loss). *Edwards.* $279/£180

DE LINT, J.G. Atlas of the History of Medicine. London: Lewis, 1926. Good. *Goodrich.* $95/£61

DE LITTLE, R.J. The Windmill Yesterday and Today. London: John Baker, 1975. VG in dj. *Hollett.* $47/£30

DE LONG, G.W. The Voyage of The Jeanette. Boston: Houghton Mifflin, 1888. 1 vol reprint. xx,911pp. Fldg map rear pocket. Good (inner hinges cracked). *Walcot.* $109/£70

DE MAFFEI, FERNANDA. Michelangelo's Lost St. John: The Story of a Discovery. NY, (1961). 1 mtd color plt. VG in dj, slipcase. *Argosy.* $60/£39

DE MASSEY, ERNEST. A Frenchman in the Gold Rush. Marguerite Eyer Wilbur (trans). SF: CA Hist Soc, 1927. Gold-stamped cl in dj (chipped). *Dawson.* $100/£65

DE MAUPASSANT, GUY. Strong as Death. D. Biddle, 1899. 1st Eng ed. NF. *Fine Books.* $50/£32

DE MICHELI, MARIO. Siqueiros. NY: Abrams, (1968). 1st ed. Fine in linen slipcase. *Karmiole.* $85/£55

DE MIOMANDRE, FRANCIS. The Love Life of Venus. D.P. Girard & T. Malcolm (trans). NY: Brentano's, 1930. 1st Amer ed. Fine in dj. *Reese.* $25/£16

DE MONFREID, HENRY. Hashish. Helen Buchanan Bell (trans). London, 1935. 1st thus. Frontis port, map. (Prelims lt browned; worn.) *Edwards.* $39/£25

DE MONTAIGNE, MICHAEL. The Essays Translated into English. London: For J. Pote et al, 1776. 8th ed. 3 vols. Orig mottled calf (all vols rebacked). Nice set. *Bickersteth.* $171/£110

DE MORGAN, AUGUSTUS. A Budget of Paradoxes. D.E. Smith (ed). Chicago, 1915. 2nd ed. 2 vols. VG. *Argosy.* $75/£48

DE MORGAN, AUGUSTUS. Differential and Integral Calculus, Containing Differentiation, Integration...Also, Elementary Illus...of Calculus. London, 1842. 1st ed. 785pp. VG (rebacked). *Argosy.* $125/£81

DE MORGAN, AUGUSTUS. Newton: His Friend: and His Niece. London: Elliot Stock, 1885. Good (2x1-inch piece torn from top edge rep; foxing) in brn cl (bumped). *Knollwood.* $125/£81

DE NAVARRO, ANTONIO. Causeries on English Pewter. London: Country Life, c. 1911. Signed presentation. (Sl foxing 1st pp.) *Petersfield.* $70/£45

DE PALOL, PEDRO and MAX HIRMER. Early Medieval Art in Spain. London: Thames & Hudson, 1967. 54 tipped in color plts, 256 b/w plts. Dj. *Edwards.* $116/£75

DE PALOL, PEDRO and MAX HIRMER. Early Medieval Art in Spain. NY, n.d. (ca 1966). 54 color illus. Good in dj. *Washton.* $100/£65

DE PALOL, PEDRO. Paleochristian Art in Spain. NY, 1969. Good in dj. *Washton.* $95/£61

DE PAOLA, TOMIE. Georgio's Village. NY: Putnams, 1982, 2nd imp. 20x27 cm. 6 pop-ups. Tomie de Paola (illus). Glazed pict bds. VG. *Book Finders.* $25/£16

DE PEREYRA, DIOMEDES. The Land of the Golden Scarabs. B-M, 1928. 1st ed. VG + in VG dj (dust soil). *Aronovitz.* $65/£42

DE PEREYRA, DIOMEDES. The Land of the Golden Scarabs. Bobbs-Merrill, 1928. 1st ed. Fine in Fine dj. *Madle.* $75/£48

DE PROROK, BYRON KHUN. Digging for Lost African Gods. NY/London: Putnam's, 1926. 1st ed. 43 plts; fldg map. Teg. Sl rubbed, o/w VG. *Worldwide.* $16/£10

DE PUTRON, P. Nooks and Corners of Old Sussex. London: Lewis, 1875. New 1/2 brown morocco. Rubber stamp, tp sl foxed, o/w Fine. *Petersfield.* $96/£62

DE QUILLE, DAN. (Pseud of William Wright). History of the Big Bonanza. Hartford/SF: Amer Pub Co/Bancroft, 1877. 1st ed, 2nd ptg. 569pp. Blue cl, pict gilt spine. VG. Howes W 710. *Schoyer.* $85/£55

DE QUILLE, DAN. (Pseud of William Wright.) History of the Comstock Silver Lode and Mines. Virginia, NV: F. Boegle, 1889. 158pp. Fine in ptd wraps. Howes W 711. *Bohling.* $200/£129

DE QUINCEY, THOMAS. Confessions of an English Opium-Eater. London, 1822. 1st ed. Lacks half-title. Old calf (joint mended). *Argosy.* $750/£484

DE QUINCEY, THOMAS. Confessions of an English Opium-Eater. Oxford: Shakespeare Head Press, 1930. LEC #1264/1520 signed by ptr and Zhenya Gay (artist). Handmade paper. 12 litho plts; teg, others uncut. Buckram-backed marbled bds. VG in slipcase (sl worn). *Cox.* $233/£150

DE QUINCEY, THOMAS. Revolt of the Tartars or, Flight of the Kalmuck Khan.... London: Dropmore Press, 1948. Ltd to 450 numbered. Stuart Boyle (illus). 3/4 brn gilt morocco over tan cl; teg. Good. *Karmiole.* $100/£65

DE REMUSAT, M. PAUL. Memoirs of Madame de Remusat. 1802-1808. Cashel Hoey & John Lillie (trans). London: Sampson et al, 1880. 3rd ed. 2 vols. Full gilt-paneled marbled calf; leather labels; speckled edges. (Sl abrasions.) *Sadlon.* $50/£32

DE RIVER, J. PAUL. The Sexual Criminal. Springfield, 1949. 1st ed. Good. *Fye.* $100/£65

DE ROO, P. History of America before Columbus.... Phila: Lippincott, 1900. 1st ed. Ltd to 1500. 2 vols. 2 frontispieces; 4 dbl-pg, 1 fldg map. Teg. Fine. *Oregon.* $120/£77

DE ROSE, CAMILLE. The Camille de Rose Story. Chicago: author, (1953). 1st ed. Promo brochure laid in. Red cl in illus dj. *Petrilla.* $25/£16

DE RUPERT, A.E.D. Californians and Mormons. NY: John Wurtele Lovell, 1881. 1st ed. 166pp. Dec brn cl (spine sl faded; extrems sl frayed). *Karmiole.* $85/£55

De Sade on Virtue and Vice. A.F. Niemoller (trans). Girard, KS: Haldeman-Julius Pub, (1946). Big Blue Book B-522. Wraps. *Hayman.* $15/£10

DE SADE, MARQUIS. Dialogue between a Priest and a Dying Man.... Chicago, 1927. 1st ed in English, ltd to 650 numbered. Teg. Gilt-stamped bds (worn; outer fr hinge splitting). *King.* $75/£48

DE SAINT-EXUPERY, ANTOINE. Flight to Arras. NY, (1942). 1st Amer ed. Lt stained, else Good in dj (price-clipped, used). *King.* $35/£23

DE SAINT-EXUPERY, ANTOINE. The Little Prince. NY: Reynal & Hitchcock, 1943. 1st ed in English. 8vo. 91pp. Peach bds, red title. VG (corners bumped) in dj (lt torn). *Davidson.* $300/£194

DE SAINT-EXUPERY, ANTOINE. The Little Prince. Katherine Woods (trans). London: Heinemann, 1951. Sm 8vo. Frontis, tp, 91pp. Orange linen on bd. VG (ink inscrip). *Hobbyhorse.* $50/£32

DE SAINT-EXUPERY, ANTOINE. The Little Prince. Katherine Woods (trans). NY: Harcourt Brace Jovanovich, 1971. Anniversary Ed. 8vo. 93pp. Glossy grn paper on bd, pict gilt titles. VF in color pict slipcase. *Hobbyhorse.* $75/£48

DE SAINT-EXUPERY, ANTOINE. Night Flight. Century, 1932. 1st ed. VG+ in VG dj. *Bishop.* $40/£26

DE SAINT-EXUPERY, ANTOINE. Wind, Sand and Stars. London: Heinemann, 1939. 1st ed. Prelims spotted, o/w Nice in dj (frayed on top, bottom edges). *Patterson.* $78/£50

DE SAULCY, F. Narrative of a Journey around the Dead Sea and in the Bible Lands. Phila: Parry & M'Millan, 1854. 2 vols. Fldg frontis map, 968pp (2pp w/tears, 1pg chipped), 2 woodcuts. (Sigs rubbed; spines chipped.) *Archaeologia.* $125/£81

DE SCHWEINITZ, EDMUND. The Life and Times of David Zeisberger.... Phila: Lippincott, 1871. Contents VG (binding frayed, hinges cracked). *Cullen.* $150/£97

DE SOUZA, BARETTO. Advanced Equitation. NY: E.P. Dutton, (1926). 1st ed. Frontis. Blue cl. VG. *Weber.* $30/£19

DE STEIN, E. The Poets in Picardy. London, 1919. (Bkpl.) Dj. *Edrich.* $39/£25

DE STOLZ, MADAME. The House on Wheels. E.F. Adams (trans). Boston: Lee & Shepard, 1871. 303pp. Aeg. Good (hinges loose). *Second Life.* $35/£23

DE TERAMOND, GUY. Mystery of Lucien Delorme. Appleton, 1915. 1st ed. VG. *Madle.* $30/£19

DE TERAN, LISA ST. AUBIN. Keepers of the House. Cape, 1982. 1st UK ed. Fine in dj. *Lewton.* $39/£25

DE TERAN, LISA ST. AUBIN. The Slow Train to Milan. Cape, 1983. 1st UK ed. Signed. Fine in dj (price-clipped). *Williams.* $39/£25

DE TOCQUEVILLE, ALEXIS. Democracy in America. Henry Reeve (trans). Cambridge: Sever & Francis, 1863. 2nd Eng ed. 2 vols. xxiii,559; xiv,499pp. Dk purple cl, gilt spine. Ends chipped, corners showing, o/w Good. *Weber.* $100/£65

DE TOLNAY, CHARLES. The Drawings of Pieter Bruegel the Elder. London, 1952. Dj (sl ragged). *Edwards.* $70/£45

DE TOLNAY, CHARLES. The Medici Chapel. Vol III orig ed. Princeton Univ Press, 1948. (Cl sl soiled.) *Edwards.* $70/£45

DE TOLNAY, CHARLES. The Sistine Ceiling. Vol II orig ed. Princeton Univ Press, 1945. Dbl-pg fldg plt. (Cl sl soiled.) *Edwards.* $70/£45

DE TOLNAY, CHARLES. The Youth of Michelangelo. Vol I, orig ed. Princeton Univ Press, 1947. 2nd ed. Frontis port (cl sl soiled). *Edwards.* $70/£45

DE TOULOUSE-LAUTREC, HENRI and MAURICE JOYANT. The Art of Cuisine. Margery Weiner (trans). London: Michael Joseph, 1966. White/red checkered cl, black spine title. Fine in dj, slipcase. *Heller.* $95/£61

DE TOULOUSE-LAUTREC, HENRI. Unpublished Correspondence of Henri de Toulouse-Lautrec. Lucien Goldschmidt & Herbert Schimmel (ed). London: Phaidon, 1969. Fldg chart, table. Fine in Mint dj. *Europa.* $23/£15

DE TROBRIAND, PHILIPPE. Army Life in Dakota. Chicago, (1941). Lakeside Classic. VG. *Schoyer.* $25/£16

DE TUBIERES, ANNE-CLAUDE-PHILIPPE. The Coachman's Story and Other Tales. Eric Sutton (trans). London: Chapman & Hall, 1927. Ltd to 1000. Teg, uncut. (Ex-lib, label stamp, blind stamps.) Cl-backed patterned bds (spine head sl frayed; sm nick). *Hollett.* $47/£30

DE VESME, ALEXANDRE. Stefano Della Bella: Catalogue Raisonne. (NY, 1971.) 2 vols. 235pp plts. VG. *Argosy.* $350/£226

DE VIGHNE, HARRY CARLOS. The Time of My Life. Phila: Lippincott, 1942. VG. *Burcham.* $35/£23

DE VINNE, THEODORE LOW. The Invention of Printing. NY: Francis Hart, 1876. 556pp. 3/4 pebbled morocco, marbled bds; marbled eps, edges. Rubbed, else VG. *Veatchs.* $200/£129

DE VINNE, THEODORE LOW. A Treatise on Title-Pages. NY: Century, 1902. 1st ed. Tape offset eps, o/w VG. *Glenn.* $55/£35

DE VINNE, THEODORE LOW. Types of the De Vinne Press. NY, 1907. Grn cl, red leather spine label, teg. Lower cvr dampstained, sl affecting margins of last leaf of text, o/w VG. *Veatchs.* $160/£103

DE VOTO, BERNARD (ed). The Journals of Lewis and Clark. Boston: Houghton Mifflin, (1953). Red cl. Fine in VG + dj (sl chipped, rubbed, spine faded). *Harrington.* $35/£23

DE VOTO, BERNARD. Across the Wide Missouri. Boston: Houghton Mifflin, 1947. 1st ed. Dj (sm stain, edges worn, fore-edge soiled). Slipcase. *Shasky.* $45/£29

DE VOTO, BERNARD. Across the Wide Missouri: Illustrated with Paintings.... Houghton Mifflin, 1947. 1st ed. 81 plts (19 color). VG in VG dj. Howes D 296. *Oregon.* $55/£35

DE VOTO, BERNARD. The Course of Empire. Boston, 1952. 1st ed. VG in Poor dj. *King.* $22/£14

DE VRIES, A.B. Jan Vermeer van Delft. London: Batsford, 1948. 73 plts (4 color). Sound in dj. *Ars Artis.* $39/£25

DE VRIES, LEONARD. Little Wide-Awake. London, 1967. Dj (sl worn). *Edwards.* $39/£25

DE VRIES, PETER. The Glory of the Hummingbird. Boston, (1974). 1st ed. Lt bumped, else Good in dj (sl rubbed, soiled). *King.* $25/£16

DE VRIES, PETER. Into Your Tent I'll Creep. Boston, (1971). 1st ed. VG in dj (sl soiled, sticker remains). *King.* $25/£16

DE VRIES, PETER. Let Me Count the Ways. Boston, 1965. 1st Amer ed. Signed. Fine (sl rubbed) in dj (sl sunned, sl rubbed, price-clipped). *Polyanthos.* $30/£19

DE VRIES, PETER. Madder Music. Boston, (1977). 1st ed. VG in dj (lt soiled, price-clipped). *King.* $25/£16

DE VRIES, PETER. Slouching Towards Kalamazoo. Boston/Toronto: Little, Brown, (1983). 1st ed. Signed. Fine in dj (price-clipped). *Bernard.* $30/£19

DE VRIES, PETER. Through the Fields of Clover. Boston, 1961. Signed presentation. Fine in NF dj (price-clipped). *Polyanthos.* $30/£19

DE VRIES, PETER. The Vale of Laughter. Boston, 1967. Signed presentation. Fine (sl bumped) in dj (nicks). *Polyanthos.* $30/£19

DE WET, OLOFF. Cardboard Crucifix. The Story of a Pilot in Spain. Edinburgh/London: Blackwood, 1938. 1st ed. Nice. *Patterson.* $194/£125

DE WILD, A.M. The Scientific Examination of Pictures. London: Bell, 1929. 46 plts, fldg chart. (Sl worn.) *Ars Artis.* $54/£35

DE WINDT, H. From Pekin to Calais by Land. London: Chapman & Hall, 1892. 2nd ed. 365pp, sm map. Butterscotch cl (shaken, worn; foxed). *Schoyer.* $40/£26

DE WINDT, HARRY. Through the Gold-Fields of Alaska to Bering Straits. London: C&W, 1898. 1st ed. viii,312pp + 32pp ads dated Jan. 1898; 32 plts; lg fldg map. (Cl mkd, bumped.) *Hollett.* $186/£120

DE WINTER, PATRICK M. European Decorative Arts 1400-1600. An Annotated Bibliography. Boston, 1988. Good. *Washton.* $60/£39

DE WITT, CLINTON. Privileged Communications Between Physician and Patient. Springfield: Thomas, 1958. NF in dj. *Goodrich.* $30/£19

DE WITT, DAVID M. The Impeachment and Trial of Andrew Johnson.... NY: Macmillan, 1903. 1st ed. (Lt wear.) Howes D 305. *Ginsberg.* $125/£81

DE WITT, WILLIAM C. Sundry Speeches and Writings. Brooklyn: Eagle Book Ptg Dept, 1881. Good. *Boswell.* $85/£55

DE ZEMLER, CHARLES. Once Over Lightly. NY: (The Author), 1939. 1st ed. Frontis. Lt blue cl. VG in dj (worn). *Weber.* $125/£81

DEACOCK, ANTONIA. No Purdah in Padam. London: Harrap, 1958. 1st ed. 11 plts; 2 maps. VG in dj. *Hollett.* $39/£25

DEADRICK, WILLIAM and LLOYD THOMPSON. The Endemic Diseases of the Southern States. Phila, 1916. 1st ed. Good. *Fye.* $150/£97

DEAM, C.C. and T.E. SHAW. Trees of Indiana. Indianapolis, 1953. 3rd ed. 114 plts, 4 full-pg maps. (Bkpl; eps browned.) *Sutton.* $35/£23

Dean's Pop-Up Book of Motor Cars. London: Dean, 1961. 23x16 cm. 3 dbl-pg pop-ups. Glazed pict bds. VG. *Book Finders.* $18/£12

DEAN, B.E. et al. Wildflowers of Alabama and Adjoining States. University, 1973. Color map. Dj. *Sutton.* $35/£23

DEAN, C.G.T. The Royal Hospital Chelsea. London: Hutchinson, 1950. Color frontis, extra plt added from other source by prev owner. Scarlet cl, gilt. Fine. *Peter Taylor.* $28/£18

DEANDREA, WILLIAM L. Killed in the Act. GC: DCC, 1981. 1st ed. Fine in dj. *Janus.* $35/£23

DEANDREA, WILLIAM L. Killed in the Ratings. NY: Harcourt Brace Jovanovich, 1978. 1st ed, 1st bk. Fine in NF dj. *Janus.* $30/£19

DEANE, SAMUEL. The New-England Farmer. Worcester, MA: Isaiah Thomas, 1790. 1st ed. viii,336pp. Orig calf (spine chipped), red calf spine label. *Karmiole.* $275/£177

DEARBORN, HENRY. Revolutionary War Journals of Henry Dearborn, 1775-1783. Chicago: Caxton Club, 1939. One of 350 by Lakeside Press. Port, 2 plts, 3 fldg maps; teg; unopened. 2-tone cl, gilt-stamped morocco spine label. Nice in slipcase (worn). *Bohling.* $200/£129

Death and Burial of Cock Robin. London: William Darton, Holborn Hill, (ca 1830). Toybook. 12mo. 13 hand-colored plts. Illus paper wrappers. Cvrs worn but complete. *Reisler.* $300/£194

Death and Burial of Cock Robin. Banbury: J.G. Rusher, n.d. (ca 1828). Chapbook. 16mo. 18 VF wood engrs. Ptd paper wrappers. VF. *Hobbyhorse.* $95/£61

Death and Burial of Cock Robin. Springfield, MA: McLoughlin Bros, n.d. (ca 1920). 8vo. 4 leaves (incl cvrs) ptd on linen-backed paper. Pict color cvr (lt soiled, rubbed). Fine. *Hobbyhorse.* $40/£26

Death of Cock Robin. NY: McLoughlin Bros, n.d. (ca 1860). (Uncle Frank's Series.) Sq 16mo. 4 leaves + 1pg list lower wrapper, lg hand-colored woodcut each pg. Pict paper wrappers. Fine. *Hobbyhorse.* $125/£81

Death Valley. Boston: Houghton Mifflin, 1939. 1st ed. Fold-out map. Fine in Fine dj. *Book Market.* $80/£52

DEATHERAGE, CHARLES P. Early History of Greater Kansas City, Missouri and Kansas. Vol 1: Early History to 1870. KC, 1927. Diamond Jubilee Ed. Lg fldg map. Pict cl. VG. Howes D 178. *Oregon.* $75/£48

DEATHERAGE, CHARLES P. Early History of Greater Kansas City.... Kansas City, MO, 1927. Diamond Jubilee Ed. Lg fldg color map (2 2-inch tears). VG. Howes D 178. *Bohling.* $150/£97

DEATHERAGE, CHARLES P. Steamboating on the Missouri River in the Sixties. Kansas City: Privately ptd, (1924). Wrappers (lt soiled). *Glenn.* $45/£29

DEBARTHE, JOE. Life and Adventures of Frank Grouard. Norman, (1958). 1st ed. Bkpl, soiled, else Good in dj (torn, spotted). *King.* $35/£23

DEBO, ANGIE. The Rise and Fall of the Choctaw Republic. Norman, 1961. 2nd ed. Fine (sig, date) in dj (sl worn). *Baade.* $47/£30

DEBO, ANGIE. The Road to Disappearance. Norman, 1941. 1st ed. NF in dj (sl chipped, price-clipped, partially split at hinges), protective cvr. *Baade.* $150/£97

DEBRAY, XAVIER BLANCHARD. A Sketch of the History of Debray's (26th) Regiment of Texas Cavalry. Waco, TX: Waco Village Press, 1961. 2nd ed. #98/300. Orig stiff tan wraps, paper label. Fine in plain paper dj (few closed tears). *Chapel Hill.* $55/£35

DEBRAY, XAVIER BLANCHARD. A Sketch of the History of Debray's 26th Regiment of Texas Cavalry. Waco, TX: Waco Village Press, 1961. Rpt ltd to 300. NF in orig ptd wrappers. *Mcgowan.* $85/£55

DEBRETT, JOHN. The Peerage of the United Kingdom of Great Britain and Ireland. London: Ptd by G. Woodfall, 1816. 10th ed. Vol 1 only. Frontis port, cvii,600pp, 88 plts (lt browned). Calf-backed marbled bds (rebound), gilt-ruled, leather spine label. *Edwards.* $93/£60

DEBS, EUGENE V. Debs: His Life, Writings and Speeches. Girard, 1908. 1st ed. Signed. (Professionally rebacked, new eps; lib stamp bottom edge, corner wear, sl edgewear.) *Baade.* $125/£81

Decorative Work of T.M. Cleland, a Record and Review. NY: Pynson Printers, 1929. 4to. 99 plts. (Extrems sl rubbed; bk ticket.) Dj (soiled; tape repaired). *Veatchs.* $100/£65

DEE, JOHN. The Private Diary of Dr..., and the Catalogue of His Library of Manuscripts.... J.O. Halliwell (ed). London, 1842. 1st ed. 102pp (endleaves waterstained). *Argosy.* $75/£48

DEERR, NOEL. Cane Sugar. London, 1911. Color frontis, 22 plts (10 color). (Foxed; worn; fr hinge cracked). *Sutton.* $75/£48

DEERR, NOEL. Cane Sugar. Manchester, 1911. 23 plts (11 color). VG. *Argosy.* $100/£65

DEERR, NOEL. Sugar and the Sugar Cane. Manchester, 1905. 11 color plts. (Worn; inner hinges sl cracked.) *Sutton.* $50/£32

Deerslayer: Or, the First Warpath: A Tale. (By James Fenimore Cooper.) Phila: Lea & Blanchard, 1841. 1st ed. 2 vols. Orig cl (rubbed, dampstained; top margin vol 1 leaves sl dampstained; top margin prelims vol 2 sl wormed; scattered foxing). 3/4 brn morocco clamshell box, linen bds, trays, raised bands, leather spine labels. BAL 3895. *Sadlon.* $800/£516

DEFENBACH, BYRON. Idaho: The Place and Its People. Chicago: Amer Hist Soc, 1933. Emb cvrs. Fine set. *Perier.* $325/£210

DEFENBACH, BYRON. Red Heroines of the Northwest. Caldwell: Caxton, 1929. 1st ed. Signed. 11 plts. VG in poor dj (stained). *Perier.* $75/£48

DEFOE, DANIEL. The Adventures of Robinson Crusoe. London: S.O. Beeton, 1864. 10th ed. xxxi,384pp. Full-pg chromolitho frontis w/plt guard, engr port, 7 full-pg engrs (some offsetting). Brn tooled cl on bds w/tooled edges, gilt. VG (ink sig, bkpl). *Hobbyhorse.* $125/£81

DEFOE, DANIEL. The Life and Adventures of Robinson Crusoe. NY: Effingham Maynard, (1891). Sm 8vo. 166pp + 3pp notes; red edges. Pict linen. Fine. *Hobbyhorse.* $150/£97

DEFOE, DANIEL. The Life and Adventures of Robinson Crusoe. London: Harrison, 1781. 1st this ed. 2 vols in 1. 289pp. Early mottled calf (rebacked), dbl leather labels. Good (wear). *Hartfield.* $395/£255

DEFOE, DANIEL. The Life and Adventures of Robinson Crusoe. London: Robert Tyas, 1840. Mtd frontis, xviii,638pp (leaf, illus detached together; hinges tender); teg. Contemp gilt-edged 1/2 morocco, marbled bds (corner repaired; corner bumped w/loss, rubbed.) Dec gilt. *Edwards.* $78/£50

DEFOE, DANIEL. The Life and Strange Surprising Adventures of Robinson Crusoe of York, Mariner. London: C. Hitch & L. Hawes et al, 1756. 12th ed. 2 vols. 8vo. (2),288; (2),275pp. Vol 1: full-pg copper engr frontis, 2 dec engr head-pieces, 6 full-pg engrs; vol 2: dbl-spread lg fldg map; 2 engr dec head-pieces, 6 full-pg copper engrs. Full leather on bds, gilt. VG (bkpl; lt frayed, corners bumped; folds rubbed; brn mks inside cvrs, eps). *Hobbyhorse.* $300/£194

DEFOE, DANIEL. The Life and Surprising Adventures of Robinson Crusoe.... London: Ernest Nister, (1895). 328pp, 6 chromolithos by Ernest Nister. Blue pict cl (rubbed, ink-stained; bkpl). Good. *Cox.* $31/£20

DEFOE, DANIEL. Moll Flanders. Hogarth Press, 1931. Alexander King (illus). VG +. *Bishop.* $20/£13

DEFOE, DANIEL. Robinson Crusoe. NY: Cosmopolitan, 1920. 1st ed. N.C. Wyeth (illus). 4to. Teg. Dk blue cl, color paste label (sl spine wear). *Reisler.* $300/£194

DEFOE, DANIEL. Romances and Narratives. London: Dent, 1895-1900. Victoria Edition. #25/150 numbered sets. 16 vols. 8vo. 3/4 gilt-stamped red morocco; teg. VG +. *Houle.* $1,500/£968

DEFOE, DANIEL. The Life and Surprising Adventures of Robinson Crusoe of York, Mariner. John Major (ed). NY: J.W. Bouton, 1884. #15/100, ptd on lg paper ed on hand-made paper, initialed by ed. xii,563pp, 31 wood engrs pasted down, 2 full-pg copper engrs, tissue guards. (Spine worn, crowns torn, hinges cracked). Internally Fine. *Hobbyhorse.* $175/£113

DEFOE, DANIEL. A Tour Thro' the Whole Island of Great Britain.... London: Peter Davies, 1927. One of 1000. 2 vols. Teg, rest uncut (fore-edges, few pp sl foxed). Djs. *Petersfield.* $248/£160

DEGENER SCHMIDT, F. and H.E. VAN GELDER. Jan Steen. London: Bodley Head, 1927. 40 plts, guards. Sm crease spine, o/w Fine. *Europa.* $65/£42

DEGOUY, LOUIS P. The Derrydale Cookbook of Fish and Game. NY: Derrydale, 1937. One of 1250 numbered sets. 2 vols. VF set in Fine orig slipcase. *Bowman.* $350/£226

DEGREGORIO, GEORGE. Joe DiMaggio. Scarborough, 1983. 1st ed. Fine in VG + dj. *Plapinger.* $45/£29

DEHN, PAUL. Quake, Quake, Quake, a Leaden Treasury of English Verse. London: Hamish, 1961. 1st ed. Fine in dj (sl worn). *Second Life.* $45/£29

DEIGHTON, LEN (ed). Drinks-man-ship. London: Hay-market Press, 1964. 1st UK ed. VG in dj (chips, edgewear, tears). *Williams.* $62/£40

DEIGHTON, LEN. Action Cookbook. London: Cape, 1965. 1st ed. VG w/o dj as issued. *Mordida.* $100/£65

DEIGHTON, LEN. Action Cookbook. Cape, 1965. 1st UK ed. Pict bds. VG. *Williams.* $74/£48

DEIGHTON, LEN. Airshipwreck. London: Cape, 1978. 1st ed. Postcard laid in. Fine in dj. *Rees.* $31/£20

DEIGHTON, LEN. Billion Dollar Brain. London: Cape, 1966. 1st UK ed. Fine in VG + metallic dj (lt dulling, scratching to spine). *Williams.* $59/£38

DEIGHTON, LEN. Bomber. London: Cape, 1970. 1st ed. VG + in dj. *Limestone.* $25/£16

DEIGHTON, LEN. Declarations of War. London: Cape, 1971. 1st UK ed. Fine in dj. *Williams.* $39/£25

DEIGHTON, LEN. An Expensive Place to Die. NY: Putnam's, 1967. 1st ed. Fine in NF dj (price-clipped). *Janus.* $45/£29

DEIGHTON, LEN. An Expensive Place to Die. London: Cape, 1967. 1st ed. In Transit Docket present. Fine in dj. *Limestone.* $95/£61

DEIGHTON, LEN. An Expensive Place to Die. Cape, 1967. 1st ed. With Docket. VG in VG dj. *Ming.* $54/£35

DEIGHTON, LEN. An Expensive Place to Die. Cape, 1967. 1st UK ed, w/wallet. Fine in dj. *Lewton.* $47/£30

DEIGHTON, LEN. Funeral in Berlin. London: Cape, 1964. 1st UK ed. Fine in dj. *Lewton.* $50/£32

DEIGHTON, LEN. Horse Under Water. Cape, 1963. 1st ed. Bkseller name tp, else Fine in dj. *Fine Books.* $85/£55

DEIGHTON, LEN. Horse Under Water. London: Cape, 1963. 1st issue, w/crossword eps. Loose crossword laid in. VG in dj. *Williams.* $147/£95

DEIGHTON, LEN. The Ipcress File. London: Hodder & Stoughton, 1962. 1st ed, 1st bk. Good (sl stained throughout; partially erased inscrip) in dj (chipped, creased). *Rees.* $47/£30

DEIGHTON, LEN. The Ipcress File. London: Hodder & Stoughton, 1962. 1st ed. Fore-edge foxed; lt spotted, o/w Fine in dj (crease, scrape; staining bottom edges). *Mordida.* $450/£290

DEIGHTON, LEN. The Ipcress File. NY: S&S, 1963. 1st Amer ed. Fine in dj (short closed tears). *Mordida.* $185/£119

DEIGHTON, LEN. The Ipcress File. NY: S&S, 1963. 1st US ed. 1st bk. NF in VG dj (soiled). *Janus.* $75/£48

DEIGHTON, LEN. London Match. London: Cape, 1985. 1st ed. Signed. VG in dj. *Rees.* $23/£15

DEIGHTON, LEN. Only When I Larf. London: Michael Joseph, 1968. 1st UK ed. Fine in VG dj. *Williams.* $132/£85

DEIGHTON, LEN. Only When I Laugh. Mysterious Press, 1987. 1st US ed. #83/250 numbered, signed. Fine in slipcase. *Williams.* $132/£85

DEIGHTON, LEN. Ou Est le Garlic: Len Deighton's French Cook Book. London: Penguin Books, 1965. Pb orig. NF. *Rees.* $31/£20

DEIGHTON, LEN. Twinkle, Twinkle, Little Spy. London: Cape, 1976. 1st ed. Fine in dj. *Mordida.* $45/£29

DEIGHTON, LEN. Violent Ward. London: Scorpion Press, 1993. One of 130 numbered, signed. Fine in special binding. *Williams.* $70/£45

DEIGHTON, LEN. Yesterday's Spy. London: Jonathan Cape, 1975. 1st ed. Fine in NF dj. *Janus.* $45/£29

DEIGHTON, LEN. Yesterday's Spy. London: Cape, 1975. 1st UK ed. Fine in dj. *Williams.* $28/£18

DEJERINE, JOSEPH and E. GAUCKLER. The Psychoneuroses and Their Treatment by Psychotherapy. Phila, 1913. 1st Eng trans. (Fr cvr spotted; fr inner hinge cracked.) *Fye.* $100/£65

DEKNATEL, FREDERICK B. Edvard Munch. Boston/London, 1950. Fine in pict dj. *Europa.* $23/£15

DEL CASTILLO, BERNAL DIAZ. The Discovery and Conquest of Mexico. Harry Block (ed). Mexico City: LEC, 1942. #904/1500 numbered, signed by Rafael Loera Chavez (printer), Block, & Miguel Covarrubias (illus). Fine in pub's slipcase (lt worn). *Hermitage.* $250/£161

DEL CHIARO, MARIO A. Etruscan Red-Figured Vase-Painting at Caere. Berkeley: Univ of CA Press, (1974). 102 plts, map. Good in dj. *Archaeologia.* $65/£42

DEL MAR, ALEXANDER. The History of Money in America. NY: Cambridge Encyclopedia Co, 1899. xxiv,121pp (blank flyleaf excised). *Schoyer.* $50/£32

DEL REY, LESTER. Marooned on Mars. Winston, 1952. 1st ed. VG. *Madle.* $20/£13

DEL REY, LESTER. Rocket from Infinity. Holt, 1966. 1st ed. Fine in dj. *Madle.* $75/£48

DEL VECCHIO, JOHN M. The 13th Valley. Toronto/NY/London/Sydney: Bantam Books, (1982). 1st ed, 1st bk. NF in white dj (internally repaired tears). *Heller.* $40/£26

DEL VECCHIO, JOHN M. The 13th Valley. NY: Bantam, (1982). 1st ptg. Fine in dj (edge tear). *Aka.* $45/£29

DEL VECCHIO, JOHN M. The 13th Valley. NY: Bantam, 1982. 1st ed. NF in NF dj (sl worn). *Revere.* $40/£26

DELACOUR, J. The Pheasants of the World. London, 1951. 1st imp. 16 color, 16 plain plts; 21 maps, diagrams. *Wheldon & Wesley.* $233/£150

DELACROIX, EUGENE. The Journal of Eugene Delacroix. Walter Pach (trans). NY: Hacker, 1980. 57 plts. Orig cl, sketch fr cvr. VF. *Europa.* $37/£24

DELAMOTTE, F. The Book of Ornamental Alphabets...From the Eighth Century.... London: C. Lockwood, 1868. 7th ed. 53 specimens ptd rectos only. VG in gold-lettered, blind-stamped brn cl. *Cox.* $54/£35

DELAND, MARGARET. An Old Chester Secret. NY: Harper, (1920). 1st ed. Stamped cl. VG in orig dj. *Second Life.* $45/£29

DELANEY, ED. Bobby Shantz. Barnes, 1953. 1st ed. VG in Good + dj. *Plapinger.* $40/£26

DELANO, ALONZO. Across the Plains and Among the Diggings. NY: Wilson-Erickson, 1936. Gold-stamped cl in dj. *Dawson.* $60/£39

DELANY, SAMUEL. The Einstein Intersection. Gollancz, 1968. 1st Eng, 1st hb ed. Fine in Fine dj (lt dust soil). *Aronovitz.* $425/£274

DELAUNAY, CHARLES. New Hot Discography. NY: Criterion, 1948. 1st thus. Fine (spine gilt dulled; name). *Beasley.* $75/£48

DELDERFIELD, R.F. Bird's Eye View. London: Constable, 1954. 1st ed. Signed presentation copy. VG in dj (sm chip missing from head of spine). *Limestone.* $65/£42

DELDERFIELD, R.F. Give Us This Day. London: Hodder & Stoughton, 1973. 1st ed. Sig, price crossed out, else VG + in dj. *Limestone.* $25/£16

DeLILLO, DON. The Day Room. NY, 1987. 1st ed. Fine in dj. *Rees.* $39/£25

DeLILLO, DON. End Zone. Houghton Mifflin, 1972. 1st ed. NF (sticker) in dj (lt rubbed; worn, 1-inch closed tear). *Stahr.* $60/£39

DeLILLO, DON. Libra. (NY): Viking, (1988). 1st ed. Fine in dj. *Reese.* $20/£13

DeLILLO, DON. The Names. NY: Knopf, 1982. 1st ed. Fine in dj. *Between The Covers.* $45/£29

DeLILLO, DON. Ratner's Star. NY: Knopf, 1976. 1st ed. NF in VG dj (edge tears; chipped). *Lame Duck.* $35/£23

DeLILLO, DON. Ratner's Star. NY: Knopf, 1976. 1st ed. Fine in Fine dj. *Between The Covers.* $65/£42

DeLILLO, DON. White Noise. Viking, 1985. 1st ed. Fine in dj. *Fine Books.* $25/£16

DELL, FLOYD. The Briary Bush. NY: Knopf, 1921. 1st ed, 3rd ptg; inscribed, signed in 1924. Sl edgeworn, soiled, else Good in dj (shelfworn). *Reese.* $40/£26

DELL, FLOYD. Love in the Machine Age. London: George Rutledge, 1930. 1st UK ed. Good (lt dampstained, shelfworn). *Gach.* $30/£19

DELL, FLOYD. An Old Man's Folly. NY: Doran, (1926). 1st ed. VG in Good dj (2 creased tears). *Reese.* $35/£23

DELLENBAUGH, FRED. The Romance of the Colorado River. Chicago: Rio Grande, (1962). VG. *Oregon.* $35/£23

Democracy. (By Henry Adams.) London: Macmillan, 1882. 1st Eng ed. 280pp(4)+24pp ads. Dk grn cl. VG (fr inner hinge sl cracked; tanned eps; sig). BAL 11. *Chapel Hill.* $200/£129

DEMPSEY, HUGH A. History in Their Blood. NY, 1982. 1st Amer ed. Fine (rmdr dot bottom edge) in dj (sl worn). *Baade.* $50/£32

DEMPSEY, HUGH A. (ed). William Parker, Mounted Policeman. Edmonton: Hurtig Pub, (1973). 1st ed. Blue cl. Fine in NF dj (sl rubbed). *Harrington.* $30/£19

DEMPSEY, PETER J.R. Freud, Psychoanalysis, Catholicism. Chicago: Henry Regnery, (1956). 1st Amer ed. Red cl. VG. *Gach.* $25/£16

DEMUS, OTTO. Byzantine Art and the West. NY, 1970. Good. *Washton.* $85/£55

DEMUS, OTTO. Byzantine Mosaic Decoration. Boston, 1955. 64pp plts. VG in dj (torn). *Argosy.* $65/£42

DEMUS, OTTO. Mosaics of Norman Sicily. London: Routledge & Kegan Paul, (1950). 120pp b/w plts. VG in dj (chipped, price-clipped). *Schoyer.* $100/£65

DEMUS, OTTO. Romanesque Mural Painting. NY, 1970. 324 plts, 103 tipped-in color. Good in dj. *Washton.* $175/£113

DENDY, WALTER C. The Philosophy of Mystery. London: Longman et al, 1841. 1st ed. (iii)-xii+443+(1)pp. Emb brn cl. VG. *Gach.* $125/£81

DENEVI, MARCO. Secret Ceremony. Harriet de Onis (trans). (NY: Time, Inc, 1961.) 1st ed thus. Fine in slipcase. *Reese.* $50/£32

DENIG, EDWIN THOMPSON. Five Indian Tribes of the Upper Missouri. John C. Ewers (ed). Norman: Univ of OK, (1961). 1st ed. VG in dj. *Laurie.* $35/£23

DENING, C.F.W. The Eighteenth-Century Architecture of Bristol. Bristol/London, 1923. 1st ed. Tipped-in frontis, 69 tipped-in plts. Fore, lower edge uncut. (Lt spotting.) *Edwards.* $155/£100

DENIS and WHITE. Water-Powers of Canada. Ottawa, 1911. *Artis.* $35/£23

DENIS, ALBERTA. Spanish Alta California. Macmillan, 1927. 1st ed. Frontis. Fine. *Oregon.* $65/£42

DENMAN, THOMAS. An Introduction to the Practice of Midwifery. London, 1805. 5th ed. 671pp; 17 engr copper plts. 1/4 antique calf; marbled bds. (Rebound; foxing; sm marginal water stain afffecting leaves.) *Fye.* $425/£274

DENNIS, GEORGE. The Cities and Cemeteries of Etruria. London, 1883. 3rd ed. 2 vols. Rubric tps, cxxviii,504; xv,579pp, fldg map. Blind emb cl, dec gilt titles (spines sl rubbed). *Edwards.* $171/£110

DENNIS, JAMES M. Karl Bitter, Architectural Sculptor, 1867-1915. London: Univ of WI, 1967. 1st ed. Frontis. Bkpl, else Fine. *Bookpress.* $35/£23

DENNIS, WESLEY. Flip. NY: Viking, 1941. 1st ed. VG in Good dj. *October Farm.* $35/£23

DENNY, ARTHUR A. Pioneer Days on Puget Sound. Seattle: C.B. Bagley, 1888. 1st ed. Errata slip. VG. Howes D 253. *Perier.* $250/£161

DENNY, EMILY INEZ. Blazing the Way. Seattle: Rainier Ptg, 1909. 1st ed. Frontis; 19 plts. VG. *Oregon.* $100/£65

DENSLOW, W.W. Denslow's House That Jack Built. NY: G.W. Dillingham, (1903). 1st ed. 4to. Color illus paper wrappers (spine chipped, marginal folds; internal marginal tears). *Reisler.* $225/£145

DENSLOW, W.W. Denslow's Humpty Dumpty. NY: G.W. Dillingham, (1903). 1st ed. 4to. Color illus paper wrappers (lt edgewear, spine chips; sm marginal tear through book). *Reisler.* $225/£145

DENSLOW, W.W. Denslow's Scarecrow and The Tin-Man and Other Stories. Chicago: M.A. Donohue, (1913). Rpt. 4to. Red cl (dknd), black lettering, color paste label. Internally Nice. *Reisler.* $685/£442

DENSMORE, FRANCES. BAE Bulletin 61. Teton Siox Music. Washington D.C.: GPO, 1918. 82 plts. VG. *Perier.* $65/£42

DENSMORE, FRANCES. BAE Bulletin 75. Northern Ute Music. Washington, 1922. 16 plts. (Ex-lib; lt dampspotting, sm tear.) *Edwards.* $23/£15

DENSMORE, FRANCES. BAE Bulletin 80. Mandan and Hidatsa Music. Washington, 1923. 19 plts. (Ex-lib.) *Edwards.* $23/£15

DENSMORE, FRANCES. BAE Bulletins 45 and 53. Chippewa Music. Washington: GPO, 1910. 2 vols. VG. *Lien.* $50/£32

DENT, C.T. Mountaineering. London: Longmans, Green, 1892. 1st ed. xx,439,(ii)pp; 13 plts. 1/2 blue roan gilt (sl rubbed, mkd). *Hollett.* $101/£65

DENT, C.T. Mountaineering. London: Longmans, Green, 1900. 3rd ed. Pict cl. VG. *Schoyer.* $65/£42

DENT, J.M. The Memoirs, 1849-1926. London: Dent, 1928. 1st ed. Frontis port, 14 plts. Maroon cl. Gilt faded, o/w VG. *Hartfield.* $45/£29

DENT, LESTER. Cry At Dusk. NY: Gold Medal, 1952. 1st ed. NF in wraps. *Beasley.* $25/£16

DENT, LESTER. Dead at the Take-Off. NY: DCC, 1946. 1st ed. Fine in dj (sm edgechips). *Else Fine.* $65/£42

DENTON, DANIEL. A Brief Description of New York, formerly called New Netherlands.... NY, 1845. 8vo. (22),57+20pp ads. Rebacked cl. Howes D 259. *Argosy.* $200/£129

DEPPE, FERDINAND. Travels in California in 1837. Gustave Arlt (trans). LA: Dawson, 1953. 1st ed. Ltd to 190 ptd. Fine. *Oregon.* $40/£26

DERBEC, ETIENNE. A French Journalist in the California Gold Rush.... A.P. Nasatir (ed). Georgetown, CA: Talisman Press, 1964. One of 750. VG+ (bkpl) in dj (dknd, lt chipped). *Bohling.* $65/£42

DERBY, J.C. Fifty Years Among Authors, Books and Publishers. NY: G.W. Carleton, 1884. 1st ed. Ltd to 500. Teg. 3/4 calf over marbled bds (extrems rubbed, fr inner hinge cracked). *Sadlon.* $30/£19

DERBY, W.L.A. The Tall Ships Pass. London, 1937. 1st ed. Eps foxed; few pp unopened, o/w VG in dj (frayed; red stain upper panel). *Edwards.* $101/£65

DERICKSEN, M. BRINKERHOFF. A Collection of Sculpture in Classical and Early Christian Antioch. NY, 1970. 78 illus on plts. Good. *Washton.* $40/£26

DERLETH, AUGUST (ed). The Arkham Sampler. Arkham House, 1949. 1st ed. NF in wraps. *Aronovitz.* $28/£18

DERLETH, AUGUST (ed). Dark Mind, Dark Heart. Sauk City: Arkham House, 1962. 1st ed. NF (lt bumped) in dj (browning; short tear). *Other Worlds.* $45/£29

DERLETH, AUGUST (ed). Dark Mind, Dark Heart. Arkham House, 1962. 1st ed. Fine in dj. *Madle.* $90/£58

DERLETH, AUGUST (ed). Fire and Sleet and Candlelight. Sauk City: Arkham House, 1961. 1st ed. NF in dj (sl browning). *Antic Hay.* $75/£48

DERLETH, AUGUST and MARK SCHORER. Colonel Markesan and Less Pleasant People. Sauk City: Arkham House, (1966). 1st ed. NF (nicked) in dj (spine lt browned, sm abrasion spots). *Other Worlds.* $35/£23

DERLETH, AUGUST. 100 Books by August Derleth. Sauk City: Arkham House, 1962. 1st ed. One of 1025. (Bkpl; notations; cvr rubbed, edgewear.) Pict wrappers. *Other Worlds.* $90/£58

DERLETH, AUGUST. Atmosphere of Houses. London: Prairie Press, 1939. One of 290. Presentation copy w/signed, inscribed holograph of Carroll Coleman (designer). Mottled sea-grn buckram, gilt spine. Corners sl bruised, o/w Very Nice. *Temple.* $202/£130

DERLETH, AUGUST. Bright Journey. NY: Scribner's, 1940. 1st ed. (Dj panel pasted to feps.) *Sadlon.* $15/£10

DERLETH, AUGUST. By Owl Light. IA City: Prairie Press, (1967). VG in dj (lt soiled). *Graf.* $40/£26

DERLETH, AUGUST. The Casebook of Solar Pons. Sauk City: Mycroft & Moran, 1965. 1st ed. Bkpl, else Fine in Fine dj (creased). *Other Worlds.* $100/£65

DERLETH, AUGUST. The Chronicles of Solar Pons. Sauk City: Mycroft & Moran, 1973. 1st ed. Fine in Fine dj (pub's price sticker). *Other Worlds.* $20/£13

DERLETH, AUGUST. The Chronicles of Solar Pons. Sauk City, WI: Mycroft & Moran, 1973. One of 4176. New in dj. *Bernard.* $25/£16

DERLETH, AUGUST. Dwellers in Darkness. Arkham House, 1976. 1st ed. Fine in dj. *Madle.* $30/£19

DERLETH, AUGUST. In Re: Sherlock Holmes. Sauk City, WI: Mycroft & Moran, 1945. One of 3604. Fine in dj. *Bernard.* $125/£81

DERLETH, AUGUST. Lonesome Places. Sauk City: Arkahm House, (1962). 1st ed. Bkpl removed, else NF in dj (spine ends, upper corners worn). *Other Worlds.* $75/£48

DERLETH, AUGUST. Lonesome Places. Sauk City: Arkham House, (1962). 1st ed. Signed. Fine in dj (sl wear). *Antic Hay.* $125/£81

DERLETH, AUGUST. The Mask of Cthulhu. Sauk City: Arkham House, 1958. 1st ed. Bkpl, else Fine in Fine dj (lt wear spine). *Other Worlds.* $125/£81

DERLETH, AUGUST. The Memoirs of Solar Pons. Arkham House, 1951. 1st ed. Fine in Mint dj. *Madle.* $175/£113

DERLETH, AUGUST. Mr. Fairlie's Final Journey. Sauk City: Mycroft & Moran, 1968. 1st ed. Fine in NF dj (pub's price sticker). *Other Worlds.* $40/£26

DERLETH, AUGUST. Mr. Fairlie's Final Journey. Arkham House, 1968. 1st ed. VF in dj. *Madle.* $50/£32

DERLETH, AUGUST. Mr. Fairlie's Final Journey. Sauk City, WI: Mycroft & Moran, 1968. One of 3493. Fine in dj. *Bernard.* $40/£26

DERLETH, AUGUST. Not Long for This World. Sauk City: Arkham House, 1948. 1st ed. Bkpl, else NF in dj (lt edgeworn). *Other Worlds.* $90/£58

DERLETH, AUGUST. Not Long for this World. Arkham House, 1948. 1st ed. VG in dj. *Madle.* $100/£65

DERLETH, AUGUST. Not Long for this World. Sauk City: Arkham House, 1948. 1st ed. Signed. Fine in dj. *Antic Hay.* $225/£145

DERLETH, AUGUST. Over the Edge. Sauk City: Arkham House, 1964. 1st ed. Top edge foxed, else VG in dj (scraped). *Other Worlds.* $45/£29

DERLETH, AUGUST. Over the Edge. Arkham House, 1964. 1st ed. VF in dj. *Madle.* $100/£65

DERLETH, AUGUST. Over the Edge. Sauk City, WI: Arkham House, 1964. One of 2520. Fine in dj. *Bernard.* $50/£32

DERLETH, AUGUST. A Praed Street Dossier. Arkham House, 1968. 1st ed. VF in dj. *Madle.* $55/£35

DERLETH, AUGUST. The Reminiscences of Solar Pons. Arkham House, 1961. 1st ed. Fine in dj. *Madle.* $85/£55

DERLETH, AUGUST. The Reminiscences of Solar Pons. Sauk City: Mycroft & Moran, 1961. 1st ed. Bkpl; staining; spine head bumped, else Fine in Fine dj. *Other Worlds.* $100/£65

DERLETH, AUGUST. Restless Is the River. Scribners, 1939. 1st ed. NF in dj (tape-repaired; frayed). *Madle.* $50/£32

DERLETH, AUGUST. Restless Is the River. Scribner's, 1939. 1st US ed. VG in dj. *Williams.* $116/£75

DERLETH, AUGUST. The Return of Solar Pons. Sauk City: Mycroft & Moran, 1958. 1st ed. Fine in dj (spine extrems lt worn). *Janus.* $135/£87

DERLETH, AUGUST. The Return of Solar Pons. Arkham House, 1958. 1st ed. Fine in Mint dj. *Madle.* $175/£113

DERLETH, AUGUST. The Shield of the Valiant. NY: Scribner's, 1945. 1st ed. Fine in NF dj. *Bernard.* $25/£16

DERLETH, AUGUST. Sleep No More. NY: Farrar & Rinehart, (1944). 1st ed. Name, date, else VG in dj (spine sl faded, sm tears, chipped). *Other Worlds.* $50/£32

DERLETH, AUGUST. Some Notes on H.P. Lovecraft. Arkham House, 1959. 1st ed. NF in wraps. *Madle.* $125/£81

DERLETH, AUGUST. Something Near. Arkham House, 1945. 1st ed. Fine in dj. *Madle.* $150/£97

DERLETH, AUGUST. Strange Ports of Call. P&C, 1948. 1st ed. Fine in dj. *Madle.* $40/£26

DERLETH, AUGUST. Thirty Years of Arkham House 1939-1969.... Sauk City: Arkham House, 1970. 1st ed. Fine in dj (lt browned). *Other Worlds.* $70/£45

DERLETH, AUGUST. Thirty Years of Arkham House 1939-1969: A History.... Sauk City, 1970. 1st ed. One of 2000. Fine in Fine dj. *Mcclintock.* $85/£55

DERLETH, AUGUST. Thirty Years of Arkham House. Arkham House, 1970. 1st ed. VF in dj. *Madle.* $85/£55

DERLETH, AUGUST. Three Problems for Solar Pons. Arkham House, 1952. 1st ed. Fine in dj (sl dusty). *Madle.* $200/£129

DERLETH, AUGUST. The Trail of Cthulhu. Jersey: Spearman, (1974). 1st ed thus. Fine in NF dj. *Other Worlds.* $35/£23

DERLETH, AUGUST. The Trail of Cthulhu. Arkham House, 1962. 1st ed. VF in dj. *Madle.* $85/£55

DERLETH, AUGUST. Travellers by Night. Sauk City: Arkham House, 1967. 1st ed. Fine in NF dj. *Other Worlds.* $50/£32

DERLETH, AUGUST. Travellers by Night. Sauk City, WI: Arkham House, 1967. One of 2486. Fine in dj. *Bernard.* $45/£29

DERLETH, AUGUST. Village Daybook. Chicago: Pellegrini & Cudahy, (1947). 1st ed. Signed. NF. *Sadlon.* $40/£26

DERLETH, AUGUST. Wilbur, The Trusting Whippoorwill. Sauk City, WI: Stanton & Lee, 1959. 1st ed. Fine in VG + dj (price-clipped; glue mk). *Bernard.* $35/£23

DERLETH, AUGUST. Wisconsin Murders. Sauk City: Mycroft & Moran, (1968). 1st ed. Fine in dj (sl wear). *Antic Hay.* $50/£32

DERLETH, AUGUST. Wisconsin Murders. Sauk City: Mycroft & Moran, (1968). 1st ed. Fine in Fine dj. *Other Worlds.* $60/£39

DERRY, RAMSAY. The Art of Robert Bateman. NY, 1982. 82 color plts. VG in dj. *Argosy.* $85/£55

DES COGNETS, LOUIS, JR. (comp). English Duplicates of Lost Virginia Records. The author, 1960. 2nd ptg. VG. *Book Broker.* $45/£29

Descendant. (By Ellen Glasgow.) NY: Harper, 1897. 1st ed. Inscribed anonymously 'With the author's sincere regards.' Name; sl cocked; foxing. *Turlington.* $300/£194

DESCHARNES, ROBERT and JEAN-FRANCOIS CHABRUN. Auguste Rodin. NY, 1967. 1st ed. VG in dj (torn). *Argosy.* $85/£55

DESCINSKY, HERBERT. English Furniture: From Gothic to Sheraton. Grand Rapids, MI: Dean-Hicks Co, 1929. 1st ed. Gilt-emb cl. 2-inch crack fr lower inner hinge, reps chipped, else Fine. *Cahan.* $85/£55

Description of Early Printed Books Owned by the Grolier Club. NY: Grolier Club, 1895. One of 400. Inscribed. 78pp. Good. *Washton.* $125/£81

Description of Three Hundred Animals.... (By Thomas Boreman.) London: J. & F. Rivington, 1774. 11th ed. Lg 12mo. Full-pg engr frontis, vi,212pp; 99 full-pg engrs (1 fldg; some restored). VG (mod binding, new eps). *Hobbyhorse.* $350/£226

Design and Construction of General Hospitals. NY: F.W. Dodge, (1953). 1st ed. Spine sunned; else VG. *Bookpress.* $35/£23

Designs for Shop-Fronts and Door-Cases. London: for E. Lumley, n.d. (ca.1830?) 4to. Engr pict title, 26 plts w/imprint of I. and F. Taylor. Orig glazed floral wrappers w/label ptd in gold on blue, cl spine (sl chipped, split). *Marlborough.* $2,093/£1,350

DESMOND, CHARLES. Naval Architecture Simplified. NY: Rudder, (1918). (2nd ed.) Fine in pub's brn jacket. *Lefkowicz.* $150/£97

DESTI, MARY. The Untold Story. NY: Liveright, 1929. 1st US ed. VG. *Second Life.* $45/£29

DEUTSCH, BABETTE. Take Them, Stranger. NY: Holt, (1944). 1st ed. Fine in dj (sl wear, soil). *Antic Hay.* $45/£29

DEUTSCH, HELENE. Confrontations with Myself.... NY: Norton, (1973). 1st ed. Cl-back gray bds. VG in dj. *Gach.* $28/£18

DEUTSCH, HELENE. Neuroses and Character Types. NY: IUP, (1965). Enlgd ed, 1st ptg. Gray cl. VG (perf stamp tp) in dj. *Gach.* $32/£21

DEUTSCH, LEO. Sixteen Years in Siberia. NY: Dutton, 1904. 3rd ptg. Frontis port. Grn cl (stained, cockled; hinges reinforced; pocket removed; foxing, internal stains). *Schoyer.* $25/£16

DEVEREUX, GEORGE. Reality and Dream: Psychotherapy of a Plains Indian. NY: IUP, (1951). 1st ed. Russet cl. VG in dj (chipped). *Gach.* $40/£26

DEVEREUX, GEORGE. A Study in Abortion in Primitive Societies. NY: Julian Press, (1955). 1st ed. Grn cl. VG. *Gach.* $28/£18

DEVOLUY, P. et al. The French Riviera. London, 1924. Clean, bright blue cvrs. *Lewis.* $25/£16

DEVONSHIRE, MRS. R.L. Rambles in Cairo. Cairo: Schindler, 1931. 2nd ed. Lg fldg color plan; 63 plts. Sl rubbed; spine torn, o/w VG. *Worldwide.* $45/£29

DEW, GWEN. Prisoner of the Japs. NY: Knopf, 1943. 1st ed. Fldg map. VG. *Petrilla.* $25/£16

DEWEES, WILLIAM. A Compendious System of Midwifery. Phila, 1826. 2nd ed. 612pp; 13 Fine engr plts. Recent 1/4 leather; new eps. *Fye.* $150/£97

DEWEES, WILLIAM. An Essay on the Means of Lessening Pain and Facilitating Certain Cases of Difficult Parturition. Phila, 1819. 2nd ed. 156pp (water stains). Orig bds; paper backstrip (cracked, worn). *Fye.* $300/£194

DEWEES, WILLIAM. Essays on Various Subjects Connected with Midwifery. Phila, 1823. 1st ed. 479pp. Orig leather. Good. *Fye.* $250/£161

DEWEES, WILLIAM. A Practice of Physic. Phila, 1833. 2nd ed. 819pp. Full leather. Good. *Fye.* $50/£32

DEWEES, WILLIAM. A Treatise on the Diseases of Females. Phila, 1828. 2nd ed. 542pp; 12 Fine engr plts. Full leather. Good. *Fye.* $200/£129

DEWEES, WILLIAM. A Treatise on the Diseases of Females. Phila, 1847. 9th ed. 532pp; 12 Fine engr plts. Full leather. Good. *Fye.* $125/£81

DEWEES, WILLIAM. A Treatise on the Physical and Medical Treatment of Children. Phila, 1833. 5th ed. 548pp. Leather. (Fep missing; water stain affecting leaves.) *Fye.* $45/£29

DEWEY, JOHN. Experience and Nature. Chicago: Open Court, 1925. 1st ed. Sl shelf wear; lt soiling pp edges, else NF. *Lame Duck.* $100/£65

DEWOLF, GORDON. Flora Exotica. Boston: Godine, 1972. Ltd to 3500. 15pp of color prints. Fine in dj. *Quest.* $45/£29

DEXTER, COLIN. The Inside Story. Pan Macmillan for American Express, 1993. 1st ed. Fine in pict wrappers. *Rees.* $31/£20

DEXTER, COLIN. Last Seen Wearing. Macmillan, 1976. 1st UK ed. Fine in VG dj (lacks sm chip). *Williams.* $612/£395

DEXTER, COLIN. Neighbourhood Watch. Moorhouse, 1992. #91/226. Fine in card cvrs. *Lewton.* $26/£17

DEXTER, COLIN. The Riddle of the Third Mile. Macmillan, 1983. 1st UK ed. Fine in dj. *Lewton.* $155/£100

DEXTER, COLIN. The Riddle of the Third Mile. Macmillan, 1983. 1st UK ed. Inscribed. Fine in NF dj. *Williams.* $186/£120

DEXTER, COLIN. Service of All the Dead. NY: St. Martin's, 1979. 1st ed. Fine in dj. *Mordida.* $150/£97

DEXTER, COLIN. The Silent World of Nicholas Quinn. NY: St. Martin's, 1977. 1st Amer ed. Fine in dj. *Mordida.* $200/£129

DEXTER, COLIN. The Way through the Woods. London: Macmillan, 1992. 1st ed. VF in dj. *Mordida.* $60/£39

DEXTER, COLIN. The Wench Is Dead. London: Macmillan, 1989. 1st ed. Signed. VF in dj. *Mordida.* $75/£48

DEXTER, COLIN. The Wench Is Dead. London: Macmillan, 1989. 1st UK ed. Fine in VG dj. *Lewton.* $19/£12

DEXTER, COLIN. The Wench Is Dead. NY: St. Martin's, 1990. 1st Amer ed. VF in dj. *Mordida.* $30/£19

DEXTER, PETE. Deadwood. NY: Random House, 1986. 1st ed. VF in dj. *Else Fine.* $45/£29

DEXTER, PETE. God's Pocket. NY: Random House, 1983. Rev copy, slip laid in. Inscribed. Fine in Fine dj. *Revere.* $100/£65

DEXTER, PETE. Paris Trout. NY: Random House, 1988. 1st ed. Signed. Fine in Fine dj. *Lame Duck.* $65/£42

DEY, MUKUL. My Pilgrimages to Ajanta and Bagh. OUP, 1950. 2nd ed. Color frontis; mod guide to Ajanta caves loosely inserted. VG in dj (defective). *Hollett.* $39/£25

DI BASSI, PIETRO ANDREA. The Labors of Hercules. Barre: Imprint Society, 1971. #107/1950 numbered. Bkpl, else Fine in pub's slipcase. *Hermitage.* $85/£55

DI CESNOLA, LOUIS PALMA. Cyprus: Its Ancient Cities, Tombs, and Temples. NY: Harper, 1878. xix,456pp. Teg. Sl rubbed, spine frayed, o/w VG. *Worldwide.* $130/£84

DI PRIMA, DIANE. Memoirs of a Beatnik. (NY: Olympia Press, 1969.) 1st ed. Fine in ptd wrappers. *Reese.* $60/£39

Diaries of Court Ladies of Old Japan. Annie Shepley Omori & Kochi Doi (trans). Boston/NY: Houghton Mifflin, (1920). Color frontis. Yellow cl (discolored, worn, bumped; foxing). *Schoyer.* $25/£16

DIBDIN, MICHAEL. Ratking. London: Faber, 1988. 1st UK ed. Fine in dj. *Lewton.* $54/£35

DIBDIN, MICHAEL. A Rich, Full Death. London: Cape, 1986. 1st UK ed. Fine in dj. *Lewton.* $54/£35

DIBDIN, MICHAEL. The Tryst. London: Faber, 1989. 1st ed. Fine in dj. *Rees.* $31/£20

DIBDIN, MICHAEL. The Tryst. London: Faber, 1989. 1st UK ed. Fine in dj. *Lewton.* $39/£25

DIBDIN, MICHAEL. Vendetta. Faber, 1990. 1st UK ed. Fine in dj. *Lewton.* $36/£23

DIBDIN, THOMAS FROGNALL. The Bibliographical Decameron. London: for author by W. Bulmer, Shakespeare Press, 1817. 1st ed. 3 vols. 4to. 19th cent full reddish-brn straight grained morocco; aeg. VG (old cat descrips tipped-in fr vol I; edges, corners rubbed; few joints starting; lacks the sample of gold ptg p417, vol II). *Chapel Hill.* $375/£242

DIBDIN, THOMAS FROGNALL. The Bibliographical Decameron. London: W. Bulmer, Shakespeare Press, 1817. 1st ed. 3 vols. 4to. 19th cent 3/4 morocco. *Chapel Hill.* $500/£323

DIBDIN, THOMAS FROGNALL. A Bibliographical, Antiquarian and Picturesque Tour in France and Germany. London: Robert Jennings & John Major, 1829. 2nd ed. 3 vols. 9 engr plts. (Internal foxing, browning.) Contemp 3/4 calf, marbled bds (ex-lib, stamp; worn; cracked joints). Overall Good. *Goodrich.* $165/£106

DIBDIN, THOMAS FROGNALL. A Bibliographical, Antiquarian and Picturesque Tour in France and Germany. London: Jennings & Major, 1829. 2nd ed. 3 vols. Frontis ports, 421; 428; 481pp, 33 autographs. Red cl (spines renewed); ptd labels. VG set (wear, sl foxing; armorial bkpls). *Hartfield.* $295/£190

DIBDIN, THOMAS FROGNALL. A Bibliographical, Antiquarian and Picturesque Tour in France and Germany. London: Robert Jennings and John Major, 1829. 2nd ed. 3 vols, complete. Blue pub's cl (respined; bkpls, pencil inscrips, newsclipping eps; cvrs sl rubbed, hinges internally strengthened.) Attractive set. *Bookpress.* $195/£126

DIBDIN, THOMAS FROGNALL. The Bibliomania or Book Madness, History, Symptoms and Cure of This Fatal Disease. Boston: Bibliophile Soc, 1903. Ltd to 483 copies. 4 vols, ptd on Bibliophile Soc watermarked paper. Full grn morocco, ribbed gilt dec spines (lt faded to brn). Teg, others uncut. *D & D.* $2,000/£1,290

DIBDIN, THOMAS FROGNALL. An Introduction to the Knowledge of Rare and Valuable Editions of the Greek and Latin Classics.... London: Longman et al, 1808. 3rd ed. 2 vols. 1/2 title, fldg facs frontis in vol 1. 3/4 maroon morocco (spine rubbed); teg. Good+ (lt foxing). *Houle.* $325/£210

DIBDIN, THOMAS FROGNALL. An Introduction to the Knowledge of Rare and Valuable Editions of the Greek and Roman Classics.... London: Harding & Lepard & G.B. Whittaker, 1827. 4th ed. 2 vols. (iv),xiii,(i),562pp, 1 plt; (iv),579,(1)pp. Contemp 1/2 leather; marbled panels, eps. (Contemp sig both bindings; vol 2 lacks 1/2 title.) *Bookpress.* $300/£194

DIBDIN, THOMAS FROGNALL. The Library Companion. London, 1825. 2nd ed. 1/2 calf (rebound), raised bands, gilt; marbled bds (new eps). Lib stamp tp, o/w Good. *Moss.* $171/£110

DIBLE, J. HENRY. Napoleon's Surgeon. London: Heineman, 1970. 1st ed. Frontis port. VG (ex-lib). *White.* $28/£18

DICEY, EDWARD. Six Months in the Federal States. London: Macmillan, 1863. 2 vols in 1. x,310; vi,326+2pp ads. Dk blue cl, gilt spine title. Good (recased; wear). Howes D 314. *Bohling.* $250/£161

DICK, GEORGE and GLADYS. Scarlet Fever. Chicago, 1938. 1st ed. Good. *Fye.* $75/£48

DICK, KAY. Ivy and Stevie. 1971. 1st UK ed. Fine in dj. *Sclanders.* $23/£15

DICK, PHILIP K. The Cosmic Puppets. (London): Severn House, (1986). 1st hb ed. Fine in dj (sl wear). *Levin.* $45/£29

DICK, PHILIP K. The Crack in Space. (Wallington, Surrey): Severn House, (1989). 1st hb ed. Fine in Fine dj. *Other Worlds.* $40/£26

DICK, PHILIP K. The Crack in Space. (Wallington): Severn House, (1989). 1st separate hb ed. Fine in dj. *Levin.* $25/£16

DICK, PHILIP K. Eye in the Sky. NY: Ace, (1957). 1st ed. Pb orig. Signed. Pp dknd, else NF in wrappers. *Between The Covers.* $375/£242

DICK, PHILIP K. Flow My Tears, the Policeman Said. Doubleday, 1974. 1st ed. Ex-lib, else VG in Fine dj. *Madle.* $65/£42

DICK, PHILIP K. Galactic Pot-Healer. Gollancz, 1971. 1st UK ed. Fine in dj. *Sclanders.* $70/£45

DICK, PHILIP K. The Game-Players of Titan. NY: Ace, (1963). Pb orig. Pp sl browned, else NF in wrappers. *Between The Covers.* $50/£32

DICK, PHILIP K. The Golden Man. Mark Hurst (ed). (NY): Berkley, (1980). 1st ed. Pb orig. Inscribed. Pp sl dknd; sl rubbed, else NF in wrappers. *Between The Covers.* $400/£258

DICK, PHILIP K. I Hope I Shall Arrive Soon. Doubleday, 1985. 1st ed. Fine in dj. *Aronovitz.* $25/£16

DICK, PHILIP K. The Man Who Japed. Eyre Methuen, 1978. 1st Eng, 1st hb ed. Fine in dj. *Aronovitz.* $225/£145

DICK, PHILIP K. The Man Whose Teeth Were All Exactly Alike. Willimantic: Ziesing, 1984. 1st ed. Fine in Fine dj (waterstaining spine head). *Other Worlds.* $75/£48

DICK, PHILIP K. Mary and the Giant. Gollancz, 1988. 1st UK ed. Fine in dj. *Williams.* $19/£12

DICK, PHILIP K. Our Friends from Frolix 8. NY: Ace Books, (1971). 1st hb ed (pub'd by The Science Fiction Book Club w/code B3 in gutter margin p184). NF in NF dj. *Levin.* $35/£23

DICK, PHILIP K. Solar Lottery. Boston: Gregg Press, 1976. 1st Amer hb ed. Bumped, o/w Fine (no dj as issued). *Levin.* $95/£61

DICK, PHILIP K. The Transmigration of Timothy Archer. NY: Timescape Books, 1982. Fine in dj. *Sclanders.* $31/£20

DICK, PHILIP K. Ubik. Doubleday, 1969. 1st ed. VG + in dj. *Aronovitz.* $525/£339

DICK, PHILIP K. Ubik: The Screenplay. Minneapolis: Corroboree Press, 1985. 1st ed, trade state. Fine in dj. *Levin.* $50/£32

DICK, PHILIP K. Valis. Kerosina Books, 1987. 1st ed. One of 1500. Fine in Fine dj. *Bishop.* $60/£39

DICK, PHILIP K. The Zap Gun. Boston: Gregg Press, 1979. 1st hb ed. Fine (no dj as issued). *Levin.* $125/£81

DICK, STEWART. The Cottage Homes of England. London: Arnold, 1909. 1st ed. 64 full-pg color plts by Helen Allingham. Grn cl, gilt. *Petersfield.* $279/£180

DICKENS, CHARLES and WILKIE COLLINS. The Lazy Tour of Two Idle Apprentices. London: Chapman & Hall, 1895. *Petersfield.* $33/£21

DICKENS, CHARLES. The Adventures of Oliver Twist; or, the Parish Boy's Progress.... London: Bradbury & Evans, 1846. 1st 8vo 1-vol ed, bound from monthly parts issue. (i-v),vi-vii,(viii-ix),x-xii,(1),2-311,(312)pp. 24 inserted plts by George Cruikshank. Full red morocco by Riviere (lt rubbed), gilt. Ptd wrappers of parts issue bound in at back. NF (bkpl removed). *Heritage.* $2,500/£1,613

DICKENS, CHARLES. The Adventures of Oliver Twist; or, the Parish Boy's Progress.... London: Bradbury & Evans, 1846. 1st 8vo 1-vol ed. Bound w/o 1/2 title. 24 plts by George Cruikshank. 1/2 brn morocco, marbled bds, matching eps; gilt spine (faded). Teg. *Heritage.* $200/£129

DICKENS, CHARLES. American Notes for General Circulation. London: Chapman & Hall, 1842. 3rd ed. Marbled edges. Forest grn 1/2 calf over marbled bds. Prelims lt foxed, else Nice. *Glenn.* $350/£226

DICKENS, CHARLES. American Notes for General Circulation.... London: Chapman & Hall, 1842. 1st ed. 2 vols. (i-xii) [(x) misnumbered xvi], (1),2-308 [internal fly-titles unnumbered]; (i-v),vi-vii,(viii),(1-3),4-306,(-312) (internal fly-titles unnumbered). (Prelims vol 1 show misnumbered pg b/c of last-minute decision to drop what Forster thought might be an ill-advised Preface.) Orig reddish brn horizontally-ribbed cl, panelled in blind w/stylized floral frame around central shield device. Spines lettered in gilt. Orig yellow eps. Good+ (smooth repair spine heads; lt rubbing, soiling). *Heritage.* $650/£419

DICKENS, CHARLES. American Notes for General Circulation.... London: Chapman & Hall, 1855. Frontis by C. Stanfield. Orig grn cl stamped in blind/gilt. (Lt rubbed, sl staining.) Text clean. *Heritage.* $125/£81

DICKENS, CHARLES. Barnaby Rudge.... Phila: E. Littell, 1842. Early Amer ed. Dbl-column text; no illus. Limp bds, cl backstrip. (Binding worn.) Protective fldg case erroneously ptd 'First American.' *Heritage.* $375/£242

DICKENS, CHARLES. The Battle of Life. NY: H.S. Nichols, (1914). Facs ed. *Heritage.* $60/£39

DICKENS, CHARLES. The Battle of Life: A Love Story. London: Bradbury & Evans, 1846. 1st ed, 4th issue. Aeg. Scarlet cl, gilt. Lt edgewear, lower hinge starting, else Fine. *Glenn.* $75/£48

DICKENS, CHARLES. Bleak House. London: Bradbury & Evans, 1853. 1st bk ed. 624pp. Grn 1/4 morocco (spine fading). VG (plts foxed). *Chapel Hill.* $200/£129

DICKENS, CHARLES. Bleak House. London, 1853. 1st book ed. 624pp. 1/2 leather, marbled bds (margins of plts sl browned; lt foxed, name; scuffed). *King.* $175/£113

DICKENS, CHARLES. Bleak House. London: Bradbury & Evans, 1853. 1st ed. Marbled edges, eps. Brn calf, gilt. VG. *Limestone.* $225/£145

DICKENS, CHARLES. Bleak House.... NY: Harper, 1853. 1st Amer ed. 2 vols. Frontis, (i-vii),viii-x,(xi)xii-xiv,(xv),xvi,(1),2-480; (ii),(481),482-936,4pp ads. 33 (of 37) wood engr plts. 1/4 crushed red-brn morocco, cl bds. Fine (sm leather bkpl). *Heritage.* $275/£177

DICKENS, CHARLES. Bleak House.... London: Bradbury & Evans, 1853. 1st ed. 8vo. (i-vii),viii-x,(xi)xii-xiv,(xv),xvi,(1),2-624pp. 40 inserted plts by Hablot Knight Browne. Pub's secondary cl binding (olive fine-diaper, blind-stamped) w/2nd vignette title. (Neat cl repair; fr hinge cracked, rear hinge repaired.) VG (lt corner dampstaining). *Heritage.* $2,000/£1,290

DICKENS, CHARLES. Charles Dickens's Letters to Charles Lever. Flora V. Livingston (ed). Cambridge: Harvard Univ, 1933. 1st ed. Fine in dj (sl dusty). *Cahan.* $40/£26

DICKENS, CHARLES. A Child's Dream of a Star. Boston: Fields, Osgood, 1871. 1st Amer ed. Aeg. Orig terra cotta cl, gilt. VG. *Macdonnell.* $100/£65

DICKENS, CHARLES. The Chimes. Phila: Lea & Blanchard, 1845. 1st Amer illus ed. 96pp; 12 illus, incl frontis, vignette title. Orig ecru cl, blocked in blind/gilt. Good. *Heritage.* $500/£323

DICKENS, CHARLES. The Chimes. London: Chapman & Hall, 1845. 1st ed. Steel engr frontis, tp by Maclise. (Sl staining.) Red cl, gilt (rebacked, orig spine laid down); aeg. VG. *Hartfield.* $295/£190

DICKENS, CHARLES. The Chimes. London: Chapman & Hall, 1845. 7th ed. Aeg. Red cl w/gilt decs. 13 illus, 5 by John Leech. VG. *Limestone.* $75/£48

DICKENS, CHARLES. The Chimes. London/NY: J.M. Dent/E.P. Dutton, 1905. Deluxe ed. Aeg. Full vellum, highly gilt. *Glenn.* $200/£129

DICKENS, CHARLES. The Chimes. London: LEC, 1931. One of 1500. Signed by Arthur Rackham (illus). Buckram over beveled bds; teg. VG (dknd; eps lt foxed; bkpl). *Cahan.* $375/£242

DICKENS, CHARLES. Christmas Books, from the Works of Charles Dickens. London/Paris: Bibliophile Soc, n.d. King Edward ed. 1/2 leather, marbled bds (spine rubbed; joints weak; 1914 inscrip). *Glenn.* $110/£71

DICKENS, CHARLES. Christmas Books. London: Chapman & Hall, 1852. 1st collected ed. Olive grn cl blocked in blind/gilt (spine faded; extrems worn). Overall Nice (eps foxed). *Glenn.* $250/£161

DICKENS, CHARLES. Christmas Books. London: Chapman & Hall, 1852. 1st collected ed. Celery grn cl blocked in blind/gilt. Lt wear, else VG. *Glenn.* $300/£194

DICKENS, CHARLES. A Christmas Carol and The Cricket on the Hearth. NY: Baker & Taylor, (1905). Color frontis (detached, laid in). Vertically ribbed black cl blocked in blind/gilt, cvr triptych of pict paper onlays. VG (bkpl). *Heritage.* $85/£55

DICKENS, CHARLES. A Christmas Carol in Prose, Being a Ghost Story of Christmas. Phila/Chicago/Toronto: John C. Winston, 1938. 1st ed thus, w/extra suite of illus by Everett Shinn. Red gilt-stamped cl. Gilt sl dimmed, else Fine in red gift box w/illus (battered, tape repairs, lacks 1 side). *Juvelis.* $350/£226

DICKENS, CHARLES. A Christmas Carol in Prose. (Phila: Robert & Samuel Dalton, 1950.) One of 600 numbered. B/w frontis. Headpieces, illus borders in red/grn. Red/grn initials. Leather-backed patterned bds. NF in slipcase (unevenly sunned). *Heritage.* $60/£39

DICKENS, CHARLES. A Christmas Carol. London: Heinemann, (1915). One of 525, signed by Arthur Rackham (illus). Lg, 4to. 12 mtd color plts; 20 b/w dwgs. Teg. White vellum, gilt, dec cvr, spine (few minor spots rear cvr; ties missing). Internally clean, bright. *Reisler.* $2,800/£1,806

DICKENS, CHARLES. A Christmas Carol. Boston: Atlantic Monthly, (1920). Facs of 1st ed. 3 color plts (incl frontis). Red cl. (Lt dampstaining several rear leaves; lt foxing eps.) *Glenn.* $100/£65

DICKENS, CHARLES. A Christmas Carol. Cleveland/NY: World, (1961). 1st ed. 6 dbl-pg illus By Ronald Searle. Fine in NF dj. *Glenn.* $150/£97

DICKENS, CHARLES. A Christmas Carol. (NY): James H. Heineman, (1967). Facing facs holograph; 4 tipped-in color plts. Red cl. Fine in VG dj. *Heritage.* $50/£32

DICKENS, CHARLES. A Christmas Carol. Boston: LEC, 1934. One of 1500. Signed by Gordon Ross (illus). Part upper fr bd rubbed through, o/w VG in Good case. *Agvent.* $75/£48

DICKENS, CHARLES. A Christmas Carol. In Prose. London: Chapman & Hall, 1843. 1st ed. (i-viii),(1),2-166,(-168)pp ads. 4 hand-colored plts by John Leech inserted. Full crimson morocco w/full gilt extra; Dickens cameo in gilt on top bd; facs Dickens sig w/full flourish in gilt on bottom bd. Fine. *Heritage.* $4,900/£3,161

DICKENS, CHARLES. The Cricket on the Hearth, a Fairy-Tale of Home. London: LEC, 1933. #904/1500 numbered. Hugh Thompson (illus). Full pict cl. Fine in pub's slipcase (sl worn). *Hermitage.* $150/£97

DICKENS, CHARLES. The Cricket on the Hearth. London: Bradbury & Evans, 1846 (i.e., Dec 1845). 1st ed. (i-viii),(1),2-174pp; engr title, frontis by Maclise. 1/2 dk purple leather, purple pebbled bds (rubbed). *Heritage.* $150/£97

DICKENS, CHARLES. The Cricket on the Hearth. London, 1846. 1st ed, 1st state. 174pp; aeg. Gilt-stamped pict cl (spine ends frayed, sl rubbed). *King.* $295/£190

DICKENS, CHARLES. Dealings with the Firm of Dombey and Son. NY: LEC, 1957. One of 1500 signed by Henry C. Pitz (illus). 2 vols. NF set in pub's slipcase (sm stain). *Cahan.* $75/£48

DICKENS, CHARLES. Dealings with the Firm of Dombey and Son.... Leipzig: Tauchnitz, 1847. 3 vols. Binder's mauve vertical wave-grain cl (backstrips faded; lack 1/2 titles; sig). *Waterfield.* $186/£120

DICKENS, CHARLES. The Dickens-Kolle Letters. Harry B. Smith (ed). Boston: Bibliophile Soc, 1910. 1st ed. One of 483 ptd. Japan vellum spine, corners; brn cl sides; spine gilt. Lt soiled, else Fine. *Hermitage.* $85/£55

DICKENS, CHARLES. Dombey and Son. London, 1848. 1st book ed (incl errata; lacks half-title). H.K. Browne (illus). 624pp (plt browned). Later 1/2 blue-grn morocco, marbled bds (sl rubbed, spine faded; foxing). *King.* $195/£126

DICKENS, CHARLES. Dombey and Son. London, 1848. 1st book ed (lacks errata leaf, possibly later issue). H.K. Browne (illus). 624pp (few loose; plts spotted). 1/2 calf, marbled bds (fr inner hinge completely detached; rubbed). *King.* $150/£97

DICKENS, CHARLES. Dombey and Son. London: Bradbury & Evans, 1848. 1st ed in bk form, bound up from orig parts pub serially between October 1846 and April 1848. Has 'capatin' misprint foot of p324, earlier (2-line) errata leaf. Etched frontis, extra title, 38 plts (foxed) by H. K. Browne ('Phiz'). Contemp 1/2 calf, gilt; marbled sides, edges (sl mks; bound w/o 1/2 title; leaf w/sm marginal tear). Nice. *Ash.* $310/£200

DICKENS, CHARLES. Dombey and Son. London: Bradbury & Evans, 1848. 1st ed. Frontis (spotted), engr title, xiv,625pp (marginal spotting); 39 plts by H.K. Browne. Contemp 1/2 calf gilt (sl rubbed). *Hollett.* $132/£85

DICKENS, CHARLES. Dombey and Son. NY: LEC, 1957. One of 1500 signed by Henry C. Pitz (illus). 2 vols. Rose buckram, paper labels. Spines sl faded, o/w NF in open-end pict box (sl shelfworn). *Heritage.* $75/£48

DICKENS, CHARLES. Dombey and Son.... London: Bradbury & Evans, 1848. 1st ed. 8vo. (i-vi),(ix-xi),xii-xiv,(xv),xvi,(1),2-624pp (i.e., bound w/o dedication leaf of prelims). 'Captain' is correct on p324. 40 inserted plts (lt foxing, browning), incl frontis, vignette title. Orig pub's grn cl variant (rebacked preserving orig backstrip; sl staining), new eps. Good. *Heritage.* $600/£387

DICKENS, CHARLES. Hard Times for These Times. NY: LEC, 1966. One of 1500 signed by Charles Raymond (illus). Orig natural buckram ove blue-grey paper bds, spine label stamped in gilt; top edge stained blue. Fine in orig cardboard open-end slipcase. *Heritage*. $60/£39

DICKENS, CHARLES. Hard Times. London, 1854. 1st book ed, orig cl bound in. 1st issue binding, priced 5/- on backstrip. 352pp (foxed spots). Full tan calf, ribbed gilt spine in 6 panels, maroon/grn gilt-lettered labels, cvrs bordered w/triple gilt fillet; teg. Nice. *King*. $350/£226

DICKENS, CHARLES. Hard Times. London: Bradbury & Evans, 1854. 1st ed, 1st binding w/5 shilling price at foot. Orig grn cl, gilt (spine crown frayed). VG (split in upper joint neatly glued). *Macdonnell*. $600/£387

DICKENS, CHARLES. Hard Times. For These Times.... London: Bradbury & Evans, 1854. 1st ed. 8vo. (i-vii),viii,(1-3),4-352pp. Orig olive moire horizontally-ribbed cl, pub's primary binding. Orig pale yellow eps. (Fading, fraying along spine; pencilling erased from rep; early ink sig dedication pg.) *Heritage*. $1,000/£645

DICKENS, CHARLES. Hard Times: For These Times. NY: LEC, 1966. One of 1500 signed by Charles Raymond (illus). Cl-backed bds. Fine in glassine wrapper, slipcase (sl faded). *Cahan*. $75/£48

DICKENS, CHARLES. The Haunted Man and the Ghost's Bargain. London: Bradbury & Evans, 1848. 1st ed. Litho frontis, title, (i-viii),(1),2-188pp. Orig red cl stamped in blind/gilt (soil). VG +. *Heritage*. $350/£226

DICKENS, CHARLES. Hunted Down. London: John Camden Hotten, (1871). 1st ed. Teg. Back panel of orig grn dj bound in. Half red morocco, gilt, w/sl raised bands over marbled bds. Marbled eps. Very Nice. *Limestone*. $285/£184

DICKENS, CHARLES. The Life and Adventures of Martin Chuzzlewit. London, 1844. 1st book ed, 1st issue. Phiz (illus). 624pp (extra title remargined; foxing; plts spotted). Full blindstamped leather, gilt borders, leather label (inner hinges cracked; rubbed). *King*. $250/£161

DICKENS, CHARLES. The Life and Adventures of Martin Chuzzlewit. London: Chapman & Hall, 1844. 1st ed in bk form, bound up from orig monthly parts pub between January 1843 and July 1844. Frontis, extra title (exhibits the misplaced pound sign), 38 etched plts by 'Phiz.' Contemp 1/2 calf, gilt (sl rubbed, dull). Good (bound w/o 1/2 title; spotting, mainly to plts). *Ash*. $310/£200

DICKENS, CHARLES. The Life and Adventures of Martin Chuzzlewit.... London: Chapman & Hall, 1844. 1st ed. (i-vii),viii,(ix),x-xii,(xiii),xiv,(xv-xvi),(1),2-624pp. 40 inserted plts by Phiz. 14-line errata. Orig pub's cl binding: variant of pebble-grained moderate blue cl w/same stamping as called for; spine w/o imprint. (Extensive cl repair, replacement along spine; hinges amateurishly fixed.) Good + (bkpl) in slipcase. *Heritage*. $650/£419

DICKENS, CHARLES. The Life and Adventures of Nicholas Nickleby. London, 1839. 1st book ed. Phiz (illus). 624pp (inscrip, lt foxed; plts heavily foxed; inner hinges cracked). 1/2 leather, marbled bds, red leather label, gilt-dec spine (heavily rubbed). *King*. $150/£97

DICKENS, CHARLES. The Life and Adventures of Nicholas Nickleby.... London: Chapman & Hall, 1839 (i.e., April 1838-Oct 1839). 1st ed, in orig monthly parts, 20 numbers bound in 19. Frontis port by Maclise, (i-vii),viii-x,(xi),xii-xiv,(xv),xvi,(1),2-624pp (lacks 2 rarest back ads, lacks 1 back ad Part IV, 'Advertiser' Part II; contemp ink sigs). 39 plts by Phiz (some w/foxing, edge browning). Orig ptd wrappers (sl spine repair, restoration ltd to last 2 parts). 4-fold chemise; pull-off box of full hunter grn morocco. *Heritage*. $3,000/£1,935

DICKENS, CHARLES. The Life and Adventures of Nicholas Nickleby.... London: Chapman & Hall, 1839. 1st ed. Frontis port by Maclise, (i-vii),viii-x,(xi),xii-xiv,(xv),xvi,(1),2-624pp. 39 inserted plts by Phiz. 1/2 morocco, grn floral pattern cl. Good. *Heritage*. $200/£129

DICKENS, CHARLES. The Life and Adventures of Nicholas Nickleby.... London: Chapman & Hall, 1839. 1st ed. Frontis port by Maclise, (i-vii),viii-x,(xi),xii-xiv,(xv),xvi,(1),2-624pp (p123 is corrected state ('sister'), p160 is 1st issue ('latter'). 39 inserted plts by Phiz; early plts bear imprint, frontis does not. Scored calf (rebacked preserving orig backstrip), black morocco labels (sm chips), gilt ruling, marbled eps; aeg; ribbon marker. VG (hinges repaired amateurishly but neatly). *Heritage*. $375/£242

DICKENS, CHARLES. The Life and Adventures of Nicholas Nickleby.... London: Chapman & Hall, 1839. 1st ed. Frontis port by Maclise, (i-vii),viii-x,(xi),xii-xiv,(xv),xvi,(1),2-624pp. Pg123 shows 1st issue misprint 'visiter', but p160 is corrected. 39 plts by Phiz (some lt foxed); early plts & frontis bear 1st issue imprint. 1/2 pebble-grain leather, marbled bds (lt rubbed), matching eps; teg. *Heritage*. $600/£387

DICKENS, CHARLES. The Life of Our Lord Written During the Years 1846-1849.... NY: S&S, 1934. #400/2387 ptd in black/red. White blind-emb 'mock-vellum' paper bds, gilt titled spine (sl sunned). *Book Block*. $70/£45

DICKENS, CHARLES. Little Dorrit. London: Bradbury & Evans, 1857. 1st ed. xiv,625pp (lacks 1/2 title), 39 illus by H.K. Browne. Contemp 1/2 calf (worn, spine faded; sl shaken, spotted, joints cracked), but Good. *Hollett*. $186/£120

DICKENS, CHARLES. Martin Chuzzlewit. NY: Knopf, 1947. 1st ed. NF in VG dj & VG slipcase. *Bishop*. $27/£17

DICKENS, CHARLES. Master Humphrey's Clock. London: Chapman & Hall, 1840, 1841. 1st ed. 3 vols, recently bound as 1. One-half morocco. Dickens centenary stamp laid in. Lacks dedication leaf, else very clean. *Glenn*. $350/£226

DICKENS, CHARLES. Master Humphrey's Clock. London: Chapman & Hall, 1840-1841. 1st bk ed. 3 vols. Lg 8vo. Frontis each vol, iv,306; vi,306; vi,426pp. Orig gilt pict, blindstamped cl. VG (bkpl each vol, sm owner stamp tps). *House*. $750/£484

DICKENS, CHARLES. Master Humphrey's Clock. London: Chapman & Hall, 1840-1841. 1st ed in bk form of both 'The Old Curiosity Shop' and 'Barnaby Rudge.' 3 vols. Dec cl, gilt, clock device; marbled eps, edges. Nice set (bkpls; wear, lt loss spine tips). *Ash*. $543/£350

DICKENS, CHARLES. Master Humphrey's Clock. London: Chapman & Hall, 1840-41. 1st bk ed, 1st issue, w/gilt-dec clock hands on fr cvrs pointing to vol #s. 3 vols. 4to, 306; 426pp. George Cattermole and Hablot Browne (illus). Brn cl (bkpl, spines lt faded; sm repair top of Vol 1 spine, sl crease in Vol 3). *Chapel Hill.* $1,200/£774

DICKENS, CHARLES. Master Humphrey's Clock. London: Chapman & Hall, 1840-41. 1st ed in bk format. 3 vols. (Browning.) 1/4 roan, marble bds (new eps; vol 1 recased, orig spine laid down; worn; corners re-tipped). Overall Good. *Goodrich.* $175/£113

DICKENS, CHARLES. The Mystery of Edwin Drood. London, 1870. 1st book ed. 190pp, port. 1/2 calf (fr hinge torn, spine faded, cvrs worn). *King.* $125/£81

DICKENS, CHARLES. The Mystery of Edwin Drood. London: Chapman & Hall, 1870. 1st ed. Pub's grn 1/2 leather binding (from orig parts w/o cvrs, most ads), marbled eps, edges, bds. VG (edgewear). *Other Worlds.* $250/£161

DICKENS, CHARLES. The Nonesuch Dickens. Bloomsbury: Nonesuch, 1937-1938. 25 vols. Orig plt by Phiz (Hablot K. Browne) p282 of Nicholas Nickleby. Teg. Various colored buckram, all w/gilt-titled and bordered black morocco spine labels (few lt worn; few spines rubbed, 1 lt sunned; offsetting of engrs.) NF. *Glenn.* $7,000/£4,516

DICKENS, CHARLES. The Old Curiosity Shop. London: Chapman & Hall, 1841. 1st ed of 1st separate issue. Frontis, (i-iii),iv,(1),2-306,(1),2-223,(224)pp (p2 numbered 2-38; p47 numbered 47-79; p96 numbered 96-102; p128 numbered 128-132). Ad expected as p(iii) has been cancelled here, replaced w/dedication pg of 1st bk form of Master Humphrey's Clock. Orig greyish-red fine diaper, dec stamped in blind, spine stamped in black/gilt. Marbled eps, matching edges. (2 sm tears fr joint cl; corners rubbed; starting to fray spine ends; sm ink stain bottom bd.) Internally bright. *Heritage.* $1,000/£645

DICKENS, CHARLES. The Old Curiosity Shop. London/NY/Toronto: Hodder & Stoughton, n.d. (1913). Deluxe ed. Ltd to 350, signed by Frank Reynolds (illus). Full vellum (foxed), gilt; silhouette port fr cvr. Lacks ties, bkpl removal, else VG. *Glenn.* $650/£419

DICKENS, CHARLES. Oliver Twist.... Cincinnati: U.P. James, 1839. Early Amer ed. 2 vols. (i-iii),iv,(5),6-216; (i-ii),(1-3),4-196pp; tps are cancels. Orig floral patterned pink cl over tan bds (extrems rubbed), paper spine labels (chipped, affecting some text). Good (foxing, browning; lib rubber stamp of Carl Pforzheimer on back pastedowns; hinges cracking). *Heritage.* $350/£226

DICKENS, CHARLES. Oliver Twist.... Phila: Lea & Blanchard, 1839. Early Amer ed. 2 vols. (i-ii),(i-iii),iv,(13),14-224; (i-iii),iv,(3),4-196pp, 16pp ads. Red cl over brn bds, paper spine labels. (Lt soiling, staining, wear, some repairs; hinges amateurishly strengthened; foxed.) *Heritage.* $550/£355

DICKENS, CHARLES. Our Mutual Friend. Harpers, 1865. 1st Amer ed. Good. *Fine Books.* $150/£97

DICKENS, CHARLES. Our Mutual Friend. London, 1865. 1st book ed. 2 vols. 320; 309pp (bkpl; many plts w/stab holes in margins; foxing; sl dampspot; lacks 1/2 titles). Early 1/2 grn calf, marbled bds (faded, scuffed; joint starting; sl frayed). *King.* $185/£119

DICKENS, CHARLES. The Personal History of David Copperfield. London: Bradbury & Evans, 1850. 1st ed. Diced emerald grn calf (newly rebacked, recased; sl foxing). Smith p76. *Glenn.* $725/£468

DICKENS, CHARLES. The Personal History of David Copperfield. London: Chapman & Hall, 1866. 2 vols. (iv),266,(2)pp ads; (iv),249,(250)pp (lt foxing; ink sigs). Orig grn pict bds (joints, corners rubbed). VG. *Heritage.* $100/£65

DICKENS, CHARLES. The Personal History of David Copperfield. London, n.d. (1870?). H.K. Browne (illus). 624pp (inscrip; inner fr hinge cracked). 1/2 red leather, marbled bds (rubbed). *King.* $150/£97

DICKENS, CHARLES. The Personal History of David Copperfield.... London: Bradbury & Evans, 1850 (i.e., May 1849-Nov 1850). 1st ed in orig monthly parts, 20 bound in 19. (i-vii),viii,(ix),x-xii,(xiii),xiv,(xv-xvi),(1),2-624pp. 40 inserted plts by Hablot Knight Browne, incl frontis and vignette title. Orig ptd wrappers. This set collates complete w/every Advertiser, every slip, and every back ad called for. (Numbers smoothly rebacked.) Chemised in 1/4 grn-black morocco slipcase. *Heritage.* $8,500/£5,484

DICKENS, CHARLES. The Posthumous Papers of the Pickwick Club. Carey, Lea & Blanchard, 1837. 1st Amer ed. Parts 2,3 & 4. Fair w/Nice contents. *Fine Books.* $200/£129

DICKENS, CHARLES. The Posthumous Papers of the Pickwick Club. London: Chapman & Hall, 1837. 1st book ed, 2nd issue, w/'Tony Weller' on signbd in engr title. Thick 8vo, 609pp. 13 colored plts. Signed envelope laid in. Full gilt-tooled polished calf, raised bands, morocco spine labels (rebacked w/orig spine laid down). *Chapel Hill.* $1,000/£645

DICKENS, CHARLES. The Posthumous Papers of the Pickwick Club. London: Chapman & Hall, 1837. 1st ed in bk form, bound up from orig monthly parts. Frontis, extra title, 41 etched plts by Seymour and 'Phiz'. Neat contemp 1/2 calf, gilt, blind (sl rubbed; minor nicks, tears). Good (leaf repaired at margin; lt browning, staining, mainly to plts). *Ash.* $388/£250

DICKENS, CHARLES. The Posthumous Papers of the Pickwick Club. London: Chapman & Hall, 1837. 1st ed, early state w/'Veller' vignette tp, 'Phiz fecit' on frontis, 7 early plts signed by Seymour, 2 plts signed by Buss. Contemp crimson 3/4 calf, raised bands, gilt. Handsome (plts foxed; marbled sides worn). *Macdonnell.* $600/£387

DICKENS, CHARLES. The Posthumous Papers of the Pickwick Club. London: Chapman & Hall, 1837. 1st ed. 43 illus by Seymour & Phiz; 2 add'l cancelled plts by Buss. 3/4 polished calf, marbled bds/eps, leather labels, silk ribbon marker; teg. Very Nice. *Hartfield.* $695/£448

DICKENS, CHARLES. The Posthumous Papers of the Pickwick Club.... NY: Hodder & Stoughton, (n.d.). Frank Reynolds (illus). Glazed red buckram, blocked in gilt/white/black. NF (staining back bd; fr hinge sl tender; leather bkpl). *Heritage.* $125/£81

DICKENS, CHARLES. The Posthumous Papers of the Pickwick Club.... London: Chapman & Hall, 1837 (i.e., April 1836-Nov 1837). 1st ed, in orig monthly parts, 20 numbers bound in 19 parts. 8vo. (i-v),vi,(vii),viii-ix,(x-xi),xii-xiv,(xv-xvi),(1),2-609,(610)pp; 43 inserted plts by R. Seymour and Phiz. Orig grn wrappers. (Part I has most wear; early #s are later issues w/o addresses and ads, though III does have supplied copy of called-for address laid in). Wrappers for I-III bear simplified illus credit; suppressed Buss plts do appear in Part III; most of later numbers have their ads. Chemised in 1/4 grn morocco slipcase. *Heritage.* $3,750/£2,419

DICKENS, CHARLES. The Posthumous Papers of the Pickwick Club.... London: Chapman & Hall, 1837. 1st ed. 8vo. (i-v),vi,(vii),viii-ix,(x-xi),xii-xiv,(xv-xvi),(1),2-609,(610)pp. 43 illus by R. Seymour and Phiz; 2nd steels of Seymour plts, Phiz replacements for Buss plts. Full smooth polished calf by Riviere, gilt, morocco spine labels; marbled eps. NF. *Heritage*. $850/£548

DICKENS, CHARLES. The Posthumous Papers of the Pickwick Club.... NY: James Turney, 1838. 1st Amer 1-vol ed. (i-v),vi,(vii),viii,(1),2-609,(610)pp (foxed, some waterstaining). 30 plts only by R. Seymour and Phiz. Orig cl (worn, repaired). *Heritage*. $200/£129

DICKENS, CHARLES. The Posthumous Papers of the Pickwick Club.... Leipzig: Bernhard Tauchnitz, 1842. Copyright ed. 2 vols. Frontis port, (i-v),vi,(vii),viii,(1),2-432; (i-iv),(1),2-427,(428)pp. Orig vertically-ribbed black cl, bordered in blind (sl rubbed, spine ends sl chipped). *Heritage*. $175/£113

DICKENS, CHARLES. The Posthumous Papers of the Pickwick Club.... Oxford: LEC, 1933. 2 vols. Fine in NF djs, orig paper slipcase (sl wear). *Heritage*. $250/£161

DICKENS, CHARLES. A Tale of Two Cities. London: Chapman & Hall, (n.d. but 1876). Amer ed of British sheets of 'Household Edition' of this title, w/D. Appleton & Co's imprint, ads on wrapper. Frontis. Pict blue wrappers (dust soiled, spine chipped, rear wrapper detached; text lt foxed). *Reese*. $50/£32

DICKENS, CHARLES. A Tale of Two Cities. London: Chapman & Hall, 1859. 1st ed w/issue pts: p(vii), Chapter VII, titled 'Monsieur the Marquis in Town' in Contents, but 'Monseigneur in Town' in text; p(vii): Chapter VIII titled 'Monseigneur the Marquis in the Country' in Contents, but "Monseigneur in the Country" in text; p(ix), 'Stryver' spelled 'Striver' in pl caption, p98 Chapter # followed by comma (?) rather than period; p134, line 12, 'affetcionately'; p166, 5 lines up 'If' correctly ptd in 'himself'; p213, correctly numbered '213'; p238, line 14, triple end quotes. H.K. Browne (illus). Pub's olive grn cl (cvrs unevenly faded) blind-stamped, gilt lettered spine (faded to brn; head, foot w w/loss). Blue open-ended slipcase. Good overall. *D & D*. $2,500/£1,613

DICKENS, CHARLES. The Works of Charles Dickens...with Introduction, General Essay, and Notes, by Andrew Lang. London: Chapman & Hall, 1903. #5/130 sets. Edition Deluxe of the Gadshill ed, w/illus on Japanese paper. 38 vols. 8vo. Teg. Brn buckram, paper spine labels. Fine in orig cl djs. *Cummins*. $1,500/£968

DICKENS, MAMIE. My Father as I Recall Him. London: Roxburgue Press, (1897). 1st ed. (vi),(7),8-128pp + 4pp ads. Untrimmed. Grn cl, pict fr cvr, gilt spine. Very Nice. *Vandoros*. $100/£65

DICKEY, JAMES. Buckdancer's Choice. Middletown, CT: Wesleyan Univ, 1965. 1st ed. Fine (except sm dent rear joint) in illus dj (sm hole, sl soil). *Cahan*. $85/£55

DICKEY, JAMES. Deliverance. Boston, 1970. 1st ed. VG in dj (top edge frayed). *Artis*. $20/£13

DICKEY, JAMES. Deliverance. Boston: Houghton Mifflin, 1970. 1st ed. Signed. Beige cl. VG in VG dj. *Chapel Hill*. $200/£129

DICKEY, JAMES. Drowning with Others. Middletown, CT: Wesleyan University, 1962. 1st ed, 1st bk. Name, else Fine in NF illus dj. *Cahan*. $150/£97

DICKEY, JAMES. Poems 1957-1967. London: Rapp & Carroll, (1967). 1st Eng ed. Signed. Fine in dj. *Juvelis*. $40/£26

DICKEY, JAMES. Poems: 1957-1967. Middletown: Wesleyan Univ, (1967). 1st ed. Fine in dj (sl wear). *Antic Hay*. $35/£23

DICKEY, JAMES. The Zodiac. NY: Doubleday, 1976. 1st ed. Signed. Fine in dj. *Sadlon*. $35/£23

DICKINSON, EMILY. Letters of Emily Dickinson. Mable Loomis Todd (ed). Boston: Roberts Brothers, 1894. 1st ed, 2nd ptg. 2 vols. VG (lt spotted). BAL 4660. *Bookpress*. $225/£145

DICKINSON, EMILY. The Pamphlet Poets. NY: S&S, (1927). 1st thus. VG in wraps. *Agvent*. $30/£19

DICKINSON, EMILY. The Poems of Emily Dickinson. Martha Dickinson Bianchi & Alfred Leete Hampson (eds). Boston: Little, Brown, 1937. 1st ed. Bkpl, else VG in dj (lg tears mended internally w/tape, long crease). BAL 4690. *Godot*. $50/£32

DICKINSON, EMILY. Poems. Second Series. T.W. Higginson and Mabel Loomis Todd (eds). Boston: Roberts Brothers, 1891. Gray cl, gilt-titled. Lt rubbing rear bd w/sl color transfer, o/w Fine. *Hermitage*. $800/£516

DICKINSON, EMILY. Poems. Second Series. T.W. Higginson and Mabel Loomis Todd (eds). Boston: Roberts Brothers, 1891. 1st ed. Sm 8vo. Pub's orig gilt dec gray-grn cl. Spine ends lt rubbed, sig fep, else VF. BAL 4661. *D & D*. $750/£484

DICKINSON, EMILY. Poems. Third Series. Mabel Loomis Todd (ed). Boston: Roberts Brothers, 1896. 1st ed, in the 1st of 2 bindings noted by Blanck, w/white ribbon marker found 'in some copies' (detached). Sm 8vo. Pub's orig gilt dec lt grn cl. Spine ends lt rubbed; dated sig fep, else VF. BAL 4656. *D & D*. $750/£484

DICKINSON, EMILY. The Single Hound. Boston: Little, Brown, 1914. 1st ed, 1st ptg. One of 595 ptd. White cl-backed bds. Corners sl rubbed, else Nice. BAL 4669. *Macdonnell*. $350/£226

DICKINSON, H.W. A Short History of the Steam Engine. Cambridge, 1938. 1st ed. Frontis port, 10 plts, 3 tables (1 fldg). (Lt wear, spine lt sunned.) *Edwards*. $39/£25

DICKINSON, J.C. Monastic Life in Medieval England. London: A&C Black, 1961. 1st ed. 57 plts, 6 plans. VG in dj (sl worn). *Hollett*. $70/£45

DICKSON, ARTHUR JEROME (ed). Covered Wagon Days. Cleveland: A.H. Clark, 1929. 1st ed. Fldg map. VG. *Lien*. $150/£97

DICKSON, ARTHUR JEROME (ed). Covered Wagon Days: A Journey Across the Plains in the Sixties, and Pioneer Days in the Northwest.... Cleveland: Clark, 1929. 1st ed. (Bkpl removed.) *Ginsberg*. $125/£81

DICKSON, CARTER. (Pseud of John Dickson Carr). Nine—And Death Makes Ten. NY: William Morrow, 1940. 1st ed. Label removed; pg edges dknd, o/w VG in dj (chipping; closed tears). *Mordida*. $100/£65

DICKSON, EDWARD. Woman and Her Diseases, From the Cradle to the Grave. Phila, 1866. 10th ed. 318pp. Good. *Fye*. $75/£48

DICKSON, GORDON. Secret Under Antarctica. Holt, 1968. 1st ed. Fine in VG dj (closed tear). *Madle*. $75/£48

DICKSON, SAMUEL. The Principles of the Chrono-Thermal System of Medicine.... NY, 1852. 15th ed. 224pp. Full leather. Good. *Fye*. $40/£26

DIDAY, P. A Treatise on Syphilis in New-Born Children and Infants at the Breast. London, 1859. 1st Eng trans. 272pp. Good. *Fye*. $150/£97

DIDAY, P. A Treatise on Syphilis in New-Born Children and Infants at the Breast. NY, 1883. 1st Amer ed. 310pp. Good. *Fye.* $100/£65

DIDAY, P. A Treatise on Syphilis.... G. Whiley (trans). London: New Sydenham Soc, 1859. xii,272pp. Emb cl (sl bumped; sunned), gilt device. *Edwards.* $101/£65

DIDION, JOAN. Play It As It Lays. NY, (1970). 1st ed. Fine in Fine dj. *Fuller & Saunders.* $25/£16

DIDION, JOAN. Slouching Towards Bethlehem. NY: FSG, (1968). 1st ed. NF in dj (lt edgewear; few tiny tears, nicks). *Antic Hay.* $75/£48

DIDSBURY, DAVID (comp). T.E. Lawrence of Arabia. A Collector's Booklist. London: Privately pub by compiler, 1972. 1st Eng ed. NF (cvrs sl mkd) in wrappers. *Ulysses.* $85/£55

DIEBENKORN, RICHARD. The Ocean Park Series: Recent Work. London: Marlborough Fine Art, (1974). Photo port; 26 color repros. VG in stiff pict wrappers; extra mylar wrapper. *Argosy.* $35/£23

DIEHL, EDITH. Bookbinding, Its Background and Technique. NY: Rinehart, 1946. 1st ed. 2 vols. 91 plts. Black cl, gilt. VG. *Shasky.* $150/£97

DIEHL, EDITH. Bookbinding, Its Background and Technique. NY: Rinehart, 1946. 1st ed. 2 vols. 91 plts. Fine (bkpl) in slipcase. *Bookpress.* $200/£129

DIEHL, EDNA GROFF. Aunt Este's Stories of the Vegetable and Fruit Children. Chicago: Albert Whitman, (1923). 1st ed. Vera Stone (illus). 8vo. 111pp. Navy cl, pict paste label; illus eps. VG. *Drusilla's.* $35/£23

DIETZ, ARTHUR ARNOLD. Mad Rush for Gold in the Frozen North. LA: Times-Mirror, 1914. Dec cl. Spine title dull, else VG. *High Latitude.* $65/£42

DIETZ, ARTHUR ARNOLD. Mad Rush for Gold in the Frozen North. LA: Times Mirror, 1914. 1st ed. Frontis, plt. Pict cl. Spotting on spine, loss of spine title gilt, o/w VG. *Oregon.* $50/£32

DIETZ, AUGUST. The Postal Service of the Confederate States of America. Richmond: Dietz Ptg, 1929. 1st ed. Signed. Color frontis. Orig grey cl. Bright, little wear. Howes D 341. *Chapel Hill.* $450/£290

DIEZ, ERNST and OTTO DEMUS. Byzantine Mosaics in Greece. Cambridge, 1931. 60 plts (15 tipped-in color). Good (spine sl sunned). *Washton.* $195/£126

DIEZ, ERNST and OTTO DEMUS. Byzantine Mosaics in Greece: Daphni and Hosios Lucas. Cambridge: Harvard Univ, 1931. 15 mtd color plts, 3 plans. Upper cvr corner sl stained, o/w Fine. *Europa.* $171/£110

DIFUSCO, JOHN et al. Tracers. NY: Hill & Wang, (1986). 1st ed. Fine in Fine dj. *Aka.* $40/£26

DIGBY, EDWARD. Private Memoirs.... London: Saunders & Otley, 1827. 1st ed. Engr frontis port of Digby, lxxxviii,328pp. 3/4 gilt morocco; raised spine panels; gilt. (Worn; mild dampstaining margins.) *Goodrich.* $150/£97

DIGBY, GEORGE WINGFIELD. The Tapestry Collection. Medieval and Renaissance. London, Victoria & Albert Museum, 1980. 108 plts. Good. *Washton.* $85/£55

DIGGES, THOMAS ATTWOOD. Letters of Thomas Attwood Digges (1742-1821). Robert H. Elias & Eugene D. Finch (eds). Columbia: Univ of SC, 1982. 1st ed. Fine in Fine dj. *Connolly.* $45/£29

DIKE, SHELDON H. The Territorial Post Offices of Colorado. (Albuquerque: S.H. Dike, 1957). Ptd wrappers, cl tape spine. *Dawson.* $30/£19

DILKE, CHARLES WENTWORTH. Great Britain: A Record of Travel.... London: Macmillan, 1868. 1st ed. Inscribed. 2 vols. 2 chromolitho frontispieces, xi,404pp, tipped-in errata, 48pp cat; 428pp; 8 plts, 6 maps. Bright grn cl. VG. *Schoyer.* $250/£161

DILL, L.V. The Obstetrical Forceps. Springfield, IL, 1953. VG. *Argosy.* $35/£23

DILLARD, ANNIE. The Living. Harper Collins, (1992). 1st ltd ed of 300 numbered, signed. New in slipcase. *Authors Of The West.* $125/£81

DILLARD, ANNIE. Pilgrim at Tinker Creek. NY: Harper's Magazine Press, 1974. 1st ed. VG in VG dj. *Revere.* $65/£42

DILLARD, ANNIE. Teaching a Stone to Talk. NY: Harper & Row, 1982. 1st ed. Fine in Fine dj. *Revere.* $40/£26

DILLARD, ANNIE. Tickets for a Prayer Wheel. (Columbia): Univ of MO, (1974). 1st ed, 1st bk. Fine in flexible bds, dj as issued. *Between The Covers.* $650/£419

DILLARD, J.L. Black English. NY: Random House, (1972). 1st ed. VG in dj. *Petrilla.* $30/£19

DILLEY, ARTHUR URBANE. Oriental Rugs and Carpets. Phila: Lippincott, (1959). 75 plts, 7 maps. Fine in dj. *Artis.* $40/£26

DILLEY, ARTHUR URBANE. Oriental Rugs and Carpets. NY/London, 1931. Color frontis; 78 plts (13 color), 7 maps; fore-edge uncut. (Dampspotting; spine sl discolored.) *Edwards.* $101/£65

DILLON, ELLIS. Death in the Quadrangle. London: Faber, 1956. 1st ed. Fine in NF dj. *Janus.* $45/£29

DILLON, RICHARD. Burnt-Out Fires, California's Modoc Indian War. Englewood Cliffs, NJ, (1973). 1st ed. Fine in dj (spine faded). *Pratt.* $30/£19

DILLON, RICHARD. The Hatchet Men. Coward-McCann, (1962). 1st ed. VG in VG dj. *Oregon.* $40/£26

DILLON, RICHARD. The Hatchet Men. NY: Coward-McCann, (1962). 1st ed. Signed. Red cl. Fine in dj (rubbed, chipped). *Harrington.* $45/£29

DILLON, RICHARD. The Legend of Grizzly Adams. Coward McCann, (1966). 1st ed. - VG in VG dj. *Oregon.* $35/£23

DILLON, RICHARD. Shanghaiing Days. Coward McCann, (1961). 1st ed. VG in VG dj. *Oregon.* $45/£29

DILLON, RICHARD. Texas Argonauts. SF: Book Club of CA, 1987. 1st ed. Ltd to 450 ptd. Color frontis. Buckram, pict bds. VF. *Oregon.* $250/£161

DILLON, RICHARD. Texas Argonauts. SF: Book Club of CA: 1987. One of 450. As New in plain dj. *Bohling.* $250/£161

DILLON, RICHARD. Wells Fargo Detective: The Biography of James B. Hume. Coward-McCann, (1969). 1st ed. Fine in Fine dj. *Oregon.* $35/£23

DIMENT, ADAM. The Great Spy Race. London: Michael Joseph, 1968. 1st ed. Fine in dj (sl dknd spine). *Mordida.* $45/£29

DIMSDALE, THOMAS J. The Vigilantes of Montana or Popular Justice in the Rocky Mountains. Helena, MT: State Publishing Co, 1915. 4th ed. Gold emb cvr. Fine. Howes D 345. *Cahan.* $85/£55

DIMSDALE, THOMAS J. The Vigilantes of Montana, or Popular Justice in the Rocky Mountains.... Helena: State Pub Co, (1915). Orig grn dec cl. Sm newspaper clipping affixed to fep w/offsetting, sm repaired tears spine top, o/w NF. *Harrington.* $100/£65

DIMSDALE, THOMAS J. The Vigilantes of Montana, or, Popular Justice in the Rocky Mountains. Helena, n.d. (ca 1915). 4th ed. Frontis; 28 plts. VG. Howes D 345. *Oregon*. $90/£58

DIMSDALE, THOMAS J. The Vigilantes of Montana. Helena, (1915). 4th ed. Name, else VG. Howes 345. *Perier*. $70/£45

DIMSDALE, THOMAS J. The Vigilantes of Montana. Butte: McKee Ptg Co, 1929. 7th ptg. 8 plts. VG in pict wraps. Howes D 345. *Schoyer*. $30/£19

DIMSDALE, THOMAS. The Present Method of Inoculating for the Small-Pox. London, 1767. 3rd ed. 160pp. Recent 1/4 leather (new eps). *Fye*. $300/£194

DINESEN, ISAK. Isak Dinesen: A Memorial. Clara Svendsen (ed). NY: Random House, 1965. 1st Amer ed. Fine in dj (price-clipped). *Virgo*. $39/£25

DINESEN, ISAK. Out of Africa. R-H, 1938. 1st ed. Fine in dj (wear; chipping). *Fine Books*. $65/£42

DINESEN, ISAK. Seven Gothic Tales. S & H, 1934. 1st Amer ed, 1st bk. One of 999 for sale; black mesh cl w/color illus. NF (sm lt stain inner hinge). *Fine Books*. $250/£161

DINGWALL, ERIC. The Girdle of Chastity. London: Routledge, 1931. 1st ed. 10 plts. Dj (soiled; back torn; cvrs damp damage). *White*. $28/£18

DINGWALL, ERIC. The Girdle of Chastity. London, 1931. 1st ed. Good. *Fye*. $200/£129

DINKINS, JAMES. 1861 to 1865, by an Old Johnnie. Cincinnati: Robert Clark, 1897. 1st ed. 280pp. Minor cvr speckling; else VG. Howes D 346. *Mcgowan*. $450/£290

DINKINS, JAMES. 1861-1865. Personal Recollections and Experiences in the Confederate Army. Cincinnati: Robert Clarke, 1897. 1st ed. Inscribed. 8vo, frontis port, 280pp. Orig red cl. Fr hinge sl tender, else VG. Howes D 346. *Chapel Hill*. $700/£452

DINNING, HECTOR. Nile to Aleppo. NY: Macmillan, 1920. 1st Amer ed, from British sheets. 13 plts. Later 3/4 polished morocco, marbled bds (tp foxed). *Schoyer*. $165/£106

Dinosaurs. NY: Random House. 17x23 cm. 4 dbl-pg pop-ups, pull tabs. Dot & Sy Barlowe (illus). Pict wraps. VG. *Book Finders*. $40/£26

DIRINGER, DAVID. The Hand-Produced Book. NY: Philosophical Lib, (1953). 1st ed. VG in dj. *Bookpress*. $110/£71

DISBROW, ALBERT. Glimpses of Chickamauga. Chicago, (1895). 1st ed. 136pp. 2 sm tears fep, o/w Fine. *Pratt*. $75/£48

DISCH, THOMAS M. 334. London: MacGibbon & Kee, 1972. 1st UK ed. VG in dj. *Williams*. $74/£48

DISCH, THOMAS M. 334. Gregg Press, 1976. 1st Amer hb ed. One of 362. NF. *Aronovitz*. $85/£55

DISCH, THOMAS M. Camp Concentration. London: Hart-Davis, 1968. 1st ed. NF in dj (sl rubbed). *Limestone*. $195/£126

DISCH, THOMAS M. Camp Concentration. London: Hart-Davies, 1968. 1st UK ed. Fine in VG dj. *Lewton*. $85/£55

DISCH, THOMAS M. Camp Concentration. London: Hart-Davies, 1968. 1st UK ed. VG in dj. *Lewton*. $93/£60

DISCH, THOMAS M. Echo Round His Bones. London: Rupert Hart-Davis, 1969. 1st hb ed. Fine in dj. *Williams*. $101/£65

DISCH, THOMAS M. The Genocides. (NY): Berkley Pub Corp, (1965). 1st ed. Ptd wraps. Fine. *Antic Hay*. $35/£23

DISCH, THOMAS M. Getting into Death. Hart-Davies, 1973. 1st UK ed. Fine in dj. *Lewton*. $43/£28

DISCH, THOMAS M. The Prisoner. London: Dennis Dobson, 1979. 1st Eng ed. NF in dj. *Limestone*. $185/£119

DISKI, JENNY. Nothing Natural. Methuen, 1986. 1st UK ed. Fine in dj. *Sclanders*. $16/£10

DISNEY, DORIS MILES. Did She Fall or Was She Pushed? GC: DCC, 1959. 1st ed. Fine in NF dj. *Janus*. $20/£13

DISNEY, WALT. Dance of the Hours from Walt Disney's Fantasia. NY: Harper, (1940). 1st ed. 8vo. Yellow cl-backed bds w/color illus (lt edgewear). Color pict dj (worn; 1-inch chip). *Reisler*. $140/£90

DISNEY, WALT. Detective Adventures. London: Juvenile Productions, (1937). 4to. Full color frontis. Cl-backed illus bds (spine ends worn). *Reisler*. $275/£177

DISNEY, WALT. Dumbo of the Circus. GC: Garden City Pub Co, (1941). Sq, sm folio. Cl-backed illus bds (edgewear). Pict dj (marginal tears). *Reisler*. $120/£77

DISNEY, WALT. Figaro and Cleo. NY: Random House, 1940. 1st ed. 8vo. Cl-backed color illus bds. Good in full color dj. *Reisler*. $175/£113

DISNEY, WALT. Hiawatha. Racine, WI: Whitman Pub Co, 1938. Lg 4to. Good in linen-like paper wrappers. *Reisler*. $125/£81

DISNEY, WALT. Honest John and Giddy. NY: Random House, 1940. 1st ed. 8vo. Cl-backed color illus bds (sl worn) in color dj (lt chipped). *Reisler*. $175/£113

DISNEY, WALT. Jiminy Cricket. NY: Random House, 1940. 1st ed. 8vo. Cl-backed color illus bds. Good in color dj (sm tears, chips). *Reisler*. $175/£113

DISNEY, WALT. The Mickey Mouse Fire Brigade. London: Collins, 1936. 1st Eng ed. Full color illus bds. Full color dj w/2 sm brn areas spine; o/w Very Nice. *Reisler*. $350/£226

DISNEY, WALT. Mickey Mouse in King Arthur's Court. NY: Blue Ribbon, (1933). 4to. 4 dble-pg pop-ups (one invisibly repaired w/separation of binding behind). Full color illus bds. Matching full color dj. *Reisler*. $1,250/£806

DISNEY, WALT. Mickey Mouse in King Arthur's Court. Blue Ribbon Books, 1933. 1st ed. Pop-up. NF. *Fine Books*. $1,000/£645

DISNEY, WALT. Mickey Mouse Story Book. Phila: McKay, (1931). 8vo. Orange pict cl, lg color label. VG. *Houle*. $950/£613

DISNEY, WALT. The Nutcracker Suite from Walt Disney's Fantasia. London: Collins, n.d. (c. 1939). 1st ed. Pict bds (corners, backstrip sl worn). Sound. *Cox*. $54/£35

DISNEY, WALT. Pinocchio. NY: Random House, 1939. 1st ed. Lg, 4to. Cl-backed color illus bds (sl corner bumping). Full color dj (marginal wear; rear lacking 2 sm pieces). *Reisler*. $250/£161

DISNEY, WALT. Santa's Workshop from the Walt Disney Silly Symphony. London/Glasgow: Collins' Cleartype Press, (1934). 1st Eng ed. 8vo. 8 color plts, 56 full-pg illus. (Foxing throughout.) Illus paper over bds (edges worn; bump; 2-inch tear fr joint paper). VG in dj (tears, sl wear). *Juvelis*. $350/£226

DISNEY, WALT. Three Little Wolves. Hollywood: Walt Disney Enterprises, 1937. Lg 4to. 14pp. Linenized paper wrappers (spine split). *Reisler*. $100/£65

DISNEY, WALT. Thumper. NY: Grosset & Dunlap, (1942). 1st ed. 8vo. Color illus bds. Good in color dj (worn; lg chip). *Reisler*. $30/£19

DISNEY, WALT. Toby Tortoise and the Hare. Hollywood: Walt Disney Enterprises, 1938. Lg 4to. 10 linenized pp. Linenized paper wrappers (spine lt chipped). *Reisler*. $165/£106

DISNEY, WALT. Walt Disney Annual. Racine, WI: Whitman Pub, (1937). 1st ed of 1st annual. 8 full-pg color plts. Illus bds (lt edgewear; pg w/marginal tear, dwg colored by owner). Full color dj (chipped, folded). *Reisler*. $850/£548

DISNEY, WALT. Walt Disney's Mickey Mouse. Hollywood: Walt Disney Enterprises, 1937. Lg 4to. Linenized stiff paper. Self cvrs (spine lt chipped). *Reisler*. $225/£145

DISNEY, WALT. Walt Disney's Pinocchio Picture Book. Racine, WI: Whitman, 1940. Lg 4to. Shapebook. Good in illus paper wrappers (sl chipped). *Reisler*. $185/£119

DISRAELI, BENJAMIN. The Dunciad of Today...and The Modern Aesop. Michael Sadleir (ed). London: Ingpen & Grant, (1928). One of 750 numbered. Bds sl soiled, faded, o/w NF. *Pharos*. $35/£23

DISRAELI, BENJAMIN. Novels and Tales. London, 1926-27. 12 vols. Pict eps; teg. Cl, blind device upper bds, gilt motifs to spines. *Edwards*. $388/£250

DISRAELI, ISAAC. Curiosities of Literature. Cambridge: Privately ptd, Riverside, 1864. 4 vols. Engr frontis port; 447; 468; 466; 447pp + 23pp index. 1/2 brn morocco, gilt; teg. VG. *Hartfield*. $295/£190

DISTURNELL, JOHN. The Great Lakes, or Inland Seas of America. NY: Scribner, 1865. 192pp; 6 plts; fldg b/w map (torn). Orig blue cl, gilt cvr title. (Sl worn; paper dknd.) Howes D 357. *Bohling*. $300/£194

DISTURNELL, JOHN. The Great Lakes, or Inland Seas of America. Phila, 1871. 270pp (lacks fep), line map. Gilt cl. Good. *Artis*. $95/£61

DITCHFIELD, P.H. London Survivals. London, 1914. Color frontis. Leather title label. (Spotting, mainly prelims; spine sl discolored.) *Edwards*. $62/£40

DITCHFIELD, P.H. The Manor Houses of England. London: Batsford, 1910. Color frontis. Pict cl (sl rubbed). *Schoyer*. $90/£58

DITCHFIELD, P.H. The Old-Time Parson. London: Methuen, 1909. Color frontis, 16 plts. Edges spotted. *Hollett*. $39/£25

DITCHFIELD, P.H. The Parish Clerk. London: Methuen, 1907. 1st ed. 31 plts. Good. *Cox*. $23/£15

DITCHFIELD, P.H. Vanishing England. London: Methuen, 1910. 1st ed. (Feps foxed; upper joint cracked; worn.) *Hollett*. $47/£30

DITCHFIELD, P.H. Vanishing England. London, 1910. 1st ed. Gilt-ruled cl (spine dknd; feps lt browned). *Edwards*. $54/£35

DITMARS, R.L. The Reptiles of North America. NY, 1936. 8 color plts. *Wheldon & Wesley*. $54/£35

DITMARS, R.L. Snakes of the World. NY, 1931. 85 plts. *Wheldon & Wesley*. $39/£25

DITMARS, R.L. and W. BRIDGES. Wild Animal World. NY/London: Appleton, 1937. 1st ed. VG. *Mikesh*. $30/£19

DITTERT, B. et al. Forerunners to Everest. London: Allen & Unwin, 1954. 1st ed. Color frontis; 24 plts; 9 maps, sketches. VG in dj (sl worn). *Hollett*. $39/£25

Dixie Cook-book Carefully Compiled from the Treasured Family Collections.... L.A. Clarkson, 1885. Rev ed. 688pp. Good (foxed; pencil, ink notes; staining; tissue repair prelims, hinges; tape repair pp240-42; new backstrip; cvr design worn). *Book Broker*. $125/£81

DIXON, C. The Bird-life of London. London, 1909. 23 plts (7 color). *Wheldon & Wesley*. $28/£18

DIXON, EDWARD H. Scenes in the Practice of a New York Surgeon. NY: Dewitt, 1855. Frontis; 407pp. (Cl worn.) *Goodrich*. $50/£32

DIXON, FRANKLIN W. Castaways of the Stratosphere. Grosset, 1935. 1st ed. Fine in dj. *Madle*. $35/£23

DIXON, FRANKLIN W. Lone Eagle of the Border. Grosset, 1929. 1st ed. VG. *Madle*. $20/£13

DIXON, FRANKLIN W. Over the Ocean to Paris. Grosset, 1927. 1st ed. VG. *Madle*. $20/£13

DIXON, GEORGE. A Voyage Round the World.... London: Geo. Goulding, 1789. 1st ed. 4to. xxvii,(iii),360,47pp, 6 fldg charts (one torn), 14 plts (1 fldg), 1 plt engr music. (Lacks frontis chart; lt damp-staining title w/short repaired tear.) Contemp full calf (rubbed, scuffed; cvrs detached). Else contents Fine. Howes D 365. *Blue Mountain*. $650/£419

DIXON, JAMES. Personal Narrative of a Tour Through a Part of the United States and Canada. NY: Lane & Scott, 1849. 1st Amer ed. Engr frontis port; 431pp (lacks half-title; damp mk to p67). Orig calf, morocco label. Soil, smudges to margins; hinges starting to crack; chipping at spine, not affecting label; edge wear; all else Good. *Connolly*. $55/£35

DIXON, ROBERT B. Fore and Aft: A Story of Actual Sea Life. Boston/NY: Lee & Shepard/Charles T. Dillingham, 1883. 1st ed. viii,325,(1 blank, 2 ads)pp. (Inner hinges tender.) *Lefkowicz*. $50/£32

DIXON, ROYAL. Signs Is Signs. Phila: George W. Jacobs, (1915). 1st ed. Red cl w/mtd cvr illus. VG (spine sl faded). *Chapel Hill*. $45/£29

DIXON, SAM HOUSTON and LOUIS W. KEMP. The Heroes of San Jacinto. Houston: Anson Jones Press, 1932. 1st trade ed. 7 ports. Red cl. Hinges cracked internally, else VG. Howes D 366. *Chapel Hill*. $85/£55

DIXON, THOMAS. The Fall of a Nation. Donohue, 1916. VG in dj (used). *Madle*. $35/£23

DIXON, THOMAS. The Fall of a Nation. NY, 1916. 1st ed. Spine sl faded, o/w VG+. *Pratt*. $30/£19

DIXON, THOMAS. The Traitor; A Story of the Fall of the Invisible Empire. NY, 1907. 1st ed. Spine label fading, o/w VG+. *Pratt*. $30/£19

DIZER, JOHN T. Tom Swift and Company: 'Boys' Books' by Stratenmeyer and Others. Jefferson/London: McFarland, 1982. 1st ed. Fine. *Cahan*. $40/£26

DJILAS, MILOVAN. Anatomy of a Moral. NY: Praeger, (1959). 1st Amer ed. Fine (sl offsetting fep) in NF dj (lt stain fr panel, extrems sl rubbed). *Between The Covers*. $50/£32

DJURKLOU, G. Fairy Tales from the Swedish. London: Heinemann, 1901. 1st Eng ed. Carl Larsson et al (illus). 8vo. Frontis, 178pp (fingering tp; 1/2 title lacks corner); 20 full-pg b/w illus. Pink cl color emb w/gilt lettering. VG (spine ends worn). *Drusilla's*. $135/£87

DOBBINS, W. Battle of Lake Erie and Reminiscences of the Flagships 'Lawrence' and 'Niagara.' Erie, 1929. VG in VG dj. *Clark*. $35/£23

DOBELL, HORACE. On Bacillary Consumption: Its Nature in Treatment in the True First Stage. London, 1889. 1st ed. 138pp. Good. *Fye.* $75/£48

DOBELL, HORACE. On Coughs, Consumption, and Diet in Disease. Phila, 1877. 1st Amer ed. 222pp. Good. *Fye.* $75/£48

DOBIE, J. FRANK and JOHN WILLIAM ROGERS. Finding Literature on the Texas Plains. Dallas: Southwest Press, 1931. 1st ed. Maroon 1/4 cl, bds, gilt. Fine. *Macdonnell.* $85/£55

DOBIE, J. FRANK and JOHN WILLIAM ROGERS. Finding Literature on the Texas Plains. Dallas, 1931. One of 300. Reading copy (ex-lib; long repaired tears frontis, tp; hinge papers cracked; soiled). *Baade.* $45/£29

DOBIE, J. FRANK and JOHN WILLIAM ROGERS. John C. Duval. Dallas, 1939. Ltd to 1000. Soiled, o/w NF in partial dj (chipped, fr panel separated). *Baade.* $200/£129

DOBIE, J. FRANK et al. Mustangs and Cow Horses. Dallas, TX, 1961. Stated 2nd ed. VF in VF dj. *Bond.* $125/£81

DOBIE, J. FRANK. The Ben Lilly Legend. Boston: Little Brown, 1950. 1st ed. Color port. *Lambeth.* $35/£23

DOBIE, J. FRANK. Bob More, Man and Bird Man. Dallas: Encino, 1965. #65/550. NF in NF slipcase. *Parker.* $150/£97

DOBIE, J. FRANK. Bob More, Man and Bird Man. Dallas: Encino Press, 1965. One of 550. Fine in slipcase. *Bohling.* $200/£129

DOBIE, J. FRANK. Coronado's Children. Dallas: Southwest, 1930. 1st ed. 2nd ptg. *Lambeth.* $20/£13

DOBIE, J. FRANK. Guide to Life and Literature of the Southwest, with a Few Observations. Univ of TX Press, 1943. 1st ed (precedes SMU ed). Softbound. Fine. *Authors Of The West.* $100/£65

DOBIE, J. FRANK. Guide to Life and Literature of the Southwest. Austin: Univ of TX, 1943. 1st ed, special ptg for University Press in Dallas, SMU. News clipping laid in w/resulting browning of eps, else VG. *Connolly.* $90/£58

DOBIE, J. FRANK. Guide to Life and Literature of the Southwest. Austin: Univ of TX Press, 1943. 1st ptg. VG in wraps. *Schoyer.* $35/£23

DOBIE, J. FRANK. Guide to Life and Literature of the Southwest. Dallas: Southern Methodist Univ, 1952. 2nd ed. Inscribed to Henry Clifford on fep. Brn-stamped cl in dj (lt stain rear panel). *Dawson.* $50/£32

DOBIE, J. FRANK. The Longhorns. Boston: Little, Brown, 1941. 1st ed. Cl ptd w/color illus (owner bkpl, sticker, # bottom edge). Dj (edgeworn). *Dawson.* $60/£39

DOBIE, J. FRANK. The Mustangs. Boston: Little Brown, (1952). 1st ed. Color frontis. Illus ep. VG in VG dj. *Oregon.* $70/£45

DOBIE, J. FRANK. The Mustangs. Boston: Little Brown, 1952. 1st ed. *Lambeth.* $45/£29

DOBIE, J. FRANK. Out of the Old Rock. Boston: Little Brown, 1972. 1st ed. Dj. *Lambeth.* $25/£16

DOBIE, J. FRANK. Rattlesnakes. Boston: Little Brown, 1965. 1st ed. Dj. *Lambeth.* $25/£16

DOBIE, J. FRANK. Some Part of Myself. Boston/Toronto: Little, Brown, (1967). 1st ed. Signed card laid in. Bkpl, else Fine in dj (lt chipped). *Glenn.* $75/£48

DOBIE, J. FRANK. Some Part of Myself. Boston: Little Brown, 1967. 1st ed. Dj. *Lambeth.* $25/£16

DOBIE, J. FRANK. Stories of Christmas and the Bowie Knife. Austin: Steck Co, (1953). Warren Hunter (illus). VG + (pg corners sl wrinkled) in glassine dj (chipped), slipcase (faded). *Bohling.* $65/£42

DOBIE, J. FRANK. Tales of the Mustang. Dallas: Book Club of TX, 1936. 1st ed, #127/300. NF in orig glassine dj (chipped). *Chapel Hill.* $1,200/£774

DOBIE, J. FRANK. Tongues of the Monte. GC: Doubleday, Doran, 1935. 1st ed. Good (erasure fr pastedown). *Lien.* $75/£48

DOBIE, J. FRANK. A Vaquero of the Brush Country. London: Hammond & Hammond, (1949). 1st Eng ed. Frontis, plt. VG in VG dj. *Oregon.* $60/£39

DOBIE, J. FRANK. The Voice of the Coyote. Boston: Little Brown, 1949. 1st ed. VG in VG dj. *Oregon.* $70/£45

DOBREE, BONAMY. The Amateur and the Theatre. Hogarth Press, 1947. 1st ed. VG. *Words Etc.* $39/£25

DOBREE, BONAMY. Rochester: A Conversation. Hogarth Press, 1926. 1st ed. Edges faded, o/w VG. *Words Etc.* $54/£35

DOBREE, VALENTINE. The Emperor's Tigers. London: Faber & Faber, (1929). 1st Eng ed. Top edge stained brn. Patterned eps. Grn cl gilt. Very Nice in pict dj. *Cady.* $25/£16

DOBSON, AUSTIN (ed). Old English Songs from Various Sources.... London: Macmillan, 1894. 1st ed. Aeg. Gilt pict cl. Bkpl, else Very Nice. *Reese.* $35/£23

DOBSON, AUSTIN. De Libris Prose and Verse. Macmillan, 1911. 13 plts. VG. *Moss.* $16/£10

DOBSON, AUSTIN. Life of Oliver Goldsmith. London: Walter Scott, 1888. 1st ed, lg paper issue. 2pp ads at back. Red/orange cl; top edge stained gray. Bkpl; spine lt fading, lt worn, o/w Fine. *Hermitage.* $100/£65

DOBSON, AUSTIN. William Hogarth. NY/London: Dodd, Mead, 1891. 1st ed. Frontis, xiv,368pp (sig); 11 photogravures, 1 facs letter, cat of prints. White cl (soiled), gilt; teg. *Weber.* $80/£52

DOBSON, AUSTIN. William Hogarth. London, 1907. New enlgd ed. 50 plts. (Cl worn, stained.) *Ars Artis.* $54/£35

DOBSON, G. et al. Russia. A&C Black, 1913. F. de Haenen (illus). Fldg map. (Pp.ix-x partly detached.) Illus cl (upper hinge cracked; sl browning; rubbed; upper joint partly split; spine chipped). *Edwards.* $70/£45

DOBSON, MRS. The Life of Petrarch. London: Bensley, 1797. 3rd ed, 1st illus. 2 vols. 388,401pp; 8 copper plts. Contemp calf. VG (fep loose). *Second Life.* $175/£113

DOBYNS, HENRY F. and ROBERT C. EULER. The Ghost Dance of 1889 Among the Pai Indians of Northwestern Arizona. (Prescott): Prescott College Press, 1967. 1st ed. Map. Pict cl. VG in dj. *Schoyer.* $50/£32

DOBYNS, STEPHEN. Concurring Beasts. Poems. NY: Atheneum, 1972. 1st ed, 1st bk. Award material laid in. VF in dj. *Reese.* $50/£32

DOBYNS, STEPHEN. A Man of Little Evils. London: Peter Davies, 1974. 1st UK ed. 1st bk. NF in NF dj. *Ming.* $47/£30

DOBYNS, STEPHEN. The Two Deaths of Senora Puccini. (NY): Viking, (1988). 1st ed. Rev material laid in. Fine in dj. *Reese.* $20/£13

DOCK, GEORGE and CHARLES BASS. Hookworm Disease: Etiology, Pathology.... St. Louis, 1910. 1st ed. Good. *Fye.* $100/£65

DOCK, LAVINIA L. A Short History of Nursing from the Earliest Times to the Present. NY, 1920. VG. *Argosy.* $35/£23

DOCKSTADER, FREDERICK J. Indian Art in Middle America. Greenwich: NYGS, (1964). 70 tipped-in color plts. Good in dj (faded). *Archaeologia.* $125/£81

DOCKSTADER, FREDERICK J. Indian Art of the Americas. NY: Museum of the Amer Indian, 1973. (Lt bumped.) *Archaeologia.* $65/£42

DOCKSTADER, FREDERICK J. Indian Art of the Americas. NY: Heye Foundation, 1973. 1st ed. Pict bds. VG. *Oregon.* $40/£26

DOCKSTADER, FREDERICK J. The Kachina and the White Man. Bloomfield Hills: Cranbrook Inst, 1954. 1st ed. NF in VG- dj. *Parker.* $45/£29

DOCKSTADER, FREDERICK J. Weaving Arts of the North American Indian. NY: Crowell, (1978). 64 color plts. Good in dj. *Archaeologia.* $65/£42

DOCTOROW, E.L. Big as Life. NY: S&S, 1966. 1st ed. NF in NF dj (closed tear at rear, sm ink #s inside fr flap). Clean, bright. *Pettler.* $300/£194

DOCTOROW, E.L. Billy Bathgate. NY: Random House, (1989). 1st ed, ltd to 300 numbered, specially bound, signed. Blue cl. Fine in pub's slipcase box. *Godot.* $85/£55

DOCTOROW, E.L. The Book of Daniel. NY: Random House, 1971. 1st ed. Fine in dj (price-clipped). *Else Fine.* $65/£42

DOCTOROW, E.L. Lives of the Poets. NY: Random House, (1984). 1st ed. Signed. Fine in dj. *Godot.* $50/£32

DOCTOROW, E.L. Ragtime. NY: Random House, 1975. 1st ed. Signed. VG (spine sl cocked) in VG dj (sm tear). *Revere.* $60/£39

DOCTOROW, E.L. Ragtime. London: Macmillan, 1976. 1st Eng ed. VF in dj. *Limestone.* $35/£23

Documents on German Foreign Policy 1918-1945. Series D, Vol III. Washington, 1950. NF. *Peter Taylor.* $112/£72

DODD, WILLIAM. Thoughts in Prison: in Five Parts. London: Edward & Charles Dilly et al, 1777. 1st ed. 8vo, (ii),iii,232pp + 1pg ad. Contemp calf (joints cracked, but firm). VG. *Marlborough.* $744/£480

DODDINGTON, GEORGE BUBB. The Diary of the Late George Bubb Doddington.... London: G. Wilkie, 1809. 4th ed. Contemp calf (rebacked; lib stamp tp; label fr cvr; bkpl); orig red morocco lettering-piece. *Waterfield.* $47/£30

DODGE, D. To Catch a Thief. R-H, 1952. 1st ed. VG + in VG + dj. *Fine Books.* $85/£55

DODGE, ERNEST S. The Polar Rosses. NY: Barnes & Noble, (1973). 1st Amer ed. VG. *Blue Dragon.* $22/£14

DODGE, GRENVILLE MELLEN. Biographical Sketch of James Bridger. NY: Unz, 1905. 3 plts (1 fldg). Few words lost p6, o/w Fine in wraps. Howes D 392. *Oregon.* $90/£58

DODGE, GRENVILLE MELLEN. Biographical Sketch of James Bridger.... NY: Unz & Co, 1905. Fldg frontis view; port; plt. VG + in ptd wraps. Howes D 392. *Bohling.* $150/£97

DODGE, IDA FLOOD. Arizona Under Our Flag. Tucson: AZ Daily Star, 1928. 1st ed. Wrinkling upper 1/2 of pp throughout w/faint damp line, else VG in ptd wrappers. *Connolly.* $25/£16

DODGE, RICHARD IRVING. The Plains of the Great West and Their Inhabitants. NY: Putnam's, 1877. 1st ed. lv,448pp, fldg map, 19 plts. Pict cl (sl soiled). Howes D 404. *Schoyer.* $135/£87

DODGE, RICHARD IRVING. The Plains of the Great West and Their Inhabitants.... NY, 1877. 1st ed. (55),448pp; fldg map. (Lib #s spine; bkpl removed.) Howes D 404. *Ginsberg.* $150/£97

DODGSON, CAMPBELL. Catalogue of Early German and Flemish Woodcuts. London, 1903, 1911. 2 vols. 36 plts (2 color). (Ex-lib, ink stamp tp, verso plts, bkpl; upper hinges tender; corners sl worn; rebacked.) *Edwards.* $155/£100

DODGSON, CAMPBELL. The Etchings of Charles Meryon. London: The Studio, 1921. 1st ed. 47 leaves of plts. Gilt parchment, gray bds (spine sl chipped, soiled). *Karmiole.* $150/£97

DODGSON, CAMPBELL. The Etchings of James McNeill Whistler. London: The Studio, 1922. 1st ed. 96 plts. Teg, rest uncut. Orig vellum-backed ptd bds, gilt. VF. *Europa.* $178/£115

DODGSON, CAMPBELL. Modern Drawings. London: The Studio, 1933. Inscrip, o/w VG. *Petersfield.* $37/£24

DODGSON, CAMPBELL. Woodcuts of the XV Century in the...British Museum. London: BM Trustees, 1934-35. 2 vols. 117 plts. Ex-lib, sm blindstamps some margins, shelf mks spine, sm stain vol 2 cvr, o/w Fine set. *Europa.* $248/£160

DODGSON, CHARLES L. The Formulae of Plane Trigonometry, Printed with Symbols.... Oxford: Ptd by James Wright, sold by J.H. and J. Parker, 1861. 1st ed. Sq 8vo, 20pp. Orig stitching; uncut, unopened as issued. Near Mint in 1/2 red morocco slipcase, ribbed gilt lettered spine. *D & D.* $3,900/£2,516

DODGSON, CHARLES L. Lawn Tennis Tournaments. London: Macmillan, 1883. 1st ed. 8vo, stitched pamphlet, 10pp. Fr, rear ptd wrap detached, edges lt browned, else Fine. *D & D.* $1,400/£903

DODGSON, CHARLES L. The New Belfry of Christ Church. London, 1872. 2nd ed (2nd thousand). Sm 8vo, (24)pp, as issued in ptd brick red wraps. VF (pencil inscrip fr cvr). *D & D.* $1,200/£774

DODGSON, CHARLES L. Sylvie and Bruno Concluded. London: Macmillan, 1893. 1st ed. Aeg. Red cl. 1893 ad slip for recall of 'Sixtieth Thousand' ed of 'Through the Looking Glass' laid in. VF. *D & D.* $60/£39

DODGSON, CHARLES L. Symbolic Logic. Part I. Elementary. London: Macmillan, 1896. 1st ed. Brick-red cl lettered in black. Vertical stain fr cvr near hinge, blank eps foxed, else Fine in red cl slipcase, gilt-lettered red morocco spine label. *D & D.* $700/£452

DODRIDGE, JOHN. The History of the Ancient and Modern Estate of the Principality of Wales, Dutchy of Cornewall, and Earldome of Chester (etc.). London: Tho. Harper for Godfrey Emondson & Thomas Alchorne, 1630. 1st ed. 4to. 142pp. (Title dusty; lt age browning; old ms notes in margins 4pp; underlining; blank corner 1 leaf torn off, sm hole edge 1 leaf, sl paper flaw 1 leaf, none affecting text.) 19th cent dk blue cl, gilt spine. *Sokol.* $310/£200

DODWELL, HENRY. The Founder of Modern Egypt. Cambridge: Univ Press, 1931. 1st ed. Sl rubbed; sl foxing, o/w VG. *Worldwide.* $45/£29

DOERNER, M. The Materials of the Artist. London: Harrap, 1949. Rev ed. 8 plts. Sound. *Ars Artis.* $33/£21

Dogs' Grand Dinner Party. (Dame Dingle's Series.) NY: McLoughlin Bros, 1869. 8vo, 6 leaves + 1pg list lower wrapper; 3/4 pg chromolithos, most signed by John Karst or Cogger; 1st, last pgs pasted down on pict chromolitho stiff paper wrappers (lt soiled, corners chipped). Good (rebacked). *Hobbyhorse*. $125/£81

DOIG, IVAN. English Creek. Atheneum, 1984. 1st ed. Inscribed, signed. Map. Fine in Fine dj. *Authors Of The West*. $60/£39

DOIG, IVAN. Ride with Me, Mariah Montana. NY: Atheneum, 1990. 1st ed. Fine in Fine dj. *Revere*. $25/£16

DOIG, IVAN. Ride with Me, Mariah Montana. Atheneum, 1990. 1st ed. Signed. New in New dj. *Authors Of The West*. $40/£26

DOIG, IVAN. The Sea Runners. NY: Atheneum, 1982. 1st ed. Fine in dj (faint crease fr flap). *Between The Covers*. $65/£42

DOKE, CLEMENT M. The Lambas of the Northern Rhodesia. London: Harrap, 1931. 1st ed. Map. VG (sl mkd). *Hollett*. $93/£60

DOLBY, ANASTASIA. Church Embroidery Ancient and Modern. London: Chapman & Hall, 1867. 176pp, 10 pp ads, fldg frontis, 20 plts. (Rear hinge cracked; rubbed, bumped, split rear joint; extrems chipped.) VG internally. *Blue Mountain*. $125/£81

DOLBY, RICHARD. The Cook's Dictionary, and Housekeeper's Directory.... London: Henry Colburn & Richard Bentley, 1832. 2nd ed. Engr frontis, (26),524,(1)leaf ads, 7 engr plans. 1/2 calf (rebacked), marbled bds, gilt. Sl spotting few leaves, else Very Nice. *Cady*. $175/£113

DOLE, MARY PHYLINDA. A Doctor in Homespun. N.p.: Privately ptd, 1941. VG. *Argosy*. $50/£32

DOLE, MARY PHYLINDA. A Doctor in Homespun. (Shelburne, MA?): Privately ptd, 1941. 1st ed. Signed. Port. Blue cl. VG. *Petrilla*. $30/£19

DOLLAR, JNO. A.W. A Handbook of Horse-Shoeing. Edinburgh: David Douglas, 1898. xxiii,438,(ii)pp. Sl worn; upper joint sl shaken. *Hollett*. $70/£45

DOLLMAN, F.T. and J.R. JOBBINS. An Analysis of Ancient Domestic Architecture.... London: Batsford, c. 1863. 2 vols. 160 plts. Mod black cl, maroon leather backs. *Petersfield*. $233/£150

DOLSON, HILDEGARDE. William Penn. NY: Random House, 1961. 1st trade ed. Leonard Everett Fisher (illus). Fine in dj. *Cattermole*. $20/£13

DOMEIER, WM. Observations on the Climate, Manners and Amusements of Malta.... London, 1810. 1st ed. 116pp. VG in wrappers. *Argosy*. $75/£48

Domestic Animals. (Bird and Animal Series.) NY: McLoughlin Bros, 1903. 4to. 5 leaves. Upper cvr illus w/title plus full-pg sheep, in dec frame w/added gold ink (lt soiled). VG (lower corner upper wrapper lt creased; lower parts of inner fold reinforced). *Hobbyhorse*. $125/£81

DOMINGUIN, LUIS MIGUEL. Toros y Toreros. NY: Abrams, (1961). 1st ed in English. VG. *Argosy*. $125/£81

Don Coronado through Kansas, 1541.... (By John Stowell.) (Seneca, KS: Don Coronado Co, 1908). 1st ed. 2 photo ports. Lt grn cl. Good (inner hinge starting). *Cullen*. $125/£81

DONAHEY, MARY DICKERSON. The Talking Bird and Wonderful Wishes of Jacky and Jean. Chicago: Albert Whitman, (1920). 1st ed. 4to. 146pp; 5 yellow/grn/blk plts by C.B. Falls. Dk grn cl, red lettering; pict paste label; illus eps. VG. *Drusilla's*. $45/£29

DONAHEY, MARY DICKERSON. The Talking Bird and Wonderful Wishes of Jacky and Jean. Chicago: Albert Whitman, 1920. 146pp + 2pp contents. 5 (of 6) VF full-pg lithos, pict eps (bkpl). Ptd grn cl on bd w/pasted pict litho label (scuffed; corners, spine edges chipped). *Hobbyhorse*. $45/£29

DONALD, DAVID. Lincoln's Herndon. NY, 1948. 1st ed. VG+ in VG+ dj. *Pratt*. $25/£16

DONALD, JAY. Life and Adventures of the James Brothers. Cincinnati: Forshee & McMakin, 1883. Later ed. Blue pict cl (worn). Howes D 415. *Glenn*. $75/£48

DONALD, JAY. Outlaws of the Border. Cobvan & Newman, 1882. 1st ed. 520pp. VG. *Bishop*. $37/£24

DONDERS, F.C. On the Anomalies of Accommodation and Refraction of the Eye. London, 1864. 1st Eng trans. 635pp. Good. *Fye*. $150/£97

DONEHOO, GEORGE P. A History of the Indian Villages and Place Names in Pennsylvania.... Harrisburg, (1928). Author's Autograph Edition, ltd to 500 numbered, signed. *Hayman*. $60/£39

DONISTHORPE, ST. J.K. British Ants, Their Life-History and Classification. Plymouth, 1915. 1st ed. 17 plts. *Bickersteth*. $56/£36

DONLEAVY, J.P. DeAlfonce Tennis. NY: Dutton, (1984). 1st ed. Fine in Fine dj. *Book Market*. $30/£19

DONLEAVY, J.P. Fairy Tales of New York. London: Penguin, 1961. 1st ed. Pb orig. Signed. Edges browned, o/w NF. *Rees*. $47/£30

DONLEAVY, J.P. The Ginger Man. Paris: Olympia Press, (1955). 1st ed. Signed. Sl rubbed, sm crease, lacks fep, else Fine in ptd wraps. *Polyanthos*. $200/£129

DONLEAVY, J.P. The Ginger Man. Paris: Olympia Press, 1958. 1st unexpurgated hb ed. Fine in dj. *Williams*. $39/£25

DONLEAVY, J.P. Leila. Further in the Destinies of Darcy Dancer, Gentleman. PA: Franklin Lib, 1983. 1st Amer ed. Signed. Aeg. Full leather, gilt. Fine. *Polyanthos*. $45/£29

DONLEAVY, J.P. The Onion Eaters. NY: Delacorte, (1971). 1st Amer ed. Rev copy w/rev slip & photo laid in. VG in dj. *Hermitage*. $30/£19

DONLEAVY, J.P. A Singular Man. Boston, 1963. 1st Amer ed. Fine (sl rubbed) in dj (sm tear, sl rubbed, price-clipped). *Polyanthos*. $25/£16

DONLEAVY, J.P. A Singular Man. London: Bodley Head, 1965. 1st Eng ed. Fine in dj (sm nick). *Ulysses*. $70/£45

DONLEAVY, J.P. What They Did in Dublin with the Ginger Man. London: MacGibbon & Kee, 1961. 1st UK ed. VG+ in dj. *Williams*. $56/£36

DONNE, JOHN. Complete Poetry and Selected Prose. John Hayward (ed). London: Nonesuch, 1932. Red cl, gilt fillets, titling. Sig, else NF. *Hartfield*. $85/£55

DONNE, JOHN. The Courtier's Library, or Catalogus Librorum Aulicorum.... (London): Nonesuch, 1930. One of 950 numbered. Paper-cvrd bds. (Spine sunned, lacks piece.) Pub's slipcase (sl dusty). *Hermitage*. $125/£81

DONNE, JOHN. The Courtier's Library.... London: Nonesuch, 1930. One of 950 numbered. Spine sunned, 2 sm nicks, else Nice in slipcase. *Reese.* $45/£29

DONNELLY, IGNATIUS. The American People's Money. Chicago: Laird & Lee, 1895. 1st ed. Fine (spine dull; name erased). BAL 4819. *Beasley.* $125/£81

DONOHOE, THOMAS. The Iroquois and the Jesuits. Buffalo, 1895. 1st ed. 276pp, 3 plts, fldg map. Good + (marginal dampstain). *Oregon.* $40/£26

DONOVAN, ROBERT J. PT 109. John F. Kennedy in World War II. NY, (1961). 1st ed. VG. *Argosy.* $75/£48

DOOLEY, JOHN. John Dooley, Confederate Soldier. Joseph T. Durkin (ed). Georgetown, DC: Georgetown Univ, 1945. 1st ed. Frontis port. Blue cl. NF in dj (worn, tape-reinforced, 2 long closed tears). *Chapel Hill.* $125/£81

DOOLITTLE, JEROME. Bombing Officer. NY: Dutton, (1982). 1st ed. Fine in Fine dj. *Aka.* $40/£26

DOOLITTLE, JUSTUS. Social Life of the Chinese. London: Sampson et al, 1868. 1st ed. xxxii,633,(i,vi)pp. Full black calf, gilt, extra prize binding. VG. *Hollett.* $186/£120

DORAN, MR. The History of Court Fools. London: Richard Bentley, 1858. 1st ed. (viii),389pp. Prize binding: contemp calf, gilt; marbled eps, all edges marbled. Prize certificate tipped in. Very Nice. *Cady.* $100/£65

DORE, J.R. Old Bibles. Eyre & Spottiswoode, 1888. 395pp; 17 plts (1 fldg). 2-color cl. Sl nick, o/w Good. *Moss.* $34/£22

DORE, J.R. Old Bibles. London: Eyre & Spottiswoode, 1888. 2nd ed. VG + . *Bishop.* $22/£14

DORIVAL, BERNARD. Paul Cezanne. Boston, 1949. 166 plts. VG in dj. *Argosy.* $85/£55

DORN, EDWARD and JENNIFER DUNBAR. Manchester Square. London/NY: Permanent Press, 1975. 1st ed. Ltd to 500 unnumbered. Sl bumped, else Fine in wrappers. *Godot.* $45/£29

DORN, EDWARD. Abhorrences. Black Sparrow, 1990. #46/150 signed. Fine in orig transparent dj. *Poetry.* $40/£26

DORN, EDWARD. Geography. Fulcrum, 1965. 1st ed. NF in dj (sl rubbed). *Poetry.* $23/£15

DORNAN, S.S. Pygmies and Bushmen of the Kalahari. London: Seeley, 1925. Map. (Backstrip faded; climate mkd.) *Petersfield.* $81/£52

DORNER, ALEXANDER. The Way Beyond Art—The Work of Herbert Bayer. NY: Wittenborn, 1947. 1st ed. Spine crown lt worn, o/w Fine in dj (lt frayed, chip). *Reese.* $85/£55

DORRENCE, WARD ALLISON. Three Ozark Streams: Log of the Moccasin and the Wilma. Richmond, MO: Missourian Press, 1938. 2nd ed. Inscribed, author photo laid in. Emb cl; gilt. VG. *Cahan.* $100/£65

DORRINGTON, ALBERT. The Radium Terrors. London: Eveleigh Nash, 1912. 1st ed. 16pp pub's cat at end. Internally Fine (gilt dulled; edges sl worn; label removed fep). *Temple.* $40/£26

DORRIS, MICHAEL. A Yellow Raft in Blue Water. NY: Henry Holt, (1987). 1st ed. Fine in dj. *Hermitage.* $35/£23

DORSETT, LYLE W. The Pendergast Machine. NY: Oxford Univ, 1968. 1st ed. Fine in Fine dj. *Connolly.* $25/£16

DORSEY, ELLA LORAINE. Pocahontas. Howard Press, 1906. 2nd ed. Contents Sound (paper cvr chipped, detached). *Book Broker.* $25/£16

DORSEY, FLORENCE L. Master of the Mississippi. Boston: Houghton Mifflin, 1941. 1st ed. 4 color plts. VG (spine sl scuffed). *Graf.* $25/£16

DORSEY, JAMES OWEN. The Cegiha Language. Washington: GPO, 1890. Presentation copy. 2 parts in 1 vol. VG. *Laurie.* $150/£97

DORSON, RICHARD M. Jonathan Draws the Long Bow. Cambridge: Harvard, 1946. Frontis. VG in dj (chipped). *Schoyer.* $30/£19

DOS PASSOS, JOHN. 1919. NY, 1932. 1st ed. Orange cl. VG in dj (repaired on verso w/tape). *Argosy.* $150/£97

DOS PASSOS, JOHN. Adventures of a Young Man. NY: Harcourt, 1939. 1st ed. Fine in dj (lt edgewear, creasing). *Else Fine.* $110/£71

DOS PASSOS, JOHN. Facing the Chair: Story of the Americanization of Two Foreignborn Workmen. Boston: Sacco-Vanzetti Defence Committee, 1927. 1st ed. Ptd wrappers lt stained, o/w VG. *Heller.* $125/£81

DOS PASSOS, JOHN. The Fourteenth Chronicle: Letters and Diaries of John Dos Passos. Boston: Gambit, 1973. 1st ed. Fine in dj. *Cahan.* $25/£16

DOS PASSOS, JOHN. The Grand Design. H-M, 1949. 1st ed. Fine in dj. *Fine Books.* $35/£23

DOS PASSOS, JOHN. The Head and Heart of Thomas Jefferson. GC: Doubleday, 1954. 1st ed. VG (sig) in dj (rubbed). *Cahan.* $25/£16

DOS PASSOS, JOHN. Number One. Boston: Houghton Mifflin, 1943. 1st ed. Rev slip laid in. VG in dj (lt worn, nicked). *Hermitage.* $75/£48

DOS PASSOS, JOHN. One Man's Initiation—1917. London: Allen & Unwin, (1920). 1st ed, 1st bk. One of the traditionally preferred copies, w/type blur 35:32, general misalignment other places, none of which has relevance to status of issue. Pale blue cl stamped in black. Spine extrems sl sunned, to sl shelf-rubbed, o/w Very Nice in dj. *Reese.* $750/£484

DOS PASSOS, JOHN. One Man's Initiation—1917. London: George Allen & Unwin, (1920). 1st ed, 1st state, with 'flat' obliterated p35, line 32. Blue cl. Fine in grey ptd dj. *Chapel Hill.* $500/£323

DOS PASSOS, JOHN. Orient Express. Harpers, 1927. 1st ed (1st issue binding). Fine in VG dj (lt wear). *Fine Books.* $195/£126

DOS PASSOS, JOHN. A Pushcart at the Curb. NY: George H. Doran, (1922). 1st ed, 1st ptg w/pub's monogram on copyright pg. Black cl-backed color pict bds. Very Nice. *Cady.* $85/£55

DOS PASSOS, JOHN. A Pushcart at the Curb. NY: Doran, (1922). 1st ed. Cl backed pict bds. Fine in dj (internally mended). *Argosy.* $275/£177

DOS PASSOS, JOHN. The Villages Are the Heart of Spain. Chicago, 1937. 1st ed, ltd. Dec cl. Spine sl worn, else Good. *Whiteson.* $70/£45

DOSTOEVSKY, FYODOR. The Brothers Karamazov. Constance Garnett (trans). Boston: LEC, 1933. Ltd to 1500—this 'out of series'. Signed by Alexander King (illus). 18 ports. Fine in glassine djs, pub's slipcase (sl shelfworn). *Sadlon.* $100/£65

DOSTOEVSKY, FYODOR. The Brothers Karamazov. NY: LEC, 1949. Ltd to 1500 numbered, signed by Fritz Eichenberg (illus). 2 vols. 48 litho plts. Good in slipcase (sl rubbed). *Karmiole.* $85/£55

DOSTOEVSKY, FYODOR. The Diary of a Writer. Boris Brasol (trans). NY: Scribner's, 1949. 1st Amer ed. 2 vols. Black cl stamped in gilt/red. Name, lt pencil marginalia, else NF in VG pub's slipcase. *Chapel Hill.* $125/£81

DOSTOEVSKY, FYODOR. A Gentle Spirit. Constance Garnett (trans). Harrison of Paris, 1931. One of 495 numbered. Prospectus. Black cl. As New in like paper slipcase. *Dermont.* $100/£65

DOSTOEVSKY, FYODOR. A Raw Youth. Constance Garnett (trans). Verona: LEC, 1974. 2 vols. #807/2000 signed by Fritz Eichenberg (15 wood engrs). Orig cl, spine labels. Slipcase. *Edwards.* $78/£50

DOTEN, ALFRED. The Journals of Alfred Doten, 1849-1903. Walter Van Tilburg (ed). Reno: Univ of NV Press, 1973. 3 vols. VG in orig box. *Perier.* $97/£63

DOTEN, ALFRED. Journals of...1849-1903. Walter Van Tilburg Clark (ed). Reno: Univ of NV, 1974. 3 vols. Fine in slipcase (edges splitting). *Bohling.* $75/£48

DOTHAN, TRUDE. The Philistines and Their Material Culture. New Haven: Yale Univ Press, (1982). 3 maps, 2 tables. Good in dj. *Archaeologia.* $150/£97

DOUGAL, WILLIAM. Off for California. The Letters, Log and Sketches of William H. Dougal, Gold Rush Artist. Biobooks, 1949. Ltd to 600 ptd. Fldg panorama. Fine. *Oregon.* $60/£39

DOUGHTY, CHARLES M. Mansoul or Riddle of the World. London, 1920. 1st ed. NF (offsetting feps) in dj (spine sunned; fr panel sl soiled; sm spine tear). *Polyanthos.* $35/£23

DOUGHTY, CHARLES M. Travels in Arabia Deserta. NY/London: Boni & Liveright/Cape, & Medici Soc, 1923. Amer issue of 3rd ed. 2 vols. Lg fldg map in pocket. Nice set (bkpls, spines evenly faded). *Cady.* $100/£65

DOUGHTY, CHARLES M. Wanderings in Arabia. London: Duckworth, 1908. 2 vols. xx,309; frontis, x,297pp, port. Good. *Hollett.* $62/£40

DOUGHTY, CHARLES M. Wanderings in Arabia. NY: Thomas Seltzer, 1924. 2 vols. Fldg map. Spines discolored; rubbed, worn on edges. *Schoyer.* $40/£26

DOUGHTY, CHARLES M. Wanderings in Arabia.... London: Duckworth, 1924. 4th ed. 2 vols. Frontis; fldg map. Internally VG (sl rubbed, soiled). *Worldwide.* $35/£23

DOUGHTY, CHARLES M. Wanderings in Arabia.... London: Duckworth, 1927. 2nd ptg of 1-vol ed. Frontis; fldg map. Sl rubbed; lacks fr flyleaf, o/w VG. *Worldwide.* $20/£13

DOUGHTY, J.H. Hill-Writings. Collected by H.M. Kelly. Manchester: Rucksack Club, 1937. 1st ed. 2 ports. VG (reps spotted) in dj. *Hollett.* $70/£45

DOUGHTY, MARION. Afoot Through the Kashmir Valleys. London, 1902. Teg. Gilt device upper bd. (Feps lt foxed; sl paint mks upper bd.) *Edwards.* $132/£85

Douglas County Tales and Towns. Armour (SD), 1938. 1st ed. Foxed, o/w Fine in pict wraps. *Baade.* $50/£32

DOUGLAS, ALFRED. The True History of Shakespeare's Sonnets. Martin Secker, 1933. 1st Eng ed. Frontis port. Grey cl (sl sunned). VG. *Dalian.* $54/£35

DOUGLAS, BYRD. Steamboatin' on the Cumberland. Nashville, (1961). Top edge spotted, else VG in dj (frayed, spotted). *King.* $75/£48

DOUGLAS, C.L. Cattle Kings of Texas. Dallas: Baugh, 1939. 1st ed, 2nd ptg. Howes D 434. *Ginsberg.* $100/£65

DOUGLAS, DAVID C. English Scholars. Cape, 1943. Pub's cl (sl tired). Sound. *Peter Taylor.* $20/£13

DOUGLAS, F.C.R. Land-Value Rating. Hogarth Press, 1936. 1st ed. VG in dj (tears). *Words Etc.* $65/£42

DOUGLAS, GEORGE M. Lands Forlorn. NY: Putnam's, 1914. Color frontis, fldg map. Orig dec cl, teg. VG. *High Latitude.* $300/£194

DOUGLAS, HOWARD. A Treatise on Naval Gunnery. London: John Murray, 1855. 4th ed. Frontis, viii,645pp + 30pp ads; 2 fldg plts. (Sl stained, rubbed.) *Lefkowicz.* $200/£129

DOUGLAS, KEITH. Alamein to Zem Zem. Poetry London, 1946. 1st Eng ed. Bkpl; bumped, o/w VG. *Edrich.* $39/£25

DOUGLAS, LANGDON. Fra Angelico. London, 1902. 6 photogravure plts, guards; 67 photo plts. Teg. (Foxing; ex-lib.) *Argosy.* $125/£81

DOUGLAS, MARJORY STONEMAN. The Everglades: River of Grass. Rinehart, (c. 1947). 1st ed. Inscribed presentation. VG. *Book Broker.* $50/£32

DOUGLAS, NORMAN (ed). Venus in the Kitchen. (By Pilaff Bey.) London: Heinemann, 1952. 1st UK ed. NF in dj (sl worn). *Williams.* $47/£30

DOUGLAS, NORMAN. An Almanac. London: C&W, (1945). 1st trade ed. (Sm stain backstrip.) Dj (torn). *Petersfield.* $40/£26

DOUGLAS, NORMAN. An Almanac. London: C&W/Martin Secker, 1945. 1st UK ed. VG in dj (soiled, sl chipped). *Virgo.* $47/£30

DOUGLAS, NORMAN. Alone. London: Chapman & Hall, 1921. 1st ed. Good (foxed, few pp sl stained; sl mks, worn; lacks dj). *Virgo.* $28/£18

DOUGLAS, NORMAN. Alone. London: Chapman & Hall, 1921. 1st ed. (Lt foxing; faded.) *Petersfield.* $31/£20

DOUGLAS, NORMAN. Alone. McBride, 1922. 1st Amer ed. Sl worn, else VG+. *Fine Books.* $45/£29

DOUGLAS, NORMAN. Birds and Beasts of the Greek Anthology. (Florence: Franceschini), 1927. 1st ed. One of 500 numbered, signed. Uncut, unopened. Blue bds (papers sl torn along hinge). VG. *Second Life.* $75/£48

DOUGLAS, NORMAN. Birds and Beasts of the Greek Anthology. London: Chapman & Hall, 1928. 1st UK ed. One of 1425. Partly unopened. VG (fore-edges speckled, bds sl soiled; lacks dj). *Virgo.* $31/£20

DOUGLAS, NORMAN. Experiments. London: Chapman & Hall, 1925. 1st Eng ed. Good (bkpl; faded, worn; lacks dj). *Virgo.* $39/£25

DOUGLAS, NORMAN. Fountains in the Sand. London: Martin Secker, 1921. 2nd ed. One of 1000. Sl faded, rubbed, o/w VG. Lacks dj. *Virgo.* $23/£15

DOUGLAS, NORMAN. How About Europe? London: C&W, 1930. 1st trade ed. (Sl foxed; backstrip faded; sl grubby.) *Petersfield.* $22/£14

DOUGLAS, NORMAN. In the Beginning. London: C&W, 1928. 1st UK ed. One of 2570. Edges sl dusty, o/w VG. Lacks dj. *Virgo.* $31/£20

DOUGLAS, NORMAN. In the Beginning. London: Folio Soc, 1953. Fine in dj (sl frayed; spine dknd). *Temple.* $33/£21

DOUGLAS, NORMAN. Late Harvest. London: Lindsay Drummond, 1946. 1st ed. Name, date, price on fep; top edges sl faded, o/w VG in dj (spine faded). *Virgo.* $31/£20

DOUGLAS, NORMAN. London Street Games. London: St. Catherine Press, 1916. 1st ed. Ltd to 500. Edges uncut (dusty). Good (sl foxed; scratched, rubbed; lacks dj). *Virgo.* $233/£150

DOUGLAS, NORMAN. London Street Games. London: C&W, 1931. 2nd ed, rev, enlgd. Cream pict bds ptd in maroon. Backstrip sl browned, else Very Nice. *Cady.* $30/£19

DOUGLAS, NORMAN. Looking Back, an Autobiographical Excursion. London: C&W, (1934). 1st (single vol) ed. (Sl foxed; faded.) *Petersfield.* $28/£18

DOUGLAS, NORMAN. Looking Back. London, 1933. 1st ed, one of 535 numbered, signed. 2 vols. (Bkpl; binding worn.) *Argosy.* $150/£97

DOUGLAS, NORMAN. Nerinda (1901). Florence: G. Orioli, 1929. #267/475 signed. Fine in bd slipcase (chipped). *Schoyer.* $85/£55

DOUGLAS, NORMAN. Nerinda (1901). Florence: G. Orioli, 1929. #412/475 signed. Uncut. Fine (spine sl sunned). *Polyanthos.* $75/£48

DOUGLAS, NORMAN. Nerinda (1901). Florence: Orioli, 1929. 1st ed. One of 475 lg paper copies, signed. Uncut, unopened. NF. *Second Life.* $125/£81

DOUGLAS, NORMAN. Nerinda. Florence: Orioli, 1929. #112/475 signed. Unopened. Name, address, o/w Fine in new slipcase, orig title laid on. *Virgo.* $109/£70

DOUGLAS, NORMAN. Old Calabria. London: Martin Secker, 1920. 2nd ed. One of 1000. VG (sl faded, rubbed, bumped; lacks dj). *Virgo.* $31/£20

DOUGLAS, NORMAN. Paneros. C&W, 1931. 1st ed. One of 650. NF. *Fine Books.* $95/£61

DOUGLAS, NORMAN. Paneros. London: C&W, 1931. 1st UK ed. #615/650. Paper-patterned bds (soiled, mkd, faded; nameplt). Lacks dj. Good. *Virgo.* $78/£50

DOUGLAS, NORMAN. Paneros. NY: Robert M. McBride, 1932. 1st Amer ed, ltd to 750 numbered. Vellum stamped in gold. Ink name; spine lt browned; outer hinge cracking, else VG. *Godot.* $65/£42

DOUGLAS, NORMAN. Some Letters of Pino Orioli to Mrs. Gordon Crotch. Edinburgh: Tragara Press, 1974. #16/120. Dec paper bds. Fine. *Virgo.* $116/£75

DOUGLAS, NORMAN. South Wind. London: Secker, (1922). #23/150 lg-paper copies, signed. Unopened. Spine cocked, o/w Fine in dj (chipped). *Schoyer.* $150/£97

DOUGLAS, NORMAN. South Wind. London, 1917. 1st ed. (Fore-edge foxed; mks.) *Petersfield.* $147/£95

DOUGLAS, NORMAN. South Wind. D-M, 1918. 1st Amer ed. One of 500 (of 1000). Inner hinges cracked; lt soil to orange cvrs, else VG. *Fine Books.* $85/£55

DOUGLAS, NORMAN. Summer Islands. London: Harmsworth, 1931. #282/500. Spine faded, o/w VG in dj (soiled, torn, lacks pieces); spare spine label. *Virgo.* $62/£40

DOUGLAS, NORMAN. They Went. London: Chapman & Hall, 1920. 1st ed. Good (bkpl; fr joint sl cracked, worn, spine frayed; lacks dj). *Virgo.* $78/£50

DOUGLAS, NORMAN. Three of Them. London: C&W, 1930. 1st ed. (Sl foxed; backstrip faded, sl torn; sl mkd.) *Petersfield.* $23/£15

DOUGLAS, NORMAN. Together. London, 1923. 1st ed. (Lt browning; sm dent; spine faded, chipped, sm tear.) *Edwards.* $23/£15

DOUGLAS, ROY. Who Is Nemo? Lippincott, 1937. 1st ed. Lt soiling pg edges, else NF in dj (lt nicked). *Murder.* $75/£48

DOUGLAS, WALTER. Manuel Lisa. Argosy-Antiquarian, 1964. 1st thus. 8 plts. Fine. *Oregon.* $50/£32

DOUGLASS, FREDERICK. My Bondage and My Freedom.... NY, 1855. 1st ed. 464pp, port (lacks fep; frontis, tp detached). Cl (spine dknd; worn; stained). *King.* $95/£61

DOURNOVO, LYDIA A. Armenian Miniatures. London: Thames & Hudson, 1961. 97 tipped-in color plts. Dj (sl chipped). *Edwards.* $93/£60

DOUTHIT, MARY OSBORN. The Souvenir of Western Women. Portland, 1905. 1st ed. VG in wraps. *Perier.* $75/£48

DOUTHIT, MARY OSBORN. The Souvenir of Western Women. Portland, 1905. 2nd ed. Grn cl. Fine. *Perier.* $150/£97

DOVE, RITA. Fifth Sunday. Lexington: Univ of KY, 1985. 1st ed. Fine in pict wraps. *Revere.* $75/£48

DOVE, RITA. Through the Ivory Gate. NY, 1992. Signed presentation. Fine in Fine dj. *Polyanthos.* $55/£35

DOVETON, F.B. Maggie in Mythica. Swan Sonnenschein, 1890. 1st ed. VG in pict cl. *Fine Books.* $125/£81

DOW, GEORGE FRANCIS and JOHN HENRY EDMONDS. The Pirates of the New England Coast 1630-1730. Salem, 1923. 1st ed. (Sl soiled.) Howes D 437. *Lefkowicz.* $100/£65

DOW, GEORGE FRANCIS. Slave Ships and Slaving. Salem: Marine Research Soc, 1927. VG. *Argosy.* $125/£81

DOW, GEORGE FRANCIS. Slave Ships and Slaving. Salem, MA, 1927. 1st ed, ltd to 250. Orig cl (sl rubbed). VG. Howes D 438. *Mcgowan.* $250/£161

DOW, H.J. The Art of Alex Colville. Toronto, 1972. Sound in dj (sl frayed). *Ars Artis.* $54/£35

DOW, LORENZO. History of Cosmopolite...To Which Is Added, the 'Journey of Life,' by Peggy Dow. Cincinnati: Anderson, Gates & Wright, 1860. 720pp. Leather (rubbed). *Hayman.* $35/£23

DOWD, JEROME. The Negro in American Life. NY: Century, (1926). 1st ed. VG. *Petrilla.* $65/£42

DOWDEY, CLIFFORD. Experiment in Rebellion. GC: Doubleday, 1946. 1st ed. Orig cl. VG in VG dj. *Mcgowan.* $45/£29

DOWDEY, CLIFFORD. The Great Plantation. NY, 1957. Berkeley Plantation Ed. Lt dj wear, chipping, o/w Fine. *Pratt.* $27/£17

DOWDEY, CLIFFORD. The Land They Fought For. GC, (1955). 1st ed. Signed. Dj chipped, o/w VG + . *Pratt.* $42/£27

DOWDEY, CLIFFORD. The Seven Days. Boston: Little, Brown, (1964). 1st ed. Blue cl. Fine in dj (spine sunned). *Chapel Hill.* $60/£39

DOWDEY, CLIFFORD. The Virginia Dynasties: The Emergence of King Carter and the Golden Age. Little, Brown, (c. 1969). 1st ed. VG in VG- dj. *Book Broker.* $25/£16

DOWELL, COLEMAN. Mrs. October Was Here. (NY): New Directions, (1974). 1st ed. Fine in dj (sl dknd). *Reese.* $20/£13

DOWLING, ALFRED E.R. RAYMOND. The Flora of the Sacred Nativity. London: Kegan Paul et al, 1900. Uncut. Buckram. Eps browned, else VG (bkpl). *Quest.* $150/£97

DOWLING, HARRY. Fighting Infection. Cambridge, 1977. 1st ed. Good in dj. *Fye.* $35/£23

DOWN, ROBERT HORACE. A History of the Silverton Country. Portland: Berncliff, 1926. 1st ed. Lt stain fr cvr, else VG. Howes D 445. *Perier.* $125/£81

DOWNES, KERRY. English Baroque Architecture. London, 1966. VG in dj. *Washton.* $125/£81

DOWNES, KERRY. Hawksmoor. London: Thames & Hudson, 1969. 1st ed thus. Dj illus mtd on fep, o/w Fine. *Europa.* $22/£14

DOWNES, RANDOLPH CHANDLER. Frontier Ohio, 1788-1803. Columbus, OH: OH State Archaeological & Hist Soc, 1935. 1st ed. Dk burgundy cl. Fine. *Chapel Hill.* $85/£55

DOWNEY, BILL. Tom Bass, Black Horseman. St. Louis: Saddle & Bridle, 1975. 1st ed. Fine in VG dj. *Oregon.* $22/£14

DOWNEY, FAIRFAX. Indian-Fighting Army. NY, 1941. 1st ed. Good (bkpl, sig, place, date of artist Harold Smith; back of dj carefully affixed to fr pastedown, lt edgewear). *Baade.* $60/£39

DOWNING, A.J. The Fruits and Fruit Trees of America. NY, 1845. 1st ed. Signed in blindstamp by binder. xiv,594pp + (14pp ads). (Even browning; lt foxing to prelims; ink note.) Cl, gilt-dec spine (wear; stain to spine). *Sutton.* $400/£258

DOWNING, A.J. The Fruits and Fruit Trees of America. Charles Downing (rev). NY, 1858. Third thousand, w/corrections. xix,760pp (even browning; foxing). Cl, gilt-dec spine (worn; spine dulled). *Sutton.* $200/£129

DOWNING, A.J. Treatise on the Theory and Practice of Landscape Gardening.... NY: A.O. Moore, 1859. 6th ed. W/supplement by Henry Winthrop Sargent. 34 plts (6 steel engrs, 4 lithos, 24 wood engrs). Marbled edges. 1/2 morocco, marbled bds (rebound; lt foxing; stains first 2, last 10ff; new eps; all plts but 1 clean). *Quest.* $220/£142

DOWNING, C.T. Neuralgia. London, 1851. 1st ed. 375pp. Orig cl (rebacked). *Fye.* $300/£194

DOWNING, E.R. A Naturalist in the Great Lakes Region. Chicago: Univ of Chicago, 1922. 1st ed. Good+ (sm blindstamp). *Mikesh.* $27/£17

DOWSETT, J. MOREWOOD. Big Game and Big Life. London: John Bale, Sons & Danielsson, (1925). 174 photos, map. (Faded, joints torn.) *Petersfield.* $87/£56

DOXIADIS, CONSTANTINOS. Architecture in Transition. London: Hutchinson, 1968. Fine in dj. *Europa.* $31/£20

DOXTATER, LEE WALTER. Procedures in Modern Crown and Bridgework. NY, 1931. (Lib ink stamp; spine faded.) *Edwards.* $39/£25

DOYLE, A. CONAN et al. Strange Secrets. Fenno, 1895. 1st ed. VG. *Fine Books.* $125/£81

DOYLE, A. CONAN. The Adventures of Gerard. NY: McClure, Phillips, 1903. 1st Amer ed. 8vo. (x),297pp + 12pp ads dated 1903 at end. 16 full-pg plts. Dk grn cl lettered in lighter grn, blocked in gilt/black/lt grn. Very Nice. *Cady.* $50/£32

DOYLE, A. CONAN. The Adventures of Sherlock Holmes, together with Memoirs. London: George Newnes, 1892. 1st ed, 1st issue, w/no name on street sign on fr cvrs. 8vo. Blue cl stamped in black/gilt; aeg. Good (hinges sprung; ends worn). *Juvelis.* $3,500/£2,258

DOYLE, A. CONAN. Adventures of Sherlock Holmes. NY: Harper & Bros, Franklin Square, (1892). 1st Amer ed, 2nd issue w/'if he had' on line 4, p65. 307pp. Sl cocked; spine darkened w/head sl chipped, else VG. *Mcgowan.* $300/£194

DOYLE, A. CONAN. Adventures of Sherlock Holmes. Harper, 1892. 1st Amer ed. 1st issue w/'if had' on pg 65 line 4. VG+. *Fine Books.* $1,500/£968

DOYLE, A. CONAN. The Adventures of Sherlock Holmes. London: Newnes, 1892. 1st ed. Orig 'Strand' pale blue cl (neatly rebacked; sl mkd; lt foxing title, margins; name). *Petersfield.* $341/£220

DOYLE, A. CONAN. The Adventures of Sherlock Holmes. London: George Newnes, 1892. 1st ed. Spine dknd; cvrs soiled; corners worn, o/w VG. *Mordida.* $950/£613

DOYLE, A. CONAN. Adventures of Sherlock Holmes. GC: Doubleday, 1930. 'Crowborough Edition.' Vol XVII only. Teg, uncut, partly unopened. Natural linen over lt brn bds, ptd paper label. VG. *Houle.* $125/£81

DOYLE, A. CONAN. Beyond the City. Chicago/NY: Rand, McNally, (1892). 1st Amer ed. Teg, uncut. Grn cl, spine heavily gilt. Fine. *Macdonnell.* $150/£97

DOYLE, A. CONAN. The British Campaign in France and Flanders, 1914-1918. London, 1916-1919. 1st eds. 6 vols. VG. *Argosy.* $400/£258

DOYLE, A. CONAN. The Case Book of Sherlock Holmes. Doran, 1927. 1st Amer ed. Good. *Fine Books.* $55/£35

DOYLE, A. CONAN. The Croxley Master and Other Tales of the Ring and Camp. NY: George H. Doran, n.d. (1925). 1st Amer ed, 2nd issue. Orange cl pict dec in dk grn. Fine in NF dj. *Sumner & Stillman.* $150/£97

DOYLE, A. CONAN. Danger! and Other Stories. Doran, 1919. 1st ed. Lt dust soil, else VG-. *Fine Books.* $55/£35

DOYLE, A. CONAN. A Desert Drama. Phila: Lippincott, 1898. 1st ed. NF in pict cvrs. *Else Fine.* $65/£42

DOYLE, A. CONAN. The Doings of Raffles Haw. Cassell, 1892. 1st ed. VG+. *Fine Books.* $375/£242

DOYLE, A. CONAN. A Duet. NY, 1899. 1st Amer ed. Fine (sl rubbed). *Polyanthos.* $100/£65

DOYLE, A. CONAN. A Duet. Appleton, 1899. 1st US ed. 336pp + ads. Gilt/silver dec cl. Sl faded, else VG. *Whiteson.* $31/£20

DOYLE, A. CONAN. The Edge of the Unknown. Putnam, 1930. 1st ed. Spine faded, else Good. *Fine Books.* $40/£26

DOYLE, A. CONAN. The Exploits of Brigadier Gerard. London: Newnes, 1896. 1st UK ed, 1st issue, w/ads dated 10.2.96. 24 full-pg illus. Good (stained, worn, sl cocked). *Williams.* $93/£60

DOYLE, A. CONAN. The Great Shadow and Beyond the City. Bristol/London: Arrowsmith/Simpkin et al, (1893). 1st ed of Beyond the City, 1st issue thus. Bkpl, back panel sl spotted, else Very Nice. *Limestone.* $155/£100

DOYLE, A. CONAN. The Hound of the Baskervilles. NY, 1902. 1st Amer ed, 3rd issue w/tipped-in tp. Spine lettering mostly gone, cvrs dknd, else Good. *King*. $125/£81

DOYLE, A. CONAN. The Hound of the Baskervilles. M-P, 1902. 1st Amer ed, later issue w/'illustrated' on canceled tp. White spine lettering mostly gone, else VG +. *Aronovitz*. $285/£184

DOYLE, A. CONAN. The Hound of the Baskervilles. London: George Newnes, 1902. 1st ed, 1st issue, w/misprint 'you' for 'your' p13, line 3. 26 plts. Pub's gilt-dec red cl. Fine + (occasional lt foxing; spine lt sunned). *D & D*. $1,900/£1,226

DOYLE, A. CONAN. The Land of Mist. Hutchinson, 1926. 1st ed, 1st issue in grn cl, w/24pp ads inserted to rear. Inscribed. VG (spine hinges, extrems worn). *Williams*. $1,387/£895

DOYLE, A. CONAN. The Land of Mist. Doran, 1926. 1st US ed. Good. *Madle*. $40/£26

DOYLE, A. CONAN. The Lost World. Burt, (1912). Good. *Fine Books*. $38/£25

DOYLE, A. CONAN. The Lost World. H&S, 1912. 1st Amer ed. 16 illus by Joseph Clement Coll. 2nd state Burt binding. Spine sl bumped, else NF. *Fine Books*. $65/£42

DOYLE, A. CONAN. The Lost World. H&S, 1912. 1st Amer ed. This bk bound red cl, has title, author & pub (being Doran only) stamped in gold on spine, has title, author stamped in black fr cvr; measures only 1-1/6 inch across top pg edges & contains 2 photo plts. VG-. *Aronovitz*. $150/£97

DOYLE, A. CONAN. The Memoirs of Sherlock Holmes. London: George Newnes, 1894. 1st Eng ed. Blue cl (faded; crudely colored spots; spine gilt rubbed; inner hinges repaired; corner worn). *Glenn*. $1,100/£710

DOYLE, A. CONAN. The Memoirs of Sherlock Holmes. London: Newnes, 1894. 1st UK ed. VG (sl worn spot; hinges repaired). *Williams*. $659/£425

DOYLE, A. CONAN. The Memoirs of Sherlock Holmes. Harper, 1894. New, rev ed (omitting the cardboard box). Spine sl dknd, fraying, else VG. *Fine Books*. $125/£81

DOYLE, A. CONAN. Our American Adventure. NY: George H. Doran, (1923). 1st Amer ed. Yellow cl, grn title. (Ink name.) Ptd dj (chipped; creased). *Hermitage*. $125/£81

DOYLE, A. CONAN. The Refugees. NY: Harper, 1893. 1st ed. 27 plts. Dec blue cl cvrs (worn). VG. *Else Fine*. $225/£145

DOYLE, A. CONAN. Rodney Stone. NY: Appleton, 1896. 1st Amer ed. Gilt dec cl. Spine sunned, hinge sl cracked, else Good. *Reese*. $25/£16

DOYLE, A. CONAN. Rodney Stone. NY: D. Appleton, 1896. 1st Amer ed. Red cl, silver/gold dec. Tape mks ep; ink inscrip, o/w VG. *Hermitage*. $175/£113

DOYLE, A. CONAN. Rodney Stone. London: Smith, Elder, 1896. 1st ed. viii,366pp,5pp ads at end; 8 plts. Untrimmed. Fine. *Bickersteth*. $217/£140

DOYLE, A. CONAN. Sherlock Holmes, the Complete Long Stories. London: John Murray, (1929). 1st ed. Red cl (spine sl faded), gold lettering. *Glenn*. $125/£81

DOYLE, A. CONAN. The Sign of the Four. London: George Newnes, 1893. 3rd ed. VG in variant cl: brn, not red. *Glenn*. $350/£226

DOYLE, A. CONAN. Songs of Action. London: Smith, Elder, 1898. 1st ed, ltd to 1000. Blue cl, gilt. Fine. *Sumner & Stillman*. $165/£106

DOYLE, A. CONAN. Songs of the Road. London: Smith, Elder, 1911. 1st ed, ltd to 2000. 2pp undated ads. Blue cl. Fine (sig). *Sumner & Stillman*. $145/£94

DOYLE, A. CONAN. The Stark Munro Letters. London: Longmans, 1895. 1st ed. Nice (bkpl, internal foxing; cvrs lt spotted, wrinkled). *Limestone*. $65/£42

DOYLE, A. CONAN. A Study in Scarlet. Chicago: Donohue, Henneberry, n.d. (fr wrapper dated May 13, 1895). A vol in the Chicago pub's 'The Ideal Library,' this being No. 209. 4pp undated ads. Ptd wrappers. VG (fr cvr sl discolored; sl shelfwear). *Sumner & Stillman*. $95/£61

DOYLE, A. CONAN. Through the Magic Door. London: Smith Elder, 1907. Teg; marbled eps. 1/2 morocco (sl rubbed; head upper joint sl split), raised bands, gilt motifs. (Spotting; hinges sl tender; spine worn, sl loss.) *Edwards*. $39/£25

DOYLE, A. CONAN. The Tragedy of the Korosko. London: Smith, Elder, 1898. 1st ed in bk form. 40 full-pg illus. Pub's gilt-dec red cl. Spine lt soiled; inner hinges cracked, else Fine. *D & D*. $60/£39

DOYLE, A. CONAN. The Tragedy of the Korosko. London: Smith, Elder, 1898. 1st ed. xii,333,vipp ads. Sydney Paget (illus). Red cl gilt. VG (joints tender). *Hollett*. $217/£140

DOYLE, A. CONAN. The Valley of Fear. NY, (1914). 1st ed. (Sl cocked; spine dknd; extrems fraying.) *King*. $95/£61

DOYLE, A. CONAN. The Valley of Fear. NY: George H. Doran, 1914. 1st Amer ed. Pub's gilt-lettered red cl. Sm lt spot cvr; foxing 1st few leaves, else Fine. *D & D*. $175/£113

DOYLE, A. CONAN. The Valley of Fear. Doran, 1914. 1st ed. VG +. *Fine Books*. $135/£87

DOYLE, A. CONAN. Visit to Three Fronts. London et al: Hodder & Stoughton, 1916. 3rd ed. White ptd wraps (soiled). *Schoyer*. $15/£10

DOYLE, A. CONAN. The White Company. McKay, (ca 1925). 1st ed thus. 14 full-pg color plts by N.C. Wyeth. VG +. *Fine Books*. $85/£55

DOYLE, A. CONAN. The White Company. London: Smith, Elder, 1903. One of 1000 numbered, signed. Internally Fine (cvrs worn). *Glenn*. $400/£258

DOYLE, ADRIAN CONAN and JOHN DICKSON CARR. The Exploits of Sherlock Holmes. London: John Murray, 1954. 1st ed. NF in VG + dj (lt chipped). *Janus*. $120/£77

DOYLE, ADRIAN CONAN and JOHN DICKSON CARR. The Exploits of Sherlock Holmes. Murray, 1954. 1st UK ed. VG (bkpl; newsclipping pasted to flyleaf) in dj. *Williams*. $109/£70

DOYLE, H.W. Alfalfa in Kansas. Topeka, 1916. Wrappers (edges soiled; backstrip partly missing; corner creased). *Sutton*. $43/£28

DOYLE, HELEN MACKNIGHT. Mary Austin: Woman of Genius. NY: Gotham House, (1939). 1st ed. Fine in dj (lt soiled). *Hermitage*. $40/£26

DOYLE, J.A. English in America. London: Longmans, 1882. 1st ed. 1st vol of 5 vol work. (16),556,(24 ads)pp, fldg color map. Howes D 454. *Ginsberg*. $100/£65

DOYLE, RICHARD. Bird's Eye Views of Society. London: Smith, Elder, 1864. 1st British ed. Engr title; 16 plts. Mod buckram. VG (contemp sig). *Agvent.* $85/£55

DOYLE, RICHARD. The Foreign Tour of Messrs. Brown, Jones and Robinson.... NY: D. Appleton, 1877. (4),80pp. Aeg. Gilt-pict grn cl (extrems worn; joints rubbed). VG. *House.* $110/£71

DOYLE, RICHARD. In Fairyland. London: Longmans, Green, 1875. 2nd ed. 31pp; 16 color plts (lt foxing, plts still bright). Pict grn cl (rubbing, sm ink stain on fr). *Schoyer.* $350/£226

DOYLE, RICHARD. Jack the Giant Killer. London: Eyre & Spottiswoode, (1888). 1st ed, 1st issue. 4to. Richard Doyle (illus). Pub's intro laid in. Orange-red cl, black dec (lt sun-faded area). *Reisler.* $400/£258

DOYLE, RODDY. Paddy Clarke Ha Ha Ha. London: Secker & Warburg, 1993. 1st UK ed. Fine in dj. *Moorhouse.* $62/£40

DOYLE, RODDY. The Van. London: Secker & Warburg, 1991. 1st ed. NF in dj. *Rees.* $39/£25

DRABBLE, MARGARET. The Garrick Year. London: Weidenfeld & Nicolson, 1964. 1st British ed. Fine in VG dj. *Pettler.* $45/£29

DRABBLE, MARGARET. The Radiant Way. London: Weidenfeld & Nicholson, (1987). 1st ed. Fine in Fine dj. *Robbins.* $25/£16

DRAGO, HARRY SINCLAIR. Following the Grass. Macaulay, (1924). 1st ed. Frontis. NF in dj (chipped). *Authors Of The West.* $35/£23

DRAGO, HARRY SINCLAIR. Wild, Wooley and Wicked. NY: Clarkson N. Potter, 1960. 1st ed. VG in Good+ dj (sl chipped). *Connolly.* $30/£19

DRAKE, BENJAMIN and EDWARD D. MANSFIELD. Cincinnati in 1826. Cincinnati: Morgan, Lodge, & Fisher, Feb 1827. 1st ed. 100,(1)pp; 2 engr plts. Later paper-cvrd bds. Spine faded; bkpl residue, else VG. Howes D 458. *Felcone.* $250/£161

DRAKE, DANIEL. Malaria in the Interior Valley of North America. Urbana: Univ of IL, 1964. Good. *White.* $23/£15

DRAKE, DANIEL. Malaria in the Interior Valley of North America.... Univ of IL Press, 1964. Fine in dj. *Glaser.* $35/£23

DRAKE, DANIEL. Practical Essays on Medical Education and the Medical Profession in the United States. Balt, 1952. Rptg. Frontis. (Ex-lib.) *Goodrich.* $35/£23

DRAKE, EMMA. Purity and Truth: What a Young Wife Ought to Know. Phila, 1902. 1st ed. Good. *Fye.* $50/£32

DRAKE, EMMA. What a Woman of Forty-Five Ought to Know. Phila, 1902. 1st ed. Good. *Fye.* $40/£26

DRAKE, FRANCIS S. Tea Leaves. Boston: Crane, 1884. 375pp. Pict cl. (Stamp edges; rear pocket removed.) *Schoyer.* $60/£39

DRAKE, LEAH BODINE. A Hornbook for Witches. Sauk City: Arkham House, 1950. 1st ed. Fine (sm stain top edge) in Fine dj. *Beasley.* $1,200/£774

DRAKE, LEAH BODINE. A Hornbook for Witches. Arkham House, 1950. 1st ed. Fine in dj. *Aronovitz.* $1,325/£855

DRAKE, SAMUEL ADAMS. Nooks and Corners of the New England Coast. NY: Harper, (1875). 1st ptg. 459pp. Pict cl. VG. *Schoyer.* $35/£23

DRAKE, SAMUEL ADAMS. Old Boston Taverns and Tavern Clubs. Boston: W.A. Butterfield, 1917. 1st ed. New illus ed. Frontis; 22 plts; fldg map at rear. Paper spine label; partially unopened. VG (lt foxing, shelfwear). *Connolly.* $37/£24

DRAKE, SAMUEL ADAMS. The Pine-Tree Coast. Boston: Estes & Lauriat, 1891. 1st ed. Grn cl stamped in black/silver. Fine in tan dj w/title stamped in black on spine, pine cone bough illus (chipped, some text loss). *Juvelis.* $250/£161

DRAPER, LYMAN C. King's Mountain and Its Heroes. Marietta, GA: Continental Book Co, 1954. Rpt of 1st ed of 1881. Pict grn cl. VG (spotting). Howes D 485. *Chapel Hill.* $70/£45

Drawings by Fragonard in North American Collections. Washington, D.C.: Nat'l Gallery of Art, 1978. Good in wrappers. *Washton.* $25/£16

DREANY, E. JOSEPH. Bible Stories from the Old Testament in Pop-Up Action Pictures. London: Publicity, 1953. 27x21cm. 4 dbl-pg pop-ups. Spiral bound. Glazed pict wraps. VG-. *Book Finders.* $80/£52

DREANY, E. JOSEPH. Cowboys in Pop-Up Action Pictures. London: Publicity, 1951. 26x21cm. 5 dbl-pg pop-ups. Spiral bound. Glazed pict wraps. VG-. *Book Finders.* $80/£52

DREANY, E. JOSEPH. Indians in Pop-Up Action Pictures. London: Publicity, 1951. 27x21cm. 5 dbl-pg pop-ups. Spiral binding; glazed pict wraps. VG. *Book Finders.* $70/£45

DREER, HENRY. Dreer's Grasses and Clovers. Phila: Dreer, 1897. 2nd ed. 123pp. Pict wraps (sm stain). *Schoyer.* $30/£19

DREIER, KATHERINE S. Shawn: The Dancer. NY: A.S. Barnes, 1933. 1st ed. Color frontis w/guard. Sl bump spine top, else Fine. *Cahan.* $125/£81

DREISER, THEODORE. An American Tragedy. NY: Boni & Liveright, 1925. #644/795 numbered, signed. Blue paper bds, linen spine. Fine in orig slipcase (worn). *Cummins.* $400/£258

DREISER, THEODORE. An American Tragedy. NY: Boni & Liveright, 1925. 1st ed, 1st issue, w/Boni & Liveright impt. 2 vols. Black cl. VG set in djs (tape mends vol 1); pub's slipcase (repaired). *Chapel Hill.* $400/£258

DREISER, THEODORE. Chains. B&L, 1927. 1st ed. One of 440 signed. Sl corner wear, else Fine. *Fine Books.* $265/£171

DREISER, THEODORE. Dawn. Liveright, 1931. 1st ed. One of 275 signed. NF. *Fine Books.* $285/£184

DREISER, THEODORE. Epitaph. NY: Heron Press, (1929). Ltd ed, signed by author & Robert Fawcett (decs). Black linen, gold lettering. Fine. *Appelfeld.* $100/£65

DREISER, THEODORE. Epitaph. NY: Heron, 1929. 1st ed. One of 1100 signed. Fine in plain tissue (lt chipped) in box (sl worn). *Beasley.* $275/£177

DREISER, THEODORE. The Financier. NY, 1912. 1st ed, 1st state. Blue mottled cl. Fine. *Bond.* $35/£23

DREISER, THEODORE. The Financier. NY: Harper, 1912. 1st ed. Blue mottled cl (lt worn). VG. *Hermitage.* $50/£32

DREISER, THEODORE. A Gallery of Women. NY, 1929. 1st Amer ed. 2 vols. Fine (sm stain vol 1) in djs (spines sunned, sl chipped), box (chipped). *Polyanthos.* $100/£65

DREISER, THEODORE. Moods Cadenced and Declaimed. NY: Boni & Liveright, 1928. 1st trade ed. Fine in dj (spine lt chipped; rubbing, sm stains). *Antic Hay*. $75/£48

DREISER, THEODORE. Moods, Cadenced and Declaimed. NY: Boni & Liveright, 1928. 1st trade ed. Orig brn bds w/blue cl spine. Bright, crisp in equally Fine dj (price-clipped). *Chapel Hill*. $250/£161

DREISER, THEODORE. Plays of the Natural and the Supernatural. NY/London: John Lane/Bodley Head, 1916. 1st ed, 1st issue, w/o 4-pg essay tipped in at back. Lt grn bds; linen cl spine; paper spine label. VG. *Antic Hay*. $75/£48

DREISER, THEODORE. Sister Carrie. NY: LEC, 1939. #162/1500 signed by Reginald Marsh (illus). Fine in slipcase. *Williams*. $186/£120

DREISER, THEODORE. The Titan. NY: John Lane, 1914. 1st ed. 1st binding of blue mottled cl. VG (lt worn). *Hermitage*. $50/£32

DREISER, THEODORE. The Titan. NY, 1914. 1st issue binding (mottled blue cl). VG. *Fuller & Saunders*. $35/£23

DREISER, THEODORE. A Traveler at Forty. NY, 1913. 1st ed. Frontis. Spotted, shelfwear, o/w Good. *Artis*. $25/£16

DREISEWERD, EDNA. The Catcher Was a Lady. Exposition, 1978. 1st ed. Fine in VG+ dj. *Plapinger*. $65/£42

DRESDEN, DONALD. The Marquis De Mores, Emperor of the Bad Lands. Norman: Univ of OK, (1970). 1st ed. Fine in dj (sl chipped). *Laurie*. $45/£29

DRESEL, GUSTAV. Gustav Dresel's Houston Journal.... Max Freund (ed). Austin: Univ of TX, 1954. 1st ed. Frontis port. Rubbed, else NF. *Cahan*. $40/£26

DRESSER, CHRISTOPHER. Principles of Decorative Design. London: Cassell, Petter & Galpin, n.d. (ca 1874). 2nd ed. viii,167,(1),(4)pp; 2 chromolitho plts. VG. *Bookpress*. $475/£306

DRESSES, ELIA. A Masque of Days. London: Cassell, 1901. 1st ed. 4to, unpaginated, double-fold pgs. Walter Crane (illus). Cl-backed pict bds. VG (sm foxing tp, fep). *Davidson*. $325/£210

DRESSLER, ALBERT (ed). Letters to a Pioneer Senator. (By James W. Mandeville.) SF: H.S. Crocker, 1925. 1st ed. #1/525. Limp leather, gilt (pict cvr bound in). VG. *Shasky*. $50/£32

DRESSLER, FLORENCE. Feminology: A Guide for Womankind. Chicago, 1911. 6th ed. 702pp. Good. *Fye*. $100/£65

DREW, JANE B. (ed). Architect's Year Book 1. London, 1945. (Ex-lib.) *Edwards*. $39/£25

DREXEL-BIDDLE, ANTHONY J. The Madeira Islands. Phila: Drexel-Biddle & Bradley, 1896. 1st ed. Frontis, 112,(4)pp; 2 maps. Tan cl, gilt. Good. *Karmiole*. $40/£26

DREXLER, ARTHUR. The Drawings of Frank Lloyd Wright. NY, (1962). VG in dj (chipped). *Argosy*. $75/£48

DREXLER, ARTHUR. The Drawings of Frank Lloyd Wright. NY: Horizon Press, (1965). 2nd ptg. Fine in dj (chipped, rubbed). *Bookpress*. $100/£65

DREYFUS, ALFRED. The Letters of Captain Dreyfus to His Wife. L.G. Moreau (trans). Harpers, 1899. 1st ed. VG+. *Fine Books*. $45/£29

DRIBERG, J.H. Initiation, Translations from Poems of the Didinga and Lango Tribes. London: Golden Cockerel Press, (1932). #207/325 signed. (Sl faded.) *Petersfield*. $65/£42

DRIBERG, TOM. Ruling Passions. London: Cape, 1977. 1st ed. Nice in dj. *Patterson*. $47/£30

DRIGGS, HOWARD. Westward America. Lippincott, (1942). Trails Ed. Color ep maps. VG (sig, address) in Good+ dj. *Oregon*. $40/£26

DRINKWATER, G.C. and T.R.B. SANDERS. The University Boat Race. C. Guron (ed). London, 1929. 1st ed. Fldg map. Teg. Orig gilt-edged cl, gilt device (lt browning, sl soiled, spine sl chipped). *Edwards*. $233/£150

DRINKWATER, JOHN. Tides. Beaumont Press, 1917. Ltd to 270 numbered. Canvas-backed patterned bds. VG. *Edrich*. $54/£35

DRINKWATER, JOHN. The World's Lincoln. NY: Bowling Green Press, 1928. One of 800. Parchment-backed bds. *Cox*. $28/£18

DRINNON, RICHARD. White Savage. The Case of John Dunn Hunter. Schocken, (1972). 1st ed. 3 maps, ep map. Fine in Fine dj. *Oregon*. $30/£19

DRISCOLL, LIEUTENANT. The Brighton Boys at St. Mihiel. Winston, 1919. 1st ed. Good. *Madle*. $10/£6

DRISCOLL, LIEUTENANT. Brighton Boys in the Radio Service. Winston, 1918. 1st ed. Good. *Madle*. $10/£6

DRIVER, CARL S. John Sevier. Chapel Hill: Univ of NC Press, 1932. 1st ed. Beige cl. NF. *Chapel Hill*. $65/£42

DRIVER, HAROLD E. Indians of North America. Chicago: Univ of Chicago, 1961. 1st ed. VG- in Good dj (spine stained; sm name stamps). *Parker*. $40/£26

DRIVER, HAROLD E. Indians of North America. Chicago, 1961. 1st ed. Rev copy. Fldg map in pocket; errata slip laid in. Dec cl. NF in dj (partially faded, tear repaired). *Baade*. $50/£32

DRUCKER, PHILIP. BAE Bulletin 144. The Northern and Central Nootkan Tribes. Washington, 1951. 1st ed. Frontis, fldg map. VG in wraps. *Oregon*. $40/£26

DRUERY, C.T. Choice British Ferns. London, 1888. iv,167pp + ads, 7 plts. (Lt wear, stained, edges dknd.) *Sutton*. $37/£24

DRUITT, HERBERT. A Manual of Costume as Illustrated by Monumental Brasses. London: De La More, 1906. Teg, others uncut. Pub's cl gilt (sl rubbed; inner hinges tender). *Peter Taylor*. $60/£39

DRUITT, HERBERT. A Manual of Costume as Illustrated by Monumental Brasses. London, 1906. Teg, rest uncut. (Text spotted; ex-libris; sl damp-spotted upper bd; spine sl bumped, mkd.) *Edwards*. $70/£45

DRUITT, ROBERT. The Principles and Practice of Modern Surgery. Phila, 1844. 568pp; 153 woodcuts. Full leather (scuffed). *Fye*. $100/£65

DRUMHELLER, DAN. Uncle Dan Drumheller Tells Thrilling Stories of Western Trails in 1854. Spokane: Inland American Printing, 1925. 1st ed. VG. *Perier*. $125/£81

DRUMMOND-HAY, JOHN H. Western Barbary. London: John Murray, 1844. 1st ed. vi,(178)pp. 3/4 calf (rubbed; foxed). *Schoyer*. $85/£55

Drums and Shadows, Survival Studies among the Georgia Coastal Negroes. (WPA). Athens: Univ of GA, 1940. 1st ed. Gilt cl. VG (blindstamp 5 leaves). *Reese*. $100/£65

DRURY, CLIFFORD. The Diaries and Letters of Henry H. Spalding and Asa Bowen Smith.... Clark, 1958. 1st ed. 9 plts, 3 maps (1 fldg); prospectus sheet laid in. Uncut; unopened. Fine. *Oregon.* $60/£39

DRURY, CLIFFORD. Elkanah and Mary Walker. Caldwell: Caxton, 1940. 1st ed. Fine in dj (tape repaired). *Perier.* $75/£48

DRURY, CLIFFORD. First White Women Over the Rockies. Glendale: Clark, 1963. 1st ed. Vol 1 only. VG. *Oregon.* $50/£32

DRURY, CLIFFORD. Henry Harmon Spalding. Caldwell: Caxton, 1936. 1st ed, w/Timothy on dj rather than Spalding. VG in dj (edgeworn). *Perier.* $80/£52

DRURY, CLIFFORD. Henry Harmon Spalding. Caxton, 1936. 1st ed. Rev copy. Frontis. VG. *Oregon.* $70/£45

DRURY, CLIFFORD. Marcus and Narcissa Whitman and the Opening of Old Oregon. Glendale: Clark, 1973. 1st ed. 2 vols. VG set. *Perier.* $97/£63

DRURY, CLIFFORD. Nine Years with the Spokane Indians. Clark, 1976. 1st ed. Color frontis port, map. Fine. *Oregon.* $45/£29

DRURY, JOHN. Old Chicago Houses. Chicago: Univ of Chicago Press, (1941). 1st ed. Rust cl; gilt spine. Good. *Karmiole.* $35/£23

DRYDEN, CECIL. Mr. Hunt and the Fabulous Plan. Caxton, 1958. 1st ed. Color frontis. Fine in VG dj. *Oregon.* $30/£19

DRYDEN, CECIL. Up the Columbia for Furs. Caxton, 1950. 2nd ptg. Color frontis, 3 color plts. VF in VF dj. *Oregon.* $35/£23

DRYDEN, JOHN. The Poetical Works. London: William Pickering, 1852. 5 vols. Port. Lighter fine diaper cl, paper labels. VG. *Cox.* $70/£45

DRYDEN, JOHN. Songs and Poems. London: Golden Cockerel Press, 1957. One of 500, this unnumbered. 8 color collotypes; unopened. Red morocco-backed grey canvas bds. VG in slipcase. *Cox.* $233/£150

DU BOIS, CHARLES G. Kick the Dead Lion. Billings, 1954. 1st ed. Pict wraps. Sig, browning to cvrs, pencil check mks in text, o/w Fine. *Baade.* $27/£17

DU BOIS, THEODORA. Death Sails in a High Wind. GC: DCC, 1945. 1st ed. NF in VG dj (price-clipped; chipped). *Janus.* $25/£16

DU BOIS, W.E.B. Darkwater: Voices from within the Veil. NY: Harcourt, Brace & Howe, 1920. 1st ed. (Eps lt foxed.) *Sadlon.* $100/£65

DU BOIS, W.E.B. Dusk of Dawn. NY: Harcourt, 1940. 1st ed. Fine (sl corner bump; bkpl) in dj (sl worn, chipped). *Beasley.* $125/£81

DU BOIS, W.E.B. The Souls of Black Folk. Chicago: A.C. McClurg, 1903. 1st ed. Good (ink name, dated 1904; fr hinge archivally mended w/Japanese tissue; binding dull, spine lt faded, frayed). *Godot.* $475/£306

DU BOIS, W.E.B. The World and Africa. NY: Viking, (1947). 1st ed. Patterned bds. VG in dj (chipped, stained). *Petrilla.* $40/£26

DU BOIS, W.E.B. The World and Africa. NY: Viking, 1947. 1st ed. VG in dj (chipped, price-clipped). *Pettler.* $40/£26

DU BOIS, WILLIAM PENE. Otto at Sea. NY: Viking, 1936. 1st ed. 16mo, unpaginated. Good (lt soil throughout, not interfering w/text; edges worn, bds soiled). *Davidson.* $125/£81

DU BOIS, WILLIAM PENE. The Three Policemen. NY: Viking, 1938. 1st ed. 8vo, 92pp. Grn cl, yellow title. VG (sm soil throughout, edges worn) in Good dj (frayed). *Davidson.* $135/£87

DU CHAILLU, PAUL B. Explorations and Adventures in Equatorial Africa. London, 1861. Map. Gilt dec brn cl (neatly rebacked). *Petersfield.* $87/£56

DU CHAILLU, PAUL B. Explorations and Adventures in Equatorial Africa. NY: Harper, 1861. 1st US ed. 532 + 4pp ads; 80 engrs, incl dbl-pg frontis, lg fldg map (repaired tear). Rust cl, gilt spine. (Sl rubbed.) *Karmiole.* $150/£97

DU CHAILLU, PAUL B. Explorations and Adventures in Equatorial Africa; With Accounts of the Manners.... NY, 1868. 2nd Amer ed. Dbl frontis; 531pp + ads; fldg map (torn). Orig gilt pict cl (worn). *Argosy.* $75/£48

DU CHAILLU, PAUL B. The Land of the Midnight Sun. NY, 1881. 2 vols. xvi,441; xvi,474pp; fldg map in rear pocket. Gilt/red illus cl (spines rubbed w/loss heads). *Edwards.* $194/£125

DU CHAILLU, PAUL B. The Land of the Midnight Sun. London: George Newnes, 1899. New ed. vii,759pp; fldg map. 1/2 maroon levant morocco gilt. Aeg. VG. *Hollett.* $186/£120

DU MAURIER, DAPHNE. The Infernal World of Branwell Bronte. London: Gollancz, 1960. 1st ed. 3 plts. Gilt cl (spine sl mkd, top faded). *Hollett.* $19/£12

DU MAURIER, DAPHNE. My Cousin Rachel. London: Gollancz, 1951. 1st ed. Sl foxing pg edges, else Fine in dj (minor edgewear). *Else Fine.* $135/£87

DU MAURIER, GEORGE. The Martian. NY: Harper, 1897. 1st Amer ed. Dec cl. NF (sm remnant name label fep). *Antic Hay.* $60/£39

DU MAURIER, GEORGE. The Martian. London/NY: Harper, 1898. Deluxe issue; one of 250 numbered. 1/2 vellum (sl soiled). Good (edges sunned). *Reese.* $75/£48

DU MAURIER, GEORGE. Peter Ibbetson. NY: Harper, 1892. 1st Amer ed. Dec grn cl. About VG (wear; ink name; fore-edge spotting). *Antic Hay.* $40/£26

DU MAURIER, GEORGE. Trilby. NY: Harper, 1894. 1st Amer ed. Dk blue 3/4 morocco leather; marbled bds; 5 raised bands on spine w/gilt-worked title; teg; marbled eps. Fine. *Antic Hay.* $125/£81

DU MAURIER, GEORGE. Trilby. London: Osgood, McIlvaine, 1895. 1st Eng 1-vol ed. x,447,(v)pp, teg. Sl rubbed. *Hollett.* $70/£45

DU MAURIER, GEORGE. Trilby. NY: Harper, 1895. Ltd ed of 600 numbered. Dec paper vellum; teg. VG (rear cvr spotted, soiled). *Antic Hay.* $85/£55

DU MAURIER, GEORGE. Trilby. London: Folio Soc, 1947. 6 plts. 1/4 dk red cl. Rear pastedown sl creased, o/w Fine in dj (strengthened w/tissue verso). *Temple.* $33/£21

DU PETIT-THAURS, ABEL. Voyage of the Venus: Sojourn in California. Charles N. Rudkin (trans). LA: Glen Dawson, 1956. 1st ed. Red cl over tan dec bds, paper spine label. Good. *Karmiole.* $50/£32

DU-PLAT-TAYLOR, F.M. Docks, Wharves and Piers. London, 1949. 3rd ed. Dj (chipped, spine sl browned). *Edwards.* $116/£75

DUBIN, LOIS SHERR. The History of Beads from 30,000 B.C. to the Present. London: Thames & Hudson, (1987). Good in dj. *Archaeologia.* $125/£81

DUBNOW, S.M. History of the Jews in Russia and Poland...until the Present Day. J. Friedlaender (trans). Phila, 1916. 1st Amer ed. 3 vols. VF set. *Bond.* $65/£42

DUBOIS, FELIX. Timbuctoo the Mysterious. Diana White (trans). London: Heinemann, 1897. 1st ed. xii,377pp; 11 maps, plans. Mod 1/2 levant morocco gilt. Nice (sl fingering; sm lib stamp). *Hollett.* $116/£75

DUBOIS, PAUL. Reason and Sentiment. NY, 1911. 1st Eng trans. Good. *Fye.* $75/£48

DUBON, DAVID. Tapestries from the Samuel H. Kress Collection at the Philadelphia Museum of Art. London, 1964. 75 plts. Good. *Washton.* $65/£42

DUBON, DAVID. Tapestries from the Samuel H. Kress Collection.... London: Phaidon, 1964. Tipped-in color frontis, 4 tipped-in color plts. Dj. *Edwards.* $31/£20

DUBOS, RENE. The Bacterial Cell in Its Relation to Problems of Virulence, Immunity and Chemotherapy. Cambridge, 1945. New cl (ex-lib). *Goodrich.* $35/£23

DUBOS, RENE. The Bacterial Cell in its Relation to Problems of Virulence, Immunity and Chemotherapy. Cambridge, 1945. 1st ed. Good. *Fye.* $35/£23

DUBOS, RENE. Louis Pasteur: Freelance of Science. Boston, 1950. 1st ed. Good. *Fye.* $25/£16

DUBUS, ANDRE. Finding a Girl in America. Boston: Godine, 1980. 1st ed. Signed, inscribed. Fine in Fine dj (sl wear). *Revere.* $100/£65

DUBUS, ANDRE. Land Where My Fathers Died. Stuart Wright/Palaemon, 1984. 1st ed. One of 200. Signed. Fine w/o dj as issued. *Lame Duck.* $100/£65

DUBUS, ANDRE. The Last Worthless Evening. Boston: Godine, 1986. 1st ed. NF in NF dj. *Pettler.* $45/£29

DUBUS, ANDRE. Separate Flights. Boston: Godine, 1975. 1st ed. NF in dj. *Lame Duck.* $100/£65

DUCANE, FLORENCE. The Flowers and Gardens of Japan. London: A&C Black, 1908. 1st ed. 50 color plts. Fine. *Quest.* $65/£42

DUCHARTRE, PIERRE LOUIS. The Italian Comedy. Randolph T. Weaver (trans). NY, (1929). 1st ed in English. Fine in dj. *Argosy.* $75/£48

DUCHAUSSOIS, PIERRE. Mid Snow and Ice. The Apostles of the North-West. Ottawa Univ, 1937. Fldg map. VG (dknd paper) in wraps. *Oregon.* $40/£26

DUCLAUX, E. Pasteur: The History of a Mind. Phila, 1920. 1st ed. Good. *Fye.* $50/£32

DUCOUDRAY-HOLSTEIN, H.L.V. Memoirs of Gilbert M. Lafayette. Geneva: John Greves, 1835. 2nd ed. 300pp. (Sunned, scuffed.) *Schoyer.* $45/£29

DUCROQUET, ROBERT. Walking and Limping: A Study.... Phila, 1968. 1st Eng trans. Good. *Fye.* $100/£65

DUDEK, LOUIS. The Searching Image. Toronto: Ryerson, (1952). 1st ed, ltd to 350. Fine in ptd wrappers. *Reese.* $200/£129

DUDLEY, HENRY WALBRIDGE. Autobiography. Menasha, WI, (ca 1913-14). Inscribed, signed 'The Author.' Gilt-titled navy cl. VG. *Bohling.* $200/£129

DUFF, E. GORDON. A Century of the English Book Trade. Bibliographical Soc, 1905. Teg; rest uncut. Half morocco, marbled bds (upper hinge sl tender; margins lt browned). *Edwards.* $54/£35

DUFF, E. GORDON. Early Printed Books. London: Kegan Paul, 1893. 1st ed. Frontis. Unopened. Gilt polished buckram. Spine faded, o/w VG. *Reese.* $50/£32

DUFF, JOHN J. A. Lincoln, Prairie Lawyer. Indianapolis, (1960). 1st ed. Sl dj wear, o/w Fine. *Pratt.* $25/£16

DUFFERIN, LORD. Letters from High Latitudes. London: OUP, (1910). Teg. Good +. *Blue Dragon.* $25/£16

DUFFERIN, LORD. Letters from High Latitudes. London, 1857. 1st ed. xx,424pp; 3 maps. Mod 1/2 calf. *Lewis.* $70/£45

DUFFERIN, LORD. Letters from High Latitudes. London: Murray, 1857. 1st ed. 8vo. xvii,(iii),424pp; 3 fldg charts, maps (sm repair margin 1 map); fldg diag, 11 engr plts (1 fldg). Contemp grn 1/2 morocco (joints cracking), gilt edges, spine. *Morrell.* $93/£60

DUFFERIN, LORD. Letters from High Latitudes. Boston: Ticknor & Fields, 1859. x,1 leaf,406pp + 16pp ads, fldg map facs (lacks frontis). Brn emb cl (spine faded). *Parmer.* $45/£29

DUFFERIN, LORD. Letters from High Latitudes. Toronto: Adam Stevenson, 1873. 1st Canadian ed. xxiii,248pp. Good. *Walcot.* $47/£30

DUFFIELD, KENNETH GRAHAM. The Four Little Pigs That Didn't Have Any Mother. Phila: Henry Altemus, (1919). 24mo. 61pp; illus eps. Red cl, gray emb bds (spine restored, strengthened internally). NF. *Drusilla's.* $50/£32

DUFFUS, R.L. The Santa Fe Trail. NY: Tudor Pub Co, (March 1936, c. 1930). 16 plts. Navy cl, gilt stamped. VG + in dj (chipped, edgeworn). *Bohling.* $35/£23

DUFFUS, R.L. The Santa Fe Trail. Longmans, 1930. 1st ed. Frontis, 15 plts. Pict gilt-stamped cl. Fine. *Oregon.* $50/£32

DUFFY, JOHN. The Sword of Pestilence. Baton Rouge: LA State Univ, 1966. 1st ed. Good. *White.* $19/£12

DUFFY, MAUREEN. The Erotic World of Faery. Hodder & Stoughton, 1972. Dj (sm tear spine). *Edwards.* $31/£20

DUFRESNE, FRANK. My Way Was North. NY: Holt, Rinehart & Winston, (1966). 1st ed. VG in dj (price-clipped). *Perier.* $25/£16

DUFRESNE, JOHN. The Way That Water Enters Stone. NY: Norton, (1991). 1st ed, 1st bk. Fine in Fine dj. *Robbins.* $25/£16

DUGDALE, FLORENCE E. The Book of Baby Birds. London: Hodder & Stoughton, (1912). 1st ed. 4to. Edward J. Detmold (illus). Cl-backed bds, color paste label. Overall Nice (edges lt foxed; fr cvr mkd; 1 pg folded). *Reisler.* $350/£226

DUGDALE, FLORENCE E. The Book of Baby Birds. NY: Hodder & Stoughton, n.d. (1912). 4to. 120pp; 19 color plts by E.J. Detmold. Sage grn cl, lt grn pict bds, shaped pict paste label. NF. *Drusilla's.* $125/£81

DUGGAR, B.M. Mushroom Growing. NY: OJ, 1915. Frontis, 15 plts (ptd both sides). Grn cl, gilt stamped. VG + (spine sl dull, ends rubbed). *Bohling.* $45/£29

DUGMORE, A. RADCLYFFE. The Romance of the Newfoundland Caribou. London, 1913. Frontis; 63 plts; fldg map. *Wheldon & Wesley.* $54/£35

DUGMORE, A. RADCLYFFE. The Romance of the Newfoundland Caribou. Phila/London: Lippincott/Heinemann, 1913. 1st Amer ed. 64 plts, 2 maps (1 fldg). (Bumped, rubbed; some foxing; pulled sig.) VG. *Blue Mountain.* $110/£71

DUGMORE, A. RADCLYFFE. The Romance of the Newfoundland Caribou. London: Heinemann, 1913. 1st ed. Fldg map. Orig gilt dec cl. Good. *Walcot.* $54/£35

DUGMORE, A. RADCLYFFE. The Romance of the New-foundland Caribou. Phila, 1913. 1st ed. Color frontis; lg fldg map. (New eps.) VG. *Artis.* $75/£48

DUGUID, J. Green Hell. NY, 1934. VG. *Trophy Room.* $45/£29

DUIS, E. The Good Old Times in McLean County, Illinois. Bloomington, 1874. xvi,865pp + (19)pp ads. Mod buckram. (Lt smudges.) *Bohling.* $150/£97

DUKE, BASIL WILSON. History of Morgan's Cavalry. Cincinnati: Miami Ptg & Pub Co, 1867. 1st ed. 578pp. Spine extrems, corners scuffed; hinges sl tender, else VG. Howes D 548. *Mcgowan.* $350/£226

DUKE, BASIL WILSON. Morgan's Cavalry. NY: Neale Pub. Co, 1906. 1st ed thus. NF. Howes D 548. *Mcgowan.* $450/£290

DUKE, BASIL WILSON. Morgan's Cavalry. NY/Washington: Neale, 1909. 2nd ed. 8vo. Frontis port. Orig grn cl. Spine sl faded, else NF in dj (tape at verso edges). Howes D 548. *Chapel Hill.* $550/£355

DUKE, JOSHUA. Kashmir and Jammu. Calcutta: Thacker, 1910. 2nd ed. Map in pocket. Grn cl. Clean. *Gretton.* $54/£35

DUKE, OSBORN. Sideman. NY: Criterion Books, (1956). 1st ed. VG in dj (nicked, sunned). *Reese.* $35/£23

DUKE, WILLIAM. Allergy: Asthma, Hayfever, Urticaria and Allied Manifestations of Reaction. St. Louis, 1925. 1st ed. Good. *Fye.* $100/£65

DUKE-ELDER, STEWART. The Neurology of Vision, Motor and Optical Anomalies. 1949. 1st Amer ed. (Ink notations.) *Fye.* $40/£26

DULAC, EDMUND. Edmund Dulac's Picture Book for the French Red Cross. London/NY/Toronto: Hodder & Stoughton, (ca 1916). 19 full color tipped-in plts, tipped-in port. Yellow cl. VG. *Cullen.* $125/£81

DULAC, EDMUND. Lyrics Pathetic and Humorous from A to Z. NY: Frederick Warne, (1908). 1st ed. 4to. Cl-backed illus bds (fr edge chipped; lt dusting, esp spine; sl mks title pg). Overall clean. *Reisler.* $600/£387

DUMAS, ALEXANDRE. The Black Tulip. NY: LEC, 1951. One of 1500. Signed by Frans Lammers (engr) and Jan Van Kimpen (designer). Full morocco. Partly unopened. VG (spine, edges dknd) in VG slipcase. *Agvent.* $75/£48

DUMAS, ALEXANDRE. Camille. Edmund Gosse (trans). London: LEC, 1937. #904/1500 numbered, signed by Marie Laurencin (illus). Dj (sl chipped) & pub's slipcase (sl sunned, dusty). *Hermitage.* $600/£387

DUMAS, ALEXANDRE. The Count of Monte Cristo. NY: LEC, 1941. #904/1500 numbered, signed by Lynd Ward (illus). 4 vols. Fine in pub's slipcase (lt rubbed). *Hermitage.* $125/£81

DUMAS, ALEXANDRE. A Gil Blas in California. M.E. Wilbur (trans). L.A.: Primavera Press, 1933. 1st complete ed in English. Inscribed, signed by Paul Landacre (engrs). Sig; sm spot, nick spine label, o/w VG (w/o dj). *Reese.* $85/£55

DUMAS, ALEXANDRE. The Man in the Iron Mask. NY: LEC, 1965. One of 1500. Signed by Edy Legrand (artist). Fine in glassine. VG case. *Agvent.* $75/£48

DUMAS, ALEXANDRE. The Three Musketeers. Maastricht: LEC, 1932. One of 1500. Signed by Pierre Falke (illus). 2 vols. Full yellow linen. NF in case (sunned, lt worn). *Agvent.* $125/£81

DUMAS, ALEXANDRE. Twenty Years After. NY: LEC, 1958. One of 1500. Signed by Edy Legrand (artist). Fine in glassine (lt worn). VG case. *Agvent.* $75/£48

DUMAS, FRANCOIS RIBADEAU. Cagliostro. London: Allen & Unwin, (1967). 1st Eng ed. VG + in VG dj. *Blue Dragon.* $40/£26

DUN, JOHN. No New Frontiers-Eleven Stories Inspired by Arizona Sunshine. East Aurora, NY: Roycrafters, (1938). Very Nice in denim binding. *Perier.* $40/£26

DUNAWAY, WAYLAND FULLER. Reminiscences of a Rebel. NY: Neale, 1913. 1st ed. Blue-gray cl. Lib bkpl, blindstamp, cvrs lt soiled, else VG. *Chapel Hill.* $200/£129

DUNAWAY, WAYLAND FULLER. Reminiscences of a Rebel. NY: Neale, 1913. 1st ed. Blue-grey cl. Lt offsetting of dj to eps, else Fine in dj (chipped, lacks 1/4-inch top spine, 1.5-inch bottom spine). *Chapel Hill.* $475/£306

DUNBAR, EDWARD E. The Romance of the Age. NY: D. Appleton, 1867. Frontis, 134pp + 10pp ads. Gold-stamped cl. *Dawson.* $60/£39

DUNBAR, HORACE. Marcy's Mill. San Diego: Privately ptd, 1944. 1st ed. Fine (inscrip). *Connolly.* $50/£32

DUNBAR, PAUL LAURENCE. The Fanatics. NY, 1901. 1st ed. (Fr hinge cracked; cvrs worn, dknd.) *King.* $195/£126

DUNBAR, PAUL LAURENCE. Folks from Dixie. NY: Dodd, Mead, 1898. 1st ed. Color frontis;263pp. E.W. Kemble (illus). Dec brn cl w/mtd cvr illus; teg. NF (sig). *Chapel Hill.* $450/£290

DUNBAR, PAUL LAURENCE. Folks from Dixie... NY: Dodd, Mead, 1898. 1st ed. Brn cl, pict onlay. Spine lt rubbed, endsheets sl foxed, o/w Very Nice. BAL 4921. *Reese.* $350/£226

DUNBAR, PAUL LAURENCE. In Old Plantation Days. NY: Dodd, Mead, 1903. 1st ed, 1st ptg, w/2 leaves after p307. Binding A, w/ampersand in 1st line of spine imprint. Brn cl, mtd cvr illus. Bkpl, insrip; inner hinges starting, o/w VG +. BAL 4946. *Chapel Hill.* $375/£242

DUNBAR, PAUL LAURENCE. Joggin' Erelong. NY: Dodd, Mead, 1906. 1st ed. Red calico cl w/ photo cvr label, paper spine label, teg. Fine. *Chapel Hill.* $350/£226

DUNBAR, PAUL LAURENCE. Lyrics of Lowly Life. NY: Dodd Mead, 1908. 1st Amer ed. Dec cl. Wear spine top corner, o/w Fine. *Agvent.* $125/£81

DUNBAR, PAUL LAURENCE. The Strength of Gideon and Other Stories. NY, 1900. 1st ed. E.W. Kemble (illus). Pict cl (spine bottom stained; sl wear). *King.* $195/£126

DUNBAR, SEYMOUR. A History of Travel in America. Indianapolis: Bobbs-Merrill, 1915. 4 vols. 2 maps, 12 color plts. Blue leather spines, marbled paper over bds (lt shelfwear). Overall attractive set (erasure on tp; stamps). *Parmer.* $250/£161

DUNBAR, WILLIAM. Life, Letters and Papers of.... Jackson, MS: MS Dept of Archives & Hist, 1930. 1st ed. 2 ports, 2 plts. VG. *Schoyer.* $65/£42

DUNCAN, ALASTAIR and GEORGES de BARTHA. Art Nouveau and Art Deco Bookbinding. NY: Abrams, (1989). 1st ed. Fine in dj. *Bookpress.* $110/£71

DUNCAN, ALASTAIR. Art Nouveau and Art Deco Lighting. Thames & Hudson, 1978. 1st ed. Dj. *Edwards.* $70/£45

DUNCAN, ANDREW. Observations on the Distinguishing Symptoms of Three Different Species of Pulmonary Consumption, the Catarrhal, the Apostematous, and the Tuberculous.... Edinburgh, 1816. 2nd ed. 195pp. Recent 1/4 leather. *Fye.* $100/£65

DUNCAN, ARCHIBALD. The Life of the Late Most Noble Lord Horatio Nelson.... London, 1806. 1st ed. Frontis port, 370pp; 9 plts (5 fldg). Bound w/A Correct Narrative of the Funeral of Horatio Lord Viscount Nelson.... London, 1806. 1st ed. Frontis, 48pp + index; 2 fldg plts laid down on Japanese paper. Dk full calf (recently rebound; worn, soiled), most of earlier spine laid down w/label. *Edwards.* $194/£125

DUNCAN, BOB. Buffalo Country. NY, 1959. 1st ed. Fine in Fine dj. *Pratt.* $25/£16

DUNCAN, BOB. Buffalo Country. Dutton, 1959. 1st ed. Fine in Fine dj. *Oregon.* $25/£16

DUNCAN, CHARLES. A Campaign with the Turks in Asia. London: Smith, Elder, 1855. 1st ed. 2 vols. 8vo. xii,308; iv,282,(2) + 16 pub's list, engr map. Grn blind-stamped cl (spines faded; tape mks foot of each vol). Internally VG (lib mks on titles; 2 lib stamps carefully removed from leaf each vol). *Morrell.* $527/£340

DUNCAN, D. The Madrone Tree. MacMillan, 1949. 1st ed. Fine in NF dj. *Fine Books.* $30/£19

DUNCAN, DAVID DOUGLAS. Picasso's Picassos. London: Macmillan, 1961. 1st ed. NF in NF dj. *Bishop.* $90/£58

DUNCAN, DAVID DOUGLAS. War without Heroes. NY: Harper & Row, (1970). 1st ed. NF in dj (edgetears; sm pieces rubbed away at corners). *Aka.* $200/£129

DUNCAN, HARRY et al. BR: A Panel Discussion at Bruce Rogers Centenary Held at Purdue University. SF: Book Club of CA, 1981. 650 ptd. Mint in plain dj. *Graf.* $45/£29

DUNCAN, JAMES (ed). Beetles. The Naturalist's Library. Vol II. Edinburgh: Lizars, 1835. 1st ed. Frontis port engr, 269pp, 31 plts. VG +. *Mikesh.* $100/£65

DUNCAN, JAMES. The Natural History of British Moths, Sphinxes, Etc. Edinburgh, 1836. 268pp + 2 leaves ads, port, add'l litho title, 30 color plts; all uncut. Maroon cl (spine faded). *Bickersteth.* $43/£28

DUNCAN, STANLEY and GUY THORNE. The Complete Wildfowler. NY: Outing, 1912. 1st ed. Teg. Orig tan cl. VG +. *Bowman.* $200/£129

DUNCAN, THOMAS D. Recollections of Thomas D. Duncan, a Confederate Soldier. Nashville: McQuiddy Ptg, 1922. 1st, only ed. Orig stiff ptd wrappers. Edges sl bumped, else Fine. *Chapel Hill.* $275/£177

DUNDONALD, THOMAS. The Autobiography of a Seaman. London: Richard Bentley, 1860. 2nd ed. 2 vols. Uncut (sig loose vol 1). *Petersfield.* $93/£60

Dune. A Pop-Up Panorama Book. NY: Grosset and Dunlap, 1984. 23x17 cm. 4 dbl-pg pop-ups; unused press-outs. Daniel Kirk (illus). Glazed pict bds. VG. *Book Finders.* $25/£16

DUNGLISON, ROBLEY. History of Medicine.... Phila, 1872. 286pp. New cl. (Stamp on tp crossed out.) *Goodrich.* $135/£87

DUNGLISON, ROBLEY. On the Influence of Atmosphere and Locality.... Phila: Carey, Lea & Blanchard, 1835. 1st ed. xi,514pp (1st/last few pp spotted); 6pg pub's cat bound at end. Contemp sheep (rubbed; upper joint split), lettering piece. Internally Fine. *Hemlock.* $150/£97

DUNHAM, JACOB. Journal of Voyages. NY, 1851 (c. 1850). Frontis port, (iii),8-243pp; 10 plts. Brn cl, gilt-stamped spine. (Sl worn, shaken, extrems frayed, lt foxing.) Howes D 567. *Bohling.* $250/£161

DUNHAM, N.J. A History of Jerauld County, South Dakota. Wessington Spgs, SD: N.p., 1910. 1st ed. Brn cl (gouge lower spine; inner hinges reinforced w/linen tape). *Karmiole.* $65/£42

DUNLAP, JOSEPH R. The Book That Never Was. NY: Oriole, 1971. As New in dj & slipcase. *Veatchs.* $40/£26

DUNLAP, WILLIAM. A History of the American Drama. NY: J&J Harper, 1832. 1st ed, w/ads. Generally VG (extrems worn; label rubbed; spine sunned; sl foxing). Howes D 570 *Dramatis Personae.* $200/£129

DUNLAY, THOMAS W. Wolves for the Blue Soldiers. Lincoln: Univ of NE, 1982. 1st ed. VG in dj. *Lien.* $40/£26

DUNLEVY, A.H. History of the Miami Baptist Association. Cincinnati: Geo. S. Blanchard, 1869. 193pp. Cvrs sl flecked, o/w VG. *Hayman.* $50/£32

DUNLOP, O. JOCELYN. English Apprentice-Ship and Child Labour. London, 1912. 1st ed. Teg. (Feps, last leaves lt foxed; bkpl remains.) Orig cl (lt spotted, spine chipped, sm label stain). *Edwards.* $78/£50

DUNN, DOROTHY. American Indian Painting of the Southwest and Plains Areas. Univ of NM Press, 1968. 1st ed. Sl cocked, else VG in dj (rubbed, soiled, edge-torn). *King.* $200/£129

DUNN, DOUGLAS. Night. London: Poem-of-the-Month Club, (1971). 1st ed. Fine. *Polyanthos.* $25/£16

DUNN, DOUGLAS. Night. London: Poem-of-the-Month Club Ltd, 1971. 1st Eng ed. Signed. VG (sl creased; sm ink mk verso). *Ulysses.* $54/£35

DUNN, J.P., JR. Massacres of the Mountains. NY: Harper, 1886. 1st ed. 784pp, fldg map. VG in dk blue buckram (rebound). Howes D 575. *Lien.* $65/£42

DUNN, J.P., JR. Massacres of the Mountains. NY, 1886. 1st ed. 784pp (occasional foxing; minor chip); fldg map. Professionally restored (rebacked, orig faded and edge-flaked spine cl over new backing; resewn). (Edgewear, soiling to cvrs.) *Baade.* $225/£145

DUNN, KATHERINE. Geek Love. NY: Knopf, 1989. 1st ed. Signed. Mint in dj. *Jaffe.* $125/£81

DUNN, NELL. Up the Junction. London: MacGibbon & Kee, 1963. 1st UK ed. Virtually Fine in dj. *Williams.* $47/£30

DUNN, ROBERT. The Shameless Diary of an Explorer. NY: Outing Pub., 1907. 1st ed. 2 fldg maps. Burgundy cl, gilt cvr titles. Spine faded, sm spot on fore-edge, else VG. *Parmer.* $495/£319

DUNNE, J.W. The New Immortality. London: Faber & Faber, 1938. 1st ed. Lower edges rough-trimmed. Fine in dj. *Temple.* $22/£14

DUNNE, J.W. The Serial Universe. London: Faber & Faber, (1934). 1st ed. Fore-edge sl spotted, o/w NF. *Sadlon.* $15/£10

DUNNE, PETER MASTEN. Black Robes in Lower California. Berkeley, Univ of CA, 1952. 1st ed. Fldg map tipped to rear. VG. *Oregon.* $45/£29

DUNNE, PETER MASTEN. Early Jesuit Missions in Tarahumara. Berkeley, 1948. 1st ed. Fldg map. Fine in dj. *Baade.* $50/£32

DUNNE, PETER MASTEN. Pioneer Black Robes on the West Coast. Berkeley/L.A.: Univ of CA, 1940. 1st ed. Gold-stamped cl. *Dawson.* $60/£39

DUNNETT, DOROTHY. The Disorderly Knights. London: Cassell, 1966. 1st ed. Lower rear corner lt bumped, else Fine in dj. *Else Fine*. $90/£58

DUNNING, JOHN. Booked to Die. NY: Scribner's, (1992). 1st Amer ed. Inscribed. Fine in dj. *Between The Covers*. $185/£119

DUNNING, JOHN. Booked to Die. NY: Scribner's, (1992). 1st ed. Fine in Fine dj. *Unger*. $150/£97

DUNNING, JOHN. Booked to Die. NY: Scribner's, 1992. 1st ed. Fine in Fine dj. *Janus*. $125/£81

DUNNING, JOHN. Booked to Die. NY: Scribner's, 1992. 1st ed. VF in dj. *Mordida*. $150/£97

DUNNING, JOHN. The Holland Suggestions. Indianapolis: Bobbs-Merrill, 1975. 1st ed. Inscribed. Fine in dj. *Mordida*. $250/£161

DUNRAVEN, EARL OF. Hunting in the Yellowstone. Horace Kephart (ed). NY: Macmillan, 1925. VG+ in dj. *Bowman*. $85/£55

DUNSANY, EDWARD. The Compromise of the King of the Golden Isles. NY: Grolier Club, 1924. Ed ltd to 300 numbered. Tp illus. Good. *Karmiole*. $100/£65

DUNSANY, LORD. The Fourth Book of Jorkens. Arkham House, 1948. 1st ed. VF in dj. *Madle*. $100/£65

DUNSANY, LORD. Guerrilla. Indianapolis: Bobbs-Merrill, (1944). 1st US ed. Top edge dusty, o/w NF in dj (lacks sm pieces). *Aka*. $20/£13

DUNSANY, LORD. His Fellow Men: A Novel. London: Jarrolds Publishers, 1952. 1st ed. Fine in dj. *Temple*. $85/£55

DUNSANY, LORD. A Journey. London, (1944). 1st Eng ed. VG in dj (soiled, sl damaged). *Edrich*. $19/£12

DUNSANY, LORD. Man Who Ate the Phoenix. London, n.d. 1st ed. Fine in dj (sl frayed). *Madle*. $75/£48

DUNSANY, LORD. My Talks with Dean Spanley. London: Heinemann, 1936. 1st ed. Frontis. Dk grn buckram, gilt. Prelims, last few leaves, edges lt foxed; o/w Fine in dj. *Temple*. $85/£55

DUNSANY, LORD. Plays of Gods and Men. Dublin: Talbot Press, 1917. 1st ed. Port. Linen, bds. Spine gilt dull, sl foxing, o/w VG. *Reese*. $50/£32

DUNSANY, LORD. Plays of Gods and Men. Luce, 1917. 1st ed. Fine in dj. *Madle*. $85/£55

DUNSANY, LORD. Rory and Bran. London: Heinemann, 1936. 1st ed. Spine sl worn; sides lt damp-spotted; ep margins sl browned; o/w Fine. *Temple*. $19/£12

DUNSANY, LORD. The Sirens Wake. Hutchinson, 1945. 1st Eng ed. VG in dj (closed tear). *Edrich*. $25/£16

DUNSANY, LORD. Strange Journeys Colonel Polders. London, 1950. 1st ed. VG in most of dj. *Madle*. $50/£32

DUNSANY, LORD. Tales of Three Hemispheres. Boston: John W. Luce, (1919). 1st Amer ed. Dec cl. VG. *Antic Hay*. $75/£48

DUNSANY, LORD. Tales of Three Hemispheres. Boston, (1919). 1st Amer ed. Fine. *Polyanthos*. $85/£55

DUNSANY, LORD. Tales of War. Dublin: Talbot Press, 1918. 1st ed. Cl-backed bds. NF in dj. *Limestone*. $195/£126

DUNSANY, LORD. The Travel Tales of Mr. Joseph Jorkens. London: Putnam's, April 1931. 1st ed. Fore-edges uncut. Dk blue buckram. Copper lettering sl oxidized affecting 4 letters; 1st, last gathering foxed; o/w very Nice. *Temple*. $70/£45

DUNSANY, LORD. While the Sirens Slept. London, (1944). 1st Eng ed. NF in VG dj. *Edrich*. $25/£16

DUNSANY, LORD. The Year. London, 1946. 1st Eng ed. VG in dj. *Edrich*. $19/£12

DUNTHORNE, GORDON. Flower and Fruit Prints of the 18th and Early 19th Centuries. Washington, 1938. 1st ed. One of 750 w/fldg color plt subs list. 4to. 34 full-pg color, 37 full-pg b/w plts. Buckram, labels. Fine in VG slipcase. *Shifrin*. $700/£452

DUNTHORNE, GORDON. Flower and Fruit Prints of the 18th and Early 19th Centuries...with a Catalogue Raisonne.... Washington, D.C., 1938. One of 2500. Fine in buckram slipcase. *Argosy*. $450/£290

DUNTHORNE, GORDON. Flowers and Fruit Prints of the 18th and Early 19th Centuries. Washington, DC: By Author, 1938. Ltd to 2500, this being one of 750 w/color plt listing subs. 73 plts (35 color, 1 fldg), color illus title, 1/2 title. Good (spine sl faded) in slipcase. *Karmiole*. $375/£242

DUPAY, R. ERNEST. St. Vith: Lion in the Way. Washington: Infantry Journal, 1949. 1st ed. VG in VG dj. *Bishop*. $25/£16

DUPLAIX, GEORGES. Popo the Hippopotamus. Racine: Whitman, (1935). 12mo. (28pp.) Color pict bds (spine rubbed). Internally NF; o/w VG. *Drusilla's*. $40/£26

DURAN-REYNALS, M.L. The Fever Bark Tree. London: W.H. Allen, 1947. 1st ed. Good in dj. *White*. $16/£10

DURANG, MARY. Love and Pride: Being the Histories of Julia Maydew.... Phila: Fisher, n.d. (ca 1845). Sq 12mo. Wood engr frontis, 108pp; 5 hand-colored engrs. Tooled red linen, gilt. Good (lt soiled, chipped; dry seal). *Hobbyhorse*. $95/£61

DURANT, JOHN. The Dodgers. Hastings House, 1948. 1st ed. Good+. *Plapinger*. $50/£32

DURAS, MARGUERITE. The Sailor from Gibraltar. Barbara Bray (trans). NY: Grove, (1966). 1st Amer ed. Fine in dj (lt soiled). *Hermitage*. $35/£23

DURER, ALBRECHT. Sketchbook of His Journey to the Netherlands 1520-1521.... London: Elek, 1971. Orig emb cl. Fine in slipcase. *Europa*. $37/£24

DURKIN, JOSEPH THOMAS. Stephen R. Mallory: Confederate Navy Chief. Chapel Hill: Univ of NC Press, (1987). 2nd ed. Fine in Fine dj. *Mcgowan*. $35/£23

DUROCHER, LEO with ED LINN. Nice Guys Finish Last. S&S, 1975. 1st ed. Fine in VG+ dj. *Plapinger*. $35/£23

DUROCHER, LEO. The Dodgers and Me. Chicago, (1948). 1st ed. VG (spine sun-struck). *Fuller & Saunders*. $25/£16

DURRELL, GERALD M. The Overloaded Ark. NY: Viking, 1953. 1st Amer ed, 1st bk. NF in dj. *Hermitage*. $40/£26

DURRELL, GERALD. How to Shoot an Amateur Naturalist. London: Collins, 1984. 1st ed. NF in dj. *Limestone*. $30/£19

DURRELL, LAWRENCE and HENRY MILLER. Lawrence Durrell and Henry Miller, A Private Correspondence. Dutton, 1963. 1st ed. Fine in Fine dj (spine fading). *Fine Books*. $35/£23

DURRELL, LAWRENCE and HENRY MILLER. Lawrence Durrell/Henry Miller. A Private Correspondence. George Wickes (ed). London: Faber & Faber, (1963). 1st ed. Red cl. Sl soil, else VG in VG ptd dj (sl wear). *Juvelis*. $50/£32

DURRELL, LAWRENCE. The Alexandria Quartet. London: Faber, 1962. #270/500 of the 1st 1 vol ed, signed. Fine (spine sl faded; bkpl) in slipcase (sl rubbed). *Williams.* $581/£375

DURRELL, LAWRENCE. In Arcadia. London: Turret Books, 1968. One of 100, signed by Durrell & Wallace Southam (composer), this copy unnumbered. Fine in wrappers (sl creased). *Ulysses.* $233/£150

DURRELL, LAWRENCE. The Big Supposer—A Dialogue with Mark Alyn. London: Abelard-Schuman, 1973. 1st UK ed. NF (bkpl) in dj. *Williams.* $28/£18

DURRELL, LAWRENCE. Bitter Lemons. Faber, 1957. 1st ed. Dj (chipped w/loss, soiled). *Edwards.* $47/£30

DURRELL, LAWRENCE. The Black Book. Paris: Olympia Press, 1959. 2nd ed, 1st issue w/grn border tp. VG in wraps, dj. *Sclanders.* $23/£15

DURRELL, LAWRENCE. Cities, Plains and People. London, 1946. 1st Eng ed. (Eps lt foxed.) *Edrich.* $19/£12

DURRELL, LAWRENCE. Clea. London: Faber, 1960. 1st UK ed. NF in dj (short closed tears). *Williams.* $43/£28

DURRELL, LAWRENCE. Clea. London: Faber, 1960. 1st UK ed. NF in dj. *Lewton.* $57/£37

DURRELL, LAWRENCE. The Greek Islands. Faber, 1978. 1st ed. Dj (sl chipped). *Edwards.* $31/£20

DURRELL, LAWRENCE. The Ikons. London: Faber, 1966. 1st UK ed. Fine (2 stamps) in VG + dj (lt mkd). *Williams.* $19/£12

DURRELL, LAWRENCE. Justine. London: Faber, 1957. 1st UK ed. Fine (bkpl). *Williams.* $39/£25

DURRELL, LAWRENCE. Prospero's Cell and Reflections on a Marine Venus. Dutton, 1960. 1st ed. Fine in dj. *Fine Books.* $45/£29

DURRELL, LAWRENCE. Prospero's Cell. London: Faber & Faber, 1945. 1st ed. Yellow cl (soiled), gold-lettered grn label. VG in pict dj (worn; lacks 1/3-inch spine top). *Vandoros.* $85/£55

DURRELL, LAWRENCE. The Red Limbo Lingo. London: Faber, 1971. #304/500. Fine (bkpl) in slipcase. *Williams.* $62/£40

DURRELL, LAWRENCE. The Red Limbo Lingo: A Poetry Notebook. NY: E.P. Dutton, 1971. 1st ed. One of 200 signed. Fine in orig acetate dj, cl slipcase. *Cahan.* $200/£129

DURRELL, LAWRENCE. Reflections on a Marine Venus. Faber, 1953. 2nd imp. (Feps lt browned.) Dj (chipped w/loss). *Edwards.* $31/£20

DURRELL, LAWRENCE. Sauve Qui Peut. London: Faber & Faber, (1966). 1st ed. Fine in dj. *Hermitage.* $40/£26

DURRELL, LAWRENCE. Sauve Qui Peut. London: Faber & Faber, 1966. 1st ed. Fine in dj (price-clipped). *Cahan.* $25/£16

DURRELL, LAWRENCE. Spirit of Place. London: Faber & Faber, (1969). 1st ed. VG in dj. *Schoyer.* $35/£23

DURRELL, LAWRENCE. Stiff Upper Lip. London: Faber, 1958. 1st UK ed. Fine (bkpl) in dj. *Williams.* $19/£12

DURRELL, LAWRENCE. Stiff Upper Lip. NY, 1959. 1st Amer ed. Sl faded, else VG in dj (soiled, rubbed, price-clipped). *King.* $20/£13

DURRELL, LAWRENCE. The Tree of Idleness and Other Poems. London, 1955. 1st ed. Fine (sl offsetting fep) in Fine dj. *Polyanthos.* $65/£42

DURRELL, LAWRENCE. Tunc. Faber, 1968. 1st UK ed. Fine in dj. *Lewton.* $23/£15

DURSO, JOSEPH. Casey. Prentice-Hall, 1967. 1st ed. Fine in VG dj. *Plapinger.* $25/£16

DURSO, JOSEPH. Yankee Stadium—50 Years of Drama. Houghton-Mifflin, 1972. 1st ed. Fine in VG + dj. *Plapinger.* $50/£32

DUSTIN, FRED. Report on Indian Earthworks in Ogemaw County, Michigan. Bloomfield Hills, MI: Cranbrook Inst of Science, 1932. 1-inch tape on cvr, tp; cvr creased, spotted; else Good in grn wraps. *Peninsula.* $37/£24

Dutch Landscape. The Early Years. Haarlem and Amsterdam 1590-1650. London: Nat'l Gallery, 1986. Good in wrappers. *Washton.* $40/£26

Dutch Masterpieces from the Eighteenth Century: Paintings and Drawings 1700-1800. Minneapolis, 1971. 106 plts. Good in wrappers. *Washton.* $40/£26

DUTT, G.S. Woman of India. Hogarth Press, 1929. 2nd ed. VG in pict dj (chipped). *Words Etc.* $54/£35

DUTTON, C.E. Report on the Geology of the High Plateaus of Utah. Washington: GPO, 1880. 1st ed. xxxii,308pp, 11 photogravure plts (1 fldg), 3 lg fldg charts. Black cl. Text vol only; Atlas vol not present. Good. *Karmiole.* $150/£97

DUTTON, E.A.T. Kenya Mountain. London: Cape, 1930. 1st ed. 56 collotype plts; 4 maps (1 lg fldg color). Blue gilt cl. Good in ptd dj (chipped, soiled). *Karmiole.* $150/£97

DUTTON, RALPH. The Chateaux of France. London: Batsford, 1957. Map. Pub's cl. Spine sl faded, o/w Good. *Europa.* $17/£11

DUVALL, MARIUS. A Navy Surgeon in California, 1846-1847. Fred Blackburn Rogers (ed). SF: John Howell, 1957. Ltd to 600. 7 illus; frontis port; 4 fldg facs. Good. *Karmiole.* $50/£32

DUVALL, MARIUS. A Navy Surgeon in California, 1846-1847. Fred Blackburn Rogers (ed). SF: John Howell, 1957. One of 600. Port, 4 fldg facs. Maroon cl; unopened. Fine in plastic wrapper. *Bohling.* $50/£32

DWIGGINS, W.A. Marionette in Motion. Detroit: Puppetry Imprints, 1939. 1/4 cl, binder's bd. NF in dw (chipped; 2/3 spine panel gone). *Veatchs.* $125/£81

DWIGGINS, W.A. Millenium 1. NY: Knopf, 1945. 1st ed. One of 1750 ptd. NF in dj (sl dusty). *Hermitage.* $35/£23

DWIGGINS, W.A. Millennium 1. NY: Knopf, 1945. 1st ed, ltd to 1750. 8 full-pg plts. Fine in dj (soiled; chipped). *Oak Knoll.* $45/£29

DWIGHT, H.G.O. Memoir of Mrs. Elizabeth B. Dwight. NY: Dodd, 1840. Frontis engr port, 323pp (foxed). Dk brn cl, blind/gilt-stamped (spine worn, cocked). *Schoyer.* $75/£48

DWIGHT, H.W. Constantinople Old and New. NY: Scribner's, 1915. 1st ed. Teg. Rubbed, o/w VG ex-lib. *Worldwide.* $65/£42

DWIGHT, MARIANNE. Letters from Brook Farm 1844-1847. Amy L. Reed (ed). Poughkeepsie, NY: Vassar College, 1928. 6 plts. Good (spine dknd, scuffed). *Bohling.* $35/£23

DWIGHT, THOMAS. Frozen Sections of a Child. NY, 1881. 1st ed. 66pp. Good. *Fye.* $300/£194

DWORKIN, ANDREA. Ice and Fire. NY: Weidenfeld & Nicholson, 1987. 1st Amer ed. Fine in Fine dj. *Revere.* $25/£16

DWYER, K.R. (Pseud of Dean Koontz.) Dragonfly. NY, (1975). 1st ed. Fine in NF dj (lt handling rub). *Mcclintock.* $100/£65

DWYER, K.R. (Pseud of Dean Koontz.) Dragonfly. Random House, 1975. 1st ed. Fine in dj (closed tear). *Madle.* $200/£129

DYCE, ALEXANDER (comp). Recollections of the Table-Talk of Samuel Rogers. London: Richards Press, 1952. Frontis port, plt. Brn cl, gilt. VG. *Hartfield.* $45/£29

DYE, DANIEL SHEETS. A Grammar of Chinese Lattice. Cambridge: Harvard Univ Press, 1937. 1st ed. 2 vols. Fine set in djs (sl edge-chipped). *Cahan.* $175/£113

DYE, HAROLD E. The Weaver. Nashville: Broadman, 1952. VG. *Burcham.* $30/£19

DYE, JOHN. Painless Childbirth: Or Healthy Mothers and Healthy Children. Buffalo, 1888. 7th ed. 451pp. Good. *Fye.* $50/£32

DYER, ISAAC WATSON. A Bibliography of Thomas Carlyle's Writings and Ana. Portland, ME: Southworth Press, 1928. Ltd to 600. Gravure frontis port. Black cl (faded). Good. *Karmiole.* $85/£55

DYER, JOHN P. The Gallant Hood. Indianapolis: Bobbs-Merrill, (1950). 1st ed. Red cl. VG. *Chapel Hill.* $45/£29

DYER, KATE GAMBOLD. Turkey Trott and the Black Santa. NY: Platt & Munk, 1942. 1st ed. Janet Robson (illus). Emb cl. Sig, presentation, else VG in dj (worn, torn). *Cahan.* $125/£81

DYER, THOMAS H. The Ruins of Pompeii.... London: Bell and Daldy, 1867. (8),111,(36)pp. 18 orig mtd photos. Orig cl gilt (sl worn), gilt edges. *Marlborough.* $372/£240

DYK, WALTER. A Navaho Autobiography. NY, 1947. 1st ed. VG in stiff wraps. *Oregon.* $50/£32

DYKES, JEFF. Billy the Kid, the Bibliography of a Legend. Albuquerque: Univ of NM Press, 1952. 1st ed, 2nd ptg w/corrections. Red cl. Back cvr sl soiled, o/w Fine. *Glenn.* $150/£97

DYKES, JEFF. High Spots in Western Illustrating. Kansas City: K.C. Posse of the Westerners, (1964). 1st ed. Tan buckram over bds. Fine. *Glenn.* $30/£19

DYKES, JEFF. My Dobie Collection. College Station, 1971. 1st ed. Pict wraps. *Baade.* $35/£23

DYKES, W.R. The Genus Iris. Cambridge, 1913. 48 color plts by F.H. Round, R.M. Cardew; 30 dwgs by C.W. Johnson. 1/2 morocco. Sl worn (neatly repaired); plt 34 sl spotted, o/w Good. *Wheldon & Wesley.* $659/£425

DYKES, W.R. A Handbook of Garden Irises. London, 1924. 24 b/w plts. Sl foxing, else VG. *Brooks.* $37/£24

DYKSTRA, ROBERT R. The Cattle Towns. NY: Knopf, (1968). 1st ed. Good in dj. *Lien.* $30/£19

DYKSTRA, ROBERT R. The Cattle Towns. NY: Knopf, 1968. 1st ed. Fine in Fine dj. *Glenn.* $45/£29

DYLAN, BOB. Tarantula. NY: Macmillan, (1971). 1st ed. NF in dj (rubbing). *Antic Hay.* $35/£23

DYLAN, BOB. Tarantula. MacGibbon & Kee, 1971. 1st UK ed. NF in dj (lt worn). *Sclanders.* $23/£15

DYOTT, G.M. Silent Highways of the Jungle. NY: Putnam's, 1922. 1st ed. Map. Blue cl. VG. *House.* $65/£42

DYRENFORTH, JAMES and MAX KESTER. Adolf in Blunderland. Toronto: McClelland & Stewart, (1940). 64pp. N. Mansbridge (illus). VG. *Davidson.* $85/£55

DYRENFORTH, JAMES and MAX KESTER. Adolf in Blunderland. London: Frederick Muller, (1940). 5th ed. 8vo. Norman Mansbridge (illus). Illus bds (minor wear). Dj (dusty); blue wrap-around ad incl. *Reisler.* $110/£71

E

EADMER. History of Recent Events in England. Geoffrey Bosanquet (trans). London: Cresset Press, 1964. Fine in dj. *Peter Taylor.* $23/£15

EAGER, J.M. The Early History of Quarantine. Washington, 1903. 1st ed. Good in wrappers. *Fye.* $30/£19

EAMES, JANE ANTHONY. Budget Closed. Boston: Ticknor & Fields, 1860. (xvi),368pp. Brn pebble cl, gilt/blind-stamped. VG. *Schoyer.* $75/£48

EAMES, PENELOPE. Medieval Furniture. London, 1977. 72 plts. Good in wrappers. *Washton.* $40/£26

EARLAND, ADA. John Opie and His Circle. London, 1911. 1st ed. Frontis port, 2 facs. (Spine lt rubbed; hinges sl shaken.) *Edwards.* $56/£36

EARLE, ALICE MORSE. China Collecting in America. NY: Empire State Book Co, 1924. Later ed. (Worn, soiled; hinges starting.) *Glenn.* $30/£19

EARLE, ALICE MORSE. Curious Punishments of Bygone Days. Chicago: Herbert Stone, 1896. 1st ed. 149pp. Uncut. Nice. *Second Life.* $75/£48

EARLE, ALICE MORSE. Customs and Fashions in Old New England. NY: Scribner's, 1893. 1st ed. *Bishop.* $15/£10

EARLE, ALICE MORSE. Sundials and Roses of Yesterday. NY, 1902. Grn dec cl. *Petersfield.* $54/£35

EARLE, ALICE MORSE. Two Centuries of Costume in America MDCXX-MDCCCXX. NY, 1903. 1st ed. 2 vols. (Sl stained.) *Argosy.* $125/£81

EARLE, JOHN. Microcosmography. London: Ptd for John Harding, 1811. New Ed. xx,340pp, 1/2 title present. Orig bds (sl rubbed), paper spine label. *Edwards.* $85/£55

Early Venetian Printing Illustrated. Venice/London/NY: Ongania/Nimmo/Scribner's, 1895. 228pp. Pict cl (soiled; bkpl). *Schoyer.* $125/£81

EARLY, ALICE K. English Dolls, Effigies and Puppets. Batsford, 1955. 1st ed. Color frontis. (Sl foxing.) Dj (sl chipped). *Edwards.* $34/£22

EARLY, JUBAL ANDERSON. Lieutenant General Jubal Anderson Early, C.S.A., Autobiographical Sketch.... Phila/London: Lippincott, 1912. 1st ed. Frontis port. Orig red cl. Name, else NF. *Chapel Hill.* $350/£226

EARLY, JUBAL ANDERSON. Lieutenant General Jubal Anderson Early, C.S.A., Autobiographical Sketch.... Phila: J.P. Lippincott, 1912. 1st ed. Sl extrem rubbing; 1913 inscrip, else VG. Howes E 12. *Mcgowan.* $350/£226

EASDALE, JOAN ADENEY. Amber Innocent. Hogarth Press, 1939. 1st ed. VG in dj (sl browned; chip). *Words Etc.* $62/£40

EASDALE, JOAN ADENEY. A Collection of Poems. Hogarth Press, 1931. 1st ed. Spine sl faded, o/w VG. *Words Etc.* $47/£30

EAST, WILLIAM and WILLIAM F. GLEASON. The 409th Infantry in World War II. Washington, (1947). 1st ed. Cl (rubbed, discolored, frayed; name). *King.* $75/£48

Eastern Archipelago. (By William H. Davenport Adams.) London: Nelson, 1880. 1st ed. 8vo. xii,(13)-576pp, incl frontis, map. Red cl, beveled edges, dec in black/gilt. Good (ink inscrip fep; spine faded, rubbed). *Morrell.* $116/£75

EASTLAKE, CHARLES L. Hints on Household Taste in Furniture, Upholstery and Other Details. London: Longmans, Green, 1868. 1st ed. xiv,269pp; 33 plts. Pub's cl. Sl cvr wear; sl spotting on early, later leaves, else very Bright. *Bookpress.* $450/£290

EASTLAKE, CHARLES L. Hints on Household Taste in Furniture, Upholstery, and Other Details. London: Longmans, Green, 1878. 4th 'revised' ed. 304pp, 29 plts (6 color), 8 color wallpaper samples. Blind-stamped cl (spine faded, shaken). *Marlborough.* $171/£110

EASTLAKE, CHARLES L. Hints on Household Taste. Boston: Osgood, 1872. 1st Amer ed. xxxvi,300pp, 34 plts. Pub's cl. Fine. *Bookpress.* $325/£210

EASTLAKE, CHARLES L. Hints on Household Taste.... London: Longmans, Green, 1872. 3rd ed. xviii,306pp; 32 plts. Pub's cl. Fine. *Bookpress.* $325/£210

EASTLAKE, CHARLES L. A History of the Gothic Revival. London: Longmans, Green, 1872. 1st ed. Frontis; xvi,427,(3)pp; 35 plts. Pub's blindstamped, gilt cl (sl edgewear, spotting; rear hinge internally cracked, else VG. Nathaniel Lloyd's copy. *Bookpress.* $350/£226

EASTMAN, CHARLES. Indian Boyhood. NY: McClure Phillips, 1902. 1st ed. Blumenschein (illus). Good + (worn; spine torn); Internally VG + . *Parker.* $75/£48

EASTMAN, CHARLES. Indian Boyhood. NY: McClure, Phillips, 1902. 1st ptg. Mtd cvr illus. VG. *Schoyer.* $85/£55

EASTMAN, ELAINE GOODALE. Pratt: The Red Man's Moses. Norman: Univ of OK, 1935. 1st ed. Good (spine lt worn). *Lien.* $50/£32

EASTMAN, MARY. The Biography of Dio Lewis. NY, 1891. 1st ed. 398pp. Good. *Fye.* $70/£45

EASTMAN, MARY. East of the White Hills. North Conway, NH, (1900). 1st ed. NF. *Mcgowan.* $45/£29

EASTMAN, MAX. Art and the Life of Action. NY: Knopf, 1934. 1st ed. Nice. *Second Life.* $20/£13

EASTMAN, MAX. Artists in Uniform. NY: Knopf, 1934. 1st ed. Grn cl. Fine in VG dj (edge tears). *Dermont.* $45/£29

EASTMAN, MAX. Artists in Uniform. NY: Knopf, 1934. 1st ed. Fine in dj (sl worn). *Second Life.* $45/£29

EASTMAN, MAX. Artists in Uniform. NY: Knopf, 1934. 1st ed. Fine in dj (lt used; internal mends; dknd spine). *Beasley.* $85/£55

EASTMAN, MAX. Child of the Amazons and Other Poems. NY: Kennerley, 1913. 1st ed. VG (foxed) *Second Life.* $45/£29

EASTMAN, MAX. Great Companions. NY, (1959). 1st ed. VG in dj. *Argosy.* $50/£32

EASTMAN, MAX. Leon Trotsky. The Portrait of a Youth. NY: Greenberg, 1925. 1st ed. NF. *Beasley.* $40/£26

EASTMAN, MAX. Understanding Germany.... NY: Kennerley, 1916. 1st ed. Good (fr hinge tender) *Second Life.* $40/£26

EASTON, JOHN. An Unfrequented Highway. NY: Knopf, 1929. 1st Amer ed. Cvrs lt spotted; pale foxing, else VG in VG dj (edgeworn, 1/2 inch clipped). *Chapel Hill.* $40/£26

EATON, ALLEN H. Handicrafts of the Southern Highlands. NY: Russell Sage Foundation, (1943). Doris Ulmann (photos). Illus eps. Gilt-emb cl. VG in dj (lt worn). *Cahan.* $45/£29

EATON, CLEMENT. Freedom of Thought in the Old South. Durham, NC: Duke Univ Press, 1940. 1st ed. Blue-grey/red cl. VG. *Chapel Hill.* $65/£42

EATON, CLEMENT. A History of the Southern Confederacy. NY: Macmillan, 1954. 1st ed. Fine in dj (lt chipped). *Cahan.* $25/£16

EATON, ELON HOWARD. Birds of New York. Albany: Univ of State of NY, 1910-14. 2nd ed. Parts 1 & 2 in 2. 106 full-pg color photolith plts. Grn cl (loose; shelfwear). VG. *Shifrin.* $100/£65

EATON, ELON HOWARD. Birds of New York. Albany: Univ of State of NY, 1910. 1st ed. 2 vols. 3 sm spots fr bds vol 2, o/w Fine. *Hermitage.* $200/£129

EATON, FRANK. Pistol Pete. London: Arco, 1953. 1st British ed. (Old stain cvr edges.) Dj. *Schoyer.* $25/£16

EBAN, ABBA. The Tide of Nationalism. NY: Horizon, 1959. 1st ed. Signed. NF (eps sl browned) in dj (lt soil; sm tear). *Antic Hay.* $75/£48

EBELING, WALTER. Handbook of Indian Foods and Fibers of Arid America. Berkeley: Univ of CA Press, 1986. 1st ed. Fine in Fine dj. *Book Market.* $150/£97

EBERHART, RICHARD. Burr Oaks. London, 1947. 1st ed. Signed. VG + in VG dj (sl edgeworn). *Fuller & Saunders.* $45/£29

EBERHART, RICHARD. The Quarry. NY: OUP, 1964. 1st ed. Signed presentation. Fine in VG dj (wear). *Antic Hay.* $50/£32

EBERLE, JOHN. A Treatise on the Diseases and Physical Education of Children. Cincinnati, 1834. 2nd ed. 559pp. Full leather. Good. *Fye.* $75/£48

EBERLEIN, HAROLD and CORTLANDT VAN DYKE HUBBARD. American Georgian Architecture. Bloomington: Indiana Univ Press, 1952. 1st Amer ed. 64 plts. Text sl yellowed, spine sl rubbed, else VG. *Bookpress.* $50/£32

EBERLEIN, HAROLD and CORTLANDT VAN DYKE HUBBARD. Glass in Modern Construction. NY/London, 1937. 62 b/w plts. (Ex-lib.) *Edwards.* $78/£50

EBERLEIN, HAROLD and CORTLANDT VAN DYKE HUBBARD. Historic Houses of George-Town and Washington City. Richmond: Dietz Press, (1958). 1st ed. Frontis. VG. *Bookpress.* $185/£119

EBERLEIN, HAROLD and CORTLANDT VAN DYKE HUBBARD. The Practical Book of Garden Structure and Design. Phila: Lippincott, 1937. 1st ed. VG in dj (chipped). *Bookpress.* $110/£71

EBERS, GEORGE. The Elixer and Other Tales. Gottsberger, 1890. 1st US ed. VG. *Madle.* $50/£32

EBERS, GEORGE. Homo Sum; A Novel. NY: William S. Gottsberger, 1880. (viii),299pp. (Bkpl.) Wraps (chipped). *Archaeologia.* $25/£16

EBERSTADT, EDWARD. Americana Catalogue. NY, 1966. Ltd to 750 sets. 4 vols. *Ginsberg.* $375/£242

EBERSTADT, EDWARD. The William Robertson Coe Collection of Western Americana. New Haven: Privately ptd, 1948. 1st ed, ltd to 100. Signed. Cl-backed bds; cvr label. VG. *Petrilla.* $185/£119

EBIN, DAVID (ed). The Drug Experience. NY: Orion, (1961). 1st ed. VG in VG dj. *Blue Dragon*. $37/£24

EBY, CECIL. The Siege of the Alcazar. London: Bodley Head, 1965. 1st ed. Fine in dj. *Patterson*. $47/£30

EBY, HENRY H. Observations of an Illinois Boy in Battle, Camp and Prisons—1861 to 1865. Mendota, IL: Privately ptd, 1910. 1st ed. Red cl. Spine lettering sl dull, else NF. *Chapel Hill*. $100/£65

ECCLES, JOHN. The Physiology of Nerve Cells. Balt, 1957. 1st ed. Good. *Fye*. $50/£32

ECKENRODE, HAMILTON J. List of the Revolutionary Soldiers of Virginia, Supplement. V.S.L., 1913. VG (rebound, worn). *Book Broker*. $45/£29

ECKENRODE, HAMILTON J. List of the Revolutionary Soldiers of Virginia. V.S.L., 1912. VG (pp browned; rebound, wear). *Book Broker*. $45/£29

ECKENRODE, HAMILTON J. and BRYAN CONRAD. George B. McClellan: The Man Who Saved the Union. Chapel Hill: Univ of NC, 1941. 1st ed. Frontis port. Fine in dj. *Cahan*. $45/£29

ECKENRODE, HAMILTON J. and BRYAN CONRAD. James Longstreet. Lee's War Horse. Chapel Hill: Univ of NC, 1936. 1st ed. Frontis port. Orig red cl. Bkpl, else NF in dj (price-clipped, few tape repairs on verso). *Chapel Hill*. $200/£129

ECKSTEIN, GUSTAV. Noguchi. NY, 1931. 1st ed. Good. *Fye*. $25/£16

ECO, UMBERTO. Foucault's Pendulum. London: Secker & Warburg, 1989. 1st Eng ed. Fine in dj. *Mordida*. $45/£29

ECO, UMBERTO. Foucault's Pendulum. London: S&W, 1989. 1st UK ed. Fine in dj. *Lewton*. $19/£12

ECO, UMBERTO. The Name of the Rose. San Diego: HBJ, (1983). 1st Amer ed. Fine in dj. *Between The Covers*. $125/£81

ECO, UMBERTO. Postscript to the Name of the Rose. NY: Harcourt, 1984. 1st ed. Fine in NF dj (sm tears; edges lt stained). *Beasley*. $25/£16

ECO, UMBERTO. Postscript to the Name of the Rose. Harcourt, Brace & Jovanovich, 1984. 1st ed. NF in NF dj. *Bishop*. $25/£16

ECO, UMBERTO. Travels in Hyper Reality. Harcourt, Brace & Jovanovich, 1986. 1st ed. NF in NF dj. *Bishop*. $22/£14

EDDIS, WILLIAM. Letters from America. Aubrey C. Land (ed). Cambridge, MA: Belknap Press, 1969. 2nd ed. Lt brn cl. Fine in dj (spine sunned). Howes E 41. *Chapel Hill*. $35/£23

EDDISON, E.R. A Fish Dinner in Memison. Dutton, 1941. 1st ed. One of 998. VG + in VG dj (lt wear, tear). *Aronovitz*. $150/£97

EDDISON, E.R. Mistress of Mistresses. London, (1935). 1st ed. VG in dj (piece missing spine). *Argosy*. $175/£113

EDDISON, E.R. The Worm Ouroboros. Cape, 1922. 1st ed. VG +. *Aronovitz*. $125/£81

EDDY, ARTHUR J. Recollections and Impressions of James A. McNeill Whistler. Phila: Lippincott, 1903. 1st ed. Port. Teg. Full contemp tan morocco, gilt extra (edges sl rubbed). VG. *Reese*. $75/£48

EDDY, DANIEL C. Walter's Tour in the East: Walter in Constantinople. NY: Crowell, 1864. 1st ed. 4 plts. Sl rubbed, o/w VG. *Worldwide*. $45/£29

EDDY, MARY BAKER. Science and Health with Key to the Scriptures. Boston: Eddy, 1886. 16th ed. Frontis (tape repair verso). Dk brn cl stamped in gilt/black (edges rubbed; corners bumped). *Houle*. $125/£81

EDE, CHARLES. The Art of the Book. London/NY, 1951. 1st ed. NF. *Baade*. $30/£19

EDEL, LEON. Henry James, the Untried Years 1843-1870. With the Conquest of London 1870-1883. With the Middle Years 1884-1894. London: Rupert Hart-Davis, 1953-63. 1st British ed. 3 vols. Ink name vol 1; spine toes worn, dknd; else Good set. *Reese*. $35/£23

EDELSON, JULIE. No News Is Good. SF: North Point, 1986. Fine in Fine dj. *Aka*. $35/£23

Eden Versus Whistler. The Baronet and the Butterfly.... Paris, 1899. 1st ed. 79pp, unopened. Ochre cl-backed bds (corners sl bumped, sl edgewear). Nice. *Europa*. $73/£47

EDEN, CECIL H. Black Tournai Fonts in England. London, 1909. (Feps sl browned; worn, faded.) *Edwards*. $31/£20

EDEN, LIZZIE SELINA. A Lady's Glimpse of the Late War in Bohemia. London, 1867. Frontis, illus tp, viii,305pp + (viii)pub's ads (feps lt browned). Gilt-dec cl (spine chipped, dknd). *Edwards*. $62/£40

EDEN, ROBERT C. The Sword and Gun, A History of the 37th Wis. Volunteer Infantry. Madison, WI: Atwood & Rublee, 1865. 1st ed. 120pp. VG. *Mcgowan*. $275/£177

EDGAR, WALTER B. (ed). The Letterbook of Robert Pringle. Columbia: SC Hist Soc, 1972. 1st ed. 2 vols. Cl-backed illus paper over bds. NF. *Cahan*. $45/£29

EDGE, WILLIAM. The Main Stem. NY: Vanguard, (1927). 1st ed. Sl external wear, o/w Nice in orange pub's cl. *Second Life*. $45/£29

EDGERTON, CLYDE. The Floatplane Notebooks. Chapel Hill: Algonquin, 1988. 1st ed. Fine in NF dj. *Aka*. $28/£18

EDGERTON, CLYDE. The Floatplane Notebooks. Chapel Hill, 1988. 1st ed. Signed. Fine in Fine dj. *Fuller & Saunders*. $45/£29

EDGERTON, CLYDE. Understanding the Floatplane. Chapel Hill: Mud Puppy Press, (1987). One of 500 signed. NF in wrappers. *Robbins*. $50/£32

EDGERTON, CLYDE. Walking Across Egypt. Chapel Hill, (1987). 1st ed. Fine in Fine dj. *Fuller & Saunders*. $35/£23

EDGERTON, CLYDE. Walking Across Egypt. Chapel Hill: Algonquin Books, 1987. 1st ed. Fine in Fine dj. *Dermont*. $35/£23

EDIS, ROBERT W. Decoration and Furniture of Town Houses. London: C. Kegan Paul, 1881. 2nd ed. Frontis,xvi,292pp (pencil underlining), 28 plts. Pub's gilt cl; teg. VG (hinges internally cracked, sl edgewear). *Bookpress*. $325/£210

EDLIN, H.L. British Plants and Their Uses. Batsford, 1951. 1st ed. Color frontis, 51 plts. Dj (spine lt faded). *Edwards*. $39/£25

EDLIN, H.L. Trees, Woods and Man. London, 1956. 1st ed. (Feps lt browned.) Dj (sl browning). *Edwards*. $59/£38

EDLIN, H.L. Woodland Crafts in Britain. Batsford, 1949. 1st ed. Color frontis. Dj (sl rubbed). *Edwards*. $39/£25

EDMONDS, EMMA. Nurse and Spy in the Union Army. Hartford, 1865. 1st ed. 384pp. Good. *Fye*. $125/£81

EDMONDS, ROBERT L. (ed). Analysis of Coniferous Forest Ecosystems in the Western United States. Stroudsburg, PA, 1982. Fine. *Brooks.* $41/£26

EDMONDS, WALTER D. Drums along the Mohawk. Boston: Little, Brown, 1936. 1st ed. Gilt-dec cl (spine sl lightened). *Sadlon.* $25/£16

EDMUNDS, MURRELL. Sojourn Among Shadows. Caldwell, ID: Caxton, 1936. 1st ed. Rev copy, slip tipped in. Fine in dj (sl edgeworn). *Sadlon.* $15/£10

EDMUNDS, WILL H. Pointers and Clues to the Subjects of Chinese and Japanese Art. London: Sampson, Low, Marston, n.d. (but ca 1934). 1st ed. Ltd to 1000. Table. Fine in dj (sl dusty). *Hermitage.* $100/£65

EDSON, LELAH JACKSON. The Fourth Corner. (Bellingham): by the Author, (1951). 1st ed. #1336/1500. Signed. VG in Poor dj (torn). *Perier.* $45/£29

EDWARDES, TICKNER. The Bee-Master of Warrilow. London, 1920. 2nd ed. (Sl foxing; spine sl discolored, chipped.) *Edwards.* $23/£15

EDWARDS, AMELIA B. Debenham's Vow. London: Hurst & Blackett, 1870. 1st ed. 3 vols. Contemp 1/2 crimson roan over marbled bds. Sl foxing, cvrs rubbed but Sound. *Limestone.* $135/£87

EDWARDS, AMELIA B. Egypt and Its Monuments.... NY, (1891). 325pp. (Bkpl; cvrs soiled.) *King.* $35/£23

EDWARDS, AMELIA B. A Thousand Miles up the Nile. London, 1889. 2nd ed. 499pp. (Stamped names; blind-stamp title; inner hinges cracked; staining.) *King.* $95/£61

EDWARDS, AMELIA B. Untrodden Peaks and Unfrequented Valleys. London: George Routledge & Sons, 1890. 2nd ed. xxiv,389pp; fldg map (sl creased); aeg. Pict cl gilt (sl mks, wear; 1/2 title, feps spotted; joints tender). *Hollett.* $116/£75

EDWARDS, BRYAN. The History...of the British Colonies in the West Indies. Dublin: Luke White, 1793. 2 vols. xxiv,491pp, fldg map; x,474pp, 5 tables (4 fldg). Buckram (rebound). Fine set. *Cahan.* $250/£161

EDWARDS, EDWARD. A Practical Treatise of Perspective.... London: Leigh, Sotheby, 1803. Engr frontis, xii,316pp, errata leaf, 40 engr plts. Contemp 1/2 leather, marbled bds (worn; tears to spine). *Ars Artis.* $388/£250

EDWARDS, G.B. The Book of Ebenezer le Page. London: Hamish Hamilton, 1981. 1st ed. Orig red cl. Fine in dj. *Rees.* $23/£15

EDWARDS, GAWAIN. The Earth-Tube. Appleton, 1929. 1st ed. VG. *Madle.* $35/£23

EDWARDS, JOHN N. Noted Guerillas, or the Warfare of the Border. St. Louis/Chicago/SF: Bryan, Brand, 1877. 1st ed. Brick-red cl. Inscrips, sm sticker; rubbed, chipped, else VG. Howes E 53. *Glenn.* $200/£129

EDWARDS, JOHN N. Shelby's Expedition to Mexico. Austin, TX: Steck Co, (1964). Facs rpt of 1872 ed. NF. Howes E 55. *Mcgowan.* $65/£42

EDWARDS, JONATHAN. History of Redemption. NY: T. & J. Swords, 1793. 1st ed. xii,574,(18)pp, frontis port (waterstained). Orig calf (top of spine chipped; generally rubbed, but sound), red spine label. *Karmiole.* $125/£81

EDWARDS, K.C. The Peak District. London, 1962. 1st ed. Dj. *Edwards.* $101/£65

EDWARDS, RALPH and MARGARET JOURDAIN. Georgian Cabinet-Makers. London, 1946. Frontis. VG. *Argosy.* $125/£81

EDWARDS, RICHARD and M. HOPEWELL. Edwards's Great West and Her Commercial Metropolis. St. Louis: Edwards's Monthly, (1860). Signed presentation. (iv),(53)-604,(1)pp + (30)pp ads. Aeg. Orig pict cl. VG. Howes E 69. *Schoyer.* $150/£97

EDWARDS, WILLIAM H. Football Days. NY: Moffat-Yard Co, 1916. 1st ed. NF. *Bishop.* $75/£48

EDWARDS, WILLIAM J. Twenty-Five Years in the Black Belt. Boston: Cornhill, (1918). 1st ed. Port; 7 plts. Dk-red cl, gilt. Signed, typed postscript mtd in fr. VG. *Petrilla.* $200/£129

EDWORDS, CLARENCE E. Camp-Fires of a Naturalist. London: Sampson Low, Marston, 1893. x,304pp. Teg. (Worn, dknd; labels roughly removed.) *Hollett.* $47/£30

EELLS, ELSIE SPICER. The Brazilian Fairy Book. NY: Stokes, 1926. 1st ed. 8vo. Color frontis, guard; 193pp; 5 color plts by George W. Hood. Gold cl, gilt lettering (sl dknd, worn). VG-. *Drusilla's.* $35/£23

EELLS, MYRON. Marcus Whitman, Pathfinder and Patriot. Seattle, 1909. 1st ed. 20 plts, double-pg map. VG. *Oregon.* $75/£48

EELLS, MYRON. A Reply to Professor's 'The Whitman Legend.' Walla Walla, WA: Statesman, 1902. VG in wraps. *Perier.* $60/£39

EGAN, BERESFORD and BRIAN DE SHANE. De Sade. London: Fortune, n.d. (1929). Ltd to 1600. (Plt spotted; bumped; rubbed.) *King.* $95/£61

EGAN, CONSTANCE. Epaminondas and the Lettuces. London: Collins. 1st ed. 12mo. A.E. Kennedy (illus). VG in VG dj (price-clipped). *Davidson.* $125/£81

EGAN, CONSTANCE. Epaminondas Helps in the Garden. London: Collins, n.d. A.E. Kennedy (illus). Sm 16mo. Paper-cvrd bds; pict label. VG (lt stains ep hinges). *Book Adoption.* $125/£81

EGAN, FEROL. The El Dorado Trail. McGraw Hill, (1970). 1st ed. Map. Fine in Fine dj. *Oregon.* $35/£23

EGAN, HOWARD. Pioneering the West.... Richmond: Egan, 1917. 1st ed. Hinge starting, else VG +. Howes E 76. *Parker.* $100/£65

EGAN, HOWARD. Pioneering the West...Major Howard Egan's Diary. Salt Lake, 1917. 1st ed. Frontis. VG (name; sl wear). *Benchmark.* $95/£61

EGAN, PIERCE. Pilgrims of the Thames, in Search of the National! London: W. Strange, 1838. 1st ed. (vi),375pp, 24 plts. Orig cl (possibly recased; spotting, but clean, tight); protective cl dj, leather labels; slipcase. *Schoyer.* $225/£145

EGERTON, GEORGE. Fantasies. London, 1898. 1st ed. VG. *Madle.* $30/£19

EGERTON, LADY FRANCIS. Journal of a Tour in the Holy Land, in May and June, 1840.... London: Ptd by Harrison, 1841. 1st, only ed. 8vo. vii,(i)blank,(1),(1)blank,(1)blank,(1)imprint,half title, 4 tinted litho plts. Grn blind-stamped cl, gilt spine. VG (sl foxing, browning to some margins). *Morrell.* $140/£90

EGGLER, ALBERT. The Everest-Lhotse Adventure. Hugh Merrick (trans). London: Allen & Unwin, 1957. 1st ed. 25 plts. VG in dj. *Hollett.* $47/£30

EGGLESTON, E.H. American Squab Culture. Warrenton, 1921. 2nd ed. Frontis port. *Sutton.* $37/£24

EGGLESTON, EDWARD. The Hoosier School-Boy. Scribners, 1883. 1st ed. Pict cl. VG. *Fine Books.* $125/£81

EGGLESTON, EDWARD. The Hoosier School-Master. NY: OJ, (1871). 1st ed, 2nd issue. Cl stamped in gilt/blind (spine gilt sl dull; rubbed, sm chips; smudges mainly to margins; lacks lower half rep). BAL 5096. *Sadlon.* $15/£10

EGGLESTON, EDWARD. The Mystery of Metropolisville. NY: OJ, (1873). 1st ed. Cl stamped in gilt/blind (rubbed; ex-lib w/sm label; label removal lower spine; eps lt foxed). BAL 5103. *Sadlon.* $15/£10

EGGLESTON, GEORGE. The Big Brother. Putnam's, 1875. 1st ed. Frontis; 182pp + 2pp ads; 4 plts. Pict gilt-stamped cl. Fine. *Oregon.* $45/£29

EGGLESTON, GEORGE. The First of the Hoosiers. Phila, 1903. 1st ed. VF. *Bond.* $40/£26

EGGLESTON, GEORGE. A Rebel's Recollections. NY: Hurd & Houghton, 1875. 1st ed. vi,(1),260pp. Brn cl. Fine. *Chapel Hill.* $175/£113

EGGSTON, ANDREW A. and DOROTHY WOLFF. Histopathology of the Ear, Nose, and Throat. Balt, 1947. 28 color plts. (Shaken.) *Argosy.* $50/£32

EHRLICH, LEONARD. God's Angry Man. NY: S&S, 1932. 1st ed. Fine (sl soiling rear bd) in dj (chipped). *Beasley.* $40/£26

EHRLICH, PAUL and S. HATA. The Experimental Chemotherapy of Spirilloses. NY, 1911. 1st Eng trans. Good. *Fye.* $400/£258

EICHELBERGER, R. Our Jungle Road to Tokyo. NY, 1950. VG in Good dj. *Clark.* $50/£32

EICKEMEYER, CARL. Over the Great Navajo Trail. NY, 1900. 1st ed. (New eps.) *Heinoldt.* $25/£16

EIDE, INGVARD. Oregon Trail. Rand McNally, (1973). 1st ed. VF in VG dj. *Oregon.* $45/£29

EIGNER, LARRY. On My Eyes. Highlands: Jonathan Williams, 1960. 1st ed. One of 500. 8 full-pg b/w photos. Pict stiff wrappers. Good (bumped, wear). *Cahan.* $125/£81

EIGNER, LARRY. What You Hear. (London): Edible Magazine, 1972. Ltd to 220. Fine in ptd wraps. *Antic Hay.* $25/£16

EILAND, MURRAY L. Chinese and Exotic Rugs. Boston: NYGS, 1979. 1st ed. VG in dj. *Argosy.* $85/£55

EILAND, MURRAY L. Chinese and Exotic Rugs. London, 1979. 1st ed. 52 color plts. (Ex-lib, ink stamp, label.) Dj (spine faded). *Edwards.* $85/£55

EINSTEIN, ALBERT. Einstein on Peace. Otto Nathan & Heinz Norden (eds). NY: S&S, 1960. 1st ed thus. Fine in dj (lt frayed). *Hermitage.* $30/£19

EINSTEIN, ALBERT. Out of My Later Years. NY, (1950). 1st ed. VG in dj (sl torn). *King.* $35/£23

EINSTEIN, CHARLES (ed). The Second Fireside Book of Baseball. S&S, 1958. 1st ed. VG in Good+ dj. *Plapinger.* $65/£42

EINSTEIN, CHARLES (ed). The Third Fireside Book of Baseball. S&S, 1968. Ltr ptg. VG+ in VG dj. *Plapinger.* $85/£55

EISEN, GUSTAVUS A. The Great Chalice of Antioch. NY, 1933. Buckram. VG. *Argosy.* $100/£65

EISENHOWER, DWIGHT D. Crusade in Europe. GC: Doubleday, 1948. 1st ed. Ltd to 1426 specially ptd, bound, signed. 8vo. Fine in acetate dj; slipcase. *Jaffe.* $1,250/£806

EISENHOWER, DWIGHT D. Mandate for Change 1953-1956. GC: Doubleday, 1963. 1st ed of 1st vol of 'The White House Years,' published separately. Ltd to 1500 signed. VF in slipcase. *Jaffe.* $650/£419

EISENHOWER, DWIGHT D. The White House Years: Waging Peace. GC: Doubleday, (1965). 1st ed. One of 1434 numbered, signed. Fine in pub's slipcase (sl soiled). *Unger.* $600/£387

EISENSCHIML, OTTO and E.B. LONG. As Luck Would Have It. Chance and Coincidence in the Civil War. Indianapolis: Bobbs-Merrill, (1948). 1st ed. Orig cl. VG. *Mcgowan.* $45/£29

EISENSCHIML, OTTO. The American Iliad. Indianapolis: Bobbs Merrill, 1947. 1st ed. VG+. *Bishop.* $15/£10

EISENSCHIML, OTTO. Why the Civil War? Indianapolis: Bobbs-Merrill, (1958). 1st ed. VG. *Mcgowan.* $35/£23

EISENSCHIML, OTTO. Why the Civil War? Indianapolis, (1958). 1st ed. Signed. VG+. *Pratt.* $50/£32

EISENSTAEDT, ALFRED. Eisenstaedt's Guide to Photography. Viking, 1978. 1st ed. Signed. NF in NF dj. *Bishop.* $30/£19

EISLER, C. The Master of the Unicorn. The Life and Work of Jean Duvet. NY: Abaris, 1977. 73 plts. Sound in dj. *Ars Artis.* $132/£85

EISLER, COLIN. Paintings from the Samuel H. Kress Collection. European Schools Excluding Italian. London, 1977. 16 color plts. (2 corners sl bumped.) *Washton.* $475/£306

EISLER, ROBERT. Man into Wolf. NY, (1952). 1st Amer ed. Good in dj (stained, sl tear). *King.* $25/£16

EISSLER, KURT R. Discourse on Hamlet and Hamlet: A Psychoanalytic Study. NY: IUP, (1971). 1st ed. Gray cl. VG in dj. *Gach.* $50/£32

EISSLER, KURT R. Leonardo Da Vinci: Psychoanalytic Notes.... NY: IUP, (1961). 1st ed. Blue cl. VG. *Gach.* $40/£26

EKSTEIN, RUDOLF. Children of Time and Space of Action and Impulse. NY: Appleton-Century-Crofts, (1966). 1st ed. Blue cl. VG in dj. *Gach.* $40/£26

ELAND, G. (ed). Purefoy Letters 1735-1753. London: Sidgwick, 1931. 2 vols. Uncut. *Petersfield.* $33/£21

ELDER, WILLIAM. Biography of Elisha Kent Kane. Phila: Childs & Peterson, 1858. 416pp + ads; marbled edges. 3/4 leather, marbled paper over bds (worn). *Parmer.* $55/£35

ELDREDGE, ZOETH SKINNER. The Beginnings of San Francisco from the Expedition of Anza.... SF: Zoeth S. Eldredge, 1912. 2 vols paged continuously. Teg; gilt spine titles. Spines faded, else VG set. *Parmer.* $125/£81

ELDRIDGE, ZOETH SKINNER. The Beginnings of San Francisco from the Expedition of Anza, 1774 to the City Charter of April 15, 1850. SF: Zoeth S. Eldridge, 1912. 1st ed. 2 vols. Teg. Grn buckram, gilt (spines faded; 1 hinge cracked). Nice set. *Shasky.* $115/£74

Elements of Medicine. (By John Brown). Phila, 1790. 1st Amer ed. Fldg chart. Old speckled calf, red label (spine eroded, hinges broken; names). *King.* $350/£226

ELGOOD, GEORGE S. and GERTRUDE JEKYLL. Some English Gardens. London: Longmans, 1904. 1st ed. Frontis; 49 color plts. Lower bd spotted, o/w VG. *Bookpress.* $375/£242

ELGOOD, P.G. Bonaparte's Adventure in Egypt. OUP, 1936. 1st thus. Frontis port, 16 other plts, fldg map, plan in pocket. VG in dj (sl worn). *Edwards.* $70/£45

ELGOOD, ROBERT (ed). Islamic Arms and Armour. London: Scolar Press, 1979. 1st ed. 2 maps. NF in dj. *Worldwide.* $200/£129

ELIOT, ELLSWORTH, JR. West Point in the Confederacy. NY, 1941. 1st ed. (Ink names; spine rubbed, sl dknd.) *King.* $45/£29

ELIOT, GEORGE. (Pseud of Mary Ann Evans.) Adam Bede. Edinburgh: Blackwood, 1859. 1st ed. 8vo. 3 vols. 16pp pub's cat end vol 3. Gilt/blind-stamped brn cl. VG in 1/2 tan calf slipcase. Sadleir 812. *Houle.* $3,500/£2,258

ELIOT, GEORGE. (Pseud of Mary Ann Evans.) Daniel Deronda. Edinburgh: Blackwood, 1876. 1st ed. 8vo. 4 vols. Later 3/4 dk blue calf over red/brn patterned bds, gilt-stamped brn morocco spine labels. VG (lacks erratum end Vol III). *Houle.* $950/£613

ELIOT, GEORGE. (Pseud of Mary Ann Evans.) George Eliot's Life as Related in Her Letters and Journals. J.W. Cross (ed). NY: Harper, 1885. 1st Amer ed. 3 vols. Grn pebble grain cl; gilt. Ink name, else Very Nice. *Hermitage.* $125/£81

ELIOT, GEORGE. (Pseud of Mary Ann Evans.) Impressions of Theophrastus Such. Edinburgh/London: Blackwood, 1879. 1st ed. 357pp; pub's slip tipped in before 1/2 title. Pub's cl (sm tear spine edge; inner joints tender; worn). *Second Life.* $75/£48

ELIOT, GEORGE. (Pseud of Mary Ann Evans.) Middlemarch. London: Folio Soc, 1972. Frontis. Brn silk over bds; oval illus on yellow paper set into fr cvr. Dec eps. Fine in yellow slipcase. *Heller.* $40/£26

ELIOT, GEORGE. (Pseud of Mary Ann Evans.) The Mill on the Floss. Edinburgh: Blackwood, 1860. 1st ed. 8vo. 3 vols. 16pp pub's cat end vol 3. Gilt/blind-stamped brn cl (edgeworn). VG in fldg brn cl slipcase by Sangorski & Sutcliffe. Sadleir 816. *Houle.* $1,750/£1,129

ELIOT, GEORGE. (Pseud of Mary Ann Evans.) The Mill on the Floss. (NY): LEC, 1963. One of 1500 numbered, signed by Wray Manning (illus). Fine in pub's slipcase. *Hermitage.* $75/£48

ELIOT, GEORGE. (Pseud of Mary Ann Evans.) The Novels of George Eliot. London: Blackwood, (ca 1904). 7 vols. 8vo. 1/2 gilt-stamped vellum over red cl; teg. Fine. *Houle.* $895/£577

ELIOT, GEORGE. (Pseud of Mary Ann Evans.) Romola. London: Smith, Elder, 1863. 1st ed. 8vo. 3 vols. 2pp ads end vol 2. Gilt/blind-stamped dk grn cl. VG in 1/2 tan morocco panelled slipcase. Sadlier 817. *Houle.* $2,750/£1,774

ELIOT, GEORGE. (Pseud of Mary Ann Evans.) Scenes of Clerical Life. London: Macmillan, 1906. 16 color plts, guards, 35 dwgs by Hugh Thomson. Black cl, gilt; aeg. Excellent. *Hartfield.* $85/£55

ELIOT, GEORGE. (Pseud of Mary Ann Evans.) Silas Marner. LEC, 1953. One of 1500, this unnumbered, unsigned. Lynton Lamb (illus). 1/2 buckram, dec bds. VG. *Cox.* $54/£35

ELIOT, GEORGE. (Pseud of Mary Ann Evans.) The Spanish Gypsy. London: William Blackwood, 1868. 1st ed. 358pp; 1/2 title (spotted). Mod 1/2 calf gilt, spine label. *Hollett.* $186/£120

ELIOT, GEORGE. (Pseud of Mary Ann Evans.) The Works of.... NY: Jenson Soc, 1910. 1st ed thus, #349/1000 registered sets. 20 vols complete. Color frontispieces. 3/4 dk blue calf, tan marbled bds (sl rubbing), gilt-stamped spines; matching eps; teg; uncut. VG. *Houle.* $650/£419

ELIOT, T.S. After Strange Gods. London: Faber, (1934). 1st ed. Fine in dj (torn). *Second Life.* $30/£19

ELIOT, T.S. Ash-Wednesday. London: Faber & Faber, 1930. 1st ed. One of 2000. Orange-brn cl. Fine in Fine dj (crease). *Sumner & Stillman.* $350/£226

ELIOT, T.S. The Classics and the Man of Letters. OUP, 1942. 1st ed. VG in wrappers. *Rees.* $16/£10

ELIOT, T.S. The Cocktail Party. London: Faber & Faber, (1950). 1st ed in verse form. This copy w/misprint 'here' for 'her' p29. Grn cl. Fine in Fine dj. *Sumner & Stillman.* $225/£145

ELIOT, T.S. Collected Poems 1909-1962. London: Faber & Faber, (1963). 1st ed. Fine in VG dj. *Godot.* $65/£42

ELIOT, T.S. The Confidential Clerk. NY: HB, (1954). 1st Amer ed. Advance rev copy w/slip tipped in. Lt offsetting from rev slip, else Fine in NF dj (lt rubbed). *Between The Covers.* $100/£65

ELIOT, T.S. The Confidential Clerk. London: Faber & Faber, 1954. 1st ed. W/misprint 'Ihad' for 'I had' p7. Fine in blue cl, gold-lettered spine. VG dj. *Vandoros.* $65/£42

ELIOT, T.S. The Cultivation of Christmas Trees. NY: Farrar, Straus & Cudahy, (1956). 1st ed. Ptd bds. NF. *Antic Hay.* $20/£13

ELIOT, T.S. The Cultivation of Christmas Trees. Ariel Poem. London, 1954. 1st ed. Fine in Fine envelope. *Polyanthos.* $60/£39

ELIOT, T.S. Dante. London: Faber & Faber, (1929). 1st ed. Ptd bds (sl chipped). Good (spine repaired). *Second Life.* $35/£23

ELIOT, T.S. The Elder Statesman. London: Faber & Faber, (1959). 1st Eng ed. Fine in dj. *Antic Hay.* $50/£32

ELIOT, T.S. Essays Ancient and Modern. London: Faber & Faber, (1936). 1st ed. Blue cl. Lt erasure mks in text, ink name, else VG in dj (spine faded, short tears, else VG). *Godot.* $150/£97

ELIOT, T.S. For Lancelot Andrewes, Essays on Style and Order. London: Faber & Gwyer, (1928). 1st ed. Fine in dj (chipped). *Second Life.* $75/£48

ELIOT, T.S. For Lancelot Andrewes. Essays on Style and Order. GC: Doubleday, 1929. 1st Amer ed, ltd to 2000. Purple cl, stamped in silver. Early, later bkpls of Paul Horgan. NF in VG dj (chips). *Reese.* $100/£65

ELIOT, T.S. Four Quartets. NY: Harcourt Brace, (1943). 2nd imp of 1st Amer ed in presumed 3rd state of dj w/$2.00 price, 9 titles ending in 'Old Possum's Book of Practical Cats,' and 'New York,' instead of 'New York, 17.' Fine in dj (sl aged; narrow chip). *Pharos.* $95/£61

ELIOT, T.S. The Idea of a Christian Society. NY: Harcourt, Brace, (1940). 1st Amer ed. VG in dj (rubbed). *Hermitage.* $45/£29

ELIOT, T.S. Journey of the Magi. (London: Faber & Gwyer, 1927). 1st trade ed. Ptd wraps. *Second Life.* $20/£13

ELIOT, T.S. Knowledge and Experience in the Philosophy of F.H. Bradley. London: Faber & Faber, (1964). 1st published ed. Fine in VG dj. *Godot.* $50/£32

ELIOT, T.S. Little Gidding. London: Faber & Faber, (1942). 1st ed, 1st issue. 16pp sewn. Spine faded, else NF in ptd wrappers. *Godot.* $65/£42

ELIOT, T.S. Little Gidding. London: Faber, 1942. 1st issue. Wrappers sl sunned, o/w Fine. *Rees.* $23/£15

ELIOT, T.S. Marina. London: Faber & Faber, 1930. One of 400 numbered, signed. E. McKnight Kauffer (illus). NF (bds lt soiled). *Beasley.* $350/£226

ELIOT, T.S. Murder in the Cathedral. London: Faber & Faber, (1935). 1st complete ed. Fep foxed, else VF in virtually As New dj. *Godot.* $385/£248

ELIOT, T.S. Notes Towards the Definition of Culture. London: Faber & Faber, (1948). 1st ed. Blue cl. Fine in Fine dj. *Sumner & Stillman.* $165/£106

ELIOT, T.S. Old Possum's Book of Practical Cats. London: Faber, 1939. 2nd imp. VG in dj (sl dusty). *Hollett.* $70/£45

ELIOT, T.S. On Poetry and Poets. NY: FSC, 1957. 1st Amer ed. Advance rev copy w/slip laid in. Fine in Fine dj (lt rubbed). *Between The Covers.* $100/£65

ELIOT, T.S. Poems 1909-1925. London: Faber & Gwyer, 1925. 1st ed. Dk blue cl, ptd spine label. VG (spine sl discolored). *Sumner & Stillman.* $195/£126

ELIOT, T.S. Poems 1909-1925. London: Faber & Gwyer, 1925. 1st ed. One of 1460. Dk blue cl, ptd spine label. Fine in NF dj. *Sumner & Stillman.* $675/£435

ELIOT, T.S. Poems. NY: Knopf, 1920. 1st US ed. Ptd bds (spine top chipped). VG. *Second Life.* $150/£97

ELIOT, T.S. Poetry and Drama. Cambridge: Harvard Univ, 1951. 1st ed. VG in dj (sl wrinkled). *Hermitage.* $65/£42

ELIOT, T.S. Prufrock and Other Observations. London: Egoist Ltd, 1917. 1st ed, 1st bk. One of 500 ptd. Buff wrappers. (Spine sl rubbed.) Cl clamshell case. *Sumner & Stillman.* $4,750/£3,065

ELIOT, T.S. The Rock. London: Faber & Faber, (1934). 1st ed. Bkpl, spine lt browned, else VG in grey ptd wrappers. *Godot.* $135/£87

ELIOT, T.S. The Rock. NY, 1934. 1st Amer ed. Fine in dj (sl rubbed, soiled, price-clipped). *Polyanthos.* $100/£65

ELIOT, T.S. The Sacred Wood. London: Methuen, (1920). 1st ed, 1st state, w/'Methuen' on spine in caps, w/no ads. Blue cl. VG (sl rubbed, faded). *Sumner & Stillman.* $145/£94

ELIOT, T.S. Selected Essays 1917-1932. NY: Harcourt, Brace; (1932). 1st Amer ed, 2nd ptg. Signed. Blue cl. Sig; faded, spine dulled; else VG. *Chapel Hill.* $250/£161

ELIOT, T.S. Sweeney Agonistes. London: Faber & Faber, 1932. 1st ed. Blue bds. Good in dj (lt soiled, frayed; sm loss along top margin). *Cox.* $62/£40

ELIOT, T.S. Thoughts after Lambeth. London: Faber & Faber, (1931). 1st ed, clothbound issue. Grey cl. Eps lt foxed, else VG. *Godot.* $85/£55

ELIOT, T.S. Thoughts after Lambeth. London: Faber & Faber, (1931). 1st ed. Prospectus laid in. Ptd wrapper over stiff wrapper. VG (sm imperfections rear wrapper). *Reese.* $30/£19

ELIOT, T.S. To Criticize the Critic. London: Faber & Faber, (1965). 1st ed. Blue cl. Fine in NF dj. *Sumner & Stillman.* $115/£74

ELIOT, T.S. The Value and Use of Cathedrals in England To-Day. (Chichester: Friends of the Chichester Cathedral, 1952). 1st ed. VG in white ptd wrappers. *Godot.* $85/£55

ELIOT, T.S. The Waste Land. NY: Boni & Liveright, 1922. #764/1000 numbered, the entire ed. 12mo. A copy from the second half, w/dropped 'a' from the word 'mountain' on pg 41. (Sm bkpl fr pastedown; fr endsheet removed, leaving: blank leaf, half title, title, half title, text.) O/w clean, tight in black cl; spine, fr bd gilt stamped (sl fading to spine). *Dermont.* $750/£484

ELIOT, T.S. What Is a Classic? London: Faber & Faber, (1945). 1st ed, Virgil Soc issue, ltd to 500. Sm edge tears, else NF in grn ptd wrappers. *Godot.* $275/£177

ELIOT, T.S. and GEORGE HOELLERING. The Film of Murder in the Cathedral. London: Faber & Faber, (1952). 1st ed. Blue cl stamped in red/silver. Fine in dj (sticker mk over price, else Fine). *Godot.* $45/£29

ELIOVSON, SIMA. South African Flowers for Gardens. Capetown: Howard Timmins, 1955. 1st ed. Contents Fine (cvr worn, spotted). *Quest.* $45/£29

ELISOFON, ELIOT. The Nile. NY: Viking, 1964. 1st ed. 38 plts; fldg map. NF in dj. *Worldwide.* $45/£29

Elizabethan Image. Painting in England 1540-1620. London: Tate Gallery, 1969. Good. *Washton.* $25/£16

ELKIN, R.H. The Children's Corner. London: Augener, (1914). Oblong, 4to. 16 full-pg color plts (incl tp) by H. Willebeek Le Mair. Tan cl, color paste label, gilt. Very Nice in pict dj (marginal tears; fr lacking piece). *Reisler.* $350/£226

ELKIN, R.H. Old Dutch Nursery Rhymes. London: Augener, (1917). Oblong, 4to. 16 full-pg color plts by H. Willebeek Le Mair; (blank ep foxed). Blue cl, color paste label, gilt. Pict dj (dusty; tears rear cvr). *Reisler.* $375/£242

ELKIN, STANLEY. Criers and Kibitzers. Blond, 1965. 1st Eng ed. Fine in NF dj. *Fine Books.* $50/£32

ELKIN, STANLEY. George Mills. NY: Dutton, (1982). 1st ed. Fine in dj. *Between The Covers.* $50/£32

ELKIN, STANLEY. Searches and Seizures. NY: Random House, (1973). 1st ed. Lt foxing fore-edge, else Fine in dj. *Between The Covers.* $65/£42

ELKINS, AARON J. A Deceptive Clarity. NY: Walker, 1987. 1st ed. Fine in dj (sl edgewear). *Janus.* $35/£23

ELKINS, AARON. A Deceptive Clarity. NY: Walker, 1987. 1st ed. Signed. VF in dj. *Mordida.* $75/£48

ELKINS, JOHN M. Indian Fighting on the Texas Frontier. Amarillo, 1929. Port, 3 plts. Gray wraps, black stamping. VG + . *Bohling.* $100/£65

ELLERMAN, J.R. The Families and Genera of Living Rodents.... London, 1940-41. 1st ed. 2 vols. Good. *Henly.* $194/£125

ELLET, CHARLES, JR. The Mississippi and Ohio Rivers: Containing Plans for the Protection of the Delta.... Phila: Lippincott, Grambo & Co, 1853. 1st ptg. Inscribed. 367pp. 12 plts (2 fldg). Orig cl (spine end cleanly chipped). *Schoyer.* $200/£129

ELLET, ELIZABETH F. The Pioneer Women of the West. Phila: Coates, n.d. (ca 1880s). Frontis. Dec cl (lt wear). *Petrilla.* $25/£16

ELLET, ELIZABETH F. The Women of the American Revolution. NY: Baker & Scribner, 1849. 5th ed vols 1 & 3; 1st ed vol 2. 348; 312; 396pp. Good set (spine wear). Howes E 93. *Second Life.* $125/£81

ELLICOTT, ANDREW. The Journal of Andrew Ellicott...During Part of the Year 1796, the Years 1797, 1798, 1799, and Part of the Year 1800.... Phila: Thomas Dobson, 1803. 1st ed. 4to. viii,299,151,(1); 14 fldg maps, charts. Contemp calf (joints cracked; cvr wear). (Lacks blank 1/2 of errata leaf w/no loss of text.) *Bookpress.* $3,000/£1,935

ELLINGTON, CHARLES G. The Trial of U.S. Grant. The Pacific Coast Years: 1852-1854. Glendale, CA: Clark, 1987. As New in As New dj. *Glenn.* $35/£23

ELLIOT, DANIEL GIRAUD. The Life and Habits of Wild Animals. London: Macmillan, 1874. 1st ed. (ii),72pp, 20 Fine full-pg woodcut plts by Joseph Wolf. Aeg. Grn pebble-grained cl, beveled bds (neatly recased), gilt. 1/2title margins sl creased, repaired; eps foxed, o/w very attractive. *Hollett.* $233/£150

ELLIOT, DON. (Pseud of Robert Silverberg.) Gang Girl. N.p.: Nightside Books, (1959). 1st ed. Sl tear tp, else Nice in pict wraps. *King.* $75/£48

ELLIOTT, F.R. Hand-Book for Practical Landscape Gardening. Rochester, NY: D.M. Dewey, 1885. 2nd ed. Frontis, 96pp (1st, last leaves browned), 15 color plts. Dec eps. Gilt-emb dec cl (lt worn, soiled; spine strengthened). VG. *Quest.* $250/£161

ELLIOTT, HENRY W. Report upon the Condition of Affairs in Territory of Alaska. Washington: GPO, 1875. 277pp; eps, edges marbled. 3/4 leather (rubbed). *Heinoldt.* $75/£48

ELLIOTT, MARY. Early Seeds, to Produce Spring Flowers. London: William Darton, n.d. (ca 1825). 1st ed. 24pp + 1pg list lower wrapper, 24 numbered copper engrs. VG (ink dedication verso frontis; sl internal spotting) in wrappers (dusted, rubbed). *Hobbyhorse.* $375/£242

ELLIOTT, MARY. Plain Things for Little Folks; Seasoned with Instruction Both for the Mind and the Eye. London: William Darton, n.d. (ca 1825-30). 12mo. 24pp + 1pg ad back wrapper, 24 engrs; plt numbered 21-22 w/imp reading: 6th. Month 14th. 1823. Sl rip frontis; inside detached from cvr; lt foxing; ink spot pg 7; dated ink sig; corner chipped; else Fine. *Hobbyhorse.* $225/£145

ELLIOTT, MARY. The Rose, Containing Original Poems for Young People. London: William Darton, n.d. (ca 1824). 12mo. 36pp, 12 engrs, some dated 1823 and 1824, section of 1 hand-colored (2 w/sl trimming of text, top edge). 3/4 morocco, new marbled eps, flyleaves. Bound w/o orig wrappers. VG. *Hobbyhorse.* $250/£161

ELLIOTT, MARY. Rural Employments. London: William Darton, 1820. 1st ed. 12mo. Frontis, 72pp; 17 full-pg copper engrs. 3/4 mod leather marbled paper on bds (lacks orig cvrs), gilt. Fine (dated ink sig recto frontis). *Hobbyhorse.* $300/£194

ELLIOTT, MARY. Rural Employments; or, A Peep into Village Concerns. London: William Darton, 1820. 1st ed. 24mo. 72pp w/pub's ad leaf of special merit at rear; 18 copperplt engrs (1 loose). Grn calf spine, gilt lettering; marbled bds. Lt foxing, o/w VG. *Drusilla's.* $350/£226

ELLIOTT, MARY. The Wax-Taper; or Effects of Bad Habits. London: William Darton, Jun, 1819. 1st ed. 12mo. 60pp + 2pp booklist, copper plt frontis (folded in 3) plus 2 full-pg engrs w/dated imp Oct. 7, 1819. Orig ptd buff paper on bds (lt soiling cvrs; spine sl chipped). Fine. *Hobbyhorse.* $450/£290

ELLIOTT, RICHARD SMITH. Notes Taken in Sixty Years. St. Louis: R.P. Studley, 1883. Frontis port, (4),336pp. Grn cl, gilt spine title. VG+. Howes E 111. *Bohling.* $225/£145

ELLIOTT, RICHARD SMITH. Notes Taken in Sixty Years. St. Louis: R.P. Studley, 1883. 1st ed. VG- (fep torn; note pasted ep). Howes E 111. *Parker.* $195/£126

ELLIOTT, W.G. (ed). Amateur Clubs and Actors. London: Edward Arnold, 1898. 1st ed. xv,320pp, uncut, 19 plts. Gilt, blind-dec grn cl (sl nicks, scratches, joints cracked; bkpl). *Hollett.* $101/£65

ELLIOTT, WM. Carolina Sports by Land and Water. London: Richard Bentley, 1867. 1st Eng ed. 292pp. Pub's grn cl. Rubberstamp, else VG. Howes E 112. *Bookpress.* $275/£177

ELLIS, E.S. Ancient Anodynes. London, 1946. (Eps, tp sl spotted; edges, spine lt faded.) *Edwards.* $31/£20

ELLIS, G. Modern Practical Joinery. London: Batsford, 1924. 5th ed. 20 dbl-pg plts, 41 photo plts. VG. *Willow House.* $101/£65

ELLIS, HAVELOCK. The Criminal. NY: Scribner & Welford, 1890. 1st Amer ed. Maroon cl; gilt. Sound (worn). *Boswell.* $75/£48

ELLIS, HAVELOCK. Man and Woman.... Boston/NY: Houghton Mifflin, 1929. Last ed, 1st ptg. Thatched grn cl. Good (lacks paper spine label). *Gach.* $30/£19

ELLIS, HAVELOCK. Sonnets. Boston/NY: Houghton Mifflin, 1925. 1st US ed. Ltd to 750. NF (bkpl) in dec bds. *Williams.* $39/£25

ELLIS, HAVELOCK. Studies in the Psychology of Sex. Phila: F.A. Davis, 1928. Various ptgs. 7 vols. Brn cl. Hinges cracked, else Good (shelfwear). *Gach.* $150/£97

ELLIS, MRS. The Wives of England. London: Griffin, n.d. (c. 1860). 371pp. VG (lt wear). *Willow House.* $47/£30

ELLIS, ROBERT. Asiatic Affinities of the Old Italians. London: Trubner, 1870. (iv),155pp. Grn cl stamped in gilt (ex-lib, pocket removed). *Schoyer.* $45/£29

ELLIS, WILLIAM. Billy Sunday—The Man and His Message. Winston, 1914. 1st ed. Good+. *Plapinger.* $65/£42

ELLIS, WILLIAM. Narrative of a Tour Through Hawaii. London, 1826. 1st ed. (8),442pp; fldg map, 7 plts. 1/2 calf (rebound). *Lewis.* $566/£365

ELLIS, WILLIAM. Polynesian Researches, During a Residence of Nearly Eight Years.... NY, 1833. 1st ed. 4 vols. 4 frontis plts, 316; 321; 300; 343pp; 3 charts, 4 vignettes. Orig maroon cl (fading, foxing). *Lewis.* $496/£320

ELLIS, WILLIAM. Three Visits to Madagascar...1853, 1854, 1856.... NY: Harper, 1859. 1st Amer ed. 514,(2 ads)pp; 15 plts, 1 map. Orig cl (insect damage). *Lefkowicz.* $150/£97

ELLISON, HARLAN. Alone Against Tomorrow. Macmillan, 1970. 1st ed. Signed. Fine in dj. *Aronovitz.* $40/£26

ELLISON, HARLAN. Angry Candy. Boston: Houghton Mifflin, 1988. 1st trade hb ed. Fine in dj. *Other Worlds.* $35/£23

ELLISON, HARLAN. Approaching Oblivion. Walker, 1974. 1st ed. Signed. Fine in dj. *Aronovitz.* $40/£26

ELLISON, HARLAN. The Fantasies of Harlan Ellison. Boston: Gregg Press, 1979. 1st ptg. VG; no dj as issued. *Bishop.* $42/£27

ELLISON, HARLAN. Love Ain't Nothing but Sex Misspelled. Trident, 1968. 1st ed. Signed. VG- in VG dj. *Aronovitz.* $165/£106

ELLISON, HARLAN. Strange Wine. Harper, 1978. 1st ed. Fine in dj. *Madle.* $70/£45

ELLISON, HARLAN. A Touch of Infinity and The Man with Nine Lives. Ace Double D-413, 1960. 1st ed. Fine in wraps. *Madle.* $65/£42

ELLISON, JAMES WHITFIELD. Summer after the War. NY: Dodd Mead, (1972). 1st ed. Fine in NF dj (price blocked out). *Aka.* $45/£29

ELLISON, RALPH. Going to the Territory. NY: Random House, (1986). 1st ed. VF in dj. *Reese.* $35/£23

ELLROY, JAMES. The Big Nowhere. NY: Mysterious, 1988. 1st ed. Fine in dj. *Janus.* $25/£16

ELLROY, JAMES. The Big Nowhere. Hastings-On-Hudson: Ultramarine Publishing, 1988. 1st ed. One of 300 numbered, cl-bound, signed. VF in slipcase w/o dj as issued. *Mordida.* $100/£65

ELLROY, JAMES. The Black Dahlia. NY: Mysterious, 1987. 1st ed. Signed. Fine in Fine dj. *Beasley.* $60/£39

ELLROY, JAMES. Brown's Requiem. London: Allison & Busby, 1984. 1st hb ed. Inscribed. VF in dj. *Mordida.* $150/£97

ELLROY, JAMES. Clandestine. London: Allison & Busby, 1984. 1st hb ed. Lower corner sl bumped; staining fore-edge, o/w Fine in dj. *Mordida.* $75/£48

ELLROY, JAMES. Silent Terror. L.A.: Blood & Guts Press, 1987. 1st ed. One of 350 numbered, signed. VF in dj. *Mordida.* $125/£81

ELLROY, JAMES. Suicide Hill. NY: Mysterious, 1986. 1st ed. Signed. Fine (sl spine wear) in Fine dj. *Beasley.* $60/£39

ELLSWORTH, LINCOLN. Beyond Horizons. NY: Doubleday, Doran, (1938). 1st ed. VG. *High Latitude.* $30/£19

ELMER, ROBERT P. Target Archery. NY, 1946. 1st ed. Uncut. VG in dj. *Argosy.* $50/£32

ELMES, JAMES and THOMAS H. SHEPHERD. Metropolitan Improvements. London: Jones & Co, 1827. 1st ed. Frontis, engr tp (sl foxed), (ii),viii,172pp; 78 plts. Contemp 1/2 sheep, marbled bds (rehinged). *Bookpress.* $650/£419

ELMES, JAMES. Memoirs of the Life and Works of Sir Christopher Wren. London: Priestley & Weale, 1823. 1st ed. 4to. Frontis port, xxxvi,532,147,(1)(4ads)pp; 12 plts (4 dbl-pg). 19th cent 1/2 morocco. Port frontis heavily offset on tp, o/w Nice. *Bookpress.* $850/£548

ELON, AMOS. The Holy Land from the Air. NY/Jerusalem: Abrams/Domino Press, 1987. 1st ed. NF in dj. *Worldwide.* $40/£26

ELSEN, ALBERT. Paul Jenkins. NY: Abrams, (c 1975). 56 hand-tipped plts. Fine in pict dj. *Cahan.* $125/£81

ELSENSOHN, ALFREDA. Pioneer Days in Idaho County. Cottonwood, ID: Benedictine Sisters, (1978). 3rd ptg. Signed. Vol 1 only. Frontis. Fine in VG dj. *Oregon.* $45/£29

ELSENSOHN, ALFREDA. Pioneer Days in Idaho County. Caldwell: Caxton, 1947/1951. 1st ed. 2 vols. Name, else VG in dj (edge torn). *Perier.* $135/£87

Elson Basic Reader—Dick and Jane. Scott Foresman, 1936. 12mo, 40pp. Wraps in grn/black w/pict of girl on swing. Fine. *Davidson.* $85/£55

ELSON, HENRY WILLIAM. The Civil War through the Camera.... NY, (1912). 1/2 leather. Extrems worn, 2 tears to spine, o/w VG + . *Pratt.* $60/£39

ELSON, HENRY WILLIAM. The Civil War Through the Camera...Together with Elson's New History...of the Civil War. Springfield, MA: Patriot Pub Co, 1938. 1st ed thus. All 16 parts bound together in 1 vol period cl. *Mcgowan.* $125/£81

ELSTOB, PETER. Spanish Prisoner. London: Macmillan, 1939. 1st ed. Very Nice. *Patterson.* $155/£100

ELWELL, N.W. Colonial Silverware of the 17th and 18th Centuries. Boston: Geo. H. Polley, 1899. 40 loose collotype plts laid in cl portfolio w/ties. Plt w/closed tear, lt edgewear, no loss, o/w VG. *Cahan.* $175/£113

ELWES, HENRY JOHN and AUGUSTINE HENRY. The Trees of Great Britain and Ireland. Edinburgh, 1906-13. 4to. 7 vols. 7 color tps, 5 color frontis port, 414 plts. Grn binder's cl (soiled, flecked, faded). Overall Nice set. *Sutton.* $1,850/£1,194

ELWES, HENRY JOHN and AUGUSTINE HENRY. The Trees of Great Britain and Ireland. Edinburgh: Privately ptd, 1906-13. 8 vols incl index vol. 4to. 6pp subs list. 5 color frontispieces, frontis port, 412 plts. Marbled eps; teg. (Prelims lt spotted, sl spotting fore-edge, ex-libris.) 1/2 grn morocco, grn cl bds; gilt-ruled raised bands, compartments, leaf motifs, lettering. Orig upper wraps bound into rear. (Spines lt sunned.) *Edwards.* $2,325/£1,500

ELWES, HENRY JOHN. Memoirs of Travel, Sport, and Natural History. E.G. Hawke (ed). London, 1930. 18 plts. (Spine dulled; soiled.) *Sutton.* $68/£44

ELWIN, MALCOLM. The Noels and the Milbankes: Their Letters....1767-1792. Macdonald, 1967. 1st ed. NF in dj (sl chipped). *Poetry.* $23/£15

ELWOOD, JOHN W. Elwood's Stories of the Old Ringgold Cavalry 1847-1865.... Coal Center, PA: The Author, 1914. 1st ed. VG (spine gilt dull, sl rubbed). *Mcgowan.* $165/£106

ELY, JAMES W., JR. The Crisis of Conservative Virginia: The Byrd Organization and the Politics of Massive Resistance. Univ of TN, (c. 1976). Frontis. VG in VG- dj. *Book Broker.* $25/£16

ELY, LEONARD. Inflammation in Bones and Jones. Phila, 1923. 1st ed. Good. *Fye.* $50/£32

ELY, LEONARD. Joint Tuberculosis. NY, 1911. 1st ed. 72 photo, x-ray illus. Good. *Fye.* $75/£48

ELY, SCOTT. Starlight. NY: Weidenfeld & Nicolson, (1987). 1st ed. Fine in Fine dj. *Aka.* $30/£19

ELY, SIMS. The Lost Dutchman Mine. NY: W. Morrow, 1953. 1st ed. VG- in dj (worn). *Parker.* $35/£23

ELY, WILMER M. The Boy Chums in Mystery Land. Burt, 1916. 1st ed. VG in dj (frayed). *Madle.* $17/£11

EMERSON, ALICE B. Ruth Fielding in the Great Northwest.... NY: Cupples & Leon, (1921). 1st ed. Red/navy pict cl. NF in dj (lt rubbed). *Sadlon.* $35/£23

EMERSON, EARL W. Poverty Bay. NY: Avon, 1985. 1st ed, pb orig. NF. *Janus.* $20/£13

EMERSON, ELLEN RUSSELL. Masks, Heads, and Faces. Boston/NY, 1891. xxvi,312pp; teg. (Soiled, hinge cracked.) *Edwards.* $62/£40

EMERSON, RALPH WALDO et al. Memoirs of Margaret Fuller Ossoli. Boston: Roberts, 1852. 1st ed, 1st issue, binding 2. 2 vols. 351,8pp ads; 352pp. Nice (both vols lack feps; spine extrems worn). BAL 6500. *Second Life.* $150/£97

EMERSON, RALPH WALDO. The Complete Works and Journals. Cambridge: Riverside Press, 1903-14. Autograph Century ed, signed by pub. 22 vols. #310/600 sets w/orig pg of mss tipped into vol 1 of the Works. Teg, others uncut. Full red morocco, ribbed gilt dec spines; gilt cvr decs, dentelles; blue morocco doublures; red silk moire eps. *D & D.* $6,900/£4,452

EMERSON, RALPH WALDO. English Traits. Boston: Phillips, Sampson, 1856. 1st ed, 1st ptg. Orig black cl, gilt. NF. BAL 5226. *Macdonnell.* $165/£106

EMERSON, RALPH WALDO. English Traits. Boston: Phillips, Sampson & Co, 1856. 1st ed. Orig brn cl. Fine. BAL 5226. *Chapel Hill.* $300/£194

EMERSON, RALPH WALDO. The Essays of Ralph Waldo Emerson. SF: LEC, 1934. #904/1500 numbered, signed by John Henry Nash (printer). Cl-backed paper-cvrd bds. Fine in pub's slipcase (sl cracked). *Hermitage.* $100/£65

EMERSON, RALPH WALDO. Letters and Social Aims. Boston: James R. Osgood, 1876. 1st ed, 1st ptg. Gray-brn cl (lt worn). NF (ink name tp). BAL 5272. *Juvelis.* $150/£97

EMERSON, RALPH WALDO. Letters of Emerson to a Friend. Charles Eliot Norton (ed). Boston: Houghton, Mifflin, 1899. 1st ed, regular format. Ltd to 1500. Grn cl, gilt. Nice (few pencilings). BAL 5307. *Macdonnell.* $45/£29

EMERSON, RALPH WALDO. Poems. NY: LEC, 1945. One of 1500. Signed by Richard & Doris Beer (artists). Full black sheepskin. (Few scuff mks; spine gilt faded.) VG case. *Agvent.* $60/£39

EMERSON, RALPH WALDO. Representative Men.... Boston: Phillips, Sampson, 1850. 1st ptg. Brn cl. VG (bkpl; sig; spine head chipped). BAL 5219. *Agvent.* $250/£161

EMERSON, RALPH WALDO. Uncollected Lectures.... NY: Rudge, 1932. VG (ink notes; inscrip). BAL 5330: 1100 copies. *Agvent.* $25/£16

EMERSON, W.D. History and Incidents of Indian Corn.... Cincinnati, 1878. 464,(1)pp (staining 2pp; yellowed, gnawing to few pp). Cl (spine faded, lt spotting). *Sutton.* $85/£55

EMERY, WALTER B. Nubian Treasure. London: Methuen, 1948. 48 plts. Gilt-emb cl. (Ink stamp.) *Archaeologia.* $65/£42

EMGELMANN, GEORGE. Labor Among Primitive Peoples.... St. Louis, 1884. 3rd ed. 227pp. Good. *Fye.* $250/£161

EMMET, THOMAS. The Principles and Practice of Gynaecology. Phila, 1879. 1st ed. 855pp. Recent 1/4 leather; marbled bds (new eps). Good. *Fye.* $300/£194

EMMETT, CHRIS. Shanghai Pierce. Norman: Univ of OK, (1953). 1st ed. VG. *Lien.* $50/£32

EMMETT, CHRIS. Texas Camel Tales. Austin: Steck, 1969. Rpt. Dj. *Lambeth.* $45/£29

EMMITT, ROBERT. The Last War Trail. Norman, 1954. 1st ed. Pict cl. Fine (sig, date) in dj (sl worn). *Baade.* $40/£26

EMMONS, EBENEZER. Agriculture of New-York. Vol 1. Albany, 1846. Tinted frontis, xi,371pp, 21 plts. (Pp dampstained; 1 map torn.) *Sutton.* $65/£42

EMMONS, EBENEZER. Agriculture of New-York. Vol 1. Albany, 1846. xi,371pp (foxing), 21 plts (1 browned), color fldg map (torn w/o loss), plan. Gilt device. (spine sl chipped, corners worn.) *Edwards.* $132/£85

EMMONS, SAMUEL FRANKLIN (ed). Geological Guide-Book for an Excursion to the Rocky Mountains. NY: Wiley, 1894. 255-485pp, 13 plts, fldg color map. Orig cl (old ex-lib). *Schoyer.* $60/£39

EMORY, W.H. Notes of a Military Reconnaissance, from Fort Leavenworth...to San Diego.... Washington: Wendell & Van Benthuysen, 1848. 1st ed. 614pp, 61 plts, 2 fldg maps. Pub's cl (rubbed; spine, ptd label chipped; lt foxing). Howes E 145. *Bookpress.* $400/£258

EMPSON, PATIENCE (ed). Wood Engravings of Robert Gibbings. London, 1959. 1st ed. Color frontis. Dj. *Edwards.* $155/£100

EMSLEY, H.H. Visual Optics. London, 1936. Frontis plt. Lt pencil mks few pp; cl sl crinkled, o/w VG. *Whitehart.* $23/£15

EMSLIE, MARGARET. Breast-Feeding. Oxford, 1931. 1st ed. Good. *Fye.* $75/£48

Encyclopaedia of Islam. Leiden: Brill, 1960. New ed. Vol 1 only. Sl rubbed, o/w VG. *Worldwide.* $250/£161

ENDICOTT, WENDELL. Adventures in Alaska and Along the Trail. NY: Frederick A. Stokes, 1928. 1st ed. VG in dj (spine torn). *Laurie.* $100/£65

ENDICOTT, WENDELL. Adventures in Alaska and Along the Trail. NY: Stokes, 1928. 1st ed. Signed presentation. Teg. Orig grn cl. VG +. *Bowman.* $75/£48

ENDICOTT, WENDELL. Adventures with Rod and Harpoon Along the Florida Keys. NY: Stokes, 1925. 1st ed. Signed presentation. Teg. Orig grn cl. VG +. *Bowman.* $80/£52

ENDO, SHUSAKU. The Sea and Poison. NY, 1972. 1st Amer ed. Fine in dj. *Polyanthos.* $25/£16

ENDORE, GUY. The Werewolf of Paris. NY: Farrar & Rinehart, (1933). 1st ed. Signed presentation note tipped in. Yellow cl. VG (bkpl). *Chapel Hill.* $40/£26

ENFIELD, J.E. Man from Packsaddle. Hollywood: House-Warven, 1951. 1st ed. VG in dj (sl worn). *Lien.* $75/£48

ENGEL, CLAIRE ELIANE. A History of Mountaineering in the Alps. London: Allen & Unwin, 1950. 1st ed. 24 plts. VG in dj (sl used). *Hollett.* $39/£25

ENGEL, DAVID H. Japanese Gardens for Today. Rutland: Chas Tuttle, 1962. Tp color illus tipped in, 279 monochrome plts. Pict cl. Fine in dj. *Quest.* $45/£29

ENGELHARDT, ALEXANDER PLATONOVICH. Russian Province of the North. Westminster: Constable, 1899. (xx),356pp, 3 maps (2 fldg). Grn dec cl (sl shaken, spine rubbed, sl stained; pocket removed). *Schoyer.* $65/£42

ENGELHARDT, ZEPHYRIN. Franciscans in Arizona. Harbor Springs, MI: Holy Childhood Indian School, 1899. vi,237,(8)pp; 2 maps (1 fldg). VG + (spine faded). Howes E 152. *Bohling.* $200/£129

ENGELHARDT, ZEPHYRIN. The Franciscans in California. Harbor Springs, MI, 1897. 1st ed. 516pp. Howes E 153. *Ginsberg.* $175/£113

ENGELHARDT, ZEPHYRIN. Missions and Missionaries of California. Santa Barbara: 1929, 1930, 1913, 1915, 1916. Vols 1-2 2nd ed, vols 3-5 1st eds. 5 vols. Brn cl, gilt spine titles. Overall VG +. Howes E 154. *Bohling.* $450/£290

ENGLAND, GEORGE ALLAN. The Air Trust. St. Louis: Phil Wagner, 1915. 1st ed. VG (owner label; tape offsetting eps). *Beasley.* $250/£161

ENGLAND, GEORGE ALLAN. Cursed. Boston: Small, Maynard, 1919. 1st ed. NF. *Beasley.* $85/£55

ENGLAND, GEORGE ALLAN. The Golden Blight. Fly, 1916. 1st ed. VG-. *Madle.* $125/£81

ENGLAND, GEORGE ALLAN. Vikings of the Ice. NY: Doubleday Page, 1924. 1st ed. Good + (spine sl rubbed, spine title chipped; fep missing). *Walcot.* $31/£20

ENGLAND, GEORGE ALLAN. Vikings of the Ice. GC: Doubleday, Page, 1924. 1st ed. Blue cl, ptd lettering piece. VG. *House.* $65/£42

ENGLEBERT, OMER. The Last of the Conquistadors— Junipero Serra. Katherine Woods (trans). NY: Harcourt, Brace, 1956. Stated 1st ed. Orange cl, black titles. VG + in dj (dknd, lt chipped). *Parmer.* $25/£16

ENGLISH, WILLIAM HAYDEN. Conquest of the Country Northwest of the River Ohio 1778-1783.... Indianapolis: Bowen-Merrill, 1896. 1st ed. 2 vols. Pub's orig brn pebbled cl, stamped in gilt. VG. *Laurie.* $200/£129

ENGLISH, WILLIAM HAYDEN. Conquest of the Country Northwest of the River Ohio 1778-1783.... Indianapolis/Kansas City: Bowen-Merrill, 1896. 1st ed. 2 vols. 586; (587)-1186pp. Brn cl. Blind/ink stamps tps, else VG. Howes E 157. *Chapel Hill.* $225/£145

Englishman in China. London: Saunders, Otley, 1860. x,272,(viii)pp, later eps. Gilt cl (hinges sl cracked, repaired; bumped). *Hollett.* $70/£45

Englishwoman in Russia. NY: Scribner's, 1855. Frontis, 316pp + 8pp pub's ads, 6 plts. Brn cl, blindstamped (spine faded, worn; sig pulled). *Schoyer.* $40/£26

Engravings from the Pictures of the National Gallery. London: Associated Engravers, 1840. Tp, dedication (i),contents(i), 29 engr plts w/text. (Lt spotting throughout.) Marbled eps, aeg. 1/2 morocco w/marbled bds (edges sl soiled, worn); dec gilt spine (rubbed). *Edwards.* $1,008/£650

ENGSTROM, J. ERIC. Coins in Shakespeare. NH: Dartmouth College, 1964. VG in glassine dj. *Hollett.* $54/£35

ENGVICK, WILLIAM (ed). Lullabies and Night Songs. London: Bodley Head, 1969. 1st Eng ed. Maurice Sendak (plts). Dec bds. VF in Fine dj. *Dalian.* $54/£35

ENO, HENRY. Twenty Years on the Pacific Slope. W. Turrentine Jackson (ed). New Haven: Yale Univ Press, 1965. 1st ed. VG in dj. *Laurie.* $50/£32

ENOCK, C. REGINALD. The Secret of the Pacific. NY: Scribner's, 1912. 1st ed. 2 fldg maps. Teg. Gilt-pict blue cl. NF. *House.* $70/£45

ENTRIKIN, F.W. Woman's Monitor. Green Springs, OH, 1881. 1st ed. 400pp. Good. *Fye.* $100/£65

ENTWISLE, E.A. The Book of Wallpaper. London, 1954. 1st ed. Color frontis, 2 color plts. Dj (sl rubbed, chipped). *Edwards.* $62/£40

EPICURUS. The Extant Remains of the Greek Text. Cyril Bailey (trans). NY: LEC, 1947. #904/1500 numbered, signed by Bruce Rogers. Fine in pub's slipcase. *Hermitage.* $175/£113

EPPS, JOHN. The Life of John Walker, M.D. London: Whittaker, Treacher, (1832). 2nd ed. viii,342pp. 1/2 calf, gilt; marbled bds. (Lt spotting.) *White.* $70/£45

EPPS, JOHN. The Life of John Walker. London, 1831. viii,342pp. Bkpl; cl spine, bds worn; spine top defective, o/w Good. *Whitehart.* $47/£30

EPSTEIN, BEN. Yogi Berra—The Muscle Man. Barnes, 1951. 1st ed. Pict cvr. Lt cvr wear, fading, o/w Fine; no dj as issued. *Plapinger.* $150/£97

EPSTEIN, JACOB. Let There Be Sculpture. London, 1940. 1st ed. Dj (sl ragged). *Edwards.* $70/£45

EPSTEIN, LAWRENCE and ARTHUR FEINER (eds). Countertransference. NY: Aronson, (1979). 1st ed. Red cl. VG in dj. *Gach.* $57/£37

Equality or A History of Lithconia. Prime Press, 1947. One of 500. Fine in dj (sl dust-soil). *Aronovitz.* $40/£26

ERASMUS, DESIDERIUS. Moriae Encomium, an Oration Spoken by Folly in Praise of Herself. NY: LEC, 1943. #904/1500 numbered, signed by Lynd Ward (illus). Full leather (sl rubbed). Fine in pub's slipcase (sl rubbed). *Hermitage.* $100/£65

ERASMUS, DESIDERIUS. Pilgrimages to Saint Mary of Walsingham and Saint Thomas of Canterbury. Westminster: ptd by John Bowyer Nichols & Son, 1849. Frontis; xxiii,248pp. Blind emb cl (sl discolouring; spine chipped; sl wrinkling lower bd; fore-edges dented; sl rubbed; ex-libris; sl spotting.) *Edwards.* $39/£25

ERBEN, WALTER. Joan Miro. London: Lund Humphries, 1959. 8 tipped-in color plts, 68 monochrome plts. VF in dj (sl worn). *Europa.* $34/£22

ERBSTEIN, C. The Show Up. P-C, 1926. 1st ed. Fine in pict dj (chipping; dust soil). *Fine Books.* $95/£61

ERDMANN, KURT. Oriental Carpets. Charles Grant Ellis (trans). London, 1960. 8 color, 179 b/w plts. (Leading corner bds sl damp-stained). *Edwards.* $74/£48

ERDOES, RICHARD. Saloons of the Old West. NY, 1979. 1st ed. Fine (faint rmdr stamp bottom edge) in dj. *Baade.* $45/£29

ERDRICH, LOUISE and MICHAEL DORRIS. Route 2. Northridge: Lord John Press, 1991. One of 275 numbered, signed. Red cl. Fine. *Robbins.* $75/£48

ERDRICH, LOUISE. The Beet Queen. NY: Henry Holt, (1986). 1st ed. Fine in dj. *Hermitage.* $40/£26

ERDRICH, LOUISE. The Beet Queen. NY: Henry Holt, 1986. 1st ed. Signed. Fine in Fine dj. *Revere.* $100/£65

ERDRICH, LOUISE. The Beet Queen. London: Hamish Hamilton, 1987. 1st UK ed. Top, fore-edges sl browned, o/w NF in dj (lt crease). *Moorhouse.* $12/£8

ERDRICH, LOUISE. Jacklight. NY: Holt, Rinehart & Winston, 1984. 1st ed, 1st bk. Wrappers (sm abrasion; spine rubbed; rmdr mk). *Moorhouse.* $54/£35

ERDRICH, LOUISE. Love Medicine. NY: Holt Rinehart & Winston, 1984. 1st ed. Signed. Fine in Fine dj. *Revere.* $200/£129

ERDRICH, LOUISE. Tracks. NY: Henry Holt, 1988. 1st ed. Signed. Fine in Fine dj. *Revere.* $40/£26

ERICHSEN, JOHN. Observations on Aneurysms Selected from the Works of the Principal Writers.... London: Sydenham Soc, 1844. xii; 524pp. Binding worn, else Good. *Goodrich.* $125/£81

ERICHSEN, JOHN. The Science and Art of Surgery. Phila, 1878. Rev from 7th Eng ed. 2 vols. 947; 989pp; 862 woodcut illus. (Binding extrems rubbed.) *Fye.* $100/£65

ERICKSON, STEVE. Days Between Stations. NY: Poseidon, 1985. 1st ed, 1st bk. Fine in Fine dj. *Revere.* $40/£26

ERICKSON, STEVE. Leap Year. NY: Poseidon, 1989. 1st ed. Fine in Fine dj. *Revere.* $30/£19

ERICKSON, STEVE. Tours of the Black Clock. NY: Poseidon, 1989. 1st ed. Fine in Fine dj. *Revere.* $25/£16

ERICSON, ERIC E. A Guide to Colored Steuben Glass. Loveland, CO: Lithographic Press, (1963), (1965). 1st ed, later ptg. 2 vols. Fine in wrappers. *Glenn.* $20/£13

ERIKSON, ERIK HOMBURGER. Insight and Responsibility. NY: Norton, (1964). Later ptg. Signed. Black cl. VG. *Gach.* $35/£23

ERMATINGER, FRANCIS. Fur Trade Letters of Frances Ermatinger Written to His Brother...1818-1853. Glendale: Clark, 1980. Blue cl, gilt. Fine in dj. *Laurie.* $40/£26

ERNEST, EDWARD. Animated Animals. Akron, OH: Saalfield, 1934. 26x20cm. 3pp w/moveable illus by Julian Wehr. Pict bds, spiral binding. Lt wear, o/w VG-. *Book Finders.* $120/£77

ERNST, MARGARET S. In a Word. London: Hamish Hamilton, 1939. 1st Eng ed. James Thurber (illus). Grey cl. NF in dj (sl soiled, chipped). *Dalian*. $39/£25

ERNST, MAX. Beyond Painting. NY: Wittenborn, Schultz, 1948. 1st ed. VG in illus wrappers (lt wear). *Cahan*. $75/£48

ERSKINE, JOHN. Peter Kills the Bear. London: Elkin Mathews & Marrot, 1930. 1st ed. One of 530 signed. Unopened. Fine in dj (chipped, split along spine). *Cahan*. $35/£23

ERSKINE, MRS. STEUART. Lady Diana Beauclerk. London: T. Fisher Unwin, 1903. 6 color plts. Gilt dec red buckram (back faded). *Petersfield*. $65/£42

ESAU, K. Plant Anatomy. NY, (1953). 85 plts. (Lt soiled; pp yellowed.) *Sutton*. $50/£32

Escape of a Confederate Officer from Prison. (By Samuel B. Davis.) Norfolk, VA: Landmark Pub. Co., 1892. 1st ed. 72pp, errata. Sl minor chipping, else NF in orig ptd wrappers. Howes D 134. *Mcgowan*. $450/£290

ESDAILE, KATHERINE A. English Church Monuments 1510 to 1840. London: Batsford, 1946. 1st ed. Spine sl faded, o/w Fine. *Europa*. $28/£18

ESHER, REGINALD. Journals and Letters. Maurice V. Brett (ed). London: Nicholson & Watson, 1934. 1st ed. 2 vols. Color frontis, 12 plts. Teg. (Fore-edges vol 1 damp-faded.) *Cox*. $28/£18

ESKEW, GARNETT. The Pageant of the Packets. NY: Henry Holt, (1929). 1st ed. VG in dj. *Laurie*. $100/£65

ESKEW, GARNETT. Salt, The Fifth Element. Chicago, 1948. 1st ed. Fine in VG dj. *Oregon*. $20/£13

ESPINOSA, CARMEN. Shawls, Crinolines, Filigree. El Paso: TX Western Press/Univ of TX, 1970. Fine in NF dj. *Connolly*. $42/£27

ESPINOSA, JOSE E. Saints in the Valleys. Albuquerque, 1967. Rev ed. Fine in dj (sl worn). *Baade*. $50/£32

ESPY, JAMES P. The Philosophy of Storms. Boston, 1841. 1st ed. 552pp, fldg map. Dec cl. VG. *Argosy*. $350/£226

ESSIG, E.O. Insects of Western North America. NY, 1926. Various ptgs. Grn cl (worn). *Brooks*. $49/£32

ETCHISON, DENNIS. The Dark Country. Scream Press, 1982. 1st ed. NF in dj. *Madle*. $135/£87

ETHERTON, P.T. and A. DUNSCOMBE ALLEN. Through Europe and the Balkans. London: Cassell, 1928. 1st ed. 32 plts. (Sl rubbed; top lower bd faded; upper joint cracked; eps sl stained.) *Hollett*. $39/£25

ETHERTON, P.T. and H. HESSELL TILTMAN. Manchuria: The Cockpit of Asia. London: Jarrolds, 1934. VG in dj (defective). *Hollett*. $39/£25

EURIPIDES. Three Plays: Medea, Hippolytus, the Bacchae. (NY): LEC, 1967. One of 1500 numbered, signed by Michael Ayrton (illus). Fine in pub's slipcase. *Hermitage*. $90/£58

EUWER, ANTHONY H. Cristopher Cricket on Cats. NY: Little Book Concern, 1909. 2nd ed. 4to, unpaginated. VG. *Davidson*. $95/£61

EVANS, ALBERT. A La California. Bancroft, 1873. 1st ed. Frontis, 379pp; 24 plts (rebound, orig cl laid on). *Oregon*. $75/£48

EVANS, ARTHUR. The Mycenaean Tree and Pillar Cult and Its Mediterranean Relations. London: Macmillan, 1901. 1 color plt. Gilt-lettered cl (spine lt faded; eps foxed; sig). *Archaeologia*. $175/£113

EVANS, ARTHUR. The Ring of Nestor. London: Macmillan, 1925. 5 plts (1 color). Good in dj (tattered). *Archaeologia*. $150/£97

EVANS, AUGUSTA. Inez: A Tale of the Alamo. NY: Dillingham, 1888. (Yellowed paper; broken inner hinges; fray at corners.) *Burcham*. $50/£32

EVANS, BARBARA. Caduceus in Saigon: A Medical Mission to Viet-Nam. London: Hutchinson, (1968). NF in VG dj (lt soiling; discoloring edges). *Aka*. $40/£26

EVANS, BESSIE and MAY. American Indian Dance Steps. NY: A.S. Barnes, 1931. 1st ed. Rebound, one released lib stamp, else VG. *Parker*. $200/£129

EVANS, C.S. Cinderella. London: Heinemann, 1919. One of 300 signed. Arthur Rackham (illus). Mtd color frontis, 4 silhouette dwgs (3 double-pg), 13 full-pg silhouettes. Teg. Japanese vellum (sl fingered, lt damped), gilt. *Hollett*. $1,008/£650

EVANS, CARADOC. Nothing to Pay. London: Faber & Faber, 1930. 1st ed. Sig; cl faded, stained, else VG in dj (spine lacks pieces; chipped). *Cahan*. $35/£23

EVANS, CLIFFORD and BETTY J. MEGGERS. BAE Bulletin 177. Archaeological Investigations in British Guiana. Washington, 1960. 68 plts. (Ex-lib.) *Edwards*. $25/£16

EVANS, DAVID. A Bibliography of Stained Glass. Woodbridge: Boydell & Brewer, 1982. Rexine. Fine in Mint dj. *Europa*. $36/£23

EVANS, DORINDA. Benjamin West and His American Students. Washington: Smithsonian Institute, 1980. 1st ed. Bkpl; wrappers sl sunned; else Fine. *Bookpress*. $50/£32

EVANS, E. EVERETT. Alien Minds. Fantasy, 1955. 1st ed. Fine in dj. *Madle*. $45/£29

EVANS, ELI N. Judah P. Benjamin, the Jewish Confederate. NY, (1988). 1st ed. Fine in Fine dj. *Mcgowan*. $35/£23

EVANS, G.H. A Guide to Malta and Gozo. Valetta: W. Watson, n.d. (1900). 1st ed. 8vo. Fldg map, 4 plts, ad slip tipped in. (Lt foxing to margins.) Blue cl, ptd in gilt (hinges cracked, spine rubbed, cockled). *Morrell*. $39/£25

EVANS, G.P. Big-Game Shooting in Upper Burma. London: Longmans Green, 1912. Lg fldg color map at rear. Grn cl, gilt elephant head. VG+ (prelims lt foxed). *Bowman*. $125/£81

EVANS, HENRY OLIVER. Iron Pioneer: Henry W. Oliver, 1840-1904. NY: Dutton, 1942. VG in VG dj. *Peninsula*. $50/£32

EVANS, I.O. Cigarette Cards: And How to Collect Them. London, 1937. Color frontis. (Newspaper cutting inserted.) Dj (sl ragged). *Edwards*. $39/£25

EVANS, J. Letters Written During a Tour Through South Wales, in the Year 1803.... London: for C. & R. Baldwin, 1804. 1st ed. xii,449pp + (ii)pub's ads (few pp w/sl loss upper margin not affecting text; lt browned; ex-libris). Contemp calf bds (lt wear; rebacked, orig spine laid down). *Edwards*. $186/£120

EVANS, JOAN. Art in Mediaeval France 987-1498. OUP, 1948. 11 plans. Pub's blue cl gilt (sl faded). Fine. *Peter Taylor*. $70/£45

EVANS, JOAN. Art in Mediaeval France 987-1498. Oxford, 1948. 281 plts. (Sl soiled, shaken.) *Washton*. $100/£65

EVANS, JOAN. English Art 1307-1461. Oxford, 1949. 96 plts. Good. *Washton*. $65/£42

EVANS, JOAN. A History of Jewellery, 1100-1870. NY: Pitman, (1953). 10 full-color plts. Plain eps foxed, else VG in dj (chipped). *Bookpress.* $135/£87

EVANS, JOAN. Life in Medieval France. London: Phaidon, 1957. Mtd frontis, 5 color plts, 91 monochrome plts. Fine. *Europa.* $28/£18

EVANS, JOAN. Pattern. A Study of Ornament in Western Europe from 1180-1900. OUP, 1931. 2 vols. (Feps lt browned.) Dj (sl soiled, ragged). *Edwards.* $248/£160

EVANS, JOAN. Pattern: A Study of Ornament in Western Europe, 1180-1900. Vol 2: The Renaissance to 1900. London: Dacapo, 1976. Pict card cvrs (sl wear). Good+. *Willow House.* $16/£10

EVANS, JOE M. A Corral Full of Stories. El Paso: By author, (1939). Signed. Fine in VG wraps, dj. *Perier.* $30/£19

EVANS, JOHN. Ancient Stone Implements, Weapons, and Ornaments of Great Britain. NY, 1872. 640pp. Dec cl. Mint. *Argosy.* $100/£65

EVANS, JOHN. Charles Coulson Rich. NY: Macmillan, 1936. Signed presentation. Maroon cl. VG. *Laurie.* $45/£29

EVANS, JOHN. The Endless Web: John Dickinson and Co, 1804-1954. London: Jonathan Cape, 1955. 49 plts. Fine in dj (sl shelfworn), red cl case. *Heller.* $50/£32

EVANS, JOHN. Message and Characters of the Book of Mormon.... Salt Lake, 1929. 1st ed. Near VG. *Benchmark.* $25/£16

EVANS, LADY. Lustre Pottery. London: Methuen & Co, 1920. 1st ed. 24 plts. Fore, lower edges uncut. (Spotting; feps browned, lib bkpl). *Edwards.* $186/£120

EVANS, M.W. Medieval Drawings. London, 1969. 132 plts. Good in dj. *Washton.* $75/£48

EVANS, MAX. Shadow of Thunder. Chicago: Swallow, 1969. 1st ed. Signed. Fine in VG+ dj (sl worn). *Parker.* $50/£32

EVANS, MYFANWY. No Rubbish Here. London: Collins, (1936). 1st ed. 4to. Margaret Tempest (illus). Grn dec bds (sl worn). *Reisler.* $90/£58

EVANS, OLIVER. The Young Mill-Wright and Miller's Guide. Phila: For author, 1795. 1st ed. 8vo. 160,178,90,10pp,(9)pp subscribers list; errata leaf. 25 full-pg plts (3-inch closed tear 1plt; sm tears). Contemp full mottled calf (lt rubbed; hinges starting but sound). VG+. *Chapel Hill.* $900/£581

EVANS, R.M. An Introduction to Color. NY/London: Wiley, 1961. 15 color plts. Sound. *Ars Artis.* $33/£21

EVANS, ROBERT FRANK. Notes on Lands and Sea. Boston: Badgor, (1922). 1st ed. (Rubber private lib stamps.) *Ginsberg.* $150/£97

EVANS, ROSALIE. The Rosalie Evans Letters from Mexico. Daisy Caden Pettus (ed). Indianapolis: Bobbs-Merrill, (1926). 1st ed. Red cl, gilt-titled. VG (lacks dj). *Hermitage.* $20/£13

EVANS, THOMAS SCATTERGOOD. Memoirs of Thomas Scattergood.... London: Charles Gilpin, 1845. 1st Eng ed. xii,464pp. (Rebacked.) *Bickersteth.* $39/£25

EVANS, W.J. The Sugar-Planter's Manual.... Phila: Lea & Blanchard, 1848. 1st Amer ed. 264pp; 2 fldg plts; pub's 24pp cat bound in. Cvrs blocked in blind, spine gilt-lettered. (Cl sl defective at spine head, foot & upper joint foot.) *Bickersteth.* $132/£85

EVANS, WALKER. American Photographs. NY: MOMA, 1938. 1st ed. 87 photo plts. (Eps lt foxed, lib stamp tp; fr hinge starting; rubbed.) *Cahan.* $50/£32

EVANS, WALKER. American Photographs. NY: MOMA, 1938. 1st ed. 87 photo plts, errata slip. Orig cl, ptd spine label. Lt spotted, eps lt foxed, else VG in dj (sl aged). *Cahan.* $250/£161

EVANS, WALKER. First and Last. NY: Harper & Row, 1978. 1st ed. Rmdr dot lower edge. NF in dj (rubbed). *Cahan.* $150/£97

EVANS, WALKER. First and Last. London: Secker & Warburg, 1978. 1st Eng ed. Fine in dj (sl rubbed). *Cahan.* $150/£97

EVANS, WALKER. Havana 1933. NY: Pantheon, (1989). 1st Amer ed. Fine in dj. *Godot.* $75/£48

EVANS, WALKER. Walker Evans: The Museum of Modern Art. MOMA, 1971. 1st ed. NF in VG+ dj. *Bishop.* $50/£32

EVANS, WILBUR and BILL LITTLE. Texas Longhorn Baseball. Strode, 1983. 1st ed. Fine in VG+ dj (shelfwear). *Plapinger.* $35/£23

EVANS-PRITCHARD, E.E. Witchcraft, Oracles and Magic Among the Azande. Oxford: Clarendon Press, 1937. 1st ed. 34 photo plts, 2 maps. Blue gilt cl. (Bkpl.) *Karmiole.* $100/£65

EVANS-WENTZ, W.Y. The Fairy-Faith in Celtic Countries. NY: University Books, (1961). 1st rpt ed. NF in VG dj. *Blue Dragon.* $40/£26

EVANSON, RICHARD T. and HENRY MAUNSELL. A Practical Treatise on the Management and Diseases of Children. Dublin, 1842. 4th ed. 570pp+ads. Partly unopened. Orig cl (bumped; few sigs loose). *Argosy.* $125/£81

EVELYN, JOHN. Diary and Correspondence.... William Bray (ed). London: Henry Colburn, 1854. New ed. 4 vols. Teg. 3/4 dk blue polished calf, marbled bds, spines gilt, raised bands, leather labels. Thin sl lightened strip top cvr edges 3 vols, o/w Clean. *Sadlon.* $175/£113

EVELYN, JOHN. The Diary of John Evelyn...from 1641 to 1705-6. William Bray (ed). London: W.W. Gibbings, 1890. 619pp. (Spine sl faded.) *Hollett.* $54/£35

EVELYN, JOHN. Diary. London: Bickers, 1879. 4 vols. Fldg table. 3/4 leather, gilt. Teg, others untrimmed. Unopened. VG. *Schoyer.* $200/£129

EVELYN, JOHN. The Life of Mrs. Godolphin. London: William Pickering, 1847. 1st ed. Engr frontis, xviii,266pp; uncut. 19th cent blind-dec grn cl-backed bds, new paper label. *Cox.* $54/£35

EVELYN, JOHN. The Life of Mrs. Godolphin. London: William Pickering, 1847. 1st ed. Engr frontis, xviii,266pp. Brn cl, paper label (rubbed; sl wear). *Cox.* $62/£40

EVELYN, JOHN. The Miscellaneous Writings. London: Colburn, 1825. 1st ed. 875pp, 4 plts (1 mezzotint). Bds, tan morocco spine, raised bands, dbl leather labels. Nice. *Hartfield.* $395/£255

EVELYN, JOHN. Silva, or a Discourse of Forest-Trees.... London: For Robert Scott, 1706. 4th ed. 2 vols. Engr frontis port, (34),384; (4),275,(5)pp. 1/2 mod calf. Sl browning, foxing; sm lib blindstamp tp, o/w Good. *Reese.* $350/£226

Evening in Autumn; or, the Useful Amusement. London: Harvey and Darton, 1821. 1st ed. Frontis (ink dedication verso), 110pp + 2pp ad, 3 full-pg copper engrs. Orig leather spine, marble paper on bd (worn, rubbed), gilt spine title. Internally sound, clean. *Hobbyhorse*. $95/£61

EVERETT, EDWARD. Report of the Secretary of State Communicating...Encroachments of the Indians of the United States upon the Territories of Mexico. Washington, 1853. 135pp. 1st pg torn along binding; sl cvr wear; internal spotting, o/w VG in wraps. *Pratt*. $75/£48

EVERETT, GEORGE and SUSAN EVERETT. Health Fragments, or, Steps Toward a True Life. NY, 1876. 3rd ed. 258; 52pp. Good. *Fye*. $60/£39

EVERETT, PERCIVAL. Suder. NY: Viking, 1983. 1st ed, 1st bk. NF in NF dj. *Revere*. $35/£23

EVERITT, CHARLES P. Adventures of a Treasure Hunter. London: Gollancz, 1952. 1st Eng ed. VG in VG + dj. *Limestone*. $45/£29

EVERSON, WILLIAM. Black Hills. (SF): Didymus Press, (1973). 1st ed. Ltd to 285 signed. As New. *Jaffe*. $100/£65

EVERSON, WILLIAM. The Masks of Drought. Black Sparrow Press, 1980. 1st trade ed, one of 500. Fine in glassine dj. *Authors Of The West*. $50/£32

EVERSON, WILLIAM. River-Root. Berkeley: Oyez, 1976. 1st ed. Ltd to 250 signed. Calf-backed cl. As New. *Jaffe*. $100/£65

EVERSON, WILLIAM. The Springing of the Blade. (Reno: Black Rock, 1968.) Ltd to 180 signed. Dec grn cl. Fine. *Antic Hay*. $125/£81

EVERSON, WILLIAM. Tendril in the Mesh. (Aromas): Cayucos Books, 1973. 1st ed. One of 250 signed. 1/4 leather, paste-paper bds. As New. *Jaffe*. $150/£97

EVERSON, WILLIAM. Tendril in the Mesh. (Aromas, CA): Cayucos Books, 1973. Ltd to 250 numbered, signed. Bds, leather spine. Fine. *Antic Hay*. $125/£81

EVJEN, JOHN OLUF. The Life of J.H.W. Stuckenberg. Minneapolis: Lutheran Free Church Pub Co, 1938. 1st ed. NF in VG dj. *Mcgowan*. $150/£97

EWALD, CARL. The Queen Bee and Other Nature Tales. G.C. Moore Smith (trans). London: Thomas Nelson, 1908. Color frontis, 125pp; 7 color plts. Gilt-dec pict cl. Mint. *Quest*. $85/£55

EWAN, J. Rocky Mountain Naturalists. Denver: Univ of Denver, 1950. 1st ed. NF in VG dj. *Mikesh*. $35/£23

EWBANK, THOMAS. A Descriptive and Historical Account of Hydraulic and Other Machines for Raising Water, Ancient and Modern.... NY: Greeley, 1847. 2nd ed, 1st bk. (16),608pp. *Ginsberg*. $125/£81

EWELL, JAMES. The Medical Companion, or Family Physician.... Balt: The Proprietors, 1822. 6th ed. (Bkpl; text waterstained, foxed.) *Bookpress*. $275/£177

EWEN, C. L'ESTRANGE. Witch Hunting and Witch Trials. London: Frederick Muller, 1971. Facs ed. 7 plts. Rexine gilt. VG in dj. *Hollett*. $54/£35

EWERS, H.H. The Sorceror's Apprentice. J. Day, 1927. 1st ed. One of 2000. NF. *Fine Books*. $65/£42

EWERS, J.K. Tales from the Dead Heart. Currawong, (ca 1940). 1st ed. VG in pict dj (lt wear). *Fine Books*. $55/£35

EWERS, JOHN C. The Horse in Blackfoot Indian Culture. Washington: Smithsonian Bulletin 159, 1955. VG. *October Farm*. $40/£26

EWERS, JOHN C. Indian Life on the Upper Missouri. Norman: Univ of OK, (1968). (1st ed). Map. VG + in dj (price-clipped). *Bohling*. $37/£24

EWERS, JOHN C. Indian Life on the Upper Missouri. Univ of OK, (1968). 1st ed. Fine in Fine dj. *Oregon*. $45/£29

EWERS, JOHN C. (ed). Adventures of Zenas Leonard, Fur Trader. Norman, (1959). 1st ed. Good (bkpl) in dj (spotted, sl torn). *King*. $35/£23

EWING, JULIANA HORATIA. The Mill Stream. London: SPCK, (1885). 16mo. 16 chromos, 16 grn/brn illus by R. Andre. Chromo w/gilt cvrs (spine restored); new but correct eps. VG. *Drusilla's*. $65/£42

EWING, JULIANA HORATIA. Mother's Birthday Review. London: SPCK, (1885). 16mo. (32pp); 16 chromos, 16 grn/brn illus by R. Andre. Gilt chromo w/gilt cvrs (hinges repaired w/archival cl; spine repaired). VG. *Drusilla's*. $45/£29

EWING, WILLIAM A. The Photographic Art of Hoyningen-Huene. London, 1986. 11 color plts. Dj. *Edwards*. $31/£20

EXLEY, FREDERICK. A Fan's Notes. H&R, 1968. 1st ed, 1st bk. Fine in NF dj. *Fine Books*. $90/£58

EXLEY, FREDERICK. Pages from a Cold Island. Random House, 1975. 1st ed. Fine in dj. *Stahr*. $15/£10

EXLEY, FREDERICK. Pages from a Cold Island. NY: Random House, 1975. 1st ed. NF in NF dj. *Revere*. $25/£16

Expedition of Humphry Clinker. (By Tobias Smollett.) London: W. Johnston & B. Collins, 1771. 1st ed, 1st ptg; misdated imprint Vol 1. George Cruikshank (illus). Engr frontis port. These illus were for 1831 London ed. 3 vols. 8vo. 250; 249; 275pp. Contemp full calf w/morocco spine labels. Very clean (sig clipped from top of Vol 1 half-title; sigs, bkseller's stamp, label). *Chapel Hill*. $1,800/£1,161

Experiences of a Deputy U.S. Marshall of the Indian Territory. (By W.F. Jones.) (Tulsa, OK, 1937.) VG in wraps. *Cullen*. $75/£48

Experiences of Flagellation. London, 1885. 1930s rprnt. 80pp, 4 plts. Cl (heavily soiled; roughly opened). *King*. $25/£16

Extraordinary Black Book: An Exposition of Abuses in Church and State.... London: Effingham Wilson, 1832. New ed. Frontis. Later 1/2 morocco (joints rubbed; lib stamp tp; lib label fr cvr). *Waterfield*. $109/£70

Eye-Witness; or, Life Scenes in the Old North State.... (By A.O. Wheeler.) Boston, 1865. 1st ed. 276pp. (Spine mended.) Howes W 314. *Ginsberg*. $125/£81

EYLES, DESMOND. Good Sir Toby. London, 1955. 1st ed. Nice in dj (sl chipped). *Edwards*. $62/£40

EYLES, DESMOND. Royal Doulton 1815-1965, the Rise and Expansion of the Royal Doulton Potteries. Hutchinson, 1965. Fine in dj (chipped, tape-repaired). *Petersfield*. $217/£140

EYRE, ALICE. The Famous Fremonts and Their America. N.p. (Santa Ana): Fine Arts Press, 1948. 1st ed. Inscribed. 24 plts, 6 maps (5 dbl-pg). VF in VF dj. *Oregon*. $125/£81

EYRE, J. The Stomach and Its Difficulties. London, 1852. 2nd ed. xvi,154pp. Orig cl (worn, dust-stained; spine ends defective). Lib stamp; marginal pencil mks, o/w Good. *Whitehart*. $54/£35

EYRE, JOHN. The European Stranger in America. NY, 1839. 1st ed. 84pp. Dbd. Howes E 253. *Ginsberg*. $100/£65

Ezra Pound. His Metric and Poetry. (By T.S. Eliot.) NY: Knopf, 1917. 1st ed. One of 1000. Frontis port. Rose paper-cvrd bds. VG (bkpl; spine sl worn). *Sumner & Stillman.* $450/£290

F

F., M.T. My Chinese Marriage. (Ghostwritten by Katherine Ann Porter.) NY: Duffield, 1921. 1st ed. Teg. Ink inscrip, 2 corners bumped, sl soiled, else VG (dj fr flap laid in). *Godot.* $75/£48

FABER, M.D. (ed). The Design Within: Psychoanalytic Approaches to Shakespeare. NY: Science House, 1970. 1st ed. Cl-backed dec bds. VG in dj (lt worn). *Gach.* $40/£26

FABES, GILBERT H. D.H. Lawrence. His First Editions: Points and Values. London: W & G Foyle Ltd, (1933). 1st ed ltd to 500 numbered. Blue cl; gilt. Spine bit rubbed. *Karmiole.* $30/£19

FABES, GILBERT H. The First Editions of Ralph Hale Mottram. London: Myers, 1934. 1st ed ltd to 300, this unnumbered. 3 plts. Cl (backstrip faded). *Cox.* $23/£15

Fable for Critics. (By James Russell Lowell.) (NY): Putnam's, 1848. 1st ed, State C (w/pg63 misnumbered). 78pp. 3/4 leather. Teg, rest untrimmed. VG. BAL 13062. *Schoyer.* $65/£42

FABRE, J. The Heavens. E.E. Fournier d'Albe (trans). London: T. Fisher, 1924. 1st Eng ed. 19 plts. Good (lt foxing 1st, last pp, fore-edge) in grn cl. *Knollwood.* $25/£16

FABRE, J. et al. Fabre's Book of Insects. London: Hodder & Stoughton, (1921). 1st ed. Lg, 4to. 12 mtd color plts by E.J. Detmold. White cl, gilt. Good in dj w/color paste label (worn w/holes). *Reisler.* $320/£206

FABRE, J. et al. Fabre's Book of Insects. Tudor, 1935. 12 tipped-in full color plts. Dampstaining rear cvr, else NF in dj (worn). *Fine Books.* $65/£42

FAENSEN, HUBERT and VLADIMIR IVANOV. Early Russian Architecture. NY, 1975. 420 plts (86 color). VG in dj, slipcase. *Argosy.* $100/£65

Faeries Pop-Up Book. London: Kestrel/Penguin, 1980. 19x27 cm. 6 dbl-pg pop-ups, pull-tabs. Glazed bds. VG. *Book Finders.* $40/£26

FAGAN, LOUIS. Collectors' Marks. London, 1883. 1st ed. Frontis, 128pp. Gilt vellum. Teg. VG. *Argosy.* $100/£65

FAGG, W.P. Afro-Portuguese Ivories. London, (n.d.). VG in dj (chipped). *Argosy.* $100/£65

FAGGE, CHARLES HILTON. The Principles and Practice of Medicine. London: J.&A. Churchill, 1886. 1st ed. 2 vols. xv,(i),1024; xi,836pp + (16)pp pub's cat. Morocco cl, blind-stamped (both vols rebacked; orig eps preserved). *Bickersteth.* $186/£120

FAHEY, HERBERT. Early Printing in California. SF: Book Club of CA, 1956. Ltd to 400. 16 plts of facs. Bkpl, o/w Fine. *Karmiole.* $250/£161

FAHEY, JOHN. The Ballyhoo Bonanza. Univ WA, (1971). 1st ed. 3 maps. Fine in VG dj. *Oregon.* $35/£23

FAHIE, J.J. Galileo. London, 1903. 1st ed. Photogravure frontis port, fldg facs. Gilt dec cl. VG. *Argosy.* $60/£39

Fair France, Impressions of a Traveller by the Author of John Halifax Gentleman. (By Mrs. Craik.) London: Hurst & Blackett, 1871. 1st ed. Calf, full gilt, grn label. Name, o/w Fine. *Petersfield.* $74/£48

FAIR, A.A. (Pseud of Erle Stanley Gardner.) All Grass Isn't Green. NY: William Morrow, 1970. 1st ed. NF (bd edges sl worn) in VG + dj. *Janus.* $25/£16

FAIR, A.A. (Pseud of Erle Stanley Gardner.) Bachelors Get Lonely. NY: Morrow, 1961. 1st ed. VG in dj (nicks). *Houle.* $75/£48

FAIR, A.A. (Pseud of Erle Stanley Gardner). Fish or Cut Bait. Morrow, 1963. 1st ed. Fine in dj (lt soiled). *Murder.* $27/£17

FAIR, A.A. (Pseud of Erle Stanley Gardner.) Fish or Cut Bait. NY: William Morrow, 1963. 1st ed. Fine in NF dj (price-clipped; lt soiling). *Janus.* $35/£23

FAIRBAIRN, W. RONALD D. Psychoanalytic Studies of the Personality. London: Routledge & Kegan Paul, (1972). 4th ptg. Black cl. VG in dj. *Gach.* $45/£29

FAIRBANK, ALFRED. Renaissance Hand Writing. Faber & Faber, 1960. 1st ed. 96 plts. Eps sl browned, else Fine in dj. *Michael Taylor.* $85/£55

FAIRBROTHER, NAN. New Lives, New Landscapes. London: Architectural Press, 1970. 2nd imp. As New. *Quest.* $55/£35

FAIRCHILD, DAVID. Exploring for Plants. NY, (1930). Frontis, map. (Worn, faded; eps tanned.) *Sutton.* $70/£45

FAIRCHILD, DAVID. Garden Islands of the Great East. NY, 1943. 1st ed. (Upper hinge cracked; spine lt sunned.) *Edwards.* $59/£38

FAIRCHILD, DAVID. The World Grows Round My Door. NY/London, 1947. *Edwards.* $59/£38

FAIRCHILD, DAVID. The World Was My Garden. London, 1947. 1st ed. (Sm dent.) *Edwards.* $59/£38

FAIRCHILD, LUCIUS. California Letters of Lucius Fairchild. WI Hist Soc, 1931. 1st ed. Frontis, 27 plts. Fine. *Oregon.* $50/£32

FAIRCHILD, LUCIUS. California Letters of Lucius Fairchild. Joseph Schafer (ed). Madison: State Hist Soc of WI, 1931. 1st ed. 28 photo plts. Blue cl, gilt (extrems lt worn). Nice. *Shasky.* $45/£29

FAIRCHILD, M. AUGUSTA. Woman and Health: A Mother's Hygienic Hand Book. Quincy, IL, 1890. 1st ed. 384pp. Good. *Fye.* $75/£48

FAIRHOLT, F.W. Costume in England: A History of Dress...til the Close of the Eighteenth Century. London, 1846. xiv,619pp (lt spotting); marbled eps, edges. 1/2 morocco w/marbled bds (sl rubbed; gilt spine faded). *Edwards.* $116/£75

FAIRHOLT, F.W. Gog and Magog. London: James Camden Hotten, 1859. Color frontis, xii,152pp. (Upper hinge sl cracked; chip; lower bd sl soiled; sl rubbed.) *Edwards.* $93/£60

FAIRLIE, GERARD. Captain Bulldog Drummond. London: Hodder & Stoughton, 1945. 1st ed. Inscription, o/w Fine in dj (lt soiled spine). *Mordida.* $75/£48

Fairy Book. GC: Doubleday, Page, 1923. 1st ed thus. 8vo. 11 color plts, 20 dwgs by Arthur Rackham. Dk blue cl, gilt. Color dj (rubbed, edges chipped). *Reisler.* $200/£129

FAKHRY, AHMED. The Pyramids. Chicago: Univ of Chicago Press, 1962. 2nd imp. 2 maps. NF in dj. *Worldwide.* $45/£29

FALCONER, J.D. On Horseback through Nigeria. London, 1911. 1st ed. Fldg map. Teg. Gilt-illus cl (spine faded; mks; extrems sl worn; mainly marginal foxing). *Edwards.* $116/£75

FALCONER, THOMAS. On the Discovery of the Mississippi.... (Austin): Shoal Creek Pub, (1975). Facs ed. Fldg map. Fine. Howes F 16. *Harrington.* $40/£26

FALCONER, WILLIAM. Mushrooms. NY: OJ, 1891. 169,(3)pp + 6pp ads. Orig maroon cl, gilt stamped. Spine lt faded, else VG. *Bohling.* $45/£29

FALCONER, WILLIAM. Observations Respecting the Pulse. 1796. 1st ed. 158pp. 1/2 leather (rubbed). *Fye.* $250/£161

FALCONER, WILLIAM. The Poetical Works. London: William Pickering, 1836. 1st Aldine ed. Uncut, partly unopened. Dk blue cl; paper label. VG (sl rubbed). *Cox.* $31/£20

FALES, MARTHA GANDY. Joseph Richardson and Family, Philadelphia Silversmiths. Middletown: Wesleyan Univ Press, (1974). 1st ed. Frontis. Bkpl; else VG in (sl sunned) dj. *Bookpress.* $110/£71

FALKNER, W.C. Rapid Ramblings in Europe. Phila: Lippincott, 1884. 1st ed. Frontis port, 566pp. Pict blue cl, beveled edges. VG (spine ends worn). *Chapel Hill.* $350/£226

FALLACI, ORIANA. Egotists: 16 Surprising Interviews. Chicago: Regnery, (1968). 1st ed. NF in VG+ dj (price-clipped). *Aka.* $35/£23

FANNING, EDMUND. Voyages and Discoveries in the South Seas 1792-1832. Salem: Marine Research Soc Pub 6, 1924. 1st ed thus. (Lt foxing 1st, last leaves.) Howes F 28. *Lefkowicz.* $95/£61

FANNING, PETE. Great Crimes of the West. SF: by Author, (1929). 1st ed. Frontis. Good. *Lien.* $35/£23

FANTHORPE, U.A. Standing To. Liskeard: Harry Chambers/Peterloo Poets, 1982. Inscribed presentation. NF in wrappers. *Moorhouse.* $23/£15

FARADAY, MICHAEL. A Course of Six Lectures on the Chemical History of a Candle.... William Crookes (ed). NY: Harper & Bros, 1861. 1st Amer ed. 223pp. Blocked in blind, spine gilt-lettered. Fine. *Bickersteth.* $271/£175

FARAGO, LADISLAS. Arabian Antic. NY: Sheridan, 1938. 1st ed. VG in dj (torn). *Worldwide.* $18/£12

FARBER, JAMES. Texas, C.S.A. A Spotlight on Disaster. NY: Jackson Co., (1947). 1st ed. One of 1000 (this copy not signed or numbered as called for). Blue cl. Few pp creased, pencil notes, underlining, else VG in dj (sl worn). *Chapel Hill.* $50/£32

FARINA, RICHARD. Been Down So Long It Looks Like Up to Me. NY: Viking, (1983). 1st ed thus (w/Thomas Pynchon intro). Clbound issue. Fine in dj. *Godot.* $50/£32

FARIS, JOHN T. Old Gardens In and About Philadelphia and Those Who Made Them. Indianapolis: Bobbs-Merrill, (1932). 1st ed. Frontis, 53 illus on plts. Fr hinge internally cracked; foxing; cvr lt worn, else VG. *Bookpress.* $110/£71

FARIS, JOHN T. The Romance of Forgotten Towns. NY: Harper, 1924. 1st ed. Pict cl, silver. VG. *Connolly.* $40/£26

FARISH, THOMAS EDWIN. The Gold Hunters of California. Chicago: M.A. Donohue, 1904. 1st ed. Dec grn cl. NF. Howes F 36. *Harrington.* $125/£81

FARJEON, ELEANOR. Edward Thomas: The Last Four Years. London: OUP, 1958. Grn buckram, gilt spine title. Inscrip, else Fine. *Heller.* $45/£29

FARJEON, ELEANOR. Edward Thomas: The Last Four Years. OUP, 1958. 1st ed. Fine in Fine dj. *Whiteson.* $47/£30

FARJEON, ELEANOR. Kaleidoscope. London: OUP, 1963. 1st thus. Edward Ardizzone (illus). 5.5x8.75. 158pp. Fine in dj. *Cattermole.* $45/£29

FARJEON, ELEANOR. The Little Bookroom. London: OUP, 1955. 1st ed. Edward Ardizzone (illus). 5.5x8.75. 302pp. Fine in dj. *Cattermole.* $75/£48

FARJEON, JEFFERSON. The Complete Smuggler. Indianapolis: Bobbs-Merrill, (1938). 1st ed. VG. *Blue Dragon.* $25/£16

FARLEIGH, JOHN. Engraving on Wood. Dryad Press, 1954. Dec bds. VG. *Moss.* $31/£20

FARLEIGH, JOHN. Engraving on Wood. London, 1954. 1st ed. Pict bds. NF. *Willow House.* $31/£20

FARLEIGH, JOHN. Graven Image: An Autobiobiographical Textbook. London: Macmillan, 1940. Fine (bkpl) in dj; paper bd slipcase w/ engr matching dj. *Heller.* $85/£55

FARLEY, JOHN. The London Art of Cookery, and Housekeeper's Complete Assistant. London: John Barker, 1800. 9th ed. Frontis, xxiv, 12 engr plts, 448pp. New 1/2 speckled calf; gilt. Very Nice. *Cady.* $225/£145

FARLEY, WALTER. The Black Stallion's Filly. NY: Random House, 1952. 1st ed. VG in Good+ dj. *October Farm.* $25/£16

FARLEY, WALTER. The Island Stallion. NY: Random House, 1948. 1st ed. VG in Good dj. *October Farm.* $25/£16

Farm. London: Bancroft, n.d. (195?). 19x23 cm. 4 pull-down panels, 4 dbl-pg pop-ups. N. Dear (illus). Pict wraps, spiral binding. VG. *Book Finders.* $80/£52

FARMAN, ELBERT E. Along the Nile with General Grant. NY: Grafton Press, 1904. 1st ed. 64 plts. Unopened. Rubbed; spine sl frayed; marginal dampstaining few leaves, o/w VG. *Worldwide.* $65/£42

FARMBOROUGH, FLORENCE. Nurse at the Russian Front, A Diary. 1914-18. London, 1974. Good in dj. *Fye.* $40/£26

Farmer's Guide in Hiring and Stocking Farms. (By Arthur Young.) Dublin: Exshaw et al, 1771. 1st Dublin ed. 2 vols. 336; 380pp; 4 figs; 8 engr plts (2 fldg). Contemp calf. VG (hinge sl tender). *Second Life.* $425/£274

Farmer's Instructor; or Every Man His Own Lawyer. Buffalo: Oliver Spafford, 1824. 2nd ed. Contemp calf (worn, stained). Usable. *Boswell.* $150/£97

Farmer's Kalendar.... (By Arthur Young.) London: Robinson et al, 1771. 1st ed. 8vo. 399pp; tp tipped in before 1/2 title. Orig paste paper bds (rubbed). Uncut. Very Nice (spine worn; fr hinge very loose; sigs). *Second Life.* $600/£387

FARMER, PHILIP JOSE. The Adventure of the Peerless Peer by John H. Watson, M.D. Boulder: Aspen Press, 1974. 1st ed. Fine in NF dj (closed tear spine). *Janus.* $45/£29

FARMER, PHILIP JOSE. Behind the Walls of Terra. Huntington Woods: Phantasia, 1982. 1st ltd ed. One of 250 numbered, signed. Map laid in. Fine in dj & slipcase. *Hermitage.* $60/£39

FARMER, PHILIP JOSE. Dark Is the Sun. Granada, 1981. 1st Eng ed. NF in dj. *Temple.* $16/£10

FARMER, PHILIP JOSE. Dayworld. NY: Putnam, (1985). 1st ed. Fine in NF dj. *Other Worlds*. $20/£13

FARMER, PHILIP JOSE. Dayworld. NY, 1985. 1st Amer ed. Signed presentation. Fine in Fine dj. *Polyanthos*. $35/£23

FARMER, PHILIP JOSE. Doc Savage. GC, 1973. 1st ed. VG in dj (sl worn, sm abrasion). *King*. $35/£23

FARMER, PHILIP JOSE. The Fabulous Riverboat. Putnam, 1971. 1st hb ed. Fine in dj. *Madle*. $325/£210

FARMER, PHILIP JOSE. A Feast Unknown. North Hollywood: Essex House, (1969). 1st ed. Sl bumped, sl rubbed, o/w Fine in wrappers. *Levin*. $100/£65

FARMER, PHILIP JOSE. A Feast Unknown. N. Hollywood: Essex House, (1969). Pb orig. Paper wraps. VG (tiny tear; sm crease fr panel). *Antic Hay*. $50/£32

FARMER, PHILIP JOSE. Flesh. London: R&W, 1968. 1st ed. Signed. Fine in dj (lt rubbed). *Else Fine*. $75/£48

FARMER, PHILIP JOSE. The Gates of Creation. NY: Ace, (1966). Pb orig. Ptd wraps. VG. *Antic Hay*. $25/£16

FARMER, PHILIP JOSE. Gods of Riverworld. NY: Putnam's, 1983. 1st ed. Fine in Fine dj. *Revere*. $20/£13

FARMER, PHILIP JOSE. Gods of Riverworld. Phantasia, 1983. 1st ed. One of 650 numbered, signed, boxed. Fine in dj. *Madle*. $50/£32

FARMER, PHILIP JOSE. The Green Odyssey. Ballantine, 1957. 1st ed, 1st bk. Signed. Fine in dj. *Aronovitz*. $1,250/£806

FARMER, PHILIP JOSE. Inside Outside. Boston: Gregg Press, 1980. 1st hb ed. Fine (no dj as issued). *Levin*. $75/£48

FARMER, PHILIP JOSE. Love Song. Dennis McMillan, 1983. 1st hb ed. One of 500 numbered, signed. Fine in dj. *Madle*. $75/£48

FARMER, PHILIP JOSE. Love Song. Macmillan, 1983. 1st hb ed. One of 500 signed. As New in dj. *Aronovitz*. $65/£42

FARMER, PHILIP JOSE. The Lovers. NY: Ballantine, (1961). 1st ed. Pb orig. Ptd wraps. Fine. *Antic Hay*. $30/£19

FARMER, PHILIP JOSE. The Lovers. NY, (1979). 1st hb ed, 1st complete ed. Signed. New in dj. *Mcclintock*. $25/£16

FARMER, PHILIP JOSE. The Maker of Universes. NY: Ace, (1965). Pb orig. Ptd wraps. VG. *Antic Hay*. $25/£16

FARMER, PHILIP JOSE. River of Eternity. HW: Phantasia, 1983. 1st ed, signed, ltd. #150/500. VF in dj, cl slipcase. *Else Fine*. $50/£32

FARMER, PHILIP JOSE. River of Eternity. Phantasia, 1983. 1st ed. One of 500 numbered, signed, boxed. Fine in dj. *Madle*. $35/£23

FARMER, PHILIP JOSE. Tarzan Alive. GC: Doubleday, 1972. 1st ed. Fine (sl bumped) in NF dj (lt soiled). *Between The Covers*. $65/£42

Farmyard Friends with Pop-Up Pictures. England: Birn Bros, n.d. (196?). 23x17 cm. 4 dbl-pg pop-ups. Glazed pict bds. VG. *Book Finders*. $30/£19

FARNHAM, ELIZA W. California, In-Doors and Out. NY: Dix, Edwards, 1856. 1st ed. 506pp + ads. Orig cl (sl rubbed, foxed; bkpl; pasted cvr remnants ep). VG. *Second Life*. $400/£258

FARNHAM, THOMAS. Travels in the Great Western Prairies, the Anahuac and Rocky Mountains, and in the Oregon Territory. 1843. 112pp. Full red morocco (rebound), gilt-stamped. VG. Howes F 50. *Oregon*. $375/£242

FARNSWORTH, DEWEY and EDITH WOOD (eds). Book of Mormon Evidences in Ancient America. Salt Lake City, 1953. Name; used. *King*. $35/£23

FAROVA, ANNA (ed). Andre Kertesz. NY: Paragraphic Books, 1966. 1st ed. Signed presentation. 66 full-pg b/w photos. Pict stiff wrappers. VG. *Cahan*. $150/£97

FARQUAR, GEORGE. The Beaux Stratagem: A Comedy. Bristol: Douglas Cleverdon, 1929. #181/527. 7 copper engrs; teg. Buckram-backed bds (sl soiled). Good. *Cox*. $85/£55

FARQUHAR, FRANCIS P. Exploration of the Sierra Nevada. SF: CA Hist Soc, 1925. Ltd to 270. Inscribed. Fine in ptd wrappers (sl bumped, browned). *Weber*. $200/£129

FARQUHAR, FRANCIS P. History of the Sierra Nevada. Berkeley/L.A., 1965. 1st ed w/errata slip. Cvrs bumped, else Good in dj. *King*. $45/£29

FARQUHAR, FRANCIS P. History of the Sierra Nevada. Berkeley: Univ of CA Press/Sierra Club, 1965. 1st ed. 4to. Color frontis. VG. *Houle*. $75/£48

FARQUHAR, FRANCIS P. Yosemite, the Big Trees and the High Sierra; A Selective Bibliography. Berkeley: Univ of CA Press, 1948. 1st ed. Signed. Engr tp. VG+ in dj (sm restored tears top edge). *Shasky*. $200/£129

FARQUHAR, FRANCIS P. (ed). Ralston-Fry Wedding and the Wedding Journey to Yosemite May 20, 1858. Berkeley: Friends of Bancroft, 1961. 1st ed. Color frontis, color plt. Paper spine label. Fine. *Oregon*. $50/£32

FARQUHAR, FRANCIS P. and MILDRED P. ASHLEY. A List of Publications Relating to the Mountains of Alaska. NY: Amer Alpine Club, 1934. 1st ed. Fine in ptd wrappers. *Weber*. $250/£161

FARQUHAR, GEORGE. The Complete Works.... Charles Stonehill (ed). London: Nonesuch, 1930. One of 900. 2 vols. Buckram-backed bds (spines faded; bumped; paper labels; partly unopened. Good set (edges, eps sl spotted). *Waterfield*. $233/£150

FARQUHAR, GEORGE. The Works.... Ptd for J & J Knapton, G Strahan, et al, 1742. 8th ed. 2 vols. Contemp mottled calf; red morocco lettering pieces (vol 2 lacks pieces). *Waterfield*. $78/£50

FARR, WILLIAM E. and K. ROSS TOOLE. Montana: Images of the Past. Boulder, 1978. 1st ed. NF in dj (sl chipped). *Baade*. $75/£48

FARR, WILLIAM. A Medical Guide to Nice. London, 1841. 1st ed. 177pp. *Fye*. $300/£194

FARRAN, RICHARD M. (Pseud of John Betjeman.) Ground Plan to Skyline. London: Newman Neame, 1960. 1st ed. Fine in wrappers. *Rees*. $70/£45

FARRAR, EMMIE FERGUSON. Old Virginia Houses along the James. NY: Bonanza, (1957). Lower tip chewed, else VG in dj (torn). *Bookpress*. $35/£23

FARRAR, GUY B. The Feathered Folk of an Estuary. London: Country Life, 1938. 1st ed. 32 plts. VG in dj (creased, price-clipped, tape-repaired verso). *Hollett*. $31/£20

FARRAR, MRS. JOHN. The Young Lady's Friend. NY: Samuel S. & William Wood, 1845. Later ed. xi,432pp (foxed). Orig brn blind-emb cl (ends worn, corners showing; bkpl). *Weber*. $45/£29

FARRAR, REGINALD. On the Eaves of the World. London: Edward Arnold, 1926. 'Second Impression.' 2 vols. 64 plts, fldg map. Blue gilt cl. Fine set. *Karmiole.* $125/£81

FARRELL, HENRY. What Ever Happened to Baby Jane? NY: Rinehart, 1960. 1st ed. Fine in NF dj (lt wear; tear spine). *Beasley.* $60/£39

FARRELL, HENRY. What Ever Happened to Baby Jane? NY: Rinehart, 1960. 1st ed. Fine (pgs lt tanned) in dj (corners lt rubbed). *Else Fine.* $65/£42

FARRELL, HENRY. What Ever Happened to Baby Jane? Rinehart, 1960. 1st ed. Fine in VG + dj. *Fine Books.* $70/£45

FARRELL, J.G. The Siege of Krishnapur. London: Weidenfeld & Nichols, 1973. 1st Eng ed. Fine in dj. *Limestone.* $85/£55

FARRELL, J.G. The Siege of Krishnapur. London: Weidenfeld, 1973. 1st UK ed. VG in dj (price-clipped). *Williams.* $56/£36

FARRELL, JACK W. and MIKE PEARSALL. North American Steam Locomotives: The Northerns. Edmonds: Pacific Fast Mail, 1975. 1st ed. Fldg frontis; pict eps. Dec grn cl. Fine in NF dj, VG + slipcase. *Harrington.* $60/£39

FARRELL, JAMES T. Calico Shoes and Other Stories. NY, (1934). Signed presentation. NF (sl sunned, sl rubbed). *Polyanthos.* $125/£81

FARRELL, JAMES T. It Has Come to Pass. NY: Theodor Herzl Press, 1958. 1st ed. NF in dj. *Cahan.* $40/£26

FARRELL, JAMES T. A Misunderstanding. NY: House of Books, 1949. Ltd to 300. Signed. Gilt-stamped cl (brown spots). Glassine dj. *Sadlon.* $50/£32

FARRELL, JAMES T. My Baseball Diary. NY: A.S. Barnes, (1957). 1st ed. Very Nice in dj. *Cady.* $60/£39

FARRELL, JAMES T. My Baseball Diary. Barnes, 1957. 1st ed. Fine in VG dj. *Plapinger.* $50/£32

FARRELL, JAMES T. The Silence of History. NY: Doubleday, 1963. 1st ed. Fine in VG dj (spine lt faded; crease). *Hermitage.* $40/£26

FARRELL, WALTER. A Companion to the Summa. NY: Sheed & Ward, (1956-ca 1960). 4 vols. VG in djs. *Houle.* $275/£177

FARRER, R. In Old Ceylon. London, 1908. 1st ed. 16 plts. Pict gilt cl. Fine. *Henly.* $205/£132

FARRER, REGINALD. The English Rock Garden, with Present Day Rock Garden by Sampson Clay. London, 1948-54. 3 vols. (Owner stamps tps.) Djs. *Henly.* $101/£65

FARRER, REGINALD. The Rainbow Bridge. London: Arnold, 1921. 1st ed. 16 plts; map. VG (lower hinge sl rubbed; spine lt marked; spotting). *Hollett.* $132/£85

FARRER, REGINALD. The Rainbow Bridge. London, 1926. 3rd imp. Map, 16 plts. Fine. *Henly.* $81/£52

FARRINGTON, HARRY WEBB. The Liberty of Lincoln. Bradley Beach, NJ, (1925). 1st ed. Orig cl. NF. *Mcgowan.* $45/£29

FARRINGTON, OLIVER C. Meteorites, Their Structure, Composition, and Terrestrial Relations. Chicago, 1915. Good in grn cl (spine title faded, corners bumped). *Knollwood.* $125/£81

FARRIS, JOHN. The Fury. Playboy Press, 1976. 1st ed. Fine in dj (spine lt worn; sm chip missing). *Stahr.* $35/£23

FARRIS, JOHN. King Windom. Trident Press, 1967. 1st ed. Fine in dj (tope edge lt worn; fr flyleaf fold lt rubbed). *Stahr.* $60/£39

FARRIS, JOHN. King Windom. NY: Trident Press, 1967. 1st ed. Fine in dj (lt wear, soil). *Antic Hay.* $75/£48

FARRIS, JOHN. The Long Light of Dawn. Putnam, 1962. 1st ed. NF in dj (spine sunned). *Stahr.* $45/£29

FARRIS, JOHN. The Long Light of Dawn. Putnam, 1982. 1st ed. Fine in dj (sl soiled). *Madle.* $125/£81

FARROW, G.E. Pixie Pickles. London: Skeffington, (1904). 1st ed. Lg, 4to. 20 full-pg illus by Harry B. Neilson. Cl-backed illus bds (wear, mks; hinges cracked). *Reisler.* $175/£113

FARROW, G.E. The Wallypug at Play. London: Raphael Tuck, (ca 1905). Alan Wright (illus). Folio. Cl-backed illus bds (edgewear). *Reisler.* $750/£484

FARSHLER, EARL. The American Saddle Horse. Louisville, 1934. 2nd ptg. Signed presentation. (Edges worn.) *October Farm.* $58/£37

FARSHLER, EARL. The American Saddle Horse. Louisville: Standard, 1938. 3rd ed. (Spine faded.) *October Farm.* $45/£29

FASSETT, F.G. (ed). The Shipbuilding Business in the United States of America. NY, 1948. 1st ed. 2 vols. *Lefkowicz.* $125/£81

FAST, HOWARD. The American. NY: Duell, Sloan & Pearce, 1947. 1st ed. Fine (sl wear) in NF dj. *Revere.* $50/£32

FAST, HOWARD. Intellectuals in the Fight for Peace. NY: Masses & Mainstream, 1949. 1st ed. NF (few passages underlined) in wraps. *Beasley.* $30/£19

FAST, HOWARD. The Passion of Sacco and Vanzetti. London: Bodley Head, 1954. 1st Eng ed. Red cl. Fine in dj (sl dusty). *Dalian.* $31/£20

FATOUT, PAUL. Mark Twain on the Lecture Circuit. Bloomington: IN Univ, 1960. 1st Amer ed. NF in VG dj. *Agvent.* $45/£29

FAULKNER, WILLIAM et al. The Segregation Decisions Papers Read at a Session of the Twenty-First Annual Meeting of the Southern Historical Association, Memphis, Tennessee, November 10, 1955. Atlanta, 1956. 1st ed, 1st ptg. NF in orig ptd wrappers. *Mcgowan.* $250/£161

FAULKNER, WILLIAM. Absalom, Absalom! C&W, 1936. 1st Eng ed. One of 1750. White cl. Fine (lacks glassine dj). *Fine Books.* $295/£190

FAULKNER, WILLIAM. As I Lay Dying. London: C&W, 1935. 1st Eng ed. NF in VG dj (soiled). *Limestone.* $650/£419

FAULKNER, WILLIAM. Big Woods. NY, (1955). 1st ed. VG in dj (frayed; 1-inch clean tear). *King.* $95/£61

FAULKNER, WILLIAM. Doctor Martino and Other Stories. London: C&W, 1934. 1st Eng ed. NF in VG + dj (lt soiled). *Limestone.* $550/£355

FAULKNER, WILLIAM. A Fable. (NY): Random House, (1954). 1st ed. #360/1000, signed. 8vo. Grey blue cl, beveled edges. NF in glassine dj (edgeworn), pub's slipcase (lt browned). *Chapel Hill.* $650/£419

FAULKNER, WILLIAM. A Fable. NY: Random House, (1954). One of 1000 signed. 2 sm spots, else VG in slipcase (dusty). *Bookpress.* $450/£290

FAULKNER, WILLIAM. A Fable. R-H, 1954. 1st ed. NF in dj. *Fine Books.* $80/£52

FAULKNER, WILLIAM. A Fable. London: Chatto, 1955. 1st UK ed. VG in dj (spine sl faded). *Williams.* $37/£24

FAULKNER, WILLIAM. Father Abraham. NY: Random House, (1983). 1st trade ed. Fine in dj. *Reese*. $30/£19

FAULKNER, WILLIAM. Faulkner's County. C&W, 1955. 1st ed. NF in VG dj (chipping). *Fine Books*. $85/£55

FAULKNER, WILLIAM. Flags in the Dust. NY: Random House, (1973). 1st ed. Fine in Fine dj. *Dermont*. $50/£32

FAULKNER, WILLIAM. Flags in the Dust. Douglas Day (ed). NY: Random House, (1973). 1st ed. Fine in NF dj. *Second Life*. $45/£29

FAULKNER, WILLIAM. Go Down Moses and Other Stories. R-H, 1942. 1st ed. Fine in NF dj. *Fine Books*. $450/£290

FAULKNER, WILLIAM. Go Down Moses and Other Stories. London: C&W, 1942. 1st Eng ed. Spot on fore edge, else Fine in NF dj (lacks rear flap). *Limestone*. $300/£194

FAULKNER, WILLIAM. A Green Bough. NY: Harrison Smith & Robert Haas, 1933. 1st ed. #30/350 (of 360) signed. 8vo. Wood-engr frontis, tailpiece, 2 mtd wood engrs upper cvr by Lynd Ward. Grey linen. Upper cvr, spine sl dknd, o/w Fine. *Cummins*. $750/£484

FAULKNER, WILLIAM. A Green Bough. NY: Smith & Haas, 1933. One of 360 numbered, signed. NF (bottom corner sl bumped; spine, bd edges sl tanned). *Between The Covers*. $950/£613

FAULKNER, WILLIAM. The Hamlet. NY: Random House, 1940. 1st ed. #217/250 specially bound, signed. 8vo. Teg. 1/2 grn cl, paper-cvrd bds. Fine (edges sl faded) in orig glassine dj. *Chapel Hill*. $3,200/£2,065

FAULKNER, WILLIAM. The Hamlet. R-H, 1940. 1st ed. #45/250 signed. VG+. *Fine Books*. $1,675/£1,081

FAULKNER, WILLIAM. Hunting Stories. NY: LEC, 1988. 1/850 numbered, signed by Neil Welliver (illus). 1/4 grn morocco. VG in cl box. *Argosy*. $500/£323

FAULKNER, WILLIAM. Idylls of the Desert. NY: Random House, 1931. #379/400, signed. Marbled bds, title label. Issued w/o dj. VG. *Schoyer*. $700/£452

FAULKNER, WILLIAM. Intruder in the Dust. NY, (1948). 1st ed. Sm spot fep, bumped, else Good in dj (chipped, soiled, sl torn, tape-reinforced on reverse). *King*. $95/£61

FAULKNER, WILLIAM. Knight's Gambit. NY: Random House, (1949). 1st ed. Fine in dj. *Jaffe*. $250/£161

FAULKNER, WILLIAM. Light in August. NY: Harrison Smith & Robert Haas, (1932). 1st ed, 1st ptg. 8vo. Cream buckram lettered in orange/blue. VG in dj (2 sm chips, spine sl faded). *Cummins*. $600/£387

FAULKNER, WILLIAM. Light in August. (NY): Harrison Smith & Robert Haas, (1932). 1st ed. 8vo. Tan cl stamped in orange/blue. Fine in ptd dj (lt wear, few closed tears repaired on verso); VG orig glassine dj (edge chips). *Chapel Hill*. $900/£581

FAULKNER, WILLIAM. Light in August. Smith & Haas, 1932. 1st ed. NF in VG dj (lt chipping). *Fine Books*. $495/£319

FAULKNER, WILLIAM. Light in August. London: C&W, 1933. 1st (UK) ed. (Sl foxed; backstrip faded; sl grubby.) *Petersfield*. $78/£50

FAULKNER, WILLIAM. The Mansion. NY: Random House, (1959). 1st ed. Fine in VG dj (price-clipped; edges sl worn). *Bernard*. $75/£48

FAULKNER, WILLIAM. The Mansion. London: C&W, 1961. 1st British ed. Fine in dj (lt soiled). *Glenn*. $85/£55

FAULKNER, WILLIAM. The Mansion. C&W, 1961. 1st UK ed. Dj (sm tears). *Edwards*. $39/£25

FAULKNER, WILLIAM. Mirrors of Chartres Street. Minneapolis: Faulkner Studies, (1953). 1st ed. One of 1000 numbered. VF in dj. *Jaffe*. $350/£226

FAULKNER, WILLIAM. Mosquitoes. NY: Boni & Liveright, 1927. 1st ed. One of 3047. 8vo. Blue cl (spine lettering sl rubbed). Fine in 1st issue dj w/'mosquitoes' design (lt rubbed, soiled). *Chapel Hill*. $3,200/£2,065

FAULKNER, WILLIAM. Mosquitoes. C&W, 1964. 1st Eng ed. NF in dj. *Fine Books*. $85/£55

FAULKNER, WILLIAM. New Orleans Sketches. S&J, 1959. 1st Eng ed. Lt foxing, else NF in VG+ dj. *Fine Books*. $65/£42

FAULKNER, WILLIAM. Pylon. NY: Harrison Smith & Robert Haas, 1935. 1st ed. 8vo. Blue cl. NF in Nice pict dj (chips). *Chapel Hill*. $550/£355

FAULKNER, WILLIAM. Pylon. NY: Smith & Haas, 1935. 1st ed. #27/300 'for sale' from special ed of 310, numbered, signed. 8vo. 3/4 blue cl, silver bds (spine sl faded); top edge silver; uncut. VG. *Houle*. $1,350/£871

FAULKNER, WILLIAM. The Reivers. NY: Random House, (1962). 1st ed. Gilt-stamped cl. VG in dj (sl rubbed, creased; sl waterstain to rear panel). *Sadlon*. $50/£32

FAULKNER, WILLIAM. The Reivers. NY: Random House, (1962). 1st ed. #127/500 signed. 8vo. Maroon cl. Fine. *Cummins*. $650/£419

FAULKNER, WILLIAM. The Reivers. NY: Random House, 1962. 1st ed. Fine in dj. *Cahan*. $50/£32

FAULKNER, WILLIAM. The Reivers. London: C&W, 1962. 1st Eng ed. Fine in dj. *Hermitage*. $50/£32

FAULKNER, WILLIAM. Requiem for a Nun. NY: Random House, (1951). 1st ed. #643/750 specially bound, signed. 8vo. Half black cl, marbled bds. Sl worn, else Fine in Fine acetate dj (chip). *Chapel Hill*. $600/£387

FAULKNER, WILLIAM. Requiem for a Nun. NY: Random House, (1959). Rev copy w/slip tipped to fep. Paper-cvrd bds. VG (sm ink stamp) in dj (soiled; nicks; 2 internally repaired tears). *Antic Hay*. $75/£48

FAULKNER, WILLIAM. Requiem for a Nun. R-H, 1951. 1st ed. NF in dj. *Fine Books*. $135/£87

FAULKNER, WILLIAM. Requiem for a Nun. London: Chatto, 1953. 1st UK ed. VG+ in dj (tiny stains rear panel; closed tears). *Williams*. $39/£25

FAULKNER, WILLIAM. Salmagundi...and a Poem by Ernest M. Hemingway. Milwaukee: Casanova Press, 1932. 1st ed. One of 525 numbered. Neat bkpl, else Very Nice in stiff ptd wrappers, slipcase (worn, cracked). *Reese*. $550/£355

FAULKNER, WILLIAM. Sanctuary. NY: Cape & Smith, (1931). 1st ed. Nice (w/o dj). *Reese*. $85/£55

FAULKNER, WILLIAM. Sanctuary. NY: Jonathan Cape & Harrison Smith, (1931). 1st ed. 8vo. Burgundy paper bds, grey cl spine lettered in red. Fine in dj (spine head, foot sl chipped; sl soiled; spine sl faded). *Cummins*. $1,500/£968

FAULKNER, WILLIAM. Sanctuary. NY: Jonathan Cape & Harrison Smith, (1931). 8vo. 1st ed. 1st binding state, w/magenta eps, grey pattern. Magenta bd, grey cl spine. Fine in dj (two short clean tears head, tail jacket spine archivally reinforced verso). *Chapel Hill*. $3,500/£2,258

FAULKNER, WILLIAM. Sanctuary. London: C&W, 1931. 1st (UK) ed. (Backstrip faded, torn; repaired tear fr cvr.) *Petersfield.* $65/£42

FAULKNER, WILLIAM. Sanctuary. London: C&W, 1931. 1st Eng ed. 1st binding (later issued in bright red cl stamped in black). One of 2000. Orig rose cl stamped in gilt. VG in Good dj (browned, chipped spine ends, separated along both spine folds). *Chapel Hill.* $350/£226

FAULKNER, WILLIAM. Sartoris. NY: Harcourt, Brace, (1929). 1st ed. 8vo. Black cl stamped in orange. Fine in NF dj (chipping head spine). *Chapel Hill.* $3,600/£2,323

FAULKNER, WILLIAM. Selected Letters of William Faulkner. Joseph Blotner (ed). NY: Random House, (1977). 1st trade ed. Tan bds, burgundy cl spine. Rmdr mk top edge, else Fine in NF dj. *Chapel Hill.* $35/£23

FAULKNER, WILLIAM. Soldier's Pay. London: C&W, 1930. 1st Eng ed. NF (cl sl soiled). *Blue Mountain.* $125/£81

FAULKNER, WILLIAM. The Sound and the Fury. NY: Jonathan Cape & Harrison Smith, (1929). 1st ed. 8vo. Patterned bds, white cl spine (inner hinges repaired) in facs dj. *Chapel Hill.* $500/£323

FAULKNER, WILLIAM. The Sound and the Fury. London: C&W, 1931. 1st (UK) ed. (Sl foxed; backstrip faded; sl rubbed.) *Petersfield.* $93/£60

FAULKNER, WILLIAM. The Sound and the Fury. Chatto, 1931. 1st ed. Good. *Whiteson.* $31/£20

FAULKNER, WILLIAM. These Thirteen Stories. London: C&W, 1933. 1st (UK) ed. (Sl foxed; backstrip faded; sl mkd.) *Petersfield.* $62/£40

FAULKNER, WILLIAM. These Thirteen Stories. London: C&W, 1933. 1st Eng ed. Blue cl, gilt. Top edges grn. NF in VG dj (lt chipped). *Limestone.* $600/£387

FAULKNER, WILLIAM. The Town. NY: Random House, (1957). 1st ed. NF in 1st issue dj w/'5/57' on fr flap (lt soiled). *Chapel Hill.* $100/£65

FAULKNER, WILLIAM. The Town. NY, (1957). 1st issue. VG (inscrip) in Good+ 1st issue dj (chipped). *Fuller & Saunders.* $25/£16

FAULKNER, WILLIAM. The Town. R-H, 1957. 1st ed. NF in NF dj. *Fine Books.* $55/£35

FAULKNER, WILLIAM. The Town. NY: Random House, 1957. 1st ed. Fine in dj (extrems sl nicked). *Second Life.* $75/£48

FAULKNER, WILLIAM. The Town. London: C&W, 1958. 1st Eng ed. NF in dj. *Limestone.* $85/£55

FAULKNER, WILLIAM. The Town. C&W, 1958. 1st UK ed. Fine in dj. *Lewton.* $43/£28

FAULKNER, WILLIAM. Uncollected Stories of.... Joseph Blotner (ed). NY: Random House, (1979). 1st ed. Fine in dj. *Second Life.* $45/£29

FAULKNER, WILLIAM. The Unvanquished. NY: Random House, (1938). 1st ed, 1st ptg. Grey cl stamped in black/red. VF in dj. *Macdonnell.* $800/£516

FAULKNER, WILLIAM. The Unvanquished. NY: Random House, (1938). 1st ed. #150/250 specially bound, signed. Edward Shenton (illus). 8vo. Teg. Patterned bds, red cl spine. NF (inner gutters sl browned); no dj or slipcase as issued. *Chapel Hill.* $2,500/£1,613

FAULKNER, WILLIAM. The Unvanquished. NY: Random House, (1938). 1st ed. One of 250 signed. VF in orig glassine dj (sl torn); cl fldg box. *Jaffe.* $3,500/£2,258

FAULKNER, WILLIAM. The Unvanquished. NY: Random House, 1938. 1st ed. #223/250 signed. 8vo. Teg. Ptd paper bds, burgundy buckram spine. Fine. *Cummins.* $1,250/£806

FAULKNER, WILLIAM. The Unvanquished. NY: Random House, 1938. One of 250 numbered, signed. Nice (spine sl faded) w/o dj or slipcase, as issued. *Lame Duck.* $2,500/£1,613

FAULKNER, WILLIAM. The Wild Palms. NY: Random House, (1939). 1st ed. #193/250 specially bound, signed. Also signed by Harold Arlen. 8vo. Teg. Fine in orig glassine dj. *Chapel Hill.* $2,250/£1,452

FAULKNER, WILLIAM. The Wild Palms. NY: Random House, (1939). 1st trade ed. 8vo. Tan cl. Fine (sl wear spine crown) in dj (lt rubbed spine ends). *Chapel Hill.* $550/£355

FAULKNER-HORNE, SHIRLEY. Pat and Her Polo Pony. London: Country Life, 1939. 1st ed. VG. *October Farm.* $25/£16

FAUNTLEROY, A.M. Report on the Medico-Military Aspects of the European War From Observations.... Washington, 1915. 1st ed. Good. *Fye.* $150/£97

FAURE, GABRIEL. The Gardens of Rome. Frank Kemp (trans). London: Medici Soc, (1926). 14 watercolors tipped in. Teg. Fine. *Quest.* $150/£97

FAUST, ALBERT B. German Element in the United States. Boston, 1909. 2 vols. (Cl worn.) *Ginsberg.* $75/£48

FAUST, IRVIN. Roar Lion Roar. NY: Random House, (1964). 1st ed. VG (lt soil) in dj (sl wear). *Antic Hay.* $35/£23

FAVOUR, ALPHEUS H. Old Bill Williams Mountain Man. Norman: Univ of OK, (1962). Pub's grn cl. Fine in dj. *Laurie.* $40/£26

FAWCETT, HENRY. Pauperism: Its Causes and Remedies. London: Macmillan, 1871. Cl worn, foxing, but Nice. *Boswell.* $125/£81

FAWKES, F.A. Horticultural Buildings. London: Batsford, n.d. (1881). 1st ed. Frontis; (ii),ii,255,(1),xvii pp. Pub's cl. Sl rubbing spine; pencil inscrip, else VG. *Bookpress.* $385/£248

FAWLEY, W. Shuddering Castle. Macaulay-Green Circle, 1936. 1st ed. NF in VG+ pict dj. *Aronovitz.* $65/£42

FAY, BERNARD. Revolution and Freemasonry 1680-1800. Boston: Little, Brown, 1935. 1st ed. Frontis. VG. *Blue Dragon.* $35/£23

FAY, CHARLES EDEY. Mary Celeste. The Odyssey of an Abandoned Ship. Salem: Peabody Museum, 1942. 1st ed. One of 850 numbered. VG in pub's box. *Lefkowicz.* $125/£81

FAZAKAS, RAY. The Donnelly Album. Canada: Macmillan, (1977). 1st ed. VG in Good+ dj. *Oregon.* $40/£26

FEA, ALLAN. The Real Captain Cleveland. London: Martin Secker, (1912). Good. *Cullen.* $60/£39

FEARING, KENNETH. Angel Arms. NY: Coward McCann, 1929. 1st ed, 1st bk. Very Nice (spine worn) in dj (spine sl used). *Reese.* $125/£81

FEARING, KENNETH. Clark Gifford's Body. NY: Random, 1942. 1st ed. Fine in pict dj (lt wear spine top). *Else Fine.* $65/£42

FEARING, KENNETH. Stranger at Coney Island and Other Poems. NY: Harcourt, Brace, (1948). 1st ed. NF. *Sadlon.* $15/£10

FEARN, JOHN RUSSELL. The Amazon Strikes Again. London, 1954. 1st ed. Fine in dj (sl frayed). *Madle.* $40/£26

FEARN, JOHN RUSSELL. Golden Amazon's Triumph. London, 1953. 1st ed. Fine in dj (sl frayed). *Madle.* $40/£26

FEARN, JOHN RUSSELL. Liners of Time. London, 1947. 1st ed. Fine in dj (sl nicked). *Madle.* $40/£26

FEATHER, LEONARD. From Satchmo to Miles. NY: Stein & Day, 1972. 1st ed. Fine in dj (lt used). *Beasley.* $35/£23

FEATHERSTONAUGH, G.W. A Canoe Voyage Up the Minnay Sotor. London, 1847. 1st ed. 2 vols. 2 maps, 2 plts. Orig cl. Howes F 67. *Ginsberg.* $850/£548

FEAVER, WILLIAM. Masters of Caricature. Knopf, 1981. 1st ed. Fine in Fine dj. *Bishop.* $37/£24

FEDER, STUART et al (eds). Psychoanalytic Explorations in Music. Madison, CT: IUP, (1990). 1st ed. Black cl. VG. *Gach.* $40/£26

FEHLANDT, AUGUST. A Century of Drink Reform in the United States. Cincinnati, 1904. 1st ed. Good. *Fye.* $50/£32

FEIBUSCH, HANS. Mural Painting. London, 1946. 1st ed. Prelims lt browned. Dj (tape repaired). *Edwards.* $47/£30

FEIFFER, JULES. Passionella and Other Stories. NY: McGraw-Hill, (1959). 1st ed. VG in pict stiff wrappers (sticker residue rear). *Reese.* $25/£16

FEILER, SEYMOUR (ed). Jean-Bernard Bossu's Travels in the Interior of North America 1751-1762. Norman, 1962. 1st ed. (Sig, date; lower cvr corners sl bumped), o/w Fine in dj (sl edgeworn). Howes B 626. *Baade.* $50/£32

FEININGER, ANDREAS. The Face of New York. NY: Crown, (1954). 1st ed. Signed. Fine in dj (lt shelfworn, nicks). *Reese.* $55/£35

FEININGER, ANDREAS. The Face of New York. Crown, 1954. 1st ed. Signed. VG+ in VG+ dj. *Bishop.* $50/£32

FEIST, RAYMOND E. Magician. GC: Doubleday, 1982. 1st ed, inscribed. NF in dj (lt wear). *Other Worlds.* $175/£113

FEITZ, LELAND. Myers Avenue. Colorado Springs, 1967. 1st ed. Pict wraps. Fine. *Baade.* $17/£11

FELD, CHARLES. Picasso, His Recent Drawings 1966-1968. NY, (1969). Pict cl. Name, sl frayed, else Good in glassine dj (dknd, sm tear). *King.* $95/£61

FELD, CHARLES. Picasso, His Recent Drawings, 1966-1968. NY: Abrams, n.d. (ca 1977). 1st ed. Fine in orig glassine dj (yellowed). *Hermitage.* $65/£42

FELDMAN, GENE and MAX GARTENBERG (eds). The Beat Generation and The Angry Young Man. NY: Citadel, 1958. 1st ed. Fine in NF dj (sm chips). *Beasley.* $60/£39

FELL, H. GRANVILLE. The Art of H. Davis Richter. Benfleet, 1935. 1st ed. Tipped-in color frontis, 44 plts (20 color). (Ex-lib; rebound.) *Edwards.* $39/£25

FELLINI, FEDERICO. Fellini on Fellini. (NY): Delacorte, (1976). 1st Amer ed. Fine in dj (2 short tears). *Between The Covers.* $50/£32

FELLOW, R. (Pseud of H. Scudder.) The Game of Croquet; Its Appointment and Laws. NY, 1868. New ed. 48pp. Pub's limp grn cl, fr cvr gilt dec, back cvr blind-tooled (sm stain, fraying lower right corner). Fine+. *D & D.* $590/£381

FELLOWES, P.F.M. et al. First Over Everest! NY, 1934. 1st ed. VG in dj (chipped). *King.* $75/£48

FELSTEAD, SIDNEY THEODORE. Sir Richard Muir, A Memoir.... London: John Lane, Bodley Head, 1927. *Boswell.* $50/£32

FELTON, MRS. Life in America. Hull: Hutchinson, 1838. 1st ed. 129pp; 2-pg map. Aeg. Pub's cl (fr hinge repaired). VG (sl foxing). *Second Life.* $350/£226

FENICHEL, OTTO. The Collected Papers of.... NY: Norton, (1953, 1954). Later ptgs. 2 vols. Grn cl. VG set (sm tear crown of vol 2). *Gach.* $40/£26

FENN, G.M. (ed). The Khedive's Country. London, 1904. (Lt spotted; 1/2-inch spine tear.) *Sutton.* $36/£23

FENN, JOHN (ed). Paston Letters. London, 1787-1789-1823. 1st eds. 5 vols. Add'l title w/vignette each vol, 46 engr plts (5 hand-colored). Uniformly bound in early 19th cent calf, matching spines gilt, red morocco labels (1st 4 vols rebacked). Nice set. *Bickersteth.* $698/£450

FENNER, BALL. Raising the Veil; or, Scenes in the Courts. Boston: James French & Co, 1856. Emb cl (chipped, worn). *Boswell.* $225/£145

FENOLLOSA, ERNEST F. Epochs of Chinese and Japanese Art. NY: Frederick A. Stokes, (1913). 2nd ed. (Sig sprung vol 1; all hinges internally cracked; sunned, rubbed, lt foxing.) *Bookpress.* $150/£97

FENOLLOSA, ERNEST F. Epochs of Chinese and Japanese Art. London: Heinemann, 1912. 1st ed. Frontispiece. Cvrs sl sunned, minor edgewear, bkpls, tips worn; else VG. *Bookpress.* $175/£113

FENSKA, RICHARD R. The Complete Modern Tree Experts Manual. NY, 1964. Good. *Brooks.* $29/£19

FENTON, JAMES. Children in Exile. Salamander, 1983. 1st ed. Fine in orig transparent dj. *Poetry.* $19/£12

FENTON, JAMES. Children in Exile. Salamander Press, 1983. 1st ed. NF in glassine dj. *Rees.* $39/£25

FENTON, JAMES. Dead Soldiers. Sycamore Press, 1981. One of 400. VG in orig wraps. *Edrich.* $39/£25

FENTON, JAMES. The Memory of War. Poems 1968-82. London, 1982. Ltd to 3000. VG in dj. *Edrich.* $25/£16

FENTON, REGINALD. Peculiar People in a Pleasant Land. Girard, KS: Pretoria Pub Co, 1905. 1st ed. Frontis port. VG (sm nick fr cover, t.p.) in dec wrappers. *Connolly.* $65/£42

FENTON, ROBERT W. The Big Swingers. Englewood Cliffs, NJ, (1967). 1st ed. VG in dj (worn, soiled, sticker removed). *King.* $25/£16

FENTON, ROBERT W. The Big Swingers. Prentice-Hall, 1967. 1st ed. Fine in dj (sl rubbed). *Madle.* $40/£26

FERBER, EDNA. Buttered Side Down. NY: Frederick A. Stokes, (1912). 1st ed. Color frontis. Fine. *Hermitage.* $40/£26

FERBER, EDNA. Giant. NY: Doubleday, 1952. 1st ed. Bkseller label, else Fine in dj (price-clipped; lt worn). *Hermitage.* $45/£29

FERBER, EDNA. Saratoga Trunk. GC: Doubleday, Doran & Co, 1941. One of 562 numbered, signed. Blue cl. Fine in pub's slipcase. *Dermont.* $150/£97

FERBER, EDNA. Show Boat. NY: Doubleday, Doran, 1926. 1st trade ed. Yellow cl. Fine (w/o dj). *Macdonnell.* $35/£23

FERGUSON, ALBERT. Orthopedic Surgery in Infancy and Childhood. Balt, 1957. 1st ed. Good. *Fye.* $100/£65

FERGUSON, CHARLES. California Gold Fields. Biobooks, 1948. 1st thus. Ltd to 750 ptd. VG. *Oregon.* $40/£26

FERGUSON, HENRY LEE. English Springer Spaniel in America. NY: Derrydale, 1932. 1st ed. Ltd to 850. Spine ends rubbed, bkpl, else NF. *Cahan.* $85/£55

FERGUSON, JAMES. Astronomy Explained Upon Sir Isaac Newton's Principles.... London: W. Strahan et al, 1770. 4th ed. Fldg frontis, 17 fldg plts. Good in full leather (worn, spotted, scraped; rebacked; new eps), orig red leather spine label laid down, raised bands. *Knollwood.* $600/£387

FERGUSSON, ALEXANDER (ed). Letters and Journals of Mrs. Calderwood of Polton. Edinburgh: David Douglas, 1884. 1st ed. lviii,386pp. Contemp 1/2 grn morocco. Edges sl spotted; tp smudged, else VG. *Bookpress.* $185/£119

FERGUSSON, ERNA. Murder and Mystery in New Mexico. Albuquerque: Merle Armitage Editions, (1948). 1st ed. VG in dj. *Schoyer.* $50/£32

FERGUSSON, JAMES. History of Indian and Eastern Architecture. London, 1876. xviii,756pp (edges, some text foxed; feps foxed, intruding onto prelims, rear pp). Teg. Morocco-backed cl (ex-libris; lower bd sl soiled; chipped; spine faded, sl scratched; upper joint splitting; lower joint wormed). *Edwards.* $78/£50

FERGUSSON, W.N. Adventure Sport and Travel on the Tibetan Steppes. London: Constable, 1911. 2 maps. Grn pict cl, gilt (foxing). *Petersfield.* $194/£125

FERMI, ENRICO. Elementary Particles. London: OUP, 1951. VG. *Argosy.* $75/£48

FERMI, ENRICO. Thermodynamics. NY, 1937. 1st ed. Ex-lib. *Argosy.* $350/£226

FERMOR, PATRICK LEIGH. Between the Woods and the Water. London, 1986. 1st ed. Signed. Dbl-pg map. Dj. *Edwards.* $70/£45

FERMOR, PATRICK LEIGH. Between the Woods and the Water. John Murray, 1986. 1st Eng ed. Blue cl. VF in dj. *Dalian.* $54/£35

FERMOR, PATRICK LEIGH. Mani. London, 1958. 1st ed. Frontis. Dj (chipped w/loss). *Edwards.* $54/£35

FERMOR, PATRICK LEIGH. Mani. London: John Murray, 1958. 1st ed. VG in dj (sl browned, sl creased). *Virgo.* $54/£35

FERMOR, PATRICK LEIGH. Roumeli. NY: Harper & Row, (1966). 1st Amer ed. VG in dj (price-clipped). *Schoyer.* $30/£19

FERMOR, PATRICK LEIGH. Roumeli. London, 1966. 1st ed. Dbl-pg map. Dj (sl worn). *Edwards.* $54/£35

FERMOR, PATRICK LEIGH. Roumeli. John Murray, 1966. 1st Eng ed. Blue cl. VF in Fine dj. *Dalian.* $101/£65

FERMOR, PATRICK LEIGH. A Time to Keep Silence. London, 1957. 1st trade ed. Dj (chipped w/loss). *Edwards.* $39/£25

FERNIE, F. Dry-Fly Fishing in Border Waters. London: Black, 1912. 1st ed. 2 plts. Fine in VG dj. *Bowman.* $45/£29

FERNOW, BERTHOLD. The Ohio Valley in Colonial Days. Albany, 1890. 1st ed. 299pp. Uncut, unopened. VG (lt chipping at extrems). Howes F 92. *Oregon.* $125/£81

FERRANDINO, JOSEPH. Firefight. NY: Soho, (1987). Fine in NF dj. *Aka.* $35/£23

FERRARS, ELIZABETH. In at the Kill. London: Collins, 1978. 1st ed. Fine in dj (internally reinforced). *Janus.* $25/£16

FERRARS, ELIZABETH. Murders Anonymous. London: Collins, 1977. 1st ed. NF in NF dj (price-clipped). *Ming.* $39/£25

FERRARS, ELIZABETH. No Peace for the Wicked. London: Collins, 1966. 1st ed. NF in NF dj (internally reinforced). *Janus.* $25/£16

FERRARS, ELIZABETH. The Pretty Pink Shroud. London: Collins, 1977. 1st ed. NF in NF dj. *Ming.* $39/£25

FERRARS, ELIZABETH. Witness Before the Fact. London: Collins, 1979. 1st ed. NF in NF dj. *Ming.* $31/£20

FERREE, BARR. American Estates and Gardens. NY: Munn, 1904. Pict cl. VG. *Schoyer.* $275/£177

FERRELL, MALLORY HOPE. Silver San Juan: The Rio Grande Southern Railroad. Boulder: Pruett Pub Co, (1973). (1st ed). 7 color plts, fldg pocket map. Fine in dj (lt edgeworn). *Bohling.* $75/£48

FERRELL, PAUL. Michigan Mossback, from Green Pine Woods and Logging Roads to Big City Rackets. Minneapolis: By Author, 1938. Good. *Peninsula.* $55/£35

FERREY, BENJAMIN. Recollections of N. Welby Pugin and His Father...With Notices of Their Works. London: Edward Stanford, 1861. 1st ed. Frontis; xv,(i),473,(1)pp; 7 plts. Pub's blue blindstamped cl. Lt cvr wear; sig; foxing on early, later leaves, else VG. *Bookpress.* $385/£248

FERRIAR, JOHN. An Essay Towards a Theory of Apparitions. London: J & J Haddock, 1813. 1st ed. 8vo. (2),x,(2),(13)-139pp. 1/4 calf, leatherette w/spine lettered in gilt; marbled eps; teg; uncut. Foxed; lt soiled, o/w VG. *Laurie.* $275/£177

FERRIDAY, PETER. Victorian Architecture. Phila: Lippincott, 1964. 1st ed. 97 illus on plts. Cvrs lt rubbed, else Fine. *Bookpress.* $45/£29

FERRIS, WARREN ANGUS. Life in the Rocky Mountains, 1830-1835. Salt Lake City: Rocky Mountain Book Shop, (1940). 2 plts, fldg map. Brn cl (lt stain). Overall very clean. Howes F 100. *Schoyer.* $125/£81

FERRIS, WARREN ANGUS. Life in the Rocky Mountains, 1830-1835. Salt Lake City, (1940). 3 plts, fldg map. VG. Howes F 100. *Oregon.* $165/£106

FERRIS, WARREN ANGUS. Life in the Rocky Mountains. Denver: Fred A. Rosenstock, 1983. Fldg facs map in rear pocket. Plastic cvr guard. Fine. *Laurie.* $75/£48

FERRIS, WARREN ANGUS. Life in the Rocky Mountains. LeRoy Hafen (ed). Denver: Old West, 1983. Rev ed. Frontis; fldg map in pocket. VF. Howes F 100. *Oregon.* $35/£23

FERRIS, WARREN ANGUS. Life in the Rocky Mountains: A Diary of Wanderings.... Paul C. Phillips (ed). Denver: Old West Pub Co, 1940. 1st bk ed. 2 maps (1 fldg), 3 facs plts. Red cl. Fine (spine gilt sl worn) in VG+ dj (sl chipped, evenly soiled). Howes F 100. *Harrington.* $325/£210

FERRISS, HUGH. The Metropolis of Tomorrow. NY: Ives Washburn, 1929. 1st ed. Frontis. Cvrs sl rubbed; rubberstamp fep, tp, else VG. *Bookpress.* $235/£152

FESSIER, M. Fully Dressed and in His Right Mind. Gollancz, 1935. 1st Eng ed, 1st bk. NF in VG dj (lt dust soil; price neatly excised from spine). *Fine Books.* $95/£61

FEVAL, PAUL. (Pseud of H. Bedford-Jones.) Salute to Cyrano. Longmans, 1931. 1st ed. Fine in dj (sl chipped). *Madle*. $40/£26

FEWKES, JESSE WALTER. Antiquities of the Mesa Verde National Park: Cliff Palace. Washington: GPO, 1911. 1st ed. Fldg plan. Grn cl (spine dknd, corners sl bumped). Internally Fine; overall VG +. *Harrington*. $45/£29

FEWKES, JESSE WALTER. BAE Bulletin 41. Antiquities of the Mesa Verde National Park. Spruce Tree House. Washington: GPO, 1909. 1st ed. 21 plts. Red calf over red cl; gilt spine (sl rubbed). *Karmiole*. $45/£29

FEWKES, JESSE WALTER. BAE Bulletin 50. Preliminary Report on a Visit to the Navaho National Monument, Arizona. Washington: GPO, 1911. Fine. *Perier*. $20/£13

FEWKES, JESSE WALTER. BAE Bulletin 51. Antiquities of the Mesa Verde National Palace Cliff Place. Washington: GPO, 1916. Fine. *Perier*. $20/£13

FEYNMAN, RICHARD. The Character of Physical Law. London: BBC, 1965. 1st ed. Name fr pastedown, else NF in dj (sl extrem wear). *Lame Duck*. $65/£42

FIALA, ANTHONY. Fighting the Polar Ice. NY: Doubleday, Doran, 1907. 2nd ed. Fldg map. Orig cl, teg. VG. *High Latitude*. $95/£61

FIDDLE, SEYMOUR. Portraits from a Shooting Gallery. NY: Harper, 1967. 1st ed. Fine in Fine dj. *Beasley*. $35/£23

FIDLER, ISAAC. Observations on Professions...and Emigration in the United States and Canada...in 1832.... NY: J&J Harper, 1833. 1st Amer ed. 247pp+ads. Good (margins, text water stained; rebacked, orig cl laid down; worn, mkd; label stained). *Hermitage*. $150/£97

FIEBER, FRIEDRICH. The Treatment of Nervous Diseases by Electricity. George M. Schweig (trans). NY, 1874. 1st ed in English. 64pp. (Ex-lib; fep loose.) *Argosy*. $100/£65

FIELD, EDWARD. Revolutionary Defences in Rhode Island: A Historical Account.... Providence: Preston & Rounds, 1896. 1st ed. xvi,161,(1 blank, 10 ads)pp. (Inner hinges weak.) *Lefkowicz*. $75/£48

FIELD, EUGENE. The Gingham Dog and the Calico Cat. Newark: Charles E. Graham, (1926). 4to. Pict paper over cl bds, orange spine. VG (edges, corners lt worn) in VG dj (lt torn). *Davidson*. $200/£129

FIELD, EUGENE. How One Friar Met the Devil and Two Pursued Him. Chicago: F.M. Morris, 1900. 1st ed. One of 300. Dec initial caps. Gilt-titled leather emblem inset. NF. BAL 5782. *Cahan*. $135/£87

FIELD, EUGENE. The Love Affairs of a Bibliomaniac. NY: Scribner's, 1896. 1st ed, 2nd state. Gilt-stamped cl; teg (dknd, sl rubbed; fr inner hinge strengthened w/book tape). BAL 5771. *Sadlon*. $20/£13

FIELD, EUGENE. Nonsense for Old and Young. Boston, 1901. 1st ed thus. Dec cl. VG. *Bond*. $25/£16

FIELD, EUGENE. Poems of Childhood. London: John Lane, 1904. 1st Eng ed. 4to. 8 full-pg color plts by Maxfield Parrish. Lobster eps; teg. Red cl, gold lettering, decs. Good in ptd dj (edge chips). *Reisler*. $775/£500

FIELD, EUGENE. Verse and Prose. Henry A. Smith (ed). Boston: Bibliophile Soc, 1917. 1st ed. Port. Japan vellum spine, corners; cl sides; gilt. Lt soiled; bkpl, else Fine. *Hermitage*. $75/£48

FIELD, HENRY. Arabs of Central Iraq. Berthold Laufer (ed). Chicago, 1935. 156 plts; 3 maps. (Crudely re-backed w/orig upper wrapper mtd.) *Argosy*. $275/£177

FIELD, HORACE and MICHAEL BUNNEY. English Domestic Architecture. London, 1905. 118 plts. (Margins sl thumbed.) Teg, rest uncut. 2-tone cl (hinges repaired; sl soiled, rubbed). *Edwards*. $116/£75

FIELD, ISOBEL. This Life I've Lived. NY: Longmans, Green, 1937. 1st ed. Frontis; 7 plts; illus eps. VG in Good+ dj. *Oregon*. $25/£16

FIELD, MICHAEL. Prevailing Wind: Witness in Indo-China. London: Methuen, (1965). (Bump spine foot.) Dj (lamination bubbling; piece missing; edgewear). *Aka*. $40/£26

FIELD, MICHAEL. (Pseud of Katherine Bradley & Edith Cooper.) Underneath the Bough. London, 1893. Probable 1st ed, but lacks pg before title. 100pp. Blue linen (worn, discolored.) *King*. $50/£32

FIELD, RACHEL. Hepatica Hawks. NY: Macmillan, 1932. 1st ed. Cl sl faded, else VG in dj (sl chipped). *Hermitage*. $35/£23

FIELD, SARA BARD. The Vintage Festival. A Play Pageant. SF: Book Club of CA, 1920. 1st ed. #459/500. Full-pg signed presentation. VG. *Perier*. $97/£63

FIELD, THOMAS W. An Essay Towards an Indian Bibliography. Columbus, OH: Long's College Book Co, 1951. 1st ed. Blue cl, spine stamped red/gold. Good. *Karmiole*. $125/£81

FIELD, THOMAS W. Pear Culture. NY: Saxton, 1863. viii,(13)-286pp. Emb cl. Spine dull, else Fine. *Quest*. $95/£61

FIELDER, MILDRED. Wild Bill and Deadwood. Seattle: Superior Pub Co, (1965). 1st ed. VG in dj (sun mks). *Schoyer*. $35/£23

FIELDING, GABRIEL. Twenty-Eight Poems. London, 1955. 1st Eng ed. (Edges sl faded.) *Edrich*. $12/£8

FIELDING, HENRY. The Adventures of Joseph Andrews. London: James Cochrane, 1832. xi,336pp, 4 plts by George Cruikshank. 3/4 red morocco, gilt spine panels. *Schoyer*. $125/£81

FIELDING, HENRY. Amelia. London: A. Millar, 1752. 1st British ed. 4 vols. 12mo. All blank leaves present w/ad leaf vol 2. Contemp speckled calf; gilt borders, #s. Nice (bkpls; old ink name titles; internal dkng; binding wear; joints starting). *Agvent*. $850/£548

FIELDING, HENRY. An Apology for the Life of Mrs. Shamela Andrews. (Berkshire): Golden Cockerel, 1926. Ltd to 450 numbered. Linen-backed bds. Bkpl; note penned 1st pg, else Fine. *Pharos*. $95/£61

FIELDING, HENRY. A Clear State of the Case of Elizabeth Canning.... London: Ptd for A. Millar, 1753. 2nd ed. Mod 1/4 calf. Tp sl soiled, else clean. *Boswell*. $350/£226

FIELDING, HENRY. An Enquiry into the Causes of the Late Increase of Robbers.... London: A. Millar, 1751. 1st ed. Early 1/4 calf. Exceedingly Nice. *Boswell*. $1,250/£806

FIELDING, HENRY. An Enquiry into the Causes of the Late Increase of Robbers.... London: A. Millar, 1751. 2nd ed. (xxxii),203pp; half title present. Recent morocco spine, linen bds, gilt. VG. *Hartfield*. $425/£274

FIELDING, HENRY. The History of the Adventures of Joseph Andrews and His Friend Mr. Abraham Adams.... Ptd for A. Millar, 1751. 5th ed, rev & corrected. 2 vols. 12 plts. Contemp calf (rubbed; vol 2 joint cracked; used, browned within). *Waterfield*. $116/£75

FIELDING, HENRY. The History of the Adventures of Joseph Andrews. And An Apology for the Life of Mrs. Shamela Andrews. London: Fraser, 1970. #484/1500. Full crushed maroon morocco, gilt; aeg. Mint in acetate dj. *Hartfield.* $125/£81

FIELDING, HENRY. The History of the Adventures of Joseph Andrews.... London/NY: John Lane/Dodd, Mead, (1929). 1st ed thus. Norman Tealby (illus). Dec black cl. NF in dj, slipcase (worn). *Chapel Hill.* $50/£32

FIELDING, HENRY. The History of the Life of the Late Mr. Jonathan Wild the Great. NY: LEC, 1943. #904/1500 numbered, signed by T.M. Cleland (illus). Cl-backed dec bds. Fine in pub's slipcase (sl mkd). *Hermitage.* $125/£81

FIELDING, HENRY. The History of Tom Jones, a Foundling. London: A. Millar, 1749. 3rd ed. 4 vols. Orig plain calf, spines numbered, gilt rules. Chip vol 1, else Excellent set (contemp bkpl). *Macdonnell.* $600/£387

FIELDING, HENRY. The History of Tom Jones, a Foundling. Ptd for A. Millar, 1750/1749. Vol 2 dated 1749 is 3rd ed, other vols dated 1750 are 4th ed. 4 vols. Contemp calf; red, dk blue spine labels. (Sig each tp, inked out 1st 2 vols; joints cracked; sl wear spine head, foot; spine label vol 2 renewed.) *Bickersteth.* $279/£180

FIELDING, HENRY. The History of Tom Jones. London, 1763. 4 vols. Full calf bindings (sl nibbling). Fine (fr hinges Vols 1-2 yielding; bkpl). *Bond.* $1,000/£645

FIELDING, HENRY. The Journal of a Voyage to Lisbon. London: A. Millar, 1755. 1st issued ed. 12mo. (iv),iv,240,193-288pp (mispaginated as issued). Contemp calf (rebacked; bkpl; cvr wear). *Bookpress.* $750/£484

FIELDING, HENRY. The Letter-Writers. London: J. Watts et al, 1750. 2nd ed. 48pp (sl browned). 1/2 red morocco. *Marlborough.* $310/£200

FIELDING, THEODORE H. Synopsis of Practical Perspective.... London, 1829. 1st ed. 136pp, 17 engr plts. 1/2 leather (neatly rebacked). *Ars Artis.* $116/£75

FIELDING, THEODORE H. Synopsis of Practical Perspective.... London: The Author, 1843. 3rd ed. Hand-colored frontis, 126pp + (i)ads, 18 plts (17 fldg). (Sl spotted; margins lt browned; cl faded.) *Edwards.* $155/£100

FIELDS, ANNIE. A Shelf of Old Books. NY: Scribner's, 1894. 1st ed. Teg, uncut. Tan silk, gilt (edges worn). *Macdonnell.* $45/£29

FIELDS, JOSEPH. The Ponder Heart. NY: Random House, (1956). 1st ed. Paper-cvrd bds. NF in dj (lt soil; browning; chip, mk). *Antic Hay.* $45/£29

FIELDS, W.C. Fields for President. NY: Dodd, Mead, 1940. 1st ed, 1st bk. 10 illus by O. Soglow. VG in dj (sm chip spine top; nicks). *Houle.* $850/£548

FIENNES, CELIA. The Journeys of Celia Fiennes. London: Cresset Press, 1949. 2 pedigrees. (Eps lt spotted.) Dj (chipped, torn). *Hollett.* $47/£30

FIENNES, CELIA. The Journeys of Celia Fiennes. C. Morris (ed). London: Cresset Press, 1949. (Eps foxed; backstrip sl faded.) *Petersfield.* $22/£14

FIENNES, R. Hell on Ice. London: Hodder & Stoughton, (1979). 1st ed. VG in VG dj. *Blue Dragon.* $22/£14

FIFIELD, LIONEL. Infections of the Hand. NY, 1927. 1st Amer ed. Good. *Fye.* $150/£97

Fifty Years in Chains; or, The Life of an American Slave. (By Charles Ball.) NY: H. Dayton, 1859. 430pp + 23pg cat (sigs pulled; foxed, stained). Red cl (heavily worn; cocked; joints split); gilt-titled spine. Fair. Howes B 65. *Blue Mountain.* $25/£16

FIGGESS, FUJIO KOYAMA JOHN. Two Thousand Years of Oriental Ceramics. London, 1961. 54 hand tipped-in color plts. (Ex-libris.) Dj (sl soiled, ragged, sl loss). *Edwards.* $101/£65

FIGGIS, DARRELL. The Mount of Transfiguration. Dublin: Maunsel, 1915. 1st ed. Teg. Parchment, bds. Fine in dj. *Reese.* $65/£42

FIGGIS, DARRELL. The Return of the Hero. NY, 1930. 1st Amer ed. NF (spine sl sunned). *Polyanthos.* $30/£19

Fighting 36th—A Pictorial History—The Texas Division in Combat. Austin: 36th Division Assoc, n.d. VG. *Perier.* $125/£81

FILIPINI, ALESSANDRO. One Hundred Ways of Cooking Fish. NY: Webster, 1892. 121pp + 4pp ads. Pict cl. VG. *Schoyer.* $65/£42

FILIPINI, ALESSANDRO. The Table: How To Buy Food, How To Cook It, and How To Serve It. NY, 1889. 1st ed. Port. White enamelled cl (sl stained, heavily worn; text browned, inscrip). *King.* $50/£32

FILLEY, WILLIAM. Life and Adventures of William Filley. Chicago, 1867. 2nd ed. 110pp; 8 plts. Wraps. (Foxed; fr cvr chipped; lacks pp 111-112, supplied in facs, & rear wrap.) *King.* $150/£97

FILSON, JOHN. Kentucke and the Adventures of Col. Daniel Boone. Louisville: John P. Morton, 1934. Ltd to 1200. Frontis map. Gilt-dec cl. As New. *Cahan.* $60/£39

FINBERG, A.J. A Complete Inventory of the Drawings of the Turner Bequest. London: HMSO, 1909. 2 vols. Fldg sketch plan. (Marginal browning tps; upper hinges cracked; sl bumped.) *Edwards.* $194/£125

FINBERG, A.J. Early English Watercolour Drawings by the Great Masters. Geoffrey Holme (ed). London: The Studio, 1919. 44 full-pg tipped-in plts (12 color), guards. Blue cl, gilt, beveled bds (faded, lt wear). Good+ (foxing). *Willow House.* $31/£20

FINCH, C. Gamut and Time-Table in Verse. London: A.K. Newman, (ca 1825). Toybook. 12mo. 35 numbered pp, 12 hand-colored engrs. Illus paper wrappers (rear cvr, spine replaced). *Reisler.* $400/£258

FINCH, CHRISTOPHER. The Art of Walt Disney. NY, (1973). Cl w/applied die-cut Mickey. VG in glassine dj (tear). *King.* $150/£97

FINCH, EDWIN W. The Frontier, Army and Professional Life of Edwin W. Finch, M.D. (New Rochelle, NY, 1909). 1st ed. Photo frontis port. Orig red cl. VG. *Chapel Hill.* $125/£81

FINCH, FRANK. The Los Angeles Dodgers. Jordan, 1977. 1st ed. Fine in VG+ dj. *Plapinger.* $30/£19

FINCH, GEORGE INGLE. The Making of a Mountaineer. London: Arrowsmith, 1924. 1st ed. 56 plts. VG (fore-edge sl spotted) in dj (torn, defective). *Hollett.* $47/£30

FINCH, JEREMIAH S. Sir Thomas Browne. NY: Schuman, 1950. Frontis. Nice in dj. *Goodrich.* $25/£16

FINDEN, WILLIAM and EDWARD FRANCIS. Finden's Illustrations of the Life and Works of Lord Byron. London: John Murray, 1833-34. 3 vols. 126 b/w engr plts. Gilt-stamped morocco, gilt spines, raised bands; aeg (extrems rubbed; inner hinges cracking vols 1, 3; starting vol 2). *Sadlon.* $225/£145

FINDLAY, ALEXANDER GEORGE. Memoir...of the Northern Atlantic Ocean.... London: Richard Holmes Laurie, (1878). 14th ed. 14 charts and plts. *Lefkowicz.* $175/£113

FINDLEY, PALMER. The Story of Childbirth. GC, NY, 1934. 1st ed. Good. *Fye.* $100/£65

FINERTY, JOHN F. War-Path and Bivouac. Chicago, (1955). Lakeside Classic. VG. *Schoyer.* $25/£16

FINGER, CHARLES J. Foot-Loose in the West. NY: William Morrow, 1932. 1st ed. Orange cl titled in blue (sl bumped). VG (sl foxing). *Blue Mountain.* $20/£13

FINGER, CHARLES J. Frontier Ballads: Heard and Gathered. GC: Doubleday Page, 1927. Ltd & 1st ed. #29/201. Inscribed by Finger, signed by Paul Honore (artist). 3 color woodcuts; teg. Imitation vellum spine, paper-cvrd sides. Fine. *Graf.* $45/£29

FINGER, CHARLES J. High Water in Arkansas. NY: Grosset & Dunlap, 1943. 1st ed. Henry C. Pitz (illus). Lg 8vo, 28pp. Fine in dj. *Godot.* $45/£29

FINGER, ERNEST. Gonorrhoea. NY, 1894. 3rd ed, 1st Eng trans. 324pp. Good. *Fye.* $100/£65

FINK, AUGUSTA. Time and the Terraced Land. Berkeley: Howell-North, 1966. 1st ed. Pict eps. Fine in NF dj. *Connolly.* $35/£23

FINLAY, IAN. Scottish Crafts. London, 1948. Good. *Washton.* $35/£23

FINLAY, IAN. Scottish Gold and Silver Work. London: C&W, 1956. 1st ed. 96 plts. Dj (sl ragged). *Edwards.* $85/£55

FINLAY, V. Virgil Finlay. Grant, 1971. 1st ed. One of 1000. Fine in dj. *Aronovitz.* $85/£55

FINLEY, J.B. History of the Wyandott Mission, at Upper Sandusky, Ohio. Cincinnati, 1840. 1st ed. 432pp. Contemp full calf. Howes F 144. *Ginsberg.* $350/£226

FINLEY, JAMES B. Autobiography of Rev. James B. Finley. W.P. Strickland (ed). Cincinnati: R.P. Thompson, 1853. 1st ed. Good (foxing; rebound, using orig spine, cvrs). Howes F 143. *Lien.* $125/£81

FINLEY, M.I. and DENIS MACK SMITH. A History of Sicily. London, 1968. 1st ed. 3 vols. Djs (chipped). *Edwards.* $70/£45

FINLEY, MERRILL L. Christ and the Colonel. Girard, KS: Haldeman-Julius, (1948). Wraps. *Hayman.* $15/£10

FINLEY, RUTH E. Old Patchwork Quilts and the Women Who Made Them. Phila: Lippincott, (1929). 3rd ptg. 96 plts. VG in dj (lt chipped). *Bookpress.* $45/£29

FINNEY, C.G. The Character, Claims, and Practical Workings of Freemasonry. Cincinnati: Western Tract & Book Soc, 1869. 1st ed. 272 pp (lacking ffep). Orig gilt-stamped cl. VG (lt foxing). *Connolly.* $65/£42

FINNEY, CHARLES G. The Circus of Dr. Lao. Abramson, 1946. 1st ed thus. Fine in dj (sl chipped, soiled). *Madle.* $45/£29

FINNEY, CHARLES G. The Circus of Dr. Lao. NY: LEC, 1982. One of 2000 numbered, signed by Claire Van Vliet (illus). Dec cl over bds. VF in slipcase. *Reese.* $95/£61

FINNEY, GUY W. The Great Los Angeles Bubble. (N.p.: Guy W. Finney, 1929). Mustard-brn cl, paper cvr label. Good. *Karmiole.* $30/£19

FINNEY, JACK. Good Neighbor Sam. S&S, 1963. 1st ed. Stain fr cvr, else VG+ in dj (lt dust soil). *Aronovitz.* $45/£29

FINNEY, JACK. Time and Again. NY: S&S, (1970). 1st ed. NF in dj. *Antic Hay.* $175/£113

FINNEY, JACK. Time and Again. NY: S&S, 1970. 1st ed. Faint trace of glue ep, else Fine in 1st state dj. *Else Fine.* $150/£97

FINNEY, JACK. The Woodrow Wilson Dime. NY: S&S, 1968. 1st ed. Fine in dj (price-clipped, sm stain fr corner). *Else Fine.* $50/£32

FINNEY, JACK. The Woodrow Wilson Dime. S&S, 1968. 1st ed. Fine in dj. *Fine Books.* $80/£52

FINNIE, RICHARD. Lure of the North. Phila, (1940). *Artis.* $30/£19

FINOT, JEAN. Problems of the Sexes. NY, 1913. 1st Eng trans. Good. *Fye.* $75/£48

FINSTERBUSCH, C.A. Cock Fighting All Over the World. Gaffney, SC: Grit & Steel, 1929. 1st ed. Author photo tipped in. VG. *Mcgowan.* $250/£161

FIOCCO, GIUSEPPE. Giovanni Bellini. NY: McGraw-Hill, (1960). 1st ed. Frontis, 46 tipped-in color plts. Red cl. Good in dj. *Karmiole.* $50/£32

FIRBANK, RONALD. Five Novels. New Directions, (1949). 1st ed. Offsetting fep, else NF in VG+ dj (dust soil rear panel). *Fine Books.* $35/£23

FIRBANK, RONALD. The Flower Beneath the Foot. London: Grant Richards, 1923. 1st ed. One of 1000. Black cl. Corner bumped, o/w Nice in Good dj (extrems chipped; tears at joints mended on verso). *Reese.* $250/£161

FIRBANK, RONALD. The New Rythum and Other Pieces. London: Duckworth, (1962). 1st ed. Fine in dj. *Hermitage.* $35/£23

FIRBANK, RONALD. The New Rythum and Other Pieces. London: Duckworth, 1962. 1st ed. NF in dj. *Limestone.* $30/£19

FIRBANK, RONALD. Odette. G. Richards, 1916. 1st ed. Contents Good (dec wraps dull). *Whiteson.* $28/£18

FIRBANK, RONALD. Prancing Nigger. NY: Brentano's, (1924). 1st Amer ed. Spine title almost rubbed off. *Sadlon.* $20/£13

FIRBANK, RONALD. Prancing Nigger. NY, (1924). 1st Amer ed. Fine (sl sunned, sl rubbed) in dj (sunned; spine lacks top, heel; chipped). *Polyanthos.* $75/£48

FIRBANK, RONALD. The Princess Zoubaroff. London: Grant Richards, 1920. 1st ed. VG in dj (sm chips, short tears, else VG). *Godot.* $100/£65

FIRBANK, RONALD. Santal. (NY): Bonacio & Saul w/Grove Press, (1955). 1st Amer ed. Rev slip laid in. Fine in dj (nicks). *Reese.* $50/£32

FIRBANK, RONALD. Sorrow in Sunlight. Brentanos, n.d., c. 1924. Ltd ed. Dec eps. VG in dj (sl worn). *Whiteson.* $31/£20

FIRBANK, RONALD. Valmouth. NY: New Directions, (1956). 1st illus ed, Amer issue of Duckworth ptg (one of 250 thus), w/ND sticker title, dj. Cvrs sl bowed, else Fine in dj (sl frayed; edges mended verso). *Reese.* $40/£26

FIREBAUGH, ELLEN. The Physician's Wife and the Things that Pertain to Her Life. Phila, 1894. 1st ed. 186pp. (Inner hinges cracked; rubbed.) *Fye.* $100/£65

First (and Second) Report(s) of the Commissioners for Inquiring into the State of Large Towns and Populous Districts. London, 1844-1845. 1st eds. Inscribed by William Brewer. 2 vols. 351; 266pp. Orig cl (rebacked). *Fye.* $300/£194

First Century of Printmaking 1400-1500. Chicago: Art Institute, 1941. Good in wrappers. *Washton*. $25/£16

First Steps in Grammar, for Very Young Children. London: Darton, n.d. (ca 1860). 4to. 8 pp + 1pg list lower wrapper. Tp vignette, repeated on upper wrapper (lt soiled, edges chipped; rebacked w/matching paper). Internally Fine. *Hobbyhorse*. $120/£77

FISCHEL, OSKAR and MAX VON BOEHN. Modes and Manners of the Nineteenth Century.... London: Dent, Dutton, 1909. 3 vols. Dec cl binding, gilt (backstrips faded). *Petersfield*. $65/£42

FISCHEL, OSKAR and MAX VON BOEHN. Modes and Manners of the Nineteenth Century.... London/NY: Dent/Dutton, 1909. 1st Amer ed. 3 vols. Teg. Dec grn cl, gilt (cvr wear; water damage vol 1; foxing, mostly prelims). *Glenn*. $325/£210

FISCHEL, OSKAR. Raphael. London: Kegan Paul, 1948. 2 vols. 302 plts. Sound in dj (torn). *Ars Artis*. $163/£105

FISCHEL, OSKAR. Raphael. London: Kegan Paul, 1948. 2 vols. 302 plts. Blue cl bds, gilt spine title. Fine (spines faded). *Heller*. $250/£161

FISCHEL, OSKAR. Raphael. London, 1948. 2 vols. xiii + 302 plts. (Sl shelf-rubbed.) *Washton*. $75/£48

FISCHER, BOBBY. Games of Chess. NY, 1959. 1st ed. Extrems sl worn, else VG in dj (edgetorn, rubbed). *King*. $20/£13

FISCHER, BRUNO. The Dead Men Grin. Phila: David McKay, 1945. 1st ed. Lt soiled, else VG in dj (lt worn). *Murder*. $75/£48

FISCHER, G.W. The Smut Fungi. NY, 1951. (Call # sticker; lib stamp.) *Sutton*. $42/£27

FISCHER, LOUIS. Infant-Feeding in Its Relation to Health and Disease. Phila, 1901. 2nd ed. Good. *Fye*. $30/£19

FISH, DONALD. Airline Detective. London: Collins, 1962. 1st UK ed. VG in VG dj (sl rubbed). *Lewton*. $34/£22

FISH, JOSEPH. The Pioneers of the Southwest and Rocky Mountain Regions. Vol 5: Mormon Migrations and Related Events. Seymour Fish (ed). N.p., n.d. (1972). 1st ed. Inscribed. Lg fldg map in rear envelope. Fine in NF dj. *Connolly*. $45/£29

FISHBEIN, MORRIS. A Bibliography of Infantile Paralysis 1789-1944. Phila: Lippincott, 1946. 1st ed. Blue cl. VG. *House*. $120/£77

FISHBERG, A.M. Heart Failure. London, 1937. 25 engrs. Ink sig; pencil mks in margins, o/w Good. *Whitehart*. $28/£18

FISHEL, WESLEY R. (ed). Vietnam: Anatomy of a Conflict. Itasca: F.E. Peacock, (1968). Fine in dj (tears; 1/3 rear flap clipped; sl faded). *Aka*. $40/£26

FISHER, DOROTHY CANFIELD. Paul Revere. NY: Random House, 1950. 1st trade ed. Norman Price (illus). Dec eps. VG in dj. *Cattermole*. $20/£13

FISHER, DOROTHY CANFIELD. Vermont Tradition. Boston: Little Brown, 1953. 1st ed. VG in Good dj. *October Farm*. $25/£16

FISHER, H. A Dream of Fair Women. B-M, 1907. 1st ed. VG. *Fine Books*. $75/£48

FISHER, H.D. The Gun and the Gospel. Chicago: Kenwood, 1896. 1st ed. (Text browned, sl brittle.) Blue cl (sl worn). *Glenn*. $95/£61

FISHER, HENRY. Abroad with Mark Twain and Eugene Field.... NY: N. Brown, 1922. 1st Amer ed. Good + (foxing cvrs; sm stain gutter 1st few pp; leather bkpl). *Agvent*. $40/£26

FISHER, JAMES. The Fulmar. London: Collins, 1952. Couple rubber stamps, else VG. *High Latitude*. $35/£23

FISHER, M.F.K. The Art of Eating. Cleveland, 1954. 1st Amer ed. Signed. NF (sl edge rubbed) in dj (sm tear, few edge chips, sl rubbed; price-clipped). *Polyanthos*. $40/£26

FISHER, M.F.K. A Cordiall Water. Boston: Little, Brown, (1961). 1st ed. Dec orange paper over bds. VG (rubbed) in dec orange dj (lt used; spine rubbed; 1/2-inch tear; tape reinforcement). *Juvelis*. $125/£81

FISHER, M.F.K. A Cordiall Water. Boston: Little, Brown, 1961. 1st ed. NF in dj (lt used, short tears). *Beasley*. $45/£29

FISHER, M.F.K. Map of Another Town. Boston: Little, Brown, 1964. 1st ed. Purple linen cl. VG in dj (used; lt stain; price-clipped). *Juvelis*. $75/£48

FISHER, M.F.K. Not Now, But Now. NY: Viking, 1947. 1st ed. Grn wove cl. NF in pict dj (lt used). *Juvelis*. $250/£161

FISHER, M.F.K. Spirits of the Valley. (NY): Targ Editions, 1985. Signed ed ltd to 250. Tan linen over dec grn bds. Fine in glassine. *Karmiole*. $100/£65

FISHER, MARGERY and JAMES. Shackleton and the Antarctic. Boston: Houghton Mifflin, Riverside Press, 1958. 1st ed. 1/2 title. Blue cl. VG in dj. *Weber*. $75/£48

FISHER, P. (Pseud of William Andrew Chatto.) The Angler's Souvenir. London: Charles Tilt, (1835). 1st ed. x,192pp, engr title, dedication, 32 plts in proof state. Green cl (fr hinge cracked; bumped, rubbed, stained; split rear joint; spine darkened, chipped; fr joint repaired). Nice internally. *Blue Mountain*. $475/£306

FISHER, RICHARD SWAINSON. A Chronological History of the Civil War in America. NY: Johnson & Ward, 1863. 160pp; 8 dbl-pg hand-colored maps, 2 fldg hand-colored maps. Cl stamped in gilt/blind. Fine. *Schoyer*. $200/£129

FISHER, RICHARD. Introduction to a Catalogue of the Early Italian Prints in the British Museum. London: Chiswick Press, 1886. viii,470pp. (Worn; ex-lib, label, cardholder, label; soiling few pp; upper hinge cracked, sl tender; joints splitting). *Edwards*. $78/£50

FISHER, ROBERT LEWIS. The Odyssey of Tobacco. CT: Prospect Press, 1939. (Spine lt browned; edges rubbed.) *Edwards*. $31/£20

FISHER, ROY. The Cut Pages. Fulcrum, 1971. 1st trade ed. Fine in dj. *Poetry*. $19/£12

FISHER, VARDIS and OPAL LAUREL HOLMES. Gold Rushes and Mining Camps of the Early American West. Caldwell: Caxton Printers, 1968. 1st ed. Signed by both authors. Gold-stamped buckram. Dj. *Dawson*. $75/£48

FISHER, VARDIS and OPAL LAUREL HOLMES. Gold Rushes and Mining Camps of the Early American West. Caldwell: Caxton, 1979. Rpt. NF in NF dj. *Parker*. $45/£29

FISHER, VARDIS. April: A Fable of Love. Caldwell/GC: Caxton/Doubleday, Doran, 1937. 1st ed. Dj. *Dawson*. $30/£19

FISHER, VARDIS. April: A Fable of Love. Caxton, 1937. 1st ed. Fine in Nice dj (sl chipped). *Authors Of The West*. $75/£48

FISHER, VARDIS. Darkness and the Deep. Vanguard, (1943). 1st ed. Fine in dj (chipped). *Authors Of The West.* $35/£23

FISHER, VARDIS. Forgive Us Our Virtues. Caldwell: Caxton, 1938. 1st ed. Fine in NF dj (sm spine chip). *Beasley.* $35/£23

FISHER, VARDIS. In Tragic Life. Caldwell: Caxton, 1932. 1st ed. VG. *Parker.* $60/£39

FISHER, VARDIS. The Mothers, an American Saga of Courage. NY: Vanguard, (1943). 1st ed. VG in dj (worn, chipped). *Hermitage.* $75/£48

FISHER, VARDIS. No Villain Need Be. Caldwell: Caxton, 1936. 1st ed. VG. *Graf.* $40/£26

FISHER, VARDIS. Passions Spin the Plot. Caxton, 1934. 1st ed. Fine in VG+ dj. *Authors Of The West.* $50/£32

FISHER, VARDIS. Pemmican. Novel of Hudson's Bay Co. Doubleday, (1956). 1st ed. Rev copy slip laid in. Fine in VG dj. *Oregon.* $40/£26

FISHER, VARDIS. Tale of Valor. A Novel of the Lewis and Clark Expedition. Doubleday, 1958. 1st ed. Ep maps. Fine in Fine dj. *Oregon.* $45/£29

FISHER, VARDIS. We Are Betrayed. Caldwell/GC: Caxton/Doubleday, 1935. 1st ed. NF in dj (lt used; shallow chips; internal tape mends). *Beasley.* $45/£29

FISHER, WILLIAM A. One Hundred and Fifty Years of Music Publishing in the United States. Boston: Ditson, 1933. 1st ed. Orig ptd wrappers. *Ginsberg.* $50/£32

FISK, DOROTHY. Dr. Jenner of Berkeley. London, 1959. 1st ed. Good in dj. *Fye.* $30/£19

FISKE, DORSEY. Academic Murder. London: Cassell, 1980. 1st ed. Fine (bd bottoms lt scraped) in Fine dj. *Janus.* $35/£23

FISKE, JOHN. The American Revolution. Boston/NY: Houghton, Mifflin, 1896. 2nd ed. 2 vols. 351; 321pp; teg. Grn cl. Fine set. *Chapel Hill.* $150/£97

FISKE, JOHN. The Letters of John Fiske. Ethel F. Fiske (ed). NY: Macmillan, 1940. 1st ed. Frontis port, 9 plts. VG in Good dj. *Connolly.* $47/£30

FITCH, JAMES M. and F.F. ROCKWELL. Treasury of American Gardens. NY: Harper, (1956). 1st ed. Lt foxing edges, eps, else VG in dj (used). *Bookpress.* $25/£16

FITCH, MICHAEL H. The Chattanooga Campaign. N.p., 1911. 1st ed ltd to 2500. Spine lt soiled, discolored, o/w VG+. *Pratt.* $60/£39

FITCH, MICHAEL H. Ranch Life and Other Sketches. Pueblo, 1914. 1st ed. One of 150 ptd. Howes F 157. *Ginsberg.* $600/£387

FITCH, NOEL RILEY. Sylvia Beach and the Lost Generation. Souvenir Press, 1984. 1st UK ed. NF in dj. *Sclanders.* $23/£15

FITCH, NOEL RILEY. Sylvia Beach and the Lost Generation. London: Souvenir, 1984. 1st UK ed. Sl scratch fr cvr, o/w VG in dj. *Virgo.* $31/£20

FITCH, SAMUEL SHELDON. Diseases of the Chest. Phila, 1841. 1st ed. Cl-backed bds, paper label. (Lacks fep.) *Argosy.* $150/£97

FITCH, WILLIAM EDWARD. Some Neglected History of North Carolina. NY: By Author, 1914. 2nd ed. 10 plts, 2 facs maps. VG. *Schoyer.* $60/£39

FITHIAN, PHILIP VICKERS. Journal of Philip Vickers Fithian, 1773-1774.... Hunter Dickinson Farish (ed). Williamsburg: Colonial Williamsburg, 1943. 2nd ed. 7 plts. Uncut. Ink name, text lt yellowed, else VG in dj (tattered). *Bookpress.* $45/£29

FITTS, JAMES FRANKLIN. A Sharp Night's Work. Chicago: Laird & Lee, (1888). 170pp + ads. Cl (sm spots back cvr; fr inner hinges sl weak). *Hayman.* $50/£32

FITZ-ADAM, ADAM. The World. London: Ptd for J. Parsons, 1794. 4 vols. Contemp diced calf. VG. *Argosy.* $175/£113

FITZGERALD, E.A. The Highest Andes. London, 1899. 1st ed. xvi,390pp, 2 fldg maps, fldg panorama. Teg. Gilt-ruled cl (spine sl faded; ex-libris). *Edwards.* $194/£125

FITZGERALD, E.A. The Highest Andes. London: Methuen, 1899. 1st ed. xvi,390pp; 51 plts; 2 maps; panorama. (Sl spotted; prelims, reps foxed; upper joint tender; cl sl mottled.) *Hollett.* $279/£180

FITZGERALD, ED (ed). The Book of Major League Baseball Clubs. Barnes, 1952. 1st ed. 2 vols. Vol 1 VG in VG dj; vol 2 Fine in Fine dj. *Plapinger.* $40/£26

FITZGERALD, EDWARD (trans). Rubaiyat of Omar Khayyam. London: Hodder, (1910). 20 tipped-in color plts by Edmund Dulac. Gilt-dec white buckram (sl mks). Fine (name). *Petersfield.* $279/£180

FITZGERALD, EDWARD (trans). Rubaiyat of Omar Khayyam. NY/London: Hodder & Stoughton, (ca. 1910). 1st Amer ed w/these illus. #181/200. Edmund Dulac (illus). Teg, rest untrimmed. Full gilt-dec parchment. VG (lacks ribbon tie; spine sl soiled). *Chapel Hill.* $400/£258

FITZGERALD, F. SCOTT. Afternoon of an Author. Princeton Univ Press, 1957. 1st ed. VG+. *Fine Books.* $35/£23

FITZGERALD, F. SCOTT. All the Sad Young Men. NY: Scribner's, 1926. 1st ed. NF. *Sadlon.* $225/£145

FITZGERALD, F. SCOTT. All the Sad Young Men. NY: Scribner, 1926. 1st ptg w/ Scribner seal on copyright pg, Scribner's sig on frep. Gilt letters faded, but Good. *Limestone.* $115/£74

FITZGERALD, F. SCOTT. The Beautiful and Damned. NY: Scribner's, 1922. 1st ed, 1st ptg, w/leaf of ads at rear. 8vo. Grn cl. NF in dj (staining, sl chipped, 2 tears). *Cummins.* $2,250/£1,452

FITZGERALD, F. SCOTT. The Beautiful and Damned. NY: Scribner, 1922. 1st ed, 1st ptg; w/'Printed at the Scribner Press' and no seal on copyright pg, no ads at rear. 8vo. Grn cl. Fine in VG 1st issue dj (lt soiled; 1-inch chip, 4-inch separation fr panel; fold; minor clean tears). *Chapel Hill.* $3,200/£2,065

FITZGERALD, F. SCOTT. The Beautiful and Damned. Scribners, 1922. 1st ed. Sl worn, else VG. *Fine Books.* $95/£61

FITZGERALD, F. SCOTT. The Crack-Up. London: New Directions, 1945. 1st ed. VG in dj (chipped, price-clipped). *Rees.* $31/£20

FITZGERALD, F. SCOTT. The Crack-Up. Edmund Fitzgerald (ed). NY: New Directions, 1945. 1st ed, 1st issue. Fine w/o dj. *Else Fine.* $25/£16

FITZGERALD, F. SCOTT. Flappers and Philosophers. Scribners, 1920. 1st ed. VG. *Fine Books.* $185/£119

FITZGERALD, F. SCOTT. The Great Gatsby. (NY): LEC, 1980. One of 2000 numbered, signed by Fred Meyer (illus). Pict cl. Fine in pub's slipcase. *Hermitage.* $125/£81

FITZGERALD, F. SCOTT. The Great Gatsby. SF: Arion, 1984. One of 350 signed by Graves (artist). 97 photo engrs. Blue-grn cl spine, corners; grey paper over bds; dec eps. Fine in pub's slipcase. *Juvelis.* $400/£258

FITZGERALD, F. SCOTT. The Great Gatsby: A Facsimile of the Manuscript. Matthew J. Bruccoli (ed). Washington: Microcard Editions, 1973. 1st ed, #1634/2000. Black cl stamped in silver. Fine in pub's white cl slipcase. *Chapel Hill.* $250/£161

FITZGERALD, F. SCOTT. The Last Tycoon. Scribners, 1941. 1st ed. Fine in VG- dj (wear; lt chipping). *Fine Books.* $285/£184

FITZGERALD, F. SCOTT. The Letters.... Andrew Turnbull (ed). London, (1964). 1st Eng ed. Good in dj (chipped). *Waterfield.* $39/£25

FITZGERALD, F. SCOTT. The Pat Hobby Stories. Scribners, 1962. 1st ed. NF in dj (short tear). *Fine Books.* $55/£35

FITZGERALD, F. SCOTT. The Preface to This Side of Paradise. Windhover Press, 1976. 1st ed. One of 150. Photo laid in. Fine w/o dj as issued. *Fine Books.* $150/£97

FITZGERALD, F. SCOTT. Tales of the Jazz Age. Toronto, 1922. 1st Canadian ed. 2 misprints on verso of tp, giving dates of both copyright & publication as 1902, not found in Amer ed. Fr inner hinge repaired, o/w VG. *Rees.* $310/£200

FITZGERALD, F. SCOTT. Tales of the Jazz Age. NY: Scribner's, 1922. 1st ed, 1st ptg, w/'and' (not 'an') on p232, line 6; w/no type batter pp22, 27, 166, 217, 224, 252. Dk grn cl. VG. *Chapel Hill.* $250/£161

FITZGERALD, F. SCOTT. Tales of the Jazz Age. NY, 1922. 1st ed. Cl (worn, frayed; bkpl; few pp roughly opened, hinges loose). *King.* $35/£23

FITZGERALD, F. SCOTT. Tales of the Jazz Age. Scribners, 1922. 1st ed. VG +. *Fine Books.* $135/£87

FITZGERALD, F. SCOTT. Taps at Reveille. Scribners, 1935. 1st ed (pp 349-352 on a stub). Fine. *Fine Books.* $95/£61

FITZGERALD, F. SCOTT. Tender Is the Night. (NY): LEC, (1982). One of 2000 numbered, signed by Charles Scribner III (intro) & Fred Meyer (illus). Pict cl. Fine in pub's slipcase. *Hermitage.* $125/£81

FITZGERALD, F. SCOTT. Tender Is the Night. (NY): LEC, (1982). One of 2000 signed by Fred Meyer (illus) and Charles Scribner III (intro). Litho frontis, 8 gouaches. Blue/ochre/cream floral dec cl. Fine in glassine wrappers, black slipcase. *Heller.* $150/£97

FITZGERALD, F. SCOTT. Tender Is the Night. NY: Scribner's, 1932. 1st ed. Dk grn cl; scarcer of 2 cl bindings, w/vertical lines rather than linen-like grain. VG + (bkpl). *Chapel Hill.* $350/£226

FITZGERALD, F. SCOTT. Tender Is the Night. London: C&W, 1934. 1st UK ed. VG (spine faded). *Williams.* $78/£50

FITZGERALD, F. SCOTT. This Side of Paradise. NY, 1920. 1st Amer ed. NF (top spine mended, new eps; corners sl rubbed; fr cvr sl faded). *Polyanthos.* $250/£161

FITZGERALD, F. SCOTT. Thoughtbook of Francis Scott Key Fitzgerald. NJ: Princeton Univ Lib, 1965. 1st ed, ltd to 300. Bkpl, paper-clip mk fep, white cvrs lt dust soiled, else Fine. Issued w/o ptd dj. *Godot.* $125/£81

FITZGERALD, F. SCOTT. The Vegetable. NY: Scribner, 1923. 1st ed. 8vo. Grn cl. NF in VG pict dj (price-clipped, dampstained fr panel, chipped). *Chapel Hill.* $650/£419

FITZGERALD, NIGEL. Affairs of Death. London: CCC, 1967. 1st ed. NF in dj (sl soiled; lt wear along spine). *Murder.* $45/£29

FITZGERALD, PERCY. The Life of David Garrick.... London: Simpkin, et al, 1899. New, rev ed. VG. *Dramatis Personae.* $25/£16

FITZGERALD, PERCY. London City Suburbs as They Are Today. London, 1893. xvi,349pp + 54pp subs. Teg. (Spine rubbed, sl discolored). *Edwards.* $70/£45

FITZGERALD, SYBIL. Naples. A&C Black, 1904. 1st ed. #205/250 signed by Augustine Fitzgerald (illus). 80 color plts. Teg. Dec cl (lt soiling; spine dknd; marginal browning; fep w/corner cut out). *Edwards.* $271/£175

FITZGERALD, ZELDA. Save Me the Waltz. London: Grey Walls Press, 1953. 1st Eng ed. NF in dj. *Limestone.* $115/£74

FITZGIBBON, CONSTANTINE. Norman Douglas, a Pictorial Record. NY: McBride, 1953. 1st Amer ed. Ltd to 364. Frontis, 17 photo plts. Fine in dj. *Cahan.* $45/£29

FITZGIBBON, CONSTANTINE. When the Kissing Had to Stop. London: Cassell, 1960. 1st ed, 1st issue (in subsequent issues, reference on pg3 to Don Juan Club was suppressed and replaced w/cancel). Very Nice in VG dj (sm mk). *Virgo.* $39/£25

FITZGIBBON, MAURICE. Arts Under Arms. London, 1901. 1st ed. Frontis port, 5 other plts. Lt foxed, o/w VG in khaki cl (sl soiled). *Edwards.* $116/£75

FITZPATRICK, J.P. Transvaal from Within. NY: Stokes, 1899. 1st Amer ed. (xvii),452pp. Grn cl (rubbed). *Schoyer.* $45/£29

FITZPATRICK, JOHN C. (ed). The Diaries of George Washington. Houghton Mifflin, 1925. 4 vols. VG (few nicks to spines). *Book Broker.* $85/£55

FITZPATRICK, JOHN C. (ed). George Washington. Colonial Traveller 1732-1775. Indianapolis: Bobbs-Merrill, (1927). 1st ed. Blue cl. NF in VG dj (closed tears). *Chapel Hill.* $55/£35

FITZPATRICK, T.J. Rafinesque. Des Moines: Historical Dept of IA, 1911. 1st ed. Frontis port. Untrimmed. VG. *Glaser.* $150/£97

FITZROY, ALMERIC. Memoirs. NY: George H. Doran, 1924. 1st Amer ed. 2 vols. Frontispieces. Grn emb cl, gilt. Fore-edge uncut (foxing). VF set. *Great Epic.* $150/£97

FITZSIMONS, CECILIA. My First Birds. NY: Harper and Row, 1985. 18x18 cm. 5 dbl-pg pop-ups, last pg w/pop-up birds. Glazed pict bds. VG. *Book Finders.* $20/£13

FITZURSE, R. It Was Not Jones. Hogarth Press, 1928. 1st ed. Spine sl faded, o/w VG. *Words Etc.* $54/£35

FITZWILLIAMS, DUNCAN. The Tongue and Its Diseases. London, 1927. 1st ed. (Backstrip spotted.) *Fye.* $100/£65

Five Little Pigs. London: Bancroft, 1964. 11x11 cm. 6 dbl-pg pop-ups. V. Kubasta (illus). Illus wraps. VG. *Book Finders.* $80/£52

Five Years in the West. (By William Allen.) Nashville: Southern Methodist Pub House, 1884. 211pp. Blind-stamped cl (sl bumped; Lib of Congress copy w/copyright & duplicate stamps t.p., verso). *Dawson.* $500/£323

FLACK, MARJORIE. Away Goes Jonathan Wheeler. GC: GC Publ, 1944. 1st ed. 8x8.25. Pict paper-cvrd bds. Fine. *Book Adoption.* $50/£32

FLACK, MARJORIE. Walter the Lazy Mouse. NY: Doubleday, Doran, 1937. 1st ed. Sm 4to. Emb cl. NF in VG + dj (sm tears). *Book Adoption.* $75/£48

FLADER, LOUIS and J.S. MERTLE. Modern Photo-Engraving. Chicago/Cincinnati, 1948. (Ex-lib.) *Edwards.* $39/£25

FLAGG, EDMUND. The Far West. NY: Harper, 1838. 1st ed. 2 vols. (16),13-263; (12),9-241pp. (Vol 1 joints worn; spine label faded, worn.) Howes F 169. *Ginsberg.* $375/£242

FLAGG, WILSON. Studies in the Field and Forest. Boston: Little, Brown, 1857. vi,(ii),330pp. Textured cl (rubbed; faded, soiled; head, tail chipped). VG. *Blue Mountain.* $65/£42

FLAHERTY, ROBERT J. with FRANCES H. My Eskimo Friends 'Nanook of the North.' London: Wm. Heinemann, 1924. 9 photogravure plts; 3 color plts; 6 plts from dwgs; 6 maps. Orig cl. Fine. *High Latitude.* $165/£106

FLAKE, CHAD (ed). A Mormon Bibliography, 1830-1930. Salt Lake, 1978. NF. *Benchmark.* $250/£161

FLAM, JACK. Matisse. The Man and His Art 1869-1918. London, 1986. 1st UK ed. 101 color plts; in dj. *Edwards.* $70/£45

FLAMMARION, CAMILLE. Lumen. Mershon, 1892. Pict stamped cl. (Lt foxing fr cvr; spine sl sunned.) *Aronovitz.* $85/£55

FLANAGAN, HALLIE. Arena. NY: Duell, Sloane & Pearce, (1940). 1st ed. Pict blue cl. VG. *Petrilla.* $30/£19

Flanders in the Fifteenth Century. Detroit: Institute of Arts, 1960. Good in wrappers. *Washton.* $45/£29

FLANNAGAN, ROY C. The Story of Lucky Strike. London, 1938. 1st ed. (Feps lt stained; wear, discoloring; spine chipped.) *Edwards.* $19/£12

FLANNER, JANET. An American in Paris. Hamish Hamilton, (1940). 1st British ed. Dj (chipped). *Bickersteth.* $39/£25

FLANNER, JANET. Paris Was Yesterday 1925-1939. Irving Drutman (ed). London: Angus Robertson, 1973. 1st UK ed. Sl bruised, o/w VG in dj (sl chipped; closed tear). *Virgo.* $23/£15

FLANNER, JANET. The Stronger Sex. NY: Hyperion Press, (1941). 1st ed. #1228/1750. 24 mtd color plts by Marcel Vertes (illus). Spine lt sunned; dkned edges, else NF. *Chapel Hill.* $225/£145

FLANNER, JANET. The Stronger Sex. NY: Hyperion, (1941). One of 1750 numbered. 24 mtd plts. (Last leaf, feps waterstained in gutter; cl soiled.) *Argosy.* $350/£226

Flatland; A Romance of Many Dimensions. (By Edwin A. Abbott.) London: Seeley, 1884. 1st ed. 4to. Ptd vellum wrappers over flexible bds (lacks 1 inch to spine). *Argosy.* $150/£97

FLAUBERT, GUSTAVE. Bouvard and Pecuchet. London: H.S. Nichols, 1896. 1st ed in English. Pub's blue ribbed cl; gilt pict cvr, spine. Lt worn, hinges cracked, eps browned, else VG. *Glenn.* $250/£161

FLAUBERT, GUSTAVE. Madame Bovary. J. Lewis May (trans). London/NY: John Lane, Bodley Head/Dodd, Mead, 1928. 1st ed thus. John Austen (illus). Floral eps. Black cl, gilt. Sig fep, o/w VG. *Heller.* $55/£35

FLAUBERT, GUSTAVE. Madame Bovary. NY: LEC, 1950. #126/1500 signed by Pierre Brissaud (illus). Fine in slipcase (sl dusty). *Williams.* $70/£45

FLAUBERT, GUSTAVE. Madame Bovary. NY: LEC, 1950. #904/1500 numbered, signed by Pierre Brissaud (illus). Fine in pub's slipcase (sl sunned). *Hermitage.* $125/£81

FLAUBERT, GUSTAVE. Salaambo; A Story of Ancient Carthage. NY: Brown House, 1930. One of 800 numbered. Alexander King (illus). Full leather, silver-stamped spine. NF in pub's slipcase (sl faded; chipped). *Hermitage.* $250/£161

FLAUBERT, GUSTAVE. Salambo. E. Powys Mathers (trans). London: Golden Cockerel Press, 1931. #193/500. 18 wood engrs by Robert Gibbings; teg, others uncut. Ptd on handmade paper. Buckram-backed dec paper bds, morocco label. *Cox.* $171/£110

FLAUBERT, GUSTAVE. Salambo. NY: LEC, 1960. One of 1500 numbered, signed by Edward Bawden (illus). Fine in pub's slipcase. *Hermitage.* $100/£65

FLAUBERT, GUSTAVE. Salammbo—The Maid of Carthage. Putnam, 1900. 1st ed. Pict cl stamped grn/gold. NF. *Fine Books.* $65/£42

FLAUBERT, GUSTAVE. Salammbo. M. French Sheldon (trans). London: Saxon, 1886. 1st ed in English. Gilt bright blue cl. Good (head, toe spine frayed; lt foxing). *Reese.* $75/£48

FLAUBERT, GUSTAVE. Salammbo. London: Mandrake Press, 1930. #1/500. 50 illus by Haydn Mackey. Blue cl. VG in dj (sl worn). *Argosy.* $125/£81

FLAUBERT, GUSTAVE. The Temptation of St. Anthony. Lafcadio Hearn (trans). NY: LEC, 1943. #904/1500 numbered, signed by Warren Chappell (illus). Fine in pub's slipcase (lt rubbed). *Hermitage.* $135/£87

FLAXMAN, J. Anatomical Studies of the Bones and Muscles for the Use of Artists. London: M.A. Nattali, 1833. Port, 13pp, 21 engr plts. (Worn, spine top missing.) *Ars Artis.* $233/£150

FLEETWOOD-HESKETH, PETER. Murray's Lancashire Architectural Guide. John Betjeman & John Piper (eds). London: John Murray, 1955. 1st ed. 2 fldg maps. (Edge tears repaired.) dj (sl spotted, worn, verso repaired). *Hollett.* $54/£35

FLEITMANN, LIDA L. Hoofs in the Distance. NY: Van Nostrand, 1953. One of 985 numbered, signed. Frontis port. Red cl, gilt title, decs. Fine+ in orig red bd slipcase. *Bowman.* $50/£32

FLEMING, A.M. The Gun Sight Mine. Boston: Meador, 1929. 1st ed. VG. *Book Market.* $175/£113

FLEMING, ALEXANDER and G.F. PETRIE. Recent Advances in Vaccine and Serum Therapy. Phila, 1934. 1st Amer ed. Good. *Fye.* $150/£97

FLEMING, ALEXANDER. Penicillin, Its Practical Application. Phila, 1946. 1st Amer ed. Good. *Fye.* $150/£97

FLEMING, ALEXANDER. Penicillin, Its Practical Application. London: Butterworth, 1946. 1st ed. Grn cl. Lacks fep, o/w VG. *White.* $37/£24

FLEMING, CLINT. When the Trout are Rising. NY, (1947). 1st ed. Signed. Photo frontis. Fine in Good dj. *Artis.* $20/£13

FLEMING, G.H. The Dizziest Season. Morrow, 1984. 1st ed. Fine in VG+ dj. *Plapinger.* $40/£26

FLEMING, G.H. The Unforgettable Season. HR & W, 1981. 1st ed. Fine in VG dj. *Plapinger.* $30/£19

FLEMING, GEORGE. Travels on Horseback in Mantchu Tartary.... London: Hurst and Blackett, 1863. 1st ed. 8vo. Color frontis, xvi,579,(1)blank,(8)pub's list, half title, fldg map. (Ink sig, early Chinese stamp to half title; short tears in margin prelim leaf.) Contemp blue half calf, marbled bds (joints repaired). VG. *Morrell.* $388/£250

FLEMING, IAN. Casino Royale. Cape, 1953. 2nd imp. NF in VG dj (spine, fore-edge sl chipped). *Williams.* $233/£150

FLEMING, IAN. Chitty Chitty Bang Bang Adventure No. 2. Cape, 1964. 1st UK ed. VG in dj (spine bumped; short closed tear fr panel; sm abraded patches). *Williams.* $93/£60

FLEMING, IAN. Chitty Chitty Bang Bang. R-H, 1964. 1st Amer ed. Presentation inscrip, else NF in VG dj. *Fine Books.* $45/£29

FLEMING, IAN. The Diamond Smugglers. London: Jonathan Cape, (1957). 1st ed. Fine in VG dj. *Glenn.* $200/£129

FLEMING, IAN. The Diamond Smugglers. Cape, 1957. 1st ed. Binding sl dull; spine lettering sl chipped, else Good. *Whiteson.* $25/£16

FLEMING, IAN. The Diamond Smugglers. London: Cape, 1957. 1st ed. VG in dj. *Limestone.* $135/£87

FLEMING, IAN. Diamonds Are Forever. Taiwanese piracy, based on Pan reprint, 1964. Brn bds (sl stained). VG in dj w/design as 1st ed Moonraker dj (sl worn, creased). *Williams.* $62/£40

FLEMING, IAN. Diamonds Are Forever. London: Cape, 1956. 1st ed. NF in Fine dj. *Limestone.* $825/£532

FLEMING, IAN. Diamonds Are Forever. London: Cape, 1958. 2nd ptg. VG in dj. *Williams.* $47/£30

FLEMING, IAN. Dr. No. Macmillan, 1958. 1st Amer ed. Fine in VG dj. *Fine Books.* $125/£81

FLEMING, IAN. Dr. No. London: Cape, 1958. 1st ed. Silhouette fr panel. Fine in dj. *Limestone.* $450/£290

FLEMING, IAN. Dr. No. London: Cape, 1958. 1st UK ed. Lacking blind-stamped woman's figure on upper bd. VG (stamp). *Williams.* $47/£30

FLEMING, IAN. Dr. No. London: Cape, 1958. 1st UK ed. VG in Good dj (closed tear; repairs). *Williams.* $85/£55

FLEMING, IAN. For Your Eyes Only. Cape, 1960. 1st ed. Fine in NF dj. *Fine Books.* $165/£106

FLEMING, IAN. For Your Eyes Only. London: Jonathan Cape, 1960. 1st ed. Fine in dj (price-clipped; sl faded spine). *Mordida.* $200/£129

FLEMING, IAN. For Your Eyes Only. London: Cape, 1960. 1st UK ed. VG + (bkseller label). *Williams.* $28/£18

FLEMING, IAN. For Your Eyes Only. London: Cape, 1960. 1st UK ed. Fine in VG + dj (lt browned). *Williams.* $124/£80

FLEMING, IAN. From Russia with Love. London: Cape, 1957. 1st UK ed. VG (lettering dulled; spine sl bumped, worn; lacks dj). *Williams.* $23/£15

FLEMING, IAN. From Russia with Love. London: Cape, 1957. 1st UK ed. NF in VG- dj (rubbed, worn). *Williams.* $124/£80

FLEMING, IAN. Goldfinger. London, (1959). 1st ed. Dj. *Petersfield.* $81/£52

FLEMING, IAN. Goldfinger. London: Cape, 1959. 1st ed. Fine in dj (short closed tear spinefold). *Else Fine.* $300/£194

FLEMING, IAN. Goldfinger. London: Cape, 1959. 1st UK ed. Fine in VG + dj (chip, 2 sm pinholes). *Williams.* $124/£80

FLEMING, IAN. Goldfinger. London: Cape, 1959. NF in dj. *Limestone.* $275/£177

FLEMING, IAN. Ian Fleming Introduces Jamaica. Morris Cargill (ed). (London): Andre Deutsch, (1965). 1st ed. NF in dj. *Pharos.* $95/£61

FLEMING, IAN. Live and Let Die. London: Cape, 1954. 1st ed, 1st issue. NF in NF dj (minimally chipped). *Limestone.* $950/£613

FLEMING, IAN. Live and Let Die. Macmillan, 1955. 1st Amer ed. Fine in VG dj (sl wear). *Fine Books.* $265/£171

FLEMING, IAN. The Man with the Golden Gun. (NY): NAL, (1965). 1st Amer ed. Fine in dj (sl wear). *Antic Hay.* $45/£29

FLEMING, IAN. The Man with the Golden Gun. Cape, 1965. 1st ed. VG in VG dj. *Ming.* $39/£25

FLEMING, IAN. The Man with the Golden Gun. Cape, 1965. 1st ed. Fine in dj. *Fine Books.* $75/£48

FLEMING, IAN. The Man with the Golden Gun. London: Cape, 1965. 1st ed. Fine in dj. *Else Fine.* $95/£61

FLEMING, IAN. The Man with the Golden Gun. London: Cape, 1965. 1st UK ed. NF in dj (price-clipped). *Williams.* $19/£12

FLEMING, IAN. Moonraker. London: Cape, (1955). 1st ed. VG (w/o dj). *Reese.* $85/£55

FLEMING, IAN. Moonraker. Paper Pan, 1956. 1st ed. VG in wrappers. *Ming.* $23/£15

FLEMING, IAN. Moonraker. London: Cape, 1965. 8th ptg. Fine in VG + dj (price-clipped). *Williams.* $39/£25

FLEMING, IAN. Octopussy and The Living Daylights. Cape, 1966. 1st ed. Fine in dj. *Fine Books.* $30/£19

FLEMING, IAN. On Her Majesty's Secret Service. Cape, 1963. 1st ed. Fine in NF dj (rubbing). *Fine Books.* $110/£71

FLEMING, IAN. The Spy Who Loved Me. NY, (1962). 1st ed. NF in VG dj (worn). *Mcclintock.* $30/£19

FLEMING, IAN. The Spy Who Loved Me. London: Cape, 1962. 1st ed. Fine in dj. *Limestone.* $200/£129

FLEMING, IAN. The Spy Who Loved Me. London: Cape, 1962. 1st UK ed. VG in dj (sl dusty; staining). *Williams.* $25/£16

FLEMING, IAN. The Spy Who Loved Me. Cape, 1962. 1st UK ed. Fine in dj. *Williams.* $132/£85

FLEMING, IAN. Thrilling Cities. London: Cape, 1963. 1st ed. 223pp w/errata slip. VG in dj (price-clipped). *Hollett.* $39/£25

FLEMING, IAN. Thrilling Cities. London: Cape, 1963. 1st UK ed. NF in dj (price-clipped). *Williams.* $39/£25

FLEMING, IAN. Thunderball. Cape, 1961. 1st ed. NF in dj. *Fine Books.* $150/£97

FLEMING, IAN. Thunderball. London: Cape, 1961. 1st ed. Fine in dj (minor rubs upper corners). *Else Fine.* $200/£129

FLEMING, IAN. Thunderball. London: Cape, 1961. 1st UK ed. NF in VG dj. *Williams.* $85/£55

FLEMING, IAN. Thunderball. London: Cape, 1961. 1st ed. NF in dj. *Limestone.* $125/£81

FLEMING, IAN. You Only Live Twice. London: Jonathan Cape, (1964). 1st ed, 1st ptg. Fine in dj. *Glenn.* $125/£81

FLEMING, IAN. You Only Live Twice. Cape, 1964. 1st ed. Dec cl. Good. *Whiteson.* $25/£16

FLEMING, IAN. You Only Live Twice. Cape, 1964. 1st ed. VG in VG dj. *Ming.* $39/£25

FLEMING, IAN. You Only Live Twice. London: Cape, 1964. 1st ed. Fine in dj. *Limestone.* $75/£48

FLEMING, IAN. You Only Live Twice. London: Cape, 1964. 1st UK ed. VG in dj (price-clipped). *Williams.* $22/£14

FLEMING, K. Can Such Things Be? or The Weird of the Beresfords.... Routledge, 1890. 1st ed. Spine lt dknd, head worn, else VG. *Aronovitz.* $125/£81

FLEMING, PETER. Bayonets to Lhasa. London, 1961. 1st ed. Frontis port; 22 plts; reviews loosely inserted. VG in dj. *Edwards.* $39/£25

FLEMING, PETER. The Flying Visit. Jonathan Cape, 1940. 1st ed. Dj (lt soiled, ragged). *Edwards.* $31/£20

FLEMING, PETER. The Gower Street Poltergeist. Rupert Hart-Davis, 1958. 1st ed. Dj (lt soiled, chipped). *Edwards.* $23/£15

FLEMING, PETER. News from Tartary. London, 1936. 1st ed. Fldg map. Dj (discolored, ragged w/loss). *Edwards.* $47/£30

FLEMING, PETER. One's Company. London, 1934. 1st ed. Fldg map. Dj (sl soiled). *Edwards.* $47/£30

FLEMING, PETER. The Siege at Peking. London, 1959. 1st ed. Frontis; 22 plts. Inscrip, o/w VG in dj (sl rubbed). *Edwards.* $25/£16

FLEMING, STUART J. Authenticity in Art: the Scientific Detection of Forgery. London: Institute of Physics, 1975. (Lib stamp verso tp, lib # spine.) *Ars Artis.* $39/£25

FLEMING, STUART J. Authenticity in Art: the Scientific Detection of Forgery. London/Bristol: Inst of Physics, 1976. Fine in Mint dj. *Europa.* $28/£18

FLEMING, VIVIAN MINOR. Campaigns of the Army of Northern Virginia Including the Jackson Valley Campaign. Richmond, VA: William Byrd Press, (1928). 1st ed. Presentation copy. 2 fldg maps. Fr bd gilt sl dull, else VG. *Mcgowan.* $175/£113

FLEMING, WILLIAM HENRY. Slavery and the Race Problem of the South. With Special Reference to the State of Georgia. Boston, 1906. 1st ed. NF in orig ptd wrappers. *Mcgowan.* $85/£55

FLEMMING, LEONARD. The Call of the Veld. London, 1924. 2nd ed. Frontis port. (Ex-lib, ink stamps; prelims browned; bkpl; spine faded.) *Edwards.* $31/£20

FLEMWELL, G. The Flower-Fields of Alpine Switzerland. NY: Dodd, Mead, 1912. 25 color photolith plts tipped in (frontis reattached). Teg; partly unopened. Grn cl, gilt; color pastedown. VG. *Shifrin.* $50/£32

FLETCHER, BANISTER. A History of Architecture on the Comparative Method. London: Batsford, 1938. 10th ed. VG (wear, sl mks). *Willow House.* $39/£25

FLETCHER, F.W.F. Sport on the Nilgiris and in Wynaad. London: Macmillan, 1911. 1st ed. Fldg map frontis. Orig cl. VG. *Bowman.* $125/£81

FLETCHER, J.S. The Ransom for London. NY: Dial, 1929. 1st Amer ed. Fine in VG dj (piece missing spine base; internal tape mends). *Mordida.* $45/£29

FLETCHER, JOHN G. Paul Gauguin, His Life and Art. NY: Nicholas Brown, 1921. 1st ed. Good (sl soiling; lt foxing). *Reese.* $35/£23

FLETCHER, JOHN. Studies on Slavery. Natchez, (MS): Jackson Warner, 1852. 2nd ed (tp states 'Fourth Thousand'). 637pp. Contemp full calf. Lib bkpl, blinstamp, morocco label, else VG. *Chapel Hill.* $175/£113

FLETCHER, ROBERT H. Free Grass to Fences. The Montana Cattle Range Story. NY: Hist Soc of MT, (1960). 1st ed. Fine in Fine dj. *Book Market.* $45/£29

FLETCHER, ROBERT H. Free Grass to Fences: The Montana Cattle Range Story. NY: Hist Soc of MT, (1960). 1st ed. Pict eps. Blind-emb cl-backed bds. Fine in VG-dj (rubbed, chipped). *Harrington.* $75/£48

FLETCHER, ROBERT S. A History of Oberlin College: From Its Foundation through the Civil War. Oberlin, OH: Oberlin College, 1943. 1st ed. Signed. 2 vols. Gilt-titled cl. Fine set. *Cahan.* $45/£29

FLETCHER, W. Bookbinding in France. Seeley, 1894. 1/4 morocco (sl rubbed; lib bkpl). *Moss.* $78/£50

FLETCHER, W. The Little Grammarian. London: John Harris, 1828. 1st ed. 12mo. 175 + 1pg dedication + 4pp list, 6 plts (incl frontis) all ptd on one side, dated Aug. 1, 1828 (lt foxing edges; ink name fep). Marbled paper on bds, red roan spine w/gilt fillets, title (lt rubbing; sm bkseller label). Fine. *Hobbyhorse.* $125/£81

FLEURY, CLAUDE. A Short History of the Ancient Israelites.... Adam Clarke (ed). Burlington (NJ): Ustick, 1813. 1st ed. 304pp incl subs list; port. Flame calf; leather label. VG. *Petrilla.* $65/£42

FLEXNER, S. and J.T. FLEXNER. William Henry Welch and the Heroic Age of American Medicine. NY: Viking, 1941. 1st ed. Frontis port; 25 plts. VG in dj (sl chipped). *White.* $34/£22

FLINT, ABEL. A System of Geometry and Trigonometry, with a Treatise on Surveying.... Hartford, 1830. 6th ed. 112; 100pp (browned; notes feps). Old calf (worn, split). *King.* $35/£23

FLINT, ANNIE. Sunbeam Stories and Others. NY: Bonnell, Silver & Co, (1897). Ink author dedication ep. 8vo. 97 + 2pp ads; 8 full-pg illus incl frontis w/guard. Dec grn cl on bds; white/brn stamped dec upper cvr. Cvrs lt soiled, else VG. *Hobbyhorse.* $50/£32

FLINT, AUSTIN. A Manual of Percussion and Auscultation. Phila, 1876. 255pp + ads (prelims, endleaves waterstained; spine worn). *Argosy.* $75/£48

FLINT, AUSTIN. Phthisis: Its Morbid Anatomy, Etiology.... Phila, 1875. 1st ed. 446pp. Good. *Fye.* $200/£129

FLINT, AUSTIN. A Treatise on the Principles and Practice of Medicine. Phila, 1873. 4th ed. 1070pp. Full leather. Good. *Fye.* $75/£48

FLINT, CHARLES L. Grasses and Forage Plants.... NY/London, 1857. 1st ed. Frontis; 236pp. VG (orig cl faded). *Second Life.* $65/£42

FLINT, F.S. In the Net of the Stars. Elkin Mathews, 1909. 1st ed. Lt foxing, o/w NF in linen-backed bds (spine label sl chipped). *Poetry.* $78/£50

FLINT, RALPH. Albert Sterner: His Life and His Art. NY: Payson & Clarke, 1927. 1st ed. Frontis port, guard; 64 plts. Paper over bds (worn). Dj lacks lg piece affecting title, o/w VG. *Cahan.* $50/£32

FLINT, RALPH. Contemporary American Etching. NY, (1930). 100 repros. (Lacks frontis; cl soiled.) *Argosy.* $200/£129

FLINT, TIMOTHY (ed). The Personal Narrative of James O. Pattie of Kentucky. Chicago, (1930). Lakeside Classic. VG. *Schoyer.* $20/£13

FLINT, TIMOTHY. Indian Wars of the West. Cincinnati: E.H. Flint, 1833. 1st ed. 240pp. Orig calf. Sig, joints repaired, lt foxing, rubbed, else VG. Howes F 201. *Cahan.* $275/£177

FLINT, TIMOTHY. Recollections of the Last Ten Years in the Valley of the Mississippi. Carbondale: SIU Press, (1968). Fine in NF dj. Howes F 204. *Harrington.* $40/£26

FLINTOFT, J. Collection of Mosses and Specimens of British Mosses from the Lake District. Keswick: Flintoft, (ca1860). 2 vols. 8vo. 174 actual samples on 130ff. Blue cl. *Marlborough.* $1,163/£750

FLORES, A. Franz Kafka, A Chronology and Bibliography. Bern Porter, 1944. One of 600 numbered. VG in ptd cvrs. *Moss.* $25/£16

FLORES, ANGEL and DUDLEY POORE (eds). Fiesta in November.... Boston: Houghton Mifflin, 1942. 1st ed. NF in pict dj. *Reese.* $125/£81

Florida Seafood Cookery. Tallahassee: FL Dept of Agriculture, August 1949. Dknd, else VG in ptd wraps. *Bohling.* $65/£42

FLORIN, LAMBERT. Boot Hill. Seattle, Superior, (1966). 1st ed. Fine in Fine dj. *Book Market.* $30/£19

FLORIN, LAMBERT. Tales the Western Tombstones Tell. Seattle: Superior, n.d. (ca 1967). 1st ed. Fine in VG dj. *Oregon.* $40/£26

Flower Garden. (By Charles McIntosh.) London: Wm. S. Orr & Co, 1840. New Ed. Hand-colored frontis, tp, 515pp, 9 full-pg hand-colored plts. Aeg. Blind-stamped, gilt-dec cl (spine dknd; hinges reinforced; sl marginal foxing). *Quest.* $225/£145

FLOWER, B.O. How England Averted a Revolution of Force. Trenton: Albert Brandt, 1903. 1st ed. Sl spine wear; sm start rear hinge; sm price fep, else VG +. *Beasley.* $100/£65

Flowering Plants from Cuban Gardens. NY: Woman's Club of Havana, 1958. Bumped, else Fine in dj. *Brooks.* $29/£19

FLUGGE, C. Micro-Organisms with Special Reference to the Etiology of the Infective Diseases. London, 1890. 1st Eng trans. 826pp. Good. *Fye.* $125/£81

FLYNN, ERROL. My Wicked, Wicked Ways. Putnam's, 1959. 3rd ed. VG in VG- dj. *Bishop.* $12/£8

FLYNN, ROBERT. North to Yesterday. NY: Knopf, 1967. 1st ed, 1st bk. Fine in dj. *Reese.* $60/£39

FLYNT, JOSIAH. Tramping with Tramps. NY: Century, 1901. Frontis, 29 plts. Tan cl (soiled; spine dknd); titled in red. VG. *Blue Mountain.* $25/£16

FLYNT, JOSIAH. The World of Graft. NY: McClure, Phillips, 1901. Dec cl. VG. *Schoyer.* $25/£16

FODOR, M.W. South of Hitler. Boston: Houghton Mifflin, 1939. 2nd ed. 8 plts. Rubbed, sl frayed; leaf w/marginal tear, o/w VG. *Worldwide.* $25/£16

FOENANDER, E.C. Big Game of Malaya. London: Batchworth, 1952. VG in dj. *Bowman.* $65/£42

FOGEL, EDWIN MILLER. Beliefs and Superstitions of the Pennsylvania Germans. Phila: American Germanica Press, 1915. 1st ed. Grn cl, gilt spine (corners lt bumped). *Karmiole.* $60/£39

FOGEL, ROBERT WILLIAM and STANLEY L. ENGERMAN. Time on the Cross: The Economics of American Negro Slavery. Boston: Little, Brown, 1974. 1st ed. 2 vols. VG in djs. *Schoyer.* $45/£29

FOGG, JEREMIAH. Orderly Book Kept by Jeremiah Fogg. Exeter, NH: Rptd from Exeter News-Letter, 1903. (# in black on cvr; rear pocket removed.) *Schoyer.* $35/£23

FOLEY, EDWARD. Seventy Years. The Foley Saga. LA: Ward Ritchie, (1945). 1st ed. 5 fldg maps, diags. VG. *Oregon.* $40/£26

FOLEY, EDWIN. The Book of Decorative Furniture: Its Form, Colour and History. NY: Putnam's, 1911. 1st ed. 2 vols. 100 tipped-in color plts. Gilt-dec blue cl. VG +. *House.* $300/£194

Folios of New Writing, Spring 1940. London: Hogarth, (1940). 1st ed. Fine in dj (short tears). *Heller.* $50/£32

Folk Tales of Flanders. NY: Dodd, Mead, 1918. 1st Amer ed. 4to, 179pp, 12 full-color illus by J. de Bosshere. Grn cl, gilt; teg. VG (lt bump head, tail). *Davidson.* $275/£177

FOLMER, HENRY. Franco-Spanish Rivalry in North America, 1524-1763. Clark, 1953. 1st ed. Frontis (fldg map). Ex-lib w/spine mks, erased title pg mk, o/w VG. *Oregon.* $45/£29

FOLMER, HENRY. Franco-Spanish Rivalry in North America, 1524-1763. Glendale, CA: Clark, 1953. 1st ed. Fldg frontis map. Burgundy cl, gilt spine. Fine. *Karmiole.* $85/£55

FOLMSBEE, BEULAH. A Little History of the Horn Book. Boston: Horn Book, (1942). 1st ed. Fine. *Glenn.* $25/£16

FONERDEN, C.A. A Brief History of the Military Career of Carpenter's Battery. New Market, VA: Henkel, 1911. 1st ed. 8vo. Orig grn cl. Lt soiled, else VG. *Chapel Hill.* $650/£419

FONTANA, BERNARD et al. Papago Indian Pottery. Seattle: Univ of WA, 1962. 1st ed. Signed. *Parker.* $45/£29

Foolish Fox. Phila: Henry Altemus, (1904). 16mo. 17 color illus by John Rea Neill. Pale grn pict cl, red lettering, dk grn images. Good in color dj (marginal chips). *Reisler.* $60/£39

FOOTE, EDWARD. Medical Common Sense.... NY, 1867. 390pp. Good. *Fye.* $50/£32

FOOTE, H. Harrison, Texas. H-B, 1956. 1st ed. Fine in NF dj. *Fine Books.* $75/£48

FOOTE, HENRY S. The Bench and Bar of the South and Southwest. St. Louis, 1876. 1st ed. (8),264pp. *Artis.* $50/£32

FOOTE, HENRY S. The Bench and the Bar of the South and Southwest. St. Louis: Thomas & Wentworth, 1876. 1st ed. viii,264pp. Orig cl. VG (extrem wear; spine chipped). Howes F236. *Mcgowan.* $350/£226

FOOTE, JOHN A. Diseases of the New-Born. Phila, 1926. 1st ed, rptd. (Ex-lib.) *Fye.* $125/£81

FOOTE, JOHN TAINTOR. Jing. NY: Derrydale, 1936. One of 950 numbered. Gilt title lt flaked, o/w Fine + in plastic wrap. *Bowman.* $120/£77

FOOTE, JOHN TAINTOR. The Number One Boy. NY: Appleton, 1926. 1st ed. VG in dj. *Bowman.* $75/£48

FOOTE, SHELBY. The Civil War. NY: Random House, (1958-63-74). 1st eds vols 2-3, 2nd ptg vol 1. Grey cl. Jacket top chipped vol 1, sm dampstain bottom spine, else Fine set in NF djs. *Chapel Hill.* $250/£161

FOOTE, SHELBY. The Civil War: A Narrative. NY: Random House, (c1958-c1974). 3 vols. Vol 1: 1st ed, vols 2-3: later ptgs. NF set in NF djs. *Mcgowan.* $125/£81

FOOTE, SHELBY. Follow Me Down. NY: Dial, 1950. 1st ed. Fine in Fine dj (partially price-clipped). *Godot.* $175/£113

FOOTE, SHELBY. Love in a Dry Season. NY: Dial Press, 1951. 1st ed. Inscribed. Lower bd edges, spine extrems shelf worn, else VG + in VG + dj (sl discoloration extrems). *Lame Duck.* $250/£161

FOOTE, WILLIAM HENRY. Sketches of Virginia, Historical and Biographical. Phila: William S. Martien, 1850, 1855. 1st ed. 2 vols. (iii),568; frontis,xiv,14-596pp. Pub's blindstamped cl (edges worn; spine vol 1 torn). (Ex-lib w/mks; bkpls.) Howes F 241. *Bookpress.* $225/£145

For Her Sake. (By Frederick William Robinson.) London: Sampson Low, 1869. 1st ed. 3 vols. (Lt foxed.) *Petersfield.* $116/£75

FORBES, ALEXANDER. California: A History of Upper and Lower California. SF: John Henry Nash, 1937. Ltd to 650. 10 plts, lg fldg map. Cl-backed marbled bds. Fine in Fine dj. Howes F 242. *Harrington.* $225/£145

FORBES, ALLAN. Sport in Norfolk County. Boston: Houghton Mifflin, 1938. Ltd to 650 numbered, signed. Inscribed. NF (spine spotted) in Good slipcase. *Blue Mountain.* $150/£97

FORBES, JACK D. Apache, Navaho and Spaniard. Norman, 1960. 1st ed. NF (sig, date) in dj. *Baade.* $45/£29

FORBES, JAMES D. Norway and Its Glaciers. Edinburgh: A&C Black, 1853. 1st ed. xxiv,349pp; 10 color lithos; 2 maps (1 fldg). 1/2 calf gilt, marbled bds (nicely rebacked to match); all edges marbled. VG. *Hollett.* $403/£260

FORBES, JAMES D. Travels through the Alps. London: A&C Black, 1900. New ed. Port, 6 fldg maps (2 in pocket); uncut. *Bickersteth.* $132/£85

FORBES, T.R. Surgeons at the Bailey. New Haven: Yale Univ, 1985. 1st ed. NF in dj. *White.* $23/£15

FORBES-BOYD, ERIC. In Crusader Greece. London, 1964. 1st ed. Frontis, 16 plts. Good in dj. *Edwards.* $28/£18

FORBES-LINDSAY, C.H. India, Past and Present. Phila: Henry T. Coates, 1903. 2 vols. 50 plts. Blue cl, gilt. Fine set. *Hermitage.* $75/£48

FORBES-MITCHELL, WILLIAM. Reminiscences of the Great Mutiny 1857-59. London: Macmillan, 1895. 3rd ptg. xii,295pp + 56pp pub's cat. Red cl, gilt. VG. *Schoyer.* $45/£29

FORBUSH, EDWARD H. A History of the Gamebirds, Wildfowl and Shorebirds. Boston: MA State Board of Ag, 1916. 2nd ed. VG+. *Bowman.* $45/£29

FORBUSH, EDWARD H. and JOHN MAY. Natural History of the Birds of Eastern and Central North America. Boston: Houghton Mifflin, 1939. 1st ed thus. 96 color plts. VG (bkpl). *Bowman.* $40/£26

FORD, ALICE (ed). Audubon's Animals. NY: The Studio, (1951). 16 color plts. VG in dj. *Argosy.* $50/£32

FORD, ALICE. John James Audubon. Norman: Univ of OK Press, 1964. 1st ed. Color frontis. Fine in dj. *Cahan.* $40/£26

FORD, CHARLES HENRI. The Garden of Disorder. London: Europa, 1938. Ltd ed, #77/500. Frontis; 78pp. (Shelf #s spine foot.) *Hollett.* $31/£20

FORD, DANIEL. Incident at Muc Wa. GC: Doubleday, 1967. 1st ed. VG (sl cocked; price mks fep, 1/2 tp) in dj (edgewear). *Aka.* $40/£26

FORD, E.B. Moths. London, 1955. 1st ed. Dj (sl rubbed). *Edwards.* $93/£60

FORD, FORD MADOX. Great Trade Route. Unwin, 1937. 1st ed. Good in dj (sl rubbed). *Whiteson.* $39/£25

FORD, FORD MADOX. A Man Could Stand Up. London: Duckworth, 1926. 1st ed. Eps sl offsetting; fore-edges sl speckled, o/w Very Nice in dj (soiled, chipped; sm pieces). *Virgo.* $78/£50

FORD, FORD MADOX. A Mirror to France. London: Duckworth, 1926. 1st ed. Fine in dj (lt used; 2 sm chips; few tears; internal mend). *Beasley.* $200/£129

FORD, FORD MADOX. New Poems. NY: Rudge, 1927. 1st ed. One of 325. Inscribed. Grn batik paper over bds, gilt label. Spine extrems worn, sm chip, tips sl worn, o/w VG w/panels of orig glassine wrapper. *Reese.* $325/£210

FORD, FORD MADOX. New York Is Not America. London: Duckworth, 1927. 1st ed. VG in VG- dj (heavily chipped). *Limestone.* $75/£48

FORD, FORD MADOX. No More Parades. London: Duckworth, 1925. 1st ed. Sl bumped; top pg corners creased; lacks dj, o/w Good. *Virgo.* $47/£30

FORD, FORD MADOX. Provence, From Minstrels to the Machine. Phila: Lippincott, 1935. 1st Amer ed. VG in dj (sl chipped). *Hermitage.* $65/£42

FORD, FORD MADOX. The Rash Act. NY: Long & Smith, 1933. 1st ed. VG in dj (lt soiled). *Argosy.* $100/£65

FORD, GERALD. A Time to Heal. (NY, 1979). 1st ed. Signed. VG in dj (sl worn). *King.* $125/£81

FORD, HENRY JONES. The Scotch-Irish in America. Princeton: Princeton Univ, 1915. VG. *Schoyer.* $50/£32

FORD, HERBERT. No Guns on Their Shoulders. Nashville: Southern, (1968). Fine in Fine dj (edge tear; scrape). *Aka.* $65/£42

FORD, HUGH. Published in Paris. London: Garnstone Press, 1975. 1st UK ed. VG in dj. *Virgo.* $39/£25

FORD, JESSE HILL. The Conversion of Buster Drumwright. Nashville: Vanderbilt, 1964. 1st ed. Signed presentation. Fine in dj (sl wear; short tears). *Antic Hay.* $65/£42

FORD, LESLIE. Road to Folly. London: Scribner's, 1940. 1st ed. VG in VG dj (sl rubbed). *Ming.* $78/£50

FORD, PAUL LEICESTER. A Checked Love Affair. NY: Dodd, Mead, 1903. 1st ed. Dec cl (lt worn). Ink inscrip, o/w Fine. *Hermitage.* $75/£48

FORD, PAUL LEICESTER. The Great K and A Train Robbery. NY: Dodd, Mead, 1897. 1st ed, 1st issue. Gilt-stamped pict cl; teg (spine sl lightened). BAL 6213. *Sadlon.* $30/£19

FORD, PAUL LEICESTER. The Great K and A Train Robbery. NY: Dodd Mead, 1897. 1st ed, 1st state w/'Train' missing from tp. VG+ (names; lt sunned spine). *Janus.* $85/£55

FORD, PAUL LEICESTER. Wanted—A Chaperon. NY: Dodd Mead, 1902. 1st ed. Dec cl (lt soiled). Ink name, o/w Fine. *Hermitage.* $45/£29

FORD, R. CLYDE. Sandy MacDonald's Man. Lansing, (1929). Map. VG. *Artis.* $15/£10

FORD, RICHARD. A Piece of My Heart. NY: Harper, (1976). 1st ed. 1st bk. Fine in Fine dj (speck). *Unger.* $275/£177

FORD, RICHARD. A Piece of My Heart. H-R, 1976. 1st ed, 1st bk. Fine in dj. *Fine Books.* $185/£119

FORD, RICHARD. The Sportswriter. NY: Vintage Books, 1986. 1st ed. Signed. NF in wraps. *Revere.* $75/£48

FORD, RICHARD. The Ultimate Good Luck. London: Collins Harvill, 1989. 1st Eng ed. Signed. VF in dj. *Between The Covers.* $85/£55

FORD, ROBERT. Captured in Tibet. London: George G. Harrap, (1957). 1st ed. 2 maps. VG. *Blue Dragon.* $25/£16

FORD, SAMUEL. The American Cyclopedia of Domestic Medicine and Household Surgery. Chicago, 1883. 1st ed. 3 vols. 1215; 67pp. Good. *Fye.* $125/£81

FORD, WORTHINGTON CHAUNCEY (ed). The Controversy between Lieutenant-Governor Spotswood, and His Council and the House of Burgesses.... Historical Ptg Club, 1891. #5/250. 61pp. Paper cvr. VG. *Book Broker.* $35/£23

FORDHAM, ELIAS PYM. Personal Narrative of Travels in Virginia, Maryland.... Frederic Austin Ogg (ed). Cleveland: Clark, 1906. 1st ed. Grn cl. Inscrip, spine ends rubbed, else VG +. Howes F 257. *Chapel Hill.* $125/£81

FORDHAM, ELIAS PYM. Personal Narrative of Travels in Virginia, Maryland...1817-1818. Cleveland: Clark, 1906. 1st ed. 4 plts. Howes F 257. *Ginsberg.* $125/£81

FORDHAM, H. Some Notable Surveyors and Map Makers of the 16th, 17th, and 18th Centuries.... CUP, 1929. VG. *Moss.* $70/£45

FORDYCE, GEORGE. Five Dissertations on Fever.... Boston: Bradford & Read, 1815. 1st Amer ed. (4),442,(2)pp (stamps, bkpl; lt foxing). Contemp calf (rubbed; upper joint partially split), red lettering piece. VG. *Hemlock.* $200/£129

FOREMAN, CAROLYN THOMAS. The Cross Timbers. (Muskogee, OK: Star Printery), 1947. Presentation copy. Fldg map. Grn cl. VG +. *Bohling.* $85/£55

FOREMAN, GRANT. Advancing the Frontier, 1830-1860. Norman: Univ of OK Press, 1933. 1st ed. Red cl. Fine in NF dj (price-clipped, tears mended on verso). *Chapel Hill.* $175/£113

FOREMAN, GRANT. Adventure on Red River. Norman: Univ of OK, 1937. 1st ptg. Fldg facs map. (Sm tear inside margin, repaired w/tape). VG. *Laurie.* $60/£39

FOREMAN, GRANT. The Adventures of James Collier, First Collector of the Port of San Francisco. Chicago: Black Cat Press, 1937. 1st ed. One of 250. Blue cl, paper cvr label. NF (sl worn). *Harrington.* $85/£55

FOREMAN, GRANT. The Five Civilized Tribes. Norman: Univ of OK, 1934. 1st ed. VG +. *Parker.* $75/£48

FOREMAN, GRANT. Indians and Pioneers. New Haven: Yale Univ Press, 1930. 1st ed. Fldg map, 8 plts. Blue cl. Owner label, else Fine. Howes F 259. *Chapel Hill.* $125/£81

FOREMAN, GRANT. Indians and Pioneers. The Story of the American Southwest Before 1830. Yale, 1930. 1st ed. 8 plts, fldg map. Fine. Howes F 259. *Oregon.* $150/£97

FOREMAN, GRANT. Pioneer Days in the Early Southwest. Cleveland, 1926. 1st ed. (Joints lt worn; sm discoloration spine.) Howes F 260. *Ginsberg.* $150/£97

FOREMAN, GRANT. Sequoyah. Norman: Univ of OK Press, (1959). 2nd ptg, entirely reset. Orange cl, paper spine label. VG in dj (price-clipped). *Chapel Hill.* $35/£23

FOREMAN, GRANT. Sequoyah. Norman: Univ of OK Press, 1938. 1st ed. Orange cl, paper spine label. NF (sl worn, spine dknd). *Harrington.* $65/£42

FOREMAN, JOHN. The Philippine Islands. London: Sampson Low, Marston, 1899. 2nd enlgd, rev ed. xvi,653,half title, frontis, 19 plts, 3 maps and charts (2 fldg, incl colored map in pocket). Blue cl, gilt lettering, black/brown vignette. VG (leaf H7 torn w/o loss; lib plt; corner bumped). *Morrell.* $163/£105

Forest Arcadia of Northern New York. (By Nathaniel Wheeler Coffin.) Boston: Burnham, 1864. 224pp (edge of 2 leaves expertly repaired). 3/4 grn leather. *Schoyer.* $100/£65

FORESTER, C.S. The African Queen. Boston: Little, Brown, 1935. 1st Amer ed. 8vo. VG in pict dj (nicks, tears). *Houle.* $850/£548

FORESTER, C.S. The Bedchamber Mystery. Saunders, 1944. 1st (and only) ed. Lt soiling, else VG. *Fine Books.* $75/£48

FORESTER, C.S. The Bedchamber Mystery. Toronto: Saunders, 1944. Only ed. Pict bds. VG in dj (lt chipped, internal repair). *Limestone.* $175/£113

FORESTER, C.S. Commodore Hornblower. Boston, 1945. 1st ed. VG (fraying, shelfwear) in dj (price-clipped, chip back panel, nicks). *Mcclintock.* $20/£13

FORESTER, C.S. The Commodore. London: Joseph, 1945. 1st ed. VG + in dj. *Limestone.* $85/£55

FORESTER, C.S. Hornblower and the Atropos. London: Michael Joseph, 1953. 1st UK ed. VG in dj. *Williams.* $28/£18

FORESTER, C.S. Hornblower and the Crisis. London: Michael Joseph, 1967. 1st UK ed. Fine in NF dj. *Williams.* $31/£20

FORESTER, C.S. Hornblower and the Hotspur. London: Michael Joseph, (1962). 1st ed. Fine in Fine dj (lt rubbed). *Unger.* $125/£81

FORESTER, C.S. Hornblower and the Hotspur. Boston: Little, Brown, (1962). 1st US ed. Fine in Fine dj (sl soiled). *Unger.* $100/£65

FORESTER, C.S. Hornblower and the Hotspur. Little Brown, 1962. 1st ed. NF in VG + dj. *Bishop.* $22/£14

FORESTER, C.S. Hornblower and the Hotspur. London: Michael Joseph, 1962. 1st UK ed. NF in dj. *Williams.* $31/£20

FORESTER, C.S. Hunting the Bismarck. London: Michael Joseph, 1959. 1st UK ed. Fine in dj. *Williams.* $31/£20

FORESTER, C.S. Hunting the Bismark. London, 1959. 1st Eng ed. VG in dj. *Edrich.* $19/£12

FORESTER, C.S. Lieutenant Hornblower. London: Michael Joseph, 1952. 1st ed. Fine in dj (shallow chipping spine head). *Else Fine.* $85/£55

FORESTER, C.S. Lieutenant Hornblower. London: Michael Joseph, 1952. 1st UK ed. VG + in VG dj. *Williams.* $34/£22

FORESTER, C.S. Lord Hornblower. London: Michael Joseph, 1946. 1st UK ed. NF in VG dj (sl chipped; spine repaired). *Williams.* $23/£15

FORESTER, C.S. Lord Nelson. B-M, 1929. 1st ed. NF in VG dj (lt wear; dust soil). *Fine Books.* $285/£184

FORESTER, C.S. Mr. Midshipman Hornblower. London: Joseph, 1950. 1st ed. NF in Fine dj. *Limestone.* $75/£48

FORESTER, C.S. Napoleon and His Court. London: Methuen, 1924. 1st UK ed. VG. *Lewton.* $93/£60

FORESTER, C.S. The Nightmare. Boston: Little Brown, (1954). 1st Amer ed. Fine in VG + dj (sl rubbed; sm nicks, tears extrems). *Between The Covers.* $65/£42

FORESTER, C.S. The Nightmare. Boston: Little, Brown, 1954. 1st ed. Fine in dj (rear panel rumpled). *Beasley.* $35/£23

FORESTER, C.S. The Nightmare. London: Michael Joseph, 1954. 1st UK ed. VG + in dj (price-clipped). *Williams.* $39/£25

FORESTER, C.S. Payment Deferred. Boston: Little, Brown, 1942. 1st Amer ed. Eps lt foxed, else Fine in dj (chip, short tape-mended tears). *Godot.* $175/£113

FORESTER, C.S. Randall and the River of Time. London: Michael Joseph, 1951. 1st UK ed. VG + in dj. *Williams.* $28/£18

FORESTER, C.S. The Ship. Boston: Little, Brown, (1943). 1st ed. VG in VG dj. *Unger.* $125/£81

FORESTER, C.S. The Ship. L-B, 1943. 1st ed. Fine in NF dj. *Fine Books.* $65/£42

FORESTER, C.S. The Ship. London: Michael Joseph, 1943. 1st UK ed. VG in dj (sl rubbed, chipped). *Williams.* $54/£35

FORESTER, FRANK. (Pseud of Henry William Herbert.) The Complete Manual for Young Sportsmen. NY: Townsend & Adams, 1868. Engr tp, frontis, 480pp, 1 plt. Orig cl; spine reads Woodward w/Woodward ads bound in at rear. VG. *Bowman.* $60/£39

FORESTER, FRANK. (Pseud of Henry William Herbert.) Field Sports in the United States and the British Provinces of America. London: Richard Bentley, 1848. 1st ed. 2 vols. Pale grn cl stamped in gilt, blind. Spines sl sunned; sl rubbing, spots; o/w VG set. BAL 8108. *Reese.* $500/£323

FORESTER, FRANK. (Pseud of Henry William Herbert.) Frank Forester's Field Sports of the United States, and British Provinces of North America. NY: Stringer & Townsend, 1849. 1st US ed. 2 vols. 360; 367pp, frontis both vols. Purple cl, gilt. Worn, faded, foxed, bkpl, else Good. BAL 8112. *Cahan.* $125/£81

FORESTER, FRANK. (Pseud of Henry William Herbert.) Frank Forester's Fish and Fishing of the United States and British Provinces of North America. NY: Stringer & Townsend, 1855. Color frontis, 359pp, 86pp Supplement. (Bumped, rubbed; split fr joint, spine.) VG. *Blue Mountain.* $125/£81

FORESTER, FRANK. (Pseud of Henry William Herbert.) The Sporting Novels of Frank Forester. NY: Derrydale, 1930. One of 750 numbered sets. 4 vols. Teg, others uncut. Blue cl. Spine labels rubbed, o/w VG + set. *Bowman.* $125/£81

FORESTER, FRANK. (Pseud of Henry William Herbert.) Trouting Along the Catasauqua. NY: Derrydale, 1927. One of 423 numbered. Frontis plt. Externally VG + (eps foxed). *Bowman.* $200/£129

FORGUE, NORMAN W. Poorer Richard. Chicago: Black Cat, 1954. Ltd ed. Uncut. Ptd wrappers. VG. *Argosy.* $40/£26

FORMAN, BENNO M. American Seating Furniture 1630-1730. NY, London, 1988. 92 plts. Dj. *Edwards.* $54/£35

FORMAN, H. BUXTON. The Shelley Library: An Essay in Bibliography. Reeves & Turner, 1886. 127pp. Unopened. Orig ptd cvrs (sl worn). *Moss.* $62/£40

FORMAN, HENRY CHANDLEE. Early Manor and Plantation Houses of Maryland. Easton, MD: The Author, 1934. 1st ed. Ink inscrip, else Fine. *Bookpress.* $325/£210

FORMAN, HENRY CHANDLEE. Old Buildings, Gardens, and Furniture in Tidewater Maryland. Cambridge, MD: Tidewater Pub, 1967. 1st ed. Bkpl, else Fine in dj (sl chipped). *Bookpress.* $45/£29

FORMILLI, C.T.G. The Stones of Italy. A&C Black, 1927. 1st ed. 32 color plts, map. (Frontis detached.) *Edwards.* $62/£40

FORREST, ANTHONY. Captain Justice: Secret Agent Against Napoleon. NY: Hill & Wang, 1981. 1st ed. VF in VF dj. *Murder.* $27/£17

FORREST, EARLE R. Arizona's Dark and Bloody Ground. Caldwell: Caxton, 1936. 1st ed. VG in VG dj. Howes H 265. *Perier.* $175/£113

FORREST, EARLE R. Arizona's Dark and Bloody Ground. Caldwell: Caxton, 1950. Rev ed. VG in dj (lt worn). *Glenn.* $40/£26

FORREST, EARLE R. Missions and Pueblos of the Old Southwest. Cleveland: Clark, 1929. 1st ed. Fine. *Parker.* $175/£113

FORREST, EARLE R. Missions and Pueblos of the Old Southwest. Cleveland: Clark, 1929. 1st ed. Teg, deckle edges. Blue cl. NF. *Parmer.* $215/£139

FORREST, FELIX C. (Pseud of Cordwainer Smith.) Ria. Duell, Sloan, 1947. 1st ed, 1st bk. NF in dj. *Madle.* $125/£81

FORSTER, E.M. Alexandria: A History and a Guide. Alexandria: Whitehead Morris, 1922. 1st ed. Fldg map back pocket. Ptd tan bds. Upper corners bumped, o/w Excellent. *Argosy.* $400/£258

FORSTER, E.M. Alexandria: A History and a Guide. Alexandria: Whitehead Morris, 1922. 1st UK ed. Plan facing pg 144 incorrectly placed to face pg 44. VG (ink inscrip; little cracking spine, repaired). No dj, as issued. *Williams.* $457/£295

FORSTER, E.M. Alexandria: A History and a Guide. Alexandria, 1938. 2nd ed. Fldg map at rear. (Backstrip chipped; lower joint split; discolored.) *Edwards.* $62/£40

FORSTER, E.M. Anonymity. London: Hogarth Press, 1925. 1st ed. Paper-cvrd bds. Bkpl; pp foxed, browned; soiled, ink stain; spine cracked. *Virgo.* $47/£30

FORSTER, E.M. Anonymity. London: Hogarth Press, 1925. 1st ed. Pict bds. VG. *Argosy.* $125/£81

FORSTER, E.M. Battersea Rise. NY, (1955). 1st Amer ed. Dec bds. Fine. *Polyanthos.* $35/£23

FORSTER, E.M. Commonplace Book. London, 1985. 1st Eng ed. VG in dj. *Edrich.* $19/£12

FORSTER, E.M. The Eternal Moment. London: Sidgwick & Jackson, 1928. 1st UK ed. Maroon cl. Lt foxing eps, prelims, o/w VG in dj (chipped; lacks sm piece spine tail). *Moorhouse.* $54/£35

FORSTER, E.M. The Hill of Devi. NY: Harcourt Brace, (1953). VG in dj (sl worn). *Second Life.* $65/£42

FORSTER, E.M. The Hill of Devi. NY, 1953. 1st Amer ed. Fine (spine extrems sl rubbed) in Fine dj. *Polyanthos.* $25/£16

FORSTER, E.M. A Letter to Madam Blanchard. Hogarth Press, 1931. 1st ed. VG in wraps. *Virgo.* $31/£20

FORSTER, E.M. A Letter to Madam Blanchard. London: Hogarth Press, 1931. 1st ed. Ptd wrappers (sl soiled). *Hollett.* $39/£25

FORSTER, E.M. The Manuscripts of a Passage to India. Arnold, 1978. #961/1500. VG + in VG + dj. *Martin.* $53/£34

FORSTER, E.M. Marianne Thornton 1797-1887. Edward Arnold, (1957). 1st ed. Dj (chipped). *Bickersteth.* $39/£25

FORSTER, E.M. Nordic Twilight. Macmillan, 1940. 1st ed. Lt foxing, else NF in wraps as issued. *Fine Books.* $45/£29

FORSTER, E.M. A Passage to India. London: Edward Arnold, 1924. 1st ed. VG (bkpl; hinges starting; spine soiled). *Lame Duck.* $100/£65

FORSTER, E.M. A Passage to India. Arnold, 1924. 1st ed. VG+ in VG dj (spine dknd). *Fine Books.* $900/£581

FORSTER, E.M. A Passage to India. London: Edward Arnold, 1924. 1st UK ed. VG (sl mks fep from label removal; foxing throughout). *Williams.* $349/£225

FORSTER, E.M. Pharos and Pharillon. Hogarth Press, 1923. 1st ed. Bds w/cl spine; ptd paper label. (Cvr fore-edges lt browned.) *Bickersteth.* $47/£30

FORSTER, E.M. Pharos and Pharillon. Richmond, UK: Hogarth Press, 1923. 1st ed. One of 900. Bkpl, rep, inside rear cvr sl foxed; spine sl sunned; extrems, paper label, cvrs sl rubbed, o/w Fine. Issued w/o dj. *Polyanthos.* $150/£97

FORSTER, E.M. Two Cheers for Democracy. London: Arnold, 1951. 1st ed. Sig, else NF in dj. *Limestone.* $45/£29

FORSTER, E.M. Virginia Woolf. NY: Harcourt, Brace, (1942). 1st Amer ed. Grn cl. Fine in dj. *Macdonnell.* $100/£65

FORSTER, E.M. What I Believe. Hogarth, 1939. 1st ed. Wraps sl dull; sm hole fr wrap 1/2 title, tp, else VG. *Whiteson.* $25/£16

FORSTER, E.M. What I Believe. Hogarth Press, 1939. 1st ed. Cvr soil, else VG in wraps as issued. *Fine Books.* $65/£42

FORSTER, E.M. Where Angels Fear to Tread. Edinburgh: Blackwood, 1905. 1st ed. This copy lacks any ads. Slate blue cl (spine faded brn, 1/4 inch chip at top). *Argosy.* $500/£323

FORSTER, E.M. Where Angels Fear to Tread. NY, 1920. 1st Amer ed. Contents Fine (sunned, sl rubbed, sl soiled). *Polyanthos.* $75/£48

FORSTER, JOHANN REINHOLD. The Resolution Journal of Johann Reinhold Forster, 1772-1775. Michael E. Hoare (ed). London: Hakluyt Soc, 1982. 1st ed. 4 vols. Color frontis vol 1. Blue gilt cl. Good in djs. *Karmiole.* $65/£42

FORSTER, JOHN REINHOLD. History of the Voyages and Discoveries Made in the North. Dublin: for Luke White, 1786. 2nd ed in English. 8vo. Fldg frontis, 489,(30)pp. Orig calf (rebacked). Edges rubbed; lib bkpl, stamps; else VG. Howes F 269. *Chapel Hill.* $250/£161

FORSTER, T.I.M. Observations on the Natural History of Swallows. London, 1817. 6th ed, enlgd. Variant issue, having 'Swallows' instead of 'Swallow Tribe'; and the words 'Sixth edition enlarged' do not appear. xiv,(1),97pp; 5 plts. Calf (rebacked). Cheap copy (very used). *Wheldon & Wesley.* $47/£30

FORSYTH, FREDERICK. The Day of the Jackal. London: Hutchinson, 1971. 1st UK ed. NF in VG dj (sl edge-worn). *Williams.* $93/£60

FORSYTH, FREDERICK. The Fourth Protocol. London: Hutchinson, 1984. 1st ed. Fine in dj. *Mordida.* $45/£29

FORSYTH, FREDERICK. No Comebacks. London: Hutchinson, 1982. 1st ed. NF in dj. *Silver Door.* $30/£19

FORSYTH, FREDERICK. The Odessa File. NY: Viking Press, (1972). 1st US ed. Signed. Fine in dj. *Bernard.* $60/£39

FORSYTH, GEORGE ALEXANDER. Thrilling Days in Army Life. NY: Harper, 1900. 1st ed. Dec cl. NF. Howes F 271. *Mcgowan.* $175/£113

FORSYTH, WILLIAM H. The Entombment of Christ. French Sculptures of the Fifteenth and Sixteenth Centuries. Cambridge, 1970. 124 plts. Good. *Washton.* $135/£87

FORSYTH, WILLIAM. A Treatise on the Culture and Management of Fruit Trees. Phila, 1802. 1st Amer ed. xii,259pp (foxing, offsetting; brown stains; pencil dwg rear blank sheet), 13 engr plts (11 fldg). Contemp full calf (worn, piece missing to spine; fr cvr bowed). *Sutton.* $225/£145

FORSYTH, WILLIAM. A Treatise on the Culture and Management of Fruit Trees. NY: Ezra Sargeant, 1802. 1st Amer ed. 259pp, 13 plts. Uncut. (Bds worn, foxed throughout.) *Argosy.* $350/£226

FORSYTH, WILLIAM. A Treatise on the Culture and Management of Fruit Trees. London, 1803. 2nd ed. xxvii,523; 13 fldg plts. Tree calf (rebacked). *Henly.* $118/£76

FORSYTH, WILLIAM. A Treatise on the Culture and Management of Fruit Trees. London, 1806. 4th ed. xxviii,523pp (fep neatly repaired), 13 fldg plts (foxing). Contemp calf bds (rebacked), gilt, orig leather label. *Edwards.* $132/£85

FORT, C. New Lands. B&L, 1923. 1st ed. VG in dj (chipping, dust soil). *Fine Books.* $175/£113

FORT, GEORGE F. Medical Economy During the Middle Ages: A Contribution to the History of European Morals...to the Close of the Fourteenth Century. NY/London, 1883. 1st ed. xii,488pp (ms commentary, bk rev on fly). Gilt spine title. Uncut. Fine. *Hemlock.* $175/£113

FORTESCUE, J.W. A History of the British Army. Vol II (of XIII). London: Macmillan, 1899. xxii,629pp + 2pp ads; 10 maps. VG. *Schoyer.* $65/£42

FORTIS, ABBE ALBERTO. Travels into Dalmatia...in a Series of Letters.... London: J. Robson, 1778. 1st Eng ed. 4to. (ii),x,584, 3 fldg engr maps and charts, 16 engr plts (11 fldg). Contemp polished calf (rebacked at early date; rubbed), gilt rules on cvrs, spine gilt, red label. Internally VG (lt browning, spotting few margins; early ink inscrip). *Morrell.* $744/£480

FORTUNE, R.F. Sorcerers of Dobu. London, 1932. Map. (Sl dampstained upper bd; lower bd sl soiled.) Dj (chipped; label remains spine). *Edwards.* $93/£60

FORTUNE, ROBERT. A Residence Among the Chinese.... London: John Murray, 1857. 1st ed. Frontis, (xvi),440pp; 5 plts. Contemp 1/2-calf (rebacked). *Bickersteth.* $225/£145

Forty Thieves, Being the History of Ali Baba and His Female Slave. Devonport: W. Pollard & J. Mudge, n.d. (ca 1835). 12mo. Full-pg frontis, 35pp; 6 hand-colored wood engrs. Pict grn stiff paper wrappers. Good (dated ink inscrip, sm spot tp; cvr lt chipped). *Hobbyhorse.* $150/£97

FOSDICK, HARRY EMERSON. Jesus of Nazareth. NY: Random House, 1959. 1st trade ed. Joseph Cellini (illus). Fine in dj. *Cattermole.* $100/£65

FOSDICK, HARRY EMERSON. The Life of Saint Paul. NY: Random House, 1962. 1st trade ed. Leonard Everett Fisher (illus). Fine in dj. *Cattermole.* $30/£19

FOSKETT, D. Samuel Cooper, 1609-1672. London: Faber, 1974. 87 plts (13 color). Excellent in dj. *Ars Artis.* $54/£35

FOSTER, DAVID. The Scientific Angler. London, (1882). 1st ed. Pict gilt cl (sl loose, sm stains; sl foxing). *Petersfield.* $81/£52

FOSTER, J.J. British Miniature Painters and Their Works. London, 1898. #88/125. Lg paper ed. Frontis port, xii,146pp,(vi)index, 58 plts. Teg, rest uncut. (Feps lt browned; edge-worn; spine sl bumped, chipped.) *Edwards.* $194/£125

FOSTER, JOHN L. (ed). Love Songs of the New Kingdom. NY: Scribner's, (1974). Good in dj. *Archaeologia.* $35/£23

FOSTER, MYLES B. A Day in a Child's Life. London: George Routledge, (1881). 1st ed. Lg 4to. Kate Greenaway (illus). Pict bds. Good in pict dj (edge chipping). *Reisler.* $900/£581

FOSTER-HARRIS. The Look of the Old West. NY: Viking, 1955. 1st ed. *Book Market.* $22/£14

FOTHERGILL, E. Five Years in the Sudan. London, 1911. VG + . *Trophy Room.* $250/£161

FOTHERGILL, J. MILNER. The Antagonism of Therapeutic Agents. Phila, 1878. 1st Amer ed. 160pp + ads (ex-lib, pencil notes; spotted; backstrip chipped; hinges cracked). *Argosy.* $125/£81

FOUCAULT, MICHEL. The Birth of the Clinic. NY: Pantheon, 1973. 1st US ed. NF in dj. *Lame Duck.* $50/£32

FOUGERA, KATHERINE GIBSON. With Custer's Cavalry. Caldwell: Caxton, 1942. Good in dj (chipped). *Lien.* $85/£55

FOUNTAIN, ROBERT and ALFRED GATES. Stubbs' Dogs. London, 1984. VG in dj. *Argosy.* $75/£48

FOURNIER, ALFRED. The Treatment in Prophylaxis of Syphilis. NY, 1907. 1st Eng trans. Good. *Fye.* $150/£97

Fourth and Fifth Annual Reports of the Bureau of Animal Industry for the Year 1887 and 1888. Washington, 1889. 510pp. (Sm chips back cvr.) *Hayman.* $40/£26

FOWLER, GENE. Minutes of the Last Meeting. NY, 1954. 1st ed. Spine sl faded, else VG in dj (sl frayed). *King.* $25/£16

FOWLER, H. ALFRED. Bookplates for Beginners. Kansas City: Alfred Fowler, 1922. 1s ed. Sl dusty, chipped, worn; ink name, else Good. *Hermitage.* $35/£23

FOWLER, H. ALFRED. Lincolniana Bookplates and Collections. Kansas City: Fowler, 1913. 1st ed. Cl-backed bds stamped in blue. *Ginsberg.* $125/£81

FOWLER, JACOB. The Journal of Jacob Fowler. NY: Francis P. Harper, 1898. 1st ed. One of 950 numbered. Fldg frontis, xxiv,183pp. Later cl, leather spine label. Lt spot fore-edge few leaves, else VG. Howes F 298. *Cahan.* $145/£94

FOWLER, JACOB. The Journal of Jacob Fowler. Elliott Coues (ed). NY: Francis Harper, 1898. #790/950. Fldg frontis, xxiv,183pp, facs. Blue cl, gilt title. VG. Howes F 298. *Bohling.* $200/£129

FOWLER, JAMES and RICKMAN GODLEE. The Diseases of the Lungs. London, 1898. 1st ed. 715pp. Table of contents heavily annotated in ink, o/w VG. *Fye.* $150/£97

FOWLER, O.S. Creative and Sexual Science. Cincinnati, 1875. 1st ed. 1065pp. Good. *Fye.* $150/£97

FOWLER, O.S. Fowler's Practical Phrenology. NY, 1853. 432pp. Good. *Fye.* $50/£32

FOWLER, O.S. A Home for All, or the Gravel Wall and Octagon Mode of Building. NY: Wells, 1854. Copyright dated 1853. 192pp, 2 frontispieces, 11pp cat. (Foxing.) *Marlborough.* $147/£95

FOWLER, O.S. A Home for All, or The Gravel Wall and Octagon Mode of Building. NY: Fowlers & Wells, 1854. Rev ed. Frontis; (iii),192,11,(1)pp. Pub's blue gilt cl. Lt rubbed; pencil inscrip; text foxed, else VG. *Bookpress.* $285/£184

FOWLER, O.S. Private Lectures on Perfect Men, Women and Children, and Happy Families. Sharon Station, NY, 1883. 191pp. (Binding spotted, worn.) *Fye.* $50/£32

FOWLER, O.S. and L.N. FOWLER. Now Illustrated Self-Instructor in Phrenology and Physiology.... London: W. Tweedie, n.d. (ca 1878). 60th Thousand. Inscribed by L.N. Fowler. Chart. Grn cl, gilt. Good. *Karmiole.* $75/£48

FOWLER, O.S. and L.N. FOWLER. Phrenology Proved, Illustrated, and Applied, Accompanied by a Chart. NY, 1838. 3rd ed. 420pp. Good. *Fye.* $75/£48

FOWLES, JOHN (trans). Ourika. Austin, 1977. One of 500 specially bound, signed. Bds sl rubbed, o/w Fine. *Rees.* $140/£90

FOWLES, JOHN and HAROLD PINTER. The French Lieutenant's Woman. Boston, (1981). #64/360. Signed by Fowles and Pinter. Fine in Fine box (sl rubbed). *Polyanthos.* $150/£97

FOWLES, JOHN with FAY GODWIN. Islands. London: Cape, 1978. 1st ed. Fine in dj. *Rees.* $16/£10

FOWLES, JOHN. The Aristos. L-B, 1964. 1st ed. VF in VF dj. *Fine Books.* $150/£97

FOWLES, JOHN. The Aristos. Boston/Toronto: Little, Brown, 1964. 1st ed. Inscribed. Orig brn cl. Fine in dj. *Rees.* $388/£250

FOWLES, JOHN. The Aristos. London: Jonathan Cape, 1965. 1st Eng ed. Inscribed. Orig dk blue cl. Dj spine sl sunned, else NF. *Rees.* $465/£300

FOWLES, JOHN. The Aristos. London: Cape, 1980. 1st British rev ed. Fine in NF dj (price-clipped). *Pettler.* $35/£23

FOWLES, JOHN. A Brief History of Lyme. Lyme Regis: Friends of the Museum, 1981. 1st ed. Signed. Fine in orig wrappers. *Rees.* $47/£30

FOWLES, JOHN. A Brief History of Lyme. Lyme Regis, 1985. 1st ed. Fine in wrappers. *Rees.* $19/£12

FOWLES, JOHN. A Brief History of Lyme. Lyme Regis: Friends of the Museum, 1985. Rev ed. Signed. Fine in orig wrappers. *Rees.* $39/£25

FOWLES, JOHN. Cinderella. Boston: Little, Brown, (1974). 1st Amer ed. Fine in dj (price-clipped). *Reese.* $50/£32

FOWLES, JOHN. Cinderella. London: Cape, (1974). 1st ed. Signed. Sm label, pub's price sticker marked out, else Fine in dj (lt edge-tanned). *Reese.* $85/£55

FOWLES, JOHN. Cinderella. London: Jonathan Cape, 1974. 1st ed. Inscribed. Orig wheat-colored cl. Dj extrems lt browned, else Fine. *Rees.* $78/£50

FOWLES, JOHN. The Collector. London: Jonathan Cape, (1963). 1st ed, 1st bk. NF in dj. *Godot.* $750/£484

FOWLES, JOHN. The Collector. London, (1963). 1st ed, 1st issue dj w/no blurbs on fr flap. Fine in dj. *Argosy.* $750/£484

FOWLES, JOHN. The Collector. L-B, 1963. 1st Amer ed, 1st bk. Advance reading copy. VG + in wraps. *Fine Books.* $250/£161

FOWLES, JOHN. The Collector. Little, Brown, 1963. 1st Amer ed. NF (bkpl, stains) in dj. *Stahr.* $75/£48

FOWLES, JOHN. The Collector. Boston/Toronto: Little, Brown, 1963. 1st Amer ed. Inscribed. Orig rust-colored cl. Sm rubbed area to dj, else NF. *Rees.* $233/£150

FOWLES, JOHN. The Collector. London: Jonathan Cape, 1963. 1st ed. Inscribed. Rust-colored cl. Sl bumped, lt foxed at edges, else NF in 1st issue dj (lt rubbed, soiled). *Rees.* $465/£300

FOWLES, JOHN. The Collector. London: Cape, 1963. 1st UK ed. VG in dj. *Williams.* $271/£175

FOWLES, JOHN. Daniel Martin. Toronto: Collins Publishers, 1977. 1st Canadian ed. Orig grn cl. Fine in dj. *Rees.* $23/£15

FOWLES, JOHN. The Ebony Tower. Boston/Toronto: Little, Brown, 1974. 1st Amer ed. Inscribed. Orig mustard cl, grn cl spine. NF in dj. *Rees.* $62/£40

FOWLES, JOHN. The Enigma of Stonehenge. London: Jonathan Cape, 1980. 1st ed. Signed. Orig dk brn cl. Fine in dj. *Rees.* $54/£35

FOWLES, JOHN. The Enigma. (Helsinki): Eurographica, 1987. #217/350 signed, dated. Fine in stiff wrappers in dj as issued. *Williams.* $116/£75

FOWLES, JOHN. The French Lieutenant's Woman. London: Jonathan Cape, 1969. 1st ed. Inscribed. Orig brn cl. Fine in dj. *Rees.* $271/£175

FOWLES, JOHN. The French Lieutenant's Woman. London: Cape, 1969. 1st UK ed. VG in dj (price-clipped, sl rubbed; mks). *Williams.* $62/£40

FOWLES, JOHN. The French Lieutenant's Woman. London: Cape, 1969. 1st UK ed. VG + in dj (sl rubbed; spine browned). *Williams.* $93/£60

FOWLES, JOHN. Islands. London: Cape, (1978). 1st ed. Signed. Brn bds, gilt-stamped. Fine in dj. *Reese.* $85/£55

FOWLES, JOHN. Islands. Boston/Toronto: Little, Brown, 1978. 1st Amer ed. Inscribed. Orig brn cl. Lt offsetting to flyleaves, else Fine in dj. *Rees.* $47/£30

FOWLES, JOHN. Islands. London: Jonathan Cape, 1978. 1st ed. Inscribed. Orig dk brn cl. Fine in dj. *Rees.* $54/£35

FOWLES, JOHN. Lyme Regis Museum Curator's Report 1981. Signed. Fine in wrappers. *Rees.* $16/£10

FOWLES, JOHN. A Maggot. London: London Ltd Editions, 1985. #32/500 signed. Orig feathered bds, pale brn cl spine. Fine in pub's glassine. *Rees.* $78/£50

FOWLES, JOHN. A Maggot. Boston/Toronto: Little, Brown, 1985. 1st Amer ed. Orig brn cl. Fine in dj. *Rees.* $23/£15

FOWLES, JOHN. A Maggot. Little, Brown, 1985. 1st Amer ed. Signed. Fine in dj. *Stahr.* $60/£39

FOWLES, JOHN. A Maggot. Toronto: Collins, 1985. 1st Canadian ed. Signed. Orig brn cl. Fine in dj. *Rees.* $62/£40

FOWLES, JOHN. A Maggot. London: Jonathan Cape, 1985. 1st trade ed. Inscribed. Orig black cl. Fine in dj. *Rees.* $78/£50

FOWLES, JOHN. A Maggot. London: Cape, 1985. 1st UK ed. NF in dj. *Williams.* $19/£12

FOWLES, JOHN. The Magus. Boston: Little, Brown, (1965). 1st ed. Fine in dj. *Between The Covers.* $200/£129

FOWLES, JOHN. The Magus. London: Cape, (1966). 1st Eng ed. Fine in Fine dj (price-clipped). *Between The Covers.* $250/£161

FOWLES, JOHN. The Magus. Boston/Toronto: Little, Brown, 1965. 1st ed. Inscribed. Orig grn cl. Fine in dj. *Rees.* $271/£175

FOWLES, JOHN. The Magus. Cape, 1966. 1st Eng ed. Fine in NF dj. *Fine Books.* $145/£94

FOWLES, JOHN. The Magus. London: Jonathan Cape, 1966. 1st Eng ed. Inscribed. Orig grey bds, purple spine. Fine in dj (sl rubbed). *Rees.* $310/£200

FOWLES, JOHN. The Magus. London: Cape, 1966. 1st UK ed. Fine in VG dj. *Williams.* $78/£50

FOWLES, JOHN. The Magus: A Revised Version. London: Cape, (1977). 1st British ed thus. Fine in dj. *Reese.* $45/£29

FOWLES, JOHN. The Magus: A Revised Version. Boston: Little, Brown, (1978). 1st Amer ed. NF in dj. *Antic Hay.* $35/£23

FOWLES, JOHN. Mantissa. Boston: Little, Brown, (1982). 1st ed, ltd issue. One of 500 numbered (of 510), signed. As New in slipcase. *Reese.* $100/£65

FOWLES, JOHN. Mantissa. Boston/Toronto: Little, Brown, 1982. 1st Amer ed. Orig grn cl. NF in dj. *Rees.* $16/£10

FOWLES, JOHN. Mantissa. Toronto: Collins, 1982. 1st Canadian ed. Orig grn cl. Fine in dj. *Rees.* $23/£15

FOWLES, JOHN. Mantissa. London: Jonathan Cape, 1982. 1st ed. Inscribed. Orig grey cl. NF in dj. *Rees.* $78/£50

FOWLES, JOHN. Poems. (NY): Ecco, (1973). 1st ed. VF in dj. *Reese.* $40/£26

FOWLES, JOHN. Poems. NY: Ecco Press, 1973. 1st ed. Inscribed. Orig beige cl. Fine in dj. *Rees.* $78/£50

FOWLES, JOHN. Poor Koko. (Helsinki): Eurographica, 1987. #324/350 signed, dated. Fine in stiff cvrs in dj as issued. *Williams.* $116/£75

FOWLES, JOHN. Shipwreck. London: Jonathan Cape, 1974. 1st ed. Signed. Orig dk-blue cl. Sm mk inside dj fr flap, else NF. *Rees.* $54/£35

FOWLES, JOHN. Shipwreck. L-B, 1975. 1st Amer ed. Fine in NF dj (2 closed tears). *Fine Books.* $18/£12

FOWLES, JOHN. A Short History of Lyme Regis. Boston: Little, Brown, (1982). Amer issue of 1st ed. One of 2500. Rev slip laid in. Fine in dj. *Reese.* $40/£26

FOWLES, JOHN. A Short History of Lyme Regis. Boston/Toronto: Little, Brown, 1982. 1st Amer ed. Orig turquoise cl. Fine in dj. *Rees.* $23/£15

FOWLES, JOHN. The Tree. Boston: Little, Brown, (1980). 1st Amer ed. Rev slip laid in. Fine in dj. *Reese.* $55/£35

FOWLES, JOHN. The Tree. Aurum Press, 1979. 1st ed. Dj (sl ragged). *Edwards.* $39/£25

FOWLES, JOHN. The Tree. London: Aurum, 1979. 1st state, w/correct price and misprint on lower dj flap. Fine in dj (sl rubbed, creased). *Rees.* $54/£35

FOWLIE, J.A. The Genus Lycaste.... Pomona, 1970. 8 color, 20 plain plts. (Extrems scuffed; lt dampstained corners, few pp.) *Sutton.* $45/£29

FOX, CHARLES J. A Guide to Officers of Towns; Containing the Statutes.... Concord: Edson C. Easton, 1866. 5th ed. Contemp sheep (rubbed). Nice. *Boswell.* $100/£65

FOX, CHARLES PHILIP and TOM PARKINSON. The Circus in America. Waukesha, WI, (1969). VG in dj (chipped, torn). *King.* $40/£26

FOX, CHARLES PHILIP. Circus Parades. Watkins Glen: Century, 1953. 1st ed. VG in Fair dj. *October Farm*. $48/£31

FOX, CHARLES. The Wonderful World of Trout. Carlisle, PA, 1963. 1st ed, #1924 of signed ltd ed. VF in dj (chipped). *Bond*. $55/£35

FOX, CYRIL. Offa's Dyke. London, 1955. 1st ed. 46 plts. Dj (chipped, sl soiled). *Edwards*. $101/£65

FOX, GEORGE HENRY. Photographic Illustrations of Skin Diseases. NY, 1880. 1st ed. 102pp; 48 hand-colored photo plts. 1/2 leather (binding worn). *Fye*. $400/£258

FOX, GEORGE HENRY. Reminiscences. NY, 1926. 1st ed. VG. *Argosy*. $35/£23

FOX, GUSTAVUS VASA. Confidential Correspondence of...1861-1865. Robert Means Thompson & Richard Wainwright (eds). NY: Naval Hist Soc, 1918-1919. 1st ed. One of 1200, subs note laid in. 2 vols. Engr frontis ports; teg, others untrimmed; partially unopened. Vellum-backed bds, gilt centerpieces. Fine in glassine djs (lt used), pub's slipcases. *Chapel Hill*. $110/£71

FOX, GUSTAVUS VASA. Confidential Correspondence of...1861-1865. Robert Means Thompson and Richard Wainwright (eds). NY: De Vinne Press, 1918-1919. Ltd to 1200 numbered sets. 2 vols. Frontis in each. Good in slipcase. *Karmiole*. $100/£65

FOX, GUSTAVUS VASA. Narrative of the Mission to Russia, in 1866.... NY: Appleton, 1879. Frontis engr, (x),462pp, 12 full-pg engrs, fldg chart; review pasted to fep. Grn cl stamped in gilt/black (lib pocket removed). Very Nice. *Schoyer*. $250/£161

FOX, HELEN MORGENTHAU. Patio Gardens. NY: Macmillan, 1929. 1st ed. Good (cvrs sl soiled; water mk fore-edge most sheets). *Second Life*. $25/£16

FOX, HELEN MORGENTHAU. Patio Gardens. NY: Macmillan, 1929. 1st ed. 2 fldg plans. Fine. *Quest*. $85/£55

FOX, JOHN C. (ed). The Lady Ivie's Trial, for Great Part of Shadwell in the County of Middlesex Before Lord Chief Justice Jeffreys in 1684. Oxford: Clarendon Press, 1929. Worn but Sound. *Boswell*. $50/£32

FOX, JOHN, JR. The Little Shepherd of Kingdom Come. NY: Scribner's, 1931. 1st ed. 8vo, 322pp, 14 full-pg color plts, tp by N.C. Wyeth (illus). Black bds, pict paper label. VG. *Davidson*. $200/£129

FOX, JOHN, JR. The Little Shepherd of Kingdom Come. NY: Scribner's, 1931. 1st ed. 4to. 14 full-pg color plts by N.C. Wyeth (sm hole List of Illustrations pg). Black cl w/color paste label, tinted top. *Reisler*. $225/£145

FOX, JOHN, JR. The Trail of the Lonesome Pine. NY: Scribner, 1908. 1st ed. Frontis; 7 plts. VG. *Oregon*. $25/£16

FOX, MARGARET. The Love-Life of Dr. Kane.... NY: Carleton, 1866. x(13)288pp. Frontis port, facs. (Head of spine chipped; minor wear.) *High Latitude*. $50/£32

FOX, MARY ANNA. The Discontented Robins, and Other Stories.... Boston: Charles Fox, n.d. (1847). 12mo. 131pp; 5 full-pg wood engrs. Blind tooled cl, gilt vignette. Shelfwear, chip, else Fine. *Hobbyhorse*. $95/£61

FOX, PENELOPE. Tutankhamun's Treasure. London: OUP, 1951. 72 plts. Good. *Archaeologia*. $45/£29

FOX, TED. Showtime at the Apollo. NY: Holt, 1983. 1st ed. Fine in Fine dj. *Beasley*. $40/£26

FOX, WELLS B. What I Remember of the Great Rebellion. Lansing, MI, 1892. 278pp; 19 plts. Orig cl, gilt title. Good (worn; spine ends frayed). *Bohling*. $450/£290

FOX, WILLIAM PRICE. Dixiana Moon. NY: Viking, (1981). 1st ed. Fine in dj. *Reese*. $20/£13

FOX, WILLIAM PRICE. Southern Fried Plus Six. Phila: Lippincott, (1968). 1st (expanded) hb ed. NF in NF dj. *Reese*. $35/£23

FOX, WILSON. The Diseases of the Stomach Being the Third Edition of the 'Diagnosis and Treatment of the Varieties of Dyspepsia.' Phila, 1875. Rev, enlgd. 283pp. Good. *Goodrich*. $25/£16

FOX-DAVIES, A.C. A Complete Guide to Heraldry. London: Nelson/Jack, n.d. (c. 1930). Rev ed. 9 plts. Teg. Pict cl. VG (lt foxing) in dj (worn). *Willow House*. $19/£12

FOXON, D. Libertine Literature in England 1660-1745. University Books, 1965. 13 plts. VG in dj (sl torn). *Moss*. $37/£24

FOXX, REDD and NORMA MILLER. The Redd Foxx Encyclopedia of Black Humor. Pasadena: Ward Ritchie, 1977. 1st ed. Fine in Fine dj. *Connolly*. $25/£16

FOY, GENERAL. History of the War in the Peninsular Under Napoleon. London: Worley, 1989. Facs ed. One of 250. 3 vols. 2 frontispieces; maps, plans loosely inserted. *Petersfield*. $70/£45

FRACASTORIUS, H. Contagion, Contagious Diseases and Their Treatment. W. Wright (trans). NY, 1930. 1st Eng trans. Good. *Fye*. $125/£81

FRACASTORO, GIROLAMO. The Sinister Shepherd. L.A., 1934. 1st ed. Good. *Fye*. $100/£65

FRAENKEL, MICHAEL. The Day Face and the Night Face. London: Carrefour Press, (1947). 1st ed. Ltd to 1000. Unopened. Fine in ptd wraps (sm tear). *Polyanthos*. $30/£19

FRAENKEL, MICHAEL. The Genesis of the Tropic of Cancer. Bern Porter, 1946. Ltd ed, signed. NF, wrappers, in ptd dj. *Polyanthos*. $75/£48

FRAENKEL, OSMOND. The Sacco-Vanzetti Case. NY: Knopf, 1931. 1st ed. Fine in VG dj (sl worn). *Beasley*. $150/£97

Fragonard. NY: Metropolitan Museum, 1988. VG (ex-lib, stain from removed label). *Washton*. $45/£29

FRAIBERG, SELMA H. with LOUIS. Insights from the Blind. NY: Basic Books, (1977). 1st ed. Yellow cl. VG (hospital stamps) in dj. *Gach*. $40/£26

FRAME, JANET. Faces in the Water. NY: George Braziller, 1961. 1st ed. VG (name) in dj (worn; short tear). *Hermitage*. $30/£19

FRAME, JANET. The Reservoir. Braziller, 1963. 1st ed. Fine in dj. *Fine Books*. $45/£29

FRAMPTON, JOHN (ed). The Most Noble and Famous Travels of Marco Polo Together with the Travels of Nicolo De Conti. London: Argonaut, 1929. Ltd to 1050 numbered (this unnumbered). Teg. Vellum-backed bds. (Bkpl; cvr soiled; bumped.) *King*. $150/£97

FRANCATELLI, CHARLES ELME. A Plain Cookery Book for the Working Classes. London: Routledge, n.d. (c. 1870). New ed. Frontis,103,(1)pp + 20pp ads. Exceptional in yellow ptd wrappers (backstrip sl defective). *Cox*. $39/£25

FRANCE, ANATOLE. The Autograph Edition of the Collected Works. NY: Gabriel Wells, 1924. One of 1075 sets, signed. 30 vols. Cl-backed bds, paper labels. Good set (rubbed; few spines nicked). *Reese.* $350/£226

FRANCE, ANATOLE. The Crime of Sylvestre Bonnard. NY: LEC, 1937. #904/1500 numbered, signed by Sylvain Sauvage (illus). Fine in pub's slipcase (worn; rubbed). *Hermitage.* $85/£55

FRANCE, ANATOLE. The Crime of Sylvestre Bonnard. Lafcadio Hearn (trans). NY: LEC, 1937. One of 1500 numbered, signed by Sylvain Sauvage (illus). Teg. Dec cl. Fine in VG slipcase (sl mkd). *Reese.* $65/£42

FRANCE, ANATOLE. The Gods Are Athirst. Alfred Allinson (trans). London/NY: John Lane/Dodd, Mead, (1927). 1st ed thus. John Austen (illus). Dec black cl. NF in NF dj (spine faded). *Chapel Hill.* $45/£29

FRANCE, ANATOLE. Mother of Pearl. Frederic Chapman (trans). London/NY: John Lane/Dodd, Mead, (1929). 1st illus ed. Frank C. Pape (illus). Dec black cl. NF in dj. *Chapel Hill.* $40/£26

FRANCE, ANATOLE. Penguin Island. NY: LEC, 1947. #904/1500 numbered, signed by Malcolm Cameron (illus). Half-leather, dec bds. Fine in pub's slipcase. *Hermitage.* $75/£48

FRANCE, ANATOLE. The Revolt of the Angels. NY: LEC, 1953. One of 1500 numbered. Fine in pub's slipcase. *Hermitage.* $50/£32

FRANCE, ANATOLE. Thais. Robert B. Douglas (trans). London: John Lane, Bodley Head, (1926). 1st illus ed. Frank C. Pape (illus). Unopened. Gilt pict cl. Head of spine sl rubbed, o/w Fine. *Sadlon.* $100/£65

FRANCE, ANATOLE. The Well of Saint Clare. Alfred Allinson (trans). London/NY: John Lane/Dodd, Mead, (1928). 1st ed thus. Frank C. Pape (illus). Fine in dj. *Chapel Hill.* $40/£26

FRANCH, JOSE ALCINA. Pre-Columbian Art. I. Mark Paris (trans). NY: Abrams, (1983). 177 color plts. Pict cvr label. VG in dj. *Argosy.* $200/£129

FRANCHERE, GABRIEL. Adventure at Astoria, 1810-1814. Hoyt Franchere (ed). Univ of OK, (1967). 1st thus. Dbl-pg map. VG in VG dj. Howes F 310. *Oregon.* $30/£19

FRANCHERE, GABRIEL. Narrative of a Voyage to the Northwest Coast of America in the Years 1811, 1812, 1813 and 1814. NY, 1854. Frontis, 376pp + ads, 2 plts. Spine sl chipped, sm nick fr joint, sl foxing or tanning, else VG. Howes F 310. *Reese.* $450/£290

FRANCHERE, GABRIEL. Narrative of a Voyage to the Northwest Coast of America in the Years 1811...1814. NY: Redfield, 1854. 2nd ed. 1st ed in English. Frontis, 376pp + 8pp ads, 2 plts. Cl cvrs (rebacked, orig gilt spine laid on; orig eps, hinges reinforced). VG (corners worn, frontis lt foxed). Howes F 310. *Oregon.* $425/£274

FRANCHERE, GABRIEL. A Voyage to the Northwest Coast of America. Chicago, (1954). Lakeside Classic. VG. *Schoyer.* $25/£16

FRANCHERE, GABRIEL. A Voyage to the Northwest Coast of America. M.M. Quaife (ed). Chicago: Lakeside Classic, 1954. Frontis, 8 plts (incl 3 maps). Fine. Howes F 310. *Oregon.* $40/£26

FRANCIS, CONVERS. Historical Sketch of Watertown.... Cambridge, 1830. 151pp. Ptd wraps. (Lower corner fr wrapper, tp torn away; paper dknd; lt foxing.) Howes F 312. *Bohling.* $75/£48

FRANCIS, DICK and JOHN WELCOME. Best Racing and Chasing Stories. London: Faber, 1966. 1st UK ed. VG in dj. *Lewton.* $47/£30

FRANCIS, DICK. Blood Sport. H&R, 1968. 1st Amer ed. NF in dj. *Fine Books.* $85/£55

FRANCIS, DICK. Blood Sport. NY: Harper, 1968. 1st ed. Fine in dj. *Else Fine.* $125/£81

FRANCIS, DICK. Bolt. London: Michael Joseph, 1986. 1st ed. Fine in dj. *Mordida.* $45/£29

FRANCIS, DICK. Bonecrack. London: Michael Joseph, 1971. 1st ed. Lt edge wear; spine head cut, else VG + in dj (sm piece missing spine foot; sl wear). *Murder.* $85/£55

FRANCIS, DICK. Bonecrack. London: Michael Joseph, 1971. 1st UK ed. NF in dj. *Williams.* $39/£25

FRANCIS, DICK. Bonecrack. NY: Harper, 1972. 1st ed. Fine in dj (price-clipped). *Else Fine.* $70/£45

FRANCIS, DICK. Comeback. London: Michael Joseph, 1991. 1st ed. Signed. Fine in dj. *Murder.* $50/£32

FRANCIS, DICK. The Edge. NY: Putnam's, 1989. 1st ed. VF in dj. *Else Fine.* $30/£19

FRANCIS, DICK. Enquiry. London: Joseph, 1969. 1st ed. Fine in dj. *Limestone.* $175/£113

FRANCIS, DICK. Enquiry. London: Michael Joseph, 1969. 1st UK ed. Fine in VG dj. *Williams.* $124/£80

FRANCIS, DICK. Flying Finish. London: Joseph, 1966. 1st ed. Fine in color pict dj. *Limestone.* $250/£161

FRANCIS, DICK. Flying Finish. London: Michael Joseph, 1966. 1st UK ed. Fine in VG + dj (short closed tear; sm stain). *Williams.* $194/£125

FRANCIS, DICK. Flying Finish. London: Joseph, 1966. 2nd ed. VG in VG dj. *Ming.* $54/£35

FRANCIS, DICK. For Kicks. London: Michael Joseph, 1965. 1st UK ed. VG (nick; lacks dj). *Williams.* $39/£25

FRANCIS, DICK. Forfeit. London: Michael Joseph, 1968. 1st ed. Fine in dj (sl faded spine; sl wear; short closed tear). *Mordida.* $150/£97

FRANCIS, DICK. Forfeit. London: Joseph, 1968. 1st ed. Sig, else Fine in dj. *Limestone.* $195/£126

FRANCIS, DICK. Forfeit. London: Michael Joseph, 1968. 1st ed. Fine in dj (minor edgewear). *Else Fine.* $285/£184

FRANCIS, DICK. Forfeit. London: Joseph, 1968. Uncorrected proof copy of 1st ed. VG. Printed wrappers. *Limestone.* $185/£119

FRANCIS, DICK. Forfeit. Harper & Row, 1969. 1st Amer ed. NF in dj (spine rubbed, sunned). *Stahr.* $50/£32

FRANCIS, DICK. High Stakes. London: Joseph, 1975. 1st ed. *Ming.* $54/£35

FRANCIS, DICK. High Stakes. London: Joseph, 1975. 1st ed. Fine in dj. *Limestone.* $85/£55

FRANCIS, DICK. High Stakes. London: Michael Joseph, 1975. 1st UK ed. Fine in dj. *Williams.* $31/£20

FRANCIS, DICK. High Stakes. NY: Harper, 1976. 1st ed. NF (name) in dj. *Else Fine.* $40/£26

FRANCIS, DICK. Hot Money. Michael Joseph, 1987. 1st UK ed. Fine in dj. *Williams.* $16/£10

FRANCIS, DICK. In the Frame. NY: Harper, 1976. 1st ed. Fine in dj. *Else Fine.* $40/£26

FRANCIS, DICK. In the Frame. London: Joseph, 1976. 1st ed. NF in NF dj. *Ming.* $62/£40

FRANCIS, DICK. In the Frame. Joseph, 1976. 1st UK ed. VG in dj. *Lewton.* $23/£15

FRANCIS, DICK. Knock Down. London: Joseph, 1974. 1st ed. VG in NF dj. *Ming.* $62/£40

FRANCIS, DICK. Knock Down. London: Michael Joseph, 1974. 1st ed. Fine in dj (scrape fr panel). *Mordida.* $65/£42

FRANCIS, DICK. Knock Down. NY: Harper, 1975. 1st ed. VF in NF dj. *Else Fine.* $40/£26

FRANCIS, DICK. Lester: The Official Biography. London: Michael Joseph, 1986. 1st ed. VF in dj. *Else Fine.* $60/£39

FRANCIS, DICK. Longshot. London: Michael Joseph, 1990. 1st ed. Fine in dj. *Else Fine.* $35/£23

FRANCIS, DICK. Nerve. H&R, 1964. 1st Amer ed. NF in dj. *Fine Books.* $325/£210

FRANCIS, DICK. Nerve. London: Joseph, 1964. 1st ed. Fine in dj (sl rubbed back panel). *Limestone.* $850/£548

FRANCIS, DICK. Nerve. London: Michael Joseph, 1964. 1st ed. Fine in dj (sl dknd spine; short closed tear). *Mordida.* $850/£548

FRANCIS, DICK. Odds Against. London: Joseph, 1965. 1st ed. VG in dj. *Limestone.* $225/£145

FRANCIS, DICK. Odds Against. Michael Joseph, 1965. 1st UK ed. NF in VG dj. *Williams.* $171/£110

FRANCIS, DICK. Proof. London: Michael Joseph, 1984. 1st ed. VF in dj. *Else Fine.* $45/£29

FRANCIS, DICK. Rat Race. Harper, 1971. 1st Amer ed. NF (name) in dj (spine sunned). *Stahr.* $35/£23

FRANCIS, DICK. Risk. London: Joseph, 1977. 1st ed. VG in NF dj. *Ming.* $62/£40

FRANCIS, DICK. Slay Ride. London: Joseph, 1969. 1st ed. Signed presentation copy. *Limestone.* $140/£90

FRANCIS, DICK. Slay Ride. London: Joseph, 1973. 1st ed. Fine in dj. *Limestone.* $115/£74

FRANCIS, DICK. Smoke Screen. London: Joseph, 1972. 1st ed. Fine in dj. *Limestone.* $115/£74

FRANCIS, DICK. Smoke Screen. London: Joseph, 1972. 1st ed. Signed. Fine in dj w/orig wraparound band. *Limestone.* $150/£97

FRANCIS, DICK. Smoke Screen. Joseph, 1972. 1st UK ed. NF in dj. *Lewton.* $23/£15

FRANCIS, DICK. The Sport of Queens. London: Joseph, 1957. 1st UK ed. VG. *Lewton.* $59/£38

FRANCIS, DICK. Trial Run. London: Michael Joseph, 1978. 1st ed. Inscribed. Lt spotting pg edges, o/w Fine in dj. *Mordida.* $85/£55

FRANCIS, DICK. Twice Shy. London: Michael Joseph, 1981. 1st UK ed. VG + (sl bumped) in dj. *Williams.* $19/£12

FRANCIS-LEWIS, CECILE. The Art and Craft of Leatherwork. London: Seeley Service, 1928. 1st ed. Color frontis; 2 color, 85 b/w plts. VG +. *Willow House.* $31/£20

FRANCOME, JOHN and JAMES MACGREGOR. Eavesdropper. London: Macdonald, 1986. 1st ed. Fine in dj. *Mordida.* $45/£29

FRANK, JEROME D. Psychotherapy and the Human Predicament. NY: Schocken Books, (1978). 1st ed. Presentation copy. VG in dj (lt worn). *Gach.* $100/£65

FRANK, P. Mr. Adam. Gollancz, 1947. 1st Eng ed, 1st bk. Spine, cvrs lightened, else Fine in VG + dj. *Aronovitz.* $38/£25

FRANK, ROBERT. Zero Mostel Reads a Book. NY: NY Times, June 1963. 1st ed. Ptd paper over bds (lt rubbed). *Cahan.* $150/£97

FRANK, WALDO. America and Alfred Stieglitz. NY: Literary Guild, 1934. 1st ed. VG + in VG dj. *Bishop.* $57/£37

FRANK, WALDO. Not Heaven. NY: Hermitage, (1953). 1st ed. Fine in dj (nick). *Reese.* $30/£19

FRANKAU, GILBERT. Seeds of Enchantment. Doubleday, 1921. 1st ed. VG. *Madle.* $30/£19

FRANKEL, S. HERBERT. Capital Investment in Africa, Its Course and Effects. London: OUP, 1938. 1st ed. Fldg chart, 2 maps. Buckram (spine lt worn). *Shasky.* $37/£24

FRANKENSTEIN, ALFRED. After the Hunt.... Berkeley: Univ of CA, 1953. 1st ed. Frontis. Cvr worn, else VG. *Bookpress.* $85/£55

FRANKFORT, HENRI. The Art and Architecture of the Ancient Orient. Middlesex: Penguin, (1954). 192 plts, fldg map. (Pencil notes.) Dj (tattered). *Archaeologia.* $50/£32

FRANKFORT, HENRI. The Art and Architecture of the Ancient Orient. Balt: Penguin Books, (1955). 1st Amer ed. 192 plts. Fine in dj (lt chipped, sunned), slipcase. *Bookpress.* $85/£55

FRANKFURTER, FELIX. Mr. Justice Holmes and the Supreme Court. Cambridge: Harvard Univ, 1938. Blue cl (spine rubbed). *Boswell.* $45/£29

FRANKLIN, BENJAMIN. The Autobiography.... SF: LEC, 1931. 1st ed thus. # 575/1500, signed by John Henry Nash (ptr). 1/4 vellum, marbled bds. NF in pub's slipcase (lt rubbed). *Chapel Hill.* $85/£55

FRANKLIN, BENJAMIN. The Autobiography.... SF: LEC, 1931. One of 1500. Signed by John Henry Nash (ptr). Parchment-backed bds. NF (sl wear) in Good slipcase. *Agvent.* $250/£161

FRANKLIN, BENJAMIN. Memoirs of the Life and Writings of Benjamin Franklin.... Phila: William Duane, 1808-18. 6 vols. Mod cl. Good set (foxing). Howes F 323. *Reese.* $750/£484

FRANKLIN, BENJAMIN. Memoirs. May Farrand (ed). Berkeley, 1949. Howes F 323. *Ginsberg.* $75/£48

FRANKLIN, BENJAMIN. Political, Miscellaneous, and Philosophical Pieces.... London: J. Johnson, 1779. 1st ed. xii,568,(6)pp; fldg table; 4 plts (1 fldg). Orig calf (neatly rebacked); old spine, label laid down. Howes F 330. *Karmiole.* $1,000/£645

FRANKLIN, BENJAMIN. Poor Richard's Almanacks for the Years 1733-1758. Phila: LEC, 1964. 1st thus. One of 1500. Signed by Norman Rockwell (illus). 1/4 natural suede cowhide. Fine in glassine & slipcase. *Agvent.* $375/£242

FRANKLIN, BENJAMIN. Satires and Bagatelles. Detroit: Fine Book Circle, 1937. Ltd to 1000 numbered. Prospectus laid in. NF in dj (sl edgeworn). *Sadlon.* $30/£19

FRANKLIN, BENJAMIN. The Writings of Benjamin Franklin. Albert Henry Smyth (ed). NY, 1905. 10 vols. Mint. *Argosy.* $600/£387

FRANKLIN, JOHN. Narrative of a Journey to the Shore of the Polar Sea...1819-20-21-22. London: John Murray, 1824. 2nd ed. 2 vols. xix,(i)blank,370; (ii),iv,(ii),(i),399,(1)imprint, half titles, 4 fldg engr maps (1 colored in outline). Orig bds (spined repaired preserving orig paper labels; blue paper of upper cvr torn at one corner). Internally VG (rust mks, stain, sl foxing of maps). *Morrell.* $372/£240

FRANKLIN, JOHN. Narrative of a Journey to the Shores of the Polar Sea in the Years 1819, 20, 21, and 22. London: John Murray, 1823. 1st ed. xvi,768pp. Errata slip, 30 engr plts (10 color). 4 fldg maps. (Sl offsetting, foxing.) Contemp half calf (rebacked), marbled bds. Gilt dec spine (relaid). Good in VG dj. *Walcot.* $698/£450

FRANKLIN, JOHN. Narrative of a Journey to the Shores of the Polar Sea in the Years 1819-20-21-22. London: John Murray, 1824. 2nd ed. 2 vols. xix,370; iv,399pp, 4 fldg maps. Recent 1/2 leather. VG. *Walcot.* $233/£150

FRANKLIN, JOHN. Narrative of a Second Expedition to the Shores of the Polar Sea in the Years 1825, 1826 and 1827.... London: John Murray, 1828. 1st ed. xxiv,320,clviipp, errata, 6 maps, 31 plts (some sl foxed, margins browned; fep repaired). Good+ (rebacked). *Walcot.* $620/£400

FRANKLIN, JOHN. Narrative of a Second Expedition to the Shores of the Polar Sea...1825, 1826, and 1827.... London: John Murray, 1828. 4to. xxiv,320,clviipp. + errata leaf. 31 plts; 6 fldg maps. Orig cl bds (rebacked), paper label; uncut. VG as issued, w/prospectus leaf for series, apparently never pub. *High Latitude.* $1,100/£710

FRANKLIN, S.R. Memories of a Rear Admiral. NY: Harper & Bros, 1898. 1st ed. Frontis port, guard (foxed), xvi,398pp + 2 plts; untrimmed; teg. VG (lacks rep). *Connolly.* $40/£26

FRANKS, LUCINDA. Waiting Out a War: The Exile of Private John Picciano. NY, (1974). Fine in Fine dj (edgetear; wrinkles). *Aka.* $35/£23

FRAPRIE, FRANK (ed). The American Annual of Photography 1934. Boston, 1933. Good (shelfworn). *Artis.* $25/£16

FRARY, I.T. Early Homes of Ohio. Richmond, (1936). 1st ed. Good. *Hayman.* $50/£32

FRARY, I.T. Early Homes of Ohio. Richmond: Garrett & Massie, (1936). 1st ed. Frontis. Eps browned, else Fine in dj (used). *Bookpress.* $85/£55

FRASER, ANTONIA. A History of Toys. N.p.: Delacorte, (1966). Fine in dj. *Artis.* $25/£16

FRASER, CLAUD LOVAT. Characters from Dickens. London: T.C. & E.C. Jack, n.d. Ltd to 250. 18 tipped-in color plts. Black moire silk-backed yellow bds (silk rubbed through in few spots). *Sadlon.* $100/£65

FRASER, CLAUD LOVAT. Sixty-three Unpublished Designs. London: First Edition Club, (1924). 1st ed. #87/500. Uncut in orig cl-backed dec bds. Good (bkpls). *Cox.* $101/£65

FRASER, COLIN. Avalanches and Snow Safety. London: John Murray, 1978. VG in dj. *Hollett.* $31/£20

FRASER, DOUGLAS. Through the Congo Basin. London: Jenkins, (1927). Few pp lt foxed, backstrip sl faded, o/w Good. *Petersfield.* $54/£35

FRASER, DOUGLAS. Through the Congo Basin. London, 1927. 1st ed. 5 maps (3 fldg). (Feps lt browned; spine sl creased, lower bd soiled.) *Edwards.* $62/£40

FRASER, G.S. Leaves Without a Tree. (Tokyo): Hokuseido Press, 1953. 1st ed. VG in dj (sm chips, tears spine head). *Antic Hay.* $45/£29

FRASER, GEORGE MacDONALD. Flashman and the Dragon. London: Barrie & Jenkins, 1985. 1st ed. VF in dj. *Else Fine.* $65/£42

FRASER, GEORGE MacDONALD. Flashman and the Redskins. London: Collins, 1982. 1st British ed. Fine in Fine dj (price-clipped). *Pettler.* $45/£29

FRASER, GEORGE MacDONALD. Flashman and the Redskins. London: Collins, 1982. 1st UK ed. VG+ in dj. *Williams.* $31/£20

FRASER, GEORGE MacDONALD. Flashman at the Charge. London: Barrie & Jenkins, 1973. 1st ed. Fine in dj (closed tear spine corner). *Else Fine.* $75/£48

FRASER, GEORGE MacDONALD. Flashman at the Charge. London: Barrie & Jenkins, 1973. 1st UK ed. NF in dj (spine sl faded; nicks). *Williams.* $54/£35

FRASER, GEORGE MacDONALD. Flashman in the Great Game. London: Barrie & Jenkins, 1975. 1st ed. Fine in dj (tear, sm chip, lt wear spine corners). *Else Fine.* $60/£39

FRASER, GEORGE MacDONALD. Flashman. London: Jenkins, 1969. 1st UK ed. VG in dj (lt creased, browned). *Williams.* $70/£45

FRASER, GEORGE MacDONALD. The General Danced at Dawn. London: Barrie & Jenkins, 1970. 1st UK ed. NF in VG dj (crease). *Williams.* $54/£35

FRASER, GEORGE MacDONALD. Mr. American. London: Collins, 1980. 1st UK ed. VG in dj. *Williams.* $19/£12

FRASER, GEORGE MacDONALD. Royal Flash. Knopf, 1970. 1st Amer ed. Fine in NF dj. *Fine Books.* $45/£29

FRASER, GEORGE MacDONALD. Royal Flash. NY: Knopf, 1970. 1st Amer ed. VG in dj (short creased tear, else VG). *Godot.* $50/£32

FRASER, GEORGE MacDONALD. Royal Flash. London: Barrie & Jenkins, 1970. 1st UK ed. VG+ (sl faded) in dj (sl dampstained). *Williams.* $59/£38

FRASER, GEORGE MacDONALD. The Sheikh and the Dustbin and Other McAuslan Stories. London: Collins-Marvill, 1988. 1st ed. VF in dj (price-clipped). *Else Fine.* $45/£29

FRASER, GEORGE MACDONALD. The Steel Bonnets. London, 1971. 1st ed. Frontis, 18 plts, 2 maps (1 fldg at rear). VG in dj (sl torn). *Edwards.* $31/£20

FRASER, JOHN. Surgery of Childhood. London, 1926. 1st ed. 2 vols. Good. *Fye.* $175/£113

FRASER, JOHN. Tuberculosis of the Bones and the Joints in Children. NY, 1914. 1st ed. 51plts. *Fye.* $75/£48

FRASER, MRS. HUGH. A Diplomatist's Wife in Japan. London: Hutchinson & Co, 1899. 2nd ed. 2 vols. Frontispieces, xviii,446; x,439. Purple cl (spines, lower cvr Vol 1 faded; string mks Vol 1; sl rubbed), gilt, teg. Generally clean (sl foxing). *Morrell.* $209/£135

FRASER, RONALD. In Hiding: The Life of Manuel Cortes. London: Allen Lane, 1972. 1st ed. Fine in dj. *Patterson.* $39/£25

FRAZER, DERYK. Reptiles and Amphibians in Britain. London, 1983. 1st ed. Dj. *Edwards.* $140/£90

FRAZER, JAMES GEORGE. Anthologia Anthropologica. Robert Angus Downie (ed). London: Percy Lund Humphries, 1938-1939. 4 vols. Good (faint lib stamps; mks). *Hollett.* $248/£160

FRAZER, JAMES GEORGE. The Belief in Immortality and the Worship of the Dead. London: Macmillan, 1913-22. 1st ed. 2 vols. (Blindstamp tp.) *Petersfield.* $54/£35

FRAZER, JAMES GEORGE. The Golden Bough: A Study in Magic and Religion. NY: LEC, 1970. #727/1500. 2 vols, boxed. Signed by James Lewicki (illus). Fine. *Graf.* $105/£68

FRAZER, JAMES GEORGE. Taboo and the Perils of the Soul. London: Macmillan, 1922. 3rd ed. Rubbed, rebacked, o/w VG ex-lib (spine sticker). *Worldwide.* $30/£19

FRAZER, ROBERT W. Mansfield on the Condition of the Western Forts 1853-54. Norman, 1963. 1st ed. Sl bumped, o/w Fine in dj. *Baade.* $40/£26

FRAZIER, E. FRANKLIN. The Negro in the United States. NY: Macmillan, 1949. 1st ed. 39 tables; 22 maps; 17 diags. Brn buckram. VG. *Petrilla.* $40/£26

FRAZIER, E. FRANKLIN. The Negro in the United States. NY: Macmillan, 1949. 2nd ptg. NF. *Aka.* $35/£23

FRAZIER, HARRY. Recollections. C&O Public Relations Dept, 1938. Frontis. Stiff paper cvr. VG. *Book Broker.* $35/£23

FREDERIC, HAROLD. The Copperhead. NY: Scribner's, 1893. 1st ed. One of 1650. Lt bumped, o/w attractive. BAL 6278. *Heller.* $100/£65

FREDERIC, HAROLD. Gloria Mundi. Chicago: Stone, 1898. 1st ed. Red cl stamped in black. Good (spine dknd). BAL 6293. *Reese.* $45/£29

FREDERIC, HAROLD. March Hares. NY: Appleton, 1896. 1st published Amer ed. Dec cl. Early ink name; sl rubbed, soiled, else VG. BAL 6290. *Reese.* $30/£19

FREDERICK II. The Art of Falconry. C.A. Wood & F.M. Fyfe (eds). Stanford, (1943). 2 color, 184 plain plts. *Wheldon & Wesley.* $88/£57

FREDERICK, J.V. Ben Holladay: The Stagecoach King. Glendale, 1940. 1st ed. News clipping laid in. Teg. VG (bkpl), no dj as issued. *Baade.* $225/£145

FREE, JOHN B. and COLIN G. BUTLER. Bumblebees. London, 1959. 1st ed. 46 photos (incl color frontis). Dj (sm tear). *Edwards.* $256/£165

FREEDBERG, DAVID. Dutch Landscape Prints of the Seventeenth Century. London: British Museum, 1980. Pub's cl. Fine in dj. *Europa.* $25/£16

FREEDBERG, S.J. Painting in Italy 1500-1600. London: Penguin, (1971). Color frontis. VG (sm piece torn margin of 1 plt) in dj, orig pict box. *Petersfield.* $31/£20

FREEDBERG, S.J. Painting of the High Renaissance in Rome and Florence. Cambridge, 1961. 2 vols. Text: x,644pp; Plates: xxxiiipp, 700 plts. Good. *Washton.* $175/£113

FREEDBERG, S.J. Parmigianino, His Works in Painting. Cambridge: Harvard Univ Press, 1950. 1st ed. 167 illus on plts. Ink sig, else VG. *Bookpress.* $185/£119

FREELING, NICOLAS. Criminal Conversation. London: Gollanz, 1965. 1st ed. NF in dj (soiled). *Janus.* $45/£29

FREELING, NICOLAS. The Dresden Green. London, 1966. 1st ed. VG in dj (price-clipped). *King.* $25/£16

FREELING, NICOLAS. Dressing of Diamond. London: Hamish Hamilton, 1974. 1st ed. NF (bumps) in NF dj. *Janus.* $35/£23

FREELING, NICOLAS. The Kitchen: A Delicious Account of the Author's Years as a Grand Hotel Cook. NY: Harper, 1970. 1st US ed. Fine (name) in VG + dj. *Janus.* $35/£23

FREELING, NICOLAS. The Widow. London: Heinemann, 1979. 1st ed. Fine (sm scuff fr pastedown) in Fine dj. *Janus.* $35/£23

FREEMAN, ALBERT C. Hints on the Planning of Poor Law Buildings. London: St Brides Press, (ca 1900). 72pp, frontis. *Marlborough.* $186/£120

FREEMAN, BUD. You Don't Look Like a Musician. Detroit: Balamp, 1974. 1st ed. Fine in Fine dj. *Beasley.* $75/£48

FREEMAN, DOUGLAS SOUTHALL (ed). Lee's Dispatches. NY, 1915. New ed (1957). Signed by McWhiney (foreword). Fldg map. Fine in dj (lt wear). *Pratt.* $60/£39

FREEMAN, DOUGLAS SOUTHALL. Lee's Lieutenants. NY: Scribner's, 1942-44. 1st ed. Signed in 1st vol. 3 vols. Orig black cl. Vol 3 sl faded, else VG +. *Chapel Hill.* $350/£226

FREEMAN, DOUGLAS SOUTHALL. Lee's Lieutenants. NY: Scribner's, 1942-44. 1st ed. Vol 1 signed. 3 vols. Orig cl (spines sunned; sl rubbed). VG. Howes F349. *Mcgowan.* $250/£161

FREEMAN, DOUGLAS SOUTHALL. Lee's Lieutenants. NY: Scribner's, 1942. 1st ed. Signed. Vol II, 1949; Vol III, 1951. VG in djs (edgewear). *Cahan.* $275/£177

FREEMAN, DOUGLAS SOUTHALL. Lee's Lieutenants. NY: Scribner's, 1946. Extra-illustrated, enlgd Arlington ed. 4 vols. NF set. Howes F 349. *Mcgowan.* $275/£177

FREEMAN, DOUGLAS SOUTHALL. R.E. Lee, A Biography. NY, (1943). Rpt. 4 vols. Fine. *Pratt.* $125/£81

FREEMAN, DOUGLAS SOUTHALL. R.E. Lee. A Biography. NY: Scribner's, 1940. 1st ptg of Pulitzer Prize ed. 4 vols. Gilt spine. VG set. Howes F 350. *Mcgowan.* $275/£177

FREEMAN, DOUGLAS SOUTHALL. Robert E. Lee, A Biography. NY: Scribner's, 1935-6. 4 vols. Tls laid in. (Bkpls fr pastedowns.) Howes F 350. *Schoyer.* $100/£65

FREEMAN, DOUGLAS SOUTHALL. The South to Posterity. NY: Scribner's, 1939. 1st ed. Grn cl. NF in dj (folds rubbed). *Chapel Hill.* $150/£97

FREEMAN, EDWARD A. The History and Conquests of the Saracens: Six Lectures.... London, 1876. 3rd ed. 203pp. Polished calf, gilt spine. VG. *Argosy.* $150/£97

FREEMAN, G.D. Midnight and Noonday. Caldwell, (1890). 1st ed, 2nd issue w/the attestation on last pg and correct spelling of 'Talbot' on tp. 406pp (sm edge-tears, edge-dkng). Rebound. Facs frontis from 1892 ed bound in w/guard. Howes F 353. *Baade.* $250/£161

FREEMAN, G.D. Midnight and Noonday. Caldwell, KS: G.D. Freeman, 1892. 1st ed. 3rd issue, w/1892 on tp. Red blind-stamped cl (soiling, lt wear; 1st 15pp detached; pp chipped, browned). Howes F 353. *Glenn.* $85/£55

FREEMAN, G.J. Sketches in Wales. London: Longman et al, 1826. 1st ed. xvi,272pp + viiipp subs, 14 mtd lithos. (Lt foxing.) Contemp gilt, blind filleted diced calf (rebacked, orig dec gilt spine laid down; fore-edge sl uneven). *Edwards.* $217/£140

FREEMAN, HARRY C. A Brief History of Butte, Montana. Chicago: Henry O. Shepard, 1900. 1st ed. Good. *Lien.* $125/£81

FREEMAN, JAMES D. (ed). Prose and Poetry of the Live Stock Industry of the United States. NY: Antiquarian Press, 1959. 2nd ed. Ltd to 550. Teg. 1/2 blind emb calf, buckram; gilt. Spine foot sl bumped, o/w Fine in Fine slipcase. Howes P 636. *Harrington.* $275/£177

FREEMAN, LEWIS R. Down the Columbia. NY: Dodd, Mead, 1921. 1st ed. VG. *Perier.* $50/£32

FREEMAN, R. AUSTIN and JOHN J. PITCAIRN. The Adventures of Romney Pringle. Phila: Oswald Train, 1968. 1st Amer ed. VF in dj. *Mordida.* $75/£48

FREEMAN, WILLIAM. The Life of Lord Alfred Douglas. Herbert Joseph, 1948. 1st Eng ed. Frontis port. Red cl (spine sunned). Fine. *Dalian.* $39/£25

FREEMAN-MITFORD, A.B. The Bamboo Garden. London, 1896. Frontis, xi,(1),224pp (eps browned; lt foxing). Gilt-stamped cl (discolored, stained). *Sutton.* $115/£74

FREEMANTLE, BRIAN. Charlie Muffin's Uncle Sam. London: Cape, 1980. 1st ed. Fine in dj. *Else Fine.* $45/£29

FREEMANTLE, BRIAN. Charlie Muffin's Uncle Sam. London: Jonathan Cape, 1980. 1st ed. Fine in dj. *Mordida.* $75/£48

FREEMANTLE, BRIAN. Charlie Muffin. London: Cape, 1977. 1st ed. VF in film dj. *Silver Door.* $60/£39

FREEMANTLE, BRIAN. The Inscrutable Charlie Muffin. London: Jonathan Cape, 1979. 1st ed. Fine in dj. *Mordida.* $75/£48

FREEMANTLE, BRIAN. Madrigal for Charlie Muffin. Hutchinson, 1981. 1st ed. Fine (rmdr dot) in Fine dj. *Ming.* $31/£20

FREEMANTLE, BRIAN. Madrigal for Charlie Muffin. London: Hutchinson, 1981. 1st ed. VF in dj. *Else Fine.* $45/£29

FREEMANTLE, BRIAN. The Run Around. London: Century, 1988. 1st ed. Fine in dj (sl wear). *Mordida.* $45/£29

FREESE, STANLEY. Windmills and Mill Wrighting. CUP, 1957. 1st ed. Fldg plan, 35 plts. Fine in dj. *Hollett.* $101/£65

FREESTON, C.L. The Passes of the Pyrenees. NY: Scribner's, 1912. 1st Amer ed. Color frontis, 8 maps, 30 itineraries. Pict cl. VG. *Schoyer.* $60/£39

FREMANTLE, ARTHUR JAMES. Three Months in the Southern States: April, June, 1863. Mobile, 1864. 158pp. Mod 1/2 cl, marbled bds, leather label. Worn but sound (heavily foxed, browned; tp soiled, contemp sig tp). Howes F 361. *Reese.* $650/£419

FREMLIN, CELIA. Possession. London: Gollancz, 1969. 1st ed. Fine in dj. *Mordida.* $40/£26

FREMONT, JOHN CHARLES. Memoirs of My Life. Chicago: Belford Clarke, 1887. Vol 1. (16),656pp, 82 plts, 7 maps (2 tinted, 2 multi-colored, 4 fldg, incl 1 lg map mtd inside back cvr). 1/2 brn morocco, purple cl, gilt spine (outer hinges rubbed, sl soiled). Sound. Howes C 367. *Karmiole.* $500/£323

FREMONT, JOHN CHARLES. Memoirs of My Life. Chicago/NY: Belford, Clarke, 1887. 1st ed. xix,655pp; 82 plts; 7 maps. Pub's gilt pict cl (sl rubbed). VG (tear rear pastedown crudely repaired). Howes F 367. *Cahan.* $400/£258

FREMONT, JOHN CHARLES. Narrative of the Exploring Expedition to the Rocky Mountains in the Year 1842.... Cooperstown: H.&E. Phinney, 1846. 186pp (dampstain top 1/4 each pg, not affecting legibility). Orig 1/4 tan sheep, black cl; black morocco spine label (sl rubbed, chipped). VG- (sl soiled, worn; lt foxing; sm lib label). Howes F 370. *Harrington.* $75/£48

French Bronze 1500-1800. NY: Knoedler, 1968. 95 plts. Red buckram. VG (ex-lib). Orig wrappers bound in. *Washton.* $50/£32

FRENCH, ALBERT. Billy. (NY): Viking, (1993). 1st ed. Fine in dj. *Turlington.* $50/£32

FRENCH, ALLEN. General Gage's Informers. Ann Arbor: Univ of MI press, 1932. 1st ed. Frontis, 4 facs (1 fldg). Red cl. Name, else NF. *Chapel Hill.* $65/£42

FRENCH, GERALD (ed). Some War Diaries, Addresses, and Correspondence of...Earl of Ypres.... London, 1937. 1st ed. Frontis port; 7 plts. VG. Grn cl (sl worn, tanned at spine). *Edwards.* $70/£45

FRENCH, GILES. Cattle Country of Peter French. Portland: Binfords & Mort, 1965. 2nd ed. Signed. Brn cl. Bkpl, o/w Fine in NF dj (sl chipped). *Harrington.* $35/£23

FRENCH, HOLLIS. Jacob Hurd and His Sons, Nathaniel and Benjamin, Silversmiths, 1702-1781. Boston: Walpole Soc, (1939). One of 250 numbered. 28 plts. VG. *Argosy.* $325/£210

FRENCH, L.H. Nome Nuggets. NY: Montross et al, 1901. Pict cl (dampstain). *Schoyer.* $30/£19

FRENCH, SAMUEL GIBBS. Two Wars: An Autobiography. Nashville: Confederate Veteran, 1901. 1st ed. Frontis port; errata slip tipped in. Orig blue cl, pict centerpiece. Early inscrip, else NF. *Chapel Hill.* $475/£306

FRENCH, SAMUEL GIBBS. Two Wars: An Autobiography.... Nashville, TN: Confederate Veteran, 1901. 1st ed. Sl extrem wear, else NF. *Mcgowan.* $350/£226

FRENCH, WILLIAM. Some Recollections of a Western Ranchman: New Mexico 1883-1899. NY: Argosy-Antiquarian, 1965. One of 750. 2 vols. Spines lt sunned, else NF in box. Howes F 375. *Bohling.* $200/£129

FRENCH, WILLIAM. Some Recollections of a Western Ranchman: New Mexico, 1883-1899. London: Methuen, (1927). 1st ed. Red cl. Fine in dj (lt wear spine ends). Howes F 375. *Bohling.* $575/£371

FRENEAU, PHILIP. Poems Written and Published During the American Revolutionary War.... Phila: Lydia R. Bailey, 1809. 3rd ed. 2 vols. 2 frontis engrs; (280,iv; 302,xiipp); 2 plts. Mod cl, leather labels. Fine set. *Felcone.* $300/£194

FRENKEL, H.S. The Treatment of Tabetic Ataxia by Means of Systematic Exercise. Phila, 1902. 1st Amer ed. Good. *Fye.* $75/£48

FRERE-COOK, GERVIS. The Decorative Arts of the Mariner. Little Brown, (1966). 1st Amer ed. Pict cl. VG in VG dj. *Oregon.* $75/£48

FRESHFIELD, DOUGLAS W. Below the Snow Line. London: Constable, 1923. 1st ed. 9 maps. Grn ribbed cl gilt. Nice (few spots) *Hollett.* $70/£45

FRESHFIELD, DOUGLAS W. Travels in the Central Caucasus and Bashan.... London: Longmans, Green, 1869. 1st ed. xv,509pp; 3 fldg maps; 5 plts (1 color). 1/2 morocco, marbled bds, eps (worn, rubbed). Internally VG (lacks fr cvr; spine chipped; sl tears fep). *Worldwide.* $145/£94

Freshman Writing. Essays by Students in English 1 and 2 at Duke University, 1958-1959. (Durham, NC: Duke Univ, 1959.) 1st ed. NF in ptd self-wraps. *Chapel Hill.* $300/£194

FREUCHEN, PETER. The Legend of Daniel Williams. NY, (1956). 1st ed. Dj wear, o/w Fine. *Pratt.* $25/£16

FREUD, ERNST L. Sigmund Freud: His Life in Pictures and Words. Christine Trollope (trans). NY/London: Harcourt, Brace, Jovanovich, (1976). 1st Amer ed. Beige linen. VG in dj. *Gach.* $125/£81

FREUD, ESTHER. Peerless Flats. Hamilton, 1993. 1st UK ed. Signed. Fine in dj. *Lewton.* $28/£18

FREUD, SIGMUND. An Autobiographical Study. London: Hogarth Press, 1935. 1st ed. One of 1768. Browned; sl mkd, rubbed; cl sl bubbled, o/w VG. *Virgo.* $62/£40

FREUD, SIGMUND. Beyond the Pleasure Principle. London, 1922. 1st Eng trans. Good. *Fye.* $100/£65

FREUD, SIGMUND. Civilization and Its Discontents. London: Hogarth Press/Inst of Psycho-Analysis, 1930. 1st ed. Grn cl. VG (lt shelfwear; spine sl stained). *Gach.* $150/£97

FREUD, SIGMUND. Civilization and Its Discontents. London: Hogarth Press, 1930. 1st ed. One of 1860. Sl foxed, browned, rubbed, o/w VG. *Virgo.* $62/£40

FREUD, SIGMUND. Civilization, War and Death. John Rickman (ed). Hogarth Press, 1939. 1st ed. VG in dj (chipped; spine rubbed, browned). *Words Etc.* $47/£30

FREUD, SIGMUND. Collected Papers. Authorized Translation. London: Hogarth Press, 1950. 5 vols. Overall Good set (ex-lib). *Goodrich.* $100/£65

FREUD, SIGMUND. Collected Papers. Authorized Translation. NY: Basic Books, 1959. 1st Amer ed. 5 vols. Good in slipcase (worn). *Goodrich.* $100/£65

FREUD, SIGMUND. Group Psychology and the Analysis of the Ego. James Strachey (trans). London: Int'l Psycho-Analytic Press, 1922. 1st ed in English, 1st issue. 1st state of the binding w/o Hogarth imprint. Grn cl. (Bkpl, sig.) *Gach.* $150/£97

FREUD, SIGMUND. Inhibitions, Symptoms and Anxiety. Hogarth Press, 1936. 1st ed. VG. *Words Etc.* $43/£28

FREUD, SIGMUND. The Interpretation of Dreams. NY, 1913. 1st Amer ed. VG (upper hinge starting). *Argosy.* $1,200/£774

FREUD, SIGMUND. Introductory Lectures on Psycho-Analysis: A Course of Twenty-Eight Lectures Delivered at the University of Vienna. Joan Riviere (trans). London, (1922). 1st ed in English. Frontis. (Backstrip torn at head.) *Argosy.* $400/£258

FREUD, SIGMUND. Moses and Monotheism. London: Hogarth Press, 1939. 1st ed. Sl mkd, rubbed, o/w VG. *Virgo.* $62/£40

FREUD, SIGMUND. On Aphasia. London: Imago Publishing, (1953). 1st Eng trans. Maroon cl. Fine in dj. *Karmiole.* $35/£23

FREUD, SIGMUND. The Origins of Psycho-Analysis. London, 1954. 1st Eng trans. Good in dj. *Fye.* $50/£32

FREUD, SIGMUND. The Problem of Anxiety. Henry Alden Bunker (trans). NY, (1936). 1st ed in vol form. VG in dj (torn, taped). *Argosy.* $175/£113

FREUD, SIGMUND. Three Contributions to the Theory of Sex. NY, 1930. 4th ed. Internally VG (ex-lib, stamps). Rebacked on orig bds. *Goodrich.* $35/£23

FREUD, SIGMUND. Three Essays on the Theory of Sexuality.... London, (1949). 1st Eng ed. Fine in dj. *Waterfield.* $62/£40

FREUD, SIGMUND. Totem and Taboo. London: Routledge, 1919. 1st ed. VG (fep foxed; sl browned, dusty; rubbed, spine dull). *Virgo.* $47/£30

FRICERO, K.J. Little French People, a Picture Book for Little Folk. Glasgow: Blackie & Son, n.d. 4to. 'French-Fold' style pp (1st 2 slit); 23 color plts by Fricero. Faux vellum spine, pict paste label; illus eps. (Stapled text block detached; cvr worn.) Illus dj portion laid in. *Drusilla's.* $75/£48

FRICKER, KARL. The Antarctic Regions. London: Swan Sonnenschein, 1904. 2nd Eng ed. Orig gilt dec cl. VG. *Walcot.* $124/£80

FRIED, FREDERICK. Artists in Wood. NY: Potter, 1970. 1st ed. Signed presentation. VG in illus dj. *Cahan.* $60/£39

FRIEDLAENDER, WALTER. Claude Lorrain. Berlin, 1921. Inscribed. 1/2 leather (worn). *Argosy.* $75/£48

FRIEDLAENDER, WALTER. Nicolas Poussin; a New Approach. NY: Abrams, n.d. 48 tipped-in color plts. VG in dj. *Argosy.* $85/£55

FRIEDMAN, B. Stern. S&S, 1962. 1st ed, 1st bk. Rev copy w/slip, photo laid in. Pinholes feps, else Fine in NF dj (sl rubbing). *Fine Books.* $75/£48

FRIEDMAN, B.H. Jackson Pollock. London, 1968. (Sl mkd.) *Edwards.* $31/£20

FRIEDMAN, BRUCE JAY. Scuba Duba. NY: S&S, (1967). 1st ed. Fine (ink rmdr mk) in NF dj. *Antic Hay.* $25/£16

FRIEDMAN, BRUCE JAY. Steambath. NY: Knopf, 1971. 1st ed. Fine in dj (short tear). *Antic Hay.* $35/£23

FRIEDMAN, HERBERT. The Symbolic Goldfinch. Washington DC, 1946. (Spine sunned.) *Washton.* $65/£42

FRIEDMAN, I.K. The Autobiography of a Beggar. Boston, 1903. 1st Amer ed. Fine (sl sunned, sl rubbed). *Polyanthos.* $40/£26

FRIEDMAN, KINKY. Frequent Flyer. William Morrow, 1989. 1st ed. Inscribed. Fine in Fine dj. *Bishop.* $18/£12

FRIEDMAN, KINKY. Greenwich Killing Time. NY: Beech Tree, 1986. 1st ed, rev copy w/pub's slip laid in. VF in dj. *Silver Door.* $25/£16

FRIEDMAN, KINKY. Musical Chairs. William Morrow, 1991. 1st ed. Signed. Fine in NF dj. *Bishop.* $20/£13

FRIEDMAN, MARTIN. Hockney Paints the Stage.... NY, 1983. VG in dj. *Argosy.* $125/£81

FRIEDMAN, W. and E.S. The Shakespearean Ciphers Examined. CUP, 1957. 10 plts. Bkpl removed, o/w VG. *Moss.* $25/£16

FRIEDMANN, H. Birds Collected by the National Geographic Society's Expeditions to Northern Brazil and Southern Venezuela. Washington, 1948. 12 plts (incl fldg map). (Plts lt foxed). Wrappers (name). *Sutton.* $27/£17

FRIEND, HILDERIC. Flowers and Flower Lore. London: Swan Sonnenschein et al, 1886. 3rd ed. Pub's presentation copy. Teg. Gilt-dec pict cvr (rebound, orig dull spine relaid; new eps). NF. *Quest.* $95/£61

Friends on the Farm Pop-Up and Play Book. London: Purnell and Sons Ltd, 1968. 36x26 cm. 3 pop-ups; pull outs in slots (have not been popped out). E. Kincaid (illus). Glazed pict bds. Some glazing coming off top fr, o/w VG. *Book Finders.* $25/£16

FRIES, U.E. From Copenhagen to Okanogan. Caldwell: Caxton, 1949. 1st ed. Frontis port. Dec cl, gilt. NF in Good+ dj. *Connolly.* $35/£23

FRIESNER, ISIDORE and A. BRAUN. A Cerebellar Abcess. NY, 1916. 1st ed. Good. *Fye.* $75/£48

FRINK, MAURICE. Cow Country Cavalcade. Denver, 1954. 1st ed. Fine in dj. *Baade.* $40/£26

FRIPP, EDGAR I. Master Richard Quyny, Baliff of Stratford-upon-Avon.... OUP, 1924. *Petersfield.* $33/£21

FRISCH, FRANK. Frank Frisch. (As told to J. Roy Stockton.) Doubleday, 1962. 1st ed. Fine. *Plapinger.* $35/£23

FRISCH, MAX. Homo Faber. London: Abelard-Schuman, 1959. 1st Eng ed. Sm stains top edge, else NF in NF dj. *Lame Duck.* $65/£42

FRISON-ROCHE, ROGER and PIERRE TAIRRAZ. Mont Blanc and the Seven Valleys. (N.p.): Arthaud, (1961). 1st ed. Color frontis, fldg map. Blue cl. Fine in dj. *House*. $55/£35

FRITZ, EMANUEL. California Coast Redwood. An Annotated Bibliography to and Including 1955. SF: Foundation for Amer Resource Mgmt, 1957. 1st ed. Fine. *Oregon*. $40/£26

FRIZZELL, MRS. LODISA. Across the Plains to California in 1852. Hugo Paltsits (ed). NY: NYPL, 1915. 1st ed. Orig ptd wrappers. Howes 3824. *Ginsberg*. $125/£81

FROEBEL, JULIUS. Seven Years' Travel in Central America, Northern Mexico, and the Far West of the United States. London, 1859. xiv,(2),587pp. 8 plts (incl frontis). Contemp 3/4 calf, marbled bds, spine gilt extra, leather labels. Edgewear, few leaves spotted, else VG. Howes F 390. *Reese*. $850/£548

FROHAWK, F.W. Natural History of British Butterflies.... London, (1924). 2 vols. 60 color, 5 plain plts. (Cvrs sl stained.) Djs (pasted inside back cvrs). *Wheldon & Wesley*. $279/£180

FROHAWK, F.W. Varieties of British Butterflies. London, (1946). 2nd issue. 48 color plts. (Sl soiled.) *Wheldon & Wesley*. $101/£65

FROISSART, JOHN. Chronicles of England, France, Spain, Portugal, Scotland...and the Adjoining Countries. John Bourchier (trans). London, 1812. 2 vols. Contemp diced calf (joints worn); gilt, blind-tooled borders. *Argosy*. $200/£129

FROLOV, Y.P. Pavlov and His School. NY, 1937. 1st ed. Good. *Fye*. $50/£32

From the Hudson to the St. Johns. (By Alfred L. Dennis). (Newark, NJ: 1874). 1st ed. 104pp; aeg (rear bd mottled). *Petrilla*. $75/£48

FROMM, ERICH. Escape from Freedom. NY: F&R, 1941. 1st ed, 1st ptg. Lt foxing; top edge dusted, else VG+ in VG dj (spine-dknd; chips, tears). *Lame Duck*. $65/£42

FROMMER, HARVEY. New York City Baseball 1947-1957. Macmillan, 1980. 1st ed. Fine in VG dj. *Plapinger*. $35/£23

FROMMER, HARVEY. Rickey and Robinson. Macmillan, 1982. 1st ed. Fine in Fine dj. *Plapinger*. $30/£19

FROST, DONALD McKAY. Notes on General Ashley, the Overland Trail and South Pass. Amer Antiq. Soc, 1945. 1st ed. Fldg map. Orig wraps bound in grn cl. VG. Howes F 392. *Oregon*. $150/£97

FROST, DONALD McKAY. Notes on General Ashley, the Overland Trail and South Pass. Barre, MA: Barre Gazette, 1960. 2nd ed. Fldg map rear pocket. Blue cl. VG in dj. *Laurie*. $60/£39

FROST, DONALD MCKAY. Notes on General Ashley. Barre: Barre Gazette, 1960. 2nd ed. Fldg map. VG in dj (stained). Howes F 392. *Schoyer*. $75/£48

FROST, HOLLOWAY H. Some Stories of Old Ironsides. Annapolis: U.S. Naval Institute, 1931. 1st ed. 8 full-pg illus. 8pp appendix w/card laid in. Untrimmed. VG in overhanging wrappers w/tipped on color picture. *Connolly*. $30/£19

FROST, JOHN. The Book of the Navy.... NY: D. Appleton, 1842. 1st ed. 344pp + (12)pp ads, 3 engr ports. Orig cl (tightly rebacked, orig spine preserved). Foxing, but very Bright. *Lefkowicz*. $100/£65

FROST, LAWRENCE A. The Custer Album. Seattle, 1964. 1st ed. Fine in dj (sl chipped). *Baade*. $35/£23

FROST, LESLIE. New Hampshire's Child: The Derry Journals of Lesley Frost. Albany: State Univ of NY, 1969. 1st ed. Fine in dj (rubbing). *Antic Hay*. $25/£16

FROST, ROBERT. Book Six: A Further Range. London, (1937). 1st Eng ed. VG (sl bumped) in Good dj (faded). *Waterfield*. $47/£30

FROST, ROBERT. A Further Range. NY: Henry Holt, (1936). 1st trade ed. Gilt. Spine sl dull. Dj (sl worn). *Sadlon*. $40/£26

FROST, ROBERT. In the Clearing. NY: HRW, (1962). 1st ed. VG (fore-edges sl dknd; offsetting prelim blanks) in VG dj (sl dampstained). *Between The Covers*. $35/£23

FROST, ROBERT. Letters of Robert Frost to Louis Untermeyer. Louis Untermeyer (ed). London: Cape, 1964. 1st UK ed. Name, o/w NF in VG dj. *Virgo*. $23/£15

FROST, ROBERT. A Masque of Mercy. NY: Holt, 1947. One of 751 specially bound, numbered, signed. NF (sm owner label). *Beasley*. $200/£129

FROST, ROBERT. A Masque of Reason. NY: Holt, (1945). 1st ed. Inscribed. Dk blue cl. Fine in Fine dj (spine chip). *Chapel Hill*. $450/£290

FROST, ROBERT. A Masque of Reason. NY: Henry Holt, 1945. 1st ed. Fine in illus dj. *Cahan*. $65/£42

FROST, ROBERT. Mountain Interval. NY: Henry Holt & Co., (1916). 1st ed, 1st state, w/lines 6-7 as duplicates p88. Inscribed. 8vo. Blue cl. Fine in ptd dj (sm mends verso); blue cl chemise, matching slipcase w/black morocco spine label. *Chapel Hill*. $2,300/£1,484

FROST, ROBERT. North of Boston. NY: Henry Holt, 1915. 1st Amer ed. Blue cl (edges, spine faded; head, tail spine chipped), gilt. VG in ptd 1st issue tan dj (spine sl chipped; sm stain below title). *Blue Mountain*. $475/£306

FROST, ROBERT. Selected Poems. NY: H. Holt, (1928). Pub's grn cl spine, paper sides. (Pencil notes.) *Book Block*. $25/£16

FROST, ROBERT. West-Running Brook. NY, 1928. 1st Amer ed. Fine in dj. *Polyanthos*. $200/£129

FROST, ROBERT. A Witness Tree. NY: Henry Holt, (1942). 1st ed. Gilt. Fine in dj (lt edgeworn). *Sadlon*. $50/£32

FROTHINGHAM, ROBERT. Trails Through the Golden West. NY: McBride, (1932). Photo eps. VG in dj. *Schoyer*. $25/£16

FROUD, BRIAN. Goblins. London: Blackie and Son, 1983. 19x29 cm. 3 dbl-pg pop-ups, wheels, pull-tabs. Glazed pict bds. Fine. *Book Finders*. $40/£26

FROUD, BRIAN. Goblins. NY: Macmillan, 1983. 1st US ed. Pop-up. Sm 4to. Glazed pict paper-cvrd bds. NF. *Book Adoption*. $45/£29

FRY, G. Escort to Berlin. NY, 1980. VG in VG dj. *Clark*. $25/£16

FRY, ROGER. Cezanne. London: Hogarth, 1927. 40 b/w plts. (Tp, 1st few leaves sl spotted; feps browned; ex-libris; spine browned.) *Edwards*. $62/£40

FRY, ROGER. Characteristics of French Art. London: C&W, 1932. 1st ed. 40 plts. Nice. *Europa*. $31/£20

FRY, ROGER. Flemish Art; A Critical Survey. London: C&W, 1927. 1st ed. Fine in dj (torn, repaired). *Europa*. $37/£24

FRY, ROGER. Last Lectures. CUP, 1939. Pub's cl. Fine. *Europa*. $47/£30

FRYER, JANE EAYRE. The Mary Frances Cook Book. London: Harrap, c. 1912. 1st UK ed. Color frontis, 7 full-pg illus. Color pict onlay fr cvr. *Petersfield*. $43/£28

FRYER, P. Private Case, Public Scandal: Secrets of the British Museum Revealed. Secker & Warburg, 1966. VG in dj. *Moss.* $28/£18

FUCHS, VIVIAN and EDMUND HILLARY. The Crossing of Antarctica. Boston, (1958). 1st Amer ed. 9 maps. Fine in dj. *Artis.* $17/£11

FUCHS, VIVIAN and EDMUND HILLARY. The Crossing of Antarctica. Boston: Little, Brown, 1958. 1st Amer ed. 64pp photo-plts. Fine in NF dj. *Connolly.* $40/£26

FUENTES, CARLOS. Aura. NY: FSG, 1965. 1st ed in English. Pencil name, else NF in bright dj (spine lt faded). *Lame Duck.* $175/£113

FUENTES, NORBERTO. Hemingway in Cuba. Seacaucus, NJ: Lyle Stuart, (1984). 1st ed. New (red rmdr line bottom pg edges) in dj. *Bernard.* $35/£23

FUERTES, LOUIS AGASSIZ. Album of Abyssinian Birds and Mammals. London, 1930. 4 pp intro & 32 color lithos in card portfolio (split, detached spine) with portions of card slipcase. *Edwards.* $341/£220

FUGARD, ATHOL. Master Harold and the Boys. NY: Knopf, 1982. 1st US ed. Fine in NF dj. *Lame Duck.* $35/£23

FUGARD, SHEILA. The Castaways. Johannesburg: Macmillan, 1972. 1st ed. Pg edges lt soiled, else NF in VG dj (2-inch edge tear, crease fr panel). *Lame Duck.* $125/£81

FULAINAIN. Marsh Arab. Haji Rikkan. Phila: Lippincott, 1928. Sketch map. VG in dj (chipped). *Schoyer.* $45/£29

FULLAWAY, DAVID and NOEL L.H. KRAUSS. Common Insects of Hawaii. Honolulu: Tongg, 1945. 1st ed. 12 full color plts. VG in dj (chipped). *Connolly.* $37/£24

FULLER, ANDREW S. The Grape Culturist. NY: The Author, 1864. 1st ed. 262,(1)pp. Blue blindstamped cl. Minor edgewear, pencil inscrip fep, sm bkseller label; else VG. *Bookpress.* $110/£71

FULLER, ANDREW S. The Illustrated Strawberry Culturist. NY, (1887). 59pp + (11pp ads). (Browned; fep detached.) Flexible cl bds (lt soil). *Sutton.* $35/£23

FULLER, ANDREW S. The Illustrated Strawberry Culturist. NY: OJ, 1866. Ptd wraps (sl worn, soiled). *Bohling.* $35/£23

FULLER, ANDREW S. The Nut Culturist. NY, 1896. viii,289pp (lt browned). Gilt-dec cl (lt wear; paper to fr hinge cracked). *Sutton.* $65/£42

FULLER, ANDREW S. The Nut Culturist. NY: OJ, 1906. Grn cl, gilt spine (rubbed, spotted). *Bohling.* $35/£23

FULLER, ANDREW S. The Propagation of Plants. NY: OJ, 1907. Grn cl, gilt spine. VG (lt rubbed). *Bohling.* $30/£19

FULLER, ANDREW S. The Small Fruit Culturist. NY: OJ, 1904. Rev, enlgd ed. Grn cl, gilt. VG + (spine ends lt rubbed). *Bohling.* $30/£19

FULLER, CLAUD E. and RICHARD D. STEUART. Firearms of the Confederacy.... Huntington, WV: Standard Publications, 1944. 1st ed. NF. *Mcgowan.* $150/£97

FULLER, GEORGE (ed). Historic Michigan. Nat'l Hist Assoc, (1924). 1st ed. 3 vols. VG set. *Artis.* $95/£61

FULLER, H.B. Not on the Screen. Knopf, 1930. 1st ed. One of 3000. Spine sl sunned, cocked, else NF in dj. *Fine Books.* $45/£29

FULLER, HENRY C. Adventures of Bill Longley...Executed at Giddings, Texas, 1878. Nacagdoches, n.d. 1st ed. Lt wear, o/w Fine in wrappers. *Hermitage.* $150/£97

FULLER, HENRY. On Rheumatism, Rheumatic Gout, and Sciatica. NY, 1854. 1st Amer ed. 322pp. Good. *Fye.* $125/£81

FULLER, HORACE W. Imposters and Adventurers. Boston: Soule & Bugbee, 1882. (Cvr sl worn.) *Boswell.* $75/£48

FULLER, J.F.C. The Dragon's Teeth. London, 1932. 1st ed. Foxing, o/w VG in blue cl; gilt spine title (short splits). *Edwards.* $70/£45

FULLER, J.F.C. The Last of the Gentlemen's War. London, 1937. 1st ed. Frontis port; 11 plts; fldg map. VG (rmdr binding). *Edwards.* $39/£25

FULLER, J.F.C. Memoirs of an Unconventional Soldier. London, 1936. Reprint. 2 frontis ports, 7 plts, 17 diagrams, 5 fldg maps at rear. Red cl. VG. *Edwards.* $62/£40

FULLER, J.F.C. War and Western Civilization. London, 1932. 1st ed. 8 full-pg maps. Eps sl browned, o/w VG in variant blue cl binding. Dj (sl rubbed). *Edwards.* $93/£60

FULLER, JACK. Fragments. NY: Morrow, 1984. 1st ed. Fine in Fine dj (2 sm edgetears). *Aka.* $35/£23

FULLER, R. BUCKMINSTER. Critical Path. NY: St. Martin's, (1981). 1st ed. Signed, dated. VF in dj. *Jaffe.* $65/£42

FULLER, R. BUCKMINSTER. Untitled Epic Poem on the History of Industrialization. Jargon, 1962. 1st ed. VG in wrappers, acetate dj (sl defective). *Poetry.* $19/£12

FULLER, THOMAS. The Church History of Britain. London: William Tegg, 1868. 3 vols. VG. *Bishop.* $20/£13

FULLER, THOMAS. The History of the Worthies of England.... N.p.: F.C. and J. Rivington et al, 1811. 2 vols. Frontis, xvi,596; (iv),619pp. Contemp gilt calf (respined; foxing; ink inscrips), aeg. *Bookpress.* $110/£71

FULLER, THOMAS. The Holy State and the Profane State. London: William Pickering, 1840. 1st ed thus. viii,400pp; red edges. Contemp 'divinity' calf dec in blind (lacking label; extrems rubbed). *Cox.* $39/£25

FULLERTON, A. To Persia for Flowers. London, 1938. 12 plts. Fine in dj. *Henly.* $54/£35

Fulton's Book of Pigeons. (By Robert Brockley Fulton.) London: Cassell, 1895. 2nd ed. Blue dec cl. *Appelfeld.* $90/£58

FULTON, AMBROSE C. Life's Voyage: A Diary of a Sailor on Sea and Land.... NY: Author, 1898. 1st ed. (8),555pp. Howes F 413. *Ginsberg.* $300/£194

FULTON, ARBELLA. Tales of the Trail. Montreal: Payette Radio, 1965. VG. *Perier.* $30/£19

FULTON, FRANCES I. SIMS. To and Through Nebraska by a Pennsylvania Girl. Lincoln, NE: Journal Co., 1884. 1st ed. 273pp. Olive cl. Nice. Howes F414. *Second Life.* $150/£97

FULTON, JAMES ALEXANDER. Peach Culture. NY: OJ, 1909. New rev, enlgd ed. Grn cl, gilt. VG + (name). *Bohling.* $25/£16

FULTON, JOHN F. Harvey Cushing, A Biography. Oxford: Blackwell, 1946. 1st British ed. Frontis port; 60 plts. Blue cl. Nice (ex-lib). *White.* $34/£22

FULTON, JOHN F. Harvey Cushing. Springfield, 1946. 1st ed. Nice (bds faded) in dj. *Goodrich.* $85/£55

FULTON, JOHN F. Harvey Cushing: A Biography. Springfield, 1946. 1st ed. Good. *Fye.* $50/£32

FULTON, JOHN F. and ALLEN D. KELLER. The Sign of Babinski. Springfield: Thomas, 1932. Signed. Nice in dj. *Goodrich.* $150/£97

FULTON, JOHN. Muscular Contraction and the Reflex Control of Movement. Balt, 1926. 1st ed. Good. *Fye.* $150/£97

FULTON, MAURICE G. History of the Lincoln County War. Robert N. Mullin (ed). Tucson: Univ of AZ, (1968). 1st ed. VG in dj (sl worn, spine faded). *Lien.* $50/£32

FULTON, ROBERT (ed). Book of Pigeons. London: Cassell Petter & Galpin, n.d. (ca 1886). viii,392pp; 50 Fine chromolitho plts. Brn cl (rebound; extrems sl rubbed). *Karmiole.* $250/£161

FULTON, WILLIAM FRIERSON. Family Record and War Reminiscences. (N.p., 191?). 1st ed. 8vo, frontis port, fldg chart. Orig blue cl, gilt centerpiece. Fine (lt wear). *Chapel Hill.* $650/£419

FUME, JOSEPH. (Pseud of William Andrew Chatto.) A Paper: Of Tobacco; Treating of the Rise, Progress, Pleasures, and Advantages of Smoking.... London: Chapman & Hall, 1839. 1st ed. Phiz (illus). Orig white pict bds, plain spine (rubbing, soiling). VG. *Houle.* $295/£190

FUNNELL, WILLIAM. A Voyage Round the World Containing an Account of Captain Dampier's Expedition.... London: James Knapton, 1707. Frontis fldg map, 300pp,15pp index, 1pg ads; 4 fldg maps, 8 plts. Full panelled contemp calf. VG. *Cullen.* $1,250/£806

FURLONG, CHARLES WELLINGTON. The Gateway to the Sahara. NY: Scribner's, 1914. New, enlgd ed. Signed presentation. 36 plts (4 color); 3 maps. Rubbed, o/w VG. *Worldwide.* $75/£48

FURLONG, CHARLES WELLINGTON. Let 'Er Buck. NY: Putnam's, 1921. 1st ptg. Bright blue cl, mtd cvr illus. VG. *Schoyer.* $35/£23

FURMAN, GABRIEL. Antiquities of Long Island. NY, 1875. 2 vols in 1. 478pp. Howes F 422. *Argosy.* $200/£129

FURST, HERBERT. Original Engraving and Etching. London/Edinburgh, 1931. (Eps lt spotted.) Dj (lt spotted, ragged). *Edwards.* $116/£75

FURST, JILL LESLIE and PETER T. Columbian Art of Mexico. NY: Abbeville, (1980). Good in dj. *Archaeologia.* $45/£29

FUSSELL, G. The Exploration of England...1570-1815. Mitre Press, 1935. Ptd cvrs. Good. *Moss.* $47/£30

FUTRELLE, JACQUES. The Diamond Master. Bobbs-Merrill, 1909. 1st ed. VG. *Madle.* $45/£29

FUZZLEBUG, FRITZ. (Pseud of John J. Dunkle). Prison Life During the Rebellion. Singer's Glen, VA: Published by Author, 1869. 1st ed. 48pp. Orig ptd pink wraps. Lt dampstain, else NF. Howes D 569. *Chapel Hill.* $175/£113

FYFIELD, F. A Question of Guilt. Heinemann, 1988. 1st UK ed, 1st bk. Mint in Mint dj. *Martin.* $37/£24

G

GABRIELSON, I.N. Western American Alpines. NY, 1932. Map; 121 photos. (Cl sl used.) *Wheldon & Wesley.* $47/£30

GABRIELSON, I.N. and FREDERICK C. LINCOLN. Birds of Alaska. Harrisburg/Washington: Stackpole/Wildlife Management Inst, 1959. VG in dj (worn). *Parmer.* $350/£226

GADDIS, THOMAS E. Birdman of Alcatraz. NY, (1955). 1st ed. VG in dj (rubbed, edgeworn). *King.* $25/£16

GADDIS, WILLIAM. JR. NY: Knopf, 1975. 1st ed. Fine in NF dj (price-clipped). *Pettler.* $90/£58

GADDIS, WILLIAM. JR. Knopf, 1975. 1st ed. Fine in dj. *Fine Books.* $95/£61

GADOW, H.F. The Evolution of the Vertebral Column. Cambridge, 1933. Port. Dj (worn). *Sutton.* $65/£42

GADOW, HANS. Through Southern Mexico. London/NY: Witherby/Scribner's, 1908. Fldg map; teg. Gold-stamped pict cl (sl sunned). *Dawson.* $75/£48

GADOW, HANS. Through Southern Mexico.... London: Witherby, 1908. 1st ed. Frontis, fldg map. Maroon cl, gilt vignette, teg. VG (1st few gatherings sl loose). *Morrell.* $93/£60

GAER, JOSEPH (ed). Bibliography of California Literature. (SF): CA Literary Research, (1935). 1st ed. Blue calf spine over blue cl. Good in orig stiff wrappers. *Karmiole.* $85/£55

GAEVERNITZ, GERO. Revolt against Hitler. London, 1948. 1st Eng ed. 7 plts. Eps sl browned, o/w Good in dj (frayed, soiled). *Edwards.* $23/£15

GAEVERNITZ, GERO. They Almost Killed Hitler. Macmillan, 1947. 1st ed. VG in VG dj. *Bishop.* $20/£13

GAG, WANDA. The Funny Thing. NY: Coward-McCann, 1929. 1st ed. Ob 16mo. 32pp. Yellow pict bds. VG in dj (lt frayed). *Davidson.* $325/£210

GAG, WANDA. Gone Is Gone. NY: Coward-McCann, (1935). 1st ed. 16mo. Color frontis. Yellow-grn cl, black lettering. Good in pict dj (smudged, chipped). *Reisler.* $175/£113

GAG, WANDA. Millions of Cats. NY: Coward McCann, 1928. 1st ed, 1st bk. 15pp. VG in dj (sm piece missing spine). *Davidson.* $400/£258

GAILLARDET, FREDERIC. Sketches of Early Texas and Louisiana. James Shepherd (trans). Austin: UTP, 1966. 1st ed. Dj. *Lambeth.* $50/£32

GAINES, ERNEST J. A Gathering of Old Men. NY: Knopf, 1983. 1st ed. Rev slip, flyer, photo laid in. VF in dj. *Reese.* $35/£23

GAINES, ERNEST J. A Gathering of Old Men. NY: Knopf, 1983. 1st ed. VF in dj. *Else Fine.* $50/£32

GAINES, RICHARD V. (comp). Hand-Book of Charlotte County, Virginia. Richmond, VA: Everett Waddey, 1889. 1st ed w/map (not found in all copies). 77,(3)pp. Minor foxing, chipping to orig ptd wrappers, else VG. *Mcgowan.* $85/£55

GAINSBOROUGH, THOMAS. Letters of Thomas Gainsborough. Mary Woodall (ed). London: Lion and Unicorn Press, 1961. One of 400. Frontis port, 26 plts. Morocco-backed bds (spine lt faded). *Edwards.* $101/£65

GAIR, MALCOLM. The Burning of Troy. GC: DCC, 1958. 1st ed. Fine (bumps) in VG + dj (folds worn). *Janus.* $20/£13

GAIRDNER, JAMES (ed). Paston Letters 1422-1509 A.D. Westminster: Constable, 1900-1901. Rpt of 1872-5 ed. 4 vols. Frontis each vol. Ptd paper spine labels (upper edges sl defective; tp final vol crudely rehinged; outer side margin trimmed.) *Bickersteth.* $217/£140

GALBRAITH, JOHN S. The Hudson's Bay Company. Berkeley: Univ of CA, 1957. 1st ed. VG in VG dj. *Blue Dragon.* $70/£45

GALE, GEORGE. Upper Mississippi. Chicago, 1867. 1st ed. 460pp, 14 plts. Howes G 14. *Ginsberg.* $200/£129

GALE, JOHN. The Missouri Expedition, 1818-1820. Roger L. Nichols (ed). Norman: Univ of OK Press, (1969). 1st ed. VG in dj. *Laurie.* $40/£26

GALE, N. Orchard Songs. Putnam, 1893. 1st ed, Amer issue. Sl sunned. NF. *Fine Books.* $50/£32

GALE, STANLEY. Modern Housing Estates. London: Batsford, 1948. Color fldg frontis. Dj (chipped). *Edwards.* $39/£25

GALE, ZONA. Romance Island. Indianapolis, (1906). 1st Amer ed. 1st bk. Pict cl. NF (sl sunned). *Polyanthos.* $45/£29

GALEN, SIEGEL. Galen on Sense Perception. Basel: Karger, 1970. NF in dj. *Goodrich.* $75/£48

Galignani's New Paris Guide for 1864. Paris: A. and W. Galignani, 1863. 4,612,xiipp; lg fldg pocket map w/hand-colored outline. Emb full morocco. VG (extrems worn). *Cullen.* $165/£106

GALLAGHER, BERTRAND E. Utah's Greatest Manhunt.... Salt Lake, 1913. 1st ed. VG in wraps. *Benchmark.* $30/£19

GALLAGHER, GARY W. Stephen Dodson Ramseur: Lee's Gallant General. Chapel Hill: Univ of NC, (1985). 1st ed, 4th ptg. Fine in Fine dj. *Mcgowan.* $35/£23

GALLAGHER, RACHEL. Letting Down My Hair. NY: Arthur Fields, (1973). 1st Amer ed. VG- (lt creasing bds, dj). *Between The Covers.* $45/£29

GALLAGHER, SHARON. Inside the Personal Computer. NY: Abbeville, 1984. 31x13 cm. Fine. *Book Finders.* $60/£39

GALLAHER, JAMES. The Western Sketch-Book. Boston: Crocker & Brewster, 1850. 408pp. Blind-emb brn cl, gilt spine title. Foxing; spine chipped, else NF. *Bohling.* $150/£97

GALLANT, MAVIS. A Fairly Good Time. NY: Random House, (1970). 1st ed. VG in dj (lt soiled). *Hermitage.* $25/£16

GALLEGLY, JOSEPH. From Alamo Plaza to Jack Harris's Saloon. Mouton: The Hague, 1970. 1st ed. Dj. *Lambeth.* $75/£48

GALLICHAN, WALTER M. Women Under Polygamy. London, 1914. Teg. (Spine faded.) *Edwards.* $70/£45

GALLICO, PAUL. Farewell to Sport. NY: Knopf, 1938. 1st ed. Fine in dj (nicks, else Fine). *Godot.* $175/£113

GALLICO, PAUL. The Small Miracle. GC: Doubleday, 1952. 1st ed. Reisie Lonette (illus). 12mo. Fine in VG dj (chipped). *Book Adoption.* $40/£26

GALLIER, JAMES. Autobiography of James Gallier, Architect. NY: De Capo Press, 1973. Rpt, 1st ed thus. Frontis, 38 plts. Bkpl, else Fine. *Bookpress.* $30/£19

GALLIZIER, NATHAN. Under the Witches Moon. Boston: Page, 1917. 1st ed. VG in illus cvr. *Else Fine.* $75/£48

GALLO, MAX. The Poster in History. Alfred & Bruni Mayor (trans). NY: American Heritage, (1974). 1st US ed. Fine in dj. *Oak Knoll.* $45/£29

GALLUP, JOSEPH. Sketches of Epidemic Diseases in the State of Vermont...to the Year 1815. Boston, 1815. 1st ed. 419pp. Orig leather (rubbed). *Fye.* $300/£194

GALLY, J.W. Sand and Big Jack Small. Chicago: Belford, Clarke, 1880. 1st ed. Frontis, 243pp. Brn cl, stamped in gilt, black. Lt foxing, fep neatly excised, edges rubbed, else Good. *Reese.* $65/£42

GALPIN, FRANCIS W. The Music of the Sumerians and Their Immediate Successors, the Babylonians and Assyrians. Cambridge: CUP, 1937. 1st ed. 12 plts. (Sig.) *Archaeologia.* $175/£113

GALPIN, FRANCIS W. Old English Instruments of Music. London: Methuen, 1911. 2nd ed. Red cl, gilt. Fore-edge sl spotted, flyleaves lt browned. *Hollett.* $85/£55

GALSWORTHY, JOHN. Awakening. London: Heinemann, (1920). 1st ed, one of 7500 ptd. Color frontis, 63,(1)pp. R.H. Sauter (illus). Gilt-stamped brn bds. Fine in blue cl chemise, slipcase, morocco spine label (chipped). *Chapel Hill.* $100/£65

GALSWORTHY, JOHN. Flowering Wilderness. London: Heinemann, 1932. 1st ed. NF in grn cl lettered in gold. Dj (worn). *Vandoros.* $25/£16

GALSWORTHY, JOHN. The Forsyte Saga. London: Heinemann, 1922. 1st ed, ltd to 275 numbered, signed. Full grn leather, gilt-stamped; teg. VG in custom 1/4 leather slipcase box. *Godot.* $375/£242

GALSWORTHY, JOHN. Four Forsyte Stories. Fountain Press, 1929. 1st ed. One of 850 signed. Spine sl faded; crvs sl lightened, else NF. *Fine Books.* $60/£39

GALSWORTHY, JOHN. The Land. London: George Allen & Unwin, (1918). 1st ed. One of 2000. Fine in orig ptd self-wraps; grn cl chemise, slipcase, leather spine label. *Chapel Hill.* $40/£26

GALSWORTHY, JOHN. Loyalties: A Drama in Three Acts. London: Duckworth, 1930. One of 315 numbered, signed. Fine in dj (sl mkd, sl chipped). *Rees.* $54/£35

GALSWORTHY, JOHN. Maid in Waiting. London: Heinemann, 1931. 1st ed. NF in grn cl lettered in gold. VG pict dj. *Vandoros.* $50/£32

GALSWORTHY, JOHN. On Forsyte Change. London: Heinemann, 1930. 1st ed. NF in grn cl lettered in gold. VG dj (lacks 3/4-inch top spine). *Vandoros.* $50/£32

GALSWORTHY, JOHN. On Forsyte Change. London: Heinemann, 1930. 1st ed. Grn cl. Fine in VG dj. *Chapel Hill.* $50/£32

GALSWORTHY, JOHN. Over the River. London: Heinemann, 1933. 1st ed. Fine in grn cl lettered in gold. NF dj. *Vandoros.* $50/£32

GALSWORTHY, JOHN. The Silver Spoon. London: Heinemann, (1926). 1st ed. Grn cl (spine crown worn). VG in dj (sl dknd; creased; tape mends verso). *Chapel Hill.* $30/£19

GALSWORTHY, JOHN. Soames and the Flag. London: Heinemann, 1930. One of 1025 signed. Teg. Vellum, gilt title. Fine in new chemise, slipcase. *Heller.* $125/£81

GALSWORTHY, JOHN. Swan Song. London: Heinemann, 1928. 1st ed. Fine in grn cl lettered in gold. NF pict dj. *Vandoros.* $75/£48

GALSWORTHY, JOHN. The White Monkey. London: Heinemann, (1924). 1st ed. Grn cl. Spine head chipped, else VG in dj remnants. *Chapel Hill.* $35/£23

GALSWORTHY, JOHN. Windows. London, (1922). 1st ed. Sm lib stamp rep, else VG in dj. *King.* $25/£16

GALTON, FRANCIS (ed). Vacation Tourists and Notes of Travel in 1862-3. Macmillan, 1864. Sole ed. viii,418pp. Contemp 1/2-calf. *Bickersteth.* $132/£85

GALVIN, JOHN (ed). The First Spanish Entry into San Francisco Bay 1774. SF: John Howell, (1971). Ltd to 5000. 4 contemp maps. Fine in VG dj. *Blue Dragon.* $75/£48

GAMBIER, J.W. Links in My Life on Land and Sea. NY: Dutton, 1906. Frontis port, newspaper rev tipped to fep; teg. Dec cl (soiled). *Schoyer.* $40/£26

GAMBLE, J.S. The Bambuseae of British India. Dehra Dun, 1978. 119 plts. *Sutton.* $55/£35

GAMBRILL, RICHARD and JAMES MacKENZIE. Sporting Stables and Kennels. NY: Derrydale, 1935. Ltd to 950. (Bumped; spine ends worn.) *October Farm.* $225/£145

GAMGEE, SAMPSON. On the Treatment of Wounds and Fractures. London, 1883. 2nd ed. 364pp. Good. *Fye.* $100/£65

GANDEE, B.F. The Artist or Young Ladies' Instructor in Ornamental Painting, Drawing, etc. London: Chapman & Hall, 1835. Color litho frontis, vii,235pp + 1f ads, 16 litho plts. Blind cl (sl worn). *Ars Artis.* $233/£150

GANN, THOMAS W.F. BAE Bulletin 64. The Maya Indians of Southern Yucatan and Northern British Honduras. Washington: GPO, 1918. 1st ed. 6pp color illus. Gilt/blindstamped grn cl (sl rubbing). VG. *Houle.* $75/£48

GANN, W.D. Tunnel Through the Air. Financial Guardian, 1927. 1st ed. VG. *Madle.* $40/£26

GANNETT, HENRY. 20th Annual Report of the U.S. Geological Survey. Washington, 1900. 159 plts. Fair (shelfworn; spine wrinkled). *Artis.* $45/£29

GANS, M.H. and TH. M. DUYVENE DE WIT-KLINK-HAMMER. Dutch Silver. Oliver Van Oss (trans). Faber & Faber, 1961. 1st ed. Dbl-pg frontis; 144 plts. Dj. *Edwards.* $70/£45

GANSON, EVE. Desert Mavericks or Who's Who in the Desert. Santa Barbara: Hebberd, 1928. 1st ed. VG- in VG- dj (chipped). *Parker.* $25/£16

GANSON, LEWIS. The Art of Close-Up Magic. Bideford, 1972. Rpt. 2 vols. Djs. *Edwards.* $39/£25

GANTT, W. HORSLEY. A Medical Review of Soviet Russia. London: BMA, 1928. Stiff bds. Good. *Goodrich.* $65/£42

GANTZ, K. Not in Solitude. Doubleday, 1959. 1st ed. NF in dj. *Aronovitz.* $25/£16

GANZ, PAUL. The Drawings of Henry Fuseli. NY, 1949. Color frontis port; 106 plts. VG. *Argosy.* $125/£81

GANZ, PAUL. The Drawings of Henry Fuseli. London: Parrish, 1949. 1st ed. Color frontis port, 106 plts. *Europa.* $62/£40

GANZ, PAUL. The Paintings of Hans Holbein, First Complete Edition. London: Phaidon, 1956. 13 tipped-in color plts. VG in dj (sl torn). *Petersfield.* $65/£42

GARAVAGLIA, LOUIS and CHARLES WORMAN. Firearms of the American West 1866-1894. Albuquerque: Univ of NM, 1985. 1st ed. NF in NF dj. *Parker.* $100/£65

GARCES, FRANCISCO. On the Trail of a Spanish Pioneer. Elliott Coues (trans). NY: Harper, 1900. 1st ed. One of 950 numbered set. 2 vols. 3 fldg maps, 5 facs, 12 plts. Howes C 801. *Ginsberg.* $375/£242

GARCIA LORCA, FEDERICO. Lament for the Death of a Bullfighter and Other Poems. A.L. Lloyd (trans). London: Heinemann, 1937. 1st ed. Fine. *Patterson.* $101/£65

GARCIA LORCA, FEDERICO. Poems. Stephen Spender (trans). Dolphin, 1939. 1st ed. Sl dull, else VG. *Whiteson.* $31/£20

GARCIA MARQUEZ, GABRIEL. The Autumn of the Patriarch. London: Cape, 1977. 1st ed. Fine in dj. *Rees.* $31/£20

GARCIA MARQUEZ, GABRIEL. Chronicle of a Death Foretold. Gregory Rabassa (trans). NY: Knopf, 1983. 1st Amer ed. Fine in Fine dj. *Revere.* $35/£23

GARCIA MARQUEZ, GABRIEL. Chronicle of a Death Foretold. NY: Knopf, 1983. 1st ed. Fine in 1st state dj w/'One Hundred Days of Solitude' on upper flap (later corrected to 'One Hundred Years of Solitude'). *Moorhouse.* $54/£35

GARCIA MARQUEZ, GABRIEL. The General in His Labyrinth. London: Jonathan Cape, (1991). 1st ed. Sig, else Fine in NF dj. *Robbins.* $20/£13

GARCIA MARQUEZ, GABRIEL. The General in His Labyrinth. Edith Grossman (trans). NY: Knopf, 1990. 1st Amer ed. Fine in Fine dj. *Revere.* $20/£13

GARCIA MARQUEZ, GABRIEL. The General in His Labyrinth. NY: Knopf, 1990. 1st Amer ed. Fine in dj. *Between The Covers.* $45/£29

GARCIA MARQUEZ, GABRIEL. In Evil Hour. Gregory Rabassa (trans). NY: Harper & Row, (1979). 1st Amer ed. Fine in dj. *Hermitage.* $35/£23

GARCIA MARQUEZ, GABRIEL. In Evil Hour. London: Cape, 1980. 1st ed. Fine in dj. *Rees.* $31/£20

GARCIA MARQUEZ, GABRIEL. Innocent Erendira and Other Stories. NY: Harper & Row, (1978). 1st Amer ed. NF in dj (price-clipped). *Hermitage.* $45/£29

GARCIA MARQUEZ, GABRIEL. Leaf Storm and Other Stories. NY: Harper, (1972). 1st ed. Name, date on 1/2 title, else NF in Fine dj (spine lettering lt tanned). *Between The Covers.* $225/£145

GARCIA MARQUEZ, GABRIEL. Love in the Time of Cholera. Edith Grossman (trans). NY: Knopf, 1988. 1st Amer ed. Fine in Fine dj. *Revere.* $25/£16

GARCIA MARQUEZ, GABRIEL. Love in the Time of Cholera. Knopf, 1988. 1st Amer ed. Fine in dj (price-clipped). *Stahr.* $35/£23

GARCIA MARQUEZ, GABRIEL. Love in the Time of Cholera. Edith Grossman (trans). NY: Knopf, 1988. 1st Amer ed. #47/350 specially bound, signed. Pink/black cl. Promo postcard laid in. Fine in orig dec acetate dj, pub's slipcase. *Chapel Hill.* $500/£323

GARCIA MARQUEZ, GABRIEL. No One Writes to the Colonel and Other Stories. H&R, 1968. 1st Amer ed. Fine in dj. *Fine Books.* $475/£306

GARCIA MARQUEZ, GABRIEL. One Hundred Years of Solitude. NY/Evanston: Harper & Row, (1970). 1st ed. Fine in NF dj (edges very sl wear). *Bernard.* $650/£419

GARCIA MARQUEZ, GABRIEL. One Hundred Years of Solitude. NY: Harper, 1970. 1st ed. Fine in Fine dj (lt wear spine head). *Beasley.* $650/£419

GARCIA MARQUEZ, GABRIEL. One Hundred Years of Solitude. Cape, 1970. 1st UK ed. NF in dj. *Lewton.* $233/£150

GARCIA, ANDREW. Tough Trip Through Paradise, 1878-1879. Boston: Houghton Mifflin, 1967. 1st ptg. VG in dj. *Schoyer.* $20/£13

GARCIA, CRISTINA. Dreaming in Cuban. NY: Knopf, 1992. 1st ed. Fine in dj (sl rubbing). *Antic Hay.* $25/£16

GARD, WAYNE. The Chisholm Trail. Norman: Univ of OK, 1954. 1st ed. Inscribed, signed. Fine in dj (spine faded). *Glenn.* $125/£81

GARD, WAYNE. The Great Buffalo Hunt. Knopf, 1959. 1st ed. Fine in VG dj. *Oregon.* $35/£23

GARD, WAYNE. The Great Buffalo Hunt. NY, 1959. 1st ed. Pict cl. Sl bumped, o/w Fine in dj (sl chipped). *Baade.* $40/£26

GARDINER, A.L. Narrative of a Journey to the Zoolu Country in South Africa. London, 1836. iv,412pp; 2 maps; 26 plts (3 color). Contemp 1/2 morocco (rebacked; sl water-staining). *Wheldon & Wesley.* $372/£240

GARDINER, ALAN and KURT SETHE. Egyptian Letters to the Dead.... London: Egypt Exploration Soc, 1928. 1st ed. 17 plts. Good (loose in portfolio as issued). *Archaeologia.* $375/£242

GARDINER, ALAN. Egyptian Grammar. Oxford: Griffith Inst, (1976). 1 plt. Good. *Archaeologia.* $65/£42

GARDINER, ALAN. My Working Years. London: Coronet Press, (1962). (Sm scratch.) *Archaeologia.* $85/£55

GARDINER, ALLEN F. Narrative of a Journey to the Zoolu Country.... London: William Crofts, 1836. 1st ed. iv,412, 2 fldg maps, 26 litho plts (2 colored, incl frontis). (Margins 2 plts frayed; foxing to some plts, adjacent text.) Grn pebble cl, spine gilt (sl cockled, rubbed; upper joint cracking, tear in spine repaired). *Morrell.* $496/£320

GARDINER, HOWARD CALHOUN. In Pursuit of the Golden Dream. Stoughton, MA: Western Hemisphere, 1970. (1st trade ed.) 2 maps (1 fldg). Unopened. Gilt-stamped cl. Fine. *Bohling.* $125/£81

GARDINER, HOWARD. In Pursuit of the Golden Dream. Dale Morgan (ed). Stoughton, Western Hemisphere, 1970. 1st trade ed. Red cl. VF. *Oregon.* $60/£39

GARDINER, LINDA. Rare Vanishing and Lost British Birds. London: J.M. Dent, 1923. 1st ed. 26 color plts. Nice (few leaves lt foxed; spine sl faded). *Shasky.* $50/£32

GARDINER, WILLIAM. The Music of Nature. Boston, 1837. 1st Amer ed. Color frontis, 505pp. Cl worn. *Argosy.* $175/£113

GARDNER, DORSEY. Quatre Bras, Ligny, and Waterloo. London, 1882. 1st ed. xiii,515pp; 2 fldg plans. Eps sl foxed, sig sl pulled, o/w VG in contemp 1/2 calf, marbled bds, spine label. *Edwards.* $116/£75

GARDNER, ERLE STANLEY and A. JOHNSON. The Case of Erle Stanley Gardner. Morrow, 1947. 1st ed. NF in VG dj (sl wear). *Fine Books.* $35/£23

GARDNER, ERLE STANLEY. The Case of the Baited Hook. NY: William Morrow, 1940. 1st ed. VG+ in dj (lt chipped). *Janus.* $125/£81

GARDNER, ERLE STANLEY. The Case of the Baited Hook. NY: William Morrow, 1940. 1st ed. Inscrip, o/w Fine in dj (sm chip; tiny closed tears; sl wear spine ends). *Mordida.* $175/£113

GARDNER, ERLE STANLEY. The Case of the Black-Eyed Blonde. Morrow, 1944. 1st ed. VG+ in VG dj (worn). *Fine Books.* $65/£42

GARDNER, ERLE STANLEY. The Case of the Daring Decoy. NY: William Morrow, 1957. 1st ed, adv rev copy. Fine in NF dj (lt edgewear). *Janus.* $75/£48

GARDNER, ERLE STANLEY. The Case of the Demure Defendant. NY: William Morrow, 1956. 1st ed. Fine in VG dj (price-clipped; internal tape mends; sl faded spine; nicked). *Mordida.* $30/£19

GARDNER, ERLE STANLEY. The Case of the Green-Eyed Sister. NY: William Morrow, 1953. 1st ed. Fine in dj (sl wrinkling fr panel). *Mordida.* $50/£32

GARDNER, ERLE STANLEY. The Case of the Grinning Gorilla. Morrow, 1952. 1st ed. NF in VG dj (lt wear). *Fine Books.* $30/£19

GARDNER, ERLE STANLEY. The Case of the Half-Wakened Wife. Cassell, 1949. 1st UK ed. VG+ in VG+ dj. *Martin.* $25/£16

GARDNER, ERLE STANLEY. The Case of the Lonely Heiress. NY: William Morrow, 1948. 1st ed. Fine in NF dj (spine sunned). *Janus.* $75/£48

GARDNER, ERLE STANLEY. The Case of the Mythical Monkeys. NY: William Morrow, 1959. 1st ed. Fine in dj (sl wear; short closed tears). *Mordida.* $35/£23

GARDNER, ERLE STANLEY. The Case of the Rolling Bones. NY: William Morrow, 1939. 1st ed. NF (edges sl worn) in VG dj. *Janus.* $125/£81

GARDNER, ERLE STANLEY. The Case of the Runaway Corpse. NY: William Morrow, 1954. 1st ed. Fine in dj (sl wear spine ends; corners nicked). *Mordida.* $45/£29

GARDNER, ERLE STANLEY. The Case of the Screaming Woman. Morrow, 1957. 1st ed. Sm ring mk fr, else NF in dj (sm ring mk; couple closed tears; lt worn). *Murder.* $30/£19

GARDNER, ERLE STANLEY. The Case of the Screaming Woman. NY: Morrow, 1957. 1st ed. Fine in VG+ dj (lt rubbing, lt edgewear). *Janus.* $45/£29

GARDNER, ERLE STANLEY. The Case of the Shapely Shadow. Morrow, 1960. 1st ed. Sl shelf wear, else Fine in VG dj (couple missing pieces). *Murder.* $25/£16

GARDNER, ERLE STANLEY. The Case of the Shapely Shadow. Morrow, 1960. 1st ed. Bds sl soiling, else Fine in dj (sl wear). *Murder.* $35/£23

GARDNER, ERLE STANLEY. The Case of the Smoking Chimney. NY: William Morrow, 1943. 1st ed. Fine in VG+ dj (sm chips). *Janus.* $125/£81

GARDNER, ERLE STANLEY. The Case of the Vagabond Virgin. Morrow, 1948. 1st ed. Spine sl worn, else NF in bright dj (lt chipped). *Murder.* $55/£35

GARDNER, ERLE STANLEY. The Case of the Waylaid Wolf. Morrow, 1959. 1st ed. Lt soiled, else NF in dj (lt edgeworn). *Murder.* $45/£29

GARDNER, ERLE STANLEY. The D.A. Breaks a Seal. NY: William Morrow, 1946. 1st ed. Fine in dj (sl edgewear). *Janus.* $75/£48

GARDNER, ERLE STANLEY. The D.A. Breaks an Egg. NY: William Morrow, 1949. 1st ed. Fine in dj (lt edgewear). *Janus.* $75/£48

GARDNER, ERLE STANLEY. The D.A. Cooks a Goose. NY: William Morrow, 1942. 1st ed. Fine in NF dj (sl soiling rear panel; spine sl dknd). *Janus.* $200/£129

GARDNER, ERLE STANLEY. The D.A. Holds a Candle. NY: William Morrow, 1938. 1st ed. Fine in dj (sl soiling). *Janus.* $200/£129

GARDNER, ERLE STANLEY. The D.A. Takes a Chance. NY: William Morrow, 1948. 1st ed. NF in VG+ dj (sl edgewear). *Janus.* $65/£42

GARDNER, ERLE STANLEY. Hovering Over Baja. NY: William Morrow, 1961. 1st ed. Grn cl, black/silver dec. NF in VG dj. *Parmer.* $25/£16

GARDNER, ERLE STANLEY. Neighborhood Frontiers. Wm. Morrow, (1954). 1st ed. VG in VG dj. *Oregon.* $30/£19

GARDNER, JAMES. For Special Services. London: Cape & Hodder, 1982. 1st ed. Fine in Fine dj. *Janus.* $35/£23

GARDNER, JOHN. For Special Services. London: Jonathan Cape, 1982. 1st ed. Fine in Fine dj. *Ming.* $23/£15

GARDNER, JOHN. For Special Services. London: Cape & Hodder, 1982. 1st ed. VF in dj. *Silver Door.* $35/£23

GARDNER, JOHN. Frankenstein. Dallas, (1979). 1st ed, ltd to 250 numbered, signed. Sl discolored, worn, else VG. *King.* $150/£97

GARDNER, JOHN. Grendel. Knopf, 1971. 1st ed. Fine in dj (sl fading). *Aronovitz.* $185/£119

GARDNER, JOHN. Grendel. NY: Knopf, 1971. 1st ed. Fine (lt foxing eps) in Fine dj. *Between The Covers.* $250/£161

GARDNER, JOHN. Icebreaker. London: Jonathan Cape, 1983. 1st ed. VF in VF dj. *Ming.* $23/£15

GARDNER, JOHN. The King's Indian. NY: Knopf, 1974. 1st ed. Pict cl. Fine in dj. *Sadlon.* $35/£23

GARDNER, JOHN. Licence Renewed. London: Jonathan Cape, 1981. 1st ed. VF in VF dj. *Ming.* $23/£15

GARDNER, JOHN. Licence Renewed. London: Cape, 1981. 1st UK ed. NF in dj. *Williams.* $19/£12

GARDNER, JOHN. The Life and Times of Chaucer. NY: Knopf, 1977. 1st ed. Label fep, else VG in dj. *Hermitage.* $40/£26

GARDNER, JOHN. The Liquidator. Muller, 1964. 1st ed. VF in VF dj. *Ming.* $54/£35

GARDNER, JOHN. No Deals, Mr. Bond. London: Jonathan Cape, 1987. 1st ed. VF in VF dj. *Ming.* $23/£15

GARDNER, JOHN. Nobody Lives For Ever. London: Jonathan Cape/Hodder & Stoughton, 1986. 1st Eng ed. Fine in dj. *Ulysses.* $70/£45

GARDNER, JOHN. The Poetry of Chaucer. Carbondale: Southern IL Univ, (1977). 1st ed. Fine in Fine dj (price-clipped). *Godot.* $100/£65

GARDNER, JOHN. Role of Honour. London: Jonathan Cape, 1984. 1st ed. VF in VF dj. *Ming.* $23/£15

GARDNER, JOHN. Rumpelstiltskin. Dallas, (1979). 1st ed, ltd to 250 numbered, signed. Sl worn, discolored, else VG. *King.* $125/£81

GARDNER, JOHN. William Wilson. Dallas, (1979). 1st ed, ltd to 250 numbered, signed. Sl discolored, worn, else VG. *King.* $100/£65

GARDNER, JOHN. William Wilson. Dallas: New London, (1979). Ltd to 250 numbered, signed. Fine. *Antic Hay.* $85/£55

GARDNER, JOHN. The Wreckage of Agathon. NY: Harper & Row, (1970). 1st ed. VG in dj (worn). *Hermitage.* $90/£58

GARDNER, ROY. Hellcatraz, the Rock of Despair. (N.p., n.d. ca 1939). 1st ed. Signed. 13 photo plts. Ptd yellow photo wrappers (soiled, chipped); press clipping tipped inside fr wrapper. *Shasky.* $55/£35

GARENNE, HENRI. (Pseud of Frank Lind.) The Art of Modern Conjuring, Magic and Illusions. London: Ward, Lock, n.d. (c. 1885). 20pp pub's cat. Pict cl stamped in black/gilt. *Dramatis Personae.* $90/£58

GARFIELD, JAMES ABRAM. Oration on the Life and Character of George H. Thomas. Cincinnati: Robert Clarke, 1871. 1st ed. 52pp. Orig ptd wrappers; fr wrap w/minor damping, yet VG. *Mcgowan.* $85/£55

GARFIELD, LEON and EDWARD BLISHEN. The God Beneath the Sea. London: Longmans, 1970. 1st ed. Charles Keeping (illus). 6.5x9.25. 168pp. VG in dj. *Cattermole.* $75/£48

GARFIELD, LEON and EDWARD BLISHEN. The Golden Shadow. London: Longman, 1973. 1st ed. 6.25x9.5. 159pp. VG in dj (sl wrinkled). *Cattermole.* $40/£26

GARFIELD, VIOLA E. et al. The Tsimshian: Their Arts and Music. NY: J.J. Augustin, n.d.(1951). 1st ed. 8 photo-plts. Fine. *Connolly.* $75/£48

GARIS, HOWARD R. Three Little Trippertrots. Newark, NJ: Charles E. Graham, 1912. 4to. Full-pg color frontis, 151 + 1pg ad, (inscrip, bkpl fep). Emb grn cl on bd w/pasted on pict color label (lt rubbed, lt faded). Good. *Hobbyhorse.* $45/£29

GARIS, HOWARD R. Uncle Wiggily's Adventures. Racine: Whitman, (1946). 24mo. Color pict bds. Nice. *Reisler.* $75/£48

GARIS, HOWARD R. Uncle Wiggily's Happy Days. NY: Platt & Munk, (1947). 1st ed. 4to. 211 numbered pp, 6 full-pg color plts by Elmer Rache. Red cl, black lettering, decs; full-color pict dj (minor marginal wear). *Reisler.* $175/£113

GARIS, HOWARD R. Uncle Wiggly and His Flying Rug. Racine: Whitman, (1940). 1st Whitman ed. 12mo. 33pp. Lang Campbel (illus). Pict bds. VG in dj (spine chipped). *Davidson.* $47/£30

GARIS, HOWARD R. Uncle Wiggly and the Pirates. Racine: Whitman, (1940). 1st Whitman ed. 12mo. 33pp. Lang Campbell (illus). Pict bds. VG in VG dj. *Davidson.* $47/£30

GARIS, HOWARD R. Uncle Wiggly on Roller Skates. Racine: Whitman, (1940). 1st Whitman ed. 12mo. 33pp. Lang Campbell (illus). Pict bds. VG in VG dj. *Davidson.* $37/£24

GARIS, HOWARD R. Uncle Wiggly Plays Indian Hunter. Racine: Whitman, (1940). 1st Whitman ed. 12mo. 33pp. Lang Campbell (illus). Pict bds. VG in VG dj. *Davidson.* $47/£30

GARLAND, HAMLIN. Back-Trailers from the Middle Border. NY, 1928. 1st ed. Gilt cl. VG. *Artis.* $15/£10

GARLAND, HAMLIN. The Book of the American Indian.... NY: Harper, 1923. 1st ed, 1st ptg. Frontis. Corners sl bruised, o/w NF in VG dj (sl frayed, chips, mended tears). *Reese.* $250/£161

GARLAND, HAMLIN. The Tyranny of the Dark. Harpers, 1905. 1st ed. VG. *Madle.* $75/£48

GARNER, BESS ADAMS. Windows in an Old Adobe. Pomona: Sanders Press, (1939). 1st ed, ltd to 2000 signed, inscribed. *Book Market.* $40/£26

GARNER, ELVIRA. Ezekiel Travels. NY: Holt, (1938). 1st ed. Inscribed. Illus pict bds (crayon rear cvr; rear hinge tape-repaired). *Second Life.* $45/£29

GARNER, ELVIRA. Ezekiel Travels. NY: Henry Holt, 1938. 1st ed. Inscribed. 8vo. Unpaginated. Elvira Garner (illus). Pict bds. VG in VG dj. *Davidson.* $185/£119

GARNER, ELVIRA. Ezekiel. NY: Henry Holt, (1937). 2nd ptg. 8vo. Unpaginated. Elvira Garner (illus). Pict bds. VG (inscrip) in VG dj. *Davidson.* $120/£77

GARNER, ELVIRA. Way Down in Tennessee. NY: Julian Messner, 1941. 1st ed. 8vo. Unpaginated. Elvira Garner (illus). Pict bds. NF in NF dj. *Davidson.* $150/£97

GARNER, HARRY. Chinese and Japanese Cloisonne Enamels. London: Faber & Faber, (1962). 1st ed. 96pp plts. Grn cl, spine label stamped in blue. Good in dj. *Karmiole.* $35/£23

GARNER, HARRY. Chinese and Japanese Cloisonne Enamels. London: Faber & Faber, (1977). Frontis, 96 plts (incl 2 color). Fine. *Bookpress.* $50/£32

GARNER, THOMAS and ARTHUR STRATTON. The Domestic Architecture of England During the Tudor Period. Vol 2. London: Batsford, 1911. 1st ed. (Tear 1st 2 leaves; last 2 plts repaired; smudging, text yellowed.) *Bookpress.* $250/£161

GARNETT, DAVID. Aspects of Love. London: Chatto, 1955. 1st UK ed. VG (ink name) in dj. *Williams.* $74/£48

GARNETT, DAVID. Go She Must! London: C&W, 1927. 1st ed. Inscribed. Gilt-titled plum cl. Very Nice. *Cady.* $45/£29

GARNETT, DAVID. The Golden Echo. NY: Harcourt, Brace, (1954). 1st US ed. Fine in NF dj (spine bottom worn). *Bernard.* $20/£13

GARNETT, DAVID. The Grasshoppers Come. (NY): Brewer, Warren & Putnam, (1931). 1st US ed. Rachel Garnett (illus). Spine dknd; cvrs lt soiled, o/w VG in Fine dj. *Bernard.* $50/£32

GARNETT, DAVID. The Grasshoppers Come. London: C&W, 1931. 1st ed, one of 210 signed. Gilt-titled yellow buckram. Superb. *Cady.* $85/£55

GARNETT, DAVID. A Man in the Zoo. NY: Knopf, 1924. 1st US ed. Cl-backed dec bds; paper spine label. *Hollett.* $23/£15

GARNETT, DAVID. The Old Dovecote and Other Stories. London: Elkin Mathews & Marrott, 1928. 1st ed, one of 530 signed. Gray bds ptd in brn. Nice. *Cady.* $20/£13

GARNETT, DAVID. Pocahontas or The Nonpareil of Virginia. London: C&W, 1933. 1st ed. Frontis. Patterned bds, gilt. VG. *Hollett.* $23/£15

GARNETT, DAVID. The Sailor's Return. London: C&W, 1925. 1st ed. Frontis wood engr. Teg; rest untrimmed. Fine in patterned stiff paper bds. NF pict dj (spine sunned). *Vandoros.* $75/£48

GARNETT, DAVID. A Terrible Day. London: William Jackson, 1932. 1st ed. #373/550 signed. Frontis. Teg, others uncut. Orig buckram. Dknd, o/w VG. *Cox.* $54/£35

GARNETT, EDWARD. A Hudson Anthology. London, 1924. Frontis port, illus fr pastedown. (Spine sl chipped.) *Edwards.* $25/£16

GARNETT, LOUISE AYRES. The Merrymakers. Chicago: Rand McNally, 1918. 4to. 80pp. Full-pg color pict frontis, dec vignette tp, VF color plts by James McCracken (lacks p58 plt). Emb blue cl on bd w/pasted color pict label, gilt titles. Good (ink inscrip; edges, spine lt rubbed; pg corner chipped). *Hobbyhorse.* $50/£32

GARNETT, LUCY M.J. Women of Turkey and Their Folk-Lore. London: David Nutt, 1890-91. 1st ed. 2 vols. (lxxx),328pp + 2pp ads; xvi,616pp + 4pp ads; fldg color map. Blue cl, gilt (cockled, discolored; ex-lib, remnants of labels, pockets removed; sig). *Schoyer.* $325/£210

GARNETT, RICHARD. A Chaplet from the Greek Anthology. NY: Frederick A. Stokes, 1898. 1st Amer ed. Parchment-backed grn paper bds (sl mkd, worn). VG. *Dalian.* $39/£25

GARNETT, RICHARD. Poems from the German. London: Bell & Daldy, 1862. 1st ed. Half-title, vi,119pp; aeg. Full black morocco, gilt. (Bkpl.) *Hollett.* $186/£120

GARNETT, THOMAS. A Treatise on the Mineral Waters of Harrogate. London, 1792. x,168pp + (i)ads (marginal spotting; tp, dedication dampstained). Uncut. Calf-backed marbled bds (rebound), gilt title. *Edwards.* $194/£125

GARRARD, LEWIS. Wah-To-Yah and the Taos Trail. Ralph Bieber (ed). Clark, 1938. 4 plts, fldg map. VG. Howes G 70. *Oregon.* $100/£65

GARRETSON, MARTIN S. The American Bison. NY: NY Zoological Soc, (1938). Fine in dj. *Schoyer.* $75/£48

GARRETSON, MARTIN S. The American Bison. NY, 1938. (Faded.) *Wheldon & Wesley.* $62/£40

GARRETT, FRANKLIN M. Atlanta and Environs. Athens: Univ of GA Press, (1969). Facs rpt of 1954 ed. 2 vols. Blue cl. VG. *Chapel Hill.* $125/£81

GARRETT, GEORGE. Cold Ground Was My Bed Last Night. Columbia: Univ of MO, (1964). 1st ed. Signed. Fine in NF dj (price-clipped; short tears). *Between The Covers.* $85/£55

GARRETT, GEORGE. The Finished Man. NY: Scribners, (1959). 1st ed. Signed. NF in dj (sl faded spine). *Turlington.* $125/£81

GARRETT, GEORGE. For a Bitter Season. Columbia: Univ of MO Press, (1967). 1st ed. Signed. VG in dj (sl frayed). *Turlington.* $75/£48

GARRETT, PAT F. The Authentic Life of Billy the Kid. Norman: Univ of OK Press, (1954). 1st ed. Fine in Fine dj. *Book Market.* $25/£16

GARRETT, PAT F. The Authentic Life of Billy the Kid. NY: Atomic Books, 1946. (Stamp to tp.) Pict wraps. *Schoyer.* $25/£16

GARRICK, DAVID. Three Plays.... NY: William Edwin Rudge, 1926. 1st ed. One of 490. 1/4 cl; dec bds (corners rubbed; spine sunned). *Dramatis Personae.* $35/£23

GARRIOTT, EDWARD B. Weather Folk-Lore and Local Weather Signs. Washington: GPO, 1903. 21 charts. Blue cl, gilt spine. Good. *Karmiole.* $30/£19

GARRISON, F. A History of Medicine. Phila: Saunders, 1929. 4th ed. Orig ed, not the later rpt. Good. *Goodrich.* $145/£94

GARRISON, F. The Principles of Anatomic Illustration before Vesalius. NY, 1926. Good (ex-lib; recased; stamps; binding rubbed). *Goodrich.* $65/£42

GARRITY, JOHN. The George Brett Story. Coward McCann & Geoghegan, 1981. 1st ed. Fine in VG+ dj. *Plapinger.* $40/£26

GARSTANG, JOHN. Tombs of the Third Egyptian Dynasty at Reqaqnah and Bet Khhallaf. Westminster: Archibald Constable, 1904. 33 plts. (Bkpl.) *Archaeologia.* $275/£177

GARTMANN, HEINZ. The Men Behind the Space Rockets. Eustace Wareing & Michael Glenny (trans). London: Weidenfeld & Nicolson, 1955. 1st ed in English. Good in dj (torn, tattered). *Knollwood.* $30/£19

GARVIN, RICHARD M. The Crystal Skull. NY: Doubleday, 1973. 1st ed. VG in VG dj. *Blue Dragon.* $25/£16

GARY, GEORGE. Studies in the Early History of the Fox River Valley. Oshkosh, WI: Times Pub Co, (1901). Frontis. Pict cl (worn; bkpl). *Bohling.* $65/£42

GASCOYNE, DAVID. Poems 1937-1942. (London): Editions Poetry, (1943). 1st ed. Cl-backed pict bds. VG (ink name; reps lt foxed) in Good dj (4 chips, internal mends). *Reese.* $100/£65

GASCOYNE, DAVID. Poems 1937-1942. London: Editions Poetry, 1943. 1st ed. (Pastedowns spotted; sl shaken; sl worn.) *Poetry.* $23/£15

GASH, JONATHAN. Firefly Gadroon. St. Martins, 1982. 1st US ed. Fine in dj. *Lewton.* $39/£25

GASH, JONATHAN. Gold from Gemini. London: CCC, 1978. 1st ed. Fine in dj (sl wrinkling lower fr panel edge). *Mordida.* $350/£226

GASH, JONATHAN. The Grail Tree. London: CCC, 1979. 1st ed. Collins editorial file copy stamp on fep. Lt spots top edge, o/w Fine in dj. *Mordida.* $300/£194

GASH, JONATHAN. The Grail Tree. London: Collins, 1979. 1st UK ed. Fine in dj. *Moorhouse.* $116/£75

GASH, JONATHAN. Jade Woman. London: Collins, 1988. 1st ed, signed. VF in dj. *Limestone.* $55/£35

GASH, JONATHAN. Jade Woman. St. Martins, 1989. 1st ed. Signed. VF- in beautiful dj. *Murder.* $40/£26

GASH, JONATHAN. The Judas Pair. NY: Harper & Row, 1977. 1st Amer ed, 1st bk. Edges sl browned, o/w VG in dj (chipped, rubbed, sl browned). *Virgo.* $101/£65

GASH, JONATHAN. The Lies of Fair Ladies. London: Scorpion Press, 1991. #29/99 signed. Fine in glassine wrapper. *Virgo.* $70/£45

GASH, JONATHAN. Moonspender. London: CCC, 1986. 1st ed. Fine in dj (lt wear spine ends). *Mordida.* $45/£29

GASH, JONATHAN. Moonspender. London: Collins, 1986. 1st UK ed. Fine in dj (sl rubbed). *Moorhouse.* $34/£22

GASH, JONATHAN. Pontiff. Galleypenny, 1971. 1st UK ed. NF in dj. *Williams.* $504/£325

GASH, JONATHAN. The Tartan Ringers. London: CCC, 1986. 1st ed. Fine in dj (sl wear spine base). *Mordida.* $45/£29

GASH, JONATHAN. The Vatican Rip. London: Collins, 1981. 1st ed. NF in dj. *Limestone.* $140/£90

GASH, JONATHAN. The Vatican Rip. London: CCC, 1981. 1st ed. Fine in dj (sl spine rubbing). *Mordida.* $200/£129

GASKELL, J. Strange Evil. Hutchinson, 1957. 1st ed, 1st bk. Signed. NF in NF dj (lt soiling spine). *Fine Books.* $125/£81

GASQUET, ABBOT. English Monastic Life. London: Methuen, 1904. 2nd ed. 18 plts; 8 maps, plans. Spine sl faded. *Hollett.* $47/£30

GASQUET, ABBOT. Parish Life in Mediaeval England. London: Methuen, (1906). (Backstrip faded, sl rubbed.) *Petersfield.* $28/£18

GASQUET, ABBOT. Parish Life in Mediaeval England. London: Methuen, 1929. 7 plts. VG in dj (repaired). *Hollett.* $54/£35

GASQUET, F.A. The Great Pestilence (A.D. 1348-9), Now Commonly Known as the Black Death. London: Simpkin Marshall, Hamilton Kent, 1893. 1st ed. xx,244pp. Red cl. Good. *White.* $54/£35

GASS, PATRICK. Gass's Journal of the Lewis and Clark Expedition. James Hosmer (ed). Chicago: A.C. McClurg, 1904. 1st trade ed. VG- (lt edgewear). *Perier.* $160/£103

GASS, PATRICK. Gass's Journal of the Lewis and Clark Expedition. James Hosmer (ed). Chicago: A.C. McClurg, 1904. Ltd ed on lg paper, #49/75. Reprint of 1811 ed. Vellum spines dark; corners bumped; ink name, else VG. *Perier.* $425/£274

GASS, PATRICK. Gass's Journal of the Lewis and Clark Expedition.... McClurg, 1904. 1st thus. Frontis, 6 plts. VG (lt soiling). Howes G 77. *Oregon.* $175/£113

GASS, PATRICK. A Journal of the Voyages and Travels of a Corps of Discovery.... Pittsburgh: M'Keehan, 1807. 1st ed. 262pp. Orig bds worn, o/w VG. Howes G 77. *Oregon.* $750/£484

GASS, WILLIAM H. In the Heart of the Heart of the Country. Harper & Row, 1968. 1st US ed. VG in dj (stained). *Williams.* $43/£28

GASS, WILLIAM H. In the Heart of the Heart of the Country. London: Cape, 1969. 1st UK ed. NF (sl mks to flyleaves) in dj. *Williams.* $28/£18

GASS, WILLIAM H. Omensetter's Luck. London: Collins, 1967. 1st UK ed. 1st bk. VG in dj (sl soiled, rubbed). *Virgo.* $78/£50

GASS, WILLIAM H. On Being Blue. Godine, (1977). One of 225 numbered, signed, deluxe. Blue cl. Fine in dj, slipcase. *Dermont.* $100/£65

GASSIER, PIERRE and J. WILSON. Goya. His Life and Work. London: Thames & Hudson, 1971. 48 mtd color plts. Sound. *Ars Artis.* $302/£195

GASSIER, PIERRE. The Drawings of Goya. NY, 1975. 407 plts (9 color). (Edges soiled.) Dj (torn). *Argosy.* $85/£55

GASTON, EDWIN W. The Early Novel of the Southwest. (Albuquerque): Univ of NM, (1961). 1st ed. Blue cl. Fine in NF dj (sl worn; spine, edge dkng). *Harrington.* $40/£26

GASTON, JOSEPH. The Centennial History of Oregon, 1811-1912 with Notice of Antecedent Explorations. Chicago: S.J. Clarke, 1912. 4 vols. VG in 3/4 leather. *Perier.* $300/£194

GASTON, ROBERT H. and WILLIAM H. Tyler to Sharpsburg.... Robert W. Glover (ed). Waco, TX, 1960. 1st ed. Ltd to 1000. Signed by Glover. Ptd wrappers. Sl damping lower corner, else VG. *Mcgowan.* $37/£24

GATHORNE HARDY, ROBERT. The Tranquil Gardener. London: Thomas Nelson, 1958. 4 color plts. NF. *Quest.* $55/£35

GATTY, HAROLD. The Raft Book. NY: George Grady, 1943. VG fldg table, map. VG+ pb in Good+ pict slipcase. *Blue Dragon.* $40/£26

GATTY, MRS. ALFRED. The Book of Sun-Dials. H.K.F. Eden & Eleanour Lloyd (eds). London: George Bell, 1890. Frontis, 578pp. Dec spine (relaid), silk-cvrd bds. Lt spotted, else Fine. *Quest.* $185/£119

GATTY, MRS. ALFRED. Legendary Tales. London: Bell & Daldy, 1858. 1st British ed. 4 plts. Red cl. VF. *Agvent.* $50/£32

GATTY, MRS. ALFRED. Parables from Nature. London: Bell & Daldy, 1861. Frontis, viii,196pp + 4pp ads (sl foxing 1st, last leaves). Aeg. Gilt cl (spine ends, edges worn; inner hinge cracked). *Quest.* $85/£55

GAUGUIN, PAUL. Noa Noa: Voyage to Tahiti. NY: Reynal, n.d. 1st US ed. 47 plts. Pict cl. Fine in dj. *Schoyer.* $80/£52

GAUNT, MARY. A Broken Journey. London: T. Werner Laurie, n.d. (1919). 1st ed. Frontis, 16 plts. Blue cl. VG (spots). *Morrell.* $47/£30

GAUNT, MARY. A Woman in China. London: T. Werner Laurie, n.d. Mod 1/2 levant morocco, gilt. VG. *Hollett.* $147/£95

GAUNT, W. The Etchings of Frank Brangwyn, R.A.: A Catalogue Raisonne. London: The Studio, 1926. 331 plts (8 photogravures). Vellum-backed bds (loose in binding). *Argosy.* $150/£97

GAUNT, WILLIAM. Marine Painting, an Historical Survey. London: Secker & Warburg, 1975. Orig cl, gilt emblem. Fine in dj. *Europa.* $34/£22

GAUTIER, THEODORE. The Romance of a Mummy. J&R Maxwell, 1886. 1st Eng ed. Pict cl stamped in gold/black. VG. *Fine Books.* $95/£61

GAUTIER, THEOPHILE. Mademoiselle de Maupin. London: Golden Cockerel, 1938. #78/500. 8 copper engrs by Buckland Wright. Orig blue cl. Good (sl soiled; neatly rebacked in vellum in orig style). *Cox.* $101/£65

GAUTIER, THEOPHILE. Mademoiselle de Maupin. NY: LEC, 1943. #904/1000 numbered, signed by Andre Dugo (illus). Half leather, dec bds. Fine in pub's slipcase (sl rubbed). *Hermitage.* $75/£48

GAWSWORTH, JOHN. Out of Africa. Army Press, 1944. 1st Eng ed. VG in orig wraps. *Edrich.* $39/£25

Gay Mother Goose. NY: Scribner's, 1938. 1st ed. 8vo, 63pp. Francoise (illus). Rebound in full leather, dentelle. Fine. *Davidson.* $200/£129

GAY, JOHN. The Beggar's Opera. Paris: LEC, 1937. #162/1500 signed by Mariette Lydis (illus). Fine in slipcase. *Williams.* $78/£50

GAY, JOHN. The Beggar's Opera. Paris: LEC, 1937. #904/1500 numbered, signed by Mariette Lydis (illus). Fine in pub's slipcase (lt worn). *Hermitage.* $85/£55

GAY, JOHN. Fables by John Gay with the Life of the Author. London: Ptd for F.C. & J. Rivington et al, J. Harris et al, 1816. 1 vol complete. 12mo. Full-pg engr frontis, xvi,228pp; 70 engrs. Full leather, gilt, spine label; marbled eps, edges. Fine (sm bk dealer label; lt foxing engr tp; sl edgewear). *Hobbyhorse.* $215/£139

GAY, JOHN. The Fables of Mr. John Gay. York: Wilson et al, 1797. 12mo. Full-pg engr frontis, viii+252pp. T. Bewicke (illus). Mod red linen on bds, 2 black gilt spine labels. VG (ink names, date; lacks orig cvrs, lower eps). *Hobbyhorse.* $250/£161

GAY, JOHN. Fables. Barre: Imprint Society, 1970. One of 1950 numbered, signed by Gillian Tyler. Fine in pub's slipcase. *Hermitage.* $85/£55

GAY, JOHN. Fables. (By the Late Mr Gay.) London: C. Hitch et al, 1757. 2 vols. 8vo. xii,194; vi,137pp; copper engr port vol 1. Gilt mod full leather on bds; gilt spine title; pink/gold eps. Gilt owner name cvr. VF. *Hobbyhorse.* $200/£129

GAY, JOHN. The Flowers of English Fable. London: Edward Lacey, n.d. (ca 1870). 16mo. 178pp; 66 Fine full-pg engrs. Red tooled morocco, paper label title, grn eps (2 labels inside cvrs, line cracking at inner hinges; shelfwear). Fine. *Hobbyhorse.* $200/£129

GAY, JOHN. Gay's Fables. London: Frederick Warne, 1866. William Harvey (illus). Frontis port w/guard, xv+271pp. Grn tooled cl on spine w/gilt title vignette upper cvr, dec gilt title spine. Brn eps. Bkpl; inner hinge cracked; else VG. *Hobbyhorse.* $150/£97

GAY, JOHN. Poems on Several Occasions. London: H. Lintot, J. & R. Tonson, 1737. 2 vols in 1. 260; 260pp; engr frontis; 2 plts. Contemp paneled calf (top fr hinge beginning to crack). Very nice. *Karmiole.* $125/£81

GAY, JOHN. Rural Sports. NY: William Edwin Rudge, 1930. One of 1500. Gilt-dec black cl, red bds. Fine in dj (corner chipped). *House.* $65/£42

GAY, JOHN. Trivia: Or the Art of Walking the Streets of London. London: For Bernard Lintott, (1716). 1st ed. Later 1/2 calf, banded, gilt (sl wear; text sl spotted, browned). Prettily bound. *Ash.* $698/£450

GAY, JOHN. Trivia: Or the Art of Walking the Streets of London. London, 1922. Rpt. Frontis port, tp facs, 15 plts. Teg; illus eps. Gilt dec cl (spine, lower bd sl soiled; feps browned). *Edwards.* $59/£38

GAY, JOHN. Trivia: or, the Art of Walking the Streets of London. London: Daniel O'Connor, 1922. 16 plts and facs. Teg. White buckram, gilt. Nice. *Cady.* $50/£32

GAZE, HAROLD. The Merry Piper. London: Longmans, Green, 1925. 1st ed. 4to. 8 full-pg color plts. Grey cl, dk blue lettering, dec. Pg roughly cut along fore-edge, o/w Very Nice. *Reisler.* $110/£71

GEARE, M. and M. CORBY. Dracula's Diary. Beaufort Books, 1982. 1st ed. NF in dj. *Aronovitz.* $28/£18

GEDDES, NORMAN BEL. Horizons. Boston: Little, Brown, 1932. 1st ed. Ink inscrip, else VG. *Bookpress.* $225/£145

GEDDES, PAUL. Hangman. St. Martin, 1977. 1st Amer ed. Fine in dj. *Murder.* $27/£17

GEDDIE, JOHN. The Lake Regions of Central Africa. London: T. Nelson, 1883. 275pp, all edges, eps marbled; 32 woodcuts. Full price calf, gilt. VG. *Hollett.* $70/£45

GEE, ERNEST R. The Sportsman's Library. NY: Bowker, 1940. One of 600. Fine. *Bowman.* $175/£113

GEE, JOSHUA. The Trade and Navigation of Great-Britain Considered.... London: Ptd for J. Almon & S. Bladon, 1767. 2nd ed. 288pp. Old calf (rubbed, scraped, lacks spine label). *Hollett.* $233/£150

GEER, J.J. Beyond the Lines. Phila: J.W. Daughaday, 1864. 2nd ptg. Frontis port, 285pp + (3)pp ads, 5 plts. Orig brn cl. Good (bkpl, hinges cracked internally, scattered foxing, worn). *Chapel Hill.* $100/£65

GEER, THEODORE. Fifty Years in Oregon. Neale Pub, 1912. 1st ed. 12pp photo plts. Fine. *Oregon.* $50/£32

GEER, WALTER. Campaigns of the Civil War. NY: Brentano's, 1926. 1st ed. VG. *Mcgowan.* $125/£81

GEHRET, ELLEN. Rural Pennsylvania Clothing. York, PA: Liberty Cap Books, (1976). 1st ed. Fine. *Oregon.* $40/£26

GEIGER, MAYNARD J. The Life and Times of Fray Junipero Serra, O.F.M. Washington: Academy of Franciscan History, 1959. 1st ed. 2 vols. NF. *Parker.* $150/£97

GEIGER, VINCENT and WAKEMAN BRYARLY. Trail to California. The Overland Journal of Vincent Geiger and Wakeman Bryarly. David Potter (ed). Yale, 1945. 1st ed. Frontis, fldg map. Fine in VG dj. *Oregon.* $50/£32

GEIGER, VINCENT and WAKEMAN BRYARLY. Trail to California: The Overland Journal of.... David Potter (ed). New Haven, 1945. 1st ed. Inscribed presentation from Potter. *Ginsberg.* $50/£32

GEIKIE, A. The Ancient Volcanoes of Great Britain. London, 1897. 2 vols. xxiv,477; xv,492pp; 7 fldg colored maps; lg fldg map (torn, repaired). Cl, gilt. Fine. *Henly.* $233/£150

GEIKIE, A. A Long Life's Work. London: Macmillan, 1924. 1st ed. NF (ex-lib). *Mikesh.* $30/£19

GEIKIE, A. Text-Book of Geology. London: Macmillan, 1882. 1st ed. Fldg frontis, xi,971pp, fldg ptd sheet. VG (eps slit inner joints). *Bickersteth.* $178/£115

GEIKIE, JAMES. Fragments of Earth Lore. Edinburgh, 1893. 1st ed. (vii),428pp; 6 color fldg maps. *Bickersteth.* $74/£48

GEIKIE, JAMES. The Great Ice Age and Its Relation to the Antiquity of Man. London, 1874. xxiii,575pp, 16 plts/maps (map in pocket). Gilt cl (rebacked, preserving spine). *Henly.* $50/£32

GEIKIE, JAMES. Prehistoric Europe, a Geological Sketch. London: Edward Stanford, 1881. 1st ed. xviii,592pp + 3 ad leaves (corner cut fep); 5 color plts and maps (3 fldg). *Bickersteth.* $105/£68

GEIL, WILLIAM EDGAR. A Yankee in Pigmy Land. London: Hodder & Stoughton, 1905. 1st ed. (Worn, soiled; label removed from spine; flyleaves browned; joints cracked; sl fingering.) *Hollett.* $31/£20

GELDART, ERNEST. The Art of Garnishing Churches at Christmas and Other Times. London: Cox Sons, 1882. 1st ed. Frontis; 70,(34)pp; 25 plts. Pub's cl. Spine sl sunned; ink inscrip, else Fine. *Bookpress.* $110/£71

GELL, WILLIAM. The Topography of Rome and Its Vicinity. London: Henry G. Bonn, 1846. New ed. viii,499pp. 3/4 calf antique, 5 raised bands. (Bkpl; several pp foxed.) *Archaeologia.* $250/£161

GELLHORN, MARTHA. The Face of War. London: Hart-Davis, 1959. 1st ed. VG (cl sl mkd). *Patterson.* $70/£45

Gen. George Washington's Account with the United States. Long Island: John Hutchings, 1857. 1st ed. (iii),52,(4)pp. Contemp 1/2 black morocco (cvr, edge wear). (Fr hinge internally cracked; ex-lib w/mks). Text VG. *Bookpress.* $185/£119

GENAUER, EMILY. Chagall at the 'Met.' NY: Metropolitan Opera Assoc, 1971. Fine in dj, slipcase. *Edwards.* $155/£100

GENDERS, ROY. A History of Scent. London: Hamish Hamilton, (1972). 1st ed. VG in VG dj. *Blue Dragon.* $30/£19

GENDERS, ROY. Perfume Through the Ages. NY: Putnam's, (1972). 1st Amer ed. VG in VG dj. *Blue Dragon.* $27/£17

General Regulations and Orders for the Army. London: Adjutant-General's Office, Jan 1822. Engr dec tp (offsetting), vii,401pp, tables (foxed, browned). VG in pub's paper-cvrd bds, paper spine label (sl worn, soiled). *Edwards.* $132/£85

GENET, JEAN. The Blacks. Faber, 1960. 1st UK ed. Fine in dj. *Sclanders.* $31/£20

GENET, JEAN. The Thief's Journal. NY, (1964). 1st Amer ed. VG in dj (sl worn). *King.* $25/£16

GENINI, RONALD and R. HITCHMAN. Romualdo Pacheco. Book Club of CA, 1985. 1st ed. Ltd to 500 ptd. Frontis. Buckram w/paper spine label. VF. *Oregon.* $80/£52

GENT, PETER. North Dallas Forty. NY: Morrow, 1973. 1st ed, 1st bk. NF in dj (tiny tears). *Antic Hay.* $45/£29

GENTHE, ARNOLD. The Book of the Dance. Boston: International Publishers, 1920. Lt rubbed; paint top edge, binding tips, else VG. *Cahan.* $65/£42

GENTHE, ARNOLD. Isadora Duncan. NY: Mitchell Kennerley, 1929. 1st ed. 24 leaves of photo plts; 1 facs plt. Black gilt cl. Good. *Karmiole.* $150/£97

Gentleman Angler.... London: G. Kearsley, 1786. 12mo. Engr frontis. Dk grn 1/2 morocco; marbled bds, eps; gilt spine. Lt stains to text, o/w clean. *Glenn.* $650/£419

GEORGE, EDWIN. Following Camel Trails of Asia. NY: Knickerbocker Press, 1926. VG. *Peninsula.* $40/£26

GEORGE, HENRY. Protection or Free Trade. NY: Henry George, 1886. 1st ed. 359pp. Gilt brn cl. VG. *Reese.* $75/£48

GEORGE, HENRY. Protection or Free Trade.... NY: H. George, 1886. 1st ed. Gilt-stamped brn cl. Floral eps. VG in 1/2 brn morocco drop box. *Houle.* $425/£274

GEORGE, JEAN CRAIGHEAD. Julie of the Wolves. NY: Harper & Row, (1972). 1st ed. 8vo. John Schoenherr (illus). Illus bds. Fine in dj (edgewear, sm tears). *Reisler.* $100/£65

GEORGE, TODD MENZIES. The Conversion of Cole Younger and the Battle of Lone Jack, Early Day Stories. Kansas City, MO: Lowell, 1963. 1st ed. Signed presentation. Fine in NF dj. *Glenn.* $50/£32

GEORGE, TODD MENZIES. Just Memories and Twelve Years with Cole Younger. N.p., 1959. Grn cl. *Glenn.* $50/£32

Georgia Scenes, Characters, Incidents, Etc., in the First Half Century of the Republic. (By Augustus Baldwin Longstreet). NY: Harper & Bros, 1847. 2nd ed. 216pp; 12 engr plts. Brn cl (extrems, corners sl frayed; bkpl), gilt spine. Howes L 448. *Karmiole.* $125/£81

Georgian Poetry, 1916-1917. London: Poetry Bookshop, 1917. 1st ed. Teg. Grn bds, gilt. Fine. *Macdonnell.* $65/£42

GERARD, E. Land beyond the Forest. NY: Harper, 1888. (x),403pp, map. Grn cl. VG. *Schoyer.* $65/£42

GERARD, L. The Golden Centipede. Dutton, 1927. 1st ed. NF in VG+ dj (spine lt soiled). *Aronovitz.* $90/£58

GERASSI, JOHN. North Vietnam: A Documentary. London: George Allen & Unwin, (1968). NF in dj (edgewear; edgetears). *Aka.* $45/£29

GERBAULT, ALAIN. In Quest of the Sun. London: Hodder & Stoughton, (1930). 1st ed. 16 plts; fldg map. (Sl scratch upper bd.) *Hollett.* $31/£20

GERBER, ALBERT B. Sex, Pornography, and Justice. NY, (1965). 1st ed. VG in VG dj. *Mcclintock.* $20/£13

GERDTS, WILLIAM and RUSSELL BURKE. American Still Life Painting. NY, (1971). VG in dj. *Argosy.* $325/£210

GERHARD, PETER. Pirates on the West Coast of New Spain, 1575-1742. Glendale: Clark, 1960. 1st ed. 4 maps. Uncut, unopened. *Dawson.* $50/£32

GERHARDUS, MALY and DIETFRIED. Expressionism: From Artistic Commitment to the Beginning of a New Era. London: Phaidon, 1979. 1st British ed. 80 color plts. Glazed pict bds. NF. *Willow House.* $22/£14

GERLACH, DON R. Philip Schuyler and the American Revolution in New York 1733-1777. Lincoln: Univ of NE Press, 1964. 1st ed. Blue cl. Fine in dj (heavily faded). *Chapel Hill.* $50/£32

GERLACH, LARRY. The Men in Blue. Viking, 1980. 1st ed. Fine in VG+ dj. *Plapinger.* $45/£29

GERMAIN, BAZIN. The Baroque. Principles, Styles, Modes, Themes. Greenwich, 1968. 24 color plts. VG in dj. *Washton.* $50/£32

GERRETSON, F.C. History of the Royal Dutch. Leiden: E.J. Brill, 1953-1957. 4 vols. Blue cl stamped in gilt. NF in slipcases. *Schoyer.* $200/£129

GERRISH, THEODORE and JOHN S. HUTCHINSON. The Blue and the Gray.... Bangor, ME: Brady, Mace, 1884. 2nd ed. 816pp; 20 full-pg maps. Rear inner hinge starting, else NF. *Mcgowan.* $85/£55

GERROLD, DAVID. The Man Who Folded Himself. London: Faber & Faber, 1973. 1st Eng ed. Red cl. Fine in dj (price-clipped). *Dalian.* $39/£25

GERRY, ELBRIDGE, JR. The Diary of.... NY: Brentano's, (1927). Largely unopened. VG in dj. *Schoyer.* $25/£16

GERSON, HORST. Rembrandt Paintings. London, 1968. (Cl soiled, spotted, rubbed.) *Edwards.* $62/£40

GERSON, HORST. Rembrandt Paintings. NY: Artabras, n.d. 140 color plts. Sound in dj. *Ars Artis.* $116/£75

GERSTAECKER, FRIEDRICH. California Gold Mines. Biobooks, 1946. Ltd to 500. 5 plts, incl 2 color (1 dbl-pg); fldg map. Paper spine label. VG. Howes G 135. *Oregon.* $50/£32

GERSTAECKER, FRIEDRICH. Wild Sports in the Far West. Lippincott, 1884. 396pp. Dec cl (worn; hinges broken). Fair. *Book Broker.* $35/£23

GERSTAECKER, FRIEDRICH. The Young Gold-Digger. London: Routledge, Warne & Routledge, 1860. 1st Eng ed. Sm 8vo. viii,339PP; 4 woodcut illus. (Spotting.) Full calf gilt prize binding (sl rubbed). *Hollett.* $47/£30

GERSTER, ARPAD. The Rules of Aseptic and Antiseptic Surgery. NY, 1890. 3rd ed. 332pp. 1/2 leather (back-strip, corners rubbed). Contents Fine. *Fye.* $100/£65

GERTSCH, W.J. American Spiders. NY: Van Nost, 1949. 1st ed. VG+ in Good+ dj. *Mikesh.* $37/£24

GESTON, MARK. Lords of the Starship. M. Joseph, 1971. 1st Eng, 1st hb ed, 1st bk. NF in dj. *Aronovitz.* $85/£55

GESTON, MARK. Out of the Mouth of the Dragon. Michael Joseph, 1969. 1st Eng, 1st hb ed. Fine in NF dj. *Aronovitz.* $75/£48

GETCHELL, F.H. An Illustrated Encyclopedia of the Science and Practice of Obstetrics. Phila, 1890. 1st ed, rptd. 276pp; 84 plts. Full leather. Corner back bd water damaged; water stain affecting upper corner 30 leaves, o/w VF. *Fye.* $400/£258

GHENT, W.J. The Early Far West, a Narrative Outline 1540-1850. Longmans, 1931. 1st ed. 7 plts. VF in VG dj. *Oregon.* $45/£29

GHENT, W.J. The Road to Oregon. London/NY/Toronto: Longmans, Green, 1929. 1st ed. Frontis, 23 plts. Gray cl (bumped; spine dknd, chipped); gilt. VG. *Blue Mountain.* $20/£13

GHOSE, SUDHIN N. Folk Tales and Fairy Stories from India. London: Golden Cockerel, 1961. 1st ed. #466/500. Ptd on Milbourn mould-made paper. Title, ep vignettes. Uncut; orig brown buckram blocked in gold. VG. *Cox.* $101/£65

GIACOMOTTI, JEANNE. French Faience. Oldbourne Press, 1963. 52 tipped-in color plts. Dj (sl ragged, edges browned; sl loss). *Edwards.* $116/£75

GIANNONE, PIETRO. Civil History of the Kingdom of Naples. London, 1729, 1731. 2 vols. (x),(xviii),742,(vi); (ii),832pp, subs list, errata. Lib buckram (hinges reinforced; lt dampstains vol 1). *Schoyer.* $300/£194

GIBB, D.E.W. Lloyd's of London. London: Macmillan, 1957. 1st ed. 22 plts. VG in dj. *Hollett.* $39/£25

GIBB, GEORGE. The Laryngoscope in Diseases of the Throat; with a Chapter on Rhinoscopy. London, 1867. 2nd ed. 163pp; 46 woodcuts. (Rebacked.) *Fye.* $75/£48

GIBB, H.A.R. Ibn Battuta: Travels in Asia and Africa, 1325-1354. NY: Robert M. McBride, 1929. 3 plts, 4 maps. (Sig.) *Archaeologia.* $55/£35

GIBBINGS, ROBERT. The 7th Man. London: Golden Cockerel Press, 1930. #53/500. Yellow buckram spine, dec bds. 15 engrs. VG (lt dust, bds sl dknd). *Williams.* $132/£85

GIBBINGS, ROBERT. The 7th Man. A True Cannibal Tale.... Golden Cockerell Press, 1930. Ltd to 500. 15 wood engrs. Pict bds; aeg (spine sl lightened). *Sadlon.* $100/£65

GIBBON, EDWARD. The History of the Decline and Fall of the Roman Empire. London: A. Strahan, 1788/1790. New ed. 12 vols. Port frontis, 3 fldg engr maps vol 1. Contemp speckled calf (hinge cracked but side firm; lacks 5 lettering, 5 numeral labels). Marginal worm slit prelims vols 1, 8; marginal worm holes through vol 5, o/w Very Clean. *Cox.* $233/£150

GIBBON, EDWARD. The History of the Decline and Fall of the Roman Empire. London: For Cadell & Davies et al, 1807. New ed. 12 vols. Frontis, fldg map (sl torn). (Lt spotting; bklps.) Speckled calf bds (rebacked in mod calf, gilt, leather title label). *Edwards.* $620/£400

GIBBON, EDWARD. The History of the Decline and Fall of the Roman Empire. London: C&W, 1875. xiii,(xvi),1303pp; engr port. Full polished tree calf (sl rubbed), gilt. Lt foxing. *Hollett.* $132/£85

GIBBON, EDWARD. The History of the Decline and Fall of the Roman Empire. J.B. Bury (ed). NY: LEC, 1946. One of 1500. 7 vols. Piranesi (illus). 1/2 black morocco. Chips spine tip 3 vols, o/w Fine in glassine remnants. Fine slipcase. *Agvent.* $425/£274

GIBBON, EDWARD. The History of the Rise and Fall of the Roman Empire. London: For Lackington, Allen & Co, 1815. New Ed. 12 vols. Frontis port, 2 fldg maps. Full tree calf, gilt (sl worn; joints splitting but firm; vols 4, 8 sl chipped; spotted). *Edwards.* $388/£250

GIBBON, EDWARD. Miscellaneous Works. With Memoirs.... London, 1796. 1st ed. 2 vols. Silhouette port. Stippled calf. (Hinges reinforced.) Marbled bd slipcase. *Argosy.* $300/£194

GIBBON, EDWARD. Roman Empire. London, 1836. 4 vols. Diced calf (neatly rebacked), blind, gilt. *Petersfield.* $248/£160

GIBBON, JOHN MURRAY. Steel of Empire. Indianapolis, 1935. 1st ed. Gilt cl. VG (bkpl, sig, ink price, emblem affixed rep) in dj (badly chipped). *Baade.* $35/£23

GIBBON, THOMAS E. Mexico Under Carranza...Four Hundred Years of Misrule. NY, 1919. 1st ed. *Ginsberg.* $75/£48

GIBBONS, FELTON. Catalogue of Italian Drawings in the Art Museum, Princeton University. NJ: Princeton Univ, 1977. 2 vols. Orig uniform cl. Fine in Mint djs. *Europa.* $90/£58

GIBBONS, KAYE. A Cure for Dreams. Chapel Hill: Algonquin, 1991. 1st ed. Signed. Fine in dj. *Turlington.* $40/£26

GIBBONS, STELLA. Conference at Cold Comfort Farm. London: Longmans, Green, 1949. 1st ed. NF in VG dj (lt chipped). *Limestone.* $75/£48

GIBBONS, STELLA. The Lowland Venus and Other Poems. London: Longmans, Green, 1938. 1st ed. VG in wrappers. *Limestone.* $65/£42

GIBBONS, STELLA. The Mountain Beast and Other Poems. London: Longmans, Green, 1930. 1st ed. Inner hinges tender, pencil underlinings, else VG in wrappers. *Limestone.* $95/£61

GIBBS, GEORGE. A Dictionary of the Chinook Jargon, or Trade Language of Oregon. NY: Cramoisy, 1863. 1st ed, 2nd issue. Uncut, unopened. VG (dampstaining to margins, not affecting text) in wraps. *Oregon.* $250/£161

GIBBS, J.F. Lights and Shadows of Mormonism. (Salt Lake Tribune Pub, 1909.) 1st ed. Good (spine faded). *Lien.* $75/£48

GIBBS, JAMES. Rules for Drawing the Several Parts of Architecture.... London: W. Innys et al, 1753. 3rd ed. viii,28pp, 63 (of 64) plts (lacks plt 61). Contemp 1/4 calf. Binding substantially worn. *Bookpress.* $300/£194

GIBBS, WOLCOTT. More in Sorrow. NY, (1958). 1st ed. VG in pict dj. *Argosy.* $60/£39

GIBSON, A.H. Natural Sources of Energy. Cambridge/NY: Univ Press/Putnam, 1913. 1st ed. Red cl (sl faded). VG. *Second Life.* $75/£48

GIBSON, A.M. The Life and Death of Colonel Albert Jennings Fountain. Norman: Univ of OK, (1965). 1st ed. Navy blue cl. Fine in dj (lt worn). *Glenn.* $45/£29

GIBSON, CHARLES DANA. Americans. NY/London, 1900. Cl-backed bds. (Loose; shaken.) *Argosy.* $200/£129

GIBSON, CHARLES DANA. Americans. NY/London, 1900. Inscribed. Loose; shaken. *Argosy.* $275/£177

GIBSON, CHARLES DANA. The Education of Mr. Pipp. NY: R.H. Russell, 1899. 1st ed. Cl-backed bds. Fr bd sl bowed, white spine soiled, o/w Fine in pub's box (broken). *Hermitage.* $125/£81

GIBSON, CHARLES DANA. The Gibson Book: A Collection of the Published Works. NY, 1907. 2 vols. Red cl (rubbed; hinges weak). *Argosy.* $250/£161

GIBSON, CHARLES R. Wireless Telegraphy and Telephony Without Wires. London, 1914. 9 plts. 3/4 calf. VG. *Argosy.* $100/£65

GIBSON, FRANK. Charles Conder, His Life and Work. London: John Lane, 1914. 1st ed. Frontis; 12 color plts; cat. Linen-backed bds (spine frayed, torn). Good (bkpls; rear hinge cracked) in new slipcase. *Hermitage.* $400/£258

GIBSON, G.A. The Nervous Affections of the Heart. Edinburgh, 1904. (Bkpl.) *Whitehart.* $132/£85

GIBSON, HARRY. Tobogganing on Crooked Runs. London, 1894. Pict cl (spine soiled). *Argosy.* $60/£39

GIBSON, IAN. The English Vice. London, 1979. 2nd imp. Dj. *Edwards.* $31/£20

GIBSON, JOHN. Physician to the World. Durham, NC, 1950. 1st ed. Good. *Fye.* $50/£32

GIBSON, THOMAS. The Anatomy of Humane Bodies Epitomized. London: For T. Flesher, 1682. (8),510pp; 13 engr plts. (Foxing, staining; lacks 2 leaves.) Contemp full-paneled calf (spine ends worn). *Goodrich.* $175/£113

GIBSON, W.B. The Book of Secrets. Personal Arts, 1927. 1st ed. VG+ in VG- dj (wear). *Fine Books.* $225/£145

GIBSON, WILFRID. The Early Whistler. (London: Faber, 1927). VG in ptd wraps. *Second Life.* $20/£13

GIBSON, WILFRID. Thoroughfares. London: Elkin Mathews, 1914. 1st ed. Inscribed. Gilt-titled tan buckram. Nice. *Cady.* $25/£16

GIBSON, WILLIAM. Neuromancer. London, 1984. 1st ed. Fine in dj (sl wrinkle). *Madle.* $400/£258

GIBSON, WILLIAM. Neuromancer. West Bloomfield: Phantasia, 1986. 1st US hb ed. Trade issue. Fine in Fine dj. *Other Worlds.* $100/£65

GIDDINGS, LUTHER. Sketches of the Campaign in Northern Mexico in Eighteen Hundred Forty-Six and Seven. NY: Putnam, 1853. 1st ed. 8vo. 2 litho maps. Gilt/blindstamped brn cl. Fine in black cl slipcase. Howes G 156. *Houle.* $1,500/£968

GIDE, ANDRE. Corydon. NY: Farrar, Straus, 1950. 1st Amer ed. Offset browning from laid-in clipping 2pp of text, else VG in VG dj (price-clipped). *Godot.* $35/£23

GIDE, ANDRE. Montaigne. Blackamore Press, 1929. One of 800 signed. NF. *Rees.* $54/£35

GIDE, ANDRE. Oscar Wilde. Bernard Frechtman (trans). NY: Philosophical Lib, 1949. 1st ed. VG in dj (spine faded; sl rubbed; price-clipped). *Hollett.* $19/£12

GIDE, ANDRE. Oscar Wilde. Kimber, 1951. 1st ed. Small inscrip. VG in dj. *Rees.* $31/£20

GIDE, ANDRE. Pretexts. (US): Meridian Books, (1959). 1st ed in English. Fine in VG dj. *Godot.* $35/£23

GIDE, ANDRE. So Be It. Justin O'Brien (trans). NY: Knopf, 1959. 1st Amer ed. VG in dj (price-clipped, chip, short tears, else VG). *Godot.* $35/£23

GIDE, ANDRE. Theseus. John Russell (trans). London: Horizon, 1948. 1st Eng ed. VG in pict dj. *Houle.* $75/£48

GIEDION, SIGFRIED. Architecture and the Phenomena of Transition. Cambridge: Harvard Univ, 1971. 1st ed. Fine in dj. *Bookpress.* $65/£42

GIEDION, SIGFRIED. Space, Time and Architecture: The Growth of a New Tradition. Cambridge: Harvard Univ, 1956. 3rd ed. VG (underlining) in dj (chipped, creased). *Bookpress.* $50/£32

GIEDION-WELCKER, CAROLA. Contemporary Sculpture. NY: George Wittenborn, (1960). Rev, enlgd ed. Blue cl. Good in dj. *Karmiole.* $50/£32

GIFFEN, GUY. California Expedition. Biobooks, 1951. Ltd to 650. 1st thus. Tipped-in port, color plt. Fine. *Oregon.* $45/£29

GIFFEN, HELEN. California Mining Town Newspapers, 1850-1880. San Fernando Valley: J.E. Reynolds, 1954. 1st ed. Ltd to 400. Bkpl, o/w Fine. *Oregon.* $50/£32

GIFFORD, BARRY. Landscape with Traveler. NY: Dutton, 1980. 1st ed. NF in dj. *Lame Duck.* $75/£48

GIFFORD, BARRY. The Neighborhood of Baseball. NY: Dutton, (1981). 1st ed. Sm soiled spot fr bd, else Fine in NF dj (2 short tears). *Between The Covers.* $75/£48

GIFFORD, E.W. The Kamia of Imperial Valley. BAE bulletin #97. Washington: GPO, 1931. 1st ed. Double-pg map, photo plt. 2 sm chips at rear, else NF. Ptd wrappers. *Connolly.* $25/£16

GIFFORD, I. The Marine Botanist.... Brighton, 1853. 3rd enlgd ed. xl,357,(1)pp; 6 color, 6 plain plts. (Cl sl worn.) *Wheldon & Wesley.* $47/£30

Gift: A Christmas and New Year's Present (for) 1843. Phila: Carey & Hart, (1842). 1st ed, 1st state of binding w/1843 on spine; 1st state of vignette title w/date present in title. Aeg. Orig full grn morocco, fully gilt. Spine ends worn, else fresh. BAL 16137 and 8069. *Macdonnell.* $350/£226

GILBERT, ANTHONY. No Dust in the Attic. Random, 1963. 1st US ed. Fine in Fine dj (tiny scrape; rear panel lt soiled). *Murder.* $25/£16

GILBERT, CHRISTOPHER. English Vernacular Furniture, 1750-1900. New Haven: Yale Univ, 1991. 1st ed. Fine in dj, slipcase. *Bookpress.* $65/£42

GILBERT, MICHAEL. The Bargain. London: Constable, 1961. 1st ed: pb orig. NF. *Janus.* $50/£32

GILBERT, MICHAEL. The Black Seraphim. London: Hodder & Stoughton, 1983. 1st ed, signed. Fine in Fine dj. *Janus.* $45/£29

GILBERT, MICHAEL. The Black Seraphim. NY: Harper, 1984. 1st ed. Sl worn, sm closed tear, else Fine in dj. *Murder.* $30/£19

GILBERT, MICHAEL. The Family Tomb. Harper, 1969. 1st ed. Sm stain bottom pg edge, else NF in dj (lt soiled, nick). *Murder.* $60/£39

GILBERT, MICHAEL. Mr. Calder and Mr. Behrens. London: Hodder, 1982. 1st ed. NF in NF dj. *Ming.* $31/£20

GILBERT, MICHAEL. Petrella at Q. London: Hodder, 1977. 1st ed. VG + in dj. *Silver Door.* $25/£16

GILBERT, MICHAEL. The Shot in Question. London: Constable, 1963. 1st ed: pb orig. NF. *Janus.* $50/£32

GILBERT, O.P. Women in Men's Guise. London, 1932. 1st ed. Frontis port, 3 other plts. Prelims, fore-edge foxed, o/w VG in dj (nick). *Edwards.* $39/£25

GILBERT, VIVIAN. The Romance of the Last Crusade. NY: Feakins, 1923. 1st ed. Frontis. Sl rubbed, foxed, o/w VG. *Worldwide.* $16/£10

GILBERT, W.S. Foggerty's Fairy. London, 1890. 1st ed. VG. *Madle.* $95/£61

GILBERT, W.S. Selected Bab Ballads.... London, Christmas 1955. Ltd to 1500, card loosely inserted. Fine in greaseproof wrapper (worn). *Waterfield.* $31/£20

GILBERT, W.S. The Story of the Mikado. London: Daniel O'Connor, 1921. 1st ed. 6 color plts; 10 b/w dwgs. Paper-cvrd bds   (partly split rt spine edge). Edges soiled; bkpl, o/w VG in dj (spine ends sl chipped). *Bernard.* $125/£81

GILCHRIST, ELLEN. The Annunciation. Boston: Little-Brown, 1983. 1st ed. VF in dj. *Else Fine.* $45/£29

GILCHRIST, ELLEN. The Annunciation. Boston: Little Brown, 1983. 1st ed. Fine in Fine dj. *Revere.* $50/£32

GILCHRIST, ELLEN. Falling Through Space: Journals. Boston: Little Brown, (1987). 1st ed. Signed. Mint in dj. *Turlington.* $45/£29

GILCHRIST, ELLEN. In the Land of Dreamy Dreams. London: Faber, 1982. 1st Eng ed. Mint in dj. *Turlington.* $75/£48

GILCHRIST, ELLEN. The Land Surveyor's Daughter. (Fayetteville, AR): Lost Roads, #14, 1979. 1st ed, signed. Acknowledgement slip laid in. Fine in orig ptd photo wraps. *Chapel Hill.* $325/£210

GILCHRIST, ELLEN. Victory Over Japan. Boston: Little-Brown, 1984. 1st ed. VF in dj (minute rubs spine). *Else Fine.* $50/£32

GILCHRIST, ROBERT C. Confederate Defence of Morris Island, Charleston Harbor. (Charleston, SC: News & Courier Book Presses), 1884. 1st separate ed. 55pp, fldg plan. Orig ptd wraps. NF. *Chapel Hill.* $150/£97

GILDER, WILLIAM H. Schwatka's Search: Sledging in the Arctic in Quest of the Franklin Records. NY: Scribner's, 1881. 1st ed. xvi,316pp + (3)pp ads. Dec cl (rubbed; lacks rep, fep torn). *Lefkowicz.* $90/£58

GILDMEISTER, E. and FR. HOFFMAN. The Volatile Oils. Edward Kremers (authorized trans). Milwaukee, 1900. 4 color maps (2 double-pg, 1 fldg). 3/4 leather (joints, corners rubbed). *Argosy.* $75/£48

GILES, DOROTHY. A Candle in Her Hand. NY, (1949). VG. *Argosy.* $40/£26

GILES, HERBERT A. A Chinese Biographical Dictionary. (Taiwan): Literature House, 1962. 1st ed thus. 2 vols. Blue limp-cl oriental binding. VG in cl slipcase. *Bookpress.* $125/£81

GILES, JANICE HOLT. Six-Horse Hitch. Boston, 1969. 1st ptg. Pict cl. Fine in dj (sl edgeworn, price-clipped). *Baade.* $35/£23

GILES, JOHN. Memoirs of Odd Adventures, Strange Deliverances, Etc. Cincinnati: Spiller, 1869. One of 250. 64pp. Mod paper wrappers. Howes G 167. *Ginsberg.* $125/£81

GILES, LEONIDAS BLANTON. Terry's Texas Rangers. (Austin: Von Boeckmann-Jones, 1911.) 1st ed. Sl cvr spotting, else VG. Howes G 168. *Mcgowan.* $1,750/£1,129

GILES, ROSENA. Shasta County California, A History. Oakland: Biobooks, 1949. 1st ed. Ltd to 1000. Fldg map; illus eps. VF. *Oregon.* $60/£39

GILL, B.M. Nursery Crimes. London: Hodder, 1986. 1st ed. Signed. Fine in dj. *Silver Door.* $40/£26

GILL, CLAUDE S. The Old Wooden Walls: Their Construction, Equipment, etc. London: Foyle, 1930. 31 plts. (Sl foxed; worn, faded.) *Petersfield.* $28/£18

GILL, ERIC. Art and a Changing Civilisation. London: John Lane, 1934. 1st ed. Red cl (faded). Dj (frayed). *Cox.* $34/£22

GILL, ERIC. Art-Nonsense and Other Essays. London: Cassell & Francis Walterson, 1929. 1st ed. Uncut in orig blue buckram. Good (backstrip faded). *Cox.* $70/£45

GILL, ERIC. Clothes. London: Cape, 1931. 1st ed. Tipped-in ad. Coarse-weave cl (spine faded). *Hollett.* $101/£65

GILL, ERIC. Clothing without Cloth: An Essay on the Nude. Waltham Saint Lawrence: Golden Cockerel, 1931. 1st ed, #341/500 numbered. 4 full-pg wood engrs. Gilt stamped red cl; top, right edges gilt, lower edge uncut. VG in glassine dj. *Houle.* $250/£161

GILL, ERIC. Clothing without Cloth: An Essay on the Nude. Golden Cockerel, 1931. One of 500 numbered. 4 wood engrs. Fine. *Hermitage.* $375/£242

GILL, ERIC. First Nudes. NY: Citadel, (1954). 1st Amer ed. Red cl, gilt. VG. *Hermitage.* $65/£42

GILL, ERIC. First Nudes. London: Neville Spearman, 1954. 1st ed. 24 plts. VG in orig cl & dj (lt soiled, frayed). *Cox.* $54/£35

GILL, ERIC. The Human Person and Society. London: Peace Pledge Union, 1940. 1st ed. Orig ptd wrappers (sl soiled; tape mk at fold). *Cox.* $28/£18

GILL, ERIC. In a Strange Land. London: Jonathan Cape, 1944. 1st ed. Title vignette, 6 other wood engrs. Orig blue cl; lettered in silver. VG in dj (soiled, worn). *Cox.* $23/£15

GILL, ERIC. In a Strange Land. London: Cape, 1944. 1st ed. 3 wood engrs by Gill. Orig cl w/Gill's symbol. Fine. *Europa.* $23/£15

GILL, ERIC. Last Essays. London: Jonathan Cape, 1942. 1st ed. 4 wood engrs by Gill. Orig cl. VG in dj (lt soiled). *Cox.* $23/£15

GILL, ERIC. Last Essays. London: Cape, 1942. 2nd imp. Uncut. Fine in dj. *Willow House.* $23/£15

GILL, ERIC. Letters. Walter Shewring (ed). London: Jonathan Cape, 1947. 1st ed. Frontis, 11 other illus. VG in orig cl. *Cox.* $28/£18

GILL, ERIC. The Lord's Song. A Sermon. London: Golden Cockerel Press, 1934. 1st ed. Uncut except for top edge. White buckram (sl faded). *Petersfield.* $194/£125

GILL, ERIC. The Lord's Song. A Sermon. London: Golden Cockerel, 1934. 1st ed. #247/500. Full-pg engr. Uncut, partly unopened. Fine in gold-lettered cream buckram. *Cox.* $271/£175

GILL, ERIC. Money and Morals.... London: Faber and Faber, 1934. 1st ed. One of 1413. Good in orig cl. *Cox.* $31/£20

GILL, ERIC. The Necessity of Belief. London: Faber & Faber, 1936. 1st ed. Orig cl. VG in dj (sl frayed, soiled). *Cox.* $39/£25

GILL, ERIC. The Necessity of Belief. London: Faber, 1936. 1st UK ed. VG+. *Williams.* $23/£15

GILL, ERIC. Sacred and Secular.... London: J.M. Dent, 1940. 1st ed. Frontis. Orig red cl. Good (backstrip sl faded). *Cox.* $28/£18

GILL, ERIC. Sculpture. An Essay on Stonecutting.... Ditchling Sussex: St. Dominic's Press, n.d. (ca 1924). 1st ed. Tp illus; 2 woodcuts. Beige linen stamped in black (spine lt soiled). *Karmiole.* $200/£129

GILL, ERIC. Social Justice and the Stations of the Cross. London: James Clarke, 1939. 1st ed. Wood-engr by Gill on title (reproduced on cover). VG in variant binding of ptd green wrappers. *Cox.* $54/£35

GILL, ERIC. Twenty-five Nudes. London: J.M. Dent & Sons, 1951. 2nd ed. Extra pictorial title in red/black; 26 full-pg wood engrs. VG in orig red cl and dj (sl browned). *Cox.* $39/£25

GILL, ERIC. Unemployment. London: Faber, 1933. Wood engr frontis. Fine in orig red ptd wrappers. *Europa.* $59/£38

GILL, ERIC. Unemployment. London: Faber & Faber, 1933. 1st ed. One of 2000. Stitched in orig dark red ptd wrappers. VG (fep, rep sl foxed). *Cox.* $54/£35

GILL, ERIC. Work and Leisure. London: Faber & Faber, 1935. 1st ed. Orig red cl lettered in blue. Good (hinges sl rubbed). *Cox.* $31/£20

GILLETT, HENRY W. and ALBERT JOHN IRVING. Gold Inlays by the Indirect System. NY, 1932. (Lib ink stamp.) *Edwards.* $54/£35

GILLETT, JAMES B. Six Years with the Texas Rangers, 1875 to 1881. Chicago, (1943). Lakeside Classic. VG. *Schoyer.* $25/£16

GILLETT, JAMES B. Six Years with the Texas Rangers, 1875-1881. Milo Milton Quaife (ed). Chicago: Lakeside Classic, 1943. Fldg map, pict cl. VG+. *Pratt.* $65/£42

GILLHAM, CHARLES E. Raw North. NY: A.S. Barnes, 1947. 1st ed. Rev slip laid in. NF in dj (lt worn). *Parmer.* $45/£29

GILLIATT, PENELOPE. One by One. London: Secker & Warburg, (1965). 1st ed, 1st bk. Fine in NF dj. *Reese.* $50/£32

GILLILAND, MAUDE T. Rincon, Remote Dwelling Place.... Brownsville: Springman King, 1964. 2nd ed. Dj. *Lambeth.* $30/£19

GILLINGHAM, ROBERT C. The Rancho San Pedro. (LA: Dominguez Estate), 1961. 1st ed. VF in Fine dj. *Perier.* $125/£81

GILLMORE, FRANCES. Flute of the Smoking Mirror. Univ of NM, 1949. 1st ed. VG in VG dj. *Oregon.* $40/£26

GILLMORE, PARKER. Leaves from a Sportsman's Diary. London: Allen, 1893. 1st ed. 341pp + ads. Red cl. Spine faded, o/w VG. *Bowman.* $35/£23

GILLMORE, PARKER. Prairie Farms and Prairie Folk. Hurst & Blackett, 1872. 1st ed. 2 vols. Engr frontis each vol; 16pp pub's cat end vol 1. Mod 1/2 calf, spines gilt w/red, grn morocco labels. (Lt foxing.) *Bickersteth.* $256/£165

GILLMORE, PARKER. Ubique. All Round the World. London: Chapman & Hall, 1871. iv,270pp. Grn cl stamped in black/gilt (soiled; owner mks). *Schoyer.* $50/£32

GILLY, WILLIAM O.S. Narratives of Shipwrecks of the Royal Navy: Between 1793 and 1849. London: John W. Parker, 1851. 2nd ed. (xxvi),336pp. Orig cl (rebacked in calf; foxing). *Lefkowicz.* $300/£194

GILMAN, RICHARD. Decadence. FSG, 1979. 1st ed. Signed. NF in NF dj. *Bishop.* $17/£11

GILMOR, HARRY. Four Years in the Saddle. NY: Harper, 1866. 1st ed. Spine ends, corners scuffed; minor damping; else VG. *Mcgowan.* $250/£161

GILMORE, ANTHONY. Space Hawk. Greenberg, 1952. 1st ed. Fine in dj (spine sl frayed). *Madle.* $75/£48

GILMOUR, JOHN and MAX WALTERS. Wild Flowers. London, 1954. 1st ed. Dj (sl rubbed, sm chip). *Edwards.* $56/£36

GILPIN, LAURA. Temples in Yucatan. NY: Hastings, 1948. 1st ed. VG+ in VG- dj. *Parker.* $195/£126

GILPIN, WILLIAM. An Essay on Prints. London: For Blamire, 1792. 4th ed. xiii,174,xipp. Contemp full calf. Bkpl, upper joint splitting, sl worn, o/w Fine (new label). *Europa.* $132/£85

GILPIN, WILLIAM. Remarks on Forest Scenery and Other Woodland Views.... London: For Blamire, 1794. 2nd ed. 3 books in 2 vols. 1/2 title, tp, vii,340,viipp; 1/2 title, 310pp, 14 aquatint plts, cat, iiipp. Dbl-pg map. Uniform diced russia, gilt. Neat repair spine vol 2, gilt titling sl faded, lt internal browning, o/w Fine set. *Europa.* $264/£170

GILSON, ADRIAN. Czar and the Sultan. NY: Harper, 1853. 196pp + 8pp ads (lacks fr fly). Royal blue cl stamped in blind, gilt (pocket removed). *Schoyer.* $35/£23

GINGHER, MARIANNE. Bobby Rex's Greatest Hit. NY: Atheneum, 1986. 1st ed, 1st bk. Rev copy, pub's slip laid in. Rose bds w/grey cl spine. Sticker removed fr pastedown, else Fine in dj. *Chapel Hill.* $30/£19

GINSBERG, ALLEN. Collected Poems 1947-1980. NY: Harper, (1984). 1st ed. VF in dj. *Reese.* $30/£19

GINSBERG, ALLEN. The Fall of America. SF: City Lights, 1972. 1st ed. Spine creased, o/w NF in wrappers. *Rees.* $31/£20

GINSBERG, ALLEN. Iron Horse. SF: City Lights, 1974. 1st ed. NF in wrappers. *Rees.* $23/£15

GINSBERG, ALLEN. Journals Early Fifties, Early Sixties. Gordon Ball (ed). NY: Grove Press, 1977. 1st Amer ed. Signed. Fine in Fine dj. *Polyanthos.* $30/£19

GINSBERG, ALLEN. T.V. Baby Poems. (London): Cape Goliard, (1967). Ltd to 100 hb, signed & numbered. NF in dj. *Antic Hay.* $100/£65

GINSBERG, ALLEN. T.V. Baby Poems. London: Cape Goliard, 1967. One of 100 specially bound, numbered, signed. Fine in dj w/add'l cl jacket, slipcase. *Rees.* $194/£125

GINSBERG, ALLEN. Wales—A Visitation July 29th, 1967. Cape Goliard Press, 1968. One of 200 hors commerce. Fine in dj. *Rees.* $31/£20

GINSBERG, ALLEN. White Shroud. Poems 1980-1985. NY: Harper, 1986. 1st ed. Inscribed. Fine in Fine dj. *Beasley.* $75/£48

GINZBURG, ELI et al. The Ineffective Soldier. NY: Columbia Univ Press, 1959. 1st ed. 3 vols. Gray cl, painted spine labels. VG in djs. *Gach.* $85/£55

GIONONI-VISANI, MARIA. Giorgio Clovio: Miniaturist of the Renaissance. NY, 1980. VG in dj (torn). *Argosy.* $85/£55

GIPSON, FRED. The Home Place. NY: Harper, (1950). 1st ed ('H-Z'). VG in dj (nicks). *Houle.* $75/£48

GIRAUD, J.P. The Birds of Long Island. NY: Wiley & Putnam, 1844. 1st ed. xxii,(2),398pp. 1 plt. Brn cl, blind-stamped, gilt spine (spine extrems sl chipped; corners, lower edges frayed). *Karmiole.* $175/£113

GIRAUD, S. LOUIS (ed). Bookano Stories with Pictures That Spring Up in Model Form: No. 10. London: Strand, (1943). 4to. 5 Fine dbl-pg pop-ups. Full color illus bds. Good. *Reisler.* $225/£145

GIRAUD, S. LOUIS (ed). Bookano Stories with Pictures That Spring Up in Model Form: No. 12. London: Strand, (1945). 4to. 5 dbl-pg pop-ups (1 w/sm paper reinforcement). Full-color illus bds (lt edgewear). *Reisler.* $185/£119

GIRAUD, S. LOUIS (ed). Bookano Stories. London: Daily Sketch & Sunday Graphic, (1944). #11. 4to. 5 double-pg pop-ups (incl aquarium, plastic water intact). Very Nice. *Reisler.* $225/£145

GIRAUD, S. LOUIS (ed). Bookano Stories. London: Daily Sketch & Sunday Graphic, (1947). #14. 4to. 5 double-pg pop-ups. Very Nice. *Reisler.* $225/£145

GIRAUD, S. LOUIS (ed). Hans Andersen's Fairy Stories with Pictures That Spring to Life. London: Strand, n.d. (1938). 4 VG dbl-pg pop-ups. (Extrems, spine rubbed; spine sl crazed.) *Book Finders.* $110/£71

GIRAUD, S. LOUIS (ed). Old Rhymes and New Stories. London: Strand, n.d. (193?). 16x22cm. 3 Excellent dbl-pg pop-ups. (Spine rebacked.) *Book Finders.* $110/£71

GIRODIAS, MAURICE (ed). The Olympia Reader. NY, 1965. 1st Amer ed. Fine (spine extrems sl rubbed) in NF dj. *Polyanthos.* $30/£19

GIROUARD, MARK. Life in the English Country House. New Haven: Yale Univ Press, 1978. 1st ed. 33 color plts. Fine in dj (sl handled). *Bookpress.* $50/£32

GIROUARD, MARK. The Return to Camelot, Chivalry and the English Gentleman. New Haven: Yale Univ Press, 1981. 1st ed. Fine in dj. *Bookpress.* $65/£42

GIROUARD, MARK. The Victorian Country House. New Haven/London: Yale, 1979. Rev, enlgd ed. Fine in color dj. *Europa.* $31/£20

GIRVIN, BRENDA. Round Fairyland with Alice. Redhill, Surrey: Wells Gardner, Darton, (1948). 1st ed thus. 8vo. W. Lindsay Cable (illus). Brn cl, gilt. Good in color pict dj (edgewear). *Reisler.* $90/£58

GISBORNE, THOMAS. Walks in a Forest, and Other Poems. London: Cadell & Davies, 1813. 8th ed. No 1/2 title. VG (name) in gilt-dec tree calf (sl rubbed; joints weakening). *Poetry.* $34/£22

GISSING, GEORGE. Charles Dickens. London: Blackie, 1898. 1st ed. 244pp. Eps browned, fore-edge foxed, bkpl, spine lt faded, else Fine. *Godot.* $75/£48

GISSING, GEORGE. Charles Dickens. London: Gresham, 1902. 1st illus ed. ix,307pp; teg. (Flyleaves sl spotted.) F.G. Kitton (illus). (Spine dknd; lower hinge rubbed; sm snag.) *Hollett.* $39/£25

GISSING, GEORGE. In the Year of Jubilee. Appleton, 1895. 1st ed. Lt rubbing, else VG. *Fine Books.* $50/£32

GISSING, GEORGE. The Private Papers of Henry Ryecroft. Portland, ME: Thomas Bird Mosher, 1921. 1/700 ptd in Van Gelder paper. Uncut. VG (joints starting). *Argosy.* $75/£48

GISSING, GEORGE. Selections Autobiographical and Imaginative from the Works of George Gissing. NY, 1929. 1st Amer ed. Fine (spine extrems sl rubbed) in dj (spine sunned, edge chips). *Polyanthos.* $60/£39

GISSING, GEORGE. The Town Traveller. NY: Stokes, (1898). 1st Amer ed. Pict cl. VG. *Argosy.* $50/£32

GISSING, GEORGE. The Town Traveller. London: Methuen, 1898. 1st ed. Ribbed cl, gilt (lt soiled, sm snag). *Sadlon.* $85/£55

GISSING, GEORGE. Veranilda. London: Constable, 1904. 1st ed. VG. *Limestone.* $65/£42

GIUDICI, DAVIDE. The Tragedy of the Italia. NY: D. Appleton, 1929. Double-pg map. VG. *High Latitude.* $40/£26

GLADDEN, WASHINGTON. From the Hub to the Hudson. Boston: New England News, 1869. 149pp. Pub's cl (sl worn). VG. *Hermitage.* $50/£32

GLADDEN, WASHINGTON. From the Hub to the Hudson. Greenfield: Merriam, 1870. 149pp; 7 plts. (Spine sunned; sl spots.) *Schoyer.* $45/£29

GLADSTONE, FLORENCE M. Notting Hill in Bygone Days. London: T. Fisher Unwin, 1924. 1st ed. 55 maps. Cl over beveled bds (sl worn, mkd; lib label). *Hollett.* $54/£35

GLADSTONE, HUGH S. Record Bags and Shooting Records. London: Witherby, 1922. 12 plts. Blue cl (worn), gilt. (Spotted.) *Hollett.* $54/£35

GLADSTONE, HUGH S. (ed). Shooting with Surtees. London, 1927. 4 color plts. Teg. (Feps, edges lt foxed, some intrusion to text.) *Edwards.* $70/£45

GLADSTONE, T.H. The Englishman In Kansas. Lincoln: Univ of NE, 1971. 1st ed. Fine in Fine dj. *Connolly.* $32/£21

GLADSTONE, W.E. Ecce Homo. London, 1868. 1st ed in bk form. Dec cvrs, gilt. NF (spine professionally mended; sl chipped). *Polyanthos.* $35/£23

GLADWIN, IRENE. The Sheriff. Gollancz, 1974. Orig ptg. Pub's cl gilt. Fresh in dj. *Peter Taylor.* $37/£24

GLADWIN, IRENE. The Sheriff: the Man and His Office. London: Gollancz, 1974. Orig ptg. Fine in dj. *Peter Taylor.* $39/£25

GLAISHER, JAMES, CAMILLE FLAMMARION, et al. Travels in the Air. London, 1871. 1st ed. 398pp; frontis, guard; 11 plts (eps, prelims foxed). Pict red cl (worn, frayed; upper hinge cracked; inscrip), gilt title. *Edwards.* $116/£75

GLAISTER, GEOFFREY A. Glossary of the Book. London: George Allen & Unwin, 1960. 1st ed. 4 tipped-in specimens. 2-tone cl (neat lib stamp tp verso). *Cox.* $54/£35

GLANVILLE, BRIAN. The Reluctant Dictator. London: Werner Laurie, 1952. 1st ed. VG in dj (sl chipped). *Hollett.* $39/£25

GLASFURD, A.I.R. Musings of an Old Shikari. London, 1928. 1st ed. Color frontis. (Feps lt browned; spine lt faded, bleached parts.) Dj (ragged, loss). *Edwards.* $74/£48

GLASGOW, ALICE. Sheridan of Drury Lane. A Biography.... NY: Frederick A. Stokes, 1940. 1st ed. VG in dj. *Dramatis Personae.* $18/£12

GLASGOW, ELLEN. The Deliverance. NY: Doubleday Page, 1904. 1st ed, 1st issue w/smooth grained cl. Lt wear spine, o/w Fine. *Hermitage.* $45/£29

GLASGOW, ELLEN. Virginia. NY: Doubleday, 1913. 1st ed. VG. *Second Life.* $30/£19

GLASGOW, ELLEN. The Voice of the People. NY: Doubleday, Page, 1900. 1st ed. Fr cvr sl mkd, else VG. *Hermitage.* $40/£26

GLASGOW, ELLEN. The Wheel of Life. NY: Doubleday, Page, 1906. 1st ed. Grn cl; red binding also exists. Fine. *Pharos.* $40/£26

GLASIER, P. As the Falcon Her Bells. London: Heinemann, 1963. 1st ed. Dec eps. VG in Good+ dj. *Mikesh.* $25/£16

GLASPELL, S. Alison's House. S. French, 1930. 1st ed. VG+ in VG dj. *Fine Books.* $65/£42

GLASPELL, S. The Visioning. NY: Stokes, (1911). 1st ed. Pict cl stamped in gilt/blind. NF. *Reese.* $125/£81

GLASSCOCK, C.B. Big Bonanza, The Story of the Comstock Lode. Indianapolis: Bobbs-Merrill, (1931). (1st ed). Frontis port. Postcard laid in. VG+ in dj (lt frayed). *Bohling.* $40/£26

GLASSCOCK, C.B. Here's Death Valley. NY: Bobbs-Merrill, (1940). 1st ed. Fine in Fine dj. *Book Market.* $65/£42

GLASSER, OTTO. Wilhelm Conrad Roentgen and the Early History of the Roentgen Rays. Springfield/Balt: Charles Thomas, (1934). 1st Eng trans. Frontis port. Pub's cl. VF (presentation inscrip). *Hemlock.* $150/£97

GLASSER, RONALD. Another War, Another Peace. NY: Summit, (1985). 1st ed. As New (rmdr mk) in Fine dj. *Aka.* $25/£16

GLAZIER, WILLARD. Heroes of Three Wars: Comprising a Series of Biographical Sketches.... Phila: Hubbard Bros, 1879. 1st ed. 418pp. VG. *Mcgowan.* $45/£29

Gleanings in Europe. By An American. (By James Fenimore Cooper). Phila: Carey, Lea & Blanchard, 1837. 1st Amer ed. 2 vols. Orig cl (spines lightened; sl spotty; scattered foxing mostly to 1st, last leaves). Cl slipcase, paper spine label. BAL 3876. *Sadlon.* $200/£129

GLEASON, C.W. and H.R. BURNER. Thirty-Eight Lectures on How to Acquire and Preserve Health. 1874. 1st ed. 472pp. Good. *Fye.* $50/£32

GLEASON, H.A. and A. CRONQUIST. The Natural Geography of Plants. NY, 1964. VG+. *Brooks.* $61/£39

GLEED, CHARLES S. (ed). From River to Sea. Chicago: Rand, McNally, 1882. 240pp + 16pp ads. Pict cl (lt spots). *Schoyer.* $100/£65

GLEICHED, EDWARD. London's Open-Air Statuary. London, 1928. 45 plts. *Edwards.* $50/£32

GLENISTER, A.G. The Birds of the Malay Peninsula, Singapore and Penang. OUP, 1951. 1st ed. 16 plts. VG in dj. *Hollett.* $54/£35

GLENN, THOMAS ALLEN. Some Colonial Mansions and Those Who Lived in Them. Phila, 1900. 1st ed. Howes G 208. *Ginsberg.* $75/£48

GLENNON, J.H. Interior Ballistics. (Balt), 1894. 1st ed. Signed. 152pp, 5 tables. VG. *Argosy.* $50/£32

GLENNY, G. The Handbook to the Flower Garden and Greenhouse. London, 1862. 5th ed. Hand-colored frontis, xii,380pp. (New eps; stamp in text.) *Henly.* $47/£30

GLICK, ALLEN. Winters Coming, Winters Gone. NY: Pinnacle, (1984). 1st trade ed. NF (rmdr stripe) in NF dj. *Aka.* $30/£19

GLOAG, JOHN. The English Tradition in Architecture. London: A&C Black, (1963). 1st ed. Frontis; 48 plts. VG in dj (used). *Bookpress.* $65/£42

GLOAG, JOHN. The English Tradition in Architecture. London: A&C Black, 1963. 1st ed. Dj (sl chipped). *Edwards.* $31/£20

GLOAG, JOHN. The English Tradition in Design. London: King Penguin Books, 1947. 1st ed. 72 plts. Rubbed, margins yellowed, else Good. *Bookpress.* $35/£23

GLOAG, JOHN. Victorian Comfort. London: A&C Black, 1961. Color frontis, 16 plts. (Ex-libris, glue mks reps.) Dj (sl chipped). *Edwards.* $39/£25

Glossary of Terms Used in Grecian, Roman, Italian, and Gothic Architecture. Oxford, 1850. 5th ed, enlgd. 2 vols in 3. (Lt spotting.) Marbled eps; teg. 1/2 morocco w/cl bds (lt faded), gilt. *Edwards.* $209/£135

GLOSSOP, R. The Egyptian Venus. Regency Press, 1946. 1st ed. NF in VG dj (spine lt chipped). *Aronovitz.* $45/£29

GLOVER, EDWIN A. Bucktailed Wildcats, A Regiment of Civil War Volunteers. NY, (1960). 1st ed. VG+ in VG+ dj. *Pratt.* $42/£27

GLOVER, MICHAEL. Wellington's Peninsular Victories. Batsford, 1963. 1st ed. 15 plts (1 dbl-pg). VG in dj (sl worn; price-clipped). *Edwards.* $47/£30

GLOVER, WILLIAM. The Mormons in California. LA: Glen Dawson, 1954. 1st ed. Ltd to 197 signed by Paul Bailey (ptr, foreword). Emb pict cl, gilt-stamped spine. Fine. *Oregon.* $85/£55

GLUBB, JOHN BAGOT. Arabian Adventures. London: Cassell, (1978). 1st ed. 13 maps. VG in dj. *Schoyer.* $30/£19

GLUBB, JOHN BAGOT. A Soldier with the Arabs. NY: Harper, (1957). VG in dj (spine faded). *Schoyer.* $35/£23

GLUBB, JOHN BAGOT. A Soldier with the Arabs. London, 1957. 1st ed. Dj (sl chipped). *Edwards.* $47/£30

GLUBB, JOHN BAGOT. Soldiers of Fortune. The Story of the Mamlukes. London/Sydney: Hodder & Stoughton, 1973. 1st ed. 33 maps; 6 charts. NF in dj. *Worldwide.* $25/£16

GLUBB, JOHN BAGOT. The Story of the Arab Legion. London: Hodder & Stoughton, 1948. 1st ptg. Sl rubbed, soiled, o/w VG. *Worldwide.* $35/£23

GLUBB, JOHN BAGOT. War in the Desert. NY: Norton, (1961). 1st Amer ed. NF in dj (price-clipped). *Schoyer.* $35/£23

GLUCKMAN, ARCADI. United States Muskets, Rifles and Carbines. Buffalo, 1948. VG. *Argosy.* $75/£48

GLUECK, NELSON. Deities and Dolphins: The Story of the Nabataens. NY: FSG, (1965). 1st ed. VF in dj. *Hermitage.* $65/£42

GLUECK, NELSON. Rivers in the Desert. NY: Farrar, Straus & Cudahy, 1959. 1st ed. 48 plts, 4 maps. VG in dj. *Worldwide.* $22/£14

GOBAT, SAMUEL. Journal of Three Years' Residence in Abyssinia. NY: M.W. Dodd, 1850. Frontis port, fldg map. Black cl (spotted, chipped, worn; foxed). *Schoyer.* $50/£32

GOBEL, HEINRICH. Tapestries of the Lowlands. NY, 1974. Rpt ed. Good. *Washton.* $75/£48

GODDARD, HENRY HERBERT. The Criminal Imbecile. NY: Macmillan, (1915). 1st ed. 4 plts. Ptd blue cl. Good (sl shelfworn). *Gach.* $50/£32

GODDEN, GEOFFREY A. British Porcelain. London, 1974. 1st UK ed. 12 color plts. Dj (sl chipped). *Edwards.* $39/£25

GODDEN, GEOFFREY A. Encyclopaedia of British Porcelain Manufacturers. London, 1988. 1st UK ed. 24 color plts. Dj. *Edwards.* $62/£40

GODDEN, GEOFFREY A. Encyclopaedia of British Pottery and Porcelain Marks. NY: Crown, (1964). Fine in dj (lt creased). *Glenn.* $45/£29

GODDEN, GEOFFREY A. Minton Pottery and Porcelain of the First Period 1793-1850. London: Barrie & Jenkins, (1978). 12 color plts. *Petersfield.* $31/£20

GODDEN, GEOFFREY A. Minton Pottery and Porcelain of the First Period 1793-1850. London, 1968. 1st ed. Frontis port; 12 color, 161 b/w plts. Dj (torn, ragged, w/some loss). *Edwards.* $54/£35

GODDEN, RUMER. The Mousewife. NY: Viking, 1951. 1st Amer ed. Fine in Fine dj (price-clipped; chip). *Between The Covers.* $50/£32

GODFREY, EDWARD S. The Field Diary of Lt. Edward Settle Godfrey.... Portland: Champoeg Press, 1957. 1st ed. Ltd to 1000. Frontis, 8 plts (incl 2 fldg maps). VG. *Oregon.* $75/£48

GODFREY, F.M. Italian Sculpture 1250-1700. NY, 1967. Good. *Washton.* $40/£26

GODFREY, W.H. Gardens in the Making. London: Batsford, 1914. 1st ed. 8 dbl-pg plans. Fine. *Quest.* $75/£48

GODLEE, RICKMAN. Lord Lister. Oxford, 1917. 1st ed. *Fye.* $85/£55

GODLEE, RICKMAN. Lord Lister. Oxford, 1924. 3rd ed. Good. *Fye.* $75/£48

GODMAN, JOHN D. Addresses Delivered on Various Public Occasions.... Phila, 1829. 194pp; uncut. Orig bds (rebacked). *Goodrich.* $95/£61

GODMAN, JOHN D. Rambles of a Naturalist. Phila: Assoc of Friends for the Diffusion of Religious and Useful Knowledge, 1859. 124pp. Good (cl sl worn; ex-lib). *Second Life.* $15/£10

GODMAN, JOHN D. Rambles of a Naturalist. To which are added Reminiscences of a Voyage to India by Reynell Coates, M.D. Phila, 1833. 151pp (prelims sl spotted). Uncut. Orig linen-cvrd bds, paper label. VG (upper hinge split). *Hemlock.* $200/£129

GODSELL, PHILIP H. Pilots of the Purple Twilight. Toronto: Ryerson Press, 1955. VG in dj. *High Latitude.* $40/£26

GODWIN, GAIL. The Perfectionists. NY: Harper & Row, (1970). 1st ed. Fine in Fine in dj. *Between The Covers.* $275/£177

GODWIN, TOM. The Survivors. Hicksville: Gnome Press, (1958). 1st ed. Later? binding of grey cl, red spine lettering. NF (usual browning to poor quality paper) in dj (lt wear; sl browning; price-clipped). *Antic Hay.* $50/£32

GODWIN, TOM. The Survivors. Gnome Press, 1958. 1st ed. Fr cvr lt spotted, else NF in NF dj (sl spine wear). *Aronovitz.* $65/£42

GOETZMANN, WILLIAM H. Army Exploration in the American West, 1803-1863. New Haven: Yale, 1960. 2nd ptg. VG + (bumped) in VG- dj. *Parker.* $75/£48

GOETZMANN, WILLIAM H. Army Explorations in the American West 1803-1863. Yale, 1959. 1st ed. 5 fldg maps in rear pocket. Fine in VG dj. *Oregon.* $150/£97

GOETZMANN, WILLIAM H. and KAY SLOAN. Looking Far North. The Harriman Expedition to Alaska, 1899. NY: Viking, (1982). 1st ed. Fine in Fine dj. *Book Market.* $30/£19

GOFF, CHARLES. Legg-Calve-Perthes Syndrome and Related Osteochondroses of Youth. Springfield, 1954. 1st ed. Good in dj. *Fye.* $75/£48

GOFFEN, R. Giovanni Bellini. Yale Univ Press, 1989. 75 color plts. Dj. *Ars Artis.* $65/£42

GOFFIN, ROBERT. Horn of Plenty. NY: Allen, Towne & Heath, 1947. 1st ed. Fine (name; sl soiled) in dj (1-inch tear spine fold). *Beasley.* $65/£42

GOFFIN, ROBERT. Horn of Plenty: The Story of Louis Armstrong. NY: Allen et al, 1947. 1st ed in English. Port. VG in pict dj. *Petrilla.* $50/£32

GOFFIN, ROBERT. Jazz: From the Congo to the Metropolitan. GC: Doubleday, Doran, 1944. 1st ed, 1st bk. VG in dj. *Petrilla.* $60/£39

GOGARTY, OLIVER ST. JOHN. Perennial. Constable, 1946. 1st ed. Edges spotted, o/w VG in dj (worn). *Poetry.* $31/£20

GOGARTY, OLIVER ST. JOHN. Wild Apples. NY: Jonathan Cape & Harrison Smith, (1929). 1st ed. NF in dj (sl wear; spine, edges sunned). *Antic Hay.* $45/£29

GOGOL, NIKOLAI. Chichikov's Journeys (Dead Souls). NY: LEC, 1944. #429/1200 signed by Lucille Corcos (illus). 2 vols. Fine in orig tissue wrappers in box. *Williams.* $116/£75

GOGOL, NIKOLAI. Chichikov's Journeys. Bernard Guilbert Guerney (trans). NY: LEC, 1944. Ltd to 1200 numbered, signed by Lucille Corcos (illus). 2 vols. Good in fldg box, slipcase. *Karmiole.* $50/£32

GOGOL, NIKOLAI. The Government Inspector and Other Plays. Constance Garnett (trans). NY: Knopf, 1927. 1st Amer ed. Ink name, else VG in dj (sl chipped). *Hermitage.* $75/£48

Gold Demon; Or, Lamora, the Maid of the Canon. (By Edward S. Ellis.) NY: Beadle & Adams, (1870). Beadle's New Dime Novels, New Series, No. 113, Old Series, No. 434. 99pp. Good in color pict wrappers (worn but complete). *Hayman.* $20/£13

GOLD, HERBERT. Therefore Be Bold. NY: Dial, 1960. 1st ed. Inscribed, signed. Fine in Very Nice dj (price-clipped). *Reese.* $30/£19

GOLD, THOS. D. History of Clarke County Virginia.... (Berryville, VA, 1914). 1st ed. 8vo. Orig blue cl. Rear hinge cracked internally; lt spotted, else VG. *Chapel Hill.* $750/£484

Gold-Headed Cane. (By William MacMichael.) London: John Murray, 1827. 1st ed. (viii),179pp; 5 wood-engr ports. Contemp full calf; rebacked retaining orig spine, label; gilt. (Lt waterstaining.) *White.* $171/£110

GOLDBERG, NORMAN L. John Crome the Elder. Oxford: Phaidon, 1978. 2 vols. 16 color plts. VF set in pict djs. *Europa.* $47/£30

GOLDBERG, NORMAN L. John Crome the Elder. Oxford: Phaidon, 1978. 2 vols. 16 color plts. Sound in dj. *Ars Artis*. $93/£60

Golden Chersonese and the Way Thither. (By Isabella Lucy Bird Bishop). NY: Putnam's, 1886. (i),xiv,483pp; 10 b/w plts; foldout map. Gilt-pict brn cl. VG. *Petrilla*. $50/£32

GOLDEN, HARRY. Carl Sandburg. Cleveland/NY: World, (1961). 1st ed. Pict cl. Fine in dj (sl worn). *Sadlon*. $20/£13

GOLDER, F.A. Bering's Voyages. NY: American Geographical Soc, 1922-25. 2 vols. 1935 rpt. VG. *High Latitude*. $100/£65

Goldilocks and the Three Bears. NY: Child Guidance, n.d. (197?). 27x20 cm. 5 moving pictures. Pict bds. VG (cellophane replaced on 4 pictures). *Book Finders*. $55/£35

GOLDING, HARRY. Willie Winkie: The Tale of a Wooden Horse. London: Ward, Lock, n.d. 16mo. 96pp, 24 full-pg color illus by Margaret W. Tarrant (illus). White pict bds. Good (soiled throughout; corners worn). *Davidson*. $75/£48

GOLDING, WILLIAM. The Brass Butterfly. London: Faber, 1958. 1st UK ed. Fine in dj. *Lewton*. $155/£100

GOLDING, WILLIAM. Darkness Visible. London: Faber & Faber, 1979. 1st ed. VF in dj. *Limestone*. $40/£26

GOLDING, WILLIAM. Darkness Visible. London: Faber, 1979. 1st UK ed. Fine in dj. *Lewton*. $25/£16

GOLDING, WILLIAM. An Egyptian Journal. London, 1985. As New in dj. *Lewis*. $23/£15

GOLDING, WILLIAM. An Egyptian Journal. London: Faber, 1985. 1st UK ed. NF in dj. *Lewton*. $20/£13

GOLDING, WILLIAM. Fire Down Below. London: Faber, 1989. 1st ed. Fine in dj. *Rees*. $19/£12

GOLDING, WILLIAM. Fire Down Below. London: Faber & Faber, 1989. 1st ed. Fine in dj. *Limestone*. $25/£16

GOLDING, WILLIAM. Free Fall. NY: Harcourt, Brace, (1960). 1st Amer ed. Fine in VG dj (spine faded, worn). *Godot*. $45/£29

GOLDING, WILLIAM. Free Fall. F&F, 1959. 1st ed. VG in NF 2nd ptg dj. *Fine Books*. $35/£23

GOLDING, WILLIAM. The Hot Gates and Other Occasional Pieces. London: Faber & Faber, (1965). 1st ed. Fine in dj (price-clipped). *Hermitage*. $65/£42

GOLDING, WILLIAM. The Inheritors. Faber, 1955. 1st UK ed. Fine in VG dj (spine top sl wear). *Williams*. $171/£110

GOLDING, WILLIAM. Nobel Lecture. Sixth Chamber, 1983. One of 500. Fine in wraps. *Lewton*. $39/£25

GOLDING, WILLIAM. Nobel Lecture. Sixth Chamber Press, 1984. One of 500 trade copies. Signed. Fine in wrappers. *Rees*. $54/£35

GOLDING, WILLIAM. The Paper Men. London: Faber, 1984. 1st ed. Signed. Fine in dj. *Rees*. $54/£35

GOLDING, WILLIAM. Pincher Martin. Faber, 1956. 1st UK ed. Fine in dj (tiny specks fr flap) w/orig wraparound band. *Williams*. $457/£295

GOLDING, WILLIAM. The Pyramid. London: Faber, 1967. 1st UK ed. Fine in dj. *Lewton*. $57/£37

GOLDING, WILLIAM. Rites of Passage. London: Faber & Faber, 1980. 1st ed. Fine in dj. *Limestone*. $35/£23

GOLDING, WILLIAM. The Two Deaths of Christopher Martin. H-B, 1956. 1st Amer ed. Signed bkpl laid in. Fine in dj. *Fine Books*. $135/£87

GOLDMAN, JAMES and STEPHEN SONDHEIM. Follies. NY: Random House, (1971). 1st ed. Lt stain bottom of bds, pp, else Fine in NF dj (wrinkling fr flap). *Between The Covers*. $125/£81

GOLDMAN, JUDITH. Windows at Tiffany's: The Art of Gene Moore.... NY: Abrams, 1980. Signed by Moore. 66 color plts. VG in dj. *Argosy*. $85/£55

GOLDMAN, WILLIAM. Marathon Man. NY: Delacorte, (1974). 1st ed. Fine in dj. *Hermitage*. $30/£19

GOLDMAN, WILLIAM. Soldier in the Rain. NY, 1960. 1st Amer ed. Fine (sl rubbed) in dj (sl rubbed). *Polyanthos*. $30/£19

GOLDMAN, WILLIAM. The Temple of Gold. NY: Knopf, 1957. 1st ed, 1st bk. Fine in dj (lt edge wear). *Dermont*. $60/£39

GOLDMAN, WILLIAM. The Temple of Gold. NY: Knopf, 1957. 1st ed, 1st bk. Fine in dj (lt rubbed, short tear). *Between The Covers*. $250/£161

GOLDNER, ORVILLE and GEORGE E. TURNER. The Making of King Kong. South Brunswick: A.S. Barnes, 1975. 1st ed. Fine in Fine dj. *Beasley*. $45/£29

GOLDRING, DOUGLAS. South Lodge. London: Constable, (1943). 1st ed. Fine in dj (lt soiled; chipped). *Pharos*. $60/£39

GOLDSBOROUGH, W.W. The Maryland Line in the Confederate States Army. Balt: Kelly, Piet, 1869. 1st ed. Frontis port, 357pp + 3 ads. Eps replaced; end leaves lt foxed; rubbed, else Good. Howes G 226. *Cahan*. $275/£177

GOLDSCHEIDER, LUDWIG. Johannes Vermeer. The Paintings, Complete Edition. Phaidon, 1958. 117 plts (34 color). Sound in dj (sl frayed). *Ars Artis*. $54/£35

GOLDSCHEIDER, LUDWIG. A Survey of Michelangelo's Models in Wax and Clay. London: Phaidon, 1962. Fine. *Europa*. $31/£20

GOLDSCHEIDER, LUDWIG. Unknown Renaissance Portraits. Phaidon, 1952. 66 plts. Dj (chipped). *Edwards*. $31/£20

GOLDSMID, EDMUND. Bibliotheca Curiosa. A Complete Catalogue of All the Publications of the Elzevir Presses. Hildesheim: George Olms Verlag, 1976. Rprnt of orig. 3 vols in 1. Gold cl. Good. *Karmiole*. $50/£32

GOLDSMITH, MIDDLETON. A Report on Hospital Gangrene.... Louisville, 1863. 1st ed. 94pp; lg fldg table. (Ex-lib; rebacked.) *Argosy*. $450/£290

GOLDSMITH, OLIVER. The Collected Letters of Oliver Goldsmith. Katherine Balderston (ed). London: CUP, 1928. 1st ed. Uncut. Cl spine, gilt, marbled bds. Nice. *Hartfield*. $185/£119

GOLDSMITH, OLIVER. The Deserted Village. London: W. Griffin, 1770. 1st ed. 4to. 1/2 title, 23pp. Full reddish brn morocco (rebound), gilt fillets, raised bands, morocco spine label. Very Nice. *Chapel Hill*. $1,200/£774

GOLDSMITH, OLIVER. Essays by Mr. Goldsmith. Ptd by W. Griffin, 1765. 1st ed. Engr tp (lt spotted, ink sig); vii,236pp; ad leaf, final blank leaf. Orig calf. VG (sm chip spine top; upper joint starting to crack). *Bickersteth*. $225/£145

GOLDSMITH, OLIVER. Essays. London: for W. Griffin, 1765. 1st ed. 12mo. Engr t.p., 236pp,(2)pp ads. Contemp full calf w/raised bands. VG (bumped, joints sl worn; inscrips). *Chapel Hill.* $600/£387

GOLDSMITH, OLIVER. An History of the Earth and Animated Nature. London: J. Nourse, 1779. 2nd ed. 8 vols. Full tree calf, gilt, 7 (of 16) labels. (Marginal browning feps, ex-libris; vol 4 spine chipped; rubbing; joints tender, splitting.) *Edwards.* $217/£140

GOLDSMITH, OLIVER. The Poetical and Dramatic Works.... Ptd by H. Goldney for Messrs Rivington, 1780. 2 vols. Port. New 1/2 calf antique. False catchword to Plays at p106 Vol I. Good (sm blindstamps on titles; brown spotting). *Hill.* $132/£85

GOLDSMITH, OLIVER. The Poetical Works with a Memoir by William Spalding. London: Charles Griffen, 1866. 2nd issue. (vi),152pp + 4pp list; port; 12 steel-engr illus; 6 woodcuts; aeg. Dk red cl, gilt. VG. *Cox.* $31/£20

GOLDSMITH, OLIVER. The Poetical Works. London: William Pickering, 1853. Port. VG in lighter fine diaper cl; paper label (sl rubbed). *Cox.* $31/£20

GOLDSMITH, OLIVER. She Stoops to Conquer. NY: Hodder & Stoughton, (1912). 1st Amer ed. Thick, 4to. 25 mtd color plts by Hugh Thomson. Grey-grn cl, gilt. Good. *Reisler.* $150/£97

GOLDSMITH, OLIVER. The Vicar of Wakefield. London: Harrap, (1929). 1st ed. 4to. 12 color plts by Arthur Rackham. Teg; few pgs uncut. Pub's binding: brn leather w/gold lettering, outline of bk illus. *Reisler.* $675/£435

GOLDSMITH, OLIVER. The Vicar of Wakefield. London: R. Ackerman, 1823. 2nd issue. 8,254pp. Thomas Rowlandson (illus). Full red morocco, gilt; aeg. Fine in felt-lined red slipcase. *Schoyer.* $700/£452

GOLDSMITH, OLIVER. The Vicar of Wakefield. London: Sampson Low, 1855. 1st ed w/these illus. viii,219pp, 40 vignette wood engrs by George Thomas. Orange cl w/gilt/blind design (backstrip sl faded; sl rubbed, soiled). Lt spotted, but Good. *Cox.* $54/£35

GOLDSMITH, OLIVER. The Vicar of Wakefield. London, 1875. 1st ed w/these illus. 12 engrs w/guards by Sangster. Orig dec cl. VG. *Argosy.* $100/£65

GOLDSMITH, OLIVER. The Vicar of Wakefield. London: John C. Nimmo, 1886. xvi,291pp. V.A. Poirson (illus). Pict cl, beveled edges. *Schoyer.* $75/£48

GOLDSMITH, OLIVER. The Vicar of Wakefield. (London/Boston): Constable/Houghton Mifflin, 1926. 1st ed. 24 color plts. Engr bkpl; spine, edges sl faded, else Fine. *Pharos.* $45/£29

GOLDSMITH, OLIVER. The Vicar of Wakefield. London: George C. Harrap, 1929. 1st ed. 12 color plts by Arthur Rackham. Teg, rest uncut; dec eps. Blue cl, gilt. VG. *Cox.* $147/£95

GOLDSTEIN, SIDNEY M. Pre-Roman and Early Roman Glass in the Corning Museum of Glass. Corning: Corning Museum of Glass, 1979. 42 plts. Fine in dj. *Archaeologia.* $150/£97

GOLDWATER, BARRY M. A Journey Down the Green and Colorado Rivers. (Phoenix: H. Walker), 1940. Ltd to 300 numbered, signed. Map. Blue pebbled calf over marbled bds, gilt. Good. *Karmiole.* $125/£81

GOLDWATER, ROBERT. Paul Gauguin. London: Thames & Hudson, n.d. 48 tipped-in full-pg illus. Tan cl bds, gilt title. Fine in dj. *Heller.* $75/£48

GOMERSALL, WILLIAM. Hunting in Craven. Skipton: 'Craven Herald' Office, 1889. 69pp. Dec head, tail pieces. VG. *Hollett.* $70/£45

Good Child or Sweet Home. London: Dean and Munday, (ca 1830). Toybook. 24mo. 14 hand-colored engrs. Engr paper wrappers. Sm fold corner several pgs; o/w Nice. *Reisler.* $350/£226

GOOD, ROBERT (ed). The Thymus in Immunobiology. NY, 1964. 1st ed. (Ex-lib.) *Fye.* $75/£48

GOOD, THOMAS. The True Principles of Scientific Cutting Defined and Illustrated.... London: for the author, 1842-3. 1st ed. 4to. 177,32pp. Appendix, engr frontis, lg fldg plt, 26 engr plts. 1/4 roan (spine, edges worn). *Marlborough.* $744/£480

GOODALL, JOHN S. Paddy Finds a Job. London: Macmillan Children's, 1981. 19x15 cm. 6 dbl-pg pop-ups. Glazed pict bds. VG. *Book Finders.* $45/£29

GOODALL, JOHN S. Shrewbettina Goes to Work. NY: Atheneum, 1981. 19x15 cm. 6 pop-ups, pull-tabs. Glazed pict bds. VG. *Book Finders.* $25/£16

GOODCHILD, GEORGE. McLean Solves It. London: Rich & Cowan, 1956. 1st ed. VG in Fine dj. *Ming.* $47/£30

GOODE, GEORGE BROWN. The Fisheries and Fishery Industries of the United States.... Washington: GPO, 1884-87. 1st ed. 5 sections in 7 vols. xxxiv,895pp,xxpp, 291 plts; (x),(3)-787pp; xviii,(5)-238pp, 18 charts, 31 fldg tables, 4 plts; 178pp, 19 plts; xxii,808; xx,881pp; xvipp, 255 plts. VG set (1 plt loose; 1 vol ex-lib; sl worn). *Lefkowicz.* $800/£516

GOODE, JOHN. Recollections of a Lifetime. NY: Neale, 1906. Port. *Schoyer.* $60/£39

GOODE, JOHN. Recollections of a Lifetime. NY/Washington: Neale, 1906. 1st ed. Frontis port. Orig gray buckram. Bkpl, blindstamp; cvrs soiled. *Chapel Hill.* $75/£48

GOODE, WILLIAM H. Outposts of Zion. Cincinnati, 1864. 464pp. Howes G 236. *Ginsberg.* $150/£97

GOODEN, ARTHUR HENRY. The Long Trail. NY: Dutton, 1952. 1st Amer ed. Fine (sl wrinkle fr pastedown) in Fine dj (short tear rear panel). *Between The Covers.* $75/£48

GOODEY, JOHN. A Thrill a Minute with Jack Albany. Simon, 1967. 1st ed. Rev copy. Top pg edges lt soiled, else Fine in bright dj (lt soiled). *Murder.* $75/£48

GOODIS, DAVID. Nightfall. NY: Julian Messner, 1947. 1st ed. Sig; dampstain upper portion rear bd, else VG+ in VG dj. *Lame Duck.* $650/£419

GOODIS, DAVID. Of Missing Persons. NY: Morrow, 1950. 1st ed. NF in dj. *Else Fine.* $285/£184

GOODIS, DAVID. Of Missing Persons. NY: Morrow, 1950. 1st ed. NF in VG dj (spine faded; sm chip, hairline crease top edge fr panel; spots of loss fr panel along spine fold). *Lame Duck.* $550/£355

GOODIS, DAVID. Of Tender Sin. NY: Fawcett, 1952. 1st ed. Pb orig. Unread. VF in wraps. *Else Fine.* $125/£81

GOODISON, NICHOLS. English Barometers 1680-1860. London, 1969. 1st UK ed. Dj (sl torn, sl loss). *Edwards.* $54/£35

GOODLAND, R. A Bibliography of Sex Rites and Customs. Routledge, 1931. Good. *Moss.* $140/£90

GOODMAN, PAUL. The Copernican Revolution. (Saugatuck: 5X8 Press, 1947.) Expanded ed. NF in ptd wraps. *Antic Hay.* $25/£16

GOODMAN, PAUL. Hawkweed. NY: Random House, (1967). 1st ed. Fine in NF dj. *Sadlon.* $25/£16

GOODNOW, MINNIE. First-Year Nursing: A Text-Book for Pupils During Their First Year of Hospital Work. Phila, 1912. 1st ed. Good. *Fye.* $100/£65

GOODRICH, CALVIN. The First Michigan Frontier. Univ of MI, 1940. 1st ed. Ep maps. Fine in VG dj. *Oregon.* $45/£29

GOODRICH, CARTER. The Miner's Freedom. Boston: Marshall Jones, 1925. 4 plts. VG in dj. *Schoyer.* $30/£19

GOODRICH, CHARLES A. The Child's History of the United States. Phila: Thomas, Cowperthwait, 1843. 12mo. vi+150pp, 23 half-pg wood engrs. Black cl on bds, black roan spine w/gilt title. Good (lacks frontis, back ep; dated ink sig feps; lt foxing; edges rubbed; spine chipped). *Hobbyhorse.* $125/£81

GOODRICH, LLOYD. Edward Hopper. NY: Abrams, (1978). 1st Amer ed. Fine in dj (sm scratch). *Between The Covers.* $450/£290

GOODRICH, LLOYD. Winslow Homer. NY: Macmillan, 1944. 1st ed. 63 photo plts. Blue cl, gilt spine. Good in dj (chipped). *Karmiole.* $50/£32

GOODRICH, LLOYD. Winslow Homer. NY: Macmillan, 1944. 1st ed. 63 plts. Eps stained, else VG. *Cahan.* $50/£32

GOODRICH, S.G. Peter Parley's Geography for Beginners. NY: Huntington and Savage, 1849. Stereotyped ed. Full-pg engr frontis, 160pp + 1pg ad lower cvr. Pict paper on bds, black leather spine. Internally Fine (edges rubbed, chipped, soiled; pencil dedication fep; sm chip spine). VG. *Hobbyhorse.* $200/£129

GOODRICH-FREER, A. In a Syrian Saddle. London: Methuen, 1905. 1st ed. Edges rubbed; few leaves affected by dampness (marginally); sl tears to spine, o/w Good. *Worldwide.* $45/£29

GOODSPEED, CHARLES ELIOT. Angling in America. Boston: Houghton Mifflin, 1939. One of 750 numbered, signed. VF in orig glassine, VG+ slipcase. *Bowman.* $400/£258

GOODWIN, C.C. The Wedge of Gold. Salt Lake City: Tribune Job Ptg Co, 1893. 1st ed. Gilt blue cl. NF. *Reese.* $75/£48

GOODWIN, GORDON. British Mezzotinters: Thomas Watson, James Watson, Elizabeth Judkins. London, 1904. #359/520. Frontis port, 5 plts. Teg, rest uncut. (Spine lt faded.) *Edwards.* $70/£45

GOODWIN, GORDON. British Mezzotinters: Thomas Watson, James Watson, Elizabeth Judkins. London: Bullen, 1904. 1st ed. #253/520. 6 plts. (Ex-lib; outer hinges worn), bds still attached. *Bookpress.* $85/£55

GOODWIN, LUCY BERKLEY. From My Kitchen Window. NY: Wendell Malliet, 1942. 1st trade ed. VG in dj (worn, heavily chipped). *Godot.* $85/£55

GOODWIN, MAUD WILDER. Dolly Madison. NY: Scribner's, 1896. 1st ed. xiv,287,4pp. NF. *Mcgowan.* $45/£29

GOODWIN, THOMAS SHEPHARD. The Natural History of Secession. NY, 1864. 1st ed. 328pp. Lt worn, spine faded, o/w VG. *Pratt.* $50/£32

GOODWYN, FRANK. Life on the King Ranch. NY: Thomas Crowell, 1951. 1st ed. VG+ (owner label). *Parker.* $35/£23

Goody Two Shoes. NY: McLoughlin Bros, 1898. Cock Robin Series. 4to. 6 leaves; 1st, last text pp ptd on wrappers; 6 VF full-pg color chromolithos. Pict stiff paper wrappers (spine lt chipped). Fine. *Hobbyhorse.* $225/£145

Goody Two-Shoes. London: Griffith & Farran, 1881. Vellum-backed paper over bds (spine rubbed, soiled; spine label rubbed; endleaves browned). Contents Fine. *Glenn.* $70/£45

GOODYEAR, W.A. The Coal Mines of the Western Coast of the United States. SF: A.L. Bancroft, 1877. (1st ed). 4,(2),5-153pp. Grn cl, gilt title. VG (extrems rubbed). *Bohling.* $125/£81

GOOKIN, WARNER FOOTE. Capawack, Alias Martha's Vineyard. Edgartown: Dukes Co. Hist Soc, 1947. 1st ed. Gilt-titled cl. Promo announcement laid in. NF. *Cahan.* $35/£23

GORDIMER, NADINE. The Conservationist. London: Cape, (1974). 1st UK ed. Fine in dj. *Hermitage.* $65/£42

GORDIMER, NADINE. July's People. Taurus: Ravan Press, (1981). 1st South African ed. Fine in dj. *Hermitage.* $40/£26

GORDIMER, NADINE. Livingstone's Companions. London: Cape, 1971. 1st ed. Fine in dj. *Rees.* $19/£12

GORDIMER, NADINE. Six Feet of the Country. NY: S&S, 1956. 1st US ed. Fine in dj (price-clipped). *Cahan.* $65/£42

GORDIMER, NADINE. The Soft Voice of the Serpent and Other Stories. NY, 1952. 1st Amer ed. Fine in dj (sl sunned, sl torn, chipped). *Polyanthos.* $60/£39

GORDIMER, NADINE. Something Out There. NY: Viking, 1984. 1st US ed. Signed. Fine in dj. *Lame Duck.* $65/£42

GORDIMER, NADINE. A World of Strangers. London: Gollancz, 1958. 1st UK ed. Fine in dj (lt chipped; dknd; stain). *Hermitage.* $45/£29

GORDON, ARMISTEAD C. For Truth and Freedom: Poems of Commemoration. Neale, 1910. 1st ed. Pict cl (soiled; tear pg13/24). Good. *Book Broker.* $65/£42

GORDON, ARMISTEAD C. Jefferson Davis. Scribner's, 1918. (1st ed). Inscribed. VG *Book Broker.* $75/£48

GORDON, ARMISTEAD C. Memories and Memorials of William Gordon McCabe. Richmond, VA: Old Dominion, 1925. 1st ed. 2 vols. Sl wear spine ends, corners; else VG set. *Mcgowan.* $150/£97

GORDON, ARMISTEAD C. The Red Hills of the Piedmont. N.p., ca 1910. 1st ed. Orig self-wraps creased where folded, else VG. *Mcgowan.* $28/£18

GORDON, BENJAMIN LEE. Medicine Throughout Antiquity. Phila: Davis, 1949. Lt dampstaining lower blank margins, o/w Good. *Goodrich.* $95/£61

GORDON, CAROLINE. Aleck Maury, Sportsman. NY: Scribner, 1934. 1st ed, 1st issue binding. 8vo. Orig grn cl (spine, edges faded). VG (sig fr pastedown) in Nice pict dj (sl edgewear). *Chapel Hill.* $500/£323

GORDON, CAROLINE. The Garden of Adonis. Scribners, 1937. 1st ed. VG in VG dj (lt wear). *Fine Books.* $150/£97

GORDON, CAROLINE. The Garden of Adonis. NY: Scribner's, 1937. 1st ed. VG in dj (sl frayed). *Turlington.* $175/£113

GORDON, CAROLINE. The Glory of Hera. NY: Doubleday, 1972. 1st ed. NF (ink price fep; bottom edge spattered) in dj. *Pharos.* $25/£16

GORDON, CAROLINE. Green Centuries. NY: Scribners, 1941. 1st ed. Fine in dj (internal tape mends). *Pharos.* $85/£55

GORDON, CAROLINE. How to Read a Novel. (NY): Viking, (1957). 1st ed. Fine in dj. *Jaffe.* $100/£65

GORDON, CAROLINE. How to Read a Novel. NY: Viking, 1957. 1st ed. Fine in dj. *Cahan.* $100/£65

GORDON, CAROLINE. The Malefactors. NY: Harcourt, Brace, (1956). 1st ed. NF in dj (lt rubbed). *Hermitage.* $50/£32

GORDON, CAROLINE. The Malefactors. NY: Harcourt Brace, (1956). 1st ed. Fine in dj. *Pharos.* $60/£39

GORDON, CAROLINE. None Shall Look Back. NY: Scribner's, 1937. 1st ed. Fine in VG dj. *Mcgowan.* $85/£55

GORDON, CAROLINE. The Strange Children. NY: Scribner's, 1951. 1st ed. NF in dj (chipped; bkseller label). *Hermitage.* $75/£48

GORDON, CAROLINE. The Strange Children. NY: Scribner's, 1951. 1st ed. Name, date, place on flyleaf, o/w VG+ in dj. *Bernard.* $100/£65

GORDON, CAROLINE. The Woman on the Porch. NY: Scribners, 1944. 1st ed. Fine in dj (sm chip spine). *Pharos.* $95/£61

GORDON, CHARLES ALEXANDER. Life on the Gold Coast. London: Bailliere, Tindall, & Cox, 1874. 1st ed. vi,84,(1)ad,(1)blank,28 pub's list (sl browned). Blue cl (rebacked preserving gilt letterpieces, gilt vignette upper cvr; new eps; sl rubbed, stained; early ink sig on title). *Morrell.* $372/£240

GORDON, DUDLEY. Charles F. Lummis: Crusader in Corduroy. (L.A.): Cultural Arts Press, (1972). 1st ed. Brn fabricoid. Fine in Fine dj. *Harrington.* $30/£19

GORDON, ELIZABETH. The Tale of Johnny Mouse. Joliet: P.F. Volland, (1920). 24th ed. 8vo. Color illus bds. Good in pict pub's box (lt edgewear). *Reisler.* $125/£81

GORDON, GRANVILLE. Sporting Reminiscences. F.G. Aflalo (ed). London, 1902. 1st ed. (Feps lt browned; spine discolored, sl chipped.) *Edwards.* $47/£30

GORDON, HAMPDEN. A Key to Old Houses. London: John Murray, 1955. 1st ed. VG in dj. *Hollett.* $31/£20

GORDON, HAROLD, JR. Hitler and the Beer Hall Putsch. Princeton Press, 1972. 1st ed. NF in VG dj. *Bishop.* $20/£13

GORDON, JAN and CORA. Two Vagabonds in the Balkans. London/NY: Lane/Dodd, Mead, 1927. 1st ed. Signed. 12 plts (3 color). Unopened. Sl rubbed, o/w VG. *Worldwide.* $35/£23

GORDON, JOHN B. Reminiscences of the Civil War. NY, 1903. 1st ed. Pict cl. VG+. *Pratt.* $125/£81

GORDON, JOHN B. Reminiscences of the Civil War. NY, 1904. Lt cvr wear, o/w Fine. *Pratt.* $75/£48

GORDON, JOHN B. Reminiscences of the Civil War. NY: Scribner's, 1904. Memorial ed. Frontis port, 2 ports. Orig blue cl. VG (early inscrip; outer joints sl soiled). *Chapel Hill.* $150/£97

GORDON, JOHN J.H. The Sikhs. London, 1904. 1st ed. Color frontis. (Spine sl chipped, discolored.) *Edwards.* $70/£45

GORDON, MARY. Men and Angels. NY: Random House, 1985. 1st ed. Signed. Fine in Fine dj. *Revere.* $35/£23

GORDON, NELLY KINZIE. The Fort Dearborn Massacre. Rand McNally, (1912). 1st ed. 3 plts, 4 postcards laid in. Fine. *Oregon.* $40/£26

GORDON, R.G. (ed). A Survey of Chronic Rheumatic Diseases Contributed by Contemporary Authorities. London, 1938. 1st ed. Good. *Fye.* $75/£48

GORDON, R.G. and M.F. BROWN. Paralysis in Children. Oxford, 1933. 1st ed. Good. *Fye.* $50/£32

GORDON, ROBERT and ANDREW FORGE. Degas. London: Thames & Hudson. 4 fldg illus. Fine in Mint dj. *Europa.* $47/£30

GORDON, SETON. Amid Snowy Wastes. Cassell, 1922. 1st ed. 2 maps. (Spine faded, tiny split at head.) Good. *Walcot.* $37/£24

GORDON, SETON. The Charm of the Hills. London: Cassell, (1951). 4th ed. 32 plts. *Petersfield.* $22/£14

GORDON, THOMAS F. A Gazetteer of the State of New Jersey.... Trenton, 1834. 1st ed. 2 vols in 1 (foxing vol II). Fldg color map (3-inch tear). Contemp calf, leather label. *Argosy.* $275/£177

GORDON, W.J. Perseus the Gorgon Slayer. London: Sampson Low et al, n.d. (1883). 4to. 16 leaves. Yellow eps, red edges. Pict chromolitho paper on bds, grn cl spine (lt rubbed). Fine. *Hobbyhorse.* $175/£113

GORDON, WELCHE. Jesse James and His Band of Notorious Outlaws. Chicago: Laird & Lee, 1892. Early rpt ed. Dec cl (lt soiled, rubbed). Good (inner hinge cracked; pp browned, chipped). *Glenn.* $65/£42

GORER, EDGAR and J.F. BLACKER. Chinese Porcelain and Hard Stones. London: Bernard Quaritch, 1911. #369/1000. 2 vols. 154 Superb color plts. Teg, rest uncut. (Lt spotting.) Gilt device upper bds (cl lt soiled). *Edwards.* $1,124/£725

GORER, EDGAR and J.F. BLACKER. Chinese Porcelain and Hard Stones. London: Bernard Quaritch, 1911. 1st ed. 2 vols. Cream linen, gilt. Fine (lt foxing, not affecting plts; spines sl dknd; lt wear). *Hermitage.* $800/£516

GOREY, EDWARD. The Blue Aspic. NY: Meredith, 1968. 1st ed. Sm 12mo. Pict paper-cvrd bds. As New in As New dj. *Book Adoption.* $60/£39

GOREY, EDWARD. The Gilded Bat. NY: S&S, (1966). 1st ed. Pict bds. Fine in dj. *Pharos.* $125/£81

GOREY, EDWARD. The Hapless Child. NY: Ivan Obolensky, (1961). 1st ed. Pict wrappers. Sl rubbed, else Fine. *Pharos.* $45/£29

GOREY, EDWARD. Les Echanges Malandreux. (Worcester, MA: Metacom Press, 1985). 1st ed, #344/500 numbered, signed. 32 dwgs. Fine in dbl-stitched ochre fldg wrappers w/pict upper cvr. *Houle.* $75/£48

GOREY, EDWARD. The Prune People. NY: Albondocani, 1983. One of 400 numbered, signed. Fine in sewn illus wrappers. *Dermont.* $35/£23

GOREY, EDWARD. The Unstrung Harp: Or, Mr. Earbrass Writes a Novel. NY/Boston: Duell, Sloan, & Pearce/Little, Brown, (1953). 1st ed, 1st bk. 30 b/w illus. Fine in dj. *Houle.* $225/£145

GOREY, EDWARD. The Willowdale Handcar. NY: Bobbs-Merrill, (1962). 1st ed. Sl soiled, else NF in wrappers. *Pharos.* $40/£26

GORKY, MAXIM. The Judge. McBride, 1924. 1st ed. Rubbing, else VG+ in dj (lt chipping). *Fine Books.* $30/£19

GORKY, MAXIM. Reminiscences of Leo Nikolaevich Tolstoy. S.S. Koteliansky & Leonard Woolf (trans). NY: B.W. Heubsch, 1920. 1st Amer ed. Bkpl; corners worn, else VG. *Chapel Hill.* $50/£32

GORKY, MAXIM. Reminiscences of Leonid Andreyev. Katherine Mansfield & S.S. Koteliansky (trans). NY: Crosby Gaige, 1928. 1st ed. One of 400. Uncut, unopened. Very Nice (bds sl faded, nicked). *Second Life.* $45/£29

GORKY, MAXIM. Reminiscences of Leonid Andreyev. Katherine Mansfield & S.S. Koteliansky (trans). NY: Crosby Gaige, 1928. Ltd to 400. Corners rubbed, lt spots. Issued w/o dj. *Sadlon.* $35/£23

GORMAN, ED and MARTIN H. GREENGERG (eds). Stalkers. Arlington Hgts: Dark Harvest, 1989. 1st ed, one of 750 numbered, signed by all 20 contributors. Fine in dj, slipcase. *Other Worlds.* $100/£65

GORMAN, HARRY M. My Memories of the Comstock. L.A.: Suttonhouse, (1939). 1st ed. Ink name, else VG in dj (edgeworn). *Perier.* $85/£55

GORMAN, HERBERT S. James Joyce. NY: Farrar, (1939). 1st ed. Port. Dated sig, else Nice in dj (lt chipped). *Reese.* $55/£35

GORMAN, HERBERT S. James Joyce. His First Forty Years. NY: B.W. Huebsch, 1924. 1st ed. Navy blue cl. NF. *Glenn.* $75/£48

GORMAN, HERBERT S. James Joyce: His First Forty Years. NY: Huebsch, 1924. 1st ed. Port. Fine in Good dj (sm chips, creases, old sm internal mends, price blocked out). *Reese.* $175/£113

GORMAN, JOHN A. The Western Horse. Danville, IL: Interstate, 1939. 1st ed, 1st ptg. Brn pict cl. Fine. *Glenn.* $40/£26

GORMAN, JOHN A. The Western Horse. Danville: Interstate, 1944. 1st ed. VG-. *Parker.* $55/£35

GOSLING, PAULA. Loser's Blues. London: Macmillan, 1980. 1st ed. NF in NF dj. *Ming.* $62/£40

GOSLING, PAULA. The Woman in Red. London: Macmillan, 1983. 1st ed. NF in NF dj. *Ming.* $47/£30

GOSLING, PAULA. The Wychford Murders. London: Macmillan, 1986. 1st ed. VF in dj. *Mordida.* $40/£26

GOSS, CLAY. Homecookin'. Washington: Howard Univ, 1974. 1st ed. Fine in dj. *Godot.* $45/£29

GOSS, HELEN ROCCA. The Life and Death of a Quicksilver Mine. L.A.: Hist Soc of Southern CA, 1958. 1st ed. Silver-dec red cl. Fine in Fine dj. *Harrington.* $50/£32

GOSSE, EDMUND. A Critical Essay on the Life and Works of George Tinworth. London: Fine Art Soc, 1883. Half-title, frontis, engr title, 5-82pp, 30 photogravure plts. Art vellum gilt, teg. *Marlborough.* $543/£350

GOSSE, EDMUND. Gossip in a Library. London: Heinemann, 1892. One of 100 numbered, signed. Port. Cl, dec bds. Good (bkpl; edgeworn; corners bruised; lt foxing). *Reese.* $35/£23

GOSSE, EDMUND. Silhouettes. London: Heinemann, 1925. 1st ed. Frontis port. Brn cl, gilt; uncut. VG in acetate dj. *Hartfield.* $65/£42

GOSSE, PHILIP HENRY. Evenings at the Microscope. London: SPCK, 1859. 506pp. Good in gilt illus purple cl (fr bd, fep moisture-stained; worn). *Knollwood.* $85/£55

GOSSE, PHILIP HENRY. A Naturalist's Rambles on the Devonshire Coast. London, 1853. xvi,451pp; 12 color, 16 plain plts (sl foxing). 1/2 calf gilt (rebacked). *Henly.* $105/£68

GOSSE, PHILIP HENRY. A Naturalist's Sojourn in Jamaica. London: Longman, 1851. 1st ed. 508pp, 8 full-pg litho plts; marbled eps. 1/2 leather. NF. *Mikesh.* $150/£97

GOSSE, PHILIP HENRY. A Text-Book of Zoology, for Schools. London: SPCK, 1851. 1st ed. (ii),450pp. Orig cl (backstrip sl worn); new fep inserted. *Cox.* $47/£30

GOSSE, PHILIP HENRY. A Year at the Shore. London, 1865. 1st ed. xii,330,2pp; 36 color plts. (Ends sl foxed.) *Henly.* $112/£72

GOSSE, PHILIP HENRY. A Year at the Shore. London, 1870. 36 color plts (frontis sl spotted). *Petersfield.* $50/£32

GOSSE, PHILIP. Dr. Viper: The Querulous Life of Philip Thicknesse. London: Cassell & Co, 1952. Fr hinge cracked; in dj (chipped). *Schoyer.* $20/£13

GOSSE, PHILIP. The Squire of Walton Hall. London: Cassell, 1940. 1st ed. Frontis; 9 plts, map. Gilt cl. (Edges, flyleaves lt spotted.) Dj (spine sl spotted). *Hollett.* $39/£25

GOTCH, J. ALFRED. Early Renaissance Architecture in England. London: Batsford, 1901. 1st ed. Frontis; 87 plts. Teg. (Ink inscrip; fr hinge internally cracked; lt foxing; cvr sl worn.) *Bookpress.* $110/£71

GOTCH, J. ALFRED. The English Home from Charles I to George IV. Batsford, 1919. 2nd imp w/corrections. Dec gilt cl (spine faded, sl rubbed; sl foxing). *Edwards.* $37/£24

GOTCH, J. ALFRED. The Growth of the English House. London: Batsford, 1928. 2nd ed, rev, enlgd. 94 plts. (Sl soiled, spine lt faded.) *Edwards.* $39/£25

GOTCH, J. ALFRED. Squires' Homes and Other Old Buildings of Northamptonshire. London: Batsford, 1939. 1st ed. Frontis. (Eps lt spotted; spine faded.) *Edwards.* $70/£45

GOTHEIN, MARIE LUISE. A History of Garden Art. London: J.M. Dent, 1928. 1st ed. 2 vols. 4to. Nice set (soiling). *Bookpress.* $550/£355

GOTTFREDSON, PETER. History of Indian Depredations in Utah. Salt Lake, 1919. 1st ed. Overall sound (ex-lib, fr hinge cracked, pg torn but complete). *Benchmark.* $75/£48

GOTTFRIED, MARTIN. Broadway Musicals. NY: Abrams, 1979. VG in dj. *Argosy.* $100/£65

GOTTSCHALK, LOUIS. Lafayette and the Close of the American Revolution. Chicago: Univ of Chicago Press, (1942). 1st ed. 2 fldg facs. Blue cl. VG. *Chapel Hill.* $50/£32

GOTTSCHALK, LOUIS. Lafayette Joins the American Army. Chicago: Univ of Chicago Press, (1938). 1st ed. Blue cl. NF in VG dj (price-clipped, 3-inch closed tear). *Chapel Hill.* $65/£42

GOUDEKET, MAURICE. Close to Colette. NY: Farrar, Straus & Cudahy, 1957. 1st ed. VG in dj (browned, sl worn). *Second Life.* $25/£16

GOUDEY, C.J. Maidenhair Ferns in Cultivation. Melbourne, 1985. Frontis. Dj. *Sutton.* $59/£38

GOUDGE, ELIZABETH. The Dean's Watch. London: Hodder, 1960. 1st UK ed. VG in dj (price-clipped). *Williams.* $28/£18

GOUDGE, ELIZABETH. The Little White Horse. NY: Coward-McCann, (1947). 1st Amer ed. 8vo. 280pp; 25 line dwgs. Blue cl; silver design, lettering; map eps. VG in Good+ dj (spine ends lack pieces). *Drusilla's.* $40/£26

GOUDY, FREDERIC W. The Story of the Village Type. NY: The Press of the Wooly Whale, 1933. One of 450 on handmade paper. Prospectus. Linen-backed bds. Fine. *Veatchs.* $100/£65

GOUGH, JOHN. An Autobiography. Boston: By the Author, 1845. 1st ed. 172pp + ads. (Sm holes upper joints.) *Hayman.* $75/£48

GOUGH, JOHN. A History of the People Called Quakers. Dublin: For Robert Jackson, 1789-90. 4 vols. Full speckled calf (extrems, spine sl rubbed, chipped); gilt bands, leather labels. (Upper joint sl tender vols 1, 3; corner gilt worn.) *Edwards.* $194/£125

GOUGH, JOHN. Sunlight and Shadow. Hartford, 1881. 542pp. Gilt-stamped 1/2 leather. Fine. *Artis.* $25/£16

GOUGH, KATHLEEN. A Garden Book for Malaya. London: Witherby, 1928. Frontis, 15 b/w plts. Gilt-stamped pict cvr, spine. VG. *Quest.* $35/£23

GOUGH, MARY. Travel into Yesterday. GC: Doubleday, 1954. 1st ed. 12 plts. NF in dj. *Worldwide.* $25/£16

GOULARD, MR. A Treatise on the Effects and Various Preparations of Lead.... London, 1769. 1st Eng ed. Tp,(ii),(xi),222pp + 1pg ads; gilt edges (sl rubbed). Full speckled calf, raised bands, morocco title label. *Edwards.* $194/£125

GOULBURN, EDWARD MEYRICK and HENRY SYMONDS. The Ancient Sculptures in the Roof of Norwich Cathedral. London/Norwich, 1876. xxxiii,589pp,(i)errata leaf, 60 plts (44 autotypes, 6 lithos, incl 1 color). (Sl offsetting, foxing.) Morocco-backed cl, gilt illus (extrems rubbed; sl cl loss corners; lower bd sl dampstained, upper bd gilt loss). *Edwards.* $186/£120

GOULD, A.A. Report on the Invertebrata of Massachusetts. W.G. Binney (ed). Boston, 1870. 2nd ed. viii,524pp; 12 plts (11 colored). (Cl sl loose; spine sl defective.) *Wheldon & Wesley.* $132/£85

GOULD, ARTHUR LEE. An Airplane in the Arabian Nights. London, 1947. 1st ed. Fine in dj. *Madle.* $35/£23

GOULD, CECIL. The Paintings of Correggio. Ithaca, 1976. 204 plts, 10 color. Good. *Washton.* $90/£58

GOULD, CECIL. The Paintings of Correggio. London: Faber, 1976. 12 color plts. VF in Mint dj. *Europa.* $116/£75

GOULD, CHARLES N. Covered Wagon Geologist. Norman: Univ of OK, 1959. 1st ed. VG in dj. *Burcham.* $25/£16

GOULD, CHESTER. Dick Tracy: The Capture of Boris Arson. Chicago: Pleasure Books, (1935). Square 4to. 3 Fine pop-ups. Full color bds. Very Nice. *Reisler.* $490/£316

GOULD, CHESTER. The Pop-Up Dick Tracy. 'Capture of Boris Arson.' Chicago: Pleasure Books, 1935. 20x23cm. 3 bright dbl-pg pop-ups. Pict bds (lt wear; pg edges sl browned). *Book Finders.* $250/£161

GOULD, E.P. Anne Gilchrist and Walt Whitman. Phila: David McKay, (1900). 1st ed. Teg, uncut. Grn cl, gilt. Fine. *Macdonnell.* $65/£42

GOULD, E.W. Fifty Years on the Mississippi. St. Louis: Nixon-Jones Ptg Co, 1889. 1st ed. Frontis port, xv,749pp + errata leaf. Gilt-stamped maroon cl. VG (lt wear; leaf stain; gilt absent 1 letter fr cvr). Howes G 273. *Bohling.* $350/£226

GOULD, GEORGE and WALTER PYLE. Anomalies and Curiosities of Medicine. NY, 1956. Facs copy of 1896 ed. Good. *Goodrich.* $45/£29

GOULD, GERALD. Lady Adela. London: Cecil Palmer, 1920. 1st ed. Spine, cvrs sl rubbed, soiled, else VG. *Pharos.* $30/£19

GOULD, LAURENCE M. Cold—The Record of an Antarctic Sledge Journey. NY: Brewer et al, 1931. Inscribed. 2 maps. Blue cl over bds. Spotting, wear to cvrs, else VG. *Parmer.* $55/£35

GOULD, LAURENCE M. Cold. NY: Brewer, Warren & Putnam, 1931. 1st ed. VG. *Walcot.* $37/£24

GOULD, LUCIUS D. The New Carpenter's and Builder's Assistant.... NY: 1879. Rev, enlgd. 73pp; 27 plts. (Few nicks.) *Petrilla.* $30/£19

GOULD, ROBERT F. Gould's History of Freemasonry Throughout the World. NY: Scribner's, (1936). 6 vols. VG + set. *Blue Dragon.* $150/£97

GOULD, RUPERT T. The Marine Chronometer: Its History and Development. London: J.D. Potter, 1923. 1st ed. Good (damp damage cvrs). George W. Mixter's bkpl. *Lefkowicz.* $100/£65

GOULD, STEPHEN JAY. Ever Since Darwin. NY: Norton, 1977. 1st ed. NF in dj (price-clipped). *Lame Duck.* $65/£42

GOULD, STEPHEN JAY. The Flamingo's Smile. NY: W.W. Norton, (1985). 1st ed. Maroon cl-backed cream bds. Very Nice in dj. *Cady.* $20/£13

GOULD, STEPHEN JAY. Hen's Teeth and Horse's Toes. NY: W.W. Norton, (1983). 1st ed. Gilt-titled grn 1/2 cl, cream paper bds. Very Nice in dj. *Cady.* $20/£13

GOULD, STEPHEN JAY. The Mismeasure of Man. NY: W.W. Norton, (1981). 1st ed. 1/2 red cl, gray paperbd sides, gilt-titled. Very Nice in dj. *Cady.* $25/£16

GOULDEN, SHIRLEY. Tales from Japan. London: W.H. Allen, 1961. 64pp. Pict bds (rebacked; worn, soiled). *Hollett.* $101/£65

GOULDSBURY, C.E. Tigerland. London: Chapman Hall, 1913. 1st ed. Gilt pict grn cl. Hinges strengthened, o/w VG + . *Bowman.* $75/£48

GOULDSBURY, E. Life in the Indian Police. London, 1912. Gilt cl (lt spotted). VG. *Trophy Room.* $150/£97

GOURLEY, J.H. Text-Book of Pomology. L.H. Bailey (ed). NY, 1923. 1st ed. 8 plts. (Name inked out; pp yellowed; inch split lower spine.) *Sutton.* $40/£26

GOVAN, GILBERT E. The Chattanooga Country 1540-1951. E.P. Dutton, 1952. 1st ed. VG. *Bishop.* $17/£11

GOVAN, GILBERT E. and JAMES W. LIVINGOOD. A Different Valor, The Story of General Joseph E. Johnson, C.S.A. Indianapolis, (1956). Signed by both. Fine in dj (sl wear). *Pratt.* $70/£45

GOVE, JESSE A. The Utah Expedition 1857-1858. Letters.... Concord, 1928. 1st ed. VG. *Benchmark.* $100/£65

GOVE, JESSE A. The Utah Expedition, 1857-1858. Otis G. Hammond (ed). Concord, 1928. 1st ed. Howes G 279. *Ginsberg.* $125/£81

GOVER, ROBERT. The Maniac Responsible. NY: Grove, (1963). 1st ed. Fine in dj (lt soiled, worn). *Hermitage.* $45/£29

GOVER, ROBERT. The One Hundred Dollar Misunderstanding. NY: Grove Press, 1962. 1st ed. VG in VG dj. *Revere.* $35/£23

Governess; or the Little Female Academy. (By Sarah Fielding.) London: J.F. & C. Rivington et al, 1789. 7th ed. 12mo. x,146pp. Linen on bds. VG (ink sig inside upper wrapper, pencil mks eps; shelfwear). *Hobbyhorse.* $300/£194

GOWANS, FRED R. Rocky Mountain Rendezvous...1825-1840. Provo: Brigham Young Univ, (1976). 1st ed. Stated first ptg but also done in hb. Fldg map. VG in wraps. *Oregon.* $40/£26

GOWANS, FRED R. Rocky Mountain Rendezvous: A History of the Fur Trade Rendezvous, 1825-1840. (Provo: Brigham Young Univ Pub, 1976). 1st ed. Apparently ltd to 2000. Fldg map. VG in tan pict wrappers (sl rubbed, worn). *Harrington.* $30/£19

GOWER, R.S. George Romney. London: Duckworth, 1904. 73 1/2-tone plts, 16 photogravure plts w/tissues. Teg. (Sm spine tear.) *Ars Artis.* $116/£75

GOWER, R.S. Sir Thomas Lawrence. Paris: Goupil, 1900. One of 600 of ordinary ed. 60 plts (incl color frontis). (Waterstain lower blank margin first 14ff.) *Ars Artis.* $132/£85

GOWERS, WILLIAM RICHARD. Diagnosis of Diseases of the Brain and of the Spinal Cord. NY: William Wood, 1885. viii,293pp + 6pp ads. VG (underlining). *Goodrich.* $250/£161

GOWERS, WILLIAM RICHARD. Diagnosis of Diseases of the Brain and Spinal Cord. NY, 1885. 1st Amer ed. 293pp. Good. *Fye.* $175/£113

GOWERS, WILLIAM RICHARD. Epilepsy and Other Chronic Convulsive Diseases. NY, 1885. 1st Amer ed. 255pp. Good. *Fye.* $175/£113

GOWERS, WILLIAM RICHARD. Epilepsy and Other Chronic Convulsive Diseases. London, 1901. 2nd ed. Good. *Fye.* $125/£81

GOWERS, WILLIAM RICHARD. Lectures on the Diagnosis of Diseases of the Brain. London, 1885. Nice (cl lt blistered, worn, rubbed). *Goodrich.* $395/£255

GOWIN, EMMET. Emmet Gowin: Photographs. NY: Knopf, A Light Gallery Book, 1976. 1st ed. Fine in illus wrappers. *Cahan.* $100/£65

GOWING, LAWRENCE and SAM HUNTER. Francis Bacon. (NY, 1989.) 10 fldg illus. VG in dj. *Argosy.* $65/£42

GOWING, LAWRENCE. Vermeer. London: Faber, 1952. 1st ed. Color frontis tipped in, 79 plts, 3 tipped-in color plts. Dj torn, o/w VF. *Europa.* $37/£24

GOWING, T. A Soldier's Experience.... Nottingham, 1906. Aeg. Gilt dec cl (extrems worn; name; plt detached). *King.* $50/£32

GOYEN, WILLIAM. Arcadio. Potter, 1983. 1st ed. Fine in dj. *Stahr.* $25/£16

GOYEN, WILLIAM. The House of Breath. London: C&W, 1951. 1st Eng ed. Fine in dj. *Limestone.* $120/£77

GOYEN, WILLIAM. The House of Breath. NY, 1975. 25th anniversary ed. Signed. Inscrip, o/w Fine in dj. *Polyanthos.* $45/£29

GOYEN, WILLIAM. The Restorer. Doubleday, 1974. 1st ed. Fine in dj (price-clipped; lt rubbed). *Stahr.* $25/£16

GOYEN, WILLIAM. While You Were Away. (Houston: Houston Pub Lib, 1978). 1st ed. Sl creasing; wraps soiled, else VG. *Turlington.* $50/£32

GOYTISOLO, JUAN. Landscapes After the Battle. Helen Lane (trans). NY: Seaver Books, 1987. 1st Amer ed. Fine in Fine dj. *Revere.* $20/£13

GRABAR, ANDRE. Christian Iconography. A Study of Its Origins. Princeton Univ, 1980. 341 plts. Fine in Mint dj. *Europa.* $47/£30

GRABER, H.W. The Life Record of H.W. Graber.... (Dallas): Privately ptd, 1916. 1st ed. 8vo, frontis port. Orig gilt-tooled 1/2 morocco. Spotted, else VG. Howes G 280. *Chapel Hill.* $1,500/£968

GRABO, CARL H. Peter and The Princess. Chicago: Reilly & Lee, 1920. 1st ed. 4to. 8 full-pg color plts by John R. Neill. Teg. Grn cl, color paste label, gilt. Good. *Reisler.* $250/£161

GRACIAN, BALTASAR. A Truthtelling Manual and the Art of Wordly Wisdom. Martin Fischer (trans). Springfield, IL: Charles C. Thomas, (1942). 1st ed. Mtd frontis. Tan fabricoid stamped in black. Good in dj, slipcase. *Karmiole.* $30/£19

GRAD, BONNIE LEE. Milton Avery. Royal Oak, MI: Strathcona, (1981). 1st ed. Brn buckram. NF in color pict dj. *Blue Mountain.* $200/£129

GRAD, BONNIE LEE. Milton Avery. Royal Oak, MI, 1981. 1st ed. 48 color plts. VG in dj. *Argosy.* $100/£65

GRADLE, H. Bacteria and the Germ Theory of Disease. Chicago, 1883. 1st ed. 219pp. Good. *Fye.* $60/£39

GRADY, JOSEPH F. The Adirondacks, Fulton Chain— Big Moose Region. Little Falls: Privately ptd, 1933. 1st ed. Fine. *Bowman.* $85/£55

GRAEME, BRUCE. Hate Ship. Dodd, 1928. 1st ed. Cvrs spotted, else VG + dj (lt soiled; couple nicks). *Murder.* $35/£23

GRAFTON, SUE. A Is for Alibi. NY: Holt, 1982. 1st ed. Fine (lt scuffed fep) in Fine dj (sl edgewear). *Janus.* $600/£387

GRAFTON, SUE. A Is for Alibi. NY: Holt Rinehart Winston, 1982. 1st ed. Inscribed in year of pub. NF in NF dj. *Pettler.* $750/£484

GRAFTON, SUE. A Is for Alibi. Holt, 1982. 1st ed. Signed. VF in dj. *Murder.* $1,100/£710

GRAFTON, SUE. A Is for Alibi. London: Macmillan, 1986. 1st UK ed. Fine (name) in dj. *Williams.* $233/£150

GRAFTON, SUE. B Is for Burglar. NY: HRW, 1985. 1st ed. VF in dj. *Else Fine.* $600/£387

GRAFTON, SUE. B Is for Burglar. NY: Holt Rinehart Winston, 1985. 1st ed. Inscribed, 1986. Fine in Fine dj. *Pettler.* $550/£355

GRAFTON, SUE. C Is for Corpse. NY: Holt, 1986. 1st ed. Fine (name, date) in Fine dj. *Janus.* $350/£226

GRAFTON, SUE. C Is for Corpse. NY: Henry Holt, 1986. 1st ed. Inscribed in year of pub. Fine in Fine dj. *Pettler.* $350/£226

GRAFTON, SUE. C Is for Corpse. London: Macmillan, 1987. 1st UK ed. Fine in dj. *Williams.* $132/£85

GRAFTON, SUE. D Is for Deadbeat. NY: Henry Holt, 1987. 1st ed. Fine in Fine dj. *Pettler.* $65/£42

GRAFTON, SUE. D Is for Deadbeat. NY: Holt, 1987. 1st ed. Fine in Fine dj. *Janus.* $125/£81

GRAFTON, SUE. D Is for Deadbeat. London: Macmillan, 1987. 1st Eng ed. VF in dj. *Limestone.* $75/£48

GRAFTON, SUE. E Is for Evidence. NY: Holt, 1988. 1st ed. Fine in Fine dj. *Janus.* $100/£65

GRAFTON, SUE. E Is for Evidence. London: Macmillan, 1988. 1st UK ed. Fine in Fine dj. *Ming.* $31/£20

GRAFTON, SUE. E Is for Evidence. London: Macmillan, 1988. 1st UK ed. Fine in dj. *Williams.* $78/£50

GRAFTON, SUE. F Is for Fugitive. NY: Henry Holt, 1989. 1st ed. VF in dj. *Mordida.* $45/£29

GRAFTON, SUE. F Is for Fugitive. London: Macmillan, 1989. 1st UK ed. VF in VF dj. *Ming.* $26/£17

GRAFTON, SUE. F Is for Fugitive. London: Macmillan, 1989. 1st UK ed. NF in dj. *Williams.* $74/£48

GRAFTON, SUE. G Is for Gumshoe. NY: Holt, 1990. 1st ed. Fine in Fine dj. *Beasley.* $40/£26

GRAFTON, SUE. H Is for Homicide. Henry Holt, 1991. 1st ed. Signed. VF in dj. *Stahr.* $45/£29

GRAFTON, SUE. H Is for Homicide. Macmillan, 1991. 1st UK ed. Fine in dj. *Williams.* $16/£10

GRAFTON, SUE. I Is for Innocent. Henry Holt, 1992. 1st ed. Signed, inscribed. VF in dj. *Stahr.* $45/£29

GRAHAM, CAROLINE. Death of a Hollow Man. London: Mysterious/Century, 1989. 1st ed. Fine in dj. *Mordida.* $85/£55

GRAHAM, E. Aunt Liza's 'Praisin' Gate.' McClurg, 1916. 1st ed. Inscribed. Fine in VG + dj. *Fine Books.* $100/£65

GRAHAM, ELEANOR. Henry the Helicopter. Whitman: Racine, 1945. Ben D. Wiliams (illus). 6.5x5.5 inches. Pict bds. Sl worn, else VG in dj (torn, soiled). *King.* $20/£13

GRAHAM, FRANK. The Brooklyn Dodgers. NY, (1947). 5th ptg. VG (bkpl) in VG dj (chipped, worn). *Fuller & Saunders.* $25/£16

GRAHAM, FRANK. The Brooklyn Dodgers. Putnam's, 1945. Ltr ptg. VG in Good+ dj. *Plapinger.* $45/£29

GRAHAM, FRANK. Casey Stengel. John Day, 1958. 1st ed. Fine in VG + dj. *Plapinger.* $30/£19

GRAHAM, FRANK. Lou Gehrig—A Quiet Hero. Putnam's, 1942. Ltr ptg. VG in Good dj. *Plapinger.* $40/£26

GRAHAM, FRANK. McGraw of the Giants. Putnam's, 1944. Ltr ptg. VG in Good dj. *Plapinger.* $30/£19

GRAHAM, FRANK. The New York Yankees. Putnam's, 1943. 1st ed. VG in Good dj. *Plapinger.* $55/£35

GRAHAM, JAMES WALTER. The Palaces of Crete. Princeton Univ, 1962. 1st ed. Dj (spine sl yellowed). *Edwards.* $31/£20

GRAHAM, JERRY BENEDICT. Handset Reminiscences, Recollections of an Old-Time Printer and Journalist. Salt Lake City, 1915. Black cl, gilt title. Edges frayed, top edge soiled, bkpl, else VG. *Bohling.* $135/£87

GRAHAM, MARIA. Three Months Passed in the Mountains East of Rome During the Year 1819. London, 1820. viii,305pp; 6 engr plts. Orig plain bds w/new spine. *Lewis.* $124/£80

GRAHAM, R.B. CUNNINGHAME. Barroso, Gustavo. Mapirunga. London, 1924. #44/350 (of 375). Partly unopened. Vellum cvrs, gilt. Fine (sl foxed) in dj (spine sunned, sl rubbed, sl soiled). *Polyanthos.* $40/£26

GRAHAM, R.B. CUNNINGHAME. A Brazilian Mystic. London: Heinemann, 1920. Fldg map. (Foxing; backstrip sl faded.) *Petersfield.* $25/£16

GRAHAM, R.B. CUNNINGHAME. The Conquest of the River Plate. London: Heinemann, (1924). Map. (1st pp sl foxed; faded, sl torn.) *Petersfield.* $39/£25

GRAHAM, R.B. CUNNINGHAME. Doughty Deeds. London: Heinemann, 1925. 1st ed. 8 plts. Lt brn cl, gilt. Nice. *Cady.* $25/£16

GRAHAM, R.B. CUNNINGHAME. The Horses of the Conquest. London, 1930. (Lt foxing.) Dj (ragged, browned, torn w/loss). *Edwards.* $31/£20

GRAHAM, R.B. CUNNINGHAME. The Horses of the Conquest. Univ of OK, 1949. 1st Amer ed. *Lambeth.* $25/£16

GRAHAM, R.B. CUNNINGHAME. The Ipane. London: T. Fisher Unwin, 1899. 1st ed. Frontis; 274pp. Recent cl (orig wrappers bound in). VG. *Hollett.* $62/£40

GRAHAM, R.B. CUNNINGHAME. Jose Antonio Paez. London: Heinemann, 1929. 1st ed. 9 plts; map. (Lower bd damped; edges, title spotted.) *Hollett.* $47/£30

GRAHAM, R.B. CUNNINGHAME. Mogreb-El-Acksa. London, 1898. 1st ed. Frontis port, xi,323pp, map. (Prelims, feps sl browned; ex-libris; spine sl chipped, faded.) *Edwards.* $116/£75

GRAHAM, R.B. CUNNINGHAME. Mogreb-El-Acksa. NY: Nat'l Travel Club, 1930. 1st ed. Frontis. Sl rubbed, frayed, o/w VG. *Worldwide.* $18/£12

GRAHAM, R.B. CUNNINGHAME. Pedro de Valdivia. London: Heinemann, 1926. 1st ed. Frontis; fldg map. (Spine faded; edge lower bd sl spotted.) *Hollett.* $47/£30

GRAHAM, R.B. CUNNINGHAME. A Vanished Arcadia. London: Heinemann, 1901. Map. (Foxing; backstrip faded.) *Petersfield.* $39/£25

GRAHAM, SHIRLEY. Paul Robeson. NY: Julian Messner, (1946). 1st ed. Port. VG in dj (lt worn). *Petrilla.* $45/£29

GRAHAM, SHIRLEY. There Was Once a Slave. NY: Messner, (1947). 1st ed. VG in dj (chipped). *Petrilla.* $40/£26

GRAHAM, STEPHEN. The Gentle Art of Tramping. London: Robert Holden, 1927. 1st ed. Woodcut frontis. VG. *Hollett.* $12/£8

GRAHAM, STEPHEN. Through Russian Central Asia. NY: Macmillan, 1916. Rev copy. Dbl-pg map. Dk blue dec cl (sl rubbed; perf stamp tp; bkpl). *Schoyer.* $60/£39

GRAHAM, T.J. A Treatise on Indigestion. Phila, 1831. 1st Amer ed. Uncut. (Foxed; stains.) *Goodrich.* $45/£29

GRAHAM, W.A. The Custer Myth, A Source Book of Custeriana.... Harrisburg: Stackpole, (1953). 1st ed. VG in VG dj. *Oregon.* $65/£42

GRAHAM, W.A. The Reno Court of Inquiry. Harrisburg: Stackpole, 1954. 1st ed. Map. NF in VG- dj. *Parker.* $75/£48

GRAHAM, W.A. The Reno Court of Inquiry....13 January 1879.... Harrisburg, PA: Stackpole, (1954). 1st ed. Fldg map. Fine in dj (edges sl chipped). *Laurie.* $75/£48

GRAHAM, WINSTON. Marnie. Doubleday, 1961. 1st ed. Fine in dj. *Fine Books.* $40/£26

GRAHAME, KENNETH (ed). The Cambridge Book of Poetry for Children. NY: Putnam's, (1916). 1st ed. Maud Fuller (illus). 8vo. 288pp. Blue cl, gilt. Lt mks fore-edge, o/w NF. *Drusilla's.* $40/£26

GRAHAME, KENNETH. Bertie's Escapade. Phila: Lippincott, (1949). 12mo. 41pp. Ernest Shepard (illus). Grey cl in pict dj. *Davidson.* $60/£39

GRAHAME, KENNETH. Dream Days. London: John Lane/Bodley Head, (1930). Lg paper ed. Signed by author & Ernest Shepard (illus). Vellum-backed marbled bds. VF in slipcase. *Pharos.* $350/£226

GRAHAME, KENNETH. Dream Days. London: John Lane, Bodley Head, 1911. 1st ed. (Flyleaves lt browned.) Yellow dec cl (sl faded). *Hollett.* $47/£30

GRAHAME, KENNETH. The Golden Age. S&K, 1895. 1st Amer ed. Yellow cl lt spotted, else VG. *Aronovitz.* $85/£55

GRAHAME, KENNETH. The Golden Age. London: John Lane/Bodley Head, 1895. Correct 1st ed w/16pp of pub's ads dated 1895 at rear. Blue cl. Fine. *Pharos.* $125/£81

GRAHAME, KENNETH. The Golden Age. London: John Lane, Bodley Head, 1900. Sm 8vo. 18 plts by Maxfield Parrish. Teg. Maroon pict cl (rubbed, worn); gilt decs. VG + . *Book Adoption.* $100/£65

GRAHAME, KENNETH. The Golden Age. London/NY: John Lane, 1900. 1st ed. Maxfield Parrish (illus). Gilt maroon cl. Fine (sig). *Pharos.* $85/£55

GRAHAME, KENNETH. The Golden Age. London: John Lane, 1915. 1st ed. 4to, viii,242,(6)pp (margins lt browned), 19 color plts by R.J. Enracht-Moony. Buff ptd linen, flowered eps. VG in dj (repaired; foxed). *Cox.* $70/£45

GRAHAME, KENNETH. The Headswoman. London/NY: John Lane/Bodley Head, 1898. 1st ed. Sl dusty; fr, rear blank eps sl foxed, o/w Very Nice in wrappers. *Pharos.* $100/£65

GRAHAME, KENNETH. The Wind in the Willows. London: Methuen, (1927). 1st ed thus. 8vo. 20 full-pg yellow/black plts by Wyndham Payne. Teg. Blue cl, gilt. Good in color pict dj (minor spine wear). *Reisler.* $300/£194

GRAHAME, KENNETH. The Wind in the Willows. Scribners, 1908. 1st Amer ed. Spine faded, else VG. *Aronovitz.* $275/£177

GRAHAME, KENNETH. The Wind in the Willows. NY: Scribner's, 1908. 1st Amer ed. 8vo. Frontis, 302 numbered pp. Teg. Grn woven cl, gilt (spine sl faded). *Reisler.* $750/£484

GRAHAME, KENNETH. The Wind in the Willows. NY: Scribner's, 1913. Blue cl, pict cvr panel; spine, top edge gilt. Lt edgewear; inscrip; else Fine. *Glenn.* $150/£97

GRAHAME, KENNETH. The Wind in the Willows. NY: LEC, 1940. Ltd to 2020 ptd. Signed by Bruce Rogers (designer). Arthur Rackham (illus). Teg. Buckram-backed batik bds. VF in slipcase. *Pharos.* $1,250/£806

GRAND, GORDON. Old Man and Other Colonel Weatherford Stories. NY: Derrydale, 1934. 1st Amer ed. NF. *Polyanthos.* $60/£39

GRAND, GORDON. Old Man and Other Colonel Weatherford Stories. NY: Derrydale, 1934. One of 1150. Bright red cl. *Cullen.* $75/£48

GRAND, GORDON. Redmond C. Stewart. NY: Scribner's, 1938. 1st Amer ed. 1/4 Japan vellum over cl. Nice (eps dknd; fading, dkng). *Hermitage.* $100/£65

GRAND, W. JOSEPH. Illustrated History of the Union Stock Yards. Chicago: the Author, 1901. 1st ed. VG. *Beasley.* $100/£65

GRANDIN, EGBERT. Obstetric Surgery. Phila, 1895. 1st ed. 207pp; 15 photo plts. Good. *Fye.* $125/£81

Grandpapa's Walking Stick. London: S.W. Partridge, n.d. (ca 1865). 16mo. Full-pg wood engr frontis; tp vignette, 64 + 16pp ads, VF cuts. Dec gilt brn cl on bds, chromolitho label. VG (sl rubbed). *Hobbyhorse.* $75/£48

GRANGE, W.B. Wisconsin Grouse Problems. Madison, 1948. *Wheldon & Wesley.* $23/£15

GRANT, BARTLE (ed). The Receipt Book of Elizabeth Raper and a Portion of Her Cipher Journal. Soho: Nonesuch, 1924. Ltd to 850 numbered. Duncan Grant (illus). Blue buckram. Spine sl faded, o/w Fine in dj. *Pharos.* $125/£81

GRANT, C.P. The Syrian Desert, Caravans Travel and Exploration. London, 1937. 4 fldg maps. Brn cl (sm exlib mks). *Lewis.* $50/£32

GRANT, E.B. Beet-Root Sugar and Cultivation of the Beet. Boston, 1867. 158pp (tanned). (Lt scuffed, spotting, esp spine.) *Sutton.* $50/£32

GRANT, ELIHU. The Peasantry of Palestine. NY/Boston/Chicago: Pilgrim Press, (1907). 1st ed. 40 plts. Partly unopened; teg. Sl rubbed, o/w VG. *Worldwide.* $65/£42

GRANT, GEORGE. Ocean to Ocean, Sandford Fleming's Expedition through Canada in 1872.... Toronto/London, 1873. 1st ed. 59 plts. VG. *Oregon.* $175/£113

GRANT, GORDON. Sail Ho! Windjammer Sketches Alow and Aloft. NY: William Farquhar Payson, (c. 1931). VG in dj (sl worn). *Hayman.* $40/£26

GRANT, H. HORACE. A Text-Book of Surgical Principles and Surgical Diseases of the Face, Mouth, and Jaws. Phila, 1902. 1st ed. Good. *Fye.* $175/£113

GRANT, J. Eyes of Horus. Methuen, 1942. 1st ed. NF in VG dj (lt wear, tear; chipped). *Aronovitz.* $90/£58

GRANT, J. A Walk across Africa. Edinburgh, 1864. 1st ed. 454pp; port; fldg map in rear pocket. 1/2 leather, marbled bds. VG + . *Trophy Room.* $1,250/£806

GRANT, JAMES. The Captain of the Guard. London: Routledge, Warne, & Routledge, 1862. 1st ed. Engr frontis. (Bkpl.) VG. *Limestone.* $70/£45

GRANT, JAMES. Jack Manly. London: Routledge et al, 1861. Blue stippled pict cl; aeg. VG. *Limestone.* $65/£42

GRANT, JOHN CAMERON. The Ethiopian: A Narrative of the Society of Human Leopards. NY: Black Hawk Press, 1935. 1st trade ed. Sm lightened spots to cvrs. Dj (lt edgeworn). *Sadlon.* $30/£19

GRANT, K.A. and V. Hummingbirds and Their Flowers. NY, 1968. Dj (sm edge tears). *Sutton.* $75/£48

GRANT, K.A. and V. Hummingbirds and Their Flowers. NY/London: Columbia Univ, 1968. 1st ed. 30 color plts, 5 maps. Color pict cl. Fine in VG dj. *Mikesh.* $37/£24

GRANT, MAXWELL. The Eyes of the Shadow. Street & Smith, 1931. 1st ed. Fine. *Madle.* $175/£113

GRANT, MICHAEL. Eros in Pompeii: The Secret Rooms of the National Museum of Naples. NY, 1975. VG in dj. *Argosy.* $50/£32

GRANT, MICHAEL. The Roman Forum. London: Weidenfeld & Nicolson, 1970. 1st ed. 16pp color plts. VG in dj. *Hollett.* $47/£30

GRANT, R. The High Priestess. Scribners, 1915. 1st ed. VG + in dj (lt wear). *Fine Books.* $65/£42

GRANT, U.S. Personal Memoirs. NY: Charles Webster, 1885-86. 1st ed. 2 vols. Good (cvr wear, hinges repaired). *Parker.* $95/£61

GRANT, U.S. Personal Memoirs. NY: Charles L. Webster, 1885-86. 1st ed. Shoulder strap ed. 2 vols. 584; 647,(1)pp. 1/2 morocco w/cl bds, all edges marbled. NF set in pub's orig binding. *Mcgowan.* $150/£97

GRANT, U.S. Personal Memoirs. NY: Charles L. Webster, 1885-86. 1st ptg. 2 vols. 584; 647pp; 2 steel-engr ports, 2 steel-engr plts, 2 fldg facs, 43 maps (1 fldg). Pict cl (vol 1 sl scuffed). *Schoyer.* $100/£65

GRANT, WILLIAM. Observations on the Nature and Cure of Fevers. London: T. Cadell, 1772. Vol 1: 2nd ed; vol 2: 1st ed. 3 leaves, xv,(2),417pp; 4 leaves (incl blank), 260pp (sigs, bkpl, defect blank upper margin vol 1). Contemp calf (rubbed; hinges cracked vol 1), dentelles, red leather labels. Very Nice. *Hemlock.* $325/£210

Granta and Its Contributors 1889-1914. London, 1924. 1st ed. Fine (lt sunned). *Polyanthos.* $50/£32

GRANVILLE, A. The Fallen Race. F.T. Neeley, 1892. 1st ed. Inner fr hinge starting, else VG. *Aronovitz.* $200/£129

GRASS, GUNTER. Cat and Mouse. Ralph Manheim (trans). NY: Harcourt, (1963). 1st Amer ed. Pub's compliments card laid in. Fine in dj. *Reese.* $25/£16

GRASS, GUNTER. Dog Years. Ralph Manheim (trans). NY: Harcourt, Brace & World, (1963). 1st Amer ed. VG in dj. *Hermitage.* $45/£29

GRASS, GUNTER. The Flounder. Ralph Manheim (trans). NY: Harcourt Brace Jovanovich, (1978). 1st Amer ed. Signed. Top edge dusty, o/w Fine in dj. *Jaffe.* $100/£65

GRASS, GUNTER. The Flounder. Ralph Manheim (trans). NY: LEC, 1985. One of 1000 numbered, signed. 3 vols. Eel skin-backed cl, paper cvr labels. VG in slipcase. *Argosy.* $400/£258

GRASS, GUNTER. Kinderlied. Northridge: Lord John, 1982. One of 300 numbered (of 350), signed. Cl, pict bds. Fine (no dj as issued). *Reese.* $50/£32

GRASS, GUNTER. The Rat. Ralph Manheim (trans). NY: Harcourt, (1987). 1st Amer ed. Rev slip laid in. VF in dj. *Reese.* $20/£13

GRASS, GUNTER. Show Your Tongue. John E. Woods (trans). NY: Harcourt, (1989). 1st Amer ed. Rev material laid in. Fine in dj. *Reese.* $30/£19

GRASS, GUNTER. The Tin Drum. Pantheon Books, 1959. 1st ed. VG in VG dj. *Bishop.* $30/£19

GRASSIER, PIERRE and JULIET WILSON. The Life and Complete Work of Francisco Goya. NY, 1981. 2nd Eng ed. 48 color plts. Good in dj. *Washton.* $125/£81

GRAU, SHIRLEY ANN. The Condor Passes. NY: Knopf, 1971. 1st ed. Fine in dj. *Pharos.* $30/£19

GRAU, SHIRLEY ANN. The Hard Blue Sky. NY: Knopf, 1958. 1st ed. Signed. Fine in dj. *Pharos.* $150/£97

GRAUSTEIN, JEANETTE. Thomas Nuttall, Naturalist. Cambridge: Harvard Univ, 1967. VF in dj. *Quest.* $50/£32

GRAUSTEIN, JEANETTE. Thomas Nuttall, Naturalist. Cambridge: Harvard, 1967. 1st ed. 7 plts, 2 dbl-pg maps. Dec cl. Fine in VG + dj. *Mikesh.* $45/£29

GRAVES, ALGERNON (comp). A Dictionary of Artists.... London, 1884. vi + 265pp + (i)ads (eps, tp lt spotted). Teg, rest uncut. Morocco-backed bds (lt soiled; rubbed; worn). *Edwards.* $70/£45

GRAVES, CHARLES. Leather Armchairs. London: Cassell, (1963). 1st ed. VG in dj (nicks, short tears). *Houle.* $75/£48

GRAVES, G. The Naturalist's Companion.... London, 1824. viii,335,(7)pp; 8 plts (plt 7 surface sl damaged). 1/2 calf. *Wheldon & Wesley.* $140/£90

GRAVES, J.M. Phrenology, or the Doctrine of the Mental Phenomena.... Norwich: M.B. Young, 1838. 1st ed. 119pp; diag; chart. Orig dec brn cl. (Water staining; lt spotting; ms notes fr pastedown.) *White.* $54/£35

GRAVES, JOHN. Goodbye to a River. NY: Knopf, 1960. 1st ed. Name, o/w Fine in NF dj. *Bernard.* $75/£48

GRAVES, R.J. Clinical Lectures on the Practice of Medicine. Dublin, 1864. 2nd ed rpt. xxvii,873pp. Orig cl (rebacked, orig spine laid on). Cl mkd, o/w VG. *Whitehart.* $70/£45

GRAVES, RICHARD. The Spiritual Quixote. London: Peter Davies, 1926. 2 vols. Frontis port, tp vignettes (feps lt browned); fore, lower edges uncut. Cl-backed dec bds. *Edwards.* $85/£55

GRAVES, ROBERT (trans). The Transformations of Lucius, Otherwise Known as the Golden Ass.... NY: Farrar, (1951). 1st Amer ed. NF in dj (lt edgeworn). *Reese.* $25/£16

GRAVES, ROBERT and JOSHUA PODRO. Jesus in Rome. London: Cassell, 1957. 1st ed. VG in Good dj (lt soiled). *Virgo.* $39/£25

GRAVES, ROBERT. Advice from a Mother. Poem-of-the-Month Club, 1970. 1st UK ed. Broadsheet. Signed. Fine. *Sclanders.* $62/£40

GRAVES, ROBERT. An Ancient Castle. NY, 1981. 1st Amer ed. As New in dj. *Bond.* $30/£19

GRAVES, ROBERT. Ann at Highwood Hall. NY, 1964. 1st Amer ed. Fine in dj. *Polyanthos.* $45/£29

GRAVES, ROBERT. Antigua, Penny, Puce. London: Seizin Press, Majorca & Constable, 1936. 1st issue w/misprints on pp 100,103 & 293. Bkpl; sl offsetting eps, o/w Very Nice in VG dj (sl soiled; rubbed, nicked; cancel upper flap). *Virgo.* $310/£200

GRAVES, ROBERT. Beyond Giving—Poems. London: Privately ptd, 1969. #351/536, signed. Fine card cvrs in dj. *Williams.* $93/£60

GRAVES, ROBERT. But it Still Goes On. London: Jonathan Cape, (1930). 1st ed w/pg 157 not on stub. NF in dj (edgewear; spine darkening; interior mend). *Antic Hay.* $75/£48

GRAVES, ROBERT. Catacrack! Mostly Stories, Mostly Funny. London: Cassell, 1956. Fine in NF dj. *Limestone.* $85/£55

GRAVES, ROBERT. Clinical Lectures. Phila, 1842. 2nd Amer ed. 560pp. Leather. *Fye.* $175/£113

GRAVES, ROBERT. Contemporary Techniques of Poetry. London: Hogarth Press, 1925. 1st ed. Good (label; foxing) in wrappers (sl soiled, faded; spine split). *Virgo.* $78/£50

GRAVES, ROBERT. The Crowning Privilege. London: Cassell, 1955. 1st ed. NF in dj. *Virgo.* $54/£35

GRAVES, ROBERT. The English Ballad. London, 1927. 1st ed. (Cl faded.) *Argosy.* $75/£48

GRAVES, ROBERT. The Golden Fleece. London: Cassell, 1944. 1st UK ed. VG (ink name) in dj (rubbed, closed tears strengthened to rear). *Williams.* $31/£20

GRAVES, ROBERT. Good-Bye to All That. London: Jonathan Cape, (1929). 1st ed, 1st issue w/Sassoon's poem on pp341-343. Salmon cl. Bkpl, fep lt dust soiled, else NF in dj (spine lt browned, nicks, sm tears, else NF). *Godot.* $675/£435

GRAVES, ROBERT. Good-Bye to All That. London: Cape, 1929. 1st issue, w/Sassoon poem on pp341-343. In 2nd issue, this was replaced by asterisks. NF in VG + dj (inconspicuous closed tears top of spine hinges). *Williams.* $1,008/£650

GRAVES, ROBERT. The Green-Sailed Vessel. London: Rota, 1971. One of 500 numbered, signed from ed of 526. Fine in dj. *Rees.* $109/£70

GRAVES, ROBERT. They Hanged My Saintly Billy. London: Cassell, 1957. 1st ed. VG in dj (sl soiled, chipped; price-clipped; sm closed tear). *Virgo.* $70/£45

GRAVES, ROBERT. Homer's Daughter. London: Cassell, (1955). 1st ed. NF in dj (sl wear; short tears). *Antic Hay.* $75/£48

GRAVES, ROBERT. Homer's Daughter. NY, 1955. 1st Amer ed. NF in dj (spine sunned, edge sl rubbed, sm edge tear). *Polyanthos.* $35/£23

GRAVES, ROBERT. I, Claudius. H&H, 1934. 1st Amer ed. NF in VG dj (wear along fold; 1/4-inch piece missing spine top). *Fine Books.* $185/£119

GRAVES, ROBERT. The Isles of Unwisdom. London: Cassell, 1950. 1st ed. Edges sl foxed, o/w VG in dj. *Rees.* $47/£30

GRAVES, ROBERT. The Isles of Unwisdom. London: Cassell, 1950. 1st ed. Sig, else VG in VG+ dj. *Limestone.* $85/£55

GRAVES, ROBERT. King Jesus. NY, (1946). 1st Amer ed. Fine (sm crease) in VG dj. *Polyanthos.* $40/£26

GRAVES, ROBERT. Lars Porsena. London: Kegan Paul, Trench, Trubner, (1927). 1st ed. Purple bds w/paper labels. Lt dampstain to fr cvr; pencil sig; label, else VG. *Chapel Hill.* $100/£65

GRAVES, ROBERT. Myths of Ancient Greece. Cassell, 1961. 1st UK ed. Fine in dj (sl rubbed; short closed tear). *Sclanders.* $19/£12

GRAVES, ROBERT. New Poems 1962. London, 1962. 1st ed. Fine in Fine dj (price-clipped). *Polyanthos.* $30/£19

GRAVES, ROBERT. On English Poetry. Heinemann, 1922. 1st ed. Dj (torn). *Petersfield.* $28/£18

GRAVES, ROBERT. Over the Brazier. Poetry Bookshop, 1917. 2nd imp. (Lt foxing.) Orig wraps. *Edrich.* $78/£50

GRAVES, ROBERT. Poems 1914-1926. Heinemann, 1927. 1st ed. Dec cl. Sl wear, else VG. *Whiteson.* $37/£24

GRAVES, ROBERT. Poems 1914-1926. London: Heinemann, 1927. 1st ed. One of 1000. Eps browned; spotted; name, date; cvrs sl rubbed, o/w VG in dj (browned, chipped, cracked). *Virgo.* $101/£65

GRAVES, ROBERT. Poems 1938-1945. London, 1946. VG in dj. *Edrich.* $39/£25

GRAVES, ROBERT. Poems 1938-1945. NY: Creative Age, 1946. 1st ed. Fine (name) in dj (few tears, minor edgewear). *Else Fine.* $50/£32

GRAVES, ROBERT. Poems 1938-1945. London: Cassell, 1946. 1st UK ed. Fine in NF dj (sl creased). *Williams.* $39/£25

GRAVES, ROBERT. Poems 1965-1968. London, 1968. 1st ed. Fine in dj (price-clipped). *Polyanthos.* $30/£19

GRAVES, ROBERT. Poems. NY: LEC, 1980. 1st ed thus; one of 2000 numbered, signed by Paul Hogarth (illus) and Freeman Keith (designer). Teg. Cl, dec bds. VF in slipcase. *Reese.* $85/£55

GRAVES, ROBERT. Poems. Elaine Kerrigan (ed). NY: LEC, 1980. 1/2000 numbered, signed by Paul Hogarth (illus) & Freeman Keith (typographer). Fine in pub's box. *Argosy.* $135/£87

GRAVES, ROBERT. Proceed, Sergeant Lamb. London: Methuen, 1941. 1st ed. Spine, pg edges sl spotted, o/w NF in dj (sl chipped, mkd). *Rees.* $54/£35

GRAVES, ROBERT. Proceed, Sergeant Lamb. Methuen, 1941. 1st ed. Foxing to fore-edge, 1st few pp; spine extrems sunned, else VG in Very Nice dj (chipped). *Fine Books.* $55/£35

GRAVES, ROBERT. The Real David Copperfield. London, 1933. 1st ed. VG in dj (2 closed tears; sm tear w/loss). *Words Etc.* $101/£65

GRAVES, ROBERT. Sergeant Lamb of the Ninth. Methuen, (1940). 1st ed. (Fr cvr dj stuck to fep; backstrip sl faded.) *Petersfield.* $19/£12

GRAVES, ROBERT. Sergeant Lamb of the Ninth. London: Methuen, 1940. 1st ed. Top edges dusty, else VG in VG dj (nicked, sl rubbed). *Limestone.* $125/£81

GRAVES, ROBERT. Sergeant Lamb's America. NY, (1940). 1st ed. Wraps in dj. VG+ in VG+ dj (sl chipped, rubbed). *Fuller & Saunders.* $75/£48

GRAVES, ROBERT. Seven Days in New Crete. London: Cassell, 1949. 1st ed. Edges sl foxed, o/w VG in dj (sl chipped). *Rees.* $31/£20

GRAVES, ROBERT. The Shout. London: Elkin Mathews, 1929. 1st ed. #270/530 signed. Unopened. Sl browned, else VG in dj (sl browned, chipped). *Virgo.* $271/£175

GRAVES, ROBERT. The Shout. London: Elkin Mathews & Marrot, 1929. 1st ed. #371/500 signed. Subs slip laid in. Dec grey bds. Lt offsetting eps, spine ends bumped, else NF in NF dj (chips; edgewear). *Chapel Hill.* $300/£194

GRAVES, ROBERT. The Siege and Fall of Troy. London: Cassell, 1962. 1st ed. NF in dj. *Limestone.* $45/£29

GRAVES, ROBERT. T.E. Lawrence to His Biographers, Robert Graves and Liddell Hart. NY: Doubleday, Doran, 1938. 1st ed, Amer issue. #292/500 sets, signed by Graves, Hart. 2 vols. 8vo. Teg. Grey cl. Fine in VG djs (sl dknd spines); pub's slipcase (lt wear). *Chapel Hill.* $750/£484

GRAVES, ROBERT. They Hanged My Saintly Billy. London: Cassell, 1957. 1st ed. NF in dj. *Limestone.* $95/£61

GRAVES, ROBERT. To Whom Else? Majorca: The Seizin Press, 1931. Ltd ed, #61/200 signed. NF (staining inside cvrs, margins; spine sl soiled, corners sl rubbed). *Polyanthos.* $175/£113

GRAVES, ROBERT. Two Wise Children. NY: Quist, 1966. 1st ed. 1st state, w/bk spine lettered in black. Fine in dj (minor rubs corners, price-clipped). *Else Fine.* $65/£42

GRAVES, ROBERT. Watch the Northwind Rise. NY: Creative Age, 1949. 1st ed. Signed. VG. *Second Life.* $95/£61

GRAVES, ROBERT. Welchman's Hose. London: The Fleuron, 1925. 1st ed. Fine (lt dkng pg edges) in slipcase (sl sunned). *Beasley.* $200/£129

GRAVES, ROBERT. Welchman's Hose. London: Fleuron, 1925. 1st ed. One of 525. 1/4 cl, dec paper over bds. Sl foxing, o/w NF in glassine wrapper (chipped). *Reese.* $350/£226

GRAVES, ROBERT. Wife to Mr. Milton. London: Cassell, 1943. 1st ed. VG in dj (sl chipped, sunned). *Rees.* $31/£20

GRAVES, W.E. Studies in Eucalyptus. St. Louis: (Eucalyptus Timber Corp), 1910. Ptd wrappers. *Dawson.* $150/£97

GRAVY, WAVY. The Hog Farm and Friends. NY: Links, 1974. 1st ed. Price oblit, o/w Fine in wraps. *Beasley.* $50/£32

GRAY, A. STUART. Edwardian Architecture. Iowa City: Univ of IA, (1986). 1st ed. Fine in dj. *Bookpress.* $135/£87

GRAY, A.A. Wendeline and Her Lady-Bug. Boston: Samuel Colman, (1846). 1st ed. 12mo; 64pp. Cl-backed pict bds. VG. *Chapel Hill.* $85/£55

GRAY, A.W. Bino. NY: E.P. Dutton, 1988. 1st ed. VF in dj. *Mordida.* $35/£23

GRAY, ALASDAIR et al. Lean Tales. Cape, 1985. 1st UK ed. Fine in dj. *Williams.* $28/£18

GRAY, ALASDAIR. 1982 Janine. London: Cape, 1984. 1st ed. Fine in dj (price-clipped). *Rees.* $19/£12

GRAY, ALASDAIR. Alasdair Gray. Saltire Self-Portrait. Saltire Soc, 1988. 1st ed. Signed. Fine in wrappers. *Rees.* $16/£10

GRAY, ALASDAIR. The Fall of Kelvin Walker. Canongate, 1985. 1st UK ed. Fine in dj. *Lewton.* $23/£15

GRAY, ALASDAIR. Lanark. Canongate, 1985. One of 1000 numbered, signed, dated. 1st thus. Fine in dj. *Rees.* $54/£35

GRAY, ALASDAIR. McGrotty and Ludmilla. Dog & Bone, 1990. Pb orig. Signed. Fine in wrappers. *Rees.* $31/£20

GRAY, ALASDAIR. Old Negatives. London: Cape, 1989. One of 500 numbered, signed, dated. Errata sheet. Fine in dj (sl mkd). *Rees.* $47/£30

GRAY, ALASDAIR. Poor Things. Bloomsbury, 1992. 1st ed. Signed. Fine in dj. *Rees.* $47/£30

GRAY, ALASDAIR. Why Scots Should Rule Scotland. Canongate, 1992. 1st ed. Signed. Fine in wrappers. *Rees.* $25/£16

GRAY, ALISDAIR. Lanark. Canongate, 1985. #334/1000 signed. Fine in dj. *Lewton.* $54/£35

GRAY, ASA and GEORGE L. GOODALE. Gray's Botanical Text Book. NY, 1879-85. 6th ed. 2 vols. xii,442pp + ads; ix,499,(36)pp. VG (spines sl bumped). *Shifrin.* $60/£39

GRAY, ASA. Gray's Manual of Botany. NY, 1950. 8th ed (Upper pp edges lt spotted.) *Sutton.* $60/£39

GRAY, ASA. Gray's New Manual of Botany. NY, 1908. 7th ed. (Scuffed, spotted; eps, edges lt foxed.) *Sutton.* $25/£16

GRAY, BASIL. The English Print. London, 1937. 24 collotype plts. VG in dj. *Argosy.* $40/£26

GRAY, CAMILLA. The Great Experiment: Russian Art 1863-1922. NY, (1962). 1st ed. 257 plts (24 full color). Name, else VG in dj (shelfworn). *King.* $150/£97

GRAY, EDWARD. Leif Eriksson. Oxford, 1930. 1st ed. 16 plts, fldg map. VG in Good+ dj. *Oregon.* $85/£55

GRAY, HAROLD. Little Orphan Annie and Jumbo, the Circus Elephant. Chicago: Pleasure Books, (1935). Square, 4to. 3 Fine pop-ups. Full color bds (lt dusting; minor wear). *Reisler.* $385/£248

GRAY, HENRY. Anatomy, Descriptive and Surgical. Phila: Henry C. Lea, 1865. 2nd Amer ed. 395 wood engrs. Burgundy 1/2 calf (rebound) orig label laid down. *Glenn.* $350/£226

GRAY, HENRY. Anatomy, Descriptive and Surgical. Phila: Lea Bros, 1897. 1249pp. Red cl; paper spine label. Good (fr cvr rehinged). *Smithfield.* $23/£15

GRAY, HENRY. Anatomy, Descriptive and Surgical. T. Pickering Pick (ed). London: Longmans, 1897. 14th ed. xl,1184,16pp pub's ads. Rebacked; title lt spotted, o/w Nice. *White.* $28/£18

GRAY, HOWARD LEVI. English Field Systems. London: Harvard Univ/Merlin, 1959. Fldg map frontis, 16 maps. Dj (sl soiled). *Edwards.* $39/£25

GRAY, JAMES H. Red Lights on the Prairies. Toronto, 1971. 1st ed. Fine in dj (sl chipped). *Baade.* $30/£19

GRAY, JOHN MORGAN. Lord Selkirk of Red River. Toronto, 1963. 1st ed. 2 maps. Fine in Fine dj. *Oregon.* $30/£19

GRAY, JOHN THOMPSON. A Kentucky Chronicle. NY/Washington: Neale Pub Co, 1906. Grn cl, gilt title. Nice (pencil, ink names). *Bohling.* $65/£42

GRAY, NICOLETTE. The Painted Inscriptions of David Jones. London: Gordon Fraser, 1981. 1st ed. Fine in dj. *Michael Taylor.* $54/£35

GRAY, NICOLETTE. XIXth Century Ornamented Types and Title Pages. London: Faber & Faber, (1951). 2nd ed. Buff-colored cl. Fine. *Glenn.* $40/£26

GRAY, NICOLETTE. XIXth Century Ornamented Types and Title Pages. London: Faber, 1938. 1st ed. 8 halftone plts, 11pg chart. Good in orig cl. *Cox.* $43/£28

GRAY, THOMAS. Elegy Written in a Country Church Yard. Cincinnati: Howe's Subscription Book Concern, 1867. Sq 12mo. Frontis, 24 leaves, 2pp ads. Paper wrapper (new, w/orig title label). *Hobbyhorse.* $70/£45

GRAY, THOMAS. Elegy Written in a Country Church-Yard. London: LEC, 1938. #904/1500 numbered, signed by Agnes Miller Parker (illus). Full pict cl, silver-stamped. Fine in glassine wrapper & pub's slipcase (sl mkd). *Hermitage.* $250/£161

GRAY, THOMAS. Poems and Letters. London: Chiswick Press, 1867. 1st ed. xvi,416pp, 4 mtd photos. Orig calf, gilt-tooled; aeg. Lt rubbing, foxing; o/w very clean. *Karmiole.* $200/£129

GRAY, THOMAS. Poems. A New Edition. London: J. Dodsley, 1768. 2nd London ed. Half-title, (iv),119,(ii)pp. (Contemp transcription on 5 blank leaves; early inscrip.) Contemp polished calf (joints cracked, but firm). *Marlborough.* $271/£175

GRAY, THOMAS. The Poetical Works. London: William Pickering, 1851. Port. Dk blue cl (sl rubbed; minor wear head, tail of backstrip; paper label worn.) *Cox.* $31/£20

GRAY, W.H. A History of Oregon 1792-1849 Drawn from Personal Observation.... Portland: Harris & Holman, 1870. 1st ed. 624pp. Worming along rear gutter, else VG. Howes G 342. *Perier.* $150/£97

GRAYSON, RUPERT. Death Rides the Forest. NY: E.P. Dutton, 1938. 1st Amer ed. Fine in dj (spine crease; sl wear spine top). *Mordida.* $45/£29

Great Ones of Ancient Egypt. Portraits by Winifred Brunton. London: Hodder & Stoughton, (1929). 17 plts (15 tipped in). (Eps browned; extrems worn, shelfwear.) *Archaeologia.* $225/£145

Great Wheel. NY: Viking, (1957). 1st ed. 8vo. Robert Lawson (illus). Grn cl, black dec. Good in color pict dj. *Reisler.* $90/£58

GREATHOUSE, CHARLES H. Ranch Life in the Old West. Hollywood, 1971. Ltd to 1000. Numbered, signed. Fine in dj. *Baade.* $37/£24

GREELEY, HORACE. Hints Toward Reforms, in Lectures.... NY, 1850. 1st ed. 400pp. Good (lt foxing; spine ends worn). *Artis.* $30/£19

GREELY, ADOLPHUS W. The Polar Regions in the Twentieth Century. Boston: Little, Brown, 1928. 1st ed. 21 plts, fldg map (tear on fold line repaired w/archival tape). Blue cl (flaking to white titles on spine). Poor dj. *Parmer*. $85/£55

GREELY, ADOLPHUS W. Three Years of Arctic Service. NY: Scribners, 1886. 2 vols. xxv,428; xii,444pp. Lg fldg map in rear pocket. Dec cl (spine ends repaired). Good + . *Walcot*. $248/£160

GREELY, ADOLPHUS W. Three Years of Arctic Service. NY, 1886. 1st ed. 2 vols. Pict cl (frayed; bkpls, foxing, inner hinges loose; lacks pocket maps). *King*. $125/£81

GREELY, ADOLPHUS W. Three Years of Arctic Service. NY: Scribner's, 1886. 2 vols. xxv,428;xii(2)444pp. Lg fldg map in pocket. Orig dec cl. Generally VG (spine ends repaired; minor wrinkling of cl on spine of vol 1 only). *High Latitude*. $250/£161

GREEN, ALAN. What a Body! NY: S&S, 1949. 1st ed. Fine in dj (sl spine fading; tiny closed tears). *Mordida*. $45/£29

GREEN, ANNA KATHERINE. The Circular Study. NY, 1900. 1st binding. Dec grn cl, gilt. Fine (name; sl rubbed). *Polyanthos*. $60/£39

GREEN, ANNA KATHERINE. The Filigree Ball. Indianapolis, (1903). 1st issue w/printer's slug ptd in red. Dec cvrs, gilt. Fine (sl rubbed). *Polyanthos*. $45/£29

GREEN, ARTHUR ROBERT. Sundials. London: SPCK, 1926. 1st ed. 16pp of plts. 1/2 title, final leaf lt spotted; sm stamp; label removed upper bd. *Hollett*. $70/£45

GREEN, BEN K. Horse Tradin'. NY, 1967. 1st ed. Debossed cl. Fine (inscrip) in dj (chipped, closed tear). *Baade*. $65/£42

GREEN, BEN K. The Last Trail Drive through Downtown Dallas. Flagstaff, 1971. Ltd to 1750. Fine in dj (price-clipped). *Baade*. $110/£71

GREEN, BEN K. Some More Horse Tradin'. NY: Knopf, 1972. 1st ed. #340/350, signed. Joe Beeler (illus). Fine in plastic dj, slipcase (lt soiled). *Bohling*. $300/£194

GREEN, BEN K. Wild Cow Tales. Knopf, 1969. 1st ed. Fine in Fine dj. *Oregon*. $45/£29

GREEN, DAVID. Blenheim Palace. Country Life, 1951. 1st ed. (Eps lt spotted.) Dj (spotted, sl chipped). *Edwards*. $225/£145

GREEN, DAVID. Gardener to Queen Anne: Henry Wise (1653-1738).... London: OUP, 1956. VG in dj. *Argosy*. $60/£39

GREEN, DAVID. Grinling Gibbons. London: Country Life, 1964. 1st ed. Frontis port. (Ex-lib w/ink stamps throughout, bkpl, #s, badly cvrd in cellophane.) Dj (wrinkled). *Edwards*. $140/£90

GREEN, E. TYRRELL. Towers and Spires. London, 1908. 1st ed. 2 fldg maps. (Feps lt browned; spine sl rubbed.) *Edwards*. $47/£30

GREEN, EARL L. Biology of the Laboratory Mouse. NY: McGraw-Hill, 1966. 1st ed. Navy blue cl. VG (sm stamp) in dj (edgeworn). *Gach*. $65/£42

GREEN, F.L. Odd Man Out. London: Michael Joseph, (1945). 1st UK ed. Bkpl, o/w NF in dj. *Bernard*. $75/£48

GREEN, FRANCES H. Biography of Mrs. Semantha Mettle, the Clairvoyant.... NY: Harmonial Assoc, 1853. 1st ed. Frontis port, 115pp. Blind-stamped black cl (sl worn). VG. *Second Life*. $225/£145

GREEN, HENRY. Back. London: Hogarth, 1946. 1st ed. Dated owner sig; edges lt foxed; else Very Nice in dj. *Reese*. $100/£65

GREEN, HENRY. Doting. London: Hogarth Press, 1952. 1st ed. Fine in dj. *Pharos*. $75/£48

GREEN, HENRY. Doting. London: Hogarth, 1952. 1st ed. Trace of foxing edges, else Fine in dj. *Reese*. $100/£65

GREEN, HENRY. Nothing. NY: Viking, 1950. 1st Amer ed. Gray cl titled in red. Very Nice in dj. *Cady*. $25/£16

GREEN, HENRY. Pack My Bag. London: Hogarth, 1940. 1st ed, 1st issue binding. Red cl, gilt-lettered. VG in 2nd issue grn dj (spine browned, else VG). *Godot*. $250/£161

GREEN, HENRY. Party Going. NY: Viking, 1951. 1st Amer ed. Gilt-titled red cl. Very Nice in dj (sl rubbed). *Cady*. $25/£16

GREEN, J.R. A Short History of the English People. London, 1902-03. 1st Eng ed. 4 vols. Grn 1/2 calf (rebound). *Edrich*. $62/£40

GREEN, JONATHAN (ed). Camera Work: A Critical Anthology. Millerton: Aperture, 1973. 1st ed. NF. *Cahan*. $100/£65

GREEN, JULIAN. The Pilgrim on the Earth. Blackamore/Harper, 1929. #262/350. 12 wood engrs. Teg, rest uncut. *Petersfield*. $78/£50

GREEN, JULIAN. The Pilgrim on the Earth. London: Blackamore, 1929. #293/350. 10 full-pg illus by Ben Sussan. Teg, others uncut. Orig vellum-backed cl. VG (sl spotting). *Cox*. $70/£45

GREEN, JULIAN. The Pilgrim on the Earth. Harpers, 1929. 1st ed. One of 375. 12 color wood engrs by Rene Ben Sussan. Fine in NF dj (sunned) & slipcase (worn). *Fine Books*. $125/£81

GREEN, MASON A. Springfield Memories. Springfield, MA: Whitney & Adams, 1876. 1st ed. Frontis, 110pp. Grn cl, gilt. Fine. *Karmiole*. $30/£19

GREEN, MASON. Springfield 1636-1886. C.A. Nichols, 1888. 1st ed. Frontis, (xxii),645pp; 15 plts (incl fldg map). Gilt-stamped pict cl. VG. *Oregon*. $125/£81

GREEN, P. The Field God and In Abraham's Bosom. McBride, 1927. 1st ed. Multi-color pict bds. Lt rubbing, else Fine in VG dj (lt wear). *Fine Books*. $75/£48

GREEN, PETER. Habeas Corpus and Other Stories. Cleveland: World, (1963). 1st Amer ed. Gilt-titled grn cl. Very Nice in dj. *Cady*. $20/£13

GREEN, ROBERT M. (comp). History of the Hundred and Twenty-Fourth Regiment Pennsylvania Volunteers.... Phila: Ware Bros, 1907. 1st ed. 2 labels addressed to green, photo laid in. Orig blue cl. Fine in plain dj (worn, top of spine cut out, chipped). *Chapel Hill*. $175/£113

GREEN, ROGER LANCELYN. A.E.W. Mason. London: Max Parrish, 1952. 1st ed. NF in NF dj. *Janus*. $35/£23

GREEN, SAMUEL A. Epitaphs from the Old Burying Ground in Groton, Massachusetts. Boston: Little, Brown, 1878. Frontis, xxii,272pp, 6 plts. Grn cl, gilt. Fine. *Karmiole*. $50/£32

GREEN, SAMUEL A. Three Military Diaries Kept by Groton Soldiers in Different Wars. Groton, MA, 1901. (Sm stamp tp.) *Schoyer*. $60/£39

GREEN, THOMAS J. Journal of the Texian Expedition Against Mier.... NY: Harper, 1845. 1st ed. 487pp, 11 plts, 2 plans (1 fldg). Mod grn morocco-backed marbled bds (rebound; new eps). Old ink sig, o/w Fine. Howes G 371. *Harrington*. $650/£419

GREEN, THOMAS MARSHALL. Historic Families of Kentucky. Cincinnati: Robert Clarke, 1889. 1st ed. iv,305pp (pencil notes; 1pg repaired). VG (spine ends worn). Howes G 373. *Cahan.* $145/£94

GREENAN, RUSSELL H. Nightmare. Random, 1970. 1st ed. Pg edges lt soiled, else Fine in dj. *Murder.* $35/£23

GREENAWAY, KATE. Almanack for 1883. London: Routledge. 1st ed. 32mo. Full-pg frontis, 22 unnumbered pp; dk grn eps. Pict glazed paper on bd cvrs, yellow cl spine. Lt chipping, else VF. *Hobbyhorse.* $150/£97

GREENAWAY, KATE. Almanack for 1883. London: George Routledge, 1883. 3x4 inches. Cl-backed color illus bds (sm chip). *Reisler.* $100/£65

GREENAWAY, KATE. Almanack for 1884. London: Routledge, (1884). Edges rubbed, else VG in glazed pict wrappers. *Glenn.* $100/£65

GREENAWAY, KATE. Almanack for 1884. London: George Routledge, 1884. 3.5x5.25 inches. Illus paper wrappers (sl dusty). *Reisler.* $90/£58

GREENAWAY, KATE. Almanack for 1884. London: Routledge, 1884. (20)pp. Cream stiff card, gilt. VG. *Hollett.* $217/£140

GREENAWAY, KATE. Almanack for 1925. London: Frederick Warne. 1st ed. Cream colored glazed pict bds (4 women representing seasons), black title. VG (pencil inscrip). *Davidson.* $150/£97

GREENAWAY, KATE. A Apple Pie. Akron: Saalfield, 1907. 1st ed thus. A muslin ABC book. 11 illus. Fr cvr olive grn/yellow/white/blue/red. VG +. *Davidson.* $200/£129

GREENAWAY, KATE. A Day in a Child's Life. George Routledge & Sons, (1881). 1st ed. 4to. 29pp. Dec bds, cl spine; grn eps. Excellent (label inside fr cvr; lt stain lower bd). *Bickersteth.* $147/£95

GREENAWAY, KATE. Greenaway Pictures to Paint. NY: McLoughlin Bros, 1882-1890. Illus glazed pict wrappers. VG (partially painted, foxing). *Davidson.* $75/£48

GREENAWAY, KATE. Kate Greenaway Pictures. London: Frederick Warne, 1921. 1st ed. Lg, 4to. Frontis port, 20 mtd color plts. Beige cl spine, olive grn cl binding (loss of color fr edge), gilt. Ptd dj (sm pieces missing; line of paint). *Reisler.* $225/£145

GREENAWAY, KATE. Marigold Garden. London: George Routledge, (1885). 1st ed. 4to. All edges tinted. Cl-backed illus bds (chipped; pg bumped; hinge separated). *Reisler.* $175/£113

GREENAWAY, KATE. Mother Goose or the Old Nursery Rhymes Illustrated by.... London/NY, n.d. (1881). 1st ed, 2nd issue w/upside down 'G' on cvr. 48pp color illus. (Sl darkened; upper hinge starting.) *Argosy.* $250/£161

GREENAWAY, KATE. Queen Victoria's Jubilee Garland. London: Routledge, 1887. Obl 8vo. 6 unnumbered leaves. Gilt edges. Pict chromolitho stiff paper wrappers, orig lt blue silk ribbon. Fine. *Hobbyhorse.* $400/£258

GREENAWAY, KATE. Under the Window. London: George Routledge, (1879). 1st ed. Edmund Evans (engrs). 4to. Pict ptd paper on bds, dk blue-grn eps (ex-libris label, ink sigs, decal mks, lt foxing at margins, cvr edges rubbed). Internally Good. *Hobbyhorse.* $110/£71

GREENBERG, CLEMENT. Joan Miro. NY: Quadrangle Press, 1950. Frontis port, 6 color plts. NF in illus dj. *Cahan.* $100/£65

GREENBERG, MARTIN H. and AUGUSTUS NORTON (eds). Touring Nam: The Vietnam War Reader. NY: Morrow, (1985). 1st ed. NF in dj (lt worn). *Aka.* $40/£26

GREENBERG, SAMUEL. Making Linoleum Cuts. NY, (1947). Eps foxed, else VG in dj. *Veatchs.* $20/£13

GREENBLATT, M. and H.C. SOLOMN. Frontal Lobes and Schizophrenia. NY: Springer, 1953. Good. *Goodrich.* $50/£32

GREENE, A.C. A Personal Country. NY: Knopf, 1969. 1st ed, 1st bk. Fine in NF dj. *Bernard.* $50/£32

GREENE, A.C. A Personal Country. NY, 1969. 1st ed. Pict cl. Fine (label, stamp fep) in dj. *Baade.* $35/£23

GREENE, FRANCIS V. The Revolutionary War and the Military Policy of the United States. NY: Scribner's, 1911. 1st ed. Dk blue cl. Rear inner hinge cracked, else VG. *Chapel Hill.* $65/£42

GREENE, GEORGE WASHINGTON. Historical View of the American Revolution. Boston: Ticknor & Fields, 1865. 1st ed. 459pp. Grn cl. Spine sl sunned, else VG. *Chapel Hill.* $125/£81

GREENE, GRAHAM and HUGH (eds). The Spy's Bedside Book. London: Rupert Hart-Davis, 1957. 1st ed. Fine in VG+ dj. *Limestone.* $95/£61

GREENE, GRAHAM. 19 Stories. Heinemann, 1947. 1st ed. Good in dj (mkd; sl rubbed). *Whiteson.* $31/£20

GREENE, GRAHAM. 21 Stories. Viking, 1962. 1st ed. Fine in dj. *Fine Books.* $58/£37

GREENE, GRAHAM. The Bear Fell Free. London: Grayson & Grayson, 1935. #160/285 (250 were for sale), signed. Fine in clean dj (inconspicuous worming to spine, fore-edges). *Williams.* $1,240/£800

GREENE, GRAHAM. Brighton Rock. Albatross, 1939. 1st thus. Sm piece cut fep; sl worn, else Good in wraps. *Whiteson.* $16/£10

GREENE, GRAHAM. British Dramatists. Collins, 1942. 1st ed. Contents Good (rubbed). *Whiteson.* $22/£14

GREENE, GRAHAM. A Burnt-Out Case. NY, 1961. 1st Amer ed. VG in dj. *Argosy.* $40/£26

GREENE, GRAHAM. A Burnt-Out Case. London: Heinemann, 1961. 1st ed. VG in dj (sl rubbed, price-clipped). *Rees.* $19/£12

GREENE, GRAHAM. A Burnt-Out Case. Heinemann, 1961. 1st ed. NF in dj. *Fine Books.* $48/£31

GREENE, GRAHAM. A Burnt-Out Case. London: Heinemann, 1961. 1st ed. NF in VG dj (fold worn). *Revere.* $60/£39

GREENE, GRAHAM. The Captain and the Enemy. London: Reinhardt, 1988. 1st UK ed. Fine in dj. *Williams.* $16/£10

GREENE, GRAHAM. The Comedians. London: Bodley Head, 1966. 1st ed. Nice in VG dj (sl nicked, price-clipped). *Virgo.* $31/£20

GREENE, GRAHAM. The Comedians. London: Bodley Head, 1966. 1st ed. VG+ in dj (price-clipped; spine head worn). *Stahr.* $45/£29

GREENE, GRAHAM. The Comedians. Bodley Head, 1966. 1st UK ed. VG in dj. *Lewton.* $23/£15

GREENE, GRAHAM. The Comedians. NY: Viking, Christmas 1965. 1st ed. Ltd to 500. Gilt. Fine. *Sadlon.* $125/£81

GREENE, GRAHAM. The Complaisant Lover. London: Heinemann, 1959. 1st ed. Fine in dj (sl sunned, nicked). *Rees.* $54/£35

GREENE, GRAHAM. The End of the Affair. London: Heinemann, (1951). 1st ed, signed. 8vo. Fine in dj (spine sl tanned). *Chapel Hill*. $500/£323

GREENE, GRAHAM. The End of the Affair. London: Heinemann, (1951). 1st ed. VG in dj (short tears; tiny chips). *Antic Hay*. $75/£48

GREENE, GRAHAM. The End of the Affair. London: Heinemann, 1951. 1st ed. VG + in VG dj (sl chipped). *Limestone*. $115/£74

GREENE, GRAHAM. Getting to Know the General. Bodley, 1984. 1st ed. Fine in dj. *Whiteson*. $22/£14

GREENE, GRAHAM. The Great Jowett. London: Bodley Head, 1981. One of 525 specially bound, numbered, signed. Fine in glassine dj. *Rees*. $194/£125

GREENE, GRAHAM. The Heart of the Matter. London: Heinemann, (1948). 1st ed. VG (fore-edge foxing) in dj (worn; Book Society Choice ptd band present). *Antic Hay*. $85/£55

GREENE, GRAHAM. The Heart of the Matter. London: Heinemann, 1948. 1st UK ed. Complete w/Book Society Choice orig wrap-around band. Fine in virtually intact dj (worn, short tears, chips). *Williams*. $147/£95

GREENE, GRAHAM. The Honorary Consul. London, 1973. 1st ed. Fine in dj (sm edge tear rear end panel). *Polyanthos*. $35/£23

GREENE, GRAHAM. How Father Quixote Became a Monsignor. Sylvester & Orphanos, 1982. One of 300 (of 330) numbered, signed. Fine in glassine dj. *Rees*. $233/£150

GREENE, GRAHAM. The Human Factor. Bodley Head, 1978. 1st UK ed. Fine in dj. *Lewton*. $23/£15

GREENE, GRAHAM. In Search of a Character. Bodley, 1961. 1st ed. Fine in Good dj. *Whiteson*. $28/£18

GREENE, GRAHAM. In Search of a Character. London: Bodley Head, 1961. 1st UK ed. Fine in dj. *Williams*. $47/£30

GREENE, GRAHAM. It's a Battlefield. London: Heinemann, 1934. 1st UK ed. VG. *Williams*. $186/£120

GREENE, GRAHAM. It's a Battlefield. London: Heinemann, 1934. 1st UK ed. VG + in almost intact dj (chipped, creased, worn). *Williams*. $1,124/£725

GREENE, GRAHAM. It's a Battlefield. Penquin, 1940. 1st thus. Wraps. VG in dj (sl worn). *Whiteson*. $16/£10

GREENE, GRAHAM. J'Accuse. London: Bodley Head, 1982. 1st ed. Name, o/w VG in wrappers. *Virgo*. $16/£10

GREENE, GRAHAM. Journey without Maps. D-D, 1936. 1st Amer ed. Some loss of spine gilt, else VG + . *Fine Books*. $75/£48

GREENE, GRAHAM. Journey without Maps. Pan, 1948. 1st thus. Dec wraps. Sl dull, else Good. *Whiteson*. $16/£10

GREENE, GRAHAM. The Little Horse Bus. London: Parrish, 1952. 1st UK ed. NF in VG dj (short closed tears, sm chips). *Williams*. $426/£275

GREENE, GRAHAM. The Little Train. London: Bodley Head, (1973). 1st ed. Oblong royal 8vo, 48pp. Dj (sl torn). *Petersfield*. $31/£20

GREENE, GRAHAM. The Living Room. Heinemann, 1953. 1st ed. Spine sl dull; sl rubbed, else Good. *Whiteson*. $28/£18

GREENE, GRAHAM. Lord Rochester's Monkey. Bodley, 1974. 1st ed w/rev slip inserted. Fine in dj. *Whiteson*. $23/£15

GREENE, GRAHAM. Lord Rochester's Monkey. London: BH, 1974. 1st UK ed. Fine in dj. *Lewton*. $26/£17

GREENE, GRAHAM. Loser Takes All. London/Toronto/Melbourne, (1955). 1st ed. Fine in Fine dj. *Mcclintock*. $135/£87

GREENE, GRAHAM. Loser Takes All. London: Heinemann, 1955. 1st ed. Good in dj (frayed). *Cox*. $23/£15

GREENE, GRAHAM. The Lost Childhood and Other Essays. Eyre & Spottiswoode, 1951. 1st ed. Fine in dj. *Fine Books*. $110/£71

GREENE, GRAHAM. The Lost Childhood and Other Essays. London: Eyre & Spottiswoode, 1951. 1st UK ed. VG + in VG dj (browned, sl worn). *Williams*. $74/£48

GREENE, GRAHAM. The Man Within. Heinemann, 1929. 1st UK ed. Pub's wraparound band. NF (sl fr hinge weakness) in VG cream-colored dj (sl spine dknd) in custom-made box. *Williams*. $2,790/£1,800

GREENE, GRAHAM. May We Borrow Your Husband? London: Bodley Head, 1967. 1st ed. VG in dj. *Hollett*. $47/£30

GREENE, GRAHAM. May We Borrow Your Husband? London: Bodley Head, 1967. 1st ed. VG in dj (sl soiled). *Virgo*. $47/£30

GREENE, GRAHAM. May We Borrow Your Husband? London: Bodley Head, 1967. 1st UK ed. Fine in VG dj (sl browning to rear panel). *Williams*. $34/£22

GREENE, GRAHAM. May We Borrow Your Husband? London: Bodley Head, 1967. One of 500 specially bound, numbered, signed. Fine in glassine dj. *Rees*. $194/£125

GREENE, GRAHAM. The Ministry of Fear. Heinemann, 1943. 1st UK ed. VG (bds sl dknd). *Williams*. $54/£35

GREENE, GRAHAM. Nightmare Journey. NY, (1975). 1st ed. Fine in dj (lt rubbed). *Mcclintock*. $125/£81

GREENE, GRAHAM. Nineteen Stories. London: Heinemann, (1947). 1st ed. Blue cl. VG (lt wear) in dj (soil; spine sl browned). *Antic Hay*. $125/£81

GREENE, GRAHAM. Our Man in Havana. London: Heinemann, 1958. 1st ed. VG in dj (sl rubbed, short tear). *Hollett*. $70/£45

GREENE, GRAHAM. Our Man in Havana. London: Heinemann, 1958. 1st ed. VG in dj. *Limestone*. $75/£48

GREENE, GRAHAM. The Pleasure Dome: The Collected Film Criticism 1935-1940. Secker, 1972. 1st ed w/rev slip inserted. Fine in Fine dj. *Whiteson*. $43/£28

GREENE, GRAHAM. The Potting Shed. Heinemann, 1958. 1st UK ed. Fine in VG dj (sl edge-worn; rubbed; stain rear panel; closed tears). *Williams*. $39/£25

GREENE, GRAHAM. A Quick Look Behind. L.A.: Sylvester & Orphanos, 1983. One of 300 (of 330) numbered, signed. Fine in slipcase. *Rees*. $233/£150

GREENE, GRAHAM. The Quiet American. London: Heinemann, 1955. 1st ed. Sl faded, spotted. *Hollett*. $39/£25

GREENE, GRAHAM. The Quiet American. Heinemann, 1955. 1st UK ed. VG in dj. *Lewton*. $54/£35

GREENE, GRAHAM. The Quiet American. Viking, 1956. 1st Amer ed. Photo laid in. Fine in VG + dj (2 short closed tears). *Fine Books*. $25/£16

GREENE, GRAHAM. The Quiet American. NY: Viking, 1956. 1st ed. Inscrip, else NF in dj (lt chipped). *Murder*. $40/£26

GREENE, GRAHAM. Reflections on Travels with My Aunt. NY: Firsts & Co, 1989. #240/250 signed. Card cvrs. Fine in dj. *Williams*. $194/£125

GREENE, GRAHAM. Reflections on Travels with My Aunt. NY, 1989. One of 250 numbered, signed. Fine in integral dj, grey/white wrappers. *Rees.* $194/£125

GREENE, GRAHAM. The Revenge. London: Stellar Press, 1963. One of 300 ptd. Fine (inscrip) in wrappers. *Moorhouse.* $248/£160

GREENE, GRAHAM. A Sense of Reality. Viking, 1963. 1st Amer ed. Fine in NF dj. *Fine Books.* $35/£23

GREENE, GRAHAM. A Sense of Reality. London: Bodley Head, 1963. 1st ed. NF in dj. *Cahan.* $50/£32

GREENE, GRAHAM. A Sense of Reality. London: BH, 1963. 1st UK ed. NF in dj. *Lewton.* $62/£40

GREENE, GRAHAM. Shades of Greene. London: Bodley Head/Heinemann, 1975. 1st UK ed. Fine in laminated bds as issued. *Williams.* $23/£15

GREENE, GRAHAM. A Sort of Life. London: Bodley Head, 1971. 1st issue, w/misprint on p177. NF in dj (sl rubbed). *Rees.* $70/£45

GREENE, GRAHAM. Stamboul Train. London: Heinemann, (1932). 1st ed. (Few pp sl foxed.) *Petersfield.* $105/£68

GREENE, GRAHAM. Stamboul Train. Heinemann, 1932. 1st ed. Sl foxing; binding sl dull, else Good. *Whiteson.* $90/£58

GREENE, GRAHAM. The Third Man and The Fallen Idol. Heinemann, 1950. 1st UK ed. Fine in VG+ dj (sl creasing; closed tear spine top). *Williams.* $302/£195

GREENE, GRAHAM. The Third Man. NY, (1950). 1st ed. Fine in NF dj (sl rub to dj spine tips). *Mcclintock.* $135/£87

GREENE, GRAHAM. The Third Man. Helsinki: Eurographica, 1988. One of 500 signed, dated. Fine in dj. *Moorhouse.* $310/£200

GREENE, GRAHAM. Travels with My Aunt. London: Bodley Head, 1969. 1st ed. Inscrip. *Petersfield.* $25/£16

GREENE, GRAHAM. Ways of Escape. Bodley, 1980. 1st ed. Fine in dj. *Whiteson.* $22/£14

GREENE, GRAHAM. Ways of Escape. London: BH, 1980. 1st UK ed. Fine in dj. *Lewton.* $23/£15

GREENE, GRAHAM. Yes and No and For Whom the Bell Chimes. London, (1983). 1st ed, ltd to 750 numbered, signed. VG in glassine dj. *King.* $195/£126

GREENE, GRAHAM. Yes and No and For Whom the Bell Chimes. London: Bodley Head, 1983. One of 750 numbered, signed. Fine in glassine dj. *Rees.* $171/£110

GREENE, GRAHAM. Yes and No and For Whom the Bell Chimes. London: Bodley Head, 1983. One of 750, signed. Fine in clear plastic wrapper. *Williams.* $147/£95

GREENE, GRAHAM. Yes and No. Helsinki: Eurographica, 1984. Holograph MS reproduced in facs, 1st thus. One of 350 signed. Fine in wrappers. *Moorhouse.* $233/£150

GREENE, GRAHAM. Yours Etc: Letters to the Press 1945-89. Reinhardt, 1989. 1st ed. Fine in dj. *Whiteson.* $25/£16

GREENE, HARRY PLUNKET. Pilot and Other Stories. London: Macmillan, 1916. 8 color plts by H.J. Ford. (Sl foxed; joint sl torn; sl rubbed.) *Petersfield.* $25/£16

GREENE, HERBERT. Secret Agent in Spain. London: Robert Hale, 1938. 1st ed. Spine sl faded, o/w Nice. *Patterson.* $93/£60

GREENE, HOMER. A Lincoln Conscript. Boston, (1909). 1st ed. NF. *Mcgowan.* $25/£16

GREENE, JEROME A. Evidence and the Custer Enigma. Kansas City: K.C. Posse of the Westerners, 1973. Ltd to 500 signed. Blue cl over bds. Fine. *Glenn.* $35/£23

GREENE, MELISSA FAY. Praying for Sheetrock. Reading: Addison Wesley, 1991. 1st ed. Fine in Fine dj. *Revere.* $35/£23

GREENE, MERLE et al. Maya Sculpture from the Southern Lowlands.... Berkeley, CA, 1972. 202 photo plts. VG in dj. *Argosy.* $125/£81

GREENE, VIVIEN. English Dolls' Houses of the Eighteenth and Nineteenth Centuries. London, 1955. 1st ed. Sl water-damaged. *Argosy.* $85/£55

GREENE, W. HOWE. The Wooden Walls among the Ice Floes. London: Hutchinson, 1933. 1st ed. Good+ (corners rubbed, ex-lib w/mks). *Walcot.* $47/£30

GREENE, WELCOME ARNOLD. The Journals of...Journeys in the South. Alice E. Smith (ed). State Hist Soc of WI, 1957. 1st ed. *Heinoldt.* $20/£13

GREENEWALT, C.H. Humming Birds. NY, 1960. 1st ptg. 70 color photos. Buckram. *Wheldon & Wesley.* $186/£120

GREENFELD, HOWARD. Gertrude Stein. NY: Crown, (1973). 1st ed. (Top edge sl lightened.) Dj (2 short tears). *Sadlon.* $15/£10

GREENHILL, F.A. Incised Effigial Slabs. Faber & Faber, 1976. 1st ed. 2 vols. 340 plts. Djs & slipcase. *Edwards.* $78/£50

Greenhouse Favorites. (By Shirley Hibberd.) Groombridge, n.d. (ca 1878). 310pp, 36 Fine full-pg color plts. Marbled edges, eps. 1/2 calf over marbled bds (recased), raised bands. *Quest.* $625/£403

GREENHOW, EDWARD. On Diphtheria. NY, 1861. 1st Amer ed. 160pp. Good. *Fye.* $55/£35

GREENHOW, EDWARD. On Diphtheria. NY, 1861. 1st Amer ed. 160pp + ads. Blind-stamped cl. VG. *Argosy.* $85/£55

GREENHOW, ROBERT. The History of Oregon and California, and the Other Territories.... Boston: Little, Brown, 1845. 2nd Amer ed. (iv),xviii,(ii),492pp (foxed, ink inscrip, lacks map). Pub's cl (worn). Howes G 389. *Bookpress.* $250/£161

GREENHOW, ROBERT. The History of Oregon and California, and the Other Territories.... NY: D. Appleton, 1845. 3rd ed. xviii,492,7pp, lg fldg map (loose). Mod 1/2 blue calf, bds (rebound; new eps); gilt-lettered spine, raised bands. Sm lib rubberstamp, marginal damage to map, o/w Fine. Howes G 389. *Harrington.* $275/£177

GREENLEAF, SIMON. A Treatise on the Law of Evidence. Boston: Little, Brown, 1866-68. 3 vols. Contemp sheep (worn, rubbed). Working set. *Boswell.* $150/£97

GREENLEAF, STEPHEN. Grave Error. Dial Press, 1979. 1st ed. Top edge lt worn, else Fine in dj (sl soiled). *Murder.* $100/£65

GREENOUGH, SARAH and JUAN HAMILTON. Alfred Stieglitz: Photographs and Writings. (Washington)/NY: Nat'l Gallery of Art/Callaway Editions, 1983. 1st ed. 73 full-pg photos. Fine in pict dj. *Cahan.* $125/£81

GREENSPAN, SOPHIE. Westward with Fremont, the Story of Solomon Carvalho. Phila, 1969. 1st ed. Ep maps. VF in VF dj. *Oregon.* $40/£26

GREENWAY, JOHN. Folklore of the Great West. Palo Alto: Amer West, 1969. 1st ed. VG+ in VG+ dj. *Bishop.* $15/£10

GREENWOOD, GRACE. (Pseud of Sara Jane Clarke Lippincott.) Records of Five Years. Boston: Ticknor & Fields, 1867. 1st ptg. vi,222pp. Grn cl. *Schoyer.* $35/£23

GREENWOOD, J. Silas the Conjurer. Ward, Lock & Bowden, (ca 1899). Pict stamped cl. VG. *Aronovitz.* $65/£42

GREENWOOD, JAMES. Curiousities of Savage Life. London, 1863. 1st & 2nd series. 2 vols. xiv,418; xiv,418pp (marginal browning; prelims loose); 16 color, 32 tinted plts. Aeg. Blind-emb cl (shaken; sl chipped; hinges cracked, bkpls removed), gilt. *Edwards.* $93/£60

GREENWOOD, JOHN. The Revolutionary Services of John Greenwood...1775-1783. NY: (De Vinne Press), 1922. Ltd to 100. 6 plts. Blue cl, gilt. Good. *Karmiole.* $125/£81

GREER, GERMAINE. The Female Eunuch. NY: McGraw-Hill, (1971). 1st Amer ed. NF (lt wear) in VG dj (1-inch chip). *Hermitage.* $35/£23

GREGG, ARTHUR B. Old Hellebergh. (Altamont, NY, 1936). 188,(4)pp; fldg map. Wraps. *Hayman.* $25/£16

GREGG, JOSIAH. Commerce of the Prairies or the Journal of a Santa Fe Trader.... NY: Langley, 1845 & 1844. Vol 1-1845 2nd ed; vol 2-1st Eng ed. 2 vols. Frontis, 320pp, 2 plts; frontis, 318pp, 2 plts, map. Vol 1 spine ends, edges worn, lacking fep; vol 2 lacking rep, o/w VG. *Oregon.* $500/£323

GREGG, JOSIAH. Commerce of the Prairies or the Journal of a Sante Fe Trader.... Phila: J.W. Moore, 1851. 5th ed. 2 vols. 323; 324pp (dknd); 6 plts (sl browned); map. Gilt spine titles. Nice set (spines sunned). Howes G 401. *Bohling.* $250/£161

GREGG, JOSIAH. Diary and Letters of Josiah Gregg. Southwestern Enterprises, 1840-1847. Univ OK, 1941. 1st ed. 10 plts, 2 fldg maps. Fine. *Oregon.* $65/£42

GREGG, KATE. The Road to Santa Fe. Journal and Diaries of George Champlin Sibley...1825-1827. Univ NM, (1952). 1st ed. Ep maps. Fine in VG dj. *Oregon.* $40/£26

GREGO, JOSEPH. Rowlandson the Caricaturist. London: C&W, 1880. 2 vols. Frontis port loosely inserted, xv,378; xi,454pp, (spotting, bkpls; hinges tender). Morocco backed cl bds (bumped, sl cl loss), dec gilt (spines rubbed). *Edwards.* $217/£140

GREGO, JOSEPH. Rowlandson the Caricaturist. London: C&W, Piccadilly, 1880. 1st ed. 2 vols. xv,378; xi,454pp, frontis w/guard vol 1. 1/2 morocco, patterned cl; raised bands, gilt; marbled edges, eps. VG set (edges, hinges rubbed; spine dried; lt foxing 1st, last few leaves; bkpl). *Cahan.* $200/£129

GREGORY, ALYSE. Wheels on Gravel. London: John Lane, Bodley Head, 1938. 1st Eng ed. Red cl. Name, o/w Fine in dj (sl dusty). *Dalian.* $54/£35

GREGORY, AUGUSTA. The Image. A Play in Three Acts. Dublin: Maunsel, 1910. 1st ed. Ptd bds. Spine crown sl worn w/narrow crack, else Nice. *Reese.* $30/£19

GREGORY, AUGUSTA. Irish Folk-History Plays. NY: Putnam's, 1912. 1st Amer ed. Fine. *Hermitage.* $50/£32

GREGORY, DICK with ROBERT LIPSYTE. Nigger. NY: Dutton, (1964). 1st ed. Name, lt rubbing base of bds, sl foxing few pp, else NF in VG dj (extrems lt worn). *Between The Covers.* $40/£26

GREGORY, J. Ru the Conqueror. Scribner, 1933. 1st ed. Fine in VG+ pict dj (sm chip spine). *Aronovitz.* $85/£55

GREGORY, J.W. The Nature and Origin of Fiords. London: John Murray, 1913. 1st ed. 8pp plts. (Sl spotting 1st, last leaves; bkpl, sig, stamp.) *Hollett.* $70/£45

GREGORY, JACK and RENNARD STRICKLAND. Sam Houston with the Cherokees: 1829-1833. UTP, 1967. 1st ed. Dj. *Lambeth.* $30/£19

GREGORY, O. Meccania the Super-State. Methuen, 1918. 1st ed. VG. *Aronovitz.* $50/£32

GREGORY, T. Deer at Night in the North Woods. Springfield/Baltimore: Thomas, 1930. 1st ed. Blind-stamped dec cl. NF. *Mikesh.* $30/£19

GREIFF, CONSTANCE M. Lost America, from the Atlantic to the Mississippi. Princeton: Pyne Press, 1971. 1st ed. Dj worn, else VG. *Bookpress.* $45/£29

GREIFF, CONSTANCE M. Lost America, from the Mississippi to the Pacific. NY: Weathervane Books, (1972). 1st ed. Rubberstamp 1/2 title, tp; dj handled, else Good. *Bookpress.* $50/£32

GREIG-SMITH, P. Quantitative Plant Ecology. Berkeley, 1983. 3rd ed. Softbound. New. *Brooks.* $39/£25

GRENDON, STEPHEN. (Pseud of August Derleth.) Mr. George and Other Odd Persons. Sauk City: Arkham House, 1963. 1st ed. Bkpl removal; spots, else NF in dj. *Other Worlds.* $35/£23

GRENDON, STEPHEN. (Pseud of August Derleth.) Mr. George and Other Odd Persons. Arkham House, 1963. 1st ed. Fine in dj. *Madle.* $40/£26

GRENFELL, WILFRED. Forty Years for Labrador. London: Hodder, 1934. Few pp sl foxed, o/w VG in dj. *Petersfield.* $25/£16

GRESHEM, WILLIAM LINDSAY. Nightmare Alley. NY, (1946). 1st ed, 1st bk. Sl worn, spine dull, else Good in dj (very worn; lt attached to eps). *King.* $25/£16

GRESSLEY, GENE M. Bankers and Cattlemen. Knopf, 1966. 1st ed. Fine in Fine dj. *Oregon.* $35/£23

GRESSLEY, GENE M. Bankers and Cattlemen. NY: Knopf, 1966. 1st ed. VG in dj. *Lien.* $40/£26

GREVILLE, CHARLES C.F. The Greville Memoirs. London: Longmans, Green, 1874-87. 8 vols. 3/4 polished calf (unevenly sunned) over marbled bds, gilt spines (nicks 3 vols), raised bands, leather spine labels, marbled edges (sl abrasions). *Sadlon.* $100/£65

GREW, DAVID. Beyond Rope and Fence. Boni & Liveright, 1922. 1st ed. *Lambeth.* $25/£16

GREY, C.H. Hardy Bulbs. Vol 1. London: Williams & Norgate, (1937). 1st ed. 15 color plts. Errata slip. VG in VG dj. *Oregon.* $100/£65

GREY, C.H. Hardy Bulbs. Vol 2. London: Williams & Norgate, (1938). 1st ed. 19 color plts. Errata slip. VG in VG dj. *Oregon.* $100/£65

GREY, RICHARD. Memoria Technica; or, A New Method of Artifical Memory.... London, 1737. 3rd ed. Sm 8vo. xvi,159pp. Full gilt-edged speckled calf; spine raised bands. (Bkpl; upper joint sl tender.) *Edwards.* $140/£90

GREY, ZANE. The Deer Stalker. NY: Harper, (1949). 1st ed. NF in NF dj (lt soiled, bumped). *Unger.* $100/£65

GREY, ZANE. The Deer Stalker. NY: Harper, 1949. 1st ed. Nice in dj (sl edgewear). *Else Fine.* $120/£77

GREY, ZANE. The Deer Stalker. H&S, 1949. 1st UK ed. VG in VG dj (rubbed). *Lewton.* $31/£20

GREY, ZANE. Fighting Caravans. NY: Harper, (1929). 1st ed. VG + in VG + dj. *Unger.* $275/£177

GREY, ZANE. Fighting Caravans. NY: Harper, 1929. 1st ed w/'H-D' code letters on copyright pg. NF in dj (edgewear; internally mended). *Antic Hay.* $175/£113

GREY, ZANE. Fighting Caravans. NY/London: Harper & Bros, 1929. 1st ed. NF in Attractive dj (short, internally mended edge-tears; lt soiling rear panel). *Bernard.* $225/£145

GREY, ZANE. Forlorn River. NY, 1927. 1st Amer ed. NF (lower edges sl rubbed; inscrip). *Polyanthos.* $45/£29

GREY, ZANE. Lost Pueblo. NY: Harper, (1954). 1st ed ('H-D'). VG in dj (edges lt rubbed). *Houle.* $150/£97

GREY, ZANE. Nevada. NY, 1928. 1st Amer ed. Pict eps. NF (spine extrems sl rubbed). *Polyanthos.* $35/£23

GREY, ZANE. Rogue River Feud. NY: Harper, 1948. 1st ed. VG (name, neat ink addition of other titles to title list prelim pg) in dj (corner wear). *Else Fine.* $200/£129

GREY, ZANE. Roping Lions in the Grand Canyon. NY: G&D, 1924. Early reissue. Fine in dj (lt worn, soiled). *Else Fine.* $85/£55

GREY, ZANE. Stairs of Sand. NY: Harpers, (1943). 1st Amer ed. Fine in dj (sm tears; sm chip rear). *Agvent.* $65/£42

GREY, ZANE. Tappan's Burro. NY: Harpers, (1923). 1st Amer ed. Chapman & Street (illus). Fine in dj (lt edgewear). *Agvent.* $250/£161

GREY, ZANE. The Thundering Herd. Harper Bros, 1935. 1st ed. VG. *Bishop.* $15/£10

GREY, ZANE. To the Last Man. NY: G&D, n.d. (c.1922). Photoplay ed. Fine in pict dj (lt chipped). *Else Fine.* $45/£29

GREY, ZANE. Wyoming. NY, (1953). 1st ed. VG. *Argosy.* $45/£29

GREY, ZANE. Wyoming. NY: Harper's, 1953. 1st ed. NF in dj (wrinkle, 2-inch closed tear back panel, minor wear extrems). *Else Fine.* $85/£55

GRIBBLE, FRANCIS. Montreux. A&C Black, 1908. 1st ed. 20 color plts by J. Hardwick Lewis & May Hardwicke. Teg. Dec cl (spine sl chipped). *Edwards.* $47/£30

GRIDLEY, MARION. Indians of Yesterday. Donohue, (1940). 1st ed. Color frontis, 5 color plts. Color pict bds. Fine in VG dj. *Oregon.* $45/£29

GRIERSON, EDWARD. A Crime of One's Own. NY: Putnam's, (1967). 1st US ed. Fine in dj (sl chipping). *Oak Knoll.* $40/£26

GRIERSON, EDWARD. A Crime of One's Own. NY: Putnam, 1967. 1st US ed. Fine (bkpl) in NF dj. *Janus.* $45/£29

GRIERSON, JOHN. Air Whaler. London: Sampson, Low, Marston, 1949. VG in dj. *High Latitude.* $55/£35

GRIERSON, JOHN. Challenge to the Poles. London: G.T. Foulis, (1964). 1st ed. 29 maps. VG in VG- dj. *Blue Dragon.* $50/£32

GRIERSON, JOHN. High Failure. London: William Hodge, 1936. 1st ed. VG (lib number inked out) in dj (sl used). *Hollett.* $39/£25

GRIESINGER, WILHELM. Mental Pathology and Therapeutics. NY, 1882. 375pp. Good. *Fye.* $100/£65

GRIEVCE, MRS. M. A Modern Herbal. London, 1931. 1st ed. 2 vols. 96 plts. (Margins sl thumbed; pencil marginal ruling; eps lt spotted.) *Edwards.* $132/£85

GRIFFIN, BULKLEY S. (ed). Offbeat History. Cleveland: World, 1967. 1st ed. Dec cl. NF in Good + dj. *Connolly.* $25/£16

GRIFFIN, JAMES BENNETT. The Fort Ancient Aspect: Its Cultural and Chronological Position.... Ann Arbor: Univ of MI Press, 1943. 157 plts, 10 maps. Good. *Archaeologia.* $185/£119

GRIFFIN, JOHN JOSEPH. Chemical Handicraft: A Classified and Descriptive Catalogue.... London, 1877. 2nd ed. 479pp. Cl (worn, chipped). *King.* $225/£145

GRIFFIN, LEPEL HENRY. The Great Republic. NY: Scribner, 1884. 1st ed. 189pp (ruffled); uncut. (Cvrs stained.) *Ginsberg.* $75/£48

GRIFFIN, MARTIN I.J. The History of Commodore John Barry. Phila: Amer Catholic Hist Soc, 1897. Ltd to 200, this unnumbered. vi,261pp; 10 plts (blind-emb stamp corners). 1/2 leather (spine scuffed). Howes G 423. *Schoyer.* $50/£32

GRIFFIS, WILLIAM ELLIOT. The Fire-Fly's Lovers and Other Fairy Tales of Old Japan. NY: T.Y. Crowell, (1908). 1st ed. Lg 8vo, x,166pp. Grn pict cl. VG. *Godot.* $50/£32

GRIFFITH, F. A Collection of Hieroglyphs: A Contribution to the History of Egyptian Writing. London: Egypt Exploration Fund, 1898. xii,74pp, 9 color plts. Good. *Archaeologia.* $125/£81

GRIFFITH, G. The Gold-Finder. White, 1898. 1st ed. Pict cl. VG. *Aronovitz.* $125/£81

GRIFFITH, G. A Mayfair Magician. F.V. White, 1905. 1st ed. Sm tear spine head, else VG. *Fine Books.* $85/£55

GRIFFITH, G.W.E. My 96 Years in the Great West. L.A.: Privately ptd, 1929. 1st ed. Frontis; 2pp ports. VG. *Oregon.* $40/£26

GRIFFITH, J.W. and A. HENFREY. The Micrographic Dictionary.... London, 1875. 3rd ed. 2 vols. 48 plts (15 color). Mod buckram. (Name half-title; sl foxing.) *Wheldon & Wesley.* $124/£80

GRIFFITHS, ARTHUR. Memorials of Millbank, and Chapters in Prison History. Henry S. King, 1875. 1st ed. 2 vols. Etched frontis each vol. Cl pict blocked in black, gilt-lettered. Clean (label removed each cvr; name fr fly vol 1). *Bickersteth.* $287/£185

GRIFFITHS, JOHN W. Treatise on Marine and Naval Architecture. NY: Appleton, 1851. Reissue. 416,(2)pp; 45 plts, 4 tables. Orig cl (worn). *Lefkowicz.* $750/£484

GRIFFITHS, JOHN W. Treatise on Marine and Naval Architecture. London: George Philip, 1856. New ed. Apparently the 1st Eng ed, ptd in dbl-columns, folio. Frontis, 196,(3,3 blank)pp, 45 plts. Later cl. *Lefkowicz.* $500/£323

GRIFFITHS, WILLIAM H. The Story of the American Bank Note Company. (NY, 1959). 4to. 8 inserted double-pg plts. Corner bumped, else Fine. *Veatchs.* $125/£81

GRIFFITHS, WILLIAM H. The Story of the American Bank Note Company. (NY: American Bank Note Co, 1959). 1st ed. 9 plts. Fine. *Bookpress.* $225/£145

GRIFFITS, THOMAS E. The Rudiments of Lithography. London: Faber & Faber, (1956). Eps dknd, o/w Fine in dj. *Heller.* $40/£26

GRIGGS, NATHAN K. Lyrics of the Lariat: Poems with Notes. NY: Revell, (1893). 1st ed. 266pp (inscrip). Dec cl. *Ginsberg.* $75/£48

GRIGGS, S.E. Souls of the Infinite. Metropolitan, 1911. 1st ed. VG + . *Aronovitz.* $50/£32

GRIGSON, GEOFFREY. The Englishman's Flora. London, 1955. Buckram (spine faded). *Wheldon & Wesley.* $78/£50

GRIGSON, GEOFFREY. The Englishman's Flora. London, 1955. 1st ed. 44 full-pg b/w plts. NF (spine sl sunned). *Shifrin.* $125/£81

GRIGSON, GEOFFREY. Gardenage. London: Routledge & Kegan Paul, 1952. Fine in dj (lt worn). *Quest.* $35/£23

GRIGSON, GEOFFREY. Painted Caves. London, 1957. 1st ed. Dj. *Edwards.* $31/£20

GRIGSON, GEOFFREY. Samuel Palmer. The Visionary Years. London, 1947. 68 plts. Good. *Washton.* $50/£32

GRIGSON, GEOFFREY. Samuel Palmer. The Visionary Years. London: Kegan Paul, 1947. Color frontis, 68 plts. Sound. *Ars Artis.* $109/£70

GRIGSON, GEOFFREY. Several Observations. Cresset, (1939). 1st ed. Cl sl bubbled, sl mkd, o/w VG. *Poetry.* $23/£15

GRIGSON, GEOFFREY. Several Observations. London: Cresset Press, (1939). 1st ed. Some leaves carelessly opened, o/w Nice. *Patterson.* $70/£45

GRIMBLE, A. Highland Sport. London: Chapman & Hall, 1894. 1st ed. xii,(iv),268pp (eps foxed; joints cracked); 10 plts. Vellum-backed bds (rubbed, bumped, spine label chipped), gilt. *Hollett.* $279/£180

GRIMES, ABSALOM. Absalom Grimes, Confederate Mail Runner. M.M. Quaife (ed). New Haven, 1926. 1st ed. Illus dj worn, chipped, o/w VG + . *Pratt.* $70/£45

GRIMES, MARTHA. The Anodyne Necklace. Boston: Little, Brown, 1983. 1st ed. Fine in NF dj (lt edgewear; closed tear). *Janus.* $75/£48

GRIMES, MARTHA. The Anodyne Necklace. Boston: Little-Brown, 1983. 1st ed. VF in dj. *Else Fine.* $100/£65

GRIMES, MARTHA. The Dirty Duck. Boston: Little-Brown, 1984. 1st ed. VF in dj. *Else Fine.* $75/£48

GRIMES, MARTHA. The Old Fox Deceiv'd. Boston: Little-Brown, 1982. 1st ed. VF in dj. *Else Fine.* $125/£81

GRIMKE, ARCHIBALD. William Lloyd Garrison, the Abolitionist. NY: Funk & Wagnalls, (1891). 1st Amer ed. Red cl. Fine. *Between The Covers.* $125/£81

GRIMM, JACOB and WILHELM. (GRIMM BROTHERS.) Fairy Tales by the Brothers Grimm. Offenbach: LEC, 1931. 1st ed. One of 1500. Signed by Fritz Kredel (illus) and Rudolf Koch (designer). Full morocco. Fine in slipcase (sl worn). *Cahan.* $150/£97

GRIMM, JACOB and WILHELM. (GRIMM BROTHERS.) The Grimm Fairy Library. London/NY: George Routledge, n.d. (ca 1870). Sm 8vo. 128pp. 10 vols, all w/black stamped dec flowers on tooled cl on bds in various colors, as issued; gilt title spines. Full-pg frontis each vol. E.H. Wehnert (illus). Orig grn cl-cvrd box (lt edgeworn); fldg lid dec w/gilt flowers, insects, spider web, title; lt grn paper label w/list of titles ptd in gold, pasted down on inside of lid. Fine set (eps darkened; some sigs pulled but still attached; occasional lt foxing. Few corners creased, 2 sl torn; corner 1 leaf restored w/some loss; few chipped edges restored; edges of index label expertly restored). *Hobbyhorse.* $900/£581

GRIMM, JACOB and WILHELM. (GRIMM BROTHERS.) Grimm's Fairy Tales. Mrs. H.B. Paull (trans). London/NY: Frederick Warne, 1888. 8vo. 16 full-pg color illus. Dk blue pebbled cl (newly rebacked in morocco). *Glenn.* $150/£97

GRIMM, JACOB and WILHELM. (GRIMM BROTHERS.) Grimm's Fairy Tales. London: Constable, 1909. 1st ed thus. Thick 4to. 325pp, 40 full-pg color illus, 55 b/w illus by Arthur Rackham. Trade ed bound in red cl, gilt pict lettering, stamping. VG (lt edgewear). *Davidson.* $1,200/£774

GRIMM, JACOB and WILHELM. (GRIMM BROTHERS.) Grimm's Fairy Tales. London: Hodder & Stoughton, 1921. 1st Eng ed. 4to. 308pp (label remains prelim; foxing), 12 full-pg color plts by Elenore Abbott. Lt brn cl, gold/blue dec, lettering. Pict dj (lt marginal foxing). *Reisler.* $225/£145

GRIMM, JACOB and WILHELM. (GRIMM BROTHERS.) Grimm's Household Tales. London: Eyre & Spottiswoode, 1946. 1st ed. 8vo. 303pp, 5 color illus, 56 b/w dwgs by Mervyn Peake. Yellow cl, black title. VG in dj (tape repaired). *Davidson.* $125/£81

GRIMM, WILHELM. Dear Mili. Ralph Manheim (trans). NY: Michael di Capua, 1988. 1st ed. Oblong 4to, (40)pp, 15 full-pg color plts (3 dbl-pg) by Maurice Sendak. Fine in dj. *Cox.* $23/£15

GRIMM, WILHELM. Dear Mili. NY: Farrar Straus, 1988. 1st ed. Maurice Sendak (illus). Lg 8vo. As New in As New dj. *Book Adoption.* $45/£29

GRIMM, WILLIAM C. How to Recognize Trees. NY, 1962. Fine in dj (chipped). *Brooks.* $24/£15

GRIMSHAW, A. The Horse, A Bibliography of British Books 1851-1976. London, 1982. Ltd ed #337/1000. Signed. Good in dj. *Henly.* $51/£33

GRIMSHAW, B. The Sorcerer's Stone. Winston, 1914. 1st Amer ed. Spine sl soiled, else VG + . *Aronovitz.* $50/£32

GRINDON, LEO H. The Shakespere Flora. Manchester/London: Palmer & Howe/Simkin, Marshall, 1883. Signed. Frontis, xii,327pp, 4 plts. Teg. Morocco spine (rebacked) over silk-cvrd bds, gilt dec. NF. *Quest.* $185/£119

GRINKER, ROY. Neurology with the Assistance of Norman A. Levey.... Springfield: Thomas, 1944. 3rd ed. (Cl rubbed.) *Goodrich.* $35/£23

GRINNELL, DIXON and LINSDALE. Fur Bearing Mammals of California. Univ CA, 1937. 1st ed. 2 vols. 2 color frontispieces, 11 color plts. Bkpls removed, o/w Fine set. *Oregon.* $175/£113

GRINNELL, GEORGE BIRD et al (eds). Hunting Trails on Three Continents. NY: Derrydale, 1933. Ltd to 250 numbered. Signed by Prentice Gray (ed). 2 plts. Fine + . *Bowman.* $2,700/£1,742

GRINNELL, GEORGE BIRD. American Duck Shooting. NY: Forest & Stream Pub Co, (1901). 1st ed. 58 ports. Gilt pict maroon cl. Extrems lt rubbed, o/w Nice. *House.* $180/£116

GRINNELL, GEORGE BIRD. Beyond the Old Frontier. Adventures of Indian-Fighters.... Scribner's, 1913. 1st ed. 15 plts, map. Good + (dampstaining rear cvr, upper spine corner of 1st few pp). *Oregon.* $40/£26

GRINNELL, GEORGE BIRD. The Fighting Cheyenne. NY, 1915. 1st ed. Pict cl. Sl cvr wear, soiling, o/w VG. *Pratt.* $125/£81

GRINNELL, GEORGE BIRD. The Fighting Cheyenne. NY: Scribner's, 1915. 1st ed. Pict cl. Good (sl spotted). Howes G433. *Lien.* $200/£129

GRINNELL, JOSEPH. Gold Hunting in Alaska. Elgin, IL: David Cook, (1901). 1st ed. Gilt-stamped cl, marbled bds. Edgeworn, o/w VG. *Oregon.* $70/£45

GRINNELL, JOSEPH. Gold Hunting in Alaska. Elizabeth Grinnell (ed). Elgin, IL: David C. Cook, (1901). 3/4 red cl, marbled bds. VG. *Bohling.* $75/£48

GRINSELL, LESLIE V. Barrow, Pyramid and Tomb: Ancient Burial Customs.... London: Thames & Hudson, (1974). Good in dj. *Archaeologia.* $35/£23

GRISHAM, JOHN. The Client. NY: Doubleday, (1993). 1st ed. Signed. As New in dj. *Jaffe.* $125/£81

GRISHAM, JOHN. The Client. Century, 1993. 1st UK ed. Fine in dj. *Lewton.* $22/£14

GRISHAM, JOHN. The Firm. NY, (1991). 1st ed. Name, sl sprung, else Good in dj (sl used). *King.* $95/£61

GRISHAM, JOHN. The Pelican Brief. NY: Doubleday, 1992. 1st ed. Fine in Fine dj. *Pettler.* $35/£23

GRISHAM, JOHN. The Pelican Brief. London: Century, 1992. 1st UK ed. Fine in dj. *Lewton.* $20/£13

GRISHAM, JOHN. A Time to Kill: A Novel of Retribution. NY: Wynwood Press, (1989). True 1st ed of 1st bk, w/no reviews of subsequent books. VF in VF dj. *Between The Covers.* $2,250/£1,452

GRISWOLD, FRANK GRAY. Fish Facts and Fancies. NY: Scribner's, 1926. One of 1000. VG. *Bowman.* $50/£32

GROBER, KARL. Children's Toys of Bygone Days. NY: Frederick A. Stokes, (1928). 1st ed. 306 photo plts. Orange cl. VG in dj (worn). *Glenn.* $145/£94

GRODDECK, GEORG. Exploring the Unconscious. NY: Funk & Wagnalls, (1950). 1st Amer ed, ptd on British sheets. Ptd black cl. VG in dj (chipped). *Gach.* $35/£23

GROENWEGEN-FRANKFORT, H.A. Arrest and Movement. London: Faber & Faber, 1951. 1st ed. 94 b/w plts. Dj (ragged, sl loss). *Edwards.* $85/£55

GROESBECK, HARRY A., JR. The Process and Practice of Photo-Engraving. GC: Doubleday, Page, 1924. 1st ed. Gilt-dec cl (tips sl rubbed). NF. *Cahan.* $50/£32

GROGAN, EMMETT. Final Score. NY: Holt, Rinehart & Winston, 1976. 1st ed. NF in dj (sl rubbed, nicked). *Sclanders.* $28/£18

GROHMANN, WILL and ANTOINE TUDAL. The Intimate Sketchbooks of G. Braque. NY: Harcourt Brace, 1955. Pict bds (edges worn). *Argosy.* $450/£290

GROHMANN, WILL. Paul Klee. NY: Abrams, (1954). NF (spine sl faded) in dj. *Cahan.* $125/£81

GROHMANN, WILL. Paul Klee. NY: Abrams, (1965). 1st ed. 40 color plts. VG. *Argosy.* $125/£81

GROHMANN, WILL. Wassily Kandinsky. Life and Work. London: Thames & Hudson, 1959. 40 tipped-in color plts, 20 b/w plts. (Cl sl worn.) *Ars Artis.* $388/£250

GROHMANN, WILL. Wassily Kandinsky: Life and Work. NY: Abrams, (1958). 1st ed. 41 tipped-in color plts. Illus cl. Fine in pict dj. *Cahan.* $200/£129

GRONLUND, LAURENCE. The New Economy. Chicago: Herbert S. Stone, 1898. 1st ed. Fep gone; rear hinge starting, else VG. *Beasley.* $85/£55

GRONOW, REESE HOWELL. The Reminiscences and Recollections of Captain Gronow. London, 1892. 2 vols. xxviii,353; xiv,340pp + 22pp pub's cat; 33 hand-colored plts; teg (eps, edges sl spotted). *Edwards.* $233/£150

GRONOW, REESE HOWELL. The Reminiscences and Recollections of Captain Gronow. London: John C. Nimmo, 1892. 2 vols. xxviii,353; xiv,340pp; emb coat-of-arms mtd on flyleaf. Joseph Grego (illus). Full polished red morocco, gilt rules, blue spine labels; teg. Fine set in felt-line slipcase. *Schoyer.* $300/£194

GROOM, PERCY. Trees and Their Life Histories. London, 1909. Gilt-stamped cl (sl bumped, worn). Nice (bkpl). *King.* $50/£32

GROOM, WINSTON and DUNCAN SPENCER. Conversations with the Enemy: The Story of Pfc. Robert Garwood. NY: Putnam's, (1983). Fine in Fine dj. *Aka.* $35/£23

GROOME, FRANCIS HINDES. Kriegspiel: The War-Game. London: Ward Lock & Bowden, 1896. 1st ed. Frontis, 380pp + 12pp ads (chip 1 ad leaf; trace of old clover leaf laid in). Blue cl, gilt-lettered spine (hinges cracked but firm). *Shasky.* $65/£42

GROPIUS, WALTER and KENZO TANGE. Katsura, Tradition and Creation in Japanese Architecture. Tokyo: Zokeisha Pub, 1960. 1st Japanese ed. VG in protective box. *Bookpress.* $185/£119

GROPIUS, WALTER et al. Town Plan for the Town of Selb. Cambridge: MIT, 1969. 1st Amer ed. Frontis; 56 plans, map. VG. *Bookpress.* $125/£81

GROPMAN, DONALD. Say It Ain't So Joe! Little-Brown, 1979. 1st ed. VG + in VG dj. *Plapinger.* $50/£32

GROSS, SAMUEL D. Autobiography with Sketches of His Contemporaries. Phila: G. Barrie, 1887. 2 vols. 2 frontis engrs, xxxi,(1),407; viii,437pp. Uncut. Signed, dated holograph letter. Red/black titles. Fine (ex-libris). *Hemlock.* $300/£194

GROSS, SAMUEL W. A Practical Treatise on Impotence, Sterility and Allied Disorders of the Male Sexual Organs. Phila, 1887. 3rd ed. 172pp. Good. *Fye.* $75/£48

GROSSMAN, JULIAN. Echo of a Distant Drum. NY: Abrams, (1974). 1st ed. Frontis. (Pencil inscrip; sm puncture hole affecting most text, fr cvr; dj rubbed, sunned.) *Bookpress.* $50/£32

GROSSMAN, WILLIAM L. and JACK W. FARRELL. The Heart of Jazz. NY: NYU Press, 1956. 1st ed. Fine in dj (lt used). *Beasley.* $40/£26

GROSSMANN, F. Pieter Bruegel. Phaidon, 1974. 3rd rev ed. 149 plts (32 color). *Ars Artis.* $78/£50

GROSSMITH, GEORGE with WEEDON GROSSMITH. Diary of a Nobody. Arrowsmith, 1892. 1st UK ed. VG (sl bumping lower edge). *Williams.* $388/£250

GROSZ, GEORGE. Ecce Homo. NY, 1966. 1st Amer ed. 16 color plts; 2 supplementary color plts inserted. Fine in dj (sl edge sunned). *Polyanthos.* $150/£97

GROUP, HAROLD E. Book of Small Houses. GC: GC Pub, (1946). 1st ed. VG. *Bookpress.* $25/£16

GROVE, ALVIN R. The Lure and Lore of Trout Fishing. Harrisburg: Stackpole, 1951. 1st ed. VG in dj. *Bowman.* $60/£39

GROVE, HENRY M. Moscow. London: A&C Black, 1912. Fldg map. Blue dec cl (spine faded; foxed). *Schoyer.* $30/£19

GROVER, EULALIE OSGOOD. The Sunbonnet Babies in Italy. Chicago: Rand McNally, (1922). Bertha Corbett Melcher & James McCracken (illus). 8vo. 187pp; illus eps. Tan cl, color emb design. Spine foot sl worn, o/w VG. *Drusilla's.* $60/£39

GROVER, H.M. A Voice from Stonehenge, Part I (all ptd). London: Cleaver, 1847. iv,196pp, litho plt. (Title stained.) Cl-backed bds. *Marlborough.* $233/£150

GROWOLL, ADOLPH. Book Trade Bibliography in the United States. NY: Brick Row, 1939. One of 150. In slipcase. *Bookpress.* $135/£87

GRUBAR, F.S. William Ranney, Painter of the Early West. NY: Clarkson Potter, 1962. 55 plts (1 color). Sound in dj. *Ars Artis.* $47/£30

GRUBB, DAVIS. Ancient Lights. Viking, 1982. 1st ed. Fine in dj. *Madle.* $95/£61

GRUBB, DAVIS. The Night of the Hunter. (NY): Harper, (1953). 1st ed, 1st bk. One of 1000, signed for presentation to the book trade. VG in orig glassine (brn, brittle, torn). *Turlington.* $125/£81

GRUBB, DAVIS. The Night of the Hunter. (NY): Harper, (1953). 1st ed. 1st bk. NF in dj. *Godot.* $65/£42

GRUBB, DAVIS. The Watchman. Scribner's, 1961. 1st ed. VG + (bkpl) in VG dj. *Bishop.* $25/£16

GRUBB, E.H. and W.S. GUILFORD. The Potato, a Compilation.... GC, 1912. (Lt scuffing spine ends; soiling.) *Sutton.* $38/£25

GRUBB, NORMAN H. Cherries. London, 1949. 1st ed. 28 plts (12 color). VG in dj. *Argosy.* $75/£48

GRUBB, NORMAN H. Cherries. London, 1949. 1st ed. Signed. 12 color, 16 plain plts. Fine. *Henly.* $43/£28

GRUBE, ERNST. Islamic Painting from the 11th to the 18th Century in the Collection of Hans P. Kraus. NY: H.P. Kraus, n.d. One of 750 numbered. 54 color plts. Good. *Washton.* $375/£242

GRUBER, FRANK. The Gift Horse. NY: Farrar & Rinehart, 1942. 1st ed. Fine in dj (spine ends nicked; sl wear). *Mordida.* $100/£65

GRUBER, FRANK. The Gold Gap. NY: Dutton, 1968. Stated 1st ed. NF in dj (spine sunned). *Aka.* $35/£23

GRUBER, FRANK. The Mighty Blockhead. NY: Farrar & Rinehart, 1942. 1st ed. Fine in dj (nicks; sl wear spine ends; closed tears). *Mordida.* $85/£55

GRUBER, FRANK. The Pulp Jungle. L.A.: Sherbourne, 1967. 1st ed. Fine in Fine dj. *Janus.* $25/£16

GRUBER, FRANK. Zane Grey a Biography. Cleveland: World, (1970). 1st ed. Fine in Fine dj. *Book Market.* $35/£23

GRUELLE, JOHN B. All About Cinderella. NY: Cupples & Leon, (1916). 1st ed. 12mo. Dk brn bds w/2-color paste label. Good in pict dj (sl staining lower edge). *Reisler.* $125/£81

GRUELLE, JOHN B. The Camel with the Wrinkled Knees. Springfield: McLoughlin Bros, (1943). 1st ed thus. Justin C. Gruelle (illus). 8vo. Full color illus bds. Full color dj (minor marginal wear). *Reisler.* $90/£58

GRUELLE, JOHN B. Raggedy Ann and the Hoppy Toad. Springfield: McLoughlin Bros, (1943). 1st ed thus. 8vo. Justin C. Gruelle (illus). Full color illus bds. Good in full color dj (minor marginal wear). *Reisler.* $95/£61

GRUELLE, JOHNNY. Beloved Belindy. Chicago: M.A. Donohue, 1926. 8vo. Unpaginated. VG in dj (sl worn). *Davidson.* $175/£113

GRUELLE, JOHNNY. Friendly Fairies. Chicago/NY: M.A. Donohue, (1919). 8vo. Unpaginated. NF (inscrip) in dj (lt chipped). *Davidson.* $125/£81

GRUELLE, JOHNNY. Friendly Fairies. Chicago: M.A. Donohue, 1919. 8vo. Pict paper-cvrd bds, cl spine. VG + . *Book Adoption.* $85/£55

GRUELLE, JOHNNY. Johnny Gruelle's Golden Book. Chicago: M.A. Donohue, 1925. Lg format Golden Bk. 95pp. VG (edges worn). *Davidson.* $65/£42

GRUELLE, JOHNNY. Marcella—A Raggedy Ann Story. Chicago: M.A. Donohue, 1929. 8vo. Unpaginated. VG (lt soil few pp, bkpl; edges bumped) in dj (tattered). *Davidson.* $150/£97

GRUELLE, JOHNNY. Raggedy Ann and Andy and the Nice Fat Policeman. NY: Johnny Gruelle, 1942. 8vo. 95pp. VG (ink name) in dj (torn). *Davidson.* $100/£65

GRUELLE, JOHNNY. Raggedy Ann and Andy. Akron: Saalfield, 1944. 6 moveables w/tabs by Julian Wehr. Red spiral binding, pict paper cvr. VG (1st pg partly separated from spiral; corners bumped). *Davidson.* $185/£119

GRUELLE, JOHNNY. Raggedy Ann in the Deep Deep Woods. Chicago: M.A. Donohue, 1930. 8vo. Unpaginated. VG (corners bumped) in Good dj (chipped). *Davidson.* $100/£65

GRUELLE, JOHNNY. Raggedy Ann's Lucky Pennies. Chicago: M.A. Donohue, 1932. 8vo. 94pp. NF in NF dj. *Davidson.* $125/£81

GRUELLE, JOHNNY. Raggedy Ann's Magical Wishes. Chicago: M.A. Donohue, (1928). 8vo. 95pp. Pict bds. VG in dj (lt torn). *Davidson.* $125/£81

GRUELLE, JOHNNY. Raggedy Ann's Magical Wishes. Joliet: P.F. Volland, (1928). 1st ed. 8vo. Cl-backed illus bds (worn; pg w/marginal tear). Pict box (worn; lacks 1 side of top). *Reisler.* $225/£145

GRUELLE, JOHNNY. Wooden Willie. Chicago: M.A. Donohue, 1927. 8vo. 95pp. VG (corners bumped) in dj (lt tattered). *Davidson.* $135/£87

GRZIMEK, BERNHARD. Grzimek's Animal Life Encyclopedia. NY, 1972-75. Lg 8vo. 13 vols. Gilt dec rexine. Djs. *Sutton.* $700/£452

GUDDE, ERWIN G. Bigler's Chronicle of the West. Berkeley, 1962. 1st ed. Frontis. VG in dj. *Benchmark.* $45/£29

GUDDE, ERWIN G. Bigler's Chronicle of the West. Berkeley: Univ of CA Press, 1962. 1st ed. Map. Purple cl. NF in Good dj (losses rear panel). *Harrington.* $45/£29

GUDERIAN, HEINZ. Panzer Leader. London, 1952. 1st ed. Frontis port; 16 plts. VG in dj. *Edwards.* $54/£35

GUDIOL, J. El Greco, 1541-1614. London: Secker & Warburg, 1973. 84 color plts. Sound. *Ars Artis.* $132/£85

GUENON, FRANCIS. A Treatise on Milch Cows. N.P. Trist (trans). NY: Judd, (1856). 63rd thousand. 88pp. VG (cl sl worn). *Second Life.* $45/£29

GUERINI, V. A History of Dentistry...Until the End of the Eighteenth Century. Phila, 1909. 1st ed. Sl shaken; cl lt worn, else Good. *Goodrich.* $175/£113

GUERNSEY, HENRY. Plain Talks on Avoided Subjects. Phila, 1899. 126pp. Good. *Fye.* $30/£19

GUEST, EDGAR A. A Heap O' Livin. Chicago: Reilly & Lee, (1916). 1st ed. Full calf; teg. VF. *Sadlon.* $20/£13

GUEST, EDGAR A. Just Folks. Chicago: Reilly & Lee, (1917). 1st ed. Full calf; teg. Sl rippling to few leaves, o/w Fine. *Sadlon.* $20/£13

GUEST, EDGAR A. The Passing Throng. Chicago: Reilly & Lee, (1923). 1st ed. Aeg. NF. *Sadlon.* $20/£13

GUEST, EDGAR A. Rhymes of Childhood. Chicago, (1924). Inscribed, signed. (Cvrs sl worn.) *King.* $35/£23

GUEST, EDGAR A. When Day Is Done. Chicago: Reilly & Lee, (1921). 1st ed. Full calf. Fine. *Sadlon.* $20/£13

GUEST, MONTAGUE J. (ed). Lady Charlotte Schreiber's Journals. London/NY, 1911. 2 vols. 8 color plts, 1 photogravure. Teg, rest uncut. (Spotting; sl rubbed, bumped.) *Edwards.* $465/£300

GUGGENHEIM, PEGGY (ed). Art of This Century. NY: Art of This Century, (1942). 1st ed, ltd to 2500. Yellow cl sl browned, name, date, else NF; issued w/o dj. *Godot.* $125/£81

Guide to the County of Sussex.... Edinburgh, 1886. 7th ed. xxi,171pp + 120pp ads, fldg map. (Hinges cracked; extrems worn; lower bd stained.) *Edwards.* $23/£15

Guide to the Fourth, Fifth and Sixth Egyptian Rooms, and the Coptic Room. London: British Museum, 1922. 7 plts. Good. *Archaeologia.* $65/£42

GUILLAIME-LENEPHTY, MAUR. Hans Memling. The Shrine of St. Ursula. Paris/Brussels, 1939. 10 tipped-in color plts. (Ends sl bumped.) *Washton.* $40/£26

GUILLAUD, JACQUELINE and MAURICE. Hieronymus Bosch, the Garden of Earthly Delights. NY: Clarkson N. Potter, (1989). 1st ed in English. Frontis. Sl rubbed rear dj; else Fine. *Bookpress.* $75/£48

GUILLAUME, PAUL and THOMAS MUNRO. Primitive Negro Sculpture. NY, (1926). 1st ed. 41 plts. VG. *Argosy.* $125/£81

GUILLEMIN, AMEDEE. The World of Comets. James Glaisher (trans). London, 1877. 548pp, 5 chromolitho plts, 5 full-pg woodcuts. Contemp smooth calf, gilt spine, gilt stamped emblem. VG. *Argosy.* $250/£161

Guinness Pop-Up Book of Records. London: Guinness, 1986. 18x26 cm, 8pp pop-ups, tabs, flaps. John Farman (illus). Glazed bds. Fine. *Book Finders.* $30/£19

Guinness Alice. Dublin: St. James's Gate, 1933. 8vo. J. 24pp (sl foxing tp; cvrs dusty). J. Gilroy (illus). Illus paper wrappers, stapled binding. *Reisler.* $150/£97

GUINNESS, GERALDINE. In the Far East. London: Morgan & Scott/China Inland Mission, 1901. 18th thousand. Fldg map. VG. *Hollett.* $147/£95

GUINNESS, GERALDINE. In the Far East. London: Morgan & Scott, n.d. (1889). (xvi),120,viiipp, color map. Cl, ptd bds. VG. *Schoyer.* $45/£29

GULICK, BILL. Snake River Country. Caxton, 1971. 1st ed. Good (inscrip; sl stain middle portion causing waviness) in dj (2 lg chips, closed tears). *Baade.* $37/£24

GULLAND, W.G. Chinese Porcelain. London, 1899-1902. 2nd ed. 2 vols. (Lt spotting.) Uncut. (New eps vol 1; cl sl rubbed; fore-edge sl dampspotted; vol 2 spine discolored, sl bumped; vol 1 rebacked, orig spine laid down.) *Edwards.* $54/£35

GULLAND, W.G. Chinese Porcelain. London, 1902. 2nd ed. 2 vols. VG. *Argosy.* $60/£39

GULLANS, C. Imperfect Correspondences. Symposium Press, 1978. 1st ed. One of 300 signed. Fine in wraps. *Fine Books.* $85/£55

GULLICK, J.T. and JOHN TIMBS. Painting Popularly Explained.... London, 1885. 5th ed. Tan cl, gilt. Good+ (sl worn). *Willow House.* $47/£30

GULLICK, MICHAEL. Modern Scribes and Lettering Artists. London, 1980. 1st ed. Dj (spine lt faded). *Edwards.* $31/£20

Gulliver's Travels in Brobdingnag. NY: McLoughlin Bros, n.d. (ca 1880). 4to. 3 leaves, 1pg list lower wrapper. Full color pict wrapper (corners chipped). VG. *Hobbyhorse.* $200/£129

Gulliver's Travels. (By Jonathan Swift.) NY: John Lovell, 1883. Lovell's Lib ed. Spine sl used, o/w Nice in wrappers. *Pharos.* $45/£29

GUMBLE, THOMAS. The Life of General Monck, Duke of Albemarle.... London, 1671. 1st ed. Sm 8vo. Frontis port, tp (sm piece torn out); 6,4,8,preface,486pp + errata slip mtd on final blank. (Lt browning throughout.) Later full calf (rubbed). VG. *Edwards.* $388/£250

GUNN, JOHN C. Gunn's New Domestic Physician: Or Home Book of Health. Cincinnati, 1858. 882pp; this copy includes 88pp appendix by J.H. Jordan: Anatomy, Physiology.... Full leather. Good. *Fye.* $300/£194

GUNN, JOHN C. Gunn's New Family Physician: or Home Book of Health. Cincinnati, 1884. 200th ed. 230pp. Full leather (hinges cracked). Contents Fine. *Fye.* $60/£39

GUNN, M.J. Print Restoration and Picture Cleaning. London, 1922. 2nd ed. 18 plts. (Cl stained.) *Ars Artis.* $39/£25

GUNN, N. Highland River. Lippincott, 1937. 1st Amer ed. NF in NF dj (lt dust soil), pub's wrap-around band. *Fine Books.* $125/£81

GUNN, THOM. The Garden of the Gods. Cambridge: Pym-Randall Press, (1968). 1st ed. One of 200 numbered, signed (of 230). Fine in ptd wrappers. *Reese.* $50/£32

GUNN, THOM. Last Days at Teddington. London: Poem-of-the-Month Club Ltd, 1971. 1st Eng ed. Signed. VG (edges sl creased). *Ulysses.* $93/£60

GUNN, THOM. Touch. London: Faber, (1967). 1st ed. Fine in dj. *Reese.* $25/£16

GUNNING, HENRY. Reminiscences of the University, Town, and County of Cambridge, from the Year 1780. London/Cambridge: George Bell/Charles Wootton, 1854. 1st ed. 2 vols. Port (sm waterstain upper margin), xxvii,339; vii,375pp, errata slip vol 1. Watered blue cl (sl defective head, foot spines). *Bickersteth.* $186/£120

GUNNISON, ALMON. Rambles Overland. Boston: Universalist Pub House, 1884. Pict cl. VG. *Schoyer.* $45/£29

GUNNISON, ALMON. Rambles Overland. Boston: Universalist Pub, 1884. 1st ed. 245pp. Spine top chipped, soiled, o/w clean. *Second Life.* $65/£42

GUNNISON, J.W. The Mormons, or, Latter-Day Saints.... Phila: Lippincott, Grambo, 1852. 1st ed. Frontis engr, ix,13-168pp + 27pp pub's ads. Dec blind-stamped binding (spine ends sl worn). VG (lt foxing). Howes G 463. *Cahan.* $275/£177

GUNTER, ARCHIBALD CLAVERING. My Japanese Prince. NY: Home, (1904). 1st ed. VG (1st 2 leaves, edges foxed) in yellow wrappers (spine chipped, sl cocked; soiled). *Juvelis.* $100/£65

GUPTILL, ARTHUR L. Norman Rockwell: Illustrator. NY: Watson-Guptill Pub, 1946. 1st ed. Signed by Rockwell. Silver-titled cl. NF (1st leaves lt foxed) in pict dj. *Cahan.* $125/£81

GUPTILL, ARTHUR L. Sketching and Rendering in Pencil. NY: Pencil Points Press, 1922. 1st ed. Good (sl worn). *Bookpress.* $65/£42

GURALNICK, PETER. Lost Highway, Journeys and Arrivals of American Musicians. Boston: Godine, 1979. 1st ed. Dj. *Lambeth.* $35/£23

GURALNICK, PETER. Searching for Robert Johnson. NY: Dutton, 1989. 1st ed. Fine in Fine dj. *Beasley.* $60/£39

GURGANUS, ALLAN. Good Help. Rocky Mount: NC Wesleyan College Press, 1988. One of 1000 numbered, signed. Fine in wrappers. *Between The Covers.* $65/£42

GURGANUS, ALLAN. Oldest Living Confederate Widow Tells All. NY: Knopf, (1989). 1st ed. Fine in Fine dj. *Unger.* $50/£32

GURGANUS, ALLAN. Oldest Living Confederate Widow Tells All. Knopf, 1989. 1st ed. Signed. Fine in dj. *Stahr*. $60/£39

GURNEY, JOSEPH JOHN. Familiar Letters to Henry Clay of Kentucky.... NY: Press of Mahlon Day, 1840. 1st Amer ed. 203pp (foxed). VG internally. (Worn; chipped spine.) *Blue Mountain*. $75/£48

GUROWSKI, ADOLPHE DE. Russia as It Is. NY: Appleton, 1854. 312pp + 4pp ads. Grn cl, gilt/blind-stamped (sl rubbed, discolored, lib pocket removed). *Schoyer*. $65/£42

GUSTAFSON, A.F. Handbook of Fertilizers. NY: OJ, 1928. 1st ed. Fine in ptd dj. *Second Life*. $40/£26

GUTHRIE, A.B., JR. The Big Sky. NY, (1947). 1st ed. Ex-lib blindstamp rep, else Good in dj (tattered, incomplete). *King*. $60/£39

GUTHRIE, A.B., JR. The Big Sky. Wm Sloan, (1947). 1st ed. Fine in VG dj. *Oregon*. $75/£48

GUTHRIE, A.B., JR. The Big Sky. William Sloane, (1947). 1st ltd ed of 500 numbered, signed. Ink name ep, else Fine. *Authors Of The West*. $100/£65

GUTHRIE, A.B., JR. The Big Sky. William Sloane, (1947). 1st trade ed. Owner stamp, eps foxed, else Fine in dj (sl chipped, price-clipped). *Authors Of The West*. $50/£32

GUTHRIE, A.B., JR. Once Upon a Pond. Missoula: Mountain Press Pub, (1973). 1st ed. Carol B. Guthrie (illus). Fine in dj. *Between The Covers*. $150/£97

GUTHRIE, A.B., JR. These Thousand Hills. Boston: Houghton Mifflin, 1956. 1st ed. Signed presentation. VG in Poor dj (torn). *Perier*. $45/£29

GUTHRIE, DOUGLAS. A History of Medicine. London: Thomas Nelson, (1945). 1st ed, 2nd ptg. Signed presentation. 72 plts. Fine (bkpl) in dj (worn). *Glaser*. $60/£39

GUTHRIE, DOUGLAS. A History of Medicine. London: Thomas Nelson, 1945. 1st ed. 72 plts. VG (spine sl faded). *White*. $54/£35

GUTHRIE, DOUGLAS. Lord Lister, His Life and Doctrine. Edinburgh, 1949. 1st ed. Good. *Fye*. $60/£39

GUTHRIE, LEONARD. Functional Nervous Disorders in Childhood. London, 1907. 1st ed. Good. *Fye*. $75/£48

GUTHRIE, LORD. Robert Louis Stevenson. Edinburgh: W. Green & Sons, 1924. 1st Eng ed. 17 plts. Blue cl. VF in dj (lacks piece fr panel). *Dalian*. $39/£25

GUTKIND, LEE. The Best Seat in Baseball, but You Have to Stand. Dial, 1975. 1st ed. Fine in VG+ dj. *Plapinger*. $40/£26

GUTTMANN, PAUL. A Handbook of Physical Diagnosis Comprising the Throat, Thorax, and Abdomen. Alex Napier (trans). NY: Wood, 1880. Trans from 3rd German ed. x,344pp; colored plt; 89 wood engr. NF. *Goodrich*. $75/£48

GUTTRIDGE, LEONARD F. and JAY D. SMITH. The Commodores. NY: Harper & Row, (1969). 1st ed. Blue cl. VG in dj. *Chapel Hill*. $35/£23

Guy Fawkes Pop-Up. Burnley, England: Candlelight Production, n.d. (1940s). 19x25 cm. 1 dbl-pg pop-up. J.W.H. (illus). Pict wraps (some rusting of staples holding pop-up.) *Book Finders*. $80/£52

GUY, DAVID. The Man Who Loved Dirty Books. NAL, 1983. 1st ed. Inscribed. NF in NF dj. *Bishop*. $20/£13

GUY, ROSA. Bird at My Window. (London): Souvenir, (1965). 1st British ed, 1st bk. Fine in NF dj (lt rubbed; couple short tears). *Between The Covers*. $125/£81

GUYER, JAMES S. Pioneer Life in West Texas. Brownwood, 1938. Red cl w/black stamping. Fine. Howes G 469. *Bohling*. $75/£48

GWYNN, STEPHEN. The Happy Fisherman. London: Country Life, 1936. 1st ed. VG+ in dj (edgeworn). *Bowman*. $35/£23

GYSIN, BRION. The Process. London: Cape, 1970. 1st UK ed. NF in dj (sm patch soiling spine). *Sclanders*. $54/£35

H

H., C.W. Talpa: or the Chronicles of a Clay Farm. Buffalo: Danforth, Hawley, 1854. 1st US ed. VG. *Second Life*. $45/£29

H., H. (Helen Hunt Jackson.) Verses. Boston: Fields, Osgood, 1870. 1st ed, 1st bk, one of 948. Grn gilt-stamped cl (sl wear). NF. BAL 10413. *Juvelis*. $300/£194

HABERLY, LOYD. Pursuit of the Horizon. A Life of George Catlin. NY: MacMillan, 1948. 1st ed. VG+ in VG- dj. *Parker*. $40/£26

HACKENBROCH, YVONNE. Bronzes, Other Metalwork and Sculpture in the Irwin Untermyer Collection.... NY: Metropolitan Museum, (1962). 202 full-pg plts. Vol V of Irwin Untermyer Collection, w/errata slip. VG in dj (torn). *Argosy*. $65/£42

HACKENBROCH, YVONNE. Bronzes. London, 1962. Frontis, 201 b/w plts. (Ex-lib w/ink stamp; bkpl, tape mks.) Dj (sl chipped, spine creased). *Edwards*. $155/£100

HACKENBROCH, YVONNE. Chelsea and Other English Porcelain.... Cambridge, MA: MMA, 1957. 1st ed. Color frontis. (Inner margin tp stained.) Dj (sl edge-torn). *Edwards*. $93/£60

HACKENBROCH, YVONNE. English and Other Silver in the Irwin Untermyer Collection. (NY): MMA, (1969). Rev ed. Color frontis, 213 plts. Sig starting. Dj (torn). *Argosy*. $250/£161

HACKENBROCH, YVONNE. English and Other Silver. NY: MMA, 1963. Frontis, 180 b/w plts. Dj. *Edwards*. $116/£75

HACKENBROCH, YVONNE. English Furniture. London: Thames & Hudson, 1958. Color frontis, 358 plts (20 color). Cl-backed, gilt device (lt soiled, rubbed; ex-lib w/ink stamp tp verso, bkpl). *Edwards*. $388/£250

HACKLEY, WOODFORD B. The Little Fork Rangers. Richmond, VA: Dietz Ptg, 1927. 1st ed. Pale grey cl. Fine. *Chapel Hill*. $75/£48

HACKWOOD, F.W. William Hone, His Life and Times. London: T. Fisher Unwin, 1912. 1st ed. Orig cl. Good (backstrip faded). *Cox*. $39/£25

HADDEN, JAMES. Washington's Expeditions (1753-1754) and Braddock's Expedition (1755). Uniontown, PA: by author, 1910. 1st ed. 17 plts, map loosely inserted. Author's copy (?) w/ink editing marks. Red cl, gilt. Good (bkpl on fr pastedown, rear card pocket, few spots). *Connolly*. $50/£32

HADFIELD, MILES. Topiary and Ornamental Hedges. London: A&C Black, 1971. Frontis, 22 plts. VF in dj. *Quest*. $55/£35

HAFEN, LEROY R. Broken Hand. The Life of Thomas Fitzpatrick. Denver: Old West, (1973). 1st rev ed. Fine in dj (price-clipped). Howes H 10. *Perier.* $65/£42

HAFEN, LEROY R. Broken Hand. The Life of Thomas Fitzpatrick. Denver: Old West Pub, (1973). 1st rev ed. Fine in dj. Rpt of Howes 4352. *Laurie.* $75/£48

HAFEN, LEROY R. Mountain Men and the Fur Trade of the Far West. Glendale, CA: Clark, 1965-1972. 10 vols, complete. Fldg map. Brn linen, gilt spines. Prospectus laid in. Fine set. *Bohling.* $1,750/£1,129

HAFEN, LEROY R. The Mountain Men and the Fur Trade of the Far West. Glendale: Clark, 1969. 1st ed. Fine. *Perier.* $75/£48

HAFEN, LEROY R. The Mountain Men and the Fur Trade of the Far West. Glendale, CA: Clark, 1972. Fine. *Laurie.* $100/£65

HAFEN, LEROY R. The Mountain Men and the Fur Trade of the Far West. Vol IV. Clark, 1966. 1st ed. VG. *Oregon.* $95/£61

HAFEN, LEROY R. The Mountain Men and the Fur Trade of the Far West. Vol VIII. Clark, 1971. 1st ed. Frontis. VF. *Oregon.* $75/£48

HAFEN, LEROY R. To the Rockies and Oregon 1839-1842. Glendale: Clark, 1955. 2nd ptg. Corner bump, else VG. *Perier.* $75/£48

HAFEN, LEROY R. (ed). Letters of Lewis Granger. LA: Dawson, 1959. Ltd to 250 ptd. Frontis, 2 facs (1 fldg). Fine. *Oregon.* $50/£32

HAFEN, LEROY R. (ed). Overland Routes to the Gold Fields, 1859 from Contemporary Diaries. Clark, 1942. 1st ed. Frontis, fldg map. Uncut, unopened. VF. *Oregon.* $135/£87

HAFEN, LEROY R. and ANN W. (eds). Far West and Rockies Series. 1820-1875. Glendale: Clark, 1954-61. 15 vols. Unopened. Grn cl, gilt lettered spines. Fine set. *Parmer.* $2,950/£1,903

HAFEN, LEROY R. and ANN W. (eds). Journals of Forty-Niners: Salt Lake to Los Angeles. Glendale: Clark, 1954. VG. *Schoyer.* $100/£65

HAFEN, LEROY R. and ANN W. (eds). Old Spanish Trail. Glendale: Clark, 1954. VG. *Schoyer.* $100/£65

HAFEN, LEROY R. and ANN W. (eds). Reports from Colorado: The Wildman Letters, 1859-1865. Glendale: Clark, 1961. 1st ed. Fldg map. Teg. Grn cl. VG. *Schoyer.* $65/£42

HAFEN, LEROY R. and FRANCIS M. YOUNG. Fort Laramie and the Pageant of the West, 1834-1890. Glendale: Clark, 1938. 1st ed. (Spine sl faded.) Howes H 11. *Ginsberg.* $175/£113

HAFEN, LEROY R. and FRANCIS M. YOUNG. Fort Laramie and the Pageant of the West, 1834-1890. Glendale: Clark, 1938. Inscribed, signed, dated by Young. (Spine, edges worn.) *Parmer.* $195/£126

HAFTMANN, WERNER. Painting in the Twentieth Century. London: Lund Humphries, (1960). 1st ed. 2 vols. 395 plts (55 color, 3 fldg). Fine in djs, pub's slipcase. *Karmiole.* $85/£55

HAGEN, WILLIAM T. The Sac and Fox Indians. Norman, 1958. 1st ed. NF (sig, date) in dj (sl worn, closed tear). *Baade.* $45/£29

HAGENBECK, CARL. Beasts and Men. London: Longmans, Green, 1912. Photograv port; 99 illus. *Dramatis Personae.* $75/£48

HAGER, JEAN. The Grandfather Medicine. NY: St Martin, 1989. 1st ed. Fine in Fine dj. *Janus.* $100/£65

HAGERUP, A.T. The Birds of Greenland. Boston: Little Brown, 1891. 1st US ed. 62pp. Orig wrappers bound in. VG. *Walcot.* $62/£40

HAGGARD, H. RIDER and ANDREW LANG. The World's Desire. London: Longmans, Green, 1890. 1st ed. viii,316,16pp. Cl, gilt over beveled bds. Very Nice. *Hollett.* $70/£45

HAGGARD, H. RIDER. Allan Quatermain. Longmans Green, 1887. 1st ed. Sl wear corner tips; spine sl faded, else VG. *Aronovitz.* $325/£210

HAGGARD, H. RIDER. The Ancient Allan. NY, 1920. 1st Amer ed. Color frontis. NF (spine sl sunned). *Polyanthos.* $30/£19

HAGGARD, H. RIDER. Ayesha: The Return of She. NY: Doubleday, Page, 1905. 1st Amer ed. Lt soiling; lt cl bubbling, o/w Very Nice. *Hermitage.* $75/£48

HAGGARD, H. RIDER. Ayesha: The Return of She. NY: Doubleday Page, 1905. 1st US ed. VG. *Other Worlds.* $35/£23

HAGGARD, H. RIDER. Ayesha: The Return of She. Doubleday, 1905. 1st US ed. VG. *Madle.* $50/£32

HAGGARD, H. RIDER. The Brethren. London: Cassell, 1904. 1st UK ed. VG (fr hinge starting; ink name). *Williams.* $47/£30

HAGGARD, H. RIDER. Cleopatra. Harpers, 1889. 1st US ed. VG. *Madle.* $100/£65

HAGGARD, H. RIDER. The Days of My Life. Longmans Green, 1926. 1st ed. 2 vols. NF set. *Fine Books.* $185/£119

HAGGARD, H. RIDER. Doctor Therne. London: Longmans, Green, 1898. 1st ed. This copy w/white eps, rounded spine, reads 'Longmans & Co.' at foot of spine, has Aberdeen University Press colophon on last leaf. Tan cl. Lt mk rear cvr, o/w Fine. *Sumner & Stillman.* $145/£94

HAGGARD, H. RIDER. Eric Brighteyes. London, 1891. 1st ed. Edgeworn, else VG. *Madle.* $175/£113

HAGGARD, H. RIDER. A Farmer's Year. London, 1899. 1st ed. VG. *Madle.* $125/£81

HAGGARD, H. RIDER. Finished. Longmans, 1917. 1st ed. VG. *Madle.* $45/£29

HAGGARD, H. RIDER. A Gardener's Year. London, 1905. 2nd imp. Plan, 25 plts. Teg. (Spine faded.) *Henly.* $43/£28

HAGGARD, H. RIDER. The Ghost Kings. Cassell, 1908. 1st ed. Half-title absent; spine lightened, else VG-. *Aronovitz.* $175/£113

HAGGARD, H. RIDER. Heart of the World. London: Longmans, Green, 1896. 1st Eng ed. 24pp cat dated 4/96. VG (spine lt sunned; lt foxing). *Agvent.* $150/£97

HAGGARD, H. RIDER. Heu-Heu. Doubleday, 1924. 1st US ed. VG. *Madle.* $30/£19

HAGGARD, H. RIDER. The Ivory Child. London, 1916. 1st ed. VG. *Madle.* $125/£81

HAGGARD, H. RIDER. Jess. Smith, Elder, 1887. 1st ed. Spine lightened, spotting, else VG. *Aronovitz.* $225/£145

HAGGARD, H. RIDER. Lysbeth. Longmans, 1901. 1st ed. VG. *Fine Books.* $85/£55

HAGGARD, H. RIDER. Lysbeth. Longmans, 1901. 1st UK ed. 26 plts. Eps foxed, o/w VG. *Lewton.* $31/£20

HAGGARD, H. RIDER. Montezuma's Daughter. Longmans, Green, 1893. 1st ed. Lt wear corner tip; fr inner hinge tender; spine faded, else VG-. *Aronovitz.* $95/£61

HAGGARD, H. RIDER. Mr. Meeson's Will. Spencer-Blackett, 1888. 1st ed. Pict cl. Spine lightened; sl worn, else VG. *Fine Books.* $325/£210

HAGGARD, H. RIDER. Nada the Lilly. Longmans, Green, 1892. 1st ed. Frontis, xv,(i),295pp; pub's 24pg cat dated 2/92; 22 plts. Gilt-lettered cl. (Lt waterstain text leaf; spine faded; lt stains upper cvr.) *Bickersteth.* $59/£38

HAGGARD, H. RIDER. Pearl-Maiden. London: Longmans, 1903. 1st Eng ed. VG (lib bkpl; wear spine tips, corners; lt foxing). *Agvent.* $125/£81

HAGGARD, H. RIDER. Queen of the Dawn. GC: Doubleday, 1925. 1st Amer ed. VG (soiling). *Agvent.* $45/£29

HAGGARD, H. RIDER. Queen Sheba's Ring. Doubleday, 1910. 1st US ed. VG. *Madle.* $100/£65

HAGGARD, H. RIDER. She and Allan. NY: Longmans, Green, 1921. 1st ed. Color frontis, 3pp undated ads. Orig red cl. Fine. *Sumner & Stillman.* $115/£74

HAGGARD, H. RIDER. She. Munro, 1887. VG in wraps (lt chipping). *Fine Books.* $100/£65

HAGGARD, H. RIDER. Stella Fregelius. L-G, 1903. 1st ed. VG-. *Fine Books.* $47/£30

HAGGARD, H. RIDER. Swallow. Longmans Green, 1899. 1st ed. VG +. *Fine Books.* $135/£87

HAGGARD, H. RIDER. The Virgin of the Sun. NY, 1922. 1st Amer ed. Frontis. Fine (spine sunned). *Polyanthos.* $50/£32

HAGGARD, H. RIDER. The Virgin of the Sun. D-P, 1922. 1st ed. VG-. *Fine Books.* $33/£21

HAGGARD, H. RIDER. The Wanderer's Necklace. Longmans, Green, 1914. 1st Amer ed. VG. *Aronovitz.* $60/£39

HAGGARD, H. RIDER. A Winter Pilgrimage. London: Longmans, Green, 1901. 1st ed, ltd to 1500. 32pp ads dated April 1901. Dk blue cl. VG (few smudges, sl shelfwear). *Sumner & Stillman.* $395/£255

HAGGARD, HOWARD W. The Lame, the Halt, and the Blind. London: Heinemann, 1932. 1st ed. 4 plts. Blue cl. Sm mk fr cvr, o/w VG. *White.* $28/£18

HAGGARD, LILIAS RIDER (ed). I Walked by Night. NY: Dutton, 1936. 1st Amer ed. VG in dj. *Bowman.* $50/£32

HAGUE, MICHAEL. World of Unicorns. NY: Henry Holt, 1986. 28x20 cm. Glazed pict bds. Fine. *Book Finders.* $45/£29

HAGUE, WILLIAM. Life and Character of Adoniram Judson. Boston: Gould & Lincoln, 1851. 38pp. Blue ptd wraps (sl dampstains, sl creased). *Schoyer.* $40/£26

HAHN, EMILY. Raffles of Singapore. NY: Doubleday, 1946. (Sl rubbed; spine faded.) *Hollett.* $23/£15

HAIG-BROWN, RODERICK. Return to the River. NY: Morrow, 1941. 1st ed. VG. *Bowman.* $40/£26

HAIG-BROWN, RODERICK. A River Never Sleeps. NY: Morrow, 1946. 1st ed. Fine in VG dj. *Bowman.* $50/£32

HAIG-BROWN, RODERICK. The Whale People. London: Collins, 1962. 1st British ed. Fine in Fine dj. *Authors Of The West.* $50/£32

HAIG-THOMAS, DAVID. Tracks in the Snow. NY: OUP, 1939. . Fine in dj. *High Latitude.* $50/£32

HAIGH, RIVHARD. Life in a Tank. NY, 1918. 1st ed. Frontis, guard; 7 plts. Good + in dj (frayed w/some loss). *Edwards.* $147/£95

HAIGH, SAMUEL. Sketches of Buenos Ayres, Chile, and Peru. London: Effingham Wilson, 1831. 2nd ed. x,434pp, lg engr fldg map. Contemp gilt brn morocco over marbled bds (extrems lt rubbed; ex-lib w/bkpl, # on spine). *Karmiole.* $300/£194

HAIGHT, ANNE. Banned Books. NY: Bowker, 1935. 1st ed. One of 1000 ptd. *Ginsberg.* $100/£65

HAIGHT, ANNE. Banned Books. Allen & Unwin, 1955. VG in dj. *Moss.* $56/£36

HAIGHT, AUSTIN D. The Biography of a Sportsman. NY: Thomas Y. Crowell, 1939. 1st ed, 1st ptg. Fine in slipcase (lt worn). *Glenn.* $40/£26

HAIL, MARSHALL. Knight in the Sun. Boston: Little Brown, 1962. 1st ed. NF in VG- dj (soiled). *Parker.* $25/£16

HAIMENDORF, CHRISTOPH VON FURER. Himalayan Barbary. NY: Abelard-Schuman, (1956). Map. VG in dj (price-clipped). *Schoyer.* $35/£23

HAINAUX, RENE. Stage Design Throughout the World Since 1950. NY, 1964. VG in dj (chipped). *Argosy.* $85/£55

HAINES, FRANCIS (ed). A Bride on the Bozeman Trail. Medford, OR: Gandee Ptg, 1970. 1st ed. Ltd to 650 numbered. 3 ports. VF. *Oregon.* $75/£48

HAINES, FRANCIS. Appaloosa. Austin: Univ of TX/Amon Carter Museum, 1964. APHC Ed. VG in Fair dj. *October Farm.* $48/£31

HAINES, FRANCIS. Appaloosa: The Spotted Horse in Art and History. Austin: Univ of TX Press, 1963. VG (bkpl) in dj (torn). *Argosy.* $75/£48

HAINES, FRANCIS. The Nez Perce. Univ OK, (1955). 1st ed. 16 plts, 3 maps. Pict cl. VG in VG dj. *Oregon.* $65/£42

HAINES, FRANCIS. The Nez Perce. Norman: Univ of OK, (1955). 1st ed. VG in dj (torn). *Perier.* $75/£48

HAINES, HERBERT. A Manual of Monumental Brasses.... Oxford/London, J.H. & Jas. Parker, 1861. 2 vols. Color frontis. (Spines worn.) *Bickersteth.* $54/£35

HAINING, PETER (ed). The Gentlewomen of Evil. London: Robert Hale, (1967). 1st ed. Rev copy, pub's slip laid in. Olive cl. Fine in NF dj. *Chapel Hill.* $35/£23

HAIRE, FRANCES H. American Costume Book. NY: Barnes, 1934. 1st ed. 10 color plts. Pict cl (emb lib stamp). *Ginsberg.* $75/£48

HALBERSTAM, DAVID. Making of a Quagmire. NY: Random House, (1965). 1st ed. Fine in dj. *Aka.* $65/£42

HALBERT, H.S. and T.H. BALL. The Creek War of 1813 and 1814. Frank L. Owsley, Jr. (ed). University, AL: Univ of AL Press, (1969). Rpt. Tan cl. Fine in dj. *Chapel Hill.* $40/£26

HALDANE, A.R.B. The Drove Roads of Scotland. London: David & Charles, 1973. Color frontis, 16 plts, fldg map. VG in dj. *Hollett.* $54/£35

HALDANE, CHARLOTTE. I Bring Not Peace. London: C&W, 1932. 1st ed. Blue cl. Mint in dj. *Weber.* $250/£161

HALDAR, HIRALAL. Neo-Hegelianism. London: Heath Cranton Ltd, 1927. 1st ed. Gilt-lettered black cl. Fine in ptd dj. *House.* $75/£48

HALDEMAN, JOE W. War Year. NY: Holt Rinehart Winston, (1972). 1st ed. Signed. Fine NF dj (fr flap corner clipped). *Aka.* $125/£81

HALE, DONALD R. We Rode with Quantrill. Clinton, MO: The Printery, 1974. 1st ed. Pict wrappers, lt soiled, o/w Fine. *Glenn.* $20/£13

HALE, EDWARD E. The Brick Moon. Barre: Imprint Society, 1971. #107/1950 numbered, signed by Michael McCurdy (illus). Bkpl, else Fine in pub's slipcase. *Hermitage.* $60/£39

HALE, EDWARD E. If Jesus Came to Boston. Boston: J. Stilman Smith, (1894). 1st ed. Inscribed. 46pp. Good in orig ptd wrappers (soiled). *Karmiole.* $60/£39

HALE, EDWARD E. Kanzas and Nebraska: The History, Geographical and Physical Characteristics.... Boston, 1854. 1st ed. Tall 12mo. 256pp; fldg map. Orig cl (spine head worn; ex-lib). Howes (1954), 4371. *Argosy.* $300/£194

HALE, EDWARD E. Memories of a Hundred Years. Macmillan, 1902. 1st ed. 2 vols. 2 frontispieces. Pict tan cl stamped in red/black, gilt. Fine. *Oregon.* $60/£39

HALE, EDWARD E. Six of One by Half a Dozen of the Other. Boston: Roberts Bros, 1872. 1st ed, 1st issue. Grn gilt-stamped cl (hinges cracked; spine skewed, 1/4-inch tear; bumped; ex-libris). Contents Sound. BAL 19468. *Juvelis.* $175/£113

HALE, F. From Persian Uplands. NY: Dutton, n.d. (ca 1920). Blue cl, gilt. VG. *Schoyer.* $65/£42

HALE, JOHN (ed). Settlers. London: Faber, 1950. 1st ed. 6 maps. VG in dj (worn, chipped). *Hollett.* $39/£25

HALE, JOHN P. History and Mystery of the Kanawha Valley. Charleston, WV, 1897. 1st ed. 18pp. VG in orig ptd wrappers. *Mcgowan.* $45/£29

HALE, JOHN P. Trans-Allegheny Pioneers. Cincinnati: Graphic Press, 1886. 1st ed. 330pp; 11 plts (1 fldg). Pub's cl. Cvrs soiled; bkpl; sl foxing, else Good. Howes H 32. *Bookpress.* $150/£97

HALE, JOHN P. Trans-Allegheny Pioneers. Cincinnati: Graphic Press, 1886. 1st ptg. 330pp. Blue cl stamped in gilt. VG. Howes H 32. *Schoyer.* $175/£113

HALE, LAURA VIRGINIA. On Chester Street. Commercial Press, 1985. Inscribed presentation sheet laid in. *Book Broker.* $50/£32

HALE, MATTHEW. The History of the Common Law. London: G.G. & J. Robinson, 1794. 5th ed. 2 vols. Full calf (rebound; sl mkd), gilt. *Petersfield.* $78/£50

HALE, NATHAN CABOT. Embrace of Life: The Sculpture of Gustav Vigeland. NY: Abrams, 1968. Signed by David Finn (photos). 32 mtd color plts. VG in dj. *Argosy.* $250/£161

HALE, NATHAN CABOT. The Spirit of Man: The Sculpture of Kaare Nygaard. N.p., n.d. (1982). VG in dj. *Argosy.* $75/£48

HALE, NATHAN G., JR. Freud and the Americans...1876-1917. NY: OUP, 1971. 1st ed. Blue cl. VG in dj (lt worn). *Gach.* $50/£32

HALE, NATHANIEL. Pelts and Palisades. Richmond, VA, (1959). 1st ed. 3 plts. VG in VG dj. *Oregon.* $30/£19

HALE, NATHANIEL. Virginia Venturer: William Claiborne, 1600-1677. Dietz, (c1951). VG in VG dj. *Book Broker.* $35/£23

HALE, WILLIAM HARLAN. Horace Greeley, Voice of the People. NY: Harper, (1950). 1st ed. Fine in VG dj (sl chipped). *Mcgowan.* $45/£29

HALE-WHITE, W. Great Doctors of the Nineteenth Century. London, (1935). Pg 1 sl dust stained; marginal pencil, o/w VG. *Whitehart.* $54/£35

HALEY, ALEX. Roots. GC: Doubleday, (1974). 1st ed. One of 500 numbered, signed. Full leather. VF in pub's slipcase. *Unger.* $450/£290

HALEY, ALEX. Roots. NY: Doubleday, 1976. 1st ed, 1st ptg. 1/4 cl, gilt. Fine in dj (tears). *Macdonnell.* $100/£65

HALEY, ALEX. Roots. Doubleday, 1976. 1st ed. NF in dj. *Fine Books.* $45/£29

HALEY, ALEX. Roots. NY: Doubleday, 1976. 1st ed. Fine in dj. *Else Fine.* $100/£65

HALEY, ALEX. Roots. London: Hutchinson, 1977. 1st UK ed. Fine in dj (price-clipped). *Williams.* $54/£35

HALEY, J. EVETTS. Charles Goodnight, Cowman and Plainsman. Boston: Houghton Mifflin, 1936. 1st ed. Map. Tan cl (spine mottled, corners worn). Howes H 36. *Parmer.* $200/£129

HALEY, J. EVETTS. Charles Goodnight, Cowman and Plainsman. Norman: Univ of OK, 1949. 1st this ed. *Lambeth.* $35/£23

HALEY, J. EVETTS. Charles Schreiner. Austin, 1944. VG + in dj w/plastic cvr attached. *Bohling.* $150/£97

HALEY, J. EVETTS. Charles Schreiner. Austin: TSHA, 1944. 1st ed. Dj (torn). *Lambeth.* $65/£42

HALEY, J. EVETTS. George W. Littlefield, Texan. Norman: Univ of OK, 1943. 1st ed. VG in Fine dj w/plastic cvr. *Bohling.* $100/£65

HALEY, J. EVETTS. Jeff Milton: A Good Man with a Gun. Norman: Univ of OK, 1948. 1st ed, 1st issue w/1 line upside down in index. Tipped-in autograph note signed. VG + in dj (faded, edgeworn). *Bohling.* $150/£97

HALEY, J. EVETTS. Jeff Milton: A Good Man with a Gun. Norman: Univ of OK Press, 1948. 1st ed, 1st issue, w/line on p421 inverted. Red cl (spine sl faded). Lg inscrip, o/w Fine. Howes H 38. *Harrington.* $80/£52

HALEY, J. EVETTS. Some Southwestern Trails. El Paso: Carl Hertzog, 1948. 1st ed. Pict cl. Fine in Poor slipcase. *Oregon.* $240/£155

HALEY, J. EVETTS. The XIT Ranch of Texas. Norman, 1967. 1st ptg thus. Fldg map. Fine in dj. Howes H 39. *Baade.* $35/£23

HALFORD, FREDERIC M. Dry-Fly Fishing in Theory and Practice. London: Vinton, 1902. 4th ed. 3 color, 16 b/w plts. (Sl foxing.) *Petersfield.* $109/£70

HALFORD, FREDERIC M. The Dry-Fly Man's Handbook. London: Routledge, (1913). 1st ed. 43 plts. Mod dk 1/2 grn morocco (rebound; fore-edge sl foxed). *Petersfield.* $248/£160

HALFORD, FREDERIC M. Modern Development of the Dry Fly.... London: Routledge, (1910). 1st ed. 9 color plts, 17 color charts, 15 plts (sl foxing few pp; backstrip sl faded). *Petersfield.* $271/£175

HALFORD, FREDERIC M. Modern Development of the Dry Fly.... London: Routledge, 1910. 1st ed. (Lt foxed; cracked joints repaired.) *Glenn.* $200/£129

HALFORD, H. Essays and Orations. London, 1831. Frontis port; 192pp. New 1/2 red morocco. VG. *Whitehart.* $78/£50

HALFPENNY, WILLIAM and JOHN. Rural Architecture in the Gothick Taste. London: Robert Sayer, 1752. 1st, and only, ed. Sm 8vo. 8pp, 16 plts. Later bds. VG. *Bookpress.* $1,500/£968

HALL, ADAM. The 9th Directive. London: Heinemann, 1966. 1st ed. Fine in dj (minor rubs spine folds). *Else Fine.* $60/£39

HALL, ADAM. The 9th Directive. London: Heinemann, 1966. 1st ed. Fine in dj. *Mordida.* $65/£42

HALL, ADAM. The Berlin Memorandum. London: Collins, 1965. 1st ed. Lt spots top pg edges, o/w Fine in dj. *Mordida.* $75/£48

HALL, ADAM. The Pekin Target. London: Collins, 1981. 1st ed. VF in dj. *Mordida.* $65/£42

HALL, ADAM. The Quiller Memorandum. NY: S&S, 1965. 1st ed. Fine (bkpl) in dj (sm hole spine). *Else Fine.* $40/£26

HALL, ADAM. The Striker Portfolio. London: Heinemann, 1969. 1st ed. Pg edges lt soiled, o/w Fine in dj (sl wear along edges). *Mordida.* $45/£29

HALL, ADAM. The Striker Portfolio. London: Heinemann, 1969. 1st ed. Sm rub cvr, else Fine in dj. *Else Fine.* $65/£42

HALL, BASIL. Account of a Voyage of Discovery to the West Coast of Corea and the Great Loo-Choo Island. Phila, 1818. 1st US ed. iv,201pp + 2pp ads; 2 charts. Contemp calf (spine renewed). *Lewis.* $132/£85

HALL, BASIL. Extracts from a Journal Written on the Coasts of Chili, Peru and Mexico.... Edinburgh, 1825. 4th ed. 2 vols. Fldg frontis map (torn, offset), xx,379; xii,320pp + 80pp (lt browning; ex-libris). Contemp 1/2 calf, marbled bds (surface loss; sm crack lower joint vol 2). *Edwards.* $62/£40

HALL, BASIL. Extracts from a Journal, Written on the Coasts of Chili, Peru, and Mexico.... Edinburgh, 1824. 3rd ed. 2 vols. xx,379; xii,304,71pp, fldg chart. Contemp 1/2 calf (rubbed). Internally clean. *Lefkowicz.* $150/£97

HALL, BASIL. Extracts from a Journal. Boston: Wells & Lilly, 1824. 2 vols in 1. xxii,244; vii,230pp (lacks rep; foxed; lt dampstain upper corner of text). Contemp 3/4 calf (rubbed, chipped). *Schoyer.* $45/£29

HALL, BASIL. Voyages. Edinburgh: Constable, 1827. 1st ed. 3 vols. Name, else VG. *Limestone.* $75/£48

HALL, CARROLL D. The Terry-Broderick Duel. SF: Colt Press, (1939). 1st ed. 6 woodcuts. Cl, bds, paper spine label. VG. *Oregon.* $60/£39

HALL, CARROLL D. (ed). Donner Miscellany. 41 Diaries and Documents. SF: Book Club of CA, 1947. One of 350 ptd by Allen Press. 1/4 grn cl; dec cl bds, uncut. Fine. *Laurie.* $300/£194

HALL, CHARLES F. Arctic Researches and Life Among the Esquimaux. NY: Harper, 1865. 1st Amer ed. xxviii,(29)-595pp, fldg map. Brn cl, gilt spine titles (heavy wear head, heel of spine; foxing). *Parmer.* $250/£161

HALL, CHARLES F. Narrative of the North Polar Expedition. Washington: GPO, 1867. 1st ed. 696pp. Good + (lacks tp). *Blue Dragon.* $75/£48

HALL, CHARLES F. Narrative of the Second Arctic Expedition Made by Charles F. Hall. Washington: GPO, 1879. 1st ed. 644pp. VG- (lacks fldg pocket map). *Blue Dragon.* $150/£97

HALL, DONALD. The Alligator Bride. NY: Harper & Row, (1969). 1st ed. Fine in dj (sl wear, soil). *Antic Hay.* $25/£16

HALL, DONALD. The Onset. Concord: Wm. B. Ewert, 1986. One of 330. Signed. *Revere.* $35/£23

HALL, DONALD. String Too Short to Be Saved. Boston: Nonpareil Books, 1977. 1st ed. Inscribed. NF in pict wraps. *Revere.* $25/£16

HALL, E. RAYMOND and K.R. KELSON. The Mammals of North America. NY, 1959. 1st ed. 2 vols. (Spines faded; ink stain corner of few pp vol 1; cvrs lt spotted, scuffed vol 2.) *Sutton.* $165/£106

HALL, E. RAYMOND. Mammals of Nevada. Univ of CA Press, 1946. Color frontis, 11 plts. (Ex-lib, ink stamps, labels, accession label.) *Edwards.* $31/£20

HALL, EDNA CLARKE. Facets: A Book of Poems and Six Illustrations. London: Elkin Mathew & Marrot, 1930. 1st ed. #28/300. Signed. Uncut. Good + (worn, bumped). *Willow House.* $39/£25

HALL, FRANCIS. Travels in Canada and the United States in 1816 and 1817. Boston: Wells & Lilly, 1818. 1st Amer ed. 332pp. Later cl. Uncut. Howes H 62. *Bookpress.* $150/£97

HALL, FRANK. History of the State of Colorado. Chicago: Blakely, 1889, 1890, 1891. 1st eds. 3 vols (of 4). Leather (2 spines repaired; reinforced hinges). VG-. *Parker.* $295/£190

HALL, GRANVILLE DAVISSON. Old Gold. Chicago, 1907. Inscribed presentation signed. *Hayman.* $35/£23

HALL, H. FIELDING. People at School. London: Macmillan, 1906. 1st ed. Turquoise cl, gilt (foxing). *Schoyer.* $50/£32

HALL, H. FIELDING. Soul of a People. London: Macmillan, 1903. 4th ed. Turquoise cl, gilt. VG. *Schoyer.* $30/£19

HALL, H.M. The Ruffed Grouse. NY: Oxford, 1946. 1st ed. Dec cl. VG + . *Mikesh.* $37/£24

HALL, H.M. Woodcock Ways. NY: Oxford, 1946. 1st ed. Dec cl. VG. *Mikesh.* $32/£21

HALL, H.R. Catalogue of Egyptian Scarabs, etc. in the British Museum. London: British Museum, 1913. (Edges sl worn.) *Archaeologia.* $650/£419

HALL, H.R. The Civilization of Greece in the Bronze Age. London: Methuen, (1928). 2 maps. Good. *Archaeologia.* $65/£42

HALL, HAL (ed). Cinematographic Annual; Vol 2. Hollywood, 1931. 64 photo plts. 1-inch spine tear, o/w Good. *Artis.* $60/£39

HALL, I. WALKER and G. HERXHEIMER. Methods of Morbid Histology and Clinical Pathology. Phila, 1905. 1st ed. Good. *Fye.* $75/£48

HALL, JAMES BAKER. Minor White Rites and Passages. 1978. 1st ed. NF in NF dj. *Bishop.* $35/£23

HALL, JAMES NORMAN and CHARLES NORDHOFF. Faery Lands of the South Seas. NY: Harper, 1921. 1st ed, 1st issue (w/'K-V' on copyright pg). VG in dj (1-inch chip spine w/sl loss of lettering, nicks, short tears, else VG). *Godot.* $185/£119

HALL, JAMES NORMAN. The Far Lands. Boston: Little, Brown, 1950. 1st ed. NF in dj (sl wear; short tear). *Antic Hay.* $45/£29

HALL, JAMES NORMAN. On the Stream of Travel. Boston/NY: Houghton Mifflin, 1926. 1st ed. Fine in dj (4-inch chip; nicks, short tears, else VG). *Godot.* $75/£48

HALL, JAMES W. Paper Products. NY: Norton, 1990. 1st ed. Fine in Fine dj. *Revere.* $35/£23

HALL, JAMES W. Under Cover of Daylight. NY: Norton, 1987. 1st ed. Fine in Fine dj. *Beasley.* $50/£32

HALL, JAMES. Geological Survey of the State of New York, Palaentology, Vol VII.... Albany, NY: Charles van Benthuysen, 1888. 278pp, 129 Very Nice full-pg plts, supplement. Good in gilt illus brn blind-stamped cl (spine frayed, corners worn, sm white stain, hinges repaired). *Knollwood.* $150/£97

HALL, JAMES. Letters from the West. London: Henry Colburn, 1828. (1st ed). 16pp ads, vi,385,(1)pp; untrimmed. Orig bds (edgeworn; rebacked), spine label laid down (rubbed, dknd; bkpl). Howes H 79. BAL 6919. *Bohling.* $500/£323

HALL, JOHN (ed). Trial of Abraham Thornton. NY: John Day, 1927. Well preserved in dj. *Boswell.* $85/£55

HALL, JOHN E. The Practice and Jurisdiction of the Court of Admiralty. Balt: Ptd by Geo. Dobbin and Murphy, 1809. 1st ed. Contemp sheep (scuffed but sound). *Boswell.* $650/£419

HALL, MARSHALL. A Descriptive, Diagnostic, and Practical Essay on Disorders of the Digestive Organs and General Health.... Keene, NH, 1823. 2nd ed. 142pp. (Dampstaining inner gutters prelims.) Uncut. (Bds worn.) *Goodrich.* $95/£61

HALL, MARSHALL. Lectures on the Nervous System and Its Diseases. Phila, 1836. 1st Amer ed. 240pp (lt foxing). Recent 1/4 leather; new eps. *Fye.* $200/£129

HALL, MAUD R. English Church Needlework. London/NY, 1901. Patterns, magazine loosely inserted. (Lt spotting; fep torn w/o loss; hinges cracked; worn). *Edwards.* $39/£25

HALL, MRS. BASIL. The Aristocratic Journey. NY: Putnam's, 1931. 1st ed. 12 plts on coated stock. Blue cl, labels. VG. *Petrilla.* $30/£19

HALL, RADCLYFFE. The Well of Loneliness. London: Cape, 1928. 1st issue, w/'whip' for 'whips' on line 13, pg50. VG in VG dj (sl wear, few nicks). *Williams.* $256/£165

HALL, RALPH. The Main Trail. San Antonio: Naylor, (1971). 1st ed. VG in Good+ dj. *Oregon.* $15/£10

HALL, S.C. (ed). The Book of British Ballads. London, n.d. Blue cl, beveled edges, gold designs, lettering. Aeg. VG. *Mcclintock.* $165/£106

HALL, S.C. and MRS. The Book of the Thames. London, 1859. 1st ed. xi,516pp+(xxiv)pp pub's ads. Aeg. Dec gilt. Good (feps sl foxed, sm bkpl; spine sl worn). *Edwards.* $186/£120

HALL, SUSAN and BOB ADELMAN. Gentleman of Leisure. NY: NAL/Prairie House, 1972. 1st ed. Fine in NF dj (short tears). *Beasley.* $35/£23

HALL, THOMAS B. Medicine on the Santa Fe Trail. (Dayton): Morningside Bookshop, 1971. 1st ed. #312/1000 signed. Fldg table. Blue cl (sl soiled). NF. *Harrington.* $55/£35

HALL, TREVOR H. Old Conjuring Books. (London): Duckworth, (1972). 1st ed, ltd to 1000 numbered, signed. Fine. *Oak Knoll.* $50/£32

HALL, TREVOR H. Old Conjuring Books. (London): Duckworth, (1972). 1st ed. One of 1000. Signed. Frontis. Fine. *Bookpress.* $100/£65

HALL, TREVOR H. Sherlock Holmes and His Creator. London: Duckworth, 1978. 1st ed. Fine in NF dj (spine sl sunned). *Janus.* $35/£23

HALL, W.W. Fun Better Than Physic; or, Everybody's Life-Preserver. Springfield, MA, 1871. 1st ed. 333pp; engr port. Good. *Fye.* $50/£32

HALL, W.W. Health at Home, Or Hall's Family Doctor.... Hartford, CT, 1873. 1st ed. 846pp. Good. *Fye.* $75/£48

HALLAHAN, WILLIAM H. The Ross Forgery. Indianapolis: Bobbs-Merrill, 1973. 1st ed. Fine in dj. *Mordida.* $45/£29

HALLENBECK, CLEVE. Journey of Fray Marcos de Niza. Dallas: University Press, 1949. Ltd to 1065. Dj. *Lambeth.* $250/£161

HALLENBECK, CLEVE. Land of the Conquistadores. Caxton, 1950. 1st ed. Color frontis; fldg map. VG in VG dj. *Oregon.* $70/£45

HALLENBECK, CLEVE. Spanish Missions of the Old Southwest. GC: Doubleday, 1926. 1st ed. *Ginsberg.* $125/£81

HALLIDAY, SAMUEL B. The Lost and Found, or Life among the Poor. NY: Phinney et al, 1860. 1st ed. Frontis port, 356pp. Contemp cl (spine dull). VG. *Second Life.* $250/£161

HALLIWELL, JAMES ORCHARD. A Dictionary of Archaic and Provincial Words...From the Fourteenth Century. London: William Boone, 1855. 3rd ed. 2 vols; 8vo. 480pp; (481)-960pp. Cl-backed bds. Paper spine labels chipped; bkpls, else VG. *Chapel Hill.* $200/£129

HALLOCK, CHARLES. The Salmon Fisher. NY: Harris, 1890. 1st ed. Frontis,126pp + ads. Fine +. *Bowman.* $175/£113

HALPER, ALBERT. The Chute. NY, 1937. 1st Amer ed. Fine (spine sl sunned; cvr sl soiled). *Polyanthos.* $30/£19

HALPER, ALBERT. The Foundry. NY, 1934. 1st Amer ed. Fine (spine sunned; cvrs soiled). *Polyanthos.* $30/£19

HALPER, ALBERT. On the Shore. NY, 1934. 1st Amer ed. NF (spine sunned). *Polyanthos.* $25/£16

HALSELL, H.H. My Autobiography. (Dallas, TX: Wilkinson Ptg, 1948.) 1st ed. Signed. VG in dj (sl worn). *Lien.* $125/£81

HALSEY, ASHLEY, JR. Illustrating for the Saturday Evening Post. Boston, (1951). 1st ed. VG. *Artis.* $40/£26

HALSEY, MARGARET. Color Blind. NY, 1946. 1st ed. Name, else VG in dj. *King.* $20/£13

HALSEY, R.T.H. and ELIZABETH TOWER. The Homes of Our Ancestors. GC: Doubleday, Page, 1925. 1st ed. One of 201. Frontis, 20 plts. Teg. (Lt rubbed, shaken; text lt foxed.) *Bookpress.* $135/£87

HALSMAN, PHILIPPE. Piccoli: A Fairy Tale. NY: S&S, 1953. 1st ed. Paul Julian (illus). VG in dj. *Houle.* $125/£81

HALTIGAN, JAMES. The Irish in the American Revolution and Their Early Influence in the Colonies. Washington: Patrick J. Haltigan, 1908. 9 plts. (Emb stamp tp.) *Schoyer.* $65/£42

HALTIGAN, JAMES. The Irish in the American Revolution and Their Early Influence in the Colonies. Washington, D.C.: Patrick J. Haltigan, 1908. 1st ed. Grn cl (recased, new eps). VG. *Chapel Hill.* $175/£113

HAMBLEN, EMILY S. On the Minor Prophecies of William Blake. Dent, 1930. 1st ed. Cl damp-mottled, o/w VG. *Poetry.* $28/£18

HAMBURGER, MICHAEL. Babes in the Wood. Sceptre Press, (1974). One of 50 numbered, signed. Fine in stapled wrappers. *Dermont.* $25/£16

HAMBURGER, MICHAEL. Collected Poems 1941-1983. London, 1984. 1st Eng ed. VG in dj. *Edrich.* $16/£10

HAMBURGER, MICHAEL. Conversations With Charwomen. Sceptre Press, (1973). One of 50 numbered, signed. Fine in stapled wrappers. *Dermont.* $25/£16

HAMBURGER, MICHAEL. In Flashlight. London, 1965. 1st Eng ed. VG in orig wraps. *Edrich.* $16/£10

HAMBY, WALLACE. Intracranial Aneurysms. Springfield, 1952. 1st ed. Good. *Fye.* $50/£32

HAMERTON, PHILIP GILBERT. Etching and Etchers. London, 1868. 1st ed. xxvi,354pp (lt browning), 30 etchings (of 33), 2 dry points. Incl 5 dbl-pg, 1 fldg plt. Marbled eps; fore, lower edge uncut. 1/2 morocco, marbled bds (upper hinge cracked, almost detached; worn). *Edwards.* $388/£250

HAMERTON, PHILIP GILBERT. Etching and Etchers. London: Macmillan, 1880. 3rd ed. 48 etchings; orig 4pp prospectus loosely inserted; uncut. (Sm piece torn from text margin.) Orig cl, brn leather back (sl rubbed). *Petersfield.* $496/£320

HAMERTON, PHILIP GILBERT. The Graphic Arts. London, 1882. xvi,384pp, 54 plts (lt spotting; new eps). Uncut. Mod cl, gilt spine title (rebacked, recased; sl rubbed). *Edwards.* $116/£75

HAMIL, ALFRED E. The Decorative Work of T.M. Cleland. NY: The Pynson Printers, 1929. 1st ed. #1009/1200. Rockwell Kent litho frontisport, 99 full-pg plts. Orig black cl (rubbed). Sm portfolio w/6 examples of letterhead by Cleland laid in. VG. *Chapel Hill.* $75/£48

HAMILTON, ALEXANDER. Outlines of the Theory and Practice of Midwifery. Northampton, MA, 1797. 3rd Amer ed. 288pp. Recent cl. (Lib perforation stamp.) *Fye.* $100/£65

HAMILTON, ALLAN. A Manual of Medical Jurisprudence.... NY, 1883. 1st ed. 380pp. Good. *Fye.* $75/£48

HAMILTON, ANGUS. In Abor Jungles. London, 1912. 1st ed. Fldg map. (Lt browning; discoloring, fading; joints splitting; spine chipped, repaired.) *Edwards.* $132/£85

HAMILTON, ANTHONY. Memoirs of Count Grammont. London: T. Bensley, 1809. 2nd ed. 3 vols. 39 engr plts (offsetting). Contemp 3/4 calf over marbled bds (sl rubbed), gilt spines, speckled edges. Some foxing. *Sadlon.* $100/£65

HAMILTON, CHARLES (ed). Cry of the Thunderbird, the American Indian's Own Story. NY, 1950. 1st ed. VG in dj (chipped, torn). *King.* $35/£23

HAMILTON, CICELY. Modern Russia as Seen by an Englishwoman. NY: Dutton, 1934. 1st ed. Bds sl spotted, o/w Fine in dj (chipped). *Beasley.* $45/£29

HAMILTON, DAVID. The Monkey Gland Affair. London: C&W, 1986. 1st ed. Fine in dj. *White.* $28/£18

HAMILTON, DONALD. The Ambushers. Greenwich: Fawcett, 1963. 1st ed. Crease fr cvr; stamp, o/w Fine in wrappers. *Mordida.* $25/£16

HAMILTON, DONALD. Death of a Citizen. Greenwich: Fawcett, 1960. 1st ed. Sl cvr wear, o/w Fine in wrappers. *Mordida.* $45/£29

HAMILTON, DONALD. Line of Fire. NY: Dell, 1955. 1st ed. VF in wrappers. *Mordida.* $45/£29

HAMILTON, DONALD. The Removers. Greenwich: Fawcett, 1961. 1st ed. Crease fr cvr, o/w Fine in wrappers. *Mordida.* $25/£16

HAMILTON, E.R. The Art of Interrogation. NY/London: Harcourt, Brace/Kegan Paul, 1929. 1st US ed. Blue-grn cl. VG in dj (chipped). *Gach.* $30/£19

HAMILTON, EDMOND. The Haunted Stars. D-M, 1960. 1st ed. Fine in NF dj. *Aronovitz.* $100/£65

HAMILTON, EDMOND. The Star Kings. Fell, 1949. 1st ed. Fine in dj (nicked; edge-rubbed). *Madle.* $125/£81

HAMILTON, EDMOND. Tharkol, Lord of the Unknown. Manchester: World Publishers, (1950). 1st ed. Sm mended nick to spine, o/w NF in pict wrappers. *Reese.* $55/£35

HAMILTON, GEORGE. The Elements of Drawing.... London: Richard Phillips, 1827. 50 engr plts (9 hand-colored). 1/2 roan over marbled bds (worn). Good (few pp, incl tp, crudely tape-repaired). *Glenn.* $120/£77

HAMILTON, HOLMAN. Zachary Taylor. Indianapolis: Bobbs-Merrill, (1951). 1st ed. Fine. *Graf.* $30/£19

HAMILTON, HOLMAN. Zachary Taylor. Bobbs Merrill, 1951. 1st ed. VG +. *Bishop.* $25/£16

HAMILTON, J.C. The Prairie Province. Toronto: Belford Bros, 1876. vii,259pp(i.e. 255)+12pp ads, 2 plts, fldg plan, fldg facs map, lg fldg illus map mtd rear cvr. Orig pict cl. VG. *Schoyer.* $125/£81

HAMILTON, J.G. (ed). The Best Letters of Thomas Jefferson. Houghton Mifflin, 1926. 1st ed. Port. VG. *Book Broker.* $40/£26

HAMILTON, JAMES. The Battle of Fort Donelson. NY, (1968). 1st ed. VG + in VG + dj. *Pratt.* $55/£35

HAMILTON, JAMES. Observations on the Use and Abuse of Mercurial Medicines in Various Diseases. NY, 1821. 1st Amer ed. 216pp. Full leather (bds detached). *Fye.* $75/£48

HAMILTON, JAMES. Observations on the Utility and Administration of Purgative Medicines in Several Diseases. Edinburgh, 1815. 5th ed. xxxii,213pp. Mod 1/2 leather gilt. Notes, underlining, o/w VG. *Whitehart.* $93/£60

HAMILTON, MARY E. The Policewoman. NY: Stokes, 1924. 1st ed. Presentation copy, inscribed, signed. VG in dj. *Petrilla.* $100/£65

HAMILTON, PATRICK. The Slaves of Solitude. London: Constable, 1947. 1st ed. VG in dj (sl nicked). *Virgo.* $31/£20

HAMILTON, PATRICK. The Slaves of Solitude. London: Constable, 1947. 1st UK ed. VG in dj. *Lewton.* $45/£29

HAMILTON, ROBERT. The Naturalist's Library. Vol XXV Mammalia-Amphibious Carnivora. London: Henry G. Bohn, 1860. 336pp. Teg. Add'l engr title, 30 engr plts. Red cl, gilt. Good +. *Walcot.* $85/£55

HAMILTON, ROBERT. The Naturalist's Library. Volume XXVI Mammalia-Whales. London: Henry G. Bohn, 1861. 264pp. Teg. Add'l engr title w/handcolored vignette, 29 engr plts. Red cl. Sm tear head of spine, o/w VG. Good +. *Walcot.* $101/£65

HAMILTON, SCHUYLER. History of the National Flag of the United States of America. Phila: Lippincott, Grambo, 1852. 1st ed. 115pp; litho tp, 3 color litho plts. Pict cl. VG. Howes H 137. *Schoyer.* $100/£65

HAMILTON, THOMAS M. The Young Pioneer, When Captain was a Boy.... Washington: Library Press, (1932). 1st ed. *Ginsberg.* $75/£48

HAMILTON, VIRGINIA. Time-Ago Lost: More Tales of Jahdu. NY: Macmillan, (1973). 1st ed. Fine in dj. *Godot.* $45/£29

HAMILTON, W. Dated Book Plates (Ex Libris) with a Treatise on Their Origin and Development. A&C Black, 1895. 225pp+index. Red dec cl (rebacked; lib stamp). Text clean. *Moss.* $186/£120

HAMLEY, EDWARD. The War in the Crimea. London, 1896. 7th ed. Photolitho frontis port, vi,312pp, 3 photolitho plts, 5 maps and plans. Sl browning, o/w VG in brn cl (sl rubbed). *Edwards.* $62/£40

HAMLIN, CYRUS. Among the Turks. NY: Robert Carter, 1878. 378pp. Royal blue cl stamped in black, gilt (spine sl discolored, rubbed). *Schoyer*. $75/£48

HAMLIN, TALBOT. Benjamin Henry Latrobe. NY: OUP, 1955. 1st ed. Frontis, 40 plts. VG in dj (torn, rubbed). *Bookpress*. $65/£42

HAMLIN, TALBOT. Greek Revival Architecture in America.... London: OUP, 1944. 1st ed. Frontis; 94 plts. VG in dj (used). *Bookpress*. $75/£48

HAMMACHER, A.M. Marino Marini: Sculpture/Painting/Drawing. NY: Abrams, (n.d., circa 1970). 1st ed. 315 illus (63 color). Fine, in dj. *Godot*. $225/£145

HAMMAN, LOUIS and SAMUEL WOLMAN. Tuberculin in Diagnosis and Treatment. NY, 1912. 1st ed. Good. *Fye*. $75/£48

HAMMER, RICHARD. One Morning in the War: The Tragedy at Son My. London: Rupert Hart-Davis, (1970). 1st UK ed. Sl rust mk 2pp; sm bump bottom edge, o/w Fine in dj (lt worn). *Aka*. $35/£23

HAMMETT, DASHIELL and ROBERT COLODNY. The Battle of the Aleutians. Adak, AK: Intelligence Section, Field Force Headquarters, 1944. 1st ed. Oblong ppwrps very lt dampstained bottom margin fep, o/w VG+. *Bernard*. $275/£177

HAMMETT, DASHIELL. The Big Knockover. NY: Random House, (1966). 1st ed. NF in dj (lt used, price-clipped, spine sl faded). *Aka*. $45/£29

HAMMETT, DASHIELL. The Continental Op. NY: Lawrence E. Spivak, 1945. 1st ed. Sl wear spine ends; rubbing, o/w NF in wrappers. *Mordida*. $85/£55

HAMMETT, DASHIELL. The Dain Curse. Knopf, 1929. 1st ed. Lt dust soil, else VG. *Fine Books*. $385/£248

HAMMETT, DASHIELL. The Dashiell Hammett Omnibus. London: Cassell, 1950. Omnibus ed. Pg edges sl spotted, o/w Fine in VG dj (sl faded spine; internal tape repair; spotting; closed tear; sl edge wear). *Mordida*. $200/£129

HAMMETT, DASHIELL. Dashiell Hammett's Mystery Omnibus. Cleveland: World Publishing, (1944). 1st ed in this format. VG (sl mottling cl) in dj (lt edgewear; sm chips). *Antic Hay*. $50/£32

HAMMETT, DASHIELL. The Drain Curse. Knopf, 1929. 1st US ed. NF (bkpl). *Williams*. $302/£195

HAMMETT, DASHIELL. The Maltese Falcon. Knopf, 1930. 1st US ed. VG (bds sl dulled, mked). *Williams*. $302/£195

HAMMETT, DASHIELL. Red Harvest. Knopf, 1928. 1st US ed, 1st bk. VG (spine faded; fr hinge sl loose). *Williams*. $225/£145

HAMMETT, DASHIELL. The Return of the Continental Op. NY: Dell 154, 1947. 2nd ed. NF in wraps (lt crease). *Beasley*. $45/£29

HAMMETT, DASHIELL. The Thin Man. Knopf, 1934. 1st US ed. VG (bds sl faded; eps replaced; sl wear spine top, bottom). *Williams*. $194/£125

HAMMOND, ALEX. The Book of Chessmen. London, 1950. 1st ed. Frontis, 61 b/w plts. (Fep sl spotted, lt tape mks pastedowns.) Dj (sl soiled, ragged w/sl loss). *Edwards*. $70/£45

HAMMOND, GEORGE P. The Adventures of Alexander Barclay, Mountain Man. Denver: Old West Pub Co, 1976. 5 color plts, 3 pocket maps. Fine in dj. *Bohling*. $75/£48

HAMMOND, GEORGE P. The Adventures of Alexander Barclay, Mountain Man. Old West, 1976. 1st ed. Color frontis, 3 fldg maps in pocket. VF in VF dj. *Oregon*. $40/£26

HAMMOND, ISAAC B. Reminiscences of Frontier Life. Portland, OR: I.B. Hammond, 1904. Inscribed. Port. VG in gray wraps (edges worn), black title. Howes H 142. *Bohling*. $350/£226

HAMMOND, MRS. JOHN HAYS. A Woman's Part in a Revolution. London, 1897. 1st ed. 159pp+32pp pub's cat. Sl browned, o/w VG in maroon cl. *Edwards*. $101/£65

HAMMOND, S.T. Practical Dog Training. NY: Forest & Stream, 1882. 1st ed. 97pp+9pp ads. Orig red gilt dec cl. VG. *Bowman*. $65/£42

HAMMOND, WILLIAM. Sexual Impotence in the Male and Female. Detroit, 1887. 1st ed. 305pp. Good. *Fye*. $250/£161

HAMMOND, WILLIAM. Sleep and Its Derangements. Phila, 1880. 1st ed, rptd. 318pp. Good. *Fye*. $100/£65

HAMMOND, WILLIAM. A Treatise on Insanity in Its Medical Relations. NY, 1883. 1st ed. 767pp. Good. *Fye*. $300/£194

HAMNER, LAURA V. The No-Gun Man of Texas. Amarillo: Laura V. Hamner, 1935. 1st ed. VG in pict cl. *Lien*. $45/£29

HAMPE, ROLAND and ERIKA SIMON. The Birth of Greek Art. NY: OUP, 1981. 60 color plts. Dj. *Edwards*. $54/£35

HAMPTON, TAYLOR. The Nickel Plate Road. Cleveland: World, 1947. 1st ed. 27 plts. Silver dec cl. VG. *Connolly*. $27/£17

HANAFORD, PHEBE A. Daughters of America; or, Women of the Century. Augusta, ME: True, n.d. (ca 1882). 730pp. Dec cl. (Pulp paper sl yellowed.) *Petrilla*. $40/£26

HANCOCK, ADA. Reminiscences of Winfield Scott Hancock. NY: Webster, 1887. 340pp. Dec cl, beveled edges. *Schoyer*. $80/£52

HANCOCK, E. CAMPBELL. The Amateur Pottery and Glass Painter. London/Worcester: Chapman & Hall/Hancock, ca 1890. 2 mtd color plts. Grn cl, gilt. *Glenn*. $60/£39

HANCOCK, H. IRVING. Dave Darrin After the Mine Layers. Altemus, 1919. 1st ed. VG in dj (frayed). *Madle*. $25/£16

HANCOCK, H. IRVING. Dave Darrin in the Arctic Station. Altemus, 1919. 1st ed. VG in dj (frayed). *Madle*. $25/£16

HANCOCK, H. IRVING. Dave Darrin's Fourth Year at Annapolis. Altemus, 1911. 1st ed. VG in dj (frayed). *Madle*. $22/£14

HANCOCK, H. IRVING. Dave Darrin's Third Year at Annapolis. Altemus, 1911. 1st ed. Good+ in dj (worn). *Madle*. $20/£13

HANCOCK, RALPH. The Forest Lawn Story. LA: Academy, (1955). Promo text laid in. Illus bds. Fine (lt rubbed). *Aka*. $20/£13

HANCOCK, RICHARD RAMSEY. Hancock's Diary; or, A History of the Second Tennessee Confederate Cavalry.... Nashville, TN: Brandon Ptg, 1887. 1st ed. 2 vols in 1. Frontis, 644pp. Orig cl. NF. Howes H 152. *Mcgowan*. $550/£355

HAND, WILLIAM. The House Surgeon and Physician. New Haven, 1820. 2nd ed. 288pp. Rebound in cl-backed bds; paper label. Good. *Fye*. $100/£65

Handbook to the Egyptian Mummies and Coffins Exhibited in the British Museum. London: British Museum, 1938. 31 plts. Good in wraps. *Archaeologia*. $45/£29

HANDY, W.C. Blues. NY: Albert & Charles Boni, 1926. 1st ed, 1st ptg. Fine (sl soiled). *Beasley*. $250/£161

HANES, BAILEY C. Bill Doolin: Outlaw O.T.... Norman, 1968. 1st ed. Fine in dj (price-clipped). *Baade*. $40/£26

HANFF, HELENE. The Duchess of Bloomsbury Street. Phila, 1973. 1st ed. VF in VF dj. *Bond*. $20/£13

HANFF, HELENE. The Duchess of Bloomsbury Street. Phila/NY: Lippincott, 1973. 1st ed. VG in dj. *Limestone*. $35/£23

HANFMANN, GEORGE M.A. Roman Art: A Modern Survey of the Art of Imperial Rome. NYGS, (1964). 52 color plts. (Lt bumped.) Dj (tattered). *Archaeologia*. $45/£29

HANFORD, PHEBE. Daughters of America; or, Women of the Century. Augusta, ME, 1882. 730pp. Good. *Fye*. $100/£65

HANKE, VICTOR. The Treatment of Diseases of the Eye. J. Herbert Parsons & George Coats (trans). London: Hodder & Stoughton, 1905. 1st ed in English. Fine. *Glaser*. $40/£26

HANLEY, J. FRANK. A Day in the Siskiyous. An Oregon Extravaganza. Indianapolis: Art Press, 1916. 1st ed. 33 color plts, 5 b/w plts, fldg plt laid in as issued. Pict cl, gilt. VG + . *Shasky*. $85/£55

HANLEY, JAMES. At Bay. London: Grayson & Grayson, 1935. #155/285 signed. NF in dj. *Williams*. $70/£45

HANLEY, JAMES. The Furys. London: C&W, 1935. 1st ed. Fine (spine discoloration) in dj (chipped, worn). *Beasley*. $60/£39

HANLEY, JAMES. Herman Melville: A Man in the Customs House. Loughton: Dud Noman Press, 1971. 1st ed, ltd to 120 numbered, signed. Ptd wrappers; spine, top edge faded, else VG. *Godot*. $65/£42

HANLEY, JAMES. The Secret Journey. NY: Macmillan, 1936. 1st US ed. Fine in dj (sm chips). *Beasley*. $85/£55

HANLEY, JAMES. Stoker Bush. London: C&W, 1935. 1st ed. Stain lower edge, o/w Nice in Nice dj (dknd spine). *Beasley*. $60/£39

HANLEY, JAMES. Stoker Bush. NY: Macmillan, 1936. 1st US ed. Fine in NF dj (few tears; sl dknd spine). *Beasley*. $75/£48

HANLEY, JAMES. A Woman in the Sky. Andre Deutsch, 1973. 1st ed. Dj. *Edwards*. $23/£15

HANNAH, BARRY. Hey Jack! NY: E.P. Dutton/Seymour Lawrence, (1987). 1st ed. Fine in dj. *Godot*. $35/£23

HANNAH, BARRY. Nightwatchman. NY: Viking, (1973). 1st ed. NF in dj (creases inner flap). *Reese*. $75/£48

HANNAH, BARRY. Two Stories. (Jackson): Nouveau Press, (1982). One of 226 signed. VF in marbled wraps. *Pharos*. $50/£32

HANNEMAN, AUDRE. Ernest Hemingway...Bibliography. Princeton Univ Press, 1967. 1st ed. Beige cl. NF. *Chapel Hill*. $65/£42

HANSBERRY, LORRAINE. The Sign in Sidney Brustein's Window. NY: Random House, 1965. 1st ed. Fine (name) in NF dj. *Beasley*. $65/£42

HANSEN, HARVEY and JEANNE MILLER. Wild Oats in Eden. Santa Rosa, 1962. 1st ed. Fine. *Oregon*. $60/£39

HANSEN, JOSEPH. Fadeout. London: Harrap, 1972. 1st British ed. NF in NF dj (lt soiling rear panel). *Silver Door*. $45/£29

HANSEN, JOSEPH. The Man Everybody Was Afraid Of. NY: Holt, 1978. 1st ed. Signed. Fine in dj. *Silver Door*. $40/£26

HANSEN, THORKILD. Arabia Felix. The Danish Expedition of 1761-1767. James & Kathleen McFarlane (trans). NY/Evanston: Harper & Row, 1962. 1st ed. Dbl-pg map. NF in dj. *Worldwide*. $35/£23

HANSEN, THORKILD. Arabia Felix: The Danish Expedition of 1761-1767. NY/Evanston: Harper & Row, (1964). Good in dj. *Archaeologia*. $45/£29

HANSEN, WOODROW. The Search for Authority in California. Biobooks, 1960. Ltd to 750 ptd. Color fldg map tipped in at rear. Fine. *Oregon*. $50/£32

HANSON, ANNE COFFIN. Jacopo Della Quercia's Fonte Gaia. Clarendon, 1965. Frontis, 96 b/w photos. (Ex-lib, ink stamps.) Dj (sl faded, chipped). *Edwards*. $74/£48

HANSON, CHARLES HENRY. Stories of the Days of King Arthur. London, 1882. 271pp; 6 full-pg plts by Gustave Dore. Pict cl (corners bumped). *Argosy*. $75/£48

HANSON, KITTY. Rebels in the Streets. Englewood Cliffs, (1964). 1st ed. VG (name stamps) in dj (sl worn). *Second Life*. $35/£23

HANWAY, JONAS. An Historical Account of the British Trade Over the Caspian Sea. London: Ptd for T. Osborne et al, 1754. 2nd ed. 2 vols. xxviii,460,(viii); xx,460,(xviii)pp + ads, 13 plts, 9 fldg maps, 12 vignettes (lacks 3 ports, 2 plts; offsetting, lt foxing). Contemp gilt ruled speckled calf (lt stain, rubbed; joints cracking, though firm; spines chipped w/loss, lack labels; lib bkpl). *Edwards*. $388/£250

HAPGOOD, HUTCHINS. Types From City Streets. NY: Funk & Wagnalls, 1910. 1st ed. Fine. *Beasley*. $100/£65

HAPGOOD, HUTCHINS. A Victorian in the Modern World. NY: Harcourt, (1939). 1st ed. Bkpl, o/w VG in dj (spine sunned, old strengthening verso). *Reese*. $50/£32

Happy Family. NY: McLoughlin Bros, (ca 1880). Pop-up. Tall, 4to. Stiff color illus bds (lt edgewear). Interior pop-up w/sm reinforcement, o/w Fine. *Reisler*. $385/£248

Happy Rock. A Book About Henry Miller. (Berkeley: Bern Porter, 1945). 1st ed, ltd to 750 numbered (this copy not numbered). Grey cl spine, paper-cvrd bds. NF. *Godot*. $65/£42

HARBORD, JAMES G. The American Army in France 1917-1919. Boston: Little Brown, 1936. 1st ed. Color frontis, 9 maps (incl 1 fldg). VG. *Graf*. $20/£13

HARCOURT, HELEN. Florida Fruits and How to Raise Them. Louisville, (KY): Morton, 1886. Rev, enlgd ed. 347pp. VG. *Second Life*. $65/£42

HARDAWAY, W.A. Essentials of Vaccination; A Compilation of Facts.... St. Louis, 1886. 1st ed. 46pp. Good. *Fye*. $75/£48

HARDCASTLE, EPHRAIM. (Pseud of William Henry Pyne.) Wine and Walnuts; or After Dinner Chit-Chat. Longman, Hurst, et al, 1824. 2nd ed. 2 vols. Contemp 1/2 calf, marbled bds. *Bickersteth*. $59/£38

HARDEE, W.J. Rifle and Infantry Tactics. Raleigh, NC: John Spelman, 1862. 144,ivpp. Orig cl-backed bds. Good (private lib bkpl, blindstamp; lacks feps; fr hinge repaired, text dampstained). *Chapel Hill*. $250/£161

HARDEKER, ALFRED. A Brief History of Pawnbroking. London, 1892. Sm 8vo. viii,367pp. (Sm tear 1/2 title; upper hinge reinforced; recased; spine chipped.) Edwards. $62/£40

HARDESTY, STEVEN. Ghost Soldiers. NY: Walker, (1986). 1st ed. Fine in Fine dj. Aka. $35/£23

HARDIE, MARTIN. English Coloured Books. London, (1906). 1st ed. 28 plts (1 loose). Pub's cl; gilt spine. (Bkpl; inner hinges cracked; cvrs worn; sl staining.) King. $150/£97

HARDIE, MARTIN. John Pettie. A&C Black, 1908. 1st ed. 50 color plts. (Feps browned; lower joint sl split; sl rubbed.) Edwards. $47/£30

HARDIE, MARTIN. Water-Colour Painting in Britain. Vol I (of 3). Dudley Snelgrove et al (eds). London: Batsford, 1969. Rpt. Color frontis. Dj (torn, ragged). Edwards. $62/£40

HARDING, A.R. (ed). Fox Trapping. Columbus: Harding, 1906. 1st ed. Dec cl. VG. Mikesh. $25/£16

HARDING, ANNALIESE. German Sculpture in New England Museums. Boston, 1972. Good in dj. Washton. $75/£48

HARDING, G. LANKESTER. The Antiquities of Jordan. NY: Praeger, (1967). 30 plts. Good in dj. Archaeologia. $35/£23

HARDING, J.D. Harding's Portfolio. London: C. Tilt, 1837. Folio. 2ff letterpress, tinted litho title w/vignette view, 23 plts, all hand-colored. Orig half morocco, aeg (inner hinge broken; foxing). Marlborough. $853/£550

HARDING, J.D. Lessons on Art. London: Bogue, 1849. 1st ed. Later red 1/2 morocco, marbled bds, orig label laid down; new eps. Pg edges worn, o/w Fine. Europa. $140/£90

HARDING, J.D. Lessons on Art. London: W. Kent et al, n.d. (before 1860). 2nd ed. viii,155pp (tp foxed); 45 litho plts (lt tidemk outer edge of some). New blind cl. Ars Artis. $194/£125

HARDING, J.D. Lessons on Trees. London: David Bogue, 1850. 3ff, 30 litho plts. 1/2 leather (sl worn), marbled bds, gilt. Good. Ars Artis. $233/£150

HARDING, J.D. Lessons on Trees. London: Kent/Windsor & Newton, n.d. 5th ed. 30 litho plts. Orig cl, blind/gilt dec (rebacked, new spine label; sl foxing; inner joint strengthened). Nice. Europa. $101/£65

HARDING, J.D. The Principles and Practice of Art. London: Chapman and Hall, 1845. 156pp + ads. 24 Fine plts by Harding. (Rebacked; upper hinge splitting; leaves stained or frayed, 1 loose.) Argosy. $150/£97

HARDING, MIKE. Walking the Dales. London: Michael Joseph, 1986. 1st ed. Gilt cl. Mint in dj. Hollett. $23/£15

HARDMAN, H. and E.J. COLE. Paper-Making Practice. (Manchester): Manchester Univ, (1960). 1st ed. Fine in dj (sl wear). Oak Knoll. $45/£29

HARDWICK, ELIZABETH. The Ghostly Lover. NY: Harcourt, Brace, (1945). 1st ed, 1st bk. Fine in dj (sl rubbed). Jaffe. $275/£177

HARDWICK, MICHAEL and MOLLIE. The Charles Dickens Companion. NY: Holt, Rinehart & Winston, (1965). 1st ed. Fine in Fine dj. Glenn. $25/£16

HARDWICK, MICHAEL. The Private Life of Dr. Watson. NY: Dutton, 1983. 1st ed. VF in dj. Silver Door. $30/£19

HARDY, ALISTER C. The Open Sea. London, 1956. 1st ed. Dj. Edwards. $101/£65

HARDY, ALLISON. Kate Bender. The Kansas Murderess.... Girard, KS: Haldeman-Julius, 1944. 1st ed. VG (cvr loose) in wraps (fragile). Book Market. $20/£13

HARDY, F. Ventriloquism Made Easy. London: Frederick Warne, n.d. (c. 1870). Bijou Book edition, issue w/o color frontis. Pict cl (sm cvr stain). Internally Fine. Dramatis Personae. $90/£58

HARDY, FLORENCE EMILY. The Early Life of Thomas Hardy 1840-1891 with The Later Years of Thomas Hardy 1892-1928. London: Macmillan, 1928/1930. 1st ed. 2 vols. Both vols in grn cl, spines gilt-lettered, dec device fr cvrs. Fine in Fine djs. Vandoros. $385/£248

HARDY, G.L. The Law and Practice of Bankruptcy. London: Effingham Wilson, 1914. Grn cl, gilt (worn but sound). Boswell. $125/£81

HARDY, H.F.H. Good Gun Dogs. London/NY: Country Life/Scribner's, 1930. 1st ed. Frontis w/glassine guard, 15 plts. Bkpl, else Fine. Cahan. $60/£39

HARDY, LADY DUFFUS. Through Cities and Prairie Lands. NY: Worthington Co, 1890. 338pp. Hayman. $20/£13

HARDY, ROBIN and ANTHONY SHAFFER. The Wicker Man. London: Hamlyn, 1979. 1st UK ed. Fine in VG dj. Lewton. $23/£15

HARDY, THOMAS. A Changed Man, The Waiting Supper and Other Tales. Harpers, 1913. 1st Amer ed. Inner hinge strengthened, else VG+. Fine Books. $65/£42

HARDY, THOMAS. A Changed Man, The Waiting Supper and Other Tales. London: Macmillan, 1913. 1st ed. (Tp sl foxed, frontis sl dull.) Petersfield. $39/£25

HARDY, THOMAS. The Dynasts, an Epic Drama of the War with Napoleon. London: Macmillan, 1927. One of 525 signed. 3 vols. Uncut except for top edge. Vellum backstrips (faded; few pp sl foxed). Petersfield. $543/£350

HARDY, THOMAS. The Dynasts. London: Macmillan, 1927. 3 vols. One of 525 numbered sets, ptd in red/black on thick laid paper, signed by Hardy. Etched port signed in pencil by Francis Dodd (artist). Gilt lettered vellum spine, batik bds. Unopened set (lt wear; dust soil). Dermont. $475/£306

HARDY, THOMAS. The Famous Tragedy of the Queen of Cornwall at Tintagel in Lyonesse. Macmillan, 1923. 1st ed. 2 plts. Pict cl gilt. (Ink inscrip.) Bickersteth. $78/£50

HARDY, THOMAS. The Famous Tragedy of the Queen of Cornwall at Tintagel in Lyonnesse. London: Macmillan, 1923. 1st ed. Grn cl, gilt. NF (inscrip). Macdonnell. $25/£16

HARDY, THOMAS. The Famous Tragedy of the Queen of Cornwall at Tintagel in Lyonnesse. MacMillan, 1923. 1st ed. One of 1000. Frontis. Corner wear, else VG+. Fine Books. $85/£55

HARDY, THOMAS. Far from the Madding Crowd. Cambridge: LEC, 1958. One of 1500 numbered, signed by Agnes Miller Parker (illus) w/add'l signed plt laid in. Fine in pub's slipcase. Hermitage. $225/£145

HARDY, THOMAS. A Group of Noble Dames. London: James R. Osgood, McIlvaine, (1891). 1st ed, in primary binding, blocked in gilt top cvr. Nice (pale cl sl rubbed, worn; lower cvr sl bubbled). Ash. $302/£195

HARDY, THOMAS. A Group of Noble Dames. London: Osgood, McIlvaine, 1891. 1st ed. Spinal extrems sl bumped, else VG. Limestone. $125/£81

HARDY, THOMAS. Human Shows, Far Phantasies: Songs and Trifles. MacMillan, 1925. 1st Amer ed. VG + in VG dj (sl chipping spine). *Fine Books*. $65/£42

HARDY, THOMAS. Jude the Obscure, the Wessex Novels, vol VIII. London, 1895 (dated 1896). 1st ed. Map. *Petersfield*. $39/£25

HARDY, THOMAS. Jude the Obscure. London: Osgood, McIlvaine, (1896). 1st ed, 1st state, 1st binding. Macbeth-Raeburn frontis, map at end. Teg. Orig dk grn cl, gilt. Osgood's name appears on tp and spine; partially blank pp in sigs A-H are numbered (pp7, 16, 25, etc). Issued as Vol VIII in Wessex Novels. Fine (few mks). *Macdonnell*. $300/£194

HARDY, THOMAS. Jude the Obscure. London: Osgood, McIlvaine, (1896). 1st ed. 5 of 1st 8 gatherings are in Purdy's 1st state, w/partially blank pgs numbered. Etched frontis; teg. (Sl worn, rubbed; Mudie's label.) Good (eps cracked, sl shaken, browning, sl creases). *Ash*. $116/£75

HARDY, THOMAS. Jude the Obscure. NY: Harper, 1896. 1st Amer ed. iv,488pp, 12 plts. Dec gilt cl (lt foxing). *Karmiole*. $75/£48

HARDY, THOMAS. Jude the Obscure. NY: Harper, 1896. 1st Amer ed. 12 illus by W. Hatherell. Gilt-worked dk grn cl. VG (sl wear; sl foxing). *Antic Hay*. $150/£97

HARDY, THOMAS. Jude the Obscure. Osgood, McIlvaine, 1896. 1st ed. VG. *Fine Books*. $275/£177

HARDY, THOMAS. Jude the Obscure. London: Osgood, McIlvaine, 1896. 1st issue, mixed state, w/pp7,16 numbered; pp25,32,38,47 unnumbered. VG (bumped; lt worn). *Williams*. $116/£75

HARDY, THOMAS. Jude the Obscure. NY: LEC, 1969. 1/1500 numbered, signed by Agnes Miller Parker (illus). VG in bd slipcase. *Argosy*. $75/£48

HARDY, THOMAS. Jude the Obscure. NY: LEC, 1969. 1st ed. One of 1500 signed by Agnes Miler Parker (illus). 1/4 morocco, bds. Bkpl; envelope tipped to back pastedown, o/w Fine in slipcase. *Pharos*. $60/£39

HARDY, THOMAS. Late Lyrics and Earlier. London, 1922. 1st ed. Fine in Fine dj. *Bond*. $75/£48

HARDY, THOMAS. Late Lyrics and Earlier. London: Macmillan, 1922. 1st ed. Fine in dj. *Pharos*. $200/£129

HARDY, THOMAS. Life and Art. NY: Greenberg, 1925. 1st ed, ltd to 2000 numbered. Olive brn cl, beveled, spine label (sl rubbed). VG (sl soiled). *Sumner & Stillman*. $65/£42

HARDY, THOMAS. Life's Little Ironies. London: Osgood, McIlvaine, 1894. 1st ed. Edges sl worn, else VG. *Limestone*. $135/£87

HARDY, THOMAS. The Mayor of Casterbridge. NY: LEC, 1964. 1st ed. One of 1500 ptd, signed by Agnes Miller Parker (engrs). 1/2 leather. Fine in slipcase. *Pharos*. $125/£81

HARDY, THOMAS. Moments of Vision and Miscellaneous Verses. London: Macmillan, 1917. 1st trade ed. Unopened. VG in dj (chipped, soiled). *Schoyer*. $85/£55

HARDY, THOMAS. Old Mrs. Chundle. NY: Crosby Gaige, 1929. One of 742. Dk grn cl-backed patterned bds. Very Nice. *Cady*. $35/£23

HARDY, THOMAS. Satires of Circumstance. London: Macmillan, 1914. 1st ed. Fine. *Pharos*. $60/£39

HARDY, THOMAS. Selected Poems. London: Medici Soc, 1921. One of 1025. Color woodcut port, tp color woodcut device. Pub's holland-backed blue bds (edges sl browned), paper labels. Dj (lacks sm piece top spine). *Book Block*. $185/£119

HARDY, THOMAS. Song of the Soldiers. Rptd from 'Times,' 9 Sept, 1914. 1st separate pub. Fine in wrappers. *Pharos*. $75/£48

HARDY, THOMAS. Tess of the D'Urbervilles. London: James R. Osgood, McIlvaine, (1892). 1st ed, 2nd issue. 3 vols. Orig gilt dec cvrs. Spines sunned, sl chipped, sl soiled, else Fine set. *Polyanthos*. $950/£613

HARDY, THOMAS. Tess of the D'Urbervilles. NY: LEC, 1956. One of 1500 signed by Agnes Miller Parker (illus). Pict cl. VG. *Pharos*. $200/£129

HARDY, THOMAS. The Three Wayfarers: A Play in One Act. Dorset: Henry Ling, 1935. One of 250. Sewn in white card wraps. VG (cvrs spotted). *Heller*. $65/£42

HARDY, THOMAS. Two on a Tower. Sampson Low et al, 1882. 1st ed. 3 vols. Grn cl; gilt-stamped spines (rebound). NF. *Fine Books*. $1,500/£968

HARDY, THOMAS. The Well-Beloved. Harpers, 1897. 1st Amer ed. Sl nicks, else VG +. *Fine Books*. $110/£71

HARDY, THOMAS. Wessex Poems. London: Harper, (1898). 1st ed. One of 500 ptd. Largely unopened. Teg. Dec cl, gilt (sl wear, sl mks). VG. *Ash*. $698/£450

HARDY, THOMAS. Winter Words. NY, 1928. #261/500. Vellum, gilt spine (sl sunned, rubbed). Box (sunned, rubbed; side mended). *Polyanthos*. $40/£26

HARDY, THOMAS. The Woodlanders. London: Macmillan, 1887. 1st ed. 3 vols. 8vo. Half titles each vol, ad pg end vol 1. Orig dk green cl blocked in blind/black; gilt-lettered spines; dk brown eps (label removal each vol, spotting, vol 2 fore-edges sl discolored by damp; sl wear). *Bickersteth*. $899/£580

HARDY, THOMAS. Yuletide in a Younger World. London: Faber & Gwyer, (n.d.). #1 of Ariel Poems. Few sm smudges on fr panel else VG. Wrappers. *Limestone*. $45/£29

HARDY, W.J. Handwriting of the Kings and Queens of England. RTS, 1893. 4 photogravure plts. Aeg. Maroon cl. Fine. *Moss*. $31/£20

HARE, AUGUSTUS J.C. The Gurneys of Earlham. London: George Allen, 1895. 1st ed. 2 vols. x,343; viii,352,4pp. VG set. *Hollett*. $85/£55

HARE, AUGUSTUS J.C. The Life and Letters of Frances Baroness Bunsen. NY: Routledge, 1879. 2 vols in 1. Frontis, 1009pp, 1 plt. (Bkpl; spine faded.) *Archaeologia*. $65/£42

HARE, AUGUSTUS J.C. Paris. London: George Allen, 1900. 2nd ed. 2 vols. VG (extrems sl rubbed). *Hollett*. $70/£45

HARE, AUGUSTUS J.C. Walks in London. London: George Allen, 1901. 7th ed. 2 vols. Bkpls; sm nick vol 2. *Hollett*. $54/£35

HARE, AUGUSTUS J.C. Walks in Rome. London, 1905. 17th ed. Map, 3 fldg plans. Gilt illus upper bd. (Spine sl chipped.) *Edwards*. $23/£15

HARE, AUGUSTUS J.C. and ST. CLAIR BADDELEY. Sicily. London: Heinemann, 1905. 1 plt (chipped edges); 6 maps, plans. VG (extrems sl rubbed). *Hollett*. $39/£25

HARE, AUGUSTUS J.C. and ST. CLAIR BADDELEY. Walks in Rome. London: Kegan Paul etc, 1913. 20th ed. 6 plans. VG. *Hollett*. $54/£35

HARE, CYRIL. He Should Have Died Hereafter. London, 1958. 1st ed. VG in dj (sm tear). *Words Etc.* $62/£40

HARE, CYRIL. That Yew Tree's Shade. London: Faber & Faber, 1954. 1st ed. Pg top edges lt soiled, o/w Fine in dj (sl dknd spine; closed tear). *Mordida.* $85/£55

HARE, CYRIL. With a Bare Bodkin. London: Faber & Faber, 1946. 1st ed. Eps, pg edges spotted, o/w VG in dj (dknd spine; chips; closed tears). *Mordida.* $45/£29

HARE, LLOYD C.M. Lucretia Mott. NY: Amer Hist Soc, 1937. 1st ed. Grn cl. VG in pict dj (sl worn, rubbed, spine dknd). *Juvelis.* $75/£48

HARGRAVE, CARRIE GUERPHAN. African Primitive Life as I Saw It in Sierra Leone, British West Africa. (Wilmington, NC, 1944). 1st ed. Orig cl. Bkpl removed, else NF. *Mcgowan.* $150/£97

HARGRAVE, CATHERINE PERRY. A History of Playing Cards and a Bibliography of Cards and Gaming. Boston: Houghton Mifflin, 1930. 1st ed. Gilt-titled red buckram. Clippings loosely laid in. Very Nice. *Cady.* $250/£161

HARGREAVES, REGINALD. The Bloodybacks. London: Rupert Hart-Davis, 1968. VG in dj. *Schoyer.* $30/£19

HARKEY, DEE. Mean as Hell. Albuquerque: Univ of NM, 1948. 1st ed, 1st state. Signed. VG + (name; dj frags pasted in eps). *Parker.* $125/£81

HARKEY, DEE. Mean as Hell. Albuquerque: Univ of NM Press, 1948. 1st ed, 2nd ptg. VG in dj. *Schoyer.* $40/£26

HARLAN, CALEB. Ida Randolph of Virginia: A Historical Novel in Verse. Phila: Ferris Bros, 1890. 2nd ed. Inscribed presentation. 101pp (several corners torn). Good + . *Book Broker.* $30/£19

HARLAN, GEORGE. Eyesight, and How to Care for It. Phila, 1879. 139pp. Good. *Fye.* $40/£26

HARLAND, MARION. Eve's Daughters or, Common Sense for Maid, Wife, and Mother. NY/Boston: Anderson/Lee & Shepard, 1882. 1st ed. 454pp. Pict cl. VG. *Petrilla.* $40/£26

HARLOW, ALVIN F. Brass-Pounders, Young Telegraphers of the Civil War. Denver, (1962). 1st ed. Dj lt worn, chipped, o/w Fine. *Pratt.* $22/£14

HARLOW, ALVIN F. Old Waybills. NY: D. Appleton-Century, 1934. Gold-stamped cl in dj. *Dawson.* $75/£48

HARLOW, FREDERICK P. The Making of a Sailor. Salem, MA: Marine Research Soc, 1928. 1st ed. VG in dj (sl worn, reinforced). *Hayman.* $45/£29

HARLOW, W.S. Duties of Sheriffs and Constables...of the State of California. SF: Sumner, Whitney, 1884. Contemp sheep. Worn, but Sound. *Boswell.* $150/£97

HARMAN, S.W. Hell on the Border. Fort Smith, (1898). 1st ed. One of 1000. (14),720pp, port. Orig ptd grn wrappers. Howes H 203. *Ginsberg.* $1,350/£871

HARMON, DANIEL W. A Journal of Voyages and Travels in the Interior of North America Between 47th and 58th Degrees N. Lat. Andover, VT, 1820. 1st ed. Frontis, 432pp; fldg map; errata slip tipped to rear pastedown (not included in all copies). Full tree calf, morocco spine label. Good + (foxed). Howes H 205. *Oregon.* $850/£548

HARMON, DANIEL W. A Journal of Voyages and Travels in the Interior of North America.... Andover, 1820. 1st ed. 432pp, errata slip, engr fldg map (in facs), port. Orig full calf, leather spine label. Howes H 205. *Ginsberg.* $750/£484

HARMON, WILLIAM. Treasury Holiday. Middletown: Wesleyan, (1970). 1st ed, 1st bk. Fine in dj. *Pharos.* $35/£23

Harmony Society in Pennsylvania. Phila: William Penn Assoc, 1937. 1st ed. VG in illus wrappers. *Cahan.* $35/£23

HARNED, T.B. (ed). The Letters of Anne Gilchrist and Walt Whitman. NY: Doubleday, Page, 1918. 1st ed. Grn cl, gilt. Fine. BAL 21463. *Macdonnell.* $65/£42

HARNESS, CHARLES. Flight into Yesterday. Bourgey & Curl, 1953. 1st ed. Fine in dj. *Madle.* $85/£55

HARNEY, GEORGE E. Stables, Outbuildings and Fences. NY: Geo. E. Woodward, (1870). 1st ed. 4to.(vi),90pp; 62 plts; Pub's cl. Fr inner hinge strengthened; cvrs rubbed; spine worn; rubberstamps tp, eps, still Clean. *Bookpress.* $750/£484

HARPENDING, ASBURY. The Great Diamond Hoax and Other Stirring Incidents in the Life of Asbury Harpending. James Wilkins (ed). SF: J.H. Barry, 1913. 1st ed. Frontis; 24 port plts. Good + (edgeworn). *Oregon.* $55/£35

HARPER, CHARLES G. From Paddington to Penzance. London, 1893. xxiv,272pp (lt spotting). Marbled eps. Gilt-filleted 1/2 calf, raised bands, gilt spine (extrems sl rubbed, surface loss). *Edwards.* $93/£60

HARPER, CHARLES G. The North Devon Coast. Chapman & Hall, 1908. 1st ed. Map. Illus blue cl (spine sl sunned; bkpl). *Edwards.* $93/£60

HARPER, CHARLES G. The South Devon Coast. Chapman & Hall, 1907. 1st ed. Map. Illus blue cl. (Feps lt foxed.) *Edwards.* $93/£60

HARPER, HARRY. Dawn of the Space Age. London: Sampson Low, Marston, n.d. ca 1945. 12 plts. Good (stain top corner pp) in dj remnants. *Knollwood.* $40/£26

HARPER, HENRY HOWARD. Library Essays about Books, Bibliophiles, Writers and Kindred Subjects. Boston: Privately ptd, 1924. 1st ed. One of unspecified #. Blue cl, bds. NF (spine sl soiled) in pub's slipcase (lt used). *Juvelis.* $75/£48

HARPER, ROBERT H. Lincoln and the Press. NY, (1951). 1st ed. VG + in VG + dj. *Pratt.* $30/£19

HARPSTER, JOHN W. (ed). Pen Pictures of Early Western Pennsylvania. Pittsburgh: Univ of Pittsburgh Press, 1938. 1st ed. *Argosy.* $75/£48

HARPSTER, JOHN W. (ed). Pen Pictures of Early Western Pennsylvania. Pittsburgh: Univ of Pittsburgh Press, 1938. 1st ed. One of 2000. Map. Black cl. Name, else NF in dj (worn). *Chapel Hill.* $60/£39

HARRADEN, BEATRICE. A New Book of the Fairies. London: Griffith Farran Browne, (1897). 8vo. Frontis, xii,179pp. Gilt edges. Pict gilt blue cl. Dated ink inscrip, lt rubbed, else VG. *Hobbyhorse.* $70/£45

HARRE, T. EVERETT. Not at Night! NY, (1928). 1st Amer ed. VG. *Mcclintock.* $65/£42

HARRER, HEINRICH. Seven Years in Tibet. Richard Graves (trans). London, 1953. 1st UK ed. Color frontis, dbl-pg map. Dj (chipped, loss). *Edwards.* $23/£15

HARRER, HEINRICH. The White Spider. Hugh Merrick (trans). London, 1959. 1st Eng ed. Fldg map. Dj (chipped w/loss). *Edwards.* $34/£22

HARRILL, LAWSON. Reminiscences 1861-1865 Lawson Merrill Captain Company I, 56th Regiment North Carolina Troops, General M.W. Ransom's Brigade. Statesville, NC: Brady, 1910. 1st ed. Ink corrections, else NF in orig stiff ptd wrappers. *Mcgowan.* $350/£226

HARRINGTON, ALAN. The Revelations of Dr. Modesto. NY: Knopf, 1955. 1st ed, 1st bk. Fine in dj (lt used). *Beasley.* $100/£65

HARRINGTON, H.D. Manual of the Plants of Colorado. Denver, 1954. (Extrems scuffed; sl shaken; underlinings, check mks; bkpl.) *Sutton.* $60/£39

HARRINGTON, MILTON. Wish-hunting in the Unconscious. NY: Macmillan, (1934). Early ptg. Inscribed. Ptd red cl. VG. *Gach.* $25/£16

HARRIS, A.C. Alaska and the Klondike Gold Fields. Chicago: H.J. Smith & Simon, (1897). 556pp; map. VG in dec cl. *Perier.* $75/£48

HARRIS, A.C. Alaska and the Klondike Gold Fields. (Jones, 1897). 528pp, map (torn, lacks lg piece). New buckram (rebound). *Heinoldt.* $35/£23

HARRIS, A.M. Pirate Tales from the Law. L-B, 1923. 1st ed. Pict cl. NF in VG pict dj (lt dust soil). *Fine Books.* $85/£55

HARRIS, ALBERT W. The Cruise of a Schooner. (Chicago): Privately ptd, (1958). 36 plts. Pict cl (spine lt faded). Howes H 221. *Ginsberg.* $125/£81

HARRIS, ANN SUTHERLAND. Andrea Sacchi. Oxford, 1977. 179 plts (4 color). Sound in dj. *Ars Artis.* $116/£75

HARRIS, ANN SUTHERLAND. Andrea Sacchi. Complete Edition of the Paintings.... Princeton, 1977. Good in dj. *Washton.* $90/£58

HARRIS, BENJAMIN BUTLER. The Gila Trail. Norman: Univ of OK, 1960. 1st ed. Fine in VG + dj. *Parker.* $25/£16

HARRIS, BILL. Virginia: Land of Many Dreams. Crescent Pub, (c. 1983). 1st ed. Unpaged. VG (cvrs warped) in Fine dj. *Book Broker.* $35/£23

HARRIS, BURTON. John Colter, His Years in the Rockies. Scribner's, 1952. 1st ed. 3 maps on 4pp. Fine in Good + dj. *Oregon.* $145/£94

HARRIS, CHARLES K. Complete Songster...150 Latest Popular Songs. Chicago: Frederick J. Drake, (1903). 1st ed. Pict brn cl (rear bd sl discolored). *Petrilla.* $65/£42

HARRIS, CHARLES TOWNSEND. Memories of Manhattan in the Sixties and Seventies. NY: Derrydale, 1928. 1st Amer ed. NF. *Polyanthos.* $50/£32

HARRIS, FOSTER. The Look of the Old West. NY: Viking, 1955. 1st ed. Fine in NF dj. *Glenn.* $20/£13

HARRIS, FRANK. Bernard Shaw. London: Victor Gollancz, 1931. 1st ed. Black cl. Spine top worn, else NF in VG dj (spine browned; heavy chipping; 2-inch tear). *Chapel Hill.* $75/£48

HARRIS, FRANK. Elder Conklin and Other Stories. London, 1895. 1st ed. 241pp, rubric tp. (Spine discolored, chipped; corners rubbed.) *Edwards.* $54/£35

HARRIS, FRANK. My Reminiscences as a Cowboy. NY: Charles Boni Paper Books, 1930. 1st ed. Dec eps. Spine dknd, o/w NF in pict wrappers. *Harrington.* $30/£19

HARRIS, FRANK. Oscar Wilde, His Life and Confessions. NY, 1918. 2 vols. VG set (paper browned; eps removed). *Mcclintock.* $15/£10

HARRIS, FRANK. Unpath'd Waters. London: John Lane, 1913. 1st Eng ed, 1st issue binding. Blind-, gilt-blocked grn cl. Very Nice. *Cady.* $30/£19

HARRIS, GARRARD. Elements of Conservation. Johnson Pub, (c. 1924). VG. *Book Broker.* $25/£16

HARRIS, GEORGE WASHINGTON. Sut Lovingood Travels with Old Abe Lincoln. Chicago: Black Cat Press, 1937. One of 150. Fine. *Graf.* $50/£32

HARRIS, HYDE. Kyd for Hire. London: Gollancz, 1977. 1st British, hb ed. VG + in dj (lt wear). *Silver Door.* $35/£23

HARRIS, J. Talks on Manures. NY, 1893. 2nd ed. xxii,(9-)366pp. (Foxing, marginal sticking to 2pp w/sl loss.) *Sutton.* $36/£23

HARRIS, J.R. Egyptian Art. London: Spring Books, (1966). 48 color plts. (Inscrip.) Dj. *Archaeologia.* $35/£23

HARRIS, JAMES E. and EDWARD F. WENTE (eds). An X-Ray Atlas of the Royal Mummies. Chicago/London: Univ of Chicago Press, (1980). 13 tables, 5 microfiches in rear pocket. (Sig.) Dj. *Archaeologia.* $75/£48

HARRIS, JAMES. Hermes; or A Philosophical Inquiry Concerning Universal Grammar. London, 1806. 6th ed. Frontis; xx,442pp,(xxvi) index. (Last few leaves spotted.) 1/2 crushed morocco, marbled bds (extrems sl worn; upper joint tender). *Edwards.* $85/£55

HARRIS, JOEL CHANDLER. Balaam and His Master. Boston: Houghton, Mifflin, 1891. 1st Amer ed. Dec brn cl. Fine (sig fr blank). BAL 7125. *Agvent.* $285/£184

HARRIS, JOEL CHANDLER. Free Joe and Other Georgian Sketches. NY: Scribner's, 1887. 1st ed. One of 3200. Tan pict cl, gilt. Fine. BAL 7114. *Macdonnell.* $150/£97

HARRIS, JOEL CHANDLER. Gabriel Tolliver. NY: McClure, Phillips & Co., 1902. 1st ed. Dec red cl. Sm dampstain upper corner, else Fine in ptd dj (lacks most of spine). BAL 7149. *Chapel Hill.* $300/£194

HARRIS, JOEL CHANDLER. Nights with Uncle Remus. Boston: James R. Osgood, 1883. 1st ed. 416pp. Orig aqua blue cl. NF. BAL 7109. *Chapel Hill.* $750/£484

HARRIS, JOEL CHANDLER. Nights with Uncle Remus. C&W, 1913. Color frontis; 7 colored plts. Pict cl. *Bickersteth.* $39/£25

HARRIS, JOEL CHANDLER. Plantation Pageants. Boston, 1899. 1st Amer ed. Pict cvrs, gilt. Fine (sl sunned, sl rubbed). *Polyanthos.* $125/£81

HARRIS, JOEL CHANDLER. Sister Jane. Boston: HMCO, 1896. 1st ed. Grn cl. NF. *Dermont.* $75/£48

HARRIS, JOEL CHANDLER. Tales from Uncle Remus. Boston, (1935). 62pp, 12 full-pg color plts by Milo Winter. Inscrip, sl worn, sm stain, ex-lib blindstamp fep, else Good in dj (frayed). *King.* $25/£16

HARRIS, JOEL CHANDLER. Uncle Remus, His Songs and His Sayings. NY: Appleton, 1881. 1st ed, 3rd state w/rev of Uncle Remus 1st pg ads. 1st bk. 231pp,(8)pp ads. Pict blue cl. VG. BAL 7100. *Chapel Hill.* $275/£177

HARRIS, JOEL CHANDLER. Uncle Remus, His Songs and His Sayings. NY: D. Appleton & Co., 1881. 1st ed, 3rd state, w/review of Uncle Remus on 1st ad pg. Eps w/floral design, not butterfly design; variation not noted in BAL 7100. 231pp,(8)pp ads. Pict powder blue cl. VG (inscrip; spine sl dknd, nicks). *Chapel Hill.* $400/£258

HARRIS, JOEL CHANDLER. Uncle Remus, His Songs and Sayings. NY: D. Appleton, 1881. 1st ed, 2nd state, w/last line p9 reading 'presumptuous' and ad at p(233) starting 'New Books. A Treatise on the Practice of Medicine....' Frontis, 7 plts inserted. Grn cl (sl rubbed, sl waterstaining affecting outer margins, sl shaken). BAL 7100. *Cummins.* $350/£226

HARRIS, JOEL CHANDLER. Uncle Remus, His Songs and Sayings. NY: LEC, 1957. One of 1500. Signed by Seong Moy (artist). Rough blue cl, stamped. Fine in case. *Agvent.* $150/£97

HARRIS, JOEL CHANDLER. Uncle Remus, or Mr. Fox, Mr. Rabbit, and Mr. Terrapin. Grant Richards, 1902. 2nd imp. Frontis; 8 color plts by J.A. Shepherd. Pict cl, rebacked w/plain matching cl spine; new eps. (Text leaf sl spotted; upper margin strengthened.) *Bickersteth.* $39/£25

HARRIS, JOEL CHANDLER. Wally Wanderoon and His Story-Telling Machine. NY: McClure, Phillips, 1903. 1st ed, probable 1st state w/8pp of ads. 294pp,(8)pp ads. Pict tan cl. 10pp dampstained; rear hinge cracked internally, else VG. BAL 7152. *Chapel Hill.* $150/£97

HARRIS, JOHN and JILL LEVER. Illustrated Glossary of Architecture 850-1830. London: Faber, 1966. 1st ed. 224 plts. Orig cl; in dj (sl chipped). *Edwards.* $39/£25

HARRIS, JOHN BRICE. From Old Mobile to Fort Assumption. Nashville, TN: Parthenon Press, (1959). 1st ed. Red cl. Spine lettering dulled, else NF. *Chapel Hill.* $40/£26

HARRIS, LAURA. The Animated Noah's Ark. NY: Grosset & Dunlap, 1945. 4 moveables (1 tab worn) by Julian Wehr. Spiral bind. VG (lt soil, name) in dj (lt worn). *Davidson.* $225/£145

HARRIS, MARK. A Ticket for a Seamstitch. Knopf, 1957. 1st ed. VG in dj (chipped). *Stahr.* $60/£39

HARRIS, ROBERT. Fatherland. London: Hutchinson, 1992. 1st UK ed. Fine in dj. *Lewton.* $47/£30

HARRIS, SARAH HOLLISTER. An Unwritten Chapter of Salt Lake, 1851-1901. NY: Ptd privately, 1901. Teg. Grn cl, gilt stamping. VG (lt rubbing, etching). Howes H 231. *Bohling.* $500/£323

HARRIS, STANLEY. Playing the Game. Stokes, 1925. 1st ed. Good + . *Plapinger.* $75/£48

HARRIS, T. Goya: Engravings and Lithographs. Wofsy, 1983. Rpt. 2 vols. Sound in dj. *Ars Artis.* $233/£150

HARRIS, THOMAS. Red Dragon. NY: Putnam, (1981). 1st ed. NF in dj. *Antic Hay.* $45/£29

HARRIS, THOMAS. Red Dragon. NY: Putnam's, 1981. 1st ed. Fine in dj (price-clipped). *Else Fine.* $50/£32

HARRIS, THOMAS. Red Dragon. Bodley, 1982. 1st UK ed. Fine in Fine dj. *Martin.* $31/£20

HARRIS, THOMAS. Red Dragon. Bodley Head, 1982. 1st UK ed. Fine in dj. *Lewton.* $39/£25

HARRIS, THOMAS. Red Dragon. London: Bodley Head, 1982. 1st UK ed. NF in dj. *Williams.* $47/£30

HARRIS, THOMAS. The Silence of the Lambs. NY: St. Martin's, 1988. 1st ed. Fine in dj. *Else Fine.* $50/£32

HARRIS, THOMAS. The Silence of the Lambs. NY: St. Martins, 1988. 1st ed. Fine in Fine dj. *Beasley.* $60/£39

HARRIS, THOMAS. The Silence of the Lambs. Heinemann, 1988. 1st UK ed, 1st issue. Fine in dj. *Lewton.* $39/£25

HARRIS, THOMAS. The Silence of the Lambs. London: Heinemann, 1989. 1st ed. NF in VG dj (price-clipped). *Ming.* $70/£45

HARRIS, W.R. The Catholic Church in Utah.... Salt Lake City: Intermountain Catholic Press, (1909). 1st ed. Dbl-pg map. Grn gilt cl. Good. *Karmiole.* $75/£48

HARRIS, W.R. The Catholic Church in Utah.... Salt Lake City: Intermountain Catholic Press, (1909). 1st ed. Gilt-stamped grn cl, beveled edges (rubbed; spine ends frayed). Good. *Houle.* $85/£55

HARRIS, W.S. Life in a Thousand Worlds. Minter, 1905. 1st ed. VG in homemade dj. *Madle.* $75/£48

HARRIS, WALTER B. East Again. The Narrative of a Journey in the Near, Middle and Far East. NY: Dutton, 1934. 2nd imp. 31 plts. Spine sl faded, o/w VG. *Worldwide.* $20/£13

HARRIS, WALTER B. Tafilet. The Narrative of a Journey of Exploration in the Atlas Mountains and the Oases of the North-West Sahara. Edinburgh/London: Blackwood, 1895. 1st ed. xiv,379,32pp; 2 maps (1 fldg). Sl rubbed, soiled; fr flyleaf torn; map torn at folds, o/w VG ex-lib. *Worldwide.* $65/£42

HARRIS, WALTER KILROY. Outback in Australia. Letchworth, 1913. Frontis port (partly detached), map. (Mainly marginal foxing; corner rubbed, sl loss; spine sl rubbed.) *Edwards.* $70/£45

Harrison's Description of England in Shakspere's Youth. London: New Shakespeare Soc, 1878. Full leather (dull). *Petersfield.* $37/£24

HARRISON, CHIP. (Pseud of Lawrence Block). Make Out With Murder. Greenwich: Fawcett, 1974. 1st ed. Fine in wrappers. *Mordida.* $45/£29

HARRISON, CONSTANCE CARY. Woman's Handiwork in Modern Homes. (NY): Scribner's, 1881. xii,242pp; 5 color litho plts, 4 uncolored plts. Pict cl (rebound in plain cl), orig upper cvr, spine (rubbed). *Bickersteth.* $171/£110

HARRISON, CONSTANCE CARY. Woman's Handiwork in Modern Homes. (NY): Scribner's, 1882. 1st ed. xii,242pp. 5 color ptd plts. Dec brn cl (sl frayed). *Karmiole.* $85/£55

HARRISON, CUTHBERT WOODVILLE. An Illustrated Guide to the Federated Malay States. London, 1911. 2nd imp. Map in pocket. Yellow cl. VG-. *Gretton.* $47/£30

HARRISON, DAVID L. Cinderella. Kansas City: Hallmark, n.d. (1970). 17x23 cm. 4 VG dbl-pg pop-ups, pull tabs. Arlene Noel (illus). Blue illus bds (scuffed). *Book Finders.* $45/£29

HARRISON, F. The Painted Glass of York. London: S.P.C.K., 1927. 1st ed. 56 plts (2 color). Sm edgetears. Dj. *Hollett.* $47/£30

HARRISON, FLORENCE. Elfin Song. London: Blackie, 1912. 1st ed. 8vo. 12 full-pg mtd color plts; teg (lt foxing). White cl (sl dkng), gold dec, lettering. *Reisler.* $290/£187

HARRISON, FREDERIC. Annals of an Old Manor-House, Sutton Place, Guildford. London: Macmillan, 1893. 9 color plts, 37 b/w plts; newspaper cutting tipped to tp. Uncut except for top edge. Few pp sl foxed, o/w Good. *Petersfield.* $194/£125

HARRISON, FREDERICK. Medieval Man and His Notions. John Murray, 1947. Good (cl faded) in dj (rubbed). *Peter Taylor.* $20/£13

HARRISON, G.B. and R.A. JONES. De Maisse. London: Nonesuch, 1931. Uncut. VG in dj. *Hollett.* $70/£45

HARRISON, GODFREY. Bristol Cream. Batsford, 1955. 1st ed. Color frontis. Dj (sl chipped). *Edwards.* $23/£15

HARRISON, HARRY. The Daleth Effect. NY: Putnam's, (1970). 1st ed. Fine in NF dj. *Antic Hay.* $50/£32

HARRISON, HARRY. Make Room! Make Room! Doubleday, 1966. 1st ed. Signed. Fine in Fine dj. *Aronovitz*. $225/£145

HARRISON, HARRY. The Men from P.I.G. and R.O.B.O.T. London: Faber & Faber, 1974. 1st Eng ed. Black cl. Fine in dj. *Dalian*. $39/£25

HARRISON, HARRY. Plague from Space. Doubleday, 1965. 1st ed. Signed. Fine in NF dj (sl rubbing). *Aronovitz*. $35/£23

HARRISON, J. The Life of the Archpriest Avvakum by Himself. Hope Mirrlees (trans). Hogarth Press, 1924. 1st ed. VG. *Words Etc.* $56/£36

HARRISON, J.E. and D.S. MacCOLL. Greek Vase Paintings. London, 1894. Frontis, 32pp, 43 b/w plts (2 dbl-pg). (Lt spotting, feps sl browned; bkpl; hinges cracked; worn, chipped.) *Edwards*. $116/£75

HARRISON, J.E. and D.S. MacCOLL. Greek Vase Paintings. London: T. Fisher Unwin, 1894. 32pp, 43 plts. (Bkpl.) *Archaeologia*. $150/£97

HARRISON, JAMES M. The Birds of Kent. London, 1953. 1st ed. 2 vols. Color frontis, 79 plts, map. *Edwards*. $78/£50

HARRISON, JANE ELLEN. Reminiscences of a Student's Life. Hogarth, 1925. 1st ed. VG. *Whiteson*. $25/£16

HARRISON, JANE ELLEN. Reminiscences of a Student's Life. London: Hogarth Press, 1925. 1st ed. One of 1000 ptd. 6 half-tone plts. Top edge red, rest uncut. Red/black marbled buckram. Label chipped, o/w Nice. *Temple*. $31/£20

HARRISON, JANE ELLEN. Reminiscences of a Student's Life.... Hogarth, 1926. 3rd imp, 750 ptd. 6 plts. Red/black mottled cl, paper label. Nice. *Waterfield*. $39/£25

HARRISON, JIM. Farmer. NY: Viking, 1976. 1st ed. VF in dj. *Else Fine*. $95/£61

HARRISON, JIM. Farmer. NY: Viking, 1976. 1st ed. Inscribed. Fine in Fine dj (nick). *Beasley*. $175/£113

HARRISON, JIM. Legends of the Fall. London: Collins, 1980. 1st ed. Fine in dj (price-clipped). *Rees*. $16/£10

HARRISON, JIM. Locations. NY: Norton, 1968. 1st ed. Fine in dj. *Else Fine*. $150/£97

HARRISON, JIM. Wolf. NY: S&S, 1971. 1st ed. Inscribed. Fine in Fine dj (sl soiled). *Beasley*. $200/£129

HARRISON, JIM. The Woman Lit by Fireflies. Boston: Houghton-Mifflin, 1990. 1st ed. VF in dj. *Else Fine*. $35/£23

HARRISON, JIM. The Woman Lit by Fireflies. Boston: Houghton Mifflin, 1990. 1st ed. Signed. Fine in Fine dj. *Revere*. $60/£39

HARRISON, JIM. The Woman Lit by Fireflies. London: Weidenfield & Nicholson, 1991. 1st British ed. Fine in Fine dj. *Revere*. $25/£16

HARRISON, JOHN and PETER LASLETT. The Library of John Locke. Oxford Bib Soc, 1965. Port. Linen-backed bds. Dj. *Petersfield*. $56/£36

HARRISON, JUANITA. My Great Wide Beautiful World. NY: Macmillan, 1936. VG. *Petrilla*. $40/£26

HARRISON, JUANITA. My Great Wide Beautiful World. NY, 1936. 1st ed, 6th ptg. Orig cl. VG. *Mcgowan*. $27/£17

HARRISON, M. The Brain. Cassell, 1953. 1st ed. Fine in NF dj (sl rubbed). *Aronovitz*. $35/£23

HARRISON, M. Brian Clarke. London: Quartet Books, 1981. Sound in dj. *Ars Artis*. $47/£30

HARRISON, MICHAEL. The Exploits of Chevalier Dupin. Arkham House, 1968. 1st ed. VF in dj. *Madle*. $65/£42

HARRISON, MICHAEL. The Exploits of the Chevalier Dupin. Sauk City: Mycroft & Moran, 1968. 1st ed, ltd to 1917. NF in dj (sl browning; price-clipped). *Antic Hay*. $50/£32

HARRISON, MICHAEL. In the Footsteps of Sherlock Holmes. NY: Drake, 1972. 1st rev US ed. Fine in VG + dj. *Janus*. $35/£23

HARRISON, MICHAEL. The London of Sherlock Holmes. NY: Drake, 1972. 1st US ed. Fine in NF dj (price-clipped, lt creased, worn). *Janus*. $35/£23

HARRISON, MICHAEL. The World of Sherlock Holmes. London: Muller, 1973. 1st ed. Fine in NF dj (spine sun-faded). *Janus*. $30/£19

HARRISON, MICHAEL. The World of Sherlock Holmes. NY: Dutton, 1975. 1st US ed. Fine in Fine dj. *Janus*. $45/£29

HARRISON, REGINALD. Clinical Lectures on Stricture of the Urethra and Other Disorders of the Urinary Organs. London, 1878. 1st ed. 193pp. Good. *Fye*. $150/£97

HARRISON, T. The Bookbinding Craft and Industry. London: Sir Isaac Pitman, n.d. (ca 1935). 2nd ed. Grn cl stamped in black. Good. *Karmiole*. $35/£23

HARRISON, TONY. A Kumquat for John Keats. Bloodaxe, 1981. 1st UK ed. Fine in wraps. *Sclanders*. $31/£20

HARRISON, TONY. The Mysteries. London: Faber, 1985. 1st ed. Fine in dj. *Rees*. $31/£20

HARRISON, WILMOT. Memorable London Houses. London, 1889. Fldg frontis map, viii,168pp (feps foxed; edges browned). Gilt-ruled cl (sl soiled; spine chipped, browned; upper joint split; rubbed w/loss). *Edwards*. $78/£50

HARRISS, JOSEPH. The Tallest Tower, Eiffel and the Belle Epoque. Boston: Houghton Mifflin, 1975. 1st ed. Fine in dj (lt chipped). *Bookpress*. $35/£23

HARROCKS, JAMES. My Dear Parents. San Diego, (1982). 1st Amer ed. Fine in Fine dj. *Mcgowan*. $35/£23

HARROP, DOROTHY A. A History of the Gregynog Press. Private Libraries Assoc, 1980. 1st ed. VG. *Cox*. $54/£35

HARSHA, D.A. The Life of Charles Sumner...and His Great Speech on Kansas. NY: Dayton & Burdick, 1856. 1st ed. 329pp; tinted port, view. Emb purple cl (spine sunned). VG. *Petrilla*. $45/£29

HARSHBERGER, JOHN W. Vegetation of the New Jersey Pine-Barrens. Phila, 1916. 1st ed. Fldg fig, lg fldg map in back. Bright. *Heinoldt*. $65/£42

HART, BERTHA SHEPPARD. Introduction to Georgia Writers. Macon: J.W. Burke, (1929). 1st ed. Grn cl. NF. *Chapel Hill*. $50/£32

HART, HENRY C. The Dark Missouri. Madison: Univ of WI, 1957. 1st ed. Tan cl. Fine in NF pict dj. *Glenn*. $30/£19

HART, HENRY. A Relevant Memoir. The Story of the Equinox Cooperative Press. NY: Three Mountains Press, 1977. 1st ed. Fine in dj. *Sadlon*. $25/£16

HART, HERBERT M. Old Forts of the Northwest. Seattle: Superior Pub Co, (1963). VG in dj. *Schoyer*. $25/£16

HART, HERBERT M. Old Forts of the Southwest. Seattle: Superior Pub Co, (1964). Stated 1st ed. Fine in dj. *Schoyer*. $25/£16

HART, HERBERT M. Pioneer Forts of the West. Seattle, (1967). 1st ed. Lt dj wear, o/w VG +. Pratt. $22/£14

HART, HORACE. Bibliotheca Typographica. Rochester, 1933. Fine in dj. Veatchs. $50/£32

HART, J. COLEMAN. Designs for Parish Churches, in the Three Styles of English Architecture. NY: Dana & Co., 1857. 1st ed. 111pp; 42 plts. Pub's cl, teg. (Ink inscrip; fr hinge internally cracked; text foxed.) Bookpress. $425/£274

HART, JAMES D. The Private Press Ventures of Samuel Lloyd Osbourne and R.L.S. SF: Book Club of CA, 1966. 1st ed. One of 500. Frontis, 11 full-pg facs, 13 add'l facs in rear pocket. Dec beige cl. Fine. Harrington. $65/£42

HART, JEROME. Argonaut Letters. SF: Payot, Upham, 1901. 1st ed. 60 plts. Sl rubbed; spine sl frayed, o/w VG. Worldwide. $30/£19

HART, JOSEPH C. The Romance of Yachting. Voyage the First. NY: Harper, 1848. 1st ed. 332,(26 ads)pp. (Text lt foxed.) Orig cl, gilt spine title, dec cvr. Very Attractive. Lefkowicz. $400/£258

HART, SCOTT. The Moon is Waning. NY: Derrydale Press, (1939). 1st ed, #926/950. Orig cl. NF. Mcgowan. $125/£81

HART-DAVIS, H.V. Chats on Angling. London, 1906. (Feps lt browned, upper hinge sl tender, cl lt soiled.) Edwards. $132/£85

HARTE, BRET. Ah Sin: A Dramatic Work. Frederick Anderson (ed). SF: Book Club of CA, 1961. Ltd to 450. VG. Shasky. $95/£61

HARTE, BRET. Colonel Starbottle's Client and Some Other People. Boston/NY: Houghton, Mifflin, 1892. 1st ed. Grn-coated eps. Brn cl (lt wear; sl squint). BAL 7362. Glenn. $95/£61

HARTE, BRET. East and West Poems. Boston: Osgood, 1871. 1st ed. Brn cl, gilt-stamped. 1st gathering ptd, trimmed sl out of register, o/w Very Nice (early name). BAL 7256. Reese. $40/£26

HARTE, BRET. East and West Poems. James R. Osgood, 1871. 1st ed. Fine (name, address). BAL 7256. Authors Of The West. $50/£32

HARTE, BRET. Jeff Briggs's Love Story and Other Sketches. London: C&W, 1880. 1st ed. 128,32pp. (Sl fingering; sl rubbed). Hollett. $23/£15

HARTE, BRET. The Letters of Bret Harte. Houghton Mifflin, 1926. 1st ed. Fine. Authors Of The West. $30/£19

HARTE, BRET. The Luck of Roaring Camp and Other Sketches. Boston: Fields, Osgood, 1870. 1st ed, preceding addition of 'Brown of Calaveras.' 238pp. Orig grn cl. Lt foxing; name; cvrs lt silverfished, else VG in custom cl folder & slipcase w/morocco label. BAL 7246. Chapel Hill. $600/£387

HARTE, BRET. The Luck of Roaring Camp and Other Sketches. Boston: Fields, Osgood, 1870. 2nd Amer ed, contains story 'Brown of Calaveras'. Emb grn cl. NF (bkpl; pencil presentation; few sl spots). BAL 7247. Antic Hay. $285/£184

HARTE, BRET. The Luck of the Roaring Camp and Other Sketches. Boston: Osgood, 1872. Grn cl, gilt (worn). BAL 7444. Glenn. $100/£65

HARTE, BRET. The Queen of the Pirate Isle. London: C&W, (1886). 1st ed. 8vo, 58 numbered pp, 28 color engrs by Kate Greenaway. Edges red. Illus cl. Reisler. $275/£177

HARTE, BRET. The Queen of the Pirate Isle. London: C&W, n.d. (1886). 1st ed. 58pp. Kate Greenaway (illus). Beige cl, edges stained gold. Overall VG (soiling). BAL 7337. Schoyer. $250/£161

HARTE, BRET. San Francisco in 1866. SF: Book Club of CA, 1951. 1st ed. Ltd to 400. Fldg plt; prospectus laid in. VG. BAL 7415. Shasky. $65/£42

HARTE, BRET. Tales of the Gold Rush. NY: LEC, 1944. One of 1200. Signed by Fletcher Martin (artist). Fine in glassine (worn). VG gold clamshell box. Agvent. $150/£97

HARTE, BRET. A Waif of the Plains. Boston: Houghton, Mifflin, 1890. 1st Amer ed. Blue cl. Fine. BAL 7350. Agvent. $75/£48

HARTE, BRET. A Waif of the Plains. London: C&W, 1890. 1st Eng ed. Very Nice (back panel sl spotted). Limestone. $75/£48

HARTE, BRET. A Ward of the Golden Gate. Boston: Houghton, Mifflin, 1890. 1st Amer ed. Grn cl. NF. BAL 7355. Agvent. $50/£32

HARTE, BRET. The Wild West. (Paris): Harrison of Paris, (1930). 1st thus. One of 840 numbered. VG (spine dknd) in case (soiled). BAL 7559. Agvent. $125/£81

HARTHAN, JOHN. The Book of Hours. NY, 1982. 89 plts (72 color). VG. Argosy. $85/£55

HARTING, JAMES EDMUND. The Birds of Middlesex. London, 1866. 1st ed. Tinted frontis, xvi,284pp (margins lt browned, ex-libris). Edwards. $54/£35

HARTING, JAMES EDMUND. British Animals Extinct within Historic Times.... London, 1880. 1st ed. Lg paper copy. x,258pp, uncut. (Rebacked, preserving spine; soiled, label chipped.) Henly. $93/£60

HARTING, JAMES EDMUND. Essays on Sport and Natural History. London, 1883. 1st ed. Frontis port, x,485pp. (Spine sl faded.) Edwards. $54/£35

HARTING, JAMES EDMUND. Hints on Shore Shooting. London: Van Voorst, 1871. 1st ed. Frontis, 88pp + 8pp ads; errta slip. Maroon cl, gilt title. VG +. Bowman. $75/£48

HARTLAND, MICHAEL. Down Among the Dead Men. London: Hodder & Stoughton, 1983. 1st ed. VF in dj. Mordida. $65/£42

HARTLEY, DOROTHY. Food in England. Macdonald, 1954. (Backstrip faded.) Dj (torn, rubbed). Petersfield. $31/£20

HARTLEY, FLORENCE. The Ladies' Book of Etiquette, and Manual of Politeness. Boston: Lee & Shepard, 1882. 340pp. Dec cl. VG. Petrilla. $45/£29

HARTLEY, L.P. The Hireling. H-H, 1957. 1st ed. Fine in NF dj. Fine Books. $18/£12

HARTLEY, L.P. Night Fears. London: Putnam's, 1924. 1st ed, 1st bk. Fine (spine sl browned; lt foxed). Williams. $116/£75

HARTLEY, L.P. The Traveling Grave and Other Stories. Sauk City: Arkham House, 1948. 1st ed, one of 2047. Fine in pict dj (sl age-darkening). Else Fine. $100/£65

HARTLEY, L.P. The Traveling Grave. Arkham House, 1948. 1st ed. Fine in dj. Madle. $135/£87

HARTLEY, MARIE and JOAN INGILBY. Life and Tradition in the Yorkshire Dales. London: J.M. Dent, 1968. 1st ed. 261 photos, map. Gilt cl. VG in dj. Hollett. $47/£30

HARTLEY, MARIE and JOAN INGILBY. The Old Hand-Knitters of the Dales. London: Dalesman, 1951. 1st ed. Gilt cl. VG in dj. Hollett. $54/£35

HARTLEY, MARSDEN. Adventures in the Arts: Informal Chapters on Painters, Vaudeville and Poets. NY: Boni & Liveright, (c 1921). 1st ed. 1st bk. Ink name, date, backstrip lt mkd, o/w VG. *Heller.* $125/£81

HARTLEY, WILLIAM and ELLEN. Osceola, the Unconquered Indian. NY: Hawthorn Books, (1973). 2nd ptg. Brn cl. Fine in dj (spine faded). *Chapel Hill.* $35/£23

HARTMAN, C.G. Possums. Austin: Univ of TX, 1952. 1st ed. Gilt dec cl. NF in VG dj. *Mikesh.* $40/£26

HARTMAN, FRANK E. Sunlight and Shadow. Chicago: Black Cat Press, 1934. Pattern paper over bds, blue leather spine. VG. *Graf.* $25/£16

HARTMANN, GEORGE. Wooed by a Sphinz of Aztlan. Prescott: Hartmann, 1907. Mtd cvr illus. VG. *Schoyer.* $65/£42

HARTMANN, SADAKICHI. Japanese Art. Boston: Page, 1904. Teg. Dk grn dec cl (sig; rubbed). *Schoyer.* $45/£29

HARTNELL, NORMAN. Silver and Gold. London: Evans Bros, 1955. 1st ed. 46 plts, full-pg dwgs. VG. *Cox.* $28/£18

HARTSHORNE, ALBERT. Old English Drinking Glasses. London: Edward Arnold, 1897. xxiii, 490pp; 67 plts (2 color). Teg. 1/2 dec japon bds (lt rubbed). VG. *Hollett.* $271/£175

HARTSHORNE, C.H. The Book Rarities in the University of Cambridge. Longman et al, 1829. xiv,559pp, frontis, title vignette. Recently rebound in 1/2 morocco. Text clean, unused. *Moss.* $326/£210

HARTT, FREDERICK. Drawings of Michelangelo. London: Thames & Hudson, 1971. 16 mtd color illus. Sound in dj. *Ars Artis.* $132/£85

HARTT, FREDERICK. Florentine Art under Fire. Princeton: Princeton Univ, 1949. 1st ed. 3 fldg maps. Blue bds (extrems, corners sl bumped). Dj (sl chipped, soiled). *Karmiole.* $35/£23

HARTT, FREDERICK. Michelangelo, the Complete Sculpture. NY: Abrams, (1968). 1st ed. Frontis, 17 tipped-in color plts. (Ink name; spine lt sunned; notes, underlining in pencil, ink.) *Bookpress.* $45/£29

HARVESTER, SIMON. Epitaph for Lemmings. London: Macmillan, 1944. 1st ed. VG in VG dj. *Ming.* $39/£25

Harvey Cushing Collection of Books and Manuscripts. NY, 1943. 1st ed. (Ex-lib w/ink notation fr cvr; lib stamps.) *Fye.* $100/£65

HARVEY, A.G. Douglas of the Fir.... Cambridge, MA, 1947. 4 maps; 2 ports; 4 plts. (Sl damage spine.) *Wheldon & Wesley.* $54/£35

HARVEY, ALFRED. The Castles and Walled Towns of England. London: Methuen, 1925. 2nd ed. Spine sl faded, corner damped. *Hollett.* $39/£25

HARVEY, DANIEL G. The Argyle Settlement in History and Story. (Rockford, IL, 1924.) Port; 3 plts. Good (cl spotting). *Bohling.* $75/£48

HARVEY, FRED. American Indians. Kansas City: Fred Harvey, 1928. 4th ed. VG- (extrems sl worn) in stiff wraps. *Parker.* $75/£48

HARVEY, FRED. Great Southwest Along the Santa Fe. Kansas City: Fred Harvey, 1927. 9th ed. VG- in stiff wraps (soil, wear). *Parker.* $85/£55

HARVEY, HENRY. History of the Shawnee Indians, from the Year 1681 to 1854, Inclusive. Cincinnati: Ephraim Morgan, 1855. 1st ed, 1st issue. x,11-316pp (lacks frontis port). 1/4 morocco, marbled bds. Rubbed, else Fine. Howes H 275. *Cahan.* $200/£129

HARVEY, J.R. Victorian Novelists and Their Illustrators. NY: NY Univ Press, 1971. 1st Amer ed. 76 illus. Fine in dj. *Bookpress.* $95/£61

HARVEY, JOHN. English Mediaeval Architects. London: Batsford, 1954. 1st ed. *Edwards.* $47/£30

HARVEY, JOHN. English Medieval Architects. Gloucester: Sutton, 1987. Rev ed. Mint in dj. *Europa.* $50/£32

HARVEY, JOHN. Gothic England. London: Batsford, (1947). 1st ed. Frontis; 176 illus on plts (6 color). VG in dj (worn). *Bookpress.* $65/£42

HARVEY, JOHN. Lonely Hearts. London: Viking, 1989. 1st ed. Fine in dj (sl wear corners). *Mordida.* $65/£42

HARVEY, L.A. and D. ST. LEGER-GORDON. Dartmoor. London, 1953. 1st ed. Dj. *Edwards.* $93/£60

HARVEY, ROWLAND HILL. Samuel Gompers. Stanford Univ Press, 1935. 1st ed. Inscribed. Frontis port. VG in dj (chipped, lt soiled). *Connolly.* $65/£42

HARVEY, WILLIAM. The Anatomical Exercises of Dr. William Harvey. London: Nonesuch, 1928. #405/1450. Fldg plt. Niger morocco. Good. *Goodrich.* $175/£113

HARVEY, WILLIAM. Movement of the Heart and Blood in Animals. Kenneth J. Franklin (trans). Oxford: Blackwell, 1957. Colored frontis. Good. *Goodrich.* $45/£29

HARVEY, WILLIAM. The Works. London: Sydenham Soc, 1847. 1st ed in English. xcvi,624pp (2 sections loose, 1 w/creased corners; paper peeling upper inner joint). *Bickersteth.* $62/£40

HARWELL, RICHARD B. Confederate Music. Chapel Hill, (1950). 1st ed. Dj w/faded spine, lt wear, o/w Fine. *Pratt.* $65/£42

HARWELL, RICHARD B. Confederate Music. Chapel Hill: Univ of NC Press, (1950). 1st ed. Frontis. Grey cl. NF in VG dj (price-clipped). *Chapel Hill.* $100/£65

HARWELL, RICHARD B. Cornerstones of Confederate Collecting. Charlottesville: Univ of VA Press, 1953. 2nd ed. Tan cl. VG. *Chapel Hill.* $60/£39

HARWELL, RICHARD B. (ed). The Confederate Reader. NY, 1957. 1st ed. VG. *Pratt.* $27/£17

HARWELL, RICHARD B. (ed). The Confederate Reader. NY: Longmans, Green, 1957. 1st ed. Grey cl. NF in VG dj. *Chapel Hill.* $60/£39

HARWELL, RICHARD B. (ed). The Union Reader. NY: Longmans, Green, 1958. 1st ed. Blue cl. NF in dj (price-clipped, sl chipped). *Chapel Hill.* $35/£23

HASEK, JAROSLAV. The Good Soldier Schweik. Paul Selver (trans). London: Heinemann, (1930). 1st ed in English. VG (cl rubbed, stained, sl warped). *Blue Mountain.* $65/£42

HASELTON, SCOTT. Epiphyllum Handbook. Pasadena, CA: Abbey Garden, 1946. 11 full-pg color plts. Fine. *Quest.* $35/£23

HASELTON, SCOTT. Epiphyllum Handbook. Pasadena, 1946. 1st ed. 11 color plts. (Sl insect holes gutter feps.) *Sutton.* $47/£30

Hasheesh Eater. (By Fitz Hugh Ludlow.) NY: Harper, 1857. 1st ed, 1st bk. Orig slate grn cl, gilt. Spotting, esp rear cvr, else fresh, tight. *Macdonnell.* $300/£194

HASKELL, FRANKLIN ARETAS. The Battle of Gettysburg. (Madison: Democrat Print Co, 1910.) 2nd ed. VG. *Mcgowan.* $85/£55

HASKELL, JOHN. The Haskell Memoirs. Gilbert E. Govan & James M. Livingood (eds). NY, (1964). 1st ed. VG+ in VG+ dj. *Pratt.* $37/£24

HASKETT SMITH, W.P. Climbing in the British Isles 1-England. London: Longmans, Green, 1894. 1st ed. xii,162,(ii,ads)pp (piece torn from top of 1/2 title), 5 plans. Faded, stained. *Hollett.* $70/£45

HASKIN, LESLIE L. Wild Flowers of the Pacific Coast. Portland, OR: Binfords & Mort, 1934. 1st ed. 182 full-pg illus. VG in dj (chipped). *Connolly.* $32/£21

HASKINS, JAMES. The War and The Protest: Vietnam. GC: Doubleday, (1971). 1st ed. VG in dj (price-clipped; edgewear). *Aka.* $35/£23

HASKINS, SAM. Cowboy Kate and Other Stories. NY: Crown Pub, 1965. 1st ed. Eps sl foxed, else Fine in illus dj. *Cahan.* $75/£48

HASLEM, JOHN. The Old Derby China Factory. London: George Bell & Sons, 1876. 1st ed. Frontis; xvi,255pp; 12 color plts. Contemp 1/2 morocco (wear along spine, edges). (Text sl browned, brittle, thumbed; feps detached; ink inscrip.) *Bookpress.* $250/£161

HASLUCK, PAUL N. Glass Working by Heat and by Abrasion. London: Cassell, 1899. 1st ed. Spine sunned, eps yellowed, corners bumped; else VG. *Bookpress.* $110/£71

HASLUCK, PAUL N. Harness Making with Numerous Engravings and Diagrams. NY: Funk & Wagnalls w/their label pasted over orig pub, (1904?). Stain fr cvr, else VG. *Perier.* $45/£29

HASLUCK, PAUL N. (ed). Wood Carving: ...Instructions, Examples and Designs. London: Cassell, 1910. Internally VG+ (amateurish rebind, no lettering). *Willow House.* $37/£24

HASLUND, HENING. Men and Gods in Mongolia (Zayagan). Elizabeth Sprigge & Claude Napier (trans). NY: Dutton, (1935). 1st Amer ed. Map. Brn cl, gilt (spine discolored). *Schoyer.* $40/£26

HASSALL, A.G. and W.O. Treasures from the Bodleian Library. NY: Columbia Univ Press, 1976. 37 color plts. VG in bd slipcase. *Argosy.* $150/£97

HASSALL, CHRISTOPHER. Edward Marsh: Patron of the Arts. London: Longmans, 1959. 1st ed. Frontis, 7 dbl-sided plts. Dk blue cl, gilt. Very Nice in laminate dj (sl frayed). *Temple.* $34/£22

HASSANEIN BEY, A.M. The Lost Oases. London: Butterworth, 1925. 1st ed. Map. VG (sl rubbed, scuffed; spine sl torn; bumped; foxed, spotted). *Worldwide.* $50/£32

HASSE, CHARLES EWALD. An Anatomical Description of the Diseases of the Organs of Circulation and Respiration. W.E. Swaine (trans). London: Sydenham Soc, 1846. xiv,400pp (feps lt foxed). Blind emb cl (joints splitting, spine chipped). *Edwards.* $23/£15

HASSLEQUIST, FREDERICK and CHARLES LINNAEUS. Voyages and Travels in the Levant. London, 1766. Fldg map.(Sl foxed throughout; few wormholes to margins.) Full contemp calf (rebacked). *Petersfield.* $496/£320

HASSLER, JON. Four Miles to Pinecone. NY: Warne, 1977. 1st ed. 1st bk. Fine (bkpl) in dj (1/4-inch chip on rear). *Else Fine.* $125/£81

HASSLER, WARREN W. General George B. McClellan, Shield of the Union. Baton Rouge, (1957). Signed. Dj faded, sl chipped, o/w Fine. *Pratt.* $50/£32

HASTINGS, JOHN. Lectures on Yellow Fever. Phila: Lindsay & Blakiston, 1848. 69pp + 6pp pub's cat. Blind-stamped brn/gilt cl. New matched eps. Scattered foxing, o/w VG. *Savona.* $70/£45

HASTINGS, JOHN. Lectures on Yellow Fever. Phila: Lindsay & Blakiston, 1848. 1st ed. (4),(17)-69,(6 ads)pp. Orig emb cl. Fine. *Glaser.* $250/£161

HASTINGS, LANSFORD W. The Emigrants' Guide to Oregon and California. Princeton: Princeton Univ, 1932. Facs ed w/add'l notes. Red cl. NF. *Glenn.* $45/£29

HASTINGS, MAURICE. Parliament House. London: Architectural Press, (1950). 1st ed. VG. *Bookpress.* $45/£29

HASTINGS, MICHAEL. The Unknown Soldier. NY: Macmillan, (1986). 1st ed. Fine in Fine dj. *Aka.* $30/£19

HATCHER, EDMUND N. The Last Four Weeks of the War. Columbus: 1892. 416pp; 8 plts photo-views. Dec cl. VG. *Petrilla.* $45/£29

HATFIELD, R.G. The American House-Carpenter: A Treatise on the Art of Building, and the Strength of Materials. NY: Wiley & Halstead, 1857. 7th ed. Signed presentation. x,398,36pp. Pub's blindstamped cl. Bkpl; text lt browned; sl rubbed, sunned, else VG. *Bookpress.* $275/£177

HATHAWAY, ERNEST. The Story of the Old Fort at Toronto. Macmillan of Canada, 1934. Rpt. 3 plts. Fine in stiff wraps. *Oregon.* $25/£16

HATTERAS, OWEN. (Pseud of H.L. Mencken and George Nathan.) Pistols for Two. NY: Knopf, 1917. 1st ed. Heavy rose paper wraps ptd in black. Superb (spine sl faded). *Cady.* $125/£81

HATTON, RICHARD G. The Craftsman's Plant Book. London, 1909. 1/2 calf, gilt. VG. *Shifrin.* $350/£226

HATTON, RICHARD G. The Craftsman's Plant Book. London, 1909. 1st ed. Color frontis. Teg. Generally VG (sl foxing; spine sl faded, fr hinge pulled, lt wear). *Willow House.* $186/£120

HATTON, THOMAS and ARTHUR H. CLEAVER. A Bibliography of the Periodical Works of Charles Dickens. London: Chapman & Hall, 1933. Lg paper ed ltd to 250 numbered, signed by both. This copy also inscribed by Hatton. 31 plts. Grn gilt cl; teg. Text foxing, o/w very bright. *Karmiole.* $250/£161

HAULTAIN, T. ARNOLD. The War in the Soudan.... Toronto, 1885. 137pp, fldg map (torn; sigs loose). Cl (worn, sl erosion). *King.* $100/£65

HAUSER, ARNOLD. Mannerism. London, 1965. 1st ed. 2 vols. 322 plts. Djs (chipped). *Edwards.* $78/£50

HAVEN, SAMUEL F. Archaeology of the United States. (Washington. Accepted for publication January, 1855. i.e. 1856.) Issued as Vol VIII in 'Smithsonian Contributions to Knowledge' series. (2),168pp, errata slip. Mod ptd bds. Tanned, else VG. Howes H 309. *Reese.* $350/£226

HAVERFIELD, F.J. and WILLIAM GREENWELL. A Catalogue of the Sculptured and Inscribed Stones in the Cathedral Library.... Durham, 1899. iv + 156pp, 13 plts. (Eps lt spotted.) *Edwards.* $54/£35

HAVIGHURST, WALTER. The Long Ships Passing. NY: MacMillan, 1942. 1st ptg. Fine in dj. *Artis.* $17/£11

HAVIGHURST, WALTER. Vein of Iron; The Pickands Mather Story. OH/NY, (1958). 1st ed. Map. Good in dj (chipped). *Artis.* $18/£12

HAVILAND, MAUD D. Summer on the Yenesei. London: Edward Arnold, 1915. Grn cl stamped in black/gilt (spine cocked, bumped, spots; foxed). *Schoyer.* $85/£55

HAWEIS, MRS. H.R. The Art of Beauty. NY: Harper, 1878. 1st Amer ed. Frontis; xiv,298,6pp. Pub's cl. Sl wear spine tips, extrems; inscrips, else very Bright. *Bookpress.* $300/£194

HAWEIS, MRS. H.R. The Art of Beauty. Piccadilly: C&W, 1883. 2nd ed. Frontis,xiv,298,(1)pp. Fr hinge internally cracked, spine sunned, eps browned, rubber-stamp fep; else VG. *Bookpress.* $300/£194

HAWES, CHARLES H. In the Uttermost East. London, 1903. 1st ed. Frontis port, 3 maps. Teg; marbled eps. 1/2 calf, marbled bds (spine faded, chipped; ex-libris). *Edwards.* $116/£75

HAWES, CHARLES H. In the Uttermost East. London: Harper, 1904. 2nd ed. Flyleaves lt browned; spine faded. *Hollett.* $186/£120

HAWKER, PETER. Colonel Hawker's Shooting Diaries. NY: Derrydale, (1931). 1st ed. Frontis port. Lt foxing top, fore-edge, 1st, last few leaves; bkpl, else VG. *Cahan.* $50/£32

HAWKES, JACQUETTA. A Land. R-H, 1951. 1st ed. 18 plts (2 color). Fine in VG dj (spine wear). *Fine Books.* $25/£16

HAWKES, JOHN. The Blood Oranges. (NY): New Directions, (1971). 1st ed. Fine in dj. *Cahan.* $40/£26

HAWKES, JOHN. The Blood Oranges. New Directions, 1971. 1st ed. Rev copy. Fine in dj. *Fine Books.* $55/£35

HAWKES, JOHN. The Goose on the Grave and the Owl. New Directions, 1954. 1st ed. Fine in VG+ dj. *Fine Books.* $70/£45

HAWKES, JOHN. The Passion Artist. (NY): New Directions, (1979). Ltd to 200. Signed. Fine in slipcase. *Sadlon.* $60/£39

HAWKES, JOHN. The Passion Artist. NY: New Directions, 1979. One of 200 signed. Fine in Fine slipcase. *Revere.* $75/£48

HAWKES, JOHN. Travesty. Chatto, 1976. 1st UK ed. NF in dj (sl mks flyleaves). *Williams.* $14/£9

HAWKING, STEPHEN. A Brief History of Time. NY: Bantam, 1988. 1st US ed, 1st ptg. Fine in dj. *Lame Duck.* $45/£29

HAWKINS, CORA FREAR. Buggies, Blizzards and Babies. IA State Univ, 1971. 1st ed. VG in dj. *Burcham.* $25/£16

HAWKINS, JOHN. The Life of Samuel Johnson, LL.D. London: J. Buckland, 1787. 2nd ed. Frontis port laid in, 605pp, full-pg engr. Chestnut leather spine, marbled bds (rebound), gilt. Excellent. *Hartfield.* $395/£255

HAWKS, ELLISON. Pioneers of Wireless. London, 1927. 1st ed. 24 plts, 45 diags. Foxing. *Argosy.* $60/£39

HAWLEY, FLORENCE. Tree-Ring Analysis and Dating in the Mississippi Drainage. Univ of Chicago, (1941). 1st ed. 7 plts (2 fldg). VG in stiff wraps. *Oregon.* $25/£16

HAWLEY, WALTER A. Early Days of Santa Barbara, California. Santa Barbara, 1910. (1st ed.) 4 plts. VG (lt wear) in ptd wraps. Howes H 332. *Bohling.* $150/£97

HAWORTH-BOOTH, MICHAEL. The Hydrangeas. London, 1975. 4th ed. VG+ in dj. *Brooks.* $25/£16

HAWTHORN, F. HORDERN. Abiding Memories. Privately ptd, 1919. 1st Eng ed. VG. *Edrich.* $25/£16

Hawthorne's Wonder Book. NY: George H. Doran, (1922). 1st Amer ed. 4to. 16 mtd full color plts, 8 tricolor full-pg illus, 20 b/w dwgs by Arthur Rackham. Gilt pict cl. Fine in pict dj (2 sm chips, o/w Fine). *Reisler.* $275/£177

HAWTHORNE, HILDEGARDE. The Lure of the Garden. NY, 1911. 48 plts (16 color). Teg. Blind-stamped, pict grn cl (dknd, fraying). *Brooks.* $61/£39

HAWTHORNE, JULIAN. True Stories of Modern Magic. NY: The Review of Reviews Co, 1908. Frontis. *Dramatis Personae.* $40/£26

HAWTHORNE, NATHANIEL (ed). Journal of an African Cruiser. (By Horatio Bridge.) NY/London: Wiley & Putnam, 1845. viii,179pp. 3/4 leather, marbled bds; orig wrappers bound in. VG. BAL 593. *Schoyer.* $175/£113

HAWTHORNE, NATHANIEL. Doctor Grimshawe's Secret. Boston: James R. Osgood, 1883. 1st ed, 1st ptg, 1st binding w/Osgood's logo at foot. Orig grn pict cl, gilt. Spine sl dknd, rubbed; early inscrip, else Nice. BAL 7642. *Macdonnell.* $75/£48

HAWTHORNE, NATHANIEL. The House of the Seven Gables. NY: LEC, 1935. #503/1500 signed by Valenti Angelo (illus). Fine in slipcase (sl rubbed). *Williams.* $93/£60

HAWTHORNE, NATHANIEL. The Marble Faun. Boston: Ticknor & Fields, 1860. 1st Amer ed, 1st ptg. 2 vols. 283pp,16pp ads; 284pp. Orig brn cl (sl rubbed). Very Nice set (bkpl). BAL 7621. *Chapel Hill.* $300/£194

HAWTHORNE, NATHANIEL. The Marble Faun. Boston: Ticknor & Fields, 1860. 1st ed, 4th ptg w/Conclusion added. 2 vols. Orig brn cl, gilt. Spine tips lt frayed, else Nice set. BAL 7624. *Macdonnell.* $100/£65

HAWTHORNE, NATHANIEL. Mosses from an Old Manse. NY: Wiley and Putnam, 1846. 1st ed, 1st ptg. 2 parts in 1 vol. 207,211pp. Contemp 3/4 leather, cl bds. VG. BAL 7598. *Schoyer.* $200/£129

HAWTHORNE, NATHANIEL. Our Old Home. Boston: Ticknor & Fields, 1863. 1st ed, 1st state. Blind-stamped cl (spine ends sl chipped). BAL 7626. *Sadlon.* $175/£113

HAWTHORNE, NATHANIEL. Our Old Home: A Series of English Sketches. Boston: Ticknor & Fields, 1863. 1st ed, 2nd ptg. One of 2000 ptd. Brn cl, gilt. This variant w/o inserted cat at end, but w/'myterious' reading still not corrected to 'mysterious.' Fine. BAL 7626. *Macdonnell.* $125/£81

HAWTHORNE, NATHANIEL. Passages from the American Note-Books of Nathaniel Hawthorne. Boston: Ticknor and Fields, 1868. 1st Amer ed. 2 vols. Both in 1st state binding. Grn cl, blindstamped; spine ornamented, lettered in gilt. Fine (lt dampstaining to lower outer margins vol 1, extrems of spines sl rubbed). BAL 7632. *Polyanthos.* $200/£129

HAWTHORNE, NATHANIEL. Passages from the English Note-Books of Nathaniel Hawthorne. Sophia Hawthorne (ed). Boston: Fields, Osgood, 1870. 1st Amer ed. 2 vols. Grn cl, blindstamped; spine ornamented, lettered in gilt. Fine (extrems of spine sl worn). BAL 7634. *Polyanthos.* $150/£97

HAWTHORNE, NATHANIEL. The Scarlet Letter. NY: George H. Doran, (1920). 1st Amer ed. Thick, 4to. 31 mtd color plts by Hugh Thomson. Cl-backed dec bds w/red A in center (spine letters lt faded). Pub's box (corners tape repaired). *Reisler.* $300/£194

HAWTHORNE, NATHANIEL. The Scarlet Letter. Ticknor et al, 1850. 2nd ed of 2500. Bound w/1st state March 1st, 1850 ads. Lt wear at corner tips, spine extrems, else VG. *Fine Books.* $675/£435

HAWTHORNE, NATHANIEL. The Scarlet Letter. NY: Heritage, 1935. 1st Heritage Press ed. Signed by W.A. Dwiggins (illus). Frontis. Full red leather. Sl rubbed, else Nice in pub's slipcase (sl worn). *Hermitage.* $125/£81

HAWTHORNE, NATHANIEL. The Scarlet Letter. NY: LEC, 1941. One of 1500. Signed by Henry Varnum Poor (lithos). Sheepskin. NF (lt scuff mks spine) in case. *Agvent.* $125/£81

HAWTHORNE, NATHANIEL. Septimius Felton. Boston: James R. Osgood & Co., 1872. 1st Amer ed. One of 3000. 229pp,(1)p ads. Dec grn cl. (Sl bubbling rear cvr). NF (sig). BAL 7638. *Chapel Hill.* $250/£161

HAWTHORNE, NATHANIEL. Septimius Felton. Osgood, 1872. 1st ed. VG. *Madle.* $100/£65

HAWTHORNE, NATHANIEL. The Seven Vagabonds. Boston/NY: Houghton Mifflin, 1916. 1st separate ed. Grn paper-cvrd bds, mtd cvr illus. Fine in NF dj (browning). BAL 7718. *Chapel Hill.* $75/£48

HAWTHORNE, NATHANIEL. The Snow-Image, and Other Twice-Told Tales. Boston, 1852. 1st Amer ed. Teg. 1/2 calf, gilt spine, raised bands. NF (name, pp foxed; sl rubbed). *Polyanthos.* $75/£48

HAWTHORNE, NATHANIEL. Tanglewood Tales. Phila: Penn Pub. Co., 1921. 1st ed thus. 4to. 261pp, 10 color illus w/guards. Illus blue cl, pict paper onlay, gilt title. VG (sm hole fr fly). *Davidson.* $375/£242

HAWTHORNE, NATHANIEL. Twice-Told Tales. Boston: James Munroe, 1842. 2nd ed, 1st issue. 2 vols. iv,331; 356pp. Full grn morocco, gilt. Teg, rest untrimmed. VG (bkpls). *Schoyer.* $250/£161

HAWTHORNE, NATHANIEL. A Wonder Book for Girls and Boys. Cambridge: Riverside, 1893. #159/250. 8vo. 210pp. Walter Crane (illus). Vellum, gilt; teg. VG (pin hole top of spine). Grn dj. *Davidson.* $750/£484

HAWTHORNE, NATHANIEL. A Wonder Book for Girls and Boys. Boston, 1893. Deluxe Edition, 1/250 numbered. x,210pp; 19 mtd color plts. Full vellum, gilt (spine sl worn; upper joint cracking, corners bumped); teg. Internally pristine. *Argosy.* $850/£548

HAY, CECILE B. and MILDRED B. History of Derby. Littleton, NH, 1967. 1st ed. Fine. *Mcgowan.* $45/£29

HAY, HELEN. Verses for Jock and Joan. NY: Fox, Duffield, 1905. 1st ed. Folio. 32pp; 6 color plts by Charlotte Harding. Yellow cl, color pict bds (rubbed). VG+. *Drusilla's.* $175/£113

HAY, IAN. The Royal Company of Archers 1676-1951. Edinburgh: Blackwood, 1951. 1st ed. Grn cl, gilt titles, crests. VG+. *Bowman.* $75/£48

HAY, JOHN. Jim Bludso of the Prairie Bell, and Little Britches. Boston: Osgood, 1871. 1st bk. 8 plts by Sol Eytinge. Orange wraps sl chipped, o/w VG. BAL 7739. *Schoyer.* $85/£55

HAY, JOHN. Jim Bludso.... Boston, 1871. 1st ed, 1st bk. Fine in wrappers. BAL 7739. *Pharos.* $100/£65

HAY, THOMAS ROBSON. Hood's Tennessee Campaign. NY: Neale, 1929. 1st ed. 4 maps (2 fldg). Orig blue cl. Spine sl bumped, eps lt foxed, o/w VG. *Chapel Hill.* $175/£113

HAY, THOMAS ROBSON. Hood's Tennessee Campaign. NY: Neale, 1929. 1st ed. 4 maps (2 fldg). Orig blue cl. NF in VG dj (chipped). *Chapel Hill.* $350/£226

HAYCOX, ERNEST. The Earthbreakers. Boston: 1952. 1st ed. Pict cl. VG in dj (spine chipped, lg piece from top back panel). *Baade.* $50/£32

HAYDEN, ARTHUR. Chats on English China. London, (1922). 10th imp. Stamped name, else Good in dj (tattered). *King.* $30/£19

HAYDEN, ARTHUR. Spode and His Successors. A History of the Pottery Stoke-on-Trent 1765-1865. London: Cassell, (1925). 1st ed. 24 mtd color plts, guards. Blue illus cl. Nice. *Karmiole.* $175/£113

HAYDEN, ARTHUR. Spode and His Successors. A History of the Pottery Stoke-on-Trent 1765-1865. London, 1925. 1st ed. Color frontis, 23 color plts tipped-in. (Upper hinge cracked.) Dj (sl soiled). *Edwards.* $101/£65

HAYDEN, F.V. Report of the United States Geological Survey of the Territories. Vol XII. Washington, 1879. xi,324pp, 43 color plts. (Ex-lib w/ink stamps, stain, #, labels; hinges cracked.) *Edwards.* $62/£40

HAYES, ALBERT. Diseases of the Nervous System. Boston, 1875. 204pp. Good. *Fye.* $50/£32

HAYES, BILLY and WILLIAM HOFFER. Midnight Express. NY: Dutton, 1977. 1st ed. NF in dj. *Worldwide.* $18/£12

HAYES, C. (ed). The Complete Guide to Painting and Drawing Techniques and Materials. Oxford: Phaidon, 1979. Sound. *Ars Artis.* $33/£21

HAYES, C.W. Handbook for Field Geologists in the United States Geological Survey. Washington: GPO, 1908. VG. *Schoyer.* $20/£13

HAYES, HARRIET. The Home Nurse and Nursery. NY, 1888. 1st ed. 366pp. Good. *Fye.* $100/£65

HAYES, I.I. An Arctic Boat Journey in the Autumn of 1854. Boston: Brown, Taggard & Chase, 1860. 1st ed. xvii,375pp, 2 fldg maps (fr internal hinge cracked, cl torn at head, tail of spine). *Walcot.* $62/£40

HAYES, I.I. The Land of Desolation. NY: Harper, 1872. 1st ed. 357pp. Good+ (spine sl dknd, fr inner hinge cracked). *Walcot.* $62/£40

HAYES, I.I. The Open Polar Sea. NY: Hurd & Houghton, 1867. 1st ed. xxiv,454pp. Good. *Walcot.* $85/£55

HAYES, JEFF W. Autographs and Memoirs of the Telegraph. Adrian, MI, 1916. Stated 1st ed. *Hayman.* $20/£13

HAYES, JOHN. Catalogue of the Oil Paintings in the London Museum. London: HMSO, 1970. Frontis, 12 plts; in dj. *Edwards.* $39/£25

HAYES, JOHN. Catalogue of the Oil Paintings in the London Museum. London: HMSO, 1970. 182 plts; pict eps. Fine in Mint dj. *Europa.* $62/£40

HAYES, JOHN. The Drawings of Thomas Gainsborough. London: Zwemmer, 1970. 2 vols. 462 plts. Sound in dj. *Ars Artis.* $163/£105

HAYES, JOHN. The Drawings of Thomas Gainsborough. London: Paul Mellon Centre, 1971. 2 vols. 462 b/w plts. Djs (sl chipped). *Edwards.* $194/£125

HAYES, JOHN. Gainsborough as Printmaker. New Haven, 1972. 95 illus. Good in dj. *Washton.* $50/£32

HAYES, RICHARD. Interest at One View Calculated to a Farthing.... Ptd for W. Meadows, 1747. 7th ed w/additions. Contemp calf (rebacked, corners repaired). *Waterfield.* $116/£75

HAYGOOD, ATTICUS G. Our Brother in Black. NY/Cincinnati: 1881. 1st ed. 252pp. Dec cl. VG. *Petrilla.* $125/£81

HAYMAKER, WEBB and BARNES WOODHALL. Peripheral Nerve Injuries, Principles of Diagnosis. Phila, 1947. 1st ed. Good. *Fye.* $150/£97

HAYMAKER, WEBB. The Founders of Neurology. Springfield, 1953. 1st ed. (Ex-lib.) *Fye.* $60/£39

HAYNES, GIDEON. Pictures from Prison Life: An Historical Sketch of the Massachusetts State Prison. Boston: Lee, 1869. 1st ed. 290pp. *Ginsberg.* $125/£81

HAYNES, LOUISE MARSHALL. Over the Rainbow Bridge. Chicago: P.F. Volland, (1920). 12mo. Carmen L. Browne (illus). Pict bds (lt dusted). Color pict box (edges broken). *Reisler.* $115/£74

HAYTER, ALETHEA. A Voyage in Vain. Faber, 1973. 1st ed. Fine in dj (price-clipped). *Poetry.* $16/£10

HAYTER, CHARLES. An Introduction to Perspective, Drawing, and Painting.... London: Kingsbury, n.d. (1825?). 4th ed. Engr frontis, xxii,294pp, 20 engr plts (18 fldg). Contemp bds (sl worn; internal browning, spotting). *Europa.* $54/£35

HAYTER, CHARLES. An Introduction to Perspective. London: The author, 1813. 1st ed. Engr frontis, 168pp, 14 engr plts. New plain wrappers. Sound. *Ars Artis.* $116/£75

HAYTER, CHARLES. An Introduction to Perspective. London, 1844. 6th ed. Port, xiv,276pp (lacks tp; lib stamps 1/2 title, plts); 4 (of 5) color plts. (Spine torn.) *Ars Artis.* $62/£40

HAYWARD, HELENA and PAT KIRKHAM. William and John Linnell. London, 1980. 2 vols. 19 color plts. (Ex-lib w/ink stamps, remains of labels, #s; spines lt faded.) *Edwards.* $39/£25

HAYWARD, J.F. Viennese Porcelain of the Du Paquier Period. Rockliff, London, 1952. 1st ed. Color frontis; 3 color, 72 b/w plts. (Feps sl browned). Orig cl (upper hinge sl cracked; sl soiled) in dj (sl ragged; repaired). *Edwards.* $140/£90

HAYWARD, JOHN. The First Part of the Life and Raigne of King Henrie the IIII. London: John Wolfe, 1599 (i.e. M. Parsons, 1638?). 4th ed. 4to. (viii),150pp. 1/2 calf gilt, aeg (bkst label upper cvr). Good (author's name on tp   completed in later ms; few headlines, 1 fore-edge shaved). Bkpl, sig of Granville C. Cunningham. *Sokol.* $543/£350

HAYWARD, JOHN. A Gazetteer of the United States of America. Hartford: Case, Tiffany, 1853. 861pp. VG. *Schoyer.* $50/£32

HAYWARD, JOHN. The New England Gazetteer. Concord, NH/Boston: Israel S. Boyd & William White/John Hayward, 1839. 8th ed. 3 plts. Brn calf (bumped, rubbed; lower fr joint split; spine chipped). Fair (foxed; dampstaining). *Blue Mountain.* $25/£16

HAYWARD, OLIVER S. and ELIZABETH H. THOMSON (eds). The Journal of William Tully.... NY: Science History Pub, 1977. 1st ed. Frontis port. 2-tone cl, gilt. Fine. *Glaser.* $25/£16

HAYWOOD, C. ROBERT. Trails South. Norman: Univ of OK, 1986. 1st ed. VG+ in VG+ dj. *October Farm.* $35/£23

HAYWOOD, GAR ANTHONY. Fear of the Dark. St. Martin, 1988. 1st ed. Fine in dj (sl rubbing). *Murder.* $40/£26

HAYWOOD, GAR ANTHONY. Fear of the Dark. London: Macmillan, 1988. 1st Eng ed. VF in dj. *Mordida.* $45/£29

HAYWOOD, JOHN. The Civil and Political History of the State of Tennessee.... Nashville, TN: Methodist Episcopal Church, South, 1915. 2nd ptg of 2nd ed of 1891. Dk brn cl. Lg lib inkstamp fep, tp, else Fine. Howes H 358. *Chapel Hill.* $125/£81

HAYWOOD, JOHN. The Natural and Aboriginal History of Tennessee.... Mary U. Rothrock (ed). Jackson, TN: McCowat-Mercer Press, 1959. 2nd ed. Blue cl. Sig, else NF in acetate dj (dusty). Howes H 359. *Chapel Hill.* $100/£65

HAZARD, THOMAS R. The Johnny-Cake Papers of 'Shepherd Tom' Together with Reminiscences of Narragansett Schools of Former Days.... Boston, 1915. 1st ed. One of 600 ptd. Inscribed presentation slip pasted fep. Map; 6 plts. Howes H 367. *Ginsberg.* $100/£65

HAZARD, THOMAS R. Report on the Poor and Insane in Rhode Island...1851. Providence: Knowles, 1851. Engr frontis. (Newly rebacked.) Good. *Goodrich.* $125/£81

HAZELTON, JOHN ADAMS. The Hazelton Letters. Mary Geneva Bloom (ed). Stockton: College of the Pacific, 1958. Tipped-in photo frontis. Bds faded, else Fine. *Parmer.* $65/£42

HAZEN, ALLEN T. A Bibliography of the Strawberry Hill Press.... Dawsons of Pall Mall, 1973. Frontis, 48 facs. VG in dj (lt soiled, frayed, owner label). *Cox.* $39/£25

HAZEN, ALLEN T. A Catalogue of Horace Walpole's Library with Horace Walpole's Library by W.S. Lewis. New Haven/London: Yale Univ, 1969. 3 vols. Blue cl bds, gilt spine titles. Fine in djs. *Heller.* $125/£81

HAZEN, WILLIAM BABCOCK. History of the Signal Service with a Catalogue of Publications, Instruments and Stations. Washington, DC, 1884. 1st ed. 39pp. VG in orig ptd wrappers. *Mcgowan.* $75/£48

HAZLETT, JAMES C. et al. Field Artillery Weapons of the Civil War. Newark, (1983). 1st ed. Inscribed by Hazlett. Dj sl worn, chipped, o/w Fine. *Pratt.* $60/£39

HAZLITT, W. CAREW. The Confessions of a Collector. London: Ward & Downey, 1897. 1st ed. viii,360pp. VG (spine label darkened; fr cvr lt spotted; bkpl). *Graf.* $45/£29

HAZLITT, W. CAREW. Gleanings in Old Garden Literature. London, 1892. vii,263pp. *Wheldon & Wesley.* $39/£25

HAZLITT, W. CAREW. Mary and Charles Lamb: Poems, Letters, and Remains. London: C&W, 1874. Lg 8vo. Frontis port; 307,31pp. Half morocco gilt (bds faded; spine scraped, rubbed; joints cracked). *Hollett.* $70/£45

HAZLITT, W. CAREW. Memoirs of William Hazlitt. London: Richard Bentley, 1867. 2 vols. xxxiii(foxed),317; 312pp; 2 engr ports. Contemp 1/2 calf gilt, raised bands, spine labels. VG. *Hollett.* $116/£75

HAZLITT, W. CAREW. Old Cookery Books and Ancient Cuisine. London: Elliot Stock, 1886. 1st ed, deluxe issue. (4),272pp. Gilt spine. Nice (sl rubbed). *Cady.* $45/£29

HAZLITT, WILLIAM. Selected Essays. Geoffrey Keynes (ed). London: Nonesuch, 1930. 1st ed. Grn buckram, beveled bds. VG. *Cox.* $31/£20

HEAD, FRANCIS. Life in Germany or a Visit to the Springs of Germany by 'An Old Man' in Search of Health (Bubbles From Brunnen). NY: Leavitt, Trow, 1848. 228pp. Sm tear foot of spine, no rep, o/w VG. *Artis Books.* $25/£16

HEAD, FRANCIS. A Narrative. London, 1839. 1st ed. (6),488+38pp. (Cl worn; new leather spine; tp corner clipped 1 inch). *Artis.* $125/£81

HEAD, FRANKLIN H. Shakespeare's Insomnia and the Causes Thereof. Chicago: Caxton Club, 1926. One of 275 ptd at Lakeside Press. Teg, others untrimmed. Patterned bds. Bottom edge sl rubbed, o/w Fine. *Cahan.* $100/£65

HEAD, HENRY. Studies in Neurology. Oxford, 1920. 2 vols. (Lib stamp on title.) *Goodrich.* $275/£177

HEAD, RICHARD and FRANCIS KIRKMAN. The English Rogue. London, 1928. 12 plts. (Sl rubbed, bumped.) *Edwards.* $62/£40

HEAD, THOMAS A. Campaigns and Battles of the Sixteenth Regiment, Tennessee Volunteers.... Nashville, TN: Cumberland Presbyterian Publ. House, 1885. 1st ed. Frontis port, 488pp. Orig dk brn cl. Cvrs soiled, else VG. *Chapel Hill.* $300/£194

HEADLAM, CECIL. The Inns of Court. A&C Black, 1909. 1st ed. 20 color plts, fldg map. Teg. Dec cl. (Sl browning.) *Edwards.* $116/£75

HEADLAND, F.W. An Essay on the Action of Medicines in the System. London, 1855. 2nd ed. x,394pp (prelims lt foxed). Orig cl (rebacked). *Whitehart.* $93/£60

HEADLEY, J.T. The Adirondack; or Life in the Woods. NY: Baker and Scribner, 1849. 1st ed. (x)288pp + 4pp cat, 8 plts (inner edge frontis lt dampstained; color clipping pasted fr pastedown). Brn cl (rubbed, bumped, stained; spine head chipped); gilt. VG. *Blue Mountain.* $125/£81

HEADLEY, J.T. Letters From Italy. NY: Baker & Scribner, 1848. New, rev ed. Frontis port, tissue. xvi,224; viii,138,(6)pp. Stamped cl. Worn; foxing few pp, else Good. *Connolly.* $45/£29

HEALY, JEREMIAH. Blunt Darts. NY: Walker, 1986. 1st ed. Fine in dj. *Mordida.* $250/£161

HEALY, JEREMIAH. Staked Goat. NY: Harper & Row, (1986). 1st ed. Fine in Fine dj. *Aka.* $25/£16

HEALY, JOHN T. An Adventure in the Idaho Mines. Clyde McLemore (ed). Missoula, 1938. Rpt. (Lib stamp cvr.) *Bohling.* $45/£29

HEALY, M.A. Report of the Cruise of the Revenue Marine Steamer Corwin...1884. Washington: GPO, 1889. Signed presentation. 128pp, 40 plts (2 chromolithos). VG. *Schoyer.* $125/£81

HEALY, WILLIAM. Mental Conflicts and Misconduct. Boston: Little, Brown, 1917. 1st ed. Signed. Brn cl. VG. *Gach.* $75/£48

HEANEY, SEAMUS. The Cure at Troy. (Derry): Field Day, (1990). 1st ed, ltd to 500 numbered, signed. Errata slip laid in. Fine in dj. *Godot.* $150/£97

HEANEY, SEAMUS. The Cure at Troy. NY: FSG, 1991. 1st Amer ed. Fine in Fine dj. *Revere.* $30/£19

HEANEY, SEAMUS. Death of a Naturalist. London: Faber, 1966. 1st UK ed. Fine in VG+ dj (spine sl faded; fore-edge lt scuffed). *Williams.* $388/£250

HEANEY, SEAMUS. The Fire I' the Flint. OUP, 1975. 1st UK ed. Fine in wrappers. *Lewton.* $26/£17

HEANEY, SEAMUS. Gravities. Newcastle Upon Tyne: Charlotte Press Publications, 1979. 1st ed, trade issue. VG in pict wrappers. *Godot.* $65/£42

HEANEY, SEAMUS. The Haw Lantern. NY: FSG, (1987). 1st Amer ed. Ltd to 250 signed. New in slipcase. *Jaffe.* $100/£65

HEANEY, SEAMUS. In Responses. Nat. Book League, 1971. 1st ed, ltd to 500. Fine. *Whiteson.* $39/£25

HEANEY, SEAMUS. Poems and a Memoir. (NY): LEC, 1982. One of 2000 signed by Heaney, Thomas Flanagan (intro), and Henry Pearson (illus). Teg. Full brn calf, blind motif. 2 imperfections rear bd, o/w Fine in slipcase. *Cahan.* $200/£129

HEANEY, SEAMUS. Station Island. London: Faber, 1984. 1st ed. Fine in dj. *Rees.* $31/£20

HEANEY, SEAMUS. Station Island. London: Faber & Faber, 1984. 1st ed. VF in dj. *Limestone.* $65/£42

HEANEY, SEAMUS. Sweeney Astray. Derry: Field Day Pub, 1983. 1st ed. Fine in dj. *Godot.* $85/£55

HEANEY, SEAMUS. Sweeney Astray. Derry: Field Day Pub, 1983. 1st ed. As New in like dj. *Dermont.* $100/£65

HEARD, H.F. The Great Fog: And Other Weird Tales. NY: Vanguard, (1944). 1st ed. Bkpl; foxing, bd edges stained, else VG+ in dj (price-clipped; sl corner chipping; foxing). *Other Worlds.* $30/£19

HEARD, H.F. The Notched Hairpin. NY: Vanguard, 1949. 1st ed. Fine in dj. *Mordida.* $75/£48

HEARD, H.F. A Taste for Honey. NY: Vanguard, 1941. 1st ed. VG in dj (piece missing spine top; sm chips). *Mordida.* $150/£97

HEARN, LAFCADIO. Books and Habits. London: Heinemann, 1922. 1st British issue, ptd in US. Gilt blue cl. Lt foxing prelims, terminal leaves, else NF. BAL 7971. *Reese.* $85/£55

HEARN, LAFCADIO. Books and Habits. Heinemann, 1922. 1st Eng ed. NF in VG+ dj (lt chipping). *Fine Books.* $95/£61

HEARN, LAFCADIO. Chita: A Memory of Last Island. NY: Harper, 1889. 1st ed. viii,204pp + ads. Salmon cl. Sl rubbed, else Fine+. BAL 7918. *Godot.* $350/£226

HEARN, LAFCADIO. Editorials. H-M, 1926. 1st ed. NF in NF dj (spine head lacks sm piece). *Fine Books.* $95/£61

HEARN, LAFCADIO. Editorials. Charles Wodward Hutson (ed). Boston: Houghton Mifflin, 1926. 1st ed. VG in dj (top edge sl chipped; short tears). BAL 7994. *Houle.* $300/£194

HEARN, LAFCADIO. Essays on American Literature. Sanki Ichikawa (ed). Kanda, Tokyo, Japan: Hokuseido Press, 1929. 1st ed. Red cl. Ep fore-edges stained, else Fine. BAL 8011. *Godot.* $85/£55

HEARN, LAFCADIO. Glimpses of Unfamiliar Japan. Boston, 1895. 2nd ed. 2 vols. (11),699pp. Silver-stamped cl. VG. *Artis.* $75/£48

HEARN, LAFCADIO. Insects and Greek Poetry. NY: Rudge, 1926. 1st bk issue. One of 550. VG. BAL 7995. *Schoyer.* $75/£48

HEARN, LAFCADIO. Japan: An Attempt at Interpretation. NY: Macmillan, 1904. 1st ed ('September, 1904'). Color frontis. VG in dj (nicks; tears). BAL 7941. *Houle.* $350/£226

HEARN, LAFCADIO. Japan: An Attempt at Interpretation. NY: Macmillan, 1904. 1st ed. Color frontis. Brn dec cl, gilt top. Fine. *Appelfeld.* $175/£113

HEARN, LAFCADIO. The Japanese Letters of.... Boston: Houghton, 1910. 1st trade ed. Port; teg. Name; lt rubbed, sm crack inner rear hinge, else Good. *Reese.* $45/£29

HEARN, LAFCADIO. A Japanese Miscellany. Boston: Little, Brown, 1901. 1st ed. State A, w/o 'October 1901' on copyright pg. Teg. Pict grn cl. VG (fep excised; sig; lt stain bottom frontis, tp). BAL 7936. *Chapel Hill.* $75/£48

HEARN, LAFCADIO. Kokoro. Boston: Houghton Mifflin, 1896. 1st ed. Sl soiling, sunning; bkpl, o/w Nice. *Beasley.* $75/£48

HEARN, LAFCADIO. Kotto. NY: Macmillan, 1902. 1st ed, 1st issue w/cinnamon colored background on tp ptd upside down. Olive cl stamped in black/grn/gilt. Lt soil, o/w VF. *Hermitage.* $300/£194

HEARN, LAFCADIO. Kotto. NY/London: Macmillan, 1902. 1st ed, 1st state w/background tp ptd upside down; artist's monograph in upper rt corner. Pict olive cl. Bright in dj (lt sunned; 1/2-inch chip top fr panel; spine lt rubbed). BAL 7938. *Chapel Hill.* $900/£581

HEARN, LAFCADIO. Kwaidan. Tokyo: Shimbi Shoin, 1932. Ltd to 1500. Signed by Yasumasa Fujita (illus). Brocaded silk-covered bds, spine tied in Japanese manner; teg. Label sl rubbed along spine edges, inscrip, o/w Fine in glassine wrapper. Silk-covered folder w/wraparound label, ivory clasps. *Sadlon.* $225/£145

HEARN, LAFCADIO. Shadowings. Boston: Little, Brown, 1900. 1st ed. 8vo. Teg. Pict blue cl. Fine (inscrip, bkseller's label) in Fine ptd blue dj. BAL 7935. *Chapel Hill.* $1,200/£774

HEARN, LAFCADIO. Some Chinese Ghosts. Boston: Roberts Bros, 1887. 1st ed. iv,185pp. Red cl. Cvrs lt soiled, spotted; name, else VG. BAL 7916. *Chapel Hill.* $400/£258

HEARN, LAFCADIO. Some Chinese Ghosts. Boston: Little, Brown, 1906. Teg. Aqua dec cl (lacks fep; fr hinge awkwardly repaired). Rpt of BAL 7916. *Schoyer.* $25/£16

HEARN, LAFCADIO. Some Chinese Ghosts. Boston: Little, Brown, 1906. 1st ed thus, 'Library Edition.' Grn pict cl. Bkpl, else NF. *Godot.* $75/£48

HEARN, LAFCADIO. Stray Leaves from Strange Literature. Boston: James R. Osgood, 1884. 1st ed, 1st bk. Grn cl. Cvrs creased, sl rubbed; inner hinges reglued; sig, o/w Clean. *Pharos.* $250/£161

HEARN, LAFCADIO. Two Years in the French West Indies. NY: Harper, 1890. 1st ed. Lt grn dec cl, gilt. NF (early inscrip). BAL 7920. *Macdonnell.* $125/£81

HEARN, SAMUEL. Coppermine Journey. Account of a Great Adventure. McClelland & Stewart, (1958). 1st thus. Ep maps. Fine in Fine dj. *Oregon.* $35/£23

HEARNE, SAMUEL. A Journey from Prince of Wales's Fort in Hudson's Bay to the Northern Ocean.... London: Strahan & Cadell, 1795. 1st ed. Folding frontis map, xliv,458pp, 4 plts, 4 fldg maps (foxed to varying degrees; title pg repaired; 2 sheets torn w/piece missing in margin). Modern binding. *Oregon.* $2,000/£1,290

HEARNE, SAMUEL. A Journey from Prince of Wales's Fort in Hudson's Bay to the Northern Ocean...1769, 1770, 1771, and 1772. Edmonton: Hurtig, c.1971. Facs rpt of 1795 orig ed. Fine in dj. *High Latitude.* $65/£42

HEARON, SHELBY. Armadillo in the Grass. NY: Knopf, 1968. 1st ed, 1st bk. Lt offsetting eps, else VG in dj (chip back panel). *Turlington.* $75/£48

HEARST, JAMES. Country Men. Muscatine: Prairie Press, 1937. One of 250. Good (binding, spine label soiled; shelf wear), contents Fine. *Graf.* $17/£11

HEAT MOON, WILLIAM LEAST. Blue Highways. Boston, 1982. 1st ed. Inscribed. Debossed dec cl. Upper corners sl bumped, o/w Fine in dj (lt worn). *Baade.* $40/£26

HEATH ROBINSON, W. Uncle Lubin. NY: Brentano's, 1902. 1st Amer ed. 8vo. W. Heath Robinson (illus). Dec cl binding w/image of Uncle Lubin and pelican w/baby (recased; sl rubbed spine edges); highlighted w/iridescent blue. *Reisler.* $1,250/£806

HEATH ROBINSON, W. (comp). Heath Robinson's Book of Goblins. London: Hutchinson, (1934). 1st ed. 4to. 7 full-pg color plts by Robinson. Dk blue cl, gold lettering; blind-stamped (lt worn). *Reisler.* $485/£313

HEATH ROBINSON, W. and CECIL HUNT. How to Run a Communal Home. London: Hutchinson, (1943). 1st ed. 12mo. Dec red cl, black lettering (sl bowed). Pict dj (edge chips). *Reisler.* $110/£71

HEATH, ARTHUR H. Sketches of Vanishing China. London: Butterworth, (1927). Frontis, 23 tipped-on repros. Yellow cl stamped in red (sl discolored; foxing). *Schoyer.* $50/£32

HEATH, FRANCIS GEORGE. The English Peasantry. Frederick Warne, 1874. 1st ed. Frontis, x,(ii),271pp + 2 ad leaves. Pict cl gilt (spine faded, dk stain; sm defective spot lower cvr). *Bickersteth.* $124/£80

HEATH, FRANCIS GEORGE. Our Woodland Trees. London, 1878. 3rd ed. xx,572pp (prelims sl foxed; bkpl removed), 8 color plts. Marbled eps, inner gilt dentelles. Aeg. Gilt ruled morocco. *Edwards.* $62/£40

HEATH, FRANCIS GEORGE. Where to Find Ferns. London, 1885. iv,153pp. Pict cl (lt wear, sm spots). *Sutton.* $35/£23

HEATH-STUBBS, JOHN. Collected Poems 1943-1987. Manchester: Carcanet, 1988. 1st Eng ed. Fine in dj. *Ulysses.* $47/£30

HEATHCOTE, J.M. et al. Skating and Figure-Skating. London, 1892. Frontis, tp, xiv,464pp, 11 plts. Illus cl (sl rubbed; ex-libris). *Edwards.* $54/£35

HEATHCOTE, J.M. et al. Skating and Figure-Skating. Boston/London: Little, Brown/Longmans, Green, 1892. 1st US ed. xiv,464pp. Pict cl. VG. *Schoyer.* $85/£55

HEATON, E.W. Everyday Life in Old Testament Times. London: Batsford, (1956). Good. *Archaeologia.* $25/£16

HEBARD, GRACE RAYMOND and E.A. BRININSTOOL. The Bozeman Trail. Cleveland: Clark, 1922. 1st ed. 2 vols. Fldg map end each vol. Uncut; teg. (Pencil marginalia; bottom tips bumped.) *Dawson.* $275/£177

HEBARD, GRACE RAYMOND and E.A. BRININSTOOL. The Bozeman Trail. Glendale: Clark, 1960. Rpt. 2 fldg maps. VG. Howes H 382. *Schoyer.* $100/£65

HEBER, REGINALD. Narrative of a Journey Through the Upper Provinces of India.... London, 1829. 4th ed. 3 vols. lxvii,450; vii,564; vii,525pp + subs list; errata slip, 27 wood engrs. Orig 1/2 calf. Nice set. *Lewis.* $240/£155

HEBER, REGINALD. Narrative of a Journey Through the Upper Provinces of India...an Account of a Journey to Madras.... Phila, 1828. 1st Amer ed. 2 vols. Fldg frontis map. Orig cl-backed bds (sl stained), paper spine labels; uncut, partly unopened. Lt foxing. *Argosy.* $175/£113

HEBERDEN, M.V. Drinks on the Victim. GC: DCC, 1948. 1st ed. VG + (bumped; pp browned) in VG + dj (lt chipped). *Janus.* $20/£13

HEBERDEN, W. Commentaries on the History and Cure of Diseases. London, 1803. 2nd Eng ed. xii,514pp (tp edge repaired; foxing). New 1/4 blue morocco. *Whitehart.* $217/£140

HEBERDEN, W. Commentaries on the History and Cure of Diseases. London, 1816. 4th ed. xii,432pp (edges dust-stained; lt foxing). Old leather (rebacked). *Whitehart.* $279/£180

HEBERT, WALTER H. Fighting Joe Hooker. Indianapolis, (1944). 1st ed. Dj worn, lacks sm pieces, o/w VG +. *Pratt.* $65/£42

HECHT, ANTHONY. A Summoning of Stones. NY: Macmillan, 1954. 1st ed, 1st bk. Bkpl, else Fine in dj (sl used). *Pharos.* $95/£61

HECHT, ANTHONY. A Summoning of Stones. NY: Macmillan, 1954. 1st ed, 1st bk. Fine in dj (lt foxed). *Jaffe.* $175/£113

HECHT, BEN and MAX BODENHEIM. Cutie, a Warm Mama. Hechtshaw Press, 1924. 1st ed. One of 200. Lt worn, else NF in plain wrapper (lt wear). *Fine Books.* $75/£48

HECHT, BEN and MAX BODENHEIM. Cutie, a Warm Mama. Chicago: Hechtshaw Press, 1924. One of 200. Fine (sl rubbed) in dj (spine, fr panel mended; torn, lacks pieces). *Polyanthos.* $35/£23

HECHT, BEN. 1001 Afternoons in New York. NY: Viking, 1941. 1st ed. Gilt pict cl. NF in dj (chipped). *Sadlon.* $45/£29

HECHT, BEN. The Bewitched Tailor. Viking, 1941. 1st ed. One of 850. Signed by author & George Grosz (illus). NF in wraps as issued. *Fine Books.* $285/£184

HECHT, BEN. Erik Dorn. NY/London: Putnam's/Knickerbocker Press, 1921. 1st ed. Lt rubbed. *Sadlon.* $20/£13

HECHT, BEN. Fantazius Mallare. Covici-McGee, 1922. 1st ed (2nd state binding). One of 2025. Fine in VG + dj. *Fine Books.* $125/£81

HECHT, BEN. Fantazius Mallare. Chicago: Covici-McGee, 1922. Ltd to 2025. Gilt (dknd). Spine sl lightened. *Sadlon.* $25/£16

HECHT, BEN. Gaily, Gaily. NY, 1963. 1st Amer ed. Fine in dj (sl rubbed). *Polyanthos.* $30/£19

HECHT, BEN. The Kingdom of Evil. Covici, 1924. 1st ed. One of 2000. VG + in VG dj (chip fr panel; inner reinforcement). *Fine Books.* $125/£81

HECHT, BEN. Letters from Bohemia. GC: Doubleday, 1964. 1st ed. VG in dj. *Hermitage.* $35/£23

HECKER, J.F.C. The Black Death in the Fourteenth Century. B.G. Babington (trans). London: A. Schloss, 1833. 1st ed in English. xii,205pp. Orig dk grn cl; rebacked preserving spine. *White.* $85/£55

HECKER, J.F.C. The Epidemics of the Middle Ages. B.G. Babington (trans). London, 1846. 1st Eng trans. 380pp. Good. *Fye.* $150/£97

HECKER, J.F.C. The Epidemics of the Middle Ages. B.G. Babington (trans). London: Trubner, 1859. 3rd ed. xxiv,360pp, errata slip. Mod cl. *Bickersteth.* $116/£75

HECKSCHER, WILLIAM S. Rembrandt's Anatomy of Dr. Nicolaas Tulp. NY, 1958. Good. *Washton.* $85/£55

HECKSCHER, WILLIAM S. Rembrandt's Anatomy of Dr. Nicolaas Tulp. NY, 1958. 1st ed. Sl bumped, inner hinges cracked, else Good in dj (frayed, rubbed, soiled, price-clipped). *King.* $95/£61

HECOX, MARGARET H. California Caravan. San Jose: (Harlan-Young Press), 1966. 1st ed. NF in dj (edge-worn). *Hermitage.* $35/£23

HECTOR, L.C. The Handwriting of English Documents. London: Edward Arnold, 1958. 1st ed. 32 plts. Eps sl spotted. Dj. *Hollett.* $39/£25

HEDGECOE, JOHN (ed). Henry Moore. NY, (1968). VG in box. *Argosy.* $200/£129

HEDGES, WILLIAM HAWKINS. Pike's Peak...Or Busted! Herbert O. Brayer (ed). Evanston: Branding Iron Press, 1954. 1st ed. Ltd to 750. Frontis. VG in dj. *Lien.* $45/£29

HEDIN, SVEN. Across the Gobi Desert. London: Routledge, (1928). 3 maps. (Binding sl faded, sm mks.) *Petersfield.* $39/£25

HEDIN, SVEN. Across the Gobi Desert. London, 1931. 1st UK ed. 3 maps (2 fldg). (Feps lt browned; spine sl faded; label removed upper bd.) *Edwards.* $78/£50

HEDIN, SVEN. Central Asia and Tibet. London: Hurst & Blackett, 1903. 1st Eng ed. 2 vols. 5 maps on 4 sheets, 8 color plts. Sm lib stamps, #s, joint tender, sl faded, rubbed, but Good set. *Hollett.* $302/£195

HEDIN, SVEN. Flight of 'Big Horse.' The Trail of War in Central Asia. F.H. Lyon (trans). NY: Dutton, 1936. 1st Amer ed. Bds (sl sunned). *Schoyer.* $40/£26

HEDIN, SVEN. Overland to India. London: Macmillan, 1910. 1st ed. 2 vols. (Spine sl dulled; hinges sl rubbed; eps vol 1 sl marked.) *Hollett.* $233/£150

HEDIN, SVEN. Through Asia. London, 1898. 1st ed. 2 vols. Frontis ports, 2 fldg maps. (Lt browning; joints chipped; spines faded, chipped w/loss; sl loss upper bd vol 1.) *Edwards.* $194/£125

HEDIN, SVEN. The Wandering Lake. F.H. Lyon (trans). NY: E.P. Dutton, 1940. 1st US ed. 10 maps. VG in dj (worn). *Hollett.* $186/£120

HEDIN, T. The Sculptures of Gaspard and Balthazard Marsy. Univ MO Press, 1983. Sound in dj. *Ars Artis.* $70/£45

HEDLEY, FENWICK Y. Marching Through Georgia. Chicago: Donohue, Henneberry & Co, 1890. 490pp. Dec cl. NF. *Mcgowan.* $65/£42

HEDLEY, W.S. Therapeutic Electricity and Practical Muscle Testing. London, 1899. 1st ed. 278pp. Good. *Fye.* $100/£65

HEDRICK, U.P. The Cherries of New York. Albany, 1915. Port, 56 full color plts. VG. *Cullen.* $85/£55

HEDRICK, U.P. The Cherries of New York. Albany, 1915. 56 color plts, b/w port. (1pg marginal smudges, gutter staining; hinges starting, lt wear.) *Sutton.* $140/£90

HEDRICK, U.P. The Cherries of New York. Albany, 1915. Frontis; 56 full-pg color plts. Gilt-dec cl (bumped; few stains; spine ends frayed; fr inner hinge starting; lt foxing). VG. *Shifrin.* $175/£113

HEDRICK, U.P. The Cherries of New York. Albany, 1915. 1st ed. Frontis port. Buckram. Mint. *Argosy.* $100/£65

HEDRICK, U.P. The Grapes of New York. Albany: J.B. Lyon, 1908. Port, 101 chromolitho plts. Grn buckram. VG. *Cullen.* $200/£129

HEDRICK, U.P. The Grapes of New York. Albany, 1908. Frontis port, 101 color plts. (Lt wear extrems, cvrs stained, hinges starting.) *Sutton.* $220/£142

HEDRICK, U.P. Manual of American Grape-Growing. L.H. Baiely (ed). NY, 1919. 32 plts. (Pp tanned; extrems lt scuffed.) *Sutton.* $45/£29

HEDRICK, U.P. The Peaches of New York. Albany, 1917. 92 color plts, map (rear pastedown scraped; inner joint cracked; scuffed). *Sutton.* $160/£103

HEDRICK, U.P. The Peaches of New York. Albany, 1917. Frontis; 92 full-pg color plts. Grn cl, gilt. VG (lt foxing). *Shifrin.* $200/£129

HEDRICK, U.P. The Pears of New York. Albany, 1921. 80 full-pg color plts. Grn cl, gilt. VG (bumped). *Shifrin.* $200/£129

HEDRICK, U.P. The Plums of New York. Albany, 1911. Frontis, 98 color plts (lacks 'October' plt; lt foxing, mostly marginal; sm scrapes; spotted). *Sutton.* $160/£103

HEDRICK, U.P. (ed). Sturtevant's Notes on Edible Plants. Albany, 1919. Port. Gilt-stamped buckram (rubbed, worn; inner hinges cracked; sm tears, cl tape to gutter edge of tp). *Sutton.* $85/£55

HEDRICK, U.P. et al. The Vegetables of New York. Vol 1, Pts 1-4. Albany, 1928-31-34-37. 1 vol in 4. 136 color plts. Stiff wrappers (lt soiled; dampstaining Pt 3). Overall VG set. *Sutton.* $225/£145

Heedless Harry's Day of Disasters. London: Darton & Co, n.d. (ca 1850). Sm 4to. Hand-colored full-pg wood engr frontis pasted down on upper wrapper; 15pp; Fine hand-colored engrs. Pict stiff paper self-wrappers. Title on cvr reads: Fun for Little Folks. Wrapper edges lt dknd, else VF. *Hobbyhorse.* $300/£194

HEFFRON, RODERICK. Pneumonia with Special Reference to Pneumococcus Lobar Pneumonia. NY, 1939. 1st ed. (Ex-lib.) *Fye.* $100/£65

HEFNER, HUGH. That Toddlin' Town. Chicago: CHI Publishers, 1951. 1st ed, 1st bk. Fine in wraps (rubbed). *Beasley.* $200/£129

HEG, H.C. The Civil War Letters of Colonel Hans Christian Heg. Theodore C. Blegen (ed). Northfield, MN: Norwegian-American Hist Assoc, 1936. 1st ed. VG in dj (sl worn). *Lien.* $35/£23

HEGGEN, THOMAS and JOSHUA LOGAN. Mister Roberts. A Play. NY: Random House, (1948). 1st ed. Nice in dj (lt chipped). *Reese.* $25/£16

HEHN, V. The Wanderings of Plants and Animals from their First Home. J.S. Stallybrass (ed). London, 1888. 523pp. (Spine head sl worn; tp foxed.) *Wheldon & Wesley.* $62/£40

Heidenmauer. (By James Fenimore Cooper.) Phila: Carey & Lea, 1832. 1st Amer ed, 2nd ptg, w/2 bl leaves end Vol 2. 2 vols. 8vo. 226; 248pp. Orig grey-blue bds paper spine labels. Sl soiled, Vol 2 spine sl worn, else NF set. BAL 3858. *Chapel Hill.* $950/£613

HEILBRUN, CAROLYN G. The Garnett Family. London: Allen & Unwin, 1961. 1st ed. Fore-edge sl spotted, o/w VG in dj (price-clipped; spine sl faded). *Virgo.* $39/£25

HEILNER, VAN CAMPEN. Our American Game Birds. NY: Doubleday, (1946). Early rpt ed. Red cl. Fine in pict dj (soiled; lacks 3-inch piece rear panel). *Glenn.* $45/£29

HEILPRIN, ANGELO. The Eruption of Pelee. Geog Soc of Phila, 1908. 1st ed. 93 plts. Good. *Artis Books.* $50/£32

HEIM, ARNOLD and AUGUST GANSSER. The Throne of the Gods. NY: Macmillan, 1939. 1st ed. 220 photogravure plts, 2 fldg panoramas, 1 lg fldg map; teg. Grn cl. Fine. *House.* $120/£77

HEIN, O.L. Memories of Long Ago by an Old Army Officer. NY: Putnam's, 1925. 1st ed. VG. *Lien.* $85/£55

HEINE, HEINRICH. Poems. Louis Untermeyer (trans). NY: LEC, 1957. One of 1500. Signed by Fritz Kredel (illus). 1/2 grn calf, dec paper. NF (spine tips rubbed) in NF case. *Agvent.* $100/£65

HEINEMANN, LARRY. Close Quarters. NY: FSG, (1977). 1st ed. NF (sl browning to top, fore-edge) in dj. *Antic Hay.* $85/£55

HEINEMANN, LARRY. Paco's Story. NY: FSG, (1986). 1st ed. Mint in dj. *Jaffe.* $45/£29

HEINEMANN, LARRY. Paco's Story. NY, 1986. 1st ed. VG in VG dj. *Clark.* $23/£15

HEINLEIN, ROBERT A. Assignment in Eternity. Reading, PA: Fantasy Press, (1953). 1st ed. Currey's binding A. Brick red cl. Fine in dj (sl wear; abraded spine base). *Antic Hay.* $150/£97

HEINLEIN, ROBERT A. Assignment in Eternity. Fantasy Press, 1953. 1st ed. One of 500 subs issue signed. Spine lightened, else NF in dj. *Fine Books.* $500/£323

HEINLEIN, ROBERT A. Cat Who Walks Through Walls. Putnam, 1985. 1st ed, w/errata slip. Fine in dj. *Madle.* $30/£19

HEINLEIN, ROBERT A. Citizen of the Galaxy. NY: Scribner's, (1957). 1st ed. Fine in dj (1-inch closed tear, else Fine). *Godot.* $325/£210

HEINLEIN, ROBERT A. Citizen of the Galaxy. Scribners, 1957. 1st ed. VG in dj. *Madle.* $375/£242

HEINLEIN, ROBERT A. Double Star. Doubleday, 1956. 1st ed. Fine in NF dj (sm tears). *Fine Books.* $1,250/£806

HEINLEIN, ROBERT A. Farmer in the Sky. Scribners, 1950. 1st ed. Fine in dj (sm chip). *Madle.* $250/£161

HEINLEIN, ROBERT A. Farnham's Freehold. NY: Putnam's, (1964). 1st ed. Ink inscrip, o/w Fine in dj (price-clipped; spine worn). *Hermitage.* $350/£226

HEINLEIN, ROBERT A. Friday. NY: Holt Rinehart & Winston, (1982). 1st ed. Fine in dj. *Other Worlds.* $30/£19

HEINLEIN, ROBERT A. Friday. NY: Holt, (1982). 1st ed. One of 500 numbered, specially bound, signed. Gilt cl. Fine in slipcase. *Reese.* $125/£81

HEINLEIN, ROBERT A. Friday. NY: Holt Rinehart & Winston, (1982). 1st ed. One of 500 signed, numbered. Fine in slipcase (no dj as issued). *Other Worlds.* $275/£177

HEINLEIN, ROBERT A. The Green Hills of Earth. Shasta, 1951. 1st ed. Fine in dj (spine age-dknd). *Madle.* $200/£129

HEINLEIN, ROBERT A. Have Space Suit—Will Travel. Scribners, 1958. 1st ed. NF in dj (frayed). *Madle.* $375/£242

HEINLEIN, ROBERT A. I Will Fear No Evil. NY: Putnam, (1970). 1st ed. Spine cocked, else NF in VG + dj. *Other Worlds.* $75/£48

HEINLEIN, ROBERT A. I Will Fear No Evil. NY: Putnam's, (1970). 1st ed. Fine in dj (sl wear). *Levin.* $450/£290

HEINLEIN, ROBERT A. Job: A Comedy of Justice. NY: Ballantine, (1984). 1st ed. VF in dj. *Reese.* $20/£13

HEINLEIN, ROBERT A. Job: A Comedy of Justice. NY: Ballantine Books, (1984). Ltd ed one of 750. Signed. Fine; issued w/o dj in slipcase. *Bernard.* $150/£97

HEINLEIN, ROBERT A. The Man Who Sold the Moon. London: S&J, 1953. 1st UK ed. Fine in VG dj. *Lewton.* $57/£37

HEINLEIN, ROBERT A. The Moon is a Harsh Mistress. NY: Putnam's, (1966). 1st ed. 8vo. VG (fep browned) in dj (lt wear; few tiny tears). *Antic Hay.* $850/£548

HEINLEIN, ROBERT A. The Number of the Beast. NEL, 1980. 1st UK ed. Fine in dj. *Lewton.* $36/£23

HEINLEIN, ROBERT A. Orphans of the Sky. Putnams, 1964. 1st ed. NF in dj (sl edge-rubbed). *Madle.* $300/£194

HEINLEIN, ROBERT A. Podkayne of Mars. NY: Putnam's, (1963). 1st ed. Sl rubbing verso last text pg, o/w Fine in dj (sl wear). *Levin.* $850/£548

HEINLEIN, ROBERT A. Red Planet. Scribners, 1949. 1st ed. VG in dj (worn). *Madle.* $200/£129

HEINLEIN, ROBERT A. Rocket Ship Galileo. Scribners, 1947. 1st ed. Fine in dj (frayed). *Madle.* $750/£484

HEINLEIN, ROBERT A. The Rolling Stones. NY: Scribner's, (1952). 1st ed. Fine in dj (price-clipped, spine sl chipped, else Fine). *Godot.* $275/£177

HEINLEIN, ROBERT A. Sixth Column. Gnome, 1949. 1st ed. Fine in NF dj. *Aronovitz.* $285/£184

HEINLEIN, ROBERT A. Sixth Column. Gnome, 1949. 1st ed. Fine in Mint dj. *Madle.* $375/£242

HEINLEIN, ROBERT A. The Star Beast. NY: Scribner's, (1954). 1st ed. Fine in VG dj (snag rear panel; price-clipped; sm chip fr panel). *Antic Hay.* $150/£97

HEINLEIN, ROBERT A. The Star Beast. Scribners, 1954. 1st ed. Lt brn stain 1/2 pp, else VG + in NF dj. *Aronovitz.* $135/£87

HEINLEIN, ROBERT A. The Star Beast. Scribners, 1954. 1st ed. Fine in dj (sl soiled, frayed). *Madle.* $250/£161

HEINLEIN, ROBERT A. Starman Jones. Scribners, 1953. 1st ed. VG + in VG dj (lt wear, tear). *Aronovitz.* $165/£106

HEINLEIN, ROBERT A. Starman Jones. Scribners, 1953. 1st ed. NF in dj (sl rubbed, frayed). *Madle.* $225/£145

HEINLEIN, ROBERT A. Starship Troopers. NY: Putnam's, (1959). 1st ed. 8vo. Fine in dj (sl wear). *Antic Hay.* $950/£613

HEINLEIN, ROBERT A. Starship Troopers. Putnam, 1959. 1st ed. Signed post card laid in. Fine in dj. *Fine Books.* $1,375/£887

HEINLEIN, ROBERT A. Stranger in a Strange Land. Putnam, 1961. 1st ed. Pg edges trimmed, o/w VG in dj (frayed; spine faded). *Madle.* $300/£194

HEINLEIN, ROBERT A. Stranger in a Strange Land. NEL, 1975. 1st Eng hb ed. Fine in dj. *Fine Books.* $250/£161

HEINLEIN, ROBERT A. Time Enough for Love. NY: S&S, (1973). 1st ed. NF (sl cocked) in VG dj (short tears). *Between The Covers.* $100/£65

HEINLEIN, ROBERT A. Time Enough for Love: The Lives of Lazarus Long. NY: Putnam's, 1973. 1st ed. Fine in dj (sl wear, sm chip). *Levin.* $500/£323

HEINLEIN, ROBERT A. Tunnel in the Sky. Scribners, 1955. 1st ed. VG in NF dj (spine lifted off from sticker removal). *Aronovitz.* $125/£81

HEINLEIN, ROBERT A. The Unpleasant Profession of Jonathan Hoag. Hicksville: Gnome, (1959). 1st ed. Pg sl browned, o/w Fine in dj (sl wear). *Levin.* $80/£52

HEINLEIN, ROBERT A. Waldo and Magic, Inc. Doubleday, 1950. 1st ed. VF in NF dj. *Aronovitz.* $285/£184

HEISKELL, S.G. Andrew Jackson and Early Tennessee History. Nashville, TN: Ambrose Ptg Co, 1920-21. 2nd ed. 3 vols. Brn cl (spines dulled). VG set (offsetting, 2 names fep vol 3). *Chapel Hill.* $200/£129

HEISTER, LORENZ. Medical, Chirurgical, and Anatomical Cases and Observations.... George Wigman (trans). London: J. Reeves for C. Hitch et al, 1755. 1st ed in English. xxxii,708pp, 8 fldg plts. Contemp calf (recently rebacked; tp mtd w/loss of 2 letters, title vignette excised; lt dampstaining, foxing internally). *Goodrich.* $395/£255

HELD, JULIUS S. The Oil Sketches of Peter Paul Rubens. Princeton Univ Press, 1980. 2 vols. 71 plts; 528 plts (24 color). Sound in dj (sl torn). *Ars Artis.* $219/£141

HELD, JULIUS S. The Oil Sketches of Peter Paul Rubens. A Critical Catalogue. NJ: Princeton Univ, 1980. 2 vols. 24 color plts, 504 monochrome plts. VF set in Mint djs. *Europa.* $194/£125

HELD, RAY E. Public Libraries in California, 1849-1878. Berkeley/L.A.: Univ of CA, 1963. Gold-stamped cl. *Dawson.* $50/£32

HELFRITZ, HANS. The Yemen, A Secret Journey. M. Heron (trans). London: Allen & Unwin, 1958. 1st ed. VG in dj. *Worldwide.* $30/£19

HELLE, ANDRE. Big Beasts and Little Beasts. Frederick A. Stokes, 1924. 12mo. 80pp, 20 color plts by Andre Helle. Brown cl, pict onlay. Good (fr fly creased, erasures, corners worn). *Davidson.* $150/£97

HELLER, JOSEPH. Catch-22: A Dramatization. NY: Delacorte, 1973. 1st ed. VG + in VG + dj (price-clipped). *Lame Duck.* $200/£129

HELLER, JOSEPH. Good as Gold. NY: S&S, (1979). 1st ed, trade issue. Fine in dj. *Godot.* $30/£19

HELLER, JOSEPH. Good as Gold. NY: S&S, 1979. 1st ed. Signed. Fine in dj. *Cady.* $25/£16

HELLER, JOSEPH. Something Happened. NY: Knopf, 1974. 1st ed. Signed. Fine in dj. *Cady.* $30/£19

HELLER, JOSEPH. We Bombed in New Haven. NY: Knopf, 1968. 1st ed. Fine in VG dj. *Revere.* $40/£26

HELLER, JOSEPH. We Bombed in New Haven. NY: Knopf, 1968. 1st ed. Signed. Fine in dj. *Antic Hay.* $75/£48

HELLER, JULES. Papermaking. NY: Watson Guptill, (1978). 1st ed. Fine in dj. *Oak Knoll.* $45/£29

HELLERMAN, TONY. Words, Weather and Wolfmen. Gallup: Southwesterner/Books, 1989. 1st ed. One of 350 numbered, signed by author, Franklin, Bulow. VF in dj. *Mordida.* $125/£81

HELLMAN, GEORGE S. The True Stevenson. A Study in Clarification. Boston, 1925. #173/250. Uncut. Fine (sl sunned, bkpl). *Polyanthos.* $50/£32

HELLMAN, LILLIAN. Candide. A Comic Operetta. NY: Random House, (1957). 1st ed. Fine in dj (lt used). *Dermont.* $45/£29

HELM, MacKINLEY. Fray Junipero Serra. The Great Walker. Stanford Univ Press, 1956. 1st ed. Frontis port. Dec cl. Fine in Good+ dj. *Connolly.* $65/£42

HELMERS, DOW. Historic Alpine Tunnel. Denver: Sage Books, (1963). 1st ed. #363 of unstated limitation. Signed. Brn cl. Fine in VG + dj. *Harrington.* $45/£29

HELMUTH, WILLIAM. A Treatise on Diphtheria. St. Louis, 1842. 1st ed. 125pp. VF. *Fye.* $100/£65

HELPRIN, MARK. A Dove of the East and Other Stories. London: Hamish Hamilton, (1976). 1st Eng ed, 1st bk. As New in dj. *Heller.* $55/£35

HELPRIN, MARK. A Dove of the East. Knopf, 1975. 1st ed, 1st bk. NF in NF dj. *Bishop.* $60/£39

HELPRIN, MARK. Swan Lake. Houghton Mifflin, 1989. 1st ed. Fine. *Bishop.* $25/£16

HELPS, A. Realmah. Roberts Brothers, 1869. 1st Amer ed. Few pp opened w/lt loss of margins, else VG. *Aronovitz.* $90/£58

HELPS, ARTHUR. The Life of Hernando Cortes. London, 1896. 2 vols. xiv,277pp + (xii)pub's list; vii,307pp + (xii)pub's list. (Spines sl rubbed.) *Edwards.* $28/£18

HELVENSTON, HAROLD. Scenery. A Manual of Scene Design. Stanford, CA: Stanford Univ, 1931. 1st ed. Beige cl. Good in dj (sl chipped, soiled). *Karmiole.* $45/£29

HEMINGWAY, ERNEST. Across the River and into the Trees. London: Cape, (1950). Pict dj, sl edge chipping, o/w VG (inscrip). *Schoyer.* $125/£81

HEMINGWAY, ERNEST. Across the River and into the Trees. Cape, 1950. 1st ed, Australian issue. VG in VG dj (wear; spine chipped). *Fine Books.* $85/£55

HEMINGWAY, ERNEST. Across the River and into the Trees. Scribners, 1950. 1st ed. Photo laid in. NF in VG + dj (short closed tears). *Fine Books.* $90/£58

HEMINGWAY, ERNEST. Across the River and Into the Trees. Cape, 1950. 1st UK ed. VG in dj (sl rubbed, browned). *Williams.* $85/£55

HEMINGWAY, ERNEST. By-Line. London: Collins, 1968. 1st UK ed. NF in dj (price-clipped). *Williams.* $47/£30

HEMINGWAY, ERNEST. By-Line: Selected Articles and Dispatches of Four Decades. William White (ed). London: Collins, 1968. 1st ed. Nice in dj. *Patterson.* $54/£35

HEMINGWAY, ERNEST. Collected Poems. SF, 1960. Pirated ed. Port opposite tp. '50 cents' ptd on back cvr. VG in ptd wraps (sticker shadow). *Revere.* $30/£19

HEMINGWAY, ERNEST. Death in the Afternoon. NY: Scribner's, 1932. 1st ed. Frontis. 1979 invoice laid in. Gilt cl. Bkpl, edges lt rubbed, o/w VG in Good dj (old external tape mends top edge; crack along joint). *Reese.* $400/£258

HEMINGWAY, ERNEST. Death in the Afternoon. NY: Scribner, 1932. 1st ed. 4to. Color frontis. Black cl, gilt-dec spine. Fine in Fine pict dj (corner-clipped; lt rubbed). *Chapel Hill.* $1,500/£968

HEMINGWAY, ERNEST. Death in the Afternoon. Cape, 1932. 1st Eng ed. VG + in VG dj (sl worn). *Fine Books.* $375/£242

HEMINGWAY, ERNEST. Death in the Afternoon. Jonathan Cape, 1933. (2nd imp.) Frontis; 63 plts. (Ink name, date fr fly.) Dj (sl defective spine head, foot). *Bickersteth.* $54/£35

HEMINGWAY, ERNEST. A Farewell to Arms. Jonathan Cape, (1929). 1st British ed. (Spine faded; 2 lt spots lower cvr.) *Bickersteth.* $70/£45

HEMINGWAY, ERNEST. A Farewell to Arms. London, (1929). 1st Eng ed. *Waterfield.* $31/£20

HEMINGWAY, ERNEST. A Farewell to Arms. NY: Scribner's, 1929. 1st ed, 1st state w/o disclaimer added in 2nd ptg at Hemingway's request. Black cl, gold labels. Fine in Nice 1st state dj (chips). *Macdonnell.* $850/£548

HEMINGWAY, ERNEST. A Farewell to Arms. NY: Scribner, 1929. 1st ed. #184/510 specially bound; signed. 8vo. Unopened. Half vellum, bds w/morocco spine label. Fine in orig glassine dj (lacks top pieces), pub's slipcase (lt worn). *Chapel Hill.* $6,000/£3,871

HEMINGWAY, ERNEST. A Farewell to Arms. NY: Scribner, 1929. 1st ed. #448/510 numbered, signed. 3/4 vellum, grn bds, gilt. VG + in glassine dj, pub's black cl slipcase (worn). *Houle.* $3,750/£2,419

HEMINGWAY, ERNEST. A Farewell to Arms. NY: Scribner's, 1948. 1st illus ed. Dennis Rasmusson (illus). Paper spine label edge sl rubbed, else Fine in VG slipcase (lt sticker shadow). *Between The Covers.* $100/£65

HEMINGWAY, ERNEST. A Farewell to Arms. Scribners, 1948. 1st illus ed. D. Rasmusson (illus). Fine in slipcase as issued. *Fine Books.* $125/£81

HEMINGWAY, ERNEST. The Fifth Column and The First 49 Stories. Cape, 1939. 1st Eng ed. Contents Good (sl dull; back sl stained). *Whiteson.* $19/£12

HEMINGWAY, ERNEST. The Fifth Column and the First Forty Nine Stories. Cape, 1939. 1st Eng ed. NF in VG dj (wear; chip rear panel). *Fine Books.* $375/£242

HEMINGWAY, ERNEST. The Fifth Column and the First Forty-Nine Short Stories. London: Cape, 1939. 1st ed. Fine in Fine pict dj. *Patterson.* $155/£100

HEMINGWAY, ERNEST. The Fifth Column and the First Forty-Nine Stories. NY: Scribner's, 1938. 1st ed. 8vo. Red cl. Very bright in dj (minor wear along edges; sm repaired edge tear). *Dermont.* $850/£548

HEMINGWAY, ERNEST. For Whom the Bell Tolls. Scribners, 1940. 1st ed. Moisture staining few pp, else VG. *Fine Books.* $45/£29

HEMINGWAY, ERNEST. For Whom the Bell Tolls. NY: Scribner's, 1940. 1st ed. VF in 1st issue dj (modest wear; sm chip rear left corner). *Dermont.* $175/£113

HEMINGWAY, ERNEST. For Whom the Bell Tolls. London: Cape, 1941. 1st ed. Fine in Fine pict dj. *Patterson.* $194/£125

HEMINGWAY, ERNEST. For Whom the Bell Tolls. London: Cape, 1941. 1st Eng ed. Sig, else VG in dj. *Limestone.* $385/£248

HEMINGWAY, ERNEST. For Whom the Bell Tolls. Princeton: Princeton Univ, 1942. One of 1500 numbered, signed. Spine sl sunned, o/w Fine in orig glassine remnants; slipcase (lt sunned). *Reese.* $250/£161

HEMINGWAY, ERNEST. The Garden of Eden. NY: Scribner's, 1986. 1st ed. Lt brn bds, beige cl spine. NF in dj. *Chapel Hill.* $40/£26

HEMINGWAY, ERNEST. Green Hills of Africa. NY/London, 1935. 1st ed. VG + (spine, edges lt faded) in VG dj (price-clipped; shelfworn edges, rubs at folds; age, handling soil to spine). *Mcclintock.* $235/£152

HEMINGWAY, ERNEST. The Hemingway Reader. NY, 1953. 1st collected ed. Fine in dj. *Argosy.* $60/£39

HEMINGWAY, ERNEST. In Our Time. Cape, 1926. 1st Eng ed. Spine extrems lightened, else VG + in dj (chipping spine extrems, corners). *Fine Books.* $1,250/£806

HEMINGWAY, ERNEST. Islands in the Stream. NY: Scribner's, (1970). 1st ed, rev copy w/slip tipped in (as issued). NF in dj (sl edgewear, faded; tiny nick spine head). *Antic Hay.* $85/£55

HEMINGWAY, ERNEST. Islands in the Stream. London: Collins, 1970. 1st ed. Fine in NF dj. *Dermont.* $40/£26

HEMINGWAY, ERNEST. Islands in the Stream. NY: Scribner's, 1970. 1st ed. Fine in dj (price-clipped). *Else Fine.* $50/£32

HEMINGWAY, ERNEST. Men Without Women. NY: Scribner's, 1927. 1st ed, 1st state. VG (name; corners lt bumped, faint cvr spots). *Else Fine.* $75/£48

HEMINGWAY, ERNEST. Men Without Women. Scribners, 1927. 1st ed. VG + in VG 2nd issue dj (3 sm chips). *Fine Books.* $875/£565

HEMINGWAY, ERNEST. A Moveable Feast. NY, (1964). 1st ed. Inscrip, else VG in dj (sl worn). *King.* $60/£39

HEMINGWAY, ERNEST. A Moveable Feast. NY: Scribners, (1964). 1st ed. Fine in NF dj (extrems lt rubbed). *Between The Covers.* $100/£65

HEMINGWAY, ERNEST. A Moveable Feast. London: Cape, 1964. 1st UK ed. Fine in dj (price-clipped). *Williams.* $28/£18

HEMINGWAY, ERNEST. The Nick Adams Stories. Scribners, 1972. 1st ed. Fine in NF dj. *Fine Books.* $65/£42

HEMINGWAY, ERNEST. The Old Man and the Sea. NY: Scribner's, 1952. 1st ed. VG (spine sl cocked) in VG dj (chipped; sl wear). *Revere.* $175/£113

HEMINGWAY, ERNEST. The Old Man and the Sea. NY: Scribner's, 1952. 1st ed. Sl spotted, else VG in dj. *Godot.* $275/£177

HEMINGWAY, ERNEST. The Old Man and the Sea. NY: Scribner's, 1952. 1st ed. Extrems lt worn, else VG in dj (lt worn, price-clipped). *Glenn.* $275/£177

HEMINGWAY, ERNEST. The Old Man and the Sea. London: Cape, 1952. 1st Eng ed, 1st state. Fine in color pict dj. *Limestone.* $95/£61

HEMINGWAY, ERNEST. The Old Man and the Sea. Cape, 1952. 1st Eng ed. Fine in dj. *Fine Books.* $125/£81

HEMINGWAY, ERNEST. Selected Letters: 1917-1961. Carlos Baker (ed). NY: Scribner's, (1981). 1st trade ed. NF in dj (tear; sl fade). *Antic Hay.* $35/£23

HEMINGWAY, ERNEST. Selected Letters: 1917-1961. Carlos Baker (ed). NY: Scribner's, (1981). Ltd ed of 500 numbered, signed by ed. Fine in glassine dj & slipcase. *Antic Hay.* $175/£113

HEMINGWAY, ERNEST. The Spanish War. London: Fact Monographs, #16, July 1938. 1st ed. Unusually Fine. *Patterson.* $147/£95

HEMINGWAY, ERNEST. The Sun Also Rises. Scribners, 1926. 1st ed. 2nd issue w/'stoppped' on pg 181 corrected. Good. *Fine Books.* $125/£81

HEMINGWAY, ERNEST. To Have and Have Not. Scribners, 1937. 1st ed. VG (sm scrape spine). *Fine Books.* $60/£39

HEMINGWAY, ERNEST. To Have and Have Not. NY: Scribner's, 1937. 1st ed. NF in VG dj (short tears, lt edgewear, else VG). *Godot.* $450/£290

HEMINGWAY, ERNEST. To Have and Have Not. NY: Scribner, 1937. 1st ed. 8vo. Black cl. Fine in Fine dj (price-clipped, lt rubbing). *Chapel Hill.* $750/£484

HEMINGWAY, ERNEST. To Have and Have Not. NY: G&D, n.d. (ca.1942). Reissue. Orange cl. Fine in dj. *Else Fine.* $75/£48

HEMINGWAY, ERNEST. The Torrents of Spring. London: Cape, (1933). 1st (UK) ed. (Sl foxed; backstrip faded; grubby.) *Petersfield.* $39/£25

HEMINGWAY, ERNEST. The Torrents of Spring. Crosby Continental Editions, 1931. 1st European ed. As New in glassine wraps. *Fine Books.* $325/£210

HEMINGWAY, ERNEST. Winner Take Nothing. NY/London: Scribner's, 1933. 1st ed. Gilt spine (lt rubbed), cvr labels. *Sadlon.* $60/£39

HEMINGWAY, ERNEST. Winner Take Nothing. Scribners, 1933. 1st ed. NF in VG+ dj. *Fine Books.* $495/£319

HEMINGWAY, ERNEST. Winner Take Nothing. NY: Scribner, 1933. 1st ed. 8vo. Black cl, gold paper labels. NF in VG dj (lt edgeworn, chips, tears). *Chapel Hill.* $500/£323

HEMINGWAY, ERNEST. Winner Take Nothing. NY: Scribner's, 1933. 1st ed. Sm insect holes fr outer hinge, rear bd, else Fine in NF dj. *Lame Duck.* $750/£484

HEMMINGS, JOHN. Monuments of the Incas. Boston: Little Brown/NYGS, (1982). 1st ed. Fine in dj. *Pharos.* $45/£29

HEMON, LOUIS. Maria Chapeldaine, a Tale of the St. John Country... W.H. Blake (trans). NY, 1924. 1st ed. *Hayman.* $15/£10

HEMSLEY, W.B. Handbook of Hardy Trees, Shrubs, and Herbaceous Plants. Boston, 1873. 1st Amer ed. xliii,687pp (foxed). Gilt-stamped cl (worn; frayed; fr inner joint cracked). *Sutton.* $90/£58

HEMSWORTH, H.W. (ed). Cuneorum Clavis. Chiswick Press, 1875. 160pp; 7 plts (3 fldg). Blue cl (spine age-dknd). *Moss.* $70/£45

HENDERSON, ALICE PALMER. The Ninety-First—The First at Camp Lewis. By Author, (1918). VG. *Perier.* $60/£39

HENDERSON, ARCHIBALD. Is Bernard Shaw a Dramatist? NY/London: Mitchell Kennerley, 1929. 1st ed. #142/1000. Grn cl, paper spine label. Sl faded, else Fine in glassine dj (chipped); VG pub's slipcase. *Chapel Hill.* $35/£23

HENDERSON, ARCHIBALD. Washington's Southern Tour 1791. Boston: Houghton Mifflin, 1923. 1st ptg. Cl, pict bds. VG. *Schoyer.* $65/£42

HENDERSON, CHARLES. Henderson's Picturesque Gardens and Ornamental Gardening Illustrated. NY: Peter Henderson, 1908. 1st ed. Mtd color illus. Sm dampstains fr cvr, else VG. *Cahan.* $75/£48

HENDERSON, DAVID. De Major of Harlem. NY: E.P. Dutton, 1970. 1st ed. Fine in dj. *Heller.* $35/£23

HENDERSON, EBENEZER. Iceland; or the Journal of a Residence in that Island, During the Years 1814 and 1815. Edinburgh: Oliphant, Waugh & Innes, 1818. 1st ed. 2 vols. (iii)-xvi,lxi,(1 blank),377; (iii-viii), 412,(1 directions to binder)pp; 15 plts, fldg map. (Lt foxing, lacks 1/2 titles.) Antique style 1/4 calf. Attractive set. *Lefkowicz.* $550/£355

HENDERSON, GEORGE C. Keys to Crookdom. NY: Appleton, 1924. 1st ed. Gilt foil law badge pasted to fep. Pict cl. VG. *Connolly.* $37/£24

HENDERSON, GEORGE FRANCIS ROBERT. Stonewall Jackson and the American Civil War. London: Longman's, Green, 1898. 1st ed. 2 vols. 2 ports, 26 maps. Later cl, lacks several maps, else NF. Presentation inscrip from Austen Chamberlain (Eng statesman) to Senator Frederic Hale. Howes H 408. *Mcgowan.* $150/£97

HENDERSON, J.T. Manual on Cattle. Atlanta, 1880. 191,(1)pp (paper dknd). Gilt-titled cl (recased, new end leaves); orig cl laid down. *Bohling.* $135/£87

HENDERSON, MRS. L.R. The Magic Aeroplane. Chicago: Reilly & Britton, (1911). 4to. 96pp, 6 color plts by Emile A. Nelson. Good (sl foxing, soil throughout; edges worn) in dj (torn). *Davidson.* $185/£119

HENDERSON, PETER. Garden and Farm Topics. NY, 1884. 1st ed. Gilt-stamped cl. VG. *Argosy.* $40/£26

HENDERSON, PETER. Gardening for Profit. NY: OJ, 1884. 276pp. Blue cl, gilt (spotted). *Bohling.* $35/£23

HENDERSON, PETER. Practical Floriculture. NY: OJ, 1928. New, enlgd ed. Fine in dj. *Second Life.* $35/£23

HENDERSON, ROBERT W. Early American Sport. NY: Grolier, 1937. One of 400. Fine. *Bowman.* $145/£94

HENDERSON, ROBERT W. Early American Sport. NY: A.S. Barnes, 1953. 2nd ed. 12 facs plts. Gray cl (spine dknd). VG. *House.* $75/£48

HENDERSON, W.A. The Housekeeper's Instructor. For Thomas Kelly, c. 1850. 17th ed. Frontis; 10 engr plts (sl foxed, margins soiled). Contemp sheep neatly re-backed w/red leather (corner rubbed). *Petersfield.* $152/£98

HENDERSON, WILLIAM. My Life as an Angler. London: W. Satchell, Peyton, 1879. (Damp spotted.) *Petersfield.* $81/£52

HENDERSON, ZENNA. Holding Wonder. Doubleday, 1971. 1st ed. Fine in dj. *Madle.* $65/£42

HENDLEY, GEORGE. Narratives of Pious Children. NY: Amer Tract Soc, n.d. (ca 1850). 12mo. 62pp. Gilt edges. Blind tooled cl, gilt dec. Fine (inscrip, lt foxing). *Hobbyhorse.* $55/£35

Hendrick Terbrugghen in America. Dayton: Dayton Art Inst, 1965. 16 illus. Good in wrappers. *Washton.* $30/£19

HENDRICK, BURTON J. The Lees of Virginia. Boston: Little, Brown, 1935. 1st ed. NF. *Mcgowan.* $85/£55

HENDRICKS, GORDON. Albert Bierstadt. NY: Abrams, 1973. 1st ed. 63 color plts. Name, else Fine in illus dj. *Cahan.* $175/£113

HENDRICKS, ROBERT J. Bethel and Aurora. NY: Press of Pioneers, 1933. 1st ed. Name, else VG. *Perier.* $60/£39

HENDRICKS, STANLEY. Astronauts on the Moon. Kansas City: Hallmark, n.d. (197?). 17x23 cm. 4 dbl-pg pop-ups, 7pp w/turn-wheels, pull-tabs. Al Muenchen (illus). Black illus bds. Dj. *Book Finders.* $80/£52

HENDRICKSON, HENRY. Out from the Darkness. Chicago: Western Sunday-School Pub Co, 1879. 399pp; port. (Cl rubbed.) *Schoyer.* $25/£16

HENDRIX, JOHN. If I Can Do It Horseback. Austin: Univ of TX, 1964. 1st ed. Dj. *Lambeth.* $35/£23

HENDY, PHILIP. Art Treasures of the National Gallery, London. NY: Abrams, (1958). 100 mtd color plts. VG in dj (torn); slipcase. *Argosy.* $75/£48

HENKER, O. Introduction to the Theory of the Spectacles. R. Kanthack (trans). Jena School of Optics, 1924. *Whitehart.* $62/£40

HENLE, FRITZ. The American Virgin Islands: A Photographic Essay. NY: Macmillan, 1971. 1st ed. 24 heliogravure photos tipped onto loose pp. Fine in cl emb folder (sl rubbed). *Cahan.* $75/£48

HENLEY, BETH. Crimes of the Heart. A Play. NY: Viking, (1982). 1st trade ed, clothbound issue. VF in dj. *Reese.* $45/£29

HENLEY, W.E. For England's Sake. David Nutt, 1900. 1st Eng ed. 12pp ads at rear. (Bkpl.) *Edrich.* $19/£12

HENNACY, AMMON. The Autobiography of a Catholic Anarchist. NY: Catholic Worker, 1946. One of 3000. NF in dj (lt used). *Beasley.* $50/£32

HENNEBERG, FREIHERR ALFRED VON. The Art and Craft of Old Lace. NY: Weyhe, (1931). 1st ed. 181 plts. Early leaves lt foxed, else VG in dj (rubbed), else VG in box (tattered). *Bookpress.* $235/£152

HENNESSY, E.F. and T.A. HEDGE. The Slipper Orchids. Randburg, RSA, 1989. 104 color plts. Fine in dj. *Brooks.* $65/£42

HENNIKER, FREDERICK. Notes, During a Visit to Egypt, Nubia, the Oasis, Mount Sinai, and Jerusalem. London: Murray, 1823. 1st ed. xi,340pp; engr tp; 3 plts (2 fldg). Recent 1/2 cl, marbled bds. 1st few leaves sl spotted, o/w VG ex-lib (emb stamp tp). *Worldwide.* $265/£171

HENOCH, EDWARD. Lectures on Children's Diseases. John Thomson (trans). London: New Sydenham Soc, 1889. 1st Eng ed. 2 vols. xv,493,(1); viii,455,(1)pp. Orig cl (crudely rebacked in cl tape). Good. *Glaser.* $95/£61

HENOCH, EDWARD. Lectures on Diseases of Children. NY, 1882. 1st Eng trans. 357pp. Good. *Fye.* $75/£48

HENREY, BLANCHE. British Botanical and Horticultural Literature Before 1800. London: OUP, 1975. 3 vols. 32 color plts. NF in slipcase. *Schoyer.* $400/£258

Henry Moore. Vol 2. Sculpture and Drawing Since 1948. London, 1955. 1st ed. (Ex-lib; tape mks.) Dj (sl soiled). *Edwards.* $62/£40

Henry Moore. Vol 2. Sculpture and Drawings 1949-1954. London, 1965. 2nd ed. (Ex-lib w/ink stamps, bkpl.) Dj (sl chipped). *Edwards.* $62/£40

Henry Moore. Vol 3. Sculpture 1955-64. Alan Bowness (ed). London, 1965. 1st ed. 179 plts, incl fldg color frontis. (Ex-lib w/ink stamp, bkpl.) Dj (sl chipped). *Edwards.* $62/£40

HENRY, ALFRED JUDSON. Climatology of the United States. Washington: GPO, 1906. Blind-stamped grn cl. (Worn, stained, hinges repaired, lib stamp, o/w Good.) *Knollwood.* $50/£32

HENRY, GERRIT. Janet Fish. NY, (1987). 70 tipped-in plts. VG. *King.* $150/£97

HENRY, J.T. The Early and Later History of Petroleum.... Phila, 1873. 1st ed. 607pp; 5 plts, 28 photo ports. Howes H 421. *Ginsberg.* $1,750/£1,129

HENRY, JOHN FRAZIER. Early Maritime Artists of the Pacific Northwest Coast, 1741-1841. Seattle: Univ of WA, (1984). VF in Fine dj. *Perier.* $35/£23

HENRY, JOHN JOSEPH. An Accurate and Interesting Account of the Hardships and Sufferings of That Band of Heroes.... Lancaster, (PA): William Greer, 1812. 1st ptg. 255pp. Full tree calf; joints split (but holding). Howes H 423. *Schoyer.* $175/£113

HENRY, MARGUERITE. Mustang. Chicago, 1966. 1st ed. VG. *October Farm.* $20/£13

HENRY, MARGUERITE. One Man's Horse. Chicago, 1977. 1st ed. Welsey Dennis (illus). VG. *October Farm.* $25/£16

HENRY, O. (Pseud of William Sydney Porter.) Cabbages and Kings. NY: McClure, Phillips, 1904. 1st ed, 1st issue, w/'McClure Phillips & Co.' on spine. 1st bk. Pict cl (spotting). Overall Good in leather/cl slipcase. BAL 16270. *Schoyer.* $150/£97

HENRY, O. (Pseud of William Sydney Porter.) Heart of the West. NY: McClure, 1907. 1st ed. Pict cl (spine lettering sl flaked). Overall VG in fldg case, leather/cl slipcase. *Schoyer.* $100/£65

HENRY, O. (Pseud of William Sydney Porter.) O. Henryana. GC: Doubleday, Page, 1920. 1st ed, ltd to 375. Parchment-backed bds, gilt. Nice. *Cady.* $50/£32

HENRY, O. (Pseud of William Sydney Porter.) Options. NY/London: Harper, 1909. 1st ed. (Spine sl lightened.) *Sadlon.* $30/£19

HENRY, O. (Pseud of William Sydney Porter.) Postscripts. NY: Harper, 1923. 1st ed. Spine sl faded, else Very Nice. *Hermitage.* $40/£26

HENRY, O. (Pseud of William Sydney Porter.) Rolling Stones. NY, 1912. 1st ed, 1st state. VG (sl color loss back cvr). *Bond.* $65/£42

HENRY, O. (Pseud of William Sydney Porter.) The Stories of O. Henry. LEC, 1965. 1st numbered ed of 1500 signed by John Groth (illus). Cl, gilt-stamped leather spine label. Fine in VG slipcase. *Authors Of The West.* $50/£32

HENRY, O. (Pseud of William Sydney Porter.) Strictly Business. NY: Doubleday, Page, 1910. 1st ed. Red ribbed cl, gilt, blind-stamped. Nice. *Cady.* $25/£16

HENRY, O. (Pseud of William Sydney Porter.) The Trimmed Lamp and Other Stories of the Four Million. NY: McClure, Phillips, 1907. 1st ed, 1st issue. (Spine sl lightened.) *Sadlon.* $35/£23

HENRY, O. (Pseud of William Sydney Porter.) The Trimmed Lamp and Other Stories of the Four Million. NY: McClure, Phillips, 1907. 1st ed. Frontis. Fine in fldg traycase, gilt red leather spine. BAL 16273. *Schoyer.* $150/£97

HENRY, O. (Pseud of William Sydney Porter.) The Voice of the City and Other Stories. NY: LEC, 1935. #1020/1500 signed by George Grosz (illus). Fine in slipcase. *Williams.* $248/£160

HENRY, O. (Pseud of William Sydney Porter.) The Voice of the City and Other Stories. NY: LEC, 1935. #904/1500 numbered, signed by George Grosz (illus). Fine in tissue wrapper & pub's slipcase. *Hermitage.* $350/£226

HENRY, O. (Pseud of William Sydney Porter.) The Voice of the City. NY: McClure, 1908. 1st ed, 1st issue. (Lt rubbed.) *Sadlon.* $40/£26

HENRY, O. (Pseud of William Sydney Porter.) Whirligigs. NY: Doubleday, Page, 1910. 1st ed. VG. *Hermitage.* $45/£29

HENRY, ROBERT S. The Armed Forces Institute of Pathology, Its First Century. Washington, 1964. *Bickersteth.* $39/£25

HENRY, ROBERT SELPH. Story of the Confederacy. Indianapolis, (1931). Gray cl. VG + . Howes H 426. *Bohling.* $40/£26

HENRY, STUART OLIVER. Conquering Our Great American Plains. NY: Dutton, (1930). Map. VG in dj (torn). Howes H 427. *Schoyer.* $65/£42

HENRY, W.S. Campaign Sketches of the War with Mexico. NY: Harper, 1847. 1st ed. Frontis, 331pp, 2 dbl-pg maps. 1/2 calf, marbled bds, morocco spine label. (19th cent bkpl, lt foxing.) Howes H 429. *Chapel Hill.* $175/£113

HENRY, WILL. From Where the Sun Now Stands. Random House, (1960). 1st ed. Dbl-pg map. Lt soiling, o/w VG in VG dj. *Oregon.* $50/£32

HENRY, WILL. The Gates of the Mountains. Random House, (1963). 1st ed. VG in VG dj. *Oregon.* $45/£29

HENRY, WILL. I, Tom Horn. Phila: Lippincott, (1975). 1st ed. NF (edges sl faded) in NF dj (spine sl faded). *Harrington.* $85/£55

HENRY, WILL. I, Tom Horn. Phila: Lippincott, (1975). 1st ed. VF in VF dj. *Oregon.* $95/£61

HENRY, WILL. One More River to Cross. NY: Random House, (1967). 1st ed. NF in NF dj. *Unger.* $100/£65

HENRY, WILL. Who Rides with Wyatt. NY: Random House, (1955). 1st ed. NF in NF dj (edge tear, soil). *Unger.* $100/£65

HENSON, JIM and J. BURNS. The Muppet Show Book. Abrams, 1978. 1st ed. Fine in dj. *Fine Books.* $75/£48

HENTY, G.A. Both Sides the Border, a Tale of Hotspur and Glendower. London: Blackie, 1899. 1st ed. 32pp ads at back. 12 illus by Ralph Peacock. Blue pict cl, gilt, beveled edges. Tp, eps sl foxed, o/w VG. *Petersfield.* $78/£50

HENTY, G.A. The Dash for Khartoum. London: Blackie, (n.d.). 10 full pg illus. VG. *Limestone.* $75/£48

HENTY, G.A. Redskin and Cow-Boy: A Tale of the Western Plains. Scribner's, 1891. 1st ed. Alfred Pearse (illus). Pict cvr. VG. *Authors Of The West.* $50/£32

HENTY, G.A. To Herat and Cabul. London: Blackie, 1902. 1st ed. 352,32pp, 8 plts by Charles M. Sheldon, map. Pict cl (sl rubbed), gilt. *Hollett.* $116/£75

HENTY, G.A. Under Wellington's Command. London: Blackie, 1899. 1st ed. 12 illus by Walter Paget. Pict blue cl (sl rubbing) stamped in gilt/red/white/black; edges stained grn. VG. *Houle.* $150/£97

HENTY, G.A. With Kitchener in the Soudan. London: Blackie, 1903. 1st ed. 384,32pp, 10 plts by William Rainey, 3 maps. Pict cl (lt faded, hinge cracked, repaired). *Hollett.* $132/£85

HENTY, G.A. Won by the Sword. London: Blackie, 1900. 1st ed. xvi,(iv),383,32pp, 12 plts by Charles M. Sheldon, 4 plans. Pict cl (sl rubbed), gilt. (Prelims sl spotted.) *Hollett.* $101/£65

HENTY, G.A. (ed). Yule Tide Yarns. NY: Longmans, Green, 1899. 1st ed, Amer issue. 45 plts. Pict-blocked terra cotta cl. Nice. *Cady.* $35/£23

HENTZ, J.P. Twin Valley: Its Settlement and Subsequent History, 1798-1882. Dayton, OH: Christian Pub House, 1883. 1st ed. xi,(xii),13-288pp; aeg. Later full morocco, gilt. Pp soiled, short tear 1 leaf repaired w/no loss, o/w VG. Howes H 432. *Cahan.* $150/£97

HEPBURN, IAN. Flowers of the Coast. London, 1952. 1st ed. 16 color, 40 plain plts. Good in dj. *Henly.* $74/£48

HEPBURN, IAN. Flowers of the Coast. London, 1952. 1st ed. Dj. *Edwards.* $93/£60

HEPPENSTALL, RAYNER. The Shearers. Hamish Hamilton, 1969. 1st ed. VG in dj. *Rees.* $16/£10

HEPWORTH, G.H. !!!. NY: Harper, 1881. 1st ed. Gilt dec cl (spine, extrems sl faded). Nice. *Reese.* $45/£29

HEPWORTH, GEORGE H. Through Armenia on Horseback. NY: Dutton, 1898. 1st ed. xii,355pp; engr tp; 25 plts; fldg map. Teg. Sl rubbed, o/w VG ex-lib (spine #). *Worldwide.* $85/£55

HERBERT, A.P. Holy Deadlock. London: methuen, (1934). 1st Eng ed. Red cl titled in blue. Nice. *Cady.* $15/£10

HERBERT, A.P. The Water Gipsies. London: Methuen, (1930). 1st ed. Fine in pict dj. *Pharos.* $60/£39

HERBERT, A.P. The Water Gipsies. London: Methuen, 1930. 1st ed, 1st issue w/#330 bottom last ad pg. (Edges spotted; cl sl faded). Pict red/grn dj (extrems sl worn). *Hollett.* $47/£30

HERBERT, AGNES. Casuals in the Caucasus. London: Lane, 1912. 1st ed. Teg. Blue pict cl. VG + (3 lib stamps). *Bowman.* $130/£84

HERBERT, AGNES. Two Dianas in Alaska. London: Lane, 1909. 1st ed. Teg. Pale grn cl, gilt title, horn decor. VG + (3 lib stamps removed). *Bowman.* $180/£116

HERBERT, AGNES. Two Dianas in Somaliland. London: Lane, 1908. 1st ed. Teg. Red cl, gilt title, dec. VG + (3 lib stamps removed). *Bowman.* $80/£52

HERBERT, EDWARD. The Autobiography.... London: Gregynog Press, 1928. #121/300 on handmade paper. 9 wood engrs by Horace Bray; teg, others uncut. Brn buckram, gilt. VG in slipcase. *Cox.* $465/£300

HERBERT, FRANK. Children of Dune. Putnam, 1976. 1st ed. NF in VG dj (wear, tear). *Aronovitz.* $100/£65

HERBERT, FRANK. Dune. Chilton, 1965. 1st ed. NF in VG dj (sl soiled; 4-inch closed tear). *Madle.* $900/£581

HERBERT, FRANK. Dune. Gollancz, 1966. 1st Eng ed. NF in dj (chip spine). *Fine Books.* $175/£113

HERBERT, FRANK. The God Makers. Putnam, 1972. 1st ed. Fine in VG + dj (sl wear). *Aronovitz.* $55/£35

HERBERT, FRANK. Soul Catcher. Putnam, 1972. 1st ed. Fine in dj. *Fine Books.* $48/£31

HERBERT, GEORGE B. Anecdotes of the Rebellion. Springfield, OH, 1894. 1st ed. 110,(2)pp. Orig ptd wrappers, loose, yet VG. *Mcgowan.* $37/£24

HERBERT, GEORGE. The Remains.... London: Pickering, 1841. 2nd Pickering ed w/half-title, allowing it to stand as vol 1 of the Works. Frontis. Orig cl, paper label. Good (sl mkd). *Cox.* $23/£15

HERBERT, GEORGE. The Temple. London: Pickering, 1844. 3rd Pickering ed. Frontis (sl spotted). With half-title, making it vol 2 of the Works. Blue cl (sl worn at backstrip), paper label (browned). *Cox.* $28/£18

HERBERT, GEORGE. The Temple. London: Bell & Daldy, 1857. Engr frontis; xiv, 350pp (label pasted-down). Contemp blind-ruled calf, gilt, beveled bds; raised bands, spine label. *Hollett.* $47/£30

HERBERT, JAMES. The Spear. London: New English Library, 1978. 1st UK ed. Fine in dj (price-clipped). *Williams.* $50/£32

HERBERT, WILLIAM. The History of the Twelve Great Livery Companies of London. London: by author, 1836-7. 2 vols. viii,(v-xii),496; 683pp. (Lacks 2pp Vol 1.) Uncut. Mod 1/2 calf, marbled bds (rebound, new eps). *Edwards.* $233/£150

HERBERTSON, AGNES GROZIER. Tinkler Johnny. London: Blackie & Son, n.d. 12mo. 239pp; 4 color plts, 20 text illus by Florence Harrison. Sage grn cl, pict paste label over bds. NF. *Drusilla's.* $75/£48

HERBST, JOSEPHINE. The Executioner Waits. NY: Harcourt, Brace, (1934). 1st ed. Bkpl, offset browning from clipping to feps, else VG in dj (soiled, nicks, else VG). *Godot.* $125/£81

HERBST, JOSEPHINE. Rope of Gold. NY: Harcourt, 1939. 1st ed. Fine in Fine dj (2 soiled spots rear panel). *Beasley.* $125/£81

HERFORD, OLIVER and JOHN CECIL HAY. Cupid's Almanac.... Boston: Houghton-Mifflin, (1908). Correct 1st ed w/o the date on tp. Fine in dj (soiled; circular cut-out). *Pharos.* $75/£48

HERFORD, OLIVER. An Alphabet of Celebrities. Boston: Small Maynard, 1899. 1st ed. NF. *Pharos.* $100/£65

HERGESHEIMER, JOSEPH. Cytherea. NY, 1922. #37/250 (of 270) signed. Uncut. NF (spine sunned). *Polyanthos.* $30/£19

HERGESHEIMER, JOSEPH. Tampico. NY: Knopf, 1926. 1st ed. Gilt-titled blue cl. NF in dj. *Cady.* $25/£16

HERING, OSWALD C. Concrete and Stucco Houses. NY: McBride, Nast & Co, 1912. 1st ed. Dec cl (sl rubbed; pencil scribbles fep). *Karmiole.* $45/£29

HERITAGE, LIZZIE. Cassell's Universal Cookery Book. London, 1901. 12 color plts. (Upper hinge sl cracked; feps lt browned; sl bumped.) *Edwards* $132/£85

HERLIHY, JAMES LEO. Midnight Cowboy. NY: S&S, (1965). 1st ed. VG in dj. *Houle.* $125/£81

HERLIHY, JAMES LEO. Midnight Cowboy. NY, 1965. 1st ed. Sl rubbed, o/w VG in dj. *Rees.* $47/£30

HERLOTS, G.A.C. Hong Kong Birds. (Hong Kong, 1967.) 2nd ed. Fine in dj. *Petersfield.* $62/£40

HERMAN, VICTOR. Coming Out of the Ice, an Unexpected Life. NY: Harcourt, 1979. Inscribed. VG in VG dj. *Peninsula.* $37/£24

HERMAN, ZVI. Peoples, Seas, and Ships. London: Phoenix House, (1966). 10 color plts. (Sig.) Dj. *Archaeologia.* $95/£61

HERMANN, LUKE. British Landscape Painting of the Eighteenth Century. NY, 1974. 136 plts (16 color). Good. *Washton.* $90/£58

Hermit: Or, the Unparallel'd Sufferings and Surprising Adventures of Mr. Philip Quarll.... (By Peter Longueville). London, 1780. 12th ed. xii,262pp. Contemp calf, leather label. VG (lt foxing, soiling). *Reese.* $500/£323

HERNDON, SARAH RAYMOND. Days on the Road. Crossing the Plains in 1865. NY: Burr Ptg House, 1902. Frontis port. VG (extrems lt rubbed). Howes H 439. *Bohling.* $200/£129

HERNDON, SARAH RAYMOND. Days on the Road. Crossing the Plains in 1865. NY: Burr, 1902. 1st ed. Good (hinge cracked; edgeworn). Howes H 439. *Parker.* $150/£97

HERNDON, SARAH RAYMOND. Days on the Road. Crossing the Plains in 1865. NY: Burr Ptg House, 1902. 1st ed. Frontis port. Eps, 1/2 title very browned, o/w VG. Howes H 439. *Second Life.* $265/£171

HERNDON, WM. LEWIS and LARDNER GIBBON. Exploration of the Valley of the Amazon. Washington: Robert Armstrong (vol 2, A.O.P. Nicholson), 1854. 2 vols. iv,417; xi,339pp, 52 litho plts, 2 map cases (one w/3 fldg engr maps, one w/2 lg fldg maps). Blind-stamped cl (spines sunned; dampstains through 1st 3rd vol 1). *Schoyer.* $300/£194

HERNMARCK, CARL. The Art of the European Silversmith 1430-1830. London/NY, 1977. 2 vols. 1001 plts (some worn due to previous adhesion to opposite pg). Djs. *Edwards.* $155/£100

HEROLD, J. CHRISTOPHER. Bonaparte in Egypt. London: Hamish Hamilton, (1963). 4 maps. (Sig.) Dj (tattered). *Archaeologia.* $35/£23

HERON-ALLEN, ED. Violin Making, as It Was and Is.... London/Melbourne: Ward, Locke, (1885). 2nd ed. Fine in dj. *Glenn.* $120/£77

HERR, MICHAEL. Dispatches. NY: Knopf, 1977. Taiwan piracy issue. VG in dj. *Aka.* $35/£23

HERRELL, WALLACE. Penicillin and Other Antibiotic Agents. Phila, 1945. 1st ed. Good. *Fye.* $50/£32

HERRICK, C.L. The Mammals of Minnesota. Minneapolis, 1892. 301pp; 8 plts (1 color). Good (sl faded; ex-lib). *Wheldon & Wesley.* $31/£20

HERRICK, ROBERT. The Memoirs of an American Citizen. NY: Macmillan, 1905. 1st ed. VG (hinges going). *Beasley.* $65/£42

HERRIGEL, EUGEN. Zen in the Art of Archery. NY: Pantheon, (1953). 1st ed. VG in Good dj. *Blue Dragon.* $30/£19

HERRING, P.F. (ed). Joyce's Notes and Early Drafts for Ulysses. Charlottesville: Univ Press of VA, (1977). 1st ed. Gilt cl. Fine, as issued, w/o dj. *Reese.* $30/£19

HERRING, P.F. (ed). Joyce's Ulysses Notesheets in the British Museum. Charlottesville: Univ Press of VA, (1972). 1st ed. Fine in dj (sl rubbed). *Reese.* $30/£19

HERRING, PAUL. The Midnight Murder. Phila: Lippincott, 1932. 1st Amer ed. Fine in dj (closed tears; sl corner wear). *Mordida.* $40/£26

HERRING, RICHARD. Paper and Paper Making, Ancient and Modern. London: Longman et al, 1863. 3rd ed. xix,134,(2)pp (prelims foxed; lt rubbed). *Oak Knoll.* $300/£194

HERRLINGER, ROBERT. History of Medical Illustration from Antiquity to A.D. 1600. (NY): Medicina Rara, (1970). 1st Amer ed. 32 plts. Linen. VF in slipcase. *Glaser.* $150/£97

HERRLINGER, ROBERT. History of Medical Illustration from Antiquity to A.D. 1600. NY: Medicina Rara, 1970. Nice in slipcase (sl sunned). *Goodrich.* $135/£87

HERRMANN, JOHN. The Salesman. NY: S&S, 1939. 1st ed. Fine in NF dj (sl wear spine ends). *Beasley.* $150/£97

HERRMANN, LUKE. Ruskin and Turner. London: Faber, 1968. 4 color plts, 48 monochrome. Ex-lib, sm stamp tp, sticker cvr, o/w Fine. *Europa.* $19/£12

HERROD-HEMPSALL, WILLIAM. Bee-Keeping, New and Old. London: Bee Journal, 1930. Vol 1 (only). Frontis port. (Eps lt spotted, content leaf detached; upper hinge cracked, sl shaken; spine lt faded, dampstained.) *Edwards.* $47/£30

HERSEY, JOHN. A Bell for Adano. NY, 1944. 1st ed. VG in dj. *Argosy.* $75/£48

HERSEY, JOHN. A Bell for Adano. London: Gollancz, 1945. 1st British ed. VG in dj (chipped). *Pettler.* $22/£14

HERSEY, JOHN. Hiroshima. Knopf, 1946. 1st ed. VG in VG dj. *Bishop.* $37/£24

HERSEY, JOHN. Hiroshima. NY: Knopf, 1946. 1st ed. Sm smudge to fr 2 blank pp, else Fine in NF dj (sl rubbing). *Between The Covers.* $65/£42

HERSEY, JOHN. Hiroshima. NY: LEC, 1983. One of 1500. Signed by Hersey, Robert Penn Warren (intro), and Jacob Lawrence (illus). 8 silk-screens. Emb title, full black leather. Fine in cl slipcase. *Cahan.* $650/£419

HERSEY, JOHN. The Marmot Drive. Knopf, 1953. 1st ed. VG + in VG dj. *Bishop.* $20/£13

HERSEY, JOHN. Men on Bataan. Knopf, 1942. 1st ed, 1st bk. VG + (name) in VG dj. *Bishop.* $120/£77

HERSEY, JOHN. A Single Pebble. NY: Knopf, 1956. 1st ed. Dec cl. NF in dj. *Sadlon.* $35/£23

HERSEY, JOHN. The Wall. NY: Knopf, 1950. 1st ed. Teal cl. Name, else Fine in NF dj. *Chapel Hill.* $30/£19

HERSEY, JOHN. The Wall. NY: LEC, 1957. One of 1500 numbered, signed by William Sharp (illus). 12 aquatints. VG in slipcase. *Argosy.* $100/£65

HERTZ, HEINRICH. Electric Waves.... D.E. Jones (authorized English trans). London, 1893. 1st ed in English. 279pp. VG. *Argosy.* $175/£113

HERVEY, HARRY. Barracoon. London, n.d. 1st ed. Fine in Fine dj. *Mcgowan.* $37/£24

HERVEY, JOHN. The American Trotter. NY: Coward McCann, 1947. 1st ed. VG in Good dj. *October Farm.* $125/£81

HERZOG, MAURICE. Annapurna. Nea Morin & Janet Adam Smith (trans). London: Cape & The Book Soc, 1952. 28 plts. VG in dj (sl worn). *Hollett.* $39/£25

HERZSTEIN, ROBERT. The War That Hitler Won. Putnam's, 1977. 1st ed. NF in NF dj. *Bishop.* $20/£13

HESS, ALFRED. Rickets Including Osteomalacia and Tetany. Phila, 1929. 1st ed. 485pp. *Fye.* $175/£113

HESS, HANS. George Grosz. London: Studio Vista, 1974. 1st Eng ed. 10 b/w photos. Fine in dj. *Ulysses.* $85/£55

HESS, THOMAS. Willem de Kooning. NY: MOMA, 1968. VG in stiff ptd wrappers. *Argosy.* $50/£32

HESSE, ERICH. Narcotics and Drug Addiction. NY, 1946. Good in dj. *Fye.* $35/£23

HESSE, HERMANN. The Glass Bead Game. NY, 1969. 1st Amer ed. NF in dj (sm mended tear, price-clipped). *Polyanthos.* $60/£39

HESSE, HERMANN. Klingsor's Last Summer. Cape, 1971. 1st Eng ed. Good in dj (torn). *Whiteson.* $19/£12

HESSE, HERMANN. Siddhartha. Hilda Rosner (trans). (NY: New Directions, 1951.) 1st Amer ed. Fine in dj (edges lt rubbed). *Reese.* $125/£81

HETHERINGTON, A.L. The Early Ceramic Wares of China. London, 1922. Color frontis, 44 plts. Fore, lower edges uncut. (Cl sl sunned lower bd, edges; spine head sl chipped.) Internally VG. *Edwards.* $132/£85

HEUSINGER, EDWARD W. Early Explorations and Mission Establishments in Texas. San Antonio: Naylor Co, 1936. 1st ed. Dk red cl. Bkpl, inkstamps fep, else VG in dj (worn, soiled). *Chapel Hill.* $100/£65

HEUTERMAN, T. Moveable Type: Biography of Legh R. Feeman. IA State Univ Press, 1979. Fine in dj. *Moss.* $25/£16

HEUVELMANS, BERNARD. On the Track of Unknown Animals. NY: Hill & Wang, 1959. 1st ed. Grn cl. Fine in VG dj. *House.* $75/£48

HEWARD, CONSTANCE. Ameliaranne Goes Touring. London: Harrap, 1941. 1st Eng ed. 8vo. Unpaginated, 29 full-pg color illus by S.B. Pearse. VG in dj (lt torn). *Davidson.* $75/£48

HEWER, H.R. British Seals. London, 1974. 1st ed. Dj. *Edwards.* $90/£58

HEWETT, EDGAR L. The Chaco Canyon and Its Monuments. (Albuquerque): Univ of NM, (1936). Frontis map. Navy cl. VG in VG + dj. *Bohling.* $85/£55

HEWETT, EDGAR L. The Chaco Canyon and Its Monuments. (N.p.): Univ of NM, (1936). 1st ed. Blue cl. Fine; fr panel, flap orig dj laid in. *Harrington.* $70/£45

HEWETT, EDGAR L. and BERTHA P. DUTTON. The Pueblo Indian World. (Albuquerque): Univ of NM Press, 1945. 1st ed. 2 fldg maps. Blue cl. Fine in VG + dj (lt chipped, spotted). *Harrington.* $60/£39

HEWISON, JAMES KING. Covenanters: A History of the Church in Scotland from the Reformation to the Revolution. Glasgow: John Smith, 1908. 1st ed. 2 vols. Frontis,16 plts; frontis,18 plts. Edges, spines faded; lt rubbed, else VG. *Cahan.* $85/£55

HEWITSON, WILLIAM C. Coloured Illustrations of the Eggs of British Birds. London, 1846. 2nd ed. 2 vols. xvi,223; 243pp, 131 color plts. Marbled eps, edges (lt foxed). Orig 1/2 calf (surface loss), raised bands, gilt (vol 2 chipped spine; sl rubbed). *Edwards.* $155/£100

HEWLETT, MAURICE. Songs and Meditations. Westminster: Constable, 1896. 1st ed, probable 1st binding. Polished brn buckram, gilt. VG (extrems sl rubbed). *Reese.* $50/£32

HEWSON, J.B. A History of the Practice of Navigation. Glasgow: Brown, Son & Ferguson, (1951). 1st ed. *Lefkowicz.* $50/£32

HEWSON, JAMES. Every Man His Own Lawyer.... Newark: Aaron Guest, 1841. Contemp sheep (worn). Decent. *Boswell.* $150/£97

HEWSON, WILLIAM. The Works. George Gulliver (ed). London: Sydenham Soc, 1846. Engr frontis port, lvi,360pp; 8 plts. Orig dk grn cl, rebacked preserving spine. Lt spotting frontis, plts; sm lib stamps, o/w Very Clean. *White.* $116/£75

HEWSON, WILLIAM. The Works. George Gulliver (ed). London: Sydenham Soc, 1846. Port; 8 plts. VG. *Argosy.* $150/£97

HEYDENREICH, LUDWIG. Leonardo da Vinci. London/NY/Basel, 1954. 1st Eng ed. Fine in dj. *Europa.* $70/£45

HEYE, GEORGE G. Certain Artifacts from San Miguel Island, California. NY: Museum of Amer Indian, Heye Foundation, 1921. Ptd wrappers (spine repaired, orig spine laid down). *Dawson.* $100/£65

HEYEN, WILLIAM. Long Island Light. NY: Vanguard, (1979). Ltd to 250 numbered, signed. Fine in dj & slipcase. *Antic Hay.* $50/£32

HEYEN, WILLIAM. My Holocaust Songs. Concord, NH: William B. Ewert, 1980. Ltd to 180 numbered, signed. Mint in acetate dj. *Antic Hay.* $45/£29

HEYEN, WILLIAM. The Swastika Poems. NY: Vanguard, (1977). 1st ed. Fine in dj. *Antic Hay.* $20/£13

HEYERDAHL, THOR. The Art of Easter Island. GC: Doubleday, 1975. 1st ed. 336 plts. Lt grn linen. Good in dj. *Karmiole.* $150/£97

HEYLIGA, WILLIAM. Fighting Blood. Goldsmith, 1936. 1st ed. Fine in dj (sl chipped). *Madle.* $20/£13

HEYMAN, THERESE THAU. Celebrating a Collection: The Work of Dorothea Lange. Oakland: Oakland Museum, 1978. 1st ed. Fine in stiff wrappers. *Cahan.* $40/£26

HEYWARD, DuBOSE. Angel. Doran, 1926. Carolina ed w/tipped in plt, signed. #5 of unknown #. Corner wear; spine label chip, else VG. *Fine Books.* $125/£81

HEYWARD, DuBOSE. Porgy. NY: Doran, (1925). 1st ed. Inscribed. Black cl stamped in gold. Sm dent top rear cvr, else NF. *Chapel Hill.* $200/£129

HEYWARD, DuBOSE. Skylines and Horizons. NY: Macmillan, 1924. 1st ed, inscribed. Blue cl, paper cvr label. Fine in dj (sm chips spine ends). *Chapel Hill.* $325/£210

HEYWARD, DuBOSE. Skylines and Horizons. NY, 1929. Mild ep tanning, else Fine. *Bond.* $35/£23

HIAASEN, CARL and WILLIAM D. MONTALBANO. A Death in China. NY: Atheneum, 1984. 1st ed. Fine in dj. *Mordida.* $175/£113

HIAASEN, CARL and WILLIAM D. MONTALBANO. Trap Line. NY: Atheneum, 1982. 1st Amer ed. Fine in dj. *Between The Covers.* $350/£226

HIAASEN, CARL. Double Whammy. NY: Putnam's, 1987. 1st ed. VF in dj (1/2-inch edgetear rear). *Else Fine.* $60/£39

HIAASEN, CARL. Skin Tight. NY: Putnam's, 1989. 1st ed. Fine in Fine dj. *Revere.* $30/£19

HIAASEN, CARL. Skin Tight. NY: Putnam's, 1989. 1st ed. Review copy. VF in dj. *Else Fine.* $95/£61

HIAASEN, CARL. Tourist Season. NY: Putnam, 1986. 1st ed. Fine (sm spot fep) in dj (2 lt creases). *Janus.* $50/£32

HIAASEN, CARL. Tourist Season. NY: Putnam's, 1986. 1st ed. VF in dj. *Mordida.* $100/£65

HIBBARD, HOWARD. Michelangelo. NY, n.d. (ca 1978). Good in dj. *Washton.* $45/£29

HIBBEN, FRANK C. Prehistoric Man in Europe. Norman: Univ of OK, 1958. 1st ed. 24 plts. Fine in Good+ dj. *Connolly.* $27/£17

HIBBEN, PAXTON. Henry Ward Beecher: An American Portrait. NY: Geo. H. Doran, 1927. 1st ed. Frontis port, 22 plts. Textured cl (wear). Pencil notes rear blank ep, else VG. *Connolly.* $42/£27

HIBBERD, SHIRLEY. The Fern Garden. London: Groombridge, n.d. (1850). New Ed. vi,148pp + 6pp ads, 2 color plts. Gilt-dec cvr, spine. *Quest.* $60/£39

HIBBERD, SHIRLEY. Field Flowers. London: Groombridge & Sons, 1870. 1st ed. iv,156pp, 8 color plts, 90 wood engrs. Aeg. Gilt-dec cl. Hinge starting, else Fine. *Quest.* $115/£74

HIBBERD, SHIRLEY. The Rambling Botanist. London: Groombridge, n.d. (1870). 148pp + 4pp ads, 16 color plts. Aeg. Gilt-dec pict cvr. Inner hinge cracked; fep neatly removed, else VG. *Quest.* $165/£106

HIBBERT, CHRISTOPHER (ed). The Wheatley Diary. London, 1964. 1st ed. Frontis; 16 plts (6 colored). VG in dj. *Edwards.* $47/£30

HICHBORN, PHILIP. Report on European Dockyards. Washington: GPO, 1889. 90pp; 53 plts (25 fldg). 1/2 sheep (dried). Good. *Lefkowicz.* $200/£129

HICHENS, ROBERT. Egypt and Its Monuments. NY: Century, 1908. 1st ed. Orange cl, gilt; teg. Fine. *Karmiole.* $50/£32

HICKERSON, THOMAS FELIX. The Faulkner Feuds. Chapel Hill, NC: Colonial Press, ca 1964. 1st ed. VG in orig ptd wrappers. *Mcgowan.* $45/£29

HICKIN, N.E. The Natural History of an English Forest: the Wild Life of Wyre. London, 1971. *Wheldon & Wesley.* $31/£20

HICKMAN, PEGGY. Silhouettes. NY: St. Martin's, 1975. 1st ed. Fine in Fine dj. *Glenn.* $25/£16

HICKMAN, WILLIAM. Brigham's Destroying Angel. NY: Geo. A. Crofutt, 1872. 1st ed. 219pp + 5pp ads. Black/gold-stamped cl (worn, spotted; rep, final leaf excised; marginal tears). *Dawson.* $100/£65

HICKMAN, WILLIAM. Brigham's Destroying Angel. Salt Lake, 1904. Frontis. Dec wraps. Sm piece missing fr wrap; sl cocked, o/w VG+. *Benchmark.* $47/£30

HICKS, EDWIN P. Belle Starr and Her Pearl. Little Rock: Pioneer, 1963. 1st ed. Signed, inscribed. Purple cl (lt soil, edgewear). *Glenn.* $65/£42

HICKS, GRANVILLE. One of Us. The Story of John Reed. NY: Equinox Cooperative Press, (1935). 1st ed. 30 lithos by Lynd Ward. Fine in dj (sl tanned). *Reese.* $125/£81

Hide and Seek, A National Geographic Action Book. Nat'l Geographic Soc, 1985. 22x23 cm. 6 pop-ups, pull-tabs, Barbara Gibson (illus). Glazed pict bds. VG. *Book Finders.* $35/£23

HIEOVER, HARRY. (Pseud of Charles Bindley). The Hunting-Field. London: Longman et al, 1850. 1st ed. xvi,222 + ,(2),32pp ads, 2 engr plts. Red leather-backed grn ribbed bds; gilt vignette; patterned eps. Plts sl foxed, else Very Nice. *Cady.* $60/£39

HIEOVER, HARRY. (Pseud of Charles Bindley.) Practical Horsemanship. London: Longman, 1850. xix,213,32pp pub's ads; engr frontis, 1 other plt (both lt spotted). Orig 1/4 leather w/grn cl cvrs; gilt emb fr cvr; rebacked w/spine laid down. *White.* $54/£35

HIEOVER, HARRY. (Pseud of Charles Bindley). The Sportsman's Friend in a Frost. London, 1857. 416pp. (Spine repaired.) *Argosy.* $85/£55

Hieroglyphick Bible; or Selected Passages in the Old and New Testaments.... Hartford: S. Andrus, 1847. 12mo. vii,125pp. Woodcut 1/2 title, full-pg frontis. Cuts VF. New eps. Tooled grn cl on bds, dec gilt title upper bd. VG (edges, corners rubbed; spine crowns soiled, chipped). *Hobbyhorse.* $175/£113

HIGGINBOTHAM, DON. Daniel Morgan. Chapel Hill: UNC Press, (1961). 1st ed. Frontis port. Brn cl. NF in VG dj (closed tears). *Chapel Hill.* $55/£35

HIGGINS, ANTHONY. New Castle, Delaware: 1651-1939. Boston: Houghton Mifflin, 1939. 1st ed. Ltd to 765 signed. 48 collotype plts. Fine. *Cahan.* $100/£65

HIGGINS, C. Harold and Maude. Lippincott, 1971. 1st ed. Fine in VG + dj (3 closed tears). *Fine Books.* $37/£24

HIGGINS, GEORGE V. The Friends of Eddie Coyle. NY: Knopf, 1972. 1st ed. Signed. VG in NF dj. *Revere.* $40/£26

HIGGINS, GEORGE V. The Friends of Eddie Coyle. Knopf, 1972. 1st US ed. NF in dj. *Lewton.* $65/£42

HIGGINS, GEORGE V. A Year Or So with Edgar. Harper & Row, 1979. 1st US ed. NF in dj. *Williams.* $23/£15

HIGGINS, JACK. Day of Judgment. London: Collins, 1978. 1st ed. Fine in dj (price-clipped). *Else Fine.* $50/£32

HIGGINS, JACK. The Eagle Has Landed. London, 1975. 1st Eng ed. VG in dj. *Edrich.* $34/£22

HIGGINS, JACK. Luciano's Luck. London: Collins, 1981. 1st ed. Fine in dj. *Silver Door.* $40/£26

HIGGINS, JOSEPH T. The Whale Ship Book. NY: Rudder Pub Co, (1927). Good. *Hayman.* $20/£13

HIGGINS, R.A. Greek and Roman Jewellery. London, 1961. 1st ed. 4 color, 64 b/w plts. Dj (sl chipped, spotted). *Edwards.* $47/£30

HIGGINS, R.A. Greek Terracottas. London: Methuen, 1967. 1st ed. 68 plts (4 tipped-in color). Dj (sl chipped). *Edwards.* $74/£48

HIGGINSON, A. HENRY. British and American Sporting Authors. London: Hutchinson, 1951. 1st ed. VG. *Bookpress.* $225/£145

HIGGINSON, MARY POTTER. Thomas Wentworth Higginson, the Story of His Life. Boston/NY: Houghton Mifflin, 1914. 1st ed. Orig cl. Spine sunned, else NF. *Mcgowan.* $75/£48

HIGGINSON, THOMAS WENTWORTH. Army Life in a Black Regiment. Boston: Fields, Osgood, 1870. 1st ed. iv,296pp. Spine sunned, else VG. *Mcgowan.* $275/£177

HIGGINSON, THOMAS WENTWORTH. Margaret Fuller Ossoli. Boston: Houghton Mifflin, 1884. 1st ed. Frontis port; 323pp. Lt grn 3/4 calf (lt faded). Very nice. BAL 8338. *Second Life.* $50/£32

HIGGINSON, THOMAS WENTWORTH. Part of a Man's Life. Boston: Houghton, Mifflin, 1905. 1st ed. Maroon cl, gilt. Lt mks, else Fine. BAL 8472. *Macdonnell.* $75/£48

High Times Encyclopedia of Recreational Drugs. NY: Stonehill, 1978. 1st ed. VG + (sl coffee staining to fore-edge) in wraps. *Sclanders.* $101/£65

HIGHSMITH, PATRICIA. The Animal-Lovers' Book of Beastly Murder. London: Heinemann, 1975. 1st ed. Fine in Fine dj. *Janus.* $30/£19

HIGHSMITH, PATRICIA. The Blunderer. NY: Coward-McCann, 1954. 1st ed. Fine in dj (sl wear spine base, corners). *Mordida.* $250/£161

HIGHSMITH, PATRICIA. The Man Who Wrote Books in His Head and Other Stories. (Helsinki): Eurographica, 1986. One of 350 signed, dated. Fine in card cvrs in dj as issued. *Williams.* $74/£48

HIGHSMITH, PATRICIA. Mermaids on the Golf Course. London: Heinemann, 1985. 1st ed. Fine in dj (price-clipped). *Janus.* $20/£13

HIGHSMITH, PATRICIA. The Snail Watcher and Other Stories. NY, 1970. 1st ed. VG in dj. *Argosy.* $45/£29

HIGHSMITH, PATRICIA. Strangers on a Train. Harper, 1950. 1st ed, 1st bk. Spine sl faded, else VG. *Fine Books.* $65/£42

HIGHSMITH, PATRICIA. The Talented Mr. Ripley. NY: Coward-McCann, (1955). 1st ed. Black cl (lt shelf worn). Dj (edges worn). *Argosy.* $100/£65

HIGHSMITH, PATRICIA. Those Who Walk Away. London: Heinemann, 1967. 1st Eng ed. Fine in NF dj (internally reinforced). *Janus.* $30/£19

HIGHSMITH, PATRICIA. The Two Faces of January. GC: Doubleday, 1964. 1st ed. VG in dj (sl chipped head spine). *Limestone.* $40/£26

HIGHSMITH, PATRICIA. Where the Action Is and Other Stories. (Helsinki): Eurographica, 1989. One of 350 signed, dated. Fine in card cvrs in dj as issued. *Williams.* $74/£48

HIGHTON, HUGH P. Shooting Trips in Europe and Algeria. London: H.F. & G. Witherby, 1921. 1st ed. (Cl on lower bd sl cockled along hinge; lt spotting.) *Hollett.* $171/£110

HIJUELOS, OSCAR. The Mambo Kings Play Songs of Love. NY: FSG, 1989. 1st ed. VF in dj. *Else Fine.* $50/£32

HIJUELOS, OSCAR. The Mambo Kings Play Songs of Love. FSG, 1989. 1st ed. Signed, inscribed. NF in dj. *Stahr.* $50/£32

HIJUELOS, OSCAR. The Mambo Kings Play Songs of Love. London: Hamilton, 1989. 1st UK ed. Signed. Fine in dj. *Lewton.* $39/£25

HIJUELOS, OSCAR. Our House in the Last World. NY: Persea Books, (1983). 1st ed. 1st bk. Fine in dj. *Godot.* $100/£65

HIJUELOS, OSCAR. Our House in the Last World. Serpents Tale, 1987. 1st UK ed. Fine in wrappers. *Lewton.* $23/£15

HILBERG, RAUL. The Warsaw Diary of Adam Czerniakow. Stein & Day, 1979. 1st ed. VG + in VG dj. *Bishop.* $22/£14

HILBERT, DAVID. The Foundations of Geometry. Chicago: Open Court, 1902. 1st US ed. VG (fraying spine head, foot). *Lame Duck.* $65/£42

HILDRETH, R. The White Slave. London, 1852. 1st British ed. 237pp (lt foxing). Contemp 3/4 calf, bds (edgewear; joints starting). Good. *Ginsberg.* $75/£48

HILDRETH, SAMUEL P. Contributions to the Early History of the North-West, Including the Moravian Missions in Ohio. Cincinnati: Poe & Hitchcock, 1864. 1st ed. 240pp. (Rubbed; lt foxed.) VG. Howes H 474. *Cahan*. $200/£129

HILER, HILAIRE. From Nudity to Rainment. An Introduction to the Study of Costume. London: W.&G. Foyle, 1929. 1st ed. 12 color plts, 12 b/w plts. Blue cl. Fine in ptd dj. *House*. $250/£161

HILEY, RICHARD W. Memories of Half a Century. London: Longmans, Green, 1899. 1st ed. xx,411pp, port. Joint cracked. *Hollett*. $39/£25

HILGER, M. INEZ. BAE Bulletin 148. Arapaho Child Life and Its Cultural Background. Washington: GPO, 1952. VG in wraps. *Lien*. $30/£19

HILL, ALFRED. The History of the Reform Movement in the Dental Profession...During the Last Twenty Years. London, 1877. xvi,400pp (spine chipped). *Edwards*. $70/£45

HILL, ALICE POLK. Tales of the Colorado Pioneers. Denver: Pierson & Gardner, 1884. 1st ed. Signed. 319pp. Fair. Howes H 480. *Lien*. $130/£84

HILL, CONSTANCE. Good Company in Old Westminster and the Temple. London: William Clowes, 1925. *Boswell*. $50/£32

HILL, DANIEL HARVEY. Bethel to Sharpsburg. Raleigh: Edwards & Broughton, 1926. 1st ed. 2 vols. Gilt-titled cl. Fine set. *Cahan*. $300/£194

HILL, G.F. Pisanello. London: Duckworth, 1905. Frontis, 74 plts. Dec upper cvr. Spine sl faded, o/w Fine. *Europa*. $39/£25

HILL, GEOFFREY. Preghiere. London, 1964. 1st Eng ed. NF in orig wraps. *Edrich*. $47/£30

HILL, GEORGE BIRBECK. Footsteps of Dr. Johnson (Scotland). London: Sampson Low, 1890. 1st ed. xviii,318pp, 23 plts, port, map. Teg, uncut. Signed note, clippings, full-pg port tipped in. Orig 3/4 calf, gilt titles, decs, silk ribbon marker. Nice. *Hartfield*. $295/£190

HILL, GEORGE BIRKBECK. The Life of Sir Rowland Hill. London, 1880. 2 vols. Frontis port; xxii,543,8pp ads; x,516pp; 4 plts; facs letter. Grn cl (sl worn; hinges cracked.) *Edwards*. $93/£60

HILL, HAMLIN. Mark Twain and Elisha Bliss. Columbia, MO: Univ of MO Press, (1964). 1st ed. Brn cl, gilt. Fine in dj. *Macdonnell*. $75/£48

HILL, HERBERT (ed). Soon, One Morning. NY: Knopf, 1963. VG in dj (chipped). *Petrilla*. $45/£29

HILL, J.L. The End of the Cattle Trail. Long Beach, CA: George W. Moyle Pub Co, (1925?). Wrappers (sl wrinkled; 1st text pg not ptd). *Schoyer*. $50/£32

HILL, J.L. The End of the Cattle Trail. Long Beach: George Moyle, n.d. 1st ed. VG in wraps. *Parker*. $60/£39

HILL, JASON. The Curious Gardener. London: Faber & Faber, 1932. 1st ed. Signed. Fine. *Quest*. $85/£55

HILL, LOUISE BILES. Joseph E. Brown and the Confederacy. Chapel Hill: Univ of NC Press, 1939. 1st ed. Grn cl. VG in dj. *Chapel Hill*. $105/£68

HILL, OLIVER. Scottish Castles of the Sixteenth and Seventeenth Centuries. London: Country Life, 1953. 1st ed. (Ex-libris; loss lower edge bds.) Dj (ragged, incomplete). *Edwards*. $194/£125

HILL, PAUL. Dialogue with Photography. FSG, 1979. 1st ed. NF in NF dj. *Bishop*. $24/£15

HILL, RALPH NADING. Sidewheeler Saga. NY: Rinehart, (1953). 1st ed. VG in Good dj. *Blue Dragon*. $25/£16

HILL, REGINALD. Another Death in Venice. London: CCC, 1976. 1st ed. Fine in dj (sl wear spine ends, corners). *Mordida*. $100/£65

HILL, REGINALD. Deadheads. London: CCC, 1983. 1st ed. Fine in dj (sl corner wear). *Mordida*. $50/£32

HILL, REGINALD. Exit Lines. London: Collins, 1984. 1st ed. Fine in dj. *Murder*. $50/£32

HILL, REGINALD. Under World. London: CCC, 1988. 1st ed. NF in NF dj. *Ming*. $31/£20

HILL, ROWLAND. Village Dialogues. London: For Thomas Tegg, 1827. 27th ed. 2 vols. Frontis port (sl waterstained edges). Mod cl-backed bds (rebound); leather labels. *Edwards*. $56/£36

HILL, S.S. The Dominions of the Pope and Sultan.... London: Madden & Malcolm, n.d. (1870). 1st ed. 2 vols in one, as issued. Engr frontis (lt stain),(iv),xii,349,(1)imprint; iv,364. 4 plts, 2 colored costume plts. Red cl, gilt (ink inscrip fep; hinges cracked, sl rubbed). *Morrell*. $124/£80

HILL, SARAH JANE FULL. Mrs. Hill's Journal, Civil War Reminiscences. Mark M. Krug (ed). Chicago: (Lakeside Classic), 1980. Fldg map. Brn cl; gilt stamping, top. Fine. *Bohling*. $30/£19

HILL, SARAH JANE FULL. Mrs. Hill's Journal, Civil War Reminiscences. Mark M. Krug (ed). Chicago: Lakeside Classics, 1980. 1st ed. Pict cl. Fine. *Pratt*. $37/£24

HILL, SUSAN. Do Me a Favour. Hutchinson, 1963. 1st UK ed. Fine in VG dj (spine faded). *Lewton*. $101/£65

HILL, W.B. Experiences of a Pioneer Minister of Minnesota. Minneapolis: J.A. Folsom, 1892. 185pp. Black cl, gilt title (sl worn, spotted, spine frayed). *Bohling*. $65/£42

HILL, W.C. Osman. Comparative Anatomy and Taxonomy Primates. Edinburgh Univ Press, 1953-1960. 4 vols. Good in orig djs. *Goodrich*. $125/£81

HILLABY, JOHN. Within the Streams. London: Harvey & Blythe, 1949. 1st ed. VG in dj (price-clipped). *Hollett*. $47/£30

HILLARD, GEORGE STILLMAN. Six Months in Italy. Boston: Ticknor, Reed, & Fields, 1854. 3rd ed. 2 vols. 432; vi,455,(5),8pp. Pub's blindstamped cl. Pencil sig; extrems rubbed, torn, stained, else VG. *Bookpress*. $85/£55

HILLARY, EDMUND. High Adventure. NY, 1955. 1st Amer ed. Cl-backed bds. VG in dj (sl rubbed). *King*. $50/£32

HILLARY, EDMUND. No Latitude for Error. London: Hodder & Stoughton, 1961. 1st UK ed. VG in dj (worn). *Parmer*. $35/£23

HILLDRUP, ROBERT LEROY. An American Missionary to Meiji Japan. Privately ptd, 1970. Port. Paper cvr. VG. *Book Broker*. $25/£16

HILLDRUP, ROBERT LEROY. The Life and Times of Edmund Pendleton. Univ of NC Press, 1939. VG in Good dj. *Book Broker*. $25/£16

HILLER, O. PRESCOTT. American National Lyrics, and Sonnets. Boston: Otis Clapp, 1860. 1st ed. vi,80pp (marginal blind stamps; stamp; top edges sl dusty; joints cracked.) Blind-stamped cl gilt (sm stains; spine top, bottom chipped). *Hollett*. $62/£40

HILLERMAN, TONY. The Blessing Way. NY: Harper & Row, (1970). 1st Amer ed, 1st bk. Fine in NF dj (spine lettering faded; rubbing). *Between The Covers.* $1,100/£710

HILLERMAN, TONY. The Blessing Way. (London): Macmillan, (1970). 1st Eng ed. Blue paper-cvrd bds. Fine in dj (sm sticker mk, else Fine). *Godot.* $385/£248

HILLERMAN, TONY. The Blessing Way. Armchair Detective Lib, (1990). Signed. Photo inset on cvr. New. *Authors Of The West.* $60/£39

HILLERMAN, TONY. The Blessing Way. Macmillan, 1970. 1st Eng ed, 1st bk. Fine in NF dj. *Fine Books.* $375/£242

HILLERMAN, TONY. The Blessing Way. NY: Armchair Detective Lib, 1990. 1st thus. One of 100 signed, numbered. VF in slipcase. *Murder.* $175/£113

HILLERMAN, TONY. Coyote Waits. NY: Harper & Row, (1989). 1st ed. Ltd to 350 signed. As New in slipcase. *Perier.* $200/£129

HILLERMAN, TONY. Coyote Waits. NY: Harper Row, 1990. 1st ed. Fine in Fine dj. *Revere.* $15/£10

HILLERMAN, TONY. Coyote Waits. London: Joseph, 1991. 1st British ed. Fine in dj. *Silver Door.* $40/£26

HILLERMAN, TONY. Dance Hall of the Dead. Armchair Detective Lib, (1991). 1st ADL trade ed. Signed. New in New dj. *Authors Of The West.* $60/£39

HILLERMAN, TONY. Dance Hall of the Dead. NY: Harper, 1973. 1st ed. NF (label) in dj (price-clipped, short closed tear). *Janus.* $400/£258

HILLERMAN, TONY. Dance Hall of the Dead. London: Pluto Press, 1985. 1st British ed. Fine in dj. *Murder.* $95/£61

HILLERMAN, TONY. Dance Hall of the Dead. London: Pluto Press, 1985. 1st Eng ed. Signed. VF in dj. *Mordida.* $125/£81

HILLERMAN, TONY. The Dark Wind. Harper, 1982. 1st ed. Fine in dj. *Murder.* $125/£81

HILLERMAN, TONY. The Fly on the Wall. NY: Harper & Row, (1971). 1st Amer ed. Fine (fore-edge sl soiled) in NF dj (sl rubbing; 2 faint smudges). *Between The Covers.* $1,250/£806

HILLERMAN, TONY. The Fly on the Wall. NY: Harper & Row, 1971. 1st ed. Sig, else VG in dj (lt chipped). *Limestone.* $550/£355

HILLERMAN, TONY. The Ghostway. London: Gollancz, 1985. 1st British ed. Fine in dj. *Murder.* $50/£32

HILLERMAN, TONY. The Ghostway. London: Gollancz, 1985. 1st Eng ed. VF in dj. *Limestone.* $40/£26

HILLERMAN, TONY. The Ghostway. London: Gollancz, 1985. 1st Eng ed. Signed. VF in dj. *Mordida.* $65/£42

HILLERMAN, TONY. The Ghostway. NY: Harper & Row, 1985. 1st trade ed. VF in dj. *Mordida.* $100/£65

HILLERMAN, TONY. Listening Woman. London: Macmillan, (1979). 1st British ed. Fine in Fine dj. *Authors Of The West.* $100/£65

HILLERMAN, TONY. Listening Woman. (London): Macmillan, (1979). 1st UK ed. NF in dj (lt soiled). *Bernard.* $125/£81

HILLERMAN, TONY. Listening Woman. NY: Harper, 1978. 1st ed. Fine (name) in Fine dj (lt crease). *Janus.* $300/£194

HILLERMAN, TONY. Listening Woman. NY: Harper & Row, 1978. 1st ed. Fine in dj (closed tears; crease). *Mordida.* $350/£226

HILLERMAN, TONY. People of Darkness. NY: Harper, 1980. 1st ed. NF in NF dj (lt edgewear). *Janus.* $185/£119

HILLERMAN, TONY. People of Darkness. NY: Harper & Row, 1980. 1st ed. VF in dj. *Mordida.* $400/£258

HILLERMAN, TONY. Rio Grande. Portland, 1975. 1st ed. Fine in Fine dj (publ price present but prepubl price clipped). *Janus.* $150/£97

HILLERMAN, TONY. Rio Grande. Portland, 1975. 1st ed. Robert Reynolds (photos). VF in dj. *Mordida.* $200/£129

HILLERMAN, TONY. Sacred Clowns. Harper Collins, (1993). 1st ltd ed of 500 numbered, signed. New in slipcase. *Authors Of The West.* $100/£65

HILLERMAN, TONY. Skinwalkers. NY: Harper & Row, 1986. 1st ed. VF in dj. *Mordida.* $45/£29

HILLERMAN, TONY. Skinwalkers. London: Michael Joseph, 1988. 1st Eng ed. Fine in dj. *Mordida.* $45/£29

HILLERMAN, TONY. Skinwalkers. London: Joseph, 1988. 1st UK ed. NF in NF dj. *Ming.* $62/£40

HILLERMAN, TONY. Talking God. NY: Harper & Row, (1989). 1st ed. As New in dj. *Sadlon.* $35/£23

HILLERMAN, TONY. Talking God. NY: Harper, 1989. 1st ed, one of 300 numbered, signed. As New in slipcase. *Janus.* $150/£97

HILLERMAN, TONY. Talking God. London: Harper & Row, 1989. 1st ed. NF in NF dj. *Ming.* $31/£20

HILLERMAN, TONY. Talking God. NY: Harper & Row, 1989. 1st ed. One of 300 specially bound, numbered, signed. VF in slipcase w/o dj as issued. *Mordida.* $125/£81

HILLERMAN, TONY. A Thief of Time. Harper, 1988. 1st ed. One of 250 signed. VF in slipcase. *Murder.* $275/£177

HILLERMAN, TONY. A Thief of Time. NY: Harper & Row, 1988. 1st ed. One of 250 specially bound, numbered, signed. VF in slipcase w/o dj as issued. *Mordida.* $200/£129

HILLERMAN, TONY. A Thief of Time. London: Michael Joseph, 1989. 1st British ed. Fine in dj. *Murder.* $45/£29

HILLGROVE, THOMAS. A Complete Practical Guide to the Art of Dancing. NY: Dick & Fitzgerald, (1863). Early ed. Woodcut frontis, 238pp + 10 leaves ads. Dec cvr. Nice (sl wear). *Cady.* $75/£48

HILLIARD, JOHN NORTHERN. Greater Magic, a Practical Treatise.... Minneapolis, (1938). 1st ed. Name, spine top sl faded, else Good in dj (defective). *King.* $495/£319

HILLIER, BEVIS. Austerity Binge. Studio Vista, 1975. 1st UK ed. Dj (sl chipped; spine faded). *Edwards.* $39/£25

HILLIER, JACK. Suzuki Harunobu: A Selection of His Color Prints and Illustrated Books. Phila: Phila Museum of Art, (1970). Color frontis. Fine in dj. *Argosy.* $75/£48

HILLIER, JACK. Utamaro. Phaidon, 1961. Tipped-in color frontis, 16 tipped-in color plts. Dj (faded, sl torn, repaired). *Edwards.* $39/£25

HILLIER, JACK. Utamaro. (London): Phaidon, 1961. 17 color plts. VG. *Argosy.* $75/£48

HILLIER, MARY. Automata and Mechanical Toys: An Illustrated History. London, 1976. VG. *Argosy.* $40/£26

HILLS, JOHN WALLER. River Keeper. NY: Scribner's, 1936. 1st Amer ed. VG. *Bowman.* $60/£39

HILLS, PATRICIA. Alice Neel. NY: Abrams, 1983. VG in dj. *Argosy.* $85/£55

HILLYER, ROBERT. The Five Books of Youth. NY: Brentano's, (1920). 1st ed. Ptd bds. NF (sm loss spine head) in dj (tears, chips; spine browning). *Antic Hay.* $50/£32

HILLYER, ROBERT. The Suburb by the Sea. NY: Knopf, 1952. 1st ed. Fine in dj (chips, tears; price-clipped). *Antic Hay.* $20/£13

HILPRECHT, HERMAN V. (ed). Recent Research in Bible Lands: Its Progress and Results. Phila: John D. Wattles, 1897. Fldg map. Teg. Gilt-pict cl. Good. *Archaeologia.* $85/£55

HILTON, JAMES. The Dawn of Reckoning. Thornton-Butterworth, 1925. 1st ed. Spine sl lightened, else NF. *Fine Books.* $75/£48

HILTON, JAMES. The Meadows of the Moon. Thornton-Butterworth, 1926. 1st ed. Spine sl lightened, else VG. *Fine Books.* $60/£39

HILTON, JAMES. To You Mr. Chips. H&S, 1938. 1st ed. Extrems sl lightened; lt foxing to pp edges, else VG + in VG dj (sl dust soiled). *Fine Books.* $75/£48

HILTON, JOHN. On Rest and Pain: A Course of Lectures.... NY: Wood, 1879. 2nd ed. 299pp. (Ex-lib; spine worn.) Internally Good. *Goodrich.* $35/£23

HILTON-SIMPSON, M.W. Among the Hill-Folk of Algeria. NY, 1921. Map. (Marginal browning; spine sl frayed.) *Edwards.* $93/£60

HIMES, CHESTER. All Shot Up. NY: Avon, 1960. 1st ed. NF (musty odor) in wraps. *Beasley.* $40/£26

HIMES, CHESTER. Black on Black. GC: Doubleday, 1973. 1st ed. Fine in dj (sl browning; sl edgewear). *Antic Hay.* $200/£129

HIMES, CHESTER. Blind Man with a Pistol. NY: Morrow, 1969. 1st ed. Fine in NF dj (lamination bumps). *Janus.* $85/£55

HIMES, CHESTER. Blind Man with a Pistol. London: Hodder & Stoughton, 1969. 1st Eng ed. Fine in dj (sl wear). *Mordida.* $85/£55

HIMES, CHESTER. A Case of Rape. NY: Targ Editions, (1980). 1st Amer ed, 1st ed in English. One of 350 ptd, signed. Fine in glassine wrapper. *Reese.* $65/£42

HIMES, CHESTER. A Case of Rape. Washington: Howard Univ, (1984). 1st trade ed. Fine in Fine dj. *Murder.* $35/£23

HIMES, CHESTER. Cotton Comes to Harlem. London: Frederick Muller, 1966. 1st Eng ed. Fine in dj. *Mordida.* $85/£55

HIMES, CHESTER. If He Hollers Let Him Go. GC: Doubleday, 1945. 1st ed, 1st bk. Top edge soiled; bds lt spotted, else VG in VG- dj (chipped). *Lame Duck.* $125/£81

HIMES, CHESTER. My Life of Absurdity. GC: Doubleday, 1976. 1st ed. Fine (rmdr spray) in Fine dj. *Beasley.* $50/£32

HIMES, CHESTER. Pinktoes. NY: Putnam/Stein & Day, 1965. 1st ed. Crease fep, o/w Fine in dj (sl spine fading). *Else Fine.* $125/£81

HIMES, CHESTER. The Real Cool Killers. London: Allison & Busby, 1985. 1st hb ed. Fine in dj. *Mordida.* $45/£29

HIMES, CHESTER. Run Man Run. London: Muller, 1967. 1st UK ed. Fine in dj (sl rubbed). *Williams.* $37/£24

HINCKLEY, BRYANT S. Daniel Hanmer Wells and Events of His Time. Salt Lake, 1942. 1st ed. Frontis. Bkpl, o/w VG + in VG- dj. *Benchmark.* $45/£29

HIND, ARTHUR M. A Catalogue of Rembrandt's Etchings. London: Methuen, 1923. 2nd ed. 2 vols. Photograv frontis. (Margins lt browned; cl lt soiled; spines bumped, sl chipped.) Vol 2 in dj (worn, torn). *Edwards.* $155/£100

HIND, ARTHUR M. A History of Engraving and Etching.... London, 1923. 3rd ed. Photograv frontis. (Eps spotted; spine faded.) *Edwards.* $85/£55

HIND, ARTHUR M. A History of Engravings and Etching from the 15th Century to the Year 1914. London, 1923. 3rd rev ed. (Backstrip sl sunned; sl foxing.) *Washton.* $75/£48

HIND, ARTHUR M. A Short History of Engraving and Etching for the Use of Collectors and Students. London, 1911. 2nd ed, rev. Photograv frontis. Fore, lower edges uncut. (Eps, text lt spotted; cl spine sl discolored.) *Edwards.* $54/£35

HIND, ARTHUR M. Wenceslaus Hollar and His Views of London and Windsor in the Seventeenth Century. London: Bodley, 1922. Frontis port, 45 plts (1 fldg). Pub's cl. Sig, spine sl faded, o/w Fine (orig dj tipped in). *Europa.* $132/£85

HIND, ARTHUR M. Wenceslaus Hollar.... London, 1922. Frontis port, 96 plts. Fore-edge uncut. (Prelims lt spotted; upper bd sl bumped, damp-spotted.) *Edwards.* $109/£70

HIND, C. LEWIS. Adventures Among Pictures. A&C Black, 1904. 1st ed. 24 plts (8 color); teg. (Sl spotting; hinges sl cracked; cl faded, rubbed; spine chipped.) *Edwards.* $39/£25

HIND, C. LEWIS. Days With Velasquez. A&C Black, 1906. 1st ed. 25 plts (8 color). (Feps sl browned; spotting upper bd; spine sl soiled.) *Edwards.* $39/£25

HIND, C. LEWIS. Rembrandt. A&C Black, 1905. 16 color plts. (Lt browned feps.) Teg. *Edwards.* $47/£30

HIND, C. LEWIS. Turner's Golden Visions. London/Edinburgh, n.d. Tipped-in color frontis, 49 tipped-in color plts; gilt eps (sl discolored). Teg, rest uncut (ms note taped fr pastedown). Japon bds (sl rubbed, spotted), gilt. *Edwards.* $116/£75

HIND, H.L. and W.B. RANDLES. Handbook of Photomicrography. London: Routledge, 1927. 2nd ed. 44 plts (8 color). VG. *Savona.* $39/£25

HIND, HENRY YOULE. Narrative of the Canadian Red River Exploring Expedition of 1857.... London: Longman, Green et al, 1860. 2 vols. 494; 472pp; fldg map each vol. Good. *Lien.* $700/£452

HINDEMITH, PAUL. The Craft of Musical Composition. NY: Associated Music, 1941. 1st ed. Sig fep, else NF in VG dj (sm chips). *Lame Duck.* $50/£32

HINDLEY, CHARLES. The Life and Times of James Catnach, Balladmonger. Reeves & Turner, 1878. 230 woodcuts. 1/2 calf. Teg. Good (sm lib stamp t.p.). *Moss.* $93/£60

HINDS, JOHN. The Veterinary Surgeon. London: Sherwood et al, 1827. xvi,571pp + (i)pub's ad, 4 fldg plts (3 partially hand-colored). 1/2 calf (rebound; staining, soiling), marbled bds, gilt bands, leather label. *Edwards.* $194/£125

HINDS, JOHN. The Veterinary Surgeon.... Phila: Grigg & Elliott, 1845. Leatherbound (worn; part frontis missing). *October Farm.* $35/£23

HINDS, WILLIAM ALFRED. American Communities. Oneida: Amer Socialist, 1878. 1st ed. VG+ (sm home-made label; bump lower rt corner). *Beasley*. $300/£194

HINES, DAVID T. Life, Adventures and Opinions of David Theo. Hines of South Carolina. NY: Bradley, 1840. 1st ed. 195pp. Muslin-backed bds (joints worn; paper label almost disintegrated). Howes H 504. *Ginsberg*. $150/£97

HINES, GORDON. Alfalfa Bill. Oklahoma City, 1932. 1st ed. Pict cl. Fine in dj. *Baade*. $45/£29

HINES, H.K. An Illustrated History of the State of Oregon. Chicago: Lewis Pub., 1893. 1300pp. Full leather. VG. *Perier*. $175/£113

HINES, J.W. Touching Incidents in the Life and Labors of a Pioneer on the Pacific Coast Since 1853. San Jose: Eaton & Co, 1911. 1st ed. VG. *Perier*. $85/£55

HINGSTON, R.W.G. A Naturalist in Hindustan. London, 1923. 1st ed. 8 plts. (Lower hinge cracked, lower bd sl spotted.) *Edwards*. $62/£40

HINKLE, JAMES F. Early Days of a Cowboy on the Pecos. Roswell, NM: James F. Hinkle, 1937. Pict wrappers (sm sticker t.p.). *Dawson*. $100/£65

HINKS, ROGER. Carolingian Art. London: Sidgwick & Jackson, 1935. 1st ed. 24 plts. Fine. *Europa*. $25/£16

HINKS, ROGER. Michelangelo Merisi da Caravaggio; His Life, His Legend, His Works. London: Faber, 1953. Color frontis, 96 plts. Spine sl faded, nicked, o/w Fine. *Europa*. $40/£26

HINKSON, KATHARINE TYNAN. Cuckoo Songs. London: Elkin Mathew & John Lane, 1894. 1st ed. Ltd to 500. Rose-colored cl bds, gilt-stamped. Fore, bottom edges untrimmed. VG (spine bumped, faded). *Hermitage*. $150/£97

HINSDALE, B.A. The Old Northwest. NY: Townsend Mac Coun, 1888. vi,(ii),440pp. Blue cl (rubbed, bumped; tear spine; fr hinge cracked); ptd spine label (dampstained, faded). Contents VG. *Blue Mountain*. $25/£16

HINSDALE, HARRIET (ed). Frank Merriwell's 'Father.' Norman, (1964). Stated 1st ed. Good in dj (sl worn). *Hayman*. $25/£16

HINSDALE, S.B. Trial of D.M. Bennett in the United States Circuit Court...Upon the Charge of Depositing Prohibited Matter in the Mail. NY: Truth Seeker Office, 1879. Reddish-brn cl, gilt (sl rubbed). Good. *Boswell*. $150/£97

HINTON, RICHARD J. The Handbook to Arizona. SF/NY: Payot, Upham/Amsterdam News Co, 1878. 431,101pp + 43pp ads, 21 litho plts, 5 maps (2 fldg), litho ad. Orig cl (sl rubbed). Howes H 513. *Schoyer*. $150/£97

HINTON, RICHARD J. The Handbook to Arizona. Tucson, 1954. 1st rpt ed. Fine in dj (edgeworn). Howes H 513. *Baade*. $75/£48

HINTON, S.E. Rumble Fish. NY: Delacorte, 1975. 1st ed. Fine (sm abrasion fep) in Fine dj (paperclip mks). *Beasley*. $50/£32

HINZ, CHRISTOPHER. Liege-Killer. NY: St. Martins, (1987). 1st ed. Corners bumped, else Fine in dj. *Other Worlds*. $60/£39

HIPPOCRATES. The Genuine Works.... Francis Adams (trans). London: Sydenham Soc, 1848. 2 vols. 872pp (sm piece cut away each half-title); 8 plts. Mod grn cl. VG. *White*. $70/£45

HIRSCH, ARTHUR HENRY. The Huguenots of Colonial South Carolina. Durham, NC: Duke Univ Press, 1928. 1st ed. Frontis port. Black cl. VG in dj (chipped). *Chapel Hill*. $85/£55

HIRSCHFIELD, MAGNUS. The Sexual History of the World War. 1934. VG (cvrs sl soiled). *Clark*. $45/£29

HIRSH, SHARON L. Ferdinand Holder. NY, (1982). 41 mtd color plts. VG in dj. *Argosy*. $50/£32

HIRSHBERG, AL. From Sandlots to League President. Messner, 1962. Ltr ptg. Fine in VG dj. *Plapinger*. $50/£32

HIRSHBERG, AL. Henry Aaron—Quiet Superstar. Putnam's, 1974. 1st ptg, rev ed. Fine in Good+ dj. *Plapinger*. $30/£19

HIRSHBERG, AL. The Red Sox: The Bean and The Cod. Boston, (1947). 1st ed. VG (lt spotted, sl insect damage to fr hinge). *Fuller & Saunders*. $20/£13

HIRSHBERG, AL. What's the Matter with the Red Sox. Dodd-Mead, 1973. 1st ed. Fine in VG dj. *Plapinger*. $40/£26

HIRST, BARTON (ed). A System of Obstetrics. Phila, 1888. 1st ed. 2 vols. 808; 854pp. Full leather. VF. *Fye*. $250/£161

HIRST, BARTON. Atlas of Operative Gynaecology. Phila, 1919. 1st ed. 164 plts. Good. *Fye*. $150/£97

HIRST, L. FABIAN. The Conquest of Plague. Oxford: Clarendon, 1953. 6 plts. Dj. *Bickersteth*. $78/£50

HISLOP, HERBERT R. An Englishman's Arizona. Tucson, 1965. Ltd to 510. Fine; no dj as issued. *Baade*. $75/£48

HISSEY, JAMES JOHN. On Southern English Roads. London, 1896. 423pp + 8pp pub's ads, fldg map. Dec eps. Gilt device upper bd, spine. (Prelims lt foxed; cl sl dampstained; sl rubbed.) *Edwards*. $39/£25

HISSEY, JAMES JOHN. On the Box Seat from London to Land's End. London: Richard Bentley, 1886. xviii,404pp; 16 wood-engr plts. Contemp 1/2-calf (sl worn). *Bickersteth*. $28/£18

HISSEY, JAMES JOHN. On the Box Seat from London to Land's End. London, 1886. xiii,404pp (feps lt foxed), 2 facs. Illus cl (spine chipped, discolored, sm stain, sl rubbed). *Edwards*. $47/£30

HISSEY, JAMES JOHN. Over Fen and Wold. London, 1898. xv,447pp (feps lt spotted), 2pp map. Gilt device upper bd, spine. (Sl bubbling; spine chipped, sm puncture.) *Edwards*. $47/£30

HISSEY, JAMES JOHN. Through Ten English Counties. London, 1894. xiv,406pp + 2pp pub's ads (feps lt browned), fldg map. Dec eps. Dec gilt upper bd. (Hinges sl cracked; spine chipped; lower joint splitting; sl bumped.) *Edwards*. $43/£28

HISSEY, JAMES JOHN. A Tour in a Phaeton. London, 1889. 403pp + 4pp pub's ads, fldg map. Illus cl (spine discolored, chipped; sl rubbed; hinges cracked). *Edwards*. $54/£35

Historical Account of Bouquet's Expedition Against the Ohio Indians in 1764. (By William Smith.) Cincinnati: Robert Clarke, 1907. Later ed. Dk red cl. Owner emb stamp, spine lt sunned, else NF. Howes S 693. *Chapel Hill*. $95/£61

Historie of Great Britannie. (By John Clapham). London: Ptd by Valentine Simmes, 1606. 2nd ed, rev, enlgd. (12),302,(2)pp; chart. Mod grn cl over marbled bds (rebound), grn morocco spine label. *Karmiole*. $300/£194

History 31st Regiment Illinois Volunteers, Organized.... (By John A. Logan.) (Evansville, IN: Keller Ptg, 1902). 1st ed. Long inscrip fr flyleaf, else VG. *Mcgowan.* $350/£226

History and Gallant Achievements of the Seven Champions of Christendom. (London: Didier & Tebbett, Jan 1, 1808.) Pub's name appears only on orig wrapper (missing). Sq 12mo. 10pp; 10 (of 12) 3/4pg hand-colored copper engrs. Later dec wrappers. Lt soiling along margins, leaf repaired, else Fine. *Hobbyhorse.* $175/£113

History of Birds. Portland: Bailey & Noyes, n.d. (ca 1830). Chapbook. 16mo. 16pp, wood engr vignette tp; lg cut of bird fr cvr, 2 on back cvr. VF. *Hobbyhorse.* $55/£35

History of Butler and Bremer Counties, Iowa. Springfield, IL: Union Pub Co, 1883. Fldg map frontis, 1323pp. 3/4 leather (scuffed). VG + . *Bohling.* $110/£71

History of Cinderella, or, the Little Glass Slipper. Glasgow: Ptd for Booksellers, n.d. (ca 1830). Chapbook. 12mo. 22pp (of 24). Pict ptd paper wrappers; upper wrapper (rebound in) illus w/wood engr vignette of lg house in dec frame. Good (lacks lower wrapper, incl last pg of text; sl chipping). *Hobbyhorse.* $35/£23

History of Cinderella. London: Sold by the Booksellers, n.d. (ca 1875). 12mo. 8pp + 1pg ad back cvr; eight 3/4pg wood engrs. Dec grn paper wrappers (chipped; spine reinforced). Fair. *Hobbyhorse.* $75/£48

History of England. London: John Wallis, 1800. Tall 24mo. Full-pg copper engr frontis, 64pp; 31 round wood engr ports (crudely hand-colored). Gray paper on bds (soiled; rebacked), blue ptd title label upper cvr. VG (sm color spot 2pp). *Hobbyhorse.* $150/£97

History of Fiction: Being a Critical Account.... (By J. Dunlop.) Longman, Hurst et al, 1816. 2nd ed w/new material added. 3 vols. Orig bds separated or separating in vols 1,3, else Good set. *Fine Books.* $125/£81

History of Goody Two Shoes. Cooperstown: H. and E. Phinney, 1829. Chapbook. 31pp. Frontis at verso of 1/2 title, VF wood-engr on tp, 10 in text. Pict yellow paper wrappers; upper wrapper ptd w/repeat of last engr of text; 2 figs ptd on lower wrapper. Cvr title reads: Goody Two Shoes. Dated imprint on cvr reads 1830. *Hobbyhorse.* $225/£145

History of Goody Two Shoes. Edinburgh: Oliver Boyd, n.d. (ca 1830). 12mo. Full-pg wood engr frontis, 40pp; 12 Fine 1/2pg wood engrs. Pict buff stiff paper wrappers. Ex-libris, spine sl rubbed, else VF. *Hobbyhorse.* $250/£161

History of Guy, Earl of Warwick. London: Ptd for Bksellers, n.d. (ca 1750). 12mo. 24pp. 1/2 pg woodcut tp; last pg w/full-pg woodcut representing armored gentleman riding horse, carrying pike w/boar's head; 1/2 pg woodcut upper wrapper of gentleman riding horse in countryside. Fine in orig pict yellow stiff paper wrappers (lt dusted). *Hobbyhorse.* $775/£500

History of Joseph. New Haven: S. Babcock, n.d. (ca 1840). Chapbook. 16mo. 16pp + 1pg ad back cvr. Wood engr vignette on cvr of Christ disputing in Temple (lt spotting); lg vignette tp of 3 wise men and star in East; (sig). Pict pink paper wrappers. Fine. *Hobbyhorse.* $55/£35

History of King Pippin. London: Dean & Munday, n.d. (ca 1840). Sq 12mo. Frontis, 15pp + 1pg list on lower wrapper. Pict yellow paper wrappers. Ink sig, lt soil, else Fine. *Hobbyhorse.* $125/£81

History of Little Fanny. Phila: Morgan & Yeager, 1825. 2nd ed. Sq 12mo. 15pp + 7 leaves. Ptd buff paper on bds. In all, VG (spotted, chipped, reinforced spine). *Hobbyhorse.* $350/£226

History of Los Angeles County, California. Oakland, CA: Thompson & West, 1880. (Berkeley: Howell-North, 1959.) Rpt ed. (4),192pp. Black gilt cl. Good. *Karmiole.* $50/£32

History of Middlesex County, Connecticut. NY: Beers, 1884. 579pp; 62 plts. Orig cl (newly rebacked in leather). *Schoyer.* $125/£81

History of Pompey the Little. (By Francis Coventry.) London: for M. Cooper et al, 1751. 1st ed. Engr frontis (inscrip), viii,272pp. (1pg torn, no loss; sl spotting). Recent 1/2 calf. *Marlborough.* $349/£225

History of Quadrupeds, for the Use of Children. Concord, NH: Rufus Merrill, 1843. Chapbook. 24mo. 8pp + 1pg ad back cvr; 5 wood engrs. Dec yellow paper wrappers (sm holes; loss of corner), spine handstitched. Fair (ink name, date). *Hobbyhorse.* $15/£10

History of Sandford and Merton. (By Thomas Day.) London: J. Wallis & E. Newbery, n.d. (ca 1794). 3rd ed. 12mo. iv,173pp; 6 full-pg copper engrs (incl frontis). Marbled paper on bds, 3/4 grn cl. Fine (dated ink sig; new eps; rebacked; lt rubbed). *Hobbyhorse.* $325/£210

History of Sandford and Merton.... (By Thomas Day.) London: John Stockdale, 1786/1786/1789. 3rd ed. 3 vols. 8vo. Full-pg engr frontis vol 1, 281pp + 3pp list; frontis, 306 + 6pp list; 308 + 4pp list. Orig 3/4 leather, marbled paper (rubbed, chipped). Good set (ragged edges; 1 pg corner restored w/loss; repaired tears; sl foxing; lib label). *Hobbyhorse.* $200/£129

History of the Art of Engraving in Mezzotinto.... (By Joseph Chelsum.) Winchester, 1786. 2ff,100pp,6ff. Old calf (rebacked, title dusty, foxing). *Marlborough.* $388/£250

History of the Bible. Concord, NH: Rufus Merrill, 1843. Chapbook. 16mo. 16pp + 1pg ad back cvr. Dec yellow paper wrappers. Fine w/Excellent engrs. *Hobbyhorse.* $50/£32

History of the Fifteenth Regiment, Iowa Veteran Volunteer Infantry. (By William Worth Belknap.) Keokuk: R.B. Ogden & Son, 1887. 1st ed. 644pp. NF. *Mcgowan.* $300/£194

History of the Fifteenth United States Army, 21 August 1944 to 11 July 1945. N.p., n.d. (1945). Cl-backed bds (worn, spotted; lt foxing.) *King.* $95/£61

History of the First Troop, Philadelphia City Cavalry 1774-1874. (By William S. Stryker). Phila, 1875. 194pp + 19pp appendix, 17 engr plts, 1 litho color plt. New buckram (rebound). *Heinoldt.* $60/£39

History of the Great Lakes, Illustrated. Chicago: J.H. Beers, 1899. 2 vols. xvi,928; iv,1213pp; 5 dbl maps. Aeg. Full leather, gilt stamping. Nice set (vol 1 spine ends chipped, glued repairs; vol 2 NF). Howes M 266. *Bohling.* $450/£290

History of the Great Plague in London, in the Year 1665.... (By Daniel Defoe.) London: Renshaw, 1832. New ed. vii,311,4pp pub ads; port. Brn cl. VG (port, title spotting). *White.* $70/£45

History of the Great Plague in London, in the Year 1665...by a Citizen, Who Lived the Whole Time in London. (By Daniel Defoe.) London, 1819. 505pp. 3/4 calf (cvrs detached). *Argosy.* $125/£81

History of the House that Jack Built. London: W.S. Fortey, n.d. (ca 1855). Chapbook. 12mo. 4 leaves + 1pg ad, 11 lt wood engrs (some crudely hand-colored), incl 1 on tp, which is repeated on upper wrapper. Untrimmed, uncut as issued. Pict yellow paper wrappers. Fine. *Hobbyhorse*. $150/£97

History of the Indian Wars.... (By Daniel Clark Sanders.) Montpelier, VT: Wright and Sibley, 1812. 1st ed. 12mo. 320pp. Contemp calf, leather spine label. Some leaves trimmed bit close as is case w/all copies, but overall Very Nice. Howes S 84. *Karmiole*. $1,000/£645

History of the Jesuits.... (By John Poynder.) 1816. 2 vols. Contemp calf (sl rubbed). *Bickersteth*. $54/£35

History of the Late Conspiracy Against the King and the Nation. (By James Abbadie). London: ptd for Daniel Brown & Thomas Bennet, 1696. 1st ed. (2),196pp. Full calf (rebound), spine label. Good. *Karmiole*. $200/£129

History of the Life and Adventures of Mr. Duncan Campbell, a Gentleman.... (By Daniel Defoe.) London: E. Curll, 1720. 1st ed. 4 copper engrs. 1/2 calf. VG. *Argosy*. $500/£323

History of the Philadelphia Almshouses and Hospitals...to the Ending of the Nineteenth Centuries.... Phila, 1905. New bds. Internally Fine. *Goodrich*. $90/£58

History of the Raising of the First American Flag on the Capitol of Mexico. Washington: 1856. 1st ed. 34pp. Pink wraps (spine wear). *Petrilla*. $125/£81

History of the Seventeenth Virginia Infantry. (By George Wise.) Balt: Kelly, Piet, 1870. 1st ed. Minor wear extrems, else VG. Howes W 592. *Mcgowan*. $450/£290

History of the Theatres of London.... (By Walley C. Oulton.) London: Martin & Bain, 1796. 1st ed. 2 vols in 1. Later 1/2 calf; leather label; emb stamps 5 leaves (1 repaired). *Dramatis Personae*. $175/£113

History of Tommy and Harry. York: J. Kendrew, n.d. (ca 1815). Chapbook. 32mo. Full-pg frontis, 1pg ad back cvr, 6 wood engrs. Dec buff wrappers. VG. *Hobbyhorse*. $100/£65

History of Valentine and Orson. (Nottingham): Ptd for Company of Walking Stationers, n.d. (ca 1790). Chapbook. 12mo. 16pp, woodcut tp, 2 tail-pieces. Uncut. Pict self wrappers. Lt marginal tears, o/w Fine. *Hobbyhorse*. $275/£177

History of Valentine and Orson. Otley: William Walker, n.d. (ca 1830). Chapbook. 12mo. 24pp. Pict ptd paper wrappers; 1/3 pg woodcut, dec frame upper wrapper (edges chipped). VG. *Hobbyhorse*. $80/£52

History of Whittington and His Cat. York: J. Kendrew, n.d. (ca 1815). Chapbook. 32mo. Full-pg woodcut frontis, 1pg ad back cvr; nine 1/2pg woodcuts (perfect state). Maroon dec wrappers. *Hobbyhorse*. $150/£97

HITCHCOCK, A.S. Manual of the Grasses of the United States. Washington, 1935. *Wheldon & Wesley*. $54/£35

HITCHCOCK, A.S. Manual of the Grasses of the United States. Washington, 1935. 1st ed. Cl (scuffed; sl shaken; pp yellowed, bkpl). *Sutton*. $65/£42

HITCHCOCK, ETHAN A. Fifty Years in Camp and Field. NY: Putnam's, 1909. 1st ed. (Lib stamps inside; sm discoloration spine.) Howes H 529. *Ginsberg*. $150/£97

HITCHCOCK, ETHAN A. A Traveler in Indian Territory. The Journal of.... Cedar Rapids: Torch Press, 1930. 1st ed. Inscribed, signed by Grant Foreman (ed). Fldg map, 5 plts. VG- (eps foxed). Howes H 537. *Parker*. $150/£97

HITCHCOCK, F. Saddle Up. London, 1959. Good +. *October Farm*. $22/£14

HITCHCOCK, FREDERICK LYMAN. War from the Inside. Phila: Lippincott, 1904. 1st ed. Sl cvr speckling, sm split fr outer hinge, else VG. *Mcgowan*. $150/£97

HITCHCOCK, HENRY-RUSSELL. The Architecture of H.H. Richardson and His Times. NY: MOMA, 1936. 1st ed. Gray cl, gilt. Good. *Karmiole*. $65/£42

HITCHCOCK, HENRY-RUSSELL. Early Victorian Architecture in Britain. London: Architectural Press, 1954. 1st ed. 2 vols. 522 illus on plts. VG in djs (chipped). *Bookpress*. $175/£113

HITCHCOCK, HENRY-RUSSELL. Rococo Architecture in Southern Germany. (NY): Phaidon, (1968). 1st ed. 218 plts. Ex-lib, else VG in dj (lt rubbed). *Bookpress*. $95/£61

HITCHCOCK, HENRY-RUSSELL. Rococo Architecture in Southern Germany. London, 1968. VG in dj. *Washton*. $85/£55

HITCHEN, DOLORES. Nets to Catch the Wind. NY: CCD, 1952. 1st ed. Pp browning, else NF in dj. *Murder*. $35/£23

HITTELL, THEODORE. The Adventures of James Capen Adams, Mountaineer and Grizzly Bear Hunter. NY: Scribner's, 1912. 3rd ptg. 11 plts. Fine. *Oregon*. $45/£29

HOAGLAND, EDWARD. Cat Man. Boston: Houghton Mifflin, 1956. 1st ed, 1st bk. Fine in dj (lt worn). *Hermitage*. $75/£48

HOAGLAND, EDWARD. Notes From the Century Before. Random House, (1969). 1st ed. 3 maps. VF in VF dj. *Oregon*. $20/£13

HOAGLAND, EDWARD. Seven Rivers West. Summit Books, 1986. 1st ed. Fine in Fine dj. *Bishop*. $15/£10

HOAGLAND, EDWARD. Tugman's Passage. Random House, 1982. 1st ed. NF in NF dj. *Bishop*. $15/£10

HOARE, CLEMENT. A Practical Treatise on the Cultivation of the Grape Vine on Open Walls. London: Longman, 1841. 3rd ed. ix,210pp + 1p ads. Orig blind-stamped cl, gilt spine title. Fine (eps browned; spine defective; hinges cracked). *Quest*. $85/£55

HOARE, CLEMENT. A Practical Treatise on the Cultivation of the Grape Vine on Open Walls. NY: H. Long, 1847. (v),14-209pp (complete). Blindstamped cl (text foxed, waterstained; cvrs worn). *Bookpress*. $85/£55

HOBAN, RUSSELL. Kleinzeit. NY: Viking, 1974. 1st ed. VF in dj. *Else Fine*. $40/£26

HOBAN, RUSSELL. The Lion of Boaz-Jachin and Jachin-Boaz. NY: Stein & Day, 1973. 1st ed. Fine in dj. *Else Fine*. $55/£35

HOBAN, RUSSELL. The Mouse and His Child. London: Faber, 1969. 1st UK ed. Fine in dj. *Lewton*. $47/£30

HOBAN, RUSSELL. Riddley Walker. London: Jonathan Cape, 1980. 1st ed. Nice. *Temple*. $37/£24

HOBAN, RUSSELL. Riddley Walker. London: Cape, 1980. 1st ed. Fine (emb owner stamp) in dj. *Else Fine*. $75/£48

HOBBS, EDWARD W. How to Make Old-Time Ship Models. Glasgow: Brown, Son, & Ferguson, 1934. 2nd ed. 5 lg fldg plans in pocket. Blue cl. Good. *Cox*. $43/£28

HOBBS, JAMES. Wild Life in the Far West. Hartford: Wiley, Waterman & Eaton, 1872. 1st ed. Color frontis, 488pp. Fair (new inner hinges). Howes H 550. *Lien*. $200/£129

HOBBS, WILLIAM H. Exploring About the North Pole of the Winds. NY: Putnam's, 1930. VG in dj (torn, frayed). *High Latitude*. $40/£26

HOBBS, WILLIAM H. Exploring About the North Pole of the Winds. NY: Putnam's, 1930. 1st ed. VG. *Blue Dragon*. $30/£19

HOBBS, WILLIAM H. Exploring About the North Pole of the Winds. NY: Putnam's, 1930. 1st ed. Blue cl over bds, black titles. NF (bumped) in VG dj. *Parmer*. $65/£42

HOBBS, WILLIAM H. Peary. NY: Macmillan, 1936. Inscribed. VG in dj (tattered). *High Latitude*. $40/£26

HOBDAY, FREDERICK T.G. Surgical Diseases of the Dog and Cat. London: Bailliere et al, 1906. 2nd ed, rev, enlgd. Gilt grn cl. Good. *Karmiole*. $35/£23

HOBSON, ELIZABETH CHRISTOPHERS. Recollections of a Happy Life. NY, 1914. 1st ed, ltd to 250. Untrimmed. Corners lt bumped, sm rubbed spot rear bd; else VG. Howes H 552. *Mcgowan*. $250/£161

HOBSON, G.D. Thirty Bindings.... First Edition Club, 1926. 1st ed. #94/600 ptd. 30 plts (16 color, 2 tinted); teg, others uncut. Buckram, gilt (backstrip faded). Good. *Cox*. $310/£200

HOBSON, R.L. Chinese Pottery and Porcelain. London, 1915. 2 vols. 40 color, 96 b/w plts; teg. (Eps, margins spotted; lt soiled cl; ink mk upper bd vol 1.) *Edwards*. $155/£100

HOBSON, R.L. Chinese Pottery and Porcelain. London, 1915. #815/1500. 2 vols. 40 color, 96 b/w plts. (Eps, mainly marginal spotting.) Teg, gilt illus title. (Cl lt soiled; sm red ink? mk upper bd vol 1.) *Edwards*. $217/£140

HOBSON, R.L. Chinese, Corean and Japanese Potteries. NY, 1914. #1171/1500. Color frontis, 24 plts (1 color). Fore, lower edges uncut. (Bds sl soiled, corners worn.) *Edwards*. $116/£75

HOBSON, R.L. Handbook of the Pottery and Porcelain of the Far East. London: British Museum, 1948. 20 plts. Bds (faded, esp spine). *Edwards*. $23/£15

HOBSON, R.L. The Later Ceramic Wares of China. London, 1925. Color frontis, 75 plts (8 fldg). (Lt spotting; edge-rubbed.) *Edwards*. $155/£100

HOBSON, R.L. The Wares of the Ming Dynasty. London: Tuttle, 1962. Facs ed. Color frontis, 9 color, 50 b/w plts. (Spine faded.) *Edwards*. $62/£40

HOBSON, R.L. Worcester Porcelain: A Description of the Ware from the Wall Period to the Present Day.... London: Bernard Quaritch, 1910. 92 collotypes; 17 chromolithos. Uncut. VG in dj. *Argosy*. $350/£226

HOBSON, R.L. et al. Chinese Ceramics in Private Collections. London, 1931. #291/625. 32 tipped-in color plts, 361 b/w. Teg, rest uncut. Red cl (bkpl; spine sunned). *Edwards*. $287/£185

HOBSON, WILDER. American Jazz Music. NY: W.W. Norton, 1939. 1st ed. NF in NF dj. *Beasley*. $150/£97

HOCH, EDWARD D. The Quests of Simon Ark. NY: Mysterious, 1984. 1st ed. VF in dj. *Mordida*. $35/£23

HOCHMAN, SANDRA. Voyage Home. Paris: Two Cities, 1960. 1st ed, 1st bk. Fine in wraps. *Second Life*. $75/£48

HOCHWALT, A.F. The Modern Pointer. N.p.: Hochwalt, 1923. 2nd ed. NF. *Artis*. $35/£23

HOCKEN, EDWARD OCTAVIUS. A Treatise on Amaurosis and Amaurotic Affections. Phila: Waldie, 1842. vi,201pp. (Leaf vi misbound in back; faint damp-staining affecting lower third last 25 leaves). 1/4 calf (rebacked). *Goodrich*. $175/£113

HOCKING, JOSEPH. The Man Who Found Out. London: Ward-Locke, 1933. 1st ed. Fine in pict dj (sm chips spine corners). *Else Fine*. $45/£29

HODAPP, WILLIAM (ed). The Pleasures of the Jazz Age. NY: Farrar, Straus, 1948. 1st ed. Name, else NF in dj (lt worn). *Chapel Hill*. $50/£32

HODDER, W.R. The Daughter of the Dawn. Page, 1903. 1st Amer ed. Spine lettering flaked; fr inner hinge starting, else VG + . *Aronovitz*. $100/£65

HODDINOTT, R.F. Early Byzantine Churches in Macedonia and Southern Serbia. London, 1963. 8 color, 64 b/w plts; 3 fldg maps. Dj. *Edwards*. $90/£58

HODGE, E.W. The Northern Highlands. Edinburgh: Scottish Mountaineering Club, 1953. 3rd ed. Map. (Bds sl damped.) Dj (sl frayed). *Hollett*. $31/£20

HODGE, FREDERICK W. BAE Bulletin 30. Handbook of American Indians North of Mexico, Part 1. Washington D.C.: GPO, 1907. VG. *Perier*. $60/£39

HODGE, FREDERICK W. BAE Bulletin 30. Handbook of American Indians North of Mexico, Part 2. Washington D.C.: GPO, 1907. Good (worn). *Perier*. $40/£26

HODGE, FREDERICK W. BAE Bulletin 30. Handbook of American Indians North of Mexico. Washington, 1907-10. 2 parts in 2 vols. Fldg map. (Sl shaken, extrems rubbed, spines sl chipped.) *Edwards*. $124/£80

HODGE, FREDERICK W. Handbook of American Indians North of Mexico. Washington: GPO, 1911. 2 vols. Color fldg map rear vol 1. Grn cl. Lt wear to extrems both vols, o/w VG. *Laurie*. $150/£97

HODGE, FREDERICK W. and THEODORE H. LEWIS (eds). Spanish Explorers in the Southern United States, 1528-1543. NY: Scribner's, 1907. 1st ed. 2 fldg maps. Dk grn cl. Rear hinge starting, lib stamps, else VG. *Chapel Hill*. $75/£48

HODGE, HUGH. On Diseases Peculiar to Women Including Displacements of the Uterus. Phila, 1868. 2nd ed. 531pp. Good. *Fye*. $50/£32

HODGE, HUGH. The Principles and Practice of Obstetrics. Phila, 1866. 550pp. Full leather. Fr hinge broken, o/w VG. *Fye*. $400/£258

HODGES, GEORGE. Fountains Abbey. London: John Murray, 1904. 1st ed. 8 plts, 2 fldg plans (1 color). Teg, uncut. Gilt cl-backed bds (spine sl dknd). *Hollett*. $39/£25

HODGES, NATH. Loimologia: or, an Historical Account of the Plague in London in 1655. London: For E. Bell & J. Osborn, 1721. 3rd ed. v,224pp, fldg table. Old marbled bds (rebacked). *Bickersteth*. $132/£85

HODGES, RICHARD. On the Nature, Pathology and Treatment of Puerperal Convulsions. London, 1864. 1st ed. 96pp. (Backstrip missing; bds detached; ex-lib.) Contents Fine. *Fye*. $200/£129

HODGKIN, HOWARD. Indian Leaves. Petersburg Press, 1982. 1st ed. Fine in integral wrappers. *Rees*. $31/£20

HODGKIN, JAMES B. Southland Stories. Manassas, VA: Journal Press, 1903. 1st ed. Grn cl. VG. *Chapel Hill*. $60/£39

HODGKIN, R.H. A History of the Anglo-Saxons. OUP, 1939. 2nd ed. 2 vols. Buckram. Djs (sl torn). *Petersfield*. $56/£36

HODGKIN, THOMAS. The History of England...to the Norman Conquest. Longmans, Green, 1906. 1st ed. 2 pull-out color maps. Cl gilt (sl rubbed, faded). Sound. *Peter Taylor.* $22/£14

HODGSON, ADAM. Remarks During a Journey Through North America in the Years 1819, 1820, and 1821.... NY: Samuel Whiting, 1823. 1st ed. 355pp (lacks fep); untrimmed. Contemp bds (worn). Good (lib bkpl, blindstamp). Howes H 560. *Chapel Hill.* $400/£258

HODGSON, MRS. WILLOUGHBY. Old English China. London, 1913. 16 color plts. Fore, lower edge uncut. (Lt spotting; soiled; spine sl bumped.) *Edwards.* $101/£65

HODGSON, W. EARL. Salmon Fishing. London: A&C Black, 1906. 1st ed. Color frontis, 6 color plts. *Petersfield.* $54/£35

HODGSON, W. EARL. Trout Fishing. London: A&C Black, 1904. Color frontis, 7 color plts (eps, 1/2 title foxed). Pict cl, gilt. *Hollett.* $54/£35

HODGSON, W. EARL. Trout Fishing. Black, 1930. 3rd ed. 7 color plts. (Sl foxing; sl spotted.) *Petersfield.* $19/£12

HODGSON, WILLIAM HOPE. Carnacki the Ghost Finder. Arkham House, 1947. 1st ed. NF in dj. *Madle.* $100/£65

HODGSON, WILLIAM HOPE. The House on the Borderland and Other Novels. Sauk City: Arkham House, 1946. 1st thus. Bkpl; corners bumped, worn, else NF in dj (lt edgeworn; clear tape corner). *Other Worlds.* $250/£161

HODGSON, WILLIAM HOPE. The House on the Borderland. Arkham House, 1946. 1st ed. VG in dj (wear, tear; chipping; inner tape reinforcement). *Aronovitz.* $165/£106

HODINOTT, R.F. Early Byzantine Churches in Macedonia and Southern Serbia. London, 1963. Good in dj (worn). *Washton.* $100/£65

HODNETT, EDWARD. English Woodcuts 1480-1535. London: Bibliographical Soc, 1935. Holland-backed bds. *Waterfield.* $54/£35

HODNETT, EDWARD. English Woodcuts 1480-1535. London: OUP, 1973. 251 woodcuts. (Ex-lib.) *Edwards.* $39/£25

HODNETT, EDWARD. English Woodcuts 1480-1535. Oxford, 1973. 251 facs woodcuts. Orig cl. New. *Cox.* $47/£30

HODNETT, EDWARD. English Woodcuts, 1480-1535. Oxford: OUP, 1973. Blue buckram, gilt spine title. Fine. *Heller.* $60/£39

HODNETT, EDWARD. English Woodcuts, 1480-1535. Oxford: OUP, 1973. 2nd ed. Fine. *Bookpress.* $85/£55

HODNETT, EDWARD. Francis Barlow. London, 1978. Good. *Washton.* $45/£29

HOEGH, L. Timberwolf Tracks: 104th Infantry Division. Washington, 1946. Good. *Clark.* $85/£55

HOEHLING, ADOLF A. Last Train from Atlanta. NY, (1958). 1st ed. NF in VG dj. *Mcgowan.* $45/£29

HOESS, RUDOLF. Commandant of Auschwitz. World, 1960. 1st ed. VG+ in VG+ dj. *Bishop.* $25/£16

HOFER, PHILIP. Baroque Book Illustration. Cambridge: Harvard Univ, 1970. 149 plts. Fine. *Europa.* $96/£62

HOFER, PHILIP. Edward Lear as a Landscape Draughtsman. Cambridge: Belknap Press of Harvard Univ Press, 1967. 1st ed. Color frontis. Fine in illus dj (chip). *Cahan.* $50/£32

HOFF, EBBE C. and J.F. FULTON. Bibliography of Aviation Medicine w/Supplement. Springfield, IL, 1942. Washington, 1944 (suppl). VG. *Argosy.* $150/£97

HOFFMAN, ABBIE. Steal This Urine Test. NY, 1987. 1st Amer ed. Signed. Fine in pict wraps. *Polyanthos.* $60/£39

HOFFMAN, ALICE. Angel Landing. NY: Putnam's, 1980. 1st ed. Lt erasure ep, else Fine in Fine dj. *Pettler.* $40/£26

HOFFMAN, ALICE. Illumination Night. NY: Putnam, (1987). 1st ed. Fine in dj. *Robbins.* $25/£16

HOFFMAN, ALICE. Property of. London: Hutchinson, (1978). 1st Eng ed, 1st bk. Fine in dj. *Heller.* $75/£48

HOFFMAN, ARNOLD. Free Gold. The Story of Canadian Mining. NY, (1947). 1st ed. VG-. *Artis.* $15/£10

HOFFMAN, E.T.A. Nutcracker. NY: Crown, (1984). Signed ltd ed w/signed, numbered litho laid in. Lg, square 4to. Maurice Sendak (illus). Dk blue cl, silver lettering cvr, spine; matching slipcase. As New. *Reisler.* $1,500/£968

HOFFMAN, E.T.A. The Tales of Hoffman. NY: LEC, 1943. #904/1500 numbered, signed by Hugo Steiner-Prag (illus). Fine in pub's slipcase (sl sunned). *Hermitage.* $95/£61

HOFFMAN, FREDERICK J. et al. The Little Magazine. Princeton: Princeton Univ, 1946. 1st ed. NF (stressed fr hinge) in dj (lt used). *Beasley.* $60/£39

HOFFMAN, FREDERICK J. et al. The Little Magazine. Princeton Univ, 1947. 2nd ed. VG. *Argosy.* $60/£39

HOFFMANN, HEINRICH. Slovenly Peter (Der Struwwelpeter). Mark Twain (trans). NY: LEC, 1935. 1st ed thus. #138/1500. H. Hoffmann (illus). VG in slipcase (lt torn). *Davidson.* $600/£387

HOFFMANN, PROFESSOR. (Pseud of Angelo John Lewis.) Drawing-Room Conjuring. London: George Routledge & Sons, n.d. (1887). 2nd ptg; Yellow pict stiff-paper bds (sl spine wear). *Dramatis Personae.* $125/£81

HOFFMANN, PROFESSOR. (Pseud of Angelo John Lewis.) More Magic by Professor Hoffmann. Phila: McKay, (ca 1920). Early Amer ed. Dk blue pict cl. VG. *Houle.* $150/£97

HOFLAND, BARBARA. The Young Cadet. London: John Harris, (1827). 1st ed. Fine hand-inked dedication fep dated 1825. 12mo. Full-pg copper engr x2 frontis, xi,232pp; 5x2 full-pg numbered engrs. Pict blue paper on bd, red roan spine, gilt. In all, Fine (spine crown lt rubbed; corners bumped). *Hobbyhorse.* $270/£174

HOFLAND, MRS. The Blind Farmer and His Children. London: J. Harris, 1816. 1st ed. Sm 8vo. VF full-pg copper engr frontis, iv,183 + 8pp list. Rebacked w/orig leather on bds; gilt spine title. VG (sl spotting in text; edges lt rubbed). *Hobbyhorse.* $195/£126

HOFLAND, T.C. The British Angler's Manual. London: Whitehead, 1839. 1st ed. xvi,410pp (foxing). Marbled eps. Orig gilt-edged blind emb calf (ex-libris; hinges cracked; fr hinge crudely repaired w/tape; upper joint splitting; rubbed), gilt dec raised bands (chipped, sl faded). *Edwards.* $93/£60

HOFMANN, E. Kokoschka. Life and Works with Two Essays by Oskar Kokoschka. London: Faber, 1947. 88 plts (5 color). (Cl sl worn.) *Ars Artis.* $93/£60

HOFSTATTER, HANS H. Art Nouveau Prints, Illustrations and Poster. London, 1984. Dj (sl soiled). *Edwards.* $43/£28

Hog Cholera: Its History, Nature.... Washington, 1889. 1st ed. 197pp. (Ex-lib.) *Fye.* $50/£32

HOGABOAM, JAMES J. The Bean Creek Valley. Hudson, MI: Jas. M. Scarritt, 1876. 140,iv pp. VG (lt soiled, chipped) in yellow ptd wraps. *Bohling.* $65/£42

HOGABOAM, JAMES J. The Bean Creek Valley. Hudson, MI: Jas. M. Scarritt, 1876. 1st ed. 140,ivpp. Good in ptd wrappers (sm tear). *Karmiole.* $75/£48

HOGAN, JOHN JOSEPH. On the Mission in Missouri 1857-1868. Kansas City, MO, 1892. 1st ed. 221pp. Howes H 573. *Ginsberg.* $150/£97

HOGAN, RAY. Johnny Ringo: Gentleman Outlaw. London: John Long, (1964). 1st ed. VG in dj (sl worn). *Lien.* $22/£14

HOGARTH, BASIL (ed). Trial of Robert Wood. Toronto: Canada Law Book Co, 1936. *Boswell.* $75/£48

HOGARTH, DAVID G. Wandering Scholar in the Levant. NY: Scribner's, 1896. (xii),206pp, fldg map. Olive cl stamped in gilt, black (ex-lib w/mks). *Schoyer.* $65/£42

HOGARTH, MARY. Modern Embroidery. The Studio, Special # Spring 1933. 8 mtd color plts. Good (worn). *Willow House.* $39/£25

HOGBEN, LANCELOT, T. The Pigmentary Effector System. Edinburgh, 1924. Good. *Goodrich.* $35/£23

HOGG, J. The Microscope, Its History, Construction and Application. London, 1883. 10th ed. xx,764pp; 9 plts (8 color). Orig cl (crudely refixed). In case (used). *Wheldon & Wesley.* $62/£40

HOGG, J. The Microscope.... London, 1883. 11th ed. xx,764pp; 9 plts (8 color). Pict cl, gilt; new eps. (3pp torn, repaired w/o loss; spotting.) *Henly.* $59/£38

HOGG, JAMES. The Private Memoirs and Confessions of a Justified Sinner. London: Cresset Press, 1947. Facs frontis; xvi,230pp. Orig cl gilt. VG in dj (top edge sl creased; sm tear). *Hollett.* $19/£12

HOGG, JAMES. The Queen's Wake: A Legendary Poem. Edinburgh, 1815. 4th ed. (viii),iv,(ii),362pp; marbled eps. Contemp brn morocco, ruled gilt, red morocco spine label. Good (joints starting). *Bickersteth.* $39/£25

HOGG, JAMES. The Works of the Ettrick Shepherd. London: Blackie & Son, 1869. 2 vols. Sm 4to. viii,712; xl,468pp; 2 engr titles; 28 steel-engr plts. Blind-stamped cl (bkpls), gilt, over bevelled bds. *Hollett.* $132/£85

HOHMAN, ELMO PAUL. The American Whaleman. NY: 1928. 1st ed. NF in dj remains. *Lefkowicz.* $125/£81

HOIG, STAN. The Western Odyssey of John Simpson Smith. Glendale, 1974. 1st ed. Minor shelf wear, o/w Fine. *Pratt.* $40/£26

HOIG, STAN. The Western Odyssey of John Simpson Smith. Glendale, CA: Clark, 1974. 1st ed. Red cl, gilt. Fine in dj. *Laurie.* $60/£39

HOKE, HELEN and JOHN. Music Boxes. NY, (1957). 10-inch Mint lp record in back pocket. Fine in Good dj. *Artis.* $45/£29

HOLBROOK, J. Ten Years among the Mail Bags. Phila: Cowperthwait, 1874. 432pp. Grn cl dec stamped in black/gilt (bumped; spine chipped). *Hermitage.* $85/£55

HOLBROOK, M.L. Parturition without Pain. NY, 1871. 1st ed. 159pp. Good. *Fye.* $75/£48

HOLBROOK, STEWART H. The Old Post Road. NY: McGraw-Hill, (1962). (1st ptg). Double map. VG + (sl dent) in dj. *Bohling.* $30/£19

HOLBROOK, STEWART H. Tall Timber. NY: Macmillan, 1941. 1st ed. VG. *Peninsula.* $35/£23

HOLBROOK, STEWART H. Wild Bill Hickok. NY: Random House, 1952. Stated 1st ptg trade. Dec eps. VG in dj. *Cattermole.* $25/£16

HOLCOMBE, JAMES P. Barton's History of a Suit in Equity, From Its Commencement to Its Final Termination. Cincinnati: Derby, Bradley & Co, 1847. *Boswell.* $125/£81

HOLCOMBE, W.H. In Both Worlds. Lippincott, 1870. 1st ed. Spine head fraying, else VG. *Aronovitz.* $75/£48

HOLDEN, EDWARD S. et al. Meteors and Sunsets.... Contributions from Lick Observatory #5, 1895. 17 plts. Brn cl. Ex-lib w/mks; fep corner torn, o/w Good. *Knollwood.* $45/£29

HOLDEN, HORACE. A Narrative of the Shipwreck, Captivity and Sufferings of Horace Holden and Benj. H. Nute. Boston, 1836. Woodcut frontis, 133pp. Contemp cl (extrems sl rubbed). Good (fep excised; lt foxing). *Reese.* $425/£274

HOLDEN, MOLLY. The Speckled Bush. London: Poem-of-the-Month Club Ltd, 1974. 1st Eng ed. Signed. VG (corner sl creased). *Ulysses.* $28/£18

HOLDEN, WILLIAM CURRY. The Espuela Land and Cattle Company. Austin: TSHA, 1970. 1st ed. Dj. *Lambeth.* $30/£19

HOLDEN, WILLIAM CURRY. The Spur Ranch. Boston: Christopher, (1934). Gold-stamped cl (bkpl, notes rep; sticker fep). *Dawson.* $175/£113

HOLDER, CHARLES F. The Boy Anglers. NY: Appleton, 1904. 1st ed. Pict cl. Fine. *Bowman.* $85/£55

HOLDER, CHARLES F. Life in the Open. NY: Putnam's, 1906. 1st ed. Grn cl, gilt dec. Fine. *Bowman.* $60/£39

HOLDERLIN, FRIEDRICH. Selected Poems. J.B. Leishman (trans). Hogarth Press, 1944. 1st ed. Sl foxed, o/w VG. *Words Etc.* $39/£25

HOLDICH, T. HUNGERFORD. The Indian Borderland 1880-1900. London: Methuen, 1902. 1st ed. 22 plts (lacks map). Teg. Spotted, sl worn. *Hollett.* $70/£45

HOLDICH, THOMAS. Tibet, The Mysterious.... London: Alston Rivers, n.d. (1906). 1st ed. 33 plts, maps (incl frontis, 2 double-pg), lg fldg colored map (torn, repaired). (Lt browning.) Orig grn cl, (hinges cracked; spine, corners sl rubbed), gilt. *Morrell.* $155/£100

HOLE, CHRISTINA. Witchcraft in England. London: Batsford, 1945. 1st ed. Mervyn Peake (illus). VG in dj (worn, defective). *Hollett.* $54/£35

HOLE, S. REYNOLDS. A Book about the Garden and the Gardener. London: Thomas Nelson, (ca 1892). Frontis, 372pp + xii pp ads. Dec eps. Gilt-dec limp reversed calf cvrs. Spine ends clipped, else VG. *Quest.* $40/£26

Holiday Book by Theodore Thinker. NY: Clark, Austin & Smith, 1854. 16mo. Red emb cl, gold spine (faded, worn; pencil mks; blank rep missing; foxing). *Reisler.* $60/£39

Holiday Tales. Providence: Weeden & Peek, 1849. 3 vols in 1. Sq 12mo. 16 + 15 + 16pp + 1pg list lower wrapper. 6 VF full-pg wood engr vignettes. Fine in pict buff paper wrappers. *Hobbyhorse.* $100/£65

HOLLAMS, JOHN. Jottings of an Old Solicitor. London: John Murray, 1906. Grn cl (worn, stained). *Boswell.* $50/£32

HOLLAND, BOB, DAN, and RAY. Good Shot! NY: Knopf, 1946. 1st ed, 1st ptg. Burgundy cl. Spine sl rubbed, else Fine in dj (lt worn). *Glenn.* $60/£39

HOLLAND, CLIVE. Warwickshire. A&C Black, 1906. Sketch map; 75 color plts by Frederick Whitehead. Teg. (Sl foxing few pp; few tears backstrip.) *Petersfield.* $70/£45

HOLLAND, CLIVE. Warwickshire. A&C Black, 1906. Color frontis, 74 color plts, fldg map. Marbled eps; teg. 1/2 morocco (rebound), marbled bds (extrems, spine lt rubbed). *Edwards.* $70/£45

HOLLAND, G.A. History of Parker County and the Double Log Cabin. Weatherford: Herald, 1937. 1st ed. (Fep removed.) *Lambeth.* $135/£87

HOLLAND, HENRY. Medical Notes and Reflections. London: Longman etc, 1839. 1st ed. vii,628pp. Contemp full calf. (Old reback, cvrs scuffed.) Very Clean internally. *White.* $70/£45

HOLLAND, IRMA RAGAN. The Pages from Virginia to North Carolina: The Lewis Page Line. The author, (c. 1981). 2nd ed. Paper cvr, spiral bound. VG (cvr wear, soil). *Book Broker.* $50/£32

HOLLAND, J.G. The Life of Abraham Lincoln. Springfield, MA: Bill, 1866. 544pp + 2pp ads (frontis stain); 4 steel-engr plts. Full blind-emb leather. VG. *Schoyer.* $65/£42

HOLLAND, MARY. Our Army Nurses. Boston, 1897. 1st ed. 600pp. Good. *Fye.* $150/£97

HOLLAND, RAY P. Bird Dogs. NY: A.S. Barnes, (1948). Ltd to 250 signed by Holland and Fred McCaleb (illus). Teg. Red cl, gilt. Beautiful in slipcase. *Glenn.* $125/£81

HOLLAND, RAY P. Scattergunning. NY: Knopf/Borzoi, 1951. 1st ed. VG + in dj. *Bowman.* $60/£39

HOLLAND, RAY P. Shotgunning in the Uplands. NY: A.S. Barnes, (1944). 1st ed. Fine. Fr panel pict dj laid in. *Glenn.* $85/£55

HOLLAND, VYVYAN. An Explosion of Limericks with Explanatory Drawings by Sprod. London: Cassell, (1967). 1st ed. Silver-lettered blue bds. Very Nice in pict dj. *Cady.* $25/£16

HOLLAND, VYVYAN. Hand Coloured Fashion Plates 1770 to 1899. London: Batsford, 1955. 1st ed. 5 color plts. Lt spotted. Dj (sl worn). *Edwards.* $101/£65

HOLLAND, VYVYAN. Hand Coloured Fashion Plates 1770-1899. Batsford, 1955. 1st ed. Fine in dj. *Moss.* $62/£40

HOLLAND, VYVYAN. Son of Oscar Wilde. London, 1954. 2nd ptg. VG in VG dj. *Mcclintock.* $20/£13

HOLLAND, W.J. The Butterfly Book. NY, 1945. Rev ed. 77 plts. (Ex-lib; sl stained; lacks fep.) *Wheldon & Wesley.* $28/£18

HOLLAND, W.J. The Moth Book.... NY, 1903. 48 color plts. 1/2 morocco (sl rubbed). *Wheldon & Wesley.* $78/£50

HOLLAND, W.J. To the River Plate and Back. NY: Putnam's, 1913. 1st ed. Full color frontis, tissue, 38 plts. Pict cl. VG (inner hinge paper cracking, sl edge wear). *Connolly.* $45/£29

HOLLEN, W. EUGENE. Beyond the Cross Timbers. Norman: Univ of OK, (1955). 1st ed. VG in VG dj. *Perier.* $30/£19

HOLLENBACK, FRANK R. The Laramie Plains Line. Denver: Sage Books, (1960). One of 300 signed. Fldg map. Fine in dj (lt soiled). *Bohling.* $125/£81

HOLLEY, MARIETTA. Around the World with Josiah Allen's Wife. NY, 1905. 1st ed. VG. *Bond.* $35/£23

HOLLEY, WILLIAM C. et al. The Plantation South, 1934-1937. Washington: GPO, 1940. 1st ed. 13 full-pg b/w photos. Illus wrappers. Spine chipped, splits; edges faded, else VG. *Cahan.* $60/£39

HOLLIDAY, C.W. The Valley of Youth. Caldwell: Caxton, 1948. 1st ed. Signed. 51 full-pg photos. *Artis.* $29/£19

HOLLIDAY, J.S. The World Rushed In. S&S, (1981). 1st ed. 13 maps. VG in VG dj. *Oregon.* $30/£19

HOLLIDAY, J.S. The World Rushed In. NY, (1981). 1st ed. Inscribed. VG + in VG + dj. *Pratt.* $35/£23

HOLLING, HOLLING C. Tree in the Trail. Boston: HMCo, 1942. 1st Amer ed. Fine in NF dj (lt rubbed; sl edgewear). *Between The Covers.* $75/£48

HOLLINGHURST, ALAN. Confidential Chats with Boys. Sycamore Press, 1982. One of 300. 1st bk. Fine in wraps. *Sclanders.* $23/£15

HOLLINGHURST, ALAN. The Swimming Pool Library. NY, (1988). 1st Amer ed. VG in VG dj (lt wear). *Mcclintock.* $20/£13

HOLLINGHURST, ALAN. The Swimming-Pool Library. London: C&W, 1988. 1st UK ed. Fine in dj. *Williams.* $39/£25

HOLLIS, CHRISTOPHER. A Study of George Orwell. Chicago: Henry Regnery, 1956. 1st ed. Blue cl. Owner label, offsetting reps from laid-in newspaper article, else NF in VG dj. *Chapel Hill.* $35/£23

HOLLISTER, OVANDO J. Boldly They Rode. Lakewood, CO: Golden Press, 1949. 1st ed thus. Rpt of Denver 1863 ed. Howes C 601. *Mcgowan.* $85/£55

HOLLISTER, OVANDO J. Colorado Volunteers in New Mexico. Chicago, (1962). Lakeside Classic. VG. *Schoyer.* $25/£16

HOLLISTER, PAUL. Glass Paperweights. NY, 1974. 120 color plts. (Ex-lib w/ink stamp; lt tape mks.) Dj (sl chipped). *Edwards.* $39/£25

HOLLOWAY, LAURA C. The Hearthstone; or, Life at Home. Phila: Bradley, Garretson, 1883. 1st ed. Engr frontis, 582pp; 10 plts. Pict grn cl; gilt pict inset. (Fep removed.) *Petrilla.* $40/£26

HOLLOWELL, J.M. War-Time Reminiscences and Other Selections. (Goldsboro, NC): Goldsboro Herald, June 1939. 1st ed. Frontis port. Orig brn ptd wraps. Fine. *Chapel Hill.* $300/£194

HOLLY, H. HUDSON. Modern Dwellings in Town and Country. NY: Harper, (1878). 1st ed. Frontis, 219pp. Pub's gilt cl. Sig sprung, else VG + . *Bookpress.* $425/£274

HOLMAN, C. HUGH. Thomas Wolfe. Minneapolis: Univ of MN Press, (1960). 1st ed. Fine in ptd grn wraps. *Chapel Hill.* $25/£16

HOLMAN, FREDERICK. Dr. John McLoughlin, the Father of Oregon. Clark, 1907. 1st ed. Frontis port, plt. Teg. VG. *Oregon.* $90/£58

HOLMAN, FREDERICK. Dr. John McLoughlin, the Father of Oregon. Cleveland: Clark, 1907. One of 1047. Bkpl, else NF. *Perier.* $100/£65

HOLME, C. GEOFFREY (ed). Applied Art, 1921. The Studio, 1921. 10 color plts. Teg. (Spotting; cl lt spine faded.) *Edwards.* $78/£50

HOLME, C. GEOFFREY (ed). Children's Toys of Yesterday. London: The Studio, 1932. 12 color plts. VG in pict card wrappers. *Hollett.* $101/£65

HOLME, C. GEOFFREY (ed). Decorative Art, 1923. The Studio, n.d. (ca 1923). 9 color plts. Mod cl (rebound), leather title label. *Edwards.* $78/£50

HOLME, C. GEOFFREY (ed). Decorative Art. The Studio, 1935. (Ex-lib.) Dj (lt soiled, chipped). *Edwards.* $78/£50

HOLME, C. GEOFFREY (ed). Decorative Art. The Studio, 1938. 8 tipped-in color plts. (Ex-lib.) Dj (lt soiled, ragged). *Edwards.* $78/£50

HOLME, C. GEOFFREY (ed). Decorative Art. The Studio, 1942. (Ex-lib.) Dj (lt soiled, ragged). *Edwards.* $62/£40

HOLME, C. GEOFFREY (ed). Drawings in Pen and Pencil from Durer's Day to Ours. London: The Studio, Spring 1922. Dec card. Lt foxing to fore-edges, o/w Superb. *Willow House.* $31/£20

HOLME, C. GEOFFREY (ed). Lettering of Today. London: The Studio, 1937. Special autumn number. Eps lt browned, else VG in dj (torn); gray cl case. *Heller.* $75/£48

HOLME, C. GEOFFREY (ed). Thomas Girtin's Water-Colours. London: The Studio, 1924. #2/200. 96 plts (16 mtd, color); marbled eps. Teg, rest uncut. Japon bds (lt soiled); gilt title; leather label. *Edwards.* $233/£150

HOLME, C. GEOFFREY and SHIRLEY B. WAINWRIGHT (eds). Decorative Art, 1927. The Studio, n.d. (ca 1927). Color frontis, 7 color plts. Mod cl (rebound), leather title label. *Edwards.* $78/£50

HOLME, C. GEOFFREY and SHIRLEY B. WAINWRIGHT (eds). Decorative Art, 1928. The Studio, n.d. (ca 1928). 6 color plts. Orig limp paper wraps (lacks lower wrap, some of spine). *Edwards.* $39/£25

HOLME, C. GEOFFREY and SHIRLEY B. WAINWRIGHT (eds). Decorative Art, 1930. The Studio, 1930. 6 color plts. (Lt browned; fore-edge 1st leaves thumbed; cl sl faded; spine worn w/sl loss.) *Edwards.* $78/£50

HOLME, CHARLES (ed). Art in Photography. London: The Studio, 1905. 101 plts. (Prelims, margins spotted.) Pub's cl (sl soiled); teg. *Edwards.* $194/£125

HOLME, CHARLES (ed). Masters of English Landscape Painting. Studio Special Summer #1903. Gilt, beveled bds. Good+ (sl wear, foxing, stamp mks). *Willow House.* $47/£30

HOLME, CHARLES (ed). Modern British Domestic Architecture and Decoration. London: The Studio, 1901. (Tp lt spotted, new eps.) Teg, rest uncut. (Sl rubbed, faded; mod reback w/contemp bds.) Paper title label. *Edwards.* $39/£25

HOLME, CHARLES (ed). Modern Etchings, Mezzotints and Drypoints. London: The Studio, 1913. 1st ed. 195 plts (7 color). Tan buckram over bds (sl rubbed). *Karmiole.* $35/£23

HOLME, CHARLES (ed). Modern Pen Drawings: European and American. London: Offices of the Studio, 1901. 1st ed. Ltd to 300. Blind-stamped vellum. Prelims foxed; bds bowed; hinges, joints starting, o/w Good. *Hermitage.* $150/£97

HOLME, CHARLES (ed). Old English Country Cottages. The Studio, 1906. (Ex-libris; sl rubbed.) *Edwards.* $39/£25

HOLME, CHARLES (ed). Old English Country Cottages. London: The Studio, 1906. 15 color plts (1 loose; some spotting). Teg. Orig cl (worn; upper joint sl split; spine chipped w/sl loss). *Edwards.* $47/£30

HOLME, CHARLES (ed). Sketches by Samuel Prout.... London: The Studio, 1915. 55 plts (fore-edge last plt repaired). (Lt thumbed; corners sl creased or reinforced.) Lib morocco-backed bds (rebound; #s), gilt. *Edwards.* $39/£25

HOLME, CONSTANCE. He-Who-Came? London: Chapman & Hall, 1930. 1st ed. Blind-, gilt-stamped blue cl. NF in dj w/pict onlay. *Cady.* $30/£19

HOLME, RATHBONE and KATHLEEN M. FROST (eds). Decorative Art. The Studio, n.d. (ca 1948). 16 color plts. Dj (sl ragged, spine faded). *Edwards.* $93/£60

HOLMES, BAYARD. The Surgery of the Head. NY, 1903. 1st ed. Good. *Fye.* $150/£97

HOLMES, CLARA H. Floating Fancies Among the Weird and the Occult. London, (1898). 248pp. *Heinoldt.* $18/£12

HOLMES, J.M. Colour in Interior Decoration. London/NY: Architectural Press/Scribner's, 1931. 13 color plts, 20 mtd color plts. Sound in dj (torn). *Ars Artis.* $70/£45

HOLMES, JOHN CLELLON. Get Home Free. NY: Dutton, 1964. 1st ed. Fine in dj. *Pharos.* $75/£48

HOLMES, JOHN CLELLON. Go. NY: Scribners, 1952. 1st ed, 1st bk. 8vo. Fine in dj (sl rubbed). *Pharos.* $500/£323

HOLMES, JOHN CLELLON. The Horn. NY: Random House, (1958). 1st ed. Fine in dj. *Pharos.* $150/£97

HOLMES, JOHN CLELLON. The Horn. NY: Thunder's Mouth, (1988). Re-issue. VF in dj. *Pharos.* $20/£13

HOLMES, JOHN CLELLON. Nothing More to Declare. NY: Dutton, 1967. 1st ed. Orig 1/2 cl over bds. VG in dj (lt rubbed, edgeworn). *Sadlon.* $15/£10

HOLMES, KENNETH L. (ed). Covered Wagon Women: Diaries and Letters... 1840-1890. Glendale, CA/Spokane, WA: Clark, 1983-93. #6/33 specially bound in leather. Signed, w/keepsake. 11 vols, all as issued, 9 w/plain djs. Fldg map vol 11. Includes signed Cisneros print. *Bohling.* $3,000/£1,935

HOLMES, MAURICE G. From New Spain by Sea to the Californias, 1519-1668. Glendale: Clark, 1963. VG. *Perier.* $47/£30

HOLMES, MAURICE G. From New Spain by Sea to the Californias, 1519-1668. Glendale: Clark, 1963. 1st ed. 7 maps, plts. (Sl bumped.) *Dawson.* $100/£65

HOLMES, OLIVER W. Astraea: The Balance of Illusions.... Boston: Ticknor, Reed & Fields, 1850. 1st ed. Spine worn; few spots eps, o/w Nice. *Pharos.* $250/£161

HOLMES, OLIVER W. Astraea: The Balance of Illusions.... Boston: Ticknor, Reeds & Fields, 1850. 1st ed. Earliest binding state. Glazed bds (lacks backstrip). BAL 8757. *Goodrich.* $65/£42

HOLMES, OLIVER W. The Autocrat of the Breakfast Table. Boston: Phillips, Samson, 1858. 1st ed, 1st state. 373pp. Brn pebble cl (worn; rear joint split). Internally Good. BAL 8781. *Goodrich.* $95/£61

HOLMES, OLIVER W. Border Lines of Knowledge in Some Provinces of Medical Science. Boston: Ticknor & Fields, 1862. 1st ed, primary binding w/Ticknor & Fields imprint. One of 1500. Orig purple cl, gilt. Fep excised, else Nice. BAL 8814. *Macdonnell.* $100/£65

HOLMES, OLIVER W. Border Lines of Knowledge in Some Provinces of Medical Science.... Boston: Ticknor & Fields, 1862. 1st ed. Gilt cl (BAL's binding 2). Sl loss spine crown, owner stamps, else Nice. BAL 8814. *Reese.* $25/£16

HOLMES, OLIVER W. Boylston Prize Dissertations for the Years 1836 and 1837. Boston, 1838. 1st ed. 371pp. Recent cl. Lib stamp on title, o/w VG. *Fye.* $250/£161

HOLMES, OLIVER W. Boylston Prize Dissertations...1836 and 1837. Boston: Little, Brown, 1838. Fldg litho map. (Foxing; stamp; rebacked, orig backstrip.) BAL 8732. *Goodrich.* $195/£126

HOLMES, OLIVER W. The Collected Works of Oliver Wendell Holmes. Boston: Riverside Press, 1890s. 14 vols. Uniform red cl; leather labels. (Lt wear.) *Goodrich.* $95/£61

HOLMES, OLIVER W. A Dissertation on Acute Pericarditis. Boston, 1937. 1st ed. Full vellum. Good. *Fye.* $75/£48

HOLMES, OLIVER W. Dorothy Q. Boston: Houghton Mifflin, 1893. 1st trade ed w/Pyle illus. 1st issue w/p50, line 8 reading '...flashed...' Grey cl stamped in silver. NF. BAL 9042. *Second Life.* $45/£29

HOLMES, OLIVER W. Elsie Venner. Boston: Ticknor & Fields, 1861. 1st ed. 2 vols. Victorian cl (rubbed; sig lt sprung). Good. *Goodrich.* $125/£81

HOLMES, OLIVER W. The Guardian Angel. Boston: Ticknor & Fields, 1867. 1st Amer ed. Brn cl, gilt-, blind-stamped. Bkpl, spine toe sl worn, few sigs sl starting, corner creased, else VG. BAL 8857. *Reese.* $85/£55

HOLMES, OLIVER W. The Guardian Angel. Boston, 1867. 1st ed. 420pp. Internally Fine. (Sl rubbed.) *Goodrich.* $85/£55

HOLMES, OLIVER W. Homeopathy, and its Kindred Delusions. Boston, 1842. 1st ed ltd to 1000. (Lt foxing, spine sl worn.) BAL 8736. *Goodrich.* $295/£190

HOLMES, OLIVER W. Homeopathy, and Its Kindred Delusions. Boston: W.D. Ticknor, 1842. 1st ed. v,1 leaf, 72pp (sl foxing first few leaves). Orig bds, paper spine label. VG (sm defects at ends; hinges split). BAL 8736. *Hemlock.* $225/£145

HOLMES, OLIVER W. A Mortal Antipathy. Boston: Houghton Mifflin, 1885. 1st ed. Nice (bkpl). *Hermitage.* $75/£48

HOLMES, OLIVER W. The One-Hoss Shay: With Its Companion Poems. Boston: Houghton Mifflin, 1905. 1st ed thus. 66 color illus by Howard Pyle. Gilt stamped grn cl; teg. VG. *Houle.* $175/£113

HOLMES, OLIVER W. The Professor at the Breakfast Table. Boston: Ticknor & Fields, 1860. 1st ed, 1st issue. 410pp. Brn pebble cl. Good (lt wear). *Goodrich.* $95/£61

HOLMES, OLIVER W. The Professor at the Breakfast Table. Boston, 1860. 1st ed. Brn cl. Sl wear spine, else Fine. BAL 7891. *Pharos.* $125/£81

HOLMES, OLIVER W. The Vision of Sir Launfal. Cambridge: Nichols, 1948. 1st ed. Yellow bds soiled; spine rebacked, else Nice. BAL 13069. *Pharos.* $200/£129

HOLMES, PETER. Mountains and a Monastery. London: Bles, 1958. 2 fldg maps. VG in dj (chipped). *Schoyer.* $30/£19

HOLMES, T.R.E. A History of the Indian Mutiny.... London, 1885. 2nd ed, rev. xx,576+48pp pub's cat; 2 fldg maps; 6 plans (5 fldg). VG in brn cl (sl worn). *Edwards.* $132/£85

HOLMES, TIMOTHY. A Treatise on Surgery. Phila, 1876. 1st Amer ed. 960pp. Good. *Fye.* $100/£65

HOLMES, TOMMY. Dodger Daze and Knights. McKay, 1953. 1st ed. VG in Good dj. *Plapinger.* $60/£39

HOLROYD, JAMES E. Baker Street By-Ways. London: Allen & Unwin, 1959. 1st ed. Fine in NF dj (price-clipped). *Janus.* $85/£55

HOLROYD, MICHAEL. Lytton Strachey. NY, 1967. 1st ed. 2 vols. As New in djs, slipcase. *Bond.* $22/£14

HOLROYD, MICHAEL. Lytton Strachey: A Critical Biography. London: Heinemann, 1967/68. 1st ed. 2 vols. Bumped, sl speckled, o/w VG in dj (sl soiled, rubbed, nicked, faded). *Virgo.* $47/£30

HOLT, A.J. Pioneering in the Southwest. Nashville: So. Bapt. Conv, (1923). 1st ed. VG. *Oregon.* $60/£39

HOLT, E. EMMETT. The Diseases of Infancy and Childhood. NY: Appleton, 1898. 1st ed, 2nd issue. 1117pp (leaves rubbed, creased; lt dampstaining). 1/2 calf (rebacked). Good. *Goodrich.* $150/£97

HOLT, EDWIN BISSELL. The Freudian Wish and Its Place in Ethics. NY: Henry Holt, 1915. 1st ed, 1st ptg. Inscribed. Blue cl. *Gach.* $75/£48

HOLT, GAVIN. Black Bullets. London: Hodder & Stoughton, 1935. 1st ed. VG in Good dj. *Ming.* $31/£20

HOLT, GAVIN. The Theme Is Murder. S&S, 1939. 1st US ed. VG in Good dj. *Ming.* $31/£20

HOLT, L. EMMETT. Diseases of Infancy and Childhood. NY, 1898. 1st ed, 2nd ptg. 1117pp. VF. *Fye.* $200/£129

HOLT, LUTHER E. The Care and Feeding of Children. NY, 1907. 4th ed. (Pencilling; news clipping pinned to fep; cl spotted). *Argosy.* $400/£258

HOLT, ROY. Heap Many Chiefs. San Antonio: Naylor, 1966. 1st ed. Dj. *Lambeth.* $45/£29

HOLT, SIMMA. Terror in the Name of God. Crown, 1965. 1st Amer ed (?). 75 photos. *Bishop.* $25/£16

HOLTON, ISAAC F. New Granada. Twenty Months in the Andes. NY, 1857. 1st ed. 16,605pp, 2 maps, errata slip. New buckram (rebound). *Heinoldt.* $45/£29

HOLTZCLAW, B.C. Ancestry and Descendants of the Nassau-Siegen Immigrants to Virginia 1714-1750. Memorial Foundation of the Germanna Colonies, 1964. VG. *Book Broker.* $65/£42

HOLWAY, JOHN. Voices from the Great Black Baseball Leagues. Dodd Mead, 1975. 1st ed. VG+ in VG dj. *Plapinger.* $110/£71

Holy Bible Reprinted According to the Authorised Version 1611. Together with: The Apocrypha. Bloomsbury: Nonesuch, 1924-1927. Ltd to 1000; Apocrypha ltd to 1250. 5 vols. 4to. Stephen Gooden (plts). Partly uncut. Cream paper-cvrd bds blocked in gilt (dknd, edgewear; spine vol 2 repaired). *Glenn.* $700/£452

HOLYOAKE, GEORGE J. Among the Americans and a Stranger in America. Chicago, 1881. 1st Amer ed. 246pp (lacks blank leaf). *Ginsberg.* $75/£48

HOLZWORTH, JOHN M. The Wild Grizzlies of Alaska. NY: Putnam's, 1930. 1st ed. Blue cl. VG+. *Bowman.* $45/£29

HOLZWORTH, JOHN M. The Wild Grizzlies of Alaska. NY: Putnam's, 1930. 1st ed. 84 photos, map. VG. *Blue Dragon.* $85/£55

HOMANN-WEDEKING, E. The Art of Archaic Greece. J.R. Foster (trans). NY: Crown, 1968. 1st ed. VG in dj (torn). *Worldwide.* $24/£15

Home Pictures. NY: McLoughlin Bros, n.d. (ca 1890). Uncle Ned's Picture Books Series. Sm 4to. 8 leaves + 1pg list lower wrapper. (Sl offsetting.) Fine in pict stiff paper wrappers (lt rubbed). *Hobbyhorse.* $185/£119

Home Primer. NY: McLoughlin Bros, n.d. (ca 1865). Sq 8vo. 14 leaves + 1pg list lower wrapper. Pict orange paper wrappers (rebacked; lt soiled, creased). Name, leaf repaired, nicks, else VG. *Hobbyhorse.* $175/£113

HOME, GORDON. The Motor Routes of England. A&C Black, 1909. 1st ed. 24 color plts, fldg map. Teg. Dec cl (edges sl rubbed). *Edwards.* $54/£35

HOME, GORDON. Old London Bridge. London, (1931). VG. *Argosy.* $100/£65

HOME, GORDON. Old London Bridge. London, 1931. 6 fldg plans. (Head sl dented; sl rubbed; ex-libris.) *Edwards.* $54/£35

HOME, GORDON. Yorkshire Dales and Fells Painted and Described. London: A&C Black, 1906. 1st ed. 20 color plts. Red cl (spine faded). Fr flyleaf spotted, inscrip laid in, o/w Nice. *Hollett.* $70/£45

HOME, GORDON. Yorkshire Vales and Wolds, Painted and Described. London: A&C Black, 1908. 1st ed. 20 color plts, fldg map. Dec blue cl gilt (extrems worn, label removed spine; lt spotting). *Hollett.* $54/£35

HOME, GORDON. Yorkshire, Painted and Described. London: A&C Black, 1908. 1st ed. 71 color plts, map. Teg (fore-edge spotted). Pict cl. *Hollett.* $70/£45

HOME, GORDON. Yorkshire. A&C Black, 1908. 1st ed. 71 color plts, fldg map. Dec cl (sl rubbed; sl waterstaining corner prelims). *Edwards.* $62/£40

HOMER. Hymns to Aphrodite. Jack Lindsay (trans). N.p.: Fanfrolico Press, n.d. One of 500 numbered. 4 photogravure plts. Uncut. VG. *Argosy.* $125/£81

HOMER. The Odyssey. T.E. Shaw (trans). (N.p.): LEC, (1981). One of 2000 signed by Barry Moser (illus). 24 wood engrs. Tan cl. Fine in slipcase. *House.* $120/£77

HONE, NATHANIEL J. The Manor and Manorial Records. London: Methuen, 1925. 3rd ed. Red cl, gilt. VG. *Hollett.* $54/£35

HONE, PHILIP. The Diary of...1828-1851. Allan Nevins (ed). NY, 1927. 2 vols. Howes H 620. *Ginsberg.* $50/£32

HONEY, WILLIAM BOWYER. The Ceramic Art of China.... London: Faber & Faber/Hyperion, 1945. 1st ed. 3 tipped-in color plts. (Fore-edge 1st, last few leaves sl waterstained.) Dj (soiled, chipped). *Edwards.* $43/£28

HONEY, WILLIAM BOWYER. German Porcelain. London: Faber & Faber, 1947. 1st ed. 4 color, 96 b/w plts. (Eps lt spotted.) Dj (sl chipped, sl wrinkled). *Edwards.* $31/£20

HONIG, DONALD. Baseball Between the Lines. Coward, McCann, 1976. 1st ed. Fine in VG dj. *Plapinger.* $30/£19

HONIG, DONALD. Mays, Mantle, Snider. MacMillan, 1987. 1st ed. VG+ in VG+ dj. *Plapinger.* $35/£23

HONIG, LOUIS O. James Bridger. Kansas City: Brown-White-Lowell, 1951. #110/525 signed. Frontis port. Purple fabricoid. Fine. *Glenn.* $150/£97

HONOUR, HUGH. Cabinet Makers and Furniture Designers. NY: Putnam's, (1969). 1st Amer ed. White cl. Fine in VG color dj (2-inch seamed tear). *House.* $40/£26

HOOD, J.B. Advance and Retreat. New Orleans: G.T. Beauregard, 1880. 1st ed. Frontis port, 358pp, fldg map. Orig pub's 1/2 morocco. VG (lt foxing, bkpl). *Chapel Hill.* $400/£258

HOOD, ROBERT E. 12 at War: Great Photographers under Fire. NY: Putnam, (1967). Illus bds, as issued. NF. *Aka.* $50/£32

HOOD, ROBERT. To the Arctic by Canoe 1819-1821. C. Stuart Houston (ed). Arctic Institute of N.A., 1974. 1st ed. 5 maps. VF in VF dj. *Oregon.* $60/£39

HOOD, T.H. Notes of a Cruise in H.M.S. 'Fawn'...in the Year 1862. Edinburgh, 1863. xii,268pp; track chart; 8 color, 6 plain plts. (Ex-lib, used, loose; foxed.) *Wheldon & Wesley.* $140/£90

HOOD, THOMAS. The Comic Annual. London: Charles Tilt, 1834. xvi,175pp + 16pp ads, 49 full-pg plts. Leather, pict bds (rubbed, spine sl chipped). *Schoyer.* $125/£81

HOOD, THOMAS. Memorials of Thomas Hood. London: Edward Moxon, 1860. 1st ed. 2 vols. Frontispieces, xx,343; vii,357pp, ad leaf end vol 2. Cl blocked in blind, gilt-lettered spines. Fine (short slit). *Bickersteth.* $78/£50

Hoofs, Claws and Antlers of the Rocky Mountains by the Camera. Denver: F.S. Thayer, 1894. 1st ed. One of 1000. 35 full-pg plts. Aeg. Pub's full morocco, gilt. VG. *Cullen.* $300/£194

HOOG, MICHEL. Paul Gauguin. London, 1987. 1st UK ed. 150 color plts. Dj. *Edwards.* $70/£45

HOOKE, N. The Roman History.... London: Ptd for J. & R. Tonson, 1766-71. Vols 1-6 4th eds; rest 1st eds. 11 vols. Early mottled calf (joints cracked), gilt, leather labels to spines (chipped; vol 6 lacks label). *Edwards.* $194/£125

HOOKER, JOHN. Some Reminiscences of a Long Life. Hartford: Belknap & Warfield, 1899. 1st ed. 351pp. Pub's cl. VG. *Second Life.* $125/£81

HOOKER, JOSEPH DALTON and JOHN BALL. Journal of a Tour in Marocco and the Great Atlas. London: Macmillan, 1878. 1st ed. xvi,499pp, fldg panorama (sl worn), lg fldg map, fldg chart, 6 woodcut plts. 20th cent 1/2 crimson levant morocco, gilt, raised bands, marbled bds. Spots, but attractive. *Hollett.* $349/£225

HOOKER, JOSEPH DALTON. Himalayan Journals. London: John Murray, 1855. New ed. 2 vols. Frontispieces, xvi,348; xii,345pp + (ii)pub's ads, 1 red plt. Vol 2 unopened. Gilt illus cl (extrems rubbed, sl chipped; sm stains spines; lib mks feps; hinges cracked vol 1). *Edwards.* $194/£125

HOOKER, JOSEPH DALTON. Himalayan Journals. London: Minerva Lib, 1891. (Sl stained.) *Petersfield.* $37/£24

HOOKER, RICHARD. The Works. John Keble (ed). OUP, 1845. 3rd ed. 3 vols. Marbled eps, edges; gilt. (Upper hinge sl tender vol 1; spines sl rubbed.) *Edwards.* $85/£55

HOOKER, W.J. A Century of Ferns. London: William Pamplin, 1854. Lg 8vo. vii,200pp. 100 VF hand-colored plts. Teg. 1/2 morocco over marbled bds (edges rubbed). VF (fep lacks sm piece). *Quest.* $700/£452

HOOKER, W.J. and C.A.W. ARNOTT. The British Flora. London, 1850. 6th ed. xliv,604pp; 12 color plts. (Cl sl stained.) *Wheldon & Wesley.* $47/£30

HOOKER, WILLIAM FRANCIS. The Prairie Schooner. Chicago: Saul Bros, 1918. Orig pict cl. VG. *Schoyer.* $45/£29

HOOPER, C.L. Report of the Cruise of the U.S. Revenue Steamer Corwin in the Arctic Ocean.... Washington: GPO, 1881. 71(2)pp. 10 plts, 4 fldg tables (1 repaired), fldg map. New stiff wrapper; orig ptd fr wrapper present. Generally Good. *High Latitude.* $125/£81

HOOPER, CHARLES E. The Country House. London: Batsford, 1906. 1st ed. Frontis, teg. (Hinges internally cracked; rubbed.) *Bookpress.* $110/£71

HOOPER, E.J. Hooper's Western Fruit Book. Cincinnati, 1857. Engr frontis, ii,333pp + ads; 4 color plts (dull). Last 40pp margins dampstained; chipped. *Brooks.* $125/£81

HOOPER, JOHN and RODNEY. Modern Furniture and Fittings. London: Batsford, 1955. 2nd rev ed. 70 plts. Lacks fep, wear, mks, o/w VG. *Willow House.* $43/£28

HOOPER, R. Lexicon Medicum. London, 1831. 6th ed. 2 vols. viii,644; 645-1311pp (prelims lt foxed). 1/2 leather (rebacked, orig spines preserved). *Whitehart.* $140/£90

HOOPES, JOSIAH. The Book of Evergreens. NY, 1868. 435pp + ads. Emb gilt-dec cl (spine ends rubbed, starting; bumped; lt spotting). VG. *Shifrin.* $40/£26

HOOTON, EARNEST ALBERT. The Indians of Pecos Pueblo. New Haven: Yale, 1930. 1st ed. Plts in rear pocket. VG- (spine wear). *Parker.* $150/£97

HOOVER, H.A. Early Days in the Mogollons (Muggyyones). El Paso: TX Western Press, 1958. 1st ed. Spine, back cvr sunned, o/w VG in pict wrappers. *Laurie.* $60/£39

HOOVER, HERBERT C. A Remedy for Disappearing Game Fishes. NY: Huntington Press, 1930. One of 990 numbered. Signed presentation. Cl-backed marbled bds. Fine in orig glassine, VG+ slipcase. *Bowman.* $275/£177

Hopalong Cassidy and Lucky at the Double X Ranch. NY: Garden City Publishing, 1950. 20x27 cm. 3 Good dbl-pg pop-ups. Jack Rowe (illus). Illus bds (rubbed; spine frayed). *Book Finders.* $75/£48

HOPE, A.R. Surrey. A&C Black, 1912. Rpt. 75 color plts, fldg map. Dec cl (spine sl faded; lt browning). *Edwards.* $70/£45

HOPE, ANTHONY. The Dolly Dialogues. London: Westminster Gazette, 1894. 4th ed. Arthur Rackham (illus). VG (inscrip) in orig wrappers (sl mkd; spine replaced w/tape). *Williams.* $93/£60

HOPE, ANTHONY. The Prisoner of Zenda. NY: Henry Holt, 1894. 1st Amer ed. Tipped in engr. Buckram cl stamped in red; teg. VG. *Antic Hay.* $125/£81

HOPE, ANTHONY. The Prisoner of Zenda. London: Arrowsmith, Bristol, 1894. 2nd issue, w/18 rather than 17 titles listed as part of Arrowsmith 3/6 series after last pg of text. Extra title is this bk. VG (spine sl faded, extrems sl rubbed, flyleaf hinges starting). *Williams.* $116/£75

HOPE, BOB. They Got Me Covered. (Hollywood, 1941). 1st ed. Couple creases on fr of orig ptd wrappers, else VG. *Mcgowan.* $45/£29

HOPE, JAMES BARRON. A Wreath of Virginia Bay Leaves. West, Johnston, 1895. Inscribed by Janey Hope Marr (ed, daughter). Frontis, 159pp. VG-. *Book Broker.* $35/£23

HOPF, ALBRECHT. Oriental Carpets and Rugs. London, 1962. 62 color plts. (Marginal browning.) Dj (chipped). *Edwards.* $93/£60

HOPKINS, G.H.E. and M. ROTHSCHILD. An Illustrated Catalogue of the Rothschild Collection of Fleas (Siphonaptera) in the British Museum. Vol 1. London: British Museum, 1953. 45 plts. Fine. *Savona.* $43/£28

HOPKINS, GERARD MANLEY. The Correspondence with Richard Watson Dixon. Claude Colleer Abbott (ed). London, 1935. 1st ed. (Cl faded.) *Argosy.* $45/£29

HOPKINS, GERARD MANLEY. Further Letters including His Correspondence with Coventry Patmore. Clause Colleer Abbott (ed). London, 1938. 1st ed. VG in dj. *Argosy.* $75/£48

HOPKINS, JOHN A. Economic History of the Production of Beef Cattle in Iowa. Iowa City, 1928. One of 600. Unopened. VF in glassine wrapper, orig mailing box. *Bohling.* $42/£27

HOPKINS, LEE BENNETT. I Think I Saw a Snail: Young Poems for City Seasons. NY: Crown, (1969). 1st ed. Harold James (illus). Tall, thin 4to. Lt sticker removal mk fr pastedown, else Fine in pict bd. NF dj (short tear, sl soiled). *Between The Covers.* $75/£48

HOPKINS, LINTON C. Black Buck. Boston: Little Brown, 1931. 1st ed. Spotting pg edges, o/w VG in dj (tape repairs). *Mordida.* $35/£23

HOPKINS, R. THURSTON. Moated Houses of England. NY, 1935. (Spine faded.) *Edwards.* $31/£20

HOPKINS, SARAH WINNEMUCCA. Life Among the Piutes: Their Wrongs and Claims. Mrs. Horace Mann (ed). Boston: Cupples, Upham, 1883. 1st ed. 268pp. Dec yellow cl, gilt-lettered spine (ends sl worn). VG+ (sl rubbed). *Harrington.* $165/£106

HOPLEY, GEORGE. (Pseud of Cornell Woolrich.) Night Has a Thousand Eyes. NY/Toronto: Farrar & Rinehart, (1945). 1st ed. Inked out name flyleaf, o/w VG+ in dj (spine ends sl chipped). *Bernard.* $200/£129

HOPLEY, GEORGE. (Pseud of Cornell Woolrich). Night Has a Thousand Eyes. NY: Farrar & Rinehart, 1945. 1st ed. Fine in VG dj (closed crease-tear; internal tape mends; sl wear). *Mordida.* $235/£152

HOPPING, RICHARD C. A Sheriff-Ranger in Chuckwagon Days. (NY): Pageant Press, (1951). 1st ed. Ink inscrip, else VG. *Perier.* $17/£11

HORAN, JAMES D. Across the Cimarron. NY, (1956). 1st ed. Fine in dj (sl wear, staining). *Pratt.* $35/£23

HORAN, JAMES D. The Authentic Wild West—The Outlaws. NY, (1977). 1st ed. Dj spine faded, o/w VG+. *Pratt.* $25/£16

HORAN, JAMES D. Confederate Agent, a Discovery in History. NY, (1954). 1st ed. Dj. *Heinoldt.* $15/£10

HORAN, JAMES D. The Life and Art of Charles Schreyvogel. NY, (1969). 36 color plts. VG in dj. *Argosy.* $185/£119

HORGAN, PAUL. The Centuries of Santa Fe. NY: Dutton, 1956. 1st ed, trade issue. Fine in NF dj. *Reese.* $30/£19

HORGAN, PAUL. The Centuries of Santa Fe. E.P. Dutton, 1956. 1st ed. Ep maps. Fine in Good+ dj. *Oregon.* $25/£16

HORGAN, PAUL. Citizen of New Salem. NY: Farrar, Straus and Cudahy, (1961). 1st ed. NF in NF dj. *Mcgowan.* $15/£10

HORGAN, PAUL. The Devil in the Desert. NY: Longmans, Green, 1952. 1st ed. Fine in dj (corners sl used). *Reese.* $50/£32

HORGAN, PAUL. Encounters with Stravinsky. NY: FSG, (1972). 1st ed. Fine in VG dj. *Godot.* $35/£23

HORGAN, PAUL. Everything to Live For. NY: FSG, (1968). 1st ed. Fine in dj. *Godot.* $35/£23

HORGAN, PAUL. The Fault of Angels. NY: Harper, 1933. 1st ed. Sl sunned, o/w VG in foil dj (sm chips, lg chip, spine lt rubbed, tarnished streak fr flap). *Reese.* $85/£55

HORGAN, PAUL. Figures in a Landscape. NY, 1940. 1st ed. VG- (date stamp) in dj (lt worn, sl chipped). *Baade.* $75/£48

HORGAN, PAUL. Give Me Possession. NY: Farrar, Straus & Cudahy, (1957). 1st ed. Fine in dj. *Godot.* $35/£23

HORGAN, PAUL. Lamy of Santa Fe. NY: FSG, 1975. 1st ed. NF in NF dj. *Parker.* $30/£19

HORGAN, PAUL. Men of Arms. Phila: David McKay, (1931). 1st ed. 5000 ptd; all but 500 destroyed. Red cl, gold dec. Spine evenly faded, sl worn, else VG. *Godot.* $350/£226

HORGAN, PAUL. The Peach Stone. NY: FSG, (1967). 1st ed. Fine in dj. *Godot.* $45/£29

HORGAN, PAUL. Rome Eternal. Farrar, Straus & Cudahy, (1959). 1st ltd ed of 350 numbered, signed. Sm erasure, else Fine in slipcase (foxed). *Authors Of The West.* $100/£65

HORGAN, PAUL. The Saintmaker's Christmas Eve. NY: Farrar, (1955). 1st ed. NF in VG dj (sl nicked). *Reese.* $45/£29

HORGAN, PAUL. Things as They Are. NY: Farrar, (1964). 1st ed. Sm label, else Fine in dj (price-clipped). *Reese.* $25/£16

HORLER, SYDNEY. The Curse of Doone. NY: Mystery League, 1930. 1st Amer ed. NF (name; chip) in dj (torn; chipped). *Polyanthos.* $25/£16

HORLER, SYDNEY. High Stakes. Little, 1935. 1st ed. Pp edges foxed, else NF in dj (spine head, foot worn; lt soiled). *Murder.* $40/£26

HORN, TOM. Life of Tom Horn, Government Scout and Interpreter. Chicago: (Lakeside Classic #85), 1987 (1st pub 1904). Color map. Brn cl; gilt stamping, top. Fine. *Bohling.* $35/£23

HORN, TOM. Life of Tom Horn, Government Scout and Interpreter. Doyce Nunis (ed). Chicago, 1987. Lakeside Classic. Frontis, map. VG. *Oregon.* $35/£23

HORNADAY, WILLIAM T. Our Vanishing Wild Life. NY: NY Zoological Soc, 1913. 1st ed. 84 photos, 10 maps. Heavy, glossy paper. Shelfwear, else Fine. *Connolly.* $47/£30

HORNADY, JOHN R. Atlanta. Yesterday, Today and Tomorrow. (Atlanta?): Amer Cities Book Co, 1922. 1st ed. Dk grn cl. Lt foxing, lacks mtd cvr label, o/w VG. *Chapel Hill.* $40/£26

HORNBEIN, THOMAS. Everest, the West Ridge. Sierra Club, (1965). 1st ed. VG in VG dj. *Oregon.* $135/£87

HORNE, HERBERT P. The Binding of Books. London: Kegan Paul, 1894. 1st ed. Frontis. Gilt polished buckram. Text block damp-wrinkled at edges, else Good. *Reese.* $30/£19

HORNE, HERBERT P. The Bindings of Books. Kegan Paul, Trench, 1915. 9 plts. Good. *Moss.* $40/£26

HORNEY, KAREN. The Collected Works of Karen Horney. NY, 1964. 1st ed, reprinted. 2 vols. Good. *Fye.* $75/£48

HORNIBROOK, M. Dwarf and Slow Growing Conifers. London, 1923. 1st ed. Frontis port; 24 plts. Canvas-backed bds (sl foxed). *Henly.* $59/£38

HORNIBROOK, M. Dwarf and Slow-Growing Conifers. London, (1938). 2nd ed. *Wheldon & Wesley.* $31/£20

HORNSBY, ROGERS. My Kind of Baseball. McKay, 1953. 1st ed. VG in Fair dj (top third fr panel gone). *Plapinger.* $35/£23

HORNUNG, CLARENCE P. Handbook of Early Advertising Art, Mainly from American Sources. NY: Dover Pub, (1956). 3rd ed. 2 vols. 237 full-pg plts; 310 full-pg plts. VG in djs. *Bookpress.* $150/£97

HORNUNG, E.W. The Amateur Cracksman. Scribner's, 1899. 1st Amer ed. Teg. Good (spotted, soiled). *Murder.* $30/£19

HORRAX, GILBERT. Neurosurgery. Springfield, 1952. (Ex-lib; rubbed.) *Goodrich.* $75/£48

HORRICKS, RAYMOND et al. These Jazzmen of Our Time. London: Gollancz, 1959. VG in dj (edgeworn; chipped). *Aka.* $25/£16

HORSLEY, VICTOR and MARY STURGE. Alcohol and the Human Body: An Introduction.... London, 1908. 2nd ed. Good. *Fye.* $150/£97

HORTON, PHILIP. Hart Crane. W.W. Norton, 1937. 1st ed. VG + in VG- dj. *Bishop.* $15/£10

HORTON, WILLIAM ELLIS. Driftwood of the Stage. Detroit: Winn & Hammond, 1904. 1st ed. (Lt discoloration, rubbing.) *Dramatis Personae.* $75/£48

HORTON, WINIFRED M. Wooden Toy-Making. Leicester: Dryad Press, (1936). 1st ed. Fine in dj (lt soiled, chipped). *Glenn.* $40/£26

HOSE, CHARLES. The Field-Book of a Jungle-Wallah. London, 1929. 1st ed. Color frontis. Gilt device upper bd. (Lt foxing; lower edge dampstained intruding internally.) *Edwards.* $47/£30

HOSIE, ALEXANDER. Three Years in Western China. London: George Philip, 1890. 1st ed. xxxiv,302,(iv)pp (fr flyleaf replaced), fldg map. Pict cl (bumped, label removed), matching blue levant morocco (rebacked), gilt. *Hollett.* $341/£220

HOSIE, DOROTHEA. Brave New China. London: Hodder & Stoughton, 1938. 1st ed. Fep map. Cl sl mkd. *Hollett.* $70/£45

HOSIE, DOROTHEA. Portrait of a Chinese Lady. London: Hodder & Stoughton, 1929. 1st ed. 24 plts. Spine faded. *Hollett.* $70/£45

HOSKINS, W.G. The Making of the English Landscape. London: Hodder, (1956). *Petersfield.* $23/£15

HOSKINS, W.G. and L. DUDLEY STAMP. The Common Lands of England and Wales. London, 1963. 1st ed. Dj. *Edwards.* $105/£68

HOSMER, JAMES. History of the Expedition of Captains Lewis and Clark. Chicago: A.C. McClurg, 1902. 1st trade ed. 2 vols. Fldg map. Ink name, bkpl, else VG set. *Perier.* $175/£113

HOSMER, JAMES. The Life of Young Sir Henry Vane.... Boston: Houghton, Mifflin, 1889. 1st ed. Frontis port, xxxii,582,(4)pp. Blue cl, gilt. Good. *Karmiole.* $35/£23

HOSMER, JAMES. A Short History of the Mississippi Valley. Boston/NY: Houghton, Mifflin, (1901). Presumed later ptg. Blue cl, gilt. VG. *Chapel Hill.* $45/£29

HOTCHKISS, CHARLES F. On the Ebb: a Few Long-Lines from an Old Salt. New Haven: Tuttle, Moorehouse & Taylor, 1878. 1st ed. 127pp. *Lefkowicz.* $95/£61

HOTCHNER, A.E. Papa Hemingway. NY: Random House, (1966). 1st ed. VG + in Fine dj. *Bernard.* $25/£16

HOTSON, J. LESLIE. The Death of Christopher Marlowe. London: Nonesuch, 1925. Fldg frontis facs. Buckram. VG. *Argosy*. $75/£48

HOTSON, J. LESLIE. The Death of Christopher Marlowe. London: Nonesuch, 1925. 1st ed, 1st ptg. Cancel tp (1st issue point). Japon vellum. (Sl edgewear; gilt spine title faded.) *Glenn*. $150/£97

HOTSON, J. LESLIE. The Death of Christopher Marlowe. London: Nonesuch, 1925. 1st ed. Lg fldg facs frontis. Uncut in orig buckram. Good. *Cox*. $31/£20

HOTTEN, JOHN CAMDEN. Abyssinia and Its People.... London: Hotten, 1868. 1st ed. vi,384,(8)pub's list, lg fldg colored map, ad slip inserted (lt browning outer margin). Blue marbled cl. Generally VG (lower joint split, extrems sl rubbed). *Morrell*. $147/£95

HOUCK, GEORGE F. The Church in Northern Ohio and in the Diocese of Cleveland, from 1749 to September, 1887. Cleveland, 1888. 2nd ed. Inscribed. 301pp. (Foxing; sm spine snag; cvr sl discolored.) *Hayman*. $25/£16

HOUDINI, HARRY. Miracle Mongers and Their Methods. Dutton, (1920). 1st ed. *Dramatis Personae*. $125/£81

HOUGH, EMERSON. Mother of Gold. NY: D. Appleton, 1924. 1st ed. Good+. *Connolly*. $15/£10

HOUGH, EMERSON. The Story of the Cowboy. NY: D. Appleton, 1905. Early ed. VG-. Howes 673. *Parker*. $50/£32

HOUGH, LEWIS. The Science of Man Applied to Epidemics. Boston, 1849. 1st ed. 290pp. Good. *Fye*. $75/£48

HOUGHTON, CLAUDE. The Tavern of Dreams. London, 1919. 1st Eng ed. Signed. Excellent in dj. *Edrich*. $39/£25

HOUGHTON, W. British Fresh-Water Fishes. London: Hull & York, 1895. 2nd ed. *Petersfield*. $70/£45

HOURWICH, ISAAC A. Immigration and Labor, the Economic Aspects.... NY: Putnam's, 1912. Worn, rear hinge cracked, else Good. *Boswell*. $65/£42

House Beautiful Gardening Manual. Boston: Atlantic Monthly, (1926). 1st ed. Text lt yellowed, edgewear, sl rubbed, else Fine. *Bookpress*. $35/£23

House of Arden. (By E. Nesbit.) London: T. Fisher Unwin, 1908. 1st ed. 8vo. Teg H.R. Millar (illus). Illus red cl, gilt (spine sl faded). *Reisler*. $350/£226

House That Jack Built. NY: McLoughlin Bros, n.d. (ca 1870). (Cinderella Series.) Sm 4to. 4 leaves, 11 half-pg chromolithos. Pict paper wrappers. Fine (sig). *Hobbyhorse*. $200/£129

HOUSE, HOMER D. Wild Flowers of New York. Albany, 1918. 1st ed. 2 vols. 264 full-pg color plts. Gold-stamped cl (bumped). VG. *Shifrin*. $125/£81

HOUSE, HOMER D. Wild Flowers of New York. Albany, 1918. 1st ed. 2 vols. Cl (sl worn, sl bumped; stamped name; ends lt foxed). *King*. $150/£97

HOUSE, HOMER D. Wild Flowers of New York. Albany, 1923. 2nd ptg. 2 vols. 264 color photo plts. VG. *Argosy*. $150/£97

HOUSE, HOMER D. Wild Flowers. NY, 1961. Re-issue of 'Wild Flowers of New York' 1923. 364 color plts. *Wheldon & Wesley*. $54/£35

HOUSE, JOHN. Monet. Yale Univ Press, 1986. 2nd ptg. Dj. *Edwards*. $39/£25

HOUSEHOLD, GEOFFREY. The Exploits of Xenophon. NY: Random House, 1955. 1st trade ed. Leonard Everett Fisher (illus). Fine in dj. *Cattermole*. $35/£23

HOUSER, M.L. Abraham Lincoln, Student. (Peoria: M.L. Houser, 1932). 1st ed. Frontis port; 14 illus. Good in dec ptd wrappers. Vincent Starrett's copy, signed by him. *Karmiole*. $30/£19

HOUSMAN, A.E. The Letters. Henry Maas (ed). Hart-Davis, 1971. 1st ed. Few pg corners turned, o/w VG. *Poetry*. $19/£12

HOUSMAN, A.E. More Poems. Cape, 1936. 1st ed. NF in dj (chipped, price-clipped; spine tanned). *Poetry*. $28/£18

HOUSMAN, A.E. More Poems. London: Cape, 1936. 1st ed. Fine in navy blue cl lettered in gold. VG+ dj. *Vandoros*. $95/£61

HOUSMAN, A.E. A Morning with the Royal Family. London: Privately ptd, Christmas 1955. Stapled ptd wrappers. VG. *Hollett*. $54/£35

HOUSMAN, A.E. A Shropshire Lad. London: Philip Lee Warner, 1914. #766/1000. Teg. Uncut; orig ribbon marker. Very Nice. *Limestone*. $125/£81

HOUSMAN, A.E. A Shropshire Lad. Riccardi Press, 1914. #768/1000. Sl wear, o/w Fine. *Poetry*. $54/£35

HOUSMAN, A.E. A Shropshire Lad. NY: Heritage, 1935. 1st Heritage Press ed. Initialed by Edward A. Wilson (illus). Frontis. Full leather. Fine in pub's slipcase (sl sunned). *Hermitage*. $150/£97

HOUSMAN, CLEMENCE. The Were-Wolf. London/Chicago: John Lane/Way & Williams, 1896. 1st ed, 2nd binding. 124pp; frontis, 5 plts inserted. Brn cl stamped in black. Nicks, sl foxing eps, o/w Fine. *Second Life*. $200/£129

HOUSMAN, LAURENCE. The Blue Moon. London: Murray, 1904. 1st ed. (Few pp lt foxed; backstrip sl faded.) *Petersfield*. $33/£21

HOUSMAN, LAURENCE. Echo de Paris. A Study from Life. London, 1923. #11/250 signed. Uncut. Dec cvrs. Fine (bkpl; label rubbed). *Polyanthos*. $50/£32

HOUSMAN, LAURENCE. Little Plays of Saint Francis. London, 1935. 1st ed. 3 vols. NF in VG djs (spines rubbed, sunned). *Polyanthos*. $45/£29

HOUSMAN, LAURENCE. Princess Badoura, A Tale from the Arabian Nights. (London): Hodder & Stoughton, n.d. ca 1907. 10 tipped-in color plts by Edmund Dulac. Bds lt soiled, else VG. *Cullen*. $175/£113

HOUSTON, ANDREW JACKSON. Texas Independence. Houston: Anson Jones, 1938. 1st ed. Blue cl. Dampstain lower fr cvr, else VG in dj (lt chipped). *Chapel Hill*. $125/£81

HOUSTON, ELEANOR JORDAN. Death Valley Scotty Told Me. Louisville: (privately ptd), (1954). 1st ed. VG in wraps. *Book Market*. $25/£16

HOUSTON, MARY G. Medieval Costume in England and France. London: A&C Black, 1939. 1st ed. 8 color plts. Flyleaves browned. Dj (worn, chipped). *Hollett*. $47/£30

Houston, A History and Guide. Houston: Anson Jones, 1942. 1st ed. 2 maps. Pict cl. VG in Fine dj (lt dknd, edgeworn). *Bohling*. $60/£39

HOVDENAKK, P. Christo Complete Editions 1964-1982. NY University Press, 1982. 66 color plts. Sound. *Ars Artis*. $54/£35

HOVEY, W.R. Treasures of the Frick Art Museum. Pittsburgh, 1975. VF in dj (sl frayed). *Europa*. $23/£15

How to Get a Farm and Where to Find One. (By James Miller.) NY: James Miller, 1864. 1st ed. 345pp+ads. Pub's cl (sl worn). VG. *Second Life*. $125/£81

How to Play Baseball. Crowell, 1913. Rpt. Pict cvr. VG+; no dj as issued. *Plapinger.* $125/£81

How-to-Get-There (Barkan System) Street Directory of New York City, Manhattan and Bronx. NY, (1932). Fldg map. Red ptd wraps (worn). *Bohling.* $35/£23

HOWARD, BENJAMIN. Prisoners of Russia. NY: Appleton, 1902. Grn dec cl (rubbed, pocket removed; fep creased). *Schoyer.* $30/£19

HOWARD, EDWARD. Outward Bound, or, A Merchant's Adventures. Phila: E.L. Carey and A. Hart, 1838. 1st Amer ed. 2 vols. Cvr soiled; labels sl rubbed; fr inner hinge starting vol 1; lt foxing. Slipcase. *Sadlon.* $50/£32

HOWARD, EDWIN L. Chinese Garden Architecture. NY: Macmillan, 1931. Color frontis. 2-color cl, pict inset. Fine (lg inscrip fep). *Quest.* $70/£45

HOWARD, F. Colour as a Means of Art. London: Henry Bohn, 1849. 108pp (sm tear margin 1f, few paint spots in margins), 18 color litho plts. Orig cl (worn, loose). *Ars Artis.* $116/£75

HOWARD, F.E. The Mediaeval Styles of the English Parish Church. NY, 1936. 180 illus on plts. Good. *Washton.* $60/£39

HOWARD, F.E. and F.H. CROSSLEY. English Church Woodwork. Batsford, 1917. Gilt-edged cl, gilt titles. (Eps lt spotted; ex-libris.) *Edwards.* $70/£45

HOWARD, F.E. and F.H. CROSSLEY. English Church Woodwork. London: Batsford, 1933. 2nd ed. 16 collotype plts. Eps sl spotted. *Hollett.* $116/£75

HOWARD, F.E. and F.H. CROSSLEY. English Church Woodwork. London, n.d. (ca 1917). (Backstrip worn.) *Washton.* $40/£26

HOWARD, F.E. and F.H. CROSSLEY. English Church Woodwork...the Mediaeval Period 1250-1550. London: Batsford, 1927. 2nd ed. 16 full-pg collotypes. Full blue cl, gilt. Good (ex-lib, stamp mks, chipped, wear). *Willow House.* $70/£45

HOWARD, FRANCIS. Reminiscences, 1848-1890. London, 1924. 1st ed. Frontis port. Eps browned; inscrip, o/w VG in grn cl (bumped; spine head, tail crumpled). *Edwards.* $31/£20

HOWARD, H.E. A Waterhen's Worlds. Cambridge, 1940. 2 plts. Good (sm stamps eps; cvr lower edge sl faded). *Wheldon & Wesley.* $70/£45

HOWARD, JAMES H. (ed, trans). The Warrior Who Killed Custer. Lincoln: Univ of NE Press, (1969). 2nd ed. 16 color plts, 39 b/w plts. Fine in dj. *Graf.* $40/£26

HOWARD, JAMES McHENRY. Recollections of a Maryland Confederate Soldier...under Johnston, Jackson and Lee. Balt: William & Wilkins, 1914. 1st ed. 11 plts; fldg map. Cl sl soiled, else VG. Howes H 706. *Mcgowan.* $350/£226

HOWARD, JOHN H. A History of Herring Lake with Introductory Legend the Bride of Mystery. Boston: Christopher Publishing House, 1929. Grn cl. VG in VG dj. *Peninsula.* $45/£29

HOWARD, JOHN. The State of the Prisons in England and Wales.... London: J. Johnson, 1792. 4th ed. 4to. (viii),540,(1)pp, 22 plts. Contemp calf (rehinged). *Bookpress.* $650/£419

HOWARD, MARTIN. Victorian Grotesque. London, 1977. 1st ed. Dj (lt yellowed). *Edwards.* $39/£25

HOWARD, McHENRY. Recollections of a Maryland Confederate Soldier and Staff Officer. Balt: Williams & Wilkins, 1914. 1st ed. Frontis port, facs, map. Orig red cl. Name, fr hinge starting, else NF. *Chapel Hill.* $450/£290

HOWARD, OLIVER OTIS. Autobiography of Oliver Otis Howard.... NY: Baker & Taylor, 1908. 2nd ed. 2 vols. Orig red cl. Lib bkpls, blndstamps; hinges starting; lt soiled, else VG. *Chapel Hill.* $275/£177

HOWARD, ROBERT E. Almuric. West Kingston: Grant, 1975. 1st thus. Bkpl removed, else Fine in NF dj. *Other Worlds.* $25/£16

HOWARD, ROBERT E. Always Comes Evening. Arkham House, 1957. 1st ed. Fine in dj. *Madle.* $500/£323

HOWARD, ROBERT E. The Coming of Conan. NY: Gnome Press, (1953). 1st ed. NF in dj (edges sl worn). *Bernard.* $100/£65

HOWARD, ROBERT E. The Coming of Conan. Gnome, 1953. 1st ed. Fine in dj (sl soiled; spine chip). *Madle.* $95/£61

HOWARD, ROBERT E. Conan the Barbarian. NY: Gnome Press, (1954). 1st ed. NF in dj (sl chipped spine ends, fr corner tips). *Bernard.* $100/£65

HOWARD, ROBERT E. Conan the Barbarian. NY: Gnome Press, (1954). 1st ed. NF (poor quality paper browned on edges; 1 pg roughly opened resulting in 1-inch tear) in dj. *Antic Hay.* $125/£81

HOWARD, ROBERT E. Conan the Conqueror. Gnome, (1950). 1st ed. Stained, else Good in dj (worn, chipped). *Other Worlds.* $50/£32

HOWARD, ROBERT E. Conan the Conqueror. NY: Gnome Press, (1950). 1st ed. Fine in dj (few rubbed spots; lt fading). *Antic Hay.* $150/£97

HOWARD, ROBERT E. The Dark Man and Others. Arkham House, 1963. 1st ed. VG in dj (sl rubbed). *Madle.* $150/£97

HOWARD, ROBERT E. Echoes from an Iron Harp. Donald Grant, 1972. 1st ed. Fine in dj. *Madle.* $75/£48

HOWARD, ROBERT E. A Gent from Bear Creek. Grant, 1965. 1st Amer ed, 1st bk. One of 732. Fine in dj. *Aronovitz.* $85/£55

HOWARD, ROBERT E. A Gent from Bear Creek. Donald Grant, 1965. 1st ed. NF in dj (sl soiled). *Madle.* $65/£42

HOWARD, ROBERT E. King Conan. NY: Gnome, (1953). 1st ed. Sl offset eps from dj, else Fine in dj (lt rubbed). *Reese.* $60/£39

HOWARD, ROBERT E. King Conan. Gnome, 1953. 1st ed. VG in dj (waterstaining). *Madle.* $40/£26

HOWARD, ROBERT E. People of the Black Circle. Donald Grant, 1974. 1st ed. Fine in dj. *Madle.* $50/£32

HOWARD, ROBERT E. The Pride of Bear Creek. Donald Grant, 1966. 1st ed. Fine in dj. *Madle.* $90/£58

HOWARD, ROBERT E. The Pride of Bear Creek. Grant, 1966. 1st ed. One of 812. Fine in dj. *Aronovitz.* $65/£42

HOWARD, ROBERT E. Red Shadows. Donald Grant, 1968. 1st ed. Fine in dj (sl dusty). *Madle.* $125/£81

HOWARD, ROBERT E. Skull-Face and Others. Arkham House, 1946. 1st ed. VG in dj (frayed). *Madle.* $575/£371

HOWARD, ROBERT E. The Sword of Conan. NY: Gnome Press, (1952). 1st ed. NF in VG dj (edges worn). *Bernard.* $125/£81

HOWARD, ROBERT E. The Sword of Conan. Gnome, 1952. 1st ed. VG in dj (waterstaining cvrs, bottom). *Madle.* $50/£32

HOWARD, ROBERT E. and L. SPRAGUE DE CAMP. Tales of Conan. Gnome, 1955. 1st ed. Fine in dj (sl dusty). *Madle.* $75/£48

HOWARD, ROBERT E. and RICHARD CORBEN. Bloodstar. Morningstar Press, 1976. 1st ed. One of 1500 numbered, signed by Corben. Fine in dj. *Madle.* $85/£55

HOWARD, ROBERT E. and T.C. SMITH. Red Blades of Black Cathay. West Kingston: Grant, 1971. 1st ed. Bkpl removal; blank leaf folded, sm edge chip, else NF in Fine dj. *Other Worlds.* $45/£29

HOWARD, ROBERT E. and T.C. SMITH. Red Blades of Black Cathay. West Kingston: Donald Grant, 1971. 1st ed. Fine in dj. *Reese.* $50/£32

HOWARD, ROBERT M. Reminiscences. Columbus, GA: Gilbert Ptg, 1912. 1st ed. Frontis port (lt foxed). Orig tan cl. Spine ends sl worn, ink underlining, o/w NF. *Chapel Hill.* $275/£177

HOWARD, T. On the Loss of Teeth. London, 1857. Color plt. (Cl stained, sl worn; back hinge spine damaged.) *Whitehart.* $62/£40

HOWARD, TIMOTHY EDWARD. A History of St. Joseph County, Indiana. Chicago/NY: Lewis Pub Co, 1907. 2 vols. Frontis; dbl map; 59 plts & ports; 131 plts & ports. 3/4 leather; gilt edges. (Plt torn; vol 1 fr hinge split, backstrip chipped; vol 2 hinges repaired). *Bohling.* $110/£71

HOWARD, WILLIAM T. Public Health Administration and The Natural History of Disease in Baltimore, 1797-1920. Washington, 1924. 1st ed. Good in wrappers. *Fye.* $75/£48

HOWAY, FREDERICK W. Dixon-Meares Controversy. Toronto: Ryerson Press, (1929). 1st ed. One of 500. Gilt-stamped blue cl. VG+ (spine faded, name). Howes H 714. *Bohling.* $125/£81

HOWAY, FREDERICK W. (ed). Voyages of the 'Columbia' to the Northwest Coast 1787-1790 and 1790-1793. MA Hist Soc, 1941. Cl backed bds (spine dull). VG. *High Latitude.* $200/£129

HOWAY, FREDERICK W. (ed). Voyages of the 'Columbia' to the Northwest Coast, 1787-1790 and 1790-1793. (Boston): MA Hist Soc, 1941. 1st ed. 14 plts. Black cl over bds. Sl rubbed, o/w Very Nice. *Karmiole.* $175/£113

HOWAY, FREDERICK W. et al. British Columbia and the United States. The North Pacific Slope from Fur Trade to Aviation. Toronto: Ryerson, 1942. 1st ed. Ep maps. Uncut, unopened. VG (sm nick) in VF dj. *Oregon.* $150/£97

HOWE, E.W. The Mystery of the Locks. Boston: Osgood, 1885. 1st ed. VF in dec binding. *Else Fine.* $100/£65

HOWE, EDGAR F. and WILBUR J. HALL. The Story of the First Decade in Imperial Valley, California. Imperial: Edgar F. Howe, 1910. Recent fabricoid w/orig gold-stamped buckram sides laid down; leather spine label. (Marginal stain 1st 38 pp, sl affecting text.) *Dawson.* $100/£65

HOWE, ELLIC. A List of London Bookbinders, 1648-1815. London: Bibliographical Soc, 1950. 1st ed. Uncut, unopened. Fine. *Bookpress.* $100/£65

HOWE, GEORGE F. The Battle History of the 1st Armored Division.... Washington, (1954). 1st ed. Few pp wrinkled, else Good in dj (tear repaired w/tape). *King.* $75/£48

HOWE, HENRY. Memoirs of the Most Eminent American Mechanics; Also, Lives of Distinguished European Mechanics.... NY, 1840. 482pp, 50 woodcuts. Good (corners worn). *Artis Books.* $45/£29

HOWE, JAMES VIRGIL. The Modern Gunsmith. NY, 1934-1941. Vol 1 inscribed. 3 vols, incl supplement. 2 tone cl. VG in dj (torn). *Argosy.* $200/£129

HOWE, JULIA WARD. A Trip to Cuba. Boston: Ticknor & Fields, 1860. 1st ed. 251pp (marginal water staining 1st 50pp). Good (dusty). BAL 9414. *Second Life.* $65/£42

HOWE, MARK DE WOLF (ed). Holmes-Laski Letters. Cambridge, MA, 1953. 1st ed. 2 vols. 2-tone cl. Good in djs (frayed). *King.* $65/£42

HOWE, MAUDE. The San Rosario Ranch. Boston: Roberts Bros, 1884. 1st ed. 390pp. Pale grn cl stamped in gilt/black (extrems sl rubbed). VG. *Reese.* $50/£32

HOWE, OCTAVIUS T. and F.C. MATTHEWS. American Clipper Ships 1833-1858. Salem, 1927. 1st ed. 2 vols. Fine set. Howes H 726. *Lefkowicz.* $300/£194

HOWE, OCTAVIUS T. and F.C. MATTHEWS. American Clipper Ships, 1833-1858. Salem: Marine Research Soc, 1926-27. 1st ed. 2 vols. 2 color frontispieces. Buckram. Fine. *Argosy.* $225/£145

HOWELL, H. GRADY. Going to Meet the Yankees. Jackson, (1981). 1st ed. Fine in dj (lt wear). *Pratt.* $65/£42

HOWELL, PETER and IAN SUTTON (eds). The Faber Guide to Victorian Churches. London: Faber, 1989. 1st ed. VG in dj. *Hollett.* $47/£30

HOWELLS, JOHN MEAD. The Architectural Heritage of the Piscataqua. NY: Architectural Book Pub, (1937). 1st ed. Dbl frontis. Inscrip, rep discolored from clipping, else VG in dj (used). *Bookpress.* $110/£71

HOWELLS, JOHN MEAD. Lost Examples of Colonial Architecture. NY: William Helburn, 1931. One of 1100. 244 plts. 2pp subs list. Fine in dj (tattered). *Bookpress.* $175/£113

HOWELLS, W.D. A Boy's Town. NY: Harper, 1890. 1st ed, 1st ptg. Gilt. Sl rubbed; fr inner hinge sl tender, o/w bright, clean. BAL 9654. *Sadlon.* $50/£32

HOWELLS, W.D. Certain Delightful English Towns. NY: Harpers, 1906. 1st Amer ed. VG (sl soiled, worn). BAL 9774. *Agvent.* $35/£23

HOWELLS, W.D. Italian Journeys. Cambridge, (MA): Riverside Press, 1901. Lg paper ed, #273/300. Tipped-on engr headpieces. Joseph Pennell (illus). Smudgy finger mks. BAL 9743. *Schoyer.* $60/£39

HOWELLS, W.D. My Mark Twain. NY/London: Harper, 1910. 1st ed, 1st ptg, 1st state of frontis port. Teg. Sage grn cl, gilt. Fine. BAL 9803. *Macdonnell.* $85/£55

HOWELLS, W.D. My Mark Twain. Reminiscences and Criticisms. NY, 1910. 1st Amer ed. Teg, rest uncut. Fine. BAL 9803 binding A. *Polyanthos.* $35/£23

HOWELLS, W.D. My Year in a Log Cabin. NY: Harper's, 1893. 1st ed. White cl soiled, else VG. *Pharos.* $20/£13

HOWELLS, W.D. New Leaf Mills: A Chronicle. NY: Harper, 1913. 1st ed, 3rd ptg (dated 1913 on tp, but w/code letter 'F-O' on copyright pg. Grn cl stamped in black. Bkpl, fr hinge started; lt faded, else VG in dj (dust soiled, 1/2-inch chip, else VG). BAL 9825. *Godot*. $85/£55

HOWELLS, W.D. Ragged Lady. NY/London: Harper, 1899. 1st ed. Gilt. Extrems sl rubbed. BAL 9723. *Sadlon*. $30/£19

HOWELLS, W.D. The Register. Boston/NY: Houghton, Mifflin, 1899. Ltr ptg. Inscribed. 91pp. Dec grn cl. Sm label fr pastedown, else Fine. BAL 9613 (1st ptg). *Chapel Hill*. $85/£55

HOWELLS, W.D. The Rise of Silas Lapham. Boston: Ticknor, 1885. 1st ed, 1st state. Cl stamped in gilt/black (rubbed, stained spots; sm holes through fep, flyleaf). BAL 9619. *Sadlon*. $45/£29

HOWELLS, W.D. The Seen and Unseen at Stratford-on-Avon. NY/London: Harper, 1914. 1st ed. Gilt; teg. Minor rubbing. BAL 9829. *Sadlon*. $25/£16

HOWELLS, W.D. The Seen and Unseen at Stratford-On-Avon. NY: Harper, 1914. 1st ed. Dec grn cl; teg. NF. BAL 9829. *Antic Hay*. $35/£23

HOWELLS, W.D. Seven English Cities. NY/London: Harper, 1909. 1st ed. Variant binding of grn cl stamped in black. Bkpl, else Fine in VG dj (dust soiled, sm chip, else VG). *Godot*. $125/£81

HOWELLS, W.D. Tuscan Cities. Boston, 1886. 1st ed. v,251pp + (ii)ads. Illus cl, gilt emblem (spine sl chipped, soiled; ex-libris); aeg. *Edwards*. $47/£30

HOWELLS, W.D. The Undiscovered Country. Boston: Houghton, Mifflin, 1880. 1st ed, 1st ptg (probable sequence). Binding B, w/fr cvr unlettered, brn eps (probable sequence, brn eps not noted by Blanck). Dec grn cl. NF (rubbing; ink names). BAL 9589. *Antic Hay*. $65/£42

HOWELLS, W.D. Venetian Life. NY: Hurd & Houghton, 1866. 1st Amer ed. Bound using British sheets w/60pp cancelled (30 leaves; 15 conjugate pairs) using Amer cancels. Purple cl, gilt. BAL 9547. *Macdonnell*. $150/£97

HOWELLS, W.D. Venetian Life. Cambridge: Riverside Press, 1907. Autograph ed; #214/550 signed by author, Edmund H. Garret (illus), publisher. Unopened. Patterned bds w/white cl spines, paper spine labels. Fine set (bkpl) in pub's cardboard slipcase. BAL 9784. *Chapel Hill*. $450/£290

HOWES, PAUL GRISWOLD. The Great Cactus Forest and Its World. NY: Duell et al, (1954). 1st ed. Color plt. VG in dj (torn). *Schoyer*. $25/£16

HOWGATE, HENRY W. The Cruise of the Florence; or Extracts from the Journal of the Preliminary Arctic Expedition of 1877-78. Washington: James C. Chapman, 1879. 183pp. Orig cl (very minor soil). VG. *High Latitude*. $300/£194

HOWITT, MARY. Hope On! Hope Ever! Boston: James Munroe, 1840. 12mo. 225pp. 1/2 title reads 'Tales for the People and their Children.' Brn blind-tooled cl on bds, gilt spine title. Good (foxing; lacks eps; chipped gold label internal lower bd; spine lt sunned; edges dusted). *Hobbyhorse*. $55/£35

HOWITT, MARY. Hope On, Hope Ever! London/Sedbergh: Simpkin, Marshall, etc/Jackson and Son, 1910. 2nd ed. Frontis photo; uncut. (Piece cut from flyleaf.) Grn cl gilt. *Hollett*. $70/£45

HOWITT, MARY. Our Cousins in Ohio. NY: Collins & Bro, 1849. 1st US ed. 251pp. Dec purple cl (sl faded). *Petrilla*. $25/£16

HOWITT, WILLIAM. The Book of the Seasons. London: Colburn & Bentley, 1831. 1st ed. xviii,404pp; teg. Half calf (sl rubbed), gilt. *Hollett*. $85/£55

HOWITT, WILLIAM. The Rural Life of England. London: Longman, Orme, etc, 1838. 1st ed. 2 vols. xx,396; xii,386, (xviii, ads)pp; 2 half-titles (bkpls; sigs). Blind-stamped ribbed cl (spines faded; worn), gilt. Very Nice. *Hollett*. $341/£220

HOWITT, WILLIAM. The Rural Life of England. Phila, 1841. Frontis, 509pp + (vi). Blind-emb cl, dec gilt title. (Lt browning; gathering detached; spine chipped.) *Edwards*. $39/£25

HOWITT, WILLIAM. Visits to Remarkable Places: Old Halls, Battle Fields.... London, 1840. Vignettes; teg; new eps. Dk blue 1/2 morocco (rebound; sm stain), gilt backstrip. *Petersfield*. $70/£45

HOWLAND, ARTHUR (ed). Materials toward a History of Witchcraft Collected by Henry Charles Lea. Phila, 1939. 1st ed. 3 vols. Good. *Fye*. $200/£129

HOWLETT, W.J. Life of the Right Reverend Joseph P. Machebeuf. Pueblo: D.D. Franklin Press, 1908. 1st ed. VG- (cvrs faded, soiled). Howes H 743. *Parker*. $100/£65

HOWLEY, M.F. Ecclesiastical History of Newfoundland. Boston: Doyle & Whittle, 1888. 1st ed. 426pp, 2 fldg maps (1 color). Grn cl, gilt (sl rubbed; ex-lib, pocket mounted rep, few mks). *Karmiole*. $65/£42

HOYLE, EDMOND. Hoyle's Games Improved.... London: W. Wood, 1782. Thomas Jones (rev). xii,216pp (lacks rep; fep torn). Contemp calf (spine extrems rubbed). *Karmiole*. $225/£145

HOYLE, EDMOND. Mr. Hoyle's Games.... London: For J. Rivington et al, n.d. (ca 1790). 16th ed. Mod speckled calf; label. VG. *Dramatis Personae*. $85/£55

HOYT, EDWIN P. Mutiny on the Globe. NY, (1975). 1st ed. Fine in dj. *Lefkowicz*. $30/£19

HOYT, HENRY F. A Frontier Doctor. Chicago, (1979). Lakeside Classic. VG. *Schoyer*. $15/£10

HOYT, HENRY F. A Frontier Doctor. Doyce B. Nunis, Jr. (ed). NY, 1929. 1979 reprint, Lakeside Classic #77. Pict cvr. Fine. *Pratt*. $37/£24

HRDLICKA, ALES. BAE Bulletin 33. Skeletal Remains Suggesting or Attributed to Early Man in North America. Washington: GPO, 1907. Good (ink underlining). *Lien*. $25/£16

HRDLICKA, ALES. BAE Bulletin 33. Skeletal Remains Suggesting or Attributed to Early Man in North America. 1907. 1st ed. 21 plts. VG. *Oregon*. $35/£23

HRDLICKA, ALES. BAE Bulletin 33. Skeletal Remains Suggesting...Early Man in North America. Washington: GPO, 1907. 21 photolithos. Good. *Goodrich*. $95/£61

HRDLICKA, ALES. BAE Bulletin 34. Physiological and Medical Observations Among the Indians of Southwestern United States and Northern Mexico. Washington: GPO, 1908. 28 plts. Good. *Goodrich*. $135/£87

HRDLICKA, ALES. BAE Bulletin 34. Physiological and Medical Observations among the Indians of Southwestern United States and Northern Mexico. Washington, 1908. 1st ed. Good. *Fye*. $100/£65

HRDLICKA, ALES. BAE Bulletin 42. Tuberculosis Among Certain Indian Tribes of the United States. Washington, 1909. 22 plts. *Edwards*. $23/£15

HRDLICKA, ALES. BAE Bulletin 42. Tuberculosis Among Certain Indian Tribes of the United States. Washington, 1909. 22 plts. NF. *Goodrich.* $65/£42

HRDLICKA, ALES. BAE Bulletin 52. Early Man in South America. Washington, 1912. 68 plts. (Ex-lib.) *Edwards.* $31/£20

HRDLICKA, ALES. BAE Bulletin 52. Early Man in South America. Washington: GPO, 1912. Good. *Goodrich.* $125/£81

HRDLICKA, ALES. BAE Bulletin 52. Early Man in South America. 1912. 1st ed. VG. *Oregon.* $50/£32

HRDLICKA, ALES. BAE Bulletin 66. Recent Discoveries Attributed to Early Man in America. Washington, 1918. 14 plts. (Ex-lib; sm tear tp; corner sl creased.) *Edwards.* $19/£12

HUBBACK, T. Elephant and Seladang Hunting in the Federated Malay States. London, 1905. Red cl, gilt. *Trophy Room.* $750/£484

HUBBARD, BERNARD R. Mush, You Malemutes. NY: America Press, 1932. 1st ed. Signed. VG in Good dj. *Blue Dragon.* $15/£10

HUBBARD, ELBERT. The Complete Writings of Elbert Hubbard. East Aurora, NY, 1908-15. Author's ed. One of 1000 sets. Each vol signed. 20 vols. 2 mss leaves tipped in. 1/2 morocco. *Argosy.* $1,500/£968

HUBBARD, ELBERT. Little Journeys to the Homes of Famous Women. East Aurora, 1898. One of 470 numbered, signed. 4to. 193pp. 3/4 suede, bds (edges rubbed); teg, others untrimmed. Contents Fine (edges untrimmed). *Veatchs.* $200/£129

HUBBARD, GEORGE. On the Site of the Globe Playhouse of Shakespeare. CUP, 1923. 1st ed. Author's compliments slip tipped in to fep. Frontis; 12 plts in rear pocket. (Feps lt browned, ex-libris.) Dj (chipped). *Edwards.* $54/£35

HUBBARD, JOHN MILTON. Notes of a Private. Memphis, TN: E.H. Clarke & Bro, 1909. 1st ed. 2 plts. VG (sl soiling; sl extrem wear). Howes H 751. *Mcgowan.* $275/£177

HUBBARD, JOHN N. Sketches of Border Adventures in the Life and Times of Major Moses Van Campen. Bath, NY: Underhill, 1842. 310pp (foxed). Full leather. Howes H 752. *Schoyer.* $165/£106

HUBBARD, JOHN N. Sketches of Border Adventures, in the Life and Times of Major Moses Van Campen.... Bath, NY: R.L. Underhill & Co., 1842. 1st ed. 310pp. Orig calf (rebacked in lt calf) red morocco spine label. (Spine extrems chipped; corners worn; bkpl; some internal foxing.) Howes H752. *Karmiole.* $150/£97

HUBBARD, L. RON. From Death to the Stars. Fantasy Pub, 1948. 1st ed. VG in dj (chipped, worn). *Madle.* $400/£258

HUBBARD, L. RON. Slaves of Sleep. Shasta Press, 1948. 1st ed. Fine in dj. *Aronovitz.* $325/£210

HUBBARD, L. RON. Slaves of Sleep. Shasta, 1948. 1st ed. Fine in dj. *Madle.* $350/£226

HUBBARD, L. RON. Slaves of Sleep. Chicago: Shasta, 1948. 1st ed. Sub's copy, signed. VG+ in dj (price-clipped, closed tear, chip). *Other Worlds.* $2,000/£1,290

HUBBARD, L. RON. Triton. F.P.C.I., 1949. 1st ed. NF in VG+ dj. *Aronovitz.* $235/£152

HUBBARD, L. RON. Triton. Fantasy Pub, 1949. 1st ed. Fine in Mint dj (sl trimmed). *Madle.* $300/£194

HUBBARD, L. RON. Typewriter in the Sky/Fear. NY: Gnome Press, (1951). 1st ed. Fine in VG dj (lt soiled; price-clipped). *Bernard.* $225/£145

HUBBARD, L. RON. Typewriter in the Sky/Fear. Gnome, 1951. 1st ed. NF in dj (sl frayed). *Madle.* $275/£177

HUBBARD, RALPH. Queer Person. NY: Doubleday, 1930. 1st ed. VG in VG- dj. *Parker.* $35/£23

HUDDLESTON, SISLEY. Paris Salons, Cafes, Studios. Phila: Lippincott, 1928. 1st ed. Frontis, 50 illus on plts. Ink, pencil sigs; spine sl sunned; cvrs sl rubbed; else VG. *Bookpress.* $35/£23

HUDSON, DEREK. Arthur Rackham. Heinemann, 1974. Re-issue. 33 color tipped-in illus. Dj (spine sl faded). *Edwards.* $101/£65

HUDSON, DEREK. Lewis Carroll. NY: Clarkson N. Potter, 1977. 1st ed. 271pp. VG (name stamp in fly) in VG dj. *Davidson.* $65/£42

HUDSON, JOSHUA HILARY. Sketches and Reminiscences. Columbia, SC: State Co, 1903. 1st ed. VG (minor cvr speckling; ex libris). Howes H 764. *Mcgowan.* $250/£161

HUDSON, THOMSON JAY. The Law of Psychic Phenomena.... London: Putnam's, 1903. 8th ed. (Worn; some pencilling.) *Boswell.* $65/£42

HUDSON, W.H. Afoot in England. London: Hutchinson, 1909. 1st ed. Gilt grn cl (rear cvr sl soiled; edges sl rubbed). Good (ink # endsheet). *Reese.* $35/£23

HUDSON, W.H. Birds in a Village. London: Chapman & Hall, 1893. 1st ed. (viii),232,(8)pp ads. Orig buckram, gilt. Uncut, unopened. *Cox.* $39/£25

HUDSON, W.H. Birds in London. London, 1898. 1st ed. xvi,339pp; 17 plts. Grn cl. *Wheldon & Wesley.* $54/£35

HUDSON, W.H. Birds of La Plata. London/Toronto/NY: J.M. Dent & Sons/E.P. Dutton, 1920. 1st ed, Amer issue ltd to 1500 sets. 2 vols. Tan cl-backed grn bds, bkpls). Nice set (sl mkd; bkpls). *Cady.* $135/£87

HUDSON, W.H. Birds of La Plata. London: Dent, 1920. Lg paper ed. 2 vols. 21 tipped-in color plts. Gilt-stamped red cl over grn cl (spines sl faded), glazed top edge; uncut. VG. *Houle.* $650/£419

HUDSON, W.H. Birds of La Plata. Penguin Books, 1952. 1st ed. 16 color plts. Dj. *Edwards.* $39/£25

HUDSON, W.H. British Birds.... London: Longmans, Green, 1895. 1st ed. Frontis, 8 chromolithos; teg. Gilt grn cl. Extrems sl rubbed, o/w VG+. *Reese.* $175/£113

HUDSON, W.H. Far Away and Long Ago. London: Dent, 1918. 1st ed. Port. Good (sl rubbed, endsheets lt foxed). *Reese.* $75/£48

HUDSON, W.H. Far Away and Long Ago. Buenos Aires: LEC, 1943. #904/1500 numbered, signed by Alberto Kraft (designer) & Ral Rosarivo (illus). Cowhide binding. Fine in pub's slipcase. *Hermitage.* $175/£113

HUDSON, W.H. Far Away and Long Ago. Buenos Aires: LEC, 1943. One of 1500 numbered, signed by Raul Rosarivo (illus) and Alberto Kraft (designer). 32 full-pg lithos. Cowhide (partly untanned); suede eps. (Upper hinge repaired.) *Argosy.* $100/£65

HUDSON, W.H. Green Mansions, a Romance of the Tropical Forest. NY: LEC, 1935. #904/1500 numbered, signed by Edward A. Wilson. Cl-backed dec bds. Fine in pub's slipcase. *Hermitage.* $85/£55

HUDSON, W.H. Green Mansions. London: Duckworth, 1904. 1st ed. In the more elaborate variant binding, w/pub's device lower cvr. Sl nick, top edge sl dusty, o/w VG. *Ash.* $147/£95

HUDSON, W.H. Idle Days in Patagonia. London: Chapman & Hall, 1893. 1st ed. Ltd to 1750. vi,256pp+40pp ads (foxing), 27 engrs. Orig buckram, gilt, blind pub's device back cvr (spine worn; hinges cracked). *Shasky.* $90/£58

HUDSON, W.H. The Naturalist in La Plata. London: Chapman & Hall, 1892. 1st ed. viii,388,40pp. Mod cl, leather spine label. VG. *Hollett.* $47/£30

HUDSON, W.H. Ralph Hearne. NY: Knopf, 1923. 1st ed. Ltd to 950 ptd. Cl-backed orange paper bds (sl worn). *Shasky.* $45/£29

HUDSON, WILSON M. (ed). The Healer of Los Olmos and Other Mexican Lore. Dallas: SMU, 1951. 1st ed. Dj. *Lambeth.* $45/£29

HUDSON, WILSON M. and ALLEN MAXWELL (eds). The Sunny Slopes of Long Ago. Dallas: Southern Methodist Univ, (1966). Fine in dj (rubbed). *Glenn.* $25/£16

HUEFFER, FORD MADOX. The Cinque Ports, a Historical and Descriptive Record. London: Blackwood, 1900. 14 photogravure plts. Teg. *Petersfield.* $54/£35

HUEFFER, FORD MADOX. The Fifth Queen! London: Alson Rivers, 1906. 1st ed. Red cl (spine faded, 2 sm spots; eps browned, foxed; fore-edge sl spotted), gilt. VG (lacks dj). *Virgo.* $78/£50

HUEFFER, FORD MADOX. High Germany. London: Duckworth, 1911. 1st ed. VG (inscrip; foxing; spine rubbed) in wrappers. *Virgo.* $194/£125

HUEPPE, FERDINAND. The Methods of Bacteriological Investigation. NY, 1886. 1st Eng trans. 218pp. Good. *Fye.* $150/£97

HUFELAND, OTTO. Westchester County During the American Revolution, 1775-1783. N.p.: Privately ptd, 1926. 1st ed, one of 250. Signed. 4 fldg maps. *Argosy.* $150/£97

HUFF, BOYD. El Puerto de Los Balleneros. LA: Dawson, 1957. Ltd to 200. Frontis. Fine. *Oregon.* $40/£26

HUFFAKER, CLAIR. Nobody Loves a Drunken Indian. NY: David McKay, (1967). 1st ed. Fine in dj (sl faded; lt worn). *Hermitage.* $40/£26

HUFHAM, JAMES DUNN. Memoir of the Rev. John L. Prichard. Raleigh, 1867. 1st ed. 182pp. VG (sl rubbed). *Mcgowan.* $75/£48

HUGES, DELBERT LITTRELL as told to LENORE HARRIS HUGES. Give Me Room. El Paso: Huges Pub, 1971. 1st ed, ltd #575. Signed by Lenore. Errata sheet. Ink name, else Fine in VG dj. *Perier.* $40/£26

HUGGINS, E.L. Winona, a Dakota Legend. NY: Putnam's, 1890. vi,176pp. Orig cl (pocket removed). *Schoyer.* $35/£23

HUGH-JONES, PHILIP (ed). Health and Disease in Tribal Societies. NY, 1977. 1st ed. Good in dj. *Fye.* $30/£19

HUGHES, DOROTHY B. The Delicate Ape. NY: Duell, Sloan & Pearce, 1944. 1st ed. Fine (sm label fep) in dj (sl wear). *Mordida.* $45/£29

HUGHES, DOROTHY B. The Expendable Man. NY: Random House, 1963. 1st ed. Fine in dj. *Mordida.* $45/£29

HUGHES, DOROTHY B. Ride the Pink Horse. NY: Duell, Sloan & Pearce, 1946. 1st ed. Pp dknd, o/w VF in dj (tiny tears). *Mordida.* $85/£55

HUGHES, G. BERNARD. English Glass for the Collector 1660-1860. London: Lutterworth, 1958. Frontis, 46 plts. Dj (sl soiled, chipped, some loss; adhered to bds). *Edwards.* $31/£20

HUGHES, G. BERNARD. Small Antique Silverware. London: Batsford, 1957. 1st ed. Dj (ragged). *Edwards.* $56/£36

HUGHES, G. BERNARD. Victorian Pottery and Porcelain. London: Country Life, 1959. 1st ed. Color frontis. Dj (chipped w/sl loss). *Edwards.* $39/£25

HUGHES, LANGSTON and ARNA BONTEMPS (eds). The Poetry of the Negro, 1746-1949. GC: Doubleday, 1949. 1st ed. VG in dj (lt worn). *Petrilla.* $165/£106

HUGHES, LANGSTON and ROY DECARAVA. The Sweet Flypaper of Life. NY: S&S, 1955. 1st ed, simultaneous pb issue. Fine in pict wrappers. *Jaffe.* $125/£81

HUGHES, LANGSTON. Ask Your Mama: 12 Moods for Jazz. NY: Knopf, 1961. 1st ed. White buckram-backed colored bds. NF in color pict dj (edges sl rubbed, sm hole spine). *Blue Mountain.* $110/£71

HUGHES, LANGSTON. Black Misery. NY: Paul S. Eiksson, 1969. 1st ed. VG in dj. *Cahan.* $65/£42

HUGHES, LANGSTON. The First Book of Jazz. NY: Franklin Watts, (1955). (8th ptg). Pict cl. VG in pict dj. *Petrilla.* $50/£32

HUGHES, LANGSTON. The First Book of Jazz. NY, 1955. 1st Amer ed. VG (sl rubbed). *Polyanthos.* $30/£19

HUGHES, LANGSTON. Five Plays. IN Univ Press, 1963. 1st ed. Inscribed. Fine in dj (3 short tears, sm wrinkle fr panel). *Fine Books.* $425/£274

HUGHES, LANGSTON. I Wonder As I Wonder. NY: Rinehart, (1956). 1st Amer ed. NF (lt spotting fr bd) in NF dj (extrems sl rubbed; tiny nicks). *Between The Covers.* $250/£161

HUGHES, LANGSTON. The Langston Hughes Reader. NY: George Braziller, 1958. 1st ed. Fine in VG+ dj (sm chip spine base). *Pettler.* $60/£39

HUGHES, LANGSTON. The Langston Hughes Reader. Braziller, 1958. 1st ed. Fine in NF dj. *Fine Books.* $65/£42

HUGHES, LANGSTON. Laughing to Keep from Crying. NY: Holt, (1952). 1st Amer ed. NF in VG dj (sl soiled; extrems dknd). *Between The Covers.* $100/£65

HUGHES, LANGSTON. Shakespeare in Harlem. NY: Knopf, 1942. 1st ed. Black/orange cl. Fine in NF dj (edges sl rubbed). *Chapel Hill.* $300/£194

HUGHES, LANGSTON. Simple Speaks His Mind. (NY): S&S, (1950). 1st ed. Blue-grn cl. Fine in NF dj (edges, spine sl sunned). *Chapel Hill.* $200/£129

HUGHES, LANGSTON. Simple Stakes a Claim. NY/Toronto: Rinehart, (1957). 1st ed. Grey bds. Pp edges browned, else Fine in dj (spine sl rubbed). *Chapel Hill.* $150/£97

HUGHES, LANGSTON. Simple's Uncle Sam. NY: Hill & Wang, (1965). 1st ed. Yellow cl. Sig, else Fine in NF dj. *Chapel Hill.* $100/£65

HUGHES, LANGSTON. The Ways of the White Folks. NY: Knopf, 1934. 1st ed. VG (spine sunned, frayed). *Beasley.* $85/£55

HUGHES, RICHARD. Gipsy-Night and Other Poems. Waltham St. Lawrence: Golden Cockerel, (1922). 1st ed, 1st bk. One of 750. Walter de la Mare's copy w/dated sig. Litho port. Sm erasure endsheet, o/w Nice in dj (sl nicked, tanned). *Reese.* $200/£129

HUGHES, RICHARD. A High Wind in Jamaica. Chatto, 1929. #131/157 numbered, signed. VG (spine sl faded; sm bkpl). *Williams.* $194/£125

HUGHES, RICHARD. The Innocent Voyage. NY: LEC, 1944. One of 1500 signed by Lynd Ward (illus). NF in dec cardbd sleeve & pub's slipcase. *Hermitage.* $100/£65

HUGHES, RICHARD. The Wooden Shepherdess. London: C&W, 1973. 1st UK ed. Fine in dj. *Lewton.* $14/£9

HUGHES, RUPERT. The Triumphant Clay. Hollywood: House-Warven, 1951. 1st ed. Lib stamp fep, o/w Fine in dj. *Hermitage.* $35/£23

HUGHES, T. Memoir of Daniel Macmillan. Macmillan, 1883. 308pp. Contemp 1/2 black morocco, red morocco label; aeg. *Moss.* $37/£24

HUGHES, T. HAROLD. and E.A.G. LAMBORN. Towns and Town Planning, Ancient and Modern. Oxford: Clarendon Press, 1923. 1st ed. Frontis. Bkpl; cvrs lt sunned, rubbed; tips worn, else VG. *Bookpress.* $125/£81

HUGHES, TED. Cave Birds. NY: Viking, (1978). 1st ed, Amer issue, ptd in Britain. Fine in Good dj (shelfworn, 2 internal mends, inked-out price sticker fr flap). *Reese.* $20/£13

HUGHES, TED. The Coming of the Kings. Chicago, 1972. 1st ed. VG in wrappers. *Words Etc.* $25/£16

HUGHES, TED. Crow. London: Faber, 1970. 1st ed. Inscrip, else Mint in dj (cutting taped to turn-in). *Hollett.* $54/£35

HUGHES, TED. Crow. NY: Harper & Row, 1971. 1st Amer ed. Fine in Fine dj. *Revere.* $40/£26

HUGHES, TED. Gaudete. NY, 1977. 1st Amer ed. Fine (spine top sl rubbed) in Fine dj (sl soiled; price-clipped). *Polyanthos.* $30/£19

HUGHES, TED. Season Songs. London: Faber & Faber, 1976. 1st Eng trade ed. Fine in dj. *Limestone.* $40/£26

HUGHES, TED. A Solstice. London: Sceptre Press, 1978. #115/350 numbered. Fine (stamp) pamphlet as issued. *Williams.* $23/£15

HUGHES, TED. Sunstruck. London: Sceptre Press, 1977. #142/300. Fine (stamp) pamphlet as issued. *Williams.* $23/£15

HUGHES, THOMAS. The Scouring of the White Horse. Cambridge: Macmillan, 1859. 1st ed, 1st issue. Dbl-pl frontis, xi,228pp. Richard Doyle (illus). Dk grn morocco, gilt; aeg. Orig pict cl cvr bound in at end. Fine. *Schoyer.* $200/£129

HUGHES, TREVOR A. A Short Essay on Aldine Bembo. London School of Ptg, 1948. Sl dusty. *Hollett.* $39/£25

HUGO, RICHARD. Duwamish Head. (Port Townsend, WA): Copperhead, (1976). 1st ed. Ltd to 1000. Fine in wrappers. *Jaffe.* $65/£42

HUGO, RICHARD. The Lady in Kicking Horse Reservoir. NY: W.W. Norton, (1973). 1st ed. Fine in dj. *Jaffe.* $50/£32

HUGO, RICHARD. Selected Poems. NY: W.W. Norton, (1979). 1st ed. Fine in dj. *Jaffe.* $45/£29

HUGO, RICHARD. The Triggering Town. NY: W.W. Norton, (1979). 1st ed. Fine in dj. *Jaffe.* $50/£32

HUGO, T. The Bewick Collector. London, 1866/8. 2 vols. xxiv,562; xxv,352pp; 180 woodcuts. (Lib stamps in few blank margins.) New blind cl. *Ars Artis.* $233/£150

HUGO, VICTOR. Les Miserables. NY: LEC, 1938. #904/1500 numbered sets signed by Lynd Ward (illus). Fine in pub's slipcase. *Hermitage.* $175/£113

HUGO, VICTOR. Notre-Dame De Paris. Paris: LEC, 1930. One of 1500. Signed by Frans Masereel (artist). 2 vols. Wrappers. Fine in glassine (torn). *Agvent.* $250/£161

HUGO, VICTOR. The Toilers of the Sea. David Glixon (ed). Verona: LEC, 1960. One of 1500. Signed by Tranquillo Marangoni (artist) and Giovanni Mardersteig (designer). Cl-backed dec bds. Fine (spine sunned) in Fine slipcase. *Agvent.* $125/£81

HUIE, WILLIAM BRADFORD. 3 Lives for Mississippi. NY: WCC, 1965. 1st ed. Fine in dj (nicked). *Turlington.* $50/£32

HUIE, WILLIAM BRADFORD. Can Do! The Story of the Seabees. NY, 1944. VG in Good dj. *Clark.* $23/£15

HUIE, WILLIAM BRADFORD. The Execution of Private Slovik. NY: Duell Sloan & Pearce, (1954). 1st ed. Fine in dj (lt worn). *Turlington.* $75/£48

HUIE, WILLIAM BRADFORD. He Slew the Dreamer. NY: Delacorte, 1968. 1st ed. NF in NF dj (chips, tears). *Aka.* $35/£23

HUIE, WILLIAM BRADFORD. Hotel Mamie Stover. NY: Potter, (1963). 1st ed. Fine in dj (lt worn). *Turlington.* $30/£19

HUISH, M.B. Happy England as Painted by Helen Allingham. A&C Black, 1904. 1st ed. Port; 80 color plts. Blue dec cl (sl damp mks). *Petersfield.* $279/£180

HUISH, MARCUS B. Japan and Its Art. London: Fine Art Soc, 1889. 1st ed. Frontis; xii,254,(2),4pp. Pub's cl (cvrs worn). Text VG. *Bookpress.* $325/£210

HUISMAN, P. and M.G. DORTU. Lautrec by Lautrec. NY, (1964). Eps, cvrs sl spotted, else Good in dj (price-clipped, rubbed, discolored). *King.* $95/£61

HULANISKI, F.J. (ed). The History of Contra Costa County California. Berkeley: Elms Pub, 1917. 1st ed. 1/2 calf over black cl (spine rebacked, old calf spine laid down). *Karmiole.* $175/£113

HULBERT, ARCHER BUTLER and DOROTHY. Marcus Whitman, Crusader. Part One 1802 to 1839. (Denver): Stewart Commission, (1936). 1st ed. VG. *Perier.* $70/£45

HULBERT, ARCHER BUTLER and DOROTHY. Marcus Whitman, Crusader. Part Two 1839 to 1843. (Denver): Stewart Commission, (1938). 1st ed. VG in VG dj. *Perier.* $75/£48

HULBERT, ARCHER BUTLER. Forty-Niners, A Chronicle of the California Trail. Boston, 1931. 1st ed. Pict cl. VG+ in VG+ dj. *Pratt.* $27/£17

HULBERT, ARCHER BUTLER. Forty-Niners. Boston: Little, Brown, 1932. VG (sm mks; stamp on flyleaf). *Hollett.* $39/£25

HULBERT, ARCHER BUTLER. Historic Highways of America. Cleveland: Clark, 1902-05. Inscribed vol 1; long presentation vol 5. 16 vols. Navy cl. Fine set. Howes H 773. *Bohling.* $950/£613

HULBERT, HOMER B. The Passing of Korea. NY, 1906. 1st ed. Teg. Cl (rubbed, spotted, bumped; ends foxed; hinges loose). *King.* $45/£29

HULKE, J.W. On Fractures and Dislocations of the Vertebral Column. London, 1892. 57pp. Good. *Goodrich.* $60/£39

HULL, D.B. Hounds and Hunting in Ancient Greece. Chicago/London: Univ of Chicago, 1964. 1st ed. Dec cl. Fine in NF dj. *Mikesh.* $40/£26

HULL, EDWARD. A Treatise on the Building and Ornamental Stones of Great Britain and Foreign Countries.... London: Macmillan, 1872. 1st ed. 333pp; 2 tipped-in photos. (Corners, spine worn; ex-lib; bkpls, stamps.) *Second Life*. $150/£97

HULLMANDEL, CHARLES. Three Views and a Plan of the Chateaux des Rochers.... London: The Author, 1819. 1f letterpress, 4 litho plts. Orig ptd wrappers. *Marlborough*. $581/£375

HULME, F. EDWARD and SHIRLEY HIBBERD. Familiar Garden Flowers. Second Series. London, n.d. (c. 1880). 160+4pp ads; 40 color lithos, guards. Aeg. Gilt-stamped cl (bumped; inner hinges cracked); floral window insert (faded) fr cvr. VG. *Shifrin*. $110/£71

HULME, F. EDWARD. Familiar Swiss Flowers. London: Cassell, 1907. 100 full-pg color photolith plts. Grn cl, blind stamp, gilt spine. VG (bumped). *Shifrin*. $50/£32

HULME, F. EDWARD. Familiar Wild Flowers. London: Cassell, n.d. (1890s). 8 vols, each viii,(160)pp; 40 colored plts. Grn dec cl (extrems rubbed). Sound. *Cox*. $85/£55

HULME, F. EDWARD. Familiar Wild Flowers. First Series. London, n.d. (c. 1880). 160pp (eps sl foxed); 40 color lithos, guards. Aeg. Gilt-stamped dec cl. VG (lt soiling). *Shifrin*. $110/£71

HULME, F. EDWARD. Principles of Ornamental Art. London: Cassell, (1875). 1st ed. xiii,(i),137pp, 32 plts. Fr hinge internally cracked; lt foxing; minor cvr wear; else VG. *Bookpress*. $275/£177

HULME, F. EDWARD. Principles of Ornamental Art. London: Cassell Petter & Galpin, n.d. Signed. 32 plts. (Lt spotting.) Dec cl, gilt (lt soiled, rubbed; lower joint sl split; spine chipped). *Edwards*. $140/£90

HULME, F. EDWARD. Suggestions in Floral Design. London: Cassell, n.d. (1878-1879). 1st ed. 52pp, 52 plts. Pub's cl. *Bookpress*. $1,400/£903

HULME, T.E. Speculations. Herbert Read (ed). London: Kegan Paul, 1924. 1st ed. Extrems lt worn; offsetting, lt foxing to eps, else NF. *Lame Duck*. $150/£97

HULSKER, JAN. The Complete Van Gogh: Paintings—Drawings—Sketches. NY: Abrams, 1980. VG in dj. *Argosy*. $150/£97

HUMANA, CHARLES. The Keeper of the Bed. Arlington Books, 1973. 1st ed. Dj (sl chipped, rubbed). *Edwards*. $31/£20

HUMBLE, RICHARD. The Illustrated History of the Civil War. NY, 1986. 1st ed. Fine in dj (sm tear). *Pratt*. $30/£19

HUMBOLDT, ALEXANDER and AIME BONPLAND. Personal Narrative of Travels to the Equinoctial Regions of America, During the Years 1799-1804.... Thomasina Ross (trans). London: George Bell, 1884. Rpt. 3 vols. (2-16 ads),xii,505,(17-31 ads); (2-16 ads),vi,521,(17-31 ads); (2-16 ads),vi,442,(17-29 ads)pp. 1890 cat tipped in vol 3. *Lefkowicz*. $75/£48

HUME, ALLAN O. Nests and Eggs of Indian Birds. Eugene William Oates (ed). London: R.H. Porter, 1889. 2nd ed. Vol 1 (of 3). (xviii),397pp + 2pp ads, tipped-on woodbury photo. Red cl (soiled, worn). *Schoyer*. $50/£32

HUME, CYRIL. The Golden Dancer. Doran, 1926. 1st ed. NF in dj (chipped, frayed). *Madle*. $35/£23

HUME, DAVID. Dialogues concerning Natural Religion.... London, 1779. 2nd ed. New eps. Contemp tree calf (rebacked; sig). *Waterfield*. $543/£350

HUME, F. Aladdin in London. H-M, 1892. 1st ed. VG. *Aronovitz*. $75/£48

HUME, FERGUS. The Mystery of a Hansom Cab. NY/Chicago: J.S. Ogilvie, March, 1888. Issued as Red Cover Series, No. 17. 238,(1)pp. Neat horizontal 2-inch tear in frontis w/no loss, o/w Good in wrappers. *Hayman*. $125/£81

HUME, FERGUS. The Mystery Queen. London: Ward Lock, 1913. 1st ed. Spine dull, worn, o/w VG w/o dj. *Mordida*. $65/£42

HUME, H. HAROLD. Camellias in America. Harrisburg: J. Horace McFarland, 1946. 1st ed. 49 full-pg color plts. Fine. *Quest*. $70/£45

HUME, H. HAROLD. Citrus Fruits and Their Culture. NY: OJ, 1915. (6th ed). Glossy paper. Orig cl. Spine dull, soiled, else VG. *Bohling*. $45/£29

HUME, H.H. Hollies. NY, 1960. Cl (lt spotted). Dj (edges worn). *Sutton*. $40/£26

HUME, IVOR NOEL. Historical Archaeology. NY: Knopf, 1969. 1st ed. Frontis. Fine in Fine dj. *Connolly*. $30/£19

HUMPHREY, MARY A. The Squatter Sovereign, or Kansas in the '50s. Chicago: Coburn & Newman, 1883. Inscribed. 354pp, 2 ports laid in, each signed by author and her husband. *Cullen*. $125/£81

HUMPHREY, WILLIAM D. Findlay (Ohio): The Story of a Community. (Findlay, OH: Findlay Ptg, 1961). 1st ed. Red cl stamped in b/w. Good in photo illus dj (chipped). *Karmiole*. $35/£23

HUMPHREY, WILLIAM. Home from the Hill. NY, 1958. 1st ed. VG+ in VG dj (lt wear, 1/2-inch punctured tear at fr gutter). *Fuller & Saunders*. $25/£16

HUMPHREY, WILLIAM. Home from the Hill. NY: Knopf, 1958. 1st ed. VG in VG- dj (chipped). *Revere*. $70/£45

HUMPHREY, WILLIAM. My Moby Dick. GC, 1978. 1st ed. VG in dj (sl yellowed). *King*. $35/£23

HUMPHREY, WILLIAM. The Ordways. NY: Knopf, 1965. 1st ed. Fine in dj. *Turlington*. $25/£16

HUMPHREY, WILLIAM. Proud Flesh. NY: Knopf, 1973. 1st ed. Fine in dj. *Turlington*. $25/£16

HUMPHREY, WILLIAM. The Spawning Run. NY: Knopf, 1970. 1st ed. Fine in Fine dj. *Pettler*. $25/£16

HUMPHREYS, CHRISTMAS. The Great Pearl Robbery of 1913. London: Heinemann, (1929). (Sl foxed; backstrip faded.) *Petersfield*. $25/£16

HUMPHREYS, FREDERICK. Manual of Veterinary Specific Homoeopathy. NY, 1860. 1st ed. 240pp. Orig stamped cl (backstrip chipped; upper hinge split). *Argosy*. $125/£81

HUMPHREYS, HENRY NOEL. The Coinage of the British Empire. London: David Bogue, 1855. 1st ed. 160pp; 24 plts (12 chromographic). Pub's cl w/gold coins stamped on fr cvr. Fine (internal foxing). *Bookpress*. $385/£248

HUMPHREYS, HENRY NOEL. A History of the Art of Printing.... London: Bernard Quaritch, 1868. 2nd issue. xii,errata,216pp, 106 plts. Good in dec cl (rebacked, retaining orig faded backstrip). *Cox*. $279/£180

HUMPHREYS, JOHN S. Bermuda Houses. Boston, (1923). 118 plts. Cl (rubbed; ex-lib blindstamp eps). *King*. $175/£113

HUMPHREYS, JOSEPHINE. Dreams of Sleep. London: Collins Harvill, 1985. 1st UK ed, 1st bk. NF in NF dj. *Robbins*. $40/£26

HUMPHREYS, LAUD. Tearoom Trade: Impersonal Sex in Public Places. Chicago: Aldine Pub., (1970). 1st ed. Very Nice in dj. *Cady.* $25/£16

HUMPHREYS, W.J. Fogs and Clouds. Balt: Williams & Wilkins, 1926. 95 plts. Good (bkpl removed; stains bottom margin last 50pp) in 1/4 cl, paper-cvrd bds (spotted, stained; nick). *Knollwood.* $35/£23

HUNEKER, JAMES. Painted Veils. NY: Boni & Liveright, (1920). Ltd to 1200. Signed. Cvr edges sl lightened. *Sadlon.* $35/£23

HUNGERFORD, EDWARD. Wells Fargo. NY, (1949). 1st ed. VG in dj (top edges frayed). *Heinoldt.* $25/£16

HUNNISETT, BASIL. Steel-Engraved Book Illustration in England. Boston, (1980). 1st Amer ed. VG in dj. *Argosy.* $50/£32

HUNT, CORNELIUS E. The Shenandoah; or the Last Confederate Cruiser. NY: Carleton, 1867. Frontis, 273pp. (Sl ink stain spine edge.) Howes H 799. *Schoyer.* $85/£55

HUNT, CORNELIUS E. The Shenandoah; or, The Last Confederate Cruiser. NY, 1867. 1st ed. 270pp. Howes H 799. *Ginsberg.* $125/£81

HUNT, ELVID. Fort Leavenworth 1827-1927. Fort Leavenworth: General Services School, 1926. 1st ed. Lt edge stains 1st few pp, else VG in dj (edgeworn). Howes H 800. *Perier.* $97/£63

HUNT, FRAZIER. Cap Mossman. Last of the Great Cowmen. NY: Hastings House, 1951. 1st ed. VG+ in VG- dj (chips). *Parker.* $50/£32

HUNT, GAILLARD (ed). The First Forty Years of Washington Society.... NY: Scribner, 1906. 1st ed. Pub's cl (worn). Good. *Second Life.* $45/£29

HUNT, JOHN WARREN. Wisconsin Gazetteer. Madison: B. Brown, 1853. 255pp + 1pg errata, fldg color map (tear in margin). Orig 1/2 leather (lt wear, foxing, writing on ep). Overall Nice. Howes H 807. *Bohling.* $350/£226

HUNT, L. The Wishing Cap Papers. L&S, 1873. 1st ed. Sl wear spine extrems, else VG. *Fine Books.* $65/£42

HUNT, LEIGH. The Autobiography of Leigh Hunt. Roger Ingpen (ed). NY: Dutton, 1903. 2 vols. Teg. Vellum-backed cl bds, vellum bd tips, gilt spines. Nice set. *Cady.* $40/£26

HUNT, LEIGH. The Feast of the Poets. London: James Cawthorn, 1814. 1st ed, 1st issue, w/ms correction p158 (line 5). (xvi),(158)pp + 2pp ads. 3/4 leather, marbled bds. VG. *Schoyer.* $200/£129

HUNT, LEIGH. Imagination and Fancy. London: Smith, Elder, 1845. 2nd ed. xii,345pp (title edges worn, dusty). Old half calf (worn), gilt. *Hollett.* $54/£35

HUNT, LEIGH. The Indicator, a Miscellany for the Fields and the Fireside. NY: Wiley & Putnam, 1845. 1st Amer ed. 2 vols bound in 1 as issued. Orig brn cl, gilt (sl rubbed). VG. *Macdonnell.* $85/£55

HUNT, LEIGH. Jar of Honey From Mount Hybla. London, 1848. 1st ed. Richard Doyle (illus). Glazed bds (rebacked), orig spine laid down. VG (sig; cvrs sl worn). *Pharos.* $100/£65

HUNT, LEIGH. Men, Women, and Books. London: Smith, Elder, 1847. 1st ed. 2 vols. Port. Orig cl stamped in blind, gilt. Sound reading set. *Reese.* $50/£32

HUNT, LEIGH. Stories from the Italian Poets. London: Chapman & Hall, 1846. 1st ed. 2 vols. Sound reading set (spine extrems frayed, nicked; inner hinges cracking). *Reese.* $50/£32

HUNT, LEIGH. Table-Talk. London: Smith, Elder, 1851. 1st ed. 3/4 19th cent calf; teg. Bound w/half-title, w/o cat. Good (extrems worn). *Reese.* $55/£35

HUNT, LEIGH. The Town; Its Memorable Characters and Events. London: Smith, Elder, 1848. 1st ed. 2 vols. Frontis. 3/4 19th cent gilt calf, 1/2 titles bound in. Early ink name, joints worn, sm chip label, else Good set. *Reese.* $60/£39

HUNT, P.F. and MARY GRIERSON. The Country Life Book of Orchids. London: Country Life, 1978. 30 full-pg color plts. Mint in slipcase. *Quest.* $85/£55

HUNT, ROCKWELL DENNIS and WILLIAM SHEFFIELD AMENT. Oxcart to Airplane. L.A.: Powell, 1929. (Spine faded; cvrs spotted, worn.) *Parmer.* $35/£23

HUNT, VIOLET. White Rose of Weary Leaf. London: Heinemann, 1908. 1st ed. VG. *Second Life.* $75/£48

Hunter's and Trapper's Complete Guide.... NY: Hurst, (1875). Frontis, ad, 81pp, 11pg pub's cat. (Minor stain few pgs). NF in color pict wraps (spine head sl chipped; cvr flaps pasted inside cvr). *Blue Mountain.* $125/£81

HUNTER, ALAN. Gently by the Shore. London: Cassell, 1956. 1st ed. VG in Good dj. *Ming.* $47/£30

HUNTER, ALAN. Gently Where the Birds Are. London: Cassell, 1976. 1st ed. VG+ in VG+ dj. *Ming.* $70/£45

HUNTER, DARD. My Life with Paper, An Autobiography. NY: Knopf, 1958. Tipped-in samples of Chinese spirit paper & Hunter's Lime Rock paper. Good in dj (faded; sl chipped). *Veatchs.* $75/£48

HUNTER, DARD. My Life with Paper. NY: Knopf, 1958. 1st ed. Fine in dj. *Graf.* $75/£48

HUNTER, DARD. My Life with Paper. NY: Knopf, 1958. 1st ed. Fine in Fine dj (ink inscrip). *Dermont.* $100/£65

HUNTER, DARD. Paper-Making in the Classroom. Peoria, IL: Manual Arts Press, (1931). 1st ed. Fine externally (offset on fep from stamp). *Oak Knoll.* $375/£242

HUNTER, DARD. Papermaking in Pioneer America. Phila: Univ of PA Press, 1952. 1st ed. 22 illus. Beige cl over mauve bds. Good. *Karmiole.* $125/£81

HUNTER, DARD. Papermaking in Pioneer America. Phila: Univ of PA, 1952. 1st ed. Fine. *Oak Knoll.* $125/£81

HUNTER, DARD. Papermaking through Eighteen Centuries. NY: Rudge, 1930. Leather spine label; teg. NF in ptd dj (dknd). *Veatchs.* $175/£113

HUNTER, DARD. Papermaking through Eighteen Centuries. NY: William Edwin Rudge, 1930. 1st ed. Prospectus, piece of Hunter's port watermarked paper, other ephemera loosely inserted. Buckram, leather spine label; teg. Ink inscrip, else Fine in dj. *Oak Knoll.* $250/£161

HUNTER, DARD. Papermaking, the History and Technique of an Ancient Craft. NY: Knopf, 1943. 1st ed. Fldg map. Well preserved in dj. *Oak Knoll.* $145/£94

HUNTER, DARD. Papermaking, the History and Technique.... NY: Knopf, 1943. 1st ed. 2 paper specimens. VG in dj (chipped). *Argosy.* $150/£97

HUNTER, DARD. Papermaking. NY: Knopf, 1957. 2nd ed, rev, enlgd. Frontis, fldg diag, fldg map. Blue cl, gilt spine. Good in dj (lt chipped). *Karmiole.* $125/£81

HUNTER, EVAN. (Pseud of Ed McBain). A Matter of Conviction. NY: S&S, 1959. 1st ed. Pp dknd, o/w Fine in dj (sl wear; corners chipped). *Mordida.* $35/£23

HUNTER, GEORGE LELAND. Decorative Furniture. Phila: Lippincott, 1923. 1st ed. 23 color plts. Gilt-titled blue cl, color plt on cvr. Fine. *House.* $180/£116

HUNTER, GEORGE LELAND. The Practical Book of Tapestries. Phila, 1925. 1st ed. VG. *Argosy.* $50/£32

HUNTER, GEORGE LELAND. The Practical Book of Tapestries. Phila/London, 1925. One of Limited Subscription Edition of 300. Color frontis; 7 color, 220 dbl-tone plts; this ed w/4 add'l color illus, 16 in dbl-tone. Teg, rest uncut. 2-tone cl bds. *Edwards.* $109/£70

HUNTER, J. MARVIN and NOAH H. ROSE. The Album of Gunfighters. Bandera, TX, (1955). 2nd ed. VG in pict cvrs. Howes H 814. *Lien.* $125/£81

HUNTER, J. MARVIN. Trail Drivers of Texas. NY: Argosy-Antiquarian, 1963. One of 97 numbered sets, signed by Harry Sinclair Drago (intro). 2 vols. 1/2 leather, tan bds; gilt. Fine in slipcase (lt soil). Howes H 816. *Bohling.* $350/£226

HUNTER, JOHN D. Manners and Customs of Several Indian Tribes Located West of the Mississippi.... Phila: For author, 1823. 1st ed. vii,(11)-402pp. 3/4 calf w/ruled borders, marbled bds. Foxing throughout, else NF. Howes H 813. *Mcgowan.* $450/£290

HUNTER, JOHN D. Memoirs of a Captivity Among the Indians of North America.... London: Longman, Hurst, 1823. New ed w/frontis port. ix, 447pp. Leather, marbled bds, gilt-stamped spine. VG. Howes H 813. *Oregon.* $450/£290

HUNTER, JOHN. Essays and Observations on Natural History, Anatomy, Physiology, Psychology, and Geology. London, 1861. 2 vols. xvii,403; xii,507pp, frontis port. (Lib ink stamps.) *Edwards.* $194/£125

HUNTER, JOHN. A Treatise on the Blood, Inflammation and Gun-Shot Wounds. Phila: James Webster, 1817. (26),514pp (foxed), 8 engr plts. Orig sheep (newly rebacked). *Goodrich.* $250/£161

HUNTER, JOHN. A Treatise on the Blood, Inflammation, and Gunshot Wounds. London: Richardson for Nicol, 1794. 1st ed. 4to. lxvii,575pp; facs port; plt one in facs on old laid paper; 8 other plts; ad leaf laid down. (Sl worming margins of leaves.) 19th cent morocco; tooled; gilt (rebacked; new eps of old laid paper). *Goodrich.* $1,175/£758

HUNTER, JOHN. A Treatise on the Venereal Disease. London, 1788. 2nd ed. Tp,(x),398pp,index, 7 engr plts (ink stamp to pastedowns, tp; lacks feps; hinges repaired; spotting; recently rebacked; corners sl worn). *Edwards.* $465/£300

HUNTER, JOHN. A Treatise on the Venereal Disease. Phila, 1841. 347pp. Foxed. *Fye.* $150/£97

HUNTER, JOHN. A Treatise on the Venereal Disease. Freeman Bumstead (ed). Phila, 1859. 2nd ed. 552pp. Good. *Fye.* $250/£161

HUNTER, MILTON. Utah Indian Stories. Salt Lake: privately ptd, 1946. 1st ed. VG. *Oregon.* $60/£39

HUNTER, ROWLAND C. Old Houses in England. NY/London: Wiley/Chapman & Hall, 1930. 114 plts. Dj (soiled). *Schoyer.* $125/£81

HUNTER, SAM. American Art of the 20th Century. NY: Abrams, (1972). VG in dj. *Argosy.* $75/£48

HUNTER, SAM. Hans Hofmann. NY: Abrams, (1963). 2nd ed. 51 mtd color illus. VG in dj (torn). *Argosy.* $500/£323

HUNTER, STEPHEN. The Master Sniper. NY: William Morrow, 1980. 1st ed. Fine in dj. *Mordida.* $40/£26

HUNTER, W. Historical Account of Charing Cross Hospital.... London, 1914. 39 plts. (Worn, dull; ex-lib w/stamps.) *Whitehart.* $62/£40

HUNTER, WILLIAM S., JR. Chisolm's Panoramic Guide from Niagara to Quebec. Montreal: C.R. Chisolm, n.d. (ca 1868). (8),viii,66,(8)pp; fldg panorama. Brn cl, gilt. Very Nice. *Karmiole.* $200/£129

HUNTFORD, ROLAND (ed). The Amundsen Photographs. NY: Atlantic Monthly, (1987). 1st US ed. Fine in Fine dj. *Blue Dragon.* $50/£32

HUNTINGTON, A.O. Studies of Trees in Winter. Boston, (1901). 12 color plts. (Spine worn; lt dampstained; hinges starting; lt foxed.) *Sutton.* $30/£19

HUNTINGTON, DAVID C. The Landscapes of Frederic Edwin Church. NY: George Braziller, (1966). 1st ed. Bkpl, sl rubbed cvrs; else Fine. *Bookpress.* $45/£29

HUNTINGTON, DWIGHT W. Our Big Game. NY: Scribner's, 1904. 1st ed. Dec cl (spotted, discolored; hinges repaired). *Schoyer.* $30/£19

HUNTON, JOHN. John Hunton's Diary. Wyoming Territory. Vol 6, 1885-89. L.G. Flannery (ed). Glendale: Clark, 1970. 1st ed. *Heinoldt.* $35/£23

HUNTRESS, KEITH (ed). Narratives of Shipwrecks and Disasters, 1586-1860. Ames, IA: IA State Univ, 1974. 1st ed. Dj. *Lefkowicz.* $50/£32

HUNTRESS, KEITH. A Checklist of Narratives of Shipwrecks and Disasters at Sea to 1860.... Ames, IA: IA State Univ, 1979. 1st ed. Frontis. (Spine sl faded.) *Lefkowicz.* $125/£81

HURD-MEAD, KATE CAMPBELL. A History of Women in Medicine...to the Beginning of the Nineteenth Century. Haddam, CT: Haddam Press, 1938. 1st ed. 39 plts. (Spine faded; ink name.) *Bickersteth.* $202/£130

HURLBUTT, FRANK. Bow Porcelain. London, 1926. 1st ed. 56 b/w, 8 color plts. (Worn; chipped spine.) *Edwards.* $78/£50

HURLBUTT, FRANK. Bow Porcelain. London: G. Bell & Sons, 1926. 1st ed. 8 color plts, 56 half-tone plts. Teg. Blind-stamped, gilt-lettered red cl. NF. *House.* $200/£129

HURLEY, FRANK. Pearls and Savages. NY: Putnam's, 1924. 1st ed. viii,414pp. Good. *Karmiole.* $100/£65

HURLIMAN, MARTIN. Traveller in the Orient. London: Thames & Hudson, 1960. 1st Eng ed. 223 photogravure plts (41 color). 1/4 blue cl. Sl faded, o/w Fine in dj (chipped, torn). *Dalian.* $70/£45

HURRELL, JOHN WEYMOUTH. Measured Drawings of Old Oak English Furniture.... London: Batsford, 1902. 110 plts. Grn binder's cl (sl stained, faded; sl smoke stain top edge margins). *Petersfield.* $124/£80

HURST, RANDLE M. The Smoke Jumpers. Caldwell: Caxton, 1966. 1st ed. Fine in VG dj. *Perier.* $30/£19

HURSTON, ZORA NEALE. Dust Tracks on a Road. Phila: Lippincott, (1942). 1st ed. 8vo. Tan cl. NF in pict dj (lt rubbed). *Chapel Hill.* $950/£613

HUSMANN, GEORGE. American Grape Growing and Wine Making. NY: OJ, 1915. Grn cl, gilt spine. VG (hinges tender). *Bohling.* $50/£32

HUSSEIN, TAHA. Stream of Days: A Student at the Azhar. Hilary Wayment (trans). London: Longmans, (1948). 2nd ed. Lt pencil mks margins. Dj (sm tears). *Aka.* $17/£11

HUSSEY, CHRISTOPHER. English Country Houses Open to the Public. (London): Country Life, (1957). Color frontis. Grn cl, color plt mtd fr cvr. Fine in color dj. *House.* $55/£35

HUSSEY, CHRISTOPHER. English Country Houses: Early Georgian 1715-1760.... London: Country Life, (1955-1958). 1st ed. 3 vols. Grn cl, color plt mtd fr cvrs. Fine in pict djs (lt chipping). *House.* $250/£161

HUSSEY, CHRISTOPHER. The Life of Sir Edwin Lutyens. London: Country Life, 1953. 1st ed. Frontis, 178 plts. Sl rubbed, else VG. *Bookpress.* $185/£119

HUSSEY, CHRISTOPHER. The Story of Ely House. London: Country Life, 1953. 37 plts. Aeg. Full soft blue calf (sl scraped), gilt. *Hollett.* $70/£45

HUSSEY, CHRISTOPHER. Tait McKenzie. A Sculptor of Youth. London: Country Life, 1929. 1st ed. 93 plts. Cl (snag). VG in dj (worn). *Cahan.* $100/£65

HUSSEY, L.D.A. South with Shackleton. London: Sampson Low, new impression 1951. VG. *High Latitude.* $50/£32

HUSSEY, TACITUS. Beginnings: Reminiscences of Early Des Moines. Des Moines, 1919. Map. Gilt-titled cl. VG + . *Bohling.* $45/£29

HUSTON, CLEBURNE. Deaf Smith, Incredible Texas Spy. Waco: Texian, 1973. 1st ed. Dj. *Lambeth.* $50/£32

HUTCHESON, MARTHA BROOKES. The Spirit of the Garden. Boston: Atlantic Monthly, 1923. Gilt-dec buckram. Sl scuffed, else Fine. *Quest.* $70/£45

HUTCHINGS, JAMES MASON. Scenes of Wonder and Curiosity in California. NY/SF: A. Roman, 1870. 3rd ed, 1st ptg. Frontis, 292pp + 4pp ads at end. Gold-stamped cl (spine ends worn; nick fr cvr fore-edge). *Dawson.* $100/£65

HUTCHINGS, W.W. London Town, Past and Present. Cassell, 1909. 2 vols. Gilt-ruled cl, gilt devices (sl staining upper bd vol 1; sl bumped; spines chipped w/loss). *Edwards.* $70/£45

HUTCHINS, PATRICIA. Ezra Pound's Kensington. An Exploration 1885-1913. London: Faber & Faber, 1965. 1st Eng ed. Fine in dj (sl rubbed, creased edges). *Ulysses.* $54/£35

HUTCHINSON, BENJAMIN. Biographica Medica.... London: J. Johnson, 1799. 1st ed. 2 vols. 19th cent 1/2 calf (rebound). Clean set (lt foxing; lib stamp tps). *Goodrich.* $595/£384

HUTCHINSON, C.C. Resources of Kansas. Topeka, 1871. Frontis, 287,(1)pp; fldg map (outer fold splitting). Gilt-titled blue cl. VG. *Bohling.* $150/£97

HUTCHINSON, H.G. Golf. London: Longmans, 1898. 6th ed. 1/2 blue morocco, lt brn sides (few pp sl foxed). *Petersfield.* $140/£90

HUTCHINSON, H.G. (ed). Fishing, the 'Country Life' Library of Sport. London: Country Life, 1904. 2 vols. (Backstrips sl faded.) *Petersfield.* $39/£25

HUTCHINSON, H.G. (ed). Shooting. London: Country Life, 1903. 2 vols. (Backs sl faded.) *Petersfield.* $74/£48

HUTCHINSON, H.N. Marriage Customs in Many Lands. London: Seeley & Co, 1897. *Boswell.* $250/£161

HUTCHINSON, J., JR. The Surgical Treatment of Facial Neuralgia. London, 1905. 1st ed. Good. *Fye.* $150/£97

HUTCHINSON, JONATHAN. Syphilis. London, 1887. 1st ed. 532pp. 1/4 leather. Good. *Fye.* $150/£97

HUTCHINSON, THOMAS J. Ten Years Wandering Among the Ethiopians.... London: Hurst & Blackett, 1861. 1st ed. Tinted litho frontis, xx,329,(1)blank, 16 ads, half title, vignette on title. (Spotting.) Orig blue cl. VG. *Morrell.* $372/£240

HUTCHINSON, W.H. Bar Cross Liar. Stillwater: Redlands, 1959. 1st ed. NF in VG + dj. *Parker.* $125/£81

HUTCHINSON, W.H. A Bar Cross Man: The Life and Personal Writings of Eugene Manlove Rhodes. Norman: Univ of OK Press, (1956). 1st ed. Grn cl. Fine in VG + dj (sl chipped, rubbed). *Harrington.* $45/£29

HUTCHINSON, W.H. One Man's West. Chico: (W.H. Hutchinson, 1948). Inscribed. Ptd wrappers. *Dawson.* $40/£26

HUTCHISON, I.R. Reminiscences, Sketches and Addresses Selected from My Papers.... Houston, TX: Cushing, 1874. 1st ed. 218pp. Howes H 856. *Ginsberg.* $175/£113

HUTCHISON, ISOBEL WYLIE. Stepping Stones from Alaska to Asia. London: Blackie, 1937. 1st ed. 20 plts (4 color), 2 maps. Blue cl (edges spotted). *Hollett.* $39/£25

HUTTON, EDWARD. The Cosmati. London, 1950. Color frontis, 64 b/w plts. (Ex-lib, ink stamp, labels, cardholder remains, #s.) *Edwards.* $31/£20

HUTTON, EDWARD. The Cosmati. London, 1950. 64 plts. VG. *Washton.* $50/£32

HUTTON, EDWARD. The Cosmati. The Roman Marble Workers of the XIIth and XIIIth Centuries. London, 1950. 64 plts. Good. *Washton.* $90/£58

HUTTON, HAROLD. Vigilante Days, Frontier Justice Along the Niobrara. Chicago, (1978). 1st ed. Fine in dj (chipped). *Pratt.* $25/£16

HUTTON, S.K. Among the Eskimos of Labrador. Toronto: Musson, 1912. 1st ed. Frontis map, lg fldg map at rear; teg. Blue cl, gilt title. VG + . *Bowman.* $100/£65

HUTTON, W. History of Derby, from the Remote Ages of Antiquity to 1791. London, 1791. 1st ed. Map. 1/2 morocco (joints worn). *Argosy.* $200/£129

HUTTON, WILLIAM RICH. Glances at California 1847-1853. San Marino: Huntington Lib, 1942. 1st ed. Grn cl. Good in dj. *Karmiole.* $30/£19

HUTTON, WILLIAM RICH. Glances at California, 1847-1853. San Marino: Huntington Lib, 1942. 1st ed. Fine. *Oregon.* $50/£32

HUXHAM, JOHN. An Essay on Fevers, and Their Various Kinds, as Depending on Different Constitutions on the Blood. London, 1750. 2nd ed. 288pp. Recent cl; new eps. *Fye.* $250/£161

HUXLEY, ALDOUS (ed). An Encyclopaedia of Pacifism. London: C&W, 1937. 1st ed. VG in Wrappers. *Limestone.* $55/£35

HUXLEY, ALDOUS. Along the Road. London: C&W, 1925. 1st ed, 1st issue, w/top stained grn. Grn cl, paper spine label. Fine in NF dj (spine lt sunned). *Chapel Hill.* $200/£129

HUXLEY, ALDOUS. Along the Road. London: C&W, 1925. 1st ed. Spine sl lightened; mild foxing. Dj (spine dknd). *Sadlon.* $25/£16

HUXLEY, ALDOUS. Ape and Essence. NY: Harper, 1948. 1st Amer ed. Gilt. Dj (sl edgeworn). *Sadlon.* $25/£16

HUXLEY, ALDOUS. Ape and Essence. Harpers, 1948. 1st ed. Fine in NF gold dj (short tears). *Fine Books.* $35/£23

HUXLEY, ALDOUS. Ape and Essence. London: C&W, 1949. 1st ed. NF in dj (sl foxed, edgeworn). *Sadlon.* $15/£10

HUXLEY, ALDOUS. Arabia Infelix and Other Poems. NY/London: Fountain Press/C&W, 1929. 1st ed. Ltd to 692. Signed. Few minor lightened spots to spine. *Sadlon.* $125/£81

HUXLEY, ALDOUS. Arabia Infelix and Other Poems. NY: Fountain Press, 1929. Signed ltd ed of 692 numbered. Fine in acetate dj. *Antic Hay.* $175/£113

HUXLEY, ALDOUS. The Art of Seeing. NY: Harper, 1942. 1st ed. VG in dj (lt wear; sm tears). *Antic Hay.* $45/£29

HUXLEY, ALDOUS. Beyond the Mexique Bay. London: C&W, 1934. Signed ltd ed of 210 numbered. Grn cl & patterned bds; teg. NF. *Antic Hay.* $375/£242

HUXLEY, ALDOUS. Brave New World Revisited. London: C&W, 1959. 1st Eng ed. Gilt. Fine in dj (spine sl dknd, edgeworn). *Sadlon.* $40/£26

HUXLEY, ALDOUS. Brave New World. D-D, 1932. 1st Amer ed. Good. *Fine Books.* $40/£26

HUXLEY, ALDOUS. Brave New World. London: C&W, 1932. 1st ed. VG in dj (sl chipped). *Limestone.* $675/£435

HUXLEY, ALDOUS. Brave New World. C&W, 1932. 1st ed. VG in VG dj (lt chipping spine head; lt wear, tear). *Aronovitz.* $750/£484

HUXLEY, ALDOUS. Brave New World. London: C&W, 1932. 1st ed. Ltd to 324. Signed. Recent cl over beveled bds, leather spine label; teg. Clamshell box. *Sadlon.* $500/£323

HUXLEY, ALDOUS. Brave New World. London: C&W, 1932. 1st trade ed. Blue cl. VG (bkpl) in dj (neatly repaired on verso along fold). *Chapel Hill.* $500/£323

HUXLEY, ALDOUS. Brave New World. London: Chatto, 1932. 1st UK ed. VG (bkpl). *Williams.* $93/£60

HUXLEY, ALDOUS. Brave New World. (NY): LEC, 1974. One of 2000 numbered, signed by Mara McAfee (illus). *Hermitage.* $125/£81

HUXLEY, ALDOUS. Brief Candles. London: C&W, 1930. 1st ed. Red cl, gilt spine (soiled, sl chipped). Ptd dj. *Karmiole.* $50/£32

HUXLEY, ALDOUS. Brief Candles. NY/London: Fountain Press/C&W, 1930. 1st ed. Ltd to 842. Signed. Recent black cl, spine gilt. Clamshell box. *Sadlon.* $125/£81

HUXLEY, ALDOUS. Brief Candles. London: C&W, 1930. 1st trade ed. Gilt. NF in dj (spine dknd). *Sadlon.* $65/£42

HUXLEY, ALDOUS. The Cicadas and Other Poems. NY: Doubleday, Doran, 1931. 1st Amer ed. Dj (spine dknd, sl edgeworn). *Sadlon.* $40/£26

HUXLEY, ALDOUS. The Cicadas and Other Poems. London: C&W, 1931. 1st trade ed. Fine in dj (sl lightened). *Sadlon.* $40/£26

HUXLEY, ALDOUS. Crome Yellow. London: C&W, 1921. 1st ed. Top edge grn. Yellow cl. Extra spine label tipped in at rear as issued. Spine, label dknd, else VG. *Chapel Hill.* $100/£65

HUXLEY, ALDOUS. The Defeat of Youth and Other Poems. London, 1918. Ltd to 250. Dec paper bds (sl rubbed; hinge sl tender). *Edrich.* $155/£100

HUXLEY, ALDOUS. The Devils of Loudun. NY, (1952). 1st Amer ed. VG in dj. *Argosy.* $35/£23

HUXLEY, ALDOUS. The Discovery: A Comedy in Five Acts. London: C&W, 1924. Special ed, ltd to 210 numbered. Cl & patterned bds. Fine in purple dj (lt wear; few tears; spine sunned). *Antic Hay.* $200/£129

HUXLEY, ALDOUS. Do What You Will. London: C&W, 1929. 1st ed. Edges sl foxed, else VG in dj. *Limestone.* $135/£87

HUXLEY, ALDOUS. The Doors of Perception. London: C&W, 1954. 1st ed. NF in dj. *Sclanders.* $47/£30

HUXLEY, ALDOUS. The Elder Peter Breughel. NY: Willey Book Co, 1938. 1st ed. 30 full-pg plts (6 color). Mustard-yellow bds. VG in dj. *Chapel Hill.* $35/£23

HUXLEY, ALDOUS. An Encyclopaedia of Pacifism. London: C&W, 1937. 1st ed. VG in ptd yellow wraps. *Chapel Hill.* $40/£26

HUXLEY, ALDOUS. Ends and Means. London: C&W, 1937. 1st ed. VG in dj (soiled, nicked, browned). *Virgo.* $47/£30

HUXLEY, ALDOUS. Ends and Means. London: C&W, 1937. 1st ed. Gilt. Sl foxing to fore-edges, o/w Fine in NF dj. *Sadlon.* $50/£32

HUXLEY, ALDOUS. Essays New and Old. NY: George H. Doran, (1927). 1st Amer ed, 1st trade ed. Blue cl. Fine in white ptd dj (sl soiled, long closed tears tape mended on verso, else VG). *Godot.* $65/£42

HUXLEY, ALDOUS. Essays New and Old. London: C&W, 1926. 1st ed. Ltd to 650. Signed. Teg. Marbled bds (rebacked). Clamshell box. *Sadlon.* $125/£81

HUXLEY, ALDOUS. Eyeless in Gaza. London: C&W, 1936. 1st ed. Ltd to 200. Signed. Teg. Dec bds (minor scuffs; lightened spots; thin, black mk upper cvr). *Sadlon.* $225/£145

HUXLEY, ALDOUS. Eyeless in Gaza. London: C&W, 1936. 1st trade ed. NF in NF dj. *Sadlon.* $100/£65

HUXLEY, ALDOUS. The Genius and the Goddess. NY: Harper, 1955. 1st Amer ed. Fine in dj (sl edgeworn). *Sadlon.* $25/£16

HUXLEY, ALDOUS. The Genius and the Goddess. London: C&W, 1955. 1st ed. Name, else NF in VG dj. *Virgo.* $31/£20

HUXLEY, ALDOUS. The Genius and the Goddess. London: C&W, 1955. 1st Eng ed. Fine in dj (sl edgeworn). *Sadlon.* $25/£16

HUXLEY, ALDOUS. Holy Face and Other Essays. London, 1929. #226/300. Teg, rest uncut. Gilt cvrs. NF (sl sunned, sl rubbed). *Polyanthos.* $125/£81

HUXLEY, ALDOUS. Jesting Pilate, an Intellectual Holiday. NY: George H. Doran, (1926). 1st Amer ed. Cl-backed dec bds. Ep gutters sl discolored, else VG. *Hermitage.* $35/£23

HUXLEY, ALDOUS. Jesting Pilate: The Diary of a Journey. London: C&W, 1926. 1st Eng ed. Blue cl. NF (sl wear) in dj (tears, sm chip spine head). *Antic Hay.* $100/£65

HUXLEY, ALDOUS. Leda. NY: Doubleday, Doran, 1929. 1st Amer ed. Ltd to 361. Signed. White linen, leather spine label (spine sl dknd, few sm yellowed spots at edge). Slipcase. *Sadlon.* $200/£129

HUXLEY, ALDOUS. Little Mexican and Other Stories. London: C&W, 1924. 1st ed. Top edge red. Red cl. NF in dj (spine dknd). *Chapel Hill.* $150/£97

HUXLEY, ALDOUS. Little Mexican and Other Stories. London: C&W, 1924. 1st Eng ed. NF in white dj (lt soil). *Antic Hay.* $175/£113

HUXLEY, ALDOUS. Mortal Coils. London: C&W, 1922. 1st ed. Spine sl lightened. Dj (spine sl dknd, foxed; repaired tears). *Sadlon.* $50/£32

HUXLEY, ALDOUS. Mortal Coils. London: C&W, 1922. 1st ed. Fine in dj (foxed). *Pharos.* $125/£81

HUXLEY, ALDOUS. Music at Night and Other Essays. NY: Fountain Press, 1931. 1st ed. #652/842 signed. Buckram-backed marbled bds, silver decs, paper label. VG. *Cox.* $116/£75

HUXLEY, ALDOUS. Music at Night and Other Essays. London: C&W, 1931. 1st trade ed. Gilt. Lower cvr edge sl lightened; few foxed spots. Dj (spine dknd). *Sadlon.* $25/£16

HUXLEY, ALDOUS. Point Counter Point. London: C&W, 1928. 1st Eng ed. Orange cl. Fine in white dj (lt edgewear; soiled; faint stain). *Antic Hay.* $225/£145

HUXLEY, ALDOUS. Point Counter Point. London: C&W, 1928. 1st trade ed. NF in dj (spine sl dknd, sl chipped). *Sadlon.* $125/£81

HUXLEY, ALDOUS. Point Counter Point. Leipzig: Bernard Tauchnitz, 1929. 2 vols. Spines dknd, reinforced breaks to spine edges. Ptd wrappers. *Sadlon.* $15/£10

HUXLEY, ALDOUS. Proper Studies. London: C&W, 1927. 1st trade ed. Mild foxing. Dj (spine dknd, sm spots to fr panel). *Sadlon.* $45/£29

HUXLEY, ALDOUS. Science, Liberty and Peace. NY/London, Harper, 1946. 1st ed. Fine in Fine dj. *Sadlon.* $45/£29

HUXLEY, ALDOUS. Selected Poems. NY: Appleton, 1925. 1st Amer ed. Sl rubbed, few lightened spots. *Sadlon.* $30/£19

HUXLEY, ALDOUS. Selected Poems. Oxford: Basil Blackwell, 1926. Later (?2nd Eng) ed. Signed. Dec bds. (sl rubbed; lt foxing; last 2 leaves carelessly opened). *Sadlon.* $50/£32

HUXLEY, ALDOUS. Texts and Pretexts: An Anthology. London: C&W, 1932. 1st trade ed. NF in NF dj. *Sadlon.* $50/£32

HUXLEY, ALDOUS. Those Barren Leaves. London: C&W, 1925. 1st ed. Ochre cl, paper spine label. Prelims lt foxed, else NF. *Chapel Hill.* $50/£32

HUXLEY, ALDOUS. Time Must Have a Stop. NY/London: Harper, 1944. 1st Amer ed. Blue cl. NF in VG dj (creasing). *Chapel Hill.* $45/£29

HUXLEY, ALDOUS. Tomorrow and Tomorrow and Tomorrow and Other Essays. NY: Harper, (1956). 1st Amer ed. NF in dj (sl edgeworn). *Sadlon.* $45/£29

HUXLEY, ALDOUS. Two or Three Graces and Other Stories. London: C&W, 1926. 1st ed. NF in dj (sl browned). *Sadlon.* $50/£32

HUXLEY, ALDOUS. Two or Three Graces and Other Stories. London: C&W, 1926. 1st ed. VG in dj (browned, sl nicked). *Limestone.* $125/£81

HUXLEY, ALDOUS. Two or Three Graces. London: C&W, 1926. 1st Eng ed. Blue cl. Fine in NF dj (sl soil). *Antic Hay.* $125/£81

HUXLEY, ALDOUS. Vulgarity in Literature. London: C&W, 1930. 1st ed. Ltd to 260. Signed. Teg. Fine. *Sadlon.* $175/£113

HUXLEY, ALDOUS. Vulgarity in Literature. London: C&W, 1930. 1st trade ed. Pict bds. NF in dj (spine sl dknd). *Sadlon.* $40/£26

HUXLEY, ALDOUS. The World of Light. London, 1931. 1st ed. Fine (sl offsetting fep) in dj (spine sl sunned, top sl chipped). *Polyanthos.* $50/£32

HUXLEY, ALDOUS. The World of Light. London: C&W, 1931. 1st trade ed. 4pg leaflet laid in. NF in dj (spine dknd). *Sadlon.* $50/£32

HUXLEY, E. Murder at Government House. Harpers, 1937. 1st Amer ed, 1st bk. VG in dj (lt worn; chipped). *Fine Books.* $85/£55

HUXLEY, J. Memories. London, 1970. 22 ports. *Wheldon & Wesley.* $28/£18

HUXLEY, JULIAN. Essays of a Biologist. London: C&W, 1923. 1st ed. Red cl (faded). *White.* $19/£12

HUXLEY, L. Life and Letters of Thomas Henry Huxley by His Son. London, 1900. 1st ed. 2 vols. 11 plts. Good. *Henly.* $124/£80

HUXLEY, T.H. Lay Sermons, Addresses and Reviews. London: Macmillan, 1887. xi,300pp. Good. *White.* $28/£18

HUXLEY, T.H. The Oceanic Hydrozoa.... London: Ray Society, 1859. x,143pp; 12 plts. 1/2 morocco. (Worn; ex-lib.) *Wheldon & Wesley.* $78/£50

HUYGHE, RENE. Delacroix. London, 1963. 56 color plts. Dj (sl chipped). *Edwards.* $132/£85

HUYSMANS, J.K. Against the Grain. Lieber & Lewis, 1922. 1st Amer ed. Fine in VG dj (sl wear). *Aronovitz.* $250/£161

HUYSMANS, J.K. Against the Grain. Paris, 1926. 'Private, Limited Edition,' numbered. (Sl bumped, worn, speckled.) *King.* $45/£29

HUYSMANS, J.K. Crowds of Lourdes. NY, 1925. 1st Amer ed. Port. (Extrems worn.) *King.* $35/£23

HUYSMANS, J.K. Down There. A&C Boni, 1924. 1st Amer ed. NF in VG+ dj. *Fine Books.* $375/£242

HYAMS, EDWARD and A.A. JACKSON (eds). The Orchard and Fruit Garden. London: Longmans, Green, 1961. 1st ed. 80 Excellent full-pg color plts. Teg. NF in slipcase. *Quest.* $135/£87

HYAMS, EDWARD and A.A. JACKSON (eds). The Orchard and Fruit Garden.... London, 1961. 80 Fine color plts (sl edgewear). Dj. *Sutton.* $135/£87

HYAMS, EDWARD and WILLIAM MacQUITTY. Irish Gardens. NY: Macmillan, 1967. 1st Amer ed. 15 color plts, 88 half-tones. NF in dj. *Quest.* $65/£42

HYAMS, EDWARD. The English Garden. London, 1964. 17 mtd color plts, 171 plain plts. Fine in dj. *Henly.* $56/£36

HYAMS, EDWARD. The English Garden. London: Thames & Hudson, 1964. 1st ed. 188 photogravure plts (17 tipped-in color). Few margins sl browned, else Fine in dj. *Quest.* $95/£61

HYAMS, EDWARD. A History of Gardens and Gardening. London, 1971. Fine in dj & slipcase. *Henly.* $54/£35

HYAMS, EDWARD. Pleasure from Plants. London, 1966. Fine in dj. *Brooks.* $22/£14

HYDE, A. et al. The Frozen Zone and Its Explorers. Hartford: Columbia Book Co, 1875. xv,800pp. Orig gilt dec cl (sl rubbed). Good. *Walcot.* $85/£55

HYDE, DAYTON O. The Last Free Man—The True Story behind the Massacre of Shoshone Mike and His Band of Indians in 1911. NY: Dial, 1973. 1st ed. Fine in Fine dj. *Perier.* $32/£21

HYDE, H. MONTGOMERY. The Story of Lamb House Rye. Rye, Sussex: Adams of Rye, 1966. 1st ed. Fine in stapled wrappers. *Pharos.* $30/£19

HYDE, H. MONTGOMERY. The Three Trials of Oscar Wilde. Univ Books, 1956. 1st Amer ed. Fine in NF dj. *Fine Books.* $20/£13

HYDE, J.A. LLOYD. Oriental Lowestoft—Chinese Export Porcelain—Porcelaine de la Cie. des Indes. Newport, Monmouthshire, 1954. One of 1500 of the 2nd ed. 4 color, 32 monochrome plts. (Bumped.) *Argosy.* $85/£55

HYDE, J.A. LLOYD. Oriental Lowestoft. NY, 1936. 1st ed. #211/1000. Signed. Color frontis, 30 b/w plts. Teg; fore-edge uncut. (Spine sl discolored.) Card slipcase (sl soiled, worn). *Edwards.* $85/£55

HYDE, JAMES. A Practical Treatise on Diseases of the Skin. Phila, 1888. 2nd ed. 676pp; 2 chromolithos. Full leather (binding rubbed). *Fye.* $30/£19

HYDE, MARY. The Impossible Friendship. Boswell and Mrs. Thrale. Cambridge: Harvard, 1972. 1st ed. Inscribed. Pub's slip attached fep. NF in dj. *Reese.* $35/£23

HYDE, PHILIP. Drylands. The Deserts of North America. San Diego: Yolla Bolly Press, (1987). 1st ed. Fine in Fine dj. *Book Market.* $125/£81

HYLL, THOMAS. The Gardeners Labyrinth. Milford, CT: Herb Lovers Book Club, 1939. Rpt. Uncut; moire-like eps. Stippled paper-cvrd bds. VF. *Quest.* $35/£23

HYMAN, MAC. Take Now Thy Son. NY: Random House, (1965). 1st ed. VG in VG dj. *Chapel Hill.* $50/£32

HYMAN, S. Edward Lear's Birds. London, 1980. 40 color plts. *Wheldon & Wesley.* $78/£50

HYNE, C.J. CUTCLIFFE. Adventures of Capt Kettle. Dillingham, 1898. 1st ed. VG-. *Madle.* $30/£19

HYNE, C.J. CUTCLIFFE. Atoms of Empire. Macmillan, 1904. 1st US ed. VG. *Madle.* $35/£23

HYNE, C.J. CUTCLIFFE. The Lost Continent. Harper, 1900. 1st US ed. VG. *Madle.* $40/£26

Hyperion. (By Henry Wordsworth Longfellow.) NY: Samuel Colman, 1839. 1st ed. 2 vols. 8vo. 213; 226pp. Brn eps. Tan bds w/paper spine labels. Excellent (sl cracks along external joints; lt foxing; bkpl Vol 2). Brn cl chemises, 1/4 morocco dbl slipcase. BAL 12064. *Chapel Hill.* $650/£419

HYSLOP, JAMES H. Borderland of Psychical Research. Boston: Herbert B. Turner, (1906). 1st ed. Blue cl, spine gilt. Fine. *Gach.* $40/£26

HYSLOP, JAMES H. Enigmas of Psychical Research. Boston, 1906. 1st ed. Good. *Fye.* $75/£48

I

IBSEN, HENRIK. The Doll's House. Henrietta Frances Lord (trans). NY: Appleton, 1889. 1st Amer ed. Uncut. White cl-backed grn paper bds, ptd in dk grn. Nice (lt rubbing). *Macdonnell.* $165/£106

IBSEN, HENRIK. A Doll's House. London: Walter Scott, 1892. 1st ed thus. 5 photos. 1/2 cl. *Dramatis Personae.* $50/£32

IBSEN, HENRIK. Peer Gynt. GC: Doubleday, Doran, 1929. 1st ed thus. Elizabeth MacKinstry (illus). Cl-backed grn bds (edge lt faded), paste label. Dj (sl wear). *Reisler.* $150/£97

IBSEN, HENRIK. Peer Gynt. GC: Doubleday, Doran, 1929. 1st ed. Cl-backed bds, labels. NF. *Hermitage.* $85/£55

IBSEN, HENRIK. Peer Gynt. London: Harrap, 1936. 1st trade ed. Arthur Rackham (illus). Fine (bkpl) in NF dj. *Williams.* $457/£295

IBSEN, HENRIK. Peer Gynt: A Dramatic Poem. Phila: Lippincott, (1936). 1st trade ed. Frontis w/guard, 11 color plts, illus eps. Loss of brightness on spine; name, else Fine. *Cahan.* $150/£97

ICKES, HAROLD L. The Autobiography of a Curmudgeon. NY: Reynal & Hitchcock, 1943. 1st ed. Frontis port. NF in dj (chipped). *Connolly.* $35/£23

ICKIS, ALONZO F. Bloody Trails along the Rio Grande.... Nolie Mumey (ed). Denver: Old West, 1958. 1st ed. One of 500 numbered, signed by Mumey. Frontis; lg fldg map. Pict dj. *Ginsberg.* $125/£81

IDE, SIMEON. A Biographical Sketch of the Life of William B. Ide.... Glorieta, NM: Rio Grande Press, (1967). Rpt. VG. Howes I 4 & 5. *Oregon.* $45/£29

IDES, E. YSBRANTS. Three Years Travels, from Moscow Over-land to China.... London: Ptd for W. Freeman et al, 1706. 1st ed in English. Extra engr title (corner torn; inking here, elsewhere); lg fldg map, 31 fldg full-pg copper plts (some crudely colored, 1 lacking outer 1/2). Calf-backed bds (worn, joints cracked, hinges reinforced). *Argosy.* $1,000/£645

IDLE, CHRISTOPHER. Hints on Shooting and Fishing. Longman, Brown, 1855. Orig cl (sl discolored). *Petersfield.* $87/£56

IGNATOW, DAVID. Poems. Prairie City, IL: Decker Press, (1948). 1st ed. 1st bk. VG. *Godot.* $175/£113

ILES, FRANCIS. Before the Fact. London: Gollancz, 1932. 1st ed. VG. *Ming.* $62/£40

ILLINGWORTH, A. HOLDEN. More Reminiscences. Bradford/London: Privately ptd, 1936. 32 engr plts (18 color). Orig smooth tan cl, gilt titles. Fine+. *Bowman.* $120/£77

Illustrated History of Klickitat, Yakima, and Kittitas Counties. Chicago: Interstate Pub., 1904. Full leather. VG. *Perier.* $375/£242

Illustrated History of North Idaho. Embracing Nez Perces, Idaho, Latah, Kootenac, and Shoshone Counties. Western Hist Pub., 1903. Full leather. VG. *Perier.* $550/£355

Illustrated History of Stevens, Ferry, Okanagan, and Chelan Counties, State of Washington. Western Pub., 1904. Full leather. VG. *Perier.* $475/£306

Illustrated History of the Big Bend Country—Embracing Lincoln, Douglas, Adams and Franklin Counties. Western Hist Pub., 1904. Facs ed. Fine. *Perier.* $140/£90

Illustrated History of Whitman County, State of Washington. W.H. Lever, 1901. Full leather (rebacked). Good. *Perier.* $400/£258

ILTON, PAUL. Digging in the Holy Land. London: W.H. Allen, 1959. 8 plts. Good in dj. *Archaeologia.* $35/£23

IMBS, BRAVIG. Confessions of Another Young Man. NY: Henkle-Yewdale House, (1936). 1st ed. White cl sl soiled at edges, o/w VG in dj (edgeworn; chips). *Reese.* $45/£29

IMES, BIRNEY. Juke Joint. Univ Press of MS: 1990. 1st Amer ed. Signed by Richard Ford (intro). Folio. Mint in dj. *Polyanthos.* $60/£39

IMISON, JOHN. Elements of Science and Art.... London: Cadell & Davies, 1808. New ed. 2 vols. ix,581pp, 25 plts; xii,611pp, 7 plts (tears to 3 neatly repaired). Contemp leather (joint vol 1 split, sl chafed). *Ars Artis.* $233/£150

IMPEY, JOHN. The Practice of the Office of Sheriff and Under Sheriff.... London: for W. Clarke and Sons, 1817. 4th ed. Contemp calf (sl worn). *Boswell.* $350/£226

Importance of Being Earnest. (By Oscar Wilde.) London: Leonard Smithers, 1899. 1st ed. Lilac cl, gilt. Variant state w/more elaborate double-loop tendril version of gilt motif (sl bumped, sunned; sl mks; prelims, edges sl browned). Good. *Ash.* $767/£495

IMRAY, JAMES and SON. The Atlantic Navigator, Being a Nautical Description.... London: James Imray and Son, 1855. 4th ed. xxii,(viii),532pp + 38pp pub's ads, 12 charts. (Sig.) *Lefkowicz.* $150/£97

INCHBALD, ELIZABETH. Animal Magnetism. A Farce.... Dublin: Ptd by C. Lewis, 1789. 1st Irish ed. 34pp. Fine in recent paper wrapper. *Hemlock.* $325/£210

Incidents of a Trip through the Great Platte Valley. (By Silas Seymour.) NY, 1867. 1st ed. Inscribed. 129pp. Article tipped in. Brn cl. Nice. Howes S 315. *Bohling.* $350/£226

Incredible Hulk. London: Pan, 1981. 20x27 cm. 3 dbl-pg pop-ups, pull-tabs. Glazed pict bds. VG. *Book Finders.* $40/£26

INDERWICK, F.A. (ed). A Calendar of the Inner Temple Records, 1505-1714. London: By Order of the Masters of the Bench, 1896-1901. 3 vols. Later 1/2 sheep. Good set (sl dusty). *Boswell.* $350/£226

Indexed County and Township Pocket Map and Shippers' Guide of Missouri. Chicago, (1904). Color map. Folder (worn, spine splitting; paper dknd). *Bohling.* $50/£32

Infant's Annual. Phila/NY/Balt: Fisher & Brother, n.d. (ca 1830). Sq 16mo. Full-pg wood engr frontis, 66pp. Tooled cl, gilt title. Spine lt faded, else Fine. *Hobbyhorse.* $90/£58

Infant's Battledore. Castle Cary: S. Moore, n.d. (ca 1830). 12mo. 2pp + 1 flap. Pink dec cvr (lt fading along fold). *Hobbyhorse.* $150/£97

Infant's Cabinet of Birds and Beasts. London: Harvey & Darton, 1820. Obl 12mo. 16 leaves, 32 engrs. Mod cvr folder. VG (pg chipped). *Hobbyhorse.* $150/£97

INGALLS, FAY. About Dogs—And Me. Hot Springs, VA, 1939. 1st ed. Tipped-in frontis. Spine dknd, bkpl, else Fine. *Cahan.* $225/£145

INGALLS, R. Theft. Faber & Faber, 1970. 1st ed, 1st bk. Fine in dj. *Fine Books.* $100/£65

INGALLS, RAYMOND. Tumors of the Orbit and Allied Pseudo Tumors, and Analysis of 216 Case Histories. Springfield, 1953. 1st ed. Good in dj. *Fye.* $50/£32

INGE, WILLIAM. The Dark at the Top of the Stairs. NY: Random House, (1958). 1st ed. Fine in dj (lt used). *Dermont.* $40/£26

INGE, WILLIAM. The Dark at the Top of the Stairs. NY, 1958. 1st Amer ed. Fine in Fine dj. *Polyanthos.* $45/£29

INGE, WILLIAM. Picnic. R-H, 1953. 1st ed. Fine in VG + dj (lt dust soil; sl chipping spine). *Fine Books.* $85/£55

INGERSOLL, L.D. A History of the War Department of the United States. Washington: Mohun, 1879. 613pp; 2 plts. VG. *Schoyer.* $85/£55

INGERSOLL, ROBERT G. The Works of Robert G. Ingersoll. NY, (1990). New Dresden ed. 12 vols. NF (spines sunned). *Polyanthos.* $175/£113

INGLIS, JAMES. Our Australian Cousins. London: Macmillan, 1880. (xvi),466pp + 44pp pub's ads. Grn cl stamped in gilt, black (chipped; bkpl, owner stamps; some early leaves creased). *Schoyer.* $85/£55

INGOLDSBY, THOMAS. (Pseud of Richard Harris Barham.) The Ingoldsby Legends or Mirth and Marvels. London: Dent, 1922. Rpt. 12 color plts by Arthur Rackham. (Sl foxed throughout.) *Petersfield.* $39/£25

INGOLDSBY, THOMAS. (Pseud of Richard Harris Barham.) The Ingoldsby Legends. London, 1864. xii,428pp (lt foxed, hinges tender); aeg. Gilt filleted cl, gilt devices (rubbed, sl cl loss; spine sl chipped, sm split). *Edwards.* $56/£36

INGOLDSBY, THOMAS. (Pseud of Richard Harris Barham.) The Ingoldsby Legends. London, 1870. xiv,512pp; marbled eps, aeg. Inner gilt dentelles, full gilt-ruled morocco (corners rubbed, sl loss; spine sl rubbed). *Edwards.* $85/£55

INGOLDSBY, THOMAS. (Pseud of Richard Harris Barham.) The Jackdaw of Rheims. London: Gay & Hancock, 1913. One of 100, signed by Charles Folkard (illus). Illus tipped-in. Full vellum, gilt design. Bds lt soiled, warped, o/w VG. *Cullen.* $325/£210

INGRAHAM, FRANC and DONALD MATSON. Neurosurgery of Infancy and Childhood. Springfield, 1954. Spine dull, o/w VG. *Fye.* $75/£48

INGRAHAM, HENRY A. American Trout Streams. NY: Angler's Club of NY, 1926. One of 350 numbered. White linen backed gray/grn bds. Fine. *Bowman.* $325/£210

INGRAHAM, PRENTISS. Buffalo Bill's Trump Card. NY: Street & Smith, (1908). Later issue. Color pict wraps (pulpy paper). *Schoyer.* $25/£16

INGRAM, JOHN H. Christopher Marlowe and His Associates. London: Grant Richards, 1904. 1st ed. Teg; others rough cut. Imitation vellum spine; paper-cvrd bds. VG (ink initials). *Hermitage.* $75/£48

INGSTAD, HELGE. East of the Great Glacier. NY: Knopf, 1937. VG in dj. *High Latitude.* $30/£19

INGSTAD, HELGE. East of the Great Glacier. NY: Knopf, 1937. 1st ed. (Sl dusty; spine faded.) Poor dj. *Parmer.* $35/£23

INGWERSEN, WILL. Alpine and Rock Plants. London, 1983. Fine in dj (spine faded). *Brooks.* $25/£16

INGWERSEN, WILL. Classic Garden Plants. London: Hamlyn, 1975. 48 color repros. Inscrip fep, else Fine in dj. *Quest.* $40/£26

INMAN, HENRY and WILLIAM CODY. The Great Salt Lake Trail. Topeka: Crane, 1899. Early rpt. G + (cvr worn, hinge repaired). *Parker.* $60/£39

INMAN, HENRY and WILLIAM CODY. The Great Salt Lake Trail. Ross & Haines, 1966. Frontis, 7 plts, fldg map. VF in VF dj. Howes I 55. *Oregon.* $45/£29

INMAN, HENRY and WILLIAM CODY. The Great Salt Lake Trail. Minneapolis: Ross & Haines, 1966. One of 1500. Fldg map. Fine in dj. Rpt of Howes I 55. *Bohling.* $35/£23

INMAN, HENRY and WILLIAM F. CODY. The Great Salt Lake Trail. NY: Macmillan, 1898. 1st ed. 529pp, map. Good. Howes I 55. *Lien.* $75/£48

INMAN, HENRY. The Delahoydes. Topeka: Crane, 1899. Apparently 1st ed. 283pp. Orig pict cl. VG. *Schoyer.* $30/£19

INMAN, HENRY. The Great Salt Lake Trail. NY, 1898. 1st ed. 13,529pp, port, 7 plts. (Cvr faded.) *Heinoldt.* $85/£55

INNES, HAMMOND. The Angry Mountain. London: Collins, 1950. 1st ed. Foxing pg edges; erasure fep, o/w VG in dj (price-clipped; sl faded spine; wear spine ends). *Mordida*. $45/£29

INNES, HAMMOND. Atlantic Fury. Collins, 1962. 1st UK ed. NF in dj (closed tear). *Williams*. $19/£12

INNES, MICHAEL and RAYNER HEPPENSTALL. Three Tales of Hamlet. London: Gollanz, 1950. 1st ed. Fine in NF dj. *Janus*. $50/£32

INNES, MICHAEL. Appleby at Allington. London: Gollanz, 1968. 1st ed. VG + (name) in VG + dj. *Janus*. $30/£19

INNES, MICHAEL. Appleby on Ararat. NY: Dodd Mead, 1941. 1st Amer ed. VF in Fine dj (sl wear). *Mordida*. $85/£55

INNES, MICHAEL. Appleby's Answer. NY: Dodd, Mead, 1973. 1st US ed. Fine in VG + dj. *Janus*. $18/£12

INNES, MICHAEL. The Daffodil Affair. NY: Dodd Mead, 1942. 1st Amer ed. VG in dj (chipped, frayed; wear). *Mordida*. $75/£48

INNES, MICHAEL. Money from Holme. London: Gollancz, 1964. 1st ed. Fine in NF dj (price-clipped). *Janus*. $35/£23

INNES, MICHAEL. Old Hall, New Hall. London: Gollancz, 1956. 1st ed. Pg edges browned, lt soiled, else VG in dj (lt chipped, soiled). *Murder*. $35/£23

INNES, MICHAEL. The Open House. London: Gollanz, 1972. 1st ed. NF (name) in NF dj. *Janus*. $30/£19

INNIS, HAROLD A. The Cod Fisheries. Yale Univ Press, 1940. 1st ed. 7 maps. *Edwards*. $70/£45

INNIS, HAROLD A. The Fur Trade in Canada. Univ Toronto, 1927. 1st ed. Lg fldg table. VG (rubberstamp on feps). *Oregon*. $75/£48

Instructions Relative to Self-Preservation During the Prevalence of Contagious Diseases. London, 1801. 1st ed. 14pp. Good in wrappers (sm hole). *Fye*. $50/£32

Interesting Life, Travels, Voyages and Daring Engagements of the Celebrated Paul Jones. NY: W. Borradaile, 1823. 12mo. Copper engr fldg frontis (chips; folds reinforced), 28pp (pg corner restored w/loss). Rebound in antique marbled paper. VG (lt marginal foxing). Howes J 225. *Hobbyhorse*. $275/£177

IOBST, RICHARD W. The Bloody Sixth the Sixth North Carolina Regiment Confederate States of America. (Durham, NC: Chrisitian Ptg Co, 1965). 1st ed. Fldg chart. NF in orig stiff ptd wrappers. *Mcgowan*. $150/£97

Ionica. (By William Johnson Cory.) London, 1858. 1st ed. VG (fr flyleaf excised). *Mcclintock*. $90/£58

Irish Emigrant. An Historical Tale Founded on Fact, by an Hibernian. Winchester, VA: John T. Sharrocks, 1817. 1st ed. Vol 1 (of 2) only. 200pp. Orig full calf. Good (pp foxed; top margin tp clipped; cvrs worn). *Mcgowan*. $150/£97

IRISH, WILLIAM. (Pseud of Cornell Woolrich.) Deadline at Dawn. Phila: Lippincott, 1944. 1st ed. Fine in dj (minor edgewear, sm chips spine top). *Else Fine*. $250/£161

IRISH, WILLIAM. (Pseud of Cornell Woolrich.) Deadline at Dawn. Cleveland/NY: World Publishing, 1946. Motion picture ed. 1st thus. VG in pict dj (lt chipped). *Limestone*. $45/£29

IRISH, WILLIAM. (Pseud of Cornell Woolrich.) Deadline at Dawn. Cleveland: World, 1946. Tower Books Motion Picture ed. Pp dknd, o/w Fine in dj (price-clipped; sl wear spine ends). *Mordida*. $45/£29

IRISH, WILLIAM. (Pseud of Cornell Woolrich.) I Married a Dead Man. Phila: Lippincott, 1948. 1st ed. NF in dj (corner wear, dust soiling back panel). *Else Fine*. $125/£81

IRISH, WILLIAM. (Pseud of Cornell Woolrich.) Waltz into Darkness. Phila: J.B. Lippincott, 1947. 1st ed. Corner sl bumped, o/w VG in dj (chip panel; internally mended tears). *Bernard*. $95/£61

IRISH, WILLIAM. (Pseud of Cornell Woolrich.) You'll Never See Me Again. NY: Dell, (1939). Pict wraps (sl worn, sl corner crease). *King*. $75/£48

IRONSIDE, ROBIN. Pre-Raphaelite Painters, with a Descriptive Catalogue by John Gere. London: Phaidon, 1948. Color frontis, 97 plts (3 color). Pub's cl. Spine sl faded, o/w Fine. *Europa*. $78/£50

IRVING, C. Daughter of Egypt. Allan, 1937. 1st ed. NF in color pict dj (wear, tear, chipping). *Aronovitz*. $110/£71

IRVING, JOHN. The 158-Pound Marriage. NY: Random House, (1974). 1st ed. Fine in NF dj (lt wear). *Between The Covers*. $150/£97

IRVING, JOHN. The 158-Pound Marriage. R-H, 1974. 1st ed. NF in dj. *Fine Books*. $100/£65

IRVING, JOHN. The Hotel New Hampshire. NY: E.P. Dutton, (1981). 1st trade ed. Signed. NF in dj. *Godot*. $65/£42

IRVING, JOHN. A Prayer for Owen Meaney. NY: Wm. Morrow, 1989. 1st ed. Fine in Fine dj. *Revere*. $25/£16

IRVING, JOHN. Setting Free the Bears. NY: Random, (1968). 1st ed, 1st bk. Sig, else Fine in dj (lt wear). *Robbins*. $400/£258

IRVING, JOHN. Setting Free the Bears. NY: Random House, (1968). 1st ed. 1st bk. Fine in white ptd dj (sl creased, else Fine). *Godot*. $450/£290

IRVING, JOHN. The Water-Method Man. R-H, 1972. 1st ed. VG + in Fine dj. *Fine Books*. $90/£58

IRVING, JOHN. The Water-Method Man. NY: Random House, 1972. 1st ed. NF (name) in VG + dj. *Pettler*. $120/£77

IRVING, JOHN. The World According to Garp. NY: Dutton, (1978). 1st ed. Inscribed. Lt foxing fore-edge, o/w Fine in Fine dj (lt rubbing to gold stamping fr panel). *Between The Covers*. $200/£129

IRVING, JOHN. The World According to Garp. Dutton, 1978. 1st ed. NF in dj (rubbed, stains). *Stahr*. $35/£23

IRVING, JOHN. The World According to Garp. NY: Dutton, 1978. 1st ed. NF in NF dj (short closed tear). *Pettler*. $55/£35

IRVING, JOHN. The World According to Garp. Gollancz, 1978. 1st UK ed. VG in dj (ink inscrip). *Williams*. $23/£15

IRVING, R.L.G. The Romance of Mountaineering. London, 1935. 1st ed. 41 collotype repros. Dj. *Bickersteth*. $23/£15

IRVING, ROLAND DUER. The Copper-Bearing Rocks of Lake Superior. Washington: GPO, 1883. 464pp w/index (lt stained; pg torn; cvrs rubbed); 29 plts (tissues rough). *King*. $95/£61

IRVING, THEODORE. The Conquest of Florida, by Hernando de Soto. NY: Putnam's, 1851. 2nd ed. 457pp, fldg map (short tear inner edge, fold darkened, torn). (Scattered foxing; sm hole fep; cl rubbed, bumped, stained.) VG. Howes I 80. *Blue Mountain*. $85/£55

IRVING, WASHINGTON. The Alhambra. N.p.: LEC, 1969. #330/1500 signed by Lima de Freitas (illus). Fine in pub's slipcase. *Hermitage*. $85/£55

IRVING, WASHINGTON. Astoria, or Anecdotes of an Enterprise beyond the Rocky Mountains. Phila: Carey, Lea, & Blanchard, 1836. 1st ed. 2 vols. 285; 279pp, 8pp ads, fldg map. Pebbled plum cl, gilt-stamped spine. Good+ (cl worn, cracking at spine edges; bkpl). Howes I 81. *Oregon.* $450/£290

IRVING, WASHINGTON. Astoria, or Anecdotes of an Enterprise Beyond the Rocky Mountains. Phila: Carey, Lea & Blanchard, 1836. Vol 1: 1st state, w/copyright notice and imprint on verso of title; Vol 2: 2nd state, w/o footnote p239. 285; 279pp + 8pp ads; fldg map. Patterned cl (sunned, spotted, extrems frayed, foxed; inner hinges vol 2 cracked, contents shaken; rear inner hinge vol 1 starting). Contemp ink sig each tp, sm bkpl each vol, else Good set. Howes I 81. *Reese.* $750/£484

IRVING, WASHINGTON. Astoria. Phila, 1836. 1st ed, 1st issue. 2 vols. Fldg map. Orig blue cl. Howes I 81. *Ginsberg.* $600/£387

IRVING, WASHINGTON. Astoria.... Putnam's, 1897. Tacoma Ed. 2 vols. xxi,389; xvi,391pp, 2 frontispieces, 26 plts. Gilt dec buckram, gilt lettering; teg. VG. *Oregon.* $165/£106

IRVING, WASHINGTON. Bracebridge Hall, or the Humourists. NY/London: Putnam's, 1896. 2 vols. Gilt; teg (spines yellowed, starting to fray). *Sadlon.* $35/£23

IRVING, WASHINGTON. Bracebridge Hall. NY, 1858. New Ed. Engr frontis, engr tp, 465pp, 12 orig designs by Schmolze; aeg. Inner gilt dentelles, contemp gilt-ruled morocco, dec gilt filleted raised bands. *Edwards.* $101/£65

IRVING, WASHINGTON. A Chronicle of the Conquest of Granada. J. Murray, 1829. 1st Eng ed. 2 vols. Orig bds (3 cvrs separated; spine wear). Contents Nice in custom made slipcase. *Fine Books.* $200/£129

IRVING, WASHINGTON. A Chronicle of the Conquest of Granada. NY: Putnam's, 1893. Agapida ed. 2 vols. xxx,380; xiv,406pp. Gilt dec white cl. Good in blue cl djs. *Karmiole.* $85/£55

IRVING, WASHINGTON. A History of the Life and Voyages of Christopher Columbus. NY: G&C Carvill, 1828. 1st Amer ed. 3 vols. xvi,399; viii,367; viii,420pp, fldg map. Contemp mottled calf, spines gilt. Good set (foxing; joints sl worn). *Lefkowicz.* $100/£65

IRVING, WASHINGTON. A History of the Life and Voyages of Christopher Columbus. NY: G. & C. Carvill, 1828. 1st Amer ed. 3 vols. Lg fldg map vol 1 (sm mend at tab). Contemp 3/4 gilt calf; 1/2 titles bound in. Edges rubbed, lt foxing, lt stains, dust smudging, else Good set. BAL 10124. *Reese.* $250/£161

IRVING, WASHINGTON. The Journals of Washington Irving. W.P. Trent (ed). Boston: Bibliophile Society, 1919. One of 430. 3 vols. Teg; uncut. Fine (extrems, spine sl rubbed). *Polyanthos.* $75/£48

IRVING, WASHINGTON. Knickerbocker Papers, Being Rip Van Winkle and the Legend of Sleepy Hollow. London: Philip Lee Warner, 1914. #655/1000. Teg, others uncut. Orig linen-backed bds. VG. *Cox.* $28/£18

IRVING, WASHINGTON. The Legend of Sleepy Hollow. Phila: David McKay, (1928). 1st Amer ed. 4to. 8 full-pg color plts by Arthur Rackham; teg. Brn cl, color paste label, gold spine lettering. Good in pict dj (worn, lacks pieces). *Reisler.* $175/£113

IRVING, WASHINGTON. The Legend of Sleepy Hollow. Phila, (1928). 1st ed, 1/125 numbered of Amer issue, ptd on handmade paper & signed by Arthur Rackham (illus). 8 mounted color plts; 30 b/w dwgs. Teg; uncut. VG. *Argosy.* $1,500/£968

IRVING, WASHINGTON. The Life and Voyages of Christopher Columbus. Boston, 1839. 1st Amer ed. Foxing; rubbed, sl soiled. *Polyanthos.* $135/£87

IRVING, WASHINGTON. Rip Van Winkle. Phila: David McKay, (1921). 1st ed. 4to. 8 color plts by N.C. Wyeth. Teg. Brn cl (spotted), color paste label. Color dj (fr cvr missing piece; marginal tears). *Reisler.* $275/£177

IRVING, WASHINGTON. Rip Van Winkle. London: Heinemann, 1905. 1st ed. 4to. 51 mtd color plts by Arthur Rackham; tinted edges. Grn cl (shelfwear, lt scratches), gold lettering, illus. *Reisler.* $350/£226

IRVING, WASHINGTON. Rip Van Winkle. London: Heinemann, 1905. 1st trade ed. 51 color plts by Arthur Rackham, mtd on grn card. Pict cl gilt (worn, bumped, stained). *Hollett.* $233/£150

IRVING, WASHINGTON. Rip Van Winkle. NY/London: Doubleday/Heinemann, 1905. 1st US ed. 51 tipped-in color plts by Arthur Rackham. Grn gilt cl. VG. *Davidson.* $400/£258

IRVING, WASHINGTON. Rip Van Winkle. Phila: David McKay, 1921. 1st ed. 8vo. 86pp, 8 full-pg color illus by N.C. Wyeth. Purple cl w/pict onlay; teg. VG (spine gilt faded, lt spots). *Davidson.* $200/£129

IRVING, WASHINGTON. Rip Van Winkle. NY: McLoughlin Bros, n.d. ca 1880. 4to. 6 full-pg chromos by Thomas Nast. Pict wraps. VG (edges worn, lt soil). *Davidson.* $285/£184

IRVING, WASHINGTON. Rip Van Winkle: A Posthumous Writing of Diedrich Knickerbocker. NY: LEC, 1930. 1/1500 numbered, signed by Frederick W. Goudy (ptr). Felix Darley (illus). Full calf (rubbed). Bd slipcase. *Argosy.* $100/£65

IRVING, WASHINGTON. The Rocky Mountains: or, Scenes, Incidents, and Adventures in the Far West.... Phila: Carey, Lea & Blanchard, 1837. 1st Amer ed, preceding British pub under the title, 'Adventures of Captain Bonneville.' 2 vols. xvi,(17)-248; vii,(1),(17)-248pp, lg fldg map each vol. Orig blue pub's muslin, ptd paper spine labels (sl worn). Offsetting from maps; closed tear 1 map, no loss, o/w VG (bkpl each vol) in 1/2 morocco, cl clamshell box. BAL 10151; Howes I 85. *Reese.* $850/£548

IRVING, WASHINGTON. Western Journals of Washington Irving. John McDermott (ed). Univ OK, 1944. 1st ed. 8 plts, fldg map. VG. *Oregon.* $35/£23

IRVING, WASHINGTON. Wolfert's Roost and Other Papers.... NY: Putnam's, 1855. 1st ed. Engr frontis, 384 + 12pp pub's ads; illus tp. Orig grn cl; dec gilt, blind-stamped (extrems sl frayed). *Karmiole.* $40/£26

IRVING, WASHINGTON. Wolfert's Roost. NY: Putnam's, 1855. 1st ptg. Frontis; engr title. NF. BAL 10188: Primary binding. *Agvent.* $125/£81

IRWIN, B.P. In Menehune Land. Printshop, 1936. 1st ed. Pict cl. VG+. *Fine Books.* $55/£35

IRWIN, MARJORY FELICE. The Negro in Charlottesville and Albemarle County.... Charlottesville, VA, 1929. 1st ed. NF in orig stiff ptd wrappers. *Mcgowan.* $75/£48

IRWIN, RICHARD B. History of the Nineteenth Army Corps. NY, 1892. 1st ed. 528pp. Gilt edge. Pict cl. Lt worn, faded, o/w VG+. *Pratt.* $150/£97

ISAACS, EDITH J.R. The Negro in the American Theatre. NY: Theatre Arts, 1947. 1st ed. VG in dj (lt chipped). *Petrilla.* $120/£77

ISADORA, RACHEL. Ben's Trumpet. NY: Greenwillow, 1979. 1st ed. 10x8.25. 32pp. Fine in dj. *Cattermole.* $125/£81

ISBELL, F.A. Mining and Hunting in the Far West 1852-1870. Burlingame: Wm. Wreden, 1948. One of 200. Port. Cl-backed bds, ptd spine label. Fine. Howes I 87. *Bohling.* $90/£58

ISHAM, NORMAN and ALBERT BROWN. Early Connecticut Houses.... Providence: Preston & Rounds, 1900. 1st ed. 7 plts. Edgewear, else VG. *Bookpress.* $225/£145

ISHERWOOD, CHRISTOPHER. The Berlin Stories. New Directions, 1945. 1st thus. VG in dj (sl rubbed). *Whiteson.* $25/£16

ISHERWOOD, CHRISTOPHER. The Condor and the Cows. NY: Random House, (1949). 1st ed. Fine in dj (sl rubbed). *Jaffe.* $65/£42

ISHERWOOD, CHRISTOPHER. The Condor and the Cows. London: Methuen, 1949. 1st UK ed. VG in dj (sl browned, mkd; spine strengthened to rear). *Williams.* $39/£25

ISHERWOOD, CHRISTOPHER. Down There on a Visit. S&S, 1962. 1st ed. Fine in NF dj (sl wear, spine fading). *Fine Books.* $30/£19

ISHERWOOD, CHRISTOPHER. A Meeting by the River. London: Methuen, 1967. 1st ed. VG in dj. *Hollett.* $39/£25

ISHERWOOD, CHRISTOPHER. A Meeting by the River. London: Methuen, 1967. 1st UK ed. Fine in NF dj (price-clipped). *Williams.* $23/£15

ISHERWOOD, CHRISTOPHER. My Guru and His Disciple. NY: FSG, (1980). 1st ed. Signed, inscribed. Fine in dj. *Houle.* $175/£113

ISHERWOOD, CHRISTOPHER. Prater Violet. NY, (1945). 1st ed. VG in VG dj (lt edgewear, soil). *Mcclintock.* $20/£13

ISHERWOOD, CHRISTOPHER. Prater Violet. R-H, 1945. 1st ed. NF in VG dj (4 short tears). *Fine Books.* $65/£42

ISHERWOOD, CHRISTOPHER. Sally Bowles. Hogarth, 1937. 1st ed. Sl rubbed, else Good. *Whiteson.* $62/£40

ISHERWOOD, CHRISTOPHER. A Single Man. London: Methuen, 1964. 1st UK ed. Fine in dj (price-clipped). *Williams.* $23/£15

ISHERWOOD, CHRISTOPHER. The World in the Evening. Methuen, 1954. 1st ed. Fading, else Good in dj (sl rubbed). *Whiteson.* $23/£15

ISHERWOOD, CHRISTOPHER. The World in the Evening. R-H, 1954. 1st ed. VG+ in Nice dj (worn). *Fine Books.* $25/£16

ISHERWOOD, CHRISTOPHER. The World in the Evening. London: Methuen, 1954. 1st UK ed. Fine in dj (sl edgeworn). *Williams.* $28/£18

ISHIGURO, KAZUO. An Artist of the Floating World. NY: Putnam's, 1986. 1st ed. VF in dj. *Else Fine.* $50/£32

ISHIGURO, KAZUO. An Artist of the Floating World. Putnam, 1986. 1st ed. Fine (name) in dj (nick). *Stahr.* $60/£39

ISHIGURO, KAZUO. An Artist of the Floating World. London: Faber, 1986. 1st issue. NF in dj (sl mkd). *Rees.* $93/£60

ISHIGURO, KAZUO. An Artist of the Floating World. London: Faber, 1986. 1st UK ed. Fine in dj (price-clipped). *Williams.* $43/£28

ISHIGURO, KAZUO. A Pale View of Hills. Faber, 1982. 1st UK ed, 1st bk. Signed. VF in VF dj. *Sclanders.* $465/£300

ISHIGURO, KAZUO. The Remains of the Day. NY: Knopf, 1989. 1st ed. VF in dj. *Else Fine.* $65/£42

ISHIGURO, KAZUO. The Remains of the Day. London: Faber, 1989. 1st UK ed. NF in dj. *Lewton.* $39/£25

ISNARD, H. Algeria. Paris/London: Arthaud/Nicolas Kaye, (1955). Color frontis, fldg map laid in. Foxed. Dj. *Schoyer.* $20/£13

ISSAC, FRANK. English and Scottish Printing Types 1501-34, 1508-41. London, 1930. 4to. 98 facs. Linen, bds; teg. Tips worn, else Fine. *Veatchs.* $100/£65

Italy, Spain, and Portugal. (By William Beckford.) NY: Wiley & Putnam, 1845. 2 vols in 1. xxii,174; xii,256pp (marginal notes). Contemp 3/4 brn morocco (rubbed). *Schoyer.* $65/£42

Italy: With Sketches of Spain and Portugal. (By William Beckford.) Phila: Key & Biddle, 1834. 1st Amer ed. 2 vols. 255; 257 (misnumbered as 357)pp (vol 1 lacks feps; foxing). Orig floral-pattern violet cl (faded), grn morocco spine labels (chipped). *Schoyer.* $125/£81

ITOH, TEIJI and YUKIO FUTAGAWA. The Elegant Japanese House. NY: Walker/Weatherhill, (1969). 1st ed in English. 129pp photos; 25pp dwgs. VG in dj (chipped). *Bookpress.* $185/£119

IVERS, LARRY E. British Drums on the Southern Frontier. Chapel Hill: UNC Press, (1974). 1st ed. Red cl. Fine in dj. *Chapel Hill.* $40/£26

IVES, BURL. The Wayfaring Stranger's Notebook. Indianapolis, 1962. 1st Amer ed. Fine (sl rubbed) in dj (rubbed; tears). *Polyanthos.* $25/£16

IVY, JUDY CROSBY. Constable and the Critics 1802-1837. Woodbridge, 1991. 9 plts. Good. *Washton.* $45/£29

IZLAR, WILLIAM VALMORE. A Sketch of the War Record of the Edisto Rifles, 1861-65. Columbia, SC: August Kohn, 1914. 1st ed. Frontis port. Orig gilt-stamped grey cl. VG+. *Chapel Hill.* $450/£290

IZZARD, RALPH. The Abominable Snowman Adventure. London: Hodder & Stoughton, 1955. 1st ed. VG in dj (sl rubbed). *Hollett.* $31/£20

IZZARD, RALPH. The Hunt for the Buru. London, 1951. 15 plts. *Wheldon & Wesley.* $23/£15

J

J., M.N. Bygone Days in the March Wall of Wales. London, 1926. (Ex-libris; lt foxing; upper bd sl scratched.) *Edwards.* $93/£60

JACCACI, AUGUST F. On the Trail of Don Quixote. NY: Scribner's, 1896. (240)pp (lacks fep); teg. Red cl, gilt (spine rubbed). *Schoyer.* $25/£16

Jack and Jill and Old Dame Gill. London: W.S. Fortey, (ca 1860). Toybook. 12mo. 8pp. Hand-colored paper wrappers (spine split, folds). *Reisler.* $125/£81

Jack and the Bean-Stalk. To which is added Little Jane and Her Mother. Boston: J. Reynolds, 1848. 12mo, 70pp. Dec dk blue paper wrappers (rebacked). Good (inscrip, internal foxing). *Hobbyhorse.* $90/£58

Jack and the Beanstalk. NY: Duenewald, (1944). 8vo. 5 tab moveables by Julian Wehr. Full color illus bds, spiral binding (corner sl worn); in dj (spine, edges worn). *Reisler.* $120/£77

Jack Daw 'At Home.' (By a Young Lady of Rank.) London: Didier and Tebbett, 1809. 3rd ed. 12mo. 16pp. Full-pg frontis, 5 Fine plts; 1st pg ptd on paper watermarked 1808 (occasional foxing). Mod full leather, gilt title. VG. *Hobbyhorse.* $200/£129

Jack Spratt and Other Rhymes. NY: McLoughlin Brothers, n.d. (ca 1860). Aunt Mary's Little Series. 12mo. 8 leaves, 1p list lower wrapper. Color pict paper wrappers. Fine. *Hobbyhorse.* $85/£55

Jack Spratt. (Gems from Mother Goose Series.) NY: McLoughlin Bros, 1898. 4to. 8 leaves. 6 VF full-pg chromolithos; 1st, last pgs ptd on wrappers. Fine (spine sl rubbed). *Hobbyhorse.* $135/£87

Jack the Giant Killer. (Robin Hood Series.) NY: McLoughlin Bros, 1889. 4 leaves. 4 full-pg wood engrs; 1st, last pgs of text ptd on pict wrapper. In all, Good (lt spotting lower part 3 leaves). *Hobbyhorse.* $40/£26

Jack the Giant Killer. A Pop-Up Edition. NY: Blue Ribbon, 1933. 17x22cm. 1 dbl-pg pop-up by Harold B. Lentz. Pict bds (fading, wear edges, spine). VG. *Book Finders.* $200/£129

JACK, ROBERT. Arctic Living. London: Hodder & Stoughton, 1957. 1st ed. 2 sketch maps. VG in dj (sl rubbed). *Hollett.* $39/£25

JACKER, CORINNE. The Black Flag of Anarchy: Antistatism in the United States. NY: Scribner's, (1968). 1st ed. NF in dj (corner clipped). *Aka.* $25/£16

JACKMAN, E.R. and R.A. LONG. The Oregon Desert. Caldwell: Caxton, 1964. 1st ed. Frontis, 8pp color plts. VG in Good+ dj. *Oregon.* $40/£26

JACKMAN, W.J. and T.H. RUSSELL. Flying Machines. Chicago: Chas C. Thompson, 1910. 1st ed. Gilt-lettered red cl (worn). Contents VG (hinges taped). *Smithfield.* $98/£63

JACKSON, C. PAUL. Clown at Second Base. Crowell, 1952. 1st ed. Fine in dj. *Madle.* $20/£13

JACKSON, CHARLES JAMES. An Illustrated History of English Plate.... London: Batsford, 1911. 1st ed. 2 vols. Lg 4to. Frontis, 76 plts. Teg. 1/2 grn morocco. Sl rubbed, else Fine. *Bookpress.* $725/£468

JACKSON, CHEVALIER. The Life of Chevalier Jackson—An Autobiography. NY, 1938. 1st ed. Signed. Good. *Fye.* $75/£48

JACKSON, CLARENCE S. Picture Maker of the Old West: William H. Jackson. NY, 1947. 1st ed. NF (bkpl) in dj (top, bottom of backstrip chipped away). *Baade.* $125/£81

JACKSON, DONALD DALE. Gold Dust. NY: Knopf, 1980. 1st ed. Fine in Fine dj. *Book Market.* $35/£23

JACKSON, E.P. A Demigod. Harpers, 1887. 1st ed. Corner tips, spine extrems worn, else VG-. *Aronovitz.* $60/£39

JACKSON, EDWARD. Skiascopy and Its Practical Application to the Study of Refraction. Phila, 1895. 1st ed. 112pp; author's ptd card tipped in. Good. *Fye.* $70/£45

JACKSON, F.G. The Great Frozen Land. London: Macmillan, 1895. 1st ed. xviii,297pp. Good (bkpl; sl rubbed). *Walcot.* $62/£40

JACKSON, F.G. A Thousand Days in the Arctic.... London: Harper & Bros, 1899. 1st ed. 2 vols. xii,551; xv,580pp. (Bumped, mrkd; spine sl worn, torn.) Good. *Walcot.* $233/£150

JACKSON, F.G. A Thousand Days in the Arctic.... London: Harper & Bros, 1899. 2 vols. xii,551; xv,580pp. Orig dec cl, teg. Generally VG (minor repair to head of spine, vol II, very minor bubbling of cl, vol I). *High Latitude.* $300/£194

JACKSON, GEORGE PULLEN (ed). White and Negro Spirituals. NY: J.J. Augustin, (1943). 1st ed. Frontis; map. Rose buckram. VG. *Petrilla.* $45/£29

JACKSON, GEORGE PULLEN. White Spirituals in the Southern Uplands. Chapel Hill: Univ of NC, 1933. 1st ed. Sl insect damage, names, else VG. *Cahan.* $75/£48

JACKSON, GRACE. Cynthia Ann Parker. San Antonio: Naylor, 1959. 1st ed. Inscribed. VG- in VG- dj. *Parker.* $50/£32

JACKSON, HELEN HUNT. A Century of Dishonor. Harper, 1881. 1st ed. NF. BAL 10444. *Authors Of The West.* $150/£97

JACKSON, HELEN HUNT. A Century of Dishonor: A Sketch of the United States Government's Dealings with Some of the Indian Tribes. Boston: Robert Bros, 1886. New ed, enlgd. x,514pp, (4)pub ads. Gray cl; stamped gilt/red. (Edges lt rubbed.) *Petrilla.* $65/£42

JACKSON, HELEN HUNT. Ramona. Roberts Bros, 1884. 1st ed. Gilt. Fine (name; tears or chips 6pp, no loss). BAL 10456. *Authors Of The West.* $500/£323

JACKSON, HELEN HUNT. Ramona. Boston: Little Brown, 1900. Monterey ed. 2 vols. VG (bkpl). *Parker.* $95/£61

JACKSON, HELEN HUNT. Zeph. Boston: Roberts, 1885. 1st ed. 253pp. VG. BAL 10460. *Second Life.* $35/£23

JACKSON, HOLBROOK (comp). Bookman's Pleasure: A Recreation for Booklovers. NY: Farrar, Straus, 1947. 1st US ed. VG in dj (lt soiled). *Graf.* $20/£13

JACKSON, HOLBROOK. The Anatomy of Bibliomania. London: Soncino Press, 1930. 1st ed. One of 1000 numbered. 2 vols. Red cl (spine faded). Fine set. *Second Life.* $250/£161

JACKSON, HOLBROOK. The Anatomy of Bibliomania. NY: Scribner's, 1932. 3rd ed. Cl lt faded, o/w Fine. *Glenn.* $65/£42

JACKSON, HOLBROOK. The Anatomy of Bibliomania. Faber, 1950. VG. *Moss.* $31/£20

JACKSON, HOLBROOK. Bernard Shaw. London: Grant Richards, 1907. 1st Eng ed. 4 ports; teg. Grn cl. Sl dusty; prelims foxed, lacks fep, o/w VG. *Dalian.* $31/£20

JACKSON, HOLBROOK. The Fear of Books. London: Soncino Press, 1932. 1st ed. Spine sl faded, else Fine. *Bookpress.* $85/£55

JACKSON, HOLBROOK. The Fear of Books. London: Soncino Press, 1932. 1st ed. #446/2000. Teg. VG. *Graf.* $50/£32

JACKSON, HOLBROOK. The Fear of Books. London/NY: Soncino/Scribner's, 1932. 1st ed. One of 2000 numbered. Teg. Fine in fldg 2-piece case. *Other Worlds.* $95/£61

JACKSON, J. HUGHLINGS. Selected Writings of John Hughlings Jackson. NY, 1958. (Facs of 1931 ed). 2 vols. Good. *Fye.* $200/£129

JACKSON, JAMES C. How to Treat the Sick without Medicine. Dansville, NY, 1874. 1st ed. 537pp. Good. *Fye.* $100/£65

JACKSON, JAMES et al. A Report on Spasmodic Cholera. Boston, 1832. 1st ed. 190pp; fldg map. Cl-backed bds (ex-lib). *Fye.* $200/£129

JACKSON, JOHN and W.A. CHATTO. A Treatise on Wood Engraving, Historical and Practical. London: Henry G. Bohn, 1861. 2nd ed, enlgd. Frontis, 664pp. Brn cl. VG (Emb institutional stamp, bkpl removed; spine ends worn, hinge cracked). *Chapel Hill.* $200/£129

JACKSON, JON A. The Blind Pig. NY: Random House, 1978. 1st ed. Name fr pastedown, o/w Fine in dj (spine top nicked). *Mordida.* $45/£29

JACKSON, JOSEPH HENRY (ed). Gold Rush Album. NY: Scribner's, 1949. 1st ed. Fine in Good+ slipcase. *Oregon.* $40/£26

JACKSON, JOSEPH HENRY. Bad Company. Harcourt, (1949). 1st ed. VG. *Oregon.* $35/£23

JACKSON, JOSEPH HENRY. Tintypes in Gold, Four Studies in Robbery. Macmillan, 1939. 2nd ptg. VG. *Oregon.* $15/£10

JACKSON, JOSEPH HENRY. (ed). Gold Rush Album. NY, 1949. 1st ed. Fine in box (worn). *Heinoldt.* $25/£16

JACKSON, JOSEPH. American Colonial Architecture. Phila: McKay, (1924). 1st ed. (Worn.) *Bookpress.* $25/£16

JACKSON, LEROY F. Rimskittle's Book. Chicago/NY: Rand McNally, (1926). 4to, 58 leaves. Ruth Eger (illus). (Sm tear bottom margin title.) Red cl (bumped), gilt; color illus by Milo Winter mtd fr cvr. NF. *Blue Mountain.* $75/£48

JACKSON, M. To America and Back; A Holiday Run. London: McCorquodale, 1886. 1st ed. 246pp; fldg map. New cl, paper spine label. *Ginsberg.* $125/£81

JACKSON, MRS. F. NEVILL. A History of Hand-Made Lace. London/NY: L. Upcott Gill/Scribner's, 1900. 1st ed. 4to. 19 plts, 12 tipped-in samples. Aeg. Full brn crushed morocco, gilt. *Cady.* $575/£371

JACKSON, ROBERT. A Systematic View of the Formation, Discipline, and Economy of Armies. London: ptd for author, 1804. 4to. xxxi,347pp. Contemp bds (rebacked) uncut. *Goodrich.* $325/£210

JACKSON, ROBERT. A Treatise on the Fevers of Jamaica.... Phila: Robert Campbell, 1795. 1st Amer ed. xi,276,19,(12 ads)pp. Contemp tree calf. VG (fr hinge started). *Glaser.* $225/£145

JACKSON, ROBERT. A Treatise on the Fevers of Jamaica.... Phila: Ptd for Robert Campbell, 1795. 1st US ed. xi,276,19pp notes+ (iv)pub's ads (lower margins waterstained; eps spotted; browning). Full calf (rebacked, hinges repaired). Orig leather label laid down. *Edwards.* $209/£135

JACKSON, SHELDON. Alaska, and Missions on the North Pacific Coast. NY, 1880. Frontis port, 400pp (marginal soiling; 2pp neatly repaired margin), fldg color map. Red morocco (rebound), red cl bds. *Edwards.* $93/£60

JACKSON, SHIRLEY. The Bad Children. Chicago: Dramatic Pub Co, (1959). 1st ed. Ink name, else Fine in ptd wrappers. *Godot.* $175/£113

JACKSON, SHIRLEY. Come Along With Me. Viking, 1968. 1st ed. NF in dj. *Aronovitz.* $45/£29

JACKSON, SHIRLEY. The Haunting of Hill House. M. Joseph, 1960. 1st Eng ed. NF in NF dj (rear panel sunned). *Aronovitz.* $150/£97

JACKSON, SHIRLEY. The Lottery. NY: Farrar-Straus, 1949. 1st ed, w/colophon. Fine (few short closed tears, minor rubbing). *Else Fine.* $300/£194

JACKSON, SHIRLEY. The Lottery. F&S, 1949. 1st ed. Fine in VG dj (sl worn). *Fine Books.* $195/£126

JACKSON, SHIRLEY. The Lottery. Farrar, Straus, 1949. 1st ed. VG in Fine dj. *Madle.* $300/£194

JACKSON, SHIRLEY. Raising Demons. NY, (1957). 1st ed. VG in dj (sl worn). *King.* $50/£32

JACKSON, SHIRLEY. The Road Through the Wall. NY: Farrar-Straus, 1948. 1st ed. 1st bk. Pg browning, else Fine in dj (extrems lt worn). *Else Fine.* $225/£145

JACKSON, SHIRLEY. The Sundial. NY: FSC, 1958. 1st ed. VF in dj. *Else Fine.* $165/£106

JACKSON, SHIRLEY. We Have Always Lived in the Castle. Viking, 1962. 1st ed, rev copy w/rev slip laid in. VG+ in VG dj. *Aronovitz.* $125/£81

JACKSON, W. TURRENTINE. Wagon Roads West. Berkeley, 1952. 1st ed. 20 maps + eps. Fine (sig, date) in dj (sl soiled). *Baade.* $35/£23

JACKSON, WILLIAM H. Time Exposure. NY, 1940. 1st ed. VG-. *Baade.* $50/£32

JACKSON, WILLIAM. The New and Complete Newgate Calendar. London: Alex. Hogg, (1800-1820). Early ed. 7 vols; 8vo. 74 full-pg plts. Early marbled bds w/turn of cent calf spines, morocco spine labels. Lib bkpl, stamps; foxing; cat descrip pasted to fep in Vol I, else VG. *Chapel Hill.* $550/£355

Jacob van Ruisdael. Cambridge: Fogg Art Museum, 1982. Good in dj. *Washton.* $45/£29

JACOB, GILES. The Clerk's Remembrancer. (London): J. Nutt, Assignee of Edward Sayer et al, 1714. Contemp calf. Worn, browned, but Sound. *Boswell.* $450/£290

JACOB, GILES. The Complete Court-Keeper. London, 1741. 4th ed. Full contemp calf (joint sl cracked; lacks eps). *Petersfield.* $39/£25

JACOB, H.E. The Saga of Coffee. London, 1935. 27 plts. (Spine fraying; dknd.) *Sutton.* $55/£35

JACOB, JOHN J. Biographical Sketch of the Life of the Late Captain Michael Cresap. Cincinnati: William Dodge, 1866. 2nd ed w/additions. Lg paper copy. 158pp, untrimmed. 1/2 brn morocco, marbled bds (top spine worn). VG (joints, extrems rubbed). Howes J 32. *Chapel Hill.* $165/£106

JACOBI, ABRAHAM. The Intestinal Diseases of Infancy and Childhood. Detroit, 1887. 1st ed. 301pp. Good. *Fye.* $250/£161

JACOBI, ABRAHAM. A Treatise on Diphtheria. NY: Wood, 1880. x,252pp. Nice. *Goodrich.* $85/£55

JACOBI, ABRAHAM. A Treatise on Diphtheria. NY, 1880. 1st ed. 252pp. Good. *Fye.* $150/£97

JACOBI, CARL. Portraits in Moonlight. Arkham House, 1964. 1st ed. VF in dj. *Madle.* $75/£48

JACOBI, CARL. Revelations in Black. Arkham House, 1947. 1st ed. Fine in dj. *Madle.* $115/£74

JACOBI, CHARLES. Some Notes on Books and Printing. London: Chiswick Press, 1912. 4th ed. 21 paper specimens. *Veatchs.* $65/£42

JACOBS, BELA. A Voice from the West. Boston, 1833. 27,(1)pp (lt foxed). Howes J 36. *Bohling.* $350/£226

JACOBS, JIM and WARREN CASEY. Grease. NY: Winter House, (1972). 1st ed. Fine in dj. *Between The Covers*. $250/£161

JACOBS, JOSEPH (ed). Celtic Fairy Tales. London: David Nutt, 1892. xiv,268pp, 8 plts by John D. Batten. Dec grn cl (sl rubbed). *Hollett*. $39/£25

JACOBS, JOSEPH (ed). Indian Fairy Tales. London: David Nutt, 1903. xiv,255pp, 9 plts by John D. Batten. Dec grn cl. VG. *Hollett*. $39/£25

JACOBS, JOSEPH (ed). More Celtic Fairy Tales. London: David Nutt, 1894. 1st trade ed. xii,234,(ii)pp, 8 plts by John D. Batten. Dec grn cl. VG. *Hollett*. $39/£25

JACOBS, JOSEPH (ed). More English Fairy Tales. London: David Nutt, 1894. 1st trade ed. xiv,243,(ii)pp, 8 plts by John D. Batten. Dec cl (discolored; spotted). *Hollett*. $39/£25

JACOBS, M. Notes on the Rebel Invasion of Maryland and Pennsylvania and the Battle of Gettysburg...1863. Phila: J.B. Lippincott, 1864. 1st ed. 48pp; lg fldg color map. (Repaired tear to map; foxing.) Purple cl, gilt (spine extrems sl rubbed; faded). *Karmiole*. $85/£55

JACOBS, ORANGE. Memoirs of Orange Jacobs. Seattle, 1908. 1st ed. VG. Howes J 37. *Perier*. $125/£81

JACOBS, ORANGE. Memoirs of Orange Jacobs. Seattle, 1908. 1st ed. Inscribed, signed. Howes J 37. *Ginsberg*. $125/£81

JACOBS, W.W. The Lady of the Barge. Harpers, 1902. 1st ed. VG. *Aronovitz*. $75/£48

JACOBS-BOND, CARRIE. Tales of Little Cats. Joliet: P.F. Volland, (1918). 43rd ed. 12mo. Katherine Sturges Dodge (illus). Illus dk blue bds (sl edgewear). *Reisler*. $40/£26

JACOBS-BOND, CARRIE. Tales of Little Dogs. Chicago: Volland, (1921). 12mo. Katharine Sturges Dodge (illus). Color dec bds. (Sl edgewear; finger mks within.) Pict box (sides broken but present). *Reisler*. $90/£58

JACOBSEN, A. Frederic Cozzens. Marine Painter. NY: Alpine Fine Arts, 1982. Sound in dj. *Ars Artis*. $93/£60

JACOBSON, DAN. The Trap. NY: Harcourt Brace, 1955. VG in dj. *Hollett*. $31/£20

JACOBUS, JOHN. Henri Matisse. NY: Abrams, (1972). 48 hand-tipped color plts. VG in dj (torn). *Argosy*. $85/£55

JACOBY, ERICH H. Agrarian Unrest in Southeast Asia. NY: Columbia Univ, 1949. VG (name; lacks dj). *Aka*. $50/£32

JACQUEMART, ALBERT. A History of Furniture. London: Reeves & Turner, (1878). 1st ed in English. xvii,470pp; teg. Gilt/black pict maroon cl (backstrip faded). VG (rear hinge cracked). *House*. $250/£161

JAEGER, B. and H.C. PRESTON. The Life of North American Insects. NY, 1859. 319pp; 69 engrs. (Sl used.) *Wheldon & Wesley*. $28/£18

JAEGER, EDMUND C. Denizens of the Desert. Boston: Houghton Mifflin, 1922. 1st ed. VG +. *Bishop*. $20/£13

JAFFE, HANS L.C. Piet Mondrian. NY, n.d. 48 tipped-in color plts. Dj. *Edwards*. $78/£50

JAFFE, IRMA B. John Trumbull: Patriot-Artist of the American Revolution. Boston, 1975. VG in dj. *Argosy*. $100/£65

JAFFE, IRMA B. The Sculpture of Leonard Baskin. NY: Viking, (1980). 1st ed. VG in dj. *Bookpress*. $65/£42

JAFFE, IRMA B. The Sculpture of Leonard Baskin. NY: Viking, 1980. Dj. *Ars Artis*. $54/£35

JAFFE, MICHAEL. Van Dyck's Antwerp Sketchbook. London: Macdonald, (1966). 1st ed. 2 vols. Frontis. Teg. Fr hinge vol 2 internally cracked, else VG in matching slipcase (worn). *Bookpress*. $225/£145

JAGO, WILLIAM. A Text-Book of the Science and Art of Bread-Making.... London: Simpkin et al, 1895. 1st ed. 648pp, xliv ads bound fr, back (foxing, soiling), 14 plts (1 color, 4 fldg). Burgundy cl (rubbed, bumped, soiled). VG. *Blue Mountain*. $125/£81

JAHIER, ALICE. France Remembered. Sylvan Press/Nicholson & Watson, 1944. 1st UK ed. VG (name) in dj (sl rubbed, torn). *Sclanders*. $39/£25

JAHNS, PAT. The Frontier World of Doc Holliday. NY, (1957). 1st ed. Dj sl worn, chipped, o/w Fine. *Pratt*. $40/£26

JAHR, G.H.G. The Homoeopathic Treatment of the Diseases of Females, and Infants at the Breast. Phila, 1856. 1st Eng trans. 422pp. Recent buckram. *Fye*. $250/£161

JAHSS, BETTY and MELVIN. Inro and Other Miniature Forms of Japanese Lacquer Art. Rutland: Charles E. Tuttle, (1971). 1st ed. VF in dj. *Hermitage*. $175/£113

JAKES, JOHN. Holiday for Havoc. Armchair Detective Lib, 1991. 1st hb ed. One of 100 numbered, signed. Fine in slipcase (no dj as issued). *Murder*. $100/£65

JAKOB, CHRISTFRIED. Atlas of the Nervous System. Phila, 1901. 84 chromolitho plts. Good. *Fye*. $100/£65

James Barry. The Artist as Hero. London: Tate Gallery, 1983. 8 color plts. Good in wrappers. *Washton*. $30/£19

James Conner...in Memoriam. (Charleston, SC: Walker, Evans & Cogswell Print, 1883.) 1st ed. Frontis, 113pp (lt foxing). VG (sl damping upper corner carrying through prelims). *Mcgowan*. $350/£226

JAMES, BESSIE and MARQUIS. Six Feet Six, The Heroic Story of Sam Houston. Bobbs, Merrill, (1931). 1st ed. Frontis. Lacks fep, o/w VG in VG dj. *Oregon*. $15/£10

JAMES, C.H. and F.R. YERBURY. Small Houses for the Community. London, 1924. 140 plts and plans, 6 fldg plans (margins sl thumbed). 2-tone cl (soiled). *Edwards*. $70/£45

JAMES, C.L. History of the French Revolution. Chicago: Abe Isaak, 1902. 1st ed. VG (fr hinge repaired). *Beasley*. $150/£97

JAMES, DAVID A. Oliver Pollock. NY/London: D. Appleton-Century, 1937. 1st ed. Blue cl. NF in VG dj (price-clipped, tape repair verso spine). *Chapel Hill*. $65/£42

JAMES, E.O. From Cave to Cathedral. London: Thames & Hudson, 1965. 1st ed. 152 plts, gilt. VG in dj. *Hollett*. $62/£40

JAMES, EDWIN. Account of an Expedition from Pittsburgh to the Rocky Mountains...1819, 1820. London: Longman et al, 1823. 1st Eng ed in 3 vols. 1047pp total, 2 hand-colored frontis plts, 1 color plt. 3/4 black morocco, marbled bds, edges. NF (lt foxed, lt edgewear). *Bowman*. $1,500/£968

JAMES, EDWIN. Narrative of the Captivity and Adventures of John Tanner.... London, 1830. 1st Eng ed. 426pp. Contemp 1/2 morocco. Howes J 42. *Ginsberg*. $1,250/£806

JAMES, F. CYRIL. The Growth of Chicago Banks. NY, 1938. 1st ed. 2 vols. *Ginsberg*. $75/£48

JAMES, F.L. The Unknown Horn of Africa. London: George Philip, 1888. 1st ed. Frontis, xiv,344,half title. 22 litho plts, lg fldg map in pocket. Maroon cl, gilt. VG. *Morrell*. $372/£240

JAMES, G.P.R. A History of the Life of Richard Coeur-de-Lion, King of England. London: Bohn, 1854. 4 vols in 2. Pub's ads at end. Gilt/blindstamped maroon cl; uncut, unopened. VG (prelims, edges foxed). *Houle.* $95/£61

JAMES, GEORGE WHARTON. California—Romantic and Beautiful. Boston: Page Co, 1914. 1st ed. Fldg color map. Edgeworn, else VG. *Parker.* $85/£55

JAMES, GEORGE WHARTON. Indian Basketry. NY: Malkan, 1901. 1st ed. Good+ (name; hinge loose; worn). *Parker.* $150/£97

JAMES, GEORGE WHARTON. Indian Blankets and Their Makers. Chicago: A.C. McClurg, 1914. 1st ed. Teg. Tan dec cl. NF (sl worn). Howes J 43. *Harrington.* $250/£161

JAMES, GEORGE WHARTON. Indian Blankets and Their Makers. NY, 1937. New ed. (Ex-lib w/ink stamp, label, #s; upper hinge tender; worn.) *Edwards.* $74/£48

JAMES, GEORGE WHARTON. Indian Blankets and Their Makers. NY: Tudor Pub, 1937. New ed. 32 color plts. Red dec cl. Eps browned; sl bumped, rear bd lt spotted, o/w NF. *Harrington.* $75/£48

JAMES, GEORGE WHARTON. Indians of the Painted Desert Region. Boston: Little Brown, 1903. 1st ed. VG- (ink name; edgeworn; hinge starting). *Parker.* $85/£55

JAMES, GEORGE WHARTON. Indians of the Painted Desert. Boston: Little Brown, 1907. Spine faded, else VG. *Perier.* $37/£24

JAMES, GEORGE WHARTON. Reclaiming the Arid West. NY: Dodd, Mead, 1917. 1st ed. (Sl bumped.) *Dawson.* $125/£81

JAMES, GEORGE WHARTON. Utah: The Land of Blossoming Valleys. Boston, 1922. 1st ed. Dec cl. Fr hinge cracked, spine sl discolored, lt water damage, o/w VG+. *Benchmark.* $50/£32

JAMES, GRACE. Green Willow and Other Japanese Fairy Tales. London: Macmillan, 1910. 1st ed. 8vo. 281pp, 40 tipped-in color plts by Warwick Goble; brn backing sheets, lettered guards. Blue cl, gilt. VG (lt foxing). *Davidson.* $450/£290

JAMES, GRACE. Green Willow and Other Japanese Fairy Tales. London: Macmillan, 1910. 1st ed. Thick, 4to. 40 mtd color plts by Warwick Goble. All edges tinted. Blue cl (lt worn), gold lettering, illus. *Reisler.* $550/£355

JAMES, H. Travelling Companions. B&L, 1919. 1st ed. VG+. *Fine Books.* $70/£45

JAMES, HAROLD and DENNIS SHEIL-SMALL. Gurkhas. (Harrisburg, PA): Stackpole Books, (1966). VG in dj. *Schoyer.* $25/£16

JAMES, HENRY. The Ambassadors. (NY): LEC, 1963. One of 1500 numbered, signed by Leslie Saalburg. Fine in pub's slipcase. *Hermitage.* $85/£55

JAMES, HENRY. The Author of Beltraffio. Boston: James R. Osgood, 1885. 1st Amer ed. Brn cl. (Spine chipped.) *Hermitage.* $150/£97

JAMES, HENRY. The Better Sort. NY: Scribners, 1903. 1st ed. NF (spine, edges sunned; owner stamps). *Beasley.* $150/£97

JAMES, HENRY. The Complete Plays.... Leon Edel (ed). Phila: Lippincott, (1949). 1st ed. Fine in dj (sl used; pencil name). BAL 10728. *Pharos.* $60/£39

JAMES, HENRY. Confidence. Boston: Houghton, Osgood, 1880. 1st Amer ed, later state binding. Orig dk brn dec cl, gilt (speckling). Houghton, Mifflin imprint; floral pattern glazed eps. Fine. BAL 10549. *Macdonnell.* $150/£97

JAMES, HENRY. Confidence. Boston: Houghton, Osgood, 1880. 1st Amer ed. Grn cl; 'Houghton, Osgood' on spine. Sl cocked; wear to extrems, else VG. *Juvelis.* $300/£194

JAMES, HENRY. Confidence. Boston, 1880. 1st ed, preferred binding w/Houghton Osgood on spine. Grn cl (lt binding wear). *Argosy.* $250/£161

JAMES, HENRY. Daisy Miller: A Study. Cambridge: LEC, 1969. #330/1500 signed by Gustave Nebel (illus). Red morocco. Fine in pub's slipcase. *Hermitage.* $125/£81

JAMES, HENRY. Daumier—Caricaturist. (Emmaus): Rodale Press, (1954). Correct 1st ed. Fine in orig glassine. *Pharos.* $40/£26

JAMES, HENRY. Essays in London and Elsewhere. NY: Harper, 1893. 1st ed. Sm name fep, tp; rubbing, else Fine. BAL 10605. *Between The Covers.* $100/£65

JAMES, HENRY. The Golden Bowl. London: Methuen, (1905). 1st British ed, w/earlier ads, dated Feb rather than March. One of 3000 ptd. Dec cl, gilt (sl worn; edges dusty, spotted; fep cracked). Good. *Ash.* $155/£100

JAMES, HENRY. The Ivory Tower. NY: Scribner's, 1917. 1st Amer ed. Teg. VG in dj (lt bumped, sm chip, else VG). *Godot.* $650/£419

JAMES, HENRY. Letters. Leon Edel (ed). Cambridge: Harvard Univ Press, 1974-1984. 1st eds. 4 vols. VG. *Argosy.* $150/£97

JAMES, HENRY. A Little Tour in France. Boston: James R. Osgood, 1885. 1st ed, 1st binding. Dk brn cl, gilt. VG. BAL 10570. *Macdonnell.* $250/£161

JAMES, HENRY. A London Life. London/NY, 1889. 2nd ed, Amer issue. Blue cl; gilt stamped. VG. *Argosy.* $85/£55

JAMES, HENRY. The Middle Years. NY: Scribner's, 1917. 1st Amer ed. (Pencil inscrip; spine frayed; dull.) *Hermitage.* $75/£48

JAMES, HENRY. Notes of a Son and Brother. London: Macmillan, 1914. 1st Eng ed. Scuff mark rear panel, interior foxing, else VG. *Limestone.* $150/£97

JAMES, HENRY. A Passionate Pilgrim. Boston: James R. Osgood, 1875. 1st ed, 1st ptg, 1st binding, 1st bk. Orig grn cl, gilt. 2 sm rubbed spots spine foot, o/w NF. BAL 10529. *Macdonnell.* $1,250/£806

JAMES, HENRY. The Portrait of a Lady. Boston: Houghton, Mifflin, 1882. 1st Amer ed. Tan pict cl. VG in 1/2 gilt-stamped brn morocco slipcase. *Houle.* $750/£484

JAMES, HENRY. The Portrait of a Lady. NY: LEC, 1967. One of 1500 numbered, signed by Colleen Browning (illus). Fine in pub's slipcase. *Hermitage.* $100/£65

JAMES, HENRY. The Princess Casamassima. NY: Macmillan, 1886. 1st US, 1st 1-vol ed. VG- (name, date; inner hinges weakened; spine ends worn w/sl loss; cl worn through at tips). *Lame Duck.* $375/£242

JAMES, HENRY. The Princess Casamassima. NY: Macmillan, 1948. 1st ed thus. 2 vols. Fine in orig pub's slipcase. *Hermitage.* $50/£32

JAMES, HENRY. The Princess Casamassima.... NY: Macmillan, 1948. 1st ptg thus. 2 vols. Cl, marbled bds. VG set in slipcase (lt soiled). *Reese.* $45/£29

JAMES, HENRY. The Private Life, Lord Beaupre, The Visits. NY: Harper, 1893. 1st Amer ed, 2nd binding state B. vi,232pp + 4pp ads. Maroon cl stamped in gold on spine. VG in dj (soiled; 3-inch chip rear panel, 2 1-inch chips fr panel; lt edge wear). *Godot.* $975/£629

JAMES, HENRY. The Question of Our Speech, the Lesson of Balzac. Boston/NY: Houghton, Mifflin, 1905. 1st ed, trade issue. One of 2000 ptd. Teg. Red cl, gilt. NF. BAL 10660. *Macdonnell.* $65/£42

JAMES, HENRY. Short Stories of Henry James. Clifton Fadiman (ed). NY: Random House, (1945). 1st ed. Blue-gray cl. Sm owner label, else NF in VG dj (spine sunned, chipped). BAL 10806. *Chapel Hill.* $30/£19

JAMES, HENRY. A Small Boy and Others. NY: Scribner's, 1913. 1st ed, 1st state w/integral, unaltered p. (ii). Port; teg. Gilt cl. Spine, top edge sunned, o/w Nice. *Reese.* $125/£81

JAMES, HENRY. A Small Boy and Others. London: Macmillan, 1913. 1st Eng ed. Presentation copy. Covers sl rubbed, prelim lt foxed, else VG. *Limestone.* $150/£97

JAMES, HENRY. Terminations. NY: Harper, 1895. 1st Amer ed. Lt soiling, staining, o/w Fine. *Hermitage.* $150/£97

JAMES, HENRY. The Tragic Muse. Boston: Riverside Press, 1890. 1st ed. 2 vols. NF (name both vols; bottom bds sl rubbed). *Between The Covers.* $450/£290

JAMES, HENRY. The Turn of the Screw. (NY): LEC, 1949. One of 1500 numbered. Mariette Lydis (illus). Fine in pub's slipcase (lt rubbed). *Hermitage.* $85/£55

JAMES, HENRY. The Wings of the Dove. NY: Scribner's, 1902. 1st ed. 2 vols. Spines lt faded, o/w Fine. *Hermitage.* $225/£145

JAMES, JESSE, JR. Jesse James, My Father. Cleveland: Economy Book League, (1933). Limp red calf (soiled, worn; top inch spine missing; prelims stained). Reading copy. Howes J 48. *Glenn.* $20/£13

JAMES, M.E. How to Decorate Our Ceilings, Walls, and Floors. London: George Bell & Sons, 1883. 1st ed. Frontis; x,86,(i)pp; 5 plts. Pub's pink cl. Rubbed; spine sunned; eps lt foxed, else VG. *Bookpress.* $265/£171

JAMES, M.R. Abbeys. London, 1926. 7 color, 100 b/w plts; color fldg map. (Feps sl spotted.) Dj (ragged; spine faded). *Edwards.* $31/£20

JAMES, M.R. The Sculptures in the Lady Chapel at Ely. London: D. Nutt, 1895. Tp,preface,68pp, 55 collotype plts. Teg, rest uncut. (Hinges repaired; cl sl damp-spotted, bumped; spine recased, repaired.) *Edwards.* $155/£100

JAMES, M.R. A Thin Ghost and Others. NY, 1919. 1st ed. VG. *Fuller & Saunders.* $75/£48

JAMES, MARQUIS. Andrew Jackson, the Border Captain. Indianapolis: Bobbs-Merrill, (1933). 1st ed. Signed on tipped-in leaf. Red cl. VG in dj (worn, chipped). *Chapel Hill.* $75/£48

JAMES, MARQUIS. The Life of Andrew Jackson. Indianapolis, 1938. Fine in dj (chipped). *Baade.* $35/£23

JAMES, MARQUIS. The Raven, a Biograpphy of Sam Houston. London: Hutchinson, (1929). 1st Eng ed. VG (sm spots back cvr). *Shasky.* $60/£39

JAMES, NORAH. Hail! All Hail! London: Scholartis Press, 1929. 1st ed. Bds spotted, o/w Fine in dj (lt used, chips). *Beasley.* $45/£29

JAMES, NORAH. Sleeveless Errand. Paris, 1929. 1st ed. Fine (sl sunned, sl rubbed). *Polyanthos.* $50/£32

JAMES, P.D. Bad Language in Church. London: Prayer Book Soc, 1988. 1st ed. Signed. Fine in wrappers. *Rees.* $39/£25

JAMES, P.D. Death of an Expert Witness. London: Faber, 1977. 1st ed. Fine in dj. *Else Fine.* $95/£61

JAMES, P.D. Death of an Expert Witness. London: Faber & Faber, 1977. 1st ed. Fine in dj. *Mordida.* $125/£81

JAMES, P.D. Death of an Expert Witness. London: Faber & Faber, 1977. 1st ed. Signed. NF in dj. *Limestone.* $155/£100

JAMES, P.D. Devices and Desires. London: Faber & Faber, 1989. 1st ed. Signed. Fine in dj. *Limestone.* $85/£55

JAMES, P.D. Devices and Desires. London: Faber, 1989. 1st UK ed. Signed. Fine in dj. *Lewton.* $22/£14

JAMES, P.D. Innocent Blood. London: Faber, 1980. 1st ed. Fine in dj. *Else Fine.* $60/£39

JAMES, P.D. Innocent Blood. London: Faber, 1980. 1st ed. Signed, inscribed. Lt browning, o/w NF in dj. *Silver Door.* $55/£35

JAMES, P.D. Innocent Blood. London: Faber & Faber, 1980. 1st ed. Signed. Fine in dj. *Mordida.* $125/£81

JAMES, P.D. A Mind to Murder. London: Faber & Faber, 1963. 1st ed. VG in dj (soiled; closed tears; corner wear). *Mordida.* $750/£484

JAMES, P.D. Shroud for a Nightingale. London: Faber & Faber, 1971. 1st ed. VG- (tape mks panels, fr pastedown) in VG dj (rubbed). *Limestone.* $195/£126

JAMES, P.D. Shroud for a Nightingale. London: Faber, 1971. 1st UK ed. Signed. Good in dj (rubbed). *Williams.* $147/£95

JAMES, P.D. The Skull Beneath the Skin. London: Faber & Faber, 1982. 1st ed. Inscribed. VF in dj. *Mordida.* $125/£81

JAMES, P.D. The Skull Beneath the Skin. NY: Scribner's, 1982. 1st ed. Signed. Fine in dj. *Else Fine.* $65/£42

JAMES, P.D. The Skull Beneath the Skin. London: Faber & Faber, 1982. 1st ed. Signed. NF in dj. *Limestone.* $135/£87

JAMES, P.D. A Taste for Death. London: Faber & Faber, 1986. 1st ed. Signed. Fine in dj. *Mordida.* $100/£65

JAMES, P.D. A Taste for Death. Faber, 1986. 1st UK ed. Fine in dj. *Lewton.* $28/£18

JAMES, P.D. An Unsuitable Job for a Woman. London: Faber & Faber, 1972. 1st ed. VG in dj. *Limestone.* $140/£90

JAMES, P.D. An Unsuitable Job for a Woman. London: Faber, 1972. 1st UK ed. NF in VG dj (spine sl discolored). *Williams.* $132/£85

JAMES, PATRICIA (ed). The Travel Diaries of Thomas Robert Malthus. CUP, 1966. Frontis port, 12 plts, 3 sketch maps, fldg family tree at rear. Dj. *Edwards.* $74/£48

JAMES, PHILIP. A Butler's Recipe Book 1719. London: CUP, 1935. Pink paper over bds; blue linen-backed spine. Fine (edges lt worn; lt spotting fore-edge). *Heller.* $95/£61

JAMES, PHILIP. A Butler's Recipe Book 1719. Cambridge: CUP, 1935. 1st ed. 12 woodcuts. Fr panel, dj flap laid in. Very Nice. *Cady.* $60/£39

JAMES, PHILIP. Children's Books of Yesterday. London/NY: The Studio, 1933. 128pp. Grn cl. VG (2 bkpls, corners bumped). *Davidson.* $75/£48

JAMES, PHILIP. Henry Moore on Sculpture. London, 1966. 1st ed. 128 plts. Dj (sl browned). *Edwards.* $74/£48

JAMES, THOMAS. Three Years Among the Indians and Mexicans. Chicago, (1953). Lakeside Classic. VG. *Schoyer.* $25/£16

JAMES, THOMAS. Three Years Among the Indians and Mexicans. Lippincott, (1962). 2 maps. Fine in VG dj. Howes J 49. *Oregon.* $20/£13

JAMES, THOMAS. Three Years Among the Indians and Mexicans. St. Louis: MO Hist Soc, 1916. #30/365. Corners chipped, else VG. Howes J 49. *Bohling.* $300/£194

JAMES, THOMAS. Three Years Among the Indians and Mexicans. St. Louis: MO Hist Soc, 1916. One of 365 numbered. Howes J 49. *Ginsberg.* $250/£161

JAMES, VINTON LEE. Frontier and Pioneer Recollections of Early Days in San Antonio and West Texas. Artes Graficas, 1938. 1st ed. Emb dec brn fabricoid. *Lambeth.* $300/£194

JAMES, WILL. Dark Horse. NY: Scribner's, 1939. 1st ed. Sm 8vo. Pict cl (sl faded). VG + in VG + dj (sm repair spine head; rough edges). *Book Adoption.* $100/£65

JAMES, WILL. Lone Cowboy, My Life Story. NY: Scribner's, 1930. 1st ed. Dj. *Lambeth.* $75/£48

JAMES, WILL. Lone Cowboy. NY, 1930. 1st ed. Pict cl. Good (label, stamp; pencil #s; worn). *Baade.* $35/£23

JAMES, WILL. Lone Cowboy. Scribners, 1930. 1st ed. Soiling, fading to spine, else VG. *Fine Books.* $40/£26

JAMES, WILLIAM. Human Immortality. Boston/NY: Houghton, Mifflin, 1898. 1st ed. (vi) + 70 + (4)pp. Beveled blue cl (sl scratched; sig). *Gach.* $50/£32

JAMES, WILLIAM. The Varieties of Religious Experience. NY: Longmans, Green, 1902. 1st ed. VG + (occasional clean severing along spine edges; spine tanned; spine label rubbed). *Lame Duck.* $650/£419

JAMES, WILLIAM. The Varieties of Religious Experience. NY: Longmans, Green, 1902. 1st ed. 8vo. Grn-gray cl (lt rubbed), paper spine label (chipped, rubbed). VG. *Gach.* $750/£484

JAMES, WILLIAM. The Will to Believe. NY: Longmans, Green, 1897. 1st ed. Spine label dknd, else VG + . *Lame Duck.* $350/£226

JAMES, WINIFRED. Mulberry Tree. NY: Dodd, Mead, n.d. (ca 1930). Frontis port, fldg map. Violet cl stamped in gilt (spine sl faded). *Schoyer.* $45/£29

JAMESON, HENRY. Heroes by the Dozen. Abilene, 1961. 1st ed. Fine in Good dj. *Oregon.* $30/£19

JAMESON, HORATIO GATES. A Treatise on Epidemic Cholera. Phila: Lindsay & Blakiston, 1855. xvi,286pp. (Lt foxing; stamps.) New antique style bds. *Goodrich.* $135/£87

JAMESON, MALCOLM. Bullard of Space Patrol. World, 1951. 1st ed. NF in dj (frayed). *Madle.* $100/£65

JAMESON, STORM. The Georgian Novel and Mr. Robinson. NY: Morrow, 1929. 1st US ed. Fine in NF dj (spine sunned; tiny chips). *Beasley.* $40/£26

Jane's Fighting Ships. London, 1938. (Backstrip split; bumped.) *Petersfield.* $155/£100

JANE, CECIL (ed). The Voyages of Christopher Columbus. London: Argonaut, 1930. Ltd to 1050 numbered, this one unnumbered. 5 maps. Vellum-backed cl (bumped; cvrs dknd). *King.* $150/£97

JANE, FRED T. The World's Warships. London: Sampson Low, Marston, (1915). 1st ed. Navy blue cl (newly recased, rebound). Pp lt yellowed, lt foxing, else VG (pencil inscrip; contemp sticker fep). *Glenn.* $150/£97

JANES, HURFORD. The Red Barrel. A History of Watney Mann. London: Murray, 1963. Fine in dj. *Peter Taylor.* $22/£14

JANEWAY, ELIZABETH. The Vikings. NY: Random House, 1951. Stated 1st ptg trade. Henry C. Pitz (illus). Dec eps. VG in dj. *Cattermole.* $25/£16

JANIS, SIDNEY. Abstract and Surrealist Art in America. NY: Reynal & Hitchcock, 1944. 1st ed. Soiled, else VG. *Cahan.* $35/£23

JANOWITZ, TAMA. American Dad. NY: Putnam, 1981. 1st ed, 1st bk. Fine in NF dj. *Beasley.* $60/£39

JANOWITZ, TAMA. Slaves of New York. London: Picador, 1986. 1st ed. VG in wrappers. *Rees.* $31/£20

JANSEN, MURK. On Bone Formation. Its Relation to Tension and Pressure. Manchester, 1920. Cl sl worn, else VG. *Goodrich.* $75/£48

JANSON, C.W. The Stranger in America, 1793-1806. NY: Press of the Pioneers, 1935. Rpt. VG. Howes J 59. *Schoyer.* $45/£29

JANVIER, CHARLES. Practical Ceramics for Students. London: C & W, 1880. 1st ed. (ii),xi,(i),258,(32)pp. Pub's cl. (Margins lt browned; edges, spine rubbed; fr hinge internally cracked; 1/2-title almost detached; ink inscrips tp.) *Bookpress.* $110/£71

JAQUES, F.P. Francis Lee Jaques, Artist of the Wilderness World. GC, 1973. (Spine lt sunned; bkpl.) Slipcase (lt faded, spotted). *Sutton.* $265/£171

JARDINE, DAVID. A Narrative of the Gunpowder Plot. London, 1857. xvi,344pp (prelims spotted). Marbled eps, edges; blind inner dentelles. Full calf, gilt; leather title label. *Edwards.* $54/£35

JARDINE, DOUGLAS. The Mad Mullah of Somaliland. London: Jenkins, 1923. (Fore-edge foxed.) *Petersfield.* $31/£20

JARDINE, DOUGLAS. The Mad Mullah of Somaliland. London, 1923. 1st ed. Frontis port, 18 plts. Hinges tender, eps browned, foxing, o/w VG in grn cl (lt rubbed), emb title. *Edwards.* $39/£25

JARDINE, WILLIAM. The Natural History of Humming-Birds. Edinburgh: W.H. Lizars, & Stirling & Kenney, 1834. 2 vols in 1. 2 frontis ports, 2 half-titles, (6),148; (4),166pp + 6pp ads. 64 Fine hand-colored plts w/guards; aeg. Grn silk (rebacked, orig spine laid down; extrems worn). *Karmiole.* $600/£387

JARDINE, WILLIAM. The Naturalist's Library. Vol VIII (only). Henry G. Bohn, n.d. Engr frontis, engr port, 30 color plts. Red cl blocked in blind/gilt. (Lg lib stamp foot of title; 8 other pp; sm stamp title; lib # spine.) *Bickersteth.* $70/£45

JARDINE, WILLIAM. The Naturalist's Library. Volume VII. Mammalia-Whales. Edinburgh: W.H. Lizars, 1843. 264pp, 29 engr plts (few sl shaved). 1/2 calf. VG. *Walcot.* $109/£70

JARMAN, W. U.S.A., Uncle Sam's Abscess, or Hell Upon Earth for U.S. Uncle Sam. Exeter, England, 1884. 194,(2)pp incl wraps. Nice (spine top chipped). *Bohling.* $125/£81

JARRATT, VERNON. The Italian Cinema. London: Falcon, (1951). Good (spine top torn). *Artis.* $15/£10

JARRELL, RANDALL. Blood for a Stranger. NY: Harcourt, Brace, (1942). 1st ed, 1st bk. 8vo. Red cl. Fine in Fine dj. *Chapel Hill.* $550/£355

JARRELL, RANDALL. The Juniper Tree. Lore Segal (trans). NY: FSG, 1973. 1st ed. Maurice Sendak (illus). 5.5x7.25. 332pp. Cl. Fine in dj, slipcase. *Cattermole.* $90/£58

JARRELL, RANDALL. Pictures from an Institution. NY, 1954. 1st Amer ed. Fine (name) in dj (sl torn, rubbed). *Polyanthos.* $50/£32

JARRELL, RANDALL. A Sad Heart at the Supermarket. NY: Atheneum, 1962. 1st ed. NF in dj. *Hermitage.* $45/£29

JARRY, MADELEINE. The Carpets of Aubusson. Leigh-on-Sea: Lewis, 1969. 92 plts. *Petersfield.* $70/£45

JARRY, MADELEINE. World Tapestry from Its Origins to the Present. NY, 1969. Good. *Washton.* $60/£39

JARVES, JAMES J. Kiana: A Tradition of Hawaii. Boston, 1857. 1st ed. 12mo. 277pp. Spine ends worn. *Argosy.* $200/£129

JASEN, DAVID A. The Theatre of P.G. Wodehouse. London: Batsford, (1979). 1st ed. 5 color plts. VG in dj. *Houle.* $65/£42

Jasper Johns. 17 Monotypes. NY, 1982. Color frontis; unpaginated; 17 color plts. Dj (sl torn). *Edwards.* $70/£45

JAVELLE, EMILE. Alpine Memories. London: T. Fisher Unwin, 1899. 1st ed. vii,444pp; 4 plts. (Hinges sl rubbed.) *Hollett.* $85/£55

JEAN, ELSIE and GEORGE H. GARTLAN. Singing As We Go. NY: Hinds, Hayden & Eldredge, (1925). 4to. Color frontis, 68 + (i)pp; 12 color plts by Mabel Betsy Hill (sm tears bottom margin 6 leaves). Blue cl, gilt, color pict paper label. VG in pict dj (chipped, sm edgetears). *Blue Mountain.* $100/£65

JEAN, MARCEL and ARPAD MEZEI. The History of Surrealist Painting. NY: Grove, 1960. 1st ed, 1st ptg. Fine in NF die-cut dj. *Beasley.* $250/£161

JEAN-AUBRY, G. and ROBERT SMITH. Eugene Boudin. Greenwich, CT: NYGS, (1968). 50 mtd color illus. VG. *Argosy.* $85/£55

JEANS, J.H. Astronomy and Cosmogony. CUP, 1929. 2nd ed. 14 plts. Good in bevel-edged blue cl (spotted, scuffed, worn; sl warped). *Knollwood.* $75/£48

JEANS, J.H. The Dynamical Theory of Gases. Cambridge, 1904. 1st ed. Hinges cracked. *Argosy.* $150/£97

JEANS, J.H. The Mathematical Theory of Electricity and Magnetism. Cambridge: CUP, 1908. 1st ed. VG. *Argosy.* $175/£113

JEFFCOAT, PERCIVAL R. Nooksack Tales and Trails. Ferndale, WA: Sedro-Woolley Courier Times, 1949. Memorial ed. Fine. *Perier.* $50/£32

JEFFERIES, RICHARD. Greene Ferne Farm. London: Smith, Elder, 1880. 1st ed, one of 1000 ptd; primary binding. Olive cl (spine sl sunned, sl rubbed). Good (internal spotting, browning; sl tears 1/2 title, ad leaf; creases; sl shaken). *Ash.* $194/£125

JEFFERIES, RICHARD. Hodge and His Masters. London: Smith, Elder, 1880. 1st ed. 2 vols. vii,359; 312,(iv)pp (pencil marginalia; spots). Dec cl (extrems sl rubbed), gilt. Very Nice. *Hollett.* $217/£140

JEFFERIES, RICHARD. Round About a Great Estate. London: Smith, Elder, 1880. 1st ed. x,204pp + 4pp ads. Blue cl, gilt. Backstrip rubbed, sl worn, o/w Good. *Cox.* $59/£38

JEFFERIES, RICHARD. Round About a Great Estate. London: Smith, Elder, 1880. 1st ed. x,204,(iv, ads)pp (edges spotted; mkd; rubbed; label partially removed upper bd). *Hollett.* $62/£40

JEFFERIES, RICHARD. The Toilers of the Field. London: Longmans, Green, 1892. 1st ed. Frontis port; viii,327,24pp ads. (Joints tender; spine, edges sl browned; paper spine label chipped, browned.) *Hollett.* $93/£60

JEFFERIES, RICHARD. Wild Life in a Southern Country. London: Smith, Elder, 1879. 2nd ed. xii,387pp (few spots; joints cracking). Dec cl (hinges rubbed; corner upper bd dented, damaged), gilt. *Hollett.* $47/£30

JEFFERIES, RICHARD. Wood Magic. London: Cassell et al, 1881. 1st ed. Miller & Matthews' variant (b), w/prelim blank in vol ii. 2 vols. Dec cl (sl bumped, shaken; sl mks, creases; nicks). Nice set. *Ash.* $310/£200

JEFFERS, ROBINSON. The Beginning and the End. NY: Random House, (1963). 1st ed. Fine in dj. *Antic Hay.* $45/£29

JEFFERS, ROBINSON. Californians. NY: Macmillan, 1916. 1st ed, one of 1200. Teg. Blue cl. Fine. *Chapel Hill.* $350/£226

JEFFERS, ROBINSON. Descent to the Dead. NY: Random House, (1931). 1st ed. #399/500 (of 550), signed. Paper-cvrd bds, parchment spine. Fine (bkpl) in pub's slipcase. *Chapel Hill.* $400/£258

JEFFERS, ROBINSON. Descent to the Dead. NY: Random House, (1931). Ltd to 500 numbered, signed. Vellum, bds. NF in slipcase (sm piece missing lower edge). *Antic Hay.* $350/£226

JEFFERS, ROBINSON. Give Your Heart to the Hawks and Other Poems. NY, 1933. 1st Amer ed. Fine in dj (sunned, sl chipped, sm edgetear). *Polyanthos.* $75/£48

JEFFERS, ROBINSON. Hungerfield and Other Poems. NY: Random House, (1954). 1st ed. Fine in dj (interior repair spine tear, chip). *Antic Hay.* $50/£32

JEFFERS, ROBINSON. Not Man Apart, Lines from Robinson Jeffers. David Brower (ed). SF: Sierra Club, (1965). 1st ed. Fine in VG dj. *Oregon.* $70/£45

JEFFERS, ROBINSON. The Selected Letters of Robinson Jeffers. Ann N. Ridgeway (ed). Balt: John Hopkins, (1968). 1st ed. Signed. Fine in dj. *Antic Hay.* $50/£32

JEFFERS, ROBINSON. Songs and Heroes. Robert J. Brophy (ed). Arundel Press, 1988. #233/250. Fine. *Poetry.* $147/£95

JEFFERS, ROBINSON. Such Counsels You Gave to Me and Other Poems. NY: Random House, (1937). 1st ed, trade issue. Red cl stamped in gold. VG in dj (price-clipped, sm chip, short tears mended w/archival tape). *Godot.* $85/£55

JEFFERS, ROBINSON. Thurso's Landing and Other Poems. Liveright, (1932). 1st trade ed. Fine (name). *Authors Of The West.* $40/£26

JEFFERSON, ISAAC. Memoirs of a Monticello Slave: As Dictated to Charles Campbell in the 1840s by Isaac.... Charlottesville: 1951. 1st ed, ltd to 1000. Port. Orig cl; deckled edges. VG. *Petrilla.* $75/£48

JEFFERSON, JOSEPH. The Autobiography of Joseph Jefferson. NY: Century Co, (1890). Inscribed presentation copy. xvi,502pp, 77 plts, index. Teg. Blind-stamped vellum-like bds (sl frayed, soiled). *Karmiole.* $40/£26

JEFFERSON, THOMAS. The Life and Morals of Jesus of Nazareth.... Washington: GPO, 1904. Full crimson straight-grained calf, gilt. Nice (sl rubbed). *Book Block.* $175/£113

JEFFREYS, JOHN GWYN. British Conchology. London: John Van Voorst, 1862-9. 1st ed. 5 vols. Color frontispieces, 30 b/w plts, 102 color plts, all by W. & G.B. Sowerby. (Recased w/unattractive reinforcing; hinges taped; sl loss to spine lettering vol 3.) *Edwards.* $930/£600

JEFFREYS, JULIUS. Views Upon the Statics of the Human Chest, Animal Heat, and Determinations of Blood to the Head. London: Longman, et al, 1843. 233pp. Uncut, unopened. Good (worn; fr fly torn out; browning). *Goodrich.* $75/£48

JEFFRIES, B. JOY. Color-Blindness: Its Dangers and Its Detection. Boston, 1879. 1st ed. 312pp. Good. *Fye.* $150/£97

JEFFRIES, SUSAN HERRING. Papa Wore No Halo. Winston-Salem: John F. Blair, 1963. Signed. Frontis port. *Schoyer.* $35/£23

JEKYLL, FRANCIS and C.G. TAYLOR (eds). A Gardener's Testament. London: Country Life, 1937. 1st ed. Fine. *Quest.* $80/£52

JEKYLL, FRANCIS. A Memoir. London: Cape, 1934. Frontis port, 19 photos. Fine in dj. *Quest.* $85/£55

JEKYLL, GERTRUDE and CHRISTOPHER HUSSEY. Garden Ornament. London/NY: Country Life/Scribner's, 1927. 2nd ed. VG (sl rubbed; lt damage to 2 plts from sticking together). *Cahan.* $325/£210

JEKYLL, GERTRUDE and EDWARD MAWLEY. Roses for English Gardens. London, 1902. (Binding faded, sl worn.) *Wheldon & Wesley.* $47/£30

JEKYLL, GERTRUDE and EDWARD MAWLEY. Roses for English Gardens. London: Country Life, 1902. 1st ed. Gilt-dec buckram (lt soiled). *Quest.* $110/£71

JEKYLL, GERTRUDE and LAWRENCE WEAVER. Gardens for Small Country Houses. London, (1927). 6th ed. Color frontis. (Cl sl used.) *Wheldon & Wesley.* $93/£60

JEKYLL, GERTRUDE and LAWRENCE WEAVER. Gardens for Small Country Houses. London: Country Life, 1924. 5th ed. Gilt-stamped cl. Spine head sl worn, lt edgewear, else Fine. *Quest.* $145/£94

JEKYLL, GERTRUDE. Children and Gardens. London, 1908. *Wheldon & Wesley.* $47/£30

JEKYLL, GERTRUDE. Children and Gardens. London: Country Life, 1908. 1st ed. Gilt-stamped cl. NF (sm marginal tear 1 leaf). *Quest.* $115/£74

JEKYLL, GERTRUDE. Colour Schemes for the Flower Garden. London: Country Life, 1925. 6th ed. 4 fldg plts. Fep neatly removed, else Fine. *Quest.* $65/£42

JEKYLL, GERTRUDE. Old English Household Life. London: Batsford, 1925. 1st ed. Gilt-stamped dec cl. Fine (lt marginal foxing). *Quest.* $90/£58

JEKYLL, GERTRUDE. Old West Surrey. London: Longmans Green, 1904. 1st ed. Gilt-dec buckram (rebacked, orig spine relaid). *Quest.* $195/£126

JEKYLL, GERTRUDE. Some English Gardens. London: Longmans, Green, 1905. 3rd ed. 50 full-pg color plts. Teg. Gilt-stamped cl. 1st, last leaves browned, else VG. *Quest.* $200/£129

JEKYLL, GERTRUDE. Wall, Water and Woodland Gardens.... London, 1933. 8th ed. (Cl sl mkd.) *Wheldon & Wesley.* $62/£40

JEKYLL, GERTRUDE. Wood and Garden. London, 1899. 4th imp. xvi,286pp. Orig buckram (spine faded). *Wheldon & Wesley.* $70/£45

JEKYLL, GERTRUDE. Wood and Garden. London, 1899. 5th imp in yr of pub. Frontis, xvi,286pp, 71 plts. Gilt-dec buckram. Cvr mottled, else Fine. *Quest.* $95/£61

JELLICOE, G.A. Garden Decoration and Ornament for Smaller Houses. London: Country Life, (1936). 1st ed. Contents Fine (lt edgewear; cl soiled). *Quest.* $125/£81

JELLICOE, G.A. The Gardens of Europe. London/Glasgow: Blackie & Sons, 1937. 1st ed. Fine in dj. *Quest.* $120/£77

JENKIN, A.K. HAMILTON. The Cornish Miner. London: Allen & Unwin, 1948. 2nd ed. Pub's cl, gilt (sl faded). VG (sm tear fep). *Peter Taylor.* $23/£15

JENKINS, J. GERAINT. The English Farm Wagon. Newton Abbott: David & Charles, 1981. 3rd ed. Fine in Fine dj. *October Farm.* $45/£29

JENKINS, J. GERAINT. Nets and Coracles. London: David & Charles, 1974. 1st ed. Fine in Fine dj. *Willow House.* $31/£20

JENKINS, JAMES TRAVIS. A History of the Whale Fisheries...to the Hunting of the Finner Whale at the Present Date. London: H.F. & G. Witherby, 1921. 12 plts. Minor pull at head of spine else VG. *High Latitude.* $150/£97

JENKINS, JAMES TRAVIS. Whales and Modern Whaling. London: Witherby, 1932. 1st ed. VG. *Walcot.* $59/£38

JENKINS, JOHN (ed). Recollections of Early Texas: Memoirs of John Holland Jenkins. Austin, 1958. 1st ed. Good (ex-lib) in dj. *Baade.* $25/£16

JENKINS, OLAF P. Geologic Guidebook Along Highway 49—Sierran Gold Belt. SF: State of CA, Nov, 1959. Centennial ed, 5th ptg. 2 color photo plts; 10 color maps. NF. *Connolly.* $35/£23

JENKINS, OLAF P. Geologic Guidebook of the San Francisco Bay Counties. SF, 1951. 1st ed. VG. *Oregon.* $30/£19

JENKINS, OLAF P. Geologic Guidebook of the San Francisco Bay Counties. SF: State of CA, Dec, 1951. 1st ed. Lg fldg chart. NF. *Connolly.* $75/£48

JENKINS, OLAF P. The Mother Lode Country: Geologic Guidebook Along Highway 49—Sierran Gold Belt. SF: CA Division of Mines, 1948 (1959). 5th ptg. Tan cl. Extrems sl worn, o/w NF. *Harrington.* $35/£23

JENKINS, STEPHEN. The Old Boston Post Road. NY: Putnam's, 1913. 3rd ptg. Frontis, 65 plts, 4 fldg maps; teg. Good (worn, dull). *Bohling.* $30/£19

JENKINS, THOMAS. The Man of Alaska, Peter Trimble Rowe. NY: Morehouse-Gorham, 1943. 1st ed, 2nd ptg. Fine in VG dj. *Perier.* $30/£19

JENKINSON, HILARY. The Later Court Hands in England. From the Fifteenth to the Seventeenth Century. NY: Frederick Ungar, 1969. Rprnt of 1927 ed. 2 vols. 49 plts. Blue cl. Fine in dj (lt soiled). *Karmiole.* $100/£65

JENKINSON, HILARY. The Later Court Hands in England.... CUP, 1927. 2 vols. 44 plts, 5pp alphabets. (Feps lt browned; lower bd sl soiled.) Vol 2 unbound as issued, in cl-backed folder. *Edwards.* $116/£75

JENNER, EDWARD. An Inquiry into the Causes and Effects of Variolae Vaccinae. Milan, 1923. Facs of 1798 ed. Paper-cvrd bds (rebacked; ex-lib). *Fye.* $60/£39

JENNESS, JOHN SCRIBNER. The Isle of Shoals. NY/Cambridge: Hurd & Houghton/Riverside Press, 1873. 1st ed. Frontis, 182pp, 3 fldg maps. Red-brn cl, gilt. Nice. *Cady.* $40/£26

JENNETT, SEAN. The Making of Books. London: Faber & Faber, 1973. 5th ed. (Ex-lib). Dj. *Edwards.* $31/£20

JENNINGS, ELIZABETH. Hurt. London: Poem-of-the-Month Club Ltd, 1970. 1st Eng ed. Signed. VG (corner creased; sl soiled verso). *Ulysses.* $56/£36

JENNINGS, JOHN. Clipper Ship Days. NY: Random House, 1952. 1st trade ed. Edwin A. Wilson (illus). Dec eps. VG in dj. *Cattermole.* $15/£10

JENNINGS, JOHN. Tattered Ensign. NY: Crowell, (1966). 1st ed. Black cl. NF in dj (rubbed). *Chapel Hill.* $40/£26

JENNINGS, N.A. A Texas Ranger. NY: Scribner's, 1899. 1st ed. x,321pp. Pict cl (sl soiled). Howes J 100. *Schoyer.* $250/£161

JENNINGS, O.E. Wild Flowers of Western Pennsylvania and the Upper Ohio Basin. Pittsburgh, 1953. 2 vols. Inscrip, else Good in djs (chipped, torn). *King.* $250/£161

JENNINGS, PRESTON J. A Book of Trout Flies. NY: Crown, (1935). Rpt ed. Fine in VG slipcase. *Glenn.* $50/£32

JENSEN, JAY. Six Years in Hell. Bountiful, UT: Horizon, (1974). 1st ed. Fine in Fine dj. *Oregon.* $35/£23

JENYNS, SOAME. Later Chinese Porcelain. Faber & Faber, 1959. 2nd ed. Color frontis, 3 color plts, 120 b/w plts. (Cl lt faded.) *Edwards.* $31/£20

JENYNS, SOAME. Ming Pottery and Porcelain. London, 1988. 2nd ed. 18 color plts. Dj. *Edwards.* $54/£35

JEPHSON, R. MOUNTENEY. The Girl He Left Behind Him. London: Routledge, 1877. 1st ed. 382pp (bkpl; sm tear 1 leaf; 1 section proud; joints cracking). Later half calf gilt (spine sl faded). *Hollett.* $47/£30

JERDAN, WILLIAM. The Autobiography. London, 1852-3. Als laid in. 4 vols. Frontis port each vol. Crimson 1/2 calf. VG. *Argosy.* $200/£129

JEREMY, HENRY. The Law of Carriers, Inn-Keepers, Warehousemen, and Other Depositories of Goods for Hire. NY: I. Riley, 1816. 1st US ed. vii,(8),163,(5)pp. Full contemp sheep (scuffed, rubbed). Text foxed, marginal dampstain, else Good. *Cahan.* $85/£55

JEROME, CHAUNCEY. History of the American Clock Business.... New Haven, 1860. Frontis port, 144 pp (foxing; ex-libris). Blind-emb cl (rubbed, spine faded). *Edwards.* $54/£35

JEROME, JEROME K. The Diary of a Pilgrimage. Bristol, (1891). 1st ed. Pub's dec cl (sl mkd; sig; note tp). Pub's cat bound at end. *Waterfield.* $70/£45

JEROME, JEROME K. Three Men in a Boat, to Say Nothing of the Dog! Ipswich: LEC, 1975. One of 2000 numbered, signed by John Griffiths (illus). Dec cl w/shelf back. Fine in pub's slipcase (sl dusty). *Hermitage.* $75/£48

JEROME, JEROME K. Three Men in a Boat. Bristol: J.W. Arrowsmith, 1889. 1st ed. 1st issue, w/unnumbered address on tp, ads datable to 1889 at rear. Fr ads headed w/pub's address, the initial 'T' to chapter one is unflawed, and ornamental capitals on pgs 77 and 95 are not inverted. Orig cl (expertly restored; sl mks, creases; sl bubbled). Nice. *Ash.* $302/£195

JEROME, JEROME K. Three Men in a Boat.... LEC, 1975. One of 2000 signed by John Griffiths (illus). 14 color plts. Buckram-backed striped bds. VG in slipcase. *Cox.* $54/£35

JEROME, JEROME K. Three Men on the Bummel. Arrowsmith's, 1900. 1st UK ed. VG+. *Sclanders.* $47/£30

JEROME, JEROME K. Told After Supper. Leadenhall Press, 1891. 1st UK ed. VG- (bkpl; spine sl marked; edges sl bumped). *Sclanders.* $39/£25

JERROLD, BLANCHARD. The Life of George Cruikshank in Two Epochs. London: C&W, 1882. 1st ed. 2 vols. (xvi),1-284; (viii),1-280pp + 32pp list. Brn pict cl stamped in gold/black. VG. *Vandoros.* $200/£129

JERROLD, W. The Autoclycus of the Bookstalls. London: Dent, 1902. 1st ed. Teg. Lt spotted, else VG. *Limestone.* $55/£35

JERROLD, W. (ed). The Book of Living Poets. London: Alston Rivers, 1907. 1st ed. Teg. Gilt dec cl. Nice (lt foxing). *Reese.* $50/£32

JERVOISE, E. The Ancient Bridges of the North of England. London: Architectural Press, 1931. 1st ed. (Corner sl creased.) *Hollett.* $39/£25

JESSE, CAPTAIN. The Life of George Brummell, Esq. London, 1886. One of 500. 2 vols. xxxii;363; xv,364,19pp ads; 40 color plts (sl offset; marginal staining text, plts; eps browned); partially unopened. Gilt upper bd; leather title label spines (rubbed; dampstaining lower bd). *Edwards.* $101/£65

JESSE, E. Gleanings in Natural History. London, 1838. 5th ed. 2 vols. Engr tps (sm lib stamps verso), 1 plt. *Henly.* $78/£50

JESSE, E. Scenes and Tales of Country Life.... London, 1844. viii,395pp; 4 plts (foxed); 4pp music. Binder's cl. *Wheldon & Wesley.* $39/£25

JESSE, F. TENNYSON. Moonraker, or The Female Pirate and Her Friends. NY: Knopf, 1927. 1st ed. Fine (sunned spine) in dj (sl used). *Beasley.* $35/£23

JESSIE, EDWARD. An Angler's Rambles. London: Van Voorst, 1836. Orig cl (back faded). *Petersfield.* $81/£52

JESSUP, RICHARD. The Cincinnati Kid. Boston: Little Brown, (1963). 1st ed, 1st bk. Fine in dj (lt used; price-clipped). *Turlington.* $45/£29

JETER, J.B. The Life of Rev. Daniel Witt, D.D. of Prince Edward County, Va. J.T. Ellyson, 1875. 276pp. VG-. *Book Broker.* $25/£16

JETER, J.B. Reflections of a Long Life. Richmond: Religious Herald, 1891. 325pp; port. VG. *Book Broker.* $35/£23

JEWETT, SARAH ORNE. A Country Doctor. Boston: Houghton, Mifflin, 1884. 1st ed. One of 1500. 351pp + ads. NF (lacks fep) in grn cl. BAL 10882. *Second Life.* $85/£55

JEWETT, SARAH ORNE. The Queen's Twin and Other Stories. Boston, 1899. 1st ed. One of 3020. 232pp. Blue/grn cl. Nice (closed tear fep; contemp inscrip). BAL 10913. *Second Life.* $75/£48

JEWETT, SARAH ORNE. Tales of New England. Boston/NY: Houghton, Mifflin, 1895. Ltd ptg. 276pp. Dec blue cl, teg. Sig; lt foxing tp, foredge, else NF. BAL 10937. *Chapel Hill.* $25/£16

JEWETT, SARAH ORNE. A White Heron and Other Stories. Boston: Houghton Mifflin, 1896. 1st ed. VG. *Bond.* $150/£97

JHABVALA, RUTH PRAWER. Get Ready for Battle. Murray, 1962. 1st UK ed. Fine in dj. *Williams.* $70/£45

JHABVALA, RUTH PRAWER. Heat and Dust. Murray, 1975. 1st ed. Fine in dj. *Poetry.* $39/£25

JHABVALA, RUTH PRAWER. Heat and Dust. Murray, 1975. 1st UK ed. Fine in dj. *Lewton.* $29/£19

JHABVALA, RUTH PRAWER. Heat and Dust. London: John Murray, 1975. 1st UK ed. NF in dj (price-clipped). *Williams.* $54/£35

JHABVALA, RUTH PRAWER. Like Birds Like Fishes and Other Stories. Murray, 1963. 1st ed w/rev slip inserted. VG in dj (dull; sl mkd). *Whiteson.* $23/£15

JILLSON, WILLARD ROUSE. The Legrande Oil Pool. Frankfort, KY: KY Geological Survey, 1930. 1st ed. 31 maps. Cl-backed illus bds (dusty). VG. *Cahan.* $50/£32

JIVAKA, LOBZANG. Imji Getsul: An English Buddhist in a Tibetan Monastery. London: Routledge & Kegan Paul, (1962). Map. VG in dj (rubbed). *Schoyer.* $30/£19

JOAN, NATALIE. Cosy-Time Tales. London: Thomas Nelson, (1922). 1st ed. 4to. 8 full-pg color plts by Anne Anderson. Cl-backed illus bds (sl edgewear, mks). *Reisler.* $250/£161

JOAN, NATALIE. Lie-Down-Stories. London: Blackie, 1919. 1st ed. 4to. 8 color plts by Anne Anderson. Cl-backed bds, color paste label. (Edgewear; foxing, esp prelims.) *Reisler.* $150/£97

Joaquin Murieta: The Brigand Chief of California. SF: Grabhorn, 1932. Frontis, fldg facs broadside (margin creased). Dec bds, cl spine, paper spine label (sl wear). *Dawson.* $150/£97

JOCELYN, STEPHEN PERRY. Mostly Alkali. Caldwell, 1953. 1st ed. Pict cl. Fine in dj. *Baade.* $75/£48

JOHN, AUGUSTUS. Chiaroscuro. London: Cape, (1952). 1st ed. Fine in dj. *Pharos.* $45/£29

JOHN, ELIZABETH A.H. Storms Brewed in Other Men's Worlds. College Station: TX A&M, (1975). 1st ed. 4 maps (3 double-pg). Fine in VG dj. *Oregon.* $50/£32

JOHN, ELIZABETH A.H. Storms Brewed in Other Men's Worlds. College Station, 1975. 1st ed. Pict cl. VG (sl soiled) in dj. *Baade.* $60/£39

JOHN, H.J. Jan Evangelista Purkyne. Phila: American Philosophical Soc, 1959. Good. *Goodrich.* $50/£32

JOHN, W.D. Pontypool and Usk Japanned Wares.... Newport: Ceramic Book Co, 1953. 1st ed. Color frontis, 27 plts (5 color). Teg, full gilt-edged leather (eps sl spotted; upper hinges sl tender; sl rubbed). *Edwards.* $78/£50

JOHN, W.D. and JACQUELINE SIMCOX. English Decorated Trays (1550-1850). Newport: Ceramic Book Co, 1964. 1st ed. 6 color plts. Full buckram. *Edwards.* $78/£50

JOHN, W.D. et al. Nantgarw Porcelain. Newport, England, 1948. Uncut. Gilt grn leather (edges, spine worn). *Argosy.* $150/£97

JOHNS, C.A. British Birds in Their Haunts. London: SPCK, 1862. 1st ed. xxxii,626pp, 190 lg woodcuts. Contemp 1/2 dk grn morocco; marbled bds, eps. All edges marbled. *Cady.* $125/£81

JOHNS, C.A. (ed). Gardening for Children. London: Charles Cox, (1849). 2nd ed. Wood-engr frontis, viii,182pp. Aeg. Blind-stamped cl, (unevenly faded), gilt device. Hinge cracked, else Fine. *Quest.* $75/£48

JOHNSGARD, P.A. Handbook of Waterfowl Behavior. Ithaca, 1965. 11 plts. (Spine bumped.) Dj (worn). *Sutton.* $47/£30

JOHNSON, ALFRED (trans). Ships and Shipping...Many American Vessels Painted by Antoine Roux and His Sons. Salem: Marine Research Soc Pub 9, 1925. 1st ed. Frontis, 9 plts. Fine. *Lefkowicz.* $130/£84

JOHNSON, AMANDUS. The Journal and Biography of Nicholas Collin, 1746-1831. Phila: NJ Soc of PA, 1936. 1st ed. Gilt. Good. *Karmiole.* $30/£19

JOHNSON, AMANDUS. The Swedes on the Delaware, 1638-1664. Phila: Swedish Colonial Society, 1915. 2nd ed. Frontis, 33 plts, 1 map. Teg; uncut. Lt foxing early leaves; else Fine. *Bookpress.* $95/£61

JOHNSON, AMANDUS. The Swedish Settlements on the Delaware, 1638-1664. Phila: Swedish Colonial Soc, 1911. 1st ed. 2 vols. Color frontis, 6 maps (3 fldg). Presentation letter tipped-in. (Rear inner hinge vol 2 starting.) Howes J 124. *Karmiole.* $200/£129

JOHNSON, AMANDUS. The Swedish Settlements on the Delaware, 1638-1664.... (Phila), 1911. 1st ed. 2 vols. 6 maps, 88 plts. Howes J 124. *Ginsberg.* $200/£129

JOHNSON, B.S. Albert Angelo. London: Constable, 1964. 1st ed. Nice in VG dj (sl soiled, closed tears). *Virgo.* $78/£50

JOHNSON, B.S. Albert Angelo. Constable, 1964. 1st UK ed. Fine in dj. *Sclanders.* $101/£65

JOHNSON, B.S. See the Old Lady Decently. London: Hutchinson, 1975. 1st ed. Fine in dj. *Rees.* $39/£25

JOHNSON, BRITA ELIZABETH. Maher-Shalal-Hash-Baz or Rural Life in Old Virginia. Claremont, VA, (1923). 1st ed. Orig cl. Fine in NF dj (minor chipping extrems). *Mcgowan.* $150/£97

JOHNSON, C.P. and J.E. SOWERBY. The Useful Plants of Great Britain. London, (1862). 324pp; 25 hand-colored plts. (Cl refixed.) *Wheldon & Wesley.* $233/£150

JOHNSON, C.W. Fauna of New England, 13, List of the Mollusca. Boston: Nat. Hist. Soc., 1915. Map. *Wheldon & Wesley.* $39/£25

JOHNSON, CECIL (comp). A Bibliography of the Writings of George Sterling. SF: Windsor Press, 1931. Ltd to 300. Marked 'Review copy'. Blue cl, gilt. Good. *Karmiole.* $60/£39

JOHNSON, CECIL and JAMES JOHNSON. A Printer's Garland. (SF): Book Club of CA, 1935. Ltd to 300 ptd by Windsor Press. Vellum-like spine over bds. Good. *Karmiole.* $100/£65

JOHNSON, CHARLES and HILARY JENKINSON. English Court Hand A.D. 1066 to 1500.... Oxford: Clarendon, 1915. Orig ed. 44 plts in separate vol. Very Nice set (sl rubbed). *Boswell.* $350/£226

JOHNSON, CHARLES. British Poisonous Plants. London, 1856. 28 color plts. *Petersfield.* $87/£56

JOHNSON, CLARENCE RICHARD. Constantinople To-Day. NY: Macmillan, 1922. 1st ed. 16 plts; 5 maps, charts (1 dbl-pg). Spine sl torn, frayed, o/w VG. *Worldwide.* $65/£42

JOHNSON, CLIFTON. The Country School in New England. NY: D. Appleton, 1893. 1st ed. Brn dec cl, photo insert fr cvr. Few pp lt foxed, else Fine. *Godot.* $125/£81

JOHNSON, DIANE. Fair Game. NY: Harcourt Brace, 1965. 1st ed, 1st bk. NF in NF dj. *Pettler.* $65/£42

JOHNSON, DOROTHY M. The Bloody Bozeman. McGraw Hill, (1971). 1st ed. 2 maps. VG in dj (dampstained). *Oregon.* $25/£16

JOHNSON, DOROTHY M. The Bloody Bozeman. NY, 1971. 1st ed. Fine in dj. *Baade.* $40/£26

JOHNSON, EDWARD. The Domestic Practice of Hydropathy. NY, 1849. 1st Amer ed. 467pp. Good. *Fye.* $60/£39

JOHNSON, EDWARD. History of Negro Soldiers in the Spanish-American War.... Raleigh: Capital Ptg Co, 1899. (Lacks 1 plt.) *Schoyer.* $50/£32

JOHNSON, EDWARD. History of Negro Soldiers in the Spanish-American War.... Raleigh, NC: Capital Ptg Co., 1899. 1st ed. Frontis, 228,(2)pp; 40 plts (waterstains reps; soiled). Blue-grn cl stamped in gold/black. *Karmiole.* $125/£81

JOHNSON, ELIZABETH L. For Your Amusement and Instruction. Bloomington: IN Univ, 1987. Mint. *Hobbyhorse.* $70/£45

JOHNSON, GEORGE W. The Gardeners' Dictionary. London: Bell, 1877. 916pp. Grn cl (ex-lib; hinges loose). *Second Life.* $45/£29

JOHNSON, GUION GRIFFIS. Ante-Bellum North Carolina; A Social History. Chapel Hill: Univ of NC Press, 1937. 1st ed. Edges, eps lt foxed, else VG. *Cahan.* $100/£65

JOHNSON, H.U. From Dixie to Canada: Romances and Realities of the Underground Railroad. Orwell, OH: H.U. Johnson, 1896. 2nd ed. Vol I (all published). Pict brn cl. NF (sl spotting). *Between The Covers.* $150/£97

JOHNSON, HARRY. My Home on the Range. St. Paul, 1942. 1st ed. Pict cl. Fine in dj (sl chipped). *Baade.* $45/£29

JOHNSON, HARRY. Night and Morning in Dark Africa. London: London Missionary Soc, n.d. 1st ed. (Sl dknd; lacks fr flyleaf; erased inscrip; eps sl spotted, browned.) *Hollett.* $54/£35

JOHNSON, HARRY. Standing the Gaff. Parthenon, 1935. 1st ed. Good +. *Plapinger.* $125/£81

JOHNSON, HENRY LEWIS. Historic Design in Printing. Boston: Graphic Arts Co, 1923. 1st ed. Maroon blind/gilt-lettered cl (sl wear). VG +. *House.* $100/£65

JOHNSON, HOMER URI. From Dixie to Canada.Romances and Realities of the Underground Railroad. Buffalo, NY: Charles Wells Moulton, 1894. 1st ed. 194pp. Orig cl. Minor cvr soiling, else NF. *Mcgowan.* $250/£161

JOHNSON, IRVING. Shamrock V's Wild Voyage Home.... Springfield, MA: Milton Brabley, (1933). 1st ed. Blue cl, stamped in orange (sl soiled). Dj. *Karmiole.* $30/£19

JOHNSON, JAMES WELDON. Black Manhattan. NY: Knopf, 1930. 1st ed. Lt rubbing spine lettering, sm tear 1 pg edge, else Fine in VG dj (shallow chip, spine sl tanned). *Between The Covers.* $750/£484

JOHNSON, JAMES WELDON. The Book of American Negro Spirituals. NY: Viking, (1926). VG. *Petrilla.* $40/£26

JOHNSON, JAMES WELDON. The Second Book of Negro Spirituals. NY: Viking, 1926. 1st ed. NF (sl soiled spine). *Beasley.* $75/£48

JOHNSON, JAMES. Change of Air, or the Philosophy of Travelling...to which is prefixed, The Wear and Tear of Modern Babylon.... NY: Samuel Wood & Sons, 1831. 1st Amer ed. viii,326pp + 2pp pub's cat. (Contemp sig, lt foxing). Orig pebbled cl, paper spine label. VG (hinges split, reinforced w/tape). *Hemlock.* $175/£113

JOHNSON, JOSEPH FORSYTH. The Natural Principles of Landscape Gardening.... Belfast: for the Author, (1874). Lg 8vo. Half-title, title, 12ff, viii,152pp, 6ff ads, 11 litho plts. Grn cl (cvrs faded, spotted; corners rubbed). *Marlborough.* $698/£450

JOHNSON, JOSEPHINE. Now in November. NY: S&S, 1934. 1st ed. 1st bk. Fine in dj (spine lt faded). *Godot.* $75/£48

JOHNSON, KENNETH. The Life and Times of Edward Robeson Taylor.... SF: Book Club of CA, 1968. 1st ed. Ltd to 400. Frontis, 3 plts, tipped-in fldg facs. Prospectus laid in. VF. *Oregon.* $50/£32

JOHNSON, KENNETH. The New Almaden Quicksilver Mine. Georgetown, CA: Talisman Press, 1963. 1st ed. Ltd to 750. Fine in dj (sm chip). *Oregon.* $75/£48

JOHNSON, LAURENCE. A Medical Formulary based on the United States and British Pharmocopoeias.... NY: Wood, 1881. vii,4022pp. NF. *Goodrich.* $50/£32

JOHNSON, LEROY and JEAN. Escape From Death Valley as Told by William L. Manly and Other '49ers. Reno: Univ of NV Press, 1987. 1st ed, ltd to 500. Fine in Fine dj. *Book Market.* $52/£34

JOHNSON, LIONEL. Poems. London/Boston: Elkin Mathews/Copeland & Day, 1895. 1st trade ed. One of 750. Pale blue bds. Loss to spine foot, sm chip crown, sm bkpl, sig, o/w Good. *Reese.* $125/£81

JOHNSON, LIONEL. Some Poems. Elkin Mathews, 1912. 1st ed. Pencil notes, o/w VG in wrappers (soiled, frayed). *Poetry.* $39/£25

JOHNSON, LUTHER B. Eighty Years of It. 1869-1949. Randolph, VT: Author, 1949. 1st ed. Inscribed, signed. Frontis; 30 photo plts. VG +. *Connolly.* $35/£23

JOHNSON, MERLE. You Know These Lines! NY: G.A. Baker, 1935. 1st ed. One of 1000 numbered. Tan cl, gilt (sl oxidized). *Macdonnell.* $85/£55

JOHNSON, PATRICIA GIVENS. James Patton and the Appalachian Colonists. McClure, (c. 1973). VG in VG dj. *Book Broker.* $25/£16

JOHNSON, PHILIP C. Mies Van Der Rohe. NY: MOMA, 1947. Card wraps (sl soiled; edges rubbed). *Edwards.* $93/£60

JOHNSON, PHILIP. Philip Johnson, Writings. NY: OUP, 1979. 1st ed. Frontis. 3 sm stains to dj (lt chipped), else Fine. *Bookpress.* $85/£55

JOHNSON, ROBERT UNDERWOOD and CLARENCE CLOUGH BUELL (eds). Battles and Leaders of the Civil War. NY: Century Co, (1887). 2nd ed. 4 vols. 1/2 leather w/cl bds. Sl wear spine extrems, else VG set. *Mcgowan.* $350/£226

JOHNSON, ROBERT UNDERWOOD and CLARENCE CLOUGH BUELL (eds). Battles and Leaders of the Civil War. NY: Yoseloff, 1956. #93/100. 4 vols. Blue morocco. NF set in cl slipcase. *Mcgowan.* $275/£177

JOHNSON, ROSSITER. Campfires and Battlefields, History of...the Great Civil War. NY, (1894). 551pp. Orig emb, dec leather. *Heinoldt.* $75/£48

JOHNSON, ROSSITER. Campfires and Battlefields. NY: Blue & Grey Press, 1958. VG in VG dj. *Mcgowan.* $50/£32

JOHNSON, S.W. How Crops Grow. NY, 1868. 394pp. (Tanned; spotted, faded spine.) *Sutton.* $45/£29

JOHNSON, SAMUEL. The Beauties of Johnson. William Cook (ed). London: Ptd for G. Kearsley, 1782. 2 vols in 1. Engr title, (6),xv,(3),228; x,(2),204pp. Full grn pseudo leather. Lt foxing, discoloration toward end, else Good. *Reese.* $85/£55

JOHNSON, SAMUEL. A Dictionary of the English Language. London: W. Strahan et al, 1773. 5th ed. 2 vols. 4to. Full polished calf (rebacked, corners repaired, new endleaves). Internally clean (marginal soiling). *Glenn.* $850/£548

JOHNSON, SAMUEL. A Dictionary of the English Language. Balt: Fielding Lucas Jr. et al, 1814. 16mo. Full-pg copper engr frontis w/engr pub impt, 259pp. Full leather on bds (edges lt worn; spine fold cracking; gilt label, decs spine. Ink sigs; uniform lt browning; sl chipping corner few leaves; else Good. *Hobbyhorse*. $125/£81

JOHNSON, SAMUEL. A Dictionary of the English Language. London: Offor et al, 1822. Wide 4tos. 2 vols. Frontis port engr. (Offsetting on tp; foxing.) 3/4 polished calf, linen bds (rebound). Handsome. *Hartfield*. $1,650/£1,065

JOHNSON, SAMUEL. A Dictionary of the English Language.... Ptd for Longman, Hurst, et al, 1818. 1st Todd ed, 1st issue. 4 vols. Port vol 1. Contemp diced calf; all vols rebacked; orig marbled eps preserved. *Bickersteth*. $349/£225

JOHNSON, SAMUEL. A Dictionary of the English Language...to Which Are Added Walker's Principles of English Pronunciation. Phila: James Maxwell, 1819. 1st Amer ed, from 11th London ed. 2 vols. Tall, wide 4tos. Frontis port. Chestnut calf spines, marbled bds (rebound), raised bands, tooled spines. Excellent set (sl foxing). *Hartfield*. $1,950/£1,258

JOHNSON, SAMUEL. Johnson and Queeney, Letters.... London: Cassell, 1932. 1st ed. #228/500. Frontis, 11 plts. Teg. Marbled cl, gilt on red leather label. Fine. *Hartfield*. $95/£61

JOHNSON, SAMUEL. A Journey to the Western Islands of Scotland. London: Strahan & Cadell, 1775. 1st ed, 1st issue w/12-line errata. 8vo. 384,(1)pp w/cancels at D8 and U4, and leaf U4 verso misnumbered 222 for 296. 3/4 calf, marbled bds (rebound, orig label laid down). Nice. *Hartfield*. $765/£494

JOHNSON, SAMUEL. A Journey to the Western Islands of Scotland. Balt/Boston/Albany/Phila: Nicklin Co. et al, 1810. 1st Amer ed. (1),184pp. (Prelim edges dknd; some foxing.) Calf bds (worn; skillfully rehinged), red leather label. Contents VG. *Hartfield*. $395/£255

JOHNSON, SAMUEL. A Journey to the Western Islands of Scotland. London: Ptd for T. Cadell & W. Davies, 1816. New ed. Mod 1/2 calf, marbled bds. Good (damp mks 1st few leaves). *Reese*. $40/£26

JOHNSON, SAMUEL. Letters to and from the Late Samuel Johnson, LL.D. Ptd for A. Strahan & T. Cadell, 1788. 1st ed. 2 vols. (ii),xv,397; xi,424pp; initial blank leaf before title vol 1. Contemp calf, red morocco spine labels (w/o errata slip vol 1; sl wear top vol 2). *Bickersteth*. $310/£200

JOHNSON, SAMUEL. The Lives of the Most Eminent English Poets. London: J. Rivington, 1790-1791. 4 vols. Engr frontis port. Orig polished calf, gilt rules, dbl leather labels. Nice set (lib bkpl; spine wear). *Hartfield*. $550/£355

JOHNSON, SAMUEL. The Lives of the Most Eminent English Poets. London: Ptd for T. Longman, 1794. New ed. 4 vols. Port vol 1. 1/2 titles bound in vols 1-2. Contemp tree calf (rebacked), gilt spines, red morocco labels. Pencil mks in text, o/w Handsome set. *Reese*. $350/£226

JOHNSON, SAMUEL. The Poetical Works. London: W. Osborne & T. Griffin, 1785. 1st collected ed. viii,152pp; half title present. Contemp grn stained calf w/burgundy spine label (spine chipped; hinges cracked but holding). (Bkpl.) *Karmiole*. $300/£194

JOHNSON, SAMUEL. The Rambler. Phila: J.J. Woodward, 1827. New ed. 4 vols. 12mo. Full-pg copper engr frontis each vol; v,257; vii,230; vii,259; vii,235 + 2pp list. Mottled calf on bds, gilt, added handwritten lib labels. Good set (sl wear, lt foxing, lt splitting; handwritten lib pocket, card pasted inside back cvr each vol; call # label spine). *Hobbyhorse*. $250/£161

JOHNSON, SAMUEL. The Works of Samuel Johnson.... Phila: H.C. Carey & I. Lea, 1825. 6 vols. Contemp mottled sheep; red, black spine labels. Nice set (hinges cracking; extrems rubbed). *Felcone*. $275/£177

JOHNSON, SAMUEL. The Works. Dublin: Luke White, 1793. 1st Dublin ed. 6 vols. Tall, thick 8vo. Engr frontis port. Full tree calf, panelled spine gilt, dbl gilt on black labels (3 replaced). VG set (armorial bkpls; sl flaws). *Hartfield*. $895/£577

JOHNSON, SIDNEY SMITH. Texans Who Wore Gray. (Tyler, TX, 1907). 1st ed. Orig cl. Minor rubbing, else VG. Howes J152. *Mcgowan*. $750/£484

JOHNSON, T. BROADWOOD. Tramps Round the Mountains of the Moon.... Boston, 1909. Fldg map. Illus cl (sl rubbed; spine, lower joint sl chipped; marginal spotting). *Edwards*. $116/£75

JOHNSON, VIRGINIA WEISEL. The Unregimented General: A Biography of Nelson A. Miles. Boston: Houghton Mifflin, 1962. 1st ed. VG in dj (sl worn). *Lien*. $50/£32

JOHNSON, WARREN B. From the Pacific to the Atlantic, Being an Account of a Journey Overland from Eureka, Humboldt, CO.... Webster, MA, 1887. 1st ed. 369pp. *Ginsberg*. $100/£65

JOHNSON, WENDELL. The Influence of Stuttering on the Personality. Iowa City, 1932. 1st ed. (Ex-lib.) *Fye*. $30/£19

JOHNSON, WILLIAM and LOUIS NEWKIRK. Leathercraft. St. Paul: Webb, 1945. 1st ed. *Lambeth*. $30/£19

JOHNSON, WILLIAM S. (ed). Lafcadio Hearn; Selected Writings 1872-1877. Woodruff, IN, 1979. 1st ed. #338/750. 2 ports. Fine in dj. *Artis*. $25/£16

JOHNSON, WILLIAM S. (ed). W. Eugene Smith. Millerton, NY: Aperture, 1981. 1st ed. Name, else NF in dj. *Cahan*. $150/£97

JOHNSON, WILLIS FLETCHER. Life of Wm. Tecumseh Sherman, Late Retired General, U.S.A. (Phila): Edgewood Pub Co, (1891). 1st ed. 607pp. VG. *Mcgowan*. $45/£29

JOHNSTON, ALVA. The Case of Erle Stanley Gardner. NY: Morrow, (1947). VG in dj (sm chips). *Houle*. $95/£61

JOHNSTON, ANNIE FELLOWS. Miss Santa Claus of the Pullman. NY: Century, 1913. 1st ed. VG. *Bishop*. $10/£6

JOHNSTON, ANNIE FELLOWS. Old Mammy's Torment. Boston: L.C. Page, 1897. 1st ed. 118pp. Pict yellow/beige cl. VG. *Chapel Hill*. $40/£26

JOHNSTON, CHARLES. Incidents Attending the Capture, Detention, and Ransom of Charles Johnston of Virginia. Cleveland: Burrows, 1905. Rpt. Frontis map. Dec cl. Howes J 158. *Ginsberg*. $125/£81

JOHNSTON, CHARLES. A Narrative of the Incidents Attending the Capture, Detention, and Ransom of Charles Johnston...in the Year 1790.... NY, 1827. 1st ed. 264pp. Linen-backed bds; paper spine label. Spotting; label sl chipped; rear flyleaf wanting, else Good. Howes J 158. *Felcone*. $300/£194

JOHNSTON, CHARLES. The Valley of the Six Nations. Univ of Toronto, 1964. 1st trade ed. Frontis, 2 fldg maps. VF in Good+ dj. *Oregon.* $45/£29

JOHNSTON, FRANCES BENJAMIN. The Early Architecture of North Carolina, a Pictorial Survey. Chapel Hill: Univ of NC, (1947). 2nd ed. Fine in pub's box (tattered). *Bookpress.* $325/£210

JOHNSTON, H. The Negro in the New World. London, (1910). 1st ed. 2 fldg maps. (Inner hinges cracked; cvrs worn.) *King.* $95/£61

JOHNSTON, H. The Uganda Protectorate. NY: Dodd, Mead, 1902. 2 vols. (xx),479; (xiv)480-1018pp (ex-lib; spines sunned, lacks frontis vol 1). *Schoyer.* $135/£87

JOHNSTON, H. The Uganda Protectorate. London: Hutchinson, 1902. 1st ed. 2 vols. 48 plts (47 colored), 9 fldg colored maps. Black cl, teg; gilt/white vignettes. Generally VG (spines rubbed, cvrs sl cockled). *Morrell.* $209/£135

JOHNSTON, HENRY P. The Storming of Stony Point on the Hudson. NY: White, 1900. Fldg color map. VG. *Schoyer.* $45/£29

JOHNSTON, HENRY P. The Yorktown Campaign and the Surrender of Cornwallis 1781. NY: Harper, 1881. 1st ed. Frontis, 206pp. Blue cl. Spine top chipped, else Fine. *Chapel Hill.* $100/£65

JOHNSTON, JOSEPH EGGLESTON. Narrative of Military Operations, Directed during the Late War between the States. NY: D. Appleton, 1874. 1st ed. 602,(6)pp. Spine extrems sl worn, else VG. Howes J 167. *Mcgowan.* $250/£161

JOHNSTON, JOSEPH EGGLESTON. Narrative of Military Operations. NY: Appleton, 1874. 1st ed. Frontis port, 602pp + 6pp ads, fldg map. Orig grn cl stamped in black/gilt. Bkpl, else bright. *Chapel Hill.* $375/£242

JOHNSTON, MARY. Audrey. NY: Houghton Mifflin, 1902. 1st ed. Spine lt faded, torn, o/w VG. *Hermitage.* $30/£19

JOHNSTON, MARY. To Have and to Hold. Boston: Houghton, Mifflin, 1900. 1st ed. Frontis. (Pencil inscrips fep, leaf 1; lt wear extrems; some corners creased; rear hinge internally cracked.) *Bookpress.* $85/£55

JOHNSTON, PAUL. Ship and Boat Models in Ancient Greece. Annapolis: Naval Inst Press, (1985). Good in dj. *Archaeologia.* $45/£29

JOHNSTON, RICHARD W. Follow Me! The Story of the Second Marine Division in World War II. NY: Random House, (1948). 1st ed. Orig cl. NF. *Mcgowan.* $125/£81

JOHNSTON, WILLIAM G. Overland to California. Oakland: Biobooks, 1948. 2nd ed. One of 1000. Lg fldg map; pict ep. Grn cl, grey cl spine, paper label. Fine. Howes J 173. *Harrington.* $60/£39

JOHNSTON, WILLIAM G. Overland to California. Oakland, 1948. Reissue. Fldg blue map. Howes J 173. *Ginsberg.* $50/£32

JOHNSTON, WILLIAM G. Overland to California. By...A Member of the Wagon Train First to Enter California.... Biobooks, 1948. Fldg map; illus fep, rep map. VF. Howes J 173. *Oregon.* $55/£35

JOHNSTON, WILLIAM PRESTON. The Life of Gen. Albert Sidney Johnston, Embracing His Service.... NY: Appleton, 1879. 2nd ed. xviii,755,(2)pp. Orig cl. VG (rear inner hinge starting; rear bd w/sl damping). Howes J175. *Mcgowan.* $125/£81

JOHNSTONE, G.H. Asiatic Magnolias in Cultivation. London: Royal Horticultural Soc, 1955. 14 full-pg color plts, fldg map. Pub's buckram gilt (lt spotted). NF (lg inscrip). *Quest.* $375/£242

JOKELSON, PAUL. Sulphides, The Art of Cameo Incrustation. (NY, 1968). VG in dj (spine scratched), slipcase (sl worn). *King.* $35/£23

JOLLIFFE, J.E.A. Angevin Kinship. London: A&C Black, 1955. 1st ed. Dj (chipped, spine sl browned). *Edwards.* $25/£16

Jolly Animal ABC. NY: McLoughlin Bros, 1900. 4to. 10 leaves; 6 full-pg chromolithos. Pict chromolitho wrappers; cvr reads 'A Nursery ABC Book.' Internally Fine (cvrs soiled, creased, chipped; sm loss of paper). *Hobbyhorse.* $55/£35

Jolly Jump-Ups Child's Garden of Verses. Springfield, MA: McLoughlin Bros, 1946. 1st ed. 8vo. 6 pop-ups by Geraldine Clyne. Glazed pict bds. Edgewear, lt soiling, else VG. *Glenn.* $125/£81

Jolly Jump-Ups Favorite Nursery Stories. Springfield, MA: McLoughlin Bros, 1942. 27x19 cm. 6 stories w/pop-ups. VG-. (extrems sl worn). *Book Finders.* $200/£129

Jolly Jump-Ups See the Circus. Springfield: McLoughlin Bros, 1944. 8vo. 6 pop-ups. Color pict bds (edges lt worn). VG. *Davidson.* $185/£119

JOLLY, RUDOLF. Atlas of Microscopic Diagnosis and Gynecology. NY, 1911. 1st Eng trans. 52 mtd color lithos. Good. *Fye.* $75/£48

JOLY, J. Radioactivity and Geology. London, 1909. 1st ed. 6 plts. Good. *Henly.* $37/£24

JONES, BILLY M. Health-Seekers in the Southwest. 1817-1900. Norman: Univ of OK, 1967. 1st ed. 16 plts; map. Fine in NF dj. *Connolly.* $35/£23

JONES, CHARLES C. General Sherman's March from Atlanta to the Coast. Augusta, GA: Chronicle Ptg, 1884. 1st ed. Signed 'Author, May 24, 1884'. 19pp. Orig ptd wraps. Sl fold, else VG. *Chapel Hill.* $125/£81

JONES, CLAUDIA. Jim-Crow in Uniform. (NY: New Age, 1940.) 1st ed. VG in pict self-wraps, side-stitched as issued. *Petrilla.* $40/£26

JONES, DAVID. The Anathemata. London, 1952. 1st Eng ed. (Name.) *Edrich.* $47/£30

JONES, DAVID. In Parenthesis. London, 1937. 1st Eng ed. VG. *Edrich.* $93/£60

JONES, DAVID. In Parenthesis. NY: Chilmark, 1961. 1st ed, 1st state. VF in dj (minor rub spine heel). *Else Fine.* $90/£58

JONES, DOUGLAS C. Elkhorn Tavern. NY: Holt, Rinehart & Winston, 1980. 1st ed. Map. NF in NF dj. *Connolly.* $25/£16

JONES, E. A Bibliography of the Dog. Library Assoc, 1971. Dec cl. Fine. *Moss.* $70/£45

JONES, E. ALFRED. The Old Silver of American Churches. Letchworth, England: Privately ptd, 1913. Ltd to 506 numbered. 145 photo plts. Grn cl, gilt; teg. Sm lib rubber stamp on lower tp, o/w exceptionally Fine. *Karmiole.* $600/£387

JONES, ERNEST. Sigmund Freud. NY: Basic, 1953. One of 250 numbered. 3 vols, each signed. Pub's buckram. Fine (lacks slipcase). *Lame Duck.* $400/£258

JONES, ERNEST. Sigmund Freud. London: Hogarth Press, 1954-57. Vol 1 New ed, rest 1st eds. 3 vols. Frontis ports. (Feps lt browned.) Djs (ragged). *Edwards.* $93/£60

JONES, FRED B. Flora of the Texas Coastal Bend. Sinton, TX, 1975. 1st ed. VG in dj. *Brooks.* $25/£16

JONES, G.N. and G.D. FULLER. Vascular Plants of Illinois. Urbana, 1955. *Sutton.* $60/£39

JONES, GAYL. Corregidora. NY: Random House, (1975). 1st ed, 1st bk. Fine in dj. *Bernard.* $45/£29

JONES, GEORGEANNA. The Management of Endocrine Disorders of Menstruation and Fertility. Springfield, IL, 1954. 1st ed. Good in dj. *Fye.* $65/£42

JONES, GWYN. The Green Island. London: Golden Cockerel, 1946. 1st ed ltd to 500 numbered. Frontis, 10 other wood-engrs by John Petts. Teg, others uncut. 2-tone cl, blocked in gold. Fine. *Cox.* $62/£40

JONES, J. WILLIAM (comp). Army of Northern Virginia Memorial Volume. Richmond: J.W. Randolph & English, 1880. 1st ed. 347pp. 1/2 tan cl, marbled bds. VG. *Chapel Hill.* $350/£226

JONES, J. WILLIAM. Christ in the Camp; or Religion in Lee's Army. Waco: James E. Yeager, n.d. (1887). 624pp, 2 color lithos. *Lambeth.* $125/£81

JONES, J. WILLIAM. Life and Letters of Robert Edward Lee. NY/Washington: Neale, 1906. 1st ed. Frontis port. Teg. Later 3/4 black levant morocco, gilt centerpieces spine, raised bands. Spine lt faded, else Fine. *Chapel Hill.* $175/£113

JONES, J. WILLIAM. Personal Reminiscences, Anecdotes, and Letters of Gen. Robert E. Lee. NY: Appleton, 1875. 2nd ed. Frontis port, 509pp. Orig pub's 1/2 morocco. VG+. *Chapel Hill.* $250/£161

JONES, J. WILLIAM. Personal Reminiscences...of Gen. Robert E. Lee. Appleton, 1875. 509pp. Good+ (new spine, headbands; foxed). *Book Broker.* $65/£42

JONES, J.B. A Rebel War Clerk's Diary at the Confederate States Capital. Phila: Lippincott, 1866. 1st ed. 2 vols. 8vo, 392; 480pp. Orig brn cl. Fine set. Howes J 220. *Chapel Hill.* $600/£387

JONES, J.B. A Rebel War Clerk's Diary. Earl Schenck Miers (ed). NY: Sagamore Press, (1958). 1st 1-vol ed. Grey cl. VG in pict dj. Howes J 220. *Chapel Hill.* $55/£35

JONES, J.W. The Salmon, the New Naturalist. London: Collins, 1959. 1st ed. 24 diags. Fine in dj. *Petersfield.* $37/£24

JONES, J.W. The Salmon. London, 1959. 1st ed. 12 plts. Good. *Henly.* $37/£24

JONES, JAMES. From Here to Eternity. Scribners, 1951. 1st ed, 1st bk. Presentation ed, signed. NF in dj. *Fine Books.* $385/£248

JONES, JAMES. From Here to Eternity. NY: Scribner's, 1951. Signed presentation ed. Gilt spine title partially rubbed, o/w Fine in dj (edgeworn, sl chipped, internal repair). *Sadlon.* $200/£129

JONES, JAMES. From Here to Eternity. London: Collins, 1952. 1st Eng ed. Lt streak back panel, else VG in dj (lt worn, chips back panel). *Limestone.* $135/£87

JONES, JAMES. The Ice-Cream Headache and Other Stories. (NY): Delacorte, (1968). 1st ed. Fine in NF dj (sl rubbed). *Reese.* $25/£16

JONES, JAMES. The Ice-Cream Headache and Other Stories. (NY, 1968). 1st ed. VG in dj (sl worn). *King.* $25/£16

JONES, JAMES. Some Came Running. NY: Scribner's, (1957). 1st ed. Very Nice in dj (creases, chips, edgetears). *Reese.* $50/£32

JONES, JENKIN LLOYD. An Artilleryman's Diary. (Madison, WI: Democrat Ptg, 1914). 1st ed. Rear inner hinge starting, else VG. *Mcgowan.* $150/£97

JONES, JOHN MATTHEW. The Naturalist in Bermuda.... London: Reeves & Turner, 1859. 1st ed. xii,(ii),200, fldg map. Grn cl. VG (lower cvr sl stained). *Morrell.* $357/£230

JONES, JOHN PAUL. Letters of John Paul Jones Printed from the Unpublished Originals in Mr. W.K. Bixby's Collection. Boston: For Bibliophile Soc, 1905. 1st ed. 3 plts. Orig bds (spine sunned). *Lefkowicz.* $65/£42

JONES, JOSEPH. Explorations of the Aboriginal Remains of Tennessee. Washington, 1876. 171pp. Uncut; unopened. (Lacks fr wrap; text dusty.) *Goodrich.* $75/£48

JONES, JOSEPH. Observations on Some of the Physical, Chemical...Phenomena of Malarial Fever. Phila, 1859. 1st ed. 419pp. Good in wraps. *Fye.* $100/£65

JONES, KATHARINE M. The Plantation South. Indianapolis: Bobbs-Merrill, (1957). 1st ed. Grn cl. NF in VG dj. *Chapel Hill.* $55/£35

JONES, L. and F.I. SCARD. The Manufacture of Cane Sugar. London, 1909. Color frontis. (Cl soiled.) *Sutton.* $95/£61

JONES, LE ROI. Dutchman and The Slave. NY: Morrow, 1964. 1st ed. Fine in NF dj. *Antic Hay.* $50/£32

JONES, M. Life and Travel in Tartary, Thibet, and China. London: T. Nelson & Sons, 1872. Chromolitho frontis; 120pp. VG. *Hollett.* $47/£30

JONES, MADISON. The Innocent. NY: Harcourt, Brace, (1957). 1st ed, 1st bk. NF in dj (lt wear). *Antic Hay.* $50/£32

JONES, MADISON. The Innocent. NY: Harcourt, 1957. 1st ed, inscribed Feb, 1957. Fine in dj (spine lt faded). *Else Fine.* $145/£94

JONES, MADISON. Season of the Strangler. NY: Doubleday, 1982. 1st ed. Fine in dj. *Pharos.* $35/£23

JONES, MARGARET BELLE (comp). Bastrop: A Compilation of Material.... Bastrop, TX, 1936. 1st ed. Black wraps. Inscrip, notes, else Fine. *Chapel Hill.* $175/£113

JONES, MICHAEL WYNN. The Cartoon History of Britain. (London, 1971). Fabricoid. VG in dj. *Argosy.* $85/£55

JONES, NARD. Wheat Women. NY: Duffield & Green, (1933). 1st ed. VG. *Perier.* $125/£81

JONES, OWEN. Ten Years of Game-Keeping. London: Arnold, 1909. 1st ed. Grn cl, gilt pheasants. VG+. *Bowman.* $45/£29

JONES, PAUL A. Quivira. Wichita: McCormick-Armstrong, (1929). 1st ed. Signed. *Glenn.* $65/£42

JONES, RAYMOND F. The Cybernetic Brains. Avalon, 1962. 1st ed. Fine in dj (sm chip). *Madle.* $25/£16

JONES, RAYMOND F. Planet of Light. Winston, 1953. 1st ed. Fine in dj. *Madle.* $125/£81

JONES, RAYMOND F. The Secret People. Avalon, 1956. 1st ed. Fine in dj. *Aronovitz.* $65/£42

JONES, RAYMOND F. Son of the Stars. Winston, 1952. 1st ed. NF in dj (frayed). *Madle.* $85/£55

JONES, RAYMOND F. The Year When Stardust Fell. Winston, 1958. 1st ed. NF in dj (spine chipped). *Madle.* $85/£55

JONES, ROBERT TYRE. Golf Is My Game. GC: Doubleday, 1960. 1st ed. Fine in VG dj (3 sm chips). *Between The Covers.* $55/£35

JONES, ROGER and NICHOLAS PENNY. Raphael. New Haven/London: Yale Univ, 1983. Pub's cl. Fine in Mint dj. *Europa.* $39/£25

JONES, ROY. Boundary Town. Vancouver, WA: Privately ptd, (1958). 1st ed. VG in Fair dj. *Oregon.* $30/£19

JONES, S.B. and A.E. LUCHSINGER. Plant Systematics. NY, 1979. Lt shelfwear. *Brooks.* $27/£17

JONES, STEPHEN. A New Biographical Dictionary.... London: Longman, Huist et al, 1811. 6th ed. 12mo. Full brn calf (sl rubbing), gilt stamped; aeg. VG. *Houle.* $125/£81

JONES, SYDNEY R. The Village Homes of England. Studio Special # Spring 1912. 12 add'l colored dwgs w/guards. Good+ (bumped, furled; lt worn) in orig paper wraps. *Willow House.* $47/£30

JONES, T. RUPERT (ed). Manual of the Natural History, Geology and Physics of Greenland and the Neighbouring Regions.... London: Eyre & Spottiswoode, 1875. 1st ed. vi,783pp. 1/2 calf, marbled bds. Good. *Walcot.* $279/£180

JONES, T. WHARTON. The Principles and Practice of Ophthalmic Medicine and Surgery. Phila, 1856. 2nd Amer ed. 500pp. Good. *Fye.* $100/£65

JONES, T.E. Leaves from an Argonaut's Note Book. SF: Whitaker & Ray, 1905. 1st ed. Frontis, 6 plts. VG. Howes J 240. *Oregon.* $175/£113

JONES, TERRY. Lee's Tigers. Baton Rouge: LSUP, 1987. 1st ed. Dj. *Lambeth.* $30/£19

JONES, THELMA. Once Upon a Lake. A History of Lake Minnetonka.... Minneapolis: Ross & Haines, 1969. Rev ed. 48 plts. NF in VG dj (lt sunned). *Connolly.* $32/£21

JONES, THOMAS. The Gregynog Press. Oxford, 1954. One of 750. Dj sl dknd, offset to eps, else Fine w/spare label at rear. *Veatchs.* $90/£58

JONES, U.J. History of the Early Settlement of the Juniata Valley.... Phila, 1856. 1st ed. 380pp. Spine gouged, dampspots fr cvr, o/w tight. Howes J 244. *Hayman.* $75/£48

JONES, VIRGIL CARRINGTON. The Civil War at Sea. NY: Holt, Rinehart & Winston, (1960-1962). 1st eds. 3 vols. Orig cl. Owner stamp, else NF VG djs (spines darkened). *Mcgowan.* $125/£81

JONES, VIRGIL CARRINGTON. Gray Ghosts and Rebel Raiders. Henry Holt, (c1956). (2nd ptg). VG. *Book Broker.* $40/£26

JONES, VIRGIL CARRINGTON. Ranger Mosby. Chapel Hill: Univ of NC, (1944). 1st ed. VG in VG dj. *Mcgowan.* $85/£55

JONES, VIRGIL CARRINGTON. Ranger Mosby. Chapel Hill: Univ of NC Press, (1944). 1st ed. Brn cl. VG in dj (edgeworn). *Chapel Hill.* $125/£81

JONES, W.F. The Experiences of a Deputy U.S. Marshall of the Indian Territory. N.p., (1937). VG+ in wraps. *Pratt.* $35/£23

JONES, WILLIAM. Finger-Ring Lore. London, 1877. xvi,545,32pp cat. (Sl faded; sl chipped.) *Edwards.* $140/£90

JONG, ERICA. Fear of Flying. Secker, 1974. 1st UK ed. NF in dj. *Williams.* $39/£25

JONG, ERICA. Fruits and Vegetables. Holt, Rinehart & Winston, (1971). 1st ed, 1st bk. Fine in NF dj. *Sadlon.* $20/£13

JONG, ERICA. Loveroot. NY, 1975. 1st Amer ed. Signed. Fine in Fine dj. *Polyanthos.* $30/£19

JONVEAUX, EMILE. Two Years in East Africa.... London: T. Nelson, 1876. 1st Eng ed. Engr frontis, xii,(13)407,(1)blank,(8)ads, 2 fldg maps. (Lt foxing.) Red cl, dec in black/gilt (presentation plt; extrms sl rubbed). *Morrell.* $186/£120

JOPPIEN, RUDIGER and BERNARD SMITH. The Art of Captain Cook's Voyages.... New Haven/London: Yale Univ Press, 1985. 4 vols. As New in djs. *Reese.* $750/£484

JORDAN, D.S. The Days of a Man. NY, 1922. One of 390 numbered sets signed in both vols. 2 vols. 8vo. Port. 1/2 morocco, blindstamped cl. Djs. *Sutton.* $500/£323

JORDAN, D.S. Fishes. NY, 1907. 18 color plts. Clean (binding sl loose). *Wheldon & Wesley.* $93/£60

JORDAN, NEIL. The Past. London: Cape, 1980. 1st UK ed. Fine in NF dj (price-clipped). *Williams.* $39/£25

JORDAN, PAT. A False Spring. Dodd & Mead, 1975. 1st ed. Fine in VG dj. *Plapinger.* $40/£26

JORDAN, TERESA. Cowgirls. GC, 1982. 1st ed. Sl bumped, o/w Fine in dj (edge worn). *Baade.* $40/£26

JORDAN, W.H. The Feeding of Animals. NY, (1901). *Sutton.* $40/£26

JOSCELYN, ARCHIE. The Golden Bowl. Cleveland: IFL, 1931. 1st ed. Illus cvr. VF in pict dj. *Else Fine.* $50/£32

JOSEPHSON, HANNAH. The Golden Threads: New England's Mill Girls and Magnates. NY: Duell, Sloan & Pearce, (1949). 1st ed. Tan cl (spine ends sl chipped). Dj (reinforced). *Petrilla.* $30/£19

JOSEPHUS, FLAVIUS. The Genuine Works of Flavius Josephus, The Jewish Historian.... William Winston (trans). Boston: Samuel Walker, 1849. 2 vols. 4to. x,(11)-572; 541,(28)pp; engr frontis, titles; 28 full-pg plts; 1 fldg plt (tear). 1/2 morocco, pebbled cl dec w/gilt borders, spine; marbled eps. Foxing; wear, bumping o/w Good. *Laurie.* $150/£97

JOSEPHUS, FLAVIUS. The Works. William Winston (trans). Edinburgh, 1815. 6 vols. 1/2 calf, marbled bds (edges sl rubbed), gilt raised bands, leather title labels. (Tp sl spotted, inner margin torn; 1st few leaves vol 1 sl browned.) *Edwards.* $116/£75

JOSEPHY, ALVIN M., JR. The Nez Perce Indians and the Opening of the Northwest. New Haven: Yale Univ Press, 1965. 1st ed. Grn cl (edges sl faded). NF (pg edges lt spotted) in NF dj. *Harrington.* $70/£45

JOSEPHY, ALVIN M., JR. The Nez Perce Indians and the Opening of the Northwest. New Haven: Yale Univ Press, 1965. 1st ed. Yale Western Americana Series #10. Ink name, else VG in VG dj. *Perier.* $80/£52

JOSLIN, ELLIOTT P. The Treatment of Diabetes Mellitus.... Phila, 1917. (Marginal dampstaining; cl worn.) *Goodrich.* $65/£42

JOST, LUDWIG. Lectures on Plant Physiology. R.J. Harvey Gibson (trans). Oxford, 1907. 1st ed in English. 1/4 morocco. VG. *Argosy.* $125/£81

JOURDAIN, MARGARET and F. ROSE. English Furniture. The Georgian Period 1750-1830. Batsford, 1953. 1st ed. Color frontis. (Ex-lib, ink stamp tp verso; label remains; tape mks.) Dj (sl soiled, ragged). *Edwards.* $78/£50

JOURDAIN, MARGARET. English Decoration and Furniture of the Early Renaissance (1500-1650). London: Batsford, 1924. 1st ed. Color frontis. (Fep lt browned; sl rubbed.) *Edwards.* $194/£125

JOURDAIN, MARGARET. English Decoration and Furniture of the Later XVIIIth Century. NY/London, n.d. (Tp sl spotted; spine faded; bd edges sl damp-stained.) Edwards. $194/£125

JOURDAIN, MARGARET. English Interiors in Smaller Houses. NY: Scribner's, n.d. (1923). 1st ed. Text lt yellowed, smudge 1/2 title, else VG. Bookpress. $125/£81

JOURDAIN, MARGARET. Regency Furniture 1795-1830. London: Country Life, 1965. Rev, enlgd. 4 color plts. Dj (ragged). Edwards. $70/£45

Journal of a Naturalist. (By J.L. Knapp.) London, 1829. 2nd ed. xvi,423pp; 7 plts (1 color). Orig cl (rebacked; spine faded). Wheldon & Wesley. $47/£30

Journal of a Voyage of Discovery to the Arctic Regions.... (By Alexander Fisher.) London: Richard Phillips, 1819. 1st ed. viii,104pp, chart, 3 diags. Recent full leather. Good+. Walcot. $171/£110

Journal of a Young Lady of Virginia, 1782. John Murphy, 1871. VG- (spine worn). Book Broker. $50/£32

Journal of an African Cruiser. (By Horatio Bridge.) NY/London: Wiley/Putnam, 1845. viii,179pp. 3/4 leather, marbled bds (orig wrappers bound in). BAL 593. Schoyer. $175/£113

Journal of Sentimental Travels in the Southern Provinces of France, Shortly Before the Revolution. (By William Combe.) London: Ackermann, 1821. 8vo. 2ff,291pp, 18 hand-colored aquatint plts from designs by Rowlandson. Rmdr binding of orange cl, gilt spine. Marlborough. $930/£600

Journal of the Constitutional Convention of the Commonwealth of Massachussetts...May, 1853. Boston: White & Potter, 1853. Contemp sheep (rubbed, worn). Boswell. $100/£65

Journal of the Life, Travels, Labours, and Religious Exercises of Isaac Martin. Phila, 1834. 160pp (lt foxing). Orig full speckled calf. Cullen. $75/£48

Journal of the Senate of the State of New York: At their Twenty-Eighth...Sixth Day of November, 1804.... Albany: John Barber. 1st ed. (ii),168+2pp index; lg fldg pg. Untrimmed. VG (sl foxing; later cl; spine ends frayed). Connolly. $165/£106

Journal, of a Young Man of Massachusetts...Who Was Captured by the British.... (By Benjamin Waterhouse.) Boston: Rowe & Hooper, 1816. 1st ed. 228pp, fldg plan. Contemp calf (soiled; fr hinge weak). Howes W 155. Lefkowicz. $450/£290

Journals of the American Congress: From 1774-1788. Washington: Way & Gideon, 1823. 4 vols. Thick 8vo. Contemp calf; leather labels (rubbed). Argosy. $400/£258

Journey to the Gold Diggins. By Jeremiah Saddlebags. Burlingame: William P. Wreden, 1950. Facs ed. One of 390. 112 illus by J.A. & D.F. Read. Red cl-backed patterned bds. Fine in NF plain blue paper wrapper. Howes R 92. Harrington. $100/£65

Journey to the Western Islands of Scotland. (By Samuel Johnson.) London: W. Strahan & T. Cadell, 1775. 2nd ed, w/6-line errata. Commonly denoted '2nd issue of 1st ed.' (2),384pp. Contemp calf (rebacked). Early ink name title, foxing, bds sl edgeworn, else VG. Reese. $225/£145

JOUTEL, HENRI. Joutel's Journal of LaSalle's Last Voyage 1684-1687. Albany: Joseph McDonough, 1906. Ltd to 500. NF. Bishop. $40/£26

JOYCE, C.R.B. and S.H. CURRY (eds). The Botany and Chemistry of Cannabis. London, 1970. Tp mkd, else VG+ in dj. Brooks. $36/£23

JOYCE, JAMES. Anna Livia Plurabelle. London: Faber & Faber, (1930). 1st British trade ed, clbound issue. Gilt cl. Label rear pastedown, o/w NF. Reese. $150/£97

JOYCE, JAMES. Anna Livia Plurabelle. London, (1930). 1st Eng ed. Sewn wraps, uncut. Plain wraps in dj (split at center fold; chipped). King. $40/£26

JOYCE, JAMES. Chamber Music. NY: Huebsch, 1923. Correct 2nd authorized Amer ed. Black bds. Laid-in news clipping of poem. Spine worn, else Good. Pharos. $45/£29

JOYCE, JAMES. Collected Poems of James Joyce. NY: Black Sun, 1936. 1st Amer ed. Frontis port. Spine sl sunned, o/w Fine in glassine dj. Polyanthos. $600/£387

JOYCE, JAMES. Dubliners. NY: Modern Library, (1926). 'First Modern Library Edition 1926.' VG-. Pharos. $30/£19

JOYCE, JAMES. Exiles. NY: B.W. Huebsch, 1918. 1st Amer ed. 8vo. Cl-backed bds. VG (bksellers' tickets rear pastedown, few pg corners creased) in dj (lt soiled; chips, tape repairs). Chapel Hill. $750/£484

JOYCE, JAMES. Finnegans Wake. Viking, 1939. 1st Amer ed. VG+ in dj (chipping upper margins). Fine Books. $295/£190

JOYCE, JAMES. Finnegans Wake. NY: Viking, 1939. 1st Amer trade ed. Orig black buckram. NF in VG dj (sunned, few sm chips). Chapel Hill. $450/£290

JOYCE, JAMES. Finnegans Wake. NY: Viking Press, 1939. 1st US trade ed. VG (no dj). Second Life. $75/£48

JOYCE, JAMES. Haveth Childers Everywhere. Paris: Henry Babou & Jack Kahane, 1930. 1st ed. #302/500. 4to. Orig ptd wraps. NF in NF orig glassine dj, pub;s slipcase (edges sl split). Chapel Hill. $900/£581

JOYCE, JAMES. Haveth Childers Everywhere. Paris/NY: Henry Babou & Jack Kahane/Fountain Press, 1930. 1st ed. One of 500 numbered (one of 250 for America). Uncut. Fine in orig white ptd wrappers (w/o slipcase). Macdonnell. $575/£371

JOYCE, JAMES. Haveth Childers Everywhere. London: Faber & Faber, 1931. 1st Eng ed. VG in wrappers. Limestone. $55/£35

JOYCE, JAMES. The Joyce Book. London: Sylvan Press, (1933). 1st ed, ltd to 500 numbered. Port. Folio. Dk blue silk stamped in silver. Lt wear at tips of spine, corners binding, else NF. Godot. $950/£613

JOYCE, JAMES. Letters of James Joyce. Stuart Gilbert (ed). London: Faber, 1957. 1st ed. Fine in NF dj (sm chips). Beasley. $65/£42

JOYCE, JAMES. The Mime of Mick, Nick and the Maggies. Hague/NY: Servire Press/Gotham Book Mart, 1934. #616/1000. VG in self wraps (lacks slipcase, tissue wrapper). Williams. $543/£350

JOYCE, JAMES. Pomes Penyeach. Paris: Shakespeare & Co., 1927. 1st ed. Errata slip tipped in at rear as issued. Ptd pale grn bds. NF (sm label at rear; edges sl dknd). Chapel Hill. $350/£226

JOYCE, JAMES. Pomes Penyeach. London: Faber & Faber, 1933. 1st Eng ed. VG in wrappers. Limestone. $95/£61

JOYCE, JAMES. A Portrait of the Artist as a Young Man. (NY): Penguin/Signet, (1948). 1st ed. Fine in wraps. Pharos. $40/£26

JOYCE, JAMES. A Portrait of the Artist as a Young Man. Leipzig: Tauchnitz, 1930. 1st thus. Vol 4937. Ads dated May 1930. VG in ptd wrappers. *Limestone.* $85/£55

JOYCE, JAMES. Two Tales of Shem and Shaun. London: Faber & Faber, 1932. 1st London ed. (Edges, backstrip sl dknd; sig, address.) Dj (spine very dknd; water stain, dust soiling). *Cox.* $47/£30

JOYCE, JAMES. Two Tales of Shem and Shaun. Faber, 1932. 1st UK ed. NF in dj (sl rubbed). *Sclanders.* $109/£70

JOYCE, JAMES. Ulysses. London: John Lane, (1936). 1st Eng ed. One of 900 on Japon vellum. Grn cl. VG in dj (torn back cvr). *Argosy.* $950/£613

JOYCE, JAMES. Ulysses. London: Egoist Press, 1922. 2nd ed (1st London). #1517/2000. Lg sq 8vo. Teg. 1/2 lt blue morocco, ribbed gilt dec spine; orig wraps bound in. *D & D.* $1,350/£871

JOYCE, JAMES. Ulysses. Paris: Shakespeare, 1927. 9th ed. Cl-backed marbled bds. VG in marbled bd slipcase. *Argosy.* $300/£194

JOYCE, JAMES. Ulysses. Paris: Shakespeare & Co, 1927. 9th ptg. Blue buckram stamped in gilt; wrappers not retained. VG. *Reese.* $75/£48

JOYCE, JAMES. Ulysses. Paris, 1930. 1st ed, 11th ptg. 3/4 burgundy leather (rubbed; lt scuffed), marbled bds (edgewear); teg; ribbon marker. Overall VG (paper lt tanned; blindstamp 1/2 title). *Mcclintock.* $125/£81

JOYCE, JAMES. Ulysses. Paris: Shakespeare and Co, 1930. Stated 11th ptg. Contemp cl; marbled bds, eps; orig blue fr wrapper bound in. Teg. VG. *Schoyer.* $175/£113

JOYCE, JAMES. Ulysses. Hamburg/Paris/Bologna: Odyssey Press, 1933. 2nd impression. 2 vols. VG (vol 1 starting fr hinge repaired) in wraps. *Else Fine.* $45/£29

JOYCE, JAMES. Ulysses. NY: Random House, 1934. 1st Amer ed. Fine (except for sm tape repair to prelim) in dj (tiny chips on one sm tape repair on verso). *Dermont.* $350/£226

JOYCE, JAMES. Ulysses. (NY: Random House, 1934.) 1st Amer ed. Lacks dj, else Fine. *Pharos.* $95/£61

JOYCE, JAMES. Ulysses. NY: LEC, 1935. One of 1500 numbered, signed by Henri Matisse (illus). 1st Amer ptg of the corrected Odyssey Press text. 4to. Gilt-stamped cl. Fine in slipcase (lt mks). *Reese.* $4,000/£2,581

JOYCE, JAMES. Ulysses. London: John Lane, 1937. 1st Eng 'trade' ed. (Sl rubbed, soiled.) *Cox.* $39/£25

JOYCE, JAMES. Ulysses. London: John Lane, Bodley Head, 1937. 1st Eng trade ed. Grn cl, gilt. Fine in Very Nice dj (sl aging, rubbing). *Macdonnell.* $375/£242

JOYCE, STANISLAUS. My Brother's Keeper. NY: Viking, 1958. 1st ed. Fine in Fine dj (sl soil; short tear). *Beasley.* $35/£23

JUAN Y SANTACILLA, JORGE and ANTONIO DE ULLOA. A Voyage to South America. Dublin: Ptd for William Williamson, 1758. 2 vols. 378; 356pp, 5 copper-engr plts (3 fldg). Nicely rebound in 20th cent calf over marbled bds, gilt. *Karmiole.* $600/£387

JUDD, DAVID W. (ed). Life and Writings of Frank Forester. NY: OJ, 1882. 1st ed. 2 vols. 300; 300pp, frontispieces w/guards. Blind borders, gold lettering. Lt worn; scrapes vol II; bkpl, inscrip, else VG. BAL 8178. *Cahan.* $75/£48

JUDD, LAURA FISH. Honolulu: Sketches of Life...from 1828-1861. Chicago, (1966). Lakeside Classic. VG. *Schoyer.* $25/£16

JUDD, LAURA FISH. Honolulu: Sketches of Life...in the Hawaiian Islands from 1828 to 1861. NY: Randolph, (1880). 2nd, enlgd ed. xiv,258pp; port w/guard. Dec cl. VG. *Petrilla.* $90/£58

JUDSON, ANN H. and JAMES D. KNOWLES. Memoir of Mrs. Ann H. Judson.... Boston: Lincoln & Edmands, 1831. 4th ed. 406pp; port w/guard; fldg map. (Lt foxing.) Calf, gilt rules, red label. *Petrilla.* $40/£26

JUDSON, EDWARD. Life of Adoniram Judson by His Son.... NY: Randolph, (1883). Signed. Frontis port, (xviii),(602)pp (sig), 2 color maps. Brn cl, gilt. *Schoyer.* $45/£29

JUDSON, PHOEBE. A Pioneer's Search for an Ideal Home. Bellingham: privately ptd, 1925. 1st ed. One of 500. Frontis. VG. Howes J 274. *Oregon.* $200/£129

JUGAKU, BUNSHO. Paper-Making by Hand in Japan. Tokyo: Meiji-Shobo, 1959. 1st ed. 24 mtd paper samples. VG in dj (worn). *Hermitage.* $500/£323

Julia and the Pet-Lamb. Portland: Shirley & Hyde, 1827. Amer rpt. 12mo. Full-pg wood engr frontis, 70pp + 1pg ad lower wrapper. Pict buff stiff paper wrappers. Good (restored corners; chipped). *Hobbyhorse.* $90/£58

JULLIAN, PHILIPPE. The Symbolists. London: Phaidon, 1973. 1st ed. VG in dj. *Argosy.* $75/£48

JUNG, C.G. Contributions to Analytical Psychology.... NY: Harcourt Brace, 1928. 1st Amer issue of 1st ed in English. VG. *Reese.* $65/£42

JUNG, C.G. Psychology and Religion: West and East...Volume 11. R.F.C. Hull (trans). London: Routledge & Kegan Paul, (1958). 1st British ed. Ptd grn cl. *Gach.* $45/£29

JUNG, C.G. The Psychology of Dementia Praecox. A.A. Brill (trans). NY, 1936. Uncut. Internally VG. Orig wrappers (frail; spine worn). *Goodrich.* $45/£29

JUNG, C.G. Symbols of Transformation: An Analysis of the Prelude to a Case of Schizophrenia. Collected Works of C.G. Jung Volume 5. Bollingen Series XX. NY: Pantheon Books, (1956). 1st ed of this trans. VG. *Gach.* $60/£39

JUNGER, ERNST. The Storm of Steel. London: C&W, 1941. 1st ed. Blue buckram. Spine faded, o/w Fine. *Temple.* $31/£20

JUNIUS. Letters. London: J. Walker, 1807. Tall 12mo. Engr frontis, title (sl browned); xx,366pp (sig). Full splashed calf, gilt. *Hollett.* $47/£30

Jurgen and the Censor. (By James Branch Cabell). NY, 1920. #419/458. Uncut. NF (bkpl; sl sunned, sl rubbed, sm stain). *Polyanthos.* $40/£26

JUST, WARD. A Soldier of the Revolution. NY: Knopf, 1970. 1st ed. NF in VG+ dj (spine sl dknd; sticker). *Lame Duck.* $150/£97

JUSTER, NORTON. The Phantom Tollbooth. NY: Epstein & Carroll, (1961). 1st Amer ed. Jules Feiffer (illus). NF (bd extrems sl dknd) in VG- dj (few tears; rubbing; faint stain). *Between The Covers.* $350/£226

JUSTICE, JEAN. Dictionary of Marks and Monograms of Delft Pottery. London: Herbert Jenkins, (1930). 1st ed. Gilt-lettered grn cl. Fine in dj (chipped). *House.* $120/£77

JUSTICE, JEAN. Dictionary of Marks and Monograms of Delft Pottery. London, 1930. 1st ed. (Feps lt spotted; damp-spotted.) Dj. *Edwards.* $101/£65

Juvenile Rambles through the Paths of Nature. (By Richard Johnson.) Swaffham: F. Skill, 1830. New ed rev by E.H. Barker. 12mo. Full-pg hand-colored wood engr frontis, engr ptd devide tp, viii + 168pp + 2pp list. Orig dk red roan back, marbled paper on bds, gilt title spine (1 cut colored by child; ink dedication; shelf wear; spine chipped; lt spotting). *Hobbyhorse.* $175/£113

K

KADAR, ISMAIL. The General of the Dead Army. Derek Coltman (trans). NY: Grossman, 1972. 1st US ed. Red mk fore-edge, o/w VG in dj. *Worldwide.* $18/£12

KADMAN, LEO. The Coins of the Jewish War of 66-73 C.E. Jerusalem: Schocken, 1960. 1st ed. 2 full-pg maps; 5 photo plts. Errata, addenda sheet. Fine in Good dj (sl chipping; closed tear). *Laurie.* $75/£48

KAEL, PAULINE. The Citizen Kane Book. Little Brown, 1971. 1st ed. VG + in VG dj. *Bishop.* $25/£16

KAESE, HAROLD. The Boston Braves. NY, (1948). 1st ed. VG + in VG dj (edgeworn). *Fuller & Saunders.* $65/£42

KAFKA, FRANZ. America. Edwin & Willa Muir (trans). London: Routledge, 1938. 1st UK ed. VG (sl production creasing to bds). *Williams.* $54/£35

KAFKA, FRANZ. The Castle. London: Secker, 1930. 1st English trans. VG in clean, largely intact dj (extensive worming). *Williams.* $147/£95

KAFKA, FRANZ. Diaries 1910-13. NY: Schocken, (1948). Adv rev copy w/slip, pub's material laid in. Fine in dj (sl dknd). *Between The Covers.* $85/£55

KAFKA, FRANZ. In the Penal Colony. Willa & Edwin Muir (trans). (NY): LEC, (1987). 1/800 numbered, signed by Michael Hafftka (illus). White flexible bds, wallet edges. Fine in linen fldg case. *Argosy.* $400/£258

KAFKA, FRANZ. Letters to Milena. NY: Schocken/FSY, (1953). Adv rev copy, slip laid in. Sl offsetting from slip, else Fine in Fine dj (sl rubbing; sm tear). *Between The Covers.* $85/£55

KAFKA, FRANZ. The Metamorphosis. A.L. Lloyd (trans). (London): The Parton Press, 1937. 1st ed in English. 8vo. Grey bds, blue cl spine, paper cvr label. Fine in glassine dj (chipped). *Chapel Hill.* $1,500/£968

KAFKA, FRANZ. The Trial. Avon: LEC, 1975. One of 2000 numbered, signed by Alan Cober (illus). Full red leather; gilt, blind titled. Fine in pub's slipcase. *Hermitage.* $175/£113

KAFTAL, GEORGE. Iconography of the Saints in Central and South Italian Schools of Painting. Florence, 1965. 1 color illus. Good (backstrip top sl bumped). *Washton.* $475/£306

KAFTAL, GEORGE. Iconography of the Saints in Tuscan Painting. Florence, 1952. One of 1000. Good. *Washton.* $400/£258

KAGANOVICH, ABRAAM L. Arts of Russia: 17th and 18th Centuries. Cleveland, (1968). Buckram. VG in dj, box. *Argosy.* $85/£55

KAHLENBERG, MARY HUNT and ANTHONY BERLANT. The Navajo Blanket. L.A.: Praeger, (1972). VG in wraps. *Perier.* $60/£39

KAHLER, HEINZ. Hagia Sophia. Ellyn Childs (trans). London, 1967. 4 tipped-in color plts, 75 b/w plts. Dj. *Edwards.* $59/£38

KAHN, E.J. The Big Drink. Random House, 1960. 1st ed. VG + in VG dj. *Bishop.* $22/£14

KAHN, EDGAR M. Andrew Smith Hallidie: A Tribute to a Pioneer California Industrialist. SF: (Edgar M. Kahn), 1953. 1st ed. One of 275. Brn cl. Fine. *Harrington.* $35/£23

KAHN, EDGAR M. Cable Car Days in San Francisco. Stanford: Stanford Univ, 1948. Rev ed. Pict cl. NF in dj (worn). *Connolly.* $25/£16

KAHN, GORDON. Hollywood on Trial. NY: Boni & Gaer, (1948). 1st ed. Ink owner stamp pastedown, else NF in VG dj (lt frayed, spine sunned, price-clipped). *Reese.* $30/£19

KAHN, HERMAN. On Thermonuclear War. Princeton, NJ: Princeton Univ, 1960. 1st ed. Good in dj (sl chipped). *Karmiole.* $35/£23

KAHN, JAMES. The Umpire's Story. Putnam's, 1953. 1st ed. VG + in VG + dj. *Plapinger.* $60/£39

KAHN, RUBEN. Tissue Immunity. Springfield, 1936. 1st ed. Good. *Fye.* $50/£32

KAHNWEILER, DANIEL-HENRY. Juan Gris. His Life and Work. Douglas Cooper (trans). London: Lund Humphries, 1947. Frontis port, 113 plts. VF. *Europa.* $81/£52

KAHNWEILER, DANIEL-HENRY. Juan Gris. His Life and Work. London: Thames & Hudson, 1969. Enlgd ed. 24 mtd color illus. Sound in dj. *Ars Artis.* $388/£250

KAIGH, FREDERICK. Witchcraft and Black Magic of Africa. London: Richard Lesley & Co, 1947. 1st Eng ed. Grn cl (ex-lib). Mkd, o/w VG. *Dalian.* $54/£35

KALLIR, OTTO. Grandma Moses. NY, (1973). VG in dj (sl dknd, sm tear). *King.* $95/£61

KALOKYRIS, KONSTANTIN. The Byzantine Wall Paintings of Crete. NY, 1973. Good in dj. *Washton.* $50/£32

KALVEN, HARRY and HANS ZEISEL. The American Jury. Chicago: Univ of Chicago Press, 1966. *Boswell.* $50/£32

KAMINSKY, STUART M. A Fine Red Rain. NY: Scribner, 1987. 1st ed. Fine in Fine dj. *Janus.* $25/£16

KAMINSKY, STUART M. The Man Who Shot Lewis Vance. NY: St. Martin, 1986. 1st ed. Fine in Fine dj. *Janus.* $30/£19

KAMINSKY, STUART M. Rostnikov's Corpse. London: Macmillan, 1981. 1st hb ed. VF in dj. *Mordida.* $150/£97

KAMM, JOSEPHINE. The Story of Emmeline Pankhurst. NY: Meredith Press, (1961). 1st US ed. Port. Grn cl. VG in pict dj. *Petrilla.* $20/£13

KAMPFER, FRITZ and KLAUS G. BEYER. Glass. Dr. Edmund Launert (trans). London, 1966. (Damp-staining.) Dj (chipped). *Edwards.* $47/£30

KANAVEL, ALLEN. Infections of the Hand.... Phila, 1914. 2nd ed. 147 engr. VG. *Goodrich.* $65/£42

KANDINSKY, WASSILY. The Art of Spiritual Harmony. M.T.H. Sadler (trans). London, 1914. 1st Eng ed. 9 plts. Uncut, paper spine label. (Few margins lt browned, hinges repaired; sl worn; rebacked, much of orig spine laid down.) *Edwards.* $388/£250

KANE, ELISHA KENT. Arctic Explorations in Search of Sir John Franklin. London: T. Nelson, 1882. Rpt of 1856 ed. Frontis, 443,(1)pp; fldg map. Contemp 1/2 calf (rubbed). *Lefkowicz.* $75/£48

KANE, ELISHA KENT. Arctic Explorations, the Second Grinnell Expedition in Search of Sir John Franklin, 1853,54,55. Phila: Childs & Peterson, 1856. 1st ed. 2 vols. 2 frontispieces; 464; 467pp; 3 maps (2 fldg); 18 plts. Pict emb cl (spine ends worn; sm chip spine top vol 1). VG. *Oregon.* $125/£81

KANE, ELISHA KENT. Arctic Explorations: The Second Grinnell Expedition in Search of Sir John Franklin 1853, '54, '55. Phila: Childs & Peterson, 1856. 2 vols. 1st ed. 464; 467pp. Extra engr titles, 20 engr plts, 2 fldg maps. Recent half calf, marbled bds. Fine. *High Latitude.* $150/£97

KANE, ELISHA KENT. The U.S. Grinnell Expedition in Search of Sir John Franklin. NY: Harper & Bros, 1854. 1st ed. 552pp; 12 plts, 3 maps (1 fldg). Brn cl, gilt. Nice, (spine extrems lt chipped; bkpl). *Karmiole.* $150/£97

KANE, ELISHA KENT. The U.S. Grinnell Expedition in Search of Sir John Franklin. NY: Harper, 1854. Rpt. 552pp; 2 maps (1 fldg), 15 plts. Orig cl. *Lefkowicz.* $125/£81

KANE, HARNETT T. The Gallant Mrs. Stonewall, A Novel Based on the Lives of General and Mrs. Stonewall Jackson. GC, 1957. Reprint. VG+ in VG+ dj. *Pratt.* $20/£13

KANE, HARNETT T. Plantation Parade. NY: Morrow, 1945. 'Louisiana Edition.' Signed. Fine in dj (sl used). *Pharos.* $20/£13

KANE, JOSEPH N. Famous First Facts; A Record...in the United States. NY, 1933. 1st ed. VG. *Argosy.* $85/£55

KANE, PAUL. Wanderings of an Artist Among the Indians of North America from Canada.... Radisson Soc, 1925. 2 ports. Upper corner of rear bd bent, o/w VG. Howes K 7. *Oregon.* $70/£45

KANNER, LEO. Child Psychiatry. Springfield, 1937. 1st ed, 2nd ptg. Signed. Good. *Fye.* $150/£97

Kansas. NY: Viking, 1939. 1st ed. Fldg map rear pocket. Grn cl. Sm owner sticker tp, lg inscrip 1/2 title, else Fine. *Glenn.* $65/£42

KANT, IMMANUEL. Critick of Pure Reason. London: William Pickering, 1838. 1st Eng translation. Mod 1/2 calf, red morocco lettering-piece. Pub's cat bound in. (Lib stamps.) *Waterfield.* $388/£250

KANTOR, MACKINLAY. Diversey. NY: Coward-McCann, 1928. 1st ed, 1st bk. Red cl. Beige ptd dj (torn, chipped; top 1/2 of back missing). *Juvelis.* $150/£97

KANTOR, McKINLEY. Turkey in the Straw. NY: Coward-McCann, 1935. 1st trade ed. 1/2 buckram; pict bds. Fine (handwritten poem fep) in dj (lg chip). *Pharos.* $75/£48

KANTOR. MacKINLAY, Lee and Grant at Appomattox. NY: Random House, 1950. 1st trade ed. Donald McKay (illus). Dec eps. VG in dj. *Cattermole.* $35/£23

KAO, MAYCHING (ed). Twentieth-Century Chinese Painting. OUP, 1988. Color frontis, 19 color plts. Dj. *Edwards.* $47/£30

KARDINER, ABRAM. The Bio-analysis of the Epileptic Reaction. Albany, NY: Psychoanalytic Quarterly Press, 1932. 1st separate ed. Presentation copy. Brn cl. VG. *Gach.* $75/£48

KAREL, LEONARD. A Dictionary of Antibiosis. NY, 1951. 1st ed. Good in dj. *Fye.* $50/£32

KARLSSON, LENNART. Medieval Ironwork in Sweden. Stockholm, 1988. 2 vols. Good (corners sl bumped). *Washton.* $200/£129

KAROUZOU, SEMNI. The Amasis Painter. Oxford: Clarendon Press, 1956. 44 plts. Fine in dj. *Archaeologia.* $300/£194

KARR, CHARLES LEE, JR. and CARROLL ROBBINS KARR. Remington Handguns. Harrisburg: Stackpole, 1951. 2nd ptg. Fine in dj (chipped). *Bowman.* $35/£23

KARR, JEAN. Zane Grey, Man of the West. NY: Greenberg, (1949). VG in VG dj. *Perier.* $50/£32

KARRAKER, CYRUS HARRELD. The Seventeenth-Century Sheriff: A Comparative Study.... Chapel Hill: Univ of NC Press, 1930. 1st ed. Unopened. Fine. *Cahan.* $40/£26

KARSH, YOUSUF. Karsh Portfolio. (Toronto, 1967). 1st ed. 48 ports. VG in dj (sl frayed). *King.* $50/£32

KARSHAN, DONALD H. Picasso Linocuts 1958-1963. NY, (1968). 1st ed w/errata. Sm defect rep, else VG in dj (edgetorn). *King.* $75/£48

KART, LAWRENCE. That Old Ball Game. David R. Phillips (ed). Regenry, 1975. 1st ed. Fine in VG+ dj. *Plapinger.* $50/£32

KASANIN, J.S. Language and Thought in Schizophrenia. Berkeley, 1944. 1st ed. Signed. Good. *Fye.* $30/£19

KASER, D. A Book for Sixpence. Beta Phi Mu, 1980. 1st ed. 5 plts. 1/4 white linen. Fine. *Moss.* $40/£26

KASHNER, RITA. Bed Rest. NY: Macmillan, (1981). 1st ed. Fine in Fine dj. *Robbins.* $25/£16

KASSNER, THEO. My Journey from Rhodesia to Egypt. London: Hutchinson, 1911. 1st ed. 3 maps (1 fldg), 40 plts ptd recto, verso. (Few leaves foxed, lt browning.) Blue cl, (cvrs sl warped, rubbed), teg. *Morrell.* $109/£70

KASTNER, ERICH. Emil and the Detectives. London: Cape, (1931). 1st Eng ed. 8vo. Illus yellow cl (dknd). *Reisler.* $175/£113

KASTNER, ERICH. The Simpletons. Richard & Clara Winston (trans). NY: Julian Messner, (1957). 1st ed thus. 4to. Red cl, black lettering, dec. Good in color dj (marginal tears; red mks). *Reisler.* $85/£55

KATZENELLENBOGEN, ADOLF. The Sculptural Programs of Chartres Cathedral: Christ—Mary—Ecclesia. Balt: Johns Hopkins Press, (1959). 1st ed. VG in dj. *Argosy.* $150/£97

KAUFFMAN, HENRY J. Early American Ironware, Cast and Wrought. Rutland: Charles E. Tuttle, (1966). 1st ed. Ex-lib, bkpl, else VG in dj. *Bookpress.* $45/£29

KAUFMAN, BOB. Golden Sardine. (SF): City Lights, (1967). 1st ed. Fine in wrappers. *Pharos.* $35/£23

KAUFMAN, BOB. Solitudes Crowded with Loneliness. (NY, 1965). 1st ed, 1st bk. VG in pict wraps (lt rubbed). *Petrilla.* $35/£23

KAUFMAN, LEWIS et al. Moe Berg—Athlete, Scholar, Spy. Little-Brown, 1974. 1st ed. VG (tape stains cvrs) in VG+ dj. *Plapinger.* $60/£39

KAUFMANN, EDGAR, JR. Fallingwater, A Frank Lloyd Wright Country House. NY: Abbeville, (1986). 1st ed. Quadruple frontis. Bkpl; else Fine. *Bookpress.* $85/£55

KAVANAGH, DAN. (Pseud of Julian Barnes.) Duffy. London: Cape, 1980. 1st ed. Fine in dj. *Rees.* $47/£30

KAVANAGH, DAN. (Pseud of Julian Barnes). Duffy. London: Cape, 1980. 1st UK ed. Fine in dj. *Lewton.* $39/£25

KAVANAGH, DAN. (Pseud of Julian Barnes). Going to the Dogs. NY, (1987). 1st ed. Fine in Fine dj. *Fuller & Saunders.* $25/£16

KAVANAGH, DAN. (Pseud of Julian Barnes.) Going to the Dogs. London: Cape, 1987. VF in dj. *Else Fine.* $65/£42

KAVANAGH, DAN. (Pseud of Julian Barnes.) Putting the Boot In. London: Cape, 1985. 1st ed. Fine in dj. *Rees.* $31/£20

KAVANAGH, DAN. (Pseud of Julian Barnes.) Putting the Boot In. Cape, 1985. 1st UK ed. Fine in dj. *Lewton.* $39/£25

KAVANAGH, H.T. Darby O'Gill and the Good People. Putnam's, 1932. VG in dj (sm chips). *Aronovitz.* $45/£29

KAVANAGH, PATRICK. A Soul for Sale. London: Macmillan, 1947. 1st ed. Fine in dj (sl rubbed). *Jaffe.* $150/£97

KAY, HELEN. Picasso's World of Children. London: Macdonald, 1965. Fine in clean dj. *Europa.* $54/£35

KAYE-SMITH, SHEILA. Joanna Godden Married and Other Stories. London: Cassell, (1926). 1st Eng ed. Gilt blue cl. Handsome in dj. *Cady.* $25/£16

KAYE-SMITH, SHEILA. Saints in Sussex. London, 1926. 1st ed. Uncut, teg. Fine (vellum spine sl sunned). *Polyanthos.* $30/£19

KAYE-SMITH, SHEILA. Susan Spray—The Female Preacher. London: Cassell, (1931). 1st trade ed. Fine in dj. *Pharos.* $60/£39

KAYNE, GEORGE and WALTER PAGEL. Pulmonary Tuberculosis: Pathology, Diagnosis.... Oxford, 1939. 1st ed. Good. *Fye.* $75/£48

KAZANTZAKIS, NIKOS. The Fratricides. London: Cassirer, 1967. 1st Eng ed. Red cl. VG in dj (lt used). *Juvelis.* $40/£26

KAZANTZAKIS, NIKOS. Freedom or Death. Jonathan Griffin (trans). NY: S&S, 1956. 1st ed. Dated rev slip laid in. Fine in dj (sl rubbed). *Pharos.* $150/£97

KAZANTZAKIS, NIKOS. The Rock Garden. Richard Howard (trans). NY: S&S, 1963. 1st ed. Nice in dj (sl soiled). *Pharos.* $125/£81

KAZANTZAKIS, NIKOS. Spain. Amy Mims (trans). NY: S&S, 1963. 1st ed. NF in pink dec dj (spine sl sunned; lt used). *Juvelis.* $40/£26

KAZANTZAKIS, NIKOS. Three Plays: Melissa, Kouros, and Christopher Columbus. Athena Gianaka Dallas (trans). NY: S&S, (1969). 1st ed. VG (sig) in dj (sl worn). *Hermitage.* $35/£23

KAZANTZAKIS, NIKOS. Toda Raba. Amy Mims (trans). NY: S&S, 1964. 1st Amer ed. NF in NF dj. *Juvelis.* $50/£32

KAZIN, ALFRED (ed). F. Scott Fitzgerald: The Man and His Work. NY, (1951). 1st ed, review copy. VG in dj. *Argosy.* $45/£29

KEAN, B.H. (ed). Tropical Medicine and Parasitology: Classic Investigations. Ithaca, NY, 1978. 1st ed. 2 vols. Good. *Fye.* $200/£129

KEAN, JAMES. Among the Holy Places: A Pilgrimage through Palestine. London: Fisher, 1891. 1st ed. (ix),386pp; 16 plts. Teg. Sl rubbed, soiled; spine sl torn, o/w VG. *Worldwide.* $75/£48

KEAN, ROBERT GARLICK HILL. Inside the Confederate Government. The Diary of.... NY: OUP, 1957. 1st ed. Fine in NF dj. *Mcgowan.* $45/£29

KEARNEY, PATRICK J. A History of Erotic Literature. London, 1982. 1st ed. Color frontis. Dj (sl chipped). *Edwards.* $39/£25

KEATE, GEORGE. An Account of the Pelew Islands in the Western Part of the Pacific Ocean.... Dublin, 1788. 1st ed. xxix,378pp; fldg chart, 16 plts. 1/2 calf (rebound). Lt internal fading. *Lewis.* $248/£160

KEATING, EDWARD M. Free Huey! Ramparts Press, 1971. 1st ed. NF in dj (rubbed, worn at edges). *Stahr.* $45/£29

KEATING, H.R.F. Inspector Ghote Draws a Line. London: Collins, 1979. 1st ed. Fine in dj (sm ink spot). *Janus.* $30/£19

KEATING, H.R.F. Inspector Ghote's Good Crusade. NY: Dutton, 1966. 1st ed. Sm tear inside cvr, else Fine in VG dj. *Murder.* $40/£26

KEATING, J.M. A History of the Yellow Fever Epidemic of 1878, in Memphis, Tennessee. Memphis, 1879. 1st ed. 454pp. Good. *Fye.* $175/£113

KEATING, J.M. A History of the Yellow Fever. Memphis: Ptd for Howard Assoc, 1879. 454pp. (Wear along joints.) *Schoyer.* $125/£81

KEATING, WILLIAM H. Narrative of an Expedition to the Source of St. Peter's River...1823. Minneapolis: Ross & Haines, 1959. One of 1500. Fldg facs map. Maroon cl, gilt. Fine in dj. Rpt of Howes 5570. *Laurie.* $40/£26

KEATS, EZRA JACK. Whistle for Willie. NY: Viking, (1964). 1st ed. Obl 4to. Sl soiling copyright pg, else Fine in VG dj (short tears; sl loss spine). *Between The Covers.* $75/£48

KEATS, JOHN. Letters of John Keats to Fanny Brawne.... H.B. Forman (ed). London: Reeves & Turner, 1878. 1st ed. Port. Gilt cl. Bkpl, ink note endsheet, lt spots upper bds, o/w VG. *Reese.* $150/£97

KEATS, JOHN. Life, Letters and Literary Remains of John Keats. Richard Monckton Milnes (ed). London: Edward Moxon, 1848. 1st ed. 2 vols. 8vo. (Half-title vol 1 bears Aug. 23, 1848 presentation, short 20th cent inscrip.) VG set (fraying to crown, inner hinges cracked 1st vol; loose sig vol 2). *Dermont.* $450/£290

KEATS, JOHN. The Poems of John Keats. Cambridge: LEC, 1966. One of 1500 numbered, signed by David Gentleman (illus). Fine in pub's slipcase. *Hermitage.* $125/£81

KEATS, JOHN. The Poetical Works. H. Buxton Forman (ed). Humphrey Milford, OUP, 1922. Full calf, gilt spine; teg. Inscrip, o/w Fine. *Sadlon.* $75/£48

KEAYS, MRS. FREDERICK LOVE. Old Roses. NY: Macmillan, 1935. 1st ed. 35 half-tone plts. (Spine faded.) *Quest.* $45/£29

KECK, LIDA M. A Silvern Secret.... Hamilton, OH: Republican Pub Co, 1894. 154pp. *Hayman.* $25/£16

KEDROV, M.S. Book Publishing Under Tzarism. The 'Zerno' Publishing House. NY: Workers Library, 1932. 1st ed. Ptd in U.K. Fine in wraps. *Beasley.* $30/£19

KEELER, CHARLES A. Birds Notes Afield. SF: D.P. Elder & Morgan Shepard, 1899. 1st ed. viii,354pp. Dec gray bds, stamped in grn. Good. *Karmiole.* $30/£19

KEELER, HARRY STEPHEN. The 16 Beans. London: Ward Lock, 1945. 1st Eng ed. VG in dj (sl wear). *Mordida.* $45/£29

KEELER, HARRY STEPHEN. The Case of Two Strange Ladies. NY: Phoenix, 1943. 1st ed. Fine in dj (internal tape mends; scrape; sl wear spine ends). *Mordida.* $50/£32

KEELER, HARRY STEPHEN. The Mysterious Mr. I. NY: E.P. Dutton, 1938. 1st ed. Fine in VG dj (spine end, corner wear; crease; internal stains). *Mordida.* $45/£29

KEELER, WILLIAM FREDERICK. Aboard the USS Florida: 1863-65. Annapolis, (1968). VG + in VG + dj. *Pratt.* $32/£21

KEELY, ROBERT N. and G.G. DAVIS. In Arctic Seas— The Voyage of the 'Kite.' Phila: Rufus C. Hartranft, 1892. vii,524pp, 2 maps (1 fldg). Dec blue cl, gilt titles; silver vignette. Rubbed, else VG. *Parmer.* $125/£81

KEELY, ROBERT N. and G.G. DAVIS. In Arctic Seas. Phila: Rufus C. Hartranft, 1898. vii,524pp. Dec cl, beveled bds (minor soil). VG. *High Latitude.* $80/£52

KEEN, A. and R. LUBBOCK. The Annotator. Putnam's, 1954. (Edges foxed.) Dj (dusty). *Moss.* $28/£18

KEEN, A. MYRA. Sea Shells of Tropical West America. Stanford, CA: Stanford Univ Press, 1958. 10 full-pg color plts. Blue cl (worn). VG. *Shifrin.* $35/£23

KEEN, WILLIAM. The Surgical Complications and Sequels of Typhoid Fever. Phila, 1898. 1st ed. 386pp. Good. *Fye.* $150/£97

KEENE, J. HARRINGTON. Fly-Fishing and Fly-Making for Trout, Etc. NY: OJ, 1887. 1st ed w/2pp of fly-tying material. Brn cl stamped in black/gold. Spine sl chipped, else VG. *Juvelis.* $225/£145

KEENE, J. HARRINGTON. Fly-Fishing and Fly-Making.... NY: Forest & Stream Pub., 1891. 2nd ed. 159,(xi)pp, 2 plts complete w/37 samples. Dec cl, gilt. Fine. *Hollett.* $426/£275

KEEP, J. West Coast Shells. SF, 1911. (Sl tears in text.) *Wheldon & Wesley.* $39/£25

Keeping One Cow. NY: OJ, 1880. (1st ed). 132pp. Brn cl, gilt spine, fr cvr stamped in black/gilt (sl rubbed, soiled, frayed). *Bohling.* $25/£16

KEES, HERMANN. Ancient Egypt: A Cultural Topography. T.G.H. James (ed). London: Faber & Faber, 1961. 25 plts, 11 maps. Good in dj. *Archaeologia.* $65/£42

KEES, WELDON. The Fall of the Magicians. NY: Reynal & Hitchcock, (1947). 1st ed. NF in dj (lt sunned, price-clipped, chip, edgetear mended to verso). *Reese.* $150/£97

KEES, WELDON. The Fall of the Magicians. NY: Reynal & Hitchcock, 1947. 1st ed. VG + in VG dj (spine lt faded; sl chipping, loss extrems). *Lame Duck.* $250/£161

KEFFER, FRANK M. History of San Fernando Valley. Glendale: Stillman Ptg, 1934. Blind, gold-stamped fabricoid (lt wear spine). *Dawson.* $125/£81

KEGLEY, F.B. Kegley's Virginia Frontier.... Southwest VA Hist Soc, 1938. #1826 of 3rd ptg. VG. *Book Broker.* $100/£65

KEILLOR, GARRISON. We Are Still Married. (NY): Viking, (1989). 1st ed. Signed. Fine in dj. *Antic Hay.* $40/£26

KEITH, ARTHUR. An Autobiography. London: Watts, (1950). Frontis port, 5 plts. (Corner lt bumped.) *Archaeologia.* $75/£48

KEITHAN, EDWARD L. Monuments in Cedar. Ketchikan: Roy Anderson, 1945. 1st ed. Fldg map, diag. Very Nice. *Parmer.* $75/£48

KEITHLEY, RALPH. Buckey O'Neill. Caldwell: Caxton Printers, 1949. VG in Fine dj. *Schoyer.* $35/£23

KELEHER, WILLIAM A. The Fabulous Frontier, Twelve New Mexico Items. Albuquerque: Univ of NM, 1962. 1st rev ed. Fine in Fair dj. Howes K 37. *Oregon.* $45/£29

KELEHER, WILLIAM A. Maxwell Land Grant. Santa Fe: (Rydal Press), 1942. 1st ed. Pict cl. Sl soiled, o/w VG. Howes K 38. *Baade.* $200/£129

KELEHER, WILLIAM A. Violence in Lincoln County, 1869-1881: A New Mexico Item. Albuquerque: Univ of NM Press, (1957). 1st ed. Fine in VG + dj (lt chipped, spine dknd). *Harrington.* $95/£61

KELEMEN, PAL. Medieval American Art. NY: Macmillan, 1944. 2nd ptg. 2 vols. 306 plts. Bkpls, else VG set in djs (worn). *Bookpress.* $250/£161

KELEMEN, PAL. Medieval American Art: A Survey in Two Volumes. NY: Macmillan, 1943. 1st ed. 306 plts. Good. *Archaeologia.* $150/£97

KELHAM, ROBERT. Domesday Book Illustrated. London, 1788. Contemp 1/2 calf (joints weak; sm stain title margin). *Petersfield.* $54/£35

KELL, JOHN McINTOSH. Recollections of a Naval Life. Washington: Neale, 1900. 1st ptg. Frontis port. Pict cl. Faint shelf mks on spine, o/w VG. Howes K 39. *Schoyer.* $200/£129

KELL, JOSEPH. (Pseud of Anthony Burgess.) One Hand Clapping. Peter Davies, 1961. 1st UK ed. NF in dj (price-clip; sl nicked, edgeworn; upper panel chipped). *Sclanders.* $233/£150

KELL, JOSEPH. (Pseud of Anthony Burgess.) One Hand Clapping. London: Peter Davies, 1961. 1st UK ed. Fine in VG + dj (lt edgewear, tiny nicks). *Williams.* $426/£275

KELLER, ALBRECHT (trans). A Hangman's Diary...Master Franz Schmidt Public Executioner of Nuremberg, 1573-1617. London: Philip Allan, 1929. *Boswell.* $50/£32

KELLER, DAVID H. Devil and the Doctor. S&S, 1940. 1st ed. VG in dj (frayed). *Madle.* $90/£58

KELLER, DAVID H. The Eternal Conflict. Phila: Prime Press, 1949. 1st ed. #92/400 signed. Partly unopened. Bkpl; closed tear; lacks slipcase, else NF. *Other Worlds.* $60/£39

KELLER, DAVID H. The Folsom Flint. Sauk City: Arkham House, 1969. 1st ed. Blemish fr pastedown, else NF in dj (closed tear). *Other Worlds.* $35/£23

KELLER, DAVID H. The Folsom Flint. Arkham House, 1969. 1st ed. Fine in dj. *Madle.* $40/£26

KELLER, DAVID H. Life Everlasting. Avalon, 1947. 1st ed. Bibliography laid in. NF in Mint dj. *Madle.* $90/£58

KELLER, DAVID H. Tales From Underwood. Arkham House, 1952. 1st ed. Fine in dj (sl nicked). *Madle.* $100/£65

KELLER, GEORGE. A Trip across the Plains and Life in California. Oakland: Biobooks, (1955). Ltd to 500. 1st ptd in 1851. Chocolate brn buckram, gilt (extrems sl worn; sm dent). Nice. Howes K 41. *Shasky.* $45/£29

KELLER, GEORGE. A Trip across the Plains and Life in California. Oakland: Biobooks, (1955). One of 500. Fine. Later ed of Howes K 41. *Bohling.* $45/£29

KELLERMAN, JONATHAN. Blood Test. NY: Atheneum, 1986. 1st ed. Inscribed. VF in dj. *Mordida.* $65/£42

KELLERMAN, JONATHAN. Over the Edge. NY: Atheneum, 1987. 1st ed, adv rev copy w/slip laid in. VF in dj. *Mordida.* $45/£29

KELLERMAN, JONATHAN. When the Bough Breaks. NY: Atheneum, 1985. 1st ed. Fine in dj (sl wear). *Mordida.* $85/£55

KELLEY, D.O. History of the Diocese of California From 1849-1914.... SF, (1915). 1st ed. *Ginsberg.* $85/£55

KELLEY, HALL J. Hall J. Kelley on Oregon. Fred Wilbur Powell (ed). Princeton: Princeton Univ, 1932. 1st ed. 5 tp repros. Red gilt cl (sl rubbed). *Karmiole.* $35/£23

KELLEY, JOSEPH. Thirteen Years in the Oregon Penitentiary. Portland, 1908. 1st ed. Frontis, 8 plts. Wraps. VG. *Oregon.* $125/£81

KELLEY, ROBERT L. Gold vs. Grain-The Hydraulic Mining Controversy in California's Sacramento Valley. Glendale: Clark, 1959. 1st ed. Fine. *Perier.* $97/£63

KELLOGG, J.H. The Household Monitor of Health. Battle Creek, 1891. 1st ed. 408pp. Good. *Fye.* $65/£42

KELLOGG, J.H. Plain Facts for Old and Young. Burlington, IA, 1892. 2nd ed. 660pp. Full leather (binding rubbed; hinges cracked). *Fye.* $75/£48

KELLOGG, LOUISE P. The British Regime in Wisconsin and the Northwest. Madison: Hist Soc WI, 1935. 1st ed. 10 plts. Fine. Howes K 50. *Oregon.* $50/£32

KELLOGG, LOUISE P. The British Regime in Wisconsin and the Northwest. Madison: WI Hist Soc, 1935. 1st ed. Red cl (spine sl faded). VG. Howes K 50. *Chapel Hill.* $125/£81

KELLOGG, LOUISE P. The French Regime in Wisconsin and the Northwest. Madison: WI Hist Soc, 1925. 1st ed. Burgundy cl (spine faded). VG. Howes K 51. *Chapel Hill.* $125/£81

KELLOGG, LOUISE P. (ed). Frontier Advance on the Upper Ohio 1778-1779. Madison: WI Hist Soc, 1916. 1st ed. One of 1250. Map. Blue cl. Internal hinges cracked, else VG. Howes K 52. *Chapel Hill.* $150/£97

KELLOGG, LOUISE P. (ed). Frontier Retreat on the Upper Ohio 1779-1781. Madison: WI Hist Soc, 1917. 1st ed. One of 1250. Blue cl. Blindstamp fep, inkstamp fr pastedown, else VG. Howes K 53. *Chapel Hill.* $150/£97

KELLOGG, SANFORD C. The Shenandoah Valley and Virginia 1861 to 1865. NY/Washington: Neale, (1903). 1st ed. Partly unopened. Orig blue cl. NF. *Chapel Hill.* $275/£177

KELLY, CHARLES. Miles Goodyear, First Citizen of Utah. Salt Lake: Privately ptd, 1937. 1st ed. Ltd to 350 numbered. Frontis. 9 plts. Bkpl, name, o/w Fine in VG dj (ink title on spine, few lines underlined on ads on back). Howes K 56. *Oregon.* $200/£129

KELLY, CHARLES. Old Greenwood, the Story of Caleb Greenwood. Salt Lake: Privately ptd, 1936. 1st ed. One of 350 numbered. VG (bkpl, name) in dj (chipped, torn). Howes K 57. *Oregon.* $200/£129

KELLY, CHARLES. Outlaw Trail: A History of Butch Cassidy and His Wild Bunch.... Salt Lake City: By Author, 1938. 1st ed. One of 1000. Signed. Gilt dec. VG (fr hinge starting; fep stained; inscrip, letter attached to 1st leaf). *Cahan.* $200/£129

KELLY, CHARLES. Salt Desert Trails. Salt Lake City: Western, 1930. Ink name, else VG. Howes K 59. *Perier.* $150/£97

KELLY, DANIEL T. and BEATRICE CHAUVENET. The Buffalo Head. Santa Fe, 1972. 1st ed. Signed presentation by pub. NF in dj (sl chipped). *Baade.* $35/£23

KELLY, DENNIS. Chicken. SF, (1979). 1st ed. VF. *Mcclintock.* $27/£17

KELLY, EBENEZER BERIAH. Ebenezer Beriah Kelly: An Autobiography. Norwich, CT, 1856. 1st ed. 100pp. Howes K 61. *Ginsberg.* $450/£290

KELLY, EMERSON. Classics of Neurology. Huntington, NY, 1971. 1st ed. Good. *Fye.* $45/£29

KELLY, FANNY. Narrative of My Captivity Among the Sioux Indians.... Cincinnati: Wilstach & Baldwin, 1871. 1st ed. 285pp. (Rebound.) Good. Howes K 62. *Hayman.* $75/£48

KELLY, FRANCIS M. and RANDOLPH SCHWABE. A Short History of Costume and Armour Chiefly in England 1066-1800. London/NY, 1931. 1st ed. 2 vols in 1. 68 plts; errata slip. VG. *Argosy.* $125/£81

KELLY, HOWARD and CHARLES NOBLE. Gynecology and Abdominal Surgery. Phila, 1908. 1st ed. 2 vols. Good. *Fye.* $150/£97

KELLY, HOWARD and ELIZABETH HURDON. The Vermiform Appendix and Its Diseases. Phila, 1905. 1st ed. Good. *Fye.* $400/£258

KELLY, HOWARD. Gynecology. NY, 1928. 1st ed. Good. *Fye.* $75/£48

KELLY, HOWARD. Medical Gynecology. NY, 1908. 1st ed. Good. *Fye.* $100/£65

KELLY, HOWARD. Medical Gynecology. NY: Appleton, 1908. 1st ed. Internally Fine (newly recased, orig spine; corners repaired). *Goodrich.* $150/£97

KELLY, HOWARD. Operative Gynecology. NY, 1898. 1st ed. 2 vols. 569; 557pp. Good. *Fye.* $250/£161

KELLY, HOWARD. Snakes of Maryland. Balt, 1936. 1st ed. Spine head, tail chipped. In wrappers. *Fye.* $100/£65

KELLY, HOWARD. Some American Medical Botanists.... NY/Troy, 1929. 43 sepia plts. VG (sl foxing). *Brooks.* $77/£50

KELLY, HUGH. Memoirs of a Magdalen. London: Harrison, 1785. 2nd ed. 2 vols in 1. 85pp. 3/4 calf. Fine. *Second Life.* $150/£97

KELLY, J. WELLS (comp). First Dictionary of Nevada Territory, 1862. Los Gatos: Talisman Press, 1962. One of 750. VG in dj. *Laurie.* $60/£39

KELLY, LAWRENCE. Navajo Roundup. Boulder, 1970. 1st ed. Fldg map in pocket. Fine in dj. *Baade.* $37/£24

KELLY, LEROY VICTOR. The Range Men. Toronto: William Briggs, 1913. Teg. Gold/white-stamped cl (glue stain inner hinges; sl loose; spine worn); 8-pg owner index inserted. *Dawson.* $400/£258

KELLY, LEROY VICTOR. The Range Men: The Story of the Ranchers and Indians of Alberta. Toronto, 1913. 1st ed. Pict cl. Howes K 66. *Ginsberg.* $850/£548

KELLY, ROB ROY. American Wood Type: 1828-1900. NY, (1969). 4to. Fine in dj. *Veatchs.* $85/£55

KELLY, ROBERT. The Scorpions. London: Calder & Boyars, (1969). 1st Eng ed. Fine in dj (short tears). *Heller.* $35/£23

KELLY, SUSAN. The Gemini Man. Walker, 1985. 1st ed. VF in VF dj. *Murder.* $75/£48

KELLY, SUSAN. The Summertime Soldiers. Walker, 1986. 1st ed. VF in VF dj. *Murder.* $45/£29

KELLY, WALT and J. O'REILLY. The Glob. Viking, 1952. 1st ed. NF in NF dj. *Aronovitz.* $150/£97

KELLY, WALT and N. MONATH. Songs of the Pogo. S&S, 1956. 1st ed. Fine in NF dj. *Aronovitz.* $88/£57

KELMAN, JAMES. The Busconductor Hines. Polygon, 1984. 1st ed. Fine in dj (sl rubbed). *Rees.* $19/£12

KELMAN, JAMES. The Busconductor Hines. London: Polygon, 1984. 1st UK ed. Signed. Fine in dj. *Lewton.* $39/£25

KELMAN, JAMES. A Chancer. Polygon, 1985. 1st ed. Fine in dj. *Rees.* $23/£15

KELSEY, ANNA M. Through the Years. San Antonio: Naylor, 1952. 1st ed. *Lambeth.* $45/£29

KELSEY, HENRY. The Kelsey Papers. Ottawa, 1929. 1st ed. Fldg map. Uncut. Fine. *Oregon.* $160/£103

KELSEY, MARY WILSON et al (comps). Robert Wilson, 1750-1826 of Blount County Tennessee.... The comp, 1987. VG (ex-lib). *Book Broker.* $50/£32

KELTON, ELMER. The Good Old Boys. GC, 1978. 1st ed. VG in dj (worn). *Baade.* $65/£42

KEMBLE, E.W. A Coon Alphabet. NY: R.H. Russell, 1898. 1st ed. 4to. Cl-backed illus grey bds, grn lettering (recased, corners worn; marginal tear 1 pg not affecting ptg). *Reisler.* $475/£306

KEMBLE, FRANCES ANN. Journal of a Residence on a Georgian Plantation in 1838-1839. NY: Harper, 1863. 1st US ed, 1st issue w/'about' repeated on line 6, p. 314. 337pp + ads. Good (spine extrems chipped). Howes K70. *Second Life.* $125/£81

KEMELMAN, HARRY. Tuesday the Rabbi Saw Red. NY: Arthur Fields, (1973). 1st ed. Fine in dj (short tear). *Sadlon.* $30/£19

KENAN, RANDALL. A Visitation of Spirits. NY: Grove Press, (1989). 1st ed, 1st bk. Lavender bds, black cl spine. Fine in pict dj. *Chapel Hill.* $35/£23

KENDALL, EDWARD AUGUSTUS. Travels Through the Northern Parts of the United States in the Years 1807 and 1808. NY: I. Riley, 1809. 1st ed. 3 vols. ix,(i)330; vi,(ii)309; vi,(ii)312pp (scattered foxing). Leather-backed bds (worn, chipped). VG internally. Howes K 74. *Blue Mountain.* $275/£177

KENDALL, ELIZABETH. Wayfarer in China. Boston/NY: Houghton Mifflin, 1913. Dbl-pg map. Turquoise dec cl (discolored; foxed; bkpl). *Schoyer.* $65/£42

KENDALL, GEORGE WILKINS. Letters from a Texas Sheep Ranch. Urbana, IL: Univ of IL Press, (1959). 1st ed. Tan cl. Fine in VG dj. *Glenn.* $45/£29

KENDALL, GEORGE WILKINS. Narrative of the Texan Santa Fe Expedition. Chicago, (1929). Lakeside Classic. VG. *Schoyer.* $30/£19

KENDALL, GEORGE WILKINS. Narrative of the Texan Santa Fe Expedition. NY: Harper, 1844. (1st ed.) 2 vols. (2),405; xii,(11)-406pp. Fldg map (short tear), 5 plts. Bright (extrems lt frayed). Howes K 75. *Bohling.* $750/£484

KENDALL, GEORGE WILKINS. Narrative of the Texan Santa Fe Expedition. Chicago: R.R. Donnelly, 1929. Frontis, fldg map. Teg. Red cl (extrems rubbed). VG +. Howes K 75. *Harrington.* $35/£23

KENDALL, GEORGE WILKINS. Wilkins. Narrative of the Texan Santa Fe Expedition. NY, 1844. 1st ed. 2 vols. Sm 8vo. 5 engrs. Orig cl. Sm piece of map margin torn; blank corner of tp lacking vol II; spines worn. Howes K 75. *Argosy.* $650/£419

KENDALL, HENRY and FLORENCE KENDALL. Muscles: Testing and Function. Balt, 1949. 1st ed. Good. *Fye.* $50/£32

KENDALL, HENRY. Posture and Pain. Balt, 1952. 1st ed. Good. *Fye.* $50/£32

KENDALL, PERCY FRY and H.E. WROOT. Geology of Yorkshire.... London, 1924. 2 vols. (Pp sl browned.) *Petersfield.* $101/£65

KENDALL, RICHARD (ed). Degas by Himself. London, 1987. 1st UK ed. Color frontis. Dj. *Edwards.* $39/£25

KENDO, T.A. Treatise on Silk and Tea Culture.... SF: A. Roman, 1870. (ii),73pp + 4pp ads at end. Gold-lettered cl (lt sunned, extrems worn). *Dawson.* $75/£48

KENDRICK, T.D. Anglo-Saxon Art to A.D. 900. NY, 1972. Rpt of 1938 ed. 104 plts. Good (spine sl sunned). *Washton.* $45/£29

KENEALLY, THOMAS. A Dutiful Daughter. Angus & Robertson, 1971. 1st ed. NF in dj. *Fine Books.* $45/£29

KENEALLY, THOMAS. Schindler's Ark. London: Hodder & Stoughton, 1982. 1st ed. Inscribed. Fine in dj (lt rubbed). *Rees.* $233/£150

KENEALLY, THOMAS. Schindler's Ark. London: Hodder, 1982. 1st UK ed. NF in dj (price-clipped). *Williams.* $116/£75

KENEALLY, THOMAS. Schindler's List. NY: Simon & Schuster, (1982). 1st Amer ed. Fine in dj (lt wear; sm tape repair rear panel). *Dermont.* $40/£26

KENEALLY, THOMAS. Three Cheers for the Paraclete. NY, 1969. 1st ed. VG (agency stamp on ep, prelim) in dj (sl rubbed, nicked). *Rees.* $19/£12

KENNAN, GEORGE. Siberia and the Exile System. NY: Century, 1891. 2 vols. xv,409; x,575pp; teg. Grey-grn cl stamped in gilt, blind (pockets removed). *Schoyer.* $125/£81

KENNAN, GEORGE. Siberia and the Exile System. NY: Century, 1891. 1st Amer ed. 2 vols. (xvi),409; (xii),575pp. Teg. Grn cl stamped in gilt/blind. Nice set. *Cady.* $150/£97

KENNAN, GEORGE. Tent Life in Siberia and Adventures Among the Koraks and Other Tribes in Kamtchatka and Northern Asia. NY: Putnam's, 1888. ix,425pp. Good (lt wear). *High Latitude.* $50/£32

KENNEDY, HARRY. Jingleman Jack. NY: Saalfield, 1901. 1st ed. Lg, 4to. Pict bds (edgewear; spine rubbed). Internally clean. *Reisler.* $350/£226

KENNEDY, J.H. Jesuit and Savage in New France. New Haven: Yale, 1950. Fldg map. VG. *Schoyer.* $35/£23

KENNEDY, JOHN F. Profiles in Courage. NY, 1956. Stated 1st ed, w/code letters M-E. Good (eps tanned). *Bond.* $60/£39

KENNEDY, JOHN F. Why England Slept. Hutchinson, (1940). 1st British ed. 16pg pub list dated Autumn, 1940 at end. Red cl (upper cvr spotted; spine faded; margin outer edges lt browned.) *Bickersteth.* $101/£65

KENNEDY, JOHN P. Memoirs of the Life of William Wirt.... Phila: Lea & Blanchard, 1849. 1st ed. 2 vols. Orig emb cl (rubbed, chipped). *Boswell.* $150/£97

KENNEDY, MARK. The Pecking Order. NY: Appleton-Century, (1953). 1st ed. NF in dj. *Godot.* $65/£42

KENNEDY, MARK. The Pecking Order. NY: Appleton-Century-Crofts, 1953. 1st ed. Fine in illus dj (sl rubbed). *Cahan.* $60/£39

KENNEDY, MICHAEL S. (ed). The Assiniboines. Norman: Univ of OK Press, (1961). 1st ptg thus. 8 repros. Fine in dj. *Schoyer.* $55/£35

KENNEDY, MILWARD. Corpse in Cold Storage. NY: H.C. Kinsey, 1934. 1st Amer ed. Bkpl, o/w Fine in VG dj (internal tape mends; sl wear). *Mordida.* $55/£35

KENNEDY, RUTH WEDGWOOD. The Renaissance Painter's Garden. NY: OUP, 1948. 60 full-pg plts. Red cl spine, blue buckram, gilt device. Fine in Fine dj. *Quest.* $90/£58

KENNEDY, WILLIAM. Billy Phelan's Greatest Game. NY: Viking, (1978). 1st ed. Fine in dj. *Jaffe*. $125/£81

KENNEDY, WILLIAM. The Ink Truck. MacDonald, 1970. 1st Eng ed, 1st bk. Fine in NF dj. *Fine Books*. $150/£97

KENNEDY, WILLIAM. O Albany! NY, 1983. 1st Amer ed. Fine (sm edge tear rear panel) in dj. *Polyanthos*. $60/£39

KENNERLY, DAVID HUME. Shooter. NY: Newsweek, (1979). 1st ed. Fine in Fine dj. *Aka*. $65/£42

KENNERLY, WILLIAM CLARK. Persimmon Hill. Univ of OK, 1948. 1st ed. Fine in VG dj. *Oregon*. $50/£32

Kenneth Grahame's The Wind in the Willows. A Pop-Up Book. NY: Holt, Rinehart, Winston, 1983. 19x27 cm. 6 pop-ups, pull-tabs. Babette Cole (illus). Glazed pict bds. VG. *Book Finders*. $45/£29

KENNEY, JAMES (ed). The Founding of Churchill. J.M. Dent, (1932). 1st ed. 3 plts. Fine in VG dj. *Oregon*. $95/£61

KENNY, CHARLES J. (Pseud of Erle Stanley Gardner.) This Is Murder. NY: Morrow, 1935. 1st ed. NF. *Janus*. $85/£55

KENNY, CHARLES. The Manual of Chess: Containing the Elementary Principles of the Game. NY: D. Appleton, 1864. 1st ed. Frontis, 122pp (sm tears feps repaired w/glassine tissue). Good (rubbed; text stains). *Cahan*. $75/£48

KENRICK, TONY. A Tough One to Lose. London: Michael Joseph, 1972. 1st ed. Fine in dj (sl wear). *Mordida*. $45/£29

KENRICK, TONY. Two for the Price of One. London: Michael Joseph, 1974. 1st ed. Fine in dj. *Mordida*. $45/£29

KENRICK, W. The New American Orchardist. Boston, (1844). 7th ed. 450pp, 2 engrs. Gilt-dec cl (worn, frayed). Overall Nice (lt foxing, offsetting). *Sutton*. $95/£61

KENT, ALEXANDER. A Tradition of Victory. London: Hutchinson, 1981. 1st ed. Signed. Fine in dj. *Else Fine*. $75/£48

KENT, ALEXANDER. Command a King's Ship. London: Hutchinson, 1973. 1st ed. VG in dj (spine sl sunned). *Limestone*. $45/£29

KENT, ALEXANDER. In Gallant Company. London: Hutchinson, 1977. 1st ed. Fine in dj. *Limestone*. $45/£29

KENT, ALEXANDER. The Inshore Squadron. London: Hutchinson, 1978. 1st ed, signed. NF in dj. *Limestone*. $60/£39

KENT, ALEXANDER. Richard Bolitho—Midshipman. London: Hutchinson, 1975. 1st ed. Fine in dj. *Limestone*. $35/£23

KENT, ALEXANDER. Sloop of War. NY: Putnam's, 1972. 1st ed. Fine in dj. *Else Fine*. $45/£29

KENT, ALEXANDER. Sloop of War. London: Hutchinson, 1972. 1st ed. NF in dj (1 closed tear). *Limestone*. $45/£29

KENT, ALEXANDER. Stand into Danger. London: Hutchinson, 1980. 1st ed. Fine in dj. *Limestone*. $35/£23

KENT, ALEXANDER. Success to the Brave. London: Hutchinson, 1983. 1st ed. Fine in dj. *Limestone*. $40/£26

KENT, ALEXANDER. A Tradition of Victory. London: Hutchinson, 1981. 1st ed. Fine in dj. *Limestone*. $40/£26

KENT, H. WATSON. The Work of Bruce Rogers. NY: OUP, 1939. 1st ed. Frontis, 22 plates & facs. VG in dj (rubbed). *Cox*. $70/£45

KENT, HENRY B. Graphic Sketches of the West. Chicago, 1890. 1st ed. 254pp. *Ginsberg*. $175/£113

KENT, ROCKWELL. An Anthology of His Work. Fridolf Johnson (ed). NY, 1982. 1st ed. VG in dj. *Argosy*. $125/£81

KENT, ROCKWELL. It's Me, O Lord. The Autobiography of.... NY: Dodd, Mead, (1955). 1st ed. Gilt title spine; vignette fr cvr. NF (cl sl rubbed edges) in VG pict dj (tape-repaired edge tears). *Blue Mountain*. $150/£97

KENT, ROCKWELL. N by E. NY: Random House, 1930. 1st ed, ltd issue. One of 900 numbered, signed. Blue cl, silver-stamped. Fine in dj (sl chipped), slipcase (sl rubbed, sunned). *Hermitage*. $250/£161

KENT, ROCKWELL. N by E. Brewer & Warren, 1930. 1st ed. Foxing eps, else VG+ in VG+ dj (sl wear). *Fine Books*. $75/£48

KENT, ROCKWELL. N by E. NY: Random House, 1930. One of 900 signed. Double-spread title; 8 inserted illus. Blue cl, silver dec. VG (spine sl faded). *Veatchs*. $150/£97

KENT, ROCKWELL. Rockwellkentiana. NY: Harcourt, Brace, 1933. 1st ed. VG. *Perier*. $60/£39

KENT, ROCKWELL. Salamina. NY: Harcourt, Brace, 1935. Inscribed. 23 full-pg illus. Blue buckram over bds, silver blind-tooling. Pict dj chipped, else VG. *Heller*. $150/£97

KENT, ROCKWELL. Salamina. NY: Harcourt, Brace, 1935. Later ptg. Blue cl. VG in dj (dampstaining; spine chip, closed tear). *Chapel Hill*. $30/£19

KENT, ROCKWELL. Voyaging Southward from the Strait of Magellen. NY: Halcyon House, 1924. VG. *Connolly*. $37/£24

KENT, ROCKWELL. Wilderness. A Journal of Quiet Adventure in Alaska. L.A.: Wilderness Press, (1970). Ltd to 1550 numbered, signed. 49 plts. Fine in slipcase. *Karmiole*. $100/£65

KENT, WILLIAM WINTHROP. Hooked Rug Design. Springfield: Pond-Ekberg, (1949). 1st ed. 144 plts. Edges, eps foxed, else VG in dj. *Bookpress*. $85/£55

KENT, WILLIAM WINTHROP. Rare Hooked Rugs.... Springfield: Pond-Ekberg, (1948). 2nd ptg. Edges, eps foxed, else VG in dj. *Bookpress*. $85/£55

KENYON, FREDERIC G. Ancient Books and Modern Discoveries. Chicago: Caxton Club, 1927. Ltd to 350. 30 collotype plts. Vellum over marbled bds. Good. *Karmiole*. $450/£290

KENYON, FREDERIC G. (ed). Facsimiles of Biblical Manuscripts in the British Museum. London, 1900. Unpaginated; uncut. 25 facs. (Margins lt thumbed; ex-lib w/ink stamps, label, #s; joint heads sl split.) *Edwards*. $85/£55

KEOWN, ANNA GORDON. Collected Poems.... Caravell Press, 1953. #93/380. 4 plts. Fine in dj. *Bickersteth*. $39/£25

KEPES, GYORGY. Sign Image Symbol. NY: George Braziller, (1966). (Worn.) Dj. *Argosy*. $50/£32

KERCHEVAL, SAMUEL. A History of the Valley or Virginia. Woodstock, VA, 1902. 3rd ed. (Sm damp area fr cvr.) *Hayman*. $35/£23

KERNER VON MARILAUN, ANTON. The Natural History of Plants. London, 1895. 2 vols. xiv,777; xiv,983pp, 16 color plts. Marbled eps, teg. 1/2 morocco, gilt (extrems sl rubbed). *Edwards.* $124/£80

KERNODLE, GEORGE. From Art to Theatre; Form and Convention in the Renaissance. Univ of Chicago, (1947). 3rd imp. VG. *Artis.* $20/£13

KEROUAC, JACK et al. Pull My Daisy. NY: Grove, 1961. 1st ed. NF (sm corner creases) in wraps. *Beasley.* $150/£97

KEROUAC, JACK. The Dharma Bums. (London): Deutsch, (1959). 1st UK ed. Copyright pg incorrectly states 'First Published 1950' but corrected by Deutsch's ptd paste-over. Fine in NF dj (spine corner sl worn; rear panel corner sl wrinkled). *Bernard.* $150/£97

KEROUAC, JACK. The Dharma Bums. NY, 1958. 1st Amer ed. Cvrs sl rubbed, o/w Fine in dj (sl rubbed). *Polyanthos.* $150/£97

KEROUAC, JACK. The Dharma Bums. NY: Viking Press, 1958. 1st ed. VG+ in dj (fr panel rubbed). *Bernard.* $175/£113

KEROUAC, JACK. Excerpts from Visions of Cody. (NY: New Directions, 1960). 1st ed. #34/750, signed. 8vo. Prospectus laid in. Ptd cream bds, purple cl spine. VG (edges browned; lacks sm piece upper corner 2 leaves) in VG acetate dj (yellowed). *Chapel Hill.* $550/£355

KEROUAC, JACK. Hymn, God Pray for Me. (Montclair, NJ): Caliban Press, (1985). Ltd to 150 numbered. VG in wraps. *King.* $35/£23

KEROUAC, JACK. Lonesome Traveler. NY: McGraw-Hill, (1960). 1st ed. VG in dj (lt edgewear; soiled; spine browned). *Antic Hay.* $75/£48

KEROUAC, JACK. Lonesome Traveler. NY, (1960). 1st ed. Cl-backed bds. Fine in pict dj. *Argosy.* $250/£161

KEROUAC, JACK. On the Road. NY: Signet, Sept 1958. 1st Signet Book ptg. NF in pict wraps. *Polyanthos.* $25/£16

KEROUAC, JACK. Rimbaud. SF: City Lights, 1960. 1st ed, 1st ptg. Folded broadside, yellow paper ptd in black. Fine. *Beasley.* $200/£129

KEROUAC, JACK. Satori in Paris. Grove, 1966. 1st ed. Fine in dj. *Fine Books.* $110/£71

KEROUAC, JACK. Satori in Paris. NY: Grove, 1966. 1st ed. NF in dj. *Lame Duck.* $150/£97

KEROUAC, JACK. The Subterraneans. (London): Deutsch, (1960). 1st UK ed. NF in dj (spine edges sl worn). *Bernard.* $100/£65

KEROUAC, JACK. Tristessa. NY: Avon, (1960). 1st ed. Pb orig. VG- (pg edges lt browned; cvr corner wrinkle). *Aka.* $35/£23

KEROUAC, JACK. Vanity of Duluoz. NY, (1968). 1st ed. VG- in dj (sl edge tears; soiled, rubbed). *King.* $100/£65

KEROUAC, JACK. Visions of Cody. New Directions, 1960. 1st ed. One of 750 signed. Fine in plastic dj. *Fine Books.* $725/£468

KEROUAC, JACK. Visions of Gerard. NY, 1963. 1st Amer ed. Fine in dj (spine sl sunned, chip, small edge tear fr panel). *Polyanthos.* $100/£65

KEROUAC, JOHN. The Town and the City. NY: Harcourt, Brace, (1950). 1st ed, 1st bk. Laid in fldg publicity release, announcing March 2nd pub date, so likely an advance rev copy. VG in dj (spine ends, corners chipped). *Bernard.* $350/£226

KERR, PHILIP. A German Requiem. Viking, 1991. 1st ed. Review slip, publicity sheets inserted. Fine in dj. *Rees.* $31/£20

KERR, PHILIP. A German Requiem. London: Viking, 1991. 1st UK ed. Fine in dj. *Lewton.* $26/£17

KERR, PHILIP. March Violets. London: Viking, 1989. 1st UK ed. Fine in dj. *Lewton.* $54/£35

KERR, PHILIP. The Pale Criminal. London: Viking, 1990. 1st UK ed. Fine in dj. *Lewton.* $47/£30

KERR, RICHARD. Nature through Microscope and Camera. London: R.T.S., 1905. Grn/gilt dec cl. VG. *Savona.* $39/£25

KERTESZ, ANDRE. Day of Paris. George Davis (ed). NY: J.J. Augustin, 1945. 1st ed. VG (sl foxing; sm stains to cl). *Cahan.* $150/£97

KERTESZ, ANDRE. From My Window. Boston: NYGS, 1981. 1st ed. 53 color photos. Fine in illus dj. *Cahan.* $85/£55

KERTESZ, ANDRE. J'Aime Paris: Photographs Since the Twenties. NY: Grossman, 1974. 1st ed. 215 full-pg b/w photos. Fine in illus dj. *Cahan.* $200/£129

KERTESZ, ANDRE. J'Aime Paris: Photographs Since the Twenties. London: Thames & Hudson, 1974. 1st Eng ed. 200 full-pg b/w photos. VG (sl foxing lower edge cl) in pict dj (price-clipped). *Cahan.* $150/£97

KERTESZ, ANDRE. Of New York. Knopf, 1976. 1st ed. NF in VG+ dj. *Bishop.* $52/£34

KESEY, KEN. One Flew Over the Cuckoo's Nest. London: Methuen, 1962. 1st UK ed. NF in dj (sl edge-worn). *Sclanders.* $186/£120

KESEY, KEN. Sailor Song. NY, 1992. 1st Amer ed. Signed, dated. Mint in Mint dj. *Polyanthos.* $40/£26

KESEY, KEN. Sometimes a Great Notion. London: Methuen, 1966. 1st UK ed. Fep sl foxed, edges sl dusty, o/w NF. Dj (internally edge-darkened). *Sclanders.* $155/£100

KESTNER, JOSEPH A. Mythology and Mysogyny. Madison, 1989. Good in dj. *Washton.* $40/£26

KESWICK, MAGGIE. The Chinese Garden. London: Academy Editions, 1978. As New. *Quest.* $55/£35

KESWICK, MAGGIE. The Chinese Garden. London, 1980. VG in dj. *Argosy.* $75/£48

KETLER, ISAAC C. Tragedy of Paotingfu. NY et al: Revell, (1902). 2nd ed. Red cl stamped in black, gilt, blind (spine sl discolored; lacks fep). *Schoyer.* $35/£23

KETTELL, RUSSELL HAWES (ed). Early American Rooms, 1650-1858. Portland: Southworth-Anthoensen Press, 1936. 1st ed. Frontis. Partly uncut. Ink name, else Fine. *Bookpress.* $175/£113

KETTELL, THOMAS PRENTICE. Southern Wealth and Northern Profits.... NY: George W. & John A. Wood, 1860. 1st ed. 173pp + (16)pp ads (fep lacks corner). Orig brn cl (lt faded). VG. *Chapel Hill.* $75/£48

KETTLE, JERRY and ED ADDEE. Low and Outside. Coward McCann, 1965. 1st ed. VG+ in Good+ dj (sm chips, spine faded). *Plapinger.* $30/£19

KEYES, E.D. From West Point to California. Oakland: Biobooks, (1950). Ltd ed. *Heinoldt.* $25/£16

KEYES, E.L. Diseases of the Genito-Urinary Organs.... NY: Appleton, 1910. 7 colored plts. *Goodrich.* $75/£48

KEYES, E.L. Lewis Atterbury Stimson, M.D. NY: Knickerbocker, 1918. 1st ed. Frontis port. Orig blue cl. NF. *Chapel Hill.* $150/£97

KEYES, E.L. The Surgical Diseases of the Genito-Urinary Organs Including Syphilis. NY, 1895. 1st ed. 704pp. 1/2 leather. Good. *Fye.* $50/£32

KEYES, E.L. The Tonic Treatment of Syphilis. NY, 1877. 1st ed. 83pp. Good. *Fye.* $100/£65

KEYES, E.L. The Venereal Diseases Including Stricture of the Male Urethra. NY, 1880. 348pp. Good. *Fye.* $50/£32

KEYES, E.L. The Venereal Diseases.... NY, 1880. 1st ed. xiii,348pp (lt marginal browning, ex-libris). *Edwards.* $39/£25

KEYES, LEONHARD A. Lineage of the Ninth Regiment of the State of New York. NY, 1953. 1st ed. Fldg map. VG + . *Pratt.* $45/£29

KEYNES, GEOFFREY (ed). Apologie and Treatise of Ambroise Pare. London: Falcon, 1951. Good. *White.* $37/£24

KEYNES, GEOFFREY (ed). Blake's Pencil Drawings. Second Series. London: Nonesuch Press, 1956. #1427/1440. Dj. *Bickersteth.* $93/£60

KEYNES, GEOFFREY (ed). Engravings by William Blake, the Separate Plates. Dublin: Emery Walker, 1956. One of 500. 45 plts. Fine. *Bookpress.* $235/£152

KEYNES, GEOFFREY (ed). Pencil Drawings by William Blake. London: Nonesuch, 1927. #1164/1550. 82 plts. (Eps sl browned.) Uncut; 1/2 cl. *Edwards.* $233/£150

KEYNES, GEOFFREY. A Bibliography of Dr. John Donne. Cambridge, 1958. 3rd ed. Ltd to 750. 2 line dwgs, 12 collotype, 28 facs illus. Good (lib bkpl, stamp). *Cox.* $50/£32

KEYNES, GEOFFREY. A Bibliography of Sir Thomas Browne. Oxford, 1968. 2nd ed, rev & augmented. (Exlib.) Dj (torn). *Goodrich.* $135/£87

KEYNES, GEOFFREY. A Bibliography of the Writings of William Harvey. Cambridge, 1953. 2nd ed, rev, ltd to 750. Good (bds sunned; ex-lib). *Goodrich.* $125/£81

KEYNES, GEOFFREY. Blake Studies. Clarendon, 1971. 2nd ed. Fine in dj (sl chipped). *Poetry.* $62/£40

KEYNES, GEOFFREY. Blood Transfusion. London: Henry Frowde/Hodder & Stoughton, 1922. 1st ed. Red cl. VG (spine faded; lib stamp). *White.* $116/£75

KEYNES, GEOFFREY. Dr. Timothy Bright, 1550-1615. London: Wellcome Hist Medical Lib, 1962. 17 plts. Sm # stamped top of title, o/w Fine. *Bickersteth.* $56/£36

KEYNES, GEOFFREY. Henry James in Cambridge. Cambridge: Heffer & Sons, (1967). 1st ed in bk form. One of 1000 ptd. Port. Pict bds. Fine in NF dj (lt sunned, price-clipped). *Reese.* $30/£19

KEYNES, GEOFFREY. John Ray, a Bibliography. Faber & Faber, (1951). One of 650. 4 plts. Dj. *Bickersteth.* $132/£85

KEYNES, GEOFFREY. The Personality of William Harvey. Cambridge, 1949. 8 port plts. NF in dj. *Goodrich.* $65/£42

KEYNES, GEOFFREY. The Portraiture of William Harvey. London, 1949. 12 plts. (Spine sunned.) *Goodrich.* $45/£29

KEYNES, GEOFFREY. The Portraiture of William Harvey. London: Keynes Press, 1985. Ltd ed of 300. Fine. *Goodrich.* $65/£42

KEYNES, GEOFFREY. William Blake's Engravings. London: Faber, 1950. Pict eps. Pub's cl. VF. *Europa.* $70/£45

KEYNES, GEOFFREY. William Blake's Engravings. Faber, 1950. 1st ed. VG. *Poetry.* $43/£28

KEYNES, GEOFFREY. William Blake's Engravings. London: Faber & Faber, 1950. 1st ed. (Eps sl spotted.) Dj (chipped, sl loss spine). *Edwards.* $70/£45

KEYNES, GEOFFREY. William Pickering, Publisher. A Memoir and a Check-List.... London: Galahad Press, (1969). Rev ed. 37 facs tps. Cl (lt mkd). Good in dj (repaired, soiled). *Cox.* $47/£30

KEYNES, GEOFFREY. William Pickering, Publisher. A Memoir and a Handlist of His Editions. London, 1924. 1/350. 37 facs. Paper spine label, extra label tipped in; teg, uncut. VG. *Argosy.* $125/£81

KEYNES, JOHN MAYNARD. The General Theory of Employment, Interest and Money. London: Macmillan, 1936. 1st ed. Dj (faded, sl frayed). *Bickersteth.* $287/£185

KEYNES, JOHN MAYNARD. The General Theory of Employment, Interest and Money. NY: Harcourt Brace, 1936. 1st US ed. VG (rep gutter stained) in dj (sl worn). *Second Life.* $250/£161

KEYNES, JOHN MAYNARD. Laissez-Faire and Communism. New Republic, 1926. 1st ed. Chipping; cvrs lt worn, else VG in wraps. *Fine Books.* $150/£97

KEYNES, JOHN MAYNARD. A Short View of Russia. Hogarth, 1925. 1st ed. 3/4 leather (sl rubbed). Contents Good (bds sl faded). *Whiteson.* $171/£110

KEYS, THOMAS E. The History of Surgical Anesthesia. NY: Schuman, 1945. Good. *Goodrich.* $75/£48

KEYSER, SARAH. Who Lives Here? NY: Questor, n.d. (197?). 27x20 cm. 5pp changing pictures. Glazed pict bds. VG. *Book Finders.* $35/£23

KHAYYAM, OMAR. Rubaiyat of Omar Khayyam. London: Hodder & Stoughton, (1913). 1st ed. Lg, 4to. Rene Bull (illus). Rust-brn cl, gilt/navy decs. Edges, prelims lt foxed, o/w Fine. *Reisler.* $650/£419

KHAYYAM, OMAR. Rubaiyat of Omar Khayyam. NY: George H. Doran, n.d. (ca 1920). 1st ed. Edward Fitzgerald (rendered by). 12 tipped-in color plts by Edmund Dulac; teg. Pub's delux binding of brn morocco (spine faded); dec gilt. *Karmiole.* $150/£97

KHAYYAM, OMAR. The Rubaiyat. Edward Fitzgerald (trans). (NY): LEC, 1935. #904/1500 numbered, signed by Valenti Angelo (illus). Full yellow leather. Fine in glassine wrapper, card liner & pub's slipcase. *Hermitage.* $175/£113

KIDD, DUDLEY. The Essential Kafir. London: A&C Black, 1925. 2nd ed. 63 plts; fldg map. VG. *Hollett.* $132/£85

KIDDER, FREDERIC. History of the Boston Massacre. Albany: Joel Munsell, 1870. 1st ed. Frontis, (2),292pp, double-pg map. Grn cl, gilt. Fine. *Karmiole.* $75/£48

KIDDER, J. EDWARD, JR. The Birth of Japanese Art. NY, (1965). 1st Amer ed. 12 mtd color plts; 2 maps. VG. *Argosy.* $65/£42

KIDDLE, C. Edgar Wallace — A Guide to His First Editions. Ivory Head Press, 1981. VG in dec laminated cvrs. *Moss.* $25/£16

KIEFER, OTTO. Sexual Life in Ancient Rome. NY: Dutton, 1935. 1st ed. 16 full-pg plts. Chipped cl at spine, o/w VG. *Second Life.* $35/£23

KIESSLING, NICOLAS K. The Library of Robert Burton. Oxford Bibliographical Soc, 1988. 1/4 tan buckram, blue paper over bds. Fine. *Heller.* $35/£23

KIJEWSKI, KAREN. Katapult. St. Martin, 1990. 1st ed. Fine in dj (sm rubbed spot). *Murder.* $55/£35

KIKUCHI, SADAO. A Treasury of Japanese Wood Block Prints Ukiyo-E. NY: Crown, (1968). 1st ed. 100 color plts. Black cl. Fine in dj. *House.* $120/£77

KILBOURNE, FREDERICK W. Alterations and Adaptations of Shakespeare. Boston: Poet Lore Co, 1906. 1st ed. Pub's cl. VG. *Dramatis Personae.* $25/£16

KILBRIDE-JONES, H.E. Zoomorphic Penannular Brooches. Soc of Antiquities of London, 1980. Dj (sl chipped). *Edwards.* $31/£20

KILGORE, D.E. A Ranger Legacy. Austin, 1973. 1st ed. Fine in dj (lt soiled). *Baade.* $35/£23

KILGORE, WILLIAM H. The Kilgore Journal of an Overland Journey to California in the Year 1850. Joyce R. Muench (ed). Hastings House, 1949. 1st ed. Ltd to 1000 numbered. Bds, paper labels. VF in VG slipcase. *Oregon.* $60/£39

KILGOUR, FREDERICK G. The Library of the Medical Institution of Yale College and Its Catalogue of 1865. New Haven: Yale Univ Press, 1960. 1st ed. Fine. *Glaser.* $25/£16

KILHAM, WALTER H. Mexican Architecture of the Vice-Regal Period. NY: Longmans, Green, 1927. 1st ed. 84 photos. Red cl; gilt. Good. *Karmiole.* $75/£48

KILVERT, FRANCIS. Diary. London: Cape, (1977). 1st illus ed. 3 vols in slipcase. *Petersfield.* $116/£75

KIM, CHEWON and G. ST. G.M. GOMPERTZ. The Ceramic Art of Korea. London: Faber & Faber, 1961. 1st ed. 100 plts. Dj (sl chipped). *Edwards.* $54/£35

KIMBALL, NELL. Nell Kimball, Her Life as an American Madam. Stephen Longstreet (ed). (NY): Macmillan, (1970). 1st ed. VG in dj. *Second Life.* $35/£23

KINAHAN, G.H. Manual of the Geology of Ireland. London, 1878. xx,444pp; color fldg map; 8 plts. (Cl sl used.) *Wheldon & Wesley.* $78/£50

KINCAID, JAMAICA. Annie John. NY, (1985). 1st ed. Fine (sm security strip rear pastedown) in Fine dj. *Fuller & Saunders.* $35/£23

KINCAID, JAMAICA. Annie John. NY: FSG, 1985. 1st ed. VF in dj (price-clipped). *Else Fine.* $40/£26

KINCAID, JAMAICA. At the Bottom of the River. NY, (1983). 1st ed, 1st bk. Fine in VG + dj (1.5-inch punctured tear fr gutter). *Fuller & Saunders.* $45/£29

KINCAID, JAMAICA. A Small Place. NY, (1988). 1st ed. Rev slip, promo letter laid in. Fine (blindstamp) in Fine dj. *Fuller & Saunders.* $45/£29

King Ranch. 100 Years of Ranching. Corpus Christi: CC Caller Times, 1953. 1st ed. Internally VG + (cvr soiled). *Parker.* $75/£48

KING, ANTHONY D. The Bungalow. London, 1984. 1st ed. Orig cl; in dj. *Edwards.* $39/£25

KING, C.W. Handbook of Engraved Gems. London: George Bell, 1885. 2nd ed. Frontis, xii,287pp, 88 plts. (Extrems worn; spine chipped; ink stain spine, top bd; foxing.) *Archaeologia.* $45/£29

KING, CHARLES. An Apache Princess. NY: Hobart, 1903. 1st ed. Frontis (tear). Spine sl skewed; fr hinge starting, o/w Fine. *Hermitage.* $65/£42

KING, CHARLES. By Land and Sea. Phila, 1891. 1st ed. 198pp (ex-lib blindstamp rep). Cl (rubbed, sl stained). *King.* $45/£29

KING, CHARLES. The Colonel's Daughter. Phila: Lippincott, 1883. 1st ed. Good (cocked; shaken). *Parker.* $225/£145

KING, CHARLES. A Daughter of the Sioux. Hobart, 1903. 1st ed. Teg. Pict cvr. Sm snag cvr photo, else Fine. *Authors Of The West.* $60/£39

KING, CHARLES. The Fifth Cavalry in the Sioux War of 1876. Milwaukee: Sentinel, 1880. VG in wraps (tape repaired). Howes K 147. *Parker.* $1,750/£1,129

KING, CHARLES. Sunset Pass. NY: J.W. Lovell, 1890. 1st ed. VG. *Parker.* $175/£113

KING, CHARLES. Trials of a Staff-Officer. Phila, 1891. 1st ed. 214pp (ex-lib blindstamp rep). Cl (lt stained, rubbed). *King.* $35/£23

KING, CHARLES. A War-Time Wooing. NY, (1888). 1st ed. Pict cl. Spine extrems worn, o/w VG + . *Pratt.* $27/£17

KING, CHARLES. Warrior Gap, A Story of the Sioux Outbreak of '68. NY, (1898). 277pp (ex-lib blindstamp rep). Pict cl (dknd, rubbed). *King.* $20/£13

KING, CLARENCE. Mountaineering in the Sierra Nevada. Boston, 1872. 1st ed, 2nd issue. 292pp; teg. (Stamped name; inner fr hinge cracked; spine chipped, rubbed, frayed; cvrs dknd.) *King.* $150/£97

KING, CONSTANCE EILEEN. The Collector's History of Dolls' Houses.... London: Hale, (1983). Dj. *Petersfield.* $78/£50

KING, FRANCIS. The Rites of Modern Occult Magic. Macmillan, 1971. 1st ed. NF in VG + dj. *Bishop.* $22/£14

KING, FRANCIS. To the Dark Tower. Van Thal, 1946. 1st ed, 1st bk. Sl browned, else Good in dj (dull; sl worn). *Whiteson.* $54/£35

KING, GRACE. Creole Families of New Orleans. NY: Macmillan, 1921. 1st ed. Color frontis, 3 b/w plts. Pict grn cl (lt smudged). *Petrilla.* $35/£23

KING, GRACE. Memories of a Southern Woman of Letters. NY: Macmillan, 1932. 1st ed. VG in dj (sl worn). *Second Life.* $65/£42

KING, GRACE. Mount Vernon on the Potomac. NY: Macmillan, 1929. 1st ed. Blue cl, gilt. Fine. *Pharos.* $35/£23

KING, H.G.R. (ed). Diary of the 'Terra Nova' Expedition to the Antarctic 1910-1912. London: Blandford, 1972. 1st ed. VG in Fine dj. *Walcot.* $37/£24

KING, HENRY. The Poems.... John Sparrow (ed). London: Nonesuch, 1925. Ltd to 900. Vellum bds (buckled; short splits, sl loss backstrip, affecting 1st letter.) *Waterfield.* $70/£45

KING, IRENE MARSCHALL. John O. Meusebach. Austin: Univ of TX, 1967. VG. *Burcham.* $30/£19

KING, JAMES. Interior Landscapes: A Life of Paul Nash. London: Weidenfeld & Nicolson, 1987. Fine in dj, black case. *Heller.* $35/£23

KING, JOHN. The American Family Physician; or, Domestic Guide to Health. Indianapolis, 1864. 794; 333pp. Full leather. Good. *Fye.* $200/£129

KING, LARRY L. The One-Eyed Man. (NY): NAL, (1966). 1st ed, 1st bk. Fine in VG dj (lt used). *Reese.* $50/£32

KING, MARTIN LUTHER, JR. Beyond Vietnam. (Palo Alto, CA: Altoan Press, 1967). 1st ed. 2-inch stain fr cvr, else VG in wrappers. *Godot.* $45/£29

KING, MARTIN LUTHER, JR. Letter from a Birmingham Jail. (N.p.): Amer Friends Service Committee, 1963. 5th ptg. Wraps (stamp; vertical crease). *Aka.* $20/£13

KING, MARTIN LUTHER, JR. Stride Towards Freedom. Harper, 1958. 1st ed, 1st bk. Fine in VG + dj. *Fine Books.* $125/£81

KING, MARTIN LUTHER, JR. Why We Can't Wait. NY: Harper & Row, (1964). 1st ed. Fine in dj. *Godot.* $85/£55

KING, MOSES. King's Handbook of New York City. Boston: Moses King, 1893. 2nd ed. 1008pp. *Bishop.* $20/£13

KING, RUFUS. Malice in Wonderland. GC: DCC, 1958. 1st ed. Fine in dj (fr panel scrapes). *Mordida.* $50/£32

KING, RUFUS. Murder Masks Miami. GC: DCC, 1939. 1st ed. Fine in pict dj (minor edgewear, rubbing). *Else Fine.* $50/£32

KING, RUFUS. Museum Piece No. 13. GC: DDCC, 1946. 1st ed. NF in VG dj (tears, sm chips). *Beasley.* $30/£19

KING, RUFUS. Museum Piece No. 13. GC: DCC, 1946. 1st ed. VG in dj (stamped inner fr flap; short closed tears; chips; wear). *Mordida.* $35/£23

KING, RUFUS. A Variety of Weapons. GC: DCC, 1943. 1st ed. Fine in dj (sm stain spine base; sl corner wear). *Mordida.* $45/£29

KING, RUFUS. A Variety of Weapons. GC: DCC, 1943. 1st ed. Fine in pict dj (lt wear spine corners). *Else Fine.* $50/£32

KING, STEPHEN and PETER STRAUB. The Talisman. Harmondsworth: Viking, 1984. 1st ed. Fine in dj. *Temple.* $37/£24

KING, STEPHEN and PETER STRAUB. The Talisman. Viking, 1984. 1st ed. Signed by Straub. Uncorrected proof. Fine in wraps. *Fine Books.* $175/£113

KING, STEPHEN and PETER STRAUB. The Talisman. NY, 1984. Signed presentation, both authors. Fine in Fine dj. *Polyanthos.* $150/£97

KING, STEPHEN. The Bachman Books. NAL, 1985. 1st ed. Fine in dj. *Madle.* $75/£48

KING, STEPHEN. Carrie. GC, 1974. 1st ed, 1st bk. Fresh in dj (sl dknd, sl worn). *King.* $495/£319

KING, STEPHEN. Christine. NY: Viking, 1983. 1st ed. Fine in dj (minor rubs corners). *Else Fine.* $40/£26

KING, STEPHEN. Cujo. Viking, 1981. 1st ed. NF in dj. *Fine Books.* $23/£15

KING, STEPHEN. Cujo. London: Macdonald, 1982. 1st UK ed. Signed. NF in dj. *Lewton.* $109/£70

KING, STEPHEN. Cycle of the Werewolf. (Westland): Land of Enchantment, (1983). 1st ed. Trade issue. Bumped, else Fine in dj. *Other Worlds.* $100/£65

KING, STEPHEN. Danse Macabre. NY, 1981. 1st ed. Bkpl, o/w NF in dj (sl rubbed). *Rees.* $116/£75

KING, STEPHEN. The Dark Half. Viking, 1989. 1st ed. Signed, inscribed. Fine in dj. *Stahr.* $100/£65

KING, STEPHEN. The Dark Tower II: Drawing of the Three. Grant, 1987. 1st ed. Fine in dj. *Madle.* $60/£39

KING, STEPHEN. The Dark Tower III: The Wastelands. Grant, 1991. 1st ed. Fine in dj. *Madle.* $40/£26

KING, STEPHEN. The Dark Tower: The Gunslinger. Grant, 1982. 1st ed. Fine in dj. *Madle.* $500/£323

KING, STEPHEN. Dolan's Cadillac. CA: Lord John Press, 1989. #239/250 signed. VF. *Polyanthos.* $400/£258

KING, STEPHEN. Dolores Claiborne. (NY): Viking, (1993). 1st Amer ed. Inscribed. *Between The Covers.* $125/£81

KING, STEPHEN. Dolores Claiborne. London: Hodder & Stoughton, 1992. Special ltd Christmas gift ed w/author's facs signature. Fine in slipcase. *Rees.* $62/£40

KING, STEPHEN. Fire-Starter. NY: Viking, (1980). 1st ed. VG in dj (lt soiling). *Houle.* $85/£55

KING, STEPHEN. Fire-Starter. Viking, 1980. 1st ed. Fine in dj. *Madle.* $85/£55

KING, STEPHEN. Four Past Midnight. (NY): Viking, (1990). 1st Amer ed. Inscribed. NF (sl bump bottom fr bd) in NF dj (sl wear). *Between The Covers.* $125/£81

KING, STEPHEN. Gerald's Game. (NY): Viking, (1992). Special ed issued to American Bookseller's Assoc w/message by King. Fine in cardboard slipcase. *Antic Hay.* $100/£65

KING, STEPHEN. Gerald's Game. London: Hodder & Stoughton, 1992. 1st ed. Fine in dj. *Rees.* $23/£15

KING, STEPHEN. Misery. London: H&S, 1987. 1st UK ed. Signed. Fine in dj. *Lewton.* $93/£60

KING, STEPHEN. My Pretty Pony. Whitney Museum, 1989. 1st ed. One of 250. Signed by author & B. Kruger (illus). As New w/o dj as issued. *Fine Books.* $2,500/£1,613

KING, STEPHEN. Needful Things. Viking, 1991. 1st ed. Fine in dj. *Madle.* $25/£16

KING, STEPHEN. Nightmares and Dreamscapes. London: Hodder & Stoughton, (1993). 1st ltd ed. Fine in slipcase. *Levin.* $155/£100

KING, STEPHEN. Pet Sematary. London: Hodder & Stoughton, 1983. 1st ed. Fine in dj. *Temple.* $34/£22

KING, STEPHEN. Pet Sematary. Hodder & Stoughton, 1983. 1st UK ed. Signed. NF in dj. *Lewton.* $109/£70

KING, STEPHEN. Salem's Lot. NEL, 1975. 1st Eng ed. NF in NF dj. *Fine Books.* $385/£248

KING, STEPHEN. Salem's Lot. London: New English Lib, 1976. 1st ed. Spine creased, pg edges browned, o/w NF in dj. *Rees.* $194/£125

KING, STEPHEN. The Shining. NY, 1977. 1st ed. Fine in dj. *Argosy.* $175/£113

KING, STEPHEN. The Shining. London: NEL, 1977. 1st UK ed. NF in dj. *Lewton.* $140/£90

KING, STEPHEN. Skeleton Crew. Scream Press, 1985. 1st ed. One of 1000 numbered, boxed, signed. Fine in dj. *Madle.* $350/£226

KING, STEPHEN. The Stand. NY: Doubleday, 1978. 1st ed, 1st ptg, 1st state of dj. Orig cl, dj (priced $12.95; later state is $18.95). Fine. *Macdonnell.* $200/£129

KING, STEPHEN. Thinner. NAL, 1984. 1st ed. Stain corner all pp, else Fine in dj. *Fine Books.* $20/£13

KING, STEPHEN. The Tommyknockers. NY: Putnam's, (1987). 1st ed, 1st state. As New in dj. *Sadlon.* $35/£23

KING, STEPHEN. The Tommyknockers. Putnam, 1987. 1st ed, 1st issue w/'Permissions to come' as the last line of copyright pg. As New in dj. *Aronovitz.* $22/£14

KING, STEPHEN. The Tommyknockers. Putnam, 1987. 1st ed. Fine in dj. *Madle.* $35/£23

KING, STEPHEN. The Tommyknockers. London: H&S, 1988. 1st UK ed. Signed. Fine in dj. *Lewton.* $93/£60

KING-HALL, STEPHEN. My Naval Life, 1906-1929. London, 1952. 1st ed. Signed. 8 plts. Eps sl browned, o/w VG in dj (chipped). *Edwards.* $39/£25

KING-HALL, STEPHEN. Post-War Pirate. London: Methuen, 1931. 1st ed. Pub's 8pp cat inserted, dated '531.' Lower edges rough-trimmed. (Sl faults.) *Temple.* $19/£12

KING-HALL, STEPHEN. Posterity. London: Hogarth Press, 1927. One of 1000 ptd. VF in grey wrappers. *Temple.* $51/£33

KINGDON-WARD, FRANK. Berried Treasure. London, 1954. 1st ed. Color frontis; 24 plain plts. (Sl foxing margins.) *Henly.* $28/£18

KINGDON-WARD, FRANK. The Land of the Blue Poppy. Little Compton, RI: Theophrastus, 1973. Rpt. *Quest.* $45/£29

KINGDON-WARD, FRANK. Pilgrimage for Plants. London: George Harrap, 1960. 1st ed. 36 plts; 2 line dwgs. VG in dj (price-clipped). *Hollett.* $62/£40

KINGDON-WARD, FRANK. A Plant Hunter in Tibet. London, 1934. 1st ed. 2 fldg maps, 16 plts. Good. *Henly.* $65/£42

KINGDON-WARD, FRANK. Plant Hunting on the Edge of the World. London: Gollancz, 1930. 1st ed. 15 plts. (Spine sl faded.) *Hollett.* $132/£85

KINGDON-WARD, FRANK. Return to the Irrawaddy. London: Andrew Melrose, (1956). Frontis, fldg map. Fine. *Quest.* $80/£52

KINGDON-WARD, FRANK. Return to the Irrawaddy. London: Andrew Melrose, 1956. 1st ed. Diag; fldg map. VG in dj (edges sl creased). *Hollett.* $116/£75

KINGMAN, RALPH CLARKE. New England Georgian Architecture. NY: Architectural Book Pub, 1913. 1st ed. 55 plts. Smudges, tp yellowed, portfolio rubbed, else VG. *Bookpress.* $125/£81

KINGSFORD, CHARLES LETHBRIDGE. The Early History of Piccadilly, Leicester Square, Soho.... Cambridge: CUP, 1925. 1st ed. 16 plts, fldg plan. VG. *Hollett.* $70/£45

KINGSLEY, CHARLES. Andromeda and Other Poems. John W. Parker, 1858. 1st ed. vii,169pp + ad leaf. (Short slit lower joint.) *Bickersteth.* $31/£20

KINGSLEY, CHARLES. Glaucus; or, The Wonders of the Shore. Cambridge: Macmillan, 1855. 1st ed, 1st issue. Sm 8vo. Frontis; 165,16pp (ads dated May 1855). Ribbed cl (spine sl faded), gilt. *Hollett.* $116/£75

KINGSLEY, CHARLES. Glaucus; or, The Wonders of the Shore. London, 1873. 5th ed, corrected & enlgd. 12 color plts. (Sl foxed; cvr sl stained.) *Wheldon & Wesley.* $39/£25

KINGSLEY, CHARLES. The Heroes. Cambridge: Macmillan, 1856. 1st ed. xviii,(ii),205,(3)pp + ad; 8 plts. Ptd cl (sl soiled; hinges splitting; corners sl worn). *Cox.* $70/£45

KINGSLEY, CHARLES. Miscellanies. London: John W. Parker & Son, 1859. 1st ed. 2 vols. 407,8; 389,(i)pp. (Joints vol 1 tender; bkpls; corners bumped; spines faded; heads sl frayed.) *Hollett.* $70/£45

KINGSLEY, CHARLES. Westward Ho! Cambridge: Macmillan, 1855. 2nd ed. 3 vols. viii,303,16pp ads; vi,356; vi,373pp; 3 half titles. (Lower joint strained; bkpl; rubbed, mkd; extrems worn, frayed; 1 spine torn, repaired). *Hollett.* $186/£120

KINGSLEY, CHARLES. Westward Ho! NY, 1920. 1st Wyeth ed. 413pp, 14 full-pg color plts by N.C. Wyeth. Cl w/pict color label (rubbed, dull; inner hinge cracked, stamped name). *King.* $65/£42

KINGSLEY, CHARLES. Westward Ho! London: Harrap, 1935. 16 color plts. Sound (sl faded, sl rubbed). *Cox.* $23/£15

KINGSLEY, CHARLES. Yeast; a Problem. London: Macmillan, 1893. 4th ed. xix,378pp; edges, eps marbled. Full tree calf gilt, raised bands, gilt-dec panels. *Hollett.* $54/£35

KINGSLEY, MARY H. Travels in West Africa. London: Macmillan, 1897. 1st ed. xvi,743pp + 8pp ads; 2 litho plts. Mod 1/2 levant morocco, gilt. Excellent (lt spots, mks). *Hollett.* $186/£120

KINGSMILL, HUGH. The Return of William Shakespeare. B-M, 1929. 1st Amer ed. VG + in dj (chipped). *Aronovitz.* $50/£32

KINGSOLVER, BARBARA. The Bean Trees. London: Virago, 1989. 1st Eng ed. Signed, dated. Fine in Fine dj. *Revere.* $100/£65

KINGSOLVER, BARBARA. Homeland and Other Stories. London: Virago, 1990. 1st Eng ed. Fine pb orig. *Revere.* $25/£16

KINGSTON, CHARLES. The Bench and the Dock. London: Stanley Paul, 1925. Blue cl (worn, faded); gilt. *Boswell.* $45/£29

KINGSTON, MAXINE HONG. Through the Black Curtain. Berkeley: Friends of the Bancroft Lib, 1987. 1st ed. Ptd wraps. *Second Life.* $25/£16

KINGSTON, MAXINE HONG. The Woman Warrior. Knopf, 1955. 1st ed, 1st bk. NF in NF dj. *Bishop.* $55/£35

KINGSTON, WILLIAM H.G. Old Jack. A Man-of-War's Man and South-Sea Whaler. London, 1859. 1st ed. 296pp. (Lt foxing; extrems sl rubbed.) *Lefkowicz.* $150/£97

KINIETZ, W. VERNON. The Indians of the Western Great Lakes, 1615-1760. Univ of MI, 1940. 1st ed. Frontis map. VG in VG dj. *Oregon.* $45/£29

KINLOCH, ALEXANDER A.A. Large Game Shooting in Thibet, The Himalayas, Northern and Central India. Calcutta, 1892. 3rd ed. (Sl foxing few pp; sm stain fr cvr.) *Petersfield.* $81/£52

KINNEAR, JOHN. Cairo, Petra, and Damascus, in 1839. London: John Murray, 1841. 1st ed. xi,(i)blank,348, half title. Blue cl (spine faded; adhesive tape mk at foot), paper label. VG (lib mks on title, lib stamps removed from 3 leaves just affecting final imprint). *Morrell.* $434/£280

KINNELL, GALWAY. Black Light. London: Hart-Davis, 1967. 1st Eng ed. Signed. Fine in dj. *Jaffe.* $65/£42

KINNELL, GALWAY. Body Rags. London: Rapp & Carroll, (1969). 1st Eng ed. One of 100 numbered, signed. Fine in dj. *Jaffe.* $100/£65

KINNELL, GALWAY. Flower Herding on Mount Monadnock. Boston: Houghton Mifflin, 1964. 1st ed. (Name fep; lt edgewear.) Dj (lt soiled; short closed tears). *Aka.* $45/£29

KINNELL, GALWAY. Poems of Night. London: Rapp & Carroll, (1968). 1st ed. Fine in dj. *Jaffe.* $50/£32

KINNELL, GALWAY. Poems of Night. London, 1968. Signed. NF in dj (sm tear, sl soiled, price-clipped). *Polyanthos.* $25/£16

KINNS, S. Moses and Geology. London, 1892. 13th thousand. xxx,514pp + 18pp ads; 16 plts. Pict gilt cl. Good. *Henly.* $39/£25

KINROSS, LORD. Europa Minor. NY: Morrow, (1956). 1st Amer ed. Dbl-pg map. VG in dj (price-clipped). *Schoyer.* $35/£23

KINSELLA, THOMAS. Another September. Dublin: Dolmen Press, 1958. 1st ed. Fine in VG dj. *Godot.* $65/£42

KINSELLA, W.P. The Alligator Report. Minneapolis: Coffee House, 1985. 1st ed. Inscribed. Fine in wraps. *Beasley.* $50/£32

KINSELLA, W.P. Dance Me Outside. Boston: Godine, 1986. 1st ed. Signed. Fine in dj. *Else Fine*. $85/£55

KINSELLA, W.P. Dance Me Outside. Boston: Godine, 1986. 1st US ed. Inscribed. Fine in Fine dj. *Beasley*. $75/£48

KINSELLA, W.P. The Iowa Baseball Confederacy. Boston: Houghton Mifflin, 1986. 1st ed. Fine (sl soil) in NF dj. *Beasley*. $45/£29

KINSELLA, W.P. The Iowa Baseball Confederacy. Boston, 1986. 1st ed. Signed. Fine in Fine dj. *Fuller & Saunders*. $45/£29

KINSELLA, W.P. The Moccasin Telegraph. Godine, 1984. 1st Amer ed. VF in dj. *Stahr*. $60/£39

KINSELLA, W.P. Red Wolf, Red Wolf. Toronto: Collins, 1987. 1st ed. Signed. Fine in Fine dj. *Revere*. $60/£39

KINSELLA, W.P. Shoeless Joe. Boston: Houghton-Mifflin, 1982. 1st ed. Signed. Name neatly blacked-out fep, else Fine in dj (price-clipped). *Else Fine*. $200/£129

KINSEY, A. Sexual Behavior in the Human Female. Phila, 1953. 1st ed. Good. *Fye*. $75/£48

KINSEY, A. et al. Sexual Behavior in the Human Male. Phila, 1948. 1st ed. Good. *Fye*. $40/£26

KINZIE, JULIETTE A. Wau-Bun, the 'Early Day' in the North-West. NY: Derby & Jackson, 1856. (1st ed.) 498pp; 6 litho views. Orig brn cl, gilt-stamped spine. (Spine sl faded; extrems lt frayed; paper dknd; fore-edge of tp frayed.) Howes K 171. *Bohling*. $300/£194

KINZIE, MRS. JOHN H. Wau-Bun. The Early Day in the North-West. Derby & Jackson, 1856. Frontis, 498pp, 5 plts. Pict gilt-stamped spine, emb cvrs. VG. Howes K 171. *Oregon*. $300/£194

KINZIE, MRS. JOHN H. Wau-Bun. The Early Day in the North-West. Chicago: Lakeside Classic, 1932. 6 plts. VG. Howes K 171. *Oregon*. $25/£16

KIP, LAWRENCE. Army Life on the Pacific; A Journal.... NY: Redfield, 1859. 1st ed. 144pp. Orig cl (sl crinkled; sm chip spine crown). Howes K 172. *Ginsberg*. $325/£210

KIP, WILLIAM INGRAHAM. Early Days of My Episcopate. Oakland: Biobooks, 1954. Ltd to 500. VG. *Perier*. $30/£19

KIP, WILLIAM INGRAHAM. Early Days of My Episcopate. Oakland: Biobooks, 1954. Ltd to 500. 4 plts; dec eps. Pict cl. Fine. *Oregon*. $45/£29

KIPLING, RUDYARD (ed). The Irish Guards in the Great War. London: Macmillan, 1923. 1st ed. 2 vols. Dk red cl. NF in djs (lt used). *Chapel Hill*. $300/£194

KIPLING, RUDYARD and WALTER DE LA MARE. St. Andrews: Two Poems. London: A&C Black, (1926). Spine, cvr edges yellowed. *Sadlon*. $25/£16

KIPLING, RUDYARD. The Absent-Minded Beggar. NY: Brentano's, 1900. 1st ed. NF in ptd, sewn wrappers. *Pharos*. $75/£48

KIPLING, RUDYARD. Actions and Reactions. NY: Doubleday, Page, 1909. 1st Amer ed. Dec grn cl; teg. VG. *Antic Hay*. $25/£16

KIPLING, RUDYARD. Actions and Reactions. NY, Oct, 1909. 1st ed. Fine. *Bond*. $50/£32

KIPLING, RUDYARD. An Almanac of Twelve Sports. London: Heinemann, n.d. (1914). 2 ad leaves; calendar for 1915; 12 plts by William Nicholson (1 w/fore-edge foxed; lt offsetting to text). Linen-backed ptd paper bds (sl rubbed, lower cvr spotted). *Cox*. $310/£200

KIPLING, RUDYARD. Barrack-Room Ballads and Other Verses. London: Methuen, 1892. 1st ed. #150/225 lg paper copies signed by pubs. Red cl (spine ends worn). VG. *Chapel Hill*. $450/£290

KIPLING, RUDYARD. Barrack-Room Ballads and Other Verses. London: Methuen, 1892. 1st trade (Eng) ed. xix,208pp + 16pp pub's cat. Teg, others untrimmed. Red cl (spine sunned). *Schoyer*. $75/£48

KIPLING, RUDYARD. A Book of Words. London: St. Martin's Street, 1928. 1st ed. Pub's gilt-dec red cl, teg. VF in VF orig ptd dj. *D & D*. $15/£10

KIPLING, RUDYARD. A Book of Words. London: Macmillan, 1928. 1st ed. Red cl. NF in dj (chipping). *Chapel Hill*. $95/£61

KIPLING, RUDYARD. Captains Courageous. London: Macmillan, 1897. 1st ed. Pict cl, gilt; aeg. Inscrip, lt # tp, o/w Nice. *Ash*. $78/£50

KIPLING, RUDYARD. Captains Courageous. Macmillan, 1897. 1st Eng ed. Pub's blue cl, gilt. VG. *Waterfield*. $43/£28

KIPLING, RUDYARD. Certain Maxims of Hafiz. Badger, 1898. 1st ed. One of 500. Pict cl. Lt wear spine extrems, else VG. *Fine Books*. $150/£97

KIPLING, RUDYARD. Collected Dog Stories. London: Macmillan, 1934. 1st ed. Red cl. NF in dj (spine dknd; 1/2-inch chip affecting few letters). *Chapel Hill*. $125/£81

KIPLING, RUDYARD. The Day's Work. NY: Doubleday, McClure, 1898. 1st Amer ed (precedes Eng). Dec grn cl; teg. NF. *Antic Hay*. $45/£29

KIPLING, RUDYARD. The Day's Work. NY: Doubleday & McClure, 1898. 1st ed. Pub's gilt-dec cl (spine rumpled); 1/2 lt brn morocco slipcase. *D & D*. $20/£13

KIPLING, RUDYARD. The Day's Work. Macmillan, 1898. 1st ed. Gilt dec cl. Spine sl dull, else VG. *Whiteson*. $25/£16

KIPLING, RUDYARD. The Day's Work. Macmillan, 1898. 1st Eng ed. Pub's blue bead-grain cl, gilt. Excellent. *Waterfield*. $70/£45

KIPLING, RUDYARD. Debits and Credits. London, 1926. 1st ed. Fine in dj (sunned, chips, sm tear). *Polyanthos*. $65/£42

KIPLING, RUDYARD. Debits and Credits. GC: Doubleday, 1926. 1st ed. Fine in dj (sl chipped). *Else Fine*. $125/£81

KIPLING, RUDYARD. Debits and Credits. London: Macmillan, 1926. 1st ed. Teg. Gilt-stamped red cl (lt spotted). VG in ptd dj (chipped). *Cahan*. $125/£81

KIPLING, RUDYARD. Doctors. London, 1908. 1st ed. Frontis port. NF in wraps. *Polyanthos*. $25/£16

KIPLING, RUDYARD. The Eyes of Asia. GC: Doubleday, Page, 1918. 1st bk ed. Spine ends lt rubbed. *Sadlon*. $50/£32

KIPLING, RUDYARD. The Eyes of Asia. NY: Doubleday, Page & Co., 1918. 1st collected ed. Pub's cl-backed bds, ptd paper label. Mint in orig ptd dj (lt worn, soiled w/sm loss foot of spine), grn cl slipcase. *D & D*. $40/£26

KIPLING, RUDYARD. The Feet of the Young Men. NY: Doubleday, Page, 1920. 1st ed. #188/377 signed. (Sl soiled, sl rubbed, blindstamp tp.) *Shasky*. $110/£71

KIPLING, RUDYARD. The Five Nations. London: Methuen, 1903. 1st ed, 1st issue, w/misprint 'David' for 'Saul' on p56 line 9. Teg, others uncut. Pub's gilt-lettered red cl. Fine in grn cl slipcase. *D & D*. $20/£13

KIPLING, RUDYARD. A Fleet in Being. London: Macmillan, 1898. 1st ed. Pict wrappers (spine lt chipped); gilt lettered blue morocco-backed folder; in slipcase. D & D. $70/£45

KIPLING, RUDYARD. The Fox Meditates.... (Medici Soc, 1933). 1st Eng ed. Blank presentation slip bound in. Fine in wrappers, envelope (dusty). Waterfield. $54/£35

KIPLING, RUDYARD. From Sea to Sea: Letters of Travel. NY: Doubleday, McClure, 1899. 1st ed, 1st state, w/errors on p90, p153 of Vol 2. 2 vols. xiii,460;ix,400 pp. Emb grn-ribbed cl. NF (name, bkpl). Connolly. $125/£81

KIPLING, RUDYARD. His Apologies.... (Medici Soc, 1932.) 1st Eng ed. Blank presentation slip bound in. Fine in wrappers, envelope (dusty). Waterfield. $39/£25

KIPLING, RUDYARD. The Jungle Book and the Second Jungle Book. London: Macmillan, 1894/95. 1st eds. 2 vols. 2pp undated ads in 2nd vol. J.L. Kipling (illus). Blue cl, gilt; aeg. VG (extrems sl rubbed, lt foxing vol 2) in Fine new slipcase. Davidson. $1,500/£968

KIPLING, RUDYARD. The Jungle Books. London: Macmillan, 1894, 1895. 1st eds. 2 vols. 8vo. Pub's gilt-dec blue cl. Lt rubbing, else Fine. D & D. $1,200/£774

KIPLING, RUDYARD. Just So Stories for Little Children. London: Macmillan, 1902. 1st ed. 4to. 247pp. Pict ptd red cl on bd (lt rubbed, spine edges dulled; some foxing, thumbed edges). Good. Hobbyhorse. $115/£74

KIPLING, RUDYARD. Just So Stories. London: Macmillan, 1902. 1st ed. Pub's orig stamped red cl. D & D. $590/£381

KIPLING, RUDYARD. Kim. London, 1901. 1st Eng ed. (Extrems rubbed.) Waterfield. $93/£60

KIPLING, RUDYARD. Kim. Macmillan, 1901. 1st Eng ed. Good. Fine Books. $125/£81

KIPLING, RUDYARD. Kipling's Poems Edited...by Wallace Rice. Chicago: Star Pub Co, 1899. 1st (unauthorized) ed, 1st binding. Copies also occur w/cancel title bearing George Hill's imprint. Includes verse by other authors falsely attributed to Kipling. Teg. Port. Ink sigs, Bkseller's description tipped to rear pastedown, o/w VG. Reese. $45/£29

KIPLING, RUDYARD. Letters of Marque. Allahabad, (India): A.H. Wheeler, 1891. 1st ed. 2 purple inkstamps indicating 'A.H. Wheeler & [Co.], Ry. Bookstall Proprietor' and 'Issued 1 Jan. 92' on fep, as called for by Livingston 74. (4),154,(4)pp. Blue/red cl. Fr hinge cracked internally; spine sl soiled, else VG. Chapel Hill. $300/£194

KIPLING, RUDYARD. Letters of Travel (1892-1913). London: Macmillan, 1920. 1st ed. Pub's gilt-dec red cl. VF in orig ptd dj (head chipped, piece missing), teg. D & D. $15/£10

KIPLING, RUDYARD. Life's Handicap. London/NY: Macmillan, 1891. 1st Amer ed. Dec two-tone cl. VG (ink presentation). Antic Hay. $45/£29

KIPLING, RUDYARD. Life's Handicap. Macmillan, 1891. 1st Eng ed. Pub's blue diaper-grain cl (sl shaken). Waterfield. $47/£30

KIPLING, RUDYARD. Limits and Renewals. NY: Doubleday, Doran, 1932. 1st Amer ed. Pict cl, gilt. Spine gilt sl rubbed, o/w Fine. Sadlon. $30/£19

KIPLING, RUDYARD. Limits and Renewals. London: Macmillan, 1932. 1st Eng ed. Gilt pict cl; teg. NF. Sadlon. $50/£32

KIPLING, RUDYARD. Many Inventions. NY: Appleton, 1893. 1st Amer ed. Dec red cl. VG (sm spots cl). Antic Hay. $45/£29

KIPLING, RUDYARD. The New Army in Training. London: Macmillan, 1915. 1st ed. Orig wraps, ptd in red (mild soiling, else Fine), in pouch in cl-backed folder. D & D. $10/£6

KIPLING, RUDYARD. Plain Tales from the Hills. Calcutta: Thacker, Spink, 1888. 1st issue. Plain olive cl, gold lettering, 24pp of ads inserted at end, misplaced pg # pg192. Good (extrems rubbed, bkpl). Williams. $1,542/£995

KIPLING, RUDYARD. Puck of Pook's Hill. NY, 1906. 1st Amer ed. 4 color plts by Arthur Rackham. Teg. Cl (worn, bumped; fr hinge loose; name stamped inside fr cvr). King. $50/£32

KIPLING, RUDYARD. Rewards and Fairies. GC: Doubleday, Page, 1910. 1st Amer trade ed. Frank Craig (illus). Pict cl, gilt (spine ends sl rubbed). Sadlon. $20/£13

KIPLING, RUDYARD. Rewards and Fairies. London: Macmillan, 1910. 1st Eng ed. Dec red cl; teg. About VG (lt wear; sm repair rear hinge; bkpl). Antic Hay. $50/£32

KIPLING, RUDYARD. Sea and Sussex. NY: Doubleday, Page, 1926. 1st Amer ed. Spine sl dull, o/w Fine in dj (chipped; dknd). Hermitage. $100/£65

KIPLING, RUDYARD. Sea Warfare. Macmillan, 1916. 1st ed. VG + in dj (chipped). Fine Books. $95/£61

KIPLING, RUDYARD. A Song of the English. London: Hodder & Stoughton, (1909). 1st separate ed. 30 Fine tipped-in color plts by W. Heath Robinson. Dec cl, gilt (sl worn, sl bowed). Good. Ash. $155/£100

KIPLING, RUDYARD. A Song of the English. London: Hodder & Stoughton, n.d. (1913). 2nd separate ed. 4to, 124pp, 16 full-pg tipped-in color plts by W. Heath Robinson. Blue cl. Eps lt browned, else Fine in dj w/Robinson pl fr panel (2 sm chips, else NF). Godot. $275/£177

KIPLING, RUDYARD. Songs from Books. GC: Doubleday, Page, 1912. 1st Amer ed. Pict cl (rubbed), gilt (sl dull). Sadlon. $20/£13

KIPLING, RUDYARD. Stalky and Co. London, 1899. 1st ed. 272pp; teg. Cl, gilt elephant head (bumped, dknd; name, date; inner hinges cracked; 1/2 title, tp creased). King. $65/£42

KIPLING, RUDYARD. The Story of the Gadsbys and Under the Deodars. U.S. Book Co, 1891. 1st Amer, hb ed. Lt wear spine extrems, else VG-. Fine Books. $125/£81

KIPLING, RUDYARD. The Story of the Gadsbys. Allahabad: A.H. Wheeler, (1890). 3rd Allahabad ed, w/'Lahore' ptd bottom of fr wrap. (2)ads, 85,(1) + (2)pp ads. Ptd pale grn wraps (sm tears; tape repair verso fr wrap; bkpl). Chapel Hill. $175/£113

KIPLING, RUDYARD. They. London, 1905. 1st ed. Fine (lt sunned, name, sl crease fep). Polyanthos. $100/£65

KIPLING, RUDYARD. Traffics and Discoveries. NY: Doubleday, Page, 1904. 1st Amer ed. Pict cl (sl rubbed), gilt; teg. Sadlon. $30/£19

KIPLING, RUDYARD. Traffics and Discoveries. London: Macmillan, 1904. 1st ed. Teg. NF in dj. Cahan. $150/£97

KIPLING, RUDYARD. Twenty Poems from Rudyard Kipling. London: Methuen, 1918. 1st ed. NF in blue soft wrappers lettered in blue. Vandoros. $65/£42

KIPLING, RUDYARD. Two Forewords. GC: Doubleday, Doran, 1935. 1st ed. Ltd to 950. Unopened. Cl-backed marbled bds. Fine in orig slipcase (rubbed). *Cahan.* $50/£32

KIPLING, RUDYARD. Two Forewords. NY: Doubleday, Doran, 1935. 1st ed. One of 950. Uncut, unopened. Fine in pub's slipcase. *Second Life.* $45/£29

KIPLING, RUDYARD. With the Night Mail. NY: Doubleday-Page, 1909. 1st ed. 4 color plts, pict eps. Emb pict cvr design; hinges starting, else Fine. *Else Fine.* $175/£113

KIPLING, RUDYARD. The Years Between. London: Methuen, 1919. 1st ed. Teg, others uncut. Pub's gilt-lettered red cl (spine lt faded, else VF). *D & D.* $15/£10

KIPLING, RUDYARD. The Years Between. London: Methuen, 1919. 1st ed. Buckram. Fine in dj (sl rubbed). *Pharos.* $125/£81

KIRBY, JOSHUA. Dr. Brook Taylor's Method of Perspective Made Easy.... Ipswich: Craighton, 1755. 2nd ed. 2 vols in 1. Frontis by Hogarth, xvi,78pp, 22 engr plts; 84pp, 27 engr plts; 15pp appendix, 2 engr plts. Contemp 1/2 calf, marbled bds. Sl foxing, spotting, o/w Fine. *Europa.* $349/£225

KIRBY, W.S. The Drummer Boy of the Ozarks. (West Plains, MO, 1912?). 2nd ed. Good+ in orig ptd wrappers (repaired edge chipping). *Mcgowan.* $45/£29

KIRBY, WILLIAM and WILLIAM SPENCE. An Introduction to Entomology. London: Longman et al, 1818. 3rd ed. 2 vols. (xxiii),519pp + 2pp ads; 530pp + 4pp ads; 5 hand-colored plts. Orig bds (corner worn; rebacked in cl w/new spine labels). Untrimmed set. *Schoyer.* $250/£161

KIRBY, WILLIAM and WILLIAM SPENCE. An Introduction to Entomology.... London: Longman et al, 1843. 6th ed. 2 vols. xxiii,(3),435,32(ads); viii,(2),426pp; 5 hand-colored plts. Uncut. (Lt foxed.) Grn cl, gilt (sl mkd). Good. *Cox.* $54/£35

KIRK, JOHN FOSTER. History of Charles the Bold, Duke of Burgandy. London: John Murray, 1863-68. 3 vols. Engr frontis vols 1, 2; 2 engr plans. 3/4 polished calf, gilt, raised bands, leather labels, marbled edges (spines mellowed; lt foxing). *Sadlon.* $100/£65

KIRK, ROBERT C. Twelve Months in the Klondike. London: Heinemann, 1899. 1st ed. xii,273. VG. *Walcot.* $85/£55

KIRK, RUSSELL. Watchers at the Strait Gate. (Sauk City), (1984). 1st ed. Fine (faint line on 1/2 title) in Fine dj. *Fuller & Saunders.* $25/£16

KIRKE WHITE, HENRY. The Poetical Works. London: William Pickering, 1830. 1st Aldine ed. Orig glazed linen. Port + 4pp adverts. Sound (short splits upper hinge; paper label defective). *Cox.* $23/£15

KIRKE, EDMUND. Down in Tennessee and Back by Way of Richmond. NY: Carleton, 1864. 1st ed. 282pp + ads. VG+ (lt shelfwear). *Chapel Hill.* $60/£39

KIRKE, EDMUND. The Rear Guard of the Revolution. NY, 1886. 1st ed. Frontis, 317pp + ads, fldg map. 1-inch gouge back cvr, o/w Good. *Artis.* $15/£10

KIRKE, HENRY. Twenty-Five Years in British Guiana. London, 1898. Frontis port, x,(i),364pp (feps lt browned), fldg map (sl torn). (Spine sl faded.) *Edwards.* $70/£45

KIRKER, JAMES. Captain Don Santiago Kirker. LA: Privately ptd, 1948. Ltd to 200. Fine. *Oregon.* $50/£32

KIRKLAND, JOSEPH. The Chicago Massacre of 1812. Chicago: Dibble Pub Co, 1893. 1st ed. 218pp. 3/4 leather, marbled bds; gilt top. Good (ex-lib; scuffed; shaken; few corners chipped). Howes K 186. *Bohling.* $65/£42

KIRKPATRICK, B.J. A Bibliography of E.M. Forster. London: Rupert Hart-Davis, 1965. 1st ed. Frontis. Bkpl; else Fine in dj (rubbed). *Bookpress.* $65/£42

KIRKPATRICK, JOHN ERVIN. Timothy Flint: Pioneer, Missionary, Author, Editor, 1780-1840. Cleveland: Clark, 1911. 6 plts. (Hinges sl rough.) *Schoyer.* $75/£48

KIRKPATRICK, ORION. History of the Leesburg Pioneers. Salt Lake City: Pyramid, (1934). 1st ed. Dbl-pg map. VG. *Oregon.* $45/£29

KIRKPATRICK, W.T. Alpine Days and Nights. London, 1932. 1st ed. Dj. *Bickersteth.* $28/£18

KIRKUP, JAMES. The Drowned Sailor and Other Poems. Grey Walls, 1947. 1st ed. Sl faded, else VG. *Whiteson.* $78/£50

KIRKUP, JAMES. The Submerged Village and Other Poems. OUP, 1951. 1st ed. Dec bds. Edges sl worn, else VG. *Whiteson.* $37/£24

KIRKWOOD, J.E. Forest Distribution in the Northern Rocky Mountains. Missoula, 1922. 21 tables. Gilt-emb grn cl. VG. *Brooks.* $37/£24

KIRN, WALTER. My Hard Bargain. NY: Knopf, 1990. 1st ed. Fine in NF dj. *Lame Duck.* $35/£23

KIRSCHENBAUM, BARUCH. The Religious and Historical Paintings of Jan Steen. Oxford: Phaidon, 1977. Color frontis, 132 b/w plts. Sound in dj. *Ars Artis.* $78/£50

KIRSCHENBAUM, BARUCH. The Religious and Historical Paintings of Jan Steen. NY, 1977. Color frontis. Good (sl bumped). *Washton.* $85/£55

KIRSTEIN, LINCOLN. For My Brother. London: Hogarth, 1943. 1st ed. Last 6pp top corners creased; top edge dusty, o/w Very Nice in dj (sl soiled; chipped). *Virgo.* $101/£65

KITCHIN, C.H.B. Curtains. Oxford: Blackwell, 1919. 1st ed, 1st bk. VG (spine tanned, sl foxing) in dec stiff wrappers. *Reese.* $100/£65

KITCHINER, WILLIAM. The Art of Invigorating and Prolonging Life, by Food, Clothes.... London, 1827. New ed. vi,341pp (tp sl shaved bottom edge just touching date). Contemp roan spine, marbled bds. *Whitehart.* $93/£60

KITCHINER, WILLIAM. The Cook's Oracle. London: Robert Cadell, et al, 1831. Contemp dk grn cl, spine w/ptd paper label; uncut. VG (rubbing; lt foxing; sigs). *Houle.* $300/£194

KITCHINER, WILLIAM. The Economy of the Eyes—Part I. London, 1826. 2nd ed. viii,242pp. Cl (spine defective; hinge cracked; worm holes inside margin, not affecting text); paper spine label. *Whitehart.* $70/£45

Kitten Eleven. London: Bancroft, 1965. 11x11 cm. 5 dbl-pg pop-ups. V. Kubasta (illus). Pict wraps. VG. *Book Finders.* $70/£45

KITTEN, F.G. The Minor Writings of Charles Dickens: A Bibliography and Sketch. Elliot Stock, 1900. Good. *Moss.* $40/£26

KITTREDGE, G.L. The Old Farmer and His Almanack. Boston, 1904. (Lt worn, shaken; spine frayed.) *Sutton.* $85/£55

KLADO, NICOLAS. The Battle of the Sea of Japan. London: Hodder, (1906). 57 plts. (Sl loose; few pp sl torn). *Petersfield.* $143/£92

KLAMKIN, MARIAN. Marine Antiques. NY: Dodd, Mead, (1975). 1st ed. *Lefkowicz.* $50/£32

KLAMKIN, MARIAN. Picture Postcards. London: Newton Abbot, 1974. Dj. *Edwards.* $39/£25

KLAUBER, LAURENCE M. A Key to the Rattlesnakes with Summary of Characteristics. San Diego, 1936. Wrappers (name on cvr). *Sutton.* $25/£16

KLAUBER, LAURENCE M. Rattlesnakes. UC Press, 1956. 2 vols. VG in dj (worn; chipped). *Goodrich.* $125/£81

KLEE, PAUL. On Modern Art. London: Faber, 1948. 24 dwgs by Klee (incl self-port). Sl underlining 3pp, o/w Fine. *Europa.* $22/£14

KLEE, PAUL. Pedagogical Sketchbook. London: Faber & Faber, (1925). 1st Eng ed. Emb cl. VG in dj (chipped). *Cahan.* $45/£29

KLEIN, FREDERIC SHRIVER (ed). Just South of Gettysburg, Carroll County, Maryland in the Civil War. Westminster, MD, 1963. 1st ed. VG + in VG + dj. *Pratt.* $45/£29

KLEIN, WILLIAM. Tokyo. NY: Crown Publishers, 1964. 1st ed. VG (lacks rep). *Cahan.* $125/£81

KLEINBERG, SAMUEL. Scoliosis: Pathology, Etiology, and Treatment. Balt, 1951. 1st ed. Good. *Fye.* $75/£48

KLEMENT, FRANK L. The Copperheads in the Middle West. (Chicago): Univ of Chicago, (1960). VG in dj. *Schoyer.* $30/£19

KLEMIN, DIANA. The Illustrated Book: Its Art and Craft. NY: Clarkson N. Potter, 1970. Fine in dj. *Heller.* $40/£26

KLESSE, BRIGITTE and HANS MAYR. European Glass from 1500-1800. Vienna: Kremayr & Scheriau, (1987). 1st ed. Fine. *Bookpress.* $70/£45

KLETTE, EARNEST. The Crimson Trail of Joaquin Murieta. L.A.: Wetzel, (1928). 1st ed. Lacks rep, else VG. *Perier.* $35/£23

KLINEFELTER, WALTER. A Bibliographical Check-List of Christmas Books. Portland, ME, 1937. 1/1500. Uncut. (Marginal pencilling, underlining.) *Argosy.* $75/£48

KLINEFELTER, WALTER. More Christmas Books. Portland, ME, 1938. One of 500 ptd at Southworth-Anthoensen Press. 2 color facs (1 fldg); prospectus. VG. *Argosy.* $75/£48

KLINGBERG, FRANK J. Old Sherry: Portrait of a Virginia Family. Garrett & Massie, (c. 1938). Good + (pencil mks; owner stamps) in Good + dj. *Book Broker.* $45/£29

KLIPPART, J.H. The Wheat Plant. Cincinnati, 1860. 706pp (yellowed; inscrip, ep staining), 8 plts. (Faded, soiled, stained.) *Sutton.* $115/£74

Klondike: The Chicago Record's Book for Gold Seekers. Phila: Globe Bible Pub Co, 1897. Enlgd ed. 555pp. Pict cl (rubbed, lt worn). VG + . *Harrington.* $60/£39

KLUCKER, CHRISTIAN. Adventures of an Alpine Guide. Erwin & Pleasaunce von Gaisberg (trans). London, 1932. 1st ed in English. Port, 15 plts. Dj. *Bickersteth.* $70/£45

KLUCKER, CHRISTIAN. Adventures of an Alpine Guide. H.E.G. Tyndale (ed). London: John Murray, 1932. 1st Eng ed. VG (lt spotting) in dj (sl chipped, spotted). *Hollett.* $101/£65

KLUCKHOHN, CLYDE. To the Foot of the Rainbow. NY: Century Co, (1927). 1st ed, 1st bk. Grn cl stamped in purple/black. Good in dj (sl chipped, soiled). *Karmiole.* $75/£48

KLUCKHOHN, CLYDE. To the Foot of the Rainbow. NY: Century, 1927. 1st ed, 1st bk. VG + in VG- dj. *Lame Duck.* $85/£55

KNAPP, ARTHUR MAY. Feudal and Modern Japan. Boston: Joseph Knight, 1897. 2 vols. (xiv),224; 226pp. White cl, gilt (soiled). *Schoyer.* $50/£32

KNEALE, A.H. Indian Agent. Caldwell: Caxton, 1950. 1st ed. VG in dj (edge-chipped). *Perier.* $75/£48

KNICKERBOCKER, H.R. The Siege of the Alcazar. London: Hutchinson, 1937. 3rd imp. Nice. *Patterson.* $47/£30

KNIGHT, C.W.R. The Book of the Golden Eagle. London, (1927). Color frontis; 83 plts. (Eps soiled.) Dj (soiled). *Wheldon & Wesley.* $47/£30

KNIGHT, CHARLES. Old England: A Pictorial Museum.... London: James Sangster, n.d. (1844). 2 vols. 392; 404pp. Red linen w/blind fillets, gilt; aeg. Overall Good (spine ends fraying; inner hinges cracked; lt foxing plts). Text Excellent. *Hartfield.* $295/£190

KNIGHT, CHARLES. Shadows of the Old Booksellers. London, 1865. 320pp. (Spine chipped, sm snag; cvrs flecked.) *Hayman.* $25/£16

KNIGHT, CLIFFORD. The Affair at Palm Springs. NY: Dodd, Mead, 1938. 1st ed. NF in VG + dj (edgewear). *Janus.* $125/£81

KNIGHT, CLIFFORD. The Affair in Death Valley. NY: Dodd, Mead, 1940. 1st ed. VG (lt tape shadows cvrs) in dj (sunned spine). *Janus.* $50/£32

KNIGHT, CLIFFORD. The Affair of the Crimson Gull. NY: Dodd, Mead, 1941. 1st ed. Fine in VG dj (edges chipped). *Janus.* $100/£65

KNIGHT, CLIFFORD. The Affair of the Fainting Butler. NY: Dodd, Mead, 1943. 1st ed. Fine (X on fep) in VG dj (spine sunned; stain). *Beasley.* $40/£26

KNIGHT, CLIFFORD. The Affair of the Fainting Butler. NY: Dodd, Mead, 1943. 1st ed: advance rev copy. Fine in NF dj (sm tears). *Janus.* $100/£65

KNIGHT, CLIFFORD. The Affair of the Limping Sailor. NY: Dodd, Mead, 1942. 1st ed. Fine in VG + dj (price-clipped). *Janus.* $100/£65

KNIGHT, CLIFFORD. The Affair of the Scarlet Crab. NY: Dodd, Mead, 1937. 1st ed. Insert w/list of clues present, still sealed. NF in VG + dj. *Janus.* $250/£161

KNIGHT, CLIFFORD. The Affair of the Skiing Clown. NY: Dodd, Mead, 1941. Softbound advance copy. NF (short tear), bound in NF dj. *Janus.* $125/£81

KNIGHT, JOAN. Journey to Japan. NY: Viking Penguin, 1986. 22x26 cm, 4 pop-ups, pull-tabs. Kinuko Craft (illus). VG. *Book Finders.* $30/£19

KNIGHT, JOHN ALDEN. Woodcock. N: Knopf, 1944. One of 275 numbered, signed by author and Edgar Burke (artist). Extra color plt for the delux issue bound in at pg140; teg. 1/4 tan linen, grn paper over bds, gilt woodcock. Fine + . *Bowman.* $250/£161

KNIGHT, JOSEPH (comp). A Smoker's Reveries. NY: H.M. Caldwell, 1909. Frontis (nearly detached). *Edwards.* $23/£15

KNIGHT, KATHLEEN MOORE. Bells for the Dead. GC: DCC, 1942. 1st ed. VG in dj (price-clipped; nicks, sl wear). *Mordida.* $45/£29

KNIGHT, LAURA. Oil Paint and Grease Paint. London, 1936. Rpt. Frontis (sl loose). (Spine, joints faded.) *Edwards.* $31/£20

KNIGHT, LUCIAN L. Georgia's Landmarks, Memorials and Legends. Atlanta, 1913-1914. 1st ed. 2 vols. 54 plts. 1/2 morocco (lt crack each spine; bkpls, emb lib stamps). Howes K 215. *Ginsberg.* $175/£113

KNIGHT, OLIVER. Life and Manners in the Frontier Army. Norman, (1978). 1st ed. Fine in dj. *Pratt.* $37/£24

KNIGHT, STAN. Historical Scripts, a Handbook for Calligraphers. London: A&C Black, 1984. 1st ed. VG. *Michael Taylor.* $28/£18

KNOBLAUGH, H. EDWARD. Correspondent in Spain. London: Sheed & Ward, 1937. 1st ed. Nice. *Patterson.* $54/£35

KNOOP, DOUGLAS and G.P. JONES. The Mediaeval Mason. Manchester Univ Press, 1967. 3rd ed. Presentation copy, inscribed. VG in dj. *Hollett.* $62/£40

KNOPF, ADOLPH. The Eagle River Region of the Southeastern Alaska. Washington: GPO, 1912. Fldg map, 2 fldg maps in pocket. Good+. *Blue Dragon.* $25/£16

KNOPF, ALFRED A. Portrait of a Publisher 1915-1965. NY: The Typophiles, 1965. 1st ed. 2 vols. VF in djs, orig box. *Limestone.* $155/£100

KNOPF, ALFRED A. Sixty Photographs. Knopf, 1975. 1st ed. NF in NF dj. *Bishop.* $20/£13

KNOPF, ALFRED A. Some Random Recollections. NY: Typophiles, 1949. One of 1250. *Veatchs.* $35/£23

KNOPF, S.A. Tuberculosis: A Preventable and Curable Disease.... NY, 1913. 2nd ed. Good. *Fye.* $75/£48

KNOWLER, DONALD. The Falconer of Central Park. NY: Karz-Cohl, 1984. Fine in NF dj. *Bishop.* $25/£16

KNOWLES, DAVID. The Religious Orders in England. Vol III: The Tudor Age. CUP, 1959. 1st ed. Lt underlining, cutting pasted to 1/2 title. *Hollett.* $39/£25

KNOWLES, HORACE J. Peeps into Fairyland. London: Thornton Butterworth, (1924). 1st ed. Sm folio. 6 full-pg color plts. Tan cl, gold lettering, dec cvr, spine. Sl darkening lower edge fr cvr; o/w bright in pict dj (marginal tears; 2 sm pieces missing). *Reisler.* $1,400/£903

KNOWLES, JOHN. Morning in Antibes. NY: Macmillan, 1962. 1st ed. Cl-backed bds (sl dampstain spine bottom). VG in dj (sl edgeworn). *Cahan.* $30/£19

KNOWLES, JOHN. Morning in Antibes. NY, 1962. 1st ed. Sl extrem wear, else Nice in dj (frayed, inner cellotape repair). *King.* $95/£61

KNOWLES, JOHN. A Separate Peace. NY: Macmillan, 1960. 1st ed. VG in VG dj (chipped; closed tear; lt soiled). *Revere.* $50/£32

KNOX, A.E. Ornithological Rambles in Sussex. London, 1849. 1st ed. vi,250pp + (iv)pub's ads, 4 plts. Gilt illus to upper bd. (Frontis offset; spine discolored, chipped; upper bd sl stained; ex-libris.) *Edwards.* $47/£30

KNOX, A.E. Ornithological Rambles in Sussex. London, 1855. 3rd ed. xii,260pp; 4 plts. (Spine head worn.) *Wheldon & Wesley.* $54/£35

KNOX, BILL. In at the Kill. Doubleday, 1961. 1st US ed. 1st bk. Fine in Fine dj. *Ming.* $39/£25

KNOX, DUDLEY W. The Naval Genius of George Washington. Boston: By Riverside Press for Houghton Mifflin, 1932. #428/550. 15 plts. VG. *Schoyer.* $35/£23

KNOX, DUDLEY W. The Naval Genius of George Washington. Boston: Houghton, 1932. 1st ed. One of 550 numbered. 15 plts. Bds, muslin spine, paper labels. *Ginsberg.* $85/£55

KNOX, GEORGE. Catalogue of the Tiepolo Drawings in the Victoria and Albert Museum. London: HMSO, 1960. Orig buckram. VF. *Europa.* $47/£30

KNOX, GEORGE. Catalogue of the Tiepolo Drawings. London: HMSO, 1960. (Ex-lib w/ink stamps, bkpl, tape mks.) Dj (sl soiled, spine lt faded). *Edwards.* $59/£38

KNOX, JOHN JAY. United States Notes. London: T. Fisher Unwin, 1885. 2nd ed rev. xii,247pp + 32pp cat. 3 photo-litho facs. VG. *Schoyer.* $100/£65

KNOX, JOHN. A Tour through the Highlands of Scotland, and the Hebrides Islands, in 1786. London: Ptd for J. Walter, 1787. 1st ed. clxxii,275,(1),103,(5)pp. Contemp calf, spine gilt extra. Endsheets lt foxed; joints cracking; lt rubbing; o/w VG. Internally Fine. *Reese.* $450/£290

KNOX, KATHARINE McCOOK. The Sharples: Their Portraits of George Washington and His Contemporaries. NY, 1972. Fabricoid. VG in dj. *Argosy.* $85/£55

KNOX, RONALD A. Essays in Satire. London: Sheed & Ward, 1928. 1st ed. Good. *Ming.* $47/£30

KNOX, RONALD A. Literary Distractions. NY: Sheed & Ward, (1958). 1st Amer ed. VG in dj. *Houle.* $85/£55

KNOX, THOMAS W. Camp-Fire and Cotton-Field. NY, 1865. 1st ed. 524pp. (Lacks spine cvr.) *King.* $50/£32

KNOX, THOMAS W. The Travels of Marco Polo for Boys and Girls. NY: Putnam's, 1885. 1st Amer ed. Blue dec cl, black/gilt-stamped. Lt stain tp, frontis; spine worn, o/w VG. *Hermitage.* $100/£65

KOBER, GEORGE and WILLIAM HANSON (eds). Diseases of Occupation and Vocational Hygiene. Phila, 1916. 1st ed. Inscribed. (Ex-lib.) *Fye.* $100/£65

KOBLER, JOHN. Afternoon in the Attic. NY: Dodd, Mead, (1950). 1st ed. Charles Addams (illus). VG in dj (chipped, 2-inch chip). *Godot.* $65/£42

KOCH, ALBERT. Journey Through a Part of the United States of North America in the Years 1844-1846. Ernst Stadler (trans). Southern IL Univ, (1972). 1st ed in English. Fine in Fine dj. *Oregon.* $17/£11

KOCH, CHARLES R.E. History of Dental Surgery. Fort Wayne, 1910. (Newly rebacked, saving orig labels; ex-lib; soiled, faded.) Internally Fine. *Goodrich.* $295/£190

KOCH, ROBERT. Bacteriological Diagnosis of Cholera...in Germany During the Winter of 1892-93. Edinburgh, 1894. 1st ed. 150pp. Good. *Fye.* $175/£113

KOCH, ROBERT. Investigations into the Etiology of Traumatic Infective Diseases. London, 1880. 1st Eng trans. 101pp. Good. *Fye.* $300/£194

KOCHER, A. LAWRENCE and HOWARD DEARSTYNE. Shadows in Silver: A Record of Virginia, 1850-1900, in Contemporary Photographs.... Scribner's, 1954. 1st ed. VG (dj text pasted on fr fly) in VG dj. *Book Broker.* $65/£42

KOCHER, THEODOR. Text-Book of Operative Surgery. Harold J. Stiles, C. Balfour Paul (trans). NY: Macmillan, 1911. 3rd Eng ed. Internally Good. (Rubbed; ex-lib.) *Goodrich.* $125/£81

KOCK, CHARLES PAUL DE. Little Lise. Edith Mary Norris (trans). NY: Quinby, (1904). Ltd to 1000 numbered. 1 orig etching by William Glackens. VG. *Argosy.* $85/£55

KOCKE, JAMES. Hypnotism. Boston, 1894. 1st ed, 7th thousand. 373pp. (Ex-lib.) Fye. $50/£32

KOEBEL, W.H. Madeira: Old and New. G. Bell & Sons, 1909. (Backstrip faded.) Petersfield. $33/£21

KOEHL, HERMANN et al. The Three Musketeers of the Air.... NY: Putnam's, 1928. 1st ed. Fine in NF dj. Hermitage. $85/£55

KOEHLER, OTTO A. Ku-Winda (to Hunt). San Antonio: Clegg, 1956. 1st ed. Gilt-stamped new grn binding. Lambeth. $85/£55

KOEHN, ALFRED. Japanese Flower Symbolism. Tokyo: At the Lotus Court, 1954. Japanese style string binding, stiff paper bds. Fine. Brooks. $75/£48

KOENIG, OSKAR. Pori Tupu. NY: McGraw-Hill, 1954. 1st ed. Fine in VG dj (closed tear). Bowman. $30/£19

KOESTER, F. Under the Desert Stars. Washington Square Pub, 1923. 1st ed. Fep excised, else NF in Very Nice dj (1/4-inch chip spine head, top rear panel). Aronovitz. $135/£87

KOESTLER, ARTHUR. The Gladiators. London: Cape, 1939. 1st ed. Edges sl spotted, spine sl faded, o/w VG in VG dj (browned). Virgo. $101/£65

KOESTLER, ARTHUR. The Invisible Writing. London: Collins/Hamish Hamilton, 1954. 1st ed. Name, date, o/w VG in VG dj (sl chipped). Virgo. $54/£35

KOESTLER, ARTHUR. The Lotus and the Robot. NY: Macmillan, 1961. 1st ed. Black cl titled in orange/pink. NF in dj. Cady. $15/£10

KOESTLER, ARTHUR. Spanish Testament. London: Gollancz, Left Book Club, 1937. 1st ed. Nice. Patterson. $47/£30

KOESTLER, ARTHUR. The Trail of the Dinosaur and Other Essays. NY, 1955. 1st Amer ed. VG in dj. Argosy. $30/£19

KOKOSCHKA, OSKAR. Saul and David. NY, (1973). VG in dj (price-clipped). King. $45/£29

KOLB, E.L. Through the Grand Canyon From Wyoming to Mexico. NY: Macmillan, 1914. 1st ed. Presentation copy inscribed by Ellsworth & Emery Kolb. Color frontis; 72 photo plts. Blue cl, mtd color illus cvr. Good in dj (sl chipped, soiled). Karmiole. $60/£39

KOLDEWEY, KARL. The German Arctic Expedition of 1869-70 and a Narrative of the Wreck of the 'Hansa' in the Ice.... London: Sampson, Low, 1874. 1st Eng ed. viii,590pp. 2 maps. Dec cl (sl worn). Good+. Walcot. $256/£165

KOLDEWEY, KARL. The German Arctic Expedition of 1869-70.... H.W. Bates (ed). London: Sampson Low, Marston, 1874. 1st Eng ed. viii,590. 4 colored litho plts incl frontis, 30 engr and woodcut plts, 2 colored maps (1 fldg, torn and repaired w/o loss). (Outer margins sl browned.) Grn pebble cl; black/silver vignette upper cvr, gilt vignette spine. Good (hinges cracked, extrems rubbed). Morrell. $481/£310

KOLLE, FREDERICK STRANGE. Plastic and Cosmetic Surgery. NY: Appleton, 1911. 1st ed. 8vo. Frontis; 1 color plts. VG (bkpl, sig, rubber stamp; hinges starting; sl wear). Glaser. $500/£323

KOLMER, JOHN. Penicillin Therapy. NY, 1947. 2nd ed. Good. Fye. $45/£29

KOLPACOFF, VICTOR. Prisoners of Quai Dong. NY: NAL, (1967). 1st ed. VG in dj (worn, edgetorn). Aka. $35/£23

KOMROFF, MANUEL (ed). The Travels of Marco Polo. Rochester: Ptg House of Leo Hart, 1933. 1st ed thus. Cl, dec bds. Fine in glassine (lt worn), slipcase (sl cracked). Reese. $45/£29

KONODY, P.G. and R.H. WILENSKI. Italian Painting. London: T.C. & E.C. Jack, n.d. 48 full-pg plts. Uncut. Hayman. $50/£32

KONYOT, ARTHUR. The White Rider. Barrington: Hill & Dale, 1961. 1st trade ed. Fine in Fine dj. October Farm. $45/£29

KOONTZ, DEAN R. The Eyes of Darkness. Dark Harvest, 1989. 1st hb ed. One of 400 numbered, signed. Fine in dj & slipcase. Madle. $95/£61

KOONTZ, DEAN R. Hanging On. Evans, 1973. 1st ed. NF in VG+ dj (lt foxing). Fine Books. $165/£106

KOONTZ, DEAN R. Hanging On. Evans, 1973. 1st ed. NF in VG+ dj (lt foxing). Aronovitz. $165/£106

KOONTZ, DEAN R. The House of Thunder. Dark Harvest, 1988. 1st hb ed. One of 550 numbered, signed. Fine in dj & slipcase. Madle. $65/£42

KOONTZ, DEAN R. Lightning. NY, 1988. 1st ed. Fine in dj (sl rubbed). Rees. $23/£15

KOONTZ, DEAN R. Midnight. NY, (1989). 1st ed. Inner hinge cracked, else VG in dj. King. $35/£23

KOONTZ, DEAN R. Shadowfires. Dark Harvest, 1990. 1st hb ed. One of 600 numbered, signed. Fine in dj & box. Madle. $65/£42

KOONTZ, DEAN R. Surrounded. Bobbs-Merrill, 1974. 1st ed. VG in Fine dj. Madle. $175/£113

KOONTZ, DEAN R. Writing Popular Fiction. Cincinnati, (1972). 1st ed, rev slip, press release present. VG in dj (spine sl sunned; 3 short edge tears, spot). King. $350/£226

KOPIT, ARTHUR L. Oh Dad, Poor Dad, Mamma's Hung You in the Closet and I'm Feelin' So Sad. NY, (1960). 1st Amer ed. Fine in dj (spine extrems sl rubbed; price-clipped). Polyanthos. $30/£19

KOPP, HANS. Himalaya Shuttlecock. H.C. Stevens (trans). London: Hutchinson, 1957. 1st ed. VG in dj (sl worn; edge tears). Hollett. $31/£20

KOPPETT, LEONARD. The New York Mets—The Whole Story. McMillan, 1970. 1st ed. VG+ in VG dj. Plapinger. $45/£29

KORNBLUTH, CYRIL. Christmas Eve. M. Joseph, 1956. 1st Eng ed. Fine in VG dj (short tears). Aronovitz. $30/£19

KORNBLUTH, CYRIL. Takeoff. Doubleday, 1952. 1st ed. Fine in dj (tape-stained). Madle. $40/£26

KORNBLUTH, CYRIL. Takeoff. Doubleday, 1952. 1st ed. Fine in dj along w/NF copy of proof of dj. Aronovitz. $100/£65

KORNGOLD, RALPH. Thaddeus Stevens. NY, (1955). 1st ed. Fine in dj (tear; lt wear). Pratt. $35/£23

KORNGOLD, RALPH. Thaddeus Stevens. NY: Harcourt, Brace, (1955). 1st ed. VG in dj (chipped). Mcgowan. $45/£29

KORNGOLD, RALPH. Thaddeus Stevens. NY, (1955). Stated 1st ed. VG in dj. Hayman. $20/£13

KORNILOVICH, ABRAAM L. Arts of Russia. James Hogarth (trans). London, 1967. 2 vols. 149 color plts. Djs (chipped). Edwards. $70/£45

KORTRIGHT, FRANCIS H. The Ducks, Geese and Swans of North America. Washington, 1943. 2nd ed. 36 color plts. Sm dampstain bottom of spine, o/w VG. Hayman. $20/£13

KOSHU, TSUJII. Japanese Orthodox Flower Arrangement: Miso-Go-Ryu and Saga-Ryu Schools. NY et al: Yamanaka & Co, 1938. Accordian-style binding w/gold brocade cvr. NF in slipcase. *Schoyer.* $75/£48

KOSINSKI, JERZY. Being There. NY: Harcourt, Brace, Jovanovich, (1970). 1st ed. Paperclip mk top edge 1st pp, o/w NF in dj. *Bernard.* $40/£26

KOSINSKI, JERZY. Being There. HBJ, 1970. 1st ed. Fine in NF dj (closed tear). *Fine Books.* $40/£26

KOSINSKI, JERZY. The Painted Bird. Boston: Houghton Mifflin, 1965. 1st ed, 1st issue (w/repeated line of text p270). VG in dj (short tears, lt foxed, else VG). *Godot.* $200/£129

KOSINSKI, JERZY. The Painted Bird. London: W.H. Allen, 1966. 1st UK ed. Fine in VG+ dj (lt smudged). *Bernard.* $100/£65

KOSTOFF, SPIRO. The Orthodox Baptistry of Ravenna. New Haven, 1965. 147 illus on plts. Good. *Washton.* $65/£42

KOTZWINKLE, WILLIAM. Christmas at Fontaine's. NY: Putnam's, 1982. 1st ed. Fine (sl soiled) in NF dj. *Revere.* $30/£19

KOTZWINKLE, WILLIAM. Christmas at Fontaine's. NY: Putnam's, 1982. 1st ed. VF in dj. *Else Fine.* $35/£23

KOTZWINKLE, WILLIAM. Doctor Rat. NY: Knopf, 1976. 1st ed. Fine in dj. *Antic Hay.* $35/£23

KOTZWINKLE, WILLIAM. Doctor Rat. Knopf, 1976. 1st ed. VG in dj. *Madle.* $50/£32

KOTZWINKLE, WILLIAM. Dream of Dark Harbor. GC: Doubleday, (1979). 1st ed. Fine in NF dj. *Bernard.* $17/£11

KOTZWINKLE, WILLIAM. E.T. the Extra-Terrestrial. Putnam, 1982. 1st ed. Fine in dj. *Aronovitz.* $28/£18

KOTZWINKLE, WILLIAM. Elephant Bangs Train. NY: Pantheon Books, (1971). 1st ed. New in dj. *Bernard.* $50/£32

KOTZWINKLE, WILLIAM. The Fan Man. NY: Harmony, (1974). 1st ed. NF in Fine dj. *Bernard.* $35/£23

KOTZWINKLE, WILLIAM. Fata Morgana. NY: Knopf, 1977. 1st ed. Fine in Fine dj. *Revere.* $35/£23

KOTZWINKLE, WILLIAM. Hermes 3000. NY, (1972). 1st ed. VG in dj. *King.* $25/£16

KOTZWINKLE, WILLIAM. Hermes 3000. Pantheon, 1972. 1st ed. Fine in dj. *Aronovitz.* $38/£25

KOTZWINKLE, WILLIAM. Hermes 3000. NY: Pantheon, 1972. 1st ed. Fine in dj. *Else Fine.* $65/£42

KOTZWINKLE, WILLIAM. Herr Nightingale and the Satin Woman. NY, 1978. 1st ed. Pict bds (rubbed). *King.* $25/£16

KOTZWINKLE, WILLIAM. The Oldest Man. NY: Pantheon, 1971. 1st ed. Fine in dj. *Else Fine.* $75/£48

KOTZWINKLE, WILLIAM. The Supreme, Superb, Exalted and Delightful, One and Only Magic Building. NY, (1973). 1st ed. Good in dj (soiled, rubbed, sm tear). *King.* $35/£23

KOUFAX, SANDY with ED LINN. Koufax. Viking, 1966. 1st ed. VG. *Plapinger.* $25/£16

KOVACS, ERNIE. Zoomar. NY, 1957. 1st Amer ed. NF in dj (sm tear, chips, sl rubbed, sl soiled). *Polyanthos.* $30/£19

KOVACS, ERNIE. Zoomar. GC, 1957. 1st ed, 1st bk. VG in dj (edge-frayed). *King.* $65/£42

KOWALCZYK, GEORG (comp). Decorative Sculpture. London, 1927. 320 b/w plts. (Ex-lib w/ink stamp, bkpl; lt spotted; rubbed; spine chipped, sl split w/some loss.) *Edwards.* $54/£35

KRACAUER, S. Orpheus in Paris. NY: Knopf, 1938. 1st ed. Fine in NF dj. *Beasley.* $30/£19

KRAENZEL, CARL FREDERICK. The Great Plains in Transition. Norman, 1955. 1st ed. Fine (sig, date) in dj (corner worn). *Baade.* $50/£32

KRAEPELIN, EMIL. Lectures on Clinical Psychiatry. Birmingham, 1985. (Facs of 1913 ed). Full leather. Good. *Fye.* $50/£32

KRAMER, HILTON. Brancusi: The Sculptor as Photographer. Lyme, CT/London: Callaway Editions/David Grob Editions, 1979. 1st ed. 25 full-pg b/w plts. NF (place, date on 1/2 title) in pict stiff wrappers (lt wear). *Cahan.* $45/£29

KRAMER, HILTON. Richard Lindner. Boston: NYGS, 1975. 56 color plts. VG in dj (torn). *Argosy.* $200/£129

KRAUS, DOROTHY and HENRY. The Gothic Choir-stalls of Spain. London, 1986. Good in dj. *Washton.* $45/£29

KRAUS, GEORGE. High Road to Promontory: Building the Central Pacific...across the High Sierra. Palo Alto: Amer West Pub, (1969). 1st ed. Red cl. Fine in VG+ dj (sl rubbed). *Harrington.* $45/£29

KRAUS, H.P. A Rare Book Saga. NY: Putnam's, 1978. Buckram bds. VG in dj (sl worn). *Heller.* $35/£23

KRAUSE, FEDOR. Surgery of the Brain and Spinal Cord Based on Personal Experiences. Hermann A. Haubold (trans). NY: Rebman, 1909-12. 3 vols. Orig cl (recased, orig spines laid down; ex-lib). *Goodrich.* $595/£384

KRAUSS, ROSALIND. Terminal Iron Works: The Sculpture of David Smith. MIT Press, (1971). VG. *Argosy.* $75/£48

KRAUSS, RUTH. A Hole Is to Dig. NY: Harper, 1952. 1st ed. 1st state, lacks word 'Gr-r-r-r', bottom p13. Maurice Sendak (illus). 5.5x6.75. 32pp. Fine in dj. *Cattermole.* $125/£81

KRAUSS, RUTH. Open House for Butterflies. NY: Harper, 1960. 1st ed. Maurice Sendak (illus). 5.5x6.75. 32pp. Cl. Fine in dj. *Cattermole.* $150/£97

KRAUTHEIMER, RICHARD. Ghiberti's Bronze Doors. Princeton, 1971. 4 color plts. Good. *Washton.* $35/£23

KREH, LEFTY. Fly Fishing in Salt Water. NY: Crown, 1974. 1st ptg. VF in dj. *Bowman.* $45/£29

KREN, THOMAS (ed). Renaissance Painting in Manuscripts: Treasures from the British Library. NY, 1983. Gilt dec cl. VG in slipcase, pict label. *Argosy.* $75/£48

KREPS, E. Science of Trapping. Harding, (1909). Revised. News clippings fep. VG. *Artis.* $20/£13

KREYMBORG, ALFRED. Blood of Things: A Second Book of Free Forms. NY: Nicholas L. Brown, 1920. 1st ed. Partially unopened. Lt rubbed, else NF in dj (chipped). *Cahan.* $50/£32

KREYMBORG, ALFRED. Edna: The Girl of the Street. Guido Bruno (ed). NY, (1915). 2nd ed. Unopened. Orig ptd wrappers, stapled (sl wear upper fore-edge; short breaks spine fold). *Sadlon.* $15/£10

KRIM, SEYMOUR. Shake It for the World, Smartass. NY, 1970. 1st ed. VG in dj (sl worn). *King.* $25/£16

KRIVITSKY, W.G. I Was Stalin's Agent. London: Hamish Hamilton, 1939. 1st ed. Faint offsetting from dj lettering to cl, o/w NF in Very Nice dj. *Patterson.* $116/£75

KRMPOTIC, M.D. Life and Works of the Reverend Ferdinand Konscak, S.J. 1703-1759. Boston: Stratford, 1923. 1st ed. 6 plts; 2 fldg maps. Maroon cl; gilt. *Karmiole.* $50/£32

KROEBER, A.L. BAE Bulletin 78. Handbook of the Indians of California. Washington: GPO, 1925. 1st ed. *Book Market.* $150/£97

KROEBER, A.L. Cultural and Natural Areas of Native North America. Berkeley: Univ of CA, (1963). 18 maps. VG +. *Mikesh.* $25/£16

KROEBER, A.L. Handbook of the Indians of California. BAE Bulletin 78. Washington: GPO, 1925. VG. *Perier.* $95/£61

KROEBER, A.L. The Patwin and Their Neighbors. Berkeley: Univ of CA, 1932. 1st ed. Fldg map. Largely unopened. Edgewear, spine sl dknd, o/w Fine in grey ptd wrappers. *Harrington.* $35/£23

KROEBER, THEODORA. Ishi, Last of His Tribe. Oakland/Boston: Parnassus/Houghton Mifflin, (1964). 1st ed. Yellow cl. Sm name stamp tp, o/w Fine in NF dj (sl rubbed). *Harrington.* $25/£16

KRONFELD, PETER. The Human Eye in Anatomical Transparencies. Rochester, NY, 1943. 1st ed. (Ex-lib.) *Fye.* $30/£19

KRUMBHAAR, E.B. Isaac Cruikshank. Phila: Univ of PA Press, (1966). 1st ed. 129 plts. Brn cl. Good in dj. *Karmiole.* $50/£32

KRUSSMANN, G. Manual of Cultivated Conifers. London, 1985. 2nd ed. 160 plts. *Wheldon & Wesley.* $109/£70

KRUTCH, JOSEPH W. The Gardener's World. NY, 1959. Dec cl. VG. *Brooks.* $24/£15

KUBASTA, V. The Flying Trunk. London: Bancroft, n.d. (196?). 26x20 cm. 8 dbl-pg pop-ups, pull fr cvr. Pict wraps. (Sm tear top 1st pop-up not affecting action.) *Book Finders.* $100/£65

KUBASTA, V. Hansel and Gretel. London: Bancroft, 1961. 26x20 cm. 8 dbl-pg pop-ups, pull-tab fr cvr. Glazed pict cards. VG-. *Book Finders.* $130/£84

KUBASTA, V. Moko and Koko in the Jungle. London: Bancroft, n.d. (1961). 22x32 cm. Lg dbl-pg pop-up. Pict bds. VG. *Book Finders.* $225/£145

KUBASTA, V. Sleeping Beauty. London: Bancroft, 1961. 26x20 cm. 7 dbl-pg pop-ups, 2 pulls. Pict wraps. VG-. *Book Finders.* $130/£84

KUBASTA, V. Tip and Top Look at Ships. London: Bancroft, 1964. 25x25 cm. 6 dbl-pg pop-ups. Pict wraps. VG-. *Book Finders.* $180/£116

KUBASTA, V. The Tournament. London: Bancroft, 1961. 22x32 cm. One lg dbl-pg pop-up. Pict bds. VG. *Book Finders.* $225/£145

KUBLER, GEORGE and MARTIN SORIA. Art and Architecture in Spain and Portugal and their American Dominions 1500-1800. Balt, 1959. Inscribed by Soria. 192 plts. *Washton.* $60/£39

KUBLER, GEORGE. The Louise and Walter Arenberg Collection: Pre-Columbian Sculpture. Vol II. Phila, 1954. VG. *Argosy.* $125/£81

KUBLER, GEORGE. The Religious Architecture of New Mexico in the Colonial Period and Since American Occupation. Colorado Springs: Taylor, 1940. 1st ed. VG (issued in paper, this w/lib binding). *Parker.* $100/£65

KUGY, JULIUS. Alpine Pilgrimage. H.E.G. Tyndale (trans). London, 1934. 1st ed in English. Port, 20 plts. Dj. *Bickersteth.* $54/£35

KUGY, JULIUS. Alpine Pilgrimage. H.E.G. Tyndale (trans). London: John Murray, 1934. 1st Eng ed. 21 plts; fldg map. (Cl sl marked.) *Hollett.* $70/£45

KUGY, JULIUS. Son of the Mountains. London: Thomas Nelson, 1938. 1st ed. Map; port; 8 plts. (Spine sl rubbed.) *Hollett.* $62/£40

KUHLMAN, CHARLES. Legend into History, the Custer Mystery. Stackpole, (1952). 2nd ptg. Frontis; 5 plts; 6 maps. Fldg map, fldg table in rear envelope. Pict gilt-stamped cl. VG in Good+ dj. *Oregon.* $65/£42

KUHN, THOMAS S. The Copernican Revolution. Cambridge: Harvard, 1957. 1st ed, 1st bk. NF in VG dj. *Lame Duck.* $100/£65

KUMMER, FREDERIC ARNOLD. The Great Road. Phila, etc.: Winston, 1938. Dbl-pg plt. VG in dj. *Worldwide.* $35/£23

KUMMER, FREDERIC ARNOLD. The Scarecrow Murders. NY: Dodd-Mead, 1938. 1st ed. VF in dj (minor wear spine ends). *Else Fine.* $75/£48

KUNDERA, MILAN. The Book of Laughter and Forgetting. London: Faber, 1982. 1st ed. NF in dj. *Rees.* $31/£20

KUNDERA, MILAN. The Farewell Party. Peter Kussi (trans). (London): John Murray, (1977). 1st English ed. Fine in dj. *Godot.* $40/£26

KUNDERA, MILAN. The Farewell Party. John Murray, 1977. 1st UK ed. Fine in dj. *Sclanders.* $31/£20

KUNDERA, MILAN. The Joke. London: Macdonald, (1969). 1st Eng ed, 1st bk. *Between The Covers.* $200/£129

KUNDERA, MILAN. The Joke. NY: Harper & Row, (1982). 1st US ed, rev copy w/slip inserted. NF in dj. *Antic Hay.* $50/£32

KUNDERA, MILAN. Laughable Loves. London, (1978). 1st Eng ed. VG in dj. *Argosy.* $35/£23

KUNDERA, MILAN. Laughable Loves. NY: Knopf, 1974. 1st US ed. NF in dj. *Lame Duck.* $100/£65

KUNDERA, MILAN. The Unbearable Lightness of Being. Michael Henry Heim (trans). NY: Harper, (1984). 1st ed. NF in dj (price-clipped). *Second Life.* $30/£19

KUNHARDT, C.P. Small Yachts. Their Design and Construction Exemplified by the Ruling Types of Modern Practice. NY, 1885. vi,(3)-369pp; 63 plts. Orig dec cl (worn). Sound. *Lefkowicz.* $800/£516

KUNHARDT, DOROTHY. Brave Mr. Buckingham. Harcourt, Brace, 1935. 1st ed. 8vo. Unpaginated. Grn cl. VG (corners lt bumped). *Davidson.* $85/£55

KUNHARDT, DOROTHY. Brave Mr. Buckingham. Harcourt, Brace, 1935. 1st ed. 8vo. Unpaginated. Beige cl. VG in dj (sm tears). *Davidson.* $120/£77

KUNITZ, STANLEY. Selected Poems 1928-1958. Boston, 1958. 1st Amer ed. Signed. Fine in dj (spine extrems sl rubbed; edge nicks). *Polyanthos.* $30/£19

KUNOS, IGNACZ (trans). Forty-Four Turkish Fairy Tales. London: George G. Harrap, (1913). 1st ed. Thick 4to. Teg. Willy Pogany (illus). (Fore-edge sl foxed.) Tan cl, color decs. Dec dj. *Reisler.* $650/£419

KUNZ, GEORGE FREDERICK. The Curious Lore of Precious Stones. Phila/London, 1913. 1st ed. Color frontis. Teg, rest uncut. (Lt marginal spotting; spine sl bumped.) *Edwards.* $78/£50

KUNZ, GEORGE FREDERICK. The Curious Lore of Precious Stones. Phila/London: Lippincott, 1913. 1st ed. Blue gilt-stamped cl, gilt top. Fine. *Appelfeld.* $125/£81

KUNZ, GEORGE FREDERICK. The Curious Lore of Precious Stones. NY, 1938. 7th ptg. (6 color plts). VG. *Argosy*. $85/£55

KUNZ, GEORGE FREDERICK. History of the Gems Found in North Carolina. Raleigh: E.M. Uzzell, 1907. 1st ed. 4 color lithos, 11 b/w plts. Ptd blue-grey wraps. Sig else VG. *Chapel Hill*. $150/£97

KUPER, WINIFRED (ed). Texas Sheepman. Austin: Univ of TX, 1951. 1st ed. Dj. *Lambeth*. $25/£16

KUPFERBERG, TULI. 1001 Ways to Live Without Working. NY: Birth Press, 1961. 1st issue. Sm rust mks, o/w NF in wraps. *Sclanders*. $39/£25

KUPRIN, ALEXANDRE. Sulamith: A Romance of Antiquity. B.G. Guerney (trans). NY: Privately ptd, 1928. Ltd to 1500. Gilt. Unopened (sm snag to spine). *Sadlon*. $75/£48

KURETSKY, S.D. The Paintings of Jacob Ochtervolt (1634-1682). Oxford: Phaidon, 1979. 199 plts. (Cl sl knocked.) *Ars Artis*. $93/£60

KURTZ, DONNA C. The Berlin Painter. Oxford: Clarendon Press, 1983. Good in dj. *Archaeologia*. $125/£81

KURTZ, DONNA C. and JOHN BOARDMAN. Greek Burial Customs. Ithaca: Cornell Univ Press, (1971). 90 plts, 7 maps. Good in dj (lt shelfworn). *Archaeologia*. $95/£61

KURTZMAN, H. The Mad Reader. Ballantine, 1954. 1st ed. Fine in wraps. *Aronovitz*. $40/£26

KUSEL, SAMUEL SELIG. An Englishman's Recollections of Egypt 1863 to 1887.... London: John Lane, 1915. Frontis port, 31 plts, map. (Extrems worn; spine shelfworn.) *Archaeologia*. $45/£29

KUTAL, ALBERT. Gothic Art in Bohemia and Moravia. London, 1971. Good. *Washton*. $50/£32

KYD, THOMAS. The Works of.... Oxford: Clarendon, 1901. Teg, others uncut. Grn buckram (back faded). *Petersfield*. $54/£35

L

L'AMOUR, LOUIS. Education of a Wandering Man. Bantam, (1989). 1st ed. VF in VF dj. *Oregon*. $17/£11

L'AMOUR, LOUIS. Fair Blows the Wind. NY: Dutton, 1978. 1st ed. Inscribed. Fine in Fine dj. *Lame Duck*. $350/£226

L'AMOUR, LOUIS. Hondo. Bantam, (1983). 1st deluxe ed. Map; aeg. Leatherbound. Fine. *Authors Of The West*. $50/£32

L'AMOUR, LOUIS. Kilkenny. Wingate, 1978. 1st Eng, 1st hb ed. Fine in dj (closed tear). *Fine Books*. $125/£81

L'AMOUR, LOUIS. Sackett's Land. E.P. Dutton, 1974. 1st ed. Fine in NF dj (chip). *Authors Of The West*. $75/£48

L'AMOUR, LOUIS. Sackett's Land. NY: Dutton, 1974. 1st ed. NF in NF dj. *Lame Duck*. $250/£161

L'ENGLE, MADELINE. A Wind in the Door. FSG, 1973. 1st ed. NF in NF dj. *Fine Books*. $85/£55

L'ESTRANGE, ROGER. Fables of Aesop and Other Eminent Mythologists. London: A. Bettesworth et al, 1738. 8th ed corrected. Frontis, (xii),548pp, engr port. Good in old calf (rebacked). *Cox*. $101/£65

L'ESTRANGE, ROGER. Fables of Aesop. Paris/NY: Harrison/Minton, Balch, Aug 1931. #36/595 thus of 665. 50 dwgs by Alexander Calder. 124pp. Ptd on Auvergne hand-made paper; made in Paris. Blue paper wrappers w/title, illus in blue on fr cvr, over bds. Red paper bd chemise, blue paper spine label. Offset from loosely inserted bkmk pub's note pg; blue wrappers sl foxed, else VG in red paper bd slipcase, blue title label. *Heller*. $800/£516

LA CONDAMINE, CHARLES MARIE DE. A Succinct Abridgement of a Voyage Made in the Inland Parts of South-America.... London: Ptd by E. Withers & G. Woodfall, 1747. 1st ed in English. xii,108pp; fldg engr map. Orig calf (rebacked); old eps preserved. *Bickersteth*. $543/£350

LA FARGE, CHRISTOPHER. Each to the Other. NY: Coward-McCann, 1939. 1st ed. NF in dj (sl soil; spine browned; nick; tears). *Antic Hay*. $20/£13

LA FARGE, OLIVER. As Long as the Grass Shall Grow. NY/Toronto: Alliance Book Corp, 1940. 1st ed. NF in dj (chipped). *Cahan*. $100/£65

LA FARGE, OLIVER. The Door in the Wall.... Boston: Houghton Mifflin, 1965. 1st ed. VG in dj. *Reese*. $20/£13

LA FARGE, OLIVER. The Mother Ditch. Boston/Cambridge: Houghton Mifflin/Riverside, 1954. 1st ed. Karl Larsson (illus). VG in dj. *Houle*. $75/£48

LA FARGE, OLIVER. Santa Eulalia—The Religion of a Chuchumatan Indian Town. Chicago: Univ of Chicago Press, (1947). 1st ed. Shelfwear, else Good in VG dj. *Perier*. $40/£26

LA FARGE, OLIVER. Sparks Fly Upward. Boston: Houghton Mifflin, 1931. 1st ed. Fine in dj (internal reinforcement top edge). *Reese*. $35/£23

LA FONTAINE, JEAN DE. Fables de La Fontaine. Paris: Jules Tallandier, 1904. 4to. 160pp. Benjamin Rabier (illus). Red pict buckram. Good+ (bds faded, sm spine repair). *Davidson*. $285/£184

LA FONTAINE, JEAN DE. The Fables of Jean de la Fontaine.... NY: LEC, 1930. #1461/1500 signed by Rudolph Ruzicka (illus). 2 vols. 8vo. xi,266; xiv,399,4pp; full-pg copper engr frontis. Teg. Grn cl, gilt titles, monograms. Fine set (spine lt faded, lt shelfwear). *Hobbyhorse*. $175/£113

LA FONTAINE, JEAN DE. Forty-Two Fables of La Fontaine. Edward Marsh (trans). Heinemann, 1924. 1st Eng ed. Brn buckram. Sl tanned; fore-edge, eps foxed, o/w VG. *Dalian*. $39/£25

LA FONTAINE, JEAN DE. Selected Fables of La Fontaine. Marianne Moore (trans). London: Faber & Faber, (1955). 1st Eng ed. One of 2000 ptd. NF (fep browned) in dj (sl wear, soil; sunned). *Antic Hay*. $45/£29

LA FONTAINE, JEAN DE. Selected Fables. NY: Quadrangle, MCMXLVIII. 1st trade ed. Folio, 88pp. Alexander Calder (illus). Dec paper on bds (line crack to spine). Fine in dj (sl chipped, internally reinforced). *Hobbyhorse*. $100/£65

LA GRANGE, HELEN and JACQUES. Clipper Ships of America and Great Britain 1833-1869. NY: Putnam's, (1936). 37 wood engrs. (Tp, binding sl spotted.) *Petersfield*. $50/£32

LA GRANGE, HELEN and JACQUES. Clipper Ships of America, Great Britain 1833-1869. NY: Putnam's, 1936. #177/300 numbered. Signed by Helen and Jacques La Grange (illus). 37 tipped-in color plts; teg. 3/4 sailcloth canvas, gilt dec. Fine (lt edgewear; bkpl). *Parmer*. $275/£177

LA MONT, VIOLET. Ballet in Pop-Up Action Pictures. London: Publicity, 1953. 27x21 cm. 4 dbl-pg pop-ups. Spiral bound, glazed pict wraps (extrems very worn). Internally VG. *Book Finders*. $70/£45

LA MOTTE FOUQUE, F. DE. Undine. NY: LEC, 1930. #695/1500 signed by Allen Lewis (illus). Fine in slip-case (rubbed, worn). *Williams*. $93/£60

LA PRADE, ERNEST. Alice in Music Land. London: Bodley Head, (1952). Grace Huxtable (illus). Orange cl, purple decs, lettering. Good in color pict dj. *Reisler*. $90/£58

LA ROCHE, R. Pneumonia. Phila, 1854. 1st ed. 502pp. Good. *Fye*. $200/£129

LA ROCHE, R. Yellow Fever, Considered in its Historical...and Therapeutical Relations. Phila, 1855. 1st ed. 2 vols. 813pp. (Rebacked, new eps.) *Fye*. $350/£226

LA SPINA, GREYE. Invaders from the Dark. Arkham House, 1960. 1st ed. VF in Mint dj. *Madle*. $125/£81

LABAT, GASTON. Regional Anesthesia. Phila, 1922. 1st ed. Good. *Fye*. $200/£129

LABAUME, EUGENE. A Circumstantial Narrative of the Campaign in Russia, Embellished with Plans.... London, 1815. 1st Eng ed. 2 fldg maps. 3/4 red morocco. VG. *Argosy*. $300/£194

LABBE, JOHN T. and VERNON GOE. Railroads in the Woods. Berkeley: Howell-North, 1961. 1st ed. Pict eps. Tan cl. Fine in NF- dj (inch notch fr panel, sl affecting title). *Harrington*. $35/£23

LABOUCHERE, NORNA. Ladies' Book-Plates. London/NY: Bell, 1895. 1st ed. 358pp. Good (lacks fep; sl worn; hinges tender). *Second Life*. $125/£81

LACHAMBRE, HENRI and ALEXIS MACHURON. Andree's Balloon Expedition in Search of the North Pole. NY: Stokes, c.1898. (vi)306pp. (Minor wear.) VG. *High Latitude*. $80/£52

LACK, D. The Life of the Robin. London, 1946. 2nd ed. 8 plts (1 color). Dj (worn). *Sutton*. $35/£23

LACROIX, PAUL. The Arts of the Middle Ages and the Renaissance. NY: Ungar, 1964. Fine in dj. *Europa*. $22/£14

LACY, ED. A Deadly Affair. NY: Hillman Bks, 1960. 1st ptg, pb orig. Fine. *Janus*. $15/£10

LACY, ED. Harlem Underground. NY: Pyramid Books, 1965. 1st ed: pb orig. NF. *Janus*. $20/£13

LACY, ED. Pity the Honest. NY: Macfadden Books, 1965. 1st ed: pb orig. Fine w/no spine crease. *Janus*. $25/£16

LACY, ED. The Sex Castle. NY: Paperback Library, 1963. 1st ed: pb orig. NF. *Janus*. $20/£13

LACY, ED. Sleep in Thunder. NY: Grosset & Dunlap/Tempo Books, 1964. 1st ed: pb orig. NF. *Janus*. $20/£13

LADD, HORATIO O. The Story of New Mexico. Boston: Lothrop, 1891. 1st ed. VG- (hinge starting). *Parker*. $95/£61

LADD, J. Commandos and Rangers of WWII. NY, 1978. VG in VG dj. *Clark*. $23/£15

Ladies' Wreath. Boston: n.d. (ca 1840). Illuminated presentation plt; half-title; 4 engr plts (foxed). Dec, gilt-pict red morocco; aeg. Bright. *Petrilla*. $50/£32

Lady's Diary of the Siege of Lucknow. NY: Lyon, 1858. 1st US ed, presentation copy. 191pp. Blind-stamped brn cl; gilt title. (Spine ends lt chipped.) *Petrilla*. $35/£23

LAFFERTY, R.A. The Flame is Green. Walker, 1971. 1st ed. Signed. Fine in dj. *Aronovitz*. $55/£35

LAFORGUE, RENE. The Defeat of Baudelaire: A Psycho-Analytical Study.... Herbert Agar (trans). London: Hogarth, 1932. 1st British ed. Fine in ptd dj (sl chipped). *Cahan*. $135/£87

LAFUENTE FERRARI, ENRIQUE. El Greco: The Expressionism of His Final Years. Robert Erich Wolf (trans). NY: Abrams, 1972. 50 hinged full-pg, fldg color plts; 122 hand-mtd text illus. VG in dj, slipcase. *Argosy*. $100/£65

LAFUENTE FERRARI, ENRIQUE. Goya. Complete Etchings, Aquatints and Lithographs. London: Thames & Hudson, 1962. 292 plts. Sound in dj. *Ars Artis*. $93/£60

LAGERKVIST, PAR. The Dwarf. NY: Fischer, (1945). 1st Amer ed. VG. *Argosy*. $45/£29

LAING, ALEXANDER (ed). The Haunted Omnibus. (NY): Farrar & Rinehart, (1937). 1st ed. 15 full-pg illus. Lynd Ward (illus). VG in dj (chips, short tears; else VG). *Godot*. $50/£32

LAING, ALEXANDER GORDON. Travels in Western Africa.... London: John Murray, 1825. 1st ed. x,(ii),465, fldg engr map, 7 engr plts (sl foxing adjacent to and on plts). Contemp half calf, marbled bds, spine gilt. VG (joints cracked, spine rubbed, bkpl). *Morrell*. $450/£290

LAING, GRAHAM A. Towards Technocracy. L.A.: Angelus Press, 1933. 1st ed. NF in NF dj. *Connolly*. $55/£35

LAING, JOHN. A Voyage to Spitsbergen; Containing an Account of That Country, of the Zoology of the North.... Edinburgh: Adam Black, 1818. 2nd ed. (vi)165pp. Uncut. Orig bds (rebacked in cl; worn). Lib stamp on verso of title, last leaf, else VG. *High Latitude*. $400/£258

LAING, SAMUEL. Journal of a Residence in Norway During the Years 1834, 1835 and 1836. London: Longman, 1837. 2nd ed. xii,482pp + 32pp ads. Orig blind stamped cl gilt (recased w/new eps). VG. *Hollett*. $54/£35

LAING, SETON. The Great City Frauds of Cole, Davidson, and Gordon, Fully Exposed. London: By Author, 1856. 4th ed. Mod 3/4 morocco. Good (sl rubbed). *Boswell*. $275/£177

LAKEMAN, STEPHEN. What I Saw in Kaffir-Land. Edinburgh: Blackwood, 1880. 1st ed. xi,(i)blank,211. (Spots; leaf clumsily opened.) Brn cl (recased w/new eps; sl stained). *Morrell*. $70/£45

LALLEMAND, M. A Practical Treatise on the Causes, Symptoms, and Treatment of Spermatorrhoea. Phila, 1853. 2nd Amer ed. 328pp. Good. *Fye*. $50/£32

LAMARTINE (ed). Narrative of the Residence of Fatalla Sayeghir Among the Wandering Arabs of the Great Desert. Phila: Carey, Lea & Blanchard, 1836. 204pp (1st 30pp affected by dampness). Foxing; rebacked; rubbed, o/w Good. *Worldwide*. $65/£42

LAMB, CHARLES and MARY. Tales From Shakespeare. London: Dent, 1909. 1st thus. 12 color plts. Arthur Rackham (illus). 1/2 red morocco, gilt. VG (sl wear joints, edges). *Agvent*. $175/£113

LAMB, CHARLES. A Dissertation Upon Roast Pig. Rochester: Ptg House of Leo Hart, 1932. One of 950 numbered, signed by Wilfred Jones (illus). Pub's slip tipped in. Vellum, oriental paper over bds. Fine in foil-cvrd slipcase (rubbed). *Reese*. $35/£23

LAMB, CHARLES. Elia. Essays...In The London Magazine. London: for Taylor and Hessey, 1823. 1st ed, 2nd issue, w/'13, Waterloo Place' on tp, w/the half-title, 6pp of ads. 8vo. Blue bds (inner hinges strengthened; cvrs neatly rehinged), orig white paper spine (head, foot worn), orig ptd paper spine label priced '9s. 6d'; uncut. *D & D.* $950/£613

LAMB, CHARLES. The Essays of Elia. London: Edward Moxon, 1849. viii,376pp; edges, eps marbled. Full polished tan calf, gilt. *Hollett.* $47/£30

LAMB, CHARLES. The Essays of Elia. Edward Moxon, 1867. New ed. Grn cl. Staining top pp; cvrs sl rubbed, o/w VG. *Dalian.* $54/£35

LAMB, CHARLES. The Essays of Elia. London: Dent, 1904. Charles Brock (illus). 2 vols. Tan linen spines (sl dknd, gilt unaffected), red linen bds, ribbon markers. Teg, uncut. VG. *Hartfield.* $95/£61

LAMB, CHARLES. The Letters. E.V. Lucas (ed). London: Dent & Methuen, 1935. 3 vols. 3 ports; aeg. VG (sm crease 1 spine; 1 hinge top worn; few spots). *Hollett.* $101/£65

LAMB, CHARLES. A Masque of Days. London: Cassel, 1901. 1st ed. Walter Crane (illus). 4to. 41pp. Color litho frontis, tp. Double-leaves folded in French style, edges uncut (edge of one leaf cut); dec eps. Cvr has dk grn leaves, flowers, gilt title on tan linen (edges lt rubbed). *Hobbyhorse.* $200/£129

LAMB, CHARLES. The Poetical Works of.... London: Moxon, 1836. 1st ed thus. Orig cl (rebacked), orig gilt backstrip laid down. Good (bkpl). *Reese.* $40/£26

LAMB, CHARLES. A Tale of Rosamund Gray and Old Blind Margaret. London: Golden Cockerel Press, 1928. #156/500 on handmade paper. Frontis. Uncut. Japon-backed bds. *Cox.* $56/£36

LAMB, CHARLES. The Works. London: Ollier, 1818. 1st collected ed. Leaf of ads at end dated June 1818. Orig cl, paper labels; uncut. VG in grn 1/2 morocco solander slipcase. *Argosy.* $350/£226

LAMB, CHARLES. The Works. London: C.&J. Ollier, 1818. 1st ed. 2 vols. ix,(3),291; (6),259pp + ad leaf dated June 1818. Contemp (or sl later) 1/2 calf, dbl morocco labels (chipped; hinges, edges rubbed; eps spotted). *Cox.* $465/£300

LAMB, CHARLES. The Works. William McDonald (ed). London: J.M. Dent, 1903. 12 vols. 3/4 straight grain morocco, gilt spines, raised bands; teg. Sm chip head of spine vol 1. *Sadlon.* $1,000/£645

LAMB, DANA. Bright Salmon and Brown Trout. Barre: Barre Press, 1964. One of 1500 numbered. VF in glassine, Fine slipcase. *Bowman.* $140/£90

LAMB, DANA. Where the Pools Are Bright and Deep. NY: Winchester, 1973. One of 250 numbered, signed. 1/2 blue leather. As New in orig slipcase. *Bowman.* $300/£194

LAMB, HAROLD. Chief of the Cossacks. NY: Random House, 1959. 1st trade ed. Robert Frankenburg (illus). VG in dj. *Cattermole.* $12/£8

LAMB, HAROLD. Hannibal: One Man Against Rome. NY, 1958. 1st ed. As New in dj (price-clipped). *Bond.* $20/£13

LAMBERT, C.J. and S. Voyage of the 'Wanderer' from the Journals and Letters of C. and S. Lambert. Gerald Young (ed). London, 1883. 1st ed. Frontis, xx,335pp, fldg chart, 24 color plts. (Very rubbed.) *Lefkowicz.* $300/£194

LAMBERT, MARGARET and ENID MARX. English Popular Art. London: Batsford, 1951. 1st ed. 8 color plts by Marx, 56 plts (frontis spotted). *Hollett.* $39/£25

LAMBERT, RAYMOND and CLAUDE KOGAN. White Fury. Showell Styles (trans). London: Hurst & Blackett, 1956. 1st Eng ed. 21 plts. VG in dj (sl worn). *Hollett.* $31/£20

LAMBERT, RICHARD S. The Railway King 1800-1871. A Study of George Hudson.... London: George Allen & Unwin, (1934). 1st ed. 4 full-pg plts, 4 maps. Nice. *Cady.* $25/£16

LAMBERT, RICHARD S. (ed). Grand Tour. London: Faber & Faber, 1935. 1st Eng ed. Frontis, 28 plts, fldg map. Blue cl (later binding). Fine in dj. *Dalian.* $54/£35

LAMBERT, ROSE. Hadjin, and the Armenian Massacres. NY, (1911). 1st ed. Cl (rubbed, soiled). *King.* $50/£32

LAMBETH, MARY WEEKS. Memories and Records of Eastern North Carolina. (Nashville: Curley Ptg Co, 1957). 1st ed. Author presentation. NF in VG dj. *Mcgowan.* $75/£48

LAMOND, H. The Sea-Trout. London, 1916. 9 color, 38 plain plts (2 short tears bottom plt 1). Unopened. *Henly.* $116/£75

LAMONT, JAMES. Seasons with the Sea-Horses. NY: Harper, 1861. 1st Amer ed. 282pp + (6)pp ads, 7 plts, fldg map. (Lib bkpl, # tp.) *Lefkowicz.* $95/£61

LAMPING, CLEMENS. French in Algiers. Crusades in Africa. And a Five Months' Captivity among the Arabs. Duff Gordon (trans). NY: Leavitt, Trow, 1848. x,178pp. Blindstamped tan cl (faded). *Schoyer.* $65/£42

LAMPMAN, B. The Tramp Printer. Portland, OR: Metropolitan Press, 1934. One of 500 numbered. Uncut. 1/4 cl. Good. *Moss.* $40/£26

Lamps on the Prairie. W.P.A., Kansas (comp). Emporia Gazette Press, 1942. 1st ed. Blue fabricoid, gilt decs. Fine (fep corner clipped) in dj (chipped). *Connolly.* $45/£29

LAMSON, MARY SWIFT. Life and Education of Laura Dewey Bridgman. Boston: New England Pub, 1878. 1st ed. xi,373pp (pencil mks margins); port; 3 fldg plts. Dec cl. *Petrilla.* $30/£19

LANCASTER, CLAY. The Japanese Influence in America. NY, (1963). 8 color plts. Dec eps. Leather label. Fine. *Argosy.* $125/£81

LANCASTER, MARIE-JAQUELINE (ed). Portrait of a Failure. London: Blond, 1968. 1st ed. VG in dj (sl browned, chipped, price-clipped). *Virgo.* $54/£35

LANCASTER, OSBERT. All Done from Memory. John Murray, 1963. 1st Eng ed. Color frontis. Yellow cl. Fine in dj. *Dalian.* $31/£20

LANCASTER, OSBERT. Homes Sweet Homes. John Murray, (1939). 1st ed. 34 full-pg illus by Lancaster. Dec eps. Yellow pict cl. Dj (spine top lacks piece; sl defective at foot). *Bickersteth.* $47/£30

LANCASTER, ROBERT A. Historic Virginia Homes and Churches. Lippincott, 1915. 1st ed. Contents VG (repair; snagged spine, rubbed). *Book Broker.* $185/£119

LANCASTER, ROBERT A. Historic Virginia Homes and Churches. Phila: Lippincott, 1915. 1st ed. Extrems sl worn, else VG. *Bookpress.* $250/£161

LANCASTER, ROBERT A. Historic Virginia Homes and Churches. Phila: Lippincott, 1915. Ltd ed. Grn pict cl, gilt. Fine. *Pharos.* $125/£81

LANCASTER, SAMUEL C. The Columbia: America's Great Highway.... Portland: Samuel Lancaster, 1926. 3rd ed. Signed presentation. 26 color plts. VG in VG dj. *Perier.* $45/£29

LANCEREAUX, ETIENNE. A Treatise on Syphilis Historical and Practical. London, 1868-1869. 1st ed in Eng. 2 vols. (Lt wear; lib stamps.) *Goodrich.* $135/£87

LANCEREAUX, ETIENNE. A Treatise on Syphilis. G. Whitley (trans). London: New Sydenham Soc, Vols XXXVIII, XLI, 1868-69. 2 vols. v,405; 379pp (margins lt yellowed, tender). Emb cl (corners rubbed; rebacked w/orig spine laid down vol 2), leather labels. *Edwards.* $93/£60

LANCEREAUX, ETIENNE. A Treatise on Syphilis. London, 1868. 1st Eng trans. 2 vols. *Fye.* $250/£161

Land at War. (By Laurie Lee.) HMSO, 1945. 1st ed. Wrappers sl rubbed, nicked, o/w Fine. *Rees.* $31/£20

LAND, ANDREW. Angling Sketches. London/NY: Longmans, Green, 1891. 1st ed. xii,176pp, 4pg pub's cat (sl foxing), 3 etchings. (Rubbed, bumped.) *Blue Mountain.* $150/£97

LANDER, RICHARD and JOHN. Journal of an Expedition to Explore the Course and Termination of the Niger. NY: Harper, 1832. 1st Amer ed. 2 vols. Frontis port, 384; (338)pp (foxed) + 2pp ads; 2 maps (1 fldg), 3 engrs. Tan cl (foxed). *Schoyer.* $125/£81

Landlord's Law. (London): Ptd by E. & R. Nutt, R. Gosling, 1739. 8th ed. Full sheep. *Boswell.* $450/£290

LANDON, FRED. Lake Huron. Indianapolis: Bobbs-Merrill, 1944. *Peninsula.* $22/£14

LANDON, MELVILLE D. Kings of the Platform and Pulpit. Chicago: Werner, 1895. 570pp. VG. *Connolly.* $45/£29

LANDON, PERCEVAL. Lhasa. London: Hurst & Blackett, 1905. 2nd ed. 2 vols. Teg. Buckram gilt (spines sunned, nicks). *Hollett.* $233/£150

LANDON, PERCEVAL. The Opening of Tibet. NY: Doubleday, Page, 1905. 1st ed, US issue. Color tipped-in frontis, 48 full-pg plts. Teg. Nice (fr bd w/darker staining). *Cady.* $85/£55

LANDOR, A. HENRY SAVAGE. *See* SAVAGE-LANDOR, A. HENRY

LANDOR, WALTER SAVAGE. Letters of an American, Mainly on Russia and Revolution. London: Chapman & Hall, 1854. 1st ed. Unopened. (Bottom corners, spine worn.) Orig wrappers. *Pharos.* $100/£65

LANDOR, WALTER SAVAGE. Pericles and Aspasia. London: Saunders & Otley, 1836. 1st ed. 2 vols. Spine paper, labels chipped, cracked. Cl folder, slipcase. *Sadlon.* $150/£97

LANDSBOROUGH, D. A Popular History of British Sea Weeds. London, 1851. 2nd ed. xvi,400pp; 2 plain, 20 color plts. (Cl repaired.) *Wheldon & Wesley.* $62/£40

LANDSDELL, HENRY. Through Siberia. Boston: Houghton Mifflin, 1882. 2 vols. Tipped-on frontis photo, (xviii),(392); (xii),(404)pp, 2 fldg maps. Dec cl (discolored, rubbed, spines cocked, pockets removed, mks). *Schoyer.* $75/£48

LANDSTEINER, KARL. The Specificity of Serological Reactions. Springfield, 1936. 1st Eng trans. Good. *Fye.* $200/£129

LANDSTROM, BJORN. Ships of the Pharaohs. GC: Doubleday, (1970). 1st ed. Map. Good in dj. *Karmiole.* $45/£29

LANDSTROM, BJORN. Ships of the Pharaohs: 4000 Years of Egyptian Shipbuilding. GC: Doubleday, (1970). Good in dj. *Archaeologia.* $150/£97

LANE, JANE. Titus Oates. London, 1944. 1st ed. VF in Fine dj. *Bond.* $20/£13

LANE, LEVI. The Surgery of the Head and Neck. (SF): By the Author, (1896). 1st ed. xiii,7-1180pp. NF. *Glaser.* $350/£226

LANE, LEVI. The Surgery of the Head and Neck. Phila, 1898. 2nd ed. 1180pp. Good. *Fye.* $200/£129

LANE, LEVI. The Surgery of the Head and Neck. Phila: Blakiston, 1898. 2nd ed. xxx,7-1180pp. NF. *Glaser.* $225/£145

LANE, LYDIA S. I Married a Soldier. Phila, 1893. 1st ed. 214pp. Dec cl (spine sl faded). Howes L 68. *Ginsberg.* $300/£194

LANE, RICHARD. Hokusai. London, 1989. 1st UK ed. 93 color plts. Dj. *Edwards.* $54/£35

LANE, RICHARD. Images from the Floating World. NJ, 1978. Dj. *Edwards.* $39/£25

LANE-POOLE, STANLEY. Sir Richard Church.... London: Longmans, Green, 1890. 76pp + 24pp pub's cat, 2 maps. Sl shaken. *Schoyer.* $75/£48

LANE-POOLE, STANLEY. The Story of the Moor in Spain. NY/London: Putnam/Fisher, Unwin, 1896. xx,285pp; fldg map. Sl rubbed, o/w VG. *Worldwide.* $25/£16

LANES, SELMA G. The Art of Maurice Sendak. NY: Abrams, 1980. 1st ed. 278pp, 94 full color illus. Fine. *Davidson.* $150/£97

LANG, ANDREW (ed). All Sorts of Stories Book by Mrs. Lang. NY: Longmans Green, 1911. H.J. Ford (illus). 12mo. Aeg. Pict cl. Lang obit, tribute from G.K. Chesterton fixed to rear blank pp. NF. *Book Adoption.* $200/£129

LANG, ANDREW (ed). The Animal Story Book. London et al: Longmans, Green, 1896. 1st ed. H.J. Ford (illus). Blue pict cl, gilt. Fine. *Limestone.* $215/£139

LANG, ANDREW (ed). The Orange Fairy Book. London, 1906. 1st ed. 8 color plts by H.J. Ford. Aeg. Orange cl, gilt. Inscrip; spine sl dull, o/w bright. *Words Etc.* $101/£65

LANG, ANDREW (ed). The Orange Fairy Book. London: Longmans, Green, 1906. 1st ed. H.J. Ford (illus). 12mo. Aeg; plain eps. Pict cl (soiled; spine dknd). VG. *Book Adoption.* $140/£90

LANG, ANDREW (ed). The Orange Fairy Book. London: Longmans, Green, 1906. 1st ed. 8vo, 8 full-pg color plts, 50 b/w dwgs by H.J. Ford. Gilt dec cvr, spine. Aeg. Good. *Reisler.* $450/£290

LANG, ANDREW (ed). The Pink Fairy Book. London: Longmans Green, 1897. 1st ed. H.J. Ford (illus). 12mo. Pict cl (spine worn). VG. *Book Adoption.* $75/£48

LANG, ANDREW (ed). The Pink Fairy Book. London: Longmans, Green, 1897. 1st ed. viii,(2),360pp. H.J. Ford (illus). Full red polished calf (rebound; orig cl bound in at back); gilt spine w/black leather label signed by 'Asprey, London'; aeg. Fine. *Karmiole.* $175/£113

LANG, ANDREW (ed). Poet's Country [Scotland]. Phila: Lippincott, 1907. 1st Amer ed. 50 color plts. Pict cl dec gilt/grn/pink. Fine. *Hermitage.* $75/£48

LANG, ANDREW (ed). The Red Fairy Book. Phila: David McKay, (1924). 1st ed. 4to. 85pp; 9 color plts by Gustaf Tenggren. Red cl, pict paste label; illus eps. VG (sl water damage spine foot; hinges strengthened, slit rear hinge). *Drusilla's.* $195/£126

LANG, ANDREW (ed). Red Fairy Book. London: Longmans, Green, 1890. #54/113 ptd on lg paper. H.J. Ford and Lancelot Speed (illus). 4to. (1/2 title unevenly cut top edge). Cl-backed bds (spine, corners worn). *Reisler.* $275/£177

LANG, ANDREW (ed). The Violet Fairy Book. London: Longmans, Green, 1901. 1st ed. 8 color plts. Aeg. Pictorial cl, gilt (faint wear). *Limestone.* $195/£126

LANG, ANDREW (ed). The Yellow Fairy Book. London, 1894. 1st ed. Aeg. Yellow cl (rubbed through spine hinge), gilt. Name; sl shaken; prelims foxed; spine dknd, o/w VG. *Words Etc.* $93/£60

LANG, ANDREW. Adventures among Books. London: Longman, 1905. 1st ed. Frontis. Back panel stained, else VG. *Limestone.* $55/£35

LANG, ANDREW. The Blue Poetry Book. London: Longmans, Green, 1891. 1st ed. 8vo. H.J. Ford & Lancelot Speed (illus). Aeg. Dk blue cl (sl worn), gilt dec. *Reisler.* $175/£113

LANG, ANDREW. The Book of Romance. London: Longmans Green, 1902. 1st ed. 8vo. 384pp; 8 color, 35 b/w plts by H.J. Ford. Aeg. Blue cl, gilt. Sl loose, o/w VG. *Drusilla's.* $110/£71

LANG, ANDREW. Books and Bookmen. NY: George J. Coombes, 1886. 1st ed. Inscrip year of pub; lg bkpl w/sl offset opposite, o/w VG. *Reese.* $85/£55

LANG, ANDREW. Border Ballads. London: Lawrence & Bullen, 1895. Ltd to 750. xxv,87pp; 12 etched plts. Orig cl gilt (stained, rubbed). *Hollett.* $70/£45

LANG, ANDREW. The Brown Fairy Book. London: Longmans, Green, 1908. 350pp, 8 color plts by H.J. Ford. Brn cl, gilt; aeg. VG (name). *Davidson.* $160/£103

LANG, ANDREW. Cock Lane and Common-Sense. London: Longman's, Green, 1894. 1st ed. Corner bumped, scraped, else VG. *Hermitage.* $75/£48

LANG, ANDREW. Fairy Books. Longmans, Green, 1889-1910. 1st eds. 12 bks (complete set). H.J. Ford (illus). VG set (minor repairs, soil). *Davidson.* $3,500/£2,258

LANG, ANDREW. Homer and His Age. NY: Longmans, Green, 1906. 8 plts. (Sm tears spine.) *Archaeologia.* $45/£29

LANG, ANDREW. How to Fail in Literature. London: Field & Tuer, Leadenhall Press, 1890. 1st ed. 95,(iv)pp; uncut (edges sl dusty; lib stamp, marginal blind stamps). Limp cl (rebacked). *Hollett.* $70/£45

LANG, ANDREW. Letters to Dead Authors. NY: Scribner's, 1886. 1st Amer ed. VG (ink name, date; lt smudge, soiling). *Hermitage.* $45/£29

LANG, ANDREW. Prince Prigio and Prince Ricardo. London: J.M. Dent, (1961). 1st ed thus. 8vo. 4 full-pg color plts by D. Watkins-Pitchford. Red/beige dec cl, blue lettering. Good in color dj. *Reisler.* $50/£32

LANG, ANDREW. Prince Prigio. Boston: Little, Brown, 1942. 1st ed thus. 8vo. Robert Lawson (illus). Illus grn cl. Good in color pict dj (worn). *Reisler.* $90/£58

LANG, ANDREW. The Princess Nobody: A Tale of Fairyland. London: Longmans, Green, (1884). 1st ed thus. 4to. Richard Doyle (illus). Cl-backed illus bds (sm rubbed spot; sl edgewear). *Reisler.* $575/£371

LANG, ANDREW. The Red Romance Book. London: Longmans Green, 1905. 1st ed. 8vo. 8 color, 28 b/w plts by H.J. Ford. Aeg. Red cl, gilt. VG (sm spot spine). *Drusilla's.* $110/£71

LANG, ANDREW. Rhymes a la Mode. London: Kegan Paul, Trench, 1885. 1st ed. Frontis, viii,(2),139pp. Teg, rest uncut. Smooth grn cl, gilt, beveled edges. VG. *Cox.* $28/£18

LANG, ANDREW. A Short History of Scotland. Edinburgh: William Blackwood, 1911. 1st Eng ed. Blue cl. Eps sl browned, o/w VF in dj (sl chipped, tanned). *Dalian.* $39/£25

LANG, ANDREW. The True Story Book. London: Longman's Green, 1893. 1st ed. NF. *Bishop.* $25/£16

LANG, H.O. History of the Willamette Valley. Portland: Geo. H. Himes, 1885. 902pp. (Rebound.) *Perier.* $250/£161

LANG, JOHN D. and SAMUEL TAYLOR. Report of a Visit to Some of the Tribes of Indians, Located West of the Mississippi River. NY: M. Day, 1843. 1st ed. Mod gilt-lettered lib cl, orig ptd wrappers bound in. VG (sl internal foxing, staining; wrappers, tp chipped, stained). Howes L 72. *Harrington.* $110/£71

LANG, JOHN D. and SAMUEL TAYLOR. Report of a Visit to Some of the Tribes of Indians, Located West of the Mississippi River. NY: Mahlon Day, 1843. 1st ed. 34pp. Orig ptd wrappers (lt creased, sm stain tp, fore-edge). VG in cl folder, morocco-backed slipcase (rubbed). Howes L 72. *Cahan.* $300/£194

LANG, MRS. Princes and Princesses. London: Longmans, Green, 1908. 1st ed. 8vo. 8 full-pg color plts by H.J. Ford. Aeg. Illus blue cl, gilt. *Reisler.* $150/£97

LANG, MRS. The Red Book of Heroes. London: Longmans, Green, 1909. 1st ed. 8vo. 8 color plts by A. Wallis Mills. Aeg. Red cl, gilt (spine sl faded). *Reisler.* $100/£65

LANGDALE, C. Gwen John. New Haven/London: Yale Univ, 1987. Sound in dj. *Ars Artis.* $68/£44

LANGDON, CHARLES W. Treatise on the Civil and Criminal Jurisdiction of Justices of the Peace and Duties of Sheriffs and Constables.... SF: A.L. Bancroft, 1870. New 1/4 calf, marbled bds. VG. *Boswell.* $175/£113

LANGDON, HELEN. Claude Lorrain. Oxford: Phaidon, 1989. Fine in Mint dj. *Europa.* $34/£22

LANGDON-DAVIES, JOHN. Air Raid. The Technique of Silent Approach; High Explosive Panic. London: Routledge, 1938. 1st ed. VG. *Patterson.* $54/£35

LANGDON-DAVIES, JOHN. Behind the Spanish Barricades. London: Secker & Warburg, 1936. 1st ed. Nice in pict dj (chipped, torn, but pretty well complete). *Patterson.* $101/£65

LANGE, DOROTHEA and PAUL TAYLOR. An American Exodus. NY, (1939). (Corners bumped.) Dj (torn). *Argosy.* $75/£48

LANGE, DOROTHEA and PAUL TAYLOR. An American Exodus. NY: Reynal & Hitchcock, 1939. 1st ed. Extrems sl rubbed, else VG in dj (well worn). *Cahan.* $225/£145

LANGE, JOHN. (Pseud of Michael Crichton.) Binary. London: Heinemann, 1972. 1st British ed. NF in dj. *Silver Door.* $30/£19

LANGE, JOHN. (Pseud of Michael Crichton.) Binary. NY: Knopf, 1972. 1st ed. Fine in dj (short tear lower spine fold). *Else Fine.* $50/£32

LANGE, JOHN. (Pseud of Michael Crichton.) Binary. NY: Knopf, 1972. 1st ed. Fine in dj. *Mordida*. $65/£42

LANGER, WILLIAM. The Undeclared War 1940-1941. Harper, 1953. 1st ed. VG+ in VG dj. *Bishop*. $15/£10

LANGFELD, WILLIAM R. (comp). Washington Irving. A Bibliography. NY: NY Pub Lib, 1933. Ltd to 450. Frontis port; 8 plts. Black cl, gilt. *Karmiole*. $50/£32

LANGFORD, NATHANIEL. Diary of the Washburn Expedition to the Yellowstone and Firehole Rivers in the Year 1870. (St. Paul, 1905). 1st ed. Pict cl. VG. *Schoyer*. $85/£55

LANGFORD, NATHANIEL. Vigilante Days and Ways. Missoula: MT State, 1957. Rpt of Howes L 78. VG in dj (worn). *Parker*. $45/£29

LANGHAM, JAMES R. A Pocket Full of Clues. NY: S&S, 1941. 1st ed. Fine in dj (nicks, tears, wear). *Mordida*. $40/£26

LANGLEY, B. and T. The Builders Jewel.... London: Longman et al, 1797. Engr frontis, 46pp, 99 plts. Sheep (rubbed, dusty). *Marlborough*. $233/£150

LANGLEY, HAROLD. To Utah with the Dragoons and Glimpses of Life in Arizona and California. 1858-1958. Univ of UT, (1974). 1st ed. Frontis. VF in VF dj. *Oregon*. $35/£23

LANGRIDGE, IRENE. William Blake: A Study.... London, 1904. Teg, rest uncut. (Feps browned; lt spotting; spine faded, worn head w/sl loss.) *Edwards*. $54/£35

LANGTON, JANE. Dark Nantucket Moon. NY: Harper, 1975. 1st ed. NF in NF dj. *Janus*. $65/£42

LANHAM, EDWIN. Murder on My Street. NY: Harcourt, (1957). 1st ed. Nice (sl edgewear) in dj (sm rub). *Reese*. $55/£35

LANIER, MILDRED B. English and Oriental Carpets at Williamsburg. Williamsburg: Colonial Williamsburg Foundation, (1975). 1st ed. Frontis. Fine in dj (worn). *Bookpress*. $35/£23

LANIER, SIDNEY (ed). The Boy's Froissart. NY: Scribner's, 1879. 1st ed, 1st state w/punctuation error on tp and binding. Blue-grey pict cl, gilt. VG. BAL 11257. *Macdonnell*. $75/£48

LANIER, SIDNEY. The Marshes of Glynn.... NY: Duell, Sloan & Pearce, (1949). 1st ed. VG (lt offset from endsheets) in dj (lt edgeworn, nicked). *Reese*. $35/£23

LANIER, SIDNEY. Poems. Phila/London: Lippincott, 1877. 1st ed, 1st binding w/design present on back cvr. Brn cl, gilt. Fine. BAL 11249. *Macdonnell*. $275/£177

LANIER, SIDNEY. Poems. Phila: Lippincott, 1877. 1st ed. 94pp. Terra-cotta cl w/beveled edges (binding state A w/circular device blindstamped back cvr). VG (inscrip; spine ends sl worn). BAL 11249. *Chapel Hill*. $350/£226

LANIER, SIDNEY. Selected Poems of.... NY: Scribner's, 1947. 1st ed. Pub's dated rev slip laid in. Gilt cl. VG in dj (shelfworn). BAL 11297. *Reese*. $25/£16

LANIN, E.B. Russian Traits and Terrors. Boston: Tucker, 1891. 288pp (paper browned). Blue cl, blind-, gilt-stamped (pocket removed). *Schoyer*. $45/£29

LANKESTER, MRS. Talks About Plants. London: Griffith & Farran, 1879. 252pp + 32pp ads; 6 color plts, guards; 26 wood engrs. Aeg. Gilt-dec pict cl. *Quest*. $75/£48

LANMAN, CHARLES. Adventures of an Angler in Canada, Nova Scotia and the United States. R. Bentley, 1848. Frontis. Brn cl (sl rubbed; few tears backstrip; label fr cvr). *Petersfield*. $194/£125

LANMAN, CHARLES. Farthest North. NY: D. Appleton, 1885. (ii)333pp. Frontis port, 4 plts, fldg map. Orig dec cl. VG (spine repaired, new eps). *High Latitude*. $100/£65

LANNING, JOHN TATE. The Diplomatic History of Georgia. Chapel Hill: Univ of NC Press, 1936. 1st ed. Fldg map. Brick-red cl. NF in dj (price-clipped). *Chapel Hill*. $85/£55

LANNING, JOHN TATE. The Spanish Missions of Georgia. Chapel Hill: Univ of NC Press, (1935). 1st ed. #501/525 signed. Brn cl. Bkpl, else Fine in dj (price-clipped). Howes L 92. *Chapel Hill*. $125/£81

LANSDELL, HENRY. Through Siberia. Boston: Houghton, Mifflin, 1882. 3rd ed. Frontis, xxiv,812pp + 4pp reviews; fldg map, 15 full-pg plts. Gray cl. VG (spine, upper fr cvr sl mkd, spotted). *Cady*. $60/£39

LAPHAM, MACY H. Crisscross Trails. Berkeley: Willis E. Berg, 1949. 1st ed. VG. *Connolly*. $47/£30

LAPKOVSKAYA, E.A. Applied Art of the Middle Ages in the Collection of the State Hermitage. Moscow, 1971. Lib of Congress dup w/stamp on fep. 84 color plts. Good. *Washton*. $90/£58

LAPP, RUDOLPH M. Blacks in Gold Rush California. New Haven: Yale Univ Press, 1977. 1st ed. Inscribed. Yellow cl. Fine in NF dj. *Harrington*. $40/£26

LARCOM, LUCY. A New England Girlhood, Outlined from Memory. Boston: Houghton, Mifflin, 1890. 274pp,(2)pub ads. Dec blue cl. (Blank flyleaf excised.) *Petrilla*. $20/£13

LARDEN, WALTER. Argentine Plains and Andine Glaciers. London: T. Fisher Unwin, 1911. 1st ed. Map; teg, uncut. (Lt spotting.) Pict red cl gilt (short nick spine). *Hollett*. $217/£140

LARDEN, WALTER. Recollections of an Old Mountaineer. London: Edward Arnold, 1910. 1st ed. 17 plts. VG. *Hollett*. $101/£65

LARDNER, DIONYSIUS. The Cabinet Cyclopaedia...A Treatise on...the Manufactures in Metal. Vol 1 Iron and Steel. London: Longman et al, 1831. 1st ed. Engr tp,viii,342pp; tp at rear, errata slip tipped in. Untrimmed. Paper label on spine. VG (2 inscrips, lacks fep, extrems sl chipped). *Connolly*. $95/£61

LARDNER, DIONYSIUS. The Microscope. London, 1856. vi,81-112,112pp + 16pp ads. Good. *Henly*. $56/£36

LARDNER, JOHN. Strong Cigars and Lovely Women. NY, (1951). 1st ed. Fine in VG dj. *Fuller & Saunders*. $35/£23

LARDNER, RING and N.W. PUTNAM. Say It with Oil. Doran, 1923. 1st ed. Bound dos-a-dos w/Say It with Bricks. Lt soil to bd edges, else VG in dj (dust soiling, rubbing). *Fine Books*. $90/£58

LARDNER, RING. The Big Town. Indianapolis: Bobbs-Merrill, (1921). 1st ed. Grn cl (lt rubbed, bumped). VG. *Hermitage*. $65/£42

LARDNER, RING. The Golden Honeymoon and Haircut. Scribners/American Booksellers Assoc, 1926. 1st ed. NF. *Fine Books*. $225/£145

LARDNER, RING. Gullible's Travels. Indianapolis: Bobbs Merrill, (1917). 1st ed. Blue cl, white lettering (effaced from spine). Bright (rear hinge paper cracking). *Macdonnell*. $75/£48

LARDNER, RING. Gullible's Travels. London: C&W, 1926. 1st ed. Edges foxed, o/w VG. *Rees*. $70/£45

LARDNER, RING. The Love Nest and Other Stories. Scribners, 1926. 1st ed. Inscribed. Spine faded, else VG in Nice dw (wear, chipping). *Fine Books.* $875/£565

LARDNER, RING. The Portable Ring Lardner. NY: Viking, 1946. 1st ed. VG in dj (lt aged). *Pharos.* $30/£19

LARDNER, RING. Treat 'Em Rough. Indianapolis: Bobbs Merrill, (1918). 1st ed, 2nd ptg w/poem 'To R.W.L.' on p6. Tan cl, pict paper label. Fine. *Macdonnell.* $50/£32

LARDNER, RING. Treat 'Em Rough. Letters from Jack the Kaiser Killer. Indianapolis, 1918. 2nd issue w/poem on p6. NF (sl rubbed, lt soiled). *Polyanthos.* $30/£19

LARDNER, RING. What of It? NY: Scribner's, 1925. 1st ed, 1st issue w/pp200 & 201 transposed. Sl rubbed, o/w VG. *Hermitage.* $45/£29

LARGE, E.C. Asleep in the Afternoon. Cape, 1938. 1st Eng ed. Grn cl. Name, o/w NF in dj (sl soiled; nicked). *Dalian.* $39/£25

LARKEY, JOANN LEECH. Davisville '68. The History...of Davis, Yolo County, California. Davis Hist & Landmarks Commission, 1969. 1st ed. Fine. *Connolly.* $55/£35

LARKIN, LEW. Bingham. Fighting Artist. Kansas City: Burton Pub Co, (1954). 1st ed. Inscribed, signed. Blue cl. Fine in dj (lt worn). *Glenn.* $50/£32

LARKIN, PHILIP. All What Jazz. NY: St. Martin's, (1970). 1st Amer ed. Fine in Fine dj. *Dermont.* $75/£48

LARKIN, PHILIP. All What Jazz. A Record Diary 1961-68. London: Faber & Faber, 1970. 1st ed. Rear bd discolored, o/w Fine in NF dj. *Beasley.* $75/£48

LARKIN, PHILIP. Aubade. (Salem, OR: Charles Seluzicki, 1980). 1st ed. #68/250 initialled by author and printer. Plain wrappers in orig silver-lined envelope. Fine. *Heller.* $250/£161

LARKIN, PHILIP. Collected Poems. London: Faber, 1988. 1st issue. Fine in Fine dj (sl creasing spine head). *Lewton.* $39/£25

LARKIN, PHILIP. Femmes Damnees. Sycamore Broadsheet 27, 1978. 1st UK ed. Single sheet folded 3 times. Fine. *Sclanders.* $31/£20

LARKIN, PHILIP. High Windows. Faber, 1974. 1st ed. Fine in dj. *Poetry.* $54/£35

LARKIN, PHILIP. Jill. Fortune Press, (1946). 1st ed. Black sand-grain cl (shaken; gatherings adrift); all edges cut; top edge sprinkled orange. *Waterfield.* $318/£205

LARKIN, PHILIP. Jill. NY: St. Martin's, (1964). 1st Amer ed. VG in dj (rubbed, lt faded). *Hermitage.* $75/£48

LARKIN, PHILIP. The North Ship. Fortune Press, 1945. 1st UK ed. Black cl w/gold spine lettering. NF, lacking dj. *Sclanders.* $287/£185

LARKIN, PHILIP. The North Ship. Fortune Press, 1965. 2nd (unauthorized) ed. Fine in dj (sl rubbed; short closed tear). *Sclanders.* $116/£75

LARKIN, PHILIP. The North Ship. London: Fortune Press, 1965. 2nd, unauthorized ed. Only 280 issued w/dj. VG+ in dj (sl closed tears rear panel). *Williams.* $302/£195

LARKIN, PHILIP. Poetry from Oxford in Wartime. William Bell (ed). Fortune Press, 1945. 1st UK ed. NF in dj (short closed tear). *Sclanders.* $124/£80

LARKIN, PHILIP. Required Writing. Faber, 1983. Wrappers, preceding cl issue. Fine. *Poetry.* $23/£15

LARKIN, PHILIP. Required Writing. Faber, 1983. 1st ed. Spine creased, o/w NF. *Rees.* $39/£25

LARKIN, PHILIP. The Whitsun Weddings. London: Faber & Faber, (1964). 1st ed. Very NF in NF dj (spine sl browned). *Antic Hay.* $150/£97

LARKIN, THOMAS OLIVER. Chapters in the Early Life of Thomas Oliver Larkin. SF: CA Hist Soc, 1939. Frontis port, map. Grn cl. Spine label faded, else NF. *Parmer.* $75/£48

LARNED, CHARLES W. The History of the Battle Monument at West Point. West Point, NY, 1898. One of 1000 ptd. Linen-backed pict bds, gilt. Fine. *Pharos.* $35/£23

LARNED, WILLIAM TROWBRIDGE (adapted by). Fables in Rhyme for Little Folks. (Adapted from the French of Jean de la Fontaine.) Chicago: P.F. Volland, (1918). 1st ed. Volland Nature Children Books. John Rae (illus). 8vo. 74 + (1) index + (2)ads. Full color pict paper on bds; pict eps. VF. *Hobbyhorse.* $150/£97

LARNED, WILLIAM TROWBRIDGE (adapted by). Fairy Tales from France. Chicago: P.F. Volland, (1920). 8vo. John Rae (illus). Color illus bds (lt shelfwear). Color pub's box (edge detached but present). *Reisler.* $100/£65

LARRAZABAL, JESUS SALAS. Air War over Spain. London, 1974. 1st Eng ed. 40 plts. Good in dj. *Edwards.* $70/£45

LARSELL, OLAF. The Doctor in Oregon. Portland: Binfords & Mort, (1947). 1st ed. Errata slip tipped in. Fine. *Oregon.* $60/£39

LARSEN, ELLOUISE BAKER. American Historical Views of Staffordshire China. GC: Doubleday, 1950. New rev, enlgd ed. Signed. Color frontis. Teg. Rose buckram, color plt fr cvr. Fine in slipcase, pict label. *House.* $160/£103

LARSON, ANDREW KARL. I Was Called to Dixie. N.p.: Author, 1979. 18 plts. NF in Good+ dj. *Connolly.* $30/£19

LARSON, GUSTIVE O. Prelude to the Kingdom. Francestown: Marshall Jones, 1947. 1st ed. VG in dj (sl worn). *Lien.* $40/£26

LARSON, T.A. History of Wyoming. Lincoln: Univ of NE, 1965. 1st ed. 40pp photo plts. Fine. *Connolly.* $35/£23

LARTIGUE, JACQUES HENRI. Diary of a Century. Richard Avedon (ed). NY: Viking, 1970. 1st ed. Fine in dj. *Cahan.* $275/£177

LARWOOD, JACOB and JOHN CAMDEN HOTTEN. The History of Signboards...to the Present Day. London, n.d. (c. 1866). 6th ed. Hand-color frontis; x,536,32pp pub ads. (Margins lt browned; lt spotting; upper hinge detached; lower hinge cracked, shaken; worn, faded.) *Edwards.* $39/£25

LARWOOD, JACOB. The Story of the London Parks. London: John Camden Hotten, (1872). 1st ed. 2 vols. 331; 272,(xxxii)pp, 4 hand-colored plts by George Cruikshank. 2-tone pict cl (neatly recased), gilt. Pencil marginal lining, o/w VG. *Hollett.* $279/£180

LASDUN, SUSAN. Victorians at Home. NY: Viking Press, (1981). 1st ed. Frontis. Fine in dj. *Bookpress.* $45/£29

LASKER, EDWARD. The Adventure of Chess. GC: Doubleday, 1951. Inscribed. NF in pict dj (rubbed, edges chipped; lacks sm pieces spine). *Blue Mountain.* $45/£29

LASKI, HAROLD J. The Crisis and the Constitution. Hogarth, 1932. 1st ed. Good in wraps (sl dull). *Whiteson.* $25/£16

LASKI, HAROLD J. The Crisis and the Constitution: 1931 and After. Hogarth Press, 1932. 1st ed. Spine sl faded, o/w VG in grn ptd wrappers. *Words Etc.* $54/£35

LASKI, HAROLD J. Law and Justice in Soviet Russia. Hogarth Press, 1935. 1st ed. VG in wrappers. *Words Etc.* $31/£20

LASKI, MARGHANITA. The Victorian Chaise-Longue. London: Cresset, 1953. 1st ed. Gilt dull, sl rubbed; o/w Fine in dj (spine sl dknd). *Temple.* $54/£35

LASS, WILLIAM E. A History of Steamboating on the Upper Missouri. Lincoln, 1962. 1st ed. NF (inner hinges dk) in dj. *Baade.* $35/£23

LASSAIGNE, JACQUES. Marc Chagall. The Ceiling of the Paris Opera. Brenda Gilchrist (trans). NY: Frederick A. Praeger, (1966). 1st ed. Lg fldg color plt in rear pocket. Red cl stamped in black. Fine in illus dj. *Karmiole.* $350/£226

LASSAIGNE, JACQUES. Marc Chagall: Drawings and Watercolors for the Ballet. NY, 1969. 1 orig litho. (Cl faded.) *Argosy.* $350/£226

LASSAIGNE, JACQUES. Spanish Painting from the Catalan Frescoes to El Greco. S. Gilbert (trans). London: Skira, (1952). Fine in dj. *Petersfield.* $50/£32

LASSEK, ARTHUR. The Unique Legacy of Dr. Hughlings Jackson. Springfield, 1970. 1st ed. Good in dj. *Fye.* $75/£48

LASSWELL, MARY. One on the House. Boston, 1949. 1st ed. Fine (no dj). *Bond.* $87/£56

LAST, JEF. The Spanish Tragedy. London: Routledge, 1939. 1st ed. Nice in dj (chipped). *Patterson.* $155/£100

LAST, MURRAY. Sokoto Caliphate. (NY): Humanities Press, (1967). Sm stain on fore-edge; in dj (creased, price-clipped). *Schoyer.* $35/£23

LATHAM, CHARLES. The Gardens of Italy. London: Country Life, (1905). 2 vols. Aeg. Gilt-dec pict cvrs. Vol 1 cvr sl stained, else Fine set. *Quest.* $475/£306

LATHAM, CHARLES. In English Homes.... Covent Garden: Country Life, 1908-1909. Vol 1, 3rd ed; vol 2, 2nd ed. Frontis. Aeg. Orig dec cl, vol 1; later cl, vol 2. (Ex-lib w/mks; fr hinge vol 1 internally cracked; few leaves both vols detached.) *Bookpress.* $250/£161

LATHAM, FRANCIS. Travels in the Republic of Texas, 1842. Gerald Pierce (ed). Austin: Encino Press, 1971. Signed by Pierce. Fine. *Oregon.* $45/£29

LATHAM, JOHN WILKINSON. British Military Swords. From 1800 to the Present Day. London, 1966. 1st ed. Color frontis; 32 b/w plts. VG in dj (crumpled top-edge). *Edwards.* $54/£35

LATHAM, PHILIP. Five Against Venus. Winston, 1952. 1st ed. NF in dj. *Madle.* $75/£48

LATHAM, PHILIP. Missing Men of Saturn. Winston, 1953. 1st ed. NF in VG dj. *Aronovitz.* $40/£26

LATHAM, PHILIP. Missing Men of Saturn. Winston, 1953. 1st ed. NF in dj (rubbed, frayed). *Madle.* $65/£42

LATHAM, ROGER. Complete Book of the Wild Turkey. Harrisburg: Stackpole, 1956. 1st ed. Dj. *Lambeth.* $25/£16

LATHAM, SIMON. Falconry or the Faulcons Lure and Cure in Two Books (and) New and Second Booke of Faulconry. London: Thomas Harper for John Harrison, 1633. 1st collected ed. 4to. (xxiv),148,(iv);(xxiv),147,(i)pp, 2nd part bound 1st. Lg woodcut on title part 1 of falcon surrounded by equipment of sport; ptr's device on title part 2. Contemp Eng speckled sheep, triple line border on cvrs, red morocco label (spine chipped at head). Handsome, crisp, well margined. From Evelyn lib, w/ monogram label. *Sokol.* $4,418/£2,850

LATHROP, DOROTHY. Animals of the Bible. NY: Frederick A. Stokes, 1937. 1st ed, 2nd issue (w/name correctly spelled on spine). 4to, vi,66pp. Fine in VG dj (lt edgewear). *Godot.* $175/£113

LATHROP, DOROTHY. Presents for Lupe. NY: Macmillan, 1940. 1st ed. Signed. 4to. Unpaginated. VG in VG dj. *Davidson.* $60/£39

LATHROP, ELISE. Early American Inns and Taverns. NY: Robert McBride, 1926. 1st ed. Pict eps. VG. *Graf.* $30/£19

LATHROP, ELISE. Early American Inns and Taverns. NY: Arno Press, 1977. Rpt. VG in dj. *Bookpress.* $25/£16

LATHROP, ELISE. Historic Houses of Early America. NY, 1927. Fore-edge uncut. Cl (sl soiled). *Edwards.* $62/£40

LATHROP, ELISE. Historic Houses of Early America. NY, 1927. Inscribed presentation. VG. *Argosy.* $85/£55

LATHROP, ELISE. Historic Houses of Early America. NY: Tudor, 1936. Rpt. Fine in dj. *Artis.* $25/£16

LATROBE, CHARLES JOSEPH. The Rambler in North America. London: Seeley & Burnside, 1835. 1st ed. 2 vols. xi,321; viii,336pp. Teg, others untrimmed. Bright red 3/4 morocco. VG set. Howes L 127. *Schoyer.* $350/£226

LATTA, FRANK F. Black Gold in the Joaquin. Caldwell: Caxton, 1949. 1st ed. Fine in VG dj. *Book Market.* $35/£23

LATTA, FRANK F. Death Valley '49ers. Santa Cruz: Bear State, (1979). 1st ed. Fine. *Book Market.* $40/£26

LATTA, FRANK F. Handbook of Yokuts Indians. Oildale, CA: Bear State Books, 1949. 1st ed. Fine. *Oregon.* $60/£39

LATTA, FRANK F. Tailholt Tales. Santa Cruz: Bear State, (1976). 1st ed. Fine. *Book Market.* $30/£19

LATTIMORE, OWEN. Inner Asian Frontiers of China. NY: Amer Geographical Soc, 1940. 1st ed. VG. *Hermitage.* $65/£42

LAUBIN, REGINALD. The Indian Tipi. Univ of OK, (1957). 6th ptg. Color frontis. VG in Good dj. *Oregon.* $20/£13

LAUDERDALE, R.J. and JOHN M. DOAK. Life on the Range and on the Trail. San Antonio: Naylor, 1936. 1st ed. Pict grn cl. VG+ in ptd dj (lt chipped, sm scrape hole spine). *House.* $110/£71

LAUF, DETEF INGO. Tibetan Sacred Art. Berkeley: Shambhala, 1976. 1st ed. 86 color plts, 18 figs. Dec eps. Fine in VG dj. *Blue Dragon.* $100/£65

LAUFE, LEONARD. Obstetric Forceps. NY, 1968. 1st ed. Good. *Fye.* $75/£48

LAUFER, BERTHOLD. The Giraffe in History and Art. Chicago: Field Museum of Natural Hist, 1928. 9 plts. Wraps (spine tape-reinforced). *Archaeologia.* $55/£35

LAUFER, BERTHOLD. Jade. A Study in Chinese Archaeology and Religion. South Pasadena, 1946. 68 plts. (Ex-lib w/ink stamps, bkpl, #s; lt soiled.) *Edwards.* $70/£45

LAUFER, BERTHOLD. Paper and Printing in Ancient China. Chicago: Caxton Club, 1931. 1st ed. Ltd to 250. Fine. *Oak Knoll*. $150/£97

LAUGHLIN, JAMES. Some Natural Things. (NY): New Directions, (1945). 1st ed. VG in dj (sl stained, nicked). *Hermitage*. $75/£48

LAUGHLIN, LEDLIE IRWIN. Pewter in America: Its Makers and Their Marks. Boston: Houghton Mifflin, 1940. 1st ed. 2 vols. Frontis, 58 plts; frontis, 30 plts. 2-tone cl. Eps dknd, else Fine. *Cahan*. $250/£161

LAURENCE, JANET. A Deepe Coffyn. London: Macmillan, 1989. 1st ed. 1st bk. NF in NF dj. *Ming*. $39/£25

LAURENCE, JOHN and ROBERT MOON. A Handy-Book of Ophthalmic Surgery. Phila, 1866. 1st Amer ed. 191pp. Good. *Fye*. $125/£81

LAURENCE, ROBERT (comp). The George Walcott Collection of Used Civil War Patriotic Covers. NY: Privately ptd, 1934. 2nd ed. Orig cl. NF. *Mcgowan*. $85/£55

LAURIDSEN, PETER. Vitus Bering: The Discoverer of Bering Strait. Julius E. Olson (trans). Chicago: S.C. Griggs, 1889. xvi,223pp; 1 fldg chart supplied in facs. (Cvrs spotted.) *Parmer*. $125/£81

LAURIE, A.P. The Brush-Work of Rembrandt and His School. London: OUP, 1932. Frontis port, 127 b/w plts. Fore-edge uncut, parts unopened (pgs sl spotted). VG in dj (sl discolored w/sm nick). *Edwards*. $93/£60

LAURIE, A.P. The Painter's Methods and Materials. London: Seeley Service, 1926. 48 plts. Sound. *Ars Artis*. $28/£18

LAURING, PALLE. Land of the Tollund Man. Reginald Spink (trans). London, 1957. 1st Eng ed. 2 maps. (Feps lt spotted.) Dj (sl chipped, browned). *Edwards*. $31/£20

LAUT, AGNES. Cadillac. Knight Errant of the Wilderness.... Bobbs Merrill, (1931). 1st ed. Ep maps. VG. *Oregon*. $35/£23

LAUT, AGNES. The Conquest of Our Western Empire. McBride, 1927. 1st ed. VG in dj (chipped). *Oregon*. $45/£29

LAUT, AGNES. The Conquest of the Great Northwest.... NY: Outing Pub. Co, 1908. 1st ed. 2 vols. 38 plts. VG set. *Oregon*. $85/£55

LAUT, AGNES. The Fur Trade of America. Macmillan, 1921. 1st ed. In 2 parts. VG. *Oregon*. $50/£32

LAUT, AGNES. Pilgrims of the Santa Fe. NY: Stokes, 1931. 1st ed. VG. *Parker*. $35/£23

LAVATER, JOHN CASPAR. Essays on Physiognomy.... London: For Robinson, 1789. 3 vols. vi,240; 324; 314pp, 360 engr plts. Contemp full polished calf, gilt. Rebacked, joints weak 2 vols, o/w Very Nice set. *Europa*. $388/£250

LAVAY, JEROME B. Disputed Handwriting. Chicago: Harvard Bk Co, 1909. 1st ed. NF (2 sm tears). *Beasley*. $40/£26

LAVENDER, DAVID (ed). The Oregon Journals of David Douglas. Ashland, 1972. Ltd to 600. 2 vols. Fldg map laid in. Gold-stamped buckram. Fine (sig, date) in plain djs. Howes D 435. *Baade*. $115/£74

LAVENDER, DAVID. Bent's Fort. NY, 1954. Dj (frayed). *Artis*. $17/£11

LAVENDER, DAVID. Bent's Fort. GC: Doubleday, 1954. 1st ed. VG in dj. *Schoyer*. $25/£16

LAVENDER, DAVID. Nothing Seemed Impossible. Palo Alto: American West, (1975). 1st ed. VG in Good+ dj. *Oregon*. $35/£23

LAVENDER, DAVID. The Rockies. NY: Harper & Row, (1968). Rev ed. 1st ptg. 4 maps. VG in dj. *Schoyer*. $25/£16

LAVENDER, DAVID. The Way to the Western Sea. NY: Harper & Row, (1988). 1st ed. Fine in Fine dj. *Perier*. $30/£19

LAVER, JAMES. Art for All: London Transport Posters 1908-1949. London: Art & Technics, 1949. 1st ed. 68 plts. VG in dj (soiled, chipped). *Willow House*. $28/£18

LAVERAN, C.L.A. Paludism. London, 1893. 1st Eng trans. 197pp. Good. *Fye*. $100/£65

LAVIN, MARY. A Likely Story. Dublin: Dolmen, 1967. One of 1500. Fine in wraps. *Beasley*. $25/£16

LAVIN, MARY. The Second-Best Children in the World. Boston: Houghton Mifflin, 1972. 1st (Amer) ed. Edward Ardizzone (illus). Fine in dj. *Godot*. $75/£48

LAW, HENRY and D.K. CLARK. The Construction of Roads and Streets. London: Crosby Lockwood, 1914. 8th ed. Buff cl. VG. *Willow House*. $28/£18

LAW, HENRY I. Delaware Bookplates. Washington: Bruin, 1940. 1st ed. 3 tipped-in bkpls. Fine. *Cahan*. $125/£81

LAWALL, CHARLES H. The Curious Lore of Drugs and Medicines. GC Pub. Co., (1927). VG. *Blue Dragon*. $30/£19

LAWLER, RAY. Summer of the Seventeenth Doll. Angus & Robertson, 1957. 1st Eng ed. Grn cl. Fine in dj (sl nicked). *Dalian*. $39/£25

LAWLESS, EMILY. Grania: The Story of an Island. London: Smith Elder, 1892. 1st ed. 2 vols. Map frontis; 286; 304pp. Maroon cl. VG (lacks fep both vols). *Second Life*. $135/£87

LAWRENCE, ADA and G. STUART GELDER. Young Lorenzo. Florence: G. Orioli, (1932). One of 740 numbered. Vellum. Partially unopened. (Lt browning, soiling to covers, dj.) *Dermont*. $165/£106

LAWRENCE, ADA and G. STUART GELDER. Young Lorenzo. Florence: G. Orioli, 1931. 1st ed. One of 740, this copy unnumbered. Unopened. Fine in illus dj. *Cahan*. $250/£161

LAWRENCE, ALEXANDER A. Storm over Savannah. Athens: Univ of GA Press, (1951). 1st ed. Inscribed. Red cl. NF in VG dj (edgewear, spine faded). *Chapel Hill*. $55/£35

LAWRENCE, D.H. Aaron's Rod. London: Martin Secker, (1922). 1st British ed. Gilt cl. Endsheets tanned, else NF. *Reese*. $60/£39

LAWRENCE, D.H. Aaron's Rod. London: Martin Secker, 1922. 1st ed. (Edges lt spotted; feps lt browned; top edges bd damp-mkd.) *Hollett*. $47/£30

LAWRENCE, D.H. Aaron's Rod. NY: Thomas Seltzer, 1922. 1st ed. NF (bds sl bowed) in VG dj (2 internal repairs; sl loss spine base). *Between The Covers*. $450/£290

LAWRENCE, D.H. Amores. NY: Huebsch, 1916. 1st Amer ed. NF (spine sl sunned, extrems sl rubbed). *Polyanthos*. $75/£48

LAWRENCE, D.H. Amores. NY: B.W. Huebsch, 1916. 1st Amer ed. Brn cl stamped in gold. Ink name, else Fine. *Godot*. $100/£65

LAWRENCE, D.H. Amores. Poems. London: Duckworth, (1916). 1st ed. Variant copy w/fore, bottom edges untrimmed. Total ed of 900. 16pp cat present. Gilt blue cl. Bkpl removed fr pastedown, sl rubbed, o/w NF. *Reese*. $400/£258

LAWRENCE, D.H. Assorted Articles. London: Martin Secker, 1930. 1st ed. VG. *Hermitage*. $50/£32

LAWRENCE, D.H. Birds, Beasts and Flowers. London: Martin Secker, (1923). 1st Eng ed of 1000. (Foxing few pp.) Cl-backed bds (sl rubbed, spotted), ptd paper label spine. Ptd dj (sl soiled, top chipped). Internally NF. *Blue Mountain*. $135/£87

LAWRENCE, D.H. The Captain's Doll. NY: Thomas Seltzer, 1923. 1st Amer ed. Blue cl, gilt. Fine. *Macdonnell*. $50/£32

LAWRENCE, D.H. The Collected Letters of.... Harry T. Moore (ed). London: Heinemann, 1962. 1st ed thus. 2 vols. Pg edges sl browned, o/w VG in dj (sl soiled, chipped, spine faded). *Virgo*. $93/£60

LAWRENCE, D.H. D.H. Lawrence's Letters to Bertrand Russell. NY: Gotham Book Mart, 1948. 1st Amer ed. One of 950. VG in dj (browned, sl nicked, one-inch closed tear). *Virgo*. $116/£75

LAWRENCE, D.H. England, My England and Other Stories. NY: Seltzer, 1922. 1st ed. VG (name; sl dull). *Reese*. $45/£29

LAWRENCE, D.H. England, My England. Secker, 1924. 1st ed. Good. *Whiteson*. $23/£15

LAWRENCE, D.H. Etruscan Places. Martin Secker, 1932. 1st Eng ed. 20 plts. Blue cl. Feps browned, o/w VG in dj (spine loss). *Dalian*. $147/£95

LAWRENCE, D.H. Kangaroo. NY: Thomas Seltzer, 1923. 1st Amer ed. Gilt cl. Very Nice. *Reese*. $35/£23

LAWRENCE, D.H. Kangaroo. NY: Thomas Seltzer, 1923. 1st Amer ed. Blue cl. Lt rubbed, mkd, o/w VG. *Hermitage*. $85/£55

LAWRENCE, D.H. Lady Chatterley's Lover, Including My Skirmish with Jolly Roger.... (Paris): Privately ptd, 1929. Contemp cl, leather spine label. Paper tanned, extrems sl rubbed, else Good. *Reese*. $55/£35

LAWRENCE, D.H. Lady Chatterley's Lover. Includes 'My Skirmish with Jolly Roger' (8pp special intro). The Author's Unabridged Popular Edition. Paris: Privately ptd, 1930. 1st ed thus. Uncut. VG (eps creased) in recent brn cl, blue/gold title. *Lewton*. $101/£65

LAWRENCE, D.H. The Ladybird: The Fox: The Captain's Doll. London: Martin Secker, 1923. 1st ed. (Eps sl browned; lt damp mks bd tops). *Hollett*. $54/£35

LAWRENCE, D.H. Last Poems. Florence: Orioli, 1932. #52/750. Sl soiled; foxed; no dj. *Virgo*. $217/£140

LAWRENCE, D.H. The Letters of D.H. Lawrence. London: Heinemann, 1932. 1st UK ed. VG. *Williams*. $31/£20

LAWRENCE, D.H. The Letters of D.H. Lawrence. Aldous Huxley (ed). London: William Heinemann, (1932). One of 500 numbered. White vellum bds. Fine in pub's slipcase (cracked/repairable). *Dermont*. $150/£97

LAWRENCE, D.H. The Letters of D.H. Lawrence. Aldous Huxley (ed). London: Heinemann, 1932. 1st ed. (Upper joint tender; sm snag spine; lt wear.) *Hollett*. $54/£35

LAWRENCE, D.H. Letters to Martin Secker 1911-1930. Privately published, 1970. One of 500 numbered. Bump, o/w NF in dj (sl nicked). *Rees*. $31/£20

LAWRENCE, D.H. Love Among the Haystacks and Other Pieces. Nonesuch, 1930. 1st ed. One of 1600. Fine in NF dj. *Fine Books*. $125/£81

LAWRENCE, D.H. Love Among the Haystacks. London: Nonesuch, 1930. One of 1600 numbered. Offsetting to eps, o/w VG in dj (sl chipped, nicked). *Rees*. $140/£90

LAWRENCE, D.H. The Lovely Lady. Secker, 1932. 1st ed. Good reading copy. *Whiteson*. $20/£13

LAWRENCE, D.H. The Man Who Died. London: Martin Secker, 1931. Ltd to 2000. Untrimmed. (Label removed flyleaf.) Grn buckram, gilt, over bevelled bds (spine, lower bd faded). *Hollett*. $70/£45

LAWRENCE, D.H. The Man Who Died. London: Secker, 1931. One of 2000. Spine sunned, o/w VG. *Rees*. $47/£30

LAWRENCE, D.H. Pansies. London: Martin Secker, (1929). 1st trade ed. Deckle-edged; largely unopened (offseting fep). Cl-backed dec bds, gilt. NF in ptd dj (spotted). *Blue Mountain*. $135/£87

LAWRENCE, D.H. Phoenix. Heinemann, 1936. 1st ed. Gilt dec brn cl. Sl dull, 1-inch tear top spine, else Good. *Whiteson*. $25/£16

LAWRENCE, D.H. The Plumed Serpent. London: Martin Secker, (1926). 1st ed. Gilt cl. VG (few pp opened carelessly). *Reese*. $75/£48

LAWRENCE, D.H. Pornography and Obscenity. London: Faber & Faber, (1929). 1st ed, clbound issue. Good (bkpl stain pastedown; dkng). *Reese*. $30/£19

LAWRENCE, D.H. Pornography and Obscenity. London: Faber & Faber, 1929. 1st ed. VG in orange wrappers. *Hollett*. $47/£30

LAWRENCE, D.H. The Prussian Officer and Other Stories. London: Duckworth, 1914. 1st ed, earlier (dk blue) binding, w/apparently earlier ads. Good (lt wear; label removed top cvr; lib label rep; sl shaken). *Ash*. $147/£95

LAWRENCE, D.H. The Prussian Officer and Other Stories. NY: Huebsch, 1916. 1st US ed. NF (spine wear). *Beasley*. $75/£48

LAWRENCE, D.H. Psychoanalysis and the Unconscious. London: Martin Secker, (1923). 1st Eng ed. One of 1000. Dk red cl. Fine in fresh, bright dj. *Godot*. $375/£242

LAWRENCE, D.H. Reflections on the Death of a Porcupine and Other Essays. Phila: Centaur Press, 1925. One of 925 numbered. Cl, marbled bds. Fine in pub's slipcase. *Dermont*. $165/£106

LAWRENCE, D.H. Sea and Sardinia. NY: Thomas Seltzer, 1921. 1st Amer ed. Extrems sl rubbed. *Sadlon*. $75/£48

LAWRENCE, D.H. The Selected Letters of D.H. Lawrence. Diana Trilling (ed). NY: Farrar, Straus & Cudahy, (1958). 1st ed. VF in Fine dj. *Hermitage*. $45/£29

LAWRENCE, D.H. Sons and Lovers. London: Duckworth, 1913. 1st ed, Roberts' variant 1, w/cancel title. (Sl worn, shaken; eps sl scuffed, soiled; sl loose.) *Ash*. $302/£195

LAWRENCE, D.H. The Spirit of Place. Richard Aldington (ed). London/Toronto: Heinemann, (1935). 1st ed. Brn cl. Fine in NF buff dj ptd in blue/orange. *Juvelis*. $375/£242

LAWRENCE, D.H. St. Mawr. Secker, 1925. 1st ed. Lt foxing; sl mkd, else Good reading copy. *Whiteson*. $20/£13

LAWRENCE, D.H. The Story of Dr. Manente. Florence, (1929). #666/1000. Frontis, 2 plts. Parchment, w/dj. VG in canvas jacket, leather spine labels; slipcase. *Schoyer*. $65/£42

LAWRENCE, D.H. The Story of Dr. Manente. Florence: Orioli, 1929. #460/1000 ptd. Unopened. Good (pp, cream paper-cvrd bd edges browned, dusty; sm bkpl) in dj (browned; chipped; sm closed tear). *Virgo*. $62/£40

LAWRENCE, D.H. The Trespasser. London: Duckworth, 1912. 1st UK ed. NF (spine sl rubbed; bkpl removed fep w/sl marking). *Williams*. $496/£320

LAWRENCE, D.H. Twilight in Italy. Duckworth, 1924. 2nd imp. Blue cl. Fine in dj (frayed; tanned). *Dalian*. $54/£35

LAWRENCE, D.H. The Virgin and the Gipsy. Secker, 1930. 1st ed. Good. *Whiteson*. $25/£16

LAWRENCE, D.H. The Virgin and the Gipsy. Florence: G. Orioli, 1930. 1st ed. #101/810 ptd. Lt foxing paper bds, o/w Fine in dj. *Hermitage*. $350/£226

LAWRENCE, D.H. Women in Love. Secker, 1921. 1st ed. Sl dull, else Good. *Whiteson*. $23/£15

LAWRENCE, D.H. and M.L. SKINNER. The Boy in the Bush. London: Martin Secker, (1924). 1st ed. Tan cl stamped in black. Stamping sl rubbed, o/w Fine (w/o dj). *Reese*. $50/£32

LAWRENCE, D.H. and M.L. SKINNER. The Boy in the Bush. NY: Thomas Seltzer, 1924. 1st Amer ed. Spine sl dull; sl rubbed. *Sadlon*. $35/£23

LAWRENCE, D.H. and M.L. SKINNER. The Boy in the Bush. NY: Seltzer, 1924. 1st Amer ed. Gilt cl. Ink name, else VG. *Reese*. $45/£29

LAWRENCE, JAMES B. China and Japan, and A Voyage Thither. Hartford, CT: Case, Lockwood & Brainard, 1870. Frontis port, 444pp, 8 lithos. Ptd on browning, chipping paper (marginal pencilling). Blue buckram (rebound). *Schoyer*. $75/£48

LAWRENCE, LARS. Morning, Noon and Night. NY: Putnam's, 1954. 1st ed. VG- (rubbed, extrems soiled, worn). *Parker*. $45/£29

LAWRENCE, T.E. The Home Letters of T.E. Lawrence and His Brothers. Oxford, 1954. 1st ed. Frontis port, 37 other plts; relevant newspaper clippings loosely inserted. Good+ in dj. *Edwards*. $116/£75

LAWRENCE, T.E. The Letters of T.E. Lawrence. David Garnett (ed). London, 1938. 1st ed. 4 maps (2 fldg). (Spine lt faded.) *Edwards*. $47/£30

LAWRENCE, T.E. The Letters of T.E. Lawrence. David Garnett (ed). NY, 1939. 1st US ed. Frontis, 15 other plts, 4 maps (2 fldg). VG in dj. *Edwards*. $70/£45

LAWRENCE, T.E. The Letters of.... Heinemann, 1938. 1st ed. Spine sl sunned, else VG. *Whiteson*. $23/£15

LAWRENCE, T.E. The Mint. London: Cape, 1955. Ltd ed (2000). Orig 1/4 morocco gilt. Teg, other edges uncut. Fine. *Hollett*. $132/£85

LAWRENCE, T.E. The Mint. Jonathan Cape, 1955. One of 2000 numbered. 1st unexpurgated ed. 1/4 morocco cl bds; teg; marbled eps. Unopened. VF in slipcase. *Dalian*. $256/£165

LAWRENCE, T.E. Oriental Assembly. A.W. Lawrence (ed). London, 1939. 2nd imp. Frontis. Edges sl foxed, o/w Good in mustard cl, gilt title. *Edwards*. $54/£35

LAWRENCE, T.E. Revolt in the Desert. NY: Doran, 1927. 1st Amer trade ed. 16 ports, fldg map at rear. Fine in Very Nice dj (sm chip top rear panel). *Chapel Hill*. $150/£97

LAWRENCE, T.E. Revolt in the Desert. Cape, 1927. 1st ed. NF in VG dj (lt dust soiling; sl chipping spine). *Fine Books*. $225/£145

LAWRENCE, T.E. Secret Despatches from Arabia. London: Golden Cockerel, (1939). 1st ed. #133/1000. Frontis. Teg, others uncut. Black morocco-backed cream buckram. *Cox*. $450/£290

LAWRENCE, T.E. Seven Pillars of Wisdom. London: Jonathan Cape, (1935). Ltd to 750 numbered. Letter of authentication (signed by pub's production mgr), letters and early receipt relating to sale of bk, and related press cuttings loosely inserted. Orig 1/4 pigskin; teg; partly unopened. Exceptionally Good (leaf creased; faint spotting of edges) in dj (sl chipped, browned). *Ash*. $1,542/£995

LAWRENCE, T.E. Seven Pillars of Wisdom. NY, 1935. 1st Amer ed, ltd to 750 numbered. 1/4 pub's pigskin. Spine rubbed, sl chipped, else Good (lacks dj, slipcase). *King*. $350/£226

LAWRENCE, T.E. Seven Pillars of Wisdom. GC: Doubleday, 1935. 1st Amer trade ed. Buckram cl. NF (eps browned) in dj (sl wear). *Antic Hay*. $125/£81

LAWRENCE, T.E. Seven Pillars of Wisdom. London: Cape, 1935. 1st trade ed. 4 fldg maps. Orig brn buckram gilt. Untrimmed. Very Nice in dj (hinges chafed; loss at head, tail of spine). *Hollett*. $132/£85

LAWRENCE, T.E. Shaw—Ede. T.E. Lawrence's Letters to H.S. Ede 1927-1935. (London): Golden Cockerel, (1942). 1st ed, regular issue. One of 470 numbered, from total ed of 500. 4to. Teg. 1/2 morocco (tanning), cl. Pub's 'Notice' slip laid in. Raised bands rubbed, o/w Nice. *Reese*. $600/£387

LAWRENCE, T.E. and C. LEONARD WOOLLEY. Palestine Exploration Fund 1914. (London): Pub by order of the Committee and Sold at the Offices of the Fund, 1914. 1st ed, 2nd binding, w/o full stop after date on spine. 4to. Lg color fldg map, issued in 1921 by the PEF, laid in. Edges lt rubbed; sm spot upper bd; lt foxing endsheets; o/w NF. *Reese*. $650/£419

LAWRENCE, THOMAS. Cabinet of Gems. London, 1837. Fine engr tp; port; 12 plts. Gilt pict cl. (Offsetting.) *Argosy*. $150/£97

Laws of the United States of America. Volume I. NY: Childs & Swaine, (1791). 8vo. (viii),592pp (2 leaves torn w/no loss of text; lt foxing). Contemp calf; leather label (inner hinge strengthened). *Argosy*. $3,000/£1,935

LAWSON, A. The Modern Farrier. London: G. Virtue, 1841. 24th ed. Frontis, iv,616pp, engr title, 7 engr plts. Mod full levant blind-ruled morocco over heavy bds, french grooves, onlaid spine label. Soiled, browned, edge repairs, old mss. recipes on fr flyleaf. *Hollett*. $101/£65

LAWSON, GEORGE. Injuries of the Eye, Orbit and Eyelids. Phila, 1867. 1st Amer ed. 408pp. Good. *Fye*. $100/£65

LAWSON, JOHN HOWARD. Roger Bloomer. NY: Seltzer, 1923. 1st ed. 1st bk. Good (endsheets sl tanned) in pict dj (chipped). *Reese*. $85/£55

LAWSON, MARIE. Pocahontas and Captain John Smith. NY: Random House, 1950. 1st trade ed. William Sharp (illus). Dec eps. VG in dj. *Cattermole*. $35/£23

LAWSON, ROBERT. Ben and Me. Boston: LBCo, 1939. 1st ed. 6.5x8.5. 114pp. Good in dj. *Cattermole*. $100/£65

LAWSON, ROBERT. Capt. Kidd's Cat. Boston: Little, Brown, (1956). 1st ed. 8vo. Lime-grn cl w/dk grn lettering, cat image. Good in color pict dj (sl marginal wear). *Reisler.* $85/£55

LAWSON, ROBERT. Country Colic. Boston: LBCo, 1944. 1st ed. 6.5x8.5. 70pp. Cl. VG in dj. *Cattermole.* $60/£39

LAWSON, ROBERT. Country Colic. Boston: Little, Brown, 1944. 1st ed. Sm 8vo. Pict cl (lt soiled). VG + in VG + dj (sm tear). *Book Adoption.* $95/£61

LAWSON, ROBERT. The Fabulous Flight. Boston: Little, Brown, 1949. 1st ed. 8vo. Pict cl. VG + (tape remnants dj flaps, pastedowns) in VG dj. *Book Adoption.* $40/£26

LAWSON, ROBERT. The Fabulous Flight. Boston: LBCo, 1949. 1st ed. 6.5x9.5. 152pp. Cl. VG in dj. *Cattermole.* $40/£26

LAWSON, ROBERT. Mr. Revere and I. Boston: Little, Brown, (1953). #18/500, signed. 8vo. Accompanying set of 8 prints. Blue cl, gilt. Cardboard slipcase w/color paste label has sm split in edge; o/w Fine. *Reisler.* $335/£216

LAWSON, ROBERT. Mr. Revere and I. Boston: Little, Brown, 1953. 1st ed. Sm 8vo. Pict cl. NF in VG dj (chipped; sm tears). *Book Adoption.* $100/£65

LAWSON, ROBERT. Mr. Twigg's Mistake. Boston: LBCo, 1947. 1st ed. 9.75x9.5. 144pp. Cl. VG in dj. *Cattermole.* $50/£32

LAWSON, ROBERT. Mr. Wilmer. NY: Little, Brown, 1945. 1st ed. Lg 12mo. Pict cl (spine ends dknd). VG + in Good dj (chipped). *Book Adoption.* $45/£29

LAWSON, ROBERT. The Tough Winter. NY: Viking, 1954. 1st ed. 8vo. Blue cl, silver illus (spine sl faded). Color dj (minor spine fading). *Reisler.* $90/£58

LAWSON, WILLIAM. The New Orchard and Fruit Garden. London: Cresset, 1927. Teg. Gilt-stamped paper spine, cl bds. As New. *Quest.* $90/£58

LAWTON, MARY. A Lifetime with Mark Twain. NY: Harcourt, Brace, (1925). 1st Amer ed. Good + (spine soiled, inscrip). *Agvent.* $45/£29

LAWTON, MARY. The Queen of Cooks—And Some Kings. NY: Boni & Liveright, 1925. 1st ed. 32 plts. Red cl. Good in dj (sl chipped). *Karmiole.* $30/£19

LAYARD, AUSTEN HENRY. Discoveries among the Ruins of Nineveh and Babylon. NY: Harper, 1875. xvi,586pp; 6 fldg plans, maps. Sl rubbed; spine sl frayed; 2 maps torn w/o loss, o/w Good ex-lib. *Worldwide.* $65/£42

LAYARD, AUSTEN HENRY. Discoveries in the Ruins of Nineveh and Babylon.... NY, 1853. 686pp (rear fly stained; lacks fldg map; frontis, title foxed; blindstamped name; cvrs frayed; outer hinges reglued; spine chipped; sig sprung). *King.* $75/£48

LAYARD, AUSTEN HENRY. Nineveh and Its Remains. NY: Putnam's, 1849. 1st Amer ed. 2 vols. 2 tinted litho frontispieces, 326pp + 16pp ads; 373pp, fldg map (crease tears), 26 plts and plans. Orig blindstamped, gilt pict cl (extrems sl worn). Clean set. *House.* $250/£161

LAYARD, AUSTEN HENRY. Nineveh and Its Remains. NY: Putnam's, 1849. 1st ed. 2 vols. viii,326; 373pp. Worn; spines chipped; lt foxing, o/w Good. *Worldwide.* $145/£94

LAYARD, AUSTEN HENRY. Nineveh and Its Remains. London: John Murray, 1849. 1st ed. 2 vols complete. 890pp, lg fldg map. 3/4 red calf, 5 raised bands, marbled bds, eps, edges (extrems rubbed, shelfwear; joints starting vol 1; sig; foxing first pp each vol). *Archaeologia.* $350/£226

LAZAREV, VIKTOR. Old Russian Murals and Mosaics. From the XI to the XVI Century. Phaidon, 1966. 265 plts (9 tipped-in); map. Dj. *Edwards.* $39/£25

LE BLANC, MAURICE. Arsene Lupin, Super-Sleuth. NY: Macauley, (1927). 1st Amer ed. Lacks top 1/4 fep, else NF in VG dj (chip spine; fr panel edges rubbed). *Between The Covers.* $185/£119

LE BLANC, MAURICE. Arsene Lupin. NY: Doubleday Page, 1909. 1st ed. Minor rubs cvr illus, else Fine. *Else Fine.* $65/£42

LE BLANC, MAURICE. Arsene Lupin. NY: Doubleday, Page, 1909. 1st US ed. NF (sl rubbing). *Beasley.* $65/£42

LE BLANC, MAURICE. The Blonde Lady. Doubleday, Page, 1910. 1st Amer ed. Pg edges spotted, white lettering, border flecking, else VG + in dj (lacks piece, sm tears). *Murder.* $200/£129

LE BLOND, MRS. AUBREY. Adventures on the Roof of the World. London: T. Fisher Unwin, 1904. 1st ed. 32 plts. Teg, uncut. Pict cl gilt (worn, snagged; label stamped on upper bd; some foxing; eps sl soiled; joints cracked). *Hollett.* $54/£35

LE BLOND, MRS. AUBREY. The Old Gardens of Italy. London, 1912. 1st ed. (Prelims pasted down; spine dknd, sl frayed.) *Brooks.* $22/£14

LE BLOND, MRS. AUBREY. True Tales of Mountain Adventure for Non-Climbers Young and Old. London: T. Fisher Unwin, 1903. 1st ed. 33 plts (of 36). Pict cl (sl rubbed). *Bickersteth.* $31/£20

LE CAIN, ERROL. The Cabbage Princess. London: Faber & Faber, (1969). 1st ed. Signed. 4to. Color illus bds (sl corner wear; school stamp on fep). Color dj (sl corner wear). *Reisler.* $185/£119

LE CARRE, JOHN. Call for the Dead. London: Gollancz, 1961. 1st UK ed, 1st bk. Signed. VG (sl faded, sm mk to spine) in VG 2nd imp dj. *Williams.* $1,395/£900

LE CARRE, JOHN. Call for the Dead. NY: Walker, 1962. 1st Amer ed. Fine in dj (spine top wear). *Mordida.* $900/£581

LE CARRE, JOHN. Call for the Dead. NY: Walker, 1962. 1st US ed. 1st bk. Fine in NF dj (short closed tear). *Janus.* $650/£419

LE CARRE, JOHN. The Honourable Schoolboy. London: Hodder & Stoughton, 1977. 1st UK ed. Signed. VG in dj (sl edgeworn, short closed tears). *Williams.* $74/£48

LE CARRE, JOHN. The Little Drummer Girl. London: Hodder & Stoughton, 1983. 1st UK ed. Signed. VG + (sl stained) in dj. *Williams.* $70/£45

LE CARRE, JOHN. The Looking Glass War. NY: Coward-McCann, 1965. 1st US ed. NF in NF dj. *Janus.* $50/£32

LE CARRE, JOHN. The Looking-Glass War. London: Heinemann, 1965. 1st ed. NF in NF dj (spine sunned, lt chipped). *Beasley.* $65/£42

LE CARRE, JOHN. The Looking-Glass War. London: Heinemann, 1965. 1st ed. VF in dj (price-clipped). *Else Fine.* $75/£48

LE CARRE, JOHN. The Looking-Glass War. London: Heinemann, 1965. 1st UK ed. Signed. NF in VG dj (closed tear; spine sl faded). *Williams.* $194/£125

LE CARRE, JOHN. A Murder of Quality. NY: Walker, (1963). 1st Amer ed. Name, address, else NF in VG- dj (sl soiled; several sm chips). *Between The Covers.* $475/£306

LE CARRE, JOHN. A Murder of Quality. London: Gollancz, 1962. 1st ed. Pp sl dknd; label removed fep, o/w NF in dj (lt staining; closed tears; nicks). *Mordida.* $1,300/£839

LE CARRE, JOHN. A Murder of Quality. NY: Walker, 1963. 1st US ed. VG (lt spotting top edges) in dj (worn, sunned spine). *Janus.* $100/£65

LE CARRE, JOHN. A Murder of Quality: The Novel and the Screenplay. London: Hodder & Stoughton, 1991. 1st ed. Signed. NF in wrappers. *Rees.* $39/£25

LE CARRE, JOHN. The Naive and Sentimental Lover. London: Hodder & Stoughton, 1971. 1st ed. Fine in dj (price-clipped). *Rees.* $39/£25

LE CARRE, JOHN. The Naive and Sentimental Lover. London: Hodder & Stoughton, 1971. 1st UK ed. Signed. Fine in dj. *Williams.* $116/£75

LE CARRE, JOHN. The Night Manager. NY: Knopf, 1993. 1st Amer ed. Signed. VF in dj. *Mordida.* $75/£48

LE CARRE, JOHN. A Perfect Spy. London: Hodder & Stoughton, 1986. 1st ed. Fine in Fine dj. *Janus.* $45/£29

LE CARRE, JOHN. A Perfect Spy. Knopf, 1986. 1st US ed. Signed. Fine in dj. *Williams.* $39/£25

LE CARRE, JOHN. The Russia House. NY: Knopf, 1989. 1st ed, adv rev copy w/slip, photo, & flyer laid in. VF in dj. *Mordida.* $65/£42

LE CARRE, JOHN. The Russia House. London: Hodder & Stoughton, 1989. 1st ed. Signed. Fine in dj. *Rees.* $47/£30

LE CARRE, JOHN. The Russia House. London: Hodder & Stoughton, 1989. One of 500 specially bound. Fine in slipcase (sl rubbed). *Rees.* $54/£35

LE CARRE, JOHN. The Secret Pilgrim. Hodder & Stoughton, 1991. 1st UK ed. Signed. Fine in dj. *Lewton.* $36/£23

LE CARRE, JOHN. A Small Town in Germany. NY: Coward-McCann, (1968). 1st ed. NF in pink, white, blue variant dj (sl edgewear; tiny tears). *Antic Hay.* $50/£32

LE CARRE, JOHN. A Small Town in Germany. London: Heinemann, 1968. 1st ed. VG + in dj. *Limestone.* $45/£29

LE CARRE, JOHN. A Small Town in Germany. London: Heinemann, 1968. 1st UK ed. Signed. NF (ink name) in VG dj. *Williams.* $85/£55

LE CARRE, JOHN. Smiley's People. London: Hodder & Stoughton, 1980. 1st UK ed. Signed. Fine in dj. *Williams.* $101/£65

LE CARRE, JOHN. The Spy Who Came in from the Cold. London: Gollancz, 1963. 1st ed. NF in dj. *Limestone.* $400/£258

LE CARRE, JOHN. The Spy Who Came in from the Cold. London: Gollancz, 1963. 1st UK ed. Signed. Fine in Fine dj (price-clipped). *Williams.* $775/£500

LE CARRE, JOHN. The Spy Who Came in from the Cold. NY: Coward-McCann, 1964. 1st US ed. NF in NF dj w/orig wrap-around band quoting Graham Greene. *Janus.* $125/£81

LE CARRE, JOHN. Tinker Tailor Soldier Spy. London: Hodder & Stoughton, 1974. 1st UK ed. Signed. NF in dj. *Williams.* $124/£80

LE CONTE, CARRIE E. Yo Semite 1878. SF: Book Club of CA, 1944 (actually 1964). One of 450. Prospectus laid in. Frontis port. Cl-backed patterned bds, ptd spine label. Fine. *Bohling.* $125/£81

LE CONTE, EMMA. When the World Ended. The Diary of Emma LeConte. Earl Schenck Miers (ed). NY: OUP, 1957. 1st ed. Fine in NF dj. *Mcgowan.* $45/£29

LE CONTE, JOSEPH. The Autobiography of Joseph le Conte. W.E. Armes (ed). NY, 1903. 1st ed. VG + (ex-lib). *Mikesh.* $37/£24

LE CONTE, JOSEPH. A Journal of Ramblings through the High Sierra of California.... SF: Sierra Club, 1930. Ltd to 1500. Port. Cvr fade, wear, else Good in wraps. *King.* $75/£48

LE CONTE, JOSEPH. A Journal of Ramblings...by the University Excursion Party. SF: Sierra Club, 1930. One of 1500 ptd. 5 full-pg photos. Bds, linen spine, paper spine label (spine head, top edge sl dknd). *Dawson.* $75/£48

LE CORBEILLER, CLARE. European and American Snuff Boxes, 1730-1830. Batsford, 1966. 1st ed. 3 color plts. Dj (chipped). *Edwards.* $39/£25

LE CORBUSIER. Aircraft. London: The Studio, 1935. 1st ed. Foxed, esp eps, o/w VG in dj (sl tattered, lacks pieces, internally reinforced w/tape). *Edwards.* $310/£200

LE CORBUSIER. The City of Tomorrow and Its Planning. London: John Rodker, 1929. 1st ed in English. Frontis; fldg plan. 2 short tears left margin plan not affecting illus; spine lt sunned; mk rear cvr, else VG. *Bookpress.* $285/£184

LE CORBUSIER. Creation Is a Patient Search. NY: Praeger, 1960. 1st ed. NF in VG dj (lt faded; tear to fold). *Lame Duck.* $75/£48

LE CORBUSIER. Looking at City Planning. NY: Grossman, 1971. 1st Amer ed. VG in dj. *Bookpress.* $65/£42

LE CORBUSIER. The Nursery Schools. Eleanor Levieux (trans). NY: Orion Press, 1968. 1st ed in English. Fine in dj (1-inch tear; else NF). *Godot.* $45/£29

LE CORBUSIER. Towards a New Architecture. London: Architectural Press, 1959. Pub's cl. Fine in dj. *Europa.* $23/£15

LE CORBUSIER. UN Headquarters. NY: Reinhold, 1947. 1st ed. VG + in dj (spine faded). *Lame Duck.* $75/£48

LE CORBUSIER. When the Cathedrals Were White. NY: R&H, 1947. 1st ed. Indent 1st few pp, else NF in VG- dj (2 inch piece torn rear panel). *Lame Duck.* $75/£48

LE FANU, J. SHERIDAN. Green Tea. Arkham House, 1945. 1st ed. NF in dj. *Madle.* $185/£119

LE FANU, J. SHERIDAN. The Purcell Papers. Sauk City: Arkham House, 1975. 1st ed. One of 4000 ptd. Fine in Fine dj. *Glenn.* $15/£10

LE FANU, J. SHERIDAN. A Stable for Nightmares. New Amsterdam, 1896. 1st ed. Sl fraying, fading at spine; dust soiling yellow cl cvrs, else VG-. *Fine Books.* $175/£113

LE FANU, WILLIAM. A Bio-Bibliography of Edward Jenner 1749-1823. London, 1951. 1st ed. Good. *Fye.* $60/£39

LE FANU, WILLIAM. A Catalogue of the Portraits and Other Paintings...in the Royal College of Surgeons of England. Edinburgh, 1960. 4 color plts. Dj. *Edwards.* $31/£20

LE FORS, JOE. Wyoming Peace Officer. Laramie: Laramie Ptg Co, (1953). Gold-stamped buckram in dj (lt overall stain). *Dawson.* $200/£129

LE GALLIENNE, RICHARD. Little Dinners with the Sphinx and Other Prose Fancies. London: John Lane, Bodley Head, 1909. 1st Eng ed. Top edge red, rest uncut (sl foxed). Red buckram (spine sl faded, mkd). Nice. *Temple.* $39/£25

LE GALLIENNE, RICHARD. Pieces of Eight. London: W. Collins Sons, 1918. 1st ed. VF orange-red cl. Nice. *Temple.* $62/£40

LE GUIN, URSULA K. The Compass Rose. Underwood-Miller, 1982. 1st ed. One of 550 signed. Fine in dj. *Madle.* $60/£39

LE GUIN, URSULA K. The Compass Rose. London: Gollancz, 1983. 1st Eng ed. Blue cl. Fine in dj. *Dalian.* $39/£25

LE GUIN, URSULA K. Gwilan's Harp. Northridge: Lord John, 1981. 1st ed thus. One of 300 numbered (of 350) signed. Fine in dec wrappers. *Reese.* $45/£29

LE GUIN, URSULA K. The Lathe of Heaven. London: Gollancz, 1972. 1st UK ed. VG+ in dj. *Williams.* $93/£60

LE GUIN, URSULA K. Malafrena. Putnam, 1979. 1st ed. NF in dj. *Madle.* $20/£13

LE GUIN, URSULA K. Orsinian Tales. Harper, 1976. 1st ed. Fine in dj (sl rubbed). *Madle.* $20/£13

LE GUIN, URSULA K. Rocannon's World. Gollancz, 1979. 1st Eng ed. Red cl. VF in dj. *Dalian.* $39/£25

LE GUIN, URSULA K. The Tombs of Atuan. Atheneum, 1971. 1st ed. NF in Fine dj. *Aronovitz.* $185/£119

LE GUIN, URSULA K. Way of the Water's Going. NY: Harper & Row, 1989. 1st ed. Fine in Fine dj. *Connolly.* $30/£19

LE GUIN, URSULA K. The Word for World Is Forest. Putnam, 1972. 1st separate ed. Fine in NF dj. *Aronovitz.* $38/£25

LE MARCHAND, ELIZABETH. Death of an Old Girl. London: Hart-Davis, 1967. 1st ed, 1st bk. Fine in dj. *Limestone.* $45/£29

LE MASSENA, ROBERT A. Articulated Steam Locomotives of North America. (Silverton: Sundance Pub, 1979). 1st ed. Color pict bds, black pebble-grained gilt-lettered cl. Fine. *Harrington.* $55/£35

LE MASSENA, ROBERT A. Rio Grande...to the Pacific! Denver: Sundance Ltd, (1974). #1934 of unstated limitation. Signed. Facs booklet in rear pocket. Photo-pict bds, red cl spine. Fine. *Harrington.* $125/£81

LE MAY, ALAN. By Dim and Flaring Lamps. Harper, (1962). 1st ed. Fine in NF dj. *Authors Of The West.* $40/£26

LE MAY, ALAN. Cattle Kingdom. Farrar & Rinehart, (1933). 1st ed. VG+ in VG dj (chipped). *Authors Of The West.* $60/£39

LE MAY, ALAN. Empire for a Lady. London: Collins, 1932. 1st ed. VG+ in pict dj (lt edgewear, chipped spine top). *Else Fine.* $90/£58

LE MAY, ALAN. Winter Range. Farrar & Rinehart, (1932). 1st ed. NF in Nice dj (chipped). *Authors Of The West.* $60/£39

LE MESURIER, F. Sauces French and English. London: Faber & Faber, 1947. Pull-out table. Cream buckram. Eps browned, dj faded, chipped, o/w Good+. *Heller.* $20/£13

LE NETREL, EDMOND. Voyage of the Heros Around the World with Duhaut-Cilly in the Years 1826, 1827, 1828, and 1829.... Blanche Collet Wagner (trans). Dawson, 1951. Ltd to 200 ptd. VG. *Oregon.* $50/£32

LE PICHON, YANN. The World of Henri Rousseau. Joachim Neugroschel (trans). NY, 1982. VG in dj. *Argosy.* $125/£81

LE VAILLANT, FRANCOIS. Travels into the Interior Parts of Africa, by Way of Cape of Good Hope. Perth, R. Morrison, 1791. 2 vols in 1. 207; 204pp; 9 copper plts, incl 2 fldg scenes. (Sl foxing; cvrs detached.) *Cullen.* $200/£129

LEA, AURORA LUCERO-WHITE. Literary Folklore of the Hispanic Southwest. San Antonio: Naylor, 1953. 1st ed. VG in VG- dj (sm chips). *Parker.* $75/£48

LEA, TOM. The Brave Bulls. Boston: Little, Brown, 1949. 1st ed. VG in dj (sl worn spine). *Limestone.* $55/£35

LEA, TOM. Bullfight Manual for Spectators. Ciudad Juarez, Mexico: Plaza de Toros, (1949). VG in yellow pict wrapper. *Laurie.* $40/£26

LEA, TOM. Bullfight Manual for Spectators. Nourse: San Carlos, 1949. 1st Amer ed. Fine in pict overhanging wraps. *Connolly.* $40/£26

LEA, TOM. Bullfight Manual for Spectators. El Paso: Carl Hertzog, 1952. (2nd ed). Tls, dated. VG+ (lt soil) in pict wraps. *Bohling.* $150/£97

LEA, TOM. The Hands of Cantu. Boston: Little, Brown, (1964). 1st ed. Color frontis. Gold cl. Fine in VG+ dj (sl chipped). *Harrington.* $45/£29

LEA, TOM. The Hands of Cantu. Boston: Little, Brown, 1964. 1st ed. Color frontis. VG in Good dj. *Connolly.* $40/£26

LEA, TOM. The King Ranch. Boston: Little Brown, 1957. 1st ed, w/error in opening sentence p507. 2 vols. Slipcase. *Lambeth.* $125/£81

LEA, TOM. The Wonderful Country. Boston: Little, Brown, (1952). 1st ed. Pict eps. Pict cl. Fine in VG+ dj (spine, edges dknd; sl chipped). *Harrington.* $35/£23

LEACH, D.G. Rhododendrons of the World and How to Grow Them. London, 1962. Fldg chart. Dj (worn). *Sutton.* $100/£65

LEACOCK, STEPHEN. My Discovery of England. London, 1922. 1st ed. Fine (spine extrems sl rubbed) in dj (edge chipped, rubbed; edge tears). *Polyanthos.* $25/£16

LEACOCK, STEPHEN. Winnowed Wisdom. NY: Dodd, Mead, 1926. 1st ed. VG in dj (edgewear; lt spine browning; 2-inch tear rear panel). *Antic Hay.* $85/£55

LEAF, MUNRO. John Henry Davis. NY: Fred Stokes, 1940. 1st ed. Sm 8vo. Pict cl. VG in Good dj (chipped). *Book Adoption.* $40/£26

LEAF, MUNRO. The Story of Ferdinand. NY: Viking, 1936. 1st ed. Robert Lawson (illus). 7x8.5. 64pp. Good. *Cattermole.* $200/£129

LEAF, MUNRO. Wee Gillis. NY: Viking, 1938. 1st ed. Robert Lawson (illus). 7x10.25. 72pp. Fine in dj. *Cattermole.* $125/£81

LEAKEY, L.S.B. and P.V TOBIAS. Olduvai Gorge. Cambridge, 1967. 2 vols. Color plt; fldg map. VG in djs. *Argosy.* $150/£97

LEAR, EDWARD. Later Letters. Lady Strachey (ed). London, 1911. 1st ed. VG (spine sl faded). *Words Etc.* $74/£48

LEARY, TIMOTHY et al. The Psychedelic Experience: A Manual.... NY: University Books, 1964. 1st ed. Fine. *Sclanders.* $124/£80

LEARY, TIMOTHY. Jail Notes. NY: Douglas, 1970. 1st ed. NF in dj (sl edgeworn, lt creased). *Sclanders.* $31/£20

LEARY, TIMOTHY. The Politics of Ecstasy. London: MacGibbon & Kee, 1970. 1st UK ed. NF in dj. *Sclanders*. $39/£25

LEAVITT, DAVID. Family Dancing. Knopf, 1984. 1st ed, 1st bk. Fine in dj. *Stahr*. $45/£29

LEAVITT, DAVID. Family Dancing. Knopf, 1984. 1st ed. Fine in dj (lt sun fading). *Hermitage*. $60/£39

LEAVITT, DAVID. The Lost Language of Cranes. NY: Knopf, 1986. 1st ed. Fine in Fine dj. *Revere*. $40/£26

LEAVITT, DAVID. While England Sleeps. NY: Viking, 1993. 1st ed. Fine in Fine dj. *Revere*. $40/£26

LEBEL, R. Marcel Duchamp. London: Trianon, 1959. 122 plts. Internally Good (cl sl worn, sm lib stamp). *Ars Artis*. $233/£150

LeCLERC, CHARLES GABRIEL. The Compleat Surgeon: or, The Whole Art of Surgery Explain'd.... London, 1727. 6th ed. 392pp. Does not incl a 2nd vol on bandages. 1/2 antique calf; marbled bds (new eps). Fine. *Fye*. $400/£258

LECOMPTE, JANET. Pueblo, Hardscrabble, Greenhorn. The Upper Arkansas, 1832-1856. Univ OK, (1978). 1st ed. VF in VG dj. *Oregon*. $40/£26

LEDA, JAY. The Melville Log. NY: Harcourt, Brace, (1951). 1st ed, 1st ptg. 2 vols. Blue cl, gilt. VF set in VG box. *Macdonnell*. $125/£81

LEDER, LAWRENCE (ed). The Livingston Indian Records 1666-1723. PA Hist Assoc, 1956. 1st ed. Fldg map. Fine. *Oregon*. $25/£16

LEDFORD, PRESTON LAFAYETTE. Reminiscences of the Civil War, 1861-1865. Thomasville, NC: News Print, 1909. 1st ed. Ptd wrappers. 2 sm tape repairs, else VG in custom-made cl clamshell box w/leather spine, antique marbled paper sides. *Mcgowan*. $1,200/£774

LEDOUX, LOUIS VERNON. Songs from the Silent Land. NY: Brentano's, 1905. 1st ed, 1st bk. Tipped-in frontis. Tan bds, paper label. Fine. *Pharos*. $95/£61

LEE, ALFRED P. A Bibliography of Christopher Morley. GC: Doubleday, Doran, 1935. 1st ed. Fine in dj (sl worn). *Cahan*. $85/£55

LEE, ANDREW. (Pseud of Louis Auchincloss.) The Indifferent Children. NY: Prentice-Hall, (1947). 1st ed, 1st bk. NF in dj (lt edgewear; internal mends to sm tears). *Antic Hay*. $135/£87

LEE, ARTHUR BOLLES. The Microtomist's Vade-Mecum. London: Churchill, 1913. 7th ed. VG (bkpl). *Savona*. $39/£25

LEE, AUDREY. The Clarion People. NY: McGraw-Hill, (1963). 1st ed. Fine in dj. *Godot*. $45/£29

LEE, HANNAH FARNHAM. The Huguenots in France and America. Cambridge: Owen, 1843. 1st ed. 2 vols. (20),336; (6),302pp. (Lt wear.) Howes L 201. *Ginsberg*. $150/£97

LEE, HARPER. To Kill a Mockingbird. London: Heinemann, (1960). 1st Eng ed. Fine (contemp name, date; corners sl bumped) in dj. *Between The Covers*. $375/£242

LEE, HARPER. To Kill a Mockingbird. London: Heinemann, 1960. 1st Eng ed. Inscrip, edges lt foxed, else VG in dj. *Limestone*. $110/£71

LEE, HARPER. To Kill a Mockingbird. London: Heinemann, 1960. 1st UK ed. VG in dj. *Williams*. $93/£60

LEE, HENRY. Memoirs of the War in the Southern Department of the United States. NY: University Pub Co, 1870. 2nd ed thus. Frontis port, 620pp + (4)pp ads, 10 maps and ports. Brn cl (spotted). Good (inner hinges cracked). Howes L 202. *Chapel Hill*. $100/£65

LEE, JOHN D. A Mormon Chronicle. Robert Glass Cleland & Juanita Brooks (eds). San Marino: Huntington Lib, 1955. 2 vols. Djs. *Dawson*. $125/£81

LEE, JOHN D. A Mormon Chronicle: The Diaries of...1848-1876. San Marino, 1955. 1st eds. 2 vols. VG set. *Benchmark*. $175/£113

LEE, JOHN D. Mormonism Unveiled.... St. Louis, 1881. Frontis, 413pp. Dec cl (recased, repaired). *Benchmark*. $45/£29

LEE, JOHN THOMAS. New Found Letters of Josiah Gregg, Santa Fe Trader and Historian. Worchester: Amer Antiquarian Soc, 1931. Inscribed. Orig wraps, bound in plain cl (bkpl). *Schoyer*. $45/£29

LEE, LAURIE. As I Walked Out One Midsummer Morning. London: Deutsch, 1969. 1st UK ed. VG+ in dj. *Williams*. $23/£15

LEE, LAURIE. The Bloom of Candles. John Lehmann, 1947. 1st ed. Soiling, o/w VG in dj (soiled). *Poetry*. $23/£15

LEE, LAURIE. The Bloom of Candles. London: John Lehmann, 1947. 1st ed. VG in dj (sl soiled). *Cox*. $39/£25

LEE, LAURIE. Cider with Rosie. Century Illustrated Edition, 1984. 1st thus. Signed. Fine in dec bds. *Lewton*. $36/£23

LEE, LAWRENCE et al. Stained Glass. London: Artist's House, 1982. VG in dj. *Hollett*. $62/£40

LEE, MARGARET L. (ed). Narcissus, A Twelfe Night Merriment. London: David Nutt, 1893. 41pp. Full blue morocco, gilt. Joints sl rubbed, wear at top fr joint. Felt-lined jacket, slipcase. *Schoyer*. $100/£65

LEE, NORMAN. Klondike Cattle Drive. Vancouver, 1960. 1st trade ed. Facs tipped in. Fine in dj (sl chipped, sl soiled). *Baade*. $35/£23

LEE, ROBERT E., JR. Recollections and Letters of General Robert E. Lee by His Son. NY: Doubleday, Page, 1904. 1st ed. VG (recased, sl insect damage to spine repaired). *Mcgowan*. $85/£55

LEE, ROBERT E., JR. Recollections and Letters of General Robert E. Lee. NY: Doubleday, Page, 1904. 1st ed. Frontis port. Grey cl. VG. *Chapel Hill*. $175/£113

LEE, ROBERT E., JR. Recollections and Letters of Robert E. Lee. GC, 1904. 1926 Reprint. Spine faded; minor soiling fr cvr, o/w Fine. *Pratt*. $35/£23

LEE, ROBERT. Clinical Reports of Ovarian and Uterine Diseases. Edinburgh, 1853. 1st ed. 340pp. Good. *Fye*. $250/£161

LEE, ROBERT. Last Days of Alexander, and the First Days of Nicholas. London: Richard Bentley, 1854. 2nd ed. iv,210pp. Grn cl (spine worn, bkpl). *Schoyer*. $85/£55

LEE, RUTH WEBB. Sandwich Glass: The History of the Boston and Sandwich Glass Company. Framingham Centre, MA, 1939. Color frontis, 203 plts. VG in dj. *Argosy*. $50/£32

LEE, SHERMAN E. A History of Far Eastern Art. Englewood Cliffs, 1964. 1st ed. 60 color plts. VG. *Argosy*. $75/£48

LEE, TANITH. The Dragon Hoard. Farrar-Straus, 1971. 1st ed, 1st bk. Fine in dj (spine lt faded). *Madle*. $100/£65

LEE, WAYNE C. Scotty Philip: The Man Who Saved the Buffalo. Caldwell: Caxton Printers, 1975. 1st ed. Fine in dj. *Graf.* $35/£23

LEE, WILLIAM. (Pseud of William Burroughs.) Junkie. Bound with Narcotic Agent by M. Helbrant. Ace, 1953. 1st ed. VG in wraps. *Fine Books.* $225/£145

LEE, WILLIS T. et al. Guidebook of the Western United States. Part B: The Overland Route. Washington: GPO, 1916. 40 plts (incl fldg map), 29 fldg color sheet maps. Red cl. VG. *Schoyer.* $50/£32

LEECH, MARGARET. Reveille in Washington 1860-1865. NY, 1941. 1st ed. Dj worn, chipped, o/w VG+. *Pratt.* $35/£23

LEECH, MARGARET. Reveille in Washington, 1860-1865. NY: Harper & Bros, (1941). 1st ed. VG (rubbed; sm slit along back gutter). *Mcgowan.* $45/£29

LEECH, SAMUEL V. The Raid of John Brown at Harper's Ferry as I Saw It. Washington: By the author, 1909. *Hayman.* $40/£26

LEEPER, DAVID ROHRER. The Argonauts of 'Forty-Nine. South Bend, IN: J.B. Stoll, 1894. 1st ed. 146,xvipp. Black/gold-stamped cl (tips, spine ends worn; fr inner hinge weak; marginal soiling; owner stamps). *Dawson.* $150/£97

LEEPER, DAVID ROHRER. The Argonauts of Forty-Nine. Columbus: Long's College, 1950. Rpt. VG-. Howes L 266. *Parker.* $45/£29

LEES, J.A. and W.J. CLUTTERBUCK. B.C. 1887. London: Longmans, 1888. 1st ed. viii,387pp (foxed), sm fldg color map. Pict cl (spine type rubbed; cocked). *Schoyer.* $75/£48

LEES-MILNE, JAMES. Another Self. London: Hamish Hamilton, 1970. 1st ed. Very Nice in VG dj (sl soiled, browned). *Virgo.* $39/£25

LEES-MILNE, JAMES. Baroque in Spain and Portugal and Its Antecedents. London: Batsford, 1960. 1st ed. Dj (sl chipped). *Edwards.* $39/£25

LEES-MILNE, JAMES. Saint Peter's. London: Hamish Hamilton, 1967. 1st ed. 47 color plts. VG in dj. *Hollett.* $39/£25

LEES-MILNE, JAMES. Tudor Renaissance. London: Batsford, (1951). 1st ed. Frontis; 35 leaves of plts. Dj lt rubbed, else VG. *Bookpress.* $45/£29

LEFFINGWELL, WILLIAM B. Shooting on Upland, Marsh and Stream. Chicago: Rand McNally, 1890. Orig cl, beveled edges, gilt scene. VG. *Bowman.* $90/£58

LEFFINGWELL, WILLIAM B. Wild Fowl Shooting. Chicago: Rand McNally, 1889. Grn cl gilt pict cvr. Fine. *Bowman.* $75/£48

LEFFINGWELL, WILLIAM B. (ed). Shooting on Upland, Marsh, and Stream. Chicago/NY: Rand, McNally, 1890. 1st ed. 473,20pp ads. Gold-stamped cl. Rubbed; lacks rep, partial separation of endsheet at hinge; bkpl, else VG. *Cahan.* $100/£65

LEFREE, BETTY. Santa Clara Pottery Today. Albuquerque: Univ of NM, (1975). 1st ed. Fine in Fine dj. *Perier.* $30/£19

LEFROY, W. CHAMBERS. The Ruined Abbeys of Yorkshire. London: Seeley, Jackson & Halliday, 1883. 12 etched plts. Gilt cl (sl mkd; joints cracking; spotting, browning). *Hollett.* $54/£35

LEFTWICH, NINA. Two Hundred Years at Muscle Shoals Being an Authentic History of Colbert County 1700-1900.... Tuscumbia, AL, 1935. 1st ed. Signed. VG. *Mcgowan.* $150/£97

LEGALLOIS, JULIEN. Experiments on the Principle of Life, and Particularly on the Principle of the Motions of the Heart.... Phila, 1813. 1st Eng trans. 328pp (inner plt margins, tp repaired). Full leather (new eps). *Fye.* $500/£323

LEGER, FERNAND. Oil Paintings. November 12-December 21, 1968. NY: Perls Galleries, 1968. Mtd pict cvr illus. VG. *Argosy.* $35/£23

LEGMAN, GERSHON. Love and Death. (NY): Breaking Point, 1949. 1st ed. 1st, last pp w/red dye from wrappers, o/w Fine. *Pharos.* $75/£48

LEGROS, L.A. and J.C. GRANT. Typographical Printing Surfaces: The Technology and Mechanism of Their Production. London, 1916. 1st ed. 120 full-pg plts. Blue cl (rebound), gilt. VG+. *Willow House.* $132/£85

LEHMAN, B.B. Memoir of Major John L. Sherk, Late Surgeon of 7th Pennsylvania Cavalry. Lebanon, PA: Worth & Reinoehl, 1865. 1st ed. 12pp. Orig ptd wrappers; sl loose w/scattered foxing; else VG. *Mcgowan.* $450/£290

LEHMAN, IRVING. Benjamin Nathan Cardozo. Stamford, CT: Overbrook, 1938. Ltd to 350. Port. (Sl cvr wear.) *King.* $75/£48

LEHMANN, B. Rumour of Heaven. Methuen, 1934. 1st ed. Good. *Whiteson.* $25/£16

LEHMANN, JOHN. Down River. Cresset, 1939. 1st Eng ed. Brn cl. Fore-edge, prelims sl foxed, o/w VG. *Dalian.* $54/£35

LEHMANN, JOHN. I Am My Brother: Autobiography II. London: Longmans, 1960. 1st ed. 4 dbl-sided plts. Top edge pink. Black bds, gilt. Fine in dj. *Temple.* $23/£15

LEHMANN, JOHN. The Noise of History. Hogarth Press, 1934. 1st ed. Spine dknd, sl cocked, o/w VG. *Words Etc.* $78/£50

LEHMANN, JOHN. Photograph. London: Poem-of-the-Month Club Ltd, 1971. 1st Eng ed. Signed. VG (edges sl creased; edge sl browned). *Ulysses.* $47/£30

LEHMANN, K.B. and R.O. NEUMANN. Atlas and Principles of Bacteriology. Phila, 1901. 1st Eng trans. 2 vols. 69 chromolithos. Good. *Fye.* $75/£48

LEHMANN, ROSAMOND. Dusty Answer. NY: Holt, 1927. 1st US ed. Fine in dj. *Second Life.* $45/£29

LEHMANN, ROSAMOND. Invitation to the Waltz. NY: Henry Holt, 1932. 1st Amer ed. VG (sig; lt fading) in dj (chipped). *Hermitage.* $25/£16

LEIBER, FRITZ. The Green Millenium. Abelard, 1953. 1st ed. VG in dj. *Madle.* $50/£32

LEIBER, FRITZ. Night's Black Agents. Arkham House, 1947. 1st ed. VG in dj (frayed, repaired). *Madle.* $100/£65

LEIBER, FRITZ. Rime Isle. Whispers Press, 1977. 1st ed. Fine in dj. *Madle.* $25/£16

LEIBER, FRITZ. The Secret Songs. London: Rupert Hart-Davis, 1968. The true 1st ed. Fine in dj. *Williams.* $147/£95

LEIBER, FRITZ. Ship of Shadows. Gollancz, 1979. 1st ed. Signed. Fine in dj. *Aronovitz.* $30/£19

LEIBER, FRITZ. A Specter Is Haunting Texas. NY: Walker, (1969). 1st ed in bk form. White dj extrems sl tanned, else NF. *Reese.* $40/£26

LEIBER, FRITZ. Two Sought Adventure. Gnome, 1957. 1st ed. NF in NF dj. *Aronovitz.* $135/£87

LEIBER, FRITZ. Two Sought Adventure. Gnome, 1957. 1st ed. Fine in Mint dj. *Madle.* $175/£113

LEIBER, FRITZ. The Wanderer. Dobson, 1967. 1st Eng, 1st hb ed. Fine in NF dj (lt rubbed). *Aronovitz.* $185/£119

LEICHHARDT, LUDWIG. Journal of an Overland Expedition in Australia.... London: T.&W. Boone, 1847. 1st ed. Frontis, 10pp ads, xx,544pp, 8pp ads (hinges cracked; scattered foxing), fldg plt, 5 full-pg plts. Orig brn cl (bumped, rubbed, warped; split along joints; spine chipped). Contents VG. *Blue Mountain.* $1,250/£806

LEIDING, HARRIETTE KERSHAW. Historic Houses of South Carolina. Phila/London: Lippincott, 1921. 1st ed. Pict emb cl. VG (lt foxing). Howes L 237. *Cahan.* $100/£65

LEIDY, J. Fresh-water Rhizopods of North America. Washington, 1879. 324pp; 48 color plts. (Cl sl used.) *Wheldon & Wesley.* $116/£75

LEIGHTON, ALEXANDER H. and DOROTHEA C. The Navaho Door. Cambridge, 1944. 1st ed. Untrimmed. Pict cl. Leaf roughly opened, o/w VG in dj (sl chipped). *Baade.* $37/£24

LEIGHTON, ANN. American Gardens in the Eighteenth Century.... Boston: Houghton Mifflin, 1976. 1st ed. Fine in Fine dj. *Book Market.* $20/£13

LEIGHTON, CLARE. Country Matters. London: Gollancz, 1937. 1st ed. (Sl faded; sl foxed throughout.) *Petersfield.* $33/£21

LEIGHTON, CLARE. Four Hedges: A Gardener's Chronicle. London: Gollancz, 1935. 1st ed. 88 engrs. VG in grn/white pict dj (sl foxing). *Houle.* $125/£81

LEIGHTON, CLARE. Southern Harvest. London: Gollancz, 1943. 1st Eng ed. Fine in dj (short tears). *Houle.* $125/£81

LEIGHTON, MARIE. In God's Good Time. London: Richards, 1903. 1st ed. Good. *Ming.* $31/£20

LEINSTER, MURRAY. (Pseud of Wiliam Fitzgerald Jenkins.) City on the Moon. Avalon, 1957. 1st ed. Fine in dj. *Madle.* $35/£23

LEINSTER, MURRAY. (Pseud of William Fitzgerald Jenkins.) Colonial Survey. Gnome, 1957. 1st ed. NF in Mint dj. *Madle.* $150/£97

LEINSTER, MURRAY. (Pseud of William Fitzgerald Jenkins.) The Last Space Ship. NY: Frederick Fell, 1949. 1st ed. Fore-edges uncut. Nice. *Temple.* $70/£45

LEINSTER, MURRAY. (Pseud of William Fitzgerald Jenkins.) Operation: Outer Space. Reading: Fantasy Press, (1954). 1st paperbound trade ed. VG (rmdr mk?) in ptd wraps. *Antic Hay.* $35/£23

LEINSTER, MURRAY. (Pseud of William Fitzgerald Jenkins.) Operation: Outer Space. Fantasy Press, 1954. 1st ed, 2nd state binding. NF in dj. *Aronovitz.* $38/£25

LEINSTER, MURRAY. (Pseud of William Fitzgerald Jenkins.) Out of This World. Avalon, 1958. 1st ed. Fine in dj (spine sl faded). *Madle.* $40/£26

LEINSTER, MURRAY. (Pseud of William Fitzgerald Jenkins.) Sidewise in Time. Chicago: Shasta, 1950. 1st ed. Fine in NF dj. *Bernard.* $150/£97

LEINSTER, MURRAY. (Pseud of William Fitzgerald Jenkins.) Space Tug. Shasta, 1953. 1st ed. Fine in Mint dj. *Madle.* $100/£65

LEIPNIK, F.L. A History of French Etching from the Sixteenth Century to the Present Day. London, 1924. 1st trade ed. Frontis, 2 orig etchings. (Bds worn.) *Argosy.* $125/£81

LEISENRING, JAMES E. The Art of Tying the Wet Fly.... Dodd, Mead, 1946. Dj (sl torn). *Petersfield.* $71/£46

LEITCH, A. A Scottish Fly-Fisher. London: Alexander Gardner, 1911. 1 color, 10 b/w plts. (2 sm stains fr cvr.) *Petersfield.* $34/£22

LEITCH, A. A Scottish Fly-Fisher. Paisley: Gardner, 1911. 1st ed. 1 color plt. VG (foxed). *Bowman.* $40/£26

LEITCH, R.P. A Course of Water-Colour Painting. London: Cassell, n.d. (ca 1880). 3rd ed. 37pp, 24 mtd chromolithos. Sound. *Ars Artis.* $54/£35

LEITH-ADAMS, A. Field and Forest Rambles. London, 1871. xvi,333pp, fldg map. Good. *Henly.* $70/£45

LEITNER, IRVING. Baseball, Diamond in the Rough. Criterion, 1972. 1st ed. VG+ in VG+ dj. *Plapinger.* $30/£19

LEJARD, ANDRE (ed). Art of the French Book. London: Paul Elek, n.d. 2-tone cl bds. (Margins lt browned; edges sl rubbed.) Dj (soiled, ragged w/loss). *Edwards.* $62/£40

LEJEUNE, RITA and JACQUES STIENNON. The Legend of Roland in the Middle Ages. London: Phaidon, 1971. 2 vols. 63 mtd color plts. VG in djs. *Argosy.* $175/£113

LELAND, CHARLES G. Leatherwork. London: Pitman, 1929. 3rd ed. Navy blue emb cl. Fine. *Glenn.* $40/£26

LELAND, CHARLES G. Leatherwork: A Practical Manual.... London: Pitman, 1922. 3rd imp. Blind dec cl, gilt. VG (sl wear). *Willow House.* $23/£15

LELAND, CHARLES G. Pidgin-English Sing-Song. London: Kegan Paul et al, 1924. 10th ed. Yellow pict cl. Very Nice. *Cady.* $30/£19

LELAND, CHARLES G. Wood Carving. John J. Holtzapffel (rev). London, 1891. 2nd ed. ix,162pp; 6 plts; uncut. (Eps, tp lt spotted; dec bds lt soiled, rubbed; spine discolored, bumped, sl loss.) *Edwards.* $54/£35

LELAND, SAMUEL PHELPS. Peculiar People. Cleveland: Aust & Clark, 1891. 1st ed. 152pp. Maroon cl stamped in gilt/blind. Edges sl rubbed, early bkpl, sm hole inner hinge, o/w Very Nice. *Reese.* $350/£226

LEM, STANISLAW. The Investigation. NY: Seabury, 1974. 1st Eng trans. NF in NF- dj. *Lame Duck.* $50/£32

LEM, STANISLAW. The Invincible. Sidgwick & Jackson, 1973. 1st ed in English. Fine in dj. *Aronovitz.* $70/£45

LEM, STANISLAW. Mortal Engines. NY: Seabury, (1977). 1st ed. Fine in dj (sl rubbed). *Between The Covers.* $75/£48

LEM, STANISLAW. The Star Diaries. NY: Seabury, 1966. 1st Eng trans. Fine in NF dj (1-inch long tear fold). *Lame Duck.* $85/£55

LEMMON, KENNETH. The Covered Garden. London: Museum Press, 1962. 1st ed. Fine in dj. *Quest.* $45/£29

LEMPRIERE, J. Universal Biography. NY: Sargeant et al, 1810. 1st Amer ed. 2 vols. Contemp full calf, leather labels. VG set (wear to headbands). *Hartfield.* $225/£145

LENEHAN, J.C. The Tunnel Mystery. NY: Mystery League, 1931. 1st Amer ed. NF in dj (rubbed; edge tears; lacks piece). *Polyanthos.* $25/£16

LENFEST, SOLOMON AUGUSTUS. The Diary of...Co. G. Sixth Massachusetts Infantry...at Suffolk, Virginia. Suffolk-Nansemond Hist Soc, 1975. Paper cvr. VG. *Book Broker.* $25/£16

LENNON, JOHN. In His Own Write. Jonathan Cape, (1964). 1st ed, 1st bk. Laminated bds, photo upper cvr. Fine. *Bickersteth.* $59/£38

LENNON, JOHN. In His Own Write. London: Cape, 1964. 1st ed. Issued w/o dj. NF. *Limestone*. $85/£55

LENNON, JOHN. A Spaniard in the Works. Cape, 1965. 1st ed. Bds creased, else NF w/o dj as issued. *Fine Books*. $35/£23

LENNON, JOHN. A Spaniard in the Works. London: Cape, 1965. 1st ed. Fine in color pict bds. Issued w/o dj. *Limestone*. $55/£35

LENROOT, CLARA C. Long, Long Ago. (Appleton, WI), 1929. Signed. 13 plts. Cl-backed bds. VG +. *Bohling*. $45/£29

LENSKI, LOIS. Little Fire Engine. NY: Oxford, 1946. 1st ed. Sm 8vo. Dk red pict cl (lt rubbed; spine sl faded). VG +. *Book Adoption*. $40/£26

LENSKI, LOIS. Two Brothers and Their Baby Sister. NY: Frederick A. Stokes, 1930. 1st ed. Obl 12mo. Pink cl (sl shelfwear; sl fold frontis), color paste label. *Reisler*. $185/£119

LENT, D. GENEVA. West of the Mountains. Seattle: Univ of WA, 1963. 1st ed. 4 maps. VG in VG- dj. *Blue Dragon*. $40/£26

LENYGON, FRANCIS. (Pseud of Margaret Jourdain.) Decoration in England from 1640 to 1760. London: Batsford, 1927. 2nd ed, rev. Frontis. (Eps lt spotted, sl damp-staining upper bd; spine faded.) *Edwards*. $194/£125

LENYGON, FRANCIS. (Pseud of Margaret Jourdain.) Furniture in England From 1660 to 1760. Batsford, 1924. 2nd ed, rev. Frontis. Teg. (Spine faded.) *Edwards*. $132/£85

LEON, D. Livingstones. Hogarth, 1933. 1st ed. Binding dull, else VG. *Whiteson*. $37/£24

LEONARD, ELMORE. Cat Chaser. NY: Arbor House, (1982). 1st ed. Fine in very NF dj (tiny tear). *Antic Hay*. $45/£29

LEONARD, ELMORE. Cat Chaser. London: Viking, 1986. 1st UK ed. Fine in dj. *Lewton*. $22/£14

LEONARD, ELMORE. City Primeval: High Noon in Detroit. NY: Arbor House, 1980. 1st ed. Fine in Fine dj (lt edgewear). *Janus*. $35/£23

LEONARD, ELMORE. Dutch Treat. (NY: Mysterious Press, 1985). Signed ltd ed of 350 numbered. This mkd 'out of series.' NF, issued w/o dj (lacks slipcase). *Antic Hay*. $50/£32

LEONARD, ELMORE. Fifty-Two Pick Up. NY: Delacorte, 1974. 1st ed. Sl shaken; edges sunned, o/w Nice in dj (sl worn). *Beasley*. $85/£55

LEONARD, ELMORE. Fifty-Two Pick Up. S & W, 1974. 1st UK ed. VG in dj. *Lewton*. $70/£45

LEONARD, ELMORE. Fifty-Two Pickup. London: Secker & Warburg, 1974. 1st UK ed. NF in NF dj. *Ming*. $93/£60

LEONARD, ELMORE. Freaky Deaky. London: Viking, 1988. 1st British ed. Signed. Fine in dj. *Silver Door*. $40/£26

LEONARD, ELMORE. Freaky Deaky. London: Viking, 1988. 1st Eng ed. Signed. VF in dj. *Limestone*. $55/£35

LEONARD, ELMORE. Glitz. NY: Mysterious, 1985. 1st ed, one of 500 numbered, signed. Fine in Fine slipcase. *Janus*. $75/£48

LEONARD, ELMORE. Gold Coast. NY: Bantam Books, 1980. 1st ed: pb orig. NF in wrappers, as issued. *Janus*. $35/£23

LEONARD, ELMORE. Gunsights. NY: Bantam, 1979. 1st ed. NF in wraps. *Beasley*. $30/£19

LEONARD, ELMORE. Hombre. Armchair Detective Library, 1989. 1st Amer, 1st hb ed. One of 100 signed, numbered. New in slipcase as issued. *Fine Books*. $100/£65

LEONARD, ELMORE. Maximum Bob. NY, (1991). 1st ed, signed. VG in dj. *King*. $25/£16

LEONARD, ELMORE. The Moonshine War. NY: Doubleday, 1969. 1st ed. Fine in dj. *Else Fine*. $375/£242

LEONARD, ELMORE. Mr. Majestyk. NY, 1974. 1st ed. Pb orig. NF. *Rees*. $19/£12

LEONARD, ELMORE. Pronto. Viking, 1993. 1st UK ed. Signed. Fine in dj. *Lewton*. $31/£20

LEONARD, ELMORE. Stick. NY: Arbor House, 1983. 1st ed. Fine in dj. *Mordida*. $35/£23

LEONARD, ELMORE. Swag. NY: Delacorte, 1976. 1st ed. Fine in NF dj (spine foot sl worn). *Janus*. $65/£42

LEONARD, ELMORE. Swag. NY: Delacorte, 1976. 1st ed. VF in dj. *Mordida*. $100/£65

LEONARD, ELMORE. Swag. NY: Delacorte, 1976. 1st ed. Signed. VF in dj (few creases to flaps). *Else Fine*. $200/£129

LEONARD, ELMORE. Touch. NY: Arbor House, 1987. 1st ed. Inscribed. VF in dj. *Mordida*. $35/£23

LEONARD, WILLIAM ELLERY. Gilgamesh. Avon: LEC, 1974. #564/2000 signed by Irving Amen (illus). Good in slipcase. *Archaeologia*. $150/£97

LEONARD, ZENAS. Adventures of Zenas Leonard, Fur Trader. Norman: Univ of OK, (1959). 1st ed thus. Map, 5 plts. VG in dj. Howes L 264. *Schoyer*. $45/£29

Leonardo da Vinci. London: Hutchinson's Children's Books, 1984. 21x19 cm. 4 dbl-pg pop-ups, pull-tabs, disappearing picture. A. & M. Provensen (illus). Glazed pict bds. VG. *Book Finders*. $40/£26

LEONARDO, RICHARD A. History of Gynecology. NY: Froben Press, 1944. 25 plts. Good. *Goodrich*. $150/£97

LEOPOLD, ALDO. Round River. NY: OUP, 1953. 1st ed, 1st ptg. NF in dj (chipped, worn). *Glenn*. $30/£19

LEROUX, GASTON. The Dark Road. NY: Macaulay, 1924. 1st ed. Fine in pict dj (minor edgewear). *Else Fine*. $90/£58

LEROUX, GASTON. The Machine to Kill. Macaulay, 1935. 1st ed. VG. *Madle*. $35/£23

LEROUX, GASTON. The Man of a Hundred Faces. NY: Macaulay, 1930. 1st Amer ed. Half-title tear, o/w VG in dj (dknd spine; chipped ends; wear; short tears). *Mordida*. $35/£23

LEROUX, GASTON. The New Idol. NY: Macaulay, 1929. 1st Amer ed. Stamp eps, o/w VG in dj (sl faded spine; crease; wear). *Mordida*. $65/£42

LEROUX, GASTON. Nomads of the Night. NY: Macaulay, 1925. 1st Amer ed. Fine in VG dj (chipping; spine label removed; sl wear; short closed tears). *Mordida*. $65/£42

LEROUX, GASTON. The Phantom of the Opera. G&D, (1925). 1st ed thus, photoplay ed. VG + in VG color wrap-around dj (sm chips). *Aronovitz*. $475/£306

LEROUX, GASTON. The Phantom of the Opera. London: Mills & Boon, 1911. 1st London ed. Pub's orig black-stamped red cl (lt soiling w/lt loss to lettering; clipped corner fr blank endleave). *D & D*. $1,000/£645

LEROY-BEAULIEU, ANATOLE. Empire of the Tsars and the Russians. Zenaide A. Ragozin (trans). NY/London: Putnam's, 1893-1896. 3 vols. (xxii),588; (x),566; (xiv),601pp, 4 fldg maps; teg. Tan cl stamped in black/gilt/red (bumped, pocket removed). *Schoyer*. $100/£65

LESAGE, ALAIN-RENE. The Adventures of Gil Blas de Santillane. Oxford: LEC, 1937. #904/1500 numbered sets signed by John Austen (illus). 2 vols. Fine set in pub's djs & slipcase. *Hermitage*. $150/£97

LESLEY, LEWIS BURT (ed). Uncle Sam's Camels. Cambridge: Harvard Univ, 1929. Frontis port, 3 plts, fldg map. Unopened. VG+ in dj (worn, chipped, lt soiled). Howes B 271. *Bohling*. $135/£87

LESLEY, LEWIS BURT (ed). Uncle Sam's Camels: The Journal of May Humphreys Stacey. Supplemented by the Report of Edward...Beale (1857-1858). Cambridge, 1929. 1st ed. *Ginsberg*. $125/£81

LESLIE, C.R. Memoirs of the Life of John Constable, R.A. Andrew Shirley (ed). Medici Society, 1937. 1st ed. Color frontis; 11 color plts. Teg; gilt title (sl discolored spine). *Edwards*. $70/£45

LESLIE, J. et al. Narrative of Discovery and Adventure in the Polar Seas and Regions. Edinburgh: Oliver & Boyd, 1830. 1st ed. 424pp, fldg map. Orig bds (rebacked in calf). Good+. *Walcot*. $59/£38

LESLIE, LIONEL A.D. Wilderness Trails in Three Continents. London, 1931. (Feps, edges lt foxed; spine lt faded; chip.) *Edwards*. $47/£30

LESLIE, MISS. The Girl's Book of Diversions. London: Thomas Tegg et al, 1835. 1st Eng ed. Sq 12mo. VF full-pg copper engr frontis, 1/2pg wood engr vignette tp w/guard; xvi,223pp; VF 1/2pg wood engrs. In all, VG (dated ink sig fepp; lt cracking along inner hinge upper cvr; corners lt bumped; spine crown worn). *Hobby-horse*. $175/£113

LESLIE, SHANE. The Cantab. London, 1926. 1st ed, 1st issue. VG (spine rubbed; lt soiled). *Mcclintock*. $35/£23

LESLIE, SHANE. A Ghost in the Isle of Wight. London: Elkin Mathews & Marrot, 1929. One of 530 numbered, signed. VG in dj (chip). *Rees*. $39/£25

LESQUEREUX, LEO. Atlas to the Coal Flora of Pennsylvania.... Harrisburg: 1879. 1st ed. 18pp; 87 double plts; 1 fldg plt, tinted. Morocco, marbled bds. VG. *Petrilla*. $30/£19

LESSER, MILTON. Earthbound. Winston, 1952. 1st ed. Fine in dj. *Madle*. $135/£87

LESSING, DORIS. The Golden Notebooks. Michael Joseph, 1962. 1st Eng ed. Black cl. Fine in dj (sl chipped). *Dalian*. $194/£125

LESSING, DORIS. The Grass Is Singing. London: Joseph, 1950. 1st UK ed, 1st bk. VG in dj (edgeworn; spine chipped). *Lewton*. $147/£95

LESSING, DORIS. In Pursuit of the English. MacGibbon, Kee, 1960. 1st Eng ed. Black cl. Bkpl, o/w VG. *Dalian*. $54/£35

LESSING, DORIS. The Marriages between Zones, Three, Four and Five. London: Cape, 1980. 1st ed. Fine in dj. *Petersfield*. $19/£12

LESSING, DORIS. Martha Quest. London: Michael Joseph, 1952. 1st ed. VG (sl offsetting eps; lt spotting fore-edges; sm label removed) in VG (sl soiled, chipped; 2 sm closed tears). *Virgo*. $93/£60

LESSING, DORIS. The Summer before the Dark. London: Cape, (1973). 1st ed. Fine in dj. *Petersfield*. $33/£21

LESSING, DORIS. The Summer before the Dark. London: Cape, 1973. 1st ed. Fine in dj. *Limestone*. $55/£35

LESSING, DORIS. This Was the Old Chief's Country. Crowell, 1951. 1st ed, Amer issue. NF in dj. *Fine Books*. $100/£65

LESTER, C. EDWARDS and ANDREW FOSTER. The Life and Voyages of Americus Vespucius. New Haven: Horace Mansfield, 1852. 2nd ed. 432pp (foxing); 12 plts (1 hand-colored). Dk brn cl, blind-stamped; gilt spine (rubbed). *Karmiole*. $125/£81

LESTER, WILLIAM S. The Transylvania Colony. Spencer, IN: Samuel R. Guard, 1935. 1st ed. Red cl. Spine faded, spotting, else VG. *Chapel Hill*. $65/£42

Letters from a Young Emigrant in Manitoba. London: Kegan Paul, Trench, 1883. 181pp+44pp ads. Orig cl (pocket removed; lacks rep). *Schoyer*. $65/£42

Letters from Goethe. NY: Nelson, (1957). 1st ed. Fldg map. VF in dj. *Artis*. $20/£13

Letters from Jamaica, 'The Land of Streams and Woods.' (By Charles J.G. Rampini.) Edinburgh: Edmonston & Douglas, 1873. 1st ed. 182,24pp ads, illus tp. Extrems rubbed, else VG. *Cahan*. $85/£55

Letters from the Mountains. Boston: Greenough & Stebbins, 1809. 1st Amer ed from 3rd London ed. 2 vols. Contemp 3/4 calf. VG. *Second Life*. $150/£97

Letters from Three Continents. (By Matthew Flourney Ward.) NY: D. Appleton, 1851. 1st ed. (iv),350,(6)pp. Blindstamped cl. Sunned, else VG. *Bookpress*. $110/£71

Letters from Yorick to Eliza. (By Laurence Sterne.) Ptd for G. Kearsly & T. Evans, 1775. New ed. 104pp (lacks 1/2 title). Mod marbled bds. *Bickersteth*. $62/£40

Letters of Junius. (By Philip Francis.) Phila: M. Carey, 1807. 2nd Amer ed. (ii),317,(5)pp. Contemp sheep (worn; ex-lib; bkpl). *Bookpress*. $110/£71

LEURET, F. and H. BON. Modern Miraculous Cures. London: Peter Davies, 1957. 1st Eng ed. Good in dj. *White*. $19/£12

LEV, MAURICE. Autopsy Diagnosis of Congenitally Malformed Hearts. Springfield, 1953. 1st ed. Good. *Fye*. $60/£39

LEVER, CHARLES. The Bramleighs of Bishop's Folly. London: Chapman & Hall, 1872. New ed. Thick 8vo. ix,448,4pp (bkpl). Dec grn cl, gilt. *Hollett*. $39/£25

LEVER, CHARLES. Lord Kilgobbin. Harpers, 1872. 1st Amer ed. Sm piece missing rear panel, else VG. *Fine Books*. $65/£42

LEVER, CHARLES. Lord Kilgobbin. London: Chapman & Hall, 1873. New ed. vii,470,4pp (bkpls). Dec grn cl, gilt. *Hollett*. $39/£25

LEVER, CHARLES. Nuts and Nutcrackers. London: Orr, 1845. viii,232pp, 6 plts by Phiz (Hablot Knight Browne). Polished morocco, gilt; red pict fr cvr bound in; aeg. *Schoyer*. $150/£97

LEVERTOV, DENISE. Chekhov on the West Heath. Andes, NY: Woolmer/Brotherson, 1977. Ltd to 200 numbered, signed. Fine in marbled wraps. *Antic Hay*. $50/£32

LEVERTOV, DENISE. The Double Image. London: Cresset Press, 1946. 1st ed, 1st bk. Nice in dj (lt tanned). *Reese*. $150/£97

LEVERTOV, DENISE. The Jacob's Ladder. (NY): New Directions Paperback, (1961). 1st ed. NF (lt stain) in ptd wraps. *Antic Hay*. $25/£16

LEVERTOV, DENISE. Life in the Forest. (NY): New Directions, (1978). One of 150 numbered, signed. Fine in slipcase. *Reese*. $85/£55

LEVERTOV, DENISE. Life in the Forest. London: New Directions, 1978. One of 150 numbered, signed. Fine in slipcase. *Ulysses*. $70/£45

LEVERTOV, DENISE. Relearning the Alphabet. (NY): New Directions Book, (1970). 1st ed. VG in VG dj (price-clipped). *Godot*. $35/£23

LEVEY, MICHAEL. Canaletto Paintings in the Royal Collection. London, 1964. Good in wrappers. *Washton*. $20/£13

LEVEY, MICHAEL. The Later Italian Pictures in the Collection of Her Majesty the Queen. London: Phaidon, 1964. Tipped-in color frontis, 205 plts, 5 tipped-in color plts. (Ex-lib w/ink stamps, bkpl, tape mks.) Dj (edges lt browned). *Edwards*. $39/£25

LEVI, ELIPHAS. The History of Magic. London: Rider & Co., (1939?). 3rd ed. Frontis. Piece of envelope flap stuck to pg, else VG- in dj (worn, tattered). *Blue Dragon*. $45/£29

LEVI, ELIPHAS. Transcendental Magic. A.W. Waite (trans). London: Rider & Son, 1923. New & rev ed. Dk red cl w/gilt decs. VG. *Blue Dragon*. $85/£55

LEVI, PRIMO. If This Is a Man. NY: Orion, 1959. 1st Eng trans. Rev copy w/pub's slip laid in. Eps sl dknd, else NF in NF dj. *Lame Duck*. $250/£161

LEVI, PRIMO. The Periodic Table. Raymond Rosenthal (trans). NY: Schocken, (1984). 1st Amer ed. Fine in dj (sm crease fr panel). *Between The Covers*. $100/£65

LEVI, PRIMO. The Periodic Table. NY: Schocken, 1984. 1st Amer ed. Fine in dj (price-clipped). *Lame Duck*. $100/£65

LEVI, WENDELL MITCHELL. The Pigeon. Sumter: (The Author), 1963. 2nd ed. Color frontis, port. Dk blue buckram. VG in dj (worn). *Weber*. $40/£26

LEVI-STRAUSS, CLAUDE. The Origin of Table Manners. John & Doreen Weightman (trans). London, 1978. 1st UK ed. Dj. *Edwards*. $39/£25

LEVICK, G.M. Antarctic Penguins. London, 1914. Good (sl spotted; ex-lib). *Wheldon & Wesley*. $31/£20

LEVIE, WILLIAM ELDER. A Popular Handbook of the Law of Bankruptcy in Scotland. Edinburgh: William Hodge, 1925. 2nd ed. *Boswell*. $75/£48

LEVIN, GAIL. Edward Hopper: The Complete Prints. NY, (1979). VG in stiff pict wrappers. *Argosy*. $40/£26

LEVIN, IRA. The Boys from Brazil. London: Michael Joseph, 1976. 1st UK ed. VG in dj. *Williams*. $23/£15

LEVIN, IRA. A Kiss Before Dying. S&S, 1953. 1st ed, 1st bk. VG+. *Fine Books*. $35/£23

LEVIN, IRA. A Kiss Before Dying. London: Michael Joseph, 1954. 1st UK ed. VG in VG dj. *Ming*. $23/£15

LEVIN, IRA. No Time for Sergeants. NY: Random House, (1956). 1st ed. Fine in dj (closed edge tear). *Dermont*. $35/£23

LEVIN, IRA. Rosemary's Baby. R-H, 1967. 1st ed. Fine in dj. *Fine Books*. $60/£39

LEVIN, IRA. Rosemary's Baby. Michael Joseph, 1967. 1st UK ed. NF in dj (sl rubbed; lt creased). *Sclanders*. $31/£20

LEVIN, MEYER. Compulsion. NY: Simon & Schuster, 1959. 1st ed. Fine in Fine dj. *Dermont*. $75/£48

LEVIN, MEYER. Reporter. NY: John Day Co, (1929). 1st ed. 1st bk. Fine in dj. *Godot*. $100/£65

LEVITIN, YEVGENY. Rembrandt Etchings.... Leningrad: Aurora, 1978. 96 tipped-in plts. Orig cl, gilt monogram. VF in slipcase. *Europa*. $43/£28

LEVITT, JEFFREY S. The World of Antique Toys. London: Mint & Boxed, (1990). Ltd to 5000 numbered. Full red morocco. Fine in slipcase. *Glenn*. $95/£61

LEVY, CHARLES. Spoils of War. Boston: Houghton Mifflin, 1974. 1st ptg. VG in dj (sl edgetears; wrinkle fr panel). *Aka*. $40/£26

LEVY, M. Whistler Lithographs. An Illustrated Catalogue Raisonne. London: Jupiter, 1975. 4 color plts. Sound in dj. *Ars Artis*. $47/£30

LEVY, MATTHIAS. The History of Short-Hand Writing; to Which is Prefixed the System Used by the Author. London, 1862. 1st ed. 1/2 morocco (worn). *Argosy*. $75/£48

LEVY, MERVYN (ed). Paintings of D.H. Lawrence. London, 1964. 1st ed. 16 color plts. Dj (chipped). *Edwards*. $54/£35

LEWINS, ROBERT. Life and Mind on the Basis of Modern Medicine. London, 1877. 1st ed. 66pp. Good. *Fye*. $75/£48

LEWIS, A.G. (ed). Sport, Travel and Adventure. London: Fisher Unwin, 1915. Teg. Red cl, gilt titles. Rubbed, o/w VG. *Bowman*. $45/£29

LEWIS, A.H. The Apaches of New York. Dillingham, 1912. 1st ed. Good. *Fine Books*. $45/£29

LEWIS, C.S. The Abolition of Man. NY: Macmillan, 1947. 1st Amer ed. Blue paper bds, gilt. Fine in Nice dj. *Macdonnell*. $50/£32

LEWIS, C.S. Beyond the Bright Blur. Harcourt Brace, 1963. 1st US ed. Fine in glassine dj (sl frayed). *Lewton*. $60/£39

LEWIS, C.S. Boxen. NY: Harcourt, Brace, Jovanovich, (1985). Uncorrected proof. NF in ptd wraps. *Antic Hay*. $45/£29

LEWIS, C.S. An Experiment in Criticism. Cambridge Univ Press, 1961. 1st ed. VG. *Argosy*. $45/£29

LEWIS, C.S. The Great Divorce. London: Bles/Centenary, (1945). 1st ed ('November 1945'). VG in dj (sm chips at spine ends). *Houle*. $200/£129

LEWIS, C.S. Hero and Leander. British Academy, 1952. 1st Eng ed. VG in grey ptd wrappers (sl tanned). *Dalian*. $39/£25

LEWIS, C.S. The Horse and His Boy. London: Geoffrey Bles, (1954). 1st ed. Pauline Baynes (illus). Grey cl, silver lettering. Good in color dj (lt worn; lt smudged). *Reisler*. $675/£435

LEWIS, C.S. The Horse and His Boy. Macmillan, 1954. 1st Amer ed. NF in Nice dj (wear, tear; 2 sm chips). *Aronovitz*. $100/£65

LEWIS, C.S. Letters to an American Lady. Grand Rapids: Wm. Eerdmans, (1967). 1st ed. VG. *Argosy*. $45/£29

LEWIS, C.S. Letters to an American Lady. Clyde S. Kilby (ed). Hodder & Stoughton, 1967. 1st Eng ed. Red cl. VG in dj. *Dalian*. $31/£20

LEWIS, C.S. Letters to Malcolm Chiefly on Prayer. London: Geoffrey Bles, (1964). 1st ed. Orig paper bds, gilt. Fine in dj (chip). *Macdonnell*. $50/£32

LEWIS, C.S. Miracles. London: Bles, 1947. 1st ed. VG in dj. *Rees*. $16/£10

LEWIS, C.S. Miracles. London, 1947. 1st ed. VG in dj (spine browned). *Words Etc*. $54/£35

LEWIS, C.S. Narrative Poems. Walter Hooper (ed). Geoffrey Bles, 1969. 1st Eng ed. Black cl. VF in dj. *Dalian*. $31/£20

LEWIS, C.S. Perelandra. London: John Lane, Bodley Head, 1943. Spine faded, o/w Nice. *Temple*. $85/£55

LEWIS, C.S. Perelandra. NY: Macmillan, 1944. 1st Amer ed. Inscrip, else VG in dj (price-clipped, spine lt faded; nicks, short tears, else VG). *Godot*. $85/£55

LEWIS, C.S. Perelandra. Macmillan, 1944. 1st Amer ed. VG+ in VG+ dj (spine lightened). *Fine Books*. $110/£71

LEWIS, C.S. Reflections on the Psalms. London: Geoffrey Bles, 1958. 1st ed. Top edge grey-grn; eps grey. Maroon bds, spine lettered yellow. Fine in dj. *Temple*. $28/£18

LEWIS, C.S. Surprised by Joy. London: G. Bles, 1955. 1st ed. VG in dj (nicks, short tears). *Houle*. $125/£81

LEWIS, C.S. That Hideous Strength. London: Bodley Head, 1945. 1st UK ed. VG in dj (sl dull, sl chipped top edge; closed tear to spine). *Williams*. $271/£175

LEWIS, C.S. Till We Have Faces. NY: Harcourt Brace, (1957). 1st US ed. Spine cocked, else VG+ in dj. *Other Worlds*. $45/£29

LEWIS, C.T. COURTNEY. The Picture Printer of the Nineteenth Century, George Baxter 1804-1867. London, 1911. 1st ed. Teg. Dec cl, color label (bkpl, inner hinges taped, lacks eps, inner fr hinge cracked; rubbed, frayed). *King*. $150/£97

LEWIS, CECIL. Sagittarius Rising. London, 1937. 1st Cheap ed, 5th imp. Eps sl browned, o/w VG in dj (sl rubbed; spine chipped). *Edwards*. $39/£25

LEWIS, CHARLES LEE. Admiral Franklin Buchanan: Fearless Man of Action. Balt: Norman, Remington, 1929. 1st ed. Gilt-emb emblem. VG in dj (dusty, tape-repaired). *Cahan*. $50/£32

LEWIS, CLARENCE IRVING. The Ground and Nature of the Right. NY: Columbia Univ Press, 1955. 1st ed. Brn-lettered gold cl. Fine in orig glassine wrapper. *House*. $75/£48

LEWIS, D.B. WYNDHAM. Four Favourites. London: Evans Bros, 1948. 1st UK ed. VG in dj (sl worn, gash to rear panel). *Williams*. $19/£12

LEWIS, D.B. WYNDHAM. The Hooded Hawk. NY: Longman's, Green, 1947. 1st ed. Sl damp fore-edge, else VG in dj (nicked). *Hermitage*. $25/£16

LEWIS, DIO. Our Digestion; or, My Jolly Friend's Secret. Phila/Boston: Maclean, 1872. 1st ed. 407pp. NF. *Second Life*. $65/£42

LEWIS, DIO. Weak Lungs, and How to Make them Strong. Boston, 1863. 1st ed. 360pp. Good. *Fye*. $50/£32

LEWIS, EDITH. Willa Cather Living. NY: Knopf, 1953. 1st ed. VG (lacks fep) in dj (worn). *Second Life*. $25/£16

LEWIS, ELISHA J. The American Sportsman: Containing Hints to Sportsmen.... Phila: Lippincott, 1857. 510pp, hand-colored frontis, color illus 1/2 title. Blind-emb, gilt dec cl. Spine lt chipped, lower portion expertly reinforced, tips rubbed, presentation, else VG. *Cahan*. $150/£97

LEWIS, ELIZABETH FOREMAN. Portraits from a Chinese Scroll. London: Harrap, 1939. 1st ed. Gilt cl (spine sl creased). Dj (sl worn). *Hollett*. $39/£25

LEWIS, F. Oriental Rugs and Textiles: The Perez Collection. Leigh-on-Sea, England: F. Lewis, 1953. 1st ed. Ltd to 300. 64 tipped-in b/w plts. Pub's illus prospectus laid in. Cl lt worn, stamp, ink notation, else NF. *Cahan*. $150/£97

LEWIS, FLORENCE. China Painting. London: Cassell, 1884. 2nd ed. Frontis, 52pp, 15 plts. (Cvr dknd, spotted.) *Bookpress*. $200/£129

LEWIS, FRANK. A Dictionary of British Bird Painters. Leigh-on-Sea, 1974. (Ex-lib w/ink stamp; sl surface loss fep.) Dj (sl chipped). *Edwards*. $39/£25

LEWIS, GEORGE. The Indiana Company 1763-1789. Glendale, CA: Clark, 1941. 1st ed. 2 fldg maps, 2 ports. Blue cl. NF. *Chapel Hill*. $150/£97

LEWIS, GEORGE. The Indiana Company 1763-1798. A Study.... Clark, 1941. 1st ed. Fldg frontis map, fldg map, 2 plts. VF. *Oregon*. $95/£61

LEWIS, HENRY. The Valley of the Mississippi Illustrated. MN Hist Soc, (1967). 1st ed. #1656/2000. 78 full-pg color plts. VF in dj. *Artis*. $45/£29

LEWIS, JOHN. A Handbook of Type and Illustration. London: Faber & Faber, 1956. VG (sig) in dj (edges worn); dec cl case. *Heller*. $35/£23

LEWIS, LLOYD. Captain Sam Grant. Boston: Little, Brown, 1950. 1st ed. NF in VG dj. *Mcgowan*. $45/£29

LEWIS, LLOYD. Sherman Fighting Prophet. NY: Harcourt, Brace, (1932). 1st ed. VG. *Mcgowan*. $75/£48

LEWIS, LLOYD. Sherman: Fighting Prophet. NY, 1932. 1st ed. VG. *Clark*. $28/£18

LEWIS, LUNSFORD LOMAX. A Brief Narrative Written for His Grandchildren. Richmond, VA, 1915. 1st ed. Signed. Later cl. VG. *Mcgowan*. $150/£97

LEWIS, M. et al. The Engravings of Giorgio Chisi. NY: MMA, 1985. Sound in dj. *Ars Artis*. $70/£45

LEWIS, M.J.T. Temples in Roman Britain. Cambridge: CUP, 1966. 4 plts. Good in dj. *Archaeologia*. $125/£81

LEWIS, MARGARET. What I Have Saved from the Writings of My Husband, Thomas B. Lewis. SF: Privately pub, 1874. 64,59pp. Emb black cl, gilt titles. (Internally soiled; cvrs worn.) Howes L 323. *Parmer*. $650/£419

LEWIS, MERIWETHER and WILLIAM CLARK. History of the Expedition of Captains Lewis and Clark 1804-5-6. McClurg, 1902. 2 vols. 3 plts, 1 fldg map; frontis, 3 maps. Sm stain vol 2, o/w VG. *Oregon*. $195/£126

LEWIS, MERIWETHER and WILLIAM CLARK. The Journals of the Expedition Under the Command of Captains Lewis and Clark.... Heritage, (1962). 2 vols. 4 ports, 16 color plts, fldg map. VG in Good+ slipcases. *Oregon*. $75/£48

LEWIS, MERIWETHER and WILLIAM CLARK. Journals of the Expedition...Performed During the Years 1804-5-6.... Nicholas Biddle (ed). NY: Heritage Press, (1962). 2 vols. Fldg map. 1/2 cloth, map patterned bds. VG+ (vol 2 sm spine puncture) in slipcase (edgewear). Howes L 317. *Bohling*. $60/£39

LEWIS, MERIWETHER and WILLIAM CLARK. Travels to the Source of the Missouri River and Across the American Continent to the Pacific Ocean. London, 1814. 1st Eng ed of 'History of the Expedition.' Half-title; 663pp. Full speckled calf. Bkpl; sm stamped name; sl worming last few blank pp into rear bd; fr inner hinge cracked, else Nice. *King*. $6,000/£3,871

LEWIS, NORMAN. The Day of the Fox. London: Cape, 1955. 1st ed. Fine in pict dj. *Patterson*. $62/£40

LEWIS, NORMAN. A Dragon Apparent. Cape/Book Soc, 1951. 1st Eng ed. Red cl. Fine (bkpl) in dj (sl nicked). *Dalian.* $70/£45

LEWIS, NORMAN. The Honoured Society. Collins, 1964. 1st Eng ed. Orange cl. Fine in dj (sl dusty). *Dalian.* $70/£45

LEWIS, NORMAN. Sand and Sea in Arabia. George Routledge & Sons, 1938. 1st Eng ed. White cl (mkd; soiled). Good. *Dalian.* $132/£85

LEWIS, NORMAN. Spanish Adventure. London: Gollancz, 1935. 1st ed. VG (cl sl worn). *Patterson.* $78/£50

LEWIS, NORMAN. Spanish Adventure. Victor Gollancz, 1935. 1st Eng ed, 1st bk. Black cl (sl mkd). VG in dj (sl soiled; chip). *Dalian.* $233/£150

LEWIS, NORMAN. The Volcanoes above Us. Jonathan Cape, 1957. 1st Eng ed. Grn cl. Name label ep, o/w Fine in dj (chip). *Dalian.* $39/£25

LEWIS, OSCAR. The Big Four. NY: Knopf, 1938. 1st ed. Blue gilt-lettered, dec cl. NF in VG+ dj. *Harrington.* $40/£26

LEWIS, OSCAR. The Children of Sanchez. Random House, (1961). 1st ed. VG in VG dj. *Oregon.* $27/£17

LEWIS, OSCAR. Lola Montez. SF: Colt, (1938). One of 750 signed. Uncut. (Bds sunned.) *Argosy.* $65/£42

LEWIS, OSCAR. Sea Routes to the Gold Fields. NY: Knopf, 1949. 1st ed. Fldg map. VG in dj (sl worn). *Lien.* $25/£16

LEWIS, OSCAR. Silver Kings. NY: Knopf, 1947. 1st ed, 2nd ptg. 17 plts. VG in Good dj. *Connolly.* $25/£16

LEWIS, OSCAR. Sutter's Fort. Prentice Hall, (1966). 1st ed. Ep maps. VG in VG dj. *Oregon.* $25/£16

LEWIS, R.H. The Book Browser's Guide to Erotica. David & Charles, 1981. Fine in dj. *Moss.* $25/£16

LEWIS, R.H. Fine Bookbinding in the 20th Century. David & Charles, 1984. Fine in dj. *Moss.* $47/£30

LEWIS, R.W.B. Edith Wharton: A Biography. Harper, 1975. 1st ed. VG in dj (sl dull, sl torn). *Whiteson.* $20/£13

LEWIS, ROGER. Outlaws of America. London: Heinrich Hanau Pub, 1972. 1st ed. NF in dj. *Sclanders.* $31/£20

LEWIS, ROY HARLEY. A Cracking of Spines. NY: St. Martin's, 1982. 1st Amer ed. Fine in dj (rubbing). *Mordida.* $35/£23

LEWIS, ROY HARLEY. Where Agents Fear to Tread. NY/London: St. Martin's, Hale, 1984. 1st ed. Fine in dj. *Silver Door.* $30/£19

LEWIS, SAMUEL. Topographical Dictionary of Scotland.... London: S. Lewis, 1851. 2nd ed. 2 vols. iv,611; (ii),622pp (cancelled lib stamps reverse tp). Dec blind-stamped cl (extrems worn). Good (bkpls). *Peter Taylor.* $90/£58

LEWIS, SINCLAIR. Arrowsmith. NY: Harcourt, (1925). 1st ptg, one of 500 lg paper copies, signed. Fine. *Second Life.* $400/£258

LEWIS, SINCLAIR. Babbitt. NY: HB & Co, (1922). 1st Amer ed. Fine in NF dj (sm internally mended tears; sm spot rear panel). *Between The Covers.* $1,500/£968

LEWIS, SINCLAIR. Babbitt. NY, 1946. 1st pb ed. Unread. Nice (lt stamp top edge pp) in dj (tearing at corners). *Mcclintock.* $25/£16

LEWIS, SINCLAIR. Dodsworth. NY: Harcourt, Brace, (1929). 1st ed. Fine in dj (worn, crinkled; spine chipped). *Hermitage.* $90/£58

LEWIS, SINCLAIR. Elmer Gantry. NY, 1927. 1st ed, not 1st binding state. 'G' of Gantry corrected, o/w VG. *Bond.* $35/£23

LEWIS, SINCLAIR. Elmer Gantry. J. Cape, 1927. 1st Eng ed. VG+ in dj (professionally backed; worn). *Fine Books.* $90/£58

LEWIS, SINCLAIR. Free Air. NY, 1919. 1st ed. Name, spine discolored, rubbed, else Good. *King.* $75/£48

LEWIS, SINCLAIR. The God-Seeker. Heinemann, 1949. 1st Eng ed. Blue cl (sl rubbed). Fine in dj (sl nicked). *Dalian.* $39/£25

LEWIS, SINCLAIR. The Innocents. Harpers, 1917. 1st ed. Fine in NF dj. *Fine Books.* $1,250/£806

LEWIS, SINCLAIR. It Can't Happen Here. Jonathan Cape, 1935. 1st Eng ed. Cream cl. VF in dj (sl soiled, tanned). *Dalian.* $70/£45

LEWIS, SINCLAIR. Main Street. Chicago: LEC, 1937. #162/1500 signed by Grant Wood (illus). Fine in slipcase (sl worn, browned). *Williams.* $465/£300

LEWIS, SINCLAIR. The Man Who Knew Coolidge. H-B, 1928. 1st ed. Spine sl dulled, else VG+ in dj (lt wear). *Fine Books.* $165/£106

LEWIS, T. HAYTER. The Holy Places of Jerusalem. London: Murray, 1888. xii,130pp. Sl rubbed; spine sl frayed, o/w VG ex-lib. *Worldwide.* $90/£58

LEWIS, THOMAS. Diseases of the Heart Described for Practitioners and Students. London: Macmillan, 1933. 1st ed, rptd w/minor corrections. Ink underlining, notes few pp, o/w VG. *White.* $43/£28

LEWIS, THOMAS. Pain. NY, 1946. 1st ed, rptd. Good. *Fye.* $30/£19

LEWIS, VIRGIL A. History of the Battle of Point Pleasant...Sunday, October 10th, 1774. Charleston, WV: Tribune, 1909. 1st ed. Frontis. Red cl. Bkpl, else VG. *Chapel Hill.* $150/£97

LEWIS, W. The New Dispensatory.... London: C. Nourse, 1781. 4th ed. viii,(iv),692pp. Contemp full calf; rebacked w/new label. Clean. *White.* $147/£95

LEWIS, W.G. The Cook. London: Houlston & Stoneman, n.d. (1849). iv,332pp (1st few leaves soiled; marginal browning; sigs; marginal notes). Orig cl (rubbed, worn; hinges cracked), yellow eps. *Cox.* $54/£35

LEWIS, W.M. The People's Practical Poultry Book. NY, 1871. 2nd ed. 223pp (4pp ads). (Extrems worn; spine mostly gone; fr hinge repaired; bkpl.) *Sutton.* $35/£23

LEWIS, WILLIAM and NAOJIRO MURAKAMI. Ranald McDonald, Narrative of Early Life on Columbia under HBC's Regime.... E. Washington Hist Soc, 1923. 1st ed. Ltd to 1000 numbered. 14 plts (ex-lib w/most mks neatly removed). *Oregon.* $75/£48

LEWIS, WILLIAM. Elements of the Game of Chess.... NY: G&C Carvill, 1827. 1st Amer ed. 275pp (prelims foxed). Orig bds, uncut (rebacked in buckram; new eps, typed label). *Felcone.* $200/£129

LEWIS, WILLIE NEWBURY. Between Sun and Sod. Clarendon, TX: Clarendon Press, (1938). (2nd issue w/author's name spelled correctly on tp.) Signed. (Sl soiled, dknd; bds sl bowed at top.) *Bohling.* $85/£55

LEWIS, WILLIE NEWBURY. Between Sun and Sod. Clarendon, TX: Clarendon Press, (1939). 1st ed, 2nd ptg. Name sticker, else VG in dj (edge-torn). *Perier.* $60/£39

LEWIS, WILMARTH. Collector's Progress. NY: Knopf, (1951). 1st ed. NF in NF dj. *Hermitage.* $40/£26

LEWIS, WILMARTH. Collector's Progress. NY, 1951. 1st ed. Fine (eps sl dknd) in Fine dj. *Bond.* $25/£16

LEWIS, WILMARTH. Collector's Progress. NY: Knopf, 1951. 1st ed. VG in dj (sl tanned, nicks). *Reese.* $30/£19

LEWIS, WILMARTH. Three Tours through London in the Years 1748-1776-1797. New Haven: Yale Univ, 1941. 1st ed. Frontis. Gray cl, paper labels. VG. *Hartfield.* $95/£61

LEWIS, WYNDHAM. America and Cosmic Man. London, 1948. One of 2000. (Bkpl.) Dj (chipped). *Edrich.* $70/£45

LEWIS, WYNDHAM. The Apes of God. London, (1931). 1st trade ed. Excellent in dj (chipped). *Edrich.* $116/£75

LEWIS, WYNDHAM. The Apes of God. London: Arthur Press, 1930. 1st ed. Ltd to 750 signed. 4to. Fine in dj. *Jaffe.* $1,000/£645

LEWIS, WYNDHAM. The Apes of God. NY: McBride, 1932. 1st ed. Fine in dj (lt used; spine rubbed). *Beasley.* $175/£113

LEWIS, WYNDHAM. The Apes of God. Santa Barbara, 1981. One of 250 numbered deluxe handbound. Pict bds. VG in glassine dj. *King.* $45/£29

LEWIS, WYNDHAM. The Art of Being Ruled. London: C&W, 1926. 1st ed, 1st state. Spine sl faded; lacks dj, else VG. *Virgo.* $194/£125

LEWIS, WYNDHAM. The Art of Being Ruled. London, 1926. 1st Eng ed. 1st issue w/single blind border rule. Prelims sl foxed, o/w VG in dj (spine sunned, chipped). *Edrich.* $225/£145

LEWIS, WYNDHAM. Blasting and Bombardiering (Autobiography 1914-1926). Eyre & Spottiswoode, 1937. 1st Eng ed. Orange cl (sl rubbed). Fine. *Dalian.* $116/£75

LEWIS, WYNDHAM. Blasting and Bombardiering. London, 1937. 1st Eng ed. 1st issue binding w/top edge stained yellow. Excellent in dj. *Edrich.* $248/£160

LEWIS, WYNDHAM. The Caliph's Design. London: Egoist Press, 1919. 1st Eng ed. Marbled paper-cvrd bds (rubbed). Fine. Issued w/o dj. *Edrich.* $233/£150

LEWIS, WYNDHAM. The Childermass. NY, 1928. 1st Amer ed. As New. *Bond.* $65/£42

LEWIS, WYNDHAM. The Childermass. London, 1928. 1st Eng ed. VG. *Edrich.* $70/£45

LEWIS, WYNDHAM. Count Your Dead—They Are Alive! London, 1937. 1st Eng ed. Excellent in dj (closed tears). *Edrich.* $194/£125

LEWIS, WYNDHAM. Count Your Dead: They Are Alive! London: Lovat Dickson, 1937. 1st ed. VG. *Patterson.* $155/£100

LEWIS, WYNDHAM. The Demon of Progress in the Arts. Chicago, 1955. 1st Amer ed. Faded, else Good in dj (rubbed, spine scratched). *King.* $30/£19

LEWIS, WYNDHAM. The Diabolical Principle and the Dithyrambic Spectator. C&W, 1931. 1st Eng ed. Foreedge sl foxed; spine tip sl faded, o/w VF in dj (spine tanned; chip upper spine, back cvr tip). *Dalian.* $194/£125

LEWIS, WYNDHAM. Doom of Youth. London: C&W, 1932. 1st ed. 8vo. Sig, o/w VG in dj (lt dust-soiled; sm ring stain fr panel). *Jaffe.* $500/£323

LEWIS, WYNDHAM. Doom of Youth. London, 1932. 1st Eng ed. Cl age-dknd, o/w VG. *Edrich.* $155/£100

LEWIS, WYNDHAM. Filibusters in Barbary. London, 1932. 1st Eng ed. Dj torn, mkd, o/w Fine in pict cl. *Edrich.* $388/£250

LEWIS, WYNDHAM. The Hitler Cult. London: Dent, 1939. 1st ed. Colonial ed stamp on title, half title; foxing; trace of sig ep; o/w VG. *Rees.* $54/£35

LEWIS, WYNDHAM. The Hitler Cult. London, 1939. 1st ed. Foxing to eps, prelims, o/w VG in dj (sl browned; crumpled at spine head, tail w/chips). *Edwards.* $349/£225

LEWIS, WYNDHAM. The Hitler Cult. London, 1939. 1st Eng ed. (Eps, edges lt foxed.) *Edrich.* $101/£65

LEWIS, WYNDHAM. The Hitler Cult. London, 1939. 1st Eng ed. Eps lt foxed, o/w VG in dj (sl chipped, dust soiled). *Edrich.* $426/£275

LEWIS, WYNDHAM. Hitler. London, 1931. 1st Eng ed. 1st binding: tan cl. Dj spine, fr panel sl trimmed, lacks back panel, o/w Excellent. *Edrich.* $186/£120

LEWIS, WYNDHAM. Journey into Barbary. Santa Barbara, 1983. One of 226 deluxe numbered, handbound, signed. Pict bds. VG in glassine dj. *King.* $65/£42

LEWIS, WYNDHAM. Left Wings Over Europe. Cape, Aug 1936. 2nd imp. Fine in 2nd imp dj (sl dusty, sl wear). *Patterson.* $78/£50

LEWIS, WYNDHAM. The Letters of Wyndham Lewis. W.K. Rose (ed). Norfolk, CT, (1963). 1st Amer ed. VG in dj (sl chipped, price-clipped, rmdr mk). *King.* $25/£16

LEWIS, WYNDHAM. The Letters of Wyndham Lewis. W.K. Rose (ed). Norfolk: New Directions, 1963. 1st ed. Fine in NF dj (sm tears). *Beasley.* $35/£23

LEWIS, WYNDHAM. The Lion and the Fox. NY, (1927). One of 1000 ptd. Excellent in cl-backed marbled bds. *Edrich.* $78/£50

LEWIS, WYNDHAM. Men without Art. Cassell, 1934. 1500 ptd. Grn cl. Spine top edge sl knocked; eps sl browned, o/w VG in dj (torn; repaired). *Dalian.* $132/£85

LEWIS, WYNDHAM. Men without Art. London, 1934. 1st Eng ed. VG in VG dj (sl chipped). *Edrich.* $310/£200

LEWIS, WYNDHAM. The Mysterious Mr. Bull. London: Robert Hale, 1938. 1st ed. Sig; spine edge torn, sl rubbed, o/w VG. *Rees.* $23/£15

LEWIS, WYNDHAM. The Mysterious Mr. Bull. Robert Hale, 1938. 1st issue in salmon pink cl. Cvrs sl mkd, o/w VG. *Dalian.* $70/£45

LEWIS, WYNDHAM. The Old Gang and the New. London, 1933. 1st Eng ed. Red cl (sl faded). Name, o/w VG in dj. *Edrich.* $186/£120

LEWIS, WYNDHAM. One-Way Song. Faber, 1933. 1st Eng ed. Grey cl (back cvr mkd; name). VG. *Dalian.* $70/£45

LEWIS, WYNDHAM. One-Way Song. London, 1933. 1st Eng ed. VG in dj (chipped, browned). *Edrich.* $132/£85

LEWIS, WYNDHAM. The Red Priest. London: Methuen, 1956. 1st ed. Cerise bds, gilt spine. Nice. *Temple.* $28/£18

LEWIS, WYNDHAM. The Red Priest. London, 1956. 1st Eng ed. Fine in Fine dj. *Edrich.* $62/£40

LEWIS, WYNDHAM. The Revenge for Love. London: Cassell, 1937. 1st ed. Eps sl spotted; bds rubbed, mkd, o/w VG. *Rees.* $23/£15

LEWIS, WYNDHAM. The Revenge for Love. London, 1952. 2nd Eng ed. VG in dj. *Edrich.* $62/£40

LEWIS, WYNDHAM. Rotting Hill. London, (1951). 1st ed. Spine sl discolored, sl cocked, else Good in dj (chipped, snagged, dknd). *King.* $40/£26

LEWIS, WYNDHAM. Rotting Hill. Chicago, 1952. VG in dj (sl chipped, rubbed). *Edrich.* $39/£25

LEWIS, WYNDHAM. Rude Assignment. London: Hutchinson, (1950). 1st ed. VG in dj (torn, lg chips). *Rees.* $85/£55

LEWIS, WYNDHAM. Snooty Baronet. London, 1932. 1st issue w/gilt lettering on spine. VG in dj (damaged, repaired). *Edrich.* $233/£150

LEWIS, WYNDHAM. Tarr. NY, 1918. 1st ed, 2nd state. Chipped, else Good. *King.* $250/£161

LEWIS, WYNDHAM. Tarr. NY, 1918. 1st priority binding: cranberry red cl, top edge stained red. Precedes Eng issue. Upper bds sl cracked; stamp fep, o/w Excellent. *Edrich.* $256/£165

LEWIS, WYNDHAM. Tarr. Phoenix Library, 1928. 1st thus. (Name.) Dj (sl rubbed). *Edrich.* $39/£25

LEWIS, WYNDHAM. Tarr. C&W, 1928. Phoenix Library. New and rev (3rd) ed. Fine in NF dj w/Fine wraparound band. *Patterson.* $116/£75

LEWIS, WYNDHAM. Unlucky for Pringle. London: Vision Press, 1973. 1st UK ed. Fine in dj. *Moorhouse.* $28/£18

LEWIS, WYNDHAM. The Vulgar Streak. London, 1941. 1st Eng ed. Excellent in dj (sl chipped). *Edrich.* $558/£360

LEWIS, WYNDHAM. The Wild Body. C&W, 1927. 1st ed. 1st binding in orange cl. Fore-edge sl spotted, prelims foxed, o/w NF. *Poetry.* $54/£35

LEWIS, WYNDHAM. The Wild Body. London, 1927. 1st issue. Top edge orange. Excellent in dj. *Edrich.* $233/£150

LEWIS, WYNDHAM. The Wild Body. London, 1927. 2nd issue binding. Red cl lettered in black; top edge stained red. Pub's name in smaller letters than that on issue w/unstained top edge. Name, o/w VG. *Edrich.* $54/£35

LEWIS, WYNDHAM. The Writer and the Absolute. London, (1952). 1st ed. Bkpl, sl rubbed, else Good in dj (sl chipped, sm stain). *King.* $25/£16

LEWIS, WYNDHAM. The Writer and the Absolute. London: Methuen, 1952. 1st UK ed. Short tear fep, o/w NF in dj (sl frayed, chipped; spine sl browned). *Moorhouse.* $85/£55

LEWISOHN, LUDWIG. The Case of Mr. Crump. Paris: Edward W. Titus, 1931. 2nd ed. Heavy gray ptd wrappers ptd in blue. Very Nice in wraparound paper band. *Cady.* $25/£16

LEY-PISCATOR, MARIA. The Piscator Experiment: The Political Theatre. NY: James H. Heineman, (1967). 1st ed. Fine (fore-edge smudged) in dj (short tear). *Aka.* $30/£19

LEYDA, JAY. The Melville Log. NY: Harcourt, Brace, (1951). 1st Amer ed. 2 vols. 15 plts. VG. *Agvent.* $90/£58

LEYDA, JAY. The Melville Log. NY: Harcourt, (1951). 1st ed. 2 vols. Sm owner stamp each vol, o/w VG set. *Reese.* $65/£42

LEYMAIRIE, JEAN. Balthus. Geneva/London: Skira/Macmillan, 1979. 48 mtd color plts, 16 monochrome plts. Fine. *Europa.* $116/£75

LEYMARIE, JEAN. Balthus. Geneva: Skira, 1979. 48 tipped-in color plts, 18 dwgs. (Lib ink stamp, label remains.) Dj (sl chipped). *Edwards.* $85/£55

LEYMARIE, JEAN. The Jerusalem Windows. NY, (1962). 2 orig color lithos, 106 plts (64 color). Marc Chagall (illus). Fine in dj. *Argosy.* $1,200/£774

LEYMARIE, JEAN. Marc Chagall, the Jerusalem Windows. NY: Braziller, 1967. Sm tear dj, o/w Fine. *Europa.* $37/£24

LEYMARIE, JEAN. Van Gogh. James Emmons (trans). London, 1978. 34 color plts. (ex-lib w/ink stamp, label, tape mk.) Dj. *Edwards.* $62/£40

LEZAMA LIMA, JOSE. Paradiso. NY: FSG, 1974. 1st Eng trans. NF in NF dj. *Lame Duck.* $100/£65

LICELY, ADAM. Sing the Body Electric. C&W, 1993. 1st UK ed. Signed. Fine in dj. *Lewton.* $28/£18

LICHT, HANS. Sexual Life in Ancient Greece. NY, 1952. 1st Amer ed. VG. *Mcclintock.* $20/£13

LICHT, HANS. Sexual Life in Ancient Greece. Lawrence H. Dawson (ed). J.H. Freese (trans). NY, 1932. 32 plts. (Cl lt spotted.) *Edwards.* $31/£20

LICHTEN, FRANCES. Decorative Art of Victoria's Era. NY, 1950. Dj (chipped w/loss). *Edwards.* $62/£40

LICHTEN, FRANCES. Folk Art of Rural Pennsylvania. London/NY: Scribner's, (1946, 'A'). Good (wear; lt soil; bkpl). *Bohling.* $85/£55

LIDDELL HART, B.H. Defence of the West. London: Cassell, 1950. 1st ed. VG in dj. *Limestone.* $45/£29

LIDDELL HART, B.H. A Greater Than Napoleon. London, 1926. 1st ed. Frontis port, 7 maps. Ex-lib w/ink stamp; lt foxing, o/w VG. Red cl (worn, faded). *Edwards.* $62/£40

LIDDELL HART, B.H. Sherman. The Genius of the Civil War. London, 1930. 1st ed. Frontis port; 13 maps (7 fldg). Good+ (ex-lib; fr inner hinge cracked, re-glued; eps foxed; remains of slip). Grn cl (sl rubbed). *Edwards.* $47/£30

LIDDELL HART, B.H. The Tanks. The History of the Royal Tank Regiment...1914-1945. London, 1959. 1st ed. 2 vols. VG in djs. *Edwards.* $233/£150

LIDDELL HART, B.H. (ed). The Letters of Private Wheeler, 1809-1828. London, 1951. 1st ed. Frontis; pict eps. VG in dj (sl worn at spine). *Edwards.* $39/£25

LIDDELL, DONALD M. Chessmen. NY, 1937. 1st ed. Dj (sl chipped). *Edwards.* $74/£48

LIDSTONE, RONALD A. The Art of Fencing. London, 1930. (Edges sl foxed, sl bumped.) *Edwards.* $47/£30

LIEB, FRED and STAN BAUMGARTNER. The Philadelphia Phillies. NY, (1953). 1st ed. VG+ in VG+ dj (sl nicked, chipped). *Fuller & Saunders.* $95/£61

LIEB, FRED and STAN BAUMGARTNER. The Philadelphia Phillies. Putnam's, 1953. 1st ed. VG in Good+ dj. *Plapinger.* $175/£113

LIEB, FRED. The Baltimore Orioles. Putnam's, 1955. 1st ed. VG. *Plapinger.* $135/£87

LIEB, FRED. The Boston Red Sox. Putnam's, 1947. 1st ed. VG in Good+ dj. *Plapinger.* $65/£42

LIEB, FRED. The Detroit Tigers. Putnam's, 1946. 1st ed. VG (fr fly removed) in VG dj. *Plapinger.* $50/£32

LIEBERMAN, WILLIAM S. Max Ernst. NY, 1961. Mtd color frontis. VG in ptd wrappers. *Argosy.* $30/£19

LIEBLING, A.J. Chicago: The Second City. NY, 1952. 1st ed. Pict bds. VG in dj (sunned). *King.* $65/£42

LIEBLING, A.J. The Earl of Louisiana. NY, 1961. 1st Amer ed. Fine in Fine dj. *Polyanthos.* $30/£19

LIEBLING, A.J. Quest for Mollie. (NY: F-R Pub Co, 1945). 1st ed. Lt dust soiled, else NF in ptd wrappers. *Godot.* $150/£97

LIEBLING, A.J. The Republic of Silence. NY: Harcourt, 1947. 1st ed. VG + in VG dj (price-clipped; fr panel creased). *Pettler.* $45/£29

LIEUTAUD, JOSEPH. Synopsis of the Universal Practice of Medicine. Phila, 1816. 1st Eng trans. 642pp. Full leather (hinges cracked; backstrip rubbed). *Fye.* $200/£129

Life and Adventures of Don Quixote de la Mancia. (By Cervantes.) London: Hurst, Robinson, 1820. New Ed. 4 vols. 8vo. Full-pg frontis each vol, xx,371; iv,388; vi,367; viii,436pp; 5 full-pg copper engrs each vol by Chas. Heath. 3/4 leather (lt dried; sl chipped), marbled paper on bds; marbled eps; red speckled fore-edges. VG set (edges shelfworn; lacks orig black title labels, 3 spine labels; reattached upper bd vol 4). *Hobbyhorse.* $190/£123

Life and Adventures of Peter Wilkins, A Cornish Man. (By Robert Paltock.) London: Robinson & Dodsley, 1751. 1st ed. 2 vols. 6 engr plts. Contemp speckled calf, labels. VG (fr hinge vol 1 cracked, vol 2 sl cracked) in 1/2 morocco slipcase. *Juvelis.* $1,100/£710

Life and Adventures of Robinson Crusoe, of York, Mariner. (By Daniel Defoe.) Newburyport: John Tilton, n.d. (ca 1875). 132pp. Wood engr vignette tp, 6 full-pg engrs (ink sig fep, lt foxing; bkpl). Dec tooled blue cl, gilt title spine. VG. *Hobbyhorse.* $115/£74

Life and Reminiscences of Jefferson Davis by Distinguished Men of His Time. Balt, 1890. 1st ed. Cvr w/shelf wear; chipping at spine extrems, o/w Fine. *Pratt.* $90/£58

Life and Strange Surprising Adventures of Robinson Crusoe of York, Mariner. (By Daniel De Foe). London: Constable, 1925. Ltd to 775. 2 vols. Teg; unopened. 3/4 calf over linen, spines gilt (upper cvrs separated both vols; spine sl scuffed). Cl-cvrd slipcase. *Sadlon.* $25/£16

Life and Surprising Adventures of Robinson Crusoe, of York, Mariner.... (By Daniel Defoe.) Derby: Henry Mozley, 1824. 12mo. Full-pg wood engr frontis, iv,221 + 3pp list; 4 full-pg cuts. 3/4 leather, marbled paper (rubbed, chipped, corners rounded; spine lt cracked). Good. *Hobbyhorse.* $150/£97

Life in California. (By Alfred Robinson). NY, 1846. Bound w/Chinigchinich by Geronimo Boscana beginning on pg 227, w/separate tp, as issued. xii,(2),341pp, 9 plts. (Spine tips sl chipped; lt fox mks.) VG. Howes R 363. *Reese.* $950/£613

Life in California. (By Alfred Robinson.) NY: Wiley & Putnam, 1846. 1st ed. xiii,341pp, 9 plts. (Foxing; recased, orig cl laid down). Gilt spine title. Howes R 363. *Bohling.* $400/£258

Life of Bishop Heber.... (By Amelia Shipley Heber.) NY: Protestant Episcopal, 1830. 1st Amer ed. 2 vols. Frontis port, xii,638; vi,564pp (foxed, lt notes, tp stamps; ex-lib rebound). *Schoyer.* $125/£81

Life of Cornelius Van Tromp...from the Year 1650, to the Time of His Death. London, 1697. 1st ed. Sm 8vo. Tp,6pp,preface,533pp. Some staining, marginal worming towards end; pp167-168 torn w/sl loss, o/w Good + in contemp full calf (rebacked w/new eps). *Edwards.* $465/£300

Life of General Worth; to Which Is Added, A Sketch of the Life of Brigadier-General Wool. NY: Sheldon, Blakeman, 1856. 2nd ed. Frontis, (2),256pp; aeg. Red cl; dec gilt, blind-stamped. Good. *Karmiole.* $45/£29

Life of Mahomet. NY: Evert Duyckinck, 1813. 2nd Amer ed. 12mo. 118pp. Plain paper on bds (sm spot on cvrs), cl spine. Internally Fine. *Hobbyhorse.* $100/£65

Life of the Late General William Eaton. Brookfield: Merriam, 1913. 1st ed. Frontis. Contemp calf (rebacked). Edges repaired; sl foxing, o/w VG. *Worldwide.* $250/£161

Life of William Henry Harrison, the People's Candidate. (By Isaac R. Jackson.) Phila: (Marshall), 1840. 1st ed. 60pp. (Text lt foxed; wrappers worn; corners creased, folded.) Orig wrappers. Howes J 20. *Bookpress.* $150/£97

Life, Trial, Confession and Execution of Albert W. Hicks.... NY, (1860). 1st issue. Frontis, 68pp; port adhered fr pastedown. Later buckram. Tanned, else VG. *Reese.* $350/£226

LIFTON, ROBERT. Home from the War: Vietnam Veterans, Neither Victims Nor Executioners. NY: S&S, (1973). 1st ed. Fine in NF dj (sm edge nicks). *Aka.* $35/£23

LIGHTDOWN, R.W. Secular Goldsmith's Work in Medieval France. London, 1978. 80 plts. Good in dj. *Washton.* $100/£65

LIGHTMAN, ALAN. Einstein's Dreams. NY: Pantheon, 1993. 1st ed, 1st bk. VF in VF dj. *Pettler.* $50/£32

LIGHTON, N.C.K. The Paintings of Norman Lighton for Roberts Birds of South Africa. A.V. Bird (ed). Cape Town, (1977). 52 color plts. Gilt-stamped cl. *Sutton.* $155/£100

Lights and Shadows of African History. (By S.G. Goodrich.) Boston: Rand & Mann, 1849. Frontis, tp vignette, 336pp + 4pp ads. Brn cl, gilt/blind-stamped (spine sl faded). *Schoyer.* $30/£19

LIGON, JOHN STOKELEY. New Mexico's Birds and Where to Find Them. Albuquerque: Univ of NM, 1961. 1st ed. VG + in VG- dj. *Parker.* $75/£48

LILIENTHAL, DAVID E. The Journals of David E. Lilienthal. NY: Harper & Row, 1964. 1st eds. 2 vols. 32 plts. Fine in Fine djs. *Connolly.* $65/£42

LILJENCRANTZ, O.A. The Thrall of Leif the Lucky. McClurg, 1902. 1st ed. VG + . *Aronovitz.* $65/£42

LILLARD, RIBHARD G. The Great Forest. NY, 1947. 1st ed. 3 maps. Dj. *Heinoldt.* $22/£14

LILLIE, H.R. The Path Through Penguin City. London: Benn, 1955. 1st ed. VG. *Walcot.* $23/£15

LILLO, GEORGE. The London Merchant. NY: Grobe, 1952. 1st Amer ed w/cancel tp. Fine in dj (sl soiled). *Pharos.* $45/£29

Lilly Martin Spencer, 1822-1902, the Joys of Sentiment. Washington: National Collection of Fine Arts, 1973. 1st ed. Frontis. Hinges sl rubbed, bkpl, else VG. *Bookpress.* $35/£23

LILLYWHITE, BRYANT. London Coffee Houses. London: Allen & Unwin, (1963). Dj pieces pasted in. *Petersfield.* $25/£16

LILLYWHITE, BRYANT. London Coffee Houses. London: Allen & Unwin, 1963. 1st ed. Brn linen, gilt. Fine in dj. *Hartfield.* $95/£61

LIN, FRANK. (Pseud of Gertrude Atherton.) What Dreams May Come. Chicago/NY/SF: Belford, Clarke & Co, (1888). 1st ed. 192pp. Nice in orig ptd wraps (separating at spine; lt spotting, tape marks). Custom brn cl chemise, matching slipcase w/red morocco spine label. *Chapel Hill.* $500/£323

LIN, TSAN-PIAO. Native Orchids of Taiwan. Vol 2. Chiayi, 1977. 4 color plts. VG + in dj. *Brooks.* $45/£29

LINCOLN, ABRAHAM and STEPHEN A. DOUGLAS. Political Debates Between Hon. Abraham Lincoln and Hon. Stephen A. Douglas, in the Celebrated Campaign of 1858...; Also the Two Great Speeches of Mr. Lincoln in Ohio.... Columbus: Follett, Foster & Co, 1860. 1st ed, 2nd issue. 268pp. Orig cl. Corners scuffed; minor wear spine extrems, else VG. Howes L338. *Mcgowan.* $250/£161

LINCOLN, ABRAHAM. Collected Works. Roy Basler (ed). New Brunswick: Rutgers, 1953. 9 vols. VG. *Schoyer.* $100/£65

LINCOLN, JACKSON S. The Dream in Primitive Cultures. Balt: Williams & Wilkins, (1935). 1st ed. Frontis. Blue cl. VG (spine faded). *Gach.* $40/£26

LINCOLN, JOSEPH C. Christmas Days. NY, 1939. #302/1000 signed by Lincoln and Harold Brett (illus). Uncut. Fine (sunned, sl chipped). *Polyanthos.* $30/£19

LINCOLN, JOSEPH C. Queer Judson. NY, 1925. 1st ed. Eps, edges foxed, else Nice in dj (chipped, torn, soiled, hole). *King.* $35/£23

LIND, L.R. Studies in Pre-Vesalian Anatomy.... Phila, 1975. Mint in dj. *Goodrich.* $65/£42

LINDBERGH, ANNE MORROW. The Wave of the Future. NY: Harcourt, Brace, (1940). 1st ed. NF in dj (lt used). *Antic Hay.* $45/£29

LINDBERGH, CHARLES A. The Spirit of St. Louis. NY: Scribner's, 1953. 1st trade ed. 16pp of 1/2 tone plts, map. Top edge blue. NF in dj. *Cady.* $100/£65

LINDBERGH, CHARLES A. We. NY, 1927. 1st ed. One of 1000 numbered, signed. Dec vellum-backed bds (spine sl dknd). *Ginsberg.* $1,000/£645

LINDBERGH-SEYERSTED, BRITA (ed). The Story of a Literary Friendship. Faber, 1982. 1st UK ed. Fine in dj (sl chipped; price-clipped). *Poetry.* $29/£19

LINDEMAN, M.H. The Quarter Horse Breeder. Wichita Falls, 1959. 1st ed. Brn cl in dj. *Lambeth.* $35/£23

LINDERMAN, FRANK. Blackfeet Indians. St. Paul, 1935. 1st ed. 65 color ports. *Ginsberg.* $300/£194

LINDERMAN, FRANK. Recollections of Charley Russell. Norman: Univ of OK, (1963). 1st ed. Turquoise cl. Fine in NF dj. *Glenn.* $35/£23

LINDESAY, ROBERT. The History of Scotland; From 21 February, 1436 to March, 1565. Edinburgh, 1728. 1st ed. Folio. xviii,237pp. Contemp full calf (worn). VG (bkpls; some foxing). *Edwards.* $426/£275

LINDLEY, HARLOW (ed). Captain Cushing in the War of 1812. Columbus: OH State Archaeological & Hist Soc, 1944. 1st ed. Fine. *Cahan.* $45/£29

LINDLEY, JOHN and JOSEPH PAXTON. Paxton's Flower Garden. London, 1850-53. 1st ed. 3 vols. 4to. iv,194; 186; 178pp; 108 Fine hand-colored lithos (12 plts lt spotting). Aeg. Contemp 1/2 calf, marbled bds (bumped, sl rubbed), labels, gilt. VG. *Shifrin.* $3,250/£2,097

LINDLEY, K. The Woodblock Engravers. David & Charles, 1970. 1st ed. Good. *Moss.* $28/£18

LINDQUIST, G.E.E. The Red Man in the United States. NY: George Doran, (1923). 8 maps, 26 photo plts. Red cl. VG+. *House.* $70/£45

LINDQUIST, G.E.E. The Red Man in the United States. NY: G. Doran, 1923. 1st ed. Good (spine torn), internally VG+. *Parker.* $50/£32

LINDSAY, DAVID. Camp Fire Reminiscences, Or Tales of Hunting and Fishing in Canada and the West. Boston: Dana Estes, (1912). 1st ptg. Partially unopened. Pict cl. VG. *Schoyer.* $75/£48

LINDSAY, DAVID. A Voyage to the Arctic in the Whaler Aurora. London: Kegan Paul, Trench, Trubner, c.1911. Orig dec cl, teg. VG. *High Latitude.* $80/£52

LINDSAY, JACK. Dionysos. London: Fanfrolico Press, (1928). Ltd to 500. 12 illus. Blue patterned cl; gilt. Good. *Karmiole.* $175/£113

LINDSAY, JACK. George Meredith: His Life and Work. London: Bodley Head, 1956. 1st ed. Frontis, tipped-in dbl-sided plt. Maroon bds. Spine gilt oxidized, o/w Fine in dj (sl frayed, internally strengthened). *Temple.* $29/£19

LINDSAY, JACK. Helen Comes of Age. London: Fanfrolico Press, 1927. One of 500 ptd, this one inscribed 'Out of series Review Copy.' Uncut. Red buckram (backstrip sl faded). Good. *Cox.* $62/£40

LINDSAY, JACK. Hogarth. London, 1977. Good. *Washton.* $25/£16

LINDSAY, JACK. Men of Forty-Eight. London: Methuen, 1948. 1st ed. Yellow cl. Very Nice in dj (frayed; 2 sm tissued repairs verso). *Temple.* $28/£18

LINDSAY, JACK. The Passionate Neatherd. London: Fanfrolico Press, (1930). 1st ed. Rev copy. (Lib stamp.) Orig wrappers. *Hollett.* $47/£30

LINDSAY, JACK. Rumanian Summer. Lawrence & Wishart, 1953. 1st Eng ed. Brn cl. VG in dj (sl chipped). *Dalian.* $39/£25

LINDSAY, MARTIN. Those Greenland Days. 1930-31. London: Blackwood, 1932. 2nd imp. VG. *Walcot.* $26/£17

LINDSAY, VACHEL. The Candle in the Cabin. NY: D. Appleton, 1926. 1st ed. Signed. Grn dec cl. Dj (worn). *Appelfeld.* $50/£32

LINDSAY, VACHEL. Every Soul Is a Circus. Macmillan, 1929. 1st ed. Fine. *Authors Of The West.* $35/£23

LINDSAY, VACHEL. General William Booth Enters into Heaven and Other Poems. NY: Mitchell Kennerly, 1913. 1st ed, 1st bk. Gilt. Spine sl lightened. *Sadlon.* $45/£29

LINDSAY, VACHEL. General William Booth Enters into Heaven and Other Poems. NY: Mitchell Kennerley, 1913. 1st ed. Bkpl; lt bumped, lt mkd, o/w VG. *Heller.* $75/£48

LINDSAY, VACHEL. Rigamarole, Rigamarole. NY: Random House, 1929. 1st ed, ltd to 475. Fine in sewn ptd wraps. *Antic Hay.* $45/£29

LINDSEY, BEN B. and RUBE BOROUGH. The Dangerous Life. NY: Horace Liveright, 1931. *Boswell.* $35/£23

LINDSLEY, JOHN BARRIEN. The Military Annals of Tennessee. Nashville: J.M. Lindsley, 1886. 1st ed. 910pp; 34 steel engr plts. Orig deluxe binding of 1/2 leather, cl. Sl scuffing to leather extrems, else VG. Howes L 358. *Mcgowan.* $650/£419

LINGENFELTER, MARY R. Books on Wheels. NY/London: Funk & Wagnalls, 1938. 1st ed. Very Nice in dj (sl worn, internally repaired). *Cady.* $25/£16

LINK, MARGARET SCHEVILL. The Pollen Path. Stanford: Stanford Univ Press, 1956. 1st ed. VG in VG dj. *Perier.* $75/£48

LINKLATER, ERIC. The Art of Adventure. London, 1947. 1st ed. NF in dj (spine top chipped). *Polyanthos.* $25/£16

LINKLATER, ERIC. The Faithful Ally. London: Jonathan Cape, 1954. 1st ed. Top edge scarlet. Scarlet cl, gilt. Fine in dj. *Temple.* $28/£18

LINKLATER, ERIC. Private Angelo. Privately ptd, (Christmas 1957). Ltd to 2000, card loosely inserted. Fine. *Waterfield.* $54/£35

LINKLATER, ERIC. Robert the Bruce. Peter Davies, 1934. 1st Eng ed. Frontis; 2 maps. Black cl. VG in dj (torn). *Dalian.* $39/£25

LINKLATER, ERIC. The Sailor's Holiday. London: Jonathan Cape, 1937. 1st ed. Lower edges uncut. Edges, few leaves sl foxed, o/w Fine in dj (sl frayed). *Temple.* $26/£17

LINKLATER, ERIC. The Sailor's Holiday. Cape, 1937. 1st Eng ed. Blue cl. VF in NF dj. *Dalian.* $54/£35

LINKLATER, ERIC. The Wind on the Moon. Macmillan, 1944. 1st Eng ed. Grn cl. VG. *Dalian.* $31/£20

LINNAEUS, C. Lachesis Lapponica. London, 1811. 1st ed in English. 2 vols in 1. xvi,366; (1),306pp (bkpl). Contemp gilt-dec tree sheep (cvr detached, spine chipped; paper shelf label). *Sutton.* $465/£300

LINNEHAN, JOHN and EDWARD COGSWELL. The Driving Clubs of Greater Boston. Boston, 1914. (Tear spine bottom.) *October Farm.* $125/£81

LINSLEY, JOHN S. Jersey Cattle in America. NY: Burr, 1885. 1st ed. 744pp. Very Nice (sl worn; fr spine loose; foxing). *Second Life.* $200/£129

LINTON, W.J. Wood-Engraving, a Manual of Instruction. London: George Bell, 1884. 1st ed, ltd to 500. Frontis, x,128pp, 6 plts. Orig cl, gilt (sl rubbed, sm chip at backstrip; sig cut from ep). Bkpl of J.C. Bright, later sig of J. Brinkley. Sound. *Cox.* $54/£35

Lionel Lincoln. (By James Fenimore Cooper.) NY: Charles Wiley, 1825-24. 1st ed. 2 vols. (xii,263; 270pp). Contemp sheep. VG (1 vol sm closed tears; few corners torn off; spots, dampstains). BAL 3832. *Felcone.* $325/£210

Lionel Lincoln. (By James Fenimore Cooper.) NY: Charles Wiley. 1825-24. 1st ed. 2 vols. 263;270pp. 19th cent 1/2 calf, marbled bds, gilt-tooled spines. VG- set (bkpl removed Vol 1; sigs, foxing; worn). BAL 3832. *Chapel Hill.* $375/£242

Lionel Lincoln. (By James F. Cooper.) London: John Miller, 1825. 1st British ed. 3 vols. Contemp 3/4 lt grn calf, gilt spines, gilt purple morocco labels; 1/2 titles bound in. Bkpls; sl rubbing, sunning, o/w very pretty set. *Reese.* $450/£290

LIPMAN, JEAN and ALICE WINCHESTER. The Flowering of American Folk Art 1776-1876. NY, (1976). VG in dj. *Argosy.* $85/£55

LIPMAN, JEAN et al. Young America, a Folk-Art History. NY: Hudson Hills Press, (1986). 1st ed. Bkpl; else Fine in dj. *Bookpress.* $65/£42

LIPMAN, JEAN. American Folk Art in Wood, Metal and Stone. Pantheon, 1948. 4 color plts. Orange cl bds. VG (ink sig feps) in dj. *Heller.* $55/£35

LIPMAN, JEAN. American Folk Art in Wood, Metal and Stone. (NY): Pantheon, 1948. 1st ed. VG in illus dj. *Cahan.* $50/£32

LIPMAN, JEAN. American Folk Art in Wood, Metal, and Stone. (NY, 1948). 4 color plts. VG in dj. *Argosy.* $75/£48

LIPMAN, JEAN. American Primitive Painting. London: OUP, 1942. Good (glue mks feps; cvr edges dknd) in dj. *Heller.* $50/£32

LIPPMANN, FRIEDRICH. The Art of Wood-Engraving in Italy in the Fifteenth Century. Bernard Quaritch, 1888. Eng ed. (Lt browning.) Gilt edged cl (soiled); teg. *Edwards.* $101/£65

LIPSKY, DAVID. Three Thousand Dollars. NY: Summit, (1989). 1st ed, 1st bk. Fine in dj. *Between The Covers.* $45/£29

LIPTON, LAWRENCE. The Holy Barbarians. NY: Julian Messner, 1959. 1st ed. Fine in NF dj. *Beasley.* $50/£32

LISH, GORDON. Dear Mr. Capote. NY: Holt, (1983). 1st ed. Rev slip, flyer laid in. As New in dj. *Reese.* $30/£19

LISS, HOWARD. Triple Crown Winners. Messner, 1969. 1st ed. Fine in Good + dj. *Plapinger.* $27/£17

Lister and the Lister Ward in the Royal Infirmary of Glasgow: A Centenary Contribution. Glasgow, 1927. 1st ed. 28 plts. Good. *Fye.* $60/£39

Lister Centenary Celebration: Descriptive Catalogue of the Lister Collection. London, 1927. 1st ed. Good. *Fye.* $30/£19

LISTER, JOSEPH. The Collected Papers of Joseph, Baron Lister. Birmingham, 1979. Facs of 1909 ed. 2 vols. Full leather. *Fye.* $150/£97

LISTER, JOSEPH. The Third Huxley Lecture. London, 1907. 1st ed. Good. *Fye.* $80/£52

LISTER, R.P. A Journey in Lapland. London: Chapman & Hall, 1965. 1st ed. VG in dj. *Hollett.* $39/£25

LISTER, RAYMOND. Catalogue Raisonne of the Works of Samuel Palmer. Cambridge, 1988. Good. *Washton.* $95/£61

LISTER, RAYMOND. George Richmond. A Critical Biography. London: Garton, 1981. 68 plts. Sound in dj. *Ars Artis.* $54/£35

LISTER, RAYMOND. Samuel Palmer and His Etchings. London: Faber, 1969. Color frontis, 39 plts. Sound in dj. *Ars Artis.* $93/£60

LISTER, RAYMOND. Victorian Narrative Paintings. London, 1966. Color frontis, 60 plts (2 color). Dj (sl chipped). *Edwards.* $31/£20

LISTER, RICHARD. Joseph Lister. NY, 1977. 1st ed. Good in dj. *Fye.* $25/£16

Little Coward. Bouckville: B. Maynard, n.d. (ca 1830). Chapbook. 32mo. 8pp. Wood engr frontis of old city; wood engr vignette tp; 3 full-pg engrs. Pict grn paper wrappers. Splitting lower fold of 1 sig, lt foxing; else Very Nice. *Hobbyhorse.* $55/£35

Little Drummer. NY: McLoughlin Brothers, n.d. (ca 1865). Dame Wonders' Series. 12mo. 4 leaves, 1p book list lower wrapper. Pict stiff paper wrappers. Cvr signed by Cogger, ptd in red/black on orange background (water spots; 2 repaired rips lower wrapper, rebacked). Good. *Hobbyhorse.* $70/£45

Little Folks Library: Circus Day. Chicago: Werner Co, (1896). 1st ed. 2 x 2 3/8 inches. 128 numbered pp. John T. McCutcheon (illus). Illus blue cardbd cvrs. Nice. *Reisler.* $225/£145

Little Girl Among the Old Masters. (By Mildred Howells.) Boston: Osgood, 1884. 1st ed. 63pp; 54 plts. Pict cl (worn; sl soiled). *Petrilla.* $50/£32

Little Lays for Little Folks. (Aunt Matilda's Series.) NY: McLoughlin Bros, n.d. (ca 1875). 6 leaves + 1pg list lower wrapper; five 3/4 pg chromolithos signed Cogger, 1 signed Howard; upper wrapper ptd in full color litho. Fine (ink sig; wrappers lt soiled). *Hobbyhorse.* $180/£116

Little Man and the Little Maid. Providence: Winsor & Perrin, 1849. 12mo. 12pp + 1pg ad lower wrapper. Brn pict stiff paper wrappers (reinforced at hinge and internal hinges some sigs). In all, Very Nice (sl offsetting; lt foxing at edges; lt soiled, spotted; spine rubbed, chipped). *Hobbyhorse.* $225/£145

Little Market Woman. NY: McLoughlin Brothers, n.d. (ca 1890). Ancient Illuminated Rhymes Series. Obl 8vo, 8ff + 1p list lower wrapper, 4 full-pg litho illus. VG (sm repaired tear lower spine). *Hobbyhorse.* $140/£90

Little Nancy, or, the Punishment of Greediness. Phila: Morgan & Yeager, n.d. (ca 1824). 1st ed. 12mo. 8pp + 4 leaves + 1pg list lower wrapper, 4 full-pg copper engrs. Buff stiff paper wrappers. Fine (sl chipping spine corner; lt foxing last leaf). *Hobbyhorse.* $315/£203

Little Red Riding Hood Pop-Up Book. NY: Blue Ribbon, 1934. 20x23cm. 3 bright pop-ups. C. Carey Cloud & Harold B. Lentz (illus). Pict bds. (sl aging to edges). *Book Finders.* $220/£142

Little Red Riding Hood. NY: McLoughlin Brothers, n.d. (ca 1870). Aunt Louisa's Big Picture Series. 4to. 8 leaves; 6 full-pg lithos. Pict chromolito stiff paper wrappers, signature of Howard lower wrapper. Fine (sl edgewear). *Hobbyhorse.* $150/£97

Little Robinson Crusoe. Phila/New Haven: Loomis & Peck/Durrie & Peck, 1847. 82 x 65mm, 191pp + 1pg list, full-pg wood engr frontis, engr vignette tp, 46 full-pg engrs in text. Pict gilt grn cl on bds, dec, gilt title spine. VG (lt foxing). *Hobbyhorse.* $275/£177

Little Stories about the Chair, Bed, Boot, and Drum, in Words of One Syllable. Newark, (NJ): Benjamin Olds, 1835. Cobb's Toys, 1st series, #8. Chapbook. 32mo. 8pp. Plain yellow paper wrapper (lt soiled, inner hinges repaired). Fine. *Hobbyhorse.* $125/£81

Little Tiny's Book of Objects. London: Routledge, n.d. (ca 1880). Sq 8vo. Frontis, 95pp; 10 full-pg wood engrs (superb quality). Pict label pasted on dec, gilt brn linen (rubbed, lt shaken). VG (spotting, lt foxing, pg tear). *Hobbyhorse.* $130/£84

Little Truths, for the Instruction of Children. Vol I. London: Darton, Harvey, and Darton, 1816. 12mo. 48pp + 1pg list lower cvr, lg copper engr tp. Yellow ptd paper on bds. VG (minor chip corner of one leaf, not interfering w/text; spine restored). *Hobbyhorse.* $120/£77

Little Verses, for Good Children. Northampton (MA): J. Metcalf, 1833. Chapbook. 32mo. 8pp, lg wood engr butterfly tp. Pict yellow paper wrappers (rebacked); upper ptd w/sm vignette, dec frame; lower ptd w/large corbeille of flowers (lt foxing, soiling). Good. *Hobbyhorse.* $50/£32

LITTLE, BRYAN. The Life and Work of James Gibbs 1682-1754. London: Batsford, 1955. 1st ed. Frontis port. Dj (sl worn, sunned). *Edwards.* $31/£20

LITTLE, BRYAN. The Life and Work of James Gibbs, 1682-1754. London: Batsford, (1955). 1st ed. Frontis; 30 illus on plts. VG in dj (worn). *Bookpress.* $45/£29

LITTLE, E.L. Atlas of United States Trees. Vol 1. Washington, 1971. 200 maps; 9 overlays. *Wheldon & Wesley.* $47/£30

LITTLE, GEORGE. Life on the Ocean; or, Twenty Years at Sea.... Boston: Waite, Peirce & Co, 1845. 3rd ed. 395pp. (Gathering started.) *Lefkowicz.* $85/£55

LITTLE, JAMES A. From Kirtland to Salt Lake City. Salt Lake City: The author, 1890. 260pp. Brn cl, gilt title. Bright (bkpl remnants fep). Howes L 382. *Bohling.* $250/£161

LITTLE, JAMES A. From Kirtland to Salt Lake City. Salt Lake City, 1890. 1st ed. 260pp. Name; lt wear, o/w VG. *Benchmark.* $175/£113

LITTLEFIELD, LYMAN O. The Martyrs; A Sketch of the Lives...of Joseph and Hyrum Smith.... Salt Lake City, 1882. 1st ed. 120pp. Back hinge loose, stain, ex-lib. *Benchmark.* $40/£26

LITTLEPAGE, JOHN D. and DEMAREE BESS. In Search of Soviet Gold. London: George G. Harrap, 1939. Fine in dj. *High Latitude.* $30/£19

LITWACK, LEON F. Been So Long in the Storm. NY, (1979). 1st ed. Fine in Fine dj. *Pratt.* $35/£23

LIU, HUI-CHEN WANG. Traditional Chinese Clan Rules. Locust Valley, NY: J.J. Augustin, (1959). Fine in dj. *Schoyer.* $45/£29

LIVEING, EDWARD. Adventure in Publishing. The Story of Ward Lock 1854-1954. London: Ward Lock, 1954. 1st ed. Color frontis, 10 plts. VG in dj. *Hollett.* $39/£25

LIVELY, PENELOPE. Moon Tiger. London: Deutsch, 1987. 1st ed. Fine in dj. *Rees.* $31/£20

LIVELY, PENELOPE. Moon Tiger. London: Deutsch, 1987. 1st ed. Fine in dj. *Limestone.* $65/£42

LIVERMORE, ABIEL ABBOT. The War with Mexico Reviewed. Boston: Amer Peace Soc, 1850. 1st ed. xii,398pp. Bright orig cl (pocket removed). *Schoyer.* $50/£32

LIVERMORE, MARY. My History of the War. Hartford: A.D. Worthington, 1889. 1st ed. 8 chromolithos. Red lib buckram (rebound), orig fr cvr cl laid on fr panel. (Marginal water stains last few pp.) *Hermitage.* $85/£55

LIVERMORE, MARY. The Story of My Life With Hitherto Unrecorded Incidents and Recollections.... Hartford, 1898. 1st ed. 730pp. Good. *Fye.* $75/£48

LIVERMORE, MARY. My Story of the War. Hartford, 1890. 700pp. Good. *Fye.* $150/£97

LIVERMORE, S.T. Block Island. Hartford, 1886. (14)pp ads, 125pp; 3 plts, fldg map. Ptd wraps. (Staining, mostly wraps; creased corners.) *Bohling.* $65/£42

LIVERSIDGE, DOUGLAS. The Last Continent. London: Jarrolds, 1958. 1st ed. Fldg map. Burgundy cl. Sm section fr cvr faded, else VG in dj (worn). *Parmer.* $40/£26

Livestock Brand Book of the State of Kansas, 1965. Topeka: Livestock Brand Commission, 1965. Fine in heavy black wrappers. *Glenn.* $45/£29

LIVINGSTON, JOHN A. Birds of the Eastern Forest. Vol I. Boston: Houghton Mifflin, 1968. 1st ed. 52 color plts by J. Fenwick Lansdowne. VF in dj. *Bowman.* $75/£48

LIVINGSTON, JOHN A. Birds of the Northern Forest. Boston: Houghton Mifflin, 1966. 1st ed. 56 color plts by J. Fenwick Lansdowne. VF in dj. *Bowman.* $75/£48

LIVINGSTON, LIDA (ed). Salvador Dali. Study of His Art-in-Jewels. Greenwich, CT: NYGS, 1959. 28 mtd color plts; mtd port photo. VG in pict slipcase. *Argosy.* $85/£55

LIVINGSTON, M. Moloch. A. Dakers, 1942. 1st ed. NF in VG dj (lt dust soil). *Aronovitz.* $30/£19

LIVINGSTON, ROBERT R. Essay on Sheep: Their Varieties.... NH: Daniel Cooledge, 1813. 143pp; woodcut on title. Sheep-backed bds. Foxed, else Very Nice. *Felcone.* $225/£145

LIVINGSTON, SAMUEL. The Diagnosis and Treatment of Convulsive Disorders in Children. Springfield, 1954. 1st ed. Signed. Good. *Fye.* $100/£65

LIVINGSTONE, DAVID and CHARLES. Narrative of an Expedition to the Zambesi and Its Tributaries. NY, 1866. Dbl frontis, xxii,638pp + 6pp pub's ads, 35 engrs, fldg map. Newspaper cuttings loosely inserted (lt browning pp202-203; marginal foxing; upper hinge sl tender; cl browned). *Edwards.* $116/£75

LIVINGSTONE, DAVID. Missionary Travels and Researches in South Africa. London: John Murray, 1857. Contemp blind-stamped brn morocco-grain cl. Lib stamp; label fr cvr, o/w VG. *Waterfield.* $209/£135

LIVINGSTONE, DAVID. Missionary Travels and Researches in South Africa. London: John Murray, 1857. 1st ed. x,687pp (lacks fldg frontis; sl browning), engr port, 2 fldg maps. Mod cl (rebound; ex-lib, labels, ink stamps, cardholder). *Edwards.* $39/£25

LIVINGSTONE, DAVID. Missionary Travels and Researches in South Africa. London, 1857. 1st ed. 687pp; fldg map. Later 1/4 leather; marbled bds. Good. *Fye.* $400/£258

LIVINGSTONE, DAVID. Missionary Travels and Researches in South Africa. NY, 1858. 1st Amer ed. 732pp. Good. *Fye.* $225/£145

LIVY. The History of Rome. Verona: LEC, 1970. #330/1500 signed by Giovanni Mardersteig (printer) and Raffaele Scorzelli (illus). Cl over patterned bds. Lt bumped, o/w Fine in pub's slipcase. *Hermitage.* $150/£97

Lizzy's Poems and Pictures for Her Young Friends. London: Darton, 1857. Aeg. Red cl, gilt. Spine chipped, else VG. *Glenn.* $150/£97

LLEWELLYN, RICHARD. None but the Lonely Heart. London: Michael Joseph, (1943). 1st trade ed. Silver-stamped cl. NF in dj (chipped). *Sadlon.* $30/£19

LLEWELLYN, RICHARD. None but the Lonely Heart. Joseph, 1943. 1st ed. Signed, ltd ed of 250. Teg. Buckram. VG. *Whiteson.* $40/£26

LLOSA, MARIO VARGAS. *See* VARGAS LLOSA, MARIO

Lloyd's Register of American Yachts. NY, 1942. Addenda of May 15, 1942 bound in. Sound. *Lefkowicz.* $75/£48

Lloyd's Register of American Yachts...1936. NY, 1936. 64 color plts. *Lefkowicz.* $75/£48

LLOYD, AMBROSE and N. THOMAS. Kites and Kite Flying. London, (1978). VG in dj. *Argosy.* $20/£13

LLOYD, H. ALAN. The Collector's Dictionary of Clocks. South Brunswick, NY, 1964. Dj (upper edge ragged). *Edwards.* $39/£25

LLOYD, HAROLD and WESLEY W. STOUT. An American Comedy. NY, 1928. 1st ed. Cl (worn, sl warped). *King.* $50/£32

LLOYD, JOHN U. Etidorpha. Cincinnati, 1897. 8th ed. 386pp. (Inner hinges cracked; spine ends frayed.) *King.* $35/£23

LLOYD, JOHN U. Red-Head. NY: Dodd, Mead, 1903. 1st ed. 9 plts. Teg; untrimmed. Pict cl, gilt. VF. *Connolly.* $67/£43

LLOYD, JOHN U. Stringtown on the Pike. NY, 1900. 1st ed. Good. *Hayman.* $15/£10

LLOYD, JOHN U. Warwick of the Knobs. NY: Dodd, Mead, 1901. 1st ed. 15 plts. Port laid on fr cvr. NF. *Connolly.* $42/£27

LLOYD, L. The Game Birds and Wild Fowl of Sweden and Norway. London: Day, 1867. 2nd ed. Frontis (chipped), xviii,599pp (lacks pp xix-xx, pp593-4); 47 chromolitho plts (of 48), map (photocopy?) in pocket, 4 full-pg woodcuts. Plate of Great Grey Shrike (not called for). (2pp, 1 plt washed w/stain toward inner margin 12pp chipped to outer margin affecting 3 plts.) Aeg. Gilt, blind emb cl (recased). *Edwards.* $271/£175

LLOYD, NATHANIEL. A History of the English House from Primitive Times to the Victorian Period. London: Architectural Press, (1951). 3rd imp. (Hinges internally cracked; rubberstamps tp, fep; rubbed.) *Bookpress.* $150/£97

LLOYD, NATHANIEL. A History of the English House.... London: Architectural Press, 1949. Rpt. (Spine faded.) *Edwards.* $101/£65

LLOYDS, F. Practical Guide to Scene Painting and Painting on Distemper. London: Rowney, n.d. (ca 1860). 97pp, 13 litho plts (6 hand-colored), 41 wood-engr diags, 21 mtd color samples. Orig cl gilt. *Marlborough.* $736/£475

LOBEIRA, VASCO. Amadis of Gaul. London, 1872. 3 vols. VG. *Madle.* $40/£26

LOBEL, ARNOLD. Grasshopper on the Road. NY: Harper & Row, (1978). 1st ed. 8vo. Full color illus bds. Good in matching color dj. *Reisler.* $35/£23

LOBLEY, J.L. Mount Vesuvius. London, 1889. 400pp, 20 plts. Pict gilt cl (sl dampstained; sl foxing). *Henly.* $37/£24

Lobster's Voyage to the Brazils. London: J. Harris and B. Crosby, 1808. 1st and only ed. Sq 12mo. 16pp; 8 full-pg hand-colored copper engrs, incl frontis. Mod full leather on bds; gilt; marbled eps. (Rebound w/o orig wrappers; lt plt offsetting; edges, spine lt rubbed.) *Hobbyhorse.* $550/£355

LOCH, HENRY BROUGHAM. Personal Narrative of Occurrences during Lord Elgin's Second Embassy to China, 1860. London: John Murray, 1869. 1st ed. viii,298,32pp, map. Gilt cl (neatly recased; corners sl bumped or restored). *Hollett.* $186/£120

LOCHER, A. With Star and Crescent. Phila, 1889. 1st ed. Frontis port, 634pp (lacks 1/2 title). Pict cl (worn, bumped; spine frayed, chipped, sl loss; hinges split). *Edwards.* $39/£25

LOCKE, ALAIN (ed). The New Negro. NY: Boni, 1925. 1st ed. VG + (name; prelim pencilling). *Beasley.* $300/£194

LOCKE, ALAIN. The Negro and His Music. Washington: Associates in Negro Folk Education, 1936. 1st ed. Dec bronze bds. *Petrilla.* $75/£48

LOCKE, EDWIN. Tuberculosis in Massachusetts. Boston, 1908. 1st ed. Good. *Fye.* $100/£65

LOCKE, G.E. The Scarlet Macaw. Boston: L.C. Page, 1923. 1st ed. Color frontis. Owner emb stamp, else VG. *Hermitage.* $30/£19

LOCKE, HAROLD. A Bibliographical Catalogue of the Published Novels and Ballads of William Harrison Ainsworth. London: Elkin Mathews, 1925. 1st ed. Blue cl over black bds; paper labels. Good. *Karmiole.* $30/£19

LOCKE, JOHN. An Essay Concerning Human Understanding. London: Allen & West, 1795. 3 vols. xv,271; xv,264; xiv,308pp. Contemp full polished calf, morocco labels, numerals. Attractive set (name; hinges worn). *Hartfield.* $395/£255

LOCKE, JOHN. Some Thoughts Concerning Education. London: Sherwood et al, 1809. Engr frontis, vi,255,(8)pp. Contemp calf, gilt (rubbed; new leather label). Early name, else Nice. *Hartfield.* $195/£126

LOCKE, WILLIAM J. A Christmas Mystery. NY: John Lane, 1910. 1st ed. Grn gilt-stamped cl. Tips worn, frayed, else VG. *Juvelis.* $50/£32

LOCKER-LAMPSON, FREDERICK. London Lyrics. London: Strahan, 1870. 1st ed thus. Uncut. Grn cl, gilt. Fine. *Macdonnell.* $35/£23

LOCKETT, T.A. and G.A. GODDEN. Davenport China, Earthenware, Glass. London: Barrie & Jenkins, (1989). Dj. *Petersfield.* $109/£70

LOCKHART-MUMMERY, P. Diseases of the Rectum and Colon and Their Surgical Treatment. NY: Wood, 1923. (Sl worn; inner fr hinge splitting.) *Goodrich.* $35/£23

LOCKLEY, FRED. History of the Columbia River Valley from the Dalles to the Sea. Chicago: S.J. Clarke, 1928. 3 vols. VG. *Perier.* $225/£145

LOCKLEY, FRED. History of the Columbia River Valley from the Dalles to the Sea. S.J. Clarke, 1928. 1st ed. 3 vols. Marbled eps, all edges marbled. Fine. *Oregon.* $200/£129

LOCKWOOD, ALICE G.B. Gardens of Colony and State. NY: Garden Club of America, 1931. 1st ed. 2 vols. VG; vol 2 in dj (tattered). *Bookpress.* $650/£419

LOCKWOOD, CHARLES. Bricks and Brownstone: The New York Row House, 1783-1929. NY: Abbeville Press, (1972). Frontis. Dj rubbed, lt creased, else VG. *Bookpress.* $85/£55

LOCKWOOD, FRANK C. The Law and Lawyers of Pickwick. London: Roxburghe Press, (ca 1930). 1st ed. Nice in ptd wrappers. *Appelfeld.* $75/£48

LOCKWOOD, FRANK C. The Life of Edward C. Ayer. Chicago: A.C. McClurg, 1929. 1st ed. Frontis; 25 plts; photo eps. VF in VG slipcase. *Oregon.* $75/£48

LOCKWOOD, FRANK C. Pioneer Days in Arizona, from the Spanish Occupation to Statehood. NY: Macmillan, 1932. 1st ed. Frontis. Fine in Fine dj. Howes L 417. *Oregon.* $150/£97

LOCKWOOD, FRANK C. Tucson—The Old Pueblo. Phoenix, (1931). Navy cl w/gilt title. VG +. *Bohling.* $110/£71

LOCKWOOD, LUKE VINCENT. Colonial Furniture in America. NY: Scribner's, 1901. 1st ed. 11 plts. (Ex-lib w/mks; text lt spotted; sl worn.) *Bookpress.* $110/£71

LOCKWOOD, LUKE VINCENT. Colonial Furniture in America. NY: Scribner's, 1926. 3rd ed. 2 vols. Blind-emb cl. VG set (rubbed; lt foxing 1st, last few leaves each vol). *Cahan.* $135/£87

LODGE, DAVID. How Far Can You Go. Secker, 1980. 1st UK ed. Fine in dj. *Williams.* $54/£35

LODGE, DAVID. Language of Fiction. NY: Columbia, 1966. 1st ed. Fine in dj (price-clipped; sm chips; tiny internal puncture). *Lame Duck.* $35/£23

LODGE, DAVID. Nice Work. Secker & Warburg, 1988. 1st Eng ed. Blue cl. Fine in dj. *Dalian.* $31/£20

LODGE, DAVID. Nice Work. Secker, 1988. Proof copy. Fine in illus wraps. *Williams.* $23/£15

LODGE, EDMUND. Portraits of Illustrious Personages of Great Britain. London: Ptd for Harding and Lepard, 1835. 12 vols. 4to. 240 ports. 1/2 calf (spines spotted); gilt-ruled bands spines. *Edwards.* $620/£400

LODGE, GEORGE E. Memoirs of an Artist Naturalist. London: Gurney & Jackson, 1946. 24 plts (10 color). Teg. VG. *Hollett.* $186/£120

LODGE, HENRY CABOT. Life and Letters of George Cabot. Boston, 1877. 1st ed. (11),615pp. Howes L 421. *Ginsberg.* $125/£81

LODGE, OLIVER. Phantom Walls. London: Hodder & Stoughton, 1929. 1st ed. VG. *Ming.* $62/£40

LOEB, HANAU (ed). Operative Surgery of the Nose, Throat and Ear. St. Louis, 1918. 1st ed. 2 vols. Good. *Fye.* $200/£129

LOEB, JACQUES. Artificial Parthenogenesis and Fertilization. Chicago, 1913. 1st Eng trans. Good. *Fye.* $150/£97

LOEB, JACQUES. Comparative Physiology of the Brain and Comparative Psychology. NY, 1900. 1st ed. Good. *Fye.* $50/£32

LOEB, JACQUES. Forced Movements, Tropisms, and Animal Conduct. Phila, 1918. 1st ed. Good. *Fye.* $60/£39

LOEDERER, R.A. Voodoo Fire in Haiti. D-D, 1935. 1st trade ed. NF in 1st state pict dj (some wear, chipping). *Fine Books.* $60/£39

LOEWENSTEIN, F.E. Bernard Shaw Through the Camera. London: B. & H. White Publications, 1948. 1st Eng ed. Blue cl. Fine in dj (torn). *Dalian.* $31/£20

LOFTHOUSE, J. A Thousand Miles from a Post Office.... London/NY/Toronto: SPCK/Macmillan, 1922. (Shelfworn.) *Cullen.* $125/£81

LOFTIE, W.J. A History of London. London, 1883. 1st ed. Inscribed, dated. 2 vols. 447; 419, 32pp ads. 1/2 leather. Hinges starting; spine ends, extrems scuffed; contents thumbed; newspaper clipping affixed half-title vol 1; both vols w/paperclip mks; annotations, else Good. *King.* $75/£48

LOFTIE, W.J. London City. London, 1891. xvi,377pp (lt foxing, mainly feps). Teg. (Upper hinge sl tender; spine wear.) *Edwards.* $47/£30

LOFTING, HUGH. Doctor Dolittle in the Moon. Cape, 1929. 1st UK ed. Fine in VG dj. *Williams.* $194/£125

LOFTING, HUGH. Doctor Dolittle's Circus. NY: Stokes, (1924). 1st ed. 4to. Color frontis, guard; 379pp; 79 full-pg b/w illus by Lofting. Yellow cl, blue emb design; pict paste label. NF. *Drusilla's.* $70/£45

LOFTING, HUGH. Doctor Dolittle's Garden. Phila: Lippincott, (1955). 15th ptg. 8vo. 327pp. Grn cl. VG in VG dj. *Davidson.* $40/£26

LOFTING, HUGH. Doctor Dolittle's Garden. London: Cape, 1928. 1st ed. Color frontis. Pict eps. Grey cl. Internally Fine (sl edgewear). *Quest.* $55/£35

LOFTING, HUGH. Doctor Dolittle's Zoo. Stokes, 1925. 1st ed. VG. *Aronovitz.* $50/£32

LOFTING, HUGH. Doctor Dolittle, A Treasury. Phila: Lippincott, (1967). 3rd ptg. 4to. 246pp. Blue cl, cream bds, gilt. NF in dj, slipcase. *Drusilla's.* $30/£19

LOFTING, HUGH. Noisy Nora. NY: F.A. Stokes, (1929). 1st ed. 12mo. Yellow cl, color paste label. Nice. *Reisler.* $155/£100

LOFTING, HUGH. The Story of Doctor Dolittle. NY: Frederick A. Stokes, 1925. (17th ptg). Signed. 180pp. H. Lofting (illus). Orange cl, pict onlay. VG (fr guard missing). *Davidson.* $100/£65

LOFTING, HUGH. Tommy, Tilly and Mrs. Tubbs. London: Jonathan Cape, (1937). 1st Eng ed. Obl 12mo. Blue cl, color paste label. Ep foxed, o/w Fine. *Reisler.* $175/£113

LOFTING, HUGH. The Voyages of Doctor Dolittle. NY: Frederick A. Stokes, 1922. 1st ed. 8vo. 20 full-pg illus (2 color). Dec grey cl, black lettering, color paste label. Good in pict dj (lacks pieces). *Reisler.* $200/£129

LOGAN, C.A. Physics of the Infectious Diseases. Chicago, 1878. 1st ed. 212pp. Good. *Fye.* $100/£65

LOGAN, HERSCHEL C. Underhammer Guns. Harrisburg: Stackpole, (1960). VG in dj. *Schoyer.* $50/£32

LOGAN, JEFFREY (ed). The Complete Book of Outer Space. Gnome, 1953. Fine in dj. *Madle.* $150/£97

LOGAN, KATE VIRGINIA COX. My Confederate Girlhood: The Memoirs of.... Garrett & Massie, 1932. (1st ed). VG in Fair dj (fr flap slit off). *Book Broker.* $45/£29

LOGAN, MRS. JOHN A. Reminiscences of a Soldier's Wife, an Autobiography. NY: Scribner's, 1913. 1st ed. Frontis port. Orig blue cl. Fine. *Chapel Hill.* $50/£32

LOGAN, RAYFORD W. (ed). Memoirs of a Monticello Slave: As Dictated to Charles Campbell in the 1840's by Isaac.... Charlottesville: Univ of VA Press, 1951. 1st ed. One of 1000. Frontis port. NF in dj (dusty). *Cahan.* $75/£48

LOGUE, CHRISTOPHER. Fluff. Bernard Stone, 1984. #61/100 signed. Buckram-backed bds. Fine. *Poetry.* $39/£25

LOGUE, CHRISTOPHER. Patrocleia. Scorpion, 1962. 1st ed. Fine in dj (sl wear). *Poetry.* $23/£15

LOKVIGAND, TOR and CHUCK MURPHY. Star Trek, The Motion Picture Pop-Up Book. NY: Wanderer/S&S, 1980. 18x24 cm. 5 dbl-pg pop-ups, pull-tabs. Glazed pict bds. VG- (inscrip). *Book Finders.* $40/£26

LOMAX, ALFRED. Pioneer Woolen Mills in Oregon. Portland: Binford & Mort, (1941). 1st ed. Frontis; 8 plts. Ltd ed morocco/wool binding (sl moth-eaten). Uncut, unopened. VG. *Oregon.* $45/£29

LOMAX, JOHN A. and ALAN. Negro Folk Songs as Sung by Leadbelly. NY: Macmillan, 1936. 1st ed. Fine (spine sl dull; name). *Beasley.* $100/£65

LOMBARD, ASA COBB PAINE. East of Cape Cod. Cuttyhunk: Privately ptd, 1976. 1st ed. Signed. Frontis map. *Lefkowicz.* $50/£32

LOMBROSO, CESARE and WILLIAM FERRERO. The Female Offender. NY: Appleton, 1895. 1st US ed. Newsclipping glued to fr pastedown, else NF in VG dj (spine-dknd). *Lame Duck.* $100/£65

LOMER, G.R. Stephen Leacock—A Check-list of His Writings. Nat'l Lib of Canada, 1954. Ptd cvrs. Good. *Moss.* $54/£35

London and County Brewer. London, 1750. 6th ed. (vii),332,(iv)index,(ii)pub's ads (lt soil; eps browned). Orig calf bds (worn, rebacked), raised bands, morocco spine label. *Edwards.* $271/£175

London Characters. London/NY: Frederick Warne/Scribner, Welford & Armstrong, n.d. (ca 1880). Aunt Luisa's London Toy Books. Folio, 12ff+1pg list lower wrapper. 36 illus, all ptd in full color litho, by H.W. Petherick. All leaves text and illus linen-backed; 1st, last pg of text pasted down on wrappers (sm ink spot top edge lower wrapper; pencil mks upper wrapper; soiling). VG (occasional internal spotting, not interfering w/plts). *Hobbyhorse.* $250/£161

LONDON, CHARMIAN. The Book of Jack London. NY: Century, 1921. 1st ed. 2 vols. 8vo. Frontis port each vol. VG in djs. *Houle.* $595/£384

LONDON, JACK. The Abysmal Brute. NY: Century, 1913. 1st ed ('May, 1913'). 8vo. Frontis; upper jacket cvr illus; 1pg ads at end. Full olive grn cl; uncut. VG in pict dj (spine nicked). BAL 11945. *Houle.* $1,500/£968

LONDON, JACK. Before Adam. Macmillan, 1907. 1st ed. VG. *Madle.* $75/£48

LONDON, JACK. Before Adam. Macmillan, 1907. 1st ed. Pict cl. C.L. Bull (illus). Spine sl faded; ff-setting to feps, else VG+. *Fine Books.* $110/£71

LONDON, JACK. Burning Daylight. NY: Macmillan, 1910. 1st ed, 2nd ptg. Blue cl stamped in white (lacks spine stamping). Good. BAL 11918. *Second Life.* $65/£42

LONDON, JACK. Burning Daylight. NY: Grosset & Dunlap, n.d. 1st ed. NF in NF dj (sm chip). *Beasley.* $75/£48

LONDON, JACK. The Call of The Wild. NY, 1903. 1st ed. Vertical ribbed grn cl, pict stamped. VG. *Argosy.* $500/£323

LONDON, JACK. A Daughter of the Snows. Lippincott, 1902. 1st ed. Pict cl. Spine faded, else VG+. *Fine Books.* $250/£161

LONDON, JACK. The Faith of Men. NY: Macmillan, 1904. 1st ed. Lt blue pict cl, gilt. VG. BAL 11878. *Macdonnell.* $150/£97

LONDON, JACK. The Game. MacMillan, 1905. 1st ed. Corner of rear cvr bumped, else VG+. *Fine Books.* $85/£55

LONDON, JACK. The Game. NY: Macmillan, 1905. 1st ed. Published June 1905, w/rubber-stamped notice on copyright pg and 3/32 type. Gilt; teg (lt rubbed, sm lightened spots). BAL 11886. *Sadlon.* $75/£48

LONDON, JACK. The God of His Fathers. Ibister, 1902. 1st Eng ed. Spine lightened; eps foxed, else VG. *Fine Books.* $175/£113

LONDON, JACK. The House of Pride and Other Tales of Hawaii. MacMillan, 1912. 1st ed. White spine lettering all but gone, else VG. *Fine Books.* $125/£81

LONDON, JACK. John Barleycorn. NY: Century, 1913. 1st ed, correct 1st ptg. NF (spine sl dulled). *Beasley.* $100/£65

LONDON, JACK. The Little Lady of the Big House. NY: Macmillan, 1916. 1st ed. Published April 1916. 1st state binding w/spine lettering in gilt (extrems sl rubbed, fr inner hinge tender). BAL 11966. *Sadlon.* $75/£48

LONDON, JACK. Love of Life and Other Stories. Macmillan, 1907. 1st ed. Lightened area rear panel, else VG+. *Fine Books.* $200/£129

LONDON, JACK. Michael. Brother of Jerry. NY, 1917. 1st Amer ed. NF (sl rubbed). *Polyanthos.* $75/£48

LONDON, JACK. The Mutiny of the Elsinore. Mills & Boon, 1915. 1st Eng ed. VG. *Fine Books.* $85/£55

LONDON, JACK. The Night-Born. NY: Century, 1913. 1st ed, 1st ptg (gathered in 8s; w/last gathering in 6). Blue-grey pict cl, gilt. VG. BAL 11942. *Macdonnell.* $150/£97

LONDON, JACK. The Red One. Mills & Boon, 1919. 1st Eng ed. Spine faded, else VG. *Fine Books.* $150/£97

LONDON, JACK. The Road. NY: Macmillan, 1907. 1st ed, 2nd binding. 2pp ads at end. Orig pict cream cl, stamped wholly in black (lt rubbed). Top edge plain. Nice (sl stains eps from home-made jacket, now removed). BAL 11906. *Macdonnell.* $300/£194

LONDON, JACK. The Scarlet Plague. Mills & Boon, (1915). 1st Eng ed. Off-setting to eps; foxing to fore-edge, else NF. *Fine Books.* $125/£81

LONDON, JACK. The Sea-Wolf. NY, 1904. 1st ed w/white spine lettering. Teg. Pict cl (worn, bumped, sm spot; fr inner hinge loose, back inner hinge cracked). *King.* $95/£61

LONDON, JACK. Smoke and Shorty. Mills & Boon, 1920. 1st ed. Soiling to cvrs, else VG-. *Fine Books.* $250/£161

LONDON, JACK. Smoke Bellew. Mills & Boon, 1913. 1st Eng ed. VG + . *Fine Books.* $85/£55

LONDON, JACK. The Son of the Wolf. Leipzig, 1914. 1st Tauchnitz ed, 1st bk. NF (edge chips) in ptd wraps. *Polyanthos.* $30/£19

LONDON, JACK. The Star Rover. NY: Macmillan, 1915. 1st Amer ed ('October, 1915'). Color frontis; 8pp pub's ads at end. Blue cl. VG. BAL 11963. *Houle.* $395/£255

LONDON, JACK. The Valley of the Moon. Mills & Boon, 1914. 1st Eng ed. Blue cl. Pp browned; name, o/w VG. *Dalian.* $70/£45

LONDON, JACK. Wonder of Woman. International Magazine, 1912. 1st ed. Foxing to fr cvr, else VG in wraps as issued. *Fine Books.* $275/£177

Lone Indian; Or, the Renegade's Prisoner. (By Thomas C. Harbaugh.) NY: Beadle & Adams, (c. 1871). Beadle's Pocket Novels No. 150. 97pp + ads. Good in pict wrappers (lacks back wrapper, sl wear to fr). *Hayman.* $20/£13

Long Day. (By Dorothy Richardson). NY: Century, 1905. 1st ed. Spine dkned; sl soiling, o/w NF. *Beasley.* $200/£129

Long Live the Queen. The Coronation Book with Realistic Pop-Up Pictures. London: Juvenile, n.d. (1953). 27x21 cm. 4 dbl-pg pop-ups, coronation photo. Spiral bound, glazed pict wraps (some glazing coming off). Internally VG-. *Book Finders.* $100/£65

LONG, A.L. Memoirs of Robert E. Lee. NY: J.M. Stoddart, 1887. 2nd ed. Frontis port, 707pp. Grn cl. Lib bkpl, blindstamp; inscrip, else VG. *Chapel Hill.* $125/£81

LONG, ANDREW DAVIDSON. Stonewall's 'Foot Calvaryman (sic)'. (Austin: Ptd by Steck, Vaughn, 1965). 1st ed, 1st issue w/o pasters correcting misprint 'calvaryman.' NF. *Mcgowan.* $45/£29

LONG, BASIL S. Catalogue of the Constantine Alexander Ionides Collections. Vol I. London: Bd of Ed, 1925. 35 plts. Fine. *Europa.* $23/£15

LONG, E.B. The Saints and the Union. Univ of IL, (1981). 1st ed. VF in VF dj. *Oregon.* $30/£19

LONG, E.R. (ed). Selected Readings in Pathology. London, 1929. 25 plts. (Spine faded; sl dull; joint cracked.) *Whitehart.* $54/£35

LONG, FRANK BELKNAP. H.P. Lovecraft: Dreamer on the Night Side. Arkham House, 1975. 1st ed. Fine in dj. *Madle.* $25/£16

LONG, FRANK BELKNAP. The Horror from the Hills. Arkham House, 1963. 1st ed, 1st issue w/blank copyright pg. One of 2000. Fine in dj. *Aronovitz.* $75/£48

LONG, FRANK BELKNAP. The Hounds of Tindalos. Arkham House, 1946. 1st ed. Fine in dj. *Madle.* $225/£145

LONG, FRANK BELKNAP. John Carstairs, Space Detective. Fell, 1949. 1st ed. NF in dj (chipped). *Madle.* $75/£48

LONG, FRANK BELKNAP. The Rim of the Unknown. Arkham House, 1972. 1st ed. Fine in dj. *Madle.* $40/£26

LONG, FRANK BELKNAP. Three Steps Spaceward. Avalon, 1963. 1st ed. Fine in dj. *Madle.* $30/£19

LONG, GEORGE. The Mills of Man. London: Herbert Joseph, 1931. 1st ed. Extrems sl rubbed. *Hollett.* $101/£65

LONG, HUEY P. Every Man a King. New Orleans: National Book Co., 1933. 1st ed. Fine in gold dj (lt chipped). *Beasley.* $75/£48

LONG, HUEY P. My First Days in the White House. Telegraph Press, 1935. 1st ed. Fine in VG + dj (short tears). *Fine Books.* $250/£161

LONG, PERRIN and ELEANOR BLISS. The Clinical and Experimental Use of Sulfanilamide, Sulfapyridine and Allied Compounds. NY, 1939. 1st ed. Good. *Fye.* $100/£65

LONG, STEPHEN H. Voyage in a Six-Oared Skiff to the Falls of Saint Anthony in 1817. Phila: Henry B. Ashmead, 1860. 1st ed. Black cl over stiff paper; stamped w/blind rules, lettered in gilt. *Laurie.* $350/£226

LONG, W.J. and C.L. BULL. Wood-Folk Comedies. Harpers, 1920. 1st ed. 8 full pg, color illus. VG + in VG dj (lt chipping spine extrems). *Fine Books.* $95/£61

LONGACRE, J.J. (ed). Craniofacial Anomalies: Pathogenesis and Repair. Phila, 1968. 1st ed. Signed. Good in dj. *Fye.* $150/£97

LONGACRES, EDWARD G. From Union Stars to Top Hat. Harrisburg, (1972). 1st ed. Sl cvr wear, o/w Fine in Fine dj. *Pratt.* $45/£29

LONGFELLOW, HENRY WADSWORTH. The Courtship of Miles Standish and Other Poems. London: W.Kent, 1858. 1st ed, 1st cl issue w/earlier 40pp cat dated Jan 1858. Dec brn cl. Very Nice (bkpl; rear cvr sl scraped; lt fraying). *Hermitage.* $225/£145

LONGFELLOW, HENRY WADSWORTH. The Courtship of Miles Standish, and Other Poems. Boston: Ticknor & Fields, 1859. iv,5-215 + 16pp book adv. Orig emb cl; gilt spine (sl wear). Short splits fr hinge; damp line 1st blank pg, all else VG. *Connolly.* $45/£29

LONGFELLOW, HENRY WADSWORTH. The Hanging of the Crane. Boston: James R. Osgood, 1875. 1st Amer ed. 64pp. Aeg. Full brn morocco. Fine. BAL 12166. *Schoyer.* $75/£48

LONGFELLOW, HENRY WADSWORTH. The Hanging of the Crane. Boston/NY: Houghton, Mifflin, 1907. 1st ed thus. One of 1000 numbered. Uncut. 1/4 cl, bds, label, intaglio gilt. *Macdonnell.* $25/£16

LONGFELLOW, HENRY WADSWORTH. Hyperion, a Romance. NY, 1839. 1st ed. Orig bds; paper labels, uncut (rubbed, chipped). BAL 12064. *Argosy.* $250/£161

LONGFELLOW, HENRY WADSWORTH. Kavanagh. Boston: Ticknor, Reed & Fields, 1849. 1st ed, 1st ptg, altered state, w/May 1, 1849 ads (state A) at fr. Orig slate purple cl, gilt. Nice (fading). BAL 12096. *Macdonnell.* $85/£55

LONGFELLOW, HENRY WADSWORTH. Keramos and Other Poems. Boston: Houghton, Osgood, 1878. 1st ed. Gilt. Extrems sl rubbed. BAL 12199. *Sadlon.* $45/£29

LONGFELLOW, HENRY WADSWORTH. The Masque of Pandora. Boston: James R. Osgood, 1875. 1st ed, 1st ptg. Ed of 3030. Grn cl, gilt. Damp mk in margin, else Good. BAL 12170. *Macdonnell.* $45/£29

LONGFELLOW, HENRY WADSWORTH. The Seaside and the Fireside. Boston: Ticknor, Reed & Fields, 1850. 1st ed, 1st issue in bds. Good (fr cvr separated, lacks paper label; sm loss lower 1st pg of ads) in cl folder, 1/2 morocco slipcase. BAL 12099. *Sadlon*. $75/£48

LONGFELLOW, HENRY WADSWORTH. The Seaside and the Fireside. Boston: Ticknor, Reed & Fields, 1850. 1st ed. Gilt; aeg (sl chipped; lt dampstain fore-edge corners; mild foxing). BAL 12099. *Sadlon*. $35/£23

LONGFELLOW, HENRY WADSWORTH. The Seaside and the Fireside. Boston: Ticknor, Reed & Fields, 1850. 1st ed. Full morocco, raised bands, 'L' emb on upper cvr. 2 sm bkpls, o/w NF. BAL 12099. *Sadlon*. $75/£48

LONGFELLOW, HENRY WADSWORTH. The Song of Hiawatha. Boston: Ticknor & Fields, 1855. 1st Amer ed, 1st ptg. Blind-stamped. Extrems sl rubbed; lacks flyleaves, upper corner of 2 leaves (not affecting text). BAL 12112. *Sadlon*. $125/£81

LONGFELLOW, HENRY WADSWORTH. The Song of Hiawatha. Boston: Ticknor & Fields, 1855. 1st Amer ed. Blind-stamped brn cl. VG. BAL 12112. *Juvelis*. $350/£226

LONGFELLOW, HENRY WADSWORTH. Tales of a Wayside Inn. Boston: Ticknor & Fields, 1863. 1st Amer ed, 1st ptg w/t.p. dated 1863. Ptg A of pub's terminal cat; this title unpriced, described as 'Nearly ready' on p.11. 225pp + 22pp ads. Teg. Purple cl. Spine faded, lt foxing vignette title; sig separation; else VG in maroon cl chemise w/leather spine label, matching slipcase. BAL 12136. *Chapel Hill*. $300/£194

LONGFELLOW, HENRY WADSWORTH. Tales of a Wayside Inn. Boston: Ticknor & Fields, 1863. 1st Amer ed, 1st ptg. Gilt, blind-stamped; teg. Spine, edges sl lightened; short breaks to spine ends; minor foxing to tissue, vignette title. BAL 12136. *Sadlon*. $60/£39

LONGFELLOW, HENRY WADSWORTH. Tales of a Wayside Inn. Boston: Ticknor & Fields, 1863. 1st Amer ed, 1st ptg. Gilt (dull), blind-stamped; teg (lightened spots; minor foxing to tissue, vignette title). BAL 12136. *Sadlon*. $95/£61

LONGFELLOW, HENRY WADSWORTH. Three Books of Song. Boston: James R. Osgood, 1872. 1st ed. Maroon cl, gilt (spine sunned, lt rubbed). VG. BAL 12159. *Macdonnell*. $15/£10

LONGMAN, W. Tokens of the Eighteenth Century Connected with Booksellers and Bookmakers. London: Longmans, Green, 1916. 1st ed. (8) plts. (Cancelled stamp tp verso; cvrs lt rubbed.) *Bookpress*. $325/£210

LONGRIDGE, C. NEPEAN. The Anatomy of Nelson's Ships. London, 1955. 1st ed. VG in blue cl (sl rubbed). *Edwards*. $85/£55

LONGSTAFF, TOM. This My Voyage. NY: Scribner's, (1950). 1st Amer ed. (viii),324pp (lt foxed); author obit laid in. Dj (chipped). *Schoyer*. $40/£26

LONGSTREET, HELEN D. Lee and Longstreet at High Tide: Gettysburg in the Light of the Official Records. Gainesville, GA: Author, 1905. 2nd ed. (Spine faded, browned.) Howes L 450. *Ginsberg*. $75/£48

LONGSTREET, JAMES. From Manassas to Appomattox. Phila, 1896. 1960 rpt. Lt dj wear, o/w VG+. *Pratt*. $60/£39

LONGSTREET, STEPHEN. Sportin' House. L.A.: Sherbourne Press, 1965. 1st ed. Fine in Fine dj. *Beasley*. $45/£29

LONGUS. Daphnis and Chloe. George Moore (trans). NY: George Braziller, 1977. Marc Chagall (illus). VG in dj, slipcase. *Argosy*. $150/£97

LONGUS. The Pastoral Loves of Daphnis and Chloe. NY: LEC, 1934. Ltd to 1500 numbered, signed by Ruth Reeves (illus). Full leather, silver medallion. Fine in slipcase (worn, spotted). *Oak Knoll*. $85/£55

LONGYEAR, EDMUND J. Mesabi Pioneer; Reminiscences Of. MN Hist Soc, 1951. 1st ed. Fine in dj. *Artis*. $25/£16

LONN, ELLA. The Colonial Agents of the Southern Colonies. Chapel Hill: UNC Press, 1945. 1st ed. Maroon cl. Top spine sl faded, else NF in dj (worn). *Chapel Hill*. $60/£39

Looking-Glass for the Mind. (By Arnaud Berquin.) London: Ptd by J. Crowder for E. Newbery, 1792. New Ed. 8vo. Table of Contents lists 36 stories w/'Alfred and Dorinda' not incl. Full-pg copper engr frontis, viii,271pp; 74 cuts by John Bewick. Full tooled calf on bds, 5 raised bands, gilt title label spine; gray eps. Fine (rebacked w/orig spine). *Hobbyhorse*. $350/£226

LOOMES, BRIAN. Lancashire Clocks and Clockmakers. London: David & Charles, 1975. 1st ed. 16 plts. VG in dj (faded). *Hollett*. $62/£40

LOOMIS, F.B. Hunting Extinct Animals in the Patagonian Pampas. NY: Dodd, 1913. 1st ed. Gilt dec cl. Hinges cracked, else VG. *Mikesh*. $60/£39

LOOMIS, LEANDER V. Journal of the Birmingham Emigrating Company. Edgar M. Ledyard (ed). Salt Lake City, 1928. One of 1000. Fldg map. NF in dj (dknd, lt chipped). Howes L 464. *Bohling*. $125/£81

LOOMIS, LEANDER V. Journal of the Birmingham Emigrating Company.... Salt Lake City, 1928. 1st ltd (1000) ed. Fldg map. Sl yellowing throughout, o/w VG. *Benchmark*. $95/£61

LOOMIS, NOEL. The Texan-Santa Fe Pioneers. Univ of OK, (1958). 1st ed. 10 maps (1 fldg). Fine in VG dj. *Oregon*. $40/£26

LOOS, ANITA. But Gentlemen Marry Brunettes. Toronto, 1928. 1st Canadian ed. Patterned bds. Inscrip; spine faded, o/w VG. *Dalian*. $39/£25

LOOS, ANITA. Gigi. NY: Random House, (1952). 1st ed. Fine in NF dj. *Godot*. $45/£29

LOPEZ, BARRY. Arctic Dreams. NY: Scribner's, (1986). 1st ed. New in New dj. *Dermont*. $35/£23

LOPEZ, BARRY. Arctic Dreams. Scribner's, (1986). 1st ed. Signed. Fine in Fine dj. *Authors Of The West*. $60/£39

LOPEZ, BARRY. Arctic Dreams. NY: Scribner's, 1986. 1st ed. Fine in Fine dj. *Revere*. $35/£23

LOPEZ, BARRY. Crossing Open Ground. NY: Scribner's, 1988. 1st ed. Fine in Fine dj. *Revere*. $25/£16

LOPEZ, BARRY. Desert Notes. KC: Sheed, Andrews, McMeel, (1976). 1st ed. Fine in dj (underlining, o/w VG). *Oregon*. $120/£77

LOPEZ, BARRY. Giving Birth to Thunder. Sleeping with His Daughter. Coyote Builds North America. Kansas City: Sheed Andrews & McMeel, 1977. 1st ed. NF in VG dj. *Parker*. $125/£81

LOPEZ, BARRY. River Notes. Kansas City: Andrews & McMeel, 1979. 1st ed. Fine in VG dj (spine ends worn). *Revere*. $75/£48

LOPEZ-REY, JOSE. A Cycle of Goya's Drawings. London, 1956. (Sl shelf-rubbed.) *Washton*. $35/£23

LOPEZ-REY, JOSE. Velasquez. London: Studio Vista, 1980. Sound. *Ars Artis*. $70/£45

LOPEZ-REY, JOSE. Velazquez. A Catalogue Raisonne.... London, 1963. 231 plts. Good. *Washton.* $110/£71

LORAC, E.C.R. Murder by Matchlight. Mystery House, 1946. 1st US ed. Good in Good dj. *Ming.* $39/£25

LORAC, E.C.R. The Theft of the Iron Dogs. London: CCC, 1946. 1st ed. Good in Good dj. *Ming.* $31/£20

LORANT, STEFAN (ed). The New World: The First Pictures of America.... Duell, Sloan & Pearce, (c. 1946). 1st ed. VG. *Book Broker.* $35/£23

LORANT, STEFAN. Lincoln: A Picture Story of His Life. NY, (1952). 1st ed. Dj worn, torn, o/w Fine. *Pratt.* $40/£26

LORD, ELIOT. Comstock Mining and Miners. Howell North, 1959. Fldg plt, fldg map in pocket. VG. *Oregon.* $40/£26

LORD, FRANCES. Christian Science Healing: Its Principles and Practice. Chicago: Lily, 1888. 1st US ed. xx,471pp. Color-pict grn cl. VG. *Petrilla.* $75/£48

LORD, FRANCIS A. Civil War Collector's Encyclopedia. Harrisburg: Stackpole, 1963. 1st ed. Dj. *Lambeth.* $45/£29

LORD, FREDERICK and RODERICK HEFFRON. Pneumonia and Serum Therapy. NY, 1938. Good. *Fye.* $40/£26

LORD, WALTER (ed). The Fremantle Diary. London, 1956. 1st ed. Pub's stamp to fep, o/w VG in dj. *Edwards.* $28/£18

LORENZ, LINCOLN. John Paul Jones Fighter for Freedom and Glory. Annapolis, 1943. 1st ed. One of 500 lg paper copies, signed. Pub's box. *Lefkowicz.* $100/£65

LORENZI, HARRI J. and LARRY S. JEFFERY. Weeds of the United States and Their Control. NY, 1987. Cvrs rubbed, contents As New. *Brooks.* $55/£35

LORIE, PETER and COLIN GARRATT. Iron Horse. Doubleday/Dolphin, 1987. 1st ed. Fine in Fine dj. *Oregon.* $25/£16

Los Angeles Bench and Bar, Centennial Edition 1949-1950. L.A.: Wilson & Sons, 1950. (Sl worn.) *Boswell.* $75/£48

Los Angeles—A Guide to the City and Its Environs. NY: Hastings House, 1941. 1st ed. Fine. *Perier.* $35/£23

LOSSING, BENSON. A Biography of James A. Garfield. NY: Henry Goodspeed, (1882). Frontis; 840pp; 51 plts. Gilt-stamped cl (worn, soiled). Fair. *Oregon.* $40/£26

LOSSING, BENSON. A History of the Civil War 1861-1865.... NY: War Memorial Assoc, (1912). 1st ed thus. Good (shaken, discoloration rear bd). *Mcgowan.* $75/£48

LOSSING, BENSON. A History of the Civil War 1861-1865.... NY: War Memorial Assoc, 1912. 1st ed. Minor chipping; else NF in orig ptd wrappers. *Mcgowan.* $150/£97

Lost Child: A Christmas Tale. London: J. Harris, 1810. 2nd ed. Variant w/plts arranged as in 1st ed. (1st plt dated Dec 11, 1809, w/caption '...but haste! behold/A little sleeping Boy!') 12mo. Frontis, viii,56pp; 5 full-pg engrs. 3/4 brn leather, marbled brn paper, gilt. VG (ink sig, edges of plt lt foxed; lt rubbed, scuffed). *Hobbyhorse.* $215/£139

Lothar Meggendorfer's International Circus. London/NY: Kestrel/Viking, 1979. 22x33 cm. 6 circus scenes. Illus wraps. VG. *Book Finders.* $45/£29

Lothar Meggendorfer's International Circus. Kestrel/Penguin, 1983. 18x26 cm. 6 panels open to form circus. Glazed pict bds. VG. *Book Finders.* $50/£32

LOTHROP, ALONZO H. and FRANK B. The Beginning of the March from Atlanta to the Sea...With a Letter Written...During Sherman's Advance on Atlanta. Madison, WI: Forward Press, n.d. 1st ed. Sm chip lower margin, else NF in orig ptd wrappers. *Mcgowan.* $150/£97

LOTI, PIERRE. Egypt. W.P. Baines (trans). NY: Duffield, 1911. 8 color plts. Sl rubbed, o/w VG. *Worldwide.* $25/£16

LOTT, EMMELINE. Harem Life in Egypt and Constantinople. Phila: T.B. Peterson, n.d. (1867). 1st US ed. Frontis, 357pp, 10 ads. Grn cl, stamped in blind, gilt (sig). *Petrilla.* $65/£42

LOUDON, J.C. Arboretum et Fruticetum Britannicum. London, 1844. 2nd ed. 8 vols (4 letterpress, 4 plts). 412 plts. Partially unopened (lt foxing). Emb grn cl (several spines chipped; lower joints vols 3, 7 starting to split). *Edwards.* $326/£210

LOUDON, J.C. An Encyclopaedia of Agriculture. London: Longman et al, 1825. 1st ed. xvi,1226pp + 2pp pub's ads, 16pp pub's ads attached at fr; 823 wood engrs. Uncut. Vellum spine, ptd paper label, marbled bds (worn). Good (hinges cracked). *Quest.* $250/£161

LOUDON, J.C. An Encyclopaedia of Agriculture. London, 1857. 5th ed. xl,1375pp, 1203 wood engrs. Contemp 3/4 calf (scuffed, edgeworn; fr hinge cracked, rear hinge split; ex-lib). *Sutton.* $200/£129

LOUDON, J.C. An Encyclopaedia of Gardening. London: Longman et al, (1845). (xvi),xl,1270,(32)pp. Pub's grn blindstamped cl. Rebacked; lt edgewear, cvrs rubbed, else VG. *Bookpress.* $450/£290

LOUDON, J.C. The Green-House Companion. London: Harding, Triphook & Lepard, 1825. Hand-colored litho frontis, xii,256,204pp. Morocco-backed marbled bds. Eps sl foxed, else Fine. *Quest.* $275/£177

LOUDON, J.C. The Green-House Companion.... London, 1832. 3rd ed. Hand colored frontis; xii,408pp. Orig cl (label worn). Good. *Henly.* $93/£60

LOUDON, J.C. The Villa Gardener. London: Orr, 1850. 2nd ed. xii,516pp; 378 wood engrs. Later 1/2 calf. Early leaves lt spotted, else VG. *Bookpress.* $450/£290

LOUDON, J.S. Arboretum et Fruticetum Britannicum. London: For the author, 1844. 2nd ed. Vols V-VIII only. vi,pp, 104 engr plts (3 fldg); vi,pp, 110 engr plts (3 fldg); vi,pp, 95 engr plts (12 fldg); vii,(1 blank),8pp, index, 103 engr plts (6 fldg). Contemp grn blindstamped cl (vol VIII rebacked, orig spine title relaid; spine head vol V worn). VG set (ex-lib). *Quest.* $325/£210

LOUDON, JANE. The Ladies' Companion to the Flower Garden. London: Smith, 1841. 7pp ads, 4 ff, 316pp. Cl (spine faded). *Marlborough.* $124/£80

LOUDON, JANE. The Lady's Country Companion. London: Longman, 1845. Engr frontis, xi,396,32pp ads. *Marlborough.* $124/£80

LOUDON, MRS. British Wild Flowers. London: Orr, (1855). 2nd ed. 60 hand-colored litho plts (sl foxing, affecting some plts); aeg. 1/2 grn morocco, marbled sides, gilt backstrip. *Petersfield.* $1,178/£760

LOUDON, MRS. Gardening for Ladies. London: John Murray, 1843. 6th ed. Engr frontis, 443pp + 16pp ads (prelims lt foxed). Silk-cvrd bds (rebacked; hinges cracked), gilt device. *Quest.* $75/£48

LOUDON, MRS. The Ladies Companion to the Flower Garden. London: William Smith, 1844. 3rd ed. Hand-colored frontis (sl foxed), vii,346pp. Aeg. Blind-stamped cl gilt (unevenly faded). VG. *Quest.* $90/£58

LOUDON, MRS. The Lady's Country Companion. London: Longman et al, 1852. 4th ed. Steel engr frontis; xi,423 + 24pp ads. Grn bds (faded, shelfwear, bumped). VG. *Shifrin.* $65/£42

LOUIS, PIERRE. Anatomical, Pathological and Therapeutic Researches Upon the Disease Known Under the Name of Gastro-Enterite, Putrid, Adynamic, Ataxic, or Typhoid Fever.... Boston, 1836. 1st Eng trans. 2 vols. 395; 462pp. Good. *Fye.* $350/£226

LOUIS, PIERRE. Pathological Researches on Phthisis. Boston, 1836. 1st Eng trans. 550pp. Good. *Fye.* $200/£129

LOUIS, PIERRE. Researches on Phthisis, Anatomical, Pathological and Therapeutical. London, 1854. 2nd ed. 571pp. Good. *Fye.* $75/£48

LOUIS, S.L. (ed). Decorum. NY: Union Pub House, 1882. 414pp. Dec cl. VG. *Petrilla.* $35/£23

LOUKOMSKI, GEORGES. Charles Cameron (1740-1812). London: Nicholson & Watson, 1943. Eps spotted. Dj. *Hollett.* $93/£60

LOUYS, PIERRE. Aphrodite. (N.p.): Privately ptd, 1926. One of 650 numbered. Frontis. 3/4 orange morocco, gilt extra; batik bds. VG (lt soiling). *Reese.* $75/£48

LOUYS, PIERRE. The Twilight of the Nymphs. Phillis Duveen (trans). London: Fortune Press, (1928). 1st ed thus. One of 1200 numbered. Cecil Beaton (illus). Cl, marbled bds. Pencil sig, else NF in dj (lt used). *Reese.* $125/£81

Love Tales from the Tallemant Rendered from the French. London: Grafton, 1925. Ltd to 1000. Label, top edges sl rubbed; sm spots lower cvr. *Sadlon.* $75/£48

LOVE, ROBERTUS. The Rise and Fall of Jesse James. NY: Putnam's, 1926. Black cl (lt worn, soiled). Howes L 521. *Glenn.* $65/£42

LOVECRAFT, H.P. At the Mountain of Madness. Arkham House, 1964. 1st ed. Fine in Fine dj. *Dermont.* $75/£48

LOVECRAFT, H.P. At the Mountains of Madness. Arkham House, 1964. 1st ed. Fine in dj (sl rubbed). *Madle.* $125/£81

LOVECRAFT, H.P. Beyond the Wall of Sleep. Sauk City: Arkham House, 1943. 1st ed. Name, date, else VG in dj (lt edgeworn; shallow chipping spine ends). *Other Worlds.* $1,250/£806

LOVECRAFT, H.P. Beyond the Wall of Sleep. Sauk City, 1943. 1st ed. One of 1200. VG (spine dull, letters at base of spine worn) in dj (sm chip base of spine, 2 sm chips top edge). *Mcclintock.* $1,200/£774

LOVECRAFT, H.P. Beyond the Wall of Sleep. Sauk City, WI: Arkham House, 1943. One of 1217. Corner tips sl bumped, o/w NF in Attractive dj (sm chip spine bottom edge). *Bernard.* $2,250/£1,452

LOVECRAFT, H.P. Collected Poems. Arkham House, 1963. 1st ed. VF in dj. *Madle.* $150/£97

LOVECRAFT, H.P. Collected Poems. Arkham House, 1963. 1st ed. One of 2000. NF in VG + dj. *Aronovitz.* $125/£81

LOVECRAFT, H.P. Cry Horror! NY, (ca 1958). 1st ed this reissue. VG. *Mcclintock.* $17/£11

LOVECRAFT, H.P. Dagon and Other Macabre Tales. Arkham House, 1965. 1st ed. One of 3000. Fine in VG + dj. *Aronovitz.* $95/£61

LOVECRAFT, H.P. The Dark Brotherhood. Arkham House, 1966. 1st ed. Fine in dj. *Madle.* $125/£81

LOVECRAFT, H.P. Dreams and Fancies. Arkham House, 1962. 1st ed. VF in dj. *Madle.* $175/£113

LOVECRAFT, H.P. Dreams and Fancies. Sauk City, WI: Arkham House, 1962. One of 2030. New in dj. *Bernard.* $150/£97

LOVECRAFT, H.P. The Dunwich Horror and Other Weird Tales. NY, Armed Services Editions. Wraps. *Hayman.* $75/£48

LOVECRAFT, H.P. The Haunter of the Dark and Other Tales of Terror. Gollancz, 1951. 1st ed. Spine sl lightened, else VG + in VG + dj (spine sl faded). *Aronovitz.* $150/£97

LOVECRAFT, H.P. The Haunter of the Dark and Other Tales of Terror. Gollancz, 1951. 1st Eng ed. Orange cl (cvr top edges sl mkd). Fine in dj (sl dusty, nicked). *Dalian.* $116/£75

LOVECRAFT, H.P. The Horror in the Museum and Other Revisions. Arkham House, 1970. 1st ed. Fine in dj. *Aronovitz.* $38/£25

LOVECRAFT, H.P. Marginalia. Sauk City, WI: Arkham House, 1944. One of 2035. NF in dj (price-clipped; lt soiled). *Bernard.* $300/£194

LOVECRAFT, H.P. The Outsider and Others. Sauk City: Arkham House, 1939. 1st ed. Corners bumped; name, date, else VG + in dj (worn; spine ends chipped; head taped; separated in 2 along rear spine edge). *Other Worlds.* $1,000/£645

LOVECRAFT, H.P. The Outsider and Others. Arkham House, 1939. 1st ed. NF in VG dj (sl wear). *Fine Books.* $1,875/£1,210

LOVECRAFT, H.P. The Outsider and Others. Sauk City, WI: Arkham House, 1939. One of 1268. Corner sl bumped, o/w NF in dj (spine ends sl worn). *Bernard.* $2,500/£1,613

LOVECRAFT, H.P. Selected Letters Volume I. Arkham House, 1965. 1st ed. NF in dj. *Madle.* $45/£29

LOVECRAFT, H.P. Selected Letters Volume III. Arkham House, 1971. 1st ed. Fine in dj. *Madle.* $200/£129

LOVECRAFT, H.P. The Shuttered Room. Arkham House, 1959. 1st ed. Fine in dj. *Madle.* $200/£129

LOVECRAFT, H.P. Something About Cats. Arkham House, 1949. 1st ed. VF in dj. *Madle.* $275/£177

LOVECRAFT, H.P. Something About Cats. Sauk City, WI: Arkham House, 1949. One of 2995. NF in dj. *Bernard.* $200/£129

LOVECRAFT, H.P. The Weird Shadow Over Innsmouth and Other Stories of the Supernatural. NY, (1944). 1st ed. VG + in wraps (lt rubbed, creased). *Mcclintock.* $55/£35

LOVECRAFT, H.P. The Weird Shadow Over Innsmouth. Bart House, 1944. 1st ed thus. VG in wraps. *Madle.* $65/£42

LOVECRAFT, H.P. and AUGUST DERLETH. The Lurker at the Threshold. Arkham House, 1945. 1st ed. VG in dj (sl frayed). *Madle.* $70/£45

LOVECRAFT, H.P. and AUGUST DERLETH. The Lurker at the Threshold. Sauk City, WI: Arkham House, 1945. One of 3041. Fine in dj. *Bernard.* $150/£97

LOVECRAFT, H.P. et al. Tales of the Cthulhu Mythos. Arkham House, 1969. 1st ed. VF in dj. *Madle.* $125/£81

LOVECRAFT, H.P. et al. Tales of the Cthulhu Mythos. Sauk City, WI: Arkham House, 1969. One of 4024. Lt tanning flyleaf, o/w Fine in NF dj. *Bernard.* $75/£48

LOVEJOY, J.C. Memoir of Rev. Charles T. Torrey.... Boston: Jewett, 1847. 1st ed. (8),364pp; port. *Ginsberg.* $75/£48

LOVELACE, DELOS W. King Kong. NY: Grosset & Dunlap, n.d. (1933). 1st ed. VG in pict dj (restored chip fr panel). *Bernard.* $250/£161

LOVESEY, PETER. Abracadaver. London: Macmillan, 1972. 1st UK ed. VG + in dj (sm closed tear). *Williams.* $70/£45

LOVESEY, PETER. Bertie and the Tinman. London: Bodley Head, 1987. 1st ed. Signed. Fine (sl corner bumps) in Fine dj. *Janus.* $35/£23

LOVESEY, PETER. A Case of Spirits. London: Macmillan, 1975. 1st ed. Signed. Sl bumped head spine and dj, else Fine. *Limestone.* $55/£35

LOVESEY, PETER. A Case of Spirits. Macmillan, 1975. 1st UK ed. Fine (pp sl browned) in NF dj *Williams.* $74/£48

LOVESEY, PETER. The Detective Wore Silk Drawers. London: Macmillan, 1971. 1st ed. VG in VG dj. *Ming.* $70/£45

LOVESEY, PETER. The False Inspector Dew. London: Macmillan, 1982. 1st ed. Signed. Fine in dj. *Limestone.* $55/£35

LOVESEY, PETER. The Last Detective. London: Scorpion Press, 1991. 1st UK ed. One of 99 numbered, signed. Fine in marbled bds as issued. *Williams.* $85/£55

LOVESEY, PETER. Rough Cider. Bodley Head, 1986. 1st UK ed. Fine in dj. *Williams.* $23/£15

LOVESEY, PETER. The Staring Man and Other Stories. (Helsinki): Eurographica, 1988. Signed, dated. Fine in card cvrs in dj as issued. *Williams.* $85/£55

LOVESEY, PETER. The Staring Man and Other Stories. (Helsinki): Eurographica, 1988. Signed, dated. Fine in card cvrs in dj as issued. *Williams.* $85/£55

LOVESEY, PETER. Waxwork. London: Macmillan, 1978. 1st ed. Fine in dj. *Limestone.* $40/£26

LOVESEY, PETER. Waxwork. Macmillan, 1978. 1st UK ed. Fine in dj. *Williams.* $62/£40

LOVESEY, PETER. Wobble to Death. NY: Dodd, 1970. 1st ed. 1st bk. Fine in dj (minor rubbing). *Else Fine.* $45/£29

LOVETT, ROBERT. Infantile Paralysis in Massachusetts During 1910. Boston, 1911. Good. *Fye.* $35/£23

LOVETT, ROBERT. The Treatment of Infantile Paralysis. Phila, 1916. Good. *Fye.* $125/£81

Loving Ballad of Lord Bateman. (By William Makepeace Thackeray.) London: Bell & Daldy, 1870. Rpt of 1839 ed. 12mo. iv + 24 leaves + 13pp notes, 11 full-pg illus by George Cruikshank + pg engr music. Dec orange cl on bds, gilt title (spine sl soiled). VF. *Hobbyhorse.* $50/£32

LOW, DAVID. Low's Autobiography. NY: S&S, 1957. 1st ed. Fine in dj. *Hermitage.* $35/£23

LOW, DAVID. With All Faults. Amate Press, 1973. Fine in dj. *Moss.* $23/£15

LOW, FRANCES H. Queen Victoria's Dolls. London, 1894. (xliv)ll. Gilt dec bds (rubbed, some loss). Rebacked? in blue cl. *Edwards.* $116/£75

LOW, FRANCES H. Queen Victoria's Dolls. London: George Newnes, 1894. 1st ed. Frontis; (86)pp. Orig 1/4 black cl. Edges rubbed; cvr lt worn; text lt yellowed, else VG. *Bookpress.* $150/£97

LOW, MARY and JUAN BREA. Red Spanish Notebook. The First Six Months of the Revolution and the Civil War. London: Secker & Warburg, 1937. 1st ed. VG (cl worn). *Patterson.* $78/£50

LOWE, E.J. Ferns: British and Exotic. (8 vols.) Together with: A Natural History of New and Rare Ferns. (1 vol.) London: 1866-72. 1st eds. 9 vols. 479 color plts vols 1-8; 72 color plts vol 9. 1/2 calf, gilt. (Ex-lib; sm stamp plts, titles; bindings sl rubbed; foxing.) *Henly.* $307/£198

LOWE, E.J. Our Native Ferns. London: Bell, 1874, 1880. Reprint. 348; 492pp + ads; 79 full-pg color plts. Goldstamped grn cl. VG (hinges tender). *Second Life.* $175/£113

LOWE, F.A. The Heron. London: New Naturalist, 1954. 1st ed. Color frontis. Dj. *Wheldon & Wesley.* $109/£70

LOWE, SAMUEL E. A New Story of Peter Rabbit. Racine: Whitman, 1926. 1st ed. 16mo. 8 full-pg color plts by Allan Wright and Earnest Vetsch. Black/turquoise bds. Good in pict dj (minor dusting). *Reisler.* $135/£87

LOWELL, AMY. John Keats. Boston: Houghton Mifflin, 1925. 1st ed. 2 vols. Dj panels laid in. VG set. BAL 13006. *Reese.* $85/£55

LOWELL, AMY. Sword Blades and Poppy Seed. NY: Macmillan, 1914. 1st ed. Complimentary copy w/pub's stamp tp. Grey bds, grn cl spine, paper labels. Fine in ptd cream dj (chips). *Chapel Hill.* $350/£226

LOWELL, EDWARD J. The Hessians and Other German Auxiliaries of Great Britain in the Revolutionary War. NY: Harper, 1884. 1st ed. (xi),328pp; 8 maps/plans. (Rear pocket removed.) *Schoyer.* $40/£26

LOWELL, GUY. American Gardens. Boston: Bates & Guild, 1902. 1st ed. 112 full-pg b/w photo plts. Teg. Gilt/violet pict grn buckram (soil, wear). VG. *House.* $280/£181

LOWELL, JAMES RUSSELL. The Biglow Papers, Second Series. Boston: Ticknor & Fields, 1867. 1st ed, 1st ptg. Ed of 2500. Grn cl, gilt. Fine. BAL 13126. *Macdonnell.* $45/£29

LOWELL, JAMES RUSSELL. The Choicest Poetry of the Age. The Biglow Papers. London: John Camden Hotten, 1861. 2nd Eng ed. xiv,200pp + 8pp pub's ads; slip tipped to tp; 3 hand-colored plts by George Cruikshank. (Spine sl dknd.) BAL 13273, 13275. *Schoyer.* $100/£65

LOWELL, JAMES RUSSELL. The Rose. Boston: James R. Osgood, 1878. 1st ed. Aeg. Grn dec cl, gilt. BAL 13321. *Macdonnell.* $30/£19

LOWELL, ROBERT. Day by Day. NY: Farrar, (1977). 1st ed. Fine in dj. *Reese.* $20/£13

LOWELL, ROBERT. The Dolphin. NY: FSG, (1973). 1st ed. New in dj. *Bernard.* $30/£19

LOWELL, ROBERT. For Lizzie and Harriet. NY: FSG, (1973). 1st ed. Fine in dj. *Antic Hay.* $25/£16

LOWELL, ROBERT. For the Union Dead. NY: FSG, (1964). 1st ed. Fine in Fine dj. *Dermont.* $75/£48

LOWELL, ROBERT. For the Union Dead. Faber, 1964. 1st Eng ed. Blue cl. VF in dj (sl dusty). *Dalian.* $54/£35

LOWELL, ROBERT. History. NY: FSG, (1973). 1st ed. New in dj. *Bernard.* $25/£16

LOWELL, ROBERT. Imitations. London: Faber & Faber, 1962. 1st Eng ed. Fine in dj (sl spotted; spine head sl creased). *Ulysses*. $85/£55

LOWELL, ROBERT. Life Studies. NY: Farrar, Straus & Cudahy, (1959). 1st ed. VG + in dj (edges sl worn; sm stain rear panel corner). *Bernard*. $125/£81

LOWELL, ROBERT. Life Studies. NY, 1959. 1st ed. Mint in Fine dj. *Bond*. $50/£32

LOWELL, ROBERT. Life Studies. London, 1959. 1st ed. Fine in dj (sunned, chips, sm tear, price-clipped). *Polyanthos*. $200/£129

LOWELL, ROBERT. Lord Weary's Castle. NY: Harcourt, Brace, (1946). 1st ed. Gilt. Spine ends mildly rubbed; clipping pasted to fr flyleaf, others removed. Dj (sl edgeworn). *Sadlon*. $45/£29

LOWELL, ROBERT. Lord Weary's Castle. H-B, 1946. 1st ed. NF in dj (lt wear spine head). *Fine Books*. $225/£145

LOWELL, ROBERT. The Mills of the Kavanaughs. NY: Harcourt, Brace, (1951). 1st ed, signed. Black cl. Sl browning fep, else NF in VG dj. *Chapel Hill*. $375/£242

LOWELL, ROBERT. The Old Glory. NY: Farrar, 1965. 1st ed. Fine in Fine dj. *Beasley*. $65/£42

LOWER, A.R.M. The North American Assault on the Canadian Forest. Toronto: Ryerson, 1938. 1st ed. 11 diags, 6 maps. Partially unopened. *Edwards*. $47/£30

LOWERY, WOODBURY. The Spanish Settlements within the Present Limits of the United States. NY/London: Putnam's, 1911. 2nd ed. 2 vols. Grn cl. Fine set. Howes L 536. *Chapel Hill*. $400/£258

LOWMAN, AL. Printing Arts in Texas. (Austin, TX): Roger Beacham, (1975). Ltd to 395. Gold cl, dec paper labels. Fine. *Karmiole*. $150/£97

LOWNDES, ROBERT. Mystery of Third Mine. Winston, 1953. 1st ed. NF in dj (sl chipped). *Madle*. $65/£42

LOWNDES, WILLIAM THOMAS. The Bibliographer's Manual of English Literature. H.G. Bohn, 1900. Rev, enlgd ed. 6 vols. Ex-lib, else Good set. *Whiteson*. $101/£65

LOWNDES, WILLIAM THOMAS. The Bibliographer's Manual of English Literature.... London: George Bell & Sons, (1857-64). New ed, rev. 4 vols. Teg, others uncut. Orig morocco-backed cl. Sound set (backs rubbed w/short splits at heads of 2 vols; 40mm strip torn from head of another). *Cox*. $132/£85

LOWRIE, WALTER. Art in the Early Church. NY, 1947. 150 plts. Good. *Washton*. $40/£26

LOWRIE, WALTER. Art in the Early Church. London, 1947. 1st ed. 153 plts. Dj (ragged). *Edwards*. $54/£35

LOWRY, MALCOLM. Dark as the Grave Wherein My Friend Is Laid. Douglas Day & Margerie Lowry (eds). (NY): NAL, (1968). 1st ed. Top edge sl dusty, o/w Fine in dj. *Reese*. $40/£26

LOWRY, MALCOLM. Dark as the Grave Wherein My Friend Is Laid. Douglas Day & Margerie Lowry (eds). Cape, 1969. 1st UK ed. Fore-edge sl spotted, o/w NF in dj. *Poetry*. $23/£15

LOWRY, MALCOLM. Dark as the Grave Wherein My Friend Is Laid. Douglas Day and Margerie Lowry (eds). NY: NAL, (1968). 1st ed (precedes Eng ed). NF in dj. *Limestone*. $85/£55

LOWRY, MALCOLM. Dark as the Grave Wherein My Friend Is Laid. Douglas Day and Margerie Lowry (eds). London: Cape, 1969. 1st Eng ed. VG in dj. *Limestone*. $55/£35

LOWRY, MALCOLM. Lunar Caustic. Earle Birney & Margerie Lowry (eds). London: Cape, (1968). 1st pb ed. White wrappers. Fine in NF dj. *Sadlon*. $60/£39

LOWRY, MALCOLM. The Selected Letters of Malcolm Lowry. Harvey Breit & Margerie Bonner Lowry (eds). Cape, 1967. 1st Eng ed. Purple patterned bds. VF in Fine dj. *Dalian*. $132/£85

LOWRY, MALCOLM. Selected Poems of Malcolm Lowry. CA: City Lights, (1962). 1st Amer ed. NF in ptd wraps. *Polyanthos*. $25/£16

LOWRY, MALCOLM. Ultramarine. Phila: Lippincott, (1962). 1st Amer, 1st rev ed. NF in dj (sl rubbed, price-clipped). *Hermitage*. $125/£81

LOWRY, MALCOLM. Ultramarine. Lippincott, 1962. 1st Amer ed (rev from 1933 ed). NF in dj. *Fine Books*. $75/£48

LOWRY, MALCOLM. Ultramarine. Phila/NY: Lippincott, 1962. 1st Amer, 1st rev ed. NF in dj. *Limestone*. $125/£81

LOWRY, MALCOLM. Under the Volcano. NY: Reynal & Hitchcock, (1947). 1st ed. VG in dj (nicks, short tears, else VG). *Godot*. $375/£242

LOWRY, MALCOLM. Under the Volcano. NY: Reynal & Hitchcock, (1947). 1st ed. Name fr pastedown, else Fine in VG dj (price-clipped; several tears; lt chipping). *Between The Covers*. $600/£387

LUBBOCK, BASIL. The Blackwell Frigates. Glasgow: Brown, Son & Ferguson, (1950). 2nd ed. VG. *Blue Dragon*. $30/£19

LUBBOCK, BASIL. The China Clippers. Boston, (1925). 6th ed. Good. *Hayman*. $20/£13

LUBBOCK, BASIL. The China Clippers. Glasgow, 1946. (Shaken; name.) *Argosy*. $85/£55

LUBBOCK, BASIL. The Down Easters: American Deep-Water Sailing Ships. Boston, 1929. Stated 1st ed. 116 half-tone repros; 4 fldg plans. Fine in dj (2 sl reinforced spots). *Hayman*. $80/£52

LUBBOCK, BASIL. The Last of the Windjammers. Glasgow: Brown, Son & Ferguson, (1927, 1929). 1st eds. 2 vols. Blue cl (lt wear). *Cullen*. $150/£97

LUBBOCK, BASIL. The Western Ocean Packets. Glasgow, 1925. Good. *Hayman*. $25/£16

LUCAS, A. Ancient Egyptian Materials and Industries. London: Edward Arnold, (1962). 4th ed. Good (stamps) in dj. *Archaeologia*. $150/£97

LUCAS, A. Ancient Egyptian Materials. London: Edward Arnold, 1926. 1st ed. Good. *Archaeologia*. $85/£55

LUCAS, A. Antiques. Their Restoration and Preservation. London: Arnold, 1932. 2nd ed. Sound. *Ars Artis*. $23/£15

LUCAS, CHARLES (ed). Pitcairn Island Register Book. London: SPCK, 1929. 1st ed. Lg fldg map. Nice (sl wear). *Cady*. $50/£32

LUCAS, E.V. Edwin Austin Abbey, Royal Academician, the Record of His Life and Work. NY: Scribner's, 1921. 1st ed. 2 vols. Frontis, 18 plts; frontis, 13 plts. (Spines sl sunned; fr hinge vol 1 internally cracked; ink inscrip.) *Bookpress*. $265/£171

LUCAS, E.V. Fireside and Sunshine. London: Methuen, 1906. 1st ed. Teg, fore-edges mainly trimmed, lower edges uncut. Lt blue buckram, gilt. Lt foxing; 2pp, title leaves lt creased; o/w Fine in dj (sl chipped, frayed). *Temple*. $33/£21

LUCAS, E.V. John Constable, the Painter. London, 1924. 16 tipped-in color plts. Teg. Gilt-edged cl (edges sl rubbed). *Edwards*. $62/£40

LUCAS, E.V. John Constable, the Painter. London/NY, 1924. #21/100. Signed. 16 tipped-in color, 48 b/w plts; extra illus tipped-in fep. Teg, rest uncut. Full leather (sl soiled, spine rubbed). *Edwards.* $233/£150

LUCAS, E.V. The Life of Charles Lamb. London, (1905). 1st ed. 2 vols. VG in dj. *Argosy.* $75/£48

LUCAS, E.V. Mr. Ingleside. London: Methuen, 1910. 1st ed. Pub's cat at end dated Aug 1910. Grn linen, gilt. Sl wear spine; prelims, edges sl foxed; o/w Nice. *Temple.* $22/£14

LUCAS, E.V. Outposts of Mercy. Methuen, 1917. 1st Eng ed. VG in brn ptd wrappers (sl foxed). *Dalian.* $31/£20

LUCAS, E.V. Playtime and Company. London: Methuen, (1925). 2nd ed. E.H. Shepard (illus). Ptd pict bds (bumped, sm tears). *Petersfield.* $31/£20

LUCAS, E.V. Playtime and Company. London: Methuen, 1925. 1st ed. #67/100. Signed by Lucas and Ernest H. Shepard (illus). 4to. 95pp. Cl-backed bds, ptd paper label. VG in glassine dj. *Davidson.* $775/£500

LUCAS, E.V. The Visit to London. NY: Brentano's, (1902). 1st Amer ed. 4to. 24 full-pg color plts by Francis D. Bedford. Cl-backed illus bds (rubbed, spine replaced; new eps). *Reisler.* $185/£119

LUCAS, E.V. (ed). Charles Lamb and the Lloyds. Smith, Elder, 1898. 1st ed. VG. *Poetry.* $20/£13

LUCAS, F.A. Animals Before Man in North America. NY, 1902. 1st ed. Blind-stamped dec cl. VG. *Mikesh.* $45/£29

LUCAS, F.L. The Woman Clothed with the Sun and Other Stories. Cassell, 1937. 1st ed. Tear spine base, else VG + in VG dj (spine fading). *Aronovitz.* $95/£61

LUCAS, GEORGE. Star Wars. Del Rey, 1977. 1st trade ed. Fine in dj. *Madle.* $45/£29

LUCAS, T.J. Camp Life and Sport in South Africa.... London, 1878. xiii,258pp; 4 color plts. Plain cl (rebound), orig dec fr cvr (rubbed). *Wheldon & Wesley.* $233/£150

LUCHETTI, CATHY. Women of the West. St. George, 1982. 1st ed. Signed. Fine in dj. *Baade.* $60/£39

LUCIA, ELLIS. Head Rig. Portland: Overland West, (1965). 1st ed. VF in VF dj. *Oregon.* $30/£19

LUCIA, ELLIS. The Saga of Ben Holladay. NY: Hastings House, (1959). 1st ed. VG in dj. *Lien.* $30/£19

LUCIANI, L. Human Physiology. F.A. Welby (trans). London, 1911, 1913, 1915. 3 vols only (of 5). Spine vol 3 faded, o/w VG. *Whitehart.* $93/£60

LUCID, ROBERT F. (ed). The Journal of Richard Henry Dana, Jr. Cambridge: Harvard Univ Press, 1968. 3 vols. *Boswell.* $125/£81

LUCIEN. The True Historie of Lucien the Samosatenian. Francis Hickes (trans). London: Golden Cockerel, 1927. #38/275. 55 wood engrs by Robert Gibbings. Niger morocco-backed buckram. Fine (sig). *Cox.* $620/£400

LUDENDORFF, GENERAL. My War Memories 1914-1918. London: Hutchinson, n.d. (1919). 1st ed in English. 2 vols. 12 fldg maps. (Backstrips faded, sl worn; sides sl mkd; bumped). *Cox.* $54/£35

LUDLAM, HARRY. Captain Scott. London: W. Foulsham, (1965). VG in VG dj. *Blue Dragon.* $40/£26

LUDLOW, N.M. Dramatic Life as I Found It.... St. Louis, 1880. 733pp. (Inner hinge mended; cvrs sl spotted.) Howes L 566. *Ginsberg.* $150/£97

LUDLOW, WILLIAM. Report of a Reconnaissance from Carroll, Montana Territory on the Upper Missouri...Summer of 1875. Washington: GPO, 1876. 1st ed. 4to. 3 fldg maps; 2 plts (dampstain margin plt I). Howes L 557. *Argosy.* $175/£113

LUDLOW, WILLIAM. Report of a Reconnaissance of the Black Hills of Dakota.... Washington: GPO, 1875. 1st separate ptg. 121pp, litho plt, 3 lg fldg maps. Orig cl (sl worn). Howes L 558. *Schoyer.* $200/£129

LUDLUM, ROBERT. The Matarese Circle. Marek, 1979. 1st ed. NF in dj. *Stahr.* $25/£16

LUDLUM, ROBERT. The Parsifal Mosaic. NY: Random, 1982. 1st ed. Signed, inscribed. Fine in dj. *Silver Door.* $75/£48

LUDLUM, ROBERT. The Rhinemann Exchange. Dial, 1974. 1st ed. Fine in dj (lt wear). *Stahr.* $30/£19

LUDLUM, ROBERT. The Rhinemann Exchange. NY: Dial, 1974. 1st ed. Fine (sunned) in Fine dj (sl wear). *Beasley.* $45/£29

LUDWIG, COY. Maxfield Parrish. NY: Watson-Guptill, (1973). 1st ed. 64 color plts. Blue gilt-stamped cl. Fine in dj. *Juvelis.* $125/£81

LUDY, ROBERT B. Historic Hotels of the World, Past and Present. Phila: David McKay, 1927. 1st ed. Signed presentation. Frontis. Teg; partly uncut. Text yellowed; few mks fr cvr, else VG. *Bookpress.* $65/£42

LUEDERS, EDWARD. Carl Van Vechten and the Twenties. Univ of NM Press, 1955. 1st ed. Signed, inscribed. VG + in VG dj. *Bishop.* $30/£19

LUGARD, F.D. The Rise of Our East African Empire. London: Blackwood, 1893. 2 vols. 32pp ads vol 1. Map in pocket. Mod 1/2 tan calf, marbled sides, gilt leather labels (rebound; tps faded). *Petersfield.* $465/£300

LUHAN, MABEL DODGE. Edge of Taos Desert. NY: Harcourt, Brace, (1937). 1st ed. VG (spine sl skewed; 1st sig loose; lacks dj). *Hermitage.* $65/£42

LUHAN, MABEL DODGE. European Experiences. NY: Harcourt, (1935). 1st ed. Port. VG. *Reese.* $25/£16

LUHAN, MABEL DODGE. Lorenzo in Taos. NY, 1932. 1st ed. Dec cl. Back blank pg w/bottom chip, o/w VG in dj (lt worn). *Baade.* $150/£97

LUHAN, MABEL DODGE. Taos and Its Artists. NY: Duell et al, (1947). 1st ed. Fine in VG dj (faded, lt edgewear, short tears). *Godot.* $325/£210

LUHAN, MABEL DODGE. Winter in Taos. NY: Harcourt, Brace, (1935). 1st ed. 16 photo plts. Dj (sl chipped). *Bickersteth.* $78/£50

LUHRS, VICTOR. The Great Baseball Mystery. Barnes, 1966. 1st ed. VG + in VG dj. *Plapinger.* $60/£39

LUK-OIE, OLE. The Green Curve and Other Stories. Doubleday, 1911. 1st US ed. NF. *Madle.* $25/£16

Luke Limner. Suggestions in Design. (By John Leighton.) London: David Bogue, 1853. 1st ed. iv,26,(2)pp, 48 plts. VG (cvr lt rubbed, sl foxing). *Bookpress.* $475/£306

LUKE, HARRY and EDWARD KEITH-ROACH (eds). The Handbook of Palestine and Trans-Jordan. London: Macmillan, 1934. 3rd ed. (Tp stamp; lacks map.) *Archaeologia.* $45/£29

LUKE, HARRY. Old Turkey and the New. London: Bles, (1955). New, rev ed. Very Nice (tape stains eps) in dj. *Schoyer.* $30/£19

LUKE, PETER. Hadrian VII. NY: Knopf, 1969. 1st Amer ed. Bkpl, else Fine in NF dj (sl wrinkling fr panel). *Between The Covers.* $65/£42

LUKIS, PARDEY. Tropical Hygiene for Anglo-Indians and Indians. Calcutta, 1914. 2nd ed. Good. *Fye.* $125/£81

LULLIES, REINHARD. Greek Sculpture. NY: Abrams, (1957). 264 plts (8 color). Good in dj (tattered). *Archaeologia.* $65/£42

LUMHOLTZ, CARL. Unknown Mexico. London, 1903. 2 vols. Frontis port, dbl-pg color facs frontis, 15 color plts, 3 fldg maps. Teg. Dec cl (discoloring, lt dampstaining; sl rubbed). *Edwards.* $233/£150

LUMHOLTZ, CARL. Unknown Mexico. A Record of Five Years' Exploration.... London: Macmillan, 1903. 1st ed in English. 2 vols. Double-pg colored facs, 15 colored lithos, 56 photogravures, 4 fldg maps, frontis port. Grn cl, dec spines, upper cvrs, teg. Fine but for lib stamps on titles, facs verso; bkpls. *Morrell.* $357/£230

LUMMIS, CHARLES F. Mesa, Canon and Pueblo. NY: Century, 1925. 1st ed. VG (hinge starting). *Parker.* $50/£32

LUMMIS, CHARLES F. Some Strange Corners of Our Country. NY: Century, 1892. 1st ptg. Color frontis, xi,270pp. Pict cl. VG. *Schoyer.* $50/£32

LUMMIS, CHARLES F. Some Strange Corners of Our Country: The Wonderland of the Southwest. Century, 1892. 1st ed. Color frontis. Dec cvr. VG +. *Authors Of The West.* $60/£39

LUMPKIN, HENRY. From Savannah to Yorktown: The American Revolution in the South. Univ of SC, (c. 1981). 1st ed. 1/4 leather. VG. *Book Broker.* $45/£29

LUNDGREN, S. Off the Beaten Track.... London, 1952. *Wheldon & Wesley.* $23/£15

LUNN, ARNOLD. A Century of Mountaineering 1857-1957. London, (1957). 1st ed. VG in dj (sl used). *King.* $40/£26

LUNN, ARNOLD. Spanish Rehearsal. London: Hutchinson, (1937). 1st ed. Good (cl worn, edges spotted). *Patterson.* $39/£25

LUNN, ARNOLD. Zermatt and the Valais. London, (1955). 1st ed. VG in dj (sl rubbed, soiled). *King.* $25/£16

LURIE, ALISON. Imaginary Friends. NY: Coward-McCann, (1967). 1st Amer ed. Owner stamp, o/w Fine in dj. *Hermitage.* $40/£26

LURIE, ALISON. The War between the Tates. NY: Random House, (1974). 1st Amer ed. Erasure fep, o/w Fine in dj (price-clipped). *Hermitage.* $25/£16

LUSK, WILLIAM THOMPSON. The Science and Art of Midwifery. London: H.K. Lewis, 1887. New ed (3rd), rev & enlgd. xviii,763pp. Sl staining prelims, title, o/w VG. *White.* $39/£25

LUTRELL, ESTELLE. Newspapers and Periodicals of Arizona 1859-1911. Tucson, 1949. 1st ed. Fine in wraps. *Baade.* $25/£16

LUTZ, JOHN. Scorcher. NY: Henry Holt, 1987. 1st ed. VF in dj. *Mordida.* $25/£16

LUTZOW, FRANCIS. Bohemia. London: Chapman & Hall, 1896. xviii,438pp, 2 line maps. (Paper browned; envelope of clippings tipped in.) Grn cl (worn, lib pocket removed, mks). *Schoyer.* $40/£26

LUXMOORE, CHAS. F.C. Saltglaze. London: Holland Press, n.d. (ca 1970). Rpnt of 1924 ed. 89 plts. Black cl. Good in dj (chipped). *Karmiole.* $50/£32

LUYS, JULES. The Brain and Its Function. NY: Appleton, 1897. 327pp + ads. Emb cl. *Goodrich.* $85/£55

LYDEKKER, RICHARD. The Royal Natural History. London: Warne, 1893-94. 6 vols. 72 color plts, 1600 engrs. All edges, eps marbled. 1/2 blue calf, gilt, leather spine labels (few sm mks, scratches). Attractive set. *Hollett.* $233/£150

LYDSTON, G. FRANK. Addresses and Essays. Chicago, 1892. 2nd ed. 189pp. Good. *Fye.* $75/£48

LYELL, C. Elements of Geology. London, 1865. 6th ed. xvi,794pp. Cl, gilt. Good (lib bkpl, stamp half title). *Henly.* $74/£48

LYELL, C. The Geological Evidences of the Antiquity of Man. Phila: George W. Childs, 1863. 1st Amer ed. x,518pp; 2 plts. Blue cl, gilt. Fine (bkpl). *Karmiole.* $175/£113

LYELL, C. The Geological Evidences of the Antiquity of Man. London, 1873. 4th ed. xix,572pp; 2 plts. (Binding sl worn.) *Henly.* $74/£48

LYELL, C. A Manual of Elementary Geology. London, 1855. 5th ed. xvi,655pp + 32pp ads, 1 plt. Pict gilt cl. (New eps.) *Henly.* $47/£30

LYELL, C. Principles of Geology. London, 1847. 7th ed, rev. Frontis; xvi,(i),810pp; 7 maps; 4 plts. Full calf, gilt. Nice. *Wheldon & Wesley.* $147/£95

LYELL, C. Principles of Geology. London, 1867-68. 10th ed. 2 vols. xvi,671,32; xvii,649pp; 7 plts; map. Pict cl, gilt. (Vol 1 rebacked preserving spine; vol 2 fore-edge upper cvr sl dampstained.) *Henly.* $132/£85

LYELL, C. Principles of Geology. London, 1868-72. Vol 1, 11th ed; vol 2, 10th ed. 8 plts. Grn cl, gilt (sl used; refixed, repaired). Contents Good. *Wheldon & Wesley.* $116/£75

LYELL, C. The Student's Elements of Geology. London, 1885. 4th ed. Frontis, 20,621pp + 32pp ads. Good. *Henly.* $37/£24

LYELL, CHARLES. A Second Visit to the United States of North America. NY: Harper, 1849. 1st Amer ed. 2 vols. 273; 287pp + ads. Ptd wraps (soiled, chipped; lt dampstained). *Parmer.* $175/£113

LYELL, DENIS D. Wild Life in Central Africa. London: Field Press, (1913). Pict cl, gilt (few pp lt foxed). *Petersfield.* $102/£66

LYELL, JAMES P.R. Early Book Illustration in Spain. London: Grafton, 1926. One of 500 numbered. (Fr hinge starting; stamp rep.) *Bookpress.* $235/£152

LYFORD, CARRIE A. Quill and Beadwork of the Western Sioux. Washington, DC, 1940. 1st ed. Back cvr creased, o/w VG in wraps. *Baade.* $25/£16

LYLES, WILLIAM H. Putting Dell on the Map. Westport: Greenwood, 1983. 1st ed. Fine; issued w/o dj. *Janus.* $50/£32

LYMAN, CHESTER S. Around the Horn to the Sandwich Islands and California 1845-1850.... Frederick J. Teggart (ed). New Haven, 1924. 1st ed. Cvrs worn; few pp wrinkled, else Good. *King.* $50/£32

LYMAN, HENRY. Insomnia; and Other Disorders of Sleep. Chicago, 1885. 1st ed. 239pp. Good. *Fye.* $100/£65

LYMAN, JOSEPH B. Cotton Culture. NY: Orange Judd, 1868. Hand-colored map. Brn cl (rebacked). *Appelfeld.* $95/£61

LYMAN, THEODORE. Meade's Headquarters 1863-1865, Letters of Colonel Theodore Lyman. George R. Agassiz (ed). NY, 1956. 1st ed. VG + in clear plastic dj. *Pratt.* $60/£39

LYMAN, WILLIAM DENISON. The Columbia River, Its History, Its Myths, Its Scenery, Its Commerce. NY: Putnam's, 1911. Early ptg. 2 fldg color maps. Blue cl (spine dknd, extrems sl worn). VG. *Harrington.* $50/£32

LYNCH, GEORGE. Impressions of a War Correspondent. London, 1903. 1st ed. Frontis, 14 other plts. VG in khaki pict cl. *Edwards.* $62/£40

LYNCH, JEREMIAH. Three Years in the Klondike. Chicago, (1967). Lakeside Classic. VG. *Schoyer.* $25/£16

LYNCH, JEREMIAH. Three Years in the Klondike. Chicago: Lakeside, 1967. Map. Fine. *Blue Dragon.* $20/£13

LYNCH, JOHN ROY. Reminiscences of an Active Life. Chicago: U of Chicago Press, (1970). 1st ed. Port. VG. *Petrilla.* $30/£19

LYNCH, LAWRENCE. Against Odds. London: Ward, Lock, 1894. 1st UK ed. Good. *Ming.* $39/£25

LYNCH, LAWRENCE. A Dead Man's Step. London: Ward, Lock, 1893. 1st ed. Good. *Ming.* $47/£30

LYNCH, NANCY. The Old-Fashioned Garden. NY: Rizzoli, 1987. 22x39 cm, 4 pop-ups. Glazed pict bds. Fine. *Book Finders.* $25/£16

LYNCH, W.F. Naval Life. NY: Scribner's, 1851. 1st ed. 308pp. (Minor foxing; bumped, stained; split fr joint; spine chipped). Internally VG. *Blue Mountain.* $95/£61

LYNN-ALLEN, B.G. Shot-Gun and Sunlight. London: Batchworth, 1951. 1st ed. Fine in VG+ dj. *Mikesh.* $50/£32

LYON, DANNY. Conversations with the Dead: Photographs of Prison Life with the Letters and Drawings of Billy McCune #122054. NY: Holt et al, 1971. 1st ed. Illus stiff wrappers. Rmdr stamp, faint remnants from price sticker, else VG. *Cahan.* $125/£81

LYON, DANNY. The Destruction of Lower Manhattan. NY: Macmillan, 1969. 1st ed. 75 b/w photos. Fine in dj (sl rubbed). *Cahan.* $225/£145

LYON, G.F. The Private Journal of Captain G.F. Lyon of H.M.S. Hecla.... Imprint Soc, 1970. 1st ed. Ltd to 1950 numbered, signed by James A. Houston (illus). 1 plt, fldg map; prospectus laid in. VF in VF slipcase. *Oregon.* $75/£48

LYON, G.F. The Private Journal of Captain G.F. Lyon, of H.M.S. Hecla.... London: John Murray, 1824. 1st ed. xiii,468pp, fldg map; new eps. Mod 1/2 calf. VG. *Walcot.* $233/£150

LYON, G.F. The Private Journal of Captain G.F. Lyon...1821-1823. Barre: Imprint Society, 1970. One of 1950 numbered, signed by James A. Houston (illus). Frontis; fldg map. Cl-backed pict bds. Bkpl, else Fine in pub's slipcase. *Hermitage.* $125/£81

LYON, G.F. The Private Journal Of.... Barre: Imprint Soc, 1970. One of 1950. Signed by James A. Houston (illus). Fldg map. Cl backed bds. VG in slipcase. *High Latitude.* $70/£45

LYON, G.F. The Private Journal of...During the Recent Voyage of Discovery under Captain Parry 1821-1823. Barre, MA: Imprint Soc, 1970. 1/1950 numbered, signed by James A. Houston (illus). VG in bd slipcase. *Argosy.* $125/£81

LYON, H.M. Sardonics. Stuyvesant, 1909. 1st ed. Pict cl w/gold, orange stamping. Lt wear fr corner tips, spine extrems, else VG-. *Aronovitz.* $125/£81

LYON, WILLIAM S. Gardening in California. LA, 1904. 3rd rev ed. 8 b/w plts. Tipped-on photo fr cvr partially peeled, else VG. *Brooks.* $32/£21

LYONS, ARTHUR. The Dead Are Discreet. NY: Mason & Lipscomb, 1974. 1st ed. Fine in Fine dj. *Lame Duck.* $350/£226

LYONS, ARTHUR. Dead Ringer. Mason, 1977. 1st ed. Signed. Fine in Fine dj. *Murder.* $60/£39

LYONS, ARTHUR. The Killing Floor. NY: Mason Chartier, 1976. 1st ed. Spine slant; pg edges, cvrs lt soiled. NF dj. *Murder.* $175/£113

LYONS, ARTHUR. The Second Coming: Satanism in America. NY: Dodd, Mead, (1970). 1st ed, 1st bk. Fine in dj. *Antic Hay.* $225/£145

LYONS, SOPHIE. Why Crime Doesn't Pay. NY, (1913). Port. (Bkpls; extrems worn.) *King.* $25/£16

LYSAGHT, A.M. Joseph Banks in Newfoundland and Labrador, 1766. Univ of CA Press, 1971. Dj. *Edwards.* $132/£85

LYTLE, ANDREW NELSON. Bedford Forrest and His Critter Company. NY: Minton, Balch, 1931. 1st ed. VG (spine sunned; expertly recased). *Mcgowan.* $125/£81

LYTLE, ANDREW NELSON. Bedford Forrest and His Critter Company. NY: Minton, Balch & Co, 1931. 1st ed. Orig cl (spine sunned; expertly recased). VG. *Mcgowan.* $150/£97

LYTLE, ANDREW NELSON. The Long Night. Indianapolis: Bobbs-Merrill, (1936). 1st ed. Signed. Bkpl, o/w Fine in dj (sl used; internally mended). *Pharos.* $250/£161

LYTLE, ANDREW NELSON. The Velvet Horn. NY: McDowell-Obolensky, (1957). 1st ed. Signed. Fine in dj. *Pharos.* $95/£61

LYTTON, E. BULWER. The Caxtons. Edinburgh/London: Wm. Blackwood Sons, 1849. 1st ed. 3 vols. Comtemp 3/4 polished calf, gilt; marbled bds, eps, edges; double leather lables. Fine (bkpl). *Hartfield.* $295/£190

LYTTON, E. BULWER. A Strange Story. Boston: Gardner A. Fuller, 1862. 1st Amer ed. Frontis. Sl wear head, toe spine; nick endsheet; o/w NF. *Reese.* $85/£55

LYTTON, ROBERT. Personal and Literary Letters. Betty Balfour (ed). London: Longmans, Green, 1906. 1st ed. Each vol inscribed, presumably by ed. 2 vols. 7 plts; 1 facs. *Cox.* $31/£20

M

M'CLELLAN, R. GUY. Republicanism in America. SF: R.J. Trumbull, 1869. 1st ed. Deluxe copy, all engrs present. xii,665pp, 21 plts, guards, marbled eps. Full leather, black leather labels. NF. *Connolly.* $185/£119

M'CLURE, ROBERT, L.M. The Discovery of the North-West Passage by H.M.S. 'Investigator.' London: Longman, 1857. 2nd ed. xxxii,463pp + ads, fldg map (sl torn, repaired), 4 tinted litho plts (sl foxed). VG. *Walcot.* $279/£180

M'DIARMID, JOHN. The Scrap Book. Edinburgh: Oliver & Boyd, 1823-1824. 3rd ed. 2 vols. 512; 544pp. 19th cent 1/2 blue calf (sl worn) over marbled bds, gilt spine, teg. *Karmiole.* $125/£81

M'DOUGALL, GEORGE F. The Eventful Voyage of H.M. Discovery Ship Resolute...in Search of John Franklin.... London: Longman et al, 1857. 8vo. xl,530pp + 1pg ad, fldg map, 8 color plts. Blue emb cl (professionally rebacked w/orig spine laid on), gilt spine titles, cvr decs. (Foxing.) Arctic Biblio 10603 calls for frontis in addition to fldg map, 8 plts. However, illus list calls for only 8 plts; no copy offered for sale in last 10 yrs has had more than 8 plts. We believe this to be one of the rare cases in which the biblio is in error. *Parmer*. $850/£548

M'KEEVOR, THOMAS. A Voyage to Hudson's Bay, During the Summer of 1812. London: Richard Phillips, 1819. 1st ed. Issued in Philips' New Voyages & Travels, vol 2, #2. Frontis, 76pp, 5 plts. 1/2 leather, gilt-stamped morocco spine label. VG. *Oregon*. $450/£290

M'KEEVOR, THOMAS. A Voyage to Hudson's Bay, During the Summer of 1812. London: Richard Phillips, 1819. Issued in Phillips' New Voyages & Travels, Vol 2, #2. Frontis, 78pp, 5 plts; 79-100pp. VG (rebound). *Oregon*. $395/£255

M'KIE. JAMES. The Bibliography of Robert Burns, with...Notes.... Kilmarnock: James M'Kie, 1881. #248/600. Signed by ptr. Uncut (lt spotting 1st, last few leaves). Orig blue paper bds (spine relined w/cl, retaining orig paper spine). *D & D*. $195/£126

M'LEAN, JOHN. Notes of a Twenty-Five Years' Service in the Hudson's Bay Territory. London: Richard Bentley, 1849. 1st ed. 2 vols. 308; 328pp. Gilt-stamped spine. News clipping on reps vol 1. Spine edges worn, o/w Fine set. *Oregon*. $900/£581

M'LEOD, JOHN. Voyage of H.M.S. 'Alceste' Along the Coast of Corea to the Island of Lewchew.... London, 1818. 2nd ed. (x),323pp; port, 5 color aquatints. Orig bds, 1/2 calf w/new spine. Nice. *Lewis*. $186/£120

M'LEOD, JOHN. Voyage of His Majesty's Ship Alceste.... London: John Murray, 1818. 2nd ed. 323pp, 5 full-pg color plts. Contemp cl (rebound). VG- (lt foxing). *Blue Dragon*. $150/£97

M'LEOD, JOHN. Voyage of His Majesty's Ship Alceste.... London: John Murray, 1819. 3rd ed. vi,(ii),339pp, engr port (sl spotted), chart, 5 hand-colored aquatints. 1/2 calf, marbled bds (extrems sl rubbed, sm stain upper hinge), gilt. *Hollett*. $581/£375

M'MAHON, BERNARD. American Gardener's Calendar. Phila: T.P. M'Mahon, 1820. 4th ed. 618pp, fldg table. Contemp marbled paper over bds, 1/2 calf. Old dampstain 1st 50pp, lt foxing, calf rubbed, else VG. *Cahan*. $300/£194

M., M. Memoirs of the Foreign Legion. NY: Knopf, 1925. 1st ed. VG (bkpl; cvrs sl soiled). *Pharos*. $35/£23

MA, HO-T'IEN. Chinese Agent in Mongolia. John De Francis (trans). Balt: Johns Hopkins, 1949. Dj (chipped, browned). *Schoyer*. $45/£29

MAAS, JEREMY. Victorian Painters. NY, 1969. VG in dj. *Argosy*. $75/£48

MAASS, JOHN. The Gingerbread Age. NY: Rinehart, (1957). 1st ed. Lt cvr wear, else VG. *Bookpress*. $35/£23

MAASS, JOHN. The Victorian Home in America. NY: Hawthorne, (1972). 1st ed. Fine in dj (rubbed). *Bookpress*. $45/£29

MABBE, JAMES. The Rogue. London: Constable, 1924. Ltd to 1025. 4 vols. Buckram-backed bds (lib #'s spines), gilt. Teg, other uncut. Marginal blindstamps; accession stamp, o/w VG set. *Hollett*. $101/£65

MABEN. The Rainbow Bunnies. London/NY: Warne, (1943). 1st ed. Pict paper over bds. NF in pict dj (soiled). *Glenn*. $50/£32

MACALISTER, R.A. STEWART. Bible Side-Lights from the Mound of Gezer.... London: Hodder & Stoughton, (1906). (Lt bumped.) *Archaeologia*. $65/£42

MacANDREW, HUGH. Italian Drawings in the Museum of Fine Arts, Boston. Boston, 1983. Good in dj. *Washton*. $30/£19

MACARDLE, DOROTHY. Fantastic Summer. London, 1946. 1st British ed. VG in dj. *Madle*. $25/£16

MACARDLE, DOROTHY. The Unforseen. Doubleday, 1946. 1st ed. Fine in dj. *Madle*. $75/£48

MacARTHUR, ARTHUR. After the Afternoon. Appleton, 1941. Fine in dj. *Madle*. $50/£32

MACARTNEY, CLARENCE EDWARD. Mr. Lincoln's Admirals. NY, 1956. 1st ed. Map. VG + . *Pratt*. $25/£16

MACAULAY, JAMES. The Gothic Revival 1745-1845. London: Blackie, 1975. 1st ed. Mint in dj. *Hollett*. $116/£75

MACAULAY, KENNETH. The History of St. Kilda. Containing a Description of This Remarkable Island.... London: For T. Becket & P.A. DeHondt, 1764. Engr fldg frontis; 278pp + ads. Orig calf (upper cvr detached). Lt foxing. *Argosy*. $400/£258

MACAULAY, LORD. The History of England. NY: Harper Bros, 1879. 5 vols. VG + . *Bishop*. $50/£32

MACAULAY, LORD. Miscellaneous Works of Lord Macaulay. NY: Harper Bros, 1880. 5 vols. VG + . *Bishop*. $25/£16

MACAULAY, R. Orphan Island. Collins, 1924. 1st ed. Top edge dusty, else NF in VG + dj (lt dust soil). *Aronovitz*. $95/£61

MACAULAY, R.H.H. Trading into Hudson's Bay: A Narrative.... Winnipeg: Hudson's Bay Co, 1934. 1st ed. Map. VG- in stiff wraps. *Blue Dragon*. $45/£29

MACAULAY, ROSE. Fabled Shore. Hamish Hamilton, 1949. 1st Eng ed. Red cl. NF in dj (sl rubbed, nicked). *Dalian*. $54/£35

MACAULAY, ROSE. Fabled Shore. From the Pyrenees to Portugal. London: Hamish Hamilton, 1949. 1st Eng ed. Fine (top edge sl spotted) in dj (sl dusty; few nicks, sl creases). *Ulysses*. $85/£55

MACAULAY, ROSE. The Lee Shore. Hodder & Stoughton, 1912. 1st Eng ed. Grey cl. Inscrip, o/w VG. *Dalian*. $70/£45

MACAULAY, ROSE. Pleasure of Ruins. Weidenfeld & Nicolson, 1953. 1st Eng ed. Grn cl. VF in dj. *Dalian*. $116/£75

MACAULAY, ROSE. Potterism: A Tragi-Farcical Tract. London: W. Collins Sons, 1920. 1st ed. Mottled pink linen, gilt. Spine gilt oxidized; cl sl bubbled; o/w Very Nice. *Temple*. $33/£21

MACAULAY, ROSE. They Went to Portugal. Cape, 1946. 1st Eng ed. Grn cl. Inscrip, o/w VG in dj (sl nicked, tanned). *Dalian*. $54/£35

MACAULAY, ROSE. Three Days. London: Constable, 1919. 1st ed. Lt fox mks edges, o/w Fine in wrappers. *Reese*. $45/£29

MACAULAY, ROSE. The Two Blind Countries. Sidgwick & Jackson, 1914. 1st Eng ed. Grn cl (sl dusty; name). VG. *Dalian*. $54/£35

MACAULAY, ROSE. The Writings of E.M. Forster. Hogarth, 1938. 1st Eng ed. Blue cl. NF in dj (soiled). *Dalian*. $70/£45

MACAULAY, THOMAS BABINGTON. Biographies by Lord Macaulay Contributed to the Encylopaedia Britannica. Edinburgh: A&C Black, 1860. lvi (spotted),235pp. Full tan calf (sl scratched), gilt. *Hollett*. $70/£45

MACAULAY, THOMAS BABINGTON. Lays of Ancient Rome. London: Longman et al, 1842. 1st ed. 191pp; uncut. (Lt spotting.) Brn cl, stamped in blind, lettered in gold. VG. *Cox*. $116/£75

MACAULAY, THOMAS BABINGTON. The Works. London: Longmans, Green, 1898. Albany ed. Ltd lg paper ed of 250. 12 vols. Teg, uncut. VG (bkpls). *Hollett*. $426/£275

MacCANN, WILLIAM. Two Thousand Miles' Ride Through the Argentine Provinces. London: Smith, Elder, 1853. 1st ed. 2 vols. xiv,(ii),295,(1)imprint, 12 pub's list dated Jan 1853; x,(ii),323,(1)glossary. Half titles (early ink inscrip to one); fldg engr map; colored litho frontis; 2 sepia lithos each vol. Grn blind-stamped cl, gilt vignettes. VG (sl rubbed, faded edges, spine; short split head of spine vol 1). *Morrell*. $535/£345

MacCARTHY, DESMOND. Humanities. NY: OUP, 1954. 1st ed. Fine in dj. *Pharos*. $25/£16

MacCARTHY, DESMOND. Memories. NY: OUP, 1953. 1st ed. Fine in dj. *Pharos*. $30/£19

MacCARTHY, DESMOND. Theatre. London: MacGibbon & Kee, 1954. 1st ed. Fine in dj. *Pharos*. $30/£19

MacCLAREN, IAN. A Doctor of the Old School. NY, 1895. 1st ed. Gilt dec cl, gilt edges. VG. *Argosy*. $85/£55

MacCLURE, VICTOR. The Ark of the Covenant. Harper, 1924. 1st ed. VG. *Madle*. $50/£32

MacCLURE, VICTOR. The Crying Pig Murder. London: Harrap, 1929. 1st ed. VG (lt foxing) in Good dj. *Ming*. $31/£20

MacCORMACK, WILLIAM. Antiseptic Surgery: An Address Delivered at St. Thomas's Hospital With the Subsequent Debate.... London, 1880. 1st ed. 286pp. (Lib mk on spine.) *Fye*. $400/£258

MacCULLOCH, JOHN. An Essay on the Remittent and Intermittent Diseases, Including, Generically Marsh Fever and Neuralgia. Phila, 1830. 1st Amer ed. 474pp. Recent 1/4 leather; marbled bds. Good. *Fye*. $175/£113

MacCURDY, EDWARD (ed). The Notebooks of Leonardo Da Vinci. NY: Reynal & Hitchcock, 1938. 1st ed in English. 2 vols. Frontis, 31 plts; frontis, 31 plts. Partly uncut. Prelims lt foxed, djs browned, else VG in slipcase. *Bookpress*. $125/£81

MacDIARMID, HUGH. The Islands of Scotland. B.T. Batsford, 1939. 1st Eng ed. Purple cl. Fore-edge, prelims sl foxed, o/w NF in dj (frayed). *Dalian*. $85/£55

MacDIARMID, HUGH. A Kist of Whistles: New Poems. (Glasgow): William Maclellan, (1947). 1st ed. Name, else VG in dj (chip, short tear). *Godot*. $65/£42

MacDIARMID, HUGH. The Letters of Hugh MacDiarmid. Alan Bold (ed). Athens: Univ of GA, (1984). 1st ed, Amer issue. Fine in dj (sticker residue flap). *Reese*. $25/£16

MacDIARMID, HUGH. Penny Wheep. Edinburgh/London: William Blackwood, 1926. 1st ed. Med blue cl. Ink name, else Fine in NF dj. *Godot*. $150/£97

MacDIARMID, HUGH. To Circumjack Cencrastus or The Curly Snake. Edinburgh/London: William Blackwood, 1930. 1st ed. Dk blue cl stamped in gold. Ink name, eps lt foxed, else Fine in VG dj. *Godot*. $125/£81

MacDONALD, A.G. A Visit to America. Macmillan, 1935. 1st Eng ed. Blue cl. VF in NF dj. *Dalian*. $54/£35

MACDONALD, ALEXANDER K. In Search of El Dorado. London, 1906. 2nd imp. Frontis port. (Lt foxing; feps lt browned; bkpl; hinges cracked; sl rubbed, sm split lower joint.) *Edwards*. $39/£25

MACDONALD, ALEXANDER K. Picturesque Paraguay.... London: Charles H. Kelly, (1911). (Foxing.) *Petersfield*. $33/£21

MacDONALD, GEORGE. At the Back of the North Wind. Phila: David McKay, 1919. 1st thus ed. Lg 8vo. 8 full-pg color illus by Jessie Willcox Smith. Teg. Pict cl (spine dknd); pict label. VG+. *Book Adoption*. $175/£113

MacDONALD, GEORGE. Catalogue of Greek Coins in the Hunterian Collection. Univ of Glasgow, 1899-1905. 3 vols. 102 plts. Teg, rest uncut. (Ex-lib w/bkpls, ink stamps, #s; feps browned, lt spotting; hinges cracked, sl shaken; upper joint vol 1 splitting, rubbed.) *Edwards*. $310/£200

MacDONALD, GEORGE. Edmonton. Fort—House—Factory. Edmonton, 1959. 1st ed. Fldg map. VG. *Oregon*. $45/£29

MacDONALD, GEORGE. The Flight of the Shadow. NY: Appleton, 1891. 1st Amer ed. 298pp + 6pp ads. Blue cl stamped in white/silver/gold. Fine. *Godot*. $275/£177

MacDONALD, GEORGE. Fort Augustus—Edmonton. Northwest Trails and Traffic. Edmonton, 1954. 1st ed. Signed. Internally Fine (ex-lib, spine mks, plts removed; rough erasure fep). *Oregon*. $75/£48

MacDONALD, GEORGE. Paul Faber, Surgeon. Phila: Lippincott, 1879. 1st Amer ed. 202pp + 6pp ads. Dk brn cl, gold-stamped spine. Fine. *Godot*. $275/£177

MacDONALD, GEORGE. The Princess and Curdie. London: Blackie & Son, 1900. 1st ed thus. 8vo. 31 b/w dwgs by Helen Stratton. Turquoise cl, gilt spine. Good. *Reisler*. $225/£145

MacDONALD, GEORGE. The Princess and Curdie. Phila: David McKay, n.d. 8vo. 4 full-pg color plts by Gertrude Kay. Grn cl, color paste label. Good in color pict dj (lt edgewear). *Reisler*. $75/£48

MacDONALD, GEORGE. The Vicar's Daughter. Boston: Roberts Bros, 1872. 1st Amer ed. vi,390pp + 2pp ads. Grn cl stamped in gold. Short tears spine; lt edgewear; fr hinge cracked; name, else VG. *Godot*. $150/£97

MacDONALD, GEORGE. Wilfrid Cumbermede. NY: Scribner's, 1872. 1st Amer ed. x,498pp + 6pp ads, 14 plts (2 not listed correctly on contents pg). Grn dec cl. Name, 1872 date; rear hinge sl cracked, else Fine. *Godot*. $250/£161

MacDONALD, GEORGE. Wilfrid Cumbermede. Strahan, 1873. 2nd ed. Crimson cl. Cvrs mkd; staining lower tips 1st few pp, o/w VG. *Dalian*. $70/£45

MACDONALD, GREVILLE. The Sanity of William Blake. George Allen & Unwin, 1920. 1st Eng ed. Grey bds. Fine in dj (sl tanned, dusty, nicked). *Dalian*. $54/£35

MACDONALD, JAMES. Food from the Far West. NY: OJ, (1878). 1st Amer ed. xvi,331pp + 4pp ads. Gold/black-stamped pict cl (sl bumped; inscrip). *Dawson*. $200/£129

MacDONALD, JOHN D. Bright Orange for the Shroud. Greenwich: Fawcett, 1965. 1st ed: pb orig. NF. *Janus*. $35/£23

MacDONALD, JOHN D. Bright Orange for the Shroud. Phila: Lippincott, 1972. 1st US hb ed. Fine in bright dj. *Janus.* $250/£161

MacDONALD, JOHN D. Contrary Pleasure. NY: Appleton, Century, Crofts, 1954. 1st ed. Lt soiled, edges sl worn, else VG in dj (chipped, lt worn, 2 sm holes). *Murder.* $75/£48

MacDONALD, JOHN D. Darker Than Amber. Greenwich: Fawcett, 1966. 1st ed: pb orig. Fine w/no spine crease. *Janus.* $45/£29

MacDONALD, JOHN D. A Deadly Shade of Gold. Greenwich: Fawcett, 1965. 1st ed: pb orig. VG +. *Janus.* $20/£13

MacDONALD, JOHN D. A Deadly Shade of Gold. NY: Lippincott, 1974. 1st ed. Sm ink price corner fep. Binder's flaw: feps not wide enough, reps too wide, else Fine in dj (minor rubs upper corners). *Else Fine.* $150/£97

MacDONALD, JOHN D. A Deadly Shade of Gold. Phila: Lippincott, 1974. 1st US hb ed. Fine in NF dj (lt edgewear, closed tear). *Janus.* $200/£129

MacDONALD, JOHN D. The Deep Blue Good-by. Phila: Lippincott, (1975). 1st hb ed. Fine in dj (edges rubbed; sm tear). *Antic Hay.* $150/£97

MacDONALD, JOHN D. The Deep Blue Good-by. Phila: Lippincott, 1975. 1st separate US hb ed. Fine in Fine dj. *Janus.* $250/£161

MacDONALD, JOHN D. The Dreadful Lemon Sky. Phila: Lippincott, 1974. 1st ed. Fine in Fine dj (2 sm closed tears, crease). *Janus.* $75/£48

MacDONALD, JOHN D. The Girl in the Plain Brown Wrapper. Greenwich: Fawcett, 1968. 1st ed: pb orig. NF w/no spine crease. *Janus.* $45/£29

MacDONALD, JOHN D. The Green Ripper. NY: Lippincott, 1979. 1st ed. Few scratches fr panel, else Fine in dj. *Limestone.* $40/£26

MacDONALD, JOHN D. The House Guests. GC: Doubleday, 1965. 1st ed. Fine in VG + dj. *Janus.* $85/£55

MacDONALD, JOHN D. The Long Lavender Look. Greenwich: Fawcett, 1970. 1st ed: pb orig. Fine (lt spine crease). *Janus.* $35/£23

MacDONALD, JOHN D. The Long Lavender Look. Phila: Lippincott, 1972. 1st hb ed. Fine in NF dj (lt rubbed; lt edgewear). *Janus.* $150/£97

MacDONALD, JOHN D. Murder for the Bride. NY: Fawcett, 1951. 1st ed. Lt wear, but tight w/no spine crease. *Janus.* $45/£29

MacDONALD, JOHN D. Nightmare in Pink. Greenwich: Fawcett, 1964. 1st ed: pb orig. Fine w/no spine crease. *Janus.* $50/£32

MacDONALD, JOHN D. Nightmare in Pink. London: Robert Hale, 1966. 1st hb ed. Fine in dj (sl wear spine base). *Mordida.* $175/£113

MacDONALD, JOHN D. Nightmare in Pink. Phila: Lippincott, 1976. 1st Amer hb ed. VF in dj (price-clipped). *Mordida.* $165/£106

MacDONALD, JOHN D. One Fearful Yellow Eye. Greenwich: Fawcett, 1966. 1st ed: pb orig. NF w/no spine crease. *Janus.* $35/£23

MacDONALD, JOHN D. One Fearful Yellow Eye. Phila: Lippincott, 1977. 1st US hb ed. Fine in Fine dj. *Janus.* $225/£145

MacDONALD, JOHN D. Pale Gray for Guilt. Greenwich: Fawcett, 1968. 1st ed: pb orig. Fine (lines on top edge) w/no spine crease. *Janus.* $35/£23

MacDONALD, JOHN D. Please Write for Details. NY: S&S, 1959. 1st ed. Fine (pp edges browned) in dj (very lt wear). *Antic Hay.* $150/£97

MacDONALD, JOHN D. A Purple Place for Dying. Phila: Lippincott, 1976. 1st separate US hb ed. Fine in Fine dj. *Janus.* $225/£145

MacDONALD, JOHN D. The Quick Red Fox. Greenwich: Fawcett, 1964. 1st ed: pb orig. 3 sm inked letters on front; o/w unread w/no spine crease. *Janus.* $40/£26

MacDONALD, JOHN D. The Quick Red Fox. Lippincott, 1964. 1st US hb ed. Pp top edges sl soiled, else Fine in dj (sm rubbed spot). *Murder.* $175/£113

MacDONALD, JOHN D. The Quick Red Fox. Phila: Lippincott, 1974. 1st separate US hb ed. Fine in Fine dj (short, closed tears). *Janus.* $225/£145

MacDONALD, JOHN D. The Scarlet Ruse. London: Robert Hale, 1975. 1st hb ed. VF in dj. *Mordida.* $65/£42

MacDONALD, JOHN D. The Scarlet Ruse. Phila: Lippincott, 1980. 1st ed. Fine in dj. *Else Fine.* $200/£129

MacDONALD, JOHN D. The Scarlet Ruse. NY: Lippincott & Crowell, 1980. 1st US hb ed. Fine in Fine dj. *Janus.* $100/£65

MacDONALD, JOHN D. A Tan and Sandy Silence. Greenwich: Fawcett, 1972. 1st ed: pb orig. NF (dkng to pgs) w/ no spine crease. *Janus.* $30/£19

MacDONALD, JOHN D. A Tan and Sandy Silence. Phila: Lippincott, 1979. 1st Amer hb ed. Fine in dj (sl corner wear; lt rubbing). *Mordida.* $125/£81

MacDONALD, JOHN D. A Tan and Sandy Silence. Phila: Lippincott, 1979. 1st US hb ed. Fine in NF dj. *Janus.* $125/£81

MacDONALD, JOHN D. Wine of the Dreamers. NY: Greenberg, 1951. 1st ed. Fine in dj (sl dknd spine; rubbing fr panel; minor wear spine ends). *Mordida.* $150/£97

MacDONALD, JOHN D. Wine of the Dreamers. NY: Greenberg, 1951. 1st ed. Lt bumping upper fr corners, else Fine in dj (minor wear corners). *Else Fine.* $250/£161

MacDONALD, JOHN ROSS. (Pseud of Kenneth Millar.) Find a Victim. London: Cassell, 1955. 1st Eng ed. NF (sl spotting edges; name) in VG + dj. *Janus.* $35/£23

MacDONALD, JOHN. (Pseud of Kenneth Millar.) The Moving Target. London: Cassell, 1951. 1st UK ed. VG + in VG- dj (sl worn; top of spine, rear panel sl chipped). *Williams.* $194/£125

MACDONALD, JOHN. Rape, Offenders and Their Victims. Springfield, 1971. 1st ed. Good in dj. *Fye.* $75/£48

MACDONALD, MICHAEL. Mystical Bedlam: Madness, Anxiety...in 17th-Century England. Cambridge, 1981. 1st ed. Good in dj. *Fye.* $45/£29

MacDONALD, NORMAN. The Orchid Hunters. NY/Toronto, 1939. 1st ed. (Margins lt browned, ex-libris; lower hinge cracked; cl soiled.) *Edwards.* $28/£18

MacDONALD, PHILIP and A. BOYD CORRELL. The Dark Wheel. NY: William Morrow, 1948. 1st ed. Fine in dj (sl wear spine ends; lt soiled back panel). *Mordida.* $65/£42

MacDONALD, PHILIP. Death on My Left. NY: Crime Club, (1933). 1st Amer ed. Fine (spine top sl bumped). *Polyanthos.* $35/£23

MacDONALD, PHILIP. Persons Unknown. GC: DCC, 1931. 1st ed. Fine in dj (minor wear, sm chip rear spine corner). *Else Fine.* $95/£61

MacDONALD, PHILIP. Triple Jeopardy. GC: DCC, 1962. Omnibus ed. Owner's label fep; spotting top edge, o/w VG in dj (wear; closed tears). *Mordida.* $30/£19

MacDONALD, ROSE M.E. Then and Now in Dixie. Ginn, (c. 1933). 293pp; ep map. Good (some illus colored by owner). *Book Broker.* $15/£10

MacDONALD, ROSS. (Pseud of Kenneth Millar.) Black Money. NY: Knopf, 1966. 1st ed. NF in dj (price-clipped). *Janus.* $125/£81

MacDONALD, ROSS. (Pseud of Kenneth Millar.) The Doomsters. Cassell, 1958. 1st UK ed. VG (bds sl mked; label removed) in dj (sl worn; closed tears). *Williams.* $59/£38

MacDONALD, ROSS. (Pseud of Kenneth Millar.) The Far Side of the Dollar. NY: Knopf, 1965. 1st ed. Fine in VG dj (internal tape mends; minor color restoration; lt wear spine ends). *Mordida.* $85/£55

MacDONALD, ROSS. (Pseud of Kenneth Millar.) The Goodbye Look. NY: Knopf, 1969. 1st ed. Fine in VG + dj. *Janus.* $45/£29

MacDONALD, ROSS. (Pseud of Keneth Millar.) The Goodbye Look. London: Collins, 1969. 1st Eng ed. VG in dj. *Limestone.* $45/£29

MacDONALD, ROSS. (Pseud of Kenneth Millar.) The Instant Enemy. NY: Knopf, 1968. 1st ed. NF in NF dj. *Janus.* $75/£48

MacDONALD, ROSS. (Pseud of Kenneth Millar.) The Instant Enemy. NY: Knopf, 1968. 1st ed. Fine (lib label fr pastedown) in dj (crease inner fr flap). *Mordida.* $85/£55

MacDONALD, ROSS. The Instant Enemy. NY: Knopf, 1968. 1st ed. Fine in Fine dj. *Beasley.* $100/£65

MacDONALD, ROSS. (Pseud of Kenneth Millar.) The Name Is Archer. NY: Bantam, 1955. 1st ed: pb orig. NF w/no spine crease. *Janus.* $85/£55

MacDONALD, ROSS. (Pseud of Kenneth Millar.) On Crime Writing. Santa Barbara: Capra, 1973. 1st ed. VF in stiff paper cvrs. *Mordida.* $25/£16

MacDONALD, ROSS. (Pseud of Kenneth Millar.) On Crime Writing: The Writer as Detective Hero.... Santa Barbara: Capra Press, 1973. 1st ed, one of 250 numbered, signed. Fine; issued w/o dj. *Janus.* $150/£97

MacDONALD, ROSS. (Pseud of Kenneth Millar.) Self-Portrait. Capra, 1981. 1st ed. Fine in dj. *Stahr.* $25/£16

MacDONALD, ROSS. (Pseud of Kenneth Millar.) The Underground Man. NY: Knopf, 1971. 1st ed. Fine in Fine dj. *Janus.* $25/£16

MacDONALD, ROSS. (Pseud of Kenneth Millar.) The Underground Man. London: Collins, 1971. 1st Eng ed. Fine in dj. *Limestone.* $40/£26

MacDONALD, ROSS. (Pseud of Kenneth Millar.) The Zebra-Striped Hearse. NY: Knopf, 1962. 1st ed. Fine in VG + dj (spine lt tanned; lt chipping spine). *Lame Duck.* $150/£97

MACDONALD, W.A. A Farewell to Commander Byrd. NY: Coward-McCann, 1929. 1st ed. (Spine dknd.) Dj (lacks spine; soiled, chipped). *Parmer.* $65/£42

MacDONNELL, KEVIN. Eadweard Muybridge: The Man Who Invented the Moving Picture. Boston: Little, Brown, 1972. 1st ed. NF in VG dj (closed tears, tape repair). *Cahan.* $65/£42

MACE, AURELIA G. The Aletheia: Spirit of Truth. Farmington, ME: 1907. 2nd ed. 34 plts. Black cl. VG. *Petrilla.* $135/£87

MACE, JEAN. The History of a Mouthful of Bread. NY, 1868. 1st Amer ed. 398,(1)pp. (Sm stain few pg edges; edge-wear; lt spot rear cvr.) *Sutton.* $65/£42

MACE, JEAN. The History of a Mouthful of Bread: And Its Effect on the Organization of Men and Animals. NY, 1868. 1st Amer ed. 399pp. Good. *Fye.* $75/£48

MacEDWARD, LEACH (ed). The Book of Ballads. (Mt. Vernon): LEC, 1967. One of 1500 signed by Fritz Kredel (illus). Buckram-backed dec paper, paper spine label. VF in slipcase. *Pharos.* $75/£48

MACEWEN, WILLIAM. Pyogenic Infective Diseases of the Brain and Spinal Cord. Glasgow: Maclehose, 1893. xxv,354pp (pencil mks); uncut. Good (lt wear; recased, backstrip laid down). *Goodrich.* $695/£448

MACFALL, HALDANE. Aubrey Beardsley. London: John Lane, The Bodley Head, 1928. 1st ed. Buckram-backed bds, paper label (spare at end). Uncut. Good. *Cox.* $70/£45

MACFALL, HALDANE. The Book of Lovat Claude Fraser. London, 1923. 1st ed. Cl-backed dec bds. VG in dj. *Argosy.* $125/£81

MACFALL, HALDANE. The Wooings of Jezebel Pettyfer. Simpkin et al, reissue 1913. Yellow cl (sl mkd, faded). VG. *Dalian.* $39/£25

MacFARLANE, GWYN. Alexander Fleming. Cambridge, 1984. Good in dj. *Fye.* $25/£16

MacFIE, HARRY. Wasa-Wasa, a Tale of the Trials and Treasure in the Far North. Hans Westerlund (trans). NY: W.W. Norton, (1951). 1st ed. VG in VG dj. *Perier.* $30/£19

MACFIE, MATTHEW. Vancouver Island and British Columbia. London, 1865. Frontis, xxi,(3),574pp, 2 partially colored fldg maps. Contemp polished calf, spine gilt extra, leather label. Map split at fold; extrems rubbed, else Very Nice. *Reese.* $500/£323

MacGAHAN, J.A. The Turkish Autrocities in Bulgaria. London: Bradbury, Agnew, 1879. 1st ed. 94pp. (Worn; ex-lib.) Internally VG. *Worldwide.* $45/£29

MACGILLIVRAY, WILLIAM. A History of British Birds, Indigenous and Migratory. London, 1837-52. 5 vols. 26 plts, 435 engrs. Blind emb cl (sl worn; spines chipped; joints 3 vols splitting). *Edwards.* $155/£100

MACGILLIVRAY, WILLIAM. Lives of Eminent Zoologists from Aristotle to Linnaeus. Edinburgh, 1834. 2nd ed. 391pp; port. Orig cl, gilt. (Inscrips.) *Wheldon & Wesley.* $70/£45

MacGRATH, HAROLD. The Lure of the Mask. Indianapolis: Bobbs-Merrill, 1908. 1st ed. VG w/o dj. *Mordida.* $35/£23

MacGREGOR, JAMES G. Blankets and Beads, a History of the Saskatchewan River. Edmonton: Inst of Applied Art, 1949. 1st ed. Fine. *Oregon.* $50/£32

MacGREGOR, JESSIE. Gardens of Celebrities.... London: Hutchinson, (ca 1918). 20 color plts. (Lt wear.) *Quest.* $60/£39

MACGREGOR, MALCOLM. Mosquito Surveys: A Handbook for Anti-Malarial and Anti-Mosquito Field Workers. London, 1927. 1st ed. 3 maps. Good. *Fye.* $30/£19

MACHEN, ARTHUR (trans). The Fortunate Lovers. Twenty-Seven Novels of the Queen of Navarre.... London: Redway, 1887. 1st abridged ed, secondary binding. Engr frontis; teg. Blue cl (extrems worn; hinges cracking). *Reese.* $25/£16

MACHEN, ARTHUR. The Anatomy of Tobacco. Knopf, 1926. 1st US ed. VG in dj (sl chipped, worn). *Madle.* $75/£48

MACHEN, ARTHUR. The Bowmen and Other Legends of the War. London: Simpkin, Marshall, Hamilton, Kent, 1915. 1st Eng ed. VG in pict bds. *Antic Hay.* $45/£29

MACHEN, ARTHUR. The Bowmen. Putnam, 1915. VG. *Madle.* $35/£23

MACHEN, ARTHUR. The Chronicle of Clemendy. Privately ptd, 1923. One of 1050 numbered, signed. VG. *Madle.* $100/£65

MACHEN, ARTHUR. Dog and Duck. London: Cape, 1924. 1st ed. #528/900. VG in dj. *Limestone.* $95/£61

MACHEN, ARTHUR. Dr. Stiggins. NY: Knopf, 1925. 1st Amer ed. NF (name; sl foxing) in NF dj (sm chips). *Between The Covers.* $65/£42

MACHEN, ARTHUR. Fantastic Tales or The Way to Attain.... Carbonnek: Privately Ptd, 1923. Signed ltd ed of 1050 numbered. Paper-vellum spine, bds. NF in dj (sl wear; sunning). *Antic Hay.* $85/£55

MACHEN, ARTHUR. The Glorious Mystery. Vincent Starrett (ed). Chicago: Covici-McGee, 1924. 1st ed. Fine (spine dulled; corners sl rubbed). *Beasley.* $45/£29

MACHEN, ARTHUR. The Green Round. Sauk City: Arkham House, 1968. 1st Amer ed. VG in dj. *Argosy.* $35/£23

MACHEN, ARTHUR. The Green Round. Sauk City, WI: Arkham House, 1968. 1st US ed, one of 2058. Fine in dj. *Bernard.* $60/£39

MACHEN, ARTHUR. Hieroglyphics. London: Grant Richards, 1902. Signed. (Spine label dknd.) Leather/cl slipcase. *Schoyer.* $200/£129

MACHEN, ARTHUR. The House of Souls. Knopf, 1922. 1st ed. VG-. *Madle.* $60/£39

MACHEN, ARTHUR. The Memoirs of Jacques Casanova. London: Venetian Soc, 1929. 1st ed. Ltd to 550. 12 vols. Teg, rest uncut. Vellum. Fine (sunned, sl rubbed). *Polyanthos.* $250/£161

MACHEN, ARTHUR. Ornaments in Jade. NY: Knopf, 1924. 1st ed, ltd to 1000 signed. Blind-stamped black cl. Very Nice in pub's slipcase. *Cady.* $50/£32

MACHEN, ARTHUR. Ornaments in Jade. NY: Knopf, 1924. 1st ed. One of 1000 numbered, signed. Paper spine label dknd, else VG + . *Other Worlds.* $75/£48

MACHEN, ARTHUR. Things Near and Far. London: Martin Secker, 1923. 1st ed. Inscribed presentation. *Cox.* $39/£25

MACHETANZ, FREDERICK. On Arctic Ice. NY: Scribner's, (1940). 1st ed, 2nd? ptg (w/o an 'A' on copyright pg). 105pp. Pict cl. Fine in VG dj (lt wear). *Godot.* $50/£32

MACHETANZ, FREDERICK. Panuck, Eskimo Sled Dog. NY: Scribner's, (1939). 1st ed, 2nd? ptg (w/o 'A' on copyright pg). Signed. 95pp. Pict cl. Fine in VG dj (price-clipped). *Godot.* $65/£42

MACHIAVELLI, NICOLAS. The Works of the Famous Nicolas Machiavelli.... London: ptd for John Starkey, 1675. Folio. (xl),529,(16),(5 ad leaves)pp. (Tp remargined along inner border; final leaf tape-repaired; browned.) Recent 1/4 calf. Overall clean. *Goodrich.* $2,000/£1,290

MACILWAIN, GEORGE. Memoirs of John Abernethy, F.R.S. with a View of His Lectures.... NY, 1853. 1st Amer ed. 434pp. Good. *Fye.* $75/£48

MACINNES, COLIN. City of Spades. NY: Macmillan, 1958. 1st Amer ed. Chip, o/w VG in dj (sl rubbed; lt worn). *Hermitage.* $30/£19

MACINTOSH, JAMES. The Roman Law of Sale. Edinburgh: T. & T. Clark, 1892. Full prize calf, extra gilt. Sl rubbed, but Very Nice. *Boswell.* $275/£177

MACINTYRE, DONALD. U-Boat Killer. W.W. Norton, 1957. 1st ed. VG in VG dj. *Bishop.* $20/£13

MACKAIL, J.W. The Life of William Morris. London/NY/Bombay: Longmans, 1899. 1st ed. 2 vols. Gilt spines (sl dull vol 1). Ends rubbed. *Sadlon.* $65/£42

MACKAY, CHARLES. Memoirs of Extraordinary Popular Delusions.... London: Routledge, 1869. 2 vols in 1. vi,303; vi,322pp, edges, eps marbled. Full calf, gilt. VG set (label on pastedown). *Hollett.* $101/£65

MacKAY, DOUGLAS. The Honourable Company, a History of the Hudsons Bay Company. Toronto: McClelland & Stewart, (1936). Stated 1st ed. Pict ep. Fine in Bobbs Merrill dj. *Oregon.* $55/£35

MacKAY, DOUGLAS. The Honourable Company. Indianapolis, (1936). 1st ed. Frontis. (Worn; spine letters removed; rubber stamp tp.) *Heinoldt.* $25/£16

MACKAYE, H.S. The Panchronicon. Scribner's, 1904. 1st ed. Pict cvrs. VG. *Aronovitz.* $75/£48

MACKAYE, PERCY. Weathergoose—Woo. NY: Longmans, 1929. 1st ed. Fine in dj (chipped; spine sunned). *Beasley.* $35/£23

MACKE, AUGUSTE. Tunisian Watercolors and Drawings. NY: Abrams, (1969). VG in dj. *Argosy.* $85/£55

MacKEEVER, SAMUEL A. Glimpses of Gotham and City Characters. NY: National Police Gazette Office, (1880). Stated 2nd ed. 72pp, 8 plts, 2 illus ad leaves. VG in pink pict wraps. *Schoyer.* $100/£65

MACKELLAR, THOMAS. The American Printer: A Manual of Typography. Phila: Mackellar, Smiths & Jordan, 1882. 13th ed. (Lt wear; internal soiling.) *Glenn.* $100/£65

MACKENNA, F. SEVERNE. Cookworthy's Plymouth and Bristol Porcelain. Leigh-on-Sea, 1946. 1st ed. #162/500. 58 plts (9 color). Ink owner stamp. Dj (ragged w/loss). *Edwards.* $194/£125

MACKENZIE, ALEXANDER. Alexander Mackenzie's Voyage to the Pacific Ocean in 1793. Chicago, 1931. Lakeside Classic. Frontis port; fldg map. Dk red cl; gilt stamping, top. Very Nice (presentation card mtd on ep). *Bohling.* $60/£39

MacKENZIE, CECIL W. Donald MacKenzie, 'King of the Northwest.' LA: Ivan Deach, 1937. 1st ed. 4 plts. Exlib, o/w VG. *Oregon.* $45/£29

MACKENZIE, COMPTON. Extraordinary Women: Theme and Variations. London: Martin Secker, 1928. One of 2100. Top edge plum, others rough trimmed. Yellow buckram. Cvr edges sl dknd; eps lt foxed; o/w NF. *Temple.* $47/£30

MACKENZIE, COMPTON. For Sale. Doubleday, Doran, 1931. 1st Amer ed. VG + in VG dj. *Fine Books.* $35/£23

MACKENZIE, COMPTON. Greece in My Life. London: C&W, 1960. 1st ed. 1/2 tone frontis; 15 plts. Mottled blue cl, gilt. Fine in dj. *Temple.* $28/£18

MACKENZIE, COMPTON. Greek Memories. C&W, 1939. NF in VG+ dj. *Fine Books.* $50/£32

MACKENZIE, COMPTON. The House of Coalport 1750-1950. London, 1951. 15 color plts. Dj. *Petersfield.* $33/£21

MACKENZIE, COMPTON. My Life and Times Octave One 1883-1891. London: C&W, 1963. Signed. Dj (sl torn). *Petersfield.* $16/£10

MACKENZIE, COMPTON. My Life and Times Octave Two: 1891-1900. London: C&W, 1963. 1st ed. Frontis port, 6 plts. Top edge blue. Blue cl, gilt spine. Fine in dj. *Temple.* $23/£15

MACKENZIE, COMPTON. Our Street. Cassell, 1931. 1st Eng ed. Red cl (sl faded; fore-edge sl foxed). NF in dj (sl soiled, chipped). *Dalian.* $54/£35

MACKENZIE, COMPTON. The Seven Ages of Woman. London: Martin Secker, 1923. 1st issue, w/o Smith's 'refurbishment' sticker on fr cvr, spine of pt. Thomas, A14, erroneously recording very dk blue ruling, lettering, blocking, as black. Grey cl. Fine in dj (spine sl faded; short tear). *Temple.* $47/£30

MACKENZIE, COMPTON. Sinister Street. London: Martin Secker, 1913-14. 1st ed. 2 vols. Prelims, fore-edge lt foxed; spots vol 1; bumped, else VG set. *Cahan.* $65/£42

MACKENZIE, COMPTON. Sublime Tobacco. London, 1957. 1st ed. Dj (chipped, edges repaired, spine faded). *Edwards.* $31/£20

MACKENZIE, COMPTON. Sylvia and Michael. Martin Secker, 1919. 1st Eng ed. Blue cl. NF in dj (sl soiled, tanned, chipped). *Dalian.* $70/£45

MACKENZIE, COMPTON. West to North. London: C&W, 1940. Probable 1st issue, w/top edge brn. Lower edges uncut. Brn cl, gilt. Edges sl foxed, o/w Fine in dj (spine sl faded). *Temple.* $31/£20

MACKENZIE, COMPTON. West to North. D-M, 1941. 1st Amer ed. NF in VG+ dj. *Fine Books.* $25/£16

MACKENZIE, COMPTON. Whisky Galore. London: C&W, 1947. 1st ed. Foxing; fore-edge spotted; inscrip, o/w VG in dj (browned, spotted, chipped). *Virgo.* $39/£25

MACKENZIE, COMPTON. Whisky Galore. London: C&W, 1947. 1st ed. Top edge lake, rest uncut. Lake cl, gilt. Spine gilt sl dull, o/w Fine in dj (chip). *Temple.* $54/£35

MacKENZIE, F. The Men of Bastogne. NY, 1968. VG in VG dj. *Clark.* $27/£17

MACKENZIE, FAITH COMPTON. Mandolinata. London: Cope & Fenwick, 1931. 1st ed, ltd to 330 signed. Gilt-titled terra cotta buckram. Nice. *Cady.* $40/£26

MACKENZIE, G. HUNTER. A Practical Treatise on the Sputum with Special Reference to...Diseases of the Throat and Lungs. Edinburgh, 1886. 1st ed. 103pp. (Ex-lib; spine chipped.) *Fye.* $75/£48

MACKENZIE, GEORGE. The Institutions of the Law of Scotland. Edinburgh: For Thomas Broun, 1688. (12),408pp (contemp marginal notes). Mod calf, red morocco label. *Karmiole.* $300/£194

MACKENZIE, JAMES. Diseases of the Heart. NY: OUP, 1910. 2nd ed, Amer issue. VG (spine faded). *Glaser.* $125/£81

MACKENZIE, JAMES. The History of Health, and the Art of Preserving It. Edinburgh: William Gordon, 1759. 2nd ed. xii,436pp (lib stamp; lt foxing). Newly rebound in 1/2 morocco, marble bds. *Goodrich.* $395/£255

MACKENZIE, JAMES. Principles of Diagnosis and Treatment in Heart Affections. London, 1916. 1st ed. 26 figs. (Lt foxing.) *Whitehart.* $39/£25

MACKENZIE, JAMES. Principles of Diagnosis and Treatment in Heart Affections. London: Henry Frowde, 1917. 1st ed, 3rd imp. VG (sl foxing; bkpl). *Glaser.* $75/£48

MACKENZIE, JAMES. Symptoms and Their Interpretation. London: Shaw & Sons, 1909. 1st ed. VG (few spots spine; lib stamp). *Glaser.* $60/£39

MACKENZIE, KENNETH R.H. The Marvellous Adventures and Rare Conceits of Master Tull Owlglass. Boston: Ticknor and Fields, 1860. Frontis, (xxx),255pp; 7 hand-colored plts by Alfred Crowquill. Full red morocco, gilt; aeg. Felt-lined protective dj, cl slipcase. Fine. *Schoyer.* $225/£145

MACKENZIE, MORELL. Diphtheria; Its Nature and Treatment.... Phila, 1879. 1st Amer ed. 104pp. Good. *Fye.* $60/£39

MACKENZIE, MORELL. Hayfever and Paroxysmal Sneezing, Their Etiology and Treatment.... London, 1889. 5th ed. 96pp. Good. *Fye.* $75/£48

MACKENZIE, ROBERT HOLDEN. The Trafalgar Roll. London: G. Allen, 1913. (Few pp sl foxed; backstrip sl faded.) *Petersfield.* $23/£15

MACKENZIE, W.M. Pompeii. A&C Black, 1910. 1st ed. 20 color plts by Alberto Pisa, fldg map. Teg. Dec cl (spine sl chipped; ex-lib, ink stamps; feps foxed). *Edwards.* $43/£28

MACKENZIE, W.M. Pompeii. London: A&C Black, 1910. 1st ed. 20 color plts. (Sl rubbed.) *Hollett.* $54/£35

MACKENZIE. WILLIAM. A Practical Treatise on the Diseases of the Eye. Phila, 1855. 1027pp. Leather. Good. *Fye.* $100/£65

MACKINDER, H.J. The Rhine. London, 1908. 1st ed. 54 color plts, 2 fldg maps, 4 line maps. Teg. Gilt vignette device. (Lt browning; feps browned; spine chipped, faded; lower joint partly split.) *Edwards.* $40/£26

MACKINNON, FRANK DOUGLAS. Inner Temple Papers. London: Stevens & Sons, 1948. (Sl rubbed.) *Boswell.* $50/£32

MACKINNON, WILLIAM ALEXANDER. On the Rise, Progress and Present Stage of Public Opinion. Saunders & Otley, 1828. 2nd ed. x,343pp. Contemp diced calf gilt. *Hill.* $101/£65

MACKLEY, GEORGE. Monica Poole, Wood Engraver. Graham Williams (ed). London: Florin, 1984. #237/300 signed by Poole. 20 wood engrs. *Petersfield.* $70/£45

MACKLIN, HERBERT W. The Brasses of England. London: Methuen, 1928. 4th ed. Red gilt cl (mkd, faded; spine snagged, repaired). *Hollett.* $39/£25

MACKWORTH, CECILY. The Destiny of Isabelle Eberhardt. London: Routledge & Kegan Paul, (1951). 1st ed. VG in dj (sl worn). *Second Life.* $35/£23

MACKWORTH-PRAED, C.W. and C.H.B. GRANT. Birds of Eastern and North Eastern Africa. London, 1957-60. 2nd ed. 2 vols. 96 color, 19 b/w plts. Djs (ragged). *Edwards.* $85/£55

MACLAGAN, ERIC. Catalogue of Italian Plaquettes; Victoria and Albert Museum. London: Bd of Education, 1924. 16 plts. Fine. *Europa.* $59/£38

MACLAGAN, T.J. The Germ Theory Applied to the Explanation of the Phenomena of Disease. London, 1876. 1st ed. 258pp. (Tp, prelim leaves stained.) *Fye.* $125/£81

MACLAGAN, T.J. Rheumatism. NY: Wood, 1886. 'Wood Library Edition.' viii,277pp. Good. *Goodrich.* $95/£61

MACLAY, EDGAR STANTON. A History of American Privateers. NY, 1899. 1st ed. xl,519pp, 14 plts. Dec cl (sl stain lower joint). *Lefkowicz.* $110/£71

MACLAY, EDGAR STANTON. A History of the United States Navy from 1775 to 1893. NY: D. Appleton, 1894. 1st ed. 2 vols. xvi,640pp, 29 plts; xxxii,577,(1 blank, 4 ads)pp, 17 plts. Orig cl (rubbed; inner hinges tender). *Lefkowicz.* $50/£32

MacLEAN, A.D. (ed). Winter's Tales 12. NY: St. Martin's Press, 1966. 1st ed. Fine in NF illus dj. *Cahan.* $20/£13

MacLEAN, ALISTAIR. Captain Cook. Collins, 1972. 1st Eng ed. Blue cl. VF in dj (price-clipped). *Dalian.* $39/£25

MacLEAN, ALISTAIR. The Guns of Navarone. GC: Doubleday, 1957. 1st ed. VG in VG- dj (extrems worn; lt soiled). *Revere.* $35/£23

MacLEAN, ALISTAIR. HMS Ulysses. London: Collins, 1955. 1st Eng ed, 1st bk. NF in dj (lt chipped). *Glenn.* $95/£61

MacLEAN, ALISTAIR. HMS Ulysses. London: Collins, 1955. 1st UK ed, 1st bk. Fine in VG dj. *Lewton.* $23/£15

MacLEAN, ALISTAIR. The Last Frontier. London: Collins, 1959. 1st UK ed. VG (sl foxing) in dj. *Williams.* $23/£15

MacLEAN, ALISTAIR. Lawrence of Arabia. NY: Random House, 1962. 1st ed. NF. *Great Epic.* $15/£10

MacLEAN, ALISTAIR. Night Without End. London: Collins, 1960. 1st UK ed. NF in dj (sm tear). *Williams.* $22/£14

MacLEAN, ALISTAIR. Partisans. London: Collins, 1982. 1st ed. Fine in dj. *Silver Door.* $30/£19

MacLEAN, ALISTAIR. River of Death. Collins, 1981. 1st issue, dated on recto/verso title leaf. Grn bds, gilt. Corners sl bumped, o/w Fine in dj. *Temple.* $19/£12

MacLEAN, ALISTAIR. South by Java Head. London: Collins, 1958. 1st ed. Fine in dj (minor edgewear). *Else Fine.* $85/£55

MACLEAN, CHARLES. Practical Illustrations of the Progress of Medical Improvement, for the Last Thirty Years.... London, 1818. 1st ed. 236pp. Recent 1/4 leather; marbled bds; new eps. *Fye.* $250/£161

MacLEAN, DAVID G. (ed). Prisoner of the Rebels in Texas. The Civil War Narrative of Aaron T. Sutton.... Decatur, IN, 1978. Fine in dj. *Hayman.* $25/£16

MacLEAN, J.P. History of the Island of Mull. Vol 1: Greenville, OH, 1923; Vol 2: San Mateo, CA, 1925. Ltd eds. Rubbed, lt dampstain edges of few leaves vol 1; lt dampstain through pg60 vol 2, else VG set. *Cahan.* $60/£39

MacLEAN, J.P. The Mound Builders.... Cincinnati: Robert Clarke, 1879. 1st ed. 234pp + 3pp ads, fldg map. Burgundy cl, gilt. Fine. *Karmiole.* $65/£42

MACLEAN, NORMAN. Casey Stengel. Drake, 1976. 1st ed. Fine in VG + dj. *Plapinger.* $30/£19

MACLEAN, NORMAN. A River Runs Through It and Other Stories. Chicago/London: Univ of Chicago Press, (1976). 1st ed, 1st bk. Fine in VG + dj (price-clipped; spine sl faded). *Bernard.* $700/£452

MACLEAN, NORMAN. A River Runs Through It and Other Stories. Chicago, (1976). 1st ed. Nice in dj (sl used; sl tear rear panel top; creases.) *King.* $500/£323

MACLEAN, NORMAN. Young Men and Fire. Univ of Chicago Press, 1992. 1st ed, 1st ptg. NF in NF dj. *Bishop.* $25/£16

MACLEHOSE, JAMES. The Glasgow University Press 1638-1931... Scottish Printing in the Last Three Hundred Years. Glasgow, 1931. 7 illus (1 fldg). VG. *Argosy.* $125/£81

MacLEISH, ARCHIBALD. Air Raid. A Verse Play for Radio. London: Bodley Head, 1939. 1st ed. Fine in pict dj. *Patterson.* $70/£45

MacLEISH, ARCHIBALD. Before March. NY: Knopf, (1932). 1st ed. #3 of Borzoi Chap Books series. VG (wear, tear) in sewn ptd wraps. *Antic Hay.* $15/£10

MacLEISH, ARCHIBALD. A Continuing Journey. Boston: Houghton Mifflin, 1968. 1st ed. VG in VG dj (spine ends worn). *Revere.* $20/£13

MacLEISH, ARCHIBALD. An Evening's Journey to Conway, Massachusetts. (Conway, 1967.) 1st ed. Fine in sewn wrappers. *Pharos.* $30/£19

MacLEISH, ARCHIBALD. Frescoes for Mr. Rockefeller's City. NY: John Day, 1933. 1st ed. Fine in wrappers. *Pharos.* $60/£39

MacLEISH, ARCHIBALD. The Hamlet of Archibald MacLeish. Boston: Houghton, Mifflin, (1928). 1st ed. Fine in dj (sl used). *Pharos.* $95/£61

MacLEISH, ARCHIBALD. The Happy Marriage and Other Poems. Boston, 1924. Spine sunned, o/w NF. *Polyanthos.* $60/£39

MacLEISH, ARCHIBALD. Herakles. Boston: Houghton, Mifflin, 1967. 1st ed. Fine in dj. *Antic Hay.* $25/£16

MacLEISH, ARCHIBALD. J.B.: A Play in Verse. London: Secker & Warburg, 1959. 1st Eng ed. NF (eps browning) in dj (wear; foxing). *Antic Hay.* $17/£11

MacLEISH, ARCHIBALD. Nobodaddy. Cambridge: Dunster House, 1926. Ltd to 700. Dec black cl. VG. *Antic Hay.* $75/£48

MacLEISH, ARCHIBALD. Panic: A Play in Verse. Boston: Houghton, Mifflin, 1935. 1st ed. Signed. NF in dj (shallow chip across top panel; other tiny chips). *Antic Hay.* $125/£81

MacLEISH, ARCHIBALD. The Pot of Earth. Boston: Houghton-Mifflin, 1925. 1st ed. VG (lacks dj). *Pharos.* $35/£23

MacLEISH, ARCHIBALD. Streets in the Moon. Boston, (1926). 1st Amer ed. Fine (spine sl sunned, extrems sl rubbed). *Polyanthos.* $25/£16

MacLEOD, CHARLOTTE. Next Door to Danger. NY: Avalon Books, 1st ed. Signed. Fine in NF dj. *Janus.* $200/£129

MacLEOD, GEORGE H.B. Notes on the Surgery of the War in the Crimea, with Remarks on the Treatment of Gunshot Wounds. Phila, 1862. 1st Amer ed. 403pp. Orig cl (worn, backstrip sl chipped; sig). *Argosy.* $100/£65

MACLEOD, NORMAN. German Lyric Poetry. Hogarth Press, 1930. 1st ed. Spine sl dull, o/w VG. *Words Etc.* $23/£15

MACLEOD, RODERICK. On Rheumatism in Its Various Forms, and on the Affections of Internal Organs.... London, 1842. 1st ed. 164pp. (Ex-lib.) Fye. $250/£161

MACLISE, DANIEL. A Gallery of Illustrious Literary Characters. William Bates (ed). London: C&W, 1873. x,239pp (upper joint cracked), gilt. Hollett. $116/£75

MacMICHEAL, WILLIAM. The Gold-Headed Cane. London: Murray, 1828. 267pp. Uncut. (Bds rebacked, orig label.) Goodrich. $150/£97

MacMICHEAL, WILLIAM. The Gold-Headed Cane. NY: Hoeber, 1925. Later rptg. Nice. Goodrich. $35/£23

MacMICHEAL, WILLIAM. Lives of British Physicians. London, 1830. 341pp; 4 engr plts. (Bds sl rubbed, worn.) Goodrich. $75/£48

MacMILLAN, D. and H.M. JONES (eds). Plays of the Restoration and Eighteenth Century.... London: Allen & Unwin, 1931. VG in dj (sl worn, soiled). Petersfield. $50/£32

MACMILLAN, DONALD B. Etah and Beyond or Life within Twelve Degrees of the Pole. Boston: Houghton Mifflin, 1927. 1st ed. Frontis, map. Blue cl over bds. sl shelf wear, else VG. Parmer. $75/£48

MACMILLAN, DONALD B. Four Years in the White North. Boston: Hale, Cushman & Flint, 1933. 3rd ptg. Fine in orig dj. High Latitude. $65/£42

MacNALTY, A. SALISBURY. A Book of Crimes. London: Elkin Mathews & Marrot, 1929. 1st ed. 8 plts. Red/black cl. VG. Weber. $45/£29

MacNEICE, LOUIS. The Burning Perch. London: Faber, (1963). 1st ed. VG in dj (spine sl faded). Houle. $65/£42

MacNEICE, LOUIS. The Burning Perch. Faber, 1963. 1st ed. Fine in dj (sl faded). Whiteson. $23/£15

MacNEICE, LOUIS. The Earth Compels. Faber, 1938. 1st ed. VG in dj (spotted; stain). Poetry. $39/£25

MacNEICE, LOUIS. Holes in the Sky. NY, 1948. 1st Amer ed. Fine in dj (sunned, sm tears, lt soiled). Polyanthos. $30/£19

MacNEICE, LOUIS. Holes in the Sky: Poems 1944-1947. NY: Random House, (1949). 1st Amer ed. Dec bds. NF in dj (edge tears). Sadlon. $25/£16

MacNEICE, LOUIS. Holes in the Sky: Poems 1944-1947. Faber, 1948. 1st ed. VG in dj (soiled, worn). Poetry. $15/£10

MacNEICE, LOUIS. The Other Wing. London: Faber & Faber, 1954. 1st ed. Michael Ayrton (illus). Fine in blue wrappers, orig yellow envelope (sl faded). Heller. $45/£29

MacNEICE, LOUIS. Out of the Picture. Faber & Faber, 1937. 1st Eng ed. Brn cl. Fine in dj (repair upper cvr). Dalian. $132/£85

MacNEICE, LOUIS. Plant and Phantom. Faber, 1941. 1st ed. NF in dj (defective). Poetry. $31/£20

MacNEICE, LOUIS. Springboard. Poems 1941-1944. London, (1944). 1st ed. VG in dj. Argosy. $60/£39

MacNEICE, LOUIS. Visitations. Faber, 1957. 1st ed. Fine in Fine dj. Whiteson. $23/£15

MACNISH, ROBERT. An Introduction to Phrenology, in the Form of Question and Answer.... Boston, 1836. 1st Amer ed. 135pp. Good. Fye. $75/£48

MACNUTT, J. SCOTT. A Manual for Health Officers. NY, 1915. Good. Fye. $100/£65

MACOMB, J.N. Report of the Exploring Expedition from Santa Fe, New Mexico to the Junction of the Grand and Green Rivers...in 1859.... Washington: Engineer Dept, US Army, 1876. viii,152pp, 22 plts (11 chromolithos). Cl (spine sunned). Dawson. $600/£387

MACON, T.J. Life Gleanings. Richmond, VA: W.H. Adams, 1913. 1st ed. VG + . Chapel Hill. $75/£48

MACON, T.J. Reminiscences of the First Company of Richmond Howitzers. Richmond: Whittet & Shepperson, (ca 1909). 1st ed. Grey cl, photo centerpiece. Lt silverfishing; bumped, name, else VG. Chapel Hill. $250/£161

MACOUN, JAMES M. A List of the Plants of the Pribilof Islands.... Washington, 1899. 29pp, 8 plts. Wrappers (chipped). Brooks. $30/£19

MACOUN, JOHN and JAMES M. Catalogue of Canadian Birds. Ottawa, 1909. Orig ptd wrappers. Ginsberg. $75/£48

MACPHERSON, JAMES. The History of Great Britain...to the Accession of the House of Hanover. London: Strahan & Cadell, 1776. 2nd ed. 2 vols. Engr port (browned). Contemp sprinkled calf (joints mended; labels chipped). Argosy. $200/£129

MacQUITTY, WILLIAM. Abu Simbel. NY: Putnam's, (1965). Good in dj (tattered). Archaeologia. $35/£23

MACQUOID, PERCY and RALPH EDWARDS. Dictionary of English Furniture, from the Middle Ages to the Late Georgian Period. London: Country Life, 1924-27. 3 vols. (Upper joint vol 3 splitting.) Argosy. $350/£226

MACQUOID, PERCY. A History of English Furniture. London/NY, 1906. Teg, rest uncut. (Lt spotting, margins thumbed; worn; lower hinge cracked). Edwards. $78/£50

MACQUOID, PERCY. A History of English Furniture. London: Lawrence & Bullen, 1938. 1st ed. 4 vols. 60 color plts. VG in maroon buckram, beveled bds. Cox. $388/£250

MACY, W.H. There She Blows! Boston/NY: Lee & Shepard/Charles T. Dillingham, 1877. 1st ed. 320,(7 ads),pp, 4 plts. Orig pict cl (neatly recased, new eps). Howes M 196. Lefkowicz. $150/£97

Madame Jane, Junk and Joe. A Novel. (By Mary Bornemann). SF: A.L. Bancroft, 1876. 1st ed. 539pp. Gilt cl (shabby, soiled, nicked). Reese. $50/£32

MADAN, FALCONER. The Early Oxford Press. OUP, 1895. viii + (iii) + 365pp (feps lt browned), 7 plts. (Extrems rubbed, spine discolored.) Edwards. $93/£60

MADDEN, DAVID. The Beautiful Greed. Random House, 1961. 1st ed. Fine in dj (dknd spine). Stahr. $45/£29

MADDEN, HENRY MILLER. Xantus. Hungarian Naturalist in the Pioneer West. Palo Alto: Books of the West, 1949. 1st ed. Frontis; 6 plts. Orange cl; gilt. Good in dj (bit soiled). Karmiole. $40/£26

MADDEN, R.R. Shrines and Sepulchres of the Old and New World. London: T.C. Newby, 1851. 2 vols. Litho tps, xii,562; (ii),692pp, 5 lithos (2 tinted). Lavender blind-stamped cl (spines faded; pockets removed). Schoyer. $100/£65

MADDOCK, HENRY. A Treatise on the Principles and Practice of the High Court of Chancery. Hartford: Oliver D. Cooke, 1827. 3rd Amer ed. 2 vols. Contemp sheep (worn, rubbed; foxing); still Sound set. Boswell. $150/£97

MADDOX, ERNEST. Tests and Studies of the Ocular Muscles. Bristol, 1898. 1st ed. 427pp. Good. Fye. $100/£65

MADDOX, JOHN LEE. The Medicine Man. NY: Macmillan, 1923. Errata. Good. *Lien.* $75/£48

MADEIRA, P. Hunting in British East Africa. PA, 1909. Pull-out rear pocket maps. Orig cl (recased). *Trophy Room.* $350/£226

MADGE, CHARLES and TOM HARRISSON. Britain by Mass-Observation. Harmondsworth: Penguin, 1939. Pb orig. VG (pencil marginalia) in dj. *Sclanders.* $16/£10

MADOX, RICHARD. An Elizabethan in 1582. Elizabeth Story Donno (ed). London: Hakluyt Soc, 1976. 1st ed. 19 plts (1 fldg). Blue cl, gilt. Good in dj. *Karmiole.* $30/£19

MAETERLINCK, MAURICE. The Blue Bird. NY: Dodd, Mead, 1920. F. Cayley Robinson (illus). Deluxe ed. Pict cl, gilt. NF. *Sadlon.* $115/£74

MAETERLINCK, MAURICE. The Life of the Bee. NY: Dodd, Mead, 1912. 1st ed. 13 mtd color plts by Edward J. Detmold. Dec gilt grn cl (extrems sl rubbed, cl soiled); teg. *Karmiole.* $50/£32

MAGER, HENRI. Water Diviners and Their Methods. London, 1931. 8 plts. *Edwards.* $54/£35

Magic Books from Mexico. Harmondsworth: King Penguin Books, 1953. 1st ed. 16 color plts. Color pict bds. NF in color pict dj. *Limestone.* $65/£42

Magician's Own Book. NY, (1857). 362pp. Gilt-stamped pict cl (extrems heavily frayed, holes in spine). *King.* $250/£161

MAGINLEY, C.J. Historic Models of Early America and How to Make Them. Harcourt Brace, 1947. 1st ed. VG. *Bishop.* $22/£14

MAGINNIS, ARTHUR J. The Atlantic Ferry, Its Ships, Men and Working. London, 1892. xviii,304pp + 40pp ads (marginal browning). Gilt illus upper bd (spine sl rubbed; upper hinge cracked). *Edwards.* $116/£75

MAGNER, D. The New System of Educating Horses. Buffalo: Warren, Johnson, 1872. 10th ed. 208pp. New cl. *Schoyer.* $50/£32

MAGNONE, GUIDO. The West Face. J.F. Burke (trans). London: Museum Press, 1955. 1st Eng ed. (Cl fault across bds; spine faded; feps browned.) *Hollett.* $31/£20

MAGNUS, HUGO. Superstition in Medicine. J.L. Salinger (trans). NY, 1905. 1st ed in English. Plt. VG. *Argosy.* $100/£65

MAGNUS, HUGO. Superstition in Medicine. NY, 1908. 1st Eng trans. Good. *Fye.* $50/£32

MAGOFFIN, SUSAN SHELBY. Down the Santa Fe Trail and into Mexico. New Haven: Yale Univ Press, 1926. Frontis, 6 plts, fldg map. Blue cl. VG (bkpl, sm sticker; sl rubbed). Howes M 211. *Parmer.* $125/£81

MAGOUN, F. ALEXANDER. The Frigate Constitution and Other Historic Ships. Salem: Marine Research Soc Pub 16, 1928. 1st ed. 30 plts, 16 plans. Dj (worn). Howes M 212. *Lefkowicz.* $250/£161

MAGRIEL, PAUL (ed). Pavlova. An Illustrated Monograph. NY: Holt, (1947). 1st ed. Fine in dj (lt edgeworn). *Reese.* $45/£29

MAGURN, RUTH SAUNDERS. The Letters of Peter Paul Rubens. Cambridge, 1955. 2nd ptg, 1971. 20 plts. Good. *Washton.* $40/£26

MAHAN, ALFRED THAYER. Admiral Farragut. NY: Appleton, (1892). 1st ed. viii,333,(1,blank,10 ads)pp; 6 plts. (Cl rubbed.) *Lefkowicz.* $75/£48

MAHAN, ALFRED THAYER. Admiral Farragut. NY: D. Appleton, 1897. 333,(10)pp. NF. *Mcgowan.* $75/£48

MAHAN, ALFRED THAYER. The Life of Nelson. London, 1899. 2nd ed. Frontis port, xix,764pp; 11 other plts, maps. Teg. Blue crushed morocco (rebound, spine sunned). VG. *Edwards.* $70/£45

MAHAN, ALFRED THAYER. The Life of Nelson: The Embodiment of Sea Power of Great Britain. Boston, 1897. 1st ed. 2 vols. (xxviii),454; xvi,427pp. NF set (sm tear spine vol 1). *Lefkowicz.* $125/£81

MAHONEY, BERTHA E. et al (comp). Illustrators of Children's Books 1744-1945. Boston, 1947. Ex-lib. Mint. *Argosy.* $250/£161

MAHONY, BERTHA E. and ELINOR WHITNEY (comps). Realms of Gold in Children's Books. GC: Doubleday, Doran, (1929). 8vo. Color frontis, xv,796pp. Blue cl. Fine in dj. *Weber.* $50/£32

MAILER, NORMAN. Advertisements for Myself. NY: Putnam, (1959). 1st ed. Fine in dj (lt soiled, edgeworn). *Reese.* $60/£39

MAILER, NORMAN. Advertisements for Myself. NY: Putnam's, 1959. 1st ed. VG in VG dj. *Revere.* $40/£26

MAILER, NORMAN. An American Dream. (London): Deutsch, (1965). 1st British ed. Sm stain top edge, else Fine in NF dj. *Reese.* $25/£16

MAILER, NORMAN. An American Dream. NY, 1965. 1st ed. Blue cl. Good in dj (chipped, torn, inner tape repair bleeding through). *King.* $35/£23

MAILER, NORMAN. Ancient Evenings. Boston: Little, Brown, 1983. 1st ed. One of 350 numbered, signed. Fine in red cl-cvrd slipcase. *Lame Duck.* $250/£161

MAILER, NORMAN. Barbary Shore. NY, (1951). 1st ed (in red/black/white dj). Cvrs spotted, else Good in dj (torn, chip panel). *King.* $125/£81

MAILER, NORMAN. Barbary Shore. NY: Rinehart, (1951). 1st ed. NF in grn/black dj (lt edgeworn). *Reese.* $60/£39

MAILER, NORMAN. Barbary Shore. NY: Rinehart, 1951. 1st ed. VG- (edgewear) in VG- dj (chipped, worn, inside tape repair). *Revere.* $75/£48

MAILER, NORMAN. Barbary Shore. London: Cape, 1952. 1st UK ed. VG in dj (sl worn; strengthened). *Williams.* $28/£18

MAILER, NORMAN. Cannibals and Christians. NY: Dial Press, 1966. 1st ed. VG in VG dj. *Revere.* $25/£16

MAILER, NORMAN. Cannibals and Christians. Dial Press, 1966. 1st ed. Apparent 1st issue w/full color photo frontis. Fine in VG + dj (short tears). *Fine Books.* $35/£23

MAILER, NORMAN. Deaths for the Ladies (and Other Disasters). London: Deutsch, 1982. 1st ed. Pb orig. Wear to spine, top edge dusty; o/w NF in wrappers. *Rees.* $23/£15

MAILER, NORMAN. Existential Errands. Boston, 1972. 1st Amer ed. Fine in dj. *Polyanthos.* $40/£26

MAILER, NORMAN. The Faith of Graffiti. NY, 1974. One of 300 numbered. Signed by author, Mervyn Kurlansky & Jon Naar. Fine in Fine box. *Polyanthos.* $150/£97

MAILER, NORMAN. The Faith of Graffiti. NY: Praeger, 1974. Signed ltd ed of 350. Imitation leather bds. John Naar (photos). Fine in slipcase. *Antic Hay.* $150/£97

MAILER, NORMAN. The Fight. Boston: Little Brown, 1975. 1st ed. NF in NF dj (clip). *Revere.* $25/£16

MAILER, NORMAN. A Fragment from Vietnam. (Helsinki): Eurographica, 1985. One of 350 signed, dated. Fine in card cvrs in dj as issued. *Williams.* $74/£48

MAILER, NORMAN. Harlot's Ghost. NY: Random House, (1991). 1st ed. Fine in dj. *Antic Hay*. $30/£19

MAILER, NORMAN. The Last Night. NY: Targ Editions, 1984. 1st ed. One of 250 signed. Fine. *Juvelis*. $90/£58

MAILER, NORMAN. The Last Night. NY: Targ Editions, 1984. Signed ed ltd to 250. Fine. *Karmiole*. $100/£65

MAILER, NORMAN. Miami and the Siege of Chicago. NY/Cleveland: World, (1968). 1st clothbound ed. Fine in VG dj (lt rubbed, sm sticker mk). *Reese*. $40/£26

MAILER, NORMAN. Of a Small and Modest Malignancy, Wicked and Bristling with Dots. Northridge: Lord John, 1980. 1st ed. One of 300 numbered, signed. Cl, marbled bds. Fine in slipcase. *Reese*. $75/£48

MAILER, NORMAN. Pieces and Pontifications. Boston: Little, Brown, (1982). 1st ed. Fine in dj (sl nick). *Reese*. $20/£13

MAILER, NORMAN. St. George and the Godfather. NY: Arbor House, (1972). 1st ed. Fine in dj. *Godot*. $45/£29

MAILER, NORMAN. Tough Guys Don't Dance. PA: Franklin Lib, 1984. 1st Amer ed. Signed. Aeg. Full leather, gilt. Fine. *Polyanthos*. $45/£29

MAILER, NORMAN. Why Are We in Vietnam? NY, 1967. 1st Amer ed. Fine (spine top sl rubbed) in Fine dj. *Polyanthos*. $25/£16

MAILER, NORMAN. Why Are We in Vietnam? Weidenfeld & Nicolson, 1969. 1st Eng ed. Black cl. Fine in dj. *Dalian*. $54/£35

MAILS, THOMAS E. Dog Soldiers, Bear Men and Buffalo Women. Englewood Cliffs: Prentice-Hall, 1973. 1st ed. NF in NF dj. *Parker*. $75/£48

MAIN, EDWIN M. The Story of the Marches, Battles and Incidents of the Third United States Colored Cavalry.... Louisville, KY: Globe Ptg, 1908. 1st ed. Sl shaken, else VG. *Mcgowan*. $1,250/£806

MAIN, T. The Progress of Marine Engineering, from the Time of Watt until the Present Day. NY, 1893. 1st ed. (xviii),248pp, 6 plts. (Fep loose.) *Lefkowicz*. $75/£48

MAINE, C. Spaceways. H&S, 1953. 1st ed, 1st bk. NF in VG+ dj (lt dust soil). *Aronovitz*. $45/£29

MAINE, HENRY SUMNER. Ancient Law, Its Connection with the Early History of Society.... London: John Murray, 1930. *Boswell*. $65/£42

MAINE, HENRY SUMNER. Lectures on the Early History of Institutions. NY: Henry Holt, 1884. Russet cl; gilt. (Worn.) *Boswell*. $75/£48

MAINE, HENRY SUMNER. Village-Communities in the East and West. NY: Henry Holt, 1880. 3rd, enlgd ed. Russet cl; gilt. Nice (sl foxing). *Boswell*. $75/£48

MAIR, CHARLES. Through the Mackenzie Basin. Toronto: William Briggs, 1908. Errata. Plain brn cl w/orig dec cvr laid on. Rebound, eps renewed, else VG. *Parmer*. $55/£35

MAIR, CHARLES. Through the MacKenzie Basin. A Narrative of the Athabasca and Peace River Treaty Expedition of 1899.... Toronto: Briggs, (1908). 1st ed. Omission sheet tipped in at pg488, 23 plts, color fldg map, errata slip at pg8. Gilt-stamped cl w/2 plts on fr cvr. Rectangular piece cut from upper corner of fep, o/w Fine. *Oregon*. $90/£58

MAISSIN, EUGENE. The French in Mexico and Texas (1838-1839). James L. Shepherd, III (trans). Salado: Anson Jones, 1961. #5/500. Orig glassine. *Lambeth*. $100/£65

MAITLAND, FREDERIC WILLIAM. The Life and Letters of Leslie Stephen. London, 1906. 1st ed. (Ink note fep; blinstamp title; cvrs worn; spine ends short tears; edges, eps spotted.) *King*. $150/£97

MAJOR, HOWARD. The Domestic Architecture of the Early American Republic, the Greek Revival. Phila: Lippincott, 1926. 1st ed. Frontis. Teg. Fine in dj (chipped; spine lt rubbed, sunned). *Bookpress*. $165/£106

MAJOR, J. KENNETH and MARTIN WATTS. Victorian and Edwardian Windmills and Watermills. London: Batsford, 1977. 1st ed. 137 photos. VG in dj. *Hollett*. $47/£30

MAJOR, REGINALD. A Panther Is a Black Cat. NY: Morrow, 1971. 1st Amer ed. Fine in NF dj (sl rubbing to surface gloss). *Between The Covers*. $65/£42

MAJORS, ALEXANDER. Seventy Years on the Frontier. Prentiss Ingraham (ed). Chicago: Rand McNally, 1893. 1st ed. 325pp + 2pp ads. Gold-stamped pict cl. (Fr inner hinge weak.) *Dawson*. $150/£97

MALAMUD, BERNARD. Dubin's Lives. NY: FSG, (1979). 1st trade ed, one of 750 'special' copies. Gold-stamped red cl. NF in tissue dj (2-inch chip, else VG). *Godot*. $65/£42

MALAMUD, BERNARD. The Fixer. London: Eyre & Spottiswoode, 1967. 1st Eng ed. Olive bds, gilt. Inscrip, o/w Very Nice in laminate dj (sl frayed, dknd). *Temple*. $12/£8

MALAMUD, BERNARD. Rembrandt's Hat. NY: FSG, (1973). 1st ed. Fine in Fine dj. *Chapel Hill*. $30/£19

MALAMUD, BERNARD. Rembrandt's Hat. NY: FSG, 1973. 1st ed. Fine in Fine dj. *Revere*. $25/£16

MALAMUD, BERNARD. The Stories of Bernard Malamud. NY: FSG, 1983. Ltd signed/numbered ed. Fine in Fine slipcase (sm corner tear). *Revere*. $75/£48

MALAMUD, BERNARD. The Tenants. NY: FSG, (1971). One of approx 250 issued w/signed tipped-in sheet. Orange cl. NF (evidence of erasure fep) in dj (sm tear). *Antic Hay*. $135/£87

MALAN, A.H. (ed). Famous Homes of Great Britain and Their Stories; More Famous Homes. NY, 1900. Together, 2 vols. Crimson calf (hinges repaired). *Argosy*. $125/£81

MALAN, A.H. (ed). Other Famous Homes of Great Britain and Their Stories. NY: Putnam's, 1902. Frontis, 175 photo plts. Gilt-dec pict cl. Fine. *Quest*. $75/£48

MALCOLM, J.P. An Historical Sketch of the Art of Caricaturing. London: Longman, Hurst et al, 1813. 1st ed. iv,158pp + list of plts/ad leaf; 31 engr plts. Title sl soiled, short marginal tears, o/w VG in contemp tree calf, crimson morocco label. *Cox*. $132/£85

MALCOLMSON, ANNE (ed). Song of Robin Hood. (Boston), 1947. 1st ed. Silver dec cl (text stained, ex-lib blindstamp rep). Dj (worn, chipped, stained). *King*. $60/£39

MALCOLMSON, ANNE (ed). Song of Robin Hood. Boston: Houghton Mifflin, 1947. 1st ed. Virginia Lee Burton (illus). Black cl, silver/red dec, lettering. Good in pict dj (lt edgewear, chip). *Reisler*. $125/£81

MALDEN, R.H. Nine Ghosts. London, 1947. Fine in NF dj. *Madle*. $75/£48

MALET, CAPTAIN. Annals of the Road. London: Longmans, Green, 1876. 1st ed. xiii,(i),403pp, 10 chromolitho plts, 3 woodcuts. Gilt-edged cl (sl bubbled; loss; spine sl sunned; sl staining upper bd; ex-libris). *Edwards*. $248/£160

MALET, RAWDEN. Unforgiving Minutes, Big Game Hunting. London: Hutchinson, (1934). (Backstrip faded, chipped; joint sl torn.) *Petersfield.* $54/£35

MALINOWSKI, BRONISLAW. The Sexual Life of Savages in North-Western Melanesia. London, 1929. 1st ed. 96 full-pg plts. 2-tone cl (worn; upper hinge cracked, lower hinge tender). *Edwards.* $62/£40

MALINS, EDWARD and PATRICK BOWE. Irish Gardens and Demesnes from 1830. NY, 1980. VG in Good dj. *Shifrin.* $30/£19

MALLALIEU, H.B. Letter in Wartime and Other Poems. London: Fortune, (1940). 1st ed. Prospectus laid in. NF in dj. *Reese.* $60/£39

MALLESON, G.B. The Indian Mutiny of 1857. London: Selley, 1901. 8th ed. Port. Full red calf, gilt (backstrip sl rubbed, faded). *Petersfield.* $31/£20

MALLET, THIERRY. Glimpses of the Barren Lands. NY: Privately ptd, 1930. 1st ed. VF. *Oregon.* $25/£16

MALLET, THIERRY. Plain Tales of the North. Putnam's, 1926. 2nd ed. Fine in VG dj. *Oregon.* $25/£16

MALLIN, JAY. Terror in Vietnam. Princeton: Van Nostrand, (1966). VG in dj (edges scuffed; chipped; price-clipped). *Aka.* $65/£42

MALLISON, SAM. The Great Wildcatter. Charleston: Education Foundation of WV, 1953. 1st ed. VG+ in VG- dj. *Parker.* $40/£26

MALLOWAN, MAX. Mallowan's Memoirs. NY: Dodd, Mead, 1977. 1st Amer ed. NF in dj. *Schoyer.* $30/£19

MALMBERG, BERTIL. Ake and His World. NY: Farrar, Rinehart, 1940. 1st ed. Barbara Cooney (illus). Sm 8vo. Pict cl (dusty; blemish top corner). VG; contents NF. *Book Adoption.* $65/£42

MALONE, DUMAS. Jefferson and His Time. Little, Brown, 1948-1981. 2 vols 1st eds, rest rpts. 6 vols. VG in Good djs. *Book Broker.* $115/£74

MALONE, MICHAEL. Dingley Falls. NY: HBJ, 1980. 1st ed. Fine in dj. *Else Fine.* $65/£42

MALONE, RICHARD. The Witcheens. London, 1928. 1st ed. VG. *Madle.* $35/£23

MALONEY, T.J. (ed). U.S. Camera Annual 1936. NY: William Morrow, (1936). Spiral binding. Lt rubbed, worn, else VG. *Hermitage.* $65/£42

MALONEY, T.J. (ed). U.S. Camera 1941. NY: Duell, Sloan & Pearce, 1940. 1st ed. 2 vols. Red cl, paper labels. VG set (lib stamp fep). *Hermitage.* $65/£42

MALORY, THOMAS. King Arthur and His Knights. Winston, 1927. 1st ed. F. Godwin (illus). NF in VG pict dj (spine chipped). *Aronovitz.* $80/£52

MALORY, THOMAS. Le Morte d'Arthur. London: J.M. Dent, 1935. 3rd ed, ltd to 1600. Thick, lg 4to. Aubrey Beardsley (illus). Teg. Black cl, gilt dec. Mint in illus dj (sm tear, o/w Fine). *Reisler.* $1,750/£1,129

MALORY, THOMAS. The Romance of King Arthur and His Knights of the Round Table. London: Macmillan, 1917. 1st trade ed. 23 plts (16 color) by Arthur Rackham. 1/2 tan morocco over cl (rebound), gilt; signed by 'Asprey;' aeg. Fine. *Karmiole.* $275/£177

MALORY, THOMAS. The Romance of King Arthur and His Knights of the Round Table. Alfred W. Pollard (abridged by). London: Macmillan, 1917. 1st Arthur Rackham-illus ed. #175/500, signed by Rackham. Color frontis, 15 tipped-in color illus. Gilt dec vellum, teg. VG (traces foxing; 1918 inscrip). *Chapel Hill.* $1,500/£968

MALOUF, DAVID. Antipodes. London: C&W, 1985. 1st UK ed. Fine in dj. *Lewton.* $23/£15

MALOUF, DAVID. Child's Play, with Eustance and the Prowler. C&W, 1982. 1st Eng ed. Blue cl. VF in VF dj. *Dalian.* $54/£35

MALOUF, DAVID. Fly Away Peter. London: C&W, 1982. 1st ed. Name, sl bump, o/w VG in dj. *Virgo.* $62/£40

MALOUF, DAVID. Harland's Half Acre. NY: Knopf, 1984. 1st Amer ed. Fine in Fine dj (sl dknd). *Between The Covers.* $45/£29

MALOUF, DAVID. Johnno. NY: Braziller, (1978). 1st Amer ed. Fine in NF dj (sl soiling). *Between The Covers.* $55/£35

MALRAUX, ANDRE. Days of Hope. Stuart Gilbert & Alastair MacDonald (trans). London: Routledge, 1938. 1st ed. VG in dj (chipped, missing sm piece spine). *Patterson.* $54/£35

MALRAUX, ANDRE. Israel. NY: Orion, 1958. 2 tipped-in color plts. VG in dj (edgetorn). *Cahan.* $100/£65

MALRAUX, ANDRE. The Twilight of the Absolute. The Psychology of Art (Volume 3). Stuart Gilbert (trans). NY: Pantheon, 1950. 1st ed. Gray cl, gilt spine. Good in dj, pub's slipcase. *Karmiole.* $75/£48

MALRAUX, ANDRE. The Voices of Silence. Stuart Gilbert (trans). GC: Doubleday, 1953. 1st Amer ed. Blue cl. Ink underlining, else NF in dj, pub's slipcase. *Chapel Hill.* $45/£29

MALTBY, CHARLES. The Life and Public Services of Abraham Lincoln. Stockton, CA: Daily Independent Steam Power Print, 1884. 326pp. VG. *Schoyer.* $60/£39

MALTHUS, T.R. An Essay on the Principle of Population. George Town: J. Milligan, 1809. 1st Amer ed from 3rd London ed. 2 vols. xvi,510,xxxiv; viii,542pp. Contemp calf (rubbed; outer hinges partly cracked but holding soundly); red gilt leather spine labels. *Karmiole.* $850/£548

MALTHUS, T.R. The Travel Diaries. Patricia James (ed). CUP, 1966. Frontis port; 12 plts; 3 sketch maps; fldg family tree at rear. Dj. *Edwards.* $74/£48

MALTZ, ALBERT. Afternoon in the Jungle. NY, (1970). 1st Amer ed. Fine (spine extrems sl rubbed) in dj (top edge sl rubbed). *Polyanthos.* $30/£19

MALTZ, ALBERT. Black Pit. NY, (1935). 1st Amer ed, 1st bk. Fine (cvrs sl soiled) in dj (piece missing top spine; edge chips, rubbed). *Polyanthos.* $50/£32

MALZBERG, BARRY. Beyond Apollo. Random House, 1972. 1st ed. Fine in dj. *Madle.* $35/£23

MAMET, DAVID. Glengarry Glen Ross. Grove, 1983. 1st ed. Fine in dj. *Whiteson.* $25/£16

MAMET, DAVID. Lakeboat. NY: Grove Press, 1981. 1st ed. Fine in Fine dj. *Beasley.* $40/£26

Man of Feeling. (By Henry Mackenzie.) London: W. Strahan & T. Cadell, 1778. Engr frontis; viii,278pp. Old polished calf (rebacked in matching calf), gilt. *Hollett.* $186/£120

MAN, FELIX H. 150 Years of Artists' Lithographs 1803-1953. London, 1953. 1st ed. 125 plts (13 color). Dj (sl yellowed, edges chipped). *Edwards.* $39/£25

MANARIN, LOUIS H. (ed). Richmond at War: The Minutes of the City Council, 1861-1865. UNC, (c1965). VG. *Book Broker.* $35/£23

MANCHESTER, WILLIAM. The City of Anger. NY: Ballantine, (1953). 1st ed, hb issue. (Sl shelfwear; sm snag.) Dj (rubbed; chipped). *Hermitage.* $45/£29

MANDELSTAM, OSIP. Journey to Armenia. Next Editions, 1980. 1st ed. Orig ring binder. *Edwards.* $19/£12

MANDEVILLE, BERNARD. The Fable of the Bees. London: C. Bathurst (et al), 1795. ix,(3),534pp. Contemp calf (rebacked w/most of old backstrip; corners repaired). Title dust-soiled w/sm marginal repair, o/w Good. *Cox*. $54/£35

MANFORD, ERASMUS. Twenty Five Years in the West. Chicago: Manford, 1867. 1st ed. 359pp. (Lt soiled; spine faded.) Howes M 250. *Ginsberg*. $175/£113

MANFRED, FREDERICK. Riders of Judgment. NY: Random, 1957. 1st ed. VF in dj (sl darkened spine, foreedges). *Else Fine*. $50/£32

MANGAM, WILLIAM DANIEL. The Clarks of Montana. (NY: Silver Bow Press), 1939. 1st ed. Signed. 10 full-pg ports, fldg facs. Pub's slip pasted in. Ptd wrappers. *Dawson*. $150/£97

MANGELSDORF, PAUL C. Corn: Its Origin, Evolution, and Improvement. Cambridge: Belknap, 1974. (Inscrip.) Dj. *Archaeologia*. $85/£55

MANGLES, JAMES. Papers and Despatches Relating to the Arctic Searching Expeditions of 1850-51-52. London: Francis & John Rivington, 1852. 2nd enlgd ed. (ii)title (verso blank),(3)-94, 3 engr charts (2 colored in outline). (Sl pencil underlining, lib stamps on title, one w/paper slip overpasted.) Blue cl (lib plts, stamps upper eps), gilt lettering on cvrs (spine, inner cvr edges sl stained, rubbed; sl loose but firm). *Morrell*. $388/£250

MANHOOD, H.A. Apples by Night. Cape, 1932. 1st Eng ed. Blue cl. VF in dj (sl dusty). *Dalian*. $54/£35

MANHOOD, H.A. Bread and Vinegar. White Owl Press, 1931. 1st ed. Signed, ltd to 205. Good. *Whiteson*. $43/£28

MANHOOD, H.A. Gay Agony. London: Jonathan Cape, 1930. One of 2000 numbered. Lower edges roughtrimmed. B/w cl. Spine lt browned, o/w Fine in dj (sl chipped). *Temple*. $16/£10

MANHOOD, H.A. Gay Agony. NY: Viking, 1931. 1st US ed. NF in dj (worn, chipped). *Beasley*. $30/£19

MANIGAULT, EDWARD. Siege Train. The Journal of a Confederate Artilleryman.... Warren Ripley (ed). (Columbia): Univ of SC Press, (1986). 1st ed. Fine in Fine dj. *Mcgowan*. $35/£23

MANJE, JUAN MATEO. Unknown Arizona and Sonora 1693-1721. Tucson: AZ Silhouettes, 1954. One of 1500. Fldg pocket map. Gilt-titled black buckram. VG in Fine dj (chips). *Bohling*. $45/£29

MANKOWITZ, WOLF. Wedgwood. London: Batsford, (1953). 1st ed. 8 full-color plts. Eps foxed, else VG in dj (chipped). *Bookpress*. $125/£81

MANLEY, GORDON. Climate and the British Scene. London, 1952. 1st ed. Dj (splits, sl tape mks). *Edwards*. $62/£40

MANLEY, J.J. Notes on Fish and Fishing. London: Sampson, 1877. 363pp + 45pp ads. Orig cl. Lt wear, o/w VG. *Bowman*. $65/£42

MANLEY, J.J. Notes on Game and Game Shooting. London: 'The Bazaar,' 1880. 389pp + ads. Brn cl, gilt dec spine, fr cvr. Fine+. *Bowman*. $75/£48

MANLY, WILLIAM LEWIS. Death Valley in '49. L.A.: Borden Pub Co, (1949). Centennial ed. Fldg map; pict eps. Brn cl, vignette. Fine in Fine dj. Howes M 255. *Harrington*. $50/£32

MANLY, WILLIAM LEWIS. Death Valley in '49. San Jose: Pacific Tree & Vine Co, 1894. 1st ed. Frontis port, 498pp, 3 plts. Mustard cl; fr cvr stamped in black, rear in blind; gilt spine title. Nice (spine ends lt rubbed; lt etching). Howes M 255. *Bohling*. $250/£161

MANLY, WILLIAM LEWIS. Death Valley in '49. Chicago: Lakeside Press, 1927. Fine. *Book Market*. $50/£32

MANLY, WILLIAM LEWIS. The Jayhawkers' Oath and Other Sketches. Arthur Woodward (ed). L.A.: Lewis, 1949. Fine in Fine dj. *Book Market*. $40/£26

MANLY, WILLIAM LEWIS. The Jayhawkers' Oath and Other Sketches. Arthur Woodward (ed). L.A.: Warren F. Lewis, 1949. 1st bk ed. Fldg color map; pict eps. Tan cl, vignette. Fine in NF dj (extrems sl worn). *Harrington*. $45/£29

MANN, ALBERT W. (comp). History of the Forty-Fifth Regiment, Massachusetts Volunteer Militia. (Boston, MA: Ptd by Wallace Spooner, 1908). 1st ed. Blue cl. Fr hinge cracked, else bright. *Chapel Hill*. $150/£97

MANN, ARTHUR. Baseball Confidential. McKay, 1951. 1st ed. VG+ in VG dj. *Plapinger*. $40/£26

MANN, EDWARD. A Manual of Psychological Medicine and Allied Nervous Diseases.... Phila, 1883. 1st ed. 699pp. Good. *Fye*. $250/£161

MANN, HEINRICH. Man of Straw. London: Hutchinson, 1946. 1st Eng ed. VG+ in VG+ dj (sm chips). *Lame Duck*. $85/£55

MANN, IDA. Developmental Abnormalities of the Eye. Cambridge, 1937. 1st ed. Good. *Fye*. $100/£65

MANN, MATTHEW. A System of Gynecology by American Authors. Phila: Lea, 1887-1888. 2 vols. 3 color plts, 201 wood engrs. Full sheep (vol 2 newly rebacked, orig labels). Good set. *Goodrich*. $150/£97

MANN, MATTHEW. A System of Gynecology. Phila, 1887. 1st ed. 2 vols. 1189; 1180pp. Good. *Fye*. $250/£161

MANN, THOMAS. The Beloved Returns. NY: Knopf, 1940. 1st US ed. One of 395 lg paper copies on Rives Liampre, signed. NF in cream dj (spine tanned), pub's cardbd slipcase (worn). *Lame Duck*. $600/£387

MANN, THOMAS. Buddenbrooks. London: Secker, 1930. 1st 1-vol ed. NF (spine sl faded) in dj. *Williams*. $116/£75

MANN, THOMAS. Confessions of Felix Krull, Confidence Man. Knopf, 1955. 1st Amer ed. Fine in dj. *Fine Books*. $28/£18

MANN, THOMAS. The Holy Sinner. Knopf, 1951. 1st Amer ed. Fine in dj. *Fine Books*. $35/£23

MANN, THOMAS. The Magic Mountain. Secker, 1927. 1st ed. 2 vols. VG+ set. *Fine Books*. $85/£55

MANN, THOMAS. The Magic Mountain. NY: LEC, 1962. One of 1500 numbered, signed by Felix Hoffman (illus). 2 vols. Slipcase corner crushed, else Fine in pub's slipcase. *Hermitage*. $150/£97

MANN, THOMAS. Mario and the Magician. London: Martin Secker, 1930. 1st British ed, 1st Eng trans. Bkpl; spine cocked, else NF in VG+ dj (sl loss of color). *Lame Duck*. $150/£97

MANN, THOMAS. Mario and the Magician. NY: Knopf, 1931. 1st ed. Fine in dj (lt used). *Beasley*. $85/£55

MANN, THOMAS. A Sketch of My Life. Harrison of Paris, (1930). 1st ed. One of 695. White cl bds faded, o/w VG. *Hermitage*. $45/£29

MANN, THOMAS. Thomas Mann: Diaries 1918-1939. Richard & Clara Winston (trans). London: Deutsch, 1983. 1st UK ed. Top edge sl faded, o/w NF in dj (sl rubbed). *Virgo*. $31/£20

MANN, THOMAS. The Transposed Heads. Knopf, 1941. 1st Amer ed. Fine in dj. *Fine Books*. $45/£29

MANNERING, GEORGE EDWARD. With Axe and Rope in the New Zealand Alps. London, 1891. 1st ed. viii,139pp + 24pp pub's cat, 18 plts, color fldg map. Gilt emblem upper bd. (Ex-lib, stamps; bkpl; upper hinge tender; plt removed upper bd.) *Edwards.* $78/£50

MANNERING, GEORGE EDWARD. With Axe and Rope in the New Zealand Alps. London: Longmans, Green, 1891. 1st ed. xi,139,24pp, uncut, color fldg map. Maroon levant morocco (rebacked, sl bumped; spotted; lib stamp). *Hollett.* $256/£165

MANNERS, VICTORIA and G.C. WILLIAMSON. Angelica Kauffmann, R.A. Her Life and Her Works. NY: Brentano's, (1924). 1st ed, ltd to 1000. 10 color plts. White cl over bds; leather spine label. Good. *Karmiole.* $125/£81

MANNING, OLIVIA. The Danger Tree. Weidenfeld & Nicolson, 1977. 1st Eng ed. Blue cl; wraparound band. VF in Fine dj. *Dalian.* $54/£35

MANNING, OLIVIA. The Great Fortune. London: Heinemann, 1960. 1st ed. NF in dj. *Limestone.* $70/£45

MANNING, OLIVIA. The Remarkable Expedition. London: Heinemann, 1947. 1st ed. Sl offsetting, foxing of eps; sl rubbed, o/w VG in dj (browned, soiled, repaired internally). *Virgo.* $78/£50

MANNING, R. Book of Fruits. Salem, 1838. 120pp (9pp ads), 4 litho plts, 1 dwg. (Foxing, pencil notes, tear fr pastedown; worn, spotted.) *Sutton.* $250/£161

MANNING, SAMUEL. The Land of the Pharaohs.... London: Religious Tract Soc, 1887. Frontis, 224pp; aeg. Gilt-pict cl (faded; spine tears; bkpl). *Archaeologia.* $45/£29

MANO, D. KEITH. Bishop's Progress. Boston: Houghton Mifflin, 1968. 1st ed. Signed, dated. Fine in NF dj (sm chip). *Revere.* $60/£39

MANO, D. KEITH. The Bridge. NY: Doubleday, 1973. 1st ed. NF in dj. *Antic Hay.* $40/£26

MANRING, B.F. The Conquest of the Coeur D'Alenes, Spokanes and Palouses. Spokane: John Graham, (1912). 1st ed. Pict cl (soiled). Howes M 262. *Perier.* $160/£103

MANSFIELD, EDWARD D. The Life of General Winfield Scott. NY, 1846. 1st ed. 366pp, port (inscrip; chipped). *King.* $35/£23

MANSFIELD, KATHERINE. The Doves' Nest and Other Stories. Constable, (1923). 1st ed. (Lt spotting prelims, final pp.) *Bickersteth.* $59/£38

MANSFIELD, KATHERINE. The Journal of...1914-1922. J. Middleton Murry (ed). Constable, 1927. 1st ed. (Ink name; newspaper cutting pasted inside fr cvr.) *Bickersteth.* $47/£30

MANSFIELD, KATHERINE. Katherine Mansfield's Letters to John Middleton Murry 1913-1922. NY: Knopf, 1951. 1st Amer ed. Name, else NF in dj (lt worn). *Chapel Hill.* $35/£23

MANSFIELD, KATHERINE. Letters to John Middleton Murry 1913-1922. John Middleton Murry (ed). Constable, 1951. 1st ed. 6 ports. *Bickersteth.* $74/£48

MANSFIELD, KATHERINE. Letters. J. Middleton Murry (ed). Constable, 1928. 1st ed. 2 vols. Port in each vol. (Cvrs vol 2 sl spotted, mkd.) *Bickersteth.* $62/£40

MANSFIELD, KATHERINE. Poems. NY, 1924. 1st Amer ed. Spine extrems, edges sl rubbed, o/w NF. *Polyanthos.* $25/£16

MANSFIELD, KATHERINE. Something Childish and Other Stories. Constable, (1924). 1st ed. (Ink name fr fly.) *Bickersteth.* $54/£35

MANSON, J.B. The Life and Work of Edgar Degas. Studio, 1927. Frontis port; 81 plts. Teg. (Tissue guards creased; feps lt browned.) Japon backed bds, japon label (worn, surface loss). *Edwards.* $39/£25

MANSON, OTIS. A Treatise on the Physiological and Therapeutic Action of the Sulphate of Quinine. Phila, 1882. Inscribed. 1st ed. 164pp. Good. *Fye.* $200/£129

MANSON, PATRICK. Tropical Diseases. London, 1900. 2nd ed. Buckram. Good. *Fye.* $40/£26

MANSON, PATRICK. Tropical Diseases. London, 1909. 4th ed. Good. *Fye.* $40/£26

MANSON, PATRICK. Tropical Diseases. Birmingham, 1984. Facs of 1898 ed. Full leather. Good. *Fye.* $50/£32

MANTLE, MICKEY. Education of a Baseball Player. S&S, 1967. 1st ed. VG + in VG + dj. *Plapinger.* $50/£32

MANTLE, MICKEY. The Mickey Mantle Story. (As told to Ben Epstein.) Holt, 1953. Ltr ptg. VG. *Plapinger.* $50/£32

MANTLE, MICKEY. The Quality of Courage. Doubleday, 1964. 1st ed. VG in Good + dj. *Plapinger.* $30/£19

MANTON, JO. Elizabeth Garrett Anderson. NY, 1963. Frontis. Nice in dj. *Goodrich.* $25/£16

Manual for Courts-Martial, U.S. Army. Washington: GPO, 1927. Buckram (worn). Usable. *Boswell.* $35/£23

MAPPLETHORPE, ROBERT. Certain People: A Book of Portraits. Pasadena: Twelvetrees, 1985. 1st ed. Fine in dj. *Beasley.* $150/£97

MAPPLETHORPE, ROBERT. Flowers. Boston: Bulfinch Press/Little, Brown, (1990). 1st ed. 50 full-pg color photos. Fine in dj. *Godot.* $85/£55

MARA, BERNARD. (Pseud of Brian Moore.) A Bullet for My Lady. NY, 1955. 1st ed. Pb orig. Wrappers sl rubbed, o/w VG. *Rees.* $93/£60

MARA, BERNARD. (Pseud of Brian Moore.) French for Murder. London: L. Miller & Son, 1954. 1st Eng ed. Pb orig. Wrappers lt rubbed, o/w VG. *Rees.* $116/£75

MARA, BERNARD. (Pseud of Brian Moore.) French for Murder. Sydney, 1955. 1st Australian ed. Lg format pb orig. Edges worn, lt rubbed, o/w VG in wrappers. *Rees.* $93/£60

MARA, BERNARD. (Pseud of Brian Moore.) This Gun for Gloria. NY, 1956. 1st ed. Pb orig. NF. *Rees.* $116/£75

MARA, BERNARD. (Pseud of Brian Moore.) This Gun for Gloria. Fawcett, 1957. 1st UK ed. Pb. VG. *Williams.* $70/£45

MARAINI, FOSCO. Secret Tibet. Eric Mosbacher (trans). London: Hutchinson, 1952. 1st Eng ed. 50 duotone plts. (Spine sl worn; fep stuck to pastedown.) *Hollett.* $47/£30

MARAN, RENE. Batouala. Adele S. Seltzer (trans). NY: Thomas Seltzer, 1922. 1st Amer ed. Gilt cl. NF in Good dj (chipped, soiled). *Reese.* $30/£19

MARAN, RENE. Batouala. Alvah Bessie (trans). NY: LEC, 1932. 1st ed this trans. One of 1500 numbered, signed by Miguel Covarrubias (illus). Full blindstamped calf. NF in slipcase (sl faded). *Reese.* $150/£97

MARBURY, MARY ORVIS. Favorite Flies and Their Histories. Boston: Houghton Mifflin, 1896. 3rd ed. 32 color plts, 6 engrs. Early 1/2 morocco, gilt-tooled spine. Fine. *Glenn.* $350/£226

MARCADE, JEAN. Eros Kalos: Essay on Erotic Elements in Greek Art. Geneva, 1962. 164 plts. VG in dj, slipcase. *Argosy.* $50/£32

MARCH, WILLIAM. The Bad Seed. London: Hamish Hamilton, (1954). 1st Eng ed. Pp dknd, else Fine in Fine dj. *Between The Covers.* $85/£55

MARCH, WILLIAM. Company K. (NY): Harrison Smith & Robert Haas, 1933. 1st ed, 1st bk. Grn cl. Name, else Fine in orig glassine dj w/ptd paper flaps (tears). *Chapel Hill.* $300/£194

MARCHIAFAVA, E. and A. BIGNAMI. Two Monographs on Malaria and the Parasites of Malarial Fevers. London, 1894. 1st Eng trans. 428pp. Good. *Fye.* $100/£65

MARCHINI, G. Italian Stained Glass Windows. NY: Abrams, (1956). 1st ed. 93 mtd color plts. Blue gilt cl. Good in dj. *Karmiole.* $100/£65

MARCHINI, G. Italian Stained Glass Windows. London: Thames & Hudson, 1957. 82 color plts, 4 lg mtd color transparencies. Fine in dj. *Europa.* $85/£55

Marconi Book of Wireless. London, 1936. 1st ed. 56 plts, 14 diags. (Lower leading corner 1/2 title, frontis cut away; eps lt spotted.) *Edwards.* $496/£320

MARCOU, JULES. Life, Letters, and Works of Louis Agassiz. NY: Macmillan, 1896. 1st ed. 2 vols. xxii,302; x,318pp + 4pp ads. Blue cl, gilt; teg. Fine set in slipcase (cracked). *Karmiole.* $35/£23

MARCOY, PAUL. Travels in South America. London: Blackie, 1875. 2nd ed. 2 vols. xii,524; viii,496pp; 10 maps. Dec grn cl (extrems worn, frayed). Aeg. (Sl loose.) *Hollett.* $233/£150

MARCUSE, WALTER D. Through Western Madagascar in Quest of the Golden Bean. London, 1914. 1st ed. Fldg map. Teg. Gilt-edged calf (spine lt sunned; lt marginal spotting). *Edwards.* $93/£60

MARCY, HENRY. The Perineum: Its Anatomy, Physiology and Methods of Restoration After Surgery. 1889. 1st ed. 32pp. Good. *Fye.* $75/£48

MARCY, RANDOLPH B. The Prairie and Overland Traveller. A Companion for Emigrants.... Richard Burton (new intro). London, 1860. 1st London ed. 12mo. viii,230pp + (2)pp ads. Gilt cl (spotted, spine lettering flaked; sig starting). Good. *Reese.* $650/£419

MARDER, ARTHUR J. Dreadnought to Scapa Flow. Oxford, 1961-1970. 1st eds. 5 vols, reviews each laid in. Exceptionally Nice in djs. *Edwards.* $581/£375

MAREK, J. and H. KNIZKOVA. The Jenghiz Khan Miniatures from the Court of Akbar the Great. Olga Kuthanova (trans). London: Spring Books, 1963. 1st ed. 56 color plts. NF in dj; box. *Worldwide.* $65/£42

MARFIELD, DWIGHT. The Mandarin's Sapphire. NY: E.P. Dutton, 1938. 1st ed. Fine in dj (wear spine ends; short closed tears). *Mordida.* $45/£29

Marginalia; or, Gleanings from an Army Note-Book. By 'Personne'.... (By Felix Gregory DeFontaine). Columbia, SC: F.G. DeFontaine, 1864. 1st ed. iii,248pp. Orig 1/2 leather, cl. Leather scuffed; foxing, else VG. *Mcgowan.* $350/£226

MARGOLIOUTH, H.M. (ed). The Poems and Letters of Andrew Marvell. OUP, 1927. 2 vols. Frontis ports, 4 plts, fldg facs. (Feps, cl lt spotted.) *Edwards.* $155/£100

MARILLIER, H.C. The Early Work of Aubrey Beardsley. London/NY, 1922. Frontis port, 155 plts. (Margins thumbed; list of plts detached). Teg, rest uncut. *Edwards.* $78/£50

MARION, JOHN FRANCIS. The Charleston Story: Scenes.... (Harrisburg): Stackpole, (1978). 1st ed. Fine in dj. *Pharos.* $30/£19

Maritime History of New York. GC, 1941. 1st ed. In dj. *Argosy.* $125/£81

MARJORIBANKS, ALEXANDER. Travels in South and North America. Edinburgh, 1853. 2nd ed. Color frontis; xiv,480pp. Orig cl (sl soiled). VG. Howes M 290. *Ginsberg.* $375/£242

MARK, MARY ELLEN. Falkland Road: Prostitutes of Bombay. NY: Knopf, 1981. 1st ed. VG in illus stiff wrappers (sm rmdr hole punched through). *Cahan.* $40/£26

MARKHAM, ALBERT H. The Great Frozen Sea. London: C. Keegan Paul, 1880. 5th ed. xix,384pp, map; marbled pg edges. Full calf (rubbed). Good. *Walcot.* $59/£38

MARKHAM, ALBERT H. A Polar Reconnaissance...to Novaya Zemlya in 1879. London: C. Kegan Paul, 1881. xvi,1 leaf,361pp, 2 fldg maps. Blue cl, black/gilt (spine dknd, edges worn, hinges strengthened). *Parmer.* $400/£258

MARKHAM, ALBERT H. A Whaling Cruise to Baffin's Bay...and an Account of the Rescue of the Crew of the Polaris. London: Sampson, Low, etc., 1875. 2nd ed. xxxi,307pp. 8 plts, fldg map. Orig dec cl (new eps). VG (minor wear, soil). *High Latitude.* $185/£119

MARKHAM, BERYL. West With the Night. H-M, 1942. VG in Good dj. *Fine Books.* $65/£42

MARKHAM, C.R. Cuzco...and Lima.... London: Chapman & Hall, 1856. 1st ed. Signed by a Markham, perhaps not author. iv,419pp; 8 hand-colored litho plts (lt foxing); fldg map. Grn cl, gilt (lower hinge cracked, short split upper hinge, but cvrs secure). *Cox.* $209/£135

MARKHAM, C.R. The Lands of Silence. Cambridge Univ Press, 1921. 1st ed. Gilt-dec cl (sl mkd, spine sl faded). Good+. *Walcot.* $209/£135

MARKHAM, C.R. The Threshold of the Unknown Region. London: Sampson, Low, Marston, 1875. 3rd ed. xvi,348pp. Good+ (sl torn head spine). *Walcot.* $70/£45

MARKHAM, ROBERT. (Pseud of Kingsley Amis.) Colonel Sun. NY: Harper & Row, (1968). 1st Amer ed. Fine in dj (sl worn). *Hermitage.* $35/£23

MARKHAM, VIOLET R. South Africa, Past and Present. London: Smith, Elder & Co, 1900. 1st ed. VG. *Mcgowan.* $150/£97

MARKHAM, VIRGIL. The Devil Drives. NY, 1932. 1st Amer ed. NF (cup ring mk fr cvr) in dj (spine sl sunned; pieces missing extrems; spine sm edge chips). *Polyanthos.* $35/£23

MARKINO, YOSHIO. A Japanese Artist in London. Phila, 1910. 12 tipped-in plts (8 color). (Upper hinge sl cracked; marginal browning; spine discolored, sl chipped.) *Edwards.* $70/£45

MARKLAND, MR. Pteryplegia: The Art of Shooting—Flying. NY: Derrydale, 1931. Ltd to 300 from total ed of 500. Sl fading, sl dust-toned, lt foxing, bkpl, else VG. *Cahan.* $125/£81

MARKMAN, SIDNEY DAVID. Colonial Architecture of Antigua Guatemala. Phila, 1966. VG in dj. *Argosy.* $150/£97

MARKS, JEANETTE. Thirteen Days. NY: Boni, 1929. 1st ed. VG + . *Beasley*. $45/£29

MARKSTEIN, GEORGE. The Cooler. London: Souvenir Press, 1974. 1st ed. Fine in dj. *Mordida*. $45/£29

MARKUS, KURT. Buckaroo. Boston, 1987. 1st ed. 127 photo plts. Gilt-stamped cl. VG + (stamped 'As-Is' 3 times; soiling to bottom edge) in dj (scratch, sm tear). *Baade*. $65/£42

MARLBOROUGH, JOHN, DUKE OF. Memoirs, with Correspondence. William Coxe (ed). London, 1820. 2nd ed. 6 vols. Contemp diced calf. VG. *Argosy*. $450/£290

MARLOWE, DEREK. The Memoirs of a Venus Lackey. London: Cape, (1968). 1st ed. Fine in dj (lt worn). *Hermitage*. $45/£29

MARLOWE, GEORGE. Coaching Roads of Old New England. NY: Macmillan, 1943. 1st ed. VG. *October Farm*. $40/£26

MARMER, MILTON J. Hypnosis in Anesthesiology. Springfield: Charles C. Thomas, (1959). 1st ed. Fine in dj. *Glaser*. $60/£39

MARON, MARGARET. Corpus Christmas. NY: DCC, 1989. 1st ed. VF in dj. *Mordida*. $30/£19

MARPLES, MORRIS. White Horses and Other Hill Figures. London: Country Life, 1949. 1st ed. 54 plts. VG in dj (worn). *Hollett*. $39/£25

MARQUEZ, GABRIEL GARCIA. *See* GARCIA MARQUEZ, GABRIEL

MARQUIS, DON. Archy's Life of Mehitabel. D-D, 1933. 1st ed. Off-setting to eps, else Fine in NF dj (worn). *Fine Books*. $95/£61

MARQUIS, DON. Danny's Own Story. NY, 1912. 1st Amer ed. NF (sl rubbed). *Polyanthos*. $50/£32

MARQUIS, DON. Mr. Hawley Breaks into Song. NY: Privately ptd, 1923. 1st ed. Dec gold foil over stiff bds (worn, spine sl chipped). Good (2pp roughly opened). *Godot*. $65/£42

MARQUIS, THOMAS. Custer, Cavalry and Crows. The Story of William White. Ft. Collins, 1975. 1st ed. Fine; no dj as issued. *Baade*. $45/£29

MARRIOTT, ALICE. Hell on Horses and Women. Norman: Univ of OK Press, (1953). 1st ed. Fine in VG + dj (lt chipped, soiled, spine sl faded). *Harrington*. $40/£26

MARRIOTT, ALICE. Maria, the Potter of San Ildefonso. Norman, 1948. 1st ed. Dec cl. VG in mod dj (worn). *Baade*. $95/£61

MARRIOTT, ALICE. The Valley Below. Norman: Univ of OK, 1949. 1st ed. Bright in dj (lt wear). *Hermitage*. $35/£23

MARRIOTT, ELSIE FRANKLAND. Bainbridge Through Bifocals. Seattle: Gateway Ptg, 1941. 1st ed. Ink name, else Fine. *Perier*. $75/£48

MARRYAT, CAPTAIN. Jacob Faithful. London: Constable, 1928. 2 vols. 12 color plts. (Sl foxed throughout.) *Petersfield*. $33/£21

MARRYAT, CAPTAIN. Masterman Ready; or, The Wreck of the Pacific. Longman, Orme, et al, 1841(-1842). 1st ed. 3 vols. Sm 8vo. Wood engr frontis each vol (vol 1 lt colored); pub's cat vol 2, 3. Orig dk grn cl, pict blocked in blind, gilt-lettered. (Lower joint vol 1 partly slit, spine foot sl defective; spines vol 2,3 faded; spine top cl each vol sl worn; binder's ticket vol 2.) *Bickersteth*. $186/£120

MARRYAT, CAPTAIN. Narrative of the Travels and Adventures of Monsieur Violet.... NY: Harper, 1843. 1st Amer ptg. 133,(2)pp. (Few sm spots; lt foxing.) Early 20th cent 1/4 morocco, cl; orig wrappers bound in (spine sl sunned; sm chip fr wrap). Very Nice. Howes M 302. *Reese*. $150/£97

MARRYAT, CAPTAIN. The Phantom Ship. Boston: Little-Brown, 1913. 1st ed. Dec navy blue cl cover (sl rubbed). NF. *Else Fine*. $125/£81

MARRYAT, CAPTAIN. The Pirate, and The Three Cutters. London: Henry G. Bohn, 1854. 284pp; 20 Fine steel-engr plts. (Spots, mks.) Blind-stamped cl (spine sl rubbed, recased), gilt. *Hollett*. $101/£65

MARRYAT, FLORENCE. Dead Man's Message. Charles Reed, 1894. 1st ed. VG. *Madle*. $50/£32

MARRYAT, FRANK. Mountains and Molehills, or Recollections of a Burnt Journal. Stanford, (1952). Rpt of 1855 ed. VG in VG dj. *Oregon*. $35/£23

MARRYAT, FRANK. Mountains and Molehills. Alexandria: Time-Life, 1980. 1st ed thus (facs reprint of 1855 London ed). Color frontis; 7 color plts. Emb leather, gilt; aeg, ribbon marker. Fine. *Connolly*. $32/£21

MARRYAT, FREDERICK. The Children of the New Forest. NY/London: Scribner's, (1927). 1st ed. Pict cvr label. Stafford Good (illus). NF. *Sadlon*. $50/£32

MARRYAT, FREDERICK. A Diary in America. NY: D. Appleton, 1839. 1st Amer 1 vol ed. 12mo. 264pp (internal foxing). Grn cl over bds (extrems, paper spine label rubbed). Howes M 300. *Karmiole*. $75/£48

MARRYAT, FREDERICK. Japhet, in Search of a Father. London: Saunders & Otley, 1836. 1st ed. 3 vols. Full mottled calf. VG (sl chipped, rubbed, lt foxed). *Cahan*. $250/£161

MARRYAT, FREDERICK. Second Series of a Diary in America.... Phila, 1840. Later ed. 300pp (foxing). Orig cl (worn; fraying; lacks spine label). Internally Good. Howes M 300. *Ginsberg*. $150/£97

MARRYAT, JOSEPH. Collections Towards a History of Pottery and Porcelain in the 15th, 16th, 17th and 18th Centuries.... London: John Murray, 1850. 1st ed. 12 chromos. 1/2 brn morocco; spine stamped blind, gilt. Rubbed, o/w VG. *Hermitage*. $125/£81

MARRYAT, THOMAS. Therapeutics; or the Art of Healing.... London: Sherwood, Neely & Jones, 1813. 23rd ed. xviii,1 leaf, 220pp. Uncut. Contemp patterned bds (rubbed; spine defect). VG. *Hemlock*. $150/£97

MARS-JONES, ADAM. Lantern Lecture. London: Faber, 1981. 1st UK ed. Fine in dj. *Williams*. $23/£15

MARS-JONES, ADAM. The Waters of Thirst. Faber, 1993. 1st UK ed. Signed. Fine in dj. *Lewton*. $28/£18

MARS. Friends and Playmates. London: George Routledge, ca 1890. 4to. 49pp + 2pp contents, frontis, tp vignette. (Bkpl; lacks pp39-42; edges scuffed; inner hinge defective). *Hobbyhorse*. $95/£61

MARSH, E.A. The Evolution of Automatic Machinery as Applied to the Manufacture of Watches.... Chicago: George K. Hazlitt, 1896. 1st ed. 150pp; 4 ports. Blue cl (sl rubbed, faded); gilt. *Karmiole*. $100/£65

MARSH, EDWARD and CHRISTOPHER HASSALL. Ambrosia and Small Beer. London: Longmans, 1964. 1st ed. Frontis, 1 plt. Lt brn cl, gilt. Fine in dj. *Temple*. $34/£22

MARSH, J.B.T. The Story of the Jubilee Singers; with Their Songs. Boston: Houghton, Mifflin, 1881. Rev ed. viii,243pp, Fine port bound at fr, 3 plts. Gilt-pict brn cl. *Petrilla*. $75/£48

MARSH, J.B.T. The Story of the Jubilee Singers; with Their Songs. Hodder & Stoughton, 1888. Tipped-in photo frontis. VG-. *Fine Books.* $60/£39

MARSH, JAMES B. Four Years in the Rockies. New Castle, PA, 1884. 1st ed. Orig pict cl (worn, soiled). Good in new cl slipcase. Howes M 306. *Schoyer.* $300/£194

MARSH, NGAIO. Colour Scheme. Collins, 1943. 1st UK ed. VG (spine sl wear; fr panel tear) in VG dj. *Martin.* $28/£18

MARSH, NGAIO. Death at the Dolphin. London: Collins, 1967. 1st Eng ed. Fine in dj (price-clipped). *Janus.* $50/£32

MARSH, NGAIO. Grave Mistake. London: CCC, 1978. 1st ed. Sl spine slant, pg edge lt soiled, else NF in dj (sm stain, sm closed tear). *Murder.* $50/£32

MARSH, NGAIO. Night at the Vulcan. Little, 1951. 1st ed. NF in dj. *Murder.* $40/£26

MARSH, NGAIO. Photo-Finish. London: Collins, 1980. 1st ed. Fine in dj (sl edgewear). *Janus.* $40/£26

MARSH, NGAIO. Singing in the Shrouds. Little, 1958. 1st ed. VG+ (edges lt worn) in dj (spine creased, lt chipped). *Murder.* $35/£23

MARSH, NGAIO. Tied Up in Tinsel. Boston: Little, Brown, 1972. 1st US ed. Fine in Fine dj. *Janus.* $25/£16

MARSH, NGAIO. When in Rome. London: Collins, 1970. 1st ed. Fine in Fine dj. *Janus.* $45/£29

MARSH, O.C. Odontornithes. Washington, 1880. xv,201pp (yellowed), 34 litho plts (1 torn, most foxed). (Extrems worn, lt spotted.) *Sutton.* $215/£139

MARSH, REGINALD. The Prints of Reginald Marsh. NY: Clarkson Potter, (1976). 1st ed. NF in dj (price-clipped). *Reese.* $50/£32

MARSHAL, WILLIAM. Manila Bay. London: Secker & Warburg, 1986. 1st ed. Fine in dj. *Murder.* $30/£19

Marshall's Abridgment of English History. London: John Marshall, n.d. (ca 1802). Sq 12mo. 61pp; 28 full-pg engrs. Pink paper on bd, pub's label back cvr. VG (ink sig, spots; rubbed, discolored). *Hobbyhorse.* $200/£129

MARSHALL, A.J. Bower-Birds, Their Displays and Breeding Cycles. London, 1954. 26 plts. Good (ex-lib). *Wheldon & Wesley.* $62/£40

MARSHALL, FRANCES and HUGH. Old English Embroidery.... London, 1894. (Ex-lib w/stamps; fep, frontis detached; few pp wrinkled; hinges cracked; worn.) *Edwards.* $85/£55

MARSHALL, JAMES. George and Martha, Encore. Boston: Houghton Mifflin, 1973. 1st ptg. 8.5-inch sq. Pict cl. As New in As New dj (sl shelfwear). *Book Adoption.* $40/£26

MARSHALL, JAMES. Portly McSwine. Boston: Houghton Mifflin, 1979. 1st ed. Inscribed, w/picture. 8x7.5. Pict cl. As New in As New dj. *Book Adoption.* $50/£32

MARSHALL, JOHN. The Life of George Washington.... Phila: Crissy, 1840. 2nd ed. 2 vols. iv,460,42,viii; 448,32,vpp; port. Full leather, leather spine labels. VG (scuffing). Howes M 317. *Schoyer.* $60/£39

MARSHALL, KATHRYN. My Sister Gone. NY: Harper & Row, (1975). 1st ed, 1st bk. Fine in dj (lt rubbed, price-clipped). *Reese.* $25/£16

MARSHALL, LOGAN. Hindenburg's March into London. Winston, 1916. 1st US ed. NF in wraps. *Madle.* $75/£48

MARSHALL, NINA L. Mosses and Lichens. NY, 1907. 1st ed. 16 color plts. VG. *Argosy.* $60/£39

MARSHALL, PAULE. Brown Girl, Brownstones. NY: Random House, (1959). 1st ed, 1st bk. Sm stain spots fore-edge, o/w NF in Attractive dj. *Bernard.* $350/£226

MARSHALL, PAULE. Brown Girl, Brownstones. NY: Random House, (1959). Advance rev copy, slip laid in. 1st bk. Fine in Fine dj. *Between The Covers.* $750/£484

MARSHALL, PAULE. Praisesong for the Widow. NY: Putnams, (1983). 1st Amer ed. Fine in dj (3 short tears, internally repaired). *Between The Covers.* $50/£32

MARSHALL, PAULE. Soul Clap Hands and Sing. NY: Atheneum, 1961. 1st ed. Edges lt foxed, else NF in dj (lt foxed, worn). *Godot.* $100/£65

MARSHALL, ROBERT. The Enchanted Golf Clubs. NY: Frederick A. Stokes, (1920). 1st Amer ed. Pict bds (spine darkened, chipped). Internally NF. *Blue Mountain.* $65/£42

MARSHALL, S.L.A. Blitzkrieg. Its History.... NY, 1940. 2nd imp. Signed. 9 maps. Eps browned, o/w VG. Beige cl, red title. *Edwards.* $62/£40

MARSHALL, WILLIAM. Yellowthread Street. NY: Holt, 1976. 1st US ed. Fine in NF dj (closed tear). *Janus.* $20/£13

MARSHBURN, JOSEPH H. and ALAN R. VELIE. Blood and Knavery, a Collection.... Rutherford: Farleigh Dickinson Univ Press, 1973. Good in dj (worn). *Boswell.* $45/£29

MARSTEN, RICHARD. Danger: Dinosaurs! Winston, 1953. 1st ed. Fine in VG dj. *Madle.* $100/£65

MARSTEN, RICHARD. Runaway Black. NY: Fawcett, 1954. 1st ed: pb orig. VG+ (lt wear, sl leaned). *Janus.* $15/£10

MARSTON, R.B. Walton and Some Earlier Writers on Fish and Fishing. London: Elliot Stock, 1894. 1st ed. xxvi,264pp + (2)pp ads, index. Grn cl, gilt. Good. *Karmiole.* $50/£32

MARTEL, G. In the Wake of the Tank. London, 1931. 1st ed. 27 plts; fldg table; map. VG (ex-lib, stamp; foxed). Lettered buff cl (sl soiled, worn). *Edwards.* $78/£50

MARTELLI, GEORGE. Italy Against the World. London, 1937. 1st ed. Frontis port; 7 plts; 3 maps. Foxing to fore-edge; eps browned, o/w VG in dj (chipped). *Edwards.* $31/£20

MARTIN, A. Atlas of Obstetrics and Gynecology. Phila, 1881. 2nd ed. 98 engr plts. Recased w/orig backstrip laid down; new eps. Good. *Fye.* $300/£194

MARTIN, DOUGLAS D. Tombstone's Epitaph. Albuquerque, 1953. 1st ed. Pict cl. NF (bkseller label) in dj (sl chipped). *Baade.* $60/£39

MARTIN, E.A. A Bibliography of Gilbert White. London, 1934. Fine. *Henly.* $50/£32

MARTIN, E.A. A Bibliography of Gilbert White...of Selborne. London, 1934. *Wheldon & Wesley.* $47/£30

MARTIN, EUGENE. Randy Starr Above the Stormy Seas. Saalfield, 1931. Fine in dj. *Madle.* $25/£16

MARTIN, F. The Hunting of the Silver Fleece. NY: Greenberg, 1946. 1st ed. VG. *Mikesh.* $25/£16

MARTIN, F.R. The Miniature Painting and Painters of Persia, India, and Turkey from the 8th to the 18th Century. London, 1968. Rpt. Ltd to 500. 271 b/w, 54 color plts. Dj (ragged). *Edwards.* $271/£175

MARTIN, FRANCOIS XAVIER. The History of Louisiana, from the Earliest Period. New Orleans, 1827/29. 2 vols. 1/2 titles, lxxxiii,(1),364; xv,(1),429pp. Mod 1/2 calf, marbled bds, leather labels. Browning, foxing, heavy at times, else VG. Howes M 332. *Reese.* $1,000/£645

MARTIN, FREDERICKA. The Hunting of the Silver Fleece-Epic of the Fur Seal. NY: Greenberg Pub, (1946). 1st ed. VG in dj (edgeworn). *Perier.* $37/£24

MARTIN, HORACE T. Castorologia, or the History and Traditions of the Canadian Beaver. Montreal/London: Wm. Drysdale/Edward Stanford, 1892. 1st ed. xvi+238pp. (Clipping pasted down; fr hinge cracked; bumped, rubbed; spine chipped; cl split top, bottom rear joint.) Good. *Blue Mountain.* $100/£65

MARTIN, ISAAC. A Journal of the Life, Travels, Labours, and Religious Exercises of Isaac Martin.... Phila, 1834. 1st ed. 160pp (sm closed tear tp). Orig full leather (few mks). VG. *Mcgowan.* $75/£48

MARTIN, JAMES. The Influence of Tropical Climates on European Constitutions.... London, 1856. 2nd ed. 599pp. Recent cl; new eps. *Fye.* $250/£161

MARTIN, JAY. Nathanael West. NY: FSG, (1970). 1st ed. Beige cl. NF (label) in VG dj. *Chapel Hill.* $40/£26

MARTIN, KINGSLEY. The British Public and the General Strike. Hogarth, 1926. 1st ed. Sl faded, else Good. *Whiteson.* $37/£24

MARTIN, KINGSLEY. The British Public and the General Strike. London: Hogarth Press, 1926. 1st ed. 1/4 gray Fine buckram. Sl worn, mkd; o/w Very Nice. *Temple.* $50/£32

MARTIN, LEE. Too Sane a Murder. NY: St Martin, 1984. 1st ed. 1st bk. Fine in Fine dj (sl wrinkle). *Janus.* $65/£42

MARTIN, LOUISE. North to Nome. Chicago: Albert Whitman, 1939. 1st ed. Frontis. VG. *Oregon.* $25/£16

MARTIN, PAUL S. The Last 10,000 Years. Tucson: Univ of AZ, 1963. 1st ed. Nice (tip sl worn). *Shasky.* $50/£32

MARTIN, THOMAS S. With Fremont to California and the Southwest, 1845-1849. Ferol Egan (ed). Ashland: Lewis Osborne, 1975. 1st ed. Cl-backed patterned bds. Fine in Fine red plain paper dj. *Harrington.* $35/£23

MARTINDALE, THOMAS. With Gun and Guide. Phila, 1910. 1st ed. Teg. (Spine sl bumped.) *Edwards.* $54/£35

MARTINEAU, HARRIET. Deerbrook. NY: Harper, 1839. 1st US ed. 2 vols. 257; 252pp. Leather-backed paper bds. VG set (lib bkpls; foxing). *Second Life.* $125/£81

MARTINEAU, HARRIET. Eastern Life, Present and Past. Phila: Lea & Blanchard, 1848. 1st US ed. 523pp. VG (mod marginalia) in orig cl (sl worn). *Second Life.* $50/£32

MARTINEAU, HARRIET. A History of Thirty Year's Peace A.D. 1816-1846. London: Bohn Libraries, George Bell, 1877-1878. 4 vols. (Backstrips sl stained.) *Petersfield.* $37/£24

MARTINEAU, HARRIET. Poor Laws and Paupers Illustrated. I. The Parish, with The Hamlets, with The Town. London: Charles Fox, 1833/34. 1st eds. 3 works bound together. (4),216; (4),164; (4),170pp. Contemp 1/2 calf (sl rubbed), dbl morocco labels. *Cox.* $70/£45

MARTINEAU, HARRIET. Retrospect of Western Travel. NY: Harper, 1838. 1st Amer ed. 2 vols. (ix),14-276; (v),6-239,(5)pp (foxed). (Spines sunned, cvrs worn; paper label worn.) Howes M 348. *Bookpress.* $175/£113

MARTINEAU, MRS. PHILIP. Gardening in Sunny Lands. NY: D. Appleton, 1924. Color frontis, 16 b/w plts. (Hinges broken; spine ends worn.) *Quest.* $35/£23

MARTONE, MICHAEL. Alive and Dead in Indiana. NY: Knopf, 1984. 1st ed. Fine in dj. *Reese.* $30/£19

MARTYN, CHARLES. The Life of Artemas Ward.... NY: Artemas Ward, 1921. 1st ed. Frontis port. Unopened; teg. Red cl. Fr cvr heavily stained, o/w VG. *Chapel Hill.* $30/£19

MARTYN, THOMAS. Letters on the Elements of Botany. London: For B. & J. White, Vols I-II 1805; vol III 1799. 5th ed. Vol I: xxiv,503, indices; Vol II: xxxiii,unpag.; Vol III: 38 hand-colored plts, ii-vi,72pp. Contemp full calf, gilt. Very handsome set. *Quest.* $625/£403

MARTYN, W. Stones of Enchantment. H. Jenkins, 1948. 1st ed. Fine in VG dj (short tears). *Aronovitz.* $29/£19

MARX, GROUCHO. Beds. Farrar & Rinehart, 1930. Pict cvr. VG. *Bishop.* $100/£65

MARX, GROUCHO. Beds. NY: Farrar & Rinehart, 1930. 1st ed, 1st bk. Color tinted photo. Pub's pict bds. *Book Block.* $185/£119

MARX, GROUCHO. Beds. F&R, 1930. 1st ed, 1st bk. Photographic bds. NF in VG+ dj (dust-soil). *Fine Books.* $225/£145

MARX, GROUCHO. The Groucho Letters. NY: S&S, 1967. 1st ed. Sig, o/w VG in dj. *Hermitage.* $35/£23

MARX, HARPO. Harpo Speaks! (NY, 1961). 1st ed. VG in dj (sl worn, soiled, price-clipped). *King.* $35/£23

MARX, KARL. Capital. NY: Appleton, 1889. Amer issue of 1st ed in English, ptd from plts of 1887 Sonnenschein pub; until recently, generally referred to as the 1st Amer 'edition'. Pub's mustard yellow cl (rebacked). Internally NF. *Lame Duck.* $1,000/£645

Mary Goodchild. NY: McLoughlin Bros, n.d. (ca 1870). (Dame Wonders' Picture Book Series.) 12mo. 4 leaves+1pg list lower wrapper, full-pg wood engr title pg, seven 3/4pg hand-colored wood engrs. Pict orange paper wrappers (spine rebacked, traces of stitching along internal gutters; edges lt rubbed). VG. *Hobbyhorse.* $125/£81

Mary Putnam Jacobi, M.D. A Pathfinder in Medicine. NY, 1925. 1st ed. Good. *Fye.* $125/£81

MARZIALS, THEO. Pan Pipes, a Book of Old Songs.... London: Routledge, 1883. 1st ed. 51pp. Color dwg by Crane each pg. Cl-backed glazed pict bds (chipped; inner hinges badly cracked; inscrip). *King.* $150/£97

MASEFIELD, JOHN. Ballads and Poems. Elkin Mathews, 1910. 1st Eng ed. Grn cl bds; gilt. VG (bkpl). *Dalian.* $54/£35

MASEFIELD, JOHN. The Coming of Christ. London: Heinemann, (1928). 1st ed. NF in dj (lt dknd, repaired tear). *Sadlon.* $20/£13

MASEFIELD, JOHN. The Dream. London: Heinemann, (1922). One of 800 numbered, signed by John and Judith Masefield (illus). VG. *Rees.* $31/£20

MASEFIELD, JOHN. The Dream. NY: Macmillan, 1922. 1st Amer ed. Ltd to 750. Signed. Teg. Rubbed. *Sadlon.* $25/£16

MASEFIELD, JOHN. Eggs and Baker, or the Days of Trial. London: Heinemann, (1936). 1st ed. Spine sl lightened. Dj (spine sl dknd). *Sadlon.* $20/£13

MASEFIELD, JOHN. The Hawbucks. London: Heinemann, 1929. 1st ed. Ltd to 275. Signed. Teg. Unopened. Top corners sl bumped, o/w Fine in dj (mildly dknd). *Sadlon.* $75/£48

MASEFIELD, JOHN. In the Mill. London: Heinemann, 1941. 1st ed. Blue buckram (sl wear), gilt (sl rubbed, dull). Internally Very Nice. *Temple.* $12/£8

MASEFIELD, JOHN. King Cole and Other Poems. London: Heinemann, 1923. 1st ed. Inscribed. Als tipped in. Blue cl. VG. *Cox.* $70/£45

MASEFIELD, JOHN. A King's Daughter. London: Heinemann, n.d. 1st ed, 1st issue. NF in dj (sl dknd). *Sadlon.* $30/£19

MASEFIELD, JOHN. Martin Hyde, the Duke's Messenger. London: Wells Gardner, Darton & Co, n.d. (1910). 1st Eng ed, 1st issue. Frontis, guard (loose); 15 plts. Teg, rest rough-trimmed. Unopened. Mulberry cl, not blue as in 2nd issue. NF in dj (sl frayed). *Temple.* $85/£55

MASEFIELD, JOHN. The Midnight Folk. Heinemann, 1927. 1st ed. Sl dull; worn, else Good. *Whiteson.* $37/£24

MASEFIELD, JOHN. The Midnight Folk. London: Heinemann, 1927. 1st UK ed. Fine in NF dj (sl creasing, sm chip bottom of spine). *Williams.* $101/£65

MASEFIELD, JOHN. Midsummer Night and Other Tales in Verse. London: Heinemann, (1928). 1st ed. Eps lt foxed. Dj (sl dknd, edgeworn). *Sadlon.* $20/£13

MASEFIELD, JOHN. Minnie Maylow's Story and Other Tales and Scenes. London: Heinemann, (1931). 1st ed. Head of spine sl rubbed. 2 copies of dj (spines dknd, lt foxing; 1 w/sl chips, repaired tear). *Sadlon.* $25/£16

MASEFIELD, JOHN. Recent Prose. London: Heinemann, 1924. 1st ed. Blue buckram, gilt. Nice. *Temple.* $12/£8

MASEFIELD, JOHN. Right Royal. London: Heinemann, 1920. 1st ed. NF in dj (spine lightened). *Sadlon.* $25/£16

MASEFIELD, JOHN. Rosas (poems). NY: Macmillan, 1918. 1st ed. One of 950 signed. Fine. *Second Life.* $35/£23

MASEFIELD, JOHN. Sard Harker. London: Heinemann, 1924. 1st ed. Ltd to 380. Signed. Teg. NF in dj (spine sl dknd). *Sadlon.* $65/£42

MASEFIELD, JOHN. The Taking of Helen. London: Heinemann, 1923. One of 780 numbered, signed. 1/4 vellum. Bumped, o/w VG. *Rees.* $39/£25

MASEFIELD, JOHN. The Trial of Jesus. London: Heinemann, (1925). 1st ed. NF in dj (sl dknd). *Sadlon.* $25/£16

MASEFIELD, JOHN. The Wanderer of Liverpool. NY: Macmillan, 1930. 1st ed. One of 350 numbered, signed. Color frontis, 32 plates, 4 plans (3 fldg). (Extrems rubbed.) *Lefkowicz.* $150/£97

MASON, A. HUGHLETT. The Journal of Charles Mason and Jeremiah Dixon. Phila: Amer Philosophical Soc, 1969. 1st ed. Frontis. VF in VG dj. *Oregon.* $60/£39

MASON, A.E.W. Lawrence Clavering. A.D. Innes, 1897. 1st Eng ed. Blue cl. Cvrs mkd; eps sl foxed; name, o/w VG. *Dalian.* $54/£35

MASON, A.E.W. No Other Tiger. NY: George H. Doran, (1927). 1st Amer ed. NF in dj. *Godot.* $45/£29

MASON, A.E.W. The Prisoner in Opal. Hodder & Stoughton, (1928). 1st Eng ed. Blue cl. Spine faded; fore-edge sl foxed, o/w VG. *Dalian.* $31/£20

MASON, A.E.W. The Summons. London: Hodder & Stoughton, (1920). 1st ed. Lt blue cl. VG in dj (nicks). *Houle.* $350/£226

MASON, A.E.W. The Winding Stair. NY: George H. Doran, (1923). 1st Amer ed. NF in dj. *Godot.* $45/£29

MASON, B.F. Through War and Peace. N.p., 1891. Minor cvr staining, o/w VG + . *Pratt.* $45/£29

MASON, BOBBIE ANN and MARTHA BENNETT STILES. Landscapes. (Frankfort, KY): Frankfort Arts Foundation, (1984). 1st ed, one of 450 numbered in stitched wraps. Signed by both. Fine. *Turlington.* $75/£48

MASON, BOBBIE ANN. The Girl Sleuth. (Old Westbury, NY): Feminist Press, 1975. 1st ed. VF in pict wrappers. *Jaffe.* $350/£226

MASON, BOBBIE ANN. Shiloh and Other Stories. NY: Harper, (1982). 1st ed. Fine in dj. *Turlington.* $100/£65

MASON, BOBBIE ANN. Shiloh and Other Stories. NY: Harper, (1982). 1st ed. Signed. Fine in dj. *Jaffe.* $125/£81

MASON, C.A. The Little Green God. Revell, 1902. 1st ed. Stamped cl. Spine dknd, bowed, else VG. *Aronovitz.* $35/£23

MASON, CHARLES. Journal of Charles Mason and Jeremiah Dixon. A.H. Mason (trans). Phila: Amer Philosophical Soc, 1969. Dj. *Heinoldt.* $15/£10

MASON, EDWARD G. Chapters from Illinois History. Chicago: Herbert S. Stone, 1901. (Ex-lib.) *Schoyer.* $40/£26

MASON, FRANCIS K. Battle over Britain. London: McWhirter, 1969. Fine. *Peter Taylor.* $59/£38

MASON, GEORGE CARRINGTON. Colonial Churches of Tidewater Virginia. Whittet & Shepperson, 1945. VG. *Book Broker.* $65/£42

MASON, HERBERT I. A Flora of the Marshes of California. Berkeley: Univ of CA, 1957. 1st ed. Fine in dj. *Quest.* $65/£42

MASON, J. Bookbinding. Warne, 1936. 1st ed. Color frontis. Yellow/grn cl. VG. *Moss.* $19/£12

MASON, JEREMIAH. Memoir and Correspondence of Jeremiah Mason. Cambridge: Riverside Press, 1873. 1st ed. Presentation copy signed in 1874 by author's son. 4to. Frontis,viii,468pp. Burgundy cl, gilt (soiled). Howes M 368. *Karmiole.* $85/£55

MASON, KATHRYN HARROD. James Harrod of Kentucky. Baton Rouge: LSU Press, (1951). 1st ed. Blue cl. NF in VG dj. *Chapel Hill.* $60/£39

MASON, MIRIAM E. A Pony Called Lightning. NY: Macmillan, 1948. 1st ed. VG in Good dj. *October Farm.* $30/£19

MASON, MIRIAM E. Susannah: The Pioneer Cow. NY: Macmillan, 1941. 1st ed. Maud and Miska Petersham (illus). 8vo. Yellow cl w/brn decs, lettering. Good in color dj (minor edgewear). *Reisler.* $75/£48

MASON, OTIS TUFTON. Primitive Travel and Transportation. Washington: GPO, 1896. 25 plts. Rust-colored cl, gilt spine titles. Orig fr wrap bound in. VG + . *Parmer.* $165/£106

MASON, SAMUEL, JR. Historical Sketches of Harford County, Maryland. Darlington, MD: Little Pines Farm, 1940. 1st ed, ltd to 250. Frontis. VG. *Connolly.* $50/£32

MASON, STUART. Bibliography of Oscar Wilde. London: T. Werner Laurie, (1914). 1st ed. Orig blue gilt cl (extrems, corners lt rubbed; bkpl), teg. *Karmiole.* $100/£65

MASPERO, G. Art in Egypt. London: Heinemann, 1912. 3 color plts. Good. *Archaeologia.* $45/£29

MASPERO, G. History of Egypt, Chaldea, Syria, Babylonia, and Assyria. London: Grolier Soc, (1904). 12 vols. Maroon buckram. VG + . *House.* $400/£258

MASPERO, G. Life in Ancient Egypt and Assyria. NY: Appleton, 1892. Authorized ed. xv,376pp. VG ex-lib. *Worldwide.* $45/£29

MASPERO, G. Life in Ancient Egypt and Assyria. NY: D. Appleton, 1935. Good. *Archaeologia.* $35/£23

MASPERO, G. Popular Stories of Ancient Egypt. New Hyde Park: University Books, (1967). Good in dj. *Archaeologia.* $35/£23

MASSACHUSETTS MEDICAL SOCIETY. Acts of Incorporation and Acts Regulating the Practice of Physic and Surgery, with the By-Laws and Orders. Boston, 1832. 88,(4)pp. Early paper wraps (worn). *Goodrich.* $125/£81

MASSAR, PHYLLIS DEARBORN. Presenting Stefano della Bella, Seventeenth-Century Printmaker. NY: Metropolitan Museum, 1972. Fine (bkpl) in dj. *Europa.* $37/£24

MASSER, PHYLLIS DEARBORN. Presenting Stefano della Bella.... MMA, 1971. 1st US ed. Sm pict onlay. Fine in dj. *Willow House.* $19/£12

MASSEY, DON W. The Episcopal Churches in the Diocese of Virginia. Diocese Church Hist Pub, (c. 1989). Fine in Fine dj. *Book Broker.* $45/£29

MASSEY, G. BETTON. Electricity in the Diseases of Women.... Phila, 1890. 1st ed. 240pp. Good. *Fye.* $175/£113

MASSEY, MARY ELIZABETH. Bonnet Brigades: American Women and the Civil War. NY, 1966. 1st ed. Lt dj wear, o/w Fine. *Pratt.* $50/£32

MASSEY, MARY ELIZABETH. Ersatz in the Confederacy. Columbia: Univ of SC Press, 1952. 1st ed. Orig cl. Fine in NF dj. *Mcgowan.* $125/£81

MASSIE, CHRIS. The Green Circle. NY: Random House, 1943. 1st Amer ed. Fine in dj (price-clipped; rubbing; sl wear). *Mordida.* $45/£29

MASSON, GEORGINA. Italian Villas and Palaces. London: Thames & Hudson, 1959. 1st ed. 193 photogravure plts. Pub's buckram gilt. Sl shaken, else VG. *Quest.* $110/£71

MASSON, ROSALINE (ed). I Can Remember Robert Louis Stevenson. Edinburgh: W. & R. Chambers, 1922. 1st Eng ed. 4 plts. Red cl, gilt. Eps sl browned, o/w VG. *Dalian.* $39/£25

MASTAI, M.L. D'OTRANGE. Illusion in Art: Trompe l'Oeil.... NY, 1975. 23 color plts. Cl spotted. Dj. *Argosy.* $85/£55

MASTEROFF, JOE. Cabaret. NY: Random House, (1967). 1st ed. Fine in dj. *Between The Covers.* $175/£113

Masterpieces of Tapestry from the Fourteenth to the Sixteenth Century. NY: MMA, 1973. Good in wrappers. *Washton.* $30/£19

MASTERS, EDGAR LEE. Althea. Rooks Press, 1907. 1st ed. Sm chip spine head, else VG in wraps as issued. *Fine Books.* $175/£113

MASTERS, EDGAR LEE. Dramatic Duologues. NY: Samuel French, 1934. Stated 1st ed. Good in wrappers. *Hayman.* $15/£10

MASTERS, EDGAR LEE. Gettysburg Manila Acoma. NY: Horace Liveright, 1930. 1st ed. One of 375. Signed. Uncut, unopened. Bkpl; else Fine in (lt worn) slipcase. *Bookpress.* $60/£39

MASTERS, EDGAR LEE. The Golden Fleece of California. NY: Farrar & Rinehart, (1936). 1st ed. VG (sl browning) in dj (spine browned; chipped). *Antic Hay.* $25/£16

MASTERS, EDGAR LEE. Jack Kelso. NY: Appleton, 1928. 1st ed. VG in dj (browned; chip). *Antic Hay.* $45/£29

MASTERS, EDGAR LEE. Mark Twain, A Portrait. NY: Scribner's, 1938. 1st ed, 1st ptg. Cream cl. Nice in VG dj. *Macdonnell.* $50/£32

MASTERS, EDGAR LEE. Spoon River Anthology. NY: Macmillan, 1915. 1st ed, 1st state. Blue dec cl, gilt. Fine (early inscrip). *Macdonnell.* $375/£242

MASTERS, EDGAR LEE. Spoon River Anthology. NY: LEC, 1942. One of 1500. Signed by author & Boardman Robinson (illus). Lacks slipcase; spine sl soiled, else Fine. *Pharos.* $150/£97

MASTERS, JOHN. Bhowani Junction. NY: Viking, 1954. 1st ed. Fine in dj (sl edgewear). *Else Fine.* $40/£26

MASTERS, JOHN. Bhowani Junction. London: Joseph, 1954. 1st ed. Inscrip, else VG in dj (nicked). *Limestone.* $40/£26

MASTERS, JOHN. The Deceivers. NY: Viking, 1952. 1st ed. Fine in dj (lt wear). *Else Fine.* $45/£29

MASTERS, JOHN. Fandango Rock. NY: Harper, 1959. 1st ed. VF in dj. *Else Fine.* $35/£23

MASTERS, JOHN. Fandango Rock. London: Michael Joseph, 1959. 1st UK ed. Fine in VG dj. *Williams.* $25/£16

MASTERS, JOHN. Far, Far the Mountain Peak. NY: Viking, 1957. 1st ed. Fine in dj. *Else Fine.* $40/£26

MASTERS, JOHN. Far, Far the Mountain Peak. London: Joseph, 1957. 1st ed. VG in Fine dj w/Book Soc wraparound band. *Limestone.* $95/£61

MASTERS, JOHN. Nightrunners of Bengal. NY: Viking, 1951. 1st ed. VG (lower cvr, dj interior watermarked). *Else Fine.* $25/£16

MASTERS, JOHN. The Ravi Lancers. London: Joseph, 1972. 1st ed. Fine in dj. *Limestone.* $70/£45

MASTERS, JOHN. The Venus of Konpara. NY: Harper, 1960. 1st ed. VF in dj. *Else Fine.* $35/£23

MASTERS, WILLIAM and VIRGINIA JOHNSON. Human Sexual Response. Boston, 1966. 1st ed, 4th ptg. Good. *Fye.* $20/£13

MASTERSON, V.V. The Katy Railroad and the Last Frontier. Norman: Univ of OK, (1952). 1st ed. Ink name, else VG in VG dj. *Perier.* $35/£23

MASTERSON, V.V. The Katy Railroad and the Last Frontier. Norman, 1952. 1st ed. NF in dj (chipped). *Baade.* $65/£42

MASUDA, H. et al. The Fishes of the Japanese Archipelago. Tokyo, 1984. 2 vols. 450pp; atlas of 380 plts. *Wheldon & Wesley.* $310/£200

MASURY, JOHN. How Shall We Paint Our Houses? NY: D. Appleton, 1868. 1st ed. 216,(6)pp. Contemp ink inscrip, sl foxing, else Fine. *Bookpress.* $195/£126

MATHER, COTTON. Magnalia Christi Americana. Hartford: Silas Andrus & Son, 1855. 1st Amer ed. 2 vols. Rebound, o/w VG + . *Bishop.* $75/£48

MATHER, FRED. Men I Have Fished With. NY: Forest & Stream, 1897. 1st ed. 9 ports. Spine dknd, cvr soil, o/w VG. *Bowman.* $30/£19

MATHER, FRED. My Angling Friends. NY: Forest & Stream, 1901. 1st ed. 13 ports. Spine dknd, o/w VG. *Bowman.* $40/£26

MATHER, R.E. and F.E. BOSWELL. Hanging the Sheriff. Salt Lake City, 1987. 1st ed. Signed by both authors. Fine in dj. *Baade.* $30/£19

MATHERS, E. POWYS. The Book of the Thousand Nights and One Night. London: The Casanova Soc, 1923. #344/750. 16 vols, bound in 8. 8vo. Colored frontis each. Teg, others uncut. 1/2 red morocco, ribbed gilt dec spines. *D & D.* $890/£574

MATHERS, E. POWYS. A Circle of the Seasons. London: Golden Cockerel Press, 1929. #112/500. 4 copper engrs by Robert Gibbings; teg, others uncut. Orig buckram. VG. *Cox.* $171/£110

MATHERS, E. POWYS. Eastern Love. London, 1927-30. One of 1000. 12 vols in 4. Fore, lower edge uncut. Gilt device upper bds. (Faded; spine vol 3 sl bumped.) *Edwards.* $93/£60

MATHERS, E. POWYS. Eastern Love. NY, n.d. (1930). #132/1500 sets. Uncut. Gilt dec cvrs. NF (spines sunned, foxed). *Polyanthos.* $125/£81

MATHERS, E. POWYS. Eastern Love. NY, n.d. (1930). Ltd to 1550 numbered. 3 vols. Vellum-backed cl (spine dknd, sl worn, faded). *King.* $75/£48

MATHERS, E. POWYS. Sung to Shahryar. London: Casanova Soc, 1925. #20/50 ptd on lg paper, numbered, signed. VG. *Williams.* $233/£150

MATHERS, S.L. MacGREGOR. Fortune-Telling Cards. The Tarot. London: Kegan, Paul, Trench, Trubner, 1909. 2nd ed. Grn cl stamped in black. Good. *Karmiole.* $30/£19

MATHES, W. MICHAEL. Mexico on Stone: Lithography in Mexico, 1826-1900. SF: Book Club of CA, 1984. 1st ed. Ltd to 550. VF in buff dj (lt soiled). *Hermitage.* $150/£97

MATHESON, DON. Stray Cat. Summit, 1987. 1st ed. 1st bk. NF in dj. *Murder.* $35/£23

MATHESON, RICHARD. The Beardless Warriors. Little-Brown, 1960. 1st ed. VG in dj (frayed, dusty). *Madle.* $100/£65

MATHESON, RICHARD. Born of Man and Woman. Chamberlain, 1954. 1st ed. Fine in dj (rubbed, chipped). *Madle.* $200/£129

MATHESON, RICHARD. Hell House. NY: Viking Press, (1971). 1st ed. Name, address flyleaf, o/w NF in dj (price-clipped). *Bernard.* $175/£113

MATHESON, RICHARD. Hell House. Viking, 1971. 1st ed. Fine in dj. *Aronovitz.* $150/£97

MATHESON, RICHARD. Hell House. Viking, 1971. 1st ed. Fine in dj. *Madle.* $250/£161

MATHESON, RICHARD. Scars. LA: Scream Press, 1987. 1st ed. One of 250 numbered, signed. Fine in slipcase. *Other Worlds.* $125/£81

MATHESON, RICHARD. Third From the Sun. NY: Bantam Books, (1955). 1st ed. Fine in ptd wraps. *Antic Hay.* $45/£29

MATHESON, RICHARD. What Dreams May Come. Putnam, 1978. 1st ed. Fine in dj. *Madle.* $100/£65

MATHEWS, JOHN JOSEPH. Talking to the Moon. Chicago: Univ of Chicago, 1945. 1st ed. Inscribed. VG + in dj (chipped). *Parker.* $35/£23

MATHEWS, MRS. M.M. Ten Years in Nevada or, Life on the Pacific Coast. Buffalo: Baker, Jones, 1880. 1st ed. 343pp; 2 ports. VG. Howes M 417. *Second Life.* $350/£226

MATHEWSON, C. Second Base Sloan. D-M, 1917. 1st ed. Good. *Fine Books.* $50/£32

MATHIAS, FRED S. The Amazing Bob Davis. NY: Longmans, Green, 1944. 1st ed. 40 sketches. Fine in Good dj. *Connolly.* $27/£17

MATHIEU, P.L. Gustave Moreau. Boston: NYGS, 1976. Sound in dj. *Ars Artis.* $163/£105

MATISSE, HENRI. Jazz. NY, (1983). Facs of orig numbered, signed ltd ed of 250. 20 full-pg color plts; facs of orig colophon. Mint in dj, box. *Argosy.* $400/£258

Matrix 2. (Gloucestershire: Whittington Press), 1982. One of 40 numbered. 1/2 niger. Portfolio contains extra set of plts. Fine in slipcase. *Bookpress.* $315/£203

Matrix 2. A Review for Printers and Bibliophiles. (Andoversford): Whittington Press, 1993. Rpt. One of 475. Stiff wraps. *Veatchs.* $120/£77

Matrix 2. John and Rosalind Randle (ed). London: Whittington Press, (Summer) 1993. 2nd ed. Ltd to 400. New in stiff cvrs, dj. *Cox.* $116/£75

Matrix 6. (Andoversford, Gloucestershire: Whittington, 1986). Ltd to 950. Dec grn ptd paper bds. Fine. *Karmiole.* $185/£119

Matrix 8. Andoversford: Whittington Press, 1988. One of 900. *Bookpress.* $175/£113

Matrix 9. Gloucestershire: Whittington Press, Winter 1989. One of 820 thus of 925. Fine in pink paper wrappers. *Heller.* $185/£119

Matrix 11. Whittington Press, 1991. One of 955. Fine in wrappers. *Bookpress.* $200/£129

Matrix 11. London: Whittington Press, Winter 1991. 1st ed. Ltd to 955. Dec paper bds. New in ptd wrapper. *Cox.* $171/£110

Matrix 13. Lower Marston Farm: Whittington Press, 1990. One of 835. Fine in stiff wrappers. *Bookpress.* $175/£113

MATSON, DONALD D. The Treatment of Acute Craniocerebral Injuries due to Missiles. Springfield: Thomas, 1948. NF. *Goodrich.* $45/£29

MATSON, G. OLAF. Palestine Guide. Jerusalem: American Colony, 1930. 3rd ed. 3 fldg maps (1 lg in back pocket). Sl rubbed; pencil mks, o/w VG. *Worldwide.* $45/£29

MATSON, NEHEMIAH. French and Indians of the Illinois River. Princeton, IL: Republican Job Ptg Est, 1874. 1st ed. Signed presentation. Mtd port. Blind-emb cl, gilt title. Sm repaired chip, lt worn, lt foxing, else VG. Howes M 419. *Cahan.* $350/£226

MATSON, NEHEMIAH. Memories of Shaubena. Chicago: D.B. Cooke, 1878. 1st ed. Frontis, (8),17-269pp; 12 plts. Blue cl, gilt spine title. (Wear; extrems frayed.) Howes M 420. *Bohling.* $200/£129

MATTER, MERCEDES. Alberto Giacometti. NY: Abrams, 1987. 45 color, 180 b/w photo plts. VG in dj. *Argosy.* $75/£48

MATTES, MERRILL J. The Great Platte River Road. (Lincoln), 1969. 1st ed. NF in dj (sl worn). *Baade.* $65/£42

MATTHAEI, R. (ed). Goethe's Colour Theory. H. Aach (trans). London: Studio Vista, 1971. Sound in dj. *Ars Artis.* $70/£45

MATTHEWS, BRANDER (chosen by). Poems of American Patriotism. NY: Scribner's, 1922. 1st ed. 4to. 14 full-pg color plts by N.C. Wyeth. Black cl w/color paste label, tinted top. Nice. *Reisler.* $350/£226

MATTHEWS, FREDERICK C. American Merchant Ships 1850-1900. Salem: Marine Research Soc Pubs 21 & 23, 1930-31. 1st eds. 2 vols. Fine set in djs. Howes M 424. *Lefkowicz.* $300/£194

MATTHEWS, FREDERICK C. American Merchant Ships 1850-1900. And the same...Series Two.... Salem, MA: Marine Research Soc, 1930-1931. 2 vols. Sm broadside laid in states that 2nd vol pub in ed of 775, 1st in ed of 1250. VG in djs (vol 1 reinforced). *Hayman.* $200/£129

MATTHEWS, L.H. British Mammals. London: New Naturalist, 1952. 1st ed. 16 colored, 48 plain plts. Dj (sl used). *Wheldon & Wesley.* $39/£25

MATTHEWS, THOMAS. The Moon's No Fool. Random House, 1936. 1st US ed. Fine in dj. *Madle.* $40/£26

MATTHEWS, WASHINGTON. Ethnography and Philology of the Hidatsa Indians. Washington, 1877. vi,239pp. (Lt wear, backstrip torn, fraying, 2 bkpls.) *Bohling.* $75/£48

MATTHEWS, WILLIAM. American Diaries; an Annotated Bibliography.... Berkeley, 1945. 1st ed. Orig ptd wrappers. *Ginsberg.* $50/£32

MATTHIESSEN, PETER. In the Spirit of Crazy Horse. NY: Viking, 1983. 1st ed. Most 1st eds recalled and destroyed due to lawsuits. VF in dj. *Else Fine.* $235/£152

MATTHIESSEN, PETER. Indian Country. NY: Viking, 1984. 1st ed. NF in NF dj. *Parker.* $85/£55

MATTHIESSEN, PETER. Midnight Turning Gray. Bristol: Ampersand, 1984. 1st ed. Fine in ptd wraps. *Revere.* $45/£29

MATTHIESSEN, PETER. Oomingmak. NY: Hastings House, 1967. 1st ed. Fine in Fine dj. *Pettler.* $50/£32

MATTHIESSEN, PETER. Sal Si Puedes. NY: Random House, 1969. 1st ed. Name, else Fine in Fine dj. *Pettler.* $50/£32

MATTHIESSEN, PETER. Sand Rivers. NY: Viking, (1981). 1st ed. Signed, inscribed. Beige cl. NF (lt dampstaining) in dj. *Chapel Hill.* $125/£81

MATTHIESSEN, PETER. Sand Rivers. NY: Viking, (1981). 1st ed. Signed. NF (sl soil) in dj (few tears; tiny nick). *Antic Hay.* $75/£48

MATTHIESSEN, PETER. Under the Mountain Wall. NY: Viking, 1962. 1st ed. 1st issue, w/plts placed within body of text, rather than at end; these copies were sold to two bk clubs, which tipped in new table of contents pg, which this copy has. Fine in dj (minor corner rubs). *Else Fine.* $60/£39

MATTHIESSEN, PETER. Wildlife in America. NY: Viking, 1959. 1st ed. Signed. NF in dj (wear; sm tears). *Antic Hay.* $185/£119

MATTHIESSEN, PETER. The Wind Birds. NY: Viking, (1973). 1st Amer ed. Fine in Fine dj (price-clipped). *Between The Covers.* $200/£129

MATURIN, ANN. At Dawn Set Free. Phila: Dorrance, (1961). 1st ed, 1st bk. Signed, inscribed presentation. VG in pict dj. *Petrilla.* $40/£26

MAU, AUGUST. Pompeii, Its Life and Art. Francis W. Kelsey (trans). NY, 1899. xxii,509pp + (iii)pub's ads, 12 plts, 6 plans. (Tp partially detached; inscrip, names erased, sm hole.) Teg. Morocco-backed cl (spine rubbed, chipped, sl loss head), gilt device. *Edwards.* $39/£25

MAUCLAIR, CAMILLE. Auguste Rodin. The Man—His Ideas—His Works. London: Duckworth, 1909. 40 plts. (Sm spine tear repaired.) *Ars Artis.* $39/£25

MAUCLAIR, CAMILLE. J.M.W. Turner. E.B. Shaw (trans). London, 1939. VG in dj. *Argosy.* $100/£65

MAUDE, AYLMER. Tolstoy on Art and Its Critics. London: Humphrey Milford, OUP, 1925. 1st ed. Fine in ptd gray wraps; grn cl folder. *Chapel Hill.* $100/£65

MAUDSLAY, ROBERT. Texas Sheepman. Austin: Univ of TX Press, 1951. 1st ed. Fine in dj (poor). *Perier.* $25/£16

MAUGHAM, R.C.F. Africa as I Have Known It. London, 1929. 1st ed. Frontis port, 2 fldg maps. (Lt marginal browning; lt soiled, sm tear, dent.) *Edwards.* $78/£50

MAUGHAM, R.C.F. Portugese East Africa. London: John Murray, 1906. 1st ed. Frontis, 32 plts, fldg map. (Foxing.) Blue cl (lib plt; damp spotting), white/gilt dec upper cvr, teg. *Morrell.* $85/£55

MAUGHAM, ROBIN. Approach to Palestine. Falcon Press, 1947. 1st Eng ed. Dec red bds. VF in dj (sl dusty). *Dalian.* $70/£45

MAUGHAM, ROBIN. Line on Ginger. London: Chapman & Hall, 1949. 1st ed. Top edge brn. Grn cl. NF in dj (frayed; verso strengthened). *Temple.* $31/£20

MAUGHAM, ROBIN. The Servant. Falcon, 1948. 1st Eng ed. Orange cl. Eps sl browned, o/w VF in dj (sl soiled, chipped). *Dalian.* $101/£65

MAUGHAM, ROBIN. The Servant. NY, 1949. 1st Amer ed. VG in dj (spine rubbed). *Words Etc.* $22/£14

MAUGHAM, ROBIN. The Slaves of Timbuktu. Longmans, 1961. 1st Eng ed. Blue cl. VG in dj (sl mkd; price-clipped). *Dalian.* $54/£35

MAUGHAM, W. SOMERSET. Ah King. London: Heinemann, (1933). 1st ed. Blue cl. VG in dj. *Chapel Hill.* $130/£84

MAUGHAM, W. SOMERSET. Ashenden or The British Agent. London: Heinemann, 1928. 1st ed. VG. *Limestone.* $145/£94

MAUGHAM, W. SOMERSET. Ashenden or the British Agent. Heinemann, 1928. 1st Eng ed. Blue cl. Spine, cvrs mkd, o/w VG. *Dalian.* $132/£85

MAUGHAM, W. SOMERSET. The Book-Bag. Florence: G. Orioli, 1932. 1st separate ed. #120/725 signed. Frontis port. Unopened. Cl-backed blue bds. Edges faded, else NF in VG dj (spine sunned; lt chipped). *Chapel Hill.* $325/£210

MAUGHAM, W. SOMERSET. Books and You. London: Heinemann, (1940). 1st ed. Blue cl. VG in dj (lt worn; spine sunned). *Chapel Hill.* $60/£39

MAUGHAM, W. SOMERSET. Books and You. London: Heinemann, 1940. 1st ed. NF in VG dj (lt spotted). *Limestone.* $85/£55

MAUGHAM, W. SOMERSET. The Bread-Winner. London: Heinemann, (1930). 1st ed, 2nd issue, w/note on 'Performing Rights' inserted before text. One of 2000 ptd. Red cl. NF; issued w/o dj. *Chapel Hill.* $95/£61

MAUGHAM, W. SOMERSET. Caesar's Wife. London: Heinemann, 1922. 1st ed. One of 2000 ptd. Red cl. NF; no dj as issued. *Chapel Hill.* $95/£61

MAUGHAM, W. SOMERSET. Cakes and Ale. London: Heinemann, (1930). 1st ed, 2nd issue, w/correct reading 'won't' rather than 'won' in line 14, p147. Blue cl (rubbed; lt bowed). VG. *Chapel Hill.* $75/£48

MAUGHAM, W. SOMERSET. Cakes and Ale. London: Heinemann, (1930). 1st ed. Fine in NF dj (sm tears). *Between The Covers.* $350/£226

MAUGHAM, W. SOMERSET. Cakes and Ale. London: Heinemann, 1930. 1st ed. Stott 26. W/misprint on pg 181, line 4, & dropped letter 'I' on pg 63, line 22. Pp sl browned; spine sl rubbed, faded, else VG in dj (soiled, browned; frayed). *Virgo.* $93/£60

MAUGHAM, W. SOMERSET. Cakes and Ale. London: Heinemann, 1930. 1st UK ed. VG+ in dj (spine sl creased). *Williams.* $194/£125

MAUGHAM, W. SOMERSET. The Casuarina Tree. London: Heinemann, 1926. 1st ed. Dk blue cl (spine top rubbed). VG in dj (chips). *Chapel Hill.* $350/£226

MAUGHAM, W. SOMERSET. Christmas Holiday. London: Heinemann, (1939). 1st ed. Blue cl. Pp lt browned, tape mks eps, else NF in dj. *Chapel Hill.* $100/£65

MAUGHAM, W. SOMERSET. The Constant Wife. NY: Doran, 1926. 1st ed. NF in scarce dj (soiled, worn corners; triangular chip head of spine affecting some title lettering). *Else Fine.* $135/£87

MAUGHAM, W. SOMERSET. The Constant Wife. London: Heinemann, 1927. 1st Eng ed. Black cl, paper labels. NF in VG dj (spine dknd). *Chapel Hill.* $150/£97

MAUGHAM, W. SOMERSET. Cosmopolitans. London, (1936). 1st Eng ed, 1st issue w/1/2 title & pp5-6 cancelled. (Spine sl faded.) *Waterfield.* $28/£18

MAUGHAM, W. SOMERSET. Cosmopolitans. London/Toronto: Heinemann, (1936). 1st Eng ed. Blue cl. Eps sl faded, else NF in dj (lt wear). *Chapel Hill.* $125/£81

MAUGHAM, W. SOMERSET. Creatures of Circumstance. London: Heinemann, (1947). 1st ed. Red cl. NF in dj (worn). *Chapel Hill.* $40/£26

MAUGHAM, W. SOMERSET. Don Fernando. Heinemann, 1935. 1st ed. Pub's gold-gilt pict binding. NF in VG dj (lt wear). *Fine Books.* $125/£81

MAUGHAM, W. SOMERSET. Don Fernando. Heinemann, 1935. 1st Eng ed. Black cl; gilt. Cvrs sl mkd; bkpl, o/w VG. *Dalian.* $54/£35

MAUGHAM, W. SOMERSET. East of Suez. London: Heinemann, 1922. 1st ed. Red cl (lt fading). VG; no dj as issued. *Chapel Hill.* $125/£81

MAUGHAM, W. SOMERSET. Encore. London: Heinemann, (1951). 1st ed. Red cl. NF in dj (spine sl dknd; lt rubbed). *Chapel Hill.* $60/£39

MAUGHAM, W. SOMERSET. The Explorer. London: Heinemann, 1908. 1st UK ed. VG. *Williams.* $47/£30

MAUGHAM, W. SOMERSET. The Explorer. London: Heinemann, 1912. 1st ed. One of 2000 ptd. Ptd wraps. Spine worn, else VG. *Chapel Hill.* $45/£29

MAUGHAM, W. SOMERSET. First Person Singular. London: Heinemann, (1931). 1st Eng ed. Blue cl. VG in dj (spine dknd, damp spots). *Chapel Hill.* $175/£113

MAUGHAM, W. SOMERSET. First Person Singular. London: Heinemann, 1931. 1st UK ed. VG in dj (sl nick top of spine). *Williams.* $302/£195

MAUGHAM, W. SOMERSET. For Services Rendered. Heinemann, 1932. 1st ed. NF in VG dj (soil, fading). *Fine Books.* $95/£61

MAUGHAM, W. SOMERSET. France at War. London: Heinemann, (1940). 1st ed. NF in red/white/blue ptd wraps. *Chapel Hill.* $35/£23

MAUGHAM, W. SOMERSET. The Gentleman in the Parlour. London: Heinemann, (1930). 1st ed. Partly unopened. Gilt-stamped black cl. NF in dj (spine sunned; chips). *Chapel Hill.* $175/£113

MAUGHAM, W. SOMERSET. The Gentleman in the Parlour. Heinemann, 1930. 1st Eng ed. Black cl; gilt. Fine in dj. *Dalian.* $194/£125

MAUGHAM, W. SOMERSET. Here and There. London: Heinemann, (1948). 1st ed. Red cl. NF in VG dj (lt chipped). *Chapel Hill.* $50/£32

MAUGHAM, W. SOMERSET. Home and Beauty. London: Heinemann, 1923. 1st ed. Red cl. Bkpl, else NF; no dj as issued. *Chapel Hill.* $95/£61

MAUGHAM, W. SOMERSET. The Hour Before the Dawn. GC: Doubleday, Doran, 1942. 1st ed. Black cl. NF in VG dj (lt wear). *Chapel Hill.* $65/£42

MAUGHAM, W. SOMERSET. Jack Straw. London: Heinemann, 1912. 1st ed. One of 1500 ptd. Fine in ptd wraps. *Chapel Hill.* $75/£48

MAUGHAM, W. SOMERSET. The Land of the Blessed Virgin. London: Heinemann, 1905. 1st ed, 1st state binding. Frontis. Gilt-stamped Japan vellum, blue bds (sl rubbed; lt soiled). Good. *Houle.* $295/£190

MAUGHAM, W. SOMERSET. The Land of the Blessed Virgin. London: Heinemann, 1905. 1st ed. Frontis. Blue bds, white linen spine. VG (offsetting fep; extrems sunned). *Chapel Hill.* $200/£129

MAUGHAM, W. SOMERSET. The Land of the Blessed Virgin. London: Heinemann, 1905. 1st ed. Frontis. Unopened. Linen-backed lt blue bds. VG. *Chapel Hill.* $350/£226

MAUGHAM, W. SOMERSET. Landed Gentry. London: Heinemann, 1913. 1st ed. One of 2000 ptd. Red cl. Bkpl removed, else NF; no dj as issued. *Chapel Hill.* $65/£42

MAUGHAM, W. SOMERSET. Letter from Singapore. (CA): Stanford Univ, (1979). 1st ed, ltd to 750. Ptd protective folder, 3 loose sheets. Lt faded, else Fine. *Godot.* $40/£26

MAUGHAM, W. SOMERSET. Liza of Lambeth. London: Heinemann, (1947). Jubilee ed. #474/1000 signed. Teg, rest uncut. Vellum backstrip (faded). *Petersfield.* $54/£35

MAUGHAM, W. SOMERSET. Liza of Lambeth. London: T. Fisher Unwin, 1897. 1st ed, 1st issue, 1st bk. Later issues state 'Colonial Edition' on tp verso. 242 + (6)pp ads. Lt grn dec cl. Sound (sl cocked; rear hinge cracked internally; tear rep). *Chapel Hill.* $850/£548

MAUGHAM, W. SOMERSET. Liza of Lambeth. London: Heinemann, 1947. Jubilee ed, #173/1000, signed. Orig 1/4 vellum, gilt-lettered black leather spine label. VF. *D & D.* $200/£129

MAUGHAM, W. SOMERSET. Loaves and Fishes. London: Heinemann, 1924. 1st ed. One of 2000 ptd. Red cl. NF; issued w/o dj. *Chapel Hill.* $95/£61

MAUGHAM, W. SOMERSET. The Magician. London: Heinemann, 1908. 1st ed, 1st issue, w/o 'Colonial Edition' on 1/2 title. One of 2100 ptd. Blue cl. VG. *Chapel Hill.* $200/£129

MAUGHAM, W. SOMERSET. The Magician. NY: Duffield, 1909. 1st ed. VG + (sl corner wear; sl pg darkening). *Else Fine.* $250/£161

MAUGHAM, W. SOMERSET. The Making of a Saint. London: T. Fisher Unwin, 1898. 1st Eng ed. Grn cl (sl rubbed; inner back joint cracked), gilt. Good. *Houle.* $350/£226

MAUGHAM, W. SOMERSET. The Making of a Saint. London: T. Fisher Unwin, 1898. 1st Eng ed. One of 2500 ptd. Grn cl. VG (fr inner hinge starting; rear hinge tender). *Chapel Hill.* $400/£258

MAUGHAM, W. SOMERSET. The Merry-Go-Round. London, 1904. 1st issue w/final blank w/o ads. Bluish-grn cl (extrems rubbed; spotting). *Waterfield.* $116/£75

MAUGHAM, W. SOMERSET. The Mixture as Before. London: Heinemann, (1940). 1st ed. Blue cl. VG (eps sl browned) in dj (lt wear). *Chapel Hill.* $95/£61

MAUGHAM, W. SOMERSET. The Moon and Sixpence. NY: George H. Doran, 1919. 1st Amer ed. Grn cl. Sl mkd; name, o/w VG. *Dalian.* $132/£85

MAUGHAM, W. SOMERSET. The Moon and Sixpence. London: Heinemann, 1919. 1st ed, 2nd issue, w/o ads. Grn cl. Text browned, else VG. *Chapel Hill.* $75/£48

MAUGHAM, W. SOMERSET. The Moon and Sixpence. Heinemann, 1919. Scarce 1st issue w/2 leaves of pub's ads at end, listing 6 novels by Eden Phillpotts, 3 by Israel Zangwill. Grn cl. (Paper browned; cvrs mkd, worn.) *Dalian.* $70/£45

MAUGHAM, W. SOMERSET. The Narrow Corner. London: Heinemann, (1932). 1st ed. Blue cl. NF in dj (chips; spine lt sunned). *Chapel Hill.* $150/£97

MAUGHAM, W. SOMERSET. Of Human Bondage. Doran, 1915. 1st ed. Inner rear hinge repaired; lt rubbing, wear to spine extrems, corner tips, else VG-. *Fine Books.* $275/£177

MAUGHAM, W. SOMERSET. Of Human Bondage. LEC, 1938. 1st ed thus, one of 1500. Signed by John Sloan (artist). 2 vols. Spines sl faded, else NF set. *Fine Books.* $375/£242

MAUGHAM, W. SOMERSET. Of Human Bondage. New Haven: Yale Univ Press, 1938. Ltd to 1500. Signed by John Sloan (etchings). 2 vols bound in 1. 16 etchings. Full crushed morocco, gilt, raised bands; aeg. Spine mellowing, o/w Fine. *Sadlon.* $500/£323

MAUGHAM, W. SOMERSET. On a Chinese Screen. London, 1922. 1st Eng ed. Black cl, gilt (sl shaken, scuffed). Good. *Waterfield.* $78/£50

MAUGHAM, W. SOMERSET. On a Chinese Screen. London: Heinemann, 1922. 1st Eng ed. One of 2000. Black cl (spine top rubbed). *Chapel Hill.* $85/£55

MAUGHAM, W. SOMERSET. Orientations. London: T. Fisher Unwin, 1899. 1st ed, 1st issue, w/teg. One of 2000 ptd. 8vo. Grn cl. Fine. *Chapel Hill.* $650/£419

MAUGHAM, W. SOMERSET. Our Betters. London: Heinemann, 1923. 1st ed. One of 1500 ptd. Red cl. NF; no dj as issued. *Chapel Hill.* $95/£61

MAUGHAM, W. SOMERSET. The Painted Veil. London, (1925). 1st ed, 3rd issue w/cancel tp, 26 works listed on 1/2 title, consecutive pagination. Blue cl. VG. *Waterfield.* $70/£45

MAUGHAM, W. SOMERSET. Penelope. London: Heinemann, 1912. 1st ed. One of 2000 ptd. Red cl. NF; no dj as issued. *Chapel Hill.* $125/£81

MAUGHAM, W. SOMERSET. Points of View. London: Heinemann, (1958). 1st ed. Grn cl. Fine in NF dj. *Chapel Hill.* $60/£39

MAUGHAM, W. SOMERSET. The Razor's Edge. London: Heinemann, (1944). 1st Eng ed. Blue cl. VG in dj (chips, tears). *Chapel Hill.* $100/£65

MAUGHAM, W. SOMERSET. The Sacred Flame. London: Heinemann, 1928. 1st Eng ed from Amer sheets. Black cl, paper labels. NF in dj. *Chapel Hill.* $175/£113

MAUGHAM, W. SOMERSET. Sheppey. London: Heinemann, 1933. 1st ed. One of 2000 ptd. Brn cl. Fine in NF dj (spine dknd). *Chapel Hill.* $125/£81

MAUGHAM, W. SOMERSET. Six Stories Written in the First Person Singular. London, (1931). 1st Eng ed. (Spine sl faded; spotting.) *Waterfield.* $31/£20

MAUGHAM, W. SOMERSET. Smith. NY: Duffield, 1911. 1st ed. Mounted photo (minute rubs). NF (sl spine fade, few rubs cvr extrems). *Else Fine.* $125/£81

MAUGHAM, W. SOMERSET. Smith. London: Heinemann, 1913. 1st ed. One of 2000 ptd. Red cl. Bkpl removal, else VG; no dj as issued. *Chapel Hill.* $95/£61

MAUGHAM, W. SOMERSET. Strictly Personal. GC: Doubleday, Doran, 1941. 1st ed. #14/515 signed. Frontis. Red cl, morocco spine label. Fine in glassine dj (lacks spine); pub's slipcase (worn). *Chapel Hill.* $250/£161

MAUGHAM, W. SOMERSET. The Summing Up. Heinemann, 1938. 1st ed. VG+ in dj (chipping to spine, rear panel). *Fine Books.* $95/£61

MAUGHAM, W. SOMERSET. Theatre. London, (1937). 1st Eng ed, 2nd issue w/pp7-8 cancelled. (Sl faded; mk; name cut fep.) *Waterfield.* $23/£15

MAUGHAM, W. SOMERSET. Then and Now. London: Heinemann, (1946). 1st ed. Blue cl. NF in dj (nicks). *Chapel Hill.* $60/£39

MAUGHAM, W. SOMERSET. The Trembling of a Leaf. London: Heinemann, 1921. 1st Eng ed. Blue cl. Offsetting fep w/trace on 1/2 title, else VG. *Chapel Hill.* $85/£55

MAUGHAM, W. SOMERSET. Trio. London: Heinemann, (1950). 1st ed. Signed, dated. Red cl. NF in dj (lt wear). *Chapel Hill.* $250/£161

MAUGHAM, W. SOMERSET. The Unattainable. London: Heinemann, 1923. 1st ed. One of 1500 ptd. Red cl. Bkpl, else NF; issued w/o dj. *Chapel Hill.* $95/£61

MAUGHAM, W. SOMERSET. The Unknown. London: Heinemann, 1920. 1st ed. One of 2000. NF in ptd wraps. *Chapel Hill.* $65/£42

MAUGHAM, W. SOMERSET. Up at the Villa. NY: Doubleday, Doran, 1941. 1st ed. Black cl. Fine in NF dj (chip). *Chapel Hill.* $50/£32

MAUGHAM, W. SOMERSET. The Vagrant Mood. London: Heinemann, (1952). 1st trade ed. Red cl. Fine in VG dj (short closed tears). *Chapel Hill.* $50/£32

MAUGHAM, W. SOMERSET. A Writer's Notebook. London: Heinemann, (1949). 1st trade ed. Black cl. Fine in NF 1st issue dj (lt wear) w/'Maughamiana' advertised on rear flap. *Chapel Hill.* $50/£32

MAUGHAM, W. SOMERSET. A Writer's Notebook. GC: Doubleday, 1949. 1st Amer ed. #914/1000 signed. Frontis port. Red cl, gilt spine, labels; teg, uncut, partly unopened. VG in pub's black bd slipcase. *Houle.* $450/£290

MAUGHAM, W. SOMERSET. A Writer's Notebook. Doubleday, 1949. 1st ed, one of 1000 signed. Fine in slip-case. *Fine Books.* $195/£126

MAUNDRELL, HENRY. A Journey From Aleppo to Jerusalem at Easter, A.D. 1697. Oxford: At the Theater, 1714. 3rd ed. (16),145,(7),10pp; copper-engr vignette on title; 15 plts. Contemp calf. Good. *Karmiole.* $300/£194

MAUNDRELL, HENRY. A Journey From Aleppo to Jerusalem at Easter, A.D. 1697. Oxford: n.p., 1714. 3rd ed. 8vo. (xii),145,(7),10pp; engr fldg frontis; 9 fldg, 4 full-pg engr plts. 1/4 red goatskin; marbled bds, eps; gilt-stamped panels, title. Foxing throughout; 2-inch tear along fold 1 plt; sl wear; rubbing, o/w VG. *Laurie.* $400/£258

MAUPIN, ARMISTEAD. Further Tales of the City. NY: Harper & Row, 1982. 1st ed. Fine in dj. *Lame Duck.* $50/£32

MAURICE, FREDERICK BARTON (ed). The Life of General Lord Rawlinson of Trent.... London, 1928. 1st ed. Frontis port; 16 plts; 3 maps (1 fldg). Bkpl; eps sl browned, foxed, o/w VG. Navy cl, gilt (extrems sl scuffed). *Edwards.* $47/£30

MAURICE, FREDERICK BARTON (ed). Soldier, Artist, Sportsman. Boston: Houghton Mifflin, 1928. 1st ed. VG. *October Farm.* $30/£19

MAURICE, FREDERICK BARTON. Robert E. Lee the Soldier. Boston/NY: Houghton Mifflin, (1925). 1st ed, 2nd imp. Orig cl. NF in VG dj. *Mcgowan.* $85/£55

MAURICE, FREDERICK BARTON. Robert E. Lee, the Soldier. London: Constable, 1925. 1st Eng ed. Frontis port, fldg map. Orig red cl. VG +. *Chapel Hill.* $40/£26

MAURICE, FREDERICK BARTON. Statesmen and Soldiers of the Civil War. Boston: Little, Brown, 1926. 1st ed. VG. *Mcgowan.* $45/£29

MAURICE, M. Not in Our Stars. Lippincott, (1923). 1st Amer ed. VG + in VG dj (spine lt chipped; mended tears fr panel). *Aronovitz.* $65/£42

MAURICEAU, A.M. The Married Woman's Private Medical Companion.... NY, 1852. 238pp. Good. *Fye.* $75/£48

MAURICEAU, A.M. The Married Woman's Private Medical Companion...Discovery to Prevent Pregnancy.... NY, 1852. xiii,(1),288pp (foxing). Pub's blind-stamped cl. VG. *Hemlock.* $175/£113

MAUROIS, ANDRE. Chelsea Way. London: Elkin Mathews & Marrot, 1930. 1st ed. One of 530 signed. Cl-backed patterned bds. Fine in dj. *Cahan.* $65/£42

MAUROIS, ANDRE. The Life of Sir Alexander Fleming, Discoverer of Penicillin. NY, 1959. 1st Eng trans. Good. *Fye.* $25/£16

MAUROIS, ANDRE. Seven Faces of Love. Haakon M. Chevalier (trans). NY: Didier, (1944). 1st Amer ed. Signed. Fine in dj (spine lt browned, else Fine), wrap-around band. *Godot.* $50/£32

MAUROIS, ANDRE. The Thought Reading Machine. Harpers, 1938. 1st ed. Fine in dj (frayed). *Madle.* $35/£23

MAUROIS, ANDRE. Voyage to Island of the Articoles. Appleton, 1929. VG. *Madle.* $15/£10

MAURON, CHARLES. The Nature of Beauty in Art and Literature. Hogarth Press, 1927. 1st ed. Edges faded, o/w VG. *Words Etc.* $47/£30

MAURY, J.C. Treatise on the Dental Art, Founded on Actual Experience. J.B. Savier (trans). Phila: Lea & Blanchard, 1843. 1st Amer ed. 324pp (staining); 20 plts; 16pp pub's cat at end, 28pp bibliography. Contemp calf (hinges rubbed). VG. *Hemlock.* $475/£306

MAURY, MATTHEW FONTAINE. A New Theoretical and Practical Treatise on Navigation. NY: Harper, 1855. 3rd ed, enlgd. (Appendix added, pp275-287; o/w this ed seemingly identical to the 1st.) 287pp, 8 engr plts. (Bkpl; lt wear spine ends.) *Lefkowicz.* $125/£81

MAURY, MATTHEW FONTAINE. The Physical Geography of the Sea. NY: Harper, 1855. 3rd ed, enlgd. 8 engr plts. (Spine ends lt worn; label.) *Lefkowicz.* $125/£81

MAURY, MATTHEW FONTAINE. The Physical Geography of the Sea. London, 1860. 7th ed. xv,493pp (foxing, few marginal mks). 13 plts (9 fldg). Blue gilt-dec cl (worn, spine frayed, soiled; paper residue on spine; inner hinges reinforced). *Sutton.* $110/£71

MAURY, MATTHEW FONTAINE. Physical Geography. NY: University Publishing, 1892. 130pp. Good in grn cl (extrems worn). *Knollwood.* $20/£13

MAVERICK, M.M. Old Villita. Comp by WPA, 1939. 1st ed. Folio; wraps. *Lambeth.* $50/£32

MAVERICK, SAMUEL. Notes on the Storming of Bexar in the Close of 1835. Frederick Chabot (ed). Frederick Chabot, (1942). 1st ed. Ltd to 100 numbered. Signed by Chabot. 3 plts, map. VG. *Oregon.* $250/£161

MAVOR, WILLIAM. Catechism of Animated Nature. NY/Balt: Samuel Wood, 1821. 12mo. 70pp + 1pg ad lower wrapper. Ptd blue stiff paper wrappers (dusted, fold reinforced). VG. *Hobbyhorse.* $80/£52

MAW, THOMAS and JOHN ABERCROMBIE. Every Man His Own Gardener.... London: For the Booksellers, 1839. Engr frontis, 420pp + 18pp ads. Later cl-backed paper-cvrd bds, paper spine label. VG. *Quest.* $90/£58

MAWER, IRENE. The Art of Mime. London, 1949. 5th ed. Frontis port. Dj (spine sl browned). *Edwards.* $23/£15

MAWSON, DOUGLAS. The Home of the Blizzard. Phila: Lippincott, (1915). 2 vols. 1st US ed, bound from sheets of 1st London ed, but w/some variation in illus. 3 fldg maps in pocket. Orig silver dec cl, teg. VG. *High Latitude.* $450/£290

MAWSON, DOUGLAS. The Home of the Blizzard. London: Heinemann, 1915. 1st ed. 2 vols. Silver gilt dec cl. VG. *Walcot.* $543/£350

MAWSON, DOUGLAS. The Home of the Blizzard. London: Heinemann, 1915. 1st ed. 2 vols. 3 fldg maps. (Sl offsetting, foxing to eps.) Blue cl, silver cvr decs, gilt spine, cvr titles. Cvrs worn, hinges weak (1 repaired). *Parmer.* $950/£613

MAWSON, DOUGLAS. The Home of the Blizzard. London: Hodder & Stoughton, 1934. Rpt. Map. Good (spine faded). *Walcot.* $39/£25

MAWSON, THOMAS H. The Art and Craft of Garden Design. London: Batsford, 1926. 5th ed. Color frontis. Fine. *Quest.* $300/£194

MAWSON, THOMAS H. The Art and Craft of Garden Making. London: Batsford, 1900. 1st ed. Teg. Gilt-ruled cl (hinges sl tender, sl fading, wear). *Edwards.* $186/£120

MAXFIELD, ARCHIBALD. Observations on Ulcers of the Legs, and Other Parts, Shewing that.... London, 1842. 1st ed. 80pp. Good. *Fye.* $100/£65

MAXON, P.B. The Waltz of Death. Mystery House, 1941. 1st ed. VG in dj. *Madle.* $50/£32

MAXWELL, GAVIN. Lords of the Atlas. Longmans, 1966. 1st Eng ed. Black cl. VF in VF dj. *Dalian.* $54/£35

MAXWELL, GAVIN. A Reed Shaken by the Wind. Longmans, Green, 1957. 1st Eng ed. Blue cl. Fine in dj (sl nicked, rubbed). *Dalian.* $101/£65

MAXWELL, GILBERT. Go Looking. Humphries, (1954). 1st ed. VG in dj (rubbed). *Turlington.* $40/£26

MAXWELL, H. Scottish Gardens.... London, 1911. New ed. 32 color plts. (Cl sl used.) *Wheldon & Wesley.* $47/£30

MAXWELL, MARIUS. Stalking Big Game with a Camera in Equatorial Africa. London: Heinemann, 1925. Extending frontis; 112 plts. VG (sl mkd). *Hollett.* $54/£35

MAXWELL, R.T. Visit to Monterey in 1842. John Haskell Kemble (ed). LA: Dawson, 1955. Ltd to 200 ptd. Fine. *Oregon.* $50/£32

MAXWELL, WILLIAM. The Anxious Man. NY: Pax, 1957. 1st ed. Broadside on newsprint, folded. VG (edges sunned, creases; torn crease). *Beasley.* $40/£26

MAXWELL, WILLIAM. Lincoln's Fifth Wheel, The Political History of the U.S. Sanitary Commission. NY, 1956. 1st ed. Inscribed. Fine in Fine dj. *Pratt.* $45/£29

MAXWELL, WILLIAM. The Old Man at the Railroad Crossing and Other Tales. NY: Knopf, 1966. 1st Amer ed. Fine in dj (ink #). *Between The Covers.* $85/£55

MAXWELL, WILLIAM. Time Will Darken It. NY: Harper, (1948). 1st ed. Bottom of bds sl rubbed, else VG in VG dj (rubbed, 2 triangular chips fr panel). *Between The Covers.* $135/£87

MAXWELL, WILLIAM. Time Will Darken It. NY: Harper, 1948. 1st ed. NF in VG dj (price-clipped). *Pettler.* $60/£39

MAY, E.S. Field Artillery. With Other Arms. London, 1898. 1st ed. viii,339pp; 3 plans. Eps browned; inscrips; hinges weak, o/w VG. Red cl (soiled; bumped; sm dent; spine creased), gilt title. *Edwards.* $47/£30

MAY, EARL CHAPIN. The Canning Clan. NY: Macmillan, 1937. 1st ed. 10 plts. Cl, silver. Fine in foil-covered dj (chipped). *Connolly.* $65/£42

MAY, JOHN BICHARD. The Hawks of North America, Their Field Identification and Feeding Habits. NY: Nat'l Assoc of Audubon Soc, 1935. Dk grn cl, gilt title. VG (bkpl, notes). *Bohling.* $85/£55

MAY, JOHN BICHARD. The Hawks of North America.... NY, 1935. 4 plain, 37 color plts. *Wheldon & Wesley.* $93/£60

MAY, R. The Advantages of Early Religion. Phila: Sunday & Adult School Union, 1820. 2nd ed. Lg VF pict wood engr tp, upper wrapper. VG (ink sig, lt foxing text). *Hobbyhorse.* $55/£35

MAY, ROBERT L. Rudolf the Red Nosed Reindeer. London: Adprint, 1939. 26x20cm. 5 VG pop-ups by Marion Guild. Spiral binding. (Cvr wear; red underlining.) *Book Finders.* $90/£58

MAY, SOPHIE. Captain Horace. Boston: Lee & Shepard, 1894. (Little Prudy Series.) Sm 8vo. Full-pg frontis, full-pg engr 1/2 title, 183pp + 4pp ads. Grn pict emb, gilt-stamped cvr; gilt spine title. Inscrip, sl rubbed, o/w VF. *Hobbyhorse.* $35/£23

MAY, TRACEY. The Tabby-Fur Family. London: R.A. Pub Co, (ca 1948). 8 full-pg color illus by Hilda Boswell. Good+ in illus stiff paper wrappers. *Reisler.* $100/£65

MAYDON, H.C. Big Game Shooting in Africa. London: Seeley, 1932. (Worn, torn; pp sl browned.) *Petersfield.* $39/£25

MAYDON, H.C. Simen, Its Heights and Abysses. London: Witherby, 1925. 1st ed. Fldg sketch. Gilt dec spine. VG. *Bowman.* $250/£161

MAYER, A.G. Medusae of the World. Washington, D.C., 1910. 3 vols. 76 color plts. Good. *Wheldon & Wesley.* $620/£400

MAYER, ALFRED M. (ed). Sport with Gun and Rod in American Woods and Waters. Edinburgh: David Douglas, 1834. 2 vols. Teg, rest uncut. Pub's cl, leather backs. *Petersfield.* $264/£170

MAYER, ALFRED M. (ed). Sport with Gun and Rod in American Woods and Waters. NY: Century, 1883. 1st ed. Pict tan cl, gilt titles. VG. *Bowman.* $75/£48

MAYER, BRANTZ. Captain Canot; or, Twenty Years of an African Slaver.... NY: Appleton, 1854. 1st Amer ed. (Staining lg portion of text; spine extrems chipped; cl edges worn.) *Between The Covers.* $185/£119

MAYER, BRANTZ. Tah-Gah-Jute; or, Logan and Cresap, An Historical Essay. Albany: Joel Munsell, 1867. 2nd ed, enlgd. 204pp; errata slip. Grn cl. VG. Howes M 451. *Chapel Hill.* $150/£97

MAYER, D.M. and W.A. SWANKER. Anomalies of Infants and Children. NY, 1958. 1st ed. (Ex-lib.) *Fye.* $75/£48

MAYER, FRANK BLACKWELL. With Pen and Pencil on the Frontier in 1851: The Diary and Sketches of.... Bertha L. Heilbron (ed). St. Paul: MN Hist Soc, 1932. 1st ed. Brn cl. Spine faded, o/w NF. *Harrington.* $50/£32

MAYER, JOHN. The Sportsman's Directory; and Park and Gamekeeper's Companion. London: Simpkin, Marshall, 1845. 7th ed. viii,181pp + 2pp ads. Blind-stamped cl. Unopened. VG. *Schoyer.* $80/£52

MAYER, R. The Artist's Handbook of Materials and Techniques. NY: Viking, 1948. Sound. *Ars Artis.* $33/£21

MAYER, R. A Dictionary of Art Terms and Techniques. London: Black, 1969. 4 color plts. Sound in dj. *Ars Artis.* $39/£25

MAYER, RONALD. 1937 Newark Bears. William Wise, 1980. 1st ed. Fine in VG+ dj (lt shelfwear, o/w Fine). *Plapinger.* $45/£29

MAYER, TOM. Bubble Gum and Kipling. NY: Viking, (1964). 1st ed, 1st bk. VG in dj (lt rubbed, short tears internally reinforced w/mending tape). *Heller.* $50/£32

MAYERS, FREDERICK J. Carpet Designs and Designing. Leigh-on-Sea: F. Lewis, 1934. 1st ed. Color frontis, 32 Excellent plts. VG (ex-lib). *Willow House.* $47/£30

MAYFIELD, H. The Kirtland's Warbler. Bloomfield Hills, 1960. Signed presentation inscription. 8 b/w photo plts. (Faded, lt spotted, scuffed; dk spots pp edges.) *Sutton.* $85/£55

MAYGRIER, J.P. Midwifery Illustrated. NY, 1850. 6th ed. 180pp; 84 Fine lithos plts. Recent 1/4 leather; marbled bds (new eps). Good. *Fye.* $350/£226

MAYHEW BROTHERS. The Magic of Kindness. NY: Harper, 1849. 1st Amer ed. George Cruikshank & Kenny Meadows (illus). 16mo, 250pp + ads. Brn cl, gold-stamped. Text foxed, spine nicked, sl frayed, else VG. *Godot.* $85/£55

MAYHEW, AUGUSTUS. Paved with Gold. London: Chapman & Hall, 1858. 1st ed. H.K. Browne (illus). Frontis, viii,408pp, add'l illus tp. 1/2 brn morocco, marbled bds (orig cl bound in). *Karmiole.* $125/£81

MAYHEW, HORACE (ed). The Comic Almanack for 1848. London: David Bogue, (1847). 1st issue, w/1848 ptd in black on cvr, proper ads, w/frontis plt, 'A Good Pennyworth.' George Cruikshank (illus). 128pp + 16pp pub's cat; 6 plts. VG in grn wraps; fldg cl case. *Schoyer.* $100/£65

MAYNE, JONATHAN. Thomas Girtin. Leigh-on-Sea, Lewis, 1949. #286/500. Tipped-in frontis port, 4 tipped-in color plts, 45 monochrome plts; deckle-edged paper. Fine. *Europa.* $116/£75

MAYO, BERNARD. Thomas Jefferson and His Unknown Brother Randolph. Tracy W. McGregor Library, 1942. Paper cvrs. VG. *Book Broker.* $25/£16

MAYO, CHARLES W. The Story of My Family and My Career. London: Hodder & Stoughton, 1970. VG in dj. *White.* $19/£12

MAYO, WILLIAM J. and CHARLES H. A Collection of Papers Published Previous to 1909. Phila: Saunders, 1912. 2 vols. 4 photos. (Ex-lib.) *Goodrich.* $50/£32

MAZER, CHARLES and LEOPOLD GOLDSTEIN. Clinical Endocrinology of the Female. Phila, 1932. 1st ed. Good. *Fye.* $75/£48

MAZZANOVICH, ANTON. Trailing Geronimo. E.A. Brininstool (ed). LA: Gem Publishing, 1926. 1st ed. Exterior spots; spine fading, else Good. *Perier.* $85/£55

MAZZUCHELLI, SAMUELE. Memoirs Historical and Edifying of a Missionary Apostolic of Order of Saint Dominic.... Chicago, 1915. 1st ed in English. 1 plt, 3 maps (2 fldg). VG. Howes M 457. *Oregon.* $125/£81

McADAMS, FRANCIS MARION. Our Knapsack. Sketches for the Boys in Blue. Columbus, 1884. 136pp; 2 ports. Ptd wraps (edges chipped; fr cvr detached). *Bohling.* $135/£87

McALEER, JOHN. Rex Stout: A Biography. Boston: Little, Brown, 1977. 1st ed. Fine in dj (spine head lt wrinkled). *Janus.* $30/£19

McALEER, JOHN. Royal Decree. Ashton: Pontes, 1983. 1st ed, one of 1000 numbered, signed. Fine in wrappers (lt spot) as issued. *Janus.* $20/£13

McALMON, ROBERT. Being Geniuses Together. S&W, 1938. 1st ed. NF in VG dj (chipping to spine extrems). *Fine Books.* $1,250/£806

McALMON, ROBERT. Being Geniuses Together. An Autobiography. London: Secker & Warburg, (1938). 1st ed. Author's compliments slip laid in. Good (spine sl dull; cl sl soiled). *Reese.* $350/£226

McALMON, ROBERT. Being Geniuses Together: 1920-1930. Joseph, 1970. 1st thus. Good in dj (sl dull). *Whiteson.* $23/£15

McALPINE, DOUGLAS et al. Multiple Sclerosis. Edinburgh, 1955. 1st ed. Good in dj. *Fye.* $75/£48

McARTHUR, HARRIET NESMITH. Recollections of the Rickreall. Portland: Privately ptd, 1930. 1st ed. Signed presentation. VG. *Perier.* $85/£55

McATEE, W.L. The Ring Necked Pheasant. Washington: American Wildlife Inst, 1945. 1st ed. VG in VG- dj. *Bishop.* $22/£14

McAULEY, MILT. Wildflowers of the Santa Monica Mountains. Canoga Park, CA, 1985. Fldg map. New in dj. *Brooks.* $21/£14

McBAIN, ED. (Pseud of Evan Hunter.) The 87th Precinct. NY: S&S, 1959. 1st ed. Fine (pp browning) in NF dj. *Janus.* $50/£32

McBAIN, ED. (Pseud of Evan Hunter.) Another Part of the City. Mystery Press, 1986. 1st ed, one of 250 numbered. Signed. VF in slipcase as issued. *Murder.* $85/£55

McBAIN, ED. (Pseud of Evan Hunter.) Bread. NY: Random House, 1974. 1st ed. Fine (lt spotting edges) in dj (lt crease fr flap). *Janus.* $25/£16

McBAIN, ED. (Pseud of Evan Hunter.) Fuzz. GC: Doubleday, 1968. 1st ed. Fine in dj. *Mordida.* $50/£32

McBAIN, ED. (Pseud of Evan Hunter.) Killer's Choice. London: Boardman, 1960. 1st UK ed, 1st hb. Good. *Ming.* $54/£35

McBAIN, ED. (Pseud of Evan Hunter.) Lady Killer. NY: Permabooks, 1958. 1st ed, pb orig. VG + (sl leaned). *Janus.* $16/£10

McBAIN, ED. (Pseud of Evan Hunter.) The Mugger. NY: Permabooks, 1956. 1st ed, pb orig. VG + (sl leaned) in VG + wrappers, as issued. *Janus.* $15/£10

McBAIN, ED. (Pseud of Evan Hunter.) The Pusher. NY: Permabooks, 1956. 1st ed, pb orig. NF (sl leaned). *Janus.* $20/£13

McCABE, JAMES. The San Juan Water Boundary Question. Univ of Toronto, (1964). 1st ed. Map. Spine faded, o/w VG. *Oregon.* $65/£42

McCAFFREY, ANNE. Dragonsdrums. Atheneum, 1979. 1st ed. Fine in dj. *Madle.* $50/£32

McCAFFREY, ANNE. The Ship Who Sang. Rapp & Whiting, 1971. 1st Eng ed. Signed. NF in VG + dj. *Aronovitz.* $90/£58

McCAFFREY, ANNE. The White Dragon. Del Rey, 1978. 1st ed. Fine in dj. *Madle.* $45/£29

McCAFFREY, ANNE. The White Dragon. Del Rey, 1978. 1st ed. Signed. NF in dj. *Aronovitz.* $50/£32

McCALL, D. Three Years in the Service. Record of the Doings of the 11th Reg. Missouri Vols. Springfield: Johnson & Bradford Printers, 1864. 2nd ed, rev, corrected. 41pp. Orig salmon ptd wrappers. Sl soiled, chipped, else VG. Custom made clamshell box. *Mcgowan.* $2,500/£1,613

McCALLA, MARY. The Twin Sisters, or The Secret of Happiness. Phila: Presbyterian Board of Pub., n.d. (ca 1860). Sq 12mo. Wood-engr frontis, 90pp; 3 plts by J.H. Byram; yellow eps. Tooled grn cl, gilt titles. Fine (ink scribble, sm spot, ex-libris). *Hobbyhorse.* $130/£84

McCALLISTER, DONALD. Three Youthful Trappers. Hollywood, CA: (Donald McCallister), 1932. Ltd to 75. Signed presentation. Vellum-like paper spine, gilt, over bds (spine dinged in places). *Karmiole.* $40/£26

McCALLUM, HENRY D. and FRANCES T. The Wire that Fenced the West. Norman: Univ of OK, 1965. 1st ed. Fine in NF dj. *Parker.* $30/£19

McCALLUM, IAN. Architecture USA. Architectural Press, 1959. (Margins sl browned.) Dj. *Edwards.* $43/£28

McCALLUM, JOHN. The Tiger Wore Spikes. Barnes, 1956. 1st ed. VG + in VG dj. *Plapinger.* $45/£29

McCAMMON, ROBERT R. Bethany's Sin. London, 1989. 1st hb ed. Fine in dj. *Other Worlds.* $50/£32

McCAMMON, ROBERT R. Mystery Walk. NY: HRW, 1983. 1st ed. VF in dj (price-clipped). *Else Fine.* $65/£42

McCAMMON, ROBERT R. Stinger. London, 1988. 1st UK ed. Fine in Fine dj. *Other Worlds.* $50/£32

McCANN, IRVING GOFF. With the National Guard on the Border. St. Louis: C.V. Mosby, 1917. Orig cl. VG. *Schoyer.* $65/£42

McCARRY, CHARLES. The Miernik Dossier. NY: SRP, 1973. 1st ed. Fine in dj (spine sl faded). *Else Fine.* $50/£32

McCARRY, CHARLES. The Miernik Dossier. Saturday Review Press, 1973. 1st ed. Rev copy. Sl worn, else Fine in bright dj (lt soiled). *Murder.* $95/£61

McCARTHY, CARLTON. Detailed Minutiae of Soldier Life in the Army of Northern Virginia 1861-1865. Richmond, VA: B.F. Johnson Pub Co, (1908). 3rd ed. Orig cl (rubbed; expertly recased). Good. *Mcgowan.* $150/£97

McCARTHY, CARLTON. Detailed Minutiae of Soldier Life in the Army of Northern Virginia 1861-1865. Richmond: Carlton McCarthy, 1882. 1st ed. Frontis, 224pp. Dk tan cl (bottom spine rubbed). VG (inscrip). *Chapel Hill.* $275/£177

McCARTHY, CORMAC. All the Pretty Horses. NY: Knopf, (1992). 1st ed. Fine in Fine dj. *Unger.* $200/£129

McCARTHY, CORMAC. All the Pretty Horses. London: Picador, (1993). 1st Eng ed. Fine in Fine dj. *Unger.* $150/£97

McCARTHY, CORMAC. All the Pretty Horses. NY: Knopf, 1992. 1st ed. Fine in dj. *Lame Duck.* $200/£129

McCARTHY, CORMAC. All the Pretty Horses. London: Picador, 1993. 1st ed. Fine in dj. *Rees.* $70/£45

McCARTHY, CORMAC. All the Pretty Horses. London: Picador, 1993. 1st UK ed. Fine in dj. *Moorhouse.* $62/£40

McCARTHY, CORMAC. Blood Meridian or The Evening Redness in the West. NY: Random House, (1985). 1st ed. Fine in Fine dj. *Robbins.* $450/£290

McCARTHY, CORMAC. Blood Meridian. NY: Random House, 1985. 1st ed. Rmdr mk top edge, else Fine in NF dj. *Lame Duck.* $135/£87

McCARTHY, CORMAC. Child of God. NY: Random House, (1973). 1st ed. 8vo. Red bds, blue cl spine. VG (sticker removed fr pastedown) in VG dj (price-clipped). *Chapel Hill.* $500/£323

McCARTHY, CORMAC. Child of God. R-H, 1973. 1st ed. Fine in dj. *Fine Books.* $375/£242

McCARTHY, CORMAC. Child of God. NY: Random House, 1973. 1st ed. NF in dj (sm rumpled patch fr panel). *Lame Duck.* $650/£419

McCARTHY, CORMAC. Child of God. C&W, 1975. 1st UK ed. Fine in dj. *Sclanders.* $155/£100

McCARTHY, CORMAC. The Orchard Keeper. NY: Random House, (1965). 1st ed, 1st bk. Fine in bright white dj (traces of soiling). *Robbins.* $2,000/£1,290

McCARTHY, CORMAC. The Orchard Keeper. NY: Random House, (ca 1970). 2nd ptg. Rose bds, grn cl spine. Lt wear, else Fine in NF dj (price-clipped). *Chapel Hill.* $250/£161

McCARTHY, CORMAC. Outer Dark. NY: Random House, (1968). 1st ed. NF in black dj (tiny chip spine base; 2 closed tears spine head, 2 to rear panel). *Robbins.* $850/£548

McCARTHY, CORMAC. The Stonemason. Hopewell: Ecco, (1994). 1st ed. Fine in Fine dj. *Unger.* $65/£42

McCARTHY, CORMAC. Suttree. NY: Random House, (1979). 1st ed. Yellowish cream bds, black cl spine. Rmdr mk; sm nick, else NF in dj (1/2-inch closed tear; crease). *Chapel Hill.* $400/£258

McCARTHY, CORMAC. Suttree. NY: Random House, (1979). 1st ed. Fine in Fine dj (nicks to fore-edge). *Unger.* $650/£419

McCARTHY, JUSTIN. Reminiscences. London: C&W, 1899. 2nd ed. 2 vols. xii,444,32; vi,489,4pp, port. Spines sl faded. *Hollett.* $47/£30

McCARTHY, MARY. Cannibals and Missionaries. NY: Harcourt, (1979). 1st ed. Fine in NF dj (nick). *Reese.* $15/£10

McCARTHY, MARY. Cast a Cold Eye. H-B, 1950. 1st ed. Fine in NF dj. *Fine Books.* $45/£29

McCARTHY, MARY. Hanoi. London: Weidenfeld & Nicolson, (1968). 1st British ed. Dj (lt wear; tear rear panel; sl foxing; ink pp edges). *Aka.* $45/£29

McCARTHY, MARY. Memories of a Catholic Girlhood. NY: Harcourt, Brace, (1957). 1st ed. Black cl, paper label. VG in dj (lt worn; price-clipped). *Hermitage.* $40/£26

McCARTHY, MARY. The Oasis. R-H, 1949. 1st ed. Minor tape shadow to reps, else Fine in VG dj. *Fine Books.* $35/£23

McCARTHY, MARY. On the Contrary. NY: Farrar, Straus & Cudahy, 1961. 1st ed. VG in dj (edgetorn). *Cahan.* $15/£10

McCARTY, CLARA S. The Story of Boxwood. Dietz Press, n.d. Signed. VG. *Book Broker.* $50/£32

McCARTY, JOHN L. Maverick Town. Norman: Univ of OK, 1946. 1st ed. 16 photo-plts. Pict cl. Fine in illus dj. *Connolly.* $55/£35

McCARTY, JOHN L. Maverick Town: The Story of Old Tascosa. Norman: Univ of OK Press, 1946. 1st ed. Pict cl. VG in dj. *Schoyer.* $35/£23

McCAUSLAND, ELIZABETH. Changing New York. Berenice Abbott (photos). NY, 1939. 1st ed. VG in dj (sl chipped). *Argosy.* $375/£242

McCAUSLAND, HUGH. The English Carriage. London, 1948. 30 plts (3 color). Dj (faded, torn w/loss). *Edwards.* $25/£16

McCAWLEY, PATRICIA. Glass Paperweights. London: Charles Letts, 1975. 1st ed. VG in dj. *Hollett.* $31/£20

McCLANAHAN, ED. The Natural Man. NY: Farrar, (1983). 1st ed, 1st bk. Rev slip, promo sheet laid in. Fine in dj. *Reese.* $35/£23

McCLANAHAN, ED. The Natural Man. FSG, 1983. 1st ed, 1st bk. Fine in NF dj. *Bishop.* $20/£13

McCLANE, A.J. The Practical Fly Fisherman. NJ, (1975). 1st ed thus. 4 color plts. Fine (name) in dj. *Artis.* $25/£16

McCLEERY, E.H. The Lone Killer. Pittsburgh: St. Pierre Ptg, n.d. (ca 1929). VG in wraps. *Schoyer.* $40/£26

McCLELLAN, CARSWELL. Notes on the Personal Memoirs of P.H. Sheridan. St. Paul, MN: Wm. E. Banning, Jr, 1889. 1st ed. 77pp. Orig gilt-stamped flexible cl. Fr cvr sl bowed, fr hinge worn, else VG. *Chapel Hill.* $125/£81

McCLELLAN, GEORGE B. McClellan's Own Story. NY: Charles L. Webster, 1887. 1st ed. Frontis port, 678pp; aeg. Orig pub's emb full morocco, blindtooled borders, centerpiece, cornerpieces. VG (lt rubbed). *Chapel Hill.* $175/£113

McCLELLAN, HENRY BRAINERD. The Life and Campaign of Major-General J.E.B. Stuart.... Boston/NY: Houghton Mifflin, 1885. 1st ed. xv,468pp; 7 maps. Inner hinges starting; spine ends frayed, else VG. *Mcgowan.* $350/£226

McCLELLAND, NANCY. Duncan Phyfe and the English Regency. 1795-1830. NY, 1939. One of 1000. 295 plts. 2-tone cl bds. (Fep sl browned; spine lt faded; sl torn.) Paper title labels (repaired). *Edwards.* $310/£200

McCLINTOCK, F.H. and EVELYN GIBSON. Robbery in London. London: Macmillan, 1961. *Boswell.* $35/£23

McCLINTOCK, F.L. The Voyage of the 'Fox' in the Arctic Seas. John Murray, 1859. 1st ed. xxvii,403 + ads. Fldg map in rear pocket. (Faded patch fr cvr from sticker removal; lacks fep.) Good + . *Walcot.* $132/£85

McCLOSKEY, ROBERT. One Morning in Maine. NY: Viking, 1952. 1st ed. Lg, 4to. Grey cl w/white letters, seascape decs. Good in pict dj (spine worn; tape mk). *Reisler.* $165/£106

McCLUNG, NELLIE. The Black Creek Stopping-House. Toronto: William Briggs, 1912. 1st ed. Grn pict cl bds. VG (edgewear; gouge back panel). *Hermitage.* $125/£81

McCLURE, ALEXANDER KELLY. Abraham Lincoln and Men of War-Times.... Phila: Times Pub Co, 1892. 4th ed. 496pp. VG. *Mcgowan.* $45/£29

McCLURE, JAMES. The Steam Pig. Harper's, 1971. 1st Amer ed. 1st bk. NF in dj (lt soiled, price-clipped). *Murder.* $65/£42

McCLURE, L.C. Photo by McClure: The Railroad, Cityscape and Landscape Photographs.... Boulder, CO: Pruett Pub Co, 1983. 1st ed. 300 photos. Fine in dj (closed tears, 1 tape-repaired). *Cahan.* $50/£32

McCLURE, MICHAEL. The Adept. NY: Delacorte, 1971. 1st ed. Signed. Fine in VG dj. *Revere.* $45/£29

McCLURE, MICHAEL. Dark Brown. SF: Auerhahn, 1961. 1st ed, one of 750. NF in ptd wraps (sl fade; corner lt bumped). *Antic Hay.* $45/£29

McCLURE, MICHAEL. Gorf. NY: New Directions, 1976. 1st ed. Signed. NF in VG dj. *Revere.* $40/£26

McCLURE, MICHAEL. Hymns to St. Geryon and Other Poems. SF: Auerhahn, 1959. 1st ed. VG in ptd wraps (sl soil; browned). *Antic Hay.* $45/£29

McCLURE, MICHAEL. Jaguar Skies. NY: New Directions, 1975. 1st ed. Inscribed. Fine in NF dj. *Revere.* $40/£26

McCLURE, MICHAEL. Little Odes and the Raptors. L.A.: Black Sparrow Press, 1969. Ltd to 1000 in paper wraps. Signed presentation. Fine (sl sunned). *Polyanthos.* $30/£19

McCLURE, MICHAEL. Scratching the Beat Surface. SF: North Point Press, 1982. Signed presentation. Pub's release laid in. Fine in Fine dj. *Polyanthos.* $30/£19

McCLURE, W.K. Italy in North Africa, an Account of the Tripoli Enterprise. London: Constable, 1913. (Tp inscrip cut out; few pp sl foxed; backstrip faded; sl mkd.) *Petersfield.* $28/£18

McCOMAS, E.S. A Journal of Travel. (Portland): Champoeg Press, 1954. 1st ed. Ltd to 500. Announcement slip inserted. Fine. *Perier.* $65/£42

McCONATHY, DALE and DIANA VREELAND. Hollywood Costume. NY: Abrams, (1976). 1st ed. Silk brocade. VG in pub's ptd mylar dj. *Hermitage.* $200/£129

McCONATHY, DALE and DIANA VREELAND. Hollywood Costume. NY: Abrams, 1976. 1st ed. Gilt, floral silk over bds. Fine in ptd acetate wrapper. *Cahan.* $150/£97

McCONATHY, RUTH H. The House of Cravens. Privately ptd, 1972. Color frontis. VG. *Book Broker.* $50/£32

McCONKEY, HARRIET E. BISHOP. Dakota War Whoop. Chicago, (1965). Lakeside Classic. VG. *Schoyer.* $25/£16

McCONKEY, HARRIET E. BISHOP. Dakota War Whoop. Chicago: R.R. Donnelly, 1965. Lakeside Classic. Lakeside Classis. 1st ed thus. 3 ports, tissues. Teg. Blue cl, gilt. Fine. Howes M58. *Connolly.* $35/£23

McCONNELL, GERALD (ed). The Twentieth Annual of American Illustration. NY: Soc of Illustrators, 1979. (Exlib.) Dj (sl yellowed). *Edwards.* $31/£20

McCONNELL, H.H. Five Years a Cavalryman. Jacksboro, TX: Rogers, 1889. 1st ed. 319pp. Sl washed-out spots bd edges, spine, else Nice. Howes M 59. *Bohling.* $450/£290

McCORKLE, JILL. Ferris Beach. Chapel Hill: Algonquin Books, 1990. 1st ed. VF in VF dj. *Pettler.* $30/£19

McCORKLE, JILL. Tending to Virginia. Chapel Hill: Algonquin Books, 1987. 1st ed. Fine in dj. *Turlington.* $35/£23

McCORMICK, CYRUS. The Century of the Reaper. Boston: Houghton Mifflin, 1931. 1st ed. McCormick medallion in gilt on eps. 23 plts. Fine in Good dj. *Connolly.* $50/£32

McCORMICK, ELSIE. Audacious Angles on China. NY/London: Appleton, 1936. Blue cl, gilt (spine faded). *Schoyer.* $25/£16

McCORMICK, ROBERT R. Ulysses S. Grant, the Great Soldier of America. NY, 1934. 1st ed. Dj worn, o/w Fine. *Pratt.* $35/£23

McCORMICK, ROBERT R. The War without Grant. NY, 1950. 1st ed. Dj lt worn, o/w Fine. *Pratt.* $40/£26

McCORNISH, WILFRID. The Three-Two Pitch. Grosset, 1948. 1st ed. Fine in dj. *Madle.* $25/£16

McCOY, ALFRED W. The Politics of Heroin in Southeast Asia. NY: Harper, 1972. 1st ed. NF in dj (lt used). *Beasley.* $45/£29

McCOY, DELL and RUSS COLLMAN. The Rio Grande Pictorial, 1871-1971: One-Hundred Years of Railroading Thru the Rockies. Denver: Sundance Ltd, (1971). 1st ed. Photo-pict bds, blue cl spine. Fine. *Harrington.* $45/£29

McCOY, ESTHER. Five California Architects. NY: Reinhold, (1960). Fine in dj (lt chipped). *Quest.* $45/£29

McCOY, HORACE. I Should Have Stayed Home. NY, 1938. 1st ed. VG in dj (worn, chipped, price-clipped, spine faded). *Mcclintock.* $85/£55

McCOY, HORACE. Kiss Tomorrow Good-Bye. NY: Random House, (1948). 1st ed. Fray bottom edge fr cvr, o/w VG + in Attractive dj (price-clipped; lt worn spine ends). *Bernard.* $100/£65

McCOY, JOSEPH G. Historic Sketches of the Cattle Trade of the West and Southwest. Kansas City, MO: Ramsey et al, 1874. 1st ed, 1st ptg. 8vo. Lib binding (rebound; margins repaired w/linen tape; 3 text pp, 8 ad pp in facs, laid in; sigs frontis recto; wear, soil.) Howes M 72. *Glenn.* $550/£355

McCRACKEN, HAROLD. George Catlin and the Old Frontier. NY, 1959. VG in dj. *Argosy.* $60/£39

McCRACKEN, HAROLD. George Catlin and the Old Frontier. NY, 1959. 1st ed. Debossed cl. Fine in dj (lt worn, sl faded, price-clipped). *Baade.* $50/£32

McCRACKEN, HAROLD. George Catlin and the Old Frontier. Dial, 1959. 1st trade ed. Fine in VG dj. *Oregon.* $45/£29

McCRACKEN, HAROLD. Hunters of the Stormy Sea. GC: Doubleday, 1957. Stated 1st ed. VG in dj. *Parmer.* $55/£35

McCRACKEN, HAROLD. Portrait of the Old West. NY, (1952). 1st ed. VG in dj (rubbed; edgeworn; sm snag). *King.* $50/£32

McCRACKEN, HAROLD. Roughnecks and Gentlemen. GC: Doubleday, 1968. 1st ed. Name else VG in dj (price-clipped). *Perier.* $30/£19

McCRACKEN, HAROLD. The White Buffalo. NY: Lippincott, (1946). 1st ed. VG in VG dj. *Perier.* $45/£29

McCRACKEN, HOWARD. The Frank Johnson Tenney Book. NY: Doubleday, 1974. 1st trade ed. VG + in VG-dj. *Parker.* $75/£48

McCRAE, HUGH. Satyrs and Sunlight. London: Fanfrolico Press, 1928. Ltd to 550 numbered. 34 plts. Norman Lindsay (illus). Full grn pebbled calf; gilt. Overall Nice (spine lt rubbed). *Karmiole.* $300/£194

McCREIGHT, ISRAEL. Buffalo Bone Days. (Sykesville, PA, 1939). Ptd wraps (sl worn, faded, sm chip). *Bohling.* $85/£55

McCULLERS, CARSON. The Ballad of the Sad Cafe. Boston: Houghton Mifflin, 1951. 1st ed. Fine in dj (sl used; spine chips). *Beasley.* $85/£55

McCULLERS, CARSON. Clock Without Hands. H-M, 1961. 1st ed. Fine in dj. *Fine Books.* $75/£48

McCULLERS, CARSON. Clock Without Hands. Cresset, 1961. 1st Eng ed. Blue cl. Spine ends sl faded, o/w Fine in dj (chipped). *Dalian.* $39/£25

McCULLERS, CARSON. Clock Without Hands. London: Cresset, 1961. 1st Eng ed. Newspaper review tipped-in. VG+ (bkpl) in dj. *Limestone.* $45/£29

McCULLERS, CARSON. The Heart Is a Lonely Hunter. H-M, 1940. 1st ed, 1st bk. VG+ in VG+ dj. *Fine Books.* $425/£274

McCULLERS, CARSON. The Member of the Wedding. Cresset, 1946. 1st Eng ed. Brn cl (lettering sl dull). NF in dj (sl soiled, chipped). *Dalian.* $132/£85

McCULLERS, CARSON. The Mortgaged Heart. Boston: Houghton Mifflin, 1971. 1st ed. Fine in Fine dj (lt fading). *Hermitage.* $35/£23

McCULLERS, CARSON. The Square Root of Wonderful. Boston: Houghton Mifflin, 1958. 1st ed. Fine in dj (chipped; closed tear). *Hermitage.* $60/£39

McCULLERS, CARSON. The Square Root of Wonderful. London, 1958. 1st Eng ed. Fine in NF dj (price-clipped). *Antic Hay.* $35/£23

McCULLERS, CARSON. The Square Root of Wonderful. A Play. London: Cresset Press, 1958. 1st Eng ed. Fine in dj (sl mkd rear panel). *Ulysses.* $85/£55

McCULLEY, JOHNSTON. Captain Fly-By-Night. Watt, 1926. 1st ed. VG in dj. *Madle.* $70/£45

McCULLOH, JAMES H. Researches on America. Balt, 1817. 2nd enlgd ed. xviii,(19)-220pp. Unopened, untrimmed. Orig paper bds (lacks paper label; spine worn, chip; lt foxing). Very Nice. Howes M 79. *Reese.* $350/£226

McCULLOH, JAMES H. Researches, Philosophical and Antiquarian, Concerning the Aboriginal History of America. Balt, 1829. 3rd ed. x,(13)-535pp, fldg map (fold split); untrimmed. Mod buckram, orig ptd paper spine label (rubbed). Sig, sl tanning, lt foxing, else VG. Howes M 79. *Reese.* $475/£306

McCUNE, BILLY. The Autobiography of Billy McCune. SF: Straight Arrow Books, 1973. 1st ed. Fine in dj (sm piece missing top of spine, crease along fr panel). *Cahan.* $100/£65

McCUTCHEON, JOHN T. Bird Center Cartoons. Chicago, 1904. 1st ed. Cl-backed pict bds (worn; bkpl). *King.* $65/£42

McCUTCHEON, JOHN T. Drawn From Memory. Indianapolis: Bobbs-Merrill, (1950). VG (bkpl). *Graf.* $20/£13

McCUTCHEON, JOHN T. John McCutcheon's Book. Chicago: The Caxton Club, 1948. Ltd to 1000. Lt grn dec cl. Good. *Karmiole.* $85/£55

McDADE, THOMAS M. The Annals of Murder: A Bibliography.... Norman: Univ of OK, (1961). (1st ed). Black cl; red spattered edges. Fine in dj. *Bohling.* $150/£97

McDANIEL, EUGENE B. and JAMES L. JOHNSON. Before Honor. Phila: Lippincott, (1975). 1st ed. NF in dj (wrinkle; sm tear). *Aka.* $40/£26

McDANIEL, RUEL. Vinegarroon, The Saga of Judge Roy Bean, 'The Law West of Pecos'. Kingsport, TN, (1936). 1st ed. Pict cvr. Minor cvr wear, o/w Fine. *Pratt.* $30/£19

McDANIEL, RUEL. Vinegarroon. Kingsport, 1936. 1st ed. Pict cl. VG. *Baade.* $20/£13

McDERMOTT, ANTHONY W. A Brief History of the 69th Regiment Pennsylvania Veteran Volunteers. (Phila: D.J. Gallagher, 1889.) 1st ed. 106pp. Cl. VG. *Mcgowan.* $250/£161

McDERMOTT, JOHN F. The Early Histories of St. Louis. St. Louis: Hist. Documents Found, 1952. 1st ed. Ep maps. VF in Good+ dj. *Oregon.* $50/£32

McDERMOTT, JOHN F. The French in the Mississippi Valley. Univ IL, 1965. 1st ed. VF in VG dj. *Oregon.* $35/£23

McDERMOTT, JOHN F. Seth Eastman's Mississippi. Univ of IL, (1973). 1st ed. VF in VF dj. *Oregon.* $35/£23

McDERMOTT, JOHN F. Travelers on the Western Frontier. Univ IL, (1970). 1st ed. VF in Fine dj. *Oregon.* $35/£23

McDERMOTT, JOHN F. (ed). The Spanish in the Mississippi Valley, 1762-1804. Univ of IL, (1974). 1st ed. VF in VF dj. *Oregon.* $35/£23

McDONALD, ARCHIBALD. Peace River. Malcolm McLeod (ed). Rutland, VT: Tuttle, (1971). Lg fldg map. White spine lettering flaked away, o/w VG. *Oregon.* $20/£13

McDONALD, EDWARD D. A Bibliography of the Writings of Theodore Dreiser. Phila: Centaur Book Shop, 1928. Ltd to 350 numbered. Frontis port tipped in. Grn cl; paper spine label. Good in dj (chipped). *Karmiole.* $30/£19

McDONALD, JERRY. North American Bison, Their Classification and Evolution. Berkeley: Univ CA, (1981). 1st ed. VF in VF dj. *Oregon.* $45/£29

McDONOUGH, JAMES LEE. Chattanooga—A Death Grip on the Confederacy. Knoxville, (1984). 1st ed. Fine in Fine dj. *Pratt.* $27/£17

McDONOUGH, MARY LOU. Poet Physicians. Springfield: Thomas, 1945. (2nd ptg). (Lt wear.) *Goodrich.* $65/£42

McDOWALL, ARTHUR. Peaks and Frescoes. OUP, 1928. Partly unopened. (1 pair leaves carelessly opened w/short tear.) *Hollett.* $70/£45

McDOWELL, FRANK and CARL ENNA (eds). Surgical Rehabilitation in Leprosy and in Other Peripheral Nerve Disorders. Balt, 1974. 1st ed. Good. *Fye.* $75/£48

McELLIGOTT, JAMES N. The American Debater. Chicago: S.C. Griggs, 1863. Revised, enlgd ed. Frontis port, 360pp. Blind-stamped brn cl. Good. *Karmiole.* $50/£32

McELROY, JOHN. Si Klegg. Washington, (1910). 2nd ed. Good in wrappers. *Hayman.* $15/£10

McELROY, JOSEPH. Hind's Kidnap. NY: Harper & Row, 1969. 1st ed. Fine in dj. *Cahan.* $60/£39

McELROY, JOSEPH. Lookout Cartridge. NY: Knopf, 1974. 1st ed. Fine in Fine dj (top edge curl). *Beasley.* $50/£32

McELROY, JOSEPH. A Smuggler's Bible. NY: Harcourt, Brace and World, (1966). 1st ed, 1st bk. Fine in Fine brilliant red dj. *Dermont.* $250/£161

McELROY, JOSEPH. A Smuggler's Bible. (London): Andre Deutsch, (1968). 1st Eng ed, 1st bk. Fine in Fine dj (price-clipped). *Between The Covers.* $250/£161

McELROY, ROBERT. Jefferson Davis: The Unreal and Real. NY: Harper, 1937. 1st ed. 2 vols. Spines sl dknd, else VG in pub's slipcase. *Mcgowan.* $85/£55

McELROY, ROBERT. Kentucky in the Nation's History. NY: Moffat, Yard, 1909. 5 ports, map, 3 facs. Unopened. VG. *Schoyer*. $65/£42

McEWAN, IAN. Black Dogs. London: Jonathan Cape, (1992). 1st ed. Signed. Fine in dj. *Godot*. $50/£32

McEWAN, IAN. Black Dogs. London: Jonathan Cape, 1992. 1st ed. Signed. Fine in Fine dj. *Revere*. $45/£29

McEWAN, IAN. Black Dogs. London Limited Editions, 1992. Ltd to 150 numbered, signed. 1/4 backed brn marbled bds. VF in tissue dj. *Dalian*. $70/£45

McEWAN, IAN. The Cement Garden. London: Cape, 1978. 1st UK ed. Inscrip, o/w Fine in dj. *Lewton*. $42/£27

McEWAN, IAN. The Cement Garden. London: Cape, 1978. 1st UK ed. Signed. Fine in dj (sl fading to spine, fr panel). *Williams*. $116/£75

McEWAN, IAN. The Child in Time. London: Cape, 1987. 1st UK ed. Signed. VG+ in dj. *Williams*. $22/£14

McEWAN, IAN. The Comfort of Strangers. NY: S&S, (1981). 1st Amer ed. Rev slip laid in. Fine in dj. *Reese*. $20/£13

McEWAN, IAN. The Comfort of Strangers. London: Cape, 1981. 1st UK ed. Signed. Fine in dj. *Williams*. $70/£45

McEWAN, IAN. The Imitation Game. London: Cape, 1981. 1st ed. Inscribed by author. Fine in dj. *Rees*. $39/£25

McEWAN, IAN. In Between the Sheets and Other Stories. NY: S&S, (1978). 1st Amer ed. Fine in dj. *Reese*. $20/£13

McEWAN, IAN. In Between the Sheets. London: Cape, 1978. 1st UK ed. Sl mk on 4pp, o/w VG in dj. *Lewton*. $57/£37

McEWAN, IAN. The Innocent. London: Jonathan Cape, (1990). 1st ed. Signed. Fine in dj. *Godot*. $65/£42

McEWAN, IAN. The Innocent. NY: Doubleday, 1990. 1st Amer ed. Signed. Fine in Fine dj. *Revere*. $35/£23

McEWEN, INEZ PUCKETT. So This Is Ranching. Caldwell: Caxton, 1948. 1st ed. Ltd to 1000 numbered, signed. Frontis, 19 photo plts, illus eps (bkpl; spine lt faded). *Karmiole*. $50/£32

McFARLAND, DENNIS. The Music Room. Boston: Houghton Mifflin, 1990. 1st ed, 1st bk. Fine in Fine dj. *Revere*. $50/£32

McFARLAND, DENNIS. The Music Room. Boston: Houghton-Mifflin, 1990. 1st ed. 1st bk. Fine in dj. *Else Fine*. $50/£32

McFARLAND, J. HORACE. Getting Acquainted with the Trees. NY, 1904. 1st ed. 20 tints. Teg. Tinted pict cl, gilt lettering. Sl wear spine ends, else VG. *Brooks*. $21/£14

McFARLING, LLOYD. Exploring the Northern Plains 1804-1876. Caldwell, ID: Caxton Printers, 1955. 1st ed. Very Clean in dj. *Laurie*. $50/£32

McFEE, WILLIAM. The Beachcomber. London: Faber & Faber, 1935. 1st ed. Grey cl. Spine edges lt rubbed; sl dusty; fox spots; o/w Nice. *Temple*. $12/£8

McFEE, WILLIAM. Casuals of the Sea. NY, 1916. 1st Amer ed. Paper yellowed, o/w VF. *Bond*. $40/£26

McFEE, WILLIAM. The Harbourmaster. NY: Doubleday, Doran, 1931. 1st ed. Ltd to 377. Signed. Gilt; teg. Spine sl dull, o/w Fine in slipcase (sl shelfworn; lacks bottom panel). *Sadlon*. $65/£42

McFEE, WILLIAM. North of Suez. NY: Doubleday, Doran, 1930. 1st ed. Ltd to 350. Signed. Teg. Fine in slipcase (sl shelfworn). *Sadlon*. $75/£48

McFEE, WILLIAM. Pilgrims of Adversity. Heinemann, 1928. 1st Eng ed. Black cl. VF in dj. *Dalian*. $54/£35

McFEE, WILLIAM. Sir Martin Frobisher. NY: Harper & Bros, 1928. VG in dj (chipped). *High Latitude*. $28/£18

McFEE, WILLIAM. Spenlove in Arcady. London: Faber & Faber, 1942. 1st ed. Tangerine cl, gilt. Inscrip, o/w Fine in dj (worn). *Temple*. $11/£7

McGAHERN, JOHN. The Barracks. London: Faber, 1963. 1st ed. Trace of sticker, sl rubbed, o/w VG. *Rees*. $23/£15

McGAHERN, JOHN. The Barracks. London: Faber & Faber, 1963. 1st UK ed, 1st bk. Fine in NF dj (sl mk fr panel). *Williams*. $543/£350

McGAHERN, JOHN. The Pornographer. Faber, 1979. 1st UK ed. Fine in dj. *Williams*. $31/£20

McGEE, JOHN W. The Catholic Church in the Grand River Valley 1833-1950. Grand Rapids, 1950. 1st ed. VG. *Artis*. $35/£23

McGILL, JOSEPH (comp). The Beverley Family of Virginia: Descendants of Major Robert Beverley.... R.L. Bryan, 1956. Port. Contents Fine (cvr damage) in dj (stuck to cvr). *Book Broker*. $95/£61

McGINLEY, PHYLLIS. The Province of the Heart. NY, 1959. 1st ed. VG in dj. *Argosy*. $20/£13

McGINLEY, PHYLLIS. Stones from a Glass House. NY: Viking, 1946. NF in dj (sl wear; tears). *Antic Hay*. $27/£17

McGINLEY, PHYLLIS. Times Three. NY: Viking, 1960. 1st ed. Fine in dj (sl wear, soil). *Antic Hay*. $20/£13

McGINNIS, JOE. The Dream Team. NY: Random House, 1972. 1st ed. NF in NF dj (sm crease). *Revere*. $35/£23

McGINNIS, JOE. Going to Extremes. NY, 1980. 1st ed. Map. VG+ in VG+ dj. *Blue Dragon*. $22/£14

McGINNIS, JOE. The Selling of the President. NY: Trident Press, 1969. 1st ed, 1st bk. NF in NF dj (lt wear). *Revere*. $45/£29

McGIVERN, ED. Ed McGivern's Book on Fast and Fancy Revolver Shooting. Springfield: King, 1938. 1st ed. Fine. *Bowman*. $50/£32

McGLASHAN, C.F. History of the Donner Party. Truckee, CA: Crowley & McGlashan, (1879). 193pp (paper dknd; notes; stamps). Red cl (worn, soiled; spine ends, fr hinge frayed), gilt. Howes M 102. *Bohling*. $500/£323

McGOWAN, EDWARD. McGowan vs. California Vigilantes. Biobooks, 1946. Ltd to 675. Fldg plt, 2 facs papers in rear pocket. VG. Howes M 103. *Oregon*. $45/£29

McGOWAN, EDWARD. McGowan vs. California Vigilantes. Oakland: Biobooks, 1946. One of 675 signed by publisher. Fldg plt, map in pocket. Fine in emb cl. *Cahan*. $65/£42

McGRATH, PATRICK. Blood and Water and Other Tales. NY: Poseidon, (1988). 1st ed, 1st bk. Lt bumped, else Fine in Fine dj. *Robbins*. $50/£32

McGRATH, PATRICK. The Grotesque. NY: Poseidon Press, 1989. 1st ed. NF in dj. *Moorhouse*. $31/£20

McGRATH, RAYMOND and A.C. FROST. Glass in Architecture and Decoration. Architectural Press, 1961. New ed, rev. *Edwards*. $78/£50

McGRAW, BLANCHE. The Real McGraw. Arthur Mann (ed). McKay, 1953. 1st ed. VG+ in VG dj. *Plapinger.* $30/£19

McGUANE, THOMAS. The Bushwhacked Piano. NY: S&S, 1971. 1st ed. NF in NF dj (sm blue stain verso spine panel, partially seeped through). *Lame Duck.* $100/£65

McGUANE, THOMAS. Keep the Change. Boston: Houghton Mifflin, 1989. 1st ed. Fine in Fine dj. *Revere.* $20/£13

McGUANE, THOMAS. Keep the Change. Boston: HM/Seymour Lawrence, 1989. One of 150 numbered, signed. Fine in cl slipcase. *Dermont.* $125/£81

McGUANE, THOMAS. The Missouri Breaks. Ballantine, 1976. 1st ed. Pb. VG (reading crease). *Stahr.* $15/£10

McGUANE, THOMAS. Nothing but Blue Skies. Boston: Houghton Mifflin, 1992. 1st ed. Signed. Fine in Fine dj. *Revere.* $40/£26

McGUANE, THOMAS. An Outside Chance. NY: FSG, 1980. 1st ed. VG in VG dj (1/2-inch chip; price-clipped). *Revere.* $30/£19

McGUANE, THOMAS. Panama. FSG, 1978. 1st ed. NF in dj. *Stahr.* $25/£16

McGUANE, THOMAS. The Sporting Club. NY: S&S, (1968). 1st Amer ed, 1st bk. NF (rmdr stripe; foxing eps, fore-edge) in NF dj (extrems dknd). *Between The Covers.* $150/£97

McGUIRE, HUNTER and GEORGE L. CHRISTIAN. The Confederate Cause and Conduct in the War between the States. Richmond, VA: L.H. Jenkins, (1907). 1st ed thus. VG (sl rubbing; tears last leaf). *Mcgowan.* $85/£55

McHALE, TOM. Farragan's Retreat. NY: Viking, (1971). 1st ed. VF in VF dj. *Between The Covers.* $65/£42

McHUGH, TOM. The Time of the Buffalo. NY, 1972. 1st ed. Fine in dj. *Baade.* $30/£19

McHUGH, TOM. The Time of the Buffalo. NY: Knopf, 1972. 1st ed. VG+ in VG- dj. *Parker.* $35/£23

McILHANY, EDWARD WASHINGTON. Recollections of a '49er. Kansas City: Hailman Ptg Co, 1908. Gold-stamped pict cl. (Sm nicks text margin; marginal stain first 12pp.) *Dawson.* $60/£39

McILHANY, EDWARD WASHINGTON. Recollections of a '49er. Kansas City: Hailman Ptg, 1908. 1st ed. Gilt-dec grn cl (spine dknd; extrems sl worn). VG. Howes M 111. *Harrington.* $100/£65

McILVANNEY, WILLIAM. Laidlaw. London: Hodder & Stoughton, 1977. 1st ed. Fine in VG dj (piece missing back panel; chipping; tears). *Mordida.* $75/£48

McILVANNEY, WILLIAM. The Papers of Tony Veitch. London: Hodder & Stoughton, 1983. 1st ed. VF in dj (price-clipped; pub's price-sticker). *Mordida.* $65/£42

McINERNEY, JAY. Brightness Falls. NY: Knopf, 1992. 1st ed. Inscribed. Fine in Fine dj. *Revere.* $45/£29

McINERNY, RALPH. The Seventh Station. NY: Vanguard, 1977. 1st ed, signed. Fine in Fine dj. *Janus.* $25/£16

McINTOSH, CHARLES. The Book of the Garden. Edinburgh/London: William Blackwood & Sons, 1855. iv,867pp + 32pp pub's ads. Gilt-stamped pict cvr, spine (worn; hinges broken; lacks rep). *Quest.* $85/£55

McINTOSH, CHARLES. The New and Improved Practical Gardener and Modern Horticulturist. London: Thomas Kelley, 1839. Engr frontis (marginal foxing), 972pp; 10 hand-colored plts. Aeg. Contemp full morocco, gilt, raised bands (hinges reinforced). *Quest.* $285/£184

McINTOSH, JAMES and PAUL FILDES. Syphilis from the Modern Standpoint. London, 1911. 1st ed. Good. *Fye.* $150/£97

McINTOSH, MARIA J. Woman in America. NY: Appleton, 1850. 1st ed. 155pp. Brn cl. VG. *Second Life.* $150/£97

McINTYRE, FRED. The True Life Story of a Pioneer. Syracuse, IN, (1955). *Hayman.* $25/£16

McINTYRE, VONDA N. Dreamsnake. Boston: Houghton-Mifflin, 1978. 1st ed. Fine in dj (sl edgewear). *Else Fine.* $75/£48

McKAY, CLAUDE. Banjo, a Story without a Plot. NY: Harper, 1929. 1st ed. Cl, dec bds. Sl offset fep; rear hinge sl strained; o/w NF in pict dj (sl chipped). *Reese.* $450/£290

McKAY, RICHARD C. Some Famous Sailing Ships and Their Builder Donald McKay.... NY/London: Putnam's, 1928. 1st ed. Inscribed. 10 color plts. (Rear inner hinge tender.) *Lefkowicz.* $85/£55

McKAY, RICHARD C. Some Famous Sailing Ships and Their Builder, Donald McKay. NY/London, 1928. Stated 1st Amer ed. 10 color plts. VG in dj (sl worn). *Hayman.* $50/£32

McKEARIN, HELEN and GEORGE. Two Hundred Years of American Blown Glass. NY: Crown Pub, (1950). 8th ptg. Frontis, 10 plts. Fine in dj (lt chipped). *Bookpress.* $35/£23

McKEE, JAMES HARVEY. Back 'In War Times.' Unadilla, NY, 1903. 1st ed. 2 veterans' letters, lock of hair laid in. VG+ in slipcase. *Pratt.* $135/£87

McKELVEY, S.D. The Lilac, a Monograph. London, (1928). 4 color charts (inserted in back cvr pocket); 172 half-tone plts. *Wheldon & Wesley.* $248/£160

McKENNEY, J. WILSON. On the Trail of Peg Leg Smith's Lost Gold. Palm Desert: Desert Press, 1957. 1st ed. Fine in heavy pict wrappers. *Connolly.* $20/£13

McKENNEY, JOHN. Tack Room Tattles. NY: Scribner's, 1934. 1st ed, rev copy. VG. *October Farm.* $40/£26

McKENNEY, THOMAS L. Sketches of a Tour to the Lakes, of the Character and Customs of the Chippeway Indians.... Balt: Fielding Lucas, 1827. 1st ed. 8vo. 494pp, 29 plts (minor foxing). Contemp 1/2 calf (rebacked; cvrs lt rubbed). Howes M 137. *Bookpress.* $650/£419

McKENNEY, THOMAS L. Sketches of a Tour to the Lakes, of the Character and Customs of the Chippeway Indians.... Imprint Soc, 1972. 17 plts (6 color). VF in VF pict slipcase. Howes M 132. *Oregon.* $50/£32

McKENNEY, THOMAS L. Sketches of a Tour to the Lakes.... Balt, 1827. 1st ed. 27 plts. (Foxing; rebound.) Slipcase. *Heinoldt.* $185/£119

McKENNEY, THOMAS L. and JAMES HALL. History of the Indian Tribes of North America. Kent, OH: Volair Ltd, 1978. 1st ed thus. 2 vols. Full leather; aeg; gold dec. Beautiful. *Perier.* $300/£194

McKENNEY, THOMAS L. and JAMES HALL. The Indian Tribes of North America.... Frederick Webb Hodge (ed). Edinburgh: John Grant, 1933. 3 vols. 123 color plts; 2 fldg maps. Rubberstamp eps, tps; sl eradicated spine #; o/w Fine. Howes M 129. *Oregon.* $625/£403

McKENZIE, DAN. The Infancy of Medicine: An Enquiry into the Influence of Folk-Lore.... London: Macmillan, 1927. VG+ in VG dj. *Blue Dragon.* $60/£39

McKERROW, R. Printers' and Publishers' Devices in England and Scotland 1485-1640. Bibliographical Soc, 1913. VG. *Moss.* $186/£120

McKILLIP, PATRICIA A. The Forgotten Beasts of Eld. NY: Atheneum, 1966. 1st ed. Fine in dj. *Else Fine.* $145/£94

McKILLIP, PATRICIA A. The Riddle-Master of Hed. NY: Atheneum, 1976. 1st ed. Fine in dj (sl edgewear). *Else Fine.* $185/£119

McKIM, RANDOLPH H. A Soldier's Recollections, Leaves from the Diary of a Young Confederate.... NY, 1910. Time-Life Collector's Lib of the Civil War 1984 reprint. Leather, gilt edges. Fine. *Pratt.* $27/£17

McKIM, RANDOLPH H. The Soul of Lee. London: Longmans, Green, 1918. 1st ed. Frontis port. Blue cl. Pencilled name, notes; pale foxing, else VG. *Chapel Hill.* $125/£81

McKINLEY, CHARLES, JR. Harriet. NY: Viking, 1946. 1st ed. William Pene DuBois (illus). Lg 8vo. Pict cl. VG in VG dj. *Book Adoption.* $40/£26

McKINLEY, GEORGIA. Follow the Running Grass. Boston: Houghton Mifflin, 1969. 1st ed. Fine in NF dj. *Reese.* $30/£19

McKUEN, ROD. We Touch the Sky. London: Elm Tree Books, 1979. 1st ed. Signed. NF in NF dj. *Bishop.* $20/£13

McLAIN, JOHN. Alaska and the Klondike. NY: McClure, Phillips, 1905. 1st ed. Fldg map. VG. *Oregon.* $80/£52

McLANDBURGH, FLORENCE. The Automaton Ear and Other Sketches. Chicago: Jansen, McClurg, 1876. 1st ed. 282pp. NF. *Second Life.* $75/£48

McLAREN, JOHN. Gardening in California. SF, 1924. 3rd ed. 9 plans. Gilt dec grn buckram. VG-. *Brooks.* $65/£42

McLAURIN, TIM. The Acorn Plan. NY: Norton, (1988). 1st ed, 1st bk. Fine in dj. *Turlington.* $45/£29

McLAVERTY, MICHAEL. Lost Fields. NY: Longmans, Green, 1941. 1st Amer ed. Ink inscrip, else Fine in VG dj. *Godot.* $65/£42

McLEAN, RUARI. Victorian Book Design and Colour Printing. London: Faber & Faber, 1963. 1st ed. 8 color, 64 monochrome plts. Sound (sl rubbed; ex-lib w/stamps, labels). *Cox.* $31/£20

McLEAN, RUARI. Victorian Book Design and Colour Printing. London: Faber & Faber, 1963. 1st ed. 64 monochromes, 8 color plts. Pink cl. Fine in dec dj. *Heller.* $85/£55

McLENNAN, JOHN FERGUSON. Studies in Ancient History. Comprising a Reprint of Primitive Marriage. London: Bernard Quaritch, 1876. 1st ed. xxx,(2),508pp + (4)pp ads. Mottled brn cl, gilt. Good (bkpl). *Karmiole.* $45/£29

McLEOD, ALEXANDER. Pigtails and Gold Dust—A Panorama of Chinese Life in Early California. Caldwell: Caxton, 1948. 2nd ptg. VG in dj (edge-chipped). *Perier.* $45/£29

McLOUGHLIN, JOHN. Letters of Dr. John McLoughlin Written at Fort Vancouver 1829-1832. Burt Brown Barker (ed). Portland: Binfords & Mort, (1948). 1st ed. Fine in VG dj. *Perier.* $45/£29

McLUHAN, MARSHALL and HARLEY PARKER. Through the Vanishing Point. NY, 1968. 1st Amer ed. Pub's letter encl. Fine in Fine dj. *Polyanthos.* $30/£19

McMAHAN, ANNA BENNESON (ed). With Shelley in Italy...1818 to 1822. Chicago: McClurg, 1905. 1st ed. Frontis w/guard; 63 plts from photos. Dec grn cl; teg. VG. *Petrilla.* $25/£16

McMENEMEY, W.H. The Life and Times of Sir Charles Hastings.... Edinburgh, 1959. Frontis; 32 plts. VG. *Whitehart.* $39/£25

McMILLAN, DOUGALD. Transition. NY: George Braziller, (1976). 1st Amer ed. Fine in dj. *Reese.* $15/£10

McMILLAN, GEORGE. The Old Breed, a History of the First Marine Division in World War II. Washington, (1949). 1st ed. Well used. *King.* $75/£48

McMILLAN, TERRY. Mama. London: Jonathan Cape, (1987). 1st UK ed, 1st bk. Lower corners lt bumped, else Fine in NF dj. *Robbins.* $75/£48

McMULLEN, ROY. The World of Marc Chagall. GC, (1968). VG. *Argosy.* $75/£48

McMURTRIE, DOUGLAS C. The Book. London: OUP, 1943. 3rd ed. Dj (torn). *Argosy.* $100/£65

McMURTRIE, DOUGLAS C. The Dutch Claims to the Invention of Printing. Chicago: Privately ptd, 1928. 2nd ed. #99/200. Fine. *Graf.* $60/£39

McMURTRIE, DOUGLAS C. Early Printing in Tennessee. Chicago, 1933. 6 plts. VG (spine snagged). *Veatchs.* $30/£19

McMURTRIE, DOUGLAS C. Early Printing in Tennessee. Chicago: Chicago Club of Ptg House Craftsmen, 1933. One of 900. VG (spine lt faded). *Graf.* $65/£42

McMURTRIE, DOUGLAS C. Early Printing in Wisconsin. Seattle: Frank McCaffrey, 1931. One of 300 ptd at Dogwood Press, inscribed. Cl, leather label. (Sl water damage lower cvr.) *Veatchs.* $45/£29

McMURTRIE, DOUGLAS C. The Golden Book. Chicago: Pascal Covici, 1931. 3rd ed. Blue cl. Fine in dj. *Oak Knoll.* $50/£32

McMURTRIE, DOUGLAS C. The Pacific Typographical Society and the California Gold Rush of 1849. Chicago: Ludlow Typograph Co, 1928. 1st ed. Dec brn bds; paper spine, cvr labels (extrems sl rubbed). *Karmiole.* $30/£19

McMURTRIE, DOUGLAS C. The Pacific Typographical Society and the California Gold Rush of 1849.... Chicago: Ludlow Typograph Co, 1928. Fine. *Graf.* $20/£13

McMURTRIE, DOUGLAS C. Pioneer Printing in Ohio. Cincinnati, 1943. Faded area back wrapper, o/w VG. *Hayman.* $15/£10

McMURTRIE, DOUGLAS C. Wings for Words. NY: Rand McNally, 1940. 1st ed. Ink name, address, else VG in dj (lt worn). *Hermitage.* $35/£23

McMURTRIE, DOUGLAS C. and ALBERT H. ALLEN. Jotham Meeker, Pioneer Printer of Kansas. Chicago: Eyncourt Press, 1930. Ltd to 650 numbered, this one out-of-series. Unopened. *Schoyer.* $50/£32

McMURTRIE, DOUGLAS C. and ALBERT H. ALLEN. Jotham Meeker. Chicago: Eyncourt Press, 1930. One of 650. Mtd frontis port. Brn buckram lettered in gilt; uncut. Fine. *Laurie.* $100/£65

McMURTRIE, W. Report on the Culture of the Sugar Beet.... Washington, 1880. (1),294pp (1pg edge-worn), 32 engr plts, 2 fldg maps (1 torn). Cl (stained). *Sutton.* $65/£42

McMURTRY, LARRY. All My Friends Are Going to Be Strangers. NY: S&S, (1972). 1st ed, 1st ptg. Fine in NF dj. *Macdonnell.* $175/£113

McMURTRY, LARRY. All My Friends Are Going to Be Strangers. NY: S&S, 1972. 1st ed. NF in NF dj. *Revere.* $100/£65

McMURTRY, LARRY. Anything for Billy. NY, (1988). 1st ed, signed. VG in dj. *King.* $50/£32

McMURTRY, LARRY. Anything for Billy. NY, (1988). 1st ed. Fine in Fine dj. *Pratt.* $30/£19

McMURTRY, LARRY. Anything for Billy. NY: S&S, (1988). 1st ed. VG in dj. *Houle.* $50/£32

McMURTRY, LARRY. Film Flam: Essays on Hollywood. NY: S&S, (1987). 1st Amer ed. Sm rmdr line, else Fine in dj. *Between The Covers.* $60/£39

McMURTRY, LARRY. It's Always We Rambled. NY: Frank Hallman, 1974. One of 300 numbered, signed. NF (bds sl splayed; extrems sl sunned) in paper-cvrd bds as issued. *Between The Covers.* $475/£306

McMURTRY, LARRY. The Last Picture Show. NY: Dial Press, (1966). Book Club ed. Signed. Fine in dj. *Bernard.* $35/£23

McMURTRY, LARRY. The Last Picture Show. Dial Press, 1966. 1st ed. NF in NF dj (faint staining to spine, corner fr panel). *Fine Books.* $250/£161

McMURTRY, LARRY. The Last Picture Show. NY: Dial, 1966. 1st ed. Tan cl. NF in NF dj. *Chapel Hill.* $400/£258

McMURTRY, LARRY. Lonesome Dove. NY: S&S, 1985. 1st ed. Inscribed. NF (rmdr stripe) in NF dj. *Revere.* $200/£129

McMURTRY, LARRY. Lonesome Dove. NY: S&S, 1985. Advance rev copy. VG (sm tear back cvr). *Parker.* $300/£194

McMURTRY, LARRY. Moving On. NY: S&S, (1970). 1st ed. Signed. VG in dj (sl soiled, used). *Turlington.* $300/£194

McMURTRY, LARRY. Moving On. Weidenfeld & Nicolson, 1971. 1st Eng ed. Brn-backed bds. NF in dj (2 inner repairs). *Dalian.* $54/£35

McMURTRY, LARRY. Some Can Whistle. NY: S&S, 1989. 1st ed. Signed. Fine in Fine dj. *Revere.* $55/£35

McNAIL, STANLEY. Something Breathing. Sauk City: Arkham House, 1965. 1st ed. Lt grn binding. Fine in Fine dj (spine ends lt worn). *Other Worlds.* $225/£145

McNALLY, R.T. In Search of Dracula. NYGS, 1972. 1st ed. NF in dj. *Aronovitz.* $25/£16

McNEAL, T.A. When Kansas Was Young. NY: Macmillan, 1922. 1st ed. Red cl, gilt. VG (sl edge wear). *Connolly.* $67/£43

McNEER, MAY. Give Me Freedom. NY: Abingdon, (1964). 1st ed. Signed by McNeer and Lynd Ward (illus). 4to. Yellow cl, black stamped lettering. Fine in color pict dj w/wrap-around illus. *Reisler.* $75/£48

McNEER, MAY. Martin Luther. NY: Abingdon-Cokesbury, (1953). 1st ed. Signed presentation by McNeer and Lynd Ward (illus). 4to. Rust-brn cl, silver stamping (lower edge sl worn). Pict dj (top edge worn; piece missing spine). *Reisler.* $60/£39

McNEIL, FRED H. Wy'East 'The Mountain.' A Chronicle of Mount Hood. Portland: Metropolitan, (1937). 1st ed. VG in VG dj. *Perier.* $65/£42

McNEILL, JOHN CHARLES. Lyrics from Cotton Land. Charlotte, NC: Stone, (1922). 12 plts. Bandana cl over bds; cvr inset; white lettering (flaked). VG. *Petrilla.* $50/£32

McNEILL-MOSS, GEOFFREY. The Epic of the Alcazar. London, 1937. 1st ed. Inscribed. Frontis map; 38 plts. VG in dj (ragged w/loss). *Edwards.* $93/£60

McNICKLE, D'ARCY. Wind from an Enemy Sky. NY, (1978). 1st ed. Fine (rmdr slash) in VG+ dj. *Fuller & Saunders.* $35/£23

McNITT, FRANK. The Indian Traders. Norman: Univ of OK Press, (1962). 1st ed. Color frontis, 3 maps. Red cl. Fine in pict dj. *House.* $30/£19

McNITT, FRANK. The Indian Traders. Norman: Univ of OK Press, (1962). 1st ed. Red cl. Spine ends sl bumped, o/w Fine in NF dj. *Harrington.* $50/£32

McNULTY, KNEELAND. Peter Milton, Complete Etchings, 1960-1976. Boston: Impressions Workshop, 1977. 1st ed. Dj sl sunned; else Fine. *Bookpress.* $45/£29

McPHARLIN, PAUL. Puppets in America 1739 to Today. Birmingham, MI: Puppetry Imprints, 1936. 1st ed. One of 1000. VG (lt foxing) in illus dj. *Cahan.* $60/£39

McPHEE, JOHN. Coming into the Country. NY, (1977). 1st ed. Fine (name) in Fine dj. *Fuller & Saunders.* $25/£16

McPHEE, JOHN. Coming into the Country. London, 1978. 1st ed. Fine in Fine dj. *Polyanthos.* $45/£29

McPHEE, JOHN. The Deltoid Pumpkin Seed. NY: FSG, 1973. 1st ed. Fine in Fine dj (lt rubbed). *Revere.* $40/£26

McPHEE, JOHN. Encounters with the Archdruid. NY: FSG, 1971. 1st ed. NF in VG dj (1/2-inch closed tear; lt wear). *Revere.* $70/£45

McPHEE, JOHN. Giving Good Weight. NY: FSG, (1979). 1st ed. Fine in dj (creased rear flap). *Bernard.* $17/£11

McPHEE, JOHN. In Suspect Terrain. NY, 1983. 1st Amer ed. Fine in Fine dj. *Polyanthos.* $30/£19

McPHEE, JOHN. Levels of the Game. NY: FSG, (1969). 1st ed. Fine in Fine dj (price-clipped). *Godot.* $45/£29

McPHEE, JOHN. Levels of the Game. NY: FSG, 1969. 1st ed. Fine in dj. *Else Fine.* $60/£39

McPHEE, JOHN. Oranges. NY: FSG, (1967). 1st ed. Fine in dj. *Godot.* $85/£55

McPHEE, JOHN. Oranges. NY: FSG, 1967. As New. *Quest.* $65/£42

McPHEE, JOHN. Pieces of the Frame. NY: FSG, 1975. 1st ed. Fine (lt shelfwear) in NF dj. *Revere.* $70/£45

McPHEE, JOHN. A Roomful of Hovings. NY: FSG, 1968. 1st ed. NF in VG dj (internal tape). *Revere.* $100/£65

McPHEE, JOHN. The Survival of the Bark Canoe. NY: FSG, 1975. 1st ed. Fine in Fine dj. *Lame Duck.* $250/£161

McPHERSON, JAMES ALAN. Elbow Room. Boston: Little, Brown, (1977). 1st ed. NF in dj w/9 line blurb by Ralph Ellison (spine rubbed, else NF). *Godot.* $100/£65

McQUINN, DONALD E. Targets. NY: Macmillan, (1980). 1st ed, 1st bk. Fine in NF dj. *Aka.* $35/£23

McREYNOLDS, EDWIN C. The Seminoles. Norman: Univ of OK Press, (1957). 1st ed. Red cl. NF (corners lt dampstained) in VG dj (sl chipped, rubbed, sl dampstain). *Harrington.* $35/£23

McREYNOLDS, EDWIN C. The Seminoles. Norman, 1957. 1st ed. (Sig, date; corners sl bumped), o/w Fine in dj (sl worn). *Baade.* $47/£30

McSHERRY, JOHN. The Form Feminine. NY: Greenberg Publisher, 1936. 1st ed. 60 full-pg b/w photos. Spiral bound. Lt soil, else Fine. *Cahan.* $75/£48

McSHERRY, RICHARD. Health, and How to Promote It. NY, 1879. 1st ed. 185pp. Good. *Fye.* $75/£48

McSHINE, KYNASTON (ed). Andy Warhol: A Retrospective. NY, 1989. 460 plts (277 color). Dec bds w/ptd protective dj, as issued. *Edwards.* $93/£60

McSHINE, KYNASTON (ed). Andy Warhol: A Retrospective. NY: MOMA, 1989. Pict bds. VG in lettered mylar wrapper. *Argosy.* $100/£65

McTAGGART, M.F. Mount and Man, a Key to Better Horsemanship. Country Life, 1925. (Fr cvr sl stained; string mks edges; backstrip faded.) *Petersfield.* $28/£18

McVAUGH, ROGERS. Edward Palmer. Norman, 1956. 5 facs, 2 maps. (Ex-lib.) Dj. *Brooks.* $19/£12

McVAUGH, ROGERS. Edward Palmer.... Little Compton, RI: Theophrastus, 1977. Rpt. *Quest.* $45/£29

McVICKAR, ARCHIBALD (rev). History of the Expedition...of Captains Lewis and Clark.... NY: A.L. Fowle, 1900. 2 vols. Fldg map. Spine faded, else VG. *Perier.* $85/£55

McWATTERS, GEORGE S. (ed). Detectives of Europe and America or Life in the Secret Service. Hartford: J.B. Burr Pub Co, 1878. 40 engrs. Full leather (rebacked), leather spine labels. *Glenn.* $175/£113

McWHORTER, L.V. The Border Settlers of Northwestern Virginia From 1768 to 1795.... Hamilton, OH, 1915. Frontis; 2 plts. (Wear, rubbing; spine bumped.) *Bohling.* $250/£161

McWHORTER, L.V. Hear Me, My Chiefs! Ruth Bordin (ed). Caldwell: Caxton, 1952. 1st ed. 3 maps (1 fldg). Tan cl lettered in red/brn. Fine in VG dj (chipped, loss, spine faded). *Harrington.* $160/£103

McWILLIAMS, CAREY. Ambrose Bierce. Boni, 1929. 1st ed. VG+ in VG- dj (worn; chipped). *Fine Books.* $38/£25

McWILLIAMS, CAREY. Louis Adamic and Shadow-America. L.A.: Arthur Whipple, (1935). Cl w/paper spine, cvr labels. Dj (top edge worn). *Dawson.* $100/£65

McWILLIAMS, JOHN. Recollections of John McWilliams. (Princeton: Princeton Univ), (1919). Frontis port. Gold-stamped cl; teg. *Dawson.* $225/£145

MEAD, EDWARD C. Historic Homes of the South-West Mountains of Virginia. Lippincott, 1899. (Ltd to 750). 275pp. Contents Sound. (Cover soil w/red splotches, water-stained; tear at hinges; ex-lib w/mks.) *Book Broker.* $50/£32

MEAD, RICHARD. A Discourse on the Plague. London: Ptd for A. Millar & J. Brindley, 1744. 9th ed, corrected & enlgd. xl,164pp. Contemp speckled calf. Clean (spine ends repaired). *White.* $147/£95

MEAD, RICHARD. A Mechanical Account of Poisons in Several Essays. London: For Ralph South, 1702. 1st ed, 1st issue. 8 leaves (lt staining outer margin first 2), 175,(1)pp; fldg plt. Mod linen-backed bds, leather spine label. Excellent. *Hemlock.* $475/£306

MEAD, RICHARD. A Mechanical Account of Poisons. London: Ptd for J. Brindley, 1745. 3rd ed. xlviii,319pp, 4 plts, incl 1 fldg (lt browned). Full speckled calf (edge-worn; chipped; top 1/2 fep cut away; hinges, joints tender; ex-lib). *Edwards.* $233/£150

MEADE, GEORGE GORDON. With Meade at Gettysburg. Phila: John C. Winston, 1930. 1st ed thus. Orig cl. Fine in VG dj (sl chipped). *Mcgowan.* $150/£97

MEADE, H. A Ride Through the Disturbed Districts of New Zealand. London, 1870. 1st ed. xii,375pp, ads; 4 color chromolithos. 1/2 morocco. *Lewis.* $225/£145

MEADE, JULIAN R. Bouquets and Bitters: A Gardner's Medley. Longmans, Green, 1940. 1st ed. Signed. VG in Good dj. *Book Broker.* $25/£16

MEADER, J.W. The Merrimack River. Boston: B.B. Russell, 1869. 308pp; lg fldg map. Grn cl, dec gilt spine (spine extrems sl frayed; bkpl). *Karmiole.* $50/£32

MEADES, JONATHAN. Filthy English. London: Jonathan Cape, 1984. 1st Eng ed. Fine in dj (spine sl faded). *Ulysses.* $70/£45

MEADOWS, DON. The American Occupation of La Paz. Dawson, 1955. 1st ed. One of 300 ptd. Fine. *Oregon.* $45/£29

MEAKIN, ANNETTE M.B. Ribbon of Iron. Westminster/NY: Constable/Dutton, n.d. (ca 1902). Fldg map. Yellow cl (sl soiled; pocket removed). *Schoyer.* $30/£19

MEANS, E.K. More E.K. Means. NY: 1919. 1st Amer ed. NF (extrems sl rubbed). *Polyanthos.* $35/£23

MEANS, WILLIAM GORDON. My Guns. Dedham: Privately ptd, 1941. 1st ed. VG. *Bowman.* $60/£39

MEANY, TOM et al. Milwaukee's Miracle Braves. A.S. Barnes, 1954. (1st ed in G&D dj). VG in Good+ dj. *Plapinger.* $45/£29

MEANY, TOM. Babe Ruth. Barnes, 1947. Ltr ptg. VG+ in Good dj. *Plapinger.* $30/£19

MEANY, TOM. Baseball's Greatest Hitters. A.S. Barnes, 1950. 1st ed. VG+ in Good+ dj. *Plapinger.* $40/£26

MEANY, TOM. The Magnificent Yankees. Barnes, 1952. 1st ed. VG. *Plapinger.* $40/£26

MEANY, TOM. Stan Musial—The Man. Barnes, 1951. 1st ed. Pict cvr. Good+; no dj as issued. *Plapinger.* $45/£29

MEANY, TOM. The Yankee Story. Dutton, 1960. 1st ed. Fine in VG dj. *Plapinger.* $50/£32

MECKAUER, W. The Books of the Emperor Wu Ti. Minton, Balch, 1931. 1st Amer ed. VG in dj. *Aronovitz.* $85/£55

Medical Research Committee. An Atlas of Gas Poisoning. N.p.: American Red Cross, 1918. 13 color plts. (Marginal browning, ex-libris, soiling, upper corner rubbed w/cl loss.) *Edwards.* $23/£15

MEDWIN, THOMAS. Journal of the Conversations of Lord Byron. London: Henry Colburn, 1824. 3/4 morocco over cl, gilt spine, raised bands. Teg. (Extrems lt rubbed.) *Sadlon.* $200/£129

MEDWIN, THOMAS. Journal of the Conversations of Lord Byron. NY: Wilder & Campbell, 1824. 1st Amer ed. 304pp; facs letter fold-out. Recent 3/4 leather, marbled bds, gilt on leather label. Excellent (pencil note). *Hartfield.* $295/£190

MEECH, W.W. Quince Culture. NY, 1888. 143pp (lt dampstaining). (Spine dknd, bubbling.) *Sutton.* $37/£24

MEEHAN, THOMAS. The American Handbook of Ornamental Trees. Phila: Lippincott, Gambo, 1853. 1st ed. 257pp. Good (foxing; pencil names). *Second Life.* $135/£87

MEEHAN, THOMAS. The Native Flowers and Ferns of the United States.... Series 1. Boston, 1878-79. 2 vols. v,192; v,200pp; 48 chromolitho plts each vol (offsetting). Aeg; marbled eps. Brown morocco (sl scuffed), gilt. Good set (tp, frontis vol 1 sl scarred from separation). *Brooks*. $295/£190

MEEK, STEPHEN HALL. The Autobiography of a Mountain Man 1805-1889. Glen Dawson, 1948. 1st ed. One of 300. Fine. *Oregon*. $80/£52

MEEK, STEPHEN HALL. The Autobiography of a Mountain Man, 1805-1889. Pasadena: Glen Dawson, 1948. *Dawson*. $45/£29

MEEKE, MRS. The Birth-day Present. London: Dean and Munday, (ca 1830). 1st ed. 12mo. Handcolored frontis, 36pp. 15 handcolored in-text engrs. Stiff ptd wraps. Spine chipped, cvrs lt soiled; else VG. *Chapel Hill*. $110/£71

MEEKER, EZRA. Pioneer Reminiscences of Puget Sound. Seattle, WA: Lowman & Hanford, (1905). 1st ed. Good. Howes M 477. *Lien*. $100/£65

MEEKER, EZRA. Pioneer Reminiscences of Puget Sound. Seattle: Lowman & Hanford, 1905. 1st ed. Signed. VG. *Perier*. $95/£61

MEEKER, EZRA. Seventy Years of Progress in Washington. Seattle: Ezra Meeker, 1921. 1st ed. Signed. Frontis, 14 plts, 11 fldg illus mtd to rep. Grn cl, gilt. Good. *Karmiole*. $45/£29

MEEKS, CARROLL L.V. Italian Architecture, 1750-1914. New Haven: Yale Univ, 1966. 1st ed. Fine in dj (creased). *Bookpress*. $185/£119

MEGINNESS, J.F. Otzinachson: A History of the West Branch Valley of the Susquehanna.... Williamsport: Gazette & Bulletin, 1889. Rev ed. Vol I. Frontis; 702,vpp; fldg plan, fldg map. Leather over cl; gilt. Contents Fine (spine leather chipped; hinges cracked). Howes M 480. *Connolly*. $125/£81

MEGROZ, R.L. (ed). For Fathers. Hodder & Stoughton, (1920). 1st Eng ed. Blue cl. NF in dj (sl tanned). *Dalian*. $31/£20

MEIER-GRAEFE, JULIUS. Modern Art Being a Contribution to a New System of Aesthetics. Florence Simmonds & George W. Chrystal (trans). NY: Putnam's, 1908. 1st Amer ed. 2 vols. Photogravure frontis each vol; teg. Gilt-dec cl (edges sl rubbed, sm scrape rear cvr). VG set (end leaves sl foxed). *Reese*. $225/£145

MEIGS, ARTHUR. A Study of the Human Blood-Vessels in Health and Disease. Phila, 1907. 1st ed. Good. *Fye*. $150/£97

MEIGS, CHARLES. Observations on Certain of the Diseases of Young Children. Phila, 1850. 1st ed. 215pp. (Ex-lib.) *Fye*. $175/£113

MEIGS, CHARLES. Obstetrics: The Science and the Art. Phila, 1849. 1st ed. 685pp. Full leather (backstrip rubbed). *Fye*. $250/£161

MEIGS, CHARLES. Obstetrics: The Science and the Art. Phila, 1852. 2nd ed. 759pp. Full leather (backstrip cracked, dry; water stains). *Fye*. $40/£26

MEIGS, CHARLES. The Philadelphia Practice of Midwifery. Phila, 1842. 2nd ed. 408pp; 36 engr plts. Recent cl; leather label. (Ex-lib.) *Fye*. $125/£81

MEIGS, J. FORSYTH. A History of the First Quarter of the Second Century of the Pennsylvania Hospital.... Phila: Collins, 1877. Frontis, 145pp; 2 plts. (Bds worn; bkpls, stamp.) *Goodrich*. $95/£61

MEIGS, J. FORSYTH. A Practical Treatise on the Diseases of Children. Phila, 1858. 3rd ed. 724pp. Full leather. Good. *Fye*. $75/£48

MEIGS, JOHN (ed). The Cowboy in American Prints. Chicago: Swallow Press, (1972). Ltd to 300 numbered, signed by Meigs & Peter Hurd (litho). 75 plts. Red cl. Fine in slipcase. *Karmiole*. $375/£242

MEIGS, PEVERIL III. The Dominican Mission Frontier of Lower California. Berkeley: Univ of CA, 1935. 1st ed. Lg fldg map, 19 photoplts. VG. *Connolly*. $95/£61

MEINE, FRANKLIN J. (ed). The Crockett Almanacs, Nashville Series, 1835-1838. Chicago: Caxton Club, 1955. One of 600. Pict cl. VG +. *Bohling*. $125/£81

MEINERTZHAGEN, R. Kenya Diary 1902-1906. London: Oliver & Boyd, (1957). *Petersfield*. $62/£40

MEINERTZHAGEN, R. Nicoll's Birds of Egypt. London, 1930. 1st ed. 2 vols. Frontis port; 31 color, 6 b/w plts; 3 color fldg maps. Gilt ruling (wear; upper bds dented, sl cl loss vol 2). *Edwards*. $465/£300

MEISELAS, SUSAN. Carnival Strippers. NY: FSG, 1976. 1st ed. VG in pict wrappers (bumped). *Cahan*. $85/£55

MEISS, MILLARD. Andrea Mantegna as Illuminator. NY, 1957. Good in dj. *Washton*. $45/£29

MEISS, MILLARD. The Great Age of Fresco: Discoveries, Recoveries, and Survivals. NY: Braziller, 1970. 118 color plts, 8 halftones. VG in dj. *Argosy*. $75/£48

MEISS, MILLARD. Painting in Florence and Siena after the Black Death. Princeton: Princeton Univ Press, 1951. 1st ed. 169 plts on 42 leaves. VG. *Bookpress*. $125/£81

MELIA, PIUS. Origin, Persecutions and Doctrines of the Waldenses.... London: Toovey, 1870. xvi,138pp, 2 plts. Red cl, gilt (spine repaired; shaken; penciling). *Schoyer*. $40/£26

MELINE, JAMES F. Two Thousand Miles on Horseback. NY: Hurd & Houghton, 1867. 1st ed. x,317pp (eps stained; lt foxing); fldg map (detached; tape-repaired tears). Brn cl (bumped, rubbed, chipped). Good. *Blue Mountain*. $50/£32

MELISH, LAWSON McCLUNG. A Bibliography of the Collected Writings of Edith Wharton. NY: Brick Row, 1927. 1st ed. VG. *Argosy*. $45/£29

MELLANBY, KENNETH. Scabies. London: OUP, 1943. 1st ed. Buff cl. VG (ex-lib). *White*. $47/£30

MELLARD, RUDOLPH. South by Southwest. Denver: Sage, 1960. 1st ed. Dj. *Lambeth*. $30/£19

MELLEN, P. Jean Clouet. Complete Edition of the Drawings, Miniatures and Paintings. London: Phaidon, 1971. 193 plts (4 color). Sound in dj. *Ars Artis*. $93/£60

MELLICK, ANDREW D., JR. Lesser Crossroads. Hubert G. Schmidt (ed). Rutgers Univ Press, 1948. 1st ed. VG in Good dj. *Connolly*. $25/£16

MELLON, RALPH. Sulfanilamide Therapy of Bacterial Infections. Springfield, 1938. 1st ed. Good. *Fye*. $50/£32

MELLY, GEORGE. Khartoum, and the Blue and White Niles. London: Colburn, 1851. 1st ed. 2 vols. xii,305,26; x,309,8pp; 2 plts; map. Internally VG ex-lib. *Worldwide*. $125/£81

MELTON, A.B. Seventy Years in the Saddle and then Some. Kansas City, 1950. 2nd, best ed. Ptd pict wrappers (lacks spine). *Ginsberg*. $125/£81

MELTZER, MILTON. Mark Twain Himself, a Pictorial Biography. NY: Bonanza Books, 1960. Rpt. Dj. *Macdonnell*. $25/£16

MELVILLE, GEORGE W. In the Lena Delta. Boston: Houghton Mifflin, 1885. 1st ed. xiii,497+ ads. Mod 1/2 calf. VG. *Walcot*. $101/£65

MELVILLE, HERMAN. The Apple-Tree Table and Other Sketches. Princeton/London: Princeton Univ Press/OUP, 1922. One of issue ltd to 1500 of total ptg of 1675. All edges uncut. 1/4 tan cl, grey-grn bds. Nice. *Temple.* $109/£70

MELVILLE, HERMAN. Battle-Pieces and Aspects of the War. NY: Harper & Bros., 1866. 1st ed. 8vo, 272pp. Brn cl, beveled edges. NF. BAL 13673. *Chapel Hill.* $2,000/£1,290

MELVILLE, HERMAN. Benito Cereno. London: Nonesuch, 1926. Ltd ed of 1650. Uncut. Buckram (lt faded; pinhole dents upper bd), gilt. *Hollett.* $186/£120

MELVILLE, HERMAN. Benito Cereno. London: Nonesuch, 1926. One of 1650. 10 hand-stenciled illus by E. McKnight Kauffer. Dk red buckram, beveled bds, gilt spine title. Eps sl browned, else Fine in patterned slipcase. *Heller.* $150/£97

MELVILLE, HERMAN. Israel Potter: His Fifty Years of Exile. NY: Putnam, 1855. 1st ed, 1st ptg; heading p141 reads 'Chapter XVI.' 1st binding; initials F, Y and E on spine ornamented w/pendants. 8vo, 276pp. Purple cl (faded to brn). VG (bkpl; ink mks fep; rear hinge tender) in red cl chemise, full morocco slipcase. BAL 13667. *Chapel Hill.* $3,000/£1,935

MELVILLE, HERMAN. Journal of a Visit to Europe and the Levant, October 11, 1856-May 6, 1857. Howard C. Horsford (ed). Princeton: Princeton Univ Press, 1955. 1st this ed. Orig brn cl. VG in dj (price-clipped; spine stained). BAL 13701. *Chapel Hill.* $60/£39

MELVILLE, HERMAN. Mardi: And a Voyage Thither. NY: Harper, 1849. 1st Amer ed. 2 vols. Purple-brn cl (spines browned, sl dull; head vol 1 chipped). Good set (text sl foxed, browned). Now in slipcase. *Ash.* $543/£350

MELVILLE, HERMAN. Mardi: And a Voyage Thither. NY: Harper, 1849. 1st Amer ed. 2 vols. 8vo. 365; 387pp + 8pp ads. Brn cl. Bright (sigs, sl discolored eps) in red cl chemise, full morocco slipcase. BAL 13658. *Chapel Hill.* $5,000/£3,226

MELVILLE, HERMAN. Moby Dick or The Whale. Chicago: Lakeside, 1930. Ltd to 1000 sets. 3 vols. Rockwell Kent (illus). Uncut. Silver stamped cl. Sl wear, else VG in glassine djs & aluminum slipcase. *King.* $2,500/£1,613

MELVILLE, HERMAN. Moby Dick. NY: Random House, 1930. 1st trade ed. Signed by Rockwell Kent (illus). VG in dj (spine sl browned). *Houle.* $425/£274

MELVILLE, HERMAN. Moby-Dick; or, The Whale. NY: Harper, 1851. 1st ed. 1st state binding, grn cl, sides stamped in blind, circular device; orange coated eps. 5 oval ink stamps to text pp reading 'Mount Pleasant Academy Library' w/letter dated 1929 giving provenance & authority to sell this copy. VG (old inkstain margin 1st 13 leaves; lt staining to cl; foxing; expertly restored; lacks blank fr flyleaf). BAL 13664. *Cahan.* $10,000/£6,452

MELVILLE, HERMAN. A Narrative of Adventures in the South Seas.... London: John Murray, 1861. Colonial issue, pub'd in Murray's Colonial Home Library at 3/6. xiii,(1),321pp. Plum cl, stamped in gilt, blind. VG (spine sl dknd). *Reese.* $150/£97

MELVILLE, HERMAN. Omoo. NY: Harper, 1847. 1st Amer ed. Frontis map. Recent 1/2 morocco over marbled bds, leather spine label, gilt-ruled (foxing). BAL 13656. *Sadlon.* $500/£323

MELVILLE, HERMAN. Omoo. London: John Murray, 1849. Frontis map. Gilt, blind-stamped cl (rebacked, orig backstrip laid on; bkpl removed fr pastedown). *Sadlon.* $175/£113

MELVILLE, HERMAN. Omoo. A Narrative of Adventures in the South Seas. London: John Murray, 1847. 1st ed. State A, w/sig mk P perfectly ptd on p209. 8vo, 321pp. Contemp 1/2 calf, marbled bds. VG (lt foxing, label). BAL 13655. *Chapel Hill.* $750/£484

MELVILLE, HERMAN. Omoo: A Narrative of Adventures in the South Seas. NY: Harper & Bros, 1847. 1st Amer ed. 8vo, 389pp(9),16pp ads. Grn cl, gilt dec spine, gilt ship fr cvr. Sig; nick at head of spine, else NF. BAL 13656. *Chapel Hill.* $3,700/£2,387

MELVILLE, HERMAN. The Piazza Tales. NY, 1856. 1st ed. Pub's gilt/blind tooled brn cl (head, foot of spine lt rubbed). 1/2 blue morocco slipcase (lt worn). *D & D.* $1,500/£968

MELVILLE, HERMAN. Typee, a Romance of the South Seas. NY: LEC, 1935. One of 1500 numbered, signed by Miguel Covarrubias (illus). Tapa cl over bds. Spine sl tanned, o/w NF in slipcase (short crack lower joint). *Reese.* $150/£97

MELVILLE, HERMAN. Typee. NY/London: Wiley & Putnam/John Murray, 1846. 1st Amer bk ed, 1st bk. 2 vols in 1. xv,(1),166,(4),(167)-325pp,(4)pp ads. Orig brn cl. Binding variant A complete w/frontis map, both 1/2 titles, tps. Good (outer joints heavily repaired; closed tear to spine; ink notations tp; inkstamps; foxing). BAL 13653. *Chapel Hill.* $250/£161

MELVILLE, HERMAN. Typee. NY, 1849. Rev ed. xiv,307pp + 8pp ads; map. Grn cl (faded). *Lewis.* $256/£165

MELVILLE, HERMAN. White-Jacket. NY: Harper & Bros., 1850. 1st Amer ed, 2nd ptg; 'Note' on p(iii), correct sig mk 'Q' on p(361). Similar to 3rd cl binding described by BAL 13662 (no lettering on cvrs), but BAL notes only slate cl. 8vo, 465pp + (14)pp ads. Blue-purple cl. VG (spine ends chipped; cl dknd; labels). *Chapel Hill.* $1,200/£774

MELVILLE, JENNIE. The Hunter in the Shadows. London: Hodder, 1969. 1st ed. NF in VG dj. *Ming.* $39/£25

MELVILLE, LEWIS. The Life and Letters of William Beckford of Fonthill. London: Heinemann, 1910. 1st ed. Gilt, blind-stamped cl. Unopened (sl dknd, sl rubbed). *Sadlon.* $40/£26

MELVILLE, PHILIP. Memoirs of the Late Philip Melville.... London: J. Dennett, (1812). Only ed. Contemp full calf, gilt, morocco label. Scratches, else VG. *Limestone.* $65/£42

MELVILLE, ROBERT. Henry Moore: Sculpture and Drawings, 1921-1969. NY: Abrams, (1968). 32 mtd color illus. VG in dj (torn). *Argosy.* $125/£81

MELVIN, JEAN SUTHERLAND. American Glass Paperweights and Their Makers. Thomas Nelson, 1967. 1st ed. VG + in VG + dj. *Bishop.* $20/£13

Memoir of Pierre Toussaint, Born a Slave in St. Domingo. (By Hannah Farnham Lee.) Boston: Crosby, Nichols, 1854. 2nd ed. Frontis port, 124pp (lib labels removed fep). Blue cl. VG. *Second Life.* $65/£42

Memoirs of a Peg-Top. (By Mary Ann Kilner.) London: John Marshall, n.d. (ca 1790). 16mo. vii,108pp; 27 half-pg woodcuts, partially hand-tinted. Marble paper on bds, 3/4 black paper spine, corners. VG (lacks frontis, ink inscrip, name stamps, chips; scuffed, rubbed, rebacked). *Hobbyhorse.* $275/£177

Memoirs of an American Lady. (By Anne Grant.) London: Longmans, 1808. 1st ed. 2 vols. Orig bds (backstrips rubbed). All edges untrimmed. Very Nice. *Hollett.* $426/£275

Memoirs of an American Lady. (By Anne Grant.) London: A.K. Newman, 1817. 2 vols in 1. 322; 344pp. VG (rebound). Howes G303. *Lien.* $85/£55

Memoirs of Marshall Hall, M.D., F.R.S....by His Widow. London: Bentley, 1861. Engr frontis (foxed), xiv,518pp (lt foxed). Orig Victorian pressed cl, gilt spine (worn, recently recased saving orig spine). Good. *Goodrich.* $195/£126

Memoirs of the Harcourt Family; A Tale for Young Ladies. London: G. Walker, 1816. 1st ed. 8vo. Engr frontis; 168pp. Grey paper-cvrd bds (joints cracked but holding; initials). VG. *Chapel Hill.* $250/£161

Memoirs of the Verney Family. London: Longmans, 1892-99. 4 vols. (Stain vol 4; corners sl bumped.) *Petersfield.* $81/£52

Memorial and Biographical History of Northern California.... Chicago, 1891. Frontis, 834pp; aeg. Inner gilt dentelles. Orig gilt-dec morocco, spine gilt. Corners sl rubbed, bkpl, occasional fox mk, else Fine. *Reese.* $1,000/£645

Memories of Old Hampton. Hampton, VA: Institute Press, 1909. 1st ed. NF. *Mcgowan.* $150/£97

Men and Manners in America. (By Thomas Hamilton.) Edinburgh/London, 1833. 2 vols. ix,393; 402pp (prelims sl browned). Marbled eps, edges. Blind-emb cl, gilt (sl worn; spines faded). *Edwards.* $132/£85

Men and Manners in America. (By Thomas Hamilton.) Edinburgh: William Blackwood, 1833. 1st ed. 2 vols in 1. xii,393; iv,402pp. (Ink stain spine; cvrs lt rubbed; ink name; stain fep.) Howes H 138. *Bookpress.* $225/£145

Men O'War. Newport News Shipbuilding & Dry Dock Co, (1943). Paper cvr. VG- (pg torn). *Book Broker.* $25/£16

MENCKEN, H.L. The Artist. Boston: John W. Luce, 1912. 1st ed. Brn paper-cvrd bds, ptd dec. Early bkpl, eps lt browned, else NF. *Godot.* $225/£145

MENCKEN, H.L. Christmas Story. NY: Knopf, 1946. 1st ed. Illus blue cl (sl wear; bds sl warped). VG in pict dj (price-clipped). *Juvelis.* $125/£81

MENCKEN, H.L. Christmas Story. NY: Knopf, 1946. 1st ed. Signed. Blue cl, illus. Ink sig; edgeworn, sl soiled, else VG in dj (price-clipped; lt used). *Juvelis.* $125/£81

MENCKEN, H.L. Heathen Days, 1890-1936. NY: Knopf, 1943. 1st ed. Fine in Fine dj. *Between The Covers.* $175/£113

MENCKEN, H.L. James Branch Cabell. NY: McBride, 1927. 1st ed. Port. Fine in ptd wrappers. *Reese.* $75/£48

MENCKEN, H.L. Letters of H.L. Mencken. NY: Knopf, 1961. 1st ed. VG in dj (sl chipped, creased). *Hermitage.* $35/£23

MENCKEN, H.L. Newspaper Days, 1899-1906. NY: Knopf, 1941. 1st ed. Fine in Fine dj (sm chip, few sm tears). *Between The Covers.* $175/£113

MENCKEN, H.L. Prejudices (Sixth Series). NY: Knopf, 1927. 1st ed. VF in VG dj (spine tanned; sm tear affecting lettering). *Lame Duck.* $250/£161

MENCKEN, H.L. Prejudices Sixth Series. London: Cape, (1929). 1st Eng ed. VG in dj (spine browned). *Limestone.* $65/£42

MENCKEN, H.L. Prejudices Third Series. Knopf, 1922. 1st ed. VG+ in VG dj (some sl wear to spine). *Fine Books.* $125/£81

MENCKEN, H.L. Prejudices. Cape, 1921. 1st Eng ed. Yellow cl. Spine sl sunned; fore-edge, eps sl foxed, o/w VG. *Dalian.* $39/£25

MENCKEN, H.L. Treatise on Right and Wrong. London: Kegan Paul et al, 1934. 1st ed. Crimson cl, gilt spine. Lt foxing edges, prelims, o/w Nice. *Temple.* $22/£14

MENCKEN, H.L. Treatise on the Gods. NY: Knopf, 1930. 1st ed. Fine in NF dj (sm nicks, short tears). *Between The Covers.* $275/£177

MENDELL and HOSMER, MISSES. Notes of Travel and Life. NY: For author, 1854. 1st ed. 288pp. Good (water mk continues at spot on top of leaves throughout text; 2-inch piece eaten from side fr hinge). Howes M513. *Second Life.* $150/£97

MENDELSOHN, ISAAC. Slavery in the Ancient Near East. NY: OUP, 1949. 1st ed. Frontis. Sl rubbed; ex-lib, #, stamps, o/w VG. *Worldwide.* $30/£19

MENDELSOHN, S. The Battle of the Warsaw Ghetto. NY, 1944. Map. Wraps (stained). *King.* $25/£16

MENEN, AUBREY. The Duke of Gallodoro. London: C&W, 1952. 1st ed. Scarlet bds, gilt. Fine in dj. *Temple.* $22/£14

MENEN, AUBREY. Speaking the Language Like a Native. London: Hamish Hamilton, 1963. 1st ed. NF in dj. *Limestone.* $30/£19

MENGARINI, GREGORY. Recollections of the Flathead Mission. Glendale: Clark, 1977. Fine. *Perier.* $42/£27

MENNINGER, WILLIAM. Juvenile Paresis. Balt, 1936. 1st ed. Good. *Fye.* $50/£32

MENPES, DOROTHY (transcribed by). War Impressions. A&C Black, 1903. Rpt. 99 color plts, fldg chart. Teg. (Pp.xiii detached, feps sl browned, ex-libris; cl sl faded, worn.) *Edwards.* $70/£45

MENPES, MORTIMER. Japan, a Record in Colour. London: A&C Black, (1905). 4th ptg. 75 color plts. Blue cl, yellow decs. Bkpl, else Very Nice. *Hermitage.* $125/£81

MENPES, MORTIMER. Whistler as I Knew Him. Macmillan, 1904. 1st ed. VG. *Bishop.* $40/£26

MENZHAUSEN, JOACHIM. The Green Vaults. Leipzig: Edition Leipzig, 1968. 1st ed in English. 14 tipped-in b/w plts, 143 plts. Fine in illus dj. *Cahan.* $85/£55

MENZIE, ARCHIBALD. Menzie's Journal of Vancouver's Voyage, April to October, 1792. Victoria, B.C.: Cullin, 1923. 2 facs maps. Orig cl (pocket removed). Howes M 519. *Schoyer.* $125/£81

MERA, H.P. The Rain Bird, a Study in Pueblo Design. Santa Fe: Lab of Anthropology, 1937. 48 full-pg plts. Fine in stiff wrappers in dj (lt soiled). *Glenn.* $325/£210

Mercedes of Castile. (By James Fenimore Cooper.) Phila: Lea & Blanchard, 1840. 1st ed. 2 vols. Orig purple cl, ptd spine labels; label in Blanck's 'state B' ('sequence arbitrary'), w/the word 'BY' alone on a line. NF (sl discoloration; sl foxing). *Sumner & Stillman.* $1,100/£710

MERCER, A.S. The Banditti of the Plains. SF: Grabhorn Press, 1935. Orig cl, bds. VG. Howes M 522. *Schoyer.* $100/£65

MERCER, A.S. Powder River Invasion: War on the Rustlers in 1892. (N.p.): Privately ptd, (1923). 2nd ed. Blue cl (sl rubbed, soiled). Internally Fine. Howes M 522. *Harrington.* $90/£58

MERCER, CAVALIE. Journal of the Waterloo Campaign, Kept throughout the Campaign of 1815. London: Peter Davies, 1927. Later ptg. VG (sl shaken; lib bkpl). *Mcgowan.* $45/£29

MERCER, F.A. (ed). Gardens and Gardening. London: The Studio Annual, 1932. *Edwards.* $43/£28

Merchant Vessels of the United States...Twenty-Seventh Annual List. Washington: GPO, 1895. vi,407pp. Sound. *Lefkowicz.* $100/£65

Merchant Vessels of the United States...Forty-Fifth Annual List. Washington: GPO, 1913. *Lefkowicz.* $80/£52

Merchant Vessels of the United States 1957.... Washington: GPO, 1957. *Lefkowicz.* $40/£26

MERCHANT, W. MOELWYN. Shakespeare and the Artist. OUP, 1959. 88 plts. (Ex-lib.) Dj (sl soiled, chipped; spine repaired). *Edwards.* $74/£48

MEREDITH, GEORGE. The Amazing Marriage. Westminster: Constable, 1896. 2nd ed. 2 vols. viii,270; vi,(271)-551pp. Uncut. (Faded, sl spotted.) *Bickersteth.* $54/£35

MEREDITH, GEORGE. Ballads and Poems of Tragic Life. London: Macmillan, 1887. 1st ed. (8),160pp; uncut. Good. *Cox.* $23/£15

MEREDITH, GEORGE. Celt and Saxon. London: Constable, 1910. 1st ed. Fore, lower edges uncut. Red cl, gilt. Spine faded; eps, prelims, sl foxed; o/w Very Nice. *Temple.* $37/£24

MEREDITH, GEORGE. Diana of the Crossways. London: Chapman & Hall, 1885. 1st ed. 3 vols. viii,344; vi,336; vi,330pp; teg. 3/4 red morocco over rust bds (sl rubbed). *Karmiole.* $175/£113

MEREDITH, GEORGE. The Letters of George Meredith to Alice Meynell.... London/SF: Nonesuch Press, 1923. One of 850. Edges uncut. 1/4 grey-grn buckram; gilt spine. Fr bd sl dampstained, o/w Fine in dj. *Temple.* $37/£24

MEREDITH, GEORGE. The Letters of George Meredith to Alice Meynell...1896-1907. London/SF: Nonesuch, 1923. 1st ed. One of 850. Unopened. Fine in dj (chipped). *Cahan.* $75/£48

MEREDITH, GEORGE. A Reading from Life with Other Poems. Westminster: Archibald Constable, 1901. 1st ed. Uncut. (Spotting pp; cvrs sl faded.) *Bickersteth.* $47/£30

MEREDITH, MRS. CHARLES. (Pseud of Louisa Anne Twamley.) My Home in Tasmania; or, Nine Years in Australia. NY: Bunce & Brother, 1853. 1st US ed. 370pp, 8 ads; 6 litho plts. Dec cl (lt wear to spine ends; some foxing). *Petrilla.* $85/£55

MEREDITH, ROBERT. Around the World on Sixty Dollars.... Chicago, (1901). *Hayman.* $15/£10

MEREDITH, ROY. Mr. Lincoln's Camera Man; Mathew B. Brady. NY, 1946. 1st ed. VG. *Artis.* $30/£19

MEREDITH, WILLIAM. Ships and Other Poems. Princeton, NJ: Princeton Univ, 1948. 1st ed. Patterned bds. Fine in dj (sl soil; sm dampstain). *Antic Hay.* $85/£55

MEREDITH, WILLIAM. The Wreck of the Thresher and Other Poems. NY: Knopf, 1964. 1st ed. Rev copy, slip laid in. Fine in NF dj. *Heller.* $30/£19

MERENESS, NEWTON D. Maryland as a Proprietary Province. NY: Macmillan, 1901. 1st ed. Teg. Grn cl. 'Compliments of Author' card tipped to fep. VG+ (sig, bkpl removed, sm emb lib stamp tp). Howes M 533. *Chapel Hill.* $125/£81

MERENESS, NEWTON D. Travels in the American Colonies.... NY: Macmillan, 1916. 1st ed. (Emb #s spine; bkpl removed.) Howes M 534. *Ginsberg.* $100/£65

MERENESS, NEWTON D. (ed). Travels in the American Colonies. NY: Macmillan, 1916. 1st ed. Later red cl. VG. Howes M 534. *Chapel Hill.* $40/£26

MEREWETHER, LEE. Seeing Europe by Automobile.... NY: Baker & Taylor, 1911. 1st ed. Grn pict cl, orange/black stamped, gilt title. Fine. *Hermitage.* $45/£29

MERIMEE, PROSPER. Carmen. NY: LEC, 1941. #162/1500 signed by Jean Charlot (illus). Fine in slipcase. *Williams.* $132/£85

MERIN, PAUL. Spain between Death and Birth. London, 1938. 1st Eng ed. Frontis; 24 plts. Eps sl browned, o/w VG. Oatmeal buckram (sl rubbed; spine sl tanned). *Edwards.* $78/£50

MERINGTON, MARGUERITE. The Custer Story. Devin Adair, 1950. 1st ed. Frontis. Spotting back cvr, o/w VG. *Oregon.* $30/£19

MERINGTON, MARGUERITE. The Custer Story. NY, 1950. 1st ed. NF in dj. *Baade.* $35/£23

MERK, FREDERICK. Slavery and the Annexation of Texas. NY: Knopf, 1972. 1st ed. Blind-emb cl. NF in illus dj (lt worn). *Cahan.* $35/£23

MERKLEY, CHRISTOPHER. Biography of Christopher Merkley.... Salt Lake City: J.H. Parry, 1887. 46pp. Ptd wrappers. Howes M 537. *Dawson.* $100/£65

MERLANT, JOACHIM. Soldiers and Sailors of France in the American War for Independence (1776-1783). Mary Bushnell Coleman (trans). NY: Scribner's, 1920. 4 plts. VG. *Schoyer.* $20/£13

MERLE, WILLIAM HENRY. Odds and Ends. London: Longman et al, 1831. 1st ed, but ads not bound in. viii,148pp; 7 full-pg plts by George Cruikshank. *Schoyer.* $150/£97

MERRILL, JAMES. The Country of a Thousand Years of Peace. NY: Knopf, 1959. 1st ed. Fine in NF dj (spine sl tanned; sl rubbed). *Between The Covers.* $150/£97

MERRILL, JAMES. The Diblos Notebook. NY: Atheneum, 1965. 1st ed. Signed. VG+ (ep clipped) in VG+ dj. *Bishop.* $50/£32

MERRILL, JAMES. Divine Comedies. Poems. NY: Atheneum, 1976. 1st ed. Inscribed, signed. Rev slip laid in. Fine in dj. *Reese.* $55/£35

MERRILL, JAMES. The Fire Screen. (London): C&W/Hogarth, 1970. 1st ed. Fine in dj (sl wear; soil; price-clipped). *Antic Hay.* $20/£13

MERRILL, JAMES. The Fire Screen. London, 1970. 1st ed. Signed. Fine in NF dj. *Polyanthos.* $25/£16

MERRILL, JAMES. From the First Nine Poems 1946-1976. NY: Atheneum, 1982. 1st ed. Signed. NF in NF dj. *Bishop.* $25/£16

MERRILL, JAMES. Late Settings Poems. NY, 1985. 1st Amer ed. Signed. Fine in Fine dj. *Polyanthos.* $30/£19

MERRILL, JAMES. Mirabell: Books of Number. NY: Atheneum, 1978. 1st ed. Inscribed, signed, dated. Fine in dj. *Reese.* $65/£42

MERRILL, JAMES. The Seraglio. NY: Knopf, 1957. 1st Amer ed. Signed. Sl bump corners, else NF in VG dj (folded tear fr panel). *Between The Covers.* $225/£145

MERRILL, JAMES. The Seraglio. NY: Knopf, 1957. 1st ed. VG+ in VG+ dj. *Bishop.* $47/£30

MERRILL, JAMES. The Seraglio. London: C&W, 1958. 1st British ed. Inscribed, signed. NF in dj (price-clipped, spine sl soiled). *Reese.* $100/£65

MERRILL, JAMES. Souvenirs. NY: Nadja, 1984. 1st ed. One of 226 signed. VF in wrappers. *Jaffe.* $125/£81

MERRILL, JAMES. Spurs to Glory. Rand McNally, (1966). 1st ed. VG in VG dj. *Oregon.* $35/£23

MERRILL, JAMES. The Yellow Pages. Cambridge, MA: Temple Bar Bookshop, 1974. 1st ed, trade issue, ltd to 800. NF in wrappers. *Godot.* $40/£26

MERRILL, SELAH. East of the Jordan. NY: Scribner's, 1883. Frontis, xvi,549pp, 3 plts, fldg map. Good. *Archaeologia.* $125/£81

MERRIMAN, CHARLES EUSTACE. Letters from a Son to His Self-Made Father. Boston: Robinson, Luce, 1904. Frontis. guard; plt. Spine, edges faded, else VG. *Connolly.* $35/£23

MERRITT, A. Dwellers in the Mirage. Liveright, 1932. 1st ed. VG. *Madle.* $75/£48

MERRITT, A. The Face in the Abyss. Liveright, 1931. 1st ed. Good+. *Madle.* $30/£19

MERRITT, A. The Moon Pool. Putnam, 1919. 1st ed, 1st bk. VG. *Aronovitz.* $65/£42

MERRITT, A. The Ship of Ishtar. Putnam, 1926. 1st ed. VG+ in VG- dj (chipping spine extrems; lt wear, tear). *Aronovitz.* $395/£255

MERRITT, A. The Story behind the Story. Amer Weekly, 1942. 1st ed. Lettering dulled, else VG+. *Aronovitz.* $35/£23

MERRITT, A. Thru the Dragon Glass. Jamaica, NY: ARRA Printers, n.d. (1932). 1st ed. Folded as single gathering, unsewn as issued. Fore-edges uncut. Lt brn paper wrappers. Text Nice (corners chipped). *Temple.* $155/£100

MERRITT, A. and H. BOK. The Black Wheel. New Collector's Group, 1947. 1st ed. One of 1000. Gilt lettering fr cvr flaked, else NF. *Aronovitz.* $50/£32

MERRITT, A. and H. BOK. The Fox Woman. New Collector's Group, 1946. 1st ed. One of 1000. NF. *Aronovitz.* $50/£32

MERRITT, PERCIVAL. The True Story of the So-Called Love Letters of Mrs. Piozzi. Cambridge: Harvard Univ, 1927. One of 350. Color batik-cvrd bds; cl spine. VG. *Dramatis Personae.* $35/£23

MERSFELDER, L.C. Cowboy—Fisherman—Hunter. Kansas City: Brown-White-Lowell Press, 1951. 2nd ed, rev, enlgd. 52 plts, 2 maps (1 fldg). Pict cl, gilt. VG in Good dj. *Connolly.* $45/£29

MERSHON, WILLIAM B. (comp). The Passenger Pigeon. NY: Outing Pub Co, 1907. 1st ed. Signed. Color frontis, 8 plts (2 color). Maroon cl, gilt title. VG (corner creasing). *Bohling.* $175/£113

MERTON, THOMAS. The Asian Journal of Thomas Merton. NY: New Directions, (1973). 1st Amer ed. Fine (sl rubbed) in dj (2 sm tears, sl sunned). *Polyanthos.* $30/£19

MERTON, THOMAS. Basic Principles of Monastic Spirituality. Kentucky: Abbey of Gethsemani, 1957. 1st ed in wrappers. Orig wrappers (edges browned, lt chipped). *Glenn.* $85/£55

MERTON, THOMAS. The Christmas Sermons of Bl. Guerric of Igny. Abbey of Gethsemani, (1959). 1st ed. Cl, patterned bds. (sm stains on rear). *Dermont.* $35/£23

MERTON, THOMAS. Clement of Alexandria: an Essay and Translation. (NY): New Directions, (1962). 1st ed. Fine in wraps. *Turlington.* $55/£35

MERTON, THOMAS. Disputed Questions. NY, 1960. 1st Amer ed. Fine in Fine dj. *Polyanthos.* $30/£19

MERTON, THOMAS. Elected Silence. London: Hollis & Carter, 1949. 1st Eng ed. VG- in dj (price-clipped; chipping). *Lame Duck.* $125/£81

MERTON, THOMAS. Figures for an Apocalypse. (Norfolk: New Directions, 1947.) 1st ed. Fine in dj (edgewear; browning). *Antic Hay.* $85/£55

MERTON, THOMAS. Ishi Means Man. Greensboro, NC: Unicorn Press, (1976). 1st ed, hb issue. Fine; issued w/o dj. *Godot.* $45/£29

MERTON, THOMAS. My Argument with the Gestapo. NY, 1969. 1st Amer ed. Fine in dj (spine extrems sl rubbed). *Polyanthos.* $25/£16

MERTON, THOMAS. My Argument with the Gestapo. NY: Doubleday, 1969. 1st ed. Sig; sl shelf wear, else NF in VG dj (price-clipped; shallow chipping). *Lame Duck.* $35/£23

MERTON, THOMAS. Original Child Bomb. (Norfolk, CT): New Directions, (1962). 1st ed. Ltd to 500 signed. Black bds, ptd label. Base spine sl rubbed, o/w Fine in acetate dj. *Jaffe.* $400/£258

MERTON, THOMAS. Seasons of Celebration. NY: FSG, (1965). 1st ed. Fine in dj (lt wear; rear panel browned). *Antic Hay.* $35/£23

MERTON, THOMAS. The Secular Journal of Thomas Merton. NY: Farrar, Straus & Cudahy, (1959). 1st ed. Sl fading; ink name, else Very Nice in dj. *Hermitage.* $50/£32

MERTON, THOMAS. Seeds of Contemplation. CT: New Directions, (1949). 1st Amer ed. Fine (sl sunned, chip). *Polyanthos.* $30/£19

MERTON, THOMAS. Seeds of Contemplation. Norfolk: ND, 1949. 1st ed. Sig, address fep, else NF in VG+ dj. *Lame Duck.* $200/£129

MERTON, THOMAS. Selected Poems. Hollis & Carter, 1950. 1st Eng ed. Cream gilt bds. Fine in dj (sl rubbed; price-clipped). *Dalian.* $54/£35

MERTON, THOMAS. The Seven Story Mountain. NY: HB&Co, (1948). 1st issue white binding. Sm contemp owner name, else Fine in NF dj (short tears). *Between The Covers.* $1,500/£968

MERTON, THOMAS. The Seven Story Mountain. NY: HB, 1948. 1st ed, in 1st (white cl) binding, 1st issue dj. NF in VG+ dj (few short edge-tears; faint vertical crease fr panel). *Lame Duck.* $1,500/£968

MERTON, THOMAS. The Sign of Jonas. NY: HB, 1953. 1st ed. Sigs, else NF in VG dj. *Lame Duck.* $45/£29

MERTON, THOMAS. The Sign of Jonas. Hollis & Carter, 1953. 1st Eng ed. Brn cl. Wraparound band. Fine in dj (sl tanned). *Dalian.* $54/£35

MERTON, THOMAS. The Silent Life. NY: FS&C, 1957. 1st ed. Lt foxing fore-edge, else NF in VG dj (price-clipped; surface loss to extrems). *Lame Duck.* $45/£29

MERTON, THOMAS. Spiritual Directions and Meditation. N.p.: Liturgial Press, (1960). 1st ed. Fine in dj. *Turlington.* $75/£48

MERTON, THOMAS. The Strange Islands. Hollis & Carter, 1957. 1st Eng ed. Maroon cl. Sm label fep, o/w Fine in dj (sl dusty). *Dalian.* $39/£25

MERTON, THOMAS. The Tears of the Blind Lions. NY: New Directions, (1949). 1st Amer ed. Wrappers. Fine in dj. *Polyanthos.* $40/£26

MERTON, THOMAS. Waters of Silence. Hollis & Carter, 1950. 1st Eng ed. Blue cl. Cvr sl spotted, o/w Fine in dj (sl frayed). *Dalian*. $54/£35

MERTON, THOMAS. The Waters of Siloe. NY: Harcourt, (1949). 1st ed. 16pp b/w photos. VG in dj (sm nicks). *Houle*. $125/£81

MERTON, THOMAS. The Wisdom of the Desert. NY, (1960). 1st Amer ed. Fine (bkpl) in dj (NF). *Polyanthos*. $30/£19

MERWIN, W.S. The Drunk in the Furnace. Hart-Davis, 1960. 1st ed. NF in dj (soiled). *Poetry*. $19/£12

MERWIN, W.S. Feathers from the Hill. Iowa City: Windhover Press, (1978). 1st ed. Ltd to 270 signed. Frontis. Fine. *Jaffe*. $150/£97

MERWIN, W.S. Green with Beasts. London: Rupert Hart-Davis, 1956. 1st ed. Ptd bds (few sm bumps). NF in dj. *Antic Hay*. $100/£65

MERWIN, W.S. The Lice. London: Hart-Davis, 1969. 1st Eng ed. Fine in dj. *Antic Hay*. $25/£16

MERWIN, W.S. The Miner's Pale Children. NY: Atheneum, 1970. 1st ed. Signed. Fine in dj. *Jaffe*. $45/£29

MERWIN, W.S. Signs. Iowa City: Windhover Press, 1971. 1st ed. One of 200 signed. Gray cl. Fine. *Jaffe*. $175/£113

MERYMAN, RICHARD. Andrew Wyeth. Boston: Houghton Mifflin, 1968. 1st ed. VG+ in VG dj. *Bishop*. $147/£95

MERYMAN, RICHARD. Andrew Wyeth. Boston, 1968. 1st ed. 121 full-pg color plts. VG. *Argosy*. $200/£129

MESSERLI, DOUGLAS. Djuna Barnes: A Bibliography. N.p.: David Lewis, 1975. Ltd to 500. Tp facs. Blue cl; gilt. Good. *Karmiole*. $30/£19

MESSICK, HANK. King's Mountain. Boston/Toronto: Little, Brown, (1976). 1st ed. Review copy; slip, promo flyer laid in. Fine in NF dj. *Chapel Hill*. $40/£26

Metallick History of the Reigns of King William III, and Queen Mary, Queen Anne, and King George I. London: For John and Paul Knapton..., 1747. iv + 40pp + 22pp text. 37 engr plts. Marbled eps, edges. 1/2 calf w/marbled bds (joints splitting head, tail; extrems worn), dec gilt bands, motifs on spine (rubbed). *Edwards*. $349/£225

METCALFE, JOHN. The Feasting Dead. Arkham House, 1954. 1st ed. Fine in dj. *Madle*. $175/£113

METCALFE, JOHN. The Feasting Dead. Arkham House, 1954. 1st ed. One of 1242. Fine in NF dj (dust-soil rear panel). *Aronovitz*. $110/£71

METCALFE, JOHN. The Smoking Leg. Doubleday, 1926. 1st US ed. VG. *Madle*. $50/£32

METCHNIKOFF, ELIE. Immunity in Infective Diseases. Cambridge, 1905. 1st ed. (Corner fr bd bent.) *Fye*. $250/£161

METCHNIKOFF, ELIE. Lectures on the Comparative Pathology of Inflammation. London, 1893. 1st Eng trans. 218pp. VF. *Fye*. $500/£323

METCHNIKOFF, ELIE. The Prolongation of Life. NY, 1908. 1st Amer ed. Good. *Fye*. $75/£48

METEYARD, ELIZA. Choice Examples of Wedgwood Art. London: George Bell and Sons, 1879. Tp (lib ink stamp verso), (iv)text. 28 plts (margins lt browned, spotted, water-stained; plt sl chipped; marginal blind-stamps.) Dec gilt-edged cl (new eps; rebacked, orig spine laid down; lt soiled, bumped). *Edwards*. $233/£150

METHUEN, HENRY H. Life in the Wilderness. London, 1846. xiii,363pp; 3 plts (foxed). Good (sl faded). *Wheldon & Wesley*. $194/£125

METHUEN, HENRY H. Life in the Wilderness. London: Richard Bentley, 1848. 2nd ed. xix,(ii),364pp; 2 litho plts. Orig blind-stamped cl (extrems sl bumped, frayed). VG. *Hollett*. $186/£120

METHUEN, LORD. Normandy Diary. London, 1952. 1st ed. Inscribed; tls loosely inserted. Color frontis; 2 color plts; 102 b/w photo plts; fldg color map at rear. VG in dw. *Edwards*. $93/£60

METHVIN, J.J. Andele, or The Mexican-Kiowa Captive. Louisville, KY: Pentecostal Herald Press, 1899. 184pp (inscrip), 9 plts (1 color). Red cl (spine soiled; rubbed), black stamping. Howes M 562. *Bohling*. $150/£97

METRAUX, ALFRED. Voodoo in Haiti. NY: OUP, 1959. 1st ed. Fine in NF dj. *Beasley*. $40/£26

METZ, A. The Anatomy and Histology of the Human Eye. Phila, 1868. 1st ed. 184pp. Good. *Fye*. $100/£65

METZ, LEON CLAIRE. John Selman, Texas Gunfighter. NY: Hastings House, (1966). Map. VG in dj. *Schoyer*. $35/£23

METZ, LEON CLAIRE. John Selman, Texas Gunfighter. Univ of OK, (1980). 2nd ed. Dbl-pg frontis map. VF in Fine dj. *Oregon*. $25/£16

METZ, LEON CLAIRE. The Shooters. El Paso, 1976. Silver Bullet ed ltd to 300 signed. 1/4 suede leather & cl, bullet inset fr cvr. Assignment card, flat dj of trade ed laid in. Part of backstrip lettering gone, o/w NF in orig slipcase (spot rubbed), label. *Baade*. $225/£145

MEW, CHARLOTTE. The Rambling Sailor. Poetry Bookshop, 1929. 1st ed. Fine in dj. *Whiteson*. $34/£22

MEW, CHARLOTTE. The Rambling Sailor. Poetry Bookshop, 1929. 1st ed. VG in dj (sl discolored; tear). *Poetry*. $43/£28

MEWSHAW, MICHAEL. Year of the Gun. NY: Atheneum, 1984. 1st ed. Nick fore-edge endsheet, else NF in dj. *Reese*. $25/£16

MEYER, CARL. Bound for Sacramento. Ruth Frey Axe (trans). Claremont, CA: Saunders Studio Press, 1938. 1st ed. Tp vignette; inserted facs of orig wrappers, tp. Yellow cl stamped in grn. Good in dj (sl chipped). *Karmiole*. $75/£48

MEYER, DUANE. The Highland Scots of North Carolina. NC Dept of Arch & Hist, 1968. Paper cvr. VG. *Book Broker*. $25/£16

MEYER, FRANZ. Marc Chagall: Life and Work. NY, n.d. (1963?). 53 tipped-in color plts. VG in dj (sl used). *King*. $250/£161

MEYER, FRANZ. Mark Chagall: Life and Work. NY: Harry N. Agrams, n.d. (ca 1964). 53 tipped-in color plts. Fine in dj. *Hermitage*. $175/£113

MEYER, HOWARD N. Colonel of the Black Regiment. NY, (1967). 1st ed. Dj chipped, spine faded, o/w VG+. *Pratt*. $35/£23

MEYER, JOHANN JAKOB. Sexual Life in Ancient India. NY: Barnes & Noble, 1953. 2 vols bound in 1. Somewhat worn, but Good. *Boswell*. $65/£42

MEYER, JOSEPH. Nature's Remedies. Hammond, 1934. 1st ed. Good. *Fye*. $40/£26

MEYER, SUSAN E. America's Great Illustrators. NY, 1982. 186 color plts. Dj (sl worn). *Edwards*. $93/£60

MEYER, THOMAS. The Bang Book. N.p.: Jargon Soc, (1971). 1st Amer ed. Signed. John Furnival (illus). Sm stamp fr pastedown, else Fine in dj w/ptd acetate overjacket (2 tears). *Between The Covers*. $100/£65

MEYEROWITZ, JOEL. Cape Light. Boston: Museum of Fine Arts, NYGS, 1978. 1st ed. NF in NF dj. *Bishop.* $32/£21

MEYEROWITZ, JOEL. St. Louis and the Arch. NYGS/St. Louis Art Museum Soc, 1980. 1st ed. Signed. NF in NF dj. *Bishop.* $42/£27

MEYERS, WILLIAM H. Journal of a Cruise to California and the Sandwich Islands...1841-1844. John Haskell Kemble (ed). SF: Book Club of CA, 1955. One of 400. 11 colored views, frontis map. Red leather spine, cl-cvrd bds. Prospectus taped in. Nice (spine lt rubbed). *Bohling.* $350/£226

MEYERSTEIN, E.H.W. Of My Early Life (1889-1918). London: Neville Spearman, 1957. 1st ed. Frontis, 2 dbl-sided plts. Scarlet bds, gilt spine. Fine in dj. *Temple.* $22/£14

MEYERSTEIN, E.H.W. Robin Wastraw. London: Gollancz, 1951. 1st ed. Bright blue glazed cl, gilt-lettered spine. Top edges sl foxed, o/w Fine in dj (frayed). *Temple.* $29/£19

MEYNELL, ALICE. Essays. Burns & Oates, 1914. 1st Eng ed. Frontis. Full blue buckram (sl spotted); teg. NF in dj (sl rubbed, tanned). *Dalian.* $39/£25

MEYNELL, ALICE. The Last Poems of Alice Meynell. London: Burns, Oates & Washbourne, 1923. 1st Eng ed. Brn paper bds. Nice. *Cady.* $20/£13

MEYNELL, ALICE. The Second Person Singular and Other Essays. OUP, 1921. 1st Eng ed. Blue cl. Fine. *Dalian.* $31/£20

MEYNELL, EVERARD. The Life of Francis Thompson. London: Burns, Oates Washbourne, 1926. 1st Eng ed. Grn cl. Spine sl sunned, o/w Fine in dj (piece cut spine). *Dalian.* $31/£20

MEYNELL, FRANCIS and HERBERT SIMON (eds). Fleuron Anthology. (London/Toronto): Ernest Benn/Univ of Toronto, (1973). 1st ed. Fine in dj. *Reese.* $50/£32

MEYNELL, FRANCIS. English Printed Books. London: Collins, 1946. 8 color plts. VG (edges sl worn) in dj (chipped); brn paper bd case. *Heller.* $25/£16

MEYNELL, FRANCIS. English Printed Books. London, 1948. 2nd ed. Good in dj (shelfworn). *King.* $20/£13

MEYNELL, L. Storm Against the Wall. Lippincott, 1931. 1st ed. VG in dj (inner reinforcement). *Aronovitz.* $65/£42

MEYRINK, G. The Golem. H-M, 1928. 1st Amer ed, w/1st issue Eng sheets. VG in dj (spine extrem chipped). *Aronovitz.* $185/£119

MICHAEL, WILLIAM W. Dry Fly Trout Fishing. NY: McGraw-Hill, 1951. 1st ed. Fine in dj. *Bowman.* $50/£32

MICHALOWSKI, KAZIMIERZ. The Art of Ancient Egypt. NY: Abrams, (1968). 1st ed. Brn cl w/mounted illus fr cvr. Good in dj. *Karmiole.* $150/£97

MICHALOWSKI, KAZIMIERZ. The Art of Ancient Egypt. London, 1969. 143 color plts. Dj (sl worn). *Edwards.* $93/£60

MICHALOWSKI, KAZIMIERZ. Karnak. Praeger, NY, (1970). 90 plts. Good in dj. *Archaeologia.* $65/£42

MICHEL, EDOUARD. Flemish Painting in the XVIIth Century. Prudence Montagu-Pollock (trans). London: Hyperion, 1939. 9 mtd color plts. (Spine faded; text block starting.) *Argosy.* $75/£48

MICHEL, EDOUARD. Rembrandt. His Life, His Work, and His Time. London: Heinemann, 1894. 2 vols. xxiv,320; xi,294pp, 76 plts. (Cl sl worn; top, bottom of spine frayed vol 2.) *Ars Artis.* $116/£75

MICHEL, EDOUARD. Rubens. His Life, His Work, and His Time. London/NY: Heinemann/Scribner's, 1899. 2 vols. xx,292; xii,323pp, 40 color plts, 40 photogravures. (Waterstain in blank margin last ff vol 1.) Dec cl. *Ars Artis.* $116/£75

MICHEL, TRUDI. Inside Tin Pan Alley. NY: Fell, 1948. 1st ed. Fine in dj (worn). *Second Life.* $25/£16

MICHEL, WALTER. Wyndham Lewis: Paintings and Drawings. Thames & Hudson, 1971. 1st ed. Fine in dj (price-clipped). *Poetry.* $233/£150

MICHELANGELO. Complete Works of Michelangelo. Mario Salmi (foreword). London, 1966. 1st UK ed. 2 vols. 32 color plts. (Ex-lib w/ink stamp, labels, #s.) Djs (sl chipped spines); pict slipcase (sl worn). *Edwards.* $74/£48

MICHELANGELO. The Letters of Michelangelo. E.H. Ramsden (ed). Stanford Univ, 1963. 2 vols. 29 plts; 29 plts. Uniform orig cl. Margin imperfection p20 vol 1, o/w VF set in slipcase. *Europa.* $85/£55

MICHELANGELO. The Letters of Michelangelo. E.H. Ramsden (ed). London, 1963. 2 vols. Frontis ports, 58 plts. (Spines lt sunned.) *Edwards.* $116/£75

MICHELET, J. Martyrs of Russia. London: David Bryce, 1853. iv,96pp (sm stain fep). Cl over card, blind/gilt-stamped (faded, loose). *Schoyer.* $35/£23

MICHENER, JAMES A. About Centennial, Some Notes on the Novel. NY: Random House, (1974). 1st ed, ltd to 3200. Fine in dj. *Oak Knoll.* $15/£10

MICHENER, JAMES A. Alaska. NY: Random House, (1988). Signed ltd ed of 1000 numbered. As New in slipcase. *Antic Hay.* $225/£145

MICHENER, JAMES A. The Bridge at Andau. NY: Random House, 1957. 1st ed. VG (sticker remains fep) in VG dj (chipped). *Revere.* $45/£29

MICHENER, JAMES A. The Bridge at Andau. NY: Random, 1957. 1st ed. Fine in dj. *Else Fine.* $75/£48

MICHENER, JAMES A. The Bridge at Andau. Secker & Warburg, 1957. 1st Eng ed. Maroon cl. Sm hole tp, o/w Fine in dj. *Dalian.* $39/£25

MICHENER, JAMES A. The Bridges at Toko-Ri. (NY): Random House, (1953). 1st ed. White eps. Fine in dj (lt used; price-clipped). *Antic Hay.* $150/£97

MICHENER, JAMES A. Caravans. NY: Random House, (1963). 1st ed. VF in bright dj. *Godot.* $85/£55

MICHENER, JAMES A. Caravans. NY: Random House, 1963. 1st ed. NF in VG dj (sm chip). *Revere.* $45/£29

MICHENER, JAMES A. Caribbean. NY: Random House, (1989). Signed ltd ed of 1000 numbered. As New in orig shrink-wrap & slipcase. *Antic Hay.* $225/£145

MICHENER, JAMES A. Caribbean. Random House, 1989. 1st ed. Signed, inscribed. Fine in dj. *Stahr.* $50/£32

MICHENER, JAMES A. Chesapeake. NY: Random House, (1978). 1st ed. Signed, dated. NF (sl rubbing) in dj. *Antic Hay.* $125/£81

MICHENER, JAMES A. The Covenant. NY: Random House, (1980). Signed ltd ed of 500 numbered. Grn cl. As new in orig shrink-wrap & slipcase. *Antic Hay.* $250/£161

MICHENER, JAMES A. The Covenant. NY: Random House, 1980. One of 500 specially-bound, numbered, signed. Spine sl tanned, else NF in pub's paper-cvrd slipcase. *Lame Duck.* $150/£97

MICHENER, JAMES A. The Drifters. NY: Random House, (1971). Signed ltd ed of 500 numbered. Fine in slipcase (sl wear). *Antic Hay.* $275/£177

MICHENER, JAMES A. The Drifters. Secker & Warburg, 1971. 1st Eng ed. Maroon cl. VF in dj. *Dalian.* $54/£35

MICHENER, JAMES A. The Floating World. NY: Random House, (1954). 1st ed. Marbled bds. Fine in dj (sl wear, rubbing; spine lt faded; sm chip spine head). *Antic Hay.* $250/£161

MICHENER, JAMES A. The Floating World. R-H, 1954. 1st ed. Inscribed. NF in VG dj (lt chipping to spine extrems). *Fine Books.* $325/£210

MICHENER, JAMES A. Hawaii. NY: Random House, (1959). 1st ed w/United Artists' form laid in. NF in dj (lt used; spine sl browned). *Antic Hay.* $125/£81

MICHENER, JAMES A. Hawaii. NY: Random House, (1959). 1st ed. NF in dj (short edge tears, sl yellowed in spots). *Sadlon.* $100/£65

MICHENER, JAMES A. Hawaii. NY: Random House, (1959). Signed ltd ed of 400 numbered. Brn cl. Fine in acetate dj & slipcase (wear; sm stains). *Antic Hay.* $450/£290

MICHENER, JAMES A. The Hokusai Sketch-Books. Rutland/Tokyo: Tuttle, 1958. 1st ed, stated 1st ptg. 187 plts. Fine (sig) in silk binding. Pict dj (lt edgewear, sm triangular chip lower fr edge). *Else Fine.* $275/£177

MICHENER, JAMES A. Iberia. NY: Random House, (1968). 1st ed. NF (ink inscrip) in dj. *Antic Hay.* $25/£16

MICHENER, JAMES A. Iberia. NY: Random House, (1968). 1st ed. Signed presentation. Fine in dj. *Antic Hay.* $250/£161

MICHENER, JAMES A. Iberia. Secker & Warburg, 1968. 1st Eng ed. Red cl. Fine in dj. *Dalian.* $101/£65

MICHENER, JAMES A. Iberia: Spanish Travels and Reflections. NY: Random House, (1968). Signed ltd ed of 500 numbered. Emb white buckram. NF in illus b/w dj and slipcase (sl wear). *Antic Hay.* $450/£290

MICHENER, JAMES A. Japanese Prints, from the Early Masters to the Modern. Rutland, VT, (1959). 1st ed. 257 plts (55 mtd color). Dec silk. VG in dj. *Argosy.* $150/£97

MICHENER, JAMES A. Japanese Prints. Tuttle, 1959. 1st ed. 257 plts (55 full color). Fine in NF dj. *Fine Books.* $135/£87

MICHENER, JAMES A. Journey. NY: Random House, (1989). 1st US ed. New in dj. *Bernard.* $25/£16

MICHENER, JAMES A. Legacy. NY: Random House, (1987). 1st ed, rev copy w/inserted slip. Fine in dj. *Antic Hay.* $50/£32

MICHENER, JAMES A. Legacy. NY: Random House, (1987). Signed ltd ed of 500 numbered. As New in slipcase. *Antic Hay.* $185/£119

MICHENER, JAMES A. Poland. NY: Random House, (1983). 1st ed. Fine in dj. *Antic Hay.* $25/£16

MICHENER, JAMES A. Poland. NY: Random House, (1983). Signed ltd ed of 500 numbered. Fine in slipcase. *Antic Hay.* $225/£145

MICHENER, JAMES A. Presidential Lottery. NY: Random House, (1969). 1st Amer ed. Fine in dj. *Between The Covers.* $45/£29

MICHENER, JAMES A. The Quality of Life. (N.p.): Girard Bank, 1970. 1st ed. Fine in slipcase. *Antic Hay.* $50/£32

MICHENER, JAMES A. Sayonara. NY: Random House, (1954). 1st Amer ed. Fine in dj (sl delamination). *Between The Covers.* $150/£97

MICHENER, JAMES A. Sayonara. NY: Random House, (1954). 1st ed. NF in dj (spine lightened). *Sadlon.* $75/£48

MICHENER, JAMES A. Space. NY: Random House, (1982). Signed ltd ed of 500 numbered. As New in orig shrink-wrap and cardboard slipcase. *Antic Hay.* $225/£145

MICHENER, JAMES A. Tales of the South Pacific. NY: Macmillan, 1950. Signed ltd ed of 1500. 1st bk. Dec blue cl. NF (gilt lettering on spine sl rubbed), issued w/o dj. *Antic Hay.* $275/£177

MICHENER, JAMES A. Texas. Austin: March 2, 1986. Deluxe 2 vol 1st illus ed. Charles Shaw (illus). Buckram. As New in slipcase. *Bohling.* $125/£81

MICHENER, JAMES A. and A. GROVE DAY. Rascals in Paradise. Secker & Warburg, 1957. 1st Eng ed. Blue cl. Fore-edge sl foxed, o/w Fine in dj. *Dalian.* $54/£35

MICHENER, JAMES A. and A. GROVE DAY. Rascals in Paradise. London: Secker & Warburg, 1957. 1st Eng ed. Fine in dj. *Godot.* $65/£42

MICHIE, PETER SMITH. The Life and Letters of Emory Upton, Colonel of the Fourth Regiment of Artillery.... NY: D. Appleton, 1885. 1st ed. xxvii,511pp. NF. *Mcgowan.* $185/£119

Michigan. A Guide to the Wolverine State. NY: OUP, (1943). 2nd ptg. Good (lacks rear packet map). *Artis.* $17/£11

MICKEL, JERE C. Footlights on the Prairie. St. Cloud, MN: North Star, 1974. 1st ed. Pict ep. Marbled bds. Fine in VG dj (chipped, closed tear). *Connolly.* $35/£23

Mickey Mouse Presents His Silly Symphonies. Babes in the Woods and King Neptune. London: Dean, n.d. (1956). 19x25 cm. 4 dbl-pg pop-ups. (2pp illus colored; weakness, some separation of spine; sl weakness to few pop-ups.) *Book Finders.* $210/£135

Mickey's Underwater Adventure. London: Purnell, 1973. 23x17 cm. 3 dbl-pg pop-ups. Glazed pict bds. VG. *Book Finders.* $50/£32

MICKLE, WILLIAM ENGLISH. Well Known Confederate Veterans and Their War Records. New Orleans: Wm. E. Mickle, 1907. Minor cvr speckling, else NF. *Mcgowan.* $650/£419

MICKO, MIROSLAV (ed). Francisco Goya y Lucientes: Caprichos. Roberta Finlayson Samsour (trans). London: Spring Books, n.d. (ca 1960). 86 plts. VG in slipcase. *Argosy.* $100/£65

MICOU, PAUL. The Music Programme. Bantam Press, 1989. 1st ed. Sm bump, o/w Fine in dj. *Rees.* $16/£10

Middle Ages. Treasures from the Cloisters and the Metropolitan Museum of Art. Los Angeles County Museum of Art, 1970. (Ex-lib w/blindstamps.) Wrappers. *Washton.* $25/£16

MIDDLETON, B.C. A History of English Craft Bookbinding Technique. Hafner, 1963. 1st ed. Good in dj. *Moss.* $62/£40

MIDDLETON, B.C. The Restoration of Leather Bindings. LTP, 1979. Dec card cvrs. VG. *Moss.* $31/£20

MIDDLETON, CONYERS. The History of the Life of Marcus Tullius Cicero. London, 1757. 6th ed w/additions. 2 vols. x,564; 591pp; engr title. Contemp full polished calf (joints cracked), gilt spine, all edges marbled. *Goodrich.* $125/£81

MIDDLETON, G.A.T. Ornamental Details of the Italian Renaissance. London: Batsford, 1900. 50 plts (1 color). Binder's cl (sl smoke stain margin 1st few pp). *Petersfield.* $186/£120

MIDDLETON, RICHARD. Poems and Songs. London: T. Fisher Unwin, 1912. 1st ed. Dk blue buckram, gilt. NF. *Cady.* $35/£23

MIDDLETON, THOMAS. The Works... A.H. Bullen (ed). Boston: Houghton, Mifflin, 1885. #118/350. 8 vols. Etched frontis port. Teg. 3/4 dk blue morocco, gilt-panelled spines. Fine set. *Cummins.* $450/£290

MIDDLETON, W.E. KNOWLES. The History of the Barometer. Balt: Johns Hopkins Press, 1964. Grn cl (exlib). Lib mks, o/w Good. *Knollwood.* $55/£35

MIELCHE, HAKON. Land of the Condor. London: William Hodge, 1947. VG (extrems sl rubbed). *Hollett.* $23/£15

MIERS, EARL SCHENCK (ed). When the World Ended: The Diary of Emma Leconte. NY: OUP, 1957. 1st ed. Frontis port. NF (name) in dj (lt wear). *Cahan.* $35/£23

MIERS, EARL SCHENCK and RICHARD ELLIS (eds). Bookmaking and Kindred Amenities. New Brunswick: Rutgers Univ/Haddon Craftsmen, 1942. 1st ed. One of 1500. Dk blue buckram, gilt. Slipcase worn, else Fine. *Hartfield.* $75/£48

MIERS, EARL SCHENCK. The Great Rebellion. The Emergence of the American Conscience. Cleveland/NY: World, (1958). 1st ed. Fine in NF dj. *Mcgowan.* $45/£29

MIGHELS, HENRY R. Sage Brush Leaves. SF: Edward Bosqui & Co, 1879. 1st ed. (6),336pp; orig mtd photo port. Brn cl (extrems rubbed; spine extrems frayed). *Karmiole.* $85/£55

MIGOT, ANDRE. Tibetan Marches. Peter Fleming (trans). London, 1955. 1st UK ed. Frontis port, dbl-pg map. Dj (sl creased, chipped). *Edwards.* $23/£15

MIKKELSEN, EIJNAR. Frozen Justice. NY: Knopf, 1922. Grey cl. VG in dj (badly chipped, soiled). *Parmer.* $65/£42

MIKKELSEN, EIJNAR. Lost in the Arctic. London: Heinemann, 1913. 1st Eng ed. Fldg map. Silver gilt-dec cl. Good (sl rubbed). *Walcot.* $105/£68

MIKKELSEN, EIJNAR. Lost in the Arctic...Story of the Alabama Expedition, 1909-1912. London: Heinemann, 1913. Fldg map. VG (spine faded; minor mks). *High Latitude.* $120/£77

MILBURN, WILLIAM. The Rifle, Axe, and Saddle-Bags, and Other Lectures. Derby & Jackson, 1857. 1st ed. Frontis, 309pp. Ex-lib w/removed label, sm bkpl neatly removed, sm call #. *Oregon.* $25/£16

MILES, ALEXANDER. Surgical Ward-Work and Nursing. London, 1894. 1st ed. 197pp. Good. *Fye.* $100/£65

MILES, ALFRED H. Natural History. NY: Dodd Mead, 1895. 1st ed. Frontis, 395pp, 20pp of chromolithos; teg. Grn pict cl, gilt title. VG + . *Bowman.* $90/£58

MILES, CARLOTA (trans). Almada of Alamos. Tucson, 1962. 1st ed. Dec cl. Fine in dj (edgeworn). *Baade.* $20/£13

MILES, CHARLES. Indian and Eskimo Artifacts of North America. Chicago: Henry Regnery, 1963. 1st ed. VG. *Blue Dragon.* $30/£19

MILES, CHARLES. Indian and Eskimo Artifacts of North America. NY: Bonanza, 1963. Rpt. VG + in VG dj. *Parker.* $37/£24

MILES, EMILY WINTROP. Coventry and Other Poems. NY: Rudge, 1941. Inscribed. Frontis. Fine in glassine (chipped). *Reese.* $30/£19

MILES, HENRY A. Lowell, As It Was, and As It Is. Lowell: Powers & Bagley & Dayton, 1845. 1st ed. 234pp; fldg map. Good (sl worn). *Second Life.* $125/£81

MILES, MANLY. Silos, Ensilage and Silage. NY: OJ, 1889. 100pp + 12pp ads. Dk brn cl, gilt spine, fr cvr stamped in black. VG + . *Bohling.* $25/£16

MILES, NELSON A. Military Europe: A Narrative of Personal Observation and Personal Experience. NY: Doubleday & McClure, 1898. 1st ed. x,112pp, 13 plts. *Lefkowicz.* $60/£39

MILES, W.J. Modern Practical Farriery. London, n.d. c.(1868-9). Color frontis, tp; 96pp. Marbled edges (fore-edges worn, frayed). 1/2 calf (lower bd soiled; hinges cracked; joints rubbed w/sm hole); gilt raised bands, morocco label. (Soiling.) *Edwards.* $109/£70

MILFORD, LOUIS LeCLERC. Memoir, or a Cursory Glance at My Different Travels and My Sojourn in the Creek Nation. J.F. McDermott (ed). Lakeside Classic, 1956. 2 maps. VF. Howes M 599. *Oregon.* $27/£17

MILFORD, LOUIS LeCLERC. Memoir, or A Cursory Glance at My Different Travels.... Chicago, (1956). Lakeside Classic. VG. *Schoyer.* $25/£16

Milk and Its Relation to the Public Health. Washington, 1909. 1st ed. Buckram. Good. *Fye.* $50/£32

MILL, HUGH ROBERT. The Life of Sir Ernest Shackleton. Boston: Little, Brown, 1923. VG-. *Blue Dragon.* $50/£32

MILL, HUGH ROBERT. The Siege of the South Pole. Alston Rivers, 1905. 1st ed. Lg fldg map at rear supplied in facs. VG. *Walcot.* $70/£45

MILL, HUGH ROBERT. The Siege of the South Pole. London: Alston Rivers, 1905. 1st ed. Lg fldg colored map (short tear), 2 fldg charts, 61 plts incl frontis. Grn cl (spine faded), gilt. VG (lt foxing). *Morrell.* $163/£105

MILL, JOHN STUART. Autobiography of John Stuart Mill. NY: Columbia Univ, 1924. Brn cl. Good in dj. *Karmiole.* $35/£23

MILL, JOHN STUART. Autobiography of.... NY: Columbia Univ Press, 1924. 1st ed. Facs frontis. Gilt-lettered black cl (spine lt faded). VG (eps lt foxed). *House.* $45/£29

MILL, JOHN STUART. On Liberty. London: John W. Parker, 1859. 2nd ed. 207pp + 8pp ads. Good (spine faded, top chipped, hinges frayed, shaken, pencil mks). *Bohling.* $125/£81

MILL, JOHN STUART. On Liberty. London: Parker, 1859. 2nd ed. Spine extrems very worn; news clipping affixed w/pin fep, else VG. *Lame Duck.* $150/£97

MILL, JOHN STUART. On Liberty. Boston: Ticknor & Fields, 1863. 1st Amer ed. NF (sl spine-faded; sl foxing). *Lame Duck.* $250/£161

MILL, JOHN STUART. Principles of Political Economy. London, 1871. 7th ed. 2 vols. xvi,617,(ii)pp ads; 608pp. Contemp cl (margins lt browned; prelims sl spotted; hinges sl tender; soiled, rubbed; spine head vol 1 bumped; lacks part of label vol 2). *Edwards.* $85/£55

MILL, JOHN STUART. The Subjection of Women. Phila: Lippincott, 1869. 1st US ed. 174pp. VG (pencil mks throughout; wear). *Second Life.* $200/£129

MILL, JOHN STUART. The Subjection of Women. NY: Appleton, 1870. 2nd US ed. 188pp. VG (top of spine worn). *Second Life.* $150/£97

MILLAIS, J.G. Far Away Up the Nile. London: Longmans, 1924. (Sl marginal foxing.) *Petersfield.* $74/£48

MILLAIS, J.G. The Life and Letters of Sir John Everett Millais. London, 1899. 2 vols. xvi+446pp+xi+511pp, 9 photogravures. Gilt-dec cl, teg. (Feps lt foxed; vol 1 sl dampspotting upper bd.) *Edwards.* $116/£75

MILLAIS, J.G. Life of Frederick Selous.... London, 1918. Frontis port. (Discolored, spine creased; hinges cracked, shaken, ex-lib.) *Edwards.* $54/£35

MILLAIS, J.G. Magnolias. London, 1927. 34 plts. Binding sl faded, o/w Fine. *Henly.* $93/£60

MILLAIS, J.G. Magnolias. London, 1927. 34 plts. (Lt worn, faded, lt spotted; fep browned; lt foxing.) *Sutton.* $125/£81

MILLAIS, J.G. Newfoundland and Its Untrodden Ways. London: Longmans, 1907. (Lt dampspots backstrip.) *Petersfield.* $70/£45

MILLAIS, J.G. Newfoundland and Its Untrodden Ways. London, 1907. 86 plts (6 color); 2 maps. (Worn, loose; nail-hole cvr, 1st few pp.) *Wheldon & Wesley.* $78/£50

MILLAIS, J.G. Newfoundland and Its Untrodden Ways. London: Longmans, Green, 1907. 1st ed. 6 color plts, 6 photogravure, 2 maps (eps lt spotted). Gilt cl (spine sl faded, extrems sl worn). *Hollett.* $132/£85

MILLAIS, J.G. The Wildfowler in Scotland. London, 1901. 2 color, 19 photogravure plts. 1/2 vellum, gilt. Sl soiled, sm nick, o/w Good. *Henly.* $186/£120

MILLAR, KENNETH. Blue City. NY: Knopf, 1947. 1st ed. VG in dj (sl wear spine ends; short closed tears). *Mordida.* $200/£129

MILLAR, MARGARET. An Air That Kills. Random, 1957. 1st ed. Fine in dj (lt spotted). *Murder.* $60/£39

MILLAR, MARGARET. The Iron Gates. NY: Random House, 1945. 1st ed. VG in dj (dknd spine; sl wear). *Mordida.* $45/£29

MILLAR, OLIVER. The Queen's Pictures. London: Chancellor Press, 1984. 52 color plts. VF in dj. *Europa.* $43/£28

MILLARD, CHARLES W. The Sculpture of Edgar Degas. Princeton Univ Press, 1976. 1 color plt, 143 b/w photos. Dj (sl chipped). *Edwards.* $39/£25

MILLAY, EDNA ST. VINCENT. Aria da Capo. NY: Mitchell Kennerley, 1921. 1st ed. Black cl. Fine in dj (spine dknd). *Jaffe.* $150/£97

MILLAY, EDNA ST. VINCENT. The Buck in the Snow and Other Poems. NY, 1928. 1st Amer ed. Fine in dj (lacks sm area; sl torn). *Polyanthos.* $25/£16

MILLAY, EDNA ST. VINCENT. The Buck in the Snow and Other Poems. NY, 1928. Ltd ed, #191/479 signed. Fine in Fine glassine dj. (Box has 2 1/2-inch piece missing from spine; side split.) *Polyanthos.* $100/£65

MILLAY, EDNA ST. VINCENT. Conversation at Midnight. NY: Harper, 1937. 1st ed. VG in dj (lt worn; price-clipped). *Hermitage.* $35/£23

MILLAY, EDNA ST. VINCENT. Conversation at Midnight. NY: Harper, 1937. 1st trade ed. NF in dj (sl wear; soiling, price-clipped). *Antic Hay.* $35/£23

MILLAY, EDNA ST. VINCENT. Fatal Interview. NY: Harper, 1931. 1st trade ed. NF (eps foxed) in dj (spine lt sunned). *Antic Hay.* $35/£23

MILLAY, EDNA ST. VINCENT. Fatal Interview: Sonnets by.... NY: Harper, 1931. 1st ed. #221/479 numbered, signed. Natural linen, lt blue bds; uncut, unopened. VG in white over black patterned bd slipcase, pub's tan bd box. *Houle.* $350/£226

MILLAY, EDNA ST. VINCENT. A Few Figs from Thistles. NY/Cincinnati: Frank Shay/Stewart Kidd, (1922). 1st ptg of 'New and Enlarged Edition,' ptg 4 poems not in earlier forms of this collection. Labels dknd, o/w VG. *Reese.* $45/£29

MILLAY, EDNA ST. VINCENT. Huntsman, What Quarry? NY/London: Harper, 1939. 1st ed. One of 551. Signed. Unopened. Linen-backed blue paper over bds, ptd paper spine label. Fine in orig glassine dj, pub's slipcase (sl rubbed). *Cahan.* $225/£145

MILLAY, EDNA ST. VINCENT. The King's Henchman. NY: Harper, 1927. 1st trade ed. NF in VG dj (lt chipping; price-clipped). *Antic Hay.* $45/£29

MILLAY, EDNA ST. VINCENT. Letters of Edna St. Vincent Millay. Allan Ross Macdougall (ed). NY: Harper, (1952). 1st ed. VG in VG dj (price-clipped). *Godot.* $40/£26

MILLAY, EDNA ST. VINCENT. Make Bright the Arrows. NY: Harper, 1940. 1st ed. NF in dj (sl wear; short tears). *Antic Hay.* $35/£23

MILLAY, EDNA ST. VINCENT. The Princess Marries the Page. NY: Harper, 1932. 1st ed. NF (sl soil) in dj (short tears; lt soiling). *Antic Hay.* $35/£23

MILLAY, EDNA ST. VINCENT. Second April. NY: Mitchell Kennerley, 1921. 1st ed. Black cl. Fine in dj (spine sunned). *Jaffe.* $150/£97

MILLAY, EDNA ST. VINCENT. There Are No Islands, Any More. NY: Harper, 1940. 1st ed. Ptd bds. NF (feps lt browned). *Antic Hay.* $30/£19

MILLAY, EDNA ST. VINCENT. Wine from These Grapes. NY/London: Harper, 1934. 1st ed. 3/4 cl, bds (sl soiled), ptd paper label spine. NF in ptd dj (sm tears). *Blue Mountain.* $45/£29

Miller and His Golden Dream. (By Eliza Lucy Leonard.) London: Wellington, Salop, 1827. Sq 12mo. Full-pg frontis w/guard, 30pp; 5 hand-colored copper engrs, marble eps. Mod mottled leather binding, raised bands, gilt title. Excellent (spine lt worn). *Hobbyhorse.* $250/£161

MILLER, A.P. Tom's Experience in Dakota. Minneapolis: Miller Hale, 1883. 1st ed. Pub's brn cl; fr title lettered in gilt. VG. *Laurie.* $250/£161

MILLER, ALBERT (ed). The Pop-Up Book of Jokes. NY: Random House, n.d. (1972). 17x24 cm. 2 pop-ups, 14pp pull-tabs. Tony Walton (illus). Pict bds. VG-. *Book Finders.* $45/£29

MILLER, ALBERT (retold by). Pinocchio. NY: Random House, n.d. (1968). 19x24 cm. 5 dbl-pg pop-ups, pull tabs. Pict bds. (Sm repair to pop-up not affecting action; backing to 1st pull-tab off but tab works.) *Book Finders.* $30/£19

MILLER, ALBERT. The Pop-Up Book of Flying Machines. NY: Random House, n.d. (1969). 17x23 cm. 4 dbl-pg pop-ups, pull tabs, orig Random House ads. Dave Chambers and Gwen Gordon (illus). Glazed pict bds. VG. *Book Finders.* $70/£45

MILLER, ALBERT. Robin Hood. NY/London: Random House/Robert Schlesinger, 1969. 21x27 cm. 6 pop-ups, pull tabs. Gwen Gordon & Dave Chambers (illus). Glazed pict bds. VG. *Book Finders.* $75/£48

MILLER, AMY B. Shaker Herbs. NY, 1976. VG in dj (sl torn). *Brooks.* $39/£25

MILLER, ARTHUR. After the Fall. NY: Viking, (1964). Signed ltd ed of 500 numbered. W/add'l signed presentation. Buckram cl. Fine in slipcase. *Antic Hay.* $250/£161

MILLER, ARTHUR. The Creation of the World and Other Business. NY: Viking, (1973). 1st ed. NF in dj. *Antic Hay.* $25/£16

MILLER, ARTHUR. Death of a Salesman. NY: Viking, 1949. 1st ed. VG in dj (dust soiled, else VG). *Godot.* $100/£65

MILLER, ARTHUR. Focus. Reynal & Hitchcock, 1945. 1st ed. VG+ in Nice dj (worn). *Fine Books.* $60/£39

MILLER, ARTHUR. Focus. London: Gollancz, 1949. 1st ed. Dj (sl torn, backstrip faded). *Petersfield.* $39/£25

MILLER, ARTHUR. Focus. London: Gollancz, 1949. 1st Eng ed. Pale blue-grn cl, red-lettered spine sl faded, o/w Fine in dj (spine sl dknd). *Temple.* $42/£27

MILLER, ARTHUR. Incident at Vichy. NY, 1965. 1st Amer ed. Signed. Fine (label, sl rubbed) in dj (nicks). *Polyanthos.* $45/£29

MILLER, CHARLES CONRAD. Cosmetic Surgery. Phila: F.A. Davis, 1924. 1st ed. VG (bkpl; sl wear). *Glaser.* $225/£145

MILLER, CINCINNATUS. Joaquin, Et Al. Portland, OR: McCormick, 1869. 1st ed. 112pp. Orig gilt-lettered cl. BAL 13747. *Ginsberg.* $1,250/£806

MILLER, DAVID HUMPHREYS. Custer's Fall-The Indian Side of the Story. NY: Duell, Sloan & Pearce, (1957). 1st ed. VG in VG dj. *Perier.* $50/£32

MILLER, DAVID HUMPHREYS. Custer's Fall. NY: Duell, Sloan & Pearce, (1957). 1st ed. VG in dj (sl worn). *Lien.* $50/£32

MILLER, E.D. Modern Polo. M.H. Hayes (ed). London/NY: Hurst & Blackett/Scribner, 1902. 2nd ed. Frontis. Red cl (spine sl faded), gilt. VG. *Houle.* $125/£81

MILLER, FRANCES TREVELYAN (ed). The Photographic History of the Civil War. NY, 1911. 1st ed. 10 vols. Pict cl. Overall VG set (sl cvr wear, some spines tender). *Pratt.* $385/£248

MILLER, FRANCIS TREVELYAN (ed). The Photographic History of the Civil War. NY: Review of Reviews Co, 1912. 1st ed. 10 vols. NF set. *Mcgowan.* $450/£290

MILLER, FRED. The Training of a Craftsman. London: H. Virtue, 1901. 1st ed. Pub's cl. Spine sl sunned; lt wear edges, joints; else VG. *Bookpress.* $185/£119

MILLER, GENEVIEVE. The Adoption of Inoculation for Smallpox in England and France. Phila, 1957. 1st ed. Good. *Fye.* $50/£32

MILLER, GENEVIEVE. Letters of Edward Jenner and Other Documents Concerning the Early History of Vaccination. Balt, 1983. 1st ed. Good. *Fye.* $30/£19

MILLER, H. The Old Red Sandstone. Edinburgh, 1879. 22nd ed. 385pp; 1 color, 14 plain plts. *Wheldon & Wesley.* $31/£20

MILLER, HENRY. Account of a Tour of the California Missions 1856. Book Club of CA, 1952. One of 375 by Grabhorn Press. 19 plts. Vellum-backed patterned bds. Fine in slipcase. *Bohling.* $165/£106

MILLER, HENRY. Black Spring. Paris: Obelisk Press, (1936). 1st ed. VG in dec wrappers; buckram slipcase. *Juvelis.* $750/£484

MILLER, HENRY. The Colossus of Maroussi. Secker & Warburg, 1942. 1st Eng ed. Blue cl. Sl spotted, o/w Fine in dj (sl rubbed). *Dalian.* $132/£85

MILLER, HENRY. The Cosmological Eye. Norfolk: New Directions, (1939). 1st ed. Tan linen titled in brn, on-laid paper illus fr cvr. Very Nice. *Cady.* $30/£19

MILLER, HENRY. The Cosmological Eye. London: Editions Poetry, 1945. 1st Eng ed. Blue cl. VF in dj (sl dusty). *Dalian.* $70/£45

MILLER, HENRY. A Devil in Paradise.... (NY): Signet/NAL, (1956). 1st ed, pb orig. Paper lt tanned, o/w VF in pict wrappers. *Reese.* $25/£16

MILLER, HENRY. First Impressions of Greece. Santa Barbara: Capra Press, 1973. 1st ed, wrappered issue. VG in ptd wrappers. *Godot.* $35/£23

MILLER, HENRY. Greece. Thames & Hudson, 1964. 1st Eng ed. Blue cl. VF in dj. *Dalian.* $54/£35

MILLER, HENRY. Henry Miller's Book of Friends, a Tribute to Friends of Long Ago. London: W.H. Allen, 1978. 1st Eng ed. Fine in dj. *Hermitage.* $25/£16

MILLER, HENRY. Henry Miller's Book of Friends. London: W.H. Allen, 1978. 1st Eng ed. Fine in dj. *Godot.* $40/£26

MILLER, HENRY. Just Wild About Harry. MacGibbon & Kee, 1964. 1st Eng ed. Grn cl. Fine in dj (sl dusty). *Dalian.* $31/£20

MILLER, HENRY. My Life and Times. Gemini Smith/Playboy, (1975). 1st trade ed. VG in dj. *King.* $40/£26

MILLER, HENRY. My Life and Times. (NY): Playboy Press, (1975). 1st trade ed. Fine in NF dj. *Antic Hay.* $45/£29

MILLER, HENRY. My Life and Times. (NY): Playboy, n.d. (1975). 1st ed. Fine in dj (lt worn; price-clipped). *Hermitage.* $75/£48

MILLER, HENRY. The Nightmare Notebook. NY: New Directions, 1975. One of 700 numbered, signed. Fine (lt sticker stain fep). W/o dj as issued. *Beasley.* $175/£113

MILLER, HENRY. Nights of Love and Laughter. (NY): Signet/NAL, (1955). Sm nick spine, paper sl tanned, else Very Nice in pict wrappers. *Reese.* $25/£16

MILLER, HENRY. Quiet Days in Clichy. Paris: Olympia Press, 1958. 28 photogravure plts. Tp lt foxed; fr wrappers sl soiled, else VG. *Cahan.* $375/£242

MILLER, HENRY. Remember to Remember. (London): Grey Walls Press, (1952). 1st British ed. Nice in Good dj (lt frayed, smudged, dknd). *Reese.* $35/£23

MILLER, HENRY. Remember to Remember. NY: New Directions, 1947. 1st Amer ed. Pg edges sl browned, o/w VG in dj (sl soiled, damp stained). *Virgo.* $116/£75

MILLER, HENRY. Remember to Remember. Grey Walls Press, 1952. 1st Eng ed. NF in VG+ dj. *Fine Books.* $55/£35

MILLER, HENRY. Stand Still Like the Hummingbird. (Norfolk): New Directions, (1962). 1st ed. Fine in VG oversize dj (frayed). *Reese.* $30/£19

MILLER, HENRY. To Paint Is To Love Again. NY, 1968. 1st ed. VG in dj (wear). *Argosy.* $50/£32

MILLER, HENRY. Tropic of Cancer. NY, (1961). 1st ed. VG in dj (sl stained). *King.* $25/£16

MILLER, HENRY. Tropic of Cancer. London: John Calder, (1963). 1st Eng ed, variant? issue w/pagination correct (pg288 and 259 are not transposed) and lacking erratum. Blue cl, gold-stamped spine. VG in dj (sm chips, tears, lt spine wear, else VG). *Godot.* $45/£29

MILLER, HENRY. Tropic of Capricorn. London: Calder, 1964. 1st British ed. VG+ in dj (price-clipped, sl chipped). *Pettler.* $25/£16

MILLER, HENRY. The Wisdom of the Heart. London: Editions Poetry, 1947. 1st Eng ed. Mottled lt scarlet cl, gilt spine. Paper sl browned, o/w Very Nice. *Temple.* $22/£14

MILLER, JOAQUIN. 49. The Gold Seeker of the Sierras. NY, 1884. 1st Amer ed. Spine sl sunned, extrems sl rubbed, bkpl, o/w Fine. *Polyanthos.* $150/£97

MILLER, JOAQUIN. In Classic Shades: And Other Poems. Chicago: Belford-Clarke, 1890. 1st ed. Pict brn cl; patterned eps. VG. BAL 13821. *Houle.* $175/£113

MILLER, JOAQUIN. Memorie and Rime. NY: Funk & Wagnalls, 1884. 1st ed. 238pp. Orig ptd wrappers (bit chipped). Good. *Karmiole.* $45/£29

MILLER, JOAQUIN. The Ship in the Desert. Boston: Roberts Bros, 1875. 1st ed. 205pp; 10pp ads. VG. *Oregon.* $80/£52

MILLER, JOAQUIN. Songs of the Sierras. Roberts Bros, 1871. 1st ed. Teg. Gilt-dec cvr. NF (rubbed). BAL 13751. *Authors Of The West.* $100/£65

MILLER, JOAQUIN. Songs of the Sun-Lands. Roberts Bros, 1873. 1st ed. Teg. Gilt-dec cvr. Fine. BAL 13756. *Authors Of The West.* $50/£32

MILLER, JOAQUIN. True Bear Stories. Rand McNally, (1900). 1st ed. Frontis, 18 plts (4 color). Color pict cvr. Good+ (soil, corner wear). *Oregon.* $80/£52

MILLER, JOHN. Memoirs of General Miller, in the Service of the Republic of Peru. London: Longman et al, 1828. 389pp, 4 fldg maps; 460pp, 3 fldg maps. Full calf, gilt. Spines lt chipped; joints scuffed, o/w VG. *Hermitage.* $250/£161

MILLER, JONATHAN and DAVID PELHAM. The Facts of Life. NY: Viking Penguin, 1984. 22x31 cm. 6 dbl-pg pop-ups. Harry Willock (illus). Glazed pict bds. *Book Finders.* $75/£48

MILLER, JONATHAN and DAVID PELHAM. The Human Body. London: Cape, 1983. 21x30 cm. Harry Willock (illus). Glazed pict bds. VG. *Book Finders.* $75/£48

MILLER, LEWIS B. A Crooked Trail. The Story of a Thousand-Mile Saddle Trip Up and Down the Texas Frontier.... Pittsburgh: Axtell-Rush Pub Co, (1908). VG- (lt rubbed, soiled; interior foxed, smudged). Howes M 611. *Bohling.* $150/£97

MILLER, MAX. The Great Trek. NY: Doubleday, Doran, 1935. VG in dj. *High Latitude.* $30/£19

MILLER, NYLE H. and JOSEPH W. SNELL. Great Gunfighters of the Kansas Cowtowns, 1867-1886. Lincoln, (1963). 1st ed thus. Fine in dj (sl chipped, sl stained). *Baade.* $60/£39

MILLER, NYLE H. and JOSEPH W. SNELL. Great Gunfighters of the Kansas Cowtowns, 1867-1886. Lincoln: Univ of NE Press, (1963). 1st ed. Fine in dj (price-clipped). *Glenn.* $50/£32

MILLER, NYLE H. and JOSEPH W. SNELL. Why the West Was Wild. Topeka: KS State Hist Soc, 1963. 1st ed. Good. *Lien.* $145/£94

MILLER, OLIVE (ed). Flying Sails of My Book House. Chicago: Book House for Children, 1953. 35th ed. VG. *Burcham.* $30/£19

MILLER, OLIVE (ed). My Book House Hall of Fame. Vol 12. Chicago: Book House for Children, 1937. Scuffed pict cvr, else VG. *Burcham.* $20/£13

MILLER, OLIVE (ed). My Bookhouse. Chicago: Bookhouse for Children, (1925). 6 vols. 4to. Teg. Grn textured cl, color paste labels, gilt. Good. *Reisler.* $250/£161

MILLER, OLIVE (ed). Nursery Friends from France. Chicago: Book House for Children, 1927. Pict cvrs; dec eps. Bumped, else VG. *Burcham.* $35/£23

MILLER, PATRICK. Ana the Runner. London: Golden Cockerel Press, 1937. 1st ed. #65/100 signed. 6 full-pg wood engrs by Clifford Webb; teg, others uncut. Brn morocco-backed buckram, gilt lettering. VG. *Cox.* $116/£75

MILLER, PAUL EDUARD (ed). Esquire's 1945 Jazz Book. NY, (1945). Fldg map. VG in dj (chipped, taped). *Artis.* $20/£13

MILLER, RANDALL M. (ed). Dear Masters: Letters of a Slave Family. Univ of GA Press, (1990). 1st pb. Inscribed. VG (pencil underlining). *Book Broker.* $18/£12

MILLER, RICHARD ROSCOE. Slavery and Catholicism. Durham, NC: North State, (1957). 1st ed. NF. *Mcgowan.* $45/£29

MILLER, THOMAS, JR. The Cactus Air Force. NY, 1969. 1st ed. VG in VG dj. *Clark.* $45/£29

MILLER, VASSAR. My Bones Being Wiser. Middletown: Wesleyan, (1963). 1st ed. Signed. Fine in dj. *Turlington.* $50/£32

MILLER, VASSAR. Wage War on Silence. Middletown: Wesleyan, (1960). 1st ed. Inscribed. VG in dj (lt used; soiled). *Turlington.* $50/£32

MILLER, W. and E. STRANGE. A Centenary Bibliography of the Pickwick Papers. Argonaut Press, 1936. Teg. Good. *Moss.* $93/£60

MILLER, WALTER M. A Canticle for Leibowitz. Phila: Lippincott, 1960. 1st ed. NF in white dj (lt edgewear; soiling, dkng on exposed panels). *Antic Hay.* $375/£242

MILLER, WALTER M. A Canticle for Leibowitz. Lippincott, 1960. 1st ed. NF in dj. *Aronovitz.* $775/£500

MILLERS, GEORGE. A Description of the Cathedral Church of Ely. London: John White, 1808. 2nd ed. xii,(i),174pp, 10 plts. Recent 1/4-calf; new eps. *Bickersteth.* $59/£38

MILLET, F.D. A Capillary Crime. Harper, 1892. 1st ed. VG. *Madle.* $30/£19

MILLETT, KATE. Elegy for Sita. (NY): Targ Editions, (1979). Ltd to 350 numbered, signed. Fine in tissue dj. *Antic Hay.* $50/£32

MILLETT, KATE. Elegy for Sita. NY: Targ, 1979. 1st ed. One of 350 signed. Fine. *Juvelis.* $50/£32

MILLETT, KATE. Elegy for Sita. NY: Targ Editions, 1979. 1st ed. One of 350 signed. Fine. *Juvelis.* $60/£39

MILLETT, KATE. Sexual Politics. NY, 1970. 1st Amer ed. Signed presentation. NF in dj (spine sl sunned; edge tears, creases). *Polyanthos.* $30/£19

MILLICAN, ALBERT. Travels and Adventures of an Orchid Hunter. London, 1891. 1st ed. Color frontis, xv,222pp+(xvi)pub's ads. (Margin pg3/4 sl repaired; margins sl thumbed, prelims spotted, ex-libris; hinges tender; dampstained, soiled, worn.) *Edwards.* $59/£38

MILLICAN, ALBERT. Travels and Adventures of an Orchid Hunter. London: Cassell, 1891. 1st ed. Chromolitho frontis; xv,222,(xvi)pp. Pict blue cl. Bright (faint spots). *Hollett.* $217/£140

MILLIGAN, CLARENCE P. Death Valley and Scotty. L.A.: Ward Ritchie, 1942. 1st ed. Fine in VG dj. *Book Market.* $40/£26

MILLIGAN, MAURICE. Missouri Waltz. NY/London: Scribner's, 1948. 1st ed. Red cl. Lg bkpl, else VG. *Glenn.* $40/£26

MILLIKEN, RALPH LEROY. The Plains Over. The Reminiscences of William Jasper Stockton. Los Banos, 1939. 1st ed. Fr cvr cleanly detached but present, back cvr pulled from 2 staples. Text Fine. *Baade*. $60/£39

MILLIKEN, RALPH LEROY. The Plains Over: The Reminiscences of William Jasper Stockton. Los Banos: Los Banos Enterprise, 1939. 1st ed. Fine. Wrappers. *Harrington*. $35/£23

MILLIN, SARAH GERTRUDE. The South Africans. NY, (1927). 1st ed. Orig cl. NF. *Mcgowan*. $45/£29

MILLING, CHAPMAN J. Red Carolinians. Chapel Hill: Univ of NC, 1940. 1st ed. VG. *Cahan*. $65/£42

MILLINGEN, JAMES. Ancient Unedited Monuments. London: (privately ptd), 1822-26. 1st ed. 2 vols in 1. viii,106; ii,40pp, 62 engr plts (42 tinted, 7 fldg or double-pg). (Some plts badly folded.) Contemp half morocco, teg (edges, corners rubbed). *Marlborough*. $2,325/£1,500

MILLS, C.K. The Nursing and Care of the Nervous and the Insane. Edinburgh, 1887. 147pp. Lib stamp; lt pencil mks in margins, o/w VG. *Whitehart*. $70/£45

MILLS, CHARLES. First Lessons in Physiology and Hygiene. Phila, 1885. 254pp. Good. *Fye*. $40/£26

MILLS, CHARLES. History of the Crusades. London: Longman et al, 1822. 3rd ed. 2 vols. Engr frontis (offset), lg fldg map, 3 tables. 1/2 calf over marbled bds (spines, extrems rubbed; lt foxing). *Glenn*. $165/£106

MILLS, ENOS A. The Adventures of a Nature Guide. GC, 1920. 1st ed. VG. *Artis*. $25/£16

MILLS, ENOS A. In Beaver World. Boston/NY: Houghton Mifflin, (1913). 1st ed. Tan pict cl. Lt bumped, else Fine. *Glenn*. $45/£29

MILLS, GEORGE S. The Little Man with the Long Shadow...Frederick M. Hubbell. Des Moines, (1955). (Sm spot fr cvr.) *Hayman*. $20/£13

MILLS, L.J. (ed). The Textile Educator. London: Pitman, 1927. 3 vols. Vol 1: mkd, rubbed bds; vol 3: sl pulled hinge; o/w Good set. *Willow House*. $54/£35

MILLS, RANDALL. Stern-Wheelers Up the Columbia. Pacific Books, (1947). 1st ed. Fine in VG dj. *Oregon*. $27/£17

MILLS, STEPHEN and JAMES PHILLIPS. Sourdough Sky. Seattle: Superior, (1969). 1st ed. Fine in Fine dj. *Perier*. $40/£26

MILLS, W.W. Forty Years at El Paso 1858-1898. El Paso: Carl Hertzog, 1962. 1st trade ed. Dj. *Lambeth*. $50/£32

MILLSON, LARRY. Ballpark Figures. (Toronto): McClelland & Stewart, 1987. 1st ed. Fine in Fine dj. *Plapinger*. $45/£29

MILMAN, H.H. The Life of Edward Gibbon, Esq. London: John Murray, 1839. 1st ed. Engr frontis port, xvi,455pp; aeg. 3/4 brn morocco, pebbled bds, gilt extra, raised bands; marbled eps. Lovely. *Hartfield*. $295/£190

MILNE, A.A. Birthday Party and Other Stories. NY: E.P. Dutton, 1948. 1st ed. 256pp. Cl-backed paper over bds in blind. Name, else NF in dj (lt foxed). *Cahan*. $40/£26

MILNE, A.A. Birthday Party. NY: E.P. Dutton, 1948. 1st ed. Sm 8vo. Pict bds; cl spine. Sm repair p45-46, else Fine in VG dj (chipped). *Book Adoption*. $50/£32

MILNE, A.A. By Way of Introduction. NY: Dutton, (1929). Lg paper ed. #105/166 numbered, signed. 8vo. Gilt-stamped lt aqua cl, patterned bds; top edge stained grn; uncut. VG in pub's lt grn bd slipcase. *Houle*. $850/£548

MILNE, A.A. The Christopher Robin Birthday Book. London: Methuen, (1930). 1st ed. 12mo. E.H. Shepard (illus). Orange cl, gilt; vignette. Good in color dj (spine faded; sl edgewear). *Reisler*. $350/£226

MILNE, A.A. The Christopher Robin Story Book. Methuen, 1929. 1st Eng ed. Lt blue cl. Spine sl faded; cvrs sl sunned; name, o/w VG. *Dalian*. $70/£45

MILNE, A.A. The Christopher Robin Verses. London: Methuen, (1932). 1st combined ed. 8vo. 12 full color plts by E.H. Shepard. Blue cl; gilt dec, vignette. Good in full color dj (edgewear). *Reisler*. $550/£355

MILNE, A.A. The House at Pooh Corner. London, (1928). 1st ed. Ernest H. Shepard (illus). Pink cl (name; worn). *Waterfield*. $116/£75

MILNE, A.A. The House at Pooh Corner. London: Methuen, (1928). 1st ed. Ernest H. Shepard (illus). 8vo. 178pp. Teg; illus eps. Shrimp cl (edges faded; thin line dknd cl on fr); gilt. VG. *Drusilla's*. $225/£145

MILNE, A.A. The House at Pooh Corner. London: Methuen, (1928). 1st ed. E.H. Shepard (illus). Teg. Pink pict cl, gilt (sl sunned, mks). Good in dj (sl chipped, soiled, sl stained). *Ash*. $442/£285

MILNE, A.A. The House at Pooh Corner. London: Methuen, 1928. 1st ed. Signed by Shepard (illus) on tp. Pub's gilt-dec pink cl (spine lt faded; lt handling). Orig ptd dj (head, foot worn w/some loss; lt handling). *D & D*. $1,200/£774

MILNE, A.A. The House at Pooh Corner. London: Methuen, 1928. 1st Eng ed. 8vo. E.H. Shepard (illus). Pink cl bds, gilt; teg. VG in dj (lt soiled). *Davidson*. $475/£306

MILNE, A.A. The Hums of Pooh. NY: E.P. Dutton, 1939. 4to. 67pp, songs. E.H. Shepard (illus). VG in dj (torn, lt stained). *Davidson*. $50/£32

MILNE, A.A. Michael and Mary. London, 1930. 1st ed. Fine in dj (spine sunned, sl rubbed, sm piece heel missing). *Polyanthos*. $30/£19

MILNE, A.A. Michael and Mary: A Play. London: C&W, 1930. 1st ed. Rubbed. *Sadlon*. $25/£16

MILNE, A.A. Now We Are Six. London: Methuen, (1927). 1st ed. 8vo. E.H. Shepard (illus). VG in dj (nicks, tears; lt soiling). *Houle*. $850/£548

MILNE, A.A. Now We Are Six. London: Methuen, 1927. 1st UK ed. Ernest H. Shepard (illus). 12mo. Maroon pict cl (sl rubbed), gilt decs. VG+; contents Fine (feps lt soiled). *Book Adoption*. $200/£129

MILNE, A.A. Once Upon a Time. London: Hodder & Stoughton, 1917. 1st ed. Charles Robinson (illus). Color frontis. Blue dec cl (faded, worn, mks). Good. *Willow House*. $23/£15

MILNE, A.A. The Princess and the Apple Tree. NY: Grosset & Dunlap, 1937. 1st ed thus. 4to. 40pp, 8 full-pg color illus by Helen Sewell. VG (edges bumped) in dj (lt spotted). *Davidson*. $65/£42

MILNE, A.A. The Secret and Other Stories. NY: Fountain Press, 1929. 1st Amer ed. Signed. NF. *Sadlon*. $175/£113

MILNE, A.A. The Secret. NY/London: Fountain/Methuen, 1929. 1st ed. One of 742 numbered, signed. Good (spine label sl tanned, sl frayed). *Reese*. $55/£35

MILNE, A.A. Success. Putnam's, 1926. 1st ed. Dec cl. Fine in dj (dull, sl rubbed). *Whiteson.* $25/£16

MILNE, A.A. The Sunny Side. (London): Methuen, (1921). 1st ed. Good (name; sl soiled). *Reese.* $30/£19

MILNE, A.A. Teddy Bear and Other Songs from 'When We Were Very Young.' Methuen, 1926. 1st Eng ed. Brn paper bds. Sl stain fore-edge, o/w VG. *Dalian.* $132/£85

MILNE, A.A. Teddy Bear and Other Songs from When We Were Very Young. London: Methuen, (1926). 1st ed. Lg 4to. E.H. Shepard (decs); H. Fraser-Simon (music). Cl-backed brn bds, label. Good in illus dj (lacks pieces; worn). *Reisler.* $120/£77

MILNE, A.A. Teddy Bear and Other Songs from When We Were Very Young. Methuen, 1926. 1st ed. E.H. Shepard (illus). Lt mks fr cvr, else VG +. *Aronovitz.* $100/£65

MILNE, A.A. Those Were the Days. London: Methuen, 1929. #249/250 signed. Unopened. Rose cl, gilt. Fine in dj (worn, repaired). *Cummins.* $375/£242

MILNE, A.A. Toad of Toad Hall. London: Methuen, (1929). 1st ed. Fine in VG dj (sl soiled, short tears). *Between The Covers.* $150/£97

MILNE, A.A. When We Were Very Young. NY: E.P. Dutton, (1924). 1st Amer ed, 2nd issue. Ernest H. Shepard (illus). 8vo. 100pp. Top stained blue; illus eps. Red cl, gilt (faded). VG. *Drusilla's.* $75/£48

MILNE, A.A. When We Were Very Young. London: Methuen, (1924). 1st ed. 8vo. Teg. E.H. Shepard (illus). Blue cl, gilt (sl shelf wear spine). Nice in dj (edgewear; spine browned; 2 sm holes). *Reisler.* $1,800/£1,161

MILNE, A.A. Winnie-the-Pooh. London: Methuen, 1926. 1st ed. Orig gilt-dec grn cl. VF. *D & D.* $700/£452

MILNE, A.A. Winnie-the-Pooh. London: Methuen, 1926. 1st ed. Pub's gilt-dec grn cl; orig ptd dj. VF. *D & D.* $1,200/£774

MILNE, A.A. Winnie-the-Pooh. London: Methuen, 1926. 1st trade ed. 8vo. 158pp, pict map ep. E. Shepard (illus). Grn cl, pict gilt. VG + (spine ends lt bumped, faded). *Davidson.* $850/£548

MILNE, A.A. Year In, Year Out. NY: E.P. Dutton, 1952. 1st ed. Lt spotting, else VG in dj (spine chipped). *Cahan.* $35/£23

MILNE, A.A. Year In, Year Out. London: Methuen, 1952. 1st ed. Ernest H. Shepard (illus). Sm 8vo. VG + in VG + dj. *Book Adoption.* $50/£32

MILNE, J. The Memoirs of a Bookman. J. Murray, 1934. 1st ed. VG. *Moss.* $22/£14

MILNER, C. DOUGLAS. Rock for Climbing. London: Chapman & Hall, 1950. 1st ed. VG in dj (short tear). *Hollett.* $39/£25

MILOSZ, CZESLAW. The Captive Mind. NY: LEC, (1983). One of 1500 numbered. Signed by Milosz & Janusz Kapusta (illus). Litho frontis; add'l litho laid in. Fine in pub's slipcase. *Hermitage.* $125/£81

MILOSZ, CZESLAW. The Captive Mind. London: S&W, 1953. 1st ed. VG in dj (sl chipping; tape repair verso). *Lame Duck.* $50/£32

MILTON, GEORGE FORT. Abraham Lincoln and the Fifth Column. NY, 1942. 1st ed. Dj worn, chipped, o/w VG +. *Pratt.* $35/£23

MILTON, JOHN. Comus, a Mask. London: Gregynog Press, 1931. #246/250. Frontis, 6 full-pg engrs by Blair Hughes-Stanton. Cream buckram-backed bds. Lt damage from erasure to fep, o/w VG. *Cox.* $388/£250

MILTON, JOHN. Paradise Lost and Paradise Regain'd. SF: LEC, 1936. #904/1500 numbered, signed by Carlotta Petrina (illus). Cl-backed dec bds, paper label. Fine in pub's slipcase (cracked; worn). *Hermitage.* $100/£65

MILTON, JOHN. Paradise Regained...together with Poems.... London: J. Tonson & M. Poulson, 1725. 6th ed. Engr frontis. Contemp panelled calf (scuffed; recently rebacked), orig endleaves. *Glenn.* $300/£194

MILTON, JOHN. Poems in English with Illustrations by William Blake. London: Nonesuch Press, 1926. 1st ed thus. One of 1450 ptd. 2 vols. Parchment-backed dec bds. Eps foxed, o/w Fine set. *Jaffe.* $250/£161

MILTON, JOHN. The Poetical Works. London: William Pickering, 1839. 2nd Aldine ed. 3 vols. Port. (Spotting 1st, final leaves; sl worn head, tail of backstrips; paper labels browned, rubbed; bkpl.) *Cox.* $54/£35

MILTON, WILLIAM WENTWORTH FITZWILLIAM and W.B. CHEADLE. The North-West Passage by Land. London: Cassell, Petter & Galpin, (1865). 3rd ed. xxiv,400pp + 16pp ads; 23 plts, 2 fldg color maps (1 in fr pocket). Blue cl, gilt dec (spine extrems frayed). *Karmiole.* $175/£113

MIMS, EDWARD. History of Vanderbilt University. Nashville: Vanderbilt Univ Press, 1946. 1st ed. Brn cl. NF in VG dj (spotted; top, bottom edges reinforced w/tape on verso). *Chapel Hill.* $75/£48

MINAMOTO, H. An Illustrated History of Japanese Art. Harold G. Henderson (trans). Kyoto, 1935. 3 color frontispieces (incl 1 dbl-pg), 218 plts. Teg. Morocco-backed bds (spine rubbed; lower bd sl soiled). *Edwards.* $140/£90

MINARIK, ELSE HOLMELUND. Father Bear Comes Home. Kingswood, Surrey: World's Work, 1960. 1st Eng ed. Maurice Sendak (illus). Grey-backed pict bds. VF in dj (sl rubbed). *Dalian.* $39/£25

MINCKLER, JEFF (ed). Pathology of the Nervous System. NY, 1968. 1st ed. 3 vols. Good. *Fye.* $75/£48

MINEHAN, THOMAS. Lonesome Road. Evanston: Row, Peterson, 1941. 1st ed. Pict bds. Fine. *Beasley.* $35/£23

MINER, WARD L. The World of William Faulkner. Durham: Duke Univ Press, 1952. 1st ed. Fine in dj (sl dusty). *Cahan.* $35/£23

MINGAY, CHARLES. A Series of Lectures on the Most Approved Principles and Practices of Modern Surgery...From the Lectures Delivered by Sir Astley Cooper.... Boston, 1823. 456pp. Full leather. Good. *Fye.* $200/£129

MINGAZZINI, PAOLINO. Greek Pottery Painting. London: Paul Hamlyn, (1969). Good in dj. *Archaeologia.* $25/£16

MINNESOTA FATS with TOM FOX. The Bankshot and Other Great Robberies. NY: World, (1966). 1st ed. Top edge spotted; tape stains. Dj (worn, torn). *Aka.* $20/£13

MINNIGERODE, MEADE. Some Personal Letters of Herman Melville and a Bibliography. NY: Brick Row Bookshop, 1922. 1st ed. One of 1500 ptd. Uncut. 1/4 linen, bds, paper label. Fine. BAL 13678. *Macdonnell.* $100/£65

MINNIGERODE, MEADE. Some Personal Letters of Herman Melville and a Bibliography. NY: Edmond Bryne Hackett, The Brick Row Shop, 1922. 1st ed. One of 1500. Spine sl darkened, else NF in VG dj (edgeworn; 1/2-inch chip bottom of spine). BAL 13678. *Chapel Hill.* $150/£97

MINNIGH, L.W. Gettysburg, What They Did Here, The Standard Historical Guide.... N.p., 1924. Cvr wear, o/w VG in pict wraps. *Pratt.* $22/£14

MINNIGH, L.W. Gettysburg: What They Did Here. Gettysburg: N.A. Meligakes, 1924. 1st ed. Fldg map tipped in. VG (sl edgewear) in pict wrappers. *Connolly.* $28/£18

MINOSO, MINNIE with FERNANDO FERNANDEZ. Extra Innings. Regenry-Gateway, 1983. 1st ed. Scarce bilingual booklet w/excerpts from bk (issued as promo for Steidl's wine cooler) laid in. Fine in Fine dj. *Plapinger.* $100/£65

MINOT, CHARLES S. A Bibliography of Vertebrate Embryology. Boston, 1893. 1st ed. 128pp. Good. *Fye.* $75/£48

Miriam Coffin or the Whale-Fishermen: a Tale. (By Joseph C. Hart.) NY: Carvill et al, 1834. 1st ed. 2 vols. 209; 206pp. (Both rebacked; bindings expertly restored; neat replacement leather spine labels; lt foxing throughout, on leaf neatly inserted.) Good set. *Lefkowicz.* $600/£387

MIRSKY, JEANNETTE. Elisha Kent Kane and the Seafaring Frontier. Boston: Little, Brown, 1954. 1st ed. Inscribed. Map. Blue cl. VG+ in VG+ dj. *Parmer.* $45/£29

MISHIMA, YUKIO. After the Banquet. NY: Knopf, (1963). 1st Amer ed. Name, stamp, o/w NF in dj (sl chipped). *Hermitage.* $60/£39

MISHIMA, YUKIO. Confessions of a Mask. Norfolk: New Directions, (1958). 1st ed in English. NF in dj (price-clipped). *Hermitage.* $65/£42

MISHIMA, YUKIO. The Decay of the Angel. Secker & Warburg, 1971. 1st Eng ed. Brn cl. Fine in dj. *Dalian.* $39/£25

MISHIMA, YUKIO. The Decay of the Angel. NY: Knopf, 1974. 1st Amer ed. VF in dj. *Hermitage.* $50/£32

MISHIMA, YUKIO. Forbidden Colors. Knopf, 1968. 1st ed. NF in VG+ dj. *Bishop.* $20/£13

MISHIMA, YUKIO. Madame de Sade. NY: Grove, 1967. 1st ed. Fine (sunning) in Fine dj. *Beasley.* $50/£32

MISHIMA, YUKIO. Runaway Horses. NY: Knopf, 1973. 1st Amer ed. VF in dj. *Hermitage.* $50/£32

MISHIMA, YUKIO. Spring Snow. NY: Knopf, (1972). 1st Amer ed. 1972 ink inscrip, else Fine in dj. *Godot.* $35/£23

MISHIMA, YUKIO. Spring Snow. Knopf, 1972. 1st Amer ed. Fine in dj. *Fine Books.* $30/£19

MISHIMA, YUKIO. The Temple of Dawn. NY: Knopf, 1973. 1st Amer ed. Fine in VG dj (price-clipped). *Godot.* $40/£26

MISHIMA, YUKIO. Thirst for Love. London: Secker & Warburg, 1970. 1st ed. NF in dj (price-clipped). *Rees.* $39/£25

MISHIMA, YUKIO. The Way of the Samurai. NY: Basic Books, 1977. 1st Eng trans. Fine in Fine dj. *Lame Duck.* $50/£32

MITCHELL, ARTHUR. About Dreaming, Laughing, and Blushing. Edinburgh, 1905. 1st ed. Good. *Fye.* $80/£52

MITCHELL, C. AINSWORTH and C.T. HEPWORTH. Inks: Their Composition and Manufacture.... London: Griffin, 1904. 1st ed. 4 plts. *Veatchs.* $120/£77

MITCHELL, D.W. Ten Years in the United States. London: Smith, Elder, 1862. 1st ed. Frontis, 332pp. Orig blue cl. Good (lib bkpl, blindstamp, hinges cracked, spine worn). *Chapel Hill.* $135/£87

MITCHELL, DONALD G. My Farm of Edgewood: A Country Book. NY, 1884. Ltd to 50. viii,329pp. Uncut. (Pp edges browned; spine sunned, worn.) *Quest.* $60/£39

MITCHELL, DONALD G. Wet Days at Edgewood. NY, 1865. 1st ed. vii,324pp. Gilt spine. Fine. *Quest.* $45/£29

MITCHELL, EDWIN. The Horse and Buggy Days in New England. NY: Coward McCann, 1937. 2nd ed. VG. *October Farm.* $25/£16

MITCHELL, GLADYS. The Rising of the Moon. London: Michael Joseph, 1945. 1st ed. Inscrip fep; cvr staining, o/w VG in dj (dknd spine; soiled back panel). *Mordida.* $45/£29

MITCHELL, GLADYS. Spotted Hemlock. London: Michael Joseph, 1958. 1st ed. Lt foxing, o/w NF in dj (lt soiled). *Murder.* $45/£29

MITCHELL, J. and JOHN DICKIE. Philosophy of Witchcraft. Glasgow, 1889. VG. *Madle.* $85/£55

MITCHELL, J.A. Amos Judd. Scribners, 1901. VG-. *Madle.* $17/£11

MITCHELL, J.A. Drowsy. Stokes, 1917. 1st ed. VG. *Madle.* $32/£21

MITCHELL, J.A. The Last American. Stokes, 1902. 1st ed. VG. *Madle.* $35/£23

MITCHELL, J.L. Hanno or The Future of Exploration. Kegan Paul, Trench, Trubner, 1928. 1st ed. VG. *Aronovitz.* $50/£32

MITCHELL, J.L. The Lost Trumpet. Bobbs-Merrill, 1932. 1st US ed. Fine in dj (sm chip). *Madle.* $85/£55

MITCHELL, JOHN KEARSLEY. Five Essays. S. Weir Mitchell (ed). Phila, 1859. 1st ed. 371pp. (Spine rubbed; hinges reinforced; 1 section starting.) *Fye.* $200/£129

MITCHELL, MAIRIN. Storm Over Spain. London: Secker & Warburg, 1937. 1st ed. Fine in dj. *Patterson.* $140/£90

MITCHELL, MARGARET. Gone With the Wind. NY: Macmillan, 1939. 1st ptg of Motion Picture Ed. Pict wrappers. Spine sl lightened. *Sadlon.* $45/£29

MITCHELL, MARGARET. Margaret Mitchell's Gone with the Wind Letters, 1936-1949. Macmillan, (c1976). (1st ptg). VG in near VG dj. *Book Broker.* $35/£23

MITCHELL, PETER. European Flower Painters. A&C Black, 1973. Dbl-sided color frontis; 49 color plts. Dj. *Edwards.* $47/£30

MITCHELL, S. WEIR. The Adventures of Francois. NY, 1898. 321pp. Good. *Fye.* $40/£26

MITCHELL, S. WEIR. The Autobiography of a Quack and the Case of George Dedlow. NY, 1900. 1st ed. Good. *Fye.* $60/£39

MITCHELL, S. WEIR. The Comfort of the Hills and Other Poems. NY, 1910. 1st ed. Good. *Fye.* $75/£48

MITCHELL, S. WEIR. The Comfort of the Hills and Other Poems. NY, 1910. 1st ed. Inscribed, initialed. Good. *Fye.* $250/£161

MITCHELL, S. WEIR. Doctor and Patient. Phila, 1888. 1st ed. 177pp. Good. *Fye.* $200/£129

MITCHELL, S. WEIR. Doctor and Patient. Phila, 1889. 3rd ed. 177pp. Good. *Fye.* $75/£48

MITCHELL, S. WEIR. Doctor and Patient. Phila, 1904. 4th ed. Good. *Fye.* $50/£32

MITCHELL, S. WEIR. Dr. North and His Friends. NY, 1900. 1st ed. Good. *Fye.* $30/£19

MITCHELL, S. WEIR. Far in the Forest. Phila, 1889. 1st ed. 298pp. Good. *Fye.* $50/£32

MITCHELL, S. WEIR. Fat and Blood: An Essay on the Treatment of Certain Forms of Neurasthenia and Hysteria. Phila, 1891. 6th ed. 168pp. Good. *Fye.* $50/£32

MITCHELL, S. WEIR. Fat and Blood: And How to Make Them. Phila, 1878. 2nd ed. 109pp. Good. *Fye.* $150/£97

MITCHELL, S. WEIR. Francis Drake, a Tragedy of the Sea. Boston, 1893. 1st ed. Inscribed, signed. (Lib bkpl; bds soiled.) *Fye.* $150/£97

MITCHELL, S. WEIR. The Guillotine Club and Other Stories. Century, 1910. 1st ed. VG +. *Aronovitz.* $65/£42

MITCHELL, S. WEIR. Hugh Wynne, Free Quaker: Sometime Brevet.... NY, 1899. 2 vols. 306; 261pp. Good. *Fye.* $50/£32

MITCHELL, S. WEIR. Injuries of Nerves and Their Consequences. Phila, 1872. 1st ed. 377pp. (Spine head, tail, corners rubbed; fep stained.) *Fye.* $600/£387

MITCHELL, S. WEIR. John Sherwood, Ironmaster. NY, 1911. 1st ed. Good. *Fye.* $30/£19

MITCHELL, S. WEIR. Lectures on Diseases of the Nervous System, Especially in Women. Phila, 1881. 1st ed. 238pp. (Ex-lib; pub's ads removed.) *Fye.* $300/£194

MITCHELL, S. WEIR. Little Stories. Century, 1903. 1st ed in bk format. Good. *Goodrich.* $25/£16

MITCHELL, S. WEIR. Little Stories. NY, 1903. 1st ed. Good. *Fye.* $60/£39

MITCHELL, S. WEIR. The Red City. NY, 1908. 1st ed. Good. *Fye.* $35/£23

MITCHELL, S. WEIR. Roland Blake. Boston, 1886. 1st ed. 379pp. Good. *Fye.* $35/£23

MITCHELL, S. WEIR. Some Recently Discovered Letters of William Harvey with Other Miscellanea. Phila, 1912. 2 plts. Fine. *Goodrich.* $75/£48

MITCHELL, S. WEIR. Wear and Tear, or Hints for the Overworked. Phila, 1891. 5th ed. 76pp. (Binding loose.) *Fye.* $25/£16

MITCHELL, S. WEIR. Westways: A Village Chronicle. NY, 1913. 1st ed. Good. *Fye.* $20/£13

MITCHELL, S. WEIR. When All the Woods are Green. NY, 1894. 1st ed. 419pp. Good. *Fye.* $40/£26

MITCHELL, S. WEIR. When All the Woods Are Green. NY: The Century Co., 1894. 1st ed. 419pp. Teg. Dec grn cl. Fine (inscrip) in ptd dj (dknd). BAL 14160. *Chapel Hill.* $350/£226

MITCHELL, S. WEIR. The Youth of Washington Told in the Form of an Autobiography. NY, 1904. 1st ed. Good. *Fye.* $35/£23

MITCHELL, SAMUEL ALFRED. Eclipses of the Sun. NY: Columbia Univ Press, 1951. 5th ed. VG in blue cl (fore-edge lt foxed). *Knollwood.* $70/£45

MITCHELL, W. Structure and Growth of the Mind. London, 1907. 1st ed. Pencil underlining, o/w Fine. *Fye.* $30/£19

MITCHELL, WILLIAM ANSEL. Linn County, Kansas: A History. Kansas City, 1928. 2 plts, dbl map at rear. VG. *Bohling.* $75/£48

MITCHELL, WILLIAM. Memoirs of World War I. NY: Random House, (1960). 1st ed. Blue binding (faded). VG in dj (worn). *Graf.* $15/£10

MITCHISON, NAOMI. The Blood of the Martyrs. Constable, 1939. 1st Eng ed. Maroon cl. Cvr tips mkd; eps sl browned, o/w VG in dj (sl tanned, nicked, dusty). *Dalian.* $47/£30

MITCHISON, NAOMI. The Delicate Fire. Cape, 1933. 1st Eng ed. Yellow cl. VF in dj (sl dusty). *Dalian.* $70/£45

MITCHLET, J. The Insect. London, 1875. 368pp. Pict gilt cl. Ends foxed, o/w Fine. *Henly.* $37/£24

MITFORD, M. A Talent to Annoy. London: Hamish Hamilton, 1986. 1st ed. Fep sl scuffed, labels removed, o/w Fine in dj. *Virgo.* $31/£20

MITFORD, MARY RUSSELL. Our Village. London: Macmillan, 1910. 1st ed. 4to. Hugh Thomson (illus). Tinted top. Grn cl, gold lettering (spine cl rippled; plt w/corner folds). Grn paper dj (marginal chipping). *Reisler.* $225/£145

MITFORD, NANCY (ed). Noblesse Oblige. London: Hamish Hamilton, 1956. 1st ed. Inscrip, else VG in dj. *Limestone.* $35/£23

MITSCH, ERWIN. The Art of Egon Schiele. Phaidon, 1975. 1st UK ed. Dj (sl ragged, sl loss). *Edwards.* $39/£25

MITTELHOLZER, EDGAR. Shadows Move Among Them. Phila: Lippincott, (1951). 1st ed. VG in dj (worn). *Petrilla.* $30/£19

MITTELHOLZER, WALTER. By Airplane Towards the North Pole. An Account of an Expedition to Spitzbergen in the Summer of 1923. Boston: Houghton Mifflin, 1925. 1st US ed. 4 maps. Lt blue w/white spine, cvr titles. Announcement postmarked 1972 laid in. VG + in dj (soiled). *Parmer.* $135/£87

MITTENDORF, W.F. A Manual on Diseases of the Eye and Ear. NY, 1881. 1st ed. Good. *Fye.* $100/£65

MITTON, G.E. Cornwall. London: A&C Black, 1915. 24 color plts by G.F. Nicholls. (Sl foxed throughout.) *Petersfield.* $54/£35

MIXSON, FRANK M. Reminiscences of a Private. Columbia, SC: State Co, 1910. 1st ed. Frontis port. Orig grey cl. Bkpl, newspaper clipping tipped to rep, else Nice, bright. *Chapel Hill.* $450/£290

MIZENER, ARTHUR. The Far Side of Paradise. Eyre & Spottiswoode, 1951. 1st UK ed. NF in dj (price-clipped). *Sclanders.* $19/£12

MO, TIMOTHY. An Insular Possession. NY: Random House, 1987. 1st Amer ed. Fine in Fine dj. *Revere.* $20/£13

MO, TIMOTHY. The Monkey King. London: Deutsch, 1978. 1st ed. 1st bk. Fine in dj. *Virgo.* $186/£120

MO, TIMOTHY. The Monkey King. London: Deutsch, 1978. 1st UK ed. Fine in dj. *Lewton.* $147/£95

MO, TIMOTHY. The Redundancy of Courage. London Ltd Eds, 1990. One of 250 numbered, signed. 1/4-backed marbled cl bds. VF in tissue dj, as issued. *Dalian.* $85/£55

MO, TIMOTHY. Sour Sweet. London: Deutsch, 1982. 1st UK ed. NF in Booker dj. *Lewton.* $39/£25

MO, TIMOTHY. Sour Sweet. London: Deutsch, 1982. 1st UK ed. Fine in Chinese dj. *Lewton.* $85/£55

Modern Painters. (By John Ruskin.) Smith, Elder, 1848(-1860). 1st ed of vols 3 to 5, 4th ed vol 1, 2nd ed vol 2. 5 vols. 83 plts (numbered 1 to 84 w/o #77 which is not called for in plt list). Orig grn cl, blocked in blind, gilt-lettered spines (faded); all vols rebacked, preserving orig spines on 3 vols, most of spine on other 2; orig eps preserved. Good set (pp, plts sl spotted). *Bickersteth*. $388/£250

Modern Priscilla Home Furnishing Book. Boston: Priscilla Pub Co, (1925). 1st ed. 4 color plts. Dec floral cl; paper spine, cvr labels. Good. *Karmiole*. $30/£19

Modern Traveller. Spain and Portugal. (By Josiah Condor.) London: Ptd for James Duncan, 1826. 2 vols. Fldg frontis map, (iv,370); iv,342pp, 7 engrs (bkpls). 3/4 leather (rubbed). *Schoyer*. $50/£32

MODY, N.H.N. Japanese Clocks. Rutland: Charles E. Tuttle, (1967). 1st ed. 135 plts. Red silk cl. Bumped, else Fine in NF dj (price-clipped). *Hermitage*. $85/£55

MOFFAT, ALFRED. Our Old Nursery Rhymes. London/Phila: Augener/McKay, (1911). Apparently 1st Amer issue. H. Willebeek Le Mair (illus). 63,(1)pp, postcard laid in. (Few edge tears, repaired.) Mtd color plt fr cvr; orig pict dj (edge chipping). *Schoyer*. $125/£81

MOFFAT, ALFRED. Our Old Nursery Rhymes. Phila/London: McKay/Augener, n.d. (1912). Oval pict cvr pastedown. Upper hinge starting; lt soil, else VG. *Glenn*. $150/£97

MOFFAT, GWEN. Over the Sea to Death. Scribner's, 1976. 1st US ed. Fine in Fine dj. *Ming*. $25/£16

MOFFETT, CHARLES S. et al. The New Painting: Impressionism 1874-1886. London: Phaidon, 1986. 1st ed. Rev copy. Navy cl, gilt. Fine in Fine dj. *Willow House*. $47/£30

MOFFETT, CLEVELAND. Possessed. McCann, 1920. 1st ed. VG. *Madle*. $18/£12

MOFFITT, JOHN. This Narrow World. NY: Dodd, Mead/Editions Poetry London-NY, (1958). 1st ed. Fine (eps browning) in dj. *Antic Hay*. $25/£16

MOHOLY-NAGY, L. Vision in Motion. Chicago: Paul Theobald, (1947). 3rd ptg. Spine sunned, rear cvr sl soiled; else VG. *Bookpress*. $65/£42

MOHR, NICHOLASA. Nilda. NY: Harper & Row, (1973). 1st ed. Pict bds (sl edgewear). VG in dj (rubbed; chipped; clipped). *Hermitage*. $35/£23

MOHRT, MICHEL. The Italian Campaign. Patrick O'Brian (trans). London: Weidenfeld & Nicolson, 1967. 1st Eng ed. NF (spine tail sl bumped) in dj (extrems sl rubbed). *Ulysses*. $116/£75

MOLESWORTH, MRS. Two Little Waifs. London, 1883. 1st ed. 7 b/w plts by Walter Crane. Dec red cl. VG. *Argosy*. $65/£42

MOLL, A. Hypnotism. London, 1890. Contemporary Science Series. xii,410pp. (Spine faded, ends worn; 1 section cracked.) *Whitehart*. $39/£25

MOLL, ALBERT. Perversions of the Sex Instinct. Newark: Julian Press, 1931. 1st ed. Brn cl, gilt-lettered spine (lt spotting). Fine. *D & D*. $45/£29

MOLLOY, FITZGERALD. Russian Court in the Eighteenth Century. NY: Scribner's, 1905. 2 vols. Teg. (Paper browned; cl discolored.) *Schoyer*. $40/£26

MOLONEY, FRANCIS. The Fur Trade in New England 1620-1767. Harvard, 1931. 1st ed. Fine. *Oregon*. $40/£26

MOLYNEUX, W.C.F. Campaigning in South Africa and Egypt. London, 1896. 1st ed. viii,287pp; 4 maps (2 fldg). VG (bkpl) in maroon cl (sl worn, bubbled; label removed upper bd). *Edwards*. $116/£75

MOMADAY, N. SCOTT. The Ancient Child. NY: Doubleday, (1989). 1st ed. Signed. Fine in dj (sl rubbed, short tear). *Godot*. $50/£32

MOMADAY, N. SCOTT. House Made of Dawn. NY: Harper & Row, (1968). 1st ed. Fine in dj (sm closed tears). *Jaffe*. $125/£81

MONAGHAN, DAVID. Smiley's Circus: A Guide to the Secret World of John Le Carre. NY: St. Martins, 1986. 1st ed. Fine in dj. *Else Fine*. $40/£26

MONAGHAN, JAY (ed). The Book of the American West. NY, (1963). 1st ed. Bkpl, o/w Good. *Artis*. $35/£23

MONAGHAN, JAY. Civil War on the Western Border, 1854-1865. Boston: Little, Brown, (1955). 1st ed. Fine in NF dj. *Mcgowan*. $75/£48

MONAGHAN, JAY. Custer. Boston: Little, Brown, 1959. 1st ed. NF (sl fade on backstrip). *Connolly*. $30/£19

MONAGHAN, JAY. The Legend of Tom Horn, Last of the Bad Men. Indianapolis, (1946). 1st ed. (Cvr dull.) *Heinoldt*. $15/£10

MONAGHAN, JAY. The Legend of Tom Horn, Last of the Bad Men. Indianapolis: Bobbs-Merrill, (1946). 1st ed. (Ridge rear cvr.) Dj (chipped, taped). *Glenn*. $35/£23

MONAGHAN, JAY. The Legend of Tom Horn. Indianapolis: Bobbs-Merrill, 1946. Frontis; 14 plts. Untrimmed. VG. *Connolly*. $30/£19

MONAGHAN, JAY. Lincoln Bibliography 1839-1939. Springfield, IL: IL State Hist Soc, 1943-45. 1st ed. 2 vols. Orig blue cl. Spines sl faded, else NF. *Chapel Hill*. $150/£97

MONAGHAN, JAY. Lincoln Bibliography 1839-1939. Springfield, 1943. 1st ed. 2 vols. *Ginsberg*. $100/£65

MONCKTON, C.A.W. Last Days in New Guinea. Bodley Head, 1922. 2 maps. (Sl foxing; backstrip sl faded, sm tears; cvrs sl mkd.) *Petersfield*. $40/£26

MONCRIEFF, A.R. HOPE. The Cockpit of Europe. A&C Black, 1920. 1st ed. 32 color plts, fldg map. Dec cl (sl soiled; spine sl chipped). *Edwards*. $39/£25

MONCRIEFF, A.R. HOPE. Isle of Wight. A&C Black, 1908. 1st ed. 24 color plts, color fldg map. Teg. Dec cl (sl worn; marginal spotting; eps browned). *Edwards*. $47/£30

MONCUS, HERMAN H. Prairie Schooner Pirates. NY, 1963. 1st ed. Inscribed. Fine in mod dj (worn). *Baade*. $25/£16

MONETTE, JOHN W. History of the Discovery and Settlement of the Valley of the Mississippi.... NY: Harper, 1846. 1st ed. 2 vols. 8vo. 567; 595pp, 3 maps (2 dbl-pg), 4 plans, 2 plts. Dk brn cl. Spine ends chipped, else NF set in slipcase. Howes M 722. *Chapel Hill*. $675/£435

MONGAN, ELIZABETH et al. Fragonard. Drawings for Ariosto. NY, 1945. One of 1200. 135 plts. Good in dj. *Washton*. $75/£48

Monkey's Frolic. London: Grant & Griffith, n.d. (ca 1845). 12mo. 17pp + 1pg ad back cvr; 14 VF 1/2pg hand-colored wood engrs. Yellow stiff paper wrappers (expertly rebound w/new backstrip, internally reinforced; spotted, sl soiled). Text, illus Fine (ink inscrip). *Hobbyhorse*. $225/£145

MONKHOUSE, COSMO. The Manchester Whitworth Institute. Historical Catalogue of the Collection of Water-Colour Drawings by Deceased Artists. Manchester, 1894. xxii,122pp; teg, 22 plts. Orig cl, blind/gilt dec. Mint. *Europa.* $93/£60

MONNETT, HOWARD N. Action before Westport, 1864. Kansas City: Westport Hist Soc, 1964. Subs' ed signed; #415/525. Fine in dj (lt sunned). *Glenn.* $150/£97

Monograph of the Work of McKim, Mead, and White, 1879-1915. NY: Architectural Book Pub, (1915). 1st ed. 4 vols, complete. Folio. VG (hinges, spine extrems worn). *Bookpress.* $2,200/£1,419

Monograph of the Work of McKim, Mead, and White, 1879-1915. Vol IV. NY: Architectural Book Pub, 1915. 1st ed. 100 plts. Internally VG (cvr wear, respined). *Bookpress.* $450/£290

MONRO, A. Essays and Heads of Lectures on Anatomy, Physiology, Pathology and Surgery. Edinburgh, 1840. Frontis port; clx,132pp (prelims sl foxed); 6 engrs. Emb cl. *Whitehart.* $248/£160

MONRO, HAROLD. Strange Meetings. Poetry Bookshop, 1917. 1st ed. (Foxing.) Wraps (wear). *Poetry.* $19/£12

MONROE, HARRIET. The Difference and Other Poems.... Chicago: Covici-McGee, 1924. 1st ed. Signed. Lt dampstain edge fr bd, else VG. *Hermitage.* $35/£23

MONROE, JAMES. Papers of James Monroe. Listed in Chronological Order.... Washington D.C.: GPO, 1904. Frontis, guard. Partially unopened. Wine buckram, mylar wrapper. Fep sl wrinkled; short tears, else VG. *Connolly.* $85/£55

MONROE, MALCOLM. The Means Is the End in Vietnam. NY: Murlagan Press, 1968. VG (stamp fep; sm bump) in wraps. *Aka.* $40/£26

MONSARRAT, NICHOLAS. The Cruel Sea. London: Cassell & Co, 1951. 1st ed. Dbl-spread map. Lt blue cl, silver spine. Nice (eps sl cracked). *Temple.* $16/£10

MONSARRAT, NICHOLAS. The Cruel Sea. Cassell, 1951. 1st Eng ed. Blue cl (fore-edge sl foxed). Fine in dj (inner repair). *Dalian.* $54/£35

MONSARRAT, NICHOLAS. Three Corvettes. London: Cassell & Co, 1945. 1st collected ed. Frontis. Lt blue cl. Fine in dj (nicked). *Temple.* $29/£19

Monsieur Nongtongpaw. London: Alfred Miller, 1830. 19pp + 4pp ads, 6 plts, vignette tp. Robert Cruikshank (illus). Yellow wraps (spine chipped); cl folder. *Schoyer.* $175/£113

MONSON, RONALD A. Across Africa on Foot. London, 1936. Frontis port, 5 maps. (Extrems rubbed, chip spine.) *Edwards.* $47/£30

Monster Island. London: Hamish Hamilton Children's Books, 1981. 19x27 cm. 5 dbl-pg pop-ups, pull-tabs. Ron & Atie van der Meer (illus). Glazed pict bds. VG. *Book Finders.* $50/£32

MONTAGU, EDWARD WORTLEY. Reflections on the Rise and Fall of the Ancient Republicks. (London: J. Rivington et al, 1778.) 4th ed. 3 p.l.,392pp. Contemp tree calf, gilt; red morocco label. Marbled eps. Bkpl; corners sl bumped; sm tear base spine; backstrip sl mkd, dulled, o/w Fine. *Pirages.* $145/£94

MONTAGU, ELIZABETH. The Letters of...with Some of the Letters of Her Correspondents.... London: Mathew Montagu, 1810-1813. 4 vols. 3rd ed of 1 & 2; 1st ed of 3 & 4. Port. Orig bds (spine ends, hinges wearing, top edges dusty), orig paper labels; uncut. *Limestone.* $175/£113

MONTAGU, ELIZABETH. The Letters. Boston: Wells & Lilly, 1825. 1st Amer ed. 3 vols. 276; 276; 275pp. Grey linen, gilt (rebound, orig labels laid down). *Hartfield.* $195/£126

MONTAGU, MARY WORTLEY. Letters from the Levant During the Embassay to Constantinople 1716-18. London: Joseph Rickerby, 1838. Contemp grn calf, gilt, over marbled bds. Marbled edges, eps. Nice. *Limestone.* $95/£61

MONTAGU, MARY WORTLEY. Letters...Written During Her Travels in Europe, Asia, and Africa.... T. Becket & P.A. de Hondt, Vols I-III - 1763; Vol IV - 1767. 3rd ed. 4 vols. Old calf (rebacked; new eps). *Hill.* $132/£85

MONTAGUE, C.E. Action and Other Stories. London: C&W, 1928. 1st ed. Top edge blue. Lt blue cl. Very Nice in dj (frayed, mkd). *Temple.* $16/£10

MONTAGUE, C.E. Dramatic Values. London: Methuen, 1911. 1st ed. Teg, fore-edges rough-trimmed, lower edges uncut. Dk grn cl, gilt. Nice (edges, few leaves foxed). *Temple.* $42/£27

MONTAGUE, C.E. A Writer's Notes on His Trade. London: C&W, 1930. 1st ed. One of 750, signed. VG (spine sl sunned; sl wear). *Juvelis.* $35/£23

Montana. A State Guide Book. NY: Viking, 1939. 1st ed. 9 maps (lg fldg in rear pocket). Blue gilt cl. Good in dj (sl chipped). *Karmiole.* $45/£29

Montana: A State Guide Book. NY: Viking, 1939. 1st ed. Fldg map in pocket. Gold-stamped cl. Dj (sl edgewear). *Dawson.* $75/£48

MONTBARD, G. Among the Moors. Sketches of Oriental Life. NY/London, 1894. xxii,(282)pp. Grn cl stamped in gilt (spine dull; 2 rubbed spots). *Schoyer.* $100/£65

MONTECINO, MARCEL. The Crosskiller. NY: Arbor House/William Morrow, 1988. 1st ed. 1st bk. Fine in Fine dj. *Janus.* $125/£81

MONTEILHET, HUBERT. Murder at the Frankfurt Book Fair. GC: Doubleday, 1976. 1st Amer ed. Fine in dj (wear fr flap crease). *Mordida.* $35/£23

MONTGOMERY, CHARLES F. American Furniture. NY: Viking, (1966). 1st ed. Blue cl, gilt. Good in dj. *Karmiole.* $60/£39

MONTGOMERY, CORA. Eagle Pass. NY: Putnam's, 1852. 1st ed. 188pp. Gilt-stamped brn cl (newly bound). Howes C 251. *Lambeth.* $100/£65

MONTGOMERY, MARION. Dry Lightning. Lincoln: Univ of NE Press, 1960. 1st ed. Fine in dj (sl spine-sunned). *Turlington.* $100/£65

MONTGOMERY, RUTHERFORD G. High Country. NY: Derrydale, 1938. One of 950 numbered. VG+ in orig glassine (chipped). *Bowman.* $100/£65

MONTHAN, GUY and DORIS. Art and the Indian Individualists. Flagstaff: Northland, 1975. 1st ed. NF in VG dj. *Parker.* $60/£39

MOODIE, SUSANNA. Roughing It in the Bush. NY: Putnam's, 1852. 1st Amer ed. 2 vols in 1, as issued. 211; 224pp. (Dampstain back cvr.) *Hayman.* $25/£16

MOODY, ELLA (ed). Decorative Art in Modern Interiors. The Studio, 1961. Vol 51. 16 color photos. (Ex-lib.) Protected dj (sl chipped). *Edwards.* $47/£30

MOODY, ELLA (ed). Decorative Art in Modern Interiors. Studio Vista, 1964. Vol 54. (Ex-lib w/ink stamp, bkpl.) Dj. *Edwards.* $47/£30

MOODY, ELLA (ed). Decorative Art in Modern Interiors. Studio Vista, 1967. Vol 57. (Ex-lib.) *Edwards.* $39/£25

MOODY, ELLA (ed). Decorative Art in Modern Interiors. Studio Vista, 1973. Vol 63. (Ex-lib.) *Edwards.* $39/£25

MOODY, S.A. The Palm Tree. London: Nelson, 1864. 448pp; 6 chromolitho plts. Aeg. Dec cl (faded; crudely rebacked), gilt-lettered spine. (Fr hinge cracked.) *Quest.* $90/£58

MOON, WILLIAM LEAST HEAT. *See* HEAT MOON, WILLIAM LEAST

MOON, BUCKLIN (ed). Primer for White Folks. GC: Doubleday, 1945. 1st ed. Gray cl. Dj (chipped). *Petrilla.* $40/£26

MOONEY, CHARLES W. Doctor in Belle Starr Country. OK City, 1975. 1st ed. NF in dj (sl worn, price-clipped). *Baade.* $75/£48

MOONEY, JAMES. The Ghost-Dance Religion and the Sioux Outbreak of 1890. Washington: GPO, 1896. 643-1136pp, 38 plts (incl 5 maps, color fldg plt). Orig grn cl. VG. *Schoyer.* $125/£81

MOONEY, TED. Easy Travel to Other Planets. FSG, 1981. 1st ed, 1st bk. NF in VG + dj. *Bishop.* $22/£14

MOONEY, TED. Easy Travel to Other Planets. NY: FSG, 1981. 1st ed. Fine in Fine dj. *Revere.* $25/£16

MOORCOCK, MICHAEL. The Adventures of Una Persson and Catherine Cornelius in the Twentieth Century. London, 1976. 1st ed. Fine in Fine dj. *Polyanthos.* $40/£26

MOORCOCK, MICHAEL. The English Assassin. Harper, 1972. 1st US ed. Fine in dj. *Madle.* $20/£13

MOORCOCK, MICHAEL. The Entropy Tango: A Comic Romance. London: New English Lib, 1981. 1st ed. Fine in dj. *Temple.* $25/£16

MOORCOCK, MICHAEL. Gloriana, or The Unfulfill'd Queen. Allison & Busby, 1978. 1st ed. Signed. Fine in NF dj. *Aronovitz.* $65/£42

MOORCOCK, MICHAEL. The Hollow Lands. Harper, 1974. 1st ed. Fine in dj. *Madle.* $20/£13

MOORCOCK, MICHAEL. The Sleeping Sorceress. NEL, 1971. 1st ed. Fine in dj. *Aronovitz.* $50/£32

MOORE, ADOLPHUS WARBURTON. The Alps in 1864. E.H. Stevens (ed). Oxford: Blackwell, 1939. 2 vols. 10 maps. Edges, eps sl spotted, o/w Fine in djs. *Hollett.* $101/£65

MOORE, ADOLPHUS WARBURTON. The Alps in 1864. E.H. Stevens (ed). Oxford: Blackwell, 1939. 2 vols. 10 maps. Edges, eps sl spotted, o/w VG set. *Hollett.* $70/£45

MOORE, ALBERT BURTON. Conscription and Conflict in the Confederacy. NY: Macmillan, 1924. 1st ed. VG (lt worn). *Cahan.* $50/£32

MOORE, ALBERT BURTON. Conscription and Conflict in the Confederacy. NY: Macmillan, 1924. 1st ed. Blue cl. 2 sm tape remnants fep, else NF. Howes M 755. *Chapel Hill.* $95/£61

MOORE, ANNE CARROLL. A Century of Kate Greenaway. NY/London: Warne, (1946). 1st ed. Pict wrappers, orig glassine. Cvrs sl wrinkled, glassine chipped, else Fine. *Glenn.* $45/£29

MOORE, BRIAN. Black Robe. NY: Dutton, (1985). 1st Amer ed. Fine in dj. *Between The Covers.* $45/£29

MOORE, BRIAN. Catholics. London: Cape, 1972. 1st UK ed. NF in dj (sl edgewear). *Williams.* $31/£20

MOORE, BRIAN. The Emperor of Ice-Cream. NY: Viking, (1965). 1st Amer ed. Sl cocked, else Fine in NF dj (sm stain; sl rubbing). *Between The Covers.* $65/£42

MOORE, BRIAN. The Emperor of Ice-Cream. Toronto, 1965. 1st Canadian ed. VG in dj (sl rubbed). *Rees.* $39/£25

MOORE, BRIAN. The Executioners. Toronto: Harlequin, 1951. 1st ed. Pb orig. Wrappers worn, o/w VG. *Rees.* $116/£75

MOORE, BRIAN. Fergus. NY, 1970. 1st ed. Signed. Bumped, o/w NF in dj (sl mkd). *Rees.* $54/£35

MOORE, BRIAN. Fergus. London: Cape, 1971. 1st UK ed. VG in dj. *Williams.* $31/£20

MOORE, BRIAN. The Great Victorian Collection. NY, 1975. 1st Amer ed. Inscribed. NF (sl bumped). *Rees.* $54/£35

MOORE, BRIAN. The Great Victorian Collection. London: Cape, 1975. 1st Eng ed. Signed. NF in dj (sm chip). *Rees.* $31/£20

MOORE, BRIAN. I Am Mary Dunne. NY: Viking, (1968). 1st ed. Sm ink # fr fly, else Fine in NF dj (sm spots spine). *Between The Covers.* $45/£29

MOORE, BRIAN. I Am Mary Dunne. Viking, 1968. 1st US ed. NF in dj (price-clipped). *Williams.* $39/£25

MOORE, BRIAN. Judith Hearne. London: Deutsch, 1955. 1st UK ed. VG + (sm abrasion) in VG dj (sl dusty). *Williams.* $388/£250

MOORE, BRIAN. Lies of Silence. London: Bloomsbury, 1990. One of 150 specially bound, numbered, signed. Fine in glassine dj. *Rees.* $70/£45

MOORE, BRIAN. The Luck of Ginger Coffey. Andre Deutsch, 1960. 1st Eng ed. NF in dj (price-clipped). *Stahr.* $60/£39

MOORE, BRIAN. The Mangan Inheritance. London: Cape, 1979. 1st ed. Signed. Fine in dj. *Rees.* $39/£25

MOORE, BRIAN. The Mangan Inheritance. NY, 1979. 1st ed. Signed. NF in dj (nick). *Rees.* $39/£25

MOORE, BRIAN. The Revolution Script. NY: HRW, (1971). 1st Amer ed. Inscribed. Fine in dj. *Between The Covers.* $150/£97

MOORE, BRIAN. The Revolution Script. NY, 1971. 1st ed. NF in dj. *Rees.* $23/£15

MOORE, BRIAN. The Revolution Script. NY, 1971. 1st ed. Signed. NF in dj. *Rees.* $39/£25

MOORE, BRIAN. The Temptation of Eileen Hughes. NY: FSC, (1981). 1st ed. Fine in dj. *Between The Covers.* $35/£23

MOORE, BRIAN. Wreath for a Redhead. Toronto: Harlequin, 1951. 1st ed, 1st bk. Pb orig. Worn, 1/2-inch loss at foot, sl creased, sm M stamped to fore-edge, o/w VG. *Rees.* $388/£250

MOORE, C.L. Doomsday Morning. Doubleday, 1957. 1st ed. Fine in dj (frayed). *Madle.* $65/£42

MOORE, C.L. Judgment Night. NY: Gnome Press, (1952). 1st ed, 2nd state binding (bds). VG (sl flaws) in dj (trimmed 1/4 inch short; tape flap corners). *Other Worlds.* $35/£23

MOORE, C.L. Judgment Night. Gnome, 1952. 1st ed. VG in dj (chipped). *Madle.* $75/£48

MOORE, C.L. Judgment Night. Gnome Press, 1952. 1st ed. NF in Fine dj (tear spine head). *Aronovitz.* $80/£52

MOORE, C.L. Northwest of Earth. NY: Gnome, (1954). 1st ed. Lt foxing to top, else NF in VG + dj (sm chip, foxing). *Other Worlds.* $75/£48

MOORE, C.L. Northwest of Earth. Gnome, 1954. 1st ed. NF in dj (chipped). *Madle.* $100/£65

MOORE, C.L. Shambleau. Gnome, 1953. 1st ed. NF in dj (frayed). *Madle*. $100/£65

MOORE, CLEMENT C. The Night Before Christmas. NY: Harcourt, Brace, (1937). 1st ed thus. 12 full-pg color plts by Reginald Birch, marbled eps. 1/2 grn morocco, gilt. Teg. Very Nice. *Cady*. $45/£29

MOORE, CLEMENT C. The Night Before Christmas. London: George G. Harrap, (1939). Reasonably early ptg. Arthur Rackham (illus). Nice in orig pict wrappers (lt chipping, soiling). *Glenn*. $125/£81

MOORE, CLEMENT C. The Night Before Christmas. London: Harrap, 1939. 1st thus. Arthur Rackham (illus). Fine (inscrip) in wrappers as issued. *Williams*. $140/£90

MOORE, CLEMENT C. The Night Before Christmas. NY: Crown, 1944. 3 moveables, 1 pop-up by Meg Wohlberg. Spiral bound; cl pict wraps. VG (1/2 image of Santa missing). *Davidson*. $42/£27

MOORE, CLEMENT C. Twas the Night Before Christmas. Boston/NY: Houghton, Mifflin, (1912). 12 full-pg color illus by Jessie W. Smith, L.F. Perkins ads fr flap. Pict paper-cvrd bds (sl smaller than 1st ed). (Paper cvr worn, dj tattered). *Davidson*. $235/£152

MOORE, CLEMENT C. The Visit of St. Nicholas. London: Ernest Nister, (ca 1890). Obl 4to. Color illus paper wrappers (worn, resewn). *Reisler*. $140/£90

MOORE, EDWARD A. The Story of a Cannoneer under Stonewall Jackson. Lynchburg, VA: J.P. Bell, 1910. 2nd ed. Grn cl (recased, new eps). *Chapel Hill*. $150/£97

MOORE, EDWARD A. The Story of a Cannoneer under Stonewall Jackson. NY, 1970. 1983 Time-Life Collector's Lib of the Civil War reprint. Roster. Leather; gilt edges. Fine. *Pratt*. $27/£17

MOORE, EDWARD A. The Story of a Cannoneer under Stonewall Jackson.... NY/Washington: Neale Pub Co, 1907. 1st ed. VG (bkpl, sm lib blindstamp, spine dknd). *Mcgowan*. $250/£161

MOORE, F.F. The Secret of the Court. Hutchinson, 1895. 1st ed. Pict cl. Emb owner stamp base tp; lt #s spine base, else VG +. *Aronovitz*. $125/£81

MOORE, FRANCIS ROW. Wapello Chief. Cedar Rapids: Torch Press, (1938). 1st ed. Signed. VG. *Graf*. $25/£16

MOORE, FRANK. Women of the War; Their Heroism and Self-Sacrifice. Hartford, 1867. 1st ed. 596pp. Good. *Fye*. $100/£65

MOORE, G.E. Principia Ethica. Cambridge: Cambridge Univ Press, 1903. 1st ed. Partially unopened. VG (lt foxing eps; sm lt stain inner bottom edge). *Lame Duck*. $650/£419

MOORE, GEORGE. Aphrodite in Aulis. London/NY: Heinemann/Fountain Press, (1930). 1st ed. One of 1825, uncut, unopened, signed. Fine in pub's slipcase (worn). *Second Life*. $45/£29

MOORE, GEORGE. Avowals. London: Privately ptd, 1919. #914/1000, signed. VG in dj (spine browned; sl damage bottom rear panel). *Williams*. $70/£45

MOORE, GEORGE. The Coming of Gabrielle. NY: Boni & Liveright, 1921. 1st Amer ed. One of 895 numbered. Fine in dj. *Hermitage*. $35/£23

MOORE, GEORGE. The Coming of Gabrielle. NY: Boni & Liveright, 1921. 1st US ed, ltd ed #79/895. VG +. *Williams*. $23/£15

MOORE, GEORGE. A Communication to My Friends. Nonesuch, 1933. #27/1000. Label; sm stain spine; sl rubbed, o/w Fine. *Poetry*. $23/£15

MOORE, GEORGE. Conversations in Ebury Street. Heinemann, 1924. #754/1030, signed. VG in dj (sl edgeworn). *Williams*. $47/£30

MOORE, GEORGE. Diagnosis and Localization of Brain Tumors. Springfield, 1953. 1st ed. Good in dj. *Fye*. $40/£26

MOORE, GEORGE. Esther Waters, a Novel. London: Walter Scott, 1894. 1st ed, primary binding. Teg. Orig dk grn cl, gilt. Fine. *Macdonnell*. $100/£65

MOORE, GEORGE. Esther Waters. London: Walter Scott, 1894. 1st ed. Inscribed. Gilt. Teg. Extrems lt rubbed. Slipcase. *Sadlon*. $275/£177

MOORE, GEORGE. Evelyn Innes. London: T. Fisher Unwin, 1898. 1st ed (this copy w/o ads at end). Gilt-stamped cl. Teg. Extrems sl rubbed, sm abrasions to lower cvr. *Sadlon*. $100/£65

MOORE, GEORGE. Heloise and Abelard. London: Privately ptd, 1921. #572/1500, signed. 2 vols. VG + in dj's (sl spine browned). *Williams*. $74/£48

MOORE, GEORGE. In Single Strictness. Heinemann, 1922. #956/1030, signed. VG in dj. *Williams*. $54/£35

MOORE, GEORGE. Letters to Lady Cunard 1895-1933. London: Hart-Davis, 1957. 1st ed. Sl browned, else VG in VG dj (sl soiled, spotted). *Virgo*. $39/£25

MOORE, GEORGE. Letters...to Ed. Dujardin 1886-1922. NY: Crosby Gaige, 1929. 1st ed. One of 668 signed. Nice. *Second Life*. $45/£29

MOORE, GEORGE. Letters...to Ed. Dujardin 1886-1922. John Eglinton (trans). NY, 1929. Ltd to 668 numbered (300 for Amer), signed. Linen-backed bds (sl dusty; fr cvr mkd). *Waterfield*. $39/£25

MOORE, GEORGE. The Making of an Immortal. NY: Bowling Green Press, 1927. 1st ed. Ltd to 1240. Signed. Unopened. NF. *Sadlon*. $45/£29

MOORE, GEORGE. The Making of an Immortal. NY/London: Bowling Green Press/Faber & Gwyer, 1927. 1st ed. One of 1240 signed. VG (label chipped). *Juvelis*. $40/£26

MOORE, GEORGE. Memoirs of My Dead Life. London: Heinemann, 1906. 1st ed. Blue cl stamped in gilt, blind. Spine crown sl worn, else Fine. *Reese*. $135/£87

MOORE, GEORGE. The Mummer's Wife. London: Vitzetelly, 1885. 1st ed, 1st issue, w/cat dated Sept 1884. 438pp + 2pp ads + 20pp pub's cat. Sm pg of orig ms in envelope tipped in. 3/4 leather (worn at upper fr joint). Teg. *Schoyer*. $125/£81

MOORE, GEORGE. The Pastoral Loves of Daphnis and Chloe. London: Heinemann, 1924. 1st ed. One of 1280 signed. Uncut. *Second Life*. $45/£29

MOORE, GEORGE. Peronnik the Fool. Harrap, 1933. #82/525 signed by author and Stephen Gooden (illus). NF in full vellum slipcase (sl browned). *Williams*. $132/£85

MOORE, GEORGE. Sister Teresa. London: Unwin, 1901. 1st ed. Port; teg. Gilt cl. Hinges cracked, else Good. *Reese*. $20/£13

MOORE, GEORGE. A Story Teller's Holiday. NY: Privately ptd, 1918. 1st Amer ed. Ltd to 1250. Extrems sl rubbed. *Sadlon*. $30/£19

MOORE, GEORGE. Ulick and Soracha. London: Nonesuch, 1926. 1st ed. #54/1250 signed. Copper engr. Cream canvas (lt dust-soiled). Good. *Cox*. $39/£25

MOORE, GUY W. The Case of Mrs. Surratt Her Contro-
versial Trial and Execution for Conspiracy in the Lincoln Assassination. Norman: Univ of OK Press, (1954).
1st ed. Orig cl. Fine in NF dj. Signed by Bell I. Wiley.
Mcgowan. $45/£29

MOORE, HAROLD E., JR. The Major Groups of Palms
and Their Distribution. Ithaca, 1973. VG in photo
wrappers (soiled). *Brooks.* $27/£17

MOORE, HENRY CHARLES. Omnibuses and Cabs. London, 1902. (Spine sl faded, soiled.) *Edwards.* $132/£85

MOORE, HENRY. Heads, Figures, and Ideas. Lon-
don/NY, 1958. Auto-litho frontis (sl torn lower corner).
(Upper hinge cracked, sl shaken; lib label.) Cl-backed
pict bds (edges sl rubbed, tape mk). *Edwards.*
$155/£100

MOORE, IAN. Grass and Grasslands. London, 1966. 1st
ed. Color frontis, 28 b/w plts. Dj. *Edwards.* $116/£75

MOORE, J.P. A Short Account of Gloucester Cathedral.
Gloucester, 1877. 8pp text (browned, sl spotted; fore-
edge lt water-stained), 24 plts (some spotted). Orig cl
(ex-libris; upper hinge tender, joint split; worn). *Edwards.* $43/£28

MOORE, JAMES. Kilpatrick and Our Cavalry. NY: Wid-
dleton, 1865. 1st ed. Inscribed presentation from Mrs.
Julia E. Kilpatrick fr flyleaf. 245,(4)pp. Dec cl (faded).
Howes M 774. *Ginsberg.* $100/£65

MOORE, JOHN HAMILTON. The New Practical Navigator. London: B. Law, 1794. 10th ed. viii,309,(1),(202
tables, 6 ads)pp; 9 plts. (Early sig, bkpl.) Contemp calf
(joints cracked). *Lefkowicz.* $325/£210

MOORE, JOHN HAMILTON. The New Practical Navigator.... London: B. Law etc, 1795. 11th ed.
viii,309,(1),(202 tables, 6 ads)pp; 9 plts. Contemp calf
(rubbed; inscrip, bkpl). *Lefkowicz.* $400/£258

MOORE, JOHN TROTWOOD. The Bishop of Cotton
Town. Phila: John C. Winston, 1906. 1st ed. Frontis.
VG (spine ends lt faded; rear hinge starting) in dj
(chipped). *Cahan.* $65/£42

MOORE, JOHN. Medical Sketches. Providence, 1794.
1st Amer ed. 271pp. Recent 1/4 leather; marbled bds;
new eps. Good. *Fye.* $300/£194

MOORE, JOSEPH. Penicillin in Syphilis. Springfield,
1946. 1st ed. Good. *Fye.* $100/£65

MOORE, MARIANNE. The Fables of La Fontaine. NY:
Viking, 1954. 1st ed. NF in dj (torn). *Hermitage.*
$35/£23

MOORE, MARIANNE. Like a Bulwark. NY: Viking,
1956. 1st ed. Dec bds. NF in dj. *Reese.* $50/£32

MOORE, MARIANNE. Like a Bulwark. London: Faber,
1957. 1st ed. VG in dj. *Rees.* $23/£15

MOORE, MARIANNE. O To Be a Dragon. NY: Viking,
1959. 1st ed. One of 5000 ptd. Fine in dj (sl wear). *Antic Hay.* $50/£32

MOORE, MARIANNE. Predilections. NY: Viking, 1955.
1st ed. VG in dj (price-clipped; chipped). *Hermitage.*
$25/£16

MOORE, MARIANNE. Predilections. NY: Viking, 1955.
1st ed. Fine (ink name) in dj (sl wear; price-clipped).
Antic Hay. $60/£39

MOORE, MARIANNE. Selected Poems. NY, 1935. 1st
ed. VG in dj (edges lt chipped). *Argosy.* $100/£65

MOORE, MARIANNE. Tell Me, Tell Me. NY: Viking,
(1966). 1st ed. Fine in VG dj (nick, corner worn).
Reese. $30/£19

MOORE, MARIANNE. What Are Years. NY, 1941. 1st
ed. VG + in VG dj (sl nicked, edgeworn). *Fuller &
Saunders.* $50/£32

MOORE, McCORNACK and McCREADY. The Story of
Eugene. NY: Stratford House, 1949. 1st ed. VG. *Oregon.* $60/£39

MOORE, MERRILL. A Doctor's Book of Hours, Including Some Dimensions of the Emotions. Springfield:
Charles C. Thomas, (1955). 1st ed. Gilt cl. Endsheet
gutters tanned, o/w NF in dj (spine, edges sunned).
Reese. $65/£42

MOORE, MERRILL. A Doctor's Book of Hours, Including Some Dimensions of the Emotions. Springfield, IL,
1955. 1st ed. Good. *Fye.* $50/£32

MOORE, MRS. BLOOMFIELD. Keely and His Discoveries. London, 1893. xxviii,372pp (reps lt spotted). Partially unopened. *Edwards.* $70/£45

MOORE, N. HUDSON. Old Glass. European and American. NY: Tudor, 1935. Frontis. Gilt pict blue cl. VG.
Connolly. $27/£17

MOORE, NICHOLAS. Henry Miller. London: Opus
Press, 1943. 1st ed. Deep pink wrappers. Sm mk tail
edge, o/w Fine. *Temple.* $54/£35

MOORE, PATRICK and HEATHER COUPER. Halley's
Comet Pop-Up Book. NY: Crown, 1985. 21x30 cm. 4
dbl-pg pop-ups, pull-tabs, lift flaps. Paul Doherty (illus). Glazed pict bds. Base of spine sl rubbed, o/w VG.
Book Finders. $35/£23

MOORE, PATRICK. The Space Shuttle Action Book. London: Aurum, 1983. 20x29 cm. 6 dbl-pg pop-ups, pull-
tabs. Tom Stimpson (illus). Glazed pict bds. VG. *Book
Finders.* $50/£32

MOORE, T. STURGE. Aphrodite Against Artemis. A Tragedy. London: At the Sign of the Unicorn, 1901. 1st ed.
Gilt grn cl (sl smudged), ribbon marker. VG. *Reese.*
$75/£48

MOORE, T. STURGE. Charles Ricketts. Cassell, 1933.
1st Eng ed. Color frontis. Blue cl. Damp-mks lower
cvrs; fore-edge sl foxed, o/w Fine in dj. *Dalian.*
$70/£45

MOORE, T.W. Treatise and Hand-Book of Orange Culture in Florida.... NY/Jacksonville, 1886. 4th ed.
(2),184,(6)pp. (2pp browned by newspaper clipping.)
Orange cl (edgewear, scuffing). *Sutton.* $50/£32

MOORE, TEX. Hell Raising for Pastime. (Riverside: Tex
Moore, 1935). (Bkpl; sticker.) Ptd wrappers. *Dawson.*
$50/£32

MOORE, THOMAS. By Bendemeer's Stream. Portland,
ME: Thomas Bird Mosher, 1917. 1st thus. One of 450.
Internally Fine (lacks backstrip; lower bd virtually de-
tached). *Poetry.* $16/£10

MOORE, THOMAS. The Epicurean, A Tale. London:
John Macrone, 1839. 1st illus ed. xi,238,67pp, 4 hand-
colored plts + extra engr tp by J.M.W. Turner. Full
blue morocco, gilt, leather spine labels. Aeg. Fine.
Schoyer. $200/£129

MOORE, W.U. Glimpses of the Next State. Watts, 1911.
1st ed. VG + . *Aronovitz.* $60/£39

MOORE, WARD. Greener Than You Think. Sloane,
1947. 1st ed. Fine in dj. *Madle.* $40/£26

MOORE, WILLIAM. The Constitutional Requirements
for Tropical Climates and Observations on the Sequel
of Disease Contracted in India. London, 1890. 1st ed.
126pp. Good. *Fye.* $100/£65

MOORE-WILLSON, MINNIE. The Seminoles of Florida. NY: Moffat, Yard, 1910. 2nd ed. Red cl, mtd cvr photo. VG (pencil sig, ink date; spine faded). *Chapel Hill.* $125/£81

MOOREHEAD, ALAN. The Fatal Impact. London, 1966. 1st ed. Frontis port, 5 maps. Dj (creased). *Edwards.* $23/£15

MOOREHEAD, ALAN. The Traitors. Hamish Hamilton, 1952. 1st Eng ed. Red cl. NF in dj (sl dusty). *Dalian.* $39/£25

MOOREHEAD, ALAN. The White Nile. London: Hamish Hilton, 1960. 1st ed. 24 plts; 9 maps. VG in dj. *Worldwide.* $16/£10

MOOREHEAD, ALAN. The White Nile. London, 1960. 1st ed. 2 maps (incl ep). Dj (sl torn). *Edwards.* $23/£15

MOORHEAD, MAX L. The Apache Frontier. Norman, 1968. 1st ed. NF (sig, date) in dj (lt edgeworn). *Baade.* $40/£26

MOORHEAD, MAX L. The Presidio. Norman: Univ of OK, 1975. 1st ed. NF in NF dj. *Parker.* $37/£24

MOORHEAD, MAX. The Presidio—Bastion of the Spanish Borderlands. Norman: Univ of OK Press, (1975). 1st ed. 21 plts. Fine in Fine dj. *Oregon.* $25/£16

MOORHOUSE, GEOFFREY. The Fearful Void. London, 1974. 1st ed. 2 maps. Dj (sl chipped). *Edwards.* $25/£16

MOORMAN, J.J. Mineral Springs of North America; How to Reach, and How to Use Them. Phila: Lippincott, 1873. 1st ed. 294pp + 22pp ads, 2 fldg maps. Rubbed, lt foxing eps, sm hole rep, edges flecked, else VG. *Cahan.* $60/£39

MOORMAN, JOHN R.H. Church Life in England in the Thirteenth Century. CUP, 1945. 9 plts, sketch map. (Spine lt faded.) *Edwards.* $31/£20

MOORMAN, MADISON B. The Journal of Madison Berryman Moorman 1850-1851. SF: CA Hist Soc, 1948. 1st ed. Frontis, fldg map. Uncut, unopened. Spine faded, o/w VG. *Oregon.* $40/£26

MOOSO, JOSIAH. The Life and Travels of Josiah Mooso. Winfield, KS: Telegram Print., 1888. 1st ed. 400pp; port. Good in orig cl (new eps; lt worn). Howes M 784. *Lien.* $500/£323

MORA, JO. Trail Dust and Saddle Leather. NY: Scribner's, 1946. 1st ed. VG in pict cl. *Lien.* $50/£32

MORAGA, GABRIEL. Diary of Ensign Gabriel Moraga's Expedition...in the Sacramento Valley 1808. Donald C. Cutter (ed, trans). (L.A.): Glen Dawson, 1957. Ltd to 300. Fldg map. Nice (sm spots fr cvr). *Shasky.* $40/£26

MORAN, BENJAMIN. The Journal of Benjamin Moran 1857-1865. Volume 1. Sarah Agnes Wallace & Frances Elma Gillespie (eds). Chicago: Univ of Chicago, 1948. 1st ed. Frontis port. Fine in Good dj (sl chipped). *Connolly.* $50/£32

MORAN, JAMES. The Fortsas Hoax. London: Arborfield, (1961). 1st ed. Fine. *Bookpress.* $65/£42

MORAN, JAMES. Printing Presses, History and Development from the Fifteenth Century to Modern Times. London: Faber & Faber, (1973). 1st ed. 64 plts. Fine in dj. *Oak Knoll.* $125/£81

MORAND, PAUL. Black Magic. Hamish Miles (trans). London: Heinemann, (1929). Marbled-styled bds, gold labels. (Spine browned; chipped; bkpl.) *Weber.* $30/£19

MORANTE, ELSA. Arturo's Island. Collins, 1959. 1st Eng ed. Blue cl. VG in dj (torn). *Dalian.* $23/£15

MORASSI, ANTONIO. Art Treasures of the Medici. Abbey Library, 1969. 55 tipped-in color plts. Dj (sl torn). *Edwards.* $39/£25

MORASSI, ANTONIO. G.B. Tiepolo, His Life and Work. London: Phaidon, 1955. 9 color plts, 93 monochrome plts. VF in dj. *Europa.* $70/£45

MORASSI, ANTONIO. G.B. Tiepolo. Phaidon, 1955. Color frontis, 8 color plts tipped in; 93 b/w plts. Dj (lt soiled; spine lt faded, torn). *Edwards.* $62/£40

MORAVIA, ALBERTO. Two Women. Angus Davidson (trans). London: Secker & Warburg, 1958. 1st ed in English. Blue bds, silver. Fine in dj (frayed, torn; verso strengthened). *Temple.* $16/£10

MORE, HANNAH. Sir Eldred of the Bower, and the Bleeding Rock. London: T. Cadell, 1776. 1st ed. (ii),49,(1, ad)pp. Later blue wrappers. *Hollett.* $147/£95

MORE, R.J. Under the Balkans.... H.S. King, 1877. *Petersfield.* $28/£18

MORE, THOMAS. Utopia. Gilbert Burnet (trans). Glasgow: Ptd by Robert Foulis, 1743. Frontis port, xxiii,139,(1 ad)pp. Orig mottled calf (worn, rubbed), leather label. Contents VG. *Hartfield.* $295/£190

MORE, THOMAS. Utopia. Ralph Robynson (trans). NY: LEC, 1934. Teg, rest untrimmed. Vellum spine, brn paste-paper bds, gilt title. Pub's slipcase. *Book Block.* $165/£106

MOREAU-VAUTHIER, C. The Technique of Painting. London: Heinemann, 1912. 24 plts. Sound. *Ars Artis.* $28/£18

MORECAMP, ARTHUR. (Pseud of Thomas Pilgrim.) Live Boys; Or, Charley and Nasho in Texas. Boston/NY, (1878). Frontis, 308pp + 10pp ads; 5 plts. Mustard cl, black/gilt stamping. Nice (soil; presentation). Howes M 790. *Bohling.* $350/£226

MOREL, E.D. Red Rubber—The Story of the Rubber Slave Trade on the Congo. Nassau Print, 1906. VG-. *Fine Books.* $55/£35

MORELAND, ARTHUR. Dickens Landmarks in London. Cassell, 1931. 1st ed. (Lt spotting; spine sl faded.) *Edwards.* $47/£30

MORELY, JOHN. The Life of Richard Cobden. London, 1881. 2 vols. Frontis port, xvi,468; xi,485pp. Marbled eps; teg. 1/2 morocco, gilt. *Edwards.* $78/£50

MORETON, ANDREW. (Pseud of Daniel Defoe.) The Secrets of the Invisible World Disclos'd. London: Clarke et al, 1738. 3rd ed. Frontis engrs, xii,395pp (tp is a cancel), 5 plts. 1/2 calf, marbled bds (bumped, edgewear), red leather spine title. Good. *Hartfield.* $395/£255

MORETON, C.O. Old Carnations and Pinks. London, 1955. 8 color plts; illus eps. Pict cl-backed bds. Good in dj (torn, repaired). *Henly.* $93/£60

MORGAN, ANN LEE. Arthur Dove. Life and Work. Newark, (1984). VG in stiff pict wrappers. *Argosy.* $175/£113

MORGAN, ANNA. My Chicago. Chicago: Ralph Fletcher Seymour, (1918). 1st ed. 16 ports. Pict cl. VG. *Petrilla.* $35/£23

MORGAN, BERRY. Pursuit. London: Heinemann, (1967). 1st Eng ed, 1st bk. Fine in dj. *Turlington.* $75/£48

MORGAN, BERRY. Pursuit. Boston: Houghton Mifflin, 1966. 1st ed, 1st bk. VG in dj (lt worn). *Turlington.* $50/£32

MORGAN, CHARLES. Portrait in a Mirror. London: Macmillan, 1929. 1st ed. Gilt-titled grn cl. Pg edges sl foxed, else Very Nice in dj. *Cady.* $15/£10

MORGAN, CHARLES. Portrait in a Mirror. Macmillan, 1929. 1st Eng ed. Grn cl (fore-edge sl foxed). Fine in dj (sl tanned, nicked). *Dalian.* $39/£25

MORGAN, CHARLES. Sparkenbroke. London: Macmillan, 1936. 1st ed. Gilt-titled grn cl. NF in dj. *Cady.* $20/£13

MORGAN, CHARLES. The Voyage. London: Macmillan, 1940. 1st ed. Gilt-titled grn cl. Fine in dj (sl worn). *Cady.* $15/£10

MORGAN, DALE (ed). Overland in 1846. Georgetown, CA: Talisman Press, 1963. One of 1000. 2 vols. Errata. Fldg map in pocket vol 1; fldg map vol 2. Fine set (sl lib mks). Orig djs. *Schoyer.* $175/£113

MORGAN, DALE (ed). Santa Fe and the Far West. Dawson, 1949. One of 200. Fine. *Oregon.* $75/£48

MORGAN, DALE (ed). The West of William R. Ashley. Denver: Old West Pub Co, 1964. 1st trade ed. 15 plts, 2 facs, 3 maps (1 fldg). Pict cl. VG. *Schoyer.* $250/£161

MORGAN, DALE and CARL I. WHEAT. Jedediah Smith and His Maps of the American West. SF: CA Hist Soc, 1954. 1st ed. Ltd to 530. 4 maps bound in (3 fldg), 3 maps in rear pocket. Red cl (spine sl faded; rear cvr sl rubbed). NF. *Harrington.* $550/£355

MORGAN, DALE and ELEANOR TOWLES HARRIS (eds). The Rocky Mountain Journals of William Marshall Anderson: The West in 1834. (By William Marshall Anderson). San Marino: Huntington Lib, 1967. 1st ed. One of 1500. Frontis port. Red cl. Fine in Fine dj. *Harrington.* $125/£81

MORGAN, DALE. The Great Salt Lake. Indianapolis: Bobbs Merrill, (1947). 1st ed. 6 maps. VG in Good+ dj. *Oregon.* $45/£29

MORGAN, DALE. The Humbolt Highroad of the West. NY: Farrar & Rinehart, (1943). 1st ed. Fine in Fine dj. *Book Market.* $85/£55

MORGAN, DALE. Jedediah Smith and the Opening of the West. Bobbs-Merrill, (1953). 1st ed. Signed, dated. Ep maps. VG (fep is about 1/8th-inch short) in VG dj. *Oregon.* $135/£87

MORGAN, DALE. Jedediah Smith and the Opening of the West. Indianapolis, 1953. 1st ed. Inscribed, dated. NF (ink sig, date, info) in dj. *Baade.* $100/£65

MORGAN, DALE. Jedidiah Smith and the Opening of the West. Indianapolis: Bobbs-Merrill, 1953. 1st ed. Sm dent, o/w VG in dj. *Schoyer.* $125/£81

MORGAN, GEORGE H. Annals, Comprising Memoirs, Incidents, and Statistics of Harrisburg.... Harrisburg: Brooks, 1858. 1st ed. (2),400,(2)pp. (Joints expertly mended.) Howes M 796. *Ginsberg.* $125/£81

MORGAN, JAMES MORRIS. Recollections of a Rebel Reefer. Boston/NY: Houghton Mifflin, 1917. 1st Amer trade ptg. 17 plts. (Fore-edges spotted.) Pict cl (sl rubbed). Howes M 798. *Schoyer.* $100/£65

MORGAN, JOHN HILL. Gilbert Stuart and His Pupils. NY: NY Hist Soc, 1939. 13 plts. Gilt dec cl; teg. VG. *Argosy.* $40/£26

MORGAN, JONNIE R. The History of Wichita Falls (TX). 1931. 1st ed. Ink name, else VG. *Perier.* $75/£48

MORGAN, LADY. Lady Morgan's Memoirs. London: Allen, 1862. 1st ed. 2 vols. Frontis engrs, viii,532; 552pp. Full polished calf, raised bands, gilt, blind fillets, red leather labels. Handsome set (sl wear; bkpl). *Hartfield.* $325/£210

MORGAN, LEWIS H. The American Beaver and His Works. Phila: Lippincott, 1868. 330pp, 24 plts (one fldg). (Ex-lib, bkpl, #; rubbed, bumped; joints splitting; spine chipped). Good. *Blue Mountain.* $150/£97

MORGAN, LEWIS H. The Indian Journals 1859-62. Univ MI, (1959). 1st ed. 16 color plts. VG in VG dj. *Oregon.* $65/£42

MORGAN, LEWIS H. The Indian Journals 1859-62. Ann Arbor, 1959. 1st ed. Dec cl (soiled). Good+ (insect holes fep, 1st pp). *Baade.* $27/£17

MORGAN, LEWIS H. League of the Ho-De-No-Sau or Iroquois. Herbert M. Lloyd (ed). NY: Dodd, Mead, 1922. New ed. 2 vols in 1. Good. *Lien.* $100/£65

MORGAN, LEWIS H. League of the Hode-no-sau-nee, or, Iroquois. Rochester: Sage & Brother, 1851. 1st ed. 8vo. 477pp; fldg map (tear to margin); fldg table; 21 plts (1 fldg). Cl spotted. Howes M 804. *Argosy.* $450/£290

MORGAN, MURRAY. Puget's Sound. Univ WA, (1979). 1st ed. VF in VF dj. *Oregon.* $30/£19

MORGAN, ROBERT. Zirconia Poems. (Northwood Narrows: Lillabulero, 1969). 1st ed, one of 1000 in wraps. Fine. *Turlington.* $30/£19

MORGAN, SPEER. Belle Starr. Boston/Toronto: Little Brown, (1979). 1st ed. Rev laid in. Fine in Fine dj. *Glenn.* $20/£13

MORGAN, TED. Literary Outlaw. London: Bodley Head, 1991. 1st UK ed. NF- in dj. *Sclanders.* $20/£13

MORGAN, THOMAS HUNT. The Development of the Frog's Egg. NY, 1897. 1st ed. 192pp. Good. *Fye.* $200/£129

MORGAN, THOMAS HUNT. Experimental Zoology. NY, 1917. 1st ed, rptd. Good. *Fye.* $75/£48

MORGAN, WILLIAM HENRY. Personal Reminiscences of the War of 1861-5. Lynchburg, VA: J.P. Bell, 1911. 1st ed. NF. *Mcgowan.* $165/£106

MORGAN, WILLIAM HENRY. Personal Reminiscences of the War of 1861-5. Lynchburg, VA: J.P. Bell, 1911. 1st ed. Frontis port; unopened. Orig gray cl. Fine in ptd dj (lt soiled). *Chapel Hill.* $300/£194

MORIARTY, GERALD P. (trans). The Paris Law Courts, Sketches of Men and Manners. NY: Scribner's, 1894. (Cl rubbed, sl worn.) Sound. *Boswell.* $75/£48

MORIN, LOUIS. French Illustrators. NY: Scribner's, 1893. 1st ed. Ltd to 1030. 68pp, in 5 parts; 15 plts w/ptd guards. VG set laid in portfolio. *Cahan.* $325/£210

MORISON, A. The Sensory and Motor Disorders of the Heart. London, 1914. Lt foxing; new eps; sl nick spine, o/w VG. *Whitehart.* $39/£25

MORISON, S. The History of The Times. The Times, 1935-1952. 4 vols in 5. 140 plts & facs. VG set. *Moss.* $147/£95

MORISON, SAMUEL ELIOT. Admiral of the Ocean Sea. Boston: Little, Brown, 1942. 1st ed. 2 vols. 58 plts; fldg map; 4 dbl-pg charts. Red cl. Good in djs (sl chipped, soiled). *Karmiole.* $75/£48

MORISON, SAMUEL ELIOT. Journals and Other Documents on the Life and Voyages of Christopher Columbus. NY: LEC, 1963. One of 1500 numbered, signed by Lima de Freitas (illus). Fine in pub's slipcase (lt rubbed). *Hermitage.* $150/£97

MORISON, SAMUEL ELIOT. The Maritime History of Massachusetts 1783-1860. London, (1923). 1st British ed. VG in dj (sl worn; reinforcements). *Hayman.* $25/£16

MORISON, SAMUEL ELIOT. Old Bruin. Commodore Matthew C. Perry 1794-1858. Boston: Little, Brown/Atlantic Monthly, 1967. 1st ed. Frontis port. Fine in Good dj. *Connolly.* $45/£29

MORISON, SAMUEL ELIOT. The Story of Mount Desert Island, Maine. Boston: Little, Brown, 1960. 1st ed. 8 plts. NF in Good dj. *Connolly.* $25/£16

MORISON, STANLEY and KENNETH DAY. The Typographic Book 1450-1935. London: Benn, 1963. 350 plts. Fine in dj (closed tear), slipcase (scuffed). *Veatchs.* $115/£74

MORISON, STANLEY. The Art of the Printer.... London: Ernest Benn, 1925. 1st ed. 245 half-tone plts. Good (backstrip faded). *Cox.* $54/£35

MORISON, STANLEY. The English Newspaper. Cambridge, 1932. 1st ed. 6 collotype plts (1 fldg). Terra cotta cl (lt soiled, sl frayed; lib bkpl, #; inner hinges cracked). *Cox.* $116/£75

MORISON, STANLEY. First Principles of Typography. NY: Macmillan, 1936. 1st ed. Beige cl stamped in maroon. Good in dj. *Karmiole.* $50/£32

MORISON, STANLEY. Four Centuries of Fine Printing. NY: Farrar, Straus & Cudahy, (1957). 3rd (rev 8vo) ed. Bkpl, o/w VG in dj (lt worn). *Hermitage.* $45/£29

MORISON, STANLEY. Modern Fine Printing. London, 1925. One of 650 numbered, in English, ptd at CUP. 328 facs plts. 2-tone cl (corner worn). Dj (torn). *Argosy.* $300/£194

MORISON, STANLEY. On the Type Faces.... Medici Soc/Fleuron, 1923. One of 750. Marbled bds, linen back (eps, tp lt foxed). *Petersfield.* $124/£80

MORISOT, BERTHE. The Correspondence of...with Her Family and Her Friends.... Denis Rouart (ed). Betty W. Hubbard (trans). London, 1957. 1st ed. VG in slipcase. *Argosy.* $200/£129

MORITZ, L.A. Grain-Mills and Flour in Classical Antiquity. Oxford: Clarendon, 1958. 16 plts, 17 tables. Good in dj (tattered). *Archaeologia.* $125/£81

MORLEY, CHRISTOPHER. Another Letter to Lord Chesterfield. NY: Ben Abramson, Argus Bookshop, 1945. 1st ed. Brn paper bds. Fine in glassine wrapper. *Cady.* $25/£16

MORLEY, CHRISTOPHER. The Haunted Bookshop. Chapman & Hall, 1920. 1st Eng ed. Brn cl. Sl spotted; prelims sl foxed; name, o/w VG. *Dalian.* $54/£35

MORLEY, CHRISTOPHER. The Man Who Made Friends with Himself. GC: Doubleday, 1949. 1st ed. NF in NF dj. *Revere.* $35/£23

MORLEY, CHRISTOPHER. Mandarin in Manhattan. GC: Doubleday, Doran, 1933. 1st ed. NF (sm rubbed spot rep; faded strip spine bottom) in dj (sl wear; short tears). *Antic Hay.* $25/£16

MORLEY, CHRISTOPHER. The Middle Kingdom: Poems 1929-1944. (NY): Harcourt, Brace, 1944. 1st ed. VG in dj (sl wear; browning; price-clipped). *Antic Hay.* $25/£16

MORLEY, CHRISTOPHER. Parnassus on Wheels. Heinemann, 1921. 1st Eng ed. Blindstamped as 'presentation copy.' 1/4 cl, dec bds (soiled). *Moss.* $11/£7

MORLEY, CHRISTOPHER. Poems. GC: Doubleday, Doran, 1929. 1st ed. Fine in dj (browning). *Antic Hay.* $35/£23

MORLEY, CHRISTOPHER. Toulemonade. GC: Doubleday, Doran, 1928. 1st ed, one of 1250. Black cl, gilt. Very Nice. *Cady.* $20/£13

MORLEY, CHRISTOPHER. Where the Blue Begins. London/NY: Heinemann/Doubleday, Page, (1925). 1st Eng ed. #157/175 numbered, signed by Arthur Rackham (illus). 4to. 4 color plts. 1/2 gilt-stamped black buckram, white bds; teg; uncut. VG. *Houle.* $850/£548

MORLEY, CHRISTOPHER. Where the Blue Begins. NY, 1922. 1st ed. *Bond.* $35/£23

MORLEY, F.V. and J.S. HODGSON. Whaling North and South. NY: Century Co, (1926). 1st ed. VG. *Blue Dragon.* $25/£16

MORLEY, JOHN DAVID. Pictures from the Water Trade. London, 1985. 1st ed. Dj. *Edwards.* $23/£15

MORLEY, JOHN. An Essay on the Nature and Cure of Schrophulous Disorders, Commonly Called the Kings Evil.... London, 1774. 12th ed. 80pp; hand colored plt. Good in wrappers. *Fye.* $75/£48

MORNEWECK, EVELYN FOSTER. Chronicles of Stephen Foster's Family.... Pittsburgh, 1944. Ltd to 3000. 2 vols. (Ex-lib w/mks; lt wear.) *Hayman.* $20/£13

Morning Walk, with Other Stories for Girls and Boys. Providence: Geo. P. Daniels, 1843. 12mo. Full-pg frontis, 24pp + 1pg ad lower wrapper. Yellow pict wrappers (repaired cut; sl spotting). Good (ink inscrip, sm spot few pp). *Hobbyhorse.* $95/£61

MORRELL, DAVID. First Blood. NY: Evans, 1972. 1st ed, 1st bk. NF in VG dj (sl edge-chipping). *Pettler.* $80/£52

MORRELL, DAVID. Last Reveille. NY: Evans, 1977. 1st ed. Fine in dj. *Else Fine.* $50/£32

MORRELL, DAVID. Testament. Evans, 1975. 1st ed. Fine in dj (sl rubbed). *Madle.* $50/£32

MORRELL, DAVID. Testament. NY: Evans, 1975. 1st ed. Fine in dj (sl wear corners). *Else Fine.* $75/£48

MORRELL, J.B. Woodwork in York. London: Batsford, 1949. (Ex-lib w/ink stamps; #; spine faded; sm chip, splitting upper joint.) *Edwards.* $31/£20

MORRELL, OTTOLINE. Dear Lady Ginger. Helen Shaw (ed). Century, 1984. 1st Eng ed. White paper bds. VF in dj. *Dalian.* $54/£35

MORRELL, Z.N. Flowers and Fruits in the Wilderness. St. Louis: Commercial, 1882. 3rd ed, revised. 412pp. Orig grn cl (new eps). Howes M 819. *Lambeth.* $85/£55

MORRIS, ALICE TALWIN. The Elephant's Apology. London: Blackie & Son, n.d. Alice B. Woodward (illus). 8vo. 152pp. Aeg. Red cl, gilt. Corners sl rubbed, o/w NF. *Drusilla's.* $95/£61

MORRIS, CASPER. An Essay on the Pathology and Therapeutics of Scarlet Fever. Phila, 1858. 192pp. Good. *Fye.* $100/£65

MORRIS, CASPER. Lectures on Scarlet Fever. Phila, 1851. 1st ed. 104pp. (Ex-lib.) *Fye.* $75/£48

MORRIS, CHARLES. The Autobiography of Commodore Charles Morris.... Boston/Annapolis, 1880. 1st ed. 111pp, heliotype port. Orig ptd wrappers. Howes M 822. *Ginsberg.* $150/£97

MORRIS, D. The Colony of British Honduras.... London: Edward Stanford, 1883. 1st ed. xiii,(i)blank,152,half title (ink inscrip), fldg colored map. Grn cl, gilt (hinges, joints split; spine rubbed, but firm). *Morrell.* $93/£60

MORRIS, DESMOND. The Art of Ancient Cyprus, with a Check-List.... Oxford: Phaidon, (1985). Good in dj. *Archaeologia.* $95/£61

MORRIS, E.P. The Fore-and-Aft Rig America. New Haven, 1927. 1st ed. Ltd to 1000. Good. *Hayman.* $75/£48

MORRIS, ERNEST. Tintinnabula: Small Bells. London: Robert Hale, (1959). 1st ed. Fine in VG+ dj. *Blue Dragon.* $22/£14

MORRIS, F.O. A History of British Birds. London, 1851-57. 1st ed, 1st issue. 6 vols. Roy 8vo. 358 color plts. Contemp 1/2 calf. (Foxing; rubbed.) *Wheldon & Wesley.* $744/£480

MORRIS, F.O. A History of British Butterflies. London, 1865. 2nd ed. 169+29pp; 73 plts (71 hand-colored). 1/2 leather (crudely rebacked in buckram). *Argosy.* $300/£194

MORRIS, F.O. A History of British Butterflies. London: George Bell & Sons, 1870. 5th ed. viii,159,24pp+8pp pub's cat, 74 plts (72 hand-colored). Uncut. Purple cl blocked in blind/gold (backstrip faded, sm hole; sl wear). Good. *Cox.* $171/£110

MORRIS, F.O. A History of British Butterflies. London, 1895. 8th ed, rev & enlgd. viii,234,(1)pp; 79 hand-colored, 2 plain plts. *Wheldon & Wesley.* $109/£70

MORRIS, F.O. A History of British Butterflies. London, 1895. 8th ed. viii,235pp; 79 hand-colored, 2 plain plts. Fine. *Henly.* $132/£85

MORRIS, F.O. A History of British Moths. London, 1896. 5th ed. 4 vols. 132 hand-colored plts. *Wheldon & Wesley.* $194/£125

MORRIS, F.O. A History of British Moths. London, 1896. 5th ed. 4 vols. 132 hand-colored plts. Pict gilt cl. Good. *Henly.* $205/£132

MORRIS, F.O. A History of British Moths. London: John C. Nimmo, 1903. 6th ed. 4 vols. 132 plts. Grn cl, gilt. Very Nice set. *Karmiole.* $375/£242

MORRIS, F.O. Nests and Eggs of British Birds. W.B. Tegetmeier (reviser). London, 1896. 3 vols. 248 color plts. (Marginal inkstain vol 2.) *Wheldon & Wesley.* $93/£60

MORRIS, F.O. Series of Picturesque Views of Seats of the Noblemen and Gentlemen of Great Britain and Ireland. London: William Mackenzie, n.d. (c. 1880). 6 vols, each w/40 chromolitho plts. Aeg. Blank margin several plts Vol 2 w/lt dampstain; fr hinge vol 1 partially cracked, else Fine set. *Cahan.* $425/£274

MORRIS, FRANK and EDWARD A. EAMES. Our Wild Orchids. NY: Scribner's, 1929. 130 full-pg plts (4 color). 2 postcards pasted rep, else Fine. *Quest.* $85/£55

MORRIS, HENRY CURTIS. Desert Gold and Total Prospecting. Washington: By author, 1955. 1st ed. Signed presentation inscription. Fine in VG dj w/'anonymous' poem on fr fly, correction in author's handwriting on rear fly. *Connolly.* $50/£32

MORRIS, JAMES. As I Saw the USA. (NY), (1956). 1st ed, 1st bk. VG+ in VG+ dj (price-clipped, edgeworn). *Fuller & Saunders.* $45/£29

MORRIS, JAMES. The Hashemite Kings. NY: Pantheon, 1959. 1st ed. 16 plts. VG in dj (sl torn). *Worldwide.* $20/£13

MORRIS, JAMES. South African Winter. Faber & Faber, 1958. 1st Eng ed. Red cl. Fine in dj. *Dalian.* $54/£35

MORRIS, JAMES. Sultan in Oman. London: Faber & Faber, 1957. 1st ed. 17 plts (1 color); 2 full-pg maps. VG (pencil mks, notes) in dj. *Worldwide.* $40/£26

MORRIS, JAN. Conundrum. Faber & Faber, 1974. 1st Eng ed. Brn cl. Fine in dj. *Dalian.* $39/£25

MORRIS, JAN. Destinations. OUP, 1980. 1st ed. Fine in Fine dj. *Bishop.* $18/£12

MORRIS, RALPH. The Life and Astonishing Adventures of John Daniel. London: Robert Holden, 1926. One of 750 numbered, this unnumbered. New ed. Blue buckram, gilt. Fine (bkpl; lt sunned spine). *Beasley.* $85/£55

MORRIS, ROBERT (ed). Collections of the Wyoming Historical Society, Vol 1. WY Hist Soc, 1897. 1st ed. Comp copy signed by Morris. 353pp, frontis. Internally Fine (corners, spine label worn; eps cracking at hinges). *Oregon.* $225/£145

MORRIS, ROBERT. Freemasonry in the Holy Land. NY, 1872. Frontis port, 608pp. Gilt/blind emb cl (faded, sm chip). *Edwards.* $194/£125

MORRIS, WILLIAM and EIRIKR MAGNUSSON (trans). Volsunga Saga. H. Halliday Sparling (ed). Walter Scott, 1888. 1st thus. Red cl sl mkd; eps foxed, o/w VG. VG. *Dalian.* $54/£35

MORRIS, WILLIAM and EIRIKR MAGNUSSON. Three Northern Love Stories, and Other Tales. London: Ellis & White, 1875. 1st ed. Blue cl (lt chafed), label (sl rubbed). *Macdonnell.* $75/£48

MORRIS, WILLIAM. An Address Delivered by William Morris...to Students of the Birmingham Municipal School of Art on Feb. 21, 1894. London: Chiswick Press, 1898. 25pp; unopened. Sl soiled, o/w VF. *Europa.* $101/£65

MORRIS, WILLIAM. Art and Its Producers, and the Arts and Crafts of Today: Two Addresses.... London: Chiswick Press, 1901. Fine. *Europa.* $109/£70

MORRIS, WILLIAM. Art and the Beauty of the Earth. A Lecture...on October 13, 1881. London: Chiswick Press, 1898. 31pp. VF. *Europa.* $96/£62

MORRIS, WILLIAM. The Defense of Guenevere and Other Poems. London: John Lane, 1904. 1st ed. 8vo. 24 b/w plts by Jessie King. Teg. Red cl, gilt. Good. *Reisler.* $400/£258

MORRIS, WILLIAM. Early Poems of William Morris. London: Blackie & Son, 1914. 1st ed. 4to. 16 mtd color plts by Florence Harrison. Teg. Lt blue cl, gilt. Fine (lt foxing prelims, fore-edge) in pub's box w/ptd cvr (edgewear, browning). *Reisler.* $575/£371

MORRIS, WILLIAM. The Earthly Paradise. London: F.S. Ellism, 1870. 5th ed. 4 vols. Contemp half calf (sl rubbed), gilt. Flyleaves, half-titles lt spotted, o/w Good. *Hollett.* $116/£75

MORRIS, WILLIAM. Hopes and Fears for Art. Boston: Roberts Bros, 1882. 1st Amer ed. (viii),217pp. Spine sl sunned, chipped; bkpl; minor edgewear; else VG. *Bookpress.* $295/£190

MORRIS, WILLIAM. News from Nowhere. London: Reeves & Turner, 1891. 1st British ed. Red cl (sl rubbed, sm stain). Good (fep torn w/sl loss; few leaves roughly opened). *Ash.* $78/£50

MORRIS, WILLIAM. Some Hints on Pattern-Designing. A Lecture...on December 10, 1881. London: Chiswick Press, 1899. 45pp. VF (from lib of Paul Cooper). *Europa.* $93/£60

MORRIS, WILLIAM. The Wood beyond the World. Lawrence & Bullen, 1895. 1st trade ed. Maroon buckram. Spine, cvrs sl sunned; sl foxing fore-edge, o/w Fine. *Dalian.* $116/£75

MORRIS, WILLIE. The Courting of Marcus Dupree. GC: Doubleday, 1983. 1st ed. NF in dj (lt scuffed; edgetears). *Aka.* $40/£26

MORRIS, WILLIE. Yazoo. Integration in a Deep Southern Town. NY: Harper's Magazine Press, 1975. 1st ed. Fine in Fine dj (sl wear). *Revere.* $25/£16

MORRIS, WRIGHT. Ceremony in Lone Tree. NY: Atheneum, 1960. 1st ed. Fine in dj (lt edgeworn; price-clipped). *Reese.* $45/£29

MORRIS, WRIGHT. God's Country and My People. NY: Harper & Row, (1968). 1st ed. Fine in dj w/$10.00 price on flap. *Godot.* $65/£42

MORRIS, WRIGHT. God's Country and My People. NY: Harper & Row, (1968). 1st ed. 2nd 'issue' priced $10. Pub's rev slip laid in. Fine in dj (lt used). *Reese.* $85/£55

MORRIS, WRIGHT. Here Is Einbaum. L.A.: Black Sparrow, 1973. 1st ed. One of 200 numbered (of 226), signed. Cl, dec bds. Fine. *Reese.* $75/£48

MORRIS, WRIGHT. The Huge Season. NY: Viking, 1954. 1st ed. Pencil name, else Fine in dj (lt used). *Reese.* $30/£19

MORRIS, WRIGHT. The Inhabitants. NY: Scribner's, 1946. 1st ed. NF in VG dj (shelfworn). *Reese.* $100/£65

MORRIS, WRIGHT. The Man Who Was There. NY: Scribner's, 1945. 1st ed. Fine in dj (reinforcement verso; chip). *Reese.* $150/£97

MORRIS, WRIGHT. The Works of Love. NY: Knopf, 1952. 1st ed. Fine in VG dj (closed tear). *Reese.* $40/£26

MORRISON, ARTHUR. Cunning Murrell. NY, 1900. 1st Amer ed. Pict cvrs. Fine (spine sl soiled; 2 edge tears prelims). *Polyanthos.* $45/£29

MORRISON, JOHN H. History of the New York Ship Yards. NY, (1909). 1st ed. Good. *Hayman.* $25/£16

MORRISON, TONI. Beloved. NY: Knopf, 1987. 1st ed. Fine in dj. *Antic Hay.* $50/£32

MORRISON, TONI. Beloved. NY: Knopf, 1987. 1st ed. As New in dj. *Jaffe.* $75/£48

MORRISON, TONI. The Bluest Eye. NY: Holt, Rinehart, & Winston, (1970). 1st ed, 1st bk. Grey bds, blue cl spine. Fine in dj (2 short, clean tears, one 1/2-inch at top fr panel, other 1/4-inch top rear panel; sl browning). *Chapel Hill.* $1,000/£645

MORRISON, TONI. Song of Solomon. NY: Knopf, 1977. 1st ed, rev copy w/inserted promo material & slip laid in. Fine in dj. *Antic Hay.* $150/£97

MORRISON, TONI. Tar Baby. NY: Knopf, 1981. 1st trade ed. Fep sl foxed, else Fine in dj. *Godot.* $35/£23

MORRISON, TONI. Tar Baby. NY: Knopf, 1981. 1st trade ed. Fine in NF dj. *Beasley.* $50/£32

MORRISON, TONI. Tar Baby. NY: Knopf, 1981. 1st trade ed. Signed. Fine in Fine dj. *Chapel Hill.* $150/£97

MORRISON, TONI. Tar Baby. London: C&W, 1981. 1st UK ed. Fine in dj. *Lewton.* $39/£25

MORRISON, VENETIA. The Art of George Stubbs. (London: Quarto Publishing, 1989). 1st ed. Bkpl; else Fine in dj. *Bookpress.* $40/£26

MORROW, JOSIAH (ed). Life and Speeches of Thomas Corwin. Cincinnati, 1896. 1st ed. (10),477pp; engr port. 1/4 leather, gilt-stamped. Good. *Artis.* $20/£13

MORROW, W.C. The Ape the Idiot and Other People. Phila, 1897. 1st Amer ed. Teg; uncut; pict cvrs gilt. Fine (spine sl sunned). *Polyanthos.* $35/£23

MORROW, W.C. The Ape, the Idiot and Other People. Phila: Lippincott, 1897. 1st ed. Teg. Gilt-dec cl, gilt dragon fr cvr. Extrems sl rubbed, lt soiling, rear inner hinge sl cracking, o/w VG. *Reese.* $55/£35

MORSE, A. REYNOLDS. Dali: A Study of His Life and Work. Greenwich, (1958). 1st Amer ed. 17 mtd color plts. Pict bds. VG. *Argosy.* $125/£81

MORSE, J.T. The Life and Letters of Oliver Wendell Holmes. Boston: Riverside Press, 1896. 1st ed. 2 vols. Frontis. (Cl rubbed.) *Goodrich.* $35/£23

MORTIMER, J. The Whole Art of Husbandry. London: D. Browne et al, 1761. 6th ed. Frontis, xvi,388,(iv); viii,450,(vi)pp (prelims browned; ex-libris, sigs). Full gilt-edged speckled calf (sl wear), dec gilt; 2 (of 4) leather labels. *Edwards.* $349/£225

MORTIMER, J.R. Forty Years' Researches in British and Saxon Burial Mounds of East Yorkshire. London, 1905. Chromolitho frontis, fldg map, fldg table, 125 plts. Teg. Morocco-backed cl, gilt. *Edwards.* $248/£160

MORTIMER, JOHN. Charade. Bodley Head, 1947. 1st ed. Signed. Spine cocked, o/w VG in dj (rebacked). *Rees.* $31/£20

MORTIMER, JOHN. In Character. London: Allen Lane, 1983. 1st UK ed. Inscribed. NF in dj. *Williams.* $37/£24

MORTIMER, JOHN. Like Men Betrayed. Collins, 1953. 1st ed. Signed. Sm blindstamp; spine sl cocked, o/w VG in dj (sl chipped). *Rees.* $31/£20

MORTIMER, JOHN. The Narrowing Stream. London: Collins, 1954. 1st ed. Blue bds, gilt spine. Fine in dj (frayed, sl mkd). *Temple.* $19/£12

MORTIMER, JOHN. The Narrowing Stream. London: Collins, 1954. 1st UK ed. Signed. VG+ in dj (spine sl creased). *Williams.* $56/£36

MORTIMER, JOHN. Paradise Postponed. Viking, 1985. 1st Eng ed. Blue cl. VF in Fine dj. *Dalian.* $47/£30

MORTIMER, JOHN. Regina V. Rumpole. London: Allen Lane, 1981. 1st UK ed. Inscribed. Fine (ink name) in dj. *Williams.* $62/£40

MORTIMER, JOHN. Rumming Park. London: Bodley Head, 1948. 1st UK ed. Signed. Fine in dj (spine sl chipped). *Williams.* $70/£45

MORTIMER, PENELOPE. A Villa in Summer. London: Joseph, 1954. 1st ed, 1st bk. Inscrip, else VG in dj. *Limestone.* $55/£35

MORTIMER, RAYMOND. A Letter on the French Pictures. London: Hogarth Letters, 1932. VG in wrappers. *Virgo.* $31/£20

MORTON, A.H. A Catalogue of Early Islamic Glass Stamps in the British Museum. British Museum, 1985. 24 b/w plts. (Ex-lib, bkpl, ink stamp verso tp.) Dj (lt faded; #s). *Edwards.* $39/£25

MORTON, ANTHONY. (Pseud of John Creasey). Attack the Baron. London: Sampson Low, 1951. 1st ed. Good in Good dj. *Ming.* $47/£30

MORTON, ANTHONY. (Pseud of John Creasey). Bad for the Baron. London: Hodder & Stoughton, 1962. 1st ed. VG+ in VG+ dj. *Ming.* $39/£25

MORTON, ARTHUR. A History of the Canadian West to 1870-71. London, n.d. (1939). 1st ed. 12 maps (11 fldg). Uncut, unopened. Repair patch on fep, o/w Fine in VG dj. *Oregon*. $250/£161

MORTON, H.V. In the Steps of St. Paul. Rich & Cowan, 1936. 1st Eng ed. Black cl. VG in dj (sl tanned, dusty). *Dalian*. $31/£20

MORTON, HENRY. Genito-Urinary Diseases and Syphilis. Phila, 1902. 1st ed. Good. *Fye*. $40/£26

MORTON, JOHN C. (ed). A Cyclopaedia of Agriculture. London, 1856. 2 vols. xi,1022; 1172pp + pub's ads, 51 engr plts (spotting). Orig emb cl (recased w/new eps), gilt illus. *Edwards*. $155/£100

MORTON, KENDAL and JULIA. Fifty Tropical Fruits of Nassau. Coral Gables, 1946. Fine. *Brooks*. $31/£20

MORTON, LESLIE T. Garrison and Morton's Medical Bibliography. London: Grafton, 1954. 2nd, rev ed. Lower corners shelfworn, o/w VG. *Reese*. $50/£32

MORTON, LESLIE T. Garrison and Morton's Medical Bibliography. An Annotated Check-List.... NY: Argosy Book Stores, 1961. 2nd ed. Grn cl. Fine in dj. *House*. $125/£81

MORTON, OREN P. A History of Pendleton County, West Virginia. Dayton, VA, 1910. 1st ed. Fldg map. (Lib bkpl; perf lib stamp tp; sm paper label spine.) Howes M 850. *Ginsberg*. $100/£65

MORWOOD, WILLIAM. Traveler in a Vanished Landscape, the Life and Times of David Douglas.... Potter, (1973). 1st ed. 3 maps. VF in Fine dj. *Oregon*. $45/£29

MOSBY, JOHN SINGLETON. The Memoirs of Colonel John S. Mosby. Bloomington: IN Univ, (1959). Fine in NF dj. Howes M 854. *Mcgowan*. $85/£55

MOSBY, JOHN SINGLETON. The Memoirs of Colonel John S. Mosby. Boston: Little, Brown, 1917. 1st ed. NF. Howes M 854. *Mcgowan*. $250/£161

MOSBY, JOHN SINGLETON. Mosby's War Reminiscences and Stuart's Cavalry Campaigns. NY: Dodd, (1887). 1st ed. 264pp. Pict cl (lt worn; recased). *Ginsberg*. $175/£113

MOSBY, JOHN SINGLETON. Mosby's War Reminiscences and Stuart's Cavalry Campaigns. NY: Dodd, Mead, (1887). 1st ed. 264pp. Dec cl. Pages foxed as per usual, still Fine. *Mcgowan*. $275/£177

MOSBY, JOHN SINGLETON. Stuart's Cavalry in the Gettysburg Campaign. NY: Moffat, Yard, 1908. 1st ed. Fldg map. Lacks 1 plt, else NF. Howes M 854. *Mcgowan*. $185/£119

MOSEDALE, JOHN. The Greatest of All. Dial, 1974. 1st ed. Good in Good dj. *Plapinger*. $30/£19

MOSES, BELLE. Louisa May Alcott: Dreamer and Worker. NY: D. Appleton, 1909. 1st ed. Cinnamon cl, blindstamped. Fine. *Hermitage*. $35/£23

MOSES, HENRY. The Works of Antonio Canova.... London, 1887. Engr frontis, 142 plts. 1/2 morocco (rubbed), spine gilt. *Argosy*. $250/£161

MOSKOWITZ, IRA (ed). Great Drawings of All Time. NY, 1962. 4 vols. 2-tone cl. Fine in buckram slipcases. *Argosy*. $350/£226

MOSKOWITZ, SAM. Seekers of Tomorrow. World, 1966. Fine in dj. *Madle*. $35/£23

MOSLEY, NICHOLAS. African Switchback. Weidenfeld & Nicolson, 1958. 1st Eng ed. Blue cl. Fine in dj (frayed). *Dalian*. $54/£35

MOSLEY, WALTER. A Red Death. NY: W.W. Norton, (1991). 1st ed. Fine in dj. *Godot*. $45/£29

MOSS, HOWARD. Finding Them Lost and Other Poems. NY: Scribner's, (1965). 1st ed. NF in dj. *Reese*. $25/£16

MOSS, HOWARD. The Wound and the Weather. NY: Reynal & Hitchcock, (1946). 1st ed, 1st bk. Corner creases prelims, o/w Fine in dj. *Reese*. $65/£42

MOSSER, MARJORIE. Good Maine Food. NY: Doubleday, 1939. 1st ed. Eps lt browned, rear cvr lt foxed, else Fine in virtually As New dj (spine lt creased). *Godot*. $200/£129

MOSSMAN, ISAAC. A Pony Expressman's Recollections. Portland: Champoeg Press, 1955. 1st ed. Ltd to 500. Tipped-in frontis port, fldg map tipped inside rear cvr. Pict cl. VF. *Oregon*. $65/£42

MOSSO, ANGELO. Fatigue. M. Drummond (trans). London, 1906. (Spine, cvr edges rubbed; joint cracked.) *Whitehart*. $54/£35

MOSSO, ANGELO. Fatigue. London, 1906. 1st Eng trans. Good. *Fye*. $100/£65

Mother Goose Panorama. McLoughlin Bros, 1957. 20x25 cm. 10 reversible panels. Hvy pict bds. Julian Wehr (illus). VG-. *Book Finders*. $60/£39

Mother Goose's Rhymes, Chimes, and Jingles. NY: McLoughlin Bros, 1898. 128pp. Pict wraps. VG (lt wear fr wrap). *Davidson*. $110/£71

Mother Goose. Boston: Lothrop, Lee & Shepard, (1905). Cl-backed pict bds. Fine (sl edgewear) in Fine dj. *Glenn*. $80/£52

Mother Goose. London: Hodder & Stoughton, (1938). 4to. 12 color illus by Jessie Wilcox Smith. Grey cl w/red stamped illus carrying into bk. Dj (frayed, worn). Sl dusting, spotting pg edges; o/w Nice. *Reisler*. $250/£161

Mother Goose: The Old Nursery Rhymes. London: Heinemann, (1913). Signed, ltd ed of 1130. Lg, 4to. 13 mtd color plts by Arthur Rackham; teg. White cl, gold lettering, illus (spine sl dknd; foxed spots within). *Reisler*. $2,200/£1,419

Mother Goose: The Old Nursery Rhymes. London: Heinemann, 1913. 1st ed thus. #1039/1130. Signed by Arthur Rackham (illus). 159pp, 13 full-pg illus mtd on brn paper, 85 b/w illus. White cl, gilt lettering; teg; slip laid in. VG. *Davidson*. $2,250/£1,452

Mother's Book of Song. London: Wells Gardner, Darton, (1902). 1st ed. 8vo. Charles Robinson (illus). Teg. Blue ribbed cl, gilt dec, lettering. Good. *Reisler*. $135/£87

MOTHERSOLE, JESSIE. Hadrian's Wall. London: John Lane, Bodley Head, 1924. Gilt cl (spine sl rubbed, faded). *Hollett*. $23/£15

MOTHERWELL, R. (ed). On My Way, Poetry and Essays 1912-1947. NY: Wittenborn, 1948. 2 orig color woodcuts by Arp. Sound. *Ars Artis*. $93/£60

MOTLEY, JOHN LOTHROP. The Rise of the Dutch Republic. London: John Chapman, 1856. 1st ed. 3 vols. Orig purple cl, gilt (spines lt sunned, sm snags). VG (hinge paper cracking). BAL 14574. *Macdonnell*. $375/£242

MOTT, ABIGAIL (comp). Narratives of Colored Americans. NY, 1882. 1st ed. 276pp. Orig cl. NF. *Mcgowan*. $250/£161

MOTT, FRANK LUTHER. A History of American Magazines, 1741-1885. NY/Cambridge: Appleton/Harvard Univ Press, 1930/1938. 1st ed. 3 vols. Maroon cl, gilt. (Rear hinge vol 1 reglued, lacks dj.) Vols 2-3 Fine in VG djs. *Macdonnell*. $225/£145

MOTT, VALENTINE. Travels in Europe and the East. NY: Harper & Bros, 1842. 452pp. (Worn, rubbed; recased, orig spine; stamp tp.) *Goodrich.* $150/£97

MOTTE, JACOB RHETT. Journey into Wilderness. James F. Sunderman (ed). Gainesville: Univ of FL Press, 1963. 2nd ptg. Grn cl. Fine in VG dj. *Chapel Hill.* $45/£29

MOTTEN, CLEMENT G. Mexican Silver and the Enlightenment. Phila: Univ of PA Press, 1950. Good in dj (chipped). *Archaeologia.* $35/£23

MOTTRAM, J.C. Fly Fishing. London: The Field, n.d. (1921). Stated 2nd ed. Grn cl, gilt title. VG +. *Bowman.* $75/£48

MOTTRAM, R.H. The Crime at Vanderlyden's. London: C&W, 1926. 1st ed. Fine in NF dj (dknd spine). *Beasley.* $150/£97

MOTTRAM, R.H. The Crime at Vanderlynden's. C&W, 1926. 1st Eng ed. Red cl. Fore-edge sl foxed, o/w NF in dj (sl tanned). *Dalian.* $39/£25

MOTTRAM, R.H. Europa's Beast. London: C&W, 1930. One of 358, this copy numbered, signed. Teg, others uncut. Unopened. 1/4 blue buckram, patterned bds. Spine faded, corner bruised, o/w Fine. *Temple.* $37/£24

MOTTRAM, R.H. For Some We Loved. London, (1956). 1st ed. VG in dj. *Argosy.* $45/£29

MOTTRAM, R.H. The Spanish Farm Trilogy 1914-1918. London: C&W, 1927. 1st 1-vol ed. Fine in VG + dj. *Limestone.* $55/£35

MOTTRAM, R.H. Strawberry Time and the Banquet. London: Golden Cockerel, 1934. #71/250. 4 wood-engrs by Gertrude Hermes. Teg, rest uncut. Morocco-backed dec cl (backstrip sl faded). VG. *Cox.* $171/£110

MOTTRAM, R.H. Ten Years Ago. C&W, 1928. 1st Eng ed. Brn cl. Spine sunned; fore-edge sl foxed, o/w VG. *Dalian.* $39/£25

MOULE, THOMAS. An Essay on the Roman Villas of the Augustan Age.... London: Longman, 1833. Frontis, viii + 179pp, plan. Contemp cl bds (upper hinge repaired; spine rebacked, corners retipped), leather title label (scuffed). *Edwards.* $59/£38

Mount Hood—A Guide. Duell, Sloan and Pearce, 1940. 1st ed. 1st state binding and dj. VG in dj (edgeworn). *Perier.* $30/£19

MOUNTFIELD, DAVID. The Coaching Age. London: Hale, 1976. 1st ed. VG in VG dj. *October Farm.* $65/£42

MOUNTFORT, GUY. Portrait of a Wilderness. London: Hutchinson, 1958. 1st ed. 50 plts (8 color). VG in dj (sl worn, repaired). *Hollett.* $31/£20

MOWAT, FARLEY. Never Cry Wolf. Toronto: McClelland & Stewart, 1963. 1st ed. NF (name, address) in VG dj. *Revere.* $40/£26

MOWATT, ANNA CORA. Autobiography of an Actress. Boston: Ticknor & Fields, 1854. 1st ed, 20th thousand. 448pp + ads. VG (sl foxed; lt wear). *Second Life.* $65/£42

MOWRY, SYLVESTER. Arizona and Sonora. NY: Harper, 1864. 3rd ed. Frontis, 251pp. Cl, marbled bds (newly rebound; new eps). VG. Howes M 869. *Schoyer.* $150/£97

MOWRY, WILLIAM A. Marcus Whitman and the Early Days in Oregon. NY: Silver, Burdett, (1901). 1st ed. 6 plts, 2 maps. VG. *Perier.* $37/£24

MOYES, PATRICIA. Death and the Dutch Uncle. London: CCC, 1968. 1st ed. Fine in dj (sl wear). *Mordida.* $65/£42

MOYES, PATRICIA. Night Ferry to Death. London: CCC, 1985. 1st ed. Fine in Fine dj. *Ming.* $26/£17

MOYES, PATRICIA. Night Ferry to Death. London: CCC, 1985. 1st ed. Signed. Fine in dj. *Mordida.* $45/£29

MOYES, PATRICIA. Who Is Simon Warwick? London: Collins, 1978. 1st ed. Fine in dj (price-clipped). *Janus.* $45/£29

MOYNIHAN, BERKELEY. American Addresses. Phila, 1917. (Lt worn.) *Goodrich.* $25/£16

MOZART, W.A. The Letters of Mozart and His Family. Emily Anderson (ed). London, 1938. 3 vols. VG in djs. *Argosy.* $125/£81

Mr. Facey Romford's Hounds. (By Robert Smith Surtees). London: Bradbury & Evans, 1865. 1st ed. Frontis, 23 etched plts by John Leech and Hablot K. Browne ('Phiz'). Pict cl, gilt (spine sl worn, sunned; fr cvr splashed). Good (eps replaced; foxing). *Ash.* $310/£200

MRAZEK, J.E. Fighting Gliders of World War II. NY, 1977. VG in VG dj. *Clark.* $35/£23

Mrs. Figgs's Grand Ball. London: Dean and Munday, n.d. (ca 1850). 12mo. 10pp + 1pg list, 10 1/2pg hand-colored engrs. 1st, last pgs pasted down on pict wrappers. Fine. *Hobbyhorse.* $250/£161

Mrs. Lovechild's Golden Present, for All Good Little Boys and Girls. York: J. Kendrew, n.d. (ca 1820). Chapbook. 32mo. Full-pg frontis, 1pg ad back cvr, alphabet of 24 letters. Dec maroon wrappers. Fine. *Hobbyhorse.* $175/£113

MUDD, NETTIE (ed). The Life of Dr. Samuel A. Mudd. NY/Washington: Neale, 1906. Howes M 871. *Schoyer.* $125/£81

MUDDIMAN, BERNARD. The Men of the Nineties. London: Henry Danielson, 1920. 1st ltd ed. One of 250. Unopened, rest untrimmed. Parchment-backed bds. 1/2 title sl stained, o/w Fine. *Cahan.* $100/£65

MUELLER, BERTHA (trans). Goethe's Botanical Writings. Woodbridge, CT, 1989. Rpt. 4 plts. Fine. *Brooks.* $25/£16

MUELLER, HANS ALEXANDER. Woodcuts of New York; Pages from a Diary.... Paul Standard (trans). NY: J.J. Augustin, (1938). 1st ed. 29 woodcuts. NF (w/o dj). *Reese.* $50/£32

MUELLER, RALPH and JERRY TURK. Report after Action. (Innsbruck: Wagnersche Universitats-Buchdruck-erei, 1945). 1st ed. Spine ends, corners scuffed; minor splitting outer hinge; else VG. *Mcgowan.* $125/£81

MUENSTERBERGER, W. and W.L. Sculpture of Primitive Man. NY: Abrams, (1955). 1st ed. 138 plts (incl 2 color). Black cl. Good in dj (sl browned, chipped). *Karmiole.* $75/£48

MUHLENBERG, HENRY M. The Notebook of a Colonial Clergyman. Theodore G. Tappert and John W. Doberstein (eds). Phila: Muhlenberg Press, 1959. 1st ed thus. Name, else Fine in dj (hole; fr fold lacks sm piece). *Chapel Hill.* $40/£26

MUIR, EDWIN. First Poems. Hogarth Press, 1925. 1st ed. Sl foxed, o/w VG. *Words Etc.* $101/£65

MUIR, JOHN. The Cruise of the Corwin. Boston/NY: Houghton Mifflin, 1917. 1st ed. Pict pastedown. Contents Fine (binding worn, soiled). BAL 14775. *Glenn.* $80/£52

MUIR, JOHN. The Cruise of the Corwin. Boston & NY: Houghton Mifflin, 1917. 1st ed. #62/550 lg paper copies. 8vo. Handcolored photogravure frontis. xxxi,(1),278,(1)pp. Illus w/facs, plts. Orig grn cl-backed bds w/morocco spine label. Fine in Fine dj, pub's slipcase (lt used) w/pict label. BAL 14775. *Chapel Hill.* $700/£452

MUIR, JOHN. The Cruise of the Corwin. Houghton Mifflin, 1917. Lg Paper Ed, ltd to 550 numbered. Handcolored frontis, guard; 26 plts. Leather spine label. *Oregon.* $450/£290

MUIR, JOHN. John of the Mountains. Unpublished Journals of John Muir. Linnie Marsh Wolfe (ed). Boston: Houghton Mifflin, 1938. 1st ed. Fine in VG dj. *Book Market.* $95/£61

MUIR, JOHN. Our National Parks. Boston: Houghton Mifflin, 1909. Holiday Edition. Frontis; dbl-pg map; 31 full-pg photo illus. Pict/gilt cl; teg. (Fr inner hinge weak.) *Dawson.* $150/£97

MUIR, JOHN. Steep Trails. Boston, 1918. 1st ed. Color label. (Bkpl; photo affixed fr pastedown; cvrs worn.) *King.* $125/£81

MUIR, JOHN. Stickeen. Boston/NY: Houghton Mifflin, 1909. Tan cl (cvrs soiled, sl corner wear). *Parmer.* $195/£126

MUIR, JOHN. Stickeen. Boston/NY, Houghton Mifflin, 1909. 1st ed. Tan cl, title device. NF. BAL 14759. *Blue Mountain.* $75/£48

MUIR, JOHN. Yosemite and the Sierra Nevada. Boston, (1948). 64 photos by Ansel Adams. VG in dj (spine chipped). *King.* $75/£48

MUIR, PERCY and B. VAN THAL. Bibliographies of the First Editions of Books by A.L. Huxley and T.F. Powys. London: Dulau, 1927. 1st ed. Ltd to 550. NF in dj (sl edgeworn). *Sadlon.* $50/£32

MUIR, PERCY. Book Collecting as a Hobby. Knopf, 1947. Good in dj. *Moss.* $25/£16

MUIR, PERCY. English Children's Books 1600-1900. NY, (1954). 1st Amer ed. Fine (sl rubbed) in dj (sunned, chipped, sl rubbed). *Polyanthos.* $100/£65

MUIR, PERCY. English Children's Books 1600-1900. London, (1985). 4th ed. Fine in Fine dj. *Oregon.* $20/£13

MUIR, PERCY. Minding My Own Business. C&W, 1956. 1st ed. Good in dj. *Moss.* $37/£24

MUIR, PERCY. Points, 1874-1930 with Points, Second Series, 1866-1934. London: Constable, 1931 and 1934. 1st eds. Ltd to 500 and 750. 2 vols. 9 plts; 13 plts. Vellum spines, marbled paper over bds. (1st vol sl dusty.) *Bookpress.* $285/£184

MUIR, PERCY. Victorian Illustrated Books. Batsford, 1971. 1st ed. Fine in dj. *Moss.* $39/£25

MUIRHEAD, ARNOLD. Grace Revere Osler. OUP, MCMXXI (1931). Ltd ed of 500. Frontis. Vellum-backed bds. Good. *Goodrich.* $150/£97

MUIRHEAD, JAMES FULLARTON. The Land of Contrasts: A Briton's View.... London/NY: John Lane, 1900. Stated 2nd ed (ptg). viii, 282pp. Pict cl. VG. *Schoyer.* $80/£52

MUIRHEAD, W.A. Practical Tropical Sanitation: A Manual.... NY, 1915. 1st ed. Good. *Fye.* $50/£32

MULDER, WILLIAM and A. RUSSELL MORTENSEN (eds). Among the Mormons. NY: Knopf, 1958. 1st ed. Fine in NF dj. *Connolly.* $45/£29

MULDOON, PAUL. Madoc: A Mystery. Faber, 1990. 1st ed. Fine in dj. *Rees.* $31/£20

MULFORD, AMI FRANK. Fighting Indians in the 7th U.S. Cavalry, Custer's Favorite Regiment. Corning, NY, (1925). 2nd ed. VG, tied in ptd wraps (edgeworn). *Bohling.* $75/£48

MULFORD, ISAAC S. A Civil and Political History of New Jersey.... Phila, 1851. 8vo. 500pp (spine head frayed; corners bumped; lt foxing). Howes M 881. *Argosy.* $125/£81

MULFORD, PRENTICE. Prentice Mulford's Story.... Oakland, (1953). Howes M 882. *Ginsberg.* $30/£19

MULGARDT, LOUIS CHRISTIAN. The Architecture and Landscape Gardening of the Exposition. SF: Paul Elder, 1915. 1st ed. Uncut. Gilt-stamped buckram bds. Fine. *Quest.* $55/£35

MULLEN, STANLEY. Kinsmen of the Dragon. Chicago: Shasta Publishers, (1951). 1st ed. Signed. VG in dj (internally mended edge-tears; sl wear spine ends, corner tips). *Bernard.* $100/£65

MULLER, DAN. My Life with Buffalo Bill. Chicago: Reilly & Lee, (1948). 1st ed. Fine. *Laurie.* $40/£26

MULLER, HERBERT J. Thomas Wolfe. Norfolk, CT: New Directions, (1947). 1st ed. Beige cl. Name stamp, pencil underlining, else NF in VG dj. *Chapel Hill.* $20/£13

MULLER, MARCIA and BILL PRONZINI. Beyond the Grave. NY: Walker, 1986. 1st ed. Fine in dj (sl edgewear). *Janus.* $45/£29

MULLER, MARCIA. Edwin of the Iron Shoes. NY: McKay-Washburn, 1977. 1st ed, 1st bk. VF in VF dj. *Murder.* $60/£39

MULLETT, CHARLES (ed). The Letters of Dr. George Cheyne to the Countess of Huntingdon. San Marino, CA, 1940. 1st ed. Good. *Fye.* $45/£29

MULLIGAN, HUGH A. No Place to Die: The Agony of Vietnam. NY: Morrow, 1967. Map. VG in VG dj (sl wear). *Aka.* $50/£32

MULLIN, GERALD W. Flight and Rebellion. Slave Resistance in Eighteenth-Century Virginia. NY, 1972. 1st ed. Orig cl. Fine in NF dj. *Mcgowan.* $30/£19

MULLINER, H.H. The Decorative Arts in England. London: B.T. Batsford, 1923. (Ex-lib w/bkpl, ink stamps, #s; rebound.) *Edwards.* $124/£80

MULVANEY, CHARLES PELHAM. The History of the Northwest Rebellion of 1885. Toronto, 1886. 12th thousand. Good (edgewear; new eps). *Artis.* $60/£39

MUMEY, NOLIE (ed). Bloody Trails Along the Rio Grande. A Day-by-Day Diary of Alonzo Ferdinand Ickis (1836-1917). Denver: Old West Pub, 1958. Ltd to 500 numbered, signed. Tipped-in frontis photo, fldg map. Fine in Fine dj. *Oregon.* $125/£81

MUMEY, NOLIE. Alexander Taylor Rankin (1803-1885), His Diary and Letters. Boulder: Johnson Pub, 1966. 1st ed. Ltd to 400 numbered, signed. Frontis. Fine. *Oregon.* $70/£45

MUMEY, NOLIE. A Pioneer Denver Mint. Denver, 1950. Ltd to 800 signed, numbered. Uncut. Pict cl. NF in dj (sl chipped). *Baade.* $100/£65

MUMEY, NOLIE. Saga of 'Auntie' Stone and Her Cabin. Boulder: Johnson Pub Co, 1964. One of 500 numbered, signed. Color view; fldg plt. Unopened. Fine in glassine wrapper (chipped, torn). *Bohling.* $135/£87

MUMFORD, GEORGE SALTONSTALL. Twenty Harvard Crews. Cambridge, 1923. 1st ed. *Lefkowicz.* $85/£55

MUMFORD, JOHN KIMBERLY. Oriental Rugs. NY, 1915. Color frontis, 15 color plts, 8 planographs, 8 photo-engrs, 2 fldg maps at rear. (Lt spotting, ex-libris, upper hinge cracked; lt soiled, sl rubbed; spine sl chipped.) *Edwards.* $54/£35

MUMMERY, A.F. My Climbs in the Alps and Caucasus. Oxford: Basil Blackwell, 1936. 16 plts. (Cl sl mkd.) *Hollett.* $39/£25

MUMMERY, J. HOWARD. The Microscopic Anatomy of the Teeth. Oxford: OUP, 1919. VG (sig). *Savona.* $47/£30

MUNDY, TALBOT. Black Light. Bobbs-Merrill, 1930. 1st ed. VG. *Madle.* $30/£19

MUNDY, TALBOT. East and West. Appleton, 1937. 1st ed. NF in dj (sl edge-rubbed). *Madle.* $185/£119

MUNDY, TALBOT. Full Moon. Appleton, 1935. 1st ed. VG in dj (spine chip). *Madle.* $150/£97

MUNDY, TALBOT. The Gunga Sahib. Appleton, 1934. 1st ed. Fine in dj. *Madle.* $200/£129

MUNDY, TALBOT. The Ivory Trail. Bobbs-Merrill, 1919. 1st ed. VG. *Madle.* $35/£23

MUNDY, TALBOT. The Ivory Trail. B-M, 1919. 1st ed. VG. *Aronovitz.* $35/£23

MUNDY, TALBOT. Jimgrim. Century, 1931. 1st ed. Spine chipped, else VG-. *Madle.* $25/£16

MUNDY, TALBOT. The Lion of Petra. NY: D. Appleton-Century, 1933. 1st ed. Dec yellow cl. Good in dj (lt soiled). *Karmiole.* $75/£48

MUNDY, TALBOT. Queen Cleopatra. Indianapolis, 1929. Special ed. #212/250 (of 265) signed. Uncut, partly unopened. Fine (sl sunned, bkpl). *Polyanthos.* $275/£177

MUNDY, TALBOT. Rung Ho! Scribners, 1914. 1st ed, 1st bk. VG-. *Aronovitz.* $75/£48

MUNDY, TALBOT. The Thunder Dragon Gate. Appleton, 1937. 1st ed. VG-. *Madle.* $25/£16

MUNDY, TALBOT. Tros of Samothrace. Appleton, 1934. 1st ed. VG-. *Madle.* $40/£26

MUNKACSI. Nudes. NY: Greenberg, 1951. 1st ed. 75 photos. Silver-titled red cl. Fine in dj (chipped). *Cahan.* $150/£97

MUNN, H. WARNER. Tales of the Werewolf Clan. Grant, 1979. 1st ed. VF in dj (minor edgewear). *Else Fine.* $65/£42

MUNNINGS, ALFRED. An Artist's Life. London, 1951-2. 3 vols. Vol 1, rpt; Vol 2, 2nd ed; Vol 3, 3rd ed. Djs (chipped, repaired). *Edwards.* $155/£100

MUNRO SMITH, G. A History of the Bristol Royal Infirmary. Bristol/London, 1917. Frontis. (Pg edges lt foxed; spine ends sl worn.) *Whitehart.* $62/£40

MUNRO, DONALD. Cranio-Cerebral Injuries. London, 1938. 1st ed. Good. *Fye.* $75/£48

MUNRO, H.H. The Toys of Peace and Other Papers. London/NY: John Lane, Bodley Head/John Lane, 1919. 1st ed. Port. Brn cl, blind-stamped, gilt-lettered. *Bickersteth.* $171/£110

MUNRO, NEIL. Ayrshire Idylls. A&C Black, 1923. 16 color plts. Dj (soiled, chipped). *Edwards.* $31/£20

MUNRO, ROBERT. Archaeology and False Antiquities. London: Methuen, 1905. 1st ed. 18 plts, plan. Spotted; spine sl dknd. *Hollett.* $47/£30

MUNRO, ROBERT. Paleolithic Man and Terramara Settlements in Europe. NY: Macmillan, 1912. 1st Amer ed. 75 plts. Gilt-lettered brn cl (wear; corners worn). VG. *House.* $110/£71

MUNRO, ROBERT. Rambles and Studies in Bosnia-Herzegovina and Dalmatia. London, 1900. 2nd ed. 40 plts. Nice (feps lt foxed). *Edwards.* $132/£85

MUNROE, KIRK. The Fur-Seal's Tooth. NY: Harper, (1894). xi,267pp. Dec cvrs. VG in added,mylar dj. *Blue Dragon.* $45/£29

MUNROE, KIRK. The Fur-Seal's Tooth. A Story of Alaskan Adventure. NY/London: Harper, c. 1894. Dec lt grn cl. Generally VG (sl wear, fading). *Parmer.* $65/£42

MUNSEY, FRANK A. Under Fire; or, Fred Worthington's Campaign. NY; Frank A. Munsey, 1890. 1st ed. Signed. Pict cl, gilt. Minor soil, rubbing. *Sadlon.* $50/£32

MUNSON, JOHN W. Reminiscences of a Mosby Guerrilla. NY: Moffat, Yard, 1906. 1st ed. Frontis port. Orig grn cl. Spine sl faded, early inscrip, else VG. *Chapel Hill.* $175/£113

MUNTHE, ALEX. The Story of San Michele. John Murray, 1936. 1st illus ed. Blue cl. Cvrs sl cocked; eps sl browned, o/w VG in dj (soiled; torn). *Dalian.* $39/£25

MUNZ, LUDWIG. Bruegel, the Drawings, Complete Edition. Phaidon, 1961. 1 mtd color illus. Dj. *Ars Artis.* $116/£75

MUNZ, LUDWIG. The Etchings of Rembrandt.... London: Phaidon, (1952). 2 vols. VG in djs (sl frayed; price-clipped); slipcase (sunned, worn). *King.* $500/£323

MUNZ, LUDWIG. Rembrandt. NY: Abrams, (1954). 1st ed. 1 fldg plt. Fine in dj. *Argosy.* $125/£81

MURASE, MIYEKO. Byobu: Japanese Screens from New York Collections. (NY): Asia Soc, (1971). VG in dj. *Schoyer.* $35/£23

MURBARGER, NELL. Ghosts of the Glory Trail. Palm Desert, (1956). 1st ed. Frontis. VG in VG dj. *Oregon.* $50/£32

MURCHISON, CHARLES. A Treatise on the Continued Fevers of Great Britain. London, 1873. 2nd ed. 729pp. (Lacks feps; stamps erased tp; paper thinning; sm perforation.) *Fye.* $150/£97

MURDOCH, IRIS and J.B. PRIESTLEY. The Sea, The Sea. London: C&W, 1978. 1st UK ed. Fine in dj. *Lewton.* $45/£29

MURDOCH, IRIS and J.B. PRIESTLEY. A Severed Head. London: C&W, 1964. 1st UK ed. NF in dj. *Lewton.* $42/£27

MURDOCH, IRIS and J.B. PRIESTLEY. A Severed Head. A Play.... London: C&W, 1964. 1st ed. Fine in dj (closed nick). *Virgo.* $62/£40

MURDOCH, IRIS. Bruno's Dream. London: C&W, 1969. 1st ed. NF in dj (sl rubbed). *Rees.* $19/£12

MURDOCH, IRIS. Bruno's Dream. C&W, 1969. 1st UK ed. VG in dj. *Lewton.* $43/£28

MURDOCH, IRIS. The Existentialist Political Myth. Delos Press, 1989. One of 225. Fine in blue wrappers. *Rees.* $31/£20

MURDOCH, IRIS. The Flight from the Enchanter. Chatto, 1956. 1st UK ed. VG + in dj (sl worn; short tears; tiny stains rear panel). *Williams.* $202/£130

MURDOCH, IRIS. The Good Apprentice. Chatto, 1985. 1st ed. Signed ltd ed of 250. VG in orig glassine wrappers. *Whiteson.* $43/£28

MURDOCH, IRIS. The Italian Girl. London: Chatto, 1964. 1st UK ed. VG (ink name) in dj. *Williams.* $43/£28

MURDOCH, IRIS. The Nice and the Good. London: Chatto, 1968. 1st UK ed. Fine in NF dj. *Williams.* $47/£30

MURDOCH, IRIS. The Red and the Green. London: C&W, 1965. 1st UK ed. NF in dj. *Lewton.* $39/£25

MURDOCH, IRIS. Reynolds Stone. London: Warren, 1981. One of 300 for sale. Signed. Fine in wraps. *Williams.* $37/£24

MURDOCH, IRIS. Reynolds Stone. London: Warren Editions, 1981. One of 750 signed. Fine in wrappers. *Rees.* $47/£30

MURDOCH, IRIS. The Sandcastle. London: C&W, 1957. 1st UK ed. NF in VG+ (sm pinhole spine). *Williams.* $194/£125

MURDOCH, IRIS. Sartre: Romantic Rationalist. Cambridge: Bowes & Bowes, 1953. 1st issue, 1st bk. Top edge lake. Red cl, gilt. Nice in dj (frayed, sl chipped, dknd). *Temple.* $109/£70

MURDOCH, IRIS. The Sea, The Sea. London: Chatto, 1978. 1st UK ed. Fine in dj. *Williams.* $54/£35

MURDOCH, IRIS. A Severed Head. London: C&W, 1961. 1st ed. Signed. VG in dj (sl chipped, internally strengthened). *Rees.* $70/£45

MURDOCH, IRIS. A Severed Head. London: Chatto, 1961. 1st UK ed. Pub's rev slip laid in. NF in dj (short tears). *Williams.* $50/£32

MURDOCH, IRIS. Something Special. Four Poems and a Story. Helsinki: Eurographica, 1990. One of 350 numbered, signed, dated. Fine in stiff wrappers, dj. *Ulysses.* $101/£65

MURDOCH, IRIS. The Time of the Angels. London: Chatto, 1966. 1st UK ed. VG (flyleaf abrased) in dj (price-clipped, 3 sm closed tears; sl creased). *Williams.* $28/£18

MURDOCH, IRIS. Under the Net. London: C&W, 1954. 2nd (1st published) issue of text, w/o blurb on 1/2 tp; variant binding (usual binding pale blue-grn matt-surfaced smooth bds, similarly blocked, lettered). Grn bds, gilt. Sl wear, spine faded, edges lt foxed, o/w Nice. *Temple.* $85/£55

MURDOCH, IRIS. A Word Child. London: C&W, 1975. 1st ed. Fine in NF dj (sm tear). *Antic Hay.* $35/£23

MURDOCH, IRIS. A Year of Birds. Compton Press, 1978. Ltd ed, #183/350 signed. Reynolds Stone (engr). Marbled bds. Fine. *Williams.* $124/£80

MURDOCH, IRIS. A Year of Birds. London: C&W, 1978. One of 350 numbered, signed by author and Reynolds Stone (illus). Cl-backed bds. Fine. *Rees.* $147/£95

MURDOCH, W.G. BURN. From Edinburgh to the Antarctic. London: Longmans, Green, 1894. 1st ed. ix,364pp + ads; fldg map (creased). Good+ (sl rubbed, sm tear foot of spine). *Walcot.* $209/£135

MURDOCK, CHARLES A. A Backward Glance at Eighty. SF: Paul Elder, 1921. 1st ed. #1059 of Memorial Ed, signed. NF (sl worn, rubbed; lt foxing sl affecting tp, frontis). *Harrington.* $75/£48

MURDOCK, HAROLD. The Nineteenth of April, 1775. Boston: Houghton Mifflin, 1925. 4 plts, fldg map. VG. *Schoyer.* $35/£23

MURDOCK, MYRTLE CHENEY. Constantino Brumidi, Michaelangelo of the United States Capitol. Washington: Monumental Press, 1950. 1st ed. Signed. VG in dj (lt worn). *Hermitage.* $95/£61

MURFIN, JAMES V. The Gleam of Bayonets. NY, (1965). 1st ed. Dj worn, o/w Fine. *Pratt.* $40/£26

MURPHY, ARTHUR. The Life of David Garrick, Esq. Dublin: Messrs. Wogan, 1801. 1st Dublin ed. Contemp 1/2 sheep (hinges worn), marbled sides. *Hill.* $70/£45

MURPHY, AUDIE. To Hell and Back. NY, (1949). 1st ed. VG in dj (sl chipped, edgetorn). *King.* $20/£13

MURPHY, BAILEY SCOTT. English and Scottish Wrought Ironwork. Batsford, 1904. 80 plts. (Lt staining, wrinkling; feps foxed; rubbed; spine sl chipped; lower bd lt stained.) *Edwards.* $279/£180

MURPHY, DERVLA. Full Tilt. John Murray, 1965. 1st Eng ed. Grn cl. Name, o/w VG in dj. *Dalian.* $70/£45

MURPHY, DERVLA. In Ethiopia with a Mule. London, 1968. 1st UK ed. Dbl-pg map. Dj (sl chipped). *Edwards.* $23/£15

MURPHY, DERVLA. Muddling Through in Madagascar. London, 1985. 1st ed. Map. Dj. *Edwards.* $23/£15

MURPHY, DERVLA. Tibetan Foothold. John Murray, 1966. 1st Eng ed. Blue cl. Fine in dj. *Dalian.* $54/£35

MURPHY, DERVLA. The Ukimwi Road. London, 1983. 1st ed. 2 maps. Dj. *Edwards.* $19/£12

MURPHY, JAMES L. An Archaeological History of the Hocking Valley. Ohio: OH Univ Press, (1975). Good in dj (tattered). *Archaeologia.* $35/£23

MURPHY, JOHN MORTIMER. Sporting Adventures in the Far West. NY: 1880. 1st ed. 469pp. Dec cl. VG. *Petrilla.* $75/£48

MURPHY, MICHAEL et al. Vincent Starrett: In Memoriam. Culver City: Luther Norris, 1974. 1st publication, one of 400 numbered. Fine. *Janus.* $35/£23

MURPHY, R.C. Bird Islands of Peru.... NY, 1925. Binder's cl. Sound (ex-lib). *Wheldon & Wesley.* $70/£45

MURPHY, THOS. D. New England Highways and Byways from a Motor Car. Boston: Page, 1924. 1st ed. 25 plts, 24 halftones from photos, fldg map. Teg. Pict dk grn cl. VG. *Chapel Hill.* $40/£26

Murray's Handbook for Berkshire. London, 1902. 2 plans, 3 fldg maps in pockets. (Edges sl faded; spine discolored, chipped.) *Edwards.* $39/£25

Murray's Handbook for Travellers in Greece. London/Paris: Murray/Galignani, 1854. xi,460pp; fldg map. Rebacked; rubbed; sl shaken, o/w VG. *Worldwide.* $65/£42

Murray's Handbook for Travellers in India and Pakistan, Burma and Ceylon. London, 1949. 16th ed. Good+ (ink notes). *Gretton.* $34/£22

Murray's Handbook for Travellers in Surrey, Hampshire, and the Isle of Wight. London: Murray, 1888. 4th ed. 3 fldg maps. (Backstrip torn, faded, sl mkd.) *Petersfield.* $65/£42

Murray's Handbook for Travellers in Syria and Palestine. London: John Murray, 1899. 4th ed. lii,(404);20pp + 52pp ads, 2pp addendum (lacks both pocket maps). Red cl (spine faded, sigs). *Schoyer.* $75/£48

Murray's Handbook for Travellers in Syria and Palestine. J.L. Porter (ed). London, 1868. 2nd ed. 2 vols. Sl wear spine heads, o/w Clean. *Gretton.* $93/£60

Murray's Handbook to the Cathedrals of Wales. London: Murray, 1873. 1st ed. xix,334pp (prelims lt browned). Blind emb cl, dec gilt spine (sl rubbed, lt soiled). *Edwards.* $39/£25

Murray's Handbook. France. Part II. London, 1874. 12th ed. Map in pocket. (Cvrs dampstained.) *Gretton.* $19/£12

Murray's Handbook. North Germany and the Rhine. London, 1877. 19th ed. Map in pocket. Good+ (cl sl rubbed). *Gretton.* $28/£18

Murray's Handbook. Switzerland, Savoy and Piedmont. London, 1843. 2nd ed. (Tp, fep, ad torn out.) *Gretton.* $17/£11

Murray's Scottish Tourist. Glasgow: Thomas Murray, n.d. (ca 1869). 2nd ed. (2),128pp+28pp ads (incl eps). Burgundy cl (top corner sl chipped). *Karmiole.* $60/£39

MURRAY, A.S. The Sculpture of the Parthenon. London: John Murray, 1903. 7 plts, incl 1 fldg (1 stained at corner). Teg. 1/2 calf (rubbed; bumped). *Archaeologia.* $85/£55

MURRAY, A.S. Terracotta Sarcophagi: Greek and Etruscan in the British Museum. London: British Museum, 1898. 11 plts. 3/4 calf (top joint broken, rubbed). Interior Fine. *Archaeologia.* $150/£97

MURRAY, ALBERT. The Hero and the Blues. Univ of MO Press, 1973. 1st ed. Good (underlining) in dj (rubbed, worn). *Stahr.* $45/£29

MURRAY, ALBERT. South to a Very Old Place. NY: McGraw-Hill, (1971). 1st ed. Black cl. Pict dj. *Petrilla.* $30/£19

MURRAY, ALBERT. Train Whistle Guitar. NY: McGraw-Hill, 1973. 1st ed. Fine (minor wear at jacket spine corners). *Else Fine.* $60/£39

MURRAY, AMELIA M. Letters from the United States, Cuba, and Canada. NY: Putnam's, 1856. 1st US ed. 402pp (initials on flyleaf bled through to tp; bkpl). Pub's cl (sl worn; rear hinge tender). Howes M 912. *Second Life.* $65/£42

MURRAY, CHARLES AUGUSTUS. The Prairie-Bird. London: Richard Bentley, 1844. 1st ed. 3 vols. Gray bds (rebacked, orig ptd paper labels); uncut. VG in black cl slipcase. *Houle.* $600/£387

MURRAY, CHARLES AUGUSTUS. Travels in North America. London: Richard Bentley, 1839. 1st ed. xvi,473; xii,372pp (foxing), 2 plts. (Respined, orig used as overlay.) Howes M 913. *Bookpress.* $350/£226

MURRAY, ELIZABETH DUNBAR. My Mother Used to Say. Boston: Christopher, 1959. 1st ed. Author's personal copy w/her name, address fep. Frontis port; 6 plts. NF in dj (deeply chipped; internally repaired). *Connolly.* $37/£24

MURRAY, G.G.A. Gobi or Shamo. London, 1890. VG. *Madle.* $100/£65

MURRAY, GEORGE. The Madhouse on Madison Street. Chicago: Follet, 1965. VG in VG dj. *Connolly.* $25/£16

MURRAY, H.J.R. A History of Board-Games Other Than Chess. Oxford: Clarendon, 1952. Fine in dj (sl chipped). *Schoyer.* $50/£32

MURRAY, H.J.R. A History of Chess. OUP, 1913. 1st ed. Teg. Gilt-ruled morocco-backed cl, gilt (spine sl rubbed; ex-lib; bkpl; upper hinge tender). *Edwards.* $140/£90

MURRAY, HELEN and MARY NUTTAL (eds). A Handlist to Howard Carter's Catalogue of Objects in Tut'ankhamun's Tomb. Oxford: Griffith Inst, 1963. Good. *Archaeologia.* $35/£23

MURRAY, JOAN. The Last Buffalo. Story of Frederick Verner.... Toronto, (1984). 1st ed. VF in VF dj. *Oregon.* $65/£42

MURRAY, JOHN, IV. John Murray III, 1808-1892, a Brief Memoir. NY: Knopf, 1920. 1st US ed. Fine (eps foxed) in dj (worn; pieces missing). *Oak Knoll.* $25/£16

MURRAY, KEITH A. The Modocs and Their War. Norman, 1959. Stated 2nd ptg. Sig, sl bumped, o/w Fine in dj. *Baade.* $50/£32

MURRAY, LINDA. Michelangelo. London: Thames and Hudson, 1984. Dj. *Edwards.* $39/£25

MURRAY, LINDLEY. The English Reader.... Buffalo: R.W. Haskins, 1825. Full swirled calf binding, gilt rules on spine, orig red leather label (lt text foxing). Binding VG. *Cullen.* $120/£77

MURRAY, LOIS LOVINA. Incidents of Frontier Life. Goshen, IN: Ev. United Mennonite Pub. House, 1880. 274pp, 2 ports. Grn cl, gilt spine title. Good (etching, fraying, foxing). Howes M 918. *Bohling.* $300/£194

MURRAY, MARGARET A. Egyptian Sculpture. London: Duckworth, (1930). 55 plts. (Sig.) *Archaeologia.* $45/£29

MURRAY, MARGARET A. Egyptian Temples. London: Sampson Low, (1931). 64 plts. Good. *Archaeologia.* $45/£29

MURRAY, MARGARET A. Petra: The Rock City of Edom. London/Glasgow: Blackie, 1939. 1st ed. 2 maps. Sl foxing, o/w VG in dj. *Worldwide.* $65/£42

MURRAY, MARGARET A. The Splendour That Was Egypt. London: Sidgwick & Jackson, 1950. 3rd imp. Color frontis. VG in dj (torn). *Worldwide.* $45/£29

MURRAY, MARIAN. Circus! From Rome to Ringling. NY: Appleton, (1956). 4to. 100 b/w illus. VG in dj. *Houle.* $55/£35

MURRAY, PETER. Piranesi and the Grandeur of Ancient Rome. London, 1971. Good. *Washton.* $30/£19

MURRAY, ROBERT. Fort Laramie. 'Visions of a Grand Old Post.' Fort Collins: Old Army Press, (1974). Autographed ed of 250. Ep maps. VF in VF dj. *Oregon.* $60/£39

MURRAY, TOM (ed). Folk Songs of Jamaica. London: OUP, (1951). 1st ed. VG in stapled wrappers. *Pharos.* $45/£29

MURRAY, W.H. Mountaineering in Scotland. London, 1947. 1st ed. Dj (sl chipped; celotape repairs). *Edwards.* $39/£25

MURRAY, WILLIAM H.H. Adventures in the Wilderness. Boston: Fields, Osgood, 1869. 1st ed. 236pp, 4 ads, 8 plts. (Inner edge tp starting; some foxing.) Burgundy cl (bumped, rubbed, stained, fr bubbled), gilt. VG. *Blue Mountain.* $85/£55

MURRY, JOHN MIDDLETON. The Evolution of an Intellectual. Richard Cobden-Sanderson, 1920. 1st Eng ed. Grn cl; paper label. Spine, cvrs sl mkd, o/w VG. *Dalian.* $70/£45

MURRY, JOHN MIDDLETON. The Life of Jesus. London: Cape, (1926). 1st ed. Lt foxing, else NF in dj (aged, soiled). *Pharos.* $60/£39

MURRY, JOHN MIDDLETON. Reminiscences of D.H. Lawrence. Cape, 1933. 1st Eng ed. Brn cl. Fore-edge sl foxed, o/w NF in dj (torn; tanned). *Dalian.* $70/£45

MURRY, JOHN MIDDLETON. Son of Woman. The Story of D.H. Lawrence. Cape, 1931. 1st Eng ed. Frontis port; note facs. Black cl. Fore-edge sl foxed, o/w VG. *Dalian.* $54/£35

MURTON, R.K. Man and Birds. London, 1971. 1st ed. 32 plts. Dj. *Edwards.* $90/£58

Muse's Mirrour, Being a Collection of Poems. London: Robert Baldwin, 1778. 1st ed. 2 vols. Contemp full calf (expertly rebacked), labels, gilt. Tight, clean set. *Macdonnell.* $225/£145

MUSGRAVE, CLIFFORD. Adam and Hepplewhite and Other Neo-Classical Furniture. London: Faber & Faber, (1966). 1st ed. Frontis, 177 illus on plts; else VG. *Bookpress.* $50/£32

MUSGRAVE, CLIFFORD. Life in Brighton, from the Earliest Times to the Present. London: Faber & Faber, 1970. 1st ed. Blue linen. Fine in pict dj. *Hartfield.* $85/£55

MUSGRAVE, CLIFFORD. Regency Furniture 1800 to 1830. NY: Thomas Yoseloff, (1961). 1st ed. 96 photo plts. Gray cl. Good in dj. *Karmiole.* $45/£29

MUSGRAVE, THOMAS. Castaway on the Auckland Isles. London, 1866. Frontis, x,174pp + 16pp ads; map. Maroon cl (relaid). *Lewis.* $133/£86

MUSHIN, WILLIAM W. and L. RENDELL-BAKER. The Principles of Thoracic Anaesthesia Past and Present. Springfield: Charles C. Thomas, (1953). 1st Amer ed. Fine in dj. *Glaser.* $60/£39

MUSIL, ROBERT. The Man without Qualities. Eithne Wilkins & Ernst Kaiser (trans). NY: Coward-McCann, (1953). 1st Amer ed. Fine in dj (lt faded, chipped). *Hermitage.* $75/£48

MUSSOLINI, BENITO. My Autobiography. London, 1936. Frontis port. VG in dj (soiled). *Edwards.* $28/£18

MUSSON, SPENCER C. Sicily. A&C Black, 1911. 48 color tipped-in plts, fldg map. Teg. Dec cl (spine sl faded; hinge cracked, tender; sl spotting). *Edwards.* $62/£40

MUSSON, SPENCER C. Sicily. London: Black, 1911. 1st ed. Fldg map; 48 tipped-in color plts. Rubbed; spine frayed, torn; sl foxing; corner few leaves wrinkled, o/w VG. *Worldwide.* $45/£29

MUTER, GLADYS N. Two Wooden Soldiers and a Hobby Horse. ('Cloth-Art' Toy Book.) Chicago: P.F. Volland, (1924). 12mo. Unpaginated. V.E. Elizabeth Cadie (illus). Orange pict cl wraps. Fine. *Davidson.* $35/£23

MUYBRIDGE, EADWEARD. Animals in Motion. London: Chapman & Hall, 1899. Frontis port, x,264pp. (Hinges cracked, shaken; rubbed; sl bumped, creased, dented.) *Edwards.* $233/£150

MUYBRIDGE, EADWEARD. The Human Figure in Motion: 196 Plates...from the Famous Muybridge Collection.... NY, 1955. Good in dj. *Fye.* $75/£48

My Brimful Book. NY: Platt & Munk, (1960). 1st ed. Tudor signature tipped-in title pg. Sm folio. Tasha Tudor, Margot Austin, Wesley Dennis (illus). Color dec bds (sm split top spine). *Reisler.* $100/£65

My Cave Life in Vicksburg. (By Mary Loughborough.) NY: Appleton, 1864. 1st ed. 196pp + ads. VG (cl faded, sl worn; part 1 pg browned). *Second Life.* $150/£97

My First Alphabet. NY: McLoughlin Brothers, n.d. (ca 1860). Little Folks Series. Sq 16mo. 6ff + 1p ad lower wrapper; 6 full-pg illus. Pict litho wrappers. Fine (lt spine wear). *Hobbyhorse.* $150/£97

My First Primer. Otley: Yorkshire Joint Stock, (ca 1840). Toybook. 12mo. 12 numbered pp. Paper wrappers w/sewn binding. Nice. *Reisler.* $90/£58

My Honey's ABC. London/Paris/NY: Raphael Tuck & Sons. Rag book (soiled, fraying). *Davidson.* $285/£184

My New Battledore. Kettering: Joseph Toller, n.d. (ca 1830). 12mo. 2pp + 1 flap, 2 Fine full-pg wood engrs on pict buff self wrapper. Fine. *Hobbyhorse.* $190/£123

My Pets Library. London: Ernest Nister, (ca 1890). 6 bks, each 3 1/4 x 3 3/4 inches. 4 chromolitho plts each bk. Nice set (pencil inscrip) in box w/color paste label (sides broken). *Reisler.* $450/£290

My Pets Pop-Up Pictures. England: Juvenile, 1948. 19x25 cm. 4 dbl-pg pop-ups. Pict bds. (Extrems sl worn.) *Book Finders.* $45/£29

My Pop-Up Book of Baby Animals. London: Dean, 1982. 26x21 cm. 4 pop-ups. Anne Grahame Johnstone (illus). Glazed pict bds. (Last pop-up sl weak.) *Book Finders.* $20/£13

My Pop-Up Book of Ships. London: Brown, Watson, 1986. 25x21 cm, 6 pop-ups (sm tear to 1). J. Pavlin (illus). Glazed pict bds. *Book Finders.* $40/£26

My Secret Life. Vols. 1-11 in 2. NY: Grove, (1966). 2nd ptg. VG in djs (frayed, soiled) & box (worn). *King.* $95/£61

My Very First Book. NY: Macmillan, (1948). 1st ed. Maud and Miska Petersham (illus). 4to. Yellow cl, color paste label, grn lettering. (Names entered; o/w unused.) Color pict slipcase (spine wear; sm split lower edge). *Reisler.* $85/£55

MYERS, A. WALLIS. The Complete Lawn Tennis Player. London, 1921. 5th ed. (Feps lt browned; lower hinge cracked; worn.) *Edwards.* $43/£28

MYERS, BERNARD S. The German Expressionists. NY: Frederick A. Praeger, (1957). 1st ed. 36 tipped-in color plts. Good in dj. *Karmiole.* $125/£81

MYERS, BERNARD S. The German Expressionists. NY: McGraw-Hill, (1963). 1st ed. Rev copy. 24 plts. Bkpl; else Fine. *Bookpress.* $45/£29

MYERS, CHARLES E. Memoirs of a Hunter. Davenport, WA: By Author, (1948). 1st ed. Fine in VG dj. *Perier.* $60/£39

MYERS, CHARLES E. Memoirs of a Hunter. Davenport: Privately ptd, 1948. 1st ed. 18 plts. Fine in NF dj. *Connolly.* $50/£32

MYERS, FRANK. Soldiering in Dakota, Among the Indians.... Pierre, SD: State Hist Soc, 1936. Extra sheet of info on Myers inserted. VG in ptd wraps. Howes M 929. *Bohling.* $60/£39

MYERS, HARRY M. and WILLIAM A. Back Trails. Lapeer, MI: H.M. Myers, (1933). #168/500. Presentation copy, signed. Als tipped in. (Spine lettering dull, rear bd sl warped.) *Bohling.* $125/£81

MYERS, J. ARTHUR. Tuberculosis Among Children. Springfield, 1930. Good. *Fye.* $40/£26

MYERS, L.H. The Root and the Flower. Cape, 1935. 1st Eng ed. Grn cl. Spine faded, o/w VG in dj (mked; repaired). *Dalian.* $39/£25

MYERS, ROBERT MANSON (ed). The Children of Pride. New Haven: Yale, 1972. 1st ed. NF in dj (sl rubbed). *Cahan.* $65/£42

MYLAR, ISAAC L. Early Days at the Mission San Juan Bautista. Watsonville: Evening Pajaronian, 1929. One of 300 signed by Mylar and James G. Piratsky (comp). Gold-stamped cl. Dj (worn, tape-reinforced). *Dawson.* $50/£32

MYRES, E.D. (ed). Pioneer Surveyor, Frontier Lawyer, The Personal Narrative of O.W. Williams 1877-1902. El Paso: Texas Western College Press, 1966. Fresh in orig dj. *Boswell.* $75/£48

MYRES, L. HARRISON. Baptisteries and Fonts Past and Present. London: Preston Guardian, 1902. Pict wrappers (staples rusted). *Hollett.* $39/£25

MYRICK, HERBERT (ed). Turkeys and How to Grow Them. NY: OJ, 1897. viii,159pp + 8pp ads. Brn cl, gilt. VG (spine sl dull, inscrips). *Bohling.* $30/£19

MYRICK, HERBERT. The American Sugar Industry. NY: OJ, 1899. viii,232pp + ads. Brn cl. VG + (lt soiled). *Bohling.* $65/£42

MYRICK, HERBERT. Cache La Poudre, the Romance of a Tenderfoot in the Days of Custer. NY: OJ, 1905. (1st trade ed). Gilt stamped cl (soiled, spine sl faded, ends frayed). Howes M 935. *Bohling.* $125/£81

MYRICK, THOMAS. The Gold Rush. Mount Pleasant, MI, (1971). Good. *Hayman.* $25/£16

N

NABB, MAGDALEN. Death in Autumn. London: CCC, 1985. 1st ed. Fine in dj. *Mordida.* $45/£29

NABB, MAGDALEN. Death of a Dutchman. London: CCC, 1982. 1st ed. Fine in dj. *Mordida.* $45/£29

NABOKOFF-SIRIN, VLADIMIR. Despair. John Long, 1937. 1st UK ed. Good (fore-edge wear; bds tired, faded). *Williams.* $659/£425

NABOKOV, VLADIMIR and EDMUND WILSON. The Nabokov-Wilson Letters.... Simon Karlinsky (ed). NY: Harper & Row, (1979). 1st ed. NF in dj. *Reese.* $30/£19

NABOKOV, VLADIMIR. Ada or Ardor: A Family Chronicle. NY: McGraw-Hill, 1969. 1st ed. VG in dj. *Hermitage.* $40/£26

NABOKOV, VLADIMIR. Bend Sinister. NY: Henry Holt, 1947. 1st ed. Fine in illus dj. *Cahan.* $250/£161

NABOKOV, VLADIMIR. Conclusive Evidence. Harpers, 1951. 1st ed. NF in VG + dj (sl wear). *Fine Books.* $225/£145

NABOKOV, VLADIMIR. The Defence. London: Weidenfield & Nicolson, 1964. 1st ed. VG in dj (sl torn). *Rees.* $23/£15

NABOKOV, VLADIMIR. Despair. Putnam, 1966. 1st Amer ed. NF in VG dj (lt wear). *Fine Books.* $75/£48

NABOKOV, VLADIMIR. The Eye. NY, 1965. 1st Amer ed. Fine in dj (price-clipped). *Polyanthos.* $60/£39

NABOKOV, VLADIMIR. The Eye. NY: Phaedra, 1965. 1st ed. NF in dj (sl browned). *Moorhouse.* $54/£35

NABOKOV, VLADIMIR. The Gift. NY, (1963). 1st Amer ed. Fine in 1st issue dj priced $5.95 (spine sl sunned). *Polyanthos.* $75/£48

NABOKOV, VLADIMIR. Invitation to a Beheading. Dimitri Nabokov (trans). London: Weidenfeld & Nicolson, 1960. 1st Eng ed. Fine in NF dj (nick). *Limestone.* $75/£48

NABOKOV, VLADIMIR. King Queen Knave. London: Weidenfield & Nicolson, 1968. 1st ed. Top edge dusty, o/w VG in dj. *Rees.* $16/£10

NABOKOV, VLADIMIR. Laughter in the Dark. B-M, 1938. 1st ed. VG. *Fine Books.* $125/£81

NABOKOV, VLADIMIR. Lolita. Paris: Olympia Press, (1955). 1st ed, 1st issue w/ptd price of 900 francs on back cvr. 2 vols. NF in wrappers (nick, tiny dot fr cvr vol 1; blind scratches fr cvr vol 2). *Juvelis.* $2,500/£1,613

NABOKOV, VLADIMIR. Lolita. London, (1959). 1st Eng ed. (Sl scuffed.) *Waterfield.* $23/£15

NABOKOV, VLADIMIR. Mary. NY, (1970). 1st ed. VG in dj. *King.* $25/£16

NABOKOV, VLADIMIR. Nikolai Gogol. New Directions, 1944. 1st ed. NF in NF dj. *Fine Books.* $135/£87

NABOKOV, VLADIMIR. Pale Fire. Putnam, 1962. 1st ed. VG + in VG + dj. *Fine Books.* $125/£81

NABOKOV, VLADIMIR. The Real Life of Sebastian Knight. Editions Poetry London, 1845. 1st Eng ed. Brn cl (spine lettering dull). NF in dj (faded; sl mkd). *Dalian.* $132/£85

NABOKOV, VLADIMIR. A Russian Beauty and Other Stories. London, (1973). 1st Eng ed. Dj (sl scuffed). *Waterfield.* $23/£15

NABOKOV, VLADIMIR. Speak, Memory. NY: Putnam's, (1966). 1st rev ed, advance rev copy. Pub's rev slip, info sheets laid in. Fine in dj. *Godot.* $75/£48

NABOKOV, VLADIMIR. The Waltz Invention. NY, 1966. 1st Amer ed. Fine (sl rubbed) in 1st issue (pink) dj (sl rubbed). *Polyanthos.* $35/£23

NABOKOV, VLADIMIR. The Waltz Invention. NY: Phaedra, 1966. 1st ed, w/all points. Fine in NF dj (sm tears). *Beasley.* $75/£48

NADAL, E.S. A Virginian Village. Macmillan, 1917. VG. *Book Broker.* $35/£23

NAEF, WESTON J. The Collection of Alfred Stieglitz: Fifty Pioneers.... NY: MMA, 1978. VG in dj. *Argosy.* $200/£129

NAEF, WESTON J. with JAMES N. WOOD. Era of Exploration: The Rise of Landscape Photography in the American West, 1860-1885. Buffalo/NY: Albright-Knox Art Gallery/Metropolitan Museum of Art, 1975. 1st ed. 126 photo plts. VG in dj. *Cahan.* $75/£48

NAGLE, WALTER. Five Straight Errors on Ladies Day. (As told to Byron Reinhardt.) Caxton, 1965. 1st ed. Fine in VG + dj. *Plapinger.* $65/£42

NAIMY, MIKHAIL. The Book of Mirdad: A Lighthouse and a Haven. London: V. Stuart, (1962). 1st British ed. VG in VG dj. *Blue Dragon.* $30/£19

NAIPAUL, SHIVA. Black and White. London: Hamish Hamilton, 1980. 1st ed. Fine in dj (price-clipped). *Rees.* $16/£10

NAIPAUL, SHIVA. The Chip-Chip Gatherers. London: Deutsch, 1973. 1st ed. Top edge lt spotted, o/w NF in dj. *Rees.* $39/£25

NAIPAUL, SHIVA. The Chip-Chip Gatherers. London: Deutsch, 1973. 1st UK ed. Fine in dj. *Williams.* $101/£65

NAIPAUL, SHIVA. Fireflies. London: Deutsch, 1970. 1st UK ed, 1st bk. Sig, o/w Fine in dj. *Lewton.* $116/£75

NAIPAUL, SHIVA. A Hot Country. London: Hamish Hamilton, 1983. 1st ed. Top edge lt spotted, o/w Fine in dj. *Rees.* $16/£10

NAIPAUL, V.S. Among the Believers. NY: Knopf, 1981. 1st Amer ed. NF (name) in VG dj. *Revere.* $30/£19

NAIPAUL, V.S. An Area of Darkness. A. Deutsch, 1964. 1st ed. NF in NF dj (2 one-inch closed tears). *Fine Books.* $75/£48

NAIPAUL, V.S. A Bend in the River. London: Deutsch, 1979. 1st UK ed. VG in dj. *Lewton.* $20/£13

NAIPAUL, V.S. A Bend in the River. London: Deutsch, 1979. 1st UK ed. Fine in dj. *Williams.* $39/£25

NAIPAUL, V.S. Congo Diary. Sylvester & Orphanos, 1980. One of 300 (of 330) numbered, signed. Fine, as issued. *Rees.* $186/£120

NAIPAUL, V.S. The Enigma of Arrival. Viking, 1987. 1st UK ed. Fine in dj. *Williams.* $19/£12

NAIPAUL, V.S. Finding the Centre. (London): Deutsch, (1984). 1st ed. As New in dj. *Jaffe.* $75/£48

NAIPAUL, V.S. Guerrillas. London: Deutsch, 1975. 1st ed. NF in dj (sl rubbed, mkd). *Rees.* $31/£20

NAIPAUL, V.S. Guerrillas. London: Deutsch, 1975. 1st ed. Fine in dj. *Limestone.* $45/£29

NAIPAUL, V.S. Guerrillas. London: Deutsch, 1975. 1st UK ed. VG in dj. *Lewton.* $25/£16

NAIPAUL, V.S. A House for Mr. Biswas. (London): Deutsch, (1961). 1st ed. Fine in NF dj (sm tears spine extrems). *Between The Covers.* $350/£226

NAIPAUL, V.S. In a Free State. London: Deutsch, 1971. 1st ed. Sl bump, o/w VG in VG dj (sl browned). *Virgo.* $39/£25

NAIPAUL, V.S. India. London: Heinemann, (1990). One of 150 numbered, signed. Cl, marbled bds. Fine. *Dermont.* $100/£65

NAIPAUL, V.S. India: A Million Mutinies Now. London: Heinemann, 1990. One of 150 specially bound, numbered, signed. Fine in glassine dj. *Rees.* $78/£50

NAIPAUL, V.S. The Loss of El Dorado. London: Deutsch, 1969. 1st ed. NF in dj (sl mkd). *Rees.* $31/£20

NAIPAUL, V.S. Miguel Street. Vanguard, 1960. 1st Amer ed. Fine in dj. *Fine Books.* $125/£81

NAIPAUL, V.S. The Mimic Men. A. Deutsch, 1967. 1st ed. Tp little dusty, else Fine in dj. *Fine Books.* $85/£55

NAIPAUL, V.S. The Mimic Men. London: Deutsch, 1967. 1st UK ed. NF in dj. *Lewton.* $70/£45

NAIPAUL, V.S. Mr. Stone and The Knight's Companion. A. Deutsch, 1963. 1st ed. Fine in VG + dj. *Fine Books.* $135/£87

NAIPAUL, V.S. The Mystic Masseur. NY: Vanguard, (1959). 1st Amer ed. Adv rev copy w/slip, photo laid in. VF in Fine dj (sl soiling). *Between The Covers.* $350/£226

NAIPAUL, V.S. The Overcrowded Barracoon. London: Deutsch, 1972. 1st ed. Name, tapemks to eps, o/w NF in dj (price-clipped). *Rees.* $31/£20

NAIPAUL, V.S. The Return of Eva Peron with The Killings in Trinidad. London: Deutsch, 1980. 1st ed. NF in dj (mkd, faded). *Rees.* $16/£10

NAIPAUL, V.S. A Turn in the South. The Franklin Library, 1989. 1st Amer ed. Signed. Fine, as issued. *Rees.* $62/£40

NAIPAUL, V.S. A Turn in the South. Viking, 1989. 1st ed. Signed. Fine in dj. *Rees.* $39/£25

NAIPAUL, V.S. A Turn in the South. Viking, 1989. 1st UK ed. Fine in dj. *Williams.* $19/£12

NAISAWALD, L. VAN LOON. Grape and Canister. NY, 1960. 1st ed. Map. VG + in dj (sl wear). *Pratt.* $55/£35

NANCE, JOSEPH M. Attack and Counter-Attack: The Texas-Mexican Frontier, 1842. Austin: Univ of TX, 1964. 1st ed. Dj. *Lambeth.* $100/£65

NANGLE, E.J. Instruments and Apparatus in Orthopaedic Surgery. Oxford, 1951. (Sig.) Dj. *Whitehart.* $39/£25

NANSEN, FRIDTJOF. Farthest North—Being the Record...of the Ship Fram 1893-96.... Westminster: Archibald Constable, 1897. 1st British ed. 2 vols. xiii,510pp, 2 fldg maps; xiii,1 leaf,671pp, 2 fldg maps. 3/4 leather (some wear), blue marbled paper over bds (eps, edges marbled; internal foxing). *Parmer.* $250/£161

NANSEN, FRIDTJOF. Farthest North. NY, 1897. 1st Amer ed. 2 vols. xi,587; xi,714pp, 16 color plts, 4 fldg maps. Gilt-dec cl (lt scuffed, spotted; sm presentation card glued in vol 1). *Sutton.* $150/£97

NANSEN, FRIDTJOF. Farthest North. Westminster: Archibald Constable, 1897. 1st British ed. 2 vols. 16 color plts, etched port. Full leather, gilt. Tp lt foxed, extrems rubbed, else VG set. *Blue Dragon.* $225/£145

NANSEN, FRIDTJOF. Farthest North. London: Constable, 1897. 1st Eng ed. 2 vols. xiii,510; xiii,671pp, 4 fldg maps. Gilt. VG (fore-edge foxing, o/w bright). *Walcot.* $132/£85

NANSEN, FRIDTJOF. Farthest North. London, 1898. 2 vols. Frontis port, xv,480; viii,456pp, color plt, fldg map, 120 plts. Gilt/color illus cl (spine sl rubbed). *Edwards.* $116/£75

NANSEN, FRIDTJOF. Farthest North. Newnes, 1898. 2nd Eng ed. 2 vols. xv,480; viii,456pp. Aeg. Silver gilt dec cl. VG (few finger mks). *Walcot.* $87/£56

NANSEN, FRIDTJOF. Farthest North: Being the Record of a Voyage of Exploration of the Ship Fram 1893-96.... NY: Harper, (1897). 1st Amer ed. 2 vols. Etched frontis port, (xiv),587; (x),729pp. (Lt foxing; spine sl faded.) *Lefkowicz.* $135/£87

NANSEN, FRIDTJOF. The First Crossing of Greenland. London: Longmans, Green, 1890. 2 vols. xxii,510; x,509pp. 12 plts, 5 fldg maps. Orig silver dec cl. VG (minor scattered foxing; spines almost unfaded). *High Latitude.* $350/£226

NANSEN, FRIDTJOF. Hunting and Adventure in the Arctic. NY: Duffield, 1925. 1st Amer ed. Frontis photo port. Sm spots cvr, else VG. *Blue Dragon.* $75/£48

NANSEN, FRIDTJOF. Through Siberia, the Land of the Future. NY: Stokes, 1914. 3 fldg maps. Orig dec cl. VG in orig ptd dj (sm piece missing from top of spine). *High Latitude.* $150/£97

NANSEN, FRIDTJOF. Through Siberia. NY/London: Stokes/Heinemann, 1914. Frontis port, 3 fldg maps. Dk blue cl stamped in red/gilt (pocket removed). *Schoyer.* $100/£65

NANSEN, FRIDTJOF. Through Siberia. Arthur G. Chater (trans). NY/London, 1914. 1st Amer ed. 156 photos on 49 plts; 3 fldg maps. (Lt foxing; several pp unsewn, loose; spine faded.) *Argosy.* $75/£48

NANSEN, FRIDTJOF. Through Siberia. NY, 1914. 1st Amer ed. 3 fldg maps. Gilt/red stamped cl. Foxing, o/w Nice bright copy. *Sutton.* $135/£87

NANSEN, FRIDTJOF. Through Siberia. Heinemann, 1914. 1st ed. Good + (lt foxing). *Walcot.* $109/£70

NANSEN, FRIDTJOF. Through Siberia. Arthur G. Chater (trans). London: Heinemann, 1914. 1st Eng ed. VG (fly-leaves browned). *Hollett.* $248/£160

NAPHEGYI, G. Among the Arabs. Phila: Lippincott, 1868. 1st ed. Frontis, 252pp. Sl rubbed, soiled; sl foxing; sl shaken, o/w VG ex-lib. *Worldwide.* $75/£48

NAPHEYS, GEORGE. The Body and Its Ailments: A Handbook.... Phila, 1876. 1st ed. 438pp. Good. *Fye.* $40/£26

NAPHEYS, GEORGE. The Transmission of Life. Phila, 1896. 362pp. Good. *Fye.* $40/£26

NAPIER, HENRY EDWARD. New England Blockaded in 1814. Walter Muir Whitehill (ed). Salem: Peabody Museum, 1939. One of 1266. 8 plts, fldg facs map. (Inscrip.) *Schoyer.* $35/£23

NAPIER, ROBERT W. John Thomson of Duddingston. Edinburgh/London, 1919. Photograv frontis port, 30 plts. Fore, lower edges uncut. (Lt spotting.) Dj. *Edwards.* $116/£75

NAPTON, WILLIAM B. Over the Santa Fe Trail 1857. Santa Fe: Stagecoach Press, 1964. #3/99; Wagonmaster ed. VG in Fine dj (sl faded, soiled). *Bohling.* $75/£48

NARAYAN, R.K. Grateful to Life and Death. N.p.: MI State College, 1953. 1st ed. As New in dj. *Hermitage.* $45/£29

NARAYAN, R.K. A Horse and Two Goats. London: Bodley Head, 1970. 1st ed. Inscrip, o/w VG in dj. *Virgo.* $43/£28

NARAYAN, R.K. The Printer of Malgudi. (N.p.): MI State Univ, 1957. 1st ed. NF in dj (1-inch tear). *Hermitage.* $40/£26

NARAYAN, R.K. Swami and His Friends and The Batchelor of Arts. MI State Univ Press, 1954. 1st ed. Yellow cl. Fine in dj. *Dalian.* $39/£25

NARAYAN, R.K. Waiting for the Mahatma. N.p.: MI State Univ, (1955). 1st ed. As New in dj. *Hermitage.* $45/£29

NARES, GEORGE S. Narrative of a Voyage to the Polar Sea during 1875-76.... Sampson, Low, 1878. Vol 1, 3rd ed; vol 2, 1st ed. xl,395; viii,378+32pp ads. 6 woodbury-type real mtd photos. 2 fldg maps (repaired w/linen tape). Orig cl (recased, preserving orig eps). Good+. *Walcot.* $349/£225

Narrative of the Cruise of the Yacht Maria.... (By Samuel Rathbone and Edward Hyde Greg.) London, 1856. 2nd ed. (4),89pp, 11 tinted litho plts (1 fldg), map. Contemp 1/2 polished calf (cvrs restored; lt foxing). *Lefkowicz.* $350/£226

Narrative of the Loss of the 'Kent,' East Indiaman by Fire.... (By Duncan McGregor.) Edinburgh, 1825. 1st ed. 78pp+16pp appendix. Mod bds. *Lewis.* $302/£195

Narrative of the Wreck of the 'Favorite' on the Island of Desolation. (By John Nunn.) London: W.E. Painter, 1850. 1st ed. xx,236pp, fldg map (torn w/o loss, repaired). Good. *Walcot.* $388/£250

Narratives of the American Revolution. Chicago, (1976). Lakeside Classic. VG. *Schoyer.* $20/£13

NASH, CHARLES EDWARD. Biographical Sketches of Gen. Pat Cleburne and Gen. T.C. Hindman. Little Rock, AR: Tunnah & Pittard, 1898. 1st ed. 8vo, frontis, 300pp. Orig black cl. Cvrs sl spotted, else VG+. *Chapel Hill.* $575/£371

NASH, COREY (retold by). Benjamin Bunny Visits Peter Rabbit. Derrydale, 1986. 17x25 cm, 3 pop-ups. Glazed pict bds. Fine. *Book Finders.* $20/£13

NASH, EPHRAIM. The Farmer's Practical Horse Farriery. Auburn: Nash, 1860. 14th thousand revised. Good+. *October Farm.* $40/£26

NASH, JAY ROBERT. Bloodletters and Badmen. NY: Evans, 1973. 1st ed. Fine (sl shaken) in dj (sl chipped; sl worn). *Beasley.* $65/£42

NASH, JOSEPH. The Mansions of England in the Olden Time. London: Henry Sotheran & Co, 1869-72. 2nd ed. 4 vols. Tp (sl chipped, repaired; #s verso) each vol + 100 plts. (Rebound; ex-lib, bkpl; #s spines; spotting throughout.) *Edwards.* $465/£300

NASH, JOSEPH. The Mansions of England in the Olden Time. London: The Studio, 1906. New ed. 104 plts. (Eps, tp lt spotted; feps browned.) *Edwards.* $54/£35

NASH, OGDEN. The Christmas That Almost Wasn't. Boston: Little, Brown, (1957). 1st ed. Linell Nash (illus). VG (bkpl) in dj (edgeworn; short tears). *Antic Hay.* $17/£11

NASH, OGDEN. Collected Verse from 1929 On. London: Dent, 1961. 1st UK ed. VG in dj. *Williams.* $47/£30

NASH, OGDEN. Family Reunion. Boston: Little, Brown, 1950. 1st ed. Fine in VG dj (sm chips, tears). *Antic Hay.* $27/£17

NASH, OGDEN. Good Intentions. Boston: Little, Brown, 1942. 1st ed. VG (lt dampstain; ink presentation) in dj (browned; price-clipped). *Antic Hay.* $25/£16

NASH, OGDEN. The Private Dining Room and Other New Verses. Boston: Little, Brown, (1953). 1st ed. NF in dj (sl browning). *Antic Hay.* $20/£13

NASH, OGDEN. The Private Dining Room. Boston: Little, Brown, (1952). 1st ed. Sig, else NF in dj (sl soiled). *Pharos.* $15/£10

NASMYTH, JAMES and JAMES CARPENTER. The Moon: Considered as a Planet.... NY: Scribner & Welford, 1885. 1st Amer ed. xv,213pp; 25 Woodburytypes, 1 color litho. Silver-emb blue cl. Sl worn, else Fine. *Cahan.* $425/£274

NASON, ELIAS and THOMAS RUSSELL. The Life and Public Services of Henry Wilson. Boston: B.B. Russell, 1876. 1st ed. 452pp, engr frontis port. Contemp 1/2 black calf over purple cl, gilt (extrems rubbed). *Karmiole.* $40/£26

NASON, ELIAS. A History of the Town of Dunstable, Massachusetts.... Boston: Alfred Mudge, 1877. Steel-engr frontis, 316pp. Purple cl, gilt spine. Lt spotted, o/w Fine. *Karmiole.* $50/£32

NASON, ELIAS. Sir Charles Henry Frankland, Baronet. Albany, NY: J. Munsell, 1865. 130pp. Blue pebbled cl (sl rubbed), paper spine label. *Karmiole.* $60/£39

NASON, ELIAS. Sir Charles Henry Frankland, Baronet. Albany: J. Munsell, 1865. Lg paper issue. 129pp. VG. *Schoyer.* $100/£65

NAST, THOMAS. The Fight at Dame Europa's School. NY: Felt, (1871). 1st Amer ed. Good (fading, spotting; sig). *Agvent.* $125/£81

NATHAN, GEORGE JEAN. The Intimate Notebooks. NY, 1932. 1st ed. Fine in dj. *Argosy.* $40/£26

NATHAN, MEL C. Franks of Western Expresses. (Chicago: Collectors' Club of Chicago, 1972.) Gold-stamped cl. Slipcase. *Dawson.* $75/£48

NATHAN, ROBERT. The Green Leaf. NY: Knopf, 1950. 1st ed. One of 3500 ptd. Fine in NF dj (spine sl browned). *Antic Hay.* $35/£23

NATHAN, ROBERT. Morning in Iowa. NY: Knopf, 1944. 1st ed. NF in VG dj (sl wear). *Antic Hay.* $25/£16

NATHAN, ROBERT. Portrait of Jennie. NY, 1940. 1st ed. VG in dj. *Argosy.* $85/£55

NATHAN, ROBERT. Selected Poems of Robert Nathan. NY: Knopf, 1935. 1st ed. One of 375 thus. Blue full-cl binding. Fine in dj (sl soil). *Antic Hay.* $65/£42

NATHAN, ROBERT. Tapiola's Brave Regiment. NY: Knopf, 1941. 1st ed. NF in dj (sl dknd). *Hermitage.* $40/£26

NATION, CARRY AMELIA. The Use and Need of the Life of Carry A. Nation. Topeka: F.M. Steves, 1905. Rev ed. Frontis port. (Tp smudge; 2 sigs sl loose.) Maroon cl (rubbed), gilt. *Weber.* $20/£13

NATIONAL BOOK LEAGUE. The Bloomsbury Group. National Book League/Hogarth, 1976. 1st ed. VG in wrappers. *Words Etc.* $16/£10

National Gallery Catalogues. Early Netherlandish School. Plates. London, 1947. (4pp),121pp of plts. (Corners sl bumped.) *Washton.* $65/£42

Natural History of Birds. Concord, NH: Rufus Merrill, 1851. (Merrill's Toys series.) 12mo. 24pp + 1pg ad back cvr; 12 Fine wood engrs. Yellow pict paper wrappers (spine lt cracked; rubbed). Good (ink sigs). *Hobbyhorse.* $75/£48

Natural History of British Birds. Alnwick: W. Davison, n.d. (ca 1815). 12mo. Frontis, 36pp; 34 Fine engrs by Thomas Bewick (cvr reads 32 engrs on wood). Pict brn paper wrappers (edge chips). Fine. *Hobbyhorse.* $100/£65

NAUGHTON, BILL. A Roof Over Your Head. London: Pilot Press, 1945. 1st ed, 1st bk. Blue cl. Damp mottling fr cvr, o/w Fine in dj (defective). *Temple.* $37/£24

NAUGHTON, BILL. A Roof Over Your Head. London: Pilot, 1945. 1st ed. Edges foxed, o/w VG in dj (sl nicked, internally strengthened). *Rees.* $23/£15

Naval Battles of the United States in the Different Wars with Foreign Nations.... (By Horace Kimball.) Boston: Higgins, Bradley & Dayton, 1857. 278,(1)pp, 19 plts. (Top spine chipped.) Howes K 135. *Lefkowicz.* $50/£32

NAVILLE, EDOUARD. The Store-City of Pithom and the Route of the Exodus. London: Trubner, 1888. vii,40pp, 13 plts, 2 maps. Good. *Archaeologia.* $85/£55

NAYLOR, JAMES BALL. The Little Green Goblin. Akron, OH: Saalfield Pub Co, (1907). Good (sm chip spine; sl rubbed). *Hayman.* $50/£32

NEAL, DANIEL. The History of New-England. London: Clark et al, 1720. 1st ed. 2 vols. Fldg map. Paneled calf (rebacked; tps browned). Howes N 26. *Rostenberg & Stern.* $475/£306

NEAL, LARRY. Hoodoo Hollerin' Bebop Ghosts. Washington: Howard Univ, 1974. 1st ed. Fine in NF dj (price-clipped). *Antic Hay.* $35/£23

NEAL, MARIE C. In Honolulu Gardens. Honolulu: The Museum, 1929. 2nd rev ed, March 1929. Cl-backed bds. VG. *Second Life.* $65/£42

NEAL, MARIE C. In Gardens of Hawaii. Honolulu, 1948. 1st ed. Fine. *Brooks.* $44/£28

NEAL, W. KEITH and D.H.L. BACK. The Mantons: Gunmakers. NY: Walker, (1967). 1st Amer ed. Color frontis, 7 color plts. VG in laminated dj. *Oregon.* $50/£32

NEALE, R. The Medical Digest. London: New Sydenham Soc, 1877. xiii,650pp. VG. *Whitehart.* $39/£25

NEARING, SCOTT. The Next Step. Ridgewood: Nellie Seeds Nearing, 1922. 1st ed. Fine (sunned spine). *Beasley.* $40/£26

NEARING, SCOTT. War: Organized Destruction and Mass Murder by Civilized Nations. NY: Viking, (1931). 1st ed. VG in dj (lt wear, nicks, short tears, else VG). *Godot.* $65/£42

NEASHAM and HENLEY. The City of the Plain. Sacramento in the Nineteenth Century. Sacramento Pioneer Foundation, 1969. 1st ed. Ltd to 2000. Color frontis. Pict gilt-stamped cl. Prospectus laid in. Fine. *Oregon.* $90/£58

NEATBY, L.H. Conquest of the Last Frontier. Athens: OH Univ, (1966). 1st ed. NF in VG dj. *Blue Dragon.* $25/£16

NEEDHAM, JOSEPH. Biochemistry and Morphogenesis. Cambridge: CUP, 1942. 1st ed. 35 plts (4 color). *Bickersteth.* $85/£55

NEEDHAM, JOSEPH. Science and Civilisation in China. Vol 3. CUP, 1959. Fldg map, 19 tables (1 fldg). 2-tone cl (ex-lib w/ink stamps, label remains, #; upper hinge reinforced w/tape). Dj (tape mks). *Edwards.* $74/£48

NEEDHAM, PAUL et al. William Morris and the art of the Book. OUP, 1976. Frontis port, 114 plts. (Ex-lib; tape mks.) Dj (spine faded, tail torn). *Edwards.* $62/£40

NEEL, J.V. and W.J. SCHULL. The Effect of Exposure to the Atomic Bombs on Pregnancy Termination in Hiroshima and Nagasaki. Washington, 1956. Good. *Fye.* $50/£32

NEESE, GEORGE MICHAEL. Three Years in the Confederate Horse Artillery. By a Gunner in Chew's Battery.... NY/Washington: Neale Pub Co, 1911. 1st ed. Orig grn cl (spine darkened w/sl discoloration; minor extrem wear). Overall VG. Howes N33. *Mcgowan.* $650/£419

NEFF, ANDREW LOVE. History of Utah 1847 to 1869. Salt Lake, 1940. 1st ed. Sm scratch spine, o/w VG +. *Benchmark.* $60/£39

NEFTEL, WILLIAM. Galvano-Therapeutics. NY, 1873. 1st ed. 161pp. Good. *Fye.* $125/£81

NEGOVSKII, V.A. Resuscitation and Artificial Hypothermia. NY, 1962. 1st Eng trans. Good. *Fye.* $50/£32

NEGRI, VITALI. Psychoanalysis of Sexual Life. LA: Western Inst of Psychoanalysis Inc, 1949. 1st ed. Maroon cl, gilt spine. Good. *Karmiole.* $30/£19

Negroes of Nebraska. Lincoln, NE, 1940. 1st ed. Fine in orig stiff ptd wrappers. *Mcgowan.* $75/£48

NEGUS, VICTOR. Artistic Possessions at the Royal College of Surgeons of England. London/Edinburgh, 1967. Orig cl, gilt emblem. VF. *Europa.* $50/£32

NEGUS, VICTOR. The Comparative Anatomy and Physiology of the Nose and Paranasal Sinuses. Edinburgh/London, 1958. Sm wormhole back cvr, final 30pp, o/w Good. *Whitehart.* $54/£35

NEHRLING, HENRY. My Garden in Florida and Miscellaneous Horticultural Notes. Estero, FL: American Eagle, 1944, 1946. 1st ed. 2 vols. Frontis port. Name; eps, edges lt foxed; spines sl worn, else VG in ptd djs. *Cahan.* $85/£55

NEHRU, JAWAHARLAL. Points of View. NY: John Day, 1941. One of 1000. Fine in orig tissue (lt used). *Beasley.* $25/£16

NEIDHARD, C. Diphtheria, as it Prevailed in the United States from 1860 to 1866, Preceded by an Historical Account.... NY, 1867. 1st ed. 176pp. Good. *Fye.* $100/£65

NEIHARDT, JOHN G. Black Elk Speaks. NY: W. Morrow, 1932. 1st ed. VG- (bkpl; waterstain bottom cvr). *Parker.* $60/£39

NEIHARDT, JOHN G. A Cycle of the West. NY: Macmillan, 1947. 1st ed. Signed inscription. Fine in dj (worn). *Dermont.* $45/£29

NEIHARDT, JOHN G. Poetic Values: Their Reality and Our Need of Them. Macmillan, 1925. 1st ed. Fine. *Authors Of The West.* $50/£32

NEIHARDT, JOHN G. The Quest. NY: Macmillan, 1916. 1st ed. Blue cl. Fine in dj (darkened at spine; lt chipping). *Dermont.* $75/£48

NEIHARDT, JOHN G. The River and I. NY: Macmillan, 1927. 2nd ed. Frontis. Black/red ptd cl (sl bumped). *Dawson.* $30/£19

NEIHARDT, JOHN G. The Song of Hugh Glass. Macmillan, 1915. 1st ed. Fine. *Authors Of The West.* $40/£26

NEIHARDT, JOHN G. The Song of the Indian Wars. NY: Macmillan, 1925. 1st ed. Pict cl. *Dawson.* $75/£48

NEIHARDT, JOHN G. The Song of the Messiah. NY: Macmillan, 1935. 1st ed. Fine in Fine dj. *Dermont.* $35/£23

NEIHARDT, JOHN G. The Splendid Wayfaring. NY: Macmillan, 1920. 1st ed. Forest grn cl. Lg bkpl, else VG. *Glenn.* $45/£29

NEIHARDT, JOHN G. The Splendid Wayfaring. NY: Macmillan, 1920. 1st ed. Frontis. Dj (lt soiled; 2 tape-repaired tears). *Dawson.* $50/£32

NEILL, A.S. Summerhill. NY: Hart, 1960. 1st ed. NF in dj (sm sticker spine panel). *Lame Duck.* $50/£32

NEILL, EDWARD D. History of the Virginia Company of London with Letters to and from the First Colony Never Before Printed. Burt Franklin, 1968. VG. *Book Broker.* $35/£23

NEILL, EDWARD D. History of the Virginia Company of London. Albany: Joel Munsell, 1869. 1st ed. Frontis, xvi,432pp (underlining, notes; bkpls; foxing, browning to text); teg. Pub's cl (spotted, sunned). *Bookpress.* $200/£129

NEILL, JOHN R. Lucky Bucky in Oz. London: Hutchinson's Books for Young People, (1945). 1st British ed. 8vo. Red cl, black lettering (foxing early pgs; spots cvr). *Reisler.* $135/£87

NEILL, JOHN R. Lucky Bucky in Oz. Chicago: Reilly & Lee, 1942. 1st ed, 1st state. 16pp, gatherings. 1st state dj w/letter from 'Bucky of Oz,' ptd price of $1.50, word Oz ptd on spine with Z inside. VG in VG dj. *Davidson.* $400/£258

NEILL, JOHN R. The Scalawagons of Oz. Chicago: Reilly & Lee, (1941). 1st ed, 1st state. 4to. Brick-red cl, color paste label. Internally Fine (marginal fold/tear) in color dj (worn; lacks pieces). *Reisler.* $575/£371

NEILL, JOHN. Outline of the Nerves with Short Descriptions. Phila: Barrington, 1852. 2nd ed. 28pp; 9 plts. (Browned, foxed; ex-lib, stamps; newly rebacked.) *Goodrich.* $75/£48

NEILL, JOHN. Outlines of the Arteries: with Short Descriptions. Phila: Barrington & Haswell, 1852. 2nd ed. 28pp; 7 hand-colored plts. VG (sig). *Glaser.* $100/£65

NEILL, PATRICK. The Fruit, Flower and Kitchen Garden. Edinburgh: Black, 1845. 3rd ed. xi,364,16pp ads. *Marlborough.* $70/£45

NEILL, PATRICK. The Fruit, Flower, and Kitchen Garden. Phila, 1851. 427pp. (Ex-lib; worn, chipped; foxed.) *Sutton.* $45/£29

Nellie Grey. London: Frederick Warne, 1869. 16mo. viii,168pp, Fine color frontis by Kronheim. Blind-stamped grn cl, backstrip gilt. Browning, but Good. *Cox.* $23/£15

Nelson's Hand-Book to the Isle of Wight. London, 1863. 215pp, fldg map. (Browning; wear.) *Edwards.* $43/£28

NELSON, GEORGE and HENRY WRIGHT. Tomorrow's House. NY: S&S, 1945. 2nd ed. Good+ (sl shaky). *Willow House.* $28/£18

NELSON, JOHN LOUW. Rhythm for Rain. Boston: Houghton Mifflin, 1937. 1st ed. VG in VG dj. *Perier.* $40/£26

NELSON, LARRY E. Bullets, Ballots, and Rhetoric. Confederate Policy for the United States Presidential Contest of 1864. University, AL: Univ of AL Press, (1980). 1st ed. Fine in NF dj. *Mcgowan.* $35/£23

NELSON, MARY CARROLL. The Legendary Artists of Taos. NY: Watson-Guptill, (1980). 1st ed. Fine in VG dj. *Perier.* $50/£32

NELSON, PHILIP. Ancient Painted Glass in England 1170-1500. London: Methuen, 1913. 1st ed. Color frontis, 32 plts. Spotted. *Hollett.* $85/£55

NELSON, R. Asiatic Cholera: Its Origin and Spread.... NY, 1866. 1st ed. 206pp. Good. *Fye.* $150/£97

NELSON, RAPHAEL. Cries and Criers of Old London. London/Glasgow: Collins, 1941. Inked and dated presentation, signed. 4to. 31 unnumbered leaves. 1 pg intro, 31 VF full-pg linocuts. Linen on bd cvrs; black vignette w/title on upper cvr. VG in Fair pict dj (edges, spine chipped). *Hobbyhorse.* $125/£81

NELSON, T.H. The Birds of Yorkshire. London, 1907. 1st ed. 2 vols. Color frontispieces. (Sl wear, ex-libris.) *Edwards.* $233/£150

NELSON, WILLIAM. Alluring Arizona. SF: By author, 1929. 2nd ed. Frontis, tissue; 9 photo-plts. Pict cl, gilt. Fine. *Connolly.* $20/£13

NELSON, WILLIAM. The Laws Concerning Game. (London): Ptd by Henry Lintot, Law-Printer to the King, 1753. 5th ed. Contemp calf. VG. *Boswell.* $450/£290

NERSESSIAN, SIRARPIE DER. Armenian Manuscripts in the Walters Art Gallery. Balt, 1973. Color frontis, 7 color plts, 243 b/w. *Edwards.* $101/£65

NERSESSIAN, V. Armenian Illuminated Gospel Books. London: British Library, 1987. 1st ed. 25 color plts; dbl-pg map. Fine in dj. *Worldwide.* $40/£26

NERUDA, PABLO. A New Decade (Poems: 1958-1967). Ben Belitt (ed). NY: Grove Press, (1969). 1st ed. Rev copy, slip laid in. Fine in dj. *Sadlon.* $25/£16

NERUDA, PABLO. Twenty Love Poems and A Song of Despair. W.S. Merwin (trans). Cape, 1969. 1st Eng ed. White ptd wrappers. VF in dj (sl rubbed). *Dalian.* $31/£20

NERUDA, PABLO. Twenty Poems. N.p.: Sixties Press, 1967. 1st ed. NF (edges lt dknd) in wraps. *Beasley.* $50/£32

NERUDA, PABLO. We Are Many. Alastair Reid (trans). London: Grossman/Cape Goliard, (1972). 1st ed. NF in pict wraps. *Polyanthos.* $25/£16

NESBIT, E. Nine Unlikely Tales for Children. London: T. Fisher Unwin, 1901. 8vo. Frontis, 297pp. Red cl (faded, spotted), gilt. *Drusilla's.* $95/£61

NESBIT, E. The Railway Children. London: Gardener, (1906). 1st ed. Pict maroon cl, gilt (stained, puckered; sig). *Petersfield*. $152/£98

NESBIT, E. and ROSAMUND E. BLAND. Cat Tales. London: Ernest Nister, (1904). 1st ed. 12mo. Isabel Watkin (illus). Illus grey cl (lib stamp eps; code # 1st pg). *Reisler*. $100/£65

NESBIT, L.M. Desert and Forest. London: Cape, 1935. 3rd ptg. Lg fldg color map. Grn cl. VG. *Bowman*. $25/£16

NETTER, FRANK. A Compilation of Paintings on the Normal and Pathological Anatomy of the Reproductive System. Summit, NJ, 1954. 1st ed. Good. *Fye*. $50/£32

NEUBERGER, RICHARD. The Lewis and Clark Expedition. NY: Random House, 1951. 1st trade ed. Winold Reiss (illus). Dec eps. VG in dj. *Cattermole*. $25/£16

NEUER, RONI and LIBERTSON. Ukiyo-E. 250 Years of Japanese Art. NY/London, 1979. 377 color plts. Dj (spine lt faded). *Edwards*. $59/£38

NEUHAUS, EUGEN. The Art of the Exposition. SF: Paul Elder, 1915. 2nd ed. Uncut, partly unopened. Gilt-stamped paper-cvrd bds. Fine. *Quest*. $50/£32

NEUMANN, GEORGE. The History of Weapons of the American Revolution. NY, 1967. VG in dj (worn). *Clark*. $40/£26

Neurosurgery and Thoracic Surgery. Phila: Saunders, 1943. Good. *Goodrich*. $25/£16

Nevada; A Guide to the Silver State. Portland, (1940). 1st ed. Fldg map. Buckram. In dj (spine chip). *Argosy*. $125/£81

NEVILL, RALPH. British Military Prints. London, 1909. (Ex-lib; upper joint cracked; lower bd damp-stained, onto eps, text; corners worn w/loss.) *Edwards*. $39/£25

NEVILL, RALPH. British Military Prints. London: Connoisseur Pub Co, 1909. 1st ed. 24 color illus. Orig dec cl (spine faded, sl soiled, extrems frayed; foxing). *Karmiole*. $35/£23

NEVILL, RALPH. British Military Prints. London, 1909. 1st ed. Color frontis, 23 other color plts (1 loose). Good+ (sl shaken) in dec red cl, mtd color medallion. *Edwards*. $70/£45

NEVILL, RALPH. British Military Prints. London: Connoisseur Pub Co, 1909. 1st ed. 24 color plts, 64 b/w or tinted plts. Gilt/black pict red cl, color plt on cvr. Spine ends worn, o/w VG+. *House*. $120/£77

NEVILL, RALPH. Old English Sporting Prints and Their History. London: The Studio, 1923. One of 1500. 103 plts (47 full-color), guards. Beveled orange cl (spine faded), gold-stamped, teg. *Bookpress*. $225/£145

NEVILLE, HUGH. The Game Laws of England for Gamekeepers. London: John Van Voorst, 1884. Orig russet cl, gilt. Very Nice. *Boswell*. $150/£97

NEVIN, DAVID. The Civil War. Sheridan's March: Atlanta to the Sea. Alexandria, VA: Time-Life Bks, (1986). 1st ed. NF. *Mcgowan*. $20/£13

NEVINS, ALLAN. Fremont, the West's Greatest Adventurer. NY: Harper, 1928. 1st ed. 2 vols. Blue cl. Fine set in ptd djs, slipcase (lt worn). *House*. $180/£116

NEVINS, ALLAN. Fremont. NY: D. Appleton-Century, 1939. 1st ptg of 2nd rev ed. Fine in dj (lt worn). *Glenn*. $45/£29

NEVINS, ALLAN. Ordeal of the Union. NY: Scribner's, (1947). 1st ed. 2 vols. VG set. *Mcgowan*. $45/£29

NEVINS, ALLAN. The War for the Union. NY, 1959/1960/1971. 1st eds. Vol 1 inscribed. 4 vols. Sl dj wear, 1 dj spine faded, o/w Fine set. *Pratt*. $95/£61

NEVINS, DEBORAH and ROBERT A.M. STERN. The Architect's Eye: American Architectural Drawings from 1799-1978. NY, 1979. Emb cl. VG in dj (soiled). *Argosy*. $100/£65

New Bath Guide. Bath: ptd by C. Pope, n.d. (ca 1765). 2nd ed. iv,60pp. (Paper flaw one leaf, sl text loss.) New wrappers. *Marlborough*. $140/£90

New California Tourist's Guide. SF: Samuel Carson, 1886. vii,169pp + 7pp ads, 3 maps (2 fldg). Pict wrappers (spine worn). *Dawson*. $200/£129

New Comic Almanack for 1836. London: W. Marshall, (1835?). 1st ptg. 48,(4)pp. 9 full-pg engrs. VG in ptd wraps (sl soiled, spine chipped). *Chapel Hill*. $50/£32

New Farmer's Calendar. (By John Lawrence.) London: Ptd by C. Whitingham, 1802. 4th ed. xxxv,(i)contents,554pp,index(vi) (flyleaf lacks coner, ex-libris). Marbled eps. Contemp gilt-edged diced calf (sl rubbed), dec gilt. *Edwards*. $194/£125

New Hieroglyphic Bible. NY: Blakeman & Mason's Ed, n.d. (ca 1840). 12mo. 98pp. Full-pg wood engr 1/2 title, tp. Tooled brn cl on bds; gilt title; spine decs. VG (cvrs, spine faded; spine corners, edges lt rubbed). *Hobbyhorse*. $100/£65

New History of England, from the Invasion of Julius Caesar to the Present Time. London: W. Darton, Jun., 1818. 2 vols, each w/1818 on cvr, 1812 on tp. Each vol: 12mo. 64pp + 1pg ad, 16 half-pg VF copper engrs. Orig ptd wrappers, ads on back cvrs (soiled, worn). Good (sigs). *Hobbyhorse*. $200/£129

New London Cries, or a Visit to Town. London: J.L. Marks, n.d. (ca 1845). 12mo. 8 leaves + 1pg list lower wrapper. Dec blue paper wrappers (sl soiling). Sm repair 1 pg, else Fine. *Hobbyhorse*. $275/£177

New Natural History; Intended as a Present for Good Boys and Girls. Otley: W. Walker, n.d. (ca 1840). Chapbook. 16mo. Full-pg frontis pasted down on cvr. Pict brn stiff paper wrappers. VG. *Hobbyhorse*. $70/£45

New Poster: International Exposition of Design in Outdoor Advertising. Phila: Franklin Inst, 1937. One of 2500. Spiral bound. (Water damage 1st few pp not affecting text.) *Artis*. $22/£14

New System of Domestic Cookery. (By Maria Eliza Rundell.) Exeter: Norris & Sawyer, 1808. 3rd ed. (6),xx,297pp. Contemp sheep. Nice (sm piece torn fore-edge; scattered foxing). *Felcone*. $400/£258

New System of Domestic Cookery. (By Maria Eliza Rundle.) London, 1829. New ed. Sm 8vo. Frontis; liv,449pp; 9 plts. (Sl spotting; marginal repairs; plts 6,7 & pp 36,37 not bound as directed; hinges sl tender; cl sl soiled, rubbed.) *Edwards*. $93/£60

New System of Domestic Cookery. (By Maria Eliza Rundle.) London, 1836. 59th ed. Frontis; xlviii,448pp; 9 plts. (Spotting.) Mod calf, marbled bds (rebound). *Edwards*. $78/£50

New-England Primer...to which is added The Assembly's Catechism. Boston: James Loring, n.d. (ca 1820). 32mo. 31 leaves, incl dec self-wrappers. VG (ink name, lt browned; last leaf worn, repaired w/loss) in folder, 3/4 morocco slipcase. *Hobbyhorse*. $200/£129

NEWBERRY, JULIA. Diary. NY: Norton, (1933). 1st ed. Port. Gilt-stamped pink cl. VG in dj (soiled). *Petrilla*. $25/£16

NEWBERRY, PERCY E. Scarabs: An Introduction to the Study of Egyptian Seals and Signet Rings. London: Constable, 1908. 1st ed. 44 plts (1 color). Teg. (Lt foxing first pp, sm bkpls.) *Archaeologia*. $250/£161

NEWBERRY, PERCY E. Scarabs: An Introduction to the Study of Egyptian Seals and Signet Rings. London: Constable, 1908. Rpt ed. Frontis, 43 plts. VG-. *Blue Dragon.* $45/£29

NEWBOLT, HENRY. Aladore. London, 1914. 1st ed. VG. *Madle.* $75/£48

NEWBOLT, HENRY. Aladore. Dutton, 1915. 1st US ed. VG. *Madle.* $50/£32

NEWBOLT, HENRY. The Linnet's Nest. (London: Faber, 1927). Good in ptd wraps (sl soiled). *Second Life.* $20/£13

NEWBY, ERIC. The Last Grain Race. London, (1956). 1st ed. Dj. *Petersfield.* $16/£10

NEWBY, ERIC. The Last Grain Race. London, 1956. 1st ed, 1st bk. Dj. *Edwards.* $47/£30

NEWBY, ERIC. Love and War in the Apennines. London, 1971. 1st ed. Frontis port, map. Dj (sl rubbed). *Edwards.* $28/£18

NEWBY, ERIC. A Short Walk in the Hindu Kush. London, 1958. 1st ed. Fldg map. Dj (chipped, sl creased, sl loss). *Edwards.* $47/£30

NEWBY, ERIC. Slowly Down the Ganges. Hodder & Stoughton, 1966. 1st Eng ed. Blue cl. Fine in dj (sl nicked). *Dalian.* $85/£55

NEWCOMB, RAYMOND L. Our Lost Explorers: The Narrative of the Jeannette Arctic Expedition as Related by the Survivors.... Hartford: American Pub Co, 1883. xv,17-479pp. Orig dec cl. VG. *High Latitude.* $75/£48

NEWCOMB, RAYMOND L. Our Lost Explorers: The Narrative of the Jeannette Arctic Expedition.... Hartford, 1882. 479pp. Good (rubbed). *Walcot.* $59/£38

NEWCOMB, REXFORD. Architecture of the Old Northwest Territory. Chicago: Univ of Chicago, (1950). Ltd to 1500 numbered. 96 leaves of plts. Good. *Karmiole.* $85/£55

NEWCOMB, REXFORD. The Old Mission Churches and Historic Houses of California. Phila/London, 1925. 1st ed. Cvr dampstained along top edges. Dj (worn, torn). *Hayman.* $50/£32

NEWCOMB, REXFORD. The Old Mission Churches and Historic Houses of California. Phila: Lippincott, 1925. 1st ed. Color frontis. Blue gilt cl (lt soiled). *Karmiole.* $100/£65

NEWCOMB, REXFORD. The Spanish House for America, Its Design, Furnishing, and Garden. Phila: Lippincott, 1927. 1st ed. Frontis. Sl rubbed; ex-lib w/mks, else VG. *Bookpress.* $110/£71

NEWCOMB, W.W. The Rock Art of Texas Indians. Austin: Univ of TX Press, 1967. 32 color, 128 monochrome illus. VG in dj. *Argosy.* $85/£55

NEWCOMBE, COVELLE. The Secret Door. NY: Dodd, Mead, 1946. 1st ed. Grn cl, gilt pict cvr. Fine (lacks dj). *Glenn.* $30/£19

NEWELL, CHARLES M. The Voyage of the Fleetwing. Boston: De Wolf, Fiske & Co, (1886). 1st ed. (6),443pp. Ptd cl (lower inner hinge weak; 1 plt 'enhanced' w/red). *Lefkowicz.* $100/£65

NEWELL, GORDON and ALLAN E. SMITH. The U.S.S. Missouri. Seattle: Superior, (1969). 1st ed. Ltd to 2500. Black leatherette, gilt. Upper joint rubbed, else Fine. *Glenn.* $45/£29

NEWELL, PETER. The Rocket Book. NY: Harper, (1912). 1st ed. 4to. Blue cl, color paste label (rubbed; marginal tears, finger mks). *Reisler.* $185/£119

NEWELL, ROBERT. Robert Newell's Memoranda. Portland: Champoeg, 1959. 1st ed. NF. *Parker.* $60/£39

NEWELL, ROBERT. Robert Newell's Memoranda. Dorothy O. Johansen (ed). Portland, OR: Champoeg Press, 1959. Ltd to 1000. Frontis. Red cl. Good. *Karmiole.* $40/£26

NEWELL, ROBERT. Robert Newell's Memoranda: Travles in Teritory of Missourie.... Champoeg Press, 1959. 1st ed. One of 1000 ptd. Frontis, 2 maps (1 fldg). Fine. *Oregon.* $75/£48

NEWHALL, NANCY. The Photographs of Edward Weston. NY: MOMA, (1946). 1st ed. Frontis port, 24 photos. Dj (sl chipped). *Shasky.* $75/£48

NEWHALL, NANCY. Time in New England. NY: OUP, 1950. 1st ed. 106 b/w plts by Paul Strand. VG (ex-lib). *Cahan.* $45/£29

NEWHALL, NANCY. Time in New England. NY: OUP, 1950. 1st ed. 106 b/w plts. Paul Strand (photos). Fine in dj. *Cahan.* $150/£97

NEWHAUSER, R.D. Modern Book Ends. Milwaukee: Bruce Pub Co, (1950). 1st ed. 24 plts. (Gutters foxed.) Dj. *Oak Knoll.* $20/£13

NEWHOUSE, EDWARD. This Is Your Day. NY: Lee Furman, 1937. 1st ed. NF in dj (lt used; tears; worn; soiling lower edge). *Beasley.* $150/£97

NEWHOUSE, S. The Trapper's Guide. Mason (NY): Oakley, 1869. 3rd ed. 215pp. Orig cl (edgewear). VG. *Bowman.* $40/£26

NEWLAND, HENRY. Forest Scenes in Norway and Sweden. London: Routledge, 1854. 1st ed. 418pp. Gilt dec red cl. Chip head of spine, o/w VG+. *Bowman.* $125/£81

NEWLANDS, JOHN A.R. On the Discovery of the Periodic Law, and on Relations Among the Atomic Weights. London, 1884. Inscribed. 39pp + ads; 2 fldg tables. Fine. *Argosy.* $350/£226

NEWMAN, E. A History of British Ferns and Allied Plants. London, 1844. 1st ed. xxxii,424pp + 8pp ads. Plt, ms pg tipped in. Fine. *Henly.* $40/£26

NEWMAN, FRANCES. The Hard-Boiled Virgin. NY: Boni & Liveright, 1926. 1st ed. Signed. VG in dj (tape reinforcement top verso). *Chapel Hill.* $200/£129

NEWMAN, FRANCES. The Hard-Boiled Virgin. NY: Boni & Liveright, 1926. 1st ed. Signed. VG in dj (internally strengthened; tears). *Turlington.* $225/£145

NEWMAN, GEORGE. The Rise of Preventive Medicine. London, 1932. 1st ed. (Ex-lib.) *Fye.* $90/£58

NEWMAN, JOHN HENRY. Discourses Addressed to Mixed Congregations. London: Longman et al, 1849. 1st ed. vi,402pp. Contemp binder's cl. Early marginal mend 1 fore-edge, spine faded, mkd, o/w Good. *Reese.* $50/£32

NEWMAN, JOHN HENRY. An Essay on the Development of Christian Doctrine. London, 1845. 1st ed. 453pp (1st few pp stained; stamps). Later 1/2 leather (rubbed). *King.* $50/£32

NEWMAN, JOHN HENRY. Sermons, Chiefly on the Theory of Religious Belief.... London: J.G.F. & J. Rivington, 1843. 1st ed. viii,354,(2)pp. Bkseller stamp fr pastedown; inscrip; sl rubbed, soiled, hinges cracked, o/w Good. *Reese.* $75/£48

NEWMAN, JOHN P. The Thrones and Palaces of Babylon and Nineveh.... NY: Harper, 1876. 1st ed. 455pp + 12pp ads (sm abrasions pp83-86), dbl-pg map. Gilt pict brn cl. VG. *House.* $80/£52

NEWMARK, HARRIS. Sixty Years in Southern California 1853-1913. Boston: Houghton Mifflin, 1930. 1st ed. Fine in Fine dj. *Book Market.* $96/£62

NEWSHOLME, ARTHUR. Epidemic Diphtheria. London, 1898. 1st ed. Inscribed. Good. *Fye.* $100/£65

NEWSHOLME, ARTHUR. The Prevention of Tuberculosis. NY, 1908. 1st Amer ed. Good. *Fye.* $75/£48

NEWSOM, SAMUEL and KANTO SHIGEMORI. Japanese Gardens. Tokyo: Tokyo News Service, 1960. Dec rice paper eps. Pict bds. Fine (marginal creases) in dj. *Quest.* $85/£55

Newton Forster, or, The Merchant Service. (By Frederick Marryat.) Phila: Carey, Lea & Blanchard, 1833. 1st Amer ed. Spines lightened; rubbed; lt foxing; spot of dampstain vol 1. *Sadlon.* $40/£26

NEWTON, A. EDWARD. The Amenities of Book-Collecting and Kindred Affections. Boston: Atlantic Monthly, (1920). 1st ed, 3rd imp. Presentation. (Corners most pp stained; spotting; label chipped.) *Oak Knoll.* $20/£13

NEWTON, A. EDWARD. The Amenities of Book-Collecting and Kindred Affections. Boston: Atlantic Monthly, 1918. 1st ed, 1st issue, w/o index, but no errata slip present. Teg. Cl-backed bds, label. NF. *Macdonnell.* $60/£39

NEWTON, A. EDWARD. The Amenities of Book-Collecting and Kindred Affections. Boston: Atlantic Monthly Press, 1918. 1st ed, 1st state. Frontis, errata slip pg 268. VG (spine and label dust soiled; shelf wear). *Graf.* $25/£16

NEWTON, A. EDWARD. Derby Day: And Other Adventures. Boston: Little, Brown, 1934. 1st ed. Checked cl, ptd label. VG in illus dj (sl dknd, chipped). *Cahan.* $35/£23

NEWTON, A. EDWARD. Doctor Johnson, a Play. Boston: Atlantic Monthly, 1923. One of 585 numbered, specially ptd & bound; signed. Port. Cl, dec paper over bds. Fine in VG slipcase (chips). *Reese.* $75/£48

NEWTON, A. EDWARD. End Papers. Boston, 1933. 1/1351 numbered of Dream Children Edition, inscribed. 8 b/w plts; facs of Lamb's Dream Children ms in pocket at rear; uncut, unopened. VG in bd slipcase. *Argosy.* $75/£48

NEWTON, A. EDWARD. End Papers. Boston: Little Brown, 1933. 1st ed. Color frontis. Fine (name on ep) in dj (lt soiled). *Graf.* $35/£23

NEWTON, A. EDWARD. End Papers. Boston: Little, Brown, 1933. One of 1351. Inscribed, signed. Facs ms of 'Dream Children' in rear pocket. 1/4 cream buckram, blue paper bds, engr fr cvr. Fine in slipcase (cracked). *Heller.* $60/£39

NEWTON, A. EDWARD. The Greatest Book in the World and Other Papers. Boston: Little, Brown, (1925). 1st trade ed, 2nd issue w/'The Autograph of Cruikshank' in list of illus p334. Color frontis. Fine in dj (worn). *Oak Knoll.* $20/£13

NEWTON, A. EDWARD. The Greatest Book in the World and Other Papers. Little, Brown, 1925. 1st ed. Color frontis. 1/4 cl. VG. *Moss.* $25/£16

NEWTON, A. EDWARD. A Magnificent Farce and Other Diversions of a Book Collector. Boston: Atlantic Monthly Press, (1921). 2nd ed. VG. *Graf.* $25/£16

NEWTON, A. EDWARD. Newton on Blackstone. Phila: Univ of PA Press, 1937. 1st ed. #1091/2000, signed. VG. *Graf.* $40/£26

NEWTON, A. EDWARD. This Book-Collecting Game. Boston: Little, Brown, 1928. 1st ed, 2nd imp. (Inscrip; rubbed; worn spot.) *Oak Knoll.* $20/£13

NEWTON, A. EDWARD. This Book-Collecting Game. Boston: Little, Brown, 1928. 1st ed, trade issue. Inscribed. Frontis. Teg. Good (label sl tanned; lt shelfwear). *Reese.* $60/£39

NEWTON, A. EDWARD. This Book-Collecting Game. London: Routledge, 1930. 1st Eng ed, w/cancelled leaf (p195). White cl. Fine in dj. *Macdonnell.* $60/£39

NEWTON, A. EDWARD. A Tourist in Spite of Himself. Boston: Little, Brown, 1930. One of 525 nimbered, signed. Frontis. Cl, dec bds. Nice (spine label sl tanned) in Good slipcase (faded, worn). *Reese.* $50/£32

NEWTON, A. EDWARD. The Trollope Society.... Phila: A. Edward Newton, 1934. 1st ed. Port. Spine sunned, else Fine in sewn ptd wrappers. *Reese.* $25/£16

NEWTON, ALFRED and HANS GADOW. A Dictionary of Birds. London: A&C Black, 1896. 1st ed. 4 parts in 1 vol. xii,124; vi,1088pp; fldg map. Grn cl (rubbed; sl shaken). Good. *Cox.* $39/£25

NEWTON, C.T. Travels and Discoveries in the Levant. London: Day, 1865. 2 vols complete. xxviii,635pp, 41 plts (6 fldg). Teg. Full 19th cent morocco, 5 raised bands (extrems sl rubbed). Attractive set. *Archaeologia.* $650/£419

NEWTON, ERIC. Christopher Wood 1901-1930. London, 1938. Tipped-in frontis port; 21 tipped-in color, 17 tipped in b/w plts. (Ex-lib w/sm ink stamp margin of plts, verso tp, bkpl; rebound in lib cl; #s.) *Edwards.* $39/£25

NEWTON, HELMUT. Sleepless Nights. NY: Congreve, 1978. 1st ed. VG (lt rubbed; sl loose). *Cahan.* $75/£48

NEWTON, HUEY P. Revolutionary Suicide. NY: Harcourt, (1973). 1st ed. VG in dj. *Petrilla.* $40/£26

NEWTON, HUEY P. and ERICKA HUGGINS. Insights and Poems. City Lights, SF, 1975. 1st Amer ed. Fine in ptd wraps (sl edge rubbed). *Polyanthos.* $25/£16

NEWTON, ISAAC. The Mathematical Principles of Natural Philosophy...To Which Are Added Newton's System of the World...by W. Emerson. With the Laws of the Moon's Motion...by John Machin. W. Davis (rev). Andrew Motte (trans). London, 1803. 2nd ed. 3 vols. Frontis port; 44 fldg plts. Later calf-backed buckram (joints sl rubbed; new eps). *Argosy.* $650/£419

NEWTON, JOHN. Letters to a Wife. Phila: William Young, 1797. 1st Amer ed. 336,(10)pp. Period calf. Presentable (foxing; spine rubbed; label chipped). *Hermitage.* $200/£129

NIBLEY, PRESTON. Brigham Young: The Man and His Work. Salt Lake, 1936. 1st ed. Writing on fep, sl cocked, o/w VG in dj. *Benchmark.* $35/£23

NICELY, WILSON. The Great Southwest. St. Louis, 1867. 1st ed. 115pp + 9pp ads; lg color fldg map. Orig gold-stamped cl. Howes N 134. *Ginsberg.* $1,750/£1,129

NICOLL, ALLARDYCE. The Development of the Theatre.... London: Harrap, 1927. (Tp lt foxed.) *Petersfield.* $54/£35

NICOLL, ALLARDYCE. A History of Late Nineteenth Century Drama 1850-1900. Cambridge, 1946. 2 vols. Fine in djs. *Petersfield.* $54/£35

NICOLL, LEWIS D. The Normans in Glamorgan, Gower and Kidweli. Cardiff, 1936. 1st ed. Fldg chart. (Feps lt browned.) Dj (lt foxed, faded). *Edwards.* $54/£35

NICHOLS, ALICE. Bleeding Kansas. NY: Oxford, 1954. 1st ed. Fine in dj (tears). *Oregon.* $30/£19

NICHOLS, BEVERLEY. A Book of Old Ballads. London: Hutchinson, 1934. 16 color plts. Fore-edge uncut. Brn suede cl (sl rubbed). *Petersfield.* $50/£32

NICHOLS, BEVERLEY. A Case of Human Bondage. Secker & Warburg, 1966. 1st Eng ed. Yellow cl. Fine in dj (sl nicked). *Dalian.* $39/£25

NICHOLS, BEVERLEY. Down the Garden Path. London: Cape, 1932. 9th imp in yr of pub. Rex Whistler (decs). Fine in dj. *Quest.* $45/£29

NICHOLS, BEVERLEY. The Fool Hath Said. London: Cape, (1936). 1st ed. Wine cl. Fine in dj. *Weber.* $35/£23

NICHOLS, BEVERLEY. Green Grows the City. London: Cape, (1939). 1st ed. Grn cl. Fine in dj. *Weber.* $35/£23

NICHOLS, BEVERLEY. Green Grows the City. London: Cape, 1939. 1st ed. NF in dj. *Quest.* $40/£26

NICHOLS, BEVERLEY. News of England or A Country without a Hero. Jonathan Cape, 1938. 1st Eng ed. Grn cl. Fine in dj (frayed, worn). *Dalian.* $39/£25

NICHOLS, BEVERLEY. No Place Like Home. Cape, 1936. 1st Eng ed. Red cl (sl dusty). VG in dj (soiled; sl chipped). *Dalian.* $54/£35

NICHOLS, BEVERLEY. Patchwork. C&W, 1921. 1st Eng ed. Grn cl. Spine faded; eps sl foxed; bkpl, o/w VG. *Dalian.* $54/£35

NICHOLS, BEVERLEY. Puck at Brighton. London: Brighton Corp, n.d. (c 1933). 1st Eng ed. Color frontis; silver cvr design; 2 maps rear (1 lg, fldg). VG (cvr sl rubbed) in wrappers. *Ulysses.* $85/£55

NICHOLS, BEVERLEY. The Rich Die Hard. London: Hutchinson, (1957). 1st ed. Black cl. Fine in dj. *Weber.* $30/£19

NICHOLS, BEVERLEY. The Stream That Stood Still. London: Cape, 1948. 1st ed. Color frontis, 302pp. (Marginal tear 1pg; spine faded). *Quest.* $30/£19

NICHOLS, BEVERLEY. The Tree That Sat Down. London: Cape, 1946. Color frontis, 302pp. Contents Fine (cvr unevenly faded). *Quest.* $30/£19

NICHOLS, BEVERLEY. Verdict on India. London: Cape, (1944). 1st ed. Dk turquoise cl. Fine in dj. *Weber.* $45/£29

NICHOLS, BEVERLEY. Village in a Valley. London: Cape, (1934). 1st ed. Rex Whistler (illus). Dk grn cl. Fine (lt foxed) in dj. *Weber.* $45/£29

NICHOLS, FRANCIS. Through Hidden Shensi. NY, 1902. Map. Dec cl (spine faded; ex-lib, few pp damaged, eps loose). *Lewis.* $31/£20

NICHOLS, FREDERICK DOVETON. The Early Architecture of Georgia. Chapel Hill: Univ of NC, 1957. 1st ed. Frontis. Ink inscrip, prelims sl foxed, else Fine in pub's box (handled). *Bookpress.* $235/£152

NICHOLS, GEORGE WARD. How Pottery Is Made, Its Shape and Decoration. London: Sampson Low et al, 1878. 1st ed. Frontis; vi,(ii),142pp. Orig ptd bds. Cvr wear; fr hinge internally cracked; bkpl, else VG. *Bookpress.* $110/£71

NICHOLS, GEORGE WARD. The Story of the Great March. NY: Harper, 1865. 'Sixteenth edition.' Spine sl sunned, else VG. *Mcgowan.* $45/£29

NICHOLS, J.C.M. Birds of Marsh and Mere. London: Philpot, 1926. Color frontis. Grn cl. VG. *Bowman.* $45/£29

NICHOLS, JAMES. Now You Hear My Horn, the Journal of James Wilson Nichols, 1820-1887. Catherine McDowell (ed). Austin: Univ of TX, (1967). 1st ed. VF in VF dj. *Oregon.* $60/£39

NICHOLS, JEANNETTE PADDOCK. Alaska, A History of Its Administration...During Its First Half Century under the Rule of the United States. Cleveland: Clark, 1924. Frontis map; 2 ports; fldg map. Unopened. VG + . *Bohling.* $150/£97

NICHOLS, JOHN. A Ghost in the Music. NY: Holt, (1979). 1st ed. Fine in dj. *Reese.* $30/£19

NICHOLS, JOHN. A Ghost in the Music. NY: Holt et al, (1979). 1st ed. Fine in dj. *Sadlon.* $30/£19

NICHOLS, JOHN. The Sterile Cuckoo. NY: David McKay, (1965). 1st ed. 1st bk. Fine in bright dj. *Godot.* $125/£81

NICHOLS, LEIGH. (Pseud of Dean Koontz.) The Eyes of Darkness. Piatkus, 1981. 1st ed. Pg edges browned, o/w Fine in dj. *Rees.* $93/£60

NICHOLS, LEIGH. (Pseud of Dean Koontz.) The Servants of Twilight. Piatkus, 1984. 1st Eng, 1st hb ed. Fine in dj. *Aronovitz.* $175/£113

NICHOLS, LEIGH. (Pseud of Dean Koontz.) Shadowfires. Avon, 1987. 1st hb ed. Fine in dj. *Madle.* $50/£32

NICHOLS, M. LEONA. The Mantle of Elias. The Story of Fathers Blanchet and Demers.... Binfords & Mort, (1941). 1st ed. Signed, dated presentation copy. Fine. *Oregon.* $50/£32

NICHOLS, MARIE. Ranald McDonald, Adventurer. Caxton, 1940. 1st ed. 11 full-pg woodcuts, 5 photo plts, ep maps. VG in Fine dj. *Oregon.* $40/£26

NICHOLS, R. Fantastica—Being the Smile of the Sphinx and Other Tales of Imagination. Macmillan, 1923. 1st Amer ed. VG + in Very Nice dj. *Aronovitz.* $95/£61

NICHOLS, R. The Smile of the Sphinx. Beaumont Press, 1920. 1st ed. One of 295. NF. *Aronovitz.* $125/£81

NICHOLS, ROSE STANDISH. English Pleasure Gardens. NY/London: Macmillan, 1902. 1st ed. Frontis, 185 engrs, 10 plans. Teg; uncut. White/grn pict cl, gilt titles. Lt soil, else Fine. *Quest.* $125/£81

NICHOLS, ROSE STANDISH. Spanish and Portuguese Gardens. Boston/NY: Houghton Mifflin, 1924. Fine in dj. *Quest.* $140/£90

NICHOLS, ROSE STANDISH. Spanish and Portuguese Gardens. Boston: Houghton Mifflin, 1924. 1st ed. 2 als tipped in. VG (cvrs sl rubbed). *Second Life.* $65/£42

NICHOLS, STEPHEN G. Romanesque Signs. Early Medieval Narrative and Iconography. New Haven/London: Yale, 1983. Fine. *Europa.* $25/£16

NICHOLS, THOMAS L. Forty Years of American Life. London: John Maxwell, 1864. 1st ed. 2 vols. xii,408; xi,368pp. (Rubbed, corner wear.) *Schoyer.* $125/£81

Nicholson's New Carpenter's Guide. London: Jones, 1825. Enlgd ed. Frontis port, xii+121pp; 120 engr plts. Full calf (new spine, eps), gilt. VG (sl stains to text). *Willow House.* $233/£150

NICHOLSON, BEN. Paintings, Reliefs, Drawings. London: Lund Humphries, 1948. 1st ed. VG. *Cahan.* $75/£48

NICHOLSON, E.M. Birds and Men. London, 1951. 1st ed. (Feps sl browned; spine sl faded.) Dj. *Edwards.* $54/£35

NICHOLSON, GEORGE (ed). The Illustrated Dictionary of Gardening. NY/London: Penman, (1890). 1st ed. 4 vols. 544; 544; 537; 608pp; 19 color plts. Grn cl; aeg. VG set (loose hinges). *Second Life.* $150/£97

NICHOLSON, GEORGE (ed). The Illustrated Dictionary of Gardening.... London: L. Upcott Gill, n.d. (ca 1885). 1st ed. 8 vols. 24 Fine chromolitho plts. Dec grn cl stamped in black/gold; aeg. Good. *Karmiole.* $200/£129

NICHOLSON, HAROLD. The English Sense of Humour. London: Dropmore Press, 1946. #507/550. VG + (ink inscrip). *Williams.* $70/£45

NICHOLSON, HENRY ALLEYNE and RICHARD LYDEKKER. A Manual of Palaeontology. London, 1889. 3rd ed. 2 vols. xviii,xi,1624pp + 32pp pub's cat (tps in facs). Marbled eps. Maroon morocco-backed marbled bds (rebound), blind edged raised bands, gilt lettering (owner stamps). *Edwards.* $116/£75

NICHOLSON, JOHN. Space Ship to Venus. London, 1948. 1st ed. Fine in dj (sl frayed). *Madle.* $25/£16

NICHOLSON, MEREDITH. The Little Brown Jug at Kildare. Indianapolis: Bobbs-Merrill, (1908). 1st ed, 1st state. Pict cl (lt rubbed). *Sadlon.* $25/£16

NICHOLSON, NORMAN. The Fire of the Lord. London: Nicholson & Watson, 1944. 1st ed. (Spine, edges faded.) *Hollett.* $54/£35

NICHOLSON, NORMAN. Hard of Hearing. London: Poem-of-the-Month Club Ltd, 1974. 1st Eng ed. Signed. VG (corner sl creased). *Ulysses.* $39/£25

NICHOLSON, NORMAN. Wednesday Early Closing. London: Faber & Faber, 1975. 1st Eng ed. Fine (spine tail sl bumped) in dj (edges sl rubbed). *Ulysses.* $39/£25

NICHOLSON, PETER. The Student's Instructor in Drawing and Working the Five Orders of Architecture.... London: I. and J. Taylor, 1823. viii,39pp, 1f ad, 41 engr pts (3 double-pg). Contemp sheep (worn, rubbed, margins thumbed). *Marlborough.* $194/£125

NICHOLSON, WILLIAM. London Types. London: William Heinemann, 1898. Lg 4to. Unpaginated; 12 full-pg color plts. Pict cl (sl rubbed, mkd). *Hollett.* $891/£575

NICKERSON, HOFFMAN. The Turning Point of the Revolution. Boston/NY: Houghton Mifflin, 1928. 1st ed. Black cl. Offsetting tp from frontis, else NF in dj (edgeworn, tape reinforcements, 1/4-inch chip spine). *Chapel Hill.* $65/£42

NICOL, C.W. From the Roof of Africa. NY: Knopf, 1972. 1st ed. Gilt dec cl. Fine in VG + dj. *Mikesh.* $25/£16

NICOL, DONALD M. Meteora. The Rock Monasteries of Thessaly. Chapman & Hall, 1963. 1st ed. Dec eps; speckled edges. Rebound in cream, grey mottled morocco-backed cl bds (sm ink stamp). *Edwards.* $47/£30

NICOL, NINA and DORIS FOGLER. Rusty Pete of the Lazy AB. NY: Macmillan, 1929. 1st ed. 8vo. 14 b/w, 2 color plts by Fogler; pict eps. Orange cl (sl rubbed, soiled) in pict orange dj (edges chipped, 2 sm pieces out). NF internally. *Blue Mountain.* $85/£55

NICOLAY, C.G. The Oregon Territory. London: Charles Knight, 1846. 1st ed. Engr frontis, 226pp; 2 maps (1 fldg). Cl-backed bds (rebound). VG. Howes N 151. *Shasky.* $200/£129

NICOLL, W. ROBERTSON. A Bookman's Letters. London: Hodder & Stoughton, 1913. 2nd ed. (Fep pasted down.) *Oak Knoll.* $25/£16

NICOLSON, B. and C. WRIGHT. Georges de La Tour. London: Phaidon, 1974. 24 color plts. Lib stamps, else internally Good. (Cl sl worn.) *Ars Artis.* $349/£225

NICOLSON, BENEDICT. Joseph Wright of Derby. London: Paul Mellon Foundation, 1968. 1st UK ed. 2 vols. Tipped-in b/w frontis ports, 355 plts. (Ex-lib w/ink stamps, label remains; tape mks.) Djs. *Edwards.* $93/£60

NICOLSON, BENEDICT. Joseph Wright of Derby: Painter of Light. London: Paul Mellon Foundation for British Art, 1968. 2 vols. VG in djs in bd slipcase (soiled). *Argosy.* $125/£81

NICOLSON, BENEDICT. The Painters of Ferrara. London, (1950). 12 mtd color plts. VG in dj (chipped). *Argosy.* $60/£39

NICOLSON, BENEDICT. The Treasures of the Foundling Hospital. Oxford: Clarendon, 1972. Frontis port, 37 plts. Orig buckram. VF in pict dj. *Europa.* $54/£35

NICOLSON, HAROLD. Lord Carnock. London, 1937. 4th imp. Sl foxing to fore-edge, o/w NF in dj. *Edwards.* $31/£20

NICOLSON, JOHN. The Arizona of Joseph Pratt Allyn. Univ of AZ, (1974). 1st ed. Frontis map. VF in VF dj. *Oregon.* $25/£16

NICOLSON, NIGEL. The National Trust Book of Great Houses of Britain. NY: Putnam's, (1965). Pict eps. (Name; uneven fade.) *Quest.* $45/£29

NICOLSON, WILLIAM. The English Historical Library. London: Timothy Childe, 1714. 2nd ed. xviii,272pp. Contemp calf (worn; bkpls; hinges chipped; lt cvr wear). *Bookpress.* $400/£258

NICOULLAUD, M. CHARLES. Memoirs of the Comtesse de Boigne (1781-1814). London: Heinemann, 1907-1912. 1st ed. 4 vols. 3/4 polished calf, gilt, raised bands. Teg. Fine. *Sadlon.* $250/£161

NIEDECKER, LORINE. Collected Poems 1936-1968. Fulcrum, 1970. 1st Eng ed. Blue cl. VF in dj. *Dalian.* $70/£45

NIEMOELLER, A.F. The Story of Jazz. Girard, KS: Haldeman-Julius Pub, (1947). 1st ed. Text sl browned, else Fine in red ptd wrappers. *Godot.* $45/£29

NIETZ, JOHN A. Old Textbooks. (Pittsburgh): Univ of Pittsburgh, (1961). 1st ptg. VG. *Schoyer.* $35/£23

NIETZSCHE, FRIEDRICH. Beyond Good and Evil. Helen Zimmern (trans). NY: Macmillan, 1907. 1st US ed. Top edge dusted, else VG + . *Lame Duck.* $150/£97

NIGHTINGALE, FLORENCE. Notes on Nursing. London, 1860. 2nd ed. 8vo. 222pp (text block loose; joints worn; corners bumped). *Argosy.* $500/£323

NIGHTINGALE, FLORENCE. Notes on Nursing: What It Is, and What It Is Not. London, (1860). 1st ed. 79pp. This early ptg includes phrase, 'The right of Translation is reserved' on tp but appeared before the ptr's errors were corrected in text. Good. *Fye.* $400/£258

NIGHTINGALE, FLORENCE. Notes on Nursing: What It Is, and What It Is Not. NY, 1860. 1st Amer ed. 140pp. Good. *Fye.* $200/£129

Nightingale, or Ladies Vocal Companion. Albany: Packard & Co, 1807. 12mo. 121pp + 5pp contents, copper engr tp w/lg vignette (lt browning, foxing on text; 3 pgs, reps w/repaired tears; few pg edges chipped). Full leather on bds, gilt title spine (lt rubbed; partially faded gilt). *Hobbyhorse.* $50/£32

NIKLITSCHEK, A. Water Lilies and Water Plants. NY: Scribner's, 1933. Good + . *Mikesh.* $30/£19

NIKLITSCHEK, A. Water Lilies and Water Plants. NY: Scribner's, 1933. 12 b/w full-pg plts. VG (mks, scratches; spine lt sunned). *Shifrin*. $35/£23

NIMMO, JOSEPH, JR. Treasury Department. Report on the Internal Commerce of the United States.... Washington, 1885. 562pp; 5 fldg maps. 1/2 morocco. Howes N 158. *Ginsberg*. $1,000/£645

NIN, ANAIS. A Child Born Out of the Fog. NY: Gemor, 1947. 1st ed. Pamphlet. VG+ in stapled wraps. *Lame Duck*. $65/£42

NIN, ANAIS. Children of the Albatross. Dutton, 1947. 1st ed. NF in dj (lt worn, missing piece head spine). *Stahr*. $25/£16

NIN, ANAIS. D.H. Lawrence. Paris: Edward W. Titus, 1932. 1st ed. #361/550. 1st bk. Contains 2 facs pp from mss Lady Chatterley's Lover. Black cl. NF (bkpl) in VG dj (lt chipping; spine browned w/1-inch chip). *Chapel Hill*. $350/£226

NIN, ANAIS. The Four-Chambered Heart. Peter Owen, 1959. 1st Eng ed. Black cl. Fine in dj. *Dalian*. $39/£25

NIN, ANAIS. The House of Incest. Paris: Siana Editions (Obelisk Press), (1936). 1st ed. One of 249 numbered (this copy not signed). Internally Fine in ptd wrapper over stiff wrappers (upper wrapper, part of spine soiled). *Reese*. $250/£161

NIN, ANAIS. The House of Incest. (NY): Gemor Press, (1947). 1st Amer ed. Pict orange cl. VG (ink name; spine sl sunned). *Reese*. $40/£26

NIN, ANAIS. Ladders to Fire. NY: E.P. Dutton, 1946. 1st ed. Outside edges of pp197-200 torn, o/w VG in dj (soiled rear panel; abrasions spine ends). *Bernard*. $65/£42

NIN, ANAIS. Ladders to Fire. NY: Dutton, 1946. 1st ed. Fine in dj (sl soiling; nick). *Reese*. $65/£42

NIN, ANAIS. The Novel of the Future. NY: Macmillan, (1968). 1st ed. Signed. Fine in white dj (sl wear). *Antic Hay*. $125/£81

NIN, ANAIS. A Spy in the House of Love. NY: British Book Centre, (1954). Stated 1st Amer ed. Name, else Fine in VG dj (sl chipping; short tear). *Between The Covers*. $55/£35

NIN, ANAIS. A Spy in the House of Love. London: Spearman, 1955. 1st UK ed. Edges, eps sl foxed; spine gilt sl dull, o/w VG in dj (sl foxed). *Virgo*. $31/£20

NIN, ANAIS. Under a Glass Bell and Other Stories. NY: Dutton, 1948. 1st ed thus. Bkpl over ink name, else Fine in Good dj (edgeworn; chip). *Reese*. $35/£23

Ninth Cavalry: One Hundred and Twenty-First Regiment, Indiana Volunteers. (By Daniel Webster Comstock.) Richmond, IN: J.M. Coe, 1890. 1st ed. 56pp, fldg map. Ptd wrappers. VG (sl staining lower margin fr wrap, backstrip generally lacking). *Mcgowan*. $350/£226

NISBET, J. The Forester. London, 1905. 1st ed. 2 vols. 1/4 morocco. Fine. *Henly*. $50/£32

NISBET, J. Our Forests and Woodlands. London, 1900. 12 plts, head-, tail-pieces by Arthur Rackham. Unopened. Good. *Henly*. $70/£45

NISBET, JAMES COOPER. Four Years on the Firing Line. Bell I. Wiley (ed). (Jackson, TN): McCowat-Mercer Press, 1963. Rpt ed. NF in VG dj. Howes N 159. *Mcgowan*. $85/£55

NIVEN, LARRY and JERRY POURNELLE. The Mote in God's Eye. S&S, 1974. 1st ed. Fine in dj. *Aronovitz*. $175/£113

NIVEN, LARRY. The Integral Trees. NY: Ballantine, (1983). 1st ed. Signed. Fine in dj. *Antic Hay*. $50/£32

NIVEN, LARRY. Lucifer's Hammer. Playboy, 1977. 1st ed. NF in dj (frayed). *Madle*. $50/£32

NIVEN, LARRY. Neutron Star. MacDonald, 1969. 1st Eng, 1st hb ed. VG+ in VG+ dj (lt dust soil). *Aronovitz*. $185/£119

NIVEN, LARRY. Ringworld. Holt et al, 1977. 1st US hb ed. VG in dj. *Lewton*. $31/£20

NIVEN, LARRY. World of Ptavvs. MacDonald, 1968. 1st Eng, 1st hb ed, 1st bk. Signed. VG+ in VG dj (sl dust soil). *Aronovitz*. $125/£81

NIVEN, RICHARD. The British Angler's Lexicon. London: W.J. Cummings, 1892. *Petersfield*. $62/£40

NIXON, HOWARD M. Five Centuries of English Bookbinding. London, (1978). Dj. *Waterfield*. $31/£20

NIXON, RICHARD. The Challenges We Face. McGraw Hill, 1960. 1st ed. NF in VG+ dj. *Bishop*. $47/£30

NIXON, RICHARD. The Memoirs of.... NY, (1978). 1st ed. Inscribed, signed, dated. Spot, spine wrinkled, else Good in dj (sl used). *King*. $95/£61

NIXON, RICHARD. Six Crises. NY: Doubleday, 1962. 1st ed. Signed (autopen). Gray cl. Fine in Fine dj. *Glenn*. $145/£94

No Church. (By Frederick William Robinson.) London: Hurst & Blackett, 1861. 1st ed. Contemp 1/2 grn calf (stamp fr cvrs; sl foxing). *Petersfield*. $116/£75

NOBLE, LOUIS L. After Icebergs with a Painter. NY, 1861. Tinted litho tp, xiv,(2),336pp+8pp ads, 6 tinted litho plts. Orig cl. Spine sl sunned, edgewear; contents tanned, sig, else VG. *Reese*. $850/£548

NOBLE, THOMAS. Practical Perspective, Exemplified on Landscapes. London: Edward Orme, 1809. Mtd engr tp (sl dust soiled), 57pp (pencil mks), 2+10 engr plts (2 blank plt margins neatly strengthened). Later cl (spine torn). *Ars Artis*. $233/£150

NOEL HUME, IVOR. Here Lies Virginia. Knopf, 1968. 1st ed. VG in Good dj. *Book Broker*. $35/£23

NOEL, BAPTIST W. The Rebellion in America. London: Nesbet, 1863. 1st ed. (20),494,(2)pp. Howes N 166. *Ginsberg*. $125/£81

NOEL, RUTH S. The Mythology of Middle Earth. Boston, 1977. 1st Amer ed. Fine in NF dj. *Polyanthos*. $125/£81

NOEL, THEOPHILUS. A Campaign from Santa Fe to the Mississippi; Being a History of the Old Sibley Brigade.... Raleigh, NC: C.R. Sanders, Jr., 1961. 1st Amer ed, ltd to 500 numbered. Orig cl. NF in orig glassine, pub's slipcase. *Mcgowan*. $175/£113

NOEL, THOMAS. The City and the Saloon. Univ of NE, (1982). 1st ed. 8 maps. VF in VF dj. *Oregon*. $20/£13

NOGUCHI, HIDEYO. Laboratory Diagnosis of Syphilis. NY, 1923. 1st ed. Good. *Fye*. $40/£26

NOGUCHI, HIDEYO. Serum Diagnosis of Syphilis and Luetin Reaction Together with the Butyric Acid Test for Syphilis. Phila, 1912. 3rd ed. Good. *Fye*. $35/£23

NOGUCHI, YONE. Hiroshige. NY, 1921. 1st ed. Ltd to 750. Frontis. Soft cream bds. VG (lt wear) in pub's wrap-around chemise (heavily worn). *Hermitage*. $150/£97

NOGUCHI, YONE. Hiroshige. London: Kegan Paul et al, 1934. Ltd to 1000. 100 plts (incl 7 color, 2 orig color woodblock prints). Dec wrappers stabbed, tied. Blue cl portfolio, ivory clasps (lt frayed, faded). *Karmiole*. $200/£129

NOHL, JOHANNES. The Black Death. C.H. Clarke (trans). London: George Allen & Unwin, 1926. 1st ed. Discoloration top cvr, o/w VG. *White*. $39/£25

NOKES, G.D. A History of the Crime of Blasphemy. London: Sweet & Maxwell, 1928. *Boswell*. $65/£42

NOLAN, CYNTHIA. A Sight of China. Macmillan, 1969. 1st Eng ed. 4 dwgs. Grey cl. Fine in dj. *Dalian*. $39/£25

NOLAN, WILLIAM F. Dashiell Hammett: A Casebook. Santa Barbara: McNally & Loftin, 1969. 1st ed. Lt spotting top edge, o/w Fine in dj. *Mordida*. $65/£42

NOLEN, ORAN WARDER. Galloping Down the Texas Trail. Odem: Vanity, 1947. 1st ed. Inscribed. VG- (soiled, bumped). *Parker*. $65/£42

NOLTE, VINCENT. Fifty Years in Both Hemispheres; or, Reminiscences of a Merchant's Life. NY: Redfield, 1854. 1st Amer ed, 1st ed in English. (4),(22),(11)-484,(4)pp. Howes N 169. *Ginsberg*. $150/£97

NORBURY, JAMES. Traditional Knitting Patterns. London: Batsford, 1962. 1st ed. NF in dj (sl worn, repaired). *Willow House*. $39/£25

NORDEN, FREDERICK LEWIS. Travels through Egypt and Nubia. Dublin: For J. Smith, 1757. Engr fldg frontis map (edge too closely trimmed), (288)pp, engr fldg plt. Polished calf, gilt spine (rubbed). *Schoyer*. $125/£81

NORDENSKJOLD, A.E. The Voyage of the Vega Round Asia and Europe.... NY: Macmillan, 1882. 1st US ed. xxvi,756pp. Good (damp tidemark on frontis, tp). *Walcot*. $78/£50

NORDHOFF, CHARLES and JAMES NORMAN HALL. Botany Bay. Boston: Little, Brown, 1941. 1st ed. *Lefkowicz*. $25/£16

NORDHOFF, CHARLES and JAMES NORMAN HALL. Mutiny on the Bounty. NY: LEC, 1947. 1/1500 numbered, signed by Fletcher Martin (illus). Gilt leather; teg. VG in cl slipcase. *Argosy*. $150/£97

NORDHOFF, CHARLES and JAMES NORMAN HALL. Passage to Marseille. NY: Grosset, (1942). 1st ed thus. VG in pict dj w/ port of Humphrey Bogart upper cvr, still from film lower cvr (sm chips). *Houle*. $75/£48

NORDHOFF, CHARLES. California for Health, Pleasure, and Residence. NY: Harper, 1875. Frontis map; 255pp,appendix,4pp ads. Full dk grn linen (sl wear). Text Fine. *Hartfield*. $195/£126

NORDHOFF, CHARLES. Cape Cod and All Along the Shore. NY: Harper, 1868. 1st ed. Inscribed, signed & dated. 239pp. VG (spine worn, faded). *Connolly*. $50/£32

NORDHOFF, CHARLES. Communistic Societies of the United States.... NY, 1875. 1st ed. 439pp. Howes N 177. *Ginsberg*. $175/£113

NORDHOFF, CHARLES. Stories of the Island World. NY: Harper, 1857. 1st ed. Frontis, 315,(1 blank, 4 ads)pp; 11 plts. VG. *Lefkowicz*. $150/£97

NORDSTROM, ESTER BLENDA. Tent Folk of the Far North. E. Gee Nash (trans). London: Herbert Jenkins, 1930. 1st ed. 15 plts. VG. *Hollett*. $39/£25

NORDYKE, LEWIS. Great Roundup. NY: William Morrow, 1955. 1st ed. Dj. *Lambeth*. $30/£19

NORDYKE, LEWIS. Great Roundup. The Story of Texas and Southwestern Cowmen. NY: William Morrow, 1955. 3rd ptg. Ink name, else VG in Good dj. *Perier*. $25/£16

NORDYKE, LEWIS. John Wesley Hardin. NY: William Morrow, 1957. 1st ed. Cl-backed bds. Offsetting eps from laid-in newspaper clippings, else Fine in dj (chipped). *Glenn*. $60/£39

NORFOLK AND WESTERN RAILWAY CO. Rules Governing the Officers and Employees of the Company. Adopted 1897 Feb. 24; Amended 1897 July 14. 34pp. Paper cvr. VG. *Book Broker*. $35/£23

NORFOLK, LAWRENCE. Lempriere's Dictionary. London: Sinclair-Stevenson, 1991. 1st ed. Signed. Fine in dj. *Rees*. $54/£35

NORFOLK, LAWRENCE. Lempriere's Dictionary. London: Sinclair-Stevenson, 1991. 1st UK ed, 1st bk. NF in dj (sl bumped). *Moorhouse*. $19/£12

NORFOLK, LAWRENCE. Lempriere's Dictionary. Sinclair-Stevenson, 1991. 1st UK ed. Fine in dj. *Williams*. $31/£20

NORFOLK, LAWRENCE. Lempriere's Dictionary. London: Limited Editions, 1991. One of ltd ed of 150 numbered, signed. Marbled bds. Mint in tissue dj. *Martin*. $74/£48

NORMAN, CHARLES. Ezra Pound. NY: Macmillan, 1960. 1st ed. One of 7567 ptd. Signed presentation. Fine in NF dj. *Antic Hay*. $75/£48

NORMAN, CHARLES. Poets and People. Indianapolis: Bobbs-Merrill, (1972). 1st ed. Fine in dj. *Pharos*. $30/£19

NORMAN, DOROTHY. Albert Stieglitz, American Seer. Random House, 1973. 1st ed. VG in VG dj. *Bishop*. $37/£24

NORMAN, HENRY. All the Russias. NY: Scribner's, 1903. 1st ed. 4 maps (1 fldg). Black cl, gilt (faded, silverfished; pocket removed). *Schoyer*. $50/£32

NORMAN, HENRY. Peoples and Politics of the Far East. NY: Scribner's, 1895. xvi,608pp, 2 fldg maps. Tan dec cl (chipped, discolored from label removal, shaken; ex-lib). *Schoyer*. $45/£29

NORMAN, JOHN. (Pseud of John Lange, Jr.) Outlaw of Gor. London; Sidgwick & Jackson, (1970). 1st hb ed. NF in silver dj (bumped, sl wear). *Levin*. $75/£48

NORMAN, JOHN. (Pseud of John Lange, Jr.) Priest-Kings of Gor. London: Sidgwick & Jackson, (1971). 1st hb ed. NF in white dj (lt dust soiling; spine faded). *Levin*. $75/£48

NORMAN, M.W. A Popular Guide to the Geology of the Isle of Wight.... London: Ventnor, 1887. vii,240pp, map, 15 plts, 4 sections, 3 views. Ends browned, o/w Fine. *Henly*. $116/£75

NORMAN, WILLIAM M. A Portion of My Life. Winston-Salem, 1959. 1st ed. VG+. *Pratt*. $30/£19

NORMAN, WILLIAM M. A Portion of My Life. Being a Short and Imperfect History...1864. Winston-Salem: John F. Blair, 1959. 1st ed. Fine in NF dj. *Mcgowan*. $45/£29

NORRIS, CHARLES. Eastern Upland Shooting. Phila/NY: Lippincott, (1946). 1st ed. Pict grn cl. Fine in dj (lt worn). *Glenn*. $75/£48

NORRIS, CHARLES. Gonorrhea in Women. Phila, 1913. 1st ed. Good. *Fye*. $75/£48

NORRIS, FRANK. The Argonaut Manuscript Limited Edition of Frank Norris's Works. GC: Doubleday, Doran, 1928. One of 245 numbered sets. 10 vols. Parchment over bds, gilt. Leaf of orig working autograph ms of McTeague in envelope laid into vol 1. The leaf is numbered '177,' and is over 300 words. Top edges sl dusty, few nicks, o/w Fine set in white djs (spines tanned). BAL 15048 & 9. *Reese.* $3,250/£2,097

NORRIS, FRANK. Collected Works of.... NY, 1928. #197/245 sets. 10 vols. Teg, rest uncut. Full vellum, gilt. Contents Fine (sunned, sl chipped, cvrs foxed). *Polyanthos.* $350/£226

NORRIS, FRANK. The Letters of.... SF: Book Club of CA, 1956. Ltd to 350. Frontis port. Fine. *Polyanthos.* $75/£48

NORRIS, FRANK. The Letters of.... Franklin Walker (ed). SF: Book Club of CA, 1956. 1st ed. One of 350 ptd. Frontis. Patterned bds. Fine. *Oregon.* $135/£87

NORRIS, FRANK. McTeague: A Story of San Francisco. NY: Doubleday & McClure, 1899. 1st ed, 1st ptg, w/'moment' as the last word on p106. Red cl stamped in white. Good (spine faded, rubbed; inner hinges cracking). BAL 15031. *Reese.* $250/£161

NORRIS, FRANK. McTeague: A Story of San Francisco. SF: Colt Press, 1941. One of 500. Tan cl-backed grn beveled bds. Spine, label dknd, o/w NF. *Harrington.* $110/£71

NORRIS, FRANK. The Pit. NY: Doubleday Page, 1903. 1st ed. Fine (spine extrems sl rubbed). *Between The Covers.* $100/£65

NORRIS, FRANK. The Pit. NY: Doubleday-Page, 1903. 1st ed. Fine. *Else Fine.* $125/£81

NORRIS, FRANK. Vandover and the Brute. Charles Norris (ed). GC: Doubleday, Page, 1914. 1st trade ed. Gilt brn cl. Fine in pict dj (brn paper reinforcements verso; chip, tear; sl losses spine crown; nicks). BAL 15406. *Reese.* $250/£161

NORRIS, K.S. (ed). Whales, Dolphins, and Porpoises. Berkeley, 1966. (Pp edges lt spotted.) Dj (chipped). *Sutton.* $85/£55

NORRIS, THADDEUS. American Fish-Culture.... Phila: Porter & Coates, 1868. 1st ed. Pebble-grain cl (lt rubbed). VG (leaves sl foxed; bkpl) in fitted slipcase. *Hermitage.* $125/£81

North American Big Game. NY: Scribner's, 1939. 1st ptg. Pict cl. (Ex-lib.) *Schoyer.* $150/£97

NORTH, ERIC. The Ant Men. Winston, 1955. 1st ed. Fine in dj (spine sl faded). *Madle.* $125/£81

NORTH, F.J. et al. Snowdonia. The National Park of North Wales. London, 1949. 1st ed. 56 color plts, 48 b/w photos, 6 maps, 26 diags. (Cl lt discolored.) Dj (sl creased). *Edwards.* $62/£40

NORTH, JOSEPH. Men in the Ranks. The Story of 12 Americans in Spain. (NY, 1939). 1st ed. VG in pict self wrappers. *Argosy.* $85/£55

NORTH, JOSEPH. Men in the Ranks. The Story of 12 Americans in Spain. NY, 1939. 1st Amer ed. Fine in pict wraps. *Polyanthos.* $200/£129

NORTH, MARIANNE. The Gallery of Paintings of Plants and Their Homes, Royal Gardens, Kew. London: HMSO, 1882. 4ff,131pp. Ptd wrappers (dusty). *Marlborough.* $140/£90

NORTH, MARIANNE. Recollections of a Happy Life. London: Macmillan, 1892. 2nd ed, 2nd ptg. 2 vols. Frontispieces, (xii),(352); (ii),(344)pp, map. Bright grn cl, gilt flower. Nice. *Schoyer.* $150/£97

NORTH, ROBERT CARVER. Bob North with Dog Team and Indians. London: Putnam's, 1929. 1st ed. VG (spine sl stained). *Hollett.* $39/£25

NORTHALL, G.F. English Folk-Rhymes. London: Kegan Paul et al, 1892. 565pp; uncut. Red cl, beveled edges, gilt. Generally VG (sl wear). *Hartfield.* $95/£61

NORTHCOTE, JAMES. The Life of Titian. London, 1830. 2 vols. Frontis port (spotted), 399; 384pp, fldg table. (Spotting; pencil notes vol 1.) Marbled eps, edges. 1/2 morocco, marbled bds (edges sl rubbed; spines lt sunned). *Edwards.* $93/£60

NORTHEN, WILLIAM J. (ed). Men of Mark in Georgia. Atlanta: A.B. Caldwell, 1907-1912. 1st ed. 6 vols. 8vo. Full brn pebbled morocco (rebound), gilt centerpieces, cornerpieces, spines. Very Nice set (tape repair verso tp, offsetting few pp vol 1). *Chapel Hill.* $1,500/£968

NORTHEND, MARY H. Garden Ornaments. NY: Duffield, 1916. 1st ed. Frontis, 31 plts. 1st, last pp sl foxed; spine sl worn, else VG. *Bookpress.* $85/£55

NORTHEND, MARY H. Historic Doorways of Old Salem. Boston: Houghton Mifflin, 1926. 1st ed. Unopened, uncut. Fine in dj (lt handled). *Bookpress.* $35/£23

NORTHROP, HENRY DAVENPORT. Indian Massacres and Savage Life. N.p. (Phila), n.d. (c. 1891). 600pp (browned, inscrip). Pict cl binding (spots, lettering dull). VG. *Graf.* $20/£13

NORTHUP, SOLOMON. Twelve Years a Slave. Auburn, 1853. 5th thousand. 336pp. (Text browned; cvrs rubbed; spine ends frayed.) *King.* $150/£97

NORTON, ANDRE. Android at Arms. NY: Harcourt, Brace, Jovanovich, (1971). 1st ed. Ink checks, else Fine in NF dj. *Hermitage.* $45/£29

NORTON, ANDRE. Android at Arms. Harcourt, 1971. 1st ed. VG in NF dj. *Madle.* $60/£39

NORTON, ANDRE. Dark Piper. Harcourt, 1968. 1st ed. Fine in dj. *Madle.* $75/£48

NORTON, ANDRE. Galactic Derelict. World, 1959. 1st ed. VG (ex-lib) in NF dj. *Madle.* $50/£32

NORTON, ANDRE. Here Abide Monsters. NY: Atheneum, 1973. 1st ed. Ink name, else Fine in VG dj. *Hermitage.* $40/£26

NORTON, ANDRE. Here Abide Monsters. Atheneum, 1973. 1st ed. Signed. VF in Fine dj. *Aronovitz.* $70/£45

NORTON, ANDRE. Huon of the Horn. Harcourt, 1951. 1st ed. VG-. *Madle.* $50/£32

NORTON, ANDRE. Ice Crown. Viking, 1970. 1st ed. Fine in dj. *Madle.* $40/£26

NORTON, ANDRE. Iron Cage. NY: Viking, (1974). 1st ed. Fine in dj. *Antic Hay.* $45/£29

NORTON, ANDRE. The Jargoon Pard. Atheneum, 1974. 1st ed. Fine in dj. *Madle.* $35/£23

NORTON, ANDRE. Night of Masks. Harcourt, 1964. 1st ed. Fine in dj. *Madle.* $85/£55

NORTON, ANDRE. Ordeal in Otherwhere. Cleveland: World, (1964). 1st ed. Fine in dj (lt wear; rear panel soiled). *Antic Hay.* $100/£65

NORTON, ANDRE. Quest Crosstime. NY: Viking, (1965). 1st ed. NF in dj. *Antic Hay.* $85/£55

NORTON, ANDRE. Red Hart Magic. Crowell, 1976. 1st ed. Signed. Fine in dj. *Aronovitz.* $60/£39

NORTON, ANDRE. Space Service. World, 1953. 1st ed. NF in dj. *Madle.* $200/£129

NORTON, ANDRE. Stand to Horse. Harcourt, 1956. 1st ed. VF in VF dj. *Madle*. $200/£129

NORTON, ANDRE. Star Man's Son 2250 A.D. Staples, 1953. 1st Eng ed. NF in NF dj. *Aronovitz*. $150/£97

NORTON, ANDRE. The Toll of the Sea. Appleton, 1909. 1st ed. White spine lettering almost gone; pict fr cvr w/white loss, else VG-. *Aronovitz*. $95/£61

NORTON, ANDRE. The White Jade Fox. Dutton, 1975. 1st ed. Signed. Fine in VG+ dj (rubbing). *Aronovitz*. $40/£26

NORTON, C.L. and JOHN HABERTON. Canoeing in Kanuckia. NY: Putnam's, 1878. 1st ed. 254pp + 10pp ads. Illus blue bds. Good. *Karmiole*. $50/£32

NORTON, CHARLES ELIOT (ed). The Correspondence of Thomas Carlyle and Ralph Waldo Emerson, 1834-1872. Boston: James R. Osgood, 1883. 1st trade ed, 1st ptg. One of 2500. 2 vols. Teg. Brn cl, leather labels, gilt. Fine set. BAL 5289. *Macdonnell*. $100/£65

NORTON, CHARLES ELIOT. Letters. London/Boston, 1913. 1st ed. 2 vols. *Bickersteth*. $39/£25

NORTON, HERMAN. Record of Facts Concerning the Persecutions at Madeira in 1843 and 1846. NY: Amer Protestant Soc, 1849. Engr frontis, 228pp, engr. Brn cl, blind/gilt-stamped (rubbed). *Schoyer*. $45/£29

NORTON, J.P. Elements of Scientific Agriculture. Albany, 1850. 1st ed. x,208pp + ads (marginal dampstain few pp; pencil notes, lt foxing). (Cvrs worn, dingy.) *Sutton*. $65/£42

NORTON, MARY. The Magic Bed-Knob. NY, 1943. 1st ed. 1st bk. Pict bds. Sl spotted, soiled, sl bumped, else Good in dj (soiled, edgetorn, wrinkled). *King*. $25/£16

Notes on a Yacht Voyage to Hardanger Fjord, and the Adjacent Estuaries. (By Charles Wilson Rothery). London: Longman, Brown, Green & Longman, n.d. (ca 1855). 1st ed. Frontis; 26 plts (1 fldg map). Rust gilt cl (upper spine sl worn). *Karmiole*. $175/£113

NOTLEW, FRANCES. New Thread in an Old Track. NY: Dutton, 1882. vi,378pp. Brn cl stamped in gilt/black. VG. *Schoyer*. $40/£26

NOTLEY, ALICE. Alice Ordered Me to be Made. Chicago: Yellow Press, (1976). 1st Amer ed. Inscribed, signed. Fine in pict wraps (sl edge rubbed). *Polyanthos*. $25/£16

NOTT, SAMUEL. Slavery, and the Remedy; Or, Principles and Suggestions for a Remedial Code. Boston, 1856. 2nd ed. 118pp. NF in orig ptd wrappers. *Mcgowan*. $150/£97

NOTT, STANLEY CHARLES. Chinese Jade Throughout the Ages. London: Batsford, 1936. 1st ed. 39 color plts. Dj (lt soiled, ragged). *Edwards*. $47/£30

NOTTINGHAM, STRATTON (comp). The Marriage License Bonds of Northumberland County, Virginia from 1783 to 1850. Genealogical Pub, 1976. Facs of 1929 ed. VG. *Book Broker*. $25/£16

NOURSE, J.E. American Explorations in the Ice Zones. Boston, 1884. 578pp, engr port, dbl-pg map, fldg map (crease splits) in rear pocket. Silver illus cl (spine chipped, loss; hinges cracked, upper hinge taped). *Edwards*. $93/£60

NOVA, CRAIG. The Geek. NY: Harper, 1975. 1st ed. Fine in dj (lt edgewear; lt soiling rear panel). *Else Fine*. $65/£42

NOVA, CRAIG. Turkey Hash. NY: Harper, 1972. 1st US ed. Sl mkd, o/w NF in dj (sl soiled; nick). *Virgo*. $47/£30

NOVAK, EMIL. Menstruation and Its Disorders. NY, 1921. 1st ed. Good. *Fye*. $35/£23

NOVAK, JOSEPH. (Pseud of Jerzy Kosinski). The Future is Ours, Comrade. GC: Doubleday, 1960. 1st ed, 1st bk, signed. Grey cl. VG (sm dampstain, label at rear) in VG dj. *Chapel Hill*. $275/£177

NOVAK, JOSEPH. (Pseud of J. Kosinski.) The Future Is Ours, Comrade. Doubleday, 1960. 1st ed. NF in dj. *Fine Books*. $175/£113

NOVAK, JOSEPH. (Pseud of J. Kosinski.) No Third Path. Doubleday, 1962. 1st ed. Fine in VG+ dj. *Fine Books*. $135/£87

NOWLAN, PHIL and DICK CALKINS. The Adventures of Buck Rogers. Whitman Big Big Book, 1934. 1st ed. VG. *Madle*. $85/£55

NOYCE, WILFRID. South Col. London, 1954. 1st ed. 5 maps, 4 color plts, 48 b/w plts. Dj (chipped, sl loss). *Edwards*. $25/£16

NOYES, A.J. In the Land of the Chinook. The Story of Blaine County. Helena, MT: State Pub, (1917). VG. Howes N 218. *Perier*. $195/£126

NOYES, ALFRED. The Accusing Ghost of Roger Casement. NY: Citadel, 1957. 1st US ed. VG in dj (spine faded). *Aka*. $30/£19

NOYES, ALFRED. The Forest of Wild Thyme. Edinburgh/London: Wm. Blackwood, 1911. 1st ed. Gilt-stamped cl. Teg. Pale foxing 1st, last leaves. *Sadlon*. $30/£19

NOYES, JOHN HUMPHREY. Male Continence. Oneida, NY: Oneida Community, 1872. 1st ed. 24pp. Text Fine (fr wrap detached; sigs). Grn ptd wraps. *Cullen*. $375/£242

NUNAN, THOMAS. Diary of an Old Bohemian.... SF: Harr Wagner, 1927. 1st ed. Pict cl. Good+ (tape repair 4pp). *Connolly*. $25/£16

NUNNELEY, THOMAS. A Treatise on the Nature, Causes, and Treatment of Erysipelas. Phila, 1844. 1st Amer ed. 235pp. Good. *Fye*. $75/£48

Nursery ABC and Simple Speller. NY: McLoughlin Bros, n.d. (ca 1870). 8vo. 4 leaves. Full color pict stiff paper wrappers. Fine. *Hobbyhorse*. $200/£129

Nursery Melodies. NY: C.P. Huestis, n.d. (ca 1880). 12mo. 24pp + 1pg list lower wrapper; 12 VF 1/2pg wood engrs, tail-piece vignettes. Pict paper wrappers (rebacked, trace of previous stitching; lt dusted). VG (name). *Hobbyhorse*. $90/£58

Nursery Rhyme Pop-up Book. London: Purnell, n.d. (195?). 21x24 cm. 4 pull-down panels, 4 dbl-pg pop-ups. E.V.A. (illus). Pict wraps. VG. *Book Finders*. $70/£45

Nursery Rhymes with Pop-Up Pictures. Somerset/London: Purnell, n.d. (197?). 24x17 cm. 3 dbl-pg pop-ups. E.V.A. (illus). Glazed pict bds. VG. *Book Finders*. $35/£23

Nursery Rhymes. NY/Toronto: Random House, 1976. 15x29 cm. Antoinette Delaney (illus). Glazed pict bds (cvrs sl worn). VG. *Book Finders*. $45/£29

NUTE, GRACE. Lake Superior. Bobbs Merrill, (1944). 1st ed. Ep maps. Fine in VG dj. *Oregon*. $25/£16

NUTT, T. Humanity to Honey Bees.... Wisbech, 1839. 5th ed. Frontis; xxx,281pp. (Cl used.) *Wheldon & Wesley*. $62/£40

NUTTALL, THOMAS. A Journey of Travels into the Arkansas Territory During the Year 1819. Savoie Lottinville (ed). Univ of OK, (1980). 1st thus. VF in VF dj. *Oregon*. $35/£23

NUTTING, WALLACE. Furniture of the Pilgrim Century 1620-1720.... Boston: Marshall Jones, (1921). Gilt-titled brn cl. VG. *House.* $120/£77

NUTTING, WALLACE. Furniture Treasury.... Framingham: Old Amer Co, (1928). 2 vols. Brn cl. VG. *House.* $180/£116

NUTTING, WALLACE. Ireland Beautiful. Framingham, (1925). 1st ed. Cl (spine discolored; faded, worn; inscrip). *King.* $30/£19

NUTTING, WALLACE. Massachusetts Beautiful. GC, (1935). 1st ed. Inscrip, else VG. *King.* $30/£19

NUTTING, WALLACE. New York Beautiful. GC, (1936). VG in dj (tattered, tape-repaired). *King.* $25/£16

NUTTING, WALLACE. A Windsor Handbook.... Saugus, MA: Wallace Nutting, (1917). Good (ink inscrip; rubbed; bumped). *King.* $75/£48

NYE, W.S. Carbine and Lance, The Story of Old Fort Sill. Norman, 1937. 3rd ed (1969). Dj wear, sm piece missing from back, o/w Fine. *Pratt.* $35/£23

O

O'BRIAN, FLANN. The Dalkey Archive. London: MacGibbon & Kee, 1964. 1st Eng ed. Fine in dj (price-clipped; edges sl rubbed). *Ulysses.* $225/£145

O'BRIAN, PATRICK. The Fortune of War. London: Collins, 1979. 1st ed. Erasures fep, o/w Fine in dj. *Mordida.* $65/£42

O'BRIAN, PATRICK. Joseph Banks. A Life. London: Collins Harvill, 1987. 1st Eng ed. Fine (spine tail sl bumped) in dj (sl creased; spine sl faded). *Ulysses.* $70/£45

O'BRIAN, PATRICK. The Letter of Marque. Collins, 1988. 1st UK ed. Fine in dj. *Lewton.* $28/£18

O'BRIAN, PATRICK. The Nutmeg of Consolation. London: Collins, 1991. 1st ed. Fine in dj. *Virgo.* $47/£30

O'BRIAN, PATRICK. The Nutmeg of Consolation. London: Collins, 1991. 1st ed. VF in dj. *Limestone.* $85/£55

O'BRIAN, PATRICK. The Reverse of the Medal. London: Collins, 1986. 1st ed. NF in dj. *Limestone.* $85/£55

O'BRIAN, PATRICK. The Reverse of the Medal. London: Collins, 1986. 1st ed. Fine in dj. *Else Fine.* $110/£71

O'BRIAN, PATRICK. The Thirteen Gun Salute. London: Collins, 1989. 1st ed. Fine in dj. *Else Fine.* $85/£55

O'BRIAN, PATRICK. The Thirteen Gun Salute. London: Collins, 1989. 1st ed. VF in dj. *Limestone.* $85/£55

O'BRIAN, PATRICK. The Wine-Dark Sea. London: Harper Collins, 1993. 1st ed, signed. VF in dj. *Limestone.* $85/£55

O'BRIEN, EDNA. August Is a Wicked Month. London: Jonathan Cape, 1965. 1st ed. Fine in dj. *Temple.* $29/£19

O'BRIEN, EDNA. Casualties of Peace. London: Cape, 1966. 1st ed. Signed. NF in dj (price-clipped). *Rees.* $31/£20

O'BRIEN, EDNA. The Love Object. London: Jonathan Cape, 1968. 1st ed. Fine in NF dj. *Temple.* $22/£14

O'BRIEN, EDNA. The Rescue. London: Hodder & Stoughton, 1983. 1st ed. 4to. Fine in ilus orange bds. *Lame Duck.* $45/£29

O'BRIEN, EDWARD J. (ed). The Best Short Stories of 1919. Boston, (1920). 1st ed. Fine in dj. *Argosy.* $60/£39

O'BRIEN, EDWARD J. (ed). The Best Short Stories of 1922. Boston, (1923). 1st ed. Fine in dj. *Argosy.* $100/£65

O'BRIEN, ESSE FORRESTER. Circus: Cinders to Sawdust. San Antonio: Naylor, (1959). Pict cl. VG in Fine dj. *Schoyer.* $25/£16

O'BRIEN, FLANN. The Dalkey Archive. London: MacGibbon & Kee, 1964. 1st ed. Fine in Fine dj (lt rubbed). *Between The Covers.* $300/£194

O'BRIEN, FLANN. The Hard Life. NY: Pantheon, 1962. 1st ed. Fine in Fine dj. *Beasley.* $60/£39

O'BRIEN, FLANN. The Poor Mouth. Patrick C. Power (trans). NY: Viking, (1974). 1st ed. Ralph Steadman (illus). Top edge lt bumped, else NF in white dj (soiled; edgeworn). *Robbins.* $30/£19

O'BRIEN, FLANN. The Poor Mouth. NY: Viking, 1974. 1st ed. Fine in dj (lt sun-dknd; tiny tears). *Beasley.* $30/£19

O'BRIEN, FLANN. Stories and Plays. NY: Viking, 1976. 1st ed. Fine in NF dj (lt soiling). *Beasley.* $35/£23

O'BRIEN, FLANN. The Third Policeman. NY: Walker, (1967). 1st US ed. NF (sm erasure fep) in dj (wear, soiled; few tears; price-clipped). *Antic Hay.* $45/£29

O'BRIEN, FLANN. The Third Policeman. London: MacGibbon & Kee, 1967. 1st ed. Fine in dj. *Limestone.* $175/£113

O'BRIEN, FLANN. The Various Lives of Keats and Chapman and the Brother. London: Hart-Davis, MacGibbon, 1976. 1st ed. Fine in dj. *Rees.* $31/£20

O'BRIEN, JACK. Alone across the Top of the World. Chicago: Winston, 1935. 1st ed. Inscribed. Frontis port; 7 plts. Pict cl. Fine in Good+ dj. *Connolly.* $42/£27

O'BRIEN, JOHN EMMET. Telegraphing in Battle. Reminiscences of the Civil War. Scranton, PA: (Wilkes-Barre, Raeder Press), 1910. 1st ed. Rear inner hinge starting, else VG. *Mcgowan.* $225/£145

O'BRIEN, KATE. The Ante-Room. London: Heinemann, (1934). 1st ed. VG in dj (sl chipped; dknd). *Reese.* $30/£19

O'BRIEN, KATE. Farewell Spain. London: Heinemann, 1937. 1st ed. Nice. *Patterson.* $70/£45

O'BRIEN, LIAM. The Remarkable Mr. Pennypacker. NY: Random House, (1954). 1st Amer ed. Sm scrape to photo frontis, else NF in NF in dj (sl tear; sl rubbing). *Between The Covers.* $55/£35

O'BRIEN, PATRICK. Pablo Ruiz Picasso. A Biography. London: Collins, 1976. 1st Eng ed. Fine (spine tail sl bumped) in dj (spine sl faded). *Ulysses.* $116/£75

O'BRIEN, TIM. Going After Cacciato. NY: Delacorte/Lawrence, (1978). 1st ed. NF in NF dj. *Dermont.* $50/£32

O'BRIEN, TIM. Going After Cacciato. NY: Delacorte, 1978. 1st ed. NF (lt erasure) in NF dj. *Revere.* $90/£58

O'BRIEN, TIM. Northern Lights. London: Marion Boyars, 1976. 1st British ed. Fine in Fine dj. *Pettler.* $90/£58

O'CALLAGHAN, E.B. The Documentary History of the State of New York. Albany, 1849-1851. 1st ed. 4 vols. vii,786; vii,1211; vii,1215; xxv,1144pp. VG. Howes O 16. *Oregon.* $200/£129

O'CALLAGHAN, E.B. The Documentary History of the State of New-York. Albany, 1850-51. 4 vols. 4to. 78 fldg maps, plts (vol 3 spine bottom chipped, foxing). Howes O 16. *Argosy.* $400/£258

O'CASEY, SEAN. Oak Leaves and Lavender. London: Macmillan, 1946. 1st ed. NF in dj (spine lightened). *Sadlon.* $20/£13

O'CASEY, SEAN. The Plough and the Stars. NY: Macmillan, 1926. 1st US ed. NF in VG+ dj. *Lame Duck.* $250/£161

O'CATHASAIGH, P. (Pseud of Sean O'Casey.) The Story of the Irish Citizen Army. Dublin/London: Maunsel, 1919. 1st ed. Grey (1st state) wrappers (joints split; backstrip defective). *Waterfield.* $101/£65

O'CONNELL, JAMES F. A Residence of Eleven Years in New Holland and the Caroline Islands.... Boston, 1836. Frontis, 265pp. Mod 1/2 calf, marbled bds. Staining to title, else VG. *Reese.* $800/£516

O'CONNOR, FEARGUS. A Practical Work on the Management of Small Farms. Manchester: Heywood, 1846. 4th ed. 192pp. Pub's cl (spotted); uncut. Good. *Second Life.* $75/£48

O'CONNOR, FLANNERY. The Artificial Nigger and Other Tales. London: Neville Spearman, (1957). 1st Eng ed. Fine in pict dj (sl rubbed). *Jaffe.* $350/£226

O'CONNOR, FLANNERY. Everything That Rises Must Converge. NY, (1965). 1st ed. Bkpl remnants, else Good in dj (torn, frayed, wrinkled, price-clipped). *King.* $125/£81

O'CONNOR, FLANNERY. Everything That Rises Must Converge. NY: FSG, (1965). 1st ed. Label, o/w Fine in dj (lt soiled). *Hermitage.* $200/£129

O'CONNOR, FLANNERY. A Good Man Is Hard to Find. NY: Harcourt, Brace, 1955. 1st ed. NF in dj (sl rubbing to fr; sl discoloration, sm chip rear panel). *Lame Duck.* $950/£613

O'CONNOR, FLANNERY. The Violent Bear It Away. NY: Farrar, Straus & Cudahy, (1960). 1st ed. VG in dj (2 sm chips, sm edge tears, else VG). *Godot.* $175/£113

O'CONNOR, FLANNERY. The Violent Bear It Away. NY: Farrar, Straus & Cudahy, (1960). 1st ed. Rev copy; pub's slip laid in. 8vo. Fine in dj. *Jaffe.* $1,000/£645

O'CONNOR, FLANNERY. The Violent Bear It Away. (London): Longmans, Green, (1960). 1st UK ed. Fine in NF dj (price-clipped; lt soiled rear panel). *Bernard.* $200/£129

O'CONNOR, FRANK. The Lonely Voice. Cleveland, (1963). 1st ed. VG in dj. *Argosy.* $30/£19

O'CONNOR, FRANK. The Saint and Mary Kate. London: Macmillan, 1932. 1st ed. Lt grn cl, gilt spine. Nice. *Temple.* $62/£40

O'CONNOR, FRANK. Three Tales. Dublin: Cuala, 1941. One of 250. Linen-backed bds. Orig plain wrapper. *Petersfield.* $39/£25

O'CONNOR, JACK. The Art of Hunting Big Game in North America. Outdoor Life, (1967). 1st ed. Fine in VG dj. *Oregon.* $45/£29

O'CONNOR, JACK. Game in the Desert Revisited. Clinton: Amwell, 1977. One of 950 numbered, signed by author, publisher. Green leatherette, gilt-stamped spine. VF in slipcase. *Bowman.* $250/£161

O'CONNOR, JACK. Hunting in the Rockies. NY: Knopf/Borzoi, 1947. 1st ed. VG+ in dj. *Bowman.* $135/£87

O'CONNOR, JACK. Hunting in the Southwest. NY: Knopf/Borzoi, 1945. 1st ed. VG+ in dj. *Bowman.* $175/£113

O'CONNOR, JACK. The Last Book. Clinton: Amwell, 1984. Trade ed. VF in VF slipcase. *Bowman.* $40/£26

O'CONNOR, LESLIE. Professional Baseball in America. Chicago, 1928. 1st ed. VG+. *Fuller & Saunders.* $45/£29

O'CONNOR, RICHARD. Bat Masterson. Doubleday, 1957. 1st ed. VG in dj (soiled, worn). *Oregon.* $12/£8

O'CONNOR, RICHARD. Hood, Cavalier General. NY: Prentice-Hall, (1949). 1st ed. NF. *Mcgowan.* $65/£42

O'CONNOR, RICHARD. Iron Wheels and Broken Men. Putnam, (1973). 1st ed. VF in VF dj. *Oregon.* $35/£23

O'CONOR, J.F.X. Facts about Bookworms.... NY, 1898. 1st ed, ltd to 750 numbered. 87pp (sl discolor fep; cvrs worn.) *King.* $50/£32

O'CROULEY, PEDRO ALONSO. A Description of the Kingdom of New Spain. Sean Galvin (trans). 1972. Fine. *Perier.* $50/£32

O'DONNELL, BERNARD. The Old Bailey and Its Trials. NY: Macmillan, 1951. *Boswell.* $25/£16

O'DONNELL, E. Byways of Ghostland. Rider, 1911. 1st ed. Sl cvr discoloration, else VG. *Aronovitz.* $95/£61

O'DONNELL, E. Ghosts Helpful and Harmful. Rider, 1924. 1st ed. VG+. *Aronovitz.* $75/£48

O'DONNELL, PETER. I, Lucifer. London: Souvenir Press, 1967. 1st UK ed. VG (name) in VG dj. *Ming.* $62/£40

O'DONNELL, PETER. Modesty Blaise. London: Souvenir Press, 1965. 1st ed. VG in VG dj (lt rubbed). *Ming.* $85/£55

O'DONNELL, T.C. The Ladder of Rickety Rungs. Chicago: P.F. Volland, (1923). 8vo. Janet Laura Scott (illus). Color illus bds (lt worn, sl chipped). Pub's illus box (corners sl worn). *Reisler.* $125/£81

O'FAOLAIN, SEAN. Bird Alone. NY, 1936. 1st Amer ed. Fine in dj (spine sl sunned; edge lt rubbed). *Polyanthos.* $30/£19

O'FAOLAIN, SEAN. The Man Who Invented Sin. NY, 1948. 1st Amer ed. Fine in Fine dj. *Polyanthos.* $30/£19

O'FAOLAIN, SEAN. Midsummer Night Madness and Other Stories. London: Jonathan Cape, 1932. 1st ed, 1st bk. Lower edges uncut. Grn cl. Fine in dj. *Temple.* $147/£95

O'FAOLAIN, SEAN. A Nest of Simple Folk. London: Cape, (1933). 1st ed. VG in dj (chips, tears). *Reese.* $125/£81

O'FAOLAIN, SEAN. A Summer in Italy. NY: Devin-Adair, 1950. 1st US ed. Signed. (Bkpl.) *Second Life.* $40/£26

O'FAOLAIN, SEAN. Teresa and Other Stories. London: Jonathan Cape, 1947. 1st ed. Lower edges uncut. Grn linen. Fine in dj (nicked, scuffed). *Temple.* $54/£35

O'FLAHERTY, LIAM. The Child of God. London: E. Archer, Christmas 1926. Ltd to 100. Signed. Ptd marbled wrappers (sm chips). *Sadlon.* $50/£32

O'FLAHERTY, LIAM. The Fairy Goose and Two Other Stories. NY/London: Crosby Gaige/Faber & Gwyer, 1927. 1st ed. One of 1190 signed, ptd. Unopened. Shamrock-sprinkled paper-cvrd bds, linen spine. Sl soil, bumped, paper label sl chipped, else VG. *Juvelis.* $50/£32

O'FLAHERTY, LIAM. The House of Gold. Cape, 1929. 1st ed. Sl dull, else Good in dec dj (sl rubbed). *Whiteson.* $39/£25

O'FLAHERTY, LIAM. Insurrection. Gollancz, 1950. 1st UK ed. VG in dj. *Lewton.* $23/£15

O'FLAHERTY, LIAM. Joseph Conrad. An Appreciation. London: E. Lahr, 1930. 1st ed, trade issue. VG in ptd wrappers. *Reese.* $25/£16

O'FLAHERTY, LIAM. Joseph Conrad. An Appreciation. London: E. Lahr, n.d. but 1930. 1st ed. Fine in blue ptd paper wrappers. *Cady.* $20/£13

O'FLAHERTY, LIAM. The Martyr. London: Gollancz, 1933. 1st ed. Dk brn cl. Top, fore-edges sl foxed, o/w NF in dj (faded, frayed, sl mkd). *Temple.* $62/£40

O'FLAHERTY, LIAM. Red Barbara and Other Stories. NY/London: Crosby Gaige/Faber & Gwyer, 1928. Ltd to 600. Signed. Leather spine label. (Lt browning fep.) *Sadlon.* $75/£48

O'FLAHERTY, LIAM. Skerrett. NY: Long & Smith, 1932. 1st Amer ed. NF in dj (lt faded, used). *Reese.* $35/£23

O'FLAHERTY, LIAM. The Tent. Cape, 1926. 1st ed. Sl dull, else Good. *Whiteson.* $25/£16

O'FLAHERTY, LIAM. The Tent. Cape, 1926. 1st ed. Inscribed. NF in NF dj (closed tear; lt dust-soil). *Fine Books.* $175/£113

O'FLAHERTY, LIAM. A Tourist's Guide to Ireland. London: Mandrake Press, (1929). 1st ed. Fep removed, o/w Good. *Cox.* $19/£12

O'HANLON, REDMOND. In Trouble Again. London, 1988. 1st ed. Map. Dj. *Edwards.* $23/£15

O'HARA, FRANK. Awake in Spain. NY: American Theatre for Poets, 1960. 1st ed. NF in wraps. *Beasley.* $40/£26

O'HARA, FRANK. The Collected Poems of Frank O'Hara. Donald Allen (ed). NY: Knopf, 1971. 1st ed. Pub's rmdr stamp bottom edge, else NF in suppressed Larry Rivers dj w/nude port of author. *Lame Duck.* $100/£65

O'HARA, FRANK. Meditations in an Emergency. NY: Grove Press, (1957). 1st ed. Sl sunning to spine; sl foxing, else Nice in ptd wraps. *Antic Hay.* $50/£32

O'HARA, FRANK. Meditations in an Emergency. NY: Grove Press, (1957). One of 75 numbered. NF (sl sunned). *Polyanthos.* $600/£387

O'HARA, JOHN. Butterfield 8. London: Cresset, 1951. 1st ed. VG in dj (sl chipped). *Rees.* $16/£10

O'HARA, JOHN. Files on Parade. NY: Harcourt, Brace, (1939). 1st ed. (Bumped.) NF in dj (sl soiled). *Blue Mountain.* $85/£55

O'HARA, JOHN. From the Terrace. R-H, 1958. 1st ed. Rev copy w/slip laid in. NF in VG+ dj. *Fine Books.* $125/£81

O'HARA, JOHN. Hellbox. NY: Random House, (1947). 1st ed. NF (sm stain cvr). Ptd dj (sl rubbed; 2 pinholes). *Blue Mountain.* $45/£29

O'HARA, JOHN. Hellbox. NY, (1947). 1st ed. Sl bumped, else VG in dj (sl rubbed). *King.* $75/£48

O'HARA, JOHN. Hope of Heaven. NY: Harcourt, Brace, (1938). 1st ed. NF in dj (few short tears). *Blue Mountain.* $95/£61

O'HARA, JOHN. The Horse Knows the Way. NY: Random House, (1964). 1st ed. #46/250 signed. Dk red cl. NF. *Chapel Hill.* $75/£48

O'HARA, JOHN. The Instrument. NY: Random House, (1967). Signed ltd ed of 300 numbered. Fine in slipcase (sl wear). *Antic Hay.* $125/£81

O'HARA, JOHN. The Lockwood Concern. R-H, 1965. 1st ed. One of 300 signed. VF in slip-case. *Fine Books.* $150/£97

O'HARA, JOHN. Ourselves to Know. NY: Random House, (1960). 1st Amer ed. Inscribed. Spine lettering rubbed, o/w VG- (lacks dj). *Between The Covers.* $135/£87

O'HARA, JOHN. Ourselves to Know. NY: Random House, (1960). 1st ed. Fine in dj (sl wear). *Reese.* $30/£19

O'HARA, JOHN. Pal Joey. NY: Duell, Sloan and Pearce, (1940). 1st ed. NF (sm chip spine; lt rubbed) in Good dj (edges chipped; lacks sm pieces; sm hole spine). *Blue Mountain.* $65/£42

O'HARA, JOHN. Pipe Night. London: Faber & Faber, 1946. 1st ed. Fore-edges uncut. Grn cl, gilt spine. Spine sl faded; lt imaging fr dj to spine, fr cvr; o/w Fine in dj (sl frayed). *Temple.* $34/£22

O'HARA, JOHN. Sermons and Soda Water. NY: Random House, 1960. 1st ed, 1st ptg. 3 vols. Very Nice set in pub's slipcase. *Cady.* $20/£13

O'HARA, JOHN. Sermons and Soda-Water. London: Cresset, 1961. 1st Eng ed, ltd to 525 numbered, signed. 3 vols. Marbled paper-cvrd bds, white spines stamped in green/gold. Fine set in pub's glassine djs, pub's slipcase box (starting to split, else Fine). *Godot.* $175/£113

O'HARA, JOHN. Sweet and Sour. NY, 1954. 1st Amer ed. Fine in dj. *Polyanthos.* $30/£19

O'HARA, JOHN. Ten North Frederick. NY, 1955. 1st ed. As New in dj. *Bond.* $35/£23

O'HART, JOHN. Irish Pedigrees, or the Origin and Stem of the Irish Nation. NY: Murphy & McCarthy, 1923. 2 vols. 40 plts. Full leatherette; gilt, blind-stamped. VG. *Cullen.* $150/£97

O'KANE, WALTER COLLINS. Sun in the Sky. Norman: Univ of OK Press, (1970). VG in dj (chipped; spine tear; price-clipped). *Blue Mountain.* $15/£10

O'KEEFFE, GEORGIA and ALFRED STIEGLITZ. Georgia O'Keeffe: A Portrait by Alfred Stieglitz. Viking, 1978. 1st ed. 50 full-pg photos. Fine in dj and VG+ slipcase. *Fine Books.* $95/£61

O'KEEFFE, GEORGIA. Georgia O'Keeffe. NY: Viking, (1976). 1st ed. Fine in dj (sl rubbed, torn). *Jaffe.* $225/£145

O'KEEFFE, GEORGIA. Georgia O'Keeffe. NY: Viking, 1976. 1st Amer ed. 108 color plts. Fine in NF dj (price-clipped; few short tears). *Between The Covers.* $450/£290

O'KEEFFE, GEORGIA. One Hundred Flowers. Nicholas Callaway (ed). NY, 1987. 1st ed. 100 color plts. Fine in dj. *Argosy.* $85/£55

O'MALLEY, C.D. (ed). The History of Medical Education.... Berkeley: Univ of CA Press, 1970. 1st ed. 2-tone cl. Fine in dj. *Glaser.* $75/£48

O'MALLLY, C.D. et al. Harvey's Lectures on the Whole of Anatomy. L.A., 1961. Good. *Goodrich.* $30/£19

O'MEARA, BARRY E. Napoleon in Exile. London: W. Simpkin & R. Marshall, 1822. 4th ed. 2 vols. xxviii,512; (2),542pp; 4 plts. Contemp 1/2 calf (neatly rebacked), orig backstrips. Good (spotting; bk ticket). *Cox.* $70/£45

O'MEARA, CARRA. The Iconography of the Facade of Saint-Gilles-du Gard. NY, 1977. 95 illus on plts; 9 plans. Good. *Washton.* $75/£48

O'MEARA, WALTER. Daughters of the Country. Harcourt, (1968). 1st ed. VG in VG dj. *Oregon.* $60/£39

O'MEARA, WALTER. The Savage Country. Houghton Mifflin, 1960. 1st ed. Ep maps. Fine in dj (lt chipped). *Oregon.* $40/£26

O'NEAL, BILL. Encyclopedia of Western Gun-Fighters. Norman, 1979. 1st ed. Dec cl. Fine in dj (shelfwear). *Baade.* $75/£48

O'NEAL, BILL. Encyclopedia of Western Gunfighters. Norman: Univ of OK Press, (1979). 1st ed. NF in dj (sl tears). *Glenn.* $60/£39

O'NEAL, BILL. The Texas League. Eakin Press, 1987. 1st ed. Fine in Fine dj. *Plapinger.* $45/£29

O'NEAL, WILLIAM. Jefferson's Buildings at the University of Virginia: The Rotunda. Univ Press of VA, 1960. 22 b/w plts. VG in VG dj. *Book Broker.* $45/£29

O'NEAL, WILLIAM. Primitive into Painter: Life and Letters of John Toole. Charlottesville: Univ of VA, 1960. 1st ed. Gilt-emb cl. Fine in color illus dj. *Cahan.* $60/£39

O'NEIL, T. The Muskrat in the Louisiana Coastal Marshes, etc. N.p.: Dept WL, 1949. 1st ed. Gilt dec cl. VG. *Mikesh.* $30/£19

O'NEILL, EUGENE. Ah, Wilderness! NY, 1933. 1st Amer ed. Fine in dj (sl sunned, sl rubbed). *Polyanthos.* $100/£65

O'NEILL, EUGENE. Ah, Wilderness! NY: LEC, 1972. One of 1500 numbered, signed by Shannon Stirnweis (illus). Fine in pub's slipcase (dusty). *Hermitage.* $100/£65

O'NEILL, EUGENE. Dynamo. NY: Horace, Liveright, 1929. 1st ed. Dk grn cl; top edge stained black. VG. *Houle.* $65/£42

O'NEILL, EUGENE. Dynamo. NY: Horace Liveright, 1929. 1st ed. Fine in NF dj (lt chipped). *Hermitage.* $85/£55

O'NEILL, EUGENE. Dynamo. NY: Horace Liveright, 1929. 1st trade ed. (Spine gilt dull.) *Sadlon.* $15/£10

O'NEILL, EUGENE. The Emperor Jones. Diff'rent. The Straw. NY: Boni & Liveright, (1921). 1st ed. (Lt rubbed.) *Sadlon.* $35/£23

O'NEILL, EUGENE. The Iceman Cometh. NY: Random House, (1946). 1st ed. NF (ink name) in VG dj (sl wear; short tears). *Antic Hay.* $75/£48

O'NEILL, EUGENE. The Iceman Cometh. NY: Random House, (1946). 1st ed. Blue cl. Sig, o/w Fine in VG dj (spine faded; tears). *Chapel Hill.* $75/£48

O'NEILL, EUGENE. The Iceman Cometh. London: Cape, 1947. 1st Eng ed. VG in dj (sl browned, chipped spine extrems). *Limestone.* $35/£23

O'NEILL, EUGENE. Lazarus Laughed. NY, 1927. 1st ed, ltd to 775 numbered, signed. Partially uncut (spine stained; label chipped). *King.* $195/£126

O'NEILL, EUGENE. Long Day's Journey into Night. New Haven: Yale Univ, 1956. 1st ed. VG (sl dampstain) in dj (sl wear, soil; chipped; price-clipped; tears). *Antic Hay.* $25/£16

O'NEILL, EUGENE. Marco Millions. NY, 1927. 1st Amer ed. Fine in dj (sunned, sl chipped, sm tear, price-clipped). *Polyanthos.* $50/£32

O'NEILL, EUGENE. Marco Millions. NY, 1927. 1st ed, ltd to 440 numbered, signed. Partially uncut (spine heavily soiled, spotted). *King.* $195/£126

O'NEILL, EUGENE. A Moon for the Misbegotten. NY: Random House, (1952). 1st ed. Black/gray bds, brn cl spine. Owner label, ink date fr pastedown, else Fine in VG dj (price-clipped; faded; chipped). *Chapel Hill.* $45/£29

O'NEILL, EUGENE. A Moon for the Misbegotten. NY: Random House, (1952). 1st ed. Fine in dj (sl dusty). *Hermitage.* $50/£32

O'NEILL, EUGENE. A Moon for the Misbegotten: A Play.... London: Cape, (1953). 1st Eng ed. VG in dj (nicks). *Houle.* $55/£35

O'NEILL, EUGENE. More Stately Mansions: A Play in Three Acts. Donald Gallup (ed). London: Cape, (1965). 1st Eng ed (reset). VG in dj. *Houle.* $55/£35

O'NEILL, EUGENE. Mourning Becomes Electra. NY: Horace Liveright, 1931. 1st ed, 1st ptg. Blue cl, gilt. VF in Fine dj. *Macdonnell.* $150/£97

O'NEILL, EUGENE. Strange Interlude. NY: Boni & Liveright, 1928. One of 750 signed of 775. Unopened. Vellum uniformly speckled, o/w Fine. *Pharos.* $225/£145

O'NEILL, JOSEPH. Land Under England. London, 1935. 1st ed. Good+. *Madle.* $27/£17

O'REILLY, JOHN. The Glob. NY, 1952. 1st ed. Sm spot color loss fr cvr, o/w Fine. *Bond.* $30/£19

O'REILLY, MONTAGUE. (Pseud of Wayne Andrews). Who Has Been Tampering with These Pianos? (NY): Direction/New Directions, (1948). 1st ed. Ptd wrappers sl worn, else Very Nice. *Reese.* $50/£32

O'RIORDAN, CONAL. Soldier's End. (London): Arrowsmith, (1938). 1st ed. Inscribed. VG. *Reese.* $25/£16

O'SHEA, HENRY. Guide to Spain and Portugal, Including the Balearic Islands. A&C Black, 1868. 3rd ed. cxiv,562pp; map. Clean. *Gretton.* $78/£50

O'SHEA, HENRY. Guide to Spain and Portugal. John Lomas (ed). A&C Black, 1902. 12th ed. Map. Grn dec cl. Clean. *Gretton.* $54/£35

O'SULLIVAN, MAURICE. Twenty Years A-Growing. M.L. Davies & G. Thomson (trans). London: C&W, 1933. 1st ed. Pale grn cl (faded). Sm tape shadow endsheet, o/w VG in dj (sl tanned, spine chipped). *Reese.* $45/£29

OAKES, C.G. Sir Samuel Romilly 1757-1818.... London: George Allen, 1935. Sl worn, spotted, but Sound. *Boswell.* $50/£32

OAKES, CLIFFORD. The Birds of Lancashire. London: Oliver & Boyd, 1953. 1st ed. Untrimmed. Grn ribbed cl gilt (top edge lower bd sl faded). *Hollett.* $70/£45

OAKES, PHILIP. Notes by the Provincial Governor. London: Poem-of-the-Month Club, (1972). 1st ed. Signed. Fine. *Polyanthos.* $25/£16

OAKESHOTT, WALTER. The Two Winchester Bibles. Oxford: Clarendon, 1981. Ltd to 1000 numbered. 12 full-pg color plts, 192 monochrome repros. Red gilt cl. Fine in linen slipcase. *Karmiole.* $250/£161

OAKLY, OBADIAH. Expedition to Oregon. NY, 1914. Fine in wraps. *Perier.* $40/£26

OATES, JOYCE CAROL. Anonymous Sins and Other Poems. Baton Rouge: LA Univ Press, 1969. 1st ed. Signed. NF (bumped) in VG dj (rubbed; sm chip; price-clipped). *Revere.* $75/£48

OATES, JOYCE CAROL. The Assassins. NY: Vanguard Press, 1975. 1st ed. Signed. Fine in Fine dj. *Revere.* $50/£32

OATES, JOYCE CAROL. Bellefleur. NY, (1980). 1st ed. VG in dj. *Argosy.* $30/£19

OATES, JOYCE CAROL. Bellefleur. NY: Dutton, 1980. 1st ed. Fine in dj. *Lame Duck.* $35/£23

OATES, JOYCE CAROL. By the North Gate. NY: Vanguard, (1963). 1st ed, 1st bk. Fine in dj (spine sl tanned). *Pharos.* $150/£97

OATES, JOYCE CAROL. Crossing the Border. NY: Vanguard, 1976. 1st ed. VF in dj. *Else Fine.* $75/£48

OATES, JOYCE CAROL. Expensive People. NY: Vanguard, (1968). 1st ed. Rev slip laid in. Fine in VG dj. *Reese.* $45/£29

OATES, JOYCE CAROL. The Hostile Sun. L.A.: Black Sparrow Press, 1973. 1st ed, ltd to 300 numbered, signed. Fine in pub's acetate dj. *Godot.* $85/£55

OATES, JOYCE CAROL. I Lock My Door Upon Myself. NY: Ecco Press, 1990. 1st ed. Signed. Fine in Fine dj. *Revere.* $30/£19

OATES, JOYCE CAROL. Marriages and Infidelities. NY: Vanguard, (1972). 1st ed. Fine in NF dj. *Hermitage.* $40/£26

OATES, JOYCE CAROL. Marya: A Life. NY: Dutton, (1986). 1st ed. Fine in dj. *Between The Covers.* $35/£23

OATES, JOYCE CAROL. Nightside. NY: Vanguard, 1977. 1st ed. Fine in dj (short closed tear). *Else Fine.* $45/£29

OATES, JOYCE CAROL. The Triumph of the Spider Monkey. Santa Barbara: Black Sparrow, 1976. 1st ed in bk form. One of 350 numbered, signed. Cl, ptd bds. VF. *Reese.* $30/£19

OATES, JOYCE CAROL. The Wheel of Love and Other Stories. NY: Vanguard, (1970). 1st ed. Fine in dj (lt used). *Reese.* $30/£19

OATES, JOYCE CAROL. With Shuddering Fall. NY: Vanguard, (1964). 1st ed. Fine in dj (lt sunned; 2 sm edge tears; lt use). *Reese.* $100/£65

OATES, JOYCE CAROL. Wonderland. NY: Vanguard, 1971. 1st ed. VF in dj. *Else Fine.* $40/£26

OATES, STEPHEN. Confederate Cavalry West of the River. Austin: Univ of TX Press, (1961). 1st ed. Orig cl. Fine in NF dj. *Mcgowan.* $150/£97

OATES, STEPHEN. To Purge This Land with Blood. NY, (1970). VG+ in VG+ dj. *Pratt.* $27/£17

OBERHUBER, KONRAD. Poussin. Phaidon, 1988. 1st UK ed. 49 color plts. Dj. *Edwards.* $54/£35

OBERNDORF, CLARENCE. The Psychiatric Novels of Oliver Wendell Holmes. NY, 1944. 1st ed. Good. *Fye.* $30/£19

OBREITER, JOHN. The Seventy-Seventh Pennsylvania at Shiloh. (Harrisburg, PA), 1908. 2nd ed. Spine scuffed, else VG. *Mcgowan.* $65/£42

Observations of an Old Man in Love, Being an Interlude in the Life and Loves of F.H. (By Frank Harris.) Phila: Privately published, 1929. Ltd to 500. Joints cracked but holding. *Sadlon.* $85/£55

Observations on Modern Gardening. (By Thomas Whately.) Dublin: Williams, 1770. 4ff,207pp. Calf (joints cracking, label chipped). *Marlborough.* $465/£300

ODETS, CLIFFORD. Night Music: A Comedy in Twelve Scenes. NY: Random House, 1940. 1st ed. Fine in dj (sl soiled, chip). *Cahan.* $45/£29

ODETS, CLIFFORD. Night Music: A Comedy in Twelve Scenes. NY: Random House, 1940. 1st ed. Fine in dj (minor wear spine ends). *Else Fine.* $85/£55

ODETS, CLIFFORD. Three Plays. NY, (1935). 1st Amer ed, 1st bk. Frontis. VG (inscrip). *Polyanthos.* $45/£29

ODGSON, WILLIAM HOPE. Deep Waters. Sauk City: Arkham House, 1967. 1st ed. Label removed fep, else VG+ in dj (sl stained). *Other Worlds.* $90/£58

ODUM, HOWARD W. Rainbow Round My Shoulder. Bobbs-Merrill, 1928. 1st ed. VG in VG dj (sl wear); wrap-around band present. *Fine Books.* $85/£55

ODUM, HOWARD W. Southern Regions of the United States. Univ of NC, (1937). 2nd ptg. VG- (pencil mks; ex-lib, mks). *Book Broker.* $35/£23

ODUM, HOWARD W. Wings on My Feet. Indianapolis: Bobbs-Merrill, 1929. 1st ed. Illus eps. Spine faded, else VG in illus dj (sl chipped, spine faded). *Cahan.* $50/£32

Oeconomy of Human Life. Providence, RI: Carver & Wilkinson, 1795. 108pp. Good. *Hayman.* $50/£32

OESTERLEN, F. Medical Logic. London: Sydenham Soc, 1855. xii,438pp. (Cl faded, rubbed; joints weak.) *Whitehart.* $78/£50

OESTRELEN, F. Medical Logic. G. Whitley (ed). London: Sydenham Soc, 1855. 437pp. Internally Good. (Sunned, faded.) *Goodrich.* $45/£29

OFFENBACH, JACQUES. Offenbach in America. NY: G.W. Carleton, 1877. 1st ed in English. 211+4pp pub's cat. Grn cl (heavily rubbed); gilt-titled spine. Internally NF. *Blue Mountain.* $45/£29

Officers of Our Union Army and Navy; Their Lives, Their Portraits.... Vol I. (By Louis Prang.) Boston: L. Prang, 1862. 16mo. 148pp incl 30 ports+ads. Aeg. Gilt cl. Bright in 1/2 cl, marbled bd slipcase, leather label. *Reese.* $650/£419

Official Brand Book of the State of South Dakota. Pierre, May 15, 1943. Soft cl cvr (worn through). Good (water stains). *Perier.* $30/£19

Official Guide to Japan. Tokyo: Japanese Government Railways, 1933. 36 maps, 14 plans. Corners bumped. *Schoyer.* $75/£48

Official Guide to the Klondyke Country and the Gold Fields of Alaska, with the Official Maps. Chicago: W.B. Conkey, 1897. 1st ed. 296pp (tanned). Dec red cl, gilt-lettered. Spine, rear cvr sunned, o/w NF. Howes K 205. *Harrington.* $150/£97

OFFIT, SIDNEY (ed). The Best of Baseball. Putnam's, 1956. 1st ed. VG+ in VG dj. *Plapinger.* $55/£35

OFFNER, RICHARD. An Early Florentine Dossal. Pescia, n.d. #29 of sm edition for private distribution. 16 plts (1 fldg). Good. *Washton.* $75/£48

OFFNER, RICHARD. Italian Primitives at Yale University. New Haven, 1927. Half-cl, bds. Good. *Washton.* $45/£29

OGDEN, ADELE. The California Sea Otter Trade 1784-1848. Berkeley: Univ of CA Press, 1941. 1st ed. VG. *Book Market.* $125/£81

OGG, FREDERIC A. The Opening of the Mississippi. NY: Macmillan, 1904. 1st ed. 5 maps. Red cl (1-inch spot spine). VG (bkpl removed, illus pasted reps; rear inner hinge starting). Howes O 40. *Chapel Hill.* $150/£97

OGILVIE, W.H. War Primer on Wound Infection, Its Causes, Prevention and Treatment. London, 1940. 1st ed. Good in wrappers. *Fye.* $50/£32

OGILVY, JAMES S. A Pilgrimage in Surrey. London: Routledge, 1914. 2 vols. 94 color plts. (Backstrips faded; sl dampstained.) *Petersfield.* $302/£195

OGLESBY, CATHARINE. Modern Primitive Arts of Mexico, Guatamala and the Southwest. NY/London: Whittlesey House, (1939). 1st ed. Dec terra cotta cl. Dj (spine lacks piece; stuck to fr cvr). *Glenn.* $30/£19

Ohio Guide. OUP, 1940. 1st ed. VG+. *Bishop.* $15/£10

Ohio Officer's Guide and Clerk's Companion Relating to the Duties of Justices of the Peace. J.B. Turnbull, 1832. 1st ed. VG. *Bishop.* $47/£30

OHNET, GEORGES. Will. Vizetelly, 1888. 1st ed in English. 407pp; uncut, unopened. Lt brn cl, blocked in dk brn, gilt-lettered. *Bickersteth.* $54/£35

OHRLIN, GLENN. The Hell-Bound Train: A Cowboy Songbook. Univ of IL Press, (1973). 1st ed. Disk laid in. Fine in Fine dj (price-clipped). *Authors Of The West.* $35/£23

OKEY, T. Paris and Its Story. London: J.M. Dent, 1904. 1st ed thus. #62/150. 51 color plts, 3 maps (1 fldg). Teg. Gilt dec cl, bevelled edges. Binding soiled, clean tears, foxing; else VG. *Chapel Hill.* $105/£68

OKEY, T. Venice and Its Story. London: J.M. Dent, 1903. 1st ed thus. #159/250. 52 color plts, 2 maps (1 fldg). Gilt-dec white cl, teg. NF. *Chapel Hill.* $105/£68

OKRENT, DANIEL and HARRIS LEWINE (eds). The Ultimate Baseball Book. Houghton-Mifflin, 1979. 1st ed. Fine in VG+ dj. *Plapinger.* $100/£65

OKRI, BEN. The Famished Road. NY, (1992). 1st Amer ed. Cl-backed bds. VG in dj. *King.* $50/£32

OKRI, BEN. The Famished Road. Cape, 1991. 1st ed. Fine in dj. *Fine Books.* $50/£32

OKRI, BEN. Stars of the New Curfew. London: Secker & Warburg, 1988. 1st ed. Fine in dj. *Rees.* $31/£20

OKRI, BEN. Stars of the New Curfew. London: S&W, 1988. 1st UK ed. Fine in dj. *Lewton.* $39/£25

OLAFSEN and POVELSEN. Travels in Iceland. London: Richard Phillips, 1805. iv,162pp, fldg map, 4 plts. 1/2 calf (rebacked), marbled bds. VG. *Walcot.* $140/£90

Old Brewery and the New Mission House at the Five Points. NY: Stringer & Townsend, 1854. VG (cvr badly worn). *Burcham.* $50/£32

Old Dutch Nursery Rhymes. London/Phila, (1917). 23 color plts by H. Willebeck Le Mair. Cl, pict label (sl worn, bumped). *King.* $95/£61

Old Dutch Nursery Rhymes. London: Augener, (1917). Obl 8vo. 31pp; 15 full-pg color illus by Willebeek Le Mair. Blue cl, gilt, pict onlay. VG. *Davidson.* $200/£129

Old English Needlework of the Sixteenth and Seventeenth Centuries. London: Sidney Hand, (1920). 1st ed. 13 photo plts. 3 photo negatives, leaflet laid in. Stiff ptd wraps (chipped, fr wrap lacks corner). *Chapel Hill.* $40/£26

Old Friends with New Faces. London: Castell, (1888). Sq 8vo. Will Gibbons (illus). Cl-backed illus bds (lt edgewear; internally, sl loose). Bright. *Reisler.* $275/£177

Old Grand-Papa, and Other Poems, for the Amusement of Children. London: Darton, Harvey, & Darton, 1815. 12mo. 48pp + 1pg list back cvr, vignette tp (spotted), 20 VF 1/2pg engrs. Dec buff paper on bds (spotted, backstrip replaced). Internally VG (lt foxing). *Hobbyhorse.* $185/£119

Old King Cole. NY: J.S. Pub Co, (n.d. ca 1940s). 1st ed thus. Pop-up. Geraldine Clyne (illus). Single sheet folded into 4pp; 1 pop-up. VG. *Godot.* $35/£23

Old King Cole. Mother Goose Melodies. NY: McLoughlin Bros, 1888. Full-pg engrs signed K.G.C.; upper cvr chromolithos. 6 leaves, all interlaid w/linen; 1st, last pgs pasted down on cvrs. VG (upper cvr creased; spine rubbed). *Hobbyhorse.* $100/£65

Old Mother Goose and Her Son Jack. NY: McLoughlin Bros, n.d. (ca 1885). (Dame Trot Series.) 8vo. 11pp; 5 full-pg illus. Pict paper wrappers. Fine. *Hobbyhorse.* $70/£45

Old Sailing Ships of New England. Boston, (1927). Good. *Hayman.* $20/£13

Old Ships of New England. Boston, 1923. 4 color dwgs. Good (crease). *Hayman.* $20/£13

Old Times on the Yukon. L.A.: Wetzel Pub Co, (1928). 1st ed. Gilt-lettered grn cl (spine dkng). NF (lt foxing). *Harrington.* $25/£16

Old West Antiques and Collectibles. (Austin): Great American Pub, (1979). Separate price guide. Fine. *Perier.* $200/£129

OLDCASTLE, J. Journals and Journalism. Leadenhall Press, 1880. Full vellum (age-dknd), pigskin corners. (Pp browning.) *Moss.* $28/£18

OLDENBURG, CLAES. Notes in Hand. NY: E.P. Dutton w/Petersburg Press, (1971). 1st ed. 50 plts; 2 photos. Orange cl. Fine in dj. *Karmiole.* $60/£39

OLDER, FREMONT. My Own Story. NY: Post-Enquirer, 1925. 1st ed thus. Frontis port. Grey stiff wraps. Spine sunned, sm chip, else Fine. *Connolly.* $35/£23

OLDHAM, J. BASIL. Blind Panels of English Binders. Cambridge, 1958. 67 plts. VG in dj. *Argosy.* $275/£177

OLDHAM, J. BASIL. Blind Panels of English Binders. Cambridge, 1958. 1st ed. 67 plts. Buckram (sl bumped). VG. *Cox.* $209/£135

OLDHAM, J. BASIL. Blind Panels of English Binders. CUP, 1958. 1st ed. 67 plts. Dj (torn, chipped). *Edwards.* $233/£150

OLDHAM, J. BASIL. English Blind-Stamped Bindings. London: Cambridge, 1952. 1st ed, ltd to 750. 61 collotype plts. Orig buckram. VG in dj (frayed). *Cox.* $233/£150

OLDREY, J. The Devil's Henchmen. Methuen, 1926. 1st ed. Foxing bottom, fore edge sheets, else VG+ in VG pict dj (lt wear, tear). *Aronovitz.* $175/£113

OLDROYD, I.S. The Marine Shells of the West Coast of North America. Stanford, CA, 1924-27. 2 vols in 4. 165 plts. Wrappers. *Wheldon & Wesley.* $140/£90

OLDS, W.B. Twenty-Five Bird Songs for Children. London/NY/Boston, G. Schirmer, (c.1914). 4to. 12 tipped-in color plts (sm tears bottom edge 16 leaves). Grn cl-backed pict bds (bumped, sl stained). VG. *Blue Mountain.* $75/£48

OLERICH, HENRY. A Cityless and Countryless World. Holstein, IA: Gilmore & Olerich, 1893. 1st ed. 447pp. Gilt-stamped red cl (mks). Lt bleed to lower margin 1st few leaves, o/w NF. *Reese.* $350/£226

OLIPHANT, J. ORIN. On the Cattle Ranges of the Oregon Country. Seattle: Univ of WA, (1968). 1st ed. Dj. *Heinoldt.* $35/£23

OLIPHANT, J. ORIN. On the Cattle Ranges of the Oregon Country. Univ of WA, (1968). 1st ed. VF in VF dj. *Oregon.* $60/£39

OLIPHANT, LAURENCE. The Russian Shores of the Black Sea in the Autumn of 1852.... London, 1854. 3rd ed. xvi,380pp; fldg map, 35 engrs. Brn cl (sm repairs). *Lewis.* $121/£78

OLIPHANT, LAURENCE. The Russian Shores of the Black Sea in the Autumn of 1852.... Edinburgh/London: Blackwood, 1854. 4th ed. Frontis litho, xiv,380pp + 16pp pub's cat, 2 maps (1 fldg). Brn cl, blind/gilt-stamped. VG. *Schoyer.* $115/£74

OLIPHANT, MRS. Jerusalem the Holy City: Its History and Hope. NY/London: Macmillan, 1892. 1st US ed. xxvi,578,4pp. Teg. Sl rubbed, o/w VG. *Worldwide.* $65/£42

OLIPHANT, MRS. The Land of Darkness Along with Some Further Chapters in the Experiences of the Little Pilgrim. Macmillan, 1888. 1st ed. Cl cvrs soiled; spine dknd, else Good. *Aronovitz.* $60/£39

Oliver Twist; or, the Parish Boy's Progress. (By Charles Dickens.) London: Richard Bentley, 1838. 1st ed, 1st issue, w/tp authorship credits to 'Boz' and the 'Fireside' version of the 'Rose Maylie and Oliver' plt. 3 vols. (iv),(1),2-331,(-336); (iv),(1),2-307,(308); (iv)(no 1/2 title called for),(1),2-315,(316)pp. 24 inserted plts by George Cruikshank. Orig pub's cl: horizontally-ribbed reddish brn variant (rather than fine-diaper) w/blind; gilt-stamped spines. VG (lt foxing, esp fr/back; soiling, fading; sl cocked). *Heritage.* $5,000/£3,226

OLIVER, CHAD. The Edge of Forever. Sherbourne, 1971. 1st ed. Fine in dj. *Madle.* $25/£16

OLIVER, ELIZABETH MURPHY. Black Mother Goose Book. Balt: MD Pub Co, (1969). 1st ltd ed. Aaron Sopher (illus). 4to. NF in color pict wraps. *Drusilla's.* $45/£29

OLIVER, HARRY. Desert Rough Cuts. L.A.: Ward Ritchie, 1938. 1st ed. Cl backstrip over paper-cvrd bds dec w/woodcut. VG (spine worn). *Connolly.* $75/£48

OLIVER, JEROME. Khan, Phantom Emperor. Reklar, 1934. 1st ed. VG. *Madle.* $30/£19

OLIVER, MARY. No Voyage and Other Poems. London: J.M. Dent, (1963). 1st ed, 1st bk. Signed. Grn bds. Fine in dj (spine-darkened). *Dermont.* $200/£129

OLIVER, WADE W. The Man Who Lived for Tomorrow. NY, 1941. Frontis. Good in dj. *Goodrich.* $30/£19

OLIVER, WILLIAM. A Practical Dissertation on Bath-Waters.... London: Samuel Leake, 1764. 5th ed. Contemp sheep (rebacked). *Waterfield.* $140/£90

OLIVIER, EDITH. From Her Journals 1924-48. Penelope Middelboe (ed). London: Weidenfeld & Nicolson, 1989. 1st ed. *Virgo.* $39/£25

OLIVIER, EDITH. Night Thoughts of a Country Landlady. London: Batsford, 1943. 1st ed. Frontis, 10 Fine 1/2-tone plts. Sky-blue cl. Fr cvr, spine sl faded, mkd, o/w Fine. *Temple.* $34/£22

OLIVIER, EDITH. Night Thoughts of a Country Landlady. B.T. Batsford, 1943. 1st Eng ed. Color frontis; 9 full-pg plts. Blue cl (spine top sl faded). NF in dj (sl soiled, chipped). *Dalian.* $54/£35

OLLIVANT, ALFRED. Bob Son of Battle. NY: Doubleday & McClure, 1898. 1st Amer ed. Pict cl (sl faded; fr inner hinge cracked; leather bkpl). Typed description laid in. Cl folder; 1/2 morocco slipcase. *Sadlon.* $75/£48

OLMSTED, FREDERICK LAW. A Journey in the Seaboard Slave States, with Remarks on Their Economy. NY: Dix & Edwards, 1856. 1st ed. xv,(i),723,(1)appendix, (iv)pub's ads. Blind-stamped brn cl, gilt. *Petrilla.* $200/£129

OLMSTED, FREDERICK LAW. A Journey in the Seaboard Slave States.... NY/London: Dix & Edwards/Sampson Low, 1856. 1st ed. 723,(1)pp; unopened. Orig emb grn cl. spine lt sunned, else Fine. Howes O 78. *Chapel Hill.* $375/£242

OLMSTED, FREDERICK LAW. A Journey Through Texas. NY: Dix, Edward, 1857. 1st ed. 516pp, map. Gilt-stamped brn linen (rebound). Howes O 79. *Lambeth.* $250/£161

OLSON, ALBERT. Picture Painting for Young Artists. Chicago: Thompson & Thomas, 1906. 1st ed. Obl 8vo. Cl-backed pict bds. (Rear hinge starting, sm soil.) *Davidson.* $50/£32

OLSON, CHARLES. Call Me Ishmael. NY: Reynal & Hitchcock, 1947. 1st ed, 1st bk. Fine in ptd dj (closed tears). *Cahan.* $250/£161

OLSON, CHARLES. The Fiery Hunt and Other Plays. Bolinas: Four Seasons Foundation, (1977). Fine in ptd wraps. *Polyanthos.* $25/£16

OLSON, CHARLES. Human Universe and Other Essays. Donald Allen (ed). SF: Auerhahn Soc, 1965. 1st ed, ltd to 250. Frontis photo port. 1/4 vellum, dec paper-cvrd bds. Fine. *Godot.* $150/£97

OLSON, CHARLES. Letters for Origin 1950-1956. Albert Glover (ed). (London): Cape Goliard, (1969). 1st ed. Fine in dj (lt used). *Reese.* $30/£19

OLSON, CHARLES. Pleistocene Man. Letters from...to John Clarke During October 1965. (Buffalo: Inst of Further Studies), 1968. 1st ed. Fine in ptd wrappers. *Reese.* $25/£16

OLSON, CHARLES. The Post Office. Bolinas: Grey Fox Press, (1975). Fine in pict wraps. *Polyanthos.* $25/£16

OLSON, CHARLES. Selected Writings.... Robert Creeley (ed). (NY): New Directions, (1966). 1st ed. Fine in dj (lt rubbed). *Reese.* $25/£16

OLSON, CHARLES. Some Early Poems. Iowa City: Windhover Press, (1978). 1st ed. One of 300. Tp woodcut by Roxanne Sexauer. Fine w/o dj, as issued. *Reese.* $100/£65

OLSON, CHARLES. Spearmint and Rosemary. Berkeley: Turtle Island, 1975. Ltd to 1000. Fine in pict self-wraps. *Polyanthos.* $25/£16

OLSON, EDMUND T. Utah: A Romance in Pioneer Days. Salt Lake City: By Author, 1931. 1st ed. 4 color plts. Gilt. Nice (wear, lt spots spine). *Shasky.* $60/£39

OLSSON, JAN. Welcome to Tombstone. London: Elek Books, (1956). 1st ed. VF in VF dj. *Oregon.* $25/£16

OLSSON, JAN. Welcome to Tombstone. London, 1956. 1st ed in English. Fine (sig, date) in dj. *Baade.* $40/£26

OLSZEWSKI, GEORGE J. Restoration of Ford's Theatre. (Washington): US Dept of Interior, 1963. 1st ed. Frontis. Bkpl, sm label feps, text sl yellowed, rear cvr rubbed, else Fine. *Bookpress.* $45/£29

OLUFSEN, O. Through the Unknown Pamirs. London: Heinemann, 1904. 3 fldg maps, plans. Red cl (sl faded; ex-lib, pocket removed). *Schoyer.* $100/£65

OMAN, C.W.C. Wellington's Army 1809-1814. London: Arnold, 1912. (Backstrip faded, sl chipped.) *Petersfield*. $23/£15

OMAN, CHARLES. Castles. London: Great Western Railway, 1926. 1st ed. 2 color plts, 5 plans, 2 maps. Lower joint tender. *Hollett*. $39/£25

OMAN, CHARLES. The Coinage of England. London: OUP, 1931. 45 plts (sl foxing). *Edwards*. $54/£35

OMAN, CHARLES. A History of the Peninsular War. Oxford: Clarendon Press, 1902-1930. 7 vols. Red cl (worn; spine fading). *Glenn*. $600/£387

OMOND, GEORGE W.T. Belgium, London: A&C Black, 1908. 1st ed. 77 color plts. VG (lower bd sl marked; eps sl browned; joints cracked). *Hollett*. $62/£40

ONDAATJE, MICHAEL. The Colleccted Works of Billy the Kid. London: Boyars, 1981. 1st ed. Fine in Fine dj (price-clipped). *Revere*. $45/£29

ONDAATJE, MICHAEL. The Collected Works of Billy the Kid. London: Marion Boyars, (1981). 1st Eng ed. Signed. Fine in dj. *Between The Covers*. $65/£42

ONDAATJE, MICHAEL. The Collected Works of Billy the Kid. London: Boyars, 1981. 1st ed. Signed. Fine in dj (price-clipped). *Rees*. $47/£30

ONDAATJE, MICHAEL. Coming Through Slaughter. NY: W.W. Norton, (1976). 1st (Amer) ed. Fine in dj. *Godot*. $65/£42

ONDAATJE, MICHAEL. Coming Through Slaughter. London: Boyars, 1979. 1st ed. Signed. Fine in dj (price-clipped). *Rees*. $47/£30

ONDAATJE, MICHAEL. Coming Through Slaughter. London: Boyars, 1979. 1st ed. Signed. Fine in Fine dj (price-clipped). *Revere*. $75/£48

ONDAATJE, MICHAEL. The English Patient. (Toronto): McCelland & Stewart, (1992). 1st Canadian ed. As New in dj. *Jaffe*. $75/£48

ONDAATJE, MICHAEL. The English Patient. NY: Knopf, 1992. 1st ed, Amer issue. Signed. Fine in dj. *Godot*. $50/£32

ONDAATJE, MICHAEL. The English Patient. NY: Knopf, 1992. 1st US ed. Rev slip laid in. Fine in dj. *Reese*. $21/£14

ONDAATJE, MICHAEL. The English Patient. NY: Knopf, 1992. 1st US ed. Signed. Fine in dj. *Lame Duck*. $75/£48

ONDAATJE, MICHAEL. In the Skin of a Lion. (Toronto): McClelland & Stewart, (1987). 1st ed. Fine in dj. *Godot*. $65/£42

ONDAATJE, MICHAEL. In the Skin of a Lion. London: Secker & Warburg, 1987. 1st ed. Fine in dj. *Rees*. $31/£20

ONDAATJE, MICHAEL. Rat Jelly. London: Boyars, 1980. 1st ed. Fine in dj. *Rees*. $31/£20

ONDAATJE, MICHAEL. Running in the Family. Norton, 1982. 1st ed. Fine in dj. *Stahr*. $60/£39

ONDAATJE, MICHAEL. Running in the Family. London: Gollancz, 1983. 1st ed. Fine in dj (sl scratched). *Rees*. $31/£20

ONDAATJE, MICHAEL. Secular Love. NY: W.W. Norton, (1985). 1st Amer ed. Fine in dj. *Godot*. $45/£29

ONDAATJE, MICHAEL. There's a Trick with a Knife I'm Learning to Do: Poems 1963-78. NY: Norton, (1979). 1st Amer ed. Signed. Fine in NF dj (2 short tears). *Between The Covers*. $125/£81

One Syllable Primer. NY: McLoughlin Bros, 1878. 24 leaves + 1 pg list lower bd. Lg wood-engr vignette tp, signed by Cogger). Glazed pict chromolitho on bds, grn cl spine; brn eps. VG (dated pencil inscrip fep; edges lt rubbed). *Hobbyhorse*. $180/£116

ONIANS, JOHN. Bearers of Meaning. Princeton Univ Press, 1988. Fine in Mint dj. *Europa*. $39/£25

ONIONS, OLIVER. Tales of a Far Riding. John Murray, 1902. 1st Eng ed. Brn cl. Fore-edge sl foxed; name, o/w VG. *Dalian*. $54/£35

ONIONS, OLIVER. The Tower of Oblivion. Macmillan, 1921. 1st ed. VG. *Madle*. $50/£32

ONO, YOKO. Grapefruit. NY: S&S, (1970). 1st ed. White cl. NF in dj (sl wear; sm chip). *Antic Hay*. $25/£16

ONO, YOKO. Grapefruit. London: Peter Owen, 1970. 1st British Commonwealth ed. Rough erasure fr end sheet, else NF in dj. *Limestone*. $75/£48

OPIE, IONA and PETER (eds). The Oxford Dictionary of Nursery Rhymes. Oxford: OUP/Clarendon Press, 1952. xxvii + 467pp, 24 full-pg illus. Black cl on bds, gilt title. Fine (sm bkseller label fep) in pict dj. *Hobbyhorse*. $85/£55

OPPE, A.P. The Drawings of Paul and Thomas Sandby. London: Phaidon, 1947. 1st ed. Tipped-in color frontis; 156 plts, illus (5 tipped-in color). (Sm nameplt; sl soiled.) *Edwards*. $39/£25

OPPE, A.P. The Drawings of William Hogarth. London, 1948. 91 plts. Corner bumped. *Washton*. $45/£29

OPPE, A.P. The Water-Colours of Turner, Cox and De Wint. London/NY, 1925. 34 mtd color plts, guards. Orig cl, gilt-panelled dec. Fine in dj. *Europa*. $85/£55

OPPEN, GEORGE. Alpine. Mt. Horeb, WI: Perishable Press, 1969. 1st ed. Ltd to 250. Fine. *Jaffe*. $200/£129

OPPENHEIM, E. PHILLIPS. Envoy Extraordinary. Boston: Little Brown, 1937. 1st Amer ed. VG (name under fr flap; bds sl soiled) in VG dj (lt soiled, sm chips). *Between The Covers*. $40/£26

OPPENHEIM, LEO et al. Glass and Glassmaking in Ancient Mesopotamia. Corning: Corning Museum of Glass, 1970. 10 plts, fldg map. Good. *Archaeologia*. $150/£97

OPPENHEIMER, SEYMOUR. The Surgical Treatment of Chronic Suppuration of the Middle Ear and Mastoid. Phila, 1906. 1st ed. Good. *Fye*. $200/£129

OPTIC, OLIVER. Hope and Have; or Fanny Grant Among the Indians. Boston: Lee & Shepard, 1866. Sm 8vo. Full-pg engr frontis, tp w/guard, 283pp + 4pp ads. Emb brn cl on bd (rubbed, bumped, shaken, torn), gilt spine. Foxing, lt spotting, dated sig, else Fair. *Hobbyhorse*. $35/£23

Opus Sadicum. (By Marquis De Sade.) Paris, 1889. 1st ed of 1st Eng trans of Justine. Frontis; 392pp. Teg. 3/4 leather (stained, worn). *King*. $50/£32

ORAGE, A.R. Selected Essays and Critical Writings. Herbert Read & Denis Saurat (eds). London: Stanley Nott, (1935). 1st ed. Gold-stamped grn cl. VG in dj (states 'Library Edition'; spine faded, else VG). *Godot*. $50/£32

ORB, C. The Man in the Moon Is Talking. Warwick Press, 1946. 1st ed. Fine in dj (lt sunned). *Aronovitz*. $30/£19

ORCHARD, HARRY. The Confessions and Autobiography of Harry Orchard. NY: McClure, 1907. 1st ed. Frontis, 7 plts. Spine lettering worn, o/w VG. *Oregon*. $160/£103

ORCUTT, WILLIAM DANA. The Book in Italy During the Fifteenth and Sixteenth Centuries Shown in Facsimile.... London: Harrap, (1928). One of 750. 128 plts. 1/4 vellum, bds; teg. Dj. *Veatchs*. $150/£97

ORCUTT, WILLIAM DANA. The Kingdom of Books. Boston: Little, Brown, 1927. #175/475 signed. 1/2 vellum over bds. Fine in slipcase (lt worn). *Glenn*. $125/£81

ORCUTT, WILLIAM DANA. The Kingdom of Books. Boston: Little, Brown, 1927. 1st ed. 3/4 morocco, moire silk-cvrd bds; spine gilt; teg. Fine. *Sadlon*. $75/£48

ORCUTT, WILLIAM DANA. The Kingdom of Books. Little, Brown, 1927. 1st trade ed. Color frontis; 31 plts. Fr cvr edge dampstained, o/w Fine. *Oregon*. $15/£10

ORCUTT, WILLIAM DANA. The Magic of the Book. Boston, 1930. 1st ed, ltd to 375 numbered, signed. Teg. 1/4 vellum (stain, spine sl dknd; inscrip). *King*. $95/£61

ORCZY, BARONESS. The Gates of Kami. Dodd-Mead, 1907. 1st ed. VG-. *Madle*. $35/£23

ORCZY, BARONESS. The Man in Gray. London: Cassell, 1918. 1st ed. VG. *Ming*. $31/£20

ORCZY, BARONESS. Sir Percy Hits Back. NY: Doran, 1927. 1st ed. Fine in dj (minor edgewear, sm chip lower rear spine corner). *Else Fine*. $175/£113

ORCZY, BARONESS. The Triumph of the Scarlet Pimpernel. Doran, 1922. 1st ed. Fine in pict dj (lg chip fr panel, chip spine head). *Fine Books*. $135/£87

ORDISH, T. FAIRMAN. Early London Theatres. London, 1894. xvi,298pp, 3 fldg maps, dec head, tail-pieces; teg, rest uncut. Morocco-backed bds (dampstained, spine sl scuffed; ex-libris). *Edwards*. $54/£35

OREGON PIONEER ASSOCIATION. Transactions of the 19th Annual Reunion...1891. 1st ed. Fine. *Oregon*. $65/£42

OREGON PIONEER ASSOCIATION. Transactions of the 20th Annual Reunion...1892. Portland, 1912. 1st ed. VG in wraps. *Oregon*. $30/£19

OREGON PIONEER ASSOCIATION. Transactions of the 21st Annual Reunion...1893. 219pp. VF in orig wraps. *Oregon*. $40/£26

OREGON PIONEER ASSOCIATION. Transactions of the 33rd Annual Reunion...1905. 1st ed. Fine in orig wraps. *Oregon*. $40/£26

OREGON PIONEER ASSOCIATION. Transactions of the 40th Annual Reunion...1912. Portland, 1915. 1st ed. Fine in wraps. *Oregon*. $20/£13

OREGON PIONEER ASSOCIATION. Transactions of the 41st Annual Reunion...1913. 1st ed. 1 plt. Fine. *Oregon*. $20/£13

OREGON PIONEER ASSOCIATION. Transactions of the 47th Annual Reunion...1919. 1st ed. Fine in orig wraps. *Oregon*. $40/£26

OREGON PIONEER ASSOCIATION. Transactions of the 50th Annual Reunion...1922. 1st ed. Fine in orig wraps. *Oregon*. $35/£23

Oregon Trail. NY, 1939. 1st ed, 2nd issue. Pict cl (sig). *Baade*. $40/£26

Oregon Trail. The Missouri River to the Pacific Ocean. NY: Hastings House, (1939). 1st ed. 2nd state binding. Map. Name, else VG. *Perier*. $50/£32

Oregon: End of the Trail. Portland: Binfords & Mort, 1940. 1st ed. VG. *Perier*. $45/£29

ORIENTI, S. and P. POOL. The Complete Paintings of Manet. London: Weidenfeld, 1967. 64 color plts. Sound in dj. *Ars Artis*. $33/£21

Original Hymns for Sabbath Schools. (By Jane Taylor & Ann Gilbert.) Boston: Ptd for Samuel T. Armstrong, 1820. 1st Amer ed. 12mo. 36pp + 1pg list lower wrapper. Full-pg wood engr frontis, pasted down on wrapper; five 1/3pg woodcuts, one signed and dated 'Fisher 1812'; upper wrapper w/1/2pg cut. Red pict paper wrappers (dusted; spine chipped). VG (ink dedication; lt dampstain cvr; internal spots). *Hobbyhorse*. $200/£129

Original Mother Goose Melodies. Boston/NY: Lee & Shepard/Dillingham, 1880. 5-3/4 x 7. 50 silhouettes. J.F. Goodridge (illus). Black/brn pict cl. VG (spine ends lt rubbed). *Davidson*. $95/£61

Origins of Utah Place Names. American Guide Series. Utah Federal Writer's Project, W.P.A. (comp). Salt Lake City, December 1938. 2nd ed. Heavy screen-ptd wrappers; staple bound. VG (stamp; paper strip w/title pasted on spine; lt damp line bottom edge of leaves). *Connolly*. $75/£48

ORIGO, IRIS. Leopardi: A Biography.... London: OUP, 1935. 1st ed. Port. Lt offset title from port; bkpl; o/w Fine in VG dj (chip; lt edgewear). *Reese*. $75/£48

ORIGO, IRIS. The World of San Bernardino. NY: Harcourt, Brace & World, (1962). 1st ed. Color frontis tipped in; 32 plts. Beige cl. Good in dj. *Karmiole*. $35/£23

ORIOLI, G. Moving Along. C&W, 1934. 1st Eng ed. Fldg map. Grn cl. VF in dj (sl mkd, nicked). *Dalian*. $70/£45

ORLOVITZ, GIL. Keep to Your Belly. NY: Louis Brigante, 1952. 1st ed. Sl browned, o/w Fine in dec ptd wrappers. *Sadlon*. $20/£13

ORLOVSKY, PETER. Dear Allen: Ship Will Land Jan 23, 58. Buffalo: Intrepid Press, (1971). 1st Amer ed. One of 1000. Signed. Fine in ptd wrappers. *Polyanthos*. $30/£19

ORMSBEE, THOMAS H. Early American Furniture Makers. NY: (Bonanza), (1930). Fine in dj (lt rubbed). *Bookpress*. $35/£23

ORMSBEE, THOMAS H. English China and Its Marks. Great Neck, NY: Deerfield Editions, (1959). 1st ed. NF in NF dj. *Glenn*. $30/£19

ORMSBY, WATERMAN. The Butterfield Overland Mail. San Marino: Huntington Library, 1942. 1st ed. Fldg frontis. Fine. *Oregon*. $55/£35

Orphan Boy. Hudson: A. Stoddard, 1822. 12mo. 34pp + 1pg list lower wrapper. Pict buff paper wrappers (soiled, chipped, spine reinforced). In all, Good. *Hobbyhorse*. $50/£32

ORRIN, H.C. Fascial Grafting in Principle and Practice.... London, 1928. 1st ed. (Ex-lib.) *Fye*. $100/£65

ORRINSMITH, MRS. The Drawing Room, Its Decorations and Furniture. London: Macmillan, 1877. 1st ed. Frontis, xii,(ii),145,(1)pp. Fr hinge internally cracked, joints lt rubbed, else VG. *Bookpress*. $135/£87

ORTEGA Y GASSET, JOSE. Toward a Philosophy of History. NY: Norton, 1941. 1st US ed. VG+ in dj. *Lame Duck*. $65/£42

ORTH, DONALD J. Dictionary of Alaska Place Names. Washington: GPO, 1967. VG (ex-lib; minimal mks). *High Latitude*. $85/£55

ORTON, JAMES. Underground Treasures: How and Where to Find Them. Hartford, 1872. 1st ed. Frontis; 137pp; engr tp. Gold-stamped cl. *Ginsberg*. $200/£129

ORTON, JOE. Entertaining Mr. Sloane. London: Hamish Hamilton, 1964. 1st UK ed, 1st bk. NF in dj (sl soiled; 2 chips). *Moorhouse*. $78/£50

ORTON, JOE. Funeral Games and The Good and Faithful Servant. London: Methuen, 1970. 1st UK ed, hb issue. NF in dj (sl soiled). *Moorhouse*. $54/£35

ORTON, JOE. Head to Toe. London: Blond, 1971. 1st UK ed. VG + in VG dj (short closed tear). *Williams*. $39/£25

ORTON, VREST. Dreiserana. A Book about His Books. NY: Chocorua Bibliographies, 1929. 1st ed. Fldg facs tipped in; 2 title-pg facs. Rose cl; gilt. Good. *Karmiole*. $30/£19

ORWELL, GEORGE. (Pseud of Eric Blair.) Animal Farm Letters. Bloomington, IN: Friends of Lilly Lib, 1984. #27/200. Promo leaflet laid in. Fine in dj. *Virgo*. $70/£45

ORWELL, GEORGE. (Pseud of Eric Blair.) Animal Farm. NY: Harcourt, (1946). 1st Amer ed. Nice in dj (price-clipped; folds rubbed; lt smudges; nick). *Reese*. $100/£65

ORWELL, GEORGE. (Pseud of Eric Blair.) Animal Farm. NY, (1946). Stated 1st Amer ed. NF in NF dj. *Mcgowan*. $125/£81

ORWELL, GEORGE. (Pseud of Eric Blair.) Animal Farm. London: Secker & Warburg, 1945. 1st UK ed. VG (crease to fep, t.p.) in VG dj (lt edgewear, sm nicks). *Williams*. $922/£595

ORWELL, GEORGE. (Pseud of Eric Blair.) Animal Farm. Toronto, 1946. 1st Canadian ed. VG. *Rees*. $16/£10

ORWELL, GEORGE. (Pseud of Eric Blair.) Burmese Days. Gollancz, 1935. 1st ed. Fep renewed; stain rear cvr, else VG-. *Fine Books*. $125/£81

ORWELL, GEORGE. (Pseud of Eric Blair.) Dickens, Dali and Others. NY, 1946. 1st ed. VG. *Rees*. $16/£10

ORWELL, GEORGE. (Pseud of Eric Blair.) England Your England. London: Secker & Warburg, 1953. 1st ed. VG in dj (sl chipped; lacks sm piece lower panel). *Rees*. $31/£20

ORWELL, GEORGE. (Pseud of Eric Blair.) The English People. Collins, 1947. 1st ed. VG in dj (sl rubbed). *Whiteson*. $31/£20

ORWELL, GEORGE. (Pseud of Eric Blair.) The English People. London: Collins, 1947. 1st ed. VG in dj (sl rubbed). *Rees*. $47/£30

ORWELL, GEORGE. (Pseud of Eric Blair.) The English People. London: Collins, 1947. 1st ed. Very Nice in dj (sl wear; lt discoloration spine). *Reese*. $50/£32

ORWELL, GEORGE. (Pseud of Eric Blair.) Homage to Catalonia. London, (1938). 1st ed. Lt grn cl (dust soiled). *Argosy*. $750/£484

ORWELL, GEORGE. (Pseud of Eric Blair.) Homage to Catalonia. London: Secker & Warburg, 1938. 1st ed. Edges, prelims sl foxed, few mks to cl; o/w VG. *Rees*. $155/£100

ORWELL, GEORGE. (Pseud of Eric Blair.) Homage to Catalonia. London: Secker & Warburg, 1938. 1st UK ed. Fine in dj (heavily chipped). *Williams*. $736/£475

ORWELL, GEORGE. (Pseud of Eric Blair.) The Lion and the Unicorn. London: Secker & Warburg, 1941. 1st ed. VG. *Rees*. $16/£10

ORWELL, GEORGE. (Pseud of Eric Blair.) Nineteen Eighty-Four. NY: Harcourt Brace, (1949). 1st US ed. Top edge soiled, else VG + in 1st state (red) dj (trimmed about quarter-inch short, corner clipping, rear fold wear). *Other Worlds*. $45/£29

ORWELL, GEORGE. (Pseud of Eric Blair.) Nineteen Eighty-Four. NY, 1949. 1st Amer ed. VG in 2nd state dj (sl chipped, nicked, lower panel repaired). *Rees*. $31/£20

ORWELL, GEORGE. (Pseud of Eric Blair.) Nineteen Eighty-Four. H-B, 1949. 1st Amer ed. Photo laid in. VG + in red issue dj. *Aronovitz*. $135/£87

ORWELL, GEORGE. (Pseud of Eric Blair.) Nineteen Eighty-Four. London: S&W, 1949. 1st UK ed. Contents Fine. Grn cl (faded, sl spotted). *Lewton*. $45/£29

ORWELL, GEORGE. (Pseud of Eric Blair.) The Road to Wigan Pier. London: Gollancz, 1937. 1st ed. Top edge dusty, name, o/w VG in wrappers. *Rees*. $31/£20

ORWELL, GEORGE. (Pseud of Eric Blair.) The Road to Wigan Pier. London: Left Book Club, 1937. 1st UK ed. VG in wraps. *Lewton*. $47/£30

ORWELL, GEORGE. (Pseud of Eric Blair.) Shooting an Elephant. London: Secker & Warburg, 1950. 1st ed. Spine sunned; o/w VG in dj (sl nicked, mkd). *Rees*. $47/£30

ORWELL, GEORGE. (Pseud of Eric Blair.) Shooting an Elephant. London: Secker & Warburg, 1950. 1st ed. NF in NF dj (sl edgewear; short closed tear). *Revere*. $90/£58

OSBORN, C.B. Stray Leaves from an Arctic Journal. Edinburgh/London: William Blackwood, 1865. x,334pp, fldg map. Emb brn cl, gilt spine titles. Overall NF (corners bumped). *Parmer*. $135/£87

OSBORN, CHASE S. The Iron Hunter. NY, 1919. 1st ed. 11 plts. Emb cl. Pencil notes, o/w VG. *Artis*. $30/£19

OSBORN, EMILY F.D. (ed). Political and Social Letters of a Lady of the Eighteenth Century, 1721-1771. (By Sarah Byng Osborn.) NY: Dodd Mead, 1891. 1st Amer ed. 190pp; 4 engr plts. Tan bds; paper label. Deckle edges (binding lt rubbed). *Petrilla*. $35/£23

OSBORN, HENRY F. Men of the Old Stone Age. NY: Scribner's, 1915. 1st ed. 8 plts; fldg map. Gilt red cl. Spine faded; fr hinge repaired, else VG-. *Smithfield*. $23/£15

OSBORN, SHERARD. A Cruise in Japanese Waters. Edinburgh: William Blackwood, 1859. 2nd ed. iv,210,16 pub's list. (Lacks half title; sl foxing, soiling; lt waterstain edge 1st leaves.) Grn pebble cl (loose but firm; lower cvr cl sl pinched). *Morrell*. $217/£140

OSBORN, SHERARD. Quedah. London: Longman, Brown, 1857. 1st ed. xvi,(ii),360,fldg map, 3 tinted litho plts, 1 chromolitho. Contemp half calf, marbled bds, red label. Good (foxing, ink sig). *Morrell*. $233/£150

OSBORNE, A.L. A Dictionary of English Domestic Architecture. London: Country Life, 1954. 1st ed. Dj (sl chipped, sm tear). *Edwards*. $31/£20

OSBORNE, CHARLES FRANCIS (ed). Historic Houses and Their Gardens. Phila: John C. Winston, 1908. 1st ed. Sunned; eps foxed, else VG. *Bookpress*. $135/£87

OSBORNE, JOHN and ANTHONY CREIGHTON. Epitaph for George Dillon. Faber, 1958. 1st Eng ed. Brn cl. VG in dj. *Dalian*. $31/£20

OSBORNE, JOHN. A Better Class of Person. London: Faber, 1981. 1st ed. Sl bump, o/w Fine in dj. *Virgo*. $47/£30

OSBORNE, JOHN. A Bond Honoured. London: Faber, 1966. 1st UK ed. Fine in NF dj (price-clipped). *Williams*. $28/£18

OSBORNE, JOHN. The Entertainer. Faber, 1957. 1st ed. VG in dj. *Whiteson*. $37/£24

OSBORNE, JOHN. The Entertainer. London: Faber, 1957. 1st UK ed. NF in dj (price-clipped, short closed tear). *Moorhouse.* $54/£35

OSBORNE, JOHN. Inadmissable Evidence. London: Faber, 1965. 1st UK ed. Fine in VG dj (price-clipped). *Williams.* $28/£18

OSBORNE, JOHN. Time Present and The Hotel in Amsterdam. London: Faber, 1968. 1st UK ed. VG in dj (sl worn, price-clipped). *Williams.* $28/£18

OSBORNE, JOHN. The World of Paul Slickey. London: Faber, 1959. 1st UK ed. NF in dj. *Moorhouse.* $31/£20

OSBOURNE, LLOYD. The Grierson Mystery. London: Heinemann, 1928. 1st ed. VG in Good+ dj. *Ming.* $47/£30

OSBUN, ALBERT G. To California and the South Seas. John H. Kemble (ed). Huntington, 1966. 1st ed. Frontis, 2 maps (1 dbl-pg). Fine in Fine dj. *Oregon.* $45/£29

OSGOOD, ERNEST STAPLES. Day of the Cattleman. Univ of MN, (1954). 2nd ptg. Dj. *Heinoldt.* $25/£16

OSGOOD, ERNEST STAPLES. The Field Notes of Captain William Clark 1803-1805. Yale Univ Press, 1964. 1st ed. VG+ in VG- dj. *Bishop.* $42/£27

OSLER, WILLIAM. Aequanimitas. London: H.K. Lewis, 1928. 2nd ed w/3 add'l addresses. VG. *White.* $23/£15

OSLER, WILLIAM. An Alabama Student and Other Biographical Essays. Oxford, 1908. 1st ed. Worn; lacks frontis, fr blank, else Good. *Goodrich.* $45/£29

OSLER, WILLIAM. An Alabama Student and Other Essays. London: OUP, 1908. 1st ed. Frontis. Lt cl wear, else Good. *Goodrich.* $150/£97

OSLER, WILLIAM. Bacilli and Bullets. Oxford, 1914. 4th ptg. Pamphlet. Good. *Fye.* $30/£19

OSLER, WILLIAM. Bibliotheca Osleriana. Montreal, 1987. Ltd to 200. Sm tear spine, o/w Mint. *Whitehart.* $233/£150

OSLER, WILLIAM. Counsels and Ideals from the Writings of William Osler. London, 1929. 2nd ed. Frontis port. Sig; ink annotations in text, o/w VG in dj. *Whitehart.* $28/£18

OSLER, WILLIAM. The Evolution of Modern Medicine. New Haven, 1921. New cl, tooled. Good. *Goodrich.* $115/£74

OSLER, WILLIAM. The Old Humanities and the New Science. Boston, 1920. Good. *Fye.* $100/£65

OSLER, WILLIAM. The Old Humanities and the New Science. Boston, 1920. 1st Amer ed. Frontis. Uncut. (Sl rubbed.) *King.* $95/£61

OSLER, WILLIAM. The Old Humanities and the New Science. Boston: Houghton Mifflin, 1920. 1st ed thus. (Bkpl, lt waterstain top edge first 28 leaves, not affecting text.) *Bookpress.* $85/£55

OSLER, WILLIAM. On Chorea and Choreiform Affections. Phila, 1894. 1st ed. 125pp. VF (1/2 inch stain fr bd edge). *Fye.* $1,200/£774

OSLER, WILLIAM. On Some Points in the Etiology and Pathology of Ulcerative Endocarditis. London, 1881. 1st ed. 8pp. Trimmed. Good in wrappers. *Fye.* $150/£97

OSLER, WILLIAM. The Principles and Practice of Medicine. NY: Appleton, 1892. 1st ed, 2nd issue. Internally VG (nicely rebound). *Goodrich.* $495/£319

OSLER, WILLIAM. The Principles and Practice of Medicine. NY, 1892. 1st ed, 2nd ptg. 1079pp. 1/2 morocco; raised bands; new eps. VF (recent museum quality binding that is exact replica of pub's best orig leather binding). *Fye.* $1,000/£645

OSLER, WILLIAM. The Principles and Practice of Medicine. NY, 1903. 5th ed. (Final index leaf missing.) 1/2 leather (rebacked, new eps). *Fye.* $40/£26

OSLER, WILLIAM. The Principles and Practice of Medicine. NY: Appleton, 1905. 5th ed. Bds (newly rebacked). Internally Clean. *Goodrich.* $75/£48

OSLER, WILLIAM. The Principles and Practice of Medicine. London: Appleton, 1909. 7th ed, rev. Rebacked w/backstrip laid down. VG. *White.* $54/£35

OSLER, WILLIAM. The Principles and Practice of Medicine. London: Appleton, 1909. 7th ed. Cl (worn; shaken; sig, note). *Goodrich.* $95/£61

OSLER, WILLIAM. The Principles and Practice of Medicine. NY: Appleton, 1912. 8th ed, largely rewritten. 3/4 calf. VG. *Goodrich.* $35/£23

OSLER, WILLIAM. The Principles and Practice of Medicine. NY/London, 1915. 8th ed. 20 charts. (Margins of few leaves sl repaired; spine faded.) *Edwards.* $39/£25

OSLER, WILLIAM. The Principles and Practice of Medicine. London: Appleton, 1930. 11th ed. Good (lib stamp). *Goodrich.* $30/£19

OSLER, WILLIAM. The Principles and Practice of Medicine. Henry Christian (re-write). NY: Appleton, 1947. 16th ed. (Worn, spine soiled.) *Goodrich.* $35/£23

OSLER, WILLIAM. Science and Immorality. London, 1904. Worn bds, else Good. *Goodrich.* $45/£29

OSLER, WILLIAM. Selected Writings of Sir William Osler 12 July 1849 to 29 December 1919.... OUP, 1951. Nice in dj. *Goodrich.* $75/£48

OSLER, WILLIAM. A Way of Life.... Balt, 1932. Good in dj. *Goodrich.* $25/£16

OSLER, WILLIAM. What the Public Can Do in the Fight Against Tuberculosis. Oxford, 1909. 1st ed. Good in wrappers. *Fye.* $45/£29

OSLEY, A.S. Mercator, A Monograph on the Lettering of Maps...in 16th Century Netherlands. NY: Watson-Guptill, (1969). 1st US ed. VF in VF dj. *Perier.* $75/£48

OSLEY, A.S. Scribes and Sources. Berthold Wolpe (trans). Boston, 1980. Dj (torn w/loss). *Edwards.* $39/£25

OSTRANDER, A.B. After 60 Years. Seattle, (1925). 1st ed. Pict wraps. VG+. *Pratt.* $40/£26

Oswald Bastable and Others. (By E. Nesbit.) London: Wells Gardner, Darton, (1905). 1st ed. 8vo. Teg. Charles E. Brock and H.R. Millar (illus). Illus wine-red cl, gilt (sl wear; margin edge folded one plt). *Reisler.* $350/£226

OSWALD, FELIX L. Summerland Sketches, or Rambles in the Backwoods of Mexico and Central America. Phila: 1880. 1st ed. Frontis, 425pp. Pict cl (flecked). *Petrilla.* $90/£58

OSWALD, FELIX. Alone in the Sleeping-Sickness Country. London, 1923. 2nd imp. Fldg map. (Dent sl piercing cl top edge; spine sl sunned.) *Edwards.* $54/£35

OSWALD, JOHN CLYDE. Printing in the Americas. NY: Gregg, (1937). 1st ed. Frontis. 1/2 title torn, else Fine. *Bookpress.* $75/£48

OSWOLD, FELIX. The Poison Problem or the Cause and Cure of Intemperance. NY, 1887. 1st ed. 138pp. Good. *Fye.* $40/£26

OTIS, JAMES. When Dewey Came to Manila. Boston: Dana Estes & Co, 1899. 107pp. Dec cl. *Schoyer.* $15/£10

OTT, JONATHAN. Hallucinogenic Plants of North America. Berkeley: Wingbow, 1976. 1st ed. Fine in VG dj. *Blue Dragon.* $40/£26

OTTEWILL, DAVID. The Edwardian Garden. New Haven: Yale Univ, 1989. 1st ed. Fine in dj, slipcase. *Bookpress.* $50/£32

OTTINO DELLA CHIESA, A. The Complete Paintings of Durer. London: Weidenfeld, 1971. 64 color plts. Sound. *Ars Artis.* $39/£25

OTTLEY, W.J. With Mounted Infantry in Tibet. London, 1906. 1st ed. Frontis port. (Feps lt foxed; spine sl faded, sl chipped, spotting.) *Edwards.* $256/£165

OTTLEY, WILLIAM YOUNG. An Inquiry into the Origin and Early History of Engraving.... London, 1816. 1st ed. 2 vols. xxii,text(1-478pp); prelims,text(479-836pp), errata. (Foxing, offsetting.) Marbled eps, edges. 1/2-calf, paper bds (stained; bkpls; joints sl rubbed; spines (bumped vol 1) w/raised bands, gilt; leather title labels. *Edwards.* $543/£350

OUGHTON, FREDERICK. Grinling Gibbons and the English Woodcarving Tradition. London, 1979. Dj (spine sl chipped). *Edwards.* $62/£40

OULIE, MARTHE. Charcot of the Antarctic. London: John Murray, 1938. VG in dj (chipped). *High Latitude.* $45/£29

Our Kings and Queens; or, the History of England in Miniature, for the Use of Children. London: George Routledge, n.d. (ca 1855). 46pp + 1pg ad, dec full-pg wood engr tp, 40 VF full-pg cuts. Pict stiff paper wrappers (upper corner lower wrapper crudely repaired; spine reinforced). Good; internally Fine. *Hobbyhorse.* $85/£55

OUSPENSKY, P.D. Strange Life of Ivan Osokin. London: Stourton Press, 1947. 1st Eng ed, ltd to 357 numbered. Tan cl, gold-stamped leather spine label. Dust soiled, else NF. *Godot.* $325/£210

OUSPENSKY, P.D. Strange Life of Ivan Osokin. London: Stourton, 1947. One of 356. Teg, rest uncut. Cream buckram (sl bumped). *Petersfield.* $78/£50

OUSPENSKY, P.D. Strange Life of Ivan Osokin. Faber & Faber, 1948. 1st ed. VG + in VG dj (lt wear, tear). *Aronovitz.* $85/£55

Out of the Depths: The Story of a Woman's Life. NY: Bradburn, 1865. 370pp. VG. *Second Life.* $35/£23

OUTERBRIDGE, HENRY. Captain Jack. NY: Century, (1928). 1st ptg. VG in dj (torn). *Schoyer.* $20/£13

OUTERBRIDGE, PAUL. Photographing in Color. NY: Random House, 1940. 1st ed. 15 tipped-in color plts, fldg color chart. Fine in dj; color plt mtd fr panel. *Cahan.* $450/£290

Outlaw Days: A True History of Early-Day Oklahoma Characters. (By Mrs. Bill Tilghman.) (Oklahoma City): Harlow Pub Co, 1926. 1st ed. Fine in pict wrappers. *Glenn.* $30/£19

Outre-Mer; A Pilgrimage Beyond the Sea. (By Henry Wadsworth Longfellow.) NY: Harper & Bros., 1835. 1st complete ed, 1st state. 2 vols. 226; 252pp. Violet cl. VG (spines sl faded; lt foxing). BAL 12059. *Chapel Hill.* $350/£226

OVERTON, GRANT. American Nights Entertainment. NY: D. Appleton et al, 1923. 1st ed. Paper labels. VG. *Sadlon.* $15/£10

OVERTON, GRANT. The Women Who Make Our Novels. NY: Dodd, Mead, 1928. New, rev ed. Review slip tipped in. Grn wove cl (spine gilt dull). *Petrilla.* $25/£16

OWEN, DAVID DALE. Report of a Geological Survey of Wisconsin, Iowa and Minnesota.... Phila: Lippincott, 1852. 1st ed. 2 vols. 638pp; 3 fldg maps (1 colored); 27 litho plts; 19 sections (18 colored). Orig cl. Cvrs faded, else VG + set. *Smithfield.* $160/£103

OWEN, DAVID DALE. Report of the Geological Survey in Kentucky...1854-1859. Frankfort, 1856-61. 4 vols. Good (Vol 1 worn, frayed, foxed, lacks fldg map; vol 3 frayed, lib mks). *Bohling.* $200/£129

OWEN, F. The Wind that Tramps the World. Lantern Press, 1929. 1st ed. NF in VG dj. *Aronovitz.* $58/£37

OWEN, FRANK. The Porcelain Magician. NY: Gnome Press, (1948). 1st ed. VG + in dj (edgewear; 2 closed tears; sm plastic A to spine head). *Other Worlds.* $50/£32

OWEN, FRANK. The Porcelain Magician. Gnome, 1948. 1st ed. Fine in dj (sl chipped). *Madle.* $30/£19

OWEN, H. COLLINSON. Salonica and After. London, 1919. 1st ed. Frontis port; 12 plts. VG. Red cl (sl spine sunned). *Edwards.* $31/£20

OWEN, HAROLD. Journey from Obscurity: Memoirs of the Owen Family. London: OUP, 1963/1965. 1st ed. 3 vols. Very Nice set in Good djs. *Virgo.* $116/£75

OWEN, J.A. (ed). Within an Hour of London Town.... (By D. Jordan.) London, 1892. 314pp. *Wheldon & Wesley.* $28/£18

OWEN, RUSSELL. The Antarctic Ocean. NY: Whittlesey House, (1941). 1st ed. 12 maps. Name stamp tp, else VG in Good dj. *Blue Dragon.* $25/£16

OWEN, RUSSELL. The Conquest of the North and South Pole. NY: Random House, 1952. 1st trade ed. Lynd Ward (illus). Dec eps. Good in dj. *Cattermole.* $30/£19

OWEN, THOMAS M. (comp). Revolutionary Soldiers in Alabama. Montgomery: Brown Ptg Co, 1911. (Sm stamp tp.) Wraps. *Schoyer.* $40/£26

OWENS, BILL. Our Kind of People. (Straight Arrow Books: The Author, 1975.) 1st ed. Fine in dj (sl sunned). *Bookpress.* $50/£32

OWENS, ROBERT DALE. The Wrong of Slavery. Phila: Lippincott, 1864. 1st ed. VG + (lt chipping spine ends; mks prelim). *Beasley.* $100/£65

OWENS, WILLIAM A. Slave Mutiny: The Revolt on the Schooner Amistad. NY: John Day, (1953). 1st ed. Red bds. VG in pict dj. *Petrilla.* $35/£23

OWENS, WILLIAM O. Three Friends, Roy Bedichek, J. Frank Dobie, Walter Prescott Webb. NY: Doubleday, 1969. 1st ed. VG in dj. *Burcham.* $25/£16

OXENHAM, H.N. Memoir of Lieutenant Rudolph De Lisle.... London, 1886. 2nd ed. Inscribed. Sm 8vo. xxiv,296pp; frontis port; 3 plts. Navy blue morocco; gilt. VG. *Edwards.* $132/£85

Oxford History of English Literature. OUP, 1954-63. 6 vols. Fine in djs. *Sadlon.* $75/£48

OXLEY, J. MacDONALD. Baffling the Blockade. London/Edinburgh/NY: T. Nelson, 1896. 1st ed. Frontis, 375pp + (8)pp ads. Orig pict lavender cl (lt soiled). Lib bkpl, blindstamp, else VG. *Chapel Hill.* $150/£97

OZ, AMOS. In the Land of Israel. NY: Harcourt, (1983). 1st Amer ed. Rev material, photo laid in. Fine in dj. *Reese.* $20/£13

OZ, AMOS. Touch the Water, Touch the Wind. NY: Harcourt, (1974). 1st Amer ed. Fine in dj (price-clipped). *Reese.* $30/£19

P

PABOR, WILLIAM E. Colorado as an Agricultural State. NY: OJ, 1883. 1st ed. 213pp. Staining to eps, o/w Nice. *Second Life.* $65/£42

PACH, WALTER. Pierre Auguste Renoir. NY: Abrams, 1950. 1st ed. 49 mtd color plts. Pict cvr label. VG in lettered mylar wrapper. *Argosy.* $50/£32

PACHT, OTTO and J.J.G. ALEXANDER. Illuminated Manuscripts on the Bodleian Library, Oxford. 1. German, Dutch, Flemish, French, and Spanish Schools. Oxford, 1969. 2nd ed. 66 plts. Good (sl bumped). *Washton.* $110/£71

PACHT, OTTO. Book Illumination in the Middle Ages: An Introduction. London, 1986. 32 color plts. Good. *Washton.* $50/£32

PACKARD, A.S., JR. Guide to the Study of Insects. NY: Henry Holt, 1883. 8th ed. xii,716pp, index, 15 plts. Grn cl, gilt. Good. *Karmiole.* $35/£23

PACKARD, E.P.W. Modern Persecution, or Insane Asylums Unveiled.... Hartford, CT, 1873. 1st ed. 402pp. (Backstrip chipped w/1x1 inch piece detached but present.) *Fye.* $150/£97

PACKARD, FRANCIS R. Life and Times of Ambroise Pare (1510-1590). NY: Paul Hoeber, 1926. 2nd ed. 27 plts; 2 fldg maps. Unopened, uncut. Good. *Goodrich.* $95/£61

PACKARD, FRANCIS R. Some Account of the Pennsylvania Hospital, from Its First Rise to the Beginning of the Year 1938. Phila: Engle Press, 1938. Uncut. VG. *Argosy.* $85/£55

PACKARD, FRANK L. The Devil's Mantle. NY: Doran, 1927. 1st ed. VF in pict dj (lt edgewear). *Else Fine.* $45/£29

PACKARD, FRANK L. Two Stolen Idols. NY: Doran, (1927). 1st Amer ed. Sl paper remnant fr bd; pencil name, else VG in VG dj (lt chipped; spine soiled). *Between The Covers.* $75/£48

PACKARD, FRANK L. Two Stolen Idols. NY: Doran, 1927. 1st ed. VF in pict dj (lt edgewear). *Else Fine.* $45/£29

PACKARD, JOHN. A Hand-Book of Operative Surgery. Phila, 1870. 1st ed. 211pp. Good (extrems rubbed; sections starting). *Fye.* $300/£194

PADDACK, WILLIAM C. Life on the Ocean or Thirty-Five Years at Sea.... Cambridge: For the author, 1893. 1st ed. (xiv),242pp. NF. *Lefkowicz.* $150/£97

PADDOCK, JUDAH. A Narrative of the Shipwreck of the 'Oswego' on the Coast of South Barbary.... London, 1818. 1st ed. xvi,372pp. (Worn bds w/19th cent rebinding.) *Lewis.* $267/£172

PADDOCK, JUDAH. A Narrative of the Shipwreck of the Ship Oswego.... NY: Collins, 1818. 1st ed. 186pp. Recent buckram. Foxing; few leaves sl frayed, o/w VG. *Worldwide.* $95/£61

PADDOCK, MRS. A.G. The Fate of Madame La Tour.... NY, 1882. 3rd ed. 361pp. VG. *Benchmark.* $30/£19

PADDOCK, W. and O.B. WHIPPLE. Fruit-Growing in Arid Regions.... NY, 1910. (Lt foxed, spotted.) *Sutton.* $45/£29

PADEV, MICHAEL. Escape from the Balkans. Indianapolis: Bobbs-Merrill, (c. 1943). 1st Amer ed. Red cl, gilt. VG. *Shasky.* $35/£23

PADGETT, EARL. Surgical Diseases of the Mouth and Jaws. Phila, 1938. 1st ed. Good. *Fye.* $250/£161

PADGETT, LEWIS. The Day He Died. Duell-Sloan, 1947. 1st ed. VG in dj (frayed). *Madle.* $100/£65

PADGETT, LEWIS. A Gnome There Was. S&S, 1950. 1st ed. VG+ in VG dj (lt wear, tear). *Aronovitz.* $65/£42

PADGETT, LEWIS. A Gnome There Was. S&S, 1950. 1st ed. VG in dj (frayed). *Madle.* $90/£58

PADGETT, LEWIS. Mutant. Gnome, 1953. 1st ed. Fine in dj (sl rubbed). *Madle.* $95/£61

PADILLA, VICTORIA. Southern California Gardens. Berkeley/L.A.: Univ of CA, 1961. 1st ed. Signed. 8pp of color plts, 2 maps, 100 b/w plts. *Quest.* $155/£100

Padlocks and Girdles of Chastity. NY, 1928. #349/645. Uncut. 1/4 white cl, purple bds. *D & D.* $95/£61

PAGE, BRUCE et al. Philby: The Spy Who Betrayed a Generation. London: Andre Deutsch, 1968. 1st ed. Fine in dj (price-clipped; closed tear; internal tape mend). *Mordida.* $90/£58

PAGE, CHRISTOPHER N. Ferns. London, 1988. 1st ed. 21 color photos. Dj. *Edwards.* $59/£38

PAGE, ELIZABETH. Wild Horses and Gold. NY: Farrar, Rinehart, 1932. Fldg map. VG. *Burcham.* $40/£26

PAGE, ELIZABETH. Wild Horses and Gold. Farrar Rinehard, 1932. 1st ed. Frontis, fldg map. VG. *Oregon.* $35/£23

PAGE, HENRY. Pasadena: Its Early Years. Lorrin Morrison, 1964. 1st ed. Frontis. Fine. *Oregon.* $45/£29

PAGE, JAMES MADISON. The True Story of Andersonville Prison: A Defense of Major Henry Wirz. NY/Washington: Neale, 1908. 1st ed. Lt wear fr gutter; pencil annotations, else VG. *Mcgowan.* $185/£119

PAGE, THOMAS NELSON. The Burial of the Guns. NY: Scribner's, 1894. 1st ed, 1st ptg. Gilt dec cl. Spot upper cvr, else Good. BAL 15375. *Reese.* $15/£10

PAGE, THOMAS NELSON. Gordon Keith. NY, 1903. 1st ed. Dec cl (sl worn; name). *King.* $25/£16

PAGE, THOMAS NELSON. Pastime Stories. NY: Harper, 1894. 1st ed. Gilt pict cl. VG. BAL 15374. *Reese.* $25/£16

PAGE, THOMAS NELSON. Red Rock: A Chronicle of Reconstruction. NY, 1898. 1st ed. (15),584pp + 4pp ads. Gilt cl (rubbed). VG-. *Artis.* $20/£13

PAGE, THOMAS NELSON. Robert E. Lee, the Southerner. Scribner, 1908. 1st ed. VG. *Book Broker.* $25/£16

PAGE, THOMAS NELSON. Robert E. Lee. NY: Scribner's, 1911. 1st ed. Frontis port. Red cl. Fr hinge sl tender, else NF. BAL 15414. *Chapel Hill.* $150/£97

PAGE, THOMAS NELSON. Santa Claus's Partner. NY: Scribners, 1899. 1st Amer ed. Dec cl. NF (sig). *Agvent.* $30/£19

Pageant of Chinese Painting. (By Bizan Harada.) N.p.: Ohtsuka-Kohgeisha, 1959. 1st ed. 4to. 1000 plts. Teg. Black morocco. Cvrs, edges rubbed; ink name fep; dj torn; else VG in orig slipcase. *Bookpress.* $600/£387

PAGET, GEORGE. The Light Cavalry Brigade in the Crimea. London, 1881. 1st ed. 346pp; color fldg plan. Good (cl rubbed). *Gretton.* $23/£15

PAGLIA, CAMILLE. Sexual Personae. New Haven: Yale Univ, (1990). 1st ed. VF in dj. *Reese.* $65/£42

PAHER, STANLEY W. Las Vegas. As It Began—As It Grew. Las Vegas: Nevada Publications, 1971. 1st ed. Signed. VG. *Connolly.* $50/£32

PAHLEN, K.K. Mission to Turkestan. Richard A. Peirce (ed). London: OUP, 1964. 1st ed in English. VG in dj. *Schoyer.* $30/£19

PAIN, BARRY. The One Before. Scribners, 1902. 1st ed. Good+. *Madle.* $50/£32

PAIN, WILLIAM. The Practical Builder. London: J. Taylor, 1804. 7th ed. 4to. (20)pp (name tp), 83 plts, 4pg cat inserted. Orig bds recovered in full leather. VG, almost no foxing. *Bookpress.* $975/£629

PAINE, ALBERT BIGELOW. Mark Twain: A Biography. NY: Harper, 1912. 1st ed, later issue w/code letters 'K-M' on copyright pg. 3 vols. VG (spines sl faded). *Antic Hay.* $100/£65

PAINE, ALBERT BIGELOW. The Ship Dwellers. NY/London: Harper, 1910. 1st ed. Worn, o/w VG. *Worldwide.* $25/£16

PAINE, ALBERT BIGELOW. The Ship Dwellers. NY: Harper, 1910. 1st ed. Blue cl; pict onlay. Fine. *Hermitage.* $25/£16

PAINE, MARTYN. Letters on the Cholera Asphyxia, as It Has Appeared in the City of New-York. NY, 1832. 1st ed. 160pp. Good. *Fye.* $150/£97

PAINE, THOMAS. Common Sense. NY: Rimington & Hooper, 1928. Ltd to 376 numbered. Frontis port. Good in slipcase. *Karmiole.* $45/£29

PAINE, THOMAS. The Rights of Man. (NY): LEC, 1961. One of 1500 numbered, signed by Lynd Ward (illus). Fine in pub's slipcase. *Hermitage.* $165/£106

Painting in England, 1700-1850. Collection of Mr. and Mrs. Paul Mellon. Richmond, VA: Museum of Fine Arts, 1963. 223 plts, 1 color. Good. *Washton.* $40/£26

Painting in Italy in the Eighteenth Century: Rococo to Romanticism. Chicago: Art Inst, 1970. Good in wrappers. *Washton.* $75/£48

Painting in the South: 1564-1980. VA Museum, (c. 1983). 1st ed. Paper cvr (scratch; tape repaired). Good+ (pp warping). *Book Broker.* $45/£29

Paintings of Michelangelo. London: Phaidon Press, (1948). 145 plts. VG. *Argosy.* $40/£26

PALEY, F.A. A Manual of Gothic Moldings. London: J. van Voorst, 1865. 3rd ed. vi,(ii),93pp; 21 plts. Orig cl (lower hinges sl rubbed), gilt. VG (bkpl). *Cox.* $54/£35

PALFREY, FRANCIS WINTHROP. Memoir of William Francis Bartlett. Boston: Houghton, Osgood, 1878. 1st ed. 309pp. VG (spine tips chipped; corners scuffed). *Mcgowan.* $150/£97

PALGRAVE, FRANCIS TURNER. The Five Days Entertainments at Wentworth Grange. Boston/London: Roberts Bros/Macmillan, 1868. 1st Amer ed. Blue cl, gilt. Lt wear, prelims foxed, else VG. *Glenn.* $150/£97

PALGRAVE, FRANCIS TURNER. A Golden Treasury of Songs and Lyrics. NY: Duffield, 1921. 8 illus. Navy blue cl, gilt-bordered pict pastedown. Beautiful in pict dj (chipped, soiled). *Glenn.* $125/£81

PALGRAVE, W.G. Ulysses or Scenes and Studies in Many Lands. London: Macmillan, 1887. 385pp. Grn cl, stamped in gilt/black (lib pocket removed). *Schoyer.* $75/£48

PALLADINO, L.B. Indian and White in the Northwest. Lancaster, PA: Wichersham Pub., 1922. 2nd enlgd ed. Emb cvr. VG. Howes P 40. *Perier.* $97/£63

PALLEN, CONDE. Crucible Island. Manhattanville, 1919. 1st ed. VG. *Madle.* $50/£32

PALLIS, MARCO. Peaks and Lamas. London: Woburn, (1974). 3rd rev, enlgd ed. VG+ in VG dj. *Blue Dragon.* $40/£26

PALLISER, CHARLES. The Quincunx. Canongate, 1989. 1st ed. Top corner sl bumped; o/w NF in dj. *Rees.* $31/£20

PALLISER, MRS. BURY. History of Lace. M. Jourdain and Alice Dryden (eds). NY, 1902. (Lt spotting; margins lt browned; hinges cracked; edges rubbed.) *Edwards.* $140/£90

PALMER, A.B. A Treatise on Epidemic Cholera and Allied Diseases. Ann Arbor, 1885. 1st ed. 224pp. Good. *Fye.* $100/£65

PALMER, A.H. The Life and Letters of Samuel Palmer, Painter and Etcher. London: Seeley, 1892. One of 130 of lg paper ed. Frontis port, xv,422pp; 21 plts, orig etching. New blind cl. Sound. *Ars Artis.* $620/£400

PALMER, A.H. The Life of Joseph Wolf, Animal Painter. London: Longmans, Green, 1895. xviii,328pp, 54 plts. Foxing; sm snag, joints cracked. *Hollett.* $217/£140

PALMER, E.H. The Caliph Haroun Alraschid and Saracen Civilization. NY: Putnam, 1881. 1st ed. 228pp. Fldg table. Rubbed; spine sl chipped; bkpl, o/w VG. *Worldwide.* $45/£29

PALMER, E.H. The Desert of the Exodus. NY: Harper, 1872. 1st ed. 470pp; 5 fldg maps (2 color); 16 plts. 1/2 morocco, marbled bds, eps. Internally VG (worn; spine top missing; rubbed). *Worldwide.* $45/£29

PALMER, GEORGE. Kidnapping in the South Seas.... Edinburgh: Edmonston & Douglas, 1871. Frontis, xii,234pp. Orig brn cl (professionally rebacked, orig spine laid down). *Parmer.* $425/£274

PALMER, HARRY et al. Athletic Sports in America, England and Australia. Hubbard Bros, 1889. 1st ed. Pict cvr. VG (hinges sl worn; pp browning, still very nice; no dj as issued). *Plapinger.* $600/£387

PALMER, HERBERT E. The Judgment of Francois Villon. London: Hogarth, 1927. 1st ed. One of 400 numbered, signed. 1/2 parchment, cl. Fine in dj. *Reese.* $85/£55

PALMER, HERBERT E. Songs of Salvation, Sin and Satire. London: Hogarth, (1925). 1st ed. One of 300. Rev slip laid in. Marbled paper over bds, paper label. Fine. *Reese.* $185/£119

PALMER, S. A General History of Printing.... London: A. Bettesworth et al, 1733. 2nd ed. 4to. vii,(v),400pp. Contemp full calf (respined, using orig spine as overlay). *Bookpress.* $725/£468

PALMER, STUART and CRAIG RICE. People vs. Withers and Malone. NY: S&S, 1963. 1st ed. Pp dknd, o/w VG in dj (nicks; short closed tears; spotting fr panel). *Mordida.* $45/£29

PALMER, STUART. Cold Poison. NY: Mill/Morrow, 1954. 1st ed. NF in VG+ dj (price-clipped; short, closed tears). *Janus.* $85/£55

PALMER, THOMAS W. Detroit in 1837, Recollections of Thomas W. Palmer. Detroit: Burton Hist Collection, 1954. (Cvr edges sunned, else VG in blue wraps.) *Peninsula.* $40/£26

PALMER, WILLIAM T. The English Lakes. A&C Black, 1908. 2nd ed. 75 color plts, map. Dec cl (sl rubbed; hinges sl cracked). *Edwards.* $54/£35

PALMER, WILLIAM T. Wanderings in the Pennines. London: Skeffington, 1951. 1st ed. VG in dj (sl worn, sm piece torn top spine). *Hollett.* $31/£20

PALMER, WILLIAM. An Introduction to Early Christian Symbolism. J. Spencer Northcote and W.R. Brownlow (eds). London, 1885. Folio. iv,61pp; 32 plts (31 color). (Marginal soiling.) Half morocco (cl soiling; sl loss lower bd; surface wear; spine head lacking portion). *Edwards.* $132/£85

PALOMARES, JOSE. Memoirs of.... Thomas Workman Temple II (trans). LA: Dawson, 1955. Ltd to 205 ptd. Color plt w/2 sm maps on verso. Fine. *Oregon.* $65/£42

PALOU, FRANCISCO. Historical Memoirs of New California. Herbert Eugene Bolton (ed). Berkeley, 1926. First English trans. 4 vols. Navy cl, gilt spine titles. VG + (rubbing; bkpls). Howes P 55. *Bohling.* $250/£161

PALOU, FRANCISCO. Life of Ven. Padre Junipero Serra. J. Adam (trans). SF, 1884. Frontis; 156pp; errata at rear. VG. Howes P 56. *Oregon.* $125/£81

PANGBORN, EDGAR. Davy. St. Martins, 1964. 1st ed. Fine in dj (sl soiled). *Madle.* $85/£55

PANGBORN, EDGAR. Davy. London, 1967. 1st British ed. Fine in dj. *Madle.* $30/£19

PANGBORN, EDGAR. The Judgement of Eve. NY: S&S, (1966). 1st ed. NF in dj (sl wear; soiled). *Antic Hay.* $50/£32

PANGBORN, EDGAR. West of the Sun. Doubleday, 1953. 1st ed. Fine in dj (chipped; tape-stained). *Madle.* $30/£19

PANGBORN, EDGAR. West of the Sun. Doubleday, 1953. 1st ed. Fine in NF dj. *Aronovitz.* $48/£31

PANGBORN, EDGAR. West of the Sun. London: Robert Hale Ltd, 1954. 1st Eng ed. Fine in dj (torn, sl frayed, verso strengthened w/tissue, clear tape). *Temple.* $22/£14

PANKHURST, CHRISTABEL. Plain Facts about a Great Evil. London: Nutt, 1913. 1st ed. Grn wraps (chipped, loose). Ptd on cheap browned paper. *Second Life.* $75/£48

PANNELL, WALTER. Civil War on the Range. L.A.: Welcome News, (1943). 1st ed. Fine in wraps. *Oregon.* $50/£32

PANOFSKY, ERWIN. The Life and Art of Albrecht Durer. Princeton, 1955. 4th ed. Good. *Washton.* $45/£29

PANOFSKY, ERWIN. Problems in Titian, Mostly Iconographic. (NY): NY Univ Press, (1969). 1st ed. Frontis, 199 illus on plts. Fine in sl sunned dj. *Bookpress.* $125/£81

PANOFSKY, ERWIN. Problems in Titian. NY, 1969. Good in dj. *Washton.* $110/£71

PANSHIN, ALEXEI. Rite of Passage. S&J, 1969. 1st Eng, 1st hb ed, 1st bk. Fine in VG + dj. *Aronovitz.* $250/£161

PANUM, PETER. Observations Made During the Epidemic of Measles on the Faroe Islands in the Year 1846. NY, 1940. 1st Eng trans. Good. *Fye.* $60/£39

PANYELLA, AUGUST (ed). Folk Art of the Americas. NY: Abrams, 1981. VG in dj. *Argosy.* $125/£81

PAPADAKI, STAMO. The Work of Oscar Niemeyer. Reinhold, 1950. 1st ed. VG + in VG dj. *Bishop.* $32/£21

PAPANICOLAOU, GEORGE. The Epithelia of Woman's Reproductive Organs: A Correlative Study of Cyclic Changes. NY, 1948. 1st ed. 22 color plts. Good. *Fye.* $75/£48

PAPANIN, IVAN. Life on an Ice Floe. NY: Julian Messner, c.1939. Map as frontis. Cl. Minor spot on lower fr cvr, else VG in dj. *High Latitude.* $25/£16

PAPPAS, GEORGE S. United States Army Unit Histories. Carlisle Barracks, PA: US Army Military History Research Collection, 1971. Fine in stapled stiff paper wrappers. *Oak Knoll.* $45/£29

PAREDES, AMERICO. With His Pistol in His Hand. Austin, 1958. 1st ed. Dec cl. Fine in mod dj (worn). *Baade.* $35/£23

PARET, J. PARMLY. Methods and Players of Modern Lawn Tennis. NY: Amer Lawn Tennis, 1915. 1st ed. Red cl, gilt. Good. *Karmiole.* $75/£48

PARETSKY, SARA. Blood Shot. NY: Delacorte, 1988. 1st ed. Signed. Fine in Fine dj. *Beasley.* $45/£29

PARETSKY, SARA. Deadlock. London: Gollancz, 1984. 1st ed. Fine in dj (price-clipped). *Rees.* $70/£45

PARETSKY, SARA. Deadlock. London: Gollancz, 1984. 1st ed. Fine in Fine dj (price-clipped). *Ming.* $78/£50

PARETSKY, SARA. Deadlock. NY: Dial, 1984. 1st ed. Fine in dj (lt rubbed corners). *Else Fine.* $275/£177

PARETSKY, SARA. Deadlock. London: Gollancz, 1984. 1st UK ed. Signed, dated. Sl crease down spine, o/w Nice in dj (price-clipped). *Virgo.* $93/£60

PARETSKY, SARA. Killing Orders. NY: Morrow, 1985. 1st ed. VF in dj. *Else Fine.* $95/£61

PARETSKY, SARA. Killing Orders. NY: Morrow, 1985. 1st US ed. Signed. Fine in dj. *Virgo.* $132/£85

PARETSKY, SARA. Toxic Shock. London: Gollancz, 1988. 1st ed. Fine in dj (lt rubbed). *Rees.* $39/£25

PARETSKY, SARA. Toxic Shock. London: Gollancz, 1988. 1st ed. Bumped, o/w Very Nice in dj (price-clipped). *Virgo.* $70/£45

PARGELLIS, STANLEY M. Lord Loudoun in North America. New Haven: Yale Univ Press, 1933. 1st ed. Frontis port, 2 fldg maps. Grn cl. Fine in unptd dj (2 inches cut from spine). Howes P 68. *Chapel Hill.* $85/£55

PARGETER, EDITH. (Pseud of Ellis Peters.) The Assize of the Dying. NY: DCC, 1958. 1st ed. Fine in dj (lt wear spine ends). *Else Fine.* $150/£97

PARGETER, EDITH. (Pseud of Ellis Peters). By This Strange Fire. NY: Reynal & Hitchcock, 1948. 1st Amer ed. VG in dj (wear; internal damp staining; chipping top edge). *Mordida.* $45/£29

PARGETER, EDITH. (Pseud of Ellis Peters). Reluctant Odyssey. London: Heinemann, 1946. 1st ed. Sl spotting top pg edges, o/w Fine in dj (sl wear spine ends). *Mordida.* $150/£97

PARGETER, EDITH. (Pseud of Ellis Peters). The Soldier at the Door. London: Heinemann, 1954. 1st ed. Fine in dj (price-clipped; sl dknd spine; stain). *Mordida.* $100/£65

PARIS, J.A. A Treatise on Diet. NY: Collins, 1828. 210pp. (Heavily foxed.) Uncut. Cl-backed bds (worn). *Goodrich.* $75/£48

PARISH, H.J. Victory with Vaccines. Edinburgh, 1968. 1st ed. Good in dj. *Fye.* $50/£32

PARISOT, R.P. The Reminiscences of a Texas Missionary. San Antonio, 1899. 1st ed. Howes P 67. *Ginsberg.* $150/£97

PARKER, AL. Baseball Giant Killers. Nortex, 1976. 1st ed. Fine in VG + dj. *Plapinger*. $100/£65

PARKER, AMOS A. Trip to the West and Texas. Concord, NH: White and Fisher, 1835. 1st ed. (Tp stain). Orig green cl (joints expertly mended), red leather spine label, gilt. Howes P 74. *Ginsberg*. $1,250/£806

PARKER, ARTHUR C. Redjacket. Last of the Seneca. NY: McGraw-Hill, (1952). 1st ed. Rust cl. VG in dj. *Chapel Hill*. $35/£23

PARKER, DOROTHY. Laments for the Living. Longmans, Green, 1930. 1st Eng ed. (Cvrs sl sprung; eps spotted.) *Bickersteth*. $59/£38

PARKER, DOROTHY. Sunset Gun. NY, 1928. 1st Amer ed. NF (spine sl sunned, corners sl rubbed). *Polyanthos*. $45/£29

PARKER, EDWARD. The Handbook for Mothers; A Guide in the Care of Young Children. NY, 1866. 2nd ed. 250pp. Good. *Fye*. $35/£23

PARKER, EDWARD. The Mother's Handbook: A Guide in the Care of Young Children. NY, 1857. 1st ed. 250pp. Good. *Fye*. $75/£48

PARKER, FRANCIS J. The Story of the Thirty-Second Regiment, Massachusetts Infantry. Boston: C.W. Calkins, 1880. 1st ed. xii,260pp. Brn cl, gilt. Good. *Karmiole*. $75/£48

PARKER, FRANK. Anatomy of the San Francisco Cable Car. James Ladd Dakin, Stanford Univ, (1946). 1st ed. Ptd wrappers, mtd photo fr wrapper (dust soiled). *Shasky*. $30/£19

PARKER, GEORGE. The Elementary Nervous System. Phila, 1919. Good. *Goodrich*. $65/£42

PARKER, GEORGE. Smell, Taste, and Allied Senses in the Vertebrates. Phila, 1922. Good (worn; fr inner hinge split). *Goodrich*. $30/£19

PARKER, GILBERT. An Adventure of the North. NY: Stone & Kimball, 1896. 1st ed. Gilt-paneled cl (sm spots lower cvr). *Sadlon*. $45/£29

PARKER, GILBERT. The Judgment House. London: Methuen, 1913. 1st ed. Lower edges uncut. Red buckram (lt mottled). Fine. *Temple*. $22/£14

PARKER, GILBERT. Pierre and His People. Chicago: Stone & Kimball, 1894. 2nd ed. Fine. *Oregon*. $10/£6

PARKER, GILBERT. A Romany of the Snows. NY: Stone & Kimball, 1897. 1st ed. Teg. VG. *Cahan*. $45/£29

PARKER, HERBERT. Courts and Lawyers of New England. NY: American Historical Soc, 1931. 4 vols. Tan buckram (sl stained). Good. *Boswell*. $250/£161

PARKER, HERMAN. A Study of the Etiology of Yellow Fever. Washington, 1903. 1st ed. 43 chromolithos/microphotographs. Good in wrappers. *Fye*. $35/£23

PARKER, JAMES A. The Western Highlands. Edinburgh: Scottish Mountaineering Club, 1947. 3rd ed, rev. Map. Edges spotted, o/w Nice. *Hollett*. $47/£30

PARKER, JAMES. The Old Army: Memories, 1872-1918. Phila: Dorrance, (1929). 1st ed. Frontis port. Blue gilt cl. Good. *Karmiole*. $45/£29

PARKER, JAMES. The Old Army: Memories, 1872-1918. Phila: Dorrance, 1929. 1st ed. VG-. *Parker*. $125/£81

PARKER, JAMES. The Old Army: Memories, 1872-1918. Phila: Dorrance, 1929. 1st ed. (Spine lt worn.) *Ginsberg*. $125/£81

PARKER, JOHN HENRY (ed). The Twelve Egyptian Obelisks in Rome. Oxford: James Parker, 1879. 2nd ed. (iii),64pp, 11 plts (8 photographic, 2 fldg). (Sm tear spine.) *Archaeologia*. $85/£55

PARKER, JOHN. Great Art Sales of the Century. NY/London, 1975. 1st ed. VF. *Bond*. $35/£23

PARKER, JOSEPH HOWARD. General Edmund Kirby Smith C.S.A. Baton Rouge, (1962). (Bumped; cvrs sl soiled, rubbed.) *King*. $40/£26

PARKER, K.T. The Drawings of Antonio Canaletto. London: Phaidon, 1948. 1st ed. Frontis, 89 plts, map. (Sm nameplt; cl sl discolored.) *Edwards*. $47/£30

PARKER, K.T. The Drawings of Antonio Canaletto...at Windsor Castle. Oxford/London: Phaidon, 1948. 89 plts, map. Red buckram. Fine in illus dj. *Europa*. $37/£24

PARKER, LANGSTON. The Modern Treatment of Syphilitic Diseases, Both Primary and Secondary.... Phila, 1854. 1st Amer ed. 316pp. Good. *Fye*. $65/£42

PARKER, NATHAN H. The Missouri Handbook. St. Louis: P.M. Pinckard, 1865. 162pp; 2 fldg maps. Bottom edgewear, else Very Nice. Howes P 87. *Perier*. $175/£113

PARKER, ROBERT B. Crimson Joy. NY: Delacorte, 1988. 1st ed. One of 250 specially bound, numbered, signed. VF in slipcase w/o dj as issued. *Mordida*. $100/£65

PARKER, ROBERT B. God Save the Child. Boston: Houghton Mifflin, 1974. 1st ed. Fine in NF dj (price-clipped; spine sl faded). *Lame Duck*. $200/£129

PARKER, ROBERT B. The Judas Goat. Boston: Houghton Mifflin, 1978. 1st ed. Fine in dj. *Mordida*. $85/£55

PARKER, ROBERT B. Looking for Rachael Wallace. NY: Delacorte, 1980. 1st ed, signed. VF in dj. *Limestone*. $85/£55

PARKER, ROBERT B. Mortal Stakes. London: Deutsch, 1976. 1st ed. NF in dj. *Rees*. $31/£20

PARKER, ROBERT B. Mortal Stakes. London: Deutsch, 1976. 1st Eng ed. Fine in dj. *Limestone*. $45/£29

PARKER, ROBERT B. A Savage Place. NY: Delacorte, 1981. 1st ed. Signed, inscribed. Fine in dj. *Silver Door*. $75/£48

PARKER, ROBERT B. Surrogate. Northridge: Lord John Press, 1982. 1st ed, one of 300 numbered, signed. Fine (spine sl sunned) in Fine dj. *Janus*. $125/£81

PARKER, ROBERT B. Wilderness. Delacorte, 1979. 1st ed. Sl rubbed, else Fine in dj. *Murder*. $75/£48

PARKER, ROBERT B. Wilderness. London: Andre Deutsch, 1980. 1st Eng ed. Black cl. VF in Fine dj. *Dalian*. $39/£25

PARKER, SAMUEL. Journal of an Exploring Tour Beyond the Rocky Mountains...1835, 36, and 37. Ross & Haines, 1967. Ltd to 2000. Lg fldg map laid in. VF in VF dj. Howes P 89. *Oregon*. $40/£26

PARKER, THEODORE. Theodore Parker's Experience as a Minister.... Boston: Rufus Leighton, Jr., 1859. 182pp + 3pp ads. Good (2 lib bkpls; paper dknd; pencil mks; faded, frayed). *Bohling*. $20/£13

PARKER, THOMAS H. History of the 51st Regiment of P.V. and V.V.... Phila: King & Baird, 1869. 1st ed. xx,(9)-703pp. VG (sl wear extrems, 2 sm owner stamps, lib stamp). *Mcgowan*. $250/£161

PARKER, WILLIAM H. Recollections of a Naval Officer, 1841-1865. NY, 1883. 1st ed. (15),372,(8)pp (bkpl removed). Howes P 92. *Ginsberg*. $125/£81

PARKES, M.B. (comp). The Medieval Manuscripts of Keble College Oxford. London: Scolar Press, 1979. 1st ed. Color frontis, 16 color plts. 1/2 morocco bds w/raised bands, gilt. Fine in lined morocco-backed slipcase. *Edwards*. $194/£125

PARKES, OSCAR. British Battleships, 'Warrior' 1860 to 'Vanguard' 1950.... London: Seeley, (1956). Dj (sl torn). *Petersfield.* $101/£65

PARKINSON, C. NORTHCOTE. Devil to Pay. Boston, HMCo, 1973. 1st Amer ed. Fine in VG dj (sm chip; sl rubbing). *Between The Covers.* $35/£23

PARKINSON, C. NORTHCOTE. Devil to Pay. Boston: Houghton-Mifflin, 1973. 1st ed. Fine in dj (lt edgewear). *Else Fine.* $40/£26

PARKINSON, C. NORTHCOTE. Devil to Pay. London: John Murray, 1973. 1st ed. VF in dj (price-clipped). *Else Fine.* $60/£39

PARKINSON, C. NORTHCOTE. Mrs. Parkinson's Law and Other Stories in Domestic Science. London: John Murray, 1968. 1st ed. VG in dj. *Limestone.* $25/£16

PARKINSON, JAMES. Outlines of Oryctology. Fossil Organic Remains...with the Formation of the Earth.... London, 1822. 1st ed. vii,(1),346pp (ownership, stamp); 10 engrs. 1/2 calf. Fine. *Hemlock.* $450/£290

PARKMAN, FRANCIS. The Discovery of the Great West: An Historical Narrative. London: John Murray, 1869. 1st British ed. Map, appendices, index. Gilt-stamped orig purple cl. Spine chipped, else VG. BAL 15458. *Authors Of The West.* $60/£39

PARKMAN, FRANCIS. Francis Parkman's Works. Frontenac Edition. Toronto: Morang, 1899. Ltd to 1000 numbered sets. 16 vols. Staining to fr cvr vol 1, spine labels dknd, o/w VG. *Oregon.* $175/£113

PARKMAN, FRANCIS. A Half-Century of Conflict. Boston, 1892. 1st ed. 2 vols. (8),333; (8),395pp. Fine. *Artis.* $75/£48

PARKMAN, FRANCIS. History of the Conspiracy of Pontiac, and the War of North American Tribes Against English Colonies After Conquest of Canada. Little & Brown, 1851. xxiv,630pp, 4 maps (2 double-pg). 1/2 leather, gilt-stamped spine, raised bands. Howes P 100. *Oregon.* $175/£113

PARKMAN, FRANCIS. History of the Conspiracy of Pontiac...After the Conquest of Canada. Boston, 1851. 1st ed. (24),630pp; 2 maps, 2 dbl-pg maps. Orig gilt cl (sl worn). Good. *Artis.* $120/£77

PARKMAN, FRANCIS. The Journals of.... Mason Wade (ed). NY: Harper, 1947. 2 vols. VG in slipcase (sl worn). *Lien.* $65/£42

PARKMAN, FRANCIS. Montcalm and Wolfe. Boston, 1884. 1st ed, 1st issue. 2 vols. (16),514; (10),502pp. 9 maps, 2 engr plts. Spine tops sl chipped, o/w VG. *Artis.* $65/£42

PARKMAN, FRANCIS. The Oregon Trail. NY: LEC, 1943. #904/1500 numbered, signed by Maynard Dixon (illus). Full tooled leather. Fine in bd folder (sl worn) & pub's slipcase. *Hermitage.* $100/£65

PARKMAN, FRANCIS. The Oregon Trail. Mason Wade (ed). NY: LEC, 1943. One of 1500 numbered, signed by Maynard Dixon (illus). Full blindstamped calf. Fine in chemise, slipcase (sl worn). *Reese.* $125/£81

PARKMAN, FRANCIS. Works. Boston: Little, Brown, 1902. One of 500. 20 vols. Red cl, paper spine labels. VG set. BAL 15508. *Schoyer.* $225/£145

PARKS, GORDON. A Choice of Weapons. NY: Harper Row, (1966). 1st ed. VG+ in VG+ dj (sl wear). *Aka.* $35/£23

PARKS, GORDON. The Learning Tree. NY: Harper, (1963). 1st ed, 1st bk. (Fep corner clipped.) Dj. *Petrilla.* $50/£32

PARKS, GORDON. Shannon. Boston: Little, Brown, (1981). 1st ed. VG in dj (lt used; edgetears, sm chip). *Aka.* $30/£19

PARKS, GORDON. Whispers of Intimate Things. NY: Viking, (1971). Rev copy, slip laid in. Bkpl, else Fine in NF dj. *Robbins.* $35/£23

PARKS, TIM. Tongues of Flame. NY: Grove Press, (1986). 1st Amer ed. Fine in dj. *Godot.* $50/£32

PARKYNS, GEORGE ISHAM. Monastic and Baronial Remains...in England, Wales, and Scotland. London: Longman et al, 1816. 1st ed. 2 vols. (x),120; iv,168pp, 100 aquatint plts. Aeg. Contemp full straight-grained morocco, gilt. Very Nice set (sl wear, offsetting of plts). *Cady.* $200/£129

PARLEY, PETER. (Pseud of Smuel Griswold Goodrich.) Peter Parley's Tales about Kings and Queens. (London): Richard T. Bowyer, n.d. (ca 1840). 188pp, full-pg copper engr frontis (lt foxing), wood engr vignette tp. Gray-grn tooled cl on bds, gilt title spine (edge chipped; hairline cracking along fold). Good (pencil note pg 11; lacks rep). *Hobbyhorse.* $115/£74

PARLEY, PETER. (Pseud of Samuel Griswold Goodrich). Tales about the Sun, Moon, and Stars. London: Thomas Tegg, 1837. 1st Eng ed. xii+330pp+2pp list, wood engr tp (ink name; lacks fep, rep cut in 1/2). 3/4 leather w/corners, marbled paper on bds, gilt title spine (rubbed, cracked; corners bumped; lt rubbed). Internally Fine. VG. *Hobbyhorse.* $230/£148

PARLEY, PETER. (Pseud of Samuel Goodrich.) Wit Bought; or, the Life and Adventures of Robert Merry. London: Darton & Hodge, n.d. (1840s). 15th ed. 12mo, Fine engr frontis, iv,171pp+ad leaf (fep renewed). Dec blue cl, gilt (sl rubbed). *Cox.* $28/£18

PARMELIN, HELENE. Picasso: Women. Paris: Editions Cercle d'Art et al, n.d. (ca 1964). 1st ed. Tipped-in frontis port. Beige linen. Good in dj. *Karmiole.* $100/£65

PARRIS, P.B. Waltzing in the Attic. NY: Doubleday, 1990. 1st ed. Signed. Fine in Fine dj. *Robbins.* $35/£23

PARRISH, RANDALL. Beth Norvell: A Romance of the West. A.C. McClurg, 1907. 1st ed. Color frontis by N.C. Wyeth. Pict cvr. Fine. *Authors Of The West.* $75/£48

PARRISH, RANDALL. Bob Hampton of Placer. Chicago: McClurg, 1906. 1st ptg. Bright pict cl. VG. *Schoyer.* $30/£19

PARRISH, RANDALL. The Maid of the Forest; a Romance of St. Clair's Defeat. Chicago: A.C. McClurg, 1913. 1st ed. 5 color plts by Frank Schoonover. Pub's grn cl dec in blind/yellow. Bumped, else Fine. *Hermitage.* $45/£29

PARRISH, RANDALL. Prisoners of Chance. McClurg, 1908. 1st ed. VG. *Madle.* $65/£42

PARROT, ANDRE. Nineveh and Babylon. Stuart Gilbert & James Emmons (trans). London: Thames & Hudson, 1961. Dj. *Edwards.* $85/£55

PARROT, ANDRE. Sumer. Stuart Gilbert & James Emmons (trans). London: Thames & Hudson, 1960. Dj (sl chipped). *Edwards.* $85/£55

PARROTT, HAROLD. Lords of Baseball. Praeger, 1976. 1st ed. Fine in VG+ dj. *Plapinger.* $45/£29

PARRY, ALBERT. Garrets and Pretenders. NY: Covici-Friede, 1933. 1st ed. Fine in dj (lt chipped). *Beasley.* $85/£55

PARRY, EDWIN SATTERTHWAITE. Betsy Ross. Quaker Rebel. Chicago: John C. Winston, 1952. Anniversary ed. Color frontis; 7 plts. Gilt pict blue cl. Fine in pict dj (sl chipped). *Connolly.* $30/£19

PARRY, ERNEST GAMBIER. Sketches of a Yachting Cruise. London, 1889. viii,272pp. Blue dec cl. *Lewis.* $96/£62

PARRY, ERNEST GAMBIER. Sketches of a Yachting Cruise. London: W.H. Allen, 1889. 1st ed. (8),271pp (piece clipped top contents pg, no loss of text), 26 plts. Dec cl. *Lefkowicz.* $100/£65

PARRY, JUDGE (retold by). Don Quixote of the Mancha. NY: John Lane, 1900. 4to. xii,245pp, tp w/guard, 11 full-pg color lithos by Walter Crane. Pict cl. Tear 1pg professionally repaired; rubbed, else VG. *Hobbyhorse.* $225/£145

PARRY, THOMAS. On Diet, With Its Influence on Man. London, 1844. 1st ed. 119pp. Good. *Fye.* $100/£65

PARRY, WILLIAM EDWARD. Journal of a Second Voyage for the Discovery of a North-West Passage...1821, 1822, 1823.... London: John Murray, 1824. 1st ed. (8),(xxxii),571,(1 errata)pp; 31 plts, 4 fldg views, 4 fldg charts. Contemp calf (neatly rebacked, worn; lib bkpl, stamps few margins). VG. *Lefkowicz.* $850/£548

PARRY, WILLIAM EDWARD. Journal of a Voyage for the Discovery of a North-West Passage...1819-1820.... London: John Murray, 1821. 1st ed, 1st issue, w/errata slip. (8),(xxx),(1 1/2-title, 1 blank),310,(2),clxxix appendix,(1 blank, 1 errata)pp. 20 plts and charts. Contemp calf (neatly rebacked, sl worn). VG (lib bkpl; sl offsetting some plts). *Lefkowicz.* $900/£581

PARRY, WILLIAM EDWARD. Memoirs of Rear Admiral Sir W. Edward Parry.... London: Longman, Brown, 1858. 5th ed. Frontis, xvi,365pp; color map. Good+ (sl rubbed). *Walcot.* $56/£36

PARRY, WILLIAM EDWARD. Narrative of an Attempt to Reach the North Pole...in the Year MDCCCXXVII. London: John Murray, 1828. 4to. xxii(2)229pp. 6 plts, lg fldg map. Orig bds, paper spine label, uncut. Joints repaired, but Fine, as issued. *High Latitude.* $850/£548

PARRY, WILLIAM EDWARD. Three Voyages for the Discovery of a Northwest Passage.... NY: Harper, 1840. 2 vols. 321; 328pp. Ptd cl. *Hayman.* $45/£29

PARRY, WILLIAM EDWARD. Three Voyages for the Discovery of a Northwest Passage...and Narrative of an Attempt to Reach the North Pole. NY: Harper, 1840. 2 vols. 1st ptg this ed. 16mo. x(11)-321; vi(9)-328pp. 2 plts. Orig ptd bds. Sticker, rubber lib stamp, else VG. *High Latitude.* $45/£29

PARSEY, ARTHUR. The Art of Miniature Painting on Ivory. London: Longman, Rees, 1831. 1st ed. Inscribed. 184pp, 8 engr plts. Later 1/2 calf, hand-marbled bds, gilt dec. VF. *Europa.* $147/£95

PARSONS, C.S.M. and F.H. CURL. China Mending and Restoration. London: Faber, 1963. 78 plts. Dj (sl chipped, rubbed). *Edwards.* $93/£60

PARSONS, E.A. The Wonder and the Glory, Confessions of a Southern Bibliophile. NY: Thistle Press, 1962. 1st ed. Red cl, gilt. Fine in dj. *Macdonnell.* $45/£29

PARSONS, ELSIE CLEWS (ed). American Indian Life. NY: B.W. Huebsch, 1922. 1st ed. VG+. *Parker.* $150/£97

PARSONS, ELSIE CLEWS. Folk-Lore of the Antilles, French and English, Part I. NY: Amer Folklore Soc/G. Stechert, 1933 1st ed. Fine. *Beasley.* $75/£48

PARSONS, ELSIE CLEWS. Pueblo of Jemez. New Haven: Yale, 1925. 1st ed. Genealogies in back envelope. VG (sl soiled). *Parker.* $175/£113

PARSONS, ELSIE CLEWS. Taos Pueblo. Menasha: George Banta, 1936. 1st ed. VG+ in stiff bound wraps. *Parker.* $275/£177

PARSONS, FRANCES THEODORA. How to Know the Ferns. NY, (1899). Frontis, xiv,(1),215pp (yellowed), 42 plts. Dj (chipped, smudged). *Sutton.* $37/£24

PARSONS, FRANCES THEODORA. How to Know the Ferns. NY: Scribner's, 1899. 1st ed. xiv,215pp + ads (tear last 2 leaves; pencil notes). Brn dec cl (bumped; inner hinges weak). VG. *Shifrin.* $30/£19

PARSONS, FRANK ALVAH. The Psychology of Dress. GC: Doubleday, Page, 1921. Frontis, 47 b/w plts. Grn cl. VG in dj (soiled, chipped). *House.* $45/£29

PARSONS, J.E. The First Winchester. NY, 1955. 1st ed. (Old ads on eps.) *Artis.* $35/£23

PARSONS, JOHN HERBERT. An Introduction to the Study of Colour Vision. Cambridge, 1915. 1st ed. (Ex-lib.) *Fye.* $75/£48

PARSONS, JOHN HERBERT. An Introduction to the Theory of Perception. Cambridge, 1927. 1st ed. Good in dj. *Fye.* $150/£97

PARSONS, SAMUEL B. Landscape Gardening. NY: Putnam's, 1891. 1st ed. xxii,329pp + 2 ads. Teg. Gilt-stamped dec cvr. (Hinge cracked.) *Quest.* $90/£58

PARSONS, THEOPHILUS. The Law of Contracts. Boston: Little, Brown, 1860. 4th ed. 2 vols. Orig sheep (very worn; joints cracking); but sound. *Boswell.* $125/£81

PARTINGTON, WILFRED. Forging Ahead. The True Story of the Upward Progress of Thomas James Wise.... NY: Putnam's, (1939). 1st ed. Ep gutters sl dknd, top edge sl dust mkd, else Fine in VG dj. *Reese.* $50/£32

PARTINGTON, WILFRED. Thomas J. Wise in the Original Cloth. Hale, 1946. 1st ed. Good (binding dull; sl mkd). *Whiteson.* $23/£15

PARTON, JAMES. Life of Andrew Jackson. Boston/NY: Houghton, Mifflin, (1887). Later ed. 3 vols. Teg. Grn cl. Name, few leaves roughly opened, else NF set. Howes P 112. *Chapel Hill.* $125/£81

PARTON, JAMES. Smoking and Drinking. Boston, 1868. 1st ed. 151pp. Good. *Fye.* $100/£65

PARTRIDGE, FRANCES. Memories. London: Gollancz, 1981. 1st ed. Fine in dj. *Virgo.* $31/£20

PASCAL, BLAISE. Les Pensees. Martin Turnell (trans). LEC, 1971. #95/1500 signed by Ismar David (illus). 12 color plts. 2-tone blind-stamped buckram. Fine in slipcase. *Cox.* $70/£45

PASCOE, CHARLES EYRE. Dickens in Yorkshire. London: Sir Isaac Pitman, (c. 1912). 14 plts (3 color). Illus bds (spine faded, sl rubbed). *Hollett.* $70/£45

PASSERON, ROGER. French Prints of the 20th Century. London, 1970. 1st UK ed. 32 tipped-in color plts. Dj (sl yellowed). *Edwards.* $47/£30

PASSERON, ROGER. Impressionist Prints. London, 1988. 2nd ed. Dj (sl torn). *Edwards.* $47/£30

Passionate Child. NY: McLoughlin Bros, n.d. (ca 1880). Mother's Series. Sq 12mo. 4 leaves, 1p list lower wrapper. Pict stiff paper wrappers. VG (sm split lower wrapper, repaired, and at 1st 2 leaves; repaired rip center of cvr). *Hobbyhorse.* $60/£39

PASTERNAK, BORIS. The Blind Beauty. NY, (1969). 1st Amer ed. VG in dj (used). *King.* $20/£13

PASTERNAK, BORIS. Doctor Zhivago. (NY): Pantheon, (1958). 1st Amer ed. NF in dj (sl edgeworn). *Sadlon.* $50/£32

PASTERNAK, BORIS. Doctor Zhivago. Max Hayward & Manya Harari (trans). London: Collins & Harvill Press, 1958. 1st ed in English. Scarlet cl, gilt. Nice (inscrip) in dj (frayed, chipped). *Temple.* $22/£14

PASTERNAK, BORIS. An Essay in Autobiography. London: Collins, 1959. 1st Eng ed. Black buckram. Fine in dj (sl nicked, dusty). *Dalian.* $39/£25

PASTERNAK, BORIS. Letters to Georgian Friends. David Magarshack (trans). London: Secker & Warburg, 1967. 1st ed. Grn bds, gilt. Fine in dj (repaired). *Temple.* $12/£8

PASTERNAK, BORIS. Safe Conduct. Alec Brown (trans). London: Eleck Books, 1959. 1st Eng ed. Frontis. Black cl. VG in dj (sl mkd). *Dalian.* $23/£15

PASTEUR, LOUIS. Studies of Fermentation: The Diseases of Beer.... London, 1879. 1st Eng trans. 418pp. (Backstrip torn; inner hinges cracked.) *Fye.* $150/£97

PASTEUR, LOUIS. Studies on Fermentation: The Diseases of Beer.... NY, 1969. Facs of 1879 ed. Good. *Fye.* $25/£16

PATACKY, DENES. Master Drawings from the Collection of the Budapest Museum of Fine Arts, 19th and 20th Centuries. NY: Abrams, (1959). 94 color plts. (Prelims starting.) Dj (torn). *Argosy.* $85/£55

PATCHEN, KENNETH. First Will and Testament. NY: Padell, (1948). 2nd ed. Fine in dj (soiled). *Graf.* $25/£16

PATCHEN, KENNETH. Outlaw of the Lowest Planet. London: Grey Walls Press, 1946. 1st ed. Fine in Fine dj. *Polyanthos.* $30/£19

PATCHEN, KENNETH. Red Wine and Yellow Hair. NY: New Directions, (1949). 1st ed. VG (few bumps on edges) in yellow dj (soil; browning; few tears; sm chip). *Antic Hay.* $45/£29

PATCHEN, KENNETH. See You in the Morning. NY, (1947). 1st Amer ed. NF in dj (2 sm edge chips; 2 edge tears; rubbed). *Polyanthos.* $45/£29

PATCHEN, KENNETH. See You in the Morning. London: Grey Walls Press, 1949. 1st Eng ed. Brn cl. Tip spine sl worn, eps sl browned, o/w VG in dj (sl soiled, sl rubbed). *Dalian.* $54/£35

PATCHEN, KENNETH. They Keep Riding Down All the Time. (NY: Padell, 1946). 1st ed. Orig unptd white wraps. VG (erased pencilled marginalia) in VG dj. *Chapel Hill.* $35/£23

PATCHEN, KENNETH. They Keep Riding Down All the Time. NY: Padell, 1946. 1st ed. Fine in stiff wrappers, illus dj. *Cahan.* $60/£39

PATE, JANET. The Black Book of Villains. London: David & Charles, 1975. 1st ed. Fine (bump; sm spot half-title) in NF dj. *Janus.* $35/£23

PATERSON, KATHERINE. Jacob Have I Loved. NY: Thomas Y. Crowell, (1980). 1st ed. 8vo. Cl-backed bds, blind-stamped; gold spine lettering. Good in full color dj (sm marginal tear). *Reisler.* $60/£39

PATMORE, DEREK. Dark Places of the Heart. London: Falcon Press, 1953. 1st Eng ed. Red cl. Fine in dj (sl dusty). *Dalian.* $39/£25

PATMORE, DEREK. A Decorator's Notebook. London: Falcon Press, 1952. 1st Eng ed. Yellow cl. VG in dj (soiled, torn). *Dalian.* $31/£20

PATMORE, DEREK. A Traveller in Venice and Other Cities in North-East Italy. London: Methuen, 1951. 1st Eng ed. Red cl. Fine in dj (sl dusty, sl chipped). *Dalian.* $39/£25

PATON, ALAN. Cry, the Beloved Country. London: Cape, 1948. 1st ed. Dj (sl torn). *Petersfield.* $39/£25

PATON, ALAN. South Africa Today. London: Lutterworth Press, 1953. 1st Eng ed. 2 line maps. VG (cvrs sl dusty, mkd, sl spotted) in wrappers. *Ulysses.* $101/£65

PATON, ALAN. Too Late the Phalarope. London: Jonathan Cape, 1953. 1st Eng ed. Grn cl. Sl sunned, o/w Fine in dj (sl soiled, nicked). *Dalian.* $39/£25

PATON, DAVID. Animals of Ancient Egypt. Princeton: Princeton Univ Press, 1925. (Stained, bumped.) *Archaeologia.* $175/£113

PATON, MAGGIE WHITECROSS. Letters and Sketches from the New Hebrides. London: Hodder & Stoughton, 1894. 2nd ed. Frontis; xi,382pp + i pg ad; map. Grn cl. VG. *Hollett.* $116/£75

PATRICK, LUCILLE NICHOLS. The Best Little Town by a Dam Site, or Cody's First 20 Years. (Cheyenne: Flintlock Pub Co, 1968). 1st ed. Inscribed. Beige cl. NF in VG- dj (soiled, chipped). *Harrington.* $45/£29

PATRICK, MARSENA RUDOLPH. Inside Lincoln's Army, the Diary of Marsena Rudolph Patrick.... David S. Sparks (ed). NY, (1964). 1st ed. Dj lt worn, o/w Fine. *Pratt.* $40/£26

PATRICK, MARY MILLS. Under Five Sultans. NY/London: Century, (1929). 1st ed. Red cl, gilt (sl spotted). *Schoyer.* $45/£29

PATRICK, TED. The Thinking Dog's Man. NY: Random House, (1964). 1st ed. Blind-stamped cl. Fine in dj. *Sadlon.* $20/£13

PATRICK, VINCENT. The Pope of Greenwich Village. NY: Seaview, (1979). 1st ed. Fine in dj. *Houle.* $75/£48

PATTEE, HAROLD E. and CLYDE T. YOUNG (eds). Peanut Science and Technology. Yoakum, TX, 1982. VG. *Brooks.* $45/£29

PATTEN, BRADLEY. The Embryology of the Pig. Phila, 1927. Good. *Fye.* $40/£26

PATTEN, BRIAN. The Unreliable Nightingale. Bertram Rota, 1973. #137/335 signed. Fine in dj. *Poetry.* $43/£28

PATTERSON, AUGUSTA OWEN. American Homes of Today.... NY: Macmillan, 1924. 1st ed. Edgewear, sl rubbed, else VG. *Bookpress.* $135/£87

PATTERSON, CALEB PERRY. The Negro in Tennessee, 1790-1865. Austin, TX, 1922. 1st ed. Fine in orig ptd wrappers. *Mcgowan.* $45/£29

PATTERSON, HARRY. (Pseud of Jack Higgins.) To Catch a King. London: Hutchinson, 1979. 1st ed. Fine in dj. *Else Fine.* $55/£35

PATTERSON, JAMES LAIRD. Journal of a Tour in Egypt, Palestine, Syria and Greece.... London, 1852. 16,480pp, 5 dbl-pg lithos (foxing; text clean). Bound marbled bds, eps. *Heinoldt.* $125/£81

PATTERSON, JAMES. Black Market. NY: S&S, 1986. 1st ed. VF in dj. *Mordida.* $35/£23

PATTERSON, LAWSON B. Twelve Years in the Mines of California. Cambridge: Miles, 1862. 1st ed. 108pp (bkpl removed). Howes P 121. *Ginsberg.* $300/£194

PATTERSON, ORLANDO. Die the Long Day. NY: William Morrow, 1972. 1st ed. NF in dj. *Cahan.* $30/£19

PATTERSON, R.M. The Buffalo Head. NY: Wm. Sloane, 1961. 1st ed. VG in VG dj. *Connolly.* $27/£17

PATTON, JOHN S. Jefferson, Cabell and the University of Virginia. Neale, 1906. VG- (ex-lib). *Book Broker.* $50/£32

Patty and Her Pitcher. NY: McLoughlin Bros, n.d. (ca 1890). (Crowquill's Fairy Tales.) Sm 4to. 16pp + 1pg list lower wrapper, 11 half-pg Fine wood engrs. Pict paper wrappers (lt soiled, rubbed). Fine. *Hobbyhorse.* $115/£74

PAUL, ELLIOT. Desperate Scenery. Random House, (1954). 1st ed. Fine in VG + dj (price-clipped). *Authors Of The West.* $30/£19

PAUL, ELLIOT. My Old Kentucky Home. London: Cresset Press, 1950. 1st Eng ed. Red cl. Spine lettering dull, o/w VG in dj (sl dusty). *Dalian.* $39/£25

PAUL, LOUIS. The Man Who Left Home. Chicago: Black Cat Press, 1938. 1st ed, ltd to 149 numbered, signed (this copy not numbered). Dec paper-cvrd bds, cl spine. NF. *Godot.* $65/£42

PAUL, WILLIAM. The Rose Garden. London: Simpkin, Marshall, 1903. 10th ed. 21 color plts. 3/4 red morocco, teg (spine head chipped, cvrs dusty). *Marlborough.* $349/£225

PAULSEN, MARTHA. Toyland. NY: Duenwald/Wehr Animation, n.d. (1944). 26x20 cm. Animated by Julian Wehr. Spiral binding. Strengthened at spine, o/w VG-. *Book Finders.* $90/£58

PAULSON, RONALD. Hogarth: His Life, Art, and Times. New Haven, 1971. 2 vols. Sl bumped, else VG in djs. *King.* $295/£190

PAVLOV, I.P. Conditioned Reflexes. G.V. Anrep (ed). OUP, 1927. 1st ed in English. VG. *White.* $140/£90

PAVLOV, I.P. Conditioned Reflexes. G.V. Anrep (ed). OUP, 1927. 1st UK ed. (Sl soiled, bumped.) *Edwards.* $155/£100

PAVLOV, I.P. Lectures on Conditioned Reflexes. NY: Liveright, (1928). 1st ed in English, 1st Amer ed. Wine cl, gilt. VF in NF dj. *Macdonnell.* $450/£290

PAVLOV, I.P. Lectures on Conditioned Reflexes. NY: Liveright Pub, (1928). 1st ed in English. Red cl. Fine in dj. *House.* $150/£97

PAVLOV, I.P. Lectures on Conditioned Reflexes. W.H. Gantt (trans). London, 1928. 1st ed in English. Frontis port; 9 figs. Rebacked, orig spine laid on. *Whitehart.* $54/£35

PAVLOV, I.P. Lectures on Conditioned Reflexes. Vol 1. NY, 1941. Good. *Fye.* $50/£32

PAVLOV, I.P. The Work of the Digestive Glands. London, 1910. 2nd Eng ed. New cl. (Perf lib stamp on title.) *Goodrich.* $115/£74

PAXSON, FREDERIC. History of the American Frontier 1763-1893. Boston/NY: Houghton Mifflin, 1924. 1st ed. Dk blue cl. VG. Howes P 145. *Chapel Hill.* $85/£55

PAXSON, FREDERIC. History of the American Frontier, 1763-1893. Boston: Houghton Mifflin, (1924). 11 maps. Blue pebbled cl. VG. *Laurie.* $40/£26

PAXTON, HARRY. The Whiz Kids. McKay, 1950. 1st ed. VG in Good dj. *Plapinger.* $125/£81

PAXTON, JOHN D. Letters on Slavery Addressed to the Cumberland Congregation, Virginia. Lexington, KY: Abraham T. Skillman, 1833. 1st ed. viii,207pp. Orig cl (expertly rebacked). VG. Howes P146. *Mcgowan.* $350/£226

PAXTON, JUNE LE MERT. My Life on the Mojave. NY: Vantage, (1957). 1st ed. Fine in Fine dj. *Book Market.* $50/£32

PAYER, JULIUS. New Lands within the Arctic Circle. Macmillan, 1876. 1st Eng ed. 2 vols. xxxi,335; xiv,303. 2 maps. Gilt-dec cl (spines sl dknd, rubbed). Good. *Walcot.* $233/£150

PAYNE, DARWIN. Owen Wister, Chronicler of the West, Gentleman of the East. Dallas: SMU, 1985. 1st ed. Dj. *Lambeth.* $30/£19

PAYNE, DAVID. Confessions of a Taoist on Wall Street. Boston: Houghton-Mifflin, 1984. 1st ed. 1st bk. Fine (blindstamp fep) in dj. *Else Fine.* $65/£42

PAYNE, DORIS PALMER. Captain Jack, Modoc Renegade. Portland: Binford & Mort, (1938). 1st ed. Red cl. NF in Good dj (heavily chipped). *Harrington.* $55/£35

PAYNE, HUMFRY and GERARD MACKWORTH-YOUNG. Archaic Marble Sculpture from the Acropolis. London, 1950. 2nd ed. Frontis, 140 plts. (Ex-lib w/ink stamp, labels; faded, sl bumped.) *Edwards.* $70/£45

PAYNE, LAURENCE. Spy for Sale. London: Hodder & Stoughton, 1969. 1st ed. Fine in dj (closed tear). *Mordida.* $30/£19

PAYNE, LAURENCE. Too Small for His Shoes. NY: Hodder & Stoughton, 1962. 1st ed. Fine in dj. *Mordida.* $30/£19

PAYNE, ROBERT. The Chinese Soldier and Other Stories. London: Heinemann, 1945. 1st Eng ed. Blue cl. Fine in dj (sl nicked). *Dalian.* $23/£15

PAYNE, ROBERT. Chungking Diary. London: Heinemann, 1945. 1st Eng ed. Brn cl. Inscrip, o/w Fine in dj (sl nicked). *Dalian.* $31/£20

PAYNE-GALLWEY, RALPH. The Fowler of Ireland. London, 1882. xiii,503pp + 2pp pub's ads. (Rebacked, orig spine laid down.) *Edwards.* $132/£85

PAYNTER, JOHN H. Horse and Buggy Days with Uncle Sam. NY: Margent Press, 1943. 1st ed. VG in pict dj. *Petrilla.* $25/£16

PAYSON, W.F. John Vytal—A Tale of the Lost Colony. Harpers, 1901. 1st ed. VG +. *Aronovitz.* $27/£17

PEABODY, ELIZABETH P. Last Evening with Allston. Boston: Lothrop, (1886). 1st ed. (Spine top chipped.) *Second Life.* $125/£81

PEABODY, ELIZABETH PALMER. Letters. Bruce A. Ronda (ed). Middletown, CT, (1984). Stated 1st ed. Fine in dj. *Hayman.* $25/£16

PEABODY, JAMES BISHOP (ed). The Holmes-Einstein Letters...1903-1935. London, 1964. 1st ed. Bumped, else Good in dj (edgeworn). *King.* $35/£23

PEABODY, MARY. Zitkana Duzaban Swift Bird. Hartford, CT: Church Missions Pub, n.d. (ca 1912). 1st ed. Frontis; 5 plts. Good + (bkpl; names; edgewear). *Oregon.* $45/£29

PEABODY, ROBERT E. The Log of the Grand Turks. Boston, 1926. Good. *Hayman.* $15/£10

Peacock 'At Home.' By a Lady (Catherine Ann Dorset). London: J. Harris, 1808. Sq 12mo. 16pp, full-pg frontis + 5 copper engr plts. Mod binding: Full red leather on bds; gilt. Fine (sm repaired tear tp; orig wrappers replaced w/marbled stiff paper). *Hobbyhorse.* $200/£129

Peacock 'At Home:' A Sequel to the Butterfly's Ball. (By Catherine Ann Dorset.) London: J. Harris, 1819. 29th ed. Sq 12mo. Frontis, 21pp + 6pp notes; 7 full-pg wood engrs. Pict buff paper wrappers. Text, plts VF (ink title fr cvr, lt rubbed, part of back wrapper missing). *Hobbyhorse.* $200/£129

PEACOCK, LUCY. Ambrose and Eleanor. London: J. Johnson & J. Harris et al, 1807. 3rd ed. 12mo. 292pp. Orig leather on bds (rebacked), gilt title, black spine label. VG (lt rubbed). *Hobbyhorse.* $300/£194

PEACOCK, THOMAS LOVE. The Genius of the Thames: A Lyrical Poem, in Two Parts. Edinburgh: For T. Hookham et al, 1810. 1st ed. vi,147pp (incl 1/2 title). Later 1/2 calf. *Bickersteth.* $512/£330

PEACOCK, THOMAS LOVE. The Misfortunes of Elphin. London: Greynog Press, 1928. #29/250. 21 wood engrs. Unopened. VG in buckram-backed dec paper (sl rubbed). *Cox.* $248/£160

PEACOCK, THOMAS LOVE. The Plays of Thomas Love Peacock. A.B. Young (ed). London: David Nutt, 1910. 1st ed. Edges untrimmed; teg. *Dramatis Personae.* $75/£48

PEAKE, HAROLD. The Bronze Age and the Celtic World. NY, (1922). 14 plts. VG. *Argosy.* $75/£48

PEAKE, MERVYN. The Craft of the Lead Pencil. London: A. Wingate, 1946. 1st ed. Pict cl (sl wear). Good+ (lt foxing). *Willow House.* $78/£50

PEAKE, MERVYN. Gormenghast. London: Eyre & Spottiswoode, 1950. 1st ed. VG. *Rees.* $39/£25

PEAKE, MERVYN. Mr. Pye. London: Heinemann, 1953. 1st ed. Edges sl foxed, o/w Fine in dj (frayed, chipped). *Temple.* $62/£40

PEAKE, MERVYN. Titus Groan. NY, (1946). 1st Amer ed. Spine extrems sl rubbed, o/w NF in dj (edge pieces missing, sm tear flap fold). *Polyanthos.* $35/£23

PEAKE, ORA BROOKS. The Colorado Range Cattle Industry. Glendale: Clark, 1937. One of 1150. VG. *Schoyer.* $150/£97

PEAKE, ORA BROOKS. A History of the United States Indian Factory System, 1795-1822. Sage, 1954. 1st ed. 1 plt. VF in VF dj. *Oregon.* $75/£48

PEARCE, J.H. Drolls from Shadowland. Macmillan, 1893. 1st Amer ed. Good. *Aronovitz.* $65/£42

PEARCE, THOMAS M. and HENDON TELFAIR (eds). America in the Southwest: A Regional History. Albuquerque: University Press, 1933. 1st ed. 2 plts. Tan buckram. VF. *Connolly.* $75/£48

PEARL, CYRIL. Dublin in Bloomtime. NY: Viking, (1969). 1st Amer ed. Frontis holograph facs. Grn cl. Ink inscrip, fr hinge tender, else VG in VG dj (price-clipped). *Godot.* $45/£29

PEARL, CYRIL. The Girl with the Swansdown Seat. Indianapolis: Bobbs-Merrill, (1955). VG+ in dj (price-clipped, short tears). *Aka.* $18/£12

PEARS, TIM. In the Place of Fallen Leaves. London: Hamilton, 1993. 1st UK ed. Signed. Fine in dj. *Lewton.* $57/£37

PEARSALL, CLARENCE E. et al. The Quest for Qual-A-Wa-Loo... Oakland: Holmes, 1966. Map frontis. Blue cl, gilt. VF. *Connolly.* $45/£29

PEARSALL, W.H. Mountains and Moorlands. London, 1950. 1st ed. (Cl lt discolored.) Dj (sl rubbed, sm split). *Edwards.* $59/£38

PEARSON, D.A.G. Golden Stone. NY: E.P. Dutton, 1929. 1st ed. VG in dj (lg chips; closed tears; wear). *Mordida.* $30/£19

PEARSON, EDMUND. Dime Novels; or, Following an Old Trail in Popular Literature. Boston: Little, 1929. 1st ed. *Ginsberg.* $50/£32

PEARSON, EDMUND. Queer Books. GC: Doubleday Doran, 1928. 1st ed. 42 plts. VG. *Graf.* $30/£19

PEARSON, EDMUND. Studies in Murder. NY, 1924. 1st ed. Cl (rubbed; bkpl). *King.* $22/£14

PEARSON, JOHN. James Bond: The Authorized Biography of 007. NY: Morrow, 1973. 1st US ed. NF in NF dj. *Janus.* $45/£29

PEARSON, JOHN. Observations on the Effects of Various Articles of the Materia Medica, in the Cure of Lues Venerea.... London, 1800. 1st ed. 188pp. 1/2 leather (rubbed). *Fye.* $250/£161

PEARSON, L. and B.H. WARREN. Diseases and Enemies of Poultry. Harrisburg, 1897. 2 vols in 1. 116; xxiv,750pp; 95 color, 8 b/w plts (few show signs of pg sticking). Aeg. 3/4 leather (worn, scuffed). *Sutton.* $165/£106

PEARSON, T.R. Off for the Sweet Hereafter. NY: Linden Press/S&S, 1986. 1st ed. Grn bds, purple cl spine. As New in dj. *Chapel Hill.* $25/£16

PEARY, JOSEPHINE. My Arctic Journal. NY, 1893. 1st ed. (4),241pp. Nice. *Artis.* $75/£48

PEARY, JOSEPHINE. My Arctic Journal.... NY/Phila: Contemp Pub, 1893. 1,1,240pp; 22 plts, map. VG (lt soil to spine, lt shelfwear). *Parmer.* $175/£113

PEARY, ROBERT E. The North Pole. London: Hodder, 1910. 1st ed. (Sl foxed.) *Petersfield.* $81/£52

PEARY, ROBERT E. The North Pole. London: Hodder & Stoughton, 1910. 1st ed. (Sl scratched, bumped; spine worn, repaired; title worn at edges; lib stamp; new eps.) *Hollett.* $116/£75

PEARY, ROBERT E. The North Pole. NY: Stokes, 1910. 1st US trade ed. Fldg color map (repaired). Pict cl. *Schoyer.* $90/£58

PEARY, ROBERT E. The North Pole. London: Hodder & Stoughton, 1910. One of 500 numbered of the edition de luxe, lg paper copy signed by Peary and Bartlett. Uncut, teg. Fldg map. Vellum type cl (mks). VG-. *Walcot.* $419/£270

PEARY, ROBERT E. The North Pole. Its Discovery in 1909 Under the Auspices of the Peary Arctic Club. NY: Stokes, 1910. 8 color plts, fldg map. Orig dec cl, teg. VG in orig ptd dj (sm pieces chipped from edges, tear w/o loss). *High Latitude.* $165/£106

PEARY, ROBERT E. Northward Over the 'Great Ice.' NY: Frederick A. Stokes, 1898. 1st ed. 2 vols. lxxx,521; xiv,625pp. (Spines faded.) *Lefkowicz.* $150/£97

PEARY, ROBERT E. Northward Over the Great Ice. London: Methuen, 1898. 1st ed. 2 vols. lxxx,521; xiv,624. Teg. Fldg map. Silver gilt cl. VG. *Walcot.* $256/£165

PEASE, ALFRED E. The Book of the Lion. London: Murray, 1913. 1st ed. Teg. Red gilt dec cl. VG+. *Bowman.* $250/£161

PEASE, THEODORE and MARGUERITE. George Rogers Clark and the Revolution in Illinois, 1763-1787. IL State Hist Soc, 1929. 1st ed. 8 plts. VG in wraps. *Oregon.* $30/£19

PEASE, ZEPHANIAH W. (ed). History of New Bedford. NY, 1918. 1st ed. Lacks 1st & 3rd leaf in Vol 3, supplied in photocopy; else NF. *Lefkowicz.* $195/£126

PEATTIE, DONALD CULROSS (ed). Audubon's America: The Narratives...of John James Audubon. Boston: Houghton Mifflin, 1940. 1st ed. Frontis port; 16 dbl-pg color plts. Untrimmed. Blue cl, red/silver insets. NF. *Connolly.* $50/£32

PEATTIE, DONALD CULROSS. An Almanac for Moderns. Washington: LEC, 1938. #162/1500 signed by Asa Cheffetz (illus). Fine in slipcase. *Williams.* $54/£35

PEATTIE, DONALD CULROSS. An Almanac for Moderns. Washington: LEC, 1938. #904/1500 numbered, signed by Asa Cheffetz (illus). NF in pub's slipcase (lt worn; dusty). *Hermitage.* $75/£48

PEATTIE, DONALD CULROSS. Journey into America. Boston: Houghton, Mifflin, 1943. 1st ed. Pict ep. Red cl. Fine in dj (edgeworn; sl chipped). *Connolly.* $30/£19

PEATTIE, DONALD CULROSS. A Prairie Grove. NY: S&S, 1938. 1st ed. VG- in Good+ dj. *Parker.* $27/£17

PEATTIE, DONALD CULROSS. The Road of a Naturalist. Boston: Houghton Mifflin, 1941. 1st ed. Paul Landacre (illus). Full blue cl; top edge stained lt red. VG in dj (nicks). *Houle.* $225/£145

PEATTIE, RODERICK (ed). The Black Hills. NY: Vanguard, (1952). 1st ed. VG in dj (sl worn). *Lien.* $40/£26

PEATTIE, RODERICK (ed). The Inverted Mountains: Canyons of the West. NY: Vanguard, 1948. 1st ed. 16 plts of photos; 2 maps. Pict cl. VG. *Connolly.* $25/£16

PEATTIE, RODERICK (ed). The Pacific Coast Ranges. NY: Vanguard, 1946. 1st ed. Frontis; 16 photo plts. Pict cl. NF in dj (chipped). *Connolly.* $35/£23

PEAVEY, JOHN R. Echoes from the Rio Grand. (1963.) 1st ed. Signed. Fine in VG dj. *Perier.* $45/£29

PECIRKA, JAROMIR. The Drawings of Edgar Degas. London: Peter Nevill, 1963. 1st ed. Emb cl. NF (bkpl) in illus dj, slipcase. *Cahan.* $50/£32

PECK, ANNE MERRIMAN. The March of Arizona History. Tucson: AZ Silhouettes, 1962. 1st ed. VG (bkpl, ink name) in VG dj. *Parker.* $45/£29

PECK, B. The World a Department Store. B. Peck, 1900. 1st ed. NF. *Aronovitz.* $75/£48

PECK, ROBERT (ed). The Annual of American Illustration. NY: Soc of Illustrators, 1965. (Ex-lib w/ink stamps, bkpl.) Dj (sl creased). *Edwards.* $31/£20

PECK, WILLIAM H. Egyptian Drawings. London: Thames & Hudson, (1978). Good in dj. *Archaeologia.* $45/£29

PECKHAM, ETHEL A.S. (ed). Alphabetical Iris Check List—1939. Balt, 1940. Grn cl. VG. *Brooks.* $75/£48

PECKHAM, GEORGE W. and ELIZABETH G. Wasps Social and Solitary. Westminster: Constable, 1905. *Bickersteth.* $43/£28

PEDDER, J. The Farmer's Land-Measurer, or Pocket Companion. NY, 1861. 144pp. (Foxing, lt dampstaining; worn, spine missing piece.) *Sutton.* $35/£23

PEDIGO, VIRGINIA G. and LEWIS. History of Patrick and Henry Counties. Stone Prnt, 1933. Inscribed. *Book Broker.* $90/£58

PEDLEY, H. Looking Forward. Briggs, 1913. 1st ed. VG+. *Aronovitz.* $38/£25

PEDLEY, KATHERINE G. Moriarty in the Stacks. Berkeley: Peacock Press, 1966. 1st ed. Frontis port. NF in stiff paper wraps. *Hartfield.* $65/£42

PEDRETTI, CARLO. Leonardo da Vinci. The Royal Palace at Romorantin. Cambridge, 1972. Good in dj. *Washton.* $45/£29

PEEKE, MARGARET. Zenia the Vestal. Arena, 1893. 1st ed. VG. *Madle.* $65/£42

PEELE, W.J. Lives of Distinguished North Carolinians with Illustrations and Speeches. Raleigh, NC Publishing Soc, 1898. 1st ed. 605pp, frontis port, 13 ports w/guards. 1/2 calf, marbled bds; marbled eps. Rubbed, chipped, fr hinge starting; lt foxing eps, few guards, else VG. *Cahan.* $85/£55

Peepshow Pictures. London: Ernest Nister, (ca 1890s). 4to. 4 pop-ups. Cl-backed color illus bds (tear to fep; sl worn; hinges cracked). *Reisler.* $750/£484

PEET, T. ERIC and C. LEONARD WOOLLEY (eds). The City of Akhenaten. Parts I-III. London: EES, 1923-1951. 1st ed. 3 vols in 4 parts. (Corners bumped.) *Archaeologia.* $650/£419

PEGG, D.E. Bone Marrow Transplantation. Chicago, 1966. 1st ed. Good. *Fye.* $50/£32

PEGLER, D.N. A Preliminary Agaric Flora of East Africa. London, 1977. 131 plts. 1/2 calf (lt rubbed). *Sutton.* $90/£58

PEIRCE, PARKER I. Antelope Bill. Minneapolis: Ross & Haines, 1962. One of 550. Fine in slipcase. Howes P 180. *Bohling.* $40/£26

PEISSEL, MICHEL. The Great Himalayan Passage. London: Collins, 1974. 1st ed. 6 maps, plts. VG in dj. *Hollett.* $28/£18

Pelayo. A Story of the Goth. (By William Gilmore Simms.) NY: Harper & Bros., 1838. 1st ed. 2 vols. 213; 282pp. Blue cl, paper spine labels. VG set (cvrs lt spotted; 1/2 inch cl separation along top of one spine edge; chipping; sig; missing pieces from flyleaves; lt foxing). BAL 18063. *Chapel Hill.* $375/£242

PELZER, LOUIS. Cattleman's Frontier: A Record of the Trans-Mississippi Cattle Industry.... Glendale: Clark, 1936. 1st ed. (Bkpl removed; lt white #s lower spine; sm emb lib stamp.) Howes P 187. *Ginsberg.* $150/£97

PELZER, LOUIS. Marches of the Dragoons in the Mississippi Valley. Iowa City: IA State Hist Soc, 1917. 1st ed. Teg. Maroon cl, gilt. (Lt waterstaining, affecting 1st 12pp.) *Glenn.* $125/£81

PEMBERTON, MAX. Captain Black. London, 1911. 1st ed. VG. *Madle.* $40/£26

PEMBERTON, MAX. The Diamond Ship. Appleton, 1907. 1st ed. VG. *Madle.* $45/£29

PEMBERTON, MAX. The Giant's Gate. London, 1901. 1st ed. Cvr used, else VG. *Madle.* $40/£26

PEMBERTON, MAX. The House under the Sea. Appletons, 1902. 1st Amer ed. Nice. *Aronovitz.* $28/£18

PEMBERTON, MAX. The Impregnable City. Dodd-Mead, 1895. 1st ed. VG. *Madle.* $60/£39

PEMBERTON, MAX. Kronstadt. London, 1898. 1st ed. VG. *Madle.* $30/£19

PEMBERTON, MAX. The Queen of the Jesters. London, 1897. 1st ed. VG-. *Madle.* $35/£23

PEMBERTON, O. Clinical Illustrations of Various Forms of Cancer and of Other Diseases.... London, 1867. 128pp; 12 full-pg plts (1 color). VG. *Whitehart.* $248/£160

PEMBERTON, W. BARING. Battles of the Crimean War. Batsford, 1962. 1st ed. 21 plts. VG in dj (price-clipped). *Edwards.* $39/£25

PENDENNIS, ARTHUR. (Pseud of William Makepeace Thackeray.) The Newcomes. Memoirs of a Most Respectable Family. London: Bradbury & Evans, 1853-55. 1st ed. Richard Doyle (illus). 24 parts in 23. 8vo. Full-pg plt. Orig ptd yellow wraps. Superb in custom red cl chemise, 1/2 morocco solander box. *Chapel Hill.* $1,300/£839

PENDENNIS, ARTHUR. (Pseud of William Makepeace Thackeray). The Newcomes. Memoirs of a Most Respectable Family. London: Bradbury & Evans, 1854-55. 1st bk ed. Richard Doyle (illus). 2 vols. 380; 375pp. Dk slate grn cl. VG+ (spine ends rubbed, plts browned at edges). *Chapel Hill.* $300/£194

PENDLEBURY, J.D.S. The Archaeology of Crete, an Introduction. London: Methuen, (1939). 1st ed. 50 plts, 24 maps. Grn cl. Fine. *Weber.* $45/£29

PENDLEBURY, J.D.S. A Handbook to the Palace of Minos Knossos with Its Dependencies. London: Max Parrish, (1959). 14 plts, 9 plans. (Sig.) Dj (torn). *Archaeologia.* $25/£16

PENDLETON, LOUIS. Invisible Police. New Church, 1932. 1st ed. VG in dj. *Madle.* $40/£26

PENFIELD, WILDER and LAMAR ROBERTS. Speech and Brain: Mechanisms. Princeton, 1959. 1st ed. Good. *Fye.* $60/£39

PENFIELD, WILDER and T.C. ERICKSON. Epilepsy and Cerebral Localization. Springfield, 1941. (Rebound; tp stamp.) *Goodrich.* $95/£61

PENFIELD, WILDER and THEODORE RASMUSSEN. The Cerebral Cortex of Man: A Clinical Study.... NY, 1950. 1st ed. Good. *Fye.* $200/£129

PENFIELD, WILDER. No Man Alone: A Neurosurgeon's Life. Boston, 1977. 1st ed. Good. *Fye.* $45/£29

Penicillin Therapy and Control in Twenty-One Army Groups. (London), 1945. 1st ed. Good. *Fye.* $100/£65

PENLEY, A. Sketching from Nature in Watercolours. London: Cassell, Petter & Galpin, n.d. (ca 1880). 36pp, 1 b/w plt, 15 mtd chromolithos (incl frontis). Orig cl (stained, worn). *Ars Artis.* $233/£150

PENN, IRVING. Inventive Paris Clothes 1909-1939. NY: Viking, (1977). 1st ed. Fine in dj. *Godot.* $65/£42

PENNANT, THOMAS. A Tour in Scotland, and A Voyage to the Hebrides. London: Benjamin White, 1776. 2nd ed. 3 vols. Tall, thick 4to. 400; 439; 481pp + 34pp of Additions to the Tour. Fine engr port, 133 engr full-pg fldg illus. Full speckled calf (expertly rebacked; sl worn), raised bands, gilt, red leather labels. Fine text and plts. *Hartfield.* $1,095/£706

PENNANT, THOMAS. A Tour in Wales. London: Ptd for Benjamin White, 1784. 2 vols. 3 tp vignettes, 52 plts (10 fldg), 2 woodcuts, vignette, 10 supplemental plts (1 fldg). (Lt browning, offsetting, bkpls.) Contemp gilt-edged calf bds (rebacked in mod calf; lt wear); marbled eps. *Edwards.* $434/£280

PENNELL, E.R. and J. The Life of James McNeill Whistler. London/Phila, 1908. 2 vols. Engr frontis ports. Fore, lower edges uncut. (Spotting; sl bumped.) Djs (sl ragged, loss on spines). *Edwards.* $85/£55

PENNELL, E.R. and J. The Life of James McNeill Whistler. London/Phila: Heinemann/Lippincott, 1908. 1st ed. 2 vols. Frontis port each vol. Cl-backed gilt-titled bds. Fr hinge partially cracked vol 1; lt foxing, else VG in djs (chipped). *Cahan.* $100/£65

PENNELL, E.R. and J. The Whistler Journal. Phila: Lippincott, 1921. 1st ed. Cl-backed bds. Sl rubbed, else VG. BAL Vol 9, p14. *Cahan.* $65/£42

PENNELL, ELIZABETH ROBINS. My Cookery Books. Boston/NY: Houghton Mifflin, 1903. 1st ed. Ltd to 330 ptd. Full morocco, gilt. Teg, others uncut. Fine. *Cady.* $500/£323

PENNELL, ELIZABETH. French Cathedrals. NY, 1909. 1st ed. VG. *Bond.* $30/£19

PENNELL, JOSEPH. Adventures of an Illustrator, mostly in Following his Authors in America and Europe. Boston, 1925. 1st ed. VG. *Argosy.* $75/£48

PENNELL, JOSEPH. Adventures of an Illustrator. Boston: Little, Brown, 1925. 1st ed. Gilt-titled cl. Fine in dj. *Cahan.* $85/£55

PENNELL, JOSEPH. Etchers and Etching. NY, 1919. 1st ed. (Cl dknd.) Dj. *Argosy.* $125/£81

PENNELL, JOSEPH. Pen Drawing and Pen Draughtsmen. Macmillan, 1897. xxxvii,470pp; uncut. (Few pp loose; inner lower joint starting to crack.) *Bickersteth.* $140/£90

PENNELL, JOSEPH. The Work of Charles Keene. London, 1897. 1st ed. 289pp; copper plt. (Spine repaired.) *Argosy.* $200/£129

PENNELL, T.L. Among the Wild Tribes of the Afghan Frontier. London: Seeley, Service, 1912. 4th ed. (Rubbed, mkd.) *Hollett.* $39/£25

PENNINGTON, PATIENCE. A Woman Rice Planter. Cambridge: Harvard Univ, 1961. Grn cl. VG. *Petrilla.* $45/£29

Pennsylvania at Andersonville, Georgia. (Harrisburg, PA: C.E. Aughinbaugh, 1909). 1st ed. NF. *Mcgowan.* $45/£29

Pennsylvania at Gettysburg. (Harrisburg, PA: E.K. Meyers), 1893. 1st ed. 2 vols. 1/2 leather w/marbled bds. VG (rebacked, new eps, extrems rubbed). *Mcgowan.* $150/£97

Pennsylvania at Gettysburg. Harrisburg, 1904. Rev ed. 2 vols. Frontispieces; fldg map rear vol II. Lacks fep, frontis guard vol I, o/w VG. Blue cl (worn, soiled). *Edwards.* $194/£125

PENTECOST, HUGH. (Pseud of Judson Philips.) The Judas Freak. NY: Dodd, Mead, 1974. 1st ed. Fine in NF dj. *Janus.* $20/£13

PENZER, N.M. The Harem. London, 1936. 1st ed. Frontis port, fldg plt, 2 fldg plans. Dj (chipped). *Edwards.* $62/£40

PENZER, N.M. Nala and Damayantii. London: A.M. Philpot, 1926. 1st ed. 10 color plts. Teg. Vellum-backed cl (rubbed, soiled), gilt. *Hollett.* $39/£25

PENZER, N.M. Paul Storr. Boston: Boston Book & Art Shop, (1954). 1st ed. 81 photo plts. Gilt-lettered rose buckram. Fine in dj. *House.* $180/£116

PENZLER, OTTO. The Great Detectives. Boston: Little, Brown, 1978. 1st ed. Fine (sl bump) in dj (lt edgewear). *Janus.* $30/£19

PEPLER, H.D.C. A Letter from Sussex...about His Friend Eric G. Chicago: Cherryburn Press, 1950. VG in orig wrappers. *Cox.* $23/£15

PEPPER, ART. Straight Life. The Story of Art Pepper. NY: Schirmer Books, 1979. 1st ed. Fine (name obliterated fep) in dj (lt used; tears). *Beasley.* $85/£55

PEPPER, D. STEVEN. Guido Reni. A Complete Catalogue.... Oxford: Phaidon, 1984. 16 color plts. Pub's cl. VF in dj. *Europa.* $109/£70

PEPYS, SAMUEL. The Diary of Samuel Pepys. Robert Latham & William Matthews (eds). Berkeley: Univ of CA, (1971-1983). Some vols later ptgs. 11 vols. Good in djs. *Karmiole.* $250/£161

PEPYS, SAMUEL. The Diary.... Henry B. Wheatley (ed). NY: Croscup & Sterling, 1898-1900. Deluxe ed. Ltd to 50. 18 vols. 8 vols w/hand-colored frontispieces; fldg map. 3/4 morocco, marbled bds (rubbed; chip 1 vol); gilt. Teg; marbled eps. *Sadlon.* $400/£258

PEPYS, SAMUEL. Memoirs.... Richard Braybrooke (ed). London: Henry Colburn, 1828. 2nd ed. 8vo. 5 vols. Fldg map vol 5. 3/4 blue morocco. Aeg. Fine set. *Schoyer.* $300/£194

PERCIVAL, A. BLAYNEY. A Game Ranger on Safari. London: Nisbet, 1928. 1st ed. Fldg map. Orig red cl (spine ends worn). VG. *Bowman.* $125/£81

PERCIVAL, A.S. The Prescribing of Spectacles. Bristol/London, 1910. (Ink sigs; cl sl affected by damp.) *Whitehart.* $39/£25

PERCIVAL, G. and R. GRAHAM. Unsewn Binding. Dryad, 1956. Dec cvrs. Good. *Moss.* $9/£6

PERCIVAL, OLIVE. Our Old-Fashioned Flowers. Pasadena, 1947. Ltd to 1000. Flora paper cvrd bds, cl spine. Shelfwear, else VG. *Brooks.* $35/£23

PERCY, ADRIAN. Twice Outlawed. Chicago: W.B. Conkey, n.d. (ca 1890). 194pp + 8pp ads. Good + (lacks fep). Howes P 225. *Oregon.* $65/£42

PERCY, HUGH EARL. Letters of Hugh Earl Percy from Boston and New York, 1774-1776. Charles Knowles Bolton (ed). Boston: Goodspeed, 1902. 1st ed. *Ginsberg.* $75/£48

PERCY, WALKER. Lancelot. NY: FSG, (1977). 1st ed, Canadian issue. Rev copy, pub's slip tipped in. Orange cl. NF in price-clipped dj (sl browning, rubbing). *Chapel Hill.* $40/£26

PERCY, WALKER. The Last Gentleman. NY: FSG, (1966). 1st ed. Fore-edge sl dusty, else Fine in NF dj (spine ends lt rubbed). *Chapel Hill.* $120/£77

PERCY, WALKER. Lost in the Cosmos: The Last Self-Help Book. NY: FSG, (1983). 1st Amer ed. Signed. Fine in dj (sl rubbed). *Between The Covers.* $95/£61

PERCY, WALKER. Love in the Ruins. NY: FSG, (1971). 1st ed, 2nd ptg. Signed. VG (top, foredge sl stained) in VG dj. *Chapel Hill.* $95/£61

PERCY, WALKER. Love in the Ruins. London: Eyre & Spottiswoode, 1971. 1st Eng ed. Grn cl. VF in dj. *Dalian.* $54/£35

PERCY, WALKER. Love in the Ruins. NY: FSG, 1971. 1st ptg. Fine in dj. *Limestone.* $65/£42

PERCY, WALKER. The Message in the Bottle. NY: FSG, (1975). 1st ed. Fine in dj. *Between The Covers.* $75/£48

PERCY, WALKER. The Second Coming. NY: FSG, (1980). 1st ed. Fine in Fine dj. *Robbins.* $30/£19

PERCY, WALKER. The Second Coming. London: Secker & Warburg, 1981. 1st Eng ed. Red cl. VG in dj. *Dalian.* $39/£25

PEREIRA, J. The Elements of Materia Medica and Therapeutics. London, 1842. 2nd ed. 2 vols. xlii,870pp, 131 figs; xxxi,1056pp, 234 figs. (Rebacked; spine vol 2 sl coming away.) *Whitehart.* $93/£60

PERELMAN, S.J. Baby, It's Cold Inside. NY: S&S, 1970. 1st ed. Fine in dj. *Cahan.* $25/£16

PERELMAN, S.J. Eastward Ha! London: Eyre Methuen, 1978. 1st Eng ed. Blue cl. VF in dj. *Dalian.* $23/£15

PERELMAN, S.J. Westward Ha! or Around the World in Eighty Cliches.... London, (1949). 1st Eng ed. *Waterfield.* $23/£15

Perilous Adventures of Quintin Harewood and His Brother Brian.... NY/Boston: C.S. Francis, 1854. 254pp + 10pp list, full-pg frontis w/guard. Dec tooled blue cl on bds, gilt title, pict vignettes. VG (sm spine chip). *Hobbyhorse.* $110/£71

PERKIN, ROBERT L. The First Hundred Years. Doubleday, 1959. 1st ed. Inscribed. VF in VG dj. *Connolly.* $75/£48

PERKINS, CHARLES C. Tuscan Sculptures. Their Lives, Works, and Times. London, 1864. 2 vols. 267; 266pp. Internally Nice (ex-lib; scuffed half-leather). *Washton.* $150/£97

PERKINS, GEORGE HAMILTON. Letters of Capt. Geo. Hamilton Perkins, U.S.N. Concord, NH: Ira C. Evans, 1886. 1st ed. 267pp, 7 plts. *Lefkowicz.* $60/£39

PERKINS, J.R. Trails, Rails and War, The Life of General G.M. Dodge. Indianapolis, (1929). 1st ed. Minor cvr wear, fading, o/w Fine in Fine dj. *Pratt.* $47/£30

PERKINS, JAMES H. Annals of the West. St. Louis: James R. Albach, 1851. 2nd ed. 818pp (foxing). Grn cl (rebound, corners creased), gilt stamped. Howes P 231. *Bohling.* $60/£39

PERKINS, MAXWELL E. Editor to Author. John Hall Wheelock (ed). NY: Scribner's, 1950. 1st ed. Maroon cl gilt. Very Nice in dj. *Cady.* $25/£16

PERKINS, MAXWELL E. Editor to Author: The Letters of Maxwell E. Perkins. John H. Wheelock (ed). NY: Scribner's, 1950. 1st ed. Dk red cl. Sig, offsetting reps from laid-in review, else VG in dj (chips). *Chapel Hill.* $50/£32

PERKINS, SAMUEL. The World as It Is. Phila: Thomas Belknap, 1838. 3rd ed. 462pp, fldg map. Good in orig full leather (worn; foxed). *Knollwood.* $55/£35

PERKS, SYDNEY. Essays on Old London. Cambridge, 1927. Frontis. Partly uncut. Cl-backed bds (sl soiled). *Edwards.* $39/£25

PERLES, ALFRED. Round Trip. London, 1946. 1st ed. VG in dj (sl rubbed; chipped). *Words Etc.* $54/£35

PERLZWEIG, JUDITH. Lamps of the Roman Period, First to Seventh Century after Christ. Princeton: ASCSA, 1961. 53 plts. Good. *Archaeologia.* $150/£97

PERRAULT, CHARLES. Beauty and the Beast. (Yellow Dwarf Series.) NY: McLoughlin Bros, n.d. ca 1880. 8vo. 16pp. Howard (illus). VG in illus wraps. *Davidson.* $125/£81

PERRAULT, CHARLES. Cinderella. NY: McLoughlin Bros, 1888. 3 double-pg color lithos by R. Andre. VG in illus wraps. *Davidson.* $75/£48

PERRAULT, CHARLES. Cinderella. London: Heinemann, 1919. 1st ed. Signed by Arthur Rackham (illus). Ltd ed (850 copies—of which 525 {500 for sale}, this is #8), ptd on Eng hand-made paper, white bds, vellum back, pict stamped & spine. Fine in Fine slipcase. *Davidson.* $1,750/£1,129

PERRAULT, CHARLES. Cinderella. NY: Dial, 1985. 1st ed. Inscribed by Susan Jeffers (illus). 4to. Unpaginated. Red bds, pict dj. Mint. *Davidson.* $50/£32

PERRAULT, CHARLES. Old-Time Stories. NY: Dodd, Mead, (1921). 1st Amer ed. 4to. 6 mtd color plts by W. Heath Robinson. (Sl darkening, few smudges.) Textured blue cl, color paste label, gilt. Matching pub's box w/color paste label (edges worn). *Reisler.* $475/£306

PERRAULT, CHARLES. Puss in Boots. NY: Greenwillow, 1977. 1st US ed. 4 pop-ups by Nicola Bayley. Glazed pict bds. VG. *Davidson.* $45/£29

PERRAULT, CHARLES. The Sleeping Beauty and Other Fairy Tales. Arthur Quiller-Couch (retold by). London: Hodder & Stoughton, (1910). 1st ed. 4to. 129pp, 30 tipped-in color plts by Edmund Dulac. Rebound in full morocco, raised bands; aeg. Fine. *Davidson.* $1,200/£774

PERRIN, N. Dr. Bowdler's Legacy. Macmillan, 1970. Fine in dj. *Moss.* $19/£12

PERROT, GEORGES and CHARLES CHIPIEZ. A History of Art in Ancient Egypt. London: Chapman & Hall, 1883. 2 vols. 878pp, 598 engrs, 14 plts. Gilt pict cl (spines chipped, torn; corners rubbed, bumped; 19th cent bkpl). *Archaeologia.* $175/£113

PERROT, GEORGES and CHARLES CHIPIEZ. A History of Art in Ancient Egypt. London: Chapman & Hall, 1883. 2 vols. Dec grn cl w/red & gilt. VG set. *Blue Dragon.* $175/£113

PERROT, GEORGES and CHARLES CHIPIEZ. A History of Art in Chaldaea and Assyria. London: Chapman & Hall, 1884. 2 vols. 818pp, 452 engrs, 15 color plts. Teg. Gilt-pict cl (bumped; lt foxing throughout). *Archaeologia.* $175/£113

PERROT, GEORGES and CHARLES CHIPIEZ. A History of Art in Phoenicia and Its Dependencies. London: Chapman & Hall, 1885. 2 vols. 870pp, 10 plts (9 color). (Sm tears spines; lt chipped; stamp 1/2titles.) *Archaeologia.* $150/£97

PERRY, BLISS. Park-Street Papers. Boston/NY: Houghton, Mifflin, 1908. 1st ed. Teg. Brn pict cl, gilt. Fine. *Macdonnell.* $50/£32

PERRY, CHARLES. The Haight Ashbury; A History. NY: Random House/Rolling Stone, (1984). 1st ed. Rev slip laid in. Fine in dj. *Reese.* $25/£16

PERRY, EVAN. Collecting Antique Metalware. London: Country Life, 1979. VG in dj. *Hollett.* $47/£30

PERRY, FRANCES. Flowers of the World. NY: Crown, (1972). Contents Fine (sm cvr spots). *Quest.* $40/£26

PERRY, FREDERICK. Fair Winds and Foul. Boston, 1925. 8 mtd illus. Partly unopened. VG. *Argosy.* $85/£55

PERRY, PETTIS. Pettis Perry Speaks to the Court. NY: New Century, 1952. 1st ed. Fine in wraps. *Beasley.* $30/£19

PERRY, R. Shetland Sanctuary, Birds on the Isle of Noss. London, 1948. 2 maps; 32 plts. (Spine sl faded.) *Wheldon & Wesley.* $31/£20

PERRY, RALPH BARTON. The Thought and Character of William James. Boston: Little Brown, 1935. 1st ed. 2 vols. Grn cl, red leather lettering pieces (chipped). VG. *House.* $80/£52

PERRY, RICHARD. The Jeannette: And a Complete and Authentic Encyclopedia of All Voyages and Expeditions to the North Polar Regions.... Cincinnati: W.E. Dibble, 1883. 840pp. Full leather, marbled eps, all edges marbled. Fr hinge cracked, sm piece missing top of spine, internally VG. *Parmer.* $125/£81

PERRY, RITCHIE. Dutch Courage. London: Collins, 1978. 1st ed. Fine in Fine dj. *Ming.* $28/£18

PERSHING, JOHN. My Experiences in the World War. NY, 1931. 1st ed. 2 vols. VG set. *Clark.* $65/£42

PERSON, CARL E. The Lizard's Trail. Chicago: Lake Pub, 1918. 1st ed. Good (discolored bds; damping top edge). *Beasley.* $75/£48

PERUCHO, JUAN. Joan Miro and Catalonia. NY: Tudor, n.d. (1968). Dec cl. VG in dj. *Argosy.* $125/£81

PETERKIN, JULIA. Roll, Jordan, Roll. NY: Robert O. Ballou, (1933). 1st ed. 8vo. Blue cl. Bottom edge sl faded, else Fine in VG dj. *Chapel Hill.* $550/£355

PETERKIN, JULIA. Roll, Jordan, Roll. NY, (1933). 1st trade ed. Doris Ulmann (photos). VG in dj. *Argosy.* $350/£226

PETERKIN, JULIA. Roll, Jordan, Roll. London: Cape, (1934). 1st Eng ed. Tipped-in tp. VG+. *Chapel Hill.* $150/£97

PETERS, CHARLES. The Autobiography of Charles Peters. Sacramento: LaGrave Co, (ca 1915). Ptd wrappers. *Dawson.* $40/£26

PETERS, CHARLES. The Autobiography of Charles Peters. Sacramento: LaGrave, n.d. (ca 1915). 1st ed. Frontis photos. Ptd wrappers. VG. *Connolly.* $45/£29

PETERS, ELIZABETH. The Curse of the Pharaohs. NY: Dodd Mead, 1981. 1st ed. Fine in dj. *Mordida.* $45/£29

PETERS, ELIZABETH. The Dead Sea Cipher. NY: Dodd, 1970. 1st ed. Fine in dj (price-clipped). *Else Fine.* $85/£55

PETERS, ELIZABETH. The Jackal's Head. NY: Meridith Press, 1968. 1st ed. Signed. Fine in dj (minor wear corners). *Else Fine.* $75/£48

PETERS, ELIZABETH. Legend in Green Velvet. NY: Dodd, Mead, 1976. 1st ed. Fine in NF dj. *Janus.* $65/£42

PETERS, ELIZABETH. Legend in Green Velvet. NY: Dodd-Mead, 1976. 1st ed. VF in dj. *Else Fine.* $95/£61

PETERS, ELLIS. City of Gold and Shadows. London: Macmillan, 1973. 1st ed. Fine in dj. *Mordida.* $175/£113

PETERS, ELLIS. Death Mask. London: CCC, 1959. 1st ed. Sl pg edge spotting, o/w Fine in dj. *Mordida.* $300/£194

PETERS, ELLIS. The Devil's Novice. London: Macmillan, 1983. 1st ed. VF in dj. *Mordida.* $85/£55

PETERS, ELLIS. An Excellent Mystery. London: Macmillan, 1985. 1st ed. Fine in Fine dj. *Ming.* $47/£30

PETERS, ELLIS. An Excellent Mystery. London: Macmillan, 1985. 1st ed. Fine in dj. *Else Fine.* $75/£48

PETERS, ELLIS. An Excellent Mystery. London: Macmillan, 1985. 1st ed. VF in dj. *Mordida.* $85/£55

PETERS, ELLIS. The Heretic's Apprentice. London: Headline, 1989. 1st ed. VF in dj. *Mordida.* $45/£29

PETERS, ELLIS. The Heretic's Apprentice. London: Headline, 1989. 1st UK ed. Signed Peters bkpl laid in. Fine in dj. *Williams.* $28/£18

PETERS, ELLIS. The Hermit of Eyton Forest. London: Headline, 1987. 1st ed. VF in dj. *Mordida.* $45/£29

PETERS, ELLIS. The Hermit of Eyton Forest. London: Headline, 1987. 1st UK ed. Signed. Fine in dj. *Williams.* $31/£20

PETERS, ELLIS. The House of Green Turf. London: CCC, 1969. 1st ed. Fine in dj. *Mordida.* $200/£129

PETERS, ELLIS. The Knocker on Death's Door. London: Macmillan, 1970. 1st ed. Fine in dj. *Mordida.* $200/£129

PETERS, ELLIS. Monk's Hood. Morrow, 1981. 1st US ed. Fine in Fine dj. *Ming.* $47/£30

PETERS, ELLIS. Monk's-Hood. NY: Morrow, 1981. 1st US ed. Fine in dj (spine extrems lt worn). *Janus.* $25/£16

PETERS, ELLIS. A Morbid Taste for Bones. NY: Morrow, 1978. 1st US ed. NF (inscrip; staining) in NF dj (price-clipped). *Janus.* $45/£29

PETERS, ELLIS. Mourning Raga. London: Macmillan, 1969. 1st ed. VG in VG dj. *Ming.* $124/£80

PETERS, ELLIS. Mourning Raga. London: Macmillan, 1969. 1st ed. Pp dknd, o/w Fine in dj. *Mordida.* $200/£129

PETERS, ELLIS. One Corpse Too Many. London: Macmillan, 1979. 1st ed. VG in NF dj. *Limestone.* $275/£177

PETERS, ELLIS. One Corpse Too Many. NY: Morrow, 1980. 1st US ed. Fine in Fine dj. *Janus.* $65/£42

PETERS, ELLIS. The Piper on the Mountain. London: CCC, 1966. 1st ed. Fine in dj. *Mordida*. $250/£161

PETERS, ELLIS. The Potter's Field. London: Headline, 1989. 1st UK ed. Signed Peters bkpl laid in. Fine in dj. *Williams*. $28/£18

PETERS, ELLIS. Rainbow's End. London: Macmillan, 1978. 1st ed. Fine in dj. *Mordida*. $85/£55

PETERS, ELLIS. The Raven in the Foregate. NY: Morrow, 1986. 1st Amer ed. VF in dj. *Silver Door*. $30/£19

PETERS, ELLIS. The Raven in the Foregate. Macdonald, 1986. 1st UK ed. Fine in Fine dj. *Martin*. $25/£16

PETERS, ELLIS. The Rose Rent. London: Macmillan, 1986. 1st ed. Fine in Fine dj. *Ming*. $39/£25

PETERS, ELLIS. The Sanctuary Sparrow. NY: Morrow, 1983. 1st Amer ed. Signed. VF in dj. *Silver Door*. $65/£42

PETERS, FRED J. Clipper Ship Prints, including Other Merchant Sailing Ships by N. Currier and Currier and Ives. NY, 1930. 1st ed. Lib ed. 63 plts. Fine. *Lefkowicz*. $100/£65

PETERS, HARRY T. America on Stone. GC, 1931. One of 751 numbered. 18 Fine color, 136 b/w plts. Fine in dj, box. *Argosy*. $450/£290

PETERS, HARRY T. California on Stone. GC: Doubleday, Doran, 1935. 1st ed. #9/501. Fine with slipcase (soiled, worn, chipped; no dj). *Bohling*. $550/£355

PETERS, HARRY T. California on Stone. GC: Doubleday, Doran, 1935. 1st ed. One of 501. 112 plts. Fine in dj (tear), slipcase. *Bookpress*. $450/£290

PETERS, HARRY T. California on Stone. NY: Arno Press, 1976. Facs rpt. 112 plts. VG. *Argosy*. $125/£81

PETERS, J.L. et al. Check-List of Birds of the World. 1931-62. 1st eds. Vols 1-7, 9, 10, 12-15. Maroon cl (vol 1 shaken, inner hinge separated; pencil notes few vols, esp vol 1; 1st vols worn). *Sutton*. $425/£274

PETERSEN, WILLIAM J. Steamboating on the Upper Mississippi. Iowa City, 1937. 1st ed. VG. Howes P 263. *Oregon*. $125/£81

PETERSEN, WILLIAM J. Steamboating on the Upper Mississippi. Iowa City: State Hist Soc, 1957. *Heinoldt*. $85/£55

PETERSHAM, M. and M. The Rooster Crows. Macmillan, 1945. 1st ed. Signed by both. 4to. Unpaginated. Full-color tan cl, black title. VG in dj (tattered). *Davidson*. $75/£48

PETERSON, CYRUS A. and JOSEPH M. HANSON. Pilot Knob. NY: Neale, 1914. 1st ed. Blue cl. Bkpl removal, else NF in dj (lt soiled). *Chapel Hill*. $275/£177

PETERSON, EMIL R. and ALFRED POWERS. A Century of Coos and Curry: History of Southwest Oregon. Portland: Binfords & Mort, 1952. 1st ed. Frontis; 30 full-pg plts. VG in dj (internally repaired). *Connolly*. $60/£39

PETERSON, FRED W. Desert Pioneer Doctor and Experiences in Obstetrics. Calexico Chronicle, 1947. 1st ed. VG. *Book Market*. $60/£39

PETERSON, HAROLD L. Arms and Armor in Colonial America 1526-1783. NY, (1956). VG. *Argosy*. $75/£48

PETERSON, R.T. Sir Kenelm Digby. The Ornament of England. Harvard, 1956. Nice in dj. *Goodrich*. $65/£42

PETERSON, R.W. Only the Ball Was White. Prentice-Hall, 1970. 1st ed. NF in VG+ dj. *Fine Books*. $125/£81

PETERSON, ROBERT. Only the Ball Was White. Prentice-Hall, 1970. 1st ed. VG+ in Good+ dj. *Plapinger*. $110/£71

PETERSON, SUSAN. Lucy M. Lewis—American Indian Potter. Tokyo: Kodansha International, (1988). 1st ed. VF in dj (price-clipped). *Perier*. $85/£55

PETIEVICH, GERALD. To Live and Die in L.A. NY: Arbor House, 1984. 1st ed. VF in dj. *Mordida*. $50/£32

PETIEVICH, GERALD. Money Men and One Shot Deal. NY: HBJ, 1981. 1st ed. 1st bk. VF in dj. *Else Fine*. $65/£42

PETIEVICH, GERALD. Money Men and One-Shot Deal. NY: Harcourt Brace Jovanovich, 1981. 1st ed. Fine in dj. *Mordida*. $65/£42

PETRAKIS, HARRY MARK. Pericles on 31st Street. Chicago: Quadrangle Books, 1965. 1st ed. Inscribed. Pict bds. Fine in dj. *Sadlon*. $15/£10

PETRIDES, ANNE. State Barges on the Thames. London, 1959. 1st ed. Dj (sl chipped). *Edwards*. $54/£35

PETRIE, W.M. FLINDERS. The Arts and Crafts of Ancient Egypt. Edinburgh/London: T.N. Foulis, (1923). (Inscrip; sm holes spine; lt rubbed.) *Archaeologia*. $55/£35

PETRIE, W.M. FLINDERS. Buttons and Design Scarabs. London: BSAE, 1925. 1st ed. 30 plts. (Sig.) *Archaeologia*. $200/£129

PETRIE, W.M. FLINDERS. Egypt and Israel. London: SPCK, 1911. Gilt-pict cl (spine faded; sig). *Archaeologia*. $35/£23

PETRIE, W.M. FLINDERS. Historical Scarabs: A Series of Drawings from the Principal Collections. London: D. Nutt, 1889. 14pp, 15 fldg plts. (Spine worn.) *Archaeologia*. $450/£290

PETRIE, W.M. FLINDERS. A History of Egypt. London: Methuen, (1907). 6th ed. 6 vols. Orig gilt-stamped blue cl (sl rubbed; spine ends worn). VG. *Houle*. $350/£226

PETRIE, W.M. FLINDERS. Janus in Modern Life. London: Archibald Constable, 1907. Good. *Archaeologia*. $35/£23

PETRIE, W.M. FLINDERS. The Making of Egypt. London: Sheldon Press, (1939). 82 plts. (Sig.) *Archaeologia*. $85/£55

PETRIE, W.M. FLINDERS. The Pyramids and Temples of Gizeh. London: Field & Tuer, (1883). 1st ed. 16 plts. (Bkpl, ink stamp tp; sm tears, label removed spine.) *Archaeologia*. $650/£419

PETRIE, W.M. FLINDERS. Researches in Sinai. NY: E.P. Dutton, 1906. (Sig; inner joints amateurishly reinforced w/tape; shelfwear.) *Archaeologia*. $150/£97

PETRIE, W.M. FLINDERS. The Revolutions of Civilisation. London/NY: Harper, 1912. Good (bkpl). *Archaeologia*. $35/£23

PETRIE, W.M. FLINDERS. Roman Portraits and Memphis (IV). London: British School of Archaeology in Egypt, 1911. (Sig.) *Archaeologia*. $200/£129

PETRIE, W.M. FLINDERS. Scarabs and Cylinders with Names Illustrated by the Egyptian. London: BSAE, 1917. 1st ed. 73 plts. 3/4 cl. (Sig; ex-lib.) *Archaeologia*. $125/£81

PETROCOKINO, A. Cashmere. London, 1920. 1st ed. 25 plts, 2 fldg maps. Gilt illus upper bd. (Lib inkstamps eps; soiled.) *Edwards*. $47/£30

PETRONIUS. The Satyricon. (NY): LEC, 1964. One of 1500 numbered, signed by Antonio Sotomayor (illus). Fine in pub's slipcase. *Hermitage*. $90/£58

PETROVITCH, WOISLAV M. Serbia. London: Harrap, 1915. 1st ed. Double-pg map, 4 ports. Blue cl, dec in black/gilt (sl rubbed). *Morrell.* $31/£20

PETRY, ANN. The Street. Boston, 1946. 1st ed, 1st bk. Pict cl. VG in dj (frayed, edge-torn). *King.* $150/£97

Pets and Toys. A Saalfield Muslin Book #242G. Akron: Saalfield Pub. Co., (1918). 16mo, 6pp (incl wraps). Yellow pict self wraps. VG + . *Davidson.* $42/£27

PETTIGREW, J.B. Animal Locomotion. London, 1873. Frontis, xiii,264pp; 130 engrs. *Wheldon & Wesley.* $74/£48

PETTIGREW, THOMAS. On Superstitions Connected with the History and Practice of Medicine and Surgery. London, 1844. 1st ed. 167pp. Good. *Fye.* $200/£129

PETZE, CHARLES L., JR. The Evolution of Celestial Navigation. NY: Motor Boating, (1948). 1st ed. (Ink mks text margins; cvr edge sl faded.) *Lefkowicz.* $45/£29

PEVSNER, NIKOLAUS. A History of Building Types. London: Thames & Hudson, 1976. 1st UK ed. Dj. *Edwards.* $54/£35

PEVSNER, NIKOLAUS. The Leaves of Southwell. London: King Penguin, 1945. 1st ed. 32 plts. Pict bds. Sl wear, o/w VG. *Willow House.* $9/£6

PEVSNER, NIKOLAUS. Some Architectural Writers of the Nineteenth Century. OUP, 1972. 1st ed. 78 plts. Dj. *Edwards.* $39/£25

PEVSNER, NIKOLAUS. West Kent and the Weald. London: Penguin, 1969. 1st ed. Piece cut from fr flyleaf. Dj. *Hollett.* $23/£15

PEYREFITTE, ROGER. Special Friendships. Edward Hyams (trans). London: Secker & Warburg, 1958. 1st Eng ed. Maroon cl. VG in dj (sl nicked, sl dusty). *Dalian.* $39/£25

PFEIFFER, IDA. A Journey to Iceland, and Travels in Sweden and Norway. Charlotte Cooper (trans). NY, 1852. 1st ed. 273pp. Foxing, o/w VG. *Artis.* $75/£48

PFEIFFER, IDA. A Woman's Journey Round the World. London, 1852. 3rd ed. xii,338pp; 12 tinted engrs. Mod 1/4 calf. *Lewis.* $56/£36

PFUHL, ERNST. Masterpieces of Greek Drawing and Painting. J.D. Beazley (trans). London: C&W, 1926. Good. *Archaeologia.* $65/£42

PHAIR, CHARLES. Atlantic Salmon Fishing. NY: Derrydale, 1937. One of 950. Fldg map; teg (frontis foxed, o/w internally VF). Grn cl, gilt dec. Lt spotted, o/w Fine + . *Bowman.* $500/£323

Phantom Flowers, a Treatise on the Art of Producing Skeleton Leaves. Boston: J.E. Tilton, 1864. 96pp, 6 plts, guards. Orig pebbled plum cl, gilt. Extrems worn, else VG. *Veatchs.* $150/£97

Pharmacopoeia of the United States of America. 1820. By the Authority of the Medical Societies and Colleges. Boston, 1820. 1st ed. 8vo. 272pp. Contemp calf. (Foxed.) *Argosy.* $1,000/£645

Pharmacopoeia of the United States of America.... NY: S. Converse, Nov 1830. 2nd ed. 176pp (foxing; sig, stamp). Contemp calf (rubbed, upper hinge split). Good. *Hemlock.* $150/£97

PHARR, ROBERT DEANE. The Book of Numbers. GC: Doubleday, 1969. 1st ed, 1st bk. Fine in dj. *Bernard.* $45/£29

PHARR, ROBERT DEANE. Giveadamn Brown. GC: Doubleday, 1978. 1st ed. 1/4 cl, paper bds. Bumped, o/w VG in dj. *Heller.* $25/£16

PHELPS, CHARLES. Traumatic Injuries of the Brain and Its Membranes. NY, 1897. 1st ed. 582pp. Good. *Fye.* $250/£161

PHELPS, WILLIAM DANE. Fremont's Private Navy: The 1846 Journal of.... Briton Cooper Busch (ed). Glendale: Clark, 1987. 1st ed. Ltd to 500. VG. *Shasky.* $40/£26

PHELPS, WILLIAM LYON. A Dash at the Pole. Boston: Ball Pub Co, 1909. 1st ed. Color paste down cvr. VG. *Blue Dragon.* $45/£29

PHILBRICK, NORMAN. Of Books and the Theatre.... (SF: Grabhorn-Hoyem), 1969. One of 1000. Frontis port, facs plt. Color cvr, sewn. VG in orig wraps. *Dramatis Personae.* $35/£23

PHILBY, H. ST. JOHN. A Pilgrim in Arabia. London: Robert Hale, 1946. 1st Eng ed. Red cl. VF in dj (sl tanned, sl soiled). *Dalian.* $101/£65

PHILBY, H. ST. JOHN. Saudi Arabia. London: Ernest Benn, 1955. 1st Eng ed. Fldg map. Blue buckram. Fine in dj (sl nicked). *Dalian.* $70/£45

PHILBY, KIM. My Silent War. London, (1968). 1st ed. Fine. *Argosy.* $75/£48

Philip Thaxter: A Novel. (By Charles Ames Washburn). NY: Rudd & Carleton, 1861. 1st ed. 350,(6)pp. Orig cl, blind-, gilt-stamped. Spine sunned, inscrip, o/w VG. *Reese.* $125/£81

PHILIP, A.P.W. On the Influence of Minute Doses of Mercury.... Washington, 1834. 60pp. New antique cl. Good. *Goodrich.* $65/£42

PHILIP, A.P.W. A Treatise on Febrile Diseases, Including the Various Species of Fever.... Hartford, 1816. 2nd Amer ed. 2 vols. 387; xxvii,453pp. Full leather (hinges cracked). *Fye.* $200/£129

PHILLIMORE, JOHN GEORGE. Private Law Among the Romans from the Pandects. London: Macmillan, 1863. Emb cl, gilt. Good. *Boswell.* $225/£145

PHILLIPPO, JAMES M. Jamaica, Its Past and Present State. Phila: James Campbell, 1843. 176pp. Orig marbled bds, 1/4 calf (new backstrip). *Cullen.* $135/£87

PHILLIPPS-WOLLEY, CLIVE. Savage Svanetia. London: Richard Bentley, 1883. 1st ed. 2 vols in 1. Engr frontispieces; half-titles; (xii),272; (viii),250, 6 engr plts. Purple blind-stamped cl. VG (ink inscrip; sl faded, stained, hinges weak). *Morrell.* $271/£175

PHILLIPS, C.E.L. Cromwell's Captains. London, 1938. 1st ed. Frontis, 7 other plts, 8 maps. Foxed, esp prelims, fore-edge, o/w VG in grn cl. *Edwards.* $47/£30

PHILLIPS, C.E.L. and P.N. BARBER. The Rothschild Rhododendrons. NY, 1979. 2nd ed. 66 color plts, port, 2 maps. Dj. *Sutton.* $90/£58

PHILLIPS, CATHERINE C. Cornelius Cole: California Pioneer and United States Senator.... SF: Nash, 1929. 1st ed. One of 250. Marbled bds, boxed. Howes C 308. *Ginsberg.* $125/£81

PHILLIPS, CATHERINE C. Coulterville Chronicle. SF: Grabhorn, 1942. 1st ed. Frontis, 22 plts. VG. *Oregon.* $125/£81

PHILLIPS, CATHERINE C. Jessie Benton Fremont. SF: John H. Nash, 1935. 1st ed. Frontis. Fine in Fine dj. Howes P 310. *Oregon.* $150/£97

PHILLIPS, CATHERINE C. Jessie Benton Fremont: A Woman Who Made History. SF: John Henry Nash, 1935. 1st ed. Frontis port. Untrimmed. Fine in NF dj. Howes P 310. *Connolly.* $175/£113

PHILLIPS, CATHERINE C. Portsmouth Plaza: The Cradle of San Francisco. SF: Nash, 1932. 1st ed. One of 1000. 88 plts. Marbled bds, vellum spine. Boxed. Howes P 311. *Ginsberg.* $150/£97

PHILLIPS, D. L. Letters from California: Its Mountains, Valleys...Climate and Productions. Springfield, IL: Illinois State Journal Co, 1877. Presentation copy. (4),viii,171pp. Gilt, black-stamped cl (lt wear, soiling; ex-lib w/stamps, sm cvr label). Howes P 312. *Bohling.* $125/£81

PHILLIPS, D.L. Letters from California: Its Mountains, Valleys.... Springfield, IL, 1877. 1st ed. (8),171pp. Orig dec cl (lt spotted). Howes P 312. *Ginsberg.* $225/£145

PHILLIPS, GEORGE. A Practical Treatise on Drawing and on Painting in Watercolours. London: Baily, 1839. 48pp, color chart, 20 aquatint plts (tidemk on some). Orig cl (worn, loose). *Ars Artis.* $302/£195

PHILLIPS, GEORGE. Rudiments of Curvilinear Design.... London: Shaw and Sons, (1839). 96pp, engr frontis, 47 engr plts, 68 wood engr text illus, 5 head or tailpieces, 26 historiated initials. Later half calf, (corners, edges rubbed, some margins grubby), orig label upper cvr. *Marlborough.* $891/£575

PHILLIPS, H. RANDALL. The Book of Bungalows. London: Country Life, 1922. 2nd ed. Opening pulled, o/w NF. *Willow House.* $31/£20

PHILLIPS, JAYNE ANNE. Machine Dreams. London: Faber, 1984. 1st ed. Fine in dj. *Rees.* $16/£10

PHILLIPS, JOHN C. A Sportsman's Scrapbook. Boston/NY: Houghton Mifflin/Riverside Press Cambridge, 1928. 1st ed. Blind-emb cl. Bkpl, else Fine. *Cahan.* $60/£39

PHILLIPS, JOHN C. and FRED LINCOLN. American Waterfowl, Their Present Situation and the Outlook for Their Future. Houghton Mifflin, 1930. 1st ed. Frontis; 7 plts w/ptd overleaf; 5 maps. VG. *Oregon.* $50/£32

PHILLIPS, JOHN C. and FREDERICK C. LINCOLN. American Waterfowl. Boston: Houghton Mifflin, 1930. 1st ed. Spine lt faded, o/w Fine+. *Bowman.* $65/£42

PHILLIPS, JOHN C. and LEWIS WEBB HILL. Classics of the American Shooting Field. Boston: Houghton Mifflin, 1930. 1st trade ed. VG. *Bowman.* $50/£32

PHILLIPS, MARK. The Memoir of Marco Parenti. Heinemann, 1989. Fine in dj, case. *Peter Taylor.* $16/£10

PHILLIPS, MARTHA E. All Through the Year. A Practical Manual of Pacific Coast Gardening. SF, 1931. 11 photo plts. Eps lt browned, else VG+. *Brooks.* $19/£12

PHILLIPS, PHILIP. Song Pilgrimage Around and Throughout the World, Embracing a Life of Song Experiences.... Chicago: Fairbanks, 1880. 1st ed. 478pp. Dec cl. *Ginsberg.* $150/£97

PHILLIPS, R. RANDAL. The Modern English House. London: Country Life, (c. 1935). 1st ed. Spine defective, repaired. *Hollett.* $70/£45

PHILLIPS, ULRICH BONNELL. Life and Labor in the Old South. Boston, 1929. 11th ptg. Fldg map. Sm stain dj spine, o/w VG+. *Pratt.* $27/£17

PHILLIPS, WENDELL. Qataban and Sheba: Exploring the Ancient Kingdoms on the Biblical Spice Routes of Arabia. NY: Harcourt, Brace, (1955). 1st ed. 3 maps. Good in dj. *Archaeologia.* $45/£29

PHILLIPS, WILLIAM. The Conquest of Kansas, by Missouri and Her Allies. Boston: Phillips, Sampson, 1856. 1st ed. 414pp, 6 ads. Gilt, blind-stamped. 1st, last few leaves lt foxed, else Fine. Howes P 330. *Cahan.* $125/£81

PHILLPOTTS, EDEN. The Apes. NY: Macmillan, 1929. 1st ed. Faint damp mk one corner, else Fine in pict dj (lt wear). *Else Fine.* $60/£39

PHILLPOTTS, EDEN. Brother Man. London: Grant Richards, 1926. 1st Eng ed. Patterned bds. Prelims sl foxed, o/w VF in dj (sl foxed, sl dusty). *Dalian.* $39/£25

PHILLPOTTS, EDEN. Children of the Mist. London: A.D. Innes, 1898. 1st ed, 1st issue. (Lt foxing; spine sl dknd; lt rubbed.) *Sadlon.* $50/£32

PHILLPOTTS, EDEN. Children of the Mist. London: A.D. Innes & Co, 1898. 1st Eng ed. Frontis. Blue cl, gilt. Sl rubbed, o/w VG. *Dalian.* $54/£35

PHILLPOTTS, EDEN. The Farm of the Dagger. London: George Newnes, 1904. 1st ed. Frontis. Dk blue cl. Nice (lt foxing). *Temple.* $22/£14

PHILLPOTTS, EDEN. Tales of the Tenements. London: John Murray, 1910. 1st ed. One of 5000 ptd. Fore-edges uncut, lower mainly trimmed. Red buckram. VG (mks, dknd). *Temple.* $14/£9

PHILLPOTTS, EDEN. The Three Brothers. London: Macmillan, 1927. 1st Eng ed. Unopened. 1/4 backed grn parchment bds. Sl faded, o/w Fine. *Dalian.* $39/£25

PHILPOT, OLIVER. Stolen Journey. London: Collector's Book Club, 1950. 1st ed, one of 150 specially bound, signed. Frontis port. Teg. Black morocco-backed marbled bds, spine gilt titled. Fldg prospectus laid in. Fine. *Cady.* $60/£39

PHIN, J. Open Air Grape Culture. NY, 1876. 1st ed. 266pp (eps foxed). Gilt-dec cl (spine faded, ends worn, fr hinge cracked). *Sutton.* $85/£55

PHIPPEN, GEORGE. The Life of a Cowboy. Tucson: Univ of AZ Press, (1969). 1st ed. Brn cl, gilt. Promo material laid in. Fine in dj (lt soiled). *Glenn.* $45/£29

PHIPPS, FRANCES. Colonial Kitchens, Their Furnishings, and Their Gardens. NY: Hawthorn, (1972). 1st ed. Fine. *Bookpress.* $65/£42

Phoenix and the Carpet. (By E. Nesbit.) London: George Newnes, (1904). 1st ed. 8vo. Teg. H.R. Millar (illus). Blue-grn cl, gilt, color decs cvr, spine (foxing). *Reisler.* $375/£242

PHYSICK, J. Catalogue of the Engraved Work of Eric Gill. V&A, 1963. #993 of about 1000. Sound in dj. *Ars Artis.* $70/£45

PIAGET, JEAN. The Child's Conception of Number. London: Routledge & Kegan Paul, (1952). 1st ed in English. Gilt-lettered blue cl. Fine in Good dj (chipped; tape-reinforced to back). *House.* $120/£77

PIAGET, JEAN. The Child's Conception of Physical Causality. Marjorie Gabain (trans). London: Kegan Paul/Harcourt, Brace, 1930 1st ed in English. Inserted ads dated 1947. Grn cl. VG (sig). *Gach.* $100/£65

PIAGET, JEAN. The Child's Conception of the World. London/NY: Kegan Paul/Harcourt, Brace, 1929. 1st ed in English, later issue w/ads dated 1939. Blue-grn cl. VG. *Gach.* $125/£81

PIAGET, JEAN. The Moral Judgment of the Child. NY/London: Harcourt, Brace/Kegan Paul, Trench, Trubner, 1932. 1st Amer ed, later issue. Ads dated 1947. Grn cl (fr cvr sl stained). *Gach.* $100/£65

PIAGET, JEAN. The Moral Judgment of the Child. London: Kegan Paul, Trench, Trubner, 1932. 1st ed in English, later issue. Inserted ads dated 1944. Grn cl. VG (fr cvr sl stained). *Gach.* $100/£65

PIAGET, JEAN. The Origins of Intelligence in Children. NY: IUP, (1952). 1st ed in English. Ptd blue-gray cl. NF. *Gach.* $30/£19

PIATT, DONN. and HENRY V. BOYNTON. General George H. Thomas, a Critical Biography. Cincinnati: Robert Clarke, 1893. 1st ed. 658pp. Orig grn cl. VG. *Chapel Hill.* $75/£48

Picasso Women, Cannes and Mougins 1954-1963. Paris/Amsterdam: Editions Cercle D'Art/Harry Abrams, 1964. 1st ed. NF in NF dj. *Bishop.* $90/£58

PICASSO, PABLO. Four Themes. London: Folio Soc, 1961. 1st ed. NF. *Bishop.* $25/£16

PICCARD, JACQUES and ROBERT S. DIETZ. Seven Miles Down. London: Longmans, Green, 1962. VG in dj. *Hollett.* $19/£12

PICCOLOPASSO, CIPRIANO. The Three Books of the Potter's Art...in the Original Italian, with Translation and an Introduction by Bernard Rackham and Alfred Van de Put. London, 1934. One of 750. 80 collotype plts. Cl sl soiled. *Washton.* $225/£145

PICKARD, KATE R. The Kidnapped and the Ransomed: The Extraordinary Story of Peter Still and His Family. NY: Negro Publication of Soc of Amer, 1941. 1st ed thus. Fine in VG dj (sl nicked; chip). *Between The Covers.* $85/£55

PICKARD, SAMUEL T. Life and Letters of John Greenleaf Whittier. Boston/NY: Houghton, Mifflin, 1894. 1st ed. 2 vols. Grn cl, gilt. BAL 22172. *Macdonnell.* $35/£23

PICKARD-CAMBRIDGE, A.W. The Theatre of Dionysus in Athens. Oxford: Clarendon, (1973). 3 plans. Good. *Archaeologia.* $85/£55

PICKERING, HAROLD G. Neighbors Have My Ducks. NY: Derrydale, 1937. #19/227. Signed, inscribed. Dk burgundy pict cl. Fine. *Sadlon.* $500/£323

PICKETT, ALBERT JAMES. History of Alabama and Incidentally of Georgia and Mississippi from the Earliest Period. Sheffield, AL: Robert C. Randolph, 1896. Rpt. Frontis port. (Worn.) Howes P 346. *Glenn.* $175/£113

PICKETT, LA SALLE CORBELL. Pickett and His Men. Atlanta, GA, 1899. 1st ed. Port; 439pp. (Bkpl; ink name; spine tips sl frayed; cvrs worn.) *King.* $50/£32

Pictorial Life of Benjamin Franklin. Phila: Dill & Collins, 1923. 1st ed. Color frontis by N.C. Wyeth, 62pp. Cl spine, paper-cvrd bds. Sl bumped, lt edgewear, else VG. *Godot.* $50/£32

Picture Alphabet of Beasts. London: Thomas Nelson, n.d. (ca 1880). 4to. 8 leaves, 4 full-pg chromolithos. Pict paper wrappers (lt soiling). Fine. *Hobbyhorse.* $215/£139

Picture Book, for Little Children. Phila: Kimber & Conrad, n.d. (ca 1812). 12mo. 24pp, title pg w/woodcut pic of naval officer and gentleman at quay w/ship; 44 woodcuts; 1 pg, uncut at side edge, shows Bible w/caption. Fine in yellow wrappers. *Hobbyhorse.* $200/£129

Picture of Verdun, or the English Detained in France. London, 1810. 2nd ed. 2 vols. Sm 8vo. 292; 263pp. Uncut. Lt foxing throughout, o/w VG. Mod cl-backed paper cvrd bds w/paper spine labels (sl soiled). *Edwards.* $116/£75

Pictured Alphabet. New-Haven: Sidney's Press, 1825. Sq 12mo. 23pp. Frontis, last pg pasted down on wrappers. All wood engrs grouped by 4 each pg, in Fine condition. Pict brn paper wrappers (dusted, lt spotted); upper wrapper w/engr of group of rabbits; lower wrapper ptd w/full-pg wood engr of sultan, 2 young ladies and pavilion. VG (lt internal foxing, browning). *Hobbyhorse.* $175/£113

Picturesque Guide to the Isle of Wight. Edinburgh, 1878. x,85pp + 104pp ads, fldg map (cellotaped, detached). Gilt-dec title. (Extrems rubbed.) *Edwards.* $23/£15

PIENKOWSKI, JAN. Haunted House. NY: E.P. Dutton, 1979. Pop-up. Sm 4to. Glazed pict paper-cvrd bds. NF. *Book Adoption.* $35/£23

PIENKOWSKI, JAN. Robot. London: Heinemann, 1981. 20x29 cm. 5 dbl-pg pop-ups, center tabs w/pulls. Glazed pict bds. VG. *Book Finders.* $70/£45

PIERCE, R.V. The People's Common Sense Medical Advisor in Plain English; or, Medicine Simplified. Buffalo, 1875. 2nd ed. 888pp, engr port. Good. *Fye.* $75/£48

PIERCE, R.V. The People's Common Sense Medical Advisor in Plain English; or, Medicine Simplified. Buffalo, 1888. 15th ed. 1008pp. Good. *Fye.* $40/£26

PIERCE, RICHARD and JOHN WINSLOW. H.M.S. Sulphur at California, 1837 and 1839. Book Club of CA, 1969. Ltd to 450 ptd. Color frontis map, prospectus laid in. Gilt stamped spine. Fine. *Oregon.* $60/£39

PIERCY, FREDERICK HAWKINS. Route from Liverpool to Great Salt Lake Valley. Cambridge, 1962. VG in dj. *Benchmark.* $35/£23

PIERCY, FREDERICK HAWKINS. Route from Liverpool to Great Salt Lake Valley. Fawn M. Brodie (ed). Cambridge: Harvard, 1962. Facs of orig tp; map. Fine in VG+ dj. Howes L 359. *Bohling.* $45/£29

PIERCY, MARGE. Dance the Eagle to Sleep. GC: Doubleday, 1970. 1st ed. Fine in dj (lt wear, browning). *Antic Hay.* $45/£29

PIERCY, MARGE. Fly Away Home. London: C&W, Hogarth Press, 1984. 1st Eng ed. Brn cl. VF in dj. *Dalian.* $31/£20

PIERSON, DAVID L. History of the Oranges (New Jersey) to 1921. NY: Lewis, 1922. 1st ed. 4 vols. 3/4 leatherette, buckram. VG. *Petrilla.* $100/£65

PIESSE, G.W. SEPTIMUS. The Art of Perfumery. Phila, 1867. 2nd Amer ed. 401pp (inscrip; frayed). *King.* $35/£23

PIETROWSKI, M. RUFIN. The Story of a Siberian Exile. London, 1863. Frontis, xii,321pp + (ii) (prelims lt spotted). Blind-emb cl, gilt device upper bd (discoloring; spine faded, sl chipped; upper hinge cracked; bkpl). *Edwards.* $132/£85

PIFFARD, HENRY and GEORGE HENRY FOX. Cutaneous and Venereal Memoranda. NY, 1880. 2nd ed. 309pp. Good. *Fye.* $50/£32

PIGGOTT, THEODORE. Outlaws I Have Known. Edinburgh/London, 1930. *Edwards.* $31/£20

PIGMAN, WALTER. The Journal of Walter Griffith Pigman. Ulla S. Fawkes (ed). Mexico: Missouri, 1942. 1st ed. Ltd to 200. Blue paper bds, ptd paper label. Howes P 361. *Ginsberg.* $150/£97

PIGNATTI, TERISIO. Giorgione. Phaidon, 1971. 24 mtd color plts. Sound in dj. *Ars Artis.* $163/£105

PIGNATTI, TERISIO. Italian Drawings in Oxford. Oxford: Phaidon. 1977. 80 color plts. Dj, slipcase (sl chipped). *Edwards.* $62/£40

PIGNATTI, TERISIO. Pietro Longhi, Complete Paintings and Drawings. London: Phaidon, 1969. 24 color plts. Fine in Mint dj. *Europa.* $101/£65

PIGOT, R. Twenty-Five Years Big Game Hunting. London, 1928. *Trophy Room.* $250/£161

Pike's Peak Region—Colorado-From Original Negatives and Photographs. NY: Albertype, 1893. 36pp. Hinge repaired, else VG. *Perier.* $60/£39

PIKE, ALBERT. Albert Pike's Journeys in the Prairie 1831-1832. (Canyon, TX: Panhandle-Plains Hist Soc, 1969.) Rpt. Inscribed by J. Evetts Haley (intro). Gilt-titled grn cl. Corners bumped, else Fine. *Bohling.* $65/£42

PIKE, G.D. Jubilee Singers and Their Campaign for Twenty Thousand Dollars. Boston/NY, 1873. 1st ed. Frontis; 219,(1)pp; port. (Joints worn.) *Ginsberg.* $75/£48

PIKE, NICHOLAS. Sub-Tropical Rambles in the Land of the Aphanapteryx. NY: Harper, 1873. 1st Amer ed. xviii,511pp + 4pp ads, 3 fldg color maps, 15 plts. Grn cl (sl soiled; pocket remnants on rear pastedown). *Schoyer.* $65/£42

PIKE, ROBERT L. (Pseud of Robert L. Fish.) Bank Job: A Lieutenant Reardon Novel. GC: Doubleday, 1974. 1st ed. NF in dj (extrems lt worn). *Janus.* $20/£13

PIKE, ROBERT L. (Pseud of Robert L. Fish.) The Gremlin's Grampa. GC: Doubleday, 1972. 1st ed. Fine in NF dj. *Janus.* $20/£13

PIKE, ROBERT L. (Pseud of Robert L. Fish.) Reardon: A Police Procedural Novel. GC: Doubleday, 1970. 1st ed. Fine in dj (price-clipped). *Janus.* $20/£13

PIKE, WARBURTON. The Barren Ground of Northern Canada. London: Macmillan, 1892. (xi),300pp, errata slip, 2 fldg maps. (Newly rebacked; orig backstrip laid down; new eps.) *Schoyer.* $100/£65

PIKE, WARBURTON. The Barren Ground of Northern Canada. London: Macmillan, 1892. 1st ed. Half title, ix,(iii),300,55 pub's list, 2 fldg maps; corrigenda bound in. Grn cl, gilt lettered spine; uncut, partly unopened. VG (cvrs lt spotted). *Morrell.* $132/£85

PIKE, WARBURTON. Through the Subarctic Forests. London: Edward Arnold, 1896. xiv(2)295pp. 2 fldg maps. Orig dec cl. VG. *High Latitude.* $225/£145

PIKE, ZEBULON M. The Expedition of Zebulon Pike...in New Spain, 1805-05-07. Elliot Coues (ed). NY: Francis P. Harper, 1895. 'Best ed', #125/150 on lg paper. 3 vols. 955pp. 7 maps. (Corners bumped; edgewear; lt spotting to vellum spines). Attractive. Howes P 373. *Perier.* $595/£384

PIKE, ZEBULON M. The Expeditions of Zebulon Montgomery Pike.... NY: Harper, 1895. 3 vols. (8,114),356; (6),357-856,(6),857-955pp, 7 maps. Howes P 373. *Ginsberg.* $600/£387

PIKE, ZEBULON M. The Journals of Zebulon Montgomery Pike, with...Related Documents. Donald Jackson (ed). Norman: Univ of OK, (1966). 1st ed thus. 2 vols. Fine in NF slipcase (corner sl bumped). Howes P 373. *Harrington.* $115/£74

PILCHER, GEORGE. A Treatise on the Structure, Economy, and Diseases of the Ear. Phila, 1843. 1st Amer ed. 299pp (water stain affecting margins few leaves); 16 engr plts. Recent 1/4 leather, marbled bds. *Fye.* $100/£65

PILCHER, LEWIS. The Treatment of Wounds, Its Principles and Practice.... NY, 1883. 1st ed. 391pp; 116 engrs. Good. *Fye.* $100/£65

PILCHER, VERONA. The Searcher. London: Heinemann, (1929). 1st ed. One of 1000. Spine faded, else VG in dj (1 tape repair). *Chapel Hill.* $125/£81

PILKINGTON, M. A Dictionary of Painters, from the Revival of Art to the Present Period. London: Crowder, 1805. xx,693pp. Contemp full calf (rebacked, orig spine laid down), gilt. Fr cvr sl scuffed, o/w VF. *Europa.* $140/£90

PILLING, JAMES CONSTANTINE. Bibliography of the Eskimo Language. Washington: Smithsonian, 1887. Facs. Untrimmed. Nice in ptd wraps (lt frayed). *Bohling.* $35/£23

PILLSBURY, PARKER. Acts of the Anti-Slavery Apostles. Concord, NH, 1883. 1st ed. 503pp. Orig cl. VG. *Mcgowan.* $150/£97

PINART, ALPHONSE. Journey to Arizona in 1876. George H. Whitney (trans). L.A.: Zamorano Club, 1962. One of 500. Fldg map; facs of Fr ed tp. 1/2 cl, dec paper over bds. NF. *Parmer.* $65/£42

PINCHOT, GIFFORD. Just Fishing Talk. Harrisburg: Telegraph, 1936. 1st ed. Fine in VG + dj. *Bowman.* $65/£42

PINCKNEY, DARRYL. High Cotton. NY: Farrar Straus, 1992. 1st ed, 1st bk. VF in VF dj. *Pettler.* $65/£42

PINCKNEY, DARRYL. High Cotton. NY: Farrar, 1992. 1st ed. Fine in Fine dj. *Beasley.* $50/£32

PINCKNEY, DARRYL. High Cotton. NY: FSG, 1992. 1st ed. Fine in Fine dj. *Revere.* $75/£48

PINCKNEY, JAMES D. Reminiscences of Catskill. Catskill: Hall, 1868. 1st ed. 79pp. Gold-stamped cl (expertly rebacked, recased). Howes P 379. *Ginsberg.* $125/£81

PINCKNEY, PAULINE. Painting in Texas, the Nineteenth Century. Austin, 1967. 1st ed. Dj. *Lambeth.* $100/£65

PINDAR. Pythian Odes. H.T. Wade-Gery & C.M. Bowra (trans). London: Nonesuch, 1928. One of 1550 numbered. Teg. White spine sl tanned, else Nice in slipcase. *Reese.* $35/£23

PINKERTON, ALLAN. Model Town and Detectives: Byron as a Detective. NY: G.W. Carlton, 1876. 1st ed. 288pp; 10pp engrs. Green w/black, gilt. Sl staining, rubbing, else VG. *Connolly.* $125/£81

PINKERTON, ALLAN. The Spy of the Rebellion.... NY: Carleton, 1983. 1st ed. Frontis; 23 plts. Pict cl. Foxing, o/w VG. *Oregon.* $30/£19

PINKERTON, ALLAN. The Spy of the Rebellion; Being a True History of the Spy System.... Hartford, CT: Chas. P. Hatch, 1886. Ltr ptg. 688pp. Orig cl. VG (fr inner hinge starting; rubbed). *Mcgowan.* $45/£29

PINKERTON, ROBERT. Hudson's Bay Company. Holt, (1931). 1st Amer ed. 7 plts. VG. *Oregon.* $50/£32

PINKUS, P. Grub Street Stripped Bare. Constable, 1968. VG in dj. *Moss.* $33/£21

PINNEY, THOMAS (ed). The Letters of Thomas Babington Macaulay. 1807-1859. CUP, 1974-81. 6 vols. Frontispieces. (Newspaper cuttings loosely inserted.) Djs (sl chipped). *Edwards.* $194/£125

PINS, JACOB. The Japanese Pillar Print. London, 1982. #455/1000. Tipped-in color frontis, 16 color plts. Illus slipcase (soiled, scuffed). *Edwards.* $93/£60

PINTER, HAROLD. Monologue. (London: Covent Garden Press, 1973.) 1st ed. One of 100 signed. Fine in tan calf; linen slipcase. *Juvelis.* $150/£97

PINTER, HAROLD. The Screenplay of the French Lieutenant's Woman. London: Jonathan Cape/Eyre Methuen, 1981. 1st ed. Signed by John Fowles. Orig black cl. Fine in dj. *Rees.* $31/£20

PINTER, HAROLD. The Screenplay of The French Lieutenant's Woman. London: Cape, 1981. 1st ed. Signed. Fine in dj. *Rees.* $54/£35

Pioneering the West 1846 to 1878.... (By Howard Egan). Salt Lake City, 1917. 1st ed. VG- (shaken, worn; name, pieces torn rep). *Benchmark.* $75/£48

PIOZZI, HESTER LYNCH. Anecdotes of the Late Samuel Johnson During the Last Twenty Years of His Life. London: Cadell, 1786. 3rd ed. 307pp. Early calf (nicely rebacked), gilt on red leather label. VG (bkpl). *Hartfield.* $325/£210

PIOZZI, HESTER LYNCH. Love Letters of Mrs. Piozzi...to William Augustus Conway. London: John Russell Smith, 1843. 1st ed. 39pp. Teg. Early 20th cent mottled calf, gilt extra. Ink comments blank prelim, marginal notes in text, o/w Good (bkpl). *Reese.* $150/£97

PIOZZI, HESTER LYNCH. Observations and Reflections Made in the Course of a Journey Through France, Italy, and Germany. Dublin: Chamberlaine et al, 1789. 1st Dublin ed. 592pp. Full calf (rebacked), raised bands, gilt, grn leather label. Contents Excellent (orig bds worn; names). *Hartfield.* $485/£313

Piozziana; or, Recollections of the Late Mrs. Piozzi, with Remarks. (By Edward Mangin.) London: Edward Moxon, 1833. 1st ed. Frontis facs, 232,(2)pp. Late 19th cent calf, polished calf panelled inlays; spine gilt extra. Sl rubbed, o/w VG. *Reese.* $150/£97

PIPER, CHARLES V. Flora of the State of Washington. Washington: GPO, 1906. Full sheep. VG. *Perier.* $40/£26

PIPER, DAVID. The English Face. London: Thames & Hudson, 1957. Spine sl faded, o/w Fine. *Europa.* $28/£18

PIPER, DAVID. The English Face. London: Thames & Hudson, 1957. Dj (sl chipped corners, spine). *Edwards.* $31/£20

PIPER, H. BEAM. Murder in the Gunroom. NY: Knopf, 1953. 1st ed. NF (name) in NF dj (lt edgewear, spine lt sunned). *Janus.* $300/£194

PIPER, JOHN. Buildings and Prospects. London: Architectural Press, 1948. 1st ed. 7 plts. VG in dj (sl defective). *Cox.* $54/£35

PIPER, W. Little Black Sambo and Other Stories. NY: Platt & Munk, c. 1927. Sm 4to. Eulalie (illus). Paper-cvrd bds (dampstained, worn); pict label; cl spine. (Contents lt soiled.) *Book Adoption.* $60/£39

PIPER, W. The Little Engine That Could. NY, (1930). Lois L. Lenski (illus). 8x6 inches. Pict cl. Good in dj (torn, chipped). *King.* $35/£23

PIPER, W. The Little Engine That Could. P&M, 1930. 1st ed thus. Lois Lenski (illus). 1 pg corners chipped, else VG. *Aronovitz.* $125/£81

PIPPETT, AILEEN. The Moth and the Star. A Biography of Virginia Woolf. Boston: Little, Brown, (1955). 1st ed. Gray/blue cl. Label, offsetting reps from laid-in newspaper, else NF in VG dj (sl worn). *Chapel Hill.* $30/£19

Pirate. (By Walter Scott). Edinburgh, 1822. 1st ed. 3 vols. Contemp 1/2 tan calf, marbled sides, backstrips gilt (sl worn; inscrip). *Petersfield.* $78/£50

Pirate. (By Sir Walter Scott.) Edinburgh: Archibald Constable & Co., 1822. 1st ed. 3 vols. 322; 332; 346pp. Untrimmed. Slate blue bds, paper spine labels. Spine ends, labels chipped; hinges cracked, else VG. *Chapel Hill.* $300/£194

PIRQUET, C.P. and BELLA SCHICK. Serum Sickness. Balt, 1951. 1st Eng trans. Good. *Fye.* $90/£58

PIRSIG, ROBERT M. Zen and the Art of Motorcycle Maintenance. NY: Morrow, 1974. 1st ed, 1st bk. Name top pg edge, else Fine in Fine dj. *Pettler.* $85/£55

PIRSIG, ROBERT M. Zen and the Art of Motorcycle Maintenance. Bodley Head, 1974. 1st UK ed. NF in dj. *Williams.* $85/£55

PIRSIG, ROBERT. Zen and the Art of Motorcycle Maintenance. NY: Morrow, 1974. 1st ed. NF in dj (price-clipped). *Lame Duck.* $100/£65

PIRSIG, ROBERT. Zen and the Art of Motorcycle Maintenance. London: Bodley Head, 1974. 1st UK ed. Inscrip; aggressive erasure fep, else NF in dj (price-clipped). *Lame Duck.* $30/£19

PIRTLE, ALFRED. The Battle of Tippecanoe. Louisville, KY, 1900. 1st ed. Both orig ptd wrappers bound in cl. NF. Howes P 389. *Mcgowan.* $150/£97

PITCAIRN, ROBERT. Criminal Trials in Scotland.... Edinburgh: William Tait, 1833. 3 vols bound in 4. Contemp calf. Sound (mkd; some joints just cracking). *Boswell.* $1,250/£806

PITKIN, ELIZA. Invalid Cookery: A Manual of Recipes. Chicago, 1880. 1st ed. 127pp. Good. *Fye.* $75/£48

PITKIN, THOMAS M. The Captain Departs: Ulysses S. Grant's Last Campaign. Carbondale: Southern IL Univ, (1973). 1st ed. NF in VG dj. *Mcgowan.* $45/£29

PITT-KETHLEY, FIONA. London. Privately ptd, 1984. 1st issue, 1st book. Fine in wrappers. *Rees.* $54/£35

PITT-KETHLEY, FIONA. Rome. London: Mammon Press, 1985. 1st ed. Fine in wrappers. *Rees.* $31/£20

PITTMAN, PHILIP. The Present State of the European Settlements on the Mississippi.... Frank H. Hodder (ed). Cleveland: Clark, 1906. Facs rpt of 1st ed. One of 500. 6 fldg maps. Brn cl. Name, eps, last few leaves foxed, else VG. Howes P 396. *Chapel Hill.* $175/£113

PITZ, H.C. Howard Pyle, Writer, Illustrator.... NY: Clarkson Potter, 1975. Sound in dj. *Ars Artis.* $70/£45

PITZ, H.C. A Treasury of American Book Illustration. NY, (1947). Dj. *Veatchs.* $40/£26

PLACE, CHARLES A. Charles Bulfinch, Architect and Citizen. Boston: Houghton Mifflin, 1925. 1st ed. Frontis. (Fr inside hinge repaired; rear hinge internally cracked; lt foxing; cvr wear.) *Bookpress.* $95/£61

PLACE, CHARLES A. Charles Bulfinch, Architect and Citizen. NY: De Capo Press, 1968. Rpt, 1st ed thus. Frontis. Bkpl, else Fine. *Bookpress.* $45/£29

PLANCHE, JAMES ROBINSON. A Cyclopaedia of Costume. London: C&W, 1876-79. 2 vols. Chromolitho frontispieces, vi,527pp; xi,448pp (tp lt browned, few leaves chipped, vol 2; margins thumbed). 16 chromolitho plts, 20 numbered (7-24 inclusive, incl 2 plts #d 16, 22) b/w plts. Errata slip vol 1. Fore, lower edges uncut. Lib morocco-backed cl bds (rebound; #s, bkpl; spines sl rubbed), gilt. *Edwards.* $388/£250

PLANTE, DAVID. The Catholic. London: C&W, 1985. 1st Eng ed. Brn cl. Fine in dj. *Dalian.* $31/£20

PLANTE, DAVID. The Catholic. NY, 1986. 1st ed. VG in dj. *Argosy.* $25/£16

PLANTE, DAVID. Difficult Women. London: Gollancz, 1983. 1st Eng ed. VF in dj. *Dalian.* $23/£15

PLANTE, DAVID. Figures in Bright Air. London: Gollancz, 1976. 1st Eng ed. Black cl. Fine in dj. *Dalian.* $54/£35

PLANTE, DAVID. The Foreigner. London: Hogarth Press, 1984. 1st Eng ed. Blue cl. Fine in dj. *Dalian.* $31/£20

PLANTE, DAVID. Slides. London: Macdonald, 1971. 1st ed. NF in dj. *Rees.* $31/£20

PLANTE, DAVID. Slides. London: Macdonald, 1971. 1st UK ed. NF in dj. *Lewton*. $29/£19

PLANTE, DAVID. The Woods. London: Gollancz, 1982. 1st Eng ed. Grn cl. VF in dj. *Dalian*. $31/£20

Planter: Or, Thirteen Years in the South. (By David Brown.) Phila: H. Hooker, 1853. 1st ed. 275pp + (1)pg ads. Dk blue cl (spine sl faded). Lib bkpl, blindstamp, few leaves stained, else VG. Howes B 834. *Chapel Hill*. $285/£184

PLATH, SYLVIA. Winter Trees. London: Faber & Faber, (1971). 1st ed. Fine in dj. *Godot*. $125/£81

PLATH, SYLVIA. Winter Trees. NY: Harper, 1972. 1st US ed. Fine in dj (rubbed). *Beasley*. $40/£26

PLATO. Lysis, or Friendship: The Symposium and Phaedrus. Benjamin Jowett (trans). NY: LEC, 1968. One of 1500 numbered, signed by Eugene Karlin (illus). Fine in pub's slipcase. *Hermitage*. $125/£81

PLATT, CHARLES A. Monograph of the Work of.... NY, 1913. 183 leaves plts. (Sl marginal browning; bkpl; upper hinges tender; rubbed, sm dent.) *Edwards*. $155/£100

PLATT, COLIN. The Monastic Grange in Medieval England. London: Macmillan, 1969. 1st ed. 16 plts. VG in dj. *Hollett*. $47/£30

PLATT, P.L. and N. SLATER. Travelers' Guide Across the Plains Upon the Overland Route to California. (SF): John Howell, 1963. 2nd ed. One of 475. Tipped-in facs of orig tp; fldg map. Black paper bds imprinted w/map. Fine. Howes P 417. *Harrington*. $100/£65

PLAUT, JAMES S. Steuben Glass. NY, 1951. 2nd rev, enlgd ed. 68 plts, 11 gravure repros. (Lib ink stamps, tape mks.) Dj (sl chipped). *Edwards*. $39/£25

PLAUT, JAMES S. (ed). Oskar Kokoschka. Boston/London: Inst Contemp Art/Parrish, n.d. (1948). 56 plts (8 color), 2 orig lithos by Kokoschka. Lib stamps, spine #s, else Good. *Ars Artis*. $388/£250

PLAYER-FROWD, J.G. Six Months in California. London, 1872. 1st ed. 164pp; 32pp ads. (Soiling; hinges weak.) *Oregon*. $95/£61

PLAYFAIR, W.S. The Systematic Treatment of Nerve Prostration and Hysteria. Phila, 1883. 1st Amer ed. 111pp. Good. *Fye*. $150/£97

Playful Fairyland Pop-Ups. Londen (sic): Birn Bros, n.d. (196?). 14x22 cm. 4 pop-ups. Hvy bds. (Extrems, spine sl worn). Inside VG. *Book Finders*. $30/£19

PLEASANT, HAZEN HAYES. A History of Crawford County, Indiana. Greenfield, IN, 1926. (Bkpl; hinges weak.) *Bohling*. $85/£55

PLEASANTS, HENRY, JR. Thomas Mason, Adventurer. Chicago: John C. Winston, (1934). 1st ed. Card signed by Peter Hurd (illus) mtd fep. 12pp b/w plts. Black gilt cl. Good in dj (soiled). *Karmiole*. $50/£32

PLENDERLEITH, H.J. The Conservation of Antiquities and Works of Art. OUP, 1956. Color frontis, 55 plts. Sound. *Ars Artis*. $47/£30

PLENDERLEITH, H.J. The Conservation of Antiquities and Works of Art. OUP, 1957. Rpt. Color frontis, 55 plts. Dj (ragged; spine faded). *Edwards*. $39/£25

PLENDERLEITH, H.J. The Conversation of Antiquities and Works of Art. Oxford, 1956. VG. *Washton*. $50/£32

PLIMPTON, GEORGE. One for the Record. Harper & Row, 1974. 1st ed. Fine in VG + dj. *Plapinger*. $25/£16

PLIMPTON, GEORGE. Out of My League. Harper, 1961. 1st ed. VG in Good dj. *Plapinger*. $25/£16

PLIMSOLL, SAMUEL. Cattle Ships; Being the Fifth Chapter of Mr. Plimsoll's Second Appeal for Our Seamen.... London, 1890. 1st ed. (6),150pp. Dec cl (soil). *Lefkowicz*. $275/£177

PLOMER, HENRY R. A Dictionary of the Booksellers and Printers Who Were at Work in England, Scotland and Ireland from 1641 to 1667. Bibliographical Soc, 1907. Recent cl, brn morocco label. VG. *Moss*. $62/£40

PLOMER, HENRY R. A Dictionary of the Printers and Booksellers...1688 to 1725. Arundell Esdaile (ed). OUP, 1922. (Marginal browning; sl rubbed, soiled; spine sl chipped, discolored.) *Edwards*. $54/£35

PLOMER, HENRY R. A Short History of English Printing 1476-1900. London: Kegan Paul et al, 1927. VG in orig cl (sl soiled), paper label + spare at end. *Cox*. $28/£18

PLOMER, WILLIAM. At Home: Memoirs. London: Jonathan Cape, 1958. 1st ed. Top edge grey. Fine in dj (sl frayed). *Temple*. $22/£14

PLOMER, WILLIAM. Celebrations. London: Jonathan Cape, 1972. 1st Eng ed. Black-backed brn bds. VF in dj. *Dalian*. $31/£20

PLOMER, WILLIAM. Double Lives. NY: Noonday, (1956). 1st Amer ed. Fine in dj (lt dusty). *Hermitage*. $35/£23

PLOMER, WILLIAM. Double Lives: An Autobiography. London: Jonathan Cape, 1943. 1st ed. Lower edges rough-trimmed. Grn cl, gilt. Fine in dj (frayed). *Temple*. $29/£19

PLOMER, WILLIAM. The Fivefold Screen. Hogarth Press, 1932. 1st ed. Signed, ltd ed of 450. Good. *Whiteson*. $47/£30

PLOMER, WILLIAM. Museum Pieces. NY: Noonday, (1954). 1st Amer ed. VG in dj. *Hermitage*. $35/£23

PLOMER, WILLIAM. Notes for Poems. Hogarth, 1927. 1st ed. VG (bkpl; soiled). *Poetry*. $19/£12

PLOMER, WILLIAM. The Planes of Bedford Square. London: The Bookbag, 1971. 1st Eng ed. Single fldg sheet parchment hand-made paper. NF. *Dalian*. $39/£25

PLOMER, WILLIAM. A Shot in the Park. London: Jonathan Cape, (1955). 1st ed. NF in dj (lt edgeworn). *Sadlon*. $10/£6

PLON, EUGENE. Thorvaldsen; His Life and Works. London, 1874. 2 engr plts. Uncut, largely unopened. Pub's beveled bds, gilt dec. Fine. *Europa*. $47/£30

PLOSS, HERMANN et al. Woman: An Historical Gynaecological and Anthropological Compendium. London, 1935. 1st Eng trans. 3 vols. Good. *Fye*. $600/£387

PLOWDEN, JOAN MEREDYTH CHICHELE. Once in Sinai. London: Methuen, 1940. 1st ed. 18 plts; 8 maps. (Sl used; upper joint cracked.) *Hollett*. $39/£25

PLUES, M. British Ferns. London, 1866. 16 hand-colored plts. Dec cl (worn, frayed; eps stained). *Sutton*. $55/£35

PLUMMER, EDWARD CLARENCE. Reminiscences of a Yarmouth Schoolboy. Portland: Marks, 1926. Inscribed. VG. *Schoyer*. $35/£23

PLUMMER, JOHN. The Book of Hours of Catherine of Cleves. NY, 1964. 32 color plts. Good in slipcase. *Washton*. $75/£48

Plutarch's Lives. The Translation Called Dryden's. Boston: Little, Brown, 1895. 5 vols. Teg. Gilt/black dec brn cl. Fine. *House*. $120/£77

POBE, MARCEL. The Art of Roman Gaul. London: Gallery Press, 1961. 1st UK ed. 259 b/w photos. (Sl wrinkled; ex-lib w/label, ink stamp, #s; new eps, hinges reinforced; sl rubbed, faded.) *Edwards*. $39/£25

Pocket Memorandum Book during a Ten Weeks' Trip to Italy and Germany in 1847. (By George Palmer Putnam). N.p.(NY): n.p., n.d. (1847). 1st ed. 140pp. (Parts of binding dknd.) *Petrilla*. $50/£32

POCOCK, W.F. Designs for Churches and Chapel. London: M. Taylor, 1835. 3rd ed. 4to. 28pp; 44 plts. Pub's blindstamped cl. Worn, spine sunned, else VG. *Bookpress*. $650/£419

POCOCK, W.F. Modern Finishings for Rooms.... London: J. Taylor, 1823. 1st ed. 23pp, 85 (of 86) plts. Lacks plt 86; tp damaged, reinforced, not affecting ptd words. Poor to Good only. *Bookpress*. $450/£290

PODHORETZ, NORMAN. Making It. NY: Random House, (1967). 1st ed. Rev copy, slip laid in. Fine in dj. *Sadlon*. $15/£10

POE, EDGAR ALLAN. A Chapter on Autobiography.... D.C. Seitz (ed). NY: Dial, 1926. 1st ed thus. One of 750 numbered. Lt edgewear, else Good. BAL 16255. *Reese*. $30/£19

POE, EDGAR ALLAN. The Gold Bug. NY: Rimington & Hooper, 1928. Ltd ed, one of 377 numbered. Black cl, gilt stamped pict design. VG in pub's slipcase. *Argosy*. $125/£81

POE, EDGAR ALLAN. The Journal of Julius Rodman. SF: Colt Press, 1947. 1st ed. Ltd to 500. 7 wood engrs. Cl-backed blue/brn dec bds (extrems lt worn). BAL 16265. *Shasky*. $95/£61

POE, EDGAR ALLAN. Poe's Tales of Mystery and Imagination. London: George G. Harrap, (1935). 1st ed thus. 4to. 12 color plts by Arthur Rackham; tinted top. Black cl, gold lettering, skeleton design. Very Nice in color dj (overflap sl foxed). *Reisler*. $600/£387

POE, EDGAR ALLAN. The Poems of Edgar Allen Poe. NY: LEC, 1943. #904/1500 numbered, signed by Hugo Steiner-Prag (illus). Full leather. NF in pub's slipcase (lt worn). *Hermitage*. $175/£113

POE, EDGAR ALLAN. Poems...Complete with an Original Memoir. NY: Widdleton, 1867. Rpt. Port; aeg. Blue cl stamped in gilt, blind. Lt foxing, early reinforcement head, toe spine, else Good. BAL 16214. *Reese*. $25/£16

POE, EDGAR ALLAN. The Raven and Other Poems. (Detroit: Fine Book Circle, 1936). Ltd to 950. Inscribed by Paul McPharlin (illus). Fine in dj (lt edgeworn). *Sadlon*. $50/£32

POE, EDGAR ALLAN. Tales of Mystery and Imagination. NY: Tudor, 1933. 1st Tudor ed. Thick, 4to. 8 mtd color plts by Harry Clarke. Black cl, gold/black paste label, gilt. Good in color pict dj, pub's box w/full color paste label (edgewear). *Reisler*. $300/£194

POE, EDGAR ALLAN. Tales. Chicago: Lakeside, 1930. One of 1000. Cl, dec bds; spine gilt extra. VG in glassine; slipcase (soiled, sunned). *Reese*. $35/£23

POE, JOHN W. The Death of Billy the Kid. Boston: Houghton Mifflin, 1933. 1st ed, 1st ptg. Brn cl (soiled; head spine lt chipped). *Glenn*. $65/£42

POE, SOPHIE A. Buckboard Days. Eugene Cunningham (ed). Caldwell, 1936. 1st ed. Spine top faded, 3/8-inch dj missing, o/w Fine in mod dj (worn, soiled, nearly complete). *Baade*. $115/£74

Poems on Several Occasions by a Gentleman of Virginia. Facsimile Text Soc, 1930. VG. *Book Broker*. $25/£16

Poems on Several Occasions. (By Matthew Prior.) London: Jacob Tonson, 1709. 1st authorized ed. Engr frontis, xxiv,(iv),328pp. Orig full chestnut polished calf, panelled in blind (rebacked in period style), morocco/gilt label. Attractive. *Hartfield*. $395/£255

POESCH, JESSIE. The Art of the Old South. NY: Knopf, 1983. 1st ed. VG in dj (chipped). *Bookpress*. $75/£48

POESCH, JESSIE. Titian Ramsay Peale, 1799-1885, and His Journals of the Wilkes Expedition. Phila, 1961. VG in dj. *Argosy*. $175/£113

Poets of Tomorrow. First Selection. Hogarth Press, 1939. 1st ed. VG in dj. *Words Etc*. $59/£38

POGANY, WILLY and ELAINE. Peterkin. Phila: David McKay, 1940. 1st ed. Willy Pogany (illus). Sm 4to. Pict paper-cvrd bds (edgewear). NF in VG dj (worn). *Book Adoption*. $50/£32

POHL, FREDERIK and C. KORNBLUTH. A Town Is Drowning. Ballantine, 1955. 1st ed. Signed by Pohl. Fine in NF dj (lt rubbed). *Aronovitz*. $500/£323

POHL, FREDERIK and JACK WILLIAMSON. Rogue Star. Dobson, 1972. 1st Eng, 1st hb ed. Signed. Fine in dj. *Aronovitz*. $75/£48

POHL, FREDERIK and JACK WILLIAMSON. Undersea City. Hicksville, NY: Gnome Press, (1958). 1st ed. Gray binding, lettered in red. Fine (ink name) in dj (sl wear; sm chip). *Antic Hay*. $50/£32

POHL, FREDERIK and JACK WILLIAMSON. Undersea City. Gnome Press, 1958. 1st ed. Signed. Fine in dj (sm area scraped off rear panel). *Aronovitz*. $45/£29

POHL, FREDERIK with C.M. KORNBLUTH. A Town Is Drowning. NY: Ballantine, (1955). 1st ed. 8vo. Fine (browning to poor quality paper) in dj (lt soil). *Antic Hay*. $600/£387

POHL, FREDERIK. Beyond the Blue Event Horizon. Del Rey, 1980. 1st ed. Signed. Fine in dj. *Madle*. $55/£35

POHL, FREDERIK. Drunkard's Walk. Gnome, 1960. 1st ed. Fine in dj. *Madle*. $35/£23

POHL, FREDERIK. Man Plus. NY: Random House, (1976). 1st ed. Fine in dj (price-clipped). *Antic Hay*. $100/£65

POHL, FREDERIK. Undersea Fleet. Gnome, 1956. 1st ed. Fine in dj (sl rubbed). *Madle*. $100/£65

POHL, FREDERIK. The Way the Future Was. London: Gollancz, 1979. 1st UK ed, trade issue. Fine in dj. *Other Worlds*. $20/£13

POHL, FREDERIK. The Way the Future Was. London: Gollancz, 1979. Signed ltd ed of 500 numbered. Paper-covered bds. Fine in dj. *Antic Hay*. $50/£32

POINDEXTER, MILES. The Ayar Incas. NY: Horace Liveright, 1930. 1st ed. 2 vols. Frontis, 63 plts; frontis, 44 plts. Bkpl; else Fine. *Bookpress*. $75/£48

POINT, NICOLAS. Wilderness Kingdom. NY, (1967). 1st ed. Dj. *Heinoldt*. $45/£29

POLAND, E.B. The Friars in Sussex 1228-1928. Hove: Combridges, 1928. 1st ed. 18 plts. Cl-backed bds (sl mkd), gilt. Notes on reps. *Hollett*. $54/£35

POLAND, HENRY. Fur-Bearing Animals in Nature and in Commerce. London, 1892. 1st ed. lvi,392pp, double-pg map. VG. *Oregon*. $95/£61

Poliomyelitis. Balt, 1932. 1st ed. Good. *Fye*. $50/£32

Polite Reasoner in Letters Addressed to a Young Lady....
(By Mary Weightman.) London: W. Bent, 1787. 12mo.
viii,109 + 8pp list + 4pp ads. Full contemp leather on
bds, label on spine; marbled eps. Fine (ink initial verso
fep; lt scuffing cvrs, spine, w/loss of sm portion lower
cvr; a label missing at spine). *Hobbyhorse.* $150/£97

POLITE, C.H. The Flagellants. FSG, 1967. 1st Amer ed,
1st bk. Fine in dj. *Fine Books.* $35/£23

POLITE, CARLENE. The Flagellants. London: Faber & Faber, (1968). 1st Eng ed. Fine in dj (lt chipped). *Heller.*
$45/£29

POLITI, LEO. A Boat for Peppe. NY: Scribner's, 1950.
1st ed. 8vo. Unpaginated. NF in NF dj. *Davidson.*
$110/£71

POLITI, LEO. Pedro, the Angel of Olivera Street. NY:
Scribner's, 1946. 1st ed. 12mo. Blue cl bds. VG in VG
dj. *Davidson.* $125/£81

POLK, RALPH W. The Practice of Printing. Peoria,
(1952). New rev ed. Good. *Veatchs.* $25/£16

POLLAK, OTTO. The Criminality of Women. Phila:
Univ of PA, 1950. 1st ed. Red cl. VG. *Petrilla.* $25/£16

POLLARD, A.W. Facsimiles from Early Printed Books in
the British Museum. London, 1897. 8pp + 36 illus on
32 plts. 1/2 cl (worn, soiled). Internally VG. *Washton.*
$85/£55

POLLARD, ALFRED W. Early Illustrated Books..in the
15th and 16th Centuries. London, 1893. 1st ed.
256pp. Uncut. (Spine faded.) *Argosy.* $45/£29

POLLARD, ALFRED W. and G.R. REDGRAVE (comps).
A Short-Title Catalogue of Books Printed in England,
Scotland, and Ireland.... London: Bibliographical Soc,
1926. (Ex-lib w/stamps, bkpl, #s; margins, feps
browned; upper hinge cracked; joints splitting.) *Edwards.* $116/£75

POLLARD, E. et al. Hedges. London, 1974. 1st ed. 20
plts. Fine in dj. *Henly.* $70/£45

POLLARD, E. et al. Hedges. London, 1974. 1st ed. Dj.
Edwards. $101/£65

POLLARD, EDWARD A. Black Diamonds Gathered in
the Darkey Homes of the South. NY: Pudney &
Russell, 1860. 2nd ed. 155pp. Orig emb brn cl. Lib
bkpl, blindstamp, sm dent, else VG. Howes P 463.
Chapel Hill. $175/£113

POLLARD, EDWARD A. The Lost Cause Regained. NY:
Carleton, 1868. 1st ed. 214,(2)pp. Dec cl. Howes P
456. *Ginsberg.* $100/£65

POLLARD, EDWARD A. The Lost Cause. NY: E.B. Treat,
1866. 1st ed. 752,(4)pp (lt foxing), 24 steel engrs. 1/2
leather w/antique marbled bds (sl rubbed). VG.
Mcgowan. $125/£81

POLLARD, H.B.C. A History of Firearms. London, 1931.
41 plts. VG. *Argosy.* $150/£97

POLLARD, H.B.C. and P. BARCLAY-SMITH. British and
American Game Birds. London, 1945. 20 color plts.
Clean (ex-lib; sm stamps). *Wheldon & Wesley.* $54/£35

POLLARD, HENRY ROBINSON. Memoirs and Sketches
of the Life of Henry Robinson Pollard. Richmond: Lewis Ptg, (1923). 1st ed. Frontis port. Orig red cl. VG + .
Chapel Hill. $50/£32

POLLARD, JAMES E. Journal of Jay Cooke or the Gibraltar Records, 1865-1905. Columbus: OH State Univ,
1935. Map. Cl, gilt-stamped red morocco spine label.
Lt soiled, else VG + . *Bohling.* $65/£42

POLLARD, JOHN. Journey to the Styx. London: Christopher Johnson, (1955). 1st ed. Map. VG in dj. *Schoyer.*
$30/£19

POLLARD, JOSEPHINE. The History of the United
States; Told in One Syllable Words. NY: McLoughlin
Bros, n.d. (ca 1905). 4to. 136pp, 6 full-pg VF chromolithos (incl frontis). Upper cvr ptd in full color, illus, gilt
title (inner hinges sl cracked; lt soiling; dated ink dedication). VG. *Hobbyhorse.* $75/£48

POLLEY, J.B. A Soldier's Letters to Charming Nellie. NY:
Neale, 1908. 1st ed. 8vo. Frontis port; teg. Orig red cl.
VG (lt wear, fr hinge cracked, bkpl removal, ink-
stamp). *Chapel Hill.* $550/£355

POLLOCK, FREDERICK. Essays in Jurisprudence and Ethics. London: Macmillan, 1882. (Ex-lib; worn). *Boswell.*
$85/£55

POLLOCK, WALTER H. et al. Fencing...Boxing...Wres-
tling. Duke of Beaufort (ed). London: Longmans, 1889.
1st ed. The Badminton Library of Sports and Pastimes.
18 intaglio plts, 24 woodcuts by George Mitchell. 3/4
gilt stamped black morocco over orange cl. VG.
Houle. $125/£81

POLLOK, COLONEL. Incidents of Foreign Sport and
Travel. London: Chapman Hall, 1894. 427pp, 10 full-
pg plts. Soiled, o/w VG. *Bowman.* $90/£58

POLO, MARCO. The Travels of Marco Polo. NY: LEC,
1934. #904/1500 numbered sets signed by Nikolai
Fyodorovitch Lapshin (illus). 2 vols. Fine in pub's slipcase (sl rubbed). *Hermitage.* $100/£65

POLUNIN, NICHOLAS. Botany of the Canadian Eastern
Arctic. Part III. Vegetation and Botany. Ottawa, 1948.
107 b/w plts, 2 maps (incl fldg map in pocket). Good
in wrappers (sl chipped). *Brooks.* $24/£15

POMERANZ, HERMAN. Medicine in the Shakespearean
Plays and Dickens' Doctors. NY: Powell Pubs, 1936.
VG-. *Blue Dragon.* $60/£39

POMEROY, JESSE HARDING. Autobiography of Jesse
H. Pomeroy. Boston: J.A. Cummings, c. 1875. 32pp,
sm plan, sm port cvr, pg1. Ptd wraps (worn, corners
creased). *Bohling.* $150/£97

POMEROY, JOHN NORTON. A Treatise on Equity Jurisprudence.... SF: A.L. Bancroft, 1881. 3 vols. Contemp
full sheep (rubbed). *Boswell.* $250/£161

POMFRET, JOHN (ed). California Gold Rush Voyages,
1848-1849. San Marino: Huntington, 1954. 1st ed. 2
maps. VG in Good+ dj. *Oregon.* $45/£29

PONTEY, WILLIAM. The Forest Pruner. For the Author,
(1805). 1st ed. 277pp + 4pp ads (fr pg restored); 8 engr
plts (3 fldg, 3 w/background wash color). 1/2 calf, marbled bds (rebound; new eps). Sl cockling, else VF.
Quest. $225/£145

PONTEY, WILLIAM. The Profitable Planter. Hudders-
field: The Author, 1808. Enlgd 2nd ed. Frontis. Mod
wrappers. (Marginal notes.) *Argosy.* $100/£65

PONTING, HERBERT G. The Great White South. London: Duckworth, (1932). 3rd ed, 10th imp. (Few pp
foxed.) *Petersfield.* $19/£12

PONTING, HERBERT G. The Great White South. London: Duckworth, 1921. 1st ed. VG. *Walcot.* $147/£95

PONTING, HERBERT G. The Great White South. NY:
Robert McBride, 1922. 1st Amer ed. NF. *Blue Dragon.*
$85/£55

PONTING, HERBERT G. In Lotus-Land Japan. London:
Macmillan, 1910. 8 tipped-on color illus. Red cl
(rubbed, scuffed, spine faded), gilt. *Schoyer.* $100/£65

PONTING, KENNETH G. Leonardo da Vinci. Drawings
of Textile Machines. NJ, 1979. 55 plts. Fine in Mint dj.
Europa. $19/£12

PONTING, TOM CANDY. Life of Tom Candy Ponting, an Autobiography. Evanston: Branding Iron Press, 1952. 2nd ed. #478/500. Brn cl-backed pict bds (soiled; spine dulled; corner wear). Internally Fine, overall VG-. Howes P 469. *Harrington.* $40/£26

POOL, MARIA LOUISE. Mrs. Gerald. NY: Harper, 1896. 1st ed. 339pp + ads. Stamped orange cl. VG. *Second Life.* $45/£29

POOLE, DEWITT C. Among the Sioux of Dakota. NY: Van Nostrand, 1881. 1st ed. 235pp. Mod cl. Howes P 470. *Ginsberg.* $350/£226

POOLE, REGINALD LANE. Illustrations of the History of Medieval Thought and Learning. London, 1932. Pub's cl (sl mkd, rubbed). Good. *Peter Taylor.* $29/£19

POOR, HENRY V. Manual of the Railroads of the United States for 1890. NY: H.V. & H.W. Poor, 1890. 146,xvi,1424,61pp + tp, fldg map. Gold-stamped cl. *Dawson.* $125/£81

POORE, HENRY R. The New Tendency in Art: Post Impressionism, Cubism, Futurism. GC: Doubleday, 1913. 1st ed. Frontis. Bds, label sl mkd, o/w VG. *Reese.* $55/£35

POORTENAAR, JAN. The Technique of Prints and Art Reproduction Processes.... London: John Lane, 1933. 1st ed. Errata slip. Linen-backed bds (sl soiled, rubbed). Good. *Cox.* $54/£35

Pop-Up Airport. London: Bancroft, 1963. #509 in series. 13x18 cm. Pict wraps. VG. *Book Finders.* $25/£16

Pop-Up Book of Gnomes. London: Kestrel, 1979. 19x27 cm. 5 pop-ups, wheels, pull-tabs. Glazed pict bds. VG. *Book Finders.* $50/£32

Pop-Up Book of Magic Tricks. NY: Viking, 1983. 20x30 cm. 4 dbl-pg pop-ups. Ron & Atie van der Meer (illus). Glazed pict bds. VG-. *Book Finders.* $28/£18

Pop-Up Book of the American Revolution. NY: Scholastic, n.d. (197?). 14x20 cm. 2 pop-ups, pull tabs, date wheel. Douglas Jamieson (illus). Pict bds (dirt mks). Inside VG. *Book Finders.* $45/£29

Pop-Up Book of the Circus. NY: Random House, 1979, 2nd ptg. 17x23 cm. 4 pop-ups, 4pp pull-tabs. Glazed pict bds. VG. *Book Finders.* $30/£19

Pop-Up Minnie Mouse. NY: Blue Ribbon, 1933. 17x22cm. 3 VG pop-ups. Pict bds (edges worn, age discoloration; mks). *Book Finders.* $400/£258

Pop-Up Picture Nursery Rhymes. London: Juvenile, n.d. (1952). 27x21 cm. 5 pop-ups. Glazed pict wraps. (Spiral binding sl worn.) Internally VG. *Book Finders.* $70/£45

Pop-Up Train Book. London: Purnell, n.d. (195?). 21x25 cm. 4 pull-down panels, 4 dbl-pg pop-ups. Pict bds. (Edge-worn, sm tear one pg, not affecting pop-up.) *Book Finders.* $70/£45

POPE, ALEXANDER. An Essay on Man.... London: John & Paul Knapton, 1745. Contemp sheep (joints cracked; hinges strengthened internally). *Waterfield.* $70/£45

POPE, ALEXANDER. Letters of Mr. Pope and Several Eminent Persons from the Years 1705-1711.... London: Booksellers of London & Westminster, 1735. 2 vols in 1. Contemp panelled calf (rubbed, sl worn; joints cracked; sl waterstaining few leaves). *Waterfield.* $178/£115

POPE, ALEXANDER. Letters of Mr. Pope...from...1705 to 1711.... Booksellers, 1735 (Vol II n.d.). 2 vols in 1. Contemp mottled calf, gilt spine, orig label. (Hinges worn.) *Hill.* $543/£350

POPE, ALEXANDER. The Poetical Works. London: William Pickering, 1852. 3 vols. Port (sl spotted). Uncut in lighter blue fine diaper cl, paper labels. *Cox.* $62/£40

POPE, ARTHUR UPHAM. Persian Architecture. London: Thames & Hudson, 1965. 1st ed. 37 color, 371 b/w plts. Dj. *Edwards.* $62/£40

POPE, BERTHA CLARK (ed). The Letters of Ambrose Bierce. SF: Book Club of CA, 1922. 1st ed. #174/415. Tipped-in frontis port. Black cl-backed marbled bds, leather spine label. VG + (2 bkpls; lt edgewear). BAL 1137. *Harrington.* $120/£77

POPE, DUDLEY. The Black Ship. Phila: Lippincott, 1964. 1st ed. Map. VG in VG dj. *Blue Dragon.* $20/£13

POPE, DUDLEY. Buccaneer. London: Secker & Warburg, 1981. 1st ed. Fine in dj. *Limestone.* $45/£29

POPE, DUDLEY. Governor Ramage R.N. London: Alison Press/Secker & Warburg, 1973. 1st Eng ed. NF (edges spotted) in dj (edges sl rubbed). *Ulysses.* $85/£55

POPE, DUDLEY. The Great Gamble. NY: S&S, (1972). 1st US ptg. 4 maps. VG in VG- dj. *Blue Dragon.* $25/£16

POPE, DUDLEY. Ramage and the Drum Beat. London: Weidenfeld & Nicolson, 1967. 1st ed. NF in dj. *Limestone.* $55/£35

POPE, DUDLEY. Ramage's Diamond. London: Secker & Warburg, 1976. 1st ed. Fine in NF dj. *Limestone.* $45/£29

POPE, DUDLEY. Ramage's Prize. London: Alison Press/Secker & Warburg, 1974. 1st UK ed. Edges sl spotted, spine sl faded, o/w VG in dj (soiled, chipped, foxed, price-clipped). *Virgo.* $70/£45

POPE, MAURICE. The Story of Decipherment from Egyptian Hieroglyphic to Linear B. NY: Scribner's, (1975). (Edges foxed.) *Archaeologia.* $35/£23

POPE, SAXTON. Hunting with the Bow and Arrow. (SF: James H. Barry, 1923). 1st ed. 20 photo plts. Internally VG (extrems sl worn). *Shasky.* $60/£39

POPE-HENNESSY, JAMES. America Is an Atmosphere. London: Home & Van Thal, 1947. 1st Eng ed. Grey cl. Fine in dj (sl nicked). *Dalian.* $31/£20

POPE-HENNESSY, JAMES. The Baths of Absalom. London: Allan Wingate, 1954. 1st Eng ed. Frontis. Grn cl. Eps sl browned, o/w VG in pict dj. *Dalian.* $39/£25

POPE-HENNESSY, JAMES. Sins of the Fathers. London, 1967. 1st ed. 3 maps. Illus eps. Dj (chipped). *Edwards.* $23/£15

POPE-HENNESSY, JAMES. West Indian Summer. London: Batsford, 1943. 1st Eng ed. Grn cl. Sl faded, inscrip, o/w Fine in dj (sl nicked, sl tanned). *Dalian.* $39/£25

POPE-HENNESSY, JOHN. Cellini. NY, 1985. VG in dj. *Argosy.* $75/£48

POPE-HENNESSY, JOHN. The Complete Work of Paolo Uccello. London: Phaidon, 1950. 1st ed. 108 plts, 3 fldg plts (1 color). VF. *Europa.* $70/£45

POPE-HENNESSY, JOHN. Fra Angelico. Ithica: Cornell Univ, (1974). 2nd ed. VG. *Bookpress.* $185/£119

POPE-HENNESSY, JOHN. Fra Angelico. London: Phaidon, 1974. 2nd ed. Dj. *Ars Artis.* $163/£105

POPE-HENNESSY, JOHN. An Introduction to Italian Sculpture. 3 parts in 5 vols. London, 1955-1963. All 4to. (One spine sunned.) *Washton.* $300/£194

POPE-HENNESSY, JOHN. Italian Gothic Sculpture. Phaidon, 1955. 1st ed. 108 plts. Orig buckram. Fine. *Europa.* $50/£32

POPE-HENNESSY, JOHN. Italian Gothic Sculpture. London, 1972. Rev ed. 112 plts. Fep repaired, o/w VG in dj. *Washton.* $150/£97

POPE-HENNESSY, JOHN. Italian High Renaissance and Baroque Sculpture. London: Phaidon, 1963. 3 vols. 168 plts. (Ex-lib w/ink stamps.) Djs (sl soiled, ragged; tape mks). *Edwards.* $93/£60

POPE-HENNESSY, JOHN. Italian Renaissance Sculpture. London, 1958. 144 plts. Spine sl sunned. *Washton.* $95/£61

POPE-HENNESSY, JOHN. Italian Renaissance Sculpture. London: Phaidon, 1971. Rpt. 144 plts. Dj (sl soiled). *Edwards.* $62/£40

POPE-HENNESSY, JOHN. Luca della Robbia. Oxford: Phaidon, 1980. 32 full-pg color illus. Sound in dj, slipcase. *Ars Artis.* $93/£60

POPE-HENNESSY, JOHN. Paolo Uccello. NY/London: Phaidon, (1969). 2nd ed. VG. *Pharos.* $60/£39

POPE-HENNESSY, JOHN. Paolo Uccello. Complete Edition. London: Phaidon, 1969. 2nd ed. VG in dj. *Ars Artis.* $116/£75

POPE-HENNESSY, JOHN. The Portrait in the Renaissance. NY, 1966. Good. *Washton.* $45/£29

POPE-HENNESSY, JOHN. The Portrait in the Renaissance. NY: Pantheon, 1966. 1st ed. VG in dj. *Bookpress.* $85/£55

POPE-HENNESSY, JOHN. Renaissance Bronzes. London: Phaidon, 1965. Dj (tape repaired). *Edwards.* $74/£48

POPE-HENNESSY, JOHN. A Sienese Codex of the Divine Comedy. Oxford/London: Phaidon, 1947. Sm split upper hinge, o/w Fine in dj. *Europa.* $37/£24

POPE-HENNESSY, UNA. Three English Women in America. London: Ernest Benn, 1929. 1st Eng ed. 3 b/w plts. VG (label fep; spine head, tail sl bumped; dent bottom edge fr cvr) in dj (sl rubbed, mkd, nicked; sl dknd spine, tear). *Ulysses.* $85/£55

Popeye and Olive Oyl Pop-Up Book. London: Dean, n.d. (1963). 23x17 cm. 3 dbl-pg pop-ups. Glazed pict bds. (Spine edges sl worn.) Internally VG. *Book Finders.* $40/£26

Popeye with Pop-Up Pictures. London: Purnell, 1960. 24x18 cm. 3 dbl-pg pop-ups. Glazed pict bds. VG. *Book Finders.* $40/£26

POPHAM, A.E. The Drawings of Parmigianino. NY, 1953. 1st Amer ed. VG in dj (torn). *Argosy.* $45/£29

Popular View of the Effects of the Venereal Disease...Collected from the Best Writers. Edinburgh, 1794. 1st ed. 205pp. 1/2 leather. (Ex-lib.) *Fye.* $150/£97

Porcelain from the Frances Oliver Collection. Birmingham, AL: Birmingham Museum of Art, 1980. Good in wrappers. *Washton.* $20/£13

PORCHER, FREDERICK ADOLPHUS. The History of the Santee Canal. Moncks Corner, SC, 1950. 2nd ed. 2 fldg plans. NF in orig ptd wrappers. *Mcgowan.* $30/£19

PORCHER, JEAN. Medieval French Miniatures. NY, 1959. 90 tipped-in color plts. Good. *Washton.* $100/£65

PORTAL, PAUL. The Compleat Practice of Men and Women Midwives. London: J. Johnson, 1763. v,(5),267pp + ads. Orig full calf (spine rubbed, worn). *Goodrich.* $475/£306

PORTER, ARTHUR KINGSLEY. Medieval Architecture, Its Origins and Development. NY/London: Baker & Taylor/Batsford, 1919. Orig ptg. 2 vols. Uncut. Pub's pale grn buckram gilt. VG (lt damp spotting text) in djs (fraying). *Peter Taylor.* $147/£95

PORTER, BRUCE et al. Art in California. SF, 1916. 332 plts. New buckram (ex-lib; tp torn in gutter). Teg. *Argosy.* $500/£323

PORTER, DAVID. A Voyage in the South Seas, in the Years 1812, 1813, and 1814. London, 1823. 1st British ed, abridged. 126pp, 3 plts, fldg map. Later 3/4 calf, leather label. VG. Howes P 484. *Reese.* $850/£548

PORTER, ELIOT. Antarctica. NY: E.P. Dutton 1978. 1st ed. 158 maps and plts. VG+ in dj (lt worn). *Parmer.* $125/£81

PORTER, ELIOT. Down the Colorado, John Wesley Powell Diary of the First Trip Through the Grand Canyon. Dutton, 1969. 1st ed. Fine in VG dj. *Oregon.* $65/£42

PORTER, ELIOT. Galapagos. SF: Sierra Club, (1968). 1st ed. 2 vols. VG in dj (frayed) & slipcase. *King.* $195/£126

PORTER, HORACE. Campaigning with Grant. NY: Century, 1897. 1st ed. Blue dec cl, gilt. Nice. *Appelfeld.* $60/£39

PORTER, HORACE. Campaigning with Grant. NY: The Century Co, 1897. 1st ed. xviii,546pp. Recased w/orig spine laid down. VG. *Mcgowan.* $85/£55

PORTER, J.L. The Giant Cities of Bashan; And Syria's Holy Places. London, 1865. 1st ed. v,371pp; 6 plts. Contemp 1/2 calf (spine repaired; ex-lib). *Lewis.* $59/£38

PORTER, J.L. The Giant Cities of Bashan; And Syria's Holy Places. London: T. Nelson, 1869. Frontis, v,371pp, 6 plts. 3/4 calf (rubbed), 5 raised bands, leather label. (Lt foxing.) *Archaeologia.* $85/£55

PORTER, JANE. The Scottish Chiefs. London: Hodder & Stoughton, 1921. 1st Eng ed. 4to. 14 full-pg color plts by N.C. Wyeth. Illus red cl, black lettering (2 sm nicks). Fr picture section of dj laid in. *Reisler.* $125/£81

PORTER, JANE. Sir Edward Seaward's Narrative of His Shipwreck. London: Routledge, n.d. (1879). 1st illus ed. Frontis, xxiv,607pp; 8 plts. Leather, red label, gilt. Contents Fine (prize bkpl; edges worn; fr hinge cracked). *Connolly.* $50/£32

PORTER, JOHN W.H. Record of Events in Norfolk County, Virginia, from April 19th, 1861, to May 10th, 1862. Portsmouth, VA: W.A. Fiske, 1892. 1st ed. 366pp + (6)pp ads. Orig purple cl. VG (rear hinge starting). *Chapel Hill.* $300/£194

PORTER, KATHERINE ANNE. French Song-Book. (Paris/NY): Harrison of Paris, (1933). One of 595 numbered, signed. Orig prospectus laid in. Fine in NF dj (sm tear; early mend verso; sm spots rear panel). *Reese.* $300/£194

PORTER, KATHERINE ANNE. Hacienda. (NY): Harrison of Paris, (1934). 1st ed, late state of pp51/52 (a cancel w/error corrected), as usual. One of 895 numbered. Lt spotting first 2 blanks, o/w VF in slipcase. *Reese.* $75/£48

PORTER, KATHERINE ANNE. Hacienda. A Story of Mexico. Paris: Harrison, (1934). 1st ed. Ltd to 895. Teg. Erratum present. NF. *Sadlon.* $45/£29

PORTER, KATHERINE ANNE. Hacienda. A Story of Mexico. Paris: Harrison, 1934. #517/895. Author's signature laid in. W/p52 corrected, tipped in. Fine in Fine box. *Polyanthos.* $75/£48

PORTER, KATHERINE ANNE. The Leaning Tower and Other Stories. London: Jonathan Cape, 1945. 1st Eng ed. Brn cl. Fine in dj. *Dalian.* $39/£25

PORTER, KATHERINE ANNE. The Never-Ending Wrong. Boston: Little Brown, 1977. 1st ed. Fine in Fine dj. *Revere.* $30/£19

PORTER, KATHERINE ANNE. The Never-Ending Wrong. London: Secker & Warburg, 1977. 1st Eng ed. Fine in Fine dj. *Revere.* $25/£16

PORTER, KATHERINE ANNE. Ship of Fools. Boston: Atlantic/Little, Brown, 1962. 1st ed. Fine in Fine dj (short tear). *Beasley.* $50/£32

PORTER, WILLIAM DENNISON. State Sovereignty and the Doctrine of Coercion...Together With a Letter from Hon. J.K. Paulding.... (Charleston, SC: Evans & Cogswell, 1860). 1st ed. 36pp. Orig ptd wrappers in later protective cvrs w/cl backstrip. VG. *Mcgowan.* $45/£29

PORTERFIELD, BILL. A Loose Herd of Texans. College Station: Texas A&M, (1978). 1st ed. Rev slip laid in. Fine in VG dj (lt used). *Reese.* $25/£16

PORTERFIELD, WILLIAM HEMPSTEAD. An Adventure in Pyramids. NY: Albert & Charles Boni, 1928. 1st ed. VG in red/black dj (sl chipped). *Connolly.* $35/£23

PORTIS, CHARLES. The Dog of the South. NY: Knopf, 1979. 1st ed. Tan cl-backed bds titled in grn. Very Nice. *Cady.* $15/£10

PORTOGHESI, PAOLO. The Rome of Borromini. NY, 1968. VG in dj. *Washton.* $150/£97

PORTOGHESI, PAOLO. Rome of the Renaissance. London, 1972. (Sm tear one plt.) Dj. *Washton.* $90/£58

Portraits of Children of the Mobility. (By Percival Leigh.) London: Richard Bentley, 1841. 1st ed. Folio. 47pp, engr armorial vignette tp, 8 full-pg lithos by J. Leech (illus), numbered and incl frontis, each representing group of children, all ptd on one side of leaf only; impt at lower edge dated Feb. 1, 1841. 1/2 sheep w/corners, brown sand grain on bds, gilt title (edges worn; line crack along spine). Internally Fine. *Hobbyhorse.* $250/£161

POSNER, KATHLEEN WEIL GARRIS. Leonardo and Central Italian Art: 1515-1550. NY, 1974. Good. *Washton.* $45/£29

POST, ALBERT. Popular Freethought in America, 1825-1850. NY: Columbia Univ, 1943. 1st ed. Grn gilt cl. Good. *Karmiole.* $30/£19

POST, LOUIS F. The Deportations Delirium of Nineteen-Twenty. Chicago: Charles H. Kerr, (1923). Port. VG. *Schoyer.* $45/£29

POST, MELVILLE DAVISSON. The Revolt of the Birds. Appleton, 1927. 1st ed. Fine in dj (sl frayed). *Madle.* $45/£29

POTOCKI OF MONTALK, COUNT. Snobbery With Violence. A Poet in Gaol. Wishart, Here & Now Pamphlet #10, 1932. Stiff card wrappers. Nice in dj. *Patterson.* $39/£25

POTOCKI OF MONTALK, COUNT. The Whirling River. Melissa Press, 1964. 1st ed. Signed, inscribed. NF. *Poetry.* $19/£12

POTOK, CHAIM. The Promise. NY: Knopf, 1969. 1st ed. NF in NF dj (short closed tear). *Sadlon.* $20/£13

POTT, PERCIVALL. The Chirurgical Works. London: Hawes, W. Clark, & R. Collins, 1775. 1/2 title, (3),802pp, 12 engr plts. Full contemp calf (rebacked). Worn, o/w Nice. *Goodrich.* $1,975/£1,274

POTT, PERCIVALL. Some Few General Remarks on Fractures and Dislocations. London: L. Hawes, 1769. (2),126pp, 2 engr plts. Recent 1/4 calf, marble bds. Overall pleasing (sl browned, foxed). *Goodrich.* $1,500/£968

POTTENGER, FRANCIS. Tuberculin in Diagnosis and Treatment. St. Louis, 1913. 1st ed. Good. *Fye.* $50/£32

POTTER, BEATRIX. Cecily Parsley's Nursery Rhymes. London: Frederick J. Warne, (1922). 1st ed. Bright red bds, white lettering, color paste label; silver spine lettering (sl faded). Fine; remains of orig glassine dj present. *Reisler.* $1,250/£806

POTTER, BEATRIX. Ginger and Pickles. London: Frederick Warne, 1909. 1st ed. Orig bds (sm chip spine; sl rubbed, shaken; sl mks); pict onlay. Good (short nick 1 leaf). *Ash.* $302/£195

POTTER, BEATRIX. Ginger and Pickles. London: Frederick Warne, 1909. 1st ed. 12mo. Lt brn bds, grn lettering, color paste label. (Lt faded areas, lt worn; fingermarks, sm fold in margin.) *Reisler.* $485/£313

POTTER, BEATRIX. The Jemima Puddle Duck Pop-Up Book. England: Warne, 1985. 20x28 cm. 3 dbl-pg, 2 single pop-ups, pull-tabs. Colin Twinn (illus). Glazed pict bds. VG-. *Book Finders.* $45/£29

POTTER, BEATRIX. Peter Rabbit's Painting Book. London: Frederick Warne, (1911). 1st ed. 8vo. 12 pairs of plts (unpainted plts painted in). Limp cl-cvrd bds, color illus (rubbed, worn, spine chipped). *Reisler.* $275/£177

POTTER, BEATRIX. The Pie and the Patty Pan. London: F. Warne, n.d. (c. 1910). Frontis; 9 color illus. Maroon bds (neatly rebacked; short marginal tear repaired). *Cox.* $28/£18

POTTER, BEATRIX. The Story of Miss Moppet. London: Frederick Warne, (1916). 1st ed in bk form. Lacks period on pg 44. 24mo. Grey bds, grn lettering, color paste label. Good in glassine dj. *Reisler.* $2,000/£1,290

POTTER, BEATRIX. The Tailor of Gloucester. London: Frederick Warne, 1903. 1st ed, 1st issue. 27 color plts. Pict eps. Color plt laid down fr cvr. VG (inner fr hinges repaired; tape repair pp 63-64). *Limestone.* $400/£258

POTTER, BEATRIX. The Tailor of Gloucester. London/NY: Federick Warne, 1903. 1st ed, 1st issue. Deluxe version w/fabric cvr instead of the bds w/colored picture. This 1st issue has only one design for eps repeated 3 times. Sq 12mo. 85pp; 27 color illus. Patterned fabric cvr, gilt title, (rebacked), orig spine cl. (Cvr edges sl faded, soiled.) *Bickersteth.* $1,023/£660

POTTER, BEATRIX. The Tale of Jemima Puddle-Duck. London, 1908. 1st ed. 16mo. Grn bds, color print fr cvr. (Contemp inscrip; backstrip sl discolored.) *Petersfield.* $248/£160

POTTER, BEATRIX. The Tale of Johnny Town-Mouse. London: Frederick Warne, (1918). 1st ed, 1st issue w/letter n missing from London on tp. 16mo. Brn bds, white lettering, color paste label set in blind-stamped frame. Sm mk rear cvr, o/w Very Nice. *Reisler.* $1,250/£806

POTTER, BEATRIX. The Tale of Mr. Tod. NY, (1912). 5.5x4 inches. 94pp; 15 full-pg plts. Bds w/color pict label. (Sl bumped; spotted; sl stained, worn.) *King.* $35/£23

POTTER, BEATRIX. The Tale of Mr. Tod. London: Frederick Warne, 1912. 1st ed. 24mo. Eps w/animals posting ad for series of Peter Rabbit bks, w/Tale of Mr. Tod as next title released. Grey bds, pict paste label, dk grn lettering, spine dec. Clean, tight (sl foxed; one pg smudged). *Reisler.* $650/£419

POTTER, BEATRIX. The Tale of Pigling Bland. London: Frederick Warne, 1913. 1st ed. 16mo. Eps incl descriptive banner of bks in series w/this title listed last; has rounded spine rather than earlier flat spines; is sl larger as well. Blue-grn bds w/brn lettering, color paste label. Clean. *Reisler.* $650/£419

POTTER, BEATRIX. The Tale of Squirrel Nutkin. Frederick Warne, 1903. 1st ed. Sm sq 8vo. Frontis (upper edge sl soiled), (86)pp; 27 color illus. Grey bds, white lettering; pict upper cvr (rebacked, preserving part of orig spine). *Bickersteth.* $124/£80

POTTER, BEATRIX. The Tale of the Flopsy Bunnies. London: Frederick Warne, 1909. 1st ed. Color pict eps. 27 color illus. Color plt laid down fr cover. Very Nice (sig). *Limestone.* $225/£145

POTTER, BEATRIX. The Tale of Tom Kitten. London: Frederick Warne, 1907. 1st ed. Orig bds (sl rubbed, sl scrape), pict onlay. Good (fep cracked; sl mks). *Ash.* $302/£195

POTTER, BEATRIX. The Tale of Tom Kitten. London: F. Warne, 1907. 1st ed. 12mo. Color frontis. Skillfully rebacked in 1/2 brn morocco over orig brn bds, color pict label. VG. *Houle.* $650/£419

POTTER, DENNIS. The Changing Forest. London: Secker, 1962. 1st UK ed. VG in dec bds as issued (sl spine damage). *Williams.* $74/£48

POTTER, DENNIS. Hide and Seek. London: Quartet, 1973. 1st UK ed. Fine card cvrs in dj. *Williams.* $19/£12

POTTER, DENNIS. Waiting for the Boat. London: Faber, 1984. 1st ed. Pb orig. NF. *Rees.* $19/£12

POTTER, DONALD. My Time with Eric Gill: A Memoir. London: Walter Ritchie, 1980. 1st ed. 'Limited to 500 copies' (actually 400, of which 89 are sl imperfectly stitched; tipped-in slip to this effect). Orig cl. Fine. *Cox.* $23/£15

POTTER, ELISHA REYNOLDS, JR. Early History of Narragansett. Providence, RI: Hist Soc, 1835. xx,315pp. (Fraying; stain lower corner.) Howes P 510. *Bohling.* $65/£42

POTTER, JACK. Cattle Trails of the Old West. Clayton, NM: Laura R. Krehbiel, (1939). 2nd ed. Inscribed. Lg fldg map. Pict wrappers (bkpl; sm # corner fr wrapper). *Dawson.* $50/£32

POTTER, NATHANIEL. A Memoir on Contagion, More Especially as it Respects the Yellow Fever. Balt, 1818. 1st ed. 117pp. Later buckram. Good. *Fye.* $200/£129

POTTER, STEPHEN and LAURENS SARGENT. Pedigree. London, 1973. 1st ed. Dj. *Edwards.* $155/£100

POTTER, STEPHEN. Potter on America. London: Rupert Hart-Davis, 1956. 1st ed. Red bds, silver-blocked. Fine in dj (sl frayed). *Temple.* $14/£9

POTTER, STEPHEN. Potter on America. London: Hart-Davis, 1956. 1st ed. Sl shelfworn, else VG in dj. *Limestone.* $40/£26

POTTIER, EDMOND. Douris and the Painters of Greek Vases. Bettina Kahnweiler (trans). NY, 1916. (Sl worn, spine bumped; margins lt browned.) *Edwards.* $31/£20

POTTINGER, DAVID T. The French Book Trade in the Ancien Regime, 1500-1791. Cambridge: Harvard Univ Press, 1958. 1st ed. Fine in dj (lt chipped). *Bookpress.* $110/£71

POTTLE, FREDERICK A. Boswell and the Girl from Botany Bay. NY: Viking, 1937. 1st ed. One of 500 numbered. Cl, dec bds. Eps foxed, gutters tanned, o/w VG (lacks slipcase). *Reese.* $45/£29

POTTLE, FREDERICK A. James Boswell, the Early Years 1740-1769. London: Heinemann, (1966). 1st ed. Fine in NF dj (edgetears). *Reese.* $40/£26

POTTLE, FREDERICK A. Pride and Negligence, the History of the Boswell Papers. NY: McGraw-Hill, 1982. 1st ed. Linen spine, silver, grey bds. Near Mint in dj. *Hartfield.* $85/£55

POTTLE, FREDERICK A. (ed). Boswell in Holland, 1763-1764. London: Heinemann, 1952. Ltd to 1050. 14 plts (incl fldg map). News article mtd to rear paste-down. Teg. Good. *Karmiole.* $75/£48

POTTLE, FREDERICK A. (ed). Boswell on the Grand Tour: Germany and Switzerland, 1764. London: Heinemann, 1953. Ltd to 1000. 15 plts, 2 maps (1 fldg). Teg. Good. *Karmiole.* $75/£48

POTTLE, FREDERICK A. et al. Index to the Private Papers of James Boswell.... London/NY: OUP, 1937. 1st ed. One of 1250 ptd. Unopened. Spine sl faded, o/w NF (lacks slipcase). *Reese.* $125/£81

POUCHER, W.A. The Backbone of England. London: Country Life, 1946. 1st ed. VG in dj (edges sl worn, chipped). *Hollett.* $47/£30

POUCHER, W.A. The Magic of Skye. London: Chapman & Hall, 1949. *Petersfield.* $33/£21

POUCHER, W.A. The Magic of the Dolomites. London: Country Life, 1951. 1st ed. VG in dj (sl spotted; price-clipped). *Hollett.* $70/£45

POUCHER, W.A. The North-Western Highlands. London: Country Life, (1954). Dj (torn). *Petersfield.* $25/£16

POULIK, JOSEF. Prehistoric Art. R. Finlayson Samsour (trans). London: Spring Books, n.d. 22 color plts. Pict cl (corners worn). *Argosy.* $50/£32

POULSEN, FREDERIK. Greek and Roman Portraits in English Country Houses. Oxford: Clarendon, 1923. 112 plts. Gilt-emb cl. Sm tears spine, sl shelfwear, o/w Fine. *Archaeologia.* $350/£226

POULSON, THEODORE FREDERICK. The Flying Wig: ...A Horrifying Tale. Honolulu: Abel Skiff, 1948. 1st ed. One of 500. Fine in illus dj (lt chipped). *Cahan.* $45/£29

POUND, EZRA. ABC of Reading. London: Routledge, 1934. 1st issue in rough red cl. Fore-edge sl foxed, o/w VF in dj (sl mkd). *Dalian.* $233/£150

POUND, EZRA. Canzoni. London: Elkin Mathews, 1911. 1st ed, 2nd issue binding, w/o author's name on spine. Brn bds. VG (bkpl; spine edges splitting). *Chapel Hill.* $400/£258

POUND, EZRA. The Classic Anthology Defined by Confucius. Cambridge: Harvard Univ, 1954. 1st Amer ed. Sl sunned. *Polyanthos.* $45/£29

POUND, EZRA. Collected Shorter Poems. London, 1968. 2nd ed. NF (name, address) in NF dj. *Polyanthos.* $25/£16

POUND, EZRA. Collected Shorter Poems. London: Faber & Faber, 1968. 2nd ed. Purple cl. VF in Fine dj. *Dalian.* $54/£35

POUND, EZRA. A Draft of XXX Cantos. London: Faber & Faber, (1933). 1st Eng ed, w/ Pound's 'latest corrections.' Text lt foxed, else VG in dj (spine faded, short tear, else VG). *Godot.* $250/£161

POUND, EZRA. Drafts and Fragments of Cantos CX-CXVII. NY: New Directions, (1968). 1st Amer ed. NF in dj (price-clipped). *Polyanthos.* $30/£19

POUND, EZRA. Gaudier-Brzeska; a Memoir. Marvell Press, 1960. New (and enlgd) ed. Fine in dj. *Sclanders.* $39/£25

POUND, EZRA. Guide to Kulchur. New Directions, n.d. (1952). New ed, review copy. VG in dj. *Argosy.* $50/£32

POUND, EZRA. The Letters of Ezra Pound 1907-1941. D.D. Paige (ed). NY: Harcourt, Brace, (1950). 1st ed. Fine in dj. *Hermitage.* $45/£29

POUND, EZRA. A Lume Spento and Other Early Poems. NY: New Directions, (1965). 1st US ed, 1st bk. Fine (top edges lt foxed; sl rubbed) in glassine (lt rubbed) as issued. *Aka.* $50/£32

POUND, EZRA. A Lume Spento and Other Early Poems. NY: New Directions, 1965. 1st Amer ed. W/descriptive label set into back cvr; one of earliest copies. Fine in orig acetate dj (spine heels lacks 1/2-inch). *Polyanthos.* $60/£39

POUND, EZRA. Lustra of Ezra Pound with Earlier Poems. NY: Knopf, 1917. 1st Amer trade ed. Yellow bds. Sig, label; eps lt foxed, few leaves roughly opened, else NF in VG ptd peach dj (tape repair verso). *Chapel Hill.* $850/£548

POUND, EZRA. Personae. London, (1952). 1st Eng ed. Good in dj (spine dknd; sl dusty). *Waterfield.* $54/£35

POUND, EZRA. Personae. London: Elkin Mathews, 1909. 1st ed. 12mo. Drab brn-grey bds (spine rubbed; outer joints starting to split). VG. *Chapel Hill.* $600/£387

POUND, EZRA. Poems 1918-21. NY: Boni & Liveright, (1921). 1st ed. Initials; cvrs soiled, aged; lacks dj, else VG. *Pharos.* $125/£81

POUND, EZRA. Selected Poems. T.S. Eliot (ed). Faber & Gwyer, (1928). 1st ed. (Ink name; sm area spine head, foot faded.) Dj (lacks upper 1/2 backstrip; upper joint slit). *Bickersteth.* $74/£48

POUND, EZRA. Selected Poems. T.S. Eliot (ed). London: Faber & Faber, 1948. Reissue. Grn cl. Sl spotted, prelims sl foxed, o/w Fine in dj (badly tanned, sl chipped). *Dalian.* $70/£45

POUND, EZRA. A Selection of Poems. London: Faber & Faber, 1940. 1st Eng ed. Pale blue paper bds. Eps sl browned, o/w VF in dj (sl sunned, sl dusty). *Dalian.* $54/£35

POUND, EZRA. Ta Hio. London: Stanley Nott, 1936. 1st Eng ed. Yellow ptd paper bds. Sl mkd, o/w VG. *Dalian.* $70/£45

POUND, EZRA. Thrones 96-109 de Los Cantares. NY: New Directions, (1959). 1st Amer ed. Erratum slip present. NF in dj (sl sunned, chipped). *Polyanthos.* $75/£48

POUND, EZRA. The Translations of Ezra Pound. London: Faber, 1953. 1st ed. VG (inscrip) in dj (sl mkd, sunned). *Rees.* $39/£25

POUND, EZRA. Umbra. London: Elkin Mathews, 1920. 1st ed. One of 1000. Orig photo of Pound laid in. Orig grey bds w/beige cl spine. VG (sig; clean tear across pp. 59-62). *Chapel Hill.* $350/£226

POUND, EZRA. Women of Trachis. A Version. London, 1956. 1st ed. Frontis port. Fine (inscrip) in dj (2 sm tears, sl rubbed). *Polyanthos.* $50/£32

POUNTNEY, W.J. Old Bristol Potteries. Bristol, 1920. Color frontis, 55 plts, fldg map. (Lt spotted lower bd; spine sl chipped, lt wear; feps lt browned.) *Edwards.* $132/£85

POURADE, RICHARD F. Time of the Bells. Volume Two. The History of San Diego. San Diego: Union-Tribune, 1961. 'Special Edition' signed by author and James S. Copley. Fldg map. Tan cl (spine faded). Slipcase (soiled). *Parmer.* $62/£40

POWELL, A. VAN BUREN. Mystery of the 15 Souls. Goldsmith, 1938. 1st ed. Fine in dj. *Madle.* $30/£19

POWELL, AARON MACY. Personal Reminiscences of the Anti-Slavery and Other Reforms and Reformers. NY, 1899. 1st ed. Inscribed by pub. xxx,279pp. Orig cl. Fine. *Mcgowan.* $165/£106

POWELL, ADAM CLAYTON. Keep the Faith, Baby! NY, 1967. 1st ed. VG + in VG dj (edgeworn, nicked). *Fuller & Saunders.* $25/£16

POWELL, ADAM CLAYTON. Marching Blacks. NY, 1945. 1st Amer ed. 1st bk. VG in dj (edge sl rubbed). *Polyanthos.* $30/£19

POWELL, ANTHONY. At Lady Molly's. L-B, 1957. 1st Amer ed. NF in VG dj. *Fine Books.* $50/£32

POWELL, ANTHONY. At Lady Molly's. London: Heinemann, 1957. 1st UK ed. NF in VG + dj (short closed tear repaired to rear). *Williams.* $74/£48

POWELL, ANTHONY. A Buyer's Market. NY: Scribner's, 1953. 1st Amer ed. Red cl. Ink name, date; sm spot fr cvr, else VG in dj (spine lt faded, 1/2-inch chip lower spine, nicks, long closed tear mended w/archival tape, else VG). *Godot.* $85/£55

POWELL, ANTHONY. A Buyer's Market. Scribners, 1953. 1st ed. (Amer issue w/tipped-in tp but Eng sheets & dw). Lt stain, sl soil to spine, else VG in VG + dj. *Fine Books.* $85/£55

POWELL, ANTHONY. Casanova's Chinese Restaurant. London: Heinemann, (1960). 1st ed. Name, else Fine in dj. *Godot.* $75/£48

POWELL, ANTHONY. Casanova's Chinese Restaurant. London: Heinemann, 1960. 1st ed. Nice in dj (sl rubbed). *Patterson.* $78/£50

POWELL, ANTHONY. Casanova's Chinese Restaurant. London: Heinemann, 1960. 1st UK ed. VG in dj. *Williams.* $85/£55

POWELL, ANTHONY. The Fisher King. NY: Norton, (1986). 1st Amer ed. Fine in dj. *Dermont.* $20/£13

POWELL, ANTHONY. The Fisher King. London: Heinemann, 1986. 1st ed. Fine in dj. *Rees.* $16/£10

POWELL, ANTHONY. Hearing Secret Harmonies. London: Heinemann, 1975. 1st UK ed. Fine in dj. *Williams.* $43/£28

POWELL, ANTHONY. The Kindly Ones. London: Heinemann, 1962. 1st ed. VF in dj (price-clipped). *Else Fine.* $125/£81

POWELL, ANTHONY. The Military Philosophers. Boston: Little-Brown, 1968. 1st ed. Fine in dj (minor rubs spine ends). *Else Fine.* $45/£29

POWELL, ANTHONY. The Military Philosophers. London: Heinemann, 1968. 1st UK ed. NF in dj. *Williams.* $47/£30

POWELL, ANTHONY. A Question of Upbringing. Heinemann, 1951. 1st UK ed. NF (sl edge-foxing) in VG dj (sl browned; sl spine wear). *Williams.* $457/£295

POWELL, ANTHONY. The Soldier's Art. London: Heinemann, 1966. 1st ed. Fine in dj. *Else Fine.* $75/£48

POWELL, ANTHONY. The Soldier's Art. London: Heinemann, 1966. 1st UK ed. Fine in dj (price-clipped). *Williams.* $47/£30

POWELL, ANTHONY. Temporary Kings. London: Heinemann, 1973. 1st UK ed. Fine in dj. *Williams.* $47/£30

POWELL, ANTHONY. To Keep the Ball Rolling, the Memoirs of Anthony Powell, Volume Two, Messengers of Day. London: Heinemann, (1978). 1st ed. Fine in dj. *Oak Knoll.* $30/£19

POWELL, ANTHONY. To Keep the Ball Rolling. London, 1976/1978/1980/1982. 1st eds. 4 vols. Fine in djs. *Polyanthos.* $100/£65

POWELL, ANTHONY. The Valley of Bones. London: Heinemann, 1964. 1st ed. Scuff, o/w VG in VG dj (sl rubbed; price-clipped). *Virgo.* $101/£65

POWELL, ANTHONY. The Valley of Bones. Heinemann, 1964. 1st UK ed. VG in dj. *Lewton.* $60/£39

POWELL, DILYS. An Affair of the Heart. London: Hodder & Stoughton, 1957. 1st Eng ed. Brn cl. Fine in dj (sl nicked, sl rubbed). *Dalian.* $39/£25

POWELL, DILYS. Remembering Greece. London: Hodder & Stoughton, 1941. 1st Eng ed. Blue cl. Eps sl foxed, o/w Fine in dj (sl nicked). *Dalian.* $54/£35

POWELL, E. ALEXANDER. The End of the Trail. NY, 1914. 1st ed. Fldg map. Pict cl. Hinge cracked, o/w NF. *Baade.* $35/£23

POWELL, E.P. Hedges, Windbreaks, Shelters and Live Fences. NY: OJ, 1902. Grn cl, gilt title. VG (sl warped). *Bohling.* $20/£13

POWELL, H.M.T. The Santa Fe Trail to California, 1849-1852. Douglas S. Watson (ed). SF: Book Club of CA, (1931). Ltd to 300. Fldg frontis, 2 fldg color maps, 15 full-pg dwgs. Tan morocco backstrip, tan cl. VF (bkpl) in brn cl slipcase, calf tips. Howes P 525. *Karmiole.* $2,250/£1,452

POWELL, HARRY J. Glass-Making in England. London: CUP, 1923. Frontis, map. (Lower edges of leaves water-stained; many pp stuck together or torn, chipped where parted.) Teg, rest uncut. (Eps lt spotted; lt faded.) Remains of dj, newspaper clippings tipped-in. *Edwards.* $93/£60

POWELL, J.W. Eleventh Annual Report of the United States Geological Survey.... Washington: GPO, 1891. 2 vols. (2),xvi,758; xiv,396pp. 96 plts incl 6 fldg charts and maps (1 in rear pocket vol 1). Purple cl, dec gilt. Good. *Karmiole.* $125/£81

POWELL, J.W. Exploration of the Colorado River of the West and Its Tributaries. Washington: GPO, 1875. Variant ptg issued w/o 2 fldg maps. xi,291pp, 72 plts. Orig blue cl. VG. Howes 528. *Schoyer.* $200/£129

POWELL, J.W. Tenth Annual Report of the United States Geological Survey.... Washington: GPO, 1890. 2 vols. (2),xvi,774; viii,124pp. 98 plts incl 2 fldg maps (1 in rear pocket). Purple cl, gilt dec (sl rubbed, soiled). *Karmiole.* $100/£65

POWELL, J.W. Twelfth Annual Report of the United States Geological Survey.... Washington: GPO, 1891. 2 vols. (2),xvi,676; xviii,576pp. 146 plts (incl 1 fldg in rear pocket vol 2). Purple cl, dec gilt (sl rubbed; old waterstain lower margin vol 1). *Karmiole.* $75/£48

POWELL, JACOB W. Thrilling Moments on Palestine Tour. Malden, MA, 1937. 1st ed. 42 plts. VG. *Worldwide.* $16/£10

POWELL, JOHN. Bring Out Your Dead. Phila, 1949. 1st ed. Good. *Fye.* $40/£26

POWELL, LAWRENCE CLARK and W.W. ROBINSON. The Malibu. L.A.: Dawson's Book Shop, 1958. One of 320. Signed by both authors, Irene Robinson (illus), and Saul and Lillian Marks (printers). Fldg color map (corner creased, not affecting ptd area). Dec bds, cl spine, (sl wear; nick), paper spine label. *Dawson.* $500/£323

POWELL, LAWRENCE CLARK. Books in My Baggage. Cleveland: World Pub Co, (1960). 1st ed. Blind, gold-stamped cl. Dj (spots, sm chips; price-clipped). *Dawson.* $35/£23

POWELL, LAWRENCE CLARK. California Classics. L.A.: Ward Ritchie, (1971). 1st ed. Dj (price-clipped). *Dawson.* $50/£32

POWELL, LAWRENCE CLARK. Heart of the Southwest. L.A.: Ptd for Dawson's Book Shop, 1955. Fldg map. Ptd bds, cl spine. *Dawson.* $175/£113

POWELL, LAWRENCE CLARK. Land of Fiction. L.A.: Glen Dawson, 1952. One of 325. (Bkpl.) *Dawson.* $50/£32

POWELL, LAWRENCE CLARK. Make Mine a Small One. Berkeley: Peacock Press, 1965. 1st separate ptg. Fine in paper wrappers. *Oak Knoll.* $15/£10

POWELL, LAWRENCE CLARK. A Passion for Books. Cleveland: World Pub Co, (1958). 1st ed. Blind, gold-stamped cl (3 spots; bkpl). Dj (worn). *Dawson.* $30/£19

POWELL, LAWRENCE CLARK. A Passion for Books. Cleveland: World Pub Co, (1958). 1st ed. One of 975. Marbled bds, cl spine. Glassine dj, slipcase. *Dawson.* $75/£48

POWELL, LAWRENCE CLARK. A Passion for Books. London: Constable, (1959). 1st British ed. Signed. Dj (price-clipped; 2 short tears). *Dawson.* $40/£26

POWELL, LAWRENCE CLARK. A Southwestern Century. Van Nuys: J.E. Reynolds, (1958). One of 500 ptd. Signed. Tom Lea (illus). Ptd bds, cl spine. Dj (taped cut). *Dawson.* $200/£129

POWELL, NETTIE. History of Marion County Georgia. Columbus, GA: Historical Pub Co, (1931). 1st ed. Fine. *Mcgowan.* $85/£55

POWELL, NICOLAS. The Drawings of Henry Fuseli. London: Faber, 1951. 64 plts. Interior Fine (spine faded, sm mk fr cvr). *Europa.* $43/£28

POWELL, NICOLAS. From Baroque to Rococo. London: Faber & Faber, 1959. 4 color plts, 2 maps, 9 plans. (Feps lt browned.) Dj (chipped, browned). *Edwards.* $47/£30

POWELL, PADGETT. Edisto. NY: Farrar, (1984). 1st ed, 1st bk. Fine in dj. *Reese.* $25/£16

POWELL, PADGETT. A Woman Named Drown. NY: Farrar, (1987). 1st ed. Fine in dj. *Reese.* $20/£13

POWELL, PHILIP WAYNE. Soldiers, Indians and Silver. Berkeley, 1952. 1st ed. Dec cl. Fine (sig, date) in dj. *Baade.* $47/£30

Power of Religion on the Mind.... (By Lindley Murray.) Trenton: Isaac Collins, 1795. 7th ed. 8vo. viii + 220pp. (Ink sig; lt spotting.) Full leather on bds (scuffed, rubbed, bumped), gilt title label on spine (chipped). Good. *Hobbyhorse.* $150/£97

POWER, D'ARCY (comp). Portraits of Dr. William Harvey. Oxford, 1913. 20 plts. (Bds worn.) *Goodrich.* $135/£87

POWER, D'ARCY. Selected Writings. Oxford, 1931. Fine frontis; 16 plts; fldg map. VG. *Whitehart.* $54/£35

POWER, D'ARCY. A Short History of St. Bartholomew's Hospital 1123-1923. London, 1923. 34 plts. 2-tone cl. (Bkpl.) *Edwards.* $39/£25

POWER, RICHARD. The Hungry Grass. NY: Dial, 1969. 1st Amer ed. Fine in VG dj (sm scraped hole rear panel; spine sl faded; rubbed). *Between The Covers.* $75/£48

POWERS, ALFRED. Early Printing in the Oregon Country. Portland Club of Printing House Craftsmen, (1933). One of 500. Fine. *Veatchs.* $35/£23

POWERS, ALFRED. History of Oregon Literature. Metropolitan Press, 1935. 1st ed. Fine in Nice dj (chipped). *Authors Of The West.* $125/£81

POWERS, J.F. Morte D'Urban. GC: Doubleday, 1962. 1st ed. NF in dj (sl dknd spine). *Bernard.* $40/£26

POWERS, J.F. Morte d'Urban. GC: Doubleday, 1962. 1st ed. Fine in NF dj (nicks). *Reese.* $50/£32

POWERS, J.F. The Prescence of Grace. London: Gollancz, 1956. 1st Eng ed. Brn cl. VF in dj (sl dusty). *Dalian.* $39/£25

POWERS, RICHARD. The Gold Bug Variations. NY: William Morrow, (1991). 1st ed. Fine in dj. *Godot.* $85/£55

POWERS, RICHARD. The Gold Bug Variations. NY: Wm. Morrow, 1991. 1st ed. Fine in Fine dj. *Revere.* $90/£58

POWERS, RICHARD. The Gold Bug Variations. London: Scribner's, 1992. 1st Eng ed. Fine in Fine dj. *Revere.* $80/£52

POWERS, RICHARD. Prisoner's Dilemma. NY: Beech Tree Books, William Morrow, (1988). 1st ed. Fine in dj. *Godot.* $65/£42

POWERS, RICHARD. Three Farmers on Their Way to a Dance. NY: Beech Tree Books, 1985. 1st ed, 1st bk. Fine in Fine dj (lt worn spots). *Revere.* $150/£97

POWERS, STEPHEN. Afoot and Alone: A Walk from Sea to Sea by the Southern Route. Hartford, CT, 1872. 1st ed. 327pp. Howes P 537. *Ginsberg.* $175/£113

POWICKE, F.M. King Henry III and the Lord Edward. Oxford: Clarendon, 1947. 2 vols. Fldg map each vol. Pub's cl gilt. NF. *Peter Taylor.* $74/£48

POWLES, L.D. Land of the Pink Pearl or Recollections of Life in the Bahamas. London: Sampson Low, 1888. (xii),321pp, fldg color map. Brick cl ruled in black, gilt (spine faded; ex-lib, pocket removed). *Schoyer.* $150/£97

POWYS, JOHN COWPER. Atlantis. London: Macdonald, 1954. 1st ed. VG in dj (price-clipped). *Hollett.* $39/£25

POWYS, JOHN COWPER. Autobiography. S&S, 1934. 1st Amer ed. NF in VG dj. *Fine Books.* $30/£19

POWYS, JOHN COWPER. Autobiography. London: John Lane, Bodley Head, 1934. 1st Eng ed. Brn cl, gilt. VF in dj (sl soiled). *Dalian.* $132/£85

POWYS, JOHN COWPER. Autobiography. NY: S&S, 1934. 1st US ed. Frontis. Fine (eps sl browned). *Graf.* $35/£23

POWYS, JOHN COWPER. The Brazen Head. London: MacDonald, 1956. 1st Eng ed. Blue cl. VF in Fine dj. *Dalian.* $54/£35

POWYS, JOHN COWPER. A Glastonbury Romance. London, (1933). 1st Eng ed. (Spine faded, scuffed.) *Waterfield.* $31/£20

POWYS, JOHN COWPER. Homer and the Aether. London, 1959. 1st ed. Fine (sl rubbed; corner edge crease) in dj (sm edge tear). *Polyanthos.* $30/£19

POWYS, JOHN COWPER. In Defense of Sensuality. London, 1930. 1st Eng ed. VG in dj. *Argosy.* $100/£65

POWYS, JOHN COWPER. Letters to Louis Wilkinson, 1935-1956. London: Macdonald, 1958. 1st ed. Rev copy. Very Nice in VG dj (sl soiled, nicked). *Virgo.* $54/£35

POWYS, JOHN COWPER. Lucifer. London: Macdonald, (1956). One of 560 numbered, signed. Blue leather, gilt cl. Fine in acetate dj, as issued. *Dermont.* $150/£97

POWYS, JOHN COWPER. Obstinate Cymric: Essays 1935-47. Druid Press, 1947. 1st ed. Fine in dj (worn). *Poetry.* $47/£30

POWYS, JOHN COWPER. Porius. Macdonald, 1951. 1st ed. Fine in NF dj. *Aronovitz.* $75/£48

POWYS, JOHN COWPER. Rabelais. London, 1948. 1st ed. Fine (offsetting eps) in dj (tear rear panel; sl edge rubbed). *Polyanthos.* $25/£16

POWYS, JOHN COWPER. Rodmoor. Shaw, 1916. 1st ed. VG-. *Fine Books.* $95/£61

POWYS, JOHN COWPER. Samphire. Thomas Seltzer, 1922. 1st US ed. VG+ in dj. *Williams.* $47/£30

POWYS, JOHN COWPER. Suspended Judgments. NY: G. Arnold Shaw, 1916. 1st ed. Signed, dated April 9. Sound (spine, corners worn; white lettering flaked; sl shaken). *Reese.* $60/£39

POWYS, JOHN COWPER. Up and Out. London, 1957. 1st ed. Fine (spine extrems sl rubbed) in dj (edge nicks). *Polyanthos.* $30/£19

POWYS, JOHN COWPER. Visions and Revisions. London: Macdonald, (1955). 1st Eng ed. Fine in dj. *Hermitage.* $45/£29

POWYS, JOHN COWPER. Wood and Stone: A Romance. NY: G. Arnold Shaw, 1915. 1st ed. Navy blue buckram, gilt. Browned patch 1/2 title, o/w Very Nice. *Temple.* $233/£150

POWYS, LLEWELYN. Apples Be Ripe. NY, 1930. 1st Amer ed. VG in dj (spine sunned; 2 edge tears; price-clipped). *Polyanthos.* $30/£19

POWYS, LLEWELYN. Impassioned Clay. London: Longmans Green, 1931. 1st Eng ed. Black cl. VF in dj. *Dalian.* $132/£85

POWYS, LLEWELYN. Love and Death. London: John Lane, Bodley Head, 1939. 1st Eng ed. Brn cl. Sl rubbed, o/w VG. *Dalian.* $54/£35

POWYS, LLEWELYN. Old English Yuletide. Herrin, IL: Trovillion Private Press, (1940). 1st separate ed, ltd to 202 numbered, signed by pub. VG. *Godot.* $65/£42

POWYS, LLEWELYN. Skin for Skin. London: Cape, 1926. 1st ed. One of 900. Fine in caramel stiff paper bds, cinnamon spine lettered in gold. VG dj (1/2-inch closed tear). *Vandoros.* $85/£55

POWYS, LLEWELYN. The Twelve Months with Engravings by Robert Gibbings. London: Bodley Head, 1936. 1st ed. Dj (soiled). *Bickersteth.* $34/£22

POWYS, LLEWELYN. The Wordsworths in Dorset. Covent Garden Press, 1972. Ltd to 600. Fine in dj. *Words Etc.* $23/£15

POWYS, T.F. Black Bryony. Knopf, 1923. 1st US ed. Edges sl worn, else VG. *Whiteson.* $22/£14

POWYS, T.F. The House with the Echo. London: C&W, 1928. 1st ed. Top edge dk brn, rest uncut. Brn cl, gilt spine. Fine in dj. *Temple.* $116/£75

POWYS, T.F. Innocent Birds. London: Chatto, 1926. 1st UK ed. Fine (foxing) in VG dj. *Williams.* $54/£35

POWYS, T.F. Kindness in a Corner. London: C&W, 1930. 1st ed. Presentation copy, inscribed, dated. (Spotted.) Dj (spine sl dknd). *Hollett.* $147/£95

POWYS, T.F. Make Thyself Many. London: Grayson & Grayson, 1935. #213/285 signed. Fine in VG dj (sl dusty). *Williams.* $85/£55

POWYS, T.F. Mark Only. London, 1924. 1st ed. Fine (sl offsetting fep) in dj (spine sunned; extrems sl chipped; folds rubbed). *Polyanthos.* $30/£19

POWYS, T.F. Mark Only. London: Chatto, 1924. 1st UK ed. Fine (foxing) in dj. *Williams.* $70/£45

POWYS, T.F. Mockery Gap. London: C&W, 1925. 1st Eng ed. Blue cl. Very Nice in dj (sl worn). *Cady.* $25/£16

POWYS, T.F. Mr. Tasker's Gods. London: C&W, 1925. 1st Eng ed. Red cl. Very Nice. *Cady.* $25/£16

POWYS, T.F. Mr. Tasker's Gods. London: Chatto, 1925. 1st UK ed. Fine (foxing) in NF dj. *Williams.* $59/£38

POWYS, T.F. The Only Penitent. London: C&W, 1931. 1st Eng ed. Cream ptd paper bds. Eps sl browned, o/w VF in dj. *Dalian.* $54/£35

POWYS, T.F. Soliloquies of a Hermit. London: Andrew Melrose, 1918. 1st British ed. Nice in dj (sl chipped, browned). *Ash.* $310/£200

POWYS, T.F. Soppit's Sabbath. Sept. 2, 1937. 1st ed. NF (edge rubbed) in pict wraps. *Polyanthos.* $25/£16

POWYS, T.F. Unclay. London: C&W, 1931. 1st ed. Top edge dk brn, rest uncut. Brn cl, gilt. Edges, first, last 2 leaves sl foxed; o/w Fine in dj (sl mkd, dknd, chipped). *Temple.* $54/£35

POWYS, T.F. Unclay. London: C&W, 1931. 1st ed. Fine in dj (spine dknd). *Beasley.* $65/£42

POWYS, T.F. Unclay. London: C&W, 1931. 1st Eng ed, 1st issue binding. Gilt-titled brn cl. Very Nice in dj (sl worn). *Cady.* $25/£16

POWYS, T.F. When Thou Wast Naked. Berks: Golden Cockerel, 1931. Ltd to 500, numbered, signed. John Nash (illus). Blue morocco-backed dec white/blue bds (sl rubbed, soiled); spine gilt-titled; teg. NF. *Blue Mountain.* $135/£87

POWYS, T.F. The White Paternoster and Other Stories. London: C&W, 1930. One of 310 numbered. Signed. Teg, rest uncut. 1/4 grn buckram, white bds. Spine faded, bds sl browned, worn, o/w Nice. *Temple.* $85/£55

POWYS, T.F. The White Paternoster. London: C&W, 1930. 1st ed. Fine in dj (lt used; sl soiled spine). *Beasley.* $60/£39

POYNTER, F.N.L. (ed). Medicine and Science in the 1860's. London, 1968. 1st ed. Good. *Fye.* $70/£45

POYNTER, F.N.L. (ed). Selected Writings of William Clowes 1544-1604. London, 1948. 8 plts. Good in dj. *Goodrich.* $25/£16

POYNTON, F.J. and A. PAINE. Researches on Rheumatism. NY, 1914. 1st Amer ed. Good. *Fye.* $150/£97

POZZI, S. Treatise on Gynaecology, Medical and Surgical. NY, 1891-1892. 1st Eng trans. 581; 583pp. Full leather. VF. *Fye.* $250/£161

PRAED, MRS. CAMPBELL. Fugitive Anne. Fenno, 1904. 1st ed. VG. *Madle.* $65/£42

PRAED, MRS. CAMPBELL. The Mystery Woman. Cassell, 1913. 1st ed. VG. *Madle.* $30/£19

Praeger Encyclopedia of Art. NY, 1971. 5 vols. VG. *Argosy.* $200/£129

PRAEGER, S. ROSAMOND. The Adventures of the Three Bold Babes. London: Longmans, Green, 1897. 1st ed. Oblong, 4to. Cl-backed illus bds (corners worn). *Reisler.* $175/£113

PRANCE, C. Peppercorn Papers: A Miscellany on Books and Book Collecting. Cambridge: Golden Head Press, 1964. 1st ed. Good in dj. *Moss.* $19/£12

PRATCHETT, TERRY. The Dark Side of the Sun. London: Colin Smythe, 1976. 1st UK ed. NF in dj. *Williams.* $388/£250

PRATCHETT, TERRY. Sourcery. London: Gollancz, 1988. 1st UK ed. VG in dj. *Lewton.* $39/£25

PRATCHETT, TERRY. Strata. Smythe, 1981. 1st UK ed. Fine in Fine dj. *Martin.* $178/£115

PRATCHETT, TERRY. Strata. London: Colin Smythe, 1981. 1st UK ed. Fine in dj. *Williams.* $217/£140

PRATCHETT, TERRY. Truckers. Doubleday, 1989. 1st ed. Signed. Fine in dj. *Lewton.* $31/£20

PRATCHETT, TERRY. Wyrd Sisters. London: Gollancz, 1988. 1st UK ed. VG in dj. *Lewton.* $34/£22

PRATHER, RICHARD S. Pattern for Panic. NY: Abelard-Schuman, 1954. 1st ed. Fine in NF dj. *Janus.* $50/£32

PRATT, ANNE and THOMAS MILLER. The Language of Flowers. London: Simpkin et al, (1909). Gilt-dec cl (spine dull; spots). *Quest.* $30/£19

PRATT, ANNE. The Ferns of Great Britain. London: SPCK, (1862). 2nd ed. iv,164pp + 4pp ads; 69 full-pg color plts. Aeg. Blindstamped, gilt-ruled cl (unevenly faded; extrems worn; spine defective). Contents Fine. *Quest.* $50/£32

PRATT, E.H. Orafacial Surgery and Its Application to the Treatment of Chronic Diseases. Chicago, 1890. 1st ed. 164pp. Good. *Fye.* $150/£97

PRATT, E.J. The Witches' Brew. London, (1925). 1st ed. Frontis. VG. *Argosy.* $40/£26

PRATT, FLETCHER and L. SPRAGUE DE CAMP. The Incomplete Enchanter. Holt, 1941. 1st ed. VG. *Madle.* $60/£39

PRATT, FLETCHER. Civil War on Western Waters. NY, (1956). 1st ed. VG+ in VG+ dj. *Pratt.* $32/£21

PRATT, FLETCHER. Invaders from Rigel. NY: Avalon, (1960). 1st ed. Fine in dj (sl wear). *Antic Hay.* $40/£26

PRATT, FLETCHER. Land of Unreason. Holt, 1942. 1st ed. VG. *Madle.* $50/£32

PRATT, FLETCHER. The Monitor and the Merrimac. NY: Random House, 1951. 1st trade ed. Dec eps. VG in unmated dj. *Cattermole.* $25/£16

PRATT, FLETCHER. The Undying Fire. Ballantine, 1953. 1st ed. Fine in dj. *Madle.* $40/£26

PRATT, PARLEY P. The Autobiography of.... Chicago, 1888. 2nd ed. Frontis, 502pp. Shaken, lt worn, o/w VG. *Benchmark.* $100/£65

PRATT, PARLEY P. The Autobiography of...One of the Twelve Apostles of the Church.... NY, 1874. 1st ed. Frontis, 502pp. Aeg. Full gilt leather (scuffing, wear; hinges repaired; water-stained plts outside edges; spine re-backed w/orig leather laid down). *Benchmark.* $250/£161

PRATT, R.H. Battlefield and Classroom. New Haven/London: Yale, 1964. 1st ed. NF. *Mikesh.* $25/£16

PRATT, W.A. The Yachtman and Coaster's Book of Reference.... Hartford: Press of Case, Lockwood & Brainard, 1879. 2nd ed. 104,(2, 3 ads)pp. (Tp loose; rubbed.) *Lefkowicz.* $75/£48

PRATT, WALTER MERRIAM. Adventure in Vermont. CUP, 1943. 1st ed. Inscribed. Frontis. Paper spine label; pict paper label on cvr. Fine in dj (lt chipped). *Connolly.* $35/£23

PRAWY, MARCEL. The Vienna Opera. NY: Praeger Pub, (1969). 1st ed. White cl, gilt spine. Good in dj (lt chipped). *Karmiole.* $45/£29

PRAZ, MARIO. Conversation Pieces. London, 1971. 31 color, 349 b/w plts. Dj. *Edwards.* $85/£55

PRAZ, MARIO. The House of Life. Angus Davidson (trans). London: Methuen, 1964. 1st UK ed. Name, else NF in VG dj (edges sl rubbed). *Virgo.* $62/£40

PRAZ, MARIO. An Illustrated History of Interior Decoration from Pompeii to Art Nouveau. London: Thames & Hudson, 1982. VF in color dj. *Europa.* $39/£25

PRAZ, MARIO. An Illustrated History of Interior Decoration.... London, 1964. 1st UK ed. 65 color, 336 b/w plts. Dj. *Edwards.* $116/£75

PRAZ, MARIO. The Romantic Agony. Oxford: Oxford Univ, 1933. 1st US ed. Fine in dj. *Lame Duck.* $85/£55

PREBLE, GEORGE HENRY. A Chronological History of the Origin and Development of Steam Navigation. 1543-1882. Phila, 1883. 1st ed. (xx),484, errata, (2 ads)pp. (Extrems worn; lib pocket, bkpl, spine #s.) *Lefkowicz.* $115/£74

PREBLE, ROBERT. Pneumonia and Pneumococcus Infections. Chicago, 1905. Good. *Fye.* $45/£29

PREECE, HAROLD. The Dalton Gang, End of an Outlaw Era. NY, (1963). 1st ed. Lt dj wear, staining, o/w VG + . *Pratt.* $40/£26

PRENDERGAST, MAURICE. Water-Color Sketchbook: 1899. Cambridge: Harvard Univ Press, (1960). Note in pocket. VG in pub's slipcase. *Argosy.* $60/£39

PRENTICE, SARTELL. The Voices of the Cathedral. London, 1937. Color frontis. (Feps lt browned.) *Edwards.* $31/£20

PRENTISS, HENRY MELLEN. The Great Polar Current—De Long—Nansen—Peary. NY: Frederick A. Stokes, 1897. 153pp. Vignette dec grn cl. Teg. Lt wear, else VG. *Parmer.* $75/£48

PRESCOTT, H.F.M. Friar Felix at Large. New Haven: Yale Univ Press, 1950. Good in dj. *Archaeologia.* $35/£23

PRESCOTT, PHILANDER. The Recollections of Philander Prescott...1819-1862. Univ NE, (1966). 1st ed. VF in VF dj. *Oregon.* $35/£23

PRESCOTT, PHILANDER. The Recollections of Philander Prescott...1819-1862. Donald Dean Parker (ed). Lincoln: Univ of NE, 1966. 1st ed. VF in NF dj. *Connolly.* $37/£24

PRESCOTT, WILLIAM H. The History of the Conquest of Mexico. NY: Harper, 1843. 1st Amer ed, 1st ptg w/'track' on p5, 6th line from bottom. 3 vols. 3 engr frontis ports (foxing, offsetting). 3/4 mod morocco; marbled bds, eps; grn calf spine labels; teg. (Text sl foxed.) *Cullen.* $500/£323

PRESCOTT, WILLIAM H. History of the Conquest of Mexico. NY: Harper, 1843. 1st Amer ed, 2nd (corrected) ptg. 3 vols. Orig pub's cl (extrems worn; spine sl chipped). VG set (sl foxing). BAL 16340. *Reese.* $425/£274

PRESCOTT, WILLIAM H. History of the Conquest of Mexico. NY: Harper, 1843. 1st ed, 2nd ptg. 3 vols. Orig purple cl, gilt (sl wear, nicks, lt fading). BAL 16340. *Macdonnell.* $375/£242

PRESCOTT, WILLIAM H. History of the Conquest of Mexico.... NY: Harper, 1843. 1st ed. 3 vols. Frontis port each vol (1st blank, frontis sl foxed vol 2 & 3). Orig pub's olive grn cl stamped in blind, gilt-titled. Excellent (ink ownership fep each vol; sl splitting joint tops) in fitted drop-lid box backed in grn morocco; gilt-titled (lt rubbed). *Hermitage.* $750/£484

PRESCOTT, WILLIAM H. The History of the Conquest of Peru. NY: Harper, 1847. Correct 1st US ed, lacking period at vol II, pg 467, line 20. 2 vols. (Sl warping both vols.) *Lame Duck.* $300/£194

PRESCOTT, WILLIAM H. The History of the Reign of Ferdinand and Isabella the Catholic. NY: LEC, 1967. One of 1500. Signed by Lima de Freitas (artist). Full tan cowhide. Fine in slipcase. *Agvent.* $95/£61

PRESCOTT, WILLIAM H. History of the Reign of Ferdinand and Isabella, the Catholic. Boston: American Stationers', 1837. 1st ed. 3 vols. Frontis port each vol. Orig pub's purple cl stamped in blind, gilt-titled. Offsetting tps; ink ownership fep vol 2; spines sl faded; gathering loose vol 2, o/w Excellent set in fitted slipcase. *Hermitage.* $300/£194

PRESENCER, ALAIN. Roaring Lion Tales Pop-Up Book. London: Blackie, 1984. 23x25 cm. 4 dbl-pg pop-ups. Glazed illus bds. VG. *Book Finders.* $50/£32

Present for Infants; or, Pictures for the Nursery. London: Darton, Harvey, and Darton, 1819. 12mo. 24pp + 1pg list back cvr; each plt numbered according to text (1 engr double numbered 20-21). Internally Fine (ink presentation; lt foxing; backstrip restored). VG. *Hobbyhorse.* $200/£129

PRESTON, GEORGE R., JR. Thomas Wolfe. A Bibliography. NY, 1943. 1st Amer ed. Frontis port. Fine. *Polyanthos.* $40/£26

PRESTON, HAYTER. Windmills. NY: Dodd, Mead, (1923). 1st ed, Amer issue. 16 full-pg color plts. Frank Brangwyn (illus). Partially unopened. Fine in dj (lg chips, tears, lt edgewear). *Godot.* $150/£97

PRESTON, JACK. Heil! Hollywood. Chicago: Reilly & Lee, 1939. 1st ed. Good in dj (sm chips, tears, creases). *Houle.* $65/£42

PRESTON, LAURA. A Boy's Trip Across the Plains. NY: A. Roman & Co, 1868. Frontis, 233pp. Gold-stamped cl (cocked; lt wear, sunned; stamp). *Dawson.* $75/£48

PRESTON, LIONEL. Sea and River Painters of the Netherlands. OUP, 1937. (Lacks fep; cl sl soiled.) *Edwards.* $59/£38

PRESTON, RICHARD. Gorges of Plymouth Fort. Univ Toronto, 1953. 1st ed. VG. *Oregon.* $70/£45

PRESTON, STUART. Edouard Vuillard. NY: Abrams, 1974. VG. *Argosy.* $100/£65

PRESTON, THOMAS L. Historical Sketches and Reminiscences of an Octogenarian. B.F. Johnson, 1900. VG. *Book Broker.* $85/£55

PRESTON, THOMAS W. Historical Sketches of the Holston Valleys. Kingsport: Kingsport Press, 1926. 1st ed. 5 maps. Teg. Gilt-emb red cl. Fine in ptd dj, orig pub's box. *Cahan.* $100/£65

PRESTWICH, G.A. Life and Letters of Sir Joseph Prestwich. London, 1899. 1st ed. xv,444pp, 18 plts. Good. *Henly.* $65/£42

PREVOST, RENAN. Sundown on the Pacific Shore. N.p.: Author, 1957. 1st ed. Inscribed. Fabricoid, gilt. Fine in dj (sl chipping). *Connolly.* $65/£42

PRICE, A. GRENFELL. White Settlers in the Tropics. NY, 1939. (Cl sl soiled; spine discolored, sl chipped.) *Edwards.* $39/£25

PRICE, A. GRENFELL. The Winning of the Australian Antarctic. Australia: Angus & Robertson, 1962. 1st ed. 12 maps. VG + in dj. *Walcot.* $31/£20

PRICE, ANTHONY. The Alamut Ambush. London: Gollancz, 1971. 1st ed. Fine in dj (sm mk). *Rees.* $93/£60

PRICE, ANTHONY. The Alamut Ambush. Gollancz, 1971. 1st UK ed. Fine in NF dj (sl rubbing). *Martin.* $116/£75

PRICE, ANTHONY. Colonel Butler's Wolf. Gollancz, 1972. 1st UK ed. Fine in Fine dj. *Martin.* $74/£48

PRICE, ANTHONY. Gunner Kelly. NY: Doubleday, 1984. 1st Amer ed. Fine in dj. *Silver Door.* $27/£17

PRICE, ANTHONY. Here Be Monsters. London: Gollancz, 1985. 1st ed. Fine in dj. *Limestone.* $45/£29

PRICE, ANTHONY. A New Kind of War. Gollancz, 1987. 1st ed. VG in VG dj. *Ming.* $31/£20

PRICE, ANTHONY. October Men. Gollancz, 1973. 1st UK ed. Fine in Fine dj. *Martin.* $70/£45

PRICE, ANTHONY. Other Paths to Glory. Gollancz, 1974. 1st UK ed. Fine in Fine dj. *Martin.* $65/£42

PRICE, ANTHONY. Our Man in Camelot. London: Gollancz, 1975. 1st ed. Fine in dj. *Mordida.* $125/£81

PRICE, ANTHONY. Our Man in Camelot. Gollancz, 1975. 1st UK ed. Fine in Fine dj. *Martin.* $59/£38

PRICE, ANTHONY. Tomorrow's Ghost. Gollancz, 1979. 1st ed. VG in Good + dj (nicked spine top). *Ming.* $31/£20

PRICE, ANTHONY. Tomorrow's Ghost. London: Gollancz, 1979. 1st ed. Fine in dj. *Janus.* $45/£29

PRICE, ANTHONY. War Game. London: Gollancz, 1976. 1st ed. VF in dj. *Mordida.* $150/£97

PRICE, BARBARA WELLS. American Folk Tales. Kansas City: Hallmark, (1975). 17x23 cm. 3 dbl-pg pop-ups, 2 illus pgs w/pull-tabs. George Kaufman (illus). Glazed pict bds. VG. *Book Finders.* $60/£39

PRICE, E. HOFFMAN. Strange Gateways. Arkham House, 1967. 1st ed. VF in dj. *Madle.* $75/£48

PRICE, EMERSON. Inn of That Journey. Caldwell, 1939. 1st ed. 1st bk. Fine in dj. *Artis.* $20/£13

PRICE, FRANCIS. The British Carpenter; or, A Treatise on Carpentry. London: C. Hitch et al, 1759. 4th ed. (viii),72pp; 62 engr plts. Recent calf antique, morocco spine label, old-style eps. Good (pp, plts spotted). *Bickersteth.* $341/£220

PRICE, FREDERIC NEWLIN. Ryder (1847-1917): A Study.... NY: William Edwin Rudge, 1932. 1st ed. 71 plts. Fine in dj. *Cahan.* $135/£87

PRICE, HARRY. The End of Borley Rectory. London: Harrap, 1948. 26 plts. Worn, mkd. *Hollett.* $31/£20

PRICE, JULIUS M. My Bohemian Days in Paris. London: T. Werner Laurie, 1913. 1st ed. 32 plts. Pict cl (spine faded, spots), gilt. *Hollett.* $47/£30

PRICE, OLIVE. Rosa Bonheur, Painter of Animals. Champaign: Garrard, 1972. 1st ed. VG in Good + dj. *October Farm.* $25/£16

PRICE, REYNOLDS (trans). The Good News According to Mark. (N.p.), 1976. 1st ed, 1st state w/dk orange ep leaves. One of 300. Fine in orig ptd pict wraps. *Chapel Hill.* $50/£32

PRICE, REYNOLDS. The Annual Heron. NY: Albondocani Press, 1980. 1st ed. #211/300 signed. Fine in French marbled wraps, paper label. *Chapel Hill.* $75/£48

PRICE, REYNOLDS. The Collected Stories. NY: Atheneum, 1993. 1st ed. Signed. Fine in Fine dj. *Revere.* $45/£29

PRICE, REYNOLDS. Country Mouse, City Mouse. (Rocky Mount, NC: Friends of the Library, NC Wesleyan Coll, 1981). 1st ed. One of 500. Fine in orig ptd wraps. *Chapel Hill.* $35/£23

PRICE, REYNOLDS. The Foreseeable Future. NY: Atheneum, 1991. 1st ed. Signed. Fine in Fine dj. *Chapel Hill.* $45/£29

PRICE, REYNOLDS. The Foreseeable Future. NY: Atheneum, 1991. 1st ed. Signed. Fine in Fine dj. *Beasley.* $50/£32

PRICE, REYNOLDS. A Generous Man. NY: Atheneum, 1966. 1st ed. Signed. Fine in Fine dj (price-clipped). *Revere.* $90/£58

PRICE, REYNOLDS. Good Hearts. NY: Atheneum, 1988. 1st ed. Fine in Fine dj. *Pettler.* $20/£13

PRICE, REYNOLDS. Good Hearts. NY: Atheneum, 1988. 1st ed. Signed. Fine in Fine dj. *Beasley.* $60/£39

PRICE, REYNOLDS. Kate Vaiden. NY: Atheneum, 1986. 1st ed. Signed. Fine in Fine dj. *Beasley.* $75/£48

PRICE, REYNOLDS. A Long and Happy Life. NY: Atheneum, 1962. 1st ed, 1st bk. Brn cl. NF in NF 1st issue dj (authors' names ptd in lt grn in rear panel blurbs). *Chapel Hill.* $125/£81

PRICE, REYNOLDS. A Long and Happy Life. London: C&W, 1962. 1st Eng ed, 1st bk. Blue cl. VF in dj (sl rubbed). *Dalian.* $54/£35

PRICE, REYNOLDS. Love and Work. London: C&W, 1968. 1st Eng ed. Blue cl. Name, o/w Fine in dj. *Dalian.* $39/£25

PRICE, REYNOLDS. Permanent Errors. NY: Atheneum, 1970. 1st ed. VF in dj. *Chapel Hill.* $60/£39

PRICE, REYNOLDS. Private Contentment. NY: Atheneum, 1984. 1st ed. VF in dj. *Chapel Hill.* $40/£26

PRICE, REYNOLDS. The Source of Light. NY: Atheneum, 1981. 1st ed. Inscribed, signed. Brn cl. Fine in dj (price-clipped). *Chapel Hill.* $65/£42

PRICE, REYNOLDS. Things Themselves. NY: Atheneum, 1972. 1st ed. Cream cl. VF in VF dj. *Chapel Hill.* $55/£35

PRICE, REYNOLDS. A Whole New Life. NY, 1994. 1st Amer ed. Signed. Fine in Fine dj. *Polyanthos.* $35/£23

PRICE, RICHARD. Bloodbrothers. Boston: HM Co, 1976. 1st ed. Fine in dj. *Between The Covers.* $65/£42

PRICE, RICHARD. The Breaks. NY: S&S, 1983. 1st ed. VG in VG- dj (worn). *Revere.* $25/£16

PRICE, RICHARD. Clockers. Boston, 1992. 1st Amer ed. Signed. Mint in Mint dj. *Polyanthos.* $40/£26

PRICE, RICHARD. Ladies Man. Boston: HM Co, 1978. 1st ed. Fine in dj (lt rubbing). *Between The Covers.* $65/£42

PRICE, RICHARD. The Wanderers. Boston: HM Co, 1974. 1st ed, 1st bk. Fine in NF dj (lt crease fr panel). *Between The Covers.* $75/£48

PRICE, THOMAS W. Brief Notes Taken on a Trip to the City of Mexico in 1878. (NY: by author, 1878). 1st ed. Pub for presentation. 103pp. Dec cl. VG. *Petrilla.* $50/£32

PRICHARD, H. HESKETH. Through the Heart of Patagonia. NY: Appleton, 1902. 1st Amer ed. 3 fldg maps. Red gilt-dec cl (sm piece missing spine; soiled, foxed). Acceptable. *Parmer.* $175/£113

PRICHARD, H. HESKETH. Through Trackless Labrador. London, 1911. 1st ed. Frontis, dbl-pg map. Gilt illus upper bd. (Feps, margins browned; spine sl faded.) *Edwards.* $93/£60

PRICHARD, H. HESKETH. Through Trackless Labrador. London: Heinemann, 1911. 1st ed. Pict cl (sl faded). Nice (damp spots; fr joint cracked). *Hollett.* $155/£100

PRICHARD, JAMES. A Treatise on Insanity and Other Disorders Affecting the Mind. Phila, 1837. 1st Amer ed. 337pp. 1/2 leather. Good. *Fye.* $250/£161

Pride and Prejudice. (By Jane Austen.) London: T. Egerton, 1817. 3rd ed. 2 vols. 1/2 grn morocco, dec bds (amateur binding, author's name misspelled on spines; joint tender; spines browned). VG. *Sumner & Stillman.* $975/£629

PRIDE, W.F. The History of Fort Riley. N.p., 1926. *Cullen.* $50/£32

PRIDE, W.F. The History of Fort Riley. (Ft. Riley), 1926. 1st ed. VG-. *Baade.* $45/£29

PRIDEAUX, S.T. Bookbinders and Their Craft. NY: Scribner's, 1903. One of 500. (Sl shaken.) *Bookpress.* $325/£210

PRIEST, A. The Sculpture of Joseph Coletti. London/NY: Macmillan, 1968. 132 plts. (Cl sl worn.) *Ars Artis.* $54/£35

PRIEST, JOSIAH. American Antiquities, and Discoveries in the West.... Albany, 1833. 3rd ed, rev. 400pp; fldg frontis, map (both worn, tears). Leather (spine scuffed; foxed throughout). *Hayman.* $50/£32

PRIESTLEY, J.B. Angel Pavement. London: Heinemann, 1930. 1st ed. Very Nice in dj (sl soiled, browned, chipped, 2 sm closed tears). *Virgo.* $39/£25

PRIESTLEY, J.B. Angel Pavement. Heinemann, 1930. 1st UK ed. VG in VG dj (sm hole). *Lewton.* $54/£35

PRIESTLEY, J.B. Brief Diversions, Being Tales, Travesties and Epigrams. Cambridge, 1922. 1st ed. Cl-backed bds, paper labels. VG. *Hollett.* $194/£125

PRIESTLEY, J.B. Brief Diversions. Cambridge: Bowes & Bowes, 1922. 1st ed. Pink stiff bds, 1/4 black spine, white paper labels. Orig glassine, paper flaps. *Vandoros.* $75/£48

PRIESTLEY, J.B. Brief Diversions. Cambridge: Bowes & Bowes, 1922. 1st Eng ed. Black 1/4 leather-backed orange bds. Sl mkd, o/w VG. *Dalian.* $70/£45

PRIESTLEY, J.B. Delight. London: Heinemann, 1949. 1st ed. Blue buckram. Fine in dj (folds sl torn). *Temple.* $16/£10

PRIESTLEY, J.B. The Doomsday Men. London: Heinemann, 1938. 1st Eng ed. Blue cl. Name, o/w Fine in dj (sl torn). *Dalian.* $31/£20

PRIESTLEY, J.B. Figures in Modern Literature. London: John Lane, (1924). 1st ed. Sticker fep, else VG. *Reese.* $20/£13

PRIESTLEY, J.B. George Meredith. London: Macmillan, 1926. 1st ed. Top edge cerise, rest uncut. Cerise buckram. Fine in dj (sl frayed). *Temple.* $37/£24

PRIESTLEY, J.B. Home Is Tomorrow. London: Heinemann, 1946. 1st Eng ed. Blue cl. Fine in dj. *Dalian.* $23/£15

PRIESTLEY, J.B. Literature and Western Man. London: Heinemann, 1960. 1st Eng ed. Black cl. Name, o/w Fine in dj (rubbed, nicked). *Dalian.* $39/£25

PRIESTLEY, J.B. Man and the Machine. Hubert Williams (ed). London: Routledge, 1935. 1st Eng ed. Red cl. Sl mkd, o/w VG in dj (sl mkd). *Dalian.* $54/£35

PRIESTLEY, J.B. The Moments and Other Pieces. London: Heinemann, 1966. 1st Eng ed. Purple cl. VF in dj. *Dalian.* $23/£15

PRIESTLEY, J.B. Papers from Lilliput. Cambridge: Bowes & Bowes, 1922. 1st ed. Uncut, unopened. 1/4 unbleached linen. Grn paper-cvrd bds, cream spine label. Fine in dj (sl faded, frayed). *Temple.* $70/£45

PRIESTLEY, J.B. Saturn Over the Water. London: Heinemann, 1961. 1st Eng ed. Blue cl. VG in dj (torn). *Dalian.* $23/£15

PRIESTLEY, J.B. Sir Michael and Sir George. London: Heinemann, 1964. 1st ed. VG in dj. *Hollett.* $31/£20

PRIESTLEY, J.B. Theatre Outlook. London: Nicholson & Watson, 1947. 1st ed. Name, date, o/w Fine in NF dj (short tears). *Beasley.* $40/£26

PRIESTLEY, J.B. Thomas Love Peacock. London: Macmillan, 1927. 1st ed. Top edge cerise, rest uncut. Cerise buckram, gilt spine. Fine in dj. *Temple.* $47/£30

PRIESTLEY, J.B. The Town Major of Miraucourt. London: Heinemann, 1930. One of 525 numbered, signed, bound in vellum. Sl spotted, o/w NF in slipcase. *Rees.* $54/£35

PRIESTLEY, J.B. with HUGH WALPOLE. Farthing Hall. Macmillan, 1929. 1st UK ed. Fine in dj (browned; sl chipping). *Williams.* $54/£35

PRIESTLEY, JOSEPH. A Description of a Chart of Biography.... Ptd for J. Johnson, 1778. 7th ed. 2 fldg tables (1 sl frayed, repaired). Mod 1/4 calf. *Waterfield.* $124/£80

PRIESTLEY, RAYMOND E. Antarctic Adventure. NY: E.P. Dutton, 1915. 1st US ed, bound from sheets of 1st London ed, in same dec binding. 3 fldg maps. Teg. Orig silver dec cl. Minor stain upper edge lower cvr, else VG. *High Latitude.* $400/£258

PRIESTLEY, RAYMOND E. Antarctic Adventure; Scott's Northern Party. NY: E.P. Dutton, 1915. 1st Amer ed. 3 fldg maps. Silver dec blue cl (cvrs worn, silver flaked; sig, stamp). *Parmer.* $395/£255

PRIME, WILLIAM C. Boat Life in Egypt and Nubia. NY: Harper, 1857. 1st ed. 498,6pp. Sl rubbed, soiled, o/w VG. *Worldwide.* $45/£29

PRIME, WILLIAM C. Boat Life in Egypt and Nubia. NY: Harper, 1859. 498pp + 6pp ads. Brn cl stamped in gilt, blind (spine ends repaired). *Schoyer.* $35/£23

PRIME, WILLIAM C. Boat Life in Egypt and Nubia. NY, 1866. xiv,498pp. (Spine sl chipped.) *Edwards.* $47/£30

PRIME, WILLIAM C. Pottery and Porcelain of All Times and Nations.... NY: Harper, 1878. Frontis, 531pp + 4pp ads; teg. Gilt/black pict brn cl (extrems lt worn). VG. *House.* $90/£58

PRIME, WILLIAM C. Tent Life in the Holy Land. NY: Harper, 1857. 1st ed. 498pp; 6 plts (2 dbl-pg). Sl rubbed, worn, o/w VG. *Worldwide.* $45/£29

PRIME, WILLIAM C. Tent Life in the Holy Land. NY: Harper, 1859. 498,3pp; 6 plts (2 dbl-pg). Spine frayed; chipped; foxed, o/w Good. *Worldwide.* $25/£16

Prince Darling. Wellington: Houlston & Son, n.d. (ca 1810). 3rd ed. 16mo. Full-pg frontis, 48pp; 5 full-pg engrs. Eng dec title label, stiff yellow paper cvr (lt soiled, glue spots inside). In all, VG, internally Fine (3 ink inscrips). *Hobbyhorse.* $175/£113

Prince of Abissinia. (By Samuel Johnson.) London: R. and J. Dodsley and W. Johnston, 1759. 2nd ed. 2 vols bound in 1. 3/4 marbled calf over marbled bds (corners sl rubbed), leather spine label. *Sadlon.* $400/£258

Prince of Abissinia. (By Samuel Johnson.) London: R. & J. Dodsley, 1759. 2nd ed. 2 vols. 12mo. 159; 165pp. (Lt foxing; some eps replaced w/antique paper.) Full polished calf, gilt (both vols same size, but bindings differ in minor detail). Good set. *Hartfield.* $595/£384

Prince of Abissinia. (By Samuel Johnson.) London: J.F. & C. Rivington et al, 1786. 7th Eng ed. vii,304pp. Contemp speckled calf, gilt (extrems sl worn; outer hinges starting to crack; bkpl). Marbled eps. Very Nice. *Cady.* $75/£48

Prince of Abissinia. (By Samuel Johnson.) London: Ptd for Rivington et al, 1793. 9th ed. Orig mottled full calf, later marbled eps. Name, else VG. *Limestone.* $65/£42

Prince of Wales' Cock Robin. Leeds: Webb, Millington, n.d. (ca 1860). Sm 4to. 12pp + 1pg list on back wrapper, 12 hand-colored wood engrs by O. Jewitt. Ptd dec stiff paper wrappers (rebacked, traces of stitching; dusted). VG. *Hobbyhorse.* $125/£81

PRINCE, L. BRADFORD. A Concise History of New Mexico. Cedar Rapids: Torch, 1912. 1st ed. Cvr very worn, else VG. *Parker.* $95/£61

PRINCE, L. BRADFORD. Spanish Mission Churches of New Mexico. Cedar Rapids: Torch Press, 1915. 1st ed. VG (hinge starting). *Parker.* $100/£65

PRINCE, L. BRADFORD. Spanish Mission Churches of New Mexico. Cedar Rapids, IA: Torch, 1915. 1st ed. Pict cl. Howes P 613. *Ginsberg.* $125/£81

PRINCE, L. BRADFORD. Spanish Mission Churches of New Mexico. Rio Grande, 1977. Fldg map. VG. Howes P 613. *Oregon.* $50/£32

PRINCE, WILLIAM ROBERT and WILLIAM. The Pomological Manual. NY, 1831. 1st ed. 2 vols. viii,(9-)200; xvi,(9-)216pp. (Foxing.) Cl-backed bds (not uniform; lt wear; foxing to bds vol 2), paper labels. Unopened set. Overall, Nice. *Sutton.* $300/£194

PRINCE, WILLIAM ROBERT and WILLIAM. A Treatise on the Vine. NY, 1830. 1st ed. viii,(9-)355pp (frontis, prelims, eps spotted; foxing). Contemp 1/2 cl (worn, soiled; fr cvr partly loose). *Sutton.* $300/£194

PRINGLE, JOHN. Observations on the Diseases of the Army. Benjamin Rush (ed). Phila, 1810. 1st Amer ed. xlvii,411pp (contemp sig, bkpl). Contemp tree calf (rubbed, bumped), red morocco spine label. VG. *Hemlock.* $400/£258

PRINZING, FRIEDRICH. Epidemics Resulting from Wars. Oxford, 1916. 1st ed. (Ex-lib.) *Fye.* $150/£97

PRIOR, MATTHEW. Poems on Several Occasions. 1733. 5th ed. 2 vols. (xxvi),231,(iv); 259,(iii)pp. Contemp calf (sl worn spine head, foot; lt waterstaining 1st vol). *Bickersteth.* $47/£30

PRIOR, MATTHEW. Poems on Several Occasions. Glasgow: Robert & Andrew Foulis, 1751. 2 vols in 1. Variant 12mo in 1/2 sheet issue. Contemp calf (rubbed; backstrip worn, chipped, split). *Waterfield.* $78/£50

PRIOR, MATTHEW. Poems on Several Occasions. Ptd for J. & R. Tonson, 1766 (and) Volume the Second. Ptd for W. Strahan, 1767. 5th ed. 2 vols. Port vol 1; frontis, 2 plts vol 2. Contemp sprinkled calf (defective label). Good. *Hill.* $93/£60

PRIOR, MATTHEW. Poems on Several Occasions. (Dublin: W. & W. Smith, P. & W. Wilson, 1768.) 2 vols. Contemp sprinkled calf (sl mkd), flat spine (sl tear), gilt rules, red dbl morocco labels. (Prelim corner torn off w/sl loss.) Well-preserved set. *Pirages.* $150/£97

PRIOR, MATTHEW. The Poetical Works. London: William Pickering, 1835. 2 vols. 1st Aldine ed. Port. Orig lighter fine diaper cl; paper labels. VG. *Cox.* $47/£30

PRITCHARD, JAMES AVERY. The Overland Diary of James A. Pritchard from Kentucky to California in 1849. Dale L. Morgan (ed). (Denver): Rosenstock: Old West Pub Co, 1959. 1st ed. 2 fldg maps, chart in rear pocket. Unopened. Pict cl. Fine in NF dj (lt edgewear). *Harrington.* $135/£87

PRITCHARD, JAMES AVERY. The Overland Diary of James A. Pritchard from Kentucky to California in 1849. Dale Morgan (ed). Denver: Old West Pub., 1959. 1st ed. Port, 2 maps, chart. VG. *Oregon.* $95/£61

PRITCHARD, JAMES AVERY. Overland Diary...From Kentucky to California in 1849. Dale L. Morgan (ed). Old West Pub Co, 1959. One of 1250. Presentation by Morgan. Frontis port, 3 maps (2 fldg), fldg pocket chart. Fine in dj (soil, chips). *Bohling.* $125/£81

PRITCHARD, JAMES B. Gibeon, Where the Sun Stood Still. Princeton: Princeton Univ Press, 1962. Good. *Archaeologia.* $25/£16

PRITCHETT, JOHN PERRY. The Red River Valley 1811-1849. Yale Univ, 1942. 1st ed. Signed presentation copy. Color ep maps. Fine. *Oregon.* $75/£48

PRITCHETT, V.S. Blind Love and Other Stories. London: C&W, 1969. 1st ed. NF in dj (price-clipped). *Rees.* $31/£20

PRITCHETT, V.S. Foreign Faces. London: C&W, 1964. 1st Eng ed. Red cl. Fine in dj (sl dusty). *Dalian.* $39/£25

PRITCHETT, V.S. In My Good Books. London: C&W, 1942. 1st ed. Lt blue cl (mottled; spine sl dknd). Nice. *Temple.* $34/£22

PRITCHETT, V.S. Marching Spain. London: Benn, 1928. 1st ed. Nice. *Patterson.* $62/£40

PRITCHETT, V.S. Marching Spain. London: Ernest Benn, 1928. 1st Eng ed, 1st bk. Orange cl. Spine bruised, o/w NF. *Dalian.* $70/£45

PRITCHETT, V.S. On the Edge of the Cliff. London: C&W, 1980. 1st ed. VG in dj (sm closed tear). *Virgo.* $19/£12

PRITCHETT, V.S. Shirley Sanz. London: Victor Gollancz, 1932. 1st ed. Black buckram. Spine crease, o/w Nice. *Temple.* $62/£40

PRITCHETT, V.S. The Tale Bearers. London: C&W, 1980. 1st ed. Grn cl. Fine in dj. *Temple.* $19/£12

PRITCHETT, V.S. When My Girl Comes Home. NY, 1961. 1st Amer ed. Fine in dj. *Artis.* $20/£13

PRIVATE 19022. (Pseud of Frederic Manning.) Her Privates We. London: Davies, (1930). 1st unexpurg ed of The Middle Parts of Fortune. Pict cl. Fine in glassine dj w/ptd flaps (chipped; price-clipped). *Jaffe.* $350/£226

Proceedings and Debates of the Third National Quarantine and Sanitary Convention. NY, 1859. 1st ed. 728pp. Good. *Fye.* $75/£48

Proceedings of the First General Convention to Consider the Questions Involved in Mosquito Extermination. Brooklyn, 1904. 1st ed. Good. *Fye.* $30/£19

PROCTER, GEORGE H. The Fishermen's Memorial and Record Book. Gloucester: Procter, 1873. 1st ed. 172pp + ads. Orig cl (worn). Internally VG. Howes P 626. *Second Life.* $75/£48

PROCTER, MAURICE. Three at the Angel. London: Hutchinson, 1958. 1st ed. NF in NF dj. *Janus.* $50/£32

PROCTOR, IVAN MARRIOTT. The Life of Ivan Marriott Proctor M.D., F.A.C.S. Privately ptd. (Raleigh: Edwards & Broughton), 1964. 1st ed. Author presentation. NF. *Mcgowan.* $45/£29

PROCTOR, L.B. The Bench and Bar of New-York. NY: Diossy, 1870. viii,779pp; 2 ports. (Bkpl; spine sl sunned.) *Schoyer.* $85/£55

PROCTOR, RICHARD A. Easy Star Lessons. London: C&W, 1882. New ed. 239pp + 32pp cat. Good in gilt-illus blue cl (bumped, worn; 1/2 title foxed). *Knollwood.* $50/£32

PRODAN, MARIO. The Art of the T'ang Potter. London, 1960. 34 tipped-in color plts, 6 diags. (Ex-libris.) Dj (upper edge sl ragged). *Edwards.* $93/£60

PROKOSCH, FREDERIC. Age of Thunder. London: C&W, 1945. 1st ed. Lower edges rough-trimmed. Fine in dj (sl frayed, dusty). *Temple.* $16/£10

PROKOSCH, FREDERIC. The Asiatics. NY, 1935. 1st ed. VG in gilt dj (mended on verso). *Argosy.* $65/£42

PROKOSCH, FREDERIC. The Assassins (Poems). London: C&W, 1936. 1st ed, preceding Amer ed. Partly unopened. Brn cl-backed dec paper bds. Fore-edge, eps sl foxed, o/w Fine in dj (sl dusty). *Dalian.* $70/£45

PROKOSCH, FREDERIC. The Assassins. NY: Harper, 1936. 1st ed. Fine in dj (lt browning; sl chipping). *Antic Hay.* $50/£32

PROKOSCH, FREDERIC. A Ballad of Love. S&W, 1961. 1st UK ed. VG in dj. *Lewton.* $16/£10

PROKOSCH, FREDERIC. The Idols of the Cave. London: C&W, 1947. 1st ed. Lower edges rough-trimmed. NF in dj (sl chipped, spine dknd). *Temple.* $31/£20

PROKOSCH, FREDERIC. Night of the Poor. London: C&W, 1939. 1st ed. Top edge blue, rest rough-trimmed. Blue cl. Spine, edges sl faded; sl wear top spine, o/w Nice in dj (lacks spine). *Temple.* $16/£10

PROKOSCH, FREDERIC. The Seven Sisters. S&W, 1963. 1st UK ed. VG in dj. *Lewton.* $16/£10

PROKOSCH, FREDERIC. A Tale for Midnight. S&W, 1956. 1st UK ed. VG in dj. *Lewton.* $19/£12

PRONZINI, BILL. Cat's Paw. Richmond: Waves Press, 1983. 1st ed, one of 100. Signed. Fine. *Janus.* $45/£29

PRONZINI, BILL. Deadfall. NY: St. Martin's, 1986. 1st ed. Signed. Fine in Fine dj. *Janus.* $25/£16

PRONZINI, BILL. Panic! NY: Random House, 1972. 1st ed. Label removed fr pastedown, o/w Fine in dj (price-clipped). *Mordida.* $35/£23

PRONZINI, BILL. Quincannon. NY: Walker, 1985. 1st ed, signed. Fine in Fine dj. *Janus.* $45/£29

PRONZINI, BILL. Snowbound. NY: Putnam, 1974. 1st ed. Signed, inscribed. NF in dj. *Silver Door.* $45/£29

PRONZINI, BILL. The Stalker. NY: Random, 1971. 1st ed. Signed, inscribed. Fine in dj (lt wear; sl soiling). *Silver Door.* $50/£32

PROPERT, W.A. The Russian Ballet, 1921-1929. London, (1931). 1st ed. VG. *Argosy.* $100/£65

PROSCH, CHARLES. Reminiscences of Washington Territory. Seattle, 1904. Signed. VG. Howes P 633. *Perier.* $125/£81

PROSKAUER, J.J. Spook Crooks! Burt, 1932. 1st ed. Fr cvr wear, else VG + . *Aronovitz.* $45/£29

PROSKE, BEATRICE GILMAN. Castilian Sculpture. NY, 1951. Good. *Washton.* $45/£29

PROSKE, BEATRICE GILMAN. Castilian Sculpture. Gothic to Renaissance. NY, 1951. Good. *Washton.* $50/£32

PROSSER, WILLIAM FARRAND. A History of the Puget Sound Country. NY: Lewis Pub, 1903. 2 vols. VG set. *Perier.* $150/£97

PROULX, E. ANNIE. Heart Songs and Other Stories. NY: Scribner's, 1988. 1st ed. 1st bk. Fine in dj. *Else Fine.* $175/£113

PROULX, E. ANNIE. Postcards. NY: Scribner, (1992). 1st ed. Fine in dj (sl soiling rear panel). *Robbins.* $60/£39

PROUST, MARCEL. Cities of the Plain. Boni, 1927. 1st Amer ed. One of 2000. 2 vols. Fine in glassine dj's (worn); VG 2 section pub's slip-case. *Fine Books.* $125/£81

PROUST, MARCEL. Cities of the Plain. C.K. Scott Moncrieff (trans). Chatto, 1929. 1st UK ed. 2 vols. VG (ink names). *Williams.* $93/£60

PROUST, MARCEL. The Guermantes Way. C.K. Scott Moncrieff (trans). Chatto, 1925. 1st UK ed. 2 vols. VG (ink names). *Williams.* $101/£65

PROUST, MARCEL. Letters of Marcel Proust to Antoine Bibesco. London: Thames & Hudson, 1953. 1st Eng trans. 500 numbered. Signed by Gerard Hopkins (trans). 8 tipped-in illus. Gilt-emb cl. VG in dj (faded). *Cahan.* $50/£32

PROUST, MARCEL. Letters of Marcel Proust. M. Curtiss (ed). Chatto, 1950. 1st ed. Sl faded, else Good in dj (sl torn). *Whiteson.* $19/£12

PROUST, MARCEL. Within a Budding Grove. C.K. Scott Moncrieff (trans). Chatto, 1924. 1st UK ed. 2 vols. VG (ink names). *Williams.* $101/£65

PROUT, SAMUEL. Prout's Microcosm. London, 1841. Tp,(ii)text, 24 plts. Emb cl (rebacked, orig spine laid down; new eps; worn), gilt. *Edwards.* $140/£90

PROVOYEUR, PIERRE. Marc Chagall: Biblical Interpretations. NY, 1983. VG in dj, slipcase. *Argosy.* $125/£81

PROWN, JULES DAVID. John Singleton Copley. Cambridge: Harvard Univ Press, 1966. 1st ed. 2 vols. Fine in pub's slicase. *Hermitage.* $125/£81

PROWN, JULES DAVID. John Singleton Copley.... Harvard Univ Press, 1966. 2 vols. Color frontis. 2-tone cl (vol I spine stained). *Argosy.* $175/£113

PROWSE, D.W. A History of Newfoundland from the English, Colonial and Foreign Records. London: Macmillan, 1895. xxiii,742pp; lg fldg map (repaired). Good + (lt foxing; sl rubbed). *Walcot.* $50/£32

PRUCHA, FRANCIS (ed). Army Life on the Western Frontier. Univ of OK, (1958). 1st ed. Map. Fine in Fine dj. *Oregon.* $40/£26

PRUCHA, FRANCIS. The Sword of the Republic. London, (1969). 1st ed. VG + (name, address). *Heinoldt.* $20/£13

PRUDDEN, T. MITCHELL. Dust and Its Dangers. NY, 1894. 1st ed, reptd. 111pp. Good. *Fye.* $50/£32

PRYCE-JONES, ALAN. The Spring Journey. London: Cobden-Sanderson, 1931. 1st Eng ed. Grn cl. VG. *Dalian.* $39/£25

PRYOR, MRS. ROGER A. The Mother of Washington and Her Times. Macmillan, 1903. 1st ed. VG-. *Book Broker*. $25/£16

PRYOR, MRS. ROGER A. Reminiscences of War and Peace. NY, 1904. 1st ed. Pict cl. Spine sl faded, sm water stain, o/w VG. *Pratt*. $50/£32

Publications of the United States Book Company, Successors to John W. Lovell Co. United States Book Co, Oct 1890. 1st ed. Worn, else VG. *Fine Books*. $85/£55

PUCKLE, BERTRAM S. Funeral Customs, Their Origin and Development. London: T. Werner Laurie, 1926. 1st ed. VG. *Hollett*. $101/£65

PUDNEY, JOHN. Low Life. London: Bodley Head, 1947. 1st Eng ed. Pink ptd paper bds. VG in dj (sl faded, nicked). *Dalian*. $39/£25

PUDNEY, JOHN. Sunday Adventure: A Story for Boys and Girls. London: Bodley Head, 1951. 1st ed. Dbl post 16mo. Frontis on 1/2 title verso. Eps ptd in blue. Yellow-grn bds. Fine in dj (sl frayed, faded; chip). *Temple*. $16/£10

PUDNEY, JOHN. Thursday Adventure. The Stolen Airliner. London: Evans Bros, 1955. 1st Eng ed. Blue cl. VG in dj (sl soiled, nicked). *Dalian*. $39/£25

PUGH, P.D. GORDON. Naval Ceramics. Newport: Ceramic Books Co, 1971. 1st ed. 131 plts (13 color). *Edwards*. $70/£45

PUGH, P.D. GORDON. Staffordshire Portrait Figures and Allied Subjects of the Victorian Era. Barrie & Jenkins, 1970. 1st ed. 37 color plts. Full gilt-edged grn morocco (rebound), raised bands. *Edwards*. $116/£75

PUGIN, A. and J. and H. LE KEUX. Specimens of the Architecture of Normandy from the 11th to the 16th Century. London: Blackie, 1874. New ed. 88pp, 78 engr plts. Aeg. Good+ (lt wear, ends foxed). *Willow House*. $116/£75

PUGIN, A. WELBY. Details of Antient Timber Houses of the 15th and 16th Centuries. London: Ackermann, 1836. 1st ed. Engr title leaf, 21 engr plts (lt foxed), 1pg ads. Pub's cl (cvr worn). *Bookpress*. $250/£161

PUGIN, A. WELBY. Glossary of Ecclesiastical Ornament and Costume.... London: Bohn, 1844. 4to. xvi,222pp, chromolitho title, 73 chromolitho plts (2 double-pg). Contemp half morocco, gilt spine (rebacked w/orig spine). *Marlborough*. $465/£300

PUGIN, A. WELBY. A Treatise on Chancel Screens and Rood Lofts. London: Charles Dolman, 1851. 1st ed. viii,124pp; 14 plts. Pub's cl. VG. *Bookpress*. $225/£145

PUIG, MANUEL. Kiss of the Spider Woman. NY: Knopf, 1979. 1st ed. Fine in Fine dj (sm nick). *Beasley*. $45/£29

PUIG, MANUEL. Pubis Angelical. Elena Brunet (trans). London: Faber & Faber, (1987). 1st Eng ed. Black cl. Fine in dj. *Godot*. $35/£23

PUIG, MANUEL. Pubis Angelical. London: Faber, 1986. 1st Eng ed. Black cl. Fine in dj. *Dalian*. $31/£20

PULLAN, RICHARD POPPLEWELL. Eastern Cities and Italian Towns. London: Edward Stanford, 1879. (iv),(240)pp + 20pp ads. Grn cl stamped in blind, gilt. NF (ex-lib). *Schoyer*. $65/£42

PUMPELLY, RAPHAEL. Across America and Asia. NY: Leypoldt & Holt, 1870. 3rd ed rev. (xvi),454pp, 4 maps (3 fldg, 1 color); 12 plts. Brick cl stamped in gilt (bkseller's tag; backstrip sl creased). Howes P 650. *Schoyer*. $85/£55

PUMPHREY, ARTHUR. Pink Danube. London: Martin Secker, 1939. 1st Eng ed. Pink cl. Faded, sl spotted, rubbed, o/w VG. *Dalian*. $54/£35

PUPIN, MICHAEL. South Slav Monuments: Serbian Orthodox Church. London: Murray, 1918. 54 plts, 4 plans, fldg map; teg. Orig buckram, gilt emb design. VF. *Europa*. $109/£70

PUPPE, GEORGE et al. The Hyman: A Medico-Legal Study in Rape. NY, 1935. 1st ed. Good. *Fye*. $75/£48

PUPPI, LIONELLO. Andrea Palladio. Boston, 1975. Good in dj. *Washton*. $165/£106

PURDON, H.G. Memoirs of the Services of the 64th Regiment...1758-1881. London, n.d. (1881). 112pp; color frontis; 2 color plts. Foxing to pp facing plts; inscrip, o/w VG. Red emb cl, gilt title. *Edwards*. $116/£75

PURDY, JAMES. 63: Dream Palace. Santa Rosa: Black Sparrow Press, 1991. Ltd to 150 numbered, signed. Cl-backed pict bds. VG. *King*. $50/£32

PURDY, JAMES. Colour of Darkness. London: Secker & Warburg, 1961 1st Eng ed. Blue cl. Fine in dj. *Dalian*. $39/£25

PURDY, JAMES. Eustace Chisholm and the Works. NY: FSG, 1967. 1st ed rev copy, pub's slip laid in. Fine in Fine dj (short corner crease). *Revere*. $30/£19

PURDY, JAMES. Malcolm. London: Secker & Warburg, 1960. 1st Eng ed. Blue cl. Spine sl faded, o/w Fine in dj (sl rubbed, creased). *Dalian*. $54/£35

PURDY, JAMES. Mourners Below. NY, (1981). 1st ed. Fine in dj. *Hayman*. $15/£10

PURDY, JAMES. Pioneers of the Valley of the Maumee Rapids and Their Improvements. Mansfield, OH: Shield & Banner Otto Gas Engine Print, 1882. 32,(1)pp; errata. Good in ptd wrappers. *Hayman*. $250/£161

PURDY, RICHARD L. Thomas Hardy: A Bibliographical Study. London: OUP, 1954. 1st ed. NF (edges foxed) in dj (lt wear, tear). *Antic Hay*. $87/£56

PURSEGLOVE, J.W. Tropical Crops: Dicotyledons. London, 1968. 2 vols. VG in djs (chipped). *Brooks*. $69/£45

PURVES, DAVID and R. COCHRANE. The English Circumnavigators. Edinburgh, 1882. Frontis, 831pp, 4 double-pg maps. Full leather, gilt; gilt emblem on fr cvr; marbled edges, eps. VG. *Oregon*. $95/£61

PURVES-STEWART, J. Sands of Time: Recollections of a Physician... London, 1939. 1st ed. Good. *Fye*. $25/£16

PUSATERI, SAMUEL J. Flora of Our Sierran National Parks—Yosemite, Sequoia and Kings Canyon. Three Rivers, 1963. Signed. VG in dj (sl chipped). *Brooks*. $47/£30

PUSEY, MERLO J. Charles Evans Hughes. NY, 1951. 1st ed. 2 vols. Spines sl dull, else Good in slipcase (splitting). *King*. $35/£23

PUSEY, W. Syphilis as a Modern Problem. 1915. 1st ed. 129pp. Good. *Fye*. $75/£48

PUSHKIN, ALEXANDER. The Golden Cockerel. NY: LEC, (n.d.) but 1949. #904/1500 numbered, signed by Edmund Dulac (illus). Fine in tissue dj, dec bd liner, pub's slipcase (sl dusty). *Hermitage*. $225/£145

Puss in Boots. NY: Duenewald, (1944). 8vo. 6 tab moveables by Julian Wehr. Full color illus bds, spiral binding. Good in dj (spine worn; marginal tear). *Reisler*. $175/£113

Puss in Boots. London: Warne, n.d. 4to. 6 color plts by H.M. Brock. Good in illus paper wrappers. *Reisler.* $125/£81

PUTNAM, A.W. History of Middle Tennessee. Nashville, TN: Ptd for Author, 1859. 1st ed. Inscribed presentation. 668pp, 3 fldg maps, 9 (of 10) plts (frontis excised). Emb brn cl (spine, corners worn; rear outer joint cracked). Good (lt foxing internally). Howes P 657. *Chapel Hill.* $250/£161

PUTNAM, E. and A. BATES. Prince Vance. Roberts Bros, 1888. 1st ed. VG. *Aronovitz.* $55/£35

PUTNAM, GEORGE GRANVILLE. Salem Vessels and Their Voyages. Salem, 1924-30. 1st ed. 4 vols. Attractive. *Lefkowicz.* $200/£129

PUTNAM, GEORGE GRANVILLE. Salem Vessels and Their Voyages. Salem: Essex Institute, 1925. Paper over bds, cl spine, gilt titles, pict paste-on. Sl shelfwear, else VG. *Parmer.* $55/£35

PUTNAM, GEORGE HAVEN. Memories of My Youth 1844-1865. NY, 1914. 1st ed. VG + . *Pratt.* $45/£29

PUTNAM, GEORGE HAVEN. A Prisoner of War in Virginia, 1864-5. NY/London: Putnam's, 1912. 1st ed. Frontis port. Orig blue cl. Sm inkstamp, else VG. *Chapel Hill.* $45/£29

PUTNAM, GEORGE HAVEN. Some Memories of the Civil War, Together with an Appreciation of the Career and Character of Major General Israel Putnam. NY: Putnam's, 1924. 1st ed. Author presentation. (Bkpl; cvrs rubbed, spot.) *Oak Knoll.* $45/£29

PUTNAM, GEORGE HAVEN. Some Memories of the Civil War. NY, 1924. 1st ed. Minor cvr wear, o/w Fine. *Pratt.* $35/£23

PUTNAM, GEORGE PALMER. Death Valley and Its Country. NY: Duell, Sloan & Pearce, 1946. 1st ed. NF in Good + dj. *Connolly.* $35/£23

PUTNAM, H. PHELPS. Trinc—A Book of Poems. NY: Doran, (1927). 1st ed. Pict paper cvr label. Fine. *Pharos.* $100/£65

PUTNAM, SAMUEL (trans). Kiki's Memoirs. Paris: Edward W. Titus, 1930. 1st ed in English. One of 1000. Ptd wraps, mtd cvr illus. Fine in orig glassine wrapper, ptd red wrap-around band (lacks plain cardboard slipcase). *Chapel Hill.* $250/£161

PUTNAM, SAMUEL. The World of Jean de Bosschere. (London): Fortune Press, (1932). 1st ed. One of 900 (of 1000) numbered. Frontis. Gilt buckram. Sl mks, o/w Very Nice. *Reese.* $85/£55

PUTNEY, WILLIAM G. (ed). Behind the Guns. Carbondale, (1965). 1st ed. Blue/gray cl. Fine in slipcase. *Bohling.* $35/£23

PUZO, MARIO. The Dark Arena. Random House. 1955. 1st ed, 1st bk. NF in VG + dj (sl wear spine head). *Fine Books.* $85/£55

PUZO, MARIO. The Godfather. London: Heinemann, (1969). 1st Eng ed. VG in dj (nicks; lt soiling). *Houle.* $125/£81

PYCRAFT, W.P. The Animal Why Book. NY: Frederick A. Stokes, n.d. (ca 1910). 4to. 89pp + 2pp contents, 32 tipped-in lithos. Pasted pict color label upper bd; cl spine; pict lower bd. NF (corners lt worn). *Hobbyhorse.* $100/£65

PYCROFT, JAMES. Twenty Years in the Church. London: L. Booth, 1861. 4th ed. viii,280pp. Mod 1/2 levant morocco, gilt. VG. *Hollett.* $116/£75

PYLE, HOWARD. Howard Pyle's Book of the American Spirit. Merle Johnson (comp). NY/London, 1923. 'B-X' on copyright pg. Pict cvrs. Fine (spine chipped; sl rubbed, sm stain) in dj (chipped, closed tears, sm stains). *Polyanthos.* $200/£129

PYLE, HOWARD. The Wonder Clock or Four and Twenty Marvelous Tales. Harper, 1892. Howard Pyle (illus). Grn cl neatly rebacked in brn morocco, gilt. *Petersfield.* $70/£45

PYM, BARBARA. An Academic Question. NY, 1986. 1st Amer ed. Fine in Fine dj. *Polyanthos.* $25/£16

PYM, BARBARA. Crampton Hodnet. London: Macmillan, 1985. Review copy, slip tipped in. Brn cl. Fine in dj. *Dalian.* $31/£20

PYM, BARBARA. A Few Green Leaves. London: MacMillan, 1980. 1st Eng ed. Black cl. VF in dj. *Dalian.* $39/£25

PYM, BARBARA. Some Tame Gazelle. NY: Dutton, 1983. 1st Amer ed. Sl dampstain reps, o/w Very Nice in Good dj (sl dampstained; price-clipped). *Virgo.* $23/£15

PYM, BARBARA. An Unsuitable Attachment. London: Macmillan, 1982. 1st ed. NF in dj. *Virgo.* $47/£30

PYNCHON, THOMAS. The Crying of Lot 49. Phila/NY: Lippincott, (1966). 1st ed. Fine in dj. *Limestone.* $285/£184

PYNCHON, THOMAS. The Crying of Lot 49. Philadelphia: Lippincott, 1966. 1st ed. Fine in NF dj (short, internally mended tear w/short crease). *Beasley.* $150/£97

PYNCHON, THOMAS. The Crying of Lot 49. London: Cape, 1967. 1st UK ed. NF (ink name) in NF dj (sl discolored). *Williams.* $279/£180

PYNCHON, THOMAS. Gravity's Rainbow. NY: Viking, (1973). 1st ed. Orange cl. NF in NF dj. *Chapel Hill.* $500/£323

PYNCHON, THOMAS. Gravity's Rainbow. NY, 1973. 1st Amer ed. Fine (sl rubbed) in dj (sl rubbed). *Polyanthos.* $450/£290

PYNCHON, THOMAS. Gravity's Rainbow. Viking, 1973. 1st ed. NF in dj. *Fine Books.* $350/£226

PYNCHON, THOMAS. Gravity's Rainbow. NY: Viking, 1973. 1st ed. Fine in Fine dj (lt cockling to spine). *Beasley.* $425/£274

PYNCHON, THOMAS. Gravity's Rainbow. Cape, 1973. Pb (issued simultaneously w/hb). Fine. *Sclanders.* $47/£30

PYNCHON, THOMAS. Low-Lands. London: Aloes Books, 1978. Correct 1st ptg; one of 1500. Vignette tp; blank, followed by leaf bearing ads at end; issued w/o eps. Wire-stitched as single gathering into glazed thin card (artboard) wrappers, cut flush; fr wrapper ptd in colors. Fine. *Temple.* $22/£14

PYNCHON, THOMAS. The Secret Integration. London: Aloes Books, 1980. 1st ed. Ltd to 2500. Fine in pict wraps. *Polyanthos.* $20/£13

PYNCHON, THOMAS. Slow Learner. Boston: Little, Brown, (1984). 1st ed. Fine in dj. *Godot.* $45/£29

PYNCHON, THOMAS. V. Phila: Lippincott, 1963. 1st ed. Fine (spine lt sunned) in Fine dj (lt spine wear). *Beasley.* $475/£306

PYNCHON, THOMAS. V. London: Jonathan Cape, 1963. 1st Eng ed, 1st bk. Top edge purple. Black bds. Top edge sl faded, o/w Fine in dj. *Temple.* $171/£110

PYNCHON, THOMAS. V. Cape, 1963. 1st Eng ed, 1st bk. NF in NF dj (lt dust-soil). *Fine Books.* $250/£161

PYNCHON, THOMAS. Vineland. London: Secker & Warburg, (1990). 1st Eng ed. Fine in Fine dj. *Dermont.* $40/£26

PYPER, GEORGE D. The Romance of an Old Playhouse. Salt Lake, 1937. 2nd ed. Rubber stamp, name, o/w VG. *Benchmark.* $30/£19

Q

Q. (Pseud of A.T. Quiller-Couch.) Sir John Constantine: Memoirs of His Adventures at Home and Abroad.... London: Smith, Elder, 1906. 1st ed. Lower edges rough-trimmed. Inscrip, o/w Nice. *Temple.* $23/£15

QUACKENBOS, JOHN D. Geological Ancestors of the Brook Trout.... NY: Tobias A. Wright, 1916. Ltd to 300 numbered, signed. Inscribed presentation. Frontis port, 1 b/w, 8 color plts. Full grn calf (rubbed, scuffed), gilt. NF internally. *Blue Mountain.* $275/£177

QUAIFE, M.M. Checagou: From Indian Wigwam to Modern City 1673-1835. Chicago: Univ of Chicago, 1933. 1st ed. Frontis map. NF in Good+ dj. *Connolly.* $30/£19

QUAIFE, M.M. Chicago and the Old Northwest, 1673-1835. Chicago, IL: Univ of Chicago Press, (1913). 1st ed. Fldg map, 10 plts. Blue cl. NF (name). Howes Q 1. *Chapel Hill.* $250/£161

QUAIFE, M.M. Chicago's Highways Old and New. Chicago: D.F. Keller, 1923. 1st ed. Fldg map, 22 plts, facs. Very Nice. *Cady.* $45/£29

QUAIFE, M.M. Chicago's Highways Old and New. Chicago: Keller, 1923. 1st ed. Good+. *October Farm.* $48/£31

QUAIFE, M.M. Lake Michigan. Indianapolis: Bobbs-Merrill, 1944. 1st ed. VG in Good dj. *Peninsula.* $30/£19

QUAIFE, M.M. This Is Detroit. Wayne Univ Press, 1951. 1st ed. VG. *Artis.* $25/£16

QUAIFE, M.M. (ed). Pictures of Gold Rush California. Chicago, (1949). Lakeside Classic. VG. *Schoyer.* $25/£16

QUAIFE, M.M. (ed). Pictures of Gold Rush California. Chicago: Lakeside Classic, Christmas 1949. 1st ed. Map. Wine cl; teg. Spine lettering worn, else VG. *Connolly.* $35/£23

QUAIFE, M.M. (ed). Pictures of Illinois One Hundred Years Ago. Chicago, 1918. Frontis. Dk grn cl, gilt stamping. VG+. *Bohling.* $75/£48

QUAIFE, M.M. (ed). Southwestern Expedition of Zebulon M. Pike. Chicago: R.R. Donnelley, 1925. Frontis, fldg map. Teg. Grn cl (extrems sl worn). NF. *Harrington.* $35/£23

QUARLES, BENJAMIN. The Negro in the Civil War. Boston: Little Brown, (1953). 1st ed. Orig cl. Fine in NF dj. *Mcgowan.* $45/£29

QUAYLE, ERIC. The Collector's Book of Books. NY: Clarkson N. Potter, (1971). Blue cl bd, gilt spine title. Fine in pict dj. *Heller.* $40/£26

QUAYLE, ERIC. The Collector's Book of Books. Studio Vista, 1971. 17 color plts. Dj (sl chipped). *Edwards.* $47/£30

QUAYLE, ERIC. The Collector's Book of Books. NY: Clarkson N. Potter, 1971. 1st Amer ed. 16 full color plts. Dj. *Bookpress.* $65/£42

QUAYLE, ERIC. The Collector's Book of Boys' Stories. (London): Studio Vista, (1973). 1st ed. Fine in dj (sl rubbed). *Bookpress.* $85/£55

QUAYLE, ERIC. The Collector's Book of Children's Books. NY: Clarkson Potter, (1971). 1st ed. Fine in dj. *Pharos.* $35/£23

QUAYLE, ERIC. The Collector's Book of Children's Books. NY: Clarkson N. Potter, (1971). 1st US ed. Fine in dj. *Oak Knoll.* $85/£55

QUAYLE, ERIC. The Collector's Book of Children's Books. (London): Studio Vista, 1971. 1st ed. 14 plts. Fine. *Bookpress.* $85/£55

QUEBBEMAN, FRANCES. Medicine in Territorial Arizona. Phoenix: AZ Hist Found, 1966. 1st ed. VG- (top edge sl foxed). *Parker.* $35/£23

QUEBEDEAUX, RICHARD. Prime Sources of California and Nevada Local History. Spokane, WA: Clark, 1992. 1st ed. One of 750 ptd. *Ginsberg.* $65/£42

QUEEN, ELLERY (ed). The Queen's Awards 1946. London: Gollancz, 1948. 1st Eng ed. Grn cl. Eps sl browned, o/w Fine in dj (soiled, chipped). *Dalian.* $31/£20

QUEEN, ELLERY. Calendar of Crime. Boston: Little Brown, 1952. 1st ed. VF in dj. *Mordida.* $75/£48

QUEEN, ELLERY. Cat of Many Tails. Boston: Little, Brown, 1949. 1st Amer ed. Blue pict cl. NF in dj (repaired, soiled). *Dalian.* $39/£25

QUEEN, ELLERY. The Finishing Stroke. NY: S&S, 1958. 1st ed. Fine in dj (sl corner wear). *Mordida.* $45/£29

QUEEN, ELLERY. The Four of Hearts. London: Gollancz, 1939. 1st UK ed. VG. *Ming.* $23/£15

QUEEN, ELLERY. The Glass Village. Boston: Houghton Mifflin, 1954. 1st ed. VF in dj (sl rubbing). *Mordida.* $65/£42

QUEEN, ELLERY. In the Queen's Parlor. NY: S&S, 1957. 1st ed. Fine in dj. *Mordida.* $45/£29

QUEEN, ELLERY. The Murderer Is a Fox. London: Gollancz, 1945. 1st UK ed. VG in VG dj. *Ming.* $23/£15

QUEEN, ELLERY. The Origin of Evil. Boston: Little Brown, 1951. 1st ed. Fine in dj (wear). *Mordida.* $75/£48

QUEEN, ELLERY. (Pseud of Theodore Sturgeon.) The Player on the Other Side. NY: Random House, (1963). 1st ed. NF in dj (lt rubbed). *Hermitage.* $65/£42

QUEEN, ELLERY. Rogue's Gallery. Boston: Little, Brown, 1945. 1st ed. Fine in dj (spine head sl worn). *Pharos.* $45/£29

QUEENY, EDGAR M. Prairie Wings. NY, 1946. 1st trade ed. Color frontis. Buckram. VG. *Argosy.* $85/£55

QUENEAU, RAYMOND. Pierrot. London: John Lehmann, 1950. 1st British ed. VG+ (spine creased) in VG+ dj (spine sl worn). *Lame Duck.* $50/£32

QUENNELL, M. and C.H.B. Everyday Life in the Old Stone Age. NY/London: Putnam's, 1922. 1st ed. Color frontis, 70 plts. Spine faded, else VG. *Mikesh.* $17/£11

QUENNELL, PETER. Baudelaire and the Symbolists. London: C&W, 1929. 1st ed. Collotype frontis, 3 plts. Lower edges uncut. Gray buckram. Fine in dj (sl frayed, spine dknd). *Temple.* $31/£20

QUENNELL, PETER. Customs and Characters. London: Weidenfeld & Nicolson, 1982. 1st ed. VG in dj. *Virgo.* $16/£10

QUENNELL, PETER. Inscription on a Fountain-Head. London: Faber & Faber, 1929. 1st ed. One of 300 numbered, signed. Grn bds, gilt. Fine. *Macdonnell.* $45/£29

QUENNELL, PETER. A Letter to Mrs. Virginia Woolf. London: Hogarth Press, 1932. 1st ed. VG in wrappers (sl soiled). *Virgo.* $39/£25

QUENNELL, PETER. Masques and Poems. London: Golden Cockerel Press, (1922). #61/375. Uncut except for top edge (sl browned). White cl backstrip, lt blue sides (sl stained). *Petersfield.* $59/£38

QUENNELL, PETER. The Phoenix-Kind. London: C&W, 1931. 1st ed. 2pp pub's ads tipped in. Top edge blue, rest uncut. Blue cl. Fading, o/w Fine in dj (faded, sl chipped). *Temple.* $47/£30

QUENNELL, PETER. A Superficial Journey Through Tokyo and Peking. London: Faber & Faber, 1932. 1st Eng ed. 17 plts. Red cl. Sl faded, o/w VG. *Dalian.* $54/£35

Quest for Qual-A-Wa-Loo. (Humbolt Bay, CA). A Collection of Diaries and Historical Notes. (SF: 1943). 1st ed. Ink name, else Fine. *Perier.* $75/£48

QUICK, HERBERT and EDWARD. Mississippi Steamboatin'. NY: Henry Holt, (1926). 1st ed. VG. *Laurie.* $75/£48

QUICK, HERBERT. American Inland Waterways. NY, 1909. 1st ed. (Rebound, orig cvr transposed.) *Heinoldt.* $50/£32

QUICK, HERBERT. Virginia of the Airlines. Bobbs-Merrill, 1909. 1st ed. VG. *Madle.* $30/£19

QUIETT, GLENN CHESNEY. Pay Dirt. NY: D. Appleton-Century, 1936. 1st ed. Frontis. Gold-stamped cl. *Dawson.* $50/£32

QUIGLEY, MARTIN. The Crooked Pitch. Algonquin, 1984. 1st ed. Fine in VG+ dj. *Plapinger.* $25/£16

QUILLER-COUCH, ARTHUR (retold by). The Sleeping Beauty and Other Fairy Tales. London: Hodder & Stoughton, (1910). 1st ed. Lg, 4to. 30 mtd color plts by Edmund Dulac. Brn leatherette cl, gold stamping, lettering (sl wear). *Reisler.* $400/£258

QUILLER-COUCH, ARTHUR. In Powder and Crinoline. London: Hodder & Stoughton, 1913. 1st Eng ed. 4to. 164pp, 24 color illus w/lettered guards by Kay Nielsen. Cl-backed pict bds, gilt. Internally VG. (Spine, bds faded; corners bumped.) *Davidson.* $700/£452

QUILLER-COUCH, ARTHUR. Old Fires and Profitable Ghosts. Scribners, 1900. 1st Amer ed. Sl wear spine extrems, else VG. *Aronovitz.* $35/£23

QUILLER-COUCH, ARTHUR. The Twelve Dancing Princesses and Others. NY: Doran, c. 1913. 1st Amer ed. 244pp, 16 tipped-in color plts by Kay Nielsen. Blue cl, pict gilt. VG (bkpl, edgewear). *Davidson.* $295/£190

QUILLER-COUCH, ARTHUR. Twelve Dancing Princesses. NY: Portland House, 1988. 1st ptg. Lg 8vo. 12 color plts by Kay Nielsen. VF in VF dj. *Book Adoption.* $40/£26

QUILP, JOCELYN. Baron Verdigris. London: Henry & Co, 1894. 1st ed. Frontis by Aubrey Beardsley, 214pp + 2pp pub's ads. Dec eps. (Sl spotting, rubbing.) *Edwards.* $70/£45

QUINBY, MOSES. Mysteries of Bee-Keeping Explained. NY: Saxton, 1864. 8th ed. 384pp. VG. *Second Life.* $45/£29

QUINBY, MOSES. Quinby's New Bee-Keeping. NY: OJ, 1897. New, rev ed. 271pp + 2pp ads. Grn cl, gilt. VG (sl soiled, lt etching). *Bohling.* $35/£23

QUINCY, JOSIAH. Essays on the Soiling of Cattle. Boston: Loring, 1862. 3rd ed. 64pp. Contemp cl-backed bds. (Ex-lib.) *Second Life.* $25/£16

QUINCY, JOSIAH. Essays on the Soiling of Cattle.... NY: OJ, n.d. (c. 1859). 121pp. Brn cl, gilt spine title. VG+. *Bohling.* $30/£19

QUINCY, JOSIAH. The History of Harvard University. Cambridge: John Owen, 1840. 2 vols. Frontispieces. Overall VG (engrs heavily browned, parts of text foxed; cl worn, tear vol 2). *Goodrich.* $125/£81

QUINN, P.T. Pear Culture for Profit. NY: OJ, 1869. 136pp. Fine. *Book Market.* $30/£19

QUINN, S.J. The History of the City of Fredericksburg, Virginia. Richmond: Hermitage Press, 1908. 1st ed. VG (plts facing pg256 bound in upside down, 1 plt sl surface damage, 1 plt marked). *Cahan.* $100/£65

QUINN, SEABURY. Roads. Arkham House, 1948. 1st ed. Fine in dj (frayed). *Madle.* $125/£81

QUINN, SEABURY. Roads. Arkham House, 1948. 1st hb ed. Virgil Finlay (illus). Fine in VG dj (lt wear, tear). *Aronovitz.* $85/£55

QUINNELL, A.J. Snap Shot. Macmillan, 1982. 1st ed. Inscribed. VG in VG dj. *Ming.* $31/£20

QUINT, ALONZO H. The Potomac and the Rapidan. Boston, 1864. 1st ed. 407pp. Fldg map. Worn, extrems chipped, o/w VG. *Pratt.* $45/£29

QUINTARD, CHARLES TODD. Doctor Quintard, Chaplain C.S.A. and Second Bishop of Tennessee. Sewanee, TN: University Press, 1905. 1st ed, ltd to 375. Minor soiling, else VG. *Mcgowan.* $450/£290

QUIRKE, ARTHUR J. Forged, Anonymous, and Suspect Documents. London: Routledge, 1930. Cl unevenly faded, o/w VG. *Heller.* $35/£23

Quiz Kids Blue Book. Akron: Saalfield, (n.d. ca 1940s). 1st ed. 128pp. Cl spine, pict paper-cvrd bds. Fine in dj (spine faded, chips, lg tears). *Godot.* $35/£23

R

R.L. Polk and Co's Salt Lake City Directory, 1894-5. Salt Lake City: R.L. Polk, 1894. 952,(3)pp. Black-stamped cl bds, cl spine (rear hinge split; binding, final sig loose). *Dawson.* $175/£113

RABAN, JONATHAN. Arabia through the Looking Glass. NY: S&S, 1979. 1st ed. VG in dj. *Worldwide.* $18/£12

RABAN, JONATHAN. Arabia through the Looking Glass. London, 1979. 1st ed. Dj. *Edwards.* $28/£18

RABAN, JONATHAN. Arabia through the Looking Glass. London: Collins, 1979. 1st Eng ed. Brn cl. VF in VF dj. *Dalian.* $39/£25

RABAN, JONATHAN. For Love and Money. Collins Harvill, 1987. 1st ed. Dj (price-clipped). *Edwards.* $23/£15

RABAN, JONATHAN. Foreign Land. Collins Harvill, 1985. 1st ed. Dj. *Edwards.* $23/£15

RABAN, JONATHAN. Old Glory. Collins, 1981. 1st ed. Dj (price-clipped). *Edwards.* $23/£15

RABAN, JONATHAN. Old Glory. London: Collins, 1981. 1st ed. Fine in dj w/orig wraparound band. *Limestone.* $45/£29

RABAN, JONATHAN. Old Glory. London: Collins, 1981. 1st Eng ed. Blue cl. VF in VF dj. *Dalian*. $39/£25

Rabbit Book. Chicago: M.A. Donohue, (ca 1909). Mary Tourtel (illus). 6.5 x 1.5 inches, stump format. Yellow cl w/red lettering, illus. Ivory catch present. Good (lt mks). *Reisler*. $285/£184

RABE, DAVID. Goose and Tomtom. NY: Grove, (1986). 1st trade ed. Fine in dj. *Reese*. $35/£23

RABELAIS, FRANCIS. Works of Mr. Francis Rabelais. London: Navarre Soc, (n.d.). 2 vols. Lovely set (fep replaced vol 1; ink name vol 2). *Williams*. $194/£125

RABINOWICZ, HARRY M. The Jewish Literary Treasures of England and America. NY: Thomas Yoseloff, (1962). 1st ed. Fine in dj (rubbed). *Oak Knoll*. $35/£23

RACKHAM, ARTHUR. Arthur Rackham's Book of Pictures. NY: Century Co, n.d. (1913). 1st Amer ed. 44 mtd color plts, guards. Teg. Tan cl; gilt cvr, spine. Fine. *Glenn*. $300/£194

RACKHAM, BERNARD and HERBERT READ. English Pottery. NY: Scribner's, 1924. 1st Amer ed. Color frontis. Gray buckram (lt wear). *Glenn*. $150/£97

RACKHAM, BERNARD. The Ancient Glass of Canterbury Cathedral. London: Humphries, 1949. 1st ed. 25 color, 80 monochrome plts. Blue cl; teg. Fine. *Hermitage*. $200/£129

RACKHAM, BERNARD. Early Staffordshire Pottery. London: Faber & Faber, 1951. 1st ed. Color frontis; 3 color, 96 b/w plts (fep sl browned). Dj (sl soiled, chipped w/sl loss). *Edwards*. $54/£35

RACKHAM, BERNARD. A Guide to the Collections of Stained Glass; Victoria and Albert Museum. London, 1936. 64 plts. 1st few pp sl spotted, o/w Fine. *Europa*. $43/£28

RACKHAM, BERNARD. Islamic Pottery and Italian Maioloica. London: Faber & Faber, (1959). 1st ed. 231 plts. Fine in dj (lt worn). *Hermitage*. $75/£48

RACSTER, OLGA. Chats On Violins. London: Werner Laurie, 1905. 1st ed. 8 plts. Grn cl, gilt, blind. Good+ (cvrs sl worn, bubbled). *Willow House*. $19/£12

RADBILL, SAMUEL X. Bibliography of Medical Ex Libris Literature. LA: Hilprand, 1951. 1st ed. Proof of author's bkpl at fr. Signed by Pavel Simon (designer). VG. *Petrilla*. $75/£48

RADCLIFFE, ANN. The Italian. London: J. Limbird, 1824. (2),189pp; 8 wood-engr illus. Contemp cl (soiled), paper label. *Cox*. $54/£35

RADCLIFFE, ANN. A Journey Made in 1794, to Holland and the Western Frontier of Germany.... Dublin: Wogan et al, 1795. 1st Irish ed. vi,499pp (dkng). Early calf (rebacked), raised bands, leather label, gilt. Nice. *Hartfield*. $395/£255

RADCLIFFE, ANN. The Mysteries of Udolpho, A Romance. London: F.C. & J. Rivington, et al, 1810. 3 vols. Marbled eps, edges. Full calf w/gilt lettering, decs. Nice (rubbed). *Limestone*. $235/£152

RADCLIFFE, CHARLES et al. On Diseases of the Spine and Nerves. Phila, 1871. 1st Amer ed. 196pp. Good. *Fye*. $75/£48

RADCLIFFE, WILLIAM. Fishing from the Earliest Times. London, 1921. (Feps, edges lt foxed, some intrusion to text; sl rubbed.) *Edwards*. $132/£85

RADCLIFFE, WILLIAM. Fishing from the Earliest Times. NY: Dutton, 1926. 2nd ed. VG+. *Bowman*. $90/£58

RADISSON, PIERRE E. The Explorations of Pierre Esprit Radisson, from Original Manuscript in Bodleian Library and the British Museum. Arthur Adams (ed). Ross & Haines, 1961. 1st thus. VF in Fine dj. Howes R 6. *Oregon*. $40/£26

RADLEY, SHEILA. Who Saw Him Die? London: Constable, 1987. 1st ed. Fine in Fine dj. *Janus*. $30/£19

RAE, EDWARD. The White Sea Peninsula. London, 1881. 1st ed. xviii,347pp; map (foxed). Contemp 1/2 calf (battered). *Lewis*. $99/£64

RAE, JOHN. New Adventures of 'Alice.' Chicago: P.F. Volland, 1917. 1st ed. 4to. 12 color illus by author. Pub's binding; pict, gilt-dec cvr. Good+. *D & D*. $80/£52

RAE, W.F. Westward by Rail. London: Longmans, 1870. 1st ed. Frontis. (14),391pp; map. (Emb lib stamp.) *Ginsberg*. $100/£65

RAE, W.F. Westward by Rail. NY: Appleton, 1871. 1st Amer ed. Color frontis map, xiv,391pp. Orig cl. VG. *Schoyer*. $50/£32

Raggedy Ann and Andy with Animated Illustrations. Akron: Saalfield, 1944. 8vo. 6 tab moveables by Julian Wehr. Color illus bds, spiral binding (corners sl worn). *Reisler*. $200/£129

RAGLAN, LORD. Jocasta's Crime. London, Methuen, (1933). 1st ed. Blue cl. VG. *Gach*. $35/£23

RAGUIN, VIRGINIA CHIEFFO. Stained Glass in Thirteenth-Century Burgundy. Princeton, 1982. Good in dj. *Washton*. $50/£32

RAHT, CARLYSLE GRAHAM. The Romance of Davis Mountains and Big Bend Country. El Paso: Rahtbooks Co., (1919). 1st ed. Frontis port, dbl-pg map, 26 plts by Waldo Williams. Illus blue cl, gilt. Bright. Howes R 16. *Karmiole*. $100/£65

RAIKES, G.A. The History of the Honourable Artillery Company. London: Richard Bentley, 1878. 2 vols. Color frontispieces. (Rubbed.) *Petersfield*. $127/£82

Railway Rag Book. Dean's Rag Book #150. London: Dean's Rag Book Co, ca 1900. Obl 16mo. VG (some soil). *Davidson*. $200/£129

RAINE, KATHLEEN. The Pythoness and Other Poems. London: Hamish Hamilton, 1949. 1st ed. Ink name, else NF in VG dj (spine worn). *Lame Duck*. $45/£29

RAINEY, GEO. The Cherokee Strip, Its History. (Enid, OK, 1925.) 1st ed. Presentation inscription. 11 photos. Ptd wrappers (sl soiled). Howes R 18. *Shasky*. $100/£65

RAINEY, GEORGE. The Cherokee Strip. Guthrie, OK: Co-Operative Pub Co, 1933. 1st ed. Good (spotting). Howes R 18. *Lien*. $60/£39

RAINEY, T.C. Along the Old Trail. Vol I. Marshall, MO: Marshall Chapter, DAR, 1914. 2 ports. VG in pict wraps. Howes R 19. *Schoyer*. $100/£65

RAINEY, T.C. Along the Old Trail. Volume I. Marshall, MO: D.A.R., 1914. 1st ed. 2 plts. VG in wraps. Howes R 19. *Oregon*. $120/£77

RAINWATER, ROBERT (ed). Max Ernst, Beyond Surrealism. NY/Oxford, 1986. 15 color plts. Dj (sl torn, repaired). *Edwards*. $39/£25

RALEIGH, WALTER. The Cabinet-Council. London: For Thomas Johnson, 1658. (8),200pp (top margin, outer corner tp, 2nd leaf chipped; early marginal notes). Calf over maroon bds (rebound), black spine label. *Karmiole*. $300/£194

RALEIGH, WALTER. The History of the World, in Five Books. London: Robert White et al, 1677. Frontis, (ix),54; (86); 885pp, 8 dbl-pg maps. Ink inscrips; eps, title leaves spotted; rubbed, else Nice. *Bookpress.* $950/£613

RALEIGH, WALTER. The Marrow of History or, an Epitome of All Historical Passages.... London: John and William Place, 1662. 2nd ed. (xxiv),574pp (ink inscrips; sm wormholes few leaves). Contemp calf (bkpl; edges rubbed; spine head chipped). *Bookpress.* $225/£145

RALEIGH, WALTER. The Marrow of History. London: For John Place & William Place, 1662. 2nd ed. (24),574pp (tp browned, sl trimmed). 19th cent 1/2 brn morocco over cl (sl rubbed). *Karmiole.* $175/£113

RALPH, JULIAN. Alone in China and Other Stories. NY: Harper, 1897. (xii),282pp. Yellow cl dec in grn, gilt. VG. *Schoyer.* $45/£29

RAMADGE, FRANCIS. Consumption Curable.... NY, 1839. 1st Amer ed. 160pp. Ex-lib. *Fye.* $75/£48

RAMBLE, ROBERT. The Book of Fishes. Phila: James Crissy, 1845. 12mo, 143pp (pulled sig; some foxing), title vignette, 41 plts. Contemp black leather-backed brn cl (rubbed, bumped; leather joint split; stained); gilt-titled. VG. *Blue Mountain.* $375/£242

RAMON Y CAJAL, S. Degeneration and Regeneration of the Nervous System. NY, 1959. (Facs of 1928 ed). 2 vols. Good. *Fye.* $250/£161

RAMON Y CAJAL, S. Histology. Balt, 1933. 1st Eng trans. (Ex-lib.) *Fye.* $250/£161

RAMPLING, ANNE. (Pseud of Anne Rice.) Belinda. NY: Arbor House, (1986). 1st ed. Signed. Fine in dj. *Bernard.* $75/£48

RAMPLING, ANNE. (Pseud of Anne Rice.) Belinda. London: Macdonald, 1986. 1st ed. Fine in dj. *Rees.* $16/£10

RAMPLING, ANNE. (Pseud of Anne Rice.) Belinda. NY: Arbor, 1986. 1st ed. VF in dj. *Else Fine.* $45/£29

RAMPLING, ANNE. (Pseud of Anne Rice.) Belinda. NY: Arbor House, 1986. 1st ed. Signed. NF in NF dj (sl wear). *Revere.* $90/£58

RAMSAY, A. MAITLAND. Atlas of External Diseases of the Eye. Glasgow, 1898. 1st ed. 195pp; 18 photogravures; 30 colored lithos. Good. *Fye.* $350/£226

RAMSAY, A. MAITLAND. Eye Injuries and Their Treatment. Glasgow, 1907. 1st ed. Good. *Fye.* $175/£113

RAMSAY, DAVID. Ramsay's History of South Carolina.... Newberry, SC: By W.J. McDuffie, 1858. 2nd ed. 2 vols in 1. 274; 307pp, fldg map. Recent red lib-style buckram. VG. Howes R 34. *Chapel Hill.* $200/£129

RAMSBOTHAM, FRANCIS. The Principles and Practice of Obstetric Medicine and Surgery, in Reference to the Process of Parturition. Phila, 1851. 6th Amer ed. 553pp, 13pp supp. Good. *Fye.* $300/£194

RAMSBOTHAM, FRANCIS. The Principles and Practice of Obstetric Medicine and Surgery. Phila, 1847. 4th Amer ed. 527pp; 55 engr plts. Bds nearly detached, o/w Good. *Fye.* $125/£81

RAMSBOTTOM, JOHN. Mushrooms and Toadstools. London, 1953. 1st ed. Dj (spine sl rubbed). *Edwards.* $59/£38

RAMSEY, FRANK PLUMPTON. The Foundations of Mathematics and Other Logical Essays. London: Routledge & Kegan Paul, (1954). 3rd ptg. Gilt-lettered blue cl. Fine in blue ptd dj. *House.* $85/£55

RAMSEY, L.W. and C.H. LAWRENCE. Garden Pools, Large and Small. NY: Macmillan, (1931). VG+. *Mikesh.* $27/£17

RAMSEY, ROBERT W. Carolina Cradle. Chapel Hill: Univ of NC Press, (1964). 1st ed. Brn cl. NF (lt pencil underlining, notes) in VG dj (price-clipped). *Chapel Hill.* $40/£26

RAMSEY, STANLEY C. Small Houses of the Late Georgian Period, 1750-1820. NY: William Helburn, 1923, 1924. 3rd ptg (vol 1), 1st ed (vol 2). 2 vols. 100 plts; 100 plts. (Vol 1 cvrs spotted, sunned, extrems worn; vol 2 cvrs spotted; early leaves vol 1 sl foxed) else VG set. *Bookpress.* $150/£97

RAMSEY, STANLEY C. Small Houses of the Late Georgian Period, 1750-1820. Architectural Press, 1924. 101 plts. (Rebound.) *Edwards.* $43/£28

RAMSEYER, FRIEDRICH AUGUST and JOHANNES KUHNE. Four Years in Ashantee. Mrs. Weitbrecht (ed). NY: Robert Carter, 1875. 320pp. Grn cl stamped in black/gilt. VG. *Schoyer.* $65/£42

RANCHER. Forrard-On! London: Country Life, 1930. One of 200 signed. Lionel Edwards (illus). 16 plts. Teg, uncut. Mod 1/4 morocco (orig upper bd lettering laid in), gilt. *Hollett.* $225/£145

RAND, AUSTIN L. American Water and Game Birds. NY, 1956. 1st ed. NF in dj. *Artis.* $25/£16

RAND, AYN. Atlas Shrugged. NY, 1957. 1st Amer ed. NF (name; sl sunned, rubbed). *Polyanthos.* $45/£29

RAND, AYN. Capitalism: The Unknown Ideal. NAL, 1966. 1st ed. One of 700 specially bound, signed. Fine in slip-case. *Fine Books.* $575/£371

RAND, AYN. The Fountainhead. London: Cassell, 1947. 1st Eng ed. Black cl. Sl rubbed, name, o/w VG. *Dalian.* $132/£85

RAND, AYN. The Virtue of Selfishness. NY: Signet, 1964. 1st ed. Pb orig. NF in wraps. *Else Fine.* $15/£10

RAND, AYN. We the Living. Macmillan, 1936. 1st ed, 1st bk. Sl spine fade, else VG+. *Fine Books.* $375/£242

RAND, CLAYTON. Sons of the South. NY: Holt, Rinehart & Winston, 1961. 1st ed. 100 full-pg ports. NF in VG dj. *Connolly.* $35/£23

RAND, EDWARD SPRAGUE. The Rhododendron and 'American Plants.' NY: Hurd & Houghton, 1876. 4th ed. 188pp. VG (ex-lib; stamps). *Second Life.* $85/£55

RANDALL, E.O. The Masterpieces of the Ohio Mound Builders. Columbus, 1908. (Sm hole in tp repaired w/no loss; spine reinforced; sl wear.) Wrappers. *Hayman.* $15/£10

RANDALL, HOMER. Army Boys in the Big Drive. Sully, 1919. 1st ed. Good+. *Madle.* $15/£10

RANDALL, JAMES GARFIELD. The Civil War and Reconstruction. Boston: D.C. Heath, (c 1937). 1st ed. Orig 2-toned cl. Head of spine chipped, else VG. *Mcgowan.* $85/£55

RANDALL, ROBERT. The Dawning Light. NY: Gnome Press, 1959. 1st Amer ed. Fine (paper browned) in dj (edge tear fr panel). *Polyanthos.* $25/£16

RANDALL, ROBERT. The Dawning Light. Gnome, 1959. 1st ed. Fine in dj (closed tear; tiny chip). *Madle.* $30/£19

RANDALL, ROBERT. The Shrouded Planet. Gnome, 1957. 1st ed. Fine in dj. *Madle.* $40/£26

RANDIER, JEAN. Men and Ships around Cape Horn, 1619-1639. M.W.B. Sanderson (trans). NY: David McKay, (1969). 1st Amer ed. Blue cl; gilt. Good in dj. *Karmiole*. $35/£23

RANDOLPH, ALEXANDER. The Mailboat. NY: Henry Holt, (1954). 1st ed, 1st bk. Fine in dj (lt edgeworn). *Sadlon*. $15/£10

RANDOLPH, E.A. The Life of Rev. John Jasper. R.T.Hill, 1884. 1st ed. 167pp; port. Contents VG (spine frayed; hinges broken). *Book Broker*. $200/£129

RANDOLPH, EDMUND. Hell Among the Yearlings. Chicago, (1978). Lakeside Classic. VG. *Schoyer*. $15/£10

RANDOLPH, ISHAM. Gleanings from a Harvest of Memories. Columbia, MO: E.W. Stephens, 1937. 1st ed. NF. *Mcgowan*. $85/£55

RANDOLPH, J. RALPH. British Travelers among the Southern Indians, 1660-1763. Norman: Univ of OK Press, (1973). 1st ed. Blue bds. NF in dj (lt soiled). *Chapel Hill*. $50/£32

RANDOLPH, JOHN. Letters of John Randolph, to a Young Relative.... Phila: Carey, Lea & Blanchard, 1834. 1st ed. (v),10-254,(14)pp (foxed; underlining; bkpl). Pub's cl (worn). *Bookpress*. $150/£97

RANDOLPH, SARAH N. The Domestic Life of Thomas Jefferson. NY: Harper, 1871. 432pp; port. VG. *Schoyer*. $45/£29

RANDOLPH, VANCE. We Always Lie to Strangers. Columbia Univ, 1951. 1st ed. Fine in Good+ dj. *Oregon*. $30/£19

RANDOLPH, VANCE. Who Blowed Up the Church House? and Other Ozark Folk Tales. NY, 1952. 1st ed. Fine in dj. *Hayman*. $20/£13

Range Plant Handbook. Washington, 1937. (Name stamp.) *Sutton*. $43/£28

RANGELL, LEO. The Mind of Watergate. NY: Norton, (1980). 1st ed. Inscribed. Gray cl-backed bds. VG (institute bkpl, stamps) in dj. *Gach*. $30/£19

RANKE, LEOPOLD. The History of the Popes. London, 1878. 3 vols. Frontis port; uncut. (Sm ink stamp; lacks feps; lower joint head vol 2 split; spines bumped; repaired split vol 1.) *Edwards*. $39/£25

RANKIN, ALEXANDER TAYLOR. Alexander Taylor Rankin (1803-1885), His Diary and Letters. Nolie Mumey (ed). Boulder: Johnson Pub Co, 1966. One of 400 signed. Port. Fine in glassine wrapper (chipped). *Bohling*. $125/£81

RANKIN, HUGH F. Francis Marion. NY: Crowell, (1973). 1st ed. Map. Dk brn cl. Fine in dj (lt edgewear). *Chapel Hill*. $40/£26

RANKIN, HUGH F. The Theatre in Colonial America. Chapel Hill: Univ of NC, (1965). VG in pict dj. *Dramatis Personae*. $35/£23

RANKIN, MELINDA. Twenty Years Among the Mexicans. Cincinnati: Chase & Hall, 1875. 199pp. Brn cl, gilt back. VG+. *Bohling*. $85/£55

RANKIN, NIALL. Antarctic Isle. Wild Life in South Georgia. London: Collins, 1951. 1st ed. Map eps. VG in dj. *Walcot*. $34/£22

RANSHOFF, JOSEPH. Under the Northern Lights and Other Stories. Cincinnati, 1921. (Ex-lib.) *Goodrich*. $50/£32

RANSOM, JOHN CROWE. Chills and Fever. NY: Knopf, 1924. 1st ed, 1st issue. Color-striped cl, paper spine label. Label, else Fine in yellow dj (price-clipped). *Chapel Hill*. $400/£258

RANSOM, JOHN CROWE. Poems about God. NY, 1919. 1st ed, 1st bk. Bds; paper labels. (Spine repaired.) *Argosy*. $400/£258

RANSOM, JOHN CROWE. The World's Body. NY: Scribner, 1938. 1st ed, inscribed. Grn cl. VG in Nice dj (brn tape on verso). *Chapel Hill*. $350/£226

RANSOM, JOHN L. Andersonville Diary, Escape, and List of the Dead.... Auburn, NY: John L. Ransom, 1881. 1st ed. Grn cl stamped in black; gilt lettered spine. Minor spotting; corners bumped, o/w VG. *Laurie*. $75/£48

RANSOME, ARTHUR. Aladdin and His Wonderful Lamp in Rhyme. London: Nisbet, (1919). One of 250 signed by Thomas Mackenzie (illus). 13 x 10 1/2 inches. (124)pp. 12 full-pg color plts, guards. Uncut; teg. Orig white cl, gilt (spine extrems sl worn). *Dawson*. $850/£548

RANSOME, ARTHUR. Great Northern? London: Jonathan Cape, 1947. 1st ed. Frontis, chart. Blue-grn buckram. Fine in dj (torn, sl chipped, verso strengthened w/clear tape). *Temple*. $37/£24

RANSOME, ARTHUR. Rod and Line. London: Cape, 1935. Bright blue cl. Fine. *Bowman*. $25/£16

RANSOME, ARTHUR. The Soldier and Death. London: John G. Wilson, Jan 1920. 1st ed. 1 gathering sewn into drab wrappers; 1/2 title not called for; colophon leaf at end; issued w/o eps. Fine. *Temple*. $116/£75

RANSOME, ARTHUR. Winter Holiday. London: Cape, (1933). 1st ed. (Sl faded.) *Petersfield*. $31/£20

RAPER, ARTHUR F. Preface to Peasantry: A Tale of Two Black Belt Counties. Chapel Hill: UNC Press, 1936. 1st ed. VG in dj (chipped, worn). *Cahan*. $60/£39

RAPHAEL, MAX. Prehistoric Cave Paintings. Norbert Guterman (trans). Pantheon Books, (1945). Good in dj (worn). *Lien*. $35/£23

RAPOU, AUGUSTUS. A Treatise on Typhoid Fever, and Its Homoeopathic Treatment. NY, 1853. 1st Eng trans. 96pp. Good. *Fye*. $75/£48

RASCOE, BURTON. Belle Starr, 'The Bandit Queen.' NY: Random House, 1941. 1st ed. Gray cl (sm stain). NF (inscrip). *Glenn*. $45/£29

RASCOE, BURTON. Belle Starr, the Bandit Queen. NY, 1941. 1st ed. Overall VG in dj. *Pratt*. $45/£29

RASMO, N. Michael Pacher. London: Phaidon, 1971. 20 mtd color plts. Sound in dj. *Ars Artis*. $70/£45

RASMUSSEN, KNUD. Greenland by the Polar Sea...Thule Expedition.... London: Heinemann, 1921. 1st Eng ed. Map. VG. *Walcot*. $147/£95

RASMUSSEN, KNUD. The People of the Polar North. London: Kegan Paul, 1908. 1st Eng ed. Map. Good (damp staining head of bds, top 1cm of some pp). *Walcot*. $59/£38

RASMUSSEN, KNUD. The People of the Polar North. Kegan Paul, 1908. 1st Eng ed. Good+ (ex-lib, stamps). *Walcot*. $101/£65

RASSAM, HORMUZD. Asshur and the Land of Nimrod. NY/Cincinnati: Eaton/Curts & Jennings, 1897. 1st ed. xvi,432pp; 19 plts; 3 fldg maps (2 color). Teg. Sl rubbed; bkpl, o/w VG. *Worldwide*. $195/£126

RATCHFORD, FANNIE E. (ed). Letters of Thomas J. Wise to John Henry Wrenn. NY, 1944. 1st ed. VG. *Argosy*. $45/£29

RATCHFORD, FANNIE E. (ed). Letters of Thomas J. Wise to John Henry Wrenn. NY: Knopf, 1944. 1st ed. Port. Eps sl tanned, else Fine in paper dj (tanned, frayed). *Reese*. $60/£39

RATCHFORD, FANNIE E. (ed). Letters of Thomas J. Wise to John Henry Wrenn. NY: Knopf, 1944. 1st ed. Fine in NF dj. *Macdonnell.* $125/£81

RATCLIFF, CARTER. Red Grooms. NY: Abbeville Press, 1984. Collector's Edition, signed. Fine in illus dj, pub's slipcase. *Cahan.* $225/£145

RATCLIFF, J.D. Yellow Magic, The Story of Penicillin. NY, 1945. 1st ed. Good. *Fye.* $30/£19

RATCLIFFE, DOROTHY UNA. The Gone Away. London: John Lane, Bodley Head, 1930. 1st ed. Frontis. Red cl gilt (spine faded; lt spots). *Hollett.* $47/£30

RATCLIFFE, DOROTHY UNA. Lapwings and Laverocks. London: Country Life, 1934. 1st ed. Frontis; 4 color plts. (Sl mkd.) *Hollett.* $47/£30

RATCLIFFE, DOROTHY UNA. Mrs. Buffey in Wartime. London: Thomas Nelson, 1942. 1st ed. Frontis. (Fep removed.) Dj (sl worn, price-clipped). *Hollett.* $31/£20

RATH, IDA ELLEN. The Rath Trail. Wichita: McCormick-Armstrong, (1961). 1st ed. Fine in Fine dj. *Glenn.* $50/£32

RATH, IDA ELLEN. The Rath Trail. Non-Fiction Biography of Charles Rath, Indian Trader. Wichita, (1961). 1st ed. VF in VF dj. *Oregon.* $40/£26

RATHBONE, AUGUSTA. French Riviera Villages. NY: Mitchell Kennerley, 1938. One of 1000. 12 color plts. Burlap-style cl w/title labels on fr cover, spine. VG (bkpls). *Schoyer.* $125/£81

RATHGEBER, BOB. The Cincinnati Reds Scrapbook. JCP, 1982. 1st ed. Fine in VG+ dj. *Plapinger.* $50/£32

Rational Exhibition. London: Darton & Harvey, n.d. (1806). 12mo. 60pp + 1pg list lower wrapper; 20 half-pg copper engrs; last engr dated May 1st, 1806. Yellow dec stiff paper wrappers. VF. *Hobbyhorse.* $975/£629

RATTI, ABATE ACHILLE. Climbs on Alpine Peaks. J.E.C. Eaton (trans). London: T. Fisher Unwin, 1925. Frontis; map. (Sl bumped; spine spotted.) *Hollett.* $70/£45

RAUCH, JOHN. Public Parks: Their Effects Upon the...Inhabitants of Large Cities.... Chicago, 1869. 1st ed. 98pp. Good in wrappers. *Fye.* $150/£97

RAVEN, C.E. John Ray, Naturalist, His Life and Works. Cambridge, 1950. 2nd ed. Port. *Wheldon & Wesley.* $93/£60

RAVEN, J.J. The Bells of England. London: Methuen, 1907. 2nd ed. (Spots, lib stamp, sm label removed from pastedown; spine sl faded, shelf #s.) *Hollett.* $54/£35

RAVEN, JOHN and MAX WALTERS. Mountain Flowers. London, 1956. 1st ed. Dj. *Edwards.* $101/£65

RAVEN, JOHN. A Botanist's Garden. London: Collins, 1971. 1st ed. *Quest.* $55/£35

RAVEN, KAREN. The Hallmark Monster Pop-Up Book. Kansas City: Hallmark, n.d. (1978). 16x23 cm. 4 dbl-pg pop-ups. Marianne Smith (illus). Glazed pict bds. VG. *Book Finders.* $45/£29

RAVEN, SIMON. Brother Cain. London: Anthony Blond, 1959. 1st UK ed. Fine in dj. *Williams.* $54/£35

RAVEN, SIMON. Come Like Shadows. London: Blond & Briggs, 1972. 1st ed. Fine in dj (lt rubbed). *Temple.* $25/£16

RAVEN, SIMON. The English Gentleman. London: Anthony Blond, 1961. 1st ed. Fine in dj. *Temple.* $37/£24

RAVEN, SIMON. The English Gentleman. London: Blond, 1961. 1st UK ed. Fine in VG dj (closed tears, sl creasing, sm chip rear panel). *Williams.* $37/£24

RAVEN, SIMON. The Face of the Waters. London: Blond, 1985. 1st ed. NF in dj. *Limestone.* $50/£32

RAVEN, SIMON. Fielding Gray. London: Anthony Blond, 1967. 1st Eng ed. NF (spine tail sl bumped) in dj. *Ulysses.* $70/£45

RAVEN, SIMON. Morning Star. London: Blond & Briggs, 1984. 1st ed. Fine in dj. *Limestone.* $55/£35

RAVEN, SIMON. The Rich Pay Late. London: Blond, 1964. 1st ed. NF in dj. *Limestone.* $75/£48

RAVEN, SIMON. The Rich Pay Late. London: Anthony Blond, 1964. 1st UK ed. Fine in dj. *Williams.* $47/£30

RAVEN-HART, R. Canoe Errant on the Mississippi. London: Methuen, 1938. 1st ed. 4 sketch maps. VG in dj (worn, repaired). *Hollett.* $23/£15

RAVENEL, FLORENCE LEFTWICH. Women and the French Tradition. NY: Macmillan, 1918. 1st ed. VG (bkpl). *Second Life.* $65/£42

RAVENSTEIN, E.G. Martin Behaim, His Life and His Globe. London: George Philip, 1908. One of 500. 6 plts, 5 color plts, 4-panel color fldg map in rear pocket. (Tips worn, rear hinge cracked internally, minor cvr rubbing). *Bookpress.* $425/£274

RAVENSTEIN, E.G. Russians on the Amur. London: Trubner, 1861. xx,467pp + 4pp pub's ads (marginal pencil notes); 3 maps (1 fldg), 4 full-pg lithos (incl frontis). Grn cl, gilt (spotty). *Schoyer.* $325/£210

RAWLINGS, MARJORIE KINNAN. Cross Creek Cookery. NY: Scribner's, 1942. 1st ed, 1st issue. Pict cl. Fine in NF dj. *Hermitage.* $100/£65

RAWLINGS, MARJORIE KINNAN. Golden Apples. NY: Scribner's, 1935. 1st ed. Orange cl w/gold stamping. VF in Excellent dj. *Dermont.* $250/£161

RAWLINGS, MARJORIE KINNAN. Golden Apples. NY: Scribner's, 1935. 1st ed. Orange cl. Fine in pict dj (pencil price). *Chapel Hill.* $500/£323

RAWLINGS, MARJORIE KINNAN. The Secret River. NY: Scribner's, (1955). 1st ed. Leonard Weisgrad (illus). Pict cl. Sm grn stain spine, fr cvr, else NF in dj (price-clipped, 1/2-inch chip, lt wear, else VG). *Godot.* $125/£81

RAWLINGS, MARJORIE KINNAN. South Moon Under. NY/London: Scribner's, 1933. 1st ed, 1st bk. Grn cl stamped in blue/gilt. Fine (sm bkseller ticket) in pict dj (crease); pub's wrap-around band. *Chapel Hill.* $750/£484

RAWLINGS, MARJORIE KINNAN. South Moon Under. Scribners, 1933. 1st ed. Stained, faded spine, else Good in VG- dw. *Fine Books.* $125/£81

RAWLINGS, MARJORIE KINNAN. South Moon Under. NY: Scribner's, 1933. 1st ed. Green cl w/gold stamping. VF in dj (sl used). *Dermont.* $200/£129

RAWLINGS, MARJORIE KINNAN. When the Whippoorwill. NY: Scribner, 1940. 1st ed. Grn cl. Inscrip, else Fine in VG dj. *Chapel Hill.* $300/£194

RAWLINGS, MARJORIE KINNAN. The Yearling. NY: Scribner's, 1938. 1st ed. NF (back eps sl stained) in dj (worn; chipped). *Pharos.* $35/£23

RAWLINGS, MARJORIE KINNAN. The Yearling. NY: Scribner's, 1938. 1st ed. VG (name, date) in VG dj (edgewear, closed tear, internal tape reinforcement). *Revere.* $75/£48

RAWLINGS, MARJORIE KINNAN. The Yearling. NY: Scribner's, 1938. 1st ed. Pict cl. NF (sl wear; ink name fep) in dj (sl wear; few tears). *Antic Hay.* $150/£97

RAWLINGS, MARJORIE KINNAN. The Yearling. NY: Scribner's, 1939. 1st ed thus. 8vo. 14 full-pg color plts by N.C. Wyeth. Oatmeal buckram, brn lettering, illus. Good in color dj (marginal chips). *Reisler.* $150/£97

RAWLINSON, GEORGE. Ancient Egypt. London/NY: Fisher/Putnam, 1897. 9th ed. xxi,402pp; dbl-pg map. Sl rubbed, foxed, o/w Good. *Worldwide.* $22/£14

RAWLINSON, GEORGE. History of Ancient Egypt. Boston: S.E. Cassino, 1882. 1st Amer ed. 2 vols. Frontis color map. VG. *Hermitage.* $95/£61

RAWLINSON, GEORGE. The Seventh Great Oriental Monarchy. NY: Dodd, Mead, 1882. 1st Amer ed. 2 vols. Chromolitho frontis, fldg map vol 1. Vol 1 eps, tp, frontis border sl foxed, o/w Clean set. *Hermitage.* $85/£55

RAWLS, JAMES J. (ed). Dan de Quille of the Big Bonanza. (By William Wright.) SF: Book Club of CA, 1980. One of 650. Frontis port. Cl-backed patterned bds. Prospectus laid in. Fine in plain dj. *Bohling.* $75/£48

RAWNSLEY, MRS. WILLINGHAM. Country Sketches for City Dwellers. London: A&C Black, 1908. 1st ed. 16 color plts; teg (feps lt browned). Dec cl. *Edwards.* $39/£25

RAWSON, PHILIP (ed). Primitive Erotic Art. London, 1973. 32 pgs color plts. Dj (sl chipped). *Edwards.* $39/£25

RAY, CLARENCE E. The Border Outlaws. Chicago: Regan Pub, n.d. (ca 1900). Orig pict wraps (bkpl). *Schoyer.* $35/£23

RAY, CLARENCE E. Life of Bob and Cole Younger with Quantrell. Chicago: Regan, n.d. (ca 1900). Orig pict wraps (bkpl). *Schoyer.* $35/£23

RAY, D.N. Cholera and Its Preventive and Curative Treatment. NY, 1884. 1st ed. 128pp. Good. *Fye.* $75/£48

RAY, GORDON N. The Illustrator and the Book in England from 1790 to 1814. NY/London, (1976). 2 color plts. *Waterfield.* $93/£60

RAY, ISAAC. Mental Hygiene. Boston, 1863. 1st ed. 338pp. Good. *Fye.* $250/£161

RAY, JOHN. Further Correspondence. Robert W.T. Gunther (ed). Ray Soc, 1928. Port; 2 plts. Fine. *Bickersteth.* $62/£40

RAY, JOHN. Travels Through the Low-Countries, Germany, Italy, and France. London, 1738. 2nd ed. 2 vols.3 plts (2 fldg). Full contemp calf. VG. *Argosy.* $500/£323

RAY, JOHN. The Wisdom of God Manifested in the Works of the Creation. William & John Innys, 1722. 8th ed. (xxiv),17-405pp; 3pp ads. Orig panelled calf (rebacked; new eps). *Bickersteth.* $140/£90

RAY, MAN. Man Ray. Self Portrait. Boston, (1963). 1st ed. Sm tear dj corner, o/w VF. *Artis.* $85/£55

RAY, MAN. Self Portrait. Boston: Little, Brown, 1963. 1st Amer ed. Inscribed. Black cl. VG in dj (worn). *Cummins.* $150/£97

RAY, MICHELLE. Two Shores of Hell: A French Journalist's Life Among the Vietcong and the G.I.'s in Vietnam. Elizabeth Abbott (trans). NY: McKay, (1968). NF in Good+ (shelfworn; price-clipped; spine sunned). *Aka.* $30/£19

RAY, ROBERT. Cage of Mirrors. NY: Lippincott & Cromwell, 1980. 1st ed, 1st bk. NF in dj (lt edgewear; closed tear). *Janus.* $30/£19

RAYMOND, DORA NEILL. Captain Lee Hall of Texas. Norman: Univ of OK Press, 1950. 1st ed. Buff-colored cl. Fine. Howes R 83. *Glenn.* $65/£42

RAYMOND, JEAN PAUL and CHARLES RICKETTS. Oscar Wilde. Recollections. Bloomsbury: Nonesuch Press, 1932. 1st ed. Dj. *Jaffe.* $225/£145

RAYNE, H. The Ivory Raiders. London, 1923. 1st ed. Fldg map. (Browned; lower hinge cracked; staining; spine discolored, chipped.) *Edwards.* $39/£25

RAYNER, ARTHUR E. Accuracy in the X-Ray Diagnosis of Urinary Stone. Preston: C.W. Whitehead, 1909. 49 mtd photos. Good. *Goodrich.* $395/£255

RAYNER, B.L. Life of Thomas Jefferson. Boston: Lilly et al, 1834. 430pp; port. (Cl sl rubbed.) *Schoyer.* $60/£39

RAYNER, RICHARD. Los Angeles Without a Map. London: Secker & Warburg, 1988. 1st ed. Signed. Fine in dj. *Rees.* $23/£15

READ, HERBERT (ed). Surrealism. NY: Harcourt, Brace, n.d. (ca 1936). 1st Amer ed. 96 plts. Orange cl. Good in illus dj (lt chipped). *Karmiole.* $75/£48

READ, HERBERT. Ambush. London: Faber & Faber, 1930. 1st ed. Fine in red wrappers. *Pharos.* $35/£23

READ, HERBERT. Art and Industry; the Principles of Industrial Design. London: Faber, 1934. 1st ed. Lower hinge split, neatly repaired, o/w Fine. *Europa.* $37/£24

READ, HERBERT. Art and Society. London/Toronto: Heinemann, 1937. 1st ed. Orig buckram bds, emb gilt motif. Spine sl faded, o/w Fine. *Europa.* $25/£16

READ, HERBERT. Moon's Farm and Poems, Mostly Elegiac. London: Faber & Faber, 1955. 1st ed. Fine in purple cl, spine lettered in white. Fine dj w/wraparound. *Vandoros.* $60/£39

READ, HERBERT. Phases of English Poetry. Hogarth, 1928. 1st ed. Dec cl. Good. *Whiteson.* $23/£15

READ, OPIE. By the Eternal! Chicago, 1906. 1st ed. VF. *Bond.* $20/£13

READ, PIERS PAUL. Alive. Phila/NY: Lippincott, (1974). 1st ed. Fine in dj (lt edgeworn). *Sadlon.* $20/£13

READ, THOMAS BUCHANAN. The Wagoner of the Alleghanies. Phila: Lippincott, 1862. 1st ed. Gilt/blind-stamped cl (sl rubbed, spotty; eps sl foxed). *Sadlon.* $25/£16

READE, CHARLES. Christie Johnstone. Boston: Ticknor & Fields, 1855. 1st Amer ed. 310,(6)+(8)pp ads. Orig grn cl (faded); gilt. *Karmiole.* $85/£55

READE, CHARLES. The Course of True Love Never Did Run Smooth. London: Richard Bentley, 1857. 1st ed in bds. Pict bds (rubbed, soiled, shaken; spine split). *Sadlon.* $20/£13

READE, CHARLES. Peggy Woffington. London: George Allen, 1899. #92/200 lg-paper copies. 298pp. Hugh Thomson (illus). Untrimmed, unopened. Pict cl (scuffed, lt silverfishing, mostly rear cvr). Internally Fine. *Schoyer.* $65/£42

READING, JOSEPH H. The Ogowe Band: A Narrative of African Travel. Phila: Reading, 1890. 2nd ptg. xv,278pp, 65 plts. Pict cl. *Schoyer.* $85/£55

READING, PETER. For the Municipality's Elderly. Secker, 1974. 1st ed. Fine in dj. *Poetry.* $28/£18

READING, PETER. The Prison Cell and Barrel Mystery. Secker, 1976. 1st ed. (Sl musty.) Dj (rubbed). *Poetry.* $23/£15

REAGAN, JOHN H. Memoirs, with Special Reference to Secession and the Civil War. NY: Neale, 1906. 1st ed. Insect damage cvr, else VG. *Parker.* $175/£113

Real Life in Ireland. London: Evans, n.d. (1829). 4th ed. 296pp, 19 hand-colored plts. Grn cl. *Schoyer.* $225/£145

REBUFFAT, GASTON and PIERRE TAIRRAZ. Between Heaven and Earth. London, (1965). 1st British ed. VG in dj. *King.* $50/£32

REBUFFAT, GASTON. On Snow and Rock. London, (1963). 1st British ed. VG in dj (sl worn). *King.* $50/£32

RECHY, JOHN. City of Night. NY, 1963. 1st Amer ed. 1st bk. Fine in NF dj. *Polyanthos.* $50/£32

RECHY, JOHN. City of Night. NY: Grove, 1963. 1st ed. 1st bk. VF in dj. *Else Fine.* $45/£29

RECHY, JOHN. This Day's Death. NY: Grove Press, 1969. 1st ed. Fine in Fine dj. *Revere.* $35/£23

RECLUS, ELIE. Curious Byways of Anthropology: Sexual Savage and Esoteric Customs of Primitive People. NY: Robin House Press, 1932. 1st ed. Sl rubbed, o/w VG. *Worldwide.* $30/£19

Recollections of a Chaperon. (By Arabella Sullivan Dacre.) London: Bentley, 1833. 1st ed. 3 vols. 305; 332; 320pp. Contemp leather-backed bds (sl scuffed). Nice set (sigs pulled). *Second Life.* $300/£194

Recollections of a College Beggar, by One Who Was There. (By W.P. Burrell.) Cleveland, 1882. 277pp + 3pp ads. VG. *Schoyer.* $40/£26

Recollections of an Excursion.... (By William Beckford.) London: R. Bentley, 1835. 1st ed. Engr frontis port, 1/2 title present; xii,228pp. Uncut. Orig pub's bds (spine renewed; early bkpl). Fine. *Hartfield.* $595/£384

Record of an Obscure Man. (By Mary Traill Spence Putnam.) Boston: Ticknor & Fields, 1861. 1st ed. (4),216pp + 16pp pub's ads. Orig brn cl, gilt spine (sl rubbed). *Karmiole.* $35/£23

Red Riding Hood. NY: Modern Promotions, (1950). #20002 in series. 26x20 cm. 4 pop-ups. Pict bds (edges sl worn). *Book Finders.* $70/£45

Red Riding Hood. London: Bancroft, 1961. Pop-up. V. Kubasta (illus). Lg 8vo. Pict wraps; cl spine (corners worn). VG. *Book Adoption.* $30/£19

Red Rover, a Tale. (By James Fenimore Cooper). London: Colburn, 1827. 1st British ed. 3 vols. Contemp 1/2 maroon calf, marbled bds, blind/gilt spines. BAL 3838. *Bickersteth.* $171/£110

RED, GEORGE PLUNKETT. The Medicine Man in Texas. (Houston: Standard Ptg & Litho Co, 1930). 1st ed. Blue cl. NF (sl worn). *Harrington.* $175/£113

REDDING, M. WOLCOTT. Antiquities of the Orient Unveiled.... NY: Redding, 1873. 1st ed. 421pp; 2 color plts (1 fldg); 90 other plts (3 fldg). Lacks map of Jerusalem, fr flyleaf; rubbed, frayed; 1 plt wrinkled, 1 plt sl torn, o/w VG. *Worldwide.* $45/£29

REDFERN, DAVID. David Redfern's Jazz Album. London: Eel Pie, 1980. 1st ed. Fine in Fine dj. *Beasley.* $60/£39

REDFIELD, ROBERT. The Folk Culture of Yucatan. Chicago: Univ of Chicago, 1941. 1st ed. Brn cl, gilt spine. VG in dj (worn). *Parmer.* $55/£35

REDFORD, A.H. The History of Methodism in Kentucky. Nashville, 1868-70. 1st ed. 2 vols (3rd vol published later). Howes R 114. *Ginsberg.* $100/£65

REDFORD, ROBERT. The Outlaw Trail. NY, 1978. 1st ptg. Debossed cl. Fine in dj. *Baade.* $55/£35

REDMOND, PAT H. History of Quincy and Its Men of Mark. Quincy, 1869. 1st ed. 302pp (pp221-224 in facs; hinges split, weak). *Artis.* $35/£23

REDMOND-HOWARD, L.G. Hindenburg's March into London. London: John Long, 1916. 1st ed. 1/2 title leaf cancel tipped onto stub. Lower edges uncut. Spine sl faded; sl foxing; o/w Fine. *Temple.* $40/£26

REDPATH, JAMES. The Public Life of Capt. John Brown. Boston: Thayer & Eldridge, 1860. 1st ed. 407,(1)pp. Sl shaken, rubbed, yet VG. *Mcgowan.* $45/£29

REECE, RICHARD. The Medical Guide...Comprising a Practical Dispensatory.... London, 1814. 11th ed. xvi,484,(10)pp (lacks pp481-2); fldg engr plt; 12-pg pub's cat bound in front. Uncut. Orig bds (worn; spine split, defects), paper label remains. *Hemlock.* $225/£145

REED, CHARLES B. The Curse of Cahawba. Chicago: 1925. 1st ed. Copy #13 inscribed and signed. 10 photo views, ptd overlays. Orig cl; paper labels. VG. *Petrilla.* $45/£29

REED, CHARLES. Masters of the Wilderness. Fort Dearborn Series. Univ Chicago, (1914). 1st ed. 4 plts. Fine in Good+ dj. *Oregon.* $35/£23

REED, CHESTER A. North American Birds Eggs. NY, 1904. VG. *Argosy.* $50/£32

REED, EARL H. Etching. A Practical Treatise. NY/London: Putnam's, 1914. 1st ed. Signed. Etched frontis, 5 plts. Teg. Very Nice. *Cady.* $60/£39

REED, ISHMAEL. Conjure. (Amherst): Univ of MA, (1972). 1st ed. Fine in dj (rubbing). *Antic Hay.* $45/£29

REED, ISHMAEL. Flight to Canada. NY: Random House, (1976). 1st ed. VG in dj. *Petrilla.* $30/£19

REED, ISHMAEL. Flight to Canada. Random House, 1976. 1st ed. Fine in dj. *Stahr.* $25/£16

REED, ISHMAEL. The Free-Lance Pallbearers. NY: Doubleday, 1967. 1st ed, 1st bk. Fine in dj. *Pharos.* $100/£65

REED, ISHMAEL. The Free-Lance Pallbearers. GC: Doubleday, 1967. 1st ed. 1st bk. Fine in dj (lt wear extrems). *Else Fine.* $125/£81

REED, ISHMAEL. The Last Days of Louisiana Red. NY: Random House, (1974). 1st ed. NF in dj. *Godot.* $35/£23

REED, ISHMAEL. Shrovetide in Old New Orleans. NY: Doubleday, 1978. 1st ed. VG in dj. *Petrilla.* $25/£16

REED, JOHN CALVIN. The Old and New South. NY, 1876. 1st ed. 24pp. VG in orig ptd wrappers. *Mcgowan.* $75/£48

REED, JOHN. Daughter of the Revolution and Other Stories. NY, (1927). 1st ed. Top edge stained, stain back cvr, else Good. *King.* $20/£13

REED, JOHN. The War in Eastern Europe. NY: Scribners, 1916. 1st Amer ed. Signed. Boardman Robinson (illus). Fine (bkpl; lacks dj). *Between The Covers.* $1,750/£1,129

REED, KIT. Armed Camps. London: Faber & Faber, (1969). 1st ed. Fine in black dj (lt rubbed). *Reese.* $30/£19

REED, KIT. Mother Isn't Dead, She's Only Sleeping. Boston: Houghton Mifflin, 1961. 1st ed, 1st bk. VG in dj (sticker residue). *Reese.* $35/£23

REED, REBECCA THERESA. Six Months in a Convent. Boston: Russell, Odiorne & Metcalf, 1835. 1st ed. 192pp (lt foxing; bkpl). Orig grn blind-emb cl (expertly restored). *Weber.* $750/£484

REED, ROWENA. Combined Operations in the Civil War. Annapolis, (1978). 1st ed. VG+ in VG+ dj. *Pratt.* $27/£17

REED, S.G. A History of the Texas Railroads, and of Transportation Conditions under Spain and Mexico and the Republic and the State. Houston: St. Clair Pub Co, (1941). Stated 2nd ed. Inscribed. Blue cl (soiled, edgeworn, bumped; rear cvr, eps waterstained; spine dknd, sagging; hinges expertly repaired). Good-; internally NF. *Harrington.* $80/£52

REED, TALBOT BAINES. A History of the Old English Letter Foundries. London: Faber & Faber, 1952. New ed. Grn cl, gilt spine title. Fine in dj. *Heller.* $200/£129

REED, TALBOT BAINES. A History of the Old English Letter Foundries. London, 1952. New rev, enlgd ed. *Veatchs.* $110/£71

REED, VERNER. Lo-To-Kah. NY: Continental, 1897. 1st ed. VG- (spine worn). *Parker.* $50/£32

REED, WALT. John Clymer: An Artist's Rendezvous with the Frontier West. Flagstaff: Northland, (1976). 1st ed. VF in dj. *Hermitage.* $125/£81

REED, WILLIAM. The Phantom of the Poles. NY: Walter S. Rockey, 1906. Grn cl (worn, soiled; hinges weak). *Parmer.* $125/£81

REEDER, A.P. Around the Golden Deep: A Romance of the Sierras. SF/Boston: Samuel Carson/Cupples & Hurd, 1888. 1st ed. 495pp. Gilt-dec cl (extrems rubbed; spine cocked). *Reese.* $50/£32

REEMELIN, CHARLES. The Vine-Dresser's Manual. NY, 1856. 103pp (4pp)ads; 30 engrs. (Frontis browned; cl worn.) *Sutton.* $95/£61

REEMELIN, CHARLES. The Vine-Dressers Manual. NY: Moore, 1858. Frontis; 103pp + ads. Pub's cl. Nice. *Second Life.* $150/£97

REES, ABRAHAM. Clocks, Watches and Chronometers (1819-20). David & Charles, 1970. Dj. *Edwards.* $39/£25

REES, DIANA and MARJORIE G. CAWLEY. A Pictorial Encyclopaedia of Goss China. Newport: Ceramic Book Co, 1970. 1st ed. Color frontis, 63 plts. (Soiled lower bd, spine faded.) *Edwards.* $54/£35

REES, J. ROGERS. The Diversions of a Book-Worm. London: Elliot Stock, 1886. 1st ed. (x),258,(6)pp. Grn cl (sl rubbed), gilt, beveled edges. *Oak Knoll.* $35/£23

REESE, LIZETTE WOODWORTH. The Old House in the Country. NY: Farrar & Rinehart, (1936). 1st ed. Marbled bds (sl rubbed); paper labels. *Sadlon.* $20/£13

REESE, TREVOR R. Colonial Georgia. Athens: Univ of GA Press, (1963). 1st ed. Red cl. NF in dj (lt rubbed). *Chapel Hill.* $45/£29

REEVE, F.D. White Colors. NY: Farrar, (1973). 1st ed. Inscribed, signed in 1982. Fine in dj (sm sticker mk fr flap). *Reese.* $30/£19

REEVES, FRANCIS B. Russia Then and Now 1892-1917. NY: Putnam's, 1917. Teg. Blue cl, gilt, laid-on illus. Spine sl dknd, o/w Nice. *Schoyer.* $40/£26

REFF, THEODORE. The Notebooks of Edgar Degas. London: OUP, 1976. 2 vols. 50 b/w plts. Djs (sl chipped). *Edwards.* $155/£100

REGLER, GUSTAV. The Owl of Minerva. Norman Denny (trans). London, 1959. 1st Eng ed. Frontis port; 7 plts. VG in dj (damp mk to spine). *Edwards.* $28/£18

Regulations for the Army of the Confederate States, 1862. Richmond: J.W. Randolph, 1862. 1st ed. 420pp (soiled, dampstained). Orig cl (faded, torn), paper spine label. Good (hinges broken). *Chapel Hill.* $200/£129

REICH, S. John Marin. A Stylistic Analysis and Catalogue Raisonne. Univ AZ Press, 1970. 2 vols. Sound in slipcase. *Ars Artis.* $233/£150

REICH, WILHELM. Listen, Little Man. NY: Orgone, 1948. 1st ed. VG in VG- dj. *Lame Duck.* $150/£97

REICHARD, GLADYS A. Dezba, Woman of the Desert. NY: J.J. Augustin, 1939. 1st ed. VG-. *Parker.* $60/£39

REICHARD, GLADYS A. Navajo Shepherd and Weaver. NY: J.J. Augustin, (1936). 2nd ptg. Tan buckram. Fine in Good- dj (rubbed, chipped, closed tears). *Harrington.* $75/£48

REICHARD, M. A Descriptive Road-Book of France. London: Leigh, 1829. Title,3-565pp, 5pp ads, fldg engr map, 6 fldg town plans. Black roan gilt (edges rubbed). *Marlborough.* $194/£125

REICHLER, JOSEPH (ed). The Baseball Encyclopedia. MacMillan, 1969. 1st ed. VG (no dj as issued) in Good+ slipcase. *Plapinger.* $45/£29

REID, ALASTAIR. To Lighten My House. Scarsdale, NY: Morgan & Morgan, (1953). 1st ed, 1st bk. Fine in dj (edge darkened). *Dermont.* $25/£16

REID, B.L. The Man from New York, John Quinn and His Friends. NY: OUP, 1968. 1st ed. Rev copy, slip laid in. Fine in dj. *Sadlon.* $30/£19

REID, BERNARD. Overland to California with the Pioneer Line. Mary M. Gordon (ed). Stanford, (1983). 1st ed. VF in VF dj. *Oregon.* $30/£19

REID, DUDLEY. Ups and Downs: the Story of a Short-Legged Man and His Journey Through Life. Des Moines, 1936. Stated 1st ed. Inscribed presentation. (Fr cvr spotted.) *Hayman.* $15/£10

REID, E.G. The Great Physician. London: OUP, 1942. Later ptg. NF in dj. *Goodrich.* $30/£19

REID, FORREST. A Garden by the Sea. Dublin/London: Talbot/T. Fisher Unwin, 1918. 1st ed. VG (sm bump top edges; sl dkng). *Reese.* $100/£65

REID, FORREST. Uncle Stephen. London: Faber & Faber, 1931. 1st Eng ed. Red cl. Spine, cvrs mkd, o/w Good. *Dalian.* $54/£35

REID, MAYNE. The Boy Hunters. London: David Bogue, 1857. 5th ed. viii,464pp; 12 plts (1 edge worn, refixed). Full calf gilt prize binding. *Hollett.* $39/£25

REID, MAYNE. The Plant Hunters.... London, 1864. vii,482pp; 12 plts. (Spine foot sl worn; refixed.) Case. *Wheldon & Wesley.* $47/£30

REID, THOMAS. An Essay on the Nature and Cure of the Phthisis Pulmonalis. London, 1782. 1st ed. 155pp. Later full leather; new eps. *Fye.* $150/£97

REID, THOMAS. An Inquiry into the Human Mind. Glasgow, 1817. 400pp. Full gilt-edged calf, blind tooling, marbled eps (upper hinge, joint tender; upper bd sl loose; spine bumped w/sl loss at head). *Edwards.* $132/£85

REID, V.S. New Day. NY: Knopf, 1949. 1st ed, 1st bk. Illus bds. Sl rubbed, else NF in dj. *Cahan.* $50/£32

REIK, THEODOR. Ritual Psycho-Analytic Studies. NY, 1958. Douglas Bryan (trans). Internally Good. (Ex-lib; worn.) *Goodrich.* $30/£19

REILLY, D.R. Portrait Waxes. London: Batsford, (1953). 1st ed. Navy blue cl. Spine lt worn, else VG. *Glenn.* $70/£45

REILLY, D.R. Portrait Waxes: An Introduction for Collectors. London, (1953). 1st ed. Color frontis, 59 plts. VG in dj. *Argosy.* $125/£81

REILLY, HELEN. Murder in Shinbone Alley. NY: DCC, 1940. 1st ed. VF (bkpl pastedown) in pict dj (sm triangular chip spine head, minor wear extrems). *Else Fine.* $50/£32

REIMANN, LEWIS C. The Game Warden and the Poachers. Ann Arbor: Northwoods Pub, 1959. Grey cl. VG. *Peninsula.* $37/£24

REINAECKER, VICTOR. The Paintings and Drawings of J.B.C. Corot.... London/NY, 1929. Tipped-in color frontis, 7 tipped-in color plts, 71 b/w plts. Teg, rest uncut. (Lt faded; spine sl chipped). *Edwards.* $116/£75

REINHARDT, RICHARD (ed). Workin' on the Railroad. Palo Alto: Amer West Pub Co, (1971). 2nd ptg. Brn cl. Fine in VG + dj (sl rubbed). *Harrington.* $30/£19

REINZ, GERHARD F. Bernard Buffet. NY: Tudor, (1968). 1st ed. 4 mtd color plts. Illus tan cl. Good. *Karmiole.* $125/£81

REISS, STEPHEN. Aelbert Cuyp. Boston, 1975. 12 color plts. W/cat of works. Good in dj. *Washton.* $85/£55

REISS, STEPHEN. Aelbert Cuyp. NYGS, 1975. Sound in dj. *Ars Artis.* $116/£75

REISS, STEPHEN. Aelbert Cuyp. London: Zwemmer, 1975. 1st ed. 12 color plts. Ex-lib, tp stamp, fep sl mkd, o/w Fine. *Europa.* $74/£48

REITER, WILLIAM. A Monograph on the Treatment of Diphtheria, Based Upon a New Etiology and Pathology. Phila, 1878. 1st ed. 47pp. Good. *Fye.* $35/£23

REITLINGER, GERALD. A Tower of Skulls. London: Duckworth, 1932. 1st ed. 24 plts, fldg map. (Sl bumped.) *Hollett.* $93/£60

REITZ, DENYS. Commando, a Boer Journal of the Boer War. London: Faber, (1929). (Inscrip; backstrip faded.) *Petersfield.* $23/£15

RELANDER, CLICK. Drummers and Dreamers—The Story of Smowhala the Prophet.... Caldwell: Caxton, 1956. 1st ed. VG in VG dj. *Perier.* $125/£81

RELANDER, CLICK. Drummers and Dreamers. Caldwell, 1956. 1st ed. Frontis. Tape mks ep edges, o/w VG in dj (tape reinforced). *Oregon.* $145/£94

REMARQUE, ERICH MARIA. All Quiet on the Western Front. NY: LEC, 1969. #727/1500. Signed by John Groth (illus). 16 full-pg color dwgs. Mint in slipcase. *Graf.* $85/£55

REMARQUE, ERICH MARIA. All Quiet on the Western Front. (NY), 1969. One of 1500 numbered, signed by John Groth (illus). Fine in pub's slipcase. *Hermitage.* $100/£65

REMARQUE, ERICH MARIA. All Quiet on the Western Front. NY: LEC, 1969. One of 1500 signed by Groth (illus). VF in slipcase & glassine. *Pharos.* $95/£61

Rembrandt, Experimental Etcher. Boston: Museum of Fine Arts, 1969. Good in wrappers (corner sl bumped). *Washton.* $45/£29

REMINGTON, FREDERIC. Frontier Sketches. Chicago: Werner, 1898. 1st ed. 15 plts. Pub's pict paper-cvrd beveled bds (sl soiled; joints splitting; corners showing); black-titled. Presentable. *Hermitage.* $375/£242

REMINGTON, FREDERIC. Sundown Leflare. NY/London: Harper, 1899. 1st ed. Frontis, 115pp + ads. NF (sl offsetting eps). BAL 16492. *Cahan.* $185/£119

REMINI, ROBERT V. Andrew Jackson and the Course of American Empire, 1767-1821. NY: Harper & Row, (1977). 1st ed. Black cl. NF in dj. *Chapel Hill.* $35/£23

Reminiscences of Oregon Pioneers. Pendleton: East Oregon Pub, 1937. 1st ed. Ink name, else Fine. *Perier.* $85/£55

REMLAP, L.T. General U.S. Grant, His Life and Public Services. NY, 1888. 716pp. Pict cl. Sl cvr wear, o/w Fine. *Pratt.* $45/£29

REMONDINO, P.C. History of Circumcision from the Earliest Times to the Present. Phila: F.A. Davis, 1891. 1st ed. Frontis, x,346pp,20pp pub's ads. Blue cl, gilt spine. *Karmiole.* $50/£32

REMY, JULES and JULIUS BRENCHLEY. A Journey to Great-Salt-Lake City. London: W. Jeffs, 1861. 1st Eng ed. 2 vols. cxxi,508; vii,605pp; 10 steel engr; 1 engr fldg map. Rebound in red cl; black leather labels lettered in gilt on spines. Scattered minor foxing, o/w VG. Howes 8536. *Laurie.* $900/£581

REMY, JULES and JULIUS BRENCHLEY. A Journey to Great-Salt-Lake City.... London: W. Jeffs, 1861. 1st Eng ed. 2 vols. cxxxi,508; 605pp, 10 steel engrs, map. Blue cl. Spines dknd, top edges worn, o/w VG. Howes R 210. *Oregon.* $895/£577

REMY, JULES and JULIUS BRENCHLEY. A Journey to Great-Salt-Lake City.... London, 1861. 1st Eng ed. 2 vols. Fldg map. Howes R 210. *Ginsberg.* $750/£484

RENAN, ERNEST. The Life of Jesus. London/Paris: Trubner/M. Levy Freres, 1864. 1st ed in English. xii,311pp. Maroon cl, gilt spine. (Lt spotting; paper peeling inner joints; spine, upper cvr faded.) *Bickersteth.* $147/£95

RENARD, M. New Bodies For Old. Macaulay, 1923. 1st ed in English. VG + . *Aronovitz.* $45/£29

RENAULT, MARY. The Charioteer. London: Longmans, 1953. 1st Eng ed. Blue cl. Cvr sl mkd, eps foxed, inscrip, o/w Good. *Dalian.* $39/£25

RENAULT, MARY. North Face. London: Longmans, Green, 1949. 1st ed. Fine in dj. *Temple.* $47/£30

RENDELL, J.M. Concise Handbook of the Island of Madeira. London: Kegan Paul, 1890. Rev'd ed. Paper cvrs. *Gretton.* $15/£10

RENDELL, RUTH. The Copper Peacock. London: Hutchinson, 1991. 1st ed. Signed. Fine in dj. *Rees.* $31/£20

RENDELL, RUTH. The Face of Trespass. London: Hutchinson, 1974. 1st ed. Fine in VG dj (worn). *Mordida.* $165/£106

RENDELL, RUTH. The Fever Tree and Other Stories. London: Hutchinson, 1982. 1st ed. NF in dj. *Rees.* $39/£25

RENDELL, RUTH. The Fever Tree and Other Stories. London: Hutchinson, 1982. 1st Eng ed. Black cl. VF in dj. *Dalian.* $39/£25

RENDELL, RUTH. Going Wrong. London: Hutchinson, 1990. 1st ed. Signed. Fine in dj. *Rees.* $31/£20

RENDELL, RUTH. Heartstones. London: Hutchinson, 1987. 1st ed. Signed. Fine in dj. *Rees.* $31/£20

RENDELL, RUTH. A Judgement in Stone. London: Hutchinson, 1977. 1st ed. Fine in dj. *Rees.* $39/£25

RENDELL, RUTH. The Killing Doll. London: Hutchinson, 1984. 1st ed. VG in VG dj. *Ming.* $31/£20

RENDELL, RUTH. The Lake of Darkness. London: Hutchinson, 1980. 1st ed. Fine in dj. *Mordida.* $65/£42

RENDELL, RUTH. The Lake of Darkness. London: Hutchinson, 1980. 1st UK ed. VG (spine slant) in VG dj. *Ming.* $23/£15

RENDELL, RUTH. The Lake of Darkness. London: Hutchinson, 1980. 1st UK ed. Fine in dj (price-clipped). *Williams.* $43/£28

RENDELL, RUTH. Make Death Love Me. London: Hutchinson, 1979. 1st ed. Prelims, edges sl mkd, o/w VG in dj (sl rubbed). *Rees.* $39/£25

RENDELL, RUTH. Make Death Love Me. London: Hutchinson, 1979. 1st UK ed. Fine in NF dj (spine sl creased). *Williams.* $62/£40

RENDELL, RUTH. Matters of Suspense. (Helsinki): Eurographica, 1986. One of 350 signed, dated. Fine in card cvrs as issued. *Williams.* $85/£55

RENDELL, RUTH. Matters of Suspense. London: Eurographica, 1987. 1st thus. One of 350 numbered, signed. Fine in wrappers. *Rees.* $140/£90

RENDELL, RUTH. The New Girl Friend. London: Hutchinson, 1985. 1st ed. Signed. Fine in dj. *Rees.* $39/£25

RENDELL, RUTH. A New Lease of Death. London: John Long, 1967. 1st ed. NF in VG dj (rubbed; spine extrems chipped; sm scuff). *Janus.* $100/£65

RENDELL, RUTH. One Across, Two Down. London: Hutchinson, 1971. 1st ed. Tape mks pastedowns; label removed fep, o/w VG in Fine dj (sl wear). *Mordida.* $85/£55

RENDELL, RUTH. Put On by Cunning. London: Hutchinson, 1981. 1st ed. Spine sl cocked, o/w NF in dj. *Rees.* $39/£25

RENDELL, RUTH. Shake Hands For Ever. London: Hutchinson, 1975. 1st UK ed. VG (ink name, sm tear repaired to flyleaf) in dj (price-clipped, closed tears). *Williams.* $101/£65

RENDELL, RUTH. The Speaker of Mandarin. London: Hutchinson, 1973. 1st Eng ed. Black cl. VF in Fine dj. *Dalian.* $54/£35

RENDELL, RUTH. Talking to Strange Men. London: Hutchinson, 1987. 1st ed. Signed. Fine in dj. *Rees.* $31/£20

RENDELL, RUTH. Three Cases for Chief Inspector Wexford. (Helsinki): Eurograpica, 1990. One of 350 signed, dated. Fine in wrappers in dj as issued. *Williams.* $85/£55

RENDELL, RUTH. The Tree of Hands. London: Hutchinson, 1984. 1st ed. Signed. Fine in dj. *Rees.* $31/£20

RENDU, LOUIS. Theory of the Glaciers of Savoy. Alfred Wills (trans). London: Macmillan, 1874. 1st ed in English. (viii),216pp. Brown cl, blocked in black, gilt-lettered spine. *Bickersteth.* $202/£130

RENNER, FREDERIC G. (ed). Paper Talk. Illustrated Letters of Charles M. Russell. Ft. Worth, 1962. 1st thus in stiff pict wraps. VG. *Baade.* $75/£48

RENOIR, JEAN. My Life and My Films. Norman Denny (trans). London: Collins, 1974. 1st ed. VG+ in dj (edgeworn; torn). *Aka.* $17/£11

Renowned History of Valentine and Orson. London: D. Pratt, 1724. 12mo. 128+12pp contents, ten 1/2pg woodcuts (1st cut partially colored by child; tp, last 4 pgs restored; pg 75 missing top portion w/loss of text; various corners, edges chipped, chewed). Orig bds (rebound; new eps, fly leaves, spine) gilt title, date. Cvr edges rubbed, corners bumped; still Good w/Fine cuts. *Hobbyhorse.* $100/£65

Report of the 10th Annual Reunion of the 50th Illinois Reunion Association.... Camp Point, IL, Journal Print. Ptd wraps (worn, upper hinge torn). *Bohling.* $45/£29

Report of the Commissioner of Agriculture, 1863. Washington, 1864. 698pp (browning, marginal staining), 48 plts. (Spine split; cvrs dingy, worn.) *Sutton.* $35/£23

Report of the Commissioner of Agriculture, 1887. Washington, 1888. 724pp, 20 color plts, color fldg map. 1/2 leather (scuffed, chipped; ex-lib). *Sutton.* $27/£17

Report of the Culpeper Virginia Monument Commission of Pennsylvania. Harrisburg, PA: Wm. Stanley Ray, 1914. 1st ed. NF. *Mcgowan.* $45/£29

Report of the Proceedings of the Society of the Army of the Tennessee. Cincinnati: Charles O. Ebel, 1909. Grn emb cl. Fine. *Glenn.* $45/£29

Report of the Secretary of State on the Criminal Statistics of the State of New York. Albany, 1855. 367pp. Ptd wraps (worn, soiled, blindstamp). *Bohling.* $30/£19

Report of the Select Committee of the Senate of the United States on the Sickness and Mortality on Board Emigrant Ships. Washington, 1854. 1st ed. 147pp. (Cvrs, backstrip worn; stained; scattered foxing.) *Fye.* $125/£81

Report of the United States Commissioners to the Paris Universal Exposition, 1878. Washington: GPO, 1880. 5 vols. Lg fldg color plan, tinted view vol 1; 2 fldg color plans vol 3. Grn cl, gold-stamped. Overall VG (cvr wear). *Schoyer.* $300/£194

Report of the...Disbursement of Contributions for the Sufferers by the Chicago Fire. (Boston): Chicago Relief & Aid Soc, 1874. x,440pp; 2 fldg maps. Unopened. VG. *Schoyer.* $125/£81

Report on the Condition of Tropical and Semi-Tropical Fruits...in 1887. Washington, 1888. 149pp (3pg corners missing), 3 chromolitho plts. Orig wrappers (lt worn; tears to rear corner). *Sutton.* $65/£42

Report on Vaccination and Its Results, Based on the Evidence Taken by the Royal Commission During the Years 1889-1897. Volume I. London, 1898. 1st ed. 493pp. Good. *Fye.* $100/£65

Reports on Plague Investigations in India. Cambridge, 1911. 1st ed. 3 vols. (Backstrips detached;) ex-lib. *Fye.* $100/£65

REPS, JOHN W. Town Planning in Frontier America. Princeton: Princeton Univ Press, 1969. 1st ed. Fine in dj (chipped; sunned). *Bookpress.* $85 £55

REPTON, HUMPHRY. The Art of Landscape Gardening. John Nolen (ed). Boston/NY: Houghton Mifflin, 1907. 1st ed thus. Fldg color frontis, 22 plts. Spine label dknd, spine head sl worn, else VG. *Quest.* $165/£106

REPTON, HUMPHRY. The Landscape Gardening and Landscape Architecture.... London: for the Editor, 1840. xxi,619pp, 2 ff ads, engr port, 253 wood engr text illus (1 w/overslip). Orig cl (sl loose). *Marlborough.* $744/£480

REQUA, RICHARD S. Architectural Details, Spain and the Mediterranean. Cleveland: J.H. Jansen, 1927. 1st ed. Ex-lib w/mks; smudging; binding rubbed, else VG. *Bookpress.* $235/£152

RESTANY, PIERRE. Cesare. John Shepley (trans). NY, 1976. 40 color plts. Dj (chipped). *Edwards.* $54/£35

RETI, LADISLAO (ed). The Unknown Leonardo. NY: McGraw-Hill, (1974). 1st ed. Frontis. Ink name fep; else VG. *Bookpress.* $65/£42

Return of the Jedi. Hans Solo's Rescue. NY: Random House, 1983. 13x15 cm. 6 pop-ups. Glazed pict bds. VG. *Book Finders.* $30/£19

REUBEN, WILLIAM. The Atom Spy Hoax. NY: Action Books, (1955). 1st ed. Assoc copy, inscribed in year of pub. Spot on fore-edge; nicks fore-edges, few leaves; o/w VG in dj. *Reese.* $45/£29

REVERE, JOSEPH W. Keel and Saddle. Boston: Osgood, 1872. 1st ed. xiii,360pp. Bkpl of Carl I. Wheat. Gold-stamped cl (spine spotted). *Dawson.* $125/£81

REVERE, JOSEPH W. Naval Duty in California. Oakland: Biobooks, 1947. 1st CA ed. Ltd to 1000 ptd. Facs of letter; 5 full-color litho plts. Untrimmed. Gilt-dec buckram. Fine. *Connolly.* $85/£55

REVERE, JOSEPH W. Naval Duty in California. Oakland: Biobooks, 1947. Ltd to 1000. *Heinoldt.* $50/£32

REVERE, JOSEPH W. A Tour of Duty in California.... Joseph N. Balestier (ed). NY/Boston: C.S. Francis/J.H. Francis, 1849. 1st ed. 305 + 14pp pub's cat, 6 plts, fldg map. (Sm paper break lower corner tp; minor foxing title, frontis.) Mod grn leather-backed cl (new eps), gilt. NF. Howes R 222. *Blue Mountain.* $395/£255

Revised Code of the Laws of Mississippi, in Which Are Comprised all Such Acts...as Were in Force at the End of the Year 1823.... Natchez: Francis Baker, 1824. 1st ed. iv,743pp. Orig full leather (spine extrems chipped; bds rubbed; skin mks). VG + (foxing throughout). *Mcgowan.* $3,500/£2,258

REWALD, JOHN. Degas: Works in Sculpture, a Complete Catalogue. London, 1944. 112 plts. 2-tone cl. VG. *Argosy.* $65/£42

REWALD, JOHN. The History of Impressionism. London: Secker, 1973. 4th rev ed. VF in dj. *Europa.* $59/£38

REWALD, JOHN. The Woodcuts of Aristide Maillol. NY, 1951. 162 woodcuts. VF in dj (edgeworn). *Artis.* $35/£23

REXROTH, KENNETH. Human, Avian, Vegetable, Blood. Berkeley: Moe's Books, 1987. 1st separate ptg. Folds, else Fine. *Chapel Hill.* $25/£16

REXROTH, KENNETH. With Eye and Ear. NY, (1970). 1st ed. Fine in Fine dj. *Polyanthos.* $30/£19

REY, CHARLES F. The Romance of the Portuguese in Abyssinia. London, 1929. 1st ed. 2 fldg maps. (Lt soiled; spine lt sunned, sl chipped; plts sl chipped; prelims lt browned). *Edwards.* $39/£25

REYNARDSON, C.T.S. BIRCH. Down the Road or Reminiscences of a Gentleman Coachman. London, 1875. xxi,224pp, 13 Fine chromolitho plts. Orig gilt illus cl (sl rubbed; bkpl). *Edwards.* $310/£200

REYNOLDS, CHARLES B. Old Saint Augustine: A Story of Three Centuries. E.H. Reynolds, 1885 (c. 1884). 144pp. VG-. *Book Broker.* $35/£23

REYNOLDS, EDWARD. A Treatise of the Passions and Faculties of the Soul of Man. London: Robert Bostock, 1647. 1st ed. (16),554pp. Brn calf (spine extrems chipped, cvrs rubbed). *Karmiole.* $150/£97

REYNOLDS, FRANK with MICHAEL McCLURE. Freewheelin' Frank, Secretary of the Angels. NY: Grove Press, 1967. 1st ed. NF in dj (lt creased, rubbed). *Sclanders.* $31/£20

REYNOLDS, GARY A. and BERYL WRIGHT. Against the Odds: African-American Artists and the Harmon Foundation. NJ, 1989. 129 plts. Dj. *Edwards.* $39/£25

REYNOLDS, GEORGE W.M. The Mysteries of the Court of London. London: John Dicks, n.d. (1860?). 4 vols. Cl blocked in blind, gilt. Lower corners vols 1-2 discolored by damp, o/w clean set. *Bickersteth.* $132/£85

REYNOLDS, GRAHAM. Catalogue of the Constable Collection, Victoria and Albert Museum. London: HMSO, 1960. 310 plts. Sm mk upper cvr, dj torn, repaired, o/w Fine. *Europa.* $31/£20

REYNOLDS, GRAHAM. Catalogue of the Constable Collection. London: HMSO, 1960. 1st ed. Color frontis. Dj (ragged, loss head spine). *Edwards.* $54/£35

REYNOLDS, GRAHAM. English Portrait Miniatures. London: Black, 1952. 24 plts. Fine in dj. *Peter Taylor.* $22/£14

REYNOLDS, GRAHAM. The Later Paintings and Drawings of John Constable. Yale Univ Press, 1984. 1st ed. 2 vols. 1087 plts (250 color). Djs. *Edwards.* $194/£125

REYNOLDS, GRAHAM. Victorian Painting. Studio Vista, 1966. 39 color plts; in dj. *Edwards.* $39/£25

REYNOLDS, HENRY. Spanish Waters. Boston: Lauriat, (1924). 1st Amer ed. 4 charts. *Lefkowicz.* $35/£23

REYNOLDS, J. RUSSELL. Lectures on the Clinical Uses of Electricity. Phila, 1872. 1st Amer ed. 112pp. Good. *Fye.* $125/£81

REYNOLDS, J. RUSSELL. A System of Medicine. Phila, 1880. 1st Amer ed. 3 vols. 1127; 935; 990pp. Good. *Fye.* $200/£129

REYNOLDS, JEREMIAH N. Mocha Dick or the White Whale of the Pacific. NY/London, 1932. 1st separate ed. White cvrs (sl foxed). Dj (rubbed). *Lefkowicz.* $100/£65

REYNOLDS, JOSHUA. The Literary Works. London: T. Cadell, 1835. 2 vols. Frontis port (sl spotted), viii,463pp; 495pp. Gilt-edged calf (sl rubbed). *Edwards.* $78/£50

REYNOLDS, MACK. The Case of the Little Green Men. Phoenix Press, 1951. 1st ed. NF in VG dj (repaired). *Madle.* $100/£65

REYNOLDS, QUENTIN. Custer's Last Stand. NY: Random House, 1951. Stated 1st ptg trade. Frederick T. Chapman (illus). Dec eps. Good in dj. *Cattermole.* $25/£16

REYNOLDS, QUENTIN. The Fiction Factory or From Pulp Row to Quality Street. NY: Random House, 1955. 1st ed. NF in NF dj (price-clipped). *Janus.* $45/£29

REYNOLDS, QUENTIN. The Wright Brothers. NY: Random House, 1950. Stated 1st ptg trade. Jacob Landau (illus). Dec eps. VG in dj. *Cattermole.* $35/£23

REYNOLDS, ROBERT. Texas. Portland: Belding, (1973). 1st ed. VG in VG dj. *Oregon.* $45/£29

REYNOLDS, STEPHEN. Letters of Stephen Reynolds. Harold Wright (ed). London: Hogarth Press, 1923. 1st ed. Frontis port, 7 plts. Fore-, lower edges uncut. Blue buckram. Last text leaf badly opened w/loss of blank corner, o/w Nice. *Temple.* $74/£48

REYNOLDS, STEPHEN. Letters of Stephen Reynolds. Harold Wright (ed). Hogarth Press, 1923. 1st ed. Together w/1pg tls from Reynolds loosely inserted. Sl rubbed, o/w VG. *Words Etc.* $101/£65

REYNOLDS-BALL, EUSTACE A. Cairo. Boston, (1897). 348pp (ink inscrip; stamped names; staining bottom pp). Teg. Gilt-stamped cl. *King.* $50/£32

REZNIKOFF, C. By the Waters of Manhattan. Boni, 1930. 1st ed. Spine label lt chipped; spine little sunned, else VG + . *Fine Books.* $65/£42

REZNIKOFF, CHARLES. Separate Way. NY: Objectivist Press, (1936). 1st ed. Yellow cl. VG in dj. *Antic Hay.* $85/£55

RHAZES. A Treatise on the Small-Pox and Measles. London, 1848. 1st ed. 212pp. Good. *Fye.* $200/£129

RHEAD, LOUIS. Bold Robin Hood and His Outlaw Band. NY, 1912. 1st Amer ed. NF (spine sunned). *Polyanthos.* $50/£32

RHEES, WILLIAM JONES. The Smithsonian Institution.... Washington: GPO, 1901. 1st ed. 2 vols. (Bkpl vol II; margins lt browned; fr hinge vol I internally cracked; sl rubbed.) *Bookpress*. $110/£71

RHEES, WILLIAM JONES. The Smithsonian Institution: Documents Relative to Its Origin and History: 1835-1899. Washington: GPO, 1901. 1st ed. 2 vols. 2 fldg maps vol 2. Marbled eps; aeg. 1/2 leather, cl, gilt. Good+ (fr hinge vol I reinforced). *Connolly*. $85/£55

RHEIMS, MAURICE. The Flowering of Art Nouveau. NY: Abrams, (1966). 1st ed. Fine in pub's mylar dj. *Hermitage*. $100/£65

RHEIMS, MAURICE. The Flowering of Art Nouveau. NY: Abrams, 1966. 12 mtd color plts. Pict cl (rubbed). Lettered mylar wrapper (torn, taped). *Argosy*. $150/£97

RHIND, W. A History of the Vegetable Kingdom. London, 1868. Rev ed. Port; color tp; xvi,744pp; 23 steel-engr, 22 hand-colored plts. 1/2 calf. *Wheldon & Wesley*. $109/£70

RHODES, EUGENE MANLOVE. The Desire of the Moth. NY, 1916. 1st ed. Frontis. Pict cl (edgeworn). Good. *Artis*. $25/£16

RHODES, EUGENE MANLOVE. The Rhodes Reader: Stories of Virgins, Villains, and Varmints. Univ of OK Press, (1957). 1st ed. Pict eps, tp. Fine in Fine dj. *Authors Of The West*. $40/£26

RHODES, JAMES FORD. Lectures on the American Civil War. NY: Macmillan, 1913. 1st ed. Fldg color map. Orig cl. NF. *Mcgowan*. $45/£29

RHODES, MARYLOU. Landmarks of Richmond. Richmond, VA: Garrett & Massie, (1938). 1st ed. Blue cl. Fine in NF dj (sm chip). *Chapel Hill*. $30/£19

RHODES, NEIL. The Ancestral Face. London: Poem-of-the-Month Club, (1973). 1st ed. Fine. *Polyanthos*. $25/£16

RHODES, WILLIAM HENRY. Caxton's Book. Bancroft, 1876. 1st ed. Good. *Aronovitz*. $125/£81

RHODES, WILLIAM HENRY. Caxton's Book: A Collection of Essays, Poems.... Daniel O'Connell (ed). SF: A.L. Bancroft, 1876. 1st ed. 300pp. Gilt cl. VG. *Connolly*. $250/£161

RHONDDA, VISCOUNTESS. Leisured Women. Hogarth Press, 1928. 1st ed. VG in wrappers. *Words Etc*. $54/£35

RHYS, HORTON. A Theatrical Trip for a Wager! Vancouver, 1966. Facs rpt of London 1861 ed. One of 500 numbered, signed. Howes R 245. *Ginsberg*. $125/£81

RHYS, JEAN. Good Morning Midnight. London: Constable, 1939. 2nd issue (1st being in purple linen grain cl; lettered and taper-ruled lt grn spine; provided w/true eps at fr, end; 3 blanks left free). Grn rough buckram over very thin bds; lettered, taper-ruled purple on spine (sl wrinkled). Lacks 1/2 title, rep; edges sl foxed; o/w Very Nice. *Temple*. $42/£27

RHYS, JEAN. Jean Rhys. Letters 1931-1966. Francis Wyndham & Diana Melly (eds). London: Andre Deutsch, 1984. 1st Eng ed. Brn cl. Fine in dj. *Dalian*. $39/£25

RHYS, JEAN. The Letters of Jean Rhys. Francis Wyndham and Diana Melly (eds). NY: Viking, (1984). 1st Amer ed. VG in dj. *Hermitage*. $20/£13

RHYS, JEAN. Quartet. NY: S&S, 1929. 1st Amer ed. VG. *Cahan*. $85/£55

RIBOT, THEODULE. The Diseases of Personality. Chicago, 1891. 1st Eng trans. 157pp. Good. *Fye*. $75/£48

RIBOT, THEODULE. The Diseases of the Will. Chicago: Open Court, 1896. 137pp + pub's cat. Good in wrappers. *Hayman*. $20/£13

RIBOT, THEODULE. The Evolution of General Ideas. Frances A. Welby (trans). Chicago: Open Court, 1899. 1st ed in English. (xii) + 231 + (5)pp. VG. *Gach*. $65/£42

RICCI, CORRADO and ANTONIO MUNOZ et al. The Vatican: Its Treasures. NY: De Vinne Press, (1914). Gilt-dec vellum; white moire silk eps. VG. *Argosy*. $100/£65

RICE, ANNE. Interview with the Vampire. (London): MacDonald Raven Books, (1976). 1st Eng ed. Black cl. NF in dj. *Godot*. $125/£81

RICE, ANNE. Interview with the Vampire. NY: Knopf, 1976. 1st ed. 1st bk. NF in dj (1-inch closed tear, lt edgewear). *Godot*. $375/£242

RICE, ANNE. Interview with the Vampire. Macdonald, 1976. 1st UK ed. VG in dj. *Lewton*. $116/£75

RICE, ANNE. Lasher. NY: Knopf, 1993. 1st ed. Signed. Fine in Fine dj. *Revere*. $40/£26

RICE, ANNE. The Mummy. C&W, 1989. 1st hb ed. NF in dj. *Lewton*. $36/£23

RICE, ANNE. The Mummy. London: Chatto, 1989. 1st hb ed. Fine in dj. *Williams*. $74/£48

RICE, ANNE. The Queen of the Damned. MacDonald, 1988. 1st Eng ed. Signed. Fine in dj. *Aronovitz*. $65/£42

RICE, ANNE. The Vampire Lestat. NY: Knopf, 1985. 1st ed. Fine in dj (few short edgetears). *Else Fine*. $85/£55

RICE, ANNE. The Vampire Lestat. NY: Knopf, 1985. 1st ed. NF in Fine dj. *Bernard*. $125/£81

RICE, ANNE. The Vampire Lestat. NY: Knopf, 1985. 1st ed. Signed. Fine in NF dj (spine sl creased). *Bernard*. $175/£113

RICE, DAVID TALBOT and WALTER FRODL. Austria: Mediaeval Wall Paintings. NY: NYGS, (1964). 32 full-pg color plts. (Corners bumped.) *Artis*. $25/£16

RICE, ELMER. A Voyage to Purilia. Cosmopolitan, 1930. 1st ed. Rev slip laid in. NF in dj (frayed). *Madle*. $50/£32

RICE, GRANTLAND. Sportlights of 1923. NY, 1924. 1st ed. VG (sm spot, tips lt rubbed, sm gouge). *Fuller & Saunders*. $45/£29

RICE, HOWARD. Barthelemi Tardiveau, A French Trader in the West. Johns Hopkins, 1938. 1st ed. 4 plts, fldg map. VG. *Oregon*. $60/£39

RICE, NATHAN. Trials of a Public Benefactor, as Illustrated in the Discovery of Etherization. NY: Pudney & Russell, 1859. 1st ed. Title-leaf, xx,(13)-460pp; 3 plts (incl frontis port). Blind-stamped cl (badly soiled; spine torn, chipped, defects; hinges split, fr cvr almost detached). Internally VG. *Hemlock*. $150/£97

RICE, NORMAN L. The Sculpture of Ivan Mestrovic. Syracuse: Syracuse Univ, 1948. 1st ed. 157 b/w plts. Gilt-titled cl. NF. *Cahan*. $65/£42

Rich Storehouse or Treasurie for the Diseased Wherein are Many Approved Medicines. London: Richard Badger, 1630. 4to in 8's. (xxiv),317,(i)pp. Contemp calf (neatly rebacked). Good (lt age yellowing). *Sokol*. $1,473/£950

RICH, ARNOLD. The Pathogenesis of Tuberculosis. Springfield, 1944. 1st ed. Good. *Fye*. $150/£97

RICH, C.J. Narrative of a Residence in Koordistan, and on the Site of Ancient Nineveh.... London, 1836. 1st ed. 2 vols. xxxiii,398; viii,411pp; 2 fldg maps, 11 plts (1 lacking edge). Contemp calf w/new spine. (Contents sl unclean, used.) *Lewis.* $240/£155

RICH, E.E. (ed). Cumberland House Journals and Inland Journal 1775-82: First Series, 1775-79. London: Hudson's Bay Record Soc, 1951. VG. *Laurie.* $125/£81

RICH, E.E. (ed). London Correspondence Inward from Eden Colville, 1849-1852. London: Hudson's Bay Record Soc, 1956. VG. *Laurie.* $125/£81

RICH, E.E. (ed). Moose Fort Journals 1783-85. London: Hudson's Bay Record Soc, 1954. Fine. *Laurie.* $150/£97

RICH, JOSEPH W. The Battle of Shiloh. Iowa City, IA, 1911. 1st ed. Port. (Ink inscrip; bumped; spine discolored, frayed; sl foxing.) *King.* $60/£39

RICH, VIRTULON. Western Life in the Stirrups. Dwight L. Smith (ed). Chicago: Caxton Club, 1965. Frontis port; dbl map. Cl spine, marbled bds. Prospectus laid in. VG + . *Bohling.* $50/£32

RICHARD, MARK. The Ice at the Bottom of the World. NY: Knopf, 1989. 1st ed, 1st bk. Fine in Fine dj. *Revere.* $40/£26

RICHARD, MARK. The Ice at the Bottom of the World. London: Jonathan Cape, 1990. 1st Eng ed. Fine in Fine dj. *Revere.* $30/£19

RICHARDS, EVA ALVEY. Arctic Mood. Caldwell: Caxton, 1949. 1st ed. VG in dj (edgeworn). *Artis.* $15/£10

RICHARDS, GILBERT. Crossroads. Woodside: Gilbert Richards, 1973. 1st ed. #211/2000. Signed. Grn cl. Fine in dj (chipped, spine faded). *Harrington.* $40/£26

RICHARDS, GRANT. Author Hunting. London: Hamish Hamilton, 1934. 1st ed. Fine (few sunned spots) in dj (chipped). *Beasley.* $40/£26

RICHARDS, J.M. The Bombed Buildings of Britain. London: Architectural Press, (1942). 2nd ptg. Frontis. Fine. *Bookpress.* $45/£29

RICHARDS, J.M. High Street. London: Country Life, 1938. 1st ed. 24 color lithos by Eric Ravilious. Pict bds (sl worn). *Hollett.* $698/£450

RICHARDS, LAURA E. When I Was Your Age. Boston: Dana Estes, (1894). 1st ed. 210pp. VG. *Second Life.* $25/£16

RICHARDS, MILTON. Dick Kent in the Far North. Akron: Saalfield, (1928). Dec cvr. VG in VG dj. *Blue Dragon.* $27/£17

RICHARDS, MILTON. Dick Kent with the Mounted Police. Akron: Saalfield, (1927). Dec cvr. VG in VG dj. *Blue Dragon.* $27/£17

RICHARDS, PAUL. Modern Baseball Strategy. Prentice-Hall, 1955. 1st ed. VG in Good dj. *Plapinger.* $25/£16

RICHARDS, PRIVATE FRANK. (Pseud of Robert Graves). Old-Soldier Sahib. London: Faber, 1936. 1st UK ed. VG in dj (sl dusty, browned, sl edgewear). *Williams.* $194/£125

RICHARDS, ROBERT. Californian Crusoe; Or, The Lost Treasure Found. London/NY: J. Parker/Stanford & Swords, 1854. 1st ed. Frontis, iv,162pp (sl damage margin 6 leaves). Blind emb cl, gilt spine title. VG (spine faded). Howes R 250. *Bohling.* $275/£177

RICHARDS, SAMUEL. Diary. Phila: Pub by his great grandson, 1909. VG. *Schoyer.* $60/£39

RICHARDS, SWISHER and ARBONA. Stoneflies. Winchester Pr., (1980). 1st ed. Fine in dj. *Artis.* $29/£19

RICHARDS, T. ADDISON. Appleton's Illustrated Hand-Book of American Travel. NY: Appleton, 1857. 1st issue. 420pp + 24pp ads; 4 fldg hand-colored maps, 27 sm fldg maps. (Sunned.) *Schoyer.* $150/£97

RICHARDSON, A.E. and H. DONALDSON EBERLEIN. The Smaller English House of the Later Renaissance 1660-1830. London: Batsford, 1933. New issue. Frontis. Dj (sl ragged). *Edwards.* $78/£50

RICHARDSON, A.E. and HECTOR O. CORFIATO. Design in Civil Architecture. Vol I. London: English Universities Press, (1948). 1st ed. Text sl yellowed; else VG in dj (worn). *Bookpress.* $65/£42

RICHARDSON, ALBERT D. Beyond the Mississippi: From the Great River to the Great Ocean. Hartford, CT: American Pub, (1869). 2nd ed. Engr frontis port; 15 full pg illus. Pub's black pebbled cl. VG (lacks the 2-pg map at fr; fr inside hinge fragile). *Laurie.* $50/£32

RICHARDSON, ALBERT D. The Secret Service, the Field, the Dungeon and the Escape. Hartford, 1865. 1st ed. 512pp. Cvr worn, faded, o/w VG + . *Pratt.* $45/£29

RICHARDSON, C. Practical Farriery. London: Pitman, 1950. 1st ed. VG in VG dj. *October Farm.* $25/£16

RICHARDSON, DOROTHY M. Dawn's Left Hand. London: Duckworth, 1931. 1st ed. Chip, o/w Fine. *Cahan.* $100/£65

RICHARDSON, DOROTHY M. Deadlock. London: Duckworth, (1921). 1st ed, 1st issue in blue cl w/pub's device back cvr. Signed. Fine in pict dj (sl chipped). *Pharos.* $400/£258

RICHARDSON, DOROTHY M. Interim. London: Duckworth, (1919). 1st ed. Fine in white pict dj (used). *Pharos.* $125/£81

RICHARDSON, DOROTHY M. The Trap. London: Duckworth, 1925. 1st ed. Corner worn, spine sl faded, o/w NF. *Temple.* $43/£28

RICHARDSON, DOROTHY M. The Tunnel. London: Duckworth, 1919. 1st ed. Blue buckram. Nice. *Temple.* $50/£32

RICHARDSON, F.L. Andrea Schiavone. OUP, 1980. 237 plts. Sound in dj. *Ars Artis.* $116/£75

RICHARDSON, FREDERICK. Frederick Richard's Book for Children. Chicago: M.A. Donohue, (1938). Obl 4to. Wine red cl, color paste label. Good. *Reisler.* $125/£81

RICHARDSON, ROBERT. The Book of the Dead. London: Gollancz, 1989. 1st ed. Fine in Fine dj. *Ming.* $39/£25

RICHARDSON, SAMUEL. The History of Sir Charles Grandison. London: Rivington, etc., 1762. 4th ed. 7 vols. 12mo. Half title; ad pg; engr frontis port. Contemp calf (rebacked), gilt, leather labels. (Sigs in vol 1.) *Hartfield.* $350/£226

RICHARDSON, SAMUEL. Pamela, or Virtue Rewarded. London: Harrison, 1785. 4 vols in 1. Thick 8vo. 634pp, 12 Nice full-pg engr illus. Orig black leather spine, marbled bds, gilt. (Hinges rubbed; uniform lt foxing, spotting; old label.) *Hartfield.* $295/£190

RICHARDSON, SAMUEL. Pamela; or, Virtue Rewarded. London: 1762. 8th ed. 4 vols. 12mo. Contemp full calf over cords (hinges rubbed; head of 1 vol chipped), cvrs ruled in gilt. *D & D.* $275/£177

RICHARDSON, W. Dr. Zell and the Princess Charlotte. L. Kabis, 1892. 1st ed. NF in Fine dj. *Aronovitz.* $250/£161

RICHARDSON, WILLIS and MAY MILLER. Negro History in Thirteen Plays. Washington: Assoc Pub, (1935). 1st ed. Fr cvr discolored, else VG in dj (worn, sl chipped). *Godot.* $175/£113

RICHIE, DONALD. The Japanese Tattoo. NY, 1980. 1st ed. VG in dj. *Argosy.* $50/£32

RICHLER, MORDECAI. The Apprenticeship of Duddy Kravitz. London: Andre Deutsch, 1959. 1st Eng ed. Red cl. VG in dj (frayed). *Dalian.* $54/£35

RICHLER, MORDECAI. The Incomparable Atuk. London: Andre Deutsch, 1963. 1st Eng ed. Black cl. Fine in dj. *Dalian.* $39/£25

RICHLER, MORDECAI. Solomon Gursky was Here. NY, 1990. 1st Amer ed. Signed. Fine in Fine dj. *Polyanthos.* $35/£23

RICHMAN, IRVING BERDINE. California Under Spain and Mexico, 1535-1847. Boston: Houghton Mifflin, 1911. 22 maps, charts, plans. Teg. Gold-stamped cl, map pockets inside both cvrs. *Dawson.* $125/£81

RICHMOND, IAN A. The City Wall of Imperial Rome: An Account of Its Architectural Development.... Oxford: Clarendon, 1930. 21 plts. Good. *Archaeologia.* $175/£113

RICHTER, CONRAD. Always Young and Fair. NY: Knopf, 1947. 1st ed. Fine in dj (lt worn). *Reese.* $20/£13

RICHTER, CONRAD. The Fields. Knopf, 1946. 1st ed. Fine in VG dj (price-clipped). *Authors Of The West.* $35/£23

RICHTER, CONRAD. The Fields. NY: Knopf, 1946. 1st trade ed. Dec cl. Fine in white dj (lt soiled). *Reese.* $45/£29

RICHTER, CONRAD. The Free Man. Knopf, 1943. 1st ed. Inscribed, signed. Fine in Fine dj. *Authors Of The West.* $75/£48

RICHTER, CONRAD. A Simple Honorable Man. NY: Knopf, 1962. 1st ed. Fine in dj. *Hermitage.* $25/£16

RICHTER, CONRAD. A Simple Honorable Man. Knopf, 1962. 1st ed. Signed. 'First Edition Circle' card laid in. Fine in Fine dj. *Authors Of The West.* $50/£32

RICHTER, CONRAD. Tacey Cromwell. Knopf, 1942. 1st ed. Fine in VG dj. *Authors Of The West.* $35/£23

RICHTER, CONRAD. The Town. Knopf, 1950. 1st ed. Fine in Fine dj. *Authors Of The West.* $40/£26

RICHTER, CONRAD. The Trees. Knopf, 1940. 1st ltd advance ed of 255 numbered for pub's presentation. Bds, label. Fine in slipcase (repaired). *Authors Of The West.* $100/£65

RICHTER, ED. Making of a Big League Pitcher. Chilton, 1963. 1st ed. Fine in VG dj. *Plapinger.* $35/£23

RICHTER, GISELA M.A. The Archaic Gravestones of Attica. London: Phaidon, 1961. Dj (chipped). *Edwards.* $59/£38

RICHTER, GISELA M.A. Attic Red-Figured Vases. Yale Univ, 1958. Rev ed. Dj (spine chipped). *Edwards.* $31/£20

RICHTER, GISELA M.A. Engraved Gems of the Greeks, Etruscans and Romans. London: Phaidon, (1968-1971). 2 vols complete. (Sl marginal dampstaining few pp; vol 2 top bd stained.) Dj. *Archaeologia.* $450/£290

RICHTER, J. PAUL. The Cannon Collection of Italian Paintings of the Renaissance. Mostly of the Veronese School. Princeton, 1936. VG ex-lib (sm nearly effaced # at backstrip). *Washton.* $50/£32

RICKERT, MARGARAET. Painting in Britain. The Middle Ages. Balt, 1954. 192 plts. Good. *Washton.* $60/£39

RICKETSON, SHRADAH. Means of Preserving Health and Preventing Diseases.... NY: Collins, 1806. xi,298pp. 'David Hosack letter' present in prelims (found in only a few copies). Orig sheep (worn; foxing). *Goodrich.* $195/£126

RICKETSON, SHRADAH. Means of Preserving Health, and Preventing Diseases. NY, 1806. 1st ed. 300pp. Full leather. Eps torn, o/w Fine. *Fye.* $350/£226

RICKETT, H.W. Wild Flowers of the United States. Vol 1. The Northeastern States. NY, 1966. 1st ed. 180 plts. (Glue residue along sl open inner joint.) Slipcase (edge cracked, bottom stained). *Sutton.* $125/£81

RICKETT, H.W. Wild Flowers of the United States. Vol 2. The Southeastern States. NY, 1967. 1st ed. 241 plts. Slipcase (bottom stained). *Sutton.* $225/£145

RICKETT, H.W. Wild Flowers of the United States. Vol 5. The Northwestern States. NY, 1971. 1st ed. 218 plts. Slipcase (lt soiled). *Sutton.* $175/£113

RICKETT, H.W. Wild Flowers of the United States. Vol 6. NY, 1973. 1st ed. 262 plts. Slipcase (edgewear). *Sutton.* $195/£126

RICKETTS, CHARLES. Oscar Wilde. Recollections by Jean Paul Raymond and Charles Ricketts. London: Nonesuch, 1932. 1st ed. Ltd to 800 (this marked 'out of series for review'). Uncut in orig cream buckram blocked in gold. The only Nonesuch bk set in Linotype. (Sl soiled.) *Cox.* $287/£185

RICKETTS, CHARLES. Some Letters from Charles Ricketts and Charles Shannon to 'Michael Field' (1894-1902). J.G. Paul Delany (ed). Edinburgh: Tragara Press, 1979. Ltd to 145 numbered. Fine in brn ptd wrappers. *Dalian.* $54/£35

RICKETTS, CHARLES. Unrecorded Histories. London: Martin Secker, 1933. 1st ed, ltd to 950. 6 full-pg silhouettes. Teg, rest uncut. Good in sand buckram. Bkpl, acquisition note of Lord Kenyon. *Cox.* $101/£65

RICKETTS, H.T. Contributions to Medical Science...1870-1910. Chicago, 1911. 1st ed. (Inner hinges cracked.) *Fye.* $200/£129

RICKEY, BRANCH and ROBERT RIGER. The American Diamond. S&S, 1965. 1st ed. VG in VG dj (nicks). *Plapinger.* $110/£71

RICORD, PHILIPPE. Lectures on Venereal and Other Diseases Arising from Sexual Intercourse. Phila: Ed. Barrington & Geo. D. Haswell, 1849. 1st Amer ed. Victor De Meric (trans). 298pp + (2)pp ads. (Foxing.) Contemp calf (rubbed, outer hinges cracked, 1/2-inch chips top, bottom of spine), black leather spine label). Worn but sound. *Karmiole.* $75/£48

RICORD, PHILIPPE. A Practical Treatise on Venereal Diseases. NY, 1842. 1st Amer ed. 339pp. *Fye.* $200/£129

RICORD, PHILIPPE. A Practical Treatise on Venereal Diseases. NY, 1849. 4th Amer ed. 339pp. Good. *Fye.* $100/£65

RIDDELL, MRS. Mortomley's Estate, a Novel. London: Tinsley, 1875. New ed. 425pp. 3/4 calf, paper label. VG. *Second Life.* $65/£42

RIDDLE, DONALD W. Congressman Abraham Lincoln. Urbana: Univ of IL, 1957. 1st ed. NF (bkpl) in Good + dj. *Connolly.* $27/£17

RIDDLE, DONALD W. Lincoln Runs for Congress. New Brunswick: Rutgers Univ, 1948. 1st ed. Frontis. Fine (bkpls) in VG dj (sm chip). *Connolly.* $32/£21

Ride a Cock-Horse and Other Nursery Rhymes. London: C&W, 1940. 1st ed. 4to. 29pp. Mervyn Peake (illus). VG in VG dj. *Davidson.* $650/£419

RIDER, DAN. Adventures with Bernard Shaw. London: Morley & Mitchell Kennerley, Jr., (1929). 1st ed. Frontis. Grn cl. NF in VG dj (spine sunned, lt chipped). *Chapel Hill.* $60/£39

RIDGE, LOLA. Firehead. NY: Payson & Clarke, 1929. 1st ed. Fine (bkpl) in dj (soiled). *Pharos.* $40/£26

RIDGEWAY, WILLIAM. The Origin and Influence of the Thoroughbred Horse. Cambridge, 1905. (Foxing.) *Wheldon & Wesley.* $78/£50

RIDGEWAY, WILLIAM. The Origin and Influence of the Thoroughbred Horse. CUP, 1905. 1st ed. Gilt-lettered blue cl. Fine. *House.* $120/£77

RIDGWAY, R. The Humming Birds. Washington, 1892. (253-)383pp (tanned). Cl (lt spotted; fr hinge cracked). *Sutton.* $95/£61

RIDING, LAURA and ROBERT GRAVES. A Pamphlet Against Anthologies. NY: Doubleday, Doran, 1928. 1st Amer ed. Red cl spine, paper-cvrd bds. Lt soiled, else VG in dj (lt browned, nicked, else VG). *Godot.* $225/£145

RIDING, LAURA. Collected Poems of Laura Riding. NY: Random House, (1938). 1st ed. Fore-edge lt foxed, else Fine in Fine dj (price-clipped). *Godot.* $325/£210

RIDING, LAURA. Description of Life. NY: Targ Editions, 1980. 1st ed. One of 350 signed. Fine. *Juvelis.* $75/£48

RIDING, LAURA. (ed). Everybody's Letters. London: Arthur Barker, 1933. 1st Eng ed. Black cl. Sl faded, rubbed; fore-edge, eps sl foxed, o/w VG. *Dalian.* $70/£45

RIDING, LAURA. The World and Ourselves. London: C&W, 1938. 1st ed. Lower edges uncut. Brownish-pink cl, gilt. Spine sl faded, o/w Nice. *Temple.* $101/£65

RIDINGS, SAM P. The Chisholm Trail. Guthrie, OK: Co-Operative Pub Co, (1936). 1st ed. Fldg map. VG in dj. Howes R 281. *Lien.* $200/£129

RIDINGS, SAM. The Chisholm Trail. Guthrie: Co-Operatice Pub, 1936. 1st ed. VG + in dj (edgeworn). Howes R 281. *Parker.* $200/£129

RIDLEY, THOMAS. A View of the Civile and Ecclesiasticall Law.... Oxford: Ric. Davis, 1676. 1st ed. (12),396,(28)pp. Mod gilt calf w/red morocco spine label. (Text browned.) *Karmiole.* $200/£129

RIDPATH, JOHN. Beyond the Sierras. A Tour of Sixty Days.... Biobooks, (1963). Ltd to 650. Fine. *Oregon.* $40/£26

RIEFENSTAHL, LENI. Coral Gardens. NY: Harper & Row, 1978. 1st US ed. NF in pict dj. *Cahan.* $85/£55

RIEFENSTAHL, LENI. The Last of the Nuba. NY: Harper & Row, 1973. 1st Amer ed. VG in dj. *Cahan.* $100/£65

RIEFENSTAHL, LENI. The Last of the Nuba. Harper & Row, 1973. 1st ed. NF in VG + dj. *Bishop.* $95/£61

RIEFENSTAHL, LENI. Vanishing Africa. Katherine Talbot (trans). NY: Harmony, 1982. 1st Amer ed. Fine in dj. *Cahan.* $100/£65

RIEFSTAHL, R.M. Persian and Indian Textiles. NY: E. Weyhe, 1923. 1st ed. 36 plts. Loose sheets, plates in pub's cl-backed folder (lt wear), as issued. *Chapel Hill.* $95/£61

RIEHL, G. and V. ZUMBUSCH. Atlas of Diseases of the Skin. In 3 Parts. Phila: Blakiston, 1925. Leatherette, gilt spine titles. Fine. *Hemlock.* $475/£306

RIESENBERG, FELIX, JR. The Golden Road: The Story of California's Spanish Mission Trail. NY: McGraw-Hill, (1962). 1st ed. Black cl. Fine in NF dj. *Harrington.* $30/£19

RIESMAN, DAVID. The Lonely Crowd. NH: Yale, 1950. 1st ed. VG in dj. *Lame Duck.* $100/£65

RIEWALD, J.G.(ed). Max in Verse. Brattleboro, 1963. 1st ed. Blue cl. Fine in dj. *Heller.* $30/£19

RIGAUD, ODETTE MENNESSON. Ah Haiti, Glimpses of Voodoo. Roxbury, MA: Nat'l Center of Afro-American Artists, 1972. 1st ed. Illus wrappers faded, else VG. *Cahan.* $35/£23

RIGG, ROBERT B. How to Stay Alive in Vietnam. Harrisburg: Stackpole, (1966). Illus bds (lt rubbed). *Aka.* $65/£42

RIGGS, STEPHEN RETURN. Dakota Grammer, Texts, and Ethnography. Washington: GPO, 1893. 3 parts in 1 vol. Cvrs rubbed; corner bumped, else VG. *Laurie.* $125/£81

RIGHTS, DOUGLAS L. The American Indian in North Carolina. Durham: Duke Univ, 1947. 1st ed. Signed presentation. Lg fldg map, 110 b/w plts. NF in illus dj (edgeworn). *Cahan.* $75/£48

RIIS, JACOB A. The Battle with the Slum. NY: Macmillan, 1902. 1st ed. Illus cl-cvrd bds. NF. *Lame Duck.* $65/£42

RIIS, JACOB A. How the Other Half Lives. NY: Scribner's, 1894. Later ptg. xvi,304pp (lacks fep). Cl, pict bds. *Schoyer.* $50/£32

RIIS, JACOB A. Out of Mulberry Street. NY: Century, 1898. 1st ed. Inscribed. Fine. *Beasley.* $250/£161

RIJNHART, SUSIE CARSON. With the Tibetans in Tent and Temple. Edinburgh: Oliphant, Anderson & Ferrier, 1901. 1st ed. Fldg map, 13 plts. Grn cl, lettered in black/gilt. VG internally (mks; cvrs sl cockled). *Morrell.* $194/£125

RILEY, C.V. and L.O. HOWARD. Insect Life. Washington, 1888-95. 7 vols. 1/2 leather (extrems worn; hinge splitting 4 vols; emb stamps; ex-lib). *Sutton.* $185/£119

RILEY, JAMES WHITCOMB. All the Year Round. Indianapolis: Bobbs-Merrill, (1912). 1st ed. 12 woodcuts. 1st state binding: navy blue cl backed in white cl, gilt. Top edges uncut. Soiled, spine browned, else Fine. *Glenn.* $200/£129

RILEY, JAMES WHITCOMB. Love Letters of the Bachelor Poet to Miss Elizabeth Kahle. Boston: Bibliophile Soc, 1922. 1st ed. One of 475 ptd. Beige bds, brn buckram spine, gilt top. Fine in box. *Appelfeld.* $85/£55

RILEY, JAMES WHITCOMB. The Riley Baby Book. Indianapolis: Bobbs-Merrill, (1913). 1st ed. Mtd color frontis. Red cl, gilt. Inscrip, sm sticker fep, else Fine. *Glenn.* $150/£97

RILEY, JAMES WHITCOMB. Rubaiyat of Doc Sifers. NY, 1897. 1st ed. VF. *Bond.* $40/£26

RILEY, JAMES. An Authentic Narrative of the Loss of the American Brig Commerce, Wrecked on the Western Coast of Africa.... Lexington, KY: Author, 1823. 410,413-455pp; 7 plts. Contemp sheep. Dampstained, foxed; spine label chipped off, else Nice. *Felcone.* $200/£129

RILEY, JAMES. An Authentic Narrative of the Loss of the American Brig Commerce...August, 1815.... Elm Grove: Sycamore, 1963. Facs ed of 1859 1st ed. Pict bds. Fine. *Connolly.* $25/£16

RILEY, JAMES. Loss of the American Brig 'Commerce' Wrecked...in August 1815.... London, 1817. 1st ed. xvi,618pp; lg fldg map. Mod 1/2 calf. *Lewis.* $287/£185

RIMBAUD, ARTHUR. A Season in Hell. Norfolk: New Directions, 1939. One of 780. Fine in dj (lt soiled; sm chip top edge). *Beasley.* $100/£65

RIMBAULT, EDWARD F. The Pianoforte. London: Robert Cocks & Co, 1860. Hand-colored frontis, xvi,420pp. Blue cl (rebound, orig black cl cvrs laid down). *Karmiole.* $200/£129

RIMMEL, EUGENE. The Book of Perfumes. London: Chapman & Hall, 1871. 7th ed. Inscribed presentation. xx,266,(ii)pp. Aeg. Spine faded. *Hollett.* $78/£50

RINEHART, MARY ROBERTS. The Circular Staircase. Indianapolis, (1908). 1st ed. 1st bk, 1st issue w/September on copyright pg. Lester Ralph (illus). Grn pict cl, stamped red/black. VG. *Argosy.* $125/£81

RINEHART, MARY ROBERTS. The Man in Lower Ten.... Indianapolis: Bobbs-Merrill, (1909). 1st ed. VG. *Reese.* $50/£32

RINEHART, MARY ROBERTS. Through Glacier Park. Boston, 1916. 1st Amer ed. Pict cvrs. Spine extrems sl rubbed; name stamps, o/w NF. *Polyanthos.* $35/£23

RINEHART, MARY ROBERTS. Through Glacier Park.... Boston: Houghton Mifflin, 1916. 1st ed. Frontis port, 16 plts. Fine. *Second Life.* $45/£29

RINEHART, MARY ROBERTS. The Yellow Room. NY: Farrar & Rinehart, 1945. 1st ed. Fine (inscrip; sl edgewear) in VG+ dj (closed tear). *Janus.* $45/£29

RINGBOLT, CAPTAIN. Sailors' Life and Sailors' Yarns. NY/Boston: C.S. Francis/J.H. Francis, 1847. 1st ed. 252pp (lt foxing). Orig cl (extrems worn). *Lefkowicz.* $75/£48

RIPLEY, R.L. Believe It or Not! Paul, 1928. 1st Eng ed. VG+ in VG dj (spine extrems chipped). *Aronovitz.* $150/£97

RIPPEY, SARAH CORY. The Goody-Naughty Book. Chicago/NY: Rand McNally, (1913). 1st ed. Pict paper over bds. *Glenn.* $85/£55

RISCHBIETER, HENNING (ed). Art and the Stage in the 20th Century: Painters and Sculptors Work for the Theatre. Greenwich, (1968). 30 color plts. VG in dj. *Argosy.* $85/£55

RISK, R.T. Erhard Ratdolt, Master Printer. Francestown, NH: Typographeum, 1982. Ltd to 100 numbered, signed. 4 plts. Linen over bds, paper spine label. Fine. *Karmiole.* $75/£48

RISTER, CARL COKE. Border Captives; The Traffic in Prisoners by Southern Plains Indians, 1835-1875. Norman: Univ of OK, 1940. 1st ed. Fldg map. *Lambeth.* $65/£42

RISTIC, DRAGISA N. Yugoslavia's Revolution of 1941. University Park: PA State Univ, 1966. 1st ed. VG in dj. *Shasky.* $30/£19

RITCHIE, ANDREW CARNDUFF. Abstract Painting and Sculpture in America. NY: MOMA, (1951). 1st ed. Frontis. VG in dj. *Bookpress.* $50/£32

RITCHIE, ANDREW CARNDUFF. Abstract Painting and Sculpture in America. NY: MOMA, 1951. 7 color plts. Dj (sl browned, chipped). *Edwards.* $31/£20

RITCHIE, ANDREW CARNDUFF. Franklin C. Watkins. NY: MOMA, 1950. 2 color plts. VG in stiff ptd wrappers. *Argosy.* $30/£19

RITCHIE, ANNA CORA. Mimic Life. Boston: Ticknor & Fields, 1856. 1st ed. 408pp + ads. VG. *Second Life.* $75/£48

RITCHIE, JAMES S. Wisconsin and Its Resources. Phila: Desilver, 1858. Fldg color frontis map, 318pp + 12pp ads, fldg color map, b/w map, 5 plts. Tan cl, gilt-, blind-stamped. VG+ (sl shaken). *Bohling.* $350/£226

RITCHIE, LEITCH. Wanderings by the Seine. London: Longmans, Rees, 1834. (vi),256pp, aeg, 20 engr plts (margins lt browned, few foxed). Panelled black morocco (rubbed; joints cracked). *Hollett.* $132/£85

RITCHIE, ROBERT WELLES. The Hell-Roarin' Forty-Niners. NY: J.H. Sears, (1928). 1st ed. VG in dj (sl worn). *Lien.* $35/£23

RITCHIE, ROBERT WELLES. The Hell-roarin' Forty-Niners. NY: J.H. Sears, (1928). 1st ed. Red dec cl. Corner sl bumped, o/w Fine in NF dj (spine dknd; sl chipped). *Harrington.* $60/£39

RITCHIE, WARD. Bookmen and Their Brothels. L.A.: Zamorano Club, 1970. Ltd ed. Fine in wrappers. *Weber.* $45/£29

RITSON, JOSEPH. Robin Hood. London: John C. Nimmo, 1885. #100/100 lg paper ltd ed. 4to. cxviii + 400pp, 80 wood engrs by Thomas Bewick ptd on China paper and pasted down beginning, end of each chapter. 9 etchings from orig paintings by A.H. Tourrier, E. Buckman. Port of Ritson and 9 copper engrs given in duplicate (1 ptd on Whatman paper, the other on Japanese paper), all w/plt guards. Orig gilt grn calf (professionally rebacked retaining orig backstrip w/5 raised bands, gilt dec and title). Fine (edges, spine ends lt rubbed). *Hobbyhorse.* $600/£387

RITTENHOUSE, BENJAMIN FRANKLIN. The Battle of Gettysburg as Seen from Little Round Top. Washington, D.C.: Judd & Detweiler, 1887. 1st ed. 13pp. Orig ptd wrappers in utilitarian binding. VG. *Mcgowan.* $85/£55

RITTENHOUSE, JACK. The Santa Fe Trail. A Historical Bibliography. Univ of NM, (1971). 1st ed. Dbl-pg map. VG in VG dj. *Oregon.* $150/£97

RITTER, LAWRENCE. The Glory of Their Times. Macmillan, 1966. 1st ed. NF in NF dj. *Fine Books.* $95/£61

RITTER, LAWRENCE. The Glory of Their Times. MacMillan, 1966. Ltr ptg. Fine in VG dj. *Plapinger.* $27/£17

RIVERS, GEORGE R.R. Captain Shays. Boston: Little, Brown, 1897. 1st ed. Gilt-stamped grn cl. Fine. *Beasley.* $125/£81

RIVERS, THOMAS. The Orchard House. London: Longmans, Green, 1879. 16th ed. 256pp + 9pp ads; fldg fig. Gilt-dec cl. VF. *Quest.* $50/£32

RIVERS, THOMAS. The Rose-Amateur's Guide. London: Longmans et al, 1861. 7th ed. 223pp + 24pp ads (2 sm marginal tears). Ruled, blind-stamped cl (spine dulled). *Quest.* $70/£45

RIVERS, THOMAS. Viruses and Virus Diseases. Stanford, 1939. 1st ed. Good. *Fye.* $35/£23

RIVERS, W.H.R. The Influence of Alcohol and Other Drugs on Fatigue. London, 1908. 1st ed. (Ex-lib.) *Fye.* $50/£32

RIVES, GEORGE L. The United States and Mexico 1821-1848. NY: Scribner's, 1913. 1st ed. 2 vols. 15 maps (2 fldg). Blue cl. VG set (blindstamp tps, bkpl, release stamp). *Chapel Hill.* $275/£177

RIZZI, ALDO. The Etchings of the Tiepolos. Complete Edition. London, 1971. Good in dj (sm repaired tear fep). *Washton.* $125/£81

Roanoke: Story of County and City. W.P.A., 1942. Fldg map. Good +. *Book Broker*. $45/£29

Robber Kitten. NY: McLoughlin Bros, n.d. (ca 1860). Susie Sunshine's Series. 8vo. 8 leaves. Pict stiff paper wrappers. Sm split lower edge wrapper else VG. *Hobbyhorse*. $95/£61

ROBBINS, ARCHIBALD. A Journal, Comprising an Account of the Loss of the Brig Commerce, of Hartford.... Hartford: F.D. Bolles, 1817. 1st ed. vii,(5),258pp; fldg map. Contemp sheep. Foxing, else Very Nice. *Felcone*. $450/£290

ROBBINS, ARCHIBALD. Robbins Journal; Comprising an Account of the Loss of the Brig 'Commerce'.... Conde Nast, 1931. Rpt. #154/355 signed by Earle Winslow (illus). Vellum, slipcase (sm mks on both). *Lewis*. $81/£52

ROBBINS, HAROLD. The Betsy. NY: Trident, (1971). 1st ed. Silver-stamped cl. Fine in dj. *Sadlon*. $25/£16

ROBBINS, TOD. The Master of Murder. London, 1933. 1st ed. Cvr wear, else VG. *Madle*. $50/£32

ROBBINS, TOD. The Spirit of the Town. Ogilvie, 1912. 1st ed. VG. *Madle*. $100/£65

ROBERGE, EARL. Timber Country, Logging in the Great Northwest. Caldwell: Caxton, 1973. 1st ed. VF in VG dj. *Oregon*. $45/£29

ROBERT, MAURICE and FREDERIC WARDE. A Code for the Collector of Beautiful Books. NY: LEC, 1936. 1st ed. Sl wear, o/w NF. *Glenn*. $45/£29

ROBERTON, JOHN. A Practical Treatise on the Power of Cantharides...in Three Parts. Including an Inquiry.... Edinburgh, 1806. 1st ed. 137pp, 88pp. Good in leather-backed wrappers. *Fye*. $200/£129

ROBERTS, ARTHUR O. Tomorrow is Growing Old. Newberg, OR: Barclay Press, (1978). 1st ed. VG in VG dj. *Perier*. $75/£48

ROBERTS, AUSTIN. Birds of South Africa. G.R. McLachlan (rev). (Cape Town, 1957). 56 color plts, 5 monochrome plts. VG in dj. *Argosy*. $60/£39

ROBERTS, BRUCE. The Carolina Gold Rush. Charlotte, NC: McNally and Loftin, 1971. 1st ed. Signed. Fldg map. Fine (portions of dj laid in). *Cahan*. $45/£29

ROBERTS, CECIL. One Year of Life. London: Hodder & Stoughton, 1952. 1st Eng ed. Blue cl. Fine in dj. *Dalian*. $23/£15

ROBERTS, CECIL. Portal to Paradise. London: Hodder & Stoughton, 1955. 1st Eng ed. Grn cl. Fine in dj (sl nicked). *Dalian*. $23/£15

ROBERTS, CHARLES G.D. Around the Camp Fire. Thomas Crowell, 1896. VG. *Bishop*. $15/£10

ROBERTS, ELIZABETH MADOX. A Buried Treasure. NY: Viking, 1931. 1st ed. Inscrip, o/w NF in dj (sl rubbed). *Pharos*. $35/£23

ROBERTS, ELIZABETH MADOX. A Buried Treasure. NY: Viking, 1931. One of 200 numbered, signed. Grn cl. Fine in split slipcase. *Dermont*. $100/£65

ROBERTS, ELIZABETH MADOX. A Flying Fighter: An American Above the Lines in France. NY: Harper, (1918). 1st ed. (Spine faded; hinges mended.) *Ginsberg*. $100/£65

ROBERTS, ELIZABETH MADOX. The Great Meadow. NY: Viking, 1930. One of 295 signed. Spine faded, o/w Fine in slipcase (defective). *Pharos*. $150/£97

ROBERTS, ELIZABETH MADOX. Jingling in the Wind. NY: Viking, 1928. 1st ed. Cl-backed patterned bds. Fine in dj (chipped). *Pharos*. $35/£23

ROBERTS, ELIZABETH MADOX. The Time of Man. Cape, 1927. 1st Eng ed. NF in dj (chip spine). *Fine Books*. $85/£55

ROBERTS, H. ARMSTRONG. The Farmer His Own Builder. Phila: McKay, (1918). 1st ed. Fine in NF dj. *Second Life*. $40/£26

ROBERTS, HARRY. Euthanasia and Other Aspects of Life and Death. London, 1936. 1st ed. Good. *Fye*. $40/£26

ROBERTS, HENRY D. A History of the Royal Pavilion, Brighton. London: Country Life, 1939. 1st ed. Frontis port, 95 plts. (Feps lt browned; worn.) *Edwards*. $70/£45

ROBERTS, JANE. A Dictionary of Michelangelo's Watermarks. Olivetti, 1988. VF in ptd wraps. *Europa*. $25/£16

ROBERTS, KEITH. The Boat of Fate. London: Hutchinson, 1971. 1st ed. NF in proof dj (sl creased, nicked). *Rees*. $47/£30

ROBERTS, KEITH. The Chalk Giants. NY: Putnams, (1975). 1st US ed. NF in dj (edgeworn; 2 closed tears). *Other Worlds*. $45/£29

ROBERTS, KENNETH and ANNA M. Moreau de St. Mery's American Journey 1793-1798. GC: Doubleday, 1947. 1st ed. Foxing few pp, else VG + in VG + dj (lt chipping). *Lame Duck*. $50/£32

ROBERTS, KENNETH and PHILIP SHACKLETON. The Canoe. A History of the Craft from Panama to the Arctic. Camden, ME: Internat'l Marine, (1983). 1st ed. Color ep maps. Gilt-stamped leatherette. VF in VF dj. *Oregon*. $75/£48

ROBERTS, KENNETH and ROBERT GARLAND. The Brotherhood of Man. NY: Samuel French, 1934. 1st ed. 32pp, stapled. Lg bkpl, else Fine in orange ptd wrappers. *Godot*. $425/£274

ROBERTS, KENNETH. (ed). Antiquamania. GC: Doubleday, Doran, 1928. 1st ed. NF in VG dj (sl chipped, short tears, spine lt browned). *Godot*. $85/£55

ROBERTS, KENNETH. The Battle of Cowpens. NY, 1958. 1st ed after ltd ptg. VG in VG dj. *Clark*. $40/£26

ROBERTS, KENNETH. Black Magic. Indianapolis: Bobbs-Merrill, (1924). 1st Amer ed. VG (spine faded; extrems sl rubbed; lacks dj). *Between The Covers*. $100/£65

ROBERTS, KENNETH. Boon Island. GC: Doubleday, 1956. 1st ed, stated presentation issue, not for sale. Signed. Tan/grn cl gilt. Fine. *Cady*. $20/£13

ROBERTS, KENNETH. Boon Island. NY: Doubleday, 1956. Signed presentation ed. 2-tone cl, gilt. NF in orig glassine dj (chipped). *Sadlon*. $75/£48

ROBERTS, KENNETH. Captain Caution. Collins, 1949. 1st Eng ed. Signed. Fine in NF dj (sl wear). *Fine Books*. $45/£29

ROBERTS, KENNETH. Henry Gross and His Dowsing Rod. GC: Doubleday, 1951. 1st ed. VG + in VG- dj. *Lame Duck*. $35/£23

ROBERTS, KENNETH. I Wanted to Write. GC: Doubleday, 1949. 1st ed. Contemp news reviews laid in. VG + in VG dj (edge tears). *Lame Duck*. $45/£29

ROBERTS, KENNETH. It Must Be Your Tonsils. GC: Doubleday, 1936. 1st ed. Fine in dj (sl shelfworn). *Lame Duck*. $200/£129

ROBERTS, KENNETH. Know New England. (MA): Boston Herald Traveler Corp, (1950). 1st ed. Lt stain fr cvr, else VG in pict wrappers. *Godot*. $175/£113

ROBERTS, KENNETH. Northwest Passage. GC: Doubleday, 1937. 1st trade ed. Inscribed. VG+ in VG+ dj (short edge tears, lt chipping extrems). *Lame Duck.* $125/£81

ROBERTS, KENNETH. Northwest Passage. NY: Doubleday, Doran, 1937. 1st trade ed. Inscribed. NF in dj (spine lt foxed, short tears, 2 nicks). *Godot.* $225/£145

ROBERTS, KENNETH. Rabble in Arms. Collins, 1939. 1st Eng ed. Signed on tipped-in pg. VG+ in VG dj (spine extrems chipped). *Fine Books.* $100/£65

ROBERTS, KENNETH. Sun Hunting. Indianapolis: Bobbs-Merrill, 1922. 1st ed. NF. *Lame Duck.* $75/£48

ROBERTS, KENNETH. Trending into Maine. Boston: Little, Brown, 1938. 1st ed. 8vo. 14 full-pg color plts by N.C. Wyeth. Beige cl, grn lettering, decs; tinted top. Very Nice (fore-edge sl foxed) in color dj (sl marginal wear). *Reisler.* $175/£113

ROBERTS, KENNETH. Trending into Maine. L-B, 1938. 1st ed. One of 1075. Signed by author & N.C. Wyeth (illus). Sl wear to spine label on lt faded spine, else NF in VG slip-case (dust-soiled). *Fine Books.* $600/£387

ROBERTS, KENNETH. Why Europe Leaves Home. NY: Bobbs-Merrill, 1922. 1st ed. Frontis. Sticker, else VG+ in VG dj (2 2-inch tears rear panel edges). *Lame Duck.* $750/£484

ROBERTS, MICHELE. A Piece of the Night. Women's Press, 1978. 1st UK ed. Fine in NF dj (sm production mk rear panel). *Lewton.* $43/£28

ROBERTS, MORLEY. On the Earthquake Line. London: Arrowsmith, 1924. 6 tipped-in color repros. Blue cl (shelfwear; edges, prelims foxed). *Parmer.* $45/£29

ROBERTS, MORLEY. The Western Avernus. Westminster: Constable, 1896. 277pp, 23 plts, fldg color map. Bright pict cl. VG. *Schoyer.* $65/£42

ROBERTS, S.C. Doctor Johnson in Cambridge. London: Putnam's, 1922. 1st ed. Uncut. Marbled bds. VG (careless opening of leaves). *Limestone.* $40/£26

ROBERTS, W. The Book-Hunter in London. Chicago: A.C. McClurg, 1895. 1st ed. 333,(1)pp; teg, uncut; patterned eps. Lt grn cl, gilt, beveled edges. VG. *Hartfield.* $165/£106

ROBERTS, W. Printer's Marks. Bell, 1893. 1st ed. Frontis, tp red/black. Grn gilt cl (spine faded). *Moss.* $62/£40

ROBERTS, W. Rare Books and Their Prices, with Chapters on Pictures, Pottery, Porcelain and Postage Stamps. London: George Redway, 1895. 1st ed. xxix,156,(4)pp. Fine. *Oak Knoll.* $25/£16

ROBERTS, W. ADOLPHE. Brave Mardi Gras. Indianapolis: Bobbs-Merrill, (1946). 1st ed. VG in dj (sm chips, discoloration, else VG). *Godot.* $50/£32

ROBERTS, W. ADOLPHE. The Pomegranate. Indianapolis: Bobbs-Merrill, (1941). 1st ed. Eps lt foxed, 2 sm chips fep; cl lt spotted, else VG in defective dj (chipped, worn, splitting, else Good). *Godot.* $75/£48

ROBERTS, WARREN. A Bibliography of D.H. Lawrence. London: Rupert Hart-Davis, 1963. 1st ed. Frontis, 9 plts. VG. *Bookpress.* $100/£65

ROBERTS, WILLIAM. The Earlier History of English Bookselling. London: Sampson Low et al, 1889. xii,341pp + ads. Blue cl, gilt titles. VG. *Heller.* $60/£39

ROBERTS-JONES, PHILIPPE. Beyond Time and Place. London: OUP, 1978. Dj. *Edwards.* $39/£25

ROBERTS-JONES, PHILIPPE. Daumier: Humours of Married Life. Angus Malcolm (trans). Boston, 1968. 60 plts. VG in dj, extra mylar wrapper. *Argosy.* $200/£129

ROBERTSON, BEN. Travelers' Rest. Clemson, SC: The Cottonfield Publishers, (1938). 1st ed, 1st bk. Presentation copy. Promo flyer laid in. Blue cl. Soil, spots; spine faded; paperclip mk; else VG. *Chapel Hill.* $450/£290

ROBERTSON, BRUCE. Sopwith—The Man and His Aircraft. Letchworth: Air Review, 1970. VG in dj. *Hollett.* $101/£65

ROBERTSON, E. GRAEME. Victorian Heritage: Ornamental Cast Iron in Architecture. Melbourne, 1960. VG. *Argosy.* $85/£55

ROBERTSON, FRANK G. and BETH KAY HARRIS. Soapy Smith, King of the Frontier Con Men. NY, 1961. 1st ed. Fine in dj. *Baade.* $35/£23

ROBERTSON, GEORGE. An Outline of the Life of George Robertson, Written by Himself. Lexington: Transylvania Ptg & Pub Co, 1876. Frontis port, 209pp, errata. Good (extrems frayed; lib mks). *Bohling.* $100/£65

ROBERTSON, GEORGE. An Outline of the Life of George Robertson.... Lexington, KY, 1876. 1st ed. xii,209pp. VG (spine extrems worn; corners scuffed). Howes R 351. *Mcgowan.* $125/£81

ROBERTSON, GILES. Giovanni Bellini. Oxford, 1968. 120 plts. Good. *Washton.* $125/£81

ROBERTSON, GILES. Giovanni Bellini. OUP, 1968. 120 plts. Good in dj. *Washton.* $175/£113

ROBERTSON, JAMES A. (ed). Louisiana under the Rule of Spain, France, and the United States 1785-1807. Cleveland: Clark, 1911. 1st ed. 2 vols. Red cl (spine ends lt worn). VG set (inner fr hinge vol 1 starting). Howes R 354. *Chapel Hill.* $400/£258

ROBERTSON, JAMES A. (ed). True Relation of the Hardships Suffered by Governor Fernando de Soto...During the Discovery of the Province of Florida. DeLand: FL Hist Soc, 1933. 1st ed thus. Ltd to 360 sets. 2 vols. As New set in slipcases. *Cahan.* $175/£113

ROBERTSON, JOHN WOOSTER. Francis Drake and Other Early Explorers Along the Pacific Coast. SF: Grabhorn Press, 1927. One of 1000. Vellum-backed bds. VG+. *Bohling.* $250/£161

ROBERTSON, JOHN. Rusty Staub of the Expos. (Canada): Prentice-Hall, 1971. 1st ed. VG+ in Good+ dj. *Plapinger.* $45/£29

ROBERTSON, ROBERT. An Essay on Fevers. London, 1790. 1st ed. 286pp. Full leather (backstrip missing; exlib; once in fire). Contents VG. *Fye.* $150/£97

ROBERTSON, THOMAS A. A Southwestern Utopia. L.A.: Ward Ritchie Press, 1947. 1st ed. Brn cl. NF in Good dj (chipped). *Harrington.* $35/£23

ROBERTSON, WILLIAM. The History of America. London, 1788. 5th ed. 3 vols. Later paper bds (rebacked in cl); paper backstrips laid down (spines sunned, sl flaked). Bkpls, else VG. Howes R 358. *Ginsberg.* $100/£65

ROBERTSON, WILLIAM. The History of America. London: for A. Strahan et al, 1792. 6th ed. 3 vols. Full contemp tree calf, gilt; morocco spine labels. *D & D.* $395/£255

ROBERTSON, WILLIAM. The History of America. London: 1820. 4 vols. 2 foldout maps; fldg plt. 1/4 dk blue calf, ribbed gilt-dec spines, gilt-lettered red/grn morocco spine labels. *D & D.* $550/£355

ROBERTSON, WILLIAM. The History of the Reign of Charles V. London: for T. Cadell & W. Davies, 1802. 10th ed. 4 vols. Frontis plt. Full contemp speckled calf, gilt-dec spines, gilt-lettered black morocco spine labels. *D & D.* $325/£210

ROBERTSON, WILLIAM. The Kipling Guide. Birmingham: The Holland Co., 1899. 1st ed. Pub's black-stamped red cl. Inner hinge cracked; lt soiling, else Fine. *D & D.* $20/£13

ROBESON, ESLANDA GOODE. African Journey. NY: John Day, (1945). VG in dj (chipped). *Petrilla.* $30/£19

ROBESON, KENNETH. The Land of Terror. Street & Smith, 1933. 1st ed. NF. *Madle.* $150/£97

ROBIE, MRS. W.F. A Commonplace Life. Baldwinville, MA: Pine Terrace, n.d. (ca 1929). 1st ed. 12 plts. Grn cl. VG. *Petrilla.* $35/£23

ROBIE, VIRGINIA. Historic Styles in Furniture. Chicago: Herbert S. Stone, 1905. 1st ed. Frontis. (Spine soiled, extrems sl rubbed.) Paper spine label. *Karmiole.* $50/£32

ROBINS, EDWARD. Echoes of the Playhouse. NY/London: Putnam's, 1895. 1st ed. Frontis. Orig cl; stamped in color, gilt. VG. *Dramatis Personae.* $30/£19

Robinson Crusoe. NY: McLoughlin Bros, 1889. (Wonder-Story Series.) Tall 8vo. 6 leaves (incl cvrs), 6 full-pg Good chromolithos. Pict cvrs (ink sig; stitched spine, ragged edges, water spots). *Hobbyhorse.* $50/£32

Robinson Crusoe. NY: McLoughlin Bros, n.d. (ca 1880). Aunt Kate's Series. 4to. 6 leaves 1p list lower wrapper. Pict stiff paper wrapper. Fine (ink dedication, date along other margin upper wrapper). *Hobbyhorse.* $175/£113

ROBINSON, A.H.W. Marine Cartography in Britain. London: Leicester Univ, 1962. 1st ed. Dbl-pg color plt. VG in orig cl; dj. *Cox.* $85/£55

ROBINSON, ALBERT G. Old New England Doorways. NY: Charles Scribner's Sons, 1919. 1st ed. 80 full-pg photo plts. Dec grn cl; gilt. *Karmiole.* $45/£29

ROBINSON, BERT. The Basket Weavers of Arizona. Albuquerque: Univ of NM, 1954. 1st ed. VG in dj (edge-torn). *Perier.* $95/£61

ROBINSON, BEVERLY W. With Shotgun and Rifle in North American Game Fields. NY, 1925. 1st ed. Fine in dj (edgeworn). *Artis.* $40/£26

ROBINSON, CELIA MYROVER. Where Romance Flowered: Stories of Old Pensacola. N.p., n.d. 1st ed. NF in orig stiff ptd wrappers. *Mcgowan.* $45/£29

ROBINSON, CHARLES. The Kansas Conflict. Harper, 1892. 1st ed. Signed. xxiii,487pp. Good+ (spine ends chipped). *Oregon.* $45/£29

ROBINSON, DOANE. A History of the Dakota or Sioux Indians.... Minneapolis: Ross & Haines, 1974. VG in VG dj. *Oregon.* $50/£32

ROBINSON, DOUGLAS H. The Dangerous Sky. A History of Aviation Medicine. Seattle: Univ of WA Press, (1973). 1st ed. Fine in dj. *Glaser.* $85/£55

ROBINSON, EDWIN ARLINGTON. Cavender's House. NY: Macmillan, 1929. 1st ed. One of 500 numbered, signed. NF in slipcase (defective). *Reese.* $85/£55

ROBINSON, EDWIN ARLINGTON. Cavender's House. Hogarth Press, 1930. Rev copy w/slip. Rear bd, spine damp-mkd affecting reps, o/w VG. *Words Etc.* $78/£50

ROBINSON, EDWIN ARLINGTON. Dionysus in Doubt. NY: Macmillan, 1925. 1st ed, 2nd binding w/white paper title label fr cvr. Red cl. NF in dj (sl edgewear, soil; spine sl browned). *Antic Hay.* $50/£32

ROBINSON, EDWIN ARLINGTON. The Glory of the Nightingales. NY: Macmillan, 1930. Ltd to 500 numbered, signed. Blue cl. NF in dj & slipcase (edges lack sm pieces). *Antic Hay.* $100/£65

ROBINSON, EDWIN ARLINGTON. King Jasper. NY: Macmillan, 1935. 1st ed. NF (ep gutters browned) in dj (sl wear; edges sunned). *Antic Hay.* $25/£16

ROBINSON, EDWIN ARLINGTON. The Man Who Died Twice. NY: Macmillan, 1924. #336/500 numbered, signed. Black cl over gray bds; uncut, partly unopened. VG in pub's black bd slipcase w/ptd paper labels. *Houle.* $85/£55

ROBINSON, EDWIN ARLINGTON. The Man Who Died Twice. NY: Macmillan, 1924. Ltd to 500 numbered, signed. VG (cl mottled). *Antic Hay.* $100/£65

ROBINSON, EDWIN ARLINGTON. Matthias at the Door. NY: Macmillan, 1931. 1st trade ed, 1st issue ptd on laid paper. NF in dj (browning; nicks; price-clipped). *Antic Hay.* $50/£32

ROBINSON, EDWIN ARLINGTON. Selected Letters of Edwin Arlington Robinson. NY: Macmillan, 1940. 1st ed. NF in VG dj (sl browning). *Antic Hay.* $35/£23

ROBINSON, EDWIN ARLINGTON. Sonnets 1889-1927. NY: Crosby, Gaige, 1928. 1st ed. Ltd to 561 signed. Uncut. NF. *Second Life.* $100/£65

ROBINSON, FRANCIS. Celebration; the Metropolitan Opera. NY, (1979). VG in dj (sl worn). *Artis.* $17/£11

ROBINSON, FRANKLIN W. Gabriel Metsu (1629-1667). A Study.... NY, 1975. Good in dj. *Washton.* $195/£126

ROBINSON, H.M. The Great Fur Land or Sketches of Life in the Hudson's Bay Territory. NY: Putnam's, 1879. 1st ed. xi,348pp. Orig pict cl. Fine. *Oregon.* $125/£81

ROBINSON, H.M. The Great Fur Land. NY: Putnam's, 1879. (xi),348pp. Orig cl (lib bkpl; pocket removed). *Schoyer.* $65/£42

ROBINSON, J.H. Silver-Knife; Or the Hunters of the Rocky Mountains. Boston: Wm. Spencer, 1854. (2nd ed.) Thin 12mo. 168pp (dknd; writing on ep). Orig cl, gilt spine title. Good (extrems chipped, fr hinge cracked, sl shaken). Howes R 367. *Bohling.* $500/£323

ROBINSON, JACKIE and ALFRED DUCKETT. Breakthrough to the Big League. Harper & Row, 1965. 1st ed. Fine in VG dj. *Plapinger.* $25/£16

ROBINSON, JACKIE. I Never Had It Made. NY, (1972). 1st ed. Fine in VG + dj (lt edgeworn). *Fuller & Saunders.* $20/£13

ROBINSON, JOHN and GEORGE FRANCIS DOW. The Sailing Ships of New England 1607-1907. Salem: Marine Research Soc Pub 1, 1922. 1st ed. (Extrems rubbed.) Howes R 369. *Lefkowicz.* $150/£97

ROBINSON, MARILYNNE. Housekeeping. NY: FSG, (1980). 1st ed. Fine in dj. *Hermitage.* $75/£48

ROBINSON, P.F. Designs for Ornamental Villas. London: For Carpenter, 1827. 2nd ed. Litho title, 96 plts. Mod bds, eps. Marginal stain 1 plt, o/w Fine. *Europa.* $271/£175

ROBINSON, P.F. Rural Architecture.... London: Rodwell & Martin, 1823. 1st ed. Title, 5ff, 24ff letterpress, 96 litho plts. Half red morocco (new spine, corners). *Marlborough.* $581/£375

ROBINSON, PERCY. Toronto During the French Regime 1615-1793. Toronto: Ryerson, (1933). 1st ed. 15 plts. VG in VG dj. *Oregon.* $195/£126

ROBINSON, PETER. A Dedicated Man. Markham, Canada: Viking, 1988. 1st ed. VF in dj. *Mordida.* $125/£81

ROBINSON, PETER. With Equal Eye. Toronto: Gabbro Press, 1979. 1st ed, inscribed in yr of pub. VG + in wraps. *Else Fine.* $350/£226

ROBINSON, ROWLAND E. Uncle Lisha's Shop. NY, 1891. 5th ed. 187pp. Gilt-pict cl. Fine. *Artis.* $20/£13

ROBINSON, S. Facts for Farmers. NY, 1864. 1034pp (lt dampstaining), 22 plts (dampstain ring). Gilt-dec 1/2 morocco (worn, soiled; outer hinge split; damp-stained). *Sutton.* $115/£74

ROBINSON, SARA. Kansas: Its Interior and Exterior Life. Boston: Crosby, 1856. 1st ed. (10),366,(6)ads pp (lacks ep); 2 plts. (Spine sl faded.) *Ginsberg.* $125/£81

ROBINSON, SARA. Kansas; Its Interior and Exterior Life.... Boston: Crosby, Nichols..., 1856. 3rd ed. ix,366pp, 6 ads; 2 view-plts. Maroon cl (spine faded; fep gone). *Petrilla.* $40/£26

ROBINSON, SERJEANT. Bench and Bar, Reminiscences of One of the Last of an Ancient Race. London: Hurst & Blackett, 1889. 3/4 morocco (spine faded). Attractive. *Boswell.* $175/£113

ROBINSON, SOLON. Solon Robinson: Pioneer and Agriculturist. Indianapolis, 1936. 1st ed. 2 vols. (Sm emb lib stamps; spine #s.) *Ginsberg.* $75/£48

ROBINSON, VICTOR. Encyclopaedia Sexualis: A Comprehensive Encyclopedia-Dictionary of the Sexual Sciences. NY, 1936. 1st ed. Good. *Fye.* $100/£65

ROBINSON, VICTOR. Victory Over Pain. A History of Anesthesia. NY: Henry Schuman, (1946). 1st ed. 28 plts. VG (sl worn). *Glaser.* $35/£23

ROBINSON, W.W. Land in California. Berkeley: Univ of CA, 1948. 1st ed. VG in VG dj. *Oregon.* $45/£29

ROBINSON, WILL. The Story of Arizona. Phoenix: Berryhill Co, (1919). Ink inscrip, else VG. *Perier.* $75/£48

ROBINSON, WILL. The Story of Arizona. Phoenix: Berryhill, (1919). 1st ed. VG. *Laurie.* $50/£32

ROBINSON, WILLIAM. Alpine Flowers for Gardens. London: John Murray, 1903. 3rd ed. Gilt-dec cvr. NF. *Quest.* $85/£55

ROBINSON, WILLIAM. Alpine Flowers for Gardens.... London, 1903. 3rd ed, rev. *Wheldon & Wesley.* $39/£25

ROBINSON, WILLIAM. The English Flower Garden and Home Grounds. London, 1903. 8th ed. Rpt. Gilt device upper bd. (Feps lt browned; sl chipped.) *Edwards.* $39/£25

ROBINSON, WILLIAM. The English Flower Garden and Home Grounds. London, 1909. 11th ed. Recent cl. Good. *Henly.* $28/£18

ROBINSON, WILLIAM. The English Flower Garden, Style, Position and Arrangement. London, 1893. 3rd ed. xxii,751pp. Cl, gilt. (Sm dampstain cvr.) *Henly.* $43/£28

ROBINSON, WILLIAM. The English Flower Garden. NY, 1984. Rpt of 15th ed. VG in dj. *Brooks.* $34/£22

ROBINSON, WILLIAM. The Garden Beautiful. London: John Murray, 1907. 1st ed. Linen spine, paper label (worn). VG. *Quest.* $75/£48

ROBINSON, WILLIAM. Garden Design and Architect's Gardens. London: John Murray, 1892. 1st ed. xviii,73pp; 27 VF steel engrs. Gilt cl (spine worn). *Quest.* $190/£123

ROBINSON, WILLIAM. Gleanings from French Gardens. London, 1868. 1st ed. Frontis, xvi,291pp; 8 ads. Cl, pict gilt. (Stamp tp.) *Henly.* $81/£52

ROBINSON, WILLIAM. God's Acre Beautiful or the Cemeteries of the Future. London/NY, 1880. 128pp, 8 wood engr plts. Contemp vellum (lt foxing). *Marlborough.* $194/£125

ROBINSON, WILLIAM. The Parks and Gardens of Paris.... London, 1878. 2nd ed, 7th thousand. Frontis; xxiv,548pp; 7 plts. Morocco (rubbed). *Wheldon & Wesley.* $101/£65

ROBINSON, WILLIAM. The Parks, Promenades and Gardens of Paris. London: Macmillan, 1878. 2nd ed. xvi,548pp. Teg. Gilt cl (ends sl worn). VG (hinge cracked). *Quest.* $185/£119

ROBINSON, WILLIAM. The Subtropical Garden; or, Beauty of Form.... London, 1871. 1st ed. xi,241pp. Partly unopened. Cl, pict gilt. Good. *Henly.* $78/£50

ROBINSON, ZIRKLE. The Robinson-Rosenberger Journey to the Gold Fields of California 1849-50. IA City: Prairie Press, (1966). 1st ed. Fine in VG dj. *Oregon.* $50/£32

ROBSON, A.W.M. and J.F. DOBSON. Diseases of the Gall-Bladder and Bile-Ducts, Including Gall-Stones. London, 1904. 3rd ed. (Cl sl worn.) *Whitehart.* $28/£18

ROBSON, JOSEPH. An Account of Six Years Residence in Hudson's Bay from 1733 to 1736 and 1744 to 1747. London: J. Payne & J. Bouquet, 1752. 1st ed. vi,84pp; 95pp, 2 fldg maps, fldg plan. Contemp leather (rebacked, binding edgeworn). Internally Fine except for 1st map, which has been repaired along folds w/sm loss on 1 fold. *Oregon.* $1,250/£806

ROCH, ANDRE. On Rock and Ice. London: A&C Black, 1947. 1st ed. 87 plts. VG in dj (edges sl worn; 2 sm pieces missing). *Hollett.* $62/£40

Rock Island States Southwest. Chicago, 1903. Good in wrappers. *Hayman.* $25/£16

ROCKER, RUDOLF. The Six. L.A.: Rocker Publication Committee, 1938. 1st ed. VG (worn, shaken). *Beasley.* $50/£32

ROCKFELLOW, JOHN ALEXANDER. Log of an Arizona Trail Blazer. Tucson, (1933). Port. Tan cl. Fine. Howes R 392. *Bohling.* $125/£81

ROCKFELLOW, JOHN ALEXANDER. Log of an Arizona Trail Blazer. Tucson: Acme, (1933). 1st ed. Inscribed. Dec cl (faded). Howes R 392. *Ginsberg.* $100/£65

ROCKWELL and HURLBURT. The Improved Practical System of Educating the Horse.... NY: Fisher & Field, 1871. Frontis; 227pp. 1/2 morocco, pebbled cl (edgeworn; inner hinges reinforced w/cl tape). Good +. *Oregon.* $25/£16

ROCKWELL, NORMAN. My Adventures as an Illustrator. GC, 1960. 1st ed, w/signed tipped-in sheet. VG- (sl waterstain) in dj (badly stained). *King.* $100/£65

ROCKWELL, NORMAN. My Adventures as an Illustrator. Doubleday, 1960. 1st ed. VG in VG dj. *Bishop.* $20/£13

ROCKWELL, WILSON (ed). Memoirs of a Lawman. Denver: Sage Books, 1962. 1st ed. VG in dj. *Lien.* $50/£32

RODDENBERRY, GENE. Star Trek. S&S, 1979. 1st ed. One of 500 signed. Fine in slipcase. *Aronovitz.* $250/£161

RODGERS, RICHARD and OSCAR HAMMERSTEIN II. Oklahoma! NY: Random House, (1943). 1st ed. Eps lt foxed, else Fine in dj. *Godot.* $85/£55

RODGERS, W.R. Europa and the Bull and Other Poems. NY: Farrar, (1952). 1st ed, Amer issue. Signed carbon typescript, inscribed tearsheet laid in. NF (sig) in VG dj (sm tears). *Reese.* $85/£55

RODIER, PAUL. The Romance of French Weaving. NY: Tudor, (1936). 2 color plts. VG. *Argosy.* $50/£32

RODIER, PAUL. The Romance of French Weaving. NY: Tudor Publishing, (1936). New Ed. (Bkpl). *Karmiole.* $50/£32

RODRIGUEZ, ANTONIO. A History of Mexican Mural Painting. NY, (1969). 1st Amer ed. VG in dj. *Argosy.* $150/£97

ROE, E.G. Sporting Prints of the 18th and Early 19th Centuries. Connoisseur, 1927. 1st ed. Red cl. Good. *Whiteson.* $62/£40

ROE, FRANK GILBERT. The Indian and the Horse. Norman, 1955. 1st ed. Fine (sig, date) in dj (backstrip faded). *Baade.* $75/£48

ROE, FRED. Ancient Church Chests and Chairs in the Home Counties Round Greater London. London: Batsford, 1929. 1st ed. Map eps. VG in dj (price-clipped). *Hollett.* $70/£45

ROE, MARY A. E.P. Roe: Reminiscences of His Life. NY, 1899. 1st ed. 235pp. VG. *Hayman.* $25/£16

ROEDER, BILL. Jackie Robinson. Barnes, 1950. 1st ed. VG in Good dj (nicks, sunning). *Plapinger.* $60/£39

ROEDER, HELEN (ed). The Ordeal of Captain Roeder. NY, (1961). 1st Amer ed. Dj worn, o/w Fine. *Pratt.* $35/£23

ROEHM, MARJORIE CATLIN. The Letters of George Catlin and His Family. Berkeley, 1966. 1st ed. VF in Fine dj. *Oregon.* $35/£23

ROEHR, CHARLES. Klondike Gold Rush Letters. NY: Vantage, (1976). 1st ed. Fine in VG dj. *Perier.* $25/£16

ROETHEL, HANS K. Kandinsky. London: Phaidon, 1979. 1st UK ed. 48 tipped-in color plts. Dj. *Edwards.* $39/£25

ROETHKE, THEODORE. Praise to the End! NY, 1951. 1st Amer ed. Fine in dj (sl rubbed). *Polyanthos.* $250/£161

ROETHKE, THEODORE. Praise to the End! NY: Doubleday, 1951. 1st ed. (Paper sl browned) in dj (worn). *Bookpress.* $100/£65

ROETHLISBERGER, M. Claude Lorrain. The Drawings. Univ CA Press, 1968. 2 vols. 1244 plts. Sound. *Ars Artis.* $217/£140

ROGERS, BRUCE. Pi. Cleveland/NY: World, 1953. 1st ed. Nice in NF dj. *Second Life.* $45/£29

ROGERS, FRED B. Bear Flag Lieutenant: The Life Story of Henry L. Ford (1822-1860). SF: CA Hist Soc, 1951. 1st bk ed. #68/250. NF (sl bumped; spine sl dknd). *Harrington.* $70/£45

ROGERS, FRED B. Soldiers of the Overland. SF: Grabhorn Press, 1938. One of 1000. 2 fldg maps. Cl, dec bds. Spine label silverfished, o/w Fine. *Schoyer.* $75/£48

ROGERS, FRED B. Soldiers of the Overland.... SF, 1938. 1st ed. Ltd to 1000 ptd. *Ginsberg.* $150/£97

ROGERS, FRED B. Soldiers of the Overland...Account of the Services of General Patrick Edward Conner.... SF, 1938. 1st ed, ltd to 1000. Fldg map. Minor spotting on cvr, o/w Fine. *Pratt.* $110/£71

ROGERS, GEORGE. Memoranda of the Experience, Labors, and Travels of a Universalist Preacher.... Cincinnati, 1845. 1st ed. 400pp. Contemp full calf (hinges strengthened). Howes R 412. *Ginsberg.* $175/£113

ROGERS, H.C.B. Weapons of the British Soldier. London: Seeley Service, (1960). 25 plts. VG in dj. *Schoyer.* $40/£26

ROGERS, J.A. Nature Knows No Color-Line. NY: By Author, 1952. One of 2000. Fine (lt spine wear) in dj (lt used). *Beasley.* $45/£29

ROGERS, J.M. The Topkapi Saray Museum. Carpets. Boston: Little Brown, 1987. 1st ed. 98 color plts. Fine in dj; slipcase. *Worldwide.* $95/£61

ROGERS, JOHN C. English Furniture. London: Country Life, 1923. 1st ed. 129 plts. Marbled eps. Lt foxing, o/w VG. *Willow House.* $23/£15

ROGERS, JOHN R. Linotype Instruction Book. Brooklyn: Mergenthaler Linotype Co, 1925. 1st ed. Frontis port. Dec tan cl. *Karmiole.* $35/£23

ROGERS, JOHN WILLIAM and J. FRANK DOBIE. Finding Literature on the Texas Plains. Dallas: Southwest, 1931. 1st ed. *Lambeth.* $50/£32

ROGERS, JOHN WILLIAM. Finding Literature on the Texas Plains. Dallas: Southwest Press, (1931). Frontis port. Cl-backed bds; gilt titles. VG+ (pencil marginalia). *Bohling.* $175/£113

ROGERS, MARK. Down Thames Street. London, 1921. Illus upper bd. (Marginal browning; spine sl chipped.) *Edwards.* $39/£25

ROGERS, MARY ELIZA. Domestic Life in Palestine. Cincinnati: Poe & Hitchcock, 1865. 436pp. Brn cl (sl faded; red streak fore-edge; foxing). *Schoyer.* $150/£97

ROGERS, MICHAEL. The Spread of Islam. Oxford: Elsevier Phaidon, 1976. 1st ed. NF in dj. *Worldwide.* $30/£19

ROGERS, P.G. The Sixth Trumpeter. The Story of Jezreel and His Tower. OUP, 1963. Fine in dj. *Peter Taylor.* $20/£13

ROGERS, WILL. Letters of a Self-Made Diplomat to His President. NY: Albert & Charles Boni, 1926. 1st ed. Fine in dj (sm chip). *Godot.* $85/£55

ROGOSIN, DONN. Invisible Men. Atheneum, 1985. 1st ed. Fine in VG+ dj (spine lt faded). *Plapinger.* $60/£39

ROHDE, ELEANOUR S. Gardens of Delight Throughout the Year. Boston, 1936. 1st ptg. VG in dj. *Brooks.* $29/£19

ROHDE, ELEANOUR S. The Old English Gardening Books. London, 1924. 16 plts; 8 plans. Orig bds, linen back (sl soiled; inner joints repaired). *Wheldon & Wesley.* $116/£75

ROHDE, ELEANOUR S. The Old English Herbals. London: Longmans, 1922. (Sl foxed throughout.) *Petersfield.* $155/£100

ROHDE, ELEANOUR S. The Old English Herbals. London, 1922. Orig ed. Frontis. (Ex-lib.) *Wheldon & Wesley.* $93/£60

ROHDE, ELEANOUR S. The Old World Pleasaunce. London/NY: MacVeagh/Dial, 1925. *Quest.* $35/£23

ROHDE, ELEANOUR S. Oxford's College Gardens. London, 1932. Color frontis; 23 color, 8 plain plts. (Lt foxing; binding sl mkd.) *Wheldon & Wesley.* $39/£25

ROHDE, ELEANOUR S. Rose Recipes. London: Routledge, 1939. Black/rose cvr. Fine in dj. *Quest.* $30/£19

ROHDE, ELEANOUR S. Shakespeare's Wild Flowers. London: Medici, n.d. (1935). 5 color plts, plan. Gilt-stamped cl (soiled). Contents clean. *Quest.* $70/£45

ROHDE, ELEANOUR S. The Story of the Garden. Boston: Hale, Cushman & Flint, 1933. Color frontis, 4 color plts. *Quest.* $70/£45

ROHE, GEORGE. A Text-Book of Hygiene. Balt, 1885. 1st ed. 324pp. (Pencil underlining.) *Fye.* $150/£97

ROHLEDER, H. Test Tube Babies. Panurge Press, 1934. 1st ed. Pg edges sl spotted, else NF in VG dj (lt spine damage). *Aronovitz.* $125/£81

ROHMER, SAX. The Bat Flies Low. NY/Chicago, (1935). 1st Burt rpt ed. NF in dj (lt edgewear to spine ends). *Mcclintock.* $45/£29

ROHMER, SAX. Bat Wing. NY, (1921). 1st Burt rpt ed. Grn cl. VG in dj (chipped top of spine, tips nicked, age discoloration). *Mcclintock.* $45/£29

ROHMER, SAX. Bat Wing. GC: Doubleday Page, 1921. 1st ed. NF (lacks dj). *Else Fine.* $75/£48

ROHMER, SAX. The Dream Detective. Doubleday, 1925. 1st ed. VG. *Madle.* $25/£16

ROHMER, SAX. The Drums of Fu Manchu. Doubleday, Doran, 1939. 1st Amer ed. Fine in later Sun Dial dj. *Sadlon.* $75/£48

ROHMER, SAX. The Drums of Fu Manchu. (GC): Doubleday, Doran, 1939. 1st ed. Fine in dj. *Bernard.* $400/£258

ROHMER, SAX. The Emperor of America. NY: Doubleday, Doran, 1929. 1st Amer ed. Fore-edge foxed, else VG in Good dj (chips, edge tears, spine browned). *Godot.* $125/£81

ROHMER, SAX. Hangover House. NY: Random, 1949. 1st ed. Fine in dj (sm chip spine head, minor edgewear). *Else Fine.* $60/£39

ROHMER, SAX. The Mask of Fu Manchu. GC: DCC, 1932. 1st ed. VG (spine sl age-darkened, lower corners bumped). *Else Fine.* $45/£29

ROHMER, SAX. Moon of Madness. Doubleday, 1927. 1st ed. NF in dj (chipped). *Madle.* $125/£81

ROHMER, SAX. President Fu Manchu. NY: Sun Dial, (1936). Later ed. NF in dj (sl rubbed). *Sadlon.* $35/£23

ROHMER, SAX. President Fu Manchu. GC: Doubleday, Doran, 1936. 1st ed. Lt dampstain 1/2 title hinge, facing pg, o/w Fine in dj. *Bernard.* $400/£258

ROHMER, SAX. She Who Sleeps. Doubleday, Doran, 1928. 1st ed. Red cl. Lt wear cl bottom edge, spine; few spots, else VG+. *Murder.* $135/£87

ROHMER, SAX. Virgin in Flames. London: Jenkins, 1953. 1st ed. VG in Good+ dj (chipped). *Limestone.* $75/£48

ROHMER, SAX. The Wrath of Fu Manchu. NY: David A. Wollheim, 1976. 1st ed. Pb orig. Daw Books no. 186. VF in wrappers. *Mordida.* $50/£32

ROHMER, SAX. Yellow Shadows. NY, (1926). 1st Burt rpt ed. VG in VG dj (lt wear, nicks to corners, top edge of spine). *Mcclintock.* $45/£29

ROHRER, MARY K. The History of Seattle Stock Companies From Their Beginnings to 1934. Univ of WA, 1945. 1st ed. Frontis. Fine. *Oregon.* $60/£39

ROJAS, A.R. The Vaquero. Santa Barbara: McNally, 1964. 1st ed. Dj. *Lambeth.* $35/£23

ROKITANSKY, C. A Manual of Pathological Anatomy. London: Sydenham Soc, 1849, 1850, 1852, 1854. 4 vols. xvi,410+36pp index, 2 plts; xvi,360; xvi,468; x,398pp. (Cl faded, stained, esp vol 1.) *Whitehart.* $295/£190

ROLFE, FREDERICK and SHOLTO DOUGLAS. The Songs of Meleager Made into English with Designs by.... London: First Editions Club, (1937). 1st ed. One of 750. Teg. Grn cl, gilt extra. Corners lt bumped; sm mk spine; else Fine. *Reese.* $125/£81

ROLFE, FREDERICK. The Armed Hand and Other Stories and Pieces. Cecil Woolf (ed). London: Cecil & Amelia Woolf, 1974. 1st Eng ed. Maroon cl. VF in dj. *Dalian.* $54/£35

ROLFE, FREDERICK. The Armed Hand and Other Stories and Pieces. Cecil Woolf (ed). London: Cecil & Amelia Woolf, 1987. Ltd to 200 numbered. Full buckram. Fine. *Dalian.* $132/£85

ROLFE, FREDERICK. Hubert's Arthur. London: Cassell, 1935. 1st Eng ed. Red cl. Sl damp-mkd, o/w VG. *Dalian.* $54/£35

ROLFE, FREDERICK. In His Own Image. London: John Lane, Bodley Head, 1924. 1st ed thus. Blue cl. Mkd, soiled, o/w Good. *Dalian.* $54/£35

ROLFE, FREDERICK. Letters to James Walsh. London: Bertram Rota, 1972. Ltd to 500 numbered. Grn cl. VF in Fine dj. *Dalian.* $70/£45

ROLFS, P.H. Subtropical Vegetable-Gardening. NY, 1916. 16 plts. (Foxing; ex-lib.) *Sutton.* $35/£23

ROLIN, JEAN. Police Drugs. NY, 1956. 1st Eng trans. Good. *Fye.* $65/£42

ROLLAND, R. The Revolt of the Machines or Invention Run Wild. Dragon Press, 1932. 1st ed. One of 500. Spine label sunned, else VG+. *Aronovitz.* $150/£97

ROLLE, ANDREW F. The Road to Virginia City. The Diary of James Knox Polk Miller. Norman, 1960. 1st ed. Sig, date; sl bumped, o/w Fine in dj (edgeworn). *Baade.* $35/£23

ROLLESTON, HUMPHRY. The Right Honourable Sir Thomas Clifford Allbutt. London, 1929. 1st ed. Good. *Fye.* $60/£39

ROLLESTON, HUMPHRY. Some Medical Aspects of Old Age. London, 1922. 1st ed. (Ex-lib.) *Fye.* $100/£65

ROLLESTON, J.D. The History of the Acute Exanthemata. London, 1937. Good. *Fye.* $100/£65

ROLLINS, PHILIP ASHTON. The Cowboy; an Unconventional History.... NY: Scribner's, 1936. Rev, enlgd ed. Dj. *Lambeth.* $45/£29

ROLLINSON, JOHN K. Pony Trails in Wyoming. E.A. Brininstool (ed). Caldwell: Caxton, 1945. 3rd ptg. Brn gilt-lettered cl (rubbed, esp corners). Good (hinges starting). *Harrington.* $35/£23

ROLLINSON, JOHN. Wyoming Cattle Trails. Caxton, 1948. 1st ed. 3 maps. Fine in VG dj. *Oregon.* $90/£58

ROLLO, W.K. Fly Fishing in Northern Streams. London: Fishing Gazette, (1924). Limp ptd wrappers (sl dull). *Petersfield.* $78/£50

ROLPH, C.H. Books in the Dock. (London): Deutsch, (1969). 1st ed. Fine in dj. *Oak Knoll.* $30/£19

ROLPH, C.H. (ed). The Trial of Lady Chatterley. Privately ptd, 1961. Ltd to 2000 numbered, signed by Allen Lane. Card loosely inserted. Fine in dj (spine faded). *Waterfield.* $85/£55

ROLT-WHEELER, FRANCIS. The Book of Cowboys. Lothrop, Lee & Shepard, (1921). 1st ed. Fine in dj (chipped, esp to spine). *Authors Of The West.* $50/£32

ROLT-WHEELER, FRANCIS. In the Time of Attila. Lothrop, Lee & Shepard, 1928. 1st ed. Fine in VG dj. *Aronovitz.* $55/£35

ROMAINES, JULES. The Body's Rapture. John Rodker (trans). London: Boriswood, 1933. 1st trade ed. Brn cl. Sl sunned, o/w VF in dj (sl mkd, sl nicked). *Dalian.* $39/£25

Roman Empresses: Lives and Secret Intrigues of the Wives of the Twelve Caesars. (By J. Roergas de Serviez.) NY, 1913. 2 vols. Purple buckram. Mint. *Argosy.* $125/£81

Roman Stories; or, the History of the Seven Wise Mistresses of Rome.... (By Thomas Howard.) London: J. Hodges & W. Johnson, 1754. 25th ed. 108pp+12pp. choice Novels. Pict 1/2 titles w/9 woodcut ports; full-pg frontis w/2 woodcuts, added title; 16 half-pg woodcuts (ink names fep). Contemp full calf (worm holes; spine cracked w/sm portion missing lower part). Internally Fine. *Hobbyhorse.* $250/£161

Romance of King Arthur and His Knights of the Round Table. NY: Macmillan, (64-66 Fifth Avenue), 1917. Amer ltd, deluxe ed of 250. Thick, sm folio. 16 full-pg mtd color plts, 70 b/w dwgs by Arthur Rackham. Teg. White leather w/gold stamping spine (rebound; orig white kid w/title, gold dec, laid in); new eps. White bd slipcase w/leather spine, gold lettering, dec. *Reisler.* $650/£419

ROMIG, EMILY CRAIG. A Pioneer Woman in Alaska. Caldwell, ID: Caxton, 1948. 1st trade ed. Fine in dj. *High Latitude.* $45/£29

ROMILLY, SAMUEL. Memoirs of the Life. London: John Murray, 1840. 3 vols. Frontis port, fldg facs; teg; marbled eps (ex-libris). Gilt-ruled 1/2 morocco, marbled bds (sl rubbed), raised bands, dec gilt. *Edwards.* $116/£75

ROMM, MICHAEL. The Ascent of Mount Stalin. Alex Brown (trans). London: Lawrence & Wishart, 1936. 1st ed. 30 plts. (Sl rubbed.) *Hollett.* $132/£85

ROMMEL, ERWIN. Attacks. Vienna, VA: Athena, 1979. 1st ed. VG+ in VG dj. *Bishop.* $18/£12

RONALDS, ALFRED. The Fly-Fisher's Entomology. London: Longman Green, 1883. 9th ed. 20 hand-colored plts. Blind-stamped grn cl, ptd paper label. Bright. *Petersfield.* $209/£135

RONALDS, ALFRED. The Fly-Fisher's Entomology. Vol 1 (of 2). Liverpool: Henry Young, 1913. One of 250, signed. 20 engr plts (12 hand-colored). Teg, uncut. 1/4 morocco (spine sl rubbed, few mks), gilt. *Hollett.* $388/£250

ROOSEVELT, KERMIT. Hunting Big Game in the Eighties. NY: Scribner's, 1933. 1st trade ed. Frontis port. Fine in dj (lacks lg piece). *Bowman.* $100/£65

ROOSEVELT, THEODORE and G.B. GRINNELL (eds). American Big Game Hunting. NY: Forest & Stream, 1893. 1st ed. 345pp; teg. Full grn crushed morocco, raised bands, gilt. Fine (spine sunned). *Bowman.* $250/£161

ROOSEVELT, THEODORE and KERMIT. East of the Sun and West of the Moon. NY: Scribner's, 1927. Gilt-lettered blue cl. NF. *House.* $50/£32

ROOSEVELT, THEODORE and KERMIT. Trailing the Giant Panda. NY: Scribner's, 1929. Color frontis, fldg map. Gilt-lettered blue cl (spine gilt rubbed). VG. *House.* $50/£32

ROOSEVELT, THEODORE. Hunting Trips of a Ranchman. NY: Putnam's, 1886. 1st trade ed. 347pp. Yelow cl, red lettering, gilt spine. VG. *Bowman.* $120/£77

ROOSEVELT, THEODORE. Letters to Kermit, 1902-1908. Will Irwin (ed). NY: Scribner's, 1946. 1st ptg. Illus eps. VG. *Schoyer.* $25/£16

ROOSEVELT, THEODORE. Outdoor Pastimes of an American Hunter. NY: Scribner's, 1905. 1st ed. VG-(name; hinge starting). *Parker.* $125/£81

ROOSEVELT, THEODORE. The Rough Riders. NY: Scribners, 1899. 1st ed. xii,29pp; 44 plts. Untrimmed; teg. Backstrip sunned w/wear, 1/4-inch split at top, else VG. *Connolly.* $150/£97

ROOSEVELT, THEODORE. Theodore Roosevelt, An Autobiography. Macmillan, 1913. 1st ed. VG+. *Bishop.* $25/£16

ROOSEVELT, THEODORE. Through the Brazilian Wilderness. NY: Scribner's, 1914. Teg (sl faded). *Petersfield.* $39/£25

ROOSEVELT, WYN. Frontier Boys in the Grand Canyon. Cleveland: Arthur Westbrook, (1908). Pict wraps (smudge). *Schoyer.* $20/£13

ROOSEVELT, WYN. Frontier Boys on the Coast. Chatterton, 1909. 1st ed. NF. *Madle.* $25/£16

ROOT, FRANK A. and WILLIAM E. CONNELLEY. The Overland Stage to California. Topeka: By Authors, 1901. 1st ed. Fldg map. Brn pict cl (sl edgewear, soiling). Howes R 434. *Glenn.* $200/£129

ROOT, FRANK A. and WILLIAM E. CONNELLEY. The Overland Stage to California. Columbus, OH: Long's College Book Co, 1950. Rpt. Fldg map. Pict cl. VG. Howes R 434. *Schoyer.* $50/£32

ROOT, HENRY. Personal History and Reminiscences with Personal Opinions on Contemporary Events 1845-1921. SF: Privately ptd, 1921. 1st ed. Frontis. VG. Howes R 434. *Oregon.* $200/£129

ROOT, M.A. The Camera and the Pencil. Phila: M.A. Root/Lippincott/Appleton, 1864. Frontis w/guard, xviii,19-456pp; aeg. Gilt/blind emb cl. Rubbed, chipped, lt foxing, else VG. *Cahan.* $250/£161

ROOTHAM, JASPER. Miss Fire. London: C&W, 1946. 1st ed. Port; 7 plts; map. VG in dj (sl worn; price-clipped). *Hollett.* $39/£25

ROPES, JOHN CODMAN. The Story of the Civil War...between 1861 and 1865. NY: Putnam's Sons, 1933. 2nd ed. 3 vols in 4. 78 maps (37 fldg). Map at rear of vol 1 separated at folds, else NF. *Mcgowan.* $150/£97

ROQUELAURE, A.N. (Pseud of Anne Rice.) Beauty's Punishment. NY: Dutton, 1984. 1st ed. VF in dj (minor edgewear). *Else Fine.* $175/£113

ROSA, JOSEPH and WALDO KOOP. Rowdy Joe Lowe, Gambler with a Gun. Univ of OK, (1989). 1st ed. VF in VF dj. *Oregon.* $20/£13

ROSA, JOSEPH G. The Gunfighter. Norman, 1969. 1st ed. Fine in dj. *Baade.* $50/£32

ROSA, JOSEPH G. They Called Him Wild Bill. Norman: Univ of OK, (1964). 1st ptg. VG in dj. *Schoyer.* $45/£29

ROSAND, DAVID and MICHELANGELO MURARO. Titian and the Venetian Woodcut. 1976. Good in wrappers. *Washton.* $50/£32

ROSCOE, HENRY. Lives of Eminent British Lawyers. London: Longman, Rees et al, 1830. Mod 1/2 grn morocco (crude but serviceable). *Boswell.* $150/£97

ROSCOE, THEODORE. United States Destroyer Operations in World War II. Annapolis, MD, (1953). 1st ed. VG in dj (edgetorn; frayed). *King.* $65/£42

ROSCOE, THOMAS. The Tourist in France. London: Robert Jennings, 1834. Engr title; (viii),280pp; 25 steel-engr plts. Orig grn morocco gilt (neatly recased). Aeg. VG. *Hollett.* $132/£85

ROSCOE, THOMAS. Tourist in Spain. London: Robert Jennings, 1836. Frontis, vignette title, xii,280pp + 4pp ads, 19 plts (most foxed); teg. Grn morocco (rubbed; pocket removed; sig trimmed from tp). *Schoyer.* $85/£55

ROSCOE, THOMAS. Wanderings and Excursions in North Wales. London: C. Tilt, Simpkin, 1836. 1st ed. xviii,262,(2)pp. 51 engrs. Aeg. Pub's full grn calf, gilt (sl rubbed). *Karmiole.* $250/£161

ROSE, A. (comp). Register of Erotic Books. NY, 1965. 2 vols. VG. *Moss.* $124/£80

ROSE, BARBARA. Claes Oldenburg. NY: MOMA, (1970). 7-leaf checklist loosely inserted. Padded vinyl cvrs. VG. *Argosy.* $50/£32

ROSE, BERNICE. The Drawings of Roy Lichtenstein. NY: MOMA, 1987. VG in dj. *Argosy.* $85/£55

ROSE, F. HORACE. On the Edge of the East. London: Methuen, (1927). (xii),(246)pp + 8pp ads. Royal blue cl. *Schoyer.* $25/£16

ROSE, HAROLD WICKLIFFE. The Colonial Houses of Worship in America. NY: Hastings House, (1963). 1st ed. Good in dj. *Karmiole.* $40/£26

ROSE, HILDA. The Stump Farm. Boston: Little, Brown, 1928. 1st ed. VG in dj (chipped; fr panel separated at fold). *Blue Mountain.* $15/£10

ROSE, JAMES C. Creative Gardens. NY: Reinhold, (1958). 1st ed. Bkpl, edgewear, else VG. *Bookpress.* $45/£29

ROSE, ROBERT R. Advocates and Adversaries, the Early Life and Times of.... Gene Gressley (ed). Chicago: Lakeside Classic, 1977. 1st ed. Frontis, dbl-pg map. Fine. *Oregon.* $30/£19

ROSE, ROBERT R. Advocates and Adversaries. Chicago, (1977). Lakeside Classic. VG. *Schoyer.* $15/£10

ROSE, ROBERT SELDEN (ed). The Portola Expedition of 1769-1770. Berkeley: Univ of CA, 1911. 1st ed. Frontis plt. VG in orig ptd wrappers. *Shasky.* $45/£29

ROSE, VICTOR M. Ross' Texas Brigade. Kennesaw: Continental Book, 1960. Facs reproduction. *Lambeth.* $45/£29

ROSE, WILLIAM. The Surgical Treatment of Neuralgia of the Fifth Nerve. London: Bailliere, 1892. viii,85pp. (New spine.) *Goodrich.* $295/£190

Rose-Bud: A Flower in the Juvenile Garland. London: Baldwin & Cradock, 1834. 4th ed. Sm 12mo. 68pp + 4pp ads + 2pp contents; 32 half-pg wood engrs. Marbled paper on bd (lt rubbed, chipped). Internally Fine. *Hobbyhorse.* $175/£113

ROSEBORO, JOHN with BILL LIBBY. Glory Days with the Dodgers. Atheneum, 1978. 1st ed. Fine in VG + dj. *Plapinger.* $30/£19

ROSEN, MILTON W. The Viking Rocket Story. NY: Harper, 1955. VG in dj (chipped; corner clipped). *Knollwood.* $40/£26

ROSENAU, M.J. (ed). Proceedings of the International Congress on Health Problems in Tropical America. Boston, 1924. 1st ed. Good. *Fye.* $75/£48

ROSENAU, MILTON. Preventive Medicine and Hygiene. NY, 1913. 1st ed. Good. *Fye.* $200/£129

ROSENBACH, A.S.W. A Book Hunter's Holiday. Boston: Houghton Mifflin, 1936. 1st trade ed. Fine in dj (worn, torn). *Graf.* $40/£26

ROSENBACH, A.S.W. Books and Bidders, the Adventures of a Bibliophile. Boston: Little, Brown, 1927. One of 785 numbered of lg paper ed, signed. Teg. 1/4 brn pebble grain cl, cream paper spine label, pale brn paper over bds, upper cvr emb. Fine in slipcase (damaged). *Heller.* $150/£97

ROSENBACH, A.S.W. Books and Bidders. Boston, 1927. 1st trade ed. (Bkpl; bumped; cvrs sl dull.) *King.* $35/£23

ROSENBACH, A.S.W. Early American Children's Books. Portland: Southworth Press, 1933. One of 585 numbered, signed. 1/4 maroon leather; teg. VF in orig slipcase. *Dermont.* $475/£306

ROSENBACH, A.S.W. The Unpublishable Memoirs. London: John Castle, 1924. 1st ed. Blue cl. VG. *Moss.* $34/£22

ROSENBAUM, ART and BOB STEVENS. The Giants of San Francisco. Coward McCann, 1963. 1st ed. Fine in VG dj. *Plapinger.* $27/£17

ROSENBERG, HAROLD. Arshile Gorky: The Man, the Time, the Idea. NY: Horizon Press, 1962. 1st ed. Fine in illus dj (sm chip). *Cahan.* $50/£32

ROSENBERG, HAROLD. Saul Steinberg. NY: Knopf, 1978. 1st ed, wrappered issue. VG in pict wrappers. *Godot.* $65/£42

ROSENBERG, JAKOB. Rembrandt. Cambridge, 1948. 2 vols. Good. *Washton.* $50/£32

ROSENBERG, LOUIS CONRAD. Cottages, Farmhouses and Other Minor Buildings in England.... NY: Architectural Book Pub, 1923. 1st ed. 102 plts (margins lt smudged few plts; sm stain plts 58, 60, 61), else VG in dj (tattered). *Bookpress.* $185/£119

ROSENBERG, LOUIS CONRAD. The Davanzati Palace, Florence, Italy.... NY: Architectural Book Pub, 1922. 1st ed. Frontis. (Bkpl removed; dj missing rear cvr). *Bookpress.* $175/£113

ROSENFELD, SYBIL. Georgian Scene Painters and Scene Painting. Cambridge, 1981. Good in dj. *Washton.* $50/£32

ROSENFELD, SYBIL. Georgian Scene Painters and Scene Painting. Cambridge: CUP, 1981. Frontis; 78 plts. VG in pict dj. *Dramatis Personae.* $85/£55

ROSENFELD, SYBIL. Strolling Players and Drama in the Provinces 1660-1765. Cambridge: CUP, 1939. 1st ed. Frontis. (Edges spotted.) *Dramatis Personae.* $40/£26

ROSENGARTEN, THEODORE. Tombee, Portrait of a Cotton Planter. NY, (1986). 1st ed. VG + in VG + dj. *Pratt.* $25/£16

ROSENTHAL, ERIC. Here Are Diamonds. London: Hale, (1950). Backstrip sl faded. *Petersfield.* $31/£20

ROSENTHAL, NAN. George Rickey. NY: Abrams, 1977. 1st ed. Silver-emb cl. Fine in pict dj. *Cahan.* $325/£210

ROSETT, JOSHUA. The Mechanism of Thought, Imagery, and Hallucination. NY, 1939. 1st ed. Fine (ex-lib). *Fye.* $50/£32

ROSHWALD, MORDECAI. Level 7. NY: McGraw-Hill, 1959. 1st ed. Fine in NF dj. *Beasley.* $30/£19

ROSKE, RALPH and CHARLES VAN DOREN. Lincoln's Commando, The Biography of Commander W.B. Cushing.... NY, (1957). 1st ed. VG in dj (minor chipping). *Pratt.* $37/£24

ROSS, ALAN. The Bandit on the Billiard Table. London: Derek Verschoyle, 1954. 1st Eng ed. Red cl. Erasure fep, o/w VG in dj (torn, repaired). *Dalian.* $54/£35

ROSS, ALAN. The Bandit on the Billiard Table. A Journey through Sardinia. London: Derek Verschoyle, 1954. 1st Eng ed. VG (edges lt spotted; spine head, tail, corners sl bumped) in dj (rubbed; nicked; sl scratched, chipped). *Ulysses.* $101/£65

ROSS, ALAN. A Calcutta Grandmother. London: Poem-of-the-Month Club, (1971). 1st ed. Signed. Fine. *Polyanthos.* $25/£16

ROSS, ALAN. A Calcutta Grandmother. London: Poem-of-the-Month Club Ltd, 1971. 1st Eng ed. Signed. VG (edges sl creased, thumbed). *Ulysses.* $34/£22

ROSS, ALAN. Time Was Away. London: John Lehmann, 1948. 1st Eng ed. 8 full-pg color plts. Yellow cl. Spine lettering dull, o/w Fine in dj (sl mkd, nicked). *Dalian.* $233/£150

ROSS, ALEXANDER. Adventures of the First Settlers on the Oregon or Columbia River. M.M. Quaife (ed). Chicago: Lakeside Classic, 1923. Fldg map. VG. Howes R 448. *Oregon.* $60/£39

ROSS, ALEXANDER. The Fur Hunters of the Far West. London: Smith Elder, 1855. 2 vols. 2 frontispieces, xv,333; viii,262pp, fldg map. Contemp 1/2 leather, marbled bds, morocco spine labels, raised bands, gilt stamping. Fine set. Howes R 449. *Oregon.* $1,400/£903

ROSS, ALEXANDER. The Fur Hunters of the Far West. London: Smith, Elder & Co, 1855. 1st ed. 2 vols. Frontis, xv,333pp; fldg map (repaired); frontis, viii,262pp. 3/4 leather, marbled bds; 5 raised bands; gilt backs, tops. Nice (dull spots; spines rubbed). Howes R 449. *Bohling.* $850/£548

ROSS, ALEXANDER. The Fur Hunters of the Far West. Chicago, 1924. Lakeside Classic rpt. Pict cl. VG + . *Pratt.* $20/£13

ROSS, CHRISTIAN K. Charley Ross; the Story of His Abduction, and the Incidents of the Search for His Recovery. London: Hodder & Stoughton, 1877. 431pp + ads. Good (sl worn). *Hayman.* $35/£23

ROSS, CLYDE P. The Lower Gila Region, Arizona. Washington: USGS, 1923. 13 plts, 3 fldg pocket maps. VG + (ends rubbed). *Bohling.* $85/£55

ROSS, E. DENISON (ed). The Art of Egypt through the Ages. London: Studio, (1931). 1st ed. Blue cl. Bumped; spine faded, o/w VG. *Hermitage.* $95/£61

ROSS, FITZGERALD. A Visit to the Cities and Camps of the Confederate States. Edinburgh/London: William Blackwood, 1865. 1st ed. 8vo, 300pp + (2)pp ads, fldg map. Orig maroon cl. Spine faded, ends bumped, else VG. Howes R 453. *Chapel Hill.* $525/£339

ROSS, FREDERICK. The Ruined Abbeys of Britain. London: William Mackenzie, (1882). 1st ed. viii,288pp, aeg, 12 chromolithos. Brn cl (sl mkd, scratched), matching levant morocco (rebacked), gilt. Neat repairs prelims, o/w Attractive. *Hollett.* $271/£175

ROSS, FREDERICK. The Ruined Abbeys of Britain. London, (1882). 1st ed. 288pp; 12 color plts, guards. Gilt pict cl. VG. *Argosy.* $350/£226

ROSS, HARVEY LEE. The Early Pioneers and Pioneer Events of the State of Illinois.... Chicago: Edwards, 1899. 1st ed. Inscribed presentation. (11),199pp. (Nicks; bkpl; emb lib stamps.) Howes R 456. *Ginsberg.* $300/£194

ROSS, HUGH. Induced Cell-Reproduction and Cancer. Phila, 1911. 1st ed. Good. *Fye.* $150/£97

ROSS, J. and J.S. BURY. Peripheral Neuritis. London, 1893. vii,424pp. (Ink stamps; cl dust-stained; spine top sl defective; inner hinges cracked.) *Whitehart.* $62/£40

ROSS, J.H. (trans). (Pseud of T.E. Lawrence.) The Forest Giant. London: Cape, (1924). 1st ed. Frontis. NF in Good dj (tanned, nicks, edgetears). *Reese.* $175/£113

ROSS, JAMES CLARK. A Voyage of Discovery and Research in the Southern and Antarctic Regions during the Years 1839-43. London: John Murray, 1847. 1st ed. 2 vols. lii,366; x,447. 19th cent half calf, marbled bds (sl rubbed). Good (some foxing to prelims). *Walcot.* $1,395/£900

ROSS, JANET. Florentine Villas. London: J.M. Dent, 1901. 1st ed. Frontis; 25 plts. Lt cvr wear, else VG. *Bookpress.* $245/£158

ROSS, JOEL. Hints and Helps to Health and Happiness. Auburn, NY, 1851. 1st ed. 303pp. Full leather. Good. *Fye.* $100/£65

ROSS, JOHN and HUGH GUNN (eds). The Book of the Red Deer and Empire Big Game. London, 1925. #442/500. Teg. Color illus mtd on upper bd. (Upper hinge cracked, cl sl soiled.) *Edwards.* $132/£85

ROSS, JOHN. Narrative of a Second Voyage in Search of a North-West Passage.... London: A.W. Webster, 1835. 1st ed. xxxiii,740. 30 plts, charts. Orig cl (rebacked, orig spine relaid). Good. *Walcot.* $426/£275

ROSS, JOHN. Narrative of a Second Voyage in Search of a North-West Passage.... London: A.W. Webster, 1835. 1st ed. 2 vols. (6),errata,(1),xxxiii, plate list, 740pp, 31 plts (9 color, 5 charts), lg fldg chart bound at fr; xii,120,cxliv,cii,(1), 20 plts (12 color), sub's list. (2 plts, 1 text leaf bound out of order.) Blue cl (rebacked, corners sl bumped; foxing, eps renewed, marginal hinge tear vol 1). *Parmer.* $1,450/£935

ROSS, JOHN. A Voyage of Discovery in His Majesty's Ships Isabella and Alexander for the Purpose of Exploring Baffin Bay. London: Longmans, Hurst, 1819. 2nd ed. 2 vols. lxix,265; iv,258pp; fldg map; 2 plts. Full calf (rebacked). VG set. *Walcot.* $364/£235

ROSS, MRS. WILLIAM P. Life and Times of Hon. William P. Ross. Fort Smith, AK, 1893. (xxiii),272pp; port. Gilt-titled cl. VG + (2 leaves misplaced in binding). Howes R 462. *Bohling.* $175/£113

ROSS, RONALD. Memories with a Full Account of the Great Malaria Problem and Its Solution. London, 1923. 1st ed. Good. *Fye.* $100/£65

ROSS, RONALD. Mosquito Brigades and How to Organise Them. London, 1902. 1st ed. Good. *Fye.* $75/£48

ROSS, RONALD. Studies on Malaria. London, 1928. 1st ed. Good. *Fye.* $100/£65

ROSSETTI, CHRISTINA. Goblin Market. London: Harrap, (1933). 1st ed. 8vo. 4 full-pg color plts by Arthur Rackham. Illus cream-colored paper wrappers (browning, darkening rear cvr). *Reisler.* $110/£71

ROSSETTI, CHRISTINA. Goblin Market. London: Macmillan, 1893. 1st ed. Tall, 12mo. Laurence Housman (illus). Aeg. Grn cl, gilt dec. Lt corner wear, o/w Very Nice. *Reisler.* $550/£355

ROSSETTI, CHRISTINA. Goblin Market. London: Harrap, 1939. 1st thus. Fine (inscrip) in wrappers as issued. *Williams.* $140/£90

ROSSETTI, CHRISTINA. New Poems by Christina Rossetti. William Michael Rossetti (ed). London/NY, 1896. Frontis port (edges sl spotted), xxiv,397pp. Teg; marbled eps. 1/2 morocco, marbled bds (sl spotted), dec gilt floral spine (lt faded). *Edwards.* $39/£25

ROSSETTI, CHRISTINA. A Pageant and Other Poems. London: Macmillan, 1881. 1st ed. Blue cl, gilt. Fep sl used, tipped-in card removed, o/w NF. *Pharos.* $125/£81

ROSSETTI, CHRISTINA. The Poetical Works of Christina Georgina Rossetti. London: Macmillan, 1904. 1st ed. Lt foxing, o/w Fine. *Pharos.* $100/£65

ROSSETTI, CHRISTINA. The Prince's Progress and Other Poems. London: Macmillan, 1866. 1st ed. Frontis, add'l tp, viii,216pp. Grn cl, gilt. Fine (2 bkpls). *Bickersteth.* $388/£250

ROSSETTI, CHRISTINA. Sing-Song: A Nursery Rhyme Book. London: Routledge, 1872. 1st ed. 120 engrs by Arthur Hughes. Pict blue cl; yellow glazed eps; aeg. Good (illus p43 hand-colored by owner; sl rubbing). *Houle.* $425/£274

ROSSETTI, CHRISTINA. Sing-Song: A Nursery-Rhyme Book. London: Routledge, 1872. 1st ed. 8vo. Aeg. Arthur Hughes (illus). Illus grn cl, gilt (sl wear corners; hinges cracked; foxing within). *Reisler.* $350/£226

ROSSETTI, DANTE GABRIEL. The Ballad of Jan Van Hunks. London: Harrap, (1929). Ltd to 620 numbered. Frontis. Good in slipcase (cracked). *Karmiole.* $30/£19

ROSSETTI, DANTE GABRIEL. The Collected Works. London: Ellis & Elvey, 1888. 2 vols. xliii,528; xl,522pp. (Sl spotting; spine tops sl rubbed, 1 sl creased.) *Hollett.* $54/£35

ROSSETTI, DANTE GABRIEL. The Early Italian Poets.... London, 1861. 1st ed (w/errata). 464pp. Good (inscrip, stamped names; water spot spine, sl rubbed). *King.* $125/£81

ROSSETTI, DANTE GABRIEL. The New Life of Dante Alighieri. Portland: Thos. B. Mosher, 1899. 3rd ed. One of 925. 96pp. Vellum paper wraps (sl flaws; spine dknd), yapped edges; uncut. VG, text Fine. *Hartfield.* $45/£29

ROSSI, FERDINANDO. Mosaics.... London: Pall Mall Press, 1970. 1st UK ed. 101 plts. Dj (sl chipped). *Edwards.* $54/£35

ROSSI, FILIPPO. Italian Jeweled Arts. Elisabeth M. Borgese (trans). NY: Abrams, (1954). 133 plts (83 color, 8 gold/silver). VG in dj. *Argosy.* $75/£48

ROSSI, FILIPPO. Italian Jeweled Arts. NY: Abrams, (1954). Frontis; 83 color, 8 gold/silver mtd plts. Fine in dj (sl torn, mended). *Hermitage.* $100/£65

ROSSI, FILIPPO. Italian Jeweled Arts. London: Thames & Hudson, (1957). 1st ed. VF in dj, pub's slipcase. *Hermitage.* $100/£65

ROSSI, PAUL A. and DAVID C. HUNT. The Art of the Old West, from the Collection of the Gilcrease Institute. Knopf, (1971). 1st ed. Pict buckram. Inscrip, o/w VF in Fine dj. *Oregon.* $65/£42

ROSSI, PAUL A. and DAVID C. HUNT. The Art of the Old West. London, 1972. 300 plts (134 color). Dj (corners sl chipped). *Edwards.* $39/£25

ROSTOEVTZEFF, MICHAEL. A Large Estate in the Third Century B.C.: A Study in Economic History. Madison: Univ of WI, 1922. 3 plts. (Joints starting; corners rubbed, bumped.) *Archaeologia.* $45/£29

ROSTOVTZEFF, M. The Social and Economic History of the Hellenistic World. Oxford: Clarendon Press, 1953. 2nd imp. 3 vols. 112 photo plts. VG. *Argosy.* $175/£113

ROSTOW, EUGENE V. A National Policy for the Oil Industry. New Haven: Yale Univ Press, 1948. Good in dj (worn, chipped). *Boswell.* $65/£42

ROSWELL, GENE. The Yogi Berra Story. Messner, 1958. Ltr ptg. Fine in VG dj. *Plapinger.* $35/£23

ROTAR, PETER P. Grasses of Hawaii. Honolulu, 1968. Fine in dj. *Brooks.* $37/£24

ROTERS, EBERHARD. Painters of the Bauhaus. London, 1969. 1st UK ed. 32 color plts. (Ex-lib w/ink stamps; upper hinge tender). Dj (#s). *Edwards.* $70/£45

ROTH, HENRY. Call It Sleep. London: Michael Joseph, (1963). 1st Eng ed, 1st bk. Inscribed. Black cl stamped in gold. NF in VG dj (nicks, wear). *Juvelis.* $350/£226

ROTH, HENRY. Nature's First Green. NY: Targ Editions, 1979. #124/350 signed. Fine in dj (sm tear). *Polyanthos.* $30/£19

ROTH, HENRY. Nature's First Green. NY: Targ Editions, 1979. One of 350 numbered, signed. Fine in dj. *Dermont.* $50/£32

ROTH, HENRY. Shifting Landscapes. Phila: Jewish Publication Soc, 1987. 1st ed. VF in VF dj. *Pettler.* $45/£29

ROTH, PHILIP. The Anatomy Lesson. NY: FSG, 1983. 1st ed. Fine in Fine dj. *Revere.* $25/£16

ROTH, PHILIP. The Facts. NY: Farrar Straus, (1988). 1st ed. One of 250 signed. Mint in slipcase. *Jaffe.* $100/£65

ROTH, PHILIP. Goodbye, Columbus. (London): Deutsch, (1959). 1st Eng ed, 1st bk. Fine in dj. *Heller.* $125/£81

ROTH, PHILIP. The Great American Novel. NY: Holt, Rinehart & Winston, (1973). 1st ed. NF in dj (sm crease fr flap). *Antic Hay.* $35/£23

ROTH, PHILIP. Our Gang. NY: Random House, 1971. 1st ed. Fine in Fine dj. *Revere.* $35/£23

ROTH, PHILIP. Our Gang. London: Cape, 1971. 1st UK ed. Fine in dj. *Williams.* $19/£12

ROTH, PHILIP. Portnoy's Complaint. NY: Random House, (1969). 1st ed. VG in VG dj. *Glenn.* $30/£19

ROTH, PHILIP. Portnoy's Complaint. NY: Random House, (1969). 1st ed. Signed. NF in dj (sl edgewear). *Antic Hay.* $125/£81

ROTH, PHILIP. When She Was Good. NY, 1967. 1st ed. Fine in dj. *Pharos.* $40/£26

ROTHENSTEIN, JOHN. British Art Since 1900. London: Phaidon, 1962. Dj (sl faded, chipped spine). *Edwards.* $31/£20

ROTHENSTEIN, JOHN. Nineteenth-Century Painting. London: John Lane, Bodley Head, 1932. 1st ed. Frontis, 15 plts. Top edge cerise, rest uncut. Spine sl faded; back cvr sl mkd; o/w Fine. *Temple.* $19/£12

ROTHENSTEIN, JOHN. Paul Nash (1889-1946). London: Beaverbrook Newspapers, 1961. 1st ed. 16 tipped-in color plts. Yellow cl, black spine title. Fine (sl bumped) in dj w/color plt onlaid. *Heller.* $125/£81

ROTHENSTEIN, WILLIAM. Since Fifty. Men and Memories, 1922-1938. Faber & Faber, 1939. 1st ed. Teg, rest uncut. Newspaper clippings tipped in to reps. 2 als loosely inserted. (Lt spotting; sl soiled, rubbed.) *Edwards.* $70/£45

ROTHENSTEIN, WILLIAM. Twelve Portraits. London: Faber & Faber, 1929. 1st ed. 12 plts w/ptd glassine guards. Edges lt soiled, else VG in dj (edgeworn, foxed). *Cahan.* $50/£32

ROTHENSTEIN, WILLIAM. Twenty-Four Portraits. NY: Harcourt, Brace, 1920. 1st ed. One of 2000 ptd. 24 ports. Cl-backed bds, ptd labels. NF (sl rubbed). *Cahan.* $60/£39

ROTHENSTEIN, WILLIAM. Twenty-Four Portraits.... London: C&W, 1923. 1st ed. Ltd to 1500. Paper labels. (Lt rubbed.) *Sadlon.* $20/£13

ROTHERY, GUY CADOGAN. The ABC of Heraldry. London: Stanley Paul, (1915). Olive grn pict cl (lt soiling, wear; inscrip). *Glenn.* $60/£39

ROTHLISBERGER, MARCEL. Claude Lorraine. The Paintings. New Haven: Yale Univ, 1961. 2 vols. VF set (bkpl). *Europa.* $442/£285

Rothschild Library. Privately ptd at CUP, 1954. Orig ed. 2 vols. 62 plts. *Marlborough.* $233/£150

ROTHSCHILD, M. and T. CLAY. Fleas, Flukes and Cuckoos, a Study of Bird Parasites. London: New Naturalist, 1952. 1st ed, 2nd ptg. 40 plts, illus. Dj. *Wheldon & Wesley.* $47/£30

Rough Notes by an Old Soldier, During Fifty Years Service.... (By George Bell.) London: Day, 1867. 1st ed. 2 vols. (12),367; (8),382pp. Frontis. Gold dec red cl, gilt cl spines (lt tear spine vol 2). *Ginsberg.* $750/£484

ROUGHEAD, WILLIAM (ed). Trial of Mrs. M'Lachlan. Glasgow: William Hodge, 1911. Orig ed. Grn cl, gilt. Usable (quite worn). *Boswell.* $125/£81

ROUGHLEY, T.C. Fish and Fisheries of Australia. London, 1951. Rev, enlgd ed. 60 color, 21 b/w plts. Dj (chipped w/loss). *Edwards.* $74/£48

ROUSE, JOHN E. The Criollo, Spanish Cattle in the Americas. Norman, Univ of OK, (1977). (1st ed). Fine in dj. *Bohling.* $60/£39

ROUSE, JOHN E. The Criollo. Spanish Cattle in the Americas. Norman: Univ of OK, 1977. 1st ed. NF (label) in NF dj. *Parker.* $35/£23

ROUSE, PARKE. The Great Wagon Road from Philadelphia to the South. NY: McGraw-Hill, (1973). Double map. VG + in dj (sl edgeworn). *Bohling.* $35/£23

ROUSSEAU, J.J. Letters on the Elements of Botany. London, 1791. 3rd ed. xxiv,(vi),503pp + 2pp ads, 38 engr plts, fldg table. Recent 1/2 calf, orig label. Fine. *Henly.* $93/£60

ROUTH, E.M.G. Tangier. England's Lost Atlantic Outpost 1661-1684. London: John Murray, 1912. 1st ed. Blue gilt cl (lt frayed). *Karmiole.* $75/£48

ROUTLEDGE, MRS. SCORESBY. The Mystery of Easter Island, the Story of an Expedition. London: Sifton, Praed, (1919). *Petersfield.* $116/£75

ROWAN, ALASTAIR. Designs for Castles and Country Villas by Robert and James Adam. Oxford: Phaidon, 1985. 64 plts. Fine. *Europa.* $37/£24

ROWAN, ARCHIBALD H. Autobiography of.... Dublin, 1840. 1st ed. (16),475pp, facs, port. Contemp 1/2 morocco. Howes R 474. *Ginsberg.* $300/£194

ROWAN, CARL T. South of Freedom. NY: Knopf, 1952. 1st ed. VG in dj (lt chipped). *Petrilla.* $30/£19

ROWAN, RICHARD WILMER. The Pinkertons, a Detective Dynasty. Boston: Little, Brown, 1931. 1st ed. Frontis, 5 plts. Brn cl. Inner hinge sl cracked, o/w VG. *Weber.* $40/£26

ROWAN, THOMAS. Coal. Spontaneous Combustion and Explosions Occurring in Coal Cargoes.... London: E. & F.N. Spon, 1882. xi,45pp + lxvii. Blind-emb cl (spine chipped; sl browning; hinges cracked). *Edwards.* $39/£25

ROWE, SAMUEL. A Perambulation of the Antient and Royal Forest of Dartmoor. Exeter/London, 1896. 3rd ed. xvi,516pp (feps lt browned), 5 fldg maps. Partly unopened. (Extrems sl rubbed; tear.) *Edwards.* $101/£65

ROWE, WILLIAM HUTCHINSON. The Maritime History of Maine: Three Centuries of Shipbuilding and Seafaring. NY, (1948). 1st ed. *Lefkowicz.* $40/£26

ROWE, WILLIAM HUTCHINSON. Shipbuilding Days and Tales of the Sea in Old North Yarmouth and Yarmouth, Maine. Portland: Marks Ptg House, 1924. 1st ed. *Lefkowicz.* $75/£48

ROWLAND, ERON OPHA. Andrew Jackson's Campaign Against the British. Macmillan, 1926. 1st ed. Inscribed. VG + (ex-lib). *Bishop.* $27/£17

ROWLAND, ERON OPHA. Varina Howell, Wife of Jefferson Davis. NY: McMillan, 1927-31. 1st ed. 2 vols. Spine sl sunned vol 2, else NF. *Mcgowan.* $125/£81

ROWLAND-BROWN, H. Butterflies and Moths at Home and Abroad. London, 1912. 21 tipped-in color plts (feps, margins sl browned). Illus laid down to upper bd (spine sl rubbed). *Edwards.* $59/£38

ROWNTREE, B. SEEBOHM and MAY KENDALL. How the Labourer Lives. London: Nelson, n.d. (1913). 1st ed. Dbl-pg map, fldg chart; errata leaf after p24. (Backstrip sl soiled, rubbed.) *Cox.* $39/£25

ROWNTREE, LESTER. Hardy Californians. NY: Macmillan, 1936. Gilt-stamped titles. Fine in dj. *Quest.* $50/£32

ROWSON, MRS. Charlotte Temple. Phila: M. Carey, 1808. 7th Amer ed. 2 vols in 1. 12mo. 137pp. Full leather on wood, title on spine label (ink name; cvr lt rubbed; internal spotting, foxing; hole pg 129, paper flaw w/rip pg 62 w/loss; few pg edges chipped). Good. *Hobbyhorse.* $70/£45

Roy Rogers' Rodeo, A Pop-Up Book. London: Purnell, n.d. (1950). 27x21 cm. 5 pop-ups. George Shaw (illus). Glazed pict bds. VG. *Book Finders.* $70/£45

ROY, ANDREW. Recollections of a Prisoner of War. Columbus, OH: Ptd by J.L. Traugher, 1909. 2nd ed, rev. Frontis port. Orig blue cl. Spine sl faded, sl sig separation, else VG. *Chapel Hill.* $85/£55

ROY, GEORGE. Generalship, or How I Managed My Husband. Cincinnati: Robert Clarke, 1875. 1st ed. Gold-stamped blue cl. Sig, else Nice. *Pharos.* $45/£29

ROY, JULES. The Battle of Dienbienphu. Robert Baldick (trans). London, 1965. 1st ed. 16 plts. Good + in dj. *Edwards.* $47/£30

ROY, WILLIAM. The Military Antiquities of the Romans in Britain. London: Soc of Antiquaries, 1793. 1st ed. Elephant folio. xvi,206pp; 51 plts and maps; list of plts; list of Soc of Antiquaries. VG (foxing; last leaf sl torn at margin; plt xxxvii bound in before tp). Mod 1/2 calf on marbled bds, spine label. *Edwards.* $543/£350

Royal Recollections.... (By David Williams.) London: Ptd for James Ridgway, 1788. 4th ed. 114pp, uncut (1/2 title sl spotted, edges repaired). Mod calf-backed marbled bds, gilt. *Hollett.* $186/£120

ROYALL, WILLIAM L. Some Reminiscences. NY: Neale, 1909. 1st ed. Gilt-stamped purple cl. NF (spine faded). *Chapel Hill.* $450/£290

ROYCE, JOSIAH. The Feud of Oakfield Creek. A Novel of California Life. Boston: Houghton Mifflin, 1887. 1st ed. 483pp. Pict mustard cl. Bkpl, inscrip, sl dknd, soiled, spine worn, else Good. *Reese.* $55/£35

ROYCE, SARAH. A Frontier Lady; Recollections of the Gold Rush and Early California. Ralph Henry Gabriel (ed). New Haven: Yale, 1932. 1st ed. Map. VG (lt wear; couple leaves roughly opened; bkpls) in dj (remnants). *Bohling.* $100/£65

ROYDE-SMITH, NAOMI. The Housemaid. NY: Knopf, 1926. 1st Amer ed. Inscribed presentation dated 1926. (Spine sl discolored; lower cvr spotted.) *Bickersteth.* $78/£50

ROYDE-SMITH, NAOMI. Summer Holiday or Gibraltar. Constable, (1929). 1st ed. (Spine, fore-edge faded.) *Bickersteth.* $43/£28

ROYDE-SMITH, NAOMI. The Tortoiseshell Cat. Constable, 1925. 1st ed. (Prelims spotted.) *Bickersteth.* $47/£30

ROYKO, MIKE. I May Be Wrong But I Doubt It. Chicago: Regnery, 1968. 1st ed. NF (lt shelf wear, traces of erasure fep) in NF dj (lt wear top edge). *Beasley.* $65/£42

RUARK, ROBERT. Grenadine Etching. GC: Doubleday, 1947. 1st ed, 1st bk. Inscribed. Grey cl. VG in dj (edgeworn; rear panel sl sunned). *Chapel Hill.* $450/£290

RUARK, ROBERT. The Honey Badger. NY, (1965). 1st ed. 2 inscrips, else Good in dj (edgetorn, 1.5-inch tear). *King.* $35/£23

RUARK, ROBERT. The Honey Badger. NY: McGraw-Hill, 1965. 1st ed. Fine+ in dj. *Bowman.* $35/£23

RUARK, ROBERT. Horn of the Hunter. GC, 1953. 1st ed. VG in dj (sl stained, scratched, sm edge tear). *King.* $75/£48

RUARK, ROBERT. Horn of the Hunter. GC: Doubleday, 1953. 1st ed. VG. *Bowman.* $80/£52

RUARK, ROBERT. The Old Man and the Boy. NY, (1957). 1st ed. VF in dj. *Artis.* $65/£42

RUARK, ROBERT. The Old Man and the Boy. NY: Holt, (1957). Advance rev copy w/slip, photo, material laid in. Fine in NF dj (spine sl tanned). *Between The Covers.* $200/£129

RUARK, ROBERT. The Old Man's Boy Grows Older. NY, (1961). 1st ed. VG in dj (dknd). *Argosy.* $45/£29

RUARK, ROBERT. Something of Value. GC: Doubleday, 1955. 1st ed. VG in dj. *Bowman.* $40/£26

RUARK, ROBERT. Uhuru. NY: McGraw Hill, 1962. 1st ed. NF in NF dj (chip; sl wear). *Revere.* $50/£32

RUARK, ROBERT. Use Enough Gun. NY, (1966). 1st ed. Fine (name) in dj. *Artis.* $40/£26

RUARK, ROBERT. Use Enough Gun. NY: NAL, 1966. 1st ed. Fine in dj. *Bowman.* $60/£39

RUBENS, BERNICE. The Elected Member. London: Eyre & Spottiswoode, 1969. 1st Eng ed. Maroon cl. Fine in dj (sl nicked). *Dalian.* $54/£35

RUBENS, BERNICE. Set on Edge. London: E&S, 1960. 1st UK ed, 1st bk. Fine in dj. *Lewton.* $39/£25

RUBER, PETER. The Last Bookman. NY: Candlelight, 1968. 1st ed. Fine in VG+ dj (spine rubbed, edgewear). *Janus.* $30/£19

RUBIN, JACOB H. I Live to Tell: The Russian Adventures of an American Socialist. Indianapolis: Bobbs-Merrill, 1934. 1st ed. VG in dj (edgeworn, spine lt sunned, price-clipped). *Aka.* $25/£16

RUBIN, JAMES HENRY. Eighteenth-Century French Life Drawing. Selections from the Collection of Mathias Polakovits. Princeton, 1977. 39 plts. Good in dj. *Washton.* $45/£29

RUBIN, JERRY. Do It! NY: S&S, (1970). 1st ed. NF (edges sl dknd) in VG dj (sm tears). *Between The Covers.* $85/£55

RUBIN, JERRY. Growing (Up) at Thirty-Seven. Evans, 1976. 1st ed. Signed. Fine in dj. *Fine Books.* $65/£42

RUBIN, REUVEN. My Life My Art, An Autobiography and Selected Paintings. NY, (1974). 95 repros. VG in dj. *Argosy.* $75/£48

RUBIN, WILLIAM S. Anthony Caro. NY: MOMA, 1975. VG in dj. *Argosy.* $60/£39

RUBIN, WILLIAM S. Dada and Surrealist Art. London: Thames & Hudson, (1969). 60 hand-mtd color plts. Red velvet stamped in black. Good in dj. *Karmiole.* $275/£177

RUBINSTEIN, H.F. (ed.) Four Jewish Plays. London: Gollancz, 1948. 1st Eng ed. Grn cl. Fore-edge, eps sl foxed, o/w Fine in dj (foxed). *Dalian.* $70/£45

RUBY, ROBERT H. and JOHN A. BROWN. The Chinook Indians—Traders of the Lower Columbia River. Norman: Univ of OK, (1976). 1st ed. Ink name, else Fine in Fine dj. *Perier.* $45/£29

RUDING, WALT. An Evil Motherhood. London: Elkin Mathews, 1896. 1st ed. Aubrey Beardsley frontis, 100pp (20pp ads). Blue dec cl. Bkpl, eps lt browned, else VG. *Godot.* $65/£42

RUDKIN, CHARLES. Camille de Roquefeuil in San Francisco 1817-1818. LA: Dawson, 1954. 1st thus. Ltd to 200 ptd. Fine in Fine dj. Howes R 438. *Oregon.* $50/£32

RUELL, PATRICK. (Pseud of Reginald Hill). Death Takes the Low Road. London: Hutchinson, 1974. 1st ed. Fine in dj. *Mordida.* $75/£48

RUESS, EVERETT. On Desert Trails with Everett Ruess. El Centro: Desert Magazine Press, 1940. 1st ed, ltd to 1000. Fine. *Book Market.* $150/£97

RUGGLE, GEORGE. Ignoramus, Comoedia.... London: T. Payne, 1787. Engr frontis; facs port. 3/4 morocco, marbled bds (sl rubbed; fr joint starting); gilt; teg. *Sadlon.* $200/£129

RUHMER, B. Cosimo Tura, Paintings and Drawings. London: Phaidon, 1958. 85 plts. Sound in dj. *Ars Artis.* $93/£60

RUHMER, E. Cranach. Greenwich, CT: Phaidon, 1963. 50 color, 4 monochrome plts. VG in dj. *Argosy.* $50/£32

RUKEYSER, MURIEL. 29 Poems. London, 1972. 1st ed. Fine in Fine dj. *Polyanthos.* $25/£16

RUKEYSER, MURIEL. Breaking Open. NY: Random House, (1973). 1st ed. Fine in dj. *Godot.* $35/£23

RUKEYSER, MURIEL. Elegies. N.p.: New Directions, (1949). 1st ed. #2/300 signed. Blue paper over bds, ptd labels. Fine (bkpl) in slipcase. *Cahan.* $100/£65

RUKEYSER, MURIEL. The Green Wave. GC: Doubleday, 1948. 1st ed. Fine in dj (spine browning). *Antic Hay.* $50/£32

RUKEYSER, MURIEL. U.S. 1. NY: Covici, Friede, (1938). 1st ed. NF in dj (internally mended tear). *Pharos.* $125/£81

Rule Britannia. London: Henry Frowde/Hodder & Stoughton, (ca 1914). 4to. 8 full-pg color illus by Charles Robinson, color tp. Cl-backed illus bds (worn; lower hinge cracked). *Reisler.* $150/£97

Rules and Regulations of the Boston Medical Association. Boston: Phelps, 1820. 23; (4)pp. Orig wraps bound in 1/2 calf; gilt spine. Good. *Goodrich.* $250/£161

RUMBALL-PETRE, A.R. Rare Bibles. NY: Philip C. Duschnes, 1963. Rpt of 'Second Edition, Revised.' Red cl, gilt. Good. *Karmiole.* $30/£19

RUMBALL-PETRE, EDWIN A.R. Rare Bibles. NY: Duschnes, 1954. 1st ed. One of 600. Fine. *Bookpress.* $85/£55

RUMER, THOMAS (ed). This Emigrating Company: The 1844...Journal of Jacob Hammer. Clark, 1991. 1st ed. Ltd to 750. VF in VF dj. *Oregon.* $35/£23

RUMER, THOMAS. The Wagon Trains of '44: A Comparative View.... Clark, 1991. 1st ed. Ltd to 752. VF in VF dj. *Oregon.* $35/£23

Rummy, That Noble Game. London: Golden Cockerel Press. One of 1250. (Sl foxed; faded.) *Petersfield.* $28/£18

RUNDALL, L.B. The Ibex of Sha-Ping. London: Macmillan, 1915. 1st ed. 15 tipped-in color plts. (Sl mks; hinges sl rubbed.) *Hollett.* $116/£75

RUNES, D. (ed). The Diary and Sundry Observations of Thomas Alva Edison. NY, (1948). VF in dj. *Artis.* $20/£13

RUNYON, DAMON. The Best of Runyon. Stokes, 1938. 1st ed. Cvrs foxed, else VG+ in Nice dj (worn, lt chipped). *Fine Books.* $200/£129

RUNYON, DAMON. In Our Town. NY, (1946). 1st Amer ed. Fine (sl crease) in dj (sl rubbed). *Polyanthos.* $30/£19

RUNYON, DAMON. In Our Town. Creative Age Press, 1946. 1st ed. VG+ in VG+ dj. *Bishop.* $62/£40

RUNYON, DAMON. Short Takes. London: Constable, 1948. 1st Eng ed. VG+ in dj. *Limestone.* $55/£35

RUNYON, DAMON. Take it Easy. Constable, 1938. 1st Eng ed. VG. *Fine Books.* $75/£48

RUNYON, DAMON. The Tents of Trouble. NY: Desmond Fitzgerald, (1911). 1st ed, 1st bk. Flexible cl (rubbed, soiled). Good. *Argosy.* $100/£65

RUNYON, DAMON. The Tents of Trouble.... NY: Desmond Fitzgerald, (1911). 1st ed. Limp imitation leather cl (sl rubbed, dknd). Good (offset from clipping). *Reese.* $125/£81

RUPP, F.A. Letters of a Physician to His Daughters on the Great Black Plague. Phila, 1910. 1st ed. Good. *Fye.* $50/£32

Rural Scenes or a Peep into the Country. (By Jane Taylor & Ann Gilbert.) London: Darton, Harvey & Darton, n.d. (ca 1818). 12mo. 2 lg cuts on tp, 87 numbered copper engrs on 29 plts (3 crudely repaired; missing eps; lacks pp31-32; last plt w/impt dated Dec 24, 1813, ptd on paper watermkd 1818. Red roan spine, marbled paper on bds (rubbed, chipped; sm holes, spots; ink name). *Hobbyhorse.* $100/£65

RUSCHA, EDWARD. Crackers. Hollywood: Heavy Industry Pub, 1969. 1st ed. Fine in plain stiff wrappers; ptd dj (sl dusty). *Cahan.* $150/£97

RUSCOE, WILLIAM. English Porcelain Figures 1744-1848. London: Tiranti, 1947. 1st ed. Fine in dj. *Pharos.* $20/£13

RUSH, BENJAMIN. The Autobiography.... George W. Corner (ed). Princeton Univ Press, 1948. 1st ed, 2nd ptg. Frontis port, 12 plts. Fine in dj. *Glaser.* $60/£39

RUSH, BENJAMIN. Medical Inquiries and Observations upon the Diseases of the Mind. Phila, 1827. 3rd ed. 365pp. Full leather. (Lib stamp title; hinges reinforced.) *Fye.* $200/£129

RUSH, BENJAMIN. Medical Inquiries and Observations. Vol 2. Phila, 1793. 1st ed. 321pp; errata leaf. Recent 1/4 leather. (Tp, preface leaf strengthened; new eps, else VG.) *Fye.* $350/£226

RUSH, BENJAMIN. Medical Inquiries and Observations: Containing an Account of the Yellow Fever.... Phila, 1798. 1st ed. Vol. 5 of series. 236pp (tp worn; browned; marginal worming 1st few sigs). Mod cl-backed bds. *Argosy.* $175/£113

RUSH, BENJAMIN. Sixteen Introductory Lectures to Courses.... Phila: Bradford & Innskeep, 1811. 1st ed. 455pp. Mod lt brn cl. (Lt foxing.) *Smithfield.* $420/£271

RUSH, NORMAN. Whites. NY: Knopf, 1986. 1st ed, 1st bk. Fine in Fine dj. *Beasley.* $85/£55

RUSH, NORMAN. Whites: Stories. London: Heinemann, (1986). 1st Eng ed, 1st bk. Fine in dj. *Heller.* $75/£48

RUSH, NORMAN. Whites: Stories. NY: Knopf, 1986. 1st ed, 1st bk. Fine in dj (price-clipped). *Heller.* $65/£42

RUSH, OSCAR. The Open Range. Caldwell: Caxton, 1936. 1st ed thus. Color frontis, 27 plts. Illus eps. Pict cl. Fine. Howes R 521. *Oregon.* $75/£48

RUSH, RICHARD. A Residence at the Court of London. London: Richard Bentley, 1833. 1st ed. 16(ads),xviii,420pp. Orig bds (spine dknd). Howes R 522. *Bookpress.* $250/£161

RUSH, RICHARD. A Residence at the Court of London. London: Richard Bentley, 1833. 1st Eng ed. xviii,(ii)420pp. 3/4-grn morocco, marbled bds (sl rubbed, bumped), gilt, marbled edges, eps. NF. Howes R 522. *Blue Mountain.* $175/£113

RUSHBY, G.G. No More the Tusker. London: Allen, 1965. 1st ed. Fine in dj. *Bowman.* $225/£145

RUSHDIE, SALMAN. Grimus. London: Gollancz, 1975. 1st UK ed, 1st bk. NF in dj (top edge sl worn). *Williams.* $186/£120

RUSHDIE, SALMAN. Grimus. Woodstock: Overlook, 1979. 1st US ed. Fine (rmdr line bottom edge) in Fine dj. *Beasley.* $85/£55

RUSHDIE, SALMAN. Haroun and the Sea of Stories. Granta, 1990. One of 251 specially bound, numbered, signed. Fine. *Rees.* $271/£175

RUSHDIE, SALMAN. The Satanic Verses. (London): Viking, (1988). 1st British ed. VF in dj. *Between The Covers.* $250/£161

RUSHDIE, SALMAN. Shame. London: Cape, 1983. 1st ed. Fine in dj. *Rees.* $31/£20

RUSHDIE, SALMAN. Shame. NY: Knopf, 1983. 1st ed. Fine in dj. *Antic Hay.* $35/£23

RUSHDIE, SALMAN. The Wizard of Oz. London: British Film Institute, 1992. 1st ed. Fine in wrappers. *Rees.* $31/£20

RUSHTON, WILLIAM LOWER. Shakespeare an Archer. London: Truslove, 1897. 1st ed. Frontis dwg. Orig grn cl. Fine. *Bowman.* $125/£81

RUSHTON, WILLIAM. W.G. Grace's Last Case. London: Methuen, 1984. 1st ed. Fine in dj. *Silver Door.* $30/£19

RUSHWORTH, W.A. The Sheep. Buffalo, 1899. 496pp. (Cl lt soiled.) *Sutton.* $50/£32

RUSK, RALPH LESLIE. The Literature of the Middle Western Frontier. NY: Columbia Univ, 1925. 1st ed. 2 vols. Grn gilt cl (lt soiled). *Karmiole.* $45/£29

RUSKIN, ARTHUR. Classics in Arterial Hypertension. Springfield: Charles C. Thomas, 1956. 1st ed. Fine in dj. *Glaser.* $85/£55

RUSKIN, JOHN. The Art of England. Orpington: George Allen, 1884. 1st ed. (viii),292pp. Ptd paper spine label. *Bickersteth*. $124/£80

RUSKIN, JOHN. Ethics of the Dust. London: Smith, Elder, 1867. 1st Eng ed. Brn cl, gilt. Sl rubbed, fore-edge sl foxed, o/w VG. *Dalian*. $70/£45

RUSKIN, JOHN. Fors Clavigera. Vols I to III. Orpington: George Allen, 1871-1873. 1st eds. First 36 letters only. Plain bds, ptd paper spine labels. (2 outer joints strengthened w/tape.) *Bickersteth*. $62/£40

RUSKIN, JOHN. The King of the Golden River. London: Harrap, 1939. 1st thus. Arthur Rackham (illus). Fine (ink inscrip) in wrappers as issued. *Williams*. $140/£90

RUSKIN, JOHN. Lectures on Architecture and Painting.... London: George Allen, 1891. 1st ed. Frontis, 15 plts. Minor rubbing; faint foxing eps; else VG. *Bookpress*. $50/£32

RUSKIN, JOHN. Lectures on Art. NY: Wiley & Son, 1870. 1st Amer ed. (viii),202pp. Pub's cl. Spine extrems sl worn; rubberstamps; bottom edge tp shaved, else Bright. *Bookpress*. $150/£97

RUSKIN, JOHN. Lectures on Art. Oxford: Clarendon Press, 1870. 1st Eng ed. Maroon cl, gilt insert. Sl faded, o/w VG. *Dalian*. $54/£35

RUSKIN, JOHN. Letters to M.G. and H.G. NY/London, 1903. 1st ed. Teg. NF (sl rubbed). *Polyanthos*. $30/£19

RUSKIN, JOHN. The Pleasures of England. Orpington: George Allen, 1884. 1st ed. 169,(1)pp. Orig 4 upper wrappers bound in at end. Orig cl; brn morocco spine label (sl chipped). *Bickersteth*. $124/£80

RUSKIN, JOHN. The Poems of John Ruskin. W.G. Collingwood (ed). London: George Allen, 1891. 1st ed. 2 vols. xxviii,289; viii,(ii),360pp; 26 plts. Contents Fine (cvrs sl rubbed; sm holes joints each vol). *Bickersteth*. $78/£50

RUSKIN, JOHN. The Political Economy of Art. London: Smith, Elder, 1857. 1st ed. viii,248pp. Pub's cl (rear hinge internally cracked, pencil few leaves, cvrs sunned, spine extrems chipped). Text VG. *Bookpress*. $150/£97

RUSKIN, JOHN. The Political Economy of Art. London: Smith Elder, 1867. viii,248pp. Grn cl (sl rubbed, soiled; inner hinges cracked). *Cox*. $39/£25

RUSKIN, JOHN. Sesame and Lilies. Portland, ME: Thomas B. Mosher, 1900. 1st ed on Van Gelder paper, ltd to 925. Stiff wraps (soiled, rubbed). *King*. $20/£13

RUSKIN, JOHN. The Seven Lamps of Architecture. London: Smith, Elder, 1849. 1st ed. viii,(iv),205,(1),16pp; 14 plts. Pub's cl (respined using orig as overlay; tips worn). (Spotting; bkpl; hinges internally cracked.) *Bookpress*. $300/£194

RUSKIN, JOHN. The Seven Lamps of Architecture. London: Smith, Elder, 1855. 2nd ed. xv,(iv),206,(ii)pp, 14 engr plts. Blind-stamped cl. Marginal lines, notes, but VG. *Hollett*. $186/£120

RUSKIN, JOHN. The Stones of Venice. George Allen, 1886. 4th ed. 3 vols. 53 plts. (Spotting; fep creased, sm nick vol 3; hinges cracked vol 1; worn.) *Edwards*. $116/£75

RUSKIN, JOHN. The Two Paths. London: Smith, Elder, 1859. 1st ed. x,(2),271,(1)pp, 2 plts. Uncut. 24-pg cat inserted at end dated May 1859. Blocked in blind, gilt lettered backstrip. VG (hinges rubbed). *Cox*. $93/£60

RUSS, JOANNA. The Zanzibar Cat. Arkham House, 1983. 1st ed. Fine in dj. *Madle*. $55/£35

RUSSEL, ERIC FRANK. Three to Conquer. Avalon, 1956. 1st ed. VG in dj (lt scraped, chipped). *Madle*. $45/£29

RUSSEL, J.H. Cattle on the Conejo. Ward Ritchie Press, 1957. 1st ed. Several sm owner name stamps on eps, else VG in VG dj. *Perier*. $40/£26

RUSSEL, OLAND D. House of Mitsui. Boston: Little, Brown, 1939. Color frontis. In dj (chipped, discolored). *Schoyer*. $40/£26

RUSSELL, ALFRED (ed). Selected Essays on Syphilis and Small-Pox. London, 1906. 1st ed. Good. *Fye*. $75/£48

RUSSELL, BERTRAND and PATRICIA (eds). The Amberley Papers. London: Hogarth, 1937. 1st ed. One of 1100 sets for British dist, from total of 1675. 2 vols. Port. Good set (ink name, date each vol; edges sl rubbed; sides sl sunned). *Reese*. $35/£23

RUSSELL, BERTRAND. Authority and the Individual. London: Allen & Unwin, 1949. 1st UK ed. VG + (ink name) in dj. *Williams*. $39/£25

RUSSELL, BERTRAND. Fact and Fiction. London, 1961. 1st ed. Fine in dj (spine sl sunned; corners sl rubbed). *Polyanthos*. $30/£19

RUSSELL, BERTRAND. Human Knowledge. London: Allen & Unwin, 1948. 1st Eng ed. Grn cl. Name, o/w VG in dj (soiled, chipped). *Dalian*. $39/£25

RUSSELL, BERTRAND. Let the People Think. London: Watts, 1941. 1st Eng ed. Brn cl. VF in dj (sl tanned). *Dalian*. $31/£20

RUSSELL, BERTRAND. Satan in the Suburbs. London: Bodley Head, 1953. 1st UK ed. NF in dj (sl rubbed). *Williams*. $23/£15

RUSSELL, BERTRAND. The Scientific Outlook. London: George Allen & Unwin, 1931. 1st Eng ed. Blue cl. Sl mkd, o/w VG in dj (sl tanned, chipped). *Dalian*. $39/£25

RUSSELL, BERTRAND. What I Believe. London: Kegan Paul et al, 1925. 1st ed. Nice. *Temple*. $22/£14

RUSSELL, BERTRAND. Why I Am not a Christian. London: Watts, 1927. 1st bk ed. VG in sm wraps. *Lame Duck*. $150/£97

RUSSELL, CHARLES EDWARD. A-Rafting on the Mississip'. NY: Century, (1928). 1st ed. Pub's blue cl, gilt on spine; blind-stamped fr cvr, pict paper label inset. Fine. *Laurie*. $90/£58

RUSSELL, CHARLES EDWARD. A-Rafting on the Mississippi. NY: The Century Co., 1928. 1st ed. Fine in NF dj. *Beasley*. $100/£65

RUSSELL, CHARLES M. Good Medicine. GC: Doubleday, (1929). Dec eps. VG (cvr sl discolored). *Smithfield*. $33/£21

RUSSELL, CHARLES M. Trails Plowed Under. NY, 1936. VG in dj. *Argosy*. $75/£48

RUSSELL, CHARLIE L. Five on the Black Hand Side. NY: Third Press, (1969). 1st ed. Grey cl. NF in dj. *Godot*. $50/£32

RUSSELL, DON. The Lives and Legends of Buffalo Bill. Norman: Univ of OK, (1960). 1st ed. Advance copy, pub's card. VG (sig) in dj. *Schoyer*. $50/£32

RUSSELL, E.F. Dark Tides. Dobson, 1962. 1st ed. VG + in NF dj. *Aronovitz*. $150/£97

RUSSELL, E.F. Deep Space. Fantasy Press, 1954. 1st ed. NF in dj (chip). *Aronovitz*. $48/£31

RUSSELL, E.F. Sentinels from Space. Bouregy & Curl, 1953. 1st ed. NF in dj. *Aronovitz*. $77/£50

RUSSELL, E.F. Sinister Barrier. Fantasy Press, 1948. 1st ed. Fine in VG + dj (2 sm chips). *Aronovitz*. $65/£42

RUSSELL, FRANK (ed). A Century of Chair Design. NY: Rizzoli, (1980). 1st ed. Frontis. Bkpl else Fine in sl rubbed dj. *Bookpress.* $50/£32

RUSSELL, H.S. A Long, Deep Furrow. Hanover, 1976. (Bkpl.) Dj. *Sutton.* $45/£29

RUSSELL, HAROLD. Chalkstream and Moorland. London: Smith, 1911. 1st ed. Fine. *Bowman.* $25/£16

RUSSELL, I.C. Glaciers of North America. Boston, 1897. 22 plts. (Worn, frayed; ex-lib.) *Sutton.* $30/£19

RUSSELL, JOHN and SUZI GABLIK. Pop Art Redefined. NY: Frederick A. Praeger, (1969). 192 plts (17 color). Good in dj. *Karmiole.* $40/£26

RUSSELL, JOHN ANDREW. The Germanic Influence in the Making of Michigan. Univ of Detroit, 1927. 1st ed. Full gilt-stamped morocco, 5 raised bands. News clipping tipped in. Fine. *Artis.* $75/£48

RUSSELL, JOHN. Paris. NY: Viking, 1960. 1st ed. Owner stamp ep, few pencil notes, else VG in illus dj. *Cahan.* $85/£55

RUSSELL, MORRIS C. Uncle Dudley's Odd Hours. Lake City, MN: Privately ptd, 1904. 1st ed. 1 port plt. Uncut, partly unopened. Fine in tied wrap. Howes M 536. *Oregon.* $300/£194

RUSSELL, MORRIS C. Uncle Dudley's Odd Hours. Lake City, MN: Home Printery, 1904. Presentation copy from 'The Perpetrator.' Port. Tied in ptd wraps. VG (lt wear; spine ends torn). *Bohling.* $250/£161

RUSSELL, OSBORNE. Journal of a Trapper or Nine Years in the Rocky Mountains, 1834-1843. (Boise: Syms-York), 1921. 2nd ed. Ltd to 100. Bkpl, faint stamp, else VG. Howes R 537. *Perier.* $175/£113

RUSSELL, OSBORNE. Journal of a Trapper, or Nine Years in the Rocky Mountains 1834-1843. Boise, 1921. 2nd ed. Letter taped to fep. VG (pencil margin notes). Howes R 537. *Oregon.* $350/£226

RUSSELL, PHILLIPS. John Paul Jones, Man of Action. NY: Brentano, 1927. 1st ed. Frontis; 11 plts; illus eps. Gilt-stamped pict cl. VG. *Oregon.* $30/£19

RUSSELL, PHILLIPS. These Old Stone Walls. Chapel Hill, (1973). 1st ed, 2nd ptg. Fine in NF dj. *Mcgowan.* $37/£24

RUSSELL, R. A Dissertation on the Use of Sea-Water in the Diseases of the Glands. London, 1752. 1st Eng ed. Frontis; xii,240pp (dampstains prelims). *Whitehart.* $279/£180

RUSSELL, R. Guide to British Topographical Prints. David & Charles, 1979. Fine in dj. *Moss.* $37/£24

RUSSELL, RACHEL. Letters. London: Longman, Brown, etc, 1852. 2 vols. 2 engr frontispieces, titles; xii,289; viii,231pp. Orig cl; paper labels. (Extrems sl frayed; labels worn.) *Hollett.* $70/£45

RUSSELL, SCOTT. Mountain Prospect. London, 1946. 1st ed. 46 plts (sm spike mk through lower cvr, final 20pp). *Bickersteth.* $31/£20

RUSSELL, THOMAS. Egyptian Service 1902-1946. London: John Murray, (1949). 3 maps. (Sig; corners bumped.) Dj (tattered). *Archaeologia.* $25/£16

RUSSELL, VIRGIL Y. Indian Artifacts. (Boulder: Johnson, 1962.) Enlgd ed, 4th ptg. Ink name, else VG in dj (torn). *Perier.* $35/£23

RUSSELL, W. CLARK. The Turnpike Sailor or Rhymes on the Road. London: Skeffington & Son, 1907. 1st Eng ed. Grn pict cl. Sl rubbed, faded, o/w VG. *Dalian.* $39/£25

RUSSELL, WILLIAM HOWARD. The British Expedition to the Crimea. London, 1858. Rev ed. 629pp + ads; 4 fldg maps/plans in pocket. (Cl stained, backstrip worn at head, tail.) *Argosy.* $150/£97

RUSSELL, WILLIAM HOWARD. Complete History of the Russian War. NY: J.G. Wells, 1856. Tinted litho frontis, (185)pp (foxed) + 3pp ads, 2 lg fldg color maps (1 stained), fldg woodcut (chipped). Black cl stamped in blind, gilt (spine worn; mks). *Schoyer.* $45/£29

RUSSELL, WILLIAM HOWARD. A Diary in the East during the Tour of the Prince and Princess of Wales. London: Routledge, 1869. xv,650pp, 6 color plts. (Bkpl.) *Archaeologia.* $75/£48

RUSSELL, WILLIAM HOWARD. My Diary North and South. London: Bradbury & Evans, 1863. 1st ed. 2 vols. 424; 442pp, fldg map (crudely repaired on verso). Orig emb blue cl. Good (lib bkpls, blind-stamps; hinges broken). Howes R 540. *Chapel Hill.* $200/£129

RUSSO, DOROTHY RITTER. A Bibliography of George Ade 1866-1944. Indianapolis: IN Hist Soc, 1947. 1st ed. Inscribed. Teg. Orig 2-tone cl, spine pict gilt-stamped. NF. *Sadlon.* $45/£29

RUSSO, RICHARD. Mohawk. London: Heinemann, 1987. 1st British ed, 1st hb ptg, 1st bk. Fine in Fine dj. *Pettler.* $75/£48

RUSSO, RICHARD. Risk Pool. NY, (1988). 1st ed. Fine in Fine dj. *Fuller & Saunders.* $35/£23

RUST, BRIAN. The American Record Label Book. New Rochelle: Arlington House, 1978. 1st US ed. Fine (rmdr mk) in dj (lt rubbed). *Beasley.* $85/£55

RUST, WILLIAM. Britons in Spain. A History of the British Battalion of the XVth International Brigade. London: Lawrence & Wishart, 1939. 1st ed. Fine in dj. *Patterson.* $78/£50

RUSTON, ARTHUR G. and DENIS WITNEY. Hooton Pagnell. London: Edward Arnold, 1934. 1st ed. 11 plts. Fore-edge lt spotted, o/w Fine in dj. *Hollett.* $101/£65

RUTH, GEORGE HERMAN. Babe Ruth's Own Book of Baseball. Putnam's, 1928. 1st ed. Good+ in Good dj. *Plapinger.* $175/£113

RUTHERFORD, ERNEST. Radioactivity. Cambridge: University Press, 1904. 1st ed. Plt. Gilt cl. VG. *Argosy.* $750/£484

RUTHERFORD, JOHN. Siege of Detroit in 1763: The Journal of Pontiac's Conspiracy.... Chicago: Lakeside Press, R.R. Donnelley, 1958. 1st ed. Teg. Fine in box. Reissue of Howes R 546. *Cahan.* $30/£19

RUTHERFORD, JOHN. Troubadours. London: Smith, Elder, 1873. x,356pp. Blue cl stamped in black/gilt (soiled, stained). *Schoyer.* $55/£35

RUTLEDGE, ARCHIBALD. Collected Poems. Columbia, SC: State Co, 1925. 1st ed. Inscribed, signed. Frontis port. Blue cl. NF in VG dj (lt soiled). *Chapel Hill.* $225/£145

RUTTER, JOAN (comp). Here's Flowers. London: Golden Cockerel Press, 1937. #62/200. Teg, rest uncut. 1/4 blue morocco, marbled sides (backstrip faded). *Petersfield.* $186/£120

RUTTER, JOAN (comp). Here's Flowers: An Anthology of Flower Poems. London: Golden Cockerel, (1937). One of 200. Blue leather spine, gilt title; marbled paper bds. Spine, edges sl dknd, else Fine. *Heller.* $350/£226

RUTTLEDGE, HUGH. Everest 1933. London: Hodder & Stoughton, 1934. 1st ed. 59 plts; 4 fldg maps. (Edges spotted.) *Hollett.* $116/£75

RUTTLEDGE, HUGH. Everest: The Unfinished Adventure. London: Hodder & Stoughton, 1937. 1st ed. 2 lg fldg maps; portfolio of 63 plts. Blue cl gilt. VG. *Hollett.* $116/£75

RUXTON, GEORGE F. Life in the Far West. LeRoy Hafen (ed). Univ OK, (1951). 1st thus. 12 plts. VF in VG dj. Howes R 554. *Oregon.* $35/£23

RUXTON, GEORGE F. Life in the Far West. Leroy R. Hafen (ed). Norman, (1951). 1st ed of this rpt ed. Good in dj (sl worn). *Hayman.* $25/£16

RYAN, ALAN. Cast a Cold Eye. Dark Harvest, 1984. 1st ed. Fine in dj. *Madle.* $60/£39

RYAN, W.M. Shamrock and Cactus. San Antonio/Houston: Southern Literary Inst, 1936. 1st ed. Cl in dj. *Lambeth.* $75/£48

RYDELL, RAYMOND A. Cape Horn to the Pacific. Berkeley: Univ of CA, 1952. 1st ed. Map. Blue cl; gilt. Good in dj. *Karmiole.* $30/£19

RYDER, JONATHAN. (Pseud of Robert Ludlum.) The Cry of the Halidon. Delacorte, 1974. 1st ed. Fine in dj (edges worn, chipped). *Stahr.* $25/£16

RYDER, LILIAN. A Child's Story of Jesus in Living Pictures. (Manchester): World, n.d. (1950). 20x16 cm. 4 pop-ups. Carl Haworth (illus). VG-. *Book Finders.* $90/£58

RYDJORD, JOHN. Indian Place Names. Norman: Univ of OK, (1968). 1st ed. Fine in VG dj. *Perier.* $35/£23

RYE, E.C. British Beetles. London, 1866. xvi,280pp; 16 hand-colored plts. (Sl used.) *Wheldon & Wesley.* $54/£35

RYE, E.C. British Beetles. London, 1866. 1st ed. xv,280pp; 16 ads; 16 hand-colored plts. (Spine sl faded, worn.) *Henly.* $101/£65

RYLANDS, GEORGE. Poems. Hogarth Press, 1931. Ltd to 350 signed. Spine, edges faded, o/w VG. *Words Etc.* $116/£75

RYMILL, JOHN. Southern Lights. C&W, 1938. 1st ed. 8 maps. VG+ in dj (torn w/some loss). *Walcot.* $140/£90

RYNNING, THOMAS H. Gun Notches: The Life Story of a Cowboy-Soldier. NY: F.A. Stokes, 1931. 1st ed. Dec ep. Untrimmed. Yellow cl, grn letters. Internally Fine (spine top softened, short tear). *Connolly.* $50/£32

RYUS, WILLIAM. The Second William Penn—A True Account of Incidents That Happened along the Old Santa Fe Trail in the Sixties. Kansas City: Frank Riley, (1913). Pict cl. VG. *Perier.* $50/£32

RYUS, WILLIAM. The Second William Penn. Kansas City: Frank T. Riley, 1913. Frontis. Fine in ptd wraps. *Parmer.* $35/£23

RYWELL, MARTIN. The Trial of Samuel Colt. Harriman, TN: Pioneer Press, 1953. 1st ed. One of 1000. Gilt-emb cl. VG in dj (edgetorn). *Cahan.* $85/£55

S

S. Weir Mitchell: Memorial Addresses and Resolutions. Phila, 1914. 1st ed. Port present. Good. *Fye.* $100/£65

SAARINEN, ALINE B. (ed). Eero Saarinen on His Work. New Haven, 1962. 1st ed. Cl-backed bds. VG in slipcase (defective). *King.* $125/£81

SAARINEN, EERO. Eero Sarrinen on His Work. New Haven: Yale, 1962. 1st ed. Fine in slipcase (worn). *Bookpress.* $150/£97

SAARTO, MARTHA. Finnish Textiles. Leigh-on-Sea: F. Lewis, 1954. 1st ed. Blank leaves lt foxed, else VG in dj. *Cahan.* $50/£32

SABARTES, JAIME. Picasso, an Intimate Portrait. London: Allen, 1949. 1st British ed. Fine in dj. *Europa.* $25/£16

SABATINI, RAFAEL. Bellarion. Hutchinson, 1926. 1st ed. VG+ in pict dj (wear, chipping). *Fine Books.* $125/£81

SABATINI, RAFAEL. Columbus. Houghton Mifflin, 1942. 1st ed. Fine in dj. *Madle.* $50/£32

SABATINI, RAFAEL. Fortune's Fool. Hutchinson, 1923. 1st ed. NF in VG pict dj (lt worn, chipped). *Fine Books.* $125/£81

SABATINI, RAFAEL. Fortune's Fool. London: Hutchinson, n.d. (1923). 1st ed. Fine in pict dj (lt edge, corner wear). *Else Fine.* $295/£190

SABATINI, RAFAEL. The Historical Nights' Entertainment. London: Martin Secker, n.d. (1917). 1st ed. Label sl rubbed, chipped, o/w NF. *Temple.* $22/£14

SABATINI, RAFAEL. The Hounds of God. Hutchinson, 1928. 1st ed. NF in pict dj. *Fine Books.* $150/£97

SABATINI, RAFAEL. The Hounds of God. London: Hutchinson, n.d. (1928). 1st ed. Fine in pict dj (sl spine fade). *Else Fine.* $350/£226

SABATINI, RAFAEL. The Lost King. Boston: Houghton-Mifflin, 1937. 1st ed. NF in pict dj (lt edgewear, spine corner chipped). *Else Fine.* $50/£32

SABATINI, RAFAEL. Master-At-Arms. H-M, 1940. 1st ed. VG in VG dj (sl wear). *Fine Books.* $50/£32

SABATINI, RAFAEL. Saint Martin's Summer. Houghton Mifflin, 1924. 1st ed. Fine in dj. *Madle.* $75/£48

SABATINI, RAFAEL. The Strolling Saint. Houghton Mifflin, 1926. Fine in dj (chipped). *Madle.* $35/£23

SABATINI, RAFAEL. The Sword of Islam. Hutchinson, 1938. 1st ed. VG in VG dj (lt chipping spine head; price circle excised from spine). *Fine Books.* $85/£55

SABATINI, RAFAEL. Torquemada and the Spanish Inquisition. Houghton Mifflin, 1930. 1st rev ed. Fine in dj (sl frayed). *Madle.* $50/£32

SABATINI, RAFAEL. The Trampling of the Lilies. London: Hutchinson, 1906. 1st ed. Prelims sl foxed, but Nice. *Temple.* $37/£24

SABIN, EDWARD. Kit Carson's Days. NY: Press of Pioneers, 1935. Signed rev copy, #110/200. 2 vols. VG (stain fep) in box (worn). *Parker.* $275/£177

SABINE, E. (ed). North Georgia Gazette and Winter Chronicle. (By W.E. Parry.) London: John Murray, 1821. xii,132pp. Good+ (edges worn; bumped). *Walcot.* $271/£175

SABINE, ELLEN. American Folk Art. NY, (1958). 12 photo plts. VG in dj (soiled). *Argosy.* $40/£26

SABRETACHE. Monarchy and the Chase. London: Eyre & Spottiswoode, (1948). 1st ed. Frontis. Fine in dj. *Oregon.* $27/£17

SACHER-MASOCH, LEOPOLD. Venus in Furs. N.p., 1921. #774/1225. Fine (sl soiled, rubbed). *Polyanthos.* $35/£23

SACHS, ERNEST. The Diagnosis and Treatment of Brain Tumors. St. Louis, 1931. 1st ed. Good. *Fye.* $150/£97

SACHS, MAURICE. Day of Wrath. London: Arthur Barker, 1953. 1st Eng ed. Grey cl. Fore-edge, eps sl foxed, name stamp, o/w NF in dj (sl torn, chipped). *Dalian.* $39/£25

SACHS, MAURICE. Witches Sabbath. London: Jonathan Cape, 1965. 1st Eng ed. Grey cl. Fine in dj. *Dalian.* $47/£30

SACKETT, ROSE McLAUGHLIN. The Cousin from Clare. NY: Macmillan, 1932. 1st ed. 8vo. 4 full-pg b/w plts by Marguerite De Angeli. Grn cl, black lettering. Good in pict dj (edgetorn 3/4-inch piece missing not affecting illus). *Reisler.* $85/£55

SACKLER, HOWARD. The Great White Hope. NY: Dial, 1968. 1st ed. Fine in dj (rubbing; interior mend). *Antic Hay.* $25/£16

SACKS, OLIVER. Awakenings. NY: Doubleday, 1974. 1st ed. Offsetting eps, else NF- in VG dj (surface loss to extrems). *Lame Duck.* $100/£65

SACKVILLE-WEST, EDWARD. The Apology of Arthur Rimbaud. Hogarth Press, 1927. 1st ed. Edges faded, o/w VG. *Words Etc.* $62/£40

SACKVILLE-WEST, EDWARD. The Rescue. London: Secker & Warburg, 1945. #445/850. 6 color plts by Henry Moore. Teg, rest uncut. Good in blue buckram (faded); remains of dj. *Cox.* $70/£45

SACKVILLE-WEST, EDWARD. Simpson. London: Heinemann, 1931. 1st Eng ed. Grn cl. VF (bkpl) in dj (sl tanned, sl chipped). *Dalian.* $39/£25

SACKVILLE-WEST, VITA. Collected Poems: Vol I. Hogarth, 1933. 1st ed. VG. *Whiteson.* $43/£28

SACKVILLE-WEST, VITA. Country Notes. NY/London: Harper, 1940. 1st ed. NF. *Quest.* $80/£52

SACKVILLE-WEST, VITA. The Dark Island. Hogarth, 1934. 1st ed. VG+ in VG dj (worn, chipped). *Fine Books.* $140/£90

SACKVILLE-WEST, VITA. The Death of Noble Godavary. London: Benn, 1935. 1st UK ed. Spine sl rubbed, fep sl creased, o/w VG in wraps. *Lewton.* $19/£12

SACKVILLE-WEST, VITA. The Death of Noble Godvary and Gottfried Kunstler. London: Ernest Benn, 1936. 1st Eng ed. Blue ptd wrappers. Sl dusty, o/w VG as issued w/o dj. *Dalian.* $39/£25

SACKVILLE-WEST, VITA. The Eagle and the Dove. NY: Doubleday, Doran, 1944. 1st Amer ed. Fine in dj. *Hermitage.* $45/£29

SACKVILLE-WEST, VITA. The Edwardians. Hogarth, 1930. 1st ed. Contents VG (spine sl faded; binding sl dull). *Whiteson.* $34/£22

SACKVILLE-WEST, VITA. English Country Houses. London: Collins, 1941. 1st Eng ed. 12 color plts. Grn paper bds. Eps sl foxed, o/w Fine in dj (sl dusty, tanned). *Dalian.* $39/£25

SACKVILLE-WEST, VITA. Grand Canyon. London: Michael Joseph, 1942. 1st UK ed. Fine in VG+ dj. *Williams.* $74/£48

SACKVILLE-WEST, VITA. Grey Wethers. London: Heinemann, 1923. 1st UK ed. Grey cl. Top edge sl dusty, o/w NF. *Moorhouse.* $78/£50

SACKVILLE-WEST, VITA. Knole and the Sackvilles. London, 1922. 1st ed. Frontis port. Sackville-West's inscribed calling card tipped-in. Uncut. (Spotting; feps lt browned.) Orig cl (lt soiled). *Edwards.* $70/£45

SACKVILLE-WEST, VITA. Knole and the Sackvilles. London: Heinemann, 1923. Lg 8vo. Frontis, 24 full-pg plts. Fine (lg inscrip fep). *Quest.* $110/£71

SACKVILLE-WEST, VITA. Knoll and the Sackvilles. NY: Doran, n.d. (1922?). 1st Amer ed from British sheets w/a cancel tp. Doran imprint spine foot, pub's device back cvr. Pict cl. Existence of Doran dj uncertain. Fine. *Pharos.* $250/£161

SACKVILLE-WEST, VITA. The Land. London: Heinemann, 1926. 1st ed. Partly unopened. Dk terra cotta cl. *Cady.* $100/£65

SACKVILLE-WEST, VITA. Orchard and Vineyard. London: John Lane, Bodley Head, 1921. 1st Eng ed. Grey-backed paper bds. Mkd; fore-edge, eps foxed, browned, o/w VG. *Dalian.* $132/£85

SACKVILLE-WEST, VITA. Saint Joan of Arc. London: Cobden-Sanderson, 1936. 1st Eng ed. Orange cl. Sl dusty, o/w VG. *Dalian.* $31/£20

SACKVILLE-WEST, VITA. Seducers in Ecuador. NY: Doran, (1925). 1st US ed. Cl-backed paper bds, paper label (sl worn). Good (presentation; 1/2 title pasted to ep). *Second Life.* $35/£23

SACKVILLE-WEST, VITA. Seducers in Ecuador. London: Hogarth Press, 1924. 1st ed. Mottled red, black cl; paper label (faded). *Argosy.* $100/£65

SACKVILLE-WEST, VITA. Sissinghurst. London: Hogarth, 1931. 1st ed. One of 500 numbered, signed. Few spine nicks, o/w Very Nice. *Reese.* $225/£145

SACKVILLE-WEST, VITA. Some Flowers. London: Cobden-Sanderson, 1937. 1st ed. Dec paper cvrs (spine worn, lacks sm piece head). VG (author photo pasted tp). *Quest.* $90/£58

SACKVILLE-WEST, VITA. Twelve Days. Hogarth Press, 1928. 32 plts. (Lt browning.) Dj (sl worn, loss). *Edwards.* $194/£125

SACKVILLE-WEST, VITA. Women's Land Army. London: Michael Joseph, 1944. 1st ed. Spine sunned, else Fine. *Quest.* $40/£26

Sacramento Guide Book. Sacramento Bee, (1939). 1st ed. Fldg map. VG. *Oregon.* $45/£29

SADDLEBAGS, JEREMIAH. (Pseud of J.A. & D.F. Read.) Journey to the Gold Diggins. Burlingame, CA: Wm. Wreden, 1950. One of 390. Cl-backed patterned bds, ptd spine label. VG+ (bkpl) in plain dj (dknd, chipped, worn). Howes R 92. *Bohling.* $80/£52

SADLEIR, MICHAEL. Archdeacon Francis Wrangham, 1769-1842. Oxford: Bibliographical Soc, 1937. 1st ed. 4 plts. (Ex-lib; chipped). Wrappers. *Bookpress.* $45/£29

SADLEIR, MICHAEL. Archdeacon Francis Wrangham, 1769-1842. Oxford: Bibliographical Soc, 1937. 1st ed. 4 plts. Spine sunned, else Fine in wrappers. *Bookpress.* $65/£42

SADLEIR, MICHAEL. Authors and Publishers. London: J.M. Dent, 1939. Rpt. Marbled bds, gilt. VF in Fine dj. *Dalian.* $23/£15

SADLEIR, MICHAEL. Blessington D'Orsay. London: Constable, 1947. New, enlgd ed. Maroon cl. VF in dj. *Dalian.* $31/£20

SADLEIR, MICHAEL. Blessington-D'orsay, a Masquerade. London: Constable, (1933). 1st ed. 16 gravure plts. (Cvr lt rubbed; eps foxed.) *Oak Knoll.* $45/£29

SADLEIR, MICHAEL. Daumier; The Man and the Artist. London: Halton & Truscott, 1924. One of 700. (Bkpl.) *Argosy.* $125/£81

SADLEIR, MICHAEL. Desolate Splendour. NY: Putnam's, 1923. 1st US ed. (Lettering flaked off.) *Oak Knoll.* $15/£10

SADLEIR, MICHAEL. Excursions in Victorian Bibliography. London, 1922. 1st ed. Errata slip. Fine in dj. *Argosy.* $100/£65

SADLEIR, MICHAEL. Forlorn Sunset. London: Constable, 1947. 1st ed. Frontis, 2 maps, 2 plts. Spine sl wrinkled; top edge faded, o/w Fine in dj (frayed, dusty). *Temple.* $12/£8

SADLEIR, MICHAEL. Modern Art and Revolution. Hogarth Press, 1932. 1st ed. Sm chip upper wrapper, edges sl browned, o/w VG. *Words Etc.* $62/£40

SADLEIR, MICHAEL. Things Past. London: Constable, (1944). 1st ed. (Cvrs faded.) *Oak Knoll.* $20/£13

SADLEIR, MICHAEL. XIX Century Fiction. Cambridge Univ Press, (1951). 1st ed, one of 1025. 2 vols. VG. *Argosy.* $400/£258

SAFFIN, JOHN. John Saffin. His Book (1665-1708). NY: Harbor Press, 1928. *Boswell.* $75/£48

SAFFORD, CARLETON and ROBERT BISHOP. America's Quilts and Coverlets. NY, (1974). VG in dj. *Argosy.* $60/£39

SAGAN, FRANCOISE. Bonjour Tristesse. Irene Ash (trans). London, (1955). 1st Eng ed, 1st bk. Fine in dj (worn; loss extrems). *Waterfield.* $70/£45

SAGAN, FRANCOISE. Those without Shadows. London: John Murray, 1957. 1st Eng ed. Red cl. Fine in dj. *Dalian.* $31/£20

SAID, EDWARD. Orientalism. NY: Pantheon, 1978. 1st ed. NF in NF dj. *Lame Duck.* $75/£48

Sailor Boy. London: Religious Tract Soc, n.d. (ca 1865). 12mo. 8 leaves, 7 full-pg chromolithos (lt offset verso). Rebound w/handmade paper, old eps. VG. *Hobbyhorse.* $95/£61

SAINT-GAUDENS, HOMER. The American Artist and His Times. NY, 1941. Color frontis. (Bkpl.) Dj. *Argosy.* $100/£65

SAINTSBURY, GEORGE. A Last Scrapbook. London: Macmillan, 1924. 1st ed. Top, lower edges uncut; fore-edges rough-trimmed. Bkmk ad loosely laid in as issued. Cvrs lt mottled; lt foxing few ll, o/w Fine in dj (nicked). *Temple.* $19/£12

SAINTSBURY, GEORGE. A Primer of French Literature. Oxford, 1880. 1st ed, 1st bk. Sm 8vo. Limp cl-cvrd bds. VG- (spine top frayed; pencil notations reps). *Lame Duck.* $100/£65

SAINTSBURY, GEORGE. A Saintsbury Miscellany. NY: OUP, 1947. 1st US ed. Fine in dj. *Oak Knoll.* $35/£23

SAISSELIN, REMY G. Style, Truth, and the Portrait. (Cleveland): Cleveland Museum of Art, (1963). 1st ed. Frontis. (Bkpl; ink underlining.) Dj (sunned). *Bookpress.* $35/£23

SAJOUS, CHARLES. The Internal Secretions and The Principles of Medicine. Phila, 1903-07. 1st ed. 2 vols. (Ex-lib.) *Fye.* $125/£81

SAJOUS, CHARLES. The Internal Secretions and The Principles of Medicine. Phila, 1911. 4th ed. 2 vols. Good. *Fye.* $50/£32

SAJOUS, CHARLES. Lectures on Diseases of the Nose and Throat. Phila, 1885. 1st ed. 439pp. 1/2 leather. Good. *Fye.* $75/£48

SAKI. (Pseud of Hector H. Munro). Beasts and Super-Beasts. London/NY/Toronto: John Lane, Bodley Head/John Lane/Bell & Cockburn, 1914. 1st ed. Blind-blocked, spine gilt-lettered. (Early pp lt spotted.) *Bickersteth.* $171/£110

SAKI. (Pseud of Hector H. Munro.) The Chronicles of Clovis. London/NY: John Lane, Bodley Head/John Lane, 1912. 1st ed. Grn pict cl. Excellent (prelims, title lt spotted). *Bickersteth.* $171/£110

SAKI. (Pseud of Hector H. Munro.) Reginald in Russia and Other Sketches. London: Methuen, (1910). 1st ed. Blue cl, gilt lettering. *Bickersteth.* $171/£110

SAKI. (Pseud of Hector H. Munro.) Reginald. London: Methuen, (1904). 1st ed. Fine. *Bickersteth.* $186/£120

SAKI. (Pseud of Hector H. Monro.) The Square Egg and Other Sketches. London: John Lane, Bodley Head, 1924. 1st Eng ed. Purple cl. Mkd, rubbed, eps sl browned, o/w VG. *Dalian.* $70/£45

SAKI. (Pseud of Hector H. Munro.) The Square Egg and Other Sketches.... London: John Lane, Bodley Head, (1924). 1st ed. Port. Blind-stamped cl, gilt-lettered spine. *Bickersteth.* $174/£112

SAKI. (Pseud of Hector H. Munro.) The Unbearable Bassington. London/NY/Toronto: John Lane, Bodley Head/John Lane/Bell & Cockburn, 1912. 1st ed. Blue cl, gilt spine (faded; name). *Bickersteth.* $171/£110

SAKI. (Pseud of Hector H. Munro.) The Westminster Alice. London, 1902. 1st separate ed. Orig ptd wrappers. *Bickersteth.* $70/£45

SAKI. (Pseud of Hector H. Munro.) The Westminster Alice. London: Westminster Gazette, 1902. 1st UK ed. Good in pict wraps (foxed, browned; ink name). *Williams.* $147/£95

SAKI. (Pseud of Hector H. Munro.) When William Came. London/NY/Toronto: John Lane, Bodley Head/John Lane/Bell & Cockburn, 1914. 1st ed. Red cl, blind-blocked, gilt-lettered. Fine (lower cvr spotted). *Bickersteth.* $178/£115

Salad for the Solitary by an Epicure. (By Frederick Saunders.) London: Richard Bentley, 1853. 1st ed. iv,284pp. (Ex-lib, w/stamp, blind stamps.) Blind-stamped cl (recased; fore-edges sl damped), gilt. *Hollett.* $70/£45

SALAMAN, MALCOLM C. The Etchings of James McBey. London/NY, 1929. Frontis, 96 plts. Teg, rest uncut. (Bkpl; spotting, feps browned; upper hinge cracked; upper joint split, lower joint tender; spine chipped w/loss.) *Edwards.* $62/£40

SALAMAN, MALCOLM C. The Etchings of Sir Francis Seymour Haden. London, 1923. 96 plts, guards. Teg; uncut, partly unopened. (Backstrip chipped.) *Argosy.* $85/£55

SALAMAN, MALCOLM C. London Past and Present. London: The Studio, Winter 1915-16. VG (lt wear, foxing) in ptd paper wraps. *Willow House.* $31/£20

SALAMAN, MALCOLM C. Londoners Then and Now.... London: The Studio, 1920. 8 color plts. Generally VG in paper wraps (soiled). *Willow House.* $31/£20

SALAMAN, MALCOLM C. The New Woodcut. London: Studio Ltd, 1930. Special Spring Number, 1930. Fine in stiff paper wrappers (chipped). *Oak Knoll.* $55/£35

SALAMAN, MALCOLM C. Old English Colour-Prints. Charles Holme (ed). London: The Studio, 1909. 40 color mtd plts. (Cl rubbed, faded.) *Karmiole.* $30/£19

SALAMAN, MALCOLM C. The Woodcut of To-Day, at Home and Abroad. Geoffrey Holme (ed). London: The Studio, 1927. Tipped-in color frontis, 7 tipped-in color plts. (Margins thumbed.) Rebound lib morocco-backed cl bds (ex-lib). *Edwards.* $47/£30

SALAME, A. A Narrative of the Expedition to Algiers in 1816.... London, 1819. 1st ed. cxliv,231pp; plan, 3 fldg plts (1 color). Calf spine (rebound), marbled bds (mkd, used throughout). *Lewis.* $302/£195

SALE, EDITH TUNIS. Colonial Interiors. NY: William Helburn, 1930. 1st ed. 159 plts. (Lt foxing; inscrip; worn.) *Bookpress.* $65/£42

SALE, EDITH TUNIS. Historic Gardens of Virginia. Richmond: James River Garden Club, 1923. 1st ed. One of 1000. Color frontis w/guard. VG (sl foxing, inscrip) in pub's slipcase (worn). *Cahan.* $85/£55

SALE, EDITH TUNIS. Interiors of Virginia Houses of Colonial Times. Richmond: William Byrd, 1927. 1st ed. Lettering rubbed, else VG. Howes S 49. *Cahan.* $100/£65

SALE, EDITH TUNIS. Interiors of Virginia Houses of Colonial Times.... Richmond, VA: William Byrd Press Inc, 1927. 1st ed. 371 plts. Blue dec cl. Good in dj (chipped). *Karmiole.* $85/£55

SALE, EDITH TUNIS. Manors of Virginia in Colonial Times. Lippincott, 1909. 1st ed. Good (borders waterstained; lacks fr fly). *Book Broker.* $45/£29

SALEEBY, C. Surgery and Society, A Tribute to Listerism. NY, 1912. Good. *Fye.* $50/£32

SALINGER, J.D. The Catcher in the Rye. Boston: Little, Brown, 1951. 1st Book Club ptg. VG in earliest state dj w/photo of Salinger back panel (nicks, creases; lt soiling). *Houle.* $275/£177

SALINGER, J.D. The Catcher in the Rye. London: Hamish Hamilton, 1951. 1st ed, 1st bk. Pg torn, o/w VG in dj (sl chipped, rubbed, internally strengthened). *Rees.* $233/£150

SALINGER, J.D. The Catcher in the Rye. London: Hamish Hamilton, 1951. 1st Eng ed. Inscrip, top edges sl dusty, else VG in dj (sl worn, frayed at spine extrems; missing sm piece at head). *Limestone.* $350/£226

SALINGER, J.D. For Esme—with Love and Squalor. Hamish Hamilton, 1953. 1st ed. Edges sl dusty, o/w NF in dj. *Rees.* $271/£175

SALINGER, J.D. Franny and Zooey. Boston/Toronto: Little, Brown, (1961). 1st ed. NF in dj. *Bernard.* $100/£65

SALINGER, J.D. Raise High the Roof Beam, Carpenter and Seymour, an Introduction. Boston, 1963. 2nd state of 1st ed, i.e., w/dedication pg bound, not tipped in. Sunfaded spine, else VF. *Bond.* $13/£8

SALINGER, J.D. Raise High the Roof Beam, Carpenters and Seymour, an Introduction. Boston, (1963). 1st ed, 3rd state. Name, else VG in dj (frayed, torn). *King.* $35/£23

SALINGER, J.D. Raise High the Roof Beam, Carpenters, and Seymour, an Introduction. London: Heinemann, 1963. 1st UK ed. Fine in VG dj (partial cocktail ring). *Beasley.* $60/£39

SALINGER, J.D. Raise High the Roof Beam. Boston: Little, Brown, (1963). 1st ed, 3rd state of dedication. Fine in VG dj (lt nicked). *Reese.* $20/£13

SALISBURY, ALBERT and JANE. Two Captains West. Seattle: Superior Pub Co, (1950). 1st ed. VG. *Graf.* $25/£16

SALISBURY, ALBERT. Here Rolled the Covered Wagons. Superior, (1948). 1st ed. Ltd to 2050 numbered. Signed, inscribed presentation. VG. *Oregon.* $35/£23

SALMI, MARIO et al. Drawings of Michelangelo. NY: George Braziller, 1965. 2-tone cl. VG. *Argosy.* $150/£97

Salmon and Sea Trout Fishing. (By David Foster.) London/Derby: Bemrose & Sons, c. 1902. Ptd pict wrapper. *Petersfield.* $78/£50

SALMON, J.T. The Native Trees of New Zealand. Wellington, 1981. VG in dj. *Brooks.* $59/£38

SALMONY, ALFRED. Chinese Sculpture: Han...to Sung. (Fulton, NY, 1945.) One of 700. 29 plts. VG. *Argosy.* $65/£42

SALT, HENRY. A Voyage to Abyssinia and Travels into the Interior of That Country...in the Years 1809 and 1810...Together with Vocabularies.... London, 1814. 1st ed. 506 + lxxv pp; 37 engr plts, charts (1 hand-colored in outline). Contemp gilt calf (corners worn; recased); uncut. Foxing. *Argosy.* $850/£548

SALTEN, FELIX. The Hound of Florence. S&S, 1930. 1st US ed. VG in dj. *Madle.* $50/£32

SALTER, JAMES. The Hunters. NY: Harper, 1956. 1st ed, 1st bk. VG in VG dj (internal tape reinforcement). *Pettler.* $150/£97

SALTER, JAMES. Light Years. NY: Random House, (1975). 1st ed. Fine in dj. *Godot.* $65/£42

SALTER, T.F. The Angler's Guide. London: T. Tegg, 1815. 3rd ed. 56 engrs. 19th cent 1/2 calf (rebacked; frontis, tp sl discolored). *Petersfield.* $217/£140

SALTUS, EDGAR. The Monster. NY: Pulitzer, 1912. 1st ed, trade issue. VG. BAL 17170. *Reese.* $20/£13

SALVINI, ROBERTO. All the Paintings of Botticelli. Oldbourne, 1965. 4 vols. 309 plts (16 color). *Ars Artis.* $39/£25

SALVINI, ROBERTO. Modern Italian Sculpture. NY: Abrams, (1959). 1st ed. 46 color plts tipped in. Maroon cl. Good in dj (chipped). *Karmiole.* $65/£42

SALZMANN, C.G. Gymnastics for Youth. Phila: Ptd by William Duane, 1802. 1st Amer ed. Fldg frontis (tear at fold), xvi,432pp; 9 copper-engr plts. Contemp mottled calf; gilt red leather spine label. Overall Very Nice. *Karmiole.* $600/£387

Sammy Tickletooth. NY: McLoughlin Bros, n.d. (ca 1885). (Little Slovenly Peter series.) Sq 12mo. 4 leaves + 1pg ad back wrapper; 8 VF 1/2pg chromolithos. Pict wrappers (lower spine split). Internally Fine. *Hobbyhorse.* $75/£48

SAMPSON, EMMA SPEED. Miss Minerva's Problem. Chicago: Reilly & Lee, 1936. Clifford Benton (illus). 12mo. Pict cl. VG+ in VG dj (spine ends tattered). *Book Adoption.* $45/£29

SAMPSON, JOHN (ed). The Wind on the Heath. London, 1930. 1st ed. Color frontis. NF (spine sl sunned; bkpl) in dj (spine sunned; edge chips). *Polyanthos.* $25/£16

SAMS, CONWAY WHITTLE. The Conquest of Virginia: The Forest Primeval. Reprint Co, 1973. Good (water damage; ex-lib). *Book Broker.* $25/£16

Samson and Delilah: From the Book of Judges According to the Authorized Version. London: Golden Cockerel, 1925. One of 325. White buckram over bds; gilt spine title. Fine in dj. *Heller.* $850/£548

SAMSON, CHARLES RUMNEY. A Flight from Cairo to Cape Town and Back. London, 1931. 1st ed. Frontis; 15 plts; fldg map at rear. VG in dj (sm piece missing upper panel; spine sl frayed). *Edwards*. $70/£45

SAMUELS, EDWARD A. Ornithology and Oology of New England. Boston: Nichols & Noyes, 1867. 1st ed. viii,584pp, 4 hand-colored plts. Grn cl, gilt. Good. *Karmiole*. $100/£65

SAMUELS, EDWARD A. Ornithology and Oology of New England.... Boston: Nichols and Noyes, 1867. 1st ed. Frontis, vii,(i)583pp, 26 plts. (Fr hinge cracked; ex-lib, bkpl; rubbed, bumped; spine faded, bubbled, chipped.) VG. *Blue Mountain*. $275/£177

SAMUELS, LEE. A Hemingway Checklist. NY: Scribner's, 1951. 1st ed. One of 750. VG (lacks erratum slip, dj). *Heller*. $45/£29

SAMUELS, LEE. A Hemingway Checklist. NY: Scribners, 1951. One of 750. Fine in NF dj (soiling; tiny chip). *Beasley*. $100/£65

SAMUELS, M. Memoirs of Moses Mendelsohn, the Jewish Philosopher. London: Ptd for Sainsbury & Co, 1827. 2nd ed. vii,(1),171pp. Old calf (rebacked). Early ink inscrip; worn; spine reticulation; o/w Good. *Reese*. $35/£23

San Bernardino City Directory, 1913-1914. L.A.: San Bernardino Directory Co, 1913. Ptd cl (shaken; fr inner hinge cracked). *Dawson*. $50/£32

SANBORN, FRANK (ed). The First and Last Journeys of Thoreau.... Boston: Biblio Soc, 1905. One of 489. Uncut. 1/2 leather, bds. VG + in Fair slipcase (sl foxed). *Mikesh*. $60/£39

SANBORN, FRANK. Henry D. Thoreau. Boston: Houghton, Mifflin, 1882. 1st ed. Teg. Maroon cl, gilt (spine evenly sunned). BAL 126 and 20125. *Macdonnell*. $85/£55

SANBORN, HELEN J. A Winter in Central America and Mexico. Boston: Lee & Shepard, (1886). iv,321pp, 2 ads. Pict red cl (lt wear to spine ends; inner hinge strained). *Petrilla*. $30/£19

SANBORN, MARGARET. Robert E. Lee. Phila/NY: Lippincott, (1966-67). 1st ed. 2 vols. Lt blue cl. NF in djs (lt used). *Chapel Hill*. $95/£61

SANCHO, IGNATIUS. Letters of the Late Ignatius Sancho, An African. London: Ptd for J. Nichols & C. Dilly, 1783. 2nd ed (so stated). 2 vols. Frontis port, xvi,204; frontis port, 224pp. 12mo. Contemp full tree calf. Fine set. *Godot*. $1,500/£968

SAND, GEORGE. The Mosaic Workers. Elizabeth A. Ashurst (trans). Phila: E. Ferrett, 1845. 1st ed this trans. Drab paper over bds, orig brn cl spine, label. VG (edgewear; foxing). *Juvelis*. $750/£484

SAND, GEORGE. Winter in Majorca. Robert Graves (trans). Mallorca: Valldemosa Edition, 1956. Wrappers. VG. *Hollett*. $23/£15

SAND, GEORGE. Winter in Majorca. Robert Graves (trans). London: Cassell, 1956. 1st ed. VG in dj. *Hollett*. $31/£20

SAND, GEORGE. Winter in Majorca. Robert Graves (trans). (Mallorca): Valldemosa, 1956. 1st Majorcan ed. VG in wraps as issued. *Williams*. $23/£15

SANDBURG, CARL and FREDERICK HILL MESERVE. The Photographs of Abraham Lincoln. Harcourt Brace, 1944. 1st ed. VG + in VG dj. *Bishop*. $25/£16

SANDBURG, CARL. Abraham Lincoln, the Prairie Years. NY, (1929). 1 vol abridged ed. VG + in VG + dj. *Pratt*. $20/£13

SANDBURG, CARL. Abraham Lincoln, the Prairie Years. NY, 1927. 2 vols in 1 ed. VG + . *Pratt*. $55/£35

SANDBURG, CARL. Abraham Lincoln, the War Years. NY: Harcourt, Brace & World, (1939). 4 vols. Black cl, gilt. Internally NF in cream djs (vol 1 chipped, discolored; vols 2, 3 chipped, sm tears vol 3; each w/hole in spine). *Blue Mountain*. $50/£32

SANDBURG, CARL. Abraham Lincoln: The War Years. NY: Harcourt, Brace, (1939). Later ptg. 4 vols. Blue cl. Fine set. Howes S 82. *Chapel Hill*. $125/£81

SANDBURG, CARL. Always the Young Strangers. NY, (1953). 1st ed, ltd to 600 numbered, signed. VG in slipcase (sunned). *King*. $150/£97

SANDBURG, CARL. Home Front Memo. NY: Harcourt, Brace, (1943). 1st ed. Fine in dj (sl worn). *Sadlon*. $35/£23

SANDBURG, CARL. Honey and Salt. NY: Harcourt, Brace & World, (1963). 1st ed. (Lt rubbed.) *Sadlon*. $15/£10

SANDBURG, CARL. Honey and Salt. NY: Harcourt, Brace & World, (1963). 1st ed. Fine (ink name) in dj (wear; tears; price-clipped). *Antic Hay*. $20/£13

SANDBURG, CARL. The Letters of Carl Sandburg. Herbert Mitgang (ed). NY: Harcourt, Brace & World, (1968). 1st ed. Black cl. Owner label, ink date, else Fine in VG dj (snag). *Chapel Hill*. $30/£19

SANDBURG, CARL. A Lincoln Preface. NY: Harcourt, Brace, 1953. One of 2850 privately ptd. Preface written in 1924; first pub'd here. Pub's card (edge dusty) loosely laid in as issued. Spine edges rubbed, o/w Fine. *Temple*. $19/£12

SANDBURG, CARL. Mary Lincoln, Wife and Widow. Documents ed by Paul M. Angle. NY, (1932). 2nd ptg. Dj worn, chipped, o/w VG + . *Pratt*. $25/£16

SANDBURG, CARL. The People, Yes. NY: Harcourt, Brace, (1936). 1st ed. VG in dj (chipped). *Sadlon*. $30/£19

SANDBURG, CARL. Potato Face. H-B, 1930. 1st ed. VG + in Nice dw (spine extrems chipped). *Fine Books*. $75/£48

SANDBURG, CARL. The Sandburg Range. NY: Harcourt, Brace, (1957). 1st ed. NF in dj (sl wear; internal mends; price-clipped). *Antic Hay*. $25/£16

SANDBURG, CARL. Smoke and Steel. NY: Harcourt, Brace, 1920. 1st ed. Signed. Grn bds, red-lettered. NF (tp lt chipped, sm tear). *Antic Hay*. $225/£145

SANDEMAN, ROBERT. His Life and Work on Our Indian Frontier.... Murray, 1895. Port, map. *Petersfield*. $34/£22

SANDER, C.F., F.K., and L.L. Sanders' Orchid Guide. St. Albans, 1927. Rev ed. Frontis port. Brn buckram. Sl rubbed, else VG. *Brooks*. $37/£24

SANDERS, ALVIN HOWARD. At the Sign of the Stock Yard Inn.... Chicago: Breeder's Gazette Print, 1915. 32 plts. 3/4 leather. Nice (sl scuffing; pp creased). *Bohling*. $90/£58

SANDERS, ALVIN HOWARD. Red White and Roan.... Chicago: Amer Shorthorn Breeders Assn, 1936. 1st ed. Frontis port. Orange cl, blue lettering. VF (bkpl). *Connolly*. $80/£52

SANDERS, ALVIN HOWARD. The Story of the Herefords.... Chicago: Breeder's Gazette, 1914. 1st ed. Grn cl, gilt stamping, mtd color illus. VG in dj (soiled; very chipped; piece missing). *Bohling*. $65/£42

SANDERS, ED. Poem from Jail. (SF: City Lights, 1963.) 1st ed, 1st bk. One of 3000 ptd. VG in ptd wraps. *Antic Hay.* $45/£29

SANDERS, ED. Tales of Beatnik Glory. NY: Stonehill, 1975. 1st ed. Fine in dj (lt used; stain on verso). *Beasley.* $30/£19

SANDERS, J.H. Horse-Breeding. Chicago, (1893). 428pp. Sm stampstained area, o/w VG. *Hayman.* $20/£13

SANDERS, LAWRENCE. The Pleasures of Helen. NY: Putnam's, (1971). 1st ed. Fine in NF dj. *Antic Hay.* $50/£32

SANDERS, WILLIAM BLISS. Examples of Carved Oak Woodwork.... London: Bernard Quaritch, 1883. 1st ed. 25 plts. Smudging, cvrs worn; text Good. *Bookpress.* $185/£119

SANDERS, WILLIAM BLISS. Examples of Carved Oak Woodwork...of the 16th and 17th Centuries. London, 1883. Unpaginated. (iv)subscriber list. 25 photo-lithos plts. (Ex-lib w/stamp, bkpl; sl rubbed, bumped; corners damp-stained.) *Edwards.* $62/£40

SANDERSON, G.P. Thirteen Years Among the Wild Beasts of India. London, 1882. 3rd ed. Color frontis, 387pp; 23 plts. Gilt pict cl. VG. *Argosy.* $150/£97

SANDERSON, G.P. Thirteen Years Among the Wild Beasts of India. Edinburgh, 1912. 7th ed. Map. Gilt/black illus cl (spine chipped, upper hinge cracked; feps browned). *Edwards.* $70/£45

SANDHURST, PHILLIP T. et al. The Great Centennial Exhibition. Phila: P.W. Ziegler, (1876). 1st ed. Frontis, 544pp. Spine sl sunned; lt rubbing else Fine. *Bookpress.* $235/£152

SANDLER, IRVING. The New York School: The Painters and Sculptors of the Fifties. NY: Harper & Row, 1978. 1st ed. Fine. *Cahan.* $35/£23

SANDOE, JAMES (ed). Murder: Plain and Fancy, with Some Milder Malefactions. NY: Sheridan House, 1948. Blue cl (worn, faded). Usable. *Boswell.* $45/£29

SANDOZ, MARI. The Battle of Little Bighorn. NY: James F. Carr, 1966. Deluxe ed, #72/249 numbered, signed. Fldg map at end. Gilt-stamped black morocco over dk blue cl; top edge stained yellow; uncut. VG. *Houle.* $450/£290

SANDOZ, MARI. The Battle of the Little Bighorn. Phila: Lippincott, (1966). 1st ed. Fine in Fine dj. *Dermont.* $45/£29

SANDOZ, MARI. The Beaver Men. NY, (1964). 1st ed. VG+ in VG+ dj. *Pratt.* $20/£13

SANDOZ, MARI. The Buffalo Hunter. NY, (1975). 1st ed. Dj w/lt wear, faded spine, few water stains, o/w VG+. *Pratt.* $20/£13

SANDOZ, MARI. The Buffalo Hunters. NY: Hastings House, (1954). 1st issue of trade ed, w/Bismarck misspelled, mis-located on ep maps. VG in dj (sl chipped). *Schoyer.* $40/£26

SANDOZ, MARI. The Buffalo Hunters. Hastings, 1954. 1st ed. Ep maps. VG in VG dj. *Oregon.* $30/£19

SANDOZ, MARI. The Cattlemen, from the Rio Grande across the Far Marias. NY: Hastings House, (1958). VG in VG dj. *Perier.* $32/£21

SANDOZ, MARI. The Cattlemen, From the Rio Grande across the Far Marias. NY, (1958). 1st ed. Sl dj wear, o/w VG+. *Pratt.* $20/£13

SANDOZ, MARI. Old Jules Country. NY, 1965. 1st Amer ed. Fine in dj (sl rubbed). *Polyanthos.* $35/£23

SANDOZ, MARI. Old Jules Country. NY: Hastings House, 1965. 1st ed. VF in VG dj (lt chipped). *Connolly.* $27/£17

SANDOZ, MARI. Old Jules. Boston: Little, Brown, 1935. 1st ed. Pict eps. Yellow pict cl. Fine (owner stamp) in VG dj (chipped; tape on verso; sl loss extrems). *Harrington.* $50/£32

SANDOZ, MARI. Slogum House. Boston: Little, Brown, 1937. 1st ed. VG in dj (sl chipped, wrinkled). *Schoyer.* $25/£16

SANDOZ, MARI. Son of the Gamblin' Man. Clarkson Potter, (1960). 1st ed. VG in VG dj. *Oregon.* $50/£32

SANDOZ, MAURICE. Fantastic Memories. NY: Doubleday, 1944. Salvador Dali (illus). Fine in dj. *Williams.* $101/£65

SANDOZ, MAURICE. The Pleasures of Mexico. NY: Kamin, 1957. 1st ed, 1st bk. Fine in dj. *Cahan.* $60/£39

SANDS, BENJAMIN FRANKLIN. From Reefer to Rear-Admiral. NY: Stokes, (1899). xv,308pp; port. *Schoyer.* $50/£32

SANDWITH, HUMPHRY. Narrative of the Siege of Kars.... London: John Murray, 1856. Frontis, (x),348pp + 30pp pub's cat (lacks rep; dampstain frontis, tp), 2 fldg b/w maps. Brn cl, blindstamped (bumped, spine cocked, rubbed). *Schoyer.* $65/£42

SANDWITH, J. An Introduction to Anatomy and Physiology. London, 1825. Presentation copy. xii,192pp (eps foxed); 12 plts (foxed; bds rubbed, worn; sl spine worn). *Whitehart.* $93/£60

SANDYS, EDWIN and T.S. VAN DYKE. Upland Game Birds. NY, 1902. 1st ed. VG. *Artis.* $35/£23

SANFORD, FREDERICK R. The Bursting of a Boom. Phila: Lippincott, 1889. 1st ed. 250pp. Pict cl. Extrems lt rubbed, else VG. *Reese.* $40/£26

SANFORD, GEORGE B. Fighting Rebels and Redskins. Norman: Univ of OK, (1969). 1st ptg. 6 maps. VG in dj (tears). *Schoyer.* $30/£19

SANFORD, GEORGE B. Fighting Rebels and Redskins. Norman: Univ of OK Press, 1969. 1st ed. Color frontis, 6 maps. Fine in dj. *Graf.* $25/£16

SANFORD, JOHN. Rules of Prey. NY: Putnam's, 1989. 1st ed. Lt stains fore-edge, o/w Fine in dj. *Mordida.* $45/£29

SANFORD, LEONARD C. et al. The Water Fowl Family. NY, 1903. 1st ed. VG. *Artis.* $35/£23

SANFORD, LEONARD C. et al. The Water-Fowl Family. NY: Macmillan, 1903. 1st ptg. Pict cl. VG. *Schoyer.* $65/£42

SANFORD, MOLLIE DORSEY. Mollie: The Journal of...in Nebraska and Colorado Territories 1857-1866. N.p.: Univ of NE, 1959. 1st ed. Dec bds. Fine in VG dj. *Connolly.* $35/£23

SANFORD, PAUL. Sioux Arrows and Bullets. San Antonio: Naylor, (1969). 1st ed. VF in Fine dj. *Oregon.* $22/£14

SANGER, DONALD BRIDGMAN and THOMAS ROBSON HAY. James Longstreet. Baton Rouge: LA State Univ, (1952). 1st ed. Fine in NF dj. *Mcgowan.* $125/£81

SANGER, MARGARET H. What Every Mother Should Know. NY: Max N. Maisel, (1910). 1st ed. Good (eps browned, brittle; hinges cracked, spine worn). *Godot.* $65/£42

SANGER, MARGARET. My Fight For Birth Control. London, 1932. 1st ed. Good. *Fye.* $75/£48

SANGER, WILLIAM. The History of Prostitution. NY, 1939. Facs of 1859 ed. Good. *Fye.* $40/£26

SANGSTER, MARGARET E. The Art of Home-Making in City and Country.... NY: Christian Herald, 1898. 1st ed. 463pp; 2 ports. Dec cl. VG. *Petrilla.* $65/£42

SANGSTER, MARGARET E. Home Fairies and Heart Flowers. NY, 1887. 1st ed. 93pp, 20 ports, decs by Frank French. Gilt-pict cl, gilt edges. VG. *Argosy.* $75/£48

SANGSTER, MARGARET E. The Mother Book. Chicago: McClurg, 1912. 1st ed. Dec lavender cl signed 'K'. *Petrilla.* $50/£32

SANSOM, WILLIAM. The Cautious Heart. NY: Reynal, (1958). 1st Amer ed. NF in dj. *Hermitage.* $35/£23

SANSOM, WILLIAM. Fireman Flower and Other Stories. NY: Vanguard, n.d. (but 1944). 1st Amer ed, 1st bk. NF in dj (rubbed; sl chipped). *Hermitage.* $50/£32

SANSOM, WILLIAM. Fireman Flower, and Other Stories. London: Hogarth Press, 1944. 1st ed, 1st bk. VG in dj. *Argosy.* $175/£113

SANSOM, WILLIAM. The Passionate North. London: Hogarth Press, 1950. 1st Eng ed. Red cl. VF in dj (sl nicked). *Dalian.* $39/£25

SANSOM, WILLIAM. Pleasures Strange and Simple. London: Hogarth, 1953. 1st ed. VF in dj. *Hermitage.* $45/£29

SANSOM, WILLIAM. Three. London: Hogarth Press, 1946. 1st Eng ed. Red cl. Eps sl foxed, o/w NF in dj (frayed, lacks piece spine). *Dalian.* $39/£25

SANSOM, WILLIAM. A Touch of the Sun. London: Hogarth Press, 1952. 1st ed. VG in dj. *Argosy.* $45/£29

SANSOM, WILLIAM. A Touch of the Sun. London: Hogarth Press, 1952. 1st Eng ed. Red cl. Sm name, o/w Fine in dj (sl dusty, nicked). *Dalian.* $39/£25

SANTAYANA, GEORGE. The Last Puritan. London, (1935). 1st ed. VG in dj. *Argosy.* $40/£26

SANTAYANA, GEORGE. Lucifer, or the Heavenly Truce. Cambridge: Dunster House, 1924. 2nd ed. Ltd to 450. Gold foil dec eps. NF. *Sadlon.* $100/£65

SANTEE, ROSS. Apache Land. NY: Scribner's, 1947. 1st ed. VG+ in VG- dj (soiled, chipped). *Parker.* $65/£42

SANTEE, ROSS. Apache Land. NY: Scribner's, 1947. 1st ptg. Pict cl. VG in VG dj. *Schoyer.* $80/£52

SANTEE, ROSS. Cowboy. Cosmopolitan, 1928. 1st ed. Pict cvr. Sl blotched, else Fine. *Authors Of The West.* $35/£23

SANTEE, ROSS. Cowboy. NY: Cosmopolitan, 1928. 1st ed. Pict cl. VG. *Connolly.* $75/£48

SANTEE, ROSS. Dog Days. Scribner's, 1955. 1st ed. Fine in NF dj. *Authors Of The West.* $40/£26

SANTEE, ROSS. Hardrock and Silver Sage. Scribner's, 1951. 1st ed. Sketch by author on fep signed, dated. Fine in VG dj. *Oregon.* $400/£258

SANTEE, ROSS. Men and Horses. NY: Century, 1926. 1st ed, 1st bk. Good (cvr bowed). *Parker.* $100/£65

SANTEE, ROSS. The Rummy Kid Goes Home, And Other Stories of the Southwest. NY: Hastings House, (1965). 1st ed. Pict cl. VG in VG dj. *Schoyer.* $35/£23

SANTEE, ROSS. The Rummy Kid Goes Home. Hastings House, (1965). 1st ed. Fine in NF dj (price-clipped). *Authors Of The West.* $30/£19

SANTMYER, HELEN HOOVEN. '...And Ladies of the Club.' Columbus: OH State Univ, (1982). 1st ed. Fine in dj. *Sadlon.* $50/£32

SAPPINGTON, JOHN. The Theory and Treatment of Fevers. Arrow Rock, MO, 1844. 1st ed. 216pp. (Spine head chipped.) *Fye.* $250/£161

SARGEANT, E. (ed). Arctic Adventure by Sea and Land...in Search of Sir John Franklin. Boston: Phillips, Sampson, 1858. 2nd ed. 480pp. Good+ (lt foxing). *Walcot.* $54/£35

SARGENT, C.E. Our Home; or, The Key to a Nobler Life. Springfield, MA: W.C. King, 1885. 8vo. 432pp; engr frontis w/guard; 11 plts. Pict, dec cl; rubricated edges. VG. *Petrilla.* $40/£26

SARGENT, CHARLES SPRAGUE. Manual of the Trees of North America. Boston, 1905. 1st ed. Map. (Lt scuffed; hinges reinforced w/cl tape.) *Sutton.* $50/£32

SARGENT, CHARLES SPRAGUE. The Silva of North America. Boston/NY, 1894-98. 1st ed (vols 1-4 later issue). Folio. Vols 1-12 (of 14). 620 plts (marginal foxing 1 plt). Ptd bds, paper labels (worn, rubbed, spine bumped vol 7; some hinges tender; pp yellowed). *Sutton.* $1,750/£1,129

SARGENT, WINTHROP (ed). The History of an Expedition against Fort du Quesne, in 1755. Phila: Lippincott, 1856. 2nd ed. Frontis, 423pp, plt, 8 fldg maps and plans. Brn cl. Spine ends chipped, else VG. Howes S 112. *Chapel Hill.* $150/£97

SAROYAN, WILLIAM. The Adventures of Wesley Jackson. NY: Harcourt, Brace, (1946). 1st ed. Blue cl. Fine in bright dj. *Godot.* $85/£55

SAROYAN, WILLIAM. The Adventures of Wesley Jackson. London: Faber, 1947. 1st Eng ed. Red cl. Fine in dj (sl nicked, dusty). *Dalian.* $39/£25

SAROYAN, WILLIAM. After Thirty Years: The Daring Young Man on the Flying Trapeze. NY: Harcourt, Brace, & World, (1964). 1st ed. Black cl. Label, ink date, Saroyan obit taped to rep, else NF in dj (lt worn). *Chapel Hill.* $30/£19

SAROYAN, WILLIAM. The Beautiful People and Other Plays. London: Faber & Faber, 1943. 1st Eng ed. Grn cl. Fine in dj (sl dusty). *Dalian.* $39/£25

SAROYAN, WILLIAM. The Bicycle Rider in Beverly Hills. Scribners, 1952. 1st ed. NF in NF dj. *Bishop.* $20/£13

SAROYAN, WILLIAM. Boys and Girls Together. London: Peter Davies, 1963. 1st Eng ed. Red cl. Fine in dj (sl nicked). *Dalian.* $39/£25

SAROYAN, WILLIAM. The Daring Man on the Flying Trapeze and Other Stories. NY: Modern Age Books, 1937. 1st ed thus. Good in ptd wraps; dj (sl chipped, worn). *Second Life.* $50/£32

SAROYAN, WILLIAM. The Human Comedy. London: Faber, 1943. 1st ed. VG (name) in dj (sl chipped). *Rees.* $16/£10

SAROYAN, WILLIAM. Inhale and Exhale. NY: Random House, (1936). 1st ed. Fine in dj (sl nicked). *Second Life.* $45/£29

SAROYAN, WILLIAM. Love, Here Is My Hat and Other Short Romances. NY: Mod Age Books, (1938). 1st ed. VG. *Second Life.* $25/£16

SAROYAN, WILLIAM. My Name Is Aram. NY: Harcourt, Brace, 1940. 1st ed. Edges sl foxed, o/w Fine in dj (frayed; spine dknd). *Temple.* $31/£20

SAROYAN, WILLIAM. A Native American. SF, 1938. 1st ed, ltd to 450, signed. Pict cl (soiled, rubbed). *King.* $175/£113

SAROYAN, WILLIAM. One Day in the Afternoon of the World. NY: Harcourt, Brace & World, (1964). 1st ed. VG in dj (price-clipped, nicks, sm tears, else VG). *Godot.* $45/£29

SAROYAN, WILLIAM. The People with Light Coming Out of Them. NY: Free Company, 1941. 1st ed. VG in pict wrappers. *Argosy.* $40/£26

SAROYAN, WILLIAM. The Trouble with Tigers. NY, (1938). 1st ed. VF in dj. *Argosy.* $150/£97

SARRAUTE, NATHALIE. Portrait of a Man Unknown. NY: Braziller, 1958. 1st US ed. Inscribed. Sm patch dj adhered to rear bd, else NF in VG dj (price-clipped; water staining verso of spine, rear panels). *Lame Duck.* $250/£161

SARRIS, ANDREW. The Films of Josef von Sternberg. MOMA, (1966). VG in dj. *Artis.* $16/£10

SARTAIN, JOHN. The Reminiscences of a Very Old Man. NY: D. Appleton, 1899. 1st ed. Frontis, xi,(iii),297,(2)pp, 19 plts. Teg. Excellent (sig on 1/2 title, eps browned). *Bookpress.* $135/£87

SARTON, MAY. A Durable Fire. NY, (1972). 1st ed. VG in dj. *Argosy.* $30/£19

SARTON, MAY. Faithful Are the Wounds. London: Gollancz, 1955. 1st Eng ed. Red cl. Fine in NF dj. *Dalian.* $54/£35

SARTON, MAY. The Fur Person. NY, (1957). 1st Amer ed. Fine (offsetting feps) in dj (sl soiled). *Polyanthos.* $35/£23

SARTON, MAY. The Fur Person. NY: Rinehart, (1957). 1st ed. Edges sl dusty, else Nice in dj. *Reese.* $25/£16

SARTON, MAY. I Knew a Phoenix. NY: Rinehart, (1959). 1st ed. VG in dj (sl soiled). *Second Life.* $45/£29

SARTON, MAY. In Time Like Air. NY: Rinehart, (1958). 1st ed. Inscribed, dated 1957. Dec paper-cvrd bds. NF in dj. *Godot.* $65/£42

SARTON, MAY. The Poet and the Donkey. NY, 1969. 1st Amer ed. Fine (sl rubbed) in dj (sl rubbed, price-clipped). *Polyanthos.* $40/£26

SARTON, MAY. A World of Light. NY: Norton, 1976. 1st ed. Erratum slip laid in. Fine in dj. *Limestone.* $40/£26

SARTRE, JEAN-PAUL. Being and Nothingness. NY: Philosophical Lib, 1956. 1st US ed. NF in dj (lt spine tanned; 2 tears rear panel). *Lame Duck.* $75/£48

SARTRE, JEAN-PAUL. Literary and Philosophical Essays. London: Rider, 1955. 1st Eng ed. Black cl. Fine in dj (sl torn). *Dalian.* $23/£15

SARTRE, JEAN-PAUL. The Reprieve. Eric Sutton (trans). London: Hamish Hamilton, (c. 1948). (Edges lt browned.) Dj (price-clipped). *Hollett.* $54/£35

SARTRE, JEAN-PAUL. Troubled Sleep. NY: Knopf, 1951. 1st ed. Fine in NF dj (short closed tear). *Beasley.* $45/£29

SARTRE, JEAN-PAUL. Two Plays (The Flies and In Camera). London: Hamish Hamilton, (1946). 1st British ed. Name, else Fine in NF dj (sl soiled; sm chips). *Between The Covers.* $85/£55

SASOWSKY, N. The Prints of Reginald Marsh. An Essay and Definitive Catalog. NY: Clarkson Potter, 1976. Sound. *Ars Artis.* $78/£50

SASSE, FRED. The Dan Patch Story. Harrisburg: Stackpole, 1957. 1st ed. VG in Good dj. *October Farm.* $40/£26

SASSOON, SIEGFRIED. Memoirs of an Infantry Officer. London: Faber, 1930. 1st ed. (Spine sl faded.) *Hollett.* $47/£30

SASSOON, SIEGFRIED. Memoirs of an Infantry Officer. NY: LEC, 1981. One of 2000 numbered, signed by Paul Hogarth (illus). Fine in pub's slipcase. *Hermitage.* $85/£55

SASSOON, SIEGFRIED. Memoirs of an Infantry Officer. NY: LEC, 1981. One of 2000 numbered, signed by Paul Hogarth (illus). Fine in slipcase. *Reese.* $90/£58

SASSOON, SIEGFRIED. Nativity. (London: Faber, 1927). VG in ptd wraps. *Second Life.* $20/£13

SASSOON, SIEGFRIED. Poems Newly Selected 1916-1935. London: Faber & Faber, 1940. 1st Eng ed. Grn bds. Eps sl browned, o/w VF in dj (sl tanned). *Dalian.* $54/£35

SASSOON, SIEGFRIED. Poems. Newly Selected 1916-1935. London, 1940. 1st ed. Newspaper articles loosely inserted. Eps browned; foxing to fore-edge; sig, o/w VG in dj (unevenly sunned). *Edwards.* $28/£18

SASSOON, SIEGFRIED. The Road to Ruin. London: Faber & Faber, (1933). 1st ed. (Sl dknd.) Dj (spine sl lightened). *Sadlon.* $45/£29

SASSOON, SIEGFRIED. Satirical Poems. NY, 1926. 1st US ed. VG+ (chipped; abrasion) in VG dj (spine sunned). *Fuller & Saunders.* $50/£32

SASSOON, SIEGFRIED. Selected Poems. London: Heinemann, 1925. 1st ed. Label ep, else VG in dj (worn, chipped). *Cahan.* $30/£19

SASSOON, SIEGFRIED. Sequences. London: Faber & Faber, (1956). 1st ed. (Eps sl spotty.) Dj (spine sl lightened.) *Sadlon.* $35/£23

SASSOON, SIEGFRIED. Sherston's Progress. London: Faber, 1936. One of 300 specially bound, numbered, signed. This copy unnumbered. NF. *Rees.* $271/£175

SASSOON, SIEGFRIED. Siegfried's Journey 1916-1920. Faber, 1945. 1st ed. Spine sl pulled, o/w VG. *Poetry.* $16/£10

SASSOON, SIEGFRIED. To My Mother. London: Faber & Gwyer, 1928. 1st ed. One of 500 numbered, signed. Pink bds, gilt. Fine. *Macdonnell.* $100/£65

SASSOON, SIEGFRIED. The Weald of Youth. London: Faber, 1942. 1st UK ed. Fine in VG dj (unevenly faded). *Williams.* $54/£35

SAUDEK, ROBERT. The Psychology of Hand Writing. NY, 1926. Good. *Fye.* $35/£23

SAUER, CARL O, et al. Starved Rock State Park and its Environs. Chicago: Univ of Chicago, 1918. 1st ed. NF in VG dj. *Lame Duck.* $350/£226

SAUER, G.C. John Gould, the Bird Man: A Chronology and Bibliography. Sotheran, 1982. Illus, 32 color, 115 b/w. Fine in dj. *Moss.* $70/£45

SAUER, MARTIN. An Account of a Geographical and Astronomical Expedition to the Northern Parts of Russia.... London: T. Cadell & W. Davies, 1802. 1st ed. 4to, xxvi,1(errata),332,58pp, lg fldg map, 14 plts bound in; new eps. Mod 1/2 calf, marbled bds. Good. *Walcot.* $1,008/£650

SAUERLANDER, WILLIBALD. Gothic Sculpture in France 1140-1270. London, 1972. 4 tipped-in color plts. Good in dj. *Washton.* $200/£129

SAUNDERS, CHARLES FRANCES. Finding the Worth While in California. NY: Robert M. McBride, 1916. 1st ed. 7 photo plts, 4 maps. (Sm marginal tear 1 leaf not affecting text; fep removed.) *Shasky.* $37/£24

SAUNDERS, CHARLES FRANCES. The Southern Sierras of California. Boston: Houghton Mifflin, 1923. 1st ed. 32 photo plts. Pict cl, gilt (lt soiled, spine sl dull; 2 leaves opened unevenly). *Shasky.* $35/£23

SAUNDERS, F. The Story of Some Famous Books. Elliot Stock, 1887. VG in orig grn cl. *Moss.* $14/£9

SAUNDERS, JAMES EDMONDS. Early Settlers of Alabama. New Orleans: L. Graham & Son, 1899. 1st ed. 530,(2),xxivpp. (Recased.) VG. Howes S 119. *Mcgowan.* $250/£161

SAUNDERS, LOUISE. The Knave of Hearts. NY: Scribner's, 1925. 1st ed. Full-pg color frontis w/guard; illus eps. Maxfield Parrish (illus). Full-sized illus title mtd on fr cvr. Sl rubbing tips, lt foxing eps, else Fine. *Cahan.* $1,500/£968

SAUNDERS, PAUL. Edward Jenner: The Cheltenham Years 1795-1823. Hanover, 1982. 1st ed. Good in dj. *Fye.* $25/£16

SAUNDERS, PETER. The Mousetrap Man. London: Collins, 1972. 1st ed. Signed. Fine in VG + dj (edgewear; closed tears). *Janus.* $50/£32

Savage and Civilized Russia. (By G.W.R. Pigott.) London: Longmans, Green, 1877. (ii),(216)pp + 41pp pub's ads. Maroon cl, gilt/blind-stamped (spine faded, pocket removed). *Schoyer.* $50/£32

SAVAGE, C. The Mandarin Duck. London, 1952. Color frontis, 16 plts. *Wheldon & Wesley.* $62/£40

SAVAGE, D.S. Mysticism and Aldous Huxley. Yonkers, NY: Alicat Bookshop, 1947. Ltd to 750. Ptd black wrappers. Short tears cvr edges, o/w Fine. *Sadlon.* $50/£32

SAVAGE, G. Richard Middleton. Palmer, 1922. 1st ed. Pp foxed, else Fine in dj. *Aronovitz.* $48/£31

SAVAGE, HENRY. The Surgery, Surgical Pathology and Surgical Anatomy of the Female Pelvic Organs in a Series of Coloured Plates Taken from Nature.... London, 1882. 5th ed. 89pp (lib stamp). Recent cl; leather label. *Fye.* $300/£194

SAVAGE, HENRY. The Surgery, Surgical Pathology and Surgical Anatomy of the Female Pelvic Organs in a Series of Plates Taken from Nature. NY, 1880. 3rd ed. 115pp; 32 full pg engr plts. Good. *Fye.* $100/£65

SAVAGE, MARGARET E. Jack Horner Pop-Up. London, n.d. (194?). No. 1 Candlelight 'Pop-Up Series'. 18x24 cm. 1 pop-up. VG + (1 picture partly colored) in dj. *Book Finders.* $110/£71

SAVAGE, WILLIAM. A Dictionary of the Art of Printing. London: Longman et al, 1841. 1st ed. viii,815pp (bound w/o 1/2 title; pp soiled, spotted, 1 leaf repaired w/o loss). Full grn buckram (label). Sound. *Cox.* $279/£180

SAVAGE, WILLIAM. Food Poisoning and Food Infections. Cambridge, 1920. 1st ed. Good. *Fye.* $50/£32

SAVAGE-LANDOR, A. HENRY. Across Coveted Lands. NY, 1903. 1st ed. 2 vols. Red dec cvrs (sl bumped). *Lewis.* $132/£85

SAVAGE-LANDOR, A. HENRY. Across Unknown South America. Hodder, (1913). 2 vols. 2 maps; 8 color plts. (Sl foxing few pp.) *Petersfield.* $101/£65

SAVAGE-LANDOR, A. HENRY. Everywhere. London: T. Fisher Unwin, 1924. 1st ed. 23 plts; 8 maps, diags. (Sl rubbed.) *Hollett.* $70/£45

SAVAGE-LANDOR, A. HENRY. In the Forbidden Land: An Account of a Journey into Tibet.... NY/London: Harper, 1899. 2 vols. Photogravure frontis, (xvi),307; (xii),(250)pp; teg, 8 chromolithos (lacks fldg map). Grn dec cl (shaken, sigs pulled, hinges repaired). *Schoyer.* $75/£48

SAVILLE-KENT, W. The Great Barrier Reef of Australia. London: Allen, n.d. (1893). 1st ed. 387pp, 48 mezzotype plts. Contents VG (rubbed). *Mikesh.* $250/£161

SAVILLE-KENT, W. A Manual of the Infusoria. London, 1881-82. 3 vols. Color frontis; 52 plts. 1/2 calf. Ex-lib w/lt stamps to text, reverse of plts, o/w VG. *Wheldon & Wesley.* $233/£150

SAVORY, THEODORE H. The Biology of Spiders. London, 1928. (Frontis detached; sl spotting.) Dj (sl chipped.) *Edwards.* $70/£45

SAWARD, BLANCHE C. Decorative Painting. London: L. Upcott Gill, n.d. (1883). 1st ed w/ sheets ptd on grey paper, chapter headings ptd on orange. xx,214,(2)pp. Pub's cl. VG (few letters illuminated). *Bookpress.* $165/£106

SAWYER, CHARLES J. and F.J.H. DARTON. English Books 1475-1900. Westminster: Sawyer, (1927). 1st ed. One of 2000. 2 vols. VG (lt foxing; ep fore-edges creased). *Reese.* $125/£81

SAWYER, CHARLES J. and F.J.H. DARTON. English Books 1475-1900. Westminster/NY: Sawyer/Dutton, 1927. 1st ed, ltd to 2000. 2 vols. Red cl, gold-stamped. Spines faded, eps browned, else VG set. *Godot.* $85/£55

SAWYER, CHARLES J. and F.J.H. DARTON. English Books 1475-1900.... London: Chas. J. Sawyer/E.P. Dutton, 1927. 1st ed, ltd to 2000 sets. 2 vols. Frontis. Teg, others uncut. Buckram, gilt lettered. VG set. *Cox.* $116/£75

SAWYER, CHARLES WINTHROP. Firearms in American History: 1600-1800. Boston, 1910. Red cl. VG. *Bowman.* $60/£39

SAWYER, JAMES. Contributions to Practical Medicine. Birmingham, England, 1886. 1st ed. 128pp. Good. *Fye.* $75/£48

SAWYER, LORENZO. Way Sketches. NY: Eberstadt, 1926. 1st ed. Ltd to 385. Howes S 133. *Ginsberg.* $150/£97

SAWYER, RUTH. Maggie Rose: Her Birthday Christmas. NY: Harper, 1952. 1st ed. 12mo. Maurice Sendak (illus). Pict paper-cvrd bds (spine faded). VG. *Book Adoption.* $135/£87

SAWYER, RUTH. Maggie Rose: Her Birthday Christmas. NY: Harper, 1952. 1st ed. 12mo. 26 b/w dwgs by Maurice Sendak (illus). Rose cl w/black lettering (sm area rear cvr w/paper stuck to cl). Illus dj (marginal tears). *Reisler.* $285/£184

SAWYER, THOMAS A. Professor Hoffmann: A Bibliography. Santa Ana: Thomas A. Sawyer, 1983. 1st ed. Signed. Good in ptd wrappers, plastic spiral binding. *Karmiole.* $30/£19

SAXL, F. and R. WITTKOWER. British Art and the Mediterranean. London: OUP, 1969. *Edwards.* $70/£45

SAYER, FREDERIC. The History of Gibraltar.... London: Chapman and Hall, 1865. 2nd ed. x,(ii),520,14, fldg plan, 3 tinted lithos. (Sl browning, soiling to plts.) Grn cl (recased, joints well repaired). *Morrell.* $124/£80

SAYER, GEOFFREY R. T'ao Ya or Pottery Refinements. London, 1959. 1st ed. (Ex-lib w/sm ink stamps, bkpl.) Dj (sl creased, chipped). *Edwards.* $47/£30

SAYERS, DOROTHY L. Busman's Honeymoon. NY: Harcourt, Brace, (1937). 1st US ed. VG + in dj (sl spine faded; lt worn edges, folds). *Bernard.* $250/£161

SAYERS, DOROTHY L. Busman's Honeymoon. London: Gollancz, 1937. 1st ed. VG in dj (sl chipped, wrinkled). *Limestone.* $375/£242

SAYERS, DOROTHY L. and M. ST. CLAIR BYRNE. Busman's Honeymoon. London: Gollancz, 1937. 1st ed. Fine in dj (price-clipped; sl dknd spine). *Mordida.* $450/£290

SAYERS, DOROTHY L. Even the Parrot. London: Methuen, (1944). 1st British ed. Sillince (illus). NF (bd bottoms sl rubbed) in VG dj (sl spine loss). *Between The Covers.* $175/£113

SAYERS, DOROTHY L. Five Red Herrings. London: Gollancz, 1931. 1st UK ed. Generally VG (corners sl bumped, sm crease in spine). *Lewton.* $42/£27

SAYERS, DOROTHY L. Gaudy Night. London: Gollancz, 1935. 1st ed. Fine. (Lacks dj.) *Else Fine.* $150/£97

SAYERS, DOROTHY L. Gaudy Night. London: Gollancz, 1935. 1st ed. VG in dj (spine chipped). *Limestone.* $650/£419

SAYERS, DOROTHY L. In the Teeth of the Evidence. London: Gollancz, 1939. 1st ed. NF in dj (lt chipped upper spine corners). *Else Fine.* $750/£484

SAYERS, DOROTHY L. In the Teeth of the Evidence. NY: Harcourt, Brace, 1940. 1st ed. Top edge soiled, o/w VG in dj (sl frayed, rubbed). *Moorhouse.* $39/£25

SAYERS, DOROTHY L. The Just Vengeance. London: Gollancz, 1946. 1st Eng ed. Black cl. VG in dj (torn, soiled). *Dalian.* $31/£20

SAYERS, DOROTHY L. Lord Peter Views the Body. London: Victor Gollancz, 1928. 1st ed. Orig cl (sl rubbed, frayed; sl slack). *Ash.* $116/£75

SAYERS, DOROTHY L. Lord Peter Views the Body. Stockholm/London: Continental Book Co/Zephyr, 1946. 1st thus. Wrappers. NF in dj. *Limestone.* $45/£29

SAYERS, DOROTHY L. The Other Six Deadly Sins. London: Methuen, (1943). 1st ed. Wrappers (lt soiling). *Glenn.* $40/£26

SAYERS, DOROTHY L. The Story of Adam and Christ. London: Hamish Hamilton, (1955). 1st Eng ed. 4to. Color picture w/27 opening flaps. Fine. *Dalian.* $54/£35

SAYERS, DOROTHY L. (ed). Tales of Detection. London: J.M. Dent, 1936. 1st Eng ed. Red cl. VG (name). *Dalian.* $31/£20

SAYERS, DOROTHY L. Whose Body? NY, (1923). 1st Amer ed. VG (spine sunned, cvrs rubbed and sl soiled, names). *Polyanthos.* $100/£65

SAYERS, DOROTHY L. The Zeal of Thy House. London: Gollancz, 1937. 1st Eng ed. Blue cl. Fore-edge, pps sl foxed, cvrs sl mkd, o/w VG in dj (torn). *Dalian.* $39/£25

SAYLES, JOHN. The Anarchists' Convention. Boston: Little Brown, 1979. 1st ed. Fine in Fine dj (sl rubbing). *Pettler.* $50/£32

SAYLES, JOHN. Pride of the Bimbos. Boston, (1975). 1st ed, 1st bk. VG in dj (closed edge tears, soil). *King.* $150/£97

SAYRE, ELEANOR A. et al. The Changing Image: Prints by Francisco Goya. Boston: Museum of Fine Arts, (1974). 1st ed. Frontis port. Black cl. Good in dj. *Karmiole.* $65/£42

SAYRE, PAUL. The Life of Roscoe Pound. Iowa City: Univ of IA, 1948. Red cl (mks). *Boswell.* $50/£32

SCAMUZZI, ERNESTO. Egyptian Art in the Egyptian Museum of Turin. NY: Abrams, (1965). 1st ed. 155 mtd plts. Fine in dj. *Hermitage.* $150/£97

SCANNELL, C. Company of Women. Sceptre, 1971. 1st ed, ltd to 150, this one unnumbered. VG in wrappers. *Whiteson.* $16/£10

SCARBOROUGH, DOROTHY. On the Trail of Negro Folk-Songs. Cambridge, 1925. 1st ed. VG + (bkpl, blindstamp). *Fuller & Saunders.* $95/£61

SCARBOROUGH, DOROTHY. A Song Catcher in Southern Mountains. NY: Columbia Univ, 1937. 1st ed. Pict cl. VG in dj (lt chipped, used). *Reese.* $85/£55

SCARRON, PAUL. The Comical Romance, and Other Tales.... London: Lawrence & Bullen, 1892. One of 1000 numbered. 2 vols. Frontis. Teg. Lt foxing early & late; corner bumped; o/w Nice set. *Reese.* $65/£42

SCARRY, RICHARD. Richard Scarry's Busytown Pop-Up Book. London: Collins, 1980. 17x23 cm. 3 dbl-pg pop-ups, 3pp pull-tabs. Glazed pict bds. VG. *Book Finders.* $45/£29

Scenes and Characters from the Works of Charles Dickens. London: Chapman & Hall, 1908. (Spine sl lightened; gilt dull; extrems sl rubbed.) *Sadlon.* $50/£32

SCHAACK, MICHAEL J. Anarchy and Anarchists, A History of the Red Terror.... Chicago, 1889. 1st ed. 698pp. Dec cl. (Inner hinges cracked; cvrs worn; back cvr sl stained.) *King.* $195/£126

SCHACHNER, NAT. Space Lawyer. Gnome, 1953. 1st ed. Fine in dj (sl frayed). *Madle.* $60/£39

SCHACHNER, NATHAN. Thomas Jefferson. Appleton-Century-Crofts, (c. 1951). 2 vols. VG. *Book Broker.* $30/£19

SCHAEFER, JACK. Adolphe Francis Alphonse Bandelier. (Santa Fe): Press of the Territorian, 1966. 1st ed. One of 1000. Fine in wrappers. *Harrington.* $25/£16

SCHAEFFER, L.M. Sketches of Travels in South America, Mexico and California. NY: James Egbert, 1860. 1st ed. 247pp. (Spine ends worn.) *Petrilla.* $100/£65

SCHAEFFER, OSCAR. Anatomical Atlas of Obstetric Diagnosis and Treatment. NY, 1896. 1st Amer ed. 234pp. Good. *Fye.* $40/£26

SCHAEFFER, SAMUEL BERNARD. Pose Please. NY/London: Knopf, 1936. 1st ed. 180 b/w photogravures. VG in spiral bound pict stiff wrappers (sl worn). *Cahan.* $125/£81

SCHAEFFER, SUSAN FROMBERG. The Rhymes and Runes of the Toad. NY: Macmillan, (1975). 1st ed. Fine in dj (crease). *Antic Hay.* $20/£13

SCHAFF, MORRIS. The Battle of the Wilderness. Boston/NY: Houghton Mifflin, (1910). Later ptg. Red cl. Fine. *Chapel Hill.* $85/£55

SCHAFF, MORRIS. The Battle of the Wilderness. Boston/NY: Houghton, Mifflin, 1910. 1st ed. 5 maps (1 color). Sl rubbed, else NF. *Mcgowan.* $85/£55

SCHAFF, MORRIS. The Sunset of the Confederacy. Boston: John W. Luce, (1912). 1st ed. 3 maps. Spine sl darkened w/wear to headcap, else VG. *Mcgowan.* $85/£55

SCHAFF, MORRIS. The Sunset of the Confederacy. Boston: John W. Luce, (1912). 1st ed. Red cl. NF. *Chapel Hill.* $100/£65

SCHAFFER, MARY T.S. Old Indian Trails. NY: Putnam's, 1911. Mtd cvr illus. VG. *Schoyer.* $85/£55

SCHALDACH, WILLIAM J. Coverts and Casts. NY: A.S. Barnes, (1943). 1st ed. Brick red buckram, gilt. Fine in dj (lt chipped). *Glenn.* $125/£81

SCHALDACH, WILLIAM J. Upland Gunning. NY: A.S. Barnes, (1946). 1st ed. 56 plts. Russet cl, gilt. Fine in dj (chipped). *Glenn.* $150/£97

SCHALLER, G.B. et al. The Giant Pandas of Wolong. Chicago/London: Univ of Chicago, 1985. NF in NF dj. *Mikesh.* $30/£19

SCHAMBERG, JAY. Treatment of Syphilis. NY, 1932. 1st ed. Good. *Fye.* $75/£48

SCHANCHE, DON. Mister Pop: The Adventures of a Peaceful Man in a Small War. NY: McKay, (1970). Felt tip mk fep, o/w VG + in dj (shelfworn). *Aka.* $45/£29

SCHAPERA, I. The Bantu-Speaking Tribes of South Africa, an Ethnographical Survey. London: Routledge & Maskew Miller, 1937. VG. *Petersfield.* $54/£35

SCHARF, J. THOMAS. History of the Confederate States Navy from Its Organization to the Surrender of Its Last Vessel.... NY: Rogers & Sherwood, 1887. 1st ed. 824pp, uncut, unopened. Orig bds (extrems worn, joints broken). Howes S 147. *Lefkowicz.* $250/£161

SCHARY, EDWIN G. In Search of the Mahatmas of Tibet. London: Travel Book Club, (1938). Frontis; 15 b/w plts; map. VG. *Blue Dragon.* $35/£23

SCHAU, MICHAEL. J.C. Leyendecker. NY: Watson-Guptill, (1974). 1st ed. Fine in dj. *Hermitage.* $250/£161

SCHAUINGER, HERMAN. A Bibliography of Trovillon Private Press. Herrin, IL: Trovillon Private Press, 1943. Ltd to 277 numbered, signed by Violet & Hal Trovillon. Red cl. *Karmiole.* $40/£26

SCHECKLEY, ROBERT. The Status Civilization. Gollancz, 1976. 1st hb ed. Fine in dj. *Aronovitz.* $60/£39

SCHELL, JONATHAN. The Village of Ben Suc: The Story of the American Destruction of a Vietnamese Village.... NY: Knopf, 1968. 1st ed. VG in dj (price-clipped; 2-inch closed, tape-mended tear). *Aka.* $45/£29

SCHENCK, DAVID. North Carolina. 1780-81. Raleigh: Edwards & Broughton, 1889. 1st ed. Frontis, 498pp, fldg map, 2 ports. Brn cl. VG. Howes S 154. *Chapel Hill.* $150/£97

SCHENDLER, SYLVAN. Eakins. Boston, 1967. 2-tone cl. VG in dj (torn). *Argosy.* $85/£55

SCHEPPEGRELL, WILLIAM. Hayfever and Asthma: Care, Prevention and Treatment. Phila, 1922. 1st ed. Good. *Fye.* $75/£48

SCHERF, MARGARET. The Corpse in the Flannel Nightgown. GC: DCC, 1965. 1st ed. Fine in dj (rubbed; price-clipped; short closed tears). *Mordida.* $30/£19

SCHERF, MARGARET. Judicial Body. GC: DCC, 1957. 1st ed. Fine in dj (internal tape residue; sl wear spine base). *Mordida.* $30/£19

SCHERMAN, KATHARINE. Catherine the Great. NY: Random House, 1957. Stated 1st ptg trade. Pranas Lape (illus). VG in dj. *Cattermole.* $20/£13

SCHERZER, KARL. Narrative of the Circumnavigation of the Globe by the Austrian Frigate 'Novara'...1857, 1858 and 1859. London, 1861-63. 1st Eng ed. 3 vols. 1,485; ix,627; vi,544pp + ads, some loosely inserted; fldg map, 7 charts. Grn cl, beveled edges. *Lewis.* $690/£445

SCHEVILL, FERDINAND. Karl Bitter: A Biography. Univ of Chicago Press, 1917. Frontis port, 40 plts. (Ex-lib, ink stamp, label, cardholder remains; sl spotting; sl chipped; bumped). *Edwards.* $47/£30

SCHILLER, FRIEDRICH. William Tell. Zurich: LEC, 1951. #904/1500 numbered, signed by Charles Hug (illus). Fine in pub's slipcase. *Hermitage.* $75/£48

SCHILLING, C.G. With Flashlight and Rifle. F. Whyte (trans). London: Hutchinson, 1906. 2 vols. Pict cl cvrs (backstrips sl faded). *Petersfield.* $85/£55

SCHILLINGS, C.G. With Flashlight and Rifle. Frederick Whyte (trans). London: Hutchinson, 1906. 1st 1-vol ed. Pict gilt cl (hinges, extrems worn; joints cracked; eps sl spotted). *Hollett.* $116/£75

SCHIMMEL, JULIE. The Art and Life of W. Herbert Dunton, 1878-1936. Austin: Univ of TX Press, (1984). VG in dj. *Argosy.* $100/£65

SCHIMPELER, R. Told by a Child—The Story of the Wah-Wu-Loos. Morton, 1903. 1st ed. VG +. *Aronovitz.* $35/£23

SCHIMPER, A.F.W. Plant Geography Upon a Physiological Basis. W.R. Fisher (trans). Oxford, 1903. Orig ptg. xxx,839pp; port; 4 maps; 502 plts, illus. Orig 1/4 morocco (used, roughly refixed). Contents Good (pencil annotations). *Wheldon & Wesley.* $93/£60

SCHLARMAN, J.H. From Quebec to New Orleans. Belleville, IL: Buechler, 1929. 1st ed. Frontis. Red cl. Fine. *Chapel Hill.* $75/£48

SCHLEBECKER, JOHN T. Cattle Raising on the Plains 1900-1961. Lincoln, 1963. 1st ed. Fine in dj. *Baade.* $55/£35

SCHLEY, WINFIELD S. and J.R. SOLEY. The Rescue of Greeley. NY, 1885. 1st ed. Cl (frayed, bumped; bkpl, map torn). *King.* $50/£32

SCHLEY, WINFIELD S. and J.R. SOLEY. The Rescue of Greely. NY: Scribner's, 1885. vii,277pp. 14 plts, 5 fldg maps. VG. (minor spot on back). *High Latitude.* $90/£58

SCHLIEMANN, HENRY. Troja. NY: Harper, 1884. 1st Amer ed. Frontis color map, xl,434pp + 6pp ads, 3 fldg plans. Blue cl, gilt spine (rubbed, shaken, pocket removed). *Schoyer.* $150/£97

SCHMIDT, J.L. and D.L. GILBERT. Big Game of North America. Harrisburg: Stackpole, 1978. 1st ed. Gilt dec cl. NF in VG dj. *Mikesh.* $35/£23

SCHMIDT, MARTIN F. and DEE BROWN. The Settlers' West. NY: Scribner's, 1955. 1st ed. Fine in dj (sl worn). *Graf.* $25/£16

SCHMIDT, WILLIAM. The Flowing Bowl. When and What to Drink. NY: Charles L. Webster, 1892. 1st ed. xvi,(2),17-294,10pp ads. Blind-stamped grn cl, gilt. Very Nice (inscrip, booklet pasted in). *Cady.* $75/£48

SCHMITZ, HERMANN. The Encyclopaedia of Furniture. London, 1926. 1st ed. 320 plts. (Feps sl browned, prelims lt spotted; worn; upper bd sl warped.) *Edwards.* $62/£40

SCHMITZ, JAMES. A Nice Day for Screaming. Chilton, 1965. 1st ed. NF in dj (sl wrinkled). *Madle.* $250/£161

SCHMITZ, JAMES. The Witches of Karres. Phila: Chilton, (1966). 1st ed. VG (fep browned) in dj (lt wear; few short tears). *Antic Hay.* $150/£97

SCHMUTZLER, ROBERT. Art Nouveau. NY: Abrams, (1962). 12 mtd color plts. Good in dj. *Karmiole.* $100/£65

SCHNEIDER, GEORGE (ed). The Freeman Journal. San Rafael: Presidio Press, (1977). 1st ed. Ltd to 1000. Fine in Fine dj. *Oregon.* $45/£29

SCHNEIDER, PIERRE. Matisse. Michael Taylor & Bridget Strevens Romer (trans). NY, 1984. Fine in dj. *Argosy.* $200/£129

SCHOENBERG, WILFRED P. Jesuit Mission Presses in the Pacific Northwest...1876-1899. (Portland): Champoeg Press, 1957. 1st ed. Bkpl, else Fine. *Perier.* $75/£48

SCHONBERGER, ARNO and HALLDOR SOEHNER. The Age of Rococo. London, 1963. 2nd imp. Tipped-in color frontis port, 48 tipped-in color plts. (Ex-lib w/ink stamps; margins lt browned; cl sl soiled.) *Edwards.* $62/£40

SCHOOLCRAFT, HENRY. Narrative of an Expedition through the Upper Mississippi to Itasca Lake.... Harper, 1834. 1st ed. 308pp, 5 maps (2 fldg), errata. Ex-lib w/sm worn, faded paper spine label; remnants of label on verso of fep; lacks rep; sm dampspot lower edge of 1st few leaves. Internally VG. Howes S 187. *Oregon.* $400/£258

SCHOOLCRAFT, HENRY. Notes on the Iroquois. NY, 1846. vii,(1),285,(2)pp. Bkpl, fraying, else VG. Howes S 191. *Reese.* $425/£274

SCHOOLCRAFT, HENRY. A View of the Lead Mines of Missouri.... NY: Charles Wiley, 1819. 1st ed. 299pp; 3 plts. Mod calf-backed marbled bds. Browning, else Fine. Howes S 194. *Felcone.* $550/£355

SCHOOLING, WILLIAM. The Governor and Company of Adventurers of England Trading into Hudson's Bay.... London: Hudson's Bay Co, 1920. Fldg facs, fldg map. Full suede, gilt-stamped crest (sm stain; fr joint starting). *Schoyer.* $65/£42

SCHOOLING, WILLIAM. The Governor and Company of Adventurers of England Trading into Hudson's Bay...1670-1920. London: Hudson's Bay, 1920. Color frontis port, fldg map. Full suede, gilt spine titles, cvr dec. Presentation card laid in. Soiling to cvrs, offset on eps. *Parmer.* $165/£106

SCHOOLING, WILLIAM. The Governor and Company of Adventures of England Trading into Hudson's Bay...1760-1920. London, 1920. 1st ed. 21 plts (3 color, 1 fldg), fldg map. Stiff wraps. VG. *Oregon.* $60/£39

SCHOOR, GENE with HENRY GILFOND. Christy Mathewson. Messner, 1953. Ltr ptg. Fine in Good+ dj. *Plapinger.* $50/£32

SCHOOR, GENE. Joe DiMaggio. Doubleday, 1980. 1st ed. Fine in VG+ dj. *Plapinger.* $30/£19

SCHOOR, GENE. The Story of Ty Cobb. Messner, (1966). Ltr ptg. VG in Good+ dj. *Plapinger.* $55/£35

SCHORER, EDWIN. Vaccine and Serum Therapy Including a Study of Infections.... St. Louis, 1909. 1st ed. Good. *Fye.* $50/£32

SCHRADER, L.L. et al. South Dakota Weeds. 1950. Pb (pp browned). *Sutton.* $33/£21

SCHRIBER, FRITZ. The Complete Carriage and Wagon Painter. NY: Richardson, 1895. Later ptg. VG. *October Farm.* $95/£61

SCHREINER, OLIVE. Trooper Peter Halket of Mashonaland. Boston: Roberts Bros, 1897. 1st Amer ed. 1st state frontis of 3 African natives hung from tree. Gilt/grn-stamped cl (spine dull; lt rubbed; lt foxing). *Sadlon.* $35/£23

SCHULBERG, BUDD. Across the Everglades. NY: Random House, 1958. 1st ed. NF in NF dj (short closed tear). *Revere.* $40/£26

SCHULBERG, BUDD. The Disenchanted. London: Bodley Head, 1951. 1st Eng ed. Grey cl. Spine sl faded, o/w VG in dj (chipped, soiled). *Dalian.* $39/£25

SCHULBERG, BUDD. What Makes Sammy Run? R-H, 1941. 1st ed, 1st bk. VG+ in VG 1st issue dj. *Fine Books.* $375/£242

SCHULL, JOSEPH. The Far Distant Ships. Ottawa, 1952. 1st ed. Frontis. Navy cl, anchor motif. VG in dj (tattered). *Edwards.* $47/£30

SCHULLIAN, DOROTHY (ed). The Baglivi Correspondence from the Library of Sir William Osler. Ithaca, 1974. Fine. *Goodrich.* $45/£29

SCHULTES, RICHARD EVANS. Native Orchids of Trinidad and Tobago. NY/Oxford, 1960. Inscribed, dated. NF in VG dj. *Shifrin.* $50/£32

SCHULTHESS, EMIL. Antarctica. NY: S&S, 1960. 1st ed. VG. *Blue Dragon.* $45/£29

SCHULTZ, CHARLES M. Good Grief, More Peanuts! NY: Rinehart, (1956). 1st ed. VG in stiff red pict wrappers. *Houle.* $60/£39

SCHULTZ, GERARD. Early History of the Northern Ozarks. Jefferson City: Midland Ptg, (1937). Presentation copy. Tipped-in view. (Faded, soiled.) *Bohling.* $65/£42

SCHULTZ, L.P. et al. Fishes of the Marshall and Marianas Islands. Washington, 1953-66. 3 vols. 148 plts; 139 tables. Wrappers. *Wheldon & Wesley.* $209/£135

SCHULZ, CHARLES. Peanuts Jubilee. Holt, Rinehart & Winston, 1975. 1st ed. NF in VG- dj. *Bishop.* $27/£17

SCHULZ, ELLEN D. Cactus Culture. NY: OJ, 1932. 1st ed. Frontis, 24 plts. Dk blue cl. (Bkpl removed.) *Weber.* $20/£13

SCHULZ, JUERGEN. Venetian Painted Ceilings of the Renaissance. Berkeley, 1968. Good. *Washton.* $60/£39

SCHULZ, JUERGEN. Venetian Painted Ceilings of the Renaissance. Berkeley: Univ of CA, 1968. 151 plts. Pub's cl. Fine in Mint dj. *Europa.* $101/£65

SCHUMACHER, GOTTLIEB. Across the Jordan. London: Richard Bentley, 1886. 1st ed. xvi,342,2, 6 fldg maps. Ochre cl (hinges cracking), lettered in black; gilt vignette. Sl grubby but clean, sound internally. *Morrell.* $85/£55

SCHUSSLER, EDITH M. Doctors, Dynamite and Dogs. Caldwell: Caxton, 1956. 1st ed. Ink name, else Fine in VG dj. *Perier.* $30/£19

SCHUSTER, ARTHUR. An Introduction to the Theory of Optics. London, 1904. 1st ed. 2 plts. Pub's blue buckram. Fine (bkpl). *Hemlock.* $200/£129

SCHUYLER, HARTLEY and GRAHAM. Illustrated Catalogue of Arms and Military Goods.... N.p.: (N. Flayderman, 1967). Rpt of 1864 ed. NF. *Mcgowan.* $85/£55

SCHWAAB, DEAN J. Osaka Prints. London, 1989. Dj. *Edwards.* $39/£25

SCHWANN, T.H. Microscopical Researches into the Accordance in the Structure and Growth of Animals and Plants. H. Smith (trans). London: Sydenham Soc, 1847. xx,268pp; 4 plts. (Rebacked, spine laid down.) *Whitehart.* $194/£125

SCHWARTZ, CHARLES W. The Prairie Chicken in Missouri. MO: Conservation Comm, 1944. Gilt emb brn leatherette. VF in Fine dj. *Bowman.* $85/£55

SCHWARTZ, DELMORE. In Dreams Begin Responsibilities. Norfolk: New Directions, 1938. 1st ed. One of 1000. Rev copy. Gilt-emb pict emblem. Few leaves sl stained, else VG in dj (lt chipped, rubbed). *Cahan.* $200/£129

SCHWARTZ, DELMORE. Shenandoah. Norfolk: New Directions/Poet of the Month, (1941). 1st ed. Fine in dj (spine sl faded). *Pharos.* $85/£55

SCHWARTZ, DELMORE. Vaudeville for a Princess. NY: New Directions, 1950. 1st ed. Pencil name, else NF in NF dj (spine sl tanned). *Lame Duck.* $100/£65

SCHWARTZ, DELMORE. The World Is a Wedding and Other Stories. London: Lehmann, 1949. 1st British ed. NF in NF dj (spine lt faded). *Lame Duck.* $150/£97

SCHWARTZ, DELMORE. The World Is a Wedding. London: Lehmann, 1949. 1st ed. Top edge dusty, o/w VG in dj (sl rubbed, sunned). *Rees.* $101/£65

SCHWARTZ, G. Rembrandt: All the Etchings Reproduced in True Size. London: Oresko Bks, 1977. 3 outsize sheets in pocket. Sound in dj (sl torn). *Ars Artis.* $54/£35

SCHWARTZ, LYNNE SHARON. Rough Strife. NY: Harper, (1980). 1st ed, 1st bk. Fine in NF dj. *Robbins.* $25/£16

SCHWARZ, ARTURO. The Complete Works of Marcel Duchamp. NY: Abrams, 1970. VG in dj (frayed). *Argosy.* $875/£565

SCHWARZ, E.H.L. The Kalahari and Its Native Races. London: Witherby, 1928. (Backstrip faded.) *Petersfield.* $90/£58

SCHWATKA, FREDERICK. Along Alaska's Great River. NY: Cassell, (1885). 1st ed. 360pp, 3 maps (2 fldg). VG- (inner spine sl loose). *Blue Dragon.* $175/£113

SCHWATKA, FREDERICK. The Search for Franklin. London: T. Nelson, 1882. 1st ed. 127pp, map. Good+ (sl dull). *Walcot.* $19/£12

SCHWATKA, FREDERICK. A Summer in Alaska. St. Louis, 1893. 418pp. VG- in mylar dj. *Blue Dragon.* $60/£39

SCHWATKA, FREDERICK. A Summer in Alaska. St. Louis, MO: J.W. Henry, 1893. Blue cl (sm nick spine). Nice. *Appelfeld.* $65/£42

SCHWATKA, FREDERICK. A Summer in Alaska. St. Louis, 1893. 418pp. Inner hinges weak, o/w VG-. *Artis.* $40/£26

SCHWATKA, FREDERICK. A Summer in Alaska. St. Louis: J.W. Henry, 1894. 4th ptg. 418pp. VG. *Perier.* $60/£39

SCHWIEBERT, ERNEST. Trout. NY: Dutton, 1978. 1st ed. Signed. 2 vols. VF in Fine+ slipcase. *Bowman.* $250/£161

SCHWIMMER, ROSIKA. Tisza Tales. GC: Doubleday, 1928. 1st ed. Willy Pogany (illus). Lg 8vo. Pict cl (worn). VG. *Book Adoption.* $45/£29

SCIDMORE, ELIZA RUHAMAH. Alaska, Its Southern Coast and the Sitkan Archipelago. Lothrop, (1885). 1st ed. Fldg map frontis; viii,340pp; 7 plts. VG. *Oregon.* $85/£55

SCIDMORE, ELIZA RUHAMAH. China: The Long-Lived Empire. NY: Century Co., 1900. (xviii),466pp. Yellow cl stamped in red (sl soiled). *Schoyer.* $45/£29

SCOBEE, BARRY. Old Fort Davis. San Antonio: Naylor Co, (1947). VG in dj (lacks 1 1/2-inch square). *Perier.* $30/£19

SCOFIELD, SAMUEL. A Practical Treatise on Vaccinia or Cowpock. NY, 1810. 1st ed. 139pp. Full leather. Plt lacking, o/w Fine. *Fye.* $200/£129

SCORESBY, CAPTAIN. The Arctic Regions; Their Situation.... London: Religious Tract Soc, (1849). 192pp. Leather spine, marbled paper over bds (rubbed, worn). *Parmer.* $75/£48

SCORESBY, WILLIAM. An Account of the Arctic Regions with a History and Description of the Northern Whale Fishery. Edinburgh: Constable, 1820. 1st ed. 2 vols. xx,551,82; viii,574. 24 maps, engrs (foxing). Full contemp calf (rebacked, old spines relaid). Good. *Walcot.* $1,085/£700

SCORESBY, WILLIAM. An Account of the Arctic Regions, with a History and Description of the Northern Whale Fishery. Edinburgh: Archibald Constable, 1820. 2 vols. xx,551,82; viii,574pp. 24 plts, maps. Orig cl-backed bds, uncut, paper spine label. VG, as issued (minor scattered foxing). *High Latitude.* $1,500/£968

SCORESBY, WILLIAM. Journal of a Voyage to the Northern Whale Fishery.... Edinburgh: Constable, 1823. 1st ed. xiii,472. 6 plts, 2 fldg maps (foxing, offsetting). Full contemp calf (rebacked). Good+. *Walcot.* $457/£295

Scotland Delineated. Edinburgh, 1791. Hand-colored fldg engr map. Full calf (sl rubbed; joint sl cracked). *Petersfield.* $54/£35

SCOTT, ANNA B. Mrs. Scott's North American Seasonal Cook Book. Phila: Winston, 1921. 1st ed. Pict white oil cl. Worn. *Petrilla.* $20/£13

SCOTT, CLEMENT (comp). Drawing-Room Plays and Parlor Pantomimes. 40 London: Stanley Rivers, 1870. 1st ed. Wood engr frontis, xii,360pp. Red cl (rubbed, soiled), gilt spine. *Karmiole.* $40/£26

SCOTT, DAVID W. and E. JOHN BULLARD. John Sloan, 1871-1951. Boston, (1976). VG in dj. *Argosy.* $50/£32

SCOTT, EDWARD B. The Saga of Lake Tahoe. (Crystal Bay: Sierra-Tahoe, 1957). 1st ed. Gold-stamped cl. Dj (edgeworn, reinforced; flap corner torn off). *Dawson.* $50/£32

SCOTT, FRANK J. The Art of Beautifying Suburban Home Grounds of Small Extent. NY: Appleton, 1870. 1st ed. 618pp + 6pp ads. Pict cl. Fine. *Schoyer.* $300/£194

SCOTT, GEORGE RYLEY. Curious Customs of Sex and Marriage. Torchstream Books, 1953. 1st ed. #25/975. Color frontis, 32 plts. Dj. *Edwards.* $70/£45

SCOTT, GEORGE RYLEY. The History of Cockfighting. London, n.d. (ca 1960). #796/1095. Color frontis. Teg. (Fading.) *Edwards.* $93/£60

SCOTT, HARVEY W. History of the Oregon Country. Cambridge: Riverside Press, 1924. #338/500. Signed. 6 vols. (4 vols w/water stain fr edge of bds, not affecting text.) *Perier.* $395/£255

SCOTT, HUGH LENOX. Some Memories of a Soldier. NY, 1928. 1st ed. (Spine top faded.) *Ginsberg.* $150/£97

SCOTT, JOHN A. (ed). Fort Stanwix (Fort Schuyler) and Oriskany. Rome, NY: Rome Sentinel Co, 1927. 1st ed. Grn cl. Inscrip, inner hinges tape repaired, else VG. *Chapel Hill.* $40/£26

SCOTT, JOHN. Partisan Life with Col. John S. Mosby. NY: Harper, 1867. 1st ed. 492pp, fldg map. Orig grn cl. Spine sl loose, else VG-. *Chapel Hill.* $250/£161

SCOTT, MARY HURLBURT. The Oregon Trail Through Wyoming. A Century of History 1812-1912. Aurora, CO: Powder River, 1958. 1st ed. #21/750. Signed. 2 fldg maps laid in. VF. *Oregon.* $150/£97

SCOTT, MARY W. Houses of Old Richmond. Richmond: Valentine Museum, 1941. 1st ed. One of 1560. Signed. Pencil notes; spine sunned; lt rubbed, else Fine. *Bookpress.* $150/£97

SCOTT, MARY W. Old Richmond Neighborhoods. Richmond: Whittet & Shepperson, 1950. 1st ed. Signed. Gilt-emb cl. VG in dj. *Cahan.* $50/£32

SCOTT, PAUL. The Bender. London: Secker & Warburg, 1963. 1st Eng ed. Red cl. Fine in dj (sl nicked). *Dalian.* $39/£25

SCOTT, PAUL. The Birds of Paradise. Eyre & Spottiswoode, 1962. 1st ed. Dj (spine chipped). *Edwards.* $23/£15

SCOTT, PAUL. The Birds of Paradise. London: Eyre & Spottiswoode, 1962. 1st Eng ed. Brn cl. VG in dj. *Dalian.* $39/£25

SCOTT, PAUL. The Chinese Love Pavilion. Eyre & Spottiswoode, 1960. 1st ed. Dj (sl browned, chipped). *Edwards.* $31/£20

SCOTT, PAUL. The Jewel in the Crown. London: Heinemann, 1966. 1st ed. VG in dj (chipped, creased). *Rees.* $47/£30

SCOTT, PETER. Wild Geese and Eskimos. London: Country Life, 1951. 1st ed. Color frontis; 2 maps. VG (edges faded; inscrip) in dj (worn at folds). *Hollett.* $42/£27

SCOTT, PETER. Wild Geese and Eskimos. London/NY: Country Life/Scribner's, 1951. 1st ed. Color frontis. Lt blue cl, gilt (2 faded spots on spine). Dj (chipped, worn). *Parmer.* $95/£61

SCOTT, R.F. Scott's Last Expedition. London: Smith Elder & Co., 1913. 1st ed. 2 vols (sl rubbed). Good +. *Walcot.* $155/£100

SCOTT, R.F. Scott's Last Expedition. NY: Dodd Mead, 1913. 1st ed. 2 vols. 17 color plts, maps. VG +. *Bishop.* $190/£123

SCOTT, R.F. Scott's Last Expedition. London: Smith Elder, 1913. 3rd ed. 2 vols. Good + (sl rubbed; bumped). *Walcot.* $109/£70

SCOTT, R.F. The Voyage of the 'Discovery.' London: Smith, Elder, 1905. 2nd imp. 2 vols. xix,556; xii,508pp, 2 fldg maps in pockets. Orig gilt-dec cl. VG. *Walcot.* $271/£175

SCOTT, WALTER (ed). The Provincial Antiquities of Scotland and Picturesque Scenery of Scotland. Edinburgh, 1847. 2 vols. 208pp; 52 plts. Later 3/4 leather, marbled bds. Sm worm hole upper fr joint vol 1, o/w Fine. *Schoyer.* $225/£145

SCOTT, WALTER. The Field of Waterloo. Edinburgh, 1815. 1st ed. 1/2 title. Uncut edges frayed, dknd, stained, o/w VG in mod bds. *Poetry.* $47/£30

SCOTT, WALTER. Ivanhoe. NY: LEC, 1940. One of 1500 signed by Allen Lewis (illus). 2 vols. Fine in slipcase. *Williams.* $132/£85

SCOTT, WALTER. The Journal of Sir Walter Scott. Edinburgh: David Douglas, 1890. 1st complete ed. 2 vols. Frontispieces. Uncut edges sl spotted, o/w VG (inscrip). *Poetry.* $54/£35

SCOTT, WALTER. Kenilworth. Edinburgh: Archibald Constable, 1821. 1st ed. 3 vols. (iv),320; (iv),339; (iv),348pp w/half-titles; teg. Later 3/4 brn morocco, marbled bds, gilt-panelled backs. Very Nice set (sl wear). *House.* $400/£258

SCOTT, WALTER. The Lady of the Lake. B-M, 1910. 1st ed thus. H.C. Christy (illus). NF. *Aronovitz.* $125/£81

SCOTT, WALTER. The Lay of the Last Minstrel. London: Longman, 1807. 6th ed. Lg 8vo. 340pp, 3 ink-and-wash dwgs on card bound in. Dk blue morocco gilt, olive watered silk eps, paste-downs by Comte de Caumont w/his label (edges sl rubbed). *Marlborough.* $698/£450

SCOTT, WALTER. Letters on Demonology and Witchcraft. London: John Murray, 1831. 2nd ed. Engr frontis (lt browned); ix,396,(ii)pp. Full black calf gilt; bds blind-ruled (sl rubbed; corners worn; rebacked). *Hollett.* $101/£65

SCOTT, WALTER. The Life of Napoleon Buonaparte, Emperor of the French. Edinburgh: Longman, Rees, 1827. 1st ed. 9 vols. Contemp half calf (spine faded, sl rubbed, scuffed), gilt. Good (eps stained). *Hollett.* $233/£150

SCOTT, WALTER. The Monastery. Longman, Hurst, Rees Orme & Brown, 1820. 1st ed. 3 vols. 1/4 leather; gilt tooling, raised spines; plain bds; marbled pg edges. Good. *Aronovitz.* $175/£113

SCOTT, WALTER. Some Unpublished Letters of Walter Scott. J. Alexander Symington (ed). Oxford: Basil Blackwell, 1932. 1st ed. 14 plts; 4 facs. Uncut; prospectus signed, dated; compliments slip from ed loosely inserted. Fine in dj. *Hollett.* $116/£75

SCOTT, WALTER. The Vision of Don Roderick: A Poem. Edinburgh/London: John Ballantyne/Longman, Hurst et al, 1811. 1st ed. Brn half-calf leather; marbled bds; gilt-worked title panel on spine. VG (fr hinge sl tender). *Antic Hay.* $125/£81

SCOTT, WALTER. The Vision of Don Roderick; a Poem. Edinburgh, 1811. 1st ed. Uncut. NF (cvrs rubbed, sl soiled; edge-rubbed; corners sl chipped; bkpl). *Polyanthos.* $100/£65

SCOTT, WILLIAM HENRY. British Field Sports. London: Sherwood, Neely & Jones, 1818. 34 engr plts (incl frontis). Contemp 1/2 calf (sm crack 1 joint). Sound. *Petersfield.* $248/£160

SCOTT-MONCRIEFF, GEORGE. Edinburgh. London: Batsford, 1947. 1st ed. Spotted. Dj (price-clipped). *Hollett.* $23/£15

Scouring of the White Horse. (By Thomas Hughes.) London: Macmillan, 1859. 1st ed. 1st issue w/the 'u' not inserted in 'up' (p60, 2nd paragraph). xi,228pp (few spots). Contemp half calf (rubbed, sl scraped; upper bd stained), gilt. *Hollett.* $116/£75

Scouts of Ohio. NY: George Munroe, (1872). 99pp. Pict wraps. *Hayman.* $25/£16

SCULL, E. MARSHALL. Hunting in the Arctic and Alaska. Phila: Winston, 1914. 1st US ed. 11 maps. Spine sl rubbed. *Schoyer.* $100/£65

SCULLY, VINCENT. American Architecture and Urbanism. NY: Praeger, (1969). 1st ed. Dj lt worn, o/w VG. *Bookpress.* $95/£61

SCULLY, VINCENT. Frank Lloyd Wright. NY, 1960. 1st ed. Dj. *Edwards.* $31/£20

SEABROOK, W.B. Adventures in Arabia. London: George Harrap, 1931. Dec cl. VG (title lt spotted). *Hollett.* $31/£20

SEABROOK, WILLIAM. Witchcraft, Its Power in the World Today. NY, (1940). 1st ed. Rubbed, bumped, else Good in dj (torn, creased, inner tape repaired). *King.* $40/£26

SEABURY, SAMUEL. Letters of a Westchester Farmer (1774-1775). White Plains, NY, 1930. Howes S 252; S 253; S 254. *Ginsberg.* $35/£23

SEABY, ALLEN W. The Roman Alphabet and its Derivatives. Batsford, 1925. 1st ed. 30 plts. (Edgeworn.) *Edwards.* $54/£35

SEABY, ALLEN W. Sheltie: The Shetland Pony. London: A&C Black, (1939). 1st ed. Fine in pict dj (used; stain fr cvr). *Pharos.* $30/£19

SEAGO, EDWARD. Sons of Sawdust. London: Putnam, 1934. 1st ed. VG. *October Farm.* $35/£23

SEAGO, EDWARD. Tideline. London: Collins, 1948. 1st ed. Good (lt spotted) in pict dj (sl soiled, frayed). *Cox.* $28/£18

SEALE, WILLIAM. Texas Riverman, the Life and Times of Captain Andrew Smyth. Univ of TX, 1966. 1st ed. Signed. Dj. *Lambeth.* $35/£23

SEARS, JOSEPH H. Tennessee Printers, 1791-1945. Kingsport, TN: Privately ptd, (1945). 1st ed. Cl bds, paper label. *Ginsberg.* $50/£32

SEAVER, GEORGE. Birdie Bowers of the Antarctic. London: John Murray, 1938. 1st ed. 3 colored plts, 2 maps. VG in dj. *High Latitude.* $45/£29

SEAVER, TOM with LEE LOWENFISH. The Art of Pitching. Mountain Lion (Hearst), 1984. 1st ed. Fine in Fine dj. *Plapinger.* $40/£26

SEAVER, TOM with STEVE JACOBSON. Pitching with Tom Seaver. Prentice-Hall, 1973. 1st ed. Fine in VG dj. *Plapinger.* $35/£23

SEAWARD, A.C. Plant Life through the Ages.... Cambridge, 1931. (Bkpl.) *Henly.* $65/£42

SECKEL, DIETRICH. Emakimono. (NY): Pantheon, (1959). 1st Amer ed. One of 975. 68 color, tipped-in illus. Ink name; minor foxing; fr cvr sl rubbed; else VG in slipcase. *Bookpress.* $125/£81

Second Chapter of Accidents and Remarkable Events. (By William Darton.) Phila: Jacob Johnson, 1807. 12mo. 48pp; 12 engrs (3 hand-colored). Marbled stiff paper wrappers (soiled). VG (stamp, dedication; leaf w/chipped corner affecting 2 words). *Hobbyhorse.* $200/£129

Secrets Concerning Arts and Trades.... Dublin: Williams, 1778. Tp,3ff,xxvii,312pp,6ff; MS recipes at end. (Well-thumbed.) Sheep (worn, upper cvr off). *Marlborough.* $388/£250

Secular Spirit: Life and Art at the End of the Middle Ages. NY: MMA, 1975. All corners taped, o/w seemingly unread in wrappers. *Washton.* $40/£26

SEDGWICK, WILLIAM. Principles of Sanitary Science and the Public Health.... NY, 1902. 1st ed. Spine torn, dull, o/w VG. *Fye.* $150/£97

SEEBOHM, HENRY. A History of British Birds. London: R.H. Porter, 1883-85. 4 vols. 68 color plts. Some titles, flyleaves spotted, o/w Very Nice set. *Hollett.* $217/£140

SEEBOHM, HENRY. Siberia in Europe. London: John Murray, 1880. (xvi),(312)pp + 24pp ads, fldg map; presentation seal tp. Slate dec cl (pocket removed). *Schoyer.* $150/£97

SEEBOHN, HENRY. The Birds of Siberia. London: John Murray, 1901. Teg. Orig dec cl (minor stains). VG. *High Latitude.* $140/£90

SEEGER, PETE. How to Play the 5-String Banjo. Beacon, NY: By author, 1954. 2nd rev ed. NF in pict wraps (sl soiled). *Blue Mountain.* $35/£23

SEFERIS, GEORGE. Poems. Rex Warner (trans). Boston, 1960. 1st Amer ed. Fine (sl sunned) in NF dj. *Polyanthos.* $55/£35

SEGAR, CHARLES (ed). Official History of the National League. Jay, 1951. 1st ed. Good+ in Good+ dj. *Plapinger.* $40/£26

SEGUIN, EDWARD. Idiocy: And Its Treatment by the Physiological Method. NY, 1866. 1st ed. 457pp. Good. *Fye.* $350/£226

SEGUIN, L.G. The Black Forest: Its People and Legends. London: Hodder & Stoughton, 1885. 3rd ed. xii,428,8pp; 6 maps. (Extrems rubbed; spots, mks; joints cracking.) *Hollett.* $39/£25

SEGY, LADISLAS. African Sculpture Speaks. NY: A.A. Wyn, (1952). *Cullen.* $60/£39

SEIDENFADEN, ERIK. Guide to Bankok with Notes on Siam. Siam: Royal State Railways, 1927. 1st ed. Dec grn cl. Clean+. *Gretton.* $116/£75

SEITZ, DON CARLOS. Braxton Bragg, General of the Confederacy. Columbia, SC: State Co, 1924. 1st ed. Later cl. NF. *Mcgowan.* $150/£97

SEITZ, DON CARLOS. Braxton Bragg, General of the Confederacy. Columbia, SC: State Co, 1924. 1st ed. Frontis port. Beige cl. Corners bumped, port tipped to fep, else VG. *Chapel Hill.* $250/£161

SEITZ, DON CARLOS. Braxton Bragg, General of the Confederacy. Columbia: The State Co., 1924. 1st ptg. Frontis port. (Sm stain on fr cvr.) *Schoyer.* $125/£81

SEITZ, DON CARLOS. Braxton Bragg: General of the Confederacy. Columbia, SC: The State Co, 1924. 1st ed. NF in VG dj. *Mcgowan.* $450/£290

SEITZ, DON CARLOS. The Tryal of Capt. William Kidd.... NY: For Rufus Rockwell Wilson, 1936. 1st ed. Ltd to 650. (Gilt sl rubbed.) *Sadlon.* $20/£13

SEITZ, WILLIAM C. Abstract Expressionist Painting in America. Cambridge: Harvard Univ Press, 1983. VG in dj. *Argosy.* $85/£55

SELBY, HUBERT. Last Exit to Brooklyn. NY: Grove Press, (c 1964). 1st ed, 1st bk. Fine in dj. *Heller.* $125/£81

SELBY, PRIDEAUX JOHN. A History of British Forest Trees, Indigenous and Introduced. London, 1842. (New eps.) *Henly.* $101/£65

SELBY, PRIDEAUX JOHN. A History of British Forest-Trees, Indigenous and Introduced. London, 1842. xx,540pp. Aeg. Contemp grn leather (sl rubbed, bumped; fr inner joint starting), gilt. VG. *Shifrin.* $100/£65

SELDEN, JOHN. Table Talk. London: Joseph White, 1786. Crimson morocco (stained, rebacked). *Boswell.* $350/£226

SELDEN-GOTH, G. (ed). Felix Mendelssohn Letters. London, 1946. 1st ed. VF in Fine dj. *Bond.* $15/£10

SELDES, GEORGE. Iron, Blood and Profits. NY: Harper, 1934. 1st ed. Fine in dj (lt used). *Beasley.* $50/£32

Selections from the Court Reports Originally Published in the Boston Morning Post, from 1834 to 1837. Boston: Otis, Broaders, 1837. Orig emb cl, gilt (sl worn). *Boswell.* $225/£145

Selections from the Fancy, by an Operator. Barre: Imprint Society, 1971. #107/1950 numbered, signed by Randy Jones (illus). Bkpl, else Fine in pub's slipcase. *Hermitage.* $85/£55

SELF, WILL. Cock and Bull. Bloomsbury, 1992. 1st ed. Fine in dj. *Rees.* $31/£20

SELF, WILL. Cock and Bull. London: Bloomsbury, 1992. 1st UK ed. Fine in dj. *Lewton.* $39/£25

SELF, WILL. The Quantity Theory of Insanity. London: Bloomsbury, 1991. 1st ed, 1st state. Signed. Fine in wrappers. *Rees.* $70/£45

SELFRIDGE, THOMAS O. Reports of Explorations and Surveys to Ascertain the Practicability of a Ship-Canal between the Atlantic and Pacific.... Washington, 1874. 268pp, 17 fldg maps, 14 full-pg litho plts. Contemp 3/4 morocco, marbled bds (sl rubbed). Internally Fine. *Reese.* $450/£290

SELLERS, CHARLES COLEMAN. Charles Willson Peale. NY, (1969). 1st ed. 14 color, 102 b/w plts. VG in dj. *Argosy.* $75/£48

SELOUS, FREDERICK COURTENEY. A Hunter's Wanderings in Africa. London, 1911. Fldg map; teg (feps lt browned). Gilt device. *Edwards.* $70/£45

SELOUS, FREDERICK COURTENEY. Sport and Travel, East and West. London: Longmans, 1900. 1st ed. Bright pict cl. VG (bkpl). *Schoyer.* $300/£194

SELWYN, CECIL E. Prairie Patchwork or Western Poems for Western People. Winnipeg, 1910. 1st ed. Pict cl. Good. *Artis.* $35/£23

SELWYN-BROWN, ARTHUR. The Physician Throughout the Ages. NY, 1928. 1st ed. Emb cl. VG. *Argosy.* $150/£97

SEMMES, RAPHAEL. The Cruise of the Alabama and the Sumter. NY, 1864. 1st Amer ed. 2 vols in 1. 12mo. Frontis; 328pp. Ex-lib. *Argosy.* $300/£194

SEMMES, RAPHAEL. My Adventures Afloat. London: Richard Bentley, 1869. 1st ed. Engr frontis port; xvi,833pp; 2 engr composite port plts; 6 color lithos; map. Orig pict blue cl (sl worn; neatly recased w/new eps). VG (plts sl damp-mkd in margins or spotted, sl offsetting). *Hollett.* $349/£225

SEMMES, RAPHAEL. Service Afloat. Balt: Balt Pub. Co., 1887. 2nd ed. 833pp. Orig pict brn cl. Good (lt spotting, hinges tender). Howes S 286. *Chapel Hill.* $135/£87

SEMON, RICHARD. In the Australian Bush and on the Coast of the Coral Sea. London: Macmillan, 1899. 1st ed. xv,(i),552pp. Ribbed grn cl. Teg, untrimmed. VG. *Hollett.* $341/£220

SEMPLE, ROBERT. Memoirs on Diphtheria from the Writings of Bretonneau, Guersant.... London, 1859. 1st ed. 407pp. Good. *Fye.* $150/£97

SENCOURT, ROGER. T.S. Eliot. A Memoir. Donald Adamson (ed). Garnstone Press, 1971. 1st UK ed. Fine in dj. *Sclanders.* $31/£20

SENDAK, MAURICE and MATTHEW MARGOLIS. Some Swell Pup or Are You Sure You Want a Dog. NY: Farrar Straus, 1976. 1st ed. Maurice Sendak (illus). VF in NF dj. *Book Adoption.* $65/£42

SENDAK, MAURICE. Atomics for the Millions. NY: McGraw-Hill, (1947). 1st ed, 1st bk. 8vo. Dec blue cl (spine sl faded). *Reisler.* $300/£194

SENDAK, MAURICE. Caldecott and Co. NY: FSG, (1988). 1st ed. Inscribed. Fine in dj. *Godot.* $45/£29

SENDAK, MAURICE. Caldecott and Co. Notes on Books and Pictures. NY, 1988. 1st Amer ed. Signed. Fine in Fine dj. *Polyanthos.* $35/£23

SENDAK, MAURICE. Higglety Pigglety Pop! (NY): Harper & Row, (1967). 1st ed. Sq 12mo, 69pp. NF in dj (lt wear, else NF). *Godot.* $75/£48

SENDAK, MAURICE. Higglety Pigglety Pop! NY: Harper, 1967. 1st ed. 7x7. 69pp. Cl. Fine in dj. *Cattermole.* $100/£65

SENDAK, MAURICE. Higglety Pigglety Pop! or There Must Be More to Life. NY, (1979). 1st pb ed. Signed, dated. Sq 8vo. Rev slip laid in. Illus paper wrappers (spine lt faded, sl mkd). Nice. *Reisler.* $125/£81

SENDAK, MAURICE. In the Night Kitchen. Harper & Row, (1970). 1st ed. 4to. Unpaginated. Maurice Sendak (illus). White cl bds, pict pastedown. Price on dj $4.95. VG in VG dj (lt torn). *Davidson.* $300/£194

SENDAK, MAURICE. In the Night Kitchen. London: Bodley Head, 1971. 1st UK ed. Lg 8vo, (40)pp. VG in dj (sl frayed). *Cox.* $54/£35

SENDAK, MAURICE. In the Night Kitchen. Colouring Book. London: Bodley Head, 1972. 1st UK ed. Lg 8vo, 40pp. Laminated card cvr. VG. *Cox.* $23/£15

SENDAK, MAURICE. Posters by Maurice Sendak. NY: Harmony, 1976. 1st ed. Sm folio. Pict paper-cvrd bds. As New in As New dj. *Book Adoption.* $75/£48

SENDER, RAMON. The War in Spain. Peter Chalmers-Mitchell (trans). London: Faber, 1937. 1st ed. Fine in pict dj. *Patterson.* $124/£80

SENEFELDER, ALOIS. The Invention of Lithography. NY: Fuchs & Lang, 1911. Mtd frontis port. Burgundy cl, gilt. Sl rubbed, else Fine. *Glenn.* $150/£97

SENEFELDER, ALOIS. The Invention of Lithography. J.W. Muller (trans). NY: Fuchs & Lang, 1911. 1st ed in English. Color frontis. Maroon cl; unopened. VG (fr hinge tender; foxing). *Chapel Hill.* $120/£77

SENKEWICZ, ROBERT. Vigilantes in Gold Rush San Francisco. Stanford, 1985. 1st ed. Dbl-pg map. VF in VF dj. *Oregon.* $25/£16

SENN, NICHOLAS. Medico-Surgical Aspects of the Spanish-American War. Chicago: Amer Medical Assoc, 1900. Fldg table, fldg plan. Pict cl. VG. *Schoyer.* $100/£65

SENN, NICHOLAS. Surgical Bacteriology. Phila, 1889. 1st ed. 270pp. Good. *Fye.* $200/£129

SENN, NICHOLAS. Surgical Bacteriology. Phila, 1891. 2nd ed. 271pp. Good. *Fye.* $75/£48

SENN, NICHOLAS. Tuberculosis of Bones and Joints. Phila, 1892. 1st ed. 504pp. (Ex-lib.) *Fye.* $75/£48

Sequel to Old Jolliffe.... (By Matilda Anne Mackarness.) Boston/Cambridge: James Munroe, 1850. 12mo. 81pp + 8pp ads. Dec blind stamped cl, gilt title. Name, lt chipping, else VG. *Hobbyhorse.* $50/£32

SEREDY, KATE. Gypsy. NY: Viking, 1951. 1st ed. 8.5x11.5. 63pp. Cl. Fine in dj. *Cattermole.* $50/£32

SEREDY, KATE. Philomena. NY: Viking, 1955. 1st ed. 93pp. Beige cl. VG in VG dj. *Davidson.* $80/£52

SEREDY, KATE. The Singing Tree. London: Harrap, (1940). 1st ed. Dj (sl torn). *Petersfield.* $37/£24

SEREDY, KATE. Tenement Tree. NY: Viking, 1959. 1st ed. 6.75x10.25. 96pp. VG (ex-lib, mks) in dj. *Cattermole.* $30/£19

SEREDY, KATE. The White Stag. NY: Viking, 1937. 1st ed. 8vo. 95pp. Fine in VG dj. *Davidson.* $150/£97

SERGE, ROCHE. Mirrors. Colin Duckworth (trans). London, 1957. 1st UK ed. 13 tipped-in color figs, 281 b/w photos. Dj (ragged w/some loss). *Edwards.* $70/£45

SERT, JOSE LUIS. Can Our Cities Survive? Cambridge: Harvard Univ Press, 1942. 1st ed. Dj worn; else VG. *Bookpress.* $325/£210

SERVICE, ROBERT W. Ballads of a Cheechako. Toronto: William Briggs, 1909. Frontis. Grn cl, gilt cvr, spine titles, photo on cvr (sl wear to edges, corners bumped, hinge cracked at 2nd sig). *Parmer.* $135/£87

SERVICE, ROBERT W. The Master of the Microbe: A Fantastic Romance. London: T. Fisher Unwin, 1926. 1st ed. Red cl. Nice. *Temple.* $22/£14

SERVICE, ROBERT W. Rhymes of a Red Cross Man. Toronto, 1916. 1st ed. NF (spine sl sunned; sl edge rubbed). *Polyanthos.* $30/£19

SETH, VIKRAM. All You Who Sleep Tonight. London: Faber, 1990. 1st UK ed. Fine in dj. *Lewton.* $23/£15

SETH, VIKRAM. From Heaven Lake. London: C&W, 1983. 1st Eng ed, 1st bk. Signed. Orange cl. VF in dj. *Dalian.* $233/£150

SETH, VIKRAM. From Heaven Lake. C&W, 1983. 1st UK ed. Fine in dj. *Lewton.* $54/£35

SETH, VIKRAM. From Heaven Lake: Travels Through Sinkiang and Tibet. London: C&W/Hogarth Press, (1983). 1st ed. Fine in dj (short tear). *Heller.* $55/£35

SETH, VIKRAM. The Golden Gate. Faber, 1986. 1st UK ed. Fine in dj. *Lewton.* $31/£20

SETH, VIKRAM. The Golden Gate. NY: Random House, 1986. 1st US ed. Fine in NF dj. *Pettler.* $45/£29

SETH, VIKRAM. Mappings. (Saratoga, CA: The Author, 1980.) 1st ed, 1st bk. One of 150 signed. VF in black paper wrappers. *Jaffe.* $450/£290

SETH, VIKRAM. A Suitable Boy. London: Phoenix House, 1993. 1st trade ed, 1st issue (1500 copies w/grn eps). Lt crease last few leaves, o/w Fine in dj. *Moorhouse.* $70/£45

SETH, VIKRAM. A Suitable Boy. Phoenix, 1993. 1st UK ed, 1st issue w/grn eps. Fine in dj. *Lewton.* $70/£45

SETON, ERNEST THOMPSON. The Arctic Prairies. London: Constable, 1912. Teg. (Spine sl faded; corners sl bumped; last leaves lt spotted.) *Hollett.* $62/£40

SETON, ERNEST THOMPSON. The Biography of a Silver Fox. NY: Century, 1909. 1st ed. Good (dknd, worn). *Hermitage.* $60/£39

SETON, ERNEST THOMPSON. The Biography of a Silver-Fox. NY: Century Co., 1909. Stated 1st ed. 8vo. 209pp, 10 full b/w plts. Grey/blue cl. VG in dj (lt torn, soiled). *Davidson.* $65/£42

SETON, ERNEST THOMPSON. Lives of Game Animals. GC, 1925-1928. One of 177 numbered sets, signed by Seton, inscribed in each vol. 4 vols. Vol 2 w/orig photos reproduced in plt xxxii tipped in at plt, w/2 add'l photos not in bk. Gilt dec 2-tone cl; teg. Frontispieces loose. *Argosy.* $600/£387

SETON, ERNEST THOMPSON. Two Little Savages. NY: Doubleday, Page, 1903. 1st ed. Grn cl (lt dampstain; lt worn; sl soiled). VG. *Hermitage.* $45/£29

SETON, ERNEST THOMPSON. Two Little Savages. Doubleday, Page, 1903. 1st ed. Dec cvr. Fine. *Authors Of The West.* $75/£48

SETON, GRACE GALLATIN. Nimrod's Wife. NY: Doubleday, Page, 1907. 1st ed. Mtd cvr photo (chipped). Tan cl, stamped in grn/red (soiled); teg. *Karmiole.* $35/£23

SETON, GRACE GALLATIN. Nimrod's Wife. NY: Doubleday Page, 1907. 1st ed. Teg. Pict gray cl, red berries on pine branches, pict onlay on cvr. VG+. *Bowman.* $50/£32

SETON-THOMPSON, ERNEST. The Biography of a Grizzly. NY: Century, 1900. 1st ed. Pict cl. NF. *Glenn.* $100/£65

SETON-THOMPSON, ERNEST. The Biography of a Grizzly.... NY: Century, 1900. 1st ed. Pict buckram, gilt. Tp sl soiled, else VG. *Pharos.* $30/£19

SETON-THOMPSON, ERNEST. The Trail of the Sandhill Stag. NY: Scribner's, 1899. 1st ed. 94pp, 8 plts (1 color). Grn cl, gilt (soiled). *Karmiole.* $35/£23

SETON-THOMPSON, ERNEST. The Trail of the Sandhill Stag.... NY: Scribner's, 1899. 1st ed. Pict buckram; gilt. Cvrs soiled, o/w VG internally. *Pharos.* $45/£29

SETTLE, MARY LEE. All the Brave Promises: Memoirs of Aircraft Woman 2nd Class. NY: Delacorte, (1966). 1st ed. VF in dj (sm closed tear). *Pharos.* $60/£39

SETTLE, MARY LEE. The Killing Ground. NY: FSG, (1982). 1st ed. Ltd to 150 signed. Fine in pub's slipcase. *Sadlon.* $40/£26

SETTLE, MARY LEE. The Kiss of Kin. NY: Harpers, (1955). 1st Amer ed. Fine in dj. *Pharos.* $150/£97

SETTLE, MARY LEE. The Kiss of Kin. London: Heinemann, (1955). Correct 1st ed. Fine in dj (chipped). *Pharos.* $175/£113

SETTLE, MARY LEE. The Love Eaters. NY: Harpers, (1954). 1st Amer ed, 1st bk. Sig, o/w Fine in dj. *Pharos.* $150/£97

SETTLE, MARY LEE. The Love Eaters. NY: Harper, (1954). 1st Amer ed. Sm stamp, else Fine in NF dj (price-clipped). *Between The Covers.* $250/£161

SETTLE, MARY LEE. The Scapegoat. NY: Random House, (1980). 1st ed. Fine in dj. *Pharos.* $35/£23

SETTLE, MARY LUND and RAYMOND W. Saddles and Spurs. Harrisburg, (1955). 1st ed. VG in VG dj. *Pratt.* $35/£23

SETTLE, RAYMOND (ed). The March of the Mounted Riflemen. Glendale: Clark, 1940. 1st ed. One of 1007. Uncut. VF. *Perier.* $150/£97

SETTLE, RAYMOND (ed). The March of the Mounted Riflemen.... Glendale: Clark, 1940. 1st ed thus. Frontis. Unopened. Blue cl. VG. Howes C 923. *Chapel Hill.* $150/£97

SETTLE, RAYMOND and MARY (eds). Overland Days to Montana in 1865. Glendale: Clark, 1971. One of 1605. VG. *Perier.* $30/£19

SETTLE, RAYMOND and MARY (eds). Overland Days to Montana in 1865. The Diary of Sarah Raymond and Journal of Dr. Waid Howard. Glendale: Clark, 1971. 1st ed. Fldg map. *Heinoldt.* $35/£23

SETTLE, WILLIAM A. Jesse James Was His Name. Columbia, MO: Univ of MO, (1966). 1st ed. Blue cl (tape offset; bkpl). Dj (soiled). *Glenn.* $35/£23

SEUSS, DR. (Pseud of Theodore Seuss Geisel.) The 500 Hats of Bartholomew Cubbins. NY: Vanguard Press, (1938). 1st ed. 4to, 25 leaves. Pict eps. Red cl-backed pict black bds (bumped, edges rubbed); illus cvr. Internally NF. *Blue Mountain.* $85/£55

SEUSS, DR. (Pseud of Theodore Seuss Geisel.) The 500 Hats of Bartholomew Cubbins. NY: Vanguard, (1938). 1st ed. Lg 4to. 47pp. Red cl-backed pict bds; pict eps. Very Nice (few margins smudged) in dj (sl worn, price-clipped, internal repairs). *Cady.* $250/£161

SEUSS, DR. (Pseud of Theodore Seuss Geisel.) The 500 Hats of Bartholomew Cubbins. NY: Vanguard, 1938. 1st ed. NF in NF dj. *Davidson.* $400/£258

SEUSS, DR. (Pseud of Theodore Seuss Geisel.) Bartholomew and the Oobleck. NY: Random House, (1949). Inscribed. Red glazed bds. VG (inscrip) in VG dj. *Davidson.* $225/£145

SEUSS, DR. (Pseud of Theodore Seuss Geisel.) The Cat in the Hat Comes Back. NY: Random House, 1958. Stated 1st ed. Unpaginated. VG (spine bumped). *Davidson.* $225/£145

SEUSS, DR. (Pseud of Theodore Seuss Geisel.) The Cat's Quizzer. NY: Beginner Books, 1976. 1st ed. 4to. Color illus bds (lt edgewear). *Reisler.* $150/£97

SEUSS, DR. (Pseud of Theodore Seuss Geisel.) Dr. Seuss from Then and Now. NY: Random House, 1986. Stated 1st ed. 4to. 93pp. VG in VG dj. *Davidson.* $55/£35

SEUSS, DR. (Pseud of Theodore Seuss Geisel.) Dr. Seuss's Sleep Book. NY: Random House, 1962. (1st ed?). 4to. Unpaginated. Pict bds. VG (corners bumped) in dj (lt soiled). *Davidson.* $175/£113

SEUSS, DR. (Pseud of Theodore Seuss Geisel.) How the Grinch Stole Christmas. NY: Random House, 1957. 1st ed. Price at $2.50. VG in VG dj. *Davidson.* $550/£355

SEUSS, DR. (Pseud of Theodore Seuss Geisel.) If I Ran the Zoo. NY: Random House, 1950. 1st ed. Price at $2.50. VG (edges, corners lt bumped) in dj (lt torn). *Davidson.* $400/£258

SEUSS, DR. (Pseud of Theodore Seuss Geisel.) Pocket Book of Boners. NY: Pocket Books, July 1941. 1st thus ed. Sm 16mo. Pict pb. NF. *Book Adoption.* $35/£23

SEUSS, DR. (Pseud of Theodore Seuss Geisel.) Scrambled Eggs Super. NY: Random House, 1953. 1st ed. Price at $2.50. VG in VG dj (2-inch tear at bottom). *Davidson.* $400/£258

SEUSS, DR. (Pseud of Theodore Seuss Geisel). The Seven Lady Godivas. NY: Random House, (1939). 1st ed. 4to. Beige cl, maroon decs. Color dj (chipped; missing lg section rear cvr). *Reisler.* $225/£145

Seven Autumn Leaves from Fairyland. Boston: A. Williams, 1873. 8vo. 135pp; 13 etchings. Blue cl, gilt. Spine rubbed, o/w VG. *Drusilla's.* $85/£55

Seven Little Sisters Who Live on the Round Ball That Floats in the Air. (By Jane Andrews.) Boston: Ticknor & Fields, 1861. 1st ed. Sm 8vo. vi,127pp,1p ad, 1/2 title, full-pg title w/guard, tp, dedication, contents. 7 full-pg VF wood engrs by S.S. Kilburn. Blind-emb brn cl on bds, dec gilt titles. Fine (edges lt soiled, rubbed). *Hobbyhorse.* $325/£210

Seven Simeons. NY: Viking, 1938. 1st ed. 4to, unpaginated. Boris Artzbasheff (illus). Grn cl. VG (2 tape mks) in dj (lt soiled). *Davidson.* $70/£45

SEVERANCE, FRANK. An Old Frontier of France. NY: Dodd, Mead, 1917. 1st ed. 2 vols. Frontis. Blue cl. VG. *Chapel Hill.* $150/£97

SEVERANCE, FRANK. An Old Frontier of France. The Niagara Region.... Dodd Mead, 1917. 1st ed. 2 vols. 33 plts (incl 12 maps). Lt soiling vol 2, o/w VG. *Oregon.* $95/£61

SEVIGNE, MADAME. Letters...to the Countess de Grignon, her Daughter. London: J. Hinton, 1759. 2 vols. Contemp sprinkled calf, gilt back (worn); red/black leather labels. *Argosy.* $100/£65

SEWALL, SAMUEL. The History of Moburn. Boston: Wiggin & Lunt, 1868. 1st ed. Engr frontis port, 658pp. Grn cl, gilt. Good. *Karmiole.* $65/£42

SEWARD, ANNA. Memoirs of the Life of Dr. Darwin. London: J. Johnson, 1804. 1st ed. 430pp. Final leaf of errata, ads present. Contemp calf (rebacked). Nice. *Hartfield.* $395/£255

SEWARD, C.A. Metal Plate Lithography. NY: Pencil Points, 1931. Good. *Artis.* $27/£17

SEWELL, BROCARD. In the Dorian Mode: A Life of John Gray 1866-1934. Tabb House, 1983. 1st ed. Fine in dj. *Poetry.* $23/£15

SEXTON, ANNE. Live or Die. Boston: Houghton Mifflin, 1966. 1st ed. Fine (sm dent) in VG dj (sm dent; spine sunned). *Revere.* $45/£29

SEXTON, R.W. Interior Architecture, the Design of Interiors of Modern American Houses. NY: Architectural Book/Paul Wenzel & Maurice Krakow, (1927). Frontis. Orange cl. Fine in dj (sl worn). *Weber.* $75/£48

SEYFFERT, OSKAR. A Dictionary of Classical Antiquities, Mythology, Religion, Literature and Art. Henry Nettleship & J.E. Sandys (eds). London: Sonnenschein, 1908. Gilt-pict cl (rebacked, extrems worn; foxing). *Archaeologia.* $65/£42

SEYMOUR, E.S. Sketches of Minnesota, the New England of the West. NY: Harper, 1850. Fldg frontis map (tape-repaired), 282pp + 6pp ads (foxing). Black cl (spine extrems frayed). Howes S 313. *Karmiole.* $200/£129

SEYMOUR, E.S. Sketches of Minnesota, the New England of the West. NY: Harper, 1850. 281pp, fldg map. 1/2 morocco. (Spine faded.) Howes S 313. *Ginsberg.* $300/£194

SEYMOUR, FLORA. The Boy's Life of Kit Carson. NY: Century, 1929. 1st ed. Good + (bkstore stamp; spine tear, soil). *Parker.* $35/£23

SEYMOUR, FLORA. The Story of the Red Man. Longmans, Green, 1929. 1st ed. Signed. Frontis, 23 plts (12 maps on 6 plts). Fine in Good + dj. *Oregon.* $50/£32

SEYMOUR, HAROLD. Baseball: The Golden Age. Oxford, 1971. 1st ed. VG + in Good + dj. *Plapinger.* $65/£42

SEYMOUR, M. HOBART. A Pilgrimage to Rome. London, 1851. 4th ed. Tp,xi,484pp (spotting); marbled eps. Speckled 1/2 calf (sm dent fore-edge upper bd). *Edwards.* $47/£30

SEYMOUR, PETER. Frontier Town. NY: Holt, Rinehart, & Winston. 1982. 16x22 cm. 4 dbl-pg pop-ups. Marvin Boggs & Borge Svensson (illus). Glazed pict bds. VG. *Book Finders.* $30/£19

SEYMOUR, ROBERT. Seymour's Comic Album. London: Kidd, n.d. (1835?). 203pp, 4 plts. VG. *Schoyer.* $150/£97

SEZNEC, JEAN. The Survival of the Pagan Gods. NY, 1953. Fine in dj. *Europa.* $70/£45

SEZNEC, JEAN. The Survival of the Pagan Gods. NY, 1953. Rev ed. Good. *Washton.* $85/£55

SHAARA, MICHAEL. The Herald. McGraw-Hill Book Co, (1981). 1st ed. Fine in dj. *Sadlon.* $30/£19

SHACKELFORD, GEORGE GREEN (ed). Collected Papers to Commemorate Fifty Years of the Monticello Association of the Descendants of Thomas Jefferson. Monticello Assoc, 1984. Vol 2. Good (corner chewed). *Book Broker.* $45/£29

SHACKLEFORD, WILLIAM Y. Belle Star, the Bandit Queen. Girard, KS: Haldeman-Julius, (1946). #1846 in Little Blue Book series. 12mo. VG in wraps. *Schoyer.* $15/£10

SHACKLEFORD, WILLIAM Y. Buffalo Bill Cody, Scout and Showman. Girard, KS: Haldeman-Julius, (1944). VG in wraps (fragile). *Book Market.* $25/£16

SHACKLETON, E.H. The Heart of the Antarctic. Heinemann, 1909. 1st ed. 2 vols. Orig (?) red cl. VG (lacks feps). *Walcot.* $147/£95

SHACKLETON, E.H. Heart of the Antarctic. London: Heinemann, 1909. 1st ed. 2 vols. 3 fldg maps, panorama in pocket; 12 color, 257 b/w plts. Teg. Blue cl (spine faded) blocked in silver. VG set. *Blue Dragon.* $375/£242

SHACKLETON, E.H. South. London: Heinemann, 1919. 1st ed. Color frontis, fldg map. Orig silver dec cl. VG (some browning of edges). *High Latitude.* $275/£177

SHACKLETON, E.H. South. Heinemann, 1919. 2nd imp. Fldg map. Pict cl (sl bumped, rubbed; 2 sm spine tears). Good. *Walcot.* $50/£32

SHACKLETON, E.H. South. The Story of Shackleton's Last Expedition 1914-1917. NY: Macmillan, 1920. 1st Amer ed. Frontis, fldg map. Grn cl, gilt titles (sl wear head, heel; sl foxing). *Parmer.* $275/£177

SHACKLETON, E.H. South. The Story of Shackleton's Last Expedition. London: Heinemann, 1920. 3rd imp. Fldg map. VG. *Walcot.* $74/£48

SHACKLETON, EDWARD A. Arctic Journeys. London: Hodder & Stoughton, 1937. 1st ed. Map. Spine faded, else VG + . *Parmer.* $75/£48

SHACKLETON, KATHLEEN. Arctic Pilot. London: Thomas Nelson, 1941. Map. VG in dj (folds strengthened on reverse). *Hollett.* $39/£25

SHACOCHIS, BOB. Easy in the Islands. NY: Crown, 1985. 1st ed. 1st bk. Fine in Fine dj. *Revere.* $45/£29

SHADWELL, ARTHUR. Drink, Temperance and Legislation. NY, 1915. 1st ed, 3rd ptg. Good. *Fye.* $35/£23

SHADWELL, THOMAS. The Complete Works. Montague Summers (ed). London: Fortune Press, 1927. #282/1200 sets. 5 vols. Frontis port, ms plt vol 1; litho frontispieces other vols; uncut, unopened. Black linen spines, gilt, marbled bds. Splendid set. *Hartfield.* $395/£255

SHAFFER, PETER. Amadeus. London: Deutsch, 1980. 1st UK ed. Fine in dj. *Williams.* $74/£48

SHAFFER, PETER. Five Finger Exercise. H. Hamilton, 1958. 1st UK ed. Sl sticky patch fr flap, fep, o/w VG + in VG dj. *Martin.* $28/£18

SHAFFER, PETER. The Private Ear and the Public Eye. London: Hamilton, 1962. 1st UK ed. NF in dj. *Williams.* $47/£30

SHAFFER, PETER. The Royal Hunt of the Sun. London: Hamilton, 1964. 1st UK ed. VG + in VG dj (fore-edges sl bumped). *Williams.* $56/£36

SHAFFER, PETER. Shrivings. London: Deutsch, 1974. 1st UK ed. Fine in NF dj. *Williams.* $54/£35

SHAFTESBURY, ANTHONY. Characteristicks of Men, Manners, Opinions, Times. Birmingham: Ptd by John Baskerville, 1773. 5th ed. 3 vols. Port, general title w/vignette vol 1; engr head pieces. 19th cent polished calf; gilt spine, black labels; marbled eps. *Bickersteth.* $341/£220

SHAHN, BEN. The Complete Graphic Works. (NY): Quadrangle/NY Times Book Co, (1973). 1st ed. VG in dj. *Hermitage.* $125/£81

SHAHN, BEN. Love and Joy About Letters. NY, 1963. VG in bd slipcase. *Argosy.* $100/£65

SHAHN, BERNARDA BRYSON. Ben Shahn. NY: Abrams, n.d. (1972). VG in dj. *Argosy.* $350/£226

SHAHN, BERNARDA BRYSON. Ben Shahn. NY: Abrams, n.d. (ca 1972). 1st ed. Fine in dj (price-clipped, else Fine). *Godot.* $350/£226

SHAIRP, JOHN CAMPBELL et al. Life and Letters of James David Forbes, F.R.S..... London: Macmillan, 1873. 1st ed. xiv,578pp + (2)pp ads, 4 engrs (incl frontis port, t.p. vignette), 4 mtd photos, fldg map. Orig red pebbled gilt cl (fr cvr sl creased in 2 places, extrems sl frayed). *Karmiole.* $125/£81

SHAKESPEARE, EDWARD O. Report on Cholera in Europe and India. Washington DC: GPO, 1890. (xxvi),945pp. Sm folio (rubbed, shaken, hinges repaired). *Schoyer.* $150/£97

SHAKESPEARE, WILLIAM. As You Like It. London: Folio Soc, 1953. 7 full-pg color plts by Salvador Dali. Sl cvr discolor, else VG in Nice dj (sl edge tear; price-clipped). *King.* $25/£16

SHAKESPEARE, WILLIAM. The Comedies, Histories and Tragedies of William Shakespeare. Herbert Farejon (ed). NY: LEC, 1939-1940 & 1941. #904/1500 numbered sets. 39 vols. Gilt-stamped buckram-backed dec bds. Fine set in tissue wrappers (torn); 2 poetry vols in slipcase (sl rubbed). *Hermitage.* $1,750/£1,129

SHAKESPEARE, WILLIAM. Flowers from Shakespeare's Garden. London: Cassell, 1906. 1st ed. 8vo. 40pp. Walter Crane (illus). VG. *Davidson.* $250/£161

SHAKESPEARE, WILLIAM. Hamlet: Prince of Denmark. London: Selwyn & Blount, (1922). 1st ed. Signed, dated by John Austen (illus). 4to. Cl-backed dec bds (sl bump). Pict dj (chipped). *Reisler.* $450/£290

SHAKESPEARE, WILLIAM. The Life of King Henry V. NY: LEC, 1951. #904/1500 numbered. Fritz Kredel (illus). Fine set in pub's slipcase (sl dusty). *Hermitage.* $100/£65

SHAKESPEARE, WILLIAM. A Midsommer Nights Dreame. London: Ernest Benn, 1924. Ltd to 550. Linen-backed bds. Ink sig, o/w Fine. *Sadlon.* $125/£81

SHAKESPEARE, WILLIAM. A Midsummer Night's Dream. London: Constable, 1914. 1st ed. Lg, 4to. 12 mtd color plts by W. Heath Robinson (guards foxed). Gilt pict cl (sl dampstaining fr). *Reisler.* $550/£355

SHAKESPEARE, WILLIAM. The National Shakespeare: Comedies, Histories, and Tragedies. London: William MacKenzie, n.d. (1900). Special ed w/India proof impressions. 3 vols. Folio. Frontis port plt. Teg, others uncut. Pub's deluxe full grn morocco, ribbed gilt dec spines; tooled in gilt, blind. *D & D.* $1,200/£774

SHAKESPEARE, WILLIAM. The Poems of William Shakespeare. NY: LEC, 1941. One of 1500 signed. 2 vols. Dec bds; teg; others untrimmed. Fine in glassines. Slipcase (sl worn). *Veatchs.* $200/£129

SHAKESPEARE, WILLIAM. Shakespeare's Sonnets.... NY: Cheshire House, 1931. One of 1200 numbered. Teg. Full gilt red pub's calf. Fine in slipcase (worn). *Reese.* $35/£23

SHAKESPEARE, WILLIAM. The Tempest. London: Heinemann, (1926). #143/520, signed by Arthur Rackham (illus). Lg, 4to. 21 mtd color plts, 25 b/w dwgs. Teg. White bds, vellum back; gold stamping cvr, spine (sl edgewear). White paper dj w/red lettering, dec (marginal tears, smudges). Nice. *Reisler.* $2,800/£1,806

SHAKESPEARE, WILLIAM. The Tempest. NY/London: Doubleday, Page/Heinemann, (1926). US issue on Eng sheets. 20 tipped-in color plts by Arthur Rackham. VG (inscrip, lt foxing). *Cahan.* $125/£81

SHAKESPEARE, WILLIAM. Venus and Adonis. Paris: Harrison, 1930. #7/440. Fine in Fine box. *Polyanthos.* $75/£48

SHAKESPEARE, WILLIAM. Venus and Adonis. Rochester: Leo Hart, 1934. 1st trade ed. Rockwell Kent (illus). NF in VG white dj (sl nicked, tanned). *Reese.* $30/£19

SHAKESPEARE, WILLIAM. The Works of Shakespeare. NY: Random House, 1929-1933. #1031/1050. 7 vols. Full tan morocco (sl worn; 3 spines dknd). *Glenn.* $1,500/£968

SHAKESPEARE, WILLIAM. The Works of William Shakespeare. NY: Nonesuch, 1929. 7 vols. Teg, others uncut. Pub's full tan pig skin, ribbed gilt-lettered spine; cvrs double-ruled in gilt. VF. *D & D.* $1,600/£1,032

SHALER, WILLIAM. Journal of a Voyage Between China and the North-Western Coast of America Made in 1804 by.... Claremont, CA, 1935. 700 numbered copies. (Bkpl, sig.) Howes S 324. *Ginsberg.* $150/£97

SHALER, WILLIAM. Journal of a Voyage Between China and the North-Western Coast of America, Made in 1804.... Claremont, CA: Saunders Studio, 1935. One of 700. Fldg map, facs tp. Howes S 324. *Lefkowicz.* $150/£97

SHAND, P. MORTON. The Architecture of Pleasure. Modern Theatres and Cinemas. London: Batsford, 1930. (Feps lt foxed; upper hinge sl cracked; cl browned.) *Edwards.* $74/£48

SHAND, P. MORTON. The Architecture of Pleasure. Modern Theatres and Cinemas. London: Batsford, 1930. 1st ed. Spine sl faded, o/w Fine. *Europa.* $84/£54

SHANGE, NTOZAKE. Betsey Brown. NY: St. Martin's, (1985). 1st ed. Sig, o/w VG in dj (short tear). *Hermitage.* $20/£13

SHANGE, NTOZAKE. For Colored Girls Who Have Considered Suicide When the Rainbow Is Enuf. NY, (1977). 1st hb ed. Cl-backed bds. VG in dj. *Argosy.* $50/£32

SHANNON, BILL and GEORGE KALINSKY. The Ball Parks. Hawthorn, 1975. 1st ed. Fine in VG dj. *Plapinger.* $175/£113

SHANNON, FRED ALBERT. The Organization and Administration of the Union Army. Cleveland: Clark, 1928. 1st ed. 2 vols. Frontispieces. Orig blue cl. VF in djs (1 tattered remnants; 1 w/spine top cut away). *Chapel Hill.* $365/£235

SHANNON, MARTHA A.S. Boston Days of William Morris Hunt. Boston: Marshall Jones, 1923. 1st ed. 41 full-pg plts. Teg. Cl-backed paper over bds. VG. *Cahan.* $85/£55

SHANNON, MARTHA A.S. Boston Days of William Morris Hunt. Boston: Marshall Jones, 1923. Ltd to 1500 numbered. Fine. *Pharos.* $40/£26

SHAPIRO, KARL. White-Haired Lover. NY, 1968. 1st Amer ed. Signed presentation. Fine in dj (edge tear). *Polyanthos.* $30/£19

SHAPIRO, LARRY. Baby Animals. A Change-A-Picture Book. Discovery Toys, 1979. 17x17 cm. 7 pictures. Linda Griffith (illus). Glazed illus bds. Fine. *Book Finders.* $25/£16

SHAPIRO, M. The Screaming Eagles: The 101st Airborne. NY, 1976. VG. *Clark.* $35/£23

SHAPIRO, MILTON. Champions of the Bat. Messner, 1967. 1st ed. Fine in VG + dj. *Plapinger.* $40/£26

SHAPIRO, MILTON. Jackie Robinson of the Brooklyn Dodgers. Messner, (1968). Ltr ptg of rev ed. Fine in VG dj. *Plapinger.* $30/£19

SHAPIRO, MILTON. The Roy Campanella Story. Messner, 1958. 1st ed. Fine in VG dj. *Plapinger.* $60/£39

SHAPIRO, MILTON. Willie Mays Story. Messner, 1960. Ltr ptg. Fine in VG dj. *Plapinger.* $50/£32

SHAPIRO, NAT and NAT HENTOFF (eds). The Jazz Makers. NY: Rinehart, 1957. 1st ed. Fine in NF dj (tear rear panel). *Beasley.* $45/£29

SHAPLEY, FERN RUSK. Paintings from the Samuel H. Kress Collection: Italian Schools XV-XVI Century. London, 1968. Good in dj. *Washton.* $175/£113

SHARP, CECIL J. and A.P. OPPE. The Dance. An Historical Survey of Dancing in Europe. London: Halton & Truscott Smith, 1924. Gilt pict cl (sl rubbed); teg. *Sadlon.* $45/£29

SHARP, CECIL. English Folk-Songs from the Southern Appalachians. Maud Karpeles (ed). London: OUP, 1952. 2nd impression. 2 vols. Fine in djs (sl used; internally mended). *Pharos.* $85/£55

SHARP, MARGERY. The Rescuers. London: Collins, 1959. 1st ed. 8vo. Judith Brook (illus). Grn cl, gilt (edges sl faded). Pict dj (spine sl worn). *Reisler.* $150/£97

SHARP, SAMUEL. Letters from Italy...in the Years 1765, and 1766. Dublin: Ptd for P. Wilson, J. Exhaw, et al, (1767). vi,380pp. Orig calf (rebacked); new eps. *Bickersteth.* $85/£55

SHARP, WILLIAM. Diagnosis and Treatment of Brain Injuries. Phila: Lippincott, 1920. Colored frontis. Cl sl rubbed, else VG. *Goodrich.* $45/£29

SHARP, WILLIAM. The Life and Letters of Joseph Severn. London: Sampson, Low, 1892. 1st ed. 14pg article tipped in. Buckram, gilt. Good (lt foxing; bkpl removed; hinges weak). *Pharos.* $45/£29

SHARPE, SAMUEL. The History of Egypt under the Ptolemies. London: Edward Moxon, 1838. v,220pp. Orig bds (corners worn; newly rebacked in cl w/new spine label). Clean, unopened. *Schoyer.* $125/£81

SHARPE, TOM. Ancestral Vices. Secker, 1980. 1st UK ed. NF in dj. *Williams.* $28/£18

SHARPE, TOM. Blott on the Landscape. London: Secker & Warburg, 1975. 1st UK ed. Fine in VG + dj. *Williams.* $74/£48

SHARPE, TOM. Blott on the Landscape. London: Secker, 1975. 1st UK ed. Signed. Fine in VG + dj. *Williams.* $140/£90

SHARPE, TOM. The Great Pursuit. Secker & Warburg, 1977. 1st ed. Fine in dj. *Limestone.* $55/£35

SHARPE, TOM. The Great Pursuit. London: Secker & Warburg, 1977. 1st UK ed. NF in dj. *Williams.* $56/£36

SHARPE, TOM. The Great Pursuit. London: Secker & Warburg, 1977. 1st UK ed. Signed. NF in dj. *Williams.* $116/£75

SHARPE, TOM. Indecent Exposure. London: Secker, 1973. 1st UK ed. Signed. Fine in NF dj (price-clipped). *Williams.* $302/£195

SHARPE, TOM. Porterhouse Blue. Secker, 1974. 1st UK ed. VG in dj (sl wear spine top). *Williams.* $54/£35

SHARPE, TOM. Riotous Assembly. London: Secker & Warburg, 1971. 1st ed. NF in VG + dj (lt dampstaining verso spine; short edgetears spine). *Lame Duck.* $250/£161

SHARPE, TOM. Vintage Stuff. London: Secker, 1982. 1st UK ed. Signed. Fine in dj. *Williams.* $62/£40

SHARPE, TOM. Wilt on High. London: Secker & Warburg, 1984. 1st UK ed. Signed. Fine in 1st state Red Ranch dj. *Williams.* $62/£40

SHARPE, TOM. Wilt. London: S&W, 1976. 1st UK ed. Inscrip, o/w NF in dj. *Lewton.* $39/£25

SHARPEY, WILLIAM et al (eds). Quain's Elements of Anatomy. London: James Walton, 1867. 7th ed. 2 vols. ccxxvii,504; viii,501-1147pp. Orig 1/2 calf. VG (vol 1 rebacked retaining backstrip, label). *White.* $65/£42

SHAVER, RICHARD. I Remember Lemuria. Venture, 1948. 1st ed. VG. *Madle.* $75/£48

SHAW, ALBERT. Abraham Lincoln. NY: Review of Reviews Corp, 1929. 1st ed. 2 vols. Red cl stamped in black/gold; teg. Very Nice set in djs (spines faded). *Karmiole.* $75/£48

SHAW, BOB. The Palace of Eternity. Gollancz, 1970. 1st ed. NF in dj. *Aronovitz.* $150/£97

SHAW, C.E. and S. CAMPBELL. Snakes of the American West. NY: Knopf, 1974. 1st ed. VG in VG dj. *Mikesh.* $35/£23

SHAW, C.E. and S. CAMPBELL. Snakes of the American West. NY, 1974. 1st ed. 74 color, 5 b/w photos. (Name stamps). Dj (chipped). *Sutton.* $65/£42

SHAW, GEORGE BERNARD and G.K. CHESTERTON. Do We Agree? (London): Cecil Palmer, (1928). 1st ed. Orange cl. Name, else Fine. *Chapel Hill.* $50/£32

SHAW, GEORGE BERNARD et al. Stalin-Wells Talk. London: New Statesman & Nation, Dec 1934. 1st ed. VG in ptd orange wraps. *Chapel Hill.* $75/£48

SHAW, GEORGE BERNARD. Adventures of a Black Girl in Her Search for God. London: Constable, 1932. 1st ed, 1st issue, w/'Genises' in headpiece p59. Pict black bds. Sm hole rear bd gutter, else NF. *Chapel Hill.* $50/£32

SHAW, GEORGE BERNARD. The Adventures of the Black Girl in Her Search for God. London: Constable, (1932). 1st ed. Pict bds. Fine. *Pharos.* $85/£55

SHAW, GEORGE BERNARD. Androcles and the Lion, Overruled, Pygmalion. London: Constable, 1916. 1st ed. Ribbed grn cl, spine gilt. Stamps fep, else VG. *Hermitage.* $85/£55

SHAW, GEORGE BERNARD. The Apple Cart. London: Constable, 1930. 1st Eng ed. Pale grn cl. NF in dj (internally mended); grn cl chemise; 1/4 morocco slipcase. *Chapel Hill.* $125/£81

SHAW, GEORGE BERNARD. The Art of Rehearsal. NY: Samuel French, (1928). 1st ed. Fine in ptd purple wraps. *Chapel Hill.* $50/£32

SHAW, GEORGE BERNARD. Back to Methuselah. London: Constable, 1921. 1st Eng ed. Lt gray-grn cl. Lt mks rear pastedown, else Fine in grn cl chemise; 1/4 morocco slipcase. *Chapel Hill.* $250/£161

SHAW, GEORGE BERNARD. Back to Methuselah. NY: LEC, 1939. #904/1500 numbered, signed by John Farleigh (illus). Full cl. Fine in pub's slipcase (sl sunned). *Hermitage.* $85/£55

SHAW, GEORGE BERNARD. Back to Methuselah. OUP, 1945. Rev ed. Blue cl. Fine in dj. *Dalian.* $23/£15

SHAW, GEORGE BERNARD. Bernard Shaw's Rhyming Picture Guide to Ayot Saint Lawrence. Luton: Leagrave Press, 1967. 1st Eng ed. Fine in pict wrappers. *Dalian.* $31/£20

SHAW, GEORGE BERNARD. The Case for Equality. (London): Nat'l Liberal Club Political & Economic Circle, (1914). 1st ed. VG in orange-brn ptd wrappers. *Godot.* $175/£113

SHAW, GEORGE BERNARD. The Case for Equality. (London): Nat'l Liberal Club Political & Economic Circle, 1913. 1st ed. Fine in ptd lt red wraps; brn cl chemise; 1/2 morocco slipcase. *Chapel Hill.* $150/£97

SHAW, GEORGE BERNARD. Cashel Byron's Profession. (London): Modern Press, 1886. 1st ed, 1st bk. Fine in lt blue ptd wraps; grn cl clamshell box. *Chapel Hill.* $1,800/£1,161

SHAW, GEORGE BERNARD. The Commonsense of Municipal Trading. London: A.C. Fifield, 1908. 1st ed thus. Ptd orange wraps. 1.5-inch piece missing spine, else VG in grn cl folder. *Chapel Hill.* $75/£48

SHAW, GEORGE BERNARD. The Doctor's Dilemma, Getting Married, and the Shewing Up of Blanco Posnet. London: Constable, 1911. 1st ed. Teg; rest rough-trimmed. Fine in grn cl, gold-lettered spine. *Vandoros.* $95/£61

SHAW, GEORGE BERNARD. Ellen Terry and Bernard Shaw. NY, 1931. 1st Amer ed. NF (offsetting fep, spine sl rubbed) in VG dj. *Polyanthos.* $35/£23

SHAW, GEORGE BERNARD. Everybody's Political What's What? London: Constable, (1944). 1st ed. Reddish brn cl. Lt offsetting fep, else Fine in VG 1st issue dj. *Chapel Hill.* $75/£48

SHAW, GEORGE BERNARD. Geneva, a Fancied Page of History in Three Acts. London: Constable, 1939. 1st ed. NF in blue-grey cl, gold-lettered spine. VG dj. *Vandoros.* $75/£48

SHAW, GEORGE BERNARD. Geneva. London: Constable, (1939). 1st ed. Frontis. Teg. Blue cl. Sl cocked, else NF in VG dj. *Chapel Hill.* $50/£32

SHAW, GEORGE BERNARD. How to Become a Musical Critic. Dan H. Laurence (ed). London: Rupert Hart-Davis, 1960. 1st ed. Red cl. Fine in dj (spine lt sunned, sl chipped). *Chapel Hill.* $35/£23

SHAW, GEORGE BERNARD. How to Settle the Irish Question. London: Talbot Press, 1917. 1st Eng ed. Lt blue ptd wrappers. Pp browned, cvrs sl chipped, o/w VG. *Dalian.* $54/£35

SHAW, GEORGE BERNARD. In Good King Charles's Golden Days. London: Constable, 1939. 1st ed. Fine in red cl, gold-lettered spine. Fine dj (price-clipped). *Vandoros.* $95/£61

SHAW, GEORGE BERNARD. The Intelligent Woman's Guide to Socialism and Capitalism. London: Constable, 1928. 1st ed. Dec grn cl. NF (lacks dj). *Chapel Hill.* $45/£29

SHAW, GEORGE BERNARD. The Intelligent Woman's Guide to Socialism and Capitalism. NY: Brentano's, 1928. 1st US ed. Dec cl. VG. *Petrilla.* $25/£16

SHAW, GEORGE BERNARD. The League of Nations. London: Fabian Soc, Jan 1929. 1st ed. Fine in ptd self-wraps. *Chapel Hill.* $50/£32

SHAW, GEORGE BERNARD. Love Among the Artists. Chicago: Herbert S. Stone, 1900. 1st ed. Dec grn cl. Fine in grn cl chemise; 1/4 morocco slipcase. *Chapel Hill.* $400/£258

SHAW, GEORGE BERNARD. Man and Superman with The Revolutionist's Handbook and Pocket Companion. (NY): LEC, 1962. One of 1500 numbered, signed by Charles Mozley (illus). 2 vols. Cl-backed pict cl. Fine set in flexible cl handbk in dbl compartment slipcase. *Hermitage.* $125/£81

SHAW, GEORGE BERNARD. Misalliance, the Dark Lady of the Sonnets, and Fanny's First Play. London: Constable, 1914. 1st ed. Teg; rest rough-trimmed. NF in grn cl, gold-lettered spine. *Vandoros.* $75/£48

SHAW, GEORGE BERNARD. Misalliance, the Dark Lady of the Sonnets, and Fanny's First Play. London: Constable, 1914. 1st ed. Fine in NF dj. *Hermitage.* $150/£97

SHAW, GEORGE BERNARD. Peace Conference Hints. London: Constable, 1919. 1st ed. NF in ptd grn wraps; grn cl folder. *Chapel Hill.* $75/£48

SHAW, GEORGE BERNARD. The Perfect Wagnerite. London: Grant Richards, 1898. 1st Eng ed. One of 1100 ptd. Purple-backed linen bds. Bds, eps sl foxed, o/w VG. *Dalian.* $132/£85

SHAW, GEORGE BERNARD. The Political Madhouse in America and Nearer Home. London: Constable, 1933. 1st Eng ed. Ptd blue bds. 1/4-inch chip spine top, else VG in orig glassine remnants. *Chapel Hill.* $50/£32

SHAW, GEORGE BERNARD. Pygmalion and Candida. (NY): LEC, 1974. One of 1500 numbered, signed by Clarke Hutton (illus). Fine in pub's slipcase. *Hermitage.* $85/£55

SHAW, GEORGE BERNARD. The Quintessence of Ibsenism. London: Walter Scott, 1891. 1st ed, 1st binding. Teg. Orig blue cl, gilt. Fine. *Macdonnell.* $100/£65

SHAW, GEORGE BERNARD. The Quintessence of Ibsenism. London: Walter Scott, 1891. 1st ed. One of 2100 ptd. Grn cl. Sl rubbed, else VG. *Chapel Hill.* $200/£129

SHAW, GEORGE BERNARD. The Quintessence of Ibsenism. London: Constable, 1913. 2nd ed. Unopened. Grn cl (spine sl sunned). VG. *Chapel Hill.* $60/£39

SHAW, GEORGE BERNARD. Ruskin's Politics. Ruskin Centenary Council, 1921. 1st ed. (Title lt spotted.) Orig wrappers. *Hollett.* $23/£15

SHAW, GEORGE BERNARD. Saint Joan. London, 1924. 1st ed. Fine (sl offsetting fep). *Polyanthos.* $125/£81

SHAW, GEORGE BERNARD. The Sanity of Art. London: New Age Press, 1908. 1st ed. VG (few pp roughly opened) in ptd brn wraps; grn cl folder. *Chapel Hill.* $150/£97

SHAW, GEORGE BERNARD. Selected Passages from the Works of Bernard Shaw. London: Constable, 1912. 1st ed. One of 1500 ptd. Frontis. Dk tan cl. Fine in NF dj (spine sunned). *Chapel Hill.* $250/£161

SHAW, GEORGE BERNARD. Sixteen Self Sketches. NY, (1949). 1st Amer ed. 24pp photos. Fine in dj (2 edge tears). *Polyanthos.* $25/£16

SHAW, GEORGE BERNARD. Sixteen Self Sketches. London: Constable, 1949. 1st ed. Reddish brn cl. Fine in NF dj (spine faded; lt wear). *Chapel Hill.* $50/£32

SHAW, GEORGE BERNARD. To a Young Actress. Peter Tompkins (ed). London: Constable, 1960. 1st Eng ed. Grn cl. Cvrs sl sprung, o/w VG in dj (sl rubbed). *Dalian.* $54/£35

SHAW, GEORGE BERNARD. Too True to Be Good, Village Wooing and On the Rocks. London: Constable, 1934. 1st ed. Teg. Fine in red brick cl, gold-lettered spine. VG dj (l soiled). *Vandoros.* $60/£39

SHAW, GEORGE BERNARD. Translations and Tomfooleries. London: Constable, 1926. 1st Eng trade ed. Unopened. Pale grn cl. Fine in dj (internally mended); grn cl chemise; 1/4 morocco slipcase. *Chapel Hill.* $150/£97

SHAW, GEORGE BERNARD. Two Plays for Puritans. NY: LEC, 1966. Ltd to 1500 numbered, signed by George Him (illus). Red cl. Fine in slipcase. *Oak Knoll.* $55/£35

SHAW, GEORGE BERNARD. The Unprotected Child and the Law. (London): Six Point Group, (ca 1923). 1st ed. Ptd blue-gray wraps. Edges sunned, else Fine in grn cl folder. *Chapel Hill.* $100/£65

SHAW, HENRY. A Booke of Sundry Draughtes. London: Pickering, 1848. (8)pp, 117 litho plts. Cl-backed ptd dec bds (rubbed but sound; later ms paper label). Good (lt spotting). *Cox.* $341/£220

SHAW, HENRY. The Decorative Arts, Ecclesiastical and Civil, of the Middle Ages. London: William Pickering, 1851. 1st ed. Folio. 41 chromolitho plts. Contemp 1/2 morocco. Foxing, lt edgewear cvr; else VG. *Bookpress.* $750/£484

SHAW, HENRY. Dresses and Decorations of the Middle Ages. London: William Pickering, 1843. 2 vols. Unpaginated. 94 hand-colored plts (ink stamps verso). Orig cl (ex-lib; ink, blind stamps w/lt imprinting; bkpl; spotting; upper hinge cracked vol 2; spines rubbed), marbled eps, inner gilt dentelles. *Edwards.* $434/£280

SHAW, HENRY. The Encyclopedia of Ornament. London: William Pickering, 1842. 1st ed. 6pp; 60 plts. Contemp 1/2 calf. Edgewear; bkpl; fr hinge internally cracked; foxing, else VG. *Bookpress.* $475/£306

SHAW, HENRY. The Handbook of Mediaeval Alphabets and Devices. London: Wm. Pickering, 1853. 1st ed. 37 plts (1 is extra to those called for) on fabric hinges. Blue cl (rebound), gilt. Foxing (mainly to margins), o/w VG. *Willow House.* $93/£60

SHAW, HENRY. A Handbook of the Art of Illumination, as Practised During the Middle Ages. London: Bell & Daldy, 1866. 1st ed. viii,66pp; 16 plts. Pub's cl. Lt chipping spine base, lower tips; sl foxing, else Very Nice. *Bookpress.* $265/£171

SHAW, HENRY. Specimens of Ancient Furniture Drawn from Existing Authorities. London: William Pickering, 1836. 1st ed. (4),57,(3)pp; 73 engr plts (12 hand-colored); uncut. Contemp brn morocco (rebacked retaining old backstrip, rubbed). 12 plts browned, o/w Good. *Cox.* $186/£120

SHAW, IRWIN. Paris! Paris! NY: Harcourt Brace, 1977. 1st Amer ed. Ronald Searle (illus). Blue cl. Fine in dj. *Dalian.* $31/£20

SHAW, IRWIN. The Young Lions. London: Cape, 1949. 1st British ed. Bkpl, else VG+ in VG dj (shallow edge chipping). *Pettler.* $45/£29

SHAW, J. BYAM. Paintings by Old Masters at Christ Church Oxford. Phaidon, 1967. 6 color plts. Dj. *Edwards.* $39/£25

SHAW, JAMES. Early Reminiscences of Pioneer Life in Kansas. (Atchison): Haskell Ptg, (1886). 1st ed. (Sl edgewear.) Howes S 341. *Glenn.* $110/£71

SHAW, LUELLA. True History of Some of the Pioneers of Colorado. Hotchkiss, CO, 1909. 12 plts & ports. Good+ (wear; marginal staining; fr hinge repaired) in gray ptd wraps. Howes S 347. *Bohling.* $85/£55

SHAW, PETER (trans). Pharmacopoeia Edinburgensis.... London: William Innys, 1740. 4th ed. (xi),265pp. Contemp speckled calf; rebacked, new label. Text Clean (sm lib stamp tp). *White.* $171/£110

SHAW, REUBEN COLE. Across the Plains in Forty-nine. Chicago, (1948). Lakeside Classic. VG. *Schoyer.* $25/£16

SHAW, REUBEN COLE. Across the Plains in Forty-nine. Farmland, IN: W.C. West, 1896. 1st ed. 200pp, port (foxed, along w/guard, tp). Grn cl, gilt title. VG (spine rubbed) in VG+ dj. Howes S 349. *Bohling.* $250/£161

SHAW, REUBEN COLE. Across the Plains in Forty-nine. Farmland, IN: W.C. West, 1896. 1st ed. One of 200. Frontis port, 200pp. Pacific Union Club bkpl, bkseller cat clipping tipped in feps. Red gilt-lettered cl (sl rubbed; spine faded). Overall VG; internally Fine. Howes S 349. *Harrington.* $225/£145

SHAW, RICHARD NORMAN. Architectural Sketches from the Continent. London, (1858). 100 plts. Recent 1/2 calf gilt. *Petersfield.* $302/£195

SHAW, ROBERT. The Flag. London: C&W, 1965. 1st Eng ed. Grey cl. Fine in dj (sl dusty). *Dalian.* $39/£25

SHAW, ROBERT. The Hiding Place. London: C&W, 1959. 1st Eng ed, 1st bk. Blue cl. VF in Fine dj w/Book Soc wraparound band. *Dalian.* $54/£35

SHAW, ROBERT. Private Time, Public Time: Fifteen Poems. (London: Poet & Printer, 1969.) 1st ed. NF. *Pharos.* $45/£29

SHAW, THOMAS. Clovers and How to Grow Them. NY: OJ, 1906. Brn cl, gilt spine, fr cvr stamped in black. VG (edges soiled). *Bohling.* $25/£16

SHAW, THOMAS. Soiling Crops and the Silo. NY: OJ, 1915. Brn cl, gilt title (rubbed; lt stain lower margin of latter leaves). *Bohling.* $25/£16

SHAW, WILLIAM A. A History of the English Church. London, 1900. 2 vols. (Spines chipped; joints cracked, frayed; glue repairs; bkpls; feps browned; hinges cracked, tender.) *Edwards.* $78/£50

SHAW, WILLIAM H. History of Essex and Hudson Counties, New Jersey. Phila: 1884. 1st ed. 2 vols. 1332pp. Later buckram over heavy bds. VG. *Petrilla.* $110/£71

SHAWN, TED. Dance We Must. London: Dennis Dobson, 1946. 1st ed. VG in illus dj (edge-chipped). *Cahan.* $50/£32

SHAY, FRANK. The Bibliography of Walt Whitman. NY: Friedman's, 1920. One of 500 numbered. Frontis. *Ginsberg.* $75/£48

SHAYLOR, JOSEPH. The Fascination of Books, with Other Papers on Books and Bookselling. Simpkin Marshall, 1912. *Petersfield.* $19/£12

SHEA, JOHN G. Discovery and Exploration of the Mississippi Valley with the Original Narratives of Marquette.... Albany, 1903. 2nd, best ed. One of 500. Port; map, letter facs. Paper labels spine, fr cvr. Howes S 357. *Ginsberg.* $150/£97

SHEA, JOHN G. Discovery and Exploration of the Mississippi Valley. NY: Redfield, 1853. (2nd ptg). Frontis facs, lxxx,267,(1)pp + 4pp ads, fldg map. Brn cl (worn, puckered; foxing). Howes S 357. *Bohling.* $150/£97

SHEA, JOHN G. Early Voyages Up and Down the Mississippi by Cavelier.... Albany, 1902. Facs rpt. One of 500 numbered, ptd. Cl bds, ptd paper label. Howes S 358. *Ginsberg.* $150/£97

SHEA, JOHN G. (ed). The Lincoln Memorial. NY/Chicago: Bunce & Huntington/S.M. Kennedy, 1865. 288pp; engr port, vignette tp. VG. *Schoyer.* $30/£19

SHEARING, JOSEPH. (Pseud of Marjorie Bowen.) The Angel of Assassination. London, 1935. 1st ed. Frontis; 3 plts. Edges foxed; o/w VG in plum cl (dampstained). Dj (sl sunned). *Edwards.* $28/£18

SHEARING, JOSEPH. (Pseud of Marjorie Bowen.) The Spectral Bride. NY, (1942). 1st Amer ed. VG in Good dj (lg piece missing back panel). *Mcclintock.* $25/£16

SHEAT, W.G. Propagation of Trees, Shrubs and Conifers. London, 1948. Dj (chipped). *Sutton.* $50/£32

SHECKLEY, ROBERT. Journey Beyond Tomorrow. Gollancz, 1964. 1st Eng, 1st hb ed. Signed. VG + in NF dj (sm chip spine head). *Aronovitz.* $125/£81

SHEED, WILFRID. The Boys of Winter. NY: Knopf, 1978. 1st ed. Signed. NF in NF dj. *Lame Duck.* $25/£16

SHEED, WILFRID. The Hack. London: Cassell, (1963). 1st Eng ed. Fine in dj (lt wear). *Hermitage.* $35/£23

SHEEHAN, H.L. and H.C. MOORE. Renal Cortical Necrosis of the Kidney and Concealed Accidental Haemorrhage. Springfield, 1953. 1st ed. Good. *Fye.* $75/£48

SHEEHAN, PERLEY. The Abyss of Wonders. Fantasy, 1953. One of 1500 numbered. Fine in box. *Madle.* $30/£19

SHEFFY, LESTER FIELDS. The Francklyn Land and Cattle Company. Austin: Univ of TX, 1963. 1st ed. NF in VG-dj. *Parker.* $55/£35

SHELDON, CHARLES. The Wilderness of the North Pacific Coast Islands. Scribner's, 1912. 1st ed. Frontis, 44 plts, fldg map. Gilt-stamped pict cl. VG. *Oregon.* $175/£113

SHELDON, HAROLD P. Tranquility: Tales of Sport with the Gun. NY: Derrydale, 1936. 1st ed. One of 950 numbered. Bkpl, else Fine. *Cahan.* $150/£97

SHELDON-WILLIAMS, I. A Dawdle in Lombardy and Venice. London, 1928. Orange cl. *Lewis.* $12/£8

Shell Guide to Wiltshire. Architectural Press, April 1935. Sl worn, o/w VG in spiral-bound wrappers. *Words Etc.* $31/£20

SHELLEY, GERARD. Speckled Domes. NY: Scribner's, 1925. Frontis port. (Pocket removed.) *Schoyer.* $45/£29

SHELLEY, MARY WOLLSTONECRAFT. Frankenstein. NY: LEC, 1934. #229/1500 signed by Everett Henry (illus). VG + (sl damage spine) in slipcase (sl rubbed). *Williams.* $194/£125

SHELLEY, MARY WOLLSTONECRAFT. Frankenstein. NY: LEC, 1934. #904/1500 numbered, signed by Everett Henry (illus). Half leather, dec cl. Fine in pub's slipcase. *Hermitage.* $250/£161

SHELLEY, MARY WOLLSTONECRAFT. Frankenstein. D-M, 1983. 1st ed thus. One of 500 signed by Stephen King (intro) & Bernie Wrightson (illus). Fine in tissue dj & slipcase. *Aronovitz.* $350/£226

SHELLEY, MARY WOLLSTONECRAFT. Letters of Mary W. Shelley (Mostly Unpublished). Boston: Bibliophiles Soc, 1918. 1st ed. Ltd to 448. Teg, others untrimmed. 1/2 vellum, bds. NF. *Cahan.* $85/£55

SHELLEY, MARY WOLLSTONECRAFT. Rambles in Germany and Italy 1840-43. London: Moxon, 1844. 1st ed. Mod marbled bds, leather labels. Very Nice (lib stamp; bound w/o 1/2 titles). *Second Life.* $350/£226

SHELLEY, PERCY BYSSHE. The Esdaile Notebook. Kenneth Neill Cameron (ed). Faber, 1964. 1st ed. Fine in NF dj. *Poetry.* $31/£20

SHELLEY, PERCY BYSSHE. Essays and Letters. Ernest Rhys (ed). London: Walter Scott, 1886. 1st ed. Spine label dknd, o/w VG. *Poetry.* $16/£10

SHELLEY, PERCY BYSSHE. Letters from Percy Bysshe Shelley to Elizabeth Hitchener. London: Bertram Dobell, 1908. 1st ed. Lg paper copy. Foxing, o/w NF. *Poetry.* $116/£75

SHELLEY, PERCY BYSSHE. The Poems of Percy Bysshe Shelley. Stephen Spender (ed). Cambridge: LEC, 1971. One of 1500 numbered, signed by Richard Shirley Smith (illus). Fine in pub's slipcase. *Hermitage*. $100/£65

SHELLEY, PERCY BYSSHE. Prometheus Unbound. London: C. and J. Ollier, 1820. 1st ed. Half-title w/ads for 4 titles by Shelly on verso; 2pp pub's ads at back; contents leaf (A3) cancelled w/corrected reading 'Miscellaneous' (lt spotting throughout). Uncut in pub's orig paper-backed blue bds (rubbed; spine worn; lacks ptd label; cvr detached) in blue cl slipcase, gilt-lettered leather spine label. *D & D*. $2,900/£1,871

SHELLEY, PERCY BYSSHE. The Shelley Papers. London: Whittaker, Treacher, 1833. 1st ed. viii,180pp + 3pp ads. Uncut. (Sig, sketch; backstrip, paper label defective; hinges broken). Slipcase, morocco label. *Cox*. $171/£110

SHELLEY, PERCY BYSSHE. With Shelley in Italy. Anna Benneson McMahon (ed). T. Fisher Unwin, 1907. 1st ed. Blind-dec cl, gilt-lettered spine (faded; edges spotted). *Poetry*. $28/£18

SHELLEY, PERCY BYSSHE. Zastrozzi: A Romance. London: Golden Cockerel Press, 1955. #66/200. 8 full-pg engrs by Cecil Keeling. Morocco-backed marbled paper. VG in slipcase (sl rubbed). *Cox*. $93/£60

SHELTON, KATHLEEN J. The Esquiline Treasure. British Museum Publ, 1981. 48 plts. Fine in Mint dj. *Europa*. $40/£26

SHELTON, LOUISE. Beautiful Gardens in America. NY: Scribners, (1916). 2nd ed. Cvrs sl rubbed, o/w Nice. *Pharos*. $35/£23

SHELTON, LOUISE. Beautiful Gardens in America. NY: Scribner's, 1916. 2nd ed. Color frontis. Gilt-dec cl (rubbed; lt dampstains margin corners), pict inse. *Quest*. $40/£26

SHELTON, WILLIAM HENRY. The Jumel Mansion. Boston/NY: Houghton Mifflin, 1916. 1st ed, ltd to 750. 33 plts. NF. Howes S 382. *Mcgowan*. $175/£113

SHENSTONE, WILLIAM. The Works in Verse and Prose. London: J. Dodsley, 1773. Vols 1,2: 4th ed; vol 3: 3rd ed. 2 frontispieces. Full contemp calf, gilt (sl worn). *Petersfield*. $132/£85

SHEPARD, ERNEST H. Drawn from Memory. Phila/NY: Lippincott, (1957). 1st Amer ed. Red cl. Fine in dj. *Juvelis*. $40/£26

SHEPARD, ERNEST H. Drawn from Memory. London: Methuen, 1957. 1st ed. Frontis. VG in pict dj (frayed). *Cox*. $31/£20

SHEPARD, ERNEST H. Drawn from Memory. NY: Lippincott, 1957. 1st ed. Rev copy. 8vo. 190pp. VG in dj (sm nick top of spine). *Davidson*. $100/£65

SHEPARD, L. The History of Street Literature. David & Charles, 1973. Fine in dj. *Moss*. $25/£16

SHEPHEARD, PETER. Modern Gardens. NY: Praeger, (1958). 1st Amer ed in yr of pub. Fine in dj. *Quest*. $120/£77

SHEPHERD, HENRY E. Life of Robert Edward Lee. NY/Washington: Neale, 1906. 1st ed. Teg. Orig gray cl (faded). VG. *Chapel Hill*. $185/£119

SHEPHERD, HENRY E. Narrative of Prison Life at Baltimore and Johnson's Island, Ohio. Balt: Commercial Ptg & Sta. Co, 1917. 1st ed. 2 plts. 1/2 leather w/marbled bds. Expertly rebacked, sl wear extrems, else VG. *Mcgowan*. $750/£484

SHEPHERD, J.C. and G.A. JELLICOE. Italian Gardens of the Renaissance. London: Tiranti, 1966. Plts Fine; Good (ex-lib, stamps, fep excised). *Europa*. $47/£30

SHEPHERD, MICHAEL. (Pseud of Robert Ludlum). The Road to Gandolfo. NY: Dial, 1975. 1st ed. Fine w/Fine djs. With 2 of the 3 variant djs (purple w/ornate lettering; cartoon character w/breasts). *Aka*. $35/£23

SHEPHERD, MICHAEL. (Pseud of Robert Ludlum.) The Road to Gandolfo. NY: Dial, 1975. 1st ed. NF in 2 of 3 variant djs, purple & purple-plum (both price-clipped). *Antic Hay*. $45/£29

SHEPHERD, MICHAEL. (Pseud of Robert Ludlum.) The Road to Gandolfo. Dial Press, 1975. 1st ed. NF with 3 djs (browning on outer dj). *Stahr*. $60/£39

SHEPHERD, RICHARD H. The Bibliography of Dickens. London: Elliot Stock, (1880). 1st ed. Orig grn cl, gilt (few mks). Very Nice (pencil mks in text). *Macdonnell*. $150/£97

SHEPPARD, EDGAR. Lectures on Madness in Its Medical, Legal, and Social Aspects. London, 1873. 1st ed. 186pp. (Fr inner hinge cracked.) *Fye*. $150/£97

SHEPPARD, WILLIAM ARTHUR. Red Shirts Remembered. Atlanta, 1940. 1st ed. Inscribed. VG + . *Pratt*. $95/£61

SHEPPARD, WILLIAM. The Touch-Stone of Common Assurances.... London: W. Strahan, W. Woodfall et al, 1784. 5th ed. Mod 1/4 leather, buckram. Good. *Boswell*. $350/£226

SHEPPERSON, ARCHIBALD BOLLING. John Paradise and Lucy Ludwell of London and Williamsburg. Richmond: Dietz Press, 1942. 1st ed. Frontis. VG in dj (chipped, torn). *Bookpress*. $35/£23

SHERATON, THOMAS. The Cabinet-Maker and Upholsterer's Drawing-Book. NY, 1946. Facs of 3rd, rev London 1802 ed. Unpaginated, 122 copper plts + 104pp ads. 2-tone cl (edges sl bumped), dec gilt spine (sl rubbed). *Edwards*. $194/£125

SHERBURNE, ANDREW. Memoirs of Andrew Sherburne, A Pensioner of the Navy of the Revolution. Utica: William Williams, 1828. 1st ed. 262pp,(1,errata). Orig calf. Howes S 391. *Lefkowicz*. $150/£97

SHERBURNE, ANDREW. Memoirs of Andrew Sherburne. Providence: Brown, 1831. 2nd ed. 312pp (lacks frontis plt; eps stained). Full leather (spine mks). Howes S 391. *Schoyer*. $40/£26

SHERBURNE, JOHN HENRY. Life and Character of Chevalier John Paul Jones. Washington City, 1825. 1st ed. 364pp; port (foxing, esp title, port). VG (spine cracked). Howes S 393. *Cullen*. $150/£97

SHERIDAN, FRANCIS. Galveston Island. Austin: 1954. 1st ed. Frontis; 4 plts. VG in dj (chipped). *Petrilla*. $20/£13

SHERIDAN, P.H. Outline Descriptions of Posts in the Military Division of the Missouri.... Old Army Press, (1972). Rpt of 1876 ed. VG in VG dj. Howes S 394. *Oregon*. $60/£39

SHERIDAN, P.H. Personal Memoirs of P.H. Sheridan, General U.S. Army. NY: Webster, 1888. 1st ed. 2 vols. Grn cl. Spotting cvrs; lt foxing; 1889 sig, o/w NF. *Pharos*. $85/£55

SHERIDAN, P.H. Personal Memoirs of P.H. Sheridan, General United States Army. NY: Charles L. Webster, 1888. 1st ed. 2 vols. Orig deluxe binding of 1/2 morocco, cl. VG set (corners scuffed, edges). *Mcgowan*. $250/£161

SHERIDAN, RICHARD BRINSLEY. The School for Scandal and St. Patrick's Day. John Squire (ed). London: Century, (1948). Deluxe ed. Ltd to 300. Full pict gilt pigskin (lt rubbed); teg. *Sadlon.* $35/£23

SHERIDAN, RICHARD BRINSLEY. The School for Scandal, a Comedy. Oxford: LEC, 1934. #904/1500 numbered, signed by Rene Ben Sussan (illus). Full dec paper-cvrd bds. Fine in card liner, pub's slipcase. *Hermitage.* $125/£81

SHERIDAN, RICHARD BRINSLEY. Verses to the Memory of David Garrick. T. Evans, 1779. 1st ed, 1st issue w/'deference' in Dedication misspelled, corrected as usual in MS. 1/2 title, frontis. New bds. Fine. *Hill.* $349/£225

SHERIDAN, RICHARD BRINSLEY. The Works. London: John Murray, 1821. 1st collected ed. 2 vols. xiii,398; 408pp; uncut. Orig pub's bds (spine renewed). Name, else handsome set. *Hartfield.* $185/£119

SHERINGHAM, GEORGE. Figure Painting in Water-Colours by Contemporary British Artists. London: The Studio, 1923. 24 mtd color plts. Gilt emb cl. VG. *Argosy.* $60/£39

SHERINGHAM, HUGH and J.C. MOORE (eds). The Book of the Fly-Rod. London: Eyre & Spottiswoode, 1931. 1st ed. 4 color, 8 b/w plts. (Backstrip sl faded.) *Petersfield.* $152/£98

SHERMAN, ELEAZER. The Narrative of Eleazer Sherman.... Providence: Brown, 1832. 1st ed. 83; 72; 108pp. Full contemp calf. Bound in at rear: 'A Discourse Addressed to Christians of all Denominations'; 2nd ed. Providence, 1833. Howes S 399. *Ginsberg.* $300/£194

SHERMAN, HAROLD M. Down the Ice. Goldsmith, 1932. 1st ed. Fine in dj (sl frayed). *Madle.* $20/£13

SHERMAN, JOHN. John Sherman's Recollections of Forty Years in the House, Senate and Cabinet. Chicago, 1895. 1st ed. 2 vols. 1,239pp. Pict cl. Lt cvr wear, o/w Fine set. *Pratt.* $75/£48

SHERMAN, WILLIAM TECUMSEH. Home Letters of General Sherman. NY: Scribner's, 1909. 1st ed. Spine lt sunned, else NF. *Mcgowan.* $65/£42

SHERMAN, WILLIAM TECUMSEH. Memoirs of Gen. William T. Sherman, Written by Himself. NY: D. Appleton, 1891. Later ed, enlgd. 2 vols. VG set. *Mcgowan.* $125/£81

SHERMAN, WILLIAM TECUMSEH. The Sherman Letters: Correspondence Between General and Senator Sherman from 1837 to 1891. Rachel Sherman Thorndike (ed). NY: Scribner's, 1894. 1st ed. viii,398pp. Spine ends repaired, sl wear fr gutter; else VG. *Mcgowan.* $85/£55

SHERRILL, CHARLES HITCHCOCK. Stained Glass Tours in England. London/NY, 1909. 16 plts; 5 maps. (Spotting; upper hinge tail tender; sl bumped). Teg, rest uncut. *Edwards.* $39/£25

SHERRILL, J. GARLAND. Peritonitis. NY, 1925. 1st ed. Good. *Fye.* $40/£26

SHERRILL, WILLIAM L. Annals of Lincoln County, North Carolina. Charlotte: Observer Ptg House, 1937. 1st ed. Rear cvr unevenly faded, o/w NF. *Cahan.* $85/£55

SHERRINGTON, C. The Endeavour of Jean Fernel. Cambridge, 1946. (Bkpl, sig; spine faded.) *Whitehart.* $39/£25

SHERRINGTON, CHARLES. The Integrative Action of the Nervous System. London: Constable, 1911. 1st ed, 2nd issue w/cancelled title pg. Good (later cl; underlining). *Goodrich.* $395/£255

SHERRINGTON, CHARLES. The Integrative Action of the Nervous System. Cambridge, 1947. 1st ed as such. Engr frontis. NF. *Goodrich.* $75/£48

SHERRINGTON, CHARLES. Man on His Nature. NY, 1941. 1st ed. Good. *Fye.* $100/£65

SHERWOOD, GEORGE. American Colonists in English Records.... Genealogical Pub, 1961. VG (pencil notes). *Book Broker.* $25/£16

SHERWOOD, MRS. The History of Mrs. Catharine Crawley. Wellington, Salop: F. Houlston and Son, 1824. 1st ed. 12mo. 1pg ad, 101pp + 4pp list, full-pg copper engr frontis; pgs untrimmed. VG (rebacked w/new eps; line scratch upper bd). *Hobbyhorse.* $325/£210

SHERWOOD, ROBERT E. There Shall Be No Night. NY, 1941. 1st ed. Fine in dj. *Artis.* $20/£13

SHERWOOD, ROBERT E. This Is New York. NY: Scribner's, 1931. 1st ed. Fine in NF dj (spine lt faded). *Antic Hay.* $35/£23

SHERWOOD, RUTH. Carving His Own Destiny. The Story of Albin Polasek. Chicago: Ralph Fletcher Seymour, (1954). 1st ed. Presentation copy signed in 1957 by Polasek. Red gilt cl. Good in dj (tape reinforced). *Karmiole.* $65/£42

SHESTACK, ALAN. The Complete Engravings of Martin Schongauer. NY, 1969. Good in wrappers. *Washton.* $40/£26

SHEW, JOEL. Children, Their Hydropathic Management in Health and Disease. NY: Fowler & Wells, 1852. 432pp; 4-pg pub's cat at end. Blind-stamped cl, gilt spine title. Fine (label tp). *Hemlock.* $150/£97

SHEW, JOEL. Hydropathy; Or, the Water-Cure. NY, 1845. Frontis. Orig emb cl. VG. *Argosy.* $100/£65

SHIEL, M.P. Invisible Voices. London, 1935. 1st ed. Corner chipped, else VG. *Madle.* $75/£48

SHIEL, M.P. Lord of the Sea. Stokes, 1901. 1st US ed. VG-. *Madle.* $75/£48

SHIEL, M.P. The Lost Viol. Clode, 1905. 1st ed. VG. *Madle.* $25/£16

SHIELDS, G.O. Cruising in the Cascades. Chicago, 1889. 1st ed. 339,(12 ads)pp. Pict cl. *Ginsberg.* $175/£113

SHIELDS, G.O. Cruisings in the Cascades. Chicago: Rand McNally, 1889. 1st ed. Frontis, 339pp + 12pp ads. Pict gilt cvr. VF. *Oregon.* $125/£81

SHIELDS, G.O. Rustlings in the Rockies. Chicago: Belford, Clark, 1883. 1st ed. xv,9-306pp. Orig pict cl (spine sunned). *Schoyer.* $45/£29

SHIFFRIN, A.B. Mr. Pirate. NY: Mitchell Kennerley, 1937. 1st ed. Signed. VG in dj (sunned). *Bookpress.* $50/£32

SHIFLET, KENNETH E. The Convenient Coward. Harrisburg, PA: Stackpole, (1961). 1st ed. VG in dj. *Lien.* $35/£23

Shiloh, or The Tennessee Campaign of 1862. (By Thomas Worthington.) Washington City: M'Gill & Witherow, 1872. 1st ed. 164pp. Contemp black 1/2 morocco (sl rubbed). VG (pencil mks in margins). Howes W 685. *Chapel Hill.* $175/£113

SHINN, CHARLES and DORRIE. The Illustrated Guide to Victorian Parian China. London: Barrie & Jenkins, 1971. 1st ed. Color frontis; 2 color, 117 b/w plts. Dj (sl water-stained, adhered to bds). *Edwards.* $70/£45

SHINN, CHARLES HOWARD. The Story of the Mine. NY: D. Appleton, 1896. 1st ed. 272pp + ads. VG in pict cl. *Lien.* $50/£32

SHIPLEY, J.W. Pulp and Paper-Making in Canada. Toronto: Longmans, Green, 1929. 1st ed. VG. *Oak Knoll.* $30/£19

SHIPLEY, WILLIAM. A True Treatise in the Art of Fly Fishing, Trolling, etc. Edward Fitzgibbon (ed). London: Simpkin Marshall, 1838. 1st ed. Grn cl (spine sunned, chipped), gilt title. *Juvelis.* $150/£97

SHIPTON, ERIC. Blank on the Map. London: Hodder & Stoughton, 1938. 1st ed. 36 plts; 3 maps (1 extending). (Scattered spotting, mainly to flyleaves, fore-edge.) Black cl. Dj (head of spine sl frayed). *Hollett.* $271/£175

SHIPTON, ERIC. Land of Tempest. Travels in Patagonia 1958-1962. London: Hodder & Stoughton, 1963. 1st ed. Color frontis, 24 plts. Gilt cl (spine faded, sl scratches). *Hollett.* $39/£25

SHIPTON, ERIC. The Mount Everest Reconnaissance Expedition 1951. London: Hodder & Stoughton, 1952. 1st ed. VG in dj (sl chipped, browned). *Hollett.* $62/£40

SHIPTON, ERIC. Mountains of Tartary. London: Hodder & Stoughton, (1951). 1st ed. 29 plts. VG in dj (chipped; sl loss spine). *Hollett.* $78/£50

SHIPTON, ERIC. That Untravelled World. London: Hodder & Stoughton, 1969. 1st ed. VG. *Hollett.* $47/£30

SHIRAS, GEORGE. Hunting Wild Life with Camera and Flashlight. Washington: NGS, (1936). 2nd ed. 2 vols. Fine. *Artis.* $45/£29

SHIRAS, GEORGE. Hunting Wild Life with Camera and Flashlight. Washington, 1936. 2nd ed. 2 vols. *Edwards.* $47/£30

SHIRAS, W.H. Children of the Atom. Boardman, 1954. 1st Eng ed. VG+ in VG+ dj (sl wear). *Aronovitz.* $45/£29

SHIRER, WILLIAM L. The Rise and Fall of Adolf Hitler. NY: Random House, 1961. 1st trade ed. VG in dj. *Cattermole.* $20/£13

SHIRER, WILLIAM L. The Sinking of the Bismarck. NY: Random House, 1962. 1st trade ed. VG in dj. *Cattermole.* $20/£13

SHIRK, DAVID L. The Cattle Drives of David Shirk, from Texas to the Idaho Mines.... (Portland): Champoeg Press, 1956. 1st ed. One of 750. Tipped-in photo. Fine. *Harrington.* $90/£58

SHIRK, DAVID L. The Cattle Drives...From Texas to the Idaho Mines 1871 and 1873. Martin F. Schmitt (ed). (Portland, OR): Champoeg Press, 1956. 1st ed. One of 750. *Ginsberg.* $100/£65

SHIRLEY, ANDREW. John Constable, R.A. Medici, 1948. 12 color illus. *Petersfield.* $28/£18

SHIRLEY, EVELYN PHILIP. Some Account of English Deer Parks. London, 1867. 1st ed. Gilt-edged cl, gilt illus. VG (spine sl rubbed). *Edwards.* $233/£150

SHIRLEY, GLENN. Heck Thomas. Phila, 1962. 1st ed. Fine in dj (sl worn). *Baade.* $50/£32

SHIRLEY, GLENN. Henry Starr, Last of the Real Badmen. NY, 1965. 1st ed. NF (inscrip) in dj (chipped). *Baade.* $37/£24

SHIRLEY, GLENN. Law West of Fort Smith. NY, (1957). 1st ed. Dj sl worn, spine faded, o/w VG+. *Pratt.* $35/£23

SHIRLEY, GLENN. Law West of Fort Smith. NY: Holt, (1957). 1st ptg. Map. VG in dj. *Schoyer.* $40/£26

SHIRLEY, GLENN. Six-Gun and Silver Star. Albuquerque, 1955. 1st ed. Map. Sl dj wear, o/w Fine. *Pratt.* $35/£23

SHIRLEY, GLENN. Toughest of Them All. Albuquerque, 1953. 1st ed, 1st issue. Fine in dj (sl worn). *Baade.* $40/£26

SHIRLING, ALBERT E. Birds of Swope Park...Kansas City, MO. Kansas City, MO: McIndoo, 1920. 1st ed. Fldg map. VG. *Glenn.* $35/£23

SHIRREFF, PATRICK. A Tour through North America.... Edinburgh/London/Glasgow/Dublin: Oliver and Boyd/Simpkin, Marshall/David Robertson/William Curry, 1835. 1st ed. iv,i-v,473pp. VG (spine ends, tips lt worn; lt foxing eps). Howes S 425. *Cahan.* $300/£194

SHIVERS, LOUISE. Here To Get My Baby Out Of Jail. London: Collins, 1983. 1st Eng ed. Fine in dj. *Hermitage.* $15/£10

SHKLOVSKY, I.W. In Far North-East Siberia. Macmillan, 1916. 1st ed. Good (inner hinges cracked, rep repaired; ex-lib). *Walcot.* $39/£25

SHORE, E. TEIGNMOUTH. Kent. London: A&C Black, 1907. 1st ed. 23 color plts, fldg map, 2 fldg plans; teg (feps lt browned; upper hinge tender). Dec cl (sl rubbed, sl bleach stain lower bd). *Edwards.* $70/£45

SHORE, EVELYN BERGLUND. Born on Snowshoes. Boston: Houghton Mifflin, (1954). VG in VG dj. *Perier.* $30/£19

SHORE, H.M. Smuggling Days and Smuggling Ways.... London: Cassell, 1892. 1st ed. Sig, else VG in (faded) red cl. *Limestone.* $85/£55

SHORE, W. TEIGNMOUTH (ed). Trial of Frederick Guy Browne and William Henry Kennedy. Edinburgh: William Hodge, 1930. Red cl, faded but Sound. *Boswell.* $50/£32

Short History of Birds and Beasts. Wellington: F. Houlston, n.d. (ca 1830). 24mo. Frontis pasted down on cvr, 23pp + 1pg ad back cvr; 12 VF 1/2pg woodcuts. Ptd brn stiff paper wrappers. VG. *Hobbyhorse.* $175/£113

SHORT, ERNEST H. The Painter in History. London, 1929. (Lt spotting.) Binder monogram, date lower dentelle. Morocco (amateurish style rebind), floral motifs spine (lt sunned). *Edwards.* $101/£65

SHORTEN, M. Squirrels. London, 1954. 1st ed. 15 plts. (Ends sl foxed.) Dj (repaired). *Henly.* $56/£36

SHORTER, ALAN W. Everyday Life in Ancient Egypt. London: Sampson Low, Marston, 1932. (Sig; faded, extrems rubbed.) *Archaeologia.* $35/£23

SHORTER, ALFRED H. Paper Making in the British Isles, an Historical and Geographical Study. N.p.: David & Charles, (1971). 1st ed. Fine. *Oak Knoll.* $50/£32

SHORTRIDGE, WILSON. The Transition of a Typical Frontier. Menasha, WI, 1922. 1st ed. Wraps. Good+. *Oregon.* $45/£29

SHOTEN, KADOKAWA (ed). A Pictorial Encyclopedia of the Oriental Arts: China. NY: Crown, (1969). 1st ed. 2 vols. VF in pub's pict slipcase. *Hermitage.* $85/£55

SHRAKE, EDWIN. But Not for Love. GC: Doubleday, 1964. 1st ed. Fine in VG dj (lt edgeworn). *Reese.* $40/£26

SHUCK, OSCAR T. Bench and Bar (in) California. SF: Occident Ptg House, 1888. 1st ed thus. Orig orange cl. Sl worn, spine dkng, edges foxed, o/w NF. *Harrington.* $90/£58

SHUCK, OSCAR T. Bench and Bar in California. SF: Occident Ptg House, 1887. Blue cl, gilt (sl rubbed). Good. *Boswell.* $75/£48

SHUFELT, S. A Letter from a Gold Miner. San Marino, 1944. Ltd to 1000. Contents Fine (bds soiled, sl edgeworn). *Baade.* $40/£26

SHUFELT, S. A Letter from a Gold Miner. Placerville, California, October 1850. Huntington, 1944. 1st ed. One of 1000 numbered. VG. *Oregon.* $50/£32

SHULMAN, ALIX. To the Barricades. NY: Crowell, (1971). 1st ed. VG in dj. *Petrilla.* $30/£19

SHULMAN, HARRY MANUEL. Slums of New York. NY: Boni, 1938. VG in dj. *Schoyer.* $40/£26

SHULMAN, HARRY MANUEL. Slums of New York. NY: Boni, 1938. 1st ed. VG in VG dj. *Bishop.* $32/£21

SHULMAN, IRVING. The Big Brokers. NY: Dial, 1951. 1st ed. NF in VG pict dj (spine sunned; narrow tear). *Reese.* $35/£23

SHULMAN, IRVING. Cry Tough! NY: Dial, 1949. 1st ed. NF in VG dj (chip; sm nicks). *Reese.* $45/£29

SHULMAN, IRVING. The Square Trap. Boston: Little, Brown, (1953). 1st ed. NF in VG dj (edgeworn, sunned, price-clipped). *Reese.* $25/£16

SHUMAY, NINA PAUL. Your Desert and Mine. L.A.: Westernlore, 1960. 1st ed. Fine in Fine dj. *Book Market.* $45/£29

SHURCLIFF, W.A. Bombs at Bikini; The Official Report of Operation Crossroads. NY: Wise, 1947. 1st ed. 32 plts. Good (cl dusty). *Artis Books.* $25/£16

SHURE, DAVID S. Hester Bateman, Queen of English Silversmiths. GC: Doubleday, (1959). 1st ed. 86 plts. Beige linen. Good. *Karmiole.* $50/£32

SHURE, DAVID S. Hester Bateman. London, 1959. 87 b/w plts. (Eps lt spotted.) Dj (sl chipped; spine lt faded). *Edwards.* $132/£85

SHURTLEFF, NATHANIEL B. Records of the Colony of New Plymouth in New England.... Boston: Press of William White, 1855-1861. 1st ed. 12 vols bound in 10. Black cl, gilt. VF set. Howes S 440. *Karmiole.* $500/£323

SHUSTER, W. MORGAN. Strangling of Persia. NY: Century, 1912. Dbl-pg color map; teg. Brick-red cl stamped in gilt/black (spine dknd). *Schoyer.* $55/£35

SHUTE, HENRY A. Plupy 'The Real Boy.' Boston: Richard G. Badger, 1911. 1st ed. VG in red pict cl. *Glenn.* $50/£32

SHUTE, NEVIL. The Chequer Board. London: Heinemann, 1947. 1st ed. Fine in dj (lt wear extrems). *Else Fine.* $75/£48

SHUTE, NEVIL. In the Wet. London: Heinemann, 1953. 1st ed. NF in dj. *Limestone.* $45/£29

SHUTE, NEVIL. No Highway. London: Heinemann, 1948. 1st ed. VG in dj (chipped, missing v-shaped piece fr panel). *Limestone.* $60/£39

SHUTE, NEVIL. On the Beach. Melbourne: Heinemann, (1957). 1st ed. Foxing to fore-edge, pg edges, else NF in NF dj (lt foxing, sl rubbing). *Between The Covers.* $185/£119

SHUTE, NEVIL. On the Beach. London: Heinemann, 1957. 1st ed. Pencil sig, date, else Fine in dj. *Limestone.* $75/£48

SHUTE, NEVIL. Ordeal. NY: Morrow, 1939. 1st Amer ed. VG in dj (sl chipped). *Limestone.* $65/£42

SHUTE, NEVIL. The Rainbow and the Rose. NY, 1958. 1st Amer ed. Fine (sl sunned; name stamp) in NF dj. *Polyanthos.* $30/£19

SHUTE, NEVIL. The Rainbow and the Rose. London: Heinemann, 1958. 1st ed. Fine in dj (frayed; back panel sl dknd). *Temple.* $22/£14

SHUTE, NEVIL. The Rainbow and the Rose. London: Heinemann, 1958. 1st Eng ed. Red cl. VG in dj (sl nicked, dusty). *Dalian.* $31/£20

SHUTE, NEVIL. Slide Rule. Morrow, 1954. 1st ed. Fine in dj. *Fine Books.* $65/£42

SHUTE, NEVIL. Stephen Morris. London: Heinemann, 1961. 1st ed. Fine in dj. *Else Fine.* $60/£39

SHUTE, NEVIL. Vinland the Good. London: Heinemann, 1946. 1st ed. NF in dj (sl darkened spine, extrems sl worn). *Else Fine.* $135/£87

SHUTES, MILTON H. Lincoln and the Doctors. NY, 1933. 1st ed, ltd to 550 numbered, signed. Teg. Cl-backed bds (worn, stained). *King.* $35/£23

SHUTTER, MARION D. Rev. James Harvey Tuttle, D.D.,: A Memoir. Boston, 1905. 1st ed. *Ginsberg.* $75/£48

SHWARTZMAN, GREGORY (ed). The Effect of Acth and Cortisone Upon Infection and Resistance. NY, 1953. 1st ed. Good in dj. *Fye.* $50/£32

SHWARTZMAN, GREGORY. Phenomenon of Local Tissue Reactivity and Its Immunological, Pathological and Clinical Significance. NY, 1937. 1st ed. Good. *Fye.* $100/£65

SIBLEY, HENRY. Iron Face. The Adventures of Jack Frazer.... T. Blegen & S. Davidson (eds). Chicago: Caxton Club, 1950. 1st ed. Ltd to 500. Frontis, 4pp prospectus laid-in. Fine. *Oregon.* $125/£81

SIBLEY, HENRY. The Unfinished Autobiography of...Together with a Selection of Hitherto Unpublished Letters from the Thirties. Minneapolis, 1932. 1st ed. #11/200. 1/4 leather, cl. Fine in Good+ slipcase. Howes S 445. *Oregon.* $150/£97

SIBLIK, JIRI. Raphael: Drawings. John O'Kane (trans). St. Paul, MN, 1983. 60 collotype repros, 1 fldg. VG in dj. *Argosy.* $65/£42

SIBSON, FRANCIS. The Survivors. Doubleday, 1932. 1st US ed. VG-. *Madle.* $20/£13

SIDDONS, ANNE RIVERS. The House Next Door. NY: S&S, 1978. 1st ed. NF (rmdr stamp) in NF dj. *Revere.* $40/£26

SIDDONS, ANNE RIVERS. Peachtree Road. NY: Harper & Row, (1988). 1st ed. Fine in dj. *Sadlon.* $30/£19

SIDDONS, G.A. The Cabinet-Maker's Guide.... London: Sherwood, Gilbert and Piper, 1830. 5th ed, 'considerably augmented.' xvi,223pp, 12pp ads, engr frontis, 4 engr plts. Contemp cl-backed bds (dusty). *Marlborough.* $426/£275

SIDNEY, A. Destination Unknown. London, 1928. 1st ed. VG. *Madle.* $40/£26

SIDNEY, PHILIP. Astrophel and Stella. Mona Wilson (ed). London: Nonesuch, 1931. Ltd to 725. VG in dec paper-cvrd bds, paper label. Orig card folder, slipcase. *Cox.* $50/£32

SIDNEY, PHILIP. The Countess of Pembroke's Arcadia. London: George Calvert, 1674. 13th ed. Folio. (xxxii),624,(26)pp. Contemp calf (rebacked, corners renewed), morocco label. Fair (lower fore-edge, margins 1st 2 leaves repaired; edges of 13 leaves damaged; spotting; browning). *Cox.* $171/£110

SIEBENHARR, W. (trans). Max Havelarr or The Coffee Sales of the Netherlands Trading Company by 'Multatuli.' NY: Knopf, 1927. 1st Amer ed. Brn cl. VF (bkpl) in dj (tanned; sl chipped). *Dalian.* $132/£85

SIEBER, ROY and ARNOLD RUBIN. Sculpture of Black Africa: The Paul Tishman Collection. L.A., 1968. Addendum loose as issued. VG in stiff pict wrappers. *Argosy.* $50/£32

Siege of Detroit in 1763. Chicago, (1958). Lakeside Classic. VG. *Schoyer.* $20/£13

SIEMENS, C. WILLIAM. On the Conservation of Solar Energy. Macmillan, 1883. 1st ed. xx,111pp; plt. *Bickersteth.* $209/£135

SIENKIEWICZ, HENRYK. Quo Vadis? Jeremiah Curtin (trans). (NY): LEC, 1959. Ltd to 1500 numbered, signed by Salvatore Fiume (illus) & Mardersteig (ptr). Fine in dj, slipcase. *Oak Knoll.* $150/£97

SIEVEKING, ALBERT FORBES. The Praise of Gardens. London: J.M. Dent, 1899. xvi,423pp (few leaves foxed). Teg, uncut. Gilt-dec cl. Hinge starting, else VG. *Quest.* $90/£58

SIEVEKING, L. Stampede! (London): Cayme Press, 1924. 1st ed. Fine (eps dknd; lt bumped) w/o dj. *Heller.* $45/£29

SIEVEKING, L. The Ultimate Island. Routledge, 1925. 1st ed. Sl soiling cl panels, else VG. *Aronovitz.* $35/£23

SIGAUD, LOUIS A. Belle Boyd, Confederate Spy. Richmond, (1945). 2nd ed. VG. *Pratt.* $27/£17

SIGERIST BEESON, N. Henry E. Sigerist: Autobiographical Writings. Montreal, 1966. Tls. Frontis port; photo at back. (Label fep.) *Whitehart.* $54/£35

SIGSBEE, CHARLES D. Deep-Sea Sounding and Dredging. Washington: GPO, 1880. 1st ed. 210pp; 41 plts (8 lg fldg); 12 forms (4 fldg). Black cl, gilt (spine, corners sl worn; bkpl). *Karmiole.* $150/£97

SILKO, LESLIE MARMON. Storyteller. NY: Seavers Books, (1981). 1st ed. VG in dj (scratch, crumpled edge; short tear). *Hermitage.* $85/£55

SILKO, LESLIE MARMON. Storyteller. NY, 1981. 1st Amer ed. Fine in Fine dj. *Polyanthos.* $65/£42

SILLIMAN, BENJAMIN, JR. Principles of Physics, or Natural Philosophy. NY, (1861). 2nd ed. 710pp + ads. (Orig backstrip worn at head.) *Argosy.* $50/£32

SILLITOE, ALAN. Barbarians and Other Poems. London: Turret Books, 1973. Ltd to 100 signed. Red bds. Fine in dj. *Dalian.* $70/£45

SILLITOE, ALAN. The General. London: Allen, 1960. 1st ed. Signed. VG in dj (sl chipped). *Rees.* $39/£25

SILLITOE, ALAN. The General. London: Allen, 1960. 1st UK ed. Fine in VG dj. *Lewton.* $42/£27

SILLITOE, ALAN. Key to the Door. W.H. Allen, 1961. 1st ed. Dj (sl chipped). *Edwards.* $31/£20

SILLITOE, ALAN. The Loneliness of the Long-Distance Runner. London: W.H. Allen, 1959. 1st ed. VG + in VG + dj (sl surface loss spine extrems; shallow chips to tips). *Lame Duck.* $250/£161

SILLITOE, ALAN. The Loneliness of the Long-Distance Runner. London: W.H. Allen, 1959. 1st Eng ed. Grn cl. NF in dj (sl dusty). *Dalian.* $132/£85

SILLITOE, ALAN. Storm. New Poems. London: W.H. Allen, 1974. 1st Eng ed. Signed. Fine in dj (price-clipped). *Ulysses.* $54/£35

SILLITOE, ALAN. The Widower's Son. London: W.H. Allen, 1976. 1st Eng ed. Grey cl. Fine in dj (price-clipped). *Dalian.* $31/£20

SILTZER, FRANK. The Story of British Sporting Prints. London: Halton & Truscott Smith, 1929. Rev, enlgd ed. 8 tipped-in color plts. Gilt-lettered grn cl (sl wear). Fine. *House.* $120/£77

SILTZER, FRANK. The Story of British Sporting Prints. London, n.d. (ca 1925). Color frontis (sl loose), 3 color plts. (Upper hinge tender; rubbed corners, joints). *Edwards.* $85/£55

SILURIENSIS, LEOLINUS. (Pseud of Arthur Machen.) The Anatomy of Tobacco. London: George Redway, 1884. 1st ed. 86pp + 2pp ads. VG in leather/cl slipcase. *Schoyer.* $300/£194

SILVERBERG, ROBERT. Born With the Dead. Random House, 1974. 1st ed. NF in dj. *Madle.* $40/£26

SILVERBERG, ROBERT. Conquerors From the Darkness. HRW, 1965. 1st ed. Signed. NF in NF dj (lt wear, tear). *Aronovitz.* $38/£25

SILVERBERG, ROBERT. Deep Space. London: Abelard, 1973. 1st Eng ed. Brn cl. Fine in dj (sl rubbed). *Dalian.* $39/£25

SILVERBERG, ROBERT. Four Men Who Changed the Universe. Putnam, 1968. 1st ed. Fine in dj. *Madle.* $35/£23

SILVERBERG, ROBERT. Lord Valentine's Castle. Harper, 1980. 1st ed. One of 250 numbered, signed. Fine in dj & slipcase. *Madle.* $100/£65

SILVERBERG, ROBERT. Majipoor Chronicles. London: Gollancz, 1982. 1st Eng ed. Red cl. VF in Fine dj. *Dalian.* $39/£25

SILVERBERG, ROBERT. The Mask of Akhnaten. Macmillan, 1965. 1st ed. NF in VG dj (sl shelf wear). *Aronovitz.* $48/£31

SILVERBERG, ROBERT. Revolt on Alpha C. Crowell, 1955. 1st ed, 1st bk. Inscribed. Fine in VG dj (spine head chipped). *Aronovitz.* $125/£81

SILVERBERG, ROBERT. Sundance and Other Science Fiction Stories. London: Abelard, 1975. 1st Eng ed. Nice in dj (sl frayed). *Temple.* $40/£26

SILVERBERG, ROBERT. The Time Hoppers. GC: Doubleday, 1967. 1st ed. NF in dj. *Antic Hay.* $65/£42

SILVERMAN, JONATHAN. For the World to See. The Life of Margaret Bourke-White. NY: Viking, (1983). 1st ed. NF in dj. *Reese.* $47/£30

SIMAK, CLIFFORD. Cemetary World. NY: Putnam's, 1973. 1st ed. VF in dj. *Else Fine.* $45/£29

SIMAK, CLIFFORD. City. Gnome Press, 1952. 1st ed. Fine in Fine dj (sl dust soil rear panel). *Aronovitz.* $395/£255

SIMAK, CLIFFORD. City. Gnome, 1952. 1st ed. Fine in dj. *Madle.* $450/£290

SIMAK, CLIFFORD. The Fellowship of the Talisman. London: Sidgwick & Jackson, 1980. 1st Eng ed. Blue cl. Fine in dj. *Dalian.* $31/£20

SIMAK, CLIFFORD. Strangers in the Universe. S&S, 1956. 1st ed. Fine in dj (tape-stained). *Madle.* $30/£19

SIMAK, CLIFFORD. They Walked Like Men. Doubleday, 1962. 1st ed, rev copy w/rev slip laid in. Fine in dj. *Aronovitz.* $175/£113

SIMAK, CLIFFORD. Why Call Them Back from Heaven? Doubleday, 1967. 1st ed. NF in dj. *Madle.* $65/£42

SIMAK, CLIFFORD. The Worlds of Clifford Simak. S&S, 1960. 1st ed. Fine in dj. *Aronovitz.* $110/£71

SIME, D. Rabies. Cambridge, 1903. Rebacked. (Ex-lib w/perf mk, stamps.) *Whitehart.* $62/£40

SIMENON, GEORGES. Betty. London, (1975). 1st Eng ed. VG in dj. *King.* $25/£16

SIMENON, GEORGES. Black Rain. London: Routledge/Kegan Paul, 1949. 1st UK ed. VG in dj (torn, sl chipped). *Williams.* $23/£15

SIMENON, GEORGES. The Blue Room. London, (1965). 1st British ed. Fep corner clipped, else Good in dj (price-clipped, sl used). *King.* $25/£16

SIMENON, GEORGES. Chit of a Girl. London: Routledge & Kegan Paul, 1949. 1st UK ed. VG in dj (sl chipped). *Williams.* $40/£26

SIMENON, GEORGES. Inquest on Bouvet. H. Hamilton, 1958. 1st ed. VG in dj. *Whiteson.* $26/£17

SIMENON, GEORGES. Magnet of Doom. Routledge, 1948. 1st ed. VG in dj (sl dull). *Whiteson.* $31/£20

SIMENON, GEORGES. Maigret and the Black Sheep. London, (1976). 1st Eng ed. VG in dj. *King.* $25/£16

SIMENON, GEORGES. Maigret and the Black Sheep. Helen Thomson (trans). London: Hamish Hamilton, 1976. 1st ed in English. Fine in Fine dj. *Janus.* $35/£23

SIMENON, GEORGES. Maigret and the Burglar's Wife. H. Hamilton, 1955. 1st ed. Good in dj (sl dull). *Whiteson.* $26/£17

SIMENON, GEORGES. Maigret and the Ghost. Eileen Ellenbogen (trans). London: Hamish Hamilton, 1976. 1st ed in English. Fine in Fine dj. *Janus.* $35/£23

SIMENON, GEORGES. Maigret and the Killer. L. Moir (trans). NY: Harcourt, Brace, Jovanovich, 1971. 1st Amer ed. Fine in Fine dj. *Smithfield.* $13/£8

SIMENON, GEORGES. Maigret and the Lazy Burglar. London: Hamish Hamilton, 1963. 1st ed. Fine in dj. *Mordida.* $65/£42

SIMENON, GEORGES. Maigret and the Loner. Eileen Ellenbogen (trans). London: Hamish Hamilton, 1975. 1st ed in English. NF in NF dj. *Janus.* $30/£19

SIMENON, GEORGES. Maigret and the Loner. London: Hamish Hamilton, 1975. 1st ed. NF in NF dj (price-clipped). *Ming.* $31/£20

SIMENON, GEORGES. Maigret and the Minister. London: Hamish Hamilton, 1969. 1st ed. VG in VG dj (stained). *Ming.* $23/£15

SIMENON, GEORGES. Maigret and the Reluctant Witnesses. London: Hamish Hamilton, 1959. 1st ed. Good in Good dj. *Ming.* $23/£15

SIMENON, GEORGES. Maigret and the Reluctant Witnesses. H. Hamilton, 1959. 1st ed. VG in dj (sl dull). *Whiteson.* $26/£17

SIMENON, GEORGES. Maigret and the Saturday Caller. H. Hamilton, 1964. 1st ed. VG in VG dw. *Whiteson.* $26/£17

SIMENON, GEORGES. Maigret and the Young Girl. London: Hamish Hamilton, 1955. 1st ed. Good in Good dj. *Ming.* $23/£15

SIMENON, GEORGES. Maigret Goes to School. London: Hamish Hamilton, 1957. 1st Eng ed. Fine in VG dj (sl dknd spine; sl wear). *Mordida.* $65/£42

SIMENON, GEORGES. Maigret Hesitates. London: Hamish Hamilton, 1970. 1st ed. Fine in dj (sl corner wear). *Mordida.* $45/£29

SIMENON, GEORGES. Maigret in Society. London: Hamish Hamilton, 1962. 1st ed. Good in Good dj. *Ming.* $28/£18

SIMENON, GEORGES. Maigret in Society. London: 1962. 1st Eng ed. Fine in VG dj (lt staining fr panel; sl wear). *Mordida.* $35/£23

SIMENON, GEORGES. Maigret Travels South. London: Routledge, 1940. 1st UK ed. VG- (bds spotted, sl stained). *Williams.* $70/£45

SIMENON, GEORGES. Maigret's Failure. London: Hamish Hamilton, 1962. 1st Eng ed. Fine in dj (sl corner wear). *Mordida.* $65/£42

SIMENON, GEORGES. The Man on the Bench in the Barn. London: Hamish Hamilton, 1970. 1st Eng ed. VF in dj. *Mordida.* $45/£29

SIMENON, GEORGES. Pedigree. London: Hamilton, 1962. 1st UK ed. VG+ in dj (sl rubbed, strengthened to rear). *Williams.* $28/£18

SIMENON, GEORGES. A Sense of Guilt. H. Hamilton, 1955. 1st ed. Sl dull, else Good in dj. *Whiteson.* $26/£17

SIMENON, GEORGES. Sunday. H. Hamilton, 1960. 1st ed. VG in dj. *Whiteson.* $26/£17

SIMENON, GEORGES. Sunday. London: Hamish Hamilton, 1960. 1st Eng ed. Fine in dj. *Mordida.* $45/£29

SIMENON, GEORGES. Three Beds in Manhattan. GC: Doubleday, 1964. 1st Amer ed. Stamp fep, else NF in dj. *Hermitage.* $35/£23

SIMENON, GEORGES. The Train. H. Hamilton, 1964. 1st ed. VG in dj (dull). *Whiteson.* $25/£16

SIMENON, GEORGES. The Widower. H. Hamilton, 1961. 1st ed. VG in dj (sl dull). *Whiteson.* $26/£17

SIMENON, GEORGES. The Window Over the Way. London: Routledge/Kegan Paul, 1951. 1st UK ed. VG in dj (chipped; piece missing). *Williams.* $23/£15

SIMIC, CHARLES. What the Grass Says. Santa Cruz: Kayak, (1967). 1st ed, 1st bk. One of 1000. Fine in ptd pict wrappers. *Reese.* $65/£42

SIMMONS, ALBERT DIXON. Wing Shots. NY: Derrydale, 1936. One of 950 numbered. 83 full-pg photo plts. VG in dj (edgeworn). *Bowman.* $90/£58

SIMMONS, HERBERT A. Corner Boy. Boston: Houghton-Mifflin, 1957. 1st ed. 1st bk. Fine in dj (minor rubs corners). *Else Fine.* $45/£29

SIMMONS, HERBERT A. Man Walking on Eggshells. Boston: Houghton-Mifflin, 1962. 1st ed. Fine in dj (price-clipped, lt wear top edge). *Else Fine.* $50/£32

SIMMS, P. MARION. The Bible in America. NY: Wilson-Erickson, 1936. 1st ed, #305/500 numbered, signed. Orig cl. VG. *Mcgowan.* $85/£55

SIMMS, W. GILMORE. The Life of Francis Marion. Geo. F. Coolidge, (1844). 10th ed. Frontis; 347pp; 10 plts. VG. Howes S 472. BAL 18086. *Oregon.* $45/£29

SIMMS, W. GILMORE. The Life of Nathanael Greene. NY: George F. Cooledge, (1849). 1st ed. Frontis port, 393pp; 12 full-pg plts. Brn cl (recased); new eps. Good (inkstamp; bkpl removed; last leaf glued to flyleaf; insect damage rear gutter). BAL 18118. Howes S 473. *Chapel Hill.* $200/£129

SIMON, ANDRE (ed). In Vino Veritas. London: Grant Richards, 1913. 1st Eng ed. Grn cl, gilt. VG. *Dalian.* $39/£25

SIMON, ANDRE. The Art of Good Living. London: Constable, 1929. 1st Eng ed. Frontis. Brn cl. VG. *Dalian.* $39/£25

SIMON, ANDRE. Bibliotheca Vinaria. (London): Holland Press, (1979). One of 600. Sl rubbed, else Fine. *Bookpress.* $125/£81

SIMON, ANDRE. Cheeses of the World. Faber, 1956. 1st ed. 5 color plts. Dj (sl chipped). *Edwards.* $31/£20

SIMON, ANDRE. Dictionary of Gastronomy. McGraw Hill, 1970. 1st ed. NF in VG + dj. *Bishop.* $20/£13

SIMON, ANDRE. English Wines and Cordials. London: Gramol Publications, 1946. 1st Eng ed. Blue cl. VG in dj (sl nicked). *Dalian.* $23/£15

SIMON, ANDRE. The History of Champagne. London, 1962. 8 color plts; 2 color maps. Dj (sl chipped, torn). *Edwards.* $39/£25

SIMON, ANDRE. In the Twilight. London: Michael Joseph, 1969. 1st Eng ed. Frontis port. Maroon cl. VF in dj (sl rubbed, price-clipped). *Dalian.* $31/£20

SIMON, CHARLES. An Introduction to the Study of Infection and Immunity.... Phila, 1912. 1st ed. Good. *Fye.* $100/£65

SIMON, HOWARD. 500 Years of Art in Illustration; From Albrecht Durer to Rockwell Kent. Cleveland/NY, 1942. 2 fldg plts. VG. *Argosy.* $85/£55

SIMON, JOHN. Filth-Diseases and Their Prevention. Boston, 1876. 1st Amer ed. 96pp. Good. *Fye.* $50/£32

SIMON, NEIL et al. Promises, Promises. NY: Random House, (1969). 1st ed. Fine in dj. *Between The Covers.* $175/£113

SIMON, NEIL. Brighton Beach Memoirs. NY: Random House, (1984). 1st ed. Fine in white dj (lt soil). *Antic Hay.* $50/£32

SIMON, NEIL. The Gingerbread Lady. NY: Random House, (1971). 1st ed. Fine in dj. *Between The Covers.* $125/£81

SIMON, NEIL. Plaza Suite. R-H, 1969. 1st ed. Fine in NF dj. *Fine Books.* $55/£35

SIMON, NEIL. The Prisoner of Second Avenue. R-H, 1972. 1st ed. Fine in dj (spine faded). *Fine Books.* $45/£29

SIMON, OLIVER and JULIUS RODENBERG. Printing of To-Day. London: Peter Davies, 1938. 1st ed. 122 illus on plts. Lt wear along edges, tips; spine sl sunned, else VG. *Bookpress.* $110/£71

SIMON, ROGER L. Peking Duck. London: Deutsch, 1979. 1st British ed. Signed. NF in dj. *Silver Door.* $40/£26

SIMON, TED. Jupiter's Travels. London: Hamish Hamilton, 1979. 1st Eng ed. Grn cl. VG in dj. *Dalian.* $39/£25

SIMONS, ALBERT and SAMUEL LAPHAM, JR. (eds). Charleston, South Carolina. NY: American Inst of Architects, 1927. 1st ed. Rear cvr spotted, eps foxed, else VG. *Bookpress.* $165/£106

SIMPKINSON, JOHN NASSAU. The Washingtons. London: Longman, Green, 1860. 1st ed. Engr frontis; xvi,326,lxxxixpp. (Hinges cracked, repaired; extrems sl worn.) *Hollett.* $70/£45

SIMPSON, C.J.W. North Ice. London: Hodder & Stoughton, 1957. 1st ed. Map. VG in dj (chipped). *Walcot.* $20/£13

SIMPSON, CHARLES. Yankee's Adventures in South Africa. Chicago: Rhodes & McClure, 1897. (224)pp + 6pp ads (paper browned). Teal cl stamped in silver (sl rubbed). *Schoyer.* $25/£16

SIMPSON, F. A Series of Ancient Baptismal Fonts.... London, 1828. Engr frontis (spotted); xxvipp text (tp, margins spotted), 39 engr plts; marbled eps, teg. 1/2 morocco w/marbled bds (bkpl; upper hinge tender; extrems sl worn). *Edwards.* $116/£75

SIMPSON, G.C. Scott's Polar Journey and the Weather. Oxford: Clarendon Press, 1926. Map, 2 diags. Good in orig card wrapper (spine chipped). *Walcot.* $28/£18

SIMPSON, GEORGE. Narrative of a Journey Round the World, During the Years 1841 and 1842. London: Henry Colburn, 1847. 1st ed. 2 vols. (xii),438; (viii),469pp, 1 plt, fldg map. Orig cl (expertly recased). Fine set (frontis foxed). Howes S 495. *Lefkowicz.* $650/£419

SIMPSON, GEORGE. Narrative of a Journey Round the World...1841 and 1842. London, 1847. 2 vols. Frontis port, xi,(1),438,24pp, fldg map; vii,(1),469pp. (Spines sunned, extrems sl frayed.) Bkpls each vol, else VG. Howes S 495. *Reese.* $900/£581

SIMPSON, GEORGE. Narrative of a Voyage to California Ports in 1841-42. Thomas C. Russell (ed). SF: Thomas C. Russell, 1930. #59/250 signed by Russell. 2 plts, 3 facs, fldg map. Linen-backed blue bds, paper spine label. Fine in NF dj (spine sl dknd, chipped). Howes S 495. *Harrington.* $250/£161

SIMPSON, JAMES Y. Clinical Lectures on Diseases of Women. Phila, 1863. 1st ed. 510pp. Good. *Fye.* $300/£194

SIMPSON, JAMES Y. The Obstetric Memoirs and Contributions. Volume I. Phila, 1855. 1st ed. 756pp. Contents VG. (Backstrip missing; ex-lib.) *Fye.* $200/£129

SIMPSON, JAMES Y. The Obstetric Memoirs and Contributions. W.O. Priestley and Horatio R. Storer (eds). Edinburgh: A&C Black, 1855/56. 2 vols. xii,857; xii,819pp; uncut. Orig brn cl; rebacked w/backstrips laid down. Lib stamps, o/w Clean text. *White.* $147/£95

SIMPSON, JAMES Y. Selected Obstetrical and Gynaecological Works....J. Watt Black (ed). NY: Appleton, 1871. xiii,852pp. (Lib stamps; bds rebacked.) *Goodrich.* $125/£81

SIMPSON, KEITH. Forensic Medicine. London, 1947. 1st ed. Good. *Fye.* $100/£65

SIMPSON, LOUIS. Air with Armed Men. London, (1972). 1st Eng ed. VG in dj. *Argosy.* $35/£23

SIMPSON, W.J. A Treatise on Plague.... Cambridge, 1905. 1st ed. (Ex-lib.) *Fye.* $100/£65

SIMPSON, WALTER. Tularemia: History, Pathology, Diagnosis and Treatment. NY, 1929. 1st ed. Good. *Fye.* $50/£32

SIMPSON, WILLIAM R. et al. Hockshop. NY, (1954). 1st ed. VG + in dj (edgeworn; price-clipped). *Mcclintock.* $20/£13

SIMPSON, WILLIAM. Meeting the Sun. London: Longmans, Green, 1874. 1st ed. xii,413,(ii)pp (sm red stamp on title), 48 plts. Dec yellow cl (lt soiled), gilt. *Hollett.* $233/£150

SIMS, E.H. American Aces: Fighter Battles of WWII. NY, 1958. VG in Good dj. *Clark.* $30/£19

SIMS, G. The Devil in London. Dodge, 1909. 1st ed. Pict cl. VG. *Aronovitz.* $65/£42

SIMS, GEORGE. The Terrible Door. London: Bodley Head, 1964. 1st ed. Fine in Fine dj. *Ming.* $39/£25

SIMS, J. MARION. Clinical Notes on Uterine Surgery. NY, 1867. 1st ed, 2nd ptg. 401pp. Orig cl. Scattered foxing, o/w Fine. *Fye.* $300/£194

SIMS, JOSEPH PATTERSON and CHARLES WILLING. Old Philadelphia Colonial Details. NY: Architectural Book Pub, 1914. 1st ed. 55 plts. Inscrip, smudging; wear, else VG. *Bookpress.* $150/£97

SIMS, ORLAND L. Cowpokes, Nesters, and So Forth. Austin: Encino Press, 1970. 1st ed. One of 250 numbered, signed. 3/4 leather. Fine in pict slipcase. *Bohling.* $150/£97

SIMSON, ROBERT. The Gray Charteris. McCann, 1922. 1st ed. VG. *Madle*. $25/£16

Sinbad the Sailor. London: Hodder & Stoughton, (1914). 1st ed, 1st issue. Lg 4to. 23 mtd color plts by Edmund Dulac. Tan dec cl, gilt illus. Good in later illus slipcase. Dulac exhibit announcement laid in. *Reisler*. $1,000/£645

Sinbad the Sailor. London: Octopus, 1979. 21x21 cm. 6 fan-fld pop-ups. J. Pavlin & G. Seda (illus). Glazed pict bds. Sl wear to bottom of spine, o/w VG. *Book Finders*. $45/£29

SINCLAIR, ARTHUR. Two Years on the Alabama. Boston: Lee & Shepard, 1895. 1st ed. Frontis port, 344pp. Orig pict gray cl. NF. *Chapel Hill*. $200/£129

SINCLAIR, ARTHUR. Two Years on the Alabama. London: Gay & Bird, 1896. 1st Eng ed. Frontis port, 352pp. Orig pict grey cl. Eps foxed, else VG. *Chapel Hill*. $200/£129

SINCLAIR, GORDON. Khyber Caravan, through Kashmire, Waziristan...and Northern India. Hurst & Blackett, (1936). *Petersfield*. $19/£12

SINCLAIR, HAROLD. The Horse Soldiers. NY, 1957. 1st ed. VG + . *Pratt*. $35/£23

SINCLAIR, IAIN. The Kodak Mantra Diaries. Albion Village Press, 1971. 1st ed. NF in spiral-bound wrappers. *Rees*. $39/£25

SINCLAIR, IAIN. White Chappell, Scarlet Tracings. London: Goldmark, 1987. 1st ed. Signed. Fine in dj. *Rees*. $39/£25

SINCLAIR, M. The Thomas Splint and Its Modifications.... London, Oxford Medical Publications, 1927. 85 figs; 3 charts (1 fldg). (Lib label, remnants; stamps.) *Whitehart*. $28/£18

SINCLAIR, MAY. Fame. London: Elkin Mathews, 1929. 1st ed. One of 530 signed. Uncut. Fine in dj. *Second Life*. $45/£29

SINCLAIR, MAY. The Flaw in the Crystal. Dutton, 1912. VG. *Madle*. $40/£26

SINCLAIR, UPTON. Boston. NY: Albert & Charles Boni, 1928. 1st ed. 2 vols. Orig grn cl. Bkpl in each, else NF in djs (sm chips). *Chapel Hill*. $85/£55

SINCLAIR, UPTON. A Captain of Industry. Girard: Appeal to Reason, 1906. 1st ed. Blue cl (sl soiled). VG. *Aka*. $65/£42

SINCLAIR, UPTON. The Flivver King. Girard, KS: Haldeman-Julius, (1937). (Sm dampspot tp.) Wrappers. *Hayman*. $20/£13

SINCLAIR, UPTON. The Goslings, a Study of the American Schools. Pasadena, CA: Upton Sinclair, (1924). 1st ed. Red cl. VG. *Second Life*. $35/£23

SINCLAIR, UPTON. The Goslings. Pasadena: Upton Sinclair, (1924). 1st ed, clbound issue (5000 thus). Red cl stamped in gilt/black. VG. *Reese*. $35/£23

SINCLAIR, UPTON. The Jungle. NY: Doubleday, Page, 1906. 1st ed, 1st issue. Pict grn cl. 1906 sig, else Fine. *Pharos*. $100/£65

SINCLAIR, UPTON. Marie Antoinette. NY: Vanguard, 1939. 1st ed. Fine in NF dj (short internally mended tears). *Beasley*. $50/£32

SINCLAIR, UPTON. O Shepherd, Speak! Monrovia, CA: publ by author, (1949). 1st ed. Presentation inscription signed by Upton and Craig Sinclair. Red cl. Good in dj. *Karmiole*. $75/£48

SINCLAIR, UPTON. The Overman. NY: Doubleday, Page, 1907. 1st ed. Fine (fep fore-edge ragged). *Beasley*. $50/£32

SINCLAIR, UPTON. The Overman. NY: Doubleday, Page, 1907. 1st ed. Frontis. Orig grn cl. NF. *Chapel Hill*. $50/£32

SINCLAIR, UPTON. Presidential Mission. London: T. Werner Laurie, 1948. 1st Eng ed. Blue cl. VF in dj (sl nicked). *Dalian*. $23/£15

SINCLAIR, UPTON. Prince Hagen. Boston: L.C. Page, 1903. 1st ed. Orig blue cl. NF. *Chapel Hill*. $95/£61

SINCLAIR, UPTON. Upton Sinclair Presents William Fox. L.A.: By the Author, 1933. Frontis port. Orange cl. Sl mkd, name, o/w VG. *Dalian*. $39/£25

SINCLAIR, UPTON. The Way Out. NY: Farrar, 1933. 1st ed. Fine in Fine dj (tears). *Beasley*. $45/£29

Sing a Song of Sixpence. NY: J.S. Pub Co, (n.d. ca 1940s). 1st ed thus. Pop-up. Geraldine Clyne (illus). Single sheet folded into 4pp; 1 pop-up. VG. *Godot*. $35/£23

SINGER, CHARLES et al (eds). A History of Technology. OUP, 1957. Rpt. 5 vols. 204 plts. VG (lt stain bottom edge vol 1) in Good djs. *Knollwood*. $280/£181

SINGER, CHARLES. From Magic to Science. NY: Boni & Liverwright, 1928. 14 colored plts. Fine. *Goodrich*. $95/£61

SINGER, CHARLES. Studies in the History and Method of Science. Oxford: Clarendon, 1917-1921. 2 vols. Colored fronts, 40 plts (5 colored); Colored fronts, 54 plts (6 colored). Good (spines sunned; sl worn; ex-lib, stamp). *Goodrich*. $375/£242

SINGER, CHARLES. Studies in the History and Method of Science. Oxford: Clarendon Press, 1921. Vol 2 only (of 2). Color frontis, 54 plts (6 color). Sl scuffed, else Good. *Goodrich*. $195/£126

SINGER, DANIEL J. Big Game Fields of America. NY, 1914. Color frontis. Device upper bd. (Ex-libris; spine rubbed, repaired tear.) *Edwards*. $43/£28

SINGER, ISAAC BASHEVIS. The Collected Stories of Isaac Bashevis Singer. NY: FSG, (1982). 1st ed. Grn cl. Fine in dj (1/2-inch tear). *Chapel Hill*. $30/£19

SINGER, ISAAC BASHEVIS. Elijah the Slave. NY: FSG, (1970). 1st ed. Fine in NF dj (price-clipped). *Godot*. $45/£29

SINGER, ISAAC BASHEVIS. Lost in America. GC: Doubleday, 1981. 1st ed. VG + in VG + dj (sl worn; price sticker). *Lame Duck*. $35/£23

SINGER, ISAAC BASHEVIS. Lost in America. GC: Doubleday, 1981. 1st ed. One of 500 numbered, signed, w/numbered color print by Raphael Soyer (illus) laid in. Fine in marbled red paper-cvrd slipcase. *Lame Duck*. $350/£226

SINGER, ISAAC BASHEVIS. The Manor. NY: FSG, 1966. 1st ed. VF in dj. *Else Fine*. $45/£29

SINGER, ISAAC BASHEVIS. Nobel Lecture. London, 1979. 1st ed. Wraps. Mint in Mint dj. *Polyanthos*. $25/£16

SINGER, ISAAC BASHEVIS. Passions. NY: FSG, 1975. 1st ed. VF in dj. *Else Fine*. $55/£35

SINGER, ISAAC BASHEVIS. The Penitent. Franklin Center: Franklin Lib, 1983. 1st ed. Signed. Fine. *Revere*. $75/£48

SINGER, ISAAC BASHEVIS. The Penitent. Franklin Center, PA: Franklin Lib, 1983. Signed ltd ed. Gilt-worked blue-morocco leather; aeg. Mint. *Antic Hay*. $100/£65

SINGER, ISAAC BASHEVIS. The Penitent. London: Jonathan Cape, 1984. 1st Eng ed. Black cl. Fine in dj. *Dalian*. $23/£15

SINGER, ISAAC BASHEVIS. Reaches of Heaven. NY: FSG, 1980. 1st ed. 4to. 95pp. Ira Moskowitz (illus). Beige cl. NF in VG dj (crease at top). *Davidson.* $35/£23

SINGER, ISAAC BASHEVIS. Satan in Goray. NY: Noonday, 1955. 1st ed. Fine in dj. *Hermitage.* $200/£129

SINGER, ISAAC BASHEVIS. Yentl the Yeshiva Boy. NY: Farrar Straus, 1983. 1st ed. Antonio Frasconi (illus). As New in VF dj (blemish back panel). *Book Adoption.* $30/£19

SINGER, ISAAC BASHEVIS. Zlateh the Goat. Harper & Row, (1966). 1st ed. Inscribed by Maurice Sendak (illus). 8vo. 90pp. VG (cl lt soiled) in VG dj. *Davidson.* $195/£126

SINGER, ISAAC BASHEVIS. Zlateh the Goat. NY: Harper, 1966. 1st ed. Maurice Sendak (illus). 6.5x9.25. 90pp. Cl. Fine in dj. *Cattermole.* $100/£65

SINGER, KURT. Diseases of the Medical Profession: A Systematic Presentation.... NY, 1932. 1st Eng trans. Good. *Fye.* $250/£161

SINGLETON, ESTHER. French and English Furniture. London, 1904. 1st ed. 68 plts; teg. Cl, gilt dec title (ex-libris; sunned). *Edwards.* $56/£36

SINGLETON, ESTHER. Historic Buildings of America. NY: Dodd, Mead, 1909. 1st ed. 47 plts. Teg. Grn cl gilt (lt foxed; worn). *Bookpress.* $25/£16

SINGLETON, ESTHER. The Shakespeare Garden. NY: William Farquar Payson, 1931. Gilt-stamped cvr, spine. Fine in dj. *Quest.* $40/£26

SINH JEE, BHAGVAT. A Short History of Aryan Medical Science. London, 1896. 280pp; 10 plts. (Sig.) *Argosy.* $75/£48

SINJOHN, JOHN. (Pseud of John Galsworthy.) Jocelyn. London: Duckworth, 1898. 1st ed, 1st issue, w/misprint p257. Olive cl. Spine dknd, cvrs sl worn, else Fine in morocco-backed slipcase. *Cummins.* $275/£177

SIODMAK, CURT. Donovan's Brain. NY, 1943. 1st ed. Fine in Fine dj (price-clipped). *Mcclintock.* $95/£61

SIODMAK, CURT. F.P.1 Does Not Answer. Little, Brown, 1933. 1st ed. VG. *Madle.* $50/£32

SIPE, C. HALE. Fort Ligonier and Its Times. Harrisburg, PA: Telegraph Press, 1932. 1st ed. Inscribed. Red cl. NF. *Chapel Hill.* $125/£81

SIPE, C. HALE. The Indian Wars of Pennsylvania. Harrisburg, 1929. 1st ed. Fldg map in pocket. *Hayman.* $100/£65

SIPE, C. HALE. The Indian Wars of Pennsylvania. Harrisburg, 1931. 2nd ed. VG in dj (worn, reinforcing). *Hayman.* $65/£42

SIPE, C. HALE. The Indian Wars of Pennsylvania.... Harrisburg: Telegraph Press, 1929. 1st ed. Frontis port. Red cl. NF. *Chapel Hill.* $135/£87

SIPLE, PAUL. A Boy Scout with Byrd. NY: Putnam's, 1931. 2nd imp. VG- in Good dj. *Blue Dragon.* $27/£17

SIREN, OSVALD. Early Chinese Paintings: from A.W. Bahr Collection. London: Chiswick Press, 1938. 1st ed. Ltd to 750 numbered. Presentation from Bahr. 25 color, b/w tipped-in plts w/guards. 2 articles laid in. Gilt-emb cl. Sl edgeworn, few spots, o/w VG. *Cahan.* $225/£145

SIREN, OSVALD. Gardens of China. NY: Ronald Press, 1949. 1st ed. 208 b/w plts. VG. *Cahan.* $250/£161

SIRINGO, CHARLES A. Riata and Spurs. Boston: Houghton Mifflin, 1927. 1st 'suppressed' ed. VG. Howes S 517. *Parker.* $150/£97

SIRINGO, CHARLES A. A Texas Cowboy. NY: Sloane, 1950. Dj. *Lambeth.* $40/£26

SIRINGO, CHARLES A. A Texas Cowboy. NY: Time-Life, 1980. Facs of 1885 ed. Simulated emb leather; marbled eps. *Heinoldt.* $35/£23

SITWELL, EDITH (comp). A Book of Winter. London: Macmillan, 1950. 1st Eng ed. Maroon cl. Fine in dj (sl dusty). *Dalian.* $39/£25

SITWELL, EDITH. Collected Poems. London: Macmillan, 1957. 1st Eng ed. Blue cl. VF in dj (sl tanned). *Dalian.* $54/£35

SITWELL, EDITH. The English Eccentrics. H-M, 1933. 1st Amer ed (Eng sheets). VG+ in VG dj. *Fine Books.* $65/£42

SITWELL, EDITH. English Women. London: William Collins, 1942. 1st ed. 8 color plts. Spine sl faded, o/w NF in dj (rubbed; spine dknd). *Temple.* $16/£10

SITWELL, EDITH. Epithalamium. London: privately ptd, Christmas 1931. Signed ltd ed. VG. *Hollett.* $388/£250

SITWELL, EDITH. Five Variations on a Theme. London: Duckworth, 1933. 1st Eng ed. One of 1000 ptd. Grey mottled paper bds. Fine in dj. *Dalian.* $70/£45

SITWELL, EDITH. Gardeners and Astronomers. NY: Vanguard Press, (1953). 1st Amer ed. One of 2500 ptd. Signed presentation. Very Nice in dj. *Antic Hay.* $225/£145

SITWELL, EDITH. Gold Coast Customs. Duckworth, (1929). 1st ed. Dj. *Bickersteth.* $47/£30

SITWELL, EDITH. Green Song and Other Poems. Macmillan, 1944. 1st ed. Dj. *Bickersteth.* $39/£25

SITWELL, EDITH. Green Song and Other Poems. London: Macmillan, 1944. 1st Eng ed. Eps sl foxed, o/w VF in dj. *Dalian.* $39/£25

SITWELL, EDITH. Jane Barston 1719-1746. London: Fabers, (1931). One of 250 numbered. R.A. Davies (illus). VF. *Pharos.* $150/£97

SITWELL, EDITH. Poor Men's Music. London: Fore Pub, 1950. 1st ed. Fine (rear cvr sl soiled) in ptd wraps. *Polyanthos.* $25/£16

SITWELL, EDITH. Popular Song. (London: Faber & Gwyer, 1928.) 1st ed. Fine in pict wrappers. *Pharos.* $20/£13

SITWELL, EDITH. Rustic Elegies. Duckworth, 1927. 1st ed. Port. Dj (price cut; burn hole repaired). *Bickersteth.* $54/£35

SITWELL, EDITH. Rustic Elegies. (London): Duckworth, 1927. 1st ed. Fine in dj (sl worn). *Reese.* $85/£55

SITWELL, EDITH. The Shadow of Cain. Lehmann, 1947. 1st ed. Pastedown, fly dknd; edges sl dknd, o/w Fine in dj. *Poetry.* $19/£12

SITWELL, EDITH. Taken Care Of. NY: Atheneum, 1965. 1st Amer ed. Red/blue cl. Owner label, ink date, else Fine in NF dj (clean tears). *Chapel Hill.* $30/£19

SITWELL, EDITH. Taken Care Of: An Autobiography. London: Hutchinson, 1965. 1st ed. Photo port frontis, 8 dbl-sided plts. Top edges sl faded, o/w Fine in dj. *Temple.* $16/£10

SITWELL, EDITH. The Wooden Pegasus. Blackwell, 1920. 1st ed. Lettering sl rubbed; edges discolored, o/w VG. *Poetry.* $31/£20

SITWELL, GEORGE. On the Making of Gardens. London: Murray, 1909. 1st ed. Pict bds, teg. Dj. *Marlborough.* $233/£150

SITWELL, GEORGE. On the Making of Gardens. London: Dropmore Press, 1949. #429/1000. 2-tone frontis, five 2-tone plts (3 dbl-pg). Fore, lower edges uncut. Dj (sl worn, loss, chipped). *Edwards.* $155/£100

SITWELL, H.D.W. Crown Jewels and Other Regalia in the Tower of London... Clarence Winchester (ed). London: Dropmore Press, (1953). 8 color plts, guards. VG in dj. *Argosy.* $125/£81

SITWELL, H.D.W. The Crown Jewels. Clarence Winchester (ed). London: Viscount Kemsley, (1953). 40 plts (8 color). Purple cl. Good in dj (sl soiled, chipped). *Karmiole.* $125/£81

SITWELL, OSBERT (ed). A Free House! London: Macmillan, 1947. (Fore-edges sl foxed.) *Petersfield.* $19/£12

SITWELL, OSBERT and SACHEVERELL. All at Sea. Duckworth, 1927. 1st ed. (Ink name.) Dj (sl dusty; sm piece missing). *Bickersteth.* $43/£28

SITWELL, OSBERT. Demos the Emperor. London: Macmillan, 1949. 1st ed. Cvrs sl rubbed, else Fine in pict wraps. *Pharos.* $30/£19

SITWELL, OSBERT. Escape with Me! Macmillan, 1939. 1st ed. Dj (sl defective). *Bickersteth.* $34/£22

SITWELL, OSBERT. Escape with Me! London: Macmillan, 1939. 1st Eng ed. 16 plts. Grn cl. Fore-edge sl foxed, o/w Fine in dj (torn, soiled). *Dalian.* $54/£35

SITWELL, OSBERT. Fee Fi Fo Fum! London: Macmillan, 1959. 1st ed. Inscribed, signed presentation card laid in. NF in dj. *Reese.* $35/£23

SITWELL, OSBERT. The Four Continents. Harper, 1954. 1st Amer ed. Fine in NF dj. *Fine Books.* $25/£16

SITWELL, OSBERT. The Four Continents. London: Macmillan, 1954. 1st Eng ed. Red cl. Fore-edge sl foxed, name ep, o/w Fine in dj. *Dalian.* $39/£25

SITWELL, OSBERT. Left Hand Right Hand! Macmillan, 1945-1950. 1st Eng ed, 2nd issue vol 1, 1st Eng eds other vols. 5 vols. Djs (chipped). *Bickersteth.* $39/£25

SITWELL, OSBERT. A Letter to My Son. Home & Van Thal, 1944. 1st ed. Dj. *Bickersteth.* $31/£20

SITWELL, OSBERT. The Man Who Lost Himself. London: Duckworth, 1929. 1st ed. Cl-backed dec paper over bds. VF in dj. *Pharos.* $125/£81

SITWELL, OSBERT. The Man Who Lost Himself. C-M, 1930. 1st Amer ed. Dust-soil to cvrs, else VG. *Fine Books.* $35/£23

SITWELL, OSBERT. Open the Door! Macmillan, 1941. 1st ed. *Bickersteth.* $28/£18

SITWELL, OSBERT. A Place of One's Own. Macmillan, 1941. 1st ed. (Ink name.) Dj. *Bickersteth.* $31/£20

SITWELL, OSBERT. Sing High! Sing Low! A Book of Essays. London: Macmillan, 1944. 1st ed. Bright in dj (soiled; sl worn). *Hermitage.* $25/£16

SITWELL, OSBERT. The True Story of Dick Whittington. London, (1945). 1st ed. VG in dj. *Argosy.* $25/£16

SITWELL, OSBERT. The True Story of Dick Whittington; A Christmas Story for Cat Lovers. London: Home & Van Thal, (1945). VG in dj (lt chipped, nicked). *Hermitage.* $35/£23

SITWELL, OSBERT. Who Killed Cock-Robin. London: C.W. Daniel, 1921. 1st issue w/wrapper loose over bds, w/o printer's stamp on back. Yellow ptd wrappers. Sl mend lower cvr, o/w VG. *Dalian.* $54/£35

SITWELL, SACHEVERELL et al. Fine Bird Books 1700-1900. London/NY: Collins/Van Nostrand, 1953. One of 2295. 38 plts (16 color, 1 double). Cl spine, corners; paper bds. VG in dj (edgeworn). *Bohling.* $750/£484

SITWELL, SACHEVERELL et al. Great Flower Books 1700-1900. London, 1956. NF in VG dj (chips, sm tears). *Shifrin.* $375/£242

SITWELL, SACHEVERELL et al. Old Garden Roses. London, 1955-57. Ltd to 2160 (these are #s 1915, 1905). 2 vols. 16 full-pg color plts. VG (margins sl browned) in Good djs (aged, worn; 2-inch tear vol 2). *Shifrin.* $225/£145

SITWELL, SACHEVERELL. All at Sea. London: Duckworth, 1927. 1st Eng ed. Blue cl. Fore-edge sl foxed, o/w VG in dj (chipped, soiled). *Dalian.* $70/£45

SITWELL, SACHEVERELL. All Summer in a Day. Duckworth, 1926. 1st ed. *Bickersteth.* $54/£35

SITWELL, SACHEVERELL. Conversation Pieces. London: B.T. Batsford, (1936). 1st ed. VG in dj (rubbed, chipped). *Chapel Hill.* $50/£32

SITWELL, SACHEVERELL. For Want of the Golden City. London: Thames & Hudson, 1974. 1st Eng ed. Blue cl. VF in dj. *Dalian.* $54/£35

SITWELL, SACHEVERELL. Golden Wall and Mirador. London: Weidenfeld & Nicolson, 1961. 1st Eng ed. Brn cl. Fine (bkpl) in dj (price-clipped). *Dalian.* $54/£35

SITWELL, SACHEVERELL. Gothic Europe. NY, 1969. Good. *Washton.* $25/£16

SITWELL, SACHEVERELL. The Homing of the Winds. Faber, 1942. 1st UK ed. Fine in dj (closed tear). *Williams.* $19/£12

SITWELL, SACHEVERELL. The Hundred and One Harlequins. London: Grant Richards, 1922. 1st ed. Spine label sl age-dknd, o/w Fine. *Pharos.* $85/£55

SITWELL, SACHEVERELL. Monks, Nuns and Monasteries. London, 1965. 1st ed. Pict eps. Dj (sl chipped, spine sl discolored). *Edwards.* $39/£25

SITWELL, SACHEVERELL. Morning, Noon and Night in London. London: Macmillan, 1948. 1st Eng ed. 8 full-pg color plts. Yellow cl. VF in dj (sl tanned, dusty). *Dalian.* $54/£35

SITWELL, SACHEVERELL. The Netherlands. London: Batsford, (1948). 1st Eng ed. Orange cl. Fore-edge sl foxed, o/w Fine in dj (price-clipped, sl tanned). *Dalian.* $54/£35

SITWELL, SACHEVERELL. Primitive Scenes and Festivals. London: Faber & Faber, 1942. 1st Eng ed. Grn cl. Fore-edge sl foxed, o/w Fine in dj (chipped, sl mkd). *Dalian.* $54/£35

SITWELL, SACHEVERELL. The Red Chapels of Banteai Srei.... London: Weidenfeld & Nicolson, 1962. 1st Eng ed. Red cl. Sm # stamp tp, o/w VF in dj (sl chipped). *Dalian.* $70/£45

SITWELL, SACHEVERELL. The Romantic Ballet from Contemporary Prints. London: Batsford, 1948. 1st Eng ed. Grey bds. Eps sl browned, o/w Fine in dj (sl tanned, dusty). *Dalian.* $54/£35

SITWELL, SACHEVERELL. Roumanian Journey. London: B.T. Batsford, 1938. 1st Eng ed. Blue cl. Fore-edge, prelims sl foxed, o/w Fine in dj (sl soiled, nicked, price-clipped). *Dalian.* $70/£45

SITWELL, SACHEVERELL. Selected Poems. London: Duckworth, 1948. 1st Eng ed. Blue cl. VF in Fine dj. *Dalian.* $70/£45

SITWELL, SACHEVERELL. Touching the Orient. London: Duckworth, 1934. 1st Eng ed. Red cl. Fine in dj (sl soiled, chipped). *Dalian.* $70/£45

SIVIERO, RODOLFO. Jewelry and Amber of Italy. NY: McGraw-Hill, 1959. 1st ed. 274 plts. VG in dj (chipped). *Bookpress.* $150/£97

Six Months of a Newfoundland Missionary's Journal...to August, 1835. (By Edward Wix.) London: Smith, 1836. 1st ed. 264pp. Orig paper bds, cl spine; ptd paper spine labels. *Ginsberg.* $850/£548

Six Months Tour Through the North of England.... (By Arthur Young.) Dublin: Wilson et al, 1770. 1st Dublin ed. 3 vols. 395; 390; 402pp; 25 engr plts (12 fldg); 5 fldg charts; fldg map. Contemp full calf (rebacked w/new spines). Good (ex-lib; sm bkpl each fr paste down; lib ink name each t.p.; foxed). *Second Life.* $400/£258

SIZER, NELSON and H.S. DRAYTON. Heads and Faces, and How to Study Them.... NY, 1896. 204pp. Good. *Fye.* $50/£32

SKAGGS, JIMMY M. The Cattle-Trailing Industry: Between Supply and Demand, 1866-1890. Lawrence: Univ Press of KS, (1973). 1st ed. Fine in dj. *Graf.* $25/£16

SKEAT, WALTER W. An Etymological Dictionary of the English Language. Oxford: Clarendon Press, 1882. 1st ed. (ii),xxviii,(i),799pp. Cl bds, morocco gilt-lettered spine. *Bickersteth.* $93/£60

SKEEL, CAROLINE A.J. Travel in the First Century after Christ. Cambridge, 1901. 2 fldg maps. Blue cl, gilt (lib pocket removed). *Schoyer.* $35/£23

SKELTON, JOHN. Family Medical Advisor: A Treatise on Scientific or Botanic Medicine. London, 1884. 12th ed. 276pp. (Inner hinges cracked; backstrip rubbed.) *Fye.* $40/£26

SKENE, ALEXANDER. Medical Gynecology. NY, 1895. 1st ed. 529pp. 1/2 leather. Good. *Fye.* $125/£81

SKENE, ALEXANDER. Treatise on the Diseases of Women. NY, 1895. 2nd ed. 968pp; 251 engrs, 9 chromolithos. 1/2 leather (backstrip rubbed). *Fye.* $40/£26

SKENE, NORMAN L. Elements of Yacht Design. NY, (1935). Rev ed. Good in dj (sl worn). *Hayman.* $20/£13

SKENE, WILLIAM F. Celtic Scotland: A History of Ancient Alban. Edinburgh: David Douglas, 1886-1890. 2nd ed. 3 vols. xvii,509; xix,510; xv,530pp. Cl on vol III damp-wrinkled, ex-lib internal mks, else VG set. *Cahan.* $75/£48

Sketch of the History of the Mayo Clinic and the Mayo Foundation.... Phila: Saunders, 1926. Good. *Goodrich.* $45/£29

Sketches by Boz Illustrative of Every-Day Life and Every-Day People. (By Charles Dickens.) London: Chapman & Hall, 1839. New ed, complete. 1st bk form ed thus (1st Chapman & Hall collection & resequencing of the 3 Macrone vols—as bound from 8vo sheets of Chapman & Hall parts issue). (iii-vii)viii,(1-3)4-526 (i.e., bound w/o 1/2 title and final blank from the sheets). 40 etched plts by Cruikshank; 'Parish Engine' plt used as frontis. Full polished calf by Morrell. NF (joints, hinges repaired). *Heritage.* $450/£290

Sketches by Boz. Illustrative of Every-Day Life and Every-Day People. (By Charles Dickens.) Phila: Lea & Blanchard, 1839. New ed, complete. 1st Amer bk ed of 1839 Sketches, w/The Public Life of Mr. Tulrumble and The Pantomime of Life added. 8vo in fours. 270pp (early ink sig, address; 3 inscrips; lt foxed throughout). 20 plts by George Cruikshank (lt browned). Orig grn blind-stamped cl (lt rubbed; sig sprung; back hinge loose), gilt. Good. *Heritage.* $600/£387

Sketches by Boz: Illustrative of Every-Day Life, and Every-Day People. The Second Series. (By Charles Dickens.) London: John Macrone, 1837 (i.e. 17 Dec 1836). 1st ed. Complete in 1 vol. 12mo. (i-x) [(vi-vii) misnumbered ii-iii and (x) misnumbered viii], (1-3),4-377,(378),(20)pp pub's ads; engr title, frontis, 8 other plts by Cruikshank inserted outside pagination. Contains List of Illustrations, listing 'Vauxhall...' twice, not listing 'Mr. Minns...' Last 2 (later) plts have not been inserted. Orig moderate red/salmon bead-impressed cl (pigment fading toward tan), spine stamped/lettered in gilt over patch of black pigment; orig yellow eps. VG (rebacked, preserving orig spine; cvrs sl soiled; fr hinge repaired, back starting). Chemised in 1/4 red morocco box, lettered in gilt. *Heritage.* $1,500/£968

Sketches from My Life. (By Augustus Charles Hobart-Hampden.) London: Longman, Green, 1886. 1st ed. viii,282pp. Sl wear extrems, else VG. *Mcgowan.* $450/£290

SKETCHLEY, R.E.D. English Book-Illustrations of To-day. London, 1903. 1st ed. Rubbing, o/w VG. *Willow House.* $54/£35

SKEWES, J. HENRY. Sir John Franklin. The True Secret of His Fate, After Forty Years Silence Now Made Public.... London: Bemrose, 1889. 1st ed. xvi,243pp. Good+ (sl rubbed). *Walcot.* $78/£50

SKEY, FREDERIC. A Practical Treatise on the Venereal Disease. London, 1840. 1st ed. 195pp; 2 hand colored lithos. Good. *Fye.* $125/£81

SKIFF, FREDERICK W. Adventures in Americana. Portland, OR: Metropolitan Press, (1935). 1st ed. Pict eps. Fine. *Graf.* $25/£16

SKIFF, FREDERICK W. Adventures in Americana. Portland: Metropolitan Press, 1935. 1st ed. #265/800, signed. VG in VG dj. *Perier.* $35/£23

SKINNER, ADA and ELEANOR M. A Child's Book of Modern Stories. NY: Dial Press, 1935. 1st ed thus. 4to. 341pp; 8 color plts by Jessie Willcox Smith. Lt grn ribbed cl, pict paste label, gilt (dull). Spine ends sl rubbed, o/w VG. *Drusilla's.* $75/£48

SKIR, LEO. Boychick. NY, 1971. 1st ed. Fine in Fine dj. *Mcclintock.* $45/£29

SKRINE, HENRY. Two Successive Tours throughout the Whole of Wales. London: Ptd for Elmsley & Bremner, 1798. 1st ed. xxviii,280pp. Contemp calf (surface cracking, loss; ex-libris); emb blind stamp upper bd. *Edwards.* $70/£45

SKUES, G.E.M. Itchen Memories. London: Jenkins, 1951. 1st ed. Fine+ in dj. *Bowman.* $165/£106

SKUES, G.E.M. Minor Tactics of the Chalk Stream and Kindred Studies. London: A&C Black, 1914. 2nd ed. Flyleaves lt browned; extrems sl worn. *Hollett.* $62/£40

SKUES, G.E.M. Minor Tactics of the Chalk Stream. London: Black, 1914. 2nd ed. Brn cl (sl dull). VG. *Bowman.* $85/£55

SKUES, G.E.M. Minor Tactics of the Chalk Stream. London, 1924. 3rd ed. Color frontis. Mod 1/2 calf. *Petersfield.* $70/£45

SLACK, H.J. Marvels of Pond-Life. London, 1878. 3rd ed. xii,147pp; 7 color plts. *Wheldon & Wesley.* $39/£25

SLADE, ADOLPHUS. Records of Travels in Turkey, Greece.... Phila/Boston: Carey & Hart/Allen & Ticknor, 1833. 1st ed. 2 vols. 262; 259pp. Internally VG (worn; ex-lib w/spine label). *Worldwide.* $165/£106

SLADE, BARNARD. Same Time Next Year. NY: Delacorte, 1975. 1st ed. Sig; sl foxing top edge, else NF in NF dj. *Lame Duck.* $85/£55

SLADE, CAROLINE. Sterile Sun. NY: Vanguard, (1936). 1st ed. VG in dj (torn). *Second Life.* $25/£16

SLADEN, DOUGLAS. In Sicily. 1896-1898-1900. London: Sands & Co, 1901. 2 vols. 11 plts. 1/2 grn levant morocco, gilt (pict rounded from orig binding laid onto upper bds). Handsome set (orig eps preserved, few neat repairs). *Hollett.* $349/£225

Slang Dictionary. London: John Camden Hotten, 1865. 'Thirteenth Thousand.' Frontis, xxii,(2),306,6pp + 16pp ads. Grn cl, gilt (sl frayed; inner hinge partly cracked). *Karmiole.* $30/£19

SLATER, J. HERBERT. Engravings and Their Value. London: L. Upcott Gill, 1912. Burgundy cl, gilt. VG. *Blue Mountain.* $50/£32

SLATIN PASHA, RUDOLF C. Fire and Sword in the Sudan. F.W. Wingate (trans). London/NY: Arnold, 1896. 4th ed. Frontis, xix,636pp; 21 plts; 2 fldg maps. Sl rubbed, soiled; lacks fr flyleaf, o/w VG. *Worldwide.* $85/£55

SLATKIN, REGINA SHOOLMAN. Francois Boucher in North American Collections: 100 Drawings. Washington: Nat'l Gallery of Art, 1973. VG in ptd wrappers. *Argosy.* $35/£23

SLATKIN, W. Aristide Maillol in the 1890s. Univ MI Research Press, 1982. 36 plts. Sound. *Ars Artis.* $39/£25

SLATTERY, CHARLES LEWIS. Felix Reville Brunot, 1820-1898. NY: Longmans, Green, 1901. 1st ed. Dbl-pg map. Teg. Blue cl (lt rubbed, edgeworn). VG (hinges tender). *Harrington.* $40/£26

SLAUGHTER, FRANK. Immortal Magyar, Semmelweis, Conqueror of Childbed Fever. NY, 1950. 1st ed. Good. *Fye.* $35/£23

SLEEMAN, W.H. Rambles and Recollections of an Indian Official. Vincent Arthur Smith (ed). Westminster, 1893. New ed. 2 vols. (Feps lt browned; vol 1 sl stained.) *Edwards.* $78/£50

Sleepy-Song Book. London: George G. Harrap, n.d. 4to. Color frontis, 12 full-pg color plts by Anne Anderson. Blue cl (lt edgewear), color paste label. *Reisler.* $175/£113

SLEIGH, BERNARD. Wood Engraving Since Eighteen-Ninety. London, 1932. VG. *Argosy.* $65/£42

SLEIGHT, C.L. The Prince of the Pin Elves. Page, 1897. 1st ed. Good. *Aronovitz.* $35/£23

SLESSOR, JOHN. The Central Blue. London, 1956. 1st ed. Frontis port; 16 plts; fldg table. VG in dj. *Edwards.* $39/£25

SLIVE, SEYMOUR. Frans Hals. NY: Phaidon/Kress, 1970-74. 3 vols. 7 color plts, 352 monochrome plts. Uniform pub's cl. Vol 1 ex-lib, fep mkd, stamp tp verso, o/w VF set in djs. *Europa.* $411/£265

SLIVE, SEYMOUR. Frans Hals. London: Phaidon, 1970. Catalogue vol only (of 3 vols). Sound in dj. *Ars Artis.* $194/£125

SLOAN, JAMES PARK. War Games. Boston: Houghton Mifflin, 1971. 1st ed. Fine in NF dj (tear rear panel). *Aka.* $45/£29

SLOAN, SAMUEL. City and Suburban Architecture. NY: Da Capo, 1976. Facs of Phila 1859 ed. 136 engrs. (Lt soiled.) *Edwards.* $62/£40

SLOANE, HANS. An Account of a Most Efficacious Medicine for...Distempers of the Eyes. Dublin: James Hoey, 1762. 4th ed. (i),17(47-54)pp. Mod bds. Good. *White.* $287/£185

SLOCUM, JOSHUA. Sailing Alone Around the World. NY: Century, 1900. 1st ed. Inscribed on fep, 'Onboard Spray, Larchmont, June 3, 1900. Joshua Slocum.' Dec blue cl. VG. *Chapel Hill.* $200/£129

SLOMAN, LARRY. Reefer Madness. NY: Indianapolis, (1979). 1st ed. VG + in VG dj. *Blue Dragon.* $35/£23

SMALE, M. and J.F. COLYER. Diseases and Injuries of the Teeth. London, 1893. xiii,423pp. (Sl foxed; worn, mkd; joint cracked, few pp coming loose.) *Whitehart.* $39/£25

SMALL, A.E. Manual of Homoeopathic Practice, for the Use of Families and Private Individuals. NY, 1879. 15th ed. 831pp. 1/4 leather. Good. *Fye.* $90/£58

SMALL, AUSTIN J. The Avenging Ray. GC: DCC, 1930. 1st Amer ed. Pp sl dknd, o/w VG in dj (dknd spine). *Mordida.* $65/£42

SMALL, AUSTIN J. The Avenging Ray. GC: DCC, 1930. 1st ed. Fine (name) in VG + dj (price-clipped). *Janus.* $45/£29

SMALL, JOHN W. Ancient and Modern Furniture. Stirling, 1903. Ltd ed, #55/250. 50 plts. Teg; rest uncut. (Margins sl thumbed; eps spotted, feps browned; lower joint tail split; worn; sl loss to spine.) *Edwards.* $140/£90

SMALL, JOHN WILLIAM. Scottish Woodwork of the Sixteenth and Seventeenth Centuries. Stirling: Eneas Mackay, (1878). 2nd ed. One of 500. Teg. Pub's yellow cl (handled; short tear inner hinge; rear hinge internally cracked; margins lt yellowed). *Bookpress.* $235/£152

SMALL, SIDNEY HERSCHEL. Sword and Candle. Indianapolis: Bobbs-Merrill, (1927). 1st ed. Yellow-stamped cl. Dj. *Dawson.* $30/£19

SMALL, TUNSTALL and CHRISTOPHER WOODBRIDGE. English Wrought Ironwork, Medieval and Early Renaissance. London: Architectural Press, n.d. (ca 1930). 1st ed. 20 plts. Cvrs sunned, else VG. *Bookpress.* $95/£61

SMALL, TUNSTALL and CHRISTOPHER WOODBRIDGE. Houses of the Wren and Early Georgian Periods. London: Architectural Press, (1928). Navy cl, gilt. VG. *Willow House.* $70/£45

SMALL, TUNSTALL and CHRISTOPHER WOODBRIDGE. Mouldings of the Wren and Georgian Periods. London: Architectural Press, (n.d.). 1st ed. 20 plts. Lt worn, else VG. *Bookpress.* $110/£71

SMALLEY, EUGENE. History of the Northern Pacific Railroad. Putnam, 1883. 1st ed. Frontis; xxiv,437pp; 52 plts (5 maps—1 fldg); color fldg map rear pocket. Gilt-stamped cl. VG. Howes S 561. *Oregon.* $175/£113

SMEDES, SUSAN DABNEY. Memorials of a Southern Planter. Balt: Cusings & Bailey, 1887. 341pp. Contents sound. Top spine torn; hinges broken; some archival repair; ex-lib. *Book Broker.* $45/£29

SMEDLEY, J. Practical Hydropathy. London, 1866. 444pp + 8pp ads; 160 figs. Foxing; inscrips; fep missing; cl faded; edges sl worn; inner hinges cracked, o/w VG. *Whitehart.* $39/£25

SMEE, A. My Garden, Its Plan and Culture. London, 1872. 2nd ed. xx,650pp. 1/2 calf (rubbed). *Wheldon & Wesley.* $47/£30

SMEJKAL, FRANTISEK. Surrealist Drawings. (London): Octopus Books, (1974). Fine in dj (lt worn, soiled). *Hermitage.* $65/£42

SMELLIE, WILLIAM. The Philosophy of Natural History. Edinburgh: Heirs of Charles Elliot et al, 1790. xiv,547pp(iii) + errata leaf. Contemp full calf bds (rebacked; scuffed). Very Nice. *Cullen.* $250/£161

SMELLIE, WILLIAM. The Philosophy of Natural History. Boston: Hillyard et al, 1827. 2nd ed. 322pp, 24pp cat. Good+ (heavy foxing; piece missing ep; spine, bds worn). *Smithfield.* $39/£25

SMILES, SAMUEL. Lives of the Engineers. London: John Murray, 1862-68. 6th thousand. 3 vols. xvi,484; xi,502; lii,542pp; all edges marbled. (Feps spotted.) Full tree calf gilt; raised bands, spine labels. (Spines sl dull.) Handsome. *Hollett.* $233/£150

SMILES, SAMUEL. Robert Dick. Baker of Thurso.... London: John Murray, 1878. Frontis port, xx,436pp. Marbled eps, edges. Gilt edged tree calf (lt spotting, upper bd detached). *Edwards.* $62/£40

SMILES, SAMUEL. Robert Dick: Baker of Thurso, Geologist and Botanist. NY: Harper, n.d. (1878). 436pp. VG (cl worn; bumped). *Smithfield.* $15/£10

SMILEY, JANE. The Age of Grief. NY: Knopf, 1987. 1st Amer ed. Sm rmdr mk, else Fine in dj. *Between The Covers.* $125/£81

SMILEY, JANE. Catskill Crafts. NY: Crown, (1988). 1st ed. Fine in Fine dj. *Robbins.* $35/£23

SMILEY, JANE. Catskill Crafts: Artisans of the Catskill Mountains. NY: Crown, 1988. 1st ed. Fine in Fine dj. *Lame Duck.* $65/£42

SMILEY, JANE. Duplicate Keys. NY: Knopf, 1984. 1st ed. NF in dj (surface scratches back panel). *Hermitage.* $50/£32

SMILEY, JANE. Ordinary Love and Good Will. NY: Knopf, 1989. 1st ed. NF in Fine dj. *Robbins.* $40/£26

SMILEY, JANE. A Thousand Acres. NY: Knopf, 1991. 1st ed. Fine in Fine dj. *Lame Duck.* $65/£42

SMITH, A.L. Frederic William Maitland. Two Lectures and a Bibliography. Oxford: Clarendon Press, 1908. (Joints cracking; spine chipped.) *Boswell.* $50/£32

SMITH, ADAM. The Theory of Moral Sentiments. London/Edinburgh, W. Strahan et al/W. Creech, 1781. 5th ed. (8),478pp + (2)pp ads. Orig tree calf (rebacked in period style), raised bands, gilt, leather labels. Very Nice. *Hartfield.* $495/£319

SMITH, ALAN. The Illustrated Guide to Liverpool Herculaneum Pottery 1796-1840. London, 1970. 1st ed. Color frontis, 7 color plts, 2 maps, 2 plans; 2 pamphlets loosely inserted. Dj (sl browned). *Edwards.* $59/£38

SMITH, ALEXANDER. A Complete History of the Lives and Robberies of the Most Notorious Highwaymen. Arthur L. Hayward (ed). London, 1933. Popular ed. 16 plts. (Sl soiled, faded.) *Edwards.* $74/£48

SMITH, ALICE R. HUGER and D.E. HUGER SMITH. The Dwelling Houses of Charleston, South Carolina. Phila/London: Lippincott, 1917. 1st ed. One of 1000. Signed by both authors. Frontis w/guard. Illus cl; teg; unopened. Lt rubbed, spine sl dknd, else VG. Howes S 571. *Cahan.* $150/£97

SMITH, AMANDA. An Autobiography...The Colored Evangelist.... Chicago: Meyer, 1893. 1st ed. 506pp; port w/guard; 25 plts. Gilt-pict maroon cl. *Petrilla.* $100/£65

SMITH, ARTHUR. Village Life in China. NY, 1899. 1st ed. 360pp. Dec cl (spine faded). *Lewis.* $37/£24

SMITH, ASHBEL. Yellow Fever in Galveston...1839. Austin: Univ of TX, 1951. Fine (sig). *White.* $39/£25

SMITH, BENJAMIN T. Private Smith's Journal. Chicago, (1963). Lakeside Classic. VG. *Schoyer.* $20/£13

SMITH, BENJAMIN T. Private Smith's Journal. Clyde C. Walton (ed). Chicago: Lakeside Classic, 1963. 1st ed. Gilt edge. Plain dj sl chipped, o/w Fine. *Pratt.* $35/£23

SMITH, BERTRAM. The Whole Art of Caravanning. London: Longmans Green, 1907. 1st ed. Good+. *October Farm.* $35/£23

SMITH, BRADLEY. Erotic Art of the Masters: The 18th, 19th, and 20th Centuries. (Secaucus, NJ, 1974.) VG in dj. *Argosy.* $75/£48

SMITH, CHARLES EDWARD. From the Deep of the Sea. NY: Macmillan, 1923. 1st Amer ed. Fldg map. Dec cl. VG. *Blue Dragon.* $25/£16

SMITH, CHARLES W. Old Virginia in Block Prints. Richmond: Dale Press, 1929. 1/1000 numbered, signed. 19 full-pg plts. VG. *Argosy.* $150/£97

SMITH, CHARLIE. Shinehawk. NY: Paris Review Editions, 1988. 1st ed. VF in fragile dj (sl rubbing, ink flaking). *Else Fine.* $75/£48

SMITH, CLARK ASHTON. The Abominations of Yondo. Arkham House, 1960. 1st ed. Fine in dj. *Madle.* $190/£123

SMITH, CLARK ASHTON. The Abominations of Yondo. Arkham House, 1960. 1st ed. One of 2000. Fine in VG+ dj. *Aronovitz.* $150/£97

SMITH, CLARK ASHTON. The Dark Chateau. Arkham House, 1951. 1st ed. Fine in dj. *Madle.* $650/£419

SMITH, CLARK ASHTON. The Dark Chateau. Arkham House, 1951. 1st ed. One of 563. Fine in NF dj. *Aronovitz.* $550/£355

SMITH, CLARK ASHTON. Genius Loci and Other Tales. Sauk City: Arkham House, 1948. 1st ed. Spine head, rear corners bumped, else NF in VG+ dj. *Other Worlds.* $150/£97

SMITH, CLARK ASHTON. Genius Loci. Arkham House, 1948. 1st ed. Fine in dj. *Madle.* $190/£123

SMITH, CLARK ASHTON. The Immortals of Mercury. Stellar Pub, 1932. 1st ed. Fine in wraps (rubbed, spotted). *Madle.* $200/£129

SMITH, CLARK ASHTON. Lost Worlds. Arkham House, 1944. 1st ed. Fine in dj (sl rubbed). *Madle.* $350/£226

SMITH, CLARK ASHTON. Lost Worlds. Arkham House, 1944. 1st ed. NF in VG+ dj (sl wear spine extrems). *Aronovitz.* $375/£242

SMITH, CLARK ASHTON. Other Dimensions. Arkham House, 1970. 1st ed. NF in dj (lt rubbed). *Madle.* $85/£55

SMITH, CLARK ASHTON. Out of Space and Time. Arkham House, 1942. 1st ed. NF in VG dj (spine top chip). *Madle.* $600/£387

SMITH, CLARK ASHTON. Out of Space and Time. London: Nevil Spearman, 1971. 1st Eng ed. Brn cl. Fine in dj. *Dalian.* $39/£25

SMITH, CLARK ASHTON. Tales of Science and Sorcery. Sauk City: Arkham House, 1964. 1st ed. NF in dj. *Other Worlds.* $100/£65

SMITH, CORNELIUS C., JR. Don't Settle for Second. San Rafael: Presidio Press, (1977). 1st ed. Frontis. VF in VF dj. *Oregon.* $25/£16

SMITH, D. MURRAY. Arctic Explorations from British and Foreign Shores from the Earliest Times to the Expedition of 1875. Edinburgh: Thomas C. Jack, 1877. 1st ed. xiv,3,824pp. Full leather, gilt. Good (1st map torn, repaired; binding rubbed, sl torn but still sound). *Walcot.* $140/£90

SMITH, DAVID E. and JOHN LUCE. Love Needs Care. Boston: Little, Brown, 1971. 1st ed. VG in dj. *Sclanders.* $31/£20

SMITH, DUANE A. Rocky Mountain Mining Camps. Bloomington: IN Univ, (1967). 1st ed. Fine in dj. *Schoyer.* $30/£19

SMITH, E. BOYD. So Long Ago. Boston: Houghton Mifflin, 1944. 1st ed. Lg, 4to. Grn cl w/blue lettering, dec (spine sl faded). Color pict dj (torn, but almost complete). *Reisler.* $165/£106

SMITH, E. QUINCY. Travels at Home and Abroad. NY/Washington: Neale Pub Co, 1911. 3 vols. Frontispieces. Grn cl, gilt stamping. Gilt tops. Fine set. *Bohling.* $250/£161

SMITH, E. QUINCY. Travels at Home and Abroad. NY/Washington: Neale, 1911. 1st ed. 3 vols. Dec cl. *Ginsberg.* $150/£97

SMITH, E.B. My Village. Scribners, 1896. 1st ed, 1st bk. Pict cl. Spine sl faded, else VG +. *Fine Books.* $125/£81

SMITH, E.E. Children of the Lens. Fantasy, 1954. 1st ed, later binding. VG in dj (worn, stained). *Madle.* $65/£42

SMITH, E.E. First Lensman. Fantasy, 1950. 1st ed. One of 500 numbered, signed. Fine in dj (spine frayed). *Madle.* $225/£145

SMITH, E.E. First Lensman. Boardman, 1955. 1st Eng ed. NF in NF dj (sl wear). *Aronovitz.* $85/£55

SMITH, E.E. Galactic Patrol. Fantasy Press, 1950. 1st ed. NF in wraps. *Aronovitz.* $55/£35

SMITH, E.E. Galactic Patrol. Fantasy, 1950. 1st ed. Fine in dj (sl chipped). *Madle.* $125/£81

SMITH, E.E. Grey Lensman. Reading, PA: Fantasy Press, 1951. 1st ed. Pastedowns browned, o/w NF in dj (sm chip spine top). *Bernard.* $75/£48

SMITH, E.E. Grey Lensman. Fantasy, 1951. 1st ed. NF in dj (sl chipped). *Madle.* $80/£52

SMITH, E.E. Lord Tedric. Wingate, 1978. 1st Eng, 1st hb ed. Fine in dj. *Aronovitz.* $40/£26

SMITH, E.E. Second Stage Lensmen. Fantasy Press, 1953. 1st ed. NF in dj (chipped). *Aronovitz.* $45/£29

SMITH, E.E. The Skylark of Space. Buffalo Bk Co, 1946. 1st ed, 1st bk. One of 500. Signed. NF in NF dj (sl wear, tear). *Aronovitz.* $475/£306

SMITH, E.E. Skylark of Space. Hadley, 1946. 1st ed. Fine in dj (sl worn). *Madle.* $400/£258

SMITH, E.E. Skylark of Valeron. Fantasy, 1949. 1st ed. VG in dj (chipped). *Madle.* $60/£39

SMITH, E.E. Skylark Three. Fantasy Press, 1948. 1st ed. Cvr corner soiled, else VG in VG dj (lt wear spine head; lt dust soil). *Aronovitz.* $60/£39

SMITH, E.E. Skylark Three. Fantasy, 1948. 1st ed. VG in dj. *Madle.* $65/£42

SMITH, E.E. Subspace Explorers. Canaveral Press, 1965. 1st ed. NF in VG + dj (lt wear, tear). *Aronovitz.* $27/£17

SMITH, E.E. Subspace Explorers. Canaveral, 1965. 1st ed. Fine in dj. *Madle.* $40/£26

SMITH, E.E. Triplanetary. Fantasy, 1948. 1st ed. Fine in NF dj. *Madle.* $95/£61

SMITH, E.E. The Vortex Blaster. Fantasy Press, 1960. 1st ed. One of 341. Fine in dj. *Aronovitz.* $450/£290

SMITH, EDMUND WARE. The Further Adventures of the One-Eyed Poacher. NY: Crown, (1947). #441/750 signed. Spine sl faded, o/w VG. *Glenn.* $40/£26

SMITH, EDMUND WARE. Tall Tales and Short. NY: Derrydale, (1938). 1st ed. One of 950 numbered. NF. *Glenn.* $200/£129

SMITH, EDWARD CONRAD. The Borderlands in the Civil War. NY: Macmillan, 1927. 1st ed. Orig blue cl. NF in VG dj (price-clipped, chipped). *Chapel Hill.* $75/£48

SMITH, EUGENE. Pioneer Epic. Boulder: Johnson Pub, 1951. Pict bds. VG. *Schoyer.* $50/£32

SMITH, EUSTACE. On the Wasting Diseases of Infants and Children. Phila, 1870. 1st Amer ed. 195pp. 1/2 leather. Good. *Fye.* $45/£29

SMITH, EUSTACE. A Practical Treatise on Disease in Children. London, 1884. 1st ed. 844pp. Good. *Fye.* $150/£97

SMITH, F. HOPKINSON. Caleb West: Master Diver. Boston: Houghton Mifflin, 1898. 1st ed. Dec cl. Ink inscrip; spine lt sunned, o/w Clean. *Hermitage.* $40/£26

SMITH, F. HOPKINSON. Colonel Carter's Christmas. NY, 1903. 1st ed. Orig cl. VG. *Mcgowan.* $38/£25

SMITH, FREDERICK. Sulfonamide Therapy in Medical Practice. Phila, 1944. 1st ed. Good. *Fye.* $50/£32

SMITH, G. ELLIOT and WARREN R. DAWSON. Egyptian Mummies. London: George Allen & Unwin, (1924). (2 corners bumped.) *Archaeologia.* $225/£145

SMITH, G. ELLIOT. Elephants and Ethnologists. London: Kegan Paul et al, 1924. 52 plts. 1/2 cl (extrems rubbed). *Archaeologia.* $110/£71

SMITH, G. ELLIOT. Elephants and Ethnologists. London, 1924. 52 plts. VG. *Argosy.* $125/£81

SMITH, G. ELLIOT. Elephants and Ethnologists. London/NY: Kegan Paul et al/E.P. Dutton, 1924. 1st ed. Frontis, 52 plts. 1/4 blue cl, bds (extrems worn). *Weber.* $65/£42

SMITH, G.M. The Freshwater Algae of the United States. NY, 1950. 2nd ed. *Wheldon & Wesley.* $47/£30

SMITH, GENE. High Crimes and Misdemeanors. NY, 1977. 1st ed. Fine in NF dj. *Mcgowan.* $35/£23

SMITH, GEORGE G. The History of Georgia Methodism from 1786 to 1866. Atlanta: A.B. Caldwell, 1913. 1st ed. Maroon cl. Spine faded, else VG. *Chapel Hill.* $125/£81

SMITH, GEORGE O. Highways in Hiding. Gnome Press, 1955. 1st ed. NF in VG dj (flaking spine folds; rubbed). *Aronovitz.* $23/£15

SMITH, GEORGE O. Highways in Hiding. Gnome, 1956. 1st ed. Fine in dj (sl rubbed). *Madle.* $85/£55

SMITH, GEORGE O. Lost in Space. Avalon, 1957. 1st ed. Fine in dj (sl frayed). *Madle.* $30/£19

SMITH, GEORGE O. Troubled Star. Avalon, 1957. 1st ed. Fine in dj. *Madle*. $35/£23

SMITH, GEORGE. Essay on the Construction of Cottages, suited for the Dwellings of the Labouring Classes.... Glasgow: Blackie and Son, 1834. 1st ed. 38pp, incl engr title (stained) w/vignette, 11 fldg plts (1 w/short tear). Orig cl, ptd label upper cvr. *Marlborough*. $171/£110

SMITH, GEORGE. Essay on the Construction of Cottages.... Glasgow: Blackie & Son, 1834. 1st ed. Lg folio, (viii),38pp, 11 plts (fldg). Emb cl. *Bookpress*. $350/£226

SMITH, GEORGE. The Laboratory or School of Arts.... London: Sherwood, Neely, etc., 1810. 7th ed. 2 vols. xi,2ff,440pp, 15 engr plts; 2ff,464pp,6ff, 16 engr plts. Contemp calf (joints rubbed). *Ars Artis*. $233/£150

SMITH, H. CLIFFORD. Buckingham Palace. London/NY, 1931. 1st Coronation ed. Frontis, 3 color, 351 b/w plts. (Tape mks pastedowns; spine sl bumped.) Dj (sl soiled, torn). *Edwards*. $93/£60

SMITH, H. CLIFFORD. Sulgrave Manor and the Washingtons. Jonathan Cape, (c1933). VG. *Book Broker*. $50/£32

SMITH, H. PERRY. The Modern Babes in the Wood. Hartford: Columbian Book Co, 1872. 444pp; sm fldg map. VG. *Schoyer*. $100/£65

SMITH, H.H. Robert E. Lee. Richmond, VA: Williams Ptg, 1924. 1st ed. Orig wraps. VG. *Chapel Hill*. $75/£48

SMITH, H.H. and F.A.G. PAPE. Coco-Nuts: The Consols of the East.... London, (1912). (1/2 title yellowed; spine faded; soiled.) *Sutton*. $75/£48

SMITH, HARRISON. From Main Street to Stockholm: Letters of Sinclair Lewis 1919-1930. NY: Harcourt Brace, (1952). 1st ed. Fine in dj (worn). *Graf*. $27/£17

SMITH, HARRY B. First Nights and First Editions. Boston: Little, Brown, 1931. 1st ed, 1st ptg. Black cl, gilt. Fine. *Macdonnell*. $35/£23

SMITH, HARRY WORCESTER. Life and Sport in Aiken and Those Who Made It. NY: Derrydale, 1935. One of 950. Color frontis, fldg facs. Uncut. VG in dj (chipped). *Argosy*. $75/£48

SMITH, HERBERT H. Brazil. The Amazons and the Coast. NY: Scribner's, 1879. Fldg map. Mustard colored cl, gilt titles. Overall VG (prelims sl foxed; cvrs sl worn). *Parmer*. $110/£71

SMITH, HERNDON. Centralia, The First Fifty Years 1845-1900. Centralia, (1942). 1st ed. Frontis; xvi,368pp; fldg map. VF in Fine dj. *Oregon*. $65/£42

SMITH, HORACE. Crooks of the Waldorf. NY: Macaulay, 1929. 1st ed. Fine in dj (chips; sl wear). *Mordida*. $40/£26

SMITH, IRA L. and H. ALLEN. Low and Inside. Doubleday, 1949. 1st ed. VG+ in Good+ dj. *Plapinger*. $25/£16

SMITH, IRA L. and H. ALLEN. Three Men on Third. Doubleday, 1951. 1st ed. VG in VG dj. *Plapinger*. $27/£17

SMITH, IRA. Baseball's Famous Outfielders. NY, (1954). 1st ed. VG+ in VG+ dj. *Fuller & Saunders*. $25/£16

SMITH, IRA. Baseball's Famous Pitchers. NY, (1954). 1st ed. VG+ (browning) in VG+ dj. *Fuller & Saunders*. $25/£16

SMITH, IRA. Baseball's Famous Pitchers. Barnes, 1954. 1st ed. VG+ in VG dj. *Plapinger*. $27/£17

SMITH, IRA. Baseball's Most Famous First Baseman. NY, (1956). 1st ed. VG+ in VG+ dj. *Fuller & Saunders*. $25/£16

SMITH, J.C. Reminiscences of Early Methodism in Indiana.... Indianapolis, 1879. 322pp. (Extrems sl worn; fr inner hinges reinforced, back inner hinges cracking.) *Hayman*. $50/£32

SMITH, J.V.C. A Pilgrimage to Egypt.... Boston: Gould & Lincoln, 1852. 1st ed. Frontis, xiii,383pp + (6)pp ads; 16 plts. Blind-stamped brn cl, gilt (foxing; lt shelfwear). *Petrilla*. $65/£42

SMITH, JAMES EDWARD. A Compendium of the English Flora. London, 1829. 1st ed in English. vii,219pp (pencil notes). Orig bubble grain cl (sl bumped, rubbed; spine sunned; refixed in case); labels. VG. *Shifrin*. $40/£26

SMITH, JAMES EDWARD. The English Flora. London: Longman et al, n.d. c.(1828-30). 2nd ed. 4 vols. (Lacks feps; recased w/sl soiled orig cl; spines faded, sl chipped.) *Edwards*. $116/£75

SMITH, JAMES EDWARD. An Introduction to the Study of Botany. London: Longman, 1833. 7th ed. 504pp; 36 plts. Grn cl (rebound); leather spine label. VG-. *Smithfield*. $29/£19

SMITH, JAMES REUEL. Springs and Wells of Manhattan and the Bronx, New York City, at the End of the Nineteenth Century. NY: NY Hist Soc, 1938. 1/4 calf over linen bds, raised bands w/floral device, gilt. *Cullen*. $170/£110

SMITH, JAMES. An Account of the Remarkable Occurrences in the Life and Travels of Col. James Smith.... Cincinnati: Robert Clarke Co, 1907. Later ed. Dk blue cl. Bkpl, sig, else VG. Howes S 606. *Chapel Hill*. $200/£129

SMITH, JENNIE. The Valley of Baga. Cincinnati: Hitchcock & Walden, 1880. 288pp. VG (cl paint-speckled). *Second Life*. $75/£48

SMITH, JEROME V.C. Natural History of the Fishes of Massachusetts.... Boston: Allen and Ticknor, 1833. 1st ed. vii,(i),399,(i)pp. (Foxing; hinges cracked; binding worn, stained; joints cracked.) Ptd paper label on spine. *Blue Mountain*. $225/£145

SMITH, JEROME V.C. Trout and Angling. Being Part Two of the Fishes of Massachusetts. NY: Derrydale, 1929. Ltd to 325. 2 plts. Grn cl over bds; paper labels. *Karmiole*. $200/£129

SMITH, JOHN SIDNEY. A Treatise on the Practice of the Court of Chancery.... Phila: P.H. Nicklin & T. Johnson, 1839. 1st Amer ed. 2 vols. Contemp sheep (worn). *Boswell*. $150/£97

SMITH, JOHN THOMAS. Vagabondiana. London: The Proprietor, 1817. 1st ed. India paper frontis; viii,52pp; 32 etched plts. Contemp full grn morocco. Aeg. Newspaper cutting laid in. Lt waterstain bottom margin 4 plts; frontis lt spotted; bkpls; sm label removed ep, o/w Fine. *Cox*. $279/£180

SMITH, JOHN. A Catalogue Raisonne of the Works of the Most Eminent Dutch, Flemish, and French Painters. London, Smith & Son, 1829-1842. 9 vols, incl supplement. Frontis ports. Marbled eps; leather title labels; gilt. (Frontispieces, tps, margins few leaves water-stained; 1 leaf loose vol 9; ex-libris; cl soiled.) *Edwards*. $209/£135

SMITH, JOHN. A Catalogue Raisonne of the Works of the Most Eminent Dutch, Flemish, and French Painters.... London, 1829-1842. 9 vols (8 vols + supplement). Gilt-tooled full leather, marbled eps. Good (bkpls). *Washton*. $600/£387

SMITH, JOHN. The Generall Historie of Virginia, New England and the Summer Isles. Cleveland: World Pub Co, 1966. Facs of London 1624 ed. Full vellum, linen ties. Fine in cl clamshell box (worn). *Cahan.* $125/£81

SMITH, JOHN. The Generall Historie of Virginia, New England, and the Summer Isles.... (Cleveland: World Pub Co, 1966). Facs ed. 14-pg booklet incl. Full gilt-dec vellum, ribbon tie closures. Fine in NF fldg box. *Harrington.* $120/£77

SMITH, JOHN. A Treatise on the Growth of Cucumbers and Melons.... Ipswich: J.M. Burton, 1839. 4th ed. 95pp, fldg plt. Good (faded). *Cox.* $47/£30

SMITH, JOSEPH H. (ed). Colonial Justice in Western Massachusetts (1639-1702). Cambridge: Harvard Univ Press, 1961. *Boswell.* $65/£42

SMITH, JOSEPH. Old Redstone. Phila, 1854. 1st ed. 459pp. Gold-tooled spine. Howes S 621. *Ginsberg.* $175/£113

SMITH, JOSHUA TOULMIN. The Northmen in New England, or America in the Tenth Century. Boston: Hilliard, Gray, 1839. xii,364pp (lacks both maps). Howes S 633. *Schoyer.* $20/£13

SMITH, JULIE. Death Turns a Trick. NY: Walker, 1982. 1st ed, 1st bk. Fine in dj (lt edgewear; sm chip). *Janus.* $100/£65

SMITH, JUSTIN H. The Annexation of Texas. NY: Barnes & Noble, 1941. Corrected ed. Tan cl. Name, else Fine in NF dj (spine faded, chip). Howes S 634. *Chapel Hill.* $150/£97

SMITH, JUSTIN H. The Annexation of Texas. NY: Barnes & Noble, 1941. Corrected ed. VG + in dj (lt soiled). *Bohling.* $150/£97

SMITH, JUSTIN H. Our Struggle for the Fourteenth Colony. NY/London: Putnam's, 1907. 1st ptg. 2 vols. 23 maps. Largely unopened. Pict cl. Fine set. Howes S 635. *Schoyer.* $125/£81

SMITH, JUSTIN H. Troubadours at Home. NY/London: Putnam's, 1899. 2 vols. (xxxii),494; (viii),496pp, 2 line maps; tipped-in als. Grn cl, gilt. VG. *Schoyer.* $85/£55

SMITH, JUSTIN H. The War with Mexico. NY: Macmillan, 1919. 1st ed. 2 vols. Fldg map. Blue cl. VG. Howes S 636. *Chapel Hill.* $250/£161

SMITH, KAY NOLTE. The Watcher. NY: CM&G, 1980. 1st ed. 1st bk. Fine in dj. *Else Fine.* $60/£39

SMITH, L. WALDEN. Saddles Up. San Antonio: Naylor, 1937. 1st ed. Dj. *Lambeth.* $30/£19

SMITH, LANGDON. Evolution. A Fantasy. Boston: John W. Luce, 1909. 1st ed in bk form. Pict marbled bds (sl rubbed; spine sl dknd). *Sadlon.* $50/£32

SMITH, LAWRENCE B. Fur or Feather. NY/London: Scribner's, 1946. 1st ed. Tan cl. Fine in dj (lt chipped). *Glenn.* $45/£29

SMITH, LAWRENCE B. The Sunlight Kid and Other Western Verses. NY: E.P. Dutton, (1935). 1st ed. Pict cl, gilt. Fine in dj (corner-clipped). *Glenn.* $25/£16

SMITH, LEE. Cakewalk. NY: Putnam's, (1981). 1st ed. Signed. VF in VF dj. *Chapel Hill.* $85/£55

SMITH, LEE. Family Linen. NY: Putnam's, (1985). 1st ed. Fine in dj. *Antic Hay.* $50/£32

SMITH, LEE. Family Linen. NY: Putnam, (1985). 1st ed. Inscribed, dated. Fine in NF dj (1-inch tear spine base). *Chapel Hill.* $50/£32

SMITH, LEE. Fancy Strut. NY: Harper & Row, (1973). 1st ed. Signed. Yellow bds, black cl spine. NF in dj (lt creases). *Chapel Hill.* $150/£97

SMITH, LEE. The Last Day the Dogbushes Bloomed. NY, et al: Harper & Row, (1968). 1st ed, 1st bk. Bkpl; surface abrasions flyleaf, fr/rear pastedowns, o/w VG in Fine dj. *Bernard.* $100/£65

SMITH, LEE. Something in the Wind. NY/Evanston: Harper & Row, (1971). 1st ed. Fine in VG + dj (lt surface imp fr panel; tear fr panel corner). *Bernard.* $125/£81

SMITH, LILLIAN. Killers of the Dream. London: Cresset Press, 1950. 1st ed. Erasure, o/w Fine in dj (sl frayed). *Temple.* $14/£9

SMITH, LOGAN PEARSALL. Songs and Sonnets. London: Elkin Mathews, 1909. 1st ed. Blue cl gilt. NF in orig plain tissue wrapper. *Cady.* $40/£26

SMITH, LOGAN PEARSALL. Unforgotten Years. London: Constable, 1938. 1st ed. Collotype frontis. Teg. Lacks most of fep, o/w Nice. *Temple.* $16/£10

SMITH, M. East Coast Marine Shells. Ann Arbor, MI, 1937. Frontis; map; 74 plts. *Wheldon & Wesley.* $54/£35

SMITH, M. Panamic Marine Shells.... Winter Park, FL, 1944. (Name fr cvr.) *Wheldon & Wesley.* $39/£25

SMITH, M. Tom the Piper's Son. An Action Book. Cincinnati: Artcraft, n.d. (195?). 15x20 cm, 5 3D spring-ups. Pict bds. (Spine worn). Internally VG. *Book Finders.* $45/£29

SMITH, MALCOLM. The British Amphibians and Reptiles. London, 1951. 1st ed. Dj (sm chip). *Edwards.* $62/£40

SMITH, MARTIN CRUZ. Canto for a Gypsy. NY: Putnam, 1972. 1st ed. Fine in NF dj (short closed tear; lt soiled rear panel). *Janus.* $100/£65

SMITH, MARTIN CRUZ. Nightwing. London: Deutsch, 1977. 1st UK ed, 1st bk. Fine in dj. *Williams.* $28/£18

SMITH, MARY P. WELLS. The Young Puritans in Captivity. Boston: Little, Brown, 1899. 1st ed. 8vo. 6 b/w plts by Jessie Wilcox Smith. Illus grey cl. *Reisler.* $125/£81

SMITH, MRS. A. MURRAY. Westminster Abbey. A&C Black, 1906. 21 color plts (1 detached). Teg. Dec cl (spine sl sunned; feps lt browned; ex-libris). *Edwards.* $39/£25

SMITH, MRS. J. GREGORY. Atla: A Story of the Lost Island. NY: Harper, 1886. 1st ed. 284pp + 4pp ads. Blue pict cl. Ink name, else VG. *Godot.* $85/£55

SMITH, NATHAN. Medical and Surgical Memoirs. Balt, 1831. 1st ed. 375pp; 4 litho plts. Orig mottled calf, leather label. VG. *Argosy.* $250/£161

SMITH, NATHAN. Medical and Surgical Memoirs. Nathan R. Smith (ed). Balt, 1831. Frontis; vii,374pp; errata. (Foxing.) Calf bds (rebacked). *Goodrich.* $175/£113

SMITH, OLGA. Gold on the Desert. Albuquerque: Univ of NM, (1956). 1st ed. Good + in Good + dj. *Oregon.* $25/£16

SMITH, PATRICK MONTAGUE. The Royal Family Pop-Up Book. London: Deans Int, 1984. 22x31 cm. 5 dbl-pg pop-ups, pull-tabs. Roger Payne (illus). Glazed pict bds. VG. *Book Finders.* $50/£32

SMITH, PAUL JORDAN. A Key to the Ulysses of James Joyce. Chicago: Covici, 1927. Ltd to 960 ptd. Map. Dec cl; mostly unopened. Fine in dj (2 internal mends). *Pharos.* $150/£97

SMITH, PHILIP. The Book: Art and Object. Merstham, 1982. Fine in dj. *Moss.* $85/£55

SMITH, PHILIP. New Directions in Bookbinding. NY: Van Nostrand Reinhold, 1974. 1st US ed. Fine in dj. *Cahan.* $175/£113

SMITH, R.A. A History of Dickinson County, Iowa. Des Moines: Kenyon Ptg & Mfg Co, 1902. Orig cl (soil, fading). Howes S 659. *Schoyer.* $95/£61

SMITH, R.A.L. Bath. London: Batsford, 1944. 1st ed. Dj (sl chipped). *Hollett.* $39/£25

SMITH, RED. Strawberries in the Wintertime. Quadrangle, 1974. 1st ed. VG in VG dj. *Plapinger.* $20/£13

SMITH, RED. Views of Sport. Knopf, 1954. 1st ed. VG in Good+ dj. *Plapinger.* $30/£19

SMITH, RIXEY and NORMAN BEASLEY. Carter Glass: A Biography. Longmans, Green, 1939. 1st ed. Signed by Carter Glass. Port. VG. *Book Broker.* $35/£23

SMITH, ROBERT A. A Social History of the Bicycle.... NY: Amer Heritage, 1972. Fine in dj. *Cahan.* $25/£16

SMITH, ROBERT C. The Art of Portugal, 1500-1800. NY, 1968. 1st ed. Frontis, 15 color plts. VG. *Argosy.* $75/£48

SMITH, ROBERT. Baseball in America. Holt, Rinehart & Winston, 1961. 1st ed. VG in Good+ dj. *Plapinger.* $35/£23

SMITH, S.E. (ed). The United States Marine Corps in World War II: The One Volume History. NY, 1969. VG. *Clark.* $40/£26

SMITH, SEBA. Way Down East. NY, 1854. 1st ed. Frontis, 384pp. VG (sl wear). *Hayman.* $35/£23

SMITH, SHERRY L. Sagebrush Soldier. Norman, (1989). 1st ed. Fine in Fine dj. *Pratt.* $22/£14

SMITH, SOUTHWOOD. A Treatise on Fever. Phila, 1830. 1st Amer ed. 448pp. Good. *Fye.* $50/£32

SMITH, STEVIE. Francesca in Winter. London: Poem-of-the-Month Club Ltd, 1970. 1st Eng ed. Signed. VG (edges sl creased; corner sl browned). *Ulysses.* $116/£75

SMITH, STEVIE. Harold's Leap. London: Chapman & Hall, 1950. 1st Eng ed. Red cl. Fine in dj (sl dusty). *Dalian.* $70/£45

SMITH, STEVIE. Some Are More Human Than Others. Gaberbocchus, 1958. 1st ed. Name, date; top edge sl spotted, o/w NF in dj (sl dknd). *Poetry.* $47/£30

SMITH, SYDNEY URE (ed). Adrian Feint. Sydney, n.d. c.(1948). One of 1500. 12 tipped-in color plts. (Ex-lib; joints split w/tears.) *Edwards.* $78/£50

SMITH, SYDNEY. The Wit and Wisdom of the Rev. Sydney Smith. London: Longman, Green, 1860. viii,355,(iv)pp. (Sl mks; joints cracking.) Blind-stamped cl (sl rubbed), gilt. *Hollett.* $23/£15

SMITH, SYDNEY. The Works. London: Longman, Green, 1860. 2 vols in 1. x,368,356pp; edges marbled. Mod half levant morocco, gilt. *Hollett.* $101/£65

SMITH, T.R. (ed). Poetic Erotica. NY: Boni and Liveright, 1921. #1192/1500. 3 vols. Uncut. Fine (sl sunned, rubbed). *Polyanthos.* $75/£48

SMITH, THOMAS H. The Mapping of Ohio. Kent State Univ Press, 1977. 1st ed. NF in VG+ dj. *Bishop.* $50/£32

SMITH, W. ROY. South Carolina as a Royal Province 1719-1776. NY/London: Macmillan, 1903. 1st ed. Maroon cl. Spine sl faded, sig, else NF. Howes S 717. *Chapel Hill.* $125/£81

SMITH, WADE C. The Little Jetts Telling Bible Stories for Young Folks: Stories and Etchings. Richmond: The author, c. 1916. 4th ed. Unpaged. Paper over bd; cl spine (tear). Contents Sound (foxing, soil). *Book Broker.* $25/£16

SMITH, WALTER E. Charles Dickens in the Original Cloth.... LA: Heritage Book Shop, 1982-1983. 1st ed. 2 vols. Fine in dj. *Bookpress.* $125/£81

SMITH, WILLIAM and SAMUEL CHEETHAM (eds). A Dictionary of Christian Antiquities. London: John Murray, 1876-1880. 1st ed. 2 vols. xii,898; x,899-2060pp. 1/2 tan calf over cl (sl rubbed), gilt spines. *Karmiole.* $85/£55

SMITH, WILLIAM and SAMUEL CHEETHAM (eds). A Dictionary of Christian Antiquities.... London, 1908. 5th imp. 2 vols. (Ex-lib; ink stamp tps, feps, #s; upper hinge vol 1 cracked; spines sl chipped.) *Edwards.* $70/£45

SMITH, WILLIAM C. Queen City Yesterdays. Crawfordsville, IN: R.E. Banta, 1959. Ltd to 1000. Inscribed presentation. Good in wrappers (sm label removed). *Hayman.* $20/£13

SMITH, WILLIAM FARRAR. Autobiography of Major General William F. Smith 1861-1864. Herbert M. Schiller (ed). (Dayton, OH), 1990. 1st ed. Fine. *Mcgowan.* $35/£23

SMITH, WILLIAM HENRY. The St. Clair Papers.... Cincinnati: Clarke, 1882. 1st ed. 2 vols. Map; 2 ports. Howes S 26. *Ginsberg.* $200/£129

SMITH, WILLIAM R. The History and Debates of the Convention of the People of Alabama.... Montgomery/Tuscalsoa/Atlanta, 1861. 1st ed. (12),(9),461pp. Contemp 1/2 morocco. *Ginsberg.* $600/£387

SMITH, WILLIAM. A Yorkshireman's Trip to the United States and Canada. London, 1892. 1st ed. (16),317,(3)pp. Dec cl. Howes S 701. *Ginsberg.* $150/£97

SMITH, WILLIE and GEORGE HOEFER. Music on My Mind. GC: Doubleday, 1964. 1st ed. NF in dj (very worn; internal mending). *Beasley.* $25/£16

Smokers Guide, Philosopher and Friend. London: Hardwicke & Bogue, 1877. Fourth Thousand. Woodcut frontis, viii,184pp + 6pp ads (incl eps). Dec red cl (lt rubbed, soiled), gilt. *Karmiole.* $40/£26

SMOLLETT, TOBIAS. The Miscellaneous Works. London: Henry G. Bohn, 1850. Thick lg 8vo. xl,966pp; engr port; 19 plts (spotted). George Cruikshank (illus). Half morocco, gilt, marbled bds (edges sl rubbed). VG. *Hollett.* $116/£75

SMOLLETT, TOBIAS. Travels Through France and Italy.... London: For R. Baldwin, 1766. 1st ed. W/half-title vol 1, lacks half-title vol 2. 372; 296pp. Contemp calf. 1 bd detached, others rehinged; lt marginal dkng from calf, o/w Good set. *Reese.* $225/£145

SMYTH, CRAIG HUGH. Mannerism and Maniera. Locust Valley, n.d. (ca 1962). 33 plts. Good. *Washton.* $100/£65

SMYTH, HENRY DE W. Atomic Energy for Military Purposes. Princeton: Princeton Univ, 1945. Orange cl. VG. *Smithfield.* $35/£23

SMYTH, HENRY DE W. A General Account of the Development of Methods of Using Atomic Energy for Military Purposes.... London: HMSO, 1945. 1st Eng ed. Fine in ptd wrappers. *Hemlock.* $225/£145

SMYTH, JAMES CARMICHAEL. Precis of the Wars in Canada, from 1755 to the Treaty of Ghent in 1814. London, 1826. 1st ptg. Inscribed. xiii,(1),185pp. Very clean, untrimmed in new cl, marbled bds (new eps). Howes S 728. *Schoyer.* $850/£548

SMYTHE, FRANK S. The Adventures of a Mountaineer. London: J.M. Dent, 1941. 17 plts. (Spine sl rubbed, darkened.) *Hollett.* $23/£15

SMYTHE, FRANK S. An Alpine Journey. London, 1934. 1st ed. Map. *Bickersteth.* $28/£18

SMYTHE, FRANK S. Climbs and Ski Runs. London: Blackwood, 1929. 1st ed, 1st bk. 61 plts. (Feps dusty; 1/2 title lt spotted; spine sl dknd, rubbed.) *Hollett.* $47/£30

SMYTHE, FRANK S. Climbs in the Canadian Rockies. London: Hodder & Stoughton, 1950. 1st ed. Color frontis; 40 plts; map. VG in dj. *Hollett* $70/£45

SMYTHE, FRANK S. Climbs in the Canadian Rockies. NY, n.d. (1950). 1st Amer ed. Sl bumped, else VG in dj (sl soiled, torn). *King.* $75/£48

SMYTHE, FRANK S. Edward Whymper. London: Hodder & Stoughton, 1940. 1st ed. 24 plts. (Spine faded, sm snag at head.) Dj (sl rubbed, chipped; spine dknd). *Hollett.* $101/£65

SMYTHE, FRANK S. Mountaineering Holiday. London: Hodder & Stoughton, 1940. 1st ed. 9 plts. VG in dj (spine dknd). *Hollett.* $47/£30

SMYTHE, FRANK S. Peaks and Valleys. London: A&C Black, 1938. 1st ed. Color frontis; 75 plts; prospectus for author's 'The Mountain Scene' loosely inserted. VG in dj (sl worn). *Hollett.* $54/£35

SMYTHE, FRANK S. Rocky Mountains. London: A&C Black, 1948. 1st ed. 64 plts (16 color). VG in dj (edges sl worn, chipped). *Hollett.* $70/£45

SMYTHE, FRANK S. The Valley of Flowers. London, 1938. 1st ed. 16 color plts, 2 maps. (Sl soiled.) *Henly.* $43/£28

SMYTHE, FRANK S. The Valley of Flowers. NY: Norton, 1949. Fine. *Quest.* $30/£19

SMYTHIES, BERTRAM E. The Birds of Borneo. London, 1960. Color frontis; 51 color, 47 plain plts; map. (Sl used.) *Wheldon & Wesley.* $155/£100

SMYTHIES, BERTRAM E. The Birds of Burma. London, 1953. 2nd rev ed. 31 color plts, fldg map. (Sl staining extrems.) Dj (ragged). *Edwards.* $155/£100

SNEAD, SAM. The Driver Book. South Norwalk, CT: Golf Digest, 1963. 1st ed. Fine in dj. *Houle.* $65/£42

SNELL, EDMUND. Kontrol. Lippincott, 1928. 1st ed. NF in dj (spine chipped). *Madle.* $50/£32

SNELL, EDMUND. The Yu-Chi Stone. Macaulay, 1926. 1st ed. VG. *Madle.* $27/£17

SNELL, EDMUND. The Z Ray. Lippincott, 1932. 1st ed. VG. *Madle.* $25/£16

SNELL, ROY. The Gray Shadow. Chicago: Reilly & Lee, (1931). 1st ed. VG in dj. *Houle.* $85/£55

SNELL, ROY. The Jet Plane Mystery. Wilson & Folliett, 1946. 1st ed. Fine in dj. *Madle.* $30/£19

SNELL, ROY. Lost in the Air. Reilly & Lee, 1920. 1st ed. VG in dj (frayed). *Madle.* $40/£26

SNELLING, O.F. Double O Seven James Bond: A Report. London: Neville Spearman/Holland, 1964. 1st ed. Lt spotting pg edges, o/w Fine in dj (sl wear). *Mordida.* $75/£48

SNELLING, O.F. Double O Seven. James Bond: A Report. London: Neville Spearman, 1964. 1st Eng ed. Fine (notes; spine tail sl bumped) in dj (extrems sl rubbed). *Ulysses.* $85/£55

SNODGRASS, MAJOR. Narrative of the Burmese War.... London, 1827. 1st ed. Frontis, xii,319pp; fldg map at rear. Eps browned by paste-action; 1st pg frayed at margins w/1 tear repaired, o/w VG. Full lt tan calf (rebacked) w/double lettering pieces. *Edwards.* $310/£200

SNODGRASS, W.D. After Experience: Poems and Translations. NY: Harper & Row, (1968). 1st ed. NF in dj (browning; sm stain). *Antic Hay.* $25/£16

SNODGRASS, W.D. Heart's Needle. Marvell, 1960. 1st UK ed. Fine in dj (sl dknd). *Poetry.* $109/£70

Snow White and the Seven Dwarfs. NY: FSG, (1972). 1st ed. Lg, 4to. Nancy Elkholm Burkert (illus). Black cl, dec blind-stamping cvr. Good in color pict dj (worn; lacks sm piece back; fr flap torn at fold). *Reisler.* $125/£81

Snow White and the Seven Dwarfs. London: Octopus, 1980. 21x21 cm. 6 dbl-pg, fan-fld pop-ups. J. Pavlin & G. Seda (illus). Glazed pict bds. VG. *Book Finders.* $40/£26

Snow White. London: Brown Watson, 1981. 26x20 cm. 6 dbl-pg, fan-fld pop-ups, pull-tabs. V. Kubasta (illus). Glazed pict bds. (Sm tears 2pp not affecting pop-ups.) *Book Finders.* $40/£26

SNOW, C.P. The Affair. London: Macmillan, 1960. 1st UK ed. NF in dj (price-clipped). *Williams.* $23/£15

SNOW, C.P. A Coat of Varnish. London: Macmillan, 1979. 1st ed. Fine in dj. *Hollett.* $47/£30

SNOW, C.P. The Conscience of the Rich. London: Macmillan, 1958. 1st Eng ed. Red cl. VF in NF dj. *Dalian.* $70/£45

SNOW, C.P. Corridors of Power. London: Macmillan, 1964. 1st ed. VG in dj. *Hollett.* $23/£15

SNOW, C.P. Strangers and Brothers. London: Faber & Faber, 1940. 1st ed. Spine lettering faded, else VG. *Limestone.* $150/£97

SNOW, EDWARD ROWE. Famous New England Lighthouses. Boston: Yankee Pub Co, (1945). 1st ed. Orig color map laid in. VG in dj (lt used; 2 tears). *Juvelis.* $45/£29

SNOW, JACK. The Magical Mimics in Oz. Chicago: Reilly & Lee, (1946). 1st ed, 1st issue measuring 1 3/16 inches thick, sheets ptd on white stock, pale yellow pict eps ptd in grn. Frank Kramer (illus). 4to. 242pp. Gray cl, color pict plt fr cvr. Fine in color pict dj (w/unclipped price of $1.75; sl chipped). *House.* $350/£226

SNOW, JACK. The Shaggy Man of Oz. Chicago: Reilly & Lee, (1949). 1st ed, 1st issue measuring 1 1/8 inches thick, pict eps. Frank Kramer (illus). 4to. 254pp. Gray/grn cl, color pict plt fr cvr. VG (lt dampstain bottom back cvr) in color pict dj (w/unclipped price of $2.00; lt edge-chipped). *House.* $300/£194

SNOW, JACK. The Shaggy Man of Oz. Chicago: Reilly & Lee, (1949). 1st ed, 1st state. 32pg gatherings. Frank Kramer (illus). Grn-gray cl w/pict label. NF in pict dj (few sm tears). *Davidson.* $275/£177

SNOW, JACK. Who's Who in Oz. Chicago: Reilly & Lee, (1954). 1st ed. 4to. Lt olive cl, gilt, dk brn colored areas. Red/yellow/black illus on dj (sl wear). Fine. *Reisler.* $325/£210

SNOW, PHILIP and STEFANIE WAINE. The People From the Horizon. London: Phaidon, (1979). 1st ed. Fine in Fine dj. *Oregon.* $40/£26

SNOWMAN, A. KENNETH. The Art of Carl Faberge. London: Faber & Faber, 1953. 1st ed. Color frontis; 26 color, 380 b/w plts. (Ex-lib w/ink stamps, #s, remains of label; tape mks.) Edwards. $39/£25

SNYDER, CHARLES. The Flaw in the Sapphire. NY: Metropolitan, 1909. 1st ed. Fine in pict cvr. (Lacks dj.) Else Fine. $50/£32

SNYDER, GARY. Earth Household. London: Jonathan Cape, 1970. 1st Eng ed. One of 1000 ptd. Black cl. Fine in dj. Dalian. $101/£65

SNYDER, GARY. Manzanita. Four Seasons, Bolinas, 1972. 1st Amer ed. Fine in pict wraps. Polyanthos. $25/£16

SNYDER, GARY. Sours of the Hills. (Brooklyn, NY): Sam Charters, (1969). Ltd to 300. Fine. Antic Hay. $35/£23

SNYDER, GARY. Turtle Island. (NY): New Directions, (1974). 1st ed. Fine in white dj (margins age-dkng). Jaffe. $125/£81

So-Sli and Ho-Fi or the Wicked Husband. (A Set of China series.) NY: McLoughlin Bros, n.d. (ca 1880). 6 leaves + 1pg list lower wrapper, 6 full-pg chromolithos; illus cvr w/dec title. Near Mint in pict stiff paper wrappers. Hobbyhorse. $175/£113

SOANE, JOHN. Lectures on Architecture. Arthur T. Bolton (ed). London, 1929. 120 plts. Gilt-edged cl. Edwards. $155/£100

SOANE, JOHN. Plans, Elevations and Sections of Buildings.... London: Taylor, 1788. 1st ed. (vi),11(2)pp, 16 leaves, 47 plts. Later 1/2 calf. Sl foxed; else VG. Bookpress. $3,850/£2,484

SOBEL, BERNARD. Burleycue: An Underground History of Burlesque Days. NY, 1931. Faded, soiled; joints repaired. Argosy. $100/£65

SOBY, JAMES THRALL et al. Bonnard and His Environment. NY: MOMA, 1964. VG in stiff pict wrappers. Argosy. $35/£23

SOBY, JAMES THRALL. Georges Rouault, Paintings and Prints. NY, 1947. 3rd ed. Fine in dj. Europa. $28/£18

Soft Furnishing Workroom Manual. Roger French (preface). London, n.d. (ca 1947). Rev ed. Cl-backed bds (margins lt browned; extrems worn). Edwards. $85/£55

SOKOLOV, Y.N. Perception and the Conditioned Reflex. S.W. Waydenfeld (trans). Oxford, 1963. (Lib stamp.) Whitehart. $28/£18

Soldier and Brave. Military and Indian Affairs in the Trans-Mississippi West. NY, 1963. 1st ed. Fine in dj (sl chipped, price-clipped). Baade. $30/£19

Soldier's Story of the War. (By Napier Bartlett.) New Orleans: Clark & Hofeline, 1874. 1st ed. 252(i.e.262),13,(35)pp + (6)pp ads (lacks frontis). Blue cl. Good (bkpl; worn). Chapel Hill. $350/£226

SOLEY, JAMES RUSSELL. The Blockade and the Cruisers. NY: Scribner's, 1883. 1st ed. (x),257,(1 blank, 4 ads)pp, fldg map + 6 maps. Lefkowicz. $45/£29

SOLLID, ROBERTA BEED. Calamity Jane. N.p.: Western Press, 1958. 1st ed. #600/2000. Fine in VG dj. Perier. $50/£32

SOLLY, N. NEAL. Memoir of the Life of William James Muller.... London, 1875. Frontis port, xxii + 369pp; tp vignette, handwriting facs; 15 mtd photo illus. Teg. (Sl bumped; joints rubbed, spine faded, bumped). Edwards. $116/£75

SOLOMITA, STEPHEN. A Twist of the Knife. NY: Putnam's, 1988. 1st ed. VF in dj. Mordida. $45/£29

SOLON, M.L. A History and Description of Italian Majolica. London: Cassell, 1907. 1st ed. 24 color, 49 b/w plts. Red cl. Soiling; spine abrasion, o/w VG. Hermitage. $85/£55

SOLZHENITSYN, ALEXANDER. August 1914. Michael Glenny (trans). NY: FSG, (1972). 1st Amer ed. Orange cl. NF (price sticker; owner label) in NF dj. Chapel Hill. $45/£29

SOLZHENITSYN, ALEXANDER. August 1914. The Red Wheel/Knot I. H.T. Willetts (trans). NY: FSG, (1989). 1st ed. Ltd to 200 signed. Red cl. As New in black cl slipcase. Jaffe. $350/£226

SOLZHENITSYN, ALEXANDER. Letter to the Soviet Leaders. Hilary Sternberg (trans). NY: Harper & Row, (1974). 1st ed. Fine in dj. Sadlon. $25/£16

SOLZHENITSYN, ALEXANDER. One Day in the Life of Ivan Denisonvich. Gollancz, 1963. 1st Eng ed. VG + in VG dj (worn). Fine Books. $50/£32

SOLZHENITSYN, ALEXANDER. One Day in the Life of Ivan Denisovitch. Ralph Parker (trans). London: Victor Gollancz, 1963. 1st Eng ed. VG (tape mrks) in dj. Hollett. $47/£30

Some Remarks on the Barrier Treaty between Her Majesty and the States-General.... (By Jonathan Swift.) London: John Morphew, 1712. 2nd ed. Sewn as issued. Nice. Waterfield. $155/£100

SOMERVILLE and ROSS. French Leave. Heinemann, 1928. 1st ed. VG. Whiteson. $31/£20

SOMERVILLE and ROSS. Further Experiences of an Irish R.M. Longmans, 1908. 1st ed. Contents Good (binding dull; sl worn). Whiteson. $28/£18

SOMERVILLE and ROSS. Happy Days. Longmans, 1946. 1st ed. Signed by Somerville. Contents Good (binding dull; sl worn). Whiteson. $39/£25

SOMERVILLE and ROSS. In Mr. Knox's Country. London, 1915. 1st ed. Edges lt foxed; spine sl faded, o/w VG. Words Etc. $54/£35

SOMERVILLE and ROSS. Mount Music. Longmans, 1919. 1st ed. VG. Whiteson. $50/£32

SOMERVILLE, MARTHA. Personal Recollections, from Early Life to Old Age, of Mrs. Somerville. Boston: Roberts Bros, 1879. Frontis port (inscrip to verso), 377pp (stain last few pp). Good in brn cl (spine frayed; worn). Knollwood. $125/£81

SOMMER, FRANCOIS. Man and Beast in Africa. Edward Fitzgerald (trans). London, 1953. 1st ed. (Feps sl browned.) Dj (sl chipped). Edwards. $47/£30

SOMMERFIELD, JOHN. The Survivors. London: John Lehmann, 1947. 1st Eng ed. Blue cl. Fine in dj (sl dusty). Dalian. $31/£20

Song of Roland. NY: LEC, 1938. #162/1500 signed by Valenti Angelo (illus). Fine in slipcase (sl dusty). Williams. $132/£85

SONNICHSEN, C.L. El Paso Salt War (1877). Pass of the North: TWP & Hertzog, 1961. 1st ed. Dj. Lambeth. $85/£55

SONNICHSEN, C.L. Outlaw. Bill Mitchell, Alias Baldy Russell. Denver: Sage, 1965. 1st ed. VG in VG- dj (sl wear). Parker. $50/£32

SONNISCHSEN, C.L. and WILLIAM V. MORRISON. Alias Billy the Kid. Albuquerque: Univ of NM Press, 1955. 1st ptg. VG in dj (chipped). Schoyer. $35/£23

SONTAG, SUSAN. Against Interpretation. NY: FSG, 1966. 1st ed. Tanning to text, else VG + in VG dj. Lame Duck. $35/£23

SONTAG, SUSAN. Against Interpretations and Other Essays. London: Eyre & Spottiswoode, 1967. 1st Eng ed. Brn cl. Fine in dj. *Dalian.* $39/£25

SONTAG, SUSAN. The Benefactor. NY: Farrar, Straus & Co, 1963. 1st ed. 1st bk. Fine in dj (sl rubbed, torn; ink name). *Temple.* $31/£20

SONTAG, SUSAN. A Susan Sontag Reader. NY, 1982. 1st Amer ed. Signed. Fine in NF dj. *Polyanthos.* $30/£19

SONTAG, SUSAN. Under the Sign of Saturn. NY, 1980. 1st Amer ed. Signed. Fine in dj (sl rubbed). *Polyanthos.* $30/£19

SOPER, ALEXANDER COBURN III. The Evolution of Buddhist Architecture in Japan. Princeton: Princeton Univ, 1942. Black gilt cl. Good. *Karmiole.* $150/£97

SOPER, JACK et al. The Black Cliff. London: Kaye & Ward, 1971. 1st ed. 111 plts. VG. *Hollett.* $70/£45

SOPHIAN, ABRAHAM. Epidemic Cerebrospinal Meningitis. St. Louis, 1913. 1st ed. Good. *Fye.* $50/£32

SOPHOCLES. The Antigone of Sophocles. John Jay Chapman (trans). Boston: Riverside Press, 1930. #325/500 of 550 on Rives h.m.p. Uncut. Dec cvrs, vellum spine, gilt lettering. Fine in glassine dj (sunned, lacks 2 sm pieces), box (sl rubbed). *Polyanthos.* $60/£39

SOPHOCLES. Antigone. Elizabeth Wyckoff (trans). Haarlem: LEC, 1975. One of 2000 numbered, signed by Harry Bennett (illus). Fine in slipcase. *Hermitage.* $75/£48

SOPHOCLES. Antigone. Haarlem: Enschede, 1975. One of 2000 signed by Elizabeth Wyckoff (trans). 8 color plts by Harry Bennett. Orig dec cl. Fine in slipcase. *Cox.* $85/£55

SORGE, ERNEST. With 'Plane, Boat and Camera in Greenland. Hurst & Blackett, 1936. 1st ed. (Sm glue stain spine.) Good. *Walcot.* $59/£38

SORGE, ERNEST. With Plane, Boat and Camera in Greenland. Appleton, 1936. 1st US ed. Panorama. VG. *Walcot.* $70/£45

SORIA, MARTIN S. Francisco de Zurbaran. London: Phaidon, 1953. 9 mtd color plts. VG in dj (chipped). *Argosy.* $75/£48

SORIA, MARTIN S. The Paintings of Zurbaran, Complete Edition. London: Phaidon, 1953. 9 mtd color plts. (Cl sl faded.) *Ars Artis.* $93/£60

SORIA, MARTIN S. The Paintings of Zurbaran; Complete Edition. London: Phaidon, 1955. 9 tipped-in color plts, 100 monochrome plts. Interior Fine (spine faded, mks). *Europa.* $37/£24

SORIN, SCOTA. Blackbird, a Story of Mackinac Island. (Detroit, 1907). 1st ed. Pict cl (deep crease; frayed; worn). *King.* $35/£23

SORLIER, C. The Ceramics and Sculptures of Chagall. Monaco, 1972. Color litho frontis. 220 plts (107 color). Excellent in dj, card slipcase. *Ars Artis.* $388/£250

SORLIER, C. Chagall Lithographs 1969-1973. Vol 4. NY, 1974. 2 color lithos. Excellent in dj. *Ars Artis.* $465/£300

SORREL, GILBERT MOXLEY. Recollections of a Confederate Staff Officer. NY: Neale Pub, 1905. 1st ed. VG (spine sl dknd; smudge spine top; pencil inscrip). Howes S 767. *Mcgowan.* $300/£194

SORRENTINO, GILBERT. Aberration of Starlight. London: Calder & Boyars, 1981. 1st Eng ed. Fine in pict wrappers. *Dalian.* $23/£15

SORRENTINO, GILBERT. Black and White. NY: Totem Press, (1964). 1st ed. VG (browning; lt soil) in ptd wraps. *Antic Hay.* $35/£23

SOTHEBY, WILLIAM. The Georgics of Virgil Translated. London: J. Wright, 1800. 1st ed. 1/2 title. Uncut. Spotting, sl soiling, o/w VG in orig bds (worn; rough re-back defective; crude label). *Poetry.* $43/£28

SOULE, GARDNER. The Long Trail. NY: McGraw, 1976. 1st ed. Dj. *Lambeth.* $25/£16

SOUREK, KAREL. Folk Art in Pictures: Nature, Human Life, Work. London: Spring Books, n.d. 61 color plts. Dec cl (spine bumped). *Argosy.* $100/£65

SOUSA, JOHN PHILIP. The Fifth String. Indianapolis: Bowen-Merrill, (1902). 1st ed. Gray-grn cl, gilt-orange cvr, spine. Spine extrems lt rubbed, else Fine. *Glenn.* $125/£81

SOUSA, JOHN PHILIP. Lyrics of the Bride-Elect. Cincinnati: John Church Co, (1897). 1st ed. 28pp. VG in ptd wrappers. *Godot.* $150/£97

SOUSTELLE, JACQUES. Mexico: Pre-Hispanic Paintings. NYGS, (1958). 32 full-pg color plts. (Edges browned.) Dj (chipped). *Argosy.* $85/£55

SOUTH, J.F. Household Surgery. London, 1880. xiv,388pp (eps sl foxed). *Whitehart.* $39/£25

SOUTHARD, CHARLES ZIBEON. The Evolution of Trout and Trout Fishing in America. NY: Dutton, 1928. 1st ed. 9 color plts. Red cl. VG + . *Bowman.* $100/£65

SOUTHERN, TERRY and MASON HOFFENBERG. Candy. NY: Putnam's, (1964). 1st Amer ed. Fine in VG dj (short tears). *Between The Covers.* $85/£55

SOUTHERN, TERRY. Blue Movie. NY: World, (1970). 1st ed. VG in dj (lt foxing). *Hermitage.* $35/£23

SOUTHERN, TERRY. Blue Movie. NY, 1970. 1st ed. Sl sunned, o/w NF in dj (nick). *Rees.* $39/£25

SOUTHERN, TERRY. Flash and Filigree. NY, (1958). 1st Amer ed. Fine (sl rubbed) in NF dj. *Polyanthos.* $35/£23

SOUTHERN, TERRY. The Magic Christian. NY: Random House, (1960). 1st ed. Fine in white dj (sl soil). *Antic Hay.* $75/£48

SOUTHERN, TERRY. The Magic Christian. Deutsch, 1959. 1st ed. Sm stain fr edge, o/w NF in dj (sl rubbed, nicked). *Rees.* $31/£20

SOUTHERN, TERRY. Red-Dirt Marijuana and Other Tastes. NAL, 1967. 1st ed. Fine in dj. *Fine Books.* $35/£23

SOUTHEY, ROBERT (trans). The Chronicle of the Cid. Haarlem: LEC, 1958. One of 1500 numbered, signed by Rene Ben Sussan (illus). Dec buckram. VG. *Argosy.* $85/£55

SOUTHEY, ROBERT. Common-Place Book. Second Series. John Wood Warter (ed). London: Longman et al, 1849. 1st ed. 1/2 title. Good (dull; spine worn). *Poetry.* $39/£25

SOUTHEY, ROBERT. Letters from England. Jack Simmons (ed). London: Cresset, 1951. VG. *Hollett.* $19/£12

SOUTHEY, ROBERT. The Life of Nelson. NY: Harper, 1830. Harper's Family Library No. VI. 12mo. 309pp + 11pp ads, engr frontis w/guard. Good (ink sig, date fep; rubbed; spine lt cracked; foxing, browning edges). *Hobbyhorse.* $55/£35

SOUTHEY, ROBERT. Roderick. London: Longman et al, 1816. 4th ed. 2 vols. No 1/2 titles. Contemp diced calf (sl rubbed; vol I upper joint tender). Nice. *Poetry.* $39/£25

SOUTHEY, ROBERT. Thalaba the Destroyer. London: Longman et al, 1809. 2nd ed. 2 vols. 1/2 titles. Good (ex-lib). *Poetry.* $31/£20

SOUTHWORTH, ALVAN S. Four Thousand Miles of African Travel. NY/London: Baker, Pratt/Sampson, Low, 1875. 1st Amer ed. xi,381pp (fr hinges starting), 20 plts, 2 full-pg maps, fldg map (short tear). VG (rubbed, bumped, sl stained). *Blue Mountain.* $95/£61

SOWELL, A.J. Rangers and Pioneers of Texas. NY, 1964. Rpt ltd to 750. Fine. Howes S 801. *Baade.* $125/£81

SOWERBY, G.B. Illustrated Index of British Shells.... London, 1859. xv,(48)pp; 24 hand-colored plts. *Wheldon & Wesley.* $233/£150

SOWERBY, G.B. Popular British Conchology. London, 1854. xii,304pp; 20 hand-colored plts. (Cl sl loose; lacks fep.) *Wheldon & Wesley.* $93/£60

SOWERBY, GITHA. Poems of Childhood. London: Henry Frowde, (1912). 1st ed. 4to. 12 mtd color plts by Millicent Sowerby. Teg. White cl-backed bds; gold stamping, dec. Dj, gilt (sl edge chipping; few holes). *Reisler.* $175/£113

SOWERBY, JOHN E. and C. JOHNSON. British Wild Flowers. London: John E. Sowerby, 1860. 1st ed. Frontis, xlix,168pp; 1500 hand-colored figs on 80pp, guards. 1/2 calf, marbled bds, gilt-dec spine. Fr hinge starting, sl gap spine joint, else VG. *Quest.* $425/£274

SOWERBY, JOHN E. and C. JOHNSON. The Ferns of Great Britain. London: Privately pub, 1855. 1st ed. Hand-colored frontis, 88pp, 48 b/w engrs. Gilt dec cl. Good + . *Mikesh.* $55/£35

SOWERBY, JOHN E. and C. JOHNSON. The Grasses of Great Britain. London, n.d. (1857-61). 1st ed. xxxii,192pp; 144 full-pg hand-colored engr plts. Emb gilt-dec cl (refixed in case; new eps; bumped; sl rubbed). Cat listing, Quaritch obituary laid in. VG. *Shifrin.* $250/£161

SOWERBY, JOHN E. and C. PIERPOINT JOHNSON. British Wild Flowers. London, 1876. 3rd ed. Hand-colored frontis; lii,186pp (new eps); 89 hand-colored full-pg plts; 2 plain plts. Aeg. Gilt-dec cl (rubbed; rebacked preserving spine; bkpl; margins browned). VG. *Shifrin.* $225/£145

SOWERS, ROBERT. The Language of Stained Glass. Forest Grove, OR, (1981). 1st ed. VG in dj. *Artis.* $20/£13

SOWLS, L.K. Prairie Ducks. Harrisburg/Washington: Stackpole/WMI, 1955. 1st ed. Pict cl. VG + in Fair dj. *Mikesh.* $45/£29

SOYER, RAPHAEL. Self-Revealment: A Memoir. NY, (1969). 1st ed. VG in dj. *Argosy.* $65/£42

SOYINKA, WOLE. Ake. London, 1981. 1st Eng ed. Frontis. Blue cl. Fine in dj. *Dalian.* $31/£20

SOYINKA, WOLE. The Interpreters. London: Andre Deutsch, 1965. 1st Eng ed. Grn cl. Fine in dj. *Dalian.* $31/£20

SOYINKA, WOLE. The Man Died: Prison Notes. NY: Harper & Row, (1972). 1st US ed. NF (lt bumps) in dj (edgewear; lacks sm piece; short tear). *Aka.* $35/£23

Space Mission. London: Methuen/Walker Books, 1982. 18x22 cm. 4 pop-ups, pull-tabs, wheels. Terry Pastor (illus). Glazed pict bds. VG. *Book Finders.* $30/£19

SPAETH, SIGMUND. Barber Shop Ballads and How to Sing Them. NY, 1940. 2nd ptg. Pict cl. Good. *Artis.* $17/£11

SPAFFORD, HORATIO GATES. A Gazetteer of the State of New-York.... Albany, 1813. Fldg frontis map; 334,iipp (foxed). Contemp mottled calf (edgeworn; fr joint starting; dust soil), leather label. Good (lacks 2 plts). Howes S 802. *Ginsberg.* $75/£48

SPAFFORD, HORATIO GATES. A Gazetteer of the State of New-York.... Albany: B.D. Packard/Author, 1824. 1st enlgd ed from 1813 1st ed. 620pp; map addenda slip pasted at end. Orig leather, red morocco label. Good (wear; crack along outer back hinge; foxing; map called for but not present). *Connolly.* $75/£48

SPALDING, MARTIN JOHN. Sketches of the Life, Times, and Character of the Rt. Rev. Benedict Joseph Flaget.... Louisville: Webb, 1852. 1st ed. Frontis, 406,(8)pp, port. Howes S 809. *Ginsberg.* $275/£177

SPARGO, JOHN. Karl Marx. His Life and Work. NY: Huebsch, 1910. 1st ed. Gilt-stamped grn cl. NF (lib #s on dedication pg, thin strip of paper on rep). *Beasley.* $65/£42

SPARK, MURIEL. The Abbess of Crewe. London: Macmillan, 1972. 1st ed. Fine in dj. *Temple.* $26/£17

SPARK, MURIEL. The Bachelors. London: Macmillan, 1960. 1st UK ed. VG in dj. *Lewton.* $54/£35

SPARK, MURIEL. Child of Light: A Reassessment of Mary Wollstonecraft Shelley. London: Tower Bridge, 1951. 1st ed. VG in dj (spine sl browned; nick). *Rees.* $147/£95

SPARK, MURIEL. A Far Cry from Kensington. London: Constable, 1988. 1st ed. Fine in dj. *Rees.* $31/£20

SPARK, MURIEL. The Girls of Slender Means. London: Macmillan, 1963. 1st ed. NF in dj. *Rees.* $31/£20

SPARK, MURIEL. Girls of Slender Means. London: Macmillan, 1963. 1st UK ed. Eps sl mottled, o/w VG in dj. *Lewton.* $45/£29

SPARK, MURIEL. John Masefield. London: Peter Nevill, 1953. 1st ed. VG (inscrip) in dj (price-clipped). *Rees.* $54/£35

SPARK, MURIEL. The Mandelbaum Gate. London: Macmillan, 1965. 1st ed. VG in dj (price-clipped, sl browned). *Hollett.* $31/£20

SPARK, MURIEL. Memento Mori. London: Macmillan, 1959. 1st UK ed. VG in VG dj (sl mkd, dusty rear panel). *Lewton.* $57/£37

SPARK, MURIEL. Not to Disturb. London: Macmillan, 1971. 1st ed. VG in dj (sl chipped). *Virgo.* $39/£25

SPARK, MURIEL. Not to Disturb. London: Observer Books, 1971. One of 500 specially bound, signed by author and illus. This copy unnumbered. Fine in glassine dj (nick). *Rees.* $109/£70

SPARK, MURIEL. The Only Problem. Franklin Library, 1984. Signed, ltd 1st ed. Fine in dec binding. *Williams.* $43/£28

SPARK, MURIEL. The Portobello Road and Other Stories. Helsinki: Eurographica, 1991. One of 350 numbered, signed. Fine in wrappers. *Rees.* $140/£90

SPARK, MURIEL. The Prime of Miss Jean Brodie. London: Macmillan, 1961. 1st UK ed. Fore-edge sl foxed, o/w VG in dj. *Lewton.* $47/£30

SPARK, MURIEL. The Public Image. NY: Knopf, (1968). 1st Amer ed. Fine in dj. *Hermitage.* $25/£16

SPARK, MURIEL. The Public Image. London: Macmillan, 1968. 1st Eng ed. Blue cl. Fine in dj (sl mkd). *Dalian.* $31/£20

SPARK, MURIEL. The Very Fine Clock. London: Macmillan, 1969. 1st ed. Edward Gorey (illus). 8vo. Pict cl. As New in As New dj. *Book Adoption.* $60/£39

SPARK, MURIEL. Voices at Play. London: Macmillan, 1961. 1st Eng ed. Red cl. VF in dj (price-clipped). *Dalian.* $39/£25

SPARKS, EDWIN EARLE (ed). The English Settlement in the Illinois. London/Cedar Rapids, IA: Museum Book Shop/Torch Press, 1907. One of 200. Blue cl. VG. Howes B 466, F 219, F 220. *Schoyer.* $75/£48

SPARKS, W.H. The Memories of Fifty Years. Phila, 1870. 1st ed. 489pp. Howes S 819. *Ginsberg.* $125/£81

SPARROW, JOHN (ed). The Poems of Bishop Henry King. London: Nonesuch, 1925. Ltd to 900. Unopened. Vellum over bds. Sm tear fep, else VG. *Cahan.* $85/£55

SPARROW, WALTER SHAW. Angling in British Art. London, 1923. 1st ed. Color frontis. Fore-edge uncut. (Lt spotting; rubbed, sl faded.) *Edwards.* $116/£75

SPARROW, WALTER SHAW. A Book of British Etching from Francis Barlow to Francis Seymour Haden. London: John Lane, 1926. 1st ed. 156 etchings. Buckram. Partly unopened. VG. *Cox.* $93/£60

SPARROW, WALTER SHAW. A Book of Sporting Painters. London: John Lane, 1931. 1st ed. 136 plts (15 color). Uncut. Grn buckram, pict panel upper cvr. VG. *Cox.* $116/£75

SPARROW, WALTER SHAW. A Book of Sporting Painters. London/NY, 1931. 1st ed. 136 plts (15 color). Fore, lower edge uncut. (Lt spotting.) *Edwards.* $116/£75

SPARROW, WALTER SHAW. British Sporting Artists from Barlow to Herring. London/NY, 1922. 1st ed. 27 color, 76 b/w plts. (Ex-libris; lower joint split; bumped.) *Edwards.* $70/£45

SPARROW, WALTER SHAW. British Sporting Artists. London: John Lane, (1922). 1st ed. 103 plts (27 color). Grn cl, stamped in black/gold (lt rubbed; some text foxing). *Karmiole.* $125/£81

SPARROW, WALTER SHAW. The English House. London: Eveleigh Nash, 1908. 1st ed. Teg. Spotted; spine sl rubbed, dknd. *Hollett.* $70/£45

SPARROW, WALTER SHAW. Frank Brangwyn and His Work. London, 1910. Color frontis, 19 color plts, 16 b/w plts. Teg. (Lt marginal spotting, dedication leaf detached, feps sl browned; sl bumped.) *Edwards.* $70/£45

SPARROW, WALTER SHAW. Henry Alken. London/NY, 1927. 1st ed. 8 color, 64 b/w plts. (Feps browned; tp lt spotted; upper hinge tender; sl soiled; spine bumped.) Teg, rest uncut. *Edwards.* $93/£60

SPAULDING, EDWARD S. The Quails. NY: Macmillan, 1949. 1st ptg. Fine in VG+ dj. *Bowman.* $60/£39

SPAULDING, EDWARD S. (comp). Adobe Days Along the Channel. (Santa Barbara: Schauer Ptg Studio), 1957. 'Grizzly Edition' ltd to 1015 numbered, signed. Rust cl stamped in brn. Good in pub's box (lt soiled). *Karmiole.* $150/£97

SPEAIGHT, ROBERT. William Rothenstein: The Portrait of an Artist in His Time. London: Eyre & Spottiswoode, 1962. Color frontis, 16 b/w plts. Blue cl cords. Bkpl; dj edges worn, else Fine. *Heller.* $30/£19

SPEARS, JOHN R. Illustrated Sketches of Death Valley and Other Borax Deserts of the Pacific Coast. Chicago: Rand, McNally, 1892. 1st ed. 226pp. Fine. *Book Market.* $250/£161

Specimens of Ancient Church Plate. Cambridge, London, 1845. 10pp text, 50 plts (spotting; ex-libris). 1/2 morocco w/marbled bds (rubbed). *Edwards.* $74/£48

SPECK, GORDON. Breeds and Half Breeds. C.N. Potter, (1969). 1st ed. 15 maps. VF in VF dj. *Oregon.* $40/£26

SPECK, GORDON. Breeds and Half-Breeds. NY: Clarkson N. Potter, (1969). 1st ed. 15 maps. Fine in dj. *Schoyer.* $30/£19

Spectator. London: For J. & R. Tonson & S. Draper, 1 March 1710—20 Dec 1714. 8 vols. Full marbled calf (lt abrasions cvr vol 8; ep edges sl browned; name, bkpl); gilt; leather spine labels. Attractive set. *Sadlon.* $375/£242

Spectator. (By Richard Steele.) Ptd for J.&R. Tonson, 1739. Vols 4 & 8 dated 1738. 12 vols. Contemp panelled calf, raised bands, gilt spine #s. (Sl wear spine head, feet; vol 2 lacks fep.) *Bickersteth.* $54/£35

SPEER, EMORY. Lincoln, Lee, Grant and Other Biographical Addresses. NY/Washington: Neale Pub, 1909. 1st ed. Inscribed. VG. *Mcgowan.* $150/£97

SPEER, MARION A. Western Trails. (Huntington Beach: by Author, 1931). Signed. Gold-stamped fabricoid. *Dawson.* $35/£23

SPEER, WILLIAM. Oldest and The Newest Empire: China and the United States. Hartford, CT: Scranton & Co., 1870. 681pp + 7pp pub's ads. Lavender cl stamped in blind (faded; ex-lib w/bkpl, paper spine label). *Schoyer.* $100/£65

SPEIGHT, HARRY. Tramps and Drives in the Craven Highlands. London: Elliot Stock, 1895. 214,(xxviii)pp, fldg map. VG. *Hollett.* $50/£32

SPEKE, JOHN H. Journal of the Discovery of the Source of the Nile. NY: Harper's, 1864. 1st Amer ed. 590pp + 6pp ads, 2 maps (1 fldg). Eps on brittle paper (chipped; tp clipped, w/name; foxing). Tan cl stamped in brn (discolored). *Schoyer.* $125/£81

SPELLMAN, D. and S. Victorian Music Covers. Evelyn, Adams & Mackay, 1969. 1st ed. VG in dj. *Moss.* $28/£18

SPELMAN, W.W.R. Lowestoft China. Norwich, 1905. Color frontis, 97 plts. Blue cl (feps sl browned; upper joint tender; sl soiled, rubbed), teg. *Edwards.* $78/£50

SPELTZ, ALEXANDER. The Styles of Ornament...to the Middle of the XIXth Century. R. Phene Spiers (ed). NY: Bruno Hessling, (1910). Grn binder's cl (backstrip sl faded). *Petersfield.* $59/£38

SPENCE, BASIL and HENK SNOEK. Out of the Ashes. London, 1963. 1st ed. 47 plts. (Bds sl warped) Dj (ragged). *Edwards.* $39/£25

SPENCE, J. Lectures on Surgery. London, 1875-1876. 2nd ed. 2 vols. xxiv,469pp (sl foxing tp), 83 figs; xxvii,471-1152pp, figs 84-157. 58 color plts. Vol 1 orig cl (sl worn; sm split inner fr hinge). Vol 2 orig cl (rebacked w/orig spine laid on), o/w VG set. *Whitehart.* $90/£58

SPENCE, LEWIS. The Myths of Ancient Egypt. Harrap, 1919. Good+. *Madle.* $25/£16

SPENCE, LEWIS. The Problem of Lemuria. London, 1933. 2nd imp. Map frontis. Dj (chipped, stained). *Edwards.* $43/£28

SPENCE, S.A. Antarctic Miscellany. London, 1980. 2nd ed, ltd to 1000. *Walcot.* $34/£22

SPENCER, BETTY. The Big Blowup. Caldwell: Caxton, 1956. 1st ed. Bkpl, else VG in dj (edgetorn). *Perier.* $40/£26

SPENCER, CHARLES. Leon Bakst. NY, 1973. VG in dj. *Argosy.* $75/£48

SPENCER, CORNELIA PHILLIPS. The Last Ninety Days of the War in North Carolina. NY: Watchman Pub Co, 1866. 1st ed. 287,(2)pp. Fr inner hinge cracking, sm rubber lib stamp, else NF. Howes S 832. *Mcgowan.* $350/£226

SPENCER, ELIZABETH. Marilee. Three Stories. UMSP, 1981. #199/300 signed. Fine in orig glassine dj. *Polyanthos.* $100/£65

SPENCER, ELIZABETH. No Place for an Angel. London: Weidenfeld & Nicholson, (1968). 1st Eng ed. Fine in dj. *Pharos.* $35/£23

SPENCER, ELIZABETH. Ship Island and Other Stories. London: Weidenfeld & Nicholson, (1969). 1st Eng ed. Fine in dj. *Pharos.* $35/£23

SPENCER, HERBERT. An Autobiography. NY: Appleton, 1904. 1st ed. 2 vols. 3/4 leather; marbled paper-cvrd bds. Surface loss fr bd 1st vol, else VG +. *Lame Duck.* $100/£65

SPENCER, HERBERT. Various Fragments. London: Williams & Northgate, 1897. 1st ed. NF (sl extrem wear). *Lame Duck.* $50/£32

SPENCER, OMAR. The Story of Sauvies Island. Binfords & Mort, (1950). 1st ed. 3 maps. VG in VG dj. *Oregon.* $27/£17

SPENCER, SCOTT. Endless Love. NY: Knopf, 1979. 1st ed. Fine in Fine dj. *Revere.* $35/£23

SPENCER, SYDNEY (ed). Mountaineering. London: Seeley Service, n.d. (1927?). 1st ed. Lonsdale Library Vol XVIII. 102 plts. Brn buckram gilt. VG in dj (worn, browned). *Hollett.* $47/£30

SPENDER, HAROLD. Byron and Greece. Murray, 1924. 1st ed. Sl mkd, bowed; edges sl spotted, o/w VG. *Poetry.* $23/£15

SPENDER, HAROLD. Through the High Pyrenees. London, 1898. 1st ed. 31 plts, 5 maps. Cl (lower joint slit). *Bickersteth.* $93/£60

SPENDER, JOHN. Therapeutic Means for the Relief of Pain. London, 1874. 1st ed. 230pp. Good. *Fye.* $250/£161

SPENDER, STEPHEN (ed). W.H. Auden. A Tribute. NY: Macmillan, (1975). 1st ed, Amer issue. Fine in VG dj (price-clipped). *Reese.* $25/£16

SPENDER, STEPHEN. Chaos and Control in Poetry. Washington: Lib of Congress, 1966. 1st ed. NF in stapled wrappers. *Pharos.* $30/£19

SPENDER, STEPHEN. The Edge of Being. London: Faber, 1949. 1st ed. VG in dj. *Rees.* $39/£25

SPENDER, STEPHEN. European Witness. London: Hamish Hamilton, (1946). 1st ed. Pencil sig, else Nice in dj (sm inner mend). *Reese.* $25/£16

SPENDER, STEPHEN. Forward from Liberalism. London: Gollancz, 1937. 1st Eng ed. Scarcer issue in black cl. Spine, cvrs sl mkd, o/w VG. *Dalian.* $39/£25

SPENDER, STEPHEN. Poems. London: Faber & Faber, (1933). 1st ed, 1st trade bk. Very Nice (eps lt foxed) in dj (lt frayed, tanned, sm chip). *Reese.* $125/£81

SPENDER, STEPHEN. Poems. London, 1933. 1st ed. Fine in NF dj (sm tear edge rear panel). *Polyanthos.* $100/£65

SPENDER, STEPHEN. Poems. NY, 1934. 1st Amer ed. Fine in dj (sunned, chips, edgetear). *Polyanthos.* $35/£23

SPENDER, STEPHEN. Poems. NY: Random House, 1934. 1st Amer ed. Lt offset fep from clipping, else Fine in dj (nick). *Reese.* $75/£48

SPENDER, STEPHEN. Recent Poems. (London): Anvil Press, (1978). 1st ed. #45/400 signed. Stiff red wraps. Fine in ptd dj. *Chapel Hill.* $75/£48

SPENDER, STEPHEN. Recent Poems. (London): Anvil Press Poetry, (1978). One of 400 numbered, signed issued for subscribers. About Fine in stapled wrappers. *Dermont.* $35/£23

SPENDER, STEPHEN. Ruins and Visions. London: Faber & Faber, (1942). 1st ed. Fine in NF dj (lt spots, sm abrasion). *Reese.* $75/£48

SPENDER, STEPHEN. Ruins and Visions. London: Faber & Faber, 1942. 1st ed. Grn cl gilt. Fine in NF dj. *Cady.* $60/£39

SPENDER, STEPHEN. Trial of a Judge. London: Faber, 1938. 1st ed. VG in dj (frayed). *Cox.* $28/£18

SPENSER, EDMUND. The Faerie Queene. CUP, 1909. One of 350. 2 vols. Teg. Full vellum, gilt dec title (lt soiled, vol 1 spine chipped, sl distorted). *Edwards.* $233/£150

SPENSER, EDMUND. The Poetical Works. London: William Pickering, 1825. 5 vols, each w/1/2 title (bound w/o engr frontis). Orig (?) lt grn cl (faded, rebacked w/darker grn cl), later paper labels (1 chipped). Good set. *Cox.* $70/£45

SPENSER, EDMUND. The Poetical Works. London: William Pickering, 1839. 1st Aldine ed. 5 vols. Dk blue cl; paper labels. Sound (backstrips sl rubbed, worn at head, tail). *Cox.* $54/£35

SPENSER, EDMUND. The Works. London: Basil Blackwell, 1930. 8 vols. Rubric 1/2 titles, tps, contents; double-pg map; partially unopened. Leather-backed dec bds (sl rubbed, sl surface loss vol 1 spine). Splendid set. *Edwards.* $1,318/£850

SPERRY, ARMSTRONG. The Voyages of Christopher Columbus. NY: Random House, 1950. 1st trade ed. Dec eps. VG in dj. *Cattermole.* $30/£19

SPICER, A. DYKES. The Paper Trade. London, (1907). NF. *Veatchs.* $110/£71

Spider Man. Piccolo Pop-up Book. London: Pan, 1981. 20x27 cm. 6 dbl-pg pop-ups, pull-tabs. Glazed pict bds. VG. *Book Finders.* $40/£26

SPIEGELMAN, ART. Maus. NY: Pantheon, 1986. 1st ed. Inscribed. Fine in wraps. *Beasley.* $65/£42

SPIES, WERNER. Max Ernst: Loplop, the Artist in the Third Person. NY, 1983. 1st Amer ed. VG in dj. *Argosy.* $75/£48

SPILLANE, DANIEL. History of the American Pianoforte. NY: Spillane, 1890. 369pp + 8 ad leaves. Fair (inner hinges cracked; glue stains inner blank margins; worn). *Cullen.* $60/£39

SPILLER, BURTON L. Grouse Feathers. NY: Derrydale, 1935. 1st ed. Ltd to 950. Color illus mtd on gilt-dec cl. NF (gilt sl dull, bkpl). *Cahan.* $225/£145

SPILSBURY, WILLIAM HOLDEN. Lincoln's Inn. London: William Pickering, 1850. 1st ed. Frontis, xvi,324pp. Uncut in orig brown cl. Good (neatly rebacked; top corner of orig backstrip missing; paper label browned). *Cox.* $85/£55

SPINDLER, KARL. The Mystery of the Casement Ship with Authentic Documents. Berlin, 1931. Frontis port. VG in dj. *Argosy.* $85/£55

SPINK, WESLEY. Infectious Diseases: Prevention and Treatment.... Minneapolis, 1978. 1st ed. Good in dj. *Fye.* $50/£32

SPINRAD, NORMAN. Passing Through the Flame. Berkley, 1975. 1st ed. NF in dj. *Madle.* $50/£32

SPINSANTI, EMANUELA (ed). The Age of Correggio and the Carracci: Emilian Painting of the Sixteenth and Seventeenth Centuries. Washington, 1986. VG in dj. *Argosy.* $125/£81

SPIVAK, JOHN LOUIS. Georgia Nigger. London, 1933. 1st ed. Frontis; 26 plts. Orig cl. NF. *Mcgowan.* $250/£161

SPLAWN, A.J. Ka-Mi-Akin, the Last Hero of the Yakimas. Portland: Binfords & Mort, 1944. 2nd ed. Bkpl, else VG in dj (torn). Howes S 838. *Perier.* $50/£32

Splendid Century. French Art 1600-1715. NY, MMA, 1960. Good in wrappers. *Washton.* $35/£23

SPLITSTONE, FRED. Orcas, Gem of the San Juans. Sedro-Woolley, WA: Courier-Times, 1946. 1st ed. Frontis map. VG. *Oregon.* $40/£26

SPOFFORD, HARRIET PRESCOTT. Art Decoration Applied to Furniture. NY: Harper, 1878. 1st ed. Frontis; 237,(3)pp. Pub's gilt cl (spine, edges worn). Aeg. (Fr hinge internally cracked; portions of text loose.) *Bookpress.* $225/£145

SPOTSWOOD, ALEXANDER. Iron Works at Tuball: Terms and Conditions for the Lease. Univ of VA McGregor Library, 1945. Ltd to 1100. VG. *Book Broker.* $35/£23

SPRAGUE, CURTISS. How to Make Linoleum Blocks. Pelham, NY: Bridgman, (1928). Bkpl removed, bds lt browned, else VG in dj (worn). *Glenn.* $20/£13

SPRAGUE, MARSHALL. The Great Gates. Boston: Little Brown, (1964). 1st ed. Fine in VG dj. *Perier.* $40/£26

SPRAGUE, MARSHALL. Massacre, The Tragedy of White River. Boston, (1957). 1st ed. Dj wear, o/w VG +. *Pratt.* $25/£16

SPRATT, H. PHILIP. Transatlantic Paddle Steamers. Glasgow: Brown et al, (1951). 1st ed. 9 plts, 4 fldg tables. Fine in dj. *Lefkowicz.* $45/£29

SPRENG, SAMUEL PETER. The Life and Labors of John Seybert.... Cleveland, 1888. 1st ed. 439pp. Good + (corners, bottom edge worn). *Mcgowan.* $27/£17

SPRENGEL, K. An Introduction to the Study of Cryptogamous Plants. In Letters. London, 1807. viii,411pp (foxing), 10 fldg hand-colored plts. Contemp bds (backstrip replaced w/cl tape; cvrs worn, soiled). *Sutton.* $350/£226

SPRENGER, JAMES ALBERT and FRANKLIN SPENCER EDMONDS. Leave Areas of the American Expeditionary Forces 1918-1919. Phila: Winston, 1928. VG. *Schoyer.* $30/£19

SPRING, AGNES WRIGHT. Buffalo Bill and His Horses. (Fort Collins: Privately ptd, 1953.) 1st ed. Fine in grn pict wrappers. *Glenn.* $20/£13

SPRING, AGNES WRIGHT. Caspar Collins: The Life and Exploits of an Indian Fighter.... NY: Columbia Univ, MCMXXVII. 1st ed. Good. *Lien.* $75/£48

SPRINGER, N. The Dark River. Murray, 1929. 1st ed, colonial issue. VG in VG pict dj (sl wear, tear). *Aronovitz.* $85/£55

SPRUNT, JAMES. Chronicles of the Cape Fear River, 1660-1916. Raleigh: Edwards & Broughton, 1916. 2nd ed. 1/2 morocco (chipped, rubbed). VG (eps lt foxed). Howes S 859. *Cahan.* $250/£161

SPRUNT, JAMES. Derelicts. Wilmington, NC: (Lord Baltimore Press), 1920. 1st ed. Orig pict blue cl. Lt spine wear, else Nice, bright. *Chapel Hill.* $450/£290

SPRUYTTE, J. Early Harness Systems. Mary Littauer (trans). London: Allen, 1983. 1st ed in English. VG. *October Farm.* $25/£16

SPRY, W.J.J. The Cruise of H.M.S. 'Challenger.' London, 1878. Rpt. xx,329pp; fldg chart. Dec cl. *Lewis.* $37/£24

SPRY, W.J.J. The Cruise of Her Majesty's Ship 'Challenger'.... NY, 1877. Frontis, xviii,388pp (yellowed), fldg map. Grn gilt-dec cl. *Sutton.* $100/£65

SPURLOCK, PEARL. Over the Old Ozark Trails. Branson: White River Leader, (1942). Signed, inscribed. Pict cl. NF in dj (soiled). *Glenn.* $45/£29

SPURNY, JAN. Modern Textile Designer: Antonin Kybal. N.p.: Artia, 1960. 28 color plts (1 fldg). Dec cl. VG in dj. *Argosy.* $50/£32

SPURZHEIM, J.G. Observations on the Deranged Manifestations of the Mind. Boston: Marsh, Capen & Lyon, 1836. 3rd Amer ed. 2 engr plts. Patterned brn cl over bds (recently rebound; foxing). *Glenn.* $175/£113

SPYRI, JOHANNA. Gritli's Children. Phila: Lippincott, (1924). 1st ed thus. 4to. 14 full-pg color plts by Maria Kirk. Tinted top. Lt olive cl, red/grn lettering, dec; color paste label. Good in color dj (lacks sm pieces). *Reisler.* $150/£97

SQUIERS, GRANVILLE. Secret Hiding-Places. London: Stanley Paul, 1934. 1st ed. 41 plts. Sl rubbed. *Hollett.* $70/£45

SQUIRE, J.C. Books in General. London: Martin Secker, (1918). 1st Eng ed. Blue paper bds. Name, o/w NF. *Dalian.* $31/£20

SQUIRE, J.C. The Grub Street Nights Entertainments. London: Hodder & Stoughton, n.d. (1924). 1st ed. Partly unopened. Fore, lower edges uncut. Pencil inscrip; foxing few pp, o/w Fine in pict dj (nick). *Temple.* $62/£40

SQUIRE, J.C. A London Reverie. London: Macmillan, 1928. 1st ed. Tinted frontis, 55 plts. Teg, rest uncut. Inscrip; cvrs sl mkd, o/w Very Nice. *Temple.* $50/£32

SQUIRE, J.C. The Moon. London: Hodder & Stoughton, (1920). 1st Eng ed. Brn bds. Sl mkd, backstrip repaired, o/w VG. *Dalian.* $23/£15

SQUIRE, J.C. Sunday Mornings. London: Heinemann, 1930. 1st ed. Nice. *Temple.* $22/£14

SQUIRES, RADCLIFFE. Allen Tate. NY: Pegasus, (1971). 1st ed. Grn cl. Fine in NF dj. *Chapel Hill.* $25/£16

ST. JOHN, BRUCE. John Sloan's New York Scene. NY: Harper & Row, (1965). 1st ed. Fine in dj (lt chipped, soiled). *Hermitage.* $45/£29

ST. JOHN, C. Short Sketches of the Wild Sports and Natural History of the Highlands. London, 1846. 1st ed. vi,281pp. 1/2 calf. *Wheldon & Wesley.* $62/£40

ST. JOHN, JOHN. To the War with Waugh. London: Whittington Press, 1973. #559/600 signed. Very Nice in glassine wrapper. *Virgo.* $186/£120

ST. LEGER, S.E. War Sketches in Colour. London: A&C Black, 1903. 1st ed. Color frontis, 65 other plts, guards; teg. VG (lt browned, cat sl damp-mkd) in blue dec cl (sl worn, corner sl whitened; rebacked, orig spine laid down; new eps). *Edwards.* $62/£40

ST. MICHAEL-PODMORE, P. A Sporting Paradise. NY: Stokes, 1904. 1st ed. Teg. Red cl, gilt titles. VG. *Bowman.* $30/£19

STABLEFORD, BRIAN. Cradle of the Sun. S&J, 1969. 1st ed, 1st bk. Fine in NF dj. *Aronovitz*. $65/£42

STACK, NICOLETE. Two to Get Ready. Caldwell, ID, 1963. 1st ed. Signed, inscribed by author and Gertrude Williamson (illus). VG. *Bond*. $25/£16

STACKPOLE, EDOUARD A. The Sea-Hunters. Phila/NY, (1953). 1st ed. Signed. (Spine sl sunned.) Dj (sl worn). *Lefkowicz*. $32/£21

STACKPOLE, EDWARD J. Chancellorsville, Lee's Greatest Battle. Harrisburg, (1958). 1st ed. VG + . *Pratt*. $30/£19

STACKPOLE, EDWARD J. Chancellorsville: Lee's Greatest Battle. Harrisburg, PA: Stackpole, (1958). 1st ed. Pict cl. Spine sl faded, lt bumped, else NF in VG dj. *Chapel Hill*. $40/£26

STACKPOLE, EDWARD J. The Fredericksburg Campaign. NY, 1957. 1st ed. VG + in dj (worn). *Pratt*. $30/£19

STACKPOLE, EDWARD J. Sheridan in the Shenandoah. Harrisburg, 1961. 1st ed. VG + in dj (sl wear; sm tear). *Pratt*. $40/£26

STACKPOLE, EDWARD J. They Met at Gettysburg. Harrisburg, (1956). 1st ed. VG + in VG + dj. *Pratt*. $30/£19

STACKPOLE, EDWARD J. They Met at Gettysburg. Harrisburg, PA: Stackpole, (1959). 4th ptg. Pict cl. Fr cvr lt spotted, else NF in dj (extrems lt browned). *Chapel Hill*. $35/£23

STACPOOLE, H.D. The Blue Lagoon. Duffield, 1910. 1st Amer ed. Pict cl. VG. *Aronovitz*. $95/£61

STACTON, DAVID. Old Acquaintance. London: Faber & Faber, 1962. 1st Eng ed. Brn cl. VF in Fine dj. *Dalian*. $39/£25

STACTON, DAVID. On a Balcony. NY, (1959). 1st Amer ed. Paper browned, else Fine in VG dj (lt used). *Mcclintock*. $35/£23

STACTON, DAVID. Sir William or A Lesson in Love. London: Faber & Faber, 1963. 1st Eng ed. Red cl. Fine in dj (sl nicked). *Dalian*. $39/£25

STACTON, DAVID. The World on the Last Day. London: Faber & Faber, 1965. 1st Eng ed. Red cl. Fine in dj. *Dalian*. $54/£35

STAEHELIN, WALTER A. The Book of Porcelain. Michael Bullock (trans). London, 1966. 1st UK ed. 34 mtd color plts. (Lt wrinkling; ex-lib w/ink stamps, bkpl.) Dj (sl chipped). *Edwards*. $116/£75

STAFFORD, WILLIAM. Allegiances. NY: Harper & Row, (1970). 1st ed. NF in dj. *Godot*. $40/£26

STAFFORD, WILLIAM. The Design on the Oriole. Night Heron Press, (1977). #128/200 signed. Fine in ptd wraps. *Polyanthos*. $100/£65

STAGEMAN, P. A Bibliography of the First Editions of Phillip Henry Gosse, F.R.S. Cambridge: Golden Head Press, 1955. #85/480. Color frontis, 5 plain plts. Bkpl, sm stamp tp, o/w Fine. *Henly*. $50/£32

STAGG, ALONZA A. Touchdown. London: Longmans, 1927. 1st ed. VG (spine rebound). *Bishop*. $72/£46

STAHAN, JOHN. The Diagnosis and Treatment of Extra-Uterine Pregnancy. Phila, 1889. 1st ed. 134pp. Good. *Fye*. $100/£65

STAHL, JOHN M. The Battle of Plattsburg. (Argos, IN): Van Trump Co, (1918). Navy cl, gilt title. VG (rubbed). *Bohling*. $60/£39

STAIB, BJORN. Across Greenland in Nansen's Track. London: Allen & Unwin, (1963). 1st ed. Map. VG in VG- dj. *Blue Dragon*. $25/£16

STALL, SYLVANUS. Purity and Truth: What a Young Husband Ought to Know. Phila, 1897. 1st ed. 300pp. Good. *Fye*. $50/£32

STALLWORTHY, JON. A Dinner of Herbs. Rougemont Press, 1971. One of 300 numbered. Fine in wraps. *Sclanders*. $31/£20

STAMBAUGH, J. LEE and LILLIAN J. The Lower Rio Grande Valley of Texas. San Antonio: Naylor, 1955. 1st ed. Signed. Fldg map. Dj. *Lambeth*. $85/£55

STANARD, MARY NEWTON. The Story of Bacon's Rebellion. NY: Neale, 1907. (Rear pocket.) *Schoyer*. $25/£16

STANARD, MARY NEWTON. The Story of Virginia's First Century. Phila, 1928. 1st ed. Gilt cl. VG. *Artis*. $25/£16

STANDING, PERCY CROSS. Sir Lawrence Alma-Tadema, O.M., R.A. London: Cassell, (1905). Frontis port. (Text foxed, clipping affixed rep; cl stained.) *Cahan*. $50/£32

STANDISH, BURT L. Frank Merriwell's Ranch. NY: Street & Smith, (1908). VG in color pict wraps. *Schoyer*. $15/£10

STANDISH, ROBERT. The Three Bamboos. London: Peter Davies, 1942. 1st Eng ed. 1st bk. Cream cl. VF in dj (sl dusty, sl tear spine). *Dalian*. $39/£25

STANDLEY, P.C. Trees and Shrubs of Mexico. Parts 1-5. Washington, (1967). 2 vols. *Sutton*. $250/£161

STANGE, ALFRED. German Painting, XIV—XVI Centuries. NY: Hyperion, (1950). 127 plts (17 mtd color). VG in dj. *Argosy*. $65/£42

STANGER, FRANK M. Sawmills in the Redwoods. San Mateo County Hist Assoc, 1967. 1st ed. Lg fldg map; pict eps. Unopened. Grn pict cl. Fine. *Harrington*. $50/£32

STANHOPE, PHILIP DORMER. Letters Written by the Late Right Honourable Philip Dormer Stanhope...to His Son, Philip Stanhope.... London: Ptd for J. Dodsley, 1774. 3rd ed. 4 vols. Frontis port plt. Full contemp calf, gilt; red morocco spine labels. (Spines sl dknd, else Fine). *D & D*. $350/£226

STANHOPE, PHILIP DORMER. Letters written to His Son.... London: Ptd for J. Nichols & Son, 1806. 12th ed. 4 vols. Frontis port, 4 half-titles. Blue paper bds, white paper spines, each spine ink #'d. Uncut. Very Nice set (bkpls; 1807 sig; lt wear, soil). *Cady*. $350/£226

STANHOPE, PHILIP DORMER. Letters.... London: For P. Dodsley, 1792. 10th ed. 4 vols. Frontis port. Contemp tree calf, full gilt emb spines (sl creased, chipped; ex-libris; upper portions cut away 1/2title vols 2,4, tp vol 2 w/o loss). *Edwards*. $194/£125

STANHOPE, PHILIP DORMER. Letters...To His Son.... London: Dodsley, 1774. 2nd ed. 4 vols. Port. Tree calf; leather labels; 1/2 titles vols 1, 4. Attractive (bkpl; sig all vols; old rebacking; crease fr cvr; joints cracked). *Agvent*. $450/£290

STANLEY, ARTHUR PENRHYN. The Life and Correspondence of Thomas Arnold. London, 1844. 2 vols. Frontis port, xxiii,432; xvi,447pp (frontis, tp foxed); marbled eps. 1/2 calf (sl rubbed), marbled bds, raised bands, gilt (spine sl scuffed). *Edwards*. $54/£35

STANLEY, ARTHUR PENRHYN. Sinai and Palestine. London: John Murray, 1856. 2nd ed. xlix,548pp; 7 maps; 5 woodcuts. Mod 1/2 levant morocco gilt. VG. *Hollett*. $116/£75

STANLEY, CLARK. Life and Adventures of the American Cow-Boy. (N.p.): Stanley, 1897. 1st ed. 39,(11)pp. Dbd. Howes S 875. *Ginsberg.* $150/£97

STANLEY, E.J. Life of Rev. L.B. Stateler. Nashville: Pub House of the M.E. Church, 1916. Rev ed. Good (inner hinges repaired) in pict cl. Howes S 879. *Lien.* $65/£42

STANLEY, FATHER. The Clovis, New Mexico, Story. Pampa: Stanley, 1966. One of 500. Signed. NF in VG+ dj. *Parker.* $45/£29

STANLEY, FATHER. Fort Bascom, Comanche-Kiowa Barrier. N.p., (1961). 1st ed. Signed. Fine in dj (spine sl faded). *Pratt.* $105/£68

STANLEY, FATHER. Fort Stanton. N.p., (1964). 1st ed, ltd to 500. Signed. Fine in dj (spine sl faded). *Pratt.* $105/£68

STANLEY, FATHER. No Tears for Black Jack Ketchum. Denver: (World Press, 1958). Ltd to 500, signed. Fine in black wrappers. *Glenn.* $85/£55

STANLEY, GEORGE. The Birth of Western Canada. A History of the Riel Rebellions. London: Longmans, Green, (1936). 1st ed. 17 plts (incl 5 maps). Good+ (ex-lib w/#, sm abrasion from plt removal on fr pastedown, occasional sm blindstamp). *Oregon.* $90/£58

STANLEY, HENRY M. The Congo and the Founding of Its Free State. NY: Harper, 1885. 1st Amer ed. 2 vols. xxvii,528; x,483pp + 12pp ads, 3 fldg maps, 2 lg fldg maps in pockets (few sm crease tears). Orig gilt pict grn cl (lt worn, rubbed). Overall VG (lt stain fore-edge margin vol 2). *House.* $300/£194

STANLEY, HENRY M. In Darkest Africa, or the Quest, Rescue, and Retreat of Emin Governor of Equatoria. NY, 1890. 1st Amer ed. 2 vols. 2 steel-engr frontis ports, 3 fldg maps as issued in pockets. Pict cl. VG set. *Argosy.* $500/£323

STANLEY, HENRY M. In Darkest Africa. London, 1890. 2 vols. xv,529; xv,472pp + 2pp pub's ads (sm hole fep vol 2); 38 plts, 3 fldg maps (1 detached, foxing verso). Illus cl (sl dampstaining vol 2; spine chipped; sl rubbed; hinges sl cracked). *Edwards.* $116/£75

STANLEY, HENRY M. In Darkest Africa. NY: Scribner's, 1890. 2 vols. (xvi),547; xvi,540pp, 2 steel-engr frontis ports, 150 wood engrs, 3 fldg color maps in pockets; aeg. 3/4 brn morocco, marbled bds (sl rubbed). Aeg. *Schoyer.* $185/£119

STANLEY, HENRY M. In Darkest Africa. London: Sampson, 1890. 2 vols. 3 fldg maps. Pict gilt cvrs. Fore-edges, few pp foxed, o/w VG. *Petersfield.* $186/£120

STANLEY, HENRY M. In Darkest Africa. London: Sampson Low, Marston, etc., 1890. 1st ed. 2 vols. xv,529; xv,472pp; 150 woodcut illus; 2 lg fldg color linen-backed maps. Mod 1/2 levant morocco. VG (marginal blind stamps; accession stamp verso titles). *Hollett.* $388/£250

STANLEY, HENRY M. In Darkest Africa.... NY: Scribner's, 1890. 1st Amer ed. 2 vols. xiv,547; xvi,540pp (foxing), 3 fldg maps in pockets. 3/4 brn morocco, marbled bds (edges rubbed), gilt. Very Nice set. *Blue Mountain.* $195/£126

STANLEY, HENRY M. My Dark Companions and Their Strange Stories. London: Sampson, 1893. Pict gilt cl (backstrip sl faded). *Petersfield.* $54/£35

STANLEY, HENRY M. Through the Dark Continent. London, 1899. 2 vols. xxxii,400pp (marginal dampstaining; leaves wrinkled); 33 plts, 7 maps (1 fldg). Dec eps. 1/2 morocco (worn; staining; joints splitting; loss head spine vol 1). *Edwards.* $70/£45

STANLEY, MRS. H.M. London Street Arabs. London, 1890. 1st ed. Frontis port, 12pp (feps lt foxed), 28 plts. 2-tone cl (worn). *Edwards.* $39/£25

STANLEY, WILLIAM OWEN. Memoirs on Remains of Ancient Dwellings in Holyhead Island. London: Ptd for Author, 1871. 18 numbered plts, fldg plan. Gilt-ruled cl (upper joint split; spine sl rubbed, chipped). *Edwards.* $116/£75

STANSBURY, HOWARD. Exploration and Survey of the Valley of the Great Salt Lake of Utah. Phila, 1852. 8vo. 2 vols. 487pp; 57 plts (3 fldg) (sl browning to 2), 3 fldg maps (2 lg maps in separate portfolio). Gilt dec cl (lt wear, sm tear to spine of portfolio, inscrip; 2 bkpls, stamped released). NF set. *Sutton.* $600/£387

STANTON, RICHARD H. A Practical Treatise for the Use of Justices of the Peace, Constables...of Kentucky. Cincinnati: Clarke, 1861. 1st ed. (8),656pp. Full contemp calf. *Ginsberg.* $175/£113

STANTON, ROBERT B. Down the Colorado. Dwight L. Smith (ed). Norman: Univ of OK Press, (1965). 1st ed. Black cl. Fine in NF dj. *Harrington.* $65/£42

STANTON, ROBERT. Down the Colorado. Dwight Smith (ed). Norman: Univ of OK, (1965). 1st ed. VF in VF dj. *Oregon.* $65/£42

STAPLEDON, OLAF. Beyond the 'Isms.' London: Secker & Warburg, 1942. 1st Eng ed. Fine in cream ptd wrappers (sl dusty). *Dalian.* $70/£45

STAPLEDON, OLAF. The Flames. S&W, 1947. 1st ed. NF in dj (3 short tears). *Aronovitz.* $70/£45

STAPLEDON, OLAF. Last and First Men. London: Methuen, 1930. 1st Eng ed. Blue cl. Very Nice. *Dalian.* $132/£85

STAPLEDON, OLAF. Last and First Men. NY: Jonathan Cape & Harrison Smith, 1931. 1st Amer ed. Purple cl. Sl faded, mkd, bkpl, lacks rep, o/w VG. *Dalian.* $54/£35

STAPLEDON, OLAF. Last and First Men. Cape & Smith, 1931. 1st Amer ed. VG (lt dust soil) in dj (wear, tear, chipping). *Aronovitz.* $135/£87

STAPLEDON, OLAF. Last and First Men. London: Methuen, 1931. 2nd ed. Blue cl. Cvrs mkd, fore-edge foxed, o/w VG. *Dalian.* $39/£25

STAPLEDON, OLAF. Last Men in London. London: Methuen, 1932. 1st ed. VG in dj (sl frayed, rubbed). *Cox.* $43/£28

STAPLEDON, OLAF. Last Men in London. London, 1934. Fine in NF dj. *Madle.* $125/£81

STAPLEDON, OLAF. New Hope for Britain. London: Methuen, 1939. 1st Eng ed. 1st issue w/'5 shilling net' unclipped from fr flap. One of 841 ptd. Blue cl. VF in NF dj (spine sl chipped). *Dalian.* $132/£85

STAPLEDON, OLAF. Odd John. London, 1935. 1st ed. VG. *Madle.* $75/£48

STAPLEDON, OLAF. Odd John. Methuen, 1935. 1st ed. Foxing, else VG+. *Aronovitz.* $75/£48

STAPLEDON, OLAF. Waking World. London: Methuen, 1934. 1st Eng ed. Brn cl. Spine, cvrs mkd, o/w VG. *Dalian.* $39/£25

STAPLEDON, OLAF. Youth and Tomorrow. London: St. Botolph Pub Co, 1946. 1st Eng ed. Blue cl. VF in Fine dj. *Dalian.* $101/£65

STAPLES, FRANKLIN. Report on Diphtheria. Winona, MN, 1880. 1st ed. 44pp. Good in wraps. *Fye.* $40/£26

STAPLES, THOMAS S. Reconstruction in Arkansas, 1862-1874. NY: Columbia, 1923. 1st ed. Contemp cl, orig ptd wrappers bound in end. (Ex-lib.) Howes S 890. *Ginsberg.* $125/£81

Star Trek. The Giant in the Universe. Random House, 1977. 21x27 cm. 4 pop-ups. Glazed pict bds. VG. *Book Finders.* $30/£19

Star Wars—Return of the Jedi. NY: Random House, 1982. 17x24 cm. 4 pop-ups, 7pp pull-tabs. John Ampert (illus). Glazed pict bds. Good-. *Book Finders.* $20/£13

STARBUCK, ALEXANDER. History of the American Whale Fishery. NY, 1964. Facs rpt. One of 750 sets. 2 vols. Frontis port, 6 plts. Boxed. *Lefkowicz.* $250/£161

STARBUCK, ALEXANDER. History of the American Whale Fishery.... Washington, 1878. 1st ed. (9),768pp, 6 plts. Howes S 892. *Ginsberg.* $600/£387

STARK, FREYA. Alexander's Path. London: John Murray, 1958. 1st Eng ed. Grn cl. Sl offsetting spine, o/w VF in dj. *Dalian.* $70/£45

STARK, FREYA. Baghdad Sketches. Baghdad: Times Press Ltd, 1932. 1st bk. Red cl. Sl mkd, sl knocked, o/w VG; no dj as issued. *Dalian.* $388/£250

STARK, FREYA. Baghdad Sketches. London: Murray, 1937. 1st ed. 42 plts; dbl-pg map. Sl rubbed; spine frayed, tears, o/w Good. *Worldwide.* $20/£13

STARK, FREYA. Dust in the Lion's Paw. NY: Harcourt, Brace & World, (1962). 1st Amer ed. In dj (sl soiled). *Schoyer.* $30/£19

STARK, FREYA. Gateways and Caravans. A Portrait of Turkey. NY: Macmillan, 1971. 1st US ed. 168 plts (25 color). NF in dj. *Worldwide.* $55/£35

STARK, FREYA. Ionia. London, 1954. 1st ed. Dbl-pg map. Dj (chipped w/loss). *Edwards.* $39/£25

STARK, FREYA. Letters from Syria. London, 1942. 1st ed. *Lewis.* $9/£6

STARK, FREYA. Riding to the Tigris. London, 1959. 1st ed. Fine in dj. *Petersfield.* $25/£16

STARK, FREYA. Riding to the Tigris. London: John Murray, 1959. 1st Eng ed. Grn cl. VF in dj. *Dalian.* $70/£45

STARK, FREYA. Rome on the Euphrates. NY: Harcourt Brace & World, (1968). 2 maps (1 fldg). Red cl (spine sl damaged). Dj (chipped, price-clipped). *Schoyer.* $40/£26

STARK, FREYA. The Southern Gates of Arabia. NY: Dutton, 1936. 1st ed. 84 plts; 2 maps. Lib buckram (sl rubbed). Ex-lib sticker, #, o/w VG. *Worldwide.* $25/£16

STARK, FREYA. A Winter in Arabia. London: John Murray, 1940. 1st Eng ed. Grn cl. Sl faded, o/w VG. *Dalian.* $116/£75

STARK, FREYA. The Zodiac Arch. London, 1968. 1st ed. Frontis. Near New in Near New dj. *Lewis.* $22/£14

STARK, R.M. A Popular History of British Mosses. London, 1860. 2nd ed. 20 color plts. Dec cl. (Sl foxing.) *Petersfield.* $31/£20

STARK, RICHARD. (Pseud of Donald Westlake.) Butcher's Moon. NY: Random House, 1974. 1st ed. Fine in Fine dj. *Janus.* $65/£42

STARK, RICHARD. (Pseud of Donald Westlake.) The Dame. NY: Macmillan, 1969. 1st ed. Fine in Fine dj. *Janus.* $40/£26

STARK, RICHARD. (Pseud of Donald Westlake). Deadly Edge. NY: Random, 1971. 1st ed. Fine in dj (lt worn). *Murder.* $65/£42

STARKIE, ENID. Arthur Rimbaud. London: Faber & Faber, 1948. Rev ed. 12 full-pg plts. Red cl. Sl sunned, neat name, o/w fine in dj (sl chipped, tanned). *Dalian.* $39/£25

STARKIE, ENID. Charles Baudelaire. Norfolk: New Directions, (1958). 1st ed. Fine in dj. *Pharos.* $30/£19

STARKIE, ENID. Petrus Borel, the Lycanthrope. Faber & Faber, 1954. 1st ed. Frontis port. (Plt edges lt yellowed, spotted; feps sl browned.) Dj (sl chipped). *Edwards.* $31/£20

STARR, STEPHEN Z. Colonel Grenfell's Wars. Baton Rouge: LSU Press, (1971). 1st ed. Brn cl. Fine in NF dj. *Chapel Hill.* $45/£29

STARR, WALTER A. My Adventures in the Klondike and Alaska 1898-1900. (Lawton Kennedy, 1960.) Frontis, port, fldg map. Grn cl, gilt. VG. *Bohling.* $45/£29

STARR, WALTER. My Adventures in the Klondike and Alaska 1898-1900. Privately ptd, 1960. 1st ed. Frontis, fldg map. Fine. *Oregon.* $45/£29

STARRETT, VINCENT. Ambrose Bierce: A Bibliography. Phila: Centaur Book Shop, 1929. 1st ed. One of 300 numbered. Tipped-in frontis port. Unopened. Fine. *Cahan.* $85/£55

STARRETT, VINCENT. Born in a Bookshop. Norman: Univ of OK, 1965. 1st ed, signed. Fine in NF dj (sm closed tear). *Janus.* $50/£32

STARRETT, VINCENT. The Great All-Star Animal League Ball Game. NY, 1957. 1st ed. Kurt Wiese (illus). VF in dj (torn). *Bond.* $35/£23

STARRETT, VINCENT. Penny Wise and Book Foolish. NY: Covici Friede, 1929. 1st ed. Grn cl. Fine in dj (sl chipping). *Oak Knoll.* $75/£48

STARRETT, VINCENT. Penny Wise and Book Foolish. NY, 1929. 1st ed. #18/300 signed. Gilt emb bds; teg. *Edwards.* $85/£55

STARRETT, VINCENT. Persons from Porlock and Other Interruptions. Chicago: Normandie House, 1938. Ltd to 399 signed. Black cl-backed grn bds, gilt-titled. Sl bumped, else Fine in dj. *Cady.* $60/£39

STARRETT, VINCENT. The Quick and the Dead. Arkham House, 1965. 1st ed. Fine in dj. *Madle.* $100/£65

STARRETT, VINCENT. Seaports in the Moon. Doubleday, 1928. 1st ed. VG in dj (chipped; frayed). *Madle.* $40/£26

State Register and Year Book of Facts: For the Year 1859. SF: Henry G. Langley & Samuel A. Morison, 1859. iv,432pp. Leather-backed cl bds (expertly re-backed). *Dawson.* $300/£194

STATON, F. The Canadian North West: A Bibliography of the Sources of Information in the Public Reference Library.... Toronto, 1931. Ptd cvrs. VG. *Moss.* $40/£26

Statutes at Large of the Provisional Government of the Confederate States of America. Richmond, VA: R.M. Smith, 1862-1864. 1st eds. 6 vols. Period 1/2 leather w/marbled bds. Foxing, else NF set in ptd wrappers. *Mcgowan.* $1,750/£1,129

Statutes of the Mississippi Territory; The Constitution of the United States, with the Several Amendments Thereto; The Ordinance for the Government.... Natchez: Peter Isler, 1816. 1st ed, 1st ptg. 495,28pp. Orig full leather (skin spots; fr hinge cracking; tail of spine chipped; corners bumped). VG. *Mcgowan.* $5,000/£3,226

STAWELL, MRS. R. Fabre's Book of Insects.... London, (1935). 12 Fine color plts. (Cl sl loose; binding sl soiled; spine head worn.) *Wheldon & Wesley*. $47/£30

STEAD, CHRISTINA. For Love Alone. NY: Harcourt-Brace, 1944. 1st ed. VF in dj (price-clipped, sl spine darkening). *Else Fine*. $85/£55

STEAD, CHRISTINA. The Man Who Loved Children. NY: Holt, Rinehart & Winston, (1965). 1st ed thus. Fine in dj. *Hermitage*. $35/£23

STEADMAN, RALPH. America. (SF: Straight Arrow Books, 1974). 1st ed. Fine in dj. *Godot*. $100/£65

STEADMAN, RALPH. Scar Strangled Banger. Topsfield: Salem House, 1988. 1st ed. Fine in Fine dj. *Revere*. $40/£26

STEALINGWORTH, SLIM. Tom Wesselmann. NY, 1980. 1st ed. *Edwards*. $116/£75

STEARNS, E. Notes on Uncle Tom's Cabin.... Phila: Lippincott, Grambo, 1853. 1st Amer ed. Brn cl. NF. *Agvent*. $250/£161

STEBBING, E.P. The Forests of India. London, 1922-6. 3 vols. 2 color fldg maps. (Ex-lib w/stamps, mks, #'s, labels; sl shaken; extrems rubbed; spine split vol 3.) *Edwards*. $78/£50

STEBBING, E.P. Jungle By-Ways in India. London: John Lane, The Bodley Head, 1911. 2nd ed. Edges spotted, o/w Fine. *Hollett*. $186/£120

STECKMESSER, KENT LADD. The Western Hero in History and Legend. Norman: Univ of OK, (1965). 1st ed. Red cl. Fine in Fine dj. *Harrington*. $35/£23

STEDMAN, J.G. Narrative of a Five Years' Expedition against the Revolted Negroes of Surinam. Barre: Imprint Society, 1971. #107/1950 numbered, signed by Rudolf van Lier (intro). 2 vols. 3 fldg maps; fldg plt. Cl-backed French marbled paper-cvrd bds, paper labels. Fine set in pub's slipcase. *Hermitage*. $150/£97

STEED, NEVILLE. Tinplate. London: Weidenfeld & Nicolson, 1986. 1st ed. Fine in Fine dj. *Janus*. $35/£23

STEEDMAN, A. Wanderings and Adventures in the Interior of Southern Africa. London, 1835. Inscribed. 2 vols. Map; 12 plts. Orig cl. (Tps, plt margins badly browned; binding worn; cl bubbled; soiled.) *Wheldon & Wesley*. $271/£175

STEEDMAN, AMY. Legends and Stories of Italy for Children. London: T.C. & E.C. Jack, (1909). 1st ed. 4to. 12 full-pg mtd color plts by Katharine Cameron. Teg. Grn cl-backed brn bds, gold stamping. Good. *Reisler*. $175/£113

Steel in the War. NY: US Steel Corp, 1946. 1st ed. Pub's slip laid in. VG (rubbed). *Cahan*. $60/£39

STEEL, DAVID. The Ship-Master's Assistant and Owner's Manual. London: David Steel, 1794. 5th ed. (xvi), 320, (2nd pagination has separate title 'New and complete tables of the net duties payable....') London: D. Steel, 1792. 126pp; 2 plts. (Contemp inscrip, bkpl.) Contemp calf (joints weak, strengthened). *Lefkowicz*. $275/£177

STEEL, J.H. A Treatise on the Diseases of the Ox. London, 1881. xxii,498pp; 2 plts. (Joint cracked.) *Whitehart*. $39/£25

STEELE, JAMES W. Frontier Army Sketches. Chicago: Jansen, 1883. 329,(6)pp. Howes S 922. *Ginsberg*. $100/£65

STEELE, MATTHEW FORNEY. American Campaigns. Washington: Byron S. Adams, 1909. 1st ed. 2 vols. Later cl. Hinges repaired, else VG. *Mcgowan*. $85/£55

STEELE, MATTHEW FORNEY. American Campaigns. Washington: Byron S. Adams, 1909. 1st ed. 2 vols. 731pp; map vol. Orig red cl. VG +. *Chapel Hill*. $150/£97

STEELE, MATTHEW FORNEY. American Campaigns. Washington: U.S. Infantry Assoc, 1922. Later ptg. 2 vols. Spines sunned, else VG. *Mcgowan*. $125/£81

STEELE, OLIVER G. Steele's Book of Niagara Falls. Buffalo, 1840. 18mo. 109pp; fldg map; 7 engrs (1 fldg). Foxing; corners bumped. *Argosy*. $125/£81

STEELE, THOMAS SEDGWICK. Canoe and Camera: A Two Hundred Mile Tour Through the Maine Forests. NY: OJ, 1880. 1st ed. 139pp (tp starting), fldg map in pocket. Pict cl (sl rubbed), gilt. *Blue Mountain*. $155/£100

STEELE, TIMOTHY. Uncertainties and Rest. Baton Rouge: LSU, 1979. 1st ed, 1st bk. VF in dj. *Pharos*. $30/£19

STEELE, WILBUR DANIEL. That Girl from Memphis. GC: Doubleday, 1945. 1st ed. VG in dj (sl frayed). *Turlington*. $25/£16

STEER, G.L. The Tree of Gernika. A Field Study of Modern War. London: Hodder & Stoughton, 1938. 1st ed. 7 fldg maps. Nice. *Patterson*. $155/£100

STEERE, EDWARD. The Wilderness Campaign. NY, (1960). 1st ed. VG + in VG + dj. *Pratt*. $45/£29

STEERS, J.A. The Coastline of England and Wales. Cambridge, 1946. 117 photos (2 color). *Wheldon & Wesley*. $54/£35

STEERS, J.A. The Coastline of England and Wales. CUP, 1948. 2nd imp. 2 color plts, 115 photos. Dj (chipped, discolored). *Edwards*. $47/£30

STEERS, J.A. The Sea Coast. London, 1953. 1st ed. (Feps lt browned.) Dj (sl chipped). *Edwards*. $93/£60

STEEVENS, G.W. Egypt in 1898. NY: Dodd, Mead, 1898. 1st ed. xii,283pp. Sl rubbed, soiled, o/w Good ex-lib (spine #). *Worldwide*. $16/£10

STEEVES, SARAH HUNT. Book of Remembrance of Marion County, Oregon, Pioneers, 1840-1860. Portland: Berncliff Press, 1922. 1st ed. NF. *Perier*. $125/£81

STEFANSSON, VILHJALMUR. The Adventure of Wrangel Island. NY, 1925. Fldg map. Blue cl. *Lewis*. $65/£42

STEFANSSON, VILHJALMUR. The Adventure of Wrangel Island. London: Cape, 1926. 1st Eng ed. Good (sl rubbed). *Walcot*. $25/£16

STEFANSSON, VILHJALMUR. The Friendly Arctic. London: Harrap, (1921). 1st Eng ed. 2 fldg maps in pocket. Good (sl rubbed). *Walcot*. $74/£48

STEFANSSON, VILHJALMUR. Hunters of the Great North. NY, (1922). Fldg map. (Spine lettering flaked.) *Artis*. $35/£23

STEFANSSON, VILHJALMUR. Hunters of the Great North. NY: Harcourt Brace, c.1922. 2 fldg maps. VG (fading). *High Latitude*. $40/£26

STEFANSSON, VILHJALMUR. My Life with the Eskimo. NY: Macmillan, 1913. 1st ed, 1st bk. 2 fldg maps. Teg. Blue cl, gilt (fr hinge cracked, spine spotted, sl shelfwear). VG. *Parmer*. $165/£106

STEFANSSON, VILHJALMUR. My Life with the Eskimo. NY: Macmillan, 1913. 1st ed. Fldg map. Good in VG dj. *Bowman*. $35/£23

STEFANSSON, VILHJALMUR. My Life with the Eskimo. Macmillan, 1913. 1st Eng ed. 2 fldg maps. VG. *Walcot*. $93/£60

STEFANSSON, VILHJALMUR. The Northward Course of Empire. NY, 1924. 2nd ed. Fldg map. VG. *Artis.* $22/£14

STEFANSSON, VILHJALMUR. Ultima Thule. Harrap, 1942. 1st Eng ed. VG in dj (torn). *Walcot.* $22/£14

STEFANSSON, VILHJALMUR. Unsolved Mysteries of the Arctic. Harrap, 1939. 1st ed. Good. *Walcot.* $19/£12

STEGMAIER, MARK and DAVID MILLER. James F. Milligan. His Journal of Fremont's Fifth Expedition, 1853-1854. Clark, 1988. 1st ed. Ltd to 750. 5 maps. VF. *Oregon.* $35/£23

STEGNER, WALLACE. All the Little Live Things. NY: Viking, 1967. 1st ed. Fine in dj (lt wear extrems). *Else Fine.* $45/£29

STEGNER, WALLACE. Angle of Repose. GC: Doubleday, 1971. 1st ed. VG + in dj (lt edgewear). *Else Fine.* $85/£55

STEGNER, WALLACE. Beyond the Hundredth Meridian. Lincoln, 1982. #150/250. Signed. Fldg frontis. NF in dec slipcase (sl wear). *Benchmark.* $145/£94

STEGNER, WALLACE. Crossing to Safety. Random House, (1987). 1st ed. Sm stain ep, else Fine in Fine dj. *Authors Of The West.* $25/£16

STEGNER, WALLACE. Crossing to Safety. PA: Franklin Lib, 1987. 1st ed, ltd to unspecified # signed. Full leather, gold dec; aeg. Fine (issued w/o dj). *Godot.* $85/£55

STEGNER, WALLACE. Remembering Laughter. London: Heinemann, (1937). 1st Eng ed. Reddish-brn cl. Ink inscrip; eps browned, top edge foxed, else VG in dj (2 nicks, lt edgewear). *Godot.* $350/£226

STEGNER, WALLACE. Remembering Laughter. Little, Brown, 1937. 1st ed. VG (spine faded). *Authors Of The West.* $50/£32

STEGNER, WALLACE. Remembering Laughter. Boston: Little, Brown, 1937. 1st ed. Grn cl. Spine, extrems lt faded, else VG in dj (spine nicked, lt edgewear, else VG). *Godot.* $350/£226

STEGNER, WALLACE. Second Growth. Boston: HMCo, 1947. 1st Amer ed. Pg edges dknd, else NF in VG- dj (extrems rubbed; ends nicked). *Between The Covers.* $175/£113

STEGNER, WALLACE. A Shooting Star. NY: Viking, 1961. 1st ed. Spine lettering sl flaked, dull, else VG in dj (short tears). *Godot.* $75/£48

STEGNER, WALLACE. A Shooting Star. NY: Viking, 1961. 1st ed. Signed. VG (2pp w/quarter-inch tears) in VG dj (worn, chipped). *Revere.* $125/£81

STEGNER, WALLACE. The Spectator Bird. Franklin Mint, 1976. Ltd 1st ed. Grn leather, gilt, aeg. VF. *Oregon.* $75/£48

STEGNER, WALLACE. The Uneasy Chair. Doubleday, 1974. 1st ed. VF in VF dj. *Oregon.* $40/£26

STEGNER, WALLACE. Where the Bluebird Sings to the Lemonade Springs. NY: Random House, 1992. 1st ed. Fine in Fine dj. *Revere.* $35/£23

STEGNER, WALLACE. Wolf Willow: A History.... London: Heinemann, (1963). 1st British ed. Fine (stamp) in VG dj (price-clipped, erasure). *Authors Of The West.* $60/£39

STEGNER, WALLACE. The Women on the Wall. London: Hammond, Hammond, (1952). 1st British ed. Fine in VG dj (price-clipped). *Authors Of The West.* $75/£48

STEICHEN, EDWARD (comp). US Navy War Photographs: Pearl Harbor to Tokyo Harbor. NY: U.S. Camera, (1944). VG in wraps (sl rough). *Schoyer.* $30/£19

STEICHEN, EDWARD. Power. (NY): U.S. Camera Book, (1945). 1st ed. NF in dj. *Godot.* $175/£113

STEIG, WILLIAM. Abel's Island. NY: FSG, 1976. 1st ed. 8vo. Fine in VG + dj (wear; sm tear). *Book Adoption.* $40/£26

STEIG, WILLIAM. The Lonely Ones. NY, 1942. 1st ed. Fine in Fine dj. *Bond.* $17/£11

STEIG, WILLIAM. Tiffky Doofky. NY: FSG, 1978. 1st ed. Fine in VG dj (soiled; sm tears). *Book Adoption.* $40/£26

STEIN, AARON MARC. Kill Is a Four-Letter Word. GC: DCC, 1968. 1st ed. NF (spotting rear cvr) in VG + dj. *Janus.* $25/£16

STEIN, AUREL. On Ancient Central-Asian Tracks. Jeannette Mirsky (ed). NY: Pantheon Books, (1964). Frontis line map. VG in dj. *Schoyer.* $30/£19

STEIN, CLARENCE C. Toward New Towns for America. (Liverpool): Univ Press of Liverpool, 1951. 1st ed. Frontis. Pencil underlining few leaves, else VG in dj (torn). *Bookpress.* $85/£55

STEIN, GERTRUDE. Everybody's Autobiography. London: Heinemann, 1938. 1st Eng ed. Red cl. Fore-edge sl foxed, o/w Fine in dj (sl rubbed, soiled). *Dalian.* $132/£85

STEIN, GERTRUDE. Four in America. New Haven: Yale UP, 1947. 1st ed. Fine in dj (sl used). *Pharos.* $60/£39

STEIN, GERTRUDE. Four Saints in Three Acts. NY, 1934. 1st Amer ed. Fine in dj (sunned, 2 chips, spine heel lacks 1 inch). *Polyanthos.* $75/£48

STEIN, GERTRUDE. The Geographical History of American or the Relation of Human Nature to the Human Mind.... (NY): Random House, (1936). 1st ed. Good (spine sl tanned, sl wear). *Reese.* $125/£81

STEIN, GERTRUDE. Geography and Plays. Boston: Four Seas Co, (1922). 1st ed. 1st binding. Cl, bds (tips, edges rubbed), spine label (bit darkened). *Dermont.* $200/£129

STEIN, GERTRUDE. The Gertrude Stein First Reader and Three Plays. Dublin: Maurice Fridberg, (1946). 1st Eng ed. Fine in dj (sl wear; nick). *Antic Hay.* $75/£48

STEIN, GERTRUDE. In Savoy or Yes Is for a Very Young Man. London: Pushkin Press, 1946. 1st ed. Ptd wraps. Fine in Fine 1st issue dj w/misprint. *Polyanthos.* $100/£65

STEIN, GERTRUDE. In Savoy or Yes Is for Yes for a Very Young Man. London: Pushkin Press, 1946. 1st ed. Wrappers. NF in dj (sl dknd). *Limestone.* $85/£55

STEIN, GERTRUDE. Lectures in America. NY: Random House, (1935). 1st ed, 1st binding. Inscribed, signed. Port. Spine, endsheet gutters tanned, o/w VG (w/o dj). *Reese.* $225/£145

STEIN, GERTRUDE. Mrs. Reynolds and Five Earlier Novelettes. New Haven: Yale, 1952. 1st ed. One of 2500 ptd. Fine in NF white dj (lt dust mkd). *Reese.* $50/£32

STEIN, GERTRUDE. Narration. Four Lectures.... Chicago: Univ of Chicago, (1935). 1st ed, trade issue (872). Good (w/o dj). *Reese.* $35/£23

STEIN, GERTRUDE. Paris France. NY: Scribners, 1940. Rmdr issue of Amer ed w/o illus. Fine in dj. *Pharos.* $40/£26

STEIN, GERTRUDE. Three Lives. John Rodker, 1927. 1st UK ed. Uncut. Paper cvrd bds. Sm stain bottom edge; spine discolored, short tear, o/w VG. *Poetry.* $78/£50

STEIN, GERTRUDE. Useful Knowledge. London: John Lane, Bodley Head, (1929). 1st Eng ed. Bkpl; ink name, date, else Fine in dj. *Godot.* $225/£145

STEIN, GERTRUDE. A Village Are You Ready Yet Not Yet. Paris: Editions de la Galerie Simon, 1928. #17/100 signed by Stein & Elie Lascaux (illus). VG (sl bumped) in ptd wrappers. *Williams.* $767/£495

STEIN, GERTRUDE. Wars I Have Seen. NY: Random House, (1945). 1st ed. Blue cl, paper labels. Name stamp; offsetting last 2 text pp, else NF in dj (lt worn). *Chapel Hill.* $50/£32

STEINBECK, JOHN and EDWARD F. RICKETTS. Sea of Cortez. NY: Viking, 1941. 1st ed. 8vo. 15 color plts; 56 dwgs; 72 b/w photos; 2 charts. VG in dj (nicks, creases). *Houle.* $650/£419

STEINBECK, JOHN. Bombs Away. NY: Viking, 1942. 1st ed. Black/white-stamped cl. Inscrip, o/w Fine. *Sadlon.* $30/£19

STEINBECK, JOHN. Cannery Row. London: Heinemann, 1945. 1st ed. Yellow cl. Stamp, ink name, o/w Fine in dj (chipped, frayed). *Temple.* $11/£7

STEINBECK, JOHN. Cannery Row. Viking, 1945. 1st ed. VG in VG+ dj (spine head worn). *Fine Books.* $125/£81

STEINBECK, JOHN. Cup of Gold. NY: Covici Friede, (1936). 1st Amer ed. Blue cl. Fine (name) in dj (sunned, chips, rubbed, creased, tape-repaired tears, price-clipped). *Polyanthos.* $60/£39

STEINBECK, JOHN. Cup of Gold. NY, (1936). 2nd ed. Text yellowing; bottom edge soiled, else Good. *King.* $35/£23

STEINBECK, JOHN. East of Eden. NY: Viking, 1952. 1st ed. Fine in lt grn cl. NF pict dj. *Vandoros.* $250/£161

STEINBECK, JOHN. East of Eden. NY: Viking, 1952. 1st ed. One of 1500 signed. Fine in orig mylar cvr (torn), slipcase. *Schoyer.* $700/£452

STEINBECK, JOHN. The Forgotten Village. NY: Viking, 1941. 1st ed. (Eps lt foxed; spine sl dknd.) Dj (sl chipped). *Sadlon.* $50/£32

STEINBECK, JOHN. The Forgotten Village. NY: Viking, 1941. 1st ed. VG (sl faded, bumped, soiled, worn). *Parker.* $75/£48

STEINBECK, JOHN. The Grapes of Wrath. London: Heinemann, (1939). 1st British ed. Fep replaced; tp, 1/2 title sl scored by pricing pencil, o/w Nice in dj (lt worn). *Ash.* $194/£125

STEINBECK, JOHN. The Grapes of Wrath. NY: Viking, (1939). 1st ed, 1st ptg w/'First Published in April 1939' and no notice of ltr ptg on copyright page, and 'First Edition' on fr flap of dj. 8vo. Orig pict beige cl. Fine in NF pict dj (price-clipped; creases). *Chapel Hill.* $2,200/£1,419

STEINBECK, JOHN. The Grapes of Wrath. Viking, (1939). 1st ed. Pict cvr, song on eps. Name, else Fine. *Authors Of The West.* $150/£97

STEINBECK, JOHN. The Grapes of Wrath. London: Heinemann, 1939. 1st ed. Spine sl cocked, top edge dusty, o/w NF in dj (sl chipped). *Rees.* $271/£175

STEINBECK, JOHN. The Grapes of Wrath. NY: Viking, 1939. 1st ed. Fine in Fine dj (lt rubs; spine sl dknd). *Beasley.* $950/£613

STEINBECK, JOHN. The Grapes of Wrath. London: Heinemann, 1939. 1st Eng ed. NF in NF dj (sl chipped). *Limestone.* $250/£161

STEINBECK, JOHN. The Grapes of Wrath. London: Heinemann, 1939. 1st UK ed. NF in VG+ dj (sm nick top of spine). *Williams.* $426/£275

STEINBECK, JOHN. The Grapes of Wrath. NY: LEC, 1940. One of 1146 numbered, signed by Thomas Hart Benton (illus). 2 vols. 1/4 rawhide, grasscloth over bds. Silver stamping vol 1 sl rubbed, o/w NF set in dj (soiled, edgeworn). *Reese.* $375/£242

STEINBECK, JOHN. The Grapes of Wrath. NY: LEC, 1940. Signed by Thomas Hart Benton (illus). 2 vols. Rawhide-backed grass cl bds (shrinkage, color variation). Promo sheet laid in. NF set in slipcase (lt worn). *Glenn.* $600/£387

STEINBECK, JOHN. In Dubious Battle. Covici Friede, 1936. 1st ed. VG. *Fine Books.* $135/£87

STEINBECK, JOHN. In Dubious Battle. London: Heinemann, 1936. 1st Eng ed. Blue cl. Sl mkd, soiled, fep soiled, o/w Good. *Dalian.* $39/£25

STEINBECK, JOHN. Journal of a Novel. London: Heinemann, 1970. 1st Eng ed. Grn cl. Fine in dj. *Dalian.* $47/£30

STEINBECK, JOHN. The Log from the Sea of Cortez. NY: Viking, 1951. 1st ed. 2 ports. Brn-stamped cl gray-grn. Dj (price-clipped, lt edgeworn). *Dawson.* $150/£97

STEINBECK, JOHN. The Log from the Sea of Cortez. London: Heinemann, 1958. 1st Eng ed. VG in dj (sl soiled, chipped). *Limestone.* $85/£55

STEINBECK, JOHN. The Log from the Sea of Cortez. Heinemann, 1958. 1st Eng ed. Corner bumped, else NF in NF dj. *Fine Books.* $125/£81

STEINBECK, JOHN. The Long Valley. Viking, 1938. 1st ed. Spine faded, else VG+ in VG+ dj. *Fine Books.* $285/£184

STEINBECK, JOHN. The Long Valley. NY: Viking, 1938. 1st ed. Fine (pastedown gutters lt discolored) in dj. *Cahan.* $425/£274

STEINBECK, JOHN. The Moon Is Down. London: Heinemann, 1942. 1st Eng ed. Sig, else VG in dj (sl worn). *Limestone.* $65/£42

STEINBECK, JOHN. Of Mice and Men. C-F, 1937. 1st ed, 1st issue. Fine in NF dj. *Fine Books.* $875/£565

STEINBECK, JOHN. Of Mice and Men. NY: LEC, 1970. #330/1500 signed by Fletcher Martin (illus). Leather-backed linen. Fine in pub's slipcase. *Hermitage.* $175/£113

STEINBECK, JOHN. Once There Was a War. NY: Viking, 1958. 1st ed. Fine in NF dj (lt wear; spine, rear panel sunned). *Beasley.* $75/£48

STEINBECK, JOHN. Once There Was a War. London: Heinemann, 1958. 1st Eng ed. Black cl. Fine in dj (sl soiled). *Dalian.* $39/£25

STEINBECK, JOHN. Once There Was a War. London: Heinemann, 1959. 1st ed. NF in NF dj. *Bishop.* $60/£39

STEINBECK, JOHN. The Pastures of Heaven. Cleveland, (1946). 1st Tower Books ed. Top browned, inner rear hinge cracked, spine sl wrinkled, else Good in dj (chipped, sl torn, rubbed). *King.* $25/£16

STEINBECK, JOHN. The Pastures of Heaven. London: Philip Allan, 1933. 1st Eng ed. Grn cl. Spine faded, cvrs sl mkd, top spine worn, o/w Good. *Dalian.* $54/£35

STEINBECK, JOHN. The Red Pony. NY, 1937. 1st ed, ltd to 699, signed. Spine sl discolored, sl bumped, else Nice in slipcase (bumped, repaired, varnished?). *King.* $850/£548

STEINBECK, JOHN. A Russian Journal. NY: Viking, 1948. 1st ed. Fine in Good dj (old reinforcement verso). *Reese.* $85/£55

STEINBECK, JOHN. A Russian Journal. London: Heinemann, 1949. 1st Eng ed. Blue cl. VG in dj (chipped, soiled). *Dalian.* $70/£45

STEINBECK, JOHN. The Short Reign of Pippin IV. London: Heinemann, 1957. 1st Eng ed. Blue cl. VF in dj. *Dalian.* $54/£35

STEINBECK, JOHN. The Short Reign of Pippin IV. London: Heinemann, 1957. 1st UK ed. Fine in VG dj. *Williams.* $25/£16

STEINBECK, JOHN. Steinbeck. The Viking Portable Library. NY, 1943. 1st Amer ed. NF (name). *Polyanthos.* $20/£13

STEINBECK, JOHN. Sweet Thursday. NY: Viking, 1954. 1st ed. NF in dj (spine lt worn, else NF). *Godot.* $85/£55

STEINBECK, JOHN. Sweet Thursday. London: Heinemann, 1954. 1st Eng ed. Grey cl. Spine sl faded, gilt dull, o/w Nice. *Temple.* $11/£7

STEINBECK, JOHN. Travels with Charley. Heinemann, 1962. 1st Eng ed. Foxing to pg edges, else NF in NF dj. *Fine Books.* $70/£45

STEINBECK, JOHN. The Wayward Bus. NY, 1947. 1st ed. Owner sig, o/w Fine in Good dj. *Bond.* $35/£23

STEINBECK, JOHN. The Wayward Bus. NY: Viking, 1947. 1st ed. Brn cl, gilt. Fine in dj. *Limestone.* $75/£48

STEINBECK, JOHN. The Winter of Our Discontent. NY, 1951. 1st ed. As New (name) in VG dj (chipped). *Bond.* $85/£55

STEINBECK, JOHN. The Winter of Our Discontent. London: Heinemann, 1961. 1st ed. Plum bds. Fine in dj (sl frayed). *Temple.* $19/£12

STEINBECK, JOHN. The Winter of Our Discontent. NY: Viking, 1961. 1st ed. VG in dj. *Houle.* $125/£81

STEINBECK, JOHN. The Winter of Our Discontent. London: Heinemann, 1961. 1st Eng ed. Fine in VG+ dj. *Limestone.* $45/£29

STEINBERG, LEO. Michelangelo's Last Paintings. The Conversion of Saint Paul, and the Crucifixion of Saint Peter.... NY, 1975. 64 plts, 24 color. Cl (sl dusty). *Washton.* $75/£48

STEINBERG, RONALD M. Fra Girolamo Savonarola, Florentine Art and Renaissance Historiography. OH Univ, 1977. Fine in dec dj. *Europa.* $23/£15

STEINBERG, SAUL. All in Line. NY, (1945). 1st ed. 1st bk. VG in dj (lacks 2 inches at spine). *Artis.* $15/£10

STEINBRUNNER, CHRIS and NORMAN MICHAELS. The Films of Sherlock Holmes. Secaucus: Citadel, 1978. 1st ed. Fine in dj. *Janus.* $45/£29

STEINDLER, ARTHUR. Mechanics of Normal and Pathological Locomotion in Man. Springfield, 1935. 1st ed. Good. *Fye.* $150/£97

STEINER, A. RALPH. Dartmouth. Brooklyn: the Author, 1922. 1st ed, 1st bk. 24 collotype plts. Cl-backed bds. Name; chips bottom edge, else NF. *Cahan.* $400/£258

STEINER, JESSE F. and ROY M. BROWN. The North Carolina Chain Gang. Chapel Hill, 1927. 1st ed. Orig cl. Blood stain fr cvr, else VG. *Mcgowan.* $150/£97

STEINKE, DARCEY. Up through the Water. GC: Doubleday, 1989. 1st ed, 1st bk. VF in dj. *Else Fine.* $45/£29

STENGEL, CASEY. Casey at the Bat. (As told to Harry T. Paxton.) Random House, 1962. 1st ed. VG in VG dj. *Plapinger.* $35/£23

STEPHENS, ALEXANDER HAMILTON. A Constitutional View of the Late War between the States. Phila: National Pub Co, (c1868-70). 1st ed. 2 vols. NF set. Howes S 938. *Mcgowan.* $185/£119

STEPHENS, ANN. Mary Derwent. Wilkes-Barre, PA, 1908. 1st ed thus. VF. *Bond.* $20/£13

STEPHENS, FREDERIC GEORGE et al. Catalogue of Political and Personal Satires. London, 1870-1954. 10 vols (of 11; lacks vol IV). Black cl (ex-lib w/ink stamps, bkpls, #s; vols 1-3 rebound; few spines lt faded). *Edwards.* $853/£550

STEPHENS, H. MORSE. Portugal. NY/London: Putnam's/Fisher Unwin, 1903. Fldg map. Grn cl, gilt (lib pocket removed, bkseller tag). *Schoyer.* $20/£13

STEPHENS, J.W.W. Blackwater Fever. Univ Press of Liverpool, 1937. Frontis port, 1 plt. Dj (sl soiled, chipped). *Edwards.* $70/£45

STEPHENS, J.W.W. Blackwater Fever. Liverpool, 1937. Frontis. Internally Good. (Rubbed.) *Goodrich.* $75/£48

STEPHENS, JAMES. The Charwoman's Daughter. London: Macmillan, 1912. 1st ed. (Eps lt foxed; spine sl lightened.) Cl folder; 1/2 morocco slipcase. *Sadlon.* $100/£65

STEPHENS, JAMES. The Charwoman's Daughter. London: Macmillan, 1912. Inscribed. Pink cl (spine lt sunned). Leather/cl slipcase. *Schoyer.* $175/£113

STEPHENS, JAMES. Collected Poems. London: Macmillan, 1926. Lg paper ed. Ltd to 500 signed. Vellum-backed bds (spine rubbed; eps sl foxed). *Sadlon.* $50/£32

STEPHENS, JAMES. The Crock of Gold. London: Macmillan, 1912. 1st ed. Recent full jade morocco, extra gilt. Few leaves sl repaired, o/w Excellent. *Ash.* $388/£250

STEPHENS, JAMES. The Crock of Gold. NY: LEC, 1942. #527/1500, signed. Robert Lawson (illus). Tall, 4to. Grn woven cl w/leather labels; gold stamped dec fr label; LEC newsletter laid in. *Reisler.* $125/£81

STEPHENS, JAMES. Etched in Moonlight. NY: Macmillan, 1928. Ltd to 750 signed. Paper spine label; teg. (Spine dknd.) *Sadlon.* $50/£32

STEPHENS, JAMES. Irish Fairy Tales. London: Macmillan, 1920. 16 color plts by Arthur Rackham (binding faded, sl loose, mkd; backstrip sl torn). *Petersfield.* $186/£120

STEPHENS, JAMES. Julia Elizabeth, a Comedy in One Act. NY: Crosby Gaige, 1929. 1st ed. One of 861 numbered, signed. NF. *Reese.* $50/£32

STEPHENS, JAMES. Reincarnations. London: Macmillan, 1918. 1st ed. Inscribed. (Lt rubbed.) *Sadlon.* $50/£32

STEPHENS, JAMES. Theme and Variations. NY: Fountain, 1930. Ltd to 850 signed. Gilt-stamped cl. Fine in pub's slipcase. *Sadlon.* $100/£65

STEPHENS, JOHN L. Incidents of Travel in Central America, Chiapas, and Yucatan. NY, 1841. 2 vols. 424; 474pp + plts, fldg map. Gilt cl (extrems frayed, chip vol 2, lt foxing). Good set. *Reese.* $650/£419

STEPHENS, JOHN L. Incidents of Travel in Central America, Chiapas, and Yucatan. NY: Harper, 1841. 1st ed. 2 vols. vo. viii,(1),424; vii,(2),474pp, 69 full-pg plts, guards; fldg map. 1/2 calf, marbled bds, gilt-tooled, morocco spine labels. Fine set (bkpls). *Cahan.* $525/£339

STEPHENS, JOHN L. Incidents of Travel in Yucatan. NY, 1843. 1st ed. 2 vols. xii,(9)-459; xvi,(9)-478pp. Gilt-stamped cl (extrems worn, frayed). Sound set (couple of sigs starting; inner fr hinge vol 1 cracking; scattered foxing). *Reese.* $450/£290

STEPHENS, L. DOW. Life Sketches of a Jayhawker of '49. (N.p.), 1916. 1st ed. 6 photo plts. VG in orig ptd wrappers (edges sl worn). *Shasky.* $50/£32

STEPHENS, WILLIAM P. American Yachting. NY/London: Macmillan, 1904. 1st ed. 4 plts. *Lefkowicz.* $100/£65

STEPHENS, WILLIAM P. Traditions and Memories of American Yachting. NY: Rudder, (1945). Enlgd ed. (Sl soiled.) *Lefkowicz.* $95/£61

STEPHENSON, MARY A. Old Homes in Surry and Sussex. Richmond, VA: Dietz Press, 1942. 1st ed. VG (fr panel, flap of dj laid in). VG. *Cahan.* $75/£48

STEPHENSON, NATHANIEL WRIGHT. The Day of the Confederacy. A Chronicle of the Embattled South. New Haven: Yale Univ Press, 1920. 1st ed. Orig paper cvrd bds. VG. *Mcgowan.* $45/£29

STEPNIAK. The Russian Peasantry. NY: Harper, 1888. 1st ed. Good (binding discolored). *Beasley.* $75/£48

STEPTOE, JOE (JOHN). Jeffrey Bear Cleans Up His Act. NY: Lothrop, Lee & Shepard, 1983. 1st ed. Pict cl. Fine in dj. *Godot.* $65/£42

STEPTOE, JOE (JOHN). Train Ride. NY: Harper & Row, (1971). 1st ed. Pict paper cvrd bds. VG in dj. *Godot.* $65/£42

STERLING, CHARLES. Great French Painting in the Hermitage. NY, (1958). VG in dj. *Argosy.* $75/£48

STERLING, GEORGE. Robinson Jeffers. NY: Boni & Liveright, 1926. (Bkpl.) dj. *Argosy.* $50/£32

STERLING, SARA HAWKS. A Lady of King Arthur's Court. Phila, 1907. 1st ed. 5 full-pg plts. Teg. Leather-backed marbled bds (worn; spine chipped; sl stain bottom pp, text; no spine title). *King.* $35/£23

STERLING, SARA HAWKS. A Lady of King Arthur's Court. Phila: George W. Jacobs, 1907. 1st ed. 5 full-pg plts. Tan cl. Cl sl dknd; cvrs sl bowed, else VG. *Chapel Hill.* $45/£29

STERN, F.C. A Study of the Genus Paeonia. London: Royal Horticultural Soc, 1946. 15 full-pg color plts. Gilt-stamped buckram (corners lt creased). Fine. *Quest.* $515/£332

STERN, JOHN A. To Hudson's Bay by Paddle and Portage. N.p.: Privately ptd, 1934. 1st ed. 6 photo plts. Grn bds (soiled, waterstain), paper cvr label (gouged), spine label (chipped). *Karmiole.* $40/£26

STERN, MADELEINE B. The Life of Margaret Fuller. NY: E.P. Dutton, 1942. 1st ed. Fine in NF dj. *Hermitage.* $45/£29

STERN, MADELEINE B. Purple Passage, the Life of Mrs. Frank Leslie. Norman, OK, 1953. 2nd ed. VG in dj (red bled onto cvr). *Second Life.* $20/£13

STERN, PHILIP VAN DOREN. The Confederate Navy, a Pictorial History. NY, (1963). 1st ed. VG+ in VG+ dj. *Pratt.* $35/£23

STERN, PHILIP VAN DOREN. Secret Missions of the Civil War. NY: Rand McNally, (1959). 1st ed. VG. *Mcgowan.* $35/£23

STERN, PHILIP VAN DOREN. They Were There. NY, (1959). 1st ed. 198 plts. Dj worn, chipped, o/w Fine. *Pratt.* $45/£29

STERN, RENEE B. Standard Book of Etiquette. Chicago: Laird & Lee, (1924). 1st ed. VG in dj. *Petrilla.* $35/£23

STERN, RICHARD G. Golk. A Novel. London: MacGibbon & Kee, 1960. 1st Eng ed. 1st bk. Red cl. NF in dj (sl mkd). *Dalian.* $39/£25

STERNBERG, GEORGE (ed). Disinfection and Disinfectants: Their Application and Use.... Concord, 1888. 1st ed. 266pp. Good. *Fye.* $100/£65

STERNBERG, GEORGE. Immunity, Protective Inoculations in Infectious Diseases and Serum-Therapy. NY, 1895. 1st ed. 325pp. Good. *Fye.* $200/£129

STERNBERG, GEORGE. Malaria and Malarial Diseases. NY, 1884. 1st ed. 329pp. Good. *Fye.* $50/£32

STERNBERG, GEORGE. Report on the Etiology and Prevention of Yellow Fever. Washington, 1890. 1st ed. 271pp. (Eps loose; ex-lib.) *Fye.* $150/£97

STERNBERG, GEORGE. A Text-Book of Bacteriology. NY, 1896. 1st ed. 693pp. Good. *Fye.* $200/£129

STERNBERG, MARTHA. George Miller Sternberg, A Biography. Chicago, 1920. 1st ed. Good. *Fye.* $45/£29

STERNE, ADOLPHUS. Hurray for Texas! The Diary of. 1838-1851. Archie McDonald (ed). Waco: Texian, 1969. 1st ed. Dj. *Lambeth.* $75/£48

STERNE, EMMA GELDERS (retold by). All About Peter Pan. NY: Cupples & Leon, (1924). 1st ed. 12mo. Tan bds w/brn lettering, color paste label. Good. *Reisler.* $85/£55

STERNE, LAURENCE. The Beauties of Stern. London: For G. Kearsley et al, 1799. 13th ed. xxiv,324pp, engr port, 6 plts; aeg, marbled eps. Later mottled polished calf gilt. Fine. *Bickersteth.* $62/£40

STERNE, LAURENCE. The Beauties of Sterne. London: G. Kearsley, 1790. 11th ed. xxiv,325,(1)pp (eps yellowed, label), 6 copper plts. Contemp (? orig) 1/2 black morocco (extrems sl worn), gilt, marbled paper sides. *Cox.* $54/£35

STERNE, LAURENCE. Letters of the Late Rev. Mr. Laurence Sterne. (London: T. Becket, 1775.) 1st ed. 3 vols. 1/2 title present vol 1. Engr frontis vol 1. Fine contemp smooth calf, gilt ruled spine, red morocco labels. (1st, last leaves discolored; 18th cent sigs, bkpl; lt spots.) Well-preserved set. *Pirages.* $850/£548

STERNE, LAURENCE. The Life and Opinions of Tristam Shandy, Gentleman. NY: LEC, 1935. #904/1500 numbered, signed by T.M. Clelland (illus). Cl-backed dec bds. Fine set in pub's slipcase. *Hermitage.* $125/£81

STERNE, LAURENCE. The Life and Opinions of Tristram Shandy Gentleman. Chicago: Stone & Kimball, 1895. 1st Amer ed. 2 vols. Teg, uncut. Fine (spines sunned; bkpls; prelims foxed). *Polyanthos.* $75/£48

STERNE, LAURENCE. The Life and Opinions of Tristram Shandy.... London: Golden Cockerel, 1929/30. #189/500 sets. 3 vols. 15 copper engrs by J.E. Laboureur, 4 wood engrs by Eric Gill. Teg, rest uncut. VG set in russet buckram (backstrips uniformly faded). *Cox.* $279/£180

STERNE, LAURENCE. The Life and Opinions of Tristram Shandy.... NY: LEC, 1935. One of 1500. Signed by T.M. Cleland (illus). 2 vols. 1/2 blue linen. Fine in case (broken). *Agvent.* $100/£65

STERNE, LAURENCE. Second Journal to Eliza Hitherto Known as Letters.... London: G. Bell & Sons, 1929. One of 1000 numbered. 1st ed thus. Teg, rest uncut. Lt class mk spine; rear pastedown sl scuffed, o/w Fine in dj (chipped, frayed). *Temple.* $29/£19

STERNE, LAURENCE. A Sentimental Journey through France and Italy. London: Golden Cockerel Press, 1928. #34/500. 6 full-pg copper engrs by J.E. Laboureur; teg, others uncut. Red buckram (backstrip faded). VG. *Cox.* $209/£135

STERNE, LAURENCE. A Sentimental Journey through France and Italy. London: Golden Cockerel, 1928. One of 500 numbered. 6 copper engrs. Presentable (cl sl damp dulled) in dj (chipped; lt staining). *Hermitage.* $200/£129

STERNE, LAURENCE. A Sentimental Journey through France and Italy. LEC, 1936. Ltd to 1500 signed by Eric Gill (designer) and Denis Tegetmeier (illus). Dec tan cl; gilt. Spine sl dknd, o/w Fine in pub's slipcase. *Sadlon.* $50/£32

STERNE, LAURENCE. A Sentimental Journey Through France and Italy. LEC, 1936. One of 1500. Signed by Denis Tegetmeier (illus) & Eric Gill (designer). Dec buckram. NF (backstrip sl dknd) in NF case. *Agvent.* $200/£129

STERNE, LAURENCE. A Sentimental Journey...by Mr. Yorick. London: Peter Davies, 1927. One of 2000 ptd. 16 illus by Vera Willoughby. Uncut, partly unopened. Dec cl (backstrip faded). Good. *Cox.* $43/£28

STETSON, JAMES. Narrative of My Experiences in the Earthquake and Fire at San Francisco. Palo Alto: Lewis Osborne, 1969. Ltd to 1500 numbered. Fine. *Oregon.* $35/£23

STETTLER, MICHAEL. Stained Glass from the Early Fourteenth Century from the Church in Koenigsfelden. OUP, 1949. 16 mtd color plts. Fine. *Europa.* $25/£16

STEVENS, CHARLES W. Fly-Fishing in Maine Lakes. Boston: A. Williams, 1881. 1st ed. 201pp, 6pg cat (top edges sl dampstained). Burgundy cl (rubbed, bumped). VG. *Blue Mountain.* $125/£81

STEVENS, G.R. History of the Canadian National Railways. Macmillan, (1973). 1st ed. VG in VG dj. *Oregon.* $45/£29

STEVENS, GERALD R. Ramblings of a Rolling Stone. London: Fisher Unwin, 1924. 1st ed. Blue cl, gilt title. VG. *Bowman.* $35/£23

STEVENS, HENRY. Recollections of James Lenox and the Formation of His Library. NY Pub Lib, 1951. Ltd to 1000. Fine in blue cl gilt. *Moss.* $43/£28

STEVENS, JOAN. Old Jersey Houses. Jersey, 1966. Fine in dj. *Europa.* $47/£30

STEVENS, JOHN H. Personal Recollections of Minnesota and Its People.... Minneapolis, 1890. 1st ed. (8),432,(15)pp, 7 plts. Howes S 969. *Ginsberg.* $100/£65

STEVENS, THOMAS. Around the World on a Bicycle. London: Sampson Low, Marston, 1888. 1st London ed. xiv,(ii),477,(1)imprint,(2), incl frontis port. (Some foxing, mks.) Grn cl (recased; sl stained, spine sl rubbed; bkpl), dec in red/black, lettered in gilt. *Morrell.* $47/£30

STEVENS, THOMAS. Through Russia on a Mustang. London, 1891. xiii,334pp (feps lt browned). Roan-backed cl (spine rubbed, lacking to head; upper joint cracked). *Edwards.* $70/£45

STEVENS, WALLACE. The Man with the Blue Guitar and Other Poems. NY: Knopf, 1937. 1st ed. One of 1000 ptd. 8vo. Yellow cl. Fine in 2nd issue dj (spine sl dknd) w/word 'conjunctions' rather than 'conjunctioning' on fr inner flap. *Jaffe.* $500/£323

STEVENS, WALLACE. The Necessary Angel. NY, 1951. 1st Amer ed. Fine in dj (spine extrems sl rubbed; price-clipped). *Polyanthos.* $125/£81

STEVENS, WALLACE. The Necessary Angel. London: Faber, 1960. 1st UK ed. Eps, edges sl spotted, o/w VG in dj (sl soiled, chipped; spine faded). *Virgo.* $101/£65

STEVENS, WALLACE. Opus Posthumous, Poems, Plays, Prose. Samuel French Morse (ed). NY: Knopf, 1957. 1st ed. Fine in NF dj. *Hermitage.* $100/£65

STEVENS, WALLACE. Opus Posthumous. NY: Knopf, 1957. 1st ed. NF in VG+ dj (lt chipped). *Lame Duck.* $100/£65

STEVENS, WALLACE. Opus Posthumous. Samuel French Morse (ed). NY: Knopf, 1957. 1st ed. One of 4800 ptd. Fine in dj. *Jaffe.* $125/£81

STEVENS, WALLACE. A Primitive Like an Orb. (NY): Banyan Press, 1948. 1st ed. Ltd to 500. Fine in grn paper wrappers. *Jaffe.* $250/£161

STEVENS, WALLACE. Transport to Summer. NY: Knopf, 1947. 1st ed. Grn bds, black cl spine, paper spine label. Fine in dj (spine dkned; tear). *Chapel Hill.* $300/£194

STEVENSON, J.W. The Cottage Homes of England. London: Houlston, 1851. Frontis, 52pp, 19 engr plts. Orig ptd bds (spine chipped). *Marlborough.* $295/£190

STEVENSON, R. RANDOLPH. The Southern Side. Balt: Turnbull Bros, 1876. 1st ed. 488pp, fldg plan, facs. Orig rust cl stamped in black/gilt. Sound, bright (lt offsetting of frontis to title). *Chapel Hill.* $300/£194

STEVENSON, ROBERT LOUIS and ARTHUR QUILLER-COUCH. St. Ives, being the Adventures of a French Prisoner in England. London: Heinemann, 1898. 1st ed. Grey cl (sl bumped). *Waterfield.* $62/£40

STEVENSON, ROBERT LOUIS and LLOYD OSBOURNE. The Wrong Box. NY: Scribners, 1889. 1st Amer ed. Classified ad on fr cvr is partially removed, o/w Nice. *Pharos.* $50/£32

STEVENSON, ROBERT LOUIS and LLOYD OSBOURNE. The Wrong Box. NY: Scribner's, 1889. 1st ed. Blue cl, dbl labels, gilt. NF. *Macdonnell.* $85/£55

STEVENSON, ROBERT LOUIS and LLOYD OSBOURNE. The Wrong Box. London: Longmans, Green, 1889. 1st ed. Variant w/o ptr's ornament on contents pg. (Sl rubbed, sl mkd, spots; sl tape mks eps.) Overall Good. *Ash.* $116/£75

STEVENSON, ROBERT LOUIS. The Amateur Emigrant. Chicago: Stone & Kimball, Lakeside Press, 1895. 1st this ed. 180pp; teg, uncut. Grn cl, gilt. VG (worn). *Hartfield.* $125/£81

STEVENSON, ROBERT LOUIS. Ballads. London: C&W, 1890. 1st British ed. VG (sl rubbing edges). *Agvent.* $95/£61

STEVENSON, ROBERT LOUIS. Ballads. London: C&W, 1890. 1st Eng ed. Beveled bds; teg. (Eps sl browned.) *Sadlon.* $45/£29

STEVENSON, ROBERT LOUIS. The Black Arrow. Scribners, 1917. VG+. *Bishop.* $18/£12

STEVENSON, ROBERT LOUIS. A Child's Garden of Verses. Chicago/NY/London: Rand McNally, (1902). 2nd ed thus. Sm 4to; 93(1)pp. Pict tan cl stamped in grn/white. Sm stamp, name, else Fine in VG pict dj (chips, tears). *Chapel Hill.* $35/£23

STEVENSON, ROBERT LOUIS. A Child's Garden of Verses. NY: Dodge, (ca 1910). Frontis port. Gilt-stamped black cl (spine ends sl frayed). VG. *Houle.* $65/£42

STEVENSON, ROBERT LOUIS. A Child's Garden of Verses. London: John Lane, Bodley Head, 1896. 1st Eng ed. 8vo. Aeg. Charles Robinson (illus). Grn textured cl, gilt. Good. *Reisler.* $175/£113

STEVENSON, ROBERT LOUIS. A Child's Garden of Verses. London: John Lane, Bodley Head, 1896. 1st illus ed. Ads dated 1895. Charles Robinson (illus). Aeg. Pict cl, gilt (sl rubbed, sl bubbled; shaken, spotting). Good (short tear 1 leaf). *Ash.* $302/£195

STEVENSON, ROBERT LOUIS. A Child's Garden of Verses. Phila: Henry Altemus, 1902. 8vo. Frontis, 162pp + 16pp ads; 3 full-pg color plts. Dec cvr ptd on linen on bd. Lt spotted, else VG. *Hobbyhorse.* $70/£45

STEVENSON, ROBERT LOUIS. A Child's Garden of Verses. London: Longmans, Green, 1905. 1st Eng ed. 4to. 12 full color plts by Jessie Wilcox Smith. Teg. Dk blue cl, color paste label (chipped; rear cvr sl loose). *Reisler.* $275/£177

STEVENSON, ROBERT LOUIS. A Child's Garden of Verses. NY, 1914. Jessie Willcox Smith (illus). 12 full-pg color plts, color pict eps. Pict cvr label. (Ink inscrip 1/2 title.) *Argosy.* $60/£39

STEVENSON, ROBERT LOUIS. A Child's Garden of Verses. NY: LEC, 1944. One of 1100. Signed by Roger Duvoisin (illus). 1/2 blue leather. Fine in glassine (lt worn) & box. *Agvent.* $150/£97

STEVENSON, ROBERT LOUIS. David Balfour. Scribner's, 1893. 1st Amer ed. xiii,406pp + 4pp ads. Name, bkpl, o/w VG. *Oregon.* $45/£29

STEVENSON, ROBERT LOUIS. David Balfour. Scribners, 1935. 1st ed thus. N.C. Wyeth (illus). VG +. *Fine Books.* $75/£48

STEVENSON, ROBERT LOUIS. Fables. NY, 1914. 1st Amer ed. E.R. Herman (illus). Teg, rest uncut. Gilt dec cvrs. NF (sl rubbed). *Polyanthos.* $50/£32

STEVENSON, ROBERT LOUIS. Fables. London, 1914. 1st ed thus, ltd to 105 numbered. Frontis, 20 mtd plts (sl spotted), guards. E.R. Herman (illus). Vellum (sl dusty); teg, others uncut. Good. *Waterfield.* $147/£95

STEVENSON, ROBERT LOUIS. A Footnote to History. Cassell, 1892. 1st ed. Frontis map, viii,322pp + (xvi)pub's cat. (Feps sl browned; sl rubbed, bumped.) *Edwards.* $39/£25

STEVENSON, ROBERT LOUIS. In the South Seas. London: C&W, 1900. 1st Eng ed. Teg. Blue buckram. Fore-edge, prelims sl foxed, o/w VG. *Dalian.* $54/£35

STEVENSON, ROBERT LOUIS. In the South Seas. London: C&W, 1900. 1st separately published ed. Beveled bds (spine sl chipped); teg. *Sadlon.* $40/£26

STEVENSON, ROBERT LOUIS. Island Nights' Entertainments. London: Cassell, 1893. 1st Eng ed, 1st issue. Color map, 27 plts by Gordon Browne & W. Hatherell. Gilt-stamped pict blue cl (sl rubbed; fr inner hinge starting), patterned eps. VG. *Houle.* $175/£113

STEVENSON, ROBERT LOUIS. Kidnapped. London: Cassell, (1913). 1st Eng ed. 4to. 14 full-pg color plts by N.C. Wyeth, fldg map; tinted top. Grn cl, color paste label. Sm dents, fore-edge foxed, o/w Fine in dj (marginal chipping, waterstains). *Reisler.* $275/£177

STEVENSON, ROBERT LOUIS. Kidnapped. (London): Cassell & Co., 1886. 1st ed, 1st issue, w/'business' rather than 'pleasure' on p40, line 11; ad for illus Treasure Island p(312); 16 unnumbered pp pub ads. 8vo. 311pp; fldg map across from tp. Brn cl. VG (blind-stamp, bkpl, hinges cracked). *Chapel Hill.* $700/£452

STEVENSON, ROBERT LOUIS. Kidnapped. NY: LEC, 1938. #162/1500 signed by Hans Alexander Mueller (illus). Fine in slipcase. *Williams.* $74/£48

STEVENSON, ROBERT LOUIS. Lay Morals and Other Papers. London: C&W, 1911. 'Presentation copy' blind-stamped on title. Beveled bds (sl rubbed); teg. *Sadlon.* $45/£29

STEVENSON, ROBERT LOUIS. The Letters to His Family and Friends. Sidney Colvin (ed). Methuen, 1901. 4th & Cheaper ed. 2 vols. 2 ports; facs letter. *Bickersteth.* $43/£28

STEVENSON, ROBERT LOUIS. A Lodging for the Night. London: C&W, 1914. 1st separate ed. Teg. Gilt-stamped brn morocco. Spine, top edge sl sunned, else Fine in tissue dj. *Juvelis.* $75/£48

STEVENSON, ROBERT LOUIS. A Lowden Sabbath Morn. London: C&W, 1898. 1st ed. Square 8vo. 127pp (spotted, bkpl); teg. *Hollett.* $54/£35

STEVENSON, ROBERT LOUIS. The Merry Men. NY: Scribner's, 1887. 1st Amer ed. Yellow ptd wrappers (dust-soiling; spine ends lt chipped). *Macdonnell.* $275/£177

STEVENSON, ROBERT LOUIS. The Merry Men. London: C&W, 1887. 1st ed, w/ads at rear dated Sept 1886. 296 + 32pp ads. Dec blue cl (soiled). VG (sig). *Chapel Hill.* $150/£97

STEVENSON, ROBERT LOUIS. The Merry Men: And Other Tales and Fables. London: C&W, 1887. 1st ed, 1st state ads at end (September, 1886). Blue cl (sl rubbing), patterned eps. VG. *Houle.* $175/£113

STEVENSON, ROBERT LOUIS. New Arabian Nights. London: C&W, 1882. 2nd issue w/'warm grey floral eps' and pub's device at end of vols i & ii. Ads dated May 1882 bound in at end vol ii. 2 vols. Cvrs rubbed, scratched, else Nice set. *Pharos.* $200/£129

STEVENSON, ROBERT LOUIS. New Arabian Nights. Avon, CT: LEC, 1976. #1281/2000 signed by C. Hutton (illus). 12 full-pg color plts. Maize buckram stamped in gold. Mint in slipcase. *Graf.* $55/£35

STEVENSON, ROBERT LOUIS. The New Arabian Nights. Avon: LEC, 1976. One of 2000 numbered, signed by Clarke Hutton (illus). Fine in pub's slipcase. *Hermitage.* $85/£55

STEVENSON, ROBERT LOUIS. On the Choice of a Profession. London: C&W, 1916. 1st ed. Lilac buckram; top edge lilac, rest uncut. Reps foxed, offsetting onto facing leaf; lg uncut edges foxed; o/w NF in dj (sl chipped). *Temple.* $37/£24

STEVENSON, ROBERT LOUIS. R.L.S. to J.M. Barrie. A Vailima Portrait. SF: Book Club of CA, 1962. 1st ed, ltd to 475. Facs plt. Uncut. Fine in canvas-backed dec bds, paper label. Dj. *Cox.* $62/£40

STEVENSON, ROBERT LOUIS. The Silverado Squatters. London: C&W, 1883. 1st ed, 1st issue, variant binding. Teg, uncut; w/o ads inserted at end, w/word 'His' missing p140 (earliest state). Orig blue cl, gilt (usual binding is grn dec cl). VG (rubbing; eps foxed). *Macdonnell.* $275/£177

STEVENSON, ROBERT LOUIS. The Silverado Squatters. London: C&W, 1883. 1st ed, 1st issue, w/ads dated to the Oct of yr of pub. Orig cl, gilt (extrms sl worn; sl mks). Good (eps just cracking). *Ash.* $194/£125

STEVENSON, ROBERT LOUIS. The Silverado Squatters. NY: Scribner's, 1923. One of 380 ptd by John Henry Nash on watermarked paper. Patterned cl, ptd spine label. VG (bkpl) in slipcase (dknd, rubbed). *Bohling.* $300/£194

STEVENSON, ROBERT LOUIS. The Silverado Squatters. SF: Grabhorn Press, 1952. Cl-backed bds. Fine in dj (dknd, soiled). *Bohling.* $135/£87

STEVENSON, ROBERT LOUIS. Songs of Travel and Other Verses. London, 1896. 1st ed. Teg, rest uncut. Fine. *Polyanthos.* $50/£32

STEVENSON, ROBERT LOUIS. St. Ives. London, 1898. 1st ed. Uncut. NF (sl rubbed). *Polyanthos.* $60/£39

STEVENSON, ROBERT LOUIS. The Strange Case of Dr. Jekyll and Mr. Hyde. NY: Scribner's, 1886. Early ptg. (viii),138pp + 16pp ads, incl inside fr, rear cvrs (minor foxing). VG in ptd wraps (stained, creased; spine lacks large portion). *Blue Mountain.* $50/£32

STEVENSON, ROBERT LOUIS. The Strange Case of Dr. Jekyll and Mr. Hyde. NY: Random House, 1929. One of 1200 numbered, signed by W.A. Dwiggins (illus). NF in pict slipcase (top panel tanned). *Reese.* $65/£42

STEVENSON, ROBERT LOUIS. Travels with a Donkey in the Cevennes. London: Folio Soc, 1967. 1st ed. Pict cl. Backstrip sl dknd, o/w VG in slipcase. *Cox.* $19/£12

STEVENSON, ROBERT LOUIS. Travels with a Donkey. NY: LEC, (1957). One of 1500 numbered, signed by Roger Duvoisin (illus). Fine in pub's slipcase (scuffed). *Hermitage.* $45/£29

STEVENSON, ROBERT LOUIS. Treasure Island. London: Harrap, (1985). 1st ed thus. #32/250 numbered, inscribed by Ralph Steadman (illus). 4to. Color frontis map. Gilt-stamped black leatherette; pict eps; aeg. Fine in matching black slipcase. *Houle.* $395/£255

STEVENSON, ROBERT LOUIS. Treasure Island. Phila: Anderson Books, 1930. Lyle Justis (illus). Fine in slipcase (sl worn). *Williams.* $101/£65

STEVENSON, ROBERT LOUIS. Two Mediaeval Tales. NY: LEC, 1930. #1117/1500 signed by C.B. Falls (illus). VG+ (ink name) in slipcase. *Williams.* $93/£60

STEVENSON, ROBERT LOUIS. Vailima Letters, being Correspondence Addressed...to Sidney Colvin. Chicago: Stone & Kimball, 1895. 1st Amer ed, trade issue. 2 vols. Teg. Gilt grn cl (sl soiled, rubbed). VG. *Reese.* $45/£29

STEVENSON, ROBERT LOUIS. Vailima Letters. Chicago: Stone & Kimball, 1895. 1st ed. 2 frontispieces; 281; 275pp. VG. *Oregon.* $75/£48

STEVENSON, ROBERT LOUIS. Weir of Hermiston. London: C&W, 1896. 1st ed. Blue cl, beveled edges. Fine. *Pharos.* $80/£52

STEVENSON, ROBERT. Music in Mexico. NY: T.Y. Crowell, (1952). Frontis. VG (bumped). Good dj (top edge torn; fr panel lacks piece). *Blue Mountain.* $30/£19

STEVENSON, W.F. Wounds in War. NY, 1898. 1st Amer ed. 437pp. Good. *Fye.* $200/£129

STEVENSON, WILLIAM G. Thirteen Months in the Rebel Army. NY, 1862. 1st ed. 232pp. Faded, sm tear, sl interior spotting, o/w VG. *Pratt.* $60/£39

STEWARD, JOHN F. Lost Maramech and Earliest Chicago. Chicago: Revell, 1903. Pict cl. VG. *Schoyer.* $45/£29

STEWART, ALVAN. Writings and Speeches of Alvan Stewart, on Slavery. Luther Rawson Marsh (ed). NY: A.B. Burdick, 1860. 1st ed. Frontis port, 426 + (2)pp of ads (frontis, title lt foxed). Brn cl; blind-stamped; gilt spine. *Karmiole.* $75/£48

STEWART, ANGUS. Tangier. London: Hutchinson, 1977. 1st Eng ed. Black cl. Fine in dj. *Dalian.* $39/£25

STEWART, CECIL. Serbian Legacy. London, 1959. 1st ed. 81 plts. Dj (chipped). *Edwards.* $43/£28

STEWART, DUGALD. Elements of the Philosophy of the Human Mind. London/Edinburgh: A. Strahan, T. Cadell/W. Creech, 1792. 1st ed. 4to, xii,567pp. Contemp polished tree calf (rebacked; hinges sl worn). *Hollett.* $581/£375

STEWART, DUGALD. Philosophical Essays. Edinburgh: William Creech & Archibald Constable, 1810. 1st ed. 4to. xii,lxxxvi,500,(i)pp; half-title; errata slip. Contemp tree calf (surface abrasions), gilt. *Hollett.* $426/£275

STEWART, EDGAR I. Custer's Luck. Norman, 1955. 1st ed. Wrinkle, o/w NF in dj (worn, lacks piece). *Baade.* $65/£42

STEWART, GEORGE L. Pickett's Charge. Boston, 1959. 1st ed. Good+ in Good+ dj. *Pratt.* $47/£30

STEWART, H.L. Celery Growing and Marketing. N.p., 1891. 151pp, port, 13 plts. Gilt-dec cl (rubbed, worn). *Sutton.* $60/£39

STEWART, HENRY. The Shepherd's Manual. NY: OJ, 1898. 276pp + 12pp ads. Rust cl, gilt stamped. VG (sl rubbed, soiled). *Bohling.* $35/£23

STEWART, HUGH. Provincial Russia. A&C Black, 1913. 1st ed. 32 plts (16 color) by F. de Haenen; fldg map. Dec cl (stained; up to pp5 fore-edge lt stained). *Edwards.* $54/£35

STEWART, MARY. The Crystal Cave. London: Hodder & Stoughton, 1970. 1st ed. Fine in dj. *Temple.* $26/£17

STEWART, MARY. The Wind of Small Isles. London: Hodder & Stoughton, 1967. 1st Eng ed. Grey cl. Fine in dj (sl tanned, dusty). *Dalian.* $31/£20

STEWART, P.M. Round the World with Rod and Rifle. London: Thornton, 1924. 1st ed. VG. *Bowman.* $65/£42

STEWART, ROBERT G. Robert Edge Pine, British Portrait Painter in America 1784-1788. Washington: Smithsonian Institute, 1979. 1st ed. Bkpl; else VG in stiff wrappers. *Bookpress.* $40/£26

STEWART, W.C. The Practical Angler or the Art of Trout-Fishing. London: A&C Black, 1905. New ed. 6 color plts. Mod 1/2 morocco, marbled sides (sl foxing few pp). *Petersfield.* $50/£32

STEWART, WILL. See Tee Shock. S&S, 1950. 1st ed. Fine in dj. *Madle.* $65/£42

STEWART, WILLIAM H. The Spirit of the South. NY/Washington: Neale, 1908. 1st ed. Grn cl. Name; spine, top edge lt faded, else VG. *Chapel Hill.* $165/£106

STICKNEY, CHARLES E. A History of the Minisink Region. Middletown, NY: Finch, 1867. 1st ed. 211pp, 16 engr plts. Orig presentation 1/2 morocco. Howes S 995. *Ginsberg.* $200/£129

STIFF, DEAN. (Pseud of Nels Anderson.) The Milk and Honey Route. NY: Vanguard, 1931. 1st ed. Ernie Bushmiller (illus). NF in dj (sl used). *Beasley.* $50/£32

STIGAND, C. and D. LYELL. Central African Game and Its Spoor. London, 1906. Fldg plt. NF. *Trophy Room.* $600/£387

STILES, CHARLES. Hookworm Disease (or Ground-Itch Anemia): Its Nature.... Washington, 1910. 1st ed. Good in wrappers. *Fye.* $40/£26

STILES, HENRY R. A History of the City of Brooklyn. Brooklyn, NY: Published by Subscription, 1867-1870. 1st ed. 3 vols. viii,464; 500; viii,501-984pp. Grn gilt cl, gilt spines. Fine set. *Karmiole.* $200/£129

STILES, JOSEPH C. Modern Reform Examined; Or, the Union of the North and South on the Subject of Slavery. Phila: Lippincott, 1858. 1st ed. 310pp. Orig cl. Foxing, else VG. *Mcgowan.* $150/£97

STILL, ANDREW T. Autobiography of Andrew T. Still. Kirksville, MO: By Author, 1897. 1st ed. 460pp. Good. *Karmiole.* $50/£32

STILL, GEORGE F. Common Disorders and Diseases of Childhood. London: Henry Frowde, 1909. 1st ed. Red cl. Spine ends sl bumped, o/w VG. *White.* $147/£95

STILL, JOHN. Jungle Tide. Boston/NY: Houghton Mifflin, 1930. Frontis photo. Lt foxing. Dj. *Schoyer.* $30/£19

STILL, JOHN. The Jungle Tide. Edinburgh/London: Wm. Blackwood, 1930. 1st ed. (Lt foxing fore-edge 1st leaves.) Dj (sl worn). *Sadlon.* $20/£13

STILL, WILLIAM. The Underground Rail Road. Phila: Porter & Coates, 1872. 1st ed. 780pp. 70 engrs. Cl. Fr hinge tender, else Fine. *Godot.* $285/£184

STILLMAN, DAMIE. Decorative Work of Robert Adam. NY: St. Martin's Press, (1973). 1st Amer ed. Frontis; 173 illus on plts. Dj. *Bookpress.* $55/£35

STINE, J.H. History of the Army of the Potomac. (Washington: Gibson Bros, 1893). 2nd ed. 752pp. Orig blue cl. Names, else NF. *Chapel Hill.* $150/£97

STIRKE, D.W. Barotseland. London, n.d. c.(1922). 1st ed. Frontis port, fldg map. (Faded; bds warped.) *Edwards.* $70/£45

STIRLING, A.M.W. William De Morgan and His Wife. London: Thornton Butterworth, (1922). 1st ed. VG. *Pharos.* $95/£61

STIRLING, A.M.W. William De Morgan and His Wife. NY: Henry Holt, 1922. 1st ed. Frontis; 37 plts. VG. *Bookpress.* $45/£29

STIX, REGINE and FRANK NOTESTEIN. Controlled Fertility: An Evaluation of Clinical Service. Balt, 1940. 1st ed. (Ex-lib.) *Fye.* $50/£32

STOCKHAM, ALICE B. Tokology, a Book for Every Woman. Chicago: Stockham, 1884. Early ed. 310pp; plts bound in; incl certificate for 1 free medical consultation. (Lacks fep; 1 pg ads torn out; cvr wear.) *Second Life.* $50/£32

STOCKHAM, ALICE B. Tokology. Chicago, 1886. Rev ed. Frontis port; 374pp. Good. *Fye.* $75/£48

STOCKLEY, C. Stalking in the Himalayas and Northern India. London, 1936. *Trophy Room.* $200/£129

STOCKLEY, C.H. Stalking in the Himalayas and Northern India. London, 1936. 1st ed. (Sl rubbed, discolored.) *Edwards.* $62/£40

STOCKTON, FRANK R. The Bee-Man of Orn and Other Fanciful Tales. NY: Scribner's, 1887. 1st ed, 1st ptg. Grn cl; teg. NF (extrems sl worn). BAL 18888. *Antic Hay.* $50/£32

STOCKTON, FRANK R. The Girl at Cobhurst. NY: Scribner's, 1898. 1st ed. Dec cl (lt rubbed; sm snag spine). *Sadlon.* $30/£19

STOCKTON, FRANK R. The Griffin and the Minor Canon. London: Collins, 1968. 1st UK ed. Sm 4to, 56pp. Good in dj (rubbed, sl chipped). *Cox.* $28/£18

STOCKTON, FRANK R. The Griffin and the Minor Canon. London: Bodley Head, 1975. 1st ed thus. Maurice Sendak (illus). Pink bds. Fine in dj. *Dalian.* $23/£15

STOCKTON, FRANK R. The Late Mrs. Null. NY: Scribner's, 1886. 1st ed. Dec cvrs. NF. *Else Fine.* $125/£81

STOCKTON, FRANK R. Rudder Grange. NY: Scribner's, 1879. 1st ed, 1st ptg. Gray cl stamped in gilt/dk blue. Good (spine top sl frayed, lt edgewear). BAL 18874. *Reese.* $50/£32

STOCKTON, FRANK R. Rudder Grange. NY: Scribner, 1879. 1st ed, 1st state w/sig mark (1) p1 and 'Mrs. Frances Hodgson Burnett's Earlier Stories' advertised on p(271). 6pp pub's ads at end. Brn cl; top edge stained brn (rubbed; spine worn; lacks blank leaf at end). Good. BAL 18874. *Houle.* $100/£65

STOCKTON, FRANK R. The Squirrel Inn. NY: Century, 1891. 1st ed. Gilt stamped lt grn cl (sl rubbing); teg, uncut. VG. *Houle.* $125/£81

STOCKTON, FRANK R. The Vizier of the Two-Horned Alexander. NY: Century, 1899. 1st ed, 1st ptg. Dec grn cl. VG (sm stain rear cvr). BAL 18934. *Antic Hay.* $35/£23

STOCKTON, FRANK R. The Vizier of the Two-Horned Alexander. Century, 1899. 1st ed. VG. *Madle.* $40/£26

STOCKTON, J. ROY. The Gashouse Gang. Barnes, 1945. 1st ed. VG. *Plapinger.* $25/£16

STODDARD, HERBERT L. The Bobwhite Quail. NY: Scribner's, (1946). 69 plts. VG. *Mikesh.* $85/£55

STODDARD, HERBERT L. The Bobwhite Quail. NY: Scribner's, 1931. 1st trade ed. Color frontis w/guard. Bkpl, inscrip, else NF. *Cahan.* $125/£81

STODDARD, HERBERT L. The Bobwhite Quail. NY: Scribner's, 1950. Later ed. Fine in brn cl. Dj (worn). *Glenn.* $100/£65

STODDART, THOMAS TOD. The Art of Angling, as Practised in Scotland. Edinburgh, 1835. 1st ed. Mod full dk grn morocco (rebound). *Petersfield.* $133/£86

STOKER, BRAM. Famous Imposters. NY: Sturgis & Walton, 1910. 1st Amer ed. 8vo. Red cl. Pencil inscrip, fr hinge starting, else Nice in ptd dj (lt wear). *Chapel Hill.* $500/£323

STOKER, BRAM. Famous Impostors. NY: Sturgis & Walton, 1910. 1st Amer ed. Fr hinge neatly repaired, else NF (sm bump spine). *Between The Covers.* $150/£97

STOKER, BRAM. The Jewel of the Seven Stars. NY/London, (1904). 1st Amer ed. VG (lt shelf rub to edges; spine dull). *Mcclintock.* $185/£119

STOKER, BRAM. The Jewel of the Seven Stars. NY: Harper, 1904. 1st Amer ed. NF (spine sl rubbed; lacks dj). *Between The Covers.* $200/£129

STOKES, ADRIAN. Inside Out. London, Faber & Faber, (1947). 1st ed. Gray cl, rag paper. VG. *Gach.* $30/£19

STOKES, GEOFFREY. The Village Voice Anthology 1956-1980. William Morrow, 1982. 1st ed. NF in NF dj. *Bishop.* $17/£11

STOKES, I.N. PHELPS and DANIEL C. HASKELL. American Historical Prints, Early Views of American Cities, Etc. NY: NY Public Lib, 1933. 1st ed. Frontis; 118 plts. Cvrs sl rubbed, else Fine. *Bookpress.* $175/£113

STOKES, I.N. PHELPS and DANIEL C. HASKELL. American Historical Prints, Early Views of American Cities.... NY: NY Public Lib, 1933. 1st ed. Blue cl. Index laid in. Fine. *Hermitage.* $175/£113

STOKES, JOHN. Modern Clinical Syphilology. Sprinfield, 1927. 1st ed. Good. *Fye.* $100/£65

STOKES, TERRY. Crimes of Passion. NY, 1973. 1st Amer ed. Signed presentation. Fine in Fine dj. *Polyanthos.* $25/£16

STOKES, THOMAS L. The Savannah. NY, (1951). 1st ed. Name, else VG in dj (rubbed, soiled, snag). *King.* $25/£16

STOKES, WILLIAM. Lectures on the Theory and Practice of Physic. Phila, 1837. 1st Amer ed. 408pp. 1/2 leather. (Ex-lib; fr hinge cracked.) *Fye.* $100/£65

STOKES, WILLIAM. A Treatise on the Diagnosis and Treatment of Diseases of the Chest. Phila: Ed Barrington & George Haswell, 1844. 2nd ed. 550pp. VG. *Bishop.* $28/£18

STOLL, ROBERT. Architecture and Sculpture in Early Britain. London: Thames & Hudson, 1967. Dj. *Edwards.* $85/£55

STONE, ALBERT H. and J. HAMMOND REED (eds). Historic Lushan. Hankow: Arthington Press, 1921. 2 maps (1 lg fldg). VG (spine sl faded). *Hollett.* $233/£150

STONE, EDWIN MARTIN. The Invasion of Canada in 1775: Including the Journal of Captain Simon Thayer.... Providence, 1867. 1st ed. (24),380pp. Howes S 1031. *Ginsberg.* $100/£65

STONE, HERBERT STUART. First Editions of American Authors; A Manual for Book-Lovers. Cambridge: Stone & Kimball, 1893. 1st ed. Teg. xxiv, 223,(2)pp ads. VG to Fine. *Bookpress.* $150/£97

STONE, IRVING. Adversary in the House. London: Falcon Press, 1949. 1st Eng ed. Black cl. VG in dj (sl dusty). *Dalian.* $31/£20

STONE, IRVING. Darrow for the Defence. London: Bodley Head, 1949. 1st Eng ed. Blue cl. Fine in dj (sl dusty). *Dalian.* $23/£15

STONE, IRVING. Men to Match My Mountains. The Opening of the Far West 1840-1900. NY: Doubleday, 1956. 1st ed. Fine in VG dj. *Book Market.* $20/£13

STONE, IRVING. Those Who Love. NY: Doubleday, 1965. 1st ed. Inscribed. Fine in dj (nicks). *Sadlon.* $40/£26

STONE, LAWRENCE. Sculpture in Britain. The Middle Ages. Harmondsworth, 1972. 2nd ed. 192 plts. Good. *Washton.* $65/£42

STONE, LEE ALEXANDER. The Power of a Symbol.... Chicago, 1925. 1st ptg, ltd to 1100 numbered. Cl-backed bds (heavily soiled, cocked; inscrips). *King.* $50/£32

STONE, LEE ALEXANDER. The Story of Phallicism.... Chicago, 1927. Ltd to 1050 numbered. 2 vols. Teg. Cl (sl worn, soiled, bumped; names both vols). *King.* $65/£42

STONE, MARY (adapted by). Children's Stories That Never Grow Old. Chicago: Reilly & Lee, (n.d.). Rpt. 8vo. John R. Neill (illus). Color dec cl. Good in pict dj (lt chipped). *Reisler.* $450/£290

STONE, OLIVIA M. Tenerife and Its Six Satellites. London: Marcus Ward, 1889. New, revised ed. Frontis gravure port, vi,506,(8)pp, 8pp ads; 8 maps. Yellow dec cl (rubbed, lt soiled). *Karmiole.* $75/£48

STONE, RICHARD H. Sky Riders of the Atlantic. Cupples & Leon, 1930. 1st ed. Good+. *Madle.* $15/£10

STONE, ROBERT. Children of Light. Deutsch, 1986. 1st UK ed. Few leaves w/sm corner crease, o/w NF in dj (sl laminate lift spine head). *Sclanders.* $62/£40

STONE, ROBERT. Children of Light. NY: Knopf, 1986. 1st US ed. Fine in dj. *Reese.* $20/£13

STONE, ROBERT. Dog Soldiers. Boston: Houghton Mifflin, 1974. 1st ed. Signed. NF in NF dj (price-clipped). *Revere.* $100/£65

STONE, ROBERT. A Flag for Sunrise. Knopf, 1991. 1st ed. Fine in dj (corner worn). *Stahr.* $25/£16

STONE, ROBERT. A Hall of Mirrors. Boston, 1967. 1st ed, 1st bk. 2-tone cl (sl worn, sl stain) in dj (sl stained, rubbed). *King.* $150/£97

STONE, ROBERT. A Hall of Mirrors. Boston: HMCO, 1967. 1st ed, 1st bk. NF (sm stains to prelims) in NF dj. *Dermont.* $250/£161

STONE, ROBERT. Outerbridge Reach. London: Andre Deutsch, (1992). 1st Eng ed. Fine in Fine dj. *Dermont.* $35/£23

STONE, WILBUR FISK. History of Colorado. Chicago: S.J. Clarke, 1918. 1st ed. 3 vols. VG-. *Parker.* $175/£113

STONE, WILLIAM L. Ballads and Poems Relating to the Burgoyne Campaign. Albany: Joel Munsell's Sons, 1893. 359pp. Black cl (fr joint repaired). *Schoyer.* $80/£52

STONE, WILLIAM L. The Campaign of Lieut. Gen. John Burgoyne.... Albany: Joel Munsell, 1877. 461pp; fldg map, 12 plts. Dec cl (mottled), leather spine label. Howes S 1036. *Schoyer.* $90/£58

STONE, WILLIAM L. The Campaign of Lieut. Gen. John Burgoyne.... Albany, 1877. 1st ed. 461pp; fldg map, ports (1 loose). Orig cl (edgeworn). Inner hinge weak, o/w Good. *Artis.* $40/£26

STONE, WILLIAM L. The Life and Times of Sir William Johnson, Bart. Albany: J. Munsell, 1865. 2 vols. 555pp, fldg plan; 544pp. Fair. Howes S 1039. *Lien.* $100/£65

STONE, WILLIAM L. Life of Joseph Brant—Thayendanegea. NY: George Dearborn, 1838. 1st ed. 2 vols. Engr frontis, title leaf, xxiv,425,(3),lviii; engr frontis, title leaf, viii,537,(3),lxivpp; 6 plts. Pub's cl. Sl chipping spine extrems; sl rubbing; bkpls, else Very Nice. Howes S 1040. *Bookpress.* $325/£210

STONEHAM, C.T. Africa All Over. London: Hutchinson, (1934). (Lt spots.) *Petersfield.* $70/£45

STONEY, SAMUEL GAILLARD et al. Black Genesis. NY: Macmillan, 1930. 1st ed. Grn cl. NF in VG pict dj (chips, tears). *Chapel Hill.* $150/£97

STONEY, SAMUEL GAILLARD. Plantations of the Carolina Low Country. Charleston, SC: Carolina Art Assoc, (1939). 2nd ed. Ltd to 1500. Brn buckram. Fine in dj. *Weber.* $85/£55

STONEY, SAMUEL GAILLARD. Plantations of the Carolina Low Country. Charleston: Carolina Art Assoc, 1939. 1st ed. One of 1500. Fine in dj (lt chipped). *Bookpress.* $235/£152

STONG, PHIL. Horses and Americans. Garden City Pub, 1946. Color frontis; 64 plts. VG in dj (chipped, worn). *Connolly.* $37/£24

STONIER, G.W. The Memoirs of a Ghost. London: Grey Walls Press, 1947. 1st ed. Back cvr sl damp-spotted, o/w Fine in dj (sl chipped). *Temple.* $28/£18

STONOR, CHARLES. The Sherpa and the Snowman. London: Hollis & Carter, 1955. 1st ed. Color frontis; 36 plts. (Sl mkd.) *Hollett.* $39/£25

STOPES, MARIE. Contraception...Its Theory, History and Practice. London: Bell, 1929. 2nd ed, rpt. 5 plts. VG. *White*. $19/£12

STOPES, MARIE. Married Love. NY: Putnam, 1931. 1st US ed. VG. *Second Life*. $35/£23

STOPP, F.J. Evelyn Waugh: Portrait of an Artist. Chapman & Hall, 1958. 1st ed. Gilt-dec spine. Good in dj (sl rubbed). *Whiteson*. $19/£12

STOPPARD, TOM. After Magritte. London: Faber, 1971. 1st UK ed. VG in wrappers. *Lewton*. $34/£22

STOPPARD, TOM. Albert's Bridge and If You're Glad I'll Be Frank. London: Faber, 1969. 1st UK ed, hb issue. NF in dj (sl soiled, rubbed). *Moorhouse*. $124/£80

STOPPARD, TOM. Dirty Linen and New-Found Land. NY: Grove Press, 1976. 1st Amer ed. Black cl. Fine in dj (1-inch closed tear). *Dalian*. $31/£20

STOPPARD, TOM. Lord Malquist and Mr. Moon. (London): Anthony Blond, (1966). 1st ed, 1st bk. Fine in dj (sl soiled). *Pharos*. $225/£145

STOPPARD, TOM. Lord Malquist and Mr. Moon. London: Anthony Blond, 1966. 1st ed. VG in VG- dj (internally repaired tears). *Limestone*. $35/£23

STOPPARD, TOM. On the Razzle. London: Faber, 1981. 1st UK ed. Fine in wrappers. *Lewton*. $29/£19

STOPPARD, TOM. Rosencrantz and Guildenstern are Dead. NY: Samuel French, 1967. 1st Acting ed. Spine sl faded, o/w Fine in wraps. *Sclanders*. $31/£20

STORER, J. and H.S. Graphic and Historic Description of the Cathedrals of Great Britain. London: Rivingtons, n.d. (1814-19 on plts). 4 vols. 4to. Engr titles dated 1817-19, 256 engr plts w/letterpress in 27 sections. Contemp purple morocco gilt, aeg (by Lewis?). *Marlborough*. $891/£575

STOREY, DAVID. Pasmore. London: Longmans, 1972. 1st Eng ed. Cream cl. Fine in dj. *Dalian*. $23/£15

STOREY, DAVID. Radcliffe. London: Longmans, 1963. 1st Eng ed. Grn cl. Name, o/w VG in dj (sl mkd). *Dalian*. $31/£20

STOREY, DAVID. Savile. London: Jonathan Cape, 1976. 1st Eng ed. Grn cl. Fine in dj. *Dalian*. $39/£25

STOREY, HARRY. Hunting and Shooting in Ceylon. London, 1907. 2nd ed. Frontis port, fldg map (repaired w/cellotape). Gilt illus upper bd. (Foxing; extrems worn.) *Edwards*. $116/£75

Stories about Tom, Jane, and Ben. Northampton: E. Turner, n.d. (ca 1830). Chapbook. 16mo. 18pp. Pict pink paper wrappers. Fine. *Hobbyhorse*. $95/£61

STORM, COLTON (comp). A Catalogue of the Everett D. Graf Collection of Western America. Univ of Chicago, 1968. 1st Amer ed. Index to maps laid in. Fine in dj (crease). *Polyanthos*. $95/£61

STORM, COLTON. A Catalogue of the Everett D. Graff Collection of Western Americana. Chicago, 1968. 1st ed. Dj. *Ginsberg*. $50/£32

STORRER, WILLIAM ALLIN. The Architecture of Frank Lloyd Wright. (Cambridge: MIT Press, 1979). 2nd ed, 2nd ptg. VG in dj (rubbed). *Bookpress*. $110/£71

STORRS, AUGUSTUS and ALPHONSO WETMORE. Santa Fe Trail, First Reports: 1825. Stagecoach Press, 1960. Ltd to 550. Gilt-stamped spine. VF in VF dj. *Oregon*. $45/£29

STORRS, RONALD. Orientations. London, 1937. 2nd imp. Good+. *Gretton*. $12/£8

STORRS, RONALD. Orientations. London: Nicholson & Watson, 1943. VG. *Schoyer*. $45/£29

Story of a Needle by A.L.O.E. (By Charlotte Maria Tucker.) London: T. Nelson, 1895. Sm 8vo. 110pp + 6pp ads. Emb dec grn cl on bd (rubbed, faded), gilt spine. Good (lt foxing, water stains frontis, tp). *Hobbyhorse*. $30/£19

Story of Little Black Sambo and The Story of Peter Rabbit. A Turnover Book. Chicago: Reilly & Lee, (1910). John R. Neill (illus). 12mo. Color illus bds (edgewear, chipping). *Reisler*. $175/£113

Story of O. Paris: Olympia Press, 1965. 1st ed. Sl crease, o/w VG in wrappers. *Words Etc*. $28/£18

Story of Pinocchio. London: Octopus, 1979. 2nd imp. 21x21 cm. 6 fan-fld pop-ups. J. Pavlin & G. Seda (illus). Glazed pict bds. VG. *Book Finders*. $40/£26

Story of the Jubilee Singers; with their Songs. London: Hodder & Stoughton, 1876. Eng ed, stated 6th ed, rev. Tipped-in photo frontis. NF (Pencil name; extrems sl rubbed). *Between The Covers*. $250/£161

Story of the Statue of Liberty. NY: Holt, Rinehart, Winston, 1986. 20x28 cm, 6 pop-ups, pull-tabs. Joseph Forte (illus). Fine. *Book Finders*. $50/£32

Story of the Stick in All Ages and Lands. NY: J.W. Bouton, 1875. 1st Amer ed. x,254pp. Brn cl, gilt. Edges stained red. Sl chipped, else Very Nice. *Cady*. $50/£32

STORY, JOSEPH. Commentaries on Equity Jurisprudence, as Administered in England and America. Boston: Little, Brown, 1886. 2 vols. Tan buckram (worn). Sound. *Boswell*. $150/£97

STORY, JOSEPH. Commentaries on the Conflict of Laws.... Boston: Little, Brown, 1872. 7th ed. Contemp sheep. Ex-lib, else Good. *Boswell*. $150/£97

STORY, JOSEPH. Commentaries on the Law of Agency as a Branch of Commercial and Maritime Jurisprudence.... Boston: Little, Brown, 1882. 9th ed. Contemp sheep. (Ex-lib, taped.) Working copy. *Boswell*. $100/£65

STORY, JOSEPH. Commentaries on the Law of Bills of Exchange.... Boston: Little, Brown, 1860. 4th ed. Contemp sheep. Ex-lib, else Good. *Boswell*. $150/£97

STORY, JOSEPH. Commentaries on the Law of Promissory Notes.... Boston: Little, Brown, 1878. 7th ed. Contemp sheep. Ex-lib, else Good. *Boswell*. $150/£97

STORY, SOMMERVILLE. Rodin. NY: Phaidon, (1949). 115 plts. VG. *Argosy*. $50/£32

STORY, WILLIAM W. Castle St. Angelo and the Evil Eye. London: Chapman & Hall, 1877. 1st ed. Frontis, tp vignette; iv,(4),238pp+36pp ads (foxing), 7 plts. Red cl, gilt (sl stained, soiled, frayed). *Karmiole*. $35/£23

STORY, WILLIAM W. A Treatise on the Law of Contracts. Boston: Little, Brown, 1856. 2 vols. Contemp sheep (rubbed, worn); but sound. *Boswell*. $150/£97

STOUT, G.L. The Care of Pictures. NY: Columbia Univ, 1950. 24 plts. Sound. *Ars Artis*. $47/£30

STOUT, H.R. Our Family Physician. Peoria, IL, 1889. 477pp. Good. *Fye*. $75/£48

STOUT, HOSEA. On the Mormon Frontier: The Diary of Hosea Stout, 1844-1861, vols 1 and 2. Juanita Brooks (ed). Salt Lake, 1964. 1st ed. Map. VG in VG- djs. *Benchmark*. $100/£65

STOUT, REX. The Broken Vase. NY: Farrar & Rinehart, 1941. 1st ed. VG in dj (tape mends; faded spine; chipping; heavy wear along folds). *Mordida*. $75/£48

STOUT, REX. The Doorbell Rang. Viking, 1965. 1st ed. Fine in dj (lt rubbed; tiny nicks). *Murder*. $65/£42

STOUT, REX. A Family Affair. NY: Viking, 1975. 1st ed. Fine in dj (short crease inner fr flap). *Mordida*. $35/£23

STOUT, REX. A Family Affair. London: Collins, 1976. 1st Eng ed. Red cl. Fine in dj. *Dalian*. $39/£25

STOUT, REX. Gambit. London: The Crime Club, 1962. 1st Eng ed. VG in dj (sl worn, browned, nicked). *Hollett*. $31/£20

STOUT, REX. The Red Box. Avon Book Co, (1943). Pict wraps (sl worn, soiled, edges spotted, text yellowed). *King*. $25/£16

STOUT, REX. Some Buried Caesar. NY, 1939. 1st ed, 1st state w/paste-label acknowledgement of magazine appearance on copyright pg and 5-pg preview of 'Rex Stout's last book' (Too Many Cooks) following pg 296. VG (lacks dj). *Bond*. $450/£290

STOUT, REX. Some Buried Caesar. Collins, 1939. 1st UK ed. VG in dj (sl extrem wear; sm closed tear rear panel). *Williams*. $302/£195

STOUT, REX. Too Many Cooks. NY, 1938. 1st ed. Good (2 rubberstamps; spine frayed). Internally Fine. *Bond*. $150/£97

STOUT, REX. Too Many Women. Viking, 1947. 1st ed. Cl cvrs lt soiled, else Fine in NF dj (closed tear; lt wear spine head, rear). *Murder*. $200/£129

STOUT, REX. Too Many Women. NY: Viking, 1947. 1st ed. Due to binding error, this copy bound w/o rep. Fine in dj (spine lt rubbed, else Fine). *Godot*. $100/£65

STOUT, TOM. Montana, Its Story and Biography. Chicago: Amer Hist Soc, 1921. 3 vols. VG set. *Perier*. $425/£274

STOW, MRS. J.W. Probate Confiscation and the Unjust Laws which Govern Women. SF: Bacon & Co, (1876). 1st ed. (iii),258pp; engr port, guard. Dec grn cl (lt wear spine ends). *Petrilla*. $450/£290

STOW, RANDOLPH. The Girl Green as Elderflower. London: Secker & Warburg, 1980. 1st Eng ed. Grn cl. Fine in dj (spine sunned). *Dalian*. $23/£15

STOW, RANDOLPH. The Merry-Go-Round in the Sea. London: Macdonald, 1965. 1st Eng ed. NF (2 corners sl bumped) in dj (extrems sl rubbed). *Ulysses*. $70/£45

STOW, RANDOLPH. Visitants. London: Secker & Warburg, 1979. 1st Eng ed. Grey cl. VF in Fine dj. *Dalian*. $31/£20

STOWE, HARRIET BEECHER. Dred; A Tale of the Great Dismal Swamp. Boston: Phillips, Sampson, 1856. 1st Amer ed, 1st ptg, w/'d' in 'dictatorial' aligned under terminal 'r' in 'rather' on pg88, line 3 in vol I, and w/'The Dicksons are fewer' on pg370, line 9 up in vol II. Binding A, w/blindstamped ornamental frame w/holly-like leaves on cvrs, unptd yellow eps. Orig black-brn cl. VG set (1869 inscrip each vol; sigs sprung vol II). BAL 19389. *Chapel Hill*. $250/£161

STOWE, HARRIET BEECHER. Dred; A Tale of the Great Dismal Swamp. Boston, 1856. 1st ed. 2 vols. 329,(6); 370pp. Orig cl. Spine extrems sl worn; corners scuffed, else VG. *Mcgowan*. $150/£97

STOWE, HARRIET BEECHER. Dred; a Tale of the Great Dismal Swamp. Boston: Phillips, Sampson, 1856. 1st ed. 2 vols. vi,329; v,(5)-370pp; 3 ad leaves end 1st vol. Black ribbed cl, blocked in blind, gilt-lettered spine. Fine (pencil name title vol 1; spine foot vol 2 sl frayed). *Bickersteth*. $186/£120

STOWE, HARRIET BEECHER. Dred; A Tale of the Great Dismal Swamp. Boston: Houghton-Mifflin, 1886. ix,607pp. Sl minor cvr speckling; else NF. *Mcgowan*. $45/£29

STOWE, HARRIET BEECHER. The Key to Uncle Tom's Cabin. London: Clarke, Beeton, n.d. (1853). 2nd Eng ed, 2nd issue. viii,508pp. Contemp 3/4 leather. Sm hole fr joint, o/w Good. BAL 19357. *Schoyer*. $125/£81

STOWE, HARRIET BEECHER. Lady Byron Vindicated. Boston: Fields, Osgood, 1870. 1st ed. 482pp. (Extrems frayed, cl rubbed, faded.) *Karmiole*. $35/£23

STOWE, HARRIET BEECHER. Lady Byron Vindicated.... London: Sampson Low, Son, & Marston, 1870. 1st Eng ed. Blue gilt-stamped cl. VG (pencil sig, 1870 date; bkseller ticket; top half last 50pp browned; wear). BAL 19456. *Juvelis*. $75/£48

STOWE, HARRIET BEECHER. Little Pussy Willow. Boston: Fields, Osgood, 1870. 1st ed. NF. *Glenn*. $35/£23

STOWE, HARRIET BEECHER. Men of Our Times. Hartford: Hartford Pub Co, 1868. 1st ed. xiv,575,(3)pp ads, 18 engr ports w/guards. Teg. Gilt-stamped grn cl (wear). BAL 19449. *Petrilla*. $45/£29

STOWE, HARRIET BEECHER. Palmetto-Leaves. Boston: James R. Osgood, 1873. 1st ed, variant binding w/Houghton, Mifflin imprint at foot. Orig brn pict cl, gilt. VF. BAL 19476. *Macdonnell*. $165/£106

STOWE, HARRIET BEECHER. The Pearl of Orr's Island. Boston: Houghton-Mifflin, 1887. 437,14pp. NF. *Mcgowan*. $45/£29

STOWE, HARRIET BEECHER. Pink and White Tyranny. Boston: Roberts Bros, 1871. 1st ed, 1st ptg. Terra cotta cl, gilt. NF. BAL 19461. *Macdonnell*. $60/£39

STOWE, HARRIET BEECHER. Sunny Memories of Foreign Lands. Boston, 1854. 1st Amer ed. 2 vols. NF (sunned, sl rubbed). BAL 19375. *Polyanthos*. $75/£48

STOWE, HARRIET BEECHER. Uncle Tom's Cabin. Cassell, 1852. 1st Eng ed. 27 illus by George Cruikshank. Half-leather w/marbled eps; raised spines. VG+. *Fine Books*. $375/£242

STOWE, HARRIET BEECHER. Uncle Tom's Cabin. Boston: Houghton-Mifflin, 1881. lxvii,529pp. NF. BAL 19343. *Mcgowan*. $85/£55

STOWE, HARRIET BEECHER. We and Our Neighbors. NY: J.B. Ford, (1875). 1st ed. Gilt/black-stamped cl (sl rubbed; dknd spots). BAL 19483. *Sadlon*. $20/£13

STOWE, JOHN. The Survey of London. London: Ptd by Elizabeth Purslow, 1633. 4th ed. Lg 4to. (xv),939,(29)pp; aeg. 1/2 calf (respined, orig spine laid on). Underlining, ink notes, text browned, else Nice. *Bookpress*. $975/£629

STOWER, CALEB. The Printer's Grammar. London: B. Crosby, 1808. Frontis, facs title, xviii,530,20,10,16pp; 7 plts (2 fldg). Late 19th cent binder's cl. Marginal soiling, lt foxing, but Good. *Cox*. $132/£85

STOY, MICHAEL S. Pea-Pod Pop-Ups. NY: Playland, 1985. 23x29 cm. 6 dbl-pg pop-ups, 3 dolls. Glazed pict bds. VG. *Book Finders*. $45/£29

STRACHEY, LYTTON. Characters and Commentaries. London: C&W, 1933. 1st ed. Eps, prelims sl browned; sl faded, o/w VG in dj (soiled, frayed, chipped, sl loss). *Virgo*. $62/£40

STRACHEY, LYTTON. Elizabeth and Essex. London: C&W, 1928. 1st Eng ed. 6 plts. Terra-cotta buckram, gilt-titled. Very Nice. *Cady*. $20/£13

STRACHEY, LYTTON. Eminent Victorians. London: C&W, 1918. 1st Eng ed. 6 plts. Grey cl. Mkd, rubbed, prelims foxed, o/w Good. *Dalian*. $132/£85

STRACHEY, LYTTON. Landmarks in French Literature. London: Williams & Norgate Home Univ Lib, (1912). 1st issue w/top edge stained grn. 1st bk. Grn cl. Eps browned; sl faded, mkd, name, o/w VG. *Dalian.* $132/£85

STRACHEY, LYTTON. Pope. NY: Harcourt, Brace, 1926. 1st Amer ed. Blue-grn paper bds. Very Nice in dj. *Cady.* $20/£13

STRACHEY, LYTTON. Portraits in Miniature. London: C&W, 1931. 1st ed. Very Nice in VG dj (soiled, browned, chipped). *Virgo.* $47/£30

STRACHEY, LYTTON. Portraits in Miniature. London, 1931. Ltd 1st ed, one of 260 signed. VG. *Argosy.* $200/£129

STRACHEY, MARJORIE. Mazzini, Garibaldi and Cavour. London: Hogarth Press, 1937. 1st ed. Inserted map frontis. Red cl. Paper lt browned, o/w Fine in dj (spine sl faded). *Temple.* $48/£31

STRACK, HENRY. Brick and Terra-Cotta Work During the Middle Ages and the Renaissance in Italy. NY: Architectural Book Pub, n.d. (1914?). 1st ed. 50 plts. (Rubberstamp tp, eps; ink inscrip fep; binding worn; ink underlining). *Bookpress.* $235/£152

STRAHAN, S.A.K. Marriage and Disease. NY, 1892. 1st ed. 326pp. Good. *Fye.* $75/£48

STRAND, KENNETH A. Early Low-German Bibles. Grand Rapids, MI: Eerdmans, (1967). 1st ed. 14 facs plts. Blue cl. Good in dj. *Karmiole.* $30/£19

STRAND, MARK. The Continuous Life. NY, 1990. 1st Amer ed. Signed. Mint in Mint dj. *Polyanthos.* $25/£16

STRAND, MARK. Reasons for Moving. NY: Atheneum, 1968. 1st ed. Fine in Fine dj. *Dermont.* $75/£48

STRANGE, EDWARD F. The Colour Prints of Hiroshige. London: Cassell, 1925. 52 plts (16 color). Good. *Ars Artis.* $302/£195

STRANGE, EDWARD F. The Colour-Prints of Hiroshige. London, 1925. Color frontis; 15 color, 38 b/w plts. (Lt spotted, soiled, sl bumped.) *Edwards.* $116/£75

STRANGE, T.A. An Historical Guide to French Interiors, Furniture, Decoration, Woodwork and Allied Arts.... London, (ca 1900). 1/4 leather (rubbed). *Argosy.* $100/£65

STRATTON, ARTHUR. The English Interior. London: Batsford, n.d. c.(1920). 115 plts. Teg, rest uncut. 2-tone cl (eps lt spotted; sl soiled, worn). *Edwards.* $194/£125

STRATTON, ROYAL. Captivity of the Oatman Girls. NY, 1857. 1982 Time-Life rpt. Map. Pict cl. Fine. *Pratt.* $20/£13

STRATTON, ROYAL. Life Among the Indians or the Captivity of the Oatman Girls.... SF: Grabhorn Press, 1935. Ltd to 550. Frontis. VG. Howes S 1068. *Oregon.* $175/£113

STRATTON-PORTER, GENE. After the Flood. Indianapolis: Bobbs-Merrill Co, (1911). Special ed, signed (dated 1912). Grn suede, inlaid metal ornament on cvr (edges worn). *Karmiole.* $45/£29

STRATTON-PORTER, GENE. Laddie. A True Blue Story. NY, 1913. NF (sl sunned, rubbed, nicked, soiled; name, bkpl). *Polyanthos.* $50/£32

STRATTON-PORTER, GENE. Moths of the Limberlost. NY, 1912. Scarce orig issue. *Wheldon & Wesley.* $54/£35

STRATTON-PORTER, GENE. The Song of the Cardinal. Indianapolis, (1903). 1st ed. (Ink inscrip; cvrs worn; spine sunned; soil.) *King.* $95/£61

STRAUB, J. HAROLD. Biff, the Fire Dog. Chicago: Lyons & Carnahan, 1936. Inscribed. Sm 8vo. 90pp (sm tear tp). Pict 2-color linen on bd (lt rubbed). VG. *Hobbyhorse.* $35/£23

STRAUB, PETER. Floating Dragon. SF/Columbia: Underwood-Miller, 1982. 1st ed. One of 500 numbered, signed by author and Diane & Leo Dillon (artists). Fine in dj (sl edgewear). *Other Worlds.* $100/£65

STRAUB, PETER. Floating Dragon. Underwood-Miller, 1982. 1st ed. One of 500 numbered, signed. Fine in dj. *Madle.* $100/£65

STRAUB, PETER. Floating Dragon. London: Collins, 1983. 1st UK ed. NF in dj. *Lewton.* $22/£14

STRAUB, PETER. The General's Wife. (West Kingston, RI), 1982. 1st ed. Ltd to 1200 signed by Straub and Tom Canty (artist). VF w/o dj, as issued. *Mcclintock.* $65/£42

STRAUB, PETER. If You Could See Me Now. NY, (1977). 1st Amer ed. Fine in Fine dj. *Mcclintock.* $125/£81

STRAUB, PETER. Marriages. London: Andre Deutsch, 1973. 1st British ed. Fine in Fine dj. *Pettler.* $150/£97

STRAUB, PETER. Shadowland. London: Collins, 1981. 1st Eng ed. Blue cl. VG in dj. *Dalian.* $39/£25

STRAUSS, IVARD. Paint Powder and Make-Up. NY, 1938. Flexible cl (dusty). *Artis.* $20/£13

STRAUSS, W.L. The Intaglio Prints of Albrecht Durer. NY: Abaris, 1981. Sound. *Ars Artis.* $116/£75

STREET, ALFRED B. Woods and Waters. NY: M. Doolady, 1860. 1st ed. xx,345pp, map, pict title, 6 plts. Brn cl (hinge starting, sig pulled; cl rubbed, bumped; spine faded, head chipped). *Blue Mountain.* $150/£97

STREET, G.S. The Autobiography of a Boy. London: John Lane, 1894. 1st Eng ed. Grn silk cl bds. Sl dknd, prelims sl foxed, o/w VG. *Dalian.* $54/£35

STREET, GEORGE EDMUND. Some Account of Gothic Architecture in Spain. London, 1865. xiv,527pp. 25 ground plans. Blind emb cl (extrems rubbed w/minor loss; upper hinge cracked, lower hinge tender; fep foxed), gilt device to spine (sl faded). *Edwards.* $85/£55

STREETER, DAVID. A Bibliography of Ed Dorn. NY: Phoenix Bookshop, 1973. Fine in stiff paper wrappers. *Oak Knoll.* $25/£16

STREETER, FLOYD. The Complete and Authentic Life of Ben Thompson, Man with a Gun. NY, (1957). 1st ed. Lt dj wear, o/w VG + . *Pratt.* $35/£23

STREETER, FLOYD. The Kaw. Farrar & Rinehart, (1941). 1st ed. VG in VG dj. *Oregon.* $40/£26

STREETER, TAL. The Art of the Japanese Kite. NY, (1974). 1st ed. Pict bds. Mint in dj. *Argosy.* $35/£23

STREETER, THOMAS W. Bibliography of Texas, 1795-1845. Cambridge: Harvard, 1955-60. 1st ed. Ltd to 600 sets. 5 vols. Djs. *Ginsberg.* $1,250/£806

STREETER, THOMAS W. The Celebrated Collection of Americana. NY, 1966-70. 8 vols. All vols except 7 w/price lists loosely inserted. Vols 1-7 blue bds (spines sl rubbed; tears heads of joints vol 6); index vol blue cl. *Edwards.* $651/£420

STRIBLING, ROBERT M. Gettysburg Campaign and Campaigns of 1864 and 1865 in Virginia. Petersburg, VA: Franklin Press, 1905. 1st ed. Grn cl. Spine ends sl rubbed, else VG + . *Chapel Hill.* $150/£97

STRICKLAND, EDWARD FOUNTAIN. Publications and Memoirs of an Old Time Family Physician. Winston-Salem, 1949. 1st ed. NF. *Mcgowan.* $75/£48

STRICKLAND, SAMUEL. Twenty Seven Years in Canada West. London, 1853. 1st ed. 2 vols. (19),311; (8),344pp. *Ginsberg.* $375/£242

STRICKLAND, WILLIAM PETER. The Pioneer Bishop: The Life and Times of Francis Asbury. NY, (1858). 1st ed. 496pp. Good + (ex-libris; spine ends, outer hinges worn). *Mcgowan.* $45/£29

STRICKLAND-CONSTABLE, H. Our Medicine Men: A Few Hints. Kingston-upon-Hull, ca 1870. 689pp. VG (joints repaired). *Argosy.* $75/£48

STRIEBER, WHITLEY. The Wolfen. NY: Morrow, 1978. 1st ed, 1st novel. Fine in dj (sl wear; price-clipped). *Antic Hay.* $50/£32

STRIEBER, WHITLEY. The Wolfen. William Morrow, 1978. 1st ed. VG + in VG + dj. *Bishop.* $20/£13

STRINDBERG, AUGUST. The Inferno. NY: Putnam's, 1913. 1st Amer ed. Maroon cl, gilt. Fine. *Macdonnell.* $75/£48

STRINDBERG, AUGUST. Married: Twenty Stories of Married Life. Ellie Schleussner (trans). London: Frank Palmer, 1913. 1st ed. Spine extrems torn, o/w Nice. Internally Fine. *Temple.* $22/£14

STRINDBERG, AUGUST. Zones of the Spirit. NY, 1913. 1st Amer ed. Fine (spine sl rubbed). *Polyanthos.* $30/£19

STRINGER, GEO. ALFRED. Leisure Moments in Gough Square. Buffalo: Ulbrich & Kingsley, 1886. 1st ed. One of 300. Inscribed. 184pp + index. Grn cl, gilt (sm repair spine; inner hinge cracked). Text Excellent. *Hartfield.* $145/£94

STRODE, GEORGE (ed). Yellow Fever. NY, 1951. 1st ed. Good. *Fye.* $40/£26

STROMMENGER, EVA. The Art of Mesopotamia. London, 1964. 44 color, 280 b/w plts. Dj (soiled, nicked w/sl loss). *Edwards.* $209/£135

STRONG, ANNA LOUISE. Road to the Grey Pamir. Boston: Little Brown, 1931. Map. (Ink underlining.) Red cl. *Schoyer.* $30/£19

STRONG, D.E. Greek and Roman Gold and Silver Plate. London: Methuen, (1966). 68 plts. Good in dj (tattered). *Archaeologia.* $45/£29

STRONG, EDWARD, JR. Effects of Hookworm Disease on the Mental and Physical Development of Children. NY, 1916. 1st ed. Good in wrappers. *Fye.* $50/£32

STRONG, EMORY. Stone Age on the Columbia River. Portland: Binfords & Mort, 1960. (Ex-lib.) Dj. *Archaeologia.* $25/£16

STRONG, HENRY W. My Frontier Days and Indian Fights on the Plains of Texas. N.p. (Dallas): n.d. (1926). Signed pict of author laid in. VG in pict wraps. *Perier.* $90/£58

STRONG, ISOBEL and LLOYD OSBOURNE. Memories of Vailima. NY: Scribner's, 1902. 1st ed. Teg. Spine, edges sunned, else VG. *Reese.* $35/£23

STRONG, JAMES CLARK. Biographical Sketch of James Clark Strong.... Los Gatos, CA, 1910. Maroon cl, gilt title. VG + (soiling fr cvr). Howes S 1080. *Bohling.* $350/£226

STRONG, JAMES CLARK. Wah-Kee-Nah and Her People.... NY, 1893. 1st ed. (14),275pp. Pict cl. *Ginsberg.* $200/£129

STRONG, L.A.G. Doyle's Rock and Other Stories. Oxford: Basil Blackwell, 1925. 1st ed. Fine in VG dj (sl chipped, used). *Reese.* $50/£32

STRONG, L.A.G. Green Memory. London: Methuen, 1961. 1st Eng ed. Grn cl. VF in dj. *Dalian.* $23/£15

STRONG, L.A.G. The Last Enemy. London: Gollancz, 1936. 1st Eng ed. Blue cl. Very Nice in dj (spine sl browned). *Cady.* $15/£10

STRONG, L.A.G. The Open Sky. London: Gollancz, 1939. 1st Eng ed. Black cl. VG in dj (faded, sl tanned). *Dalian.* $39/£25

STRONG, L.A.G. Sea Wall. London: Gollancz, 1933. 1st Eng ed. Black cl. NF in dj (sl faded). *Dalian.* $31/£20

STRONG, L.A.G. The Story of Sugar. London, 1954. 12 plts. Dj. *Edwards.* $23/£15

STRONG, MOSES. History of the Territory of Wisconsin, from 1836 to 1848. Madison, 1885. Frontis port, 637pp. Grn cl. Good (spine top torn, edges snagged, fep removed). Howes S 1081. *Bohling.* $35/£23

STRONG, RICHARD P. et al. Report of First Expedition to South America 1913. Cambridge: Harvard Univ Press, 1915. Old, sm tag on backstrip (ex-lib?). *Schoyer.* $65/£42

STRONG, ROY. The National Portrait Gallery. Tudor and Jacobean Portraits. London: HMSO, 1969. 2 vols. 6 tipped-in color plts vol 1. Dec eps. Good set (rubbed; sl internal mks) in dec slipcase. *Europa.* $225/£145

STROUD, DOROTHY. Capability Brown. London: Country Life, 1950. 1st ed. Color frontis. *Quest.* $85/£55

STROUD, DOROTHY. Capability Brown. London: Country Life, 1957. 2nd ed. Color frontis. *Argosy.* $85/£55

STROYER, JACOB. My Life in the South. Salem: Newcomb & Gauss, 1898. 1st ed, new, enlgd. Inscribed, signed. Frontis port, 100pp. (Sl spine spotted.) *Petrilla.* $350/£226

STRUBBERG, FRIEDERICH. The Backwoodsman. London: Maxwell, 1864. 1st ed. (4),428pp. Orig dec grn cl. Howes S 106. *Ginsberg.* $750/£484

STRUBELL, M. and M. (trans). Trueta: Surgeon in War and Peace. London: Gollancz, 1980. 1st Eng ed. Fine in dj. *White.* $28/£18

STRUTT, EDWARD C. Fra Filippo Lippi. London: Bell, 1901. Dec gilt cl. VG (edgewear). *Willow House.* $43/£28

STRUTT, J.G. Sylva Britannica.... London, (1830). 2nd or smaller ed. Engr tp; viii,151pp; 49 engr plts. (Cl repaired; sl spotted.) *Wheldon & Wesley.* $186/£120

STRUTT, JOSEPH. A Complete View of the Dress and Habits of the People of England. London, 1970. Facs of 1842 ed. 2 vols. Frontispieces, 143 plts. (Ex-lib w/ink stamps, labels, tape mks, #s; cvrd in cellophane w/sl bubbling; joints sl tender). Djs (chipped). *Edwards.* $70/£45

STRUTT, JOSEPH. The Sports and Pastimes of the People of England. London, 1868. lxvii,420pp (margins sl thumbed); 140 engrs; marbled eps, edges. 1/2 morocco (rubbed). *Edwards.* $93/£60

STRUTT, JOSEPH. The Sports and Pastimes of the People of England.... London: T.T. & J. Tegg, 1833. New ed. Contemp 1/2 calf, black leather label. *Petersfield.* $47/£30

STRUVE, CHRISTIAN AUGUST. A Practical Essay on the Art of Recovering Suspended Animation. Albany, 1803. 1st Amer ed. 12mo. Contemp full calf (joints cracked). *Goodrich.* $150/£97

STRYKER, WILLIAM S. The Battles of Trenton and Princeton. Boston/NY: Houghton, Mifflin, 1898. 1st ed. 514pp. Red cl. Inner hinges cracked, else VG. Howes S 1090. *Chapel Hill.* $100/£65

STRZYGOWSKI, JOSEF. Early Church Art in Northern Europe. London: Batsford, 1928. 1st ed. 53 plts. *Edwards.* $74/£48

STRZYGOWSKI, JOSEF. Origins of Christian Church Art. O.M. Dalton, H.J. Braunholtz (trans). OUP, 1923. Dj (chipped, yellowed). *Edwards.* $93/£60

STUART, DABNEY. The Diving Bell. NY: Knopf, 1966. 1st ed, 1st bk. Signed on tp. Fine in dj (sl used; spine head chip). *Pharos.* $85/£55

STUART, DABNEY. Friends of Yours, Friends of Mine. Richmond: Rainmaker Press, (1974). 1st ed. Signed. VF in dj. *Pharos.* $40/£26

STUART, GRANVILLE. Forty Years on the Frontier. Paul C. Phillips (ed). Glendale: Clark, 1957. 2 vols in one. Pub's announcement laid in. Fine in plain dj (spine trimmed to show title). Howes S 1096. *Bohling.* $100/£65

STUART, J.A. ERSKINE. The Bronte Country: Its Topography, Antiquities, and History. London: Longmans, Green, 1888. 1st ed. xiii,242pp. Teg. 2-tone cl gilt (spine, edges sl dknd; sm chips spine). *Hollett.* $70/£45

STUART, JAMES and NICHOLAS REVETT. The Antiquuities of Athens.... London: Tilt and Bogue, 1841. v-xvii,156,1f, 70 engr plts. Contemp blind-stamped calf (rubbed). *Marlborough.* $233/£150

STUART, JESSE. Foretaste of Glory. NY: Dutton, 1946. 1st ed. Fine in dj. *Pharos.* $125/£81

STUART, JESSE. He'll Be Comin Down the Mountain. London: Dennis Dobson, 1946. 1st Eng ed, 1st bk. Grn cl. Fine in dj (sl torn, dusty). *Dalian.* $54/£35

STUART, JESSE. A Ride with Huey the Engineer. NY: McGraw-Hill, (1966). 1st ed. Robert Henneberger (illus). 95pp. Bkpl, else Fine in dj. *Godot.* $85/£55

STUART, RUTH McENERY. Napoleon Jackson the Gentleman of the Plush Rocker NY, 1916. 1st ed. Orig cl. VG. *Mcgowan.* $38/£25

STUART, VILLIERS. Nile Gleanings Concerning the Ethnology, History and Art of Ancient Egypt.... London: Murray, 1879. 58 plts; teg (sl foxed). Pict dk blue cl, new lighter blue morocco backstrip, gilt. *Petersfield.* $124/£80

STUBBS, GEORGE. The Anatomy of the Horse. London, 1938. Frontis. (Ex-lib w/ink stamps, bkpl, #.) *Edwards.* $155/£100

STUBBS, GEORGE. An Illustrated Lecture on Sketching from Nature in Pencil and Water Colour.... London: Day, n.d. (ca1850). 12pp, chromolitho frontis, 16 litho plts, (4 colored). Green cl (marginal dampstains). *Marlborough.* $279/£180

STUCK, HUDSON. The Ascent of Denali. NY: Scribner's, 1914. 1st ed. Fldg map. Gilt pict cl. Good (sm stain fr cvr; spine lettering sl flaked). *Artis.* $60/£39

STUCK, HUDSON. Ten Thousand Miles with a Dog Sled. NY: Scribner's, 1914. 1st ed. 60 photos, fldg map, 4 color plts. Inner hinges cracked, else VG in mylar dj. *Blue Dragon.* $145/£94

STUHLMANN, GUNTHER (ed). A Literate Passion. San Diego, 1987. 1st Amer ed. Fine in dj. *Polyanthos.* $30/£19

STURGE, JOSEPH. A Visit to the United States in 1841. London, 1842. 1st ed. viii,192,cxxii pp. Orig cl. Spine extrems chipped; old repair to spine at binder's title, else VG. *Mcgowan.* $165/£106

STURGE, JOSEPH. A Visit to the United States in 1841. London: Hamilton, Adams, 1842. 1st ed. viii,(1)errata, 192,(123)pp. Blind-stamped gray cl (worn; inner hinges glued). *Petrilla.* $175/£113

STURGEON, THEODORE and D. WARD. Sturgeon's West. Doubleday, 1973. 1st ed. NF in NF dj. *Aronovitz.* $65/£42

STURGEON, THEODORE. The Cosmic Rape. NY: Dell, (1958). 1st ed. Fine in wraps. *Artis.* $20/£13

STURGEON, THEODORE. The Dreaming Jewels. Greenberg, 1950. 1st ed. Binding, eps stained, else Good in dj. *Aronovitz.* $10/£6

STURGEON, THEODORE. The Dreaming Jewels. Greenberg, 1950. 1st ed. VG in dj (rubbed). *Madle.* $40/£26

STURGEON, THEODORE. The Dreaming Jewels. NY: Greenberg, 1950. 1st ed. Signed. NF in dj (sl edgewear). *Else Fine.* $135/£87

STURGEON, THEODORE. E Pluribus Unicorn. Abelard, 1953. 1st ed. Fine in NF dj. *Aronovitz.* $90/£58

STURGEON, THEODORE. Maturity. Rune Press, 1979. 1st ed. One of 750 signed. Fine in dj. *Aronovitz.* $45/£29

STURGEON, THEODORE. More Than Human. NY: Farrar, Straus & Young, (1953). 1st ed. VG in dj (lt soil). *Antic Hay.* $85/£55

STURGEON, THEODORE. More Than Human. Farrar, 1953. 1st ed. Fine in dj. *Madle.* $325/£210

STURGEON, THEODORE. A Touch of Strange. Doubleday, 1958. 1st ed. VG+ in VG+ dj. *Aronovitz.* $75/£48

STURGEON, THEODORE. Without Sorcery. Prime Press, 1948. 1st ed, 1st bk. Signed. Cvrs sl rubbed, else VG. *Aronovitz.* $50/£32

STURGEON, THEODORE. Without Sorcery. Prime, 1948. 1st ed. Fine in dj (sl rubbed). *Madle.* $80/£52

STURGES, ARTHUR M. Practical Beekeeping. London, 1924. Color frontis, 16 plts. (Sl foxing; spine sl discolored.) *Edwards.* $39/£25

STURGIS, RUSSELL. A Study of the Artist's Way of Working in the Various Handicrafts and Arts of Design. NY, 1905. Inscribed presentation. 2 vols. Gilt dec spine. VG. *Argosy.* $150/£97

STYRON, WILLIAM. Against Fear. Palaemon Press, (1981). One of 300 signed. Gray sewn wrappers. Fine. *Dermont.* $50/£32

STYRON, WILLIAM. As He Lay Dead, A Bitter Grief. NY: Albondocani, 1981. One of 300 numbered, signed. Fine in sewn marbled wrappers. *Dermont.* $60/£39

STYRON, WILLIAM. The Confessions of Nat Turner. NY: Random House, (1967). 1st ed. Signed. NF in dj. *Antic Hay.* $125/£81

STYRON, WILLIAM. The Confessions of Nat Turner. NY: Random House, (1967). One of 500 signed. NF in orig slipcase. *Pharos.* $250/£161

STYRON, WILLIAM. The Confessions of Nat Turner. Random House, 1967. 1st ed. NF (sticker shadow fep) in dj (chipped spine, corners). *Stahr.* $50/£32

STYRON, WILLIAM. The Confessions of Nat Turner. R-H, 1967. 1st ed. One of 500 specially bound, signed, photo laid in. Fine in VG slip-case. *Fine Books.* $285/£184

STYRON, WILLIAM. The Confessions of Nat Turner. NY: Random House, 1967. 1st ed. Signed. Fine in NF dj. *Revere.* $85/£55

STYRON, WILLIAM. The Confessions of Nat Turner. London: Cape, 1968. 1st ed. Fine in dj. *Rees.* $31/£20

STYRON, WILLIAM. The Confessions of Nat Turner. London, 1968. 1st ed. Signed. Fine in Fine dj. *Polyanthos.* $35/£23

STYRON, WILLIAM. Darkness Visible. London, 1991. 1st ed. Signed. Fine in Fine dj. *Polyanthos.* $35/£23

STYRON, WILLIAM. Darkness Visible. NY: Random House, 1991. 1st lg print ed. Signed. *Revere.* $85/£55

STYRON, WILLIAM. In the Clap Shack. NY: Random House, (1973). 1st ed. Rev slip laid in. VF in dj. *Reese.* $50/£32

STYRON, WILLIAM. In the Clap Shack. R-H, 1973. 1st ed. Signed. Fine in dj. *Fine Books.* $75/£48

STYRON, WILLIAM. Inheritance of Night. Durham: Duke Univ Press, 1993. One of 250 signed, numbered. Fine w/o djs (as issued). *Revere.* $175/£113

STYRON, WILLIAM. Lie Down in Darkness. Indianapolis/NY: Bobbs-Merrill, (1951). 1st Amer ed, 1st bk. Signed. Fine in dj (spine sl rubbed). *Between The Covers.* $450/£290

STYRON, WILLIAM. Lie Down in Darkness. Indianapolis: Bobbs Merrill, (1951). 1st ed, 1st bk. VG in Good dj (lg chips; sm snag). *Reese.* $65/£42

STYRON, WILLIAM. Lie Down in Darkness. Indianapolis: Bobbs-Merrill, (1951). 1st ed. 1st bk. VG in dj (price-clipped, 2 sm chips, short tears, else VG). *Godot.* $150/£97

STYRON, WILLIAM. Lie Down in Darkness. Hamilton, 1952. 1st UK ed. VG (eps foxed) in dj. *Lewton.* $93/£60

STYRON, WILLIAM. The Message of Auschwitz. (Blacksburg): Press de la Warr, 1979. 1st ed in bk form. One of 200 (of 226) numbered, signed. Fine in dec wrappers. *Reese.* $60/£39

STYRON, WILLIAM. Set This House on Fire. NY: Random House, (1960). 1st ed. VG in VG dj. *Chapel Hill.* $40/£26

STYRON, WILLIAM. Sophie's Choice. NY: Random House, (1979). 1st ed. Signed. VF in dj. *Pharos.* $150/£97

STYRON, WILLIAM. Sophie's Choice. London: Cape, 1979. 1st UK ed. Fine in dj (price-clipped). *Virgo.* $28/£18

STYRON, WILLIAM. Sophie's Choice. London: Cape, 1979. 1st UK ed. NF in dj. *Williams.* $31/£20

STYRON, WILLIAM. This Quiet Dust. NY: Random House, (1982). One of 250 numbered, signed. VF in dj. *Pharos.* $250/£161

Succession of the Monarchs of England. London: J. Harris, 1809. Sq 12mo. vii,64pp; 31 oval woodcut ports. Dk grey paper on bds (lt soiled), leather spine (rubbed). VG (lt foxing, dated ink dedication). *Hobbyhorse.* $250/£161

SUCKLING, E.V. The Examination of Waters and Water Supplies. London: Churchill, 1943. 5th ed. 36 plts. VG. *Savona.* $39/£25

SUCKLING, JOHN. A Ballad Upon a Wedding. Golden Cockerel Press, 1927. #42/375. 8 b/w engrs. White buckram spine, gilt title; purple/yellow batik paper bds. Dj discolored, else Fine (bkpl). *Heller.* $325/£210

SUCKLING, JOHN. The Works. Dublin: Nelson, 1766. 1st Dublin ed. 462,(2)pp. Teg. 3/4 crushed morocco, gilt extra, panelled spine; marbled eps. Sl defect tp, not affecting text, else Fine (bkpl). *Hartfield.* $295/£190

SUE, EUGENE. The Mysteries of Paris. NY: J. Winchester, 1844. 1st Amer ed. Leather-backed marbled bds (worn). *Argosy.* $100/£65

SUE, EUGENE. Paula Monti. London: Chapman & Hall, 1845. 1st Eng ed. (4),388pp + 16pp pub's cat dated August 1845; 20 plts. Blue cl (short splits but hinges sound). Uncut. Good (T gathering misbound after U but complete). *Cox.* $54/£35

SUE, EUGENE. The Rival Races; or, The Sons of Joel. London, 1863. 1st Eng ed. 3 vols. Grn cl. VG. *Argosy.* $150/£97

SUEHSDORF, A.D. The Great American Baseball Scrapbook. Random House, 1978. 1st ed. VG+ in VG+ dj. *Plapinger.* $30/£19

SUFFLING, ERNEST R. English Church Brasses From the 13th to the 17th Century. London, 1910. (Spine sl chipped.) *Edwards.* $62/£40

SUGARS, W.P. Tales of a Forgotten Village. Ypsilanti: University Lithoprinters, 1953. Signed. 5 fldg maps. Red cl. VG. *Peninsula.* $50/£32

SUGDEN, EDWARD BURTENSHAW. A Series of Letters to a Man of Property.... London: Reed, Hunter et al, 1815. 3rd ed. Orig bds; uncut. *Boswell.* $250/£161

SUGERMAN, DANNY. The Doors. The Illustrated History. Benjamin Edmonds (ed). NY: William Morrow, 1983. Special issue signed by author & 2 members of The Doors, Ray Manzarek, Robby Krieger. Fldg poster. Cl-backed paper bds. Fine in dj. *Ulysses.* $194/£125

SULLIVAN, EDWARD et al. Yachting. Vol 1 (only). London, 1901. Frontis, 20 plts. Dec eps (browned; stain upper margin last 1/2, affecting text; wrinkling; lt browning; spine rubbed, chipped). *Edwards.* $39/£25

SULLIVAN, FRANK. A Rock in Every Snowball. Boston: Little, Brown, 1946. 1st ed. Signed. Fine in dj (nicks, short tears, else VG). *Godot.* $65/£42

SULLIVAN, JAMES. The History of Land Titles in Massachusetts. Boston: By I. Thomas & E.T. Andrews, 1801. Contemp sheep (rebacked, worn, embrowned). Usable. *Boswell.* $150/£97

SULLIVAN, LOUIS H. Kindergarten Chats. NY: Wittenborn, Schultz, 1947. 1st ed thus. Wrappers lt rubbed, sl discolored bottom fr, else Fine. *Bookpress.* $225/£145

SULLIVAN, MAURICE S. Jedediah Smith, Trader and Trail Breaker. NY: Press of the Pioneers, 1936. 1st ed. Fine in VG dj. *Perier.* $225/£145

SULLIVAN, MAURICE S. Jedediah Smith. NY: Press of Pioneers, 1936. 1st ed. VG- in VG- dj. *Parker.* $195/£126

SULLIVAN, MAY KELLOGG. A Woman Who Went to Alaska. Boston: James Earle, (1903). 28 plts. Pict cl, mtd illus (2pp torn, crudely repaired). *Schoyer.* $45/£29

SULLIVAN, MICHAEL. The Meeting of Eastern and Western Art. Univ of CA Press, 1989. 24 color plts. Dj. *Edwards.* $34/£22

SULLIVAN, W.J.L. Twelve Years in the Saddle for Law and Order on the Frontiers of Texas. NY: Buffalo Head, 1966. Facs rpt of 1909 orig ed. One of 500. Howes S 1129. *Ginsberg.* $50/£32

SUMMERHAYES, MARTHA. Vanished Arizona. Chicago, (1939). Lakeside Classic. Spine type rubbed. *Schoyer.* $25/£16

SUMMERHAYES, MARTHA. Vanished Arizona: Recollections of My Army Life. Phila: Lippincott, 1908. 1st ed. Dec cl. Howes S 1132. *Ginsberg.* $125/£81

SUMMERHAYES, V.S. Wild Orchids of Britain. London, 1951. 1st ed. Cl (lt discolored) in dj (sl rubbed). *Edwards.* $74/£48

SUMMERS, FESTUS PAUL. The Baltimore and Ohio in the Civil War. NY: Putnam's, (1939). 1st ed. 16 plts, 8 maps. NF. *Mcgowan.* $150/£97

SUMMERS, FESTUS PAUL. The Baltimore and Ohio in the Civil War. NY: G.P. Putnam's Sons, (1939). 1st ed. Inscribed on dj. 16 plts; 8 maps. Fine in NF dj. *Mcgowan.* $250/£161

SUMMERS, MONTAGUE (ed). Covent Garden Drollery. London: Fortune Press, 1927. Ltd to 575 numbered on hand-made paper. Brn buckram-backed paper bds. Fine (bkpl). *Dalian.* $101/£65

SUMMERS, MONTAGUE. A Gothic Bibliography. London, n.d. 1/750, this unnumbered. 21 plts. Uncut, unopened. (Backstrip gnawed.) *Argosy.* $85/£55

SUMMERS, MONTAGUE. The Gothic Quest. London: Fortune Press, (1938). 1st Eng ed. 16 plts. Red cl. Sl mkd, sl dusty, eps sl tanned, o/w VG. *Dalian.* $116/£75

SUMMERS, MONTAGUE. The Vampire in Europe. Dutton, 1929. 1st US ed. VG. *Madle.* $50/£32

SUMMERS, MONTAGUE. The Werewolf. London, 1933. 8 plts. (Lt mainly marginal spotting; cl lt soiled, sl rubbed.) *Edwards.* $54/£35

SUMMERS-SMITH, D. The House Sparrow. London, 1963. 1st ptg. Color frontis, 32 photo plts. Cl (name). Dj (sm tears). *Sutton.* $90/£58

SUMMERSELL, CHARLES GRAYSON. CSS Alabama, Builder, Captain, and Plans. Univ of AL, (1985). 1st ed. Blueprints in ep pouch. Fine in Fine dj. *Pratt.* $50/£32

SUMNER, THOMAS H. A New and Accurate Method of Finding a Ship's Position at Sea.... Boston: Thomas Groom, 1851. 3rd ed, rev. 90,(2 ads)pp; 9 plts on 6 sheets. VG (contemp label; bkpl). *Lefkowicz.* $175/£113

SUMPTER, JESSE. Paso Del Aquila: A Chronicle of Frontier Days on the Texas Border.... Ben E. Pingenot (ed). (Austin): Encino Press, (1969). 1st ed. One of 1100. Dec bds. Fine. *Harrington.* $70/£45

SUNDER, JOHN E. Joshua Pilcher—Fur Trader and Indian Agent. Norman: Univ of OK, (1968). 1st ed. Ink name, else Fine in VG dj. *Perier.* $45/£29

SUNDKLER, BENGT G.M. Bantu Prophets in South Africa. OUP, 1961. 18 plts. VG (spine faded). *Hollett.* $31/£20

Supplement No. 1 Colorado Brand Book of 1928. May 15, 1928 to May 15, 1931. Silverfishing eps, else Very Nice. *Perier.* $60/£39

SURTEES, R.S. Handley Cross or Mr. Jorrock's Hunt. London: Edward Arnold, (ca 1920). 2 vols. 24 full-pg color plts by Cecil Aldin. (Spines faded; vol 1 starting.) *Argosy.* $150/£97

SURTEES, VIRGINIA (ed). Reflections of a Friendship; John Ruskin's Letters to Pauline Trevelyan 1848-1866. London: Allen & Unwin, 1979. 4pp creased lower margin, o/w VF in Mint dj. *Europa.* $23/£15

Sussex. A&C Black, 1913. Rpt. Wilfrid Ball (illus). 75 color plts, fldg map. Dec cl (spine sl rubbed). *Edwards.* $70/£45

SUSUNI, GIANCARLO. The Roman Stonecutter. Oxford: Basil Blackwell, (1973). 6 plts. (Ink stamp, label tp.) *Archaeologia.* $45/£29

SUTCLIFFE, A.J. On the Track of Ice Age Mammals. Cambridge: Harvard, 1985. 1st ed. Fine. *Mikesh.* $25/£16

SUTCLIFFE, G. LISTER. The Modern Carpenter, Joiner, and Cabinet-Maker. London: Gresham, 1902-1904. 1st eds. Very Nice set (sl rubbed). *Bookpress.* $750/£484

SUTCLIFFE, HALLIWELL. By Moor and Fell. London: T. Fisher Unwin, 1899. 1st ed. vi,360pp. VG. *Hollett.* $39/£25

SUTCLIFFE, HALLIWELL. The Striding Dales. London: Warne, 1929. 1st ed. 12 color plts. VG. *Hollett.* $47/£30

SUTHERLAND, CAPTAIN. A Tour up the Straits, from Gibraltar to Constantinople. London: Ptd for Author, 1790. 2nd ed. xlvii,372pp (lt water-staining tp, subsequent few pgs). Orig calf (lacks label). *Bickersteth.* $74/£48

SUTHERLAND, G.A. The Heart in Early Life. London, 1914. 1st ed. Good. *Fye.* $100/£65

SUTHERLAND, GEORGE. A Manual of the Geography and Natural and Civil History of Prince Edward Island. Charlottetown: John Ross, 1861. 1st ed. v,(i) contents, 5-164. (Browning.) Purple cl, paper label. Good (faded, head, tail of spine sl rubbed). *Morrell.* $341/£220

SUTHERLAND, J. The Adventures of an Elephant Hunter. London, 1912. 1st ed. Nice in gilt pict cl, raised pub's presentation blindstamp on title. *Trophy Room.* $575/£371

SUTHERLAND, ROBERT Q. and R.L. WILSON. The Book of Colt Firearms. Kansas City, MO: By the author, (1971). 1st ed. Signed, inscribed. Lg 4to. 39 full-pg color plts. Gray cl, gilt. Fine (bkpl) in Fine dj. *Glenn.* $600/£387

SUTHERLAND, ROBERT Q. and R.L. WILSON. The Book of Colt Firearms. Kansas City: Sutherland, 1971. 1st ed. 1258 b/w photos, dwgs. Fine+ in dj. *Bowman.* $450/£290

SUTHERLAND, W. and W.G. The Sign Writer and Glass Embosser. Manchester: Decorative Art Journals, 1898. Title, 62pp, 32 colored litho plts, numerous text illus, photographs (part loose). Dec brown cl folder (rubbed). *Marlborough.* $744/£480

SUTHREN, VICTOR. The Black Cockade. Toronto: Collins, 1977. 1st ed. 1st bk. Signed. Fine in dj (lt edgewear). *Else Fine.* $95/£61

SUTTON, DENYS et al. Woburn Abbey and Its Collections. London, 1965. Orig cream bds, gilt motif. VF. *Europa.* $22/£14

SUTTON, DENYS. French Drawings of the Eighteenth Century. London, 1949. 65 plts, 2 color. Good. *Washton.* $25/£16

SUTTON, DENYS. Nocturne: The Art of James McNeill Whistler. London: Country Life, 1963. Frontis. Blue cl over bds; gilt titles. Fine (edges faded). *Heller.* $70/£45

SUTTON, ERIC (trans). The Opportunities of a Night. (By M. de Crebillon). London: Chapman & Hall, 1925. Ltd to 1000. Teg. Cl-backed dec bds. Dj (spine dknd; worn). *Sadlon.* $25/£16

SUTTON, THOMAS. The Daniells, Artists and Travellers. London: Bodley Head, (1954). 1st ed. 31 plts (7 color); 3 maps. Blue gilt cl. Good in dj. *Karmiole.* $50/£32

SUZOR, RENAUD. Hydrophobia. An Account of M. Pasteur's System.... London, 1887. 1st ed. 231pp. (Ex-lib.) *Fye.* $150/£97

SVERDRUP, OTTO. New Land. London: Longmans, Green, 1904. 2 vols. 2 fldg maps in pocket. Silver dec cl. Minor pull at head of spine vol 1, else VG. *High Latitude.* $400/£258

SVERDRUP, OTTO. Sverdrup's Arctic Adventures. London: Longman, (1959). VG in VG dj. *Blue Dragon.* $25/£16

SWAAN, WIM. Art and Architecture of the Late Middle Ages. London, 1988. 3rd ed. Good. *Washton.* $50/£32

SWAAN, WIM. The Gothic Cathedral. NY, 1969. Good. *Washton.* $85/£55

Swallow Barn. (By John Pendleton Kennedy). Phila: Carey & Lea, 1832. 1st ed. 2 vols. (ii),x,312; iv,320pp. Pub's 1/4 cl (professionally respined using orig spines as overlays). (Foxing.) *Bookpress.* $675/£435

SWAN, JOHN. A Trip to the Gold Mines of California in 1848. John Hussey (ed). Book Club of CA, 1960. 1st ed. Ltd to 400 ptd. Port plt. Leatherette, marbled bd, gilt. VG. *Oregon.* $75/£48

SWAN, JOSEPH R. A Manual for Executors and Administrators.... Columbus: Isaac N. Whitting et al, 1843. 1st ed. 332pp. Leather. (Lacks fep, rep, else solid.) *Hayman.* $40/£26

SWANBERG, WILLIAM ANDREW. First Blood. (London, 1960). 1st British ed. Fine in NF. *Mcgowan.* $35/£23

SWANBERG, WILLIAM ANDREW. First Blood. The Story of Fort Sumter. NY: Scribner's, (1957). Book Club ed. Red cl. VG in dj (spine faded). *Chapel Hill.* $40/£26

SWANBERG, WILLIAM ANDREW. Sickles the Incredible. NY, 1956. 1st ed. Lt chipped, o/w VG in dj. *Pratt.* $50/£32

SWANBERG, WILLIAM ANDREW. Sickles the Incredible. NY, 1956. 2nd ptg. Fine. *Pratt.* $37/£24

SWANN, H.K. A Dictionary of English and Folk Names of British Birds. London, 1913. Orig ptd w/8 blank leaves at end for notes. (Sl used.) *Wheldon & Wesley.* $54/£35

SWANN, T.B. Driftwood. Vantage, 1952. 1st ed, 1st bk. Foxing eps, else Fine in VG + dj. *Aronovitz.* $85/£55

SWANN, THOMAS BURNETT. Queens Walk in the Dusk. Forest Park: Heritage, 1977. 1st ed. One of 2000 numbered. 11 tipped-in plts. VF in dj. *Else Fine.* $65/£42

SWANSON, E.B. A Century of Oil and Gas in Books: A Descriptive Bibliography. NY: Appleton, (1960). 1st ed. *Ginsberg.* $75/£48

SWANTON, JOHN R. BAE Bulletin 145. The Indian Tribes of North America. Washington D.C.: GPO, 1952. VG. *Perier.* $60/£39

SWANTON, JOHN R. BAE Bulletin 43. Indian Tribes of the Mississippi Valley and Adjacent Coast of the Gulf of Mexico. Washington: GPO, 1911. 1st ed. Fldg map (name; hinges loose; rubbed). *King.* $45/£29

SWARBRICK, JOHN. Robert Adam and His Brothers: Their Lives, Work and Influence on English Architecture, Decoration and Furniture. London, 1915. VG. *Argosy.* $150/£97

SWARZENSKI, HANNS. Monuments of Romanesque Art. London: Faber & Faber, 1967. 2nd ed. 238 b/w plts. (Ex-lib w/ink stamp, tape mks.) Dj (sl ragged). *Edwards.* $74/£48

SWAYNE, MARTIN. The Blue Germ. Doran, 1918. 1st ed. VG. *Madle.* $30/£19

SWAYSLAND, W. Familiar Wild Birds. London: Cassell, 1883. 1st ed. 4 vols. viii,160; viii,160; viii,160; viii,176pp; 160 Fine chromolitho plts. Contemp 1/2 crimson calf, dbl morocco labels (lacks 2 of 8). Sound (spotting; rubbed). *Cox.* $132/£85

SWEDENBORG, EMANUEL. Swedenborg's Works. London: Houghton Mifflin, (ca 1930). Rotch Edition. 32 vols. Teg. Blue cl, gilt. Good. *Karmiole.* $500/£323

SWEDIAUR, FRANCOIS. Practical Observations on Venereal Complaints. NY: Samuel Campbell, 1788. 1st Amer ed. 8vo.(iv),128pp. Contemp sheep (lt worn). (Paper browned.) *Bookpress.* $650/£419

SWEENEY, JAMES JOHNSON (ed). Three Young Rats and Other Rhymes. NY: Curt Valentin, 1944. 1st ed. Ltd to 700. 12 1/4 x 9 1/2. 130pp, 85 dwgs by Alexander Calder. Cl-backed pict yellow paper bds (sl dust soiling; sl bumped). *Shasky.* $175/£113

SWEENEY, JAMES JOHNSON (ed). Three Young Rats and Other Rhymes. NY: MOMA, 1946. 2nd ed. Alexander Calder (illus). VG. *Argosy.* $65/£42

SWEENEY, JAMES JOHNSON. Soulages. London: Phaidon, 1972. 117 color plts, 13 b/w plts. (Ex-lib w/ink stamp, label.) Dj. *Edwards.* $70/£45

SWEET, ALEXANDER E. and J. ARMOY KNOX. On a Mexican Mustang, through Texas.... London: C&W, 1905. New ed. Largely unopened. Pict cl. VG. *Schoyer.* $85/£55

SWEET, ALEXANDER E. and J. ARMOY KNOX. On a Mexican Mustang. London: C&W, 1884. 1st Eng ed. 672pp. Dec red cl. Fine. *Lambeth.* $85/£55

SWEETER, WILLIAM. Treatise on Consumption, Embracing an Inquiry into the Influence Exerted Upon It by Journeys, Voyages, and Changes of Climate.... Boston, 1836. VG. *Argosy.* $85/£55

SWENSON, OLAF. West of the World. NY: Dodd Mead, 1944. 2nd ptg. VG. *Artis.* $20/£13

SWIFT, DEAN. Gulliver's Travels. London, n.d. (1865) 352pp. Blind-dec, gilt; beveled bds. Good + (faded, wear; bkpl). *Willow House.* $23/£15

SWIFT, EMERSON H. Roman Sources of Christian Art. CUP, 1951. 1st ed. Frontis, 48 plts. Dj (spine yellowed). *Edwards.* $85/£55

SWIFT, GRAHAM. Ever After. London: Picador, 1992. 1st UK ed. Signed. Fine in dj. *Lewton.* $26/£17

SWIFT, GRAHAM. Out of This World. London: Viking, 1988. 1st UK ed. Fine in dj. *Lewton.* $19/£12

SWIFT, GRAHAM. Shuttlecock. London: Lane, 1981. 1st ed. Fine in dj. *Rees.* $186/£120

SWIFT, GRAHAM. Shuttlecock. London: Lane, 1981. 1st ed. Signed. Fine in dj. *Rees.* $209/£135

SWIFT, GRAHAM. The Sweet Shop Owner. London: Lane, 1980. 1st ed. Fine in dj. *Rees.* $194/£125

SWIFT, GRAHAM. The Sweet Shop Owner. London: Lane, 1980. 1st ed. Signed. Fine in dj. *Rees.* $209/£135

SWIFT, GRAHAM. Waterland. NY: Poseidon, 1983. 1st ed. Sl mk, o/w Fine in Fine dj. *Beasley.* $35/£23

SWIFT, GRAHAM. Waterland. Heinemann, 1983. 1st UK ed. VG in dj. *Lewton.* $62/£40

SWIFT, JOHN FRANKLIN. Robert Greathouse. An American Novel. NY: Carleton, 1870. 1st ed. 573pp. (Extrems torn, frayed; early bkseller label.) *Reese.* $65/£42

SWIFT, JONATHAN. Directions to Servants. Golden Cockerell Press, 1925. Ltd to 380. Vellum-backed marbled bds (corners sl rubbed). *Sadlon.* $175/£113

SWIFT, JONATHAN. Gulliver's Travels. NY: Crown, (1947). 24 orig engrs. Fine in NF dj. *Reese.* $45/£29

SWIFT, JONATHAN. Gulliver's Travels. London, 1909. 1/750 numbered, signed by Arthur Rackham (illus), w/extra color plt not in trade ed. 13 full mtd color plts; 2 full-pg b/w illus. Spine darkened; joints worn; ties missing. *Argosy.* $600/£387

SWIFT, JONATHAN. Gulliver's Travels. London/NY: Dent/Dutton, 1909. 1st ed w/12 mtd illus by Arthur Rackham. Ltd to 750 lg paper copies, signed by Rackham. Uncut. VG (lt soiling spine, rear cvrs, eps); linen ties. *Second Life.* $800/£516

SWIFT, JONATHAN. Gulliver's Travels. London, 1909. New ed. Arthur Rackham (color illus). Pict cvrs, gilt. NF (spine extrems, corners sl rubbed; sm tear side spine rear cvr). *Polyanthos.* $75/£48

SWIFT, JONATHAN. Gulliver's Travels. NY, 1913. 1st Amer ed. Louis Rhead (illus). NF (spine sunned). *Polyanthos.* $50/£32

SWIFT, JONATHAN. Selected Essays. Berkshire: Golden Cockerel, 1925. Ltd to 450. Parchment-backed bds (rubbed, dusty). VG. *Cahan.* $150/£97

SWIFT, JONATHAN. Selected Essays. Volume One. London: Golden Cockerel Press, 1925. #392/450. Uncut. Parchment-backed grn bds. Good (bkpl, pencil note). *Cox.* $194/£125

SWIFT, JONATHAN. A Tale of a Tub. Thomas Tegg, 1811. Frontis; 6 plts. 19th cent 1/2 calf; marbled sides. *Hill.* $62/£40

SWIFT, JONATHAN. Travels into Several Remote Nations of the World. London: Golden Cockerel, 1925. Ltd to 480. 2 vols. Sm 4to. 40 woodcuts; uncut. 3/4 cream buckram, gilt; black paper sides (surface damaged). *Hollett.* $1,008/£650

SWIFT, JONATHAN. Travels into Several Remote Nations of the World. In Four Parts. London: Charles Bathurst, 1742. 4th ed. Tp, (xii),351pp + 1pg ad, 6 engr plts. Contemp sprinkled calf (rebacked). *Marlborough.* $194/£125

SWIFT, JONATHAN. The Works. London: Henry G. Bohn, 1850. 2 vols. Thick lg 8vo. lxxxiv,844; iv,854pp; engr port (sl spotted); fldg facs. Half buckram (spines lt faded), gilt. *Hollett.* $132/£85

SWIGGETT, HOWARD. War out of Niagara. NY: Columbia Univ Press, 1933. 1st ed. Frontis. Blue cl. Fine in dj (spine sl dknd). *Chapel Hill.* $100/£65

Swim for Life; the True Story of One of the Author's Experiences. (By Herbert Myrick.) NY: OJ, 1904. #783/1000. Grn cl, gilt stamped cvr (age spotted, sl soiled). *Bohling.* $150/£97

SWINBURNE, ALGERNON CHARLES. Atalanta in Calydon. London: Medici Soc, 1923. #759/1025. Teg, others uncut. Holland-backed dec bds. Fine. *Cox.* $28/£18

SWINBURNE, ALGERNON CHARLES. Atalanta in Calydon. London: Medici Soc, 1923. Ltd ed to 1037. Uncut. Cl-backed dec bds, gilt. Dj (extrems sl chipped). *Hollett.* $54/£35

SWINBURNE, ALGERNON CHARLES. Ballads of the English Border. William A. MacInnes (ed). London: Heinemann, 1925. 1st ed. (Sl cockled.) *Hollett.* $47/£30

SWINBURNE, ALGERNON CHARLES. The Duke of Gandia. London: C&W, 1908. 1st Eng ed. Blue buckram. Eps sl browned, o/w VG. *Dalian.* $31/£20

SWINBURNE, ALGERNON CHARLES. Hide and Seek. London: Stourton Press, 1975. #120/250. Gilt-edged 1/2 calf. *Edwards.* $43/£28

SWINBURNE, ALGERNON CHARLES. Posthumous Poems. Edmund Gosse, C.B. and Thomas James Wise (eds). William Heinemann, 1917. *Bickersteth.* $39/£25

SWINBURNE, ALGERNON CHARLES. Rosamund. London: C&W, 1899. 1st Eng ed. Brn buckram. Spine dknd, eps sl browned, o/w VG. *Dalian.* $31/£20

SWINBURNE, ALGERNON CHARLES. The Sisters. London: C&W, 1892. 1st Eng ed. Blue cl, gilt. Eps sl browned, o/w VG. *Dalian.* $39/£25

SWINBURNE, ALGERNON CHARLES. A Song of Italy. London: John Camden Hotten, 1867. 1st ed. Fine in cl folder; 1/2 morocco slipcase. *Sadlon.* $65/£42

SWINBURNE, ALGERNON CHARLES. The Springtide of Life. London: Heinemann, (1918). 1st ed. Arthur Rackham (illus). Gilt-pict cl (sl rubbed). *Sadlon.* $150/£97

SWINBURNE, ALGERNON CHARLES. Swinburne's 'Hyperion' and Other Poems. London: Faber & Gwyer, 1927. 1st Eng ed. Brn cl. Spine sunned, o/w VG. *Dalian.* $23/£15

SWINBURNE, CHARLES ALFRED. Life and Work of J.M.W. Turner, R.A. London, 1902. Engr frontis. Teg, rest uncut. (Tp lt spotted; marginal pencil notes; feps browned; worn.) *Edwards.* $70/£45

SWINBURNE, JOHN. A Typical American. Albany, 1888. Port. VG. *Argosy.* $35/£23

SWINDLER, MARY HAMILTON. Ancient Painting...to the Period of Christian Art. London, 1929. Color frontis, 16 plts. (Lt soiled, lower bds damp-stained.) *Edwards.* $74/£48

SWINNERTON, FRANK. English Maiden. London: Hutchinson, (1945). 1st Eng ed. Black cl. Fine in dj. *Dalian.* $39/£25

SWINNERTON, FRANK. Tokefield Papers. London: Martin Secker, 1927. 1st Eng ed. Grn cl. Fore-edge sl foxed, o/w NF in dj (tanned). *Dalian.* $39/£25

SWINNERTON, FRANK. A Woman in Sunshine. London: Hutchinson, (1945). 1st Eng ed. Black cl. Fine in dj. *Dalian.* $39/£25

SWINNERTON, H.H. Fossils, the New Naturalist. London: Collins, 1960. 1st ed. 1 color plt, 133 photos. Dj. *Petersfield.* $47/£30

SWINTON, WILLIAM. Campaigns of the Army of the Potomac. A Critical History of Operations...1861-1865. NY: Scribner's Sons, 1882. Rev ed. Frontis (damping upper corner);660,8pp. Orig cl. VG (sl rubbed). *Mcgowan.* $45/£29

SWINTON, WILLIAM. The Twelve Decisive Battles of the War. NY: Dick & Fitzgerald, (1867). 1st ed. 7 engr ports; 7 maps. Gilt/blindstamped brn cl, beveled edges. Fine. *Houle.* $225/£145

SWISHER, JOHN M. The Swisher Memoirs. Rena Maverick Green (ed). San Antonio: Sigmund, 1932. 1st ed. Signed by Green. Wraps. *Lambeth.* $75/£48

SYDENHAM, THOMAS. The Entire Works etc. J. Swan (ed). London: F. Newberry, 1769. 5th ed. x,xxviii,666,(20)pp. Contemp full speckled calf; new eps. Upper joints cracked; lt waterstaining; partly removed inscrip; crayon underlining in text, o/w Crisp. *White.* $147/£95

SYDENHAM, THOMAS. The Works of Thomas Sydenham. R.G. Latham (ed). London: Sydenham Soc, 1848. 2 vols. 276; 359pp. (Rebacked, spines laid down.) *Whitehart.* $217/£140

SYDNEY, COCKERELL. Old Testament Miniatures. NY, n.d. (ca 1975). VG in dj. *Washton.* $100/£65

SYERS, EDGAR WOOD. The Poetry of Skating. London: Watts, 1905. Teg. (Lt stamp; 2 blind stamps; fr joint tender.) *Hollett.* $70/£45

SYKES, CHRISTOPHER. Stranger Wonders. London: Longmans, 1937. 1st Eng ed. Brn cl. Fine (name) in dj (sl tanned, dusty). *Dalian.* $70/£45

SYKES, CHRISTOPHER. Wassmuss. London: Longmans Green, 1936. 1st Eng ed. 12 photos. Brn linen. Sl spotted, o/w NF. *Dalian.* $70/£45

SYKES, GODFREY. Westerly Trend.... Tucson: AZ Pioneers Hist Soc, 1944. One of 2000 ptd at Lakeside Press. VG + in dj. *Bohling.* $60/£39

SYLVESTER, HERBERT MILTON. Indian Wars of New England. Boston: W.B. Clarke, 1910. 3 vols. Unopened, untrimmed; gilt tops. Orig cl, ptd spine labels (dknd, rubbed). Overall Nice (soil; bkpls). Howes S 1186. *Bohling.* $350/£226

SYMONDS, J. The Magic of Aleister Crowley. London: Frederick Muller, (1958). 1st ed. Frontis; 8 plts. VG in VG dj. *Blue Dragon.* $125/£81

SYMONDS, JOHN ADDINGTON. Giovanni Boccaccio as Man and Author. NY: Scribner's, 1895. VG. *Hermitage.* $85/£55

SYMONDS, JOHN ADDINGTON. The Letters of John Addington Symonds. Detroit, 1967-69. 1st ed. 3 vols. Fine set in VG glossy djs (lt rubbed). *Mcclintock.* $45/£29

SYMONDS, JOHN ADDINGTON. Our Life in the Swiss Highlands. A&C Black, 1907. 2nd ed. 20 color plts, fldg map. Teg. (Feps foxed, dampstained; inscrip; upper bd sl warped; spine chipped; sl rubbed.) *Edwards.* $39/£25

SYMONDS, JOHN ADDINGTON. Shelley. London: Macmillan, 1878. 1st Eng ed. Limp red cl. Sl rubbed, o/w VG. *Dalian.* $54/£35

SYMONDS, JOHN ADDINGTON. Walt Whitman. A Study. London: John C. Nimmo, 1893. 1st ed, trade issue. Frontis port, 4 plts. Grn cl stamped in gold. Fine. *Godot.* $185/£119

SYMONDS, JOHN ALDINGTON. Walt Whitman. London: John C. Nimmo, 1893. #93/208, lg paper ed. xxxv,160pp, 5 plts. Untrimmed. (Some spotting.) *Schoyer.* $85/£55

SYMONDS, MARGARET. Days Spent on a Doge's Farm. London: T. Fisher Unwin, 1893. 1st ed. Frontis. Gilt pict cl. VG (lt rubbing). *Reese.* $45/£29

SYMONDS, R.W. Masterpieces of English Furniture and Clocks. London: Batsford, 1940. 1st ed. One of 1250. 8 color plts. (Spine sl faded; ex-libris.) *Edwards.* $116/£75

SYMONDS, R.W. The Present State of Old English Furniture. NY: Frederick Stokes, n.d. (c. 1920). Gilt-, blind-dec maroon cl. NF (sl wear). *House.* $90/£58

SYMONDS, R.W. and B.B. WHINERAY. Victorian Furniture. London: Country Life, (1962). 1st ed. Color frontis. Blue cl. Fine. *House.* $55/£35

SYMONDS, R.W. and B.B. WHINERAY. Victorian Furniture. London, 1987. 20 color plts. VG in dj. *Argosy.* $50/£32

SYMONGTON, J. in a Bengal Jungle. Chapel Hill: Univ of NC, (Mar 1935). 2nd ptg. NF in VG dj. *Mikesh.* $37/£24

SYMONS, A.J.A. Ermin. Governor of Equatoria. London: Falcon Press, 1950. 1st Eng ed. Pict bds. Fine. *Dalian.* $31/£20

SYMONS, A.J.A. The Quest for Corvo. NY, 1934. 1st Amer ed. Fine in dj (2 sm tears; age-dknd; price-clipped). *Mcclintock.* $65/£42

SYMONS, A.J.A. The Quest for Corvo. London, 1934. 1st Amer ed. Fine (sl rubbed) in VG dj (spine sunned; rubbed, chipped, creased). *Polyanthos.* $75/£48

SYMONS, A.J.A. The Quest for Corvo. Cassell, 1934. 1st ed. Contents VG (sl dull). *Whiteson.* $28/£18

SYMONS, A.J.A. The Quest for Corvo. London, 1934. 1st ed. Fine (edges sl rubbed) in VG dj. *Polyanthos.* $75/£48

SYMONS, A.J.A. et al. The Nonesuch Century: An Appraisal, a Personal Note and a Bibliography.... London: Nonesuch, 1936. One of 750. Grn buckram, gilt leather spine label. VG (top edge sl spotted, spine faded). *Heller.* $750/£484

SYMONS, ARTHUR. Confessions—A Study in Pathology. London: Cape, 1930. 1st UK ed. Marbled paper cvrd bds. VG + . *Williams.* $31/£20

SYMONS, ARTHUR. Love's Cruelty. London: Martin Secker, 1923. 1st Eng ed. Blue cl. Sl mkd, rubbed; eps foxed, o/w VG. *Dalian.* $54/£35

SYMONS, JULIAN. A.J.A. Symons. His Life and Speculations. London: Eyre & Spottiswoode, 1950. 1st Eng ed. Red cl. VG in dj (sl nicked). *Dalian.* $39/£25

SYMONS, JULIAN. The Blackheath Poisonings. London: Collins, 1978. 1st ed. VF in dj. *Silver Door.* $30/£19

SYMONS, JULIAN. The Blackheath Poisonings. London: Collins, 1978. 1st ed. Fine in Fine dj. *Janus.* $35/£23

SYMONS, JULIAN. The Detective Story in Britain. Essex: Longmans, 1969. 1st rev ed, pb orig. NF (name). *Janus.* $25/£16

SYMONS, JULIAN. The Immaterial Murder Case. Gollancz, 1945. 1st UK ed. VG in VG dj (sl fading; spine wear; 3 tears). *Martin.* $85/£55

SYMONS, JULIAN. The Modern Crime Story. Edinburgh: Tragara Press, 1980. 1st ed. #30/125. Fine in stiff wraps. *Murder.* $100/£65

SYMONS, JULIAN. The Players and the Game. NY: Harper, 1972. 1st US ed. Fine in dj (lt sunned spine). *Janus.* $20/£13

SYMONS, JULIAN. The Progress of a Crime. NY: Harper, 1960. 1st US ed. VG + in dj (rubbed). *Janus.* $15/£10

SYMONS, JULIAN. A Reflection on Auden. London: Poem-of-the-Month Club, (1973). 1st ed. Signed. Fine. *Polyanthos.* $25/£16

SYMONS, JULIAN. Sweet Adelaide. London: Collins, 1980. 1st ed. Fine in NF dj. *Janus.* $25/£16

SYMONS, JULIAN. A Three-Pipe Problem. Collins, 1975. 1st ed. Fine in dj (price-clipped). *Stahr.* $45/£29

SYMONS, JULIAN. A Three-Pipe Problem. London: Collins, 1975. 1st ed. Fine in NF dj (price-clipped; short closed tears). *Janus.* $65/£42

SYMONS-JEUNE, B.H.B. Natural Rock Gardening. London, 1936. 2nd ed. 32 plts. (Ends sl foxed.) *Henly.* $25/£16

SYNGE, J.M. The Aran Islands. London: Maunsel, 1911. (Frontis, eps sl foxed.) *Petersfield.* $25/£16

SYNGE, J.M. The Playboy of the Western World. Barre: Imprint Society, 1970. #107/1950 numbered, signed by ed and Lewis le Brocquy (illus). Bkpl, else Fine in pub's slipcase. *Hermitage.* $85/£55

SYNGE, J.M. The Shadow of the Glen; Riders to the Sea. London: Elkin Mathews, 1905. 1st ed. Nice in wrappers (sl used). *Pharos.* $200/£129

SYNGE, J.M. The Works of John M. Synge. Boston, 1912. 1st Amer ed. 4 vols. Frontis ports. Uncut, teg. Fine (spines sl sunned, bkpls). *Polyanthos.* $175/£113

SYNGE, J.M. The Works of John M. Synge. Boston: Luce, 1912. 1st ed. 2 vols. Orig buckram, leather spine labels. Spines sl soiled, else Nice set. *Pharos.* $35/£23

SYNGE, P.M. Mountains of the Moon. London: Lindsay Drummond, 1937. 2 plts tipped in, 91 collotype plts, 2 maps. (Backstrip faded, sl stained.) *Petersfield.* $54/£35

SYRKIN, MARIE. Blessed Is the Match...Jewish Resistance in Europe. Gollancz, 1948. Nice in dj (sl worn, chipped). *Patterson.* $62/£40

SZARKOWSKI, JOHN. The Face of Minnesota. Minneapolis: Univ of MN, 1958. 1st ed. 24 full color photos. Illus cl. Lt foxing, else VG in dj (chipped). *Cahan.* $50/£32

T

TABB, JOHN B. Later Lyrics. NY/London: John Lane, 1902. 1st ed. Blue cl, gold-stamped. Bkpl, else Fine. *Pharos.* $35/£23

TADEMA, LAWRENCE ALMA. The Courting of Mary Smith. London: Hurst & Blackett, 1886. 1st ed. 3 vols. Binders' brn buckram, leather labels (tps spotted). *Petersfield.* $78/£50

TADEMA, LAWRENCE ALMA. The Keeper of the Keys. London: Hurst & Blackett, 1890. 1st ed. 3 vols. Orig cl. VG. *Petersfield.* $116/£75

TAFT, L.R. Greenhouse Construction. NY: OJ, 1907. Grn cl, gilt stamped spine. VG (ends rubbed; end leaves soiled). *Bohling.* $45/£29

TAFT, L.R. Greenhouse Management. NY: OJ, 1907. Grn cl, gilt title. Good (washed out spot; corner frayed). *Bohling.* $35/£23

TAFT, MARCUS LORENZO. Strange Siberia. NY/Cincinnati: (1911). Grn cl stamped in gilt/silver (stained; sl foxed). *Schoyer.* $35/£23

TAFT, ROBERT. Artists and Illustrators of the Old West 1850-1900. NY: Scribner's, (1953). Brn cl. Sm scrape back cvr dj, o/w Fine. *House.* $40/£26

TAFT, ROBERT. Artists and Illustrators of the Old West 1850-1900. NY, (1953). 1st ed. Dj (frayed, torn). *Heinoldt.* $35/£23

TAGGARD, GENEVIEVE (ed). Circumference. NY: Covice Friede, 1929. 1st Amer ed. #593/1000 for subscribers only (of 1050), signed. Uncut. Fine (vellum spine sl foxed; sm area heel of spine mended). *Polyanthos.* $45/£29

TAGGARD, GENEVIEVE. Words for the Chisel. NY: Knopf, 1926. 1st ed. Fine in NF dj (sunned spine; sm chip rear panel). *Beasley.* $85/£55

TAGORE, RABINDRANATH. Chitra: A Play in One Act. London: India Soc, 1913. One of 500. Cl sl mkd, dknd, o/w NF. *Poetry.* $23/£15

TAGORE, RABINDRANATH. The Crescent Moon. NY: Macmillan, 1913. 1st ed. VG (sm ink name stamp fep) in dj (edge chipped). *Antic Hay.* $45/£29

TAGORE, RABINDRANATH. The Crescent Moon.... London: Macmillan, 1920. xii,82,(2)pp, 8 color plts. Blue cl. Good. *Cox.* $12/£8

TAGORE, RABINDRANATH. Red Oleanders: A Drama in One Act. Macmillan, 1925. 1st ed. NF (bkpl) in dj (sl dknd). *Poetry.* $19/£12

TAILFER, PAT et al. A True and Historical Narrative of the Colony of Georgia.... Charles Town: ptd by P. Timothy for the authors, (1741). (Washington: Peter Force, 1835). xiii,80pp (lt foxing). Recent cl-backed bds. Howes T 6. *Petrilla.* $75/£48

TAILLANDIER, YVON. Indelible Miro. NY: Tudor Pub, (1972). 1st ed. 2 orig lithos pulled by hand for this publication. Fine in NF dj, pub's slipcase. *Hermitage.* $200/£129

TAINE, JOHN. The Forbidden Garden. Fantasy Press, 1947. 1st ed. Fine in VG dj (wear, tear). *Aronovitz.* $40/£26

TAINE, JOHN. Green Fire. Dutton, 1928. 1st ed. VG-. *Madle.* $40/£26

TAINE, JOHN. The Iron Star. Dutton, 1930. 1st ed. VG. *Aronovitz.* $25/£16

TAINE, JOHN. Quayle's Invention. Dutton, 1927. 1st ed. Fine. *Madle.* $45/£29

TAINE, JOHN. The Time Stream. Hadley, 1947. 1st ed. Fine in VG dj. *Madle.* $35/£23

TAIT, LAWSON. Diseases of Women. NY, 1879. 2nd Amer ed. 192pp. Good. *Fye.* $75/£48

TAIT, LAWSON. Lectures on Ectopic Pregnancy and Pelvic Haematocele. Birmingham, 1888. 1st ed. 107pp. (Ex-lib; backstrip top chipped.) *Fye.* $150/£97

TAIT, LAWSON. The Pathology and Treatment of Diseases of the Ovaries. NY, 1883. 4th ed. 357pp. Good. *Fye.* $75/£48

TAIT, SAMUEL W., JR. The Wildcatters. Princeton: Princeton Univ, 1946. Rpt. Brn marbled bds (corners worn). VG- (bkpl). *Parker.* $37/£24

TALBOT, CHARLES W. (ed). Durer in America. London/NY, 1971. *Edwards.* $43/£28

TALBOT, EDITH ARMSTRONG. Samuel Chapman Armstrong. NY: Doubleday, Page, 1904. 1st ed. VG (ex libris). *Mcgowan.* $85/£55

TALBOT, ETHELBERT. My People of the Plains. NY: Harper, 1906. 1st ed. VG- (ink name). *Parker.* $50/£32

TALBOT, EUGENE. Interstitial Gingivitis or So-Called Pyorrhoea Alveolaris. Phila, 1899. 1st ed. 192pp; 73 photomicrographs. Good. *Fye.* $150/£97

TALBOT, P. AMAURY. In the Shadow of the Bush. NY, 1912. Color frontis; fldg map. Pict cvr label. Mint. *Argosy.* $125/£81

TALBOT, P. AMAURY. In the Shadow of the Bush. London, 1912. 1st ed. Color frontis, fldg inset, fldg map. Illus laid down upper bd. (Sl browning; bumped; rebacked, orig spine laid down; wear.) Edwards. $70/£45

TALBOT, THEODORE. The Journals of Theodore Talbot 1843 and 1849-52.... Portland, OR, 1931. 1st ed. Howes T 13. Ginsberg. $125/£81

TALBOT-KELLY, R.B. The Way of the Birds. London: Collins, 1937. 1st ed. (Spine sl worn, snagged.) Hollett. $217/£140

TALCOTT, DUDLEY VAILL. Report of the Company. NY: Random House, 1936. 2nd ptg. VG-. Blue Dragon. $30/£19

Tale of a Tub. (By Jonathan Swift.) London: John Nutt, 1710. 1st illus ed, lg paper copy. 8vo, (xxxii),344pp, 8 Fine engr plts (sl dampstain lower corners); untrimmed. Orig 1/4 sheep over marbled bds, hand-written paper spine label. Lovely. Marlborough. $814/£525

Tale of a Tub. (By Jonathan Swift). London: For John Nutt, 1710. 5th ed. (xxxii),344pp, 8 engr plts. Orig calf (joints cracked at top), spine gilt (most rubbed off; lacks label). Good. Bickersteth. $341/£220

Tale of a Tub. (By Jonathan Swift.) Ptd for John Nutt, 1710. 5th ed. Frontis; 7 plts. Contemp panelled calf, gilt back; sprinkled edges. Very Fair (sl wear). Hill. $388/£250

Tale of a Tub. (By Jonathan Swift.) London: John Nutt, 1710. 5th ed. Frontis, 344pp, 7 Fine full-pg engrs. Later 3/4 crushed morocco, brn cl, gilt titling. VG (sl worming top gutter). Hartfield. $495/£319

Tale of Peter Rabbit. Sandusky, OH: American Crayon, 1943. Sm folio. 6 full-pg color illus by Fern Bisel Peat. Rose-pink bds (top edge sl faded). Very Nice in color pict dj (marginal tears). Reisler. $85/£55

TALFOURD, THOMAS NOON (ed). Final Memorials of Charles Lamb. London: Edward Moxon, 1848. 1st ed. 2 vols. 1/2 titles; 8pp ads dated July 1, 1848 vol 1. Blind-dec cl (soiled; sl shaken); gilt-lettered spines (dulled; short tears vol II; shaken). Poetry. $42/£27

TALFOURD, THOMAS NOON (ed). The Letters of Charles Lamb, with a Sketch of His Life. London, 1837. 1st ed. 2 vols. Frontis ports. VG (sl rubbed, sunned). Polyanthos. $95/£61

TALLACK, WILLIAM. The California Overland Express. Hist Soc of CA, 1935. One of 150 ptd. 4pp fldg map, 2 plts (1 map). Illus cl, bds. Fine. Oregon. $190/£123

TALLANT, ROBERT. The Louisiana Purchase. NY: Random House, 1952. 1st trade ed. Warren Chappell (illus). Dec eps. Good in dj. Cattermole. $25/£16

TALLENT, ANNIE D. The Black Hills or The Last Hunting Ground of the Dakotahs. St. Louis: Nixon-Jones Ptg, 1899. 1st ed. 713pp. Good. Howes H 14. Perier. $175/£113

TALLENT, ROBERT. Voodoo in New Orleans. NY: Macmillan, 1946. 1st ed. Signed. Fine in dj (lt used). Beasley. $45/£29

TALLENTYRE, S.G. The Life of Voltaire. London, 1904. 2nd ed. 2 vols. Frontis port. Uncut. (Lt spotting.) Edwards. $43/£28

TAMARIN, ALFRED. Japan and the United States. (NY): Macmillan, (1970). 1st ed. Dj. Lefkowicz. $45/£29

TAN, AMY. The Joy Luck Club. NY: Putnam's, (1989). 1st Amer ed, 1st bk. VF in dj. Between The Covers. $300/£194

TAN, AMY. The Joy Luck Club. Putnam, 1989. 1st ed, 2nd ptg. Signed. Fine in dj. Fine Books. $75/£48

TAN, AMY. The Kitchen God's Wife. NY: Putnam's, 1991. 1st ed. Fine in Fine dj. Revere. $25/£16

TANGYE, H. LINCOLN. In the Torrid Sudan. London: John Murray, 1910. 1st ed. Fldg map, 32 plts. Blue cl, gilt, teg. Good (extrems rubbed, upper hinge cracking; pub's sm blind stamp on title). Morrell. $54/£35

TANKERSLEY, ALLEN P. John B. Gordon: A Study in Gallantry. Atlanta: Whitehall Press, 1955. 1st ed. Frontis port. Grey cl. NF in dj (lt browned). Chapel Hill. $100/£65

TANNAHILL, REAY. Food in History. NY: Stein & Day, 1973. 1st ed. Grn/red cl. NF. Connolly. $25/£16

TANNENBAUM, FRANK. Slave and Citizen: The Negro in the Americas. NY: Knopf, 1947. 1st ed. VG in dj (lt chipped). Petrilla. $35/£23

TANNER, HELEN HORNBECK. Zespedes in East Florida 1784-1790. (Coral Gables, FL): Univ of Miami Press, (1963). 1st ed. Inscribed. Red cl. NF (lt foxing) in VG dj (spine chipped). Chapel Hill. $50/£32

TANNER, HENRY, JR. English Interior Woodwork of the VI, VII, VIIIth Centuries. London: Batsford, 1902. 50 plts. Teg. (Margins sl thumbed; hinges reinforced; new eps; sl rubbed, sunned.) Edwards. $171/£110

TANNER, HENRY, JR. English Interior Woodwork of the XVI, XVII and XVIIIth Centuries. NY, (1903). 50 plts. 1/2 cl (badly worn). Argosy. $125/£81

TANNER, T.H. A Practical Treatise on the Diseases of Infancy and Childhood. Phila, 1866. 2nd Amer ed. 464pp. Good. Fye. $75/£48

TANNER, T.H. The Practice of Medicine. London, 1875. 7th ed. 2 vols. xviii,642; (v),675pp (edges dusty; spines worn; cl faded; joint cracked vol 1). Whitehart. $39/£25

TANNER, WILLIAM. The Book of Bond. Cape, 1965. 1st ed. VG in VG dj. Ming. $31/£20

TAPLIN, WILLIAM. The Gentleman's Stable Directory. Ptd for G. Kearsley, 1788. 6th ed, corrected, enlgd. Contemp sheep (backstrip chipped; sm loss of leather rear cvr; lacks feps; sm marginal loss on T2; sig). Waterfield. $132/£85

TAPLIN, WILLIAM. The Sporting Dictionary, and Rural Repository of General Information.... London, 1803. 1st ed. 2 vols. Old calf (worn). VG. Argosy. $250/£161

TAPPLY, H.G. Tackle Tinkering. NY, (1946). 2nd ptg. Fine in dj. Artis. $19/£12

TAPPLY, WILLIAM G. Death at Charity's Point. NY: Scribner's, 1984. 1st ed. VF in dj. Mordida. $150/£97

TAPPLY, WILLIAM G. Death at Charity's Point. Scribner's, 1984. 1st ed. Fine in dj (sm spots). Murder. $175/£113

TAPPLY, WILLIAM G. The Dutch Blue Error. Scribner's, 1984. 1st ed. Fine in dj. Murder. $250/£161

TARAVAL, SIGISMUNDO. The Indian Uprising in Lower California, 1734-1737. Marguerite Eyer Wilbur (trans). L.A.: Quivira Soc, 1931. One of 665. 9 plts. Bds (extrems lt worn), paper spine label. Dawson. $150/£97

TARBEAUX, FRANK. Autobiography of.... Donald Henderson Clarke (ed). NY, 1930. 1st ed. (Cvr worn; 2 sm rubber stamps ppiv, 3.) Heinoldt. $25/£16

TARBELL, IDA M. The History of the Standard Oil Company. NY: McClure, 1904. 1st ptg. 2 vols. (Scribbling on 2 leaves; lt spotting spine.) Howes T 33. Schoyer. $150/£97

TARDE, GABRIEL. Penal Philosophy. Boston: Little, Brown, 1912. 1st ed in Eng. Crimson cl (rubbed, sl abraded); gilt. *Boswell.* $50/£32

TARG, WILLIAM (ed). Bouillabaisse for Bibliophiles. Cleveland: World, (1955). 1st ed. Fine in VG dj. *Graf.* $40/£26

TARG, WILLIAM (ed). Bouillabaisse for Bibliophiles. Cleveland, (1955). 1st ed. Name, date, bumped, else VG in dj (dknd, frayed, worn). *King.* $50/£32

TARG, WILLIAM (ed). Carrousel for Bibliophiles. NY: Philip C. Duschnes, 1947. 1st ed. Fine in VG dj. *Graf.* $40/£26

TARG, WILLIAM and HARRY F. MARKS (comps). Ten Thousand Rare Books and Their Prices. Chicago: Black Archer Press, 1936. Ltd to 370. Fldg frontis. Black cl. Good. *Karmiole.* $50/£32

TARG, WILLIAM. Indecent Pleasures. NY, 1975. 1st Amer ed. Fine in dj. *Polyanthos.* $35/£23

TARGAN, BARRY. Surviving Adverse Seasons. Urbana: Univ of IL, 1979. 1st ed. Fine in dj. *Cahan.* $45/£29

TARKINGTON, BOOTH. Beasley's Christmas Party. NY/London: Harper, 1909. 1st ed, 1st issue w/period after 1909 on copyright pg, 1st state w/spine flat w/Harper imprint 1/16-inch in orig tan dj (later issue? or variant state?) ptd in black w/no decs, blurb different from fr cvr. NF (dated ink inscrip) in dj (chipped w/loss of letter 'R' in Harper). *Juvelis.* $110/£71

TARKINGTON, BOOTH. Claire Ambler. NY: Doubleday, Doran, 1928. 1st ed. Fine in dj (lt soiled). *Hermitage.* $45/£29

TARKINGTON, BOOTH. The Fascinating Stranger and Other Stories. NY: Doubleday, Page, 1923. 1st trade ed. Very Nice in dj (sl worn). *Second Life.* $85/£55

TARKINGTON, BOOTH. His Own People. NY: Doubleday, Page, 1907. 1st ed. (Spine sl lightened.) *Sadlon.* $40/£26

TARKINGTON, BOOTH. In the Arena: Stories of Political Life. London: John Murray, 1905. Cancel tp. 1st ed, English issue, from imported sheets of Amer ed. Frontis, 7 plts. Lower edges rough-trimmed. NF. *Temple.* $22/£14

TARKINGTON, BOOTH. The Midlander. GC: Doubleday, Page, 1923. 1st ed. #121/377 signed. Spine sl sunned, else Fine in dj (spine faded, lt worn). *Chapel Hill.* $125/£81

TARKINGTON, BOOTH. An Overwhelming Saturday.... NY: Int'l Magazine Co, (1913). 1st ed. Dec ptd wrappers (thin spot; sm holes). *Sadlon.* $20/£13

TARKINGTON, BOOTH. Penrod Jashber. GC: Doubleday-Doran, 1929. 1st ed. VG+ in dj (edgeworn, chipped spine ends, drknd). *Else Fine.* $85/£55

TARKINGTON, BOOTH. Penrod Jashber. NY, 1929. 1st ed. VG (minor speckling cvrs). *Bond.* $85/£55

TARKINGTON, BOOTH. Penrod. NY: Doubleday, Page, 1914. 1st ed, 1st issue text, 1st issue binding. Cerulean blue mesh cl. Fine in dj (1-inch chip rear panel, 1/2-inch chip crown, nicks, short tears, lt wear). *Godot.* $475/£306

TARKINGTON, BOOTH. Penrod. NY, 1914. 1st ed, 1st state of binding (blue mesh cl) and 'sence' for 'sense' pg 19 but lacking Roman numeral viii on preface. VG (lacking dj). *Bond.* $350/£226

TARKINGTON, BOOTH. Seventeen. NY/London: Harper, (1916). 1st ed, 1st binding, w/gilt-stamped spine. Orange cl. Name, else Fine in dj. *Chapel Hill.* $350/£226

TARLETON, BANESTRE. A History of the Campaigns of 1780 and 1781, in the Southern Provinces of North America. London: T. Cadell, 1787. 1st ed, bound w/ad leaf (tiny hole). vii,(1),518,(2)pp; 3 fldg, 2 full-pg maps. Orig full leather (neatly rebacked w/orig spine label). Bkpl, else NF. Howes T37. *Mcgowan.* $3,500/£2,258

TARR, JOHN C. Lettering, a Source Book of Roman Alphabets. London: Crosby Lockwood, 1951. 1st ed. VG in dj. *Michael Taylor.* $20/£13

TARR, LASZLO. The History of the Carriage. Elisabeth Hoch (trans). London, 1969. Dj (celotaped). *Edwards.* $39/£25

TARTT, DONNA. The Secret History. Knopf, 1992. 1st ed. Fine in dj. *Stahr.* $35/£23

TARTT, DONNA. The Secret History. NY: Knopf, 1992. 1st ed. VF in dj. *Mordida.* $50/£32

TARTT, DONNA. The Secret History. Knopf, 1992. 1st ed. Advance readers ed. Fine in wraps. *Fine Books.* $65/£42

TASISTRO, LOUIS and HENRY COPPEE. History of the Civil War in America. Joseph H. Coates, 1876. 4 vols complete. 3100pp. VG. *Bishop.* $55/£35

TASSI, ROBERTO. Graham Sutherland; Complete Graphic Work. London: Thames & Hudson, 1978. Pub's dec cl. Mint in dj. *Europa.* $93/£60

TASSIN, RAY. Stanley Vestal, Champion of the West. Glendale: Clark, 1973. Dj. *Heinoldt.* $30/£19

TATE, ALLEN and DONALD DAVIDSON. The Literary Correspondence of Donald Davidson and Allen Tate. Athens: Univ of GA Press, (1974). 1st ed. Brn cl. Fine in dj. *Chapel Hill.* $30/£19

TATE, ALLEN. Collected Poems 1919-1976. NY, 1977. 1st Amer ed. Fine (sl rubbed) in dj (price-clipped). *Polyanthos.* $100/£65

TATE, ALLEN. The Fathers. NY: Putnams, 1938. 1st ed. NF in dj (sl used). *Pharos.* $75/£48

TATE, ALLEN. Mr. Pope and Other Poems. NY: Minton, Balch & Co., 1928. 1st ed. 8vo. Black cl, olive grn paper labels. NF (offsetting to fep, fr jacket flap) in dj (chip rear panel, nicks). *Chapel Hill.* $700/£452

TATE, ALLEN. Mr. Pope and Other Poems. NY: Minton, Balch, 1928. 1st ed. Fine in NF dj (sm chip; spine sl dknd). *Beasley.* $750/£484

TATE, ALLEN. Poems 1928-1931. NY: Scribners, 1932. 1st ed. Cvr label. Fine. *Pharos.* $75/£48

TATE, ALLEN. The Poetry Reviews of Allen Tate 1924-1944. Baton Rouge/London: LA State Univ Press, (1983). 1st ed. Lt gray-grn cl. NF in dj. *Chapel Hill.* $25/£16

TATE, ALLEN. Reactionary Essays on Poetry and Ideas. NY: Scribner's, 1936. 1st ed. Blue cl (sl faded). VG in dj (aging, worn). *Cahan.* $85/£55

TATE, ALLEN. Stonewall Jackson, the Good Soldier. NY: Minton, Balch, 1928. 1st ed. Fr inner hinge cracking; worn, else VG. *Mcgowan.* $150/£97

TATE, ALLEN. Stonewall Jackson. NY: Milton, Balch, 1928. 1st ed. Paper spine, cvr labels. Sl edgewear, o/w VG. *Pharos.* $125/£81

TATE, ALLEN. Two Conceits For the Eye to Sing, if Possible. (Cummington): The Cummington Press, 1950. 1st ed. One of 300. Stitched wraps w/paper label. (Label inside rear wrap), else Fine in orig envelope w/card-stock stiffener (ink mks). *Chapel Hill.* $380/£245

TATE, JAMES. Land of Little Sticks. Worcester: Metacom, 1981. Ltd to 300 numbered, signed. Fine in sewn wraps. *Antic Hay.* $50/£32

TATE, JAMES. The Lost Pilot. New Haven/London: Yale Univ Press, 1967. 1st ed, 1st bk. NF in dj (lt soiled). *Chapel Hill.* $150/£97

TATE, JAMES. The Torches. Santa Barbara: Unicorn, (1968). Ltd to 250 hb. Fine in acetate dj. *Antic Hay.* $50/£32

TATE, R. A Plain and Easy Account of the Land and Fresh-water Mollusks of Great Britain. London, 1866. 1st ed. 252pp; 11 color plts. *Wheldon & Wesley.* $54/£35

TATLOCK, R.R. Spanish Art: An Introductory Review of Architecture, Painting, Sculpture, Textiles.... NY, 1927. VG in dj. Fine plts. *Argosy.* $125/£81

TATTERSALL, C.E.C. A History of British Carpets. London, 1934. 1st ed. 116 plts, incl 55 color (edges sl dampstained). Orig cl (lt faded; prelims lt spotted). *Edwards.* $116/£75

TAUSSIG, FREDERICK. Abortion, Spontaneous and Induced: Medical and Social Aspects. St. Louis, 1936. 1st ed. Good. *Fye.* $75/£48

TAUSSIG, FREDERICK. Diseases of the Vulva. NY, 1924. 1st ed. Good. *Fye.* $40/£26

TAUSSIG, FREDERICK. The Prevention and Treatment of Abortion. St. Louis, 1910. 1st ed. Good. *Fye.* $125/£81

TAUSSIG, HELEN. Congenital Malformations of the Heart. 1947. 1st ed, 2nd ptg. Good. *Fye.* $150/£97

TAUSSIG, HELEN. Congenital Malformations of the Heart. Cambridge, 1960. 2nd ed. 2 vols. Good. *Fye.* $75/£48

TAVERNER, ERIC. Salmon Fishing. London: Seeley, 1931. 1st ed. Color frontis, 110 plts. (Backstrip faded.) *Petersfield.* $39/£25

TAVISTOCK, MARQUESS OF. Parrots and Parrot-Like Birds in Aviculture. London: F.V. White, (1935). 1st ed. 8 color plts. Gilt-lettered grn cl. VG. *House.* $80/£52

TAYLOR, ALFRED. Birds of a County Palatine. London: 'Wild Life' Publishing, 1913. 30 lg tipped-in photo plts. Pict cl, onlaid illus upper bd (sl rubbed, scratched), gilt. *Hollett.* $78/£50

TAYLOR, ALFRED. A Manual of Medical Jurisprudence. London: John Churchill, 1846. Contemp calf, gilt (sl rubbed). Good. *Boswell.* $225/£145

TAYLOR, BASIL. Stubbs. NY: Harper & Row, 'Icon Editions,' (1971). 1st US ed. Frontis port, 138 plts (16 color). Rust gilt cl. Good in dj. *Karmiole.* $50/£32

TAYLOR, BASIL. Stubbs. London: Phaidon, 1971. Frontis port, 120 plts. Pub's cl. Fine in Mint dj. *Europa.* $62/£40

TAYLOR, BAYARD. Lands of the Saracen; or, Pictures of Palestine.... NY: Putnam's, 1855. 1st ed. Frontis, tp, 451pp, fldg map. Grey cl stamped in blind (sig pulled; faded, w/gilt paint specks). BAL 19648. *Schoyer.* $75/£48

TAYLOR, BAYARD. Visit to India, China, and Japan. In the Year 1853. NY: Putnam, 1859. 16th ed. Frontis, 539pp, tp, fldg map. Grey cl stamped in blind, gilt (spine faded, worn; foxing). *Schoyer.* $35/£23

TAYLOR, CHARLES M. Vacation Days in Hawaii and Japan. Phila: 1898. 1st ed. Frontis, 361pp. Dec cl. Sm stain on rear bd, else Bright. *Petrilla.* $40/£26

TAYLOR, DEEMS. Walt Disney's Fantasia. NY: S&S, 1940. 2nd ptg. Fine in dj (worn, torn). *Graf.* $65/£42

TAYLOR, ELIZABETH. Blaming. London: Chatto, 1976. 1st UK ed. Fine in VG dj (nick). *Williams.* $37/£24

TAYLOR, ELIZABETH. A Game of Hide-and-Seek. NY: Knopf, 1951. 1st Amer ed. Fine in NF dj (spine sl dknd). *Reese.* $35/£23

TAYLOR, ELIZABETH. Mrs. Palfrey at the Claremont. London: C&W, 1971. 1st ed. VG in dj. *Hollett.* $47/£30

TAYLOR, ELIZABETH. Mrs. Palfrey at the Claremont. London: C&W, 1971. 1st UK ed. Fine in VG dj. *Lewton.* $34/£22

TAYLOR, ELIZABETH. The Soul of Kindness. NY: Viking, (1964). 1st Amer ed. Fine in NF dj (sm abrasion rear panel). *Reese.* $35/£23

TAYLOR, ELIZABETH. A View of the Harbour. NY: Knopf, 1947. 1st Amer ed. Fine in VG dj (lt nicked). *Reese.* $35/£23

TAYLOR, ELIZABETH. The Wedding Group. London: C&W, (1968). 1st ed. NF in dj. *Limestone.* $65/£42

TAYLOR, EVA. The Haven-Finding Art: A History of Navigation from Odysseus to Captain Cook. NY, (1957). 1st Amer ed. Dj (repaired). *Lefkowicz.* $50/£32

TAYLOR, EVA. The Mathematical Practitioners of Tudor and Stuart England. Cambridge: University Press, 1970. Rpt. 14 plts (2 fldg). VF in dj. *Lefkowicz.* $175/£113

TAYLOR, EVA. Oxcart, Chuckwagon and Jeep. San Lucas, CA, (1945). VG in wraps. *Perier.* $25/£16

TAYLOR, FITCH W. A Voyage Round the World.... New Haven, 1851. 13th ed. 2 vols in 1. 317; 650pp, color litho port. Cl (frayed; foxing). *King.* $150/£97

TAYLOR, FRANK H. Philadelphia in the Civil War 1861-1865. Pub by the City, 1913. 24 plts; fldg map. Gilt-titled cl; gilt top. Average (wear). *Bohling.* $35/£23

TAYLOR, GEORGE B. An Account of the Genus Meconopsis. London: New Flora & Silva, 1934. 1st ed. Frontis, 29 plts, 12 maps. Gilt-stamped cl. Fine. *Quest.* $75/£48

TAYLOR, GRIFFITH. With Scott: The Silver Lining. London: Smith, Elder, 1916. 2 fldg maps. Orig dec cl. VG (minor wear). *High Latitude.* $550/£355

TAYLOR, H.V. The Apples of England. London, 1946. 3rd ed. 36 color plts. (Cl sl mkd.) *Wheldon & Wesley.* $39/£25

TAYLOR, HENRY. The Mediaeval Mind. Macmillan, 1927. 4th ed. 2 vols. VG+. *Bishop.* $25/£16

TAYLOR, HENRY. Notes from Books. London: John Murray, 1849. 1st ed. 1/2 title; ad leaf. Good (fly removed; spine faded, fraying). *Poetry.* $90/£58

TAYLOR, HENRY. Old Halls in Lancashire and Cheshire. Manchester: Cornish, 1884. xxxii,164pp, 1f ad, 33 litho plts. (Spine, corners chipped.) *Marlborough.* $116/£75

TAYLOR, HILARY. James McNeill Whistler. NY, (1978). VG in dj. *Argosy.* $30/£19

TAYLOR, I. History of the Transmission of Ancient Books to Modern Times. London: Holdsworth, 1827. 1st ed. Contemp full polished calf, raised bands, gilt spine. Sm wormhole foot 1 joint, o/w Attractive. *Moss.* $50/£32

TAYLOR, ISAAC. Scenes in Africa.... NY: W.B. Gilley, 1827. 12mo. Engr frontis fldg map, 126pp; 28 full-pg VF engrs. Marbled paper on bds (soiled), 3/4 leather spine, gilt title. VG (name, 2 edges of plt leaves repaired; lt foxed). *Hobbyhorse.* $150/£97

TAYLOR, ISAAC. Scenes in America.... London: Harris & Son, 1821. 1st ed. Frontis; viii,122,(2)pp; 84 hand-colored illus on plts; fldg map (repaired). Orig 1/4 red morocco (worn). (Inscrips; foxing, browning.) *Bookpress.* $150/£97

TAYLOR, ISAAC. Scenes in America.... Hartford: Silas Andrus, 1830. 12mo. Fldg copper-engr frontis map, lg vignette tp, vi,117pp; 26 full-pg plts. Plain paper on bds, black roan, gilt title (spotted, lt rubbed). In all, VG (dated ink sig, internal foxing). *Hobbyhorse.* $125/£81

TAYLOR, J.E. Tourist's Guide to the County of Suffolk.... London: Edward Stanford, 1887. 1st ed. (4),140pp + 32pp ads, lg fldg map. Rust cl, gilt. Good. *Karmiole.* $35/£23

TAYLOR, JANE and ANN. Little Ann and Other Poems. London: George Routledge, (ptd 1882; pub 1883). 1st ed. Kate Greenaway (illus). 8vo. 64pp. 1/2 cl, illus bds (sl rubbing). Internally clean. *Reisler.* $250/£161

TAYLOR, JANE and ANN. Little Ann and Other Poems. London/NY: Frederick Warne, n.d. (ca 1900). Tall 8vo. 64pp. Full color pict paper on bd, grn cl corners, spine. Title, on glossy paper ptd on cvrs, reads: Little Ann A Book illustrated by Kate Greenaway. Good (eps lt browned; rubbed, spotted). *Hobbyhorse.* $115/£74

TAYLOR, JEFFERYS. Aesop in Rhyme, with Some Originals. Boston: Munroe & Francis, n.d. (ca 1830). 1st Amer ed. Sq 16mo. vi+263pp (few corners restored, affecting letters); 13 full-pg wood engrs (colored by child), gray eps. Black morocco on bds, gilt (lt spotting). VG. *Hobbyhorse.* $175/£113

TAYLOR, JOHN RUSSELL. The Art Nouveau Book in Britain. N.p.: MIT Press, (1966). 1st US ed. Fine in dj (tape repaired). *Oak Knoll.* $45/£29

TAYLOR, JOSEPH HENRY. Beavers, Their Ways and Other Sketches. Washburn, ND: Privately ptd, 1904. 1st ed. 18 plts (pg19 plt missing). VG. Howes T 66. *Oregon.* $250/£161

TAYLOR, JOSHUA C. William Page. The American Titian. Chicago: Univ of Chicago Press, (1957). 1st ed. Frontis port. Yellow cl. Good in dj. *Karmiole.* $60/£39

TAYLOR, KATHERINE AMES. Lights and Shadows of Yosemite. SF: H.S. Crocker Co, (1926). Dec bds, cl spine (sl dknd; sm bump). *Dawson.* $45/£29

TAYLOR, LILY ROSS. Local Cults in Etruria. Rome: American Academy, 1923. Fldg map. Maroon cl (ex-lib, pocket removed). *Schoyer.* $45/£29

TAYLOR, MARIE HANSEN. On Two Continents. NY: Doubleday, 1905. 1st ed. 8 plts. Dec cl; teg. *Petrilla.* $20/£13

TAYLOR, MARSHALL W. The Fastest Bicycle Rider in the World. Worcester, MA: Wormley Pub Co, (1928). 1st Amer ed. Gilt-stamped cl (lt rubbed). NF. *Between The Covers.* $250/£161

TAYLOR, NATHANIEL. The Coming Empire or Two Thousand Miles in Texas on Horseback. NY: A.S. Barnes, 1877. 1st ed. 389pp. Gilt-stamped linen (rebound). Howes M 81. *Lambeth.* $145/£94

TAYLOR, NATHANIEL. The Coming Empire or Two Thousand Miles in Texas on Horseback. Houston: Carlisle, 1936. Rev ed. Fldg order form. (Pencil corrections, index.) Dj. *Lambeth.* $85/£55

TAYLOR, PETER. In the Miro District and Other Stories. NY: Knopf, 1977. 1st ed. Fine in NF dj. *Chapel Hill.* $50/£32

TAYLOR, PETER. A Long Fourth and Other Stories. NY: Harcourt, Brace, (1948). 1st ed, 1st bk. Inscribed. Black cl. NF (offsetting pp72-72 from laid-in clipping) in dj (spine sl faded, tear). *Chapel Hill.* $400/£258

TAYLOR, PETER. Miss Leonora When Last Seen. NY: Ivan Obolensky, (1963). 1st ed. Signed. VG (lt dust soiling) in VG dj. *Chapel Hill.* $250/£161

TAYLOR, PETER. The Oracle of Stoneleigh Court. NY: Knopf, 1993. 1st ed. Signed. Fine in Fine dj. *Revere.* $50/£32

TAYLOR, PETER. A Stand in the Mountains. NY, (1985). One of 1000. Signed. Fine; no dj as issued. *Polyanthos.* $60/£39

TAYLOR, PETER. A Summons to Memphis. NY: Knopf, 1986. 1st ed. Signed. NF in VG dj. *Revere.* $65/£42

TAYLOR, PETER. Tennessee Day in St. Louis. NY: Random House, (1957). 1st ed. Fine in dj. *Jaffe.* $150/£97

TAYLOR, PHOEBE ATWOOD. Three Plots for Asey Mayo. NY, (1942). 1st ed. NF in dj (price-clipped, rubbed at folds, edges). *Mcclintock.* $85/£55

TAYLOR, RICHARD. Destruction and Reconstruction. NY: D. Appleton, 1879. 1st ed. 274pp + (6)pp ads. Brn cl (soiled). VG (sig). Howes T 73. *Chapel Hill.* $175/£113

TAYLOR, RICHARD. Destruction and Reconstruction: Personal Experiences of the Late War. NY: Appleton, 1879. 1st ed. 274,(6)pp. Orig cl. Sm rubbed spot on spine; minor extrem wear, else VG. Howes T73. *Mcgowan.* $225/£145

TAYLOR, ROBERT. A Practical Treatise on Sexual Disorders of the Male and Female. Phila, 1897. 1st ed. 451pp. Spine head torn, o/w Fine. *Fye.* $150/£97

TAYLOR, WALTER H. Four Years with General Lee. NY: Appleton, 1878. 2nd ed. 199pp. Orig grn cl (lt spotted). Good+ (foxing, sig; fr hinge tender). Theodore Davidson's copy, w/his sig. Howes T 74. *Chapel Hill.* $150/£97

TAYLOR, WALTER H. General Lee. Norfolk, VA: By Nusbaum Book & News Co, (1906). 1st ed. Red cl (spine faded). VG (bumped, rear inner hinge cracked). Howes T 75. *Chapel Hill.* $275/£177

TAYLOR, WILLIAM. Scenes and Adventures in Afghanistan.... London: T.C. Newby and Boone, 1842. 1st ed. Half title, (vi),iv,(ii),239,(1)blank,(10)ads. (Stamp erasure, sm ink stamp margin of title.) Partly uncut. Grn blind-stamped cl. Lt stain foot of spine, cvrs, o/w VG. *Morrell.* $450/£290

TAYLOUR, WILLIAM. Mycenean Pottery in Italy and Adjacent Areas. Cambridge: CUP, 1958. 17 plts, 2 maps. (Sig; spine sl chipped.) Dj. *Archaeologia.* $200/£129

TEAGUE, WALTER D. Design This Day. Harcourt Brace, 1940. 1st ed. Blue cl, gilt. VG+. *Willow House.* $39/£25

TEASDALE, SARA. Dark of the Moon. NY: Macmillan, 1926. 1st trade ed. (Sl rubbed.) *Sadlon.* $20/£13

TEASDALE, SARA. Dark of the Moon. NY: Macmillan, 1926. Ltd to 250 numbered, signed. Vellum, bds; teg. NF in slipcase (sl wear). *Antic Hay.* $175/£113

TEBB, WILLIAM. The Recrudescence of Leprosy and Its Causation. London, 1893. 1st ed. (Ex-lib.) *Argosy.* $75/£48

TEDLOCK, E.W., JR. The Frieda Lawrence Collection of D.H. Lawrence Manuscripts. Univ of NM Press, 1948. 1st Amer ed. Fine in dj (spine sl sunned; edge chips). *Polyanthos.* $35/£23

TEICHMANN, EMIL. A Journey to Alaska in the Year 1868. Oskar Teichmann (ed). NY, Argosy-Antiquarian, 1963. 1st ed thus; ltd to 750. Fine. *Perier.* $85/£55

TEICHMANN, EMIL. A Journey to Alaska in the Year 1868.... NY: Argosy-Antiquarian, 1963. One of 750. Port, map. Gilt-stamped cl. Fine in glassine wrapper. Rpt of Howes T 88. *Bohling.* $75/£48

TEMPLE, RICHARD CARNAC. The Itinierary of Ludovico di Varthema of Bologna from 1502 to 1508. London: Argonaut, 1928. 1st ed, #266/975. 5 maps; 2 plts. Sl rubbed, o/w VG. *Worldwide.* $175/£113

TEMPLE, RONALD. The Message from the King's Coffer. Sausalito: Temple, 1920. 1st ed. VG. *Blue Dragon.* $35/£23

TEMPLE, WILLIAM. An Introduction to the History of England... Ptd by W.S., 1708. 3rd ed. Contemp panelled calf; red morocco lettering-piece. Good. *Waterfield.* $124/£80

TEMPLE, WILLIAM. Memoirs of What Pass'd in Christendom. London: Sam Buckley, 1709. 1st ed. (6),344pp. (Title sl stained.) Contemp calf (fr outer hinge partially cracked). *Karmiole.* $125/£81

TEMPLE, WILLIAM. The Works. London: For J. Round, J. Tonson, 1731. 2 vols. Frontis port; (xvi),480; (iv),585pp. Full blind filleted, gilt ruled calf. (Loss to extrems; hinges cracked; vol 1 upper bd nearly detached; worn; bkpl; fep detached vol 1.) *Edwards.* $233/£150

Ten Little Colored Boys. NY: Howell, Soskin, 1942. Obl 4to, 10pp. Emery I. Gondor (illus). Color pict bds, spiral bound. VG (sm wear). *Davidson.* $200/£129

Ten Little Nigger Boys. London: Juvenile Productions, ca 1940s. Pict wraps (ink names fr wrap). VG. *Davidson.* $250/£161

Ten Little Teddy Bears. London: Bancroft, 1965. 11x11 cm. 5 dbl-pg pop-ups. V. Kubasta (illus). Pict wraps. VG. *Book Finders.* $70/£45

Tenant-House; or, Embers From Poverty's Hearthstone. (By Augustine Joseph Hickey Duganne.) NY: DeWitt, 1857. 1st ed. NF- (fraying, chipping cl, spine ends). *Beasley.* $300/£194

TENN, WILLIAM. Of All Possible Worlds. Ballantine, 1955. 1st ed, 1st bk. NF in VG+ dj. *Aronovitz.* $185/£119

TENN, WILLIAM. Of Monsters and Men. NY: Walker, (1968). 1st ed. NF (pgs 4 & 5 browned) in dj (sl wear; lt soil). *Antic Hay.* $100/£65

TENNANT, C.M. Peter the Wild Boy. London: James Clarke & Co, n.d. (1935). 1st Eng ed. Black cl. Fine in dj (soiled, nicked). *Dalian.* $39/£25

TENNANT, ELEANORA. Spanish Journey. London, 1936. 1st ed. Foxing to fore-edge, margins, o/w VG in dj (sl foxed). *Edwards.* $31/£20

TENNANT, EMMA. Black Marina. London: Faber & Faber, 1985. 1st ed. Fine in dj. *Temple.* $16/£10

TENNANT, EMMA. The Time of the Crack. London: Jonathan Cape, (1973). 1st ed. Fine (agent's label fep) in dj (sl edgewear). *Antic Hay.* $85/£55

TENNANT, J.E. In the Clouds above Baghdad. London, 1920. 1st ed. Frontis; 27 plts; magazine article inserted. Hinges tender; eps sl browned; heavy pencil sketches erased, o/w Good in dk grn cl. *Edwards.* $78/£50

TENNENBAUM, PAULA. Building Buildings. Staten Island Children's Mus, 1985. 11x20 cm. 21 fold-out pp. Heavy crds, in orig envelope. VG. *Book Finders.* $30/£19

TENNENT, J. EMERSON. The Wild Elephant. London: Longmans, Green, 1867. xix,198pp + (ii)pp pub's ads; 3 plts. (Newspaper cutting taped verso subtitle; lt browning.) Orig gilt dec cl (sl rubbed, spine sl chipped, sm split lower joint). *Edwards.* $194/£125

TENNEY, E.P. The New West. As Related to the Christian College. Cambridge: Riverside, 1878. 3rd ed. VG-. *Parker.* $150/£97

Tennyson's Guinevere and Other Poems. London: Blackie & Son, 1912. 1st ed. 4to. 24 mtd color plts by Florence Harrison. Teg. Olive cl, gilt. Fine (fore-edges foxed) in pub's box w/ptd cvr (edgewear; browning). *Reisler.* $575/£371

TENNYSON, ALFRED, FREDERICK, and CHARLES. Poems by Two Brothers. London: Macmillan, 1893. 2nd ed. #205/300 on hand-made paper. xx,251pp; 10 facs plts. Linen (browned; soiled; sl wear backstrip). Uncut, largely unopened. Marginal thumb-prints, o/w VG internally. *Cox.* $70/£45

TENNYSON, ALFRED. Ballads and Other Poems. London: Macmillan, 1880. 1st ed. Grn cl, gilt. NF. *Macdonnell.* $30/£19

TENNYSON, ALFRED. Ballads and Other Poems. London: C. Kegan Paul, 1880. 1st ed. (vi),(1),2-184,pp, (185-188) book-list. With 3pp bookplist of Tennyson's works in back as called for. Grn cl; gold-lettered, blind-stamped spine. (Early inscrip.) *Vandoros.* $85/£55

TENNYSON, ALFRED. The Cup and the Falcon. London: Macmillan, 1884. 1st ed. Grn cl, gilt. Fine. *Macdonnell.* $30/£19

TENNYSON, ALFRED. The Death of Oenone, Akbar's Dream, and Other Poems. London: Macmillan, 1892. 1st ed. Grn cl, gilt. Fine. *Macdonnell.* $25/£16

TENNYSON, ALFRED. The Devil and the Lady. London: Macmillan, 1930. 1st ed. One of 1500. Uncut. 1/4 parchment, batik bds, gilt. VF. *Macdonnell.* $40/£26

TENNYSON, ALFRED. The Devil and the Lady. Charles Tennyson (ed). London: Macmillan, 1930. One of 1500. Frontis. Unopened. 1/4 vellum, paste paper cvrs. Fine in dj (spotted). *Heller.* $125/£81

TENNYSON, ALFRED. Enoch Arden. Boston: Ticknor & Fields, 1864. 1st Amer ed. Brn cl, gilt. Fine. *Macdonnell.* $50/£32

TENNYSON, ALFRED. Enoch Arden. London: Edward Moxon, 1864. 1st ed (no ads in this copy). Blind-stamped cl (sl rubbed). *Sadlon.* $75/£48

TENNYSON, ALFRED. Enoch Arden. London: Moxon, 1864. 1st ed (though bound w/o ads). Aeg. Full grn calf, spine gilt extra. Good (short crack fep gutter; lt foxing, rubbing). *Reese.* $50/£32

TENNYSON, ALFRED. Enoch Arden. London: Edward Moxon, 1864. 1st ed, 1st binding. Olive grn cl, gilt (spine sl sunned). Nice. *Macdonnell.* $75/£48

TENNYSON, ALFRED. The Foresters, Robin Hood, and Maid Marian. NY: Macmillan, 1892. 1st Amer ed. Grn cl, gilt. Fine. *Macdonnell.* $25/£16

TENNYSON, ALFRED. The Foresters, Robin Hood, and Maid Marian. London: Macmillan, 1892. 1st ed. Recent cl. NF. *Sadlon.* $25/£16

TENNYSON, ALFRED. The Foresters, Robin Hood, and Maid Marian. London: Macmillan, 1892. 1st ed. Grn cl, gilt. Fine. *Macdonnell.* $25/£16

TENNYSON, ALFRED. Gareth and Lynette. London: Strahan, 1872. 1st ed. Grn cl, gilt. Nice. *Macdonnell.* $30/£19

TENNYSON, ALFRED. The Holy Grail, and Other Poems. Boston: Fields, Osgood, 1870. 1st Amer ed. Grn cl, gilt. NF. *Macdonnell.* $20/£13

TENNYSON, ALFRED. The Holy Grail, and Other Poems. London: Strahan, 1870. 1st ed. Grn cl, gilt. NF. *Macdonnell.* $40/£26

TENNYSON, ALFRED. The Holy Grail, and Other Poems. London: Strahan, 1870. 1st ed. Aeg. Full morocco (sm rubbed spots) stamped in gilt/blind. *Sadlon.* $75/£48

TENNYSON, ALFRED. Idylls of the King. London: Edward Moxon, 1859. 1st ed, 1st issue w/o printer's imprint on title verso; w/July 1859 ads (as inserts they have no priority). Orig grn cl, gilt. VG. *Macdonnell.* $45/£29

TENNYSON, ALFRED. Idylls of the King. London: Edward Moxon, 1859. 1st ed, 2nd issue w/ptr's imprint title verso. Grn cl, gilt. *Macdonnell.* $30/£19

TENNYSON, ALFRED. In Memoriam, Annotated by the Author. London: Macmillan, 1905. 1st ed thus. Grn cl, gilt. Fine. *Macdonnell.* $30/£19

TENNYSON, ALFRED. Locksley Hall Sixty Years After. London: Macmillan, 1886. 1st ed, 1st issue w/o subtitle on 1/2 title. Grn cl, gilt. Fine (inscrip). *Macdonnell.* $45/£29

TENNYSON, ALFRED. The Lover's Tale. London: G. Kegan Paul, 1879. 1st ed. Grn cl, gilt. Fine. *Macdonnell.* $35/£23

TENNYSON, ALFRED. Maud. London: Edward Moxon, 1855. 1st ed. Grn cl, gilt. NF. *Macdonnell.* $125/£81

TENNYSON, ALFRED. Poems. London: Edward Moxon, 1857. 1st ed. xiii,(3),375pp; aeg. Contemp tan morocco, gilt (faded; lt spotting). Good. *Cox.* $116/£75

TENNYSON, ALFRED. Poems. London: Edward Moxon, 1863. 15th ed. Grn cl, gilt. NF. *Macdonnell.* $45/£29

TENNYSON, ALFRED. Queen Mary, a Drama. London: Henry King, 1875. 1st ed, 1st issue w/'Behled' on p126. Grn cl, gilt. Wear, fr hinge weak, else VG. *Macdonnell.* $30/£19

TENNYSON, ALFRED. Queen Mary, a Drama. London: Henry King, 1875. 1st ed, 2nd issue w/'Beheld' on p126. Grn cl, gilt. VG. *Macdonnell.* $30/£19

TENNYSON, ALFRED. A Selection From the Poems of Alfred, Lord Tennyson. NY: Doubleday, Doran, 1944. 1st ed. Nice in dj (sl frayed). *Pharos.* $35/£23

TENNYSON, ALFRED. Tennyson's Suppressed Poems. London: Sands, 1910. 1st ed. Grn cl, gilt. NF. *Macdonnell.* $35/£23

TENNYSON, ALFRED. Tiresias and Other Poems. London: Macmillan, 1885. 1st ed, 1st issue, w/o imprint at end of text. Grn cl, gilt. Fine. *Macdonnell.* $30/£19

TENNYSON, ALFRED. Tiresias and Other Poems. London: Macmillan, 1885. 1st ed, 2nd issue, w/imprint at end of text. Grn cl, gilt. Fine. *Macdonnell.* $30/£19

TENNYSON, ALFRED. Tiresias and Other Poems. London: Macmillan, 1885. 1st ed; state w/printer's imprint fr and rear. Grn cl (sl rubbed, soiled). Good (rear hinge cracking). *Reese.* $20/£13

TENNYSON, ALFRED. The Works. London: Macmillan, 1884. 1st collected ed. 7 vols. Dk grn cl, gilt. Sm spot last vol, else Fine set. *Macdonnell.* $100/£65

TENNYSON, FREDERICK. Days and Hours. London: John W. Parker, 1854. 1st ed, 1st bk. Tan moire cl, gilt (spine dust-soiled). Nice. *Macdonnell.* $85/£55

TERHUNE, ALBERT PAYSON. Lad of Sunnybank. NY, 1929. 1st ed. Fine (lib bkpl). *Bond.* $140/£90

TERKEL, STUDS. Giants of Jazz. NY: Crowell, (1957). 1st ed. Red cl. Bkpl remnants fep, else NF in VG dj (price-clipped). *Chapel Hill.* $45/£29

TERRACE, EDWARD L.B. Egyptian Paintings of the Middle Kingdom. London: George Allen & Unwin, 1968. 57 color plts. Good in dj. *Archaeologia.* $95/£61

TERRELL, JOHN UPTON. Apache Chronicle. NY, (1972). 1st ed. Map. Fine in Fine dj. *Pratt.* $30/£19

TERRELL, JOHN UPTON. Apache Chronicle. NY: World, (1972). 1st ed. Red cl-backed bds. Fine in VG dj (few holes in spine). *Chapel Hill.* $35/£23

TERRELL, JOHN UPTON. Bunkhouse Papers. NY, 1971. 1st ed. Dj. *Heinoldt.* $25/£16

TERRELL, JOHN UPTON. War for the Colorado River. Glendale: Clark, 1965. 1st eds. 2 vols. NF in VG djs. *Parker.* $60/£39

Terrestrial Air-Breathing Mollusks of the United States, and the Adjacent Territories of North America. (By Amos Binney.) Boston, 1859. Vol 4 (of 5). 6 hand-colored lithos. VG. *Argosy.* $150/£97

TERRY, CHARLES E. and MILDRED PELLENS. The Opium Problem. NY: Committee on Drug Addiction, 1928. 1st ed. NF (repaired rear hinge; sl sunned; name, address). *Beasley.* $85/£55

TERRY, ROSE. Poems. Boston: Ticknor & Fields, 1861. 1st ed, 1st bk. 16pp ads dated Dec 1860. Brn blind-stamped cl (spine sl faded, chipped); gilt. VG. BAL 3770. *Juvelis.* $75/£48

TERRY, T.B. and A.I. ROOT. The ABC of Strawberry Culture. Medina, 1902. 2nd ed. (Lt worn, spotted.) *Sutton.* $25/£16

TERRY, WALLACE. Bloods: An Oral History of the Vietnam War by Black Veterans. NY: Random House, (1984). 1st ed. NF in dj (lt worn; corner chips). *Aka.* $35/£23

TERZIAN, JAMES. The Kid from Cuba. Doubleday, 1967. 1st ed. Fine in VG + dj. *Plapinger.* $30/£19

TEUTHOLD, PETER (trans). The Necromancer: Or the Tale of the Black Forest.... London: Robert Holden, 1927. 1st this ed. One of 1500. Variant copy, all edges trimmed. Dec pict yellow bds. *Reese.* $85/£55

TEVIS, WALTER. The Man Who Fell to Earth. Greenwich: Gold Medal Books, (1963). Paperback orig. (Paper sl aged.) *Pharos.* $60/£39

Texas; a Guide to the Lone Star State. NY, (1947). 4th ptg. Fine in Good dj. *Artis.* $29/£19

TEY, JOSEPHINE. The Daughter of Time. Peter Davies, 1951. 1st UK ed. VG + in VG dj (sl edge-worn; closed tears; sl chipping). *Williams.* $147/£95

TEY, JOSEPHINE. The Franchise Affair. NY: Macmillan, 1949. 1st Amer ed. Fine in dj (price-clipped; internal dampstain; sl wear). *Mordida.* $45/£29

TEY, JOSEPHINE. Miss Pym Disposes. NY: Macmillan, 1948. 1st Amer ed. Sm stain back cvr; pp lt spotted, o/w Fine in dj. *Mordida.* $45/£29

TEY, JOSEPHINE. The Singing Sands. NY: Macmillan, 1953. 1st Amer ed. Lower corners bumped, o/w VG in dj (price-clipped; closed tear; sl faded spine). *Mordida.* $40/£26

THACHER, JAMES. Military Journal of the American Revolution.... Hartford, CT: Hurlbut, Williams & Co, 1862. 486pp. Full sheep, morocco spine label (spine ends chipped). VG (hinges cracked). Howes T 149. *Chapel Hill.* $200/£129

THACKERAY, WILLIAM M. The Adventures of Philip on His Way through the World. London: Smith, Elder, 1862. 1st ed, 1st pub'd binding. 3 vols. Blind-stamped brn cl, gilt spines. Bkpls 2 vols, removed from 1st; 3 inner hinges cracked; sl rubbed, lt soiled, o/w Good set. *Reese.* $450/£290

THACKERAY, WILLIAM M. The Newcomes. London: Bradbury & Evans, 1854. 1st ed. 2 vols. Half-titles, titles, viii,380; viii,375pp. Richard Doyle (illus). Old watered silk cl (reacsed); leather spine labels. *Hollett.* $271/£175

THACKERAY, WILLIAM M. Punch's Prize Novelists, the Fat Contributor, and Travels in London. NY: D. Appleton, 1853. 1st ed. 306pp + ads. Brn cl. Eps foxed; early ink name; sm spot spine, else VG. *Godot.* $135/£87

THACKERAY, WILLIAM M. Sketches and Travels in London. London: Bradbury & Evans, 1856. 1st ed. iv,176pp. 3/4 leather, marbled bds. Aeg. VG. *Schoyer.* $100/£65

THACKERAY, WILLIAM M. Thackeray's Letters to an American Family. NY: Century, 1904. 1st Amer ed. VG. *Reese.* $20/£13

THACKERAY, WILLIAM M. Vanity Fair. London: Bradbury & Evans, 1848. 1st ed, 1st issue w/suppressed woodcut of 'Marquis of Steyne' p336. (W/rustic heading p1 and 'Mr. Pitt' reading p453.) Tall, thick 8vo. xvi,624pp; 40 full-pg plts. Full polished calf (rebacked, orig spine laid down; cvrs worn), gilt extra by Riviere; aeg. Contents Excellent. Custom felt-lined solander case, morocco label. *Hartfield.* $985/£635

THACKERAY, WILLIAM M. Vanity Fair. London: Bradbury & Evans, 1848. 1st ed, 1st issue, w/rustic heading (pl1) and 'Marquis of Steyne' wood engr (p336). Teg. Recent 1/2 calf, worked in gilt, blind. Nice (sl browned). *Ash.* $620/£400

THACKERAY, WILLIAM M. The Virginians. London: Bradbury & Evans, 1858-1859. 1st bk ed. 2 vols. 3/4 morocco (sl rubbed, scuffed; heavy foxing); gilt; leather spine labels. *Sadlon.* $95/£61

THACKERAY, WILLIAM M. The Virginians. London: Bradbury & Evans, 1858-59. 1st ed. 2 vols. 382,(i); viii,376pp. (Foxing; 1 section loose; bkpl; labels each vol.) Blind-stamped cl (spines sl rubbed, faded; frayed), gilt. *Hollett.* $186/£120

THACKERAY, WILLIAM M. Works. London: Smith, Elder, 1899-1906. 13 vols. 8vo. 3/4 gilt-stamped grn morocco; teg; uncut. VG. *Houle.* $1,250/£806

THALHEIMER, ROLAND. Percussion Revolvers of the United States. St. Louis: Privately ptd, (1970). 1st ed. Signed. Fine in dj (chipped). *Oregon.* $45/£29

THANET, OCTAVE. (Pseud of Alice French.) An Adventure in Photography. NY: Scribner's, 1893. 1st ed. VG (rubbed). *Cahan.* $125/£81

THANET, OCTAVE. (Pseud of Alice French.) A Book of True Lovers. Chicago: Way & Williams, 1897. 1st ed. Pict bds; teg. VG (wear; inscrip). *Hermitage.* $100/£65

THATCHER, B.B. Indian Traits. NY: Harper, 1833. 2 vols. 234; 216pp. Fair. *Lien.* $60/£39

THAW, HARRY. The Traitor. Dorrance, (1926). 1st ed. Frontis. VG in VG dj. *Oregon.* $45/£29

THAXTER, CELIA. The Cruise of the Mystery, and Other Poems. Boston/NY: Houghton, Mifflin, 1886. 1st ed. One of 1000. Partly uncut. Vegetable vellum wrappers folded over bds. NF (inscrip). BAL 19895. *Juvelis.* $150/£97

THAYER, ELI. A History of the Kansas Crusade, Its Friends and Its Foes. Harper, 1889. 1st ed. xxii,294pp; 6pp ads. Tape mks feps, o/w Fine. *Oregon.* $75/£48

THAYER, JAMES BRADLEY. A Western Journey with Mr. Emerson. Boston: Little, Brown, 1884. 1st ed. Uncut. Orig white wrappers. VF in Very Nice gray ptd dj (snag w/sm loss). *Macdonnell.* $150/£97

THAYER, JAMES BRADLEY. A Western Journey with Mr. Emerson. (SF): Book Club of CA, 1980. One of 600. Frontis. Black cl spine, gilt title; grn dec paper bds. Green eps. Fine. *Heller.* $35/£23

THAYER, JAMES BRADLEY. A Western Journey with Mr. Emerson. Shirley Sargent (ed). SF: Book Club of CA, 1980. Ltd to 600. Frontis. Gilt-stamped cl, patterned bds. VF. *Oregon.* $60/£39

THAYER, LEE. The Scrimshaw Millions. NY: Sears, 1932. 1st ed. Fine in pict dj. *Else Fine.* $75/£48

THAYER, W. Lectures on the Malarial Fevers. NY, 1897. 1st ed. 326pp. Good. *Fye.* $60/£39

THAYER, W.M. The Pioneer Boy and How He Became President. Boston, 1863. 1st ed. VG. *Bond.* $25/£16

THAYER, W.M. The Printer Boy. How Benjamin Franklin...Made His Mark.... London: Gall & Inglis, (1875). Frontis, 264pp, 6 full-pg wood engrs. Blue cl dec in black/gold (sl rubbed, mkd; label, sig). *Cox.* $28/£18

THAYER, W.R. The Life and Letters of John Hay. Boston/NY: Houghton Mifflin, (1915). 1st ed, 9th imp. 2 vols. VG set. *Mcgowan.* $85/£55

THAYER, W.R. The Life of John Hay. Boston, (1908). 1st ed. 2 vols. VG + . *Pratt.* $37/£24

THEINER, GEORGE. A Day at the Farm. London: Bancroft, 1964. 18x22 cm. 5 fan-fld moveables. Rudolph Lukes (illus). Pict bds (edges sl worn). Internally VG. *Book Finders.* $65/£42

THEOBALD, J. DAZLEY. Magic and Its Mysteries. London: Frederick Warne, n.d. (c. 1880). 65 engrs. (Edges worn; rebacked.) *Dramatis Personae.* $70/£45

THEOBALD, JOHN and LILLIAN. Arizona Territory Post Offices and Post Masters. Phoenix: Arizona Hist Foundation, 1961. 1st ed. Grn cl; gilt. Good in dj. *Karmiole.* $40/£26

There Was an Old Woman Who Lived in a Shoe. London: Ernest Nister, (ca 1890). Shapebook, oblong, 4to. Full color pict paper cvrs w/stapled binding (overall wear). *Reisler.* $150/£97

THEROUX, ALEXANDER. Darconville's Cat. NY: Doubleday, 1981. 1st ed. Signed. NF in dj. *Lame Duck.* $150/£97

THEROUX, ALEXANDER. The Great Wheadle Tragedy. Boston: Godine, 1975. 1st ed. Signed. Name, date, else NF in VG dj (price-clipped). *Lame Duck.* $100/£65

THEROUX, ALEXANDER. Three Wogs. Boston: Gambit, 1972. 1st ed, 1st bk. Signed. Fine in presumed 1st issue dj w/sepia-tone photo, mention of a 'Trappist monastery in Kentucky' on rear flap. *Lame Duck.* $300/£194

THEROUX, PAUL and BRUCE CHATWIN. Patagonia Revisited. Michael Russell, 1985. 1st ed. Signed by Theroux. Fine in dj. *Rees.* $47/£30

THEROUX, PAUL. The Black House. London: Hamish Hamilton, 1974. 1st ed. Fine in dj (price-clipped, short closed tear). *Rees.* $47/£30

THEROUX, PAUL. The Black House. London: Hamilton, 1974. 1st UK ed. Fine in VG+ dj. *Williams.* $47/£30

THEROUX, PAUL. Chicago Loop. London: Hamish Hamilton, 1990. 1st ed. Signed. NF in dj. *Rees.* $28/£18

THEROUX, PAUL. Chicago Loop. London: Hamilton, 1990. 1st UK ed. Signed. Fine in dj. *Lewton.* $25/£16

THEROUX, PAUL. The Consul's File. London: Hamilton, 1977. 1st UK ed. Fine in dj. *Lewton.* $34/£22

THEROUX, PAUL. Dr. Slaughter. London: Hamilton, 1984. 1st UK ed. Fine in dj. *Lewton.* $19/£12

THEROUX, PAUL. The Family Arsenal. London: Hamish Hamilton, 1976. 1st ed. Fine in dj. *Rees.* $47/£30

THEROUX, PAUL. The Family Arsenal. London: Hamilton, 1976. 1st UK ed. Fine in dj. *Lewton.* $37/£24

THEROUX, PAUL. Fong and the Indians. London: Hamilton, 1976. 1st UK ed. VG in dj. *Lewton.* $42/£27

THEROUX, PAUL. The Great Railway Bazaar. London: Hamish Hamilton, 1975. 1st ed. NF in dj (sl rubbed, price-clipped). *Rees.* $39/£25

THEROUX, PAUL. The Happy Isles of Oceania. NY: Putnam's, (1992). 1st ed. Signed. Fine in dj. *Godot.* $45/£29

THEROUX, PAUL. London Snow. London: Michael Russell, 1979. One of 450 specially bound, numbered, signed by Theroux and John Lawrence (illus). Fine in tissue dj. *Rees.* $93/£60

THEROUX, PAUL. London Snow. London: Hamilton, 1980. 1st trade ed. NF in dj (spine faded, short closed tear). *Williams.* $39/£25

THEROUX, PAUL. My Secret History. London: Hamilton, 1989. 1st UK ed. Signed. Fine in dj. *Lewton.* $25/£16

THEROUX, PAUL. My Secret History. Hamish Hamilton, 1989. 1st UK ed. Signed. Fine in dj. *Sclanders.* $23/£15

THEROUX, PAUL. O-Zone. London: Hamilton, 1986. 1st UK ed. Signed. Fine in dj. *Lewton.* $26/£17

THEROUX, PAUL. The Old Patagonian Express. London: Hamish Hamilton, 1979. 1st ed. Fine in dj. *Rees.* $31/£20

THEROUX, PAUL. The Old Patagonian Express. London: Hamilton, 1979. 1st UK ed. Fine in VG dj. *Lewton.* $39/£25

THEROUX, PAUL. Picture Palace. London: Hamish Hamilton, 1978. 1st ed. Signed. NF in dj. *Rees.* $31/£20

THEROUX, PAUL. Picture Palace. London: Hamilton, 1978. 1st UK ed. Fine in dj. *Lewton.* $29/£19

THEROUX, PAUL. Sailing Through China. London: Michael Russell, 1983. 1st ed. Signed. Fine in dj. *Rees.* $31/£20

THEROUX, PAUL. Sailing Through China. London: Russell, 1983. 1st trade ed. Signed. Fine in dj. *Williams.* $37/£24

THEROUX, PAUL. Saint Jack. Boston: Houghton Mifflin, 1973. 1st ed. Fine in dj (lt worn). *Hermitage.* $45/£29

THEROUX, PAUL. The Shortest Day of the Year. London: Sixth Chamber Press, 1986. One of 175 numbered, signed. Fine, as issued. *Rees.* $109/£70

THEROUX, PAUL. Sinning with Annie. Boston: Houghton, Mifflin, 1972. 1st ed. Fine in dj (lt edgewear; few sm tears). *Antic Hay.* $100/£65

THEROUX, PAUL. Sinning with Annie. Houghton, 1972. 1st US ed. Bkpl, o/w Fine in dj. *Lewton.* $107/£69

THEROUX, PAUL. Sinning with Annie. Boston: Houghton Mifflin, 1972. 1st US ed. NF in dj (sl chipped, creased). *Virgo.* $140/£90

THEROUX, PAUL. Waldo. Bodley Head, 1968. 1st UK ed. VG+ in VG dj (sl edge wear). *Martin.* $59/£38

THEROUX, PAUL. The White Man's Burden. London: Hamilton, 1987. 1st UK ed. NF in dj. *Williams.* $34/£22

THESIGER, WILFRED. Arabian Sands. NY: Dutton, 1959. 1st ed. Fldg map. VG in dj. *Worldwide.* $20/£13

THESIGER, WILFRED. Arabian Sands. NY, 1959. 1st ed. Fldg map in pocket. Dj (sm tears). *Lewis.* $37/£24

THESIGER, WILFRED. The Life of My Choice. London, 1987. 1st ed. Dj. *Edwards.* $31/£20

THESIGER, WILFRED. The Marsh Arabs. London: Longmans, 1964. 1st Eng ed. Grn cl. Sl spotted, inscrip, o/w VG in dj (sl worn). *Dalian.* $54/£35

THIAN, RAPHAEL P. Legislative History of the General Staff of the Army of the United States.... Washington, 1901. 1st ed. *Ginsberg.* $150/£97

THIERS, LOUIS ADOLPHE. The History of the French Revolution. London: Richard Bentley, 1881. New ed. 5 vols. 41 steel engrs. 3/4 burgundy leather, marbled bds. *Glenn.* $450/£290

Think Before You Speak. (By Catherine Ann Dorset.) Phila: Johnson & Warner, 1810. Imprint on cvr dated 1811. Sq 12mo. 32pp + 1pg ad lower wrapper, copper engr frontis, 5 full-pg plts (2 browned). Good (spine sl chipped) in ptd stiff paper wrappers. *Hobbyhorse.* $150/£97

THINKER, THEODORE. First Lessons in Botany, or The Child's Book of Flowers. (Pseud of Francis Channing Woodworth.) NY: Saxton & Miles, 1846. 1st ed. 12mo. 108pp. Black calf over ptd bds (sl soiled). *Karmiole.* $60/£39

Third Spira. London, 1732. 3rd ed. 104pp. Leather-backed marbled bds (rebound). Pp browned, else Good. *King.* $85/£55

THOMAS, ALAN G. Great Books and Book Collectors. London: Chancellor Press, 1975. 40 color plts. Dj. *Edwards.* $54/£35

THOMAS, ALAN G. Great Books and Book Collectors. London: Weidenfeld & Nicholson, 1975. Fine in dj; brn cl case. *Heller.* $75/£48

THOMAS, ALFRED BARNABY (ed). Teodoro de Croix and the Northern Frontier of New Spain, 1776-1783. Norman, 1941. 1st ed. Fldg map. NF in dj (sl worn). *Baade.* $45/£29

THOMAS, BERTRAM. Arabia Felix. NY, 1932. 1st ed. Lg fldg map. Red cl (fading). *Lewis.* $65/£42

THOMAS, BERTRAM. Arabia Felix. NY: Scribner's, 1932. 1st ed. Signed. Lg fldg map. Red cl. Good in dj. *Karmiole.* $85/£55

THOMAS, BERTRAM. The Arabs. GC: Doubleday, Doran, 1937. 1st ed. 18 plts; 4 maps (1 fldg). VG in dj. *Worldwide.* $65/£42

THOMAS, BOB. Walt Disney: An American Original. NY: S&S, (1976). Advance rev copy, pub's slip laid in. VG in dj. *Houle.* $95/£61

THOMAS, CHARLES W. Ice Is Where You Find It. Indianapolis/NY: Bobbs-Merrill, 1951. Blue cl. Dj worn, else VG. *Parmer.* $35/£23

THOMAS, CLARENCE. General Turner Ashby, the Centaur of the South. Winchester, VA: Eddy Press, 1907. 1st ed. NF. *Mcgowan.* $450/£290

THOMAS, D.M. Ararat. London: Gollancz, 1983. 1st Eng ed. Blue cl. VF in dj. *Dalian.* $31/£20

THOMAS, D.M. Birthstone. London, 1980. 1st ed. Signed. Fine in dj. *Words Etc.* $16/£10

THOMAS, D.M. The Devil and the Floral Dance. London: Robson Books, 1978. 1st Eng ed. Pict bds. Fine; no dj as issued. *Dalian.* $54/£35

THOMAS, D.M. The Flute Player. E.P. Dutton, 1979. 1st ed. NF in NF dj. *Bishop.* $17/£11

THOMAS, D.M. Personal and Possessive; Poems. Outposts Publications, 1964. 1st ed, 1st bk. Signed. VG in wrappers. *Words Etc.* $186/£120

THOMAS, D.M. Swallow. London, 1984. 1st ed. Inscribed. Fine in dj. *Words Etc.* $19/£12

THOMAS, D.M. The White Hotel. Viking, 1981. 1st ed. NF in NF dj. *Bishop.* $17/£11

THOMAS, DYLAN and JOHN DAVENPORT. The Death of the King's Canary. London: Hutchinson, 1976. 1st ed. Fine in dj. *Limestone.* $30/£19

THOMAS, DYLAN. Adventures in the Skin Trade. New Directions, (1955). 1st Amer ed. Fine in dj (sl lightened). *Sadlon.* $75/£48

THOMAS, DYLAN. Adventures in the Skin Trade. London, 1955. 1st ed. VG in dj (chip). *Words Etc.* $54/£35

THOMAS, DYLAN. A Child's Christmas in Wales. Norfolk, CT: New Directions, (1954). 1st separate ed. Inscrip, else VG in dj. *Limestone.* $65/£42

THOMAS, DYLAN. A Child's Christmas in Wales. Norfolk, CT: New Directions, (1954). 1st separate ed. Ptd bds. Fine in dj. *Sadlon.* $75/£48

THOMAS, DYLAN. The Collected Letters of Dylan Thomas. London, 1985. 1st ed. Fine (sm sticker) in dj. *Polyanthos.* $45/£29

THOMAS, DYLAN. The Collected Letters. Paul Ferris (ed). NY: Macmillan, (1985). 1st ed. Fine in Fine dj. *Aka.* $35/£23

THOMAS, DYLAN. Deaths and Entrances. London: Dent, (1946). 1st ed. VF in dj (sl rubbed). *Jaffe.* $350/£226

THOMAS, DYLAN. Deaths and Entrances: Poems. London, (1946). 1st ed. Good in dj (sl rubbed, chipped). *Waterfield.* $233/£150

THOMAS, DYLAN. Deaths and Entrances; Poems. London, 1946. 1st ed. VG in dj (sl rubbed). *Words Etc.* $132/£85

THOMAS, DYLAN. The Doctor and the Devils. New Directions, (1953). 1st Amer ed. (Spine sl lightened.) Dj (sl worn). *Sadlon.* $30/£19

THOMAS, DYLAN. The Doctor and the Devils. London, 1953. 1st ed. VG in dj (chips). *Words Etc.* $78/£50

THOMAS, DYLAN. In Country Sleep and Other Poems. (NY): New Directions, (1952). 1st ed, trade issue. Port. Erasure early leaf, o/w VG in dj (tanned, chips). *Reese.* $85/£55

THOMAS, DYLAN. In Country Sleep. (NY, 1952). 1st ed. Grey-grn bds. Fine in 1/2 leather clamshell case. *Argosy.* $300/£194

THOMAS, DYLAN. Letters to Vernon Watkins. Dent, 1957. 1st ed. VG in dj. *Whiteson.* $20/£13

THOMAS, DYLAN. The Map of Love. London: J.M Dent & Sons, (1939). 1st ed, 1st issue. Frontis port. Mauve cl. Spine sl faded, else NF in dj (lt sunned spine). *Chapel Hill.* $450/£290

THOMAS, DYLAN. The Poems of.... New Directions, 1971. 1st thus w/errata slip. Fine in Fine dj. *Whiteson.* $39/£25

THOMAS, DYLAN. A Prospect of the Sea and Other Stories. London, 1955. 1st ed. VG (name) in dj (torn, chipped). *Words Etc.* $28/£18

THOMAS, DYLAN. A Prospect of the Sea. Daniel Jones (ed). Dent, 1955. 1st ed. NF in dj (sl soiled; top edge sl worn). *Poetry.* $54/£35

THOMAS, DYLAN. Quite Early One Morning. New Directions, (1954). 1st Amer ed. Fine in dj (lt worn). *Sadlon.* $50/£32

THOMAS, DYLAN. Quite Early One Morning. (NY): New Directions, (1954). 1st Amer ed. Fine in dj (lt rubbed); orig wraparound band intact. *Reese.* $65/£42

THOMAS, DYLAN. Quite Early One Morning. NY, 1954. 1st Amer ed. Fine in dj. *Argosy.* $75/£48

THOMAS, DYLAN. Quite Early One Morning. London: J.M. Dent, 1954. 1st ed. Frontis port. Fine in dj (frayed, sl chipped). *Temple.* $29/£19

THOMAS, DYLAN. Under Milk Wood. New Directions, (1954). 1st Amer ed. 1st issue dj w/photo of Thomas back cvr. VG. *Argosy.* $125/£81

THOMAS, DYLAN. Under Milk Wood. London, 1954. 1st ed. VG (name, date) in dj (1-inch closed tear; sl rubbed). *Words Etc.* $78/£50

THOMAS, DYLAN. The World I Breathe. Norfolk, CT: New Directions, (1939). 1st ed, 1st issue; single star on sides of author's name on tp, spine. One of 700. Large 8vo. VG (bkpl removed; red ink initials, date fep; tape mks pastedowns) in dj (lt used). *Chapel Hill.* $500/£323

THOMAS, EDWARD. Cloud Castle and Other Poems. London: Duckworth, 1922. 1st Eng ed. Prelims sl foxed, o/w VG in dj (sl frayed). *Dalian.* $101/£65

THOMAS, EDWARD. The Heart of England. Dent, 1906. 1st ed. Teg. Dec white cl. Fr cvr stained, sl bubbled; foxing of fep, 1/2 title, else VG. *Whiteson.* $93/£60

THOMAS, EDWARD. The Heart of England. London, 1906. 1st ed. Teg. Dec cl. Name, ep foxed, bumped, dknd, else Good in dj (defective). *King.* $150/£97

THOMAS, EDWARD. A Literary Pilgrim in England.... London: Methuen, 1917. 1st ed. 8 color plts, 12 monotone. Blue cl (lt soiled, unevenly faded). *Cox.* $39/£25

THOMAS, EDWARD. Oxford. London: A&C Black, 1903. #77/300. 60 color plts; teg, rest uncut. Contents Fine (sl rubbed, sm hole fr cvr, sl bumped). *Petersfield.* $341/£220

THOMAS, EDWARD. Oxford. A&C Black, 1903. 1st ed. 60 color plts. Teg. Dec cl (edges sl rubbed; spine sl faded; hinges cracked; feps browned). *Edwards.* $62/£40

THOMAS, EDWARD. Poems. London: Selwyn & Blount, 1917. Rpt. Grey paper bds. Fore-edge, prelims sl browned, o/w VG. *Dalian.* $54/£35

THOMAS, EDWARD. Selected Poems. London: Greynog Press, 1927. #50/275. Wood-engr title vignette. VG in yellow buckram (sl soiled). *Cox.* $209/£135

THOMAS, EMORY M. The Confederate Nation 1861-1865. Harper & Row, 1979. 1st ed. VG + in VG + dj. *Bishop.* $18/£12

THOMAS, FREDERICK W. The Emigrant, or Reflections While Descending the Ohio. Cincinnati: J. Drake Spiller, 1872. 48pp. Contemp bds, ptd paper label. VG. *Cahan.* $40/£26

THOMAS, GEORGE C., JR. The Practical Book of Outdoor Rose Growing for the Home Garden. Phila: Lippincott, 1914. 1st ed. 96 full-pg color plts. Teg; uncut. Grn cl, gilt; photo cvr illus. VG (lt spotting; shelfwear). *Shifrin.* $40/£26

THOMAS, GEORGE C., JR. and GEORGE C., III. Game Fish of the Pacific. Phila: Lippincott, 1930. 1st ed. Color frontis. Blue cl, stamped in silver/blue (sl faded, soiled). Dj. *Karmiole.* $60/£39

THOMAS, HUGH. The Spanish Civil War. Harper, 1961. 1st ed. VG in dj (sl torn). *Whiteson.* $28/£18

THOMAS, ISAIAH. The Diary of Isaiah Thomas 1805-1828. Worcester: AAS, 1909. 2 vols. *Veatchs.* $150/£97

THOMAS, J.J. The American Fruit Culturist.... Auburn, 1856. Later ed. 424pp (6pp ads). (Lt foxed.) Grn cl (dingy, worn, spotted). *Sutton.* $40/£26

THOMAS, J.J. Farm Implements and Farm Machinery. NY: OJ, 1879. 312pp. Brn cl, gilt stamped. VG. *Bohling.* $50/£32

THOMAS, J.J. Rural Affairs: A Practical and Copiously Illustrated Register of Rural Economy and Rural Taste. Albany, NY, 1858-60. 2 vols. (2),xvi,336; (2),xix,332pp. Blind/gilt-stamped cl (spines faded). VG. *Shifrin.* $150/£97

THOMAS, K. BRYN. Curare, Its History and Usage. London: Pitman, 1964. 1st ed. Cvrs mkd, o/w Fine. *White.* $39/£25

THOMAS, LAURIE. 200 Years of Australian Painting. Sydney, (1971). 60 color plts. VG in dj. *Argosy.* $60/£39

THOMAS, LESLIE. The Virgin Soldiers. London: Constable, 1966. 1st Eng ed. Black cl. Name, o/w Good in dj (sl chipped). *Dalian.* $23/£15

THOMAS, LOWELL. Hungry Waters, the Story of the Great Flood. Phila, (1937). 1st ed. Pict cl (spines sunned; sl soiled, worn). *King.* $35/£23

THOMAS, LOWELL. Hungry Waters. Chicago: John C. Winston, 1937. 1st ed. Frontis. VG (eps foxed). *Connolly.* $35/£23

THOMAS, LOWELL. With Lawrence in Arabia. NY: GC, 1924. 1st ed. 15 plts; map. VG (bkpl) in dj (tattered). *Worldwide.* $16/£10

THOMAS, NICHOLAS. A Guide to Prehistoric England. Batsford, 1960. 1st ed. Dj. *Edwards.* $31/£20

THOMAS, R.H.G. The Liverpool and Manchester Railway. London: Batsford, 1980. 1st ed. Frontis. VG in dj. *Hollett.* $39/£25

THOMAS, R.S. Poetry for Supper. London: Rupert Hart-Davis, 1958. 1st Eng ed. Red bds. VF in dj (sl mkd, sl nicked) w/Poetry Book Soc wraparound band. *Dalian.* $70/£45

THOMAS, ROBERT. The Modern Practice of Physic. NY, 1813. 2nd Amer ed. 697pp. Full leather. *Fye.* $100/£65

THOMAS, ROBERT. The Modern Practice of Physic. NY, 1813. 2nd Amer ed. Contemp calf (broken; foxed). *Argosy.* $125/£81

THOMAS, ROBERT. Modern Practice of Physic.... NY: Collins, 1820. 5th Amer ed. VG in wrappers. *Argosy.* $85/£55

THOMAS, ROBERT. The Modern Practice of Physic...With an Appendix, by Edward Miller, M.D. NY, 1811. 1st Amer ed. 697pp. Full leather. Good. *Fye.* $200/£129

THOMAS, ROSEMARY HYDE. It's Good to Tell You: French Folktales from Mississippi. Univ of MO, 1981. 1st ed in English. VG in VG dj. *Book Broker.* $25/£16

THOMAS, ROSS. Briarpatch. NY: S&S, 1984. 1st ed. VF in dj. *Mordida.* $35/£23

THOMAS, ROSS. Brown Paper and Some String. Privately ptd, 1987. 1st ptg. Fine. *Janus.* $20/£13

THOMAS, ROSS. Cast a Yellow Shadow. NY: Wm. Morrow, 1967. 1st ed. NF in Attractive dj (sl crease fr flap). *Bernard.* $125/£81

THOMAS, ROSS. Cast a Yellow Shadow. NY: Morrow, 1967. 1st ed. NF in dj. *Limestone.* $175/£113

THOMAS, ROSS. Chinaman's Chance. NY: S&S, (1978). 1st ed. NF in NF dj. *Aka.* $60/£39

THOMAS, ROSS. Chinaman's Chance. NY: S&S, 1978. 1st ed. Fine in dj. *Limestone.* $75/£48

THOMAS, ROSS. The Eighth Dwarf. NY: S&S, 1979. 1st ed. Fine in Fine dj. *Janus.* $35/£23

THOMAS, ROSS. The Fools in Town Are on Our Side. London: Hodder & Stoughton, 1970. 1st ed. Edges lt spotted, o/w Fine in dj (short closed tears; wrinkling back panel). *Mordida.* $175/£113

THOMAS, ROSS. The Fools in Town Are on Our Side. NY: William Morrow, 1971. 1st Amer ed. Fine in dj. *Mordida.* $125/£81

THOMAS, ROSS. If You Can't Be Good. NY: Morrow, 1973. 1st ed. Top edges sl dusty, else VG + in dj. *Limestone.* $85/£55

THOMAS, ROSS. If You Can't Be Good. NY: William Morrow, 1973. 1st ed. Fine in dj (internal stains). *Mordida.* $100/£65

THOMAS, ROSS. The Money Harvest. NY: William Morrow, 1975. 1st ed. Signed. NF in dj (lt edgewear). *Janus.* $75/£48

THOMAS, ROSS. The Mordida Man. NY: S&S, 1981. 1st ed. Fine in dj (sl wear spine base). *Mordida.* $50/£32

THOMAS, ROSS. Out on the Rim. NY: Mysterious, 1987. 1st ed. Signed. As New in dj. *Janus.* $25/£16

THOMAS, ROSS. The Porkchoppers. NY: S&S, 1972. 1st ed. VG + in VG dj. *Limestone.* $85/£55

THOMAS, ROSS. The Porkchoppers. NY: William Morrow, 1972. 1st ed. Signed. NF (top edge sl spotted) in VG + dj (sl sunned spine; closed tears). *Janus.* $35/£23

THOMAS, ROSS. Spies, Thumbsuckers, etc. Northridge: Lord John, 1989. 1st ed, one of 300 numbered, signed. As New. *Janus.* $50/£32

THOMAS, T. GAILLARD. A Practical Treatise on the Diseases of Women. Phila, 1869. 2nd ed. 647pp. Recent cl. *Fye.* $80/£52

THOMAS, THOMAS EBENEZER. Correspondence...Mainly Relating to the Anti-Slavery Conflict in Ohio. N.p. (Dayton, OH), 1909. 1st ed. 2 ports. Blind-stamped grn cl, gilt. VG. *Petrilla.* $65/£42

THOMAS, WARD. Stranger in the Land. Boston: Houghton Mifflin, 1949. 1st ed. Fine in dj (sl edgeworn). *Reese.* $25/£16

THOMAS, WILLIAM H. A Slaver's Adventures on Land and Sea. Boston: Lee & Shepard, 1873. 1st Amer ed. Grn cl; gilt spine. NF (sl worn). *Between The Covers.* $85/£55

THOMAS, WILLIAM S. Hunting Big Game with Gun and with Kodak. NY: Putnam's, 1906. 1st ed. Teg. Photo paste-down on fr cvr. Fine. *Bowman.* $50/£32

THOMAS, WILLIAM S. Hunting Big Game with Gun and with Kodak. NY: Putnam's, 1906. 1st ptg. Pict cl (rough opening some pp; fingerprints, soil in text). *Schoyer.* $50/£32

THOMAS, WILLIAM S. Trails and Tramps in Alaska and New Foundland. NY: Putnam's, 1913. 1st ptg. Pict cl. VG. *Schoyer.* $85/£55

THOMASON, JOHN W. Jeb Stuart. Scribner's, 1930. (1st ed). VG. *Book Broker.* $40/£26

THOME, JAMES A. and J. HORACE KIMBALL. Emancipation in the West Indies. NY: Amer Anti-Slavery Soc, 1838. 1st ed. 128pp (sm stamp; lacks map). VG. *Petrilla.* $50/£32

THOMPSON, A. HAMILTON. The Cathedral Churches of England. London: S.P.C.K., 1925. 1st ed. 21 plts. Sm scratch upper bd. *Hollett.* $39/£25

THOMPSON, AMES. The Adventure Boys and the Temple of Rubies. Cupples & Leon, 1928. 1st ed. VG in dj (sl frayed). *Madle.* $17/£11

THOMPSON, ARTHUR R. Gold-Seeking on the Dalton Trail. Boston: Little, Brown, 1900. 1st ptg. Inscribed. 10 plts, map. Pict cl. VG. *Schoyer.* $125/£81

THOMPSON, C. WYVILLE. The Depths of the Sea. London: Macmillan, 1874. 2nd ed. 528pp + ads. Bkpl; short split top fr joint; lt foxing, o/w Fine. *Pharos.* $85/£55

THOMPSON, CLARA MILDRED. Reconstruction in Georgia. NY: Columbia, 1915. 1st ed. New cl, leather label. Howes T 189. *Ginsberg.* $125/£81

THOMPSON, DANIEL (comp). The Laws of Vermont, of a Public and Permanent Nature. Montpelier: Knapp and Jewett, 1835. Full sheep (rubbed, foxed). *Boswell.* $85/£55

THOMPSON, DOROTHY. Dorothy Thompson's Political Guide. NY: Stackpole, (1938). 1st ed. Fine in dj. *Godot.* $45/£29

THOMPSON, DOROTHY. Let the Record Speak. Boston: Houghton Mifflin, 1939. 1st ed. Offsetting eps, else Fine in dj. *Godot.* $45/£29

THOMPSON, DUNSTAN. The Phoenix in the Desert. London: John Lehmann, 1951. 1st ed. 16 plts. (Damp spotted.) Dj (edges sl chipped, torn). *Hollett.* $23/£15

THOMPSON, EDWARD. Cock Robin's Decease: An Irregular Inquest. London: Hogarth Press, 1928. 1st ed. Integral ad leaf, blank at end. Grey card wrappers, cut flush. Nice (spine sl dknd). *Temple.* $109/£70

THOMPSON, FRANCIS. Shelley. London: Burns & Oates, 1909. 1st ed. Buckram, gilt. Sl fading top edge cvrs, else Fine. *Pharos.* $40/£26

THOMPSON, FRED (comp). The I.W.W. Its First Fifty Years (1905-1955). Chicago: I.W.W., 1955. 1st ed, clbound issue. VG in dj (lt frayed, stained). *Reese.* $40/£26

THOMPSON, GEORGE FAYETTE. A Manual of Angora Goat Raising. Chicago: American Sheep Breeder Co, 1903. 1st ed. Grn cl, gilt. Good. *Karmiole.* $30/£19

THOMPSON, GEORGE. The Palm Land. Cincinnati: Moore, Wilstach, Keys, 1859. 3rd ed. 456pp, 15 plts, fldg map. Pict cl. VG. *Petrilla.* $45/£29

THOMPSON, HENRY. Clinical Lectures on Diseases of the Urinary Organs. London: J.&A. Churchill, 1888. 8th ed. xiv,470,(16 ads)pp. Gilt spine title. Fine. *Hemlock.* $175/£113

THOMPSON, HUNTER S. Fear and Loathing in Las Vegas. NY: Random House, (1971). 1st ed. NF (eps, pg edges foxed; bd edges faded) in NF dj (edges sl dknd). *Between The Covers.* $150/£97

THOMPSON, HUNTER S. Fear and Loathing in Las Vegas. Random House, 1971. 1st ed. VG+ in VG+ dj. *Bishop.* $135/£87

THOMPSON, HUNTER S. Fear and Loathing on the Campaign Trail '72. SF: Straight Arrow, (1973). 1st ed. Cl (sl soiled) in dj (worn). *Second Life.* $45/£29

THOMPSON, HUNTER S. Fear and Loathing on the Campaign Trail '72. Straight Arrow Press, 1973. 1st ed. VG+ in VG dj. *Bishop.* $48/£31

THOMPSON, HUNTER S. Fear and Loathing on the Campaign Trail '72. SF: Straight Arrow, 1973. 1st ed. Ralph Steadman (illus). NF in VG+ dj. *Pettler.* $75/£48

THOMPSON, HUNTER S. Fear and Loathing: on the Campaign Trail. London: Alison & Busby, 1974. 1st Eng ed. NF (spine head, tail sl bumped) in dj (sl rubbed; edges creased). *Ulysses.* $116/£75

THOMPSON, HUNTER S. The Great Shark Hunt. Gonzo Papers, vol 1. NY: Summit/Rolling Stone Press, 1979. 1st ed. Fine (shadow fep) in NF dj (price-clipped). *Revere.* $75/£48

THOMPSON, HUNTER S. Screwjack. Santa Barbara: Neville, 1991. One of 300 (of 326) numbered, signed. Gilt-stamped cl. As New. *Between The Covers.* $125/£81

THOMPSON, HUNTER. Screwjack. Santa Barbara: Neville, 1991. 1st ed. One of 300 (of 326) numbered, signed. Fine w/o dj as issued. *Lame Duck.* $150/£97

THOMPSON, J. ERIC. Ancient Maya Relief Sculpture. NY: Museum of Primitive Art, 1967. 60 plts; map. VG in ptd wrappers; slipcase. *Argosy.* $45/£29

THOMPSON, J. ERIC. Maya History and Religion. Norman: Univ of OK Press, (1970). 1st ed. 3 maps. Good in dj. *Archaeologia.* $35/£23

THOMPSON, J. HARRY. Report of Columbia Hospital for Women and Lying-In Asylum, Washington, D.C. Washington, 1873. 431pp. Contents Fine. (Spine faded, chewed.) *Fye.* $200/£129

THOMPSON, J.A. and J. CANTLIE. Prize Essays on Leprosy. London: New Sydenham Soc, 1897. 413pp; fldg map. (Sl foxing; spine faded, sl worn.) *Whitehart.* $28/£18

THOMPSON, JAMES. Poems, in the Scottish Dialect. Edinburgh: For the author, 1801. 1st ed. Engr frontis port; xxiii,215pp; uncut. (Blind stamps; lib label fr pastedown.) Very Nice in mod half levant morocco gilt solander box. *Hollett.* $457/£295

THOMPSON, JIM. Cropper's Cabin. NY, (1952). VG in pict wraps. *King.* $40/£26

THOMPSON, JIM. The Getaway. (NY): Signet, (1959). 1st Amer ed. Pb orig. Pp sl dknd; lt crease, else VG+ in wrappers. *Between The Covers.* $150/£97

THOMPSON, JIM. The Getaway. NY: Signet, 1959. 1st ed. Pb orig. NF in wraps. *Else Fine.* $125/£81

THOMPSON, JIM. Ironside. NY: Pyramid, 1967. 1st ed. Pb orig. VG+ in wraps (corner crease, minor edgerubs). *Else Fine.* $35/£23

THOMPSON, JIM. The Killer Inside Me. Lion Books #99, 1952. 1st ed. Pb orig. Pg edges lt discolored, sm creases, else Fine in wraps. *Murder.* $350/£226

THOMPSON, JIM. Now and on Earth. Dennis McMillan, 1986. 1st ed. One of 400 signed by Stephen King (intro). Fine in dj. *Madle.* $100/£65

THOMPSON, JOSEPH P. Teachings of the New Testament on Slavery. NY: Joseph H. Ladd, 1856. 1st ed. 52pp. Ptd wraps (spine lt chipped). *Petrilla.* $35/£23

THOMPSON, JOSIAH. Six Seconds in Dallas. Bernard Geis, (1967). 1st ed. Fine in VG dj. *Perier.* $65/£42

THOMPSON, JOSIAH. Six Seconds in Dallas. (NY, 1967). Cl-backed bds (dull). Dj (defective). *King.* $60/£39

THOMPSON, KAY. Eloise at Christmastime. NY: Random House, (1958). 1st ed. Hilary Knight (illus). 4to. Color illus bds (sl loss of acrylic overlay spine/fr hinge; corners bumped). VG-. *Drusilla's.* $115/£74

THOMPSON, KAY. Eloise in Moscow. NY: Random House, (1959). 1st ed. Hilary Knight (illus). 4to. Dbl fldg color spread. Orange illus bds. Good in Good+ dj (soiled, tear; lt rubbed). *Drusilla's.* $100/£65

THOMPSON, KAY. Eloise in Moscow. NY: S&S, 1959. 1st ed. Unpaginated. Hilary Knight (illus). Orange cl bds. VG in VG dj. *Davidson.* $200/£129

THOMPSON, KAY. Eloise in Paris. NY: S & S, 1957. 1st ed. 4to. 65pp. Hilary Knight (illus). Blue cl. VG (base lt faded, inscrip) in VG dj. *Davidson.* $225/£145

THOMPSON, KAY. Eloise in Paris. London: Max Rinehart, 1958. 1st UK ed. Sm 4to. Hilary Knight (illus). Pict gilt on blue cl. Fine in Fine dj (1.5-inch suntanned band top edge). *Book Adoption.* $175/£113

THOMPSON, KAY. Eloise, a Book for Precocious Grown Ups. NY: S&S, 1955. 19th ptg. Hillary Knight (illus). Pict black/red on white bds (sl soil). NF in VG+ dj (sm tear; lt soil). *Book Adoption.* $40/£26

THOMPSON, MARGARET. High Trails of Glacier National Park. Caldwell: Caxton, 1936. 1st ed. Fldg map. VG in VG dj. *Perier.* $50/£32

THOMPSON, R. The Gardeners Assistant. London, (1859). xv,774pp, 12 Fine hand-colored plts. Gilt calf. Sl rubbed, o/w Fine. *Henly.* $194/£125

THOMPSON, R. Unfit for Modest Ears. Macmillan, 1979. Fine in dj. *Moss.* $28/£18

THOMPSON, R.A. The Russian Settlement in California. Oakland: Biobooks, 1951. One of 700. Unopened. Sl offsetting eps, else Fine. *Parmer.* $95/£61

THOMPSON, ROBERT LUTHER. Wiring a Continent. Princeton, 1947. 1st ed. VG (sig, date). *Baade.* $35/£23

THOMPSON, ROBERT. The Gardener's Assistant: Practical and Scientific.... London, 1859. xv,774pp (feps sl foxed); 12 Fine full-pg hand-colored engrs. Orig calf (bumped; rubbed); marbled fore-edges, eps. VG. *Shifrin.* $500/£323

THOMPSON, RUTH PLUMLY. The Cowardly Lion of Oz. Chicago: Reilly & Lee, (1923). 1st ed. Sm 4to. 291pp; 12 color plts by John R. Neill. Grn cl, pict paste label. Label, spine ends sl rubbed; hinges cracked, o/w VG. *Drusilla's.* $175/£113

THOMPSON, RUTH PLUMLY. The Cowardly Lion of Oz. Chicago: Reilly & Lee, (1923). 1st ed. 4to. 12 color plts by John R. Neill. Dark grn cl, color pict paste label; non-standard, in pub's name on spine (rear hinge cracked; few scratches rear cvr). *Reisler.* $250/£161

THOMPSON, RUTH PLUMLY. The Giant Horse of Oz. Chicago: Reilly & Lee, (1928). 1st ed. 8vo. 281pp; 12 tipped-in plts by John R. Neill. One of earliest copies w/'r' in 'morning' undamaged, pg116, line 1. Tp margins sl browned; cl cut on heel, o/w Nice. *Second Life.* $225/£145

THOMPSON, RUTH PLUMLY. The Gnome King of Oz. Chicago: Reilly & Lee, (ca 1935). Early ptg. 4to. John R. Neill (illus). Red cl, lg color pict label. VG in dj (sm chips). *Houle.* $125/£81

THOMPSON, RUTH PLUMLY. Kabumpo in Oz. Chicago: Reilly & Lee. 1st ed, later state. 12 color plts (coated on ptd side only), Kabumpo on p199. John R. Neill (illus). Blue cl, pict cvr label. Good only (hinge cracking, soiled). *Davidson.* $285/£184

THOMPSON, RUTH PLUMLY. King Kojo. Phila: David McKay, (1938). 1st ed. 8vo. 8 color plts. Red cl, color paste label (sl spotting; rear cvr stained; bkpl; pasted descriptions on blank prelims). *Reisler.* $175/£113

THOMPSON, RUTH PLUMLY. The Lost King of Oz. Chicago: Reilly & Lee, (1925). 1st ed, 1st state. 8vo, 280pp, 12 color plts coated on 1 side. J. Neill (illus). Having top serif from letter 'K' on pg 193 (line 4). Blue cl, pict label. VG. *Davidson.* $400/£258

THOMPSON, RUTH PLUMLY. Ozoplaning with the Wizard of Oz. Chicago: Reilly & Lee, (1939). 1st ed. 4to. John R. Neill (illus). Yellow-orange cl, pict paste label (sm corner fold); in pict dj (edgewear; lacks sm piece back). *Reisler.* $675/£435

THOMPSON, RUTH PLUMLY. Pirates in Oz. Chicago, (1931). Later ptg (1946?). John R. Neill (illus). 9x6.5 inches. 280pp. Cl, pict label. Sl tape stains eps, else Nice in dj (tattered; tape stains). *King.* $35/£23

THOMPSON, RUTH PLUMLY. The Purple Prince of Oz. Chicago, (1932). 1st ed, 1st state. 9x6.5 inches. 281pp; 12 full-pg color plts. Cl, pict label. (Bkpl; inner hinges broken; spine split fr cvr; worn.) *King.* $75/£48

THOMPSON, STANBURY (ed). The Journal of John Gabriel Stedman 1744-1797.... London: Mitre Press, 1962. 1st ed. VG in dj (short edge tears). *Hollett.* $54/£35

THOMPSON, THEOPHILUS. Annals of Influenza or Epidemic Catarrhal Fever in Great Britain from 1510 to 1837. London, 1852. 1st ed. 406pp. Good. *Fye.* $150/£97

THOMPSON, THOMAS S. Coast Pilot for the Upper Lakes.... Detroit Free Press, 1869. 5th ed. 175pp + ads. Paper-cvrd bds. Fair (spine cl re-stitched; eps foxed). *Artis.* $550/£355

THOMPSON, TOMMY. The Script Letter. Studio, 1939. 1st ed. Gilt. Good+ (cvrs worn, spine lettering faded). *Willow House.* $23/£15

THOMPSON, W.C. On the Road with a Circus. London, 1903. 1st ed. Pict cl (spine sl chipped; upper joint, hinge split). *Edwards.* $31/£20

THOMPSON, WILLIAM. Reminiscences of a Pioneer. SF, 1912. 1st ed. VG. *Perier.* $50/£32

THOMS, HERBERT. Classical Contributions to Obstetrics and Gynecology. Springfield: Charles C. Thomas, 1935. 1st ed. VG in dj (spine dknd). *White.* $51/£33

THOMS, P.P. A Dissertation on the Ancient Chinese Vases of the Shang Dynasty, From 1743-1496, B.C. London: The Author, 1851. 1st ed. 64pp; 42 wood engr. Gilt stamped blue cl (spine extrems sl rubbed). *Karmiole.* $125/£81

THOMSON, ARTHUR. A Handbook of Anatomy for Art Students. Clarendon, 1915. 4th ed. 66 plts. Dj (lt soiled). *Edwards.* $39/£25

THOMSON, C.W. The Depths of the Sea.... London, 1874. 8vo. xxiii,527pp; 8 maps, plts. Dec cl. Good (ex-lib; spine head, foot sl defective). *Wheldon & Wesley.* $93/£60

THOMSON, C.W. The Voyage of the 'Challenger'—The Atlantic. NY, 1878. 2 vols. 391; 340pp; 42 plts, map. (Lt worn, scuffed; sm splits to spine; fr hinges cracked; ex-lib, #, cards removed; stamps). *Sutton.* $150/£97

THOMSON, CHRISTINE. Not at Night. London, 1926. VG. *Madle.* $45/£29

THOMSON, D. Handy Book of Fruit Culture Under Glass. Edinburgh/London, 1873. 1st ed. x,316pp. (3 lib stamps; cl worn, frayed, spine splitting, fr hinge cracked.) *Sutton.* $75/£48

THOMSON, D. The Life and Art of George Jamesone. OUP, 1974. Color frontis, 126 plts. Sound in dj. *Ars Artis.* $93/£60

THOMSON, DAVID. Oral Vaccines and Immunization by Other Unusual Routes. Balt, 1948. 1st ed. Good. *Fye.* $75/£48

THOMSON, ELIZABETH. Harvey Cushing. NY, 1950. Orig ed. Good. *Goodrich.* $35/£23

THOMSON, ELIZABETH. Harvey Cushing: Surgeon, Author, Artist. NY, 1950. 1st ed. Good. *Fye.* $30/£19

THOMSON, H. DOUGLAS (ed). The Sherlock Holmes. Northumberland Street, London. London: Whitbread & Co, (1950). 1st ed. Purple-ptd wrappers. Sl dusty, o/w VG. *Dalian.* $54/£35

THOMSON, J.J. Applications of Dynamics to Physics and Chemistry. Macmillan, 1888. 1st ed. viii,312pp + ad leaf. (Ink name, date; sm slits top spine; sm hole upper hinge.) *Bickersteth.* $116/£75

THOMSON, J.J. Conduction of Electricity through Gases. CUP, 1903. 1st ed. Uncut, unopened. (Rubber name stamp 3pp.) *Bickersteth.* $248/£160

THOMSON, J.J. Electricity and Matter. Westminster: Constable, 1904. 1st ed. (Spine sl rubbed.) *Bickersteth.* $85/£55

THOMSON, JAMES. Essays and Phantasies. London: Reeves & Turner, 1881. 1st ed. Grn cl. Fine in dj. *Argosy.* $60/£39

THOMSON, JAMES. The Poetical Works. London: Bell & Daldy, 1862. 2 vols. 2 frontispieces; clxxiv,248; 258pp; aeg. Contemp full purple morocco, gilt. *Hollett.* $54/£35

THOMSON, JAMES. The Seasons. London: For A. Millar, 1752. 4 plts. Contemp paneled calf (rubbed; chipped; browning, foxing, mainly 1st, last leaves). *Sadlon.* $85/£55

THOMSON, JAMES. The Seasons. London: Nonesuch Press, 1927. 1st thus. #1182/1500. 5 picts. Dec cvrs; uncut. NF (inscrip). *Polyanthos.* $50/£32

THOMSON, JAMES. The Works. London: A. Millar, 1766. 4 vols. Engr frontis ports. Full polished calf, raised bands, gilt on red leather labels. Attractive set (sm flaws). *Hartfield.* $375/£242

THOMSON, JOHN L. History of the Indian Wars and War of the Revolution of the United States. Phila: Lippincott, 1887. Later ed. 402pp. Brick-red cl. NF. Howes T 213. *Chapel Hill.* $75/£48

THOMSON, JOHN. Francis Thompson. London: Simpkin Marshall Hamilton Kent & Co, 1913. 2nd ed. Frontis port. Brn buckram, gilt. Eps browned, name, cvrs sl bubbled, o/w VG. *Dalian.* $39/£25

THOMSON, RICHARD. Degas. The Nudes. London, 1988. 1st ed. Dj. *Edwards.* $43/£28

THOMSON, SAMUEL. New Guide to Health; or Botanic Family Physician. Boston, 1831-32. 3rd ed. 2 vols in 1. 216; 156pp. Recent cl. *Fye.* $150/£97

THOMSON, SPENCER. Health Resorts of Britain.... London: Ward & Lock, 1860. 1st ed. xii,330pp; fldg map. Cl blocked in blind; gilt lettering (rebacked, preserving orig spine, eps). *Bickersteth.* $70/£45

THOMSON, ST. C. and L. COLLEDGE. Cancer of the Larynx. London, 1930. Inscribed by Colledge. 106 figs on plts. Ex-lib w/stamps, label removal, o/w VG. *Whitehart.* $39/£25

THOMSON, WILLIAM M. Central Palestine and Phoenicia. NY: Harper, 1882. 1st ed. xxiv,689pp; aeg. Full brn morocco (sl wear), gilt, beveled edges. Nice. *House.* $120/£77

THON, MELANIE RAE. Girls in the Grass. NY: Random House, 1991. 1st Amer ed. 1st bk. Fine in Fine dj. *Revere.* $35/£23

THOREAU, HENRY DAVID. Cape Cod. Boston: Ticknor and Fields, 1865. 1st ed. 8vo. Initial blank, pg of ads for Thoreau's writings facing tp; 24pp pub's ad dated Dec, 1864. Pub's pebble-grained slate blue cl (spine sl sunned, rubbed). *D & D.* $450/£290

THOREAU, HENRY DAVID. Cape Cod. Boston: Ticknor & Fields, 1865. 1st ed. One of 2000. 252pp + 24pp pub cat inserted at rear as issued. Grn cl. VG (1-inch split top fr spine edge; cvrs sl dulled; dampstaining first, last pp). BAL 20115. *Chapel Hill.* $450/£290

THOREAU, HENRY DAVID. The Correspondence of Henry David Thoreau. Washington Square: NY Univ Press, 1958. 1st ed, 1st ptg. One of 2000 ptd. Grn cl, gilt. Fine in dj (lt used). BAL 20164. *Macdonnell.* $150/£97

THOREAU, HENRY DAVID. A Little Book of Nature Themes. Portland: Thomas B. Mosher, 1906. 1st ed. Blue-grey ptd wrappers, tissue dj. VF. BAL 20209. *Macdonnell.* $65/£42

THOREAU, HENRY DAVID. Maine Woods. Boston: Ticknor and Fields, 1864. 1st ed. 8vo. Initial blank, pg of ads for Thoreau's writings facing tp; 23pp pub's ad dated April, 1864. Pub's vertical-grained grn cl. Beautiful. *D & D.* $950/£613

THOREAU, HENRY DAVID. Men of Concord. Boston: Houghton Mifflin, 1936. 1st ed thus. 10 color plts by N.C. Wyeth. VG. *Artis.* $45/£29

THOREAU, HENRY DAVID. Sir Walter Raleigh. Boston: Bibliophile Soc, 1905. 1st ed. Ltd to 489. Uncut. 3/4 brn morocco, gilt (sl rubbed). Attractive in box (2-inch chip lower edge). BAL 20142. *Macdonnell.* $225/£145

THOREAU, HENRY DAVID. Transmigration of the Seven Brahmans. NY: William Rudge, 1932. 1st trade ed. One of 1000. Orig 1/4 cl, gilt. Fine in dj (chipped). BAL 20155. *Macdonnell.* $125/£81

THOREAU, HENRY DAVID. Walden, or Life in the Woods. Boston: LEC, 1936. #904/1500 numbered, signed by Edward Steichen (photos). Half-leather, dec bds. Fine in pub's slipcase. *Hermitage.* $900/£581

THOREAU, HENRY DAVID. Walden, or Life in the Woods. Boston: LEC, 1936. 1st ed thus. One of 1500 signed by Edward Steichen (photos). Unopened. Sl wear to spine ends, tips, else NF. *Cahan.* $650/£419

THOREAU, HENRY DAVID. Walden; Or, Life in the Woods. Boston: Ticknor & Fields, 1854. 1st ed. 8vo. 357pp; 8pp pub's cat dated June, 1854 inserted at rear as issued. Orig emb brn cl. Sm marginal dampstain faintly visible top 1st 20pp, else NF. BAL 20106. *Chapel Hill.* $9,000/£5,806

THOREAU, HENRY DAVID. A Week on the Concord and Merrimack Rivers. Boston: LEC, 1975. One of 2000. Signed by Raymond Holden (illus). Fine in VG case. *Agvent.* $100/£65

THOREAU, HENRY DAVID. Where I Lived and What I Lived For. London: Golden Cockerel, 1924. #369/380. 5 wood engrs by Robert Gibbings. Vellum-backed blue batik bds; uncut. Fine (bkpl; pencil mks). *Cox.* $171/£110

THOREAU, HENRY DAVID. Winter: From the Journal of.... H.G.O. Blake (ed). Boston: Houghton, 1888. 1st ed. 14pp pub's cat at end. Gilt-stamped grn cl (lt rubbing); teg. VG. BAL 20131. *Houle.* $295/£190

THORN, JOHN (ed). The Armchair Book of Baseball. Scribner's, 1985. 1st ed. Fine in VG dj. *Plapinger.* $25/£16

THORN, JOHN and PETE PALMER. The Hidden Game of Baseball. Doubleday, 1984. 1st ed. Fine in VG+ dj. *Plapinger.* $40/£26

THORNBURN, ARCHIBALD. British Birds. London: Longmans, Green, 1925. 4 vols. 192 color plts. VG set (backstrips sl faded). *Cox.* $147/£95

THORNBURY, WALTER. Life in Spain. NY: Harper, 1860. 388pp + 8pp ads (foxed). Grn pebble cl (spotted). *Schoyer.* $40/£26

THORNBURY, WALTER. The Life of J.M.W. Turner, R.A. London: C&W, 1877. New ed. xix,636pp (top lt spotted), 8 plts; marbled eps; teg. 1/2 morocco w/marbled bds (upper hinge cracked), gilt. *Edwards.* $93/£60

THORNDIKE, RUSSELL. Dr. Syn Returns. London: Rich & Cowan, 1935. 1st Eng ed. Black cl. Sl mkd, o/w VG. *Dalian.* $39/£25

THORNE, R. THORNE. Diphtheria: Its Natural History and Prevention. London, 1891. 1st ed. 266pp. (Ex-lib.) *Fye.* $40/£26

THORNE, THOMAS. Fuchsias for All Purposes. London, 1959. VG in dj. *Brooks.* $24/£15

THORNHILL, J.B. Adventures in Africa Under the British, Belgian, and Portuguese Flags. London: Murray, 1915. Signed presentation. Fldg map (few pp sl foxed; binding spotted). *Petersfield.* $105/£68

THORNTON, J. QUINN. The California Tragedy. (Oakland: Biobooks, 1945). One of 1500. Inscribed by publisher. Pict cl. Fine in VG+ dj (chipped, spine dknd). Howes T 224. *Harrington.* $50/£32

THORNTON, J. QUINN. Oregon and California in 1848. NY: Harper, 1849. 1st ed. 2 vols. Frontispieces, 393; 379pp + 16pp ads, 10 plts, fldg map. Blind-emb black cl, gilt-lettered spine (cl differs sl each vol; edges, extrems, spine ends worn; corners showing). VG set (eps replaced vol 2; lt foxing). Howes T 224. *Harrington.* $650/£419

THORNTON, JOHN. John Abernethy. London, 1953. 1st ed. Good in dj. *Fye.* $45/£29

THORNTON, PETER. Seventeenth-Century Interior Decoration in England, France and Holland. New Haven/London: Yale/Mellon, 1978. Fine in Mint dj. *Europa.* $74/£48

THORNTON, R.J. Dr. Cullen's Practice of Physic. London, 1816. xxvi,534pp (lt foxing). 1/4 morocco (worn; rebound). *Whitehart.* $93/£60

THORP, JOSEPH. Early Days in the West. (Liberty, MO: Gilmer, 1924). VG in pict wraps. Howes T 231. *Schoyer.* $50/£32

THORP, JOSEPH. Early Days in the West. Liberty, MO, 1924. VG in pict wraps. Howes T 231. *Bohling.* $100/£65

THORP, N. HOWARD. Pardner of the Wind. Caxton, 1945. 1st ed. VG+ (spine sunned). *Authors Of The West.* $50/£32

THORP, N. HOWARD. Tales of the Chuck Wagon. Santa Fe, 1926. 1st ed. Wraps. *Lambeth.* $20/£13

THORP, RAYMOND W. and ROBERT BUNKER. Crow Killer. Bloomington, 1958. 1st ed. NF (sig, date) in dj (sl clipped). *Baade.* $47/£30

THORP, THOMAS BANGS. The Hive of the 'Bee-Hunter'.... NY: Appleton, 1854. 1st ed. 312pp, 9 full-pg wood engrs. Olive grn cl blocked in blind/gilt. Nice (sig, label; sl worn, sl browning to pg edges). Howes T 233. *Cady.* $225/£145

THORPE, ADAM. Mornings in the Baltic. London: Secker & Warburg, 1988. 1st ed. Presentation copy. Fine in dj, wrappers. *Rees.* $39/£25

THORPE, CARLYLE. A Journey to the Walnut Sections of Europe and Asia. L.A., 1923. (Edgewear.) *Sutton.* $35/£23

THORPE, CARLYLE. A Journey to the Walnut Sections of Europe and Asia. L.A.: Privately ptd, 1923. 1st ed. Khaki cl, ptd bds (lt soiled). *Karmiole.* $30/£19

THORPE, JAMES. Phil May. London: Harrap, 1932. Frontis port, 1 color plt. (Sl rubbed, faded, bumped; sm nick.) *Edwards.* $74/£48

Thoughts on a Pebble. (By Gideon Algernon Mantell.) London: Reeve et al, 1849. 8th ed. Engr frontis port, xiii,102pp + 4pp list; 4 chromolithos, 26 linographs. Gilt dec title. (Sl browning, soiling.) *Edwards.* $124/£80

THRAPP, DAN L. Al Sieber, Chief of Scouts. Univ of OK Press, (1964). 1st ed. Fine in dj. *Artis.* $40/£26

THRASHER, HALSEY. The Hunter and Trapper. NY: OJ, (1868). 1st ed. Frontis, iv,91,(5)pp; 5 full-pg woodcuts. Brn cl; gilt. Good. *Karmiole.* $50/£32

Three Little Pigs. L.A.: Intervisual, n.d. Carousel Book. Pop-up. Karen Acosta (illus). Lg 16mo. Glazed pict paper-cvrd bds. VG+. *Book Adoption.* $50/£32

Three Little Pigs/Goldilocks and the Three Bears. London: Bancroft, 1961. 26x20 cm. 8 dbl-pg pop-ups. V. Kubasta (illus). Pict bds w/moveable tab fr, back. VG. *Book Finders.* $140/£90

Three Young Rats and Other Rhymes. NY: Curt Valentin, 1944. 1st ed. Rev copy. One of 700. Alexander Calder (illus). 1/2 cl, illus bds. Dj repaired, o/w VG. *Davidson.* $250/£161

THROCKMORTON, ARTHUR. Oregon Argonauts: Merchant Adventures.... OR Hist Soc, 1961. 1st ed. Ltd to 1000. Pict eps. VF in Fine dj. *Oregon.* $30/£19

Through the Fire of Affliction or Fifteen Years in a Mattress Grave. (By Thomas F. Lockhart). Odessa, MO: MO Ledger Printery, n.d. (1901). Wraps. *Hayman.* $40/£26

THROWER, NORMAN J.W. (ed). The Three Voyages of Edmund Halley in the 'Paramore', 1698-1701. London: Hakluyt Soc, 1981. 1st ed. 2 vols. 15 plts (1 fldg); vol 2 consists of 3 lg map facs in portfolio. Blue cl, gilt. Good in djs. *Karmiole.* $40/£26

THUBRON, COLIN. The Hills of Adonis. London: Heinemann, 1968. 1st Eng ed. Grn cl. Fine in Fine dj (price-clipped). *Dalian.* $54/£35

THUBRON, COLIN. Journey into Cyprus. London: Heinemann, 1975. 1st Eng ed. Grn cl. VF in dj (price-clipped). *Dalian.* $70/£45

THUBRON, COLIN. Mirror to Damascus. London: Heinemann, 1967. Proof copy. 1st bk. VG in ptd wraps (stain). *Williams.* $116/£75

THUBRON, COLIN. Where Nights Are Longest. Random House, 1984. 1st ed. Fine in Fine dj. *Bishop.* $20/£13

THURBER, F.B. Coffee. NY, 1883. 3rd ed. Frontis, xv,416pp (inscrip), 2 plts. (Lt scuffed, soiled; sm spine end tear; fr hinge cracked.) *Sutton.* $95/£61

THURBER, JAMES. Alarms and Diversions. Harper, 1957. 1st ed. Inscribed. VG + in VG dj (lt flaking). *Fine Books.* $350/£226

THURBER, JAMES. Further Fables of Our Time. London: Hamish Hamilton, 1956. 1st Eng ed. Blue cl. Fine in dj (sl chip). *Dalian.* $31/£20

THURBER, JAMES. Many Moons. NY: Harcourt Brace, 1943. 1st ed. 47pp. Louis Slobodkin (illus). Fine (inscrip) in dj (lt soiled, worn). *Davidson.* $185/£119

THURBER, JAMES. The Middle-Aged Man on the Flying Trapeze. NY: Armed Services Ed, (1944). Pp browned, o/w VG in yellow ptd wrappers (sl soiled). *Dalian.* $23/£15

THURBER, JAMES. The Middle-Aged Man on the Flying Trapeze. Hamish Hamilton, 1935. 1st British ed. Pict cl (lt soiled). *Bickersteth.* $101/£65

THURBER, JAMES. The Middle-Aged Man on the Flying Trapeze. H-H, 1935. 1st Eng ed. Lt foxing to spine, else VG in VG- dj (spine head chipped; lt wear). *Fine Books.* $225/£145

THURBER, JAMES. The Thirteen Clocks. NY, (1950). 1st ed, 1st issue. Mark (sic) Simont (illus). Extrems faded, else VG in dj (price-clipped, torn, worn). *King.* $65/£42

THURBER, JAMES. The Thirteen Clocks. NY: S&S, 1950. 1st ed (Marc misspelled Mark on tp). 8vo. 124pp. Marc Simont (illus). Bds, cl. VG in VG dj. *Davidson.* $125/£81

THURBER, JAMES. The Thurber Album. NY: S&S, 1952. 1st ed. VG in dj (spine nicked, lt worn, else VG). *Godot.* $45/£29

THURBER, JAMES. The Thurber Carnival. London: Hamish Hamilton, 1945. 1st ed. Spine sl faded; cvr edges sl browned; o/w Nice in dj (frayed, sl dusty). *Temple.* $16/£10

THURBER, JAMES. Thurber Country. London, (1953). 1st British ed. Sl bumped, else VG in dj (sl soiled). *King.* $30/£19

THURBER, JAMES. A Thurber Garland. London: Hamish Hamilton, 1955. 1st Eng ed. Dec bds. VG. *Dalian.* $23/£15

THURBER, JAMES. The White Deer. NY: Harcourt, Brace, (1945). 1st ed. Ink name, else Fine in dj. *Godot.* $85/£55

THURBER, JAMES. The Years with Ross. London: Hamish Hamilton, (1959). 1st Eng ed. Name, date, else NF in VG dj (sl tanned; chip). *Between The Covers.* $45/£29

THURMAN, MICHAEL E. The Naval Department of San Blas—New Spain's Bastion for Alta California and Nootka. 1767 to 1798. Glendale: Clark, 1967. VG. *Perier.* $47/£30

THWAITE, ANTHONY. At Dunkeswell Abbey. London: Poem-of-the-Month Club Ltd, 1970. 1st Eng ed. Signed. NF (sm mk verso). *Ulysses.* $25/£16

THWAITES, REUBEN G. and LOUISE P. KELLOGG (eds). Documentary History of Dunmore's War 1774. Madison: WI Hist Soc, 1905. 1st ed. Frontis port. Brn cl. Offsetting 2pp, else NF. Howes T 254. *Chapel Hill.* $200/£129

THWAITES, REUBEN G. and LOUISE P. KELLOGG. Frontier Defense on the Upper Ohio, 1777-1778. Madison: WI Hist Soc, 1912. 1st ed. Fldg map. Brn cl. Blindstamp fep, else Fine. Howes T 256. *Chapel Hill.* $150/£97

THWAITES, REUBEN G. and LOUISE P. KELLOGG. The Revolution on the Upper Ohio, 1775-1777. Madison: WI Hist Soc, 1908. 1st ed. Fldg map. Brn cl. Inkstamp fep, else Fine. Howes T 257. *Chapel Hill.* $150/£97

TIBBLES, THOMAS HENRY. Buckskin and Blanket Days. GC: Doubleday, 1957. 1st ed. Fine in VG + dj (lt chipped, rubbed, spine sl faded). *Harrington.* $35/£23

TIBBLES, THOMAS HENRY. Buckskin and Blanket Days. Chicago: R.R. Donnelley, 1985. Map. Teg. Brn cl. Fine. *Harrington.* $30/£19

TICEHURST, CLAUD B. A History of the Birds of Suffolk. London, 1932. Color fldg map. (Label remains; lt spotting; spine faded.) *Edwards.* $70/£45

TICHY, HERBERT. Cho Oyu. London: Methuen, 1957. 1st Eng ed. 36 plts (4 color). VG in dj. *Hollett.* $70/£45

TICKNOR, CAROLINE. Glimpses of Authors. Boston/NY: Houghton, Mifflin, 1922. 1st ed. Maroon cl, heavily gilt. Spine gilt tarnished, else Fine. *Macdonnell.* $50/£32

TICKNOR, GEORGE. Life of William Hickling Prescott. London: Routledge, Warne, & Routledge, 1864. 1st Eng ed. xii,511pp; teg. 3/4 leather, raised bands, gilt titles; marbled paper over bds, eps. Overall VG + (lt shelfwear). *Parmer.* $125/£81

TICKNOR, GEORGE. Life, Letters and Journals of George Ticknor. Boston: James R. Osgood, 1876. 1st ed. 2 vols. viii, 524; 534pp, engr frontis each vol, 1 photogravure. Gray cl, gilt. Good set. *Karmiole.* $50/£32

Tiepolo. A Bicentenary Exhibition 1770-1970. Cambridge: Fogg Art Museum, 1970. 104 plts. Good in wrappers (fr wrapper sl creased). *Washton.* $30/£19

TIETJENS, EUNICE and JANET. The Jaw-Breaker's Alphabet. NY: Albert & Charles Boni, 1930. 1st ed. Oblong 4to. Hermann Post (illus). Cl-backed illus bds (edgewear). *Reisler.* $90/£58

TIETZE, CHRISTOPHER. The Condom as a Contraceptive. NY, 1960. 1st ed. Good in wrappers. *Fye.* $30/£19

TIETZE, HANS. Tintoretto. The Paintings and Drawings. London, 1948. (Sl soiled; corner sl bumped.) *Washton.* $60/£39

TIFFANY, FRANCIS. This Goodly Frame the Earth.... Boston/NY: Houghton, Mifflin, 1896. x,364,(2 blank, 4 ads)pp. *Lefkowicz.* $35/£23

TIFFIN, WALTER F. Gossip About Portraits, Including Engraved Portraits. London: John Russell Smith, 1867. 1st ed. (viii),223pp. Grn cl, blind emb cvrs, gilt. Errata slip tipped in. Very Nice. *Cady.* $35/£23

TILGHMAN, ZOE A. Marshal of the Last Frontier. Glendale: Clark, 1949. 1st ed. Frontis. Fldg map torn along 1 fold, repaired, o/w VG. *Oregon.* $145/£94

TILGHMAN, ZOE A. Marshal of the Last Frontier. Glendale: Clark, 1964. Rev. VG+ (sm discoloration spine). *Parker*. $60/£39

TILGHMAN, ZOE A. Outlaw Days, A True History of Early-Day Oklahoma Characters. (OK City): Harlow Pub Co, 1926. VG+ (pen title on spine) in pict wrappers. *Bohling*. $70/£45

TILKE, MAX. The Costumes of Eastern Europe. London: Ernest Benn, 1926. 1st ed. 96 color plts. Good in dj (sl chipped). *Karmiole*. $250/£161

TILLER, TERENCE. The Inward Animal. London: Hogarth Press, 1943. 1st Eng ed. Red cl. Fine in dj (tanned). *Dalian*. $31/£20

TILLETT, LESLIE (ed). Wind on the Buffalo Grass. NY: Thomas Y. Crowell, (1976). 1st ed. Dj (3 short tears). *Dawson*. $45/£29

TILLOTSON, HARRY S. The Beloved Spy. Caldwell, ID: Caxton Printers, 1948. 1st ed. #145/1000 signed. Frontis port. Untrimmed. Red cl. VG (bkpl, lib blindstamp, release stamp tp). *Chapel Hill*. $60/£39

TILMAN, H.W. The Ascent of Nanda Devi. Cambridge: University Press, 1937. 35 plts; 2 maps (1 fldg). VG in dj (sl worn; spine dknd). *Hollett*. $186/£120

TILMAN, H.W. Mischief in Patagonia. CUP, 1957. 1st ed. 16 plts, 2 maps. Dj (sl foxed, rubbed, sl loss). *Edwards*. $47/£30

TILMAN, H.W. Mount Everest 1938. Cambridge, 1948. 1st ed. Bumped; sl cvr fade, else Good in dj (spine chipped; worn). *King*. $65/£42

TILMAN, H.W. Mount Everest 1938. Cambridge: University Press, 1948. 1st ed. 36 plts; 4 maps. VG (flyleaves spotted) in dj. *Hollett*. $101/£65

TILMAN, H.W. Snow on the Equator. London: G. Bell, 1937. 1st ed. 20pp of plts, 4 maps. Flyleaves, prelims sl spotted. *Hollett*. $101/£65

TILT, EDWARD J. Elements of Health, and Principles of Female Hygiene. Phila, 1853. 1st Amer ed. 436pp. (Exlib.) *Fye*. $75/£48

TILT, EDWARD J. A Hand Book of Uterine Therapeutics, and of Diseases of Women. NY, 1869. 2nd ed. 345pp. Good. *Fye*. $75/£48

TIMBERLAKE, HENRY. Lieut. Henry Timberlake's Memoirs 1756-1765. Samuel Cole Williams (ed). Johnson City, TN: Watauga Press, 1927. 1st ed thus. Frontis, fldg map. Untrimmed. Later blue cl. VG; internally Fine. Howes T 271. *Chapel Hill*. $150/£97

TIMBS, JOHN. Curiosities of London. London, n.d. (c. 1867). New ed. Cl bds (sl soiling; rebacked; lt foxing), gilt device. *Edwards*. $70/£45

Times Telescope for 1832. London: Sherwood, Gilbert & Piper, 1832. 3 books in 1. 112; 172; 104pp, 9 plts. (Worm damage few pp.) Blind-stamped maroon cl (rebacked, orig spine cl laid down; chipped, bkpl). Good. *Knollwood*. $40/£26

TIMLIN, WILLIAM. The Ship that Sailed to Mars. London: Harrap, (1923). 1st ed. 48 color illus tipped in, calligraphic text tipped in. Vellum backstrip, gilt (sl faded), grey sides. (Pg edges sl browned; dampstain fore-edge; sl loose, sl bumped.) *Petersfield*. $698/£450

TIMLIN, WILLIAM. The Ship that Sailed to Mars. A Fantasy. London: George G. Harrap, (1923). Lg, thick 4to. 48 mtd pp of text; 48 mtd color plts. Gold dec vellum-backed bds. Grey paper dj (few pieces missing). *Reisler*. $2,000/£1,290

TIMM, WERNER. The Graphic Art of Edvard Munch. London, 1972. Rpt. 16 color plts. (Margins lt browned; pencil underlining; ex-lib w/ink stamp, label, tape mks.) Dj. *Edwards*. $78/£50

TIMMEN, FRITZ. Blow for the Landing...Steam Navigation on the Waters of the West. Caldwell: Caxton, 1973. 1st ed. Fine in Fine dj. *Perier*. $45/£29

TIMROD, HENRY. The Essays of Henry Timrod. Ed W. Parks (ed). Athens: Univ of GA Press, 1942. 1st Amer ed. NF (spine lt sunned). *Polyanthos*. $35/£23

TIMROD, HENRY. Poems of Henry Timrod. Boston/NY: Houghton, Mifflin, 1899. 1st ptg of Memorial Edition. 193pp. Orig blue cl, teg (binding A). Bkpl, else VG. BAL 20331. *Chapel Hill*. $35/£23

TINBERGEN, N. The Herring Gulls World. London, 1953. 1st ed. 31 plts. Good. *Henly*. $56/£36

TINGLEY, ELBERT R. Poco Loco; Sketches of New Mexico Life. Blair: Danish Lutheran Publ, 1900. 1st ed. VG-. *Parker*. $225/£145

TINKER, EDWARD LAROCQUE. Creole City. NY: Longman's, 1953. 1st ed. Fine in dj. *Pharos*. $22/£14

TINKLE, LON. Mr. De. A Biography of Everette Lee De-Golyer. Boston: Little, Brown, 1970. 1st ed. Frontis. VG in Good dj. *Connolly*. $47/£30

TINLEY, G.F. et al. Colour Planning of the Garden. London, 1924. 64 plts. Sl wear to spine head, tail, o/w Fine. *Henly*. $93/£60

TINSLEY, HENRY C. Two Christmas Stories: Little Tommy Stuffin, Patsy Bolivar. Staunton: Beverley Press, 1905. Unpaged. VG-. *Book Broker*. $25/£16

TINSLEY, JIM BOB. He Was Singin' This Song. Orlando: Univ of Central FL, (1981). Fine in Fine dj. *Perier*. $40/£26

TIPPING, H. AVRAY and CHRISTOPHER HUSSEY. English Homes. Period IV-Vol II. London, 1928. Frontis. Marbled eps, teg. 2-tone cl (sl rubbed, soiled; spine lt faded). *Edwards*. $310/£200

TIPPING, H. AVRAY. English Gardens. London/NY: Country Life/Scribner's, 1925. 1st ed. Gilt; aeg. Rubbed, sl spine wear, lt soil, else VG. *Cahan*. $200/£129

TIPPING, H. AVRAY. English Gardens. London: Country Life, 1925. 1st ed. 521 photos. (Dampstaining lower tips 2nd 1/2 of bk; spine sunned) in dj (lacks spine; chipped). *Bookpress*. $295/£190

TIPPING, H. AVRAY. English Homes. London, 1929. 2nd ed. Aeg. Marbled eps. Contents Fine (cl faded; worn; hinge weak). *Quest*. $110/£71

TIPPING, H. AVRAY. The Garden of Today. London: Martin Hopkinson, 1933. Frontis. Dec eps. Gilt-stamped cl. Fr hinge starting, else Fine. *Quest*. $35/£23

TIPPING, H. AVRAY. Grinling Gibbons and the Wood-Work of His Age (1648-1720). London: Country Life/George Newnes, 1914. 1st ed. Teg. White cl-backed wood veneered bds. Fine (lt wear) in plain dj (worn). *House*. $250/£161

TIPPING, H. AVRAY. Grinling Gibbons and the Woodwork of His Age (1648-1720). Country Life, 1914. (Ex-lib; corners bumped, torn.) *Petersfield*. $186/£120

TISCHNER, HERBERT. Oceanic Art. NY, 1954. VG in dj. *Argosy*. $65/£42

TISSOT, J. JAMES. The Life of Our Savior Jesus Christ. NY: McClure-Tissot, 1899. 1st ed. 4 vols. 4 color frontispieces. 1/2 black morocco over marbled bds, gilt. Good set. *Karmiole*. $175/£113

TISSOT, M. Onanism: or, A Treatise Upon the Disorders Produced by Masturbation.... A. Hume (trans). London: Ptd for Richardson & Urquart, 1781. 5th ed. xii,183pp. Contemp tree sheep; rebacked w/spine laid down. Lt spotting pp, o/w VG. *White.* $147/£95

TITMARSH, M.A. (Pseud of William M. Thackeray.) Doctor Birch and His Young Friends. London: Chapman and Hall, 1849. 49pp + 1pg ad, 16 uncolored plts (incl frontis, vignette tp) by Thackeray. 3/4 leather, marbled bds (sl edge rubbing). *Schoyer.* $150/£97

TITMARSH, M.A. (Pseud of William M. Thackeray.) The Kicklebury's on the Rhine. London: Smith, Elder, 1850. 87pp, 15 tinted plts (incl vignette title) by Thackeray. 3/4 leather, marbled bds (joints rubbed, sl starting). *Schoyer.* $100/£65

TITMARSH, M.A. (Pseud of William M. Thackeray.) Notes of a Journey from Cornhill to Grand Cairo. London: Chapman & Hall, 1846. 1st ed. Hand-colored frontis; xiv,301pp. Teg. Contemp half brn morocco, bds, raised bands. NF. *Chapel Hill.* $350/£226

TITMARSH, M.A. (Pseud of William M. Thackeray.) Our Street. London: Chapman & Hall, 1848. 1st ed, 1st issue (w/colored plts). 54pp, 16 hand-colored plts (incl frontis, vignette tp) by Thackeray. Full red morocco (sl wear). Aeg. Pict wraps (soiled) bound in. *Schoyer.* $300/£194

TITMARSH, M.A. (Pseud of William M. Thackeray.) Rebecca and Rowena. London: Chapman and Hall, 1850. 1st ed. viii,102pp, 8 hand-colored plts + uncolored vignette tp. Full brn morocco. Aeg. Fine. *Schoyer.* $250/£161

TITMARSH, M.A. (Pseud of William M. Thackeray.) The Rose and the Ring. London: Smith, Elder, 1855. 1st ed. iv,128pp; 8 plts by Thackeray. Full lt brn morocco. Aeg. Fine. *Schoyer.* $225/£145

TITMARSH, M.A. (Pseud of William M. Thackeray). The Second Funeral: In Three Letters to Miss Smith of London. And the Chronicle of the Drum. London, 1841. 1st ed. Sq 12mo. Frontis, 122pp, 2 plts. Sl staining, o/w Good +. Orig ptd card wraps (soiled; repairs to spine; upper wrap nearly detached). *Edwards.* $194/£125

TITOV, HERMAN and MARTIN CAIDIN. I Am Eagle! Indianapolis: Bobbs-Merrill, 1962. 1st ed. VG in dj (worn, corner clipped). *Knollwood.* $35/£23

Tity and Mirtillo. Wellington: F. Houlston, n.d. (ca 1805). Sm 12mo. Frontis, 46pp + 2pp ads; 5 full-pg oval woodcuts. Stiff paper wrappers (lt faded, soiled, chipped), engr title label. Internally VG (ink names, spot tp, frontis). *Hobbyhorse.* $175/£113

TOBIE, HARVEY E. No Man Like Joe. Portland: Binfords & Mort, (1949). 1st ed. VG in VG dj. *Perier.* $32/£21

TOBIN, TERENCE. Plays by Scots 1660-1800. Iowa City: Univ of IA, (1974). Pub's cl (lt soiled). *Dramatis Personae.* $40/£26

Toby Twirls Dilly Paddle Pop-Up Book. London: Sampson and Low, n.d. (195?). 26x20 cm. 5 pop-ups. Glazed pict bds, spiral binding. VG (label). *Book Finders.* $120/£77

TODD, CHARLES BURR. General History of the Burr Family in America. NY, 1878. 1st ed. 455,(1)pp. Gold-stamped cl. *Ginsberg.* $150/£97

TODD, EDWIN. The Neuroanatomy of Leonardo Da Vinci. Santa Barbara, CA, 1983. 1st ed. Good. *Fye.* $75/£48

TODD, F.S. Waterfowl.... NY, 1979. Signed. Dj. *Sutton.* $110/£71

TODD, FRANK. Eradicating Plague from San Francisco. SF, 1909. 1st ed. Good. *Fye.* $50/£32

TODD, FRANK. The Story of the Exposition. NY: Putnam's, 1921. 1st ed. 5 vols. 3-pg color panoramic frontis; lg fldg map; 61 color plts. Red gilt cl. Good. *Karmiole.* $185/£119

TODD, FREDERICK. Soldiers of the American Army 1775-1954. Chicago: Henry Regnery, (1954). 32 color plts. VG. *Graf.* $48/£31

TODD, FREDERICK. Soldiers of the American Army, 1775-1954. Chicago: Regnery, (1954). 1st thus. Fine in Good+ dj (sm chips). *Oregon.* $45/£29

TODD, RICHARD CECIL. Confederate Finance. Athens: Univ of GA, 1954. 1st ed. NF in dj (sm chip, 2 short closed tears). *Cahan.* $40/£26

TODD, RUTHVEN. Tracks in the Snow. NY: Scribner's, 1947. 1st ed. Nice in dj (sunned). *Pharos.* $35/£23

TODD, SERENO EDWARDS. The Apple Culturist. NY: Harper, 1871. 1st ed. 334pp + ads. Grn cl. Good (sm chip; rubbing). *Second Life.* $75/£48

TOESCA, PIETRO and FERDINANDO FORLATI. Mosaics of St. Marks. CT: NYGS, 1958. 44 color plts w/interleaved blanks. (Ink stamp.) Mod cl (rebound). *Edwards.* $62/£40

TOKE, MONROE TSA. The Peyote Ritual. SF: Grabhorn Press, (1957). Ltd to 325. 14 color plts. Pict bds. Fine in plain dj (edges shabby). *Glaser.* $300/£194

TOKLAS, ALICE B. The Autobiography of Alice B. Toklas. (By Gertrude Stein.) London: John Lane, 1933. 1st Eng ed. Sig, edges foxed, else VG in dj (spine sl browned). *Limestone.* $215/£139

TOKLAS, ALICE B. The Autobiography. London: John Lane, Bodley Head, 1935. 1st ed thus. Grn cl. VG. *Dalian.* $23/£15

TOKLAS, ALICE B. Staying on Alone: Letters of Alice B. Toklas. NY: Liveright, (1973). 1st ed. Fine in dj (chipped). *Hermitage.* $40/£26

TOKLAS, ALICE B. What Is Remembered. London: Michael Joseph, (1963). 1st Eng ed. VG in dj (sl chipped). *Hermitage.* $40/£26

TOLKIEN, J.R.R. The Adventures of Tom Bombadil and Other Verses from the Red Book. London: George Allen & Unwin, (1962). 1st ed. Signed by Pauline Baynes (illus). Tall, 8vo. Color illus bds; color dj. Fine. *Reisler.* $335/£216

TOLKIEN, J.R.R. Beowulf: the Monsters and the Critics. N.p., n.d. (1936). 1st Eng ed. VG (cvrs dusty, sl soiled; cvr edges sl rubbed; corners sl creased; upper cvr faded). *Ulysses.* $225/£145

TOLKIEN, J.R.R. Farmer Giles of Ham. London: George Allen & Unwin, 1949. 1st UK ed. NF in VG dj (sm chip; closed tears). *Williams.* $74/£48

TOLKIEN, J.R.R. The Hobbit. A&U, 1937. 1st ed. NF in VG, bright dj (lt wear, chipping). *Fine Books.* $6,500/£4,194

TOLKIEN, J.R.R. The Hobbit. H-M, 1938. 1st Amer ed, 1st issue w/o 1/2-title; w/bowing figure as opposed to H-M logo on tp. 4 color illlus. Nick spine head, else VG + in VG- dj (wear, tear; lt chipping; staining). *Aronovitz.* $1,975/£1,274

TOLKIEN, J.R.R. Pictures: By J.R.R. Tolkien. Boston: Houghton Mifflin, 1979. 1st Amer ed. 48 full-pg color plts. Gilt emblem. Fine in pub's slipcase (tips lt rubbed). *Cahan.* $60/£39

TOLKIEN, J.R.R. The Return of the King. A&U, 1955. 1st ed. Fine in VG + dj (spine lt sunned). *Aronovitz.* $750/£484

TOLKIEN, J.R.R. The Return of the King. London: George Allen & Unwin, 1955. 1st UK ed. Virtually Fine in VG + dj (sl dknd patches). *Williams.* $736/£475

TOLKIEN, J.R.R. The Road Goes Ever On. Boston: Houghton Mifflin, 1967. 1st ed. Fine in dj (sl faded). *Second Life.* $75/£48

TOLKIEN, J.R.R. The Silmarillion. London: George Allen & Unwin, (1977). 1st Eng ed. Fine in dj. *Antic Hay.* $45/£29

TOLKIEN, J.R.R. The Silmarillion. Boston: Houghton, Mifflin, 1977. 1st Amer ed, 1st issue, w/perfect type on pg 299 & w/'Father' for Farmer Giles on pg (3). Fine in NF dj. *Antic Hay.* $20/£13

TOLKIEN, J.R.R. The Silmarillion. A&U, 1977. 1st ed. As New in dj. *Aronovitz.* $30/£19

TOLKIEN, J.R.R. Sir Gawain and the Green Knight, Pearl, Sir Orfeo. Boston: Houghton, Mifflin, 1975. 1st Amer ed. Fine in NF dj (short tear). *Antic Hay.* $35/£23

TOLKIEN, J.R.R. Smith of Wootton Major. London: Allen & Unwin, 1967. 1st ed. Frontis. White glazed bds. Fine; issued w/o dj. *Temple.* $51/£33

TOLKIEN, J.R.R. The Two Towers. London: George Allen & Unwin, 1954. 1st UK ed. NF (lacks dj). *Williams.* $287/£185

TOLKIN, MICHAEL. The Player. NY: Atlantic Monthly Press, 1988. 1st ed, 1st bk. Fine in Fine dj. *Revere.* $35/£23

TOLLER, JANE. Prisoners-of-War Work 1756-1815. Cambridge: Golden Head Press, 1965. 1st ed. VF in dj. *Lefkowicz.* $75/£48

TOLLES, FREDERICK B. George Logan of Philadelphia. NY: OUP, 1953. 1st ed. Frontis port. Blue cl. Faded spots spine, else VG. *Chapel Hill.* $40/£26

TOLMIE, WILLIAM FRASER. Physician and Fur Trader. Vancouver: Mitchell Press, 1963. 1st ed. Fine in dj (torn). *Perier.* $30/£19

TOLNAY, C. DE. The Drawings of Pieter Brueghel the Elder. London, 1952. Rev ed. Cl (sl worn). *Ars Artis.* $93/£60

TOLSTOI, COUNTESS SOPHIE. Autobiography of Countess Sophie Tolstoi. S.S. Koteliansky & Leonard Woolf (trans). London: Hogarth Press, 1922. One of 1000 ptd. White marbled bds. Integral ad leaf at end. Spine ends worn, faded; edges sl rubbed, o/w Fine w/o ptd dj, as issued. *Temple.* $116/£75

TOLSTOI, LEV NIKOLAEVITCH. Anna Karenina. NY: Thomas Y. Crowell, (1886). 1st ed in English. Variant state w/o pub's device or address on title, w/o ptr's imprint on verso, w/o ads. Variant binding in blue cl (restored, strengthened, refurbished; eps replaced), smaller imperial eagle top cvr. (Wear; text sl brittle; nicks, tears; sm repaired hole 1 leaf; leaf ink-splashed.) *Ash.* $194/£125

TOLSTOY, ALEXANDRA. I Worked for the Soviet. New Haven: Yale, 1934. 1st ed. VG in dj (edgewear, chips). *Aka.* $35/£23

TOLSTOY, LEO. Anna Karenina. Moscow: LEC, 1933. #1402/1500 numbered sets, signed by Nikolas Piskariov (illus). 2 vols. Fine in new slipcase. *Hermitage.* $275/£177

TOLSTOY, LEO. Anna Karenina. Cambridge: LEC, 1951. #904/1500 numbered, signed by Barnett Freedman (illus). 2 vols. NF in pub's slipcase. *Hermitage.* $125/£81

TOLSTOY, LEO. Anna Karenina. Cambridge: LEC, 1951. One of 1500. Signed by Barnett Freedman (litho). 2 vols. NF in VG djs & slipcase. *Agvent.* $125/£81

TOLSTOY, LEO. Childhood. Boyhood. Youth. NY: Crowell, (1886). 1st Amer ed. Dec cl. Bright (bkpl; rubbing; soiling). *Agvent.* $125/£81

TOLSTOY, LEO. Resurrection. NY: LEC, 1963. One of 1500. Signed by Fritz Eichenberg (artist). Blue/tan buckram. Fine in Fine slipcase. *Agvent.* $125/£81

TOLSTOY, LEO. Sebastopol. NY: Harpers, 1887. 1st Amer ed. Port. VG (lg bkpl; rubbed; spine tips worn). *Agvent.* $75/£48

Tom Thumb's Folio.... York: J. Kendrew, n.d. (ca 1820). Chapbook. 16mo. 31pp + 1pg list. Dec ptd title on gray stiff paper wrappers. VF (lt chipped). *Hobbyhorse.* $175/£113

Tom Thumb. NY: McLoughlin Bros, 1888. Cock Robin Series. 4to. 8pp; 6 full-pg chromolithos. 1st, last pp pasted down on wrappers. Chromolitho pict glossy wrappers. (Ink dedication tp; vertical fold throughout; lt rubbing, chipping at spine, edges.) Internally VG. *Hobbyhorse.* $75/£48

Tom Thumb. NY: McLoughlin Bros, 1897. Cock Robin Series. 4to. 6 leaves; 6 full-pg chromolithos. Pict stiff paper wrappers. Fine (minor rubbing at spine). *Hobbyhorse.* $225/£145

TOMES, J. A System of Dental Surgery. London, 1906. 5th ed. (Sl stained, worn; joint sl cracked.) *Whitehart.* $39/£25

TOMKINS, CALVIN. Living Well Is the Best Revenge. Viking, 1962. 1st ed. NF in dj. *Stahr.* $25/£16

TOMLINSON, EVERETT T. Camping on the St. Lawrence. Boston, 1899. vi,412pp. Grn cl, pict cvr. Good (spine dknd). *Peninsula.* $25/£16

TOMLINSON, H.M. All Our Yesterdays. NY/London: Harper, 1930. Ltd to 350 signed. Paper label (sl rubbed; spine sl dknd). *Sadlon.* $25/£16

TOMLINSON, H.M. Gallion's Reach. NY: Harpers, 1927. Ltd to 350 numbered, signed. 4 tipped-in woodcut illus. Cl-backed bds, paper spine label (dull). 2 leaves torn, else VG. *Pharos.* $60/£39

TOMLINSON, H.M. London River. London: Cassell, 1921. 1st ed. Sm nick spine, else VG. *Reese.* $30/£19

TOMLINSON, H.M. Old Junk. London: Andrew Melrose, 1918. 1st Eng ed. Purple cl. Faded, inscrip, eps foxed, o/w VG. *Dalian.* $70/£45

TOMLINSON, H.M. Out of Soundings. London: Heinemann, 1931. 1st ed. One of 275 signed by author and H. Charles Tomlinson (illus). Unopened. Grn cl. Few bubbles spine, o/w Fine in slipcase (lt used). *Juvelis.* $75/£48

TOMLINSON, H.M. The Sea and the Jungle. London: Duckworth, (1912). 1st ed, 1st bk. Frontis; 20pp ads at end. Gilt-stamped grn cl; teg. VG in matching grn cl fldg box. *Houle.* $250/£161

TOMLINSON, H.M. The Sea and the Jungle. London, 1930. 1st ed. Uncut, partly unopened. Clare Leighton (illus). Fine (spine sl sunned). *Polyanthos.* $200/£129

TOMLINSON, H.M. The Sea and the Jungle. London: Duckworth, 1930. 1st illus ed. One of 515 signed. 7 full-pg woodcuts; teg. NF in dj (sl dusty, rubbed). *Cahan.* $250/£161

TOMLINSON, H.M. The Sea and the Jungle. Barre: Imprint Society, 1971. #107/1950 signed by Garrick Palmer (illus). Half leather-backed pict cl. Bkpl, else Fine in pub's slipcase. *Hermitage.* $85/£55

TOMLINSON, H.M. Waiting for Daylight. London: Cassell, 1922. 1st ed. Fine in dj (lt rubbed). *Pharos.* $45/£29

TOMLINSON, H.M. Waiting for Daylight. London: Cassell, 1922. 1st Eng ed. Maroon cl. Obituary cuttings tipped in. VG (blind presentation stamp tp). *Dalian.* $31/£20

TOMLINSON, J. (ed). The Paintings and the Journal of Joseph Whiting Stock. Wesleyan Univ Press, 1976. Port. Sound in dj. *Ars Artis.* $39/£25

TOMLINSON, WILLIAM WEAVER. Comprehensive Guide to Northumberland. Newcastle-on-Tyne: William H. Robinson, (c. 1930). 11th ed. 3 fldg maps; fldg map in rear pocket. VG. *Hollett.* $31/£20

Tommy Tatters. NY: McLoughlin Bros, n.d. (ca 1880). Uncle Toby's Series. Sq 16mo. 8 leaves + 1p list lower wrapper; 4 VF full-pg chromolithos. Pict stiff paper wrappers. Tp reads 'Tommy Tatter.' VG (sm split lower wrapper). *Hobbyhorse.* $85/£55

TOMORY, PETER. The Life and Art of Henry Fuseli. London, (1972). 267 plts (13 color). VG in dj. *Argosy.* $85/£55

TOMPKINS, FRANK. Chasing Villa. Harrisburg, 1934. 1st ed. Pict cvr. VG +. *Pratt.* $100/£65

TOMPKINS, PETER (ed). To a Young Actress. NY, 1960. 1st ed. As New in Perfect dj. *Bond.* $25/£16

TOMPKINS, WALKER. Santa Barbara's Royal Rancho. Berkeley: Howell North, 1960. 1st ed. Fine in Fine dj. *Oregon.* $35/£23

TOOKER, ELISABETH. An Ethnography of Huron Indians, 1615-1649. BAE Bulletin 190. 1964. 1st ed. Fine. *Oregon.* $30/£19

TOOKER, RICHARD. The Day of the Brown Horde. Payson & Clarke, 1929. 1st ed. VG in dj (lt chipped). *Madle.* $100/£65

TOOLE, JOHN KENNEDY. A Confederacy of Dunces. Baton Rouge: LA State Univ, 1980. 'Second Printing.' Rev slip laid in dated 5/31/80. Lt grn cl. VF in VF dj. *Pharos.* $60/£39

TOOLE, JOHN KENNEDY. A Confederacy of Dunces. Baton Rouge: LSU, 1980. 1st Amer ed. Fine in NF dj (spine, extrems sl rubbed). *Between The Covers.* $750/£484

TOOLE, JOHN KENNEDY. A Confederacy of Dunces. Baton Rouge: LA State Univ Press, 1980. 1st ed, 1st bk. 8vo. VF in dj (sl rubbed). *Jaffe.* $650/£419

TOOLEY, R.V. English Books with Coloured Plates 1790 to 1860. Boston: Boston Book & Art Shop, (1954). 1st ed. Blue cl. Fine in dj. *House.* $100/£65

TOOLEY, R.V. English Books with Coloured Plates 1790 to 1860. London: Batsford, 1954. 1st ed. (Ex-lib w/ink stamps, bkpl, #s). *Edwards.* $54/£35

TOOLEY, R.V. Some English Books with Colour Plates. Ingpen, 1935. 1st ed. Teg. Sl dull, else VG. *Whiteson.* $109/£70

TOOLEY, SARAH. The History of Nursing in the British Empire. London, 1906. 1st ed. (Spine head, tail worn, torn.) *Fye.* $100/£65

TOOMBS, SAMUEL. New Jersey Troops in the Gettysburg Campaign.... Orange, NJ: 1888. 1st ed. 406pp. VG. *Pratt.* $75/£48

TOOMER, JEAN. Essentials. Chicago: Private Edition, 1931. 1st ed, #429/1000. 8vo. Fine (1931 sig under fr flap; pencil check mks) in VG dj (soiled). *Chapel Hill.* $1,100/£710

TOOMER, JEAN. Essentials. Chicago: Private Ed, 1931. 1st ed. One of 1000 numbered, this unnumbered. Black cl, ptd labels. Fine in ptd dj. *Cahan.* $650/£419

TOPHAM, EDWARD. The Life of John Elwes, Esquire.... London: Thomas Davison, 1790. 1st bk ed. Etched frontis port, viii,98pp, fldg table, marbled eps. Aeg. 1/2 red morocco, gilt spine. Very Nice (tp cut sl close, not affecting text, expertly remargined; bkpl, sig). *Cady.* $125/£81

TOPLEY, W.W.C. An Outline of Immunity. Balt, 1933. 1st Amer ed. Good. *Fye.* $40/£26

TOPONCE, ALEXANDER. Reminiscences of Alexander Toponce-Pioneer 1839-1923. Ogden, 1923. VG. Howes T 299. *Perier.* $175/£113

Topsy. NY: McLoughlin Bros, ca 1900. Shape book of Topsy wearing big hat, carrying slice of watermelon. 9 inches tall. 2 full-pg, 1 double-pg chromos. Stiff pict wraps. NF. *Davidson.* $350/£226

TORCYZNER, HARRY. Magritte. Richard Miller (trans). NY, 1977. Dj (rubbed, sl torn). *Edwards.* $70/£45

TORME, MEL. The Other Side of the Rainbow. NY: Morrow, 1970. 1st ed. VG in dj (nicks). *Houle.* $37/£24

TOULOUSE-LAUTREC. Lautrec by Lautrec. NY, (1964). 1st ed. VG in dj. *Argosy.* $60/£39

Tour on the Prairies. (By Washington Irving.) London: John Murray, 1835. 1st British ed. Orig bds, cl, spine label. VG. BAL 10139. *Authors Of The West.* $500/£323

Tour on the Prairies. (By Washington Irving.) Phila: Carey, Lea & Blanchard, 1835. 1st ed, 1st issue. 'The Crayon Series, No. 1.) Prelim series tp, 'advertisement' leaf precede actual tp. 'No. 1.' does not appear on spine label. 274pp + 24pp ads. Grn cl (rubbed, soiled); paper spine label (chipped). BAL 10140. *Karmiole.* $125/£81

Tour, Through Upper and Lower Canada. (By John C. Ogden.) Litchfield, (CT), 1799. 1st ed. 12mo. 119pp. Orig full leather. VG (corner of last leaf missing, w/loss; bkpl). Howes O 38 *Schoyer.* $550/£355

TOURGEE, ALBION W. An Appeal to Caesar. NY: Fords, Howard & Hulbert, 1884. 1st ed. Pict cl. VG. *Connolly.* $50/£32

TOURNIER, MICHEL. The Fetishist. Barbara Wright (trans). GC: Doubleday, 1984. 1st Amer ed. VF in dj. *Reese.* $30/£19

TOURTOULON, PIERRE DE. Philosophy in the Development of Law. NY: Macmillan, 1922. Blue cl; gilt. (Worn.) *Boswell.* $75/£48

TOWN, L. Bookbinding by Hand. Faber, 1951. 1st ed. Signed. VG in dj. *Moss.* $47/£30

TOWN, L. Bookbinding by Hand. Faber, 1963. VG in dj. *Moss.* $37/£24

TOWNSEND, ALEX. Wooden Woman. Doubleday, Doran, 1930. 1st ed. Fine in dj. *Madle.* $50/£32

TOWNSEND, CHARLES WENDELL (ed). Captain Cartwright and His Labrador Journal. Boston, 1911. 1st ed. Fldg map. (Marginal browning; ex-libris; blind stamp fep; spine faded.) *Edwards.* $54/£35

TOWNSEND, E.D. Anecdotes of the Civil War in the United States. NY: Appleton, 1884. 1st ed. Inscribed. 287pp + (12)pp ads. Orig dec brn cl. VG (lib bkpl, # bottom of preface). *Chapel Hill.* $45/£29

TOWNSEND, E.D. The California Diary of General E.D. Townsend. Malcolm Edwards (ed). (N.p.): Ward Ritchie Press, (1970). 1st ed. Black cl. Fine in Fine slipcase. *Harrington.* $40/£26

TOWNSEND, JOHN K. Narrative of a Journey Across the Rocky Mountains, to the Columbia River.... Phila: Henry Perkins, 1839. 1st ed. 352pp. Orig brn blind-emb cl (rebacked), orig spine laid on (corners, edges showing; sm part rear bd rippled). VG (expertly re-hinged; lt rubbed, soiled; 2 clippings glued fep; lt internal foxing). Howes T 319. *Harrington.* $525/£339

TOWNSEND, PETER S. Account of the Yellow Fever, as It Prevailed in the City of New York, in the Summer and Autumn of 1822. NY, 1823. 1st ed. 383pp. New cl-backed bds. (Ex-lib; few pp torn/reinforced w/o loss; upper corner waterstained.) *Argosy.* $150/£97

TOWNSEND, W. CHARLES. Memoirs of the House of Commons, from the Convention Parliament of 1688-9 to the Passing of the Reform Bill, in 1832. London: Henry Colburn, 1844. 2nd ed. 2 vols. Full contemp calf, gilt. *Boswell.* $450/£290

TOWNSEND, WILLIAM H. Lincoln and Liquor. NY: Press of the Pioneers, 1934. Cl faded, worn, but Sound. *Boswell.* $75/£48

TOWNSHEND, CHAUNCY HARE. Facts in Mesmerism, or Animal Magnetism.... Boston, 1841. 1st Amer ed. x,(2),549pp. Orig blind-stamped cl (worn; joints partially split; bumped). Internally Excellent. *Hemlock.* $175/£113

TOWNSHEND, CHAUNCY HARE. Facts in Mesmerism.... London: Hippolyte Bailliere, 1844. 2nd ed. xxxvi,390pp. Orig grn cl (sl rubbed; lt spotting). *White.* $85/£55

TOXOPEUS, KLASS. Flying Storm. NY: Dodd, Mead, (1954). 1st ed. VG in Good+ dj. *Blue Dragon.* $22/£14

Toy-Shop; or, Sentimental Preceptor.... (By Richard Johnson.) Swaffam: F. Skill, 1830. New ed rev by E.H. Barker. 12mo. viii+172pp+4pp list, full-pg engr frontis, tp vignette. Black roan marbled paper on bds, gilt title spine (ink dedication; rubbed). Internally Fine. *Hobbyhorse.* $325/£210

TOYNBEE, J. and J. WARD PERKINS. The Shrine of St. Peter and the Vatican Excavations. London/NY/Toronto: Longmans, 1958. 32 plts. Spine sl faded, o/w Fine. *Europa.* $34/£22

TOYNBEE, J.M.C. Art in Britain under the Romans. London: OUP, 1964. (Ex-lib.) *Edwards.* $43/£28

TOYNBEE, J.M.C. Art in Britain under the Romans. Oxford: Clarendon, 1964. Pub's buckram, gilt. Fine. *Peter Taylor.* $71/£46

TOYNBEE, J.M.C. Art in Roman Britain. London: Phaidon, 1962. (Ex-lib w/ink stamps, bkpl.) Dj (sl chipped). *Edwards.* $42/£27

TRACY, CHARLES. An American Sur-Realist. Boston: Christopher Pub House, (1939). 1st ed. Fine in pict dj. *Godot.* $125/£81

TRACY, JACK with JIM BERKEY. Subcutaneously, My Dear Watson: Sherlock Holmes and the Cocaine Habit. Bloomington: James A. Rock, 1978. 1st ed. Fine in Fine dj. *Janus.* $50/£32

TRACY, JACK. The Encyclopedia Sherlockiana. NY, (1977). 1st ed. Fine (name) in dj. *Artis.* $17/£11

TRACY, LOUIS. An American Emperor. Putnam, 1897. 1st ed. VG. *Madle.* $65/£42

TRACY, LOUIS. The Final War. Putnam, 1896. 1st US ed. VG+. *Madle.* $95/£61

TRACY, LOUIS. Karl Grier. Clode, 1905. 1st ed. VG. *Madle.* $45/£29

TRACY, LOUIS. The Lost Provinces. Putnam, 1898. 1st US ed. VG. *Madle.* $90/£58

Tragi-Comic History of the Burial of Cock Robin; with the Lamentation of Jenny Wren.... Phila: Benjamin Warner, 1821. Sq 12mo. Frontis, 17pp; 7 full-pg wood engrs (sm rip frontis, last cut). Pink paper wrappers. Good (bkpl, internally browned). *Hobbyhorse.* $170/£110

Train and Bank Robbers of the West. (By Augustus C. Appler). Chicago: Belford, Clarke, (1880). 313, 287pp. 12 plts. Rear pocket present. Pict cl (worn; stamp on edges). Howes A 295. *Schoyer.* $50/£32

TRAIN, ARTHUR. The Lost Gospel. Scribners, 1925. 1st ed. VG. *Madle.* $30/£19

TRAIN, ARTHUR. The Man Who Rocked the Earth. NY: Doubleday, Page, 1915. 1st ed, binding variant A. Dk blue pict cl. Sm pencil mk fep, else Fine. *Godot.* $85/£55

TRALBAUT, MARC EDO. Vincent Van Gogh. NY: Viking, (1969). 1st Amer ed. VF in Fine dj. *Hermitage.* $85/£55

TRALL, R.T. Diphtheria: Its Nature, History, Causes.... NY, 1862. 1st ed. 276pp. Good. *Fye.* $40/£26

TRALL, R.T. Hand-Book of Hygienic Practice; Intended as a Practical Guide for the Sick-Room.... NY, 1865. 1st ed. 300pp; 49 woodcut illus. Good. *Fye.* $75/£48

TRALL, R.T. Pathology of the Reproductive Organs; Embracing All Forms of Sexual Disorders. Boston, 1862. 1st ed. 2 vols in 1. 242; 279pp. Full leather. Good. *Fye.* $150/£97

TRAMS, A. FRANCIS. More Marginalia: Based on Leigh Hunt's Copy of Henry E. Napier's 'Florentine History' 1846. Cedar Rapids: Privately ptd (Torch Press), 1931. Ltd to 325. *Graf.* $35/£23

Transactions of the 3rd Annual Re-Union of the Oregon Pioneer Association...and A Biography of Col. Jos. L. Meek. Salem: EM Waite, 1876. 1st ed. VG in wraps. *Oregon.* $40/£26

Transactions of the Horticultural Society of London. 2nd Series. Vol 1. London, 1835. xi,546,(40)pp, 22 plts. Full calf (worn, scuffed; parts of backstrip missing; outer hinges split). *Sutton.* $50/£32

Transactions of the Kansas State Historical Society, 1905-1906. Vol IX. 1906. Fldg map. VG. Howes C 301. *Oregon.* $60/£39

TRAQUAIR, RAMSAY. The Old Silver of Quebec. Toronto: Macmillan, 1940. 1st ed. 16 plts. VG. *Oregon.* $95/£61

TRASK, LEONARD. A Brief Sketch of the Life and Sufferings of Leonard Trask, the Wonderful Invalid. Portland, 1858. 48pp. (Ex-lib.) Ptd wrappers. *Argosy.* $50/£32

TRAUTMAN, MILTON B. The Birds of Buckeye Lake, Ohio. Ann Arbor, 1940. Good (orig wraps bound in). *Hayman.* $50/£32

Traveller's Guide Through the Middle and Northern States, and the Provinces of Canada.... (By M. Gideon Davison.) Saratoga Springs, 1833. Styled 'fifth edition-enlgd and improved' on tp. Frontis; 448pp. Orig 1/2 calf, marbled bds (worn, scuffed). Internally VG. Howes D 143. *Ginsberg.* $125/£81

Travels and Adventures in the Congo Free State.... (By Henry Bailey.) London: Chapman & Hall, 1894. 1st ed. 8vo. Frontis, xiv,(i)illus,(i)blank,335pp, half title (sm lib stamp), fldg map. Maroon cl. Good (lt spotting; lib plt, extrems sl rubbed). *Morrell.* $395/£255

Travels and Adventures of John Bull the Younger. London: John Harris, n.d. (1827). 12mo. 14 leaves, each ptd w/1/2pg hand-colored engr. Ptd stiff wrappers (rebound into black morocco full leather) w/gilt title; name in gilt title upper cvr misspelled 'Jhon.' Watermkd 1827. Fine. *Hobbyhorse.* $375/£242

Travels Through the Interior Parts of North America. (By Thomas Anburey.) London: William Lane, 1791. 2nd ed. 2 vols. xii,414; 492pp. Fldg map (linen backed); 6 plts. Teg, other edges untrimmed. Later (19th cent) 3/4 leather w/marbled bds. Nice set. Howes A 226. *Schoyer.* $500/£323

TRAVEN, B. The Carreta. London: C&W, 1935. 1st Eng ed. VG+. *Limestone.* $185/£119

TRAVEN, B. General From the Jungle. H&W, 1972. 1st Amer ed. Minor soil to fore-edge, else Fine in dj. *Fine Books.* $30/£19

TRAVEN, B. The Rebellion of the Hanged. Charles Duff (trans). London: Robert Hale, (1952). 1st Eng ed. Bkshp stamp fep, edges sl spotted, else VG in dj (nicked, rubbed, sl chipped, internally repaired). *Limestone.* $195/£126

TRAVEN, B. The Rebellion of the Hanged. NY: Knopf, 1952. 1st US ed. VG+ in VG+ dj. *Pettler.* $45/£29

TRAVEN, B. The Treasure of the Sierra Madre. Knopf, 1935. 1st Amer ed. Flaking to spine lettering, else VG. *Fine Books.* $125/£81

TRAVER, ROBERT. Hornstein's Boy. NY, 1962. 1st ed. Bkpl, o/w Fine in dj. *Artis.* $35/£23

TRAVER, ROBERT. The Jealous Mistress. Boston, (1967). 2nd ptg. Bkpl, o/w VF in dj. *Artis.* $30/£19

TRAVER, ROBERT. Laughing Whitefish. NY, 1965. 1st ed. Bkpl, o/w VF in dj. *Artis.* $75/£48

TRAVER, ROBERT. Trout Magic. NY, 1974. 1st ed. Bkpl, o/w Fine in dj. *Artis.* $50/£32

TRAVERS, P.L. Friend Monkey. HBJ, 1971. 1st ed. Fine in dj. *Aronovitz.* $28/£18

TRAVERS, P.L. I Go By Sea, I Go By Land. Harper, 1941. 1st ed. NF in VG dj (lt wear spine extrems). *Aronovitz.* $55/£35

TRAVERS, P.L. Mary Poppins Opens the Door. Davies, 1944. 1st ed. VG in dj. *Aronovitz.* $165/£106

TRAVERS, P.L. and C. KEEPING. About the Sleeping Beauty. M-H, 1975. 1st ed. Fine in dj. *Aronovitz.* $38/£25

TRAVIS, HELGA. The Nez Perce Trail. Yakima, WA: Franklin Press, 1967. 1st ed. VG in VG dj. *Oregon.* $35/£23

TREADWELL, EDWARD F. The Cattle King. NY: Macmillan, 1931. 1st ed. Fair. *Lien.* $60/£39

TREADWELL, EDWARD F. The Cattle King: A Dramatized Biography. NY, 1931. 1st ed. Signed. Howes T 336. *Ginsberg.* $85/£55

Treasure Island. London: Octopus, 1979. 2nd imp. 21x21 cm. 6 fan-fldg pop-ups. J. Pavlin & G. Seda (illus). Glazed pict bds. VG. *Book Finders.* $40/£26

TREAT, LAWRENCE. H as in Hangman. NY: Duell, 1942. 1st ed. Fine in VG+ dj (lt chipping; closed tears). *Janus.* $50/£32

TREAT, ROGER. Walter Johnson. Messner, 1948. 1st ed. VG+ in Good+ dj. *Plapinger.* $140/£90

TREDREY, F.D. The House of Blackwood 1804-1954. London, 1954. 1st ed. *Edwards.* $39/£25

TREECE, HENRY. 38 Poems. Fortune, (1940). 1st ed. Buckram. Eps foxed, o/w Fine in dj (short tear). *Poetry.* $43/£28

TREFUSIS, VIOLET. Don't Look Round. London: Hutchinson, 1952. 1st ed. Eps sl foxed; rubbed; spine gilt dull, o/w Good in dj (lacks back section, folds). *Virgo.* $47/£30

TREGO, FRANK H. Boulevarded Old Trails in the Great Southwest. NY: Greenberg Pub, (1929). Good. *Perier.* $25/£16

TREMLETT, MRS. HORACE. With the Tin Gods. London, 1915. 1st ed. (Lt foxing; spine faded.) *Edwards.* $47/£30

TREND, J.B. Alfonso the Sage and Other Spanish Essays. London: Constable, 1926. 1st ed. (Eps lt foxed.) Pub's red cl gilt (spine lt faded). Dj (sl frayed). *Peter Taylor.* $23/£15

TRENNERT, ROBERT A., JR. Indian Traders on the Middle Border: The House of Ewing, 1827-54. Lincoln/London: Univ of NE Press, 1981. 1st ed. Map. Fine in dj. *Cahan.* $20/£13

TRESCOT, WILLIAM HENRY. The Diplomatic History of the Administration of Washington and Adams, 1789-1801. Boston, 1857. 1st ed. Unsigned presentation copy. 8vo. 282pp. *Argosy.* $150/£97

TRESCOT, WILLIAM HENRY. The History of the Revolution. NY: Appleton, 1852. (viii),169pp. (Spine ends worn.) *Schoyer.* $30/£19

TRESEDER, NEIL G. and MARJORIE BLAMEY. The Book of Magnolias. London: Collins, 1981. 33 full-pg color plts. Inscrip, else Fine in dj. *Quest.* $85/£55

TREUB, HECTOR. The Right to Life of the Unborn Child. NY, 1903. 1st Eng trans. Good. *Fye.* $125/£81

TREVATHAN, CHARLES E. The American Thoroughbred. NY: Macmillan, 1905. 1st ed. Frontis, 12 plts. Gilt pict grn cl. VG. *House.* $50/£32

TREVELYAN, JANET PENROSE. The Life of Mrs. Humphrey Ward. London: Constable, 1923. 1st ed. Frontis port, 5 plts. Lower edges uncut. Nice. *Temple.* $31/£20

TREVELYAN, R.C. Poems and Fables. Hogarth Press, 1925. 1st ed. VG. *Words Etc.* $233/£150

TREVES, FREDERICK. Scrofula and Its Gland Diseases. NY, 1882. 1st Amer ed. 181pp. Good. *Fye.* $40/£26

TREVES, FREDERICK. The Tale of a Field Hospital. London, 1900. 1st ed. 14 plts. Good (ex-lib, bkpl removed, eps browned) in limp leather cvrd bds (worn, soiled, label removed). *Edwards.* $47/£30

TREVES, FREDERICK. Uganda for a Holiday. NY: Dutton, 1910. 1st ed. Fldg map at rear. Tan pict cl. VG. *Bowman.* $45/£29

TREVISAN, A.F. Men and Jackasses. NY: Pilgrim Press, 1938. 1st ed. Frontis; 11 plts. Fine in Good+ dj. *Oregon.* $17/£11

TREVOR, WILLIAM. Angels at the Ritz. London: Bodley Head, (1975). 1st ed. NF in dj. *Antic Hay.* $45/£29

TREVOR, WILLIAM. Beyond the Pale. London: Bodley Head, 1981. 1st ed. Fine in dj. *Rees.* $31/£20

TREVOR, WILLIAM. The Children of Dynmouth. NY: Viking, (1977). 1st ed. Fine in white dj (soiling). *Robbins.* $25/£16

TREVOR, WILLIAM. The Children of Dynmouth. Bodley Head, 1976. 1st UK ed. Inscrip, o/w Fine in dj. *Lewton.* $42/£27

TREVOR, WILLIAM. The Day We Got Drunk on Cake. London: Bodley Head, 1967. 1st UK ed. Fine in VG dj (chip bottom of spine; sl creasing). *Williams.* $543/£350

TREVOR, WILLIAM. Fools of Fortune. London: BH, 1983. 1st UK ed. Fine in dj. *Lewton.* $23/£15

TREVOR, WILLIAM. The Last Lunch of the Season. London: Covent Garden Press, 1973. One of 100 numbered, signed from ed of 600. Fine in wrappers. *Rees.* $70/£45

TREVOR, WILLIAM. The Love Department. London: Bodley Head, 1966. 1st ed. VG in dj (spine sunned). *Rees.* $78/£50

TREVOR, WILLIAM. The Love Department. London: Bodley Head, 1966. 1st UK ed. NF in VG+ dj. *Williams.* $70/£45

TREVOR, WILLIAM. Lovers of Their Time and Other Stories. London: Bodley Head, 1978. 1st ed. Fine in dj. *Limestone.* $85/£55

TREVOR, WILLIAM. Lovers of Their Time. Bodley Head, 1978. 1st UK ed. NF in dj (lt worn). *Sclanders.* $31/£20

TREVOR, WILLIAM. Miss Gomez and the Brethren. Bodley Head, 1971. 1st ed. NF in dj. *Fine Books.* $85/£55

TREVOR, WILLIAM. Miss Gomez and the Brethren. London: Bodley Head, 1971. 1st ed. Minor bump spine heel, else Fine in dj. *Else Fine.* $125/£81

TREVOR, WILLIAM. Mrs. Eckdorf in O'Neill's Hotel. London: Bodley Head, 1969. 1st ed. VG in dj (rubbed, internally strengthened, price-clipped). *Rees.* $31/£20

TREVOR, WILLIAM. Mrs. Eckdorf in O'Neill's Hotel. London: Bodley Head, 1969. 1st ed. VF in dj (minor rubbing extrems). *Else Fine.* $90/£58

TREVOR, WILLIAM. Mrs. Eckdorf in O'Neill's Hotel. Bodley Head, 1969. 1st UK ed. NF in dj. *Lewton.* $70/£45

TREVOR, WILLIAM. The News from Ireland and Other Stories. NY: Viking, (1986). 1st Amer ed. Fine in dj. *Godot.* $35/£23

TREVOR, WILLIAM. Nights at the Alexandra. London: Hutchinson, (1987). 1st ed. Fine in Fine dj. *Dermont.* $20/£13

TREVOR, WILLIAM. The Old Boys. NY: Viking, 1964. 1st ed. VF in dj (spine sl darkened). *Else Fine.* $100/£65

TREVOR, WILLIAM. The Old Boys. London: D-P, 1971. 1st UK ed. Fine in VG card wraps (bumped). *Lewton.* $29/£19

TREVOR, WILLIAM. Old School Ties. London: Lemon Tree, 1976. 1st ed. NF in dj (price-clipped). *Rees.* $78/£50

TREVOR, WILLIAM. Old School Ties. London: Lemon Tree Press, 1976. 1st UK ed. Fine in dj (price-clipped). *Williams.* $70/£45

TREVOR, WILLIAM. Other People's Worlds. London: Bodley Head, 1980. 1st ed. Fine in dj (price-clipped, sl creased). *Rees.* $31/£20

TREVOR, WILLIAM. Other People's Worlds. London: BH, 1980. 1st UK ed. Fine in dj. *Lewton.* $26/£17

TREVOR, WILLIAM. Other People's Worlds. Bodley Head, 1980. 1st UK ed. NF- (lt wear) in dj. *Sclanders.* $28/£18

TREVOR, WILLIAM. Scenes from an Album. Dublin Books, 1981. 1st ed. Fine in wrappers. *Rees.* $23/£15

TREVOR, WILLIAM. The Silence in the Garden. London: Bodley Head, 1988. One of 150 specially bound, numbered, signed. Fine in glassine dj. *Rees.* $93/£60

Trial of the Conspirators for the Assassination of President Lincoln.... Washington: GPO, 1865. Ptd sewn wraps (lt worn). *Boswell.* $225/£145

TRIGGER, BRUCE. The Children of Aataentsic. A History of the Huron People to 1660. McGill-Queens Univ, 1976. 1st ed. 2 vols. Fine in Fine djs. *Oregon.* $75/£48

TRILLING, LIONEL. E.M. Forster. Norfolk, CT: New Directions, (1943). 1st ed. VG (name; offsetting rep from laid-in newspaper article) in dj (lt wear). *Chapel Hill.* $40/£26

TRIPLER, CHARLES S. and GEORGE C. BLACKMAN. Hand-Book for the Military Surgeon. Cincinnati: Robert Clarke, 1861. 1st ed. Cl (1861 ink inscrip; worn.) *Glenn.* $950/£613

TRIPLER, CHARLES S. and GEORGE C. BLACKMAN. Hand-Book for the Military Surgeon. Cincinnati, 1862. 3rd ed. 121pp + 42pp appendix of tables. (Ex-lib; cl worn.) *Argosy.* $75/£48

TRIPLETT, FRANK. Conquering the Wilderness. NY: N.D. Thompson, 1885. 742pp. Leather binding. VG. *Perier.* $80/£52

TRIPLETT, FRANK. The Life, Times and Treacherous Death of Jesse James. Chicago: Sage/Swallow, 1970. Rpt ed. Tape offset mks eps, o/w VG. *Glenn.* $50/£32

TRIPP, C.E. Ace High, the Frisco Detective; or, the Girl Sport's Double Game. SF: The Book Club of CA, 1948. Rptd from Beadle's Half-Dime Lib, #814, Feb 28, 1893. Ltd to 500. 10 engrs by Mallette Dean. Red cl over yellow dec bds, paper spine label (spine lt rubbed). *Karmiole.* $50/£32

TRIPP, F.E. British Mosses, Their Homes, Aspects, Structure and Uses. London, 1874. 2nd ed. 2 vols. xxi,124pp + 8pp ads; 125-235pp + 8pp ads, 39 hand-colored plts. Partly unopened. Fine. *Henly.* $186/£120

TRISTRAM, H.B. The Land of Israel. London: SPCK, 1865. 1st ed. xx,651pp; 2 lg fldg maps (1 torn at folds w/o loss); 4 chromolitho plts. Contemp 1/2 blue calf, morocco label, marbled sides (rubbed), gilt. Good (sl spotting). *Cox.* $171/£110

TRISTRAM, H.B. The Land of Israel; A Journal.... London: SPCK, 1866. 2nd ed. Half title, xx,656,4 ads. 2 fldg maps (1 colored), 4 chromolithos, 8 engr plts (sl foxing, mainly adjacent to plts). Orig brown cl (recased, new eps), gilt device, spine gilt, blue labels (chipped). *Morrell.* $116/£75

TRISTRAM, W. OUTRAM. Moated Houses. London, 1910. 1st ed. Teg. (Spine faded; hinges cracked; bkpl; ink stamps; cellophane taped to pastedowns.) *Edwards.* $39/£25

TRIVAS, N.S. Frans Hals, Paintings. London: Phaidon, 1949. 2nd ed. 160 plts (4 color). (Cl sl stained.) *Ars Artis.* $70/£45

TROBRIAND, PHILIPPE REGIS DE. Military Life in Dakota. Lucile M. Kane (ed). St. Paul, 1951. 1st ed. Map. Dj (ragged, spine faded). *Edwards.* $23/£15

TROCCHI, ALEXANDER. Helen and Desire. North Hollywood: Brandon House, (1967). 1st Amer ed. NF in pict wraps. *Polyanthos.* $25/£16

TROCCHI, ALEXANDER. White Thighs. North Hollywood: Brandon House, (1967). 1st complete pb ed. Fine in dec wraps. *Polyanthos.* $25/£16

TROLLOPE, ANTHONY. Barchester Towers. NY: LEC, 1958. One of 1500 signed by Fritz Kredel (illus). Leather-backed dec bds. VF in slipcase. *Pharos.* $125/£81

TROLLOPE, ANTHONY. The Belton Estate. London: Ward Lock, n.d. (ca 1870). 329pp (20pp pub's ads). Grn pub's cl (inner hinge cracked; worn), black/gilt dec cvrs, spine. *Hartfield.* $195/£126

TROLLOPE, ANTHONY. Cicero. London: Chapman and Hall, 1880. 1st ed, 1st issue. 2 vols. 8vo. Pub's gilt-stamped maroon cl. VF+. *D & D.* $600/£387

TROLLOPE, ANTHONY. Doctor Thorne. Leipzig: Bernard Tauchnitz, 1858. Tauchnitz copyright ed. Collection of British Authors vol 449. 2 vols. Sm 8vo. Teg. 1/4 red morocco, gilt-lettered spines. *D & D.* $90/£58

TROLLOPE, ANTHONY. Doctor Wortle's School. London, 1881. 1st ed. 2 vols. Uncut. Pub's black-stamped gray cl (head, foot of spines rubbed; sm early repair to gutter of 2nd blank endleaf vol 2, else Fine). *D & D.* $1,950/£1,258

TROLLOPE, ANTHONY. An Editor's Tales. London: Chapman & Hall, 1876. 366pp. 3/4 polished olive calf, gilt; marbled bds, eps; all edges marbled. Nice. *Hartfield.* $225/£145

TROLLOPE, ANTHONY. The Eustace Diamonds. NY: Harper, 1872. 1st ed in bk form. 8vo. 351pp; 4pp ads at front. Brick red cl, gilt-titled. Attractive (corners sl worn, 1 bumped; sl shelfwear; bkpl). *Hermitage.* $750/£484

TROLLOPE, ANTHONY. The Eustace Diamonds. Harpers, 1872. 1st ed. Lt wear to corner tips, else VG. *Fine Books.* $675/£435

TROLLOPE, ANTHONY. The Last Chronicle of Barset. NY: Harper, 1867. 1st Amer ed. Gilt-stamped purple cl (faded; spine nicked). VG. *Houle.* $175/£113

TROLLOPE, ANTHONY. The Last Chronicle of Barset. London: Smith, Elder, 1867. 1st ed. 2 vols. George H. Thomas (illus). Marbled edges. Blue calf gilt w/leather gilt labels, raised bands, over contemp marbled bds. Very Nice set. *Limestone.* $375/£242

TROLLOPE, ANTHONY. Orley Farm. NY: Harper, 1862. 1st Amer ed. 338+6pp ads. Patterned cl (worn). Good. *Cullen.* $125/£81

TROLLOPE, ANTHONY. Orley Farm. London: Chapman & Hall, 1862. 1st ed. 2 vols. viii,320; 320pp; 40 engrs by J.E. Millais. Bound by Bumpus in 3/4 chestnut calf; marbled bds, eps; teg. VG (lt spotting; bkpl). *Hartfield.* $495/£319

TROLLOPE, ANTHONY. The Tireless Traveler. Bradford Allen Booth (ed). Berkeley: Univ of CA Press, 1941. 1st ed. Red cl, gilt. VG. *Hartfield.* $65/£42

TROLLOPE, ANTHONY. The Vicar of Bullhampton. London: Bradbury, Evans, 1870. 1st ed, in bk form, bound up from orig monthly parts. 35 wood-engr plts, illus. Bound w/o 1/2 title or ads in contemp 1/2 calf (rebacked), banded, ruled, labelled. Nice (sl mks, flaws, lt creases). *Ash.* $388/£250

TROLLOPE, ANTHONY. The Warden. NY: LEC, (1955). One of 1500 numbered, signed by Fritz Kredel (illus). Fine in pub's slipcase. *Hermitage.* $85/£55

TROLLOPE, ANTHONY. The Warden. NY: LEC, (1955). One of 1500 signed by Fritz Kredel (illus). Prospectus laid in. Cl-backed pict bds. Fine in Nice slipcase. *Pharos.* $125/£81

TROLLOPE, ANTHONY. The Way We Live Now. NY: Harper, 1875. 1st Amer ed. 408pp; 8pp ads at back, 4pp at fr. Brick red cl stamped in blind, gilt-titled spine. (Frayed/worn; joints, extrems sl rubbed.) *Hermitage.* $125/£81

TROLLOPE, ANTHONY. The West Indies and the Spanish Main. NY: Harper, 1860. 1st Amer ed. 8vo, 385pp,8pp ads. Brn cl, gilt. VG (sl shelfwear; sig). *Hartfield.* $325/£210

TROLLOPE, FRANCES. Domestic Manners of the Americans. London, 1832. 2nd ed. 2 vols. (12),304; (4),303pp, 24 plts. Orig cl (rebacked, sl bubbled), orig backstrips laid down, ptd paper spine labels (worn). VG (occasional fox mk; most guards intact). Howes T 357. *Reese.* $750/£484

TROLLOPE, FRANCES. Domestic Manners of the Americans. Barre: Imprint Soc, 1969. Ltd to 1950 ptd. Engr frontis, 25pg facs insert. Brn cl, gilt. Fine in slipcase. *Cady.* $25/£16

TROLLOPE, FRANCES. Jessie Phillips. London: Henry Colburn, 1844. 1st 1-vol ed. viii,352pp, port, 11 plts (lt waterstain foot some plts). Blind-stamped cl, gilt-lettered spine (faded; spot to foot). *Bickersteth.* $140/£90

TROLLOPE, FRANCES. Paris and the Parisians in 1835. Paris, 1836. 2 vols. 1/2 calf (extrems worn). *Argosy.* $60/£39

TROLLOPE, FRANCES. The Widow Barnaby. London: Richard Bentley, 1839. 1st ed. 3 vols. 1/2 titles all vols. Orig bds (rebacked; new eps), orig ptd paper spine labels preserved. Good. *Bickersteth.* $442/£285

TROLLOPE, JOANNA. Eliza Stanhope. Hutchinson, 1978. 1st UK ed. NF in dj. *Williams.* $78/£50

TROLLOPE, MRS. Belgium and Western Germany, in 1833. Brussels: Fred Wilmans, 1834. 1st ed. 2 vols in 1. 2 engr frontispieces, 252,232pp (scattered foxing). 1/2 calf, gilt-dec spine panels, marbled bds. *Hollett.* $233/£150

TROLLOPE, THOMAS ADOLPHUS. A Decade of Italian Women. London: Chapman & Hall, 1859. 1st ed. 2 vols. Frontis,410; 451pp. (Guards to ports, frontis spotted.) 3/4 brn crushed morocco; linen bds, eps; gilt. Fine. *Hartfield.* $295/£190

TROTSKY, LEON. The History of the Russian Revolution. Max Eastman (trans). London: Gollancz, 1932. 1st Eng ed. 3 vols. Black cl. Fine in yellow ptd djs. *Weber.* $350/£226

TROUP, J. ROSE. With Stanley's Rear Column. London, 1890. 2nd ed. Frontis port, xii,361pp+40pp pub's cat, 13 plts, fldg map (torn w/o loss). Lt foxed, inner hinges starting, o/w VG in grn cl (sl worn). *Edwards.* $132/£85

TROUT, KILGORE. (Pseud of Philip Jose Farmer.) Venus on the Half-Shell. NY: Dell, 1975. 1st ed, pb orig. Fine in wraps. *Else Fine.* $20/£13

TROW, M.J. Brigade: Further Adventures of Inspector Lestrade. London: Macmillan, 1986. 1st ed. VG in VG dj. *Ming.* $31/£20

TROW, M.J. Lestrade and the Leviathan. London: Macmillan, 1987. 1st ed. Fine in Fine dj. *Ming.* $31/£20

TROWBRIDGE, J.M. The Cider Makers' Hand Book. NY: OJ, 1920. Grn cl, gilt spine. VG (bumped). *Bohling.* $20/£13

TROWBRIDGE, M.E.D. Pioneer Days: The Life-Story of Gershom and Elizabeth Day. Phila: American Baptist Pub Soc, 1895. 1st ed. 160pp. Good. Howes 10413. *Lien.* $50/£32

TROWER, HAROLD E. The Book of Capri. Naples: Emil Press, 1906. Vellum (lt wear, soil). *Edwards.* $70/£45

TRUAX, CHARLES. The Mechanics of Surgery. Chicago, 1899. 1st ed. 1024pp. Orig cl. Good (ex-lib w/bkpls, stamp; tape stains to spine; hinges cracked). *Glaser.* $450/£290

TRUAX, RHODA. The Doctors Jacobi. Boston, 1952. 1st ed. Good in dj. *Fye.* $35/£23

TRUCCHI, LORENZA. Francis Bacon. John Shepley (trans). NY: Abrams, (1975). 1st ed. Fine (sig loose; p1 gutter torn) in dj (lt soiled; abrasion). *Hermitage.* $150/£97

TRUDEAU, EDWARD LIVINGSTON. An Autobiography. NY, 1916. 1st ed. Good. *Fye.* $35/£23

TRUDEAU, EDWARD LIVINGSTON. An Autobiography. Phila/NY: Lea & Febiger, 1916. 1st ed. Dk grn cl, bevelled edges. Fr joint cracking; bkpl; else VG. *Chapel Hill.* $65/£42

True and Admirable History of the Marquis of Salus, and Patient Grissel. Newcastle: George Angus, ca 1810. Chapbook. 12mo. 24pp, lg Fine woodcut tp. Pict self-wrappers (dusty, chipped, edges creased). NF. *Hobbyhorse.* $200/£129

True Stories, from Modern History.... (By Maria Elizabeth Budden.) London: Harris, 1819. 1st ed. 3 vols. 12mo. full-pg engr frontis each vol, vi,202 + 2pp list; iv,207; iv,215 + 1pg list. Marbled cvrs, red roan spine, gilt title. Fine set (sl rubbing, ink sig). *Hobbyhorse.* $255/£165

TRUE, FREDERICK W. An Account of the Beaked Whales of the Family Ziphiadae in the Collection of the United States National Museum.... Washington, 1910. 1st ed. 42 plts. Lib pamphlet binder (perf lib stamps tp; coming unbound). *Lefkowicz.* $75/£48

TRUE, FREDERICK W. The Whalebone Whales of the Western North Atlantic, Etc. Washington: Smithsonian, (1983). 50 plts. VF. *Mikesh.* $60/£39

TRUE, FREDERICK W. The Whalebone Whales of the Western North Atlantic.... Washington, 1904. 50 plts. (Ex-lib; marginal damage, esp to last plt.) *Wheldon & Wesley.* $116/£75

TRUE, FREDERICK W. The Whalebone Whales of the Western North Atlantic.... Washington, 1904. 1st ed. 50 plts. Good (lib mks; 2 gatherings loose). *Lefkowicz.* $175/£113

TRUESDALE, JOHN. The Blue Coats and How They Lived, Fought and Died for the Union. Phila, (1867). 1st ed. 510pp. Worn, stained; illus badly repaired w/tape, o/w VG. *Pratt.* $40/£26

TRUETT, RANDLE BOND. Trade and Travel around the Southern Appalachians before 1830. Univ NC, 1935. 1st ed. 5 plts. VG in Good+ dj (back reinforced w/heavy paper). *Oregon.* $45/£29

TRUITT, W.J. Nature's Secrets Revealed. Marietta, 1919. Good. *Fye.* $35/£23

TRUMAN, BEN C. Occidental Sketches.... SF: SF News Co, 1881. 1st ed. Inscribed. (Lt wear, marginal tear repaired on blank.) Howes T 365. *Shasky.* $110/£71

TRUMAN, HARRY S. Mr. Citizen. (NY): Bernard Geis, (1960). 1st ed. Signed. VG in dj (minor wear). *Houle.* $325/£210

TRUMBELL, JAMES HAMMOND. BAE Bulletin 25. Natick Dictionary. Washington, 1903. (Upper hinge cracked through; worn.) *Edwards.* $31/£20

TRUMBO, DALTON. Additional Dialogue, Letters of Dalton Trumbo 1942-1962. NY: M. Evans, (1970). 1st ed. VG in dj. *Hermitage.* $25/£16

TRUMBULL, H. CLAY. The Knightly Soldier. Boston, 1865. 1st ed. 381pp. Pict cvr. Worn, spotted, o/w VG. *Pratt.* $45/£29

TRUMBULL, HENRY. History of the Discovery of America; of the Landing of Our Forefathers...to Which is Annexed...Almost Every Important Engagement With the Savages.... Boston, 1819. Later ptg. 256pp; 2 color plts. Mod cl. Tears in 1 plt repaired, else Good+. Howes T 370. *Mcgowan.* $85/£55

TRUMBULL, M.M. The Free Trade Struggle in England. Chicago: Open Court, 1892. 2nd ed. NF. *Beasley.* $65/£42

TRUSLER, JOHN. The Progress of Man and Society. London: Ptd for Author, 1791. 1st ed. Sm 8vo. iii+v+264pp, 136 woodcuts by John Bewick, plus sm dec tail-pieces. 3/4 leather w/corners, marbled paper on bds, raised bands, gilt title labels. Fine (lt foxing to text, sm chip fore-edge pg 209). *Hobbyhorse.* $600/£387

TRUSS, SELDON. Turmoil at Brede. NY: Mystery League, 1931. 1st Amer ed. NF in dj (sl edge rubbed; lacks 2-inch piece). *Polyanthos.* $30/£19

TRYON, THOMAS. The Other. NY: Knopf, 1971. 1st ed, 1st bk. Signed presentation. Red cl. NF in dj (few sm interior reinforcements). *Antic Hay.* $65/£42

TSIEN, T.H. Written on Bamboo and Silk. Chicago: Univ of Chicago Press, 1962. 1st ed. Sig, else VG in dj (chipped). *Cahan.* $40/£26

TUBBS, COLIN R. The New Forest. London, 1986. 1st ed. Dj. *Edwards.* $70/£45

TUBBY, A.H. Deformities: A Treatise on Orthopaedic Surgery. Edinburgh, 1895. 1st ed. 374pp. (Spine head, tail chipped.) *Fye.* $300/£194

TUCKER, ELIZABETH S. Old Youngsters. NY: Frederick A. Stokes, 1897. 1st ed. Lg, 4to. 6 full-pg color plts by Maud Humphrey. Elizabeth Tucker (illus). Cl-backed pict bds (lt chipped; corners bumped). Internally clean (new blank eps). *Reisler.* $385/£248

TUCKER, GLENN. Dawn Like Thunder. NY, (1963). 1st ed. Dj worn, o/w VG+. *Pratt.* $35/£23

TUCKER, GLENN. Tecumseh. Indianapolis: Bobbs-Merrill, (1956). 1st ed. Grey/red cl. Fine in NF dj. *Chapel Hill.* $50/£32

TUCKER, GLENN. Zeb Vance: Champion of Personal Freedom. Indianapolis/Kansas City/NY: Bobbs-Merrill, 1965. 1st ed. Frontis port. NF in illus dj (sl worn). *Cahan.* $30/£19

TUCKER, ST. GEORGE. A Dissertation on Slavery.... NY, 1861. 2nd ed. One of 100. 104pp. Mod cl-backed bds, label. VG. Howes T 396. *Petrilla.* $85/£55

TUCKER, WILSON. The Chinese Doll. Rinehart, 1946. 1st ed, 1st bk. VG in dj (chipped). *Madle.* $60/£39

TUCKER, WILSON. The City in the Sea. NY/Toronto: Rinehart, (1951). 1st ed. VG+ in dj (lt dampstained rear panel). *Bernard.* $60/£39

TUCKER, WILSON. The Time Masters. Rinehart, 1953. 1st ed. Fine in dj. *Madle.* $75/£48

TUCKER, WILSON. The Time Masters. Rinehart, 1953. 1st ed. Inscribed. NF in VG dj (lt rubbing). *Aronovitz.* $75/£48

TUCKWELL, W. The Ancient Ways. London: Macmillan, 1893. 1st ed. Presentation copy. xii,171pp. Spine sl rubbed, faded. *Hollett.* $70/£45

TUDOR, TASHA (selected by). Wings from the Wind. Phila: J.B. Lippincott, (1964). 1st ed. 4to. Gold cl-backed grn bds, blind stamp dec cvr. Color dj (sm piece missing). *Reisler.* $90/£58

TUDOR, TASHA. A Is for Annabelle. NY: OUP, 1954. 1st ed. Obl 8vo. Unpaginated. VG + in dj. *Bookpress.* $125/£81

TUDOR, TASHA. A Is for Annabelle. NY: OUP, 1954. 1st ed. 8vo. Grn cl, gilt lettering. NF in NF dj (sl dusty). *Drusilla's.* $225/£145

TUDOR, TASHA. Around the Year. NY: OUP, 1957. 1st ed. Obl 8vo. Unpaginated. Fine in dj (2-inch tape stain fr panel). *Bookpress.* $125/£81

TUDOR, TASHA. Around the Year. NY: OUP, 1957. 1st ed. Obl 8vo. Yellow cl, gold lettering. Good in dec dj. *Reisler.* $185/£119

TUDOR, TASHA. A Book of Christmas. NY/London: Collins, 1979. 19x27 cm. 6 pop-ups, pull-tabs, flaps. Glazed pict bds. VG. *Book Finders.* $30/£19

TUDOR, TASHA. Corgiville Fair. NY: Thomas Y. Crowell, (1971). 1st ed. Obl 4to. Turquoise cl, gold dec. Good in color pict dj (lt stains). *Reisler.* $100/£65

TUDOR, TASHA. The County Fair. NY: OUP, (1940). 1st ed. 24mo. Red cl w/white dots (corners sl worn). Internally clean (owner box fep filled in). *Reisler.* $200/£129

TUDOR, TASHA. The County Fair. NY: OUP, 1953, 5th ptg. 24mo. Red cl w/white dots. Color pict dj (upper edge chipped). Sl edgewear; o/w Nice. *Reisler.* $135/£87

TUDOR, TASHA. Dorcas Porkus. NY: OUP, (1942). 4th ptg, 1945. 24mo. Yellow cl w/white dots. Dj (edges chipped; mks from tape removal). *Reisler.* $135/£87

TUDOR, TASHA. Favorite Stories. Phila: Lippincott, 1965. 1st ed. Lg 8vo. Pict cl. NF in NF dj. *Book Adoption.* $75/£48

TUDOR, TASHA. Mother Goose: Seventy-Seven Verses with Pictures.... NY: OUP, (c. 1944). 1st ed. 8vo. 87pp. Grn cl, gilt designs (faded). VG in dj (smudged; chipped; lacks spine portions). *Drusilla's.* $100/£65

TUDOR, TASHA. Tasha Tudor's Favorite Stories. Phila: J.B. Lippincott, (1965). 1st ed. 4to. Cl-backed aquamarine bds, red vignette. Color pict dj (sl edgewear). *Reisler.* $100/£65

TUDOR, TASHA. Tasha Tudor's Season of Delight. NY: Philomel/Putnams, 1986. 22x22 cm. VG. *Book Finders.* $40/£26

TUDOR, TASHA. A Time to Keep, the Tasha Tudor Book of Holidays. Chicago: Rand McNally, (1977). 1st ed. Signed presentation. 4to. Unpaginated. Pict bds. Fine; no dj as issued. *Bookpress.* $125/£81

TUER, ANDREW W. Forgotten Children's Books. London: Leadenhall, 1898-1899. 1st ed, later issue. Blue cl, pict gilt; teg. VG (hinges tender but tight). *Davidson.* $185/£119

TUER, ANDREW W. History of the Horn-Book. London: Leadenhall Press, 1897. 2nd ed. Frontis (foxed), xviii,486,(3)pp; pocket (foxed) w/3 facs horn bks in rear. Orig cl, leather spine label; teg. Fine. *Oak Knoll.* $350/£226

TUER, ANDREW W. Old London Street Cries, and the Cries of Today. London: Field & Tuer, Leadenhall Press, 1885. Hand-colored frontis, 137,(vii)pp. Later cl-backed bds (orig label relaid). VG. *Hollett.* $70/£45

TUER, ANDREW W. Pages and Pictures from Forgotten Children's Books. London/NY: Leadenhall/Scribner's, 1898-9. 1st trade ed. 510pp + 20pp cat. Pub's slip tipped in at end. Full blue morocco, gilt (orig pict cl binding bound at end). Teg, others untrimmed. Fine in felt-lined dj, cl slipcase. *Schoyer.* $175/£113

TUER, ANDREW W. Stories from Old Fashioned Children's Books. London, 1899-1900. xvi + 439pp + 33pp pub's ads. Illus feps (sl browned); teg, rest uncut. *Edwards.* $74/£48

TUKER, M.A.R. Rome. Black, (1905). 70 color plts. 2pp ads tipped in at back. (Binding faded.) *Petersfield.* $39/£25

TUKER, M.A.R. Rome. A&C Black, 1905. 1st ed. 70 color plts by Alberto Pisa. Dec cl (spine faded, sl chipped; feps lt browned). *Edwards.* $39/£25

TUKEY, H.B. The Pear and Its Culture. NY, 1928. 10 plts. (Pp browned; cvrs spotted, faded.) Dj (rubbed). *Sutton.* $23/£15

TULL, JETHRO. The Horse-Hoeing Husbandry. London, 1822. 1st Cobbett ed. xix,332pp (1pg ad); 1plt. (Sl stained eps, name, spot prelim.) Contemp 1/2 calf (rubbed, worn). *Sutton.* $225/£145

TULL, JETHRO. The Horse-Hoeing Husbandry. London, 1829. xxiv,466pp, largely unopened, 1 plt. (Sl spotting.) *Henly.* $209/£135

TULL, JETHRO. The Horse-Hoeing Husbandry. London: Cobbett, 1829. Later ptg of collected ed. 436pp. VG. *Second Life.* $175/£113

TULLIDGE, EDWARD W. Life of Joseph the Prophet. NY, 1878. 1st ed. 545pp, port of Hyrum (lacks port of Joseph; tp torn but complete; preface partially detached, rubber stamp; hinges cracked, wear, fading; rubbed). *Benchmark.* $200/£129

TUNNARD, CHRISTOPHER. Gardens in the Modern Landscape. London: Architectural Press, 1950. 2nd rev ed. Fine. *Quest.* $80/£52

TUNNEY, KIERAN. Tallulah: Darling of the Gods. NY: Dutton, 1973. 1st ed. Red cl. Fine in dj. *Houle.* $75/£48

TUNNICLIFFE, C.F. My Country Book. London: The Studio, (1942). 16 color plts. Dj (sl torn). *Petersfield.* $54/£35

TUPPER, HARMON. To the Great Ocean. Boston: Little Brown, (1965). 1st ed. VG in dj (chipped, price-clipped). *Schoyer.* $35/£23

TURGENEV, IVAN. The Torrents of Spring. Constance Garnett (trans). Westpost: LEC, 1976. One of 1600 signed by Lajos Szalay (illus). Cl, marbled bds. VF in acetate & slicase. *Pharos.* $75/£48

TURKIN, HY and S.C. THOMPSON. Official Encyclopedia of Baseball. Barnes, 1951. 1st ed. Fine in VG dj. *Plapinger.* $25/£16

TURNER, A. LOGAN. Joseph, Baron Lister Centenary Volume, 1827-1927. Edinburgh, 1927. 1st ed. Good. *Fye.* $60/£39

TURNER, CHARLES W. Chessie's Road. Richmond: Garrett & Massie, 1956. Frontis, 19 plts (1 fldg). Navy cl, gilt title. VG + in dj (chipped). *Bohling.* $45/£29

TURNER, DAN. The Expos Inside Out. (Canada): McClelland & Stewart, 1983. Ltr ptg. Fine in VG + dj. *Plapinger.* $30/£19

TURNER, DANIEL. Siphylis. London, 1732. 4th ed. Port, (xxvi),476pp. Contemp panelled calf (rubbed; spine top worn). *Bickersteth.* $287/£185

TURNER, DANIEL. Syphilis. A Practical Dissertation on the Venereal Disease...In Two Parts. London, 1724. 2nd ed. 16 leaves, 376pp, 4 leaves. (Bkpl, contemp sig.) Contemp blind-tooled calf, floral decs. Internally Fine (upper hinge split; upper cvr detached; short splits lower hinge). *Hemlock.* $400/£258

TURNER, E.S. The Phoney War on the Home Front. London: Michael Joseph, 1961. Fine in dj (faded). *Peter Taylor.* $22/£14

TURNER, ERNEST. Hints to Househunters and House-holders. London: Batsford, 1883. 1st ed. Frontis; xiv,161,(23)pp. Pub's gilt cl. Lt foxing; wear along joints, else VG. *Bookpress.* $185/£119

TURNER, FREDERICK JACKSON. The Significance of the Frontier in American History. Ithaca: Cornell Univ, 1956. One of 275 signed. 1st ed as such. Cl-backed bds issued w/o dj. Fine. Howes T 422. *Cahan.* $100/£65

TURNER, G. Nineteen Years in Polynesia. London, 1861. xii,548pp; map. Grn cl (ex-lib). *Lewis.* $99/£64

TURNER, G.A. (ed). The Diary of Peter Bussell (1806-1814). London: Peter Davies, 1931. 1st ed. 4 plts. VG in dj (frayed). *Hollett.* $23/£15

TURNER, HENRY SMITH. The Original Journals of Henry Smith Turner with Stephen Watts Kearny..., 1846. Dwight L. Clarke (ed). Norman: Univ of OK Press, (1966). 1st ed. VG in dj. *Laurie.* $35/£23

TURNER, J.V. Below the Clock. NY: D. Appleton/Century, 1936. 1st Amer ed. Name fep, o/w VG in dj (closed tears; chips; wear). *Mordida.* $35/£23

TURNER, J.W. CECIL. Russell on Crime. London: Stevens & Sons, 1964. 12th ed. 2 vols. *Boswell.* $50/£32

TURNER, JOHN PETER. The North-West Mounted Police 1873-1893. Ottawa: Edmond Cloutier, 1950. 2 vols. Fldg map rear vol 1. Ink names; vol 2 askew; corners creased, else VG in pub's stiff blue paper wrappers. *Hermitage.* $90/£58

TURNER, JOHN PETER. The North-West Mounted Police 1873-1893.... Ottawa, 1950. 2 vols. Fldg map. Wraps. *Hayman.* $100/£65

TURNER, JOHN. Pioneers of the West: A True Narrative. Cincinnati: Jennings, 1903. 1st ed. Howes T 424. *Ginsberg.* $150/£97

TURNER, LUCIAN M. Contributions to the Natural History of Alaska. Washington: GPO, 1886. 226pp; 26 plts (11 color). Decent (spotting, wear) in black cl. *Perier.* $195/£126

TURNER, WILLIAM (ed). William Adams An Old English Potter. London/NY, 1904. Color frontis. (Margins spotted; edges sl rubbed; spine head sl bumped.) *Edwards.* $59/£38

TURNEY, IDA VIRGINIA. Paul Bunyan, The Work Giant. Portland: Binfords & Mort, 1941. Ltd 1st ed. Pict eps. Pict cl. Fine in VG dj. *Connolly.* $45/£29

TURNOR, REGINALD. The Smaller English House 1500-1939. Batsford, 1952. 1st ed. Color frontis. Dj (sl soiled; spine head repaired). *Edwards.* $34/£22

TUROW, SCOTT. The Burden of Proof. NY, (1900). 1st Amer ed. Signed. Fine in Fine dj. *Polyanthos.* $30/£19

TUROW, SCOTT. The Burden of Proof. London: Bloomsbury, 1990. 1st UK ed. Signed. Fine in dj. *Williams.* $28/£18

TUROW, SCOTT. Presumed Innocent. London: Bloomsbury, 1987. 1st UK ed. Fine in dj. *Williams.* $39/£25

TURRILL, CHARLES B. California Notes. SF: Edward Bosqui, 1876. 1st ed. xiii,(1),2-232pp, 2 maps. Sound (lt worn; sl cracking inner margins few sigs). *Shasky.* $100/£65

TURTON, G.E. There Was Once a City. Knopf, 1927. 1st ed. NF in dj (lt chipping spine head). *Aronovitz.* $55/£35

TURTON, W. A Manual of the Land and Fresh-water Shells of the British Islands. London, 1831. viii,152,16pp; 10 hand-colored plts. *Wheldon & Wesley.* $70/£45

TUTTLE, C.R. The Golden North. Chicago: Rand, McNally, 1897. 1st ed. x,307pp. VG- (cvr lettering worn). *Blue Dragon.* $50/£32

TUTTLE, C.R. A New Centennial History of the State of Kansas. Madison, WI/Lawrence, KS: Inter-State Book Co, 1876. 1st ed. Blind-stamped cl (rebacked preserving title). *Glenn.* $200/£129

TUTTLE, DANIEL SYLVESTER. Reminiscences of a Missionary Bishop. NY, (1906). 2 ports. Gilt-stamped cl, top. VG (spine faded, fore-edge soiled; name). *Bohling.* $65/£42

TUTTLE, FRANCIS. Report of the Cruise of the U.S. Revenue Cutter Bear...in the Arctic Ocean.... Washington: GPO, 1899. iv,144pp. 48 plts, lg fldg map. VG. *High Latitude.* $100/£65

TUTUOLA, AMOS. My Life in the Bush of Ghosts. NY: Grove, 1954. 1st US ed. Fine (name) in dj (lt used). *Beasley.* $40/£26

TUTUOLA, AMOS. The Palm-Wine Drinkard. London: Faber, 1952. 1st UK ed, 1st bk. Sl bumped; eps sl spotted, o/w NF in dj (sl rubbed). *Moorhouse.* $31/£20

TUTUOLA, AMOS. The Palm-Wine Tapster in the Deads' Town. London, 1952. 1st ed. 1st bk. Fine (spine lt sunned) in dj (spine lt sunned, 2 nicks). *Polyanthos.* $50/£32

TWAIN, MARK et al. The Niagara Book. Buffalo: Underhill & Nichols, 1893. 4th ptg, issued same yr as 1st, w/copyright occupying 2 lines, and w/o ads following text. 225pp. Orig grn cl. Good (hinges cracked internally; spine dknd; lower corner fep chipped). BAL 3437. *Chapel Hill.* $50/£32

TWAIN, MARK. The $30,000 Bequest and Other Stories. NY: Harper, 1906. 1st ed, 1st state. Orig red cl, gilt. Spine sl sunned, else Fine. BAL 3492. *Macdonnell.* $250/£161

TWAIN, MARK. Adventures of Huckleberry Finn. NY: Charles L. Webster, 1855. 1st ed w/all 1st issue points but w/illus p283 in redone state C. Points: B. Copyright pg dated 1884; leaf tipped in. A. pg(13) - Him & Another Man listed as at p.88. A. p57, line 23 - with the was. A. p155, folio, final 5 missing. A. p161, sig mk (11) - not present as in all NY copies known. C. p283, illus, engr redone, leaf tipped in. A. Frontis port - ptd by Heliotype & w/cl under bust vi A. p143 - final 'l' and period absent; word nobody hyphenated lines 6-7; in line 7, 'body' has broken b. Sq 8vo. Frontis port. 336pp. E.W. Kemble (illus). Gilt/black pict grn cl (extrems worn). VG (bkpl; 2 hand stamps feps) in custom black cl slipcase. *House.* $1,500/£968

TWAIN, MARK. The Adventures of Huckleberry Finn. London: C&W, 1884. 1st Eng ed. Dec red cl. VG- (sl hinge cracks; spine wear, fading; soiling, staining cvrs). BAL 3414: Issue A. Catalog dated Nov. 1886. *Agvent.* $950/£613

TWAIN, MARK. Adventures of Huckleberry Finn. NY: Charles L. Webster & Co., 1885. 1st Amer ed, 1st issue; title-leaf a cancel; 'Him and another Man' listed as at p88; 'was' for 'saw' on p57; final '5' lacking from p155 folio; p283 in third state (a cancel leaf w/redone, not ribald, engr), but the ribald engr noted only in a prospectus and a set of advance sheets, not in any copy of the pub bk. Sm 4to, 366pp. Orig pict dk grn cl. Fine in custom grn cl chemise, slipcase w/morocco spine label. BAL 3415. *Chapel Hill.* $7,500/£4,839

TWAIN, MARK. Adventures of Huckleberry Finn. NY: Charles L. Webster, 1885. 1st Amer ed. State (1) of pp(13), 57 & 155, state (2) of port, state (3) of p283, no sig mk 11 p161. 174 b/w illus by E.W. Kemble; port photograv opposite frontis. Full orig dk grn cl, spine & upper cvr stamped gilt/black (rubbing; spine worn; corners bumped). Good. BAL 3415. *Houle.* $1,750/£1,129

TWAIN, MARK. Adventures of Huckleberry Finn. NY: Charles L. Webster, 1885. 1st ed, 1st issue, w/all 1st issue points: 1st state of plt on p283, with the bulge in Mr. Phelps pants; p.155 w/2nd '5' missing; p.13 w/illus 'Him and Another Man' listed at p.88, rather than p. 87 where it appears; p.57 w/'with the was' in the 11th line from the bottom (later corrected to 'with the saw'; p.143 w/defective 'b' in 'body' in line 7 and 'Co' in upper rt-hand corner of illus. Orig pub's deluxe binding of full sheep (neatly rebacked; cvrs worn, scuffed along edges), gilt lettered red/black spine labels. The plate on p.283 of Mr. Phelps w/sl bulge exists only in prospectus and early copies bound in pub's leather; other copies bound in pub's leather at later date show the pl on p.283 in later states. *D & D.* $5,900/£3,806

TWAIN, MARK. Adventures of Huckleberry Finn. Charles L. Webster, 1885. 1st ed, 1st issue: all 1st issue points, error on table of contents for illus title 'Him and Another Man' listed pg 88 appears pg 87; 'was' for 'saw' on pg 57, etc. E.W. Kemble (illus). Tight, clean in beautiful box. *Davidson.* $3,200/£2,065

TWAIN, MARK. Adventures of Huckleberry Finn. NY: Charles L. Webster, 1885. 1st ed. All BAL points are earliest issue for trade ed except point 4 w/this copy being state C (final 5 present in different font) and point 6 being state C (p283 engr redone, tipped in). Very bright (top, bottom spine worn; few leaves foxed or lt stained). BAL 3415. *Glenn.* $1,200/£774

TWAIN, MARK. The Adventures of Huckleberry Finn.... Bernard De Voto (ed). NY: LEC, 1942. One of 1500. Signed by Thomas Hart Benton (illus). Full butternut cl. Spine sl dknd, o/w Fine in VG case (sunned). *Agvent.* $350/£226

TWAIN, MARK. The Adventures of Tom Sawyer. Washington: Georgetown Univ Lib, (1982). 1st ed thus, ltd to 1000. Facs ed of orig ms. 2 vols. Blue cl, gilt. Fine set (eps cracked, wrinkled) in box. *Macdonnell.* $200/£129

TWAIN, MARK. The Adventures of Tom Sawyer. NY: Random House, 1930. #1222/2000. Donald McKay (illus). Leather spine, dec cl bds. VG+ in slipcase (browned, worn). *Williams.* $70/£45

TWAIN, MARK. The Adventures of Tom Sawyer. Cambridge: LEC, 1939. Ltd ed. Signed by Thomas Hart Benton (illus). (Spine sl faded.) Box (worn, repaired). *Glenn.* $450/£290

TWAIN, MARK. The American Claimant. NY: Charles L. Webster, 1892. 1st ed. xv,277pp. Pict grey/grn cl, gilt (sl soiled, extrems lt worn). BAL 3434. *Shasky.* $115/£74

TWAIN, MARK. The American Claimant. Webster, 1892. 1st ed. Pict stamped cl. Spine edges lt rubbed, else VG. *Fine Books.* $125/£81

TWAIN, MARK. The American Claimant. NY: Charles L. Webster, 1892. 1st ed. Gilt-titled, illus cl (extrems rubbed). Fine. BAL 3434. *Cahan.* $150/£97

TWAIN, MARK. The American Claimant. London: C&W, 1892. 1st Eng ed. Ads dated May 1892. Spine, top of fr panel sl faded, else VG. *Limestone.* $75/£48

TWAIN, MARK. The Celebrated Jumping Frog of Calaveras County and Other Sketches. NY: C.H. Webb, 1867. 1st ed, 2nd ptg w/broken, worn type pp66, 198 and absence of ad leaf before tp. Orig maroon cl over beveled bds; pict stamped, lettered gilt. Presentable (worn, rubbed). BAL 3310. *Hermitage.* $1,000/£645

TWAIN, MARK. The Celebrated Jumping Frog of Calaveras County, and Other Sketches. NY: C.H. Webb, 1867. 1st ed, 2nd ptg w/ad leaf not present, and broken type on pp 21, 66, and 198. 1st bk. 198pp. Orig blue cl w/beveled edges. Good (bds heavily worn, soiled; spine ends repaired; lt dampstain lower corner throughout; pencil sig). BAL 3310. *Chapel Hill.* $400/£258

TWAIN, MARK. Christian Science. NY, 1907. 1st Amer ed. NF (bkpl; tape removal mks; sl sunned). *Polyanthos.* $45/£29

TWAIN, MARK. A Connecticut Yankee in King Arthur's Court. NY: Charles Webster, 1889. 1st ed, 2nd state w/o S-like ornament at p59. Pub's 3/4 morocco, gilt (lt rubbed). Nice. BAL 3429. *Macdonnell.* $165/£106

TWAIN, MARK. Death-Disk. NY: Edgar S. Werner, 1913. 1st ed. Tp vignette. NF in paper wrappers. BAL 3676. *Cahan.* $135/£87

TWAIN, MARK. Death-Disk. NY: Edgar S. Werner, 1913. 1st Separate ed. Ptd self-wraps. NF in cl folder. BAL 3676. *Agvent.* $85/£55

TWAIN, MARK. A Double Barrelled Detective Story. NY, 1902. 1st ed. Hitchcock (illus). Teg. Gilt-stamped red cl (sl spotted, sl bumped; foxing). *King.* $100/£65

TWAIN, MARK. Following the Equator. Hartford, 1897. 1st ed, 1st issue. 712pp (names). Dec cl. Worn, else Nice. *King.* $175/£113

TWAIN, MARK. Following the Equator. Hartford: Amer Pub Co, 1897. 1st ed, single imprint, but no priority between these copies and those w/dbl imprint. Orig pict blue cl, gilt. Hinge paper sl cracking, o/w VG. BAL 3451. *Macdonnell.* $150/£97

TWAIN, MARK. Following the Equator. Hartford: American Publishing, 1897. 1st ed. 1st state w/single Hartford imprint. Blue cl, pict paper label inset on fr cvr. Fine. BAL 3451. *Cahan.* $225/£145

TWAIN, MARK. Following the Equator. Hartford: American, 1897. 1st trade ed, 1st issue. 712pp. Blue pict binding (sl rubbed, sl shaken). BAL 3351. *Schoyer.* $175/£113

TWAIN, MARK. A Horse's Tale. NY: Harper's, 1907. 1st Amer ed. Lucius Hitchcock (illus). Dec red cl. NF (contemp name, date pastedown; spine sunned; leather bkpl). BAL 3500. *Agvent.* $175/£113

TWAIN, MARK. A Horse's Tale. NY: Harper, 1907. 1st ed. Orig red pict cl. White lettering effaced from spine, else VG. BAL 3500. *Macdonnell.* $50/£32

TWAIN, MARK. A Horse's Tale. NY: Harper, 1907. 1st ed. Signed. 8vo. Frontis; 4 full-pg b/w illus by Lucius Hitchcock. Pict red cl stamped in white/brn/black (sl wear). VG. *Houle.* $1,500/£968

TWAIN, MARK. How to Tell a Story and Other Essays. NY: Harper, 1897. 1st ed. Teg, uncut. Orig red dec cl, gilt. Fine. BAL 3449. *Macdonnell*. $275/£177

TWAIN, MARK. The Innocents Abroad. NY: LEC, 1962. One of 1500 numbered, signed by Fritz Kredel (illus). Fine (bkpl) in pub's slipcase. *Hermitage*. $125/£81

TWAIN, MARK. Is Shakespeare Dead? NY: Harper, 1909. 1st Amer ed. Inscrip, else Fine in VG dj (couple tears; shallow extrem chipping). *Between The Covers*. $450/£290

TWAIN, MARK. The Jumping Frog. NY, 1903. 1st ed. F. Strothman (illus). Red pict cl. VG. *Argosy*. $350/£226

TWAIN, MARK. Letters from Honolulu. Honolulu: Thomas Nickerson, 1939. 1st bk ed. One of 1000. Grn cl, pict paper cvr, spine labels. Fine (spine, top edges sl sunned) in orig acetate wrapper. BAL 3561. *Harrington*. $110/£71

TWAIN, MARK. Life on the Mississippi. Boston: James R. Osgood & Co., 1883. 1st Amer ed, 1st state; vignette of Twain in flames p441, caption reading 'The St. Louis Hotel' p443. 8vo. 624pp. Dec brn cl, pict gilt-stamping. VG (sig; bkpl; bumped, fr hinge weak). BAL 3411. Howes C 480. *Chapel Hill*. $500/£323

TWAIN, MARK. Life on the Mississippi. Boston: James R. Osgood, 1883. 1st Amer ed. Sl stain top edge, else NF. BAL 3411. Blanck's first state, intermediate A. *Between The Covers*. $475/£306

TWAIN, MARK. Life on the Mississippi. Montreal: Dawson Bros, 1883. 1st Canadian ed. Orig lavender cl, gilt (spine faded, lt damp mk rear cvr). VG. *Macdonnell*. $150/£97

TWAIN, MARK. Life on the Mississippi. Boston: James R. Osgood, 1883. 1st ed, 1st ptg, intermediate state B. Orig pict brn cl, gilt. Foot of spine frayed, hinge paper cracked, but bright, solid copy w/o illus of Twain's head in flames p441, but reading 'St. Louis Hotel' p443. BAL 3411. *Macdonnell*. $150/£97

TWAIN, MARK. Life on the Mississippi. Boston: James R. Osgood, 1883. 1st ed, 2nd state. Orig pict brn cl, gilt (worn, hinges cracked.) BAL 3411. *Macdonnell*. $35/£23

TWAIN, MARK. Life on the Mississippi. Boston: Osgood, 1883. 1st ed, intermediate state w/'The St. Louis Hotel' on p. 443 but w/o vignette of Twain in flames p441). 8vo,624pp. Orig pub's 1/2 morocco w/gilt dec spine. NF (spine sl rubbed). BAL 3411. Howes C480. *Chapel Hill*. $750/£484

TWAIN, MARK. Life on the Mississippi. NY: LEC, 1944. #904/1500 numbered, signed by Thomas Hart Benton (illus). Half leather, pict cl. Fine in tissue dj & drop-lid box (faded; worn). *Hermitage*. $400/£258

TWAIN, MARK. The Love Letters of Mark Twain. Dixon Wecter (ed). NY: Harper, 1949. 1st trade ed, 1st ptg. Orig cl, gilt. Fine in VG dj. *Macdonnell*. $35/£23

TWAIN, MARK. The Man That Corrupted Hadleyburg. NY: Harper, 1900. 1st ed, 1st state. Orig red cl, gilt. Spine lt faded, else tight, fresh copy. BAL 3459. *Macdonnell*. $250/£161

TWAIN, MARK. The Man That Corrupted Hadleyburg. NY: Harper, 1900. 1st ed. State 3 w/plate opposite p2 not having the line '[page 2' and leaves bulking 1 inch. Gold-stamped red cl (spine sl faded). VG. BAL 3459. *Second Life*. $75/£48

TWAIN, MARK. Mark Twain's (Burlesque) Autobiography and First Romance. NY: Sheldon, (1871). 1st ed, 2nd state w/ad verso tp. Orig terra cotta cl, gilt (spine sl worn; fep neatly excised). Bright. BAL 3326. *Macdonnell*. $65/£42

TWAIN, MARK. Mark Twain's Autobiography. NY: Harper, 1924. 1st ed, 1st state. 2 vols. Teg. Orig blue cl, gilt. Fine set in attractive djs. BAL 3537. *Macdonnell*. $200/£129

TWAIN, MARK. Mark Twain's Autobiography. NY: Harpers, 1924. 2nd ptg. 2 vols. Fine in djs (lt soiled; edgeworn; lg chip 1 spine). *Agvent*. $80/£52

TWAIN, MARK. Mark Twain's Letter to William Bowen. SF: Book Club of CA, 1938. One of 400. Buckrambacked bds; paper label. Sl offsetting fep from leather bkpl, o/w NF. BAL 3560. *Agvent*. $150/£97

TWAIN, MARK. Mark Twain's Notebook. NY: Harper's, 1935. 1st Amer ed. VG (offsetting fep; spotting t.p., frontis) in dj (chips, stains). *Agvent*. $150/£97

TWAIN, MARK. Mark Twain's Sketches, New and Old. Hartford: Amer Pub Co, 1875. 1st ed, 2nd state. 320pp. Blue cl, stamped in gold/black (extrems sl worn, hinges partially cracked but firm; names scratched out, sm stain corner of fr cvr). BAL 3364. *Shasky*. $185/£119

TWAIN, MARK. Mark Twain's Speeches. NY: Harper, 1910. 1st ed, 1st state. Orig red cl, gilt. Spine lt sunned, else Fine. BAL 3513. *Macdonnell*. $125/£81

TWAIN, MARK. Mark Twain's [Date, 1601.] Conversation as It Was by the Social Fireside in the Time of the Tudors. Chicago: Mark Twain Soc of Chicago, 1939. Ltd to 550. Signed by Franklin J. Meine (intro). Natural linen, leather labels. NF. *Cahan*. $65/£42

TWAIN, MARK. Mark Twain—Howells Letters. Cambridge: Belknap Press, 1960. 1st ed. 2 vols. Orig black cl. Fine set in NF djs (nicks). *Macdonnell*. $125/£81

TWAIN, MARK. Merry Tales. NY: Charles L. Webster, 1892. 1st ed, 1st issue. Pict cl in gilt/colors (extrems rubbed). BAL 3435. *Sadlon*. $50/£32

TWAIN, MARK. Merry Tales. NY: Webster, 1892. 1st ed, 1st state. Orig olive-grn cl, gilt. This copy does not have frontis port, and has parsley-leaf patterned eps. (Sl rubbed.) Attractive. BAL 3435. *Macdonnell*. $150/£97

TWAIN, MARK. The Notorious Jumping Frog and Other Stories. NY: LEC, 1970. #330/1500 signed by Joseph Low (illus). Spine lt faded, o/w Fine in pub's slipcase (lt faded). *Hermitage*. $85/£55

TWAIN, MARK. The Notorious Jumping Frog and Other Stories. NY: LEC, 1970. One of 1500 signed by Joseph Low (illus). VF in slipcase & glassine. *Pharos*. $125/£81

TWAIN, MARK. Personal Recollections of Joan of Arc. NY: Harper, 1896. 1st ed, 1st state. Orig red cl, gilt. Spine sl dusty, o/w Fine. BAL 3446. *Macdonnell*. $200/£129

TWAIN, MARK. The Prince and the Pauper. Boston: James R. Osgood & Co., 1882. 1st Amer ed. Binding state B; w/true eps fr, rear; rosette on spine 1/16-inch scant below fillet. 411pp. Pict grn cl. VG (name; wear to spine ends, corners). BAL 3402. *Chapel Hill*. $300/£194

TWAIN, MARK. The Prince and the Pauper. (NY): LEC, 1964. One of 1500 numbered, signed by Clarke Hutton (illus). Fine in pub's slipcase. *Hermitage*. $100/£65

TWAIN, MARK. Pudd'n Head Wilson. London: C&W, 1894. 1st ed. Variant binding (also issued in pict red cl), w/pubs inserted Sept. 1898 cat at rear. BAL 3441 records blue cl copies w/cats dated Sept. 1894, June 1899. 8vo. 246pp + 32pp ads. Orig blue cl. Inscrip fr pastedown, spine crown rubbed, o/w NF. *Chapel Hill.* $650/£419

TWAIN, MARK. Punch, Brothers, Punch! NY: Clote, Woodman, (1878). Correct 1st ed, w/Twain's name ptd in roman type on tp. 140,(1)pp + 1pg ads. Orig dec blue cl (1st binding, w/o caricatures on eps). VG (spine ends, corners worn; bkpl; fr inner hinge starting; sm chip top fr fly). BAL 3378. *Chapel Hill.* $175/£113

TWAIN, MARK. Report from Paradise. NY: Harper, 1952. 1st ed. Linen-backed paper over bds. Fine in dj (lt soiled, chipped). BAL 3581. *Glenn.* $30/£19

TWAIN, MARK. Roughing It. Hartford: Amer Pub Co, 1872. 1st ed, 2nd state of p242. Orig black cl, gilt (spine ends frayed, few nicks). Bright. BAL 3337. *Macdonnell.* $150/£97

TWAIN, MARK. Roughing It. Hartford: Amer Pub Co, 1872. 1st ed, mixed state w/only one word lacking p242. Orig black cl, gilt. (Hinge paper cracked, text browning; sl rubbed.) BAL 3337. *Macdonnell.* $150/£97

TWAIN, MARK. The Stolen White Elephant. Boston: James R. Osgood, 1882. 1st ed. Orig cream pict cl, gilt (sl mkd). Attractive. (Early inscrip.) BAL 3404. *Macdonnell.* $200/£129

TWAIN, MARK. Tom Sawyer Abroad. NY: Charles L. Webster & Co., 1894. 1st ed. 8vo,219pp,(4)pp ads. Orig pict tan cl (binding variant B). Bright, clean (upper portions sl sunned; bkpl; inscrip; 1/2-inch stain rear pastedown, ep). BAL 3440. *Chapel Hill.* $800/£516

TWAIN, MARK. Tom Sawyer. Cambridge: LEC, 1939. #162/1500 signed by Thomas Hart Benton (illus). Fine in slipcase (sl split, worn). *Williams.* $388/£250

TWAIN, MARK. The Tragedy of Pudd'nhead Wilson and the Comedy Those Extraordinary Twins. Hartford, CT: American Pub Co, 1894. 1st Amer ed, 1st ptg, w/conjugate tp and sheets bulking about 1 1/8 inches. State A of frontis w/Twain's facs autograph measuring 1 7/16 inches wide. 8vo,432pp. Orig brn cl stamped in black/gold. Fine (sig). BAL 3442. *Chapel Hill.* $500/£323

TWAIN, MARK. The Tragedy of Pudd'nhead Wilson.... Hartford, CT, 1894. 1st Amer ed, 1st state. 432pp, port. Dec cl. Sl dknd, sl frayed, else Nice. *King.* $300/£194

TWAIN, MARK. A Tramp Abroad. Toronto: Rose-Belford Pub Co, (1880). 1st Canadian ed. 410pp + ads. Blue cl stamped in gold (sl worn). BAL 3626. *Second Life.* $200/£129

TWAIN, MARK. A Tramp Abroad. Hartford: Amer Pub Co, 1880. 1st ed, 2nd state of frontis captioned 'Titian's Moses;' state B of frontis port; state A of sheets; state A of cvr stamping. This copy w/'3' blindstamped beneath pub's imprint rear cvr. Pub's blindstamped gilt black cl (sl rubbed, spine sl sunned, lacks fep). BAL 3386. *Book Block.* $125/£81

TWAIN, MARK. A Tramp Abroad. CT/London, 1880. 2nd state, w/328 illus. Gilt pict cvrs. Fine (spine extrems sl chipped; sm area side spine mended; corners sl rubbed). *Polyanthos.* $200/£129

TWAIN, MARK. A Yankee at the Court of King Arthur. C&W, 1889. 1st Eng ed. Spine lightened; sm tear rear hinge, else VG + . *Aronovitz.* $185/£119

TWEEDIE, MRS. ALEC. Hyde Park. Its History and Romance. NY: James Pott, 1908. 1st ed, US issue. 29 plts. Teg. Red dec cl, gilt. Nice. *Cady.* $25/£16

TWEEDSMUIR, LORD. Hudson's Bay Trader. London: Clerke & Cockeran, 1951. 1st ed. VG (spine sl faded; stamp) in dj (sl worn, torn). *Hollett.* $39/£25

TWIFORD, WILLIAM RICHARD. Sown in Darkness. Tremayne, 1940. 1st ed. Fine in dj (sl frayed). *Madle.* $75/£48

TWITCHELL, RALPH EMERSON. The History of the Military Occupation of the Territory of New Mexico from 1846 to 1851.... Chicago: Rio Grande, 1963. Rpt. VG + (owner label). *Parker.* $35/£23

TWITE, M.L. The World's Racing Cars. London: MacDonald, (1964). 1st ed. Grn cl, gilt. Good. *Shasky.* $45/£29

Two Sisters. NY: Philip J. Cozans, n.d. (ca 1850). Chapbook. 12mo. 8pp + 1pg ad lower wrapper. Tp engr repeated on hand-colored upper wrapper. Near Mint in pict paper wrappers. *Hobbyhorse.* $80/£52

Two Years Before the Mast. (By Richard Henry Dana). London, 1841. 1st British ed. (2),124pp. Later buckram. VG (few fox mks). Howes D 49. *Reese.* $450/£290

Two Years Before the Mast. (By Richard Henry Dana Jr.) NY: Harper, 1841. 483pp. Orig brn cl (ends worn; lt foxing). Good. BAL 4434. *Lefkowicz.* $200/£129

TWYMAN, MICHAEL. Printing 1770-1970, an Illustrated History of Its Development and Uses in England. London: Eyre & Spottiswoode, 1970. 1st ed. Dj (rubbed). *Bookpress.* $125/£81

TYAS, ROBERT. The Language of Flowers. London: Routledge, 1875. 223pp; 3 chromolitho plts. Aeg. Gilt-dec cl. Fine. *Quest.* $75/£48

TYGIEL, JULES. Baseball's Great Experiment: Jackie Robinson and His Legacy. NY, 1983. 1st ed. VG + (blindstamp) in VG + dj (lt creased). *Fuller & Saunders.* $25/£16

TYLER, ANNA COGSWELL (retold by). Twenty-Four Unusual Stories for Boys and Girls. NY: Harcourt, Brace, 1921. 1st ed. 8vo. Maud & Miska Petersham (illus). Grn cl, black lettering, decs. Good in pict dj (lt edgewear; chips). *Reisler.* $135/£87

TYLER, ANNE. The Accidental Tourist. NY: Knopf, 1985. 1st ed, signed. Rev copy, pub's letter laid in. Fine in dj. *Limestone.* $215/£139

TYLER, ANNE. Breathing Lessons. NY: Knopf, 1988. 1st trade ed. Fine in dj. *Godot.* $45/£29

TYLER, ANNE. Celestial Navigation. NY: Knopf, 1974. 1st ed. Fine in dj. *Else Fine.* $300/£194

TYLER, ANNE. The Clock Winder. NY: Knopf, 1972. 1st ed. Pea grn cl. VG (sm splash-mks top edge; 2pp creased) in VG dj (spine soiled). *Chapel Hill.* $475/£306

TYLER, ANNE. Dinner at the Homesick Restaurant. NY: Knopf, 1982. 1st Amer ed. Fine in dj. *Between The Covers.* $100/£65

TYLER, ANNE. Earthly Possessions. NY: Knopf, 1977. 1st Amer ed. Fine in dj (rubbing spine foot). *Between The Covers.* $200/£129

TYLER, ANNE. Earthly Possessions. NY: Knopf, 1977. 1st ed. Fine in Fine dj (sl wear spine head). *Beasley.* $75/£48

TYLER, ANNE. Morgan's Passing. NY: Knopf, 1980. 1st ed. Fine in dj. *Else Fine.* $95/£61

TYLER, ANNE. Saint Maybe. NY: Knopf, 1991. 1st ed. Signed. Fine in Fine dj. *Revere.* $60/£39

TYLER, ANNE. Saint Maybe. London: C&W, 1991. 1st UK ed. Fine in dj. *Lewton.* $23/£15

TYLER, ANNE. A Slipping-Down Life. NY: Knopf, 1970. 1st ed. Fine in dj (lt worn). *Hermitage.* $300/£194

TYLER, ANNE. The Tin Can Tree. London: Macmillan, 1966. 1st British ed. Signed. Pg edges lt foxed, else NF in dj. *Lame Duck.* $650/£419

TYLER, ANNE. Tumble Tower. NY, 1993. 1st Amer ed. Signed bkpl laid in. Fine in Fine dj. *Polyanthos.* $30/£19

TYLER, ANNE. Tumble Tower. NY: Orchard, 1993. 1st ed. Signed by Tyler and Mitra Modaressi (illus). 4to. Fine in Fine dj. *Lame Duck.* $65/£42

TYLER, DANIEL. A Concise History of the Mormon Battalion in the Mexican War. (S.L.C.), 1881. 1st ed. (4),376pp. Full orig leather (spine repaired; new eps). Howes T 447. *Ginsberg.* $350/£226

TYLER, LYON G. The Letters and Times of the Tylers. Richmond: Whittet & Shepperson, 1884-1885. 1st ed. 2 vols. Frontis, xiii,(iii),633pp,plt; frontis, xiv,(ii),736pp,3 plts. Pub's cl (cvrs rubbed; corners vol 2 torn, bruised). (Ex-lib w/bkpl; all hinges internally cracked.) Howes T 448. *Bookpress.* $400/£258

TYMMS, W.R. and M.D. WYATT. The Art of Illumination in Europe from the Earliest Times. London: Day, (1860). 1st ed. 95 chromolithos. 3/4 gilt-stamped vellum, lt brn cl; teg. VG (sl foxing, not affecting plts). *Houle.* $325/£210

TYNAN, KATHARINE and FRANCES MAITLAND. The Book of Flowers. London: Smith, Elder, 1909. Gilt-dec pict cl. Hinges starting, else VG. *Quest.* $35/£23

TYNAN, KATHARINE. Shamrocks. London: Kegan Paul, Trench, 1887. 1st ed. Beige cl (soiled), gilt lettering. VG (bkpls; spine sunned). *Hermitage.* $150/£97

TYNDALE, WALTER. An Artist in Italy. London: Hodder & Stoughton, (1913). 1st ed. 26 tipped-in color plts, captioned guards. Dec cl, gilt. VG. *Cox.* $28/£18

TYNDALE, WALTER. An Artist in Italy. London: Hodder & Stoughton, 1913. 26 tipped-in color plts. VG. *Hollett.* $101/£65

TYNDALL, JOHN. The Glaciers of the Alps. London: John Murray, 1860. 1st ed. Frontis, xx,444pp + pub's 32pg cat dated Jan 1860; 5 color plts. Red morocco cl, blocked in blind, gilt-lettered spine (sl faded); brown eps. Fine. *Bickersteth.* $186/£120

TYNDALL, JOHN. The Glaciers of the Alps. London, 1896. 2nd ed. xxv,445pp; 3 plts (1 color); errata slip inserted. (Pencil notes.) *Henly.* $65/£42

TYRRELL, JAMES W. Across the Sub-Arctics of Canada.... Toronto, 1908. 3rd ed. Fldg map. (Inscrip; eps foxed.) *Petersfield.* $25/£16

TYRWHITT, J. et al. The Heart of the City: Towards the Humanization of Urban Life. NY: Pellegrini and Cudahy, 1952. 1st ed. Frontis. Sl waterstain margin edges, not affecting text or illus; else VG in worn dj. *Bookpress.* $250/£161

TYSON, JAMES. Diary of a Physician in California. Biobooks, 1955. 1st thus. Ltd to 500. Fine. Howes T 451. *Oregon.* $40/£26

U

U.S. Infantry Tactics...May 1, 1861.... Phila: Lippincott, 1861. 1st ptg. 450pp + (6)pp ads. Grn cl. Names, foxing, else VG + . *Chapel Hill.* $75/£48

UDELL, JOHN. Journal Kept During a Trip Across the Plains.... L.A.: N.A. Kovach, 1946. 1st ed thus. (Top spine sl faded.) *Glenn.* $40/£26

UDELL, JOHN. Journal Kept During a Trip Across the Plains.... L.A.: N.A. Kovach, 1946. Ltd to 750. 7 plts. Fine in Fine dj. Howes U 4. *Oregon.* $45/£29

UDEN, GRANT. Collector's Casebook. Constable Young, 1963. 1st ed. VG in dj. *Moss.* $14/£9

UEBERWASSER, WALTER. Rogier van der Weyden: Paintings from the Escorial and the Prado. NY: Iris Books, 1946. 7 mtd color plts. (Backstrip worn.) *Argosy.* $50/£32

UHDE, WILHELM. Vincent Van Gogh. NY: Phaidon, (1941). 120 plts (16 mtd color). VG in dj. *Argosy.* $60/£39

UHLENDORF, BERNHARD A. The Siege of Charleston. Ann Arbor: Univ of MI Press, 1938. 1st ed. Grn cl. Spot fr cvr, else NF. *Chapel Hill.* $125/£81

UKERS, W.H. All About Coffee. NY, 1922. Buckram. (Sl worming.) *Wheldon & Wesley.* $116/£75

UKERS, W.H. All About Coffee. NY, 1935. 2nd ed. Good. *Wheldon & Wesley.* $147/£95

UKERS, W.H. All About Tea. NY, 1935. 2 vols. Frontispieces. Grn gilt-dec cl. 1/2 title worn, dj panels glued to blank sheets, o/w Fine set. *Sutton.* $125/£81

ULLSTEIN, H. The Rise and Fall of the House of Ullstein. London: Nicholson & Watson, n.d. VG in dj. *Moss.* $47/£30

UMBRA. (Pseud of Charles Cavendish Clifford.) Travels. Edinburgh: Edmonston & Douglas, 1865. Frontis, illus tp, vi,278pp. Maroon cl (sl frayed). *Karmiole.* $50/£32

UMLAUFT, F. The Alps. Louisa Brough (trans). London: Kegan Paul, Trench, 1889. 1st Eng ed. xii,523pp; 2 maps. (Sl rubbed; spine dknd; spots.) *Hollett.* $116/£75

Unbeaten Tracks in Japan: An Account of Travels on Horseback in the Interior.... NY: Putnam's (ca 1880s). 2 vols in 1. Frontispieces, xxiii,407; xiii,392pp; fldg map. Gilt-pict brn cl. VG. *Petrilla.* $60/£39

Uncle Buncle's Young Friends. London: Dean & Munday, (ca 1840). 8vo. 7 full-pg hand-colored wood engrs. Illus grn paper wrappers (spine chipped). *Reisler.* $125/£81

Uncle Frank's Fables, for Good Boys and Girls. NY: Wm. H. Murphy, n.d. (ca 1850). 5 vols. 12mo. 34pp each vol + 1pg ads back cvrs, 16 wood engrs each vol. Pict paper wrappers w/wood engr pict vignette, framed. VG set (ink sig top corner vol V). *Hobbyhorse.* $225/£145

Uncle Wiggily's Woodland Games. (By Howard R. Garis.) Newark: Charles E. Graham, (1922). 1st ptg. 8vo. Lang Campbell (illus). Blue cl, color paste label, silver lettering. Good. *Reisler.* $75/£48

Uncle's Present. A New Battledore. Phila: Jacob Johnson, n.d. (ca 1810). 12mo. 4pp + 1 flap; 24 cuts. Pict buff stiff self-wrappers. (Sl internal foxing; wrappers dusted.) *Hobbyhorse.* $450/£290

Uncle's Present. A New Battledore. Phila: Jacob Johnson, n.d. (ca 1820). 12mo. 4pp + 1 flap, 24 woodcuts. 1st, last pp pasted down to pict buff stiff paper self wrappers (reinforcement at inner folds; lt chipped, browned). *Hobbyhorse.* $320/£206

UNDERHILL, E. The Gray World. Century, 1904. 1st ed. VG + . *Aronovitz.* $85/£55

UNDERHILL, HAROLD A. Masting and Rigging the Clipper Ship and Ocean Carrier. Glasgow: Brown et al, (1965). Fldg plan. Dj. *Lefkowicz.* $40/£26

UNDERHILL, RUTH M. The Navajos. Norman: Univ of OK Press, (1956). 1st ptg. 2 maps. VG in dj. *Schoyer.* $35/£23

UNDERWOOD, GEORGE C. History of the Twenty-Sixth Regiment of the Carolina Troops, in the Great War 1861-'65. Goldsboro, NC: Nash Bros, (1901). 1st ed. Frontis port. Orig red cl. Faded, spine sl loose, else Good + . Howes U 13. *Chapel Hill.* $325/£210

UNDERWOOD, JOHN. Alaska. An Empire in the Making. Dodd Mead, 1913. 1st ed. 48 plts. Pict cl. VG. *Oregon.* $50/£32

UNDERWOOD, MICHAEL. A Treatise on the Disease of Children, and Management of Infants from Birth. Boston: By David West, 1806. 2nd Amer ed. 3 vols in 1. xx,476pp. (Ex-libris.) Contemp calf (rubbed, spine bruised), red lettering piece. VG. *Hemlock.* $275/£177

UNDERWOOD, MRS. DESMOND. Grey and Silver Leaved Plants. London: Collins, 1971. 1st ed. Mint. *Quest.* $55/£35

UNDERWOOD, PAUL A. The Kariye Djami. NY: Pantheon, 1966. 1st ed. 3 vols. NF in djs; slipcase. *Worldwide.* $350/£226

UNGERER, TOMI. Crictor. NY: Harper, 1958. 1st ed. 4to. 32pp. Cl-backed pict bds, blue spine. VG in dj (torn). *Davidson.* $75/£48

UNGERER, TOMI. No Kiss for Mother. NY: Harper & Row, 1973. 1st ed. 8vo. 40pp. Fine in Fine dj. *Davidson.* $50/£32

United States 'History' as the Yankee Makes and Takes It. (By John Cussons.) Glen Allen, VA: Cussons, May 1900. '3rd ed.' Wraps (sl soiled). *Schoyer.* $40/£26

United States 'History,' as the Yankee Makes and Takes It. (By John Cussons.) Glen Allen, VA: Cussons, May, 1900. 3rd ed, so stated. Stiff yellow wraps. Good + (spine worn, water stains). *Chapel Hill.* $75/£48

United States Strategic Bombing Survey: The Effects of Atomic Bombs on Hiroshima and Nagasaki. GPO, 1946. 1st ed. 2 fldg color maps bound in rear. VG + in wraps. *Fine Books.* $150/£97

UNSWORTH, BARRY. The Partnership. London: New Authors Ltd, 1966. 1st British ed, 1st bk. NF in VG + dj. *Pettler.* $125/£81

UNSWORTH, WALT. Tiger in the Snow. London: Gollancz, 1967. 1st ed. 11 illus; 5 maps. VG in dj. *Hollett.* $31/£20

UNTERKIRCHER, FRANZ. European Illuminated Manuscripts. London: Thames and Hudson, 1967. 60 tipped-in color plts.(Ex-lib w/ink stamps, bkpl.) Dj (chipped), slipcase (worn, splitting). *Edwards.* $116/£75

UNTERMEYER, LOUIS. Burning Bush. NY, 1928. 1st ed. Frontis. Rockwell Kent (illus). VG in dj. *Argosy.* $45/£29

UNTERMEYER, LOUIS. The New Adam. NY: Harcourt, 1920. 1st ed. Fine (shelfwear) in dj (lt used). *Beasley.* $60/£39

UNWIN, J.D. Hopousia. London, 1940. 1st ed. Frontis port. (Cl lt soiled). *Edwards.* $31/£20

UP DE GRAFF, F.W. Head Hunters of the Amazon. NY: Duffield, 1923. 1st ed. Fldg map. Gilt-lettered grn cl (lt worn). VG. *House.* $45/£29

UP DE GRAFF, F.W. Head-Hunters of the Amazon. London: Jenkins, 1923. 1st ed. Fldg map. VG + . *Mikesh.* $37/£24

UPDIKE, DANIEL BERKELEY. In the Day's Work. Cambridge: Harvard Univ Press, 1924. Teg. Dj missing lg portion at spine, else VG. *Veatchs.* $40/£26

UPDIKE, DANIEL BERKELEY. Printing Types. Cambridge: Harvard, 1922. 1st ed. 2 vols. Good set (ex-lib but clean). *Reese.* $60/£39

UPDIKE, DANIEL BERKELEY. Printing Types. Cambridge: Harvard Univ, 1937. 2nd ed. 2 vols. Maroon cl (sl mkd). Good set (pencil notes). *Cox.* $132/£85

UPDIKE, DANIEL BERKELEY. Printing Types. OUP, 1937. 2nd ed. 2 vols. (Feps, vol 1 spine lt browned.) Djs (chipped). *Edwards.* $116/£75

UPDIKE, JOHN. Bath after Sailing. Monroe, CT: Pendulum, 1968. One of 125 numbered, signed. Fine in stiff cardboard wraps in cl-cvrd chemise & slipcase w/leather spine labels. *Lame Duck.* $850/£548

UPDIKE, JOHN. Bech Is Back. London: Deutsch, 1983. 1st UK ed. Fine in dj. *Williams.* $23/£15

UPDIKE, JOHN. Brother Grasshopper. Worcester, MA: Metacom Press, 1990. 1st ed. Ltd to 176 signed. Fine in dj. *Juvelis.* $125/£81

UPDIKE, JOHN. Buchanan Dying. Deutsch, 1974. 1st ed. Dec eps. VG in dj. *Whiteson.* $16/£10

UPDIKE, JOHN. The Carpentered Hen and Other Tame Creatures. Harpers, 1958. 1st ed, 1st bk. VG + in VG + 2nd ptg dj w/4 children (not 2). *Fine Books.* $195/£126

UPDIKE, JOHN. A Child's Calendar. NY: Knopf, (1965). 1st ed. Red cl. Fine in dj. *Godot.* $150/£97

UPDIKE, JOHN. The Coup. NY: Knopf, 1978. One of 350 numbered, signed. Grn cl. Fine in dj, pub's slipcase. *Dermont.* $150/£97

UPDIKE, JOHN. The Coup. London: Deutsch, 1979. 1st Eng ed. Fine in dj. *Limestone.* $25/£16

UPDIKE, JOHN. Couples. London: Deutsch, 1968. 1st UK ed. Fine in NF dj (price-clipped). *Williams.* $25/£16

UPDIKE, JOHN. Cunts. NY: Frank Hallman, (1974). 1st ed, ltd to 250 numbered, signed. Fine; issued w/o dj. *Godot.* $200/£129

UPDIKE, JOHN. Ego and Art in Walt Whitman. NY: Targ Editions, 1980. Ltd to 350 signed. Brn gilt cl over dec bds. Fine in plain paper dj. *Karmiole.* $100/£65

UPDIKE, JOHN. Facing Nature. NY: Knopf, 1985. 1st ed. Fine in NF dj (short edge tears). *Lame Duck.* $45/£29

UPDIKE, JOHN. Getting the Words Out. Lord John Press, 1988. One of 250 numbered, signed. As New. *Dermont.* $60/£39

UPDIKE, JOHN. Hawthorne's Creed. NY: Targ Editions, (1981). Ltd to 250 signed. Frontis port. Purple cl over marbled bds, sm mtd cvr illus. Fine in plain paper dj. *Karmiole.* $85/£55

UPDIKE, JOHN. Hawthorne's Creed. NY: Targ Editions, 1981. 1st ed. One of 250 signed. Frontis. Marbled paper over bds, maroon linen spine, photo repro fr cvr. New in grey wrapper. *Juvelis.* $75/£48

UPDIKE, JOHN. Hoping for a Hoopoe. London: Gollancz, 1959. 1st Eng ed, 1st bk. Rev copy w/pub's slip laid in. Black cl. VG in VG dj. *Chapel Hill.* $150/£97

UPDIKE, JOHN. Hub Fans Bid Kid Adieu. Northridge: Lord John Press, 1977. One of 300 numbered, signed. Cl, patterned bds. Fine in custom blue linen 2-part slipcase w/leather spine labels. *Dermont.* $250/£161

UPDIKE, JOHN. Iowa. A Broadside. Portland: Press-22, (1980). #24/200 (of 226) signed. Matted. Fine. *Polyanthos.* $60/£39

UPDIKE, JOHN. Marry Me. London, (1977). 1st Eng ed. Good in dj (sl scuffed). *Waterfield.* $23/£15

UPDIKE, JOHN. Marry Me. NY: Knopf, 1976. 1st US ed, 1st issue, w/code on rear panel. VG in dj. *Williams.* $19/£12

UPDIKE, JOHN. Midpoint and Other Poems. London: Deutsch, 1969. 1st UK ed. NF in dj. *Williams.* $47/£30

UPDIKE, JOHN. Midpoint and Other Poems. NY: Knopf, 1969. Ltd to 350 numbered, signed. Fine (bkpl) in dj & orig slipcase. *Antic Hay.* $135/£87

UPDIKE, JOHN. Museums and Women and Other Stories. NY: Knopf, 1972. 1st ed. Olive cl. Fine in NF dj. *Chapel Hill.* $50/£32

UPDIKE, JOHN. The Music School. NY: Knopf, 1966. 1st ed, 1st issue, w/transposed lines on pg 46. Fine in dj. *Godot.* $185/£119

UPDIKE, JOHN. Picked-Up Pieces. NY: Knopf, 1975. 1st ed, trade issue. Sm rmdr mk bottom edge, else Fine in dj. *Godot.* $50/£32

UPDIKE, JOHN. Problems and Other Stories. NY: Knopf, 1979. 1st ed. NF in dj. *Second Life.* $45/£29

UPDIKE, JOHN. Rabbit at Rest. London: Deutsch, 1990. 1st Eng ed. Fine in Fine dj. *Revere.* $30/£19

UPDIKE, JOHN. Rabbit at Rest. NY: Knopf, 1990. 1st trade ed. Fine in dj. *Godot.* $45/£29

UPDIKE, JOHN. Rabbit at Rest. Knopf, 1990. 1st trade ed. Signed. VF in dj. *Stahr.* $45/£29

UPDIKE, JOHN. Rabbit Is Rich. London: Deutsch, 1982. 1st UK ed. NF in dj (spine sl faded). *Williams.* $19/£12

UPDIKE, JOHN. Rabbit Redux. London, (1972). 1st Eng ed. Good in dj. *Waterfield.* $28/£18

UPDIKE, JOHN. Roger's Version. NY: Knopf, 1986. 1st ed. Inscribed. Fine in Fine dj. *Revere.* $75/£48

UPDIKE, JOHN. Roger's Version. Knopf, 1986. 1st trade ed. Signed. Fine in dj. *Stahr.* $45/£29

UPDIKE, JOHN. S. (London): Deutsch, (1988). 1st Eng ed. One of 75 numbered (of 97), signed. 1/4 calf; marbled bds. Fine in marbled paper-cvrd slipcase (sl rubbed). *Between The Covers.* $285/£184

UPDIKE, JOHN. Self-Consciousness. NY: Knopf, 1989. 1st ed, ltd to 350 numbered, signed. Fine in acetate dj, pub's slipcase box. *Godot.* $150/£97

UPDIKE, JOHN. Self-Consciousness. NY: Knopf, 1989. 1st trade ed. Signed. Fine in dj. *Bernard.* $65/£42

UPDIKE, JOHN. Self-Consciousness. Memoirs. NY, 1989. Signed presentation. Fine in Fine dj. *Polyanthos.* $50/£32

UPDIKE, JOHN. Spring Trio. N.p.: Paleamon, (1982). One of 150 numbered, signed. Fine in wrappers in batik dj, paper label. *Between The Covers.* $125/£81

UPDIKE, JOHN. Sunday in Boston. PA: Rook Broadsides 5, (1975). #280/300 signed. Matted. Fine. *Polyanthos.* $60/£39

UPDIKE, JOHN. Talk from the Fifties. Northridge: Lord John, 1979. One of 75 numbered, signed. Fine. *Between The Covers.* $125/£81

UPDIKE, JOHN. Trust Me. Knopf, 1987. 1st ed. Signed. Fine in dj. *Stahr.* $45/£29

UPDIKE, JOHN. Warm Wine. NY: Albondocani Press, 1973. 1st ed, #72/250 numbered, signed. Fine in orig French marbled wraps w/paper label. *Chapel Hill.* $150/£97

UPDIKE, JOHN. The Witches of Eastwick. (London): Andre Deutsch, (1984). 1st Eng ed. Fine in dj. *Antic Hay.* $35/£23

UPDIKE, JOHN. The Witches of Eastwick. NY: Knopf, 1984. 1st trade ed. Promo material laid in. Fine in dj. *Reese.* $35/£23

UPDIKE, JOHN. The Witches of Eastwick. London: Deutsch, 1984. 1st UK ed. Fine in dj. *Williams.* $28/£18

UPDIKE, JOHN. Your Lover Just Called. (England): Penguin Books, (1980). 1st Eng ed. Fine in pict wrappers. *Godot.* $45/£29

UPDIKE, WILKINS, Memoirs of the Rhode-Island Bar. Boston: Thomas H. Webb, 1842. 3/4 morocco over marbled bds. Rubbed, but Sound. *Boswell.* $150/£97

UPFIELD, ARTHUR. Bony Buys a Woman. London: Heinemann, 1957. 1st ed. NF in dj (worn; chips, tear). *Stahr.* $35/£23

UPFIELD, ARTHUR. Death of a Swagman. GC: Doubleday, 1945. 1st ed. Fine (name, address fep) in VG + dj (sm pinholes). *Janus.* $100/£65

UPFIELD, ARTHUR. Gripped by Drought. Dennis McMillan, 1990. 1st US ed. One of 450. Fine in dj. *Madle.* $35/£23

UPFIELD, ARTHUR. The House of Cain. SF: Dennis McMillan, 1983. Reprint ed. VF in dj. *Mordida.* $40/£26

UPFIELD, ARTHUR. Madman's Bend. Heinemann, 1963. 1st ed. Fine in NF dj (spine dknd; chip). *Stahr.* $50/£32

UPFIELD, ARTHUR. The Murchison Murders. Miami Beach: Dennis McMillan, 1987. 1st US ed. Fine in Fine dj. *Janus.* $25/£16

UPFIELD, ARTHUR. Murder Must Wait. GC: DDC, 1953. 1st ed. Name fep; pp dknd, o/w VG in dj (price-clipped; wear; dampstain spine base). *Mordida.* $35/£23

UPFIELD, ARTHUR. The Mystery of Swordfish Reef. London: Heinemann, 1960. 1st Eng ed. Sig, else VG in dj. *Limestone.* $75/£48

UPFIELD, ARTHUR. The New Shoe. GC: DDC, 1951. 1st ed. Pp dknd, o/w VG in dj (sl corner wear). *Mordida.* $45/£29

UPFIELD, ARTHUR. A Royal Abduction. Dennis McMillan, 1984. 1st Amer ed. VF in dj. *Mordida.* $50/£32

UPFIELD, ARTHUR. The Will of the Tribe. NY: Crime Club, 1962. 1st ed. NF in NF dj (rubbed; lt wear). *Stahr.* $45/£29

UPFIELD, ARTHUR. The Will of the Tribe. London: Heinemann, 1962. 1st ed. NF in dj. *Limestone.* $55/£35

UPFIELD, ARTHUR. The Will of the Tribe. London: Heinemann, 1962. 1st Eng ed. NF in VG dj (flyleaf folds, spine chipped; torn). *Stahr.* $35/£23

UPHAM, CHARLES W. Lectures on Witchcraft. Boston: Carter & Hendee, 1832. 2nd ed. 300pp. Orig linen (rebacked, orig spine laid down), paper label (worn); uncut. VG (bkpl). Howes U21. *Second Life.* $85/£55

UPHAM, ELIZABETH. Little Brown Bear. NY: Platt & Munk, (1942). 8vo. 8 full-pg color illus by Marjorie Hartwell. Orange cl, black lettering, illus. Good in full color dj (lt edgewear). *Reisler.* $75/£48

UPSON, ARTHUR T. High Lights in the Near East. London/Edinburgh: Marshall, Morgan & Scott, n.d. (ca 1933). Blue cl. VG. *Schoyer.* $30/£19

UPSON, WILLIAM HAZLETT. Botts in War, Botts in Peace. NY, 1944. Ltd gift ed. VG. *Bond.* $35/£23

UPSON, WILLIAM HAZLETT. Keep 'Em Crawling. Earthworms at War. NY/Toronto, (1943). 1st ed. VG in VG dj. *Mcclintock.* $45/£29

UPTON, BERTHA. The Adventures of Two Dutch Dolls. London/NY: Longmans, Green, 1898. 1st ed. 4to. 29 full-color plts by Florence Upton. Pict bds, cl spine. VG (internally soiled, corners bumped). *Davidson.* $350/£226

UPTON, BERTHA. The Golliwogg's Christmas. London: Longmans, Green, 1907. 1st ed, variant binding. Obl 4to. Florence K. Upton (illus). Cl-backed limp illus bds. (Worn; pp w/marginal tears, folds, smudges.) *Reisler.* $485/£313

UPTON, BERTHA. The Golliwogg's Circus. London/NY: Longmans, Green, 1903. 1st ed. Obl 4to. 31 illus by Florence Upton. (Pp creased, sm soil throughout, bds soiled, edges bumped, still respectable.) *Davidson.* $300/£194

UPTON, BERTHA. The Golliwogg's Desert Island. London: Longmans, Green, (1906). 1st ed. Oblong 4to. Florence K. Upton (illus). Cl-backed illus bds (lt chipping; sl mkd; few mks pgs). *Reisler.* $375/£242

UPTON, BERTHA. The Golliwogg's Desert-Island. London: Longmans, Green, 1906. 1st ed. Obl 4to. Florence K. Upton (illus). Cl-backed illus bds. (Rubbed, worn; few pp lt foxed.) *Reisler.* $375/£242

UPTON, FLORENCE K. The Adventures of Borbee and the Wisp. London: Longmans, Green, 1908. 1st ed. Lg square 4to. Florence K. Upton (illus). Pict bds (sl rubbed). *Reisler.* $585/£377

UPTON, LUCILE MORRIS. Bald Knobbers. Point Lookout, MO: S of O Press, (1970). 2nd ed. Red pebbled cl. Fine. *Glenn.* $25/£16

UPWARD, EDWARD. In the Thirties. London: Heinemann, 1962. 1st ed. VF in dj. *Else Fine.* $65/£42

UPWARD, EDWARD. In the Thirties. Heinemann, 1962. 1st UK ed. NF in dj. *Lewton.* $54/£35

UPWARD, EDWARD. The Railway Accident and Other Stories. London: Heinemann, 1969. 1st ed. Fine in dj. *Temple.* $85/£55

URBAN, JOHN W. Battle Field and Prison Pen. (Phila): Edgewood Pub Co, (1882). 1st ed. xi,(13)-486pp. NF. *Mcgowan.* $85/£55

URBINO, L.B. and HENRY DAY. Art Recreations. Boston: J.E. Tilton, 1860. Teg. Purple pebbled cl (sl worn). *Glenn.* $175/£113

URIS, LEON. The Angry Hills. NY: Random House, (1955). 1st ed. VG in dj (nicks). *Houle.* $95/£61

URIS, LEON. Battle Cry. NY: Putnam's, (1953). 1st ed, 1st bk. Fine in dj (sl rubbed). *Pharos.* $95/£61

URNER, CLARENCE H. The Thrush. Henkel Press, 1927. Brn cl. VG-. *Book Broker.* $25/£16

URQUHART, B.L. The Rhododendron. Sharpthorne, Leslie Urquhart Press, 1958-62. 2 vols. 36 color plts. As New in dj (sm tear neatly repaired). *Quest.* $375/£242

USTINOV, PETER. The Banbury Nose, a Play in Four Acts. London: Cape, (1945). 1st ed. Sm inscrip endsheet, o/w VG in dj (2 sm chips). *Reese.* $30/£19

UTLEY, ROBERT. Billy the Kid. A Short and Violent Life. Lincoln: Univ of NE Press, (1989). 1st ed. Fine in Fine dj. *Book Market.* $38/£25

UTLEY, ROBERT. Frontiersmen in Blue, The United States Army and the Indians, 1858-1865. NY, 1967. 2nd ptg (1973). VG+ in VG+ dj. *Pratt.* $35/£23

UZANNE, OCTAVE. The Book-Hunter in Paris. Chicago, 1893. 232pp. Partially unopened. Some sigs starting. *Argosy.* $50/£32

V

VACARESCO, HELENE. The Bard of the Dimbovitza. London: Osgood, McIlvaine, 1891. 130pp. (Spine, edges darkened; spine chipped, sm piece out; sm split fr joint.) Internally Fine; overall VG. *Blue Mountain.* $75/£48

VACHELL, H.A. The Other Side. London, 1910. 1st ed. Good+. *Madle.* $22/£14

VACHSS, ANDREW. Blue Belle. NY: Knopf, 1988. 1st ed. Signed. Fine in Fine dj. *Beasley.* $50/£32

VACHSS, ANDREW. Flood. NY: Fine, 1985. 1st ed. Fine in NF dj. *Silver Door.* $35/£23

VACHSS, ANDREW. Flood. London: Collins, 1986. 1st Eng ed. *Revere.* $30/£19

VACHSS, ANDREW. Flood. Collins, 1986. 1st UK ed. Fine in dj. *Sclanders.* $19/£12

VACHSS, ANDREW. Hard Candy. NY: Knopf, 1989. 1st ed. Inscribed. Fine (sl marker bleed-through from author's sig) in Fine dj. *Beasley.* $40/£26

VACHSS, ANDREW. Strega. NY: Knopf, 1987. 1st ed. Inscribed. Fine in Fine dj. *Beasley.* $50/£32

VACKETT, ORE H. Catalogue of Illinois Trade Tokens. Vol 1. Westville, IL: Vackett, 1973. 1st ed. Blue gilt cl. Good. *Karmiole.* $30/£19

VACLAVIK, ANTONIN and JAROSLAV OREL. Textile Folk Art. London: Spring Books, n.d. (ca 1965). VG in dj. *Schoyer.* $75/£48

VAIL, I.E. Three Years on the Blockade. NY: Abbey Press, (1902). 1st ed. Red cl. Faded, else VG. *Chapel Hill.* $200/£129

VAIL, R.W.G. The Voice of the Old Frontier. NY: Yoseloff, (1949). 1st ed. Blue cl. NF in dj (spine dknd, rubbed, corners chipped, tape verso). *Harrington.* $50/£32

VALCANOVER, F. All the Paintings of Titian. London: Oldbourne, 1965. 4 vols. 437 plts (16 color). Rexine. Sound. *Ars Artis.* $39/£25

VALE, ROBERT. Efficiency in Hades. Stokes, 1923. 1st ed. VG. *Madle.* $27/£17

VALENTINE, D.T. Manual of the Corporation of the City of New-York, 1863. NY: Edmund Jones, 1863. xii,852pp, 7 engr ports (incl frontis), 4 fldg maps, 19 chromolithos (7 fldg), 3 tinted lithos, 2 fldg tables, 20 facs (4 fldg). Emb cl, gilt vignette. VG (bumped, rubbed; 1st sig pulled; short closed tears on maps, no loss). *Cahan.* $125/£81

VALENTINER, W.R. The Late Years of Michel Angelo. NY, 1914. One of 300. VG in wrappers. *Argosy.* $35/£23

VALENTINER, W.R. Studies of Italian Renaissance Sculpture. London: Phaidon, 1950. (Ex-lib, ink stamps, label, #.) Blind emb stamp upper bd (spine sl discolored; lettering sl chipped). *Edwards.* $70/£45

VALIN, JONATHAN. Final Notice. NY: Dodd, 1980. 1st ed. VF in dj. *Else Fine.* $125/£81

VALIN, JONATHAN. The Lime Pit. NY: Dodd, 1980. 1st ed. 1st bk. Fine in dj. *Else Fine.* $65/£42

VALLANCE, AYMER. Greater English Church Screens. London: Batsford, 1947. 1st ed. 155 plts (incl color frontis). Spots. Dj. *Hollett.* $70/£45

VALLANCE, AYMER. William Morris. Studio Editions, 1986. Frontis port, 16 color plts. Dj. *Edwards.* $39/£25

VALLERY-RADOT, R. The Life of Pasteur. Mrs. R.L. Devonshire (trans). Westminster: Constable, 1902. 1st ed in English. 2 vols. Pp uncut. Orig cl, recased. Good. *White.* $70/£45

VALLIER, DORA. Henri Rousseau. NY: Abrams, (1962). 1st Amer ed. Fine in dj. *Cahan.* $100/£65

VALLIER, DORA. Henri Rousseau. NY: Abrams, (1962). 1st ed. Color frontis, 29 mtd color plts, 161 add'l plts, repros. Grn cl stamped in yellow. Good in dj. *Karmiole.* $100/£65

VAMBERY, ARMINIUS. History of Bokhara.... London: Henry S. King, 1873. 2nd ed. (xxxvi),(420)pp. Red cl stamped in black/gilt (lib pocket removed). *Schoyer.* $150/£97

VAN ALLSBURG, CHRIS. Jumanji. Boston: HMCo, 1981. 1st ed. 32pp. Cl. VG in dj. *Cattermole.* $200/£129

VAN ALLSBURG, CHRIS. Jumanji. Boston: Houghton Mifflin, 1981. 1st ed. 8vo. Unpaginated, 14 full-pg b/w illus. Fine in Fine dj. *Davidson.* $225/£145

VAN ALLSBURG, CHRIS. Just a Dream. Boston: HM Co, 1990. 1st ed. Signed. Fine in dj. *Between The Covers.* $85/£55

VAN ALLSBURG, CHRIS. The Stranger. Boston: Houghton Mifflin, 1986. 1st ed. Blue cl, gilt. NF in NF dj. *Davidson.* $85/£55

VAN ASH, CAY. Ten Years Beyond Baker Street. NY: Harper & Row, 1984. 1st ed. Fine in dj. *Mordida.* $45/£29

VAN BUREN, W.H. and E.L. KEYES. A Practical Treatise on the Surgical Diseases of the Genito-Urinary Organs, Including Syphilis. NY, 1874. 1st ed. 672pp. Good. *Fye.* $100/£65

VAN DE PASS, CRISPIN. Hortus Floridus. London: Minerva, 1974. 100 full-pg plts. As New. *Quest.* $90/£58

VAN DE WETERING, JANWILLEM. The Blond Baboon. Boston: Houghton Mifflin, 1978. 1st ed. Fine in NF dj. *Janus.* $25/£16

VAN DE WETERING, JANWILLEM. The Corpse on the Dike. Boston: Houghton Mifflin, 1976. 1st ed. Fine in NF dj. *Janus.* $25/£16

VAN DE WETERING, JANWILLEM. The Rattle-Rat. NY: Pantheon, 1985. 1st ed in English. Fine in Fine dj. *Janus.* $25/£16

VAN DE WETERING, JANWILLEM. Tumbleweed. Boston: Houghton Mifflin, 1976. 1st ed. Fine in NF dj. *Janus.* $25/£16

VAN DER LINDEN, FRANK. The Turning Point: Jefferson's Battle for the Presidency. Robert B. Luce, (c. 1962). Inscribed presentation. VG in Good dj. *Book Broker.* $25/£16

VAN DER MEER, RON. World's First Ever Pop-Up Games Book. NY: Delacorte, 1982. 26x22 cm. 6 revolving pictures. Glazed pict bds. VG. *Book Finders.* $45/£29

VAN DER POST, LAURENS. A Bar of Shadow. London: Hogarth Press, 1954. 1st ed. Fine in dj (lt chipped). *Glenn.* $45/£29

VAN DER POST, LAURENS. The Darkest Eye in Africa. London: Hogarth Press, 1955. 1st ed. Burgundy cl. (Edges, eps foxed.) Dj (lt soiled). *Glenn.* $45/£29

VAN DER POST, LAURENS. The Hunter and the Whale. London: Hogarth Press, 1967. 1st ed. Ink sig fep, else Fine in VG dj. *Glenn.* $40/£26

VAN DER POST, LAURENS. The Hunter and the Whale. London: Hogarth Press, 1967. 1st UK ed. VG+ (ink inscrip) in dj. *Williams.* $28/£18

VAN DER WOLK, JOHANNES. The Seven Sketchbooks of Vincent Van Gogh. NY: Abrams, 1986. Fine in Mint dj. *Europa.* $42/£27

VAN DER ZEE, JACOB. The Hollanders of Iowa. Iowa City, 1912. 1st ed. *Ginsberg.* $75/£48

VAN DINE, S.S. The Benson Murder Case. NY: Scribner's, 1926. 1st ed. 1st bk. VG (lacks dj). *Else Fine.* $150/£97

VAN DINE, S.S. The Benson Murder Case. London: Scribner's, 1927. 1st ed. VG. *Ming.* $39/£25

VAN DINE, S.S. The Bishop Murder Case. NY: Scribner's, 1929. 1st ed. Fine in dj. *Else Fine.* $275/£177

VAN DINE, S.S. The Canary Murder Case. NY: Scribner's, 1927. 1st ed. VG. *Sadlon.* $20/£13

VAN DINE, S.S. The Casino Murder Case. NY: Scribner's, 1934. 1st ed. Fine in pict dj (lt wear top corners). *Else Fine.* $285/£184

VAN DINE, S.S. The Dragon Murder Case. NY: Scribner's, 1933. 1st ed. VG in dj (edgewear, corners chipping). *Else Fine.* $90/£58

VAN DINE, S.S. The Dragon Murder Case. London: Cassell, 1934. 1st UK ed. VG. *Ming.* $39/£25

VAN DINE, S.S. The Garden Murder Case. NY: Scribner, 1935. 1st ed. 8pp pub's ads at end. VG in dj (2 sm chips). *Houle.* $275/£177

VAN DINE, S.S. The Gracie Allen Murder Case. NY: Scribner's, 1938. 1st ed. VG in dj (chipped; rubbed; closed tears, perforations). *Mordida.* $85/£55

VAN DINE, S.S. The Greene Murder Case. NY: Scribner's, 1928. 1st ed. Black cl stamped in white. Good in dj (chipped). *Karmiole.* $75/£48

VAN DINE, S.S. The Greene Murder Case. NY: Scribner's, 1928. 1st ed. VG in dj (rubbed, chipped corners, spine ends). *Else Fine.* $75/£48

VAN DINE, S.S. The Scarab Murder Case. NY: Scribner's, 1930. 1st ed. NF. (Lacks dj.) *Else Fine.* $45/£29

VAN DINE, S.S. The Scarab Murder Case. London: Cassell, 1930. 1st UK ed. VG. *Ming.* $39/£25

VAN DINE, S.S. The Winter Murder Case. NY: Scribner's, 1939. 1st ed. VG in dj (spine crease; lt frayed; wear; internal staining). *Mordida*. $175/£113

VAN DINE, S.S. The Winter Murder Case. NY: Scribner's, 1939. 1st ed. Fine in dj (sl wear). *Else Fine*. $400/£258

VAN DOREN STERN, PHILIP (ed). The Life and Writings of Abraham Lincoln. NY: Random House, (1940). 1st ed. Frontis port. VG in dj (nicks). *Houle*. $85/£55

VAN DOREN, CARL. The Great Rehearsal. NY, 1948. #314/350 (of 380) signed. Fine in Fine box. *Polyanthos*. $50/£32

VAN DOREN, CARL. Jane Mecom: The Favorite Sister of Benjamin Franklin.... NY: Viking, 1950. 1st ed. VG in dj. *Petrilla*. $20/£13

VAN DOREN, CARL. Secret History of the American Revolution. Viking, 1941. 1st ed, ltd to 590 signed. Fine in dj (frayed). *Heinoldt*. $45/£29

VAN DOREN, CARL. Secret History of the American Revolution. NY: Viking, 1941. 1st ed. One of 590, signed. Map. VG. *Cahan*. $40/£26

VAN DOREN, MARK. The Country Year. NY: Sloane, (1946). 1st ed. Pict cl. NF (eps lt browned) in VG dj (browned; price-clipped). *Antic Hay*. $25/£16

VAN DOREN, MARK. The Seven Sleepers and Other Poems. NY: Holt, (1944). 1st ed. NF (pp 86-87 browned) in dj (sl wear). *Antic Hay*. $35/£23

VAN DYKE, HENRY. The Lost Boy. NY/London: Harper, 1914. 1st ed. 44pp, 3 mtd plts by N.C. Wyeth. Grn cl, gilt. Fine in pict dj (1/2-inch chip at crown, base of spine; tears; surface tears w/loss to lettering, else VG). *Godot*. $175/£113

VAN DYKE, HENRY. The Travel Diary of an Angler. NY: Derrydale, 1929. 1st ed, ltd to 750. VG. *Mcgowan*. $250/£161

VAN DYKE, JOHN C. The Desert: Further Stories in Natural Appearances. Scribner's, 1901. 1st ed. NF (bkpl, #s on copyright pg, effaced from spine). *Authors Of The West*. $50/£32

VAN DYKE, JOHN C. The Grand Canyon of the Colorado. Scribner's, 1920. 1st ed. Fine (owner stamps). *Authors Of The West*. $60/£39

VAN DYKE, JOSEPH S. Popery: The Foe of the Church and of the Republic. Phila: Peoples, 1871. 1st ed. 304pp. *Ginsberg*. $75/£48

VAN DYKE, THEODORE S. Flirtation Camp. NY: Fords, Howard & Hulbert, 1881. 1st ed. 299pp. Gilt dec cl. Sm spot upper cvr, sm spot upper margin few leaves, o/w VG. *Reese*. $65/£42

VAN FLEET, CLARK C. Steelhead to a Fly. Boston: Little Brown, 1954. 1st ed. VF in dj. *Bowman*. $275/£177

VAN GOGH, VINCENT. The Complete Letters of Vincent Van Gogh. NYGS, 1958. 1st ed. 3 vols. NF in VG slip-case. *Fine Books*. $175/£113

VAN GOGH, VINCENT. Letters to an Artist. Rela van Messel (trans). London, 1936. 7 facs; 9 plts. (Feps lt browned.) *Edwards*. $39/£25

VAN GULIK, ROBERT. The Chinese Lake Murders. Joseph, 1960. 1st ed. VG in dj (sl nicked, rubbed). *Rees*. $70/£45

VAN GULIK, ROBERT. The Chinese Nail Murders. NY: Harper & Row, 1961. 1st Amer ed. Lt spotting, o/w Fine in dj (sl dknd spine). *Mordida*. $45/£29

VAN GULIK, ROBERT. The Chinese Nail Murders. London: Michael Joseph, 1961. 1st UK ed. VG+ in VG dj (price-clipped, closed tears). *Williams*. $56/£36

VAN GULIK, ROBERT. Judge Dee at Work. London: Heinemann, 1967. 1st ed. VG+ in dj. *Limestone*. $75/£48

VAN GULIK, ROBERT. The Monkey and the Tiger. London: Heinemann, 1965. 1st ed. Fine in dj. *Mordida*. $85/£55

VAN GULIK, ROBERT. Poets and Murder. London: Heinemann, 1968. 1st ed. Fine in NF dj (internally repaired). *Limestone*. $145/£94

VAN HORNE, THOMAS B. The Life of Major-General George H. Thomas. NY: Scribner's, 1882. 1st ed. Frontis port, 502pp + fldg maps + (6)pp ads. Orig blue cl, beveled edges. Lib bkpl, # bottom of preface, else VG. *Chapel Hill*. $75/£48

VAN LHIN, ERIC. (Pseud of Lester Del Rey.) Battle on Mercury. Winston, 1953. 1st ed. NF in VG dj (sl chipped). *Aronovitz*. $48/£31

VAN LUSTBADER, ERIC. Beneath an Opal Moon. NY: Doubleday, 1980. 1st ed. NF in dj (lt soiled). *Antic Hay*. $25/£16

VAN METER, RALPH A. Bush Fruit Production. NY: OJ, 1928. 1st ed. Fine in pict dj. *Second Life*. $45/£29

VAN MILLIGEN, ALEXANDER. Constantinople. London: A&C Black, 1906. Fldg map. Teg. Tan dec cl. VG. *Schoyer*. $125/£81

VAN MILLIGEN, ALEXANDER. Constantinople. A&C Black, 1906. 1st ed. 63 color plts, fldg map. Teg. Dec cl (lt dampstaining; feps lt browned). *Edwards*. $132/£85

VAN NOSTRAND, JEANNE. First Hundred Years of Painting in California, 1775-1875. SF: John Howell-Books, 1980. One of 2500. NF in dj (sl soiled; nicks). *Bohling*. $100/£65

VAN OSDEL, A.L. Historic Landmarks. N.p. (Yankton, SD): Privately ptd, n.d. (ca 1915). 1st ed. 22 plts. Pict cl, gilt-stamped spine. Fine. *Oregon*. $125/£81

VAN PELT, GARRETT, JR. Old Architecture of Southern Mexico. Cleveland: J.H. Jansen, 1926. 1st ed. *Bookpress*. $165/£106

VAN PUYVELDE, LEO. The Dutch Drawings in the Collection...at Windsor Castle. London/NY: Phaidon, 1944. VF in dj. *Europa*. $53/£34

VAN RAVENSWAAY, CHARLES. The Arts and Architecture of German Settlements in Missouri. Columbia: Univ of MO, 1977. 1st ed. Blue cl stamped in black/gold. Good in dj. *Karmiole*. $85/£55

VAN RENSSELAER, MARIA. Correspondence...1669-1689. A.J.F. Van Laer (ed). Albany: Univ of the State of NY, 1935. 1st ed. Blue cl; gilt. VG. *Petrilla*. $30/£19

VAN RENSSELAER, MRS. JOHN KING. Prophetical, Educational and Playing Cards. Phila, (1912). 1st ed. 16 plts. (Rebound.) *Heinoldt*. $65/£42

VAN RENSSELAER, MRS. JOHN KING. Prophetical, Educational and Playing Cards. London: Hurst & Blackett, 1912. 1st Eng ed. 16 b/w plts. Red buckram (sl rubbing), gilt. VG. *Houle*. $325/£210

VAN RENSSELAER, STEPHEN. Early American Bottles and Flasks. Peterborough, NH, 1926. Rev ed. 162 photo plts. (Hinges cracked.) *Argosy*. $75/£48

VAN VECHTEN, CARL. Peter Whiffle: His Life and Works. NY: Knopf, 1927. 1st illus ed. Fine in orig tissue dj (torn), illus slipcase. *Dermont*. $65/£42

VAN VECHTEN, CARL. Sacred and Profane Memories. NY: Knopf, 1932. One of 2000 numbered. Blue cl. VF in dj (sl sunned at spine). *Dermont*. $100/£65

VAN VOGT, A.E. Away and Beyond. P&C, 1952. 1st ed. Fine in dj (chipped). *Madle.* $35/£23

VAN VOGT, A.E. The Book of Ptath. Fantasy Press, 1947. 1st ed in dj. VG. *Cullen.* $90/£58

VAN VOGT, A.E. Children of Tomorrow. London: Sidgwick & Jackson, 1972. 1st Eng ed. Blue cl. Fine in dj. *Dalian.* $39/£25

VAN VOGT, A.E. Destination Universe. P&C, 1952. 1st ed. NF in dj (frayed). *Madle.* $25/£16

VAN VOGT, A.E. Empire of the Atom. Shasta, 1957. 1st ed. Fine in dj (rear panel sl soiled). *Madle.* $75/£48

VAN VOGT, A.E. The House That Stood Still. Greenberg, 1950. Fine in dj. *Madle.* $15/£10

VAN VOGT, A.E. Masters of Time. Fantasy, 1950. 1st ed. Fine in dj. *Madle.* $75/£48

VAN VOGT, A.E. Masters of Time. Fantasy Press, 1950. 1st ed. One of 500 signed. VG+ in NF dj. *Aronovitz.* $125/£81

VAN VOGT, A.E. The Mind Cage. NY: S&S, 1957. 1st ed. Fine (usual pp browning) in NF dj. *Antic Hay.* $35/£23

VAN VOGT, A.E. Slan. Arkham House, 1946. 1st ed. VG in dj (tape along edges). *Madle.* $150/£97

VAN VOGT, A.E. Slan. Sauk City: Arkham House, 1946. 1st ed. Signed. Bkpl, else VG+ in dj (edgeworn; clear tape corners, spine ends). *Other Worlds.* $150/£97

VAN VOGT, A.E. Slan. S&S, 1951. 1st ed thus. VG in dj. *Madle.* $25/£16

VAN VOGT, A.E. The Violent Man. NY: Farrar, Straus & Cudahy, (1962). 1st ed. Pp sl browned, else Fine in dj (lt rubbed, soiled). *Hermitage.* $45/£29

VAN VOGT, A.E. The Voyage of the Space Beagle. S&S, 1950. 1st ed. Signed. Fine in NF dj (lt soiling rear panel). *Aronovitz.* $110/£71

VAN VOGT, A.E. The Weapon Makers. Hadley, 1947. 1st ed. Signed. NF in VG+ dj (lt soiling). *Aronovitz.* $135/£87

VAN VOGT, A.E. The Weapon Shops of Isher. London, 1952. 1st British ed. NF in dj. *Madle.* $30/£19

VAN VOGT, A.E. and MAYNE HULL. The Sea Thing and Other Stories. London: Sidgwick & Jackson, 1970. 1st Eng ed. Blue cl. Fine in dj. *Dalian.* $39/£25

VAN VORST, JOHN and MARIE. The Woman Who Toils. NY: Doubleday, 1903. 1st ed. VG. *Second Life.* $85/£55

VAN WINKLE, C.S. The Printer's Guide. NY: Lakeside, 1970. Facs rpt of 1818. Foxing; bd tips bruised. *Veatchs.* $45/£29

VAN ZILE, EDWARD S. Perkins, the Fakeer. Smart Set, 1903. 1st ed. VG. *Madle.* $75/£48

VAN, MELVIN. The Big Heart. SF: Fearon Pub, 1957. 1st ed. 93 b/w photos by Ruth Bernhard. NF in illus dj. *Cahan.* $60/£39

VANBRUGH, JOHN. The Complete Works. Bloomsbury: Nonesuch, 1924. 1st this ed, #1019/1300 sets. 4 vols. Frontis port; 6 plts (2 dbl-pg); 2 dbl-pg plans vol 4. Blue cl spines, bds; uncut. NF. *Hartfield.* $395/£255

VANBRUGH, JOHN. The Complete Works. Bonamy Dobree & Geoffrey Webb (eds). Nonesuch, 1927-8. #1047/1410. 4 vols. Frontis port. Uncut. (Ex-lib, ink stamps, #s, labels removed spines.) *Edwards.* $116/£75

VANCE, JACK. Big Planet. NY: Avalon, (1957). 1st ed. Spine leaning, top edge soiled, else Fine in o/w NF dj (half-inch closed tear, creasing). *Other Worlds.* $150/£97

VANCE, JACK. Big Planet. Avalon, 1957. 1st ed. Fine in dj. *Madle.* $200/£129

VANCE, JACK. The Dirdir. London: Dennis Dobson, 1969. 1st Eng ed. Black cl. Fine in dj. *Dalian.* $31/£20

VANCE, JACK. Eight Phantasms and Magics. Macmillan, 1969. 1st ed. VG in NF dj. *Madle.* $185/£119

VANCE, JACK. The Languages of Pao. NY: Avalon, (1958). 1st ed, signed. Top edge soiled, bottom edge nicked, else NF in dj (edge worn, torn, scratch to length of spine). *Other Worlds.* $125/£81

VANCE, JACK. The Languages of Pao. Avalon, 1958. 1st ed. VF in dj (spine faded). *Madle.* $200/£129

VANCE, JACK. Vandals of the Void. Phila: Winston, (1953). 1st ed. VG+ in dj (worn). *Other Worlds.* $175/£113

VANCE, JOHN. Vandals of the Void. Winston, 1953. 1st ed. Signed. VG+ in VG+ dj (4 sm chips rear panel). *Aronovitz.* $190/£123

VANCOUVER, GEORGE. Vancouver in California 1792-1794. Marguerite Eyer Wilbur (ed). LA: Dawson, 1953-1954. Ltd to 600. 3 vols. Fine. *Oregon.* $150/£97

VANDER VEEN, HARM R.S. Jewish Characters in Eighteenth Century English Fiction and Drama. Groningen: J.B. Walters, 1935. Fldg frontis. VG. *Dramatis Personae.* $60/£39

VANDERWOOD, PAUL. Night Riders of Reelfoot Lake. Memphis: Memphis State Univ, (1969). 1st ed. Fine in VG dj. *Oregon.* $25/£16

VANDIER, JACQUES. Egypt: Paintings from Tombs and Temples. NY: NYGS, (1954). 32 color plts. Good in dj (tattered). *Archaeologia.* $85/£55

VANDIVER, FRANK E. Black Jack. College Station, (1977). 1st ed. 2 vols. Dj lt worn, o/w Fine. *Pratt.* $47/£30

VANDIVER, FRANK. Jubal's Raid. NY, (1960). 1st ed. Sl dj wear, o/w VG+. *Pratt.* $45/£29

VARBLE, RACHEL M. Jane Clemens, the Story of Mark Twain's Mother. NY: Doubleday, 1964. 1st ed, 1st ptg. 1/4 cl, gilt. Fine in VG dj. *Macdonnell.* $30/£19

VARESCHI, V. and E. KRAUSE. Mountains in Flower. London, 1939. Color frontis, 72 b/w plts. (Tape residue cvr). Dj (soiled). *Sutton.* $35/£23

VARGAS LLOSA, MARIO. The Green House. NY, 1968. 1st Amer ed. Fine (sl rubbed) in dj (chips, tears, sl rubbed). *Polyanthos.* $45/£29

VARGAS LLOSA, MARIO. The Perpetual Orgy: Flaubert and Madame Bovary. NY: FSG, (1986). 1st ed. Fine in NF dj. *Antic Hay.* $27/£17

VARGAS LLOSA, MARIO. The Storyteller. NY: FSG, (1989). 1st Amer ed. Fine in dj. *Between The Covers.* $40/£26

VARGAS LLOSA, MARIO. The Time of the Hero. NY: Grove Press, 1965. 1st ed. Fine in dj. *Moorhouse.* $78/£50

VARGAS LLOSA, MARIO. The Time of the Hero. NY, 1966. 1st Amer ed. Fine in dj (nick). *Polyanthos.* $75/£48

VARGAS LLOSA, MARIO. The War of the End of the World. NY, (1984). 1st ed. Signed. Fine in Fine dj. *Fuller & Saunders.* $45/£29

VARGAS LLOSA, MARIO. The War of the End of the World. NY, 1984. 1st Amer ed. Fine in dw. *Polyanthos*. $30/£19

VARGAS LLOSA, MARIO. Who Killed Palomino Molero? London: Faber, 1988. 1st UK ed. Fine in dj. *Williams*. $23/£15

Variety, or Amusing and Instructing Tales in Prose and Verse for Young Folks. (NY): Turner & Fisher, n.d. (ca 1835). 77mm x 65mm, 128pp, copper engr title pg, wood engr 1/2 title, full-pg engr frontis, 14 full-pg engrs. Tooled grn cl on bds (lt soiled, faded), gilt title. VG (ink name fep; internal spotting). *Hobbyhorse*. $100/£65

VARLEY, JOHN. Wizard. Berkeley: Putnam, 1980. 1st ed. NF in dj. *Madle*. $65/£42

VARLEY, TELFORD. Hampshire. A&C Black, 1909. 1st ed. 75 colored plts; fldg map. Pict cl. Nice. *Bickersteth*. $34/£22

VARNEY, ALMON C. Our Homes and Their Adornments. Detroit: J.C. Chilton, 1884. 3rd ptg. Frontis, 498,(1)pp. Gilt cl. Text margins lt browned; faint wear joints, edges; rear cvr soiled; else VG. *Bookpress*. $265/£171

VARNEY, GEORGE J. A Gazetteer of the State of Maine. Boston: Russell, 1882. 611pp. Marbled edges. 3/4 leather. VG. *Schoyer*. $65/£42

VARTANIAN, H.G. Honeymoon in a Taxicab. Detroit: Harlo Press, 1973. 1st ed. Signed. Grn cl. VG in VG dj. *Peninsula*. $35/£23

VASARI, GIORGIO. Lives of Seventy of the Most Eminent Painters, Sculptors, and Architects. London: George Bell, 1897. 1st ed thus. 4 vols, complete. Matching gilt calf. 2 hinges repaired, else Handsome set. *Bookpress*. $200/£129

VASEY, GEORGE (ed). Grasses of the Arid Districts.... Washington, 1888. 60pp + 30 full-pg plts. Good in wrappers. *Hayman*. $20/£13

VASEY, GEORGE. Grasses of the South. Washington, 1887. 63pp; 16 plts. Staple holes binding edge, o/w VG in wrappers. *Hayman*. $20/£13

VASSILIKOS, VASSILIS. Z. NY: FSG, (1968). 1st Amer ed. NF in dj. *Hermitage*. $40/£26

VASSOS, RUTH. Contempo. NY: E.P. Dutton, 1929. 1st ed. Blue cl (lt faded, soiled). *Glenn*. $50/£32

VASSOS, RUTH. Ultimo. NY: E.P. Dutton, 1930. 1st ed. Red cl (lt worn, soiled). *Glenn*. $60/£39

VAUGHAN, MALCOLM. Derain. NY: Hyperion, 1941. 1 mtd plt. VG in dj. *Argosy*. $75/£48

VAUGHN, J.W. The Battle of Platte Bridge. Norman: Univ of OK Press, (1963). 1st ed. VG in dj. *Laurie*. $40/£26

VEATCH, A.C. Quito to Bogota. NY, 1917. 2 maps (1 fldg), 2 fldg plans (edge of 1 sl chipped, browned). Dj (sl chipped, spine browned). *Edwards*. $54/£35

VECKI, VICTOR. The Pathology and Treatment of Sexual Impotence. Phila, 1899. 1st Eng trans. 291pp. Good. *Fye*. $75/£48

VEDDER, ELIHU. The Digressions of.... Boston/NY: Houghton Mifflin, 1910. 1st ptg. Pict cl. VG. *Schoyer*. $75/£48

VEECK, BILL with ED LINN. The Hustler's Handbook. Putnam's, 1965. 1st ed. VG + (inscrip) in VG dj (spine sunned). *Plapinger*. $65/£42

VEECK, BILL with ED LINN. Veeck as in Wreck. Putnam's, 1962. 1st ed. VG. *Plapinger*. $27/£17

VEITCH, J. A Manual of Orchidaceous Plants.... Chelsea, 1888. 104pp (marginal tear 1pg), 4 plts (browned), 2 fldg maps. Wrappers (chipped, brittle, names, backstrip replaced w/brn paper; shaken). *Sutton*. $40/£26

VELAZQUEZ, LORETA JANETA. The Woman in Battle. Hartford: T. Belknap, n.d. (ca 1876). Rpt ed. Frontis, 606pp. Grn dec cl stamped in black/gold (spine lt frayed). *Karmiole*. $50/£32

VELIKOVSKY, IMMANUEL. Peoples of the Sea. GC: Doubleday, 1978. 1st ed. VG in VG dj. *Blue Dragon*. $15/£10

VELIKOVSKY, IMMANUEL. Stargazer and Gravediggers. NY: Wm. Morrow, 1983. 1st ed. VG + in VG dj. *Blue Dragon*. $20/£13

VELPEAU, A. An Elementary Treatise on Midwifery. Phila, 1831. 1st Eng trans. 584pp. Full leather. Good. *Fye*. $250/£161

VELVIN, ELLEN. Rataplan, a Rogue Elephant and Other Stories. Phila: Henry Altemus, (1902). 1st ed. 328pp. Red cl, gilt dec, pict insert fr cvr. Broadside laid in. Fine (1902 inscrip) in dj (sl chipped). *Godot*. $75/£48

VENABLE, WILLIAM H. 1788-1888. Footprints of the Pioneers in the Ohio Valley: A Centennial Sketch. Cincinnati: Valley, 1888. 1st ed. (1),128pp. *Ginsberg*. $75/£48

VENABLE, WILLIAM H. The School Stage. Cincinnati/NY: Wilson, Hinkle & Co, (1873). 1st ed. vi + 234 + 9pp list. Tooled, gilt grn cl on bds; marbled edges. Fine (sl chipped, rubbed). *Hobbyhorse*. $225/£145

VENABLE, WILLIAM. Garbage Crematories in America. NY, 1906. 1st ed. Good. *Fye*. $40/£26

Venetian Drawings from the Collection of Janos Scholz. Montgomery, AL: Montgomery Museum of Fine Arts, 1976. One of 400. (Ex-lib.) Wrappers. *Washton*. $30/£19

VENTURI, ADOLFO. North Italian Painting of the Quattrocento; Lombardy, Piedmont, Liguria. Florence/Paris: Pantheon/Pegasus, 1930. 80 plts, guards; teg. Orig red 1/2 leather, gilt-panelled spine. VF. *Europa*. $78/£50

VERBECK, FRANK. Little Black Sambo and the Baby Elephant. Phila: Henry Altemus, (1925). 24mo. 62pp; 30 color illus by Verbeck. Red cl, gray emb bds; pict paste label; illus eps. NF (spine restored, strengthened internally). *Drusilla's*. $85/£55

VERBECK, FRANK. Little Black Sambo and the Baby Elephant. NY: Platt & Munk, (1935). Color pict label. VG. *Argosy*. $50/£32

VERE, ARPREY. Ancient and Modern Magic. London: George Routledge & Sons, n.d. (c. 1887). Ads on eps. VG (Hamley's stamp on half-title). *Dramatis Personae*. $125/£81

VERESSAYEV, VIKENTY. The Memoirs of a Physician. S. Linden (trans). NY, 1916. VG. *Argosy*. $45/£29

VERGA, GIOVANNI. Mastro-Don Gesualdo. D.H. Lawrence (trans). London: Jonathan Cape, (1925). 1st British ed. Few text pp foxed, else VG in dj (spine browned, else VG). *Godot*. $85/£55

VERHOEFF, MARY. The Kentucky River Navigation. Louisville: Filson Club, 1917. 3 fldg maps; 21 plts. Mod cl w/orig ptd fr wrap bound in. Nice. *Bohling*. $150/£97

VERINDER, FREDERICK. Land and Freedom. London: Hogarth Press, 1935. One of 500 ptd. 1st issue. Grn cl, gilt spine. Erratum tipped in at p176-7. Gilt sl oxidized, o/w Fine in dj (spine sl dknd). *Temple*. $33/£21

VERITY, FRANK T. et al. Flats, Urban Houses, and Cottage Homes. London: Hodder & Stoughton, (1906). 1st ed. Frontis; 18 color plts. (Text lt foxed; binding worn). *Bookpress.* $175/£113

Vermont. A Profile of the Green Mountain State. American Pictorial Guide Series. NY: Fleming, 1941. 1st ed. Signed by Roaldus Richmond (State Supervisor). VG in Fair dj. *Connolly.* $35/£23

VERNAM, GLENN. Man on Horseback. NY: Harper's, 1964. 1st ed. (Sl underlining.) Dj. *Lambeth.* $40/£26

VERNAM, GLENN. The Rawhide Years. NY: Doubleday, 1976. 1st ed. Dj. *Lambeth.* $45/£29

VERNE, JULES. Doctor Ox and Other Stories. Osgood, 1874. 1st US ed. VG. *Madle.* $350/£226

VERNE, JULES. A Voyage Around the World—South America. Routledge & Sons, 1876. 1st Eng ed. VG. *Aronovitz.* $235/£152

VERNE, JULES. The Works of.... Charles F. Horne (ed). NY, n.d. Edition D'Amiens #65/600 sets. 15 vols. Teg, rest uncut. Fine set (bkpls; sl sunned, sl soiled). *Polyanthos.* $350/£226

VERNER, ELIZABETH O'NEILL. The Stonewall Ladies. Charleston, SC: Tradd St Press, 1963. 1st ed, 2nd ptg. NF. *Mcgowan.* $37/£24

VERNER, WILLOUGHBY. History and Campaigns of the Rifle Brigade 1800-1813. London: John Dale Sons & Danielson, 1912-1919. 2 vols. 40 maps and plans; aeg. Dec cl binding. Good (inscrip t.p. vol 1). *Graf.* $75/£48

VERNER, WILLOUGHBY. Sketches in the Soudan. London: R.H. Porter, 1886. 2nd ed. Engr 1/2 title, 37 tinted lithos. Orig pict bds (stained, soiled, bumped, sl loose). *Petersfield.* $349/£225

VERNON, ARTHUR. The History and Romance of the Horse. Boston, 1939. 1st ptg. Gilt cl. Spine faded, bottom edge soiled, o/w VG. *Baade.* $40/£26

VERNON, JOSEPH S. Along the Old Trail. Cimarron: Tucker-Vernon, 1910. 1st ed. Edgeworn, spine chipped, else VG. Variant of Howes V 77. *Parker.* $85/£55

VERNON-HARCOURT, L.F. Rivers and Canals.... Oxford: Clarendon, 1896. 2nd ed, enlgd. 2 vols. (20),(12),704pp; 13 fldg plts. NF. *Artis.* $75/£48

VERRENT, ANNE. Capt. Tar and the Three Little Princesses. London: Sampson Low, Marston, n.d. (195?). 19x26 cm. 8pp pull-tab scenes. Glazed pict bds (extrems, spine worn). Internally VG. *Book Finders.* $50/£32

VERRILL, A. HYATT. The Treasure of Bloody Gut. Putnam, 1937. 1st ed. Fine in dj (sm chip). *Madle.* $95/£61

Verses on Various Occasions. (By John Henry Newman.) London, 1868. 1st ed, ends at pg 340 w/no index. (Ink inscrip; spine defective; cl rippled, dknd, worn.) *King.* $65/£42

VERTUE, GEORGE. Anecdotes of Painting in England. London: Major, 1826-28. 5 vols. Half red morocco (rubbed, vol 1 dampstained at beginning). *Marlborough.* $194/£125

VERTUE, GEORGE. A Catalogue of Engravers.... London: Ptd by J. Moore, 1794. Frontis port, 230pp,(iii)index, 15 engr ports (of 17?). Contemp tree calf (rebacked in mod calf; new eps; ex-lib w/bkpl; spotting; head of few plts sl waterstained), gilt. *Edwards.* $70/£45

VERVLIET, H.D.L. Sixteenth-Century Printing Types of the Low Countries. Harry Carter (trans). Amsterdam, 1968. Fine in dj. *Veatchs.* $125/£81

VERY, LYDIA. A Strange Disclosure. Boston: James H. Earle, (1898). 1st ed. Brn gilt-stamped cl (sl worn). NF. *Juvelis.* $150/£97

VESEY-FITZGERALD, BRIAN and F. LAMONTE (eds). Game Fish of the World. London: Nicholson, 1949. 1st ed. 80 color plts. Spine sunned, o/w VG. *Bowman.* $75/£48

VESEY-FITZGERALD, BRIAN. Rivermouth. London: Eyre & Spottiswoode, (1949). 1st ed. C.F. Tunnicliffe (engrs). Dj. *Petersfield.* $19/£12

VESTAL, STANLEY. Dobe Walls. Boston: H. Mifflin, 1929. 1st ed. Good+ (hinge repaired). *Parker.* $40/£26

VESTAL, STANLEY. Dodge City. (London): Peter Nevill, (1955). 1st Eng ed. Blue bds. VG in dj. *Schoyer.* $35/£23

VESTAL, STANLEY. Fandango, Ballads of the Old West. Boston: Houghton Mifflin, (1927). VG in dj (sl worn; dusty). *Hermitage.* $150/£97

VESTAL, STANLEY. Happy Hunting Grounds. Chicago: Lyons & Carnahan, 1938. 4 color plts. Blue cl, pict label. VG (spine worn). *Connolly.* $27/£17

VESTAL, STANLEY. Jim Bridger, Mountain Man. NY: Morrow, 1946. 1st ed. Port. VG in dj (chipped). *Schoyer.* $55/£35

VESTAL, STANLEY. Joe Meek. Caldwell: Caxton, 1952. 1st ed. Frontis, 8 plts. VG in Good+ dj. *Oregon.* $50/£32

VESTAL, STANLEY. Kit Carson, The Happy Warrior of the Old West. Boston, 1928. 1st ed. Faded spine, o/w VG. *Pratt.* $40/£26

VESTAL, STANLEY. The Missouri. NY: Farrar & Rinehart, (1945). 1st ptg. VG in dj (sl chipped). *Schoyer.* $45/£29

VESTAL, STANLEY. Queen of Cowtowns, Dodge City. NY: Harper, (1952). Early ptg. 4 plts. VG in dj. *Schoyer.* $20/£13

VESTAL, STANLEY. Sitting Bull, Champion of the Sioux. Boston: Houghton Mifflin, 1932. 1st ptg. Pict cl (type rubbed) in dj (chipped, torn). Howes V 82. *Schoyer.* $60/£39

VESTAL, STANLEY. Wagons Southwest. NY: American Pioneer Trails Assoc, 1946. 1st ed. Fine in pict wrappers (lt stained). *Glenn.* $45/£29

VESTAL, STANLEY. Warpath and Council Fire. NY: Random House, (1948). 1st ptg. 10 photos. Pict cl. VG in dj. *Schoyer.* $65/£42

VETROMILE, EUGENE. A Tour in Both Hemispheres. NY: D.&J. Sadlier, 1880. 1st ed. Pebbled cl over beveled bds (sl rubbed; sm lightened spots); pict-stamped. *Sadlon.* $100/£65

Vicar of Wakefield. (By Oliver Goldsmith.) Dublin: Pat. Wogan, 1800-1793. 2 vols in 1 (a mixed set). Later 1/2 calf (rebacked; orig lettering-piece). *Waterfield.* $78/£50

VICKERY, WILLIS. Three Excessively Rare and Scarce Books and Something of Their Author. Cleveland: For the Author, 1927. 1st ed. Rear corner sl rubbed, o/w NF. *Sadlon.* $35/£23

VICTOR, PAUL-EMILE. My Eskimo Life. London: Hamish Hamilton, 1938. 1st Eng ed. VG in dj. *Walcot.* $28/£18

VICTORIA, QUEEN. Leaves from the Journal of Our Life in the Highlands, from 1848-1861. Arthur Helps (ed). NY: Harper, 1868. 1st Amer ed. Engr frontispieces, 287pp + 8pp ads. Pebbled cl, beveled bds. Very Nice. *Cady*. $30/£19

VIDA, M. The Game of Chess. (London): Stanton Press, 1926. Ltd to 250 numbered, signed. Linen-backed bds. VG, w/extra label. *King*. $150/£97

VIDAL, A. A Treatise on Venereal Diseases. NY, 1874. 3rd ed. 499pp. Good. *Fye*. $50/£32

VIDAL, GORE. Creation. NY: Random House, (1981). 1st trade ed. Signed. Fine in dj. *Bernard*. $50/£32

VIDAL, GORE. In a Yellow Wood. NY: Dutton, 1947. 1st ed. VG (inscrip) in dj (ragged chipping bottom fr panel). *Chapel Hill*. $125/£81

VIDAL, GORE. The Judgement of Paris. London: Heinemann, 1953. 1st UK ed. VG (bkseller stamp) in dj (sl torn, chipped; repaired). *Williams*. $37/£24

VIDAL, GORE. The Ladies in the Library and Other Stories. (Helsinki): Eurographica, 1985. One of 350 signed. Fine in card cvrs in dj as issued. *Williams*. $74/£48

VIDAL, GORE. Matters of Fact and Fiction. NY: Random House, 1977. 1st ed. NF in Fine dj (sm chip). *Revere*. $30/£19

VIDAL, GORE. Myra Breckinridge. Boston: Little, Brown, (1968). 1st ed. Signed. NF (edges sl bumped; faint evidence sm label removed fep) in dj (sm tear). *Antic Hay*. $125/£81

VIDAL, GORE. Myron. NY: Random House, (1974). 1st ed. Rmdr stamp bottom edge, else Fine in dj (lt creased, else Fine). *Godot*. $35/£23

VIDAL, GORE. Reflections on a Sinking Ship. Boston: Little Brown, 1969. 1st Amer ed. Gray/black cl lettered in silver. Sl bump, else Very Nice in Fine dj. *Cady*. $20/£13

VIDAL, GORE. The Second American Revolution and Other Essays (1976-1982). NY: Random House, 1982. 1st ed. Fine in Fine dj. *Revere*. $30/£19

VIDAL, GORE. A Thirsty Evil. London: Heinemann, 1958. 1st UK ed. Signed. VG (name) in dj (sl browned; sm stains). *Williams*. $47/£30

VIDAL, GORE. Visit to a Small Planet. Boston: Little Brown, (1956). 1st Amer ed. Orange cl-backed black bds lettered in black. NF in dj. *Cady*. $60/£39

VIDAL, GORE. Washington, D.C. Boston: Houghton Mifflin, 1967. 1st ed. NF in NF dj (price-clipped; sm closed tears). *Revere*. $35/£23

VIELE, MRS. EGBERT L. Following the Drum. Phila: T.B. Peterson & Bros, (1864). 2nd ptg. Untrimmed. Orig chromolitho pict wraps (worn). Howes V 92. *Schoyer*. $150/£97

VIELE, TERESA. Following the Drum. NY, 1858. 1st ed, 1st issue. 256,(7),(1)-4pp. (Joints worn; spine crown chipped.) Howes V 92. *Ginsberg*. $250/£161

Views Natchez Mississippi. Tom L. Ketchings Co, (1930s?). Unpaged. Paper cvr. VG. *Book Broker*. $25/£16

VILAPLANA, RUIZ. Burgos Justice. London, 1938. 1st ed. Eps sl browned, o/w Good. Brn cl (bumped; spine sunned). *Edwards*. $31/£20

VILIMKOVA, MILADA. Egyptian Jewellery. London: Paul Hamlyn, (1969). Good in dj. *Archaeologia*. $95/£61

Village Annals, Containing Austerus and Humanus. Phila: Johnson & Warner, 1814. 12mo. Full-pg wood engr frontis, tp vignette, 35pp. Marbled paper on bds (spine restored). VG (browned, water spot, corners chipped, tp mended). *Hobbyhorse*. $100/£65

Village Annals, Containing Austerus and Humanus. Phila: Johnson & Warner, 1814. 35pp. Full-pg wood engr frontis, 7 lg cuts. Frontis, last pg pasted down on wrappers. Fine (ex-libris). *Hobbyhorse*. $200/£129

VILLIERS, ALAN. Give Me a Ship to Sail. London, 1958. 1st ed. Dj (sl worn). *Edwards*. $25/£16

VILLIERS, ALAN. The Making of a Sailor. London, 1938. 1st UK ed. Dj (chipped, loss). *Edwards*. $47/£30

VILLIERS, FREDERIC. Villiers: His Five Decades of Adventure. NY/London: Harper, (1920). 2 vols complete. 7 plts. Good. *Archaeologia*. $65/£42

VILLIERS, FREDERIC. Villiers: His Five Decades of Adventures. NY/London: Harper, (1920). Autographed ed, #83/100. Signed in vol 1. 2 vols. 8 plts. Teg, partially unopened. Paper spine labels. *Schoyer*. $125/£81

VILLIERS-STUART, C.M. Spanish Gardens. London: Batsford, 1929. 1st ed. 86 plts (6 color). Gilt-dec pict cl. Fine in dj. *Quest*. $145/£94

VILLON, FRANCOIS. The Lyrical Poems of Francois Villon. NY: LEC, 1979. One of 2000 signed by Stephen Harvard (designer). VF in glassine & slipcase. *Pharos*. $125/£81

VILNAY, Z. Steimatzky's Palestine Guide. Jerusalem, 1935. 5 maps in pocket. Red cl. Clean. *Gretton*. $31/£20

VINCENT, FRANK, JR. The Land of the White Elephant...(1871-2). NY: 1874. 1st ed. 316pp; dbl-plt color map; 34 engr plts, guards; 23 smaller engr. Gilt-pict cl (corners lt rubbed). *Petrilla*. $75/£48

VINCENT, LEON H. Dandies and Men of Letters. Boston: Houghton Mifflin, 1913. 1st ed. Frontis; 11 ports. 3/4 dk grn morocco, marbled bds (spine faded to tan); teg. VG. *Houle*. $150/£97

VINCENT, MRS. HOWARD. China to Peru over the Andes. London: Sampson Low, Marston, 1894. xi,333,30,(ii)pp, color fldg map. Pict yellow cl (sl rubbed), gilt. *Hollett*. $78/£50

VINCENT, WILLIAM. The Voyage of Nearchus from the Indus to the Euphrates.... London: T. Cadell and W. Davies, 1797. 1st ed. Frontis, xv,(i),530,(2)pp, 6 maps (5 fldg). Bkpl, lt foxing; else VG. *Bookpress*. $350/£226

VINE, BARBARA. (Pseud of Ruth Rendell.) The Dark-Adapted Eye. Viking, 1986. 1st ed. Fine in dj (price-clipped). *Rees*. $31/£20

VINOGRADOFF, PAUL. Villainage in England. Oxford: Clarendon Press, 1968. VG in dj. *Hollett*. $62/£40

VINTON, STALLO. John Colter, Discoverer of Yellowstone Park. NY: Eberstadt, 1926. 1st ed. Ltd to 530. Signed, inscribed presentation. Frontis, 1 plt (map). VG. Howes V 114. *Oregon*. $350/£226

VINYCOMB, JOHN. On the Processes for the Production of Ex Libris. London: A&C Black, 1894. 1st ed. Chromolitho frontis, xii,96pp + 4pp ads, 17 plts; teg, others uncut. (Sl worn, short splits; ex-lib w/small stamps on most plts.) *Cox*. $39/£25

VIRGIL. The Aeneid. John Dryden (trans). NY: LEC, 1944. Ltd to 1100 numbered, signed by Carlotta Petrina (illus). Grn calf over cl. Good in fldg box, slipcase. *Karmiole*. $65/£42

VIRGIL. The Aeneid. John Dryden (trans). NY: LEC, 1944. One of 1100 numbered, signed by Carlotta Petrina (illus). Bkpl, else Fine in tissue dj & pub's drop-lid box. *Hermitage*. $125/£81

VIRGIL. The Eclogues. C.S. Calverley (trans). NY: LEC, 1960. 1/1500 numbered, signed by Vertes (illus). VG in buckram slipcase. *Argosy*. $100/£65

VIRGIL. The Ecologues. NY: LEC, 1960. One of 1500 numbered, signed by Vertes (illus). Fine in pub's slipcase. *Hermitage*. $85/£55

VIRGIL. The Georgics. John Dryden (trans). Verona: LEC, 1952. 1st ed. Signed by Giovanni Mardersteig & Bruno Bramanti (engr). Buckram-backed dec paper over bds. Engr bkpl, else Fine in dj (sl chipped) & slipcase. *Pharos*. $250/£161

Visit to the Zoological Gardens. London: A.K. Newman, (ca 1830). 3rd ed. Toybook. 12mo. 12 hand-colored engrs (1 signed Pickering). (Foxing; inscrips, presentations.) Engr paper wrappers (worn). *Reisler*. $350/£226

VISSCHER, WILLIAM LIGHTFOOT. Poems of the South; and other Verse. Chicago, 1911. 1st ed. Full pg presentation copy. *Argosy*. $100/£65

VISSCHER, WILLIAM LIGHTFOOT. A Thrilling and Truthful History of the Pony Express. Chicago: Rand, McNally, (1908). Pict cl. *Dawson*. $45/£29

VISSCHER, WILLIAM LIGHTFOOT. A Thrilling and Truthful History of the Pony Express. Chicago: Charles T. Powner, 1946. Rpt. Fine in dj (worn). *Graf*. $25/£16

VISSCHER, WILLIAM LIGHTFOOT. A Thrilling and Truthful History of the Pony Express.... Chicago: Chas. Powner, 1946. 2nd ed. Frontis. Fine in Good+ dj. *Oregon*. $35/£23

VISSER, H.F.E. Asiatic Art. NY, (1948). 1st ed. 214 plts (8 color). VG in dj. *Argosy*. $85/£55

VITRY, PAUL. French Sculpture During the Reign of Saint Louis, 1226-1270. Florence: Pantheon, (1938). 1st ed. 90 full-pg collotype plts. Fine in dj. *Karmiole*. $250/£161

VITTORINI, E. In Sicily. (NY): New Directions, (1949). 1st ed. VG+ in dj. *Bernard*. $20/£13

VITTORINI, E. In Sicily. New Directions, 1949. 1st Amer ed. VG- in Nice dj (sm chip spine head; dust-soil rear panel). *Fine Books*. $45/£29

VIVIENNE. They Came to My Studio. London: Hall Publications, 1950s. VG+ in VG dj. *Bishop*. $30/£19

VOGE, CECIL. The Chemistry and Physics of Contraceptives. London, (1933). VG. *Argosy*. $40/£26

VOGE, CECIL. The Chemistry and Physics of Contraceptives. London, 1933. 1st ed. Good. *Fye*. $100/£65

VOIGHT, DAVID QUENTIN. America Through Baseball. Nelson-Hall, 1976. 1st ed. VG+ in VG+ dj. *Plapinger*. $30/£19

VOIGHT, DAVID QUENTIN. American Baseball—From Commissioner's to Continental Expansion. Univ of OK, 1970. 1st ed. VG+ in VG+ dj. *Plapinger*. $45/£29

VOIGHT, DAVID QUENTIN. American Baseball—From Gentleman's Sport to the Commissioner System. Univ of OK, 1966. 1st ed. Fine in VG+ dj. *Plapinger*. $50/£32

VOIGHT, DAVID QUENTIN. American Baseball—From Postwar Expansion to the Electronic Age. Penn State Univ, 1983. 1st ed. Fine in Fine dj. *Plapinger*. $50/£32

VOLANT, F. and J.R. WARREN (eds). Memoirs of Alexis Soyer. London: W. Kent & Co, 1859. 1st ed. xvi,303pp. Blue ptd bds. Good. *Cox*. $54/£35

VOLBACH, W.F. Early Christian Art. London: Thames & Hudson, 1961. 39 color, 271 b/w plts. Dj (sl worn). *Edwards*. $78/£50

Volcano Under the City. (By William Osborn Stoddard.) NY: Fords, Howard, & Hulbert, 1887. Fldg frontis map, 350pp. (Rear pocket removed; stamp on edges.) *Schoyer*. $45/£29

VOLLARD, AMBROISE. Paul Cezanne. His Life and Art. NY: Crown, 1937. Color frontis, 33 plts. Interior Fine (extrems worn). *Europa*. $37/£24

VOLLMANN, WILLIAM T. An Afghanistan Picture Show. NY: FSG, (1992). 1st ed. Fine in Fine dj. *Robbins*. $35/£23

VOLLMANN, WILLIAM T. An Afghanistan Picture Show. NY, 1992. 1st Amer ed. Signed. Fine in Fine dj. *Polyanthos*. $45/£29

VOLLMANN, WILLIAM T. Butterfly Stories. Deutsch, 1993. 1st UK ed. Pb orig. Fine in self-wrappers. *Williams*. $39/£25

VOLLMANN, WILLIAM T. Fathers and Crows. Deutsch, 1992. 1st UK ed. NF (sl creasing couple pp; bkseller's stamp fr paste-down ep) in dj. *Williams*. $171/£110

VOLLMANN, WILLIAM T. The Ice-Shirt. (NY): Viking, (1990). 1st Amer ed. Fine in dj (1-inch cut spine, else Fine). *Godot*. $40/£26

VOLLMANN, WILLIAM T. Rainbow Stories. London: Deutsch, 1989. 1st ed. signed. Fine (specks to tp) in Fine dj. *Revere*. $250/£161

VOLLMANN, WILLIAM T. The Rifles. NY: Viking, 1994. 1st ed. Signed. Fine in Fine dj. *Revere*. $45/£29

VOLLMANN, WILLIAM T. Thirteen Stories and Thirteen Epitaphs. NY, 1991. 1st Amer ed. Signed. Fine in Fine dj. *Polyanthos*. $75/£48

VOLLMANN, WILLIAM T. Whores for Gloria. NY: Pantheon, 1991. 1st US ed. VF in VF dj. *Pettler*. $30/£19

VOLLMANN, WILLIAM T. Whores for Gloria. NY, 1991. True 1st ed, signed. Fine in Fine dj. *Polyanthos*. $40/£26

VOLLMANN, WILLIAM T. You Bright and Risen Angels. London: Deutsch, 1987. 1st ed, 1st bk. One of 2500. Lt bump, o/w Fine in dj. *Rees*. $116/£75

VOLLMANN, WILLIAM T. You Bright and Risen Angels. London: Deutsch, 1987. 1st UK ed (precedes US). NF (sl bumped) in dj. *Williams*. $124/£80

VOLTAIRE, FRANCOIS MARIE AROUET DE. The Age of Louis XIV. London, 1779-81. 3 vols. 2 engr frontis ports. Contemp tree calf (rebacked; foxed; bkpls), gilt filleting, morocco spine labels. *Edwards*. $155/£100

VOLTAIRE, FRANCOIS MARIE AROUET DE. Candide and Other Romances. London/NY: John Lane/Dodd, Mead, (1929). Norman Tealby (illus). Pict black cl. NF in glassine dj, illus pub's slipcase. *Chapel Hill*. $50/£32

VOLTAIRE, FRANCOIS MARIE AROUET DE. Candide or Optimism. Richard Aldington (trans). London: Nonesuch Press, 1939. 20 color plts by Sylvain Sauvage. Cl-backed patterned bds (sl rubbed), gilt. *Hollett*. $70/£45

VOLTAIRE, FRANCOIS MARIE AROUET DE. Letters of M. De Voltaire to Several of His Friends. Rev. T. Franklin (trans). Glasgow: Robert Urie, 1770. 162pp; half-title. Old calf (sl rubbed; spine label missing), gilt. *Hollett*. $54/£35

VOLTAIRE, FRANCOIS MARIE AROUET DE. The Princess of Babylon. London: Nonesuch, 1927. Ltd ed to 1500. (Label removed fr pastedown.) Parchment-backed marbled bds, gilt. *Hollett*. $78/£50

VOLTAIRE, FRANCOIS MARIE AROUET DE. The Princess of Babylon. London: Nonesuch Press, 1927. One of 1500 numbered, ptd on handmade paper. Frontis. Teg, rest uncut. Ink price ep, o/w NF. *Temple.* $33/£21

VON BOENNINGHAUSEN, C. The Homoeopathic Treatment of (W)Hooping Cough. NY, 1870. 1st Eng trans. 199pp. (Ex-lib; backstrip chipped, torn; fr hinge cracked.) *Fye.* $75/£48

VON BOENNINGHAUSEN, C. The Homoeopathic Treatment of (W)hooping Cough. NY, 1870. 1st Eng trans. 199pp. (Ex-lib; backstrip chipped, torn; fr hinge cracked.) *Fye.* $75/£48

VON CLAUSEWITZ, KARL. On War. J.J. Graham (trans). London: Kegan Paul, Trench, Trubner, 1911. New, rev ed. 3 vols. Insect damage, but serviceable set. *Mcgowan.* $85/£55

VON ECKARDSTEIN, BARON. Ten Years at the Court of St. James' 1895-1905. George Young (ed). London: Thornton Butterworth, (1921). 1st ed. 3/4 dk blue calf, marbled bds; teg. Fine. *Sadlon.* $45/£29

VON ERFFA, H. and A. STALEY. The Paintings of Benjamin West. Yale Univ Press, 1986. Sound in dj. *Ars Artis.* $132/£85

VON HAGEN, VICTOR WOLFGANG. The Ancient Sun Kingdoms of the Americas: Aztec, Maya, Inca. Cleveland: World, (1961). Lt edgewear. Dj (price-clipped, sm tears). *Aka.* $27/£17

VON HAGEN, VICTOR WOLFGANG. The Aztec and Maya Papermakers. NY: J.J. Augustin, (1944). 39 plts. Good in dj. *Archaeologia.* $95/£61

VON HAGEN, VICTOR WOLFGANG. The Aztec and Maya Papermakers. NY: J.J. Augustin, (1944). 1st trade ed. Tipped-in sample on Huun-Paper as frontis; 39 full-pg plts at end. Fine in dj (sl chipped). *Oak Knoll.* $125/£81

VON HAGEN, VICTOR WOLFGANG. The Aztec and Maya Papermakers. NY: J.J. Augustin, (1944). 1st trade ed. Frontis; 39 photo plts. VG in dj. *Hermitage.* $150/£97

VON HAMMER, JOSEPH. The History of the Assassins. Oswald Charles Wood (trans). London: Smith & Elder, 1835. viii,240pp. Later black calf, marbled bds (spine rubbed). *Karmiole.* $85/£55

VON HELMHOLTZ, HERMANN. On the Sensations of Tone as a Physiological Basis for the Theory of Music. London, 1885. 2nd ed. 576pp. Fine. *Fye.* $150/£97

VON HELMHOLTZ, HERMANN. Sensations of Tone. London, 1895. 3rd Eng ed. xvii,567pp; 68 figs. (Cl sl dull; spine edges rubbed; ex-lib w/stamps.) *Whitehart.* $124/£80

VON HOLST, H.V. Modern American Homes. Chicago: Amer Technical Soc, 1913. 1st ed. 108 plts, rectos only. Buckram (sl darkened). *Petrilla.* $110/£71

VON JAKSCH, RUDOLF. Clinical Diagnosis: The Bacteriological, Chemical, and Microscopical Evidence of Disease. London, 1890. 1st Eng trans. 398pp. Good. *Fye.* $100/£65

VON KRAFFT-EBBING, R. Text-Book of Insanity Based on Clinical Observations. Phila, 1904. 1st Eng trans. Good. *Fye.* $100/£65

VON LANG and SIBYLL. Eichmann Interrogated. Dennys Publishing, 1983. 1st ed. Fine in Fine dj. *Bishop.* $20/£13

VON MANSTEIN, ERICH. Lost Victories. Chicago, 1958. VG. *Clark.* $35/£23

VON MEYER, GEORG HERMANN. The Organs of Speech and Their Application in the Formation of Articulate Sounds. London, 1892. 2nd ed. 349pp. Good. *Fye.* $75/£48

VON NIEMEYER, FELIX. Clinical Lectures on Pulmonary Consumption. London, 1870. 1st Eng trans. 71pp. Good. *Fye.* $45/£29

VON RIBBENTROP, JOACHIM. The Ribbentrop Memoirs. London, 1954. 1st Eng ed. Frontis port, 4 plts; newspaper article tipped in to fep. VG in dj (spine sl faded). *Edwards.* $28/£18

VON RIEDESEL, BARONESS. Baroness von Riedesel and the American Revolution. Chapel Hill: UNC Press, (1965). 1st ed this trans. Blue-grn cl. NF in dj (lt used, price-clipped). *Chapel Hill.* $40/£26

VON SACHER-MASOCH, LEOPOLD. Venus in Furs. Paris: Privately ptd for Parisian Bibliophiles, 1902. One of 300 on English Classic Antique Wove paper. Teg, others untrimmed. Full red morocco, gilt (orig fr wrapper bound in), leather spine labels. VG in felt-lined jacket, slipcase. *Schoyer.* $200/£129

VON SCHIEFNER, F. ANTON (comp). Tibetan Tales Derived from Indian Sources. London: Kegan Paul, 1906. Largely unopened. Butterscotch cl stamped in gilt/dk brn. VG. *Schoyer.* $125/£81

VON SCHILLER, FREDRICH. The History of the Thirty Years War in Germany. London: W. Simpkin & R. Marshall, 1828. 1st ed of new trans by James Mariott Duncan. 2 vols. (6),224; viii,260pp, aeg. Purple straight-grained morocco (rubbed); dec gilt. *Karmiole.* $150/£97

VON SCHLABRENDORFF, FABIAN. The Secret War Against Hitler.... Pitman, 1965. 1st ed. NF in VG+ dj. *Bishop.* $22/£14

VON SEIDLITZ, W. A History of Japanese Colour-Prints. Anne Heard Dyer, Grace Tripler (trans). London, 1910. Color frontis, 15 color plts. Fore, lower edges uncut. (Inner margin tp sl spotted; ex-libris; sl rubbed; spine lt sunned, sm split head.) *Edwards.* $116/£75

VON SEIDLITZ, W. A History of Japanese Colour-Prints. Phila: Lippincott, 1920. 16 color plts, 79 b/w plts. Gilt-dec grn cl. VG. *House.* $120/£77

VON SIMPSON, OTTO. Sacred Fortress. Chicago, 1948. 48 plts. Good (cl sl spotted). *Washton.* $50/£32

VON WINNING, HASSO. Pre-Columbian Art of Mexico and Central America. NY: Abrams, (1968). 1st ed. Signed. 175 mtd color plts. Rust/beige cl, gilt. Good in dj. *Karmiole.* $275/£177

VONNEGUT, KURT. Bluebeard. Delacorte, 1987. 1st ed. One of 500 numbered, signed, boxed. Fine. *Madle.* $100/£65

VONNEGUT, KURT. Breakfast of Champions. NY: Delacorte, 1973. 1st ed. Sm name/address sticker ep, else Fine in NF dj. *Pettler.* $35/£23

VONNEGUT, KURT. Cat's Cradle. NY: Holt Rinehart, (1963). 1st ed. Signed. (Spine sunned.) Fair dj (chip). *Cullen.* $100/£65

VONNEGUT, KURT. Fates Worse Than Death. (Nottingham: Bertrand Russell Peace Foundation, 1982). 1st ed. Fine in ptd wrappers. *Reese.* $20/£13

VONNEGUT, KURT. Galapagos. PA: Franklin Lib, 1985. 1st thus. Signed. Aeg. Full leather, gilt. Mint. *Polyanthos.* $55/£35

VONNEGUT, KURT. God Bless You Mr. Rosewater. London: Cape, 1965. 1st UK ed. 1st issue, in maroon rather than black bds. VG in dj (lt edgewear, short closed tears). *Williams.* $85/£55

VONNEGUT, KURT. Jailbird. (NY), (1979). #54/500, signed. Fine in VG+ slipcase (label scratched, rubbed). *Fuller & Saunders.* $125/£81

VONNEGUT, KURT. Mother Night. Greenwich, CT: Gold Medal Books, (1962). 1st ed. Pict wraps (soiled). *King.* $50/£32

VONNEGUT, KURT. Mother Night. NY: Harper & Row, (1966). 1st hb ed. Fine in Fine dj. *Chapel Hill.* $100/£65

VONNEGUT, KURT. Mother Night. London: Cape, (1968). 1st Eng ed. Sm name stamp, else Fine in NF dj (spine sl tanned, short tear rear panel). *Between The Covers.* $125/£81

VONNEGUT, KURT. Palm Sunday. Delacorte, 1981. 1st ed. Fine in dj. *Madle.* $15/£10

VONNEGUT, KURT. Player Piano. Scribners, 1952. 1st ed, 1st bk. Variant bound in dker grn cl. Foxing eps; mks, soiling cvrs, else VG in dj (sunning; wear, tear). *Aronovitz.* $125/£81

VONNEGUT, KURT. Player Piano. NY: Scribner's, 1952. 1st ed, 1st bk. NF (sl touches of browning to eps) in dj (sl wear; spine, edges browned). *Antic Hay.* $385/£248

VONNEGUT, KURT. Player Piano. Scribner's, 1952. 1st US ed. 1st issue, w/pub's seal on copyright pg. 1st bk. NF (spine sl lightened) in VG dj (spine browned). *Williams.* $302/£195

VONNEGUT, KURT. Player Piano. Macmillan, 1953. 1st Eng ed, 1st bk. Soiling cvrs, else VG in dj (chipped). *Aronovitz.* $125/£81

VONNEGUT, KURT. The Sirens of Titan. (NY): Dell, (1959). 1st ed, pb orig. Good (lt creasing, use) in pict wrappers. *Reese.* $35/£23

VONNEGUT, KURT. The Sirens of Titan. (NY: Dell Pub, 1959). 1st ed, pb orig. Fine in pict wrappers. *Godot.* $85/£55

VONNEGUT, KURT. The Sirens of Titan. Dell, 1959. 1st ed. VG in wraps. *Madle.* $50/£32

VONNEGUT, KURT. Slaughterhouse-Five. (NY): Lawrence/Delacorte, (1969). 1st ed. Blue cl. NF in dj (sl browning). *Antic Hay.* $175/£113

VONNEGUT, KURT. Slaughterhouse-Five. NY: Delacorte Press, 1969. 1st US ed. VG (erasure to 1/2 title, sm stain fore-edge; sl rubbed) in dj (soiled, browned, chipped). *Virgo.* $155/£100

VOORHIS, ERNEST. Historic Forts and Trading Posts of the French Regime and of the English Fur Trading Companies. Ottawa: Dept of Interior, 1930. 1st ed. 2 lg fldg maps in pocket. Pict cl, rivet-type binding. Fine. *Oregon.* $650/£419

VORONOFF, SERGE. The Conquest of Life. G.G. Rambaud (trans). London: Brentano's, 1928. VG in dj (sl grubby). *White.* $31/£20

VORONOFF, SERGE. Rejuvenation by Grafting. London: George Allen & Unwin, 1925. 1st Eng trans. 38 plts. VG. *White.* $39/£25

VORONOFF, SERGE. Rejuvenation by Grafting. Fred F. Imianitoff (ed). London, 1925. 1st Eng ed. VG (bumped) in dj. *Argosy.* $100/£65

VOUGHT, JOHN G. Treatise on Bowel Complaints. Rochester, NY: The Author, 1823. 1st ed. 204pp. (Bds crudely rebacked in cl.) *Argosy.* $175/£113

Voyages of Captain James Cook. (By Captain James Cook.) London: William Smith, 1842. 2 vols. Frontis, xx,506pp, 16pp pub's cat bound in; xi,619pp, (fr hinges cracked); engr title, 4 maps (2 fldg). (Bumped, stained; spines faded.) NF internally. *Blue Mountain.* $385/£248

VOYNICH, E.L. The Gadfly. NY: Henry Holt, 1897. 1st ed, 1st bk. Gilt/black-stamped cl (sl rubbed). *Sadlon.* $50/£32

VROMAN, A.C. Dwellers at the Source. NY: Grossman, 1973. 1st ed. VG+ in VG dj. *Parker.* $100/£65

VROOMAN, JOHN J. Forts and Firesides of the Mohawk Country New York. Phila: Elijah Ellsworth Brownell, 1943. Tan cl w/blue. VG+. *Parmer.* $150/£97

VYDRA, JOSEF and LUDVIK KUNZ. Paintings on Folk Ceramics. Roberta Finlayson Samsour (trans). London, n.d. (ca 1960). VG. *Argosy.* $75/£48

VYSE, CHARLES. The Tutor's Guide, being a Complete System of Arithmetic.... Ptd for G.G.J. & J. Robinson, 1793. 8th ed. (iv),iv,(iv),324pp (few sm ink spots). Orig sheep (sl scratched; joints cracked). *Bickersteth.* $70/£45

W

W, A.O. (A.O. WHEELER). Eye-Witness. Boston: B.B. Russell, 1865. 1st ed. Frontis, 276pp. Orig black cl. VG. Howes W 314. *Chapel Hill.* $125/£81

WACKERNAGEL, MARTIN. The World of the Florentine Renaissance Artist. Princeton Univ, 1981. VF in Mint dj. *Europa.* $28/£18

WADDELL, ALFRED MOORE. Some Memories of My Life. Raleigh: Edwards & Broughton, 1908. 1st ed. Frontis port. Orig grn cl. VG+. *Chapel Hill.* $75/£48

WADDELL, JOSEPH A. Annals of Augusta County, Virginia. (N.p., ca 1885). 1st ed. 55pp. Orig ptd brn wraps. Spine sl rubbed, o/w NF. *Chapel Hill.* $175/£113

WADDELL, L. AUSTINE. Lhasa and Its Mysteries.... London, 1905. Dec cl (relaid, stained, faded). *Lewis.* $171/£110

WADE, ELIZABETH. Ant Ventures. Rand McNally, (1924). 1st ed. 246pp, 5 full-color plts by Harrison Cady. Grn cl w/pict label. VG (corners bumped, glue mks from bkpl). *Davidson.* $95/£61

WAERZOLDT, WILHELM. Durer and His Times. Phaidon, 1955. Enlgd ed. 32 woodcuts; 151 b/w (16 tipped-in color) plts. Protected dj cellotaped to pastedowns. *Edwards.* $31/£20

WAGENHELM, KAL. Clemente. Praeger, 1973. 1st ed. VG+ in VG+ dj. *Plapinger.* $35/£23

WAGENKNECHT, EDWARD (ed). Mrs. Longfellow: Selected Letters and Journals...(1817-1861). NY: Longmans, Green, 1956. 1st ed. Fine in dj. *Sadlon.* $15/£10

Waggles. A Nodding Head Book. London: Rainbow, n.d. (195?). 18x27 cm. 4pp figs w/heads on wire springs. Pict wraps. VG. *Book Finders.* $100/£65

WAGNER, FREDERICK. Submarine Fighter of the American Revolution...David Bushnell. NY, 1963. VG in VG dj. *Clark.* $35/£23

WAGNER, GLENDOLIN DAMON. Old Neutriment. Boston: Ruth Hill, (1934). Inscribed. Frontis port. Red cl, gilt title. VG + (spine dull). Howes W 5. *Bohling.* $150/£97

WAGNER, HARR. Joaquin Miller and His Other Self. SF: Harr Wagner Pub Co, 1929. 1st ed. #50/1100. Marbled eps. 3/4 blue gilt-lettered morocco, marbled bds. Cornerwear, chip spine head, o/w NF. *Harrington.* $50/£32

WAGNER, HENRY R. The Cartography of the Northwest Coast of America to the Year 1800. Berkeley: Univ of CA, 1937. 2 vols. Inscribed vol 1. Cl (lt wear). *Dawson.* $450/£290

WAGNER, HENRY R. The Cartography of the Northwest Coast of America—to the Year 1800. Berkeley: Univ of CA, 1937. 1st ed. 2 vols. VG in djs (lt soiled). Howes W 7. *Perier.* $650/£419

WAGNER, HENRY R. The First American Vessel in California. L.A.: Dawson, 1954. 1st ed. Ltd to 325 ptd. Frontis, plt. Pict bds, paper spine label. *Oregon.* $45/£29

WAGNER, HENRY R. Juan Rodriguez Cabrillo, Discoverer of the Coast of California. SF: CA Hist Soc, 1941. One of 750. Unopened. Cl-backed patterned bds, ptd spine label. Nice (bkpl). Howes W 8. *Bohling.* $150/£97

WAGNER, HENRY R. Peter Pond: Fur Trader and Explorer. (New Haven): Yale Univ Lib, 1955. 1st ed. One of 500. 3 fldg maps in separate folder. Gilt-lettered linen-backed brn bds. Fine in Fine slipcase. *Harrington.* $175/£113

WAGNER, HENRY R. Peter Pond: Fur Trader and Explorer. (New Haven): Yale Univ Lib, 1955. One of 500. 3 fldg maps in separate folder. Slipcase. *Dawson.* $125/£81

WAGNER, HENRY R. The Plains and the Rockies, Bibliography of Original Narratives...1800-1865. SF: Grabhorn, 1937. One of 600. Gilt-stamped spine label. NF (bkpl; accession # stamped 2pp). *Bohling.* $165/£106

WAGNER, HENRY R. The Plains and the Rockies: A Bibliography of Original Narratives of Travel and Adventure, 1800-1865. SF: John Howell, 1921. 1st ed, 2nd issue. Linen spine, paper label. *Dawson.* $250/£161

WAGNER, HENRY R. The Plains and the Rockies: A Bibliography of Original Narratives of Travel and Adventure, 1800-1865. SF: Grabhorn, 1937. 2nd ed. One of 600. Inscribed. Red-ruled cl, leather spine label. (Bumped.) Wagner's bkpl. *Dawson.* $125/£81

WAGNER, HENRY R. The Plains and the Rockies: A Bibliography of Original Narratives of Travel and Adventure, 1800-1865. Columbus: Long's College Book Co, 1953. 3rd ed. (2 lt spots rear cvr.) *Dawson.* $75/£48

WAGNER, HENRY R. The Rise of Fernando Cortes. Berkeley: Cortes Soc, 1944. One of 300. Inscribed. Frontis. Fldg map. (Inner hinges strengthened; bottom tips few pp sl bent.) *Dawson.* $125/£81

WAGNER, HENRY R. Sir Francis Drake's Voyage Around the World, Its Aims and Achievements. SF: John Howell, 1926. 1st ed. Frontis port, 4 plts, 7 fldg maps. Red cl, gilt-lettered spine (dulled, sl faded). Internally Fine; overall VG + (extrems sl worn; spotted). Howes W 9. *Harrington.* $200/£129

WAGNER, HENRY R. Sir Francis Drake's Voyage Around the World. SF: Howells, 1926. 1st ed. Label over Howells imprint; sm spot fr cvr, else Fine. *Perier.* $225/£145

WAGNER, HENRY R. Spanish Explorations in the Strait of Juan de Fuca. Santa Ana: Fine Arts Press, 1933. 1st ed. VG. *Parmer.* $600/£387

WAGNER, RICHARD. The Rhinegold and the Valkyrie. London, 1910. 1st ed. Arthur Rackham (illus). Aeg. Blue calf, gilt, raised bands (orig fr cvr bound in). Fine (sl rubbed; bkpl). *Polyanthos.* $375/£242

WAGNER, RICHARD. The Ring of the Nibelung. London: Heinemann, 1939. 1st trade ed thus. Arthur Rackham (illus). Fine (bkpl) in NF dj. *Williams.* $457/£295

WAGNER, RICHARD. Siegfried and the Twilight of the Gods. London, 1911. 1st ed. Arthur Rackham (illus). Teg. 1/2 calf, gilt dec, raised bands. Oxford binding. Fine (sl sunned, sl rubbed; bkpl). *Polyanthos.* $400/£258

WAGONER, DAVID. Dry Sun, Dry Wind. IN Univ, 1953. 1st Amer ed. 1st bk. Fine in dj (sunned, lacks sm pieces, tears). *Polyanthos.* $25/£16

WAGSTAFF, A.E. Life of David S. Terry. SF, 1892. 1st ed. 526pp. Howes W 14. *Ginsberg.* $300/£194

WAHL, JAN. Pleasant Fieldmouse. NY: Harper, 1964. 1st ed. Maurice Sendak (illus). 7.25x9.25. 66pp. Pict cl. Fine in dj. *Cattermole.* $135/£87

WAHL, O.W. Land of the Czar. London: Chapman & Hall, 1875. (xvi),(384)pp + 34pp pub's ads. Brn cl, blind-stamped (rubbed, pocket removed). *Schoyer.* $75/£48

WAHL, PAUL and DON TOPPEL. The Gatling Gun. NY, (1965). 1st ed. Fine in Fine dj. *Pratt.* $75/£48

WAILES, REX. The English Windmill. London: Routledge & Kegan Paul, 1971. 32 plts. VG in dj. *Hollett.* $70/£45

WAIN, HARRY. A History of Preventive Medicine. Springfield, 1970. 1st ed. (Ex-lib.) Dj. *Fye.* $40/£26

WAIN, LOUIS. Louis Wain's Cats and Dogs. London: Raphael Tuck, (1903). 1st ed. Lg, 4to. 24 full-pg illus. (Eps chipped.) Cl-backed illus bds (corners, edges worn; hinges cracked). *Reisler.* $1,275/£823

WAIN, LOUIS. Louis Wain's Father Xmas. London: John F. Shaw, (1912). 8vo. Color frontis, 4 mtd color plts. Cl-backed bds, color paste label. Good. *Reisler.* $550/£355

WAINWRIGHT, A. The Far Eastern Fells. Kentmere: Henry Marshall, 1957. 1st ed. (Edges sl warped.) Dj (sl worn). *Hollett.* $147/£95

WAINWRIGHT, A. Wainwright in Scotland. London: Michael Joseph, 1988. 1st ed. Signed. VG in dj. *Hollett.* $54/£35

WAINWRIGHT, A. Wainwright on the Pennine Way. London: Michael Joseph, 1985. 1st ed. Signed. VG in dj (price-clipped). *Hollett.* $54/£35

WAINWRIGHT, A. Walks in the Limestone Country. Kendal: Westmorland Gazette, (c. 1976). 15th imp. Signed. Inscrip. Dj (price-clipped). *Hollett.* $54/£35

WAINWRIGHT, J.M. The Land of Bondage; Its Ancient Monuments and Present Condition. NY: Appleton, 1852. 1st ed. xx,190pp; fldg plt. 1/2 morocco, marbled bds; all edges marbled. Rubbed; sl foxing, o/w VG. *Worldwide.* $195/£126

WAITE, ARTHUR. The Book of Ceremonial Magic. University Books, 1961. Fine in dj. *Madle.* $13/£8

WAITE, CATHARINE V. Adventures in the Far West. Chicago: C.V. Waite, 1882. xi,311pp + 8pp ads. Black-stamped cl (short tear spine head; stamp erased t.p.). *Dawson.* $75/£48

WAITE, FREDERICK CLAYTON. The Story of a Country Medical College. Montpelier: Vermont Hist Soc, 1945. Color frontis port; 7 plts; 1 graph. (4pp loose.) *Argosy.* $60/£39

WAITZ, JULIA ELLEN. The Journal of Julia Le Grand, New Orleans, 1862-1863. Richmond: Everett Waddey, 1911. 1st ed. NF. *Mcgowan.* $150/£97

WAKE, WILLIAM. The Principles of the Christian Religion Explained.... Ptd by W. Bowyer, 1731. 5th ed, corrected. Contemp panelled calf; red morocco lettering-piece. Nice (scuffing). *Waterfield.* $70/£45

WAKEFIELD, H. RUSSELL. The Clock Strikes Twelve. Sauk City: Arkham House, 1946. 1st US ed. Bkpl, else VG+ in dj (price-clipped; edgeworn). *Other Worlds.* $40/£26

WAKEFIELD, H. RUSSELL. The Clock Strikes Twelve. Sauk City, WI: Arkham House, 1946. One of 4040. New in dj. *Bernard.* $65/£42

WAKEFIELD, H. RUSSELL. Strayers From Sheol. Arkham House, 1961. 1st ed. VF in dj. *Madle.* $70/£45

WAKEFIELD, H. RUSSELL. Strayers from Sheol. Sauk City, WI: Arkham House, 1961. One of 2070. Fine in NF dj. *Bernard.* $50/£32

WAKEFIELD, PRISCILLA. An Introduction to Botany. London: Darton & Harvey, 1807. 5th ed. 180pp, 11 hand-colored plts; fldg contents pg. Uncut. Calf spine over marbled bds (rebound; new eps). Fine. *Quest.* $165/£106

WAKOSKI, DIANE. Cap of Darkness. Santa Barbara: Black Sparrow, 1980. Ltd to 250 numbered, signed. Fine in acetate dj. *Antic Hay.* $45/£29

WAKOSKI, DIANE. The Fable of the Lion and the Scorpion. (Milwaukee: Pentagram, 1975.) 1st trade ed (one of 900 thus). Signed. Fine in ptd wraps. *Antic Hay.* $45/£29

WAKOSKI, DIANE. The Ring. Santa Barbara: Black Sparrow, 1977. One of 140 numbered, signed. Fine. *Reese.* $65/£42

WAKOSKI, DIANE. Waiting for the King of Spain. Santa Barbara: Black Sparrow, 1976. 1st ed. One of 250 numbered, signed. Fine. *Reese.* $50/£32

WAKOWSKI, DIANE. Media the Sorceress. Santa Rosa: Black Sparrow, 1991. One of 150 numbered, signed. VF in acetate. *Pharos.* $40/£26

WAKSMAN, SELMAN (ed). Streptomycin: Nature and Practical Applications. Balt, 1949. 1st ed. Good. *Fye.* $50/£32

Walam Olum or Red Score. Indianapolis: Indianapolis Hist Soc, 1954. Teg. 2-tone cl. Lt spotted, else VG. *King.* $95/£61

WALCOTT, CHARLES FOLSOM. History of the Twenty-First Regiment Massachusetts Volunteers.... Boston: Houghton, Mifflin, 1882. 1st ed. xiii,502pp. VG (sl rubbed). *Mcgowan.* $165/£106

WALCOTT, DEREK. Another Life. NY: FSG, (1973). 1st ed. Fine in dj. *Godot.* $75/£48

WALCOTT, DEREK. The Antilles. NY: FSG, 1992. 1st ed. Signed, dated. Fine in Fine dj. *Revere.* $50/£32

WALCOTT, DEREK. Dream on Monkey Mountain. NY: Farrar, 1970. 1st ed. VF in dj. *Else Fine.* $65/£42

WALCOTT, DEREK. Remembrance and Pantomime. NY: FSG, (1980). 1st ed. Very NF in dj (sm crease fr flap). *Antic Hay.* $50/£32

WALCOTT, DEREK. Three Plays. NY: FSG, 1986. 1st ed. Inscribed. Fine in Fine dj. *Revere.* $75/£48

WALDBERG, PATRICK. Rene Magritte. A. Wainhouse (trans). Brussels: De Rache, 1965. 1st ed. Frontis port. Dj torn, o/w VF. *Europa.* $155/£100

WALDEN, HOWARD T., II. Big Stony. NY: Macmillan, (1940). Red cl, gilt pict cvr. *Glenn.* $30/£19

WALDEN, HOWARD T., II. Upstream and Down. NY: Derrydale, (1938). 1st ed. #513/950. VG. *Mcgowan.* $225/£145

WALDEN, JANE BREVOORT. Igloo. NY/London: Putnam's, 1931. 3rd ptg. Blue cl, dog fr cvr. Overall Very Nice (bkpl; sl worn). *Parmer.* $42/£27

WALDEN, WALTER. The Voodoo Gold Trail. Small-Maynard, 1922. 1st ed. VG. *Madle.* $15/£10

WALDMAN, DIANE. Mark Rothko. London, 1978. 1st ed. (Ex-lib, ink stamps; bkpl.) Dj. *Edwards.* $140/£90

WALDMANN, E. Edouard Manet. Berlin: Cassirer, 1923. Color woodcut frontis, 50 plts. Sound. *Ars Artis.* $54/£35

WALDO, FULLERTON. Down the Mackenzie Through the Great Lone Land. Macmillan, 1923. 1st ed. Frontis; 15 plts. Pict plt fr cvr; gilt-stamped spine. Fine. *Oregon.* $45/£29

WALDO, LEWIS P. The French Drama in America in the Eighteenth Century and Its Influence.... Balt: Johns Hopkins, 1942. Frontis. Cl (spotted; spine folded; inscrip). *Dramatis Personae.* $50/£32

WALEY, ARTHUR (ed). The Year Book of Oriental Art and Culture, 1924-1925. London: Ernest Benn, 1925. 1st ed. 2 vols. 60 collotype plts. Brn gilt cl. Vol 2: fldg cl portfolio (chipped). *Karmiole.* $125/£81

WALEY, ARTHUR (trans). The Lady Who Loved Insects. London: Blackamore, 1929. #342/550. Teg, rest uncut (faded). *Petersfield.* $39/£25

WALEY, ARTHUR (trans). The Lady Who Loved Insects. London: Blackamore Press, 1929. #371/550. NF in slipcase (browned). *Williams.* $74/£48

WALEY, ARTHUR. The Opium War through Chinese Eyes. London, 1958. 1st ed. Map. Dj (sl soiled, browned, loss). *Edwards.* $34/£22

WALEY, ARTHUR. The Secret History of the Mongols. London, 1963. 1st ed. Dj (sl soiled, scratches). *Edwards.* $39/£25

WALFORD, LIONEL A. Marine Game Fishes of the Pacific Coast from Alaska to the Equator. Berkeley: Univ of CA, 1937. 1st ed. 37 color, 32 b/w plts. Gray-grn cl (lt rubbed, soiled; leaves foxed). *Glenn.* $95/£61

Walker Percy. Memorial Tributes.... (NY): FSG, 1990. 1st ed. Mint in dec wrappers. *Jaffe.* $45/£29

WALKER, A. EARL. A History of Neurological Surgery. NY, 1967. Facs rpt of 1951 orig ed. Nice in dj. *Goodrich.* $125/£81

WALKER, A. EARL. Posttraumatic Epilepsy. Springfield: Thomas, 1949. NF. *Goodrich.* $45/£29

WALKER, A. EARL. Posttraumatic Epilepsy. Springfield, 1949. 1st ed. Good. *Fye.* $100/£65

WALKER, ALDACE FREEMAN. The Vermont Brigade in the Shenandoah Valley. Burlington, VT: Free Press Assoc, 1869. 1st ed. 191pp. Sl rubbing, else VG. *Mcgowan.* $175/£113

WALKER, ALEXANDER. Beauty in Women. Glasgow, 1892. 5th ed. Frontis, 339pp + 15pp ads, 22 plts. (Eps lt spotted.) *Edwards.* $74/£48

WALKER, ALEXANDER. Intermarriage. NY, 1839. 1st Amer ed. 384pp. Good. *Fye.* $75/£48

WALKER, ALICE. The Color Purple. NY: HBJ, (1982). 1st Amer ed. VF in dj. *Between The Covers.* $675/£435

WALKER, ALICE. Good Night, Willie Lee, I'll See You in the Morning. NY: Dial Press, (1979). 1st Amer ed. Fine in dj. *Between The Covers.* $500/£323

WALKER, ALICE. Good Night, Willie Lee, I'll See You in the Morning. Dial Press, 1979. 1st ed. Fine in dj. *Fine Books.* $225/£145

WALKER, ALICE. Langston Hughes, American Poet. NY: Crowell, (1974). 1st Amer ed. Signed. Don Miller (illus). Sm rmdr mk, else Fine in dj. *Between The Covers.* $1,000/£645

WALKER, ALICE. Meridian. (London): Deutsch, (1976). 1st Eng ed. Dj spine faded, o/w Fine. *Heller.* $45/£29

WALKER, ALICE. Meridian. London: Deutsch, 1976. 1st UK ed. Fine in dj. *Lewton.* $42/£27

WALKER, ALICE. Once. NY: HB&W, (1968). 1st Amer ed, 1st bk. Signed. Sm rmdr stripe, else Fine in NF dj (sl rubbed; short tear). *Between The Covers.* $850/£548

WALKER, ALICE. The Third Life of Grange Copeland. (London): Women's Press, (1985). 1st British ed. Fine in NF dj. *Robbins.* $50/£32

WALKER, ALICE. While Love Is Unfashionable.... (Berkeley, CA): Moe's Books, 1984. Broadside. Fine. *Antic Hay.* $50/£32

WALKER, ALICE. You Can't Keep a Good Woman Down. NY: HBJ, (1981). 1st Amer ed. Signed. Fine in dj. *Between The Covers.* $350/£226

WALKER, ARDIS M. Francisco's Garces. Kernville, CA: Kern County Hist Soc, (1946). 1st ed. 7 plts. Presentation copy, inscribed by Walker and Joan Cullimore (illus). Red cl over dec pink bds (corner bit rubbed). *Karmiole.* $50/£32

WALKER, ARDIS M. Freeman Junction, the Escape Route...from Death Valley in 1849. San Bernardino, 1961. VG+ in ptd wraps. *Bohling.* $20/£13

WALKER, C.B. The Mississippi Valley, and Prehistoric Events. Burlington, IA, 1880. 784pp, 4 tinted plts (2 are maps). Black cl, gilt spine title (rebound). Good. *Bohling.* $85/£55

WALKER, C.F. The Art of Chalk Stream Fishing. London, (1968). 1st ed. Name, o/w Fine in dj. *Petersfield.* $28/£18

WALKER, C.F. Chalk Stream Flies. London: Black, 1953. 1st ed. 4 color plts. VF in Fine dj. *Bowman.* $45/£29

WALKER, E.S. Treetops Hotel. London: Hale, (Oct 1962). 12 plts. Fine in VG+ dj. *Mikesh.* $20/£13

WALKER, EGBERT H. Flora of Okinawa and the Southern Ryukyu Islands. Washington, 1976. Color frontis. As New in dj. *Brooks.* $68/£44

WALKER, ERIC ANDERSON. Great Trek. London: A&C Black, 1938. 3 maps (2 fldg). Blue cl, gilt (bumped, worn; foxed). *Schoyer.* $22/£14

WALKER, FRANCIS A. A History of the Second Army Corps in the Army of the Potomac. NY, 1886. 1st ed. Pict cvr. Letter from Quartermaster-General pasted in. Sl cvr wear, o/w VG+. *Pratt.* $95/£61

WALKER, FRANKLIN. San Francisco's Literary Frontier. Knopf, 1939. 1st ed. VG (inscrip). *Oregon.* $30/£19

WALKER, G. GOOLD. The Honourable Artillery Company 1537-1926. London: John Lane, 1926. 4 color, 40 monochrome plts. Dj (soiled, sl torn). *Bickersteth.* $37/£24

WALKER, GEORGE. The Celebrated Analysis of the Game of Chess. A.D. Philidor (trans). London: Whittaker, Treacher, 1832. xxxiii,(iii),252pp. Spine sl cocked. *Hollett.* $54/£35

WALKER, GEORGE. Venereal Disease in the American Expeditionary Forces. Balt, 1922. 1st ed. Good. *Fye.* $50/£32

WALKER, HENRY J. Jesse James 'The Outlaw.' (Des Moines, IA: Henry J. Walker, 1961.) 1st ed. Orange cl. Fine. *Glenn.* $40/£26

WALKER, J. HUBERT. Walking in the Alps. London, 1951. 1st ed. 2pp als tipped in w/cellotape. *Petersfield.* $39/£25

WALKER, JOHN. Elements of Elocution.... 1806. 3rd ed. Port; xv,354pp; 5 plts. Tree calf, rebacked w/morocco, mod paper label. *Bickersteth.* $39/£25

WALKER, MARGARET. The Ballad of the Free. Detroit: Broadside Press, 1966. Signed. Broadside. Fine. *Antic Hay.* $75/£48

WALKER, MARGARET. For My People. New Haven, 1942. 1st ed, 1st bk. VG in VG dj (loss of 1/3 of surface from adhesion to another surface; lt bumped). *Fuller & Saunders.* $125/£81

WALKER, MARY ADELAIDE. Through Macedonia to the Albanian Lakes. London: Chapman & Hall, 1864. 1st ed. 12 tinted lithos, 3 w/add'l hand-coloring. Grn cl, dec gilt-stamped. VG (foxing, affecting 1 image). *Hermitage.* $950/£613

WALKER, N. An Introduction to Dermatology. Edinburgh, 1925. 8th ed. 92 color plts. Eps sl foxed, o/w VG. *Whitehart.* $28/£18

WALKER, R.A. How to Detect Beardsley Forgeries. Bedford: R.A. Walker, 1950. 1st ed. Cvrs sl discolored, else Fine in wrappers. *Bookpress.* $65/£42

WALKER, R.A. (ed). The Best of Beardsley. London: The Bodley Head, 1948. 1st ed. Frontis; 134 plts. Dec yellow cl (lower cvr sl soiled). Good. *Cox.* $47/£30

WALKER, WILLIAM. The War in Nicaragua. Mobile: S.H. Goetzel, 1860. 1st ed. Engr frontis, 432pp; lg fldg map at rear. Brn cl (spine sl rubbed, soiled). *Karmiole.* $300/£194

WALKINGAME, FRANCIS. The Tutor's Assistant. London: Thomas Richardson, Derby, 1835. Contemp sheep (backstrip torn). *Petersfield.* $31/£20

WALL, J. CHARLES. Porches and Fonts. London: Wells et al, (1912). 1st ed. Frontis. Dec slate blue cl. Sl bumped, else Very Nice. *Cady.* $75/£48

WALL, J. CHARLES. Shrines of British Saints. London: Methuen, 1905. 1st ed. 27 plts. Spotting. *Hollett.* $70/£45

WALL, OSCAR GARRETT. Recollections of the Sioux Massacre. N.p., 1909. 1st ed w/errata. Good (lt wear cvr; spine lettering faded). Howes W 46. *Lien.* $50/£32

WALLACE, ALEXANDER. The Heather in Lore, Lyric and Lay. NY: A.T. De La Mare, 1903. Color frontis. Gilt-dec pict cvr. *Quest.* $40/£26

WALLACE, ALFRED RUSSEL. Darwinism: An Exposition of the Theory of Natural Selection.... London: Macmillan, 1889. Grn diaper-grain cl. Good (sl shaken). *Waterfield.* $101/£65

WALLACE, ALFRED RUSSEL. Island Life or the Phenomena and Causes of Insular Faunas and Floras.... London: Macmillan, 1892. 2nd ed. 3 plts. Grn sand-grain cl. VG. *Waterfield.* $101/£65

WALLACE, ALFRED RUSSEL. Island Life. London, 1880. 1st ed. xvii,526pp + 2pp pub's ads (prelims, edges sl foxed, some intrusion to text), 21 maps (incl color frontis), 5 diags. Teg. (Lib label, rebacked w/orig spine laid down, worn gilt device.) *Edwards*. $155/£100

WALLACE, ANTHONY F.C. King of the Delawares: Teedyuscung, 1700-1763. Phila: Univ of PA Press, 1949. 1st ed. Brn cl. VG in dj. *Chapel Hill*. $55/£35

WALLACE, BRENTON G. and FREDERIC G. WARNER. The Work of Wallace and Warner, Philadelphia. Phila: Franklin Ptg, 1930. 1st ed. 81 plts. NF. *Cahan*. $150/£97

WALLACE, DAVID FOSTER. The Broom of the System. NY: Viking, 1987. Hb issue, 1st bk. Fine in dj. *Lame Duck*. $100/£65

WALLACE, DILLON. Saddle and Camp in the Rockies. NY: Outing, 1911. 1st ed. VG +. *Bowman*. $40/£26

WALLACE, EDGAR. Again Sanders. NY: Doubleday-Doran, 1929. 1st ed. Fine (name). Pict dj (spine lt faded). *Else Fine*. $95/£61

WALLACE, EDGAR. Angel Esquire. NY: Henry Holt, 1908. 1st Amer ed. Spotting few pp; spine sl dknd, o/w Fine w/o dj. *Mordida*. $125/£81

WALLACE, EDGAR. The Day of Uniting. NY: Mystery League, 1930. 1st Amer ed. Fine in dj (closed tears; sl wear). *Mordida*. $65/£42

WALLACE, EDGAR. The Day of Uniting. Mystery League, 1930. 1st ed. Top edges sl dknd, sl foxed, else VG in dj (lt worn, rubbed). *Murder*. $25/£16

WALLACE, EDGAR. The Four Just Men. London, 1905. 1st ed. Frontis; competition leaf. Orange cl (dusty, mkd; faded; spotting). *Waterfield*. $93/£60

WALLACE, EDGAR. The Ringer Returns. GC: DDC, 1931. 1st Amer ed. Fine in dj (short closed tears; sl wear spine ends; sl spine fading). *Mordida*. $85/£55

WALLACE, EDGAR. Sanders of the River. London/Melbourne/Toronto: Ward, Lock, 1911. 1st UK ed. Frontis. Eps browned, o/w VG +. *Bernard*. $75/£48

WALLACE, EDGAR. Terror Keep. GC: Doubleday Page, 1927. 1st Amer ed. NF in dj (closed tears; corner chips; wear). *Mordida*. $100/£65

WALLACE, EDGAR. The Twister. GC: DCC, 1929. 1st ed. Fine (name). Pict dj (lt wear to extrems). *Else Fine*. $90/£58

WALLACE, EDGAR. Writ in Barracks. London: Methuen, 1900. 1st ed. 47pp pub's cat at end dated November 1900. Gilt- stamped red cl; uncut, partly unopened. VG (lt foxing). *Houle*. $150/£97

WALLACE, EDWARD S. The Great Reconnaissance. Boston, 1955. 1st ed. NF in dj. *Baade*. $35/£23

WALLACE, ERNEST and E. ADAMSON HOEBEL. The Comanches. Norman, 1954. 2nd ptg. Pict cl. Fine (sig, date) in dj. *Baade*. $27/£17

WALLACE, F.L. Address: Centauri. NY: Gnome Press, (1955). 1st ed. Fine in dj (lt wear). *Antic Hay*. $45/£29

WALLACE, FREDERICK W. In the Wake of the Wind-Ships. NY: George Sully, (1927). Good. *Hayman*. $40/£26

WALLACE, H. FRANK. The Big Game of Central and Western China.... London: John Murray, 1913. 1st ed. Frontis, 31 plts, 2 maps. Ochre cl, dec in black; teg. Good (lt foxing, lib plt; sl soiled). *Morrell*. $209/£135

WALLACE, H. FRANK. Big Game. London: Eyre & Spottiswoode, 1934. (Back sl faded.) *Petersfield*. $39/£25

WALLACE, H. FRANK. A Highland Gathering. NY: Century, 1932. 1st Amer ed. VG in dj. *Bowman*. $60/£39

WALLACE, HENRY. Uncle Henry's Own Story of His Life.... Des Moines: Wallace Pub Co, 1917-1918-1919. 1st ed. Fine. Howes W 52. *Graf*. $100/£65

WALLACE, IAN. Croyd. NY: Putnam, (1967). 1st ed. Rev copy w/inserted slip & promo material. Fine in dj (sl wear). *Antic Hay*. $250/£161

WALLACE, IAN. Deathstar Voyage. NY: Putnam's, (1969). 1st ed. Fine in dj (sl wear; short tears; price-clipped). *Antic Hay*. $50/£32

WALLACE, IAN. Deathstar Voyage. London: Dobson, 1972. 1st ed. VF in dj. *Else Fine*. $85/£55

WALLACE, JOHN. Carpetbag Rule in Florida: The Inside Workings of the Reconstruction.... Jacksonville, FL: Da Costa, 1888. 1st ed. 444pp, port. New 1/2 morocco. Howes W 53. *Ginsberg*. $750/£484

WALLACE, JOSEPH. The History of Illinois and Louisiana under the French Rule. Cincinnati: Robert Clarke, 1893. 1st ed. 433pp. Grn cl. Pub's prospectus laid in. NF. Howes W 55. *Chapel Hill*. $325/£210

WALLACE, JOSEPH. The History of Illinois and Louisiana under the French Rule. Cincinnati: Clark, 1899. 433pp, fldg map. Howes W 55. *Ginsberg*. $175/£113

WALLACE, PAULE A.W. Indian Paths of Pennsylvania. Harrisburg, 1965. VG in dj (sl worn). *Hayman*. $20/£13

WALLACE, PHILIP B. Colonial Churches and Meeting Houses: Pennsylvania, New Jersey. NY: Architectural Book, (1931). 1st ed. Blue buckram. Fine (bkpl) in dj. *Weber*. $100/£65

WALLACE, PHILIP B. Colonial Ironwork in Old Philadelphia. NY: Architectural Book Pub, (1930). 1st ed. 147 plts. Bkpl; eps, 1/2 title foxed, else VG in dj (spine sunned). *Bookpress*. $95/£61

WALLACE, SUSAN. Along the Bosphorus. Chicago/NY: Rand McNally, 1898. (ii),(384)pp; teg. Aqua dec cl (sl rubbed, esp spine). *Schoyer*. $45/£29

WALLACE, T. The Diagnosis of Mineral Deficiencies in Plants.... London, 1951. 2nd ed. 156 plts. (Corner bumped.) *Sutton*. $75/£48

WALLANT, EDWARD. The Pawnbroker. NY, 1961. 1st ed. VF in dj. *Pharos*. $150/£97

WALLANT, EDWARD. The Tenants of Moonbloom. NY, 1963. 1st ed. VF in dj. *Pharos*. $60/£39

WALLER, AUGUSTUS D. Lectures on Physiology. London, 1897. 1st ed. 144pp. Good. *Fye*. $300/£194

WALLER, EDMUND. Poems, Etc., Written Upon Several Occasions, and to Several Persons. London: Jacob Tonson, 1712. 9th ed. Frontis, lxvi,288pp. Contemp calf. VG. *Bookpress*. $185/£119

WALLER, JOHN AUGUSTINE. A Voyage in the West Indies. London: For Sir Richard Phillips, 1820. 106pp, map (margins foxed), 6 plts; uncut. Mod cl, red morocco back. *Petersfield*. $326/£210

WALLER, ROBERT JAMES. Love in Black and White. Sinclair-Stevenson, 1992. 1st Eng ed. Fine in dj. *Rees*. $70/£45

WALLEY, DEAN. Wheels That Work. Kansas City: Hallmark, n.d. (1970). 17x23 cm. 4 pop-ups, pull-tabs. Walter Swartz (illus). Glazed pict bds. VG. *Book Finders*. $40/£26

WALLING, GEORGE W. Recollections of a New York Chief of Police. NY: Caxton Book Concern, 1887. 608pp (edge 1 leaf torn, no loss). Sl wear rear cvr, o/w bright. *Schoyer*. $125/£81

WALLIS, GEORGE. The Art of Preventing Diseases, and Restoring Health.... London: Robinson, 1793. xx,850,(12)pp. Full tree calf (fr joint cracked). *Goodrich.* $125/£81

WALLIS, HENRY. Italian Ceramic Art: The Maiolica Pavement Tiles of the Fifteenth Century with Illustrations.... London: Bernard Quaritch, 1902. One of 250 numbered. 93 sepia plts. Cream cl (soiled). Teg; uncut, unopened. *Argosy.* $250/£161

WALLMO, O.C. (ed). Mule and Black-Tailed Deer of North America. Lincoln/London: Univ of NE, 1981. 1st ed. Gilt dec cl. Fine in VG+ dj. *Mikesh.* $30/£19

WALLY, DEAN. A Visit to the Haunted House. Kansas City: Hallmark, n.d. (1971). 17x23 cm. Arlene Noel (illus). Glazed pict bds. VG. *Book Finders.* $50/£32

WALPOLE, FRED. Four Years in the Pacific, in Her Majesty's Ship 'Collingwood,' from 1844 to 1848. London: Richard Bentley, 1850. 2nd ed. 2 vols. 2 frontispieces, xiv,(4),432; x,(2),416pp. Blue gilt cl (sl rubbed). *Karmiole.* $300/£194

WALPOLE, HORACE. The Castle of Otranto. Westerham: LEC, 1975. One of 2000 signed by W.S. Lewis (intro). Morocco patterned bds. VF in glassine & slipcase. *Pharos.* $150/£97

WALPOLE, HORACE. Constable's Edition of the Castle of Otranto and the Mysterious Mother. Montague Summers (ed). London: Constable, 1924. 1st ed thus. One of 550. Color engr frontis. Gilt dec cl. Sl rubbed, sl frayed, else Good. *Reese.* $60/£39

WALPOLE, HORACE. Journal of the Printing-Office at Strawberry Hill.... (London): Constable, 1923. 1st ed. One of 650. Parchment, bds. Eps tanned, else VG. *Reese.* $125/£81

WALPOLE, HORACE. Letters of Horace Walpole...to Sir Horace Mann.... Lord Dover (ed). London, 1833. 2nd ed. 3 vols. Frontis port (spotted). Marbled eps, edges (prelims, tps spotted). 1/2 calf, cl bds, gilt, leather label. *Edwards.* $116/£75

WALPOLE, HORACE. The Letters of.... John Wright (ed). London: Richard Bentley, 1840. 1st this ed. 6 vols. Engr frontispieces. Late 19th cent 3/4 pebbled calf (sl dknd, rubbed). Good set (sl foxing). *Reese.* $175/£113

WALPOLE, HORACE. Letters to the Rev. William Cole... Ptd for Rodwell & Martin, & Henry Colburn, 1818. 1st ed. (iv),259pp. Uncut. Mod 1/2 cl, gilt-lettered spine. *Bickersteth.* $54/£35

WALPOLE, HORACE. Letters...to George Montagu, Esq. from the Year 1736, to the Year 1770. London: For Rodwell & Martin, 1818. (i),446,(viii)pp. (Few spots; neatly repaired tear.) Near-contemp full calf (sl rubbed; hinges tender; bkpl), gilt. *Hollett.* $233/£150

WALPOLE, HORACE. Letters...to George Montague, Esq., from the Year 1736 to the Year 1770. London, 1818. 1st ed. 446pp. Contemp polished calf, gilt back (hinge reinforced). *Argosy.* $500/£323

WALPOLE, HORACE. Memoirs of the Reign of King George the Third. London, 1894. #543/740 ptd. 4 vols. 16 ports. (Spines faded, sl rubbed; lt marginal browning.) *Edwards.* $116/£75

WALPOLE, HORACE. Private Correspondence.... London, 1820. 4 vols. Frontis port. Orig 1/2 calf (loss), filleted edges, marbled bds (spines sl discolored, worn; labels sl chipped, vol 1 label partly detached, vol 4 detached). *Edwards.* $132/£85

WALPOLE, HORACE. Reminiscences. London: John Sharpe, 1818. (4),120pp; extra engr title w/vignette. Orig bds. Uncut. Backstrip, paper label partly rubbed away, o/w Good. *Cox.* $43/£28

WALPOLE, HORACE. A Selection of the Letters of.... W.S. Lewis (ed). NY/London: Harper, 1926. 1st ed. 2 vols. Paper spine labels. Fine set in djs. *Schoyer.* $75/£48

WALPOLE, HUGH. The Blind Man's House: A Quiet Story. London: Macmillan, 1941. 1st ed. Fine in dj (sl frayed, spine lt mkd). *Temple.* $26/£17

WALPOLE, HUGH. The Cathedral. NY: Doran, 1922. Lg-paper ed, one of 500 numbered, signed. Linen-backed bds. VF in plain dj & slipcase. *Pharos.* $85/£55

WALPOLE, HUGH. Hans Frost. London: Macmillan, 1929. 1st ed. Fine in grn ribbed cl, gold-lettered spine. NF dj. *Vandoros.* $85/£55

WALPOLE, HUGH. Harmer John. London: Macmillan, 1926. 1st ed. Gilt/blind-stamped cl. NF in dj (worn; internally tape-repaired). *Sadlon.* $35/£23

WALPOLE, HUGH. Harmer John. London: Macmillan, 1926. One of 250 lg-paper copies, signed. Linen-backed bds. VF in orig white ptd dj. *Pharos.* $95/£61

WALPOLE, HUGH. John Cornelius, His Life and Adventures. London: Macmillan, 1937. 1st ed. Fine in dec blind-stamped cl, gold-lettered spine. NF dj. *Vandoros.* $75/£48

WALPOLE, HUGH. A Letter to a Modern Novelist. London: Hogarth Press, 1932. 1st ed. VG in wrappers (sl soiled). *Virgo.* $39/£25

WALPOLE, HUGH. Portrait of a Man with Red Hair. London: Macmillan, 1925. Ltd to 250 signed. Paper label. (Rubbed.) *Sadlon.* $50/£32

WALPOLE, HUGH. Reading. London: Jarrolds, 1926. #10/150, signed. Frontis port. Unopened. VG. *Schoyer.* $50/£32

WALPOLE, HUGH. Wintersmoon. London: Macmillan, 1928. Ltd to 175 signed. Unopened. (Lt rubbed; top edge sl lightened.) *Sadlon.* $50/£32

WALPOLE-BOND, JOHN. A History of Sussex Birds. London, 1938. 1st ed. 3 vols. 53 color plts by Philip Rickman. Teg. (Spines sl faded.) *Edwards.* $287/£185

WALSH, CHRISTY (ed). Baseball's Greatest Lineup. Barnes, 1952. 1st ed. VG in Good+ dj. *Plapinger.* $35/£23

WALSINGHAM, LORD and RALPH PAYNE-GALLWEY. Shooting. Field and Covert and Moor and Marsh. London, 1887. 2nd ed. 2 vols. xv,357; xiii,348pp (staining corner text vol 2); dec eps (lt browned). Illus cl (spines sl rubbed, chipped; bkpl). *Edwards.* $47/£30

WALSTON, CHARLES. Alcamenes and the Establishment of the Classical Type in Greek Art. CUP, 1926. 1st ed. 24 plts. Dj (sl chipped). *Edwards.* $85/£55

Walt Disney Studios' The Black Hole. A Pop-Up Book. NY: Harmony/Crown, 1979. 19x27 cm. 6 pop-ups, pull-tabs. Glazed pict bds (corners sl worn). *Book Finders.* $30/£19

Walt Disney's Donald Duck the Pop-Up Astronaut. London: Purnell, 1970. 21x27 cm. 7 pop-ups, pull tabs. Glazed pict bds. *Book Finders.* $40/£26

Walt Disney's Donald Duck's Pop-Up Circus. London: Purnell, 1970. 21x27 cm. 6 pop-ups, tabs. Glazed pict bds. VG. *Book Finders.* $50/£32

Walt Disney's Snow White and the Seven Dwarfs. NY: Windmill Books/S&S, 1981. 21x25 cm. 4 pull-down pop-ups. Glazed pict bds. VG. *Book Finders.* $30/£19

WALTERS, H.B. Catalogue of the Terracottas.... London: British Museum, 1903. 44 plts. VG (ink stamp tp; rebound black buckram). *Edwards.* $155/£100

WALTERS, H.B. (ed). Marbles and Bronzes: Fifty-two Plates.... London: British Museum, 1928. 3rd ed. 52 collotype plts. Gilt-lettered cl. Good. *Archaeologia.* $350/£226

WALTERS, LORENZO D. Tombstone's Yesterday. Tucson, 1928. 1st ed. Pict cl. Howes W 73. *Ginsberg.* $200/£129

WALTON, ALAN HULL. Love Recipes Old and New. Torchstream Books, 1956. #38/1375. 12 plts. Dj (lt faded, chipped). *Edwards.* $70/£45

WALTON, BRYCE. Sons of the Ocean Deep. Winston, 1952. 1st ed. Fine in dj (spine faded). *Madle.* $65/£42

WALTON, EVANGELINE. Witch House. Sauk City: Arkham House, 1945. 1st ed. Bkpl, else VG in dj (price-clipped; closed tears). *Other Worlds.* $40/£26

WALTON, EVANGELINE. Witch House. Sauk City, WI: Arkham House, 1945. One of 2949. New in dj. *Bernard.* $75/£48

WALTON, IZAAK. The Compleat Angler. NY/London: Hodder & Stoughton, (1911). 1st trade ed. 25 tipped-in color plts, guards; pict eps. James Thorpe (illus). Gilt pict grn buckram (extrems sl worn). *House.* $200/£129

WALTON, IZAAK. The Compleat Angler. London, (1931). 1st ed, ltd to 775 numbered, signed by Arthur Rackham (illus). 12 mtd color plts. Full grn morocco, gilt. *D & D.* $1,400/£903

WALTON, IZAAK. The Compleat Angler. London: J. Major, 1835. 2nd Major ed. lviii,416pp, 14 copper-engr plts. Old panelled calf, broad raised bands, spine label (hinges chipped, cracked; rubbed). Some plts sl spotted, but VG. *Hollett.* $116/£75

WALTON, IZAAK. The Compleat Angler. NY: LEC, 1930. #1005/1500 signed by Douglas W. Gorsline (illus). VG + (lacks slipcase). *Williams.* $140/£90

WALTON, IZAAK. The Compleat Angler. London: Eyre & Spottiswoode, 1930. #8/450 signed by Frank Adams (illus). Vellum-backed bds. VG + (bkpl). *Williams.* $147/£95

WALTON, IZAAK. The Complete Angler. London: Wm. Pickering, 1826. 325pp + index. Orig linen, paper label (worn). Good (contemp sigs). *Second Life.* $45/£29

WALTON, IZAAK. The Complete Angler. London: C&W, 1875. (Piece cut from ep; sl foxing. *Petersfield.* $65/£42

WALTON, IZAAK. The Complete Angler. John Major (ed). Boston: Little, Brown, 1870. 3rd Little Brown ed. Gilt stamped grn cl; teg. VG. *Houle.* $125/£81

WALTON, IZAAK. The Lives of Dr. John Donne; Sir Henry Wotton; Mr. Richard Hooker; Mr. George Herbert; and Dr. Robert Sanderson. York: Wilson, Spence & Mawman, 1796. Contemp diced calf (worn; spine sl chipped; sl foxing; lt dampstain prelim corners); leather spine label; marbled edges. *Sadlon.* $75/£48

WAMBAUGH, JOSEPH. The Black Marble. NY: Delacorte, (1978). 1st ed. Fine in dj. *Antic Hay.* $25/£16

WAMBAUGH, JOSEPH. The Choirboys. NY: Delacorte, (1975). 1st ed. NF in dj (price-clipped). *Antic Hay.* $25/£16

WANDELL, SAMUEL H. and MEADE MINNIGERODE. Aaron Burr. A Biography. NY/London: Putnam, 1925. 1st ed. 2 vols. Blue cl. NF in VG djs. *Chapel Hill.* $150/£97

Wanderings of Tom Starboard. (By Isabella Jane Clarke Towers.) London: John Harris, 1830. 295pp; 6 engrs. 3/4 leather, gilt. Teg. Fine. *Schoyer.* $175/£113

WANDREI, DONALD. Dark Odyssey. Webb, 1931. 1st ed. One of 400 numbered, signed. Fine in dj. *Madle.* $250/£161

WANDREI, DONALD. Ecstasy. Recluse Press, 1928. 1st ed. One of 322. VF in tissue dj. *Madle.* $350/£226

WANDREI, DONALD. The Eye and the Finger. Arkham House, 1944. 1st ed. VG in VG dj (lt chipping spine head, flap-fold extrems). *Aronovitz.* $145/£94

WANDREI, DONALD. The Eye and the Finger. Arkham House, 1944. 1st ed. VG in dj (trimmed, reinforced). *Madle.* $150/£97

WANDREI, DONALD. Poems for Midnight. Sauk City: Arkham House, 1964. 1st ed. Name, date; spine bumped; rear bd cl blemished, else NF in Fine dj. *Other Worlds.* $125/£81

WANDREI, DONALD. Poems for Midnight. Arkham House, 1964. 1st ed. VF in Mint dj. *Madle.* $175/£113

WANDREI, DONALD. Strange Harvest. Sauk City: Arkham House, 1965. 1st ed. Heavy water mks fep, erasures, o/w VG in dj. *Glenn.* $25/£16

WANDREI, DONALD. Strange Harvest. Sauk City: Arkham House, 1965. 1st ed. Fine in dj. *Antic Hay.* $50/£32

WANDREI, DONALD. Strange Harvest. Arkham House, 1966. 1st ed. Fine in dj. *Madle.* $80/£52

WANDREI, DONALD. The Web of Easter Island. Sauk City: Arkham House, 1948. 1st ed. Bkpl, else VG + in dj (worn; tear, chipping). *Other Worlds.* $40/£26

WANDREI, DONALD. The Web of Easter Island. Arkham House, 1948. 1st ed. One of 3000. As New in dj. *Aronovitz.* $70/£45

WANDREI, DONALD. The Web of Easter Island. Sauk City, WI: Arkham House, 1948. One of 3068. New in dj. *Bernard.* $75/£48

WARBURTON, GEORGE. Hochelaga; or, England in the New World. Eliot Warburton (ed). London: Henry Colburn, 1846. 2nd ed, rev. 2 vols. Frontis, xiv,318,26; iv,368pp. VG (blindstamp fep). *Bohling.* $85/£55

WARD, A.W. and A.R. WALLER (eds). The Cambridge History of English Literature. Cambridge: University Press, 1908. 14 vols. Buckram (spine faded, worn), gilt. Good. *Hollett.* $132/£85

WARD, ARTEMUS. The Grocer's Encyclopedia. NY: Artemus Ward, (1911). 80 color plts. Grn buckram (wear, soil); leather label. *Glenn.* $250/£161

WARD, ARTEMUS. The Grocers' Hand-Book and Directory for 1883. Phila, 1882. 305pp (tanned), 14 color plts. (Worn.) *Sutton.* $150/£97

WARD, BERNHARDT. Following Abraham Lincoln, 1809-1865. NY, (1943). Signed. *Heinoldt.* $25/£16

WARD, CHARLES WILLIS. The American Carnation/How to Grow It. NY: De La Mere, 1903. 1st ed. 4 color, 108 b/w plts. Good (rubbed). *Second Life.* $40/£26

WARD, CHRISTOPHER. The Delaware Continentals 1776-1783. Wilmington: Hist Soc of DE, 1941. 1st ed. Frontis. Blue cl. Offsetting rep, else NF. *Chapel Hill.* $75/£48

WARD, CHRISTOPHER. The War of the Revolution. NY, 1952. 2 vols. VG set in box. *Clark.* $35/£23

WARD, D.B. Across the Plains in 1853. Seattle, (1911). 1st ed. VG in wraps. Howes W 94. *Perier.* $300/£194

WARD, DON (ed). Hoof Trails and Wagon Tracks. NY: Dodd Mead, 1957. 1st ed. Dj. *Lambeth.* $25/£16

WARD, EDWIN. Knapsack-Manual for the Sportsman on the Field. London, 1872. 57pp; aeg. Orig burgundy calf, gilt elephant head on cvr. Rebacked, lt edgewear, o/w VG +. *Bowman.* $75/£48

WARD, ELIZABETH. No Dudes, Few Women. Albuquerque, 1951. 1st ed. Sl fading to cvrs, o/w VG in dj (sl chipped). *Baade.* $75/£48

WARD, FAY E. The Cowboy at Work. NY: Hastings House, 1968. 1st ed. VG in dj (lt worn). *Cahan.* $50/£32

WARD, H. and W. ROBERTS. Romney, a Biographical and Critical Essay with a Catalogue Raisonne of His Works. London: Agnew, 1904. #26/350 on Japan. 2 vols. 46plts; 24 plts. 1/2 leather. Lib stamps tps, o/w Good internally (corners worn; top, bottom of spines chaffed). *Ars Artis.* $465/£300

WARD, HERBERT. Five Years with the Congo Cannibals. London, 1890. Frontis port, xxxiii,308pp. Dec cl (spine sl chipped; joints sl rubbed; ex-libris). *Edwards.* $194/£125

WARD, JAMES. Colour Harmony and Contrast. London: Chapman & Hall, 1912. 2nd ed. 16 color plts. Olive grn cl, soiled, else VG. *Glenn.* $100/£65

WARD, JOHN. A Compendium of Algebra.... London: Dan. Browne, 1724. 2nd ed. Contemp panelled calf (rebacked); orig eps. *Waterfield.* $132/£85

WARD, JOHN. Romano-British Buildings and Earthworks. London: Methuen, 1911. 1st ed. Red gilt cl (sl worn, creased). *Hollett.* $70/£45

WARD, JOHN. The Sacred Beetle. London: John Murray, 1902. 16 plts. Emb pict cl (sm nick; inscrip, pencil mks). *Archaeologia.* $150/£97

WARD, KENNETH. The Boy Volunteers with the British Artillery. NY Book Co, 1917. NF. *Madle.* $20/£13

WARD, LESTER. Young Ward's Diary. NY, (1935). 1st ed. Spine cvr faded, o/w VG. *Pratt.* $60/£39

WARD, LYND. God's Man. NY: Cape & Smith, (1930). 1st trade ed, 4th ptg ('March 1930'). Black cl over b/w pict bds (rebacked); top edge stained black; uncut; black eps. VG. *Houle.* $150/£97

WARD, LYND. Madman's Drum. London: Cape, (1930). 1st Eng ed. Black cl over b/w pict bds (sl rubbing; top corners bumped); top edge stained gray, bottom edge uncut. VG. *Houle.* $150/£97

WARD, LYND. The Silver Pony. Boston: HMCo, 1973. 1st ed. 8x9.25. 88pp. Cl. Fine in dj. *Cattermole.* $90/£58

WARD, MARTHA. Steve Carlton—Star Southpaw. Putnam's, 1975. 1st ed. Fine in VG dj. *Plapinger.* $30/£19

WARD, MARY AUGUSTA. The Writings of Mrs. Humphry Ward. Boston: Houghton Mifflin, 1909-1912. Numbered ed (limitation not stated), signed. 16 vols. Tan cl, paper spine labels. Good. *Karmiole.* $250/£161

WARD, MAY ALDEN. Old Colony Days. Boston: Roberts Bros, 1896. 1st ed, inscribed. Gold dec cl. Good (hinges cracked; wear; spine chipped). *Juvelis.* $75/£48

WARD, MRS. HUMPHRY. Fenwick's Career. London: Smith, Elder, 1906. One of 250 numbered, signed. 2 vols. Frontis, 6 plts. Uncut. Wrappers sl dknd, o/w Fine. *Temple.* $70/£45

WARD, NED. The London Spy Compleat, in Eighteen Parts. London: Casanova Soc, 1924. Ltd to 1000 numbered. Frontis. Fine. *Oak Knoll.* $45/£29

WARD, ROWLAND. Records of Big Game. 1899. 3rd ed. Mod 1/2 dk grn morocco. Fine. *Grayling.* $310/£200

WARD, ROWLAND. Records of Big Game. 1907. 5th ed. Contents Excellent (spine faded, cvrs lt mkd). *Grayling.* $155/£100

WARD, ROWLAND. Records of Big Game. 1910. 6th ed. Contents VG (cl sl rubbed). *Grayling.* $155/£100

WARD, ROWLAND. Records of Big Game. London: Ward, 1910. 6th ed. Orig zebra design cl, eps. Lt foxing, o/w Fine. *Bowman.* $170/£110

WARD, ROWLAND. Records of Big Game. 1922. 8th ed. NF in dj (repaired). *Grayling.* $388/£250

WARD, ROWLAND. Records of Big Game. London: Ward, 1928. 9th ed. Pale blue cl, gilt titles, zebra eps. Fine. *Bowman.* $225/£145

WARD, ROWLAND. Records of Big Game. 1928. 9th ed. Buckram (sl rubbed, faded). VG; contents Fine. *Grayling.* $388/£250

WARD, ROWLAND. Records of Big Game, African and Asiatic Sections.... London: Rowland Ward, 1935. 10th ed. (Sm holes back cvr.) *Petersfield.* $102/£66

WARD-JACKSON, PETER. Italian Drawings. London: HMSO, 1979-80. 1st eds. 2 vols. Djs (sl chipped). *Edwards.* $70/£45

WARD-PERKINS, JOHN B. Roman Architecture. NY: Abrams, (1977). Good in dj. *Archaeologia.* $125/£81

WARDE, FREDERIC. Bruce Rogers—Designer of Books. Harvard University, 1925. 1st ed. Cl, ptd label. VG +. *Willow House.* $70/£45

WARDELL, J.R. Contributions to Pathology.... London, 1885. x,807pp. (Lib label, ink stamp; cl dull, dust stained; sl worn.) *Whitehart.* $54/£35

WARDLAW, C.W. Banana Diseases. London, 1961. Frontis. (Soiled pg edges.) *Sutton.* $75/£48

WARDLAW, CHARLES. Fundamentals of Baseball. Scribner's, 1924. Ltr ptg. VG. *Plapinger.* $30/£19

WARDNER, JIM. Jim Wardner of Idaho. By Himself. NY: Anglo-American Pub Co, 1900. Inscribed. 3 plts. (Sm holes fr joint, but tight; soiled.) *Schoyer.* $50/£32

WARDNER, JIM. Jim Wardner of Wardner, Idaho. NY, 1900. 1st ed. (Rebound; orig fr label transposed.) *Heinoldt.* $20/£13

WARE, CAROLINE F. Greenwich Village, 1920-1930. Boston: Houghton Mifflin, 1935. VG in dj. *Schoyer.* $45/£29

WARE, CHARLES CROSSFIELD. North Carolina Disciples of Christ. St. Louis: Christian Board of Pub, 1927. 1st ed. VG. *Petrilla.* $65/£42

WARE, EUGENE F. The Indian War of 1864. NY: St. Martin's Press, (1960). Rpt. VG in VG dj. Howes W 103. *Perier.* $45/£29

WARE, GEORGE W. German and Austrian Porcelain. NY: Crown Pub, (1963). 1st ed. 178 plts (4 color), 5 mtd photos, 2 color maps. Good in dj (sl chipped). *Karmiole.* $35/£23

WARE, JOSEPH E. The Emigrants' Guide to California. Princeton: Princeton Univ, 1932. Foldout map. Ink name, else VG. Howes W 104. *Perier.* $75/£48

WARE, WILLIAM ROTCH. The Georgian Period. NY: UPC Book Co, 1901-1908. 12 parts in 3 vols, complete. 451 plts. Worn. *Bookpress.* $325/£210

WARE, WILLIAM ROTCH. The Georgian Period. NY: UPC Book Co, 1923. 6 vols, complete. 454 VG plts (loose). (Wear; title leaves smudged, lt soiled.) *Bookpress.* $500/£323

WARHOL, ANDY. Andy Warhol's Index (Book). NY: Random House, 1967. 1st ed. Pop-ups: castle, stagecoach, accordion, airplane, Hunt's tomato paste can; balloon fused to opposite pg as usual. VG in ptd silver foil stiff wrappers (sl crease). *Cahan.* $300/£194

WARING, G.E. Draining for Profit.... NY, (1879). 2nd ed. 252pp. (Yellowed, pencil notes; faded, tears, wear). *Sutton.* $65/£42

WARING, G.E. Farmer's Vacation. Boston: Osgood, 1876. (252)pp. Grn dec cl (rubbed). *Schoyer.* $65/£42

WARING, GUY. My Pioneer Past. Boston: Bruce Humphries, (1936). Unopened. Gilt lettering dull, foxing to pp facing plts, else VG + . *Bohling.* $60/£39

WARING, GUY. My Pioneer Past. Boston: Bruce Humphries, (1936). 1st ed. Fine in Poor dj. *Perier.* $45/£29

WARING, J.B. Illustrations of Architecture and Ornament. London: Blackie, 1871. 3,viii,48pp, 70 engrs and litho plts; aeg. Orig emb cl, gilt. Extrems sl worn, o/w Fine. *Europa.* $124/£80

WARING, JANET. Early American Stencils on Walls and Furniture. NY: William R. Scott, 1937. 1st ed. One of 800. Color stencil samples tipped in. Cl, stencil illus mtd on fr; gilt-titled spine. VG (bkpl, date). *Cahan.* $200/£129

WARING, JOSEPH IOOR. A History of Medicine in South Carolina, 1825-1900. SC Medical Assoc, 1967. 1st ed. Frontis port. Fine in dj. *Glaser.* $45/£29

WARING, P.A. The Peacock Country. Day, 1948. 1st ed, rev copy w/rev slip laid in. Fine in VG dj (lt wear, tear). *Aronovitz.* $37/£24

WARK, DAVID. The Practical Home Doctor for Women and Children, to Which is Added a Valuable Appendix.... NY, 1882. 1st ed. 554pp. Good. *Fye.* $75/£48

WARNER, FRANK A. Bobby Blake in Frozen North. Barse & Hopkins, 1923. 1st ed. VG in dj. *Madle.* $17/£11

WARNER, FRANK A. Bobby Blake on Auto Tour. Barse & Hopkins, 1920. 1st ed. Fine in dj (sl frayed). *Madle.* $20/£13

WARNER, FRANK A. Bobby Blake on Mystery Mountain. Barse & Hopkins, 1926. 1st ed. VG in dj. *Madle.* $17/£11

WARNER, FRANK A. Bobby Blake on the School Eleven. Barse & Hopkins, 1921. 1st ed. VG in dj. *Madle.* $17/£11

WARNER, GEORGE. Queen Mary's Psalter: Miniatures and Drawings by an English Artist of the 14th Century.... London: British Museum, 1912. 316 collotype sepia plts. Teg. 3/4 morocco (scuffed). *Argosy.* $250/£161

WARNER, LANGDON. The Craft of the Japanese Sculptor. NY, 1936. 85 plts. (Sl rubbed; spine discolored.) *Edwards.* $85/£55

WARNER, LANGDON. The Craft of the Japanese Sculptor. NY, 1936. 1st ed. 85pp of plts. Good (rubbed, edgewear). *Artis.* $45/£29

WARNER, LANGDON. Japanese Sculpture of the Tempyo Period. MA: Harvard Univ Press, 1959. Text vol, 217 unbound accompanying plts, as issued (lib ink stamps verso plts), 2 maps. Text bound in paper wraps, encl w/plts in lg worn cl-cvrd box w/pegs (top portion detached w/portion lacking). *Edwards.* $271/£175

WARNER, LUCIEN. A Popular Treatise on the Functions and Diseases of Women. NY, 1873. 1st ed. 345pp. Good. *Fye.* $75/£48

WARNER, MIKELL DE LORES W. (trans). Catholic Church Records of the Pacific Northwest. St. Paul, OR: French Prairie Press, (1972). 1st ed. *Artis.* $25/£16

WARNER, OLIVER (ed). An Account of the Discovery of Tahiti. London: Folio Soc, 1955. 1st ed. Frontis map. VG. *Hollett.* $23/£15

WARNER, OPIE L. Pardoned Lifer: Life of George Sontag, Former Member Notorious Evans-Sontag Gang Train Robbers. (San Bernardino, 1909). Frontis port. Red cl. VG (spine faded, bkpl). *Bohling.* $100/£65

WARNER, RICHARD. Literary Recollections. London: Longman et al, 1830. 2 vols. (8),398; (4),500pp, 4-pg facs al. 19th cent polished calf, gilt spine, 2 morocco spine labels each vol (vol 1 spine sl chipped; rubbed; bkpls). *Karmiole.* $85/£55

WARNER, RICHARD. A Walk Through Wales, in August 1797. Together with A Second Walk Through Wales. Bath: Ptd by R. Cruttwell, 1801/1799. 4th ed/2nd ed. 2 vols. Half title, aquatint frontis, viii,238pp; half title, aquatint frontis, x,365pp + (ii) ads (few pp w/scorch mk), aquatint plt. Marbled eps. Early mottled calf (sl rubbed; upper bd detached vol 2; lt stain upper bd, vol 1; bkpl), dec gilt, leather spine labels. *Edwards.* $147/£95

WARNER, SYLVIA TOWNSEND. The Flint Anchor. NY: Viking, 1954. 1st Amer ed. Fine in dj (lt worn). *Hermitage.* $35/£23

WARNER, SYLVIA TOWNSEND. The Innocent and the Guilty. London: C&W, 1971. 1st Eng ed. NF (spine tail sl bumped) in dj (sl rubbed, dknd spine). *Ulysses.* $54/£35

WARNER, SYLVIA TOWNSEND. The Museum of Cheats and Other Stories. London: C&W, 1947. 1st ed. Fine in dj (sl frayed, chipped). *Temple.* $39/£25

WARNER, SYLVIA TOWNSEND. A Spirit Rises. London: C&W, 1962. 1st ed. Fine in dj. *Temple.* $28/£18

WARNER, SYLVIA TOWNSEND. T.H. White, a Biography. NY: Viking, (1968). 1st Amer ed. Blue cl. Very Nice in dj (sl worn). *Cady.* $15/£10

Warren Olney, 1841-1921. (N.p.): Privately ptd, 1961. 1st ed. Fldg family tree. Red cl. Fine. *Harrington.* $30/£19

WARREN, B.H. Report on the Birds of Pennsylvania. Harrisburg, 1890. 2nd ed. xiv,434pp (prelims loose); 99 color, 1 b/w plt. Marbled eps, edges. Gilt-edged 1/2 morocco, marbled bds, gilt raised bands, lettering (upper hinge tender, surface loss extrems, spine worn). *Edwards.* $248/£160

WARREN, CHARLES. Jacobin and Junto. Cambridge: Harvard, 1931. VG in dj. *Schoyer.* $35/£23

WARREN, EDWARD. The Life of John Collins Warren, M.D..... Boston: Ticknor & Fields, 1860. 2 vols. 420; 382pp; extra engr title in each; engr frontispieces. Gold on fr bds. Lt wear, else VG set. *Goodrich.* $175/£113

WARREN, G.C. and H.J. BURLINGTON. The Outdoor Heritage of New Jersey. NJ: Fish & Game Comm, 1937. 1st ed. Fld-out map. VG. *Artis.* $20/£13

WARREN, JOHN. A View of the Mercurial Practice in Febrile Diseases. Boston, 1813. 1st ed. 187pp; errata slip. Recent cl w/leather label; untrimmed. Lib perforation stamp, o/w VG. *Fye.* $250/£161

WARREN, ROBERT PENN. All the King's Men. NY: Harcourt, Brace, (1946). 1st ed. 8vo. Dk red cl. VG in 2nd issue dj (rubbed, chipped, soiled) w/Sinclair Lewis blurb rear flap, rev excerpts rear panel. *Chapel Hill.* $500/£323

WARREN, ROBERT PENN. All the King's Men. E&S, 1948. 1st Eng ed. VG+ in VG dj (lt chipping spine extrems). *Fine Books.* $165/£106

WARREN, ROBERT PENN. At Heaven's Gate. NY: Harcourt, Brace, (1943). 1st ed. Blue cl. Fine in VG dj (lt chipped). *Chapel Hill.* $450/£290

WARREN, ROBERT PENN. At Heaven's Gate. London: E&S, (1946). 1st Eng ed. VG in dj (lt wear). *Turlington.* $250/£161

WARREN, ROBERT PENN. Band of Angels. NY: Random House, (1955). 1st ed. Fine in very bright dj. *Dermont.* $35/£23

WARREN, ROBERT PENN. Band of Angels. NY, (1955). 1st ed. VG+ in VG+ dj (sm nick). *Fuller & Saunders.* $35/£23

WARREN, ROBERT PENN. Brother to Dragons. (NY): Random House, (1953). 1st ed. Blue cl. VG (stains, inkstamp eps) in dj (soiled). *Chapel Hill.* $45/£29

WARREN, ROBERT PENN. The Gods of Mount Olympus. NY: Random House, (1959). 1st ed. Blue cl. Fine in dj (lt used). *Dermont.* $125/£81

WARREN, ROBERT PENN. Jefferson Davis Gets His Citizenship Back. KY Univ, (1980). 1st Amer ed. Fine in Fine dj. *Polyanthos.* $35/£23

WARREN, ROBERT PENN. John Brown: The Making of a Martyr. NY, 1929. 1st ed, 1st bk. VG. *Argosy.* $450/£290

WARREN, ROBERT PENN. Remember the Alamo! NY: Random House, 1958. 1st ed. Name, else Fine in dj. *Cahan.* $125/£81

WARREN, ROBERT PENN. Selected Poems 1923-1975. NY: Random House, (1975). One of 250 numbered, signed. VF in slipcase. *Pharos.* $250/£161

WARREN, ROBERT PENN. Selected Poems 1923-1975. NY: Random House, (1976). 1st trade ed. Inscribed. Sig, else Fine in Fine dj. *Chapel Hill.* $125/£81

WARREN, ROBERT PENN. Selected Poems: New and Old, 1923-1966. NY: Random House, (1966). 1st ed, #144/250 specially bound, signed. Orig beige cl. Fine in Fine dj, pub's slipcase. *Chapel Hill.* $250/£161

WARREN, ROBERT PENN. Wilderness. NY, (1961). 1st ed. Fine in Fine dj. *Pratt.* $20/£13

WARREN, ROBERT PENN. World Enough and Time. NY: Random House, (1950). Signed. Fine in dj. *Turlington.* $275/£177

WARREN, ROBERT PENN. World Enough and Time. NY: Random House, 1950. 1st ed sheets bound w/ptd pg stating this copy #42 of ltd ed esp for Booksellers of America. Gilt-emb grey cl. VG in plain acetate dj (lacks sm piece of spine). *Cahan.* $50/£32

WARREN, SAMUEL. Passages from the Diary of a Late Physician. NY, n.d. 3 vols. Orig cl. VG. *Argosy.* $50/£32

Warriors Brave, A Story of the Little Lead Soldiers. London: E. Nister, n.d. Little Mother Stories. 32mo. (56pp); 26 sm chromos by M.M. Jamieson, Jr. Illus eps (lacks fep). Brn cl (worn); color pict bds. Good+. *Drusilla's.* $55/£35

WASEURTZ AF SANDELS, G.M. A Sojourn in California by the King's Orphan,...1842-1843. SF: Book Club of CA, 1945. 1st ed. Ltd to 300. 19 plts (4 color), 3 maps. 1/2 cl, patterned bds. Fine. Howes W 125. *Harrington.* $125/£81

WASHBURN, CEPHAS. Reminiscences of the Indians. Richmond: Presbyterian Committee of Publication, (1869). 236pp. Orig cl, gilt spine title. Good+ (sl worn, frayed). Howes W 127. *Bohling.* $300/£194

WASHBURN, CHARLES. Come Into My Parlor. NY: Knickerbocker, (1934). 1st ed. VG. *Second Life.* $20/£13

WASHBURN, EMORY. A Treatise on the American Law of Easements and Servitudes. Phila: George W. Childs, 1863. New 1/4 calf (sl browned). Good. *Boswell.* $225/£145

WASHBURN, F.A. The Massachusetts General Hospital: Its Development, 1900-1935. Boston, 1939. 1st ed. (Ex-lib.) *Argosy.* $75/£48

WASHINGTON, BOOKER T. Up from Slavery. NY, 1901. 1st Amer ed. Frontis port. Teg, rest uncut. Fine (spine sl sunned, sl rubbed). *Polyanthos.* $150/£97

WASHINGTON, BOOKER T. Up from Slavery. NY: Doubleday Page, 1901. 1st ed, 1st bk. Contemp owner name, else Fine. *Between The Covers.* $200/£129

WASHINGTON, GEORGE. The Diaries of George Washington 1748-1799. John C. Fitzpatrick (ed). Boston/NY: Houghton Mifflin, (1925). 2nd ptg. 4 vols. Frontispieces. Blue cl. Fine set. *Chapel Hill.* $150/£97

WASHINGTON, GEORGE. The Diary of George Washington, from 1789 to 1791. Richmond: Press of Hist Soc, 1861. Gilt title. Ends chipped, tips rubbed, name, else Good. Howes W 132. *Cahan.* $150/£97

Washington. A Guide to the Evergreen State. Portland: Binfords & Mort, 1931. 1st rev ed. VG in VG dj. *Oregon.* $35/£23

Washington. A State Guide. Portland: Binfords & Mort, 1941. 1st ed. 2nd state binding. Map in pocket. VG in dj (worn, torn). *Perier.* $60/£39

WASSERMAN, JACK. Leonardo da Vinci. NY: Abrams, 1975. 48 hand-tipped color plts. Mint in dj. *Argosy.* $60/£39

WASSERMANN, AUGUST. Immune Sera: Haemolysins, Cytotoxins, and Precipitins. NY, 1904. 1st Eng trans. (Ex-lib.) *Fye.* $125/£81

WASSERMANN, JACOB. Kerkhoven's Third Existence. Eden & Cedar Paul (trans). NY, 1934. 1st Amer ed. Fine in dj (torn). *Bond.* $15/£10

WASSON, ROBERT GORDON. Hall Carbine Affair. Danbury, CT: Privately ptd, 1971. One of 250. Blue morocco, cl; gilt top. Fine in slipcase. *Bohling.* $250/£161

Watch with Mother Jump-Up Picture Book. London: Publicity, n.d. (1950's). 27x21 cm. 5 fan-fld dbl-pg pop-ups. Glazed pict bds. VG. *Book Finders.* $50/£32

WATERHOUSE, ELLIS. Gainsborough. London: Hulton, 1958. Orig ed. 8 color plts. (Sm spot on fr cvr.) *Ars Artis.* $132/£85

WATERHOUSE, ELLIS. Gainsborough. London, 1966. W/cat of works. Good. *Washton.* $90/£58

WATERHOUSE, ELLIS. Painting in Britain 1530 to 1790. Balt, 1962. 2nd ed. 194 plts. VG. *Washton.* $50/£32

WATERHOUSE, KEITH. Billy Liar on the Moon. London: Michael Joseph, 1975. 1st UK ed. Fine in dj. *Williams.* $28/£18

WATERMAN, JOSEPH M. With Sword and Lancet: The Life of General Hugh Mercer. Richmond: Garrett & Massie, (1941). VG. *Schoyer.* $30/£19

WATERMAN, THOMAS TILESTON and JOHN A. BARROWS. Domestic Colonial Architecture of Tidewater Virginia. NY: Scribner's, 1932. 1st ed. Name, else Fine in slipcase (tattered). *Bookpress.* $385/£248

WATERMAN, THOMAS TILESTON and JOHN A. BARROWS. Domestic Colonial Architecture of Tidewater Virginia. Chapel Hill: Univ of NC, 1947. 1st ed. Fine in slipcase (sl used). *Pharos.* $95/£61

WATERMAN, THOMAS TILESTON. The Early Architecture of North Carolina. Chapel Hill: UNC Press, 1941. 1st ed, 1st issue, ltd to 900 numbered. Illus on pg208 ptd upside-down. Foxing 1/2 title, tp, last few leaves, else VG. *Cahan.* $250/£161

WATERS, FRANK. Book of the Hopi. NY: Viking, (1963). 1st ed. Rev copy; pub's slip laid in. VF, As New in dj. *Jaffe.* $225/£145

WATERS, FRANK. The Colorado. NY: Rinehart, (1946). 1st ed, 1st imp. Fine in VG dj (sl edgetears; sm chip). *Reese.* $65/£42

WATERS, FRANK. The Colorado. NY, 1946. 1st ed. NF (bkpl) in dj (sl worn, lacks piece). *Baade.* $35/£23

WATERS, FRANK. The Earp Brothers of Tombstone. NY, 1960. 1st ed. Inscribed. Cvrs foxed, o/w NF in dj (sl chipped). *Baade.* $75/£48

WATERS, FRANK. Masked Gods. (Albuquerque): Univ of NM Press, (1950). One of 300. Signed. Fine in VG dj (2 sm chips; long seamed tear). *House.* $300/£194

WATERS, FRANK. Pike's Peak. Chicago: Swallow, (1971). 1st ed. Fine in VG dj. *Dermont.* $25/£16

WATERS, L.L. Steel Trails to Santa Fe. Lawrence, KS: 1950. 1st ed. VG. *Petrilla.* $20/£13

WATERS, L.L. Steel Trails to Santa Fe. Lawrence, 1950. 1st ed. Clipping glued in, few pp w/lower corner sl bent, o/w Fine in dj. *Baade.* $50/£32

WATERS, NAOMI (ed). Our Favourite Dish.... London: Putnam, 1952. 1st Eng ed. VG (top edge sl dusty; sl spotted; spine head, tail sl bumped) in dj (torn; creased; rubbed, worn; lacks sm piece top edge lower cvr). *Ulysses.* $101/£65

WATERS, RUSSELL. El Estranjero. Chicago: Rand McNally, 1910. 1st ed. Frontis; 25 plts. Gilt-stamped pict cl. VG. *Oregon.* $40/£26

WATERTON, CHARLES. Natural History Essays. Norman Moore (ed). London, n.d. c.(1870). Frontis port, vii,631pp. Marbled eps. 1/2 calf (sl rubbed); marbled bds, edges (worn); raised bands, gilt. *Edwards.* $39/£25

WATERTON, CHARLES. Wanderings in South America, the North-West of the United States, and the Antilles...1812, 1816, 1820, and 1824. London: J. Mawman, 1825. 1st ed. Frontis, vii,326pp. Overall VG (lt foxed; worn). Howes W 158. *Parmer.* $850/£548

WATKIN, EDWARD W. A Trip to the United States and Canada: In a Series of Letters. London: W.H. Smith, 1852. 1st ed. xii,149pp. Contemp 1/2 pebbled maroon calf, gilt titled spine. Nice. *Cady.* $60/£39

WATKINS, ALFRED. The Old Straight Track. London: Methuen, 1925. 1st ed. Fine. *Hollett.* $101/£65

WATKINS, DAMON D. Keeping the Home Fires Burning. Columbus: Ohio Co, (1937). VG in wraps. *Schoyer.* $30/£19

WATKINS, HAROLD. The Art of Gerald Moira. London, n.d. c.(1922). 36 plts, (6 color). (Margins sl browned; rebound ex-lib, label, bkpl, #s.) *Edwards.* $47/£30

WATKINS, PAUL. In the Blue Light of African Dreams. London: Hutchinson, 1990. 1st ed. Fine in dj. *Rees.* $39/£25

WATNEY, JOHN. Mervyn Peake. London: Michael Joseph, 1950. 1st Eng ed. Grn cl. Fine in dj. *Dalian.* $31/£20

WATROUS, JAMES. American Printmaking, a Century of American Printmaking 1880-1980. (Wisconsin): Univ of WI Press, (1984). 1st ed. Fine in dj. *Oak Knoll.* $50/£32

WATSON, A. Hand Bookbinding.... Bell Pub, 1963. VG in dj. *Moss.* $25/£16

WATSON, ANDREW G. The Manuscripts of Henry Savile of Banke. London: Bibliographical Soc, 1969. Good. *Washton.* $50/£32

WATSON, COLIN. Blue Murder. London: Eyre, 1979. 1st ed. Fine in Fine dj. *Ming.* $28/£18

WATSON, COLIN. Blue Murder. London: Eyre Methuen, 1979. 1st ed. Fine in dj. *Mordida.* $65/£42

WATSON, COLIN. Broomsticks over Flaxborough. London: Eyre Methuen, 1972. 1st ed. VG in dj (internally repaired). *Limestone.* $65/£42

WATSON, COLIN. Lonelyheart 4122. London: Eyre & Spottiswood, 1967. 1st ed. Fine in dj. *Else Fine.* $90/£58

WATSON, COLIN. Whatever's Been Going on at Mumblesby. London: Methuen, 1982. 1st ed. Fine in Fine dj. *Ming.* $39/£25

WATSON, DOUGLAS S. (ed). Spanish Occupation of California. SF: Grabhorn Press, 1934. One of 550. Fldg map. Cl-backed bds, ptd spine label. VG+. *Bohling.* $125/£81

WATSON, DOUGLAS S. (ed). Traits of American Indian Life and Character. (By Peter Skene Ogden.) SF: Grabhorn Press, 1933. Cl-backed bds, ptd labels. VG (lt corner wear). *Bohling.* $120/£77

WATSON, ERNEST W. Forty Illustrators and How They Work. NY: Watson-Guptill, (1947). 2nd ed. 324 repros (24 color). Fine in dj (chipped, pieces missing). *Oak Knoll.* $75/£48

WATSON, IAN. Deathhunter. St. Martin's, 1981. 1st US ed. Fine in dj. *Madle.* $40/£26

WATSON, IAN. The Embedding. Scribners, 1973. 1st ed. Signed. Fine in dj. *Madle.* $60/£39

WATSON, J. The Sexual Adventures of Sherlock Holmes. NY: Traveller's Companion, 1971. 1st ed: pb orig. NF (sm scuff; 2 sm lt letters cvr) in wrappers as issued. *Janus.* $60/£39

WATSON, JAMES D. The Double Helix. London, 1968. 1st ed, 2nd imp. Dj. *Wheldon & Wesley.* $47/£30

WATSON, JAMES D. The Double Helix. London: Weidenfeld & Nicolson, 1968. 1st ed. VG in dj (sm tear). *White.* $70/£45

WATSON, JAMES D. The Double Helix. NY: Atheneum, 1968. 1st ed. Fine in dj. *Godot.* $85/£55

WATSON, JOHN F. Annals of Philadelphia and Pennsylvania in the Olden Time. Phila: Leary, Stuart, 1927. 3 vols. (Bkpls; vol 2 spine lt worn.) *Hermitage.* $150/£97

WATSON, KENT H. (preface). The Work of Bruce Rogers. NY, OUP, 1939. Frontis port (minor spotting). Orig cl (ex-lib w/stamps, labels, #; bumped, dented). Dj remains inserted. *Edwards.* $78/£50

WATSON, MARGARET G. Silver Theatre. Glendale: A.H. Clark, 1964. 1st ed. VG in dj. *Lien.* $30/£19

WATSON, MARGARET G. Silver Theatre. Glendale, CA: Clark, 1964. 1st ed. Fldg map. VG + in dj. *Bohling.* $47/£30

WATSON, MARGARET G. Silver Theatre: Amusements of Nevada's Mining Frontier in Early Nevada, 1850 to 1864. Glendale, CA: Clark, 1964. 1st ed. Fldg map. Fine in dj (dusty). *Cahan.* $40/£26

WATSON, NORMAN and EDWARD J. KING. Round Mystery Mountain, a Ski Adventure. NY/Toronto: Longmans, Green, 1935. 1st ed. Color frontis, 32 plts, 3 maps. Lt blue cl. Fine in dj. *Weber.* $50/£32

WATSON, R. Chemical Essays. London, 1800. 7th ed. 5 vols. Fldg table vol 1. Some pp all vols unopened; 1/2 title vol 3 only. Orig speckled calf (some spines sl worn; labels sl chipped). *Bickersteth.* $287/£185

WATSON, ROBERT. Advantages of Dark. NY: Atheneum, 1966. 1st ed. Inscribed. Fine in dj (sl dknd). *Turlington.* $35/£23

WATSON, ROBERT. A Paper Horse. NY: Atheneum, 1962. 1st ed, 1st bk. VG in orig ptd wraps. *Chapel Hill.* $30/£19

WATSON, W. The Forester's Manual. Edinburgh: Stirling, Kenney, 1837. 1st ed. 146pp. Cl; paper label (worn). VG (sl foxed). *Second Life.* $75/£48

WATSON, W. and W. BEAN. Orchids, Their Cultivation and Management. London: L. Upcott Gil, 1890. 1st ed. Frontis, xi,554 + 32pp ads; 6 color chromolithos, 52 plts. Aeg. Dec cvr; gilt-lettered spine. Extrems sl worn, else Fine. *Quest.* $135/£87

WATSON, W.F. The Worker and Wage Incentives. Hogarth Press, 1934. 1st ed. VG in red ptd wrappers. *Words Etc.* $70/£45

WATSON, WILBUR J. Bridge Architecture. NY: William Helburn, (1927). 1st ed. 199 full-pg photos. Few mks, else VG. *Bookpress.* $175/£113

WATSON, WILLIAM. Life in the Confederate Army. NY: Scribner & Welford, 1888. 1st Amer ed. 456pp. Orig gold cl. Good (spine loose, sigs pulled, rear hinge cracked, descrip pasted to fr flyleaf). Howes W 173. *Chapel Hill.* $250/£161

WATSON, WILLIAM. Pencraft: A Plea for the Older Ways. London: John Lane, Bodley Head, 1917. 1st ed. Fading, o/w NF in dj (faded, worn). *Temple.* $22/£14

WATSON, WILLIAM. A Practical Treatise on the Office of Sheriff.... London: S. Sweet et al, 1848. 2nd ed. Emb cl (sl rubbed). *Boswell.* $350/£226

WATSON, WILLIAM. Sculpture of Japan. London, 1959. Dj (ragged w/loss). *Edwards.* $47/£30

WATSON, WILLIAM. Sculpture of Japan. From the 5th to the 15th Century. London, (1959). VG (shelfwear). *Artis.* $25/£16

WATSON, WILLIAM. Wordsworth's Grave. London: John Lane, 1904. Teg. Limp leather (extrems sl worn), gilt. *Hollett.* $39/£25

Watt's Songs Against Evil. (By Isaac Watts.) NY: McLoughlin Bros, n.d. (ca 1865). 12mo. 6 leaves + 1pg list lower wrappers; 5 VF 1/2pg chromolithos. Pict paper wrappers. Fine. *Hobbyhorse.* $80/£52

Watt's Songs Against Faults. (By Isaac Watts.) NY: McLoughlin Bros, n.d. (ca 1865). 12mo. 6 leaves + 1pg list lower wrappers; 4 VF 1/2pg chromolithos. Pict paper wrappers (spine reinforced). Fine. *Hobbyhorse.* $80/£52

WATT, E.A.S. The Love Letters of a Genius. London: Harrison & Sons, 1905. Teg; uncut. (Spotting; sl rubbed; corners bumped.) *Hollett.* $54/£35

WATT, GEORGE. Indian Art at Delhi 1903. London: John Murray et al, 1904. Frontis, 86 plts. Teg, rest uncut. Emb cl (ex-lib w/stamps, bkpl; lt soiled; joints rubbed; head upper joint sl split; spine faded, bumped). *Edwards.* $271/£175

WATTERS, PAT. Coca-Cola: An Illustrated History. Doubleday, 1978. 1st ed. NF in VG + dj. *Bishop.* $22/£14

WATTS, ALAN. The Meaning of Happiness. NY: Harper, 1940. 1st ed. VG in VG- dj. *Lame Duck.* $65/£42

WATTS, ISAAC. Divine and Moral Songs for Children. London: Sunday School Union, n.d. (ca 1860). Stereotype Ed. 16mo. 46pp. Contemp cvr, antique marbled paper, red roan spine. Internally Fine. *Hobbyhorse.* $95/£61

WATTS, ISAAC. Divine Songs. Hartford: Rpt by Hudson & Goodwin, 1807. 16mo. x + 120pp, 1/2pg woodcut frontis, 37 half-pg woodcuts. Gray paper on bds, gilt title on red roan spine. Fine (ink name, dedication verso of frontis, last pg; lt foxing; edges lt rubbed). *Hobbyhorse.* $400/£258

WATTS, ISAAC. The First Principles of Astronomy and Geography.... London: Longman et al, 1765. 7th ed. xiii,(13),222pp, 10pp tables, 6 fldg pp engr illus. Later full chestnut polished calf, gilt rules, decs, raised bands (orig leather label laid down). Nice. *Hartfield.* $295/£190

WATTS, ISAAC. Logic: or, The Right Use of Reason.... Boston, 1796. 'Second American Edition.' 285pp (foxed, browned; ink inscrips). Old calf. (Fr cvr detached; worn.) *King.* $60/£39

WATTS, M.S. George Frederic Watts. NY, n.d. (ca 1900). 3 vols. VG. *Argosy.* $150/£97

WATTS, W.W. Catalogue of Pastoral Staves. London: Bd of Ed, 1924. 20 plts. Spine sl faded, o/w Fine. *Europa.* $31/£20

WATTS, W.W. Old English Silver. NY, 1924. 134 plts. Uncut. VG. *Argosy.* $150/£97

WATTS-DUNTON, THEODORE. Old Familiar Faces. Herbert Jenkins, 1915. 1st Eng ed. Frontis. Grn cl (sl rubbed). VG. *Dalian.* $31/£20

WAUGH, ALEC. Fuel for the Flame. London: Cassell, 1960. 1st ed. Fine in dj (sl nicked). *Temple.* $22/£14

WAUGH, AUBERON. Consider the Lilies. London: Joseph, 1968. 1st ed. NF in dj. *Limestone.* $35/£23

WAUGH, AUBERON. The Foxglove Saga. NY: S&S, 1961. 1st Amer ed, 1st bk. NF in dj. *Hermitage.* $35/£23

WAUGH, EVELYN. A Bachelor Abroad. Cape & Smith, 1930. 1st Amer ed. Spine sl faded; yellow cl cvrs sl dusty, else VG + . *Fine Books.* $85/£55

WAUGH, EVELYN. Basil Seal Rides Again or The Rakes Regress. L-B, 1963. 1st Amer ed, one of 1000 signed. Fine in plastic dj. *Fine Books.* $295/£190

WAUGH, EVELYN. Basil Seal Rides Again. Boston: Little Brown, 1963. Ltd to 1000 signed. Buckram gilt. VG in orig acetate wrapper (sl torn). *Words Etc.* $310/£200

WAUGH, EVELYN. Basil Seal Rides Again. London: Chapman & Hall, 1963. One of 750 bound in buckram, numbered, signed. Sl bowed, spine sl sunned, o/w Fine in glassine dj (sl nicked). *Rees.* $310/£200

WAUGH, EVELYN. Black Mischief. F&R, 1932. 1st Amer ed. VG + in VG dj (spine extrems lt chipped). *Fine Books.* $275/£177

WAUGH, EVELYN. Black Mischief. London: Chapman & Hall, 1932. 1st ed. Spine sl faded, rubbed; sl browning pp; lacks dj, o/w VG. *Virgo.* $54/£35

WAUGH, EVELYN. Black Mischief. Chapman & Hall, 1932. 1st ed. Dec cl. Sl dull, else Good in dj (dull, sl worn). *Whiteson.* $209/£135

WAUGH, EVELYN. Black Mischief. London: Chapman & Hall, 1932. 1st ed. Edges sl foxed, else VG in NF dj. *Limestone.* $450/£290

WAUGH, EVELYN. Brideshead Revisited. London: Chapman & Hall, 1945. 1st UK ed. VG in dj (lt chipped, soiled, creased; spine sl tanned). *Moorhouse.* $434/£280

WAUGH, EVELYN. Brideshead Revisited. Boston: Little, Brown, 1945. Advance issue of 1st Amer ed; ltd to 600, of which 150 were for presentation. Grn cl stamped in gilt. W/ornate pencil monogram of Paul Horgan dated Los Alamos 1945, his bkpl. NF in dj (chipped, tanned). *Reese.* $400/£258

WAUGH, EVELYN. Decline and Fall. D-D, 1929. 1st Amer ed. VG-. *Fine Books.* $135/£87

WAUGH, EVELYN. Edmund Campion. London: Longmans, Green, 1935. One of 50 numbered, bound in buckram, signed for private distribution. Bkpl fr pastedown; spine dull, buckram sunned, minor bruising to corners; o/w NF. *Rees.* $1,318/£850

WAUGH, EVELYN. Edmund Campion. L-B, 1946. 1st Amer ed. NF in NF dj (closed tear). *Fine Books.* $65/£42

WAUGH, EVELYN. A Handful of Dust. F&R, 1934. 1st Amer ed. VG + in VG + dj. *Fine Books.* $375/£242

WAUGH, EVELYN. A Handful of Dust. Chapman & Hall, 1934. 1st UK ed. Signed. Fine (bkpl). *Williams.* $1,163/£750

WAUGH, EVELYN. Helena. Boston: Little, Brown, 1950. 1st Amer ed. Sl stain fr bd, else Nice in dj. *Cady.* $15/£10

WAUGH, EVELYN. Helena. Boston, 1950. 1st Amer ed. Fine in dj (sl rubbed, price-clipped). *Polyanthos.* $30/£19

WAUGH, EVELYN. Helena. London: Chapman & Hall, 1950. 1st ed. Fine in dj (sl worn; closed tears). *Sadlon.* $40/£26

WAUGH, EVELYN. Helena. London: Chapman & Hall, 1950. 1st ed. VG in dj (sl chipped w/short tears). *Limestone.* $75/£48

WAUGH, EVELYN. The Holy Places. British Book Centre, 1953. 1st ed. One of 1000. Fine in dj. *Fine Books.* $195/£126

WAUGH, EVELYN. A Little Learning. London: Chapman & Hall, 1964. 1st ed. NF in dj. *Rees.* $31/£20

WAUGH, EVELYN. A Little Learning. London: Chapman & Hall, 1964. 1st ed. Very Nice in dj (sl soiled, nicked, sm closed tear). *Virgo.* $54/£35

WAUGH, EVELYN. Love Among the Ruins. Chapman & Hall, 1953. 1st ed. Fine in NF dj. *Fine Books.* $95/£61

WAUGH, EVELYN. Love Among the Ruins. London, 1953. 1st ed. Ltd to 350 numbered, signed. Teg, others uncut. Eps sl spotted, o/w Good. *Waterfield.* $310/£200

WAUGH, EVELYN. Love Among the Ruins. Chapman & Hall, 1953. 1st UK ed. Fine in VG + dj. *Williams.* $47/£30

WAUGH, EVELYN. The Loved One. (London): Chapman & Hall, (1948). 1st trade ed. VF in dj. *Jaffe.* $125/£81

WAUGH, EVELYN. The Loved One. London: Chapman & Hall, n.d. Fine in NF dj. *Sadlon.* $75/£48

WAUGH, EVELYN. Men at Arms. L-B, 1952. 1st Amer ed. Fine in dj. *Fine Books.* $85/£55

WAUGH, EVELYN. Men at Arms. London: Chapman & Hall, 1952. 1st ed. Sig, else VG + in Fine dj. *Limestone.* $175/£113

WAUGH, EVELYN. Ninety-Two Days. London, 1934. 1st ed. VG. *Words Etc.* $194/£125

WAUGH, EVELYN. Officers and Gentlemen. Chapman & Hall, 1955. 1st ed. VG in dj (sl chipped). *Rees.* $39/£25

WAUGH, EVELYN. Officers and Gentlemen. London: Chapman & Hall, 1955. 1st UK ed. VG in dj (sl worn; closed tears). *Moorhouse.* $31/£20

WAUGH, EVELYN. The Ordeal of Gilbert Pinfold. L-B, 1957. 1st Amer ed. Fine in dj. *Fine Books.* $65/£42

WAUGH, EVELYN. The Ordeal of Gilbert Pinfold. Chapman & Hall, 1957. 1st ed. VG in dj (sl chipped). *Whiteson.* $23/£15

WAUGH, EVELYN. Put Out More Flags. London: Chapman & Hall, 1942. 1st ed. Good (pp edges, eps, cvr edges browned; sl cocked; bkpl; lacks dj). *Virgo.* $16/£10

WAUGH, EVELYN. Remote People. London: Duckworth, (1931). 1st ed. 7 plts, 2 maps. Maroon cl stamped in gold. Fine in dj (sl loss crown, base of spine, else Fine). *Godot.* $875/£565

WAUGH, EVELYN. Remote People. Duckworth, 1931. 1st ed. 2 maps. (Feps lt browned; spine faded.) *Edwards.* $93/£60

WAUGH, EVELYN. Robbery Under Law: The Mexican Object-Lesson. London: Chapman & Hall, 1939. 1st ed. Owner stamp erased from fep; top edge sl faded, o/w Fine. *Temple.* $116/£75

WAUGH, EVELYN. Scoop. L-B, 1938. 1st Amer ed. Fine in VG + dj (worn). *Fine Books.* $275/£177

WAUGH, EVELYN. Scoop. London: Chapman & Hall, 1938. 1st ed. Very Nice (sl offsetting eps; bkpl; corners sl rubbed) in dj (soiled, worn; sm pieces chipped; corner torn). *Virgo.* $465/£300

WAUGH, EVELYN. Scott-King's Modern Europe. C&H, 1947. 1st ed. NF in dj. *Fine Books.* $65/£42

WAUGH, EVELYN. Scott-King's Modern Europe. Boston: Little, Brown, 1949. 1st Amer ed. Cl faded, else VG in dj (lt rubbed). *Hermitage.* $40/£26

WAUGH, EVELYN. Tactical Exercise. L-B, 1954. 1st ed. VF in dj. *Fine Books.* $85/£55

WAUGH, EVELYN. A Tourist in Africa. London: Chapman & Hall, 1960. 1st ed. Frontis, 4 dbl-sided plts. Fine in dj (worn, dknd). *Temple.* $39/£25

WAUGH, EVELYN. A Tourist in Africa. London: Chapman & Hall, 1960. 1st ed. Edges sl spotted, o/w VG in dj (sl soiled, chipped, damp-stained). *Virgo.* $47/£30

WAUGH, EVELYN. A Tourist in Africa. London: Chapman & Hall, 1960. 1st ed. NF in dj. *Limestone.* $85/£55

WAUGH, EVELYN. A Tourist in Africa. C & H, 1960. 1st UK ed. VG in dj. *Lewton.* $39/£25

WAUGH, EVELYN. Unconditional Surrender. London: Chapman & Hall, 1961. 1st ed. Nice in dj. *Temple.* $28/£18

WAUGH, EVELYN. Unconditional Surrender. London: Chapman & Hall, 1961. 1st ed. VG in dj. *Rees.* $31/£20

WAUGH, EVELYN. Unconditional Surrender. London: Chapman & Hall, 1961. 1st UK ed. NF in dj. *Williams.* $39/£25

WAUGH, EVELYN. Vile Bodies. Cape & Smith, 1930. 1st Amer ed. Sm tears at spine head; corner tips worn, else Good. *Fine Books.* $55/£35

WAUGH, EVELYN. Vile Bodies. Harmondsworth, Middlesex: Penguin, 1938. 1st Penguin ed. Fine in orig wrappers. NF dj. *Vandoros.* $45/£29

WAUGH, EVELYN. Waugh in Abyssinia. London: Longmans, Green, 1936. 1st ed, 2nd issue w/pp163-4 a cancel, for which new copy has been pasted over fr dj flap. Inscribed. Bottom pg edges lt foxed, else VG+ in dj (spine dknd; tears upper flap fold; shallow chips extrems). *Lame Duck.* $2,850/£1,839

WAUGH, EVELYN. Waugh in Abyssinia. Longmans, Green, 1936. 1st ed. (Sm ink spot fore-edge pg 1/2, lacks fep; upper hinge tender; cl soiled, corners sl worn, spine sl bumped.) *Edwards.* $78/£50

WAUGH, EVELYN. When the Going Was Good. London: Duckworth, 1946. 1st ed. VG in dj (3-inch closed tear at fold; extrems sl worn). *Jaffe.* $250/£161

WAUGH, EVELYN. When the Going Was Good. L-B, 1947. 1st Amer ed. NF in dj. *Fine Books.* $65/£42

WAUGH, EVELYN. Work Suspended and Other Stories Written before the Second World War. London: Chapman & Hall, 1948. 1st ed. Fine in dj. *Jaffe.* $150/£97

WAUGH, F.A. The American Apple Orchard. NY, 1912. (Scuffing, bkpl removed.) *Sutton.* $35/£23

WAUGH, F.A. Plums and Plum Culture. NY: OJ, 1901. Grn cl, gilt title, black decs. Nice, bright (corner bumped). *Bohling.* $35/£23

WAUGH, F.A. Textbook of Landscape Gardening. NY: John Wiley, 1922. 1st ed. Olive gilt cl (corners sl bumped). *Karmiole.* $60/£39

WAUGH, HILLARY. Finish Me Off. GC: Doubleday, 1970. 1st ed. NF in NF dj. *Janus.* $20/£13

WAUGH, HILLARY. Madman at My Door. GC: Doubleday, 1978. 1st ed. Fine in NF dj. *Janus.* $20/£13

WAUGH, IDA. Ideal Heads. Phila: Sunshine, 1890. 1st ed. Sm folio. 24 litho plts. Prelim w/ b/w dwg of 5 little maids by Jessie Wilcox Smith. Aeg. Illus brn cl, gilt (spine, corners worn). *Reisler.* $685/£442

WAUGH, LORENZO. The Autobiography. Oakland, CA, 1883. Good (spine ends sl worn). Howes W181. *Hayman.* $75/£48

WAUGH, LORENZO. The Autobiography. SF, 1885. 3rd & enlgd ed. Frontis port, 351pp; 10 plts. (Edges rubbed; spine faded.) Later ed of Howes W 181. *Bohling.* $85/£55

Wax Flowers, How to Make Them. Boston: J.E. Tilton, 1864. 116pp + 4pp ads (lt dampstaining lower margins). Pebble cl, gilt device fr cvr (extrems worn). Good. *Quest.* $40/£26

Wax Flowers, How to Make Them. Boston: J.E. Tilton, 1864. 1st ed. Pub's cl (spine sl spotted; bkstore ticket inside fr cvr). *Bookpress.* $135/£87

WAXMAN, SAMUEL M. (ed). Nomads and Listeners of Joseph Edgar Chamberlin. Cambridge: Riverside Press, 1937. Ltd to 1000 numbered. Good. *Hayman.* $20/£13

WAY, T.R. Memories of James McNeill Whistler. London: The Artist, 1912. 1st ed. NF (sl sunned, sl rubbed, soiled). *Polyanthos.* $30/£19

WAY, VIRGIL GILMAN. History of the Thirty-Third Regiment Illinois Veteran Volunteer Infantry in the Civil War.... Gibson City, IL: Pub by the Association, 1902. 1st ed. Orig cl. NF. *Mcgowan.* $350/£226

WAYLAND, JOHN WALTER. Stonewall Jackson's Way Route Method Achievement. Staunton, VA: McClure, 1940. 1st ed. 2 sigs sl pulled, yet VG. *Mcgowan.* $350/£226

WAYMAN, JOHN HUDSON. The Diary of a Doctor on the California Trail 1852. E.W. Todd (ed). Denver, (1971). Map. *Heinoldt.* $15/£10

WAYTE, SAMUEL C. The Equestrian's Manual. London: W. Shoeberl, 1850. 1st ed. xii,171,(iv)pp, tinted plt (bottom corner lt dampstained). Good (bumped, rubbed; faded; spine head chipped, sm hole). *Blue Mountain.* $95/£61

We Ripened Fast, the Unofficial History of the Seventy-Sixth Infantry Division. Frankfurt, Germany, (1946). 1st annual reunion program, 2 copies of Onaway also present. Badly bumped, else VG in dj (worn, sl torn, stained, chipped). *King.* $125/£81

WEALE, B.L. PUTNAM. Manchu and Muscovite. Being Letters...of 1903. London: Macmillan, 1907. Fldg map. Red cl ruled in blind, gilt. VG. *Schoyer.* $65/£42

WEALE, W.H. JAMES. Hubert and John Van Eyck. London, 1907. One of 365. 41 photograv plts. (Minor browning.) *Edwards.* $116/£75

WEAR, GEORGE W. Pioneer Days and Kebo Club Nights. Boston: Meador Pub Co, 1932. Gold-stamped fabricoid (lt spotted). *Dawson.* $75/£48

Weather Warnings for Watchers, by 'the Clerk' Himself. London: Houlston & Sons, 1887. 3rd ed. 96pp, 67 engrs. VG in mod red cl, gilt spine title, new eps. *Knollwood.* $45/£29

WEATHERFORD, MARK. Bannock-Piute War. Corvallis, OR: Privately ptd, 1959. 2nd ptg. Signed presentation. VG in wraps. *Oregon.* $55/£35

WEATHERFORD, WILLIS DUKE. Negro Life in the South. NY, 1911. 2nd ed. Orig cl. VG. *Mcgowan.* $38/£25

WEAVER, EARL with BERRY STAINBACK. It's What You Learn After You Know It All That Counts. Doubleday, 1982. 1st ed. Fine in VG+ dj. *Plapinger.* $27/£17

WEAVER, JOHN D. The Brownsville Raid. NY: Norton, (1970). 1st ed. VG in dj. *Petrilla.* $30/£19

WEAVER, LAURENCE. Laminated Board and Its Uses. London, 1930. Illus laid down upper bd (extrems rubbed; spine chipped). *Edwards.* $70/£45

WEAVER, LAWRENCE. Cottages. London: Country Life, 1926. 1st ed. Lt edgewear, else VG. *Quest.* $50/£32

WEAVER, LAWRENCE. Cottages. London: Country Life, 1926. 1st ed. Frontis. Ink inscrip, else VG. *Bookpress.* $75/£48

WEAVER, LAWRENCE. Cottages. London: Country Life, 1926. 3rd ed. VG in dj. *Cox.* $39/£25

WEAVER, LAWRENCE. English Leadwork. Batsford, 1909. Frontis. Teg. Gilt-dec title upper bd, spine. *Edwards.* $310/£200

WEAVER, LAWRENCE. English Leadwork. London: Batsford, 1909. 1st ed. Gilt/black lettered gray cl. NF. *House.* $180/£116

WEAVER, LAWRENCE. The House and Its Equipment. London: Country Life, n.d. (c. 1920). VG +. *Willow House.* $85/£55

WEAVER, LAWRENCE. Houses and Gardens by E.L. Lutyens. London: Country Life, 1913. 1st ed. Buckram-backed bds (worn, bumped, sl scratched, frayed). *Hollett.* $256/£165

WEAVER, LAWRENCE. Houses and Gardens by E.L. Lutyens. London: Country Life, 1925. 3rd ptg. Sl yellowing margins; sl worn; rubberstamp fep, else VG. *Bookpress.* $375/£242

WEAVER, LAWRENCE. Lutyens' Houses and Gardens. London: Country Life, 1921. 1st ed. Cl-backed bds, gilt. VG (sl wear, opening sl pulled). *Willow House.* $70/£45

WEAVER, LAWRENCE. Luytens' Houses and Gardens. London: Country Life, 1921. 1st ed. Frontis. (2 marginal tears; sl shaken; lt worn.) *Quest.* $80/£52

WEAVER, LAWRENCE. Memorials and Monuments Old and New. London: Country Life, 1905. 1st ed. 2-tone gilt cl (spine sl dknd, mkd). *Hollett.* $85/£55

WEAVER, LAWRENCE. Small Country Houses of Today. London: Country Life, 1922. Vol 1. 3rd ed. Grn cl, gilt (spine repaired, chipped). *Willow House.* $132/£85

WEAVER, LAWRENCE. Small Country Houses of Today. London: Country Life, 1922. Vol 2. 2nd ed rev. Grn cl, gilt. Faded, o/w VG. *Willow House.* $132/£85

WEAVER, MIKE. Alvin Langdon Coburn...1882 to 1966. NY: Aperture, (1986). VF in dj. *Artis.* $17/£11

WEBB, ALEXANDER S. The Peninsula, McClellan's Campaign of 1862-Campaigns of the Civil War, Vol III. New, 1881. 1st ed. Lt cvr wear, o/w Fine in pict cl. *Pratt.* $47/£30

WEBB, BEN J. The Centenary of Catholicity in Kentucky. Louisville, 1884. 1st ed. 594pp. (Frayed.) *King.* $75/£48

WEBB, CHARLES. The Graduate. NY: NAL, 1963. 1st ed, 1st bk. NF in VG dj (lt chipping, 1-inch tear spine head). *Lame Duck.* $150/£97

WEBB, GEOFFREY. Architecture in Britain. The Middle Ages. London: Penguin, 1956. 1st ed. VG + in dj (chipped). *Willow House.* $39/£25

WEBB, GEOFFREY. Architecture in Britain. The Middle Ages. Harmondsworth, 1965. 2nd ed. 192 illus on plts. Good in dj (sl worn). *Washton.* $75/£48

WEBB, GEORGE. A Pima Remembers. Tucson, 1959. 1st ed. Dec cl, margins. NF (lt blue pencil mks in margins) in dj. *Baade.* $25/£16

WEBB, JAMES JOSIAH. Adventures in the Santa Fe Trade 1844-1847. Ralph Bieber (ed). Glendale: Clark, 1931. 1st ed. 7 plts, fldg map. Fine. *Oregon.* $150/£97

WEBB, JAMES. A Sense of Honor. Englewood Cliffs: Prentice-Hall, (1981). Adv rev copy, slip laid in. 3pp corners sl creased, else Fine in dj. *Between The Covers.* $75/£48

WEBB, KATE. On the Other Side: 23 Days with the Viet Cong. (NY): Quadrangle, (1972). 1st ed. Dust top edges, o/w Fine in dj (sl scuffing; edge tears). *Aka.* $40/£26

WEBB, M.I. Michael Rysbrack, Sculptor. London: Country Life, 1954. Frontis port. Fine in dec dj. *Europa.* $90/£58

WEBB, MARY. The Chinese Lion. London: Rota, 1937. Ltd 1st ed, one of 350 numbered. Cl-backed dec bds. (Bkpl.) Pub's box. *Argosy.* $85/£55

WEBB, MARY. Gone to Earth. London: Constable, 1917. 1st Eng ed. Dk rose cl blocked in blind/black. Name, address, date ep, else Nice. *Cady.* $25/£16

WEBB, MARY. The House in Dormer Corner. London: Hutchinson, (1920). 1st ed. Good (ink name; rear inner hinge mended). *Reese.* $30/£19

WEBB, SIDNEY and BEATRICE. The Truth about Soviet Russia. London: Longmans, Green, (1942). 1st ed. Dbl-pg frontis map. VG in ptd cream wraps. *Chapel Hill.* $75/£48

WEBB, SIDNEY and HAROLD COX. The Eight Hours Day. London: Walter Scott, (1891). Binder's red sandgrain cl. *Waterfield.* $70/£45

WEBB, TODD. Georgia O'Keeffe. The Artist's Landscape. Pasadena: Twelvetrees, 1984. 1st ed. Fine (tiny rubs) in Fine slipcase. *Beasley.* $150/£97

WEBB, WALTER PRESCOTT. The Great Plains. (N.p.): Ginn & Co, (1931). 1st ed, 2nd issue w/no error in heading chapter 2. Silver dec black cl. NF (fep creased) in dj (lt soiled). Howes W 193. *House.* $120/£77

WEBB, WALTER PRESCOTT. The Great Plains. (Boston): Ginn, (1931). 1st ed, 2nd issue. Pict cl. VG in dj (scuffed). Howes W 193. *Schoyer.* $65/£42

WEBB, WALTER PRESCOTT. The Great Plains. NY, 1931. 1st ed. Pict cl. Fine. *Pratt.* $65/£42

WEBB, WALTER PRESCOTT. History as High Adventure. E.C. Barksdale (ed). Austin: Pemberton Press, 1969. One of 350. 1/2 morocco. Fine in slipcase. *Bohling.* $75/£48

WEBB, WALTER PRESCOTT. The Texas Rangers. Austin, 1965. 2nd ed. Fine in dj (sl edgeworn, closed tear). Howes W 194. *Baade.* $50/£32

WEBBER, MALCOLM. Medicine Show. Caldwell, ID: Caxton, 1941. 1st ed. VG +. *Bishop.* $17/£11

WEBER, BRUCE. Bruce Weber. L.A.: Twelvetrees Press, 1983. 1st ed. 88 plts. Fine in pict dj. *Cahan.* $250/£161

WEBER, CARL J. The Rise and Fall of James R. Osgood. Waterville, ME: Colby College, 1959. 1st ed. Fine in Nice dj. *Macdonnell.* $45/£29

WEBER, GEORGE W. The Ornaments of Late Chou Bronzes. New Brunswick: Rutgers Univ Press, 1973. Color frontis (verso stuck to 1/2 title). Dj (sl chipped). *Edwards.* $54/£35

WEBER, H. and F.P. The Mineral Waters and Health Resorts of Europe. London, 1898. xiii,524pp (lacks map in pocket; sig; spine ends worn; cl dust stained; lt foxing). *Whitehart.* $28/£18

WEBER, MAX. Cubist Poems. London: Elkin Mathews, 1914. 1st ed, 1st bk. Blue cl w/gilt cvr illus (spine lt rubbed). *Karmiole.* $250/£161

WEBER, SARAH STILWELL. The Musical Tree. Phila: Penn Publishing, 1925. Frontis, 38 leaves, 14 plts. Tan cl. NF in Good pict dj (short tears edges; chip rear panel, spine head). *Blue Mountain.* $100/£65

WEBSTER, CAROLINE. Mr. W. and I. NY, 1942. 1st ed. VF. *Bond.* $20/£13

WEBSTER, FRANK V. Tom Taylor at West Point. Cupples & Leon, 1915. 1st ed. VG. *Madle.* $17/£11

WEBSTER, JONATHAN VINTON. Two True California Stories. SF: P.J. Thomas, 1883. 1st ed. 256pp. Gilt dec cl (rubbed, soiled). *Reese.* $55/£35

WEBSTER, KIMBALL. The Gold Seekers of '49. Manchester, NH, 1917. 16 plts/ports. (Spine faded; internal lib mks, notes.) *Bohling.* $85/£55

WEBSTER, KIMBALL. The Gold Seekers of '49. Manchester: Standard Book Co, 1917. Frontis. Black-stamped cl, paper cvr label. Dj (2 tears). *Dawson.* $100/£65

WEBSTER, W.H.B. Narrative of a Voyage to the Southern Atlantic Ocean, in the Years 1828, 29, 30. London: Richard Bentley, 1834. 2 vols. 399; 398pp, 5 aquatint plts (foxed), 2 maps (1 fldg). Grey bds (rebound) w/orig leather spines (rubbed), new morocco spine labels (lacks half-titles). *Schoyer.* $400/£258

WECHSELMANN, WILHELM. The Treatment of Syphilis with Salvarsan. NY, 1911. 1st Eng trans. 16 colored plts. *Fye.* $200/£129

WECHSLER, HERMAN. Great Prints and Printmakers. Bentveld: Abrams, (1967). 100 plts. VG. *Argosy.* $60/£39

WECTER, DIXON. Sam Clemens of Hannibal. Boston: Houghton, Mifflin, 1952. 1st ed, 1st ptg. Fine in NF dj (nicks, sl faded). *Macdonnell.* $45/£29

WECTER, DIXON. Sam Clemens of Hannibal. Boston: Houghton Mifflin, 1952. 1st ed. Frontis port. VG in pict dj. *Shasky.* $30/£19

WEDDA, JOHN. Gardens of the American South. NY, 1971. NF in VG dj. *Shifrin.* $35/£23

WEDDLE, ROBERT. Plowhorse Cavalry; the Caney Creek Boys.... Austin: Madrona, 1974. 1st ed. Dj. *Lambeth.* $40/£26

WEDECK, HARRY. Dictionary of Aphrodisiacs. NY, 1961. 1st ed. Good. *Fye.* $50/£32

WEDEL, WALDO R. An Introduction to Kansas Archaeology.... Washington, 1959. 97 full-pg plts. (Owner stamp.) *Hayman.* $50/£32

WEDGWOOD, C.V. Strafford 1593-1641. London: Cape, 1935. Frontis, 7 plts. VG. *Peter Taylor.* $23/£15

WEDGWOOD, JOSIAH C. Staffordshire Pottery and Its History. London: Sampson Low, 1913. 2 maps. Teg, rest uncut. Grn bds, white buckram backstrip (sl foxing throughout). *Petersfield.* $87/£56

WEDGWOOD, JULIA. The Personal Life of Josiah Wedgwood: The Potter. London: Macmillan, 1915. Frontis port, guard. VG. *Cahan.* $25/£16

WEDGWOOD, RALPH and EARL BENDITT (eds). Sudden Death in Infants. Washington, 1963. Good. *Fye.* $50/£32

WEDMORE, E.B. A Manual of Beekeeping.... London, 1932. (Lt foxing; cl sl soiled; spine discolored.) *Edwards.* $39/£25

WEDMORE, FREDERICK. Etching in England. London, 1895. Teg, rest uncut. (Lt spotting.) Dec bds (lt soiled, rubbed). *Edwards.* $39/£25

WEEGEE. (Pseud of Arthur Fellig). Naked City. Cincinnati: Zebra Picture Books, (1945). 1st ed thus. VG in black pict wrappers (lt worn). *Godot.* $65/£42

WEEGEE. (Pseud of Arthur Fellig.) Naked Hollywood. Mel Harris (text). NY, (1953). 1st ed. Cl-backed bds (bumped, worn). *King.* $75/£48

WEEGEE. (Pseud of Arthur Fellig.) Naked Hollywood. Mel Harris (text). NY: Pellegrini & Cudahy, 1953. 1st ed. Yellow/black cl. Extrems lt rubbed, else Fine in VG dj (chipped). *Cahan.* $85/£55

WEEGEE. (Pseud of Arthur Fellig.) Weegee's People. NY: Duell, Sloan & Pearce, 1946. 1st ed. Fine (ring on rear bd) in VG dj (chipped). *Beasley.* $100/£65

WEEKES, MARY. Trader King. Regina: School Aids & Text Co, (1949). 1st ed. Pict cl. VG. *Oregon.* $45/£29

WEEKS, DONALD. Frederick William Rolfe and Artists' Models. Edinburgh: Tragara Press, 1981. Ltd to 115 (this one of 25 add'l copies for author use). Fine in plain grn wrappers; paper label. *Dalian.* $101/£65

WEEKS, DONALD. Frederick William Rolfe, Christchurch, and the Artist. Edinburgh: Tragara Press, 1980. Ltd to 120 (this one of 25 add'l copies for author use). Fine in plain red wrappers; ptd label. *Dalian.* $101/£65

WEEKS, GEORGE F. California Copy. Washington, DC: Washington College Press, 1928. 1st ed. Inscribed by author's wife. Frontis, 10 plts. Silver-lettered yellow cl (sl soiled; spine dknd; extrems sl worn). Internally Fine; overall VG + . *Harrington.* $45/£29

WEEKS, JOHN. A Treatise on Diseases of the Eye. Phila, 1910. Good. *Fye.* $40/£26

WEEKS, STEPHEN B. Southern Quakers and Slavery. Balt: Johns Hopkins Press, 1896. 1st ed. xiv,400pp; lg fldg map. Lt staining 1st few leaves; rubbed; bkpl; rep creased, closed tears, else VG. *Cahan.* $85/£55

WEES, FRANCES SHELLEY. The Maestro Murders. NY: Mystery League, 1931. 1st Amer ed. NF in dj (tears; edge pieces missing). *Polyanthos.* $25/£16

WEGENER, E. Greenland Journey. London: 1939. 1st Eng ed. VG. *Walcot.* $54/£35

WEGMANN, EDWARD. The Design and Construction of Dams. London, 1900. 4th ed. Frontis, 11 plts, 86 fldg plts, 24 tables. Gilt illus upper bd. (Hinges tender, rebacked w/orig spine laid down, corners rubbed.) *Edwards.* $116/£75

WEHLE, HARRY B. and THEODORE BOLTON. American Miniatures, 1730-1850. GC: Garden City Publishing, (1937). 1st ed. Frontis. (Ex-lib w/mks; text browned; dj tattered.) *Bookpress.* $50/£32

WEHLE, ROBERT G. Wing and Shot. Scottsville, NY: Country Press, (1964). 1st ed. Brn cl. Fine in dj (lt chipped). *Glenn.* $75/£48

WEHR, JULIAN. Animated Antics in Playland. Ohio/NY: Saalfield, 1946. 26x20 cm. Bright pictures, movables by Julian Wehr. (Cvrs detached from spiral binding, spine now attached w/tape.) *Book Finders.* $90/£58

WEIBEL, ADELE COULIN. Two Thousand Years of Textiles. The Figured Textiles of Europe and the Near East. NY, 1952. 331 plts. Good in dj, slipcase. *Washton.* $175/£113

WEIDENMANN, J. Beautifying Country Homes. A Handbook of Landscape Gardening. NY: OJ, (1870). 1st ed. Sm folio, 40,(5)pp, 24 plts, 7 dbl-pg illus. Respined, w/new eps. Cvrs rubbed, corners sl worn; else Clean. *Bookpress.* $1,150/£742

WEIGALL, ARTHUR. The Life and Times of Akhnaton, Pharaoh of Egypt. London: Thornton Butterworth, 1933. (Bkpl removed.) *Archaeologia.* $45/£29

WEIGALL, ARTHUR. Sappho of Lesbos, Her Life and Times. NY: Stokes, 1932. 1st ed. VG w/o dj. *Second Life.* $25/£16

WEIL, GUNTHER et al (eds). The Psychedelic Reader. NY: University Books, 1965. 1st ed. VG + in dj. *Sclanders.* $47/£30

WEILER, MILTON C. The Classic Decoy Series. NY: Winchester Press, 1969. One of 1000, this copy out of series. 24 color plts. Wrappers, gilt titles, brn linen ties. Fine in slipcase. *Weber*. $295/£190

WEINBAUM, STANLEY. The Dark Other. Fantasy Pub, 1950. 1st ed. VG in dj (chipped, frayed). *Madle*. $50/£32

WEINBAUM, STANLEY. A Martian Odyssey. Fantasy, 1949. 1st ed. Fine in dj (chipped). *Madle*. $75/£48

WEINBAUM, STANLEY. The New Adam. Z-D, 1939. 1st ed. VG in dj (worn, chipped). *Aronovitz*. $48/£31

WEINBAUM, STANLEY. The New Adam. Ziff-Davis, 1939. 1st ed. NF in dj (lt chipped). *Madle*. $125/£81

WEINBERGER, MARTIN. Michelangelo the Sculptor. London/NY, 1967. 1st ed. 2 vols. 144 b/w plts. (Ex-lib w/ink stamps, label remains; tape mks.) Djs (sl chipped). *Edwards*. $78/£50

WEIR, JAMES. The Winter Lodge. Phila, 1854. 1st ed. 231pp + pub's cat. VG (foxing). *Hayman*. $75/£48

WEISBERGER, R. WILLIAM. Speculative Free Masonry and the Enlightenment. Columbia Univ Press, 1994. 1st ed. Fine in Fine dj. *Bishop*. $45/£29

WEISEL, GEORGE (ed). Men and Trade on the Northwest Frontier as Shown by the Fort Owen Ledger. Missoula: MT State Univ, (1955). 1st ed. 7 plts, fldg map. VG. *Oregon*. $40/£26

WEISENBURGER, FRANCIS PHELPS. Idol of the West—The Fabulous Career of Rollin Mallory Duggett. Syracuse: Syracuse Univ Press, (1965). 1st ed. Fine in Fine dj. *Perier*. $30/£19

WEISS, T. The Catch. NY: Twayne Publ, (c 1951). 1st ed. Ink name, o/w Fine in dj (price-clipped). *Heller*. $35/£23

WEITENKAMPF, FRANK. The Illustrated Book. Cambridge: Harvard Univ, 1938. VG in dj (torn). *Argosy*. $50/£32

WEITZMANN, KURT. Late Antique and Early Christian Book Illumination. NY, (1977). 1st ptg. 48 color plts. Fine in dj (worn). *Artis*. $22/£14

WEITZMANN, KURT. The Miniatures of the Sacra Parallela. NJ: Princeton Univ, 1979. Dbl-pg color plt, 162 b/w plts. Dj (sl soiled). *Edwards*. $70/£45

WELCH, CHARLES. History of the Big Horn Basin. Salt Lake City, 1940. 1st ed. VG+. *Benchmark*. $150/£97

WELCH, CHARLES. History of the Monument. City Lands Committee of the Corp. of the City of London, 1893. 120pp, teg, 3 lg fldg illus. Pict grn cl (edges damp-stained), gilt. *Hollett*. $47/£30

WELCH, D'ALTE A. A Bibliography of American Children's Books Printed Prior to 1821. (N.p.): American Antiquarian Soc, 1972. Buckram. VG. *Argosy*. $175/£113

WELCH, DENTON. Maiden Voyage. NY: L.B. Fischer, 1945. 1st Amer ed, 1st bk. VG in dj (chipped, creased). *Reese*. $25/£16

WELCH, DENTON. A Voice through a Cloud. Lehmann, 1950. 1st ed. Sl dull, else Good in dj (sl worn). *Whiteson*. $28/£18

WELCH, DENTON. A Voice through a Cloud. John Lehmann, 1950. 1st ed. VG in dj (sl nicked). *Words Etc*. $39/£25

WELCH, JAMES. The Death of Jim Loney. NY: Harper, 1979. 1st ed. Fine in Fine dj. *Beasley*. $65/£42

WELCH, JEFFREY EGAN. Literature and Film. An Annotated Bibliography, 1909-1977. NY: Garland, 1981. VG. *Artis*. $17/£11

WELCH, STUART CARY et al. The Emperors' Album. NY: MOMA, 1987. 100 plts. Dj. *Edwards*. $70/£45

WELCH, WILLIAM. Bacteriology. Balt, 1920. 1st ed. *Fye*. $75/£48

WELCH, WILLIAM. A Great Physician and Medical Humanist: A Review of Harvey Cushing's Life of Sir William Osler. 1925. 1st ed. Good in wrappers. *Fye*. $60/£39

WELCH, WILLIAM. Papers and Addresses. Balt, 1920. 1st ed. 3 vols. Good. *Fye*. $300/£194

WELD, H.H. (ed). A Residence of Eleven Years in New Holland and the Caroline Islands. Boston, 1836. Inscribed. xviii,265pp, 2 plts. Brn cl (signs of old damp; discoloration). *Lewis*. $457/£295

WELD, ISAAC, JR. Travels through the States of North America and the Provinces of...Canada...1795, 1796 and 1797. London, 1799. 1st ed. 24,464pp (title, frontis repaired; corner torn preface pp), 14 plts (2 plts, erratum missing); 3 contemp maps laid in. 3/4 leather. *Heinoldt*. $250/£161

WELDON, FAY. ...And the Wife Ran Away. NY: David McKay, (1968). 1st Amer ed, 1st bk. Fine in dj (lt rubbed). *Hermitage*. $85/£55

WELDON, FAY. ...And the Wife Ran Away. NY: McKay, 1968. 1st US ed, 1st bk. Fine (lt bumped corner) in NF dj (short tears, sl spine wear). *Beasley*. $75/£48

WELDON, FAY. The Fat Woman's Joke. London: MacGibbon & Kee, 1967. 1st ed, 1st bk. Sl bumped, o/w VG in dj (sl rubbed). *Rees*. $101/£65

WELDON, JOHN LEE. The Naked Heart. NY: Farrar, Straus & Young, (1953). 1st ed. Fine in dj (sl worn). *Sadlon*. $20/£13

WELLARD, JAMES HOWARD. The Snake in the Grass. NY: Dodd Mead, 1942. 1st ed. Fine in dj (sl wear). *Mordida*. $65/£42

WELLER, JAC. Wellington in the Peninsula, 1808-1814. London, 1962. 1st ed. Frontis; 48 plts; fldg map at rear. VG in dj (sl torn w/sl loss). *Edwards*. $54/£35

Wellesley Papers: The Life and Correspondence of Richard Colley Wellesley.... London: Herbert Jenkins, 1914. 1st ed. 2 vols. Gilt-stamped cl; teg. Unopened. Spines sl dknd, o/w Fine. *Sadlon*. $30/£19

WELLESLEY, GORDON. Sex and the Occult. London: Souvenir, (1973). 1st ed. Fine in VG dj. *Blue Dragon*. $35/£23

WELLMAN, MANLY WADE. The Dark Destroyers. NY: Avalon, (1959). 1st ed. NF in dj (lt wear, soiled). *Antic Hay*. $25/£16

WELLMAN, MANLY WADE. Giant in Gray, A Biography of Wade Hampton of South Carolina. NY, (1949). 1st ed. VG+ in dj (tear on back). *Pratt*. $80/£52

WELLMAN, MANLY WADE. Giant in Gray: A Biography of Wade Hampton of South Carolina. NY: Scribner's, 1949. 1st ed. NF in NF dj. *Mcgowan*. $95/£61

WELLMAN, MANLY WADE. Giants from Eternity. NY: Avalon, (1959). 1st ed. NF in dj (lt edgewear; short tear, crease). *Antic Hay*. $45/£29

WELLMAN, MANLY WADE. Island in the Sky. NY: Avalon, (1961). 1st ed. NF in dj (lt wear). *Antic Hay*. $25/£16

WELLMAN, MANLY WADE. Island in the Sky. Avalon, 1961. 1st ed. Fine in dj. *Madle*. $45/£29

WELLMAN, MANLY WADE. The School of Darkness. GC: Doubleday, 1985. 1st ed. Fine in dj. *Bernard.* $20/£13

WELLMAN, MANLY WADE. Who Fears the Devil? Arkham House, 1963. 1st ed. Fine in dj. *Madle.* $200/£129

WELLMAN, PAUL. The Buckstones. NY: Trident, 1967. 1st ed. VF in Fine dj (spine lt sunned). *Hermitage.* $35/£23

WELLMAN, PAUL. Death in the Desert. NY: Macmillan, 1935. 1st ed. Fldg map. Tan cl. Dated sig, else VG in pict dj. *Chapel Hill.* $85/£55

WELLMAN, PAUL. A Dynasty of Western Outlaws. NY, 1967. 1st ed. Lt stained, dj lt worn, o/w Fine. *Pratt.* $40/£26

WELLMAN, WALTER. The Aerial Age. NY: A.R. Keller, 1911. 1st ed. VG (sl crease in spine, o/w clean). *Walcot.* $85/£55

WELLS, CALVIN. Bones, Bodies, and Disease. London: Thames & Hudson, (1964). Good in dj. *Archaeologia.* $55/£35

WELLS, CAROLYN. The Missing Link. Phila: Lippincott, 1938. 1st ed. Lt worn, else Fine in homemade acetate dj. *Murder.* $25/£16

WELLS, CAROLYN. Spooky Hollow. Phila: Lippincott, 1923. 1st ed. Worn, bumped. *Murder.* $25/£16

WELLS, CHARLES KNOX POLK. Life and Adventures of Polk Wells. (Halls, MO): G.A. Warnica, (1907). Black/gold-stamped cl. Fine. *Dawson.* $150/£97

WELLS, E.F.V. Lions Wild and Friendly. London: Cassell, 1933. 1st ed. VG. *Mikesh.* $35/£23

WELLS, EDWARD LAIGHT. Hampton and His Cavalry in '64. Richmond: Johnson, 1899. 1st ed. 429,(24)pp. 1/2 leather, marbled bds (sl worn). VG. Howes W 245. *Mcgowan.* $275/£177

WELLS, H. GIDEON. The Chemical Aspects of Immunity. NY, 1925. 1st ed. Good. *Fye.* $100/£65

WELLS, H.G. 28 Science Fiction Stories. (NY): Dover, (1952). 1st ed, review copy. VG. *Argosy.* $50/£32

WELLS, H.G. The Adventures of Tommy. NY: Frederick A. Stokes, 1929. 1st Amer ed. Pict color label on red linen on bds. Lt rubbing corners, spine; else Excellent. *Hobbyhorse.* $175/£113

WELLS, H.G. Ann Veronica. Harpers, 1909. 1st ed. VG in pict dj (torn, chipped). *Fine Books.* $125/£81

WELLS, H.G. The Atlantic Edition of the Works of H.G. Wells. NY: Scribner's, 1924-6. One of 1050 numbered sets (of 1670 signed sets). 28 vols. VG set (labels sl tanned, lt soiled; lt edgewear). *Reese.* $1,500/£968

WELLS, H.G. The Autocracy of Mr. Parham. London: Heinemann, 1930. 1st ed. 10 dbl-pg 1/2-tone plts. Fr cvr sl spotted, o/w Fine. *Temple.* $22/£14

WELLS, H.G. The Autocracy of Mr. Parham. London: Heinemann, 1930. 1st UK ed. VG in dj (worn, chipped). *Williams.* $37/£24

WELLS, H.G. The Brothers. NY: Viking, 1938. 1st Amer ed. VG in dj (nicks). *Houle.* $125/£81

WELLS, H.G. Brynhild. London: Methuen, 1937. 1st ed. Mottled lt brn cl. VF in dj (torn, sl chipped, internally reinforced w/white paper). *Temple.* $62/£40

WELLS, H.G. Christina Alberta's Father. NY, 1925. 1st Amer ed. Fine (sl edge crease fr cvr) in dj (spine heel sl chipped, rubbed; price-clipped). *Polyanthos.* $35/£23

WELLS, H.G. The Country of the Blind and Other Stories. Nelson, (1911). 1st ed. VG + . *Aronovitz.* $150/£97

WELLS, H.G. The Dream. Macmillan, 1924. 1st US ed. VG. *Madle.* $15/£10

WELLS, H.G. Floor Games. London: Frank Palmer, (1911). 1st British ed. Few pp sl soiled; extrems rubbed, else VG. *Between The Covers.* $225/£145

WELLS, H.G. The History of Mr. Polly. London: Thomas Nelson, (1910). 1st ed, 1st issue, w/the 'Trepanned' ad on penultimate leaf. Color frontis. VG (few leaves sl bumped, edges lt spotted; enamel title panel almost completely unchipped). *Ash.* $116/£75

WELLS, H.G. The Invisible Man. London: C. Arthur Pearson, 1897. 1st ed. Pub's gilt-lettered red cl, stamped in black on cvr (spines sunned; bkpl). *D & D.* $900/£581

WELLS, H.G. The Invisible Man. NY: LEC, 1967. 1/1500 numbered, signed by Charles Mozley (illus). VG in bd slipcase. *Argosy.* $75/£48

WELLS, H.G. The Island of Doctor Moreau. Stone & Kimball, 1896. 1st Amer ed. Photo laid in. Sl rubbing spine extrems; staining lower gutters 1st several pp, else VG. *Aronovitz.* $225/£145

WELLS, H.G. The Island of Doctor Moreau. NY: Stone & Kimball, 1896. 1st Amer ed. Sm 8vo. (viii),9-250,(2)pp: colophon on recto, verso blank. Teg, rest uncut. Black cl, gilt-blocked, ruled, lettering, leaf device, circular monogram (spine sl worn; fr inner hinge paper cracked). Title in red/black. Nice. *Cady.* $250/£161

WELLS, H.G. The Island of Doctor Moreau. London: Heinemann, 1896. 1st ed, 1st issue. Orig tan pict cl (chips head, foot spine). *Macdonnell.* $225/£145

WELLS, H.G. The Island of Doctor Moreau. London: William Heinemann, 1896. 1st ed. Pub's red/yellow cl, stamped in black/red (lt handling, else Fine). *D & D.* $1,200/£774

WELLS, H.G. The Island of Doctor Moreau. London: Heinemann, 1896. 1st UK ed. Ad in rear for Wells' The Time Machine followed by 32pg inserted cat w/pg 1 headed Donovan Pasha (unrecorded variant?). Spine dknd; dampstain upper corner rear cvr, o/w VG. *Bernard.* $250/£161

WELLS, H.G. The Island of Doctor Moreau. London: Heinemann, 1896. 1st UK ed. NF (lt mks). *Williams.* $853/£550

WELLS, H.G. The King Who Was a King. London: Ernest Benn, (1929). 1st ed. Prelims lt foxed, o/w VG in VG dj (spine chipped, dknd; 1-inch closed tear fr panel). *Hermitage.* $75/£48

WELLS, H.G. Kipps. London: Macmillan, 1905. 1st UK ed, ads to rear dated 10/10/05. VG (eps sl foxed; ink name). *Williams.* $23/£15

WELLS, H.G. Meanwhile: The Picture of a Lady. London: Ernest Benn Ltd, 1927. 1st ed. Brn buckram, gilt spine. Fine in dj (sl torn; verso strengthened w/brn paper). *Temple.* $70/£45

WELLS, H.G. Men Like Gods. London: Cassell, (1923). 1st ed. VG in dj (nicks). *Houle.* $375/£242

WELLS, H.G. Men Like Gods. Macmillan, 1923. 1st US ed. Fine in dj (lt chipped). *Madle.* $200/£129

WELLS, H.G. Mind at the End of Its Tether. London: Heinemann, 1945. 1st UK ed. VG in dj. *Williams.* $39/£25

WELLS, H.G. Mr. Bletsworthy on Rampole Island. Ernest Benn, 1928. 1st ed. Good (lt spotting) in dj (sl soiled; sm creases, slits at edges). *Bickersteth*. $85/£55

WELLS, H.G. Mr. Bletsworthy on Rampole Island. London: Benn, 1928. 1st UK ed. VG in William Orpen dj. *Williams*. $39/£25

WELLS, H.G. Mr. Britling Sees It Through. London: Cassell, 1916. 1st UK ed. VG in brn paper dj ptd in blue/orange (chipped, couple stains fr panel). *Williams*. $116/£75

WELLS, H.G. The New Machiavelli. NY: Duffield, 1910. 1st ed. Red cl (lt rubbed). VG. *Hermitage*. $45/£29

WELLS, H.G. The New World Order. London: Secker & Warburg, 1940. 1st ed. NF in tan cl, red-lettered spine. VG pict dj (soiled, chipped). *Vandoros*. $50/£32

WELLS, H.G. New Worlds for Old. London: Constable, 1908. 1st UK ed. VG (label on pastedown). *Williams*. $23/£15

WELLS, H.G. The Open Conspiracy. GC: Doubleday, Doran, 1928. 1st Amer ed. NF in dj (sl stained, chipped). *Hermitage*. $50/£32

WELLS, H.G. The Research Magnificent. London: Macmillan, 1915. 8pp pub's list advertising this title w/o reviews, dated 'c.15.8.15.' 1st issue; later copies w/o inserted ads. Grn cl. Fine. *Temple*. $28/£18

WELLS, H.G. The Sea Lady. Appleton, 1902. 1st Amer ed. Pict binding. Spine sl sunned, else VG +. *Aronovitz*. $95/£61

WELLS, H.G. The Sea Lady. Appleton, 1902. 1st US ed. VG. *Madle*. $250/£161

WELLS, H.G. The Secret Places of the Heart. London: Cassell, 1922. 1st UK ed. VG + in dj (browned, sl worn, short closed tears). *Williams*. $47/£30

WELLS, H.G. Select Conversations With An Uncle.... London/NY: John Lane/Merriam Co., 1895. 1st Amer ed, 1st issue binding. 195pp + (5)pp ads. Dec lt grn cl. VG +. *Chapel Hill*. $300/£194

WELLS, H.G. Select Conversations With An Uncle.... London/NY: John Lane/Merriam Co., 1895. 1st ed. 117pp + 16pp ads. Teg. Silver-grey cl. VG (bkpl, spine dkned). *Chapel Hill*. $350/£226

WELLS, H.G. The Soul of a Bishop. Cassell, (1917). 1st ed. Grn cl; blocked, lettered in blind. *Bickersteth*. $70/£45

WELLS, H.G. Star Begotten: A Biological Fantasia. London: C&W, 1937. 1st ed, 1st state w/gilt spine lettering on black cl. VG in VG illus dj (lt chipped). *Cahan*. $75/£48

WELLS, H.G. The Stolen Bacillus. Methuen, 1895. 1st ed. Dec cl. VG (sl wear). *Aronovitz*. $685/£442

WELLS, H.G. Tales of Space and Time. Doubleday & McClure, 1899. 1st Amer ed. Spine sl dknd; fr inner hinge starting, else VG-. *Aronovitz*. $135/£87

WELLS, H.G. Tono-Bungay. London: Macmillan, 1909. 1st ed, 2nd issue w/ads dated Feb 1909. (Joints rubbed; sl worn.) *Hermitage*. $25/£16

WELLS, H.G. Tono-Bungay. Leipzig: Tauchnitz, 1909. 1st thus. 2 vols. VG (stickers). *Agvent*. $75/£48

WELLS, H.G. The Undying Fire. Macmillan, 1919. 1st US ed. Adv rev copy w/pub's stamp. NF. *Madle*. $75/£48

WELLS, H.G. The War in the Air. London: Bell, 1908. 1st UK ed, 1st issue, in blue bds lettered in gold. Good (rubbed). *Williams*. $101/£65

WELLS, H.G. The War of the Worlds. London: Heinemann, 1898. 1st UK ed, w/16pp of ads dated 1897. VG (sl damp damage top corners of bds, some pp). *Williams*. $426/£275

WELLS, H.G. The War of the Worlds. London: William Heinemann, 1898. 1st ed, 2nd issue, w/white pastedown eps. Pub's gray cl. Generally VG (lt soiling; scattered foxing; offsetting to eps). *D & D*. $900/£581

WELLS, H.G. When the Sleeper Wakes. NY: Harper, 1899. 1st Amer ed. 15 illus (Eng ed has 3). Pict cl. NF (faint, scattered spotting to cl). *Antic Hay*. $125/£81

WELLS, H.G. When the Sleeper Wakes. NY/London: Harper, 1899. 1st Amer ed. 330pp + ads. Pict cl. NF. *Godot*. $175/£113

WELLS, H.G. When the Sleeper Wakes. Harpers, 1899. 1st ed. Spine sl lightened; lt foxing, else VG. *Aronovitz*. $285/£184

WELLS, H.G. The Wonderful Visit. Macmillan, 1895. 1st Amer ed. VG. *Aronovitz*. $225/£145

WELLS, H.G. The World of William Clissold. NY: George H. Doran, (1926). 1st Amer ed. 2 vols. Bkpls, else Fine in djs (sl chipped, faded). *Hermitage*. $50/£32

WELLS, H.G. The World of William Clissold. Ernest Benn, 1926. 1st ed. 3 vols. (Upper cvr vol 3 sl spotted.) Djs (all w/sm chips, edges torn; mks). *Bickersteth*. $78/£50

WELLS, H.G. You Can't Be Too Careful. London: Secker & Warburg, 1941. 1st ed. VF in dj (closed tear). *Temple*. $56/£36

WELLS, H.P. City Boys in the Woods or a Trapping Venture in Maine. London: Chapman & Hall, 1890. Beveled edges, gilt dec cvr (sl bumped, joint sl torn; tp sl foxed). *Petersfield*. $74/£48

WELLS, H.P. Fly-Rods and Fly-Tackle. NY: Harper, 1885. True 1st ed w/1885 on tp. 364pp + ads. Gilt pict grn binding. Fine. *Bowman*. $140/£90

WELLS, J. SOELBERG. A Treatise on the Diseases of the Eye. Phila, 1873. 2nd Amer ed. 800pp; 6 color chromolithos. Full leather. Good. *Fye*. $75/£48

WELLS, J.C. The Gateway to the Polynia. London: Henry, S. King, 1876. New ed. ix,3,355pp, map, fldg section of whaling vessel. Orig gilt cl. Good (spine worn, torn at head). *Walcot*. $93/£60

WELLS, PERCY A. and JOHN HOOPER. Modern Cabinet Work; Furniture and Fitments. London/NY: Batsford/John Lane, 1910. 1st ed, US issue. Sl foxing eps, prelims, else Fine. *Cahan*. $85/£55

WELLS, ROBERT. The Pastry Cook and Confectioner's Guide.... London: Crosby Lockwood, 1889. 1st ed. xv,(i),108pp, 4 ads; 40pp, 16pp pub's cat. (Fr hinge starting; grn cl bumped, rubbed, stained.) VG. *Blue Mountain*. $150/£97

WELLS, ROLLA. Episodes of My Life. St. Louis, 1933. 1st ed. Inscribed presentation. Bds, blue leather spine. Howes W 254. *Ginsberg*. $125/£81

WELLS, SAMUEL. Wedlock. NY, 1870. 1st ed. 236pp. Good. *Fye*. $65/£42

WELLS, WILLIAM CHARLES. An Essay on Dew, and Several Appearances Connected with It. London: Taylor & Hessey, 1814. 1st ed. 8vo. 16(ads),(4),146pp. Untrimmed. 2-tone bds (bumped; fr joint starting); paper spine label (rubbed). NF in NF 1/4 morocco fldg case. *Glaser*. $950/£613

WELLS, WILLIAM CHARLES. An Essay on Dew.... Ptd for Taylor & Hessey, 1814. 1st ed. 19th cent 1/2 blue calf gilt (sl rubbed), marbled sides, gilt edges. *Hill.* $310/£200

WELSH, PETER C. Track and Road: The American Trotting Horse. Washington, 1967. Dj (price-clipped). *Edwards.* $31/£20

WELTY, EUDORA. Acrobats in a Park. Northridge: Lord John Press, 1980. One of 300 numbered, signed. Cl, marbled paper-cvrd bds. Fine. *Between The Covers.* $175/£113

WELTY, EUDORA. Acrobats in a Park. Northridge: Lord John Press, 1980. Signed ltd ed of 300 numbered. Marbled bds. Fine, issued w/o dj. *Antic Hay.* $185/£119

WELTY, EUDORA. The Bride of the Innisfallen and Other Stories. NY: Harcourt, Brace, (1955). 1st ed, 2nd issue w/5 copyright dates, grn cl-backed bds, silver-titled. (Sl shelfworn, bumped.) Dj (lt used). *Hermitage.* $250/£161

WELTY, EUDORA. The Bride of the Innisfallen and Other Stories. NY, (1955). 1st ed, 2nd issue w/multiple copyright dates. Nice in dj (insect damage). *King.* $175/£113

WELTY, EUDORA. The Bride of the Innisfallen and Other Stories. London: Hamish Hamilton, 1955. 1st Eng ed. NF in VG dj (lt chipped). *Limestone.* $95/£61

WELTY, EUDORA. The Bride of the Innisfallen. H-B, 1955. 1st ed (1st issue w/1955 the only date on copyright pg). Fine in dj. *Fine Books.* $375/£242

WELTY, EUDORA. A Curtain of Green. NY: Doubleday, Doran, 1941. 1st ed, 1st ptg, 1st bk. Ed of 2476. Orange cl, stamped in grn/white. Fine (w/o dj). *Macdonnell.* $300/£194

WELTY, EUDORA. Delta Wedding. NY: Harcourt, Brace, (1946). 1st ed, 1st ptg. Cream cl stamped in purple. Fine in dj (lt used). *Macdonnell.* $175/£113

WELTY, EUDORA. The Eye of the Story. NY: Random House, (1977). One of 300 signed. Fine in slipcase. *Pharos.* $275/£177

WELTY, EUDORA. The Golden Apples. NY: Harcourt, Brace, (1949). 1st ed, 1st ptg. Fine in NF dj. *Macdonnell.* $175/£113

WELTY, EUDORA. The Golden Apples. NY: Harcourt, Brace, (1949). 1st ed. Signed. Grn bds, mauve cl spine. Fine in Fine pict dj. *Chapel Hill.* $350/£226

WELTY, EUDORA. The Golden Apples. London: Bodley Head, 1950. 1st ed. Bds bowed, o/w NF in dj. *Rees.* $101/£65

WELTY, EUDORA. The Golden Apples. London: Bodley Head, 1950. 1st Eng ed, 1st issue (brn cl). Rev copy, slip laid in. Fine in VG dj (sl chipped, dusty). *Limestone.* $150/£97

WELTY, EUDORA. Losing Battles. NY: Random House, (1970). 1st ed. Sl dust soiling, else NF in dj (spine sunned). *Chapel Hill.* $45/£29

WELTY, EUDORA. Losing Battles. NY: Random House, (1970). 1st trade ed. (Top edge lightened; dk spot cvr.) NF dj. *Sadlon.* $20/£13

WELTY, EUDORA. Losing Battles. NY: Random House, (1970). One of 300 numbered, signed. Grn buckram. VF in orig acetate & slipcase. *Pharos.* $350/£226

WELTY, EUDORA. Music from Spain. Greenville, MS: The Levee Press, 1948. 1st ed. #52/775, signed. 8vo. Salmon bds, paper spine label. Spine bumped, edges sl dknd, else Fine. *Chapel Hill.* $600/£387

WELTY, EUDORA. On Short Stories. NY: HB & Co, (1949). One of 1500. Fine in VG orig tissue dj (few long tears). *Between The Covers.* $200/£129

WELTY, EUDORA. One Time, One Place. NY: Random House, (1971). 1st ed, ltd to 300 numbered, specially bound, signed. Fine in pub's slipcase. *Godot.* $450/£290

WELTY, EUDORA. One Time, One Place. NY: Random House, (1971). 1st ed. Ink inscrip, else VG in dj (extrems lt worn, short tear, else VG). *Godot.* $125/£81

WELTY, EUDORA. One Time, One Place. NY: Random House, (1971). 1st trade ed. Signed on 1/2 title. Brn cl. Fine in dj. *Pharos.* $150/£97

WELTY, EUDORA. One Writer's Beginning. Cambridge: Harvard Univ Press, 1984. 1st ed. Signed. Fine in dj. *Antic Hay.* $175/£113

WELTY, EUDORA. The Optimist's Daughter. NY: Random House, 1972. 1st ed. Fine in Fine dj. *Pettler.* $50/£32

WELTY, EUDORA. Photographs. London/Jackson: Univ of MI Press, (1989). 1st ed. Ltd to 375 signed. As New in matching cl slipcase. *Jaffe.* $225/£145

WELTY, EUDORA. Place in Fiction. NY: House of Books, 1957. 1st ed. #189/300, signed. 8vo. Brn cl. Prospectus laid in. Fine in Fine tissue dj. *Chapel Hill.* $550/£355

WELTY, EUDORA. The Ponder Heart. NY: Harcourt, Brace, (1954). 1st ed. VG (top edges sunned, worn; bkpl) in dj. *Hermitage.* $85/£55

WELTY, EUDORA. The Ponder Heart. Harcourt, Brace, 1954. 1st ed. VF in VF dj (lt rubbed rear panel). *Fine Books.* $125/£81

WELTY, EUDORA. The Ponder Heart. NY: Harcourt Brace, 1954. 1st ed. Inscribed. NF (lt scuffed; sm sticker) in VG dj (chip; closed tear). *Revere.* $175/£113

WELTY, EUDORA. The Ponder Heart. London: Hamish Hamilton, 1954. 1st Eng ed. NF in dj. *Limestone.* $95/£61

WELTY, EUDORA. Retreat. Palaemon Press Ltd, (1981). One of 40, hors commerce, numbered i-xl. Dec bds. Fine. *Dermont.* $200/£129

WELTY, EUDORA. The Robber Bridegroom. NY: Doubleday, Doran, 1942. 1st ed, 1st ptg. Ed of 3490. Blue-grn cl stamped in pink/white. VF in dj (nicks). *Macdonnell.* $450/£290

WELTY, EUDORA. Selected Stories. NY: Modern Library, 1954. 1st Modern Library ed. NF in VG+ dj (sl nicked). *Limestone.* $145/£94

WELTY, EUDORA. The Wide Net and Other Stories. London: John Lane, The Bodley Head, (1945). 1st Eng ed. 8vo. Grn cl. Fine (sl foxing fore-edge) in Fine dj, ptd both sides. *Chapel Hill.* $500/£323

WELTY, EUDORA. Women! Make Turban in Own Home! (Winston-Salem): Palaemon, (1979). #12/200 numbered, signed. VF. *Pharos.* $150/£97

WENDORF, FRED. Archaeological Studies in the Petrified Forest National Monument. Flagstaff: Northern AZ Soc of Science & Art, 1953. VG in dj. *Schoyer.* $45/£29

WENDT, LLOYD and HERMAN KOGAN. Bet a Million! Indianapolis: Bobbs-Merrill, (1948). 1st ed. VG in dj (sl worn). *Lien.* $35/£23

WENKAM, ROBERT. Kauai and the Park Country of Hawaii. Kenneth Brower (ed). SF: Sierra Club, 1967. 1st ed. 2 maps (incl ep). Dj (chipped, creased, loss). *Edwards.* $62/£40

WENTWORTH, EDWARD NORRIS. America's Sheep Trails: History, Personalities. Ames: Iowa State Univ, 1948. 1st ed. VG+ (sl bumped). *Bohling.* $80/£52

WENTWORTH, MAY. Fairy Tales from Gold Lands. NY/SF: A. Roman, 1868. Frontis, 237pp. Gold-stamped cl (lt worn; cocked). *Dawson.* $50/£32

WENTWORTH, PATRICIA. The Case of William Smith. London: Hodder & Stoughton, 1950. 1st Eng ed. NF in VG+ dj. *Janus.* $45/£29

WENTWORTH, PATRICIA. Ladies' Bane. Phila: Lippincott, 1952. 1st ed. NF (lt bumps) in NF dj (lt wear). *Janus.* $45/£29

WEPPNER, MARGARETHA. The North Star and the Southern Cross. (Albany, NY): Published by Author, 1882. 1st ed. 2 vols. x,506; viii,504pp, 2 tinted litho frontispieces (1 double-pg). Black cl (soiled), gilt. *Karmiole.* $50/£32

WEPPNER, MARGARETHA. The North Star and the Southern Cross...A Two Years' Journey Round the World. London: by the author, 1876. 1st ed. 2 vols. Frontispieces. x,505; vii,504pp. Grn cl (lt rubbing). *Petrilla.* $40/£26

Wept of Wish Ton-Wish. (By James Fenimore Cooper.) Phila: Carey, Lea & Carey, 1829. 1st Amer ed, 1st ed under this title. 2 vols. 8vo. 251; 234pp. Blue-grey bds, paper spine labels. Good (lower half fr joint broken Vol 1; vertical crack spine Vol 2, chipped at ends, lacks most of paper label). BAL 3844 *Chapel Hill.* $550/£355

Wept of Wish Ton-Wish. (By James Fenimore Cooper.) Phila: Carey, Lea & Carey, 1829. 1st ed. 2 vols in 1. Contemp 3/4 brn calf, marbled bds, gilt (paper peeling from bds). BAL 3488. *Macdonnell.* $75/£48

WERFEL, FRANZ. Star of the Unborn. Viking, 1946. 1st ed. Fine in dj. *Madle.* $35/£23

WERNER, ALFRED. Pascin. NY: Abrams, (1959). 1st ed. 34 tipped-in color plts. Gilt rust cl. Good in dj (sl chipped). *Karmiole.* $75/£48

WERNER, ALICE. Myths and Legends of the Bantu. London: Harrap, 1933. 1st ed. VG in dj (stained). *Hollett.* $59/£38

WERNER, HERMAN. On the Western Frontier with the United States Cavalry Fifty Years Ago. N.p., (1934). 1st ed. Orig ptd wrappers. Howes W 259. *Ginsberg.* $50/£32

WERNER, HERMAN. On the Western Frontier with the United States Cavalry...Fifty Years Ago. Pub by author, (1934). Fine in stiff wraps. Howes W 259. *Perier.* $40/£26

WERNER, M.R. Brigham Young. Harcourt, Brace, (1925). 1st ed. Frontis; 15 plts. VG. *Oregon.* $40/£26

WERPER, BARTON. Tarzan and the Abominable Snowman. Gold Star, 1965. 1st ed. Fine in wraps. *Madle.* $35/£23

WERPER, BARTON. Tarzan and the Silver Globe. (Derby): Gold Star, (1964). 1st ed. VG+ in pict wrappers. *Other Worlds.* $25/£16

WERPER, BARTON. Tarzan and the Silver Globe. Gold Star, 1964. 1st ed. NF in wraps. *Madle.* $30/£19

WERPER, BARTON. Tarzan and the Snake People. (Derby): Gold Star, (1964). 1st ed. Heavy browning, soiling, else VG+ in pict wrappers. *Other Worlds.* $20/£13

WERSTEIN, IRVING. Kearny the Magnificent, The Story of General Philip Kearny, 1815-1862. NY, (1962). 1st ed. VG+ in VG+ dj. *Pratt.* $40/£26

WERTENBAKER, THOMAS J. The Planters of Colonial Virginia. Princeton: Princeton Univ Press, 1922. 1st ed. Brn bds, grn cl spine. VG. Howes W 260. *Chapel Hill.* $85/£55

WERTENBAKER, THOMAS J. Virginia under the Stuarts 1607-1688. Princeton: Princeton Univ Press, 1914. 1st ed. Teg; partly unopened. Dk red cl. VG (bkpl, abrasion fep). Howes W 261. *Chapel Hill.* $85/£55

WERTHAM, FREDRIC. Seduction of the Innocent. NY, 1954. VG. *Polyanthos.* $45/£29

WESCHER, HERTA. Collage. Robert E. Wolf (trans). NY: Abrams, (1979). 40 hand-tipped color plts. VG in dj. *Argosy.* $125/£81

WESCHER, PAUL. Jean Fouquet and His Time. NY, 1947. Numerous illus hors texte. Cl (sl faded). *Washton.* $35/£23

WESCOTT, GLENWAY. The Babe's Bed. Paris: Harrison, 1930. 1st ed, ltd to 375 numbered, signed. Partially unopened. Eps lt browned, else Fine in VG pub's slipcase. *Godot.* $250/£161

WESCOTT, GLENWAY. The Babe's Bed. Paris: Harrison of Paris, 1930. 1st ed. One of 375 signed. Red silk, gilt. Yellow pub's box (sl soiled). *Juvelis.* $450/£290

WESCOTT, GLENWAY. A Calendar of Saints for Unbelievers. NY, 1933. 1st Amer ed. Signed. Fine (name; sl rubbed) in dj (chipped, rubbed, price-clipped). *Polyanthos.* $35/£23

WESLEY, CHARLES HARRIS. The Collapse of the Confederacy. Washington, DC: Associated Publishers, 1937. 1st ed. NF. *Mcgowan.* $85/£55

WESLEY, JOHN. The Journal. Nehemiah Curnock (ed). Epworth Press, 1938. Bicentenary issue. 8 vols. Frontis ports. Djs (sl chipped; spines browned). *Edwards.* $349/£225

WESLEY, JOHN. The Letters. 1721-1791. John Telford (ed). Epworth Press, 1931. Standard ed. 8 vols. Frontis ports. (Lacks frontis vol 4; 1/2 title, fep detached; spine lt faded; eps lt spotted.) *Edwards.* $155/£100

WESLEY, MARY. The Camomile Lawn. Macmillan, 1984. 1st UK ed. Spine sl leaned, o/w NF in dj. *Sclanders.* $39/£25

WESLEY, MARY. Haphazard House. London: Dent, 1983. 1st UK ed. NF in dj. *Moorhouse.* $34/£22

WESLEY, MARY. Harnessing Peacocks. Macmillan, 1985. 1st UK ed. NF in dj. *Sclanders.* $23/£15

WESLEY, MARY. Harnessing Peacocks. London: Macmillan, 1985. 1st UK ed. NF in dj. *Lewton.* $39/£25

WESLEY, MARY. Not That Sort of Girl. Macmillan, 1987. 1st UK ed. VG in dj. *Lewton.* $28/£18

WEST, ANTHONY. The Crusades. NY: Random House, 1954. 1st trade ed. Carl Rose (illus). VG in dj. *Cattermole.* $30/£19

WEST, CHARLES. An Inquiry into the Pathological Importance of Ulceration of the Os Uteri. Phila, 1854. 1st Amer ed. 88pp. Good. *Fye.* $200/£129

WEST, HERBERT FAULKNER. The Mind on the Wing. NY: Coward McCann, (1947). 1st ed. Fine in VG dj. *Graf.* $25/£16

WEST, HERBERT FAULKNER. Notes from a Bookman. N.p.: Westholm Pub, 1968. Ltd to 399 numbered, signed. 3 sm sketches. Blue cl over dec bds, gilt spine. Good in dj (sl soiled). *Karmiole.* $50/£32

WEST, LUTHER. The Housefly. Ithaca, NY, 1951. 1st ed. *Fye.* $35/£23

WEST, NATHANAEL. The Ancestry, Life, and Times of Hon. Henry Hastings Sibley. St. Paul: Pioneer Press, 1889. 1st ed. Frontis, x,596pp, index, errata. Fine. *Oregon.* $75/£48

WEST, NATHANAEL. A Cool Million. NY: Covici Friede, (1934). 1st ed. Tan cl lt foxed, else VG in dj (edgeworn, creased, 1.5-inch chips top, bottom spine; folds splitting, archivally mended verso). *Godot.* $550/£355

WEST, NATHANAEL. A Cool Million. London: Neville Spearman, 1954. 1st Eng ed. NF (pp edges sl browned) in dj (sl dusty, nicked; spine, edges dknd). *Ulysses.* $70/£45

WEST, NATHANAEL. The Day of the Locust. NY: Random House, (1939). 1st ed. Orig red cl w/orange paper spine label. VG (sl cocked; sl soiled) in dj (tears). *Chapel Hill.* $650/£419

WEST, NATHANAEL. The Day of the Locust. London: Grey Walls Press, (1951). 1st Eng ed. Blue cl. Sig, else NF in dj (spine sunned). *Chapel Hill.* $150/£97

WEST, NATHANAEL. Miss Lonelyhearts. NY: Liveright, (1933). 1st ed. Tan cl (fading, wear). Good (w/o dj). *Macdonnell.* $200/£129

WEST, NATHANAEL. Miss Lonelyhearts. London: Grey Walls Press, 1949. 1st Eng ed. NF in dj (sl rubbed, dusty, nicked; spine sl dknd). *Ulysses.* $70/£45

WEST, NATHANAEL. Miss Lonelyhearts. Grey Walls Press, 1949. 1st Eng ed. VG+ in VG dj (sunning to spine, rear panel). *Fine Books.* $85/£55

WEST, NATHANAEL. Miss Lonelyhearts. London: Grey Walls Press, 1949. 1st UK ed. NF in VG dj (browned, worn). *Williams.* $116/£75

WEST, PAUL. The Pearl and the Pumpkin. NY: Dillingham, 1904. 1st ed. Lg 8vo. 240pp, 16 full-color plts by W.W. Denslow. Lt grn cl, pict onlay. Fine. *Davidson.* $400/£258

WEST, PAUL. The Women of Whitechapel and Jack the Ripper. NY, 1991. 1st Amer ed. Signed. Mint in Mint dj. *Polyanthos.* $35/£23

WEST, REBECCA. Arnold Bennett Himself. NY: John Day, 1931. 1st ed. VG (sunning, soiling; edge tears) in wraps. *Beasley.* $40/£26

WEST, REBECCA. The Birds Fall Down. London, 1966. 1st ed. Fine in dj. *Argosy.* $40/£26

WEST, REBECCA. Black Lamb and Grey Falcon. Viking, 1941. 1st ed. 2 vols. NF in NF dj and VG slipcase. *Bishop.* $27/£17

WEST, REBECCA. Black Lamb and Grey Falcon...Journey Through Yugoslavia in 1937. London, 1946. 2 vols. Djs (sl wear). *Lewis.* $37/£24

WEST, REBECCA. The Court and the Castle. New Haven, 1957. 1st ed. VG in dj. *King.* $35/£23

WEST, REBECCA. Harriet Hume. Doubleday, 1929. 1st ed. VG. *Madle.* $25/£16

WEST, REBECCA. A Letter to a Grandfather. London: Hogarth, 1933. 1st ed. Good (sl worn) in cream wraps (browned). *Second Life.* $45/£29

WEST, RICHARD S. Gideon Welles, Lincoln's Navy Department. Indianapolis, 1945. 1st ed. VG in dj (worn, chipped). *Pratt.* $35/£23

WEST, RICHARD S. Lincoln's Scapegoat General. Boston, 1965. 1st ed. VG in VG dj. *Pratt.* $35/£23

WEST, WALLACE. The Everlasting Exiles. Avalon, 1967. 1st ed. Fine in dj. *Madle.* $18/£12

WESTERMANN, WILLIAM LINN. Upon Slavery in Ptolemaic Egypt. NY: Columbia Univ Press, 1929. 1st ed. Frontis. Partly unopened. Sl rubbed, soiled, o/w VG. *Worldwide.* $45/£29

WESTERMARCK, EDWARD. The History of Human Marriage. London, 1894. 2nd ed. 644pp. Good. *Fye.* $100/£65

WESTERMARCK, EDWARD. Wit and Wisdom in Morocco. A Study of Native Proverbs. London: Routledge, 1930. 1st ed. Blue cl. VG. *House.* $50/£32

WESTERMEIER, CLIFFORD P. Who Rush to Glory. Caldwell, 1958. 1st ed. Dj chipped, o/w VG+. *Pratt.* $60/£39

Western Journey with Mr. Emerson. (By James Bradley Thayer.) Boston: Little Brown, 1884. 141pp. VG in ptd wrapper w/ptd dj (chipped, dknd, soiled), laid in fldg cl case. *Bohling.* $200/£129

Western Range. Letter from the Secretary of Agriculture.... Washington: GPO, 1936. 1st ed. VG in wraps. *Oregon.* $95/£61

Western Town. London: Kestrel, 1983. 15x22 cm. 3 pop-ups. Marvin Boggs & Borge Svensson. Glazed pict bds. VG. *Book Finders.* $40/£26

Westerners Brand Book 1960. Denver Posse. Boulder: Johnson Pub Co, (1961). 1st ed. Ltd to 500. VG in VG dj. *Oregon.* $45/£29

Westerners Brand Book 1974-1975. Denver: Westerners, (1977). 1st ed. Ltd to 525. VF in VF dj. *Oregon.* $45/£29

Westerners Brand Book, Los Angeles Corral. LA: Westerners, 1947. 1st ed. Ltd to 600. Fine. *Oregon.* $160/£103

Westerners Brand Book, Los Angeles Corral. 1949. LA: Westerners, (1950). 1st ed. Ltd to 400. Vol 3. Fldg facs, lg fldg map. Fine. *Oregon.* $190/£123

Westerners Brand Book. Los Angeles Corral. Brand Book #10. L.A., 1963. Ltd to 525. Pict cl. NF in dj (sl soiled). *Baade.* $90/£58

Westerners Brand Book. Los Angeles Corral. Brand Book #12. (1966.) 1st ed. Ltd to 500. Dec eps. Black cl. Fine. *Harrington.* $75/£48

Westerners Brand Book. Los Angeles Corral. Brand Book #12. L.A., 1966. Ltd to 500. Pict cl. Fine in glassine dj. *Baade.* $75/£48

Westerners Brand Book. Los Angeles Corral. Brand Book #13. (1969.) 1st ed. Tan cl. Fine in Fine dj. *Harrington.* $50/£32

Westerners Brand Book. Los Angeles Corral. Brand Book #13. L.A., 1969. NF in dj. *Baade.* $65/£42

Westerners Brand Book. Los Angeles Corral. Brand Book #14. L.A., 1974. Ltd to 500. Fine in dj. *Baade.* $65/£42

Westerners Brand Book. Los Angeles Corral. Brand Book #14. Doyce B. Nunis, Jr. (ed). (1974.) 1st ed. Ltd to 500. Pict eps. Black cl. Fine in Fine dj. *Harrington.* $50/£32

Westerners Brand Book. Los Angeles Corral. Brand Book #6. L.A., 1956. Ltd to 400. Pict cl, 1/4 leather. Fine in dj (lt soiled, partially faded). *Baade.* $95/£61

Westerners Brand Book. Los Angeles Corral. Brand Book #7. (1957.) 1st ed. Ltd to 475. Red morocco-backed grey cl, beveled bds. NF in VG+ dj. *Harrington.* $80/£52

Westerners Brand Book. Los Angeles Corral. Brand Book #8. L.A., 1959. Ltd to 525. Pict cl. Fine in dj. *Baade.* $90/£58

WESTLAKE, DONALD E. 361. NY: Random House, (1962). 1st Amer ed. Sl cocked, else NF in NF dj (lt rubbed). *Between The Covers.* $65/£42

WESTLAKE, DONALD E. Brothers Keepers. NY: Evans, 1975. 1st ed. Fine in dj (spine ends lt worn). *Janus.* $30/£19

WESTLAKE, DONALD E. The Busy Body. NY: Random House, 1966. 1st ed. NF in dj (price-clipped). *Janus.* $45/£29

WESTLAKE, DONALD E. Castle in the Air. NY: Evans, 1980. 1st ed. Fine in Fine dj. *Janus.* $30/£19

WESTLAKE, DONALD E. Enough. NY: Evans, 1977. 1st ed. Fine in NF dj. *Janus.* $30/£19

WESTLAKE, DONALD E. God Save the Mark. NY: Random House, 1967. 1st ed. Fine in NF dj (price-clipped). *Janus.* $45/£29

WESTLAKE, DONALD E. The Hot Rock. NY: S&S, 1970. 1st ed. NF in VG dj (worn). *Janus.* $25/£16

WESTLAKE, DONALD E. The Hot Rock. NY: S&S, 1970. 1st ed. VF in dj. *Mordida.* $85/£55

WESTLAKE, DONALD E. Kahawa. NY: Viking, 1982. 1st ed. Fine in Fine dj. *Janus.* $45/£29

WESTLAKE, DONALD E. Killy. Random, 1963. 1st ed. Lt edgewear, else NF in VG dj (sm rubbed spot, lt worn). *Murder.* $50/£32

WESTLAKE, DONALD E. The Spy in the Ointment. NY: Random House, 1966. 1st ed. NF (lt sunning bd edges) in dj. *Janus.* $35/£23

WESTMACOTT, MARY. (Pseud of Agatha Christie.) Absent in the Spring. London: Collins, 1944. 1st UK ed. VG + in dj. *Williams.* $147/£95

WESTMACOTT, MARY. (Pseud of Agatha Christie.) A Daughter's a Daughter. London: Heinemann, 1952. 1st UK ed. Pub's rev slip laid in. VG + in dj (repaired closed tears, related creasing repaired). *Williams.* $54/£35

WESTMACOTT, MARY. (Pseud of Agatha Christie). A Daughter's a Daughter. London: Heinemann, 1952. 1st UK ed. VG (ink inscrip) in dj (price-clipped). *Williams.* $70/£45

WESTMACOTT, MARY. (Pseud of Agatha Christie.) The Rose and the Yew Tree. NY: Rinehart, 1948. 1st US ed. Fine (label) in VG + dj (price-clipped). *Janus.* $75/£48

WESTON, EDWARD. 50 Photographs. NY: Duell Sloan & Pearce, 1947. 1st ed. One of 1500 initialed by Weston. 51 plts. Cl-backed heavy beveled bds. Fine in ptd dj (sl edgewear). *Cahan.* $1,000/£645

WESTON, EDWARD. The Daybooks of Edward Weston. Volume 1. Mexico. Nancy Newhall (ed). Rochester: George Eastman House, (1961). 1st ed. NF in dj (lt dustmarked). *Reese.* $125/£81

WESTON, EDWARD. The Flame of Recognition. Nancy Newhall (ed). Rochester: Aperture, (1965). 1st ed. VG in dj. *Argosy.* $60/£39

WESTON, EDWARD. Seeing California with Edward Weston. (CA): Westways/Auto Club of Southern CA, (1939). 1st ed. Pict paper-cvrd bds. Text VG. (Bds bumped at extrems, lt edge-worn.) *Godot.* $375/£242

WESTWOOD, H.R. Modern Caricaturists. London, 1932. (Sl browning; cl worn, rubbed.) *Edwards.* $54/£35

WESTWOOD, T. Berries and Blossoms; A Verse-Book for Young People. London: Darton & Co, 1855. 1st ed. Color frontis, color tp,(xiii),141pp. Blocked in blind, gilt (rebacked, old eps preserved). *Bickersteth.* $56/£36

WETHEY, H.E. El Greco and His School. Princeton, 1962. 2 vols. Good in djs. *Washton.* $275/£177

WETHEY, H.E. The Paintings of Titian. Complete Edition. London: Phaidon, 1969/71. 3 vols. (Vol 3 rebound; sl kink to plts toward end vol 3.) Djs (dj to vol 3 torn, repaired). *Ars Artis.* $1,163/£750

WETMORE, ALPHONSO. Gazetteer of the State of Missouri. St. Louis: C. Keemle, 1837. Engr frontis, (5),x-xvi,(17)-382pp; map (wrinkled, repaired). Orig cl (worn, faded), ptd spine label (dknd, chipped). (Foxing.) Howes W 296. *Bohling.* $500/£323

WETMORE, HELEN CODY. Last of the Great Scouts. Duluth Press, (1899). 2nd ptg. Frontis; xiv,296pp; 15 plts. Blindstamped cvr. VG. Howes W 297. *Oregon.* $45/£29

WEYGANDT, CORNELIUS. The Dutch Country. NY, 1939. 1st ed. VF in dj (worn). *Bond.* $25/£16

WEYGANDT, CORNELIUS. The Plenty of Pennsylvania. NY, 1942. 1st ed. VF in dj (sl damaged). *Bond.* $30/£19

WEYGANDT, CORNELIUS. The Red Hills. Phila, 1929. 1st ed. VF. *Bond.* $35/£23

WEYMOUTH, A. Through the Leper Squint. London: Selwyn & Blount, n.d. (1938). (Lt spotting.) *White.* $19/£12

WHALLEY, JOYCE IRENE. The Art of Calligraphy. London, 1980. Dj. *Edwards.* $56/£36

WHARFIELD, HAROLD B. With Scouts and Cavalry at Fort Apache. John A. Carroll (ed). Tucson: AZ Pioneers' Hist Soc., 1965. Inscribed by Carroll. Blue cl. VG + . *Bohling.* $60/£39

WHARTON, ANNE. Heirlooms in Miniature. Phila: Lippincott, 1898. VG + . *Bishop.* $38/£25

WHARTON, EDITH (ed). The Book of the Homeless. Scribners, 1916. 1st ed. Sl wear to tips, else NF. *Fine Books.* $95/£61

WHARTON, EDITH and OGDEN CODMAN. The Decoration of Houses. NY, 1902. 56 plts. (Sl rubbed, spotted; upper hinge cracking.) *Argosy.* $125/£81

WHARTON, EDITH. The Age of Innocence. NY: D. Appleton, 1920. 1st ed, 1st issue, with the'(1)' on p365; p186 line 7 reading 'Forasmuch as it hath please Almighty God—,' (later changed to 'Dearly beloved, we are gathered together here—,'). Pub's black-stamped red cl (sm snag head of spine, else Fine). In orig cream dj, priced '$2.00' (lt soiling; lt fraying, rumpling along edges; chipping to spine head, affecting one letter; 1 1/2-inch piece lacking from base of spine containing the wording for the pub). *D & D.* $2,000/£1,290

WHARTON, EDITH. The Age of Innocence. (NY/London: Appleton), 1920. 1st ed, 3rd issue w/tiny #3 under last line of text. VG (ink name). *Williams.* $47/£30

WHARTON, EDITH. The Age of Innocence. NY: LEC, 1973. One of 2000 numbered, signed by Lawrence Beall Smith (illus). Fine in pub's slipcase. *Hermitage.* $125/£81

WHARTON, EDITH. Artemis to Actaeon and Other Verse. NY: Scribner's, 1909. 1st ed. Dk grn cl stamped in gilt; teg. Contemp ink inscrip dated Oct 1909; sl wear, else NF. *Juvelis.* $250/£161

WHARTON, EDITH. A Backward Glance. NY: D. Appleton-Century, 1934. 1st ed. Blue cl stamped in gold. VG (sl wear) in ptd lt grn dj (chipping; lacks 1/4-inch spine head; dkng). *Juvelis.* $275/£177

WHARTON, EDITH. The Buccaneers. NY: D. Appleton-Century, 1938. 1st Amer ed. NF (eps lt foxed; faint spotting on bds) in NF dj (lt rubbed). *Between The Covers.* $400/£258

WHARTON, EDITH. The Buccaneers. Appleton-Century, 1938. 1st ed. Fine in VG + dj (spine head sl worn). *Fine Books.* $150/£97

WHARTON, EDITH. The Buccaneers. NY: D. Appleton Century, 1938. 1st ed. Navy blue cl gilt. Fine (2 sl scratches cvr) in dj (edgewear). *Juvelis.* $450/£290

WHARTON, EDITH. Crucial Instances. NY: Scribner's, 1901. 1st ed. Binding A. Grayish olive-grn paper-cvrd bds. Ink inscrip; spine chipped, sl loss of spine lettering; fr hinge tender, else Good + . *Godot.* $45/£29

WHARTON, EDITH. The Custom of the Country. NY: Scribner's, 1913. 1st Amer ed. NF (spine sl faded; corners sl rubbed; lacks dj). *Between The Covers.* $125/£81

WHARTON, EDITH. The Custom of the Country. NY: Scribner's, 1913. 1st ed. 12mo. Red cl, gilt. (Ink sig, date.) Orig dj (1/2-inch chip spine, piece missing back panel). *Juvelis.* $1,500/£968

WHARTON, EDITH. Ethan Frome. NY: Scribner's, 1911. 1st ed, 1st issue. Red cl, gilt (lt wear). *Shasky.* $50/£32

WHARTON, EDITH. Ethan Frome. (NY): LEC, 1939. One of 1500 numbered, signed by Henry Varnum Poor (illus). Fine (bkpl) in slipcase (lt worn). *Between The Covers.* $150/£97

WHARTON, EDITH. French Ways and Their Meaning. NY: Appleton, 1919. 1st ed, 1st ptg. Grn pict cl, gilt. Fine. *Macdonnell.* $75/£48

WHARTON, EDITH. The Fruit of the Tree. NY: Scribner's, 1907. 1st ed, binding B. Red cl stamped in gold. Spine evenly faded, else VG. *Godot.* $45/£29

WHARTON, EDITH. The Gods Arrive. NY: Appleton, 1932. 1st ed. Fine in dj (lt wear, sm chips spine corners). *Else Fine.* $185/£119

WHARTON, EDITH. The Greater Inclination. NY: Scribner's, 1899. 1st ed. Fair (loss spine extrems; spine edges rubbed). *Between The Covers.* $100/£65

WHARTON, EDITH. The House of Mirth. NY: LEC, 1975. One of 1500 numbered, signed by Lily Harmon (illus). Fine in slipcase. *Hermitage.* $85/£55

WHARTON, EDITH. Hudson River Bracketed. NY: Appleton, 1929. 1st ed. (Sl dusty.) Dj (chipped; lacks word Hudson on spine front). *Second Life.* $150/£97

WHARTON, EDITH. Human Nature. NY: D. Appleton, 1933. 1st Amer ed. Offsetting eps, else Fine in VG dj (chip; couple tiny tears). *Between The Covers.* $450/£290

WHARTON, EDITH. Italian Villas and Their Gardens. Century, 1904. 1st ed. Maxfield Parrish (illus). VG + . *Fine Books.* $325/£210

WHARTON, EDITH. Italian Villas and Their Gardens. NY: Century, 1910. Teg; uncut. Maxfield Parrish (illus). Gilt-dec pict cl. Hinges cracked; spine ends sl worn, else Fine. *Quest.* $195/£126

WHARTON, EDITH. Madame de Treymes. NY: Scribner's, 1907. 1st ed. (Lt rubbed.) *Sadlon.* $45/£29

WHARTON, EDITH. The Mother's Recompense. NY: Appleton, 1925. 1st ed, 1st ptg. Maroon cl, gilt. Heavy erasure fep, else VF in Nice dj (spine evenly sunned). *Macdonnell.* $200/£129

WHARTON, EDITH. The Mother's Recompense. Appleton, 1925. 1st ed. NF in NF dj (sm chip rear panel). *Fine Books.* $85/£55

WHARTON, EDITH. The Old Maid. NY: D. Appleton, 1924. 1st Amer ed. Fine in NF dj (lt sunned; sl nicks). *Between The Covers.* $200/£129

WHARTON, EDITH. Old New York: False Dawn. NY: D. Appleton, 1924. 1st ed. Prelims lt foxed, o/w Fine. *Hermitage.* $40/£26

WHARTON, EDITH. Old New York: New Year's Day. NY: D. Appleton, 1924. 1st ed. VG (3 pin holes fr hinge, 1 affecting paper spine label). *Hermitage.* $30/£19

WHARTON, EDITH. The Reef. Appleton, 1912. 1st ed. VG. *Whiteson.* $37/£24

WHARTON, EDITH. Sanctuary. London: Macmillan, 1903. 1st Eng ed, presumed 1st issue. iv,212pp + ads. Red cl. VG. *Godot.* $85/£55

WHARTON, EDITH. Summer. NY: D. Appleton, 1917. 1st ed. Dk red cl, gold-stamped title. Very Nice (spine sl skewed; lacks dj). *Hermitage.* $100/£65

WHARTON, EDITH. Tales of Men and Ghosts. NY: Scribner's, 1910. 1st ed. Teg. Name; lt spot fr cvr, o/w VG + . *Bernard.* $175/£113

WHARTON, EDITH. The Touchstone. NY: Scribner's, 1900. 1st ed. Teg. Lt foxing, upper joint cracked, closed at earlier date, else Good. *Reese.* $60/£39

WHARTON, EDITH. The Valley of Decision. NY: Scribner's, 1902. 1st ed, 2nd ptg (by Manhattan Press; 1st issue by Merrymount Press). 2 vols. Red cl, gold-stamped; teg. Sm soil mks spines, else NF set. *Godot.* $50/£32

WHARTON, HENRY E. and R. FARQUHAR CURTIS. The Practice of Surgery.... Phila: Lippincott, 1899. Rev ed. 1242pp. Orig sheep (worn; stain). *Goodrich.* $125/£81

WHARTON, WILLIAM H. Thrilling Tales of the Frozen North. Phila: John E. Potter, 1894. 1st ed. 718pp. Dec lt blue cl. VG-. *Blue Dragon.* $30/£19

WHARTON, WILLIAM. Birdy. London: Cape, 1978. 1st UK ed. Fine in dj (price-clipped). *Williams.* $23/£15

WHARTON, WILLIAM. Birdy. NY: Knopf, 1979. 1st ed, 1st bk. Fine in dj. *Reese.* $35/£23

WHEAT, CARL I. Books of the California Gold Rush. SF: Colt Press, 1949. One of 500. 5 plts. Ptd bds, cl spine, ptd label (sl edgeworn). VG. *Bohling.* $275/£177

WHEAT, CARL I. Books of the California Gold Rush: A Centennial Selection. SF: Colt Press, 1949. One of 500. Dec ptd bds w/cl spine, paper spine label. *Dawson.* $200/£129

WHEATLEY, DENNIS. Dangerous Inheritance. London: Hutchinson, (1965). 1st ed. Fine in NF dj. *Antic Hay.* $25/£16

WHEATLEY, DENNIS. Dangerous Measures. London, 1974. 1st ed. Fine in dj. *Madle.* $40/£26

WHEATLEY, DENNIS. Evil in a Mask. London, 1969. 1st ed. Fine in dj (sl frayed). *Madle.* $30/£19

WHEATLEY, DENNIS. The Forbidden Territory. London: Hutchinson, 1933. 1st UK ed. 1st bk. VG- (bds sl mkd, warped). *Williams.* $54/£35

WHEATLEY, DENNIS. Mayhem in Greece. London, 1962. 1st ed. Fine in dj (frayed; torn). *Madle.* $30/£19

WHEATLEY, DENNIS. Saturdays with Bricks. London: Hutchinson, 1961. 1st UK ed. NF in dj (sl rubbed, chipped, closed tears). *Williams.* $47/£30

WHEATLEY, DENNIS. Strange Conflict. London: Hutchinson, 1941. 1st UK ed. NF (ink name, spine sl faded) in VG dj (price-clipped). *Williams*. $116/£75

WHEATLEY, DENNIS. Vendetta in Spain. London, 1961. 1st ed. Fine in dj (sl frayed). *Madle*. $30/£19

WHEATLEY, DENNIS. The Wanton Princess. London, 1966. 1st ed. Fine in dj. *Madle*. $40/£26

WHEATLEY, HENRY B. Round about Piccadilly and Pall Mall. London: Smith, Elder, 1870. 1st ed. Frontis, xii,405pp. Pict cl (backstrip faded), gilt. *Cox*. $31/£20

WHEATLEY, HEWITT. The Rod and Line. London: Longman, 1849. 1st ed. 9 hand-colored plts. Blind-stamped brn cl. Nick to backstrip, o/w Fine. *Petersfield*. $248/£160

WHEATLEY, RICHARD. Cathedrals and Abbeys in Great Britain and Ireland. NY: Harper, 1890. 1st ed. 44 plts (31 dbl-pg steel engrs). (Text lt yellowed; smudges, sm stain later leaves; prelims foxed; stained, worn.) *Bookpress*. $110/£71

WHEATLY, SARAH. The Christmas Fire-Side. London: Longman et al, 1806. 12mo. xii+189+2pp ads, full-pg copper engr frontis. Full calf, red label w/gilt title. Fine (ink dedication, sigs; corners lt bumped; sl crack top of spine). *Hobbyhorse*. $175/£113

WHEELER, GEORGE AUGUSTUS. Castine, Past and Present. Boston, 1896. 12mo. 112pp; 2 fldg maps. Ex-lib. *Argosy*. $100/£65

WHEELER, HOMER W. Buffalo Days. Indianapolis: Bobbs-Merrill, (1925). Good (wear). Howes W 322. *Lien*. $45/£29

WHEELER, JOHN H. Historical Sketches of North Carolina from 1584 to 1851. NY: Frederick H. Hitchcock, 1925. Rpt of 1851. 2 vols in 1. Eps foxed, else VG. *Cahan*. $45/£29

WHEELER, MONROE (ed). Modern Painters and Sculptors as Illustrators. NY: MOMA, (1936). 1st ed. One of 2500. VG in dj. *Second Life*. $45/£29

WHEELER, MONROE. Modern Painters and Sculptors as Illustrators. NY: MOMA, (1936). 1st ed. Compliments card laid in. Grey pict cl over bds, maroon spine. Fine in dj (sl browned). *Juvelis*. $90/£58

WHEELER, OLIN D. The Trail of Lewis and Clark 1804-1904. NY: Putnams, 1904. 1st ed. 2 vols. Ink name, else NF set. Howes W 325. *Perier*. $295/£190

WHEELER, R. The Bloody Battle for Suribachi. NY, 1965. (Ex-lib.) *Clark*. $24/£15

WHEELER, R.E.M. Prehistoric and Roman Wales. OUP, 1925. 1st ed. Frontis, 113 maps. (Sl faded.) *Edwards*. $43/£28

WHEELER, RICHARD. Sherman's March. NY, (1978). 1st ed. Fine in Fine dj. *Pratt*. $30/£19

WHEELER, W.A. An Explanatory and Pronouncing Dictionary of the Noted Names of Fiction.... Ticknor & Fields, 1866. 2nd ed, rev. Spine head sm tear, else VG. *Fine Books*. $75/£48

WHEELER, W.M. The Social Insects, Their Origin and Evolution. London, 1928. 48 plts. Fine in dj. *Henly*. $43/£28

WHEELER-HOLOHAN, V. (ed.) Boutell's Manual of Heraldry. London/NY: Frederick Warne, 1931. 1st ed as such. Color frontis, 31 plts. NF (sm dampstains). *Cahan*. $50/£32

WHEELOCK, JULIA S. The Boys in White. NY, 1870. 1st ed. 274pp. Gilt pict cl (hinges broken). *Argosy*. $50/£32

Wheels and Whims. (By Florine Thayer McCray & Esther Louise Smith.) Boston: Cupple & Upham, 1884. 1st ed. 288pp. VG (stamped cl sl soiled). *Second Life*. $75/£48

WHELAN, R. The Flying Tigers. NY, 1942. VG in Good dj. *Clark*. $27/£17

WHELEN, TOWNSEND. The American Rifle. NY: Century, 1920. VG. *Bowman*. $60/£39

WHELPLEY, G.F. General Letter Engraving for Watchmakers, Jewellers, and Kindred Trades. Chicago: Hazlitt, 1892. 111pp+15pp ads. Good. *Moss*. $62/£40

When the Circus Comes to Town. Racine: Whitman, (ca 1930). Oblong, 4to. 5 full color panels joined w/cl hinges form 2-sided panorama (lt rubbing; minor wear). *Reisler*. $150/£97

Where Men Only Dare to Go! (By Royal W. Figg.) Richmond: Whittet & Shepperson, 1885. 1st ed. Multiple-port frontis, 263pp. Gilt-stamped brn cl. NF. *Chapel Hill*. $400/£258

WHIFFEN, EDWIN THOMAS. Outing Lore. NY, 1928. 1st ed. Gilt cl. VG. *Artis*. $20/£13

WHINNEY, M.D. The Interrelation of the Fine Arts in England in the Early Middle Ages. London, 1930. 24 illus on plts. Good (text sl foxed). *Washton*. $40/£26

WHIPPLE, A.B.C. The Mysterious Voyage of Captain Kidd. NY: Random House, 1970. 1st trade ed. H.B. Vestal (illus). Pict cl cvr. *Cattermole*. $100/£65

WHISTLER, JAMES McNEILL. The Gentle Art of Making Enemies. London: Heinemann, 1890. 1st ed. #31/250 on lg paper. 292pp, uncut. Orig ochre cl-backed buff bds (rubbed, sl soiled; corners bumped). Interior Fine. *Europa*. $132/£85

WHISTLER, JAMES McNEILL. The Gentle Art of Making Enemies. NY: Frederick Stokes & Brother, 1890. 1st unauthorized Amer ed. Sm 8vo. Uncut, w/the 2 pp ads in rear. Gray paper wraps ptd in red. Cl folder; 1/2 red morocco slipcase, gilt. *D & D*. $395/£255

WHISTLER, JAMES McNEILL. The Gentle Art of Making Enemies. NY: Lovell, 1890. Ltd ed. One of 100 for Amer, autographed by Whistler w/his butterfly monogram. Newly bound in 3/4 blue morocco. VG. *Argosy*. $850/£548

WHISTLER, JAMES McNEILL. Ten O'Clock. Portland, ME, 1925. 2nd ed. One of 450. Frontis port, 1 fldg illus. Uncut hand-made paper. (Lower hinge sl cracked; joint heads splitting.) *Edwards*. $47/£30

WHISTLER, LAURENCE and RONALD FULLER. The Work of Rex Whistler. London: Batsford, 1960. 1st ed. 116 collotype repros, 36 letter press repros; dec eps (2 bkpls tipped in w/lt offsetting; lt browning); 4 Whistler djs (chipped, worn) loosely inserted. Dj (sl worn, soiled, sl loss). *Edwards*. $388/£250

WHISTLER, LAURENCE. The English Festivals. London: Heinemann, 1947. 1st ed. Pict cl. Offset eps, else Fine in dj (shelfworn, internally mended tears). *Reese*. $45/£29

WHISTLER, LAURENCE. The Engraved Glass of Laurence Whistler. London: Cupid Press, 1952. 1st ed. Ltd to 550 signed. 82 plts. Gilt-emb cl. 1st leaves foxed, o/w VG. *Cahan*. $100/£65

WHISTLER, LAURENCE. Sir John Vanbrugh, Architect and Dramatist, 1664-1726. London: Cobden-Sanderson, 1938. 1st ed. Frontis; 14 plts. Eps sl foxed; cvr lt worn, else Fine. *Bookpress*. $120/£77

WHITAKER, ARTHUR P. The Mississippi Question 1795-1803. NY/London: D. Appleton, (1934). 1st ed. Fldg map. Blue cl. VG. *Chapel Hill*. $50/£32

WHITAKER, CHARLES HARRIS and HARTLEY BURR ALEXANDER. The Architectural Sculpture of the State Capitol at Lincoln, Nebraska. NY: Press of Amer Inst of Architects, 1926. 1st ed. 46 photo plts. Beige cl over blue bds, paper cvr label. Good. *Karmiole*. $60/£39

WHITAKER, FESS. History of Corporal Fess Whitaker. (Louisville, 1918.) Grn cl, gilt title. VG. *Bohling*. $75/£48

WHITAKER, ROGERS E.M. and ANTHONY HISS. All Aboard with E.M. Frimbo: World's Greatest Railroad Buff. NY: Grossman (Viking), 1974. 1st ed. Very Nice in dj (price-clipped). *Cady*. $25/£16

WHITAKER, W. The Geology of London and of Part of the Thames Valley. London, 1889. 2 vols. iii,352; xi,556pp (feps lt browned; ex-lib w/labels). Blind emb cl, gilt armorial (spines chipped, joints splitting). *Edwards*. $116/£75

WHITE, A. A Bibliography of Gilbert White, the Naturalist and Antiquarian of Selborne.... Halton, 1934. Good. *Moss*. $62/£40

WHITE, ALMA. The Story of My Life. Zarephath, NJ, 1919. 1st ed. Vol 1 only. Orig cl. NF. *Mcgowan*. $45/£29

WHITE, ANNE TERRY. Prehistoric America. NY: Random House, 1951. Stated 1st ptg trade. Aldren Watson (illus). Dec eps. VG in dj. *Cattermole*. $20/£13

WHITE, ANNE TERRY. Will Shakespeare and the Globe Theater. NY: Random House, 1955. 1st trade ed. C. Walter Hodges (illus). VG in dj. *Cattermole*. $20/£13

WHITE, BENJAMIN. Silver. London, 1917. 1st ed. *Edwards*. $140/£90

WHITE, C. The Flower Drawings of Jan van Huysum. Leigh on Sea: Lewis, 1964. 64 plts. Sound. *Ars Artis*. $54/£35

WHITE, CHARLES. An Account of the Regular Gradation in Man, and in Different Animals and Vegetables. London, 1799. 1st ed. 4to. 4 engr plts (3 fldg). 1/2 calf (joints mended); uncut. Fine. *Argosy*. $750/£484

WHITE, CHARLES. Cases in Surgery, with Remarks. Part the First (all published)...to which is added, An Essay on the Ligature of Arteries, by J. Aiken. London, 1770. 1st ed. 8vo. xv,198,(4)pp (title lt browned); 7 fldg engr plts. Contemp calf (sm slits upper hinge; sl bruised); spine banded, red morocco lettering piece. VG. *Hemlock*. $875/£565

WHITE, CHRISTOPHER. Rembrandt as an Etcher. London, 1969. Good in dj. *Washton*. $175/£113

WHITE, DAVID and RICHARD AVERSON. The Celluloid Weapon; Social Comment in the American Film. Boston: Beacon, (1972). VG in dj. *Artis*. $16/£10

WHITE, E.B. Charlotte's Web. NY: Harper, (1952). 1st ed. 8vo. VF in dj. *Jaffe*. $650/£419

WHITE, E.B. Charlotte's Web. NY: Harper, 1952. 1st ed. Garth Williams (illus). Sm 8vo. Pict cl. VG. *Book Adoption*. $80/£52

WHITE, E.B. Charlotte's Web. NY: Harper, 1952. 1st ed. Garth Williams (illus). 5.5x8.25. 182pp. Cl. Fine in dj. *Cattermole*. $250/£161

WHITE, E.B. Letters of E.B. White. Dorothy Lubrano Guth (ed). NY: Harper & Row, (1976). 1st ed. Blue cl. Rmdr mk bottom edge, else NF in VG dj. *Chapel Hill*. $30/£19

WHITE, E.B. One Man's Meat. NY: Harper, (1942). 1st ed. Grn cl. Extrems sl worn, else VG in dj (short edge tears, 6 external tape repairs, else VG). *Godot*. $85/£55

WHITE, E.B. The Second Tree from the Corner. NY, (1954). 1st ed, review copy. VG in dj. *Argosy*. $85/£55

WHITE, E.B. Stuart Little. NY: Harper, (1945). 1st ed. 8vo. Pict cl. VF in dj. *Jaffe*. $500/£323

WHITE, E.B. Stuart Little. NY: Harper, 1945. 1st ed. Garth Williams (illus). Sm 8vo. Pict cl. VG. *Book Adoption*. $50/£32

WHITE, E.B. Stuart Little. NY: Harper, 1945. 1st ed. Garth Williams (illus). 5.5x8.25. 131pp. Cl. VG in dj. *Cattermole*. $150/£97

WHITE, EDMUND. The Beautiful Room Is Empty. London, 1988. 1st ed. Signed presentation. Fine in Fine dj. *Polyanthos*. $35/£23

WHITE, EDMUND. States of Desire. NY, 1980. 1st Amer ed. Signed. Fine in dj (spine heel sl rubbed). *Polyanthos*. $30/£19

WHITE, EDWARD LUCAS. Lukundoo. Doran, 1927. 1st ed. VG. *Madle*. $50/£32

WHITE, ERIC WALTER. Stravinsky's Sacrifice to Apollo. Hogarth Press, 1930. 1st ed. VG in dj. *Words Etc*. $54/£35

WHITE, ERIC WALTER. Stravinsky's Sacrifice to Apollo. London: Hogarth Press, 1930. 1st ed. One of 1000 ptd. VF in dj. *Temple*. $70/£45

WHITE, ERIC WALTER. Walking Shadows. Hogarth Press, 1931. 1st ed. Dec bds. Contents Good (sl dull; spine worn). *Whiteson*. $62/£40

WHITE, ERIC WALTER. Walking Shadows. Hogarth Press, 1931. 1st ed. Spine chipped, worn; bds sl browned, o/w VG. *Words Etc*. $93/£60

WHITE, ERNEST WILLIAM. Cameos from the Silver-Land. London: John Van Voorst, 1881. 2 vols. Map. (Foxed throughout.) *Petersfield*. $65/£42

WHITE, ETHEL LINA. Some Must Watch. NY: Harper, (1941). 1st Amer ed. Corner of half-title lacks sm piece, else Fine in dj. *Godot*. $125/£81

WHITE, FREDERICK. The Spicklefisherman and Others. NY: Derrydale, 1928. Ltd to 775. Spine darkened, yet VG. *Mcgowan*. $250/£161

WHITE, GEORGE S. Memoir of Samuel Slater, the Father of American Manufactures. Phila: Ptd at No. 46, Carpenter Street, 1836. 2nd ed. Frontis port, 448pp; 19 plts. VG (ex-lib). *Cahan*. $75/£48

WHITE, GEORGE S. Memoir of Samuel Slater.... Phila, 1836. (Cl worn, sl foxed throughout; plts Fine.) *Argosy*. $150/£97

WHITE, GILBERT. The Natural History and Antiquities of Selborne. London, 1911. 24 color plts. Gilt illus upper bd (feps lt browned; spine chipped, sm tear; ex-libris). *Edwards*. $47/£30

WHITE, GILBERT. The Natural History and Antiquities of Selborne. L.C. Miall and W.W. Fowler (eds). London, 1901. Plt. (Sl foxed.) *Wheldon & Wesley*. $23/£15

WHITE, GILBERT. The Natural History and Antiquities of Selborne. Thomas Bell (ed). London: John van Voorst, 1877. 2 vols. lix,507pp + (ii)ads; 410pp (eps spotted; margins lt browned). Notes, clippings loosely inserted. (Upper hinge cracked vol 1; cl lt soiled; sl worn.) *Edwards*. $93/£60

WHITE, GILBERT. The Natural History and Antiquities of Selborne. W. Jardine (ed). London, 1853. Frontis, xviii,342pp; map; 4 plts. *Wheldon & Wesley*. $31/£20

WHITE, GILBERT. The Natural History of Selborne. London, 1924. 1st ed. Gilt illus upper bd (spine lt faded). *Edwards*. $39/£25

WHITE, GILBERT. The Natural History of Selborne.... London, 1825. 2 vols. 351; 2,364pp, 4 plts (1 hand-colored). Uncut. (Sl worn.) *Henly.* $140/£90

WHITE, GLEESON. Children's Books and Their Illustrators. London: The Studio, 1897. 1st ed. 68pp. (Foxing; cvr lt spotted.) *Bookpress.* $110/£71

WHITE, GWEN. European and American Dolls. NY: Putnam's, (1966). 1st Amer ed. Frontis. Fine in dj (rubbed; lt chipped). *Bookpress.* $75/£48

WHITE, GWEN. European and American Dolls.... Batsford, 1966. 1st ed. Color frontis. (Ex-lib w/ink stamp, remains of label.) Dj (worn, lt faded). *Edwards.* $116/£75

WHITE, HENRY KIRKE. History of the Union Pacific Railway. Chicago: Univ of Chicago, 1895. iii,129pp. 14 charts (2 fldg). Grn cl, gilt title. VG (sl rubbed). *Bohling.* $125/£81

WHITE, JOHN. The American Railroad Passenger Car. Balt: John Hopkins Univ Press, (1978). 1st ed, 2nd ptg. VF in Fine dj. *Perier.* $50/£32

WHITE, JOHN. The Birth and Rebirth of Pictorial Space. London: Faber, 1957. 1st ed. 64 plts. Dj sl torn, o/w Fine. *Europa.* $50/£32

WHITE, JOHN. The Birth and Rebirth of Pictorial Space. NY, 1958. 64 plts. Good in dj (worn). *Washton.* $50/£32

WHITE, JOHN. Studies in Late Medieval Italian Art. London: Pindar, 1984. VF in Mint pict dj. *Europa.* $70/£45

WHITE, LAWRENCE GRANT. Sketches and Designs by Stanford White. NY: Paul Wenzel, Maurice Krakow, 1920. 1st ed. Frontis, 56 plts. Cvrs lt spotted, black leather spine label lt chipped; else Fine. *Bookpress.* $485/£313

WHITE, MINOR. Mirrors, Messages, Manifestations. NY: Aperture, 1969. 1st ed. VG in illus dj (chipped, 3-inch sliver fr panel). *Cahan.* $200/£129

WHITE, PATRICK. The Burnt Ones. NY: Viking, (1964). 1st Amer ed. NF in dj (2 short edgetears). *Godot.* $45/£29

WHITE, PATRICK. The Cockatoos. NY: Viking, (1974). 1st Amer ed. Fine in Fine dj (price-clipped; lt rubbed). *Between The Covers.* $45/£29

WHITE, PATRICK. The Twyborn Affair. London: Cape, 1979. 1st ed. NF in NF dj. *Lame Duck.* $45/£29

WHITE, PATRICK. Voss. NY: Viking, 1957. 1st ed. Fine in NF dj (spine sl tanned). *Between The Covers.* $75/£48

WHITE, PHILO. Philo White's Narrative of a Cruize in the Pacific to South America.... Charles L. Camp (ed). Denver, (1965). 1st ed. Ltd to 1000. *Ginsberg.* $100/£65

WHITE, SOL. Sol White's Official Base-Ball Guide. Camden House, 1984. Facs rpt of 1907 ed. Fine; no dj as issued. *Plapinger.* $125/£81

WHITE, STEWART EDWARD. African Camp Fires. GC, 1913. 1st ed. Pict cl (dknd, worn, sl frayed). *King.* $35/£23

WHITE, STEWART EDWARD. Conjuror's House. NY, 1903. 1st ed. Pict cl (spine rubbed, dull; worn, ex-lib blindstamp rep; name). *King.* $35/£23

WHITE, STEWART EDWARD. The Forest. NY, 1903. 1st Amer ed. Teg; pict cvrs. Fine (spine sl sunned). *Polyanthos.* $35/£23

WHITE, T.H. The Age of Scandal. NY: Putnam's, (1950). 1st Amer ed. Tan cl titled in dk brn. Very Nice in dj (sl worn). *Cady.* $25/£16

WHITE, T.H. America at Last. NY: Putnam's, 1954. 1st Amer ed. NF (spine head, tail sl bumped) in dj (sl rubbed, nicked, creased). *Ulysses.* $85/£55

WHITE, T.H. Burke's Steerage. London: Collins, 1938. 1st ed. VG in dj (faded; edges chipped; price-clipped). *Hollett.* $62/£40

WHITE, T.H. Burke's Steerage. London, 1938. 1st ed. VG in dj (chipped). *Words Etc.* $78/£50

WHITE, T.H. England Have My Bones. London: Collins, 1936. 1st ed. Edges lt foxed, else VG in dj (internally repaired). *Limestone.* $250/£161

WHITE, T.H. Farewell Victoria. London: Cape, 1960. New reset illus ed. Red cl gilt. Very Nice in dj (price-clipped). *Cady.* $15/£10

WHITE, T.H. The Godstone and the Blackymor. NY: Putnam's, 1959. 1st Amer ed. VG in dj. *Cahan.* $15/£10

WHITE, T.H. The Godstone and the Blackymor. NY: Putnam, 1959. 1st US ed. Contents Good (binding sl discolored; sl rubbed). *Whiteson.* $23/£15

WHITE, T.H. Gone to Ground. London: Collins, 1935. 1st ed. Brn cl, gilt-lettered spine. Gilt oxidized, o/w Fine. *Temple.* $62/£40

WHITE, T.H. The Goshawk. Jonathan Cape, 1951. 1st ed. Dj (sl chipped). *Edwards.* $31/£20

WHITE, T.H. The Goshawk. London: Cape, 1951. 1st ed. VG+ in dj. *Limestone.* $65/£42

WHITE, T.H. The Once and Future King. London: Collins, 1958. 1st ed, 1st state of dj, w/ad for 'King Arthur's Avalon' by Geoffrey Ashe on back panel. Blue cl, gilt. Eps sl foxed; o/w Fine in dj (sl frayed). *Temple.* $132/£85

WHITE, T.H. The Once and Future King. London: Collins, 1958. 1st UK ed. VG in dj (price-clipped). *Williams.* $62/£40

WHITE, T.H. The Scandal Monger. NY: Putnam's, 1952. 1st Amer ed. Nice in dj (spine sl browned). *Cady.* $10/£6

WHITE, W. BERTRAM. The Miracle of Haworth. London: Univ of London Press, 1937. 1st ed. 17 plts. VG. *Hollett.* $47/£30

WHITE, WALTER. A Londoner's Walk to the Land's End. London, 1855. Fldg map frontis, x,357pp (lt foxing; label remains). 1/2 calf, cl bds (soiled; rubbed; hinges cracked through). *Edwards.* $39/£25

WHITE, WALTER. Northumberland, and the Border. London: Chapman & Hall, 1859. 1st ed. xii,472,16pp, fldg map. Blind-stamped cl gilt (faded). *Hollett.* $132/£85

WHITE, WALTER. The Sea Gypsies of Malaya. Phila: Lippincott, 1922. 1st ed. 15 photo plts, fldg map. (Text foxing.) Gray cl. *Karmiole.* $75/£48

WHITE, WILLIAM ALLEN. The Martial Adventures of Henry and Me. NY: Macmillan, 1918. 1st ed. Red cl pict stamped in grey/grn, gilt-titled. NF. *Hermitage.* $35/£23

WHITE, WILLIAM CHARLES. Bone Culture of Ancient China: An Archaeological Study of Bone Material from Northern Honan.... Toronto: University Press, 1945. Inscribed presentation. Frontis; 2 maps. Buckram. VG. *Argosy.* $75/£48

WHITE, WILLIAM CHARLES. Tomb Tile Pictures of Ancient China. Univ of Toronto Press, 1939. 137 plts. VG in dj. *Argosy.* $125/£81

WHITEFORD, SIDNEY. A Guide to Porcelain Painting. London: George Rowney, n.d. (ca 1895). Aeg. Brick red cl stamped in gilt/blind. (Lacks fep; lt foxing.) *Glenn.* $50/£32

WHITEHEAD, A.N. The Aims of Education and Other Essays. NY: Macmillan, 1929. 1st ed. Red cl (lt soil). VG. *House.* $80/£52

WHITEHEAD, ALFRED NORTH. Process and Reality. NY: Macmillan, 1929. 1st ed. Sig; ink notes rep; signs of successful erasure of marginal ink notes, else VG. *Lame Duck.* $65/£42

WHITEHEAD, ALFRED NORTH. Process and Reality. Cambridge: Cambridge Univ, 1929. 1st Eng ed. Name, else NF. *Lame Duck.* $150/£97

WHITEHEAD, C.E. The Camp Fires of the Everglades or Wild Sports in the South. Edinburgh, 1891. xi,298pp, 16 plts. Teg, rest uncut. Pict gilt cl. Sl worn, short tears head spine, inner hinge cracked, o/w Good. *Henly.* $101/£65

WHITEHEAD, G. KENNETH. The Wild Goats of Great Britain and Ireland. London: David & Charles, 1972. 1st ed. VG in dj. *Hollett.* $39/£25

WHITEHEAD, HENRY. Jumbee and Other Uncanny Tales. Arkham House, 1944. 1st ed. Fine in dj. *Madle.* $300/£194

WHITEHEAD, HENRY. West India Lights. Sauk City: Arkham House, 1946. 1st ed. Bkpl, else NF in dj (browned). *Other Worlds.* $75/£48

WHITEHEAD, HENRY. West India Lights. Arkham House, 1946. 1st ed. NF in Fine dj. *Madle.* $95/£61

WHITEHEAD, JAMES. Domains. Baton Rouge: LSU, (1966). 1st ed, 1st bk. Signed. NF in dj (sl frayed). *Turlington.* $35/£23

WHITEHEAD, P.J.P. and P.I. EDWARDS. Chinese Natural History Drawings. British Museum, 1974. Ltd to 400 numbered. 20 Fine collotype color plts. 1/4 goatskin leather, dec buckram. Velvet-lined buckram portfolio box. *Sutton.* $295/£190

WHITEHOUSE, J. HOWARD. Ruskin the Painter and His Works at Bembridge. OUP, 1938. Frontis port, 67 plts. VF in dj. *Europa.* $40/£26

WHITER, LEONARD. Spode. London, 1970. 1st ed. Color frontis, 8 color plts; newspaper clippings inserted. Dj (sl ragged). *Edwards.* $93/£60

WHITFIELD, CHRISTOPHER. Together and Alone. London: Golden Cockerel Press, 1945. 1st ed. #239/500. 10 wood-engrs by John O'Connor; teg, others uncut. Cream buckram-backed marbled cl (lt soiled, faded), gilt letters. *Cox.* $74/£48

WHITING, CHARLES. The Battle of Hurtgen Forest. London: Leo Cooper, (1989). 1st ed. VF in VF dj. *Oregon.* $27/£17

WHITING, GERTRUDE. Tools and Toys of Stitchery. NY, 1928. 1st ed. (Ex-lib.) *Argosy.* $75/£48

WHITING, JOHN D. Practical Illustration: A Guide for Artists. NY/London: Harper, (1920). 1st ed. Pict cvr pastedown. Hinges repaired, else Fine in dj. *Glenn.* $65/£42

WHITING, LILIAN. Boston Days. Boston: Little, Brown, 1902. 1st ed. Frontis port; 20 plts. Untrimmed. Blue cl, spine grn/gilt/white. Sl edgewear, else Fine. *Connolly.* $42/£27

WHITING, LILIAN. The Land of Enchantment. Boston, 1906. 1st ed. Teg. Gilt pict cl. VG (sig; bumped, lt worn). *Baade.* $50/£32

WHITING, ROBERT. The Chrysanthemum and the Bat. Dodd, Mead, 1977. 1st ed. Fine in Fine dj. *Plapinger.* $45/£29

WHITLOCK, HERBERT P. and MARTIN L. EHRMANN. The Story of Jade. NY: Sheridan House, (1949). 1st ed. Rust cl (bkpl). *Karmiole.* $50/£32

WHITMAN, ALFRED. The Print-Collector's Handbook. London, 1901. (Lt spotting; lower hinge cracked; spine sl bumped). Teg, rest uncut. *Edwards.* $39/£25

WHITMAN, ALFRED. Samuel Cousins. London: Bell, 1904. One of 600. 36 plts. (Tear top of spine, sl worn.) *Ars Artis.* $78/£50

WHITMAN, ALFRED. Samuel Cousins. London, 1904. One of 600. 35 collotype plts. VG. *Argosy.* $150/£97

WHITMAN, ROBIN. The Cadfael Companion. London: McDonald, 1991. 1st ed. Fine in dj. *Murder.* $50/£32

WHITMAN, S.E. The Troopers: An Informal History of the Plains Cavalry, 1865-1890. NY: Hastings House, (1962). Fine in VG dj. *Graf.* $25/£16

WHITMAN, WALT. The Book of Heavenly Death.... Portland: Mosher, 1905. 1st ed thus. One of 500. Port. Sound (offset 2pp from clipping; upper bd sl spotted; upper joint sl cracking). *Reese.* $25/£16

WHITMAN, WALT. Good-Bye My Fancy. Phila, 1891. 1st ed. VG (cl sl bubbling; fr hinge cracked, damp mk) in fldg cl slipcase w/matching red leather labels. *Mcclintock.* $375/£242

WHITMAN, WALT. Leaves of Grass. Phila: David McKay, 1891-1892. 9th ed. 438pp; untrimmed. (Extrems sl rubbed.) *Hollett.* $116/£75

WHITMAN, WALT. Leaves of Grass. Phila: David McKay, 1891-2. 1st ed thus, 2nd issue (cl). Grn cl, gilt. VG (fr inner hinge starting; lt rubbed, sl mkd). *Hermitage.* $400/£258

WHITMAN, WALT. Leaves of Grass. NY: LEC, 1929. One of 1500 signed by Frederic Warde (designer). Frontis port; facs plt. Fine in dj & slipcase. *Pharos.* $250/£161

WHITMAN, WALT. Leaves of Grass. NY: LEC, 1942. #904/1500 signed by Edward Weston (photos). 2 vols. Full dec bds. Fine in tissue wrappers & pub's slipcase. *Hermitage.* $1,000/£645

WHITMAN, WALT. Leaves of Grass. NY: LEC, 1942. One of 1500 numbered, signed by Edward Weston (photos). 2 vols. Pict bds, leather spine labels. 1 glassine dj defective at spine, o/w VF set in slipcase (lt mkd). *Reese.* $1,000/£645

WHITMAN, WALT. Leaves of Grass. NY/London: Heritage/Nonesuch, n.d. (1940). One of 1000. Signed by Rockwell Kent (illus). Full pub's morocco. Sl bumped; sl wear, else VG in slipcase (bumped). *King.* $350/£226

WHITMAN, WALT. November Boughs. Phila: David McKay, 1888. 3rd ptg. Gilt-stamped cl. Teg; unopened. (Sl rubbed). BAL 21430. *Sadlon.* $125/£81

WHITMAN, WALT. Specimen Days in America. London: Walter Scott, 1887. 1st Eng ed, primary binding. Orig blue cl, label. Fine. BAL 21428. *Macdonnell.* $165/£106

WHITMAN, WALT. Specimen Days in America. London: Walter Scott, 1887. 1st ptg of preface, add'l note. (Few leaves soiled.) NF (bumped, rubbed; ptd paper spine label darkened). BAL 21428. *Blue Mountain.* $65/£42

WHITMAN, WALT. Walt Whitman in Camden. Hadden Craftsmen, 1938. Ltd to 1100. Fine (sl rubbed); issued w/o dj. *Polyanthos.* $35/£23

WHITMAN, WILLIAM. The Giant Sorcerer, or The Extraordinary Adventures of Raphael and Cassandra. Boston/NY: Houghton Mifflin, 1927. 1st ed. Frank Boyd (illus). 8vo. Color frontis, (xii),131pp. Dec cl, eps. Lt soil, else VG in illus dj (lt chipped, dknd, sl soiled). *Cahan.* $50/£32

WHITMORE, ELIZABETH. Ernest D. Roth. NY, 1929. 12 mtd repros. Corners worn. *Argosy.* $60/£39

WHITNEY, CASPAR. The Flowing Road. Phila/London: Lippincott, 1912. 1st ed. Name, sl wear inner hinge; else NF. *Chapel Hill.* $50/£32

WHITNEY, CASPAR. On Snow-Shoes to the Barren Grounds. NY: Harper & Bros, 1896. x324pp. Teg. Orig dec cl. VG. (minor tear at head of spine, repaired). *High Latitude.* $125/£81

WHITNEY, H. Hunting with the Eskimos. NY, 1910. NF. *Trophy Room.* $150/£97

WHITNEY, HARRY. Hunting with the Eskimos. NY: Century, 1910. 1st ed. VG + . *Bowman.* $65/£42

WHITNEY, JOSIAH DWIGHT. The Yosemite Guide-Book. (Sacramento: Geological Survey of CA), 1869. 1st ed, 1st ptg. Frontis; 155pp; 2 fldg maps in fr/rear pockets; 7 full-pg engrs. Gold-stamped pict cl (spine ends worn; rippled area rear cvr, last leaves; short tears along folds lg map). *Dawson.* $850/£548

WHITNEY, JOSIAH DWIGHT. The Yosemite Guide-Book. (Sacramento: Geological Survey of CA), 1871. 2nd ed, 1st ptg. 133pp; 2 fldg maps (1 tape-repaired). Gold-stamped cl (lt worn). *Dawson.* $450/£290

WHITNEY, ORSON F. History of Utah.... Salt Lake, 1892-1904. 1st ed. 4 vols. Frontis, 736;860;765;707pp. map. Aeg. Full leather (scuffing, bumped; vol 1 shaken, spine worn, partially detached; vol 3 shaken, spine split; vol 4 spine worn w/2 sm pieces missing); vol 2 unusually nice. Overall set VG-. *Benchmark.* $800/£516

WHITNEY, ORSON F. Life of Heber C. Kimball.... Salt Lake, 1888. 1st ed. Frontis, 520pp; aeg. Full gilt leather. Hinges tender, sm piece torn tp, o/w VG. *Benchmark.* $175/£113

WHITRIDGE, ARNOLD. No Compromise. NY: Farrar, Straus & Cudahy, 1960. 1st ed. VG + in VG + dj. *Bishop.* $17/£11

WHITT, J.F. The Strand Magazine: 1891-1950. London: Whitt, 1979. 1st ed. Errata slip. Fine in Fine wrappers as issued. *Janus.* $35/£23

WHITTEMORE, EDWARD. Jerusalem Poker. NY: Holt Rinehart Winston, 1978. 1st ed. Fine in Fine dj. *Pettler.* $35/£23

WHITTEMORE, EDWARD. Quin's Shanghai Circus. NY: Holt Rinehart Winston, 1974. 1st ed. Fine in Fine dj. *Pettler.* $35/£23

WHITTEMORE, REED. William Carlos Williams. Boston: Houghton, Mifflin, 1975. 1st ed. Black cl. NF in dj. *Chapel Hill.* $25/£16

WHITTICK, ARNOLD. European Architecture in the Twentieth Century. NY: Abelard-Schuman, 1974. 1st ed. NF in illus dj. *Cahan.* $50/£32

WHITTIER, JOHN GREENLEAF. Among the Hills. Boston: Fields, Osgood, 1869. 1st ed, 1st binding. Orig grn cl, gilt. Fine. BAL 21874. *Macdonnell.* $30/£19

WHITTIER, JOHN GREENLEAF. Literary Recreations and Miscellanies. Boston: Ticknor & Fields, 1854. 1st ed. Brn cl stamped in gilt/blind. Lt moisture mk lower edge, mk upper bd, joint cracking, o/w Good. BAL 21786. *Reese.* $35/£23

WHITTIER, JOHN GREENLEAF. Miriam and Other Poems. Boston: Fields, Osgood, 1871. 1st ed, 1st binding. Gilt grn cl. Inscrip, else Fine. BAL 21889. *Reese.* $30/£19

WHITTIER, JOHN GREENLEAF. Old Portraits and Modern Sketches. Boston: Ticknor et al, 1850. 1st ptg. 304pp + 4pp Dec 1849 pub's cat inserted. Blind-stamped cl. Unopened. VG in clamshell slipcase, red leather spine. BAL 21769. *Schoyer.* $125/£81

WHITTIER, JOHN GREENLEAF. The Panorama and Other Poems. Boston: Ticknor & Fields, 1856. 1st ed. Brn cl, gilt (spine crown frayed). VG (early inscrip). BAL 21792. *Macdonnell.* $30/£19

WHITTIER, JOHN GREENLEAF. The Pennsylvania Pilgrim. Boston: James R. Osgood, 1872. 1st ed, 2nd ptg. Grn cl, gilt. VF. BAL 21904. *Macdonnell.* $30/£19

WHITTIER, JOHN GREENLEAF. Snow-Bound. Boston/NY: Houghton, Mifflin, 1906. 1st ed thus. Teg. Dec olive grn cl, gilt. VG. *Macdonnell.* $25/£16

WHITTIER, JOHN GREENLEAF. The Tent on the Beach. Boston: Ticknor & Fields, 1867. 1st ed, 1st state. Wine cl, gilt. Good (rubbed). BAL 21866. *Macdonnell.* $15/£10

WHITTIER, JOHN GREENLEAF. Whittier's Unknown Romance: Letters.... Boston: Houghton Mifflin, 1922. 1st ed. One of 385. Cl-backed bds in orig box (worn). BAL 22203. *Second Life.* $75/£48

WHITTINGHAM, RICHARD. The White Sox—A Pictorial History. Contemporary, 1982. 1st ed. Fin ein Fine dj. *Plapinger.* $45/£29

WHITTINGTON, HARRY. Man in the Shadow. NY: Avon, 1957. 1st ed. Fine in wrappers. *Mordida.* $35/£23

WHITTINGTON, HARRY. Play for Keeps. NY: Abelard-Schuman, 1957. 1st ed. Fine in dj (crease-tears; lt spine wear). *Mordida.* $75/£48

WHITTLESEY, CHARLES. Crossing and Re-Crossing the Connecticut River.... (New Haven), 1938. Frontis. Grn cl, gilt title. VG (cvr, endleaves sl spotted). *Bohling.* $35/£23

WHITTLESEY, CHARLES. Early History of Cleveland, Ohio.... Cleveland, 1867. 1st ed. viii,(2),487pp; 6 full-pg lithos. Teg. Dec blind-emb cl. Bkpl; lt worn; sl soil, else VG. Howes W 399. *Cahan.* $225/£145

WHITTOCK, NATHANIEL. The Art of Drawing and Colouring, from Nature, Birds, Beasts, Fishes, and Insects. London: Isaac Taylor Hinton, 1830. 1st ed. 4to. (iv),100pp, 24 litho plts (12 color, 12 plain). Comntemp grn calf. Sm spots fr cvr; else Fine. *Bookpress.* $1,500/£968

Whole Duty of Man. (By Richard Allestree.) London, For Robert Pawlet, 1680. Tp,(xiv),503,9pp. Full calf (sl worn; sm hole; new morocco label; lacks fep; upper rt joint cracked, bd sl loose). *Edwards.* $109/£70

WHYMPER, EDWARD. A Guide to Zermatt and the Matterhorn. John Murray, 1899. 3rd ed. Inscribed. 306pp. Card cvrs. (Sm area print skimmed where label removed.) *Gretton.* $47/£30

WHYMPER, EDWARD. Scrambles Amongst the Alps in the Years 1860-69. John Murray, 1871. 1st ed. Neate W65-'Some copies marked 4th. Thousand....' xviii,(ii),432pp; 23 plts; 5 fldg maps. Grn cl (recased), preserving orig eps, gilt spine. (Sl defective spine top repaired; map tears repaired; lt spotting eps, half title, title.) *Bickersteth.* $310/£200

WHYMPER, EDWARD. Scrambles Amongst the Alps in the Years 1860-69. London, 1893. 4th ed. 468pp. Inner hinges cracked; sl spotted, else VG in dj (rubbed). *King.* $295/£190

WHYMPER, EDWARD. Travels Amongst the Great Andes of the Equator. NY, 1892. 1st Amer ed. 456pp (fep stained, sl chipped; 1st few pp detached); lg fldg map in pocket. Teg. Pict cl (inner fr hinge cracked; extrems worn). *King.* $100/£65

WHYMPER, EDWARD. Travels Amongst the Great Andes of the Equator. NY: Scribner's, 1892. 1st Amer ed. xxiv, 1l, frontis map, 455pp, fldg map, map in rear pocket. Dk blue/grn cl, silver titles. Sl dusty, else NF. *Parmer.* $400/£258

WHYMPER, EDWARD. Travels Amongst the Great Andes of the Equator. London: John Murray, 1892. 1st ed. xxiv,456pp; 20 plts; 4 maps (1 in rear pocket). Aeg. (Joints tender; sl rubbed.) *Hollett.* $186/£120

WHYMPER, EDWARD. Travels Amongst the Great Andes of the Equator. London, 1892. 2nd ed. xxiv,456pp, 20 plts, 4 maps (2 fldg, 1 in rear pocket). (Ex-lib, bkpl, label remains, blindstamp tp; lacks upper portion fly leaf; cl soiled, spine discolored.) *Edwards.* $85/£55

WHYMPER, FREDERICK. Travel and Adventure in the Territory of Alaska. London: John Murray, 1868. (Sl damp mkd.) *Petersfield.* $225/£145

WHYMPER, FREDERICK. Travel and Adventure in the Territory of Alaska. NY: Harper, 1869. 1st Amer ed. 353pp; fldg map; ad leaf. Gold-stamped pict cl (lt worn). *Dawson.* $100/£65

WHYTE, ADAM GOWANS. Christabel's Fairyland. London: Chapman & Hall, 1926. 1st ed. Tall 8vo, (viii),183,(1)pp, 8 plts by Pauline Gautier. White linen-backed dec paper bds, gilt backstrip. Very Nice in pict dj (rubbed, lt soiled). *Cox.* $39/£25

WHYTE-MELVILLE, G.J. The Works of.... Herbert Maxwell (ed). London: Thacker, 1899-1902. Ltd to 250 sets. 24 vols. Plum colored buckram (backs faded, sl mks). *Petersfield.* $341/£220

WICK, CARTER. (Pseud of Collin Wilcox.) The Faceless Man. NY: Saturday Review/Dutton, 1975. 1st ed. Fine (spotting top edges) in NF dj. *Janus.* $30/£19

WICKERSHAM, JAMES. Old Yukon, Tales—Trails—and Trials. Washington, DC, 1938. Blue cl (spine rubbed; hinges weak). VG. *Bohling.* $50/£32

WICKS, WILLIAM S. Log Cabins and Cottages. NY: Forest & Stream, 1908. 1st ed. 44 plts. Text sl yellowed; bkpl; rubbed, else Fine. *Bookpress.* $95/£61

WICKSON, E.J. The California Fruits and How to Grow Them. SF, 1891. 2nd ed. Color frontis, 599pp. (Yellowed; rubbed, fr inner hinge cracked.) *Sutton.* $43/£28

WIDEMAN, JOHN EDGAR. The Lynchers. NY: Harcourt, (1973). 1st ed. VG in dj. *Petrilla.* $45/£29

WIENER, LEO. Africa and the Discovery of America. Phila: Innes & Sons, 1920. 1st ed. 3 vols. 100 plts. VG. *Petrilla.* $140/£90

WIENERS, JOHN. Ace of Pentacles. Carr & Wilson, 1964. 1st ed. VG in wrappers (sl soiled). *Poetry.* $19/£12

WIENERS, JOHN. Ace of Pentacles. NY: James F. Carr/Robert A. Wilson, 1964. 1st ed. VF in orig glassine. *Pharos.* $30/£19

WIENERS, JOHN. King Solomon's Magnetic Quiz. Pleasant Valley, NY: Kriya Press, 1967. Ltd to 100 numbered. Broadside. Fine. *Antic Hay.* $35/£23

WIGGIN, KATE DOUGLAS. The Diary of a Goose Girl. Boston, 1902. 1st Amer ed. Pict cvrs. Fine (sl rubbed). *Polyanthos.* $35/£23

WIGGIN, KATE DOUGLAS. Marm Lisa. Boston, 1896. 1st Amer ed. Pict cvrs. NF. *Polyanthos.* $35/£23

WIGGIN, KATE DOUGLAS. The Romance of a Christmas Card. Boston: Houghton Mifflin, 1916. 1st ed. Alice Earle Hunt (illus). Blue cl stamped in gilt, color illus mtd fr cvr; teg. Fine in pict dj (edgeworn; 3 1/2-inch tear fr panel, 2-inch piece lacking spine foot). BAL 22675. *Juvelis.* $150/£97

WIGGIN, KATE DOUGLAS. A Summer in a Canon. A California Story. Boston: Houghton, 1889. 1st ed, ltd to 1530. Frontis. Gilt-dec cl. Inner hinges cracking, few smudges; bumped, else Good. BAL 22589. *Reese.* $55/£35

WIGGIN, KATE DOUGLAS. Susanna and Sue. Boston/NY: Houghton Mifflin, 1909. 1st ed. 225pp, 12 headpieces by N.C. Wyeth; teg. Grey dec cl. Name, else Fine in pict dj (chipped, heavy external tape repair). *Godot.* $85/£55

WIGGIN, MAURICE. The Passionate Angler. London: Theodore Brun, 1949. 1st ed. #105/300. Signed. Orig full smooth calf, gilt; ribbon marker. VG + (spine sunned). *Willow House.* $31/£20

WIGGINS, I.L. and D.M. PORTER. Flora of the Galapagos Islands. Stanford, 1971. 96 color plts. *Wheldon & Wesley.* $105/£68

WIGHT, ANDREW. Present State of Husbandry in Scotland. Edinburgh, 1778 (vols 1-2), 1784 (vols 3-4). 4 vols in 6. Calf (non-matching, sl rubbed). *Marlborough.* $1,008/£650

WIGHT, J. Mornings at Bow Street. London: Charles Baldwyn, 1824. Unstated 2nd ed. x,279pp. George Cruikshank (illus). Contemp 3/4 leather, dec spine panels. *Schoyer.* $150/£97

WIGHTMAN, WILLIAM M. Life of William Capers, D.D., One of the Bishop of the Methodist Episcopal Church.... Nashville, TN, 1859. 1st ed. 516pp; port. Contemp 1/2 morocco. *Ginsberg.* $100/£65

WIGHTWICK, GEORGE. The Palace of Architecture: A Romance of Art and History. London: James Fraser, 1840. 1st ed. Frontis,xx,219pp (text foxed; bkpl), hand-colored plt. Contemp 1/2 morocco (cvrs rubbed). *Bookpress.* $285/£184

WIGMORE, JOHN HENRY. A Panorama of the World's Legal Systems. St. Paul: West Pub Co, 1928. Ltd ed #294/1990 signed. 3 vols. Photo laid in. (Worn.) *Boswell.* $350/£226

WILBRAHAM, RICHARD. Travels in the Transcaucasian Provinces of Russia.... London: John Murray, 1839. 1st ed. Engr frontis; half title, xvii,(i),477,12 pub's list; fldg map, 4 litho plts, errata slip before 1st pg. Brn blind-stamped cl (faded, stained; bkpl; recased preserving orig eps). VG internally. *Morrell.* $326/£210

WILBUR, ANNE T. (trans). Solitary of Juan Fernandez; or, the Real Robinson Crusoe. (By Xavier Saintine.) Boston: Ticknor et al, 1851. 1st Amer ed. viii,141pp. Blind-stamped cvrs, gilt title. Nice (sl wear). *Cady.* $50/£32

WILBUR, RICHARD. The Beautiful Changes and Other Poems. NY: Reynal & Hitchcock, (1947). 1st ed, 1st bk. Orig beige cl. NF in dj (price-clipped; lt wear). *Chapel Hill.* $300/£194

WILBUR, RICHARD. A Bestiary. NY: Pantheon Books, (1955). 1st ed. #708/800 signed by Wilbur and Alexander Calder (illus). Black cl. Fine in pub's cardbd slipcase (sl worn). *Chapel Hill.* $375/£242

WILBUR, RICHARD. Lying and Other Poems. Omaha: Cummington Press, 1987. 1st ed. One of 160. Fine in wrappers. *Reese.* $45/£29

WILCOX, ARTHUR. Moon Rocket. London: Thomas Nelson, 1946. 5 plts. Good (foxing spots fore-edge) in blue cl. *Knollwood.* $45/£29

WILCOX, EARLEY VERNON. Farmer's Cyclopedia of Live Stock. NY: OJ, 1912. 5 color cut-out overlays. Grn cl, gilt spine. VG + (spot). *Bohling.* $65/£42

WILCOX, LUTE. Irrigation Farming, A Handbook.... NY: OJ, 1898. viii,311,(2)pp + 13pp ads. Grn cl, gilt spine (rubbed, spotted). *Bohling.* $45/£29

WILCOX, R. TURNER. The Mode in Furs. NY: Scribner's, 1951. 1st ed. VG in dj (back missing lg pieces). *Oregon.* $25/£16

Wild West. London: Bancroft, n.d. (195?). 19x23 cm. 4 pull-down panels, 4 dbl-pg pop-ups. N. Dear (illus). Pict wraps; spiral binding. VG. *Book Finders.* $80/£52

WILDE, JOHANNES. Italian Drawings in the Department of Prints and Drawings in the British Museum. Michelangelo and His Studio. London, 1975. 2nd ed. Good. *Washton.* $65/£42

WILDE, OSCAR. The Ballad of Reading Gaol. NY: LEC, 1937. #904/1500 numbered, signed by Zhenya Gay (illus). Full leather. NF in pub's slipcase. *Hermitage.* $100/£65

WILDE, OSCAR. A Collection of Original Manuscripts, Letters, and Books.... London: Dulau & Co, n.d. (1928). One of 2000 in total ed of 2105. Japanese vellum self-wrappers (chipped at spine; dusty; gilt dulled), French-folded over thin white card. Internally Fine. *Temple.* $57/£37

WILDE, OSCAR. De Profundis. Methuen, (1905). 1st ed, 1st issue w/ads dated February 1905. Wilde's last prose work, written in prison, published posthumously w/preface by Robert Ross. Envelope mtd inside back cvr w/orig pub's leaflet, 3 press cuttings. Blue cl gilt; teg, others untrimmed. (Lt spotting prelims; cl sl rubbed, faded at spine top.) *Bickersteth.* $62/£40

WILDE, OSCAR. De Profundis. London: Methuen, (1905). 1st ed. Blue cl. 2 sm bkpls; eps, edges lt foxed, else VG. *Godot.* $250/£161

WILDE, OSCAR. De Profundis. Second Edition with Additional Matter. NY: Putnam's, 1909. 1st Amer ptg of the expanded text. Port. 3/4 brn calf, spine gilt extra. Inscrip; upper joint sl weak, else Good. *Reese.* $35/£23

WILDE, OSCAR. A House of Pomegranates. NY: Brentano's, n.d. 1st Amer ed. 162pp, 16 mtd color plts by Jessie M. King. Red cl, pict gilt. Hinges reinforced, foxing, offsetting, rebacked, else VG. *Davidson.* $825/£532

WILDE, OSCAR. An Ideal Husband. London: Leonard Smithers, 1899. 1st ed. Ltd to 1000. Recent lt tan cl stamped in gilt. Unopened. *Sadlon.* $125/£81

WILDE, OSCAR. Impressions of America. Sunderland: Keystone, 1906. One of 500. Contemp roan, gilt cipher upper cvr; gilt-lettered spine (repaired; sl foxing). Orig ptd wrappers bound in (sl browned, chipped). *Morrell.* $147/£95

WILDE, OSCAR. Lady Windermere's Fan and The Importance of Being Earnest. London: LEC, 1973. One of 1500. Signed by Tony Walton (artist). Fine (bkpls) in case. *Agvent.* $100/£65

WILDE, OSCAR. Poems. Boston: Roberts Bros, 1881. 1st Amer ed, 1st binding w/cherub imbibing bubbly on fr cvr. Brn cl, gilt (spine tips sl rubbed, stains rear cvr). Attractive. *Macdonnell.* $250/£161

WILDE, OSCAR. The Portrait of Mr. W.H. NY: Mitchell Kennerley, 1921. One of 1000 numbered. Signed by Kennerley. VG (sig). *Agvent.* $95/£61

WILDE, OSCAR. Ravenna. Oxford: Thos. Shrimpton, 1878. 1st ed, 1st bk. Orig ptd wrappers (cracked hinges neatly reglued; chips). Nice in cl fldg case. *Macdonnell.* $450/£290

WILDE, OSCAR. Salome. R.A. Walker (trans). London: Heinemann, 1957. Aubrey Beardsley (illus). Black buckram over beveled bds; blocked in silver. Sl faded upper cvr, o/w VG. *Cox.* $43/£28

WILDE, OSCAR. The Selfish Giant and Other Stories. Phila/NY: David Mckay, 1935. 1st ed. 8vo. 86pp, 7 full-pg color illus, 1 plt (lt spot at base). Kate Seredy (illus). VG (spine soil). *Davidson.* $50/£32

WILDE, OSCAR. The Short Stories of Oscar Wilde. (Burlington): LEC, 1968. One of 1500 signed by James Hill (illus). VF in glassine & slipcase. *Pharos.* $100/£65

WILDE, OSCAR. Vera or The Nilhists. Methuen, 1927. 2nd ed, 1st trade ed. Grn cl. Fine in dj (sl nicked, rubbed). *Dalian.* $54/£35

WILDENSTEIN, GEORGES. The Paintings of Fragonard. Complete Edition. London: Phaidon, 1960. Tipped-in color frontis, 1 tipped-in color fig, 126 b/w plts, 14 tipped-in colored plts. (Ex-lib w/ink stamp, label, bkpl; spine sl faded.) *Edwards.* $194/£125

WILDENSTEIN, GEORGES. The Paintings of Fragonard. Complete Edition. London, 1960. 142 plts, 16 color. Good in slipcase. *Washton.* $200/£129

WILDENSTEIN, GEORGES. The Paintings of Fragonard. Complete Edition. London: Phaidon, 1960. Color frontis, 125 monochrome plts. VF in ptd slipcase. *Europa.* $287/£185

WILDER, DANIEL. The Annals of Kansas. Topeka: KS Pub House, 1875. 1st ed. Full leather (lt wear; ex-lib). Howes W 411. *Glenn.* $100/£65

WILDER, LAURA INGALLS. Little Town on the Prairie. NY: Harper, (1941). 1st ed. 8vo. 15 b/w illus by Helen Sewell and Mildred Boyle. Tan cl, brn dec, lettering. Nice in pict dj (edgewear; holes rear). *Reisler.* $250/£161

WILDER, LAURA INGALLS. On the Way Home.... NY: Harper, Row, (1962). 1st ed. Nice in dj (rumpled, worn). *Second Life.* $45/£29

WILDER, LOUISE BEEBE. Colour in My Garden. GC: Doubleday, Page, 1918. 1st ed. Ltd to 1500. 24 mtd color plts. VG (extrems rubbed, lt soiling, spine damp-buckled). *Cahan.* $75/£48

WILDER, THORNTON. The Bridge of San Luis Rey. Boni, 1929. 1st illus ed. One of 1100. Signed by author and Rockwell Kent (illus). VG + . *Fine Books.* $250/£161

WILDER, THORNTON. The Bridge of San Luis Rey. NY: Boni & Liveright, 1929. One of 1100 signed by Wilder & Rockwell Kent (illus). Pict cl (sl soiled), o/w Fine. *Pharos.* $225/£145

WILDER, THORNTON. The Bridge of San Luis Rey. NY: LEC, 1962. One of 1500 numbered, signed by Jean Charlot (illus). Fine in pub's slipcase. *Hermitage.* $150/£97

WILDER, THORNTON. The Cabala. NY: Boni & Liveright, 1926. 1st ed, 1st bk. Fine. *Second Life.* $75/£48

WILDER, THORNTON. The Cabala. London: Longmans, 1926. 1st Eng ed. Fine in dj (spine sl sunned). *Pharos.* $200/£129

WILDER, THORNTON. The Cabala. NY: A & C Boni, 1926. 1st issue points. Sig; lacks dj, else NF. *Pharos.* $85/£55

WILDER, THORNTON. The Cabala. NY, 1926. 1st issue. NF (sl sunned). *Polyanthos.* $100/£65

WILDER, THORNTON. The Ides of March. NY: Harpers, (1948). 1st ed. Fine in dj (sl used). *Pharos.* $45/£29

WILDER, THORNTON. Our Century. (NY): Century, 1947. #988/1000 numbered. Paper cvr label. VG (apparently issued w/o slipcase). *Pharos.* $60/£39

WILDER, THORNTON. Our Town. A Play in Three Acts. NY: Coward McCann, (1938). 1st ed. VG in VG dj. *Juvelis.* $200/£129

WILDER, THORNTON. Theophilus North. NY: Harper & Row, (1973). One of 275 numbered, signed. Blue buckram, paper spine label. VF in acetate & slipcase. *Pharos.* $300/£194

Wildflower. (By Frederick William Robinson.) London: Hurst & Blackett, 1857. 3 vols. Contemp 1/2 red leather (eps foxed). *Petersfield.* $130/£84

WILDMAN, ROUNSEVELLE. China's Open Door: A Sketch of Chinese Life and History. Boston: Lothrop, (1900). xvi,318pp + 2pp ads. Teg. Royal blue cl stamped in gilt. VG. *Schoyer.* $40/£26

WILEY, BELL IRVIN. The Life of Billy Yank. Indianapolis, (1952). 1st ed. VG+ in VG+ dj. *Pratt.* $47/£30

WILEY, BELL IRVIN. The Life of Billy Yank. Bobbs Merrill, 1952. 2 vols. VG+ in VG slipcase. *Bishop.* $30/£19

WILEY, BELL IRVIN. The Life of Johnny Reb. Indianapolis: Bobbs-Merrill, (1943). 1st ed. Red cl. VG+ (name) in VG dj (edgeworn). *Chapel Hill.* $95/£61

WILEY, GEORGE E. Plantation Tales. Broadway Pub, (c. 1906). Port, guard (torn). VG-. *Book Broker.* $50/£32

WILHELM, GALE. We Too Are Drifting. NY: Random House, (1935). 1st ed. Cl, gilt leather wraparound, ptd paper wraparound (sl rubbed). VG (owner stamp endsheet; sl dusty, spine sl tanned). *Reese.* $40/£26

WILHELM, KATE and T. THOMAS. Year of the Cloud. Doubleday, 1970. 1st ed. NF in NF dj (1 closed tear). *Aronovitz.* $85/£55

WILHELM, KATE. Fault Lines. NY: Harper, (1977). 1st ed. VG in dj. *Houle.* $50/£32

WILHELM, KATE. Margaret and I. Little Brown, 1971. 1st ed. Signed. NF in dj. *Aronovitz.* $45/£29

WILK, MAX. Yellow Submarine. World, 1968. 1st ed. Pict cl. Rubbing, else NF. *Fine Books.* $85/£55

WILKENSON, LADY. Weeds and Wild Flowers. London: John van Voorst, 1858. x,421pp + 15pp ads; 12 hand-colored engrs; 26 woodcuts. Aeg. Gilt-lettered morocco spine (rebacked over orig blind-stamped cl; new eps). Hinge cracked, else Fine. *Quest.* $185/£119

WILKES, CHARLES. Columbia River to the Sacramento. Oakland: Biobooks, 1958. Ltd to 600. Lg fldg map, dbl-pg map. *Heinoldt.* $30/£19

WILKES, CHARLES. Narrative of the United States Exploring Expedition. Phila, 1849. 5 vols. 13 maps, steel engrs. Speckled calf, gilt-stamped spines; gilt eagles fr cvr. Extrems worn, lt spot last pp vol 1; vol 4 spine chipped, else Nice set. Howes. *King.* $495/£319

WILKIE, FRANC B. Davenport Past and Present. Davenport: Luse, Lane, 1858. 1st ed. Dbl-pg frontis; 33pp, errata. Orig blind-stamped brn cl, gilt spine title. Lib bkpl; corners worn; spine chipped, else Very Clean. *Hermitage.* $165/£106

WILKINS, HENRY. The Family Advisor; Or, A Plain and Modern Practice of Physics.... Phila, 1801. 3rd ed. 106pp. Full leather. Good. *Fye.* $150/£97

WILKINS, JOHN H. Elements of Astronomy.... Boston: Hilliard, Gray, Little, & Wilkins, 1828. Fldg frontis, 152pp, 9 plts. Good in 1/4 leather, marbled bds (worn; spine chipped, bkpl, sl foxed). *Knollwood.* $40/£26

WILKINSON, DAVID. Whaling in Many Seas and Cast Adrift in Siberia.... London, n.d. (1905). Inscribed. Map. VG (lt foxing). *Walcot.* $233/£150

WILKINSON, J. GARDNER. The Manners and Customs of the Ancient Egyptians. London: John Murray, 1878. 3 vols. 1533pp. Gilt pict cl. Feps renewed, frontis vol III repaired, o/w Fine set. *Archaeologia.* $475/£306

WILKINSON, J. GARDNER. Modern Egypt and Thebes. London: John Murray, 1843. 2 vols complete. 1067pp, fldg map. (Sig, bkpl; sl discoloration spine vol 1.) *Archaeologia.* $650/£419

WILKINSON, J. GARDNER. Modern Egypt and Thebes. London: Murray, 1843. 1st ed. 2 vols. xx,476; iv,591pp; fldg map. Contemp morocco (vol 2 rebacked). Aeg. Sl rubbed, sl spotting, o/w Nice. *Worldwide.* $300/£194

WILKINSON, J. GARDNER. A Popular Account of the Ancient Egyptians. London: John Murray, 1854. 2 vols. Frontis, xvi,errata,419; frontis, x,438pp (edges yellow; eps browned). 1/2 calf, marbled sides, gilt letter pieces. *Peter Taylor.* $76/£49

WILKINSON, J. GARDNER. A Popular Account of the Ancient Egyptians. NY: Harper, 1854. 1st ed thus. 2 vols. Gilt/blindstamped brn cl (corners bumped; spine ends worn; rubbed). VG. *Houle.* $225/£145

WILKINSON, J.V.S. The Lights of Canopus. NY/London: William Edwin Rudge/Studio Ltd, n.d. (but 1929). 1st ed. 36 tipped-in repros. Ink names, else VG. *Hermitage.* $100/£65

WILKINSON, OSBORN and MAJOR-GENERAL JOHNSON. The Memoirs of the Gemini Generals. London, 1896. 1st ed. xii,441pp; partially unopened. (Sl rubbed, spine chipped.) *Edwards.* $54/£35

WILKINSON, ROBERT. Londini Illustrata. London, n.ds. (1819-25). 2 vols. 204 full-pg plts (few w/holes in margins) + engr titles. Teg. 3/4 red morocco; marbled bds (ex-lib; scuffed; lib mks removed, w/holes in margins of few plts where mks excised). *King.* $995/£642

WILKS, S. and W. MOXON. Lectures on Pathological Anatomy. London, 1889. 3rd ed. xx,672pp. (Cl sl worn, dust stained; sm label on spine; inner hinge cracked, o/w VG.) *Whitehart.* $43/£28

WILL, P. Horrid Mysteries. A Story from the German of the Marquis of Grosse. London: Robert Holden, 1927. 1st ed thus. One of 1500 sets. 2 vols. Variant copy w/edges trimmed. Illus yellow paper bds. Extrems sl rubbed, nick 1 spine, o/w VG set. *Reese.* $125/£81

WILLARD, BERTON C. Russell W. Porter, Arctic Explorer, Artist, Telescope Maker. Freeport, ME: Bond Wheelwright, 1976. 1st ed. VG in red cl. *Knollwood.* $30/£19

WILLARD, CHARLES DWIGHT. The Fall of Ulysses. NY: George H. Doran, 1912. 1st ed. 84pp; 4 full-pg color plts by Frank Ver Beck. Cl spine, paper cvrd bds, emb design fr cvr. Fine in dj. *Godot.* $85/£55

WILLARD, FRANCES E. Glimpses of Fifty Years.... Chicago: H.J. Smith, (1889). 1st ed. xvi,(1),698pp + 6pp appendix; 3 ports w/guards; 12 plts; 2 chromolitho color plts (1 dbl); 2 ms facs (1 fldg). Dec, pict grn cl. VG. *Petrilla.* $40/£26

WILLARD, FRANCES E. A Wheel within a Wheel. Chicago: Woman's Temperance Pub Co, (1898). 1st ed. 75pp. VG (cl sl soiled). *Second Life.* $125/£81

WILLARD, JOHN WARE. A History of Simon Willard, Inventor and Clockmaker. NY: Paul P. Appel, 1962. New and Corrected ed. Sl musty, else VG in dj. *Cahan.* $60/£39

WILLARD, THEODORE A. The Lost Empires of the Itzaes and Mayas. Glendale, CA: Clark, 1933. 1st ed. Color frontis, 73 plts, map. Grn cl, gilt spine, teg. Good. *Karmiole.* $75/£48

WILLARD, X.A. Willard's Practical Butter Book. NY: Rural Publishing, 1875. 1st ed. 171,(21)pp. Minor cvr wear, pencil inscrip fep; else Fine. *Bookpress.* $150/£97

WILLARD, X.A. Willard's Practical Butter Book. NY, 1875. 2nd ed. 171pp (fep stuck to pastedown), 54 engrs. Dec cl (dampstained). *Sutton.* $95/£61

WILLARD, X.A. Willard's Practical Dairy Husbandry. NY: Moore, 1872. 1st ed. 546pp + ads. Fine (private lib label; label removed ep). *Second Life.* $75/£48

WILLCOX, WILLIAM B. Portrait of a General. NY: Knopf, 1964. 1st ed. Frontis port. Blue cl. VG in dj (price-clipped). *Chapel Hill.* $45/£29

WILLEFORD, CHARLES. Everybody's Metamorphosis. Missoula: Dennis McMillan, 1988. 1st ed. One of 400 numbered, signed. VF in dj. *Mordida.* $135/£87

WILLEFORD, CHARLES. High Priest of California. NY: Royal Books, (1953). 1st ed: pb orig. VG + (creasing; spine rubbed), as issued in pb dbl w/Talbot Mundy's Full Moon. *Janus.* $100/£65

WILLEFORD, CHARLES. High Priest of California. NY: Royal, 1953. Pub in 'giant' paper ed w/Talbot Mundy's Full Moon. Ink # on fr cvr; sl creasing, edgewear, else VG + . *Lame Duck.* $125/£81

WILLEFORD, CHARLES. I Was Looking for a Street. Woodstock: Countryman, 1988. 1st ed. VF in dj. *Mordida.* $45/£29

WILLEFORD, CHARLES. Kiss Your Ass Good-Bye. London: Victor Gollancz, 1989. 1st Eng ed. VF in dj. *Mordida.* $45/£29

WILLEFORD, CHARLES. Kiss Your Ass Goodbye. (Miami Beach): Dennis McMillan, 1987. 1st hb ed. One of 400 numbered, signed. Sl bump, else As New in dj. *Between The Covers.* $150/£97

WILLEFORD, CHARLES. The Machine in Ward Eleven. NY: Belmont, 1963. Pb orig. NF in illus wraps. *Lame Duck.* $125/£81

WILLEFORD, CHARLES. New Hope for the Dead. NY: St. Martins, 1985. 1st ed. VF in dj (price-clipped). *Else Fine.* $75/£48

WILLEFORD, CHARLES. Proletarian Laughter. NY: Alicat Bookshop, 1948. One of 1000. VG + (tanning to text, wraps; spine worn at staples). *Lame Duck.* $125/£81

WILLEFORD, CHARLES. Sideswipe. NY: St. Martin's, 1987. 1st ed. Fine in dj. *Janus.* $25/£16

WILLEFORD, CHARLES. Something About a Soldier. NY: Random House, 1986. 1st ed. VF in dj. *Mordida.* $45/£29

WILLEFORD, CHARLES. Wild Wives and High Priest of California. SF: RE/Search, 1987. 1st ed. One of 250 signed, numbered. Fine in dj. *Murder.* $135/£87

WILLEFORD, CHARLES. The Woman Chaser. Chicago: Newsstand Library, 1960. 1st ed. VF in wrappers. *Mordida.* $165/£106

WILLETT, C. and PHILLIS CUNNINGTON. Handbook of English Costume in the Eighteenth Century. London, 1957. Eps sl stained, o/w VG. *Washton.* $30/£19

William Morris and the Art of the Book. NY: Pierpont Morgan Lib, 1976. 1st ed. 114 plts. Fine in dj. *Bookpress.* $125/£81

WILLIAMS, A. COURTNEY. A Dictionary of Trout Flies.... London: A&C Black, 1949. 1st ed. 16 plts (8 color). Sig; spine sl creased, lettering dulled. *Hollett.* $54/£35

WILLIAMS, ALEXANDER. Murder in the WPA. NY: Robert M. McBride, 1937. 1st ed. VG in dj (spine faded; chipped). *Cahan.* $85/£55

WILLIAMS, ALFRED B. Hampton and His Red Shirts. Charleston: Walker, Evans & Cogswell, (1935). 2nd ed. Red cl. NF in VG dj. *Chapel Hill.* $95/£61

WILLIAMS, ARCHIBALD. Petrol Peter. London: Methuen, (1906). 1st ed. 4to. A. Wallis Mills (illus). Cl-backed illus bds (worn; internal smudging; 1pg marginal tear). *Reisler.* $585/£377

WILLIAMS, BEN AMES. The Strange Woman. Houghton Mifflin, 1942. 1st ed. (Sl rubbed.) Dj (sl chipped, worn). *Sadlon.* $25/£16

WILLIAMS, BENJAMIN S. Hints on the Cultivation of British and Exotic Ferns and Lycopodiums.... London, 1852. vii,67pp (eps lt soiled; tp missing piece). (Faded, soiled.) *Sutton.* $50/£32

WILLIAMS, BENJAMIN S. The Orchid-Grower's Manual. London, 1871. 4th ed. viii,300pp (yellowed; 2pp browned), 17 plts. Contemp 1/2 calf. *Sutton.* $85/£55

WILLIAMS, BENJAMIN S. The Orchid-Grower's Manual. Weinheim, 1961. 7th ed. (Rear inner hinge cracked.) *Sutton.* $75/£48

WILLIAMS, BENJAMIN S. The Orchid-Growers Manual. London: Victoria & Paradise Nurseries, 1877. 5th ed. Fldg color frontis, 336pp + 24pp ads, 51 plts. Gilt-dec cl. NF (new eps). *Quest.* $155/£100

WILLIAMS, BENJAMIN S. The Orchid-Growers Manual. London, 1885. 6th ed. xiv,660 + 20pp ads; 68 plain plts (42 dbl-pg). Pict gilt-dec cl (bumped, sl rubbed). VG (owner stamp 1pg, verso 1 plt, fr 1 plt). *Shifrin.* $125/£81

WILLIAMS, BUTLER. A Manual for Teaching Model-Drawing.... London: Parker, 1843. xv,257pp, frontis, 13 plts. Cl (rebacked). *Marlborough.* $225/£145

WILLIAMS, C.B. Insect Migration. London, 1958. 1st ed. Dj. *Edwards*. $105/£68

WILLIAMS, C.J.B. Principles of Medicine. London, 1843. xxxvi,390pp (sig blocked out). Emb cl (back hinge sl cracked). *Whitehart*. $140/£90

WILLIAMS, C.J.B. Principles of Medicine. Phila, 1857. New Amer ed from 3rd London. 496pp. Good. *Goodrich*. $75/£48

WILLIAMS, CARRIE. Complete Instructions in Rearing Silkworms. SF: Whitaker & Ray, 1902. 1st ed. Dust worn cl, o/w VG. *Second Life*. $45/£29

WILLIAMS, CHARLES. All Hallow's Eve. NY: Pellegrini & Cudahy, (1948). 1st Amer ed, 1st issue binding and dj. Black cl gilt. Handsome in dj. *Cady*. $35/£23

WILLIAMS, CHARLES. Big City Girl. NY: Fawcett, 1951. 1st ed. Pb orig. Unread. Fine in wraps. *Else Fine*. $65/£42

WILLIAMS, CHARLES. The Diamond Bikini. NY: Fawcett, 1956. 1st ed. Pb orig. NF in wraps. *Else Fine*. $40/£26

WILLIAMS, CLARA ANDREWS. The Surprise Book, the Adventures of Jack and Betty. NY, (1911). 1st ed. George Alfred Williams (illus). 64pp. Cl-backed pict bds (worn, loose; smudges, detached pp). *King*. $95/£61

WILLIAMS, E. CRAWSHAY. Across Persia. London: Arnold, 1907. 1st ed. Lg fldg map at rear. Grn cl, gilt title. VG. *Bowman*. $25/£16

WILLIAMS, EDWARD G. Fort Pitt and the Revolution on the Western Frontier. Pittsburgh: Hist Soc of Western PA, (1978). #202/500. Signed. Fldg map. VG. *Schoyer*. $75/£48

WILLIAMS, EDWARD T. China Yesterday and Today. NY: Crowell, (1923). Fldg color map in pocket. Grn cl, gilt (sl scuffed; ex-lib, bkpls). *Schoyer*. $40/£26

WILLIAMS, FREDERICK S. Our Iron Roads. London, 1852. xii,390pp (perf blindstamp tp). 3/4 leather (deteriorated; backstrip chipped away; outer hinges split; ex-lib), marbled bds. *Bohling*. $45/£29

WILLIAMS, G.F. The Diamond Mines of South Africa. NY, 1906. 2 vols. 28 plts (3 color); 15 maps (4 color). Recent 1/2 morocco. Uncut, largely unopened. Fine. *Henly*. $341/£220

WILLIAMS, GEOFFREY and RONALD SEARLE. How to Be Topp; A Guide to Sukcess for Tiny Pupils. NY: Vanguard, (1954). 1st ed. Grn cl. Fine. *Weber*. $30/£19

WILLIAMS, GWYN (trans). Against Women. London: Golden Cockerel Press, (1953). #71/350 signed by John Petts (illus). VF in limp box. *Petersfield*. $279/£180

WILLIAMS, H. (ed). One Whaling Family. Boston: Houghton Mifflin, 1964. 1st Amer ed. VG+ in dj. *Walcot*. $14/£9

WILLIAMS, H.N. The Life and Letters of Admiral Sir Charles Napier, K.C.B. London, 1917. 1st ed. Frontis port; 23 plts. Eps very sl browned, o/w Good in grn cl (corners bumped). *Edwards*. $39/£25

WILLIAMS, HELEN MARIA. A Narrative of the Events Which Have Taken Place in France, from the Landing of Napoleon Bonaparte on the 1st of March, 1815 till the Restoration of Louis XVIII. Phila: Thomas, 1816. 1st US ed. 245pp. Ptd bds (cvrs almost separate); uncut. VG. *Second Life*. $250/£161

WILLIAMS, HENRY and OTTALIE. How to Furnish Old American Houses. NY: Pellegrini & Cudahy, (1949). 1st ed. Frontis. Fine in dj (tattered). *Bookpress*. $25/£16

WILLIAMS, HENRY T. and S. ANNIE FROST. Evening Amusements. NY: Henry T. Williams, 1878. (Extrems rubbed.) *Dramatis Personae*. $100/£65

WILLIAMS, HENRY. A Practical Guide to the Study of the Diseases of the Eye.... Boston, 1869. 3rd ed. 422pp; 7 engr plts (1 fldg). Good. *Fye*. $125/£81

WILLIAMS, J. WHITRIDGE. Obstetrics. NY, 1903. 1st ed. (Binding rubbed.) *Fye*. $500/£323

WILLIAMS, JAMES. The Rise and Fall of 'The Model Republic.' London: Richard Bentley, 1863. xiv,424pp. VG. Howes W 458. *Schoyer*. $125/£81

WILLIAMS, JAMES. Seventy-Five Years on the Border. Kansas City: Standard Ptg Co, 1912. VG+. *Bohling*. $45/£29

WILLIAMS, JAMES. Seventy-Five Years on the Border. Kansas City, 1912. 1st ed. Frontis; plt. Lt wear; new eps, o/w VG. *Oregon*. $45/£29

WILLIAMS, JOHN A. Captain Blackman. GC: Doubleday, 1972. 1st ed. Pub's comp stamp fr pastedown. VG+ in dj (price-clipped; shelfworn; sl wrinkling). *Aka*. $35/£23

WILLIAMS, JOHN A. The Man Who Cried I Am. Boston: Little Brown, (1967). 1st ed. Fine in dj (lt use; short tear). *Reese*. $30/£19

WILLIAMS, JOHN A. The Man Who Cried I Am. Boston: Little, Brown, (1967). 1st ed. VG in dj. *Godot*. $35/£23

WILLIAMS, JOHN A. This Is My Country Too. NY: NAL-World, (1965). 1st ed. VG in dj. *Petrilla*. $40/£26

WILLIAMS, JOHN G. The Adventures of a Seventeen-Year-Old Lad.... Boston, 1894. 308pp, port. Gilt cl (discolored; insect damage at joints but hinges sound). Internally VG. Howes W 465. *Reese*. $500/£323

WILLIAMS, JOHN H. The Guardians of the Columbia. Tacoma: By Author, 1912. 1st ed. VG. *Perier*. $40/£26

WILLIAMS, JOHN. Butcher's Crossing. NY: Macmillan, 1960. 1st ed. Pp browned, o/w Fine in dj. *Heller*. $45/£29

WILLIAMS, JONATHAN. An Ear in Bartram's Tree. (NY): New Directions, (1969). 1st this ed. Signed. VG in wraps. *Turlington*. $20/£13

WILLIAMS, JONATHAN. The Loco Logodaedalist in Situ. NY: Grossman, 1972. 1st trade ed, w/blue eps. Signed. Fine in dj (lt worn). *Turlington*. $50/£32

WILLIAMS, LEWIS. Chinook by the Sea. Portland: Kilham Ptg, (1924). 1st ed. Fine. *Oregon*. $100/£65

WILLIAMS, LYNNA. Things Not Seen and Other Stories. Boston: Little, Brown, (1992). 1st ed, 1st bk. Fine in Fine dj. *Robbins*. $20/£13

WILLIAMS, MARGERY. The Velveteen Rabbit. London: Heinemann, 1922. 1st ed. 4to. William Nicholson (illus). Color illus bds (spine chipped; corners worn); dec eps. *Reisler*. $1,200/£774

WILLIAMS, MARGERY. The Velveteen Rabbit. Mt. Vernon, NY: Press of A. Colish, 1974. One of 1500. 8vo. 6 mtd color plts by Marie Angel. Velvet cl cvr, gold ptd label set in. Good+. *Reisler*. $675/£435

WILLIAMS, MARY FLOYD. History of the San Francisco Committee of Vigilance of 1851. Berkeley: Univ of CA, 1921. 1st ed. Inscribed. Blue cl. NF. *Harrington*. $100/£65

WILLIAMS, MARY FLOYD. Papers of the San Francisco Committee of Vigilance of 1851. Berkeley: Univ of CA, (1919). 1st ed. 11 plts (incl map, fldg table). VG. *Oregon*. $100/£65

WILLIAMS, MONTAGU. Leaves of a Life, Being the Reminiscences of Montagu Williams, Q.C. Boston: Houghton, Mifflin, 1890. 2 vols. Good set. *Boswell.* $150/£97

WILLIAMS, R.H. With the Border Ruffians. E.W. Williams (ed). Lincoln: Univ of NE, 1982. 1st of this ed w/notes. Howes W 475. *Lambeth.* $50/£32

WILLIAMS, RUSS and C. CADIEUX. The Ways of Game Fish. Chicago: Ferguson, (1972). 1st trade ed. Fine in Fine dj. *Oregon.* $50/£32

WILLIAMS, RUSS. The Ways of Wildfowl. Chicago: Ferguson, (1971). 1st trade ed. Fine in Fine dj. *Oregon.* $60/£39

WILLIAMS, S. WELLS. History of China. NY: Scribner's, 1897. xiv,474pp + 4pp ads, map. VG. *Schoyer.* $45/£29

WILLIAMS, S.H. Voodoo Roads. Wien: Jugend/Volk, 1949. 1st ed. VG. *Mikesh.* $35/£23

WILLIAMS, SAMUEL COLE (ed). Early Travels in the Tennessee Country, 1540-1800. Johnson City, TN: Watauga Press, 1928. 1st ed. Inscribed. Teg. Blue cl. Inscrip, spine soiled, else VG. Howes W 483. *Chapel Hill.* $125/£81

WILLIAMS, SAMUEL COLE. Dawn of Tennessee Valley and Tennessee History. Johnson City, TN: Watauga Press, 1937. 1st ed. Map. Partially unopened; teg. Blue cl (spine sl soiled). Fine. Howes W 482. *Chapel Hill.* $125/£81

WILLIAMS, SAMUEL COLE. History of the Lost State of Franklin. NY: Press of the Pioneers, 1933. 2nd ed, rev. Inscribed. Frontis port. Blue cl. Prelims browned, else VG. Howes W 484. *Chapel Hill.* $200/£129

WILLIAMS, SAMUEL COLE. Tennessee During the Revolutionary War. Nashville, TN: Tennessee Hist Commission, 1944. 1st ed. Teg. Blue cl. NF. *Chapel Hill.* $100/£65

WILLIAMS, STEPHEN W. American Medical Biography, or Memoirs of Eminent Physicians.... Greenfield, 1845. 664pp; 9 engr. Victorian emb cl (head, tail pieces worn). *Goodrich.* $295/£190

WILLIAMS, SYDNEY B. Antique Blue and White Spode. London, 1987. Rpt. VG in dj. *Argosy.* $50/£32

WILLIAMS, TED with JOHN UNDERWOOD. My Turn at Bat. S&S, 1969. 1st ed. VG + in VG dj. *Plapinger.* $40/£26

WILLIAMS, TENNESSEE et al. Five Young American Poets, Third Series 1944. Norfolk: New Directions, 1944. 1st ed. NF in dj (spine dknd; sm stain). *Turlington.* $200/£129

WILLIAMS, TENNESSEE. Baby Doll. London: Secker & Warburg, 1957. 1st ed. Fine in dj. *Hermitage.* $50/£32

WILLIAMS, TENNESSEE. Collected Stories. (NY): New Directions, (1985). 1st ed. Blue cl. Fine in dj. *Chapel Hill.* $45/£29

WILLIAMS, TENNESSEE. The Glass Menagerie. NY: Random House, 1945. 1st ed. Fine in NF dj (rear panel tear; shallow chip; spine sunned). *Beasley.* $200/£129

WILLIAMS, TENNESSEE. Grand. NY: House of Books, 1964. One of 300 numbered, signed. Fine. *Beasley.* $275/£177

WILLIAMS, TENNESSEE. Hard Candy. A Book of Stories. (Norfolk): New Directions, (1954). 1st ed. Ltd to 1500. Cl-backed patterned paper over bds. VG in slipcase. *Cahan.* $75/£48

WILLIAMS, TENNESSEE. Memoirs. NY: Doubleday, 1975. 1st ed. Fine in dj. *Sadlon.* $20/£13

WILLIAMS, TENNESSEE. Memoirs. GC: Doubleday, 1975. 1st ed. Orange bds, black cl spine. Fine in dj (ring stain). *Chapel Hill.* $30/£19

WILLIAMS, TENNESSEE. Moise and the World of Reason. NY: S&S, (1975). 1st ed, 2nd ptg. Inscribed. NF in NF dj. *Chapel Hill.* $100/£65

WILLIAMS, TENNESSEE. Period of Adjustment. (NY): New Directions Book, (1960). 1st ed. VG in dj (spine lt browned, foxed, else VG). *Godot.* $75/£48

WILLIAMS, TENNESSEE. The Roman Spring of Mrs. Stone. NY: New Directions, (1950). 1st ed, ltd issue, one of 500 numbered, signed. Imitation vellum-backed tapa bds; gilt spine sl dknd, else Fine in slipcase (sl soiled). *Hermitage.* $275/£177

WILLIAMS, TENNESSEE. The Rose Tattoo. (NY: New Directions, 1950.) 1st ed. Pink cl. Fine in dj. *Appelfeld.* $85/£55

WILLIAMS, TENNESSEE. The Rose Tattoo. London: Secker & Warburg, 1954. 1st Eng ed. VG in dj (edge-worn; 1 1/2-inch chip top of spine affecting author's name; 2-inch chip upper corner rear panel). *Chapel Hill.* $50/£32

WILLIAMS, TENNESSEE. Small Craft Warnings. London: Secker & Warburg, 1973. 1st ed. NF in dj (sl browned, stained). *Rees.* $31/£20

WILLIAMS, TENNESSEE. Steps Must Be Gentle. Targ, 1980. One of 350 signed. Cl, marbled bds. As New in plain dj. *Dermont.* $150/£97

WILLIAMS, TENNESSEE. A Streetcar Named Desire. (Norfolk), (1947). 1st ed. VG (sm spot sunned, bkpl partially covering earlier removal, pp curled) in VG dj (sunned, lacking 1.5-inch at foot of spine, overall sm chips). *Fuller & Saunders.* $295/£190

WILLIAMS, TENNESSEE. A Streetcar Named Desire. Lehmann, 1949. 1st UK ed. Bkpl, o/w VG in VG dj (tear back panel). *Martin.* $22/£14

WILLIAMS, TENNESSEE. A Streetcar Named Desire. NY: LEC, 1982. #588/2000. Litho frontis. Brn leather spine, gilt title, 13-color fabric. Prospectus, invitation laid in. Fine in cream paper slipcase. *Heller.* $150/£97

WILLIAMS, TENNESSEE. Suddenly Last Summer. New Directions, 1958. 1st ed. Signed. VG + in VG + dj (sm chip spine head). *Fine Books.* $275/£177

WILLIAMS, TENNESSEE. Tennessee Williams' Letters to Donald Windham 1940-1965. Verona: n.p., 1976. 1st ed, one of 500 numbered. Fine in wraps, dj, slipcase. *Turlington.* $150/£97

WILLIAMS, TENNESSEE. The Two-Character Play. (NY): New Directions, (1969). 1st ed. One of 350 numbered, signed. Fine in slipcase. *Reese.* $350/£226

WILLIAMS, WALTER and FLOYD C. SHOEMAKER. Missouri, Mother of the West. Chicago/NY: Amer Hist Soc, 1930. 1st ed. 5 vols. Emb cl (lt edgewear). *Glenn.* $150/£97

WILLIAMS, WILLIAM CARLOS. Al Que Quiere! Boston: Four Seas, 1917. 1st ed. Sl sunning rear bd, o/w Fine in VG glassine dj. *Beasley.* $500/£323

WILLIAMS, WILLIAM CARLOS. The Autobiography. NY: Random House, 1951. 1st ed. Fine in Fine dj (short tear; sl rubbing). *Beasley.* $100/£65

WILLIAMS, WILLIAM CARLOS. The Build-Up. NY: Random House, (1952). 1st ed, 2nd issue, w/New Directions sticker over tp imprint. Fine in dj. *Reese.* $60/£39

WILLIAMS, WILLIAM CARLOS. The Build-Up. NY: Random House, (1952). 1st ed. NF in VG dj (price-clipped). *Chapel Hill.* $60/£39

WILLIAMS, WILLIAM CARLOS. The Collected Earlier Poems of.... (Norfolk): New Directions, (1952). 1st ed. Fine in dj (lt rubbed). *Reese.* $50/£32

WILLIAMS, WILLIAM CARLOS. The Collected Later Poems of.... (Norfolk): New Directions, (1950). 1st ed, 1st issue binding, w/separately ptd supplement, 'The Rose,' laid in, rather than bound in. Edges sl foxed, o/w NF in dj (sl closed tear). *Reese.* $75/£48

WILLIAMS, WILLIAM CARLOS. The Great American Novel. Paris: Three Mountains Press, 1923. 1st ed, #25/300 ptd on Rives handmade paper. Good, clean internally (cvrs, flyleaves dampstained; spine label lacking; edges browned). *Chapel Hill.* $175/£113

WILLIAMS, WILLIAM CARLOS. In the Money. Norfolk, CT, (1940). 1st ed, rev copy w/rubber-stamped pub date notice on fep. VG in dj (worn, edges chipped). *Mcclintock.* $30/£19

WILLIAMS, WILLIAM CARLOS. Journey to Love. NY: Random House, (1955). 1st ed. Fine in dj (short edge tears). *Sadlon.* $45/£29

WILLIAMS, WILLIAM CARLOS. The Knife of the Times and Other Stories. Ithaca, NY: Dragon Press, (1932). 1st ed. One of 500 ptd. 8vo. Blue cl. VF in glassine & ptd paper djs. *Jaffe.* $850/£548

WILLIAMS, WILLIAM CARLOS. The Knife of the Times and Other Stories. Ithaca, NY: The Dragon Press, (1932). 1st ed. One of 500. 8vo. Orig blue cl, paper labels. NF in orig glassine, ptd paper djs. *Chapel Hill.* $900/£581

WILLIAMS, WILLIAM CARLOS. Kora in Hell: Improvisations. Boston: Four Seas, 1920. 1st ed. One of 1000. Ptd grey bds. Near VG (spine lt dampstained w/1 1/2-inch crack at bottom neatly repaired; crack fr inner hinge; sm chip lower corner rear bd). *Chapel Hill.* $250/£161

WILLIAMS, WILLIAM CARLOS. Life Along the Passaic River. Norfolk: New Directions, 1938. 1st ed. Spine sl dknd; initials, o/w Fine in NF dj (spine dknd, worn). *Beasley.* $200/£129

WILLIAMS, WILLIAM CARLOS. Make Light of It. Random House, 1950. 1st ed. VF in Fine dj. *Fine Books.* $75/£48

WILLIAMS, WILLIAM CARLOS. Paterson (Book I). (NY): New Directions, (1946). 1st ed. One of 1063 bound. Pastedowns tanned, o/w VG in dj (tanned, chipped, split at spine fold). *Reese.* $135/£87

WILLIAMS, WILLIAM CARLOS. Paterson (Book II). (NY): New Directions, (1948). 1st ed. One of 1009 ptd. Fine in dj (edges lt tanned; sl nick). *Reese.* $275/£177

WILLIAMS, WILLIAM CARLOS. Paterson (Book III). (NY): New Directions, (1949). 1st ed. One of 999 bound. Fine in VG dj (sl tanned, sm chip). *Reese.* $250/£161

WILLIAMS, WILLIAM CARLOS. Paterson (Book Five). NY: New Directions, (1958). 1st Amer ed. Fine in Fine dj. *Polyanthos.* $25/£16

WILLIAMS, WILLIAM CARLOS. Paterson (Book Five). NY: New Directions, 1958. 1st ed. Fine in Fine dj. *Beasley.* $100/£65

WILLIAMS, WILLIAM CARLOS. The Pink Church. Columbus: Golden Goose, 1949. One of 400 numbered. Fine (sunned) in wraps. *Beasley.* $175/£113

WILLIAMS, WILLIAM CARLOS. Selected Essays. Random House, 1954. 1st ed. VF in Fine dj. *Fine Books.* $65/£42

WILLIAMS, WILLIAM CARLOS. Selected Essays. NY: Random House, 1954. One of 3350. Fine in Fine dj (crease). *Beasley.* $75/£48

WILLIAMS, WILLIAM CARLOS. A Voyage to Pagany. NY: Macaulay, 1928. 1st ed. Signed. Orig brn cl. Spine heavily rubbed; sm blindstamp, else VG in dj (worn; supplied from another copy). *Chapel Hill.* $300/£194

WILLIAMS-ELLIS, CLOUGH. Cottage Builing in Cob, Pise, Chalk and Clay, A Renaissance. London, 1920. 2nd ed. Cl-backed bds. (Pp browned; bumped; rubbed.) *King.* $35/£23

WILLIAMS-FREEMAN, J.P. An Introduction to Field Archaeology. London: Macmillan, 1915. (Sl foxed; sl stains fr cvrs.) *Petersfield.* $50/£32

WILLIAMS-WOOD, CYRIL. Staffordshire Pot Lids and Their Potters. Faber & Faber, 1972. 1st ed. Color frontis; 8 color, 72 b/w plts. Dj (spine sl chipped). *Edwards.* $70/£45

WILLIAMSON, ALEXANDER. Journeys in North China.... London: Smith, Elder, 1870. 1st ed. 2 vols. xx,444; viii,442pp, 2 fldg maps, 8 woodcut plts. Grn cl (sl worn, spines sl creased), gilt. Joints sl strained, but VG set. *Hollett.* $426/£275

WILLIAMSON, G.C. Andrew and Nathaniel Plimer. Miniature Painters. London: Bell, 1903. One of 352. 65 plts. Mod blue cl, orig title mtd on fr cvr. Tidemk blank margin last leaf, else VG. *Ars Artis.* $194/£125

WILLIAMSON, G.C. The Book of Famille Rose. London, 1927. 1st ed. One of 750. 62 plts (19 color). Teg. (Feps lt browned.) Dj (chipped; discolored to spine). *Edwards.* $271/£175

WILLIAMSON, G.C. Signed Enamel Miniatures of the XVIIth, XVIIIth and XIXth Centuries. London: Nachemsohn, 1926. #207/500. 12 plts, guards. Fine. *Europa.* $54/£35

WILLIAMSON, G.R. George Engelheart, 1750-1829. London: Bell, 1902. One of 350. 87 plts under tissues. New blind cl. (Sl tidemk in blank margin first few ff.) *Ars Artis.* $147/£95

WILLIAMSON, HENRY. As the Sun Shines. London: Faber, 1941. 1st ed. (Sl faded.) Dj. *Petersfield.* $23/£15

WILLIAMSON, HENRY. The Beautiful Years. Faber, 1929. 1st rev ed, #64/200 signed. NF (spine faded). *Williams.* $116/£75

WILLIAMSON, HENRY. The Children of Shallowford. London: Faber, (1939). 1st ed. Eps sl foxed, o/w clean in dj (sl ragged). *Petersfield.* $39/£25

WILLIAMSON, HENRY. Dandelion Days. Faber, 1930. 1st rev ed, #113/200 signed. NF. *Williams.* $116/£75

WILLIAMSON, HENRY. Genius of Friendship: T.E. Lawrence. London: Faber, 1941. 1st ed. Foxing eps; o/w VG in dj (sl worn, chip). *Rees.* $78/£50

WILLIAMSON, HENRY. The Labouring Life. Cape, 1932. 1st UK ed. VG (sl damp-spotting bds). *Williams.* $23/£15

WILLIAMSON, HENRY. Lone Swallows. Collins, 1922. 1st UK ed. VG (sl tear bottom upper bd). No dj, as issued. *Williams.* $74/£48

WILLIAMSON, HENRY. Lucifer Before Sunrise. London: Macdonald, 1967. 1st ed. Fine in dj. *Temple.* $16/£10

WILLIAMSON, HENRY. The Old Stag. Putnam, 1926. 1st UK ed. NF (sl pg browning) in VG + dj. *Williams.* $116/£75

WILLIAMSON, HENRY. The Pathway. Cape, 1931. 1st ed thus, #41/200 signed. VG + (spine sl faded). *Williams*. $116/£75

WILLIAMSON, HENRY. The Patriot's Progress. NY: E.P. Dutton, (1930). 1st Amer ed. VG in dj (chipped; torn). *Hermitage*. $35/£23

WILLIAMSON, HENRY. The Patriot's Progress. London: Geoffrey Bles, (1930). 1st Eng ed. Red buckram gilt. Very Nice in dj. *Cady*. $60/£39

WILLIAMSON, HENRY. The Scandaroon. London: Macdonald, 1972. One of 250 numbered, signed. Aeg. Full dk blue morocco-grain rexine, gilt. Fine in dk blue rexine-covered slipcase. *Temple*. $78/£50

WILLIAMSON, HENRY. The Star Born. Faber, 1933. Ltd ed, #31/70 signed. VG (sl warped damp-stained bds; spine faded). *Williams*. $171/£110

WILLIAMSON, HENRY. The Village Book. London: Cape, (1930). 1st Eng ed. Orange-tan cl, gilt. Very Nice. *Cady*. $25/£16

WILLIAMSON, HENRY. The Village Book. Cape, 1930. Ltd ed, #148/504 signed. Vellum-backed bds. VG + . *Williams*. $101/£65

WILLIAMSON, HENRY. The Wet Flanders Plain. Beaumont Press, 1929. Ltd ed, #296/400. VG + . *Williams*. $93/£60

WILLIAMSON, HENRY. The Wild Red Deer of Exmoor. Faber, 1931. 1st trade ed. VG + in dj (sl rubbed, worn). *Williams*. $39/£25

WILLIAMSON, HUGH. The History of North Carolina. Phila: Thomas Dobson, 1812. 1st ed. 2 vols. xix,289pp, errata, fldg map; viii,289pp. Recent 1/2 morocco gilt, marbled paper over bds. Fine set. Howes W 494. *Cahan*. $750/£484

WILLIAMSON, JACK and JAMES GUNN. Star Bridge. Gnome, 1955. 1st ed. Fine in dj (spine sl dknd). *Madle*. $45/£29

WILLIAMSON, JACK and MILES J. BREUER. The Girl From Mars. Stellar Pub, 1929. 1st ed. Cvrs dusty, else NF in wraps. *Madle*. $100/£65

WILLIAMSON, JACK. The Cometeers. Fantasy Press, 1950. 1st ed. Fine in VG dj (spine lt chipped). *Aronovitz*. $55/£35

WILLIAMSON, JACK. Dragon's Island. NY: S&S, 1951. 1st ed. Pub's card laid in. VG + in dj (spine ends sl worn; rear panel soiled). *Bernard*. $45/£29

WILLIAMSON, JACK. The Humanoids. S&S, 1949. 1st ed. VG + in VG dj (lt wear, tear). *Aronovitz*. $45/£29

WILLIAMSON, JACK. The Legion of Space. Fantasy, 1947. 1st ed. NF in dj (frayed, soiled). *Madle*. $45/£29

WILLIAMSON, JACK. The Legion of Space. Fantasy Press, 1947. 1st ed. One of 500 inscribed. NF in dj. *Aronovitz*. $185/£119

WILLIAMSON, JACK. Trapped in Space. Doubleday, 1968. 1st ed. Fine in dj (spine frayed). *Madle*. $85/£55

WILLIAMSON, JAMES J. Mosby's Rangers. NY: Ralph B. Kenyon, 1896. 1st ed. 8vo, frontis, 511pp. Blue-gray pebbled cl, gilt centerpiece. VG + (spine sl sunfaded, lt wear). Howes W 498. *Chapel Hill*. $575/£371

WILLIAMSON, THAMES. Hunky. NY: Coward-McCann, 1929. 1st ed. Dec cl. Pencil erasure endsheet, else Fine in pict dj. *Reese*. $30/£19

WILLINGHAM, CALDER. End as a Man. NY: Vanguard, (1947). 1st ed. (Offsetting ep.) 1st issue dj w/blank rear panel (frayed; lt chipped; internally mended). *Turlington*. $50/£32

WILLINGHAM, CALDER. The Gates of Hell. NY: Vanguard, (1951). 1st ed. VG (dusty) in dj (lt used). *Turlington*. $45/£29

WILLINGHAM, CALDER. Natural Child. NY: Dial, 1952. 1st ed. Binder's glue discoloration bds, else VG in dj (frayed). *Turlington*. $35/£23

WILLINGHAM, CALDER. Reach to the Stars. NY: Vanguard, (1951). 1st ed. Very NF in dj. *Antic Hay*. $50/£32

WILLINGHAM, CALDER. To Eat a Peach. NY: Dial, 1955. 1st ed. VG in dj (sl frayed; sm spot). *Turlington*. $35/£23

WILLIS, B. A Yanqui in Patagonia. Stanford: Stanford Univ, (Jan 1948). Blind-stamped gilt dec cl. NF in VG dj. *Mikesh*. $25/£16

WILLIS, CONNIE. Fire Watch. Bluejay Books, 1985. 1st ed. Fine in dj (spine top tear). *Madle*. $100/£65

WILLIS, CONNIE. Lincoln's Dreams. Bantam, 1987. 1st ed. Fine in dj. *Madle*. $40/£26

WILLIS, EOLA. The Charleston Stage in the XVIII Century with Social Settings of the Time. Columbia: State Co, 1924. 1st ed. Signed. Inner hinge cracked; lib mks, o/w VG. *Pharos*. $45/£29

WILLIS, N.P. American Scenery. Barre: Imprint Society, 1971. #107/1950 numbered. Frontis. Bkpl, else Fine in pub's slipcase. *Hermitage*. $90/£58

WILLIS, ROBERT and JOHN WILLIS CLARK. The Architectural History of the University of Cambridge. CUP, 1886. 4 vols. 29 double-pg or fldg plans. Teg, uncut. Buckram-backed gilt cl (extrems sl worn). Excellent set. *Hollett*. $279/£180

WILLIS, THOMAS. The Anatomy of the Brain and Nerves. William Feindel (ed). Montreal, 1965. 1st ed thus. 2 vols. Vellum. Good in slipcase. *Fye*. $250/£161

WILLIUS, FREDERICK A. and THOMAS E. KEYS. Cardiac Classics. St. Louis: Mosby, 1941. Internally Good (ex-lib, stamps). *Goodrich*. $75/£48

WILLIUS, FREDERICK A. and THOMAS E. KEYS. Cardiac Classics. St. Louis: Mosby, 1941. 1st ed. Frontis. Fine. *Glaser*. $150/£97

WILLMOTT, ERNEST. English House Design. London: Batsford, 1911. (Edges sl rubbed.) *Edwards*. $70/£45

WILLNER, SIS. A Gentleman Decides. Chicago: Black Archer, 1931. 1st ed. Fine in dj (sl wear). *Antic Hay*. $27/£17

WILLOUGHBY, HOWARD. Australian Pictures Drawn With Pen and Pencil. London: R.T.S., 1886. 1st ed. 224,8pp (illus ads); map. Aeg. Brn pict cl (neatly rebacked w/all but sm piece of orig backstrip preserved; sl damage upper cvr). *Cox*. $101/£65

WILLOUGHBY, JOHN C. East Africa and Its Big Game. London, 1889. Fldg map. Gilt dec black cl (joints repaired). *Petersfield*. $143/£92

WILLS, ALFRED. Wanderings among the High Alps. Oxford: Blackwell, 1937. 16 plts. (Fore-edge, flyleaves sl spotted). Dj. *Hollett*. $54/£35

WILLS, GEOFFREY. English Looking-Glasses. London: Country Life, 1965. Pub's gilt cl (sl mkd). Pict dj. *Peter Taylor*. $29/£19

WILLS, MARY H. A Winter in California. Norristown, PA: (Morgan R. Wills), 1889. 150pp. Pict cl. *Dawson*. $100/£65

WILLSHIRE, WILLIAM HUGHES. A Descriptive Catalogue of Playing and Other Cards. London, 1876. Frontis,x,360pp + viii + 87pp supp; 22 plts (7 hand-colored). (Ex-lib, rebound; tp sl soiled; upper hinge repaired.) *Edwards.* $116/£75

WILLSHIRE, WILLIAM HUGHES. An Introduction to the Study and Collection of Ancient Prints. London: Ellis & White, 1874. Frontis. Grn cvrs, black leather backstrip (sm tears; sl stained). *Petersfield.* $109/£70

WILLSHIRE, WILLIAM HUGHES. An Introduction to the Study and Collection of Ancient Prints. London, 1877. 2nd ed. 2 vols. xx,373pp; viii,305pp, 3 plts (2 fldg). (Ex-lib w/ink stamps, bkpls; frontis, tp vol 1 sl spotted; tape mks ep edges). Teg, rest uncut. Crushed morocco-backed cl bds (upper edges sl faded; blind lib stamp, #s; rubbing). *Edwards.* $116/£75

WILLSON, BECKLES. The Great Company (1667-1871), Being a History of...Merchants-Adventurers Trading into Hudson's Bay.... London: Smith Elder, 1900. 14 plts, fldg map, fldg facs. VG. Howes W 511. *Oregon.* $100/£65

WILLSON, BECKLES. The Great Company, Being a History of...Merchants-Adventurers Trading into Hudson's Bay. Toronto: Copp Clark, (1899). 1st ed. xxii,17-541pp, frontis, fldg map, 12 plts. Pict gilt-stamped cl. VG. Howes W 511. *Oregon.* $140/£90

WILLSON, BECKLES. The Great Company. London: Smith, Elder, 1903. 2 vols. (Ex-lib stamps tps, #s backstrips.) *Petersfield.* $65/£42

WILLSON, BECKLES. John Slidell and the Confederates in Paris (1862-1865). NY: Minton, Balch & Co, 1932. 1st ed. Orig cl. NF in dj (sl chipped). *Mcgowan.* $125/£81

WILLSON, BECKLES. Life of Lord Strathcona and Mount Royal. Boston, (1915). 2 vols. Red cl; gilt stamping, tops. Unopened. (Vol 1 dampstaining rear bd, some leaves.) Vol 2 Fine in dj (dknd, chipped). *Bohling.* $50/£32

WILLSON, DIXIE. Pinky Pup and the Empty Elephant. Joliet: P.F. Volland, 1928. Rev ed. 8vo. Erick Berry (illus). Cl-backed pict bds, black spine. NF in VG box. *Davidson.* $225/£145

WILLWERTH, JAMES. Eye in the Last Storm: A Reporter's Journal of One Year in Southeast Asia. NY: Grossman, 1972. 1st ed. Sl cocked, else NF in dj (edgeworn, torn). *Aka.* $35/£23

WILMERDING, JOHN. Fitz Hugh Lane. NY, (1971). 1st ed. 10 color plts. NF in dj. *Lefkowicz.* $80/£52

WILSON, A. PHILIPS. A Treatise on Febrile Diseases, Including Intermitting, Remitting, and Continued Fevers.... Hartford, 1809. 1st Amer ed. 5 vols in 2. Contemp calf (hinges repaired; 1st few pp waterstained). *Argosy.* $200/£129

WILSON, A.N. Kindly Light. London: S&W, 1979. 1st UK ed. Fine in dj. *Lewton.* $26/£17

WILSON, A.N. Kindly Light. London: Secker, 1979. 1st UK ed. NF (sl scuffed) in dj (sm closed tear). *Williams.* $34/£22

WILSON, A.N. The Sweets of Pimlico. London: Martin Secker, 1977. 1st ed. Rev copy, signed presentation. VG in dj (chipped, nicked, rubbed, creased). *Virgo.* $147/£95

WILSON, A.N. Unguarded Hours. London: Secker & Warburg, 1978. 1st ed. Corners bumped; o/w VG in dj. *Rees.* $23/£15

WILSON, A.N. Who Was Oswald Fish? Secker & Warburg, 1981. 1st ed. Label fr pastedown, o/w NF in dj. *Rees.* $16/£10

WILSON, A.P. An Essay on the Nature of Fever. London, 1807. iv,210pp. 1/2 antique leather. VG. *Whitehart.* $140/£90

WILSON, ADRIAN. The Design of Books. NY: Reinhold, 1967. Fine in VG dj. *Veatchs.* $65/£42

WILSON, ADRIAN. The Making of the Nuremberg Chronicle. Amsterdam: Nico Israel, (1976). 1st ptg. Signed. Fine in dj. *Bookpress.* $165/£106

WILSON, ADRIAN. The Making of the Nuremberg Chronicle. Amsterdam: Nico Israel, 1978. 2nd ptg. 12 full-pg color facs. Dj. *Dawson.* $95/£61

WILSON, ALBERT. Gardeners All in California. Menlo Park, 1953. 1st ed. Inscribed. Fine in dj. *Brooks.* $24/£15

WILSON, ALBERT. Rambles in North Africa. Boston, 1926. 48 b/w plts. (Upper hinge split; edges sl rubbed.) *Edwards.* $39/£25

WILSON, ALEXANDER and CHARLES LUCIAN BONAPARTE. American Ornithology. London/Edinburgh, 1832. 3 vols. cvii,408; vii,390; viii,523pp, port (foxed); 97 hand-colored plts (lt staining to 3; offsetting). 19th-cent 1/2 morocco, marbled bds, eps (edges, corners worn; scuffing, sm nicks backstrip vol 3). *Sutton.* $1,350/£871

WILSON, ALEXANDER and CHARLES LUCIAN BONAPARTE. American Ornithology. London, 1876. 3 vols. 8vo. cv,408; vii,495; vii,540pp; 103 hand-colored plts. Gilt dec morocco, red cl (wear; 1/2-inch tear, split vol 1; rubbed; foxing, mostly to fr, back pp). *Sutton.* $950/£613

WILSON, AMOS. The Pennsylvania Hermit. Phila, 1839. 24pp, woodcut port. Dbd. Howes W 515. *Ginsberg.* $125/£81

WILSON, ANGUS. Anglo-Saxon Attitudes. London: Secker & Warburg, 1956. 1st UK ed. VG (ink name) in dj (sl edgeworn). *Williams.* $25/£16

WILSON, ANGUS. A Bit Off the Map. London: Secker, 1957. 1st UK ed. Fine in dj. *Williams.* $39/£25

WILSON, ANGUS. Hemlock and After. S & W, 1952. 1st UK ed. VG in Good dj (spine sl rubbed; closed tears). *Lewton.* $28/£18

WILSON, ANGUS. Late Call. London: Secker & Warburg, 1964. 1st ed. Fine in dj. *Temple.* $22/£14

WILSON, ANGUS. The Middle Age of Mrs. Eliot. London, 1958. 1st ed. Fine (sm label) in dj (spine sl sunned, rear panel sl soiled). *Polyanthos.* $35/£23

WILSON, ANGUS. The Mulberry Bush. London: Secker, 1956. 1st UK ed. NF in dj (sl scuffed). *Williams.* $39/£25

WILSON, ANGUS. The Old Men at the Zoo. NY: Viking, 1961. 1st ed. Fine in dj. *Hermitage.* $30/£19

WILSON, ANGUS. The Old Men at the Zoo. London: Secker & Warburg, 1961. 1st UK ed. VG + in dj (spine sl browned). *Williams.* $39/£25

WILSON, ANGUS. The Wrong Set: And Other Stories. NY: William Morrow, 1950. 1st Amer ed, 1st bk. VG in dj (repaired, foxed). *Cahan.* $25/£16

WILSON, CALVIN DILL. The Faery Queen. Chicago: A.C. McClurg, 1906. 1st ed. 8vo. (12),143pp, grn dec borders each pg; teg. Navy levant, gilt dec back. Spine lt faded, o/w Fine. *House.* $100/£65

WILSON, CHARLES M. Ambassadors in White. NY, (1942). 1st ed. VG. *Argosy.* $35/£23

WILSON, CHARLES M. Ambassadors in White. NY, 1942. 1st ed. *Fye.* $40/£26

WILSON, CHARLES W. Picturesque Palestine, Sinai and Egypt. NY: Appleton, 1881. 1st US ed. 4 vols. 478; 474pp. Sl rubbed, o/w VG. *Worldwide.* $350/£226

WILSON, COLIN. A Book of Booze. London: Gollancz, 1974. 1st UK ed. NF (lt bumped) in dj (price-clipped). *Williams.* $28/£18

WILSON, COLIN. The Mind Parasites. Arkham House, 1967. 1st ed. VF in dj. *Madle.* $85/£55

WILSON, COLIN. The Philosopher's Stone. Crown, 1971. 1st Amer ed. Fine in VG + dj (sl wear). *Aronovitz.* $40/£26

WILSON, COLIN. The Space Vampires. NY: Random House, 1976. 1st Amer ed; precedes Eng ed. Black-backed blue paper bds. VF in Fine dj. *Dalian.* $54/£35

WILSON, COLIN. The World of Violence. London: Gollancz, 1963. 1st ed. NF in dj (sl mkd). *Rees.* $31/£20

WILSON, COLIN. The World of Violence. London: Gollancz, 1963. 1st UK ed. Fine in dj. *Williams.* $28/£18

WILSON, DANIEL. Prehistoric Man. London: Macmillan, 1876. 3rd ed. 2 vols. Color frontis each vol. Teg. Gilt/black pict brn cl. VG (lt wear). *House.* $160/£103

WILSON, DAVID M. Anglo-Saxon Art. London, 1984. 1st ed. *Edwards.* $47/£30

WILSON, DAVID M. Anglo-Saxon Art. From the Seventh Century to the Norman Conquest. Woodstock, 1984. 73 color illus. Good in dj. *Washton.* $45/£29

WILSON, DAVID M. Catalogue of Antiquities of the Later Saxon Period. London: British Museum, 1964. 64 plts. VF in dj. *Europa.* $78/£50

WILSON, DOROTHY CLARKE. Bright Eyes. NY: McGraw-Hill, (1974). VG in dj (edgeworn). *Petrilla.* $25/£16

WILSON, E.H. A Naturalist in Western China. London, 1913. 2nd ed. 2 vols. Map; 101 plts. (Cl sl used). *Wheldon & Wesley.* $217/£140

WILSON, E.H. Plant Hunting. Vol 1 (of 2). Boston, 1927. Signed presentation inscription. (Spine dknd.) *Sutton.* $150/£97

WILSON, EDMUND. The American Earthquake. NY, 1958. 1st ed. Fine in dj. *Artis.* $25/£16

WILSON, EDMUND. An Atlas of the Fertilization and Karyokinesis of the Ovum. NY, 1895. 1st ed. 32pp; 10 photo plts. (Binding, leaves waterstained; outer hinges cracked.) *Fye.* $100/£65

WILSON, EDMUND. The Bit Between My Teeth. NY: Farrar, 1965. 1st ed. Fine in NF dj (sm snag mended on verso). *Reese.* $30/£19

WILSON, EDMUND. The Cell in Development and Inheritance. NY, 1904. 2nd ed. Good. *Fye.* $75/£48

WILSON, EDMUND. The Cold War and the Income Tax; a Protest. NY: Farrar, Straus, 1963. 1st ed. NF in dj (sl torn). *Hermitage.* $40/£26

WILSON, EDMUND. The Devils and Canon Barham. NY: Farrar, (1973). 1st ed. NF in dj. *Reese.* $25/£16

WILSON, EDMUND. Europe without Baedeker. GC: Doubleday, 1947. 1st ed. VG in dj (rubbed; sl chipped). *Hermitage.* $50/£32

WILSON, EDMUND. Memoirs of Hecate County. GC: Doubleday, 1946. 1st ed. Offsetting eps, o/w Nice in dj (chip). *Reese.* $35/£23

WILSON, EDMUND. Memoirs of Hecate County. NY: Doubleday, 1946. 1st ed. NF in dj (rubbed, chipped). *Sadlon.* $45/£29

WILSON, EDMUND. Night Thoughts. NY: Farrar, (1961). 1st ed. Fine in dj. *Reese.* $25/£16

WILSON, EDMUND. Patriotic Gore, Studies in the Literature of the American Civil War. NY, 1962. 1st ed. Minor cvr wear, o/w VG + . *Pratt.* $45/£29

WILSON, EDMUND. Patriotic Gore. NY, 1962. 1st ed. VG. *Pratt.* $45/£29

WILSON, EDMUND. A Piece of My Mind. NY: Farrar, (1956). 1st ed. Fine in dj (lt mks). *Reese.* $30/£19

WILSON, EDMUND. Poets, Farewell! NY: Scribner's, 1929. 1st ed. Brn bds, black cl spine. Fine. *Chapel Hill.* $50/£32

WILSON, EDMUND. Poets, Farewell! NY: Scribners, 1929. 1st ed. NF in dj (sm chips; sl interior reinforcement; browning). *Antic Hay.* $325/£210

WILSON, EDMUND. The Triple Thinkers. NY: Harcourt, Brace, (1938). 1st ed. NF in dj (price-clipped). *Hermitage.* $250/£161

WILSON, EDMUND. Upstate. Records and Recollections of Northern New York. NY: Farrar, (1971). 1st ed. NF in dj. *Reese.* $20/£13

WILSON, EDMUND. A Window on Russia. NY: Farrar, Straus, (1972). 1st ed. Fine in dj. *Sadlon.* $35/£23

WILSON, EDWARD S. Oriental Outing. Cincinnati: Cranston & Curts, 1894. Inscribed presentation. 294pp. Blue cl stamped in gilt. *Schoyer.* $45/£29

WILSON, EPHRAIM A. Memoirs of the War.... Cleveland: W.M. Bayne Ptg Co, 1893. 1st ed. 435pp, 6 plts. 2-toned cl. Rear inner hinge starting, extrems rubbed, else VG. *Mcgowan.* $185/£119

WILSON, ERNEST H. Aristocrats of the Garden. Boston: Stratford, 1932. Frontis. Teg. (Ex-lib.) *Quest.* $25/£16

WILSON, ERNEST H. China, Mother of Gardens. Boston: Stratford, (1929). Signed. Fldg map. Black cl, dec gilt. Ink name, else VG. *Hermitage.* $350/£226

WILSON, ERNEST H. If I Were to Make a Garden. Boston: Stratford Co, (1931). 1st ed. Frontis port, 37 plts. Fine in dj. *Karmiole.* $75/£48

WILSON, ERNEST H. The Lilies of Eastern Asia. London/Boston, 1929. 2nd ed. 22 full-pg b/w photos. Gold-stamped emb cl. NF in VG dj. *Shifrin.* $100/£65

WILSON, ERNEST H. More Aristocrats of the Garden. Boston: Stratford, 1928. Frontis. Teg; uncut. VG in dj (repaired). *Quest.* $45/£29

WILSON, EVERETT B. Early Southern Towns. NY: A.S. Barnes, (1967). 1st ed. VG in dj (used). *Bookpress.* $65/£42

WILSON, FRANCIS. The Eugene Field I Knew. NY: Scribner's, 1898. 1st ed. (Sl rubbed.) *Sadlon.* $20/£13

WILSON, G. MURRAY (ed). Fighting Tanks. London, 1929. 1st ed. Frontis; 15 plts. Foxing; sl damage to fore-edges of 1/2 title, frontis, 3pp; inner hinge sl strained after ffep, o/w Good + . Blue cl (rubbed). *Edwards.* $54/£35

WILSON, G.F. A Bibliography of the Writings of W.H. Hudson. London: Bookman's Journal, 1922. 1st ed. Good. *Shasky.* $40/£26

WILSON, GAHAN. Eddy Deco's Last Caper. NY: Times Books, 1987. 1st ed. Fine. *Janus.* $20/£13

WILSON, GAHAN. Everybody's Favorite Duck. NY: Mysterious Press, 1988. 1st ed. One of 100 numbered, signed. Fine in slipcase; issued w/o dj. *Janus.* $75/£48

WILSON, GAHAN. Gahan Wilson's America. S&S, 1985. 1st ed. Fine in dj. *Madle.* $30/£19

WILSON, J. LEIGHTON. Western Africa: Its History, Condition and Prospects. NY: Harper & Bros, 1856. 1st ed. Frontis, 527pp, map. Red cl stamped in blind, paper label (owner mks, notes; spine faded). *Schoyer.* $85/£55

WILSON, J.C. (ed). Infectious Diseases. NY, 1911. 1st Eng trans. *Fye.* $50/£32

WILSON, JAMES HARRISON. Under the Old Flag. Recollections of Military Operations in the War for the Union.... NY: Appleton, 1912. 1st ed. 2 vols. Orig cl. Minor cvr spotting; rear inner hinges starting, else VG. *Mcgowan.* $150/£97

WILSON, JOB. Inquiry into the Nature and Treatment of the Prevailing Epidemic Called Spotted Fever.... Boston: Bradford & Read, 1815. 1st ed. 5 plts. Orig bds (backstrip worn; ex-lib). *Argosy.* $150/£97

WILSON, JOSEPH THOMAS. The Black Phalanx. Hartford, CT: American Pub Co, 1888. 1st ed. 528pp. Inner hinges cracking, else VG. *Mcgowan.* $275/£177

WILSON, LILLIAN M. Ancient Textiles from Egypt in the University of Michigan Collection. Ann Arbor: Univ of MI Press, 1933. 23 plts. Fine. *Archaeologia.* $150/£97

WILSON, MAY. Rheumatic Fever. Studies.... NY, 1940. 1st ed, 3rd ptg. *Fye.* $50/£32

WILSON, MONA. The Life of William Blake. Nonesuch, 1927. #24/1480. 24 b/w plts; fldg corrigenda leaf. 1/4 vellum (soiled); marbled bds (worn). Bkpl removed w/sl loss pastedown, o/w NF. *Poetry.* $116/£75

WILSON, MONA. The Life of William Blake. London: Nonesuch, 1927. 1st ed. 1/2 vellum binding, marbled bds, gilt lettered spine. *D & D.* $150/£97

WILSON, MONA. The Life of William Blake. London: Nonesuch, 1927. 1st ed. #526/1480. 24 plts. Uncut. Good in parchment-backed marbled bds (backstrip sl discolored; edges rubbed). *Cox.* $101/£65

WILSON, NEILL C. Silver Stampede. NY: Macmillan, 1937. 1st ed. VF in VF dj. *Book Market.* $75/£48

WILSON, NICHOLS FIELD (ed). Adventures in Business. Volume One, May 21, 1943...May 12, 1944. Buena Park: Ghost Town Press, 1944. 1st ed. NF. *Connolly.* $72/£46

WILSON, O.S. The Larvae of the British Lepidoptera and their Food Plants. London, 1880. xxix,367pp; 40 color plts. 1/2 morocco (sl rubbed). *Wheldon & Wesley.* $233/£150

WILSON, RICHARD L. Short Ravelings from a Long Yarn, or Camp March Sketches of the Santa Fe Trail. Benjamin F. Taylor (ed). Santa Ana: Fine Arts Press, 1936. Unopened. Gilt, 1/2 leather (deteriorating, split fr hinge, chipped base spine). Internally Fine (bkpls removed fr pastedown, fep). Howes T 45. *Bohling.* $135/£87

WILSON, ROBERT FORREST. Crusader in Crinoline. The Life of Harriet Beecher Stowe. Phila: Lippincott, (1941). 1st ed. 30 plts. Orig cl. NF in VG dj. *Mcgowan.* $45/£29

WILSON, ROMER. The Hill of Cloves. London: Heinemann, 1929. 1st ed. #216/775 signed. Uncut. Good in buckram-backed dec bds. *Cox.* $43/£28

WILSON, RUFUS. Out of the West. Press of the Pioneers, 1933. 1st ed. VF in Good dj. *Oregon.* $55/£35

WILSON, THEODORE D. An Outline of Ship Building, Theoretical and Practical. NY: John Wiley & Son, 1873. 1st ed. Frontis, (xviii),398,(91)-106 ads, pp; 3 fldg tables, 42 plts (10 fldg). (Contemp inscrip, text underlines, 5pp owner ms notes tipped in.) *Lefkowicz.* $200/£129

WILSON, WALTER. Memoirs of the Life and Times of Daniel De Foe. Hurst, Chance, 1830. 3 vols. Engr frontis port (foxed). Contemp 1/2 calf (rubbed, spotting). *Waterfield.* $124/£80

WILSON, WILLIAM L. A Borderland Confederate. Festus P. Sumners (ed). Pittsburg, (1962). 1st ed. Dj lt worn, o/w Fine. *Pratt.* $35/£23

WILSON, WILLIAM S. The Ocean as a Health Resort. London, 1881. 2nd ed. Fldg chart back pocket. (Ex-lib.) *Argosy.* $50/£32

WILSON, WOODROW. George Washington. NY, 1897. 1st Amer ed. Teg, rest uncut. Dec gilt cvrs. Fine (sunned, sl soiled). *Polyanthos.* $75/£48

WILSON, WOODROW. Guarantees of Peace. NY: Harper, (1917). 1st ed. Blue cl (lt soiled, spine faded). *Glenn.* $45/£29

WILSON, YATES. More 'Alice.' London: T.V. Boardman, (1959). 1st ed. 8vo. Ivory cl w/vertical pink/gold patterns. Good in color illus dj. *Reisler.* $85/£55

WILSON, YATES. More 'Alice.' London: T.V. Boardman, 1959. 1st ed. 8vo. Pub's pink/white cl, gilt-lettering. VF+ in orig dj. *D & D.* $65/£42

WILSTACH, PAUL. Hudson River Landings. Indianapolis: Bobbs-Merrill, 1933. 1st ed. VG. *Bowman.* $25/£16

WILSTACH, PAUL. Potomac Landings. NY: Tudor, 1937. New ed. Frontis map. Dec cl, gilt. NF. Howes W546. *Connolly.* $60/£39

WILTON, A. The Life and Work of J.M.W. Turner. London: Academy, 1979. Sound in dj. *Ars Artis.* $116/£75

WILTSEE, ERNEST A. Gold Rush Steamers of the Pacific. SF: Grabhorn, 1938. 1st ed. One of 500 ptd. Signed. Pub's cl-backed brick red cl, paper label. Fine. *Hermitage.* $350/£226

WILTSEE, ERNEST A. Gold Rush Steamers of the Pacific. SF: Grabhorn Press, 1938. One of 500. Frontis. Cl, linen spine, paper label. *Dawson.* $250/£161

WILTSEE, ERNEST A. The Pioneer Miner and the Pack Mule Express. SF: CA Hist Soc, 1931. Inscribed. Fldg map. Gold-stamped cl. Dj (lt chipped). *Dawson.* $200/£129

WILTSEE, ERNEST A. The Truth about Fremont: An Inquiry. SF: John Henry Nash, 1936. 1st ed. One of 1000. Signed. Facs frontis. Fine in NF dj. *Harrington.* $80/£52

WILTZ, CHRIS. The Killing Circle. NY: Macmillan, 1981. 1st ed. Fine (emb name fep) in Fine dj. *Janus.* $65/£42

WINCHELL, MARY E. Home by the Bering Sea. Caldwell: Caxton, 1951. 1st ed. Inscribed. VG (faded edges) in dj (worn). *Parmer.* $55/£35

WINCHELL, NEWTON H. The Aborigines of Minnesota. St. Paul: Minnesota Hist Soc, 1911. 1st ed. 36 full pg, 1/2 tone plts; 26 fldg inserts. Rebound in 1/2 black morocco, black pebbled cl bds w/spine lettered in gilt; new eps. Fine. Howes 11209. *Laurie.* $450/£290

WINCHESTER, ALICE. Versatile Yankee. The Art of Jonathan Fisher, 1768-1847. Princeton: Pyne Press, (1973). VG in dj. *Argosy.* $85/£55

WINCHESTER, CLARENCE (ed). Shipping Wonders of the World. (London, 1936-37). 1st ed. 2 vols. 30 color plts. 2 typed letters from ed laid in. *Lefkowicz.* $75/£48

WINCHESTER, J.D. Capt. J.D. Winchester's Experience on a Voyage from Lynn, Massachusetts to...the Alaskan Gold Fields. Salem, MA: Newcomb & Gauss, 1900. 27 plts. Navy cl, gilt. Good (worn, soiled, extrems frayed). Howes W 556. *Bohling.* $200/£129

WINCHESTER, J.D. Capt. J.D. Winchester's Experience on a Voyage.... Salem: Newcomb & Gauss, 1900. 1st ed. Frontis, 25 plts. Dk blue cl (worn, bumped). VG. Howes W 556. *Parmer.* $200/£129

WINCHESTER, J.D. Captain J.D. Winchester's Experience on a Voyage from Lynn, Massachusetts to San Francisco.... Salem, MA: Newcomb & Gaus, 1900. 1st ed. Frontis; 27 plts. VG. Howes W 556. *Oregon.* $190/£123

WINCKEL, FRANZ. Diseases of Women. A Handbook.... J.H. Williamson (trans). Phila: P. Blakiston, 1887. 1st ed in English. xxix,674pp + pub's 16pg cat. *Bickersteth.* $62/£40

WIND, EDGAR. Pagan Mysteries in the Renaissance. NY, 1968. Rev, enlgd ed. Red buckram binding. (Ex-lib.) *Washton.* $50/£32

WINDELL, ROLAND. Brush of Angels' Wings. San Antonio: Naylor, 1952. 1st ed. *Lambeth.* $40/£26

WINDHAM, DONALD. The Kelly Boys. NY, 1957. Ltd to 240 signed. Single French-folded sig. Fine in ptd envelope. *Cahan.* $75/£48

WINDHAM, DONALD. Two People. NY: Coward-McCann, 1965. 1st ed. Fine in dj. *Cahan.* $40/£26

WINDISCH-GRAETZ, MATHILDE. The Spanish Riding School. NY: Barnes, 1956. 1st US ed. VG. *October Farm.* $25/£16

WINDLE, BERTRAM C.A. Remains of the Prehistoric Age in England. London: Methuen, 1904. 1st ed. Inscrip; sl rubbed, faded, mkd. *Hollett.* $54/£35

WINFREE, WAVERLY K. (comp). Guide to the Manuscript Collections of the Virginia Historical Society. V.H.S., 1985. Paper cvr. VG (ink mks). *Book Broker.* $25/£16

WINGATE, A.W.S. A Cavalier in China. London: Grayson & Grayson, 1940. 1st ed. 15 plts. (Spine faded.) *Hollett.* $54/£35

WINGATE, RONALD. Wingate of the Sudan. London: John Murray, (1955). 2 maps. Good. *Archaeologia.* $35/£23

WINGER, HOWARD W. Printers' Marks and Devices. Chicago: Caxton, 1976. 1st ed, ltd to 600. Fine in glassine wrapper. *Oak Knoll.* $55/£35

WINNAN, AUDUR H. A Catalogue Raisonne of Wanda Ga'g. Washington, Smithsonian Institute. 1st ed. 4to. 315pp. Fine in Fine dj. *Davidson.* $75/£48

WINOGRAND, GARRY. Stock Photographs. Austin/London: Univ of TX, (1980). 1st ed. Fine in dj. *Godot.* $75/£48

WINOGRAND, GARRY. Stock Photographs. The Fort Worth Fat Stock Show and Rodeo. Austin: Univ of TX, 1980. 1st ed. Fine in Fine dj. *Beasley.* $65/£42

WINSHIP, GEORGE PARKER. The Merrymount Press of Boston. Vienna: Herbert Reichner, 1929. Ltd to 350 numbered. Good in slipcase (sl rubbed). *Karmiole.* $300/£194

WINSLOE, CHRISTA. The Child Manuela: The Novel of 'Maedchen in Uniform,'.... Agnes Neill Scott (trans). NY: Farrar & Rinehart, (1933). Cvrs sl age-dknd, else VG in pict dj (lt used). *Pharos.* $60/£39

WINSLOW, C. Man and Epidemics. Princeton Univ Press, 1952. 1st ed. (Erased pencilling rep.) Dj (chipped). *White.* $28/£18

WINSLOW, MIRON. Memoir of Mrs. Harriet Wadsworth Winslow.... NY/Boston: Leavitt, Lord/Crocker & Brewster, 1835. Frontis port, tp vignette, 408pp (foxing). Salmon cl (discolored, faded), blind/gilt-stamped. *Schoyer.* $60/£39

WINSOR, JUSTIN. Cartier to Frontenac; Geographical Discovery.... Boston: HM Co, 1894. 2nd ed. (8),379pp. Gilt cl, leather spine label (spine dknd, sl worn). Good. *Artis.* $65/£42

WINSOR, JUSTIN. The Mississippi Basin. Boston/NY: Houghton, Mifflin, 1895. 1st ed. Partly unopened. 2-tone cl. Spine dknd, else VG. Howes W 577. *Chapel Hill.* $135/£87

WINSOR, JUSTIN. The Mississippi Basin. The Struggle in America between England and France 1697-1763. Houghton Mifflin, 1895. 1st ed. ix,484pp. Overall VG (lt ink # lower spine, remnants of labels fr, rear). Howes W 577. *Oregon.* $85/£55

WINSOR, JUSTIN. Westward Movement: The Colonies and the Republic West of the Alleghanies, 1763-1798.... Boston, 1897. 1st ed. (8),595pp. Howes W 579. *Ginsberg.* $100/£65

WINSOR, WILLIAM. Loma: A Citizen of Venus. St. Paul, 1897. 1st ed. Gilt-pict fr cvr. Fine. *Mcclintock.* $195/£126

WINSTEN, S. Days with Bernard Shaw. London: Hutchinson, (1947). 1st Eng ed. Red cl. NF in VG dj (chipped). *Chapel Hill.* $40/£26

Winter Soldier Investigation. Boston: Beacon, (1972). 1st ed. As New in dj. *Aka.* $50/£32

WINTER, CARL. The Fitzwilliam Museum. London: Trianon Press, 1958. 1st ed. #120/1500. Frontis port, 107 plts (7 color). *Edwards.* $62/£40

WINTER, MARIAN HANNAH. The Theatre of Marvels. NY, 1964. 1st Amer ed. VG in dj. *Argosy.* $75/£48

WINTERBURN, GEORGE. The Value of Vaccination. A Non-Partisan Review.... Phila, 1886. 1st ed. 182pp. Good. *Fye.* $75/£48

WINTERICH, JOHN T. 23 Books and the Stories Behind Them. Berkeley: Univ of CA, 1938. Dj (lt chipped). *Dawson.* $60/£39

WINTERICH, JOHN T. Early American Books and Printing. NY: Houghton Mifflin, 1935. 1st ed. 300 lg paper copies. Signed. Teg, others untrimmed. Red cl, leather spine label (sl chipped). NF in slipcase (lt worn). *Cahan.* $75/£48

WINTERICH, JOHN T. A Primer of Book-Collecting. London: George Allen & Unwin, 1928. 1st ed. Red cl, gilt. VF. *Macdonnell.* $35/£23

WINTERICH, JOHN T. (ed). Pages from Earlier Editions of Horace.... NY: LEC, 1961. One of 1500 numbered. VG. *Argosy.* $100/£65

WINTERNITZ, MILTON CHARLES (ed). Collected Studies on the Pathology of War Gas Poisoning. New Haven, 1920. 41 plts. NF (sm bump fr bd) in orig plain dj. *Goodrich.* $125/£81

WINTERSON, JEANETTE. Oranges Are Not the Only Fruit. London: Bloomsbury Classics, 1991. 1st hb ed. Fine in dj. *Lewton.* $54/£35

WINTERSON, JEANETTE. The Passion. Bloomsbury, 1987. 1st UK ed. Signed. NF (ink name) in VG dj (tear spine middle). *Williams*. $54/£35

WINTERSON, JEANETTE. Sexing the Cherry. NY: Atlantic Monthly, (1989). 1st Amer ed. Fine in dj. *Between The Covers*. $35/£23

WINTERSON, JEANETTE. Sexing the Cherry. London: Bloomsbury, 1989. 1st UK ed. Fine in dj. *Lewton*. $23/£15

WINTHER, OSCAR O. The Old Oregon Country: A History.... Bloomington: Univ IN, 1950. 1st ed. 5 maps. Fine. *Oregon*. $75/£48

WINTRINGHAM, T.H. Deadlock War. London: Faber, 1940. 1st ed. VG in dj (worn, dusty). *Patterson*. $62/£40

WINTRINGHAM, T.H. English Captain. London: Faber, 1939. 1st ed. Fldg map. VG in dj (fr, spine panels, fr flap pasted on plain paper). *Patterson*. $85/£55

WIRKUS, FAUSTIN and TANEY DUDLEY. The White King of La Gonave. GC: Doubleday, Doran, 1931. 1st ed. Double-pg map. Orange cl (sl soiled). Dj. *Karmiole*. $40/£26

WIRT, WILLIAM. Sketches of the Life and Character of Patrick Henry. Phila: James Webster, 1818. 3rd ed. Frontis, xv(i),427,(i),xiipp (heavily foxed; ink inscrips; rubberstamp). Contemp sheep (worn). *Bookpress*. $125/£81

WIRT, WILLIAM. Sketches of the Life and Character of Patrick Henry. Phila: James Webster..., 1818. 3rd ed. xv,427,xiipp; port. Contemp mottled sheep. Blindstamp on flyleaf; few sigs browned, else Very Nice. Howes W 586. *Felcone*. $125/£81

WISE, DANIEL. Summer Days on the Hudson. NY: Nelson & Phillips, 1875. 1st ed. 288pp. Ornate cl, gilt. VG. *Connolly*. $75/£48

WISE, GEORGE. Campaigns and Battles of the Army of Northern Virginia. NY: Neale Pub Co, 1916. 1st ed. Recased, sl cvr speckling, else VG. *Mcgowan*. $250/£161

WISE, GEORGE. Campaigns and Battles of the Army of Northern Virginia. NY: Neale, 1916. 1st ed. Frontis port, port. Orig red buckram. Bkpl, blindstamp, else VG. *Chapel Hill*. $275/£177

WISE, GEORGE. History of the Seventeenth Virginia Infantry, C.S.A. Balt: Kelly, Piet & Co, 1870. 1st ed. 312pp. Orig purple cl. NF (lt shelfwear; name). Howes W 592. *Chapel Hill*. $450/£290

WISE, JENNINGS CROPPER. The Long Arm of Lee. Lynchburg, VA: J.P. Bell, 1915. 1st ed. 2 vols. Red cl. Inner hinges cracked vol 1, else VG. *Chapel Hill*. $275/£177

WISE, JENNINGS CROPPER. The Long Arm of Lee. Lynchburg, VA: J.P. Bell, 1915. 1st ed. 2 vols. 1st state binding. Rear inner hinge vol 2 starting, else NF set. *Mcgowan*. $250/£161

WISE, JENNINGS CROPPER. Ye Kingdome of Accawmacke. Richmond: Bell, 1911. (Rear pocket removed.) *Schoyer*. $35/£23

WISE, JOHN R. The New Forest. London: Smith, Elder, 1863. 1st ed. Walter Crane (illus). Aeg. Purple cl, gilt (extrems worn; endleaves foxed; hinges cracked). *Glenn*. $200/£129

WISE, JOHN S. Recollections of Thirteen Presidents. Doubleday, 1906. (1st ed). Teg. Text VG (rear cvr water-stained w/some red bleeding to rep; internal foxing). *Book Broker*. $45/£29

WISEMAN, ROBERT F. The Complete Horseshoeing Guide. Norman: Univ of OK, (1968). 1st ed, 1st ptg. Fine in dj. *Glenn*. $40/£26

WISLIZENUS, F.A. A Journey to the Rocky Mountains in the Year 1839. St. Louis: MO Hist Soc, 1912. Ltd to 500 numbered. Fldg map. Gilt-stamped spine. VG (corners bumped). Howes W 596. *Oregon*. $250/£161

WISTAR, CASPAR. A System of Anatomy.... Phila: Dobson, 1817. 2nd Amer ed. 2 vols. (Foxed.) Calf (rubbed; joints cracked). *Goodrich*. $125/£81

WISTAR, ISAAC JONES. Autobiography of Isaac Jones Wistar 1827-1905. Phila: Wistar Inst, 1937. 5 plts, fldg map. Uncut, unopened. VF in VG dj. *Oregon*. $65/£42

WISTAR, ISAAC JONES. Autobiography of Isaac Jones Wistar. NY, 1937. 1st ed except for prior private pub. Fldg map. Minor dj chipping, o/w Fine. *Pratt*. $47/£30

WISTAR, ISAAC JONES. Autobiography of Isaac Jones Wistar. NY, 1937. 1st ed thus. Fine in Good dj (chipped). *Bond*. $20/£13

WISTER, OWEN. A Journey in Search of Christmas. NY: Harper, 1904. 1st ed. VG. *Perier*. $30/£19

WISTER, OWEN. Lady Baltimore. NY: Macmillan, 1906. 1st ed. Pict cl (lt rubbed). *Sadlon*. $15/£10

WISTER, OWEN. Owen Wister Out West. Fanny Kemble Wister (ed). Univ of Chicago Press, 1958. 1st ed. Dj. *Lambeth*. $40/£26

WISTER, OWEN. Owen Wister Out West. Fanny Kimble Wister (ed). Chicago, (1958). 2nd ptg, same yr. Fine in dj (worn). *Pratt*. $30/£19

WISTER, OWEN. Padre Ignacio, or The Song of Temptation. NY/London: Harper, 1911. 1st ed. (Spine ends, label sl rubbed.) *Sadlon*. $15/£10

WISTER, OWEN. The Virginian. London: Macmillan, 1902. 1st British ed. 7 plts (of 8); teg. Pict cvr. VG (eps foxed, clipping removed). *Authors Of The West*. $20/£13

WISTER, OWEN. The Virginian. LEC, 1951. Ltd to 1500. Signed by William Moyers (illus). 2 laid-in promo items. Fine in NF orig slipcase. *Baade*. $125/£81

WISTER, OWEN. Watch Your Thirst. NY: Macmillan, 1923. Ltd to 1000 signed. (Sm waterstain lower cvr.) Dj (chipped, repaired). *Sadlon*. $40/£26

WISTER, OWEN. When West Was West. NY, 1928. 1st ed thus. VG- (cvrs dull). *Baade*. $30/£19

WISTER, OWEN. The Writings of Owen Wister. Macmillan, 1928. 1st ed of this set. 11 vols. Frontis each vol, 6 Remington plts. Fine set. *Authors Of The West*. $300/£194

WITHERBY, H.F. et al. The Handbook of British Birds. London: H.F. & G. Witherby, 1938-1941. 1st ed. 5 vols. 147 color plts. Blue buckram. VG in pict djs (sl frayed). *Cox*. $171/£110

WITHERBY, H.F. et al. The Handbook of British Birds. London, 1948. 5th imp. 5 vols. 157 plts. Good set in djs (sl worn). *Wheldon & Wesley*. $140/£90

WITHERS, ALEXANDER S. Chronicles of Border Warfare.... Parsons, WV, 1958. Ltd to 1000 numbered. (Sm defect top of tp, not affecting print.) *Hayman*. $25/£16

WITHERSPOON, S.J.A. The Glimerick Book. Putnam's, 1925. 1st Eng ed. Dec bds (sl mkd, faded). VG. *Dalian*. $39/£25

WITTEMANS, FR. A New and Authentic History of the Rosicrucians. Chicago: Aries, (1938). 1st ed. VG in Good dj. *Blue Dragon*. $50/£32

WITTENMYER, ANNIE. History of the Woman's Temperance Crusade. Boston: James H. Earle, (1882). 1st ed. Burgundy cl. Fine. *Karmiole*. $45/£29

WITTGENSTEIN, LUDWIG. Philosophical Investigations. G.E.M. Anscombe (trans). NY: Macmillan, (1953). 1st Amer ed. Grn-lettered brn cl. Sl bumped, o/w Fine. *House*. $350/£226

WITTGENSTEIN, LUDWIG. Remarks on the Foundations of Mathematics. G.E.M. Anscombe (trans). Oxford: Basil Blackwell, 1956. 1st ed. Gilt-lettered blue cl. VF in red ptd dj. *House*. $350/£226

WITTKOWER, RUDOLF. Gian Lorenzo Bernini. London/NY: Phaidon, 1955. 131 plts. Fine in dj. *Europa*. $84/£54

WITTROCK, WOLFGANG. Toulouse-Lautrec. The Complete Prints. Catherine E. Kuehn (trans). (London): Sotheby's, (1985). 1st ed. 2 vols. 100 color plts. Grn cl, gilt spines. Fine set in djs; pub's slipcase. *Karmiole*. $300/£194

Wizard of Oz. London: Octopus, 1980. 21x21 cm. 6 dbl-pg, fan-fld pop-ups. J. Pavlin & G. Seda (illus). Glazed pict bds. VG. *Book Finders*. $45/£29

WODEHOUSE, P.G. America, I Like You. NY: S&S, 1956. 1st ed. VG + in dj. *Limestone*. $95/£61

WODEHOUSE, P.G. Angel Cake. GC: Doubleday, 1952. 1st Amer ed. Brn cl w/grn lettering. VG in colored pict dj. *Limestone*. $155/£100

WODEHOUSE, P.G. Aunts Aren't Gentlemen. London: Barrie & Jenkins, 1974. 1st ed. Fine in dj. *Limestone*. $65/£42

WODEHOUSE, P.G. Author! Author! NY: S&S, 1962. 1st ptg. Tan cl over lt orange bds. Fine in VG color pict dj (few closed tears). *Limestone*. $175/£113

WODEHOUSE, P.G. Bachelors Anonymous. London: Jenkins, 1973. 1st UK ed. Fine in dj. *Williams*. $59/£38

WODEHOUSE, P.G. Bertie Wooster Sees It Through. NY: S&S, 1955. 1st Amer ed. Fine in tan cl spine, grey-blue dec bds. VG pict dj. *Vandoros*. $195/£126

WODEHOUSE, P.G. Biffen's Millions. NY, 1964. 1st ed. VG in dj (sl soiled, worn, price-clipped). *King*. $60/£39

WODEHOUSE, P.G. Big Money. London: Jenkins, 1931. 1st ptg of Eng 1st ed. Orange cl w/black lettering. Cvrs sl soiled, else VG. *Limestone*. $95/£61

WODEHOUSE, P.G. Bill the Conqueror. NY: Doran, 1924. 1st Amer ed. Yellow-orange cl w/grn lettering, dec. Good (pock mks fr gutter, bottom of panel) in VG dj (soiled, nicked). *Limestone*. $300/£194

WODEHOUSE, P.G. Bill the Conqueror. London: Methuen, 1924. 1st ed. Orig cl (sl soiled; neatly re-backed retaining orig backstrip). Sound (edges browned). *Cox*. $31/£20

WODEHOUSE, P.G. Bill the Conqueror. NY: Doran, 1924. 1st ed. Dec cvr. Fine in pict dj (faint dust soiling, lt edgewear). *Else Fine*. $750/£484

WODEHOUSE, P.G. Bill the Conqueror. London: Methuen, 1924. 1st in rpt 2/6 dj w/boxed statement. Red cl w/black lettering. VG in dj. *Limestone*. $115/£74

WODEHOUSE, P.G. Brinkley Manor. Boston: Little Brown, 1934. 1st Amer ed. Orange-red cl w/black lettering, dwg. VG + in VG pict dj (lt chipping at corners, spine extrems) *Limestone*. $285/£184

WODEHOUSE, P.G. The Butler Did It. NY: S&S, 1957. 1st Amer ed. NF in grn cl, black bds, silver lettering. VG pict dj (3/4-inch loss bottom spine). *Vandoros*. $170/£110

WODEHOUSE, P.G. Carry On, Jeeves. London: Jenkins, 1925. 1st ed. Grn pict cl. VG. *Limestone*. $115/£74

WODEHOUSE, P.G. Carry On, Jeeves. London: Jenkins, 1925. 1st UK ed. Fine (stamp) in VG 1st issue dj (sm closed tear to spine; lt soiled). *Williams*. $1,744/£1,125

WODEHOUSE, P.G. The Clicking of Cuthbert. London: Herbert Jenkins, 1922. 1st ed, 1st issue, in smoother cl, w/8 titles listed on verso of 1/2 title. Pict cl (sl worn). Good. *Ash*. $116/£75

WODEHOUSE, P.G. The Clicking of Cuthbert. London: Jenkins, 1922. 1st ed, 3rd issue. Fine in pict cvr. (Lacks dj.) *Else Fine*. $65/£42

WODEHOUSE, P.G. The Clicking of Cuthbert. London: Jenkins, 1922. 1st ed. Grn pict cl, grn lettering. Near VG (fading moisture spot inner corner rear panel, top edges darkened, fr edges sl foxed, corners wearing). *Limestone*. $175/£113

WODEHOUSE, P.G. Cocktail Time. London: Jenkins, 1958. 1st ed. Red cl, black lettering. VG + in VG dj (lt chipped). *Limestone*. $95/£61

WODEHOUSE, P.G. The Code of the Woosters. London: Herbert Jenkins, (1938). 1st ed. Variant turquoise cl. Nice. *Ash*. $132/£85

WODEHOUSE, P.G. The Code of the Woosters. London: Jenkins, 1938. 1st ed, 1st Eng ptg. Grn-turquoise cl w/black lettering, decs. VG in VG- colored pict 7/6 dj (chipped w/2 pieces tape top fr panel). *Limestone*. $500/£323

WODEHOUSE, P.G. The Code of the Woosters. GC: Doubleday, Doran, 1938. 1st ed. Yellow cl dec in blue. Very Nice. *Cady*. $30/£19

WODEHOUSE, P.G. Company for Henry. London: Herbert Jenkins, 1967. 1st ed. Fine in illus dj. *Cahan*. $40/£26

WODEHOUSE, P.G. Company for Henry. London: B&J, 1967. 1st UK ed. VG in dj (sm closed tear). *Lewton*. $26/£17

WODEHOUSE, P.G. The Crime Wave at Blandings. Doubleday, Doran, 1937. 1st Amer ed. VG in dw (inner reinforcement). *Fine Books*. $185/£119

WODEHOUSE, P.G. The Crime Wave at Blandings. GC: Doubleday, Doran, 1937. 1st ed. Grn cl, dk grn lettering, dwgs. VG + in dj (sl chipped at spine extrems). *Limestone*. $235/£152

WODEHOUSE, P.G. The Crime Wave at Blandings. NY: Doubleday, Doran, 1937. 1st ed. Pict cl. VG in dj (sl rubbed, sunned). *Ash*. $612/£395

WODEHOUSE, P.G. Do Butlers Burgle Banks? London: Jenkins, 1968. 1st ed. NF in dj (sl rubbed, creased, price-clipped). *Rees*. $31/£20

WODEHOUSE, P.G. Do Butlers Burgle Banks? London: Jenkins, 1968. 1st Eng ed. Fine in NF dj (few tears back panel). *Limestone*. $85/£55

WODEHOUSE, P.G. Doctor Sally. London: Methuen, 1933. 3rd ed. Blue cl w/black lettering, decs. Edges foxed, else VG in VG + color pict dj. *Limestone*. $110/£71

WODEHOUSE, P.G. Eggs, Beans and Crumpets. London: Jenkins, 1940. 1st ptg. Table of contents fails to list last story 'Ukridge and the Old Stopper,' using its pg #s for the title 'Buttercup Day.' Orange cl w/black lettering, design. VG in VG- dj (spine extrems chipped, affecting lettering). *Limestone*. $240/£155

WODEHOUSE, P.G. Enter Psmith. NY: Macmillan, (1935). 1st Amer ed. Orange cl. NF. *Godot*. $50/£32

WODEHOUSE, P.G. A Few Quick Ones. NY: S&S, 1959. 1st ed. White cl spine over gray buckram, black/pink letters; yellow/pink stripes. Bkpl, else NF in dj. *Limestone.* $75/£48

WODEHOUSE, P.G. A Few Quick Ones. London: Jenkins, 1959. 1st UK ed. Fine in VG dj (price-clipped). *Williams.* $54/£35

WODEHOUSE, P.G. Fish Preferred. NY, 1929. 1st Amer ed. NF (sl sunned, rubbed; name, foxing). *Polyanthos.* $45/£29

WODEHOUSE, P.G. French Leave. London: Herbert Jenkins, 1955. 1st ed. NF in dj (sl creased, nicked). *Rees.* $54/£35

WODEHOUSE, P.G. French Leave. London: Jenkins, 1955. 1st UK ed. NF in dj (sm nicks). *Williams.* $116/£75

WODEHOUSE, P.G. Frozen Assets. London, (1964). 1st ed. VG in dj. *Argosy.* $100/£65

WODEHOUSE, P.G. Frozen Assets. London: Jenkins, 1964. 1st ed. Red cl w/gilt lettering. NF in dj. *Limestone.* $100/£65

WODEHOUSE, P.G. Frozen Assets. London: Jenkins, 1964. 1st UK ed. VG (sl abrasion, crease fep) in dj (browned, short closed tears). *Williams.* $50/£32

WODEHOUSE, P.G. Full Moon. Doubleday, 1947. 1st ed. Fine in pict dj (dust-soil rear panel). *Fine Books.* $125/£81

WODEHOUSE, P.G. Full Moon. London: Jenkins, 1947. 1st Eng ed. Orange cl, black lettering. Fine in NF dj. *Limestone.* $125/£81

WODEHOUSE, P.G. Full Moon. London: Jenkins, 1947. 1st UK ed. VG (2 sm spots on rear cvr) in dj. *Lewton.* $47/£30

WODEHOUSE, P.G. Galahad at Blandings. London: Jenkins, 1965. 1st Eng ed. Red cl, gilt. Discoloration back panel, else VG in dj (sm interior stain, repair). *Limestone.* $85/£55

WODEHOUSE, P.G. Galahad at Blandings. London: Jenkins, 1965. 1st UK ed. Fine in VG dj (price-clipped). *Williams.* $56/£36

WODEHOUSE, P.G. The Girl in Blue. London: Barrie & Jenkins, 1970. 1st ed. Fine in dj. *Limestone.* $125/£81

WODEHOUSE, P.G. The Girl in Blue. London: Barrie & Jenkins, 1970. 1st UK ed. VG (ink name) in dj (lt wear, chipped). *Williams.* $43/£28

WODEHOUSE, P.G. The Gold Bat. London: A&C Black, 1911. 2nd ed. Red pict cl w/black/gold lettering, dwg. VG. *Limestone.* $295/£190

WODEHOUSE, P.G. Golf Without Tears. NY: Doran, 1924. 1st Amer ed of The Clicking of Cuthbert. NF. (Lacks dj.) *Else Fine.* $135/£87

WODEHOUSE, P.G. The Great Sermon Handicap. St. Hughs Press, (1933). VG. *Fine Books.* $45/£29

WODEHOUSE, P.G. He Rather Enjoyed It. NY: George H. Doran, (1925). 1st Amer ed. Red cl stamped in black. Spine sl faded, sm tear crown, else NF. *Godot.* $185/£119

WODEHOUSE, P.G. He Rather Enjoyed It. NY: Doran, 1925. 1st Amer ed. Red cl w/black lettering. Spine sl faded, sm tear, else NF. *Limestone.* $285/£184

WODEHOUSE, P.G. The Head of Kay's. London: A&C Black, 1905. 1st ed, 1st issue. Frontis, illus by T.M.R. Whitwell. Title pg foxed, else VG + . *Limestone.* $1,500/£968

WODEHOUSE, P.G. The Head of Kay's. Black, 1922. 1st thus. Dec cl. Frontis loose; sl faded, else Good. *Whiteson.* $39/£25

WODEHOUSE, P.G. Heavy Weather. London: Jenkins, 1933. 1st ed, 1st ptg. Blue cl w/orange lettering, decs. VG in dj (lt chip). *Limestone.* $675/£435

WODEHOUSE, P.G. Heavy Weather. Jenkins, 1933. 1st ed. VG + . *Fine Books.* $75/£48

WODEHOUSE, P.G. Heavy Weather. Toronto: M&S, 1933. 1st ed. Fine in dj (lt wear). *Else Fine.* $200/£129

WODEHOUSE, P.G. Heavy Weather. London: Jenkins, 1933. 1st Eng ptg. Blue cl w/orange lettering, decs. Sig, else NF. *Limestone.* $135/£87

WODEHOUSE, P.G. How Right You Are, Jeeves. NY: S&S, 1960. 1st ed. Fine in NF dj (sm closed tear). *Limestone.* $185/£119

WODEHOUSE, P.G. The Ice in the Bedroom. NY: S&S, 1961. 1st Amer ed. Signed. Bkpl, else NF in VG dj (sl chipping). *Between The Covers.* $350/£226

WODEHOUSE, P.G. The Ice in the Bedroom. NY: S&S, 1961. 1st ed, 1st ptg. Signed. Black cl, white/yellow/red lettering over paper-cvrd spine. VG in Fine dj. *Limestone.* $295/£190

WODEHOUSE, P.G. If I Were You. London: Jenkins, (1931). 1st Eng ed. Red cl w/black lettering, decs. VG- (panels sl rubbed; edges, prelims lt foxed, name). *Limestone.* $75/£48

WODEHOUSE, P.G. If I Were You. London: Jenkins, 1931. 1st ed, 1st ptg. Orange cl w/black lettering, decs. Sig, else VG in dj (lt chipped at spine extrems, corners). *Limestone.* $950/£613

WODEHOUSE, P.G. The Inimitable Jeeves. London: Herbert Jenkins, 1923. 1st ed, 1st issue, w/10 titles verso of 1/2 title. Pict cl (sl worn, few mks). Nice. *Ash.* $147/£95

WODEHOUSE, P.G. The Inimitable Jeeves. London: Jenkins, 1923. 1st ed. Sage pict cl. Top edges dusty; fr, bottom edges foxed; 2 sm spots foot of fr panel, else VG. *Limestone.* $215/£139

WODEHOUSE, P.G. The Intrusion of Jimmy. NY: Watt, (1910). 1st ed, 1st issue (w/gilt stamped spine). 8vo. Color frontis, 4 b/w illus by Will Grefe. Black cl, gilt stamped spine, upper cvr; upper cvr round color pict label (esp bright gilt stamped upper cvr). VG. *Houle.* $750/£484

WODEHOUSE, P.G. Jeeves and the Feudal Spirit. London: Jenkins, 1954. 1st ed. NF in dj. *Limestone.* $155/£100

WODEHOUSE, P.G. Jeeves and the Feudal Spirit. London: Jenkins, 1954. 1st UK ed. VG in VG dj (edgewear, strengthened to rear). *Williams.* $85/£55

WODEHOUSE, P.G. Jeeves and the Tie That Binds. NY: S&S, (1971). 1st Amer ed. Fine in dj (sl wear). *Antic Hay.* $35/£23

WODEHOUSE, P.G. Jeeves and the Tie That Binds. NY: S&S, 1971. 1st Amer ed. VF in dj. *Limestone.* $55/£35

WODEHOUSE, P.G. Jeeves in the Offing. London: Jenkins, 1960. 1st UK ed, 1st issue, w/half-title for 'A Few Quick Ones.' NF in dj (ink initials fr flap). *Williams.* $78/£50

WODEHOUSE, P.G. Laughing Gas. GC: Doubleday, Doran, 1936. 1st Amer ed. Orange cl w/black letters, dwgs. Fine in Fine pict dj. *Limestone.* $425/£274

WODEHOUSE, P.G. Laughing Gas. London: Jenkins, 1936. 1st ed. Red cl w/black letters, decs. Nice in dj (creased, repaired at bottom of fr panel, sm loss at spine tail). *Limestone.* $765/£494

WODEHOUSE, P.G. Leave It to Psmith. Doran, 1924. 1st Amer ed. VG. *Fine Books.* $125/£81

WODEHOUSE, P.G. Leave It to Psmith. London: Jenkins, 1924. 1st ed. Grn pict cl. Good (spotting, rubbed, short split lower hinge). *Limestone.* $115/£74

WODEHOUSE, P.G. The Little Nugget. NY: Watt, (1914). 1st Amer ed. Frontis, 2 illus by Will Grefe. Gilt stamped black cl. VG. *Houle.* $450/£290

WODEHOUSE, P.G. The Little Nugget. Methuen, 1913. 1st UK ed. VG (foxing; spine fading; fep replaced?). *Williams.* $1,163/£750

WODEHOUSE, P.G. The Little Nugget. London: Methuen, 1926. 12th ed. Blue cl w/black lettering. Sig, else VG in VG- 2/6 dj (soiled, chips). *Limestone.* $95/£61

WODEHOUSE, P.G. The Little Warrior. Doran, 1920. 1st US ed. VG + (spine dulling). *Williams.* $504/£325

WODEHOUSE, P.G. Love Among the Chickens. NY, 1909. 1st Amer ed. NF (name, fep lacks piece; sunned, rubbed, sl soiled). *Polyanthos.* $45/£29

WODEHOUSE, P.G. The Luck of the Bodkins. Boston: Little Brown, 1936. 1st Amer ed. Pale grn cl w/black lettering, design. Name, else Fine in NF dj (sm internal repair). *Limestone.* $350/£226

WODEHOUSE, P.G. The Mating Season. London: Jenkins, (1949). 1st ed. Orange cl w/black lettering. VG in dj. *Limestone.* $100/£65

WODEHOUSE, P.G. The Mating Season. London: Jenkins, 1949. 1st UK ed. VG (tape mks to eps) in dj (sl chipped). *Williams.* $85/£55

WODEHOUSE, P.G. Meet Mr. Mulliner. London: Herbert Jenkins, 1927. 1st ed. Clipping w/photo tipped to fep. Fine in grn cl, black lettering, decs. Lacks dj. *Vandoros.* $225/£145

WODEHOUSE, P.G. Meet Mr. Mulliner. Leipzig: Tauchnitz, 1929. 1st European ed; 1st thus. Ads dated March 1929. Sm tear top spine, else VG in orig wrappers. *Limestone.* $45/£29

WODEHOUSE, P.G. Mike and Psmith. London: Jenkins, 1953. 1st UK ed. NF in VG dj (lt edgeworn). *Williams.* $147/£95

WODEHOUSE, P.G. Mike at Wrykyn. London: Jenkins, 1953. 1st UK ed. VG in dj (sl chipped, worn, price-clipped). *Williams.* $116/£75

WODEHOUSE, P.G. Money for Nothing. GC: Doubleday, Doran, 1928. 1st Amer ed. Lt blue cl, blue lettering, orange decs. NF. *Limestone.* $95/£61

WODEHOUSE, P.G. Money for Nothing. London: Jenkins, 1928. 1st ed, 1st ptg. Red cl w/black lettering, decs. Cvrs sunned, else VG. *Limestone.* $200/£129

WODEHOUSE, P.G. Money in the Bank. GC: Doubleday Doran, 1942. 1st ed. Dk red cl w/pict dwg. VG- in dj (lt chipped spine). *Limestone.* $245/£158

WODEHOUSE, P.G. The Most of P.G. Wodehouse. NY: S&S, 1960. 1st ed. Fine in dj (lt wear spine corners). *Else Fine.* $50/£32

WODEHOUSE, P.G. The Most of P.G. Wodehouse. NY, 1960. 1st ed. VG in dj (worn, sl tears). *King.* $50/£32

WODEHOUSE, P.G. Much Obliged, Jeeves. London, (1971). 1st ed. Fine in dj (price-clipped). *Argosy.* $75/£48

WODEHOUSE, P.G. Much Obliged, Jeeves. London: Barrie & Jenkins, 1971. 1st UK ed. VG + in dj (spine lettering faded). *Williams.* $70/£45

WODEHOUSE, P.G. Mulliner Nights. Leipzig: Tauchnitz, (1935). #5218. 1st thus. Wrappers. Upper spine sl pulling, else VG. *Limestone.* $35/£23

WODEHOUSE, P.G. Mulliner Nights. London: Jenkins, (mid-1930s). 3rd ptg. Red cl w/black lettering, designs. Sig, else VG in color pict 5/ dj. *Limestone.* $75/£48

WODEHOUSE, P.G. Mulliner Omnibus. London: Jenkins, 1935. 1st ed. Fine (name). (Lacks dj.) *Else Fine.* $85/£55

WODEHOUSE, P.G. My Man Jeeves. London: George Newnes, (1919). 1st ed, 1st issue, in pink cl w/Newnes' 1/9 Novels ads at rear. Good (sl sunned, discolored; fep cracked; inscrips; sl brittle, chipped). *Ash.* $767/£495

WODEHOUSE, P.G. No Nudes Is Good Nudes. NY, (1970). 1st ed. Cl-backed bds. Sl musty odor, else VG in dj (yellowed). *King.* $35/£23

WODEHOUSE, P.G. No Nudes Is Good Nudes. NY: S&S, 1970. 1st Amer ed. Fine in NF dj. *Limestone.* $65/£42

WODEHOUSE, P.G. Nothing Serious. London: Jenkins, (1950). 1st ed. Red-orange cl w/black lettering, designs. Fr panel lt stained, else VG in VG- dj (lt chipped; missing piece fr panel, spine, back panel, affecting lettering). *Limestone.* $125/£81

WODEHOUSE, P.G. The Old Reliable. London: Jenkins, 1951. 1st ed. Orange cl w/black lettering. NF in dj. *Limestone.* $185/£119

WODEHOUSE, P.G. The Old Reliable. London: Jenkins, 1951. 1st UK ed. Fine in VG + dj (sl spine wear; sl discolored). *Williams.* $147/£95

WODEHOUSE, P.G. Pearls, Girls and Monty Bodkin. London, 1972. 1st ed. Fine in dj (sl rubbed). *Words Etc.* $31/£20

WODEHOUSE, P.G. Pearls, Girls and Monty Bodkin. London: Barrie & Jenkins, 1972. 1st ed. Fine in dj (price-clipped). *Else Fine.* $60/£39

WODEHOUSE, P.G. Pearls, Girls and Monty Bodkin. London: Jenkins, 1972. 1st UK ed. Fine in NF dj (short closed tears). *Williams.* $54/£35

WODEHOUSE, P.G. A Pelican at Blandings. London: Jenkins, 1969. 1st UK ed. Fine in dj (sm stain). *Williams.* $85/£55

WODEHOUSE, P.G. Performing Flea. London: Jenkins, 1953. 1st ed. Blue cl, gilt. VG in dj (sl rubbed, chipped). *Limestone.* $155/£100

WODEHOUSE, P.G. Pigs Have Wings. London, (1952). 1st Eng ed. (Spine faded.) *Waterfield.* $19/£12

WODEHOUSE, P.G. Pigs Have Wings. London: Jenkins, 1952. 1st ed. Red cl w/black lettering. Edges sl foxed, else VG in dj (lt chipped spine extrems). *Limestone.* $195/£126

WODEHOUSE, P.G. Pigs Have Wings. London: Jenkins, 1952. 4th ptg. Red cl w/black lettering. Fine in VG- dj (missing 1-inch piece lower fr corner). *Limestone.* $55/£35

WODEHOUSE, P.G. The Play's the Thing. Brentano's, 1927. 1st ed. NF in VG + dj (lt dust-soil to spine). *Fine Books.* $375/£242

WODEHOUSE, P.G. Plum Pie. NY: S&S, (1967). 1st Amer ed. Fine in dj. *Limestone.* $95/£61

WODEHOUSE, P.G. Plum Pie. London: Jenkins, 1966. 1st UK ed. VG (ink inscrip) in dj. *Williams.* $50/£32

WODEHOUSE, P.G. The Pothunters. London: A&C Black, 1924. Color frontis. Red cl w/black lettering, decs. Name, else VG. *Limestone.* $90/£58

WODEHOUSE, P.G. The Prince and Betty. NY: Watt, (1912). 1st ed. 8vo. Frontis, 4 illus by Will Grefe. Gilt stamped pict black cl; upper cvr w/2 oval color cameo port labels (spine sl faded); gilt stamping esp bright. VG. *Houle.* $625/£403

WODEHOUSE, P.G. The Prince and Betty. NY: W.J. Watt, 1912. Reissue. Dk blue cl, gilt titled, pict paper label. Very Nice. *Cady.* $15/£10

WODEHOUSE, P.G. Psmith in the City. London: A&C Black, 1919. 2nd ed. Blue pict cl, color lettering. VG (sig, fr panel sl creased). *Limestone.* $195/£126

WODEHOUSE, P.G. Psmith Journalist. London: A&C Black, 1915. 2nd Eng ed, 1st issue. Blue pict cl, black/gold/cream/yellow/blue lettering and drawing. 'Black' on foot of spine 1/8-inch. 12 full-pg b/w plts by T.M.R. Whitwell. Inscrip, cvrs sl rubbed, spine extrems bumped, else VG. *Limestone.* $700/£452

WODEHOUSE, P.G. The Purloined Paperweight. S&S, 1967. 1st ed. Fine in dj. *Fine Books.* $50/£32

WODEHOUSE, P.G. Quick Service. Doubleday, Doran, 1940. 1st Amer ed. VG+ in VG dj (lt wear). *Fine Books.* $195/£126

WODEHOUSE, P.G. Quick Service. NY: Doubleday Doran, 1940. 1st Amer ed. Beige cl w/black lettering, illus. VG+ in VG colored pict dj (lt chipping spine extrems, upper fr panel, back panel). *Limestone.* $235/£152

WODEHOUSE, P.G. Quick Service. Toronto: L-G, 1941. 1st ed. Fine in dj (lt wear). *Else Fine.* $150/£97

WODEHOUSE, P.G. The Return of Jeeves. NY: S&S, 1954. 1st Amer ptg. Tan cl over charcoal gray bds. NF (sig) in colored pict dj. *Limestone.* $165/£106

WODEHOUSE, P.G. Right Ho, Jeeves. London: Jenkins, 1934. 1st ed. Beige cl w/red lettering, decs. Cvrs soiled, else VG. *Limestone.* $195/£126

WODEHOUSE, P.G. Right Ho, Jeeves. London: Jenkins, 1934. 1st UK ed. NF in dj (spine bumped, creased). *Williams.* $1,395/£900

WODEHOUSE, P.G. Ring for Jeeves. London: Jenkins, 1951. 1st UK ed. NF in VG dj (closed tears; sm hole). *Williams.* $62/£40

WODEHOUSE, P.G. Sam the Sudden. London: Methuen, 1925. 1st ed, 1st issue w/ads dated 8/25 on last pg. Red cl w/black lettering. Spine ends sl bumped, else VG. *Limestone.* $135/£87

WODEHOUSE, P.G. The Small Bachelor. NY, (1927). 1st Amer ed. Spine worn, else Good. *King.* $125/£81

WODEHOUSE, P.G. Something Fishy. London: Herbert Jenkins, 1957. 1st ed. Fine in purplish-red cl lettered in black. NF color pict dj. *Vandoros.* $195/£126

WODEHOUSE, P.G. Something New. Appleton, 1915. 1st ed. Spine sl faded, else VG. *Fine Books.* $395/£255

WODEHOUSE, P.G. St. Austin's. Black, 1903. 1st UK ed. VG (sl spine dulling; lacks frontis). *Williams.* $1,473/£950

WODEHOUSE, P.G. Stiff Upper Lip, Jeeves. London: Jenkins, 1963. 1st ed. Red cl, gilt. Fine in dj. *Limestone.* $135/£87

WODEHOUSE, P.G. Stiff Upper Lip, Jeeves. London: Jenkins, 1963. 1st UK ed. Fine (fep sl rubbed) in dj. *Williams.* $59/£38

WODEHOUSE, P.G. Summer Lightning. London: Jenkins, 1929. 1st Eng ed. Red cl w/black lettering, decs. NF. *Limestone.* $135/£87

WODEHOUSE, P.G. Summer Moonshine. Doubleday, Doran, 1937. 1st Amer ed. VG+ in VG+ dj. *Fine Books.* $225/£145

WODEHOUSE, P.G. Summer Moonshine. NY: Doubleday-Doran, 1937. 1st ed. NF in 2nd state pict dj (lt spine fade, minor wear). *Else Fine.* $135/£87

WODEHOUSE, P.G. Thank You, Jeeves. London: Jenkins, 1934. 1st UK ed. Fine in VG+ 2nd issue dj w/ 2/6d price label on spine, issued 1935. This bk issued w/this wrapper. *Williams.* $233/£150

WODEHOUSE, P.G. Thank You, Jeeves. London: Jenkins, 1934. 1st ed, first printing. Grey-beige cl w/red lettering. VG+. *Limestone.* $125/£81

WODEHOUSE, P.G. Ukridge. London: Jenkins, 1924. 1st ed. Bright grn pict cl. Fr panel sl spotted, fr edges sl foxed, else VG. *Limestone.* $185/£119

WODEHOUSE, P.G. Uncle Dynamite. London: Jenkins, 1948. 1st ed. Orange-red cl, black lettering. Fine in NF dj. *Limestone.* $165/£106

WODEHOUSE, P.G. Uncle Fred in the Springtime. London: Jenkins, 1939. 1st ed, 1st Eng ptg. Dk red cvrs, gold lettering on spine. Sm Blackwell label fr pastedown, else NF in colored pict dj w/ 7/6 Net on grn spine label. *Limestone.* $665/£429

WODEHOUSE, P.G. Very Good, Jeeves. NY, 1930. 1st Amer ed. NF (sunned, rubbed). *Polyanthos.* $75/£48

WODEHOUSE, P.G. Very Good, Jeeves. Doubleday, Doran, 1930. 1st Amer ed. Near VG in dj (lt chipped, stained). *Fine Books.* $225/£145

WODEHOUSE, P.G. The Week-end Wodehouse. Doubleday, Doran, 1939. 1st ed. NF in VG pict dj (lt flaking to spine head). *Fine Books.* $195/£126

WODEHOUSE, P.G. William Tell Told Again. London: A&C Black, 1904. 1st ed, 1st issue. Lt stone-colored pict cl, gilt. 1904 inscrip; sl stain top of 1 plt; inner hinges sl tender; few ink stains fr, back panels; gilt lettering sl faded but picture quite bright. Better than acceptable. *Limestone.* $1,500/£968

WODEHOUSE, P.G. William Tell Told Again. London: A&C Black, 1904. 1st ed. 2nd, tan binding, 1904 on tp. NF (fr bd sl sprung; name fep). *Beasley.* $500/£323

WODEHOUSE, P.G. Wodehouse on Golf. Doubleday, Doran, 1940. 1st ed. VG+ in 2nd state binding, 1st state pict dj (sm chips). *Fine Books.* $285/£184

WODEHOUSE, P.G. The World of Blandings. London: Barrie & Jenkins, 1976. 1st ed. VG in dj (1 tear, sm chip). *Limestone.* $65/£42

WODEHOUSE, P.G. The World of Psmith. London: Barrie & Jenkins, 1974. 1st ed. Grn cl w/white lettering. NF in dj. *Limestone.* $85/£55

WODEHOUSE, P.G. and GUY BOULTON. Bring on the Girls! NY, 1953. 1st ed. Sl discolored, else VG in dj (rubbed, edgetorn). *King.* $85/£55

WODEHOUSE, P.G. and GUY BOULTON. Bring on the Girls! London: Jenkins, 1954. 1st Eng ed. Maroon cl, gilt. VG in sl worn dj. *Limestone.* $135/£87

WOEHRMANN, PAUL. At the Headwaters of the Maumee. Indianapolis: InHS, 1971. Frontis; 4pp plts. VG in ptd wraps. *Bohling.* $24/£15

WOIWODE, LARRY. Beyond the Bedroom Wall. NY, (1975). 1st ed. VG in dj. *King.* $50/£32

WOIWODE, LARRY. What I'm Going to Do, I Think. NY: FSG, (1969). 1st ed, 1st bk. Fine in dj (lt worn; chips). *Hermitage.* $45/£29

WOJCIECHOWSKA, MAIA. Shadow of a Bull. NY: Atheneum, 1964. 1st ed. 8vo. Alvin Smith (dwgs). Red cl, gold stamped, emb title. Good in yellow dj (pin hole; worn). *Reisler.* $75/£48

Wolf at the Door. Boston: Roberts Bros, 1877. 1st ed. Gilt-dec cl. VG (edges sl worn). *Reese.* $30/£19

WOLF, EDWIN and JOHN FLEMING. Rosenbach, a Biography. Cleveland/NY: World, (1960). 1st trade ed. VG in dj (lt used). *Juvelis.* $80/£52

WOLF, EDWIN and JOHN FLEMING. Rosenbach: The Life of One of the Greatest Book Collectors. Weidenfeld & Nicolson, 1960. Good in dj (sl torn). *Moss.* $54/£35

WOLFE, BERTRAM D. Diego Rivera. His Life and Times. London, 1939. Color frontis. (Cl lt discolored spine.) *Edwards.* $39/£25

WOLFE, GENE. The Claw of the Concilliator. S&S, 1981. 1st ed, uncorrected proof. Inscribed. VG+ in wraps. *Aronovitz.* $200/£129

WOLFE, GENE. The Devil in a Forest. Follet, 1976. 1st ed. Signed. Fine in VG+ dj. *Aronovitz.* $45/£29

WOLFE, GENE. The Fifth Head of Cerberus. NY: Scribner's, (1972). 1st ed. Fine in dj (sl wear). *Antic Hay.* $20/£13

WOLFE, GENE. The Fifth Head of Cerberus. Scribners, 1972. 1st ed. Signed. Fine in dj. *Aronovitz.* $33/£21

WOLFE, GENE. Operation Ares. Dobson, 1977. 1st Eng, 1st hb ed, 1st bk. Signed. VF in dj. *Aronovitz.* $40/£26

WOLFE, GENE. The Sword of the Lictor. Timescape, 1982. 1st ed. NF in dj. *Madle.* $50/£32

WOLFE, GEOFFREY. The Final Club. NY, 1990. 1st Amer ed. Signed. Fine in Fine dj. *Polyanthos.* $35/£23

WOLFE, HUMBERT. Notes on English Verse Satire. London: Hogarth Press, 1929. 1st ed. Edges, prelims sl foxed, o/w Fine in dj (sl chipped). *Temple.* $42/£27

WOLFE, HUMBERT. Notes on English Verse Satire. Hogarth Press, 1929. 1st ed. VF in dj. *Words Etc.* $70/£45

WOLFE, HUMBERT. Troy. London: Faber & Gwyer, 1928. 1st ed. One of 500 numbered, signed. Sugar blue bds, gilt. VF. *Macdonnell.* $75/£48

WOLFE, LINNIE MARSH. Son of the Wilderness: The Life of John Muir. Knopf, 1945. 1st ed. 3/4 black leather (rebound), gilt-stamped. Name, date, else Fine. *Authors Of The West.* $50/£32

WOLFE, SUSAN. The Last Billable Hour. NY: St Martin, 1989. 1st ed. Fine in dj (sm closed tear; lt wrinkled). *Janus.* $200/£129

WOLFE, THOMAS J. (ed). Spencer's Faerie Queen. London: George Allen, 1897. 1st ed. Walter Crane (illus). 6 vols. 4to. Teg. Gilt-stamped illus white cl, gold/red lettering. 19 parts bound together, incl paper wrappers. Lovely set (sl handled) in orig pub's box (worn, frayed, but complete). *Reisler.* $1,650/£1,065

WOLFE, THOMAS. America. Chicago: Privately ptd (at the Norman Press), 1942. 1st separate ed. Fine in dj (sm chip top corner fr panel, short tear top rear panel). *Chapel Hill.* $300/£194

WOLFE, THOMAS. The Correspondence of Thomas Wolfe and Homer Andrew Watt. NY: NY Univ Press, 1954. 2nd ptg. Rose cl. Fine in dj (spine sunned). Together, as issued, w/Thomas Clark Pollock and Oscar Cargill's Thomas Wolfe at Washington Square. NY: NY Univ Press, 1954. 2nd ptg. Grey cl. Fine in dj (spine sunned). *Chapel Hill.* $50/£32

WOLFE, THOMAS. From Death to Morning. London: Heinemann, (1936). 1st Eng ed. Ed of 1500. Fore-edge foxed, else VG in dj (spine evenly browned, else VG). *Godot.* $175/£113

WOLFE, THOMAS. From Death to Morning. NY: Scribner's, 1935. 1st ed, 1st state binding. Top edge stained orange. VG in dj (sl worn). *Sadlon.* $125/£81

WOLFE, THOMAS. From Death to Morning. NY, 1935. 1st ed. Fine (spine gilt faded). *Bond.* $50/£32

WOLFE, THOMAS. From Death to Morning. NY: Scribner's, 1935. 1st ed. Maroon cl. Fine in dj (sl nicked). *Appelfeld.* $100/£65

WOLFE, THOMAS. From Death to Morning. Heinemann, 1936. 1st Eng ed. VG in VG dj. *Fine Books.* $125/£81

WOLFE, THOMAS. Gentlemen of the Press. Chicago: William Targ, Black Archer, (1942). Ltd to 350. Grn cl; paper title label. NF. *Antic Hay.* $250/£161

WOLFE, THOMAS. Gentlemen of the Press. Chicago: William Targ: Black Archer Press, 1942. 1st ed. Ltd to 350 for subs. Grn linen, ptd paper label. Sig, else Fine w/o dj as issued. *Cahan.* $200/£129

WOLFE, THOMAS. The Letters of Thomas Wolfe. Elizabeth Nowell (ed). NY: Scribner's, (1956). 1st ed. Black cl, blue bds. Sig, date, ink indexing rep, else VG in dj (spine faded; lt worn). *Chapel Hill.* $40/£26

WOLFE, THOMAS. Look Homeward, Angel. London: Heinemann, (1930). 1st Eng ed. One of 3000. 8vo. Orig blue cl. VG (eps foxed) in VG dj (soil, tape mks). *Chapel Hill.* $600/£387

WOLFE, THOMAS. Mannerhouse. NY: Harper, 1948. 1st ed. Ltd to 500. Frontis port. Black cl, paper spine label. Fine in dj, pub's slipcase. *Cahan.* $250/£161

WOLFE, THOMAS. Mannerhouse. Harpers, 1948. 1st ed. One of 500. Fine in dj, slip-case. *Fine Books.* $150/£97

WOLFE, THOMAS. A Note on Experts: Dexter Vespasian Joyner. NY: House of Books, 1939. 1st ed. #21/300. Brn cl. NF. *Chapel Hill.* $350/£226

WOLFE, THOMAS. Of Time and the River. London: Heinemann, 1935. 1st ed. Sl warped, o/w VG in dj (chipped, frayed). *Rees.* $39/£25

WOLFE, THOMAS. Of Time and the River. NY: Scribner's, 1935. 1st ed. Fine in dj (chipped). *Second Life.* $125/£81

WOLFE, THOMAS. The Short Novels of Thomas Wolfe. Scribners, 1961. 1st ed. VF in Fine dj. *Fine Books.* $40/£26

WOLFE, THOMAS. The Story of a Novel. NY: Scribner's, (1936). 1st ed. Fine in Fine dj. *Dermont.* $75/£48

WOLFE, THOMAS. The Web and the Rock. NY, 1939. 1st ed. VG. *Bond.* $40/£26

WOLFE, THOMAS. The Web and the Rock. NY/London: Harper, 1939. 1st ed. NF in dj (sl chipped). *Sadlon.* $125/£81

WOLFE, THOMAS. The Web and the Rock. NY: Harper, 1939. 1st ed. VG in dj (sl nicked). *Second Life.* $125/£81

WOLFE, THOMAS. The Web and the Rock. Heinemann, 1947. 1st Eng ed. VG+ in VG+ dj (sl wear to spine extrems). *Fine Books.* $70/£45

WOLFE, THOMAS. You Can't Go Home Again. NY/London: Harper, (1940). 1st ed. NF in dj (sl chipped). *Sadlon.* $125/£81

WOLFE, THOMAS. You Can't Go Home Again. Harpers, 1940. 1st ed. Fine in VG+ dj (flaking to spine extrems). *Fine Books.* $125/£81

WOLFE, THOMAS. You Can't Go Home Again. Heinemann, 1947. 1st ed. VG in dj (sl chipped, worn). *Rees.* $39/£25

WOLFE, THOMAS. You Can't Go Home Again. London: Heinemann, 1947. 1st Eng ed. VG in VG dj (lt chipped). *Limestone.* $95/£61

WOLFE, TOM. The Bonfire of the Vanities. NY: FSG, (1987). 1st ed. Sl sticker residue fep, o/w As New in dj. *Jaffe.* $75/£48

WOLFE, TOM. The Bonfire of the Vanities. NY: FSG, (1987). One of 250 numbered, signed. Fine in slipcase as issued. *Between The Covers.* $350/£226

WOLFE, TOM. The Bonfire of the Vanities. London: Cape, 1988. 1st Eng ed. Fine in dj. *Limestone.* $70/£45

WOLFE, TOM. The Bonfire of the Vanities. London: Cape, 1988. 1st UK ed. VG+ in dj. *Williams.* $37/£24

WOLFE, TOM. The Electric Kool-Aid Acid Test. London: Weidenfeld & Nicolson, 1969. 1st Eng ed. Fine in dj. *Limestone.* $95/£61

WOLFE, TOM. From Bauhaus to Our House. NY, (1981). 1st ed, ltd to 350 numbered, signed. VG in slipcase. *King.* $100/£65

WOLFE, TOM. The Kandy-Kolored Tangerine-Flake Streamline Baby. NY, (1965). 1st ed, 1st bk. VG in dj (spotted, price-clipped). *King.* $95/£61

WOLFE, TOM. Mauve Gloves and Madmen, Clutter and Vine. NY, (1976). 1st ed. VG in dj (price-clipped). *King.* $35/£23

WOLFE, TOM. The Painted Word. NY: FSG, 1975. 1st ed. NF in Fine dj. *Limestone.* $45/£29

WOLFE, TOM. The Pump House Gang. NY, (1968). 1st ed. Good in dj (edgetorn, soiled, dknd). *King.* $50/£32

WOLFE, TOM. The Pump House Gang. NY, 1968. 1st Amer ed. Fine (sl rubbed; name) in Fine dj. *Polyanthos.* $50/£32

WOLFE, TOM. The Purple Decades. NY, (1982). 1st ed. VG in dj (sl dknd, short edge tears). *King.* $25/£16

WOLFE, TOM. Radical Chic and Mau-Mauing the Flak Catchers. NY, (1970). 1st ed. VG in dj. *King.* $25/£16

WOLFE, TOM. Radical Chic and Mau-Mauing the Flak Catchers. London: Michael Joseph, 1971. 1st UK ed. VG in dj (price over-written in ink). *Williams.* $54/£35

WOLFE, TOM. The Right Stuff. NY: Farrar Straus, 1979. 1st ed. Fine in Fine dj. *Pettler.* $35/£23

WOLFENSTINE, MANFRED R. The Manual of Brands and Marks. Ramon F. Adams (ed). Norman: Univ of OK Press, (1970). 1st ed. 74 plts. Brick red cl (foreedge bumped). Nice in dj (lt chipped, spine faded). *Harrington.* $35/£23

WOLFF, MARITTA. Whistle Stop. NY: Random House, 1941. VG in dj (tattered). *Peninsula.* $35/£23

WOLFF, PERRY S. A History of the 334th Infantry, 84th Division. Mannheim (Germany), (1945). 1st ed. Buckram. Nice. *King.* $75/£48

WOLFF, TOBIAS. Back in the World. London: Cape, (1986). 1st UK ed. Fine in NF dj. *Robbins.* $25/£16

WOLFF, TOBIAS. Back in the World. Cape, 1986. 1st UK ed. Fine in dj. *Sclanders.* $19/£12

WOLFF, TOBIAS. Ugly Rumours. London: Allen & Unwin, 1975. 1st UK ed. 1st bk. Ex-lib, stamps, label removed, note to ep, sl bumped, o/w VG in VG dj (sl chipped). *Virgo.* $233/£150

WOLFSON, HARRY AUSTRYN. The Philosophy of Spinoza. Harvard Univ Press, 1934. 1st ed. 2 vols. VG+ in VG dj. *Bishop.* $35/£23

WOLHUTER, HARRY. Memories of a Game Hunter. Wild Life Protection Soc of South Africa, (1950). 3rd ed. 17 plts. Dj (torn). *Petersfield.* $62/£40

WOLHUTER, HARRY. Memories of a Game-Ranger. London, 1955. 5th ed. Frontis port. Gilt device upper bd. (Spine sl faded.) *Edwards.* $39/£25

WOLHUTER, HARRY. Memories of a Game-Ranger. Johannesburg: Wild Life Protection Agency of South Africa, 1958. 6th ed. 17 plts. VG (sl spotted) in dj (sl worn). *Hollett.* $31/£20

WOLLE, F. Fresh-Water Algae of the United States. Bethlehem, 1887. 2 vols. 364pp (tanned), 157 color plts. (Lt wear extrems; white staining edges; hinges starting.) *Sutton.* $475/£306

WOLLHEIM, DONALD. The Secret of Saturn's Rings. Winston, 1954. 1st ed. VG in dj (sl frayed). *Madle.* $60/£39

WOLLHEIM, DONALD. Secret of the Martian Moons. Winston, 1955. 1st ed. VG. *Madle.* $20/£13

WOLLHEIM, DONALD. Up There and Other Strange Directions. Nesfa, 1988. 1st ed. One of 250 signed. Fine in dj & slipcase as issued. *Aronovitz.* $65/£42

WOLLSTONECRAFT, MARY. Memoirs of Mary Wollstonecraft. London: Constable, 1927. Ltd to 700. VG+ (bkpl). *Bishop.* $22/£14

WOLO. Friendship Valley. NY: William Morrow, 1946. 1st ed. Signed. 8vo. Unpaginated. Wolo (illus). VG in dj (torn). *Davidson.* $95/£61

WOLO. The Secret of the Ancient Oak. William Morrow, 1942. 1st ed. 8vo. 40pp. Wolo (illus). NF in VG dj. *Davidson.* $75/£48

WOLPE, BERTHOLD (ed). A Newe Booke of Copies 1574. London, 1962. 2nd ed. Good (bkpl). *Washton.* $40/£26

WOLSTENHOLME, G.E.W. and M. O'CONNOR. The Nature of Sleep. London, 1961. Frontis; 10 plts. VG in dj. *Whitehart.* $28/£18

Women Torch-Bearers, The Story of the Women's Christian Temperance Union. Evanston, IL, 1924. 2nd ed. Good. *Fye.* $75/£48

Wonderful Adventures of Humpty Dumpty. (By William Winter.) NY: McLoughlin Bros, (ca 1868). 4to. 12pp text, 12pp of plts by Thomas Nast. 'Office Sample' on fr cvr. Illus paper wrappers (sl spine wear). *Reisler.* $750/£484

Wonderful History of Dame Trot and Her Pig. London: Chapman & Hall, 1883. 4to. 23pp. Pict color paper on bds, cl spine; dec eps. Fine (near invisible dry seal fep; ink dated dedication tp; eps lt discolored). *Hobbyhorse.* $215/£139

WOOD JONES, F. Structure and Function as Seen in the Foot. London, 1944. (Feps lt foxed; cl dull, worn, creased; section sl cracked.) *Whitehart.* $39/£25

WOOD, BACHE et al. The Dispensatory of the United States of America. Phila: Lippincott, 1894. 17th ed. (44),1930pp. Full calf (edges worn). Good. *Artis.* $50/£32

WOOD, C.J. Reminiscences of the War. N.p., (1880). 283pp. Orig blind-emb cl, gilt spine title. VG+ (extrems lt worn). *Bohling.* $150/£97

WOOD, CASEY A. An Introduction to the Literature of Vertebrate Zoology. London: OUP, 1931. 1st ed. Color frontis. Gilt-lettered blue cl. VG+. *House.* $350/£226

WOOD, CHARLES. First, the Fields. Chapel Hill: UNC Press, 1941. 1st ed. Fine in illus dj. *Cahan.* $35/£23

WOOD, CHARLES. Lines West: A Pictorial History of the Great Northern Railway...from 1887-1967. Seattle: Superior Pub Co, (1967). 1st ed. Tan cl. Fine in VG+ dj. *Harrington.* $45/£29

WOOD, EDWARD J. Curiosities of Clocks and Watches from the Earliest Times. Richard Benley, 1866. Frontis. New 1/2 black morocco gilt. *Petersfield.* $87/£56

WOOD, ERIC. Death of an Oddfellow. London: John Hamilton, (1938). 1st ed. Fine in VG dj (soiled spine; short closed tears; short creases). *Mordida.* $65/£42

WOOD, ERSKINE. Life of Charles Erskine Scott Wood. By Author, (1978). 1st ed. Ltd to 500. VG in VG dj. *Perier.* $97/£63

WOOD, FRANCES and DOROTHY. I Hauled These Mountains in Here. Caldwell: Caxton, 1977. 1st ed. Fine in VG dj. *Perier.* $22/£14

WOOD, G. BERNARD. Bridges in Britain. London: Cassell, 1970. 1st ed. 35 plts. VG in dj. *Hollett.* $39/£25

WOOD, G.A.R. and R.A. LASS. Cocoa. London, 1985. 4th ed. Rexine. Dj. *Sutton.* $85/£55

WOOD, J.G. The Common Objects of the Microscope. London, 1861. 1st ed. iv,188pp; 12 color plts. Nice. *Wheldon & Wesley.* $70/£45

WOOD, J.G. The Common Objects of the Sea-Shore. London, 1859. viii,204pp; 21 color plts. (Lower corner waterstained.) *Wheldon & Wesley.* $39/£25

WOOD, JOHN GEORGE. The Principles and Practice of Sketching Landscape Scenery from Nature.... London, for the Author by Bensley and Son, 1816. 2nd ed. 4 parts in 1. Oblong folio. (iv)18; 16; 8; 14,2pp. 16,16,16, 16 plts (6 hand-tinted, 2 w/overslips). Half morocco (rebacked; corners, edges worn; binder's blanks creased, staining). *Marlborough.* $1,008/£650

WOOD, MORRISON. The Devil Is a Lonely Man. Crowell, 1946. 1st ed. Fine in dj. *Madle.* $25/£16

WOOD, RICHARD G. Stephen Harriman Long 1784-1864, Army Engineer, Explorer, Inventor. Glendale, 1966. 1st ed. Fine. *Pratt.* $35/£23

WOOD, RICHARD G. Stephen Harriman Long, 1784-1864.... Glendale: Clark, 1966. 1st ed. Fine. *Book Market.* $20/£13

WOOD, RICHARD. Stephen Harriman Long 1784-1864. Clark, 1966. 1st ed. Lg fldg map. VF. *Oregon.* $35/£23

WOOD, STANLEY. Over the Range to the Golden Gate. Chicago: R.R. Donnelley & Sons, 1889. 1st ed. 13pp ads. Spine sunned, else Fine. *Laurie.* $50/£32

WOOD, STANLEY. Over the Range to the Golden Gate. Chicago: R.R. Donnelley, 1901. Olive grn pict cl (rubbed, bumped; lower half rear joint split). Good. *Blue Mountain.* $25/£16

WOOD, SUMNER GILBERT. The Taverns and Turnpikes of Blandford 1733-1833. Blandford, MA: By Author, 1908. 1st ed. Frontis; tipped-in fldg map; 53 b/w plts. Olive grn cl (bumped). NF. *Blue Mountain.* $35/£23

WOOD, THOMAS. Memoirs of Mr. James H. Wood, Late Surgeon to the Dispensary and Workhouse.... London, 1816. 2nd ed. Litho frontis port. Orig bds. (Ex-lib.) *Argosy.* $60/£39

WOOD, W. BIRKBECK and J.E. EDMONDS. A History of the Civil War in the United States, 1861-5. NY: Putnam's, (1905). 1st Amer ed. 13 fldg maps, 11 plans (1 fldg). Orig blue cl. Spine starting internally, else VG. *Chapel Hill.* $95/£61

WOOD, WILLIAM. Manual of Physical Exercises: Comprising Gymnastics, Rowing.... NY, 1867. Frontis, 316pp. Orig emb cl (worn). *Goodrich.* $85/£55

WOOD-LEGH, K.L. (ed). A Small Household of the XVth Century. Manchester Univ Press, 1956. 1st ed. 2 plts. Dj (sl chipped, stained). *Edwards.* $23/£15

WOODALL, PERCY H. Intra-Pelvic Technic or Manipulative Surgery of the Pelvic Organs. Kansas City, (1926). 1st ed. *Bickersteth.* $34/£22

WOODBERRY, GEORGE E. The North Shore Watch and Other Poems. Boston: Houghton, 1890. 1st ed, ltd to 776. Teg, wallet fore-edges. VG. BAL 23190. *Reese.* $45/£29

WOODBURY, CHARLES J. Talks with Ralph Waldo Emerson. NY: Baker & Taylor, 1890. 1st ed. White cl-backed tan bds, gilt (spine aged, rubbed). Nice. *Macdonnell.* $65/£42

WOODCOCK, H.B.D. and W.T. STEARN. Lilies of the World. London/NY: Country Life/Scribner's, 1950. 1st ed. Red cl, gilt. VG in Good dj (repaired). *Shifrin.* $80/£52

WOODFORD, FRANK B. Lewis Cass, the Last Jeffersonian. Brunswick, NJ: Rutger's Univ Press, 1950. 1st ed. VG in dj (torn). *Peninsula.* $35/£23

WOODFORDE, CHRISTOPHER. The Norwich School of Glass-Painting in the Fifteenth Century. OUP, 1950. 44 plts. (Ex-lib, spine taped.) *Edwards.* $39/£25

WOODFORDE, JAMES. The Diary of a Country Parson: 1758-1781. John Beresford (ed). OUP, 1924-1927. 1st ed. Vols 1-3 (of 5). Frontis port. Orig cl, spine labels. *Edwards.* $85/£55

WOODFORDE, JAMES. The Diary of a Country Parson: the Reverend James Woodforde, 1758-1802. John Beresford (ed). OUP, 1926-1931. 3rd issue 1st vol, which was published in 1924, 1st ed other vols. 5 vols. Frontis each vol. Ptd paper spine labels (rubbed). Good set (ink name each fr fly). *Bickersteth.* $202/£130

WOODHOUSE, CHARLES. Homoeopathic Home and Self Treatment of Disease for the Use of Families and Travellers. Rutland, VT, 1868. 1st ed. 180pp. Recent buckram. Good. *Fye.* $75/£48

WOODHOUSE, JAMES. Poems on Several Occasions. London: for the author by Richardson & S. Clark, 1764. 1st ed. (vii),109pp; uncut. Orig blue-grey wrappers (spine chipped). *Marlborough.* $504/£325

WOODHOUSE, S.C. Crude Ditties. NY: E.P. Dutton, 1903. #3 in Oogley Oo series. 16mo. 24 color illus by Augusine J. Macgregor. Tan illus cl. Good. *Reisler.* $150/£97

WOODMASON, CHARLES. The Carolina Backcountry on the Eve of the Revolution. Richard J. Hooker (ed). Chapel Hill: UNC Press, 1953. 1st ed. NF in VG dj (edgeworn). *Chapel Hill.* $50/£32

WOODRELL, DANIEL. Under the Bright Lights. Holt, 1986. 1st ed. Fine in dj. *Murder.* $60/£39

WOODRUFF, C.E. The Effects of Tropical Light on White Men. NY: Rebman, 1905. 1st ed. VG (cvrs lt worn). *Smithfield.* $15/£10

WOODRUFF, MATHEW. Diary of a Union Soldier...June—December 1865. F.N. Boney (ed). Univ of AL, (1969). 1st ed. *Heinoldt.* $15/£10

WOODRUFF, MICHAEL. The Transplantation of Tissues and Organs. Springfield, 1960. 1st ed. *Fye.* $200/£129

WOODRUFF, WILLIAM EDWARD. With the Light Guns in '61-65: Reminiscences.... Little Rock, AR: Central Ptg, 1903. 1st ed. Dec red cl. Nice (lt spotted). Howes W 650. *Chapel Hill.* $500/£323

WOODS, FREDERICK. A Bibliography of the Works of Sir Winston Churchill. Univ of Toronto Press, (1963). 1st Canadian ed. Fine in dj. *Argosy.* $75/£48

WOODS, HENRY F. God's Loaded Dice, Alaska, 1897-1930. Caldwell: Caxton, 1948. 1st ed. (Spine faded.) *Heinoldt.* $25/£16

WOODS, K.S. Rural Crafts of England. London, 1949. 1st ed. Dj (spine sl chipped). *Edwards.* $23/£15

WOODS, ROBERT A. and ALBERT J. KENNEDY. Handbook of Settlements. NY: Russell Sage Foundation, 1911. Olive cl. *Schoyer.* $40/£26

WOODS, S. Lights and Shadows of Life on the Pacific Coast. NY: Funk & Wagnalls, 1910. 1st ed. Frontis port. Yellow cl (lt soiled, extrems sl worn). *Shasky.* $30/£19

WOODS, STUART. Run Before the Wind. NY: W.W. Norton, 1983. 1st ed. Cvrs stained, o/w Fine in dj. *Mordida.* $60/£39

WOODSON, CARTER G. The History of the Negro Church. DC, (1945). 2nd ed. VG (rubbed, bumped). *Fuller & Saunders.* $45/£29

Woodstock; or, The Cavalier. (By Sir Walter Scott.) Edinburgh: Ptd for Archibald Constable, 1826. 1st ed. 3 vols. Uncut; w/all 1/2, fly-titles. Orig bds; orig backstrips, labels laid down. (Age-soiling.) *Hill.* $132/£85

WOODWARD, ARTHUR. Lances at San Pasqual. SF: CA Hist Soc, 1948. 1st ed. Frontis, 2 plts. Fine. *Oregon.* $95/£61

WOODWARD, C. VANN. Mary Chestnut's Civil War. New Haven: Yale Univ, (1981). 1st thus, in 1st state dj. NF in NF dj. *Mcgowan.* $85/£55

WOODWARD, C.S. Oriental Ceramics at the Cape of Good Hope 1652-1795. Cape Town/Rotterdam, 1974. 5 color plts. Dj (sl chipped corners, spine). *Edwards.* $140/£90

WOODWARD, GEORGE E. Woodward's Country Homes. NY: American News Co, (1865). vi,(i),8-188pp. VG (bkpl removed) in pub's cl (rubbed, spotted). *Bookpress.* $135/£87

WOODWARD, GRACE STEELE. The Cherokees. Norman: Univ of OK Press, (1963). 1st ed. Tan cl. Fine in VG dj. *Chapel Hill.* $60/£39

WOODWARD, J.J. et al. The Medical and Surgical History of the War of the Rebellion. 1861-1865. Washington D.C., 1870-88. 6 vols. Mixed set w/some 2nd issue vols (binding states mixed w/some ex-lib; several vols recased; 1 vol rebound in new grn cl). *Goodrich.* $1,500/£968

WOODWARD, JOSEPH. Diarrhoea and Dysentery. Washington, 1879. 1st ed. 869pp. Vol 1 of part 2 of Medical and Surgical History of the War of the Rebellion. Good. *Fye.* $300/£194

WOODWARD, R. PITCHER. On a Donkey's Hurricane Deck. Snow Hill, MD: Chronicle Co, 1930. Inscribed. Pict cl. VG. *Schoyer.* $75/£48

WOODWARD, WILLIAM. French Quarter Etchings of Old New Orleans. New Orleans: Magnolia Press, 1938. 1st ed. Frontis, 54 plts. Eps foxed, else NF. *Cahan.* $125/£81

WOODWARD, WILLIAM. Meet General Grant. NY, 1928. 1st ed. VG. *Mcgowan.* $45/£29

WOODWORTH, JOHN. Cholera Epidemic of 1873 in the United States. Washington, 1875. 1st ed. 1025pp. (Ex-lib; backstrip crudely repaired w/binder's tape; tp discolored by scotch tape.) *Fye.* $60/£39

WOOFTER, THOMAS JACKSON. Black Yeomanry Life on St. Helena Island. NY: Henry Holt, (1930). 1st ed. Cl sl rubbed, spine sunned; yet VG. *Mcgowan.* $150/£97

WOOFTER, THOMAS JACKSON. Landlord and Tenant on the Cotton Plantation. Washington, DC, 1936. 1st ed. VG in orig stiff ptd wrappers. *Mcgowan.* $75/£48

WOOLDRIDGE, S.W. and FREDERICK GOLDRING. The Weald. London, 1953. 1st ed. (Feps lt browned.) Dj (sl chipped). *Edwards.* $93/£60

WOOLEY, L.H. California 1849-1913 or The Rambling Sketches.... Oakland: De Witt & Snelling, 1913. 1st ed. Frontis port. Very Nice in orig dec ptd wrappers (chips). *Shasky.* $55/£35

WOOLF, DOUGLAS. Wall to Wall. NY: Grove, (1962). 1st ed. Sm tape mk fep, else NF in dj (lt edgeworn, price-clipped; sl short). *Reese.* $30/£19

WOOLF, DOUGLAS. Ya! John-Juan. NY: Harper & Row, (1971). 1st ed. Inscribed, signed. Fine in dj. *Reese.* $40/£26

WOOLF, LEONARD. Downhill All the Way. NY: Harcourt, Brace & World, (1967). 1st Amer ed. Blue cl-backed bds. VG in dj (rubbed). *Chapel Hill.* $25/£16

WOOLF, LEONARD. Essays on Lit. History, Politics, etc. Hogarth, 1927. 1st ed. Good. *Whiteson.* $47/£30

WOOLF, LEONARD. Fear and Politics. Hogarth Press, 1924. 1st ed. Spine sl dknd, o/w VG in wrappers. *Words Etc.* $116/£75

WOOLF, LEONARD. The Hotel. London: Hogarth Press, 1939. 1st ed. Pink cl. NF in dj. *Karmiole.* $75/£48

WOOLF, LEONARD. Hunting the Highbrow. Hogarth Press, 1927. 1st ed. Edges, spine browned, o/w VG. *Words Etc.* $62/£40

WOOLF, LEONARD. Hunting the Highbrow. London: Hogarth Press, 1927. 1st ed. Sl faded, o/w Fine. *Temple.* $70/£45

WOOLF, LEONARD. Sowing. An Autobiography of the Years 1880 to 1904. London: Hogarth, (1960). 1st ed. Port. NF in dj (spine tanned). *Reese.* $20/£13

WOOLF, VIRGINIA. Beau Brummel. NY: Rimington & Hooper, 1930. 1st ed. One of 550 numbered, signed. Teg. Cl-backed bds, peacock label. Sm stamp rep, slipcase worn, else NF. *Veatchs.* $400/£258

WOOLF, VIRGINIA. Between the Acts. NY: Harcourt, Brace, (1941). 1st Amer ed. Blue cl. Fine in Fine dj (2 pieces of tape at foot). *Macdonnell.* $60/£39

WOOLF, VIRGINIA. Between the Acts. London: Hogarth Press, 1941. 1st ed. 8vo. Blue cl. VG (offsetting fep) in white dj (soiled). *Chapel Hill.* $500/£323

WOOLF, VIRGINIA. The Captain's Death Bed and Other Essays. NY: Harcourt, Brace, (1950). 1st ed. Blue cl, gilt. Fine in dj (lt aged). *Macdonnell.* $100/£65

WOOLF, VIRGINIA. The Captain's Death Bed and Other Essays. London: Hogarth, 1950. 1st ed. VG in dj (sl bruised). *Cox.* $54/£35

WOOLF, VIRGINIA. The Captain's Death Bed and Other Essays. London: Hogarth, 1950. 1st ed. NF in dj. *Limestone.* $135/£87

WOOLF, VIRGINIA. The Captain's Death Bed and Other Essays. London: Hogarth, 1950. 1st ed. Fine (sl rubbed) in dj (sunned, sl chipped). *Polyanthos.* $150/£97

WOOLF, VIRGINIA. The Death of the Moth and Other Essays. London: Hogarth Press, 1942. 1st ed. VG (spine faded). *Second Life.* $40/£26

WOOLF, VIRGINIA. Flush, a Biography. NY, (1933). 1st Amer ed. VG (lacks dj). *King.* $25/£16

WOOLF, VIRGINIA. Flush, a Biography. H-B, 1933. 1st Amer ed. NF in VG dj (sm chip spine extrems). *Fine Books.* $85/£55

WOOLF, VIRGINIA. Flush, a Biography. London: Hogarth, 1933. 1st ed (one of 12,680 designated as 'Large Paper Edition.' Edges sl tanned, o/w Very Nice in dj (tanned, chips, sl closed tears mended on verso). *Reese.* $85/£55

WOOLF, VIRGINIA. Flush, a Biography. London: Hogarth Press, 1933. 1st ed. Tan cl, gilt. Fine in VG dj. *Macdonnell.* $125/£81

WOOLF, VIRGINIA. Granite and Rainbow. NY: Harcourt, Brace, (1958). 1st Amer ed. Blue cl. Label, ink date, else NF in dj (spine sunned). *Chapel Hill.* $60/£39

WOOLF, VIRGINIA. Granite and Rainbow. Hogarth Press, 1958. 1st ed. VG in dj (sl foxed; tears). *Words Etc.* $70/£45

WOOLF, VIRGINIA. A Haunted House and Other Stories. NY: Harcourt, Brace, (1944). 1st Amer ed (4000 copies). Dk blue cl titled in silver. Very Nice in dj. *Cady.* $60/£39

WOOLF, VIRGINIA. Hours in a Library. Harcourt, Brace, 1957. 1st ed. Fine. *Whiteson.* $34/£22

WOOLF, VIRGINIA. Jacob's Room. London: Hogarth, 1922. 1st ed. 14pp ads inserted at end. Good (eps mkd; spine, paper label age dknd). *Pharos.* $200/£129

WOOLF, VIRGINIA. A Letter to a Young Poet. Hogarth Press, 1932. 1st ed. Spine sl browned, o/w VG in wrappers. *Words Etc.* $47/£30

WOOLF, VIRGINIA. A Letter to a Young Poet. London: Hogarth, 1932. 1st ed. VG in wrappers. *Limestone.* $75/£48

WOOLF, VIRGINIA. The Letters of Virginia Woolf. Nigel Nicolson & Joanne Trautmann (eds). NY: HBJ, 1975-1980. 1st eds. 6 vols. NF in djs (lt used). *Robbins.* $125/£81

WOOLF, VIRGINIA. The Letters of Virginia Woolf. Volume IV: 1929-1931. Nigel Nicolson & Joanne Trautmann (eds). NY/London: Harcourt Brace Jovanovich, (1979). 1st Amer ed. Cream bds, blue cl spine. Rmdr mk, owner label, else Fine in dj (1-inch tear). *Chapel Hill.* $20/£13

WOOLF, VIRGINIA. The Moment and Other Essays. London: Hogarth, 1947. 1st ed. Cvrs sl bowed, else VG in dj (sl chipped). *Limestone.* $75/£48

WOOLF, VIRGINIA. The Moment and Other Essays. London: Hogarth, 1947. 1st ed. Fine in dj (sl used). *Pharos.* $100/£65

WOOLF, VIRGINIA. Monday or Tuesday. Hogarth Press, 1921. 1st ed. Sl dust soiled, o/w VG. *Words Etc.* $581/£375

WOOLF, VIRGINIA. Monday or Tuesday. Richmond: Hogarth Press, 1921. 1st ed. One of 1000 w/illus by Vanessa Bell. NF in stiff white paper bds, brn cl spine. *Vandoros.* $1,150/£742

WOOLF, VIRGINIA. Mrs. Dalloway. London: Leonard & Virginia Woolf at Hogarth Press, 1925. 1st ed. 8vo. Orig dk red cl. NF in dj (worn, soiled, chipped, split along fr flap fold, verso tape repairs). *Chapel Hill.* $1,700/£1,097

WOOLF, VIRGINIA. Night and Day. Doran, 1920. 1st Amer ed. VG-. *Fine Books.* $125/£81

WOOLF, VIRGINIA. Reviewing. Hogarth Press, 1939. 1st ed. VG in wrappers. *Words Etc.* $28/£18

WOOLF, VIRGINIA. Reviewing. London: Hogarth Press, 1939. 1st ed. 1 gathering sewn into pale blue wrappers. Sl browned; o/w Fine. *Temple.* $31/£20

WOOLF, VIRGINIA. Roger Fry: A Biography. NY, (1940). 1st ed. Stamped 'Review Copy.' Fine (bkpl) in VG+ dj (soiled, sm chips). *Fuller & Saunders.* $125/£81

WOOLF, VIRGINIA. A Room of One's Own. NY: Harcourt Brace, 1929. 1st US ed. Excellent in dj (chipped). *Second Life.* $250/£161

WOOLF, VIRGINIA. The Second Common Reader. H-B, 1932. 1st Amer ed. NF in VG dj (dust-soil; sm chip spine head). *Fine Books.* $125/£81

WOOLF, VIRGINIA. Street Haunting. SF, 1930. 1st ed, ltd to 500 signed. Dec bds, leather spine. Spine strip sl dull; lower edge sl worn, else VG. *Whiteson.* $992/£640

WOOLF, VIRGINIA. Three Guineas. H-B, 1938. 1st Amer ed. Fine in NF dj (tiny chips fr panel). *Fine Books.* $125/£81

WOOLF, VIRGINIA. To The Lighthouse. London: Leonard & Virginia Woolf at the Hogarth Press, 1927. 1st ed. 8vo. Orig blue cl. NF (lt offsetting to spine from dj) in dj (spine-dknd, chips, tears). *Chapel Hill.* $1,750/£1,129

WOOLF, VIRGINIA. To the Lighthouse. London: Hogarth Press, 1927. One of 3000. Cvrs sl mkd, faded; gilt dull; sl foxing, mks; o/w Nice. *Temple.* $109/£70

WOOLF, VIRGINIA. Virginia Woolf and Lytton Strachey: Letters. Leonard Woolf & James Strachey (eds). (London): Hogarth/C&W, (1956). 1st ed. Fine in dj. *Pharos.* $95/£61

WOOLF, VIRGINIA. The Voyage Out. NY: Doran, (1920). 1st US ed, 1st bk. Handsome (sl wear; lacks dj). *Robbins.* $85/£55

WOOLF, VIRGINIA. Walter Sickert: A Conversation. Hogarth Press, 1934. 1st ed. Text foxed, o/w VG in wrappers. *Words Etc.* $28/£18

WOOLF, VIRGINIA. Walter Sickert: A Conversation. London: Hogarth, 1934. 1st ed. Fine in sewn pict wrappers. *Pharos.* $100/£65

WOOLF, VIRGINIA. Walter Sickert: A Conversation. London: Hogarth Press, 1934. 1st ed. VG+ in wraps as issued. *Williams.* $101/£65

WOOLF, VIRGINIA. The Waves. NY: Harcourt, Brace, (1931). 1st Amer ed. Blue cl, gilt. Fine in dj (torn, browned). *Macdonnell.* $100/£65

WOOLF, VIRGINIA. The Waves. Hogarth, 1931. 1st ed. Spine faded, else Good. *Whiteson.* $78/£50

WOOLF, VIRGINIA. The Waves. Harcourt, 1931. 1st US ed. Fine in Vanessa Bell dj. *Lewton.* $132/£85

WOOLF, VIRGINIA. A Writer's Diary. London: Hogarth Press, 1953. 1st ed. Orange cl, gilt. Fine in dj (spine lt aged). *Macdonnell.* $75/£48

WOOLF, VIRGINIA. A Writer's Diary. Leonard Woolf (ed). London: Hogarth Press, 1953. (Sl faded.) *Petersfield.* $25/£16

WOOLF, VIRGINIA. The Years. H-B, 1937. 1st Amer ed. VG+ in VG dj (worn). *Fine Books.* $95/£61

WOOLF, VIRGINIA. The Years. London: Leonard & Virginia Woolf at the Hogarth Press, 1937. 1st ed. Orig grn cl (spine, edges dknd). VG (offsetting fep) in dj (3-inch tear fr panel, chipping ends of dknd spine). *Chapel Hill.* $400/£258

WOOLF, VIRGINIA. The Years. London: Hogarth Press, 1937. 1st ed. Fine photoport loosely inserted. Fine in pale jade-grn cl, gold-lettered spine. NF pict dj. *Vandoros.* $475/£306

WOOLLEY, C. LEONARD. The Art of the Middle East including Persia, Mesopotamia and Palestine. NY: Crown, (1961). 61 color plts. Good in dj. *Archaeologia.* $35/£23

WOOLLEY, C. LEONARD. Dead Towns and Living Men. NY: OUP, 1929. 1st ed. (Sig.) *Archaeologia.* $45/£29

WOOLLEY, C. LEONARD. Dead Towns and Living Men. London, 1932. 1st ed thus. Eps very sl browned, o/w Good. Grn cl (sunned at spine). *Edwards.* $25/£16

WOOLLEY, C. LEONARD. History Unearthed. London: Ernest Benn, 1958. Good in dj (tattered). *Archaeologia.* $35/£23

WOOLLEY, C. LEONARD. Spadework. London: Lutterworth, (1953). (Spine faded.) *Archaeologia.* $25/£16

WOOLLEY, L.H. California, 1849-1913. Oakland: DeWitt & Snelling, 1913. 1st ed. Frontis port. Dec grey wrappers; sl rubbed, chipped, losses spine ends, o/w VG+. *Harrington.* $65/£42

WOOLMAN, JOHN. A Journal of the Life and Travels of John Woolman in the Service of the Gospel. Essex House Press, 1901. 1st ed. One of 250. Frontis; unopened. Full vellum. VG (spine title lt rubbed). Howes W 669. *Cahan.* $275/£177

WOOLMAN, JOHN. The Works of John Woolman. Phila: Joseph Crukshank, 1774. 1st ed. xiv,(2),436pp. Contemp sheep (bds sl scuffed; rebacked). Howes W 669. *Felcone.* $400/£258

WOOLNOUGH, C.W. The Whole Art of Marbling as Applied to Book-Edges etc. London: George Bell, 1881. 2nd, expanded ed. 82pp; 54 Fine specimens. Period-style 3/4 oasis morocco; gilt; new eps; marbled paper sides. Lib blindstamp corner tp, specimen pp. *Veatchs.* $700/£452

WOOLRICH, CORNELL. The Black Curtain. NY: Simon & Schuster, 1941. 1st ed. Offsetting to pastedown eps, else Fine in pict dj (lt edgewear, some rubbing). *Else Fine.* $250/£161

WOOLRICH, CORNELL. Hotel Room. NY: Random House, 1958. 1st ed. Eps lt discolored, else VG in illus dj. *Cahan.* $65/£42

WOOLRICH, CORNELL. Hotel Room. NY: Random House, 1958. 1st ed. Fine in NF dj (internal reinforcement). *Janus.* $125/£81

WOOLRICH, CORNELL. Rendezvous in Black. NY/Toronto: Rinehart, (1948). 1st ed. VG+ in dj (edges sl worn). *Bernard.* $175/£113

WOOLRICH, CORNELL. Rendezvous in Black. Rinehart, 1948. 1st ed. Sl edgeworn, bkpl, else NF in dj (chipped, lt rubbed). *Murder.* $85/£55

WOOLRYCH, AUSTIN. Battles of the English Civil War. Batsford, 1961. 1st ed. Frontis port; 17 plts. VG in dw. *Edwards.* $39/£25

WOOLSON, ABBA (ed). Dress-Reform: A Series of Lectures. Boston, 1874. 1st ed. 263pp. (Notations, underlining.) *Fye.* $150/£97

WOOLSON, ABBA. Woman in American Society. Boston: Roberts, 1873. 1st ed. 271pp. Nice. *Second Life.* $150/£97

WOOLSON, CONSTANCE FENIMORE. Horace Chase. NY: Harper, 1894. 1st ed. 419pp (bkpl removed fep). *Hayman.* $20/£13

WOOLSON, CONSTANCE FENIMORE. Jupiter Lights. NY, 1889. 1st ed. 347pp (lib pocket fep). *Hayman.* $20/£13

WOOLSON, CONSTANCE FENIMORE. Rodman the Keeper: Southern Sketches. NY, 1880. 1st ed. Grn cl (name title). *Argosy.* $100/£65

WOOSTER, DAVID. Alpine Plants.... London, 1872-74. 1st ed. 1st & 2nd series. 2 vols. 8vo. xii,152; 140pp (eps sl foxed; lt spotting); 108 hand-colored engr plts. Emb blue gilt-dec cl, new blue morocco spines, gilt. NF (bumped). *Shifrin.* $625/£403

WORCESTER, SAMUEL. History of the Town of Hollis, New Hampshire, From Its First Settlement to the Year 1879. Nashua, NH: O.C. Moore, 1879. 1st ed. Frontis; 393pp; 24 plts. Ends worn, o/w VG. *Oregon.* $75/£48

WORDSWORTH, CHRISTOPHER and HENRY LITTLEHALES. The Old Service-Books of the English Church. London: Methuen, 1904. 1st ed. 38 facs plts (4 color). Good. *Cox.* $39/£25

WORDSWORTH, CHRISTOPHER and HENRY LITTLEHALES. The Old Service-Books of the English Church. London: Methuen, 1904. 1st ed. Color frontis, xv,319,44pp, 37 plts. Spine sl faded. *Hollett.* $85/£55

WORDSWORTH, MARY. The Letters 1800-1855. Mary E. Burton (ed). Clarendon, 1958. 1st ed. Fly glued to pastedown, lib stamp tp verso, o/w VG (ex-lib) in dj (sl stretched; price-clipped). *Poetry.* $25/£16

WORDSWORTH, WILLIAM. Our English Lakes, Mountains, and Waterfalls.... London: A.W. Bennett, 1864. 1st ed. Illus w/orig photos by Thomas Ogle. Aeg. Dec gilt cvrs (spine professionally rebacked). NF (name). *Polyanthos.* $285/£184

WORDSWORTH, WILLIAM. Poems, Chiefly of the Early and Late Years; including The Borderers. London: Edward Moxon, 1842. 1st thus. No 1/2 title, as issued. Upper bd detached, backstrip lost, o/w VG. *Poetry.* $39/£25

WORDSWORTH, WILLIAM. The Poetical Works. London: Edward Moxon, 1836. New ed. 6 vols. Engr frontis port. Orig cl (neatly recased), gilt. *Hollett.* $279/£180

WORDSWORTH, WILLIAM. The Poetical Works. London: Edward Moxon, 1849. New ed. 6 vols. Aeg. Lacks both plts, o/w VG set in 19th cent calf (staining; spine heads dknd, chipped); recent leather labels. *Poetry.* $186/£120

WORDSWORTH, WILLIAM. The Prelude.... London: Edward Moxon, 1850. 1st ed. 8vo. 374pp. Teg. Full grn morocco, raised bands, gilt spine panels, inner dentelles. Excellent (2 bkpls fr pastedown, fr outer joint leather worn, pencil notes rear fly, foxing). Excellent binding. *Chapel Hill.* $650/£419

WORDSWORTH, WILLIAM. The Recluse. London: Macmillan, 1888. 1st ed. Uncut, unopened. Grn cl. VF. *D & D.* $140/£90

WORDSWORTH, WILLIAM. The Sonnets of.... London: Moxon, 1838. 1st ed. (iv),477,xipp. Full calf, raised band, gold stamped spine (rebacked, orig spine laid down). Issued w/o 1/2 title. Nice (contemp names). *Second Life.* $425/£274

WORDSWORTH, WILLIAM. Thanksgiving Ode, January 18, 1816. London: Longman et al, 1816. 1st ed. ix,(1),52pp. Early 1/2 red cl, patterned bds; ptd paper spine label. VG. *Chapel Hill.* $750/£484

WORDSWORTH, WILLIAM. Yarrow Revisited and Other Poems. Boston: James Munroe, 1835. 1st Amer ed. Teal cl dec in blind. Lt foxing; ink name; stamp fep; spine chipped, else Good. *Hermitage.* $100/£65

WORGAN, GEORGE. The Art of Modeling Flowers in Wax. Brooklyn: (1867). 1st ed. 39pp. Dec cl. VG. *Petrilla.* $35/£23

WORK, JOHN. Fur Brigade to the Bonaventura. Alice Maloney (ed). SF: CA Hist Soc, 1945. 1st ed. Ltd to 500. Frontis, 3 plts, fldg map. Fine. *Oregon.* $125/£81

WORK, JOHN. The Snake Country Expedition of 1830-1831. Norman: Univ of OK Press, (1971). 1st ed. Blue cl. VG in dj. *Laurie.* $40/£26

WORK, PAUL. Tomato Production. NY: OJ, 1926. 1st ed. Fine in illus dj (sl worn). *Second Life.* $45/£29

WORK, THOMAS. The Basis of Chemotherapy. London, 1948. 1st ed. *Fye.* $75/£48

World-Wide Fables. NY: McLoughlin Bros, n.d. (ca 1875). Aunt Louisa Series. 4to. 10 leaves + 1pg list lower wrapper; 1st, last pp pasted down on wrappers. Pict chromolitho paper wrappers. Fine (sl wear spine, margin). *Hobbyhorse.* $215/£139

WORLIDGE, T. A Select Collection of Drawings from Curious Antique Gems.... London: M. Worlidge, 1768. 48pp. Frontis port (spotted), 179 plts (of 180; lacks plt 31, but add'l copy plt 10 in proof state bound in; some marginal spotting; sm ink stamp). Contemp full red straight-grained morocco (edges rubbed), gilt, paper label. Ex-libris Viscount Sydney. *Edwards.* $543/£350

WORMALD, FRANCIS. English Drawings of the Tenth and Eleventh Centuries. London, 1952. 50 illus on 40 plts. Good in dj (sl worn). *Washton.* $40/£26

WORMAN, ERNEST JAMES. Alien Members of the Book-Trade During the Tudor Period. Bibliographical Soc, 1906. (Margins lt browned.) Teg; rest uncut. 1/2 morocco, marbled bds. (Fore-edge upper bd sl damaged; spine gilt sl faded.) *Edwards.* $47/£30

WORMSER, RICHARD. The Yellowlegs. GC, (1966). Dj lt worn, o/w Fine. *Pratt.* $40/£26

WORRELL, JOHN. A Diamond in the Rough.... Indianapolis, 1906. 1st ed. Howes W 679. *Ginsberg.* $200/£129

WORSHAM, JOHN H. One of Jackson's Foot Cavalry. NY, 1912. Time-Life 1982 rprnt. Leather, gilt. Fine. *Pratt.* $27/£17

WORSHAM, JOHN H. One of Jackson's Foot Cavalry. Bell I. Wiley (ed). Jackson, TN: McCowat-Mercer, 1964. 1st ed thus. Fine in NF dj. *Mcgowan.* $85/£55

WORSHAM, JOHN H. One of Jackson's Foot Cavalry.... NY: Neale, 1912. 1st ed. Frontis. Orig grey cl. Name, spine lt sunned, else NF in custom 1/4 morocco slipcase. Howes W 680. *Chapel Hill.* $425/£274

WORSLEY, ETTA B. Columbus on the Chattahoochee. Columbus, 1951. 1st ed. Author presentation. Sl shaken, else NF in dj. *Mcgowan.* $150/£97

WORSLEY, F.A. Shackleton's Boat Journey. London: Folio Soc, 1974. Fine in slipcase. *Blue Dragon.* $45/£29

WORSLEY, F.A. Under Sail in the Frozen North. Phila: David McKay, 1927. Lg fldg map. Orig cl. Bright in orig dj (chipped, sl soiled). *High Latitude.* $65/£42

WORSLEY, F.A. Under Sail in the Frozen North. London: Stanley Paul, 1927. 1st ed. VG. *Walcot.* $43/£28

WORTHINGTON, FRANK. Chiromo the Witch Doctor and Other Rhodesian Studies. London: Field Press, n.d. (c. 1930). (Sl faded, soiled; spots; flyleaves lt browned.) *Hollett.* $54/£35

WORTHINGTON, GREVILLE. A Bibliography of the Waverley Novels. London: Constable, (1931). Ltd to 500. Collotype frontis photo; 21 tp facs. Vellum over marbled bds; gilt spine (extrems sl rubbed; stamp on feps). *Karmiole.* $100/£65

WORTHINGTON, W.H. Portraits of the Sovereigns of England.... London: Pickering, 1824. Half-title, title, 36 engr plts on India Paper. Later half blue morocco, teg (rubbed, edges worn). *Marlborough.* $233/£150

WORTHINGTON-SMITH, BRIAN. Collecting and Breeding Butterflies and Moths. London: Warne, (1951). *Petersfield.* $34/£22

WORTLEY, EMMELINE STUART. Travels in the United States, etc. During 1849 and 1850. NY: Harper, 1851. 1st US ed. 463pp + ads. Cl (worn). Good (lt foxing, water stain). Howes W 687. *Second Life.* $125/£81

WOUK, HERMAN. The Caine Mutiny. GC, 1951. 1st ed. Cl (spine sl discolored; ex-lib blindstamp rep). Dj (worn, lg chip, torn). *King.* $50/£32

WOUK, HERMAN. The Caine Mutiny. NY, 1952. 1st illus ed, review copy. Lawrence Beall Smith (illus). VG in dj (price-clipped). *Argosy.* $75/£48

WOUK, HERMAN. The Caine Mutiny. PA: Franklin Lib, 1977. Ltd ed privately ptd and signed. Aeg. Full leather, gilt. Fine. *Polyanthos.* $60/£39

WOUK, HERMAN. Marjorie Morningstar. GC: Doubleday, 1955. 1st ed. VG in VG dj (extrems worn). *Revere.* $65/£42

WOUK, HERMAN. The Winds of War. Boston: Little, Brown, (1971). 1st ed. Fine in NF dj. *Antic Hay.* $75/£48

WRATISLAW, THEODORE. Oscar Wilde: A Memoir. London: Eighteen Nineties Soc, 1929. Fine in dj (short tear). *Veatchs.* $20/£13

WRAXALL, LASCELLES. Remarkable Adventures and Unrevealed Mysteries. London: Richard Bentley, 1863. 1st ed. 2 vols. 2 engr frontispieces, xii,332; viii,344pp. blind-stamped cl (frayed), gilt. *Hollett.* $70/£45

WRAXALL, NATHANIEL WILLIAM. The History of France, from the Accession of Henry the Third to the Death of Louis the Fourteenth. London: Strahan & Cahill, 1795. 1st ed. 3 vols. Full mottled calf (hinges strengthened). *Argosy.* $250/£161

WRAXALL, NATHANIEL WILLIAM. Posthumous Memoirs of His Own Time, and Historical Memoirs of My Own Time. Phila, 1836, 1837. 1st Amer ed. 2 vols. 568 + appendix,index,2pp ads; 494 + 2pp ads. Recent grn buckram, gilt on black label. VG. *Hartfield.* $145/£94

WRAXALL, PETER. An Abridgment of the Indian Affairs Contained in Four Folio Volumes.... Charles McIlwain (ed). Harvard, 1915. 1st ed. VG. *Oregon.* $60/£39

Wreck of the 'Glide' with Recollections of the Fijiis and of Wallis Island. (By James Oliver.) London, 1848. 1st ed. Frontis, 203pp (facs, ep torn; discoloration). 1/2 calf (rebound). *Lewis.* $133/£86

Wreck of the 'London.' London, (1866). 2nd ed. Frontis, vi,106pp, 16pp ads; 5 plts. Orig yellow bds (worn). *Lewis.* $70/£45

Wrecked on the Feejees. (By William S. Cary.) (Nantucket, 1928). Orig wrappers. *Lefkowicz.* $20/£13

WRENCH, G.T. Lord Lister. London, 1914. 4th ed. 4 plts. (Sm label fep; eps sl faded.) *Whitehart.* $28/£18

WRIGHT, A.E. Principles of Microscopy. London, 1906. 18 plts. Cl (sl loose). *Wheldon & Wesley.* $56/£36

WRIGHT, ALMROTH. Handbook of the Technique of the Teat and Capillary Glass Tube and Its Applications.... London, 1912. 1st ed. Good. *Fye.* $250/£161

WRIGHT, ALMROTH. Studies on Immunisation and Their Application to the Diagnosis and Treatment of Bacterial Infections. London, 1909. 1st ed. Good. *Fye.* $350/£226

WRIGHT, ANDREW. Court Hand Restored. London: Benjamin White, 1776. 1st ed. (8),100pp; 20 engr plts. Ltr 1/2 calf over marbled bds, burgundy/blue morocco spine labels. Good. *Karmiole.* $200/£129

WRIGHT, ANDREW. Court Hand Restored. London, 1778. 2nd ed. Gilt-edged calf, gilt dec spine (rubbed), morocco label (joints starting to crack; bkpl; feps sl foxed; pp1-7 lt browned). *Edwards.* $186/£120

WRIGHT, ANDREW. Court-Hand Restored. London: Reeves & Turner, 1879. 9th ed. xviii,100pp; 30 tissue-guarded plts. New eps. Later cl, gilt. VG. *Hollett.* $132/£85

WRIGHT, ANDREW. Court-Hand Restored.... London: Reeves & Turner, 1879. 9th ed. xviii,99pp, 30 plts, guards. Good (sl worn). *Cox.* $47/£30

WRIGHT, AUSTIN TAPPAN. Islandia. NY, (1958). 1st rev ed. VG in dj. *Argosy.* $75/£48

WRIGHT, AUSTIN TAPPAN. Islandia. Farrar, 1942. 1st ed. VG in dj (chipped, worn). *Madle.* $95/£61

WRIGHT, BARTON. The Unchanging Hopi. Flagstaff: Northland, 1975. 1st ed. NF in VG+ dj. *Parker.* $40/£26

WRIGHT, BRUCE. High Tide and an East Wind. Stackpole, 1954. 1st ed. Fine in Good dj. *Artis.* $30/£19

WRIGHT, CHARLES and C. ERNEST FAYLE. A History of Lloyd's. London, 1928. Frontis port. Teg. (Edges ink stamped; spine sl faded; sl worn.) *Edwards.* $62/£40

WRIGHT, CHARLES. Absolutely Nothing to Get Alarmed About. NY: FSG, (1973). 1st ed. NF in NF dj. *Aka.* $25/£16

WRIGHT, CHARLES. The Grave of the Right Hand. Middletown: Wesleyan, (1970). 1st ed. Fine in dj. *Turlington.* $75/£48

WRIGHT, CHARLES. The Grave of the Right Hand. Middletown, CT: Wesleyan Univ, 1970. 1st ed, 1st bk. Fine in dj (lt rubbed, price-clipped). *Cahan.* $65/£42

WRIGHT, CHARLES. A Journal of the Year of the Ox. Iowa City: Windhover, 1988. One of 150 signed. Black cl. Fine. *Dermont.* $75/£48

WRIGHT, CHARLES. The Messenger. NY: Farrar, (1963). 1st ed. NF in VG dj (edge tears; crease; lt rubbed). *Reese.* $30/£19

WRIGHT, CHARLES. Private Madrigals. (Madison: Abraxis, 1969.) 1st ed. Signed. Fine in stapled wraps. *Turlington.* $100/£65

WRIGHT, CHARLES. The Southern Cross. NY: Random House, (1981). 1st ed. Fine in dj. *Turlington.* $25/£16

WRIGHT, CHRISTOPHER. Poussin Paintings, a Catalogue Raisonne. London: Jupiter Books, 1984. Sound in dj. *Ars Artis.* $78/£50

WRIGHT, CHRISTOPHER. Poussin Paintings, Catalogue Raisonne. (London): Jupiter Bks, (1984). 1st ed. Contemp blue calf, gilt spine. Good in dj. *Karmiole.* $60/£39

WRIGHT, DARE. Take Me Home. NY: Random House, 1965. 1st ed. 4.5x7. 42pp. Cl. Fine in dj. *Cattermole.* $50/£32

WRIGHT, DUDLEY. Druidism. London: E.J. Burrow, 1924. 1st ed. 9 plts. VG-. *Blue Dragon.* $150/£97

WRIGHT, E.W. (ed). Lewis and Dryden's Marine History of the Pacific Northwest. Portland: Lewis & Dryden Ptg Co, 1895. 1st ed. 494pp. Gilt full morocco, beveled bds (rebacked), orig spine laid on. Restored to NF (ex-lib, sm stamps tp; hinges expertly reinforced). Howes W 693. *Harrington.* $350/£226

WRIGHT, E.W. (ed). Lewis and Dryden's Marine History of the Pacific Northwest. Portland: Lewis & Dryden Ptg, 1895. 1st ed. 494pp. Recased w/orig spine laid on. Attractive. Howes W 693. *Perier.* $525/£339

WRIGHT, E.W. (ed). Lewis and Dryden's Marine History of the Pacific Northwest.... Portland, OR: Lewis & Dryden, 1895. 1st ed. Frontis, (xxiv),494pp. Orig morocco (joints sl worn). Fine. Howes W 693. *Lefkowicz.* $500/£323

WRIGHT, FRANK LLOYD. An American Architecture. Edgar Kaufmann (ed). NY: Horizon, 1955. 1st ed. VG in dj (faded; sl worn). *Hermitage.* $150/£97

WRIGHT, FRANK LLOYD. Architecture. Man in Possession of His Earth. NY: Doubleday, 1962. 1st ed. Fine in dj (sm tear). *Glenn.* $165/£106

WRIGHT, FRANK LLOYD. An Autobiography. NY: Duell, Sloane & Pearce, (1943, 'first edition'). Port. Dec red buckram (spine sl faded). *Petrilla.* $125/£81

WRIGHT, FRANK LLOYD. Drawings for a Living Architectur. Horizon, 1959. 1st ed. NF in VG+ dj. *Bishop.* $440/£284

WRIGHT, FRANK LLOYD. Drawings for a Living Architecture. NY: Horizon Press, 1959. 1st ed. Oblong folio. Dj tattered, else VG. *Bookpress.* $950/£613

WRIGHT, FRANK LLOYD. The Future of Architecture. NY: Horizon, 1953. 1st ed. Spine sl worn, lacks fep, o/w Fine. *Europa.* $70/£45

WRIGHT, FRANK LLOYD. Genius and the Mobocracy. NY: DSP, 1949. 1st ed. Name, date, else NF in VG+ dj (lt staining bottom edge, spine). *Lame Duck.* $85/£55

WRIGHT, FRANK LLOYD. The Natural House. NY: Horizon Press, 1954. 1st ed. VG in dj (nicks, short tears, edgewear). *Godot.* $60/£39

WRIGHT, FRANK LLOYD. The Story of the Tower. NY: Horizon Press, 1956. 1st ed. *Glenn.* $160/£103

WRIGHT, FRANK LLOYD. The Story of the Tower: The Tree That Escaped the Crowded Forest. NY: Horizon, 1956. 1st ed. Frontis. (Color illus stained; text yellowing; dj tattered, torn in half.) *Bookpress.* $135/£87

WRIGHT, FRANK LLOYD. The Work of Frank Lloyd Wright. Horizon Press, 1965. (Ex-lib w/ink stamps, label, tape mks, #s; sl soiled). Lacks dj. *Edwards.* $155/£100

WRIGHT, G. FREDERICK. The Ice Age in North America and Its Bearings upon the Antiquity of Man. Oberlin, OH: Bibliotheca Sacra, 1911. 5th ed. Forntis, 3 maps (2 fldg, misbound at p202, 312, 401), 9 plts. Gray cl (inner hinges recased). VG. *Weber.* $60/£39

WRIGHT, G.F. and W. UPHAM. Greenlands Ice Fields and Life in the North Atlantic. NY: Appleton, 1896. 1st ed. pp xv, 5 maps. Silver gilt cl (one sig sl loose). Good. *Walcot.* $56/£36

WRIGHT, HAROLD BELL. The Calling of Dan Matthews. Chicago: Book Supply, 1909. 1st ed. Red cl. VG. *Antic Hay.* $27/£17

WRIGHT, HAROLD BELL. Exit. NY: D. Appleton, 1930. 1st ed. (Cl sl faded.) Dj (top chipped; fr worn). *Glenn.* $70/£45

WRIGHT, HAROLD BELL. The Mine with the Iron Door. NY: Burt, (1926). Photoplay ed. VG in dj (4 sm chips; nicks, creases). *Houle.* $65/£42

WRIGHT, HAROLD BELL. The Mine with the Iron Door. NY, 1923. 1st Amer ed. Color frontis. NF (rear hinge repaired). *Polyanthos.* $35/£23

WRIGHT, HAROLD BELL. The Mine with the Iron Door. NY/London: D. Appleton, 1923. 1st ed. VG (lt edgewear). *Glenn.* $125/£81

WRIGHT, HAROLD BELL. The Shepherd of the Hills. Chicago, 1907. 1st ed. Cl, pict label (spine sunned, worn; inscrip). *King.* $35/£23

WRIGHT, HAROLD BELL. The Winning of Barbara Worth. Chicago: Book Supply, 1911. 1st ed. 6 plts. VG. *Connolly.* $20/£13

WRIGHT, J. LEITCH. William Augustus Bowles. Athens: Univ of GA Press, (1967). 1st ed. Red cl. VG in dj (tape repair). *Chapel Hill.* $50/£32

WRIGHT, JULIA McNAIR. Among the Alaskans. Phila: Presbyterian Board of Pub, (1883). Color frontis map, 351pp. Dec cl. VG. *Schoyer.* $75/£48

WRIGHT, KENNETH. (Pseud of Lester Del Rey.) The Mysterious Planet. Winston, 1953. 1st ed. NF in VG- dj (lt chipped). *Aronovitz.* $45/£29

WRIGHT, KENNETH. (Pseud of Lester Del Rey.) The Mysterious Planet. Winston, 1953. 1st ed. Fine in dj. *Madle.* $125/£81

WRIGHT, L.R. Sleep While I Sing. NY: Viking, 1986. 1st ed. Fine in dj. *Mordida.* $40/£26

WRIGHT, L.R. The Suspect. NY: Viking, 1985. 1st ed. Fine in dj. *Mordida.* $45/£29

WRIGHT, LEWIS. The Illustrated Book of Poultry. London, 1890. New ed. vi,591pp (foxing), 50 Bright chromolitho plts. Gilt-dec cl (chipping heel of spine; paper cracking to inner hinges repaired). *Sutton.* $1,250/£806

WRIGHT, LEWIS. The Practical Poultry Keeper. Boston, 1870. Later ed. viii,243pp (yellowed, tp chipped; ex-lib); 12 plts. *Sutton.* $20/£13

WRIGHT, MRS. D. GIRAUD. (Louise Wigfall). A Southern Girl in '61, The War-Time Memoirs of a Confederate Senator's Daughter. NY, (1905). 1st ed. Frontis port missing; sm stain fr cvr, o/w VG+ in pict cl. *Pratt.* $65/£42

WRIGHT, RICHARD. 12 Million Black Voices. NY: Viking, 1941. 1st ed. Tan hopsacking (lt smudged). VG. *Petrilla.* $85/£55

WRIGHT, RICHARD. Black Boy. NY: Harper, (1945). 1st ed ('2-5...M-T'). Good in dj (sm chips, nicks, tears). *Houle.* $125/£81

WRIGHT, RICHARD. Black Boy. NY/London: Harper, (1945). Ltr ptg. Inscribed. Dk blue cl. VG in VG dj. *Chapel Hill.* $225/£145

WRIGHT, RICHARD. The Color Curtain. Cleveland, 1956. 1st Amer ed. Fine in Fine dj. *Polyanthos.* $100/£65

WRIGHT, RICHARD. The Colour Curtain. Dobson, 1956. 1st Eng ed. Fine in dj. *Fine Books.* $50/£32

WRIGHT, RICHARD. Native Son. Angus & Robertson, 1940. 1st Australian ed. Spine faded, else VG. *Fine Books.* $55/£35

WRIGHT, RICHARD. The Outsider. Angus & Robertson, 1954. 1st Australian ed. Fine in NF dj (lt dust soiling). *Fine Books.* $65/£42

WRIGHT, RICHARD. White Man, Listen! GC: Doubleday, 1957. 1st ed. Fine in NF dj (spine corners sl worn). *Bernard.* $100/£65

WRIGHT, RICHARDSON and MARGARET McELROY (eds). House and Garden's Book of Color Schemes. NY: Conde Nast, (1929). 1st ed. Frontis. Heavily rubbed; margins lt yellowed, else Good. *Bookpress.* $65/£42

WRIGHT, ROBERT. A Memoir of General James Oglethorpe.... London: Chapman, 1867. 1st ed. (16),424pp, map. (Lt wear fr cvr, lower spine.) Howes W 705. *Ginsberg.* $150/£97

WRIGHT, S. FOWLER. Deluge. Cosmopolitan, 1928. 1st Amer ed. VG in dj (lt worn). *Aronovitz.* $50/£32

WRIGHT, S. FOWLER. Dream or The Simian Maid. Harrap, 1931. 1st ed. NF in VG dj (spine sl sunned). *Aronovitz.* $125/£81

WRIGHT, S. FOWLER. Elfwin. Longmans, 1930. 1st Amer ed. NF in VG- dj. *Aronovitz.* $125/£81

WRIGHT, S. FOWLER. Elfwin. Longmans, 1930. 1st ed. VG. *Madle.* $30/£19

WRIGHT, S. FOWLER. Spiders' War. NY: Abelard, (1954). 1st ed. NF (top, fore-edge spotted) in dj (wear, soiled; price-clipped). *Antic Hay.* $25/£16

WRIGHT, S. FOWLER. The Throne of Saturn. Arkham House, 1949. 1st ed. Fine in dj. *Madle.* $45/£29

WRIGHT, S. FOWLER. The Throne of Saturn. Sauk City: Arkham House, 1949. 1st ed. VG (eps browned) in dj (sl wear; spine base chipped). *Antic Hay.* $50/£32

WRIGHT, S. FOWLER. The Throne of Saturn. London: Heinemann, 1951. 1st Eng ed. Fine in dj. *Temple.* $40/£26

WRIGHT, S. FOWLER. Vengeance of Gwa. London, 1945. Fine in dj (sl soiled). *Madle.* $25/£16

WRIGHT, S. FOWLER. The World Below. Shasta, 1949. Fine in dj (chipped). *Madle.* $35/£23

WRIGHT, S. FOWLER. The World Below. Shasta, 1949. One of 500 signed. Fine in dj (sl soiled). *Madle.* $65/£42

WRIGHT, SOLOMON A. My Rambles as East Texas Cowboy, Hunter.... Austin: TFS, 1942. 1st ed. Dj. *Lambeth.* $40/£26

WRIGHT, SOLOMON. My Rambles as East Texas Cowboy, Hunter, Fisherman, Tie-Cutter. Austin: Texas Folklore Soc, 1942. VG+ (lt bumped). *Bohling.* $60/£39

WRIGHT, THOMAS. The Life of Colonel Fred Burnaby. London, 1908. 1st ed. Frontis port, 58 plts. Teg. (Lt browning.) Rmdr cl binding (?). *Edwards.* $54/£35

WRIGHT, THOMAS. The Life of Sir Richard Burton. London, 1906. 2nd ed. 2 vols. Frontis ports, 62 plts. Contemp cl (edges dknd; lt staining vol 2; spines chipped, soiled; pp.vii-x vol 1 detached, lt foxing). *Edwards*. $116/£75

WRIGHT, THOMAS. The Life of William Blake. Olney, 1929. 1st ed. 2 vols. Inscrip; sl rubbed, o/w VG set. *Poetry*. $116/£75

WRIGHT, THOMAS. The Life of William Blake. London: Olney, 1929. 2 vols. 2 color plts. Lib cl (ex-lib; spotting throughout), gilt. *Edwards*. $101/£65

WRIGHT, W.P. Garden Trees and Shrubs. London, 1928. 2nd ed. 73 plts (24 color); fldg plan. Sl foxing at ends, edges, o/w Fine. *Henly*. $43/£28

WRIGHTSON, JOHN. The Principles of Agricultural Practice as an Instructional Subject. London: Chapman & Hall, 1893. 3rd ed. 228pp. Excellent. *Second Life*. $65/£42

Writers Take Sides. NY, 1938. 1st ed. Sl dull, else Good in wrappers. *Whiteson*. $109/£70

WU, G.D. Prehistoric Pottery in China. London: Kegan Paul et al, 1938. 1st ed. 64 plts. VG in dj. *Bookpress*. $110/£71

WUERTH, LOUIS A. Catalogue of the Lithographs of Joseph Pennell. NY, 1931. One of 425 numbered. Leather-backed buckram (spine dknd, chipped). Dj (torn). *Argosy*. $200/£129

WUNDERLICH, CARL. On the Temperature in Diseases: A Manual of Medical Thermometry. London, 1871. 1st Eng trans. 468pp. 40 woodcuts, 7 lithos. Ex-lib. *Fye*. $300/£194

WURLITZER, RUDOLPH. Nog. NY: Random House, 1968. 1st ed, 1st bk. Fine in Fine dj. *Beasley*. $60/£39

WURM, THEODORE and ALVIN C. GRAVES. The Crookedest Railroad in the World. Berkeley: Howell-North, 1960. 2nd rev ed. Dec cl. Fine in VG+ dj (1/4-inch loss spine top). *Harrington*. $30/£19

WURM, THEODORE. Hetch Hetchy and Its Dam Railroad. Berkeley: Howell-North Books, (1973). 1st ed. Yellow cl. NF (lt foxing) in VG dj (chipped, closed tears). *Harrington*. $60/£39

WYATT, M. DIGBY. The History, Theory, and Practice of Illuminating. London: Day & Son, (1861). 1st ed. (2),vi,68,66pp, 24 plts. Red cl (rebacked retaining orig backstrip; bruised). *Cox*. $47/£30

WYCHERLEY, GEORGE. Buccaneers of the Pacific. Indianapolis: Bobbs-Merrill, (1928). VG. *Blue Dragon*. $50/£32

WYCHERLEY, WILLIAM. The Complete Works. Montague Summers (ed). Nonesuch, 1924. 4 vols. Uncut. (Ex-lib, ink stamps, #s; feps lt browned; spine labels browned, one removed.) *Edwards*. $116/£75

WYCHERLEY, WILLIAM. The Complete Works. Montague Summers (ed). London: Nonesuch, 1924. #823/975. 4 vols. Cl-backed bds (corners rubbed; lt discolored; feps lt browned), paper spine labels (sl chipped vols 3&4.) *Edwards*. $194/£125

WYCHERLEY, WILLIAM. The Country Wife. London: Hutchinson, 1934. #965/1000 signed by Steven Spurrier (illus). 8 color plts. Uncut. Good in yellow linen-backed dec bds, paper label (backstrip sl rubbed, soiled). *Cox*. $39/£25

WYCHERLEY, WILLIAM. Works. Soho: Nonesuch, 1924. 4 vols. One of 900 numbered on antique paper. Prospectus. Partly unopened. VG (edgewear; foxing eps; spine labels chipped). *Agvent*. $100/£65

WYER, MALCOLM G. Western History Collection: Its Beginning and Growth. Denver, 1950. Probable 1st ed. Fine. *Baade*. $35/£23

WYETH, JOHN ALLEN. Life of General Nathan Bedford Forrest. NY: Harper & Bros, 1899. 1st ed. xix,(1),655pp. VG (rubbed; rear inner hinge starting). *Mcgowan*. $250/£161

WYETH, JOHN ALLEN. That Devil Forrest: Life of General Nathan Bedford Forrest. NY: Harper, (1959). 1st ed thus. NF in VG dj. *Mcgowan*. $85/£55

WYETH, JOHN ALLEN. With Sabre and Scalpel. NY: Harper & Bros, 1914. 1st ed. Orig cl. Minor soiling, else VG. *Mcgowan*. $250/£161

WYETH, N.C. The Wyeths: The Letters of N.C. Wyeth, 1901-1945. Betsy James Wyeth (ed). Boston: Gambit, 1971. 1st ed. Fine in dj. *Cahan*. $100/£65

WYLIE, ELINOR. Angels and Other Earthly Creatures. NY: Knopf, 1929. Patterned bds. NF (eps browned) in dj. *Antic Hay*. $45/£29

WYLIE, ELINOR. Mr. Hodge and Hazard. NY: Knopf, 1928. One of 145 numbered, signed. Blue cl w/silver stamping. Unopened. Fine in pub's slipcase. *Dermont*. $250/£161

WYLIE, ELINOR. Nets to Catch the Wind. London: Knopf, 1928. 1st Eng ed. Tan patterned bds. VG (bkpl) in dj (spine dknd). BAL 23484. *Chapel Hill*. $100/£65

WYLIE, ELINOR. The Orphan Angel. NY: Knopf, 1923. One of 160 numbered, signed on Borzoi rag paper. Cl, marbled bds. NF, unopened, w/extra spine label; in pub's orig slipcase. *Dermont*. $150/£97

WYLIE, ELINOR. Trivial Breath. NY: Knopf, 1929. 1st ed. Fine in Fine dj. *Dermont*. $35/£23

WYLIE, ELINOR. The Venetian Glass Nephew. NY, 1925. 1st ed, presentation copy. VG in dj. *Argosy*. $175/£113

WYLLY, CHARLES S. The Seed That Was Sown in the Colony of Georgia. NY: Neale, 1910. 1st ed. (Faded.) Howes W 723. *Ginsberg*. $125/£81

WYLLYS, RUFUS. Arizona. Phoenix: Hobson & Herr, (1950). 1st ed. Ink name, else Fine in VG dj. *Perier*. $60/£39

WYLLYS, RUFUS. Arizona: History of a Frontier State. Phoenix: Hobson & Herr, (1950). 1st ed. 8 plts, 9 maps, pict eps. VF in VG dj. *Oregon*. $45/£29

WYLLYS, RUFUS. Arizona: History of a Frontier State. Phoenix: Hobson Herr, 1950. 1st ed. VG in VG- dj. *Parker*. $65/£42

WYMAN, MORRILL. Autumnal Catarrh (Hay Fever), With Illustrative Maps. NY, 1876. 221pp. Good. *Fye*. $150/£97

WYMAN, WALKER D. Nothing but Prairie and Sky. Norman: Univ of OK, (1954). 1st ed. VG in dj (sl worn). *Lien*. $50/£32

WYNDHAM, JOHN. Chocky. London: Michael Joseph, 1968. 1st ed. Fine in dj. *Temple*. $40/£26

WYNDHAM, JOHN. The Chrysalids. London: Joseph, 1955. 1st UK ed. VG in VG dj. *Lewton*. $23/£15

WYNDHAM, JOHN. The Chrysalids. London: Michael Joseph, 1955. 1st UK ed. NF in dj. *Williams*. $85/£55

WYNDHAM, JOHN. Consider Her Ways and Others. London: Michael Joseph, 1961. 1st ed. NF in dj (torn, verso strengthened). *Temple*. $26/£17

WYNDHAM, JOHN. The Day of the Triffids. Joseph, 1951. 1st ed, 1st bk. Contents Good (binding sl dull; sl rubbed). *Whiteson*. $50/£32

WYNDHAM, JOHN. The Day of the Triffids. Doubleday, 1951. 1st ed. NF in dj (lt shelf wear). *Aronovitz*. $225/£145

WYNDHAM, JOHN. The Day of the Triffids. London: Joseph, 1951. 1st Eng ed. VG + in dj (sl chipped spine extrems) *Limestone*. $275/£177

WYNDHAM, JOHN. The Day of the Triffids. London: Michael Joseph, 1951. 1st UK ed. Virtually Fine (sl chipped) in VG + dj. *Williams*. $256/£165

WYNDHAM, JOHN. The Midwich Cuckoos. Ballantine, 1957. 1st ed. VG in dj (chipped, worn). *Madle*. $35/£23

WYNDHAM, JOHN. The Midwich Cuckoos. Michael Joseph, 1957. 1st ed. Lt stain cvrs, else VG + in NF dj (lt soil rear panel). *Aronovitz*. $100/£65

WYNDHAM, JOHN. The Seeds of Time. London, 1956. 1st ed. VG. *Madle*. $25/£16

WYNDHAM, RICHARD. The Gentle Savage. NY: Morrow, 1936. 1st ed. Color frontis. Sl rubbed, spine sl faded, o/w VG. *Worldwide*. $45/£29

WYNKOOP, RICHARD. Vessels and Voyages.... NY: Burr, 1886. 1st ed. (lvi),208pp. Attractive. *Lefkowicz*. $150/£97

WYNN, MARCIA RITTENHOUSE. Desert Bonanza. Story of Early Randsburg Mojave Desert Mining Camp. Culver City: Samelson, 1949. 1st ed. Fine in Fine dj. *Book Market*. $50/£32

WYON, REGINALD. The Balkans from Within. London, 1904. 1st ed. 2 fldg maps. (Browning; feps lt foxed; ink stamp fep; soiling, discoloring, stain lower joint.) *Edwards*. $116/£75

WYSS, JOHANN. The Swiss Family Robinson. Ipswich: LEC, 1963. One of 1500. Signed by David Gentleman (engrs). Imported grass-cl. Fine in soiled slipcase. *Agvent*. $100/£65

X

X, MALCOLM. (Pseud of Malcolm Little.) The Autobiography.... NY: Grove, (1965). 1st ed. VG in dj (edgeworn). *Petrilla*. $150/£97

X, MALCOLM. (Pseud of Malcolm Little.) Malcolm X Speaks. NY: Merit Pub, 1965. 1st ed, 1st ptg. Black cl. Ink name, sm erasures in text, else VG in dj (chipped, worn, else Good). *Godot*. $125/£81

X., S.M. Grandma's Stories and Anecdotes of 'Ye Olden Times.' Boston: Angel Guardian Press, 1899. 1st ed, w/type, handwritten errata slip. 139pp. Gilt-stamped tan cl; aeg. VG. *Petrilla*. $40/£26

XANTUS, JOHN. Travels in Southern California. Theodore Shoenman & Helen Benedek Shoenman (eds). Detroit: Wayne State Univ, 1976. 1st thus. Frontis; 16 plts; map. VF in VG dj. *Oregon*. $22/£14

Y

YADIN, YIGAEL. Bar-Kokhba; the Rediscovery of the Legendary Hero of the Second Jewish Revolt Against Rome. NY: Random House, (1971). 7 maps. (Sig.) Dj. *Archaeologia*. $25/£16

YADIN, YIGAEL. Masada: Herod's Fortress and the Zealot's Last Stand. NY: Random House, (1966). Good in dj. *Archaeologia*. $25/£16

Yankee Doodle: An Old Friend in a New Dress. NY: Dodd, Mead, 1881. 1st ed. Lg, 4to. Frontis (marginal ink stain, ink mks verso), 32pp (marginal ink stain tp); 8 full-pg color illus by Howard Pyle. 1937 invoice laid in. Color illus bds (edges rubbed, worn). *Reisler*. $750/£484

YARDLEY, R.B. The Samoa Express Postage Stamps. Royal Philatelic Soc, 1916. 10 photo plts. (Spine renewed to paper cvrs.) *Gretton*. $28/£18

YARRELL, WILLIAM. A History of British Birds. London: John Van Voorst, 1843. 1st ed. 3 vols. 520 wood engrs. Partially unopened. (Feps lt foxed, sl spotting edges; rebound, spines faded.) *Edwards*. $116/£75

YARRELL, WILLIAM. A History of British Birds. London, 1856. 3rd ed. 3 vols. 550 woodcut engrs. 1/2 calf. Good. *Henly*. $109/£70

YARRELL, WILLIAM. A History of British Birds. London: John van Voorst, 1871-5. 4th ed. 4 vols. 564 woodcuts. (Feps lt browned, spines sl rubbed.) *Edwards*. $171/£110

YARRELL, WILLIAM. A History of British Fishes. London, 1836. 1st ed. 2 vols. (Sl foxing; rebacked, preserving spines.) *Henly*. $116/£75

YASTRZEMSKI, CARL with AL HIRSHBERG. Batting. Viking, 1972. 1st ed. Fine in VG + dj. *Plapinger*. $25/£16

YASTRZEMSKI, CARL with AL HIRSHBERG. Yaz. Viking, 1968. 1st ed. Fine in VG + dj. *Plapinger*. $25/£16

YATES, DORNFORD. Berry and I Look Back. London: Ward, Lock, 1958. 1st ed. Very Nice in dj. *Temple*. $16/£10

YATES, DORNFORD. Red in the Morning. London: Ward, Lock, 1946. 1st ed. Top edge red. Fore-edges sl foxed; top edges sl faded; o/w Fine. *Temple*. $14/£9

YATES, GEORGE WORTHINGTON. The Body That Wasn't Uncle. NY: William Morrow, 1939. 1st ed. Fine in dj (rubbed streak on spine). *Mordida*. $65/£42

YATES, GEORGE WORTHINGTON. If a Body. NY: William Morrow, 1941. 1st ed. Fine in dj (faded spine; short closed tears). *Mordida*. $40/£26

YATO, TAMOTSU. Young Samurai. Bodybuilders of Japan. NY, (1967). 1st Amer ed. Fine in NF dj (lt edgewear). *Mcclintock*. $75/£48

YEAGER, BUNNY. Camera in Jamaica. South Brunswick: A.S. Barnes, 1967. 5 color photos. VG. *Cahan*. $45/£29

Year 1200. NY: MMA, 1970. Good in wrappers (sl rubbed). *Washton*. $55/£35

Year in Spain. (By Alexander Sidell Mackenzie). Boston, 1829. 1st ed. Lib buckram (rebound; ex-lib w/mks). *King*. $75/£48

Yearbook of the U.S. Department of Agriculture, 1905. Washington, 1906. 73 plts. (Ccl soiled.) *Sutton*. $35/£23

Yearbook of the U.S. Department of Agriculture, 1918. Washington, 1919. 62 plts (2 color). (Chipped, insect tracings, ex-lib.) *Sutton.* $25/£16

Yearbook of the U.S. Department of Agriculture. 1897. Washington, 1898. 792pp. *Hayman.* $15/£10

YEARNS, WILFRED BUCK. The Confederate Congress. Athens: Univ of GA, 1960. 1st ed. Emb cl. Pastedowns foxed, else VG in dj. *Cahan.* $40/£26

YEATS, G.D. Some Observations on the Duodenum, or Second Stomach. London, 1820. 54pp (foxing); 2 fldg plts. 1/2 cl (rebound); marbled bds. *Whitehart.* $101/£65

YEATS, J.B. The Amaranthers. Heinemann, 1936. 1st ed. VG in dec dj (sl dull). *Whiteson.* $93/£60

YEATS, J.B. Letters from Bedford Park: A Selection from Correspondence (1890-1901) of John Butler Yeats. Dublin: Cuala Press, 1972. 1st ed. One of 500. Un-opened. Fine in paper dj. *Cahan.* $60/£39

YEATS, J.B. Letters to His Son; W.B. Yeats and Others. J. Hone (ed). Faber, 1944. 1st ed. Sm corner cut fep, else VG in dj (dull, torn). *Whiteson.* $25/£16

YEATS, W.B. Autobiographies. Macmillan, 1920. 1st ed. Dec cl. Spine sl faded, else VG. *Whiteson.* $124/£80

YEATS, W.B. Autobiographies. Macmillan, 1926. 1st ed. Dec cl sl dull, else Good. *Whiteson.* $62/£40

YEATS, W.B. Autobiographies. London: Macmillan, 1955. 1st ed thus. Eps foxed, else VG in dj. *Godot.* $50/£32

YEATS, W.B. Autobiographies. London: Macmillan, 1955. New ed. Edges spotted; offsetting eps, o/w VG in dj (soiled, browned, nicked). *Virgo.* $39/£25

YEATS, W.B. The Cat and the Moon and Certain Poems. Dublin: Cuala Press, 1924. 1st ed. One of 500. Un-opened. Spine sl tanned, label sl chipped, else Nice. *Reese.* $275/£177

YEATS, W.B. Dramatis Personae 1896-1902.... NY: Macmillan, 1936. 1st collective ed. Port. gilt cl. VG (sl sunning edges; lt tanning feps) in dj (lt soiled; narrow chips). *Reese.* $85/£55

YEATS, W.B. Early Poems and Stories. London: Macmillan, 1925. 1st collective ed thus. One of 2908 ptd. Grn cl stamped in gilt/blind. Good (early bkpl; ink name; top spine sunned) in dj (worn; deep triangular chip spine crown). *Reese.* $75/£48

YEATS, W.B. Early Poems and Stories. NY: Macmillan, 1925. One of 250 numbered, specially ptd & bound, signed. Sm spots rear bd, o/w Fine (w/o slipcase). *Reese.* $500/£323

YEATS, W.B. Essays and Introductions. Macmillan, 1961. 1st ed. VG in dj (badly torn). *Whiteson.* $28/£18

YEATS, W.B. Ideas of Good and Evil. NY: Macmillan, 1903. 1st Amer ed. Uncut. Blue cl, gilt. *Macdonnell.* $175/£113

YEATS, W.B. In the Seven Woods. NY: Macmillan, 1903. 1st Amer ed. Teg, uncut. Blue cl, gilt. Fine. *Macdonnell.* $165/£106

YEATS, W.B. Last Poems and Plays. NY: Macmillan, 1940. 1st Amer ed. Pub's grn cl, blind-blocked design, gilt-titled spine. Pale grn dj (sl used). *Book Block.* $125/£81

YEATS, W.B. Later Poems. NY: Macmillan, 1924. One of 250 numbered, specially ptd & bound, signed. Lt spots label, spine; o/w VG (w/o slipcase). *Reese.* $400/£258

YEATS, W.B. Letters to W.B. Yeats. 2 vols. Macmillan, 1977. 1st eds. Fine in Fine djs. *Whiteson.* $34/£22

YEATS, W.B. Mythologies. Macmillan, 1959. 1st ed. VG in dj (sl dull, rubbed). *Whiteson.* $28/£18

YEATS, W.B. On the Boiler. Dublin: Cuala Press, (1939). 2nd ed. Pict ptd wrappers (spine cracked; chips; eps lt foxed). *Sadlon.* $50/£32

YEATS, W.B. On the Boiler. Dublin: Cuala Press, (1939). 2nd ed. VG+ (lt wear to yapp edges) in ptd blue wraps (sticker removed fr wrap). *Chapel Hill.* $150/£97

YEATS, W.B. A Packet for Ezra Pound. Dublin: Cuala Press, 1929. 1st ed. Ltd to 425 ptd. Holland-backed bds. Fine in plain dj. *Jaffe.* $350/£226

YEATS, W.B. Per Amica Silentia Lunae. Macmillan, 1918. 1st ed. Gilt dec cl. Sl dull; sl rubbed, else Good. *Whiteson.* $47/£30

YEATS, W.B. Plays for an Irish Theatre. Bullen, 1911. 1st ed. Contents VG (bds sl dull, mkd; spine label missing). *Whiteson.* $25/£16

YEATS, W.B. The Poems of W.B. Yeats. NY: LEC, 1970. One of 1500 numbered, signed by Robin Jacques (illus). Fine in pub's slipcase. *Hermitage.* $175/£113

YEATS, W.B. Poems. London: T. Fisher Unwin, 1901. 3rd ed. Gilt-stamped blue cl. VG (short tear spine base; eps tanned; incrips). *Chapel Hill.* $150/£97

YEATS, W.B. Poems. London: T. Fisher Unwin, 1904. 1st ed. Gilt-dec blue cl. NF (spine head sl rubbed, eps foxed). *Jaffe.* $175/£113

YEATS, W.B. Poems. London: T. Fisher Unwin, 1904. 4th ed. Largely unopened. Emb pict cl. NF (bkpl). *Cahan.* $175/£113

YEATS, W.B. Responsibilities and Other Poems. NY: Macmillan, 1916. 1st Amer ed. Gray bds. VG (spine dknd; edges lt browned; sig). *Chapel Hill.* $250/£161

YEATS, W.B. Responsibilities: Poems and a Play. Cuala, 1914. #35/400. Unopened. Sl abrasion tp; top edge dusty; white linen spine sl soiled, o/w VG. *Poetry.* $186/£120

YEATS, W.B. The Secret Rose. London: Lawrence & Bullen, 1897. 1st ed. J.B. Yeats (illus). Good (eps browned, sl foxed; top edges dusty; rubbed; lower edge cvr sl dampstained). *Virgo.* $194/£125

YEATS, W.B. Selected Poems. NY: Macmillan, 1921. 1st ed, grey-grn cl issue. Ink name, date; spine lt worn, corner bumped, else VG. *Godot.* $85/£55

YEATS, W.B. Selected Poems. London: Macmillan, 1929. 1st ed, 1st issue (w/o erratum slip). Teg. Blue cl. VG in dj (sl chipped, else VG). *Godot.* $175/£113

YEATS, W.B. The Shadowy Waters. London: Hodder & Stoughton, 1900. 1st ed. Beveled edges, teg. Blue cl (spine ends, corners worn; rear cvr stained). VG. *Chapel Hill.* $200/£129

YEATS, W.B. Synge and the Ireland of His Time.... Churchtown, Dundrum: Cuala Press, 1911. 1st ed. One of 350. Corners bumped, o/w NF. *Reese.* $275/£177

YEATS, W.B. The Tables of the Law; and the Adoration of the Magi. Shakespeare Head, 1914. #53/510. VG (inscrip; webbing exposed after 1st gathering). *Poetry.* $34/£22

YEATS, W.B. The Trembling of the Veil. London: T. Werner Laurie, 1922. 1st ed. Ltd to 1000 signed. Paper spine label. Fine in NF dj. *Sadlon.* $400/£258

YEATS, W.B. The Trembling of the Veil. London: By T. Werner Laurie for subs, 1922. 1st ed. One of 1000 numbered, signed. Top edge sl tanned, else Fine in dj (spine tanned, nicks, creased edge tear). *Reese.* $350/£226

YEATS, W.B. Wheels and Butterflies. Macmillan, 1934. 1st ed. Gilt dec cl sl dull, else VG. *Whiteson.* $47/£30

YEATS, W.B. Wheels and Butterflies. London: Macmillan, 1934. 1st ed. Fine (bkpl) in dj (sl rubbed; sm internal mend). *Pharos.* $75/£48

YEATS, W.B. Where There Is Nothing.... NY: Macmillan, 1903. 1st Amer trade ed. Gilt blue cl. Nick spine, sm smudge title gilt, o/w Very Nice. *Reese.* $75/£48

YEATS, W.B. (ed). Irish Fairy and Folk Tales. London/NY: Walter Scott/Scribner's, (ca. 1893). Early illus ed. 326pp,(13)pp ads, 12 plts by James Torrance. This copy w/Scribner ads at rear, binding w/Scott imprint. Pict lt grn cl, aeg. VG (bkpl removed; spine sl dkned). *Chapel Hill.* $95/£61

YEATS, W.B. (ed). Irish Fairy Tales. NY: Cassell, 1892. 1st Amer ed. viii,236pp. Blue/white cl. Dull, spine lt browned; corners sl worn, else VG. *Godot.* $375/£242

YELD, GEORGE. Scrambles in the Eastern Graians 1878-1897. London: T. Fisher Unwin, 1900. 1st ed. Map. Uncut. Pict cl gilt (extrems rubbed; spine faded; upper joint cracked; lacks fep). *Hollett.* $85/£55

Yellow Book. London, 1894-1897. 1st eds. 13 vols. Pict yellow cl. NF (spines sunned; extrem tears). *Polyanthos.* $950/£613

Yellow Dwarf. (Yellow Dwarf Series.) NY: McLoughlin Bros, n.d. (ca 1885). 5 leaves + 1pg list lower wrapper. Double-pg spread + 4 full-pg chromolithos by Justin H. Howard. Upper wrapper w/designed title, illus (spine rubbed). Internally Fine. *Hobbyhorse.* $100/£65

Yellow Dwarf. (Yellow Dwarf Series.) NY: McLoughlin Bros, n.d. ca 1880. 16pp. Howard (illus). Illus wraps. VG (few spots not affecting text). *Davidson.* $120/£77

YEO, I. BURNEY. The Therapeutics of Mineral Springs and Climates. Chicago, 1904. 1st ed. (Ex-lib.) *Argosy.* $40/£26

YEO, PETER F. Hardy Geraniums. Portland, 1985. 44 color plts. Fine in dj. *Brooks.* $45/£29

YERBY, FRANK. Benton's Row. Dial, 1954. 1st ed. NF (name) in dj (chipped, internally repaired). *Stahr.* $35/£23

YERBY, FRANK. Bride of Liberty. GC: Doubleday, 1954. 1st ed. VG in VG dj (chipped; worn; short tears). *Revere.* $35/£23

YERBY, FRANK. The Golden Hawk. NY: Dial Press, 1948. 1st ed. VG in dj (lt chipped). *Petrilla.* $35/£23

YERBY, FRANK. Griffin's Way. NY: Dial, 1962. 1st ed. Fine in NF dj (spine sl dknd). *Between The Covers.* $50/£32

YERBY, FRANK. The Vixens. Dial, 1947. 1st ed. VG+ in dj (chipped, worn). *Stahr.* $45/£29

YERBY, FRANK. A Woman Called Fancy. NY: Dial Press, 1951. 1st ed. VG- (bumped; fep clipped) in VG- dj (worn, chipped). *Revere.* $40/£26

YEUTTER, FRANK. Jim Konstanty. Barnes, 1951. Rev copy w/slip. VG in Good+ dj. *Plapinger.* $35/£23

YEVTUSHENKO, YEVGENY. A Precocious Autobiography. Andrew R. McAndrew (trans). NY: E.P. Dutton, 1963. 1st ed. Rev copy, slip laid in. Fine in dj (lt rubbed). *Sadlon.* $20/£13

YEVTUSHENKO, YEVGENY. Selected Poems. Robin Milner-Gulland & Peter Levy (trans). NY: E.P. Dutton, 1962. 1st ed. Rev copy, slip laid in. Fine in dj (lt rubbed). *Sadlon.* $20/£13

YEVTUSHENKO, YEVGENY. Stolen Apples. NY, 1971. Ltd ed of 250 numbered, signed. Fine in matching slipcase. *Sclanders.* $186/£120

YINGLING, W.A. The Experience of a Converted Catholic. Cincinnati: Walden & Stowe, 1883. 47pp. Good in ptd wrappers. *Hayman.* $20/£13

YOCH, JANE J. Landscaping the American Dream. NY: Abrams, (1989). 1st ed. Fine in Fine dj. *Book Market.* $40/£26

YOGANANDA, PARAMAHANSA. Autobiography of a Yogi. NY: Philosophical Library, (1946). 1st ed. Tape mks outside cvr, else Good+ in dj (worn). *Blue Dragon.* $55/£35

YONGE, CHARLOTTE M. Little Lucy's Wonderful Globe. London/NY, 1871. 74pp + ads; 24 wood-engr plts. Gilt-pict cl (backstrip worn). *Argosy.* $65/£42

YONGE, CHARLOTTE M. The Sea Shore, the New Naturalist. London: Collins, (1949). 1st ed. Dj. *Petersfield.* $39/£25

YONGE, CHARLOTTE M. The Sea Shore. London, 1949. 1st ed. Dj (sl creased). *Edwards.* $47/£30

YONGE, CHARLOTTE M. Unknown to History. London: Macmillan, 1882. 1st ed. 2 vols. 1/2 titles each vol (name, date to both), ad leaf end of vol 2. Gilt-lettered spine. *Bickersteth.* $124/£80

YONGE, SAMUEL H. The Site of Old 'James Towne' 1607-1698. Richmond, VA, 1926. 17 plts. *Heinoldt.* $15/£10

YORICK, MR. (Pseud of Laurence Sterne.) A Sentimental Journey through France and Italy. London: For J. Wenman, (1782). Frontis engr. Contemp polished calf (sl rubbed); gilt; leather spine label. *Sadlon.* $75/£48

YORICK, MR. (Pseud of Laurence Sterne.) A Sentimental Journey through France and Italy. Ptd for T. Becket & P.A. De Hondt, 1768. 1st ed, 1st issue, on ordinary paper. Missing ad leaf promised 2 further vols, which Sterne did not live to write. Variants are 'vaus' on p150 vol 1, and 'who have' on p133 vol 2. 2 vols. xx,203; (iv),208pp. Orig speckled calf. (Inscrip fr fly leaf each vol; spines rubbed; lacks labels; spine top vol 2 defective; upper joint vol 2 cracked.) *Bickersteth.* $442/£285

YORICK, MR. (Pseud of Laurence Sterne.) A Sentimental Journey Through France and Italy. London: T. Becket & P.A. de Hondt, 1768. 1st ed. 2 vols. 12mo; xx,203; (4),208pp; half titles present. 18th cent calf (hinges rubbed; top spine vol 2 chipped). Gilt-tooled borders on cvrs, gilt spines, red calf labels; marbled eps. Nice. *Karmiole.* $1,250/£806

YORICK, MR. (Pseud of Laurence Sterne). A Sentimental Journey through France and Italy. London: for T. Cadell, 1794. Later ed. 3 vols in one. 12mo, 311pp. Recent brn cl, red cl spine label. VG. *Chapel Hill.* $50/£32

YORICK, MR. (Pseud of Laurence Sterne.) A Sentimental Journey through France and Italy. London: West et al, 1801. New ed. (iv),155,(1)pp, 6 plts. Contemp calf (rubbed), morocco label. Good (top margin 1/2title repaired). *Cox.* $43/£28

YORKE, MALCOLME. The Spirit of Place. Nine Neo-Romantic Artists.... NY, 1988. Good in dj. *Washton.* $35/£23

YOST, FIELDING. Football for Player and Spectator. Ann Arbor: Univ Pub Co, 1905. 1st ed. VG+. *Bishop.* $100/£65

YOST, KARL and FREDERIC G. RENNER. A Bibliography of the Published Works of Charles M. Russell. Lincoln: Univ of NE, 1971. 2nd ptg. NF in illus dj. *Cahan.* $50/£32

YOST, KARL and FREDERIC G. RENNER. Charles M. Russell. A Bibliography. Lincoln: Univ of NE, (1971). 2nd ed. 42 plts (18 color). Dj. *Heinoldt*. $50/£32

YOUATT, WILLIAM. Sheep: Their Breeds, Management, and Diseases. NY: Moore, (1848). 159pp. Pub's cl (sl water-stained). *Second Life*. $75/£48

YOUMANS, ELIZA. The First Book of Botany. London: Henry S. King, 1872. New, enlgd ed. xi,201pp + 48pp ads; 300 engrs. Gilt-stamped cl. Fine. *Quest*. $50/£32

YOUMANS, ELIZA. The First Book of Botany. NY: Appleton, 1873. New, enlgd ed. 202pp + ads. Leather-backed bds. VG (foxed; rubbed). *Second Life*. $25/£16

Young Merchant. (By John Frost). Boston, 1841. 2nd stereotype ed. Frontis, extra title, 288pp. Cl (frayed, sl worn). *King*. $35/£23

YOUNG, A.S. The Mets from Mobile. Harcourt, Brace & World, 1970. 1st ed. Fine in VG dj. *Plapinger*. $40/£26

YOUNG, ART. Art Young's Inferno: A Journey through Hell 600 Years after Dante. NY, (1934). 1st ed. VG. *Argosy*. $45/£29

YOUNG, ART. Art Young: His Life and Times. NY: Sheridan House, 1939. 1st ed. Ink name; fep browning, o/w Fine. *Hermitage*. $25/£16

YOUNG, ART. On My Way. NY: Horace Liveright, (1928). 1st ed. Ltd to 1000 numbered. Japanese vellum over bds (spotting fr bd; spine lt worn), o/w VG. *Hermitage*. $45/£29

YOUNG, CHARLES E. Dangers of the Trail in 1865, a Narrative.... Geneva, NY, 1912. Map, port. VG+. *Bohling*. $150/£97

YOUNG, DOROTHY WEIR. The Life and Letters of J. Alden Weir. Lawrence W. Chisholm (ed). New Haven: Yale Univ Press, 1960. Color frontis. VG in dj (torn). *Argosy*. $85/£55

YOUNG, EDWARD. The Correspondence 1683-1765. Henry Pettit (ed). Clarendon, 1971. 1st ed. Fine in dj (price-clipped; nick). *Poetry*. $34/£22

YOUNG, EGERTON RYERSON. By Canoe and Dog Train Among the Cree and Salteaux Indians. Toronto: William Briggs, (1890). 1st ed. Frontis, 267pp. Pict cl. Fep adhered to pastedown, o/w VG. *Oregon*. $60/£39

YOUNG, EGERTON RYERSON. By Canoe and Dog-Train Among the Cree and Salteaux Indians. NY/Cincinnati: Hunt & Eaton/Cranston & Curts, 1890. 267pp. Blue-grn cl (worn, soiled). *Parmer*. $125/£81

YOUNG, EGERTON RYERSON. By Canoe and Dog-Train Among the Cree and Salteaux Indians. London: Charles H. Kelly, 1890. 4th thousand. Mtd frontis port, xii,267pp, port. Pict tan cl blocked in black/gold. VG. *Cox*. $47/£30

YOUNG, FILSON. The Relief of Mafeking. London, 1900. 1st ed. Frontis, 3 other ports; 2 maps; facs. New eps, foxing, o/w VG in red cl (sl worn). *Edwards*. $70/£45

YOUNG, FRANCIS BRETT. Black Roses. London: Heinemann, 1929. 1st ed, ltd to 525 signed. Unopened. Full vellum, gilt-titled. Very Nice. *Cady*. $60/£39

YOUNG, G. (ed). The Voyage of the 'Wanderer' from the Journals and Letters of C. and S. Lambert. London, 1883. xx,335pp; fldg chart, 23 Fine color engrs. Dec cl. Excellent. *Lewis*. $287/£185

YOUNG, GEOFFREY WINTHROP. Mountain Craft. London, 1934. 3rd ed. 9 plts. Dj. *Bickersteth*. $23/£15

YOUNG, GEOFFREY WINTHROP. On High Hills. London: Methuen, 1944. 25 plts. VG in dj (sl worn). *Hollett*. $31/£20

YOUNG, GERALD. The Wild Pigs. London: Sonnenschein, 1899. 4 plts by W. Parkinson. Gilt pig; beveled edges. *Petersfield*. $25/£16

YOUNG, HERBERT. They Came to Jerome, the Billion Dollar Copper Camp. Jerome, AZ: Hist Soc, 1972. 1st ed, ltd to 600 signed, numbered. Map. Fine. *Oregon*. $35/£23

YOUNG, HUGH. Hugh Young. NY: Harcourt Brace, 1940. 1st ed. 3 color plts. Good in dj (worn). *Goodrich*. $45/£29

YOUNG, J. RUSSELL. Around the World with General Grant. Amer News Co, 1879. 1st ed. 2 vols complete. 1262pp. VG. *Bishop*. $37/£24

YOUNG, J.P. The Seventh Tennessee Cavalry. Nashville: M.E. Church, South, 1890. 1st ed. Frontis port, 227pp. Orig dk brn cl. Good (bkpl; worn; blindstamps tp, plts). Howes Y 28. *Chapel Hill*. $300/£194

YOUNG, JENNIE J. The Ceramic Art. NY: Harper, 1879. 1st ed. (iv),499,(3)pp. Gilt cl. *Bookpress*. $275/£177

YOUNG, JESSE BOWMAN. What a Boy Saw in the Army. NY, (1894). 1st ed. 399pp, 100 dwgs by Frank Beard. Pict cl. Cvr wear, but VG. *Pratt*. $65/£42

YOUNG, KARL. The Drama of the Medieval Church. OUP, 1933. 2 vols. Frontispieces. (Emb stamps, lib labels, #s; eps soiled, dampstained; hinges cracked, tender; worn, bubbled.) *Edwards*. $85/£55

YOUNG, MARGUERITE. Miss Macintosh My Darling. NY: Scribner's, (1965). 1st ed. Fine in dj (nicked). *Hermitage*. $35/£23

YOUNG, NELLIE MAY. An Oregon Idyl. Glendale: Clark, 1961. 1st ed. VG in VG dj. *Oregon*. $35/£23

YOUNG, OTIS E. The First Military Escort on the Santa Fe Trail, 1829. Glendale: Clark, 1952. 4 plts, fldg map. Unopened. Orig cl. VG. *Schoyer*. $65/£42

YOUNG, OTIS E. The First Military Escort on the Santa Fe Trail, 1829. Glendale: Clark, 1952. 1st ed. Frontis; fldg map. Uncut, unopened. *Dawson*. $100/£65

YOUNG, OTIS E. The First Military Escort on the Santa Fe Trail, 1829. Glendale: Clark, 1952. 1st ed. Map. Mostly unopened; teg. Red cl (spine faded, bumped). VG+. *Harrington*. $100/£65

YOUNG, OTIS E. The West of Philip St. George Cook, 1809-1895. Glendale: Clark, 1955. 1st ed. VG (ex-lib). *Parker*. $75/£48

YOUNG, OTIS E. The West of Philip St. George Cooke, 1809-1895. Glendale: Clark, 1955. 1st ed. Fldg map. Dk red cl. Fine. *Harrington*. $120/£77

YOUNG, OTIS E. Western Mining. An Informal Account of Precious-Metals...1893. (Norman: Univ of OK Press, 1970). 1st ed. Fine in dj. *Laurie*. $50/£32

YOUNG, S. HALL. Hall Young of Alaska, 'The Mushing Parson.' NY: Fleming H. Revell Co, (1927). Frontis, 448pp; map; 14pp photo illus. Gold-stamped cl. (Fr hinge loose; sl warped.) *Dawson*. $100/£65

YOUNG, S.P. The Last of the Loners. Toronto/London: Macmillan, 1970. 1st ed. Blind-stamped dec cl. Fine in VG+ dj. *Mikesh*. $35/£23

YOUNG, S.P. The Wolf in North American History. Caldwell: Caxton, 1946. 1st ed. NF. *Mikesh*. $45/£29

YOUNG, S.P. and E.A. GOLDMAN. The Puma, Mysterious American Cat. Washington: Amer Wildlife Inst, 1946. 1st ed. Color frontis, 13 tables. Grn cl. VG in pict dj (chipped). *House*. $65/£42

YOUNG, S.P. and E.A. GOLDMAN. The Puma. Washington: AWI, 1946. 1st ed. 93 plts, 13 tables, 6 figs. Gilt dec cl. NF. *Mikesh*. $40/£26

YOUNG, STARK. Encaustics. NY: New Republic, 1926. 1st ed. Sm mended split spine foot, o/w NF. *Pharos.* $125/£81

YOUNG, STARK. Guenevere: A Play in Five Acts. NY: Grafton, 1906. 1st ed. NF. *Pharos.* $250/£161

YOUNG, STARK. The Torches Flare. NY: Scribner's, 1928. 1st ed. VG in illus dj (sl stains). *Cahan.* $50/£32

YOUNG, T. A Practical and Historical Treatise on the Consumptive Diseases. London, 1815. xii,496pp. 1/2 leather (joints weak; corners, spine rubbed; foxing). *Whitehart.* $372/£240

YOUNG, W. Picturesque Architectural Studies and Practical Designs.... London: E.& F.N. Spon, 1872. 1st ed. viii,37,(1)pp, 50 plts. (Lt foxing early leaves, margins illus.) Pub's gilt cl. Fr hinge internally cracked; sl wear edges, joints; else VG. *Bookpress.* $475/£306

YOUNGER, WILLIAM. Gods, Men and Wine. London, 1966. 1st ed. 16 color plts. Dj (sl chipped). *Edwards.* $39/£25

YOUNGHUSBAND, FRANCIS. The Coming Country. Dutton, 1928. 1st ed. VG. *Madle.* $30/£19

YOUNGHUSBAND, FRANCIS. Kashmir. A&C Black, 1924. New ed. 32 color plts, 2 maps. Blind-emb cl (spine rubbed; sl loss corners; lt browning; sm label fep). *Edwards.* $31/£20

YOUNGHUSBAND, G.J. The Story of the Guides. London, 1908. (Cl sl rubbed, faded.) Sound. *Gretton.* $31/£20

YOUNGMAN, W.E. Gleanings from Western Prairies. Cambridge: James Piggott, 1882. 1st ed. VG+ (mk on fep). *Parker.* $125/£81

YOURCENAR, MARGUERITE (trans). Two Lives and a Dream. (London): Aidan Ellis, (1987). 1st British ed. Nice in dj (lt smudged). *Reese.* $20/£13

YOURCENAR, MARGUERITE. The Alms of Alcippe. Edith R. Farrell (trans). NY: Targ Editions, 1982. 1st ed. One of 250 signed. Fine in glassine dj. *Juvelis.* $125/£81

Youth's Cabinet of Nature, for the Year. NY: Samuel Wood, 1814. Rpt. 12mo. 52pp + 1pg list lower wrapper, 13 half-pg engrs. Dec stiff buff paper wrappers (lt stains). Fine. *Hobbyhorse.* $120/£77

Youthful Recreations. Phila: J. Johnson, n.d. (ca 1802). 1st ed. 16mo. 16 leaves. Engr tp, 15 Fine full-pg copper engrs. Orig yellow/gold stiff paper wrappers. Fine. *Hobbyhorse.* $425/£274

YOYOTTE, JEAN. Treasures of the Pharaohs: the Early Period, the New Kingdom, the Late Period. Geneva: Skira, (1968). 120 tipped-in plts. (Bkpl; corner bumped.) *Archaeologia.* $150/£97

YZENDOORN, REGINALD. History of the Catholic Mission in the Hawaiian Islands. Honolulu, 1927. 16 plts. Pict cl (shaken, edgeworn, spine ends frayed, rubberstamps). *Bohling.* $75/£48

Z

ZACKEL, FRED. Cocaine and Blue Eyes. NY: Coward, 1978. 1st ed. Fine in Fine dj. *Beasley.* $35/£23

ZAEHENSDORF, J.W. Bookbinding. Bell & Sons, 1890. 2nd ed. Fine in grn cl. *Moss.* $109/£70

ZAMPETTI, PIETRO. Paintings from the Marches. London, 1971. 187 b/w, 40 color plts. Good in dj. *Washton.* $85/£55

ZANGWILL, ISRAEL. The Celibates' Club. NY: Macmillan, 1905. 1st thus. Good+ (cvrs rubbed). *Agvent.* $25/£16

ZANGWILL, ISRAEL. The King of Schnorees. London, 1894. 1st ed. VG. *Madle.* $75/£48

Zanita: A Tale of the Yosemite. (By Maria Therese Longworth). NY: Hurd & Houghton, 1872. 1st ed. 296pp. Plum cl stamped in gilt, blind. Good (inscrip; spine,edges faded, few marginal spots). *Reese.* $125/£81

ZANUCK, DARYL F. Habit and Other Short Stories. Times-Mirror, 1923. 1st ed. VG. *Fine Books.* $55/£35

ZAPF, HERMAN. Herman Zapf and His Design Philosophy. Chicago: Soc of Typographic Arts, 1987. Fine in dj. *Moss.* $93/£60

ZAREM, L. The Green Man From Space. Dutton, 1955. 1st ed. Fine in VG+ dj. *Aronovitz.* $35/£23

ZAROULIS, N.L. The Poe Papers. NY: Putnam, (1977). 1st ed, 1st bk. Fine (stamp fep) in dj. *Pharos.* $85/£55

ZAROULIS, N.L. The Poe Papers. NY: Putnam's, 1977. 1st ed. Fine in dj (chipped). *Oak Knoll.* $35/£23

ZEISBERGER, DAVID. Zeisberger's Indian Dictionary; English, German, Iroquois.... Cambridge: (Harvard) Univ Press, 1887. 4to. 236pp. *Argosy.* $125/£81

ZELAZNY, ROGER. The Courts of Chaos. NY: Doubleday, 1978. 1st bk ed. Fine in dj. *Sadlon.* $30/£19

ZELAZNY, ROGER. Doors of His Face, Lamps of His Mouth. Doubleday, 1971. 1st ed. Fine in dj. *Madle.* $300/£194

ZELAZNY, ROGER. For a Bereath I Tarry. Underwood-Miller, 1980. 1st ed. One of 600. Fine in wraps. *Madle.* $25/£16

ZELAZNY, ROGER. A Rose for Ecclesiastes. RHD, 1969. 1st Eng, 1st hb ed. Signed. NF in dj. *Aronovitz.* $475/£306

ZELAZNY, ROGER. To Die in Italbar. Doubleday, 1973. 1st ed. Fine in dj (sl frayed). *Madle.* $45/£29

ZEVI, BRUNO. Towards an Organic Architecture. London: Faber & Faber, (1950). 1st ed in English. Ex-lib w/mks; spine sunned, else VG. *Bookpress.* $110/£71

ZINCKE, F. BARHAM. Egypt of the Pharaohs and of the Khedive. London: Smith, Elder, 1873. 2nd ed. Map. Gilt-pict cl (extrems rubbed, sm tears spine; sig). *Archaeologia.* $65/£42

ZINSSER, HANS. Infection and Resistance. NY, 1914. 1st ed. (Fr hinge broken.) Contents VG. *Fye.* $75/£48

ZOGBAUM, RUFUS FAIRCHILD. Horse, Foot, and Dragoons. NY: Harper, 1888. 1st ptg. 176pp, frontis illus on tissue. Pict cl. VG. *Schoyer.* $200/£129

ZOLA, EMILE. The Masterpiece. Katherine Woods (trans). (NY): Howell, Soskin, 1946. 1st ed this translation. Black cl. VG in pict dj (rubbed; chips). *Chapel Hill.* $40/£26

ZOLA, EMILE. Nana. NY: LEC, 1948. #648/1500 signed by Bernard Lamotte (illus). Fine in slipcase (sl worn). *Williams.* $116/£75

ZOLA, EMILE. Paris. London, 1898. 1st Eng ed. Blue cl. VG (lt rubbed). *Mcclintock.* $25/£16

ZOLOTOW, CHARLOTTE. It's Not Fair. NY: Harper, 1976. 1st ed. William Pene DuBois (illus). Lg 12mo. Pict paper-cvrd bds. As New in As New dj (price-clipped). *Book Adoption.* $40/£26

ZOSS, JOEL and JOHN BOWMAN. Diamonds in the Rough. Macmillan, 1989. 1st ed. Mint in Mint dj. *Plapinger.* $27/£17

ZOUCH, THOMAS. Memoirs of the Life and Writings of Sir Philip Sidney. York: Ptd by Thomas Wilson, 1809. 2nd ed. Copper-engr frontis port, 400pp. 1/2 calf (ca 1900) over purple cl, black morocco spine label. (Fr outer hinge partly cracked; spine rubbed; bkpl.) *Karmiole.* $175/£113

ZUCKERMAN, SOLLY. Functional Affinities of Man, Monkeys, and Apes.... London, 1933. 1st ed. 24 plts, 11 tables. Sl foxing, o/w NF in dj. *Goodrich.* $95/£61

ZUKOFSKY, LOUIS. After I's. (Pittsburgh, PA): Boxwood Press/Mother Press, (1964). Signed. VG (sl soil) in ptd white wraps. *Antic Hay.* $45/£29

ZUKOFSKY, LOUIS. Autobiography. NY: Grossman, 1970. 1st ed. Fine in Fine dj. *Revere.* $35/£23

ZUKOFSKY, LOUIS. Prepositions. London, 1967. 1st ed. #137/150 signed. Fine in dj (price-clipped). *Polyanthos.* $100/£65

ZURCHER, BERNARD. Vincent Van Gogh. NY, 1985. 1st Eng trans. 150 color plts. Dj. *Edwards.* $54/£35

ZWEIG, STEFAN. Beware of Pity. NY, 1939. 1st Amer ed. Signed presentation. NF (spine extrems sl rubbed) in dj (spine heel sl rubbed). *Polyanthos.* $75/£48